MAR-21/86.

THE BANTAM NEW COLLEGE
GERMAN & ENGLISH DICTIONARY

The Best Low-Priced Dictionary You Can Own

With more entries than any other compact paperbound dictionary—including thousands of new words—*The Bantam New College German & English Dictionary* is the most complete budget dictionary available today.

Whether you need it at home, the office, school, or in the library, this one indispensable, authoritative volume will prove its value over and over again, every time you use it.

THE BANTAM NEW COLLEGE DICTIONARY SERIES

John C. Traupman, Author

JOHN C. TRAUPMAN received his B.A. in German and in Latin at Moravian College and his M.A. and Ph.D. in Classics at Princeton University. He is chairman of the Department of Classical Languages at St. Joseph's University (Philadelphia). He served as president of the Philadelphia Classical Society, of the Pennsylvania Classical Association, and of the Classical and Modern Language League. He has published widely in learned journals and is the author of *The New College Latin & English Dictionary* (Bantam Books, 1966) and an associate editor of *The Scribner-Bantam English Dictionary* (Scribner's, 1977; Bantam Books, 1979).

Edwin B. Williams, General Editor

EDWIN B. WILLIAMS (1891–1975), A.B., A.M., Ph.D., Doct. d'Univ., LL.D., L.H.D., was chairman of the Department of Romance Languages, dean of the Graduate School, and provost of the University of Pennsylvania. He was a member of the American Philosophical Society and the Hispanic Society of America. Among his many lexicographical works are *The Williams Spanish and English Dictionary* (Scribner's, formerly Holt) and *The Bantam New College Spanish and English Dictionary*. He created and coordinated the Bantam series of original dictionaries—English, French, German, Italian, Latin, and Spanish.

THE BANTAM NEW COLLEGE
GERMAN & ENGLISH
DICTIONARY

JOHN C. TRAUPMAN, Ph.D.
St. Joseph's University, Philadelphia

BANTAM BOOKS
TORONTO • NEW YORK • LONDON • SYDNEY • AUCKLAND

THE BANTAM NEW COLLEGE
GERMAN & ENGLISH DICTIONARY
A Bantam Book / February 1981

ISBN 0-553-14155-4

Published simultaneously in the United States and Canada

Bantam Books are published by Bantam Books, Inc. Its trade-
mark, consisting of the words "Bantam Books" and the por-
trayal of a bantam, is Registered in U.S. Patent and Trademark
Office and in other countries. Marca Registrada. Bantam
Books, Inc., 666 Fifth Avenue, New York, New York 10103.

PRINTED IN THE UNITED STATES OF AMERICA

0 9 8 7 6 5 4

CONTENTS

I wish to express my appreciation to the many persons on whose help I relied in researching and compiling this Dictionary. I am particularly indebted to Edwin B. Williams, Walter D. Glanze, Donald Reis, Rudolf Pillwein, and Helmut Kreitz.

J. C. T.

HOW TO USE
THIS DICTIONARY

HINWEISE FÜR
DEN BENUTZER

All entry words are treated in a fixed order according to the parts of speech and the functions of verbs. On the German-English side: past participle, adjective, adverb, pronoun, preposition, conjunction, interjection, transitive verb, reflexive verb, reciprocal verb, intransitive verb, impersonal verb, auxiliary verb, substantive; on the English-German side: adjective, substantive, pronoun, adverb, preposition, conjunction, transitive verb, intransitive verb, auxiliary verb, impersonal verb, interjection.

Alle Stichwörter werden in einheitlicher Reihenfolge gemäß der Wortart und der Verbfunktion behandelt. Im deutsch-englischen Teil: Partizip Perfekt, Adjektiv, Adverb, Pronomen, Präposition, Konjunktion, Interjektion, transitives Verb, reflexives Verb, reziprokes Verb, intransitives Verb, unpersönliches Verb, Hilfsverb, Substantiv; im englisch-deutschen Teil: Adjektiv, Substantiv, Pronomen, Adverb, Präposition, Konjunktion, transitives Verb, intransitives Verb, Hilfsverb, unpersönliches Verb, Interjektion.

The order of meanings within an entry is as follows: first, the more general meanings; second, the meanings with usage labels; third, the meanings with subject labels in alphabetical order; fourth, illustrative phrases in alphabetical order.

Die verschiedenen Bedeutungen sind innerhalb eines Stichwortartikels in folgender Anordnung gegeben: zuerst die allgemeinen Bedeutungen; dann die Bedeutungen mit Bezeichnung der Sprachgebrauchsebene; dann die Bedeutungen mit Bezeichnung des Sachgebietes, in alphabetischer Reihenfolge; zuletzt die Anwendungsbeispiele, in alphabetischer Reihenfolge.

Subject and usage labels (printed in roman and in parentheses) refer to the preceding entry word or illustrative phrase in the source language (printed in boldface), e.g.,

Die Bezeichnungen der Sprachgebrauchsebene und des Sachgebiets (in Antiqua und in Klammern) beziehen sich auf das vorangehende Stichwort oder Anwendungsbeispiel in der Ausgangssprache (halbfett gedruckt), z.B.

mund′tot *adj*—**j-n m. machen** (fig) silence s.o.
Pinke [′pɪŋkə] *f* (–;) (coll) dough

Words in parentheses and in roman coming after a meaning serve to clarify that meaning, e.g.,

Kursiv gedruckte Wörter in Klammern, die nach einer Bedeutung stehen, sollen diese Bedeutung illustrieren, z.B.

überschau′en *tr* look over, survey; overlook (*a scene*)

Words in parenthese and in roman type coming after or before a meaning are optional additions to the word in the target language, e.g.,

In Antiqua gedruckte Wörter in Klammern, die nach oder vor einer Bedeutung stehen, sind wahlfreie Erweiterungen des Wortes der Zielsprache, z.B.

Tanne [ˈtanə] *f* (–;–n) fir (tree)
Pap′rikaschote *f* (green) pepper

Meaning discriminations are given in the source language and are in italics, e.g.,

Bedeutungsdifferenzierungen sind in der Ausgangssprache angegeben und kursiv gedruckt, z.B.

überrei′zen *tr* overexcite; (*Augen, Nerven*) strain
earn [ʌrn] *tr* (*money*) verdienen; (*interest*) einbringen

Since vocabulary entries are not determined on the basis of etymology, homographs are listed as a single entry.

Da die Etymologie bei der Anführung der Stichwörter unberücksichtigt bleibt, sind gleichgeschriebene Wörter als ein und dasselbe Stichwort verzeichnet.

The entry word is represented within the entry by its initial letter followed by a period (if the entry word contains more than three letters), provided the form is identical. The same applies to a word that follows the parallels. The entry word is not abbreviated within the entry when associated with suspension points, e.g.,

Innerhalb eines Stichwortartikels wird das Stichwort (wenn es mehr als drei Buchstaben enthält) durch seinen Anfangsbuchstaben und einen Punkt angegeben, vorausgesetzt, daß die betreffende Form mit dem Stichwort identisch ist. Das Gleiche gilt für ein Wort, das nach den Vertikalstrichen steht. Wenn ein Stichwort innerhalb eines Stichwortartikels in Verbindung mit Auslassungspunkten angegeben ist, wird es nicht abgekürzt, z.B.

weder . . . noch

Parallels are used (a) to separate parts of speech, (b) to separate transitive, reflexive, reciprocal, intransitive, impersonal, and auxiliary verbs, (c) to separate verbs taking HABEN from those taking SEIN, (d) to indicate a change in pronunciation of the entry word, depending on the meaning, e.g.,

Es ist der Zweck der Vertikalstriche, (a) Wortarten voneinander zu trennen, (b) transitive, reflexive, reziproke, intransitive, unpersönliche Verben und Hilfsverben zu trennen, (c) Verben mit dem Hilfsverb HABEN von Verben mit dem Hilfsverb SEIN zu trennen, (d) verschiedene Aussprachen des Stichwortes je nach Bedeutung anzuzeigen, z.B.

bow [bau] *s* Verbeugung *f*; (naut) Bug *m* . . .
‖ [bo] *s* (*weapon*) Bogen *m*; . . .

(e) to show change from a strong verb to a weak verb and vice versa, (f) to show a change in the case governed by

(e) den Wechsel von einem starken zu einem schwachen Verb und umgekehrt anzuzeigen, (f) den Wechsel in einem

a preposition where the entry word is a preposition, (g) to show a shift of accent, e.g.,

von einer Präposition regierten Fall anzuzeigen, wo das Stichwort selbst eine Präposition ist, (g) unterschiedliche Stellungen des Akzents anzuzeigen, z.B.

ü′bergießen *tr* . . . ‖ **übergie′ßen** *tr* . . .

The centered period in the English word on the German-English side marks the point at which the following letters are dropped before irregular plural endings are added. The centered period in the entry word on the English-German side marks the point at which the following letters are dropped before irregular plural endings are added to nouns and inflections are added to verbs. The centered period in the phonetic spelling indicates diaeresis, e.g.,

Der auf Mitte stehende Punkt im Stichwort des deutsch-englischen Teils zeigt die Stelle an, wo die nachfolgenden Buchstaben abzutrennen sind, bevor unregelmäßige Pluralendungen angefügt werden können. Der auf Mitte stehende Punkt im Stichwort des englisch-deutschen Teils zeigt die Stelle an, wo die nachfolgenden Buchstaben abzutrennen sind, bevor unregelmäßige Pluralendungen an Hauptwörter and Flexionen an Verben angefügt werden können. Der auf Mitte stehende Punkt in der Lautschrift zeigt Diärese an, z.B.

befähigt [bə′fe·ɪçt]

On the German-English and the English-German side, in the case of a transitive verb, the meaning discrimination in parentheses before the target word is always the object of the verb. On the German-English side, in the case of an intransitive verb, the meaning discrimination in parentheses before the target word is always the subject of the verb. On the English-German side, the suggested subject of a verb is prefaced by the words "said of".

Im deutsch-englischen und im englisch-deutschen Teil ist die bei transitiven Verben in Klammern vor dem Wort in der Zielsprache angegebene Bedeutungsdifferenzierung immer das Objekt des Verbs. Im deutsch-englischen Teil ist bei intransitiven Verben die vor dem Wort in der Zielsprache angegebene Bedeutungsdifferenzierung immer das Subjekt des Verbs. Im englisch-deutschen Teil stehen vor dem beabsichtigten Subjekt eines Verbs die Worte "said of."

Inflections are generally not shown for compound entry words, since the inflections have been shown where the components are entry words. However, when the last component of a compound noun on the German-English side has various inflections depending on meaning, the inflection is shown for the compound, e.g.,

Bei zusammengesetzten Stichwörtern ist die Flexion im Allgemeinen nicht angegeben, da sie unter den als Stichwörter angeführten Teilen des Kompositums angegeben ist. Falls jedoch der letzte Teil eines deutschen Kompositums je nach der Bedeutung verschieden flektiert wird, ist die Flexion für das Kompositum angegeben, z.B.

Ton′band *n* (–[e]s;̈er) . . .

German verbs are regarded as reflexive regardless of whether the reflexive pronoun is the direct or indirect object of the verb.

Deutsche Verben gelten als reflexiv ohne Rücksicht darauf, ob das Reflexivpronomen das direkte oder indirekte Objekt des Verbs ist.

On the English-German side, when the pronunciation of an entry word is not given, stress in the entry word is shown as follows: a high-set primary stress mark ′ follows the syllable that receives the primary stress, and a high-set secondary stress mark ′ follows the syllable that receives the secondary stress. When the pronunciation of an entry word *is* provided [given in brackets], a high-set primary stress mark ‛ *precedes* the syllable that receives the primary stress, and a *low*-set secondary stress mark ‚ *precedes* the syllable that receives the secondary stress.

On the German-English side, when the pronunciation of an entry word is not given, a high-set primary stress mark ′ follows the syllable of the entry word that receives the primary stress. When the pronunciation of the entry *is* provided [given in brackets], a high-set primary stress mark ‛ *precedes* the syllable that receives the primary stress. (Because opinions on the system of secondary stress in German differ widely, secondary stress marks are not employed in this Dictionary.)

Wo die Aussprache des Stichwortes im englisch-deutschen Teil nicht angegeben ist, wird die Betonung des Stichwortes folgendermaßen angedeutet: Das stärkere, obere graphische Zeichen ′ steht nach der Silbe mit dem Haupttonakzent, und das schwächere, obere Zeichen ′ steht nach der Silbe mit dem Nebentonakzent. Wo hingegen die Aussprache des Stichwortes im englisch-deutschen Teil [in eckigen Klammern] angegeben ist, steht das stärkere, obere Zeichen ‛ *vor* der Silbe mit dem Haupttonakzent und das schwächere, *untere* Zeichen ‚ *vor* der Silbe mit dem Nebentonakzent.

Wo die Aussprache das Stichwortes im deutsch-englischen Teil nicht angegeben ist, steht das starke Zeichen ′ nach der Stichwortsilbe mit dem Haupttonakzent. Wo hingegen die Aussprache des Stichwortes im deutschenglischen Teil [in eckigen Klammern] angegeben ist, steht das starke Zeichen ‛ *vor* der Silbe mit dem Haupttonakzent. (Wegen der widersprüchlichen Theorien, die die Frage des Nebentonakzents im Deutschen umgeben, wendet dieses Wörterbuch keine Nebentonakzente für die deutschen Wörter an.)

Proper nouns and general abbreviations are listed in their alphabetical position in the main body of the Dictionary.

Eigennamen und allgemeine Abkürzungen sind in den beiden Hauptteilen des Wörterbuches in alphabetischer Reihenfolge angegeben.

This Dictionary contains approximately 75,000 "entries." As entries are counted (a) nonindented boldface headwords and (b) elements that could have been set nonindented as separate headwords, too, but that for reasons of style and typography are grouped under the nonindented headwords, namely, separate parts of speech and boldface idioms and phrases.

Dieses Wörterbuch enthält ungefähr 75.000 "Stichwörter." Die folgenden Elemente gelten als Stichwörter: (a) die nicht eingerückten fettgedruckten Wörter am Anfang eines Stichwortartikels und (b) Elemente, die man auf dieselbe Weise hatte drucken können, die aber aus Stil– und Typographiegründen eingerückt wurden, nämlich die unterschiedlichen Wortarten und die fettgedruckten Redewendungen.

PART ONE

German-English

GERMAN—ENGLISH

A

A, a [ɑ] *invar n* A, a; (mus) A; **das A und O** the beginning and the end; (*das Wichtigste*) the most important thing

Aal [ɑl] *m* (-[e]s;-e) eel; (nav) torpedo

aal′glatt′ *adj* (fig) sly as a fox

Aas [ɑs] *n* (-es;-e) carrion; (sl) louse

ab [ap] *adv* off; away; down; on, e.g., **von heute ab** from today on; (theat) exit, exeunt, e.g., **Hamlet ab** exit Hamlet; **ab und zu** now and then || *prep* (*dat*) from, e.g., **ab Frankfurt** from Frankfurt; minus, e.g., **ab Skonto** minus discount

ab′ändern *tr* alter; (*völlig*) change; (*mildern*) modify; (parl) amend

Ab′änderung *f* (-;-en) alteration; change; modification; (parl) amendment

Ab′änderungsantrag *m* (parl) (proposed) amendment

ab′arbeiten *tr* work off || *ref* work hard

Ab′art *f* variety, type

ab′arten *intr* (SEIN) deviate from type

Ab′bau *m* (-[e]s;) demolition; reduction; cutback; layoff; (chem) decomposition; (min) exploitation

ab′bauen *tr* demolish; (*Maschinen, Fabriken*) dismantle; (*Steuern, Preise, Truppen*) reduce; (*Zelt*) take down; (*Lager*) break; (*Angestellte*) lay off; (chem) decompose; (min) work, exploit

ab′beißen §53 *tr* bite off || *intr* take a bite

ab′bekommen §99 *tr* (*seinen Teil*) get; (*Schmutz*) get out; (*Deckel*) get off; **du wirst was a.!** you're going to get it!

ab′berufen §122 *tr* (dipl) recall

ab′bestellen *tr* cancel

ab′betteln *tr*—**die ganze Straße a.** beg up and down the street; **j-m etw a.** chisel s.th. from s.o.

ab′biegen §57 *tr* bend, twist off; (*Gefahr*) avert; (*Plan*) thwart; **das Gespräch a.** change the subject || *intr* (SEIN) branch off; (fig) get off the track; **in e-e Seitenstraße a.** turn down a side street; **nach links a.** turn left; **von e-r Straße a.** turn off a road

Ab′bild *n* picture, image

ab′bilden *tr* represent

Ab′bildung *f* (-;-en) illustration, figure

ab′binden §59 *tr* untie; (*Kalb*) wean; (*Arm*) apply a tourniquet to; (surg) tie off || *intr* (Zement) set

Ab′bitte *f* apology; **A. tun wegen** apologize for

ab′bitten §60 *tr* apologize for || *intr* apologize

ab′blasen §61 *tr* blow off; (fig) call off || *intr* (mil) sound the retreat

ab′blättern *intr* (SEIN) shed leaves; (*Farben, Haut*) flake, peel

ab′blenden *tr* dim; (cin) fade out; (phot) stop down || *intr* (aut) dim the lights; (nav) darken ship; (phot) stop down the lens

Ab′blendlicht *n* (aut) low-beam lights

ab′blitzen *intr* (SEIN) be unsuccessful; **j-n a. lassen** snub s.o.

ab′blühen *intr* stop blooming || *intr* (SEIN) fade

ab′böschen *tr* slope; (*Mauer*) batter

ab′brausen *tr* hose down || *ref* shower off || *intr* (SEIN) (coll) roar off

ab′brechen §64 *tr* break off; (*Belagerung*) raise; (*Gebäude*) demolish; (*Zelt*) take down; (sport) call; **das Lager a.** break camp || *intr* (SEIN) (& fig) break off

ab′bremsen *tr* slow down; (*Streik*) prevent; (*Motoren*) (aer) rev || *intr* put on the brakes; (aer) fishtail

ab′brennen §97 *tr* burn off; (*Feuerwerk*) set off; (*Geschütz*) fire; (chem) distil out; (metal) refine; (naut) bream; **ich bin vollkommen abgebrannt** (coll) I'm dead broke || *intr* (SEIN) burn down

ab′bringen §65 *tr* (*Fleck*) remove; (*gestrandetes Schiff*) refloat; **davon a. zu** (*inf*) dissuade from (*ger*); **vom rechten Weg a.** lead astray; **vom Thema a.** throw off; **von der Spur a.** throw off the scent; **von e-r Gewohnheit a.** break of the habit

ab′bröckeln *intr* crumble; (*Farbe*) peel (off); (*Preis, Aktie*) go slowly down; (*Mitglieder*) fall off

Ab′bruch *m* (-*e*s Zweiges, der Beziehungen) breaking off; (-*e*s Gebäudes) demolition; (*Schaden*) damage; **A. des Spiels** (sport) calling of the game; **A. tun** (dat) harm, spoil; **auf A. verkaufen** sell at demolition value; (*Maschinen*) sell for junk

ab′brühen *tr* (culin) scald

ab′brummen *tr* (*Strafe*) (coll) serve, do || *intr* (SEIN) (coll) clear out

ab′buchen *tr* (*abschreiben*) write off; (acct) debit

ab′bürsten *tr* brush off

ab′büßen *tr* atone for; **e-e Strafe a.** serve time; **er hat es schwer a. müssen** (coll) he had to pay for it dearly

Abc [abeˈtse] *n* (-;-) ABC's

Abc′-Schütze *m* (-n;-n) pupil

ab′danken *tr* dismiss; (*pensionieren*)

retire ‖ *intr* resign; (*Herrscher*) abdicate; (mil) get a discharge

ab'decken *tr* uncover; (*Tisch*) clear; (*Bett*) turn down; (*Vieh*) skin; (*e-e Schuld*) pay back; (mil) camouflage; (phot) mask

ab'dichten *tr* seal (off); (*Loch*) plug up; (*mit weichem Material*) pack; (naut) caulk

ab'dienen *tr* (*Schuld*) work off; (mil) serve (*one's term*)

ab'drehen *tr* twist off; (*Gas, Licht, Wasser*) turn off ‖ *intr* turn away

ab'dreschen §67 *tr* thrash

Ab'druck *m* (*-s;-e*) reprint; offprint; copy; (*Abguß*) casting; (phot, typ) proof ‖ *m* (*-s;-e*) impression, imprint

ab'drucken *tr* print

ab'drücken *tr* (*abformen*) mold; (*Gewehr*) fire; (*Pfeil*) shoot; (*umarmen*) hug; **den Hahn a.** pull the trigger ‖ *ref* leave an impression ‖ *intr* pull the trigger

ab'duschen *ref* shower off

Abend ['ɑbənt] *m* (*-s;-e*) evening; **am A.** in the evening; **bunter A.** social; (telv) variety show; **des Abends in the evening(s); zu A. essen** eat dinner

A'bendblatt *n* evening paper

A'bendbrot *n* supper, dinner

A'benddämmerung *f* twilight, dusk

A'bendessen *n* supper, dinner

abendfüllend ['ɑbəntfʏlənt] *adj* full-length (*movie*)

A'bendgesellschaft *f* party (*in the evening*)

A'bendland *n* West, Occident

abendländisch ['ɑbəntlɛndɪʃ] *adj* occidental

a'bendlich *adj* evening ‖ *adv* evenings

A'bendmahl *n* supper; **das Heilige A.** Holy Communion

abends ['ɑbənts] *adv* in the evening

Abenteuer ['ɑbəntɔɪ·ər] *s* (*-s;-*) adventure; **galantes A.** (love) affair

a'benteuerlich *adj* adventurous; (*Unternehmen*) risky

aber ['ɑbər] *adv* yet, however; (before adjectives and adverbs) really, indeed; **a. und abermals** over and over again; **hundert und a. hundert** hundreds and hundreds of ‖ *conj* but ‖ *interj*—aber, aber! now, now! ‖ **Aber** *n* (*-s;-s*) but; **hier gibt es kein A.!** no ifs and buts

A'berglaube *m* superstition

abergläubisch ['ɑbərglɔɪbɪʃ] *adj* superstitious

ab'erkennen §97 *tr*—j-m etw a. deny s.o. s.th.; (jur) dispossess s.o. of s.th.

Ab'erkennung *f* (*-;-en*) denial; (jur) dispossession

abermalig ['ɑbərmɑlɪç] *adj* repeated

abermals ['ɑbərmɑls] *adv* once more

ab'ernten *tr* reap, harvest

ab'fahren §71 *tr* cart away; (*Strecke*) cover; (*Straße*) wear out; (*Reifen*) wear down ‖ *intr* (SEIN) depart; drive off

Ab'fahrt *f* departure

Ab'fall *m* (*der Blätter*) falling; (*Bö-*

schung) steep slope; (*von e-m Glauben*) falling away; (*von e-r Partei*) defection; (*Sinken*) drop, decrease; **Abfälle** garbage, trash; chips, shavings

ab'fallen §72 *intr* (SEIN) fall off; (*von e-r Partei*) defect; (*vom Glauben*) fall away; (*abnehmen*) decrease, fail; (*Kunden*) stay away; (sport) fall behind; **a. gegen** compare badly with; **es wird etw für dich a.** there'll be s.th. in it for you; **körperlich a.** lose weight; **stell a.** drop away

abfällig ['ɑpfɛlɪç] *adj* disparaging

Ab'fallprodukt *n* by-product

ab'fangen §73 *tr* catch; (*Angriff*) foil; (*Brief*) intercept; (aer) pull out of a dive; (*U-Boot*) (nav) trim; (sport) catch (up with); **j-m die Kunden a.** steal s.o.'s customers

ab'färben *intr* (*Farben*) run; (*Stoff*) fade; **a. auf** (*acc*) stain; (fig) rub off on

ab'fassen *tr* compose, draft; (*erwischen*) catch

Ab'fassung *f* (*-;-en*) wording; composition

ab'faulen *intr* (SEIN) rot away

ab'fegen *tr* sweep off, whisk off

ab'fertigen ['ɑpfɛrtɪgən] *tr* get ready for sending off; (*Gepäck*) check; (*Zollgüter*) clear; (*Kunden*) wait on; (*abweisen*) snub; (*verwaltungsmäßig*) (adm) process;

Ab'fertigung *f* (*-;-en*) dispatch; snub; zollamtliche A. clearance

ab'feuern *tr* fire; (rok) launch

ab'finden §59 *tr* (*Gläubiger*) satisfy; (*Partner*) buy off; (*entschädigen*) (für) compensate (for) ‖ *ref*—sich a. lassen settle for a lump-sum payment; **sich a. mit** put up with; come to terms with

Ab'findung *f* (*-;-en*) satisfaction; lump-sum settlement

Ab'findungsvertrag *m* lump-sum settlement

abflachen ['ɑpflɑxən] *tr* level; (*abschrägen*) bevel ‖ *ref* flatten out

abflauen ['ɑpflau·ən] *intr* (SEIN) slack off; (*Interesse*) flag; (*Preis*) go down; (st. exch.) ease off

ab'fliegen §57 *intr* (SEIN) take off

ab'fließen §76 *intr* (SEIN) flow off, drain off

Ab'flug *m* takeoff, departure

Ab'fluß *m* discharge; drain, gutter, gully; **See ohne A.** lake without outlet

Ab'flußrinne *f* drainage ditch

Ab'flußrohr *n* drainpipe; soil pipe; (*vom Dach*) downspout

ab'fordern *tr*—j-m etw a. demand s.th. from s.o.

ab'fragen *tr*—j-n etw a. question s.o. about s.th.; quiz s.o. on s.th.

ab'fressen §70 *tr* eat up; crop, chew off; (*Metall*) corrode

ab'frieren §77 *intr* (SEIN) be nipped by the frost; **abgefroren** frostbitten

Abfuhr ['ɑpfur] *f* (*-;-en*) removal; (*Abweisung*) (coll) cold shoulder, snub

ab'führen *tr* lead away; *(festnehmen)* arrest; *(fencing)* defeat ‖ *intr* cause the bowels to move

Abführmittel ['apfʏrmɪtəl] *n* laxative

ab'füllen *tr* (*Wein, Bier*) bottle

Ab'gabe *f* (*Auslieferung*) delivery; (*Verkauf*) sale; (*Steuer*) tax; (*Zoll*) duty; (*der Wahlstimme*) casting; (*e-s Urteils*) pronouncing; (*e-r Meinung*) expressing; (fb) pass; **Abgaben** taxes, fees

ab'gabenfrei *adj* tax-free, duty-free

abgabenpflichtig ['apgɑːbənpflɪçtɪç] *adj* taxable, subject to duty

Ab'gang *m* departure; (*von e–m Amt*) retirement; (*von der Schule*) dropping out; (*Verlust*) loss; (*Abnahme*) decrease; (gym) finish; (pathol) discharge; (pathol) miscarriage; (theat) exit; **guten A. haben** sell well

abgängig ['apgɛŋɪç] *adj* lost, missing; (com) marketable

Ab'gangsprüfung *f* final examination

Ab'gangspunkt *m* point of departure

Ab'gas *n* (aut) exhaust; (indust) waste gas

ab'geben §80 *tr* (*Paß*) hand over; (*Gepäck*) check; (*abliefern*) deliver; (*Schulheft*) hand in; (*Urteil*) pass; (*Meinung*) express; (*Gutachten*) give; (*Amt*) lay down; (*gute Ernte*) yield; (*Schuß*) fire; (*Wahlstimme*) cast; (*Waren*) sell, let go; (*sich eignen als*) act as, serve as; be cut out to be; (elec) deliver; (fb) pass; (phys) give off; **e–e Offerte a.** (jur) make an offer; **e–n Narren a.** play the fool; **er würde e–n guten Vater a.** he would make a good father; **j–m eins a.** (coll) let s.o. have it; **j–m von etw a.** share s.th. with s.o. ‖ *ref*—**sich a. mit** bother with; associate with; spend time on

abgebrannt ['apgəbrant] *adj* (coll) broke

abgebrüht ['apgəbryːt] *adj* (fig) hardened

abgedroschen ['apgədrɔʃən] *adj* trite, hackneyed; (*Witz*) stale

abgefeimt ['apgəfaɪmt] *adj* cunning; out-and-out

abgegriffen ['apgəgrɪfən] *adj* well-thumbed

abgehackt ['apgəhakt] *adj* jerky

abgehärmt ['apgəhɛrmt] *adj* careworn, drawn

ab'gehen §82 *intr* (SEIN) leave, depart; (*Brief*) go off; (*Knopf*) come off; (*Schuß*) go off; (*Farbe*) fade; (*Seitenweg*) branch off; (*vom Gesprächsgegenstand*) digress, go off; (*vom rechten Wege*) stray; (*aus e–m Amt*) resign, retire; (*von der Bühne*) retire; (*von der Schule*) drop out; graduate; (com) sell; (theat) exit; **bei Barzahlung gehen fünf Prozent ab** you get a five-percent reduction for paying cash; **davon kann ich nicht a.** I must insist on it; **er geht mir sehr ab** I miss him a lot; **nicht a. von** stick to; **reißend a.** sell like hotcakes; ‖ *ref*—**sich** [dat] **nichts a.**

lassen deny oneself nothing ‖ *impers* —**es geht ihm nichts ab** he lacks for nothing; **es gehen mir zehn Dollar ab** I am ten dollars short; **es ist alles glatt abgegangen** everything went well

ab'gehend *adj* (*Post, Beamte*) outgoing; (*Zug*) departing

abgekämpft ['apgəkɛmpft] *adj* exhausted

abgekartet ['apgəkartət] *adj* (*Spiel*) fixed; **abgekartete Sache** put-up job

abgeklappert ['apgəklapərt] *adj* hackneyed

abgeklärt ['apgəklɛrt] *adj* mellow, wise

abgelebt ['apgəlept] *adj* decrepit

abgelegen ['apgəleːgen] *adj* out-of-the-way, outlying

ab'gelten §83 *tr* meet, satisfy

abgemacht ['apgəmaxt] *adj* settled ‖ *interj* agreed!

abgemagert ['apgəmaːgərt] *adj* emaciated

abgemessen ['apgəmɛsən] *adj* measured; (*genau*) exact; (*Rede*) deliberate; (*Person*) stiff, formal

abgeneigt ['apgənaɪkt] *adj* reluctant; (dat) averse to; **ich bin durchaus nicht a.** (coll) I don't mind if I do

Ab'geneigtheit *f* (–;) aversion

abgenutzt ['apgənʊtst] *adj* worn out

Abgeordnete ['apgəˌɔrdnətə] §5 *mf* delegate; (pol) representative; deputy (*member of the Bundestag*); (Brit) Member of Parliament

Ab'geordnetenhaus *n* House of Representatives; (Brit) House of Commons

abgerissen ['apgərɪsən] *adj* torn; (*zerlumpt*) ragged; (*ohne Zusammenhang*) incoherent, disconnected

Abgesandte ['apgəzantə] §5 *mf* envoy

abgeschieden ['apgəʃiːdən] *adj* secluded; (*verstorben*) deceased, late

Ab'geschiedenheit *f* (–;) seclusion

abgeschliffen ['apgəʃlɪfən] *adj* polished

abgeschlossen ['apgəʃlɔsən] *adj* isolated; (*Leben*) secluded; (*Ausbildung*) completed

abgeschmackt ['apgəʃmakt] *adj* tactless, tasteless; (fig) insipid

abgesehen ['apgəzeː-ən] *adj*—**a. davon, daß** not to mention that; **a. von** aside from, except for

abgespannt ['apgəʃpant] *adj* tired out

abgestanden ['apgəʃtandən] *adj* stale

abgestorben ['apgəʃtɔrbən] *adj* (*Pflanze, Gewebe*) dead; (*Glied*) numb

abgestumpft ['apgəʃtʊmpft] *adj* blunt; (*Kegel*) truncated; (fig) dull; (gegen) indifferent (to)

abgetakelt ['apgətaːkəlt] *adj* (*Person*) seedy; (*Schiff*) unrigged

abgetan ['apgətuːn] *adj* settled

abgetragen ['apgətraːgən] *adj* threadbare

abgetreten ['apgətreːtən] *adj* worn-down

ab'gewinnen §52 *tr* win; **e–r Sache Geschmack a.** acquire a taste for s.th.; **e–r Sache Vergnügen a.** derive pleasure from s.th.; **j–m e–n Vorteil a.** gain an advantage over s.o.

abgewirtschaftet [ˈapgəvɪrt/aftət] *adj* run-down

ab′gewöhnen *tr*—**ich kann es mir nicht a.** I can't get it out of my system; **j–m etw a.** break s.o. of s.th.

abgezehrt [ˈapgətseːrt] *adj* emaciated

ab′gießen §76 *tr* pour off; (*Statue*) cast; (chem) decant; (culin) strain off

Ab′glanz *m* reflection

ab′gleiten §86 *intr* (SEIN) slip off; (**an** *dat*) glance off (*s.th.*); (aer, aut) skid; (st. exch.) decline

Ab′gott *m* idol

Abgötterei [apgœtəˈraɪ] *f* (–;-en) idolatry; **A. treiben** worship idols; **mit j–m A. treiben** idolize s.o.

abgöttisch [ˈapgœtɪ/] *adj* idolatrous ‖ *adv*—**a. lieben** idolize

Ab′gottschlange *f* boa constrictor

ab′graben §87 *tr* (*Bach*) divert; (*Feld*) drain; (*Hügel*) level

ab′grämen *ref* eat one's heart out

ab′grasen *tr* (*Wiese*) graze on; (fig) scour, search

ab′greifen §88 *tr* wear out (*by constant handling*); (*Buch*) thumb

ab′grenzen *tr* mark off, demarcate; delimit; (fig) differentiate

Ab′grund *m* abyss; precipice

abgründig [ˈapgryndɪç] *adj* precipitous; (fig) deep, unfathomable

ab′gucken *tr* (coll) copy, crib; (coll) **pick up a habit from** ‖ *intr* (coll) copy, crib

Ab′guß *m* (sculp) cast; **A. in Gips** plaster cast

ab′hacken *tr* chop off; (*Baum*) chop down

ab′haken *tr* unhook, undo; (*in e-r Liste*) check off; (telp) take off (*the receiver*)

ab′halftern *tr* unharness; (fig) sack

ab′halten §90 *tr* hold off; (*Vorlesung*) give; (*Regen*) keep out; (*Versammlung, Parade*) hold; (**von**) keep (from)

Ab′haltung *f* (–;-en) hindrance; (*e-r Versammlung*) holding; (*e-s Festes*) celebration

ab′handeln *tr* (*Thema*) treat; (*erörtern*) discuss; **er läßt sich nichts a.** he won't come down (*in price*); **etw vom Preise a.** get s.th. off the price (*by bargaining*)

abhanden [apˈhandən] *adv*—**a. kommen** get lost; **a. sein** be missing

Ab′handlung *f* (–;-en) essay; (*Vortrag in e–m gelehrten Verein*) paper; (*Doktorarbeit*) thesis, dissertation; (*mündlich*) discourse, discussion

Ab′hang *m* slope

ab′hängen *tr* (*vom Haken*) take off; (*e-n Verfolger*) shake off; (rr) uncouple ‖ *intr* (telp) hang up; **a. von** depend on; be subject to (*s.o.'s approval*)

abhängig [ˈaphɛŋɪç] *adj* (*Stellung*) subordinate; (*Satz*) dependent; (*Rede*) indirect; (*Kasus*) oblique; (**von**) dependent (on), contingent (upon)

Ab′hängigkeit *f* (–;-en) dependence; (gram) subordination; **gegenseitige A.** interdependence

ab′härmen *ref* pine away; **sich a. wegen** (or **über** *acc*) fret about

ab′härten *tr* harden; (gegen) inure (to) ‖ *ref* (gegen) become hardened (to)

ab′hauen §93 *tr* cut off; chop off ‖ §109 *intr* (SEIN) (coll) scram, get lost

ab′häuten *tr* skin, flay

ab′heben §94 *tr* lift off; (*Rahm*) skim; (*Geld*) withdraw; (*Dividende*) collect; (*Haut*) (surg) strip off ‖ *ref* become airborne; (**von**) contrast (with)

Ab′hebung *f* (–;-en) lifting; (*vom Bankkonto*) withdrawal; (cards) cutting

Ab′hebungsformular *n* withdrawal slip

ab′heften *tr* (*Briefe*) file; (sew) tack

ab′heilen *intr* (HABEN & SEIN) heal up

ab′helfen §96 *intr* (dat) (*e–m Unrecht*) redress; (*e-r Schwierigkeit*) remove; (*e–m Mangel*) relieve; **dem ist nicht abzuhelfen** that can't be helped

ab′hetzen *tr* drive hard, work to death; (hunt) hunt down ‖ *ref* rush; tire oneself out

Ab′hilfe *f* remedy, redress; **A. schaffen** take remedial measures; **A. schaffen für** remedy, redress

ab′hobeln *tr* plane (down)

abhold [ˈaphɔlt] *adj* (dat) ill-disposed (towards), averse (to)

Abholdienst [ˈaphɔldiːnst] *m* pickup service

ab′holen *tr* fetch, call for, pick up

ab′holzen *tr* clear (of trees), deforest

Abhörapparat [ˈaphøːraparaːt] *m* (mil, nav) listening device

ab′horchen *tr* overhear; (med) sound; (rad, telp) monitor

ab′hören *tr* overhear, eavesdrop on; (*Studenten*) quiz; (*Schallplatte, Tonband*) listen to; (mil) intercept; (telp) monitor

Ab′hörgerät *n* bugging device

Ab′hörraum *m* (rad, telv) control room

Ab′irrung *f* (–;-en) deviation; (opt) aberration

Abitur [abiˈtuːr] *n* (–s;-e) final examination (*at end of junior college*); **das A. bestehen** graduate

Abiturient –in [abituˈriˈent(ɪn)] §7 *mf* graduate (*of a junior college*)

Abitur′zeugnis *n* diploma (*from senior high school or junior college*)

ab′jagen *tr* drive hard; **j–m etw a.** recover s.th. from s.o. ‖ *ref* run one's head off

abkanzeln [ˈapkantsəln] *tr* (coll) give (*s.o.*) a good talking to

ab′kauen *tr* chew off ‖ *ref*—**sich** [*dat*] **die Nägel a.** bite one's nails

ab′kaufen *tr*—**j–m etw a.** buy s.th. from s.o.

Abkehr [ˈapkeːr] *f* (–;) turning away; estrangement; (*Verzicht*) renunciation

ab′kehren *tr* turn away, avert; (*mit dem Besen*) sweep off ‖ *ref* turn away; become estranged

ab′klappern *tr* (coll) scour, search

ab'klatschen *tr* imitate slavishly; make an exact copy of; (*beim Tanzen*) cut in on; (typ) pull (*a proof*)

ab'klingen §142 *intr* (SEIN) (*Farbe*) fade; (*Töne*) die away; (*Schmerz*) ease off

ab'klopfen *tr* beat off, knock off; (*Teppich*) beat; (med) tap, percuss || *intr* stop the music (*with the rap of the baton*)

ab'knabbern *tr* (coll) nibble off

ab'knallen *tr* fire off; (sl) bump off

ab'knicken *tr* snap off || *intr* (SEIN) snap off

ab'knipsen *tr* pinch off, snip off; (*Film*) use up

ab'knöpfen *tr* unbutton; **j-m Geld a.** squeeze money out of s.o.

ab'knutschen *tr* (coll) pet

ab'kochen *tr* boil; (*Obst*) stew; (*Milch*) scald || *intr* cook out

ab'kommandieren *tr* detach, detail

ab'kommen §99 *intr* (SEIN) (**von**) get away (from); (*Mode*) go out of style; (naut) become afloat (again); **auf zwei Tage a.** get away for two days; **gut** (or **schlecht**) **a.** (sport) get off to a good (or bad) start; **hoch** (or **tief**) **a.** aim too high (or low); **vom Kurs a.** go off course; **vom Boden a.** become airborne; **vom Thema a.** get off the subject; **vom Wege a.** lose one's way, stray; **von der Wahrheit a.** deviate from the truth; **von e-r Ansicht a.** change one's views || **Abkommen** *n* (**-s;-**) (com, pol) agreement; (jur) settlement

abkömmlich ['apkœmlɪç] *adj*—**a. sein** be able to get away

Abkömmling ['apkœmlɪŋ] *m* (**-s;-e**) descendant; scion

ab'koppeln *tr* uncouple

ab'kratzen *tr* scratch off; (*Schuhe*) scuff up || *intr* (*sterben*) (sl) croak; (*abhauen*) (sl) beat it; **kratz ab!** drop dead!

ab'kriegen *tr* (coll) get off or out

ab'kühlen *tr, ref & intr* cool off

Abkunft ['apkunft] *f* (**-;**) lineage

ab'kürzen *tr* shorten; (*Inhalt*) abridge; (*Wort*) abbreviate; (math) reduce

Ab'kürzung *f* (**-;-en**) shortening; abridgement; abbreviation; (*kürzerer Weg*) shortcut

ab'küssen *tr* smother with kisses

ab'laden §103 *tr* unload; (*Schutt*) dump

Ab'ladeplatz *m* dump; (mil) unloading point

Ab'lage *f* (*für Kleider*) cloakroom; (*Lagerhaus*) depot, warehouse; (*abgelegte Akten*) files; (mil) dump

ab'lagern *tr* (*Wein, usw.*) age; (geol) deposit || *ref* (geol) be deposited || *intr* a. lassen age, season

Ab'laß *m* (**-lasses;-lässe**) outlet, drain; (com) deduction; (eccl) indulgence

ab'lassen §104 *tr* leave off; (*Bier*) tap; (*Dampf*) let off; (*Teich, Faß*) drain; (*Waren*) sell; **etw vom Preise a.** knock s.th. off the price; **j-m etw billig a.** (com) let s.o. have s.th. cheaply || *intr* desist, stop; **a. von** let go of, give up

Ablativ ['ablatif] *m* (**-s;-e**) ablative

Ab'lauf *m* overflow; (*e-r Frist, e-s Vertrags*) expiration; (*der Ereignisse*) course; (sport) start

ab'laufen §105 *tr* (*Strecke*) run; (*Stadt*) scour; (*Schuhe*) wear out; **j-m den Rang a.** get the better of s.o.; outrun s.o. || *intr* (SEIN) run away; (*Zeit*) expire; (*ausfallen*) turn out; (com) fall due; (sport) start

Ab'laut *m* ablaut

Ab'leben *n* demise, decease

ab'lecken *tr* lick (off)

ab'legen *tr* (*Last, Waffen*) lay down; (*ausziehen*) take off; (*Schwert*) lay aside; (*die alte Haut*) slough; (*Karten*) discard; (*Akten, Dokumente*) file; (*Briefe*) sort; (*Namen*) drop, stop using; (*Sorgen, Kummer*) put away; (*Prüfung, Gelübde, Eid*) take; (*Predigt*) deliver; (*Gewohnheit*) give up; (*Rechenschaft*) render, give; **Bekenntnis a.** make a confession; **die Maske a.** (fig) throw off all disguise; **die Trauer a.** come out of mourning; **ein volles Geständnis a.** come clean; **Probe a.** furnish proof; **seine Fehler a.** mend one's ways; **Zeugnis a.** (für or gegen) testify (for or against) || *intr* take off one's coat or hat (and coat); **bitte, legen Sie ab!** please take your things off

Ab'leger *m* (**-s;-**) (bot) shoot; (com) subsidiary; (hort) slip, cutting

ab'lehnen *tr* refuse, turn down; (*Antrag*) reject; (*Zeugen*) challenge; (*Erbschaft*) renounce; **durch Abstimmung a.** vote down

ab'lehnend *adj* negative

Ab'lehnung *f* (**-;-en**) refusal

ab'leiern *tr* recite mechanically

ab'leisten *tr* (*Eid*) take; **den Militärdienst a.** (mil) serve one's time

ab'leiten *tr* lead away; (*Herkunft*) trace back; (*Fluß, Blitz*) divert; (*Wasser*) drain off; (*Wärme*) conduct; (chem) derive; (elec) shunt; (gram, math) derive; **abgeleitetes Wort** derivative || *ref* (aus, von) be derived (from)

Ab'leitung *f* (**-;-en**) (*e-s Flusses*) diversion; (*des Wassers*) drainage; (elec, phys) conduction; (gram, math) derivation; (phys) convection

ab'lenken *tr* turn away, divert; (*Gefahr, Verdacht*) ward off; (fencing) parry; (opt, phys) deflect

Ab'lenkung *f* (**-;-en**) diversion; distraction; (opt) refraction

ab'lernen *tr*—**j-m etw a.** learn s.th. from s.o.

ab'lesen §107 *tr* read off; (*Zähler*) read; (*Obst*) pick; **es j-m vom Gesicht a., daß** tell by looking at s.o. that

ab'leugnen *tr* deny, disown; (*Glauben*) renounce

Ab'leugnung *f* (**-;-en**) denial, disavowal

ab'liefern *tr* deliver, hand over, surrender

Ab'lieferung *f* (**-;-en**) delivery; (*der Schußwaffen*) surrender

ab'liegen §108 *intr* (*Wein*) mature; (*Obst*) ripen ‖ *intr* (SEIN) be remote

ab'löschen *tr* extinguish; (*Stahl*) temper; (*Tinte*) blot; (*Kalk*) slake

ab'lösen *tr* loosen, detach; (*Posten*) relieve; (*Schuld*) discharge; (*Pfand*) redeem; (*Haut*) peel off ‖ *ref* (*bei*) take turns (at)

Ab'lösung *f* (-;-en) loosening; relief; discharge

ab'machen *tr* undo, untie; (*erledigen*) settle, arrange; (*Vertrag*) conclude; (*Rechnung*) close

Ab'machung *f* (-;-en) settlement

abmagern ['apmɑgərn] *intr* (SEIN) grow thin, thin down

Ab'magerung *f* (-;) emaciation

ab'mähen *tr* mow

ab'malen *tr* portray; (fig) depict

Ab'marsch *m* departure

ab'marschieren *intr* (SEIN) march off

Ab'mattung *f* (-;) fatigue

ab'melden (*Besuch*) (coll) call off; der ist bei mir abgemeldet (coll) I've had it with him; j-n bei der Polizei a. give notice to the police that s.o. is leaving town ‖ *ref* (mil) report off duty

ab'messen §70 *tr* measure (off); (*Worte*) weigh; (*Land*) survey

ab'montieren *tr* dismantle; (*Geschütz*) disassemble; (*Reifen*) take off ‖ *ref* (aer) (coll) disintegrate in the air

ab'mühen *ref* exert oneself, slave

ab'murksen *tr* (sl) do in

ab'nagen *tr* gnaw (off); (*Knochen*) pick

Ab'nahme *f* (-;-n) (*Verminderung*) (an dat) reduction (in), drop (in); (*des Gewichts*) loss; (*des Mondes*) waning; (*des Tages*) shortening; (*e-s Eides*) administering; (*e-r Rechnung*) auditing; (indust) final inspection; (surg) amputation; **A. der Geschäfte** decline in business; **A. e-r Parade** reviewing of the troops; **A. finden** be sold; **in A. geraten** decline, wane

ab'nehmen §116 *tr* take off, remove; (*Wäsche*) take down; (*Schnurrbart*) shave off; (*wegnehmen*) take away; (*Hörer*) lift, unhook; (*Strom*) use; (*Obst*) pick; (*Eid*) administer; (*Waren*) purchase; (*Rechnung*) audit; (*prüfen*) inspect and pass; (*Verband*) remove; (phot) take; (surg) amputate; **aus Berichten a.** gather from reports; **das kann ich dir nicht a.** I can't accept what you are saying; **die Parade a.** inspect the troops; **j-m die Arbeit a.** take the work off s.o.'s shoulders; **j-m die Beichte a.** hear s.o.'s confession; **j-m die Maske a.** unmask s.o., expose s.o.; **j-m die Verantwortung a.** relieve s.o. of responsibility; **j-m ein Versprechen a.** make s.o. make a promise; **j-m zuviel a.** charge s.o. too much ‖ *intr* diminish; (*Preise*) drop; (*Wasser*) recede; (*Kräfte*) fail; (*Mond*) be on the wane; **an Dicke a.** taper; **an Gewicht a.** lose weight; **an Kräften a.** lose strength ‖ **Abnehmen**

n (-s;) decrease; **im A. sein** be on the decrease

Ab'nehmer -in §6 *mf* buyer, consumer; (*Kunde*) customer; (*Hehler*) fence

Ab'neigung *f* (-;-en) (gegen, vor dat) aversion (to, for), dislike (of)

abnorm [ap'nɔrm] *adj* abnormal

Abnormität [apnɔrmi'tɛt] *f* (-;-en) abnormity, monstrosity

ab'nötigen *tr* (dat) extort (from)

ab'nutzen, ab'nützen *tr* wear out ‖ *ref* wear out, become worn out

Ab'nutzung *f* (-;-en) wear and tear; (*Abrieb*) abrasion; (mil) attrition

Ab'öl *n* (-s;-e) used oil

Abonnement [abɔn(ə)'mã] *n* (-s;-s) (auf acc) subscription (to)

Abonnements'karte *f* commutation ticket

Abonnent -in [abɔ'nɛnt(ɪn)] §7 *mf* subscriber

abonnieren [abɔ'nirən] *tr* subscribe to; **abonniert sein auf** (acc) have a subscription to ‖ *intr* (auf acc) subscribe (to)

ab'ordnen *tr* delegate, deputize

Ab'ordnung *f* (-;-en) delegation

Abort [a'bɔrt] *m* (-s;-e) toilet ‖ [a'bɔrt] *m* (-s;-e) abortion

ab'passen *tr* measure, fit; (*abwarten*) watch for; (*auflauern*) waylay

ab'pfeifen §88 *tr* (sport) stop

ab'pflücken *tr* pluck off

ab'placken, ab'plagen *ref* work oneself to death, slave

ab'platzen *intr* (SEIN) come loose

Abprall ['apral] *m* rebound; (*Geschoß*) richochet

ab'prallen *intr* (SEIN) rebound; ricochet

ab'pressen *tr* extort

ab'putzen *tr* clean (off); (*polieren*) polish; (*Mauer*) roughcast, plaster

ab'raten §63 *intr—*j—*m von etw a.* advise s.o. against s.th.

Ab'raum *m* (-es;) rubble; (min) overburden

ab'räumen *tr* clear away; (*Tisch*) clear

ab'reagieren *tr* (*Spannung, Erregung*) work off ‖ *ref* (coll) calm down

ab'rechnen *tr* subtract; (*Spesen*) account for; (com) deduct ‖ *intr* settle accounts

Ab'rechnung *f* (-;-en) (*von Konten*) settlement; (*Abzug*) deduction; **A. halten** balance accounts

Ab'rede *f* agreement, arrangement; **in A. stellen** deny

ab'reden *intr—*j—*m von etw a.* dissuade s.o. from s.th.

ab'reiben *tr* rub off; (*Körper*) rub down

Ab'reise *f* departure

ab'reisen *intr* (SEIN) (nach) depart (for)

ab'reißen §53 *tr* tear off; (*Haus*) tear down; (*Kleid*) wear out ‖ *intr* (SEIN) tear off

ab'richten *tr* (*Tier*) train; (*Pferd*) break in; (*Brett*) dress

Ab'richter -in §6 *mf* trainer

ab'riegeln *tr* (*Tür*) bolt; (mil) seal off

ab'ringen §142 *tr*—j-m etw a. wrest s.th. from s.o.

ab'rinnen §121 *intr* (SEIN) run off, run down

Ab'riß *m* summary, outline; (*Skizze*) sketch

ab'rollen *tr & ref* unroll, unwind || *intr* (SEIN) unroll, unwind

ab'rücken *tr* push away, move back || *intr* (SEIN) clear out; (fig) dissociate oneself; (mil) march off

Ab'ruf *m* recall; **auf A.** on call

ab'rufen §122 *tr* call away; (*Zug*) call out, announce

ab'runden *tr* round off

ab'rupfen *tr* pluck (off)

ab'rüsten *tr & intr* disarm

Ab'rüstung *f* (–;) disarmament

ab'rutschen *intr* (SEIN) slip (off)

absacken ['apzakən] *intr* (SEIN) sink; (*Flugzeug*) pancake

Ab'sage *f* cancellation; (*Ablehnung*) refusal

ab'sagen *tr* cancel || *intr* decline; (*dat*) renounce, repudiate

ab'sägen *tr* saw off

ab'sahnen *tr* (& fig) skim (off)

Ab'satz *m* stop, pause, break; (*Zeileneinrückung*) indentation; (*Abschnitt*) paragraph; (*des Schuhes*) heel; (*der Treppen*) landing; (*Vertrieb*) market, sale(s); **ohne A.** without a break

ab'satzfähig *adj* marketable

Ab'satzgebiet *n* territory (*of a salesman*)

Ab'satzmarkt *m* (com) outlet

Ab'satzstockung *f* slump in sales

ab'saugen *tr* suck off; (*Teppich*) vacuum

Ab'saugventilator *m* exhaust fan

ab'schaben *tr* scrape off

ab'schaffen *tr* abolish, do away with; (*Mißbrauch*) redress; (*Diener*) dismiss

ab'schälen *tr* peel

ab'schalten *tr* switch off

ab'schätzen *tr* (*Wert*) estimate; (*für die Steuer*) assess, appraise

abschätzig ['apˌʃɛtsɪç] *adj* disparaging

Ab'schaum *m* (–[e]s;) (& fig) scum

ab'scheiden §112 *tr* part, sever; (physiol) excrete; (physiol) secrete || *intr* (SEIN) pass away, pass on

Ab'scheu *m* (–[e]s;) (vor *dat*, gegen) abhorrence (of), disgust (at)

ab'scheuern *tr* scrub off, scour; (*Haut*) scrape; (*abnutzen*) wear out

abscheu'lich *adj* atrocious

ab'schicken *tr* send away; (*Post*) mail

ab'schieben §130 *tr* shove off; deport

Abschied ['apˌʃit] *m* (–[e]s;–e) (*Weggang*) departure; (*Entlassung*) dismissal; (mil) discharge; **A. nehmen von** take leave of; (*e–m Amt*) resign, retire from

Ab'schiedsfeier *f* farewell party

Ab'schiedsrede *f* valediction

Ab'schiedsschmaus *m* farewell dinner

ab'schießen §76 *tr* (*Gewehr*) fire, shoot; (*Flugzeug*) shoot down; (*Panzer*) knock out; (rok) launch; **j-n a.** bring about s.o.'s downfall

ab'schinden §167 *tr* skin || *ref* slave

ab'schirmen *tr* screen (off); (gegen) guard (against)

ab'schlachten *tr* butcher; (fig) massacre

Ab'schlag *m* discount; (golf) tee shot; **auf A.** in part payment, on account

ab'schlagen §132 *tr* knock off; (*Baum*) fell; (*Angriff*) repel; (*Bitte*) refuse; **das Wasser a.** pass water || *intr* (golf) tee off

abschlägig ['apˌʃlɛgɪç] *adj* negative; **a. bescheiden** turn down

Ab'schlagszahlung *f* installment

ab'schleifen §88 *tr* grind off; (fig) refine, polish || *ref* become refined

ab'schleppen *tr* drag away, tow away

Ab'schleppwagen *m* tow truck

ab'schleudern *tr* fling off, catapult

ab'schließen §76 *tr* lock (up); (*Straße*) close off; (*Rechnung*) close, settle; (*Bücher*) balance; (*Vertrag*) conclude; (*Rede*) wind up; (*Wette*) wager || *ref* seclude oneself, shut oneself off || *intr* conclude

ab'schließend *adj* definitive; (*Worte*) concluding || *adv* definitively; (*schließlich*) in conclusion

Ab'schluß *m* completion; (*e–s Vertrags*) conclusion; (*Geschäft*) transaction, deal; (*Verkauf*) sale; (*Rechnungs-, Konto-, Buch-*) closing; (mach) seal

ab'schmeicheln *tr*—j-m etw a. coax s.th. out of s.o.

ab'schmelzen §133 *tr* (*Erz*) smelt; (*Schnee*) melt || *intr* (SEIN) melt

ab'schmieren *tr* copy carelessly; (coll) beat up; (aut) lubricate || *intr* (SEIN) (aer) (coll) crash

ab'schnallen *tr* unbuckle, unstrap

ab'schnappen *intr* (SEIN) (coll) stop dead; (coll) die

ab'schneiden §106 *tr* cut (off); (*Hecke*) trim; **den Weg. a.** take a shortcut; **j-m das Wort a.** cut s.o. short; **j-m die Ehre a.** steal s.o.'s good name || *intr*—gut a. do well

Ab'schnitt *m* cut, cutting; (*Teilstück*) part, section; (*im Scheckbuch*) stub; (*Kapitel*) section, paragraph; (math) segment; (mil) sector

ab'schnüren *tr* untie; (surg) ligature; **j-m den Atem a.** choke s.o.

ab'schöpfen *tr* skim off

ab'schrägen *tr & ref* slant, slope

ab'schrauben *tr* unscrew

ab'schrecken §134 *tr* scare off; (*abbringen*) deter

ab'schreiben §62 *tr* copy; (*Schularbeit*) crib; (*uneinbringliche Forderung*) write off; (*Literaturwerk*) plagiarize; (*Wert*) depreciate || *intr* send a refusal

Ab'schreiber –in §6 *mf* plagiarist

Ab'schreibung *f* (–;–en) write-off

ab'schreiten §86 *tr* pace off; (mil) review; **die Front a.** review the troops

Ab'schrift *f* copy, transcript; (com, jur) duplicate

ab'schriftlich *adj & adv* in duplicate

ab'schuften *ref* work oneself to death

ab'schürfen *ref*—**sich** [*dat*] **die Haut a.** skin oneself

Ab'schürfung f (-;-en) abrasion
Ab'schuß m (e-r Waffe) firing; (e-r Rakete) launching; (e-s Panzers) knocking out; (e-s Flugzeugs) downing, kill; (hunt) kill
abschüssig ['apʃ ʏsiç] adj sloping; (steil) steep
Ab'schußrampe f launch pad
ab'schütteln tr shake off
ab'schwächen tr weaken; (vermindern) diminish, reduce; (Farben) tone down || ref (Preis) decline
ab'schweifen intr (SEIN) stray, digress
Ab'schweifung f (-;-en) digression
ab'schwellen §119 intr (SEIN) go down; (Lärm, Gesang) die down
ab'schwenken intr (SEIN) swerve
ab'schwören intr (dat) (dem Glauben) deny; (dem Trunk) swear off
ab'segeln intr (SEIN) set sail
absehbar ['apzeɓar] adj foreseeable
ab'sehen §138 tr foresee; es abgesehen haben auf (acc) be out to get || intr—a. von disregard; refrain from
ab'seifen tr soap down
abseits ['apzaɪts] adv aside; (sport) offside || prep (genit) off
ab'senden §140 tr send (off), dispatch; (Post) mail; (befördern) forward
Ab'sender -in §6 mf sender, dispatcher
Ab'sendung f (-;-en) sending, dispatching; mailing, shipping
ab'sengen tr singe off
Absentismus [apzen'tɪsmʊs] m (-;) absenteeism
ab'setzen tr (Betrag) deduct; (Last) set down; (entwöhnen) wean; (Beamten) remove; (König) depose; (Fallschirmtruppen, Passagiere) drop; (com) sell; (typ) set up || ref settle, set; (mil) disengage || intr stop, pause
Absetzung f (-;-en) dismissal
Ab'sicht f intention, purpose; in der A. with the intention; mit A. on purpose; ohne A. unintentionally
ab'sichtlich adj intentional || adv on purpose, intentionally
ab'sitzen §144 tr (Strafzeit) serve, do || intr (SEIN) (vom Pferde) dismount; a. lassen (chem) let settle
absolut [apzo'lut] adj
absolvieren [apzɔl'virən] tr absolve; (Studien) finish; (Hochschule) graduate from; (Prüfung) pass
abson'derlich adj peculiar, strange
ab'sondern tr separate, segregate; (Kranken) isolate; (physiol) secrete || ref keep aloof
absorbieren [apzɔr'birən] tr absorb
ab'speisen tr feed; j-n mit schönen Worten a. put s.o. off with polite words
abspenstig ['apʃpɛnstɪç] adj—a. machen lure away; j-m a. werden desert s.o.
ab'sperren tr shut off, block off; (Tür) lock; (Strom) cut off; (Gas) turn off
ab'spielen tr play through to the end; (Schallplatte, Tonband) play; (Tonbandaufnahme) play back || ref take place
ab'sprechen §64 tr dispute, deny; (ab-

machen) arrange; j-m das Recht a. zu (inf) dispute s.o.'s right to (inf)
ab'sprechend adj (Urteil) unfavorable; (Kritik) adverse; (tadelnd) disparaging
ab'springen §142 intr (SEIN) jump down, jump off; (Ball) rebound; (Glasur) chip; (abschweifen) digress; (aer) bail out, jump; a. von quit, desert
Ab'sprung m jump; (ins Wasser) dive; (des Balles) rebound
ab'spulen tr unwind, unreel
ab'spülen tr rinse (off)
ab'stammen intr (SEIN) (von) be descended (from); (von) be derived (from)
Abstammung f (-;-en) descent, extraction; (gram) derivation
Ab'stand m distance; (räumlich und zeitlich) interval; A. nehmen von refrain from; A. zahlen pay compensation
abstatten ['apʃtatən] tr (Besuch) pay; (Bericht) file; (Dank) give, return
ab'stauben tr dust off; (sl) swipe
ab'stechen §64 tr (töten) stab; (Rasen) cut; (Hochofen) tap; (Karten) trump || intr—gegen (or von) etwa a. contrast with s.th.
Ab'stecher m (-s;-) side trip; (Umweg) detour; (fig) digression
ab'stecken tr (Haar) unpin, let down; (Kleid) pin, fit; (surv) mark off
ab'stehen §146 intr (entfernt sein) (von) be, stand away (from); (Ohren, usw.) stick out || intr (HABEN & SEIN) (von) refrain (from)
ab'steigen §148 intr (SEIN) get down, descend; in e-m Gasthof a. stay at a hotel
ab'stellen tr (Last) put down; (Radio, Gas, usw.) turn off; (Motor) switch off; (Auto) park; (Mißstand) redress; (mil) detach, assign; a. auf (acc) gear to
Ab'stellraum m storage room
ab'stempeln tr stamp
ab'sterben §149 intr (SEIN) die off; (Pflanzen) wither; (Glieder) get numb
Abstieg ['apʃtik] m (-[e]s;) descent
ab'stimmen tr tune; (com) balance; a. auf (acc) (fig) attune (to) || intr (über acc) vote (on)
Abstinenzler -in [apstɪ'nɛntslər(ɪn)] §6 mf teetotaler
ab'stoppen tr stop; (sport) clock
ab'stoßen §150 tr push off; (Waren) get rid of, sell; (Schulden) pay off; (Geweih) shed; (fig) disgust, sicken; (phys) repel || ref—sich [dat] die Hörner a. (fig) sow one's wild oats || intr (SEIN) shove off
ab'stoßend adj repulsive
abstrakt [ap'ʃtrakt] adj abstract
ab'streichen tr (abwischen) wipe off; (Rasiermesser) strop; (abhaken) check off; (bact) swab; (com) deduct
ab'streifen tr (Handschuh, usw.) take off; (Haut) slough off; (Gewohnheit) break || intr (SEIN) deviate, stray
ab'streiten §86 tr contest, dispute

Ab'strich m (beim Schreiben) down-stroke; (Abzug) cut; (bact) swab
ab'stufen tr (Gelände) terrace; (Farben) shade off
abstumpfen ['apstumpfən] tr blunt
Ab'sturz m fall; (Abhang) precipice; (aer) crash
abstürzen intr (SEIN) fall down; (aer) crash
ab'suchen tr (Gebiet) scour, comb
Ab-szeß [ap'stses] m (-szesses; -szesse) abscess
Abt [apt] m (-[e]s;ⁿe) abbot
ab'takeln tr unrig; (coll) sack, fire
ab'tasten tr probe; (rad) scan
Abtei [ap'taɪ] f (-;-en) abbey
Ab'teil m compartment
ab'teilen tr divide, partition
Ab'teilung f (-;-en) department, division; (im Krankenhaus) ward; (arti) battery; (mil) detachment, unit
Ab'teilungsleiter -in §6 mf department head, section head
Ab'teilungszeichen n hyphen
Äbtissin [ep'tɪsɪn] f (-;-nen) abbess
ab'tönen tr tone down, shade off
ab'töten tr (Bakterien) kill; (das Fleisch) mortify
Abtrag ['aptrak] m (-[e]s;ⁿe)—j-m A. leisten compensate s.o.; j-m A. tun hurt s.o.
ab'tragen §132 tr carry away; (Gebäude) raze; (Kleid) wear out; (Schuld) pay
abträglich ['aptreklɪç] adj detrimental
ab'treiben §62 tr drive away; (Leibesfrucht) abort || intr (SEIN) drift away; vom Kurs a. drift off course
Ab'treibung f (-;-en) abortion
ab'trennen tr separate, detach; (Glied) sever; (Genähtes) unstitch
ab'treten §152 tr wear out (by walking); (aufgeben) cede, turn over || intr (SEIN) retire, resign; (theat) exit
Ab'treter m (-s;-) doormat
Ab'tretung f (-;-en) (von Grundeigentum) transfer; (pol) cession
ab'trocknen tr dry || intr (SEIN) dry
ab'tropfen intr (SEIN) trickle, drip
ab'trudeln intr (SEIN) go into a tailspin; (coll) toddle off, saunter off
abtrünnig ['aptrʏnɪç] adj unfaithful; (eccl) apostate; a. werden defect
Ab'trünnigkeit f (-;) desertion, defection; (eccl) apostasy
ab'tun §154 tr (ablegen) take off; (beiseite schieben) get rid of; (töten) kill; (erledigen) settle; a. als dismiss as; kurz a. make short work of; mit e-m Achselzucken a. shrug off
ab'urteilen tr pass final judgment on
ab'verlangen tr—j-m etw a. demand s.th. of s.o.
ab'wägen §156 tr weigh
ab'wälzen tr roll away; (Schuld) shift
ab'wandeln tr (Thema) vary; (Hauptwort) (gram) decline; (Zeitwort) (gram) conjugate
ab'wandern intr (SEIN) wander off; (Bevölkerung) migrate; (Arbeitskräfte) drift away
Ab'wanderung f (-;-en) exodus, migration

Ab'wandlung f (-;-en) variation; (e-s Hauptwortes) declension; (e-s Zeitwortes) conjugation
ab'warten tr wait for; (Anweisung) await; das bleibt abzuwarten! that remains to be seen! s-e Zeit a. bide one's time || intr wait and see
abwärts ['apverts] adv down, downwards; mit ihm geht es a. (coll) he's going downhill
ab'waschen §158 tr wash (off)
ab'wechseln tr & intr alternate
ab'wechselnd adj alternate
Ab'wechs(e)lung f (-;-en) variation; (Mannigfaltigkeit) variety; (Zerstreuung) diversion, entertainment
Ab'weg m wrong way; auf Abwege führen mislead; auf Abwege geraten go wrong
Ab'wehr f (-;-en) defense; (e-s Stoßes, usw.) warding off; (mil) counter-espionage service
ab'wehren tr ward off, avert
ab'weichen §85 intr (SEIN) deviate, diverge; (verschieden sein) differ
Ab'weichung f (-;-en) deviation; difference; (math) divergence
ab'weiden tr graze on
ab'weisen §118 tr refuse, turn down; (Angriff) repel; (Berufung) deny
ab'weisend adj (gegen) unfriendly (to)
Ab'weisung f (-;-en) refusal; (jur) denial; (mil) repulse
ab'wenden tr turn away, turn aside; (Augen) avert; (Aufmerksamkeit) divert; (Krieg, Gefahr) prevent || §140 & 120 ref (von) turn away (from)
ab'werfen §160 tr throw off; (Bomben) drop; (Blätter, Geweih) shed; (Gewinn) bring in, yield; (Zinsen) bear; (Karten) discard; (Joch) shake off
ab'werten tr devaluate
Ab'wertung f (-;-en) devaluation
abwesend ['apvezənt] adj absent, missing; (fig) absent-minded
Ab'wesenheit f (-;) absence; (fig) absent-mindedness
ab'wickeln tr unwind, unroll; (Geschäfte) transact; (Schulden) settle; (Aktiengesellschaft) liquidate || ref unwind; (fig) develop sich gut a. (com) turn out well
ab'wiegen §57 tr weigh
ab'wischen tr wipe off, wipe clean
Abwurf ['apvurf] m drop(ping); (Bomben) release; (Ertrag) yield
ab'würgen tr wring the neck of; (aut) stall
ab'zahlen tr pay off
ab'zählen tr count off
Ab'zahlung f (-;-en) payment in installments; (Rate) installment; auf A. on terms
Ab'zahlungsgeschäft n deferred-payment system
ab'zapfen tr (Bier) tap; (Blut) draw
Ab'zehrung f emaciation; consumption
Ab'zeichen n distinguishing mark; badge; (mil) decoration
ab'zeichnen tr copy, draw, sketch;

(*Dokument*) initial || *ref* become apparent; (*gegen*) stand out (against)

Ab′ziehbild *n* decal

ab′ziehen §163 *tr* pull off; (*Kunden*) lure away; (*Reifen*) take off; (*Bett*) strip; (*vom Preise*) deduct, knock off; (*vervielfältigen*) run off; (*Abziehbild*) transfer; (*Schlüssel vom Loch*) take out; (*Rasiermesser*) strop; (*Wein*) draw; (*Truppen*) withdraw; (*Aufmerksamkeit*) divert; (arith) deduct; (phot) print; (typ) pull || *intr* (SEIN) depart; (*abmarschieren*) march off; (*Rauch*) disperse

Ab′zug *m* (*e–r Summe*) deduction; (*Rabatt*) rebate, allowance; (*Skonto*) discount; (*am Gewehr*) trigger; (*Weggang*) departure; (*für Wasser*) outlet; (*für Rauch*) escape; (mil) withdrawal; (phot) print; (typ) proof sheet

abzüglich [′aptsyklɪç] *prep* (*genit* or *acc*) less, minus

Ab′zugsbogen *m* proof sheet

Ab′zugspapier *n* duplicating paper; (phot) printing paper

Ab′zugsrohr *n* drainpipe

ab′zweigen *tr* divert || *intr* (SEIN) branch off

ach [ax] *interj* oh!; ah!; **ach so!** oh, I see!; **ach was!** nonsense!; **ach wo!** of course not!

Achse [′aksə] *f* (*–;–n*) axis; (*am Wagen*) axle; (mach) shaft; **auf der A.** on the move; **per A.** by truck; by rail

Achsel [′aksəl] *f* (*–;–n*) shoulder; **auf die leichte A. nehmen** make light of; **mit den Achseln zucken** shrug one's shoulders; **über die Achseln ansehen** look down on

Ach′selbein *n* shoulder blade

Ach′selgrube *f*, **Ach′selhöhle** *f* armpit

Ach′selträger –in §6 *mf* opportunist

acht [axt] *adj* eight; **alle a. Tage** once a week; **in a. Tagen** within a week; **über a. Tage** a week from today || **Acht** *f* (*–;–en*) eight || *f* (*–;*) (*Bann*) outlawry; (*Obacht*) care, attention; **in die A. erklären** outlaw; (fig) ostracize; **sich in a. nehmen vor** (*dat*) watch out for

achtbar [′axtbar] *adj* respectable

achte [′axtə] §9 *adj & pron* eight

achteckig [′axtekɪç] *adj* octagonal

Achtel [′axtəl] *n* (*–s;–*) eighth (part)

achten [′axtən] *tr* (*beachten*) respect; (*schätzen*) esteem; (*erachten*) consider || *intr*—**a. auf** (*acc*) pay attention to; **a. darauf, daß** see to it that

ächten [′eçtən] *tr* outlaw, proscribe; (*gesellschaftlich*) ostracize

ach′tenswert *adj* respectable

achter(n) [′axtər(n)] *adv* aft, astern

acht′geben §80 *intr* (*auf acc*) pay attention (*to*); **gib acht!** watch out!

acht′los *adj* careless

Acht′losigkeit *f* (*–;*) carelessness

acht′sam *adj* [′axtzam] cautious; (*auf acc*) attentive (to); (*auf acc*) careful (of)

Acht′samkeit *f* (*–;*) carefulness

---

achttägig [′axttegɪç] *adj* eight-day; eight-day old; one-week

Ach′tung *f* (*–;*) attention; (**vor** *dat*) respect (for); **A.!** watch out!; (mil) attention!

ach′tungsvoll *adj* respectful; (*als Briefschluß*) Yours truly

acht′zehn *adj & pron* eighteen || **Achtzehn** *f* (*–;–en*) eighteen

acht′zehnte §9 *adj & pron* eighteenth

achtzig [′axtsɪç] *adj* eighty

achtziger [′axtsɪgər] *invar adj* of the eighties; **die a. Jahre** the eighties || **Achtziger –in** §6 *mf* octogenarian

achtzigste [′axtsɪçstə] §9 *adj* eightieth

ächzen [′eçtsən] *intr* groan, moan

Acker [′akər] *m* (*–s;±*) soil, (arable) land, field; (*Maß*) acre

Ackerbau (**Ak′kerbau**) *m* farming

ackerbautreibend [′akərbautraibənt] *adj* agricultural

Ackerbestellung (**Ak′kerbestellung**) *f* cultivation, tilling

Ackerland (**Ak′kerland**) *n* arable land

ackern [′akərn] *tr & intr* plow

addieren [a′dirən] *tr & intr* add

Addiermaschine [a′dirma/inə] *f* adding machine

Addition [adɪ′tsjon] *f* (*–;–en*) addition

ade [a′de] *interj* farewell!; bye-bye!

Adel [′adəl] *m* (*–s;*) nobility, noble birth; (*edle Gesinnung*) noble-mindedness

ad(e)lig [′ad(ə)lɪç] *adj* noble, titled; nobleman's || **Ad(e)lige** §5 *m* nobleman || §5 *f* noblewoman

A′delsstand *m* nobility

Ader [′adər] *f* (*–;–n*) vein

adieu [a′djø] *interj* adieu!

Adjektiv [′atjektif] *n* (*–s;–e*) adjective

Adjutant –in [atju′tant(ɪn)] §7 *mf* adjutant; (*–s Generals*) aide(-de-camp)

Adler [′adlər] *m* (*–s;–*) eagle

Ad′lernase *f* aquiline nose

Admiral [atmɪ′ral] *m* (*–[e]s;–e*) admiral

Admiralität [atmɪralɪ′tet] *f* (*–;*) admiralty

adoptieren [adɔp′tirən] *tr* adopt

Adoption [adɔp′tsjon] *f* (*–;–en*) adoption

Adoptiv– [adɔp′tif] *comb. fm.* adoptive

Adressat –in [adre′sat(ɪn)] §7 *mf* addressee; (*e–r Warensendung*) consignee

Adresse [a′dresə] *f* (*–;–n*) address; **an die falsche A. kommen** (fig) bark up the wrong tree; **per A.** care of

adressieren [adrə′sirən] *tr* address; (*Waren*) consign

adrett [a′dret] *adj* smart, neat

Advent [at′vent] *m* (*–s;–e*) Advent

Adverb [at′verp] *n* (*–[e]s;–ien* [-ɪ-ən]) adverb

Advokat –in [atvo′kat(ɪn)] §7 *mf* lawyer

Affäre [a′ferə] *f* (*–;–n*) affair

Affe [′afə] *m* (*–s;–n*) ape, monkey; **e–n Affen haben** (sl) be drunk

Affekt [a′fekt] *m* (*–[e]s;–e*) emotion; (*Leidenschaft*) passion

affektiert [afek′tirt] *adj* affected

Affektiert'heit f (-;-en) affectation
äffen ['ɛfən] tr ape, mimic
Af'fenliebe f doting
Af'fenpossen pl monkeyshines
Af'fenschande f crying shame
Af'fentheater n farce, joke
affig ['afɪç] adj affected; (geckenhaft) foppish
Äffin ['ɛfɪn] f (-;-nen) female ape, female monkey
Afrika ['afrɪka] n (-s;) Africa
afrikanisch [afrɪ'kanɪʃ] adj African
After ['aftər] m (-s;-) anus
AG, A.G., A.-G. abbr (Aktiengesellschaft) stock company
ägäisch [ɛ'ge·ɪʃ] adj Aegean
Agende [a'gendə] f (-;-n) memo pad
Agent -in [a'gent(ɪn)] §7 mf agent, representative; (Geheim-) secret agent
Agentur [agen'tur] f (-;-en) agency
aggressiv [agrɛ'sif] adj aggressive
Ägide [ɛ'gidə] f (-;-n) aegis
Agio ['aʒi·o] n (-s;-s) premium
Agitation [agɪta'tsjon] f (-;-en) agitation, rabble-rousing
Agi-tator [agɪ'tator] m (-s;-tatoren [ta'torən] (& mach) agitator
agitatorisch [agɪta'torɪʃ] adj inflammatory
agitieren [agɪ'tirən] intr agitate
Agraffe [a'grafə] f (-;-n) clasp
agrarisch [a'grorɪʃ] adj agrarian
Ägypten [ɛ'gyptən] n (-s;) Egypt
Ägypter -in [ɛ'gyptər(ɪn)] §6 mf Egyptian
ägyptisch [ɛ'gyptɪʃ] adj Egyptian
ah [ɑ] interj ah!
Ahle ['alə] f (-;-n) awl, punch
Ahn [ɑn] m (-(e)s & -en;-en) ancestor
ahnden ['andən] tr (strafen) punish; (rächen) avenge
Ahn'dung f (-;) revenge
ähneln ['ɛnəln] intr (dat) resemble
ahnen ['anən] tr have a premonition of, suspect; (erfassen) divine
Ah'nentafel f family tree
ähnlich ['ɛnlɪç] adj alike; (dat) similar (to), analogous (to): das sieht ihm ä. that's just like him; j-m ä sehen look like s.o.
Ähn'lichkeit f (-;-en) (mit) resemblance (to)
Ah'nung f ['anʊn] f (-;-en) (Vorgefühl) presentiment, hunch; (böse) misgiving; (Argwohn) suspicion; keine A. haben have no idea
ah'nungslos adj unsuspecting
ah'nungsvoll adj full of misgivings
Ahorn ['ahorn] m (-[e]s;-e) maple
Ähre ['ɛrə] f (-;-n) (Korn) ear; (e-r Blume) spike; Ähren lesen glean
Als ['a·ɪs] n (-;-) (mus) A sharp
Akade-mie [akadə'mi] f (-;-mien ['mi·ən] academy; university
Akademiker -in [aka'demɪkər(ɪn)] §6 mf university graduate
akademisch [aka'demɪʃ] adj academic; university
Akazie [a'katsjə] f (-;-n) acacia
akklimatisieren [aklimatɪ'zirən] tr acclimate || ref become acclimated
Akkord [a'kort] m (-[e]s;-e) chord;

(Vereinbarung) accord; (com) settlement; im A. arbeiten do piecework
Akkord'arbeit f piecework
Akkordeon [a'kordɛ·ɔn] n (-s;-s) accordion
akkreditieren [akredɪ'tirən] tr accredit; open an account for
Akkreditiv [akredɪ'tif] n (-[e]s;-e) (Beglaubigungsschreiben) credentials; (com) letter of credit
Akkumula·tor [akumu'lator] m (-s; -toren ['torən]) storage battery
akkurat [aku'rat] adj accurate
Akkusativ ['akuzatif] m (-[e]s;-e) accusative (case)
Akrobat [akro'bat] §7 m acrobat
Akrobatik [akro'batɪk] f (-;) acrobatics
Akrobatin [akro'batɪn] §7 f acrobat
Akt [akt] m (-[e]s;-e) act, action; (paint) nude; (theat) act
Akte ['aktə] f (-;-n) document; record, file; (jur) instrument; zu den Akten legen file; (fig) shelve
Ak'tendeckel m file folder
Ak'tenklammer f paper clip
Ak'tenmappe f brief case, portfolio
ak'tenmäßig adj documentary
Ak'tenschrank m file cabinet
Ak'tentasche f brief case
Ak'tenzeichen n file number
Aktie ['aktsjə] f (-;-n) stock
Ak'tienbesitzer -in §6 mf stockholder
Ak'tienbörse f stock exchange
Ak'tiengesellschaft f corporation
Ak'tieninhaber -in §6 mf stockholder
Ak'tienmakler -in §6 mf stockbroker
Ak'tienmarkt m stock market
Ak'tienschein m stock certificate
Aktion [ak'tsjon] f (-;-en) action; (Unternehmung) campaign, drive; (polizeiliche) raid; (mil) operation; Aktionen activity
Aktionär -in [aktsjo'ner(ɪn)] §8 mf stockholder
aktiv [ak'tif] adj active; (Bilanz) favorable; (chem) activated; (gram) active; a. werden become a member (of a student club) || Aktiv n (-s;) (gram) active voice
Aktiva [ak'tiva] pl assets; A. und Passiva assets and liabilities
Aktiv'posten m asset
aktuell [aktu'ɛl] adj current, topical || Aktuelle pl (journ) newsbriefs
Akustik [a'kustɪk] f (-;) acoustics
akustisch [a'kustɪʃ] adj acoustic(al)
akut [a'kut] adj acute
Akzent [ak'tsent] m (-[e]s;-e) accent (mark); (Nachdruck) emphasis; (phonet) stress
akzentuieren [aktsentu'irən] tr accent; (fig) stress, accentuate
akzeptieren [aktsep'tirən] tr accept
Alabaster [ala'bastər] m (-s;) alabaster
Alarm [a'larm] m (-[e]s;-e) alarm; A. blasen (or schlagen) (mil & fig) sound the alarm; blinder A. false alarm
Alarm'anlage f alarm system; warning system (in civil defense)
alarm'bereit adj on the alert

Alarm′bereitschaft *f* (state of) readiness; **in A.** on the alert

alarmieren [alar′miːrən] *tr* alert; alarm

Alaun [a′laun] *m* (-s;-e) alum

Alaun′stift *m* steptic pencil

Albanien [al′banjən] *n* (-s;) Albania

albanisch [al′banɪʃ] *adj* Albanian

albern [′albərn] *adj* silly

Al-bum [′album] *n* (-s;-ben [bən]) album

Alchimist [alçɪ′mɪst] §7 *m* alchemist

Alge [′algə] *f* (-;-n) alga; seaweed

Algebra [′algebra] *f* (-;) algebra

algebraisch [algə′braɪʃ] *adj* algebraic

Algerien [al′gerjən] *n* (-s;) Algeria

algerisch [al′gerɪʃ] *adj* Algerian

Algier [′alʒir] *n* (-s;) Algiers

Alibi [′alibi] *n* (-s;-s) alibi

Alimente [alɪ′mɛntə] *pl* child support

alimentieren [alɪmɛn′tirən] *tr* pay alimony to; (*Kind*) support

Alkohol [′alkohol] *m* (-s;-e) alcohol

al′koholfrei *adj* non-alcoholic

Alkoholiker –in [alkə′holikər(ɪn)] §6 *mf* alcoholic

alkoholisch [alkə′holɪʃ] *adj* alcoholic

all [al] *adj* all; (*jeder*) every; (*jeder beliebige*) any; **alle beide** both (of them); **alles Gute!** take care!; (*im Brief*) best wishes; **alle zehn Minuten** every ten minutes; **alle zwei Tage** every other day; **auf alle Fälle** in any case ‖ *indef pron* each, each one; everyone, everything; all; **aller und jeder** each and every one; **in allem** all told; **vor allem** above all, first of all

alle [′alə] *adv* all gone; **a. machen** finish off; **a. sein** be all gone; **a. werden** run low

Allee [a′le] *f* (-;-n) (tree-lined) avenue; (tree-lined) walk

Allego-rie [alego′ri] *f* (-;-rien [′ri-ən]) allegory

allegorisch [ale′gorɪʃ] *adj* allegoric(al)

allein [a′laɪn] *adj* alone ‖ *adv* alone; only; however; no fewer than, no less than; **schon a. der Gedanke** the mere thought

Allein′berechtigung *f* exclusive right

Allein′flug *m* solo flight

Allein′handel *m* monopoly

Allein′herrschaft *f* autocracy

Allein′herrscher –in §6 *mf* autocrat

allei′nig *adj* (*ausschließlich*) sole, exclusive; (*einzig*) only

allein′stehend *adj* alone in the world; (*unverheiratet*) single; (*Gebäude*) detached

Allein′verkauf *m*, **Allein′vertrieb** *m* franchise

al′lemal *adv* every time; **ein für a.** once and for all

al′lenfalls *adv* if need be; (*vielleicht*) possibly; (*höchstens*) at most

allenthalben [′alənt′halbən] *adv* everywhere

al′lerart *invar adj* all kinds of

al′lerbe′ste §9 *adj* very best; **aufs a.** in the best possible manner

al′lerdings′ *adv* (*gewiß*) certainly (*strong affirmative answer*); (*zugestehend*) admittedly, I must admit

al′lerer′ste §9 *adj* very first, first ... of all

Aller·gie [aler′gi] (-;-gien [′gi-ən]) allergy

allergisch [a′lergɪʃ] *adj* allergic

al′lerhand′ *invar adj* all kinds of; (*viel*) a lot of ‖ *indef pron* —**das ist a.!** that's great!; **das ist doch a.!** the nerve!

Allerhei′ligen *invar n* All Saints' Day

allerlei [′alər′laɪ] *invar adj* all kinds of ‖ **Allerlei** *n* (-s;-s) hotchpotch; (mus) medley

al′lerlet′zte §9 *adj* very last, last of all; latest

al′lerliebste [′alər′lipstə] §9 *adj* dearest ... of all; (*Kind*) sweet

al′lermei′ste §9 *adj* most; **am allermeisten** most of all; chiefly

al′lernäch′ste §9 *adj* very next

al′lerneu′este §9 *adj* latest, newest

Allersee′len *invar n* All Souls' Day

allesamt [alə′zamt] *adv* all together

al′lezeit *adv* always

Allge′genwart *f* omnipresence

all′gemein *adj* general, universal

All′gemeinheit *f* universality; (*Öffentlichkeit*) public

Allheil′mittel *n* cure-all

Allianz [alɪ′ants] *f* (-;-en) alliance

alliieren [alɪ′irən] *ref*—**sich a. mit** ally oneself with

alliiert [alɪ′irt] *adj* allied ‖ **Alliierte** §5 *mf* ally

alljähr′lich *adj* annual, yearly

All′macht *f* omnipotence

allmäch′tig *adj* omnipotent, almighty

allmählich [al′meliç] *adj* gradual

allnächt′lich *adj* nightly

allseitig [′alzaitɪç] *adj* all-round ‖ *adv* from all sides, on all sides

All′tag *m* daily routine

alltäg′lich *adj* daily; (fig) everyday

all′tags *adv* daily; (*wochentags*) weekdays

All′tags- *comb.fm.* everyday; (fig) commonplace

All′tagsmensch *m* common man

All′tagswort *n* (-[e]s;-er) household word

allwissend [al′vɪsənt] *adj* omniscient

allwö′chentlich *adj & adv* weekly

allzu- *comb.fm.* all too

all′zumal *adv* one and all, all together

all′zusammen *adv* all together

Alm [alm] *f* (-;-en) Alpine meadow

Almanach [′almanax] *m* (-[e]s;-e) almanac

Almosen [′almozen] *n* (-s;-) alms

Alp [alp] *m* (-[e]s;-e) elf, goblin; (*Alptraum*) nightmare

Alp′druck *m* (-[e]s;), **Alp′drücken** *n* (-s;) nightmare

Alpen [′alpən] *pl* Alps

Alphabet [alfa′bet] *n* (-[e]s;-e) alphabet

alphabetisch [alfa′betɪʃ] *adj* alphabetical

alpin [al′pin] *adj* alpine

als [als] *adv* as, like ‖ *conj* than; when, as; but, except; **als ob** as if

alsbald′ *adv* presently, immediately

alsdann′ *adv* then, thereupon

also ['alzo] *adv* so, thus; therefore, consequently; **na a.!** well then!

alt [alt] *adj* (**älter** ['eltər], **älteste** ['eltəstə] §9) *adj* old; (*bejahrt*) aged; (*gebraucht*) second-hand; (*gestanden*) stale; (*antik*) antique; (*Sprache*) ancient || **Alt** *m* (-[e]s;-e) contralto || **Alte** §5 *m* (coll) old man; **die Alten** the ancients; **mein Alter** (coll) my husband || **Alte** §5 *f* (coll) old woman; **meine Alte** (coll) my wife

Altan [al'tɑn] *m* (-[e]s;-e), **Altane** [al'tɑnə] *f* (-;-n) balcony, gallery

Altar [al'tɑr] *m* (-[e]s;ːe) altar

alt'bewährt *adj* long-standing

Alt'eisen *n* scrap iron

Alt'eisenhändler *m* junk dealer

Alter ['altər] *n* (-s;-) age; (*Greisen-*) old age; (*Zeit-*) epoch; (*Dienst-*) seniority; **er ist in meinem A.** he is my age; **im A. von** at the age of; **mittleren Alters** middle-aged

altern ['altərn] *intr* (SEIN) age

Alternative [alterna'tivə] *f* (-;-n) alternative

Al'tersgrenze *f* age limit; (*für Beamte*) retirement age

Al'tersheim *n* home for the aged

Al'tersrente *f* old-age pension

al'tersschwach *adj* decrepit; senile

Al'tersschwäche *f* (feebleness of) old age

Al'tersversorgungskasse *f* old-age pension fund

Altertum ['altərtum] *n* (-s;) antiquity

altertümlich ['altərtymlɪç] *adj* ancient; (*Möbel*) antique; (*veraltet*) archaic

Al'tertumsforscher -in §6 *mf* archaeologist; (*Antiquar*) antiquarian

Al'tertumskunde *f*, **Al'tertumswissenschaft** *f* study of antiquity; classical studies

althergebracht ['alt'hergəbraxt] *adj* long-standing, traditional

alther'kömmlich *adj* ancient, traditional

Altist [al'tɪst] §7 *m* alto (*singer*)

Altistin [al'tɪstɪn] §7 *f* contralto (*female singer*)

alt'klug *adj* precocious

ältlich ['eltlɪç] *adj* elderly

Alt'meister *m* past master; (sport) ex-champion

alt'modisch *adj* old-fashioned

Alt'stadt *f* old (part of the) city

Alt'stadtsanierung *f* urban renewal

Alt'stimme *f* alto; contralto (*female voice*)

altväterlich ['altfetərlɪç], **altväterisch** ['altfetərɪʃ] *adj* old-fashioned; old-time

Alt'warenhändler -in §6 *mf* second-hand dealer

Altweibersommer [alt'vaɪbərzɔmər] *m* Indian summer; (*Spinnweb*) gossamer

Aluminium [alu'minjum] *n* (-s;) aluminum

am [am] *contr* **an dem**

amalgamieren [amalga'mirən] *tr* amalgamate

Amateur [ama'tør] *m* (-s;-e) amateur

Amazone [ama'tsonə] *f* (-;-n) Amazon

Am-boß ['ambɔs] *m* (-bosses;-bosse) anvil

ambulant [ambu'lant] *adj* ambulatory || *adv*—**a. Behandelte** out-patient

Ambulanz [ambu'lants] *f* (-;-en) out-patient clinic; (*Krankenwagen*) ambulance

Ameise ['amaɪzə] *f* (-;-n) ant

Amerika [a'merɪka] *n* (-s;) America

Amerikaner -in [amerɪ'kɑnər(ɪn)] §6 *mf* American

amerikanisch [amerɪ'kɑnɪʃ] *adj* American

Ami ['ami] *m* (-s;-s) (sl) Yank || *f* (-;-s) American cigarette

Amme ['amə] *f* (-;-n) nurse, wet-nurse

Amnes•tie [amnes'ti] *f* (-;-tien ['ti·ən]) amnesty

amnestieren [amnes'tirən] *tr* pardon

A•mor ['amɔr] *m* (-s;-moren ['morən]) (myth) Cupid

Amortisation [amɔtiza'tsjon] *f* (-;-en) amortization

Amortisations'kasse *f* sinking fund

amortisieren [amɔrti'zirən] *tr* amortize

Ampel ['ampəl] *f* (-;-n) hanging lamp; (*Verkehrs-*) traffic light

Ampere [am'per] *n* (-s;-) ampere

Amphibie [am'fibjə] *f* (-;-n) amphibian

Amphi'bienpanzerwagen *m* amphibious tank

Amphitheater [am'fite·atər] *n* (-s;-) amphitheater

Ampulle [am'pulə] *f* (-;-n) phial

Amputation [amputa'tsjon] *f* (-;-en) amputation

amputieren [ampu'tirən] *tr* amputate

Amputierte [ampu'tirtə] §5 *mf* amputee

Amsel ['amzəl] *f* (-;-n) blackbird

Amt [amt] *n* (-[e]s;ːer) office; (*Pflicht*) duty, function; (dipl) post; (eccl) divine service; (telp) exchange

amtieren [am'tirən] *intr* be in office, hold office; (eccl) officiate

amt'lich *adj* official

Amts- comb.fm. official, of (an) office

Amts'antritt *m* inauguration

Amts'befugnis *f* competence

Amts'bereich *m* jurisdiction

Amts'bewerber -in §6 *mf* office seeker

Amts'bezirk *m* jurisdiction

Amts'blatt *n* official bulletin

Amts'eid *m* oath of office

Amts'enthebung *f* dismissal

Amts'führung *f* administration

amts'gemäß *adj* official || *adv* officially

Amts'gericht *n* district court

Amts'gerichtsrat *m* (official rank of) district-court judge

Amts'geschäfte *pl* official duties

Amts'gewalt *f* (official) authority

Amts'handlung *f* official act

Amts'niederlegung *f* resignation

Amts'schimmel *m* bureaucracy; (coll) red tape

Amts'siegel *n* seal of office

Amts'sprache f official language; (coll) officialese, gobbledygook
Amts'tracht f robes
Amts'träger –in §6 mf officeholder
Amts'verletzung f misconduct in office
Amts'weg m—**auf dem Amtswege** through official channels
Amts'zeichen n (telp) dial tone
Amulett [amu'let] n (–[e]s;–e) amulet
amüsant [amy'zant] adj amusing
amüsieren [amy'zirən] tr amuse, entertain || ref amuse oneself; (sich gut unterhalten) enjoy oneself
an [an] adv on; onward || prep (dat) at, against, on, upon, by, to; (Grad, Maß) in; **an sich** per se; **an und für sich** properly speaking; **es ist an dir zu** (inf) it's up to you to (inf) || prep (acc) at, on, upon, against, to
analog [ana'lok] adj analogous
Analo·gie [analo'gi] f (–;–gien ['gi·ən]) analogy
Analphabet –in [analfa'bet(ın)] §7 mf illiterate
Analphabetentum [analfa'betəntum] n (–s;), **Analphabetismus** [analfabe-'tısmus] m (–;) illiteracy
analphabetisch [analfa'betıʃ] adj illiterate
Analyse [ana'lyzə] f (–;–n) analysis; (gram) parsing; **durch A.** analytically
analysieren [analy'zirən] tr analyze; (gram) parse
Analy·sis [a'nɑlyzıs] f (–;–sen [ana-'lyzən]) (math) analysis
Analytiker –in [ana'lytıkər(ın)] §6 mf analyst
analytisch [ana'lytıʃ] adj analytic(al)
Anämie [anɛ'mi] f (–;) anemia
anämisch [an'ɛmıʃ] adj anemic
Ananas ['ananas] f (–;–se) pineapple
Anarchie [anar'çi] f (–;) anarchy
anästhesieren [anɛste'zirən] tr anesthetize
Anästheti·kum [anɛs'tetıkum] n (–s; –ka [ka]) anesthetic
an'atmen tr breathe on
Anato·mie [anato'mi] f (–;–mien ['mi·ən]) anatomy
anatomisch [ana'tomıʃ] adj anatomical
an'backen §50 tr bake gently || intr (HABEN & SEIN) cake on
an'bahnen tr pave the way for
anbandeln ['anbandəln] intr—**a. mit** flirt with
An'bau m (–[e]s;) cultivation || m (–[e]s;–bauten) annex, new wing
an'bauen tr cultivate; (Gebäudeteil) add on
An'baufläche f (arable) acreage
An'baumöbel pl sectional furniture
An'beginn m outset
an'behalten §90 tr keep (garment) on
anbei [an'baɪ] adv enclosed (herewith)
an'beißen §53 tr bite into, take the first bite of || intr nibble at the bait; (fig) bite
an'belangen tr—**was mich anbelangt** as far as I am concerned, as for me
an'bellen tr bark at
anberaumen ['anbəraumən] tr schedule
an'beten tr (& fig) worship

An'betracht m—**in A.** (genit) in consideration of, in view of
an'betteln tr bum, chisel
An'betung f (–;) worship
an'betungswürdig adj adorable
an'bieten §58 tr offer || ref offer one's services
an'binden §59 tr tie (up) || intr—**mit j–m a.** pick a quarrel with s.o.
an'blasen §61 tr blow at, blow on
An'blick m look, view, sight
an'blicken tr look at; (besehen) view; (mustern) eye
an'blinzeln tr wink at
an'brechen §64 tr (Vorräte) break into; (Flasche, Kiste) open || intr (SEIN) (Tag) dawn; (Nacht) come on
an'brennen §97 tr light || intr (SEIN) catch fire; (Speise) burn
an'bringen §65 tr bring, fetch; (befestigen) (an acc) attach (to): (Bitte) make; (Klage) lodge; (Geld) invest; (Tochter) marry off; (Waren) sell, get rid of; (Bemerkung) insert; (Licht, Lampe) install; (Geld) (coll) blow
An'bruch m break; **bei A. der Nacht** at nightfall; **bei A. des Tages** at daybreak
an'brüllen tr roar at
Andacht ['andaxt] f (–;–en) devotion; (Gottesdienst) devotions
andächtig ['andɛçtıç] adj devout
an'dauern intr continue, last; (hartnäckig sein) persist
An'denken n (–s;–) remembrance; souvenir; **zum A. an** (acc) in remembrance of
andere ['andərə] §9 adj & pron other; (folgend) next; **ein anderer** another; another one; **kein anderer** no one else
ändern ['endərn] tr change; (Wortlaut) modify || ref change
andernfalls ['andərn'fals] adv (or) else
anders ['andərs] adj else; (als) different (from); **a. werden** change || adv otherwise differently
an'dersartig adj of a different kind
anderseits ['andər'zaɪts] adv on the other hand
an'derswo adv somewhere else
anderthalb ['andərt'halp] invar adj one and a half
Än'derung f (–;–n) change, variation; modification
Än'derungsantrag m amendment
anderwärts ['andər'verts] adv elsewhere
anderweitig ['andər'vaɪtıç] adj other, further || adv otherwise; elsewhere
an'deuten tr indicate, suggest; (anspielen) hint at, allude to; (zu verstehen geben) imply, intimate
an'deutungsweise adv by way of suggestion
an'dichten tr—**j–m etw a.** impute s.th. to s.o.
An'drang m rush; crowd; heavy traffic; (von Arbeit) pressure
an'drehen tr turn on; **j–m etw a.** palm s.th. off on s.o.

an'drohen *tr*—j—m etw a. threaten s.o. with s.th.

an'drücken *tr*—etw a. an (*acc*) press s.th. against

an'eignen *ref*—**sich** [*dat*] **a.** appropriate; (*Gewohnheit*) acquire; (*Meinungen*) adopt; (*Sprache*) master; (*widerrechtlich*) appropriate, usurp

aneinan'der *adv* together

aneinan'dergeraten §63 *intr* (SEIN) come to blows

Anekdote [anɛk'dotə] *f* (-;-n) anecdote

an'ekeln *tr* disgust, nauseate

an'empfehlen §147 *tr* recommend

An'erbieten *n* (-s;-) offer, proposal

an'erkennbar *adj* recognizable

an'erkennen §97 *tr* (**als**) recognize (as); (**als**) acknowledge (as); (*Schuld*) admit; (*billigen*) approve; (*lobend*) appreciate; (*Anspruch*) allow; **nicht a.** repudiate, disown; (*sport*) disallow

An'erkennung *f* (-;-en) acknowledgement; recognition; appreciation; admission; **lobende A.** honorable mention

anfachen ['anfaxən] *tr* (*Feuer*) fan; (*Gefühle*) inflame; (*Haß*) stir up

an'fahren §71 *tr* (*herbeibringen*) carry, convey; (*anstoßen*) run into; (fig) snap at; (naut) run afoul of ‖ *intr* (SEIN) drive up; (*losfahren*) start off

An'fall *m* attack

an'fallen §72 *tr* attack, assail ‖ *intr* (SEIN) accumulate, accrue

anfällig ['anfɛlɪç] *adj* (**für**) susceptible (to)

An'fang *m* beginning, start; **von A. an** from the very beginning

an'fangen §73 *tr & intr* begin, start

Anfänger –**in** ['anfɛŋər(ɪn)] §6 *mf* beginner; (*Neuling*) novice

anfänglich ['anfɛŋlɪç] *adj* initial

an'fangs *adv* at the start, initially

An'fangsbuchstabe *m* initial (letter)

An'fangsgründe *pl* rudiments, elements

an'fassen *tr* take hold of; (*behandeln*) handle, touch ‖ *intr* lend a hand

an'faulen *intr* (SEIN) begin to rot

anfechtbar ['anfɛçtbar] *adj* debatable, questionable; (jur) contestable

an'fechten §74 *tr* (*Richtigkeit*) contest; (*beunruhigen*) trouble; (jur) challenge

An'fechtung *f* (-;-en) (eccl) temptation; (jur) challenge

an'fertigen *tr* make, manufacture

an'feuchten *tr* moisten, wet

an'feuern *tr* inflame; (sport) cheer

an'flehen *tr* implore

an'fliegen §57 *tr* (aer) approach

An'flug *m* (*Anzeichen*) suggestion, trace; (*oberflächliche Kenntnis*) smattering; (*dünner Überzug*) film; **A. von Bart** down; **leichter A. von** slight case of

an'fordern *tr* call for, demand; (mil) requisition

an'fragen *intr* (über *acc*, wegen, nach) ask (about *s.th.*); (**bei**) inquire (of *s.o.*)

an'fressen §70 *tr* gnaw; (*Metall*) corrode

anfreunden ['anfrɔɪndən] *ref* (**mit**) make friends (with)

an'frieren §77 *intr* (SEIN) begin to freeze; **a. an** (*acc*) freeze onto

an'fügen *tr* (an *acc*) join (to)

an'fühlen *tr & ref* feel

Anfuhr ['anfur] *f* (-;-en) delivery

an'führen *tr* lead; (*Worte*) quote; (*Grund*) adduce; (*täuschen*) take in, fool; (mil) lead, command

An'führer –**in** §6 *mf* leader; (mil) commander; (pol) boss

An'führung *f* quotation

An'führungszeichen *n* quotation mark

an'füllen *tr & ref* fill up

An'gabe *f* (*Erklärung*) statement; (*beim Zollamt*) declaration; (coll) showing off; Angaben data; directions; **nähere Angaben machen** give particulars; **wer hat die A.?** whose serve is it?

an'geben §80 *tr* (*mitteilen*) state; (*bestimmen*) appoint; (*anzeigen*) inform against; (*vorgeben*) pretend; (*Preis*) quote ‖ *intr* (coll) show off; (cards) deal first; (tennis) serve

An'geber –**in** §6 *mf* informer; (*Prahler*) show-off

angeblich ['angeblɪç] *adj* alleged

an'geboren *adj* innate, natural

An'gebot *n* offer; (*bei Auktionen*) bid; **A. und Nachfrage** supply and demand

angebracht ['angəbraxt] *adj* advisable; **es für a. halten zu** (*inf*) see fit to (*inf*); **gut a.** appropriate; **schlecht a.** ill-timed

angegossen ['angəgosən] *adj*—**wie a. sitzen** fit like a glove

angeheiratet ['angəhaɪratət] *adj* related by marriage

angeheitert ['angəhaɪtərt] *adj* tipsy

an'gehen §82 *tr* charge, attack; (*Problem*) tackle; **das geht dich gar nichts an** that's none of your business; **j—n um etw a.** approach s.o. for s.th. ‖ *intr* (SEIN) begin; (*zulässig sein*) be allowable; (*leidlich sein*) be tolerable; **das geht nicht an** that won't do

an'gehend *adj* future, prospective

an'gehören *intr* (*dat*) be a member (of)

Angehörige ['angəhørɪgə] §5 *mf* member; **nächste Angehörigen** next of kin; **seine Angehörigen** his relatives

Angeklagte ['angəklaktə] §5 *mf* defendant; (*wenn verhaftet*) suspect

Angel ['anəl] *f* (-;-n) fishing tackle; (*e-r Tür*) hinge; **aus den Angeln heben** (& fig) unhinge

an'gelangen *intr* (SEIN) (**an** *dat*, **bei**) arrive (at)

an'gelegen *adj*—**sich** [*dat*] **etw a. sein lassen** make s.th. one's business

An'gelegenheit *f* (-;-en) affair, business

angelehnt ['angələnt] *adj* ajar

An'gelgerät *n* fishing tackle

An'gelhaken *m* fish(ing) hook

angeln ['anəln] *tr & intr* (**nach**) fish (for)

An'gelpunkt *m* pivot, central point

An'gelrute *f* fishing rod

angelsächsisch [ˈaŋəlzeksɪʃ] *adj* Anglo-Saxon

An'gelschnur *f* fishing line

angemessen [ˈaŋɡəmesən] *adj* suitable (*ausreichend*) adequate; (*annehmbar*) reasonable; (*Benehmen*) proper; (*dat*) in keeping (with); **für a. halten** think fit

angenehm [ˈaŋɡənem] *adj* pleasant; **sehr a! pleased to meet you!**

angeregt [ˈaŋɡərekt] *adj* lively

angeschlagen [ˈaŋɡəˌlagən] *adj* chipped; (*Boxer*) groggy; (*mil*) hard-hit

angesehen [ˈaŋɡəze-ən] *adj* respected; (*ausgezeichnet*) distinguished

An'gesicht *n* countenance, face; **von A.** by sight

an'gesichts *prep* (*genit*) in the presence of; (*fig*) in view of

angestammt [ˈaŋɡəʃtamt] *adj* hereditary

Angestellte [ˈaŋɡəʃteltə] §5 *mf* employee; **die Angestellten** the staff

angetan [ˈaŋɡətan] (**mit**) clad (in); **a. sein von** have a liking for; **ganz danach a. zu** (*inf*) very likely to (*inf*)

angetrunken [ˈaŋɡətruŋkən] *adj* tipsy

angewandt [ˈaŋɡəvant] *adj* applied

angewiesen [ˈaŋɡəvizən] *adj—***a. sein auf** (*acc*) have to rely on

an'gewöhnen *tr—***j—m etw a.** accustom s.o. to s.th.

An'gewohnheit *f* (–;-en) habit

an'gleichen §85 *tr* adapt, adjust

Angler –in [ˈaŋlər(ɪn)] §6 *mf* fisher

an'gliedern *tr* link, attach; (*Gesellschaft*) affiliate

an'greifen §88 *tr* (*anfassen*) handle; (*Vorräte*) draw on, dip into; (*Körper*) affect; (*mil*) attack

an'greifend *adj* aggressive, offensive

An'greifer –in §6 *m* aggressor

an'grenzen *intr* (**an** *acc*) be adjacent (to), border (on)

An'griff *m* attack

An'griffskrieg *m* war of aggression

an'griffslustig *adj* aggressive

Angst [aŋst] *f* (–;-ﬂe) fear, anxiety

ängstigen [ˈɛŋstɪɡən] *tr* alarm || *ref* (**vor**) be afraid (of); (**um**) be alarmed (about)

ängstlich [ˈɛŋstlɪç] *adj* uneasy, jittery; (*besorgt*) anxious; (*sorgfältig*) scrupulous; (*schüchtern*) timid

Angst'zustände *pl* jitters

an'haben §89 *tr* have on; **j—m etw a.** have s.th. on. s.o.; **j—m etw a. können** be able to harm s.o.

an'haften *intr* (*dat*) stick (to)

an'haken *tr* check off; (**an** *acc*) hook (onto)

an'halten §90 *tr* stop; (*Atem, Ton*) hold; || *intr* stop; (*andauern*) continue, last

an'haltend *adj* continuous

An'halter *m—***per A. fahren** hitch-hike

An'haltpunkt *m* clue, lead

An'hang *m* (–[e]s;-ﬂe) appendix; (*Gefolgschaft*) following; (*jur*) codicil

an'hängen §92 & §109 *tr* (*Hörer*) hang up; (*hinzufügen*) add on; **j—m e-e Krankheit a.** infect s.o. with a disease; **j—m e-n Prozeß a.** bring suit

against s.o.; j—m etw a. pin s.th. on s.o. || §92 *intr* (**an** *dat*) adhere (to)

An'hänger –in §6 *mf* follower || *m* (*Schmuck*) pendant; (*aut*) trailer

anhänglich [ˈanhɛŋlɪç] *adj* (**an** *acc*) attached (to), devoted (to)

Anhängsel [ˈanhɛŋzəl] *m* (–s;-) appendage, adjunct

an'hauchen *tr* breathe on

an'häufen *tr* & *ref* pile up

An'häufung *f* (–;-en) accumulation

an'heben §94 *tr* lift (up); (*Lied*) strike up; (*aut*) jack up

an'heften *tr* fasten; (*annähen*) stitch

an'heilen *tr* & *intr* heal up

anheim'fallen §72 *intr* (SEIN) (*dat*) devolve (upon)

anheim'stellen *tr* (*dat*) leave (to)

An'höhe *f* rise, hill

an'hören *tr* listen to, hear || *ref* **—sich gut a.** sound good

Anilin [anɪˈlin] *n* (–s;) aniline

Animier/dame *f* B-girl

animieren [anɪˈmirən] *tr* encourage

Anis [aˈnis] *m* (–es;-e) anise

an'kämpfen *intr* (**gegen**) struggle (against)

An'kauf *m* purchase

an'kaufen *tr* purchase

Anker [ˈaŋkər] *m* (–s;-) anchor; (*elec*) armature; **vor A. gehen** drop anchor

ankern [ˈaŋkərn] *intr* anchor

an'ketten *tr* (**an** *acc*) chain (to)

An'klage *f* accusation, charge; (*jur*) indictment; **A. erheben** prefer charges; **die A. vertreten** be counsel for the prosecution; **unter A. stellen** indict

an'klagen *tr* (**wegen**) accuse (of), charge (with), indict (for)

An'kläger –in §6 *mf* accuser; (*jur*) prosecutor

An'klageschrift *f* (bill of) indictment

an'klammern *tr* (**an** *acc*) clip (to) || *ref* (**an** *acc*) cling (to)

An'klang *m* (**an** *acc*) reminiscence (of), trace (of); **A. finden** be well received, catch on

an'kleben *tr* (**an** *acc*) paste (on), stick (on) || *intr* (HABEN & SEIN) stick

an'kleiden *tr* & *ref* dress

an'klingeln *tr* ring, call up || *intr—***bei j—m a.** ring s.o.'s doorbell

an'klopfen *intr* (**an** *acc*) knock (on)

an'knipsen *tr* switch on

an'knüpfen *tr* tie, attach; (*Gespräch*) start || *intr* (**an** *acc*) link up (with)

an'kommen §99 *intr* (SEIN) (**in** *dat*) arrive (at); (**bei**) be well received (by); (**bei**) get a job (with); **es darauf a. lassen** take one's chances; **es kommt ganz darauf an, ob it** (all) depends on whether

Ankömmling [ˈankœmlɪŋ] *m* (–s;-e) newcomer, arrival

an'kündigen *tr* announce, proclaim; **j—m etw a.** notify s.o. of s.th.

An'kündigung *f* (–;-en) announcement

Ankunft [ˈankunft] *f* (–;-ﬂe) arrival

an'kurbeln *tr* crank up; **die Wirtschaft a.** prime the economy

an'lachen *tr* laugh at

An'lage *f* (*Anordnung*) plan, layout;

(*Bau*) construction; (*Errichtung*) installation; (*Fabrik*) plant, works; (*Garten*) park, grounds; (*Fähigkeit*) ability, aptitude (*im Brief*) enclosure; **in der A.** enclosed

An'lagekapital *n* invested capital; permanent assets

an'langen *tr*—**was mich anlangt** as far as I'm concerned ‖ *intr* (SEIN) arrive

An-laß ['anlas] *m* (**-lasses;-lässe**) occasion; (*Grund*) reason, motive; **S. geben zu** give rise to; **ohne allen A.** without any reason

an'lassen §104 *tr* (*Kleid*) keep on; (*Motor*) start (up); (*Wasser*) turn on; (*Pumpe*) prime; (*Stahl*) temper; **j-n hart a.** rebuke s.o. sharply ‖ *ref* **sich gut a.** shape up

Anlasser ['anlasər] *m* (**-s;-**) starter

anläßlich ['anleslɪç] *prep* (*genit*) on the occasion of

An'lauf *m* run, start

an'laufen §105 *tr* run at; (*Hafen*) put into ‖ *intr* (SEIN) (*Motor*) start up; (*Brille*) fog up; (*Metall*) tarnish; (*anwachsen*) accumulate; (*Schulden*) mount up; (*Film*) start, come on; **angelaufen kommen** come running up; **ins Rollen a.** (fig) get rolling; **rot a.** blush

an'legen *tr* (an *acc*) put (on), lay (on); (*Garten*; *Geld*) lay out; (*Kapital*) invest; (*Leitung*) install; (*Verband*) apply; (*Kolonie*) found ‖ *ref*—**sich a. mit** have a run-in with ‖ *intr* put ashore; moor

An'legeplatz *m* pier

an'lehnen *tr* (an *acc*) lean (against); (*Tür*) leave ajar ‖ *ref* (an *acc*) lean (against); (fig) be based (on), rely (on)

Anleihe ['anlaɪə] *f* (**-;-n**) loan

an'leiten *tr* (zu) guide (to); **a. in** (*dat*) instruct in

An'leitung *f* (**-;-en**) guidance; (*Lehre*) instruction

an'lernen *tr* train, break in

an'liegen §108 *intr* (*passen*) fit; (an *dat*) lie near, be adjacent (to); **eng a.** fit tight; **j-m a.** pester s.o. ‖ **Anliegen** *n* (**-s;-**) request; **ein A. an j-n haben** have a request to make of s.o.

an'liegend *adj* adjacent; (*Kleid*) tight-fitting; (*Brief*) enclosed

an'locken *tr* lure (on)

an'machen *tr* (*Licht*) switch on; (*Feuer*) light; (*zubereiten*) prepare; (an *acc*) attach (to)

an'malen *tr* paint

an'marschieren *intr* (SEIN) approach

anmaßen ['anmasən] *ref*—**sich** [*dat*] **etw a.** usurp s.th.; **sich** [*dat*] **a., etw zu sein** pretend to be s.th.

an'maßend *adj* arrogant

An'meldeformular *n* registration form

an'melden *tr* announce; report; (*Anspruch*, *Berufung*) file; (*Konkurs*) declare; (*Patent*) apply for; (*educ*) register; (sport) enter ‖ *ref* make an appointment (with); (zu) enroll (in); (mil) report in

an'merken *tr* note down; **j-m etw a.** notice s.th. in s.o.

an'messen §70 *tr*—**j-m etw a.** measure s.o. for s.th.

An'mut *f* (**-;**) charm, attractiveness

an'mutig *adj* charming

an'nageln *tr* (an *acc*) nail (to)

an'nähen *tr* (an *acc*) sew on (to)

annähernd ['anne·ərnt] *adj* approximate

An'näherung *f* (**-;-en**) approach

An'näherungsversuch *m* (romantic) pass; attempt at reconciliation

an'näherungsweise *adv* approximately

An'nahme *f* (**-;-n**) acceptance; (*Vermutung*) assumption

annehmbar ['annembar] *adj* acceptable

an'nehmen §116 *tr* accept, take; (*vermuten*) assume, suppose, guess; (*Glauben*) embrace; (*Gewohnheit*) acquire; (*Gesetz*) pass; (*Kind*) adopt; (*Arbeiter*) hire; (*Farbe*, *Gestalt*) take on; (*Titel*) assume; **etw als erwiesen a.** take s.th. for granted ‖ *ref* (*genit*) take care of

annektieren [anek'tirən] *tr* annex

Annexion [ane'ksjon] *f* (**-;-en**) annexation

Annonce [a'nõsə] *f* (**-;-n**) advertisement

annoncieren [anõ'sirən] *tr* advertise

anöden [a'nø:dən] *tr* bore to death

anonym [ano'nym] *adj* anonymous

an'ordnen *tr* arrange; (*befehlen*) order

an'packen *tr* grab hold of, seize; (*Problem*) tackle

an'passen *tr* fit; (*Worte*) adapt; ‖ *ref* (*dat* or an *acc*) adapt oneself (to)

an'passungsfähig *adj* adaptable

an'pflanzen *tr* plant, cultivate

an'pflaumen *tr* (coll) kid

anpöbeln ['anpøbəln] *tr* mob

an'pochen *tr* (an *acc*) knock (on)

An'prall *m* impact; (**e-s** *Angriffs*) brunt

an'prallen *intr* (SEIN) (gegen, an *acc*) collide (with), run (into)

an'preisen *tr* praise; **j-m etw a.** recommend s.th. to s.o.

An'probe *f* fitting, trying on

an'probieren *tr* try on

an'pumpen *tr*—**j-n a. um** hit s.o. for

an'quatschen *tr* talk the ears off

an'raten §63 *tr* advise, recommend

an'rechnen *tr* charge; **hoch a.** appreciate; **j-m etw a.** charge s.o. for s.th.

An'recht *n* (auf *acc*) right (to)

An'rede *f* address

an'reden *tr* address, speak to

an'regen *tr* stimulate; suggest

An'reiz *m* incentive

an'reizen *tr* stimulate; spur on

an'rennen §97 *intr* (SEIN) (gegen) run (into); **angerannt kommen** come running

an'richten *tr* (*Schaden*) cause, do; (culin) prepare

anrüchig ['anrʏçɪç] *adj* disreputable

an'rücken *intr* (SEIN) approach

An'ruf *m* (telephone) call

an'rufen §122 *tr* call; (*Gott*) invoke; (*Schiff*) hail; (jur) appeal to; (mil) challenge; (telp) call up

an'rühren *tr* touch; (*Thema*) touch on; (*mischen*) stir

An'sage *f* announcement

an'sagen *tr* announce; *(Trumpf)* declare

An'sager –in §6 *mf* announcer

an'sammeln *tr* gather; *(anhäufen)* amass; *(Truppen)* concentrate ‖ *ref* gather; *(Zinsen)* accumulate

ansässig ['anzesɪç] *adj* residing; **a. werden** (or **sich a. machen**) settle ‖ **Ansässige** §5 *mf* resident

An'satz *m* start; *(Mundstück)* mouthpiece; *(Spur)* trace; *(in e-r Rechnung)* charge; *(Schätzung)* estimate; (geol) deposit; (mach) attachment; (math) statement

an'saugen §125 *tr* suck in; *(Pumpe)* prime

an'schaffen *tr* procure; *(kaufen)* get, purchase; **Kinder a.** (coll) have kids

an'schalten *tr* switch on

an'schauen *tr* look at

an'schaulich *adj* graphic

An'schauung *f* outlook, opinion; *(Vorstellung)* perception; *(Auffassung)* conception; *(Erkenntnis)* intuition; *(Betrachtung)* contemplation

An'schauungsbild *n* mental image

An'schauungsmaterial *n* visual aids

An'schein *m* appearance

an'scheinend *adj* apparent, seeming

an'scheinlich *adv* apparently

an'schicken *ref* get ready

an'schieben §130 *tr* give *(s.th.)* a push

anschirren ['anʃɪrən] *tr* harness

An'schlag *m* (an *acc*, gegen) striking (against); *(Anprall)* impact; *(Attentat)* attempt; *(Bekanntmachung)* notice; *(e-r Uhr)* stroke; *(e-r Taste)* hitting; *(Berechnung)* calculation; *(e-s Gewehrs)* firing position; *(Komplott)* plot; (mach) stop *(for arresting motion)*; (mus) touch; (tennis) serve; **A. spielen** play tag

An'schlagbrett *n* bulletin board

an'schlagen §132 *tr* (an *acc*) fasten (to); *(Plakat)* post; *(Gewehr)* level; *(Tasse, usw.)* chip; *(Taste)* hit; *(einschätzen)* estimate; *(Gegner)* (box) have in trouble; **e-n anderen Ton a.** (fig) change one's tune ‖ *ref* bump oneself ‖ *intr (Wellen)* (an *acc*) beat against); *(Hund)* let out a bark; *(Arznei)* work

An'schlagzettel *m* notice; poster

an'schließen §76 *tr* padlock; *(anketten)* chain; *(verbinden)* connect; *(anfügen)* join; (com) affiliate; (elec) plug in ‖ *ref (dat, an acc)* join, side with ‖ *intr (Kleid)* be tight

an'schließend *adj* (an *acc*) subsequent (to); adjacent (to) ‖ *adv* next, then

An'schluß *m* connection; (pol) annexation, union; **sie sucht A.** (coll) she is looking for a man

An'schlußbahn *f* (rr) branch line

An'schlußdose *f* (elec) receptacle

An'schlußschnur *f* (elec) cord

An'schlußzug *m* connection, connecting train

an'schmachten *tr* make eyes at

an'schmiegen *ref* (an *acc*) nestle up (to); *(Kleid)* (an acc) cling (to)

anschmiegsam ['anʃmiːkzam] *adj* accommodating; cuddly

an'schmieren *tr* smear; (coll) bamboozle

an'schnallen *tr* buckle ‖ *ref* fasten one's seat belt

an'schnauzen *tr* snap at, bawl out

an'schneiden §106 *tr* cut into; *(Thema)* take up

An'schnitt *m* first cut

an'schrauben *tr* (an *acc*) screw on (to)

an'schreiben §62 *tr* write down; *(Spielstand)* mark; *(dat)* charge (to); (com) write to; **etw a. lassen** buy s.th. on credit

An'schreiber –in §6 *mf* scorekeeper

An'schreibetafel *f* scoreboard

an'schreien §135 *tr* yell at

An'schrift *f* address

An'schriftenmaschine *f* addressograph

anschuldigen ['anʃʊldɪgən] *tr* accuse

an'schwärzen *tr* blacken, disparage

an'schwellen *tr* cause to swell; *(Unkosten, usw.)* swell ‖ §119 *intr* (SEIN) swell up, puff up; increase

an'schwemmen *tr* wash *(s.th.)* ashore; (geol) deposit

an'sehen §138 *tr* look at; (fig) regard ‖ **Ansehen** *n* (–s;–) appearance; *(Achtung)* reputation; *(Geltung)* prestige, authority; **von A.** by sight; of high repute

ansehnlich ['anzenlɪç] *adj* good-looking; *(beträchtlich)* considerable; *(eindrucksvoll)* imposing

An'sehung *f* (–;–)—**in A.** (genit) in consideration of

anseilen ['anzaɪlən] *tr* rope together

an'setzen *tr* (an *acc*) put (on), apply (to): *(zum Kochen)* put on; *(Frist, Preis)* set; *(abschätzen)* rate; *(berechnen)* charge; *(Knospen)* put forth ‖ *intr* begin; *(fett werden)* get fat

An'sicht *f* view; *(Meinung)* opinion; **zur A.** on approval

an'sichtig *adj*—**a. werden** (genit) catch sight of

An'sichtspostkarte *f* picture postcard

An'sichtssache *f* matter of opinion

An'sichtsseite *f* frontal view, façade

An'sichtssendung *f* article(s) sent on approval

ansiedeln *ref* & *ref* settle

An'siedler –in §6 *mf* settler

An'siedlung *f* (–;–en) settlement

An'sinnen *n* (–s;–) unreasonable demand

an'spannen *tr* stretch; *(Pferd)* hitch up; (fig) exert, strain

An'spannung *f* (–;–en) exertion, strain

an'speien §135 *tr* spit on

an'spielen *tr* (cards) lead with ‖ *intr* **(auf acc)** allude (to); (mus) start playing; (sport) kick off, serve, break

An'spielung *f* (–;–en) allusion, hint

an'spitzen *tr* sharpen *(to a point)*

An'sporn *m* spur, stimulus

an'spornen *tr* spur

An'sprache *f* (an *acc*) address (to); **e-e A. halten** deliver an address

an'sprechen §64 *tr* speak to, address; *(Ziel, Punkt)* make out; **a. als** regard as; **j–n a. um** ask s.o. for ‖ *intr (dat)* appeal to, interest; **(auf acc)** respond (to)

an′sprechend *adj* appealing
an′springen §142 *tr* leap at ‖ *intr* (SEIN) (*Motor*) start (up); **angesprungen kommen** come skipping along
an′spritzen *tr* sprinkle, squirt
An′spruch *m* claim; **A. haben auf** (*acc*) be entitled to; **A. machen** (or **erheben**) **auf** (*acc*), **in A. nehmen** demand, require, claim; **große Ansprüche stellen** ask too much
an′spruchslos *adj* unpretentious
an′spruchsvoll *adj* pretentious; (*wählerisch*) choosey, hard to please
an′spucken *tr* spit on
an′spülen *tr* wash ashore; (geol) deposit
an′stacheln *tr* goad on
Anstalt [′an/talt] *f* (–;–en) institution, establishment; **Anstalten treffen zu** make preparations for
An′stand *m* (*Schicklichkeit*) decency; (*Bedenken*) hesitation; (*Einwendung*) objection; (hunt) blind
anständig [′an/tendiç] *adj* decent
An′standsbesuch *m* formal call
An′standsdame *f* chaperone
An′standsgefühl *n* tact
an′standshalber *adv* out of politeness, out of human decency
an′standslos *adv* without fuss
an′starren *tr* stare at, gaze at
anstatt [an′/tat] *prep* (genit) instead of
an′stauen *tr* dam up ‖ *ref* pile up
an′staunen *tr* gaze at (in astonishment)
an′stecken *tr* stick on; (*Ring*) put on; (*anzünden*) set on fire; (*Zigarette, Feuer*) light; (pathol) infect ‖ *ref* become infected
an′steckend *adj* infectious; (*durch Berührung*) contagious
An′steckung *f* (–;–en) infection; (*durch Berührung*) contagion
an′stehen §146 *intr* (**nach**) line up (for): (*zögern*) hesitate; **j–m gut a.** fit s.o. well, become s.o.
an′steigen §148 *intr* (SEIN) rise, ascend; (*zunehmen*) increase, mount up
an′stellen *tr* (**an** *acc*) place (against); (*beschäftigen*) hire; (*Versuch, usw.*) (*Vergleich*) draw; (*Heizung, Radio*) turn on ‖ *ref* (**nach**) line up (for); **sich a., als ob** act as if; **stell dich nicht so dumm an!** don't play dumb!
anstellig [′an/teliç] *adj* skillful
An′stellung *f* (–;–en) hiring; job
an′steuern *tr* steer for
Anstieg [′an/tik] *m* (–[e]s;–e) rise; (*e–s Weges*) grade
an′stieren *tr* stare at, glower at
an′stiften *tr* instigate
An′stifter –in §6 *mf* instigator
an′stimmen *tr* (*Lied*) strike up; (*Geheul*) let out
An′stoß *m* impact; (*Antrieb*) impulse; (*Ärgernis*) offense; (sport) kickoff; **den A. geben zu** start
an′stoßen §150 *tr* bump against; (*Ball*) kick off; (*Wagen*) give a push; (*mit dem Ellbogen*) nudge, poke ‖ *intr* clink glasses; **a. an** (*acc*) adjoin; **bei j–m a.** shock s.o.; **mit den Gläsern a.** clink glasses; **mit der Zunge a.** lisp ‖

intr (SEIN)—**mit dem Kopf a. an** (*acc*) bump one's head against
an′stoßend *adj* adjoining
anstößig [′an/tøsiç] *adj* shocking
an′strahlen *tr* beam on; (fig) beam at; (*mit Scheinwerfern*) floodlight
an′streben *tr* strive for
an′streichen §85 *tr* paint; (*Fehler*) underline; (*anhaken*) check off
An′streicher *m* house painter
an′streifen *tr* brush against, graze
an′strengen *tr* exert; (*Geist*) tax; **e–n Prozeß a.** file suit ‖ *intr* be a strain
an′strengend *adj* strenuous, trying
An′strengung *f* (–;–en) exertion, effort
An′strich *m* (*Farbe*) paint; (*Überzug*) coat (*of paint*); (fig) tinge
An′sturm *m* assault, charge
antarktisch [ant′arktiʃ] *adj* antarctic
an′tasten *tr* touch, finger
An′teil *m* share, portion; (*Quote*) quota; (st. exch.) share; **A. nehmen an** (*dat*) take part in; (fig) sympathize with
an′teilmäßig *adj* proportional
An′teilnahme *f* (–;) (**an** *dat*) participation (in); (*Mitleid*) sympathy
Antenne [an′tenə] *f* (–;–n) antenna, aerial; (orn) antenna, feeler
Antibioti·kum [antibi′otikum] *n* (–s; –ka [ka]) antibiotic
antik [an′tik] *adj* ancient; classical ‖ **Antike** *f* (–;–n) (classical) antiquity; (*Kunstwerk*) antique
Anti′kenhändler –in §6 *mf* antique dealer
Antilope [anti′lopə] *f* (–;–n) antelope
Antipa·thie [antipa′ti] *f* (–;–thien [′ti·ən]) antipathy
an′tippen *tr* & *intr* tap
Antiqua [an′tikva] *f* (–;) roman (type)
Antiquar –in [anti′kvar(in)] §8 *mf* antique dealer; second-hand book-dealer
Antiquariat [antikva′rjat] *n* (–[e]s;–e) second-hand bookstore
antiquarisch [anti′kvariʃ] *adj* second-hand
Antiquität [antikvi′tet] *f* (–;–en) antique
Antlitz [′antlits] *m* (–es;–e) (Bib, poet) countenance
Antrag [′antrak] *m* (–[e]s;ᵉe) (*Angebot*) offer; (*Vorschlag*) proposal; (*Gesuch*) application; (pol) motion
an′tragen §132 *tr* offer; (*vorschlagen*) propose ‖ *intr*—**a. auf** (*acc*) make a motion for; propose, suggest
An′tragsformular *n* application form
Antragsteller –in [′antrak/telar(in)] §6 *mf* applicant; (parl) mover
an′treffen §151 *tr* meet; find at home
an′treiben §62 *tr* drive on, urge on; (*Schiff*) propel; (*anreizen*) egg on ‖ *intr* (SEIN) wash ashore
an′treten §152 *tr* (*Amt, Erbschaft*) enter (upon); (*Reise*) set out on; (*Motorrad*) start up ‖ *intr* (SEIN) take one's place; (mil) fall in; (sport) enter
An′trieb *m* (–s;–e) (*Beweggrund*) motive; (*Anreiz*) incentive; (mech) drive, impetus; **aus eigenem A.** on

one's own initiative; **neuen A. verleihen** (*dat*) give fresh impetus to
An'tritt *m* (-[e]s;-e) beginning, start;
(*e-s Amtes*) entrance upon
an'tun §154 *tr* (*Kleid*) put on; **j-m
etw a.** do s.th. to s.o.
Antwort ['antvɔrt] *f* (-;-en) answer
antworten ['antvɔrtən] *intr* (**auf** *acc*)
reply (to), answer; **j-m** a. answer s.o.
an'vertrauen *tr* entrust; (*mitteilen*)
tell, confide
an'verwandt *adj* related ‖ **Anver-
wandte** §5 *mf* relative
an'wachsen §155 *intr* (SEIN) begin to
grow; grow together; (*Wurzel schlagen*) take root; (*zunehmen*) increase
Anwalt ['anvalt] *m* (-[e]s;-̈e) attorney
An'waltschaft *f* legal profession, bar
an'wandeln *tr*—**mich wandelte die Lust
an zu** (*inf*) I got a yen to (*inf*); **was
wandelte dich an?** what got into
you?
An'wandlung *f* (-;-en) impulse, sudden feeling; (*von Zorn*) fit
An'wärter **-in** §6 *mf* candidate; (*mil*)
cadet, officer candidate
Anwartschaft ['anvart/aft] *f* (-;) expectancy; (*Aussicht*) prospect
an'wehen *tr* blow on ‖ *intr* (SEIN)
drift
an'weisen §118 *tr* (*beauftragen*) instruct; (*zuteilen*) assign; (*Geld*) remit
An'weisung *f* (-;-en) instruction; assignment; (fin) money order
anwendbar ['anventbar] *adj* (**auf** *acc*)
applicable (to); (**für, zu**) that can be
used (for)
an'wenden §140 *tr* (**auf** *acc*) apply
(to); (**für, zu**) use (for)
An'wendung *f* (-;-en) application;
use
an'werben §149 *tr* recruit
an'werfen §160 *tr* (*Motor*) start up
An'wesen *n* estate, property; presence
anwesend ['anvezənt] *adj* present ‖
Anwesende §5 *mf* person present;
verehrte Anwesende! ladies and
gentlemen!
An'wesenheit *f* (-;) presence
an'wurzeln *ref & intr* (SEIN) take root;
wie angewurzelt rooted to the spot
An'zahl *f* (-;) number, quantity
an'zahlen *tr* pay down ‖ *intr* make a
down payment
an'zapfen *tr* tap
An'zeichen *n* indication, sign; (*Vorbe-
deutung*) omen; (pathol) symptom
Anzeige ['antsaɪgə] *f* (-;-n) (*Ankündigung*) announcement, notice; (*Reklame*) ad; (med) advice; **kleine
Anzeigen** classified ads
an'zeigen *tr* announce; notify; (*Symp-
tome, Fieber*) show, indicate; (*bei
der Polizei*) report, inform against;
(*inserieren*) advertise
An'zeigenvermittlung *f* advertising
agency
an'zetteln *tr* (*Verschwörung*) hatch
an'ziehen §163 *tr* pull; (& fig) attract;
(*Kleid*) put on; (*e-e Person*) dress;
(*Riemen, Schraube*) tighten; (*Bremse*)
apply; (*Beispiele, Quellen*) quote ‖

intr pull, start pulling; (*Preis*) go up;
(chess) go first
An'ziehung *f* (-;-en) attraction; (*Zitat*)
quotation
An'ziehungskraft *f* appeal; (& phys)
attraction; (astr) gravitation
An'zug *m* suit; (mil) uniform; **in A.
sein** (*Armee*) be approaching;
(*Sturm*) be gathering; (*Gefahr*) be
imminent
anzüglich ['antsylɪç] *adj* offensive; **a.
werden** become personal
an'zünden *tr* set on fire; (*Feuer*) light
an'zweifeln *tr* doubt, question
apart [a'part] *adj* charming; (coll)
cute
Apathie [apa'ti] *f* (-;) apathy
apathisch [a'patɪʃ] *adj* apathetic
Apfel ['apfəl] *m* (-s;-̈) apple
Ap'felkompott *n* stewed apples
Ap'felmus *n* applesauce
Ap'felsaft *m* apple juice
Apfelsine [apfəl'zinə] *f* (-;-n) orange
Ap'feltorte *f* apple tart; **gedeckte A.**
apple pie
Ap'felwein *m* cider
Apostel [a'pɔstəl] *m* (-s;-) apostle
Apostroph [apo'strof] *m* (-[e]s;-e)
apostrophe
Apotheke [apo'tekə] *f* (-;-n) phar-
macy
Apotheker **-in** [apo'tekər(ɪn)] §6 *mf*
druggist
Apothe'kerwaren *pl* drugs
Apparat [apa'rat] *m* (-[e]s;-e) ap-
paratus, device; (phot) camera; (rad,
telv) set; (telp) telephone; **am A.!**
speaking
Appell [a'pɛl] *m* (-[e]s;-e) appeal;
(mil) roll call; (mil) inspection
appellieren [ape'lirən] *intr* (& jur)
(**an** *acc*) appeal (to)
Appetit [ape'tit] *m* (-[e]s;-e) appetite
Appetit'brötchen *n* canapé
appetit'lich *adj* appetizing; (*Mädchen*)
attractive
applaudieren [aplau'dirən] *tr & intr*
applaud
Applaus [a'plaus] *m* (-es;-e) applause
Appretur [apre'tur] *f* (-;-en) (tex)
finish
Aprikose [aprɪ'kozə] *f* (-;-n) apricot
April [a'prɪl] *m* (-[s];-e) April
Aquarell [akva'rɛl] *n* (-[e]s;-e) water-
color; watercolor painting
Aqua-rium [a'kvarjum] *n* (-s;-rien
[rɪ-ən]) aquarium
Äqua-tor [e'kvator] *m* (-s;-toren
['torən]) equator
Ära ['era] *f* (-;Ären ['erən]) era
Araber **-in** ['arabər(ɪn)] §6 *mf* Arab
Arabien [a'rabjən] *n* (-s;) Arabia
arabisch [a'rabɪʃ] *adj* Arabian; (*Zif-
fer*) Arabic
Arbeit ['arbaɪt] *f* (-;-en) work
arbeiten ['arbaɪtən] *tr & intr* work
Arbeiter ['arbaɪtər] *m* (-s;-) worker;
A. und Unternehmer *pl* labor and
management
Ar'beiterausstand *m* walkout, strike
Ar'beitergewerkschaft *f* labor union
Arbeiterin ['arbaɪtərɪn] *f* (-;-nen)
working woman, working girl

Ar'beiterschaft *f* (–;) working class
Arbeitertum ['arbaɪtərtum] *n* (–s;)
working class, workers
Ar'beitgeber –in §6 *mf* employer
Ar'beitnehmer –in §6 *mf* employee
arbeitsam ['arbaɪtzam] *adj* industrious
Ar'beitsanzug *m* overalls; (mil) fatigue
clothes, fatigues
Ar'beitseinkommen *n* earned income
Ar'beitseinstellung *f* work stoppage
ar'beitsfähig *adj* fit for work
Ar'beitsgang *m* process; operation
(*single step of a process*)
Ar'beitsgemeinschaft *f* team; (educ)
workshop
Ar'beitsgerät *n* equipment, tools
Ar'beitskommando *n* (mil) work detail
Ar'beitskraft *f* labor force; Arbeits-
kräfte personnel
Ar'beitslager *n* work camp
Ar'beitsleistung *f* (work) quota; (*e-r
Maschine, Fabrik*) output
Ar'beitslohn *m* wages, pay
ar'beitslos *adj* unemployed
Ar'beitslosenunterstützung *f* unemploy-
ment compensation
Ar'beitslosigkeit *f* unemployment
Ar'beitsmarkt *m* labor market
Ar'beitsminister *m* secretary of labor
Ar'beitsministerium *n* department of
labor
Ar'beitsnachweis *m*, Ar'beitsnachweis-
stelle *f* employment agency
Ar'beitsniederlegung *f* walkout, strike
ar'beitsparend *adj* labor-saving
Ar'beitspause *f* break, rest period
Arbeitspferd *n* (& *fig*) workhorse
Ar'beitsplatz *m* job, place of employ-
ment
Ar'beitsrecht *n* labor law
ar'beitsscheu *adj* work-shy, lazy
Ar'beitsschicht *f* shift
Ar'beitsstätte *f* place of employment;
workshop; yard
Ar'beitsstelle *f* job, position
Ar'beitstag *m* workday
Ar'beitsvermittlung *f* employment
agency
Ar'beitsversäumnis *n* absenteeism
Ar'beitszeug *n* tools
Ar'beitszimmer *n* study; workroom
archaisch [ar'çaːɪʃ] *adj* archaic
Archäologe [arçɛ·ɔ'loːgə] *m* (–n;–n) ar-
chaeologist
Archäologie [arçɛ·ɔlɔ'giː] *f* (–;) archaeology
Archäologin [arçɛ·ɔ'loːgɪn] *f* (–;–nen)
archaeologist
archäologisch [arçɛ·ɔ'loːgɪʃ] *adj* archae-
ological
Architekt –in [arçɪ'tɛkt(ɪn)] §7 *mf*
architect
Architektur [arçɪtɛk'tuːr] *f* (–;–en) architecture
Ar·chiv [ar'çiːf] *n* (–[e]s;–chive
['çivə]) archives; (*für Zeitungen*)
morgue
Areal [are'aːl] *n* (–s;–e) area
Are·na [a'reːna] *f* (–;–nen [nən]) arena
arg [ark] *adj* (ärger ['ɛrgər]; ärgste
['ɛrkstə] §9) bad, evil, wicked; (coll)
awful; (*schlimm*) grave; (*Raucher*)

heavy ‖ Arg *n* (–s;) malice, cunning
‖ Arge §5 *m* Evil One ‖ §5 *n* evil
Argentinien [argɛn'tiːnjən] *n* (–s;) Argentina
Argentinier –in [argɛn'tiːnjər(ɪn)] §6
mf Argentinean
Ärger ['ɛrgər] *m* (–s;) irritation; mit
j–m Ä. haben have trouble with s.o.
är'gerlich *adj* (auf *acc* or über *acc*)
annoyed (at); irritating, annoying
ärgern ['ɛrgərn] *tr* annoy ‖ *ref* (über
acc) be annoyed (at)
Ärgernis ['ɛrgərnɪs] *n* (–ses;–se) scandal, offense; (*Mißstand*) nuisance
Arg'list *f* craft, cunning
arg'listig *adj* crafty, cunning
arg'los *adj* guileless; (*nichtsahnend*)
unsuspecting
Argwohn ['arkvoːn] *m* (–s;) suspicion
argwöhnen ['arkvøːnən] *tr* suspect
argwöhnisch ['arkvøːnɪʃ] *adj* suspicious
Arie ['arjə] *f* (–;–n) aria
Arier –in ['arjər(ɪn)] §6 Aryan
arisch ['arɪʃ] *adj* Aryan
Aristokrat [arɪstɔ'kraːt] *m* (–en;–en)
aristocrat
Aristokra·tie [arɪstɔkra'tiː] *f* (–;–tien
['tiː·ən]) aristocracy
Aristokratin [arɪstɔ'kraːtɪn] *f* (–;–nen)
aristocrat
Arithmetik [arɪt'meːtɪk] *f* (–;) arithmetic
Arktis ['arktɪs] *f* (–;) Arctic
arktisch ['arktɪʃ] *adj* arctic
arm [arm] *adj* (ärmer ['ɛrmər],
ärmste ['ɛrmstə] §9 (an *dat*) poor
in) ‖ Arm *m* (–[e]s;–e) arm; (*e–s
Flusses*) branch
Armatur [arma'tuːr] *f* (–;–en) arma-
ture; Armaturen fittings, mountings
Armatu'renbrett *n* instrument panel;
(aut) dashboard
Arm'band *n* (–[e]s;–er) bracelet;
watchband; (*Armabzeichen*) brassard
Arm'banduhr *f* wrist watch
Arm'binde *f* brassard; (med) sling
Ar·mee [ar'meː] *f* (–;–meen ['me·ən])
army
Ärmel ['ɛrməl] *m* (–s;–) sleeve
Är'melaufschlag *m* cuff
Är'melkanal *m* English Channel
är'mellos *adj* sleeveless
Armen– [armən] *comb.fm.* for the
poor
Ar'menhaus *n* poorhouse
Armenien [ar'meːnjən] *n* (–s;) Armenia
armenisch [ar'meːnɪʃ] *adj* Armenian
Ar'menpflege *f* public assistance
Ar'menunterstützung *f* public assist-
ance, welfare
Ar'menviertel *n* slums
Armesün'dermiene *f* hangdog look
Arm'lehne *f* arm, armrest
Arm'leuchter *m* candelabrum
ärmlich ['ɛrmlɪç] *adj* poor, humble
arm'selig *adj* poor, wretched; (*kläg-
lich*) paltry
Armut ['armuːt] *f* (–;) poverty
Arm'zeichen *n* semaphore
Aro·ma [a'roːma] *n* (–s;–men [mən],
–mata [mata]) aroma
aromatisch [aro'maːtɪʃ] *adj* aromatic
Arrest [a'rɛst] *m* (–[e]s;–e) arrest;

(in der Schule) detention; (jur) impounding, seizure

Arsch [arʃ] m (-es;⁼e) (sl) ass

Arsch'backe f (sl) buttock

Arsch'kriecher m (sl) brown-noser

Arsch'lecker m (sl) brown-noser

Arsen [ar'zen] n (-s;) arsenic

Arsenal [arze'nɑl] (-s;-e) arsenal

Art [art] f (-;-en) sort, kind; nature; (Rasse) race, breed; species; (Weise) manner; (Verfahren) procedure; (Muster) model; **das ist keine Art!** that's no way to behave!

art'eigen adj true to type

arten ['artən] intr (SEIN)—**a. nach** take after

Arterie [ar'terjə] f (-;-n) artery

artig ['artıç] adj (brav) good, well-behaved; (höflich) polite

Artikel [ar'tikəl] (-s;-) (com, gram, journ) article

Artillerie [artıle'ri] f (-;) artillery

Artillerie'aufklärer m artillery spotter

Artischocke [artı'ʃɔkə] f (-;-n) artichoke

Artist –in [ar'tɪst(ın)] §7 mf artist; (beim Zirkus) performer

Arznei [arts'naı] f (-;-en) medicine, medication, drug

Arznei'kraut n herb, medicinal plant

Arznei'kunde f, **Arznei'kunst** f pharmaceutics; pharmacology

Arznei'mittel n medication

Arzt [artst] m (-[e]s;⁼e) doctor

Ärztin ['ertstɪn] f (-;-nen) doctor

ärztlich ['ertstlıç] adj medical

As [as] n (Asses; Asse) ace ‖ n (-s;-) (mus) A flat

Asbest [as'best] m (-[e]s;-e) asbestos

asch'bleich adj ashen, pale

Asche ['aʃə] f (-;-n) ash(es), cinders

Aschen– comb.fm. ash; cinder; funerary

A'schenbahn f cinder track

A'schenbecher m ashtray

Aschenbrödel ['aʃənbrødəl] n (-s;-) Cinderella; drudge

Aschermittwoch [aʃər'mıtvɔx] m (-s; -e) Ash Wednesday

asch'fahl adj ashen, pale

äsen ['ezən] intr graze, feed

asiatisch [azı'atıʃ] adj Asiatic

Asien ['azjən] n (-s;) Asia

Asket [as'ket] m (-en;-en) ascetic

asketisch [as'ketıʃ] adj ascetic

Asphalt [as'falt] m (-[e]s;) asphalt

asphaltieren [asfal'tirən] tr asphalt

Asphalt'pappe f tar paper

aß [as] pret of essen

Assistent –in [asıs'tent(ın)] §7 mf assistant

Assistenz [asıs'tents] f (-;-en) assistance

Assistenz'arzt m, **Assistenz'ärztin** f intern

Ast [ast] m (-es;⁼e) bough, branch; (im Holz) knot, knob

ästhetisch [es'tetıʃ] adj esthetic(al)

Asthma ['astma] n (-s;) asthma

ast'rein adj free of knots; **nicht ganz a.** (coll) not quite kosher

Astrologe [astro'logə] m (-n;-n) astrologer

Astrologie [astrolo'gi] f (-;) astrology

Astronaut [astro'naut] m (-en;-en) astronaut

Astronom [astro'nom] m (-en;-en) astronomer

Astronomie [astrono'mi] (-s;) astronomy

astronomisch [astro'nomıʃ] adj astronomic(al)

Astrophysik [astrofy'zik] f (-;) astrophysics

Asyl [a'zyl] n (-[e]s;-e) asylum, sanctuary; (Obdach) shelter; **ohne A.** homeless

Atelier [ate'lje] n (-s;-s) studio

Atem ['atəm] m (-s;) breath

A'tembeklemmung f shortness of breath

A'temholen n (-s;) respiration

a'temlos adj breathless

A'temnot f breathing difficulty

A'tempause f breathing spell

a'temraubend adj breath-taking

A'temzug m breath

Atheismus [ate'ısmus] m (-s;) atheism

Atheist –in [ate'ıst(ın)] §7 mf atheist

Äther ['etər] m (-s;) ether

Athlet [at'let] m (-en;-en) athlete

Athletik [at'letık] f (-;) athletics

Athletin [at'letın] f (-;-nen) athlete

athletisch [at'letı/] adj athletic

Atlantik [at'lantık] m (-s;) Atlantic

At·las ['atlas] m (-'-;) (myth) Atlas ‖ m (-lasses; -lanten ['lantən] & -lasse) atlas ‖ m (- & -lasses;-lasse) satin

atmen ['atmən] tr & intr breathe

Atmosphäre [atmo'sferə] f (-;-n) (& fig) atmosphere

atmosphärisch [atmo'sferı/] adj atmospheric; **atmosphärische Störungen** (rad) static

At'mung f (-;) breathing

Atom [a'tom] n (-s;-e) atom

Atom– comb. fm. atom, atomic

Atom'abfall m fallout; atomic waste

atomar [ato'mar] adj atomic

Atom'bau m atomic structure

atom'betrieben adj atomic-powered

Atom'bombe f atomic bomb

Atom'bombenversuch m atomic test

Atom'-Epoche f atomic age

Atom'kern m atomic nucleus

Atom'müll m atomic waste

Atom'regen m fallout

Atom'schutt m atomic waste

ätsch [etʃ] interj (to express gloating) serves you right!, good for you!

Attentat [aten'tat] n (-s;-e) attempt (on s.o.'s life); assassination

Attentäter –in [aten'tetər(ın)] §6 mf assailant, would-be assassin; assassin

Attest [a'test] n (-es;-e) certificate

attestieren [ates'tirən] tr attest (to)

Attrappe [a'trapə] f (-;-n) dummy

Attribut [atrı'but] n (-[e]s;-e) attribute; (gram) attributive

atzen ['atsən] tr feed

ätzen ['etsən] tr corrode; (med) cauterize (typ) etch

ät'zend adj corrosive; caustic

Au [au] f (-;-en) (poet) mead, meadow

au *interj* ow!, ouch!; oh!

Aubergine [ober'ʒin(ə)] *f* (-;-n) eggplant

auch [aux] *adv* also, too; *(selbst)* even

Audienz [au'djents] *f* (-;-en) audience; *(jur)* hearing

auf [auf] *adv up*; **auf und ab** up and down; **von Kind auf** from childhood on ‖ *prep (dat)* on, upon; **auf der ganzen Welt** in the whole world; **auf der Universität** at the university ‖ *prep (acc)* on; up; to; **auf den Bahnhof gehen** go to the station; **auf deutsch** in German; **drei aufs Dutzend** three to a dozen; **es geht auf vier Uhr** zu it's going on four; **Monat auf Monat verging** month after month passed ‖ *interj* get up! ‖ **Auf** *n*—**das Auf und Nieder** the ups and downs

auf'arbeiten *tr (Rückstände)* catch up on; *(verbrauchen)* use up; *(erneuern)* renovate; *(mach)* recondition ‖ *ref* work one's way up

auf'atmen *intr* breathe a sigh of relief

aufbahren ['aufbarən] *tr* lay out

Auf'bau *m* (-[e]s;) construction; structure; organization; *(Anlage)* arrangement, setup; (chem) synthesis ‖ *m* (-[e]s;-ten) structure; (aer) framework; (aut) body; (naut) superstructure

auf'bauen *tr* erect; *(Organization)* establish; (chem) synthesize; (mach) assemble ‖ *ref*—**er baute sich vor mir auf** he planted himself in front of me; **sich** [*dat*] **e-e Existenz a.** make a life for oneself

auf'bäumen *ref* rear; *(fig)* rebel

auf'bauschen *tr* puff up; *(fig)* exaggerate

auf'begehren *intr* flare up; *(gegen)* protest (against), rebel (against)

auf'behalten §90 *tr* keep on; keep open

auf'bekommen §99 *tr (Tür)* get open; *(Knoten)* loosen; *(Hausaufgabe)* be assigned

auf'bereiten *tr* prepare, process

auf'bessern *tr (Gehalt)* improve, raise

auf'bewahren *tr* keep, store; **das Gepäck a. lassen** check one's baggage

auf'bieten §58 *tr* summon; *(Brautpaar)* announce the banns of; (mil) call up

auf'binden §58 *tr* tie up; *(lösen)* untie; **j-m etw a.** put s.th. over on s.o.

auf'blähen *tr* inflate, distend

auf'blasen §61 *tr* inflate ‖ *ref* get puffed up

auf'bleiben §62 *intr* (SEIN) *(Tür)* stay open; *(wachen)* stay up

auf'blenden *intr* turn on the high beam

auf'blicken *intr* glance up

auf'blitzen *intr* (HABEN & SEIN) flash

auf'blühen *intr* (SEIN) begin to bloom

auf'bocken *tr* (aut) jack up

auf'brauchen *tr* use up

auf'brausen *intr* (HABEN & SEIN) bubble, seethe; *(Wind)* roar; *(fig)* flare up

auf'brausend *adj* effervescent; irascible

auf'brechen §64 *tr* break up; break open; (hunt) eviscerate ‖ *intr* (SEIN) burst open; *(fortgehen)* (nach) set out (for)

auf'bringen §65 *tr* bring up; *(Geld, Truppen)* raise; *(Schiff)* capture; *(Kraft)* gather; *(Mut)* get up; *(erzürnen)* infuriate

Auf'bruch *m* departure

auf'brühen *tr* bring to a boil

auf'bügeln *tr* iron, press; refresh (*one's knowledge of s.th.*)

aufbürden ['aufbyrdən] *tr—*j-m etw a. saddle s.o. with s.th.

auf'decken *tr* uncover; *(Bett)* turn down; *(Tischtuch)* spread

auf'drängen *tr* force open; **j-m etw a.** force s.th. on s.o.

auf'drehen *tr* turn up; *(Uhr)* wind; *(Hahn)* turn on; *(Schraube)* unscrew; *(Strick)* untwist ‖ *intr (Wagen)* increase speed; (coll) step on it, get a move on

auf'dringlich *adj* pushy; *(Farben)* gaudy

Auf'druck *m* print, imprint

auf'drücken *tr* impress, imprint, affix; *(öffnen)* squeeze open

aufeinan'der *adv* one after the other

Aufeinan'derfolge *f* succession; series

aufeinan'derfolgen *intr* (SEIN) follow one another

aufeinan'derfolgend *adj* successive

Aufenthalt ['aufenthalt] *m* (-[e]s;-e) holdup, delay; **ohne A.** nonstop

Auf'enthaltsgenehmigung *f* residence permit

Auf'enthaltsort *m (Wohnsitz)* residence; *(Verbleib)* whereabouts

Auf'enthaltsraum *m* lounge

auf'erlegen *tr* impose ‖ *ref—sich* [*dat*] **die Pflicht a. zu** (*inf*) make it one's duty to (*inf*); **sich** [*dat*] **Zwang a. müssen** have to restrain oneself

auf'erstehen §146 *intr* (SEIN) rise (from the dead)

Auf'erstehung *f* (-;) resurrection

auf'erwecken *tr* raise from the dead

auf'erziehen §163 *tr* bring up, raise

auf'essen §70 *tr* eat up

auf'fädeln *tr (Perlen)* string

auf'fahren §71 *tr (Fahrzeuge)* park; *(Geschütze)* bring up; *(Wein, Speisen)* serve up ‖ *intr* (SEIN) rise, mount; *(im Auto)* pull up; *(in Erregung)* jump (up); (arti) move into position; **a. auf** (*acc*) run into

Auf'fahrt *f* ascent; *(Zufahrt)* driveway

auf'fallen §72 *intr* (SEIN) be conspicuous; **j-m a.** strike s.o.

auf'fallend, auf'fällig *adj* striking; noticeable; *(Farben)* loud, gaudy

auf'fangen §73 *tr (Ball, Worte)* catch; *(Briefe, Nachrichten)* intercept

auf'fassen *tr* comprehend; *(deuten)* interpret; *(Perlen)* string

Auf'fassung *f* (-;-en) understanding, interpretation; *(Meinung)* view

auf'finden §59 *tr* find *(after searching)*

auf'fliegen §57 *intr* (SEIN) fly up; *(Tür)* fly open; *(scheitern)* fail; **a. lassen** break up (*e.g., a gang*)

auf'fordern *tr* call upon, ask

Auf'forderung *f* (-;-en) invitation; *(jur)* summons

auf'frischen tr freshen up, touch up
auf'führen tr (Bau) erect; (Schauspiel) present; (eintragen) enter; (Zeugen) produce; (anführen) cite; (mil) post; **einzeln a.** itemize || ref behave, act
Auf'führung f (-;-en) erection; performance; entry; specification; behavior
auf'füllen tr fill up
Auf'gabe f task, job; (e-s Briefes) mailing; (des Gepäcks) checking; (e-r Bestellung) placing; (e-s Amtes, e-s Geschäfts) giving up; (educ) homework; (jur) waiver; (math) problem; (mil) assignment
auf'gabeln tr (& coll) pick up
Auf'gang m ascent; (Treppe) stairs; (astr) rising
auf'geben §80 tr give up; (Amt) resign; (Post) mail; (Gepäck) check in; (Anzeige) place; (Preis) quote; (Arbeit) assign; (Telegramm) send
auf'geblasen adj (fig) uppity
Auf'gebot n public notice; (eccl) banns; (mil) call-up
auf'gebracht adj angry, irate
auf'gedonnert adj (coll) dolled up
auf'gehen §82 intr (SEIN) rise; (Tür) open; (Pflanzen) come up; (arith) go into; **genau a.** come out exactly
auf'geklärt adj enlightened
auf'geknöpft adj (coll) chatty
auf'gekratzt adj (coll) chipper
Auf'geld n surcharge; premium
auf'gelegt adj (zu) disposed (to)
auf'geräumt adj (fig) good-humored
auf'geschlossen adj open-minded; (für) receptive to
auf'geschmissen adj (coll) stuck
auf'gestaut adj pent-up
auf'geweckt adj smart, bright
auf'geworfen adj (Lippen) pouting; (Nase) turned-up
auf'gießen §76 tr (auf acc) pour (on); (Tee, Kaffee) make, brew
auf'graben §87 tr dig up
auf'greifen §88 tr pick up; (Dieb) catch; (fig) take up
auf'haben §98 tr (Hut) have on; (Tür, Mund) have open; (Aufgabe) have to do
auf'hacken tr hoe up
auf'haken tr unhook
auf'halten §90 tr hold up; (Tür) hold open; (anhalten) stop, delay || ref stay; (wohnen) live; **sich über etw a.** find fault with s.th.
Auf'hängeleine f clothesline
auf'hängen §92 tr hang up; **j-m etw a.** push s.th. on s.o.; (Wertloses) palm s.th. off on s.o.
auf'häufen tr & ref pile up
auf'heben §94 tr lift up, pick up; (bewahren) preserve; (ungültig machen) cancel; (Gesetz) repeal; (ausgleichen) cancel out, offset; (Strafe, Belagerung) lift; **gut aufgehoben sein** be in good hands
auf'heitern tr cheer up || ref cheer up; (Gesicht) brighten; (Wetter) clear up
auf'hellen ref & intr brighten
auf'hetzen tr incite, egg on

auf'holen tr hoist; (Verspätung) make up for || intr catch up
auf'horchen intr prick up one's ears
auf'hören intr stop, quit
auf'jauchzen intr shout for joy
auf'kaufen tr buy up; (Markt) corner
auf'klären tr clear up; enlighten; (mil) reconnoitre || ref clear up; (Gesicht) light up, brighten
Auf'klärer m (-s;-) (aer) reconnaissance plane; (mil) scout
Auf'klärung f (-;-en) explanation; enlightenment; (mil) reconnaissance
Auf'klärungsbuch n sex-education book
Auf'klärungsspähtrupp m reconnaissance patrol
auf'kleben tr (auf acc) paste (onto)
auf'klinken tr unlatch
auf'knacken tr crack open
auf'knöpfen tr unbutton
auf'knüpfen tr (lösen) untie; (hängen) (coll) string up
auf'kochen tr & intr boil
auf'kommen §99 intr (SEIN) come up, rise; (Gedanke) occur; (Mode) come into fashion; (Schiff) appear on the horizon; **a. für** answer for; (Kosten) defray; **a. gegen** stand up against, cope with; **a. von** recover from ||
Aufkommen n (-s;) rise; recovery
auf'krempeln tr roll up
auf'kreuzen intr (coll) show up
auf'kriegen tr see **aufbekommen**
auf'lachen intr burst out laughing
auf'laden §103 tr load up; (Batterie) charge || ref-sich [dat] etw a. saddle oneself with s.th.
Auf'lage f edition, printing; (e-r Zeitung) circulation; (Steuer) tax; (Stütze) rest, support
auf'lassen §104 tr leave open; (Fabrik, Bergwerk) abandon
auf'lauern intr (dat) lie in wait (for)
Auf'lauf m gathering, crowd; (Tumult) riot; (com) accumulation; (culin) soufflé
auf'laufen §105 intr (SEIN) rise; (anwachsen) accrue; (Schiff) get stranded; (Panzer) get stuck
auf'leben intr (SEIN) revive
auf'lecken tr lick up
auf'legen tr (auf acc) put (on); (Steuer) impose; (Hörer) hang up; (Buch) publish; (Karten) lay on the table; (Liste) make available for inspection; (Anleihe) float; (Faß Bier) put on || intr (telp) hang up
auf'lehnen tr (auf acc) lean (on) || ref (auf acc) lean (on); (gegen) rebel (against)
Auf'lehnung f (-;-en) rebellion; resistance
auf'lesen §107 tr pick up, gather
auf'liegen §108 intr (auf dat) lie (on); (zur Ansicht) be displayed
auf'lockern tr loosen; (Eintönigkeit, Vortrag) break (up)
auf'lösbar adj soluble; solvable
auf'lösen tr untie; (öffnen) loosen; (entwirren) disentangle; (Versammlung) break up; (Heer) disband; (Ehe) dissolve; (Verbindung) sever; (Firma) liquidate; (Rätsel) solve;

(*zerlegen*) break down; dissolve; (*entziffern*) decode; **ganz aufgelöst** all out of breath

Auf'lösung f (-;-en) solution; disentanglement; (*e-r Versammlung, Ehe*) breakup; (*Zerfall*) disintegration; (*von Beziehungen*) severance; (com) liquidation

auf'machen tr open (up); (*Geschäft*) open; (*Dampf*) get up; (coll) do up (*e.g., big, tastefully*) || *ref* (*Wind*) rise; (**nach**) set out (for)

Auf'machung f (-;-en) layout, format; (*Kleidung*) outfit

Auf'marsch m parade; (mil) concentration; (*zum Gefecht*) (mil) deployment

auf'marschieren intr (SEIN) parade; (*strategisch*) assemble; (*taktisch*) deploy

auf'merken tr (auf acc) pay attention (to)

aufmerksam ['aufmɛrkzam] adj (auf acc) attentive (to)

Auf'merksamkeit f (-;) attention

auf'möbeln tr (coll) dress up; (*anherrschen*) (sl) chew out; (*aufmuntern*) (coll) pep up || *ref* (coll) doll up

auf'muntern tr cheer up

Auf'nahme f (-;-n) taking up; (*Empfang*) reception (*Zulassung*) admission; (*von Beziehungen*) establishment; (*Inventur*) stock-taking; (electron) recording; (phot) photograph

Auf'nahmeapparat m camera; recorder

Auf'nahmegerät n camera; recorder

Auf'nahmeprüfung f entrance exam

auf'nehmen §116 tr take up; (*erfassen*) grasp; (*Diktat*) take down; (*Gast*) receive; (*Inventar*) take; (*Geld*) borrow; (*Anleihe*) float; (*Spur*) pick up; (*Beziehungen*) establish; (*eintragen*) enter; (*durch*) *Tonband, Schallplatte* record; (geog) map out; (phot) take

auf'opfern tr offer up, sacrifice

auf'päpeln tr spoon-feed

auf'passen intr pay attention; look out; **paß auf!** watch out!

auf'pflanzen tr set up; (*Seitengewehr*) fix

auf'platzen intr (SEIN) burst (open)

auf'polieren tr polish up

auf'prägen tr (auf acc) (& fig) impress (on)

auf'prallen intr (auf acc) crash (into)

auf'pumpen tr pump up

auf'putschen tr incite; (coll) pep up

auf'putzen tr dress up; clean up || *ref* dress up

auf'raffen tr pick up || *ref* stand up; (fig) pull oneself together

auf'räumen tr (*Zimmer*) straighten up; (*wegräumen*) clear away || *intra*—a. **mit** do away with, get rid of

Auf'räumungsarbeiten pl clearance

auf'rechnen tr add up; (acct) balance

auf'recht adj upright, erect

auf'rechterhalten §90 tr maintain

auf'regen tr excite, stir up; (*unruhig machen*) disturb, upset

Auf'regung f (-;-en) excitement

auf'reiben §62 tr rub off; (*wundreiben*) rub sore; (*vertilgen*) destroy; (*Heer*) grind up; (*Kräfte*) sap; (*Nerven*) fray || *ref* worry onself to death

auf'reibend adj wearing, exhausting

auf'reihen tr string, thread

auf'reißen §53 tr tear open; (*Straße*) tear up; (*Tür*) fling open; (*Augen*) open wide; (*zeichnen*) sketch || *intr* (SEIN) split open, crack

auf'reizen tr provoke, incite; (*stark erregen*) excite

auf'reizend adj provoking, annoying; (*Rede*) inflammatory; (*Anblick*) sexy

auf'richten tr erect, set up; (*trösten*) comfort || *ref* sit up

auf'richtig adj upright, sincere

Auf'richtigkeit f sincerity

auf'riegeln tr unbolt

Auf'riß m front view

auf'rollen tr roll up; (*entfalten*) unroll

auf'rücken intr (SEIN) advance; (**zu**) be promoted (to)

Auf'ruf m (*Aufschrei*) outcry; (*Aufforderung*) call; (mil) call-up

auf'rufen §122 tr call on; (*appellieren an*) appeal to; (*Banknoten*) call in

Auf'ruhr m uproar; (*Tumult*) riot

auf'rühren tr stir up

aufrührerisch ['aufryrərɪʃ] adj inflammatory, rebellious; (mil) mutinous

auf'runden tr round out

auf'rüsten tr & intr arm; rearm

Auf'rüstung f (-;-en) rearmament

auf'rütteln tr wake up (*by shaking*)

auf'sagen tr recite; (*ein Ende machen mit*) terminate

auf'sammeln tr gather up

aufsässig ['aufzɛsɪç] adj hostile; (*widerspenstig*) rebellious

Auf'satz m superstructure; (*auf dem Tische*) centerpiece; (*Schularbeit*) essay, composition; (*in der Zeitung*) article; (golf) tee; (mil) gun sight

auf'saugen §125 tr suck up; absorb

auf'schauen intr look up

auf'scheuchen tr scare up

auf'scheuern tr scrape

auf'schichten tr stack (up), pile (up)

auf'schieben §130 tr push up; (*Tür*) push open; (*verschieben*) postpone

auf'schießen §76 intr (SEIN) shoot up

Auf'schlag m (auf acc) striking (upon), impact (on); (*an Kleidung*) cuff, lapel; (*Steuer-*) surtax; (*Preis-*) price hike; (tennis) service, serve

auf'schlagen §132 tr (*öffnen*) open; (*Ei*) crack; (*Karte, Ärmel*) turn up; (*Zelt*) pitch; (*Wohnung*) take up; (*Preis*) raise; (*Knie, usw.*) bruise; (*Ball*) serve || *intr* (SEIN) (*Tür*) fly open; (*Flugzeug*) crash; (*Ball*) bounce; (tennis) serve

auf'schließen §76 tr unlock, open || *ref* (dat) pour out one's heart (to) || *intr* (mil) close ranks

auf'schlitzen tr slit open

Auf'schluß m information; (chem) decomposition

auf'schlußreich adj informative

auf'schnallen tr buckle; unbuckle

auf'schnappen tr snap up; (*Nachricht*) pick up

Auf′schneidemaschine *f* meat slicer
auf′schneiden §106 *tr* cut open; (*Fleisch*) slice ‖ *intr* (coll) talk big
Auf′schneider *m* boaster
Auf′schnitt *m*—**kalter A.** cold cuts
auf′schnüren *tr* untie, undo
auf′schrauben *tr* unscrew; (**auf** *acc*) screw (on)
auf′schrecken §134 *tr* startle; (*Wild*) scare up ‖ *intr* (SEIN) be startled
Auf′schrei *m* scream, yell; (fig) outcry
auf′schreiben §62 *tr* write down
auf′schreien §135 *intr* scream, yell
Auf′schrift *f* inscription; (*Anschrift*) address; (*e-r Flasche*) label
Auf′schub *m* deferment, postponement; (*Verzögerung*) delay; (jur) stay
auf′schürfen *tr* scrape; (*Bein*) skin
auf′schwellen §119 *intr* (SEIN) swell up; (*Fluß*) rise
auf′schwemmen *tr* bloat
auf′schwingen §142 *ref* (& fig) soar; **sich ~, etw zu tun** bring oneself to do s.th.
Auf′schwung *m* (& fig) upswing
auf′sehen §138 *intr* look up ‖ **Aufsehen** *n* (-**s**;) sensation, stir
auf′sehenerregend *adj* sensational
Auf′seher –**in** §6 *mf* supervisor; (*im Museum*) guard; (*im Geschäft*) floorwalker
auf′sein §139 *intr* (SEIN) be up; (*Tür*) be open
auf′setzen *tr* put on; (*aufrichten*) set up; (*schriftlich*) compose, draft ‖ *ref* sit up ‖ *intr* (aer) touch down; (rok) splash down
Auf′sicht *f* inspection, supervision
Auf′sichtsbeamte *m*, **Auf′sichtsbeamtin** *f* inspector, supervisor
Auf′sichtsbehörde *f* control board
Auf′sichtsdame *f* floorwalker
Auf′sichtsherr *m* floorwalker
Auf′sichtsrat *m* board of trustees; (*Mitglied*) trustee
auf′sitzen §144 *intr* (SEIN) sit up; (**auf** *dat*) sit (on), rest (on); **j–m a.** be taken in by s.o.; **j–n a. lassen** stand s.o. up
auf′spannen *tr* stretch, spread; (*Regenschirm*) open
auf′sparen *tr* save (up)
auf′speichern *tr* store (up)
auf′sperren *tr* unlock; (*Augen, Tür*) open wide
auf′spielen *tr* strike up ‖ *ref* (**mit**) show off (with) ‖ *intr* play dance music
auf′spießen *tr* spear, pierce
auf′sprengen *tr* force open; (*mit Sprengstoff*) blow up
auf′springen §142 *intr* (SEIN) jump up; (*Tür*) fly open; (*Ball*) bounce; (*Haut*) chap, crack
auf′spritzen *tr* (*Farbe*) spray on; (sl) shoot up ‖ *intr* (SEIN) squirt up
auf′sprudeln *intr* (SEIN) bubble (up)
auf′spulen *tr* wind up
auf′spüren *tr* track down, ferret out
auf′stacheln *tr* goad; (fig) stir up
auf′stampfen *intr*—**mit dem Fuß a.** stamp one′s foot
Auf′stand *m* insurrection, uprising

aufständisch [′aʊfʃtɛndɪʃ] *adj* insurgent ‖ **Aufständischen** *pl* insurgents
auf′stapeln *tr* stack up, pile up
auf′stechen §64 *tr* puncture; (surg) lance
auf′stecken *tr* (*Flagge*) plant; (*Haar*) pin up; (coll) give up; **j–m ein Licht a.** enlighten s.o.
auf′stehen §146 *intr* (HABEN) stand open ‖ *intr* (SEIN) stand up, get up; (*gegen*) revolt (against)
auf′steigen §148 *intr* (SEIN) climb; (*Reiter*) mount; (*Rauch*) rise; (*Gewitter*) come up; (*Tränen*) well up; **a. auf** (*acc*) get on
auf′stellen *tr* set up, put up; (*Beispiel*) set; (*Behauptung*) make; (*Wachposten*) post; (*Bauten*) erect; (*Leiter*) raise (*Waren*) display; (*Maschine*) assemble; (*als Kandidaten*) nominate; (*Regel, Problem*) state; (*Lehre*) propound; (*Rekord*) set; (*Liste*) make out; (*Rechnung*) draw up, make out; (*Stühle*) arrange; (*Falle*) set; (*Bedingungen, Grundsätze*) lay down; (*Beweis*) furnish ‖ *ref* station oneself
Auf′stellung *f* (-;-**en**) erection; assertion; list, schedule; (mil) formation; (pol) nomination; (sport) lineup
auf′stemmen *tr* pry open ‖ *ref* prop oneself up
Auf′stieg *m* climb; (*Steigung*) slope; (fig) advancement
auf′stöbern *tr* ferret out; (fig) unearth
auf′stoßen §150 *tr* push open ‖ *ref*—**sich |dat| das Knie a.** skin one′s knee ‖ *intr* (HABEN) (sl) belch ‖ *intr* (HABEN & SEIN) bump, touch; (*Schiff*) touch bottom ‖ *intr* (SEIN)—**j–m a.** strike s.o., cross s.o.′s mind
auf′streichen §85 *tr* (*Butter*) spread
auf′streuen *tr* (**auf** *acc*) sprinkle (on)
Auf′strich *m* upstroke; (*auf Brot*) spread
auf′stützen *tr* prop up
auf′suchen *tr* search for; (*nachschlagen*) look up; (*Ort*) visit; (*aufsammeln*) pick up; (*Arzt*) go to see
Auf′takt *m* upbeat; (fig) prelude
auf′tauchen *intr* (SEIN) turn up, appear; (*Frage*) crop up; (*U-Boot*) surface; (*Gerücht*) arise
auf′tauen *tr* & *intr* (SEIN) thaw
auf′teilen *tr* divide up
Auf′trag [′aʊftrak] *m* (-[e]s;⁼e) (*Anweisung*) orders, instructions; (*Bestellung*) order, commission; (*Sendung*) mission; **in A. von** on behalf of
auf′tragen §132 *tr* instruct, order; (*Speise*) serve; (*Farben, Butter*) put on; (*Kleidungsstück*) wear out; (surv) plot; **j–m etw a.** impose s.th. on s.o. ‖ *intr*—**dick** (or **stark**) **a.** put it on thick
Auf′traggeber –**in** §6 *mf* employer; (*Besteller*) client, customer
Auf′tragsformular *n* order blank
auf′tragsgemäß, **auf′trag(s)mäßig** *adv* as ordered, according to instructions
auf′treffen §151 *intr* (SEIN) strike
Auf′treffpunkt *m* point of impact
auf′treiben §62 *tr* (*Staub; Geld*) raise;

(Wild) flush; *(aufblähen)* distend; *(Teig)* cause to rise

auf′trennen *tr* rip, undo, unstitch

auf′treten §152 *tr (Tür)* kick open ‖ *intr* (SEIN) step, tread; *(erscheinen)* appear; *(handeln)* act, behave; *(eintreten)* occur, crop up; *(pathol)* break out; *(theat)* enter ‖ **Auftreten** *n* (–s;) appearance; occurrence; behavior; **sicheres A.** poise

Auf′trieb *m* drive; buoyancy; *(aer & fig)* lift; *(agr)* cattle drive; **j—m A. geben** encourage s.o.

Auf′tritt *m (Streit)* scene, row; *(theat)* entrance *(of an actor)*; *(theat)* scene

auf′trumpfen *intr* play a higher trump; **gegen j—n a.** go to s.o. better

auf′tun §154 *tr & ref* open

auf′türmen *tr & intr* pile up

auf′wachen *intr* (SEIN) awaken, wake up

auf′wachsen §155 *intr* (SEIN) grow up

auf′wallen *intr* (SEIN) boil, seethe; *(fig)* surge, rise up

Auf′wallung *f* (–;–en) *(fig)* outburst

Aufwand [′aufvant] *m* (–[e]s;⁻e) *(an dat)* expenditure (of); *(Prunk)* show

auf′wärmen *tr* warm up; *(fig)* drag up

Auf′wartefrau *f* cleaning woman

auf′warten *intr (dat)* wait on; **a. mit** oblige with, offer

Auf′wärter –in §6 *mf* attendant ‖ *f* cleaning woman

aufwärts [′aufverts] *adv* upward(s)

Auf′wärtshaken *m* (box) uppercut

Auf′wartung *f* (–;) attendance; *(bei Tisch)* service; *(Besuch)* call; **j—m seine A. machen** pay one's respects to s.o.

Aufwasch [′aufvaʃ] *m* (–es;) washing; dirty dishes

auf′waschen §158 *tr & intr* wash up

auf′wecken *tr* wake (up)

auf′weichen *tr* soften; soak ‖ *intr* (SEIN) become soft; become sodden

auf′weisen §118 *tr* produce, show

auf′wenden §140 *tr* spend, expend; **Mühe a.** take pains

auf′werfen §160 *tr* throw up; *(Tür)* fling open; *(Graben)* dig; *(Frage)* raise ‖ *ref*—**sich a. zu** set oneself up as

auf′wickeln *tr* wind up; *(Haar)* curl; *(loswickeln)* unwind

aufwiegeln [′aufviːɡəln] *tr* instigate

Aufwiegler –in [′aufviːɡlər(ɪn)] §6 *mf* instigator

aufwieglerisch [′aufviːɡlərɪʃ] *adj* inflammatory

Auf′wind *m* updraft

auf′winden §59 *tr* wind up; *(Anker)* weigh ‖ *ref* coil up

auf′wirbeln *tr (Staub)* raise; **viel Staub a.** (coll) make quite a stir

auf′wischen *tr* wipe up

auf′wühlen *tr* dig up; *(Wasser)* churn up; *(fig)* stir up

auf′zählen *tr* enumerate, itemize

auf′zäumen *tr* bridle

auf′zehren *tr* consume

auf′zeichnen *tr* make a sketch of; *(notieren)* write down, record

aufzeigen *tr* point out

auf′ziehen §163 *tr* pull up; *(öffnen)* pull open; *(Uhr)* wind; *(Saite)* put on; *(Perlen)* string; *(Kind)* bring up; *(Tier)* breed; *(Pflanzen)* grow; *(Flagge, Segel)* hoist *(Anker)* weigh; *(Veranstaltung)* arrange, organize; *(coll)* kid ‖ *intr* (SEIN) approach, pull up

Auf′zucht *f* breeding, raising

Auf′zug *m* elevator; *(e–r Uhr)* winder; *(Aufmarsch)* parade, procession; *(gym)* chin-up; *(theat)* act

auf′zwingen §142 *tr*—**j—m etw a.** force s.th. on s.o.; **j—m seinen Willen a.** impose one's will on s.o.

Augapfel [′aukapfəl] *m* eyeball; *(fig)* apple of the eye

Auge [′auɡə] *n* (–s;–n) eye; *(auf Würfeln)* dot; *(hort)* bud; *(typ)* face

äugeln [′ɔɪɡəln] *intr*—**ä. mit** wink at

Augen– [auɡən] *comb.fm.* eye, of the eye(s), in the eye(s); visual; *(anat)* ocular, optic(al)

Au′genblick *m* moment, instant

au′genblicklich *adj* momentary; *(sofortig)* immediate, instantaneous

Au′genblicksmensch *m* hedonist; impulsive person

Au′genbraue *f* eyebrow

Au′genbrauenstift *m* eyebrow pencil

au′genfällig *adj* conspicuous, obvious

Au′genhöhle *f* eye socket

Au′genlicht *n* eyesight

Au′genlid *n* eyelid

Au′genmaß *n* sense of proportion; **ein gutes A. haben** have a keen eye; **nach dem A.** by eye

Au′genmerk *n* attention

Au′gennerv *m* optic nerve

Au′genschein *m* inspection; *(Anschein)* appearances; **in A. nehmen** inspect

au′genscheinlich *adj* obvious

Au′genstern *m* pupil; iris

Au′gentäuschung *f* optical illusion

Au′gentrost *m* sight for sore eyes

Au′genwasser *n* eyewash

Au′genweide *f* sight for sore eyes

Au′genwimper *f* eyelash

Au′genwinkel *m* corner of the eye

Au′genzeuge *m*, **Au′genzeugin** *f* eyewitness

–äugig [ɔɪɡɪç] *comb.fm.* –eyed

August [au′ɡust] *m* (–[e]s & –s;–e) August

Auktion [auk′tsjon] *f* (–;–en) auction

Auktio·nator [auktsjo′natɔr] *m* (–s; –natoren [na′toːrən]) auctioneeer

auktionieren [auktsjo′niːrən] *tr* auction off, put up for auction

Au·la [′aula] *f* (–;–s & –len [lən]) auditorium

aus [aus] *adv* out; **von … aus** from, e.g., **vom Fenster aus** from the window ‖ *prep (dat)* out of, from; because of

aus′arbeiten *tr* elaborate; finish ‖ *ref* work out, take physical exercise

Aus′arbeitung *f* (–;–en) elaboration; *(schriftlich)* composition; *(körperlich)* workout; *(tech)* finish

aus′arten *intr* (SEIN) get out of hand; **(in** *acc)* degenerate (into)

aus′atmen *tr* exhale

aus'baden tr (coll) take the rap for
aus'baggern tr dredge
Aus'bau m (–[e]s;) completion; expansion, development
aus'bauen tr complete; (erweitern) expand, develop
aus'bedingen tr stipulate
aus'bessern tr repair; (Kleid) mend; (Bild) retouch
aus'beulen tr take the dents out of
Aus'beute f (Ertrag) output; (Gewinn) profit, gain
ausbeuten ['ausbɔɪtən] tr exploit
aus'biegen §57 tr bend out || intr (SEIN) curve; (dat, vor dat) make way (for)
aus'bilden tr develop; (lehren) train, educate; (mil) drill || ref train
Aus'bilder m (mil) drill instructor
aus'bitten §60 ref–sich [dat] etw a. ask for s.th.; insist on s.th.
aus'bleiben §62 intr (SEIN) stay out; stay away; be missing
aus'bleichen §85 tr & intr (SEIN) bleach; fade
aus'blenden tr (cin, rad) fade-out
Aus'blick m (auf acc) view (of); (fig) outlook
aus'bohren tr bore (out), drill (out)
aus'borgen ref–sich [dat] etw a. von borrow s.th. from
aus'brechen §64 tr break off || intr (SEIN) (aus) break out (of)
aus'breiten tr & ref spread; extend
aus'brennen §97 tr burn out, gut; (Sonne) parch; (med) cauterize || intr (SEIN) burn out; (Haus) be gutted
Aus'bruch m outbreak; (e-s Vulkans) eruption; (e-s Gefangenen) breakout; (des Gelächters) outburst
aus'brüten tr incubate; hatch
Ausbuchtung ['ausbuxtʊŋ] f (–;-en) bulge
ausbuddeln ['ausbudəln] tr (coll) dig out
aus'bügeln tr iron out
Aus'bund m (von) very embodiment (of)
ausbürgern ['ausbyrgərn] tr expatriate
aus'bürsten tr brush out
Aus'dauer f perseverance
aus'dauern intr persevere, persist
aus'dauernd adj persevering; (bot) perennial
aus'dehnen tr & ref stretch, expand; (Organ) dilate
aus'denken §66 tr think out; think up; **nicht auszudenken** inconceivable
aus'deuten tr interpret, explain
aus'dienen intr serve one's time
aus'dorren intr (SEIN) dry up; wither
aus'dörren tr dry up, parch
aus'drehen tr turn out; turn off
Aus'druck m expression
aus'drücken tr squeeze out; (fig) express
ausdrücklich ['ausdryklɪç] adj express, explicit
aus'druckslos adj expressionless
aus'drucksvoll adj expressive
Aus'drucksweise f way of speaking
aus'dünsten tr exhale, give off || intr evaporate; (schwitzen) sweat

auseinan'der adv apart; separately
auseinan'derfallen §72 intr (SEIN) fall apart
auseinan'dergehen §82 intr (SEIN) part; (Versammlung) break up; (Meinungen) differ; (Wege) branch off; (auseinanderfallen) come apart
auseinan'derhalten §90 tr keep apart
auseinan'derlaufen §105 intr (SEIN) (Menge) disperse; (Wege) diverge
auseinan'dernehmen §116 tr take apart
auseinan'dersetzen tr explain || ref– sich mit etw a. come to grips with s.th.; sich mit j–m a. have it out with s.o.; (gütlich) come to an understanding with s.o.
Auseinan'dersetzung f explanation; (Erörterung) discussion, controversy; (Übereinkommen) arrangement
aus'erkoren adj chosen; predestined
aus'erlesen adj choice || §107 tr choose, select
aus'ersehen §138 tr destine
aus'erwählen tr pick out, choose
aus'fahren §71 tr (Straße, Gleis) wear out; (aer) let down; **den Motor a.** (coll) open it up; **die Kurve a.** not cut the corner || intr (SEIN) drive out; (naut) put to sea; (rr) pull out
Aus'fahrt f departure; exit; (Spazierfahrt) ride, drive; (Torweg) gateway
Aus'fall m falling out; (Ergebnis) result; (Verlust) loss; (fencing) lunge; (mach) breakdown; (mil) sally
aus'fallen §72 intr (SEIN) fall out; (nicht stattfinden) fail to take place; (ausgelassen werden) be omitted; (versagen) go out of commission; (Ergebnis) turn out; (mil) sortie
aus'fallend adj aggressive, insulting
aus'fechten §74 tr (Kampf) fight; (Streit) settle (by fighting)
aus'fegen tr sweep (out)
aus'fertigen tr finish; (Paß) issue; (Scheck) write out; (Schriftstück) draw up, draft; **doppelt a.** draw up in duplicate
aus'findig adj—a. machen find out; (aufspüren) trace
aus'fliegen §57 intr (SEIN) fly out; (wegfliegen) fly away; (von Hause wegziehen) leave home; go on a trip
aus'fließen §76 intr (SEIN) flow out
Aus'flucht f evasion; **Ausflüchte machen** dodge, beat around the bush
aus'fluchten tr align
Aus'flug m trip, outing
Ausflügler ['ausflyglər] m (–s;–) tourist, vacationer
Aus'fluß m outflow; (Eiter) discharge; (Ergebnis) outcome; (Mündung) outlet
aus'folgen tr hand over
aus'forschen tr investigate; sound out
aus'fragen tr interrogate, quiz
aus'fressen §70 tr empty (by eating); (chem) corrode; (geol) erode; **was hast du denn ausgefressen?** (coll) what were you up to?
Ausfuhr ['ausfur] f (–;-en) export
Aus'fuhrabgabe f export duty
ausführbar ['ausfyrbar] adj feasible

aus'führen *tr* carry out; export, ship; (*Auftrag*) fill; (*darlegen*) explain

Aus'fuhrhändler –*in* §6 *mf* exporter

ausführlich ['ausfy:rlɪç] *adj* detailed ‖ *adv* in detail, in full

Aus'führung *f* (–;–en) carrying out, performance; (*Qualität*) workmanship; (*Darlegung*) explanation; (*e–s Gesetzes, Befehls*) implementation; (*Fertigstellung*) completion; (*e–s Verbrechens*) perpetrations; (*typ*) type, model; copy

Aus'fuhrwaren *pl* exports

aus'füllen *tr* fill out; (*Zeit*) occupy; (*Lücke; Stellung*) fill

Aus'gabe *f* (*Verteilung*) distribution; (*von Geldern*) expenditure; (*von Briefen*) delivery; (*e–s Buches*) edition; (*von Aktien*) issue

Aus'gang *m* exit; (*Auslaß*) outlet; (*Ergebnis*) result; (*Ende*) close, end; (*aer*) gate

Aus'gangspunkt *m* starting point

Aus'gangssprache *f* source language

aus'geben §80 *tr* give out, distribute; (*Aktien; Befehl*) issue; (*Geld*) spend; (*Briefe*) deliver; (*Karten*) deal ‖ *ref*—**sich a. für** pass oneself off as

ausgebeult ['ausgəbɔɪlt] *adj* baggy

Aus'geburt *f* figment

aus'gedehnt *adj* extensive

aus'gedient *adj* retired; (*educ*) emeritus

aus'gefallen *adj* (fig) eccentric, odd

aus'gefeilt *adj* (fig) flawless

aus'geglichen *adj* (*Person*) well-balanced; (*Styl*) balanced

aus'gehen §82 *intr* (SEIN) go out; (*Vorräte, Geld, Geduld*) run out; (*Haar*) fall out; (*Farbe*) fade; **a. auf** (*acc*) aim at, be bent on; **a. von** proceed from; **die Sache ging von ihm aus** it was his idea; **frei a.** get off scot-free; **gut a.** turn out well; **leer a.** come away empty-handed; **wenn wir davon a., daß** going on the assumption that

Aus'gehverbot *n* curfew

aus'gekocht *adj* (*Lügner*) out-and-out; (*Verbrecher*) hardened

aus'gelassen *adj* boisterous

aus'geleiert *adj* trite; worn-out; (*Gewinde*) stripped

aus'gemacht *adj* settled; downright

ausgenommen *prep* (acc) except; **niemand a.** bar none

aus'gepicht *adj* inveterate

aus'gerechnet *adv* just, of all ...; **a. Sie!** you of all people!

aus'geschlossen *adj* out of the question, impossible

Ausgesiedelte ['ausgəzi:dəltə] §5 *mf* evacuee, displaced person

aus'gestalten *tr* make arrangements for

aus'gesucht *adj* choice

aus'gezeichnet *adj* excellent

ausgiebig ['ausgi:bɪç] *adj* abundant; (*ergiebig*) productive

aus'gießen §76 *tr* pour out, pour away

Aus'gleich *m* (–s;–e) (*Ersatz*) compensation; (*Vergleich*) compromise; (acct) settlement; (tennis) deuce

aus'gleichen §85 *tr* level, smooth out; (*Konten*) balance; (*Verlust*) compensate for ‖ *ref* cancel one another out

Ausgleichs– *comb.fm.* balancing, compensating

Aus'gleichung *f* (–;–en) equalization; settlement; compensation

aus'gleiten §86 *intr* (SEIN) slip

aus'graben §87 *tr* dig out, dig up; (*Leiche*) exhume; (archeol) excavate

aus'greifen §88 *intr* reach out; **weit ausgreifend** far-reaching

Ausguck ['ausguk] *m* (–s;–e) lookout

aus'gucken *intr* (nach) be on the lookout (for)

Aus'guß *m* sink; (*Tülle*) spout, nozzle

aus'haken *tr* unhook

aus'halten §90 *tr* endure, stand ‖ *intr* persevere, stick it out

aus'handeln *tr* get by bargaining

aushändigen ['aushɛndɪgən] *tr* hand over, surrender

Aus'hang *m* notice, shingle

Aus'hängeschild *n* (–[e]s;–er) sign board, shingle; (fig) front, cover

aus'harren *intr* hold out, last

aus'hauchen *tr* breathe out, exhale

aus'heben §94 *tr* lift out; (*Tür*) lift off its hinges; (*Truppen*) recruit

aushecken ['aushɛkən] *tr* (fig) hatch

aus'heilen *tr* heal completely ‖ *intr* (SEIN) heal up

aus'helfen §96 *intr* (dat) help out

Aus'hilfe *f* (temporary) help; (temporary) helper; makeshift

Aushilfs– *comb.fm.* temporary, emergency

Aus'hilfsarbeit *f* part-time work

Aus'hilfslehrer –*in* §6 *mf* substitute teacher

aus'hilfsweise *adv* temporarily

aus'höhlen *tr* hollow out

aus'holen *tr* (*ausfragen*) sound out ‖ *intr* (beim Schwimmen) stroke; **mit dem Arm a.** raise the arm (before striking); **weit a.** start from the beginning

aus'horchen *tr* sound out, pump

aus'hülsen *tr* (*Bohnen, usw.*) shell

aus'hungern *tr* starve (out)

aus'husten *tr* cough up

aus'kehlen *tr* groove

Aus'kehlung *f* (–;–en) groove

aus'kehren *tr* sweep (out)

aus'kennen §97 *ref* know one's way; (in e–m Fach) be well versed

Aus'klang *m* end, close

aus'klappen *tr* pull out (a fold-away bed)

aus'kleiden *tr* line, panel; (*ausziehen*) undress ‖ *ref* undress

aus'klopfen *tr* beat the dust out of

ausklügeln ['auskly:gəln] *tr* figure out (ingeniously)

aus'kneifen §88 *intr* (SEIN) beat it

aus'knipsen *tr* (coll) switch off

ausknobeln ['auskno:bəln] *tr* figure out

aus'kochen *tr* boil out; boil clean

aus'kommen §99 *intr* (SEIN) come out, get out; (*ausreichen*) manage ‖ **Auskommen** *n* (–s;) livelihood

auskömmlich ['auskœmlɪç] *adj* adequate

aus'kosten *tr* relish

aus'kramen ['auskrɑ:mən] *tr* (aus Schubladen) drag out; (fig) show off

aus′kratzen *tr* scratch out; (surg) curette

aus′kriechen §102 *intr* (SEIN) be hatched

aus′kugeln *ref*—sich [*dat*] den Arm a. dislocate the shoulder

aus′kundschaften *tr* explore; (mil) scout

Auskunft [′auskunft] *f* (–;ᵈᵉe) information, piece of information

Auskunftei [auskunf′taɪ] *f* (–;-en) private detective agency

Aus′kunftschalter *m* information desk

aus′kuppeln *tr* uncouple; (*die Kupplung*) release ‖ *intr* disengage the clutch

aus′lachen *tr* laugh at ‖ *ref* have a good laugh

aus′laden §103 *tr* unload; (*Gast*) put off ‖ *intr* project, jut out ‖ **Ausladen** *n* (–;) unloading; projection

Aus′lage *f* (*von Geld*) outlay; (*Unkosten*) expenses; (*von Waren*) display; (*Schaufenster*) display window

Aus′land *n* foreign country, foreign countries; **im A. leben** live abroad; **ins A. gehen** go abroad

Ausländer -in [′auslendər(ɪn)] §6 *mf* foreigner, alien

aus′ländisch *adj* foreign, alien

Auslands- *comb.fm.* foreign

Aus′laß [′auslas] *m* (–lasses;-lässe) outlet

aus′lassen §104 *tr* let out; (*weglassen*) omit; (*Wut*) (*an dat*) vent (on) ‖ *ref* express one's opinion

Aus′lassung *f* omission; (*Bemerkung*) remark

Aus′lassungszeichen *n* (gram) apostrophe; (typ) caret

Aus′lauf *m* sailing; room to run

aus′laufen §105 *intr* (SEIN) run out; (*Schiff*) put out to sea; (*Farbe*) run; **a. in** (*acc*) end in; (*Straße*) run into

Aus′läufer *m* (geol) spur; (hort) runner

aus′leben *tr* live out ‖ *ref* make the most of one's life ‖ *intr* die

aus′lecken *tr* lick clean

aus′leeren *tr* empty ‖ *ref* have a bowel movement

aus′legen *tr* lay out; (*Waren*) display; (*erklären*) construe; (*Geld*) advance; (*Fußboden*) cover (*with carpeting*); (*Minen*) lay; (*Schlinge*) set; **falsch a.** misconstrue, misinterpret

Aus′leger -in §6 *mf* interpreter ‖ *m* outrigger; (*e-s Krans*) boom

aus′leihen §81 *tr* lend (out) ‖ *ref*—sich [*dat*] etw a. borrow s.th.

aus′lernen *intr* finish one's apprenticeship; **man lernt nie aus** one never stops learning

Aus′lese *f* pick, choice

aus′lesen §107 *tr* pick out; (*Buch*) finish reading

aus′liefern *tr* deliver, turn over; (*verteilen*) distribute; (*Verbrecher*) extradite; **j-m ausgeliefert sein** be at s.o.'s mercy

aus′liegen §108 *intr* (SEIN) be on display

aus′löffeln *tr* spoon out; **etw a. zu ha-**

ben have to face the consequences of s.th.

aus′löschen *tr* (*Feuer*) extinguish; (*Licht*) put out; (*Schreiben*) erase

aus′losen *tr* draw lots for

aus′lösen *tr* loosen, release; (*Gefangegen*) ransom; (*Pfand*) redeem

Aus′löser *m* (–s;–) release

aus′loten *tr* (naut & fig) plumb

aus′lüften *tr* air, ventilate

aus′machen *tr* (*Feuer*) put out; (*sichten*) make out; (*betragen*) amount to; (*Fleck*) remove; (*Licht*) turn out; (*bilden*) constitute; (*vereinbaren*) agree upon; **es macht nichts aus** it doesn't matter

aus′malen *tr* paint ‖ *ref*—sich [*dat*] etw a. picture s.th.

aus′marschieren *intr* (SEIN) march out

Aus′maß *n* measurement; dimensions; **in großem A.** on a large scale; (fig) to a great extent

ausmergeln [′ausmergərln] *tr* exhaust

ausmerzen [′ausmertsən] *tr* reject; (*ausrotten*) eradicate

aus′messen §70 *tr* measure; survey

aus′misten *tr* (*Stall*) clean; (fig) clean up

aus′mustern *tr* discard; (mil) discharge

Aus′nahme *f* (–;-n) exception

Aus′nahmezustand *m* state of emergency

aus′nahmslos *adj & adv* without exception

aus′nahmsweise *adv* by way of exception

aus′nehmen §116 *tr* take out; (*Fisch, Huhn*) clean; (*ausschließen*) exclude; (sl) clean out (of money) ‖ *ref*—sich gut a. look good

aus′nutzen, aus′nützen *tr* utilize; (*Gelegenheit*) take advantage of

aus′packen *tr* unpack; (*Geheimnis*) disclose ‖ *intr* (coll) unburden oneself, open up

aus′pfeifen §88 *tr* hiss (off the stage)

aus′plappern *tr* blurt out, blab out

aus′plaudern *tr* blab out

aus′plündern *tr* ransack; (coll) clean out (of money)

aus′polstern *tr* stuff, pad

aus′posaunen *tr* (coll) broadcast

aus′probieren *tr* try out, test

Aus′puff *m* (–[e]s;-e) exhaust

Aus′puffleitung *f* (aut) manifold

Aus′puffrohr *n* exhaust pipe

Aus′pufftopf *m* (aut) muffler

aus′pumpen *tr* pump out; **ausgepumpt** (coll) exhausted

aus′putzen *tr* (*reinigen*) clean out; (*schmücken*) adorn ‖ *ref* dress up

aus′quartieren *tr* put out (*of s.o.'s room*)

aus′radieren *tr* erase

aus′rangieren *tr* (coll) scrap

aus′rauben *tr* rob, ransack

aus′räumen *tr* (*Schrank*) clear out; (*Möbel*) remove; (med) clean out

aus′rechnen *tr* figure out

aus′recken *tr* stretch ‖ *ref*—sich [*dat*] den Hals a. crane one's neck

Aus′rede *f* evasion, excuse

aus′reden *tr*—j-m etw a. talk s.o. out

of s.th. ‖ *ref* make excuses ‖ *intr* finish speaking

aus'reiben §62 *tr* rub out; (mach) ream

aus'reichen *tr* suffice, be enough

aus'reichend *adj* sufficient

Aus'reise *f* departure; way out

aus'reißen §53 *tr* tear out ‖ *ref—er reißt sich* [*dat*] *dabei kein Bein aus* he's not exactly killing himself ‖ *intr* (SEIN) run away

Aus'reißer *m* runaway

aus'renken *tr* dislocate

aus'richten *tr* straighten; (in *e-e Linie bringen*) align; (*vollbringen*) accomplish; (*Botschaft, Gruß*) convey

aus'roden *tr* root out; (*Wald*) clear

aus'rollen *tr* roll out ‖ *intr* (SEIN) (aer) taxi to a standstill

ausrotten ['ausrɔtən] *tr* root out; (*Volk, Tierrasse*) exterminate; (*Übel*) eradicate

aus'rücken *tr* (*Kupplung*) disengage ‖ *intr* (SEIN) march off; run away

Aus'ruf *m* outcry; (*öffentlich*) proclamation; (gram) interjection

aus'rufen §122 *tr* call out; exclaim; **a. als** (*or* **zum**) proclaim

Aus'rufungszeichen *n* exclamation point

aus'ruhen *ref* & *intr* rest

aus'rupfen *tr* pluck

aus'rüsten *tr* equip, fit out; arm

aus'rutschen *intr* (SEIN) slip (out)

Aus'saat *f* sowing; (& fig) seed(s)

aus'säen *tr* sow; (fig) disseminate

Aus'sage *f* statement; (gram) predicate; (jur) affidavit

aus'sagen *tr* state ‖ *intr* give evidence, make a statement

Aus'sagesatz *m* declarative sentence

Aus'sageweise *f* (gram) mood

Aus'satz *m* leprosy

Aussätzige ['auszɛtsɪɡə] §5 *mf* leper

aus'saugen §125 *tr* suck dry; (fig) bleed white

Aus'sauger **-in** §6 *mf* (coll) bloodsucker

aus'schalten *tr* (*Licht, Radio, Fernseher*) turn off; (fig) shut out

Aus'schalter *m* circuit breaker

Aus'schank *m* sale of alcoholic drinks; (*Kneipe*) bar, taproom

aus'scharren *tr* dig up

Aus'schau *f—A.* **halten nach** be on the lookout for

aus'schauen *intr—a.* **nach** look out for; look like; **gut schaust du aus!** what a mess you are!

aus'scheiden §112 *tr* eliminate; (physiol) excrete, secrete ‖ *intr* (SEIN) retire, resign; (sport) drop out; **das scheidet aus!** that's out!

Aus'scheidung *f* (-;-en) elimination; retirement; (physiol) excretion, secretion

Aus'scheidungskampf *m* elimination bout

aus'schelten §83 *tr* scold, berate

aus'schenken *tr* pour (*drinks*)

aus'scheren *intr* (aus) veer away (from)

aus'schiffen *tr* disembark; (*Ladung*) unload ‖ *ref* disembark

aus'schimpfen *tr* scold, take to task

aus'schirren *tr* unharness

aus'schlachten *tr* cut up; (*Flugzeuge, usw.*) cannibalize; (*ausnutzen*) make the most of

aus'schlafen §131 *tr* sleep off ‖ *ref* & *intr* get enough sleep

Aus'schlag *m* rash; (e-s *Zeigers*) deflection; **den A. geben** turn the scales

aus'schlagen §132 *tr* knock out; (*Feuer*) beat out; (*Metall*) hammer out; (*Innenraum*) line; (*Angebot*) refuse ‖ *intr* bud; sprout; (*Pferd*) kick; (*Pendel*) swing; (*Zeiger*) move ‖ *intr* (SEIN) turn out

aus'schlaggebend *adj* decisive

aus'schließen §76 *tr* lock out; (*von der Schule*) expel; (*ausscheiden*) exclude; (sport) disqualify

aus'schließlich *adj* exclusive, sole ‖ *adv* exclusively, only ‖ *prep* (*genit*) exclusive of

aus'schlürfen *tr* sip

aus'schmieren *tr* grease; (**mit**) smear (with); (fig) pull a fast one on; (mas) point

aus'schmücken *tr* adorn, decorate; (*Geschichte*) embellish

aus'schnaufen *intr* get one's wind

aus'schneiden §106 *tr* cut out; **tief ausgeschnitten** low-cut, low-necked

Aus'schnitt *m* cut; (*Zeitungs-*) clipping; (*Kleid*) neckline; (*literarisch*) extract; (geom) sector

aus'schreiben §62 *tr* write out (in full); finish writing; (*ankündigen*) announce; (*Formular*) fill out; (*Rezept*) make out

aus'schreiten §86 *tr* pace off ‖ *intr* (SEIN) walk briskly

Aus'schreitung *f* (-;-en) excess

Aus'schuß *m* waste, scrap; (*Komitee*) committee

Aus'schußware *f* (indust) reject

aus'schütten *tr* pour out, spill; (*Dividende*) pay ‖ *ref—sich vor Lachen a.* split one's sides laughing

aus'schwärmen *intr* (SEIN) swarm out; (*Truppen*) deploy

aus'schwatzen *tr* blab out, blurt out

aus'schweifend *adj* (*Phantasie*) wild; (*liederlich*) wild, dissolute

Aus'schweifung *f* (-;-en) excess; curve; digression

aus'schwemmen *tr* rinse out; wash out

aus'schwenken *tr* rinse

aus'schwitzen *tr* sweat out; exude

aus'sehen §138 *intr* look; **nach j-m a.** look out for s.o.; **nach Regen a.** look like rain; **wie sieht er aus?** what does he look like? ‖ **Aussehen** *n* (-s;) look(s); appearance(s)

außen ['ausən] *adv* outside; **nach a.** out(wards)

außen-, Außen- *comb.fm.* external; outer; exterior; outdoor; foreign

Au'ßenaufnahme *f* (phot) outdoor shot

Au'ßenbahn *f* (sport) outside lane

aus'senden §140 *tr* send out

Au'ßenfläche *f* outer surface

Au'ßenminister *m* Secretary of State; (Brit) Foreign Secretary

Au'ßenpolitik *f* foreign policy

Au'ßenseite *f* outside

Außenseiter ['ausənzaɪtər] *m* (-s;-) dark horse, long shot; (*Einzelgänger*) loner; (*Nichtfachmann*) layman

Außenstände ['ausənʃtɛndə] *pl* accounts receivable

Au'ßenstelle *f* branch office

außer ['ausər] *prep* (*genit*)—a. **Landes** abroad || *prep* (*dat*) outside, out of; except, but; besides, in addition to; **a. Hause** not at home; **a. sich sein** be beside oneself

au'ßeramtlich *adj* unofficial, private

außerdem ['ausərdem] *adv* also, besides; moreover, furthermore

au'ßerdienstlich *adj* unofficial, private; (*mil*) off duty

äußere ['ɔɪsərə] §9 *adj* outer, exterior, external || **Äußere** §5 *n* exterior

au'ßerehelich *adj* extra-marital; (*Kind*) illegitimate

au'ßergewöhnlich *adj* extraordinary

außerhalb ['ausərhalp] *prep* (*genit*) outside, out of

äußerlich ['ɔɪsərlɪç] *adj* external, outward; (*oberflächlich*) superficial

Äu'ßerlichkeit *f* superficiality; (*Formalität*) formality; **Äußerlichkeiten** externals; formalities

äußern ['ɔɪsərn] *tr* express || *ref* (*über acc*) express one's views (about); (*in dat*) be manifested (in)

au'ßerordentlich *adj* extraordinary; **außerordentlicher Professor** associate professor

äußerst ['ɔɪsərst] *adj* outermost; (*fig*) extreme, utmost || *adv* extremely, highly || **Äußerste** §5 *n* extremity, extreme(s); **aufs Ä.** to the utmost; **bis zum Äußersten** to extremes; to the bitter end

außerstande ['ausərʃandə] *adj* unable

Äu'ßerung (-;-en) (*Ausdruck*) expression; (*Bemerkung*) remark

aus'setzen *tr* set out, put out; (*an der Küste*) maroon; (*Kind*; *dem Wetter*) expose; (*Boot*) lower; (*Wachen*) post; (*Belohnung*) hold out, promise; (*Tätigkeit*) discontinue; **auszusetzen haben an** (*dat*) find fault with || *intr* stop, halt

Aus'sicht *f* (*auf acc*) view (of); (*fig*) (*auf acc*) hope (of); **in A. nehmen** consider, plan

aus'sichtslos *adj* hopeless

Aus'sichtspunkt *m* vantage point

aus'sichtsreich *adj* promising

Aus'sichtsturm *m* lookout tower

aussichtsvoll *adj* promising

aus'sieben *tr* sift out; (*fig*) screen

aus'siedeln *tr* evacuate by force

Aus'siedlung *f* (-;-en) forced evacuation

aus'sinnen §121 *tr* think up, devise

aussöhnen ['auszønən] *tr* reconcile

aus'sondern *tr* (*trennen*) separate; (*auswählen*) single out; (*physiol*) excrete

aus'spähen *n* spy out || *intr* (*nach*) keep a lookout (for), reconnoiter

aus'spannen *tr* stretch; extend; (*Zugtiere*) unhitch || *intr* relax

Aus'spannung *f* (-;-en) relaxation

aus'speien §135 *tr* spit out

aus'sperren *tr* lock out, shut out

aus'spielen *tr* (*Karten*) lead with; (*Preis*) play for || *intr* lead off

aus'spionieren *tr* spy out

Aus'sprache *f* pronunciation; (*Erörterung*) discussion, talk

aus'sprechen §64 *tr* pronounce; (*deutlich*) articulate; (*ausdrücken*) express || *ref* (*über acc*) speak one's mind (about); (*für*; *gegen*) declare oneself (for; against); **sich mit j—m über etw a.** talk s.th. over with s.o. || *intr* finish speaking

Aus'spruch *m* statement

aus'spülen *tr* rinse

aus'spüren *tr* trace (down)

aus'staffieren *tr* fit out, furnish

aus'stampfen *tr* stamp out

Aus'stand *m* walkout

aus'ständig *adj* on strike, striking; (*fin*) in arrears, outstanding

ausstatten ['ausʃtatən] *tr* furnish, equip; (*Tochter*) give a dowry to

Aus'stattung *f* (-;-en) furnishings; equipment; trousseau

aus'stechen §64 *tr* cut out; (*Auge*) poke out; (*fig*) outdo

aus'stehen §146 *tr* endure, stand || *intr* still be expected, be overdue

aus'steigen §148 *intr* (SEIN) get out, get off

aus'stellen *tr* exhibit; (*Wache*) post; (*Quittung, Scheck*) make out; (*Paß*) issue

Aus'stellung *f* (-;-en) exhibit; issuance; criticism

Aus'stellungsdatum *n* date of issue

aus'sterben §149 *intr* die out

Aus'steuer *f* hope chest, dowry

aus'stopfen *tr* stuff, pad

Aus'stoß *m* (indust) output

aus'stoßen §150 *tr* knock out; (*vertreiben*) eject; (*Seufzer, Schrei, Fluch*) utter; (*Torpedo*) launch; (math) eliminate; (phonet) elide; (phys) emit

Aus'stoßrohr *n* torpedo tube

Aus'stoßung *f* (-;-en) ejection; utterance; (gram) elision

Aus'stoßzahlen *pl* (indust) production figures

aus'strahlen *tr & intr* radiate

aus'strecken *tr & ref* stretch out

aus'streichen §85 *tr* cross out; (*glätten*) smooth out; (*Bratpfanne*) grease

aus'streuen *tr* strew, scatter, spread

aus'strömen *tr & intr* (SEIN) pour out

aus'studieren *tr* study thoroughly

aus'suchen *tr* pick out

Aus'tausch *m* exchange

aus'tauschbar *adj* exchangeable; interchangeable

aus'tauschen *tr* exchange; interchange

Aus'tauschstoff *m* substitute

Aus'tauschstück *n* spare part

aus'teilen *tr* distribute, deal out

Auster ['austər] *f* (-;-n) oyster

aus'tilgen *tr* exterminate, wipe out

aus'toben *tr* give vent to || *ref* (*Person*) let one's hair down; (*Kinder*) raise a rumpus; (*Gewitter*) stop raging

aus'tollen *ref* make a racket

Austrag ['austrak] *m* (-[e]s;)—**bis zum A. der Sache** until the matter is decided; **zum A. bringen** bring to a head; (jur) settle; **zum A. kommen** come up for a decision

aus'tragen §132 *tr* carry out; (*Briefe*) deliver; (*Kleider*) wear out; (*Meisterschaft*) decide; (*Klatschereien*) spread; (acct) cancel

Aus'träger *m* deliveryman

Australien [aus'traljən] *n* (-s;) Australia

Australier –in [aus'traljər(ɪn)] §6 *mf* Australian

aus'treiben §62 *tr* drive out; exorcise

aus'treten §152 *tr* (*Feuer*) tread out; (*Schuhe, Treppen*) wear out || *intr* (SEIN) step out; (*Blut*) come out; (coll) go to the bathroom; **a. aus** leave (*school, a company, club*)

aus'trinken §143 *tr* drink up, drain

Aus'tritt *m* withdrawal

aus'trocknen *tr & intr* (SEIN) dry up

aus'tüfteln *tr* puzzle out

aus'üben *tr* (*Aufsicht, Macht*) exercise; (*Beruf*) practice; (*Pflicht*) carry out; (*Einfluß, Druck*) exert; (*Verbrechen*) commit; **ausübende Gewalt** executive power

Aus'verkauf *m* clearance sale

aus'verkaufen *tr* sell out; close out

aus'wachsen §155 *tr* outgrow

Aus'wahl *f* choice, selection

aus'wählen *tr* select, pick out

Aus'wanderer –in §6 *mf* emigrant

aus'wandern *intr* (SEIN) emigrate

auswärtig ['ausvertɪç] *adj* out-of-town; (*ausländisch*) foreign

auswärts ['ausverts] *adv* outward(s); out, away from home; (*außer der Stadt*) out of town; (*im Ausland*) abroad

Aus'wärtsspiel *n* away game

aus'wechselbar *adj* interchangeable

aus'wechseln *tr* exchange, interchange; (*ersetzen*) replace

Aus'weg *m* way out; escape

Ausweich– *comb.fm.* evasive; alternate; substitute; emergency; reserve

aus'weichen §85 *intr* (SEIN) (*dat*) make way (for), get out of the way (of); (*dat*) evade; **a. auf** (*acc*) switch to

aus'weichend *adj* evasive

Aus'weichklausel *f* escape clause

Aus'weichlager *n* emergency store

Aus'weichstelle *f* passing zone

Aus'weichstraße *f* bypass

Aus'weichziel *n* secondary target

aus'weinen *ref* have a good cry || *intr* stop crying

Ausweis ['ausvais] *m* (-s;-e) identification (card); (com) statement

aus'weisen §118 *tr* expel; (*aus Besitz*) evict; (*verbannen*) banish, deport; (*zeigen*) show || *ref* prove one's identity

Aus'weispapiere *pl* identification papers

Aus'weisung *f* (-;-en) expulsion; eviction; deportation

aus'weiten *tr & ref* widen, expand

auswendig ['ausvendɪç] *adj* outer || *adv* outside; outwardly; by heart

aus'werfen §160 *tr* throw out; (*Graben*) dig; (*Summe*) allocate; (*Lava*) eject; (*Blut, Schleim*) spit up; (angl) cast

aus'werten *tr* evaluate; (*ausnützen*) utilize; (*Statistik*) interpret

aus'wickeln *tr* unwrap

aus'wiegen §57 *tr* weigh out

aus'wirken *tr* knead || *ref* take effect; **sich a. auf** (*acc*) affect; **sich** [*dat*] **etw bei j–m a.** obtain s.th. from s.o.

Aus'wirkung *f* (-;-en) effect

aus'wischen *tr* wipe out; wipe clean; **j–m eins a.** play a dirty joke on s.o.

aus'wittern *tr* season || *intr* weather

aus'wringen §142 *tr* wring out

Aus'wuchs *m* outgrowth; (pathol) tumor

Aus'wurf *m* throwing out; (fig) scum; (mach) ejection

aus'zacken *tr* indent; (*wellenförmig*) scallop

aus'zahlen *tr* pay out; pay off || *ref*— **es zahlt sich nicht aus** it doesn't pay

aus'zählen *tr* count out

aus'zanken *tr* scold

aus'zehren *tr* consume, waste

Aus'zehrung *f* (-;) consumption

aus'zeichnen *tr* mark, tag; (*ehren*) honor; (fig) distinguish

Aus'zeichnung *f* (-;-en) labeling; decoration, honor; distinction

aus'ziehen §163 *tr* pull out; (*Kleid*) take off; (*Stelle*) excerpt; (*Zeichnung*) ink in; (chem) extract || *ref* undress || *intr* (SEIN) set out; (aus e–r Wohnung) move out

aus'zischen *tr* hiss off the stage

Aus'zug *m* departure; moving; excerpt; (*Abriß*) summary; (Bib) Exodus; (chem) extract; (com) statement

aus'zugsweise *adv* in summary form

aus'zupfen *tr* pluck out

authentisch [au'tentɪʃ] *adj* authentic

Auto ['auto] *n* (-s;-s) auto(mobile)

Au'tobahn *f* superhighway

Au'tobus *m* bus

Autodidakt [autodɪ'dakt] *m* (-en;-en) self-educated person

Au'todroschke *f* taxi

Au'tofahrer –in §6 *mf* motorist

Au'tofahrschule *f* driving school

Au'tofahrt *f* car ride, drive

Au'tofalle *f* speed trap

Autogramm [auto'gram] *n* (-[e]s;-e) autograph

Autogramm'jäger –in §6 *mf* autograph hound

Au'tokino *n* drive-in movie

Au'tokolonne *f* motorcade

Autokrat [auto'krat] *m* (-en;-en) autocrat

autokratisch [auto'kratɪʃ] *adj* autocratic

Automat [auto'mat] *m* (-en;-en) vending machine; (*Musik–*) jukebox; (*Spiel–*) slot machine

Automa'tenrestaurant *n* automat

automatisch [auto'matɪʃ] *adj* automatic

Automobil [automo'bil] *n* (-[e]s;-e) automobile

autonom [auto'nom] *adj* autonomous

Autonomie [autono'mi] *f* (-;) autonomy

Au•tor ['autor] *m* (-s;-toren ['torən]) author

Autoreparatur'werkstatt *f* auto repair shop, garage
Autorin [au'torɪn] *f* (-; -nen) authoress
autorisieren [autorɪ'zirən] *tr* authorize
autoritär [autorɪ'ter] *adj* authoritarian
Autorität [autorɪ'tet] *f* (-; -en) authority
Au'toschlosser *m* automobile mechanic
Au'toschuppen *m* carport

Au'tounfall *m* automobile accident
avancieren [avã'sirən] *intr* (SEIN) advance; (zu) be promoted (to)
avisieren [avɪ'zirən] *tr* advise, notify
Axt [akst] *f* (-; ⸚e) ax
Azalee [atsa'le·ə] *f* (-; -n) azalea
Azetat [atse'tɑt] *n* (-[e]s; -e) acetate
Azeton [atse'ton] *n* (-s;) acetone
Azetylen [atsety'len] *n* (-s;) acetylene
azurn [a'tsurn] *adj* azure, sky-blue

B

B, b [*be*] *invar n* B, b; (mus) B flat
babbeln ['babəln] *intr* babble
Baby ['bebi] *n* (-s; -s) baby
Babysitter ['bebɪzɪtər] *m* (-s; -) baby-sitter
Bach [bax] *m* (-[e]s; ⸚e) brook, creek
Backe ['bakə] *f* (-; -n) cheek; jaw (*of a vise*); (mach) die
backen ['bakən] §50 (& *pret* **backte**) *tr* bake; (*in der Pfanne*) fry ‖ (*pret* **backte;** *pp* **gebacken**) *intr* bake ‖ §109 *intr* (HABEN & SEIN) cake; stick
Backenbart (**Bak'kenbart**) *m* side whiskers
Backenstreich (**Bak'kenstreich**) *m* slap
Backenzahn (**Bak'kenzahn**) *m* molar; kleiner (or vorderer) B. bicuspid
Bäcker ['bekər] *m* (-s; -) baker
Bäckerei [bekə'raɪ] *f* (-; -en) bakery
Back'fett *n* shortening
Back'fisch *m* fried fish; (fig) teenager
Back'fischalter *n* teens (*of girls*)
Back'form *f* cake pan
Back'hähnchen *n* fried chicken
Back'hendel *n* (Aust) fried chicken
Back'huhn *n* fried chicken
Back'obst *n* dried fruit
Back'ofen *m* baking oven
Back'pfeife *f* slap in the face, smack
Back'pflaume *f* prune
Back'pulver *n* baking powder
Back'stein *m* brick
Back'trog *m* kneading trough
Back'waren *pl* baked goods
Back'werk *n* pastries
Bad [bɑt] *n* (-[e]s; ⸚er) bath; bath-room; (*Badeort*) spa
Ba'deanstalt *f* public baths; public pool
Ba'deanzug *m* swim suit
Ba'dehaube *f* bathing cap
Ba'dehose *f* bathing trunks
Ba'dekappe *f* bathing cap
Ba'demantel *m* bathrobe
baden ['badən] *tr & ref* bathe ‖ *intr* take a bath; **b. gehen** go swimming
Ba'deort *m* bathing resort; spa
Ba'destrand *m* bathing beach
Ba'detuch *n* bath towel
Ba'dewanne *f* bathtub
Badende ['badəndə] §5 *mf* bather
Ba'dewärter -n §6 *mf* lifeguard; bath-house attendant
Ba'dezimmer *n* bathroom
baff [baf] *adj* dumbfounded

Bagage [ba'gɑʒə] *f* (-;) (fig) rabble; (mil) baggage
Bagatelle [baga'telə] *f* (-; -n) trifle
Bagatel'lesache *f* petty offense
bagatellisieren [bagatelɪ'zirən] *tr* minimize, make light of
Bagger ['bagər] *m* (-s; -) dredge
baggern ['bagərn] *tr & intr* dredge
bähen ['be·ən] *intr* bleat
Bahn [bɑn] *f* (-; -en) way, path; (aer) runway; (astr) orbit; (aut) lane; (rr) railroad; (sport) course, track; (*Eis-*) (sport) rink; **auf die schiefe B. geraten** go astray; **B. brechen** (*dat*) pave the way (for); **mit der B. fahren** travel by train
bahn'brechend *adj* pioneering, epoch-making
Bahn'brecher -in §6 *mf* pioneer
Bahn'damm *m* railroad embankment
bahnen ['banən] *tr*—**e-n Weg. b.** clear a path, open up a path
Bahn'fahrt *f* train trip
bahn'frei *adj* free on board, f.o.b.
Bahn'hof *m* railroad station
Bahn'hofshalle *f* concourse
Bahn'hofsvorsteher *m* stationmaster
Bahn'linie *f* railroad line
Bahn'schranke *f* (rr) barrier
Bahn'steig *m* (rr) platform
Bahn'strecke *f* (rr) line, track
Bahn'übergang *m* railroad crossing
Bahn'wärter *m* (rr) signalman
Bahre ['barə] *f* (-; -n) stretcher; bier
Bahr'tuch *n* pall
Bai [baɪ] *f* (-; -en) bay
Baiser [be'ze] *m & n* (-s; -s) meringue cookie
Baisse ['besə] *f* (-; -n) (com) slump
Bais'sestimmung *f* downward trend
Baissier [bes'je] *m* (-s; -s) (st.exch.) bear
Bajonett [bajo'net] *n* (-s; -e) bayonet
Bake ['bakə] *f* (-; -n) beacon
Bakterie [bak'terjə] *f* (-; -n) bacterium
Bakte'rienforscher -in §6 *mf* bacteriologist
Bakte'rienkunde *f* bacteriology
Balance [ba'lɑ̃sə] *f* (-;) balance
balancieren [balã'sirən] *tr & intr* balance
bald [balt] *adv* (eher ['e·ər]; eheste ['e·əstə] §9 soon; (*beinahe*) nearly
baldig ['baldɪç] *adj* speedy; (*Antwort*) early

baldigst ['baldɪgst] *adv* very soon; at the earliest possible moment

Balg [balk] *m* (-[e]s;⁌e) skin, pelt; (*Hülse*) shell, husk; **Bälge** bellows; **j-m den B. abziehen** fleece s.o. ‖ *m & n* (-[e]s;⁌er) (coll) brat

balgen ['balgən] *ref* roll around, romp; (*raufen*) scuffle ‖ **Balgen** *m* (-s;-) (phot) bellows

Balgerei [balgə'raɪ] *f* (-;-en) scuffle

Balken ['balkən] *m* (-s;-) beam, rafter

Bal'kenwerk *n* framework

Balkon [bal'kon] *m* (-s;-e) balcony

Ball [bal] *m* (-[e]s;⁌e) ball; (*Tanz*) ball

Ballade [ba'ladə] *f* (-;-n) ballad

Ballast ['balast] *m* (-[e]s;-e) ballast; (fig) drag; (coll) padding

ballen ['balən] *tr*—**die Faust b.** clench one's fist ‖ *ref* form a cluster ‖ **Ballen** *m* (-s;-) (anat) ball; (com) bale; (pathol) bunion

ballern ['balərn] *intr* (coll) bang away

Ballett [ba'let] *n* (-[e]s;-e) ballet

Ballistik [ba'lɪstɪk] *f* (-;) ballistics

Ballon [ba'lon] *m* (-s;-s) balloon

Ball'saal *m* ballroom

Ball'schläger *m* (sport) bat

Ball'spiel *n* ball game

Bal'lung *f* (-;-en) (mil) massing (of troops)

Balsam ['balzam] *m* (-s;-e) balm, balsam; (fig) balm

balsamieren [balza'mirən] *tr* embalm

balzen ['baltsən] *intr* perform a mating dance

Bambus ['bambʊs] *m* (-;- & -ses;-se) bamboo

Bam'busrohr *n* bamboo, bamboo cane

banal [ba'nɑl] *adj* banal

Banane [ba'nɑnə] *f* (-;-n) banana

Banause [ba'nauzə] *f* (-n;-n) philistine

banausisch [ba'nauzɪʃ] *adj* narrow-minded

Band [bant] *m* (-[e]s;⁌e) volume; (*Einband*) binding ‖ *n* (-[e]s;-e) bond, tie; **Bande** chains, shackles ‖ *n* [-[e]s;⁌er) (*e-s Hutes, usw.*) band; (*Bindfaden*) string; (*zum Schmuck*) ribbon; tape; (anat) ligament; (electron) recording tape; (rad) band; **am laufenden B.** continuously

Bandage [ban'daʒə] *f* (-;-n) bandage

bandagieren [banda'ʒirən] *tr* bandage

Bande ['bandə] *f* (-;-n) band, gang, crew; (billiards) cushion

Ban'denkrieg *m* guerilla war(fare)

Ban'denmitglied *n* gangster; (mil) guerilla

Ban'denunwesen *n* gangsterism; partisan activities

bändigen [bendɪgən] *tr* tame; (fig) subdue, overcome; master

Bandit [ban'dit] *m* (-en;-en) bandit

Band'maß *n* tape measure

Band'säge *f* band saw

Band'scheibe *f* (anat) disk

Band'scheibenquetschung *f* slipped disk

Band'wurm *m* tapeworm

bang(e) [baŋ(ə)] *adj* scared, anxious; (*Gefühl*) disquieting; **j-m b. machen** scare s.o. ‖ **Bange** *f* (-;) fear

Bangigkeit ['baŋɪçkaɪt] *f* (-;) fear

Bank [baŋk] *f* (-;⁌e) bench; pew; (geol) layer, bed ‖ *f* (-;-en) bank

Bank'anweisung *f* check

Bank'ausweis *m* bank statement

Bank'einlage *f* bank deposit

Bankett [baŋ'ket] *n* (-s;-e) banquet

bank'fähig *adj* negotiable

Bank'guthaben *n* bank balance

Bank'halter –in §6 *mf* banker (*in games*)

Bankier [baŋk'je] *m* (-s;-s) banker

Bank'konto *n* bank account

bank'mäßig *adj* by check

bankrott [baŋk'rət] *adj* bankrupt ‖ *m* (-[e]s;-e) bankruptcy

Bank'verkehr *m* banking (*activity*)

Bank'wesen *n* banking

Bann [ban] *m* (-[e]s;-e) ban; (*Zauber*) spell; (eccl) excommunication

bannen ['banən] *tr* banish; (*Geister*) exorcize; (eccl) excommunicate

Banner ['banər] *n* (-s;-) banner; standard

Ban'nerträger *m* standard-bearer

Bann'fluch *m* anathema

Bann'kreis *m* spell; **in j-s B. geraten** come under s.o.'s spell

Bann'meile *f* (fig) city limits

Bann'ware *f* contraband

bar [bar] *adj* bare; (*rein*) pure, sheer; (fin) cash ‖ *adv* cash ‖ *prep* (*genit*) devoid of, lacking ‖ **Bar** *f* (-;-s) bar, taproom

Bär [ber] *m* (-en;-en) bear; (astr) Dipper; **j-m e-n B. aufbinden** tell s.o. a fish story

Bar– *comb.fm.* cash

Baracke [ba'rakə] *f* (-;-n) barrack; (wooden) hut

Barbar –in [bar'bar(ɪn)] §7 *mf* barbarian

Barbarei [barba'raɪ] *f* (-;-en) barbarism; (*Grausamkeit*) barbarity

barbarisch [bar'barɪʃ] *adj* barbarous; barbaric, primitive

bärbeißig ['berbaɪsɪç] *adj* surly

Bar'bestand *m* cash on hand

Bar'betrag *m* amount in cash

Barbier [bar'bir] *m* (-s;-e) barber

barbieren [bar'birən] *tr* shave; (fig) fleece

Barett [ba'ret] *n* (-[e]s;-e) beret

barfuß ['barfus] *adv* barefoot

barfüßig ['barfysɪç] *adj* barefooted

barg [bark] *pret* of **bergen**

Bar'geld *n* cash

barhäuptig ['barhɔɪptɪç] *adj* bareheaded

Bar'hocker *m* bar stool

Bariton ['barɪton] *m* (-s;-e) baritone

Barkasse [bar'kasə] *f* (-;-n) launch

Bärme ['bermə] *f* (-;) yeast, leaven

barmherzig [barm'hertsɪç] *adj* merciful

Bar'mittel *pl* cash

barock [ba'rok] *adj* baroque ‖ **Barock** *m & n* (-s;) baroque; baroque period

Barometer [barə'metər] *n* (-s;-) barometer

Baron [ba'ron] *m* (-s;-e) baron

Baronin [ba'ronɪn] *f* (-;-nen) baroness

Barre ['barə] f (-;-n) bar
Barren ['barən] m (-s;-) bar; ingot; (gym) parallel bars
Barriere [bar'jerə] f (-;-n) barrier
barsch [barʃ] adj gruff, rude ‖ **Barsch** m (-es;-e) (ichth) perch
Barschaft ['barʃaft] f (-;) cash
barst [barst] pret of bersten
Bart [bart] m (-[e]s;Ʝe) beard; (e-r Katze) whiskers; (e-s Fisches) barb; **der B. ist ab!** the jig is up!; **sich** [dat] **e-n B. wachsen lassen** grow a beard
bärtig ['bertɪç] adj bearded
bart'los adj beardless
Bar'verlust m straight loss
Basalt [ba'zalt] m (-[e]s;-e) basalt
Basar [ba'zar] m (-s;-e) bazaar
Ba·sis ['bazɪs] f (-;-sen [zən]) basis; (archit, math, mil) base
Baß [bas] m (Basses;Bässe) (mus) bass
Baß'geige f bass viol, contrabass
Bassin [ba'sɛ̃] n (-s;-s) reservoir; swimming pool; (naut) dock, basin
Baß'schlüssel m bass clef
Baß'stimme f bass (voice), basso
basta ['basta] interj—**und damit b.!** and that's that!
Bastard ['bastart] m (-[e]s;-e) bastard; (bot) hybrid
Bastei [bas'taɪ] f (-;-en) bastion
basteln ['bastəln] intr tinker
Bast'ler –in §6 mf hobbyist
bat [bat] pret of bitten
Bataillon [batal'jon] n (-s;-e) battalion
Batte·rie [batə'ri] f (-;-rien ['ri·ən] battery
Bau [bau] m (-[e]s;) erection, construction, building; (Bauart) structure, design; (Körper-) build; **er ist beim Bau** he is in the building trade; **er ist vom Bau** (coll) he's in the racket; **im Bau** under construction ‖ m (-[e]s;-ten) building; **auf dem Bau** at the construction site ‖ m (-[e]s;-e) burrow, hole; (min) mine
–bau m comb.fm. –construction, –building; –culture; –mining
Bau'abnahme f building inspection
Bau'arbeiter m construction worker
Bau'art f build; structure; type, model
Bauch [baux] m (-[e]s;Ʝe) belly, stomach; (Leib) bowels; (coll) pot-belly
Bauch– comb.fm. abdominal
bauchig ['bauxɪç] adj bulging; convex
Bauch'klatscher m belly flop
Bauch'laden m vendor's tray
Bauch'landung f belly-landing
Bauch'redner –in §6 mf ventriloquist
Bauch'speicheldrüse f pancreas
Bauch'weh n stomach ache, bellyache
bauen ['bau·ən] tr build; erect; make, manufacture; (ackern) till; (an-bauen) grow ‖ intr build; (an dat) work (at); (auf acc) depend (on), trust
Bauer ['bau·ər] m (-s & -n;-n) farmer; (cards) jack; (chess) pawn ‖ m (-s;-) builder ‖ m & n (-s;-) bird-cage
Bäuerchen ['bɔɪ·ərçən] n (-s;-) small farmer; (baby's) burp

Bäuerin ['bɔɪ·ərɪn] f (-;-nen) farmer's wife
bäuerisch ['bɔɪ·erɪʃ] adj boorish
Bau'erlaubnis f building permit
bäuerlich ['bɔɪ·erlɪç] adj rural
Bau'ernbursche m country lad
Bau'erndirne f country girl
Bauernfänger ['bau·ərnfɛŋər] m (-s;-) confidence man
Bau'erngut n, **Bau'ernhof** m farm
Bau'fach n architecture
bau'fällig adj dilapidated
Bau'genehmigung f building permit
Bau'gerüst n scaffold(ing)
Bau'gewerbe n building trade
Bau'gewerkschule f school of architecture and civil engineering
Bau'grundstück n building site
Bau'holz n lumber
Bau'kasten m building set
Bau'kunst f architecture
bau'lich adj architectural; structural; **in gutem baulichen Zustand** in good repair
Baum [baum] m (-[e]s;Ʝe) tree; (mach) shaft, axle; (naut) boom
Bau'meister m building contractor, builder; architect
baumeln ['bauməln] intr dangle
bäumen ['bɔɪmən] ref rear
Baum'garten m orchard
Baum'grenze f timber line
Baum'krone f treetop
Baum'schere f pruning shears
Baum'schule f nursery (of saplings)
Baum'stamm m tree trunk
baum'stark adj strong as an ox
Baum'muster n model (number)
Baum'wolle f cotton
Baum'wollkapsel f cotton boll
Baum'wollsamt m velveteen
Bau'plan m ground plan
Bau'platz m building lot
Bau'rat m (-[e]s;Ʝe) building inspector
Bausch [bauʃ] m (-[e]s;Ʝe) pad, wad; (e-s Segels) bulge, belly; **in B. und Bogen** wholesale
bauschen ['bauʃən] tr, ref & intr bulge, swell
bauschig ['bauʃɪç] adj puffy; baggy
Bau'schule f school of architecture and civil engineering
Bau'sparkasse f building and loan association
Bau'stahl m structural steel
Bau'stein m building stone; brick
Bau'stelle f building site; road construction
Bau'stoff m building material
Bau'techniker m construction engineer
Bau'unternehmer m contractor
Bau'unternehmung f building firm, building contractors
Bau'werk n building, edifice
Bau'wesen n building industry
Bau'zaun m hoarding
Bau'zeichnung f blueprint
Bayer –in ['baɪ·ər(ɪn)] §6 mf Bavarian
bayerisch ['baɪ·erɪʃ] adj Bavarian
Bayern ['baɪ·ərn] n Bavaria
Bazillenträger [ba'tsɪləntregər] m germ carrier

Bazil·lus [ba'tsɪlʊs] *m* (-ȝ-len [lən]) bacillus

be- [bə] *insep pref*

beabsichtigen [bə'apzɪçtɪgən] *tr* intend; (mit) mean (by)

beach'ten *tr* pay attention to; (*merken*) note, notice; (*befolgen*) observe; (*berücksichtigen*) consider

beach'tenswert *adj* noteworthy

Beach'tung *f* (-ȝ) attention; notice; observance; consideration

Beamte [bə'amtə] *m* (-nȝ-n) official

Beam'tenherrschaft *f* bureaucracy

Beam'tenlaufbahn *f* civil service career

Beamtentum [bə'amtəntum] *n* (-[e]sȝ) officialdom, bureaucracy

Beamtin [bə'amtɪn] *f* (-ȝ-nen) official

beäng'stigen *tr* make anxious, alarm

beanspruchen [bə'an/pruxən] *tr* claim; (*Zeit, Raum*) require; **zu stark beansprucht werden** be worked too hard

beanstanden [bə'an/tandən] *tr* object to, find fault with; (*Waren*) reject; (*Wahl*) contest; (*Recht*) challenge

Bean'standung *f* (-ȝ-en) objection; complaint

bean'tragen *tr* propose; (**bei**) apply for (to)

beant'worten *tr* answer

Beant'wortung *f* (-ȝ-en) answer

bear'beiten *tr* work; (*Land*) cultivate; (*Buch, Text*) revise; (*Wörterbuch*) compile; (*für die Bühne*) adapt; (*ein Manuskript*) prepare; (*Thema; Kunden*) work on; (*Person*) try to influence; (chem) treat; (*Auftrag*) (com) handle; (*Fall*) (jur) handle; (metal) machine, tool; (mus) arrange

bearg'wöhnen *tr* be suspicious of

beaufsichtigen [bə'aufzɪçtɪgən] *tr* supervise; (*Arbeiten*) superintend; (*Kinder*) look after; (educ) proctor; **streng b.** keep a sharp eye on

beauf'tragen *tr* commission, appoint; (mit) entrust (with)

Beauftragte [bə'auftraktə] §5 *mf* representative; (com) agent

bebau'en *tr* cultivate; (*Gelände*) build up

beben ['bebən] *intr* (vor) tremble (with), shake (with); (*Erde*) quake

bebrillt [bə'brɪlt] *adj* bespectacled

Becher ['beçər] *m* (-sȝ-) cup, mug

bechern ['beçərn] *intr* (coll) booze

Becken ['bekən] *n* (-sȝ-) basin, bowl; (anat) pelvis; (mus) cymbal

bedacht [bə'daxt] *adj* (**auf** *acc*) intent (on); **auf alles b. sein** think of everything; **darauf b. sein zu** (*inf*) be anxious to (*inf*) || **Bedacht** *m*—**B. nehmen auf** (*acc*) take into consideration; **mit B. deliberately**; with caution

bedächtig [bə'deçtɪç], **bedachtsam** [bə'daxtzam] *adj* cautious, deliberate

bedan'ken *ref*—**ich würde mich bestens b., wenn** (iron) I would be most indignant if; **sich b. bei j—m für** thank s.o. for

Bedarf [bə'darf] *m* (-[e]sȝ) demand; requirement; (**an** *dat*) need (of); **bei B.** if required; **den B. decken** meet the demand; **nach B.** as required;

seinen B. decken an (*dat*) get one's supply of

Bedarfs'artikel *pl* needs, supplies

Bedarfs'fall *m*—**im B.** in case of need

Bedarfs'güter *pl* consumer goods

Bedarfs'haltestelle *f* optional bus or trolley stop

Bedarfs'träger *m* consumer

bedauerlich [bə'dau·ərlɪç] *adj* regrettable

bedau'erlicherweise *adv* unfortunately

bedauern [bə'dau·ərn] *tr* pity, feel sorry for; regret, deplore || **Bedauern** *n* (-sȝ) (**über** *acc*) regret (over); (*Mitleid*) (mit) pity (for)

bedau'ernswert *adj* pitiful, pitiable

bedecken (bedek'ken) *tr* cover; bedeckt overcast

Bedeckung (Bedek'kung) *f* (-ȝ-en) cover; escort; (mil) escort; (nav) convoy

beden'ken §66 *tr* consider; (*beachten*) bear in mind; (*im Testament*) provide for || *ref* deliberate, think a matter over; **sich e—s anderen b.** change one's mind || **Bedenken** *n* (-sȝ-) (*Erwägung*) consideration, reflection; (*Einwand*) objection; (*Zweifel*) doubt, scruple

bedenk'lich *adj* (*ernst*) serious, critical; (*gefährlich*) risky; (*heikel*) ticklish; (*Charakter*) questionable

bedeu'ten *tr* mean; **das hat nichts zu b.** that doesn't matter; **j—m b., daß** make it clear to s.o. that

bedeu'tend *adj* important; (*beträchtlich*) considerable

bedeutsam [bə'dɔɪtzam] *adj* significant; (*Blick*) meaningful

Bedeu'tung *f* (-ȝ-en) meaning; (*Wichtigkeit*) importance

bedeu'tungsvoll *adj* significant

bedie'nen *tr* wait on, serve; (*Maschine*) operate || *ref* (*genit*) make use of; **bedienen Sie sich** help yourself || *intr* wait on people; (cards) follow suit

Bedie'nung *f* (-ȝ) service; servants; waitresses

Bedienungs- *comb.fm.* control

Bedie'nungsanweisung *f* instructions

Bedie'nungsmannschaft *f* gun crew

bedingen [bə'dɪŋən] *tr* condition, stipulate; (*in sich schließen*) imply; **bedingt** conditioned, conditional

bedin'gungsweise *adv* conditionally

bedrän'gen *tr* press hard; (*beunruhigen*) pester; **bedrängte Lage** state of distress; **bedrängte Verhältnisse** financial difficulties

Bedrängnis [bə'drɛnnɪs] *f* (-ȝ-se) distress; **in ärgster B.** in dire straits

bedro'hen *tr* threaten, menace

bedroh'lich *adj* threatening

bedrucken (bedruk'ken) *tr* print on; (*Stoff*) print

bedrücken (bedrük'ken) *tr* oppress

bedür'fen §69 *intr* (*genit*) require

Bedürfnis [bə'dʏrfnɪs] *n* (-sesȝ-se) need, requirement; (*Wunsch*) desire; **Bedürfnisse** necessities; **das dringende B. haben zu** (*inf*) have the urge to (*inf*)

Bedürf′nisanstalt f comfort station
bedürf′nislos adj having few needs
bedürftig [bə′dʏrftɪç] adj needy; **b.
sein** (genit) be in need of
Beefsteak [′bifstek] n (-s;-s) steak;
Deutsches B. hamburger
beehren [bə′eːrən] tr honor ‖ ref—
sich b. zu (inf) have the honor of
(ger)
beei′len ref hurry (up)
beein′drucken tr impress
beeinflussen [bə′aɪnflusən] tr influence
Beein′flussung f (-;) (genit) influence
(on), effect (on); (pol) lobbying
beeinträchtigen [bə′aɪntrɛçtɪgən] tr
(Ruf) damage; (Wert) detract from;
(Rechte) encroach upon; (Aussichten) hurt, spoil
been′den, been′digen tr end, conclude;
(Arbeit) complete
beengen [bə′ɛŋən] tr confine, cramp;
sich beengt fühlen feel cramped;
(fig) feel restricted
beer′ben tr—j—n **b.** inherit s.o.'s estate
beerdigen [bə′erdɪgən] tr bury, inter
Beer′digung f (-;-en) burial
Beere [′beːrə] f (-;-n) berry
Beet [bet] n (-[e]s;-e) (agr) bed
befähigen [bə′fɛ·ɪgən] tr enable,
qualify
befähigt [bə′fɛ·ɪçt] adj able, capable
Befä′higung f (-;-en) qualification;
(Fähigkeit) ability
befahl [bə′faːl] pret of **befehlen**
befahrbar [bə′faːrbar] adj (Weg) passable; (Wasser) navigable
befah′ren §51 tr travel; (Meer) sail;
(Fluß) navigate; (Küste) sail along;
(Schacht) go down into
befal′len §72 tr strike, attack; infest
befan′gen tr embarrassed; (schüchtern) shy; (voreingenommen) prejudiced; (parteiisch) partial
befas′sen tr touch, handle ‖ ref—sich
b. mit concern oneself with
befehden [bəfedən] tr make war on
Befehl [bə′fel] m (-[e]s;-e) order, command; **auf B.** (genit) by order of
befeh′len §51 tr order, command; **was
b. Sie?** what is your pleasure?
befehligen [bə′feːlɪgən] tr command,
be in command of
Befehls′form f imperative mood
Befehlshaber [bə′feːlshabər] m (-s;-)
(mil) commanding officer; (nav)
commander in chief; **oberster B.**
supreme commander
befehlshaberisch [bə′feːlshabərɪʃ] adj
imperious
Befehls′stelle f command post
befe′stigen tr (an dat) fasten (to), attach (to); (mil) fortify
Befe′stigung f (-;-en) fortification
befeuchten [bə′fɔɪçtən] tr moisten, wet
befeu′ern tr (aer, naut) mark with
lights; (mil) fire on, shoot at
befin′den §59 tr deem ‖ ref be, feel ‖
Befinden n (-s;) judgment, view;
(state of) health; **je nach B.** according to taste
befindlich [bə′fɪntlɪç] adj present, to

be found; **all die im Hafen befind-
lichen Schiffe** the ships (present) in
the harbor; **b. sein** happen to be
beflecken (beflek′ken) tr stain, taint
beflissen [bə′flɪsən] adj (genit) keen
(on), interested (in) ‖ **Beflissene** §5
mf (genit) student (of)
befohlen [bə′foːlən] pp of **befehlen**
befol′gen tr obey, comply with
Befol′gung f (-;) observance
beför′dern tr ship; (spedieren) forward; (im Rang) promote; (fördern)
further
Beför′derungsmittel n means of transportation
befra′gen tr question, interrogate;
poll; (um Rat) consult
befrakt [bə′frakt] adj in tails
befrei′en tr free; liberate; (vom Militärdienst) exempt; (von e-r Aufgabe)
excuse; (von Sorgen, e-r Last) relieve
Befrei′ung f (-;-en) freeing; liberation;
exemption; rescue
befremden [bə′fremdən] tr surprise,
astonish; strike as odd ‖ **Befremden**
n (-s;) surprise, astonishment
befreunden [bə′frɔɪndən] ref—sich
mit etw b. reconcile oneself to s.th.;
sich mit j—m b. make friends with
s.o.
befrieden [bə′friːdən] tr pacify
befriedigen [bə′friːdɪgən] tr satisfy
befrie′digend adj satisfactory
befristen [bə′frɪstən] tr set a time
limit on
Befri′stung f (-;-en) time limit
befruchten [bə′fruxtən] tr (Land)
make fertile; (schwängern) impregnate; (Ei) fertilize; **künstlich b.** in-
seminate; (bot) pollinate
befugt [bə′fukt] adj authorized
befüh′len tr feel, touch
Befund m (-[e]s;-e) findings, facts
befürch′ten tr fear, be afraid of
Befürch′tung f (-;-en) apprehension
befürworten [bə′fyːrvortən] tr support;
(anraten) recommend
begabt [bə′gaːpt] adj gifted, talented
Bega′bung f (-;-en) aptitude; (natural)
gift, talent
Bega′bungsprüfung f intelligence test
begann [bə′gan] pret of **beginnen**
begatten [bə′gatən] tr mate with ‖
ref copulate, mate
bege′ben §80 tr (Anleihen) float, place;
(Wertpapiere) sell ‖ ref go; occur;
es begab sich (Bib) it came to pass;
sich an die Arbeit b. set to work;
sich auf die Flucht b. take to flight;
sich auf die Reise b. set out on a
trip; **sich b.** (genit) renounce; **sich
in Gefahr b.** expose oneself to danger
Bege′benheit f (-;-en) event, incident
begegnen [bə′geɡnən] intr (SEIN) (dat)
meet, come upon; (Schwierigkeiten,
Feind) encounter; (Gefahr) face
bege′hen §82 tr walk on; walk along;
(Verbrechen, Irrtum) commit; (Fest)
celebrate
Begehr [bə′ger] m & n (-s;) desire; request; (econ) demand
begehren [bə′gerən] tr wish for; crave;

(Bib) covet; *etw von* ‖-m b. ask s.o. for s.th. ‖ *intr* (nach) yearn (for)
begeh′renswert *adj* desirable
begehr′lich *adj* covetous
begehrt [bə′gert] *adj* in demand
begeistert [bə′gaɪstərt] *adj* enthusiastic
Begei′sterung *f* (–;) enthusiasm
Begier [bə′gir] *f* (–;) var of **Begierde**
Begierde [bə′girdə] *f* (–;-n) desire; (fleshly) appetite; eagerness; craving
begierig [bə′giriç] *adj* eager; (*Augen*) hungry; (nach, auf *acc*) desirous (of); **b. zu** (*inf*) eager to (*inf*)
begie′ßen §76 *tr* water; (culin) baste; **das wollen wir b.** we want to celebrate it (*by drinking*)
Beginn [bə′gɪn] *m* (–[e]s;) beginning; (*Ursprung*) origin
beginnen [bə′gɪnən] §52 *tr & intr* begin
beglaubigen [bə′glaʊbɪgən] *tr* certify, authenticate; (*Gesandten*) accredit
Beglau′bigung *f* (–;) authentication; accreditation
Beglau′bigungsschreiben *n* (dipl) credentials
beglei′chen §85 *tr* balance; (*Rechnung*) pay in full; (*Streit*) settle
begleiten [bə′glaɪtən] *tr* accompany; escort; see (*e.g., off, home*); **hinaus b.** see to the door
Beglei′ter -in §6 *mf* companion
Begleit′erscheinung *f* concomitant
Begleit′musik *f* background music
Begleit′schreiben *s* covering letter
Beglei′tung *f* (–;-en) company; escort; (*Gefolge*) retinue; (mus) accompaniment
beglück′wünschen *tr* (zu) congratulate (on)
Beglück′wünschung *f* (–;-en) congratulation
begnadet [bə′gnadət] *adj* highly gifted
begnadigen [bə′gnadɪgən] *tr* pardon; (pol) grant amnesty to
Begna′digung *f* (–;-en) pardon; amnesty
begnügen [bə′gnygən] *ref* (mit) content oneself (with), be satisfied (with)
begonnen [bə′gɔnən] *pp* of **beginnen**
begra′ben §87 *tr* bury
Begräbnis [bə′grepnis] *n* (–ses;-se) burial; funeral
Begräb′nisfeier *f* funeral
Begräb′nisstätte *f* burial place
begradigen [bə′gradɪgən] *tr* straighten; (tech) align
begrei′fen §88 *tr* touch, handle; (*verstehen*) grasp; (*enthalten*) comprise
begreif′lich *adj* understandable
begreif′licherweise *adv* understandably
begren′zen *tr* bound; limit, restrict
Begren′zung *f* (–;-en) limitation
Begriff [bə′grɪf] *m* (–[e]s;-e) idea, notion; (*Ausdruck*) term; (philos) concept; **im B. sein zu** (*inf*) be on the point of (*ger*)
begriffen [bə′grɪfən] *adj*—**b. sein in** (*dat*) be in the process of
begrün′den *tr* found, establish; (*Behauptung*) substantiate, prove
Begrün′der -in §6 *mf* founder

Begrün′dung *f* (–;-en) establishment; proof; (*Grund*) ground, reason
begrüßen *tr* greet; welcome
begünstigen [bə′gynstɪgən] *tr* favor; (*fördern*) promote, support; (jur) aid and abet
Begün′stiger *m* (–s;–) accessory after the fact
Begünstigte [bə′gynstɪçtə] §5 *mf* (ins) beneficiary
Begün′stigung *f* (–;-en) promotion, encouragement; support, backing; (jur) aiding and abetting
begut′achten *tr* give an expert opinion on; **b. lassen** obtain expert opinion on
begütert [bə′gytərt] *adj* well-to-do
begütigen [bə′gytɪgən] *tr* appease
behaart [bə′hart] *adj* hairy
behäbig [bə′hebɪç] *adj* comfort-loving; (*beleibt*) portly
behaftet [bə′haftət] *adj* afflicted
behagen [bə′hagən] *intr* (dat) please, suit ‖ **Behagen** *n* (–s;) pleasure
behaglich [bə′haklɪç] *adj* pleasant; (*traulich*) snug, cozy
behal′ten §90 *tr* keep, retain; **Recht b.** turn out to be right
Behälter [bə′heltər] *m* (–s;–) container; box; (*für Öl, usw.*) tank
behan′deln *tr* treat; deal with; handle
behän′gen §92 *tr* hang; deck out
beharren [bə′harən] *intr* remain (unchanged); (in *dat*) persevere (in); (auf *dat*) persist (in), stick (to)
beharrlich [bə′harlɪç] *adj* steadfast
behau′en §93 *tr* hew
behaupten [bə′haʊptən] *tr* declare, assert; (*festhalten*) maintain, retain; allege ‖ *ref* stand one's ground; (*Preise*) remain steady
behausen [bə′haʊzən] *tr* lodge, house
Behau′sung *f* (–;-en) dwelling
behe′ben §94 *tr* (*Schwierigkeiten*) remove; (*Zweifel*) dispel; (*Schaden*) repair; (*Lage*) remedy; (*Geld*) withdraw; (*Schmerzen*) eliminate
beheimatet [bə′haɪmatət] *adj*—**b. sein in** (dat) reside in; come from
Behelf [bə′helf] *m* (–[e]s;-e) expedient; makeshift
behel′fen §96 *tr* (mit) make do (with)
Behelfs– comb.fm. temporary
behelfs′mäßig *adj* temporary, makeshift
behelligen [bə′helɪgən] *tr* bother
Behel′ligung *f* (–;-en) bother, trouble
behende [bə′hendə] *adj* agile, quick; (*gewandt*) handy; (*geistig*) smart
beherbergen [bə′herbergən] *tr* take in, put up (*as guest*)
beherr′schen *tr* (*Land*) rule; (*Sprache*) master; (*Gefühle*) control; (*überragen*) tower over; **den Luftraum b.** (mil) have air supremacy
Beherr′scher -in §6 *mf* ruler ‖ *m* master ‖ *f* mistress
beherzigen [bə′hertsɪgən] *tr* take to heart, remember
beherzt [bə′hertst] *adj* courageous
behe′xen *tr* bewitch; (fig) captivate
behilflich [bə′hɪlflɪç] *adj* helpful
behin′dern *tr* hinder; hamper; block
behor′chen *tr* overhear

Behörde [bə'hørdə] f (-;-n) authority, board; *die Behörden* the authorities

behördlich [bə'hørtlıç] *adj* official

behü'ten *tr* (vor *dat*) protect (against); **Gott behüte!** God forbid!

behutsam [bə'hutzam] *adj* wary

bei [baɪ] *prep* (*dat*) (Ort) by, beside, at, with, in; (*in Anschriften*) in care of, c/o; (*Zeit, Umstände*) at, by, during, on; (*Zustände, Eigenschaften*) at, while, in; **bei mir haben** have on me; **bei meiner Ehre** upon my honor; **bei Schiller** in the works of Schiller; **bei uns** at our house; **bei weitem** by far

bei'behalten §90 *tr* retain, keep

Bei'blatt n supplement

bei'bringen §65 *tr* obtain, procure; (*Beweise, Zeugen*) produce; (*Arznei, Gift*) administer; (*Wunde, Niederlage, Schlag, Verluste*) inflict; **j-m die Nachricht schonend b.** break the news gently to s.o.; **j-m etw b.** teach s.o. s.th., make s.th. clear to s.o.

Beichte ['baɪçtə] f (-;-n) confession

beichten ['baɪçtən] *tr* (eccl) confess

Beicht'kind n (eccl) penitent

Beicht'stuhl m (eccl) confessional

beide ['baɪdə] *adj* both; two || *pron* both; two; **keiner von beiden** neither of them

beiderlei ['baɪdər'laɪ] *invar adj* both kinds of

beiderseitig ['baɪdər'zaɪtıç] *adj* bilateral; (*gemeinsam*) mutual

beiderseits ['baɪdər'zaɪts] *adv* on both sides; mutually, reciprocally || *prep* (*genit*) on both sides of

beieinan'der *adv* together; **gut b. sein** (coll) be in good shape

Bei'fahrer -in §6 *mf* relief driver; passenger (*next to the driver*)

Bei'fall m approval; applause

bei'fällig *adj* approving; (*Bericht*) favorable || *adv* approvingly

Bei'fallklatschen n clapping, applause

Bei'fallsgeschrei n loud cheering

Bei'fallsruf m cheer

Bei'film m (cin) second feature

bei'folgend *adj* enclosed

bei'fügen *tr* add; (*e-m Brief*) enclose

bei'fügend *adj* (gram) attributive

Bei'fügung f (-;-en) addition; enclosure; (gram) attributive

Bei'gabe f extra; funerary gift

bei'geben §80 *tr* add; assign || *intr* give in; **klein b.** knuckle under

Bei'geschmack m taste, flavor; tinge

Bei'hilfe f aid; (*Stipendium*) grant; (*Unterstützung*) subsidy; allowance; (jur) aiding and abetting

bei'kommen § 99 *intr* (SEIN) (dat) get the better of; (*dat*) reach; *e-r Schwierigkeit*) overcome

Beil [baɪl] n (-[e]s;-e) hatchet

Bei'lage f (*im Brief*) enclosure; (*e-r Zeitung*) supplement; **Fleisch mit B.** meat and vegetables

beiläufig ['baɪlɔɪfıç] *adj* incidental; casual || *adv* by the way, incidentally; **b. erwähnen** mention in passing

bei'legen *tr* add; (*Titel*) confer; (*Wichtigkeit*) attach; (*Streit*) settle; etw

e-m Brief b. enclose s.th. in a letter || *intr* heave to

Bei'leid n (-s;) condolence(s)

bei'liegen §108 *intr*—**e-m Brief b.** be enclosed in a letter; **j-m b.** lie with s.o

beim *abbr* bei dem

bei'messen §70 *tr* attribute, impute

bei'mischen *tr* mix in

Bein [baɪn] n (-[e]s;-e) leg; (*Knochen*) bone; (fig) foot; **j-m ein B. stellen** trip s.o.

beinahe ['baɪna·ə], [baɪ'na·e] *adv* almost, nearly

Bei'name m appellation; (*Spitzname*) nickname

Bein'bruch m fracture, broken leg

Bein'schiene f (surg) splint; (sport) shin guard

Bein'schützer m (sport) shin guard

Bein'stellen n (sport) tripping

bei'ordnen *tr* assign, appoint (s.o.) as assistant; (*dat*) place (s.th.) on a level (with)

beipflichten ['baɪpflıçtən] *intr* (dat) agree with (s.o.), agree to (s.th.)

Bei'programm n (cin) second feature

Bei'rat m (-s;-e) adviser, counselor; (*Körperschaft*) advisory board

beir'ren *tr* mislead

beisammen [baɪ'zamən] *adv* together

Beisam'mensein n (-s;) being together; gathering, reunion; **geselliges B.** social; informal reception

Bei'satz m addition; (*bei Legierung*) alloy; (gram) appositive

Bei'schlaf m sexual intercourse

bei'schließen §76 *tr* enclose

Bei'schluß m—**unter B. von allen Dokumenten** with all documents attached

bei'schreiben §62 *tr* write in the margin; add as a postscript

Bei'schrift f postscript

Bei'sein n (-s;) presence

beisei'te *adv* aside; **b. schaffen** remove; (coll) do (s.o.) in

bei'setzen *tr* bury, inter

Bei'sitzer m associate judge

Bei'spiel n example; **zum B.** for example

bei'spielhaft *adj* exemplary

bei'spiellos *adj* unparalleled

bei'spielsweise *adv* by way of example

bei'springen §142 *intr* (dat) come to the aid of

beißen ['baɪsən] §53 *tr & intr* bite

bei'ßend *adj* biting; stinging, pungent, acrid; (*Reue*) bitter

Beiß'korb m muzzle

Beiß'zahn m (anat) incisor

Beiß'zange f pincers, nippers

Bei'stand m aid, support; (*Person*) assistant

bei'stehen §146 *intr* (dat) stand by, back, support

Bei'steuer f contribution

bei'steuern *tr* contribute

bei'stimmen *intr* (dat) agree with

Bei'stimmung f (-s;) approval

Bei'strich m comma

Beitrag ['baɪtra:k] m (-[e]s;-e) contribution; (*e-s Mitglieds*) dues

bei'tragen §132 *tr & intr* contribute
bei'treiben §62 *tr* collect; (*Abgaben*) exact; (mil) commandeer, requisition
bei'treten §152 *intr* (SEIN) (*dat*) join; (*j-s Meinung*) concur in
Bei'tritt *m* joining; concurrence
Bei'wagen *m* (aut) sidecar
Bei'werk *n* (-[e]s) accessories
bei'wohnen *intr* (*dat*) attend; (*e-m Ereignis*) be witness to; (*j-m*) have intercourse with (*s.o.*)
Bei'wort *n* (-[e]s;⁻er) epithet; (gram) adjective
Beize ['baɪtsə] *f* (-;-n) corrosive; (wood) stain; (*Falken-*) falconry; (culin) marinade
beizeiten [baɪ'tsaɪtən] *adv* on time; (*frühzeitig*) early
beizen ['baɪtsən] *tr* (*ätzen*) corrode; (*Holz*) stain; (*Wunde*) cauterize; (hunt) go hawking
bejahen [bə'jɑ·ən] *tr* say 'yes' to
beja'hend *adj* affirmative
bejahrt [bə'jɑrt] *adj* aged
bekämp'fen *tr* fight, oppose
bekannt [bə'kant] *adj* known; familiar; (*berühmt*) well-known || **Bekannte** §5 *mf* acquaintance
Bekannt'gabe *f* announcement
bekannt'geben §80 *tr* announce
bekannt'lich *adv* as is well known
bekannt'machen *tr* announce; (*Gesetz*) promulgate
Bekannt'machung *f* (-;-en) publication, announcement; (*Plakat*) poster
Bekannt'schaft *f* (-;) acquaintance; (coll) acquaintances
bekeh'ren *tr* convert || *ref* (zu) become a convert (to)
Bekehrte [bə'kertə] §5 *mf* convert
beken'nen §97 *tr* (*Sünde*) confess; (*zugestehen*) admit; **Farbe b.** follow suit; (fig) put one's cards on the table || *ref*—**sich schuldig b.** plead guilty; **sich zu e-r Religion b.** profess a religion; **sich zu e-r Tat b.** own up to a deed; **sich zu j-m b.** stand by s.o., believe in s.o.
Bekennt'nis *n* (eccl) confession; (*Konfession*) denomination
bekla'gen *tr* deplore; (*Tod*) mourn || *ref* (*über acc*) complain (about), find fault (with)
bekla'genswert *adj* deplorable
Beklagte [bə'klaktə] §5 *mf* defendant
beklat'schen *tr* applaud
bekle'ben *tr* paste; (*mit Etiketten*) label; **e-e Mauer mit Plakaten b.** paste posters on a wall
beklei'den *tr* clothe, dress; (*Mauer*) face, cover; (*Amt*) hold
beklem'men *tr* stifle, oppress
Beklem'mung *f* (-;-en) worry, anxiety; **Beklemmungen** claustrophobia
beklommen [bə'kləmən] *adj* uneasy
bekom'men §99 *tr* get; obtain; receive; (*Schnupfen*) catch; (*Risse*) develop || *intr* (*dat*) do good; **j-m schlecht b.** do s.o. harm; **wohl bekomm's!** to your health!
bekömmlich [bə'kœmlɪç] *adj* digestible; (*gesund*) healthful; (*zuträglich*) wholesome

beköstigen [bə'kœstɪgən] *tr* board, feed || *ref*—**sich selbst b.** do one's own cooking
bekräf'tigen *tr* (*Vorschlag*) support; (*bestätigen*) substantiate; **mit e-m Eid b.** seal with an oath
bekrän'zen *tr* wreath, crown
bekreu'zen, bekreu'zigen *ref* cross oneself, make the sign of the cross
bekrie'gen *tr* make war on
bekrit'teln *tr* criticize, pick at
bekrit'zeln *tr* scribble on, doodle on
beküm'mern *tr* worry, trouble || *ref* (um) concern onself (with), bother (about)
beküm'mert *adj* (*über acc*) worried (about)
bekunden [bə'kundən] *tr* manifest, show; (*öffentlich*) state publicly
bela'den §103 *tr* load; (fig) burden
Belag [bə'lak] *m* (-[e]s;⁻) covering; coat(ing); flooring; layer; surface
bela'gern *tr* besiege, beleaguer
Bela'gerung *f* (-;-en) siege
Belang [bə'laŋ] *m* (-[e]s;-e) importance, consequence; **Belange** interests
belan'gen *tr* (jur) sue; **was mich belangt** as far as I am concerned
belang'los *adj* unimportant
bela'sten *tr* load (down); (*Grundstück*) encumber; (fig) burden; (acct) charge; (jur) incriminate
belästigen [bə'lestɪgən] *tr* annoy, bother; (*mit Fragen*) pester; (*unabsichtlich*) inconvenience
Bela'stung *f* (-;-en) load; encumbrance; (fig) burden; (acct) debit; **die Zeiten größter B.** the peak hours
Bela'stungsprobe *f* (fig) acid test
Bela'stungszeuge *m* witness for the prosecution
belau'fen §105 *ref*—**sich b. auf** (*acc*) amount to, come to
belau'schen *tr* overhear
bele'ben *tr* animate; (*Getränk*) spike; **wieder b.** revive
belebt [bə'lept] *adj* animated, lively
Bele'bungsmittel *n* stimulant
Beleg [bə'lek] *m* (-s;-e) (*Beweisstück*) evidence; (*Unterlage*) voucher; (*Beispiel*) example; (jur) exhibit
bele'gen *tr* cover; (*Platz*) take, occupy; (*bemannen*) man; (*beweisen*) verify; (*Vorlesung*) register for; **ein Brötchen mit Schinken b.** make a ham sandwich; **mit Beispielen b.** exemplify; **mit Fliesen b.** tile; **mit Steuern b.** tax; **mit Teppichen b.** carpet || *ref* become coated
Beleg'schaft *f* (-;-en) crew; personnel; shift
Beleg'schein *m* voucher; receipt
Beleg'stelle *f* reference
belegt [bə'lekt] *adj* (*Platz*) reserved; (*Zunge*) coated; (*Stimme*) husky; (telp) busy; **belegtes Brot** sandwich
beleh'ren *tr* instruct || *ref*—**sich b. lassen** listen to reason
beleh'rend *adj* instructive
Beleh'rung *f* (-;-en) instruction; (*Lehre*) lesson; (*Rat*) advice; **zu Ihrer B.** for your information

beleibt [bə'laɪpt] *adj* stout
beleidigen [bə'laɪdɪgən] *tr* offend
belei'digend *adj* offensive
bele'sen *adj* well-read
beleuch'ten *tr* light (up), illuminate; (fig) throw light on
Beleuch'ter *m* (aer) pathfinder; (theat) juicer
Beleuch'tung *f* (-;-en) lighting, illumination; (fig) elucidation
Beleuch'tungskörper *m* lighting fixture
Belgien ['bɛlgjən] *n* (-s;) Belgium
Belgier –in ['bɛlgjər(ɪn)] §6 *mf* Belgian
belgisch ['bɛlgɪʃ] *adj* Belgian
belichten [bə'lɪçtən] *tr* (phot) expose
Belich'tung *f* (-;-en) exposure
belie'ben *intr* please ‖ *impers* (*dat*)— wenn es Ihnen beliebt if you please ‖ **Belieben** *n* (-s;) liking; es steht in Ihrem B. it's up to you; nach B. as you like
beliebig [bə'libɪç] *adj* any (you please) ‖ *adv* as ... as you please
beliebt [bə'lipt] *adj* favorite; (bei) popular (with)
Beliebt'heit *f* (-;) popularity
belie'fern *tr* supply, furnish
bellen ['bɛlən] *intr* bark
belob(ig)en [bə'lob(ɪg)ən] *tr* praise; commend; (mil) cite
beloh'nen *tr* reward
belü'gen §111 *tr* lie to, deceive
belustigen [bə'lustɪgən] *tr* amuse
bemächtigen [bə'mɛçtɪgən] *intr* (*genit*) seize, get hold of; (mil) seize
bemi'keln *tr* criticize, carp at
bema'len *tr* paint; decorate
bemängeln [bə'mɛŋəln] *tr* criticize
bemannen [bə'manən] *tr* man
Beman'nung *f* (-;-en) (nav) crew
bemänteln [bə'mɛntəln] *tr* gloss over; (*Fehler, Fehltritt*) cover up
bemei'stern *tr* master ‖ *ref* control oneself; (*genit*) get hold of
bemerk'bar *adj* perceptible
bemer'ken *tr* notice; (*äußern*) remark
bemer'kenswert *adj* remarkable
Bemer'kung *f* (-;-en) note; remark
bemes'sen §70 *tr* measure; proportion
bemit'leiden *tr* pity, feel sorry for
bemittelt [bə'mɪtəlt] *adj* well-to-do
bemogeln [bə'mogəln] *tr* cheat
bemü'hen *tr* trouble, bother; **bemüht sein zu** (*inf*) take pains to (*inf*) ‖ *ref* bother, exert oneself; **sich für j-n b.** intervene for s.o.; **sich um etw b.** make an effort to obtain s.th.; **sich um j-n b.** attend to s.o.; **sich zu j-m b.** go to s.o.
Bemü'hung *f* (-;-en) bother; effort
bemüßigt [bə'mysɪçt] *adj*—**sich b. fühlen zu** (*inf*) feel obliged to (*inf*)
bemu'stern *tr*—**ein Angebot b.** (com) send samples of an offer
bemuttern [bə'mutərn] *tr* mother
benachbart [bə'naxbart] *adj* neighboring; (*Fachgebiet*) related, allied
benachrichtigen [bə'naxrɪçtɪgən] *tr* notify; put on notice
Benach'richtigung *f* (-;-en) notification; notice
benachteiligen [bə'naxtaɪlɪgən] *tr*

place at a disadvantage, handicap; discriminate against
benebelt [bə'nebəlt] *adj* covered in mist; (fig) groggy
benedeien [bene'daɪ-ən] *tr* bless
beneh'men §116 *tr*—**j-m etw b.** take s.th. away from s.o. ‖ *ref* behave ‖ **Benehmen** *n* (-s;) behavior
beneiden [bə'naɪdən] *tr*—**j-n um etw b.** begrudge s.o. s.th.
benei'denswert *adj* enviable
benen'nen §97 *tr* name, term
Bengel ['bɛŋəl] *m* (-s;-) rascal
benommen [bə'nomən] *adj* dazed
benö'tigen *tr* need
benutz'bar *adj* usable
benut'zen, benüt'zen *tr* use, make use of
Benut'zerkarte *f* library card
Benzin [bɛnt'sin] *n* (-s;-e) gasoline
Benzin'behälter *m* gas tank
beobachten [bə'obaxtən] *tr* observe; (*polizeilich*) keep under surveillance; (med) keep under observation
Beob'achtung *f* (-;-en) observation; (*e-s Gesetzes*) observance
beor'dern *tr* order (*to go to a place*)
bepacken (bepak'ken) *tr* load (down)
bepfian'zen *tr* plant
bequem [bə'kvem] *adj* comfortable; cozy; (*Stellung*) soft; (*Raten, Lösung*) easy; (*faul*) lazy; **b. zur Hand haben** have handy
berappen [bə'rapən] *tr* (coll) shell out
bera'ten §63 *tr* (*über acc*) advise (on); discuss ‖ *ref* & *intr* (*über acc*) confer (about), deliberate (on)
bera'tend *adj* advisory, consulting
beratschlagen [bə'rat/lagən] *intr* (*über acc*) consult (on); **mit j-m b.** consult s.o., confer with s.o.
berat'schlagend *adj* advisory
Bera'tung *f* (-;-en) advice; (jur, med) consultation; **in B. sein** be under consideration
Bera'tungsstelle *f* counseling center
berau'ben *tr* (*genit*) rob (of); (*genit*) dispossess (of); (*genit*) deprive (of); (*genit*) bereave (of)
berech'nen *tr* calculate, figure out; (*schätzen*) estimate; (com) charge
berech'nend *adj* calculating
Berech'nung *f* (-;-en) calculation
berechtigen [bə'rɛçtɪgən] *tr* authorize; justify, warrant; (**zu**) entitle (to)
Berech'tigung *f* (-;-en) right, authorization; justification; (**zu**) title (to)
bereden [bə'redən] *tr* talk over, discuss; **j-n zu etw b.** talk s.o. into s.th. ‖ *ref*—**sich mit j-m über etw b.** confer with s.o. on s.th.
beredsam [bə'retzam] *adj* eloquent
beredt [bə'ret] *adj* eloquent
Bereich *m* & *n* (-[e]s;-e) region; range; (fig) field, sphere; **es fällt nicht in meinen B.** it's not within my province
bereichern [bə'raɪçərn] *tr* enrich
berei'fen *tr* cover with frost; (aut) put tires on
berei'nigen *tr* (*Streit, Konto*) settle; (*Mißverständnis*) clear up
berei'sen *tr* tour

bereit [bə'raɪt] *adj* ready
bereiten [bə'raɪtən] *tr* prepare; (*Kaffee*) make; (*Freude*) give
Bereit'schaft *f* (-;) readiness; team, squad; (mil) alert
bereit'stellen *tr* make available
Berei'tung *f* (-;-en) preparation; (*Herstellung*) manufacture
bereit'willig *adj* ready, willing
bereu'en *tr* rue, regret
Berg [bɛrk] *m* (-[e]s;-e) mountain; (*Hügel*) hill; **über alle Berge sein** be off and away; **zu Berge stehen** stand on end
bergab' *adv* downhill, down the mountain
bergauf' *adv* uphill; up the mountain
Berg'bahn *f* mountain railroad
Berg'bau *m* (-[e]s;) mining
Berg'bewohner -in §6 *mf* mountaineer
bergen ['bɛrgən] §54 *tr* rescue; (*enthalten*) hold; (*Gefahr*) involve; (*Segel*) take in; (naut) salvage; (poet) conceal; (rok) recover ‖ *ref*—**in sich b. involve**
bergig ['bɛrgɪç] *adj* mountainous
Berg'kessel *m* gorge
Berg'kette *f* mountain range
Berg'kluft *f* ravine, gully
Berg'kristall *m* rock crystal, quartz
Berg'land *n* hill country
Berg'mann *m* (-[e]s;-leute) miner
Berg'predigt *f* Sermon on the Mount
Berg'recht *n* mining law
Berg'rücken *m* ridge
Berg'rutsch *m* landslide
Berg'schlucht *f* gorge, ravine
Berg'spitze *f* mountain peak
Berg'steiger -in §6 *mf* mountain climber
Berg'steigerei *f* mountain climbing
Berg'sturz *m* landslide
Ber'gung *f* (-;-en) rescue; (naut) salvage; (rok) recovery
Ber'gungsarbeiten *pl* salvage operations
Ber'gungsschiff *n* salvage vessel; (rok) recovery ship
Berg'wacht *f* mountain rescue service
Berg'werk *n* mine
Berg'wesen *n* mining
Bericht [bə'rɪçt] *m* (-[e]s;-e) report
berichten [bə'rɪçtən] *tr & intr* report
Berichterstatter -in [bə'rɪçtɛr,tatər (ɪn)] §6 *mf* reporter; correspondent; (rad) commentator
Bericht'erstattung *f* (-;) reporting
berichtigen [bə'rɪçtɪgən] *tr* rectify; (*Text*) emend; (*Schuld*) pay off
berie'chen §102 *tr* sniff at; (fig) size up ‖ *recip* (coll) sound each other out
Berlin [bɛr'lin] *n* (-s;) Berlin
Bernstein ['bɛrn,taɪn] *m* amber
bersten ['bɛrstən] §55 *intr* (SEIN) (vor *dat*) burst (with)
berüchtigt [bə'rʏçtɪçt] *adj* notorious
berücken (berük'ken) *tr* captivate
berücksichtigen [bə'rʏkzɪçtɪgən] *tr* (*erwägen*) consider; (*in Betracht ziehen*) make allowance for
Berück'sichtigung *f* (-;-en) consideration

Beruf' *m* (-[e]s;-e) vocation; profession; (*Gewerbe*) trade; (*Tätigkeit*) occupation; (*Laufbahn*) career
beru'fen *adj* called; authorized ‖ §122 *tr* call; (*ernennen*) appoint; (*Geister*) conjure up ‖ *ref*—**sich auf ein Gesetz b.** quote a law (*in support*); **sich auf j-n b.** use s.o.'s name as a reference
beruf'lich *adj* professional; vocational
Berufs– *comb.fm.* professional; vocational
Berufs'diplomat *m* career diplomat
Berufs'genossenschaft *f* professional association; trade association
Berufs'heer *n* regular army
Berufs'schule *f* vocational school
Berufs'sportler -in §6 *mf* professional
berufs'tätig *adj* working
Beru'fung *f* (-;-en) call; vocation; appointment; (jur) appeal; **B. einlegen** (jur) appeal; **unter B. auf** (*acc*) referring to
Beru'fungsgericht *n* appellate court
beru'hen *intr* (auf *dat*) be based (on); (auf *dat*) be due (to); **e-e Sache auf sich b. lassen** let a matter rest
beruhigen [bə'ru·ɪgən] *tr* calm; appease
beru'higend *adj* soothing; reassuring
Beru'higung *f* (-;) calming; appeasement, pacification; (*der Lage*) stabilization; **zu meiner großen B.** much to my relief
Beru'higungsmittel *n* sedative
berühmt [bə'rymt] *adj* (wegen) famous (for)
Berühmt'heit *f* (-;-en) renown; (*berühmte Persönlichkeit*) celebrity
berüh'ren *tr* touch; (*erwähnen*) touch on; (*wirken auf*) affect; (*Zug*) pass through ‖ *ref* come in contact, meet
Berüh'rung *f* (-;-en) touch; contact
besä'en *tr* sow; (*bestreuen*) strew; **mit Sternen besät** star-spangled
besa'gen *tr* say; (*bedeuten*) mean
besagt [bə'zakt] *adj* aforesaid
besänftigen [bə'zɛnftɪgən] *tr* calm; appease ‖ *ref* calm down
Besatz' *m* trimming
Besat'zung *f* (-;-en) garrison; occupation; army of occupation; (aer, nav) crew
Besat'zungsarmee *f* army of occupation
Besat'zungsbehörde *f* military government
besau'fen §124 *ref* (coll) get drunk
beschä'digen *tr* damage ‖ *ref* injure oneself
beschaf'fen *adj*—**ich bin eben so b.** that's the way I am; **übel b. sein** be in bad shape ‖ *tr* get, procure; (*Geld*) raise
Beschaf'fenheit *f* (-;-en) quality, property; (*Zustand*) state; (*Art*) nature; (*Anlage*) design
Beschaf'fung *f* (-;-en) procuring; (*Erwerb*) acquisition
beschäftigen [bə'ʃɛftɪgən] *tr* occupy; keep busy; (*anstellen*) employ; **beschäftigt sein bei** work for (*a company*); **beschäftigt sein mit** be busy with

beschä′men *tr* shame, make ashamed; **beschämt sein** be ashamed

Beschau′ *f* inspection

beschau′en *tr* look at; inspect

beschau′lich *adj* contemplative

Bescheid [bə′ʃaɪt] *m* (-[e]s;-e) answer; (*Anweisung*) instructions, directions; (*Auskunft*) information; (*jur*) decision; **B. hinterlassen bei** leave word with; **B. wissen** be well-informed; **j-m B. geben** (or **sagen**) give s.o. information or directions

beschei′den *adj* modest; (*Preise*) moderate; (*Auswahl*) limited; (*einfach*) simple, plain || §112 *tr* inform; (*beordern*) order, direct; (*vorladen*) summon; (*zuteilen*) allot; **abschlägig b.** turn down; **es ist mir beschieden** it fell to my lot || *ref* be satisfied

Beschei′denheit *f* (-;) modesty

bescheinigen [bə′ʃaɪnɪgən] *tr* (*Empfang*) acknowledge; (*bezeugen*) certify

Beschei′nigung *f* (-;-en) acknowledgement; certification; (*Schein*) certificate; (*im Brief*) to whom it may concern

beschei′ßen §53 *tr* (sl) cheat

beschen′ken *tr*—**j-n b. mit** present s.o. with

bescheren [bə′ʃerən] *tr* give gifts to

Besche′rung *f* (-;-en) distribution of gifts (*especially at Christmas*); **e-e schöne B.** (coll) a nice mess

beschicken (beschik′ken] *tr* (*mit Waren*) supply; (*Messe*) exhibit at, send exhibits to; (*Kongreß*) send delegates to; (*Hochofen*) feed, charge

beschie′ßen §76 *tr* shoot up; (mil, phys) bombard

beschimp′fen *tr* insult, call (*s.o.*) names

beschir′men *tr* shield, protect

beschla′fen *tr* (*e-e Frau*) sleep with; (*e-e Sache*) sleep on

Beschlag′ *m* (-s;-e) hardware; (*Huf-*) horse shoes; (*auf Fensterscheiben*) steam, vapor; (*Überzug*) thin coating; **in B. nehmen** confiscate; (*Schiff*) seize; (*Gehalt*) attach

beschla′gen *adj*—**b. in** (dat) well-versed in || §132 *tr* cover, coat; (*Metallverzierungen*) fit, mount; (*Pferd*) shoe || *ref & intr* steam up; (*Mauer*) sweat; (*Metall*) oxidize

beschlagnahmen [bə′ʃlaknamən] *tr* confiscate; (*Schuldnervermögen*) attach; (mil) requisition; (naut) seize

beschlei′chen §85 *tr* stalk, creep up on

beschleunigen [bə′ʃlɔɪnɪgən] *tr* accelerate, speed up

Beschleu′niger *m* (-s;-) accelerator

beschlie′ßen §76 *tr* end, wind up; (*sich entschließen*) decide

Beschluß′ *m* conclusion; decision; resolution; (jur) order; **unter B.** under lock and key; **zum B.** in conclusion

beschluß′fähig *adj*—**b. sein** have a quorum; **beschlußfähige Anzahl** quorum

beschmie′ren *tr* smear, coat; grease

beschmut′zen *tr* soil, dirty

beschnei′den §106 *tr* clip, trim; (fig) curtail; (surg) circumcise

beschneit [bə′ʃnaɪt] *adj* snow-covered

beschönigen [bə′ʃønɪgən] *tr* (*Fehler*) whitewash, cover up, gloss over

beschrän′ken *tr* limit

beschränkt′ *adj* limited; (*Verhältnisse*) straitened; (*geistig*) dense

beschrei′ben §62 *tr* describe; use up (*in writing*)

Beschrei′bung *f* (-;-en) description

beschrei′ten §86 *tr* walk on; **den Rechtsweg b.** take legal action

beschriften [bə′ʃrɪftən] *tr* inscribe; (*Kisten*) mark; (*mit Etikett*) label

Beschrif′tung *f* (-;-en) inscription; lettering; (*erläuternde*) caption

beschuldigen [bə′ʃʊldɪgən] *tr* (*genit*) accuse (of), charge (with)

beschummeln [bə′ʃʊməln] *tr* (coll) (*um*) cheat (out of)

Beschuß′ *m* test firing

beschüt′zen *tr* protect, defend

beschwat′zen *tr* gossip about; **j-n dazu b. zu** (*inf*) talk s.o. into (*ger*)

Beschwerde [bə′ʃverdə] *f* (-;-n) trouble; (*Klage*, *Krankheit*) complaint

beschweren [bə′ʃverən] *tr* burden || *ref* (*über acc*) complain (about)

beschwer′lich *adj* troublesome

beschwichtigen [bə′ʃvɪçtɪgən] *tr* appease; (*Hunger*) satisfy; (*Gewissen*) soothe

beschwin′deln *tr* (**um**) swindle (out of)

beschwingt [bə′ʃvɪŋt] *adj* lively

beschwipst [bə′ʃvɪpst] *adj* tipsy, high

beschwö′ren *tr* swear to; (*Geister*) conjure up; (*bitten*) implore, entreat

Beschwö′rungsformel *f* incantation

beseelen [bə′zelən] *tr* inspire, animate

beseelt′ *adj* animated; (*von Hoffnungen*) filled; (*Spiel*) inspired

bese′hen §138 *tr* look at; inspect

beseitigen [bə′zaɪtɪgən] *tr* eliminate, remove, clear away; (*Übel*, *Fehler*) redress; (*Schwierigkeit*) overcome; (*töten*) do away with; (pol) purge

Besen [′bezən] *m* (-s;-) broom

Be′senstiel *m* broomstick

besessen [bə′zesən] *adj* (**von**) obsessed (by); (*vom Teufel*) possessed

Beses′senheit *f* (-;-en) obsession; (*vom Teufel*) possession

beset′zen *tr* occupy; (*mit Juwelen*) set off; (*Amt*, *Rolle*) fill; (*Hut*) trim

besetzt′ *adj* (*Platz*, *Abort*) occupied; (*Stelle*) filled; (*Kleid*) trimmed, set off; (telp) busy

Besetzt′zeichen *n* (telp) busy signal

Beset′zung *f* (-;-en) decoration; (*e-r Stelle*) filling; (mil) occupation; (theat) cast

besichtigen [bə′zɪçtɪgən] *tr* view; tour; inspect; (mil) inspect, review

Besich′tigung *f* (-;-en) sightseeing; inspection; (mil) inspection, review

besie′deln *tr* colonize; populate

besie′geln *tr* seal

besie′gen *tr* defeat; (*Widerstand*) overcome; (*Gefühle*) master

besin′nen §121 *ref* consider; (**auf** *acc*) think (of); **sich anders b.** change one's mind; **sich e-s Besseren b.** think better of it

besinn'lich *adj* reflective

Besin'nung *f* (-;) consciousness; reflection; **j-n zur B. bringen** bring s.o. to his senses

besin'nungslos *adj* unconscious; (*unüberlegt*) senseless

Besitz' *m* (-es;-e) possession; **in B. nehmen** take possession of

besitz'anzeigend *adj* possessive

besit'zen §144 *tr* own, possess

Besit'zer -in §6 *mf* possessor, owner

Besitz'ergreifung *f* (-;-en) occupancy; seizure

Besitz'stand *m* ownership; (fin) assets

Besitztum [bə'zɪtstum] *n* (-s;-"er) possession

Besit'zung *f* (-;-en) possession, property; (*Landgut*) estate

besoffen [bə'zɔfən] *adj* (coll) soused

besohlen [bə'zolən] *tr* sole

besolden [bə'zoldən] *tr* pay

Besol'dung *f* (-;-en) pay, salary

beson'dere §9 *adj* particular, special

Beson'derheit *f* (-;-en) peculiarity; (com) specialty

beson'ders *adv* especially; separately

besonnen [bə'zɔnən] *adj* prudent; (*bedacht*) considerate; level-headed

besor'gen *tr* take care of; (*beschaffen*) procure, get; (*befürchten*) fear

Besorgnis [bə'zɔrknɪs] *f* (-;-se) concern; (*Furcht*) fear

besorg'niserregend *adj* alarming

besorgt [bə'zɔrkt] *adj* (**um**) worried (about), anxious (for)

Besor'gung *f* (-;-en) care; procurement; (*Auftrag*) errand; **Besorgungen machen** run errands

bespre'chen §64 *tr* discuss; (*Buch*) review; **e-e Schallplatte b.** make a recording || *ref* confer

Bespre'cher -in §6 *mf* reviewer, critic

bespren'gen *tr* sprinkle

besprit'zen *tr* splash; spray

besser ['besər] *adj & adv* better

bessern ['besərn] *tr* better, improve || *ref* improve

Bes'serung *f* (-;-en) improvement; **baldige B.** speedy recovery

Bes'serungsanstalt *f* reform school

Bestand' *m* (-[e]s;-"e) existence; (*Vorrat*) stock, inventory; (*Kassen-*) cash on hand; (*Baum-*) stand; **B. an** (*dat*) number of; **B. an kampffähigen Truppen** effective strength; **B. haben, von B. sein** have endurance, be lasting

bestän'dig *adj* constant, steady

Bestands'aufnahme *f* inventory

Bestand'teil *m* component; ingredient

bestär'ken *tr* strengthen, fortify

bestätigen [bə'ʃtɛtɪgən] *tr* confirm; (*Zeugnis*) corroborate; (*Empfang*) acknowledge; (*Vertrag*) ratify || *ref* prove true, come true

bestatten [bə'ʃtatən] *tr* bury, inter

Bestat'tungsinstitut *n* funeral home

bestau'ben, bestäuben [bə'ʃtɔɪbən] *tr* cover with dust; sprinkle; (bot) pollinate

beste ['bestə] §9 *adj* best; **am besten**

best (of all); **auf dem besten Weg sein zu** be well on the way to; **aufs b.** in the best way; **der erste b.** anybody

beste'chen §64 *tr* bribe; (fig) impress

beste'chend *adj* fascinating, charming

bestech'lich *adj* open to bribery

Beste'chung *f* (-;) bribery

Beste'chungsgeld *n* bribe

Besteck [bə'ʃtɛk] *n* (-[e]s;-e) kit; (*Tisch-*) single service; (aer, naut) reckoning, position; (med) set of instruments

bestecken (*bestek'ken*) *tr* stick; (culin) garnish

beste'hen §146 *tr* undergo; (*Prüfung*) pass || *intr* exist, be; (gegen) hold one's own (against); (*in e-r Prüfung*) pass; **b. auf** (*dat*) insist on; **b. aus** consist of; **b. in** (*dat*) consist in

beste'hend *adj* existing, extant; present

besteh'len §147 *tr* (**um**) rob (of)

bestei'gen §148 *tr* climb; (*Schiff*) board; (*Pferd*) mount; (*Thron*) ascend

Bestell'buch *n* order book

bestel'len *tr* order; (*Zimmer*) reserve; (*Zeitung*) subscribe to; (*ernennen*) appoint; (*Briefe*) deliver; (*Feld*) till; (*kommen lassen*) send for

Bestell'zettel *m* order slip

be'stenfalls *adv* at best

besteu'ern *tr* tax

bestialisch [best'jalɪʃ] *adj* beastly

Bestie ['bestjə] *f* (-;-n) beast

bestim'men *tr* determine; (*Zeit, Preis*) set; (*ernennen*) appoint; (*Begriff*) define; (gram) modify; (math) find; **j-n b. zu** (or **für**) destine s.o. for; talk s.o. into || *intr* decree; **b. in** (*dat*) have a say in; **b. über** (*acc*) dispose of

bestimmt' *adj* determined; definite; particular || *adv* definitely

Bestim'mung *f* (-;-en) determination; (*e-r Zeit, e-s Preises*) setting; destination; mission, goal; (*e-s Begriffs*) definition; (*Schicksal*) fate; (*Vorschrift*) regulation; (*e-s Vertrags*) provision; (gram) modifier; **mit B. nach** (naut) heading for; **seiner B. übergeben** dedicate, open

bestra'fen *tr* punish

bestrah'len *tr* irradiate; (med) give radiation treatment to

bestre'ben *tr* strive, endeavor || **Bestreben** *n* (-s;) tendency

Bestre'bung *f* (-;-en) effort

bestrei'chen §85 *tr* spread; (*mit Feuer*) rake; **mit Butter b.** butter

bestrei'ken *tr* strike

bestrei'ten §86 *tr* contest; fight; (*Ausgaben*) defray; (*Recht*) deny; **e-e Unterhaltung allein b.** do all the talking

bestreu'en *tr* (**mit**) strew (with)

bestricken (*bestrik'ken*) *tr* (fig) charm

bestücken [bə'ʃtykən] *tr* arm, equip

bestür'men *tr* storm; (fig) bombard

Bestür'mung *f* (-;-en) storming

bestür'zen *tr* dismay

Besuch [bə'zux] *m* (-[e]s;-e) visit; (*Besucher*) visitor(s), company;

(*genit*) visit (to); **auf B. gehen** pay a visit

besu'chen *tr* visit; (*Gasthaus, usw.*) frequent; (*Schule, Versammlung*) attend; (*Kino*) go to

Besu'cher **–in** §6 *mf* visitor, caller

Besuchs'zeit *f* visiting hours

besudeln *tr* soil, stain

betagt [bə'takt] *adj* advanced in years

beta'sten *tr* finger, touch, handle

betätigen [bə'tetıgən] *tr* set in operation; (*Maschine*) operate; (*Bremse*) apply || *ref*—**sich nützlich b.** make oneself useful; **sich politisch b.** be active in politics

betäuben [bə'tɔıbən] *tr* deafen; stun; (*Schmerz*) deaden; (*durch Rauschgift*) drug, dope; (*med*) anesthetize

Betäu'bungsmittel *n* drug; painkiller; (med) anesthetic

Bete ['betə] *f* (–;-n) beet

beteiligen [bə'taılıgən] *tr* (**an** *dat*, **bei**) give (*s.o.*) a share (in) || *ref* (**an** *dat*) participate (in)

Betei'ligung *f* (–;-en) participation; (*Teilhaberschaft*) partnership; (*Teilnehmerzahl*) attendance

beten ['betən] *tr & intr* pray

beteuern [bə'tɔı-ərn] *tr* affirm

betiteln [bə'titəln] *tr* entitle

Beton [be'tɔn] *m* (–s;) concrete

betonen [bə'tonən] *tr* (*Silbe*) stress, accent; (*nachdrücklich*) emphasize

betonieren [betə'nirən] *tr* cement

Betonmisch'maschine *f* cement mixer

betören [bə'tørən] *tr* infatuate

Betracht' *m* (–[e]s;) consideration; **außer B. lassen** rule out; **es kommt nicht in B.** it is out of the question; **in B. ziehen** take into account, consider

betrachten [bə'traxtən] *tr* look at; consider

beträchtlich [bə'treçtlıç] *adj* considerable

Betrach'tung *f* (–;-en) observation; consideration; meditation; **Betrachtungen anstellen über** (*acc*) reflect on

Betrag [bə'trak] *m* (–[e]s;⁼e) amount; **über den B.** von in the amount of

betra'gen §132 *tr* amount to || *ref* behave || **Betragen** *n* (–s;) behavior

betrau'en *tr* entrust

betrau'ern *tr* mourn for

Betreff [bə'tref] *m* (–[e]s;) re; (**am Briefanfang**) re; **in B.** (*genit*) in regard to

betref'fen §151 *tr* befall; (*berühren*) affect, hit; (*angehen*) concern; **betrifft** (*acc*) re; **was das betrifft** as far as that is concerned; **was mich betrifft** I for one

betreffs [bə'trefs] *prep* (*genit*) concerning

betrei'ben §62 *tr* carry on; (*leiten*) manage; (*Beruf*) practice; (*Studien*) pursue; (*Maschine*) operate

betre'ten *adj* embarrassed || §152 *tr* step on; set foot on or in; (*Raum*) enter; (*unbefugt*) trespass on

betreuen [bə'trɔı-ən] *tr* look after

Betrieb [bə'trip] *m* (–s;-e) operation,

running; (*Unternehmen*) business; (*Anlage*) plant; (*Werkstatt*) workshop; (fig) rush, bustle; **aus dem B. ziehen** take out of service; **außer B.** out of order; **großer B.** hustle and bustle; **in vollem B.** in full swing

betriebsam [bə'tripzam] *adj* enterprising, active

Betrieb'samkeit *f* (–;) hustle

betriebs'fähig *adj* in working order

betriebs'fertig *adj* ready for use

Betriebs'ingenieur *m* production engineer

Betriebs'kosten *pl* operating costs

Betriebs'leiter *m* superintendent

Betriebs'material *n* (rr) rolling stock

Betriebs'prüfer **–in** §6 *mf* auditor

Betriebs'ruhe *f*—**heute B.** (public sign) closed today

Betriebs'stoff *m* fuel

Betriebs'störung *f* breakdown

Betriebs'wirtschaft *f* industrial management

betrin'ken §143 *ref* get drunk

betroffen [bə'trɔfən] *adj* shocked, stunned; (*heimgesucht*) afflicted

betrü'ben *tr* sadden, distress

betrüb'lich *adj* sad, distressing

betrübt [bə'trypt] *adj* sad, sorrowful

Betrug [bə'truk] *m* (–[e]s;) fraud, swindle; **frommer B.** white lie

betrü'gen §111 *tr* cheat, swindle

Betrügerei [bətrygə'raı] *f* (–;-en) deceit, cheating

betrü'gerisch *adj* deceitful; fraudulent

betrunken [bə'truŋkən] *adj* drunk

Bett [bet] *n* (–[e]s;-en) bed

Bett'decke *f* bedspread

Bettelei [betə'laı] *f* (–;) begging

betteln ['betəln] *intr* (**um**) beg (for)

betten ['betən] *tr* put to bed || *ref* make oneself a bed; bed down

Bett'genosse *m* bedfellow

Bett'gestell *n* bedstead

Bett'himmel *m* canopy (over a bed)

bettlägerig ['betlegərıç] *adj* bedridden

Bett'laken *n* bed sheet

Bettler **–in** ['betlər(ın)] §6 *mf* beggar

Bett'stelle *f* bedstead

Bettuch (Bett'tuch) *n* sheet

Bet'tung *f* (–;-en) bedding; (mil) emplacement; (rr) bed

Bett'vorleger *m* bedside rug

Bett'wäsche *f* bed linen

Bett'zeug *n* bedding

betupfen [bə'tupfən] *tr* dab (at); (surg) swab

beugen ['bɔıgən] *tr* bend; (fig) humble; (gram) inflect || *ref* bend; bow

Beu'gung *f* (–;-en) bending; bowing; (gram) inflection

Beule ['bɔılə] *f* (–;-n) lump; (*Geschwür*) boil; (*kleiner Blechschaden*) dent

beunruhigen [bə'unru·ıgən] *tr* make uneasy, worry, disturb

Beun'ruhigung *f* (–;-en) anxiety, uneasiness; disturbance

beurkunden [bə'urkundən] *tr* authenticate

beurlauben [bə'urlaubən] *tr* grant leave of absence to; (*vom Amt*) suspend; (mil) furlough; **sich b. lassen**

ask for time off ‖ *ref* (**bei**) take one's leave (of)

beur'teilen *tr* evaluate; (**nach**) judge (by); **falsch b.** misjudge

Beute ['bɔɪtə] *f* (–;) booty, loot; **zur B. fallen** (*dat*) fall prey to

Beutel ['bɔɪtəl] *m* (–s;–) bag, pouch; purse; (billiards) pocket

beu'telig *adj* baggy

Beu'tezug *m* raid

bevölkern [be'fœlkərn] *tr* populate

Bevöl'kerung *f* (–;–en) population

bevollmächtigen [be'fɔlmεçtɪgən] *tr* authorize; (*jur*) give (*s.o.*) power of attorney

Bevoll'mächtigte §5 *mf* authorized agent; proxy; (*pol*) plenipotentiary

bevor [bə'for] *conj* before; **bevor ... nicht** until

bevormunden [be'formundən] *tr* treat in a patronizing manner

bevor'raten *tr* stock; stockpile

bevorrechtet [bə'forrεçtət] *adj* privileged

bevor'stehen §146 *intr* be imminent, be on hand; **bevorstehend** forthcoming; **j–m b.** be in store for s.o.

bevorzugen [bə'fortsugən] *tr* prefer

bevor'zugt *adj* preferential; high-priority; privileged; favorite

bewa'chen *tr* guard, watch over

bewach'sen §155 *tr* overgrow, cover

Bewa'chung *f* (–;–en) guard, custody

bewaff'nen *tr* arm

Bewaff'nung *f* (–;) armament, arms

Bewahr'anstalt *f* detention home

bewah'ren *tr* keep, preserve; (**vor** *dat*) save (from), protect (against)

bewäh'ren *tr* prove ‖ *ref* prove one's worth; **sich nicht b.** prove a failure

Bewah'rer §6 *mf* keeper

bewahrheiten [bə'varhaɪtən] *tr* verify ‖ *ref* come true

bewährt [bə'vεrt] *adj* tried, trustworthy

Bewah'rung *f* (–;) preservation

Bewäh'rung *f* (–;–en) testing, trial; (*jur*) probation

Bewäh'rungsfrist *f* (*jur*) probation; **j–m B. zubilligen** put s.o. on probation

Bewäh'rungsprobe *f* test

bewaldet [bə'valdət] *adj* woody

bewältigen [bə'vεltɪgən] *tr* (*Hindernis*) overcome; (*Lehrstoff*) master

bewandert [bə'vandərt] *adj* experienced

Bewandtnis [bə'vantnɪs] *f* (–;) circumstances, situation

bewäs'sern *tr* water, irrigate

bewegen [bə'vegən] *tr* move, stir ‖ *ref* move, stir; (*von der Stelle*) budge; (*Temperatur*) vary; (*exerzieren*) take exercise; (*astr*) revolve ‖ §56 *tr* prompt, induce

Beweg'grund *m* motive; incentive

beweg'lich *adj* movable; (*behend*) agile; (*Geist*) versatile; (*Zunge*) glib

Beweg'lichkeit *f* (–;) mobility; agility; versatility

bewegt [bə'vεkt] *adj* agitated; (*ergreifend*) stirring; (*Stimme*) trembling; (*Unterhaltung*) lively; (*Leben*) eventful; (*unruhig*) turbulent

Bewe'gung *f* (–;–en) movement; mo-

tion; move; (*Gebärde*) gesture; (*fig*) emotion; **in B. setzen** set in motion

Bewe'gungsfreiheit *f* room to move; (*fig*) leeway, freedom of action

bewe'gungslos *adj* motionless

beweh'ren *tr* arm; (*Beton*) reinforce

beweihräuchern [bə'vaɪrɔɪçərn] *tr* (*fig*) flatter; (*eccl*) incense

bewei'nen *tr* mourn, shed tears over

Beweis [bə'vaɪs] *m* (–es;–e) (**für**) proof (of), evidence (of)

beweisen [bə'vaɪzən] §118 *tr* prove, demonstrate; (*bestätigen*) substantiate

Beweis'führung *f* argumentation

Beweis'grund *m* argument

Beweis'kraft *f* cogency, force

beweis'kräftig *adj* convincing

Beweis'last *f* burden of proof

Beweis'stück *n* exhibit

bewen'den *intr*—**es dabei b. lassen** leave it at that ‖ **Bewenden** *n*—**damit hat es sein B.** there the matter rests

bewer'ben §149 *ref*—**sich b. um** apply for; (*kandidieren*) run for; (*Vertrag*) bid for; (*Preis*) compete for; (*Frau*) court

Bewer'ber –**in** §6 *mf* applicant; candidate; bidder; competitor ‖ *m* suitor

Bewer'bungsformular *n* application form

Bewer'bungsschreiben *n* written application

bewer'fen §160 *tr* pelt; (*Mauer*) plaster

bewerkstelligen [bə'vεrk/tεlɪgən] *tr* manage, bring off

bewer'ten *tr* (**auf** *acc*) value (at), appraise (at); **b. mit fünf Punkten** give five points to (*e.g., a performance*); **zu hoch b.** overrate

Bewer'tung *f* (–;–en) valuation

bewilligen [bə'vɪlɪgən] *tr* approve, grant

Bewil'ligung *f* (–;–en) approval; permit

bewillkommnen [bə'vɪlkɔmnən] *tr* welcome

bewir'ken *tr* cause, occasion, effect

bewir'ten *tr* entertain

bewirt'schaften *tr* (*Acker*) cultivate; (*Betrieb*) manage; (*Mangelware*) ration

Bewir'tung *f* (–;) hospitality

bewitzeln [bə'vɪtsəln] *tr* poke fun at

bewog [bə'vok] *pret* of **bewegen**

bewogen [bə'vogən] *pp* of **bewegen**

bewoh'nen *tr* inhabit, occupy

Bewoh'ner –**in** §6 *mf* (*e–s Landes*) inhabitant; (*e–s Hauses*) occupant

bewölken [bə'vœlkən] *tr* cloud ‖ *ref* cloud over, get cloudy

bewölkt *adj* cloudy, overcast

Bewöl'kung *f* (–;) clouds

bewun'dern *tr* admire

bewun'dernswert, bewun'dernswürdig *adj* admirable

bewußt [bə'vust] *adj* conscious; **die bewußte Sache** the matter in question

bewußt'los *adj* unconscious

Bewußt'sein *n* consciousness; **bei B. sein** be conscious

Bewußt'seinsspaltung *f* schizophrenia

bezah'len *tr* pay; (*Gekauftes*) pay for

Bezah′lung *f* (-;-en) payment; (*Lohn*) pay

bezäh′men *tr* tame; (fig) control

bezau′bern *tr* bewitch; (fig) fascinate

bezeich′nen *tr* (*zeichnen*) mark; (*bedeuten*) signify; (*benennen*) designate; (*kennzeichnen*) characterize; (*zeigen*) point out

bezeich′nend *adj* characteristic

Bezeich′nung *f* (-;-en) marking, mark; (*Name*) name; (*Ausdruck*) term

bezei′gen *tr* show, manifest, express

bezeu′gen *tr* attest; (jur) testify to

bezichtigen [bə′tsɪçtɪgən] *tr* accuse

bezieh′bar *adj* (*Ware*) obtainable; (*Wohnung*) ready for occupancy; (auf *acc*) referable (to)

bezie′hen §163 *tr* (*Polstermöbel*) cover; (*Wohnung*) move into; (*Universität*) go to; (*geliefert bekommen*) get; (*Gehalt*) draw; (auf *acc*) relate (to), refer (to); **das Bett frisch b.** change the bed linens; **die Stellung b.** (mil) occupy the position; **die Wache b.** (mil) go on guard duty ‖ *ref* become overcast; **sich auf j-n b.** use s.o.'s name as a reference

Bezie′hung *f* (-;-en) relation, connection, respect; **in B. auf** (*acc*) in respect to; **in guten Beziehungen stehen zu** be on good terms with

bezie′hungslos *adj* unrelated; irrelevant

Bezie′hungssatz *m* relative clause

bezie′hungsweise *adv* respectively

Bezie′hungswort *n* [-[e]s; ̈er] (gram) antecedent

beziffern [bə′tsɪfərn] *tr* (auf *acc*) estimate (at) ‖ *ref*—**sich b. auf** (*acc*) amount to, number

Bezirk [bə′tsɪrk] *m* (-s;-e) district, ward, precinct; (*Bereich*) sphere

Bezug′ *m* (-[e]s; ̈e) cover, case; (von *Waren*) purchase; (von *Zeitungen*) subscription; (*Auftrag*) order; **Bezüge** earnings; **B. nehmen auf** (*acc*) refer to; **in B. auf** (*acc*) in reference to

bezüglich [bə′tsyklɪç] *adj* (auf *acc*) relative (to); **bezügliches Fürwort** relative pronoun ‖ *prep* (*genit*) concerning, as to, with regard to

Bezugnahme [bə′tsuknamə] *f*—**unter B. auf** (*acc*) with reference to

Bezugs′anweisung *f* delivery order

bezugs′berechtigt *adj* entitled to receive ‖ **Bezugsberechtigte** §5 *mf* (ins) beneficiary

bezwecken [bə′tsvekən] *tr* aim at, have in mind; (**mit**) intend (by)

bezwei′feln *tr* doubt, question

bezwin′gen §142 *tr* conquer; (fig) control, master

Bibel [′bibəl] *f* (-;-n) Bible

Bi′belforscher –in §6 *mf* Jehovah's Witness

Biber [′bibər] *m* (-s;-) beaver

Bibliothek [bibliˈotek] *f* (-;-en) library

Bibliothekar –in [bɪbliˌoteˈkar(ɪn)] §8 *mf* librarian

biblisch [′biblɪʃ] *adj* biblical

bieder [′bidər] *adj* honest; (*leichtgläubig*) gullible

Bie′dermann *m* (-[e]s; ̈er) honest man

biegen [′bigən] §57 *tr* bend; (gram) inflect ‖ *ref*—**sich vor Lachen b.** double up with laughter ‖ *intr* (SEIN) bend; **um die Ecke b.** go around the corner

biegsam [′bikzam] *adj* flexible

Bie′gung *f* (-;-en) bend, bending; (gram) inflection

Biene [′binə] *f* (-;-n) bee

Bie′nenfleiß *m*—**mit B. arbeiten** work like a bee

Bie′nenhaus *n* beehive

Bie′nenkorb *m* beehive

Bie′nenstich *m* bee sting; (culin) almond pastry

Bie′nenstock *m* beehive

Bie′nenzucht *f* beekeeping

Bier [bir] *n* (-[e]s;-e) beer

bie′ten [′bitən] §58 *tr* offer; **b. auf** (*acc*) bid for ‖ *ref* present itself; **das läßt er sich nicht b.** he won't stand for it

Bigamie [bɪgaˈmi] *f* (-;) bigamy

bigott [bɪˈgot] *adj* bigoted

Bigotterie [bɪgotəˈri] *f* (-;) bigotry

Bilanz [biˈlants] *f* (*acct*) balance; (acct) balance sheet

Bilanz′abteilung *f* auditing department

bilanzieren [bilanˈtsirən] *intr* balance

Bild [bɪlt] *n* (-es;-er) picture; image; (*Bildnis*) portrait; (in e-m *Buch*) illustration; (*Vorstellung*) idea; (rhet) metaphor, figure of speech; **im Bilde sein** be in the know

Bild′band *m* (-[e]s; ̈e) picture book ‖ *n* (-[e]s; ̈er) (telv) video tape

Bild′bandgerät *n* video tape recorder

Bild′betrachter *m* slide viewer

Bildchen [′bɪltçən] *n* (-s;-) small picture; (cin) frame

Bild′einstellung *f* (-;-en) focusing

bilden [′bɪldən] *tr* form, fashion, create; (*entwerfen*) design; (*gründen*) establish; (*Geist*) educate, develop; (*Gruppe*) constitute ‖ *ref* form, be produced; develop; educate oneself

bil′dend *adj* instructive; **bildende Künste** fine arts, plastic arts

bil′derreich *adj* (*Buch*) richly illustrated; (*Sprache*) picturesque, ornate

Bil′derschrift *f* picture writing

Bil′dersprache *f* imagery

Bil′derstürmer *m* iconoclast

Bild′frequenz *f* camera speed

Bild′funk *m* television

bild′haft *adj* pictorial; graphic

Bildhauer [′bɪlthau̯ˌər] *m* (-s;-) sculptor

Bildhauerei [′bɪlthau̯ˌarai] *f* (-;) sculpture

Bildhauerin [′bɪlthau̯ˌərɪn] *f* (-;-nen) sculptress

bild′hübsch *adj* pretty as a picture

Bild′karte *f* photographic map; (cards) face card

bild′lich *adj* pictorial; figurative

Bildner –in [′bɪldnər(ɪn)] §6 *mf* sculptor ‖ *m* (fig) molder ‖ *f* sculptress

Bildnis [′bɪltnɪs] *n* (-ses;-se) portrait

Bild′röhre *f* picture tube, TV tube

bildsam [′bɪltzam] *adj* plastic; (fig) pliant

Bild'säule f statue
Bild'schirm m television screen
bild'schön adj very beautiful
Bild'schriftzeichen n hieroglyph
Bild'seite f head, obverse
Bild'signal n video signal
Bild'stock m wayside shrine
Bild'streifen m filmstrip; (journ) comic strip
Bild'sucher m (phot) viewfinder
Bild'teppich m tapestry
Bild'ton`kamera f sound-film camera
Bil'dung f (-;-en) formation; shape; education, culture
Bil'dungsanstalt f educational institution
Bild'werfer m projector
Bild'werk n sculpture; imagery
Billard ['bɪljart] n (-s;) billiards
Bil'lardkugel f billiard ball
Bil'lardloch n pocket
Bil'lardstab, Bil'lardstock m cue
Billett [bɪl'jet] m (-s;-e) ticket
Billett'ausgabe f, **Billett'schalter** m ticket office; (theat) box office
billig ['bɪlɪç] adj cheap; (Preis) low; (Ausrede, Trost) poor
billigen ['bɪligən] tr approve
Bil'ligung f (-;) approval
Billion [bɪl'jon] f (-;-en) trillion; (Brit) billion
bimbam ['bɪm'bam] interj ding-dong || **Bimbam** m—**heiliger B.!** holy smokes!
bimmeln ['bɪməln] intr (coll) jingle; (telp) ring
Bimsstein ['bɪms/taɪn] m (-s;-e) pumice stone
Binde ['bɪndə] f (-;-n) band; (Krawatte) tie; (Armschlinge) sling; (für Frauen) sanitary napkin; (med) bandage
Bin'deglied n link; (fig) bond, tie
binden ['bɪndən] §59 tr bind, tie
Bin'destrich m hyphen; **mit B. schreiben** hyphenate
Bin'dewort n (-[e]s;-er) conjunction
Bind'faden m string, twine; **es regnet Bindfäden** it's raining cats and dogs
Bin'dung f (-;-en) binding; tie, bond; obligation; (mus) ligature
binnen ['bɪnən] prep (genit & dat) within; **b. kurzem** before long
Binnen- comb.fm. inner; internal; inland; domestic, home
Bin'nengewässer n inland water
Bin'nenhandel m domestic trade
Bin'nenland n inland; interior; **im B.** inland
Binse ['bɪnzə] f (-;-n) rush, reed; **in die Binsen gehen** (coll) go to pot
Bin'senwahrheit f truism
Biochemie [bɪ·oçe'mi] f (-;) biochemistry
Biogra•phie [bɪ·ogra'fi] (-;-phien [fi·ən] biography
biographisch [bɪ·o'grafɪ/] adj biographic(al)
Biologie [bɪ·o'gi] f (-;) biology
biologisch [bɪ·o'logɪ/] adj biological
Biophysik [bɪ·ofy'zik] f (-;) biophysics
Birke ['bɪrkə] f (-;-n) birch
Birma ['bɪrma] n (-s;) Burma

Birne ['bɪrnə] f (-;-n) pear; (elec) bulb; (Kopf) (sl) bean
bis [bɪs] prep (acc) (zeitlich) till, until; (örtlich) up to, to; **bis an** (acc) up to; **bis auf** (acc) except for; **bis nach** as far as || conj until, till
Bisamratte ['bizamratə] f (-;-n) muskrat
Bischof ['bɪ/əf] m (-s;̈e) bishop
bischöflich ['bɪ/øflɪç] adj episcopal
Bi'schofsamt n episcopate
Bi'schofsmütze f miter
Bi'schofssitz m episcopal see
Bi'schofsstab m crosier
bisher [bɪs'her] adv till now
bisherig [bɪs'herɪç] adj former, previous; (Präsident) outgoing
Biskuit [bɪs'kvit] m & n (-[e]s;-e) biscuit
bislang' adv till now
biß [bɪs] pret of **beißen** || **Biß** m (Bisses; Bisse) bite; sting
bißchen ['bɪsçən] n (also used as invar adj & adv) bit, little bit
Bissen ['bɪsən] m (-s;-) bit, morsel
bissig ['bɪsɪç] adj biting, snappish
Bistum ['bɪstum] n (-s;̈er) bishopric
bisweilen [bɪs'vaɪlən] adv sometimes
Bitte ['bɪtə] f (-;-n) request; **e-e B. einlegen bei** intercede with
bitten ['bɪtən] §60 tr ask || intr **b. für** intercede for; **b. um** ask for; **wie bitte?** I beg your pardon? || interj please!; you are welcome!
bitter ['bɪtər] adj bitter
bit'terböse adj (coll) furious
Bit'terkeit f (-;) bitterness
bit'terlich adv bitterly; deeply
Bit'tersalz n Epsom salts
Bittgang ['bɪtgaŋ] m (-[e]s;̈e) (eccl) procession
Bittsteller ['bɪt/telər] m (-s;-) petitioner, suppliant
Biwak ['bivak] n (-s;-s) bivouac
biwakieren [biva'kirən] intr bivouac
bizarr [bɪ'tsar] adj bizarre
blähen ['ble·ən] tr inflate, distend || ref swell || intr cause gas
blaken ['blakən] intr smolder
Blamage [bla'maʒə] f (-;-n) disgrace
blamieren [bla'mirən] tr embarrass || ref make a fool of oneself
blank [blaŋk] adj bright; (Schuh) shiny; (bloß) bare; (Schwert) drawn; (sl) broke; **blanke Waffe** side arms; **b. ziehen** draw one's sword
Blankett [blaŋ'ket] n (-s;-e) blank
blanko ['blaŋko] adv—**b. lassen** leave blank; **b. verkaufen** sell short
Blan'koscheck m blank check
Blan'kovollmacht f blanket authority
Blank'vers m blank verse
Bläschen ['blesçən] n (-s;-) small blister; small bubble
Blase ['blazə] f (-;-n) blister; bubble; (coll) gang; (anat) bladder; **Blasen werfen** (Farbe) blister; **Blasen ziehen** (Haut) blister
Bla'sebalg m pair of bellows
blasen ['blazən] tr blow; (Instrument) play || intr blow
Bla'senleiden n bladder trouble
Bläser ['blezər] m (-s;-) blower

blasiert [bla'zirt] *adj* blasé

blasig ['blazıç] *adj* blistery; bubbly

Blas'instrument *n* wind instrument

Blasphe·mie [blasfe'mi] *f* (-;-mien ['mi·ən]) blasphemy

blasphemieren [blasfe'mirən] *intr* blaspheme

Blas'rohr *n* blowpipe; peashooter

blaß [blas] *adj* pale; keine blasse Ahnung not the foggiest notion

Blässe ['blɛsə] *f* (-;) paleness, pallor

Blatt [blat] *n* (-;=er) leaf; (*Papier-*) sheet; (*Gras-*) blade

Blatter ['blatər] *f* (-;-n) pustule; die Blattern smallpox

blätterig ['blɛtərıç] *adj* leafy; scaly

blättern ['blɛtərn] *intr*—in e-m Buch b. page through a book

Blat'ternarbe *f* pockmark

Blät'terwerk *n* foliage

Blatt'gold *n* gold leaf, gold foil

Blatt'laus *f* aphid

Blatt'pflanze *f* house plant

blättrig ['blɛtrıç] *adj var* of blätterig

Blatt'zinn *n* tin foil

blau [blau] *adj* (& *fig*) blue; (*coll*) drunk; blaues Auge black eye; keinen blauen Dunst haben (*coll*) not have the foggiest notion; mit e-m blauen Auge davonkommen (*coll*) get off easy || Blau *n* (-s;-s) blue; blueness

blau'äugig *adj* blue-eyed

Blau'beere *f* blueberry

Bläue ['blɔɪ·ə] *f* (-;) blue; blueness

bläuen ['blɔɪ·ən] *tr* dye blue

bläulich ['blɔɪlıç] *adj* bluish

blau'machen *intr* (*coll*) take off from work

Blech [blɛç] *n* (-[e]s;-e) sheet metal; (*sl*) baloney; (*mus*) brass

Blech'büchse *f* tin can

blechen ['blɛçən] *tr* (*coll*) pay out || *intr* (*coll*) cough up the dough

Blech'instrument *n* brass instrument

blecken ['blɛkən] *tr*—die Zähnen b. bare one's teeth

Blei [blaɪ] *n* (-[e]s;) lead

Bleibe ['blaɪbə] *f* (-;-n) place to stay

bleiben ['blaɪbən] §62 *intr* (SEIN) remain, stay; am Leben b. survive; bei etw b. stick to s.th.; dabei bleibt es! that's final!; für sich b. keep to oneself; sich [*dat*] gleich b. never change; und wo bleibe ich? (*coll*) and where do I come in?

blei'bend *adj* lasting, permanent

bleich [blaɪç] *adj* pale || Bleiche *f* (-;) bleaching; paleness

blei'chen *tr* bleach; make pale || *intr* (SEIN) bleach; (*verblassen*) fade

Bleich'gesicht *n* paleface

Bleich'mittel *n* bleach

bleiern ['blaɪ·ərn] *adj* leaden

Blei'soldat *m* tin soldier

Blei'stift *m* pencil

Bleistiftspitzer ['blaɪ/tıft/pıtsər] *m* (-s;-) pencil sharpener

Blende ['blɛndə] *f* (-;-n) window blind; shutter; (*phot*) diaphragm

blen'den *tr* blind; (*bezaubern*) dazzle

blen'dend *adj* fabulous

Blen'der *m* (-s;-) (*coll*) fourflusher

Blendling ['blɛntlıŋ] *m* (-s;-e) (*Mischling*) mongrel; (*bot*) hybrid

Blick [blık] *m* (-[e]s;-e) glance, look; (*auf acc*) view (of)

blicken (blık'ken) *intr* (auf *acc*, nach) glance (at), look (at); sich b. lassen show one's face

Blick'fang *m* (*coll*) eye catcher

blieb [blip] *pret* of bleiben

blies [blis] *pret* of blasen

blind [blınt] *adj* (für, gegen) blind (to); (*Spiegel*) clouded; (*trübe*) dull; (*Alarm*) false; (*Patrone*) blank; blinder Passagier stowaway

Blind'band *m* (-[e]s;=e) (*typ*) dummy

Blind'boden *m* subfloor

Blind'darm *m* appendix

Blind'darmentzündung *f* appendicitis

Blind'darmoperation *f* appendectomy

Blin'denheim *n* home for the blind

Blin'denhund *m* Seeing-Eye dog

Blin'denschrift *f* braille

Blind'flug *m* blind flying

Blind'gänger *m* (*mil*) dud

Blind'landung *f* instrument landing

blindlings ['blıntlıŋs] *adv* blindly

Blind'schreiben *n* touch typing

blinken ['blıŋkən] *intr* blink, twinkle; (*Sonne*) shine; (*mil*) signal

Blin'ker *m*, Blink'licht *n* (*aut*) blinker

blinzeln ['blıntsəln] *intr* blink, wink

Blitz [blıts] *m* (-es;-e) lightning; (*fig* & *phot*) flash

Blitz'ableiter *m* lightning rod

blitz'blank' *adj* shining; spick and span

Blitz'krieg *m* blitzkrieg

Blitz'licht *n* (*phot*) flash

Blitz'lichtaufnahme *f* (*phot*) flash shot

Blitz'lichtbirne *f* (*phot*) flash bulb

Blitz'lichtgerät *n* flash gun

Blitz'lichtröhre *f* (*phot*) electronic flash, flash tube

Blitz'schlag *m* stroke of lightning

blitz'schnell' *adj* quick as lightning

Blitz'strahl *m* flash of lightning

Block [blɔk] *m* (-s;=e) block, log; (*Stück Seife*) cake; (*von Schokolade*) bar; (*von Löschpapier*) pad; (*geol*) boulder; (*metal*) ingot; (*pol*) bloc

Blockade [blɔ'kadə] *f* (-;-n) blockade

Blocka'debrecher *m* blockade runner

blocken (blɔk'ken) *tr* (*sport*) block

Block'haus *n* log cabin

blockieren [blɔ'kirən] *tr* block up; (*mil*) blockade

Block'kalender *m* tear-off calendar

Block'schrift *f* block letters

blöd(e) ['blød(ə)] *adj* stupid, idiotic; feeble-minded; (*schüchtern*) shy

Blöd'heit *f* (-;) stupidity, idiocy

Blö'digkeit *f* (-;) shyness

Blöd'sinn *m* idiocy; nonsense

blöd'sinnig *adj* idiotic || *adv* idiotically; (*sehr*) (*coll*) awfully

blöken ['bløkən] *intr* bleat; (*Kuh*) moo

blond [blɔnt] *adj* blond, fair || Blonde §5 *m* blond || *f* blonde

blondieren [blɔn'dirən] *tr* bleach

Blondine [blɔn'dinə] *f* (-;-n) blonde

bloß [blos] *adj* bare; (*nichts als*) mere *adv* only; barely

Blöße ['bløsə] *f* bareness; nakedness; (*fig*) weak point

bloß'legen *tr* lay bare
bloß'stellen *tr* expose
blühen ['bly·ən] *intr* blossom, bloom; (*Backen*) be rosy; (*fig*) flourish
Blume ['blumə] *f* (*-;-n*) flower; (*des Weins*) bouquet; (*des Biers*) head
Blu'menbeet *n* flower bed
Blu'menblatt *n* petal
Blu'mengewinde *n* garland, festoon
Blu'menhändler –in §6 *mf* florist
Blu'menkelch *m* calyx
Blu'menkohl *m* cauliflower
Blu'menstaub *m* pollen
Blu'mentopf *m* flowerpot
Bluse ['bluzə] *f* (*-;-n*) blouse
Blut [blut] *n* (*-[e]s*) blood; **bis aufs B.** almost to death; **B. lecken** taste blood; **heißes B.** hot temper
Blut'andrang *m* (*pathol*) congestion
blut'arm *adj* anemic
Blut'armut *f* anemia
Blut'bahn *f* bloodstream
Blut'bild *n* blood count
blut'dürstig *adj* bloodthirsty
Blüte ['blytə] *f* (*-;-n*) blossom, flower, bloom; (*fig*) prime
Blut'egel *m* leech
bluten ['blutən] *intr* bleed
Blü'tenblatt *n* petal
Blü'tenstaub *m* pollen
Blut'erguß *m* bruise
Blu'terkrankheit *f* hemophilia
Blü'tezeit *f* blooming period; (*fig*) heyday
Blut'farbstoff *m* hemoglobin
Blut'gerinnsel *n* blood clot
Blut'hund *m* bloodhound
blutig ['blutɪç] *adj* bloody
blut'jung *adj* very young, green
Blut'körperchen *n* corpuscle
Blut'kreislauf *m* blood circulation
blut'leer, blut'los *adj* bloodless
Blut'pfropfen *m* blood clot
Blut'probe *f* blood test
Blut'rache *f* blood feud
Blut'rausch *m* mania to kill
blutrünstig ['blutrynstɪç] *adj* gory
Blut'sauger *m* bloodsucker, leech
Blut'schande *f* incest
blutschänderisch ['blut/ɛndərɪʃ] *adj* incestuous
Blut'spender –in §6 *mf* blood donor
blut'stillend *adj* coagulant
Blut'sturz *m* hemorrhage
Bluts'verwandte §5 *mf* blood relation
Blut'übertragung *f* blood transfusion
blut'unterlaufen *adj* bloodshot
Blut'vergießen *n* (*-s*) bloodshed
blut'voll *adj* lively, vivid
Blut'wasser *n* lymph
Blut'zeuge *m*, **Blut'zeugin** *f* martyr
Bö [bø] *f* (*-;-en*) gust, squall
Bob [bɔb] *m* (*-s;-s*) bobsled
Bock [bɔk] *m* (*-[e]s; ̈-e*) buck; ram; he-goat; (*Kutsch-*) driver's seat; (*tech*) horse; **B. springen** play leapfrog; **e-n B. schießen** pull a boner
bockbeinig ['bɔkbaɪnɪç] *adj* stubborn
bocken ['bɔkən] *intr* buck; (*sich aufbäumen*) rear; (*ausschlagen*) kick; (*brunsten*) be in heat; (*aut*) hesitate
bockig ['bɔkɪç] *adj* thickheaded
Bock'sprung *m* caper; leapfrog

Boden ['bodən] *m* (*-s; ̈*) (*Erd-*) ground, soil; (*Meeres-*) bottom; (*Fuß-*) floor; (*Dach-*) attic; (*Trocken-*) loft; **B. fassen** get a firm footing; **zu B. drücken** crush
Bo'denertrag *m* (*agr*) yield
Bo'denfenster *n* dormer window
Bo'denfläche *f* floor space; (*agr*) acreage
Bo'denfliese *f* floor tile
Bodenfräse ['bodənfrɛzə] *f* (*-;-n*) Rotortiller
Bo'denhaftung *f* roadability
Bo'denkammer *f* attic
bo'denlos *adj* bottomless; (*fig*) unmitigated
Bo'denmannschaft *f* (*aer*) ground crew
Bo'denreform *f* agrarian reform
Bo'densatz *m* grounds, sediment
Bodenschätze ['bodən/ɛtsə] *pl* mineral resources
Bo'densee *m* (*-s*) Lake Constance
bo'denständig *adj* native, indigenous
bog [bok] *pret* of **biegen**
Bogen ['bogən] *m* (*-s; ̈*) bow; (*Kurve*) curve; (*Papier-*) sheet; (*beim Schilaufen*) turn; (*beim Eislaufen*) circle; (*archit*) arch; (*math*) arc; **den B. raushaben** have the hang of it; **den B. überspannen** (*fig*) go too far; **e-n großen B. um j–n machen** give s.o. wide berth
Bo'genfenster *n* bow window
bo'genförmig *adj* arched
Bo'gengang *m* arcade; archway
Bo'genschießen *n* (*-s*) archery
Bo'genschütze *m* archer
Bo'gensehne *f* bowstring
Bohle ['bolə] *f* (*-;-n*) plank
Böhme ['bømə] *m* (*-n;-n*) Bohemian
Böhmen ['bømən] *n* (*-s*) Bohemia
Bohne ['bonə] *f* (*-;-n*) bean; **blaue Bohnen** bullets; **grüne Bohnen** string beans
Boh'nermasse *f* polish; floor polish
bohnern ['bonərn] *tr* wax, polish
Boh'nerwachs *n* floor wax
Bohr– [bor] *comb.fm.* drill, drilling, bore, boring
bohren ['borən] *tr* drill, bore
Bohrer ['borər] *m* (*-s;-*) drill; (*ent*) borer
Bohr'insel *f* offshore drilling platform
Bohr'presse *f* drill press
Bohr'turm *m* derrick
böig ['bø·ɪç] *adj* gusty; (*aer*) bumpy
Boje ['bojə] *f* (*-;-n*) buoy
Böller ['bœlər] *m* (*-s;-*) mortar
böllern ['bœlərn] *intr* fire a mortar
Bollwerk ['bɔlverk] *n* (*-s;-e*) bulwark
Bolzen ['bɔltsən] *m* (*-s;-*) bolt; dowel
Bombardement [bombardə'mã] *n* (*-s; -s*) bombardment
bombardieren [bombar'dirən] *tr* bombard
Bombe ['bɔmbə] *f* (*-;-n*) bomb, bombshell; (*coll*) smash hit
Bomben– *comb.fm.* bomb, bombing; huge
Bom'benabwurf *m* bombing; **gezielter B.** precision bombing
Bom'benerfolg *m* (*theat*) smash hit
bom'benfest *adj* bombproof
Bom'benflugzeug *m* bomber

Bom′bengeschäft n (coll) gold mine

Bom′benpunktzielwurf m precision bombing

Bom′benreihenwurf m stick bombing

Bom′bensache f (coll) humdinger

Bom′benschacht m bomb bay

Bom′benschütze m bombardier

Bom′bentrichter m bomb crater

Bom′benzielanflug m bombing run

Bom′benzielgerät n bombsight

Bon [bõ] m (-s;-s) sales slip; (*Gutschein*) credit note

Bonbon [bõˈbõ] m & n (-s;-s) piece of candy; **Bonbons** candy

Bonbonniere [bõbɔnɪˈɛrə] f (-;-n) box of candy

Bonze [ˈbɔntsə] m (-;-n) (coll) big shot, bigwig; (pol) boss

Boot [bot] n (-[e]s;-e) boat

Boots′mann m (-es;-leute) boatswain; (nav) petty officer

Bord [bɔrt] m (-es;e) edge; bookshelf; (naut) board, side; **an B.** aboard, on board; **von B. gehen** leave the ship

Bordell [bɔrˈdɛl] n (-s;-e) brothel

Bord′karte f boarding pass

Bord′schütze m aerial gunner

Bord′schwelle f curb

Bord′stein m curb

Bord′waffen pl (aer, mil) armament

Bord′wand f ship's side

Borg [bɔrk] m (-s;) borrowing; **auf B.** on credit; on loan

borgen [ˈbɔrgən] tr (von, bei) borrow (from); loan out, lend

Borke [ˈbɔrkə] f (-;-n) bark

Born [bɔrn] m (-es; -e) (poet) fountain

borniert [bɔrˈnirt] adj narrow-minded

Borsäure [ˈbɔrzɔɪrə] f (-;) boric acid

Börse [ˈbœrzə] f (-;-n) purse; stock exchange

Bör′senkurs m market price; quotation

Bör′senmakler –in §6 mf stockbroker

Bör′senmarkt m stockmarket

Bör′sennotierung f (st.exch.) quotation

Bör′senpapiere pl stocks, shares, securities

Borste [ˈbɔrstə] f (-;-n) bristle

borstig [ˈbɔrstɪç] adj bristly; (fig) crusty

Borte [ˈbɔrtə] f (-;-n) trim; braid; (*Saum*)

bös [bøs] var of **böse**

bös′artig adj nasty; (*Tier*) vicious; (pathol) malignant

Böschung [ˈbœʃʊŋ] f (-;-en) slope; (*e-s Flusses*) bank; (rr) embankment

böse [ˈbøzə] adj bad, evil, nasty; angry || **B.** §5 mf wicked person || m devil || n evil; harm

Bösewicht [ˈbøzəvɪçt] m (-s;-e) villain

boshaft [ˈboshaft] adj malicious; wicked; (*tückisch*) spiteful

bossieren [bɔˈsirən] tr emboss

bös′willig adj malicious, willful

bot [bot] pret of **bieten**

Botanik [boˈtanɪk] f (-;) botany

Botaniker –in §6 mf botanist

botanisch [boˈtanɪʃ] adj botanic(al)

Bote [ˈbotə] m (-n;-n) messenger

Bo′tengang m errand

Botin [ˈbotɪn] f (-;-nen) messenger

Bot′schaft f (-;-en) message, news; (*Amt*) embassy; (*Auftrag*) mission

Botschafter –in [ˈbotʃaftər(ɪn)] §6 ambassador

Bottich [ˈbɔtɪç] m (-s;-e) tub; vat

Bouillon [bʊlˈjõ] f (-;) bouillon

Bowle [ˈbolə] f (-;-n) punch

boxen [ˈbɔksən] tr & intr box

Bo′xer m (-s;-) boxer

Box′kampf m boxing match

Boykott [bɔɪˈkɔt] m (-s;-e) boycott

boykottieren [bɔɪkɔˈtirən] tr boycott

brach [brax] pret of **brechen** || adj fallow

brachte [ˈbraxtə] pret of **bringen**

brackig [ˈbrakɪç] adj brackish

Branche [ˈbrɑ̃ʃə] f (-;-n) line of business; (com) branch

Brand [brant] m (-[e]s;̈e) burning; fire; (coll) thirst; (agr) blight; (pathol) gangrene **in B. geraten** catch fire; **in B. setzen** (or **stecken**) set on fire

Brand′blase f blister

Brand′bombe f incendiary bomb

Brand′brief m urgent letter

Brand′direktor m fire chief

branden [ˈbrandən] intr surge, break

Brand′fackel f firebrand

brandig [ˈbrandɪç] adj (agr) blighted; (pathol) gangrenous

Brand′mal n brand; (fig) moral stigma

brand′marken tr stigmatize

Brand′mauer f fire wall

brandschatzen [ˈbrant/atsən] tr sack

Brand′stifter –in §6 mf arsonist

Brand′wunde f burn

Brand′zeichen n brand

brannte [ˈbrantə] pret of **brennen**

Branntwein [ˈbrantvaɪn] m brandy

Brasilien [braˈziljən] n (-s;) Brazil

Bratapfel [ˈbrɑːtapfəl] m baked apple

braten [ˈbrɑːtən] §63 tr & intr roast; (*im Ofen*) bake; (*auf dem Rost*) broil, grill; (*in der Pfanne*) fry || **Braten** m (-s;-) roast

Bra′tensoße f gravy

Brat′fisch m fried fish

Brat′huhn n broiler

Brat′kartoffeln pl fried potatoes

Brat′pfanne f frying pan, skillet

Bratsche [ˈbratʃə] f (-;-n) viola

Bräu [brɔɪ] m & n (-[e]s;) brew

Brauch [braux] m (-[e]s;̈e) custom

brauchbar [ˈbrauxbar] adj useful

brauchen [ˈbrauxən] tr need; (*Zeit*) take; (*gebrauchen*) use

Brauchtum [ˈbrauxtum] n (-s;) tradition

Braue [ˈbrau·ə] f (-;-n) eyebrow

brauen [ˈbrau·ən] tr brew

Brau′er m (-s;-) brewer

Brauerei [brau·əˈraɪ] f (-;-en), **Brau′haus** n brewery

braun [braun] adj brown; (*Pferd*) bay

Bräune [ˈbrɔɪnə] f (-;) brown; sun tan; (pathol) diphtheria

bräunen [ˈbrɔɪnən] tr tan; (culin) brown || ref & intr tan

bräunlich [ˈbrɔɪnlɪç] adj brownish

Braus [braus] m (-es;) noise; revelry

Brause ['brauzə] f (-;-n) soda, soft drink; (*Duschbad*) shower; (*an Gieß-kannen*) nozzle
Brau'sebad n shower
Brau'sekopf m hothead
Brau'selimonade f soda, soft drink
brau'sen intr spray, water || intr bubble; (*toben*) roar || intr (SEIN) rush
Braut [braut] f (-;⁀e) fiancée; bride
Braut'ausstattung f trousseau
Braut'führer m usher
Bräutigam ['brɔɪtɪgam] m (-s;-e) fiancé; bridegroom
Braut'jungfer f (-;-n) bridesmaid; er-ste B. maid of honor
Braut'kleid n bridal gown
Braut'leute pl engaged couple
bräutlich ['brɔɪtlɪç] adj bridal; nuptial
Braut'schatz m dowry
Braut'werber -in §6 mf matchmaker
Braut'werbung f courting
Braut'zeit f period of engagement
Braut'zeuge m best man
brav [braf] adj well-mannered, good, honest
Brav'heit f good behavior
Bravour [bra'vur] f (-;) bravado
Brech'eisen n crowbar, jimmy
brechen ['brɛçən] §64 tr break; (*Pa-pier*) fold; (*Steine*) quarry; (*Blumen*) pick; (coll) vomit; (opt) refract; die Ehe b. commit adultery || ref break; (opt) be refracted || intr (SEIN) break; (coll) vomit
Brech'reiz m nausea
Brech'stange f crowbar
Bre'chung f (-;-en) (opt) refraction
Brei [braɪ] m (-s;-e) paste; pap, gruel; zu B. schlagen beat to a pulp
breit [braɪt] adj broad, wide
breitbeinig ['braɪtbaɪnɪç] adv with legs outspread
breit'drücken tr flatten (out)
Brei'te f (-;-n) width; latitude
Brei'tengrad m degree of latitude
breit'machen ref take up (too much) room; (fig) throw one's weight around
breit'schlagen §132 tr (coll) persuade
breitschulterig ['braɪtʃultərɪç] adj broad-shouldered
breitspurig ['braɪtʃpurɪç] adj (coll) pompous; (rr) broad-gauge
breit'treten §152 tr belabor
Breit'wand f (cin) wide screen
Bremsbelag ['brɛmsbəlak] m brake lining
Bremse ['brɛmzə] f (-;-n) brake; (ent) horsefly
bremsen ['brɛmzən] tr brake; (fig) curb; (atom phys) slow down || intr brake
Brem'ser m (-s;-) brakeman
Brems'flüssigkeit f brake fluid
Brems'fußhebel m brake pedal
Brems'klotz m wheel chock
Bremsleuchte ['brɛmslɔɪçtə] f, **Brems'-licht** n (aut) brake light
Brems'rakete f (rok) retrorocket
Brems'schuh m brake shoe
brems'sicher adj skidproof
Brems'spur f skid mark
Brems'wagen m (rr) caboose

Brems'weg m braking distance
Brennapparat ['brɛnaparat] m still
brennbar ['brɛnbar] adj inflammable, combustible
brennen §97 tr burn; (*Branntwein*) dis-til; (*Kaffee*) roast; (*Haar*) curl; (*Ziegel*) fire || intr burn; smart
Bren'ner m (-s;-) burner; distiller
Brennerei [brɛnə'raɪ] f (-;-en) distil-lery
Brenn'holz n firewood
Brenn'material n fuel
Brenn'ofen m kiln
Brenn'punkt m focus; im B. stehen be the focal point
Brenn'schere f curler
Brenn'schluß m (rok) burnout
Brenn'spiegel m concave mirror
Brenn'stoff m fuel
brenzlig ['brɛntslɪç] adj (*Geruch*) burnt; (*Situation*) precarious
Bresche ['brɛʃə] f (-;-n) breach; e-e B. schlagen make a breach
Brett [brɛt] n (-[e]s;-er) board; plank; (*für Bücher, Geschirr*) shelf; **Bretter** (coll) skis; (theat) stage; **Schwarzes B.** bulletin board
Bret'terbude f shack
Bret'terverschlag m wooden partition
Brett'säge f ripsaw
Brezel ['brɛtsəl] f (-;-n) pretzel
Brief [brif] m (-[e]s;-e) letter; **Briefe wechseln** correspond
Brief'ausgabe f mail delivery
Briefbeschwerer ['brifbəʃverər] m (-s;-) paperweight
Brief'bestellung f mail delivery
Brief'beutel m mail bag
Brief'bogen m piece of notepaper
Brief'bote m mailman, postman
Briefchen ['brifçən] n (-s;-) note; **B. Streichhölzer** book of matches
Brief'einwurf m slot in a mailbox; let-terdrop; mailbox
Brief'fach n pigeonhole; post-office box
Brief'freund -in §8 mf pen pal
Brief'hülle f envelope
Brief'kasten m mailbox
Brief'klammer f paper clip
Brief'kopf m letterhead
Brief'kurs m (st.exch.) selling price
brief'lich adj written; **brieflicher Ver-kehr** correspondence || adv by letter
Brief'mappe f folder
Brief'marke f postage stamp
Brief'markenautomat m stamp ma-chine
Brief'ordner m ring binder
Brief'papier n stationery; note paper
Brief'porto n postage
Brief'post f first-class mail
Brief'schaften pl correspondence
Brief'stempel m postmark
Brief'tasche f billfold, wallet
Brief'taube f carrier pigeon
Brief'träger m mailman, postman
Brief'umschlag m envelope
Brief'verkehr m correspondence
Brief'waage f postage scales
Brief'wahl f absentee ballot
Brief'wechsel m correspondence
briet [brit] pret of braten

Brigade [brɪ'gɑdə] f (-;-n) brigade
Briga'degeneral m brigadier general; (Brit) brigadier
Brikett [brɪ'kɛt] n (-[e]s;-s) briquette
brillant [brɪl'jant] adj brilliant || **Brillant** m (-en;-en) precious stone (esp. diamond)
Brille ['brɪlə] f (-;-n) eyeglasses; (für Pferde) blinkers; (Toilettenring) toilet seat; **B. mit doppeltem Brennpunkt** bifocals
Bril'lenbügel m sidepiece (of glasses)
Bril'lenfassung f eyeglass frame
Bril'lenschlange f cobra
bringen ['brɪŋən] §65 tr bring, take; **an sich b.** acquire; **es mit sich b., daß** bring it about that; **es zu etw b.** achieve s.th.; **etw hinter sich b.** get s.th. over and done with; **etw über sich** (or **übers Herz**) **b.** be able to bear s.th.; **j-n auf etw b.** put s.o. on to s.th.; **j-n außer sich b.** enrage s.o.; **j-n dazu b. zu** (inf) get s.o. to (inf); **j-m um etw b.** deprive s.o. of s.th.; **j-n zum Lachen b.** make s.o. laugh; **unter die Leute b.** circulate
brisant [brɪ'zant] adj high-explosive
Brise ['brizə] f (-;-n) breeze
Britannien [brɪ'tanjən] n (-s;) Britain
Brite ['brɪtə] m (-n;-n) Briton, Britisher; **die Briten** the British
Britin ['brɪtɪn] f (-;-nen) Briton, British woman
britisch ['brɪtɪʃ] adj British
Broché [bro'ʃe] n (-s;) broché; brocaded fabric
Bröckchen ['brœkçən] n (-s;-) bit; morsel, crumb; fragment
bröck(e)lig ['brœk(ə)lɪç] adj crumbly
bröckeln ['brœkəln] tr & intr crumble
brocken ['brɔkən] tr—**Brot in die Suppe b.** break bread into the soup || **Brocken** m (-s;-) piece, bit; lump; **Brocken** pl scraps, bits and pieces; **harter B.** (coll) tough job
brockenweise [brok'kenweise] adv bit by bit
brodeln ['brodəln] intr bubble, simmer
Brokat [bro'kɑt] m (-s;-e) brocade
Brombeere ['brombeerə] f (-;-n) blackberry
Bromid [bro'mit] n (-[e]s;-e) bromide
Bronchitis [brɔn'çitɪs] f (-;) bronchitis
Bronze ['brõsə] f (-;-n) bronze
Brosche ['broʃə] f (-;-n) brooch
broschieren [brɔ'ʃirən] tr stitch; brocade; **broschiert with stapled binding**
Broschüre [brɔ'ʃyrə] f (-;-n) brochure
Brösel ['brøzəl] m (-s;-) crumb
Brot [brot] n (-[e]s;-e) bread; loaf; **geröstetes B.** toast
Brot'aufstrich m spread
Brötchen ['brøtçən] n (-s;-) roll
Brot'erwerb m livelihood, living
Brot'geber m, **Brot'herr** m employer
Brot'kasten m breadbox
brot'los adj unemployed; unprofitable
Brot'neid m professional jealousy
Brot'röster m (-s;-) toaster
Brot'schnitte f slice of bread
Brot'studium n bread-and-butter courses
Brot'zeit f breakfast

Bruch [brux] m (-[e]s;⁻e) breaking; break, crack; breakage; (aer) crash; (geol) fault; (math) fraction; (min) quarry; (pathol) hernia; (surg) fracture; **B. machen** crash-land; **in die Brüche gehen** go to pot; **zu B. gehen** break || [brux] m & n (-s;⁻e) bog
Bruch'band n (-s;⁻er) (surg) truss
Bruch'bude f shanty
brüchig ['brʏçɪç] adj fragile, brittle
Bruch'landung f crash landing
Bruch'rechnung f fractions
Bruch'stück n fragment, chip; **Bruchstücke** (fig) scraps, snatches
bruch'stückhaft adj fragmentary
Bruch'teil m fraction; **im B. e-r Sekunde** in a split second
Bruch'zahl f fractional number
Brücke ['brʏkə] f (-;-n) bridge; (Teppich) small (narrow) rug; (gym) backbend
Brückenkopf (Brük'kenkopf) m bridgehead
Brückenpfeiler (Brük'kenpfeiler) m pier of a bridge
Brückenwaage (Brük'kenwaage) f platform scale
Brückenzoll (Brük'kenzoll) m bridge toll
Bruder ['brudər] m (-s⁻) brother; (Genosse) companion; (eccl) lay brother
brüderlich ['brydərlɪç] adj brotherly
Brüderschaft ['brydər/aft] f (-;-en) brotherhood; fraternity
Brühe ['bry-ə] f (-;-n) broth; (Fleisch-) gravy; **in der B. stecken** be in a jam
brühen ['bry-ən] tr boil; scald
brüh'heiß adj piping hot
Brüh'kartoffeln pl potatoes boiled in broth
Brüh'würfel m bouillon cube
brüllen ['brʏlən] tr & intr roar, bellow; (Sturm) howl; (Ochse) low; **b. vor Lachen** roar with laughter
Brummbär ['brumbɛr] m (-en;-en) grouch
brummen ['brumən] tr mumble; grumble; growl || intr mumble; grumble; growl; (summen) buzz, hum; (Orgel) boom; (im Gefängnis) do time, do a stretch
brummig ['brumɪç] adj grouchy
brünett [bry'nɛt] adj brunet(te) || **Brünette** §5 brunette
Brunft [brunft] f (-;) rut
Brunft'zeit f rutting season
Brunnen ['brunən] m (-s;-) well; (Spring-) spring
Brunnenkresse ['brunənkresə] f (-;-n) watercress
Brunst [brunst] f (-;) rut, heat; (fig) ardor, passion
brunsten ['brunstən] intr be in heat
brünstig ['brʏnstɪç] adj in heat; (fig) passionate
brüsk [brusk] adj brusque
brüskieren [brus'kirən] tr snub
Brust [brust] f (-;⁻e) breast, chest
Brust'bein n breastbone, sternum
Brust'bild n portrait; (sculp) bust
brüsten ['brʏstən] ref show off

Brust′fellentzündung f pleurisy

Brust′kasten m, **Brust′korb** m thorax

Brust′schwimmen n breast stroke

Brust′stück n (culin) brisket

Brust′ton m —**im B. der Überzeugung** with utter conviction

Brust′umfang m chest measurement; (*bei Frauen*) bust measurement

Brü′stung f (-;-en) balustrade

Brust′warze f nipple

Brust′wehr f breastwork

Brut [brut] f (-;-en) brood; (pej) scum

brutal [bru′tɑl] adj brutal

Brut′apparat m, **Brut′ofen** m incubator

brüten [′brytən] tr hatch; (fig) plan || intr incubate; **b. auf** (*dat*) (fig) sit on; **b. über** (*dat*) brood over; pore over

brutto [′bruto] adj (com) gross

Brut′tosozialprodukt n gross national product

Bube [′bubə] m (-n;-n) boy; (*Schurke*) rascal; (cards) jack

Bu′benstreich m, **Bu′benstück** n prank; dirty trick

bübisch [′bybɪʃ] adj rascally

Buch [bux] n (-[e]s;⁀er) book; (cards) straight

Buch′besprechung f book review

Buchbinderei [′buxbɪndərɑɪ] f (-;-en) bookbindery; (*Gewerbe*) bookbinding

Buch′binderleinwand f buckram

Buch′deckel m book cover

Buch′drama n closet drama

Buch′druck m printing, typography

Buch′drucker m printer

Buch′druckerei f print shop; (*Gewerbe*) printing

Buche [′buxə] f (-;-n) beech

Buchecker [′buxekər] f (-;-n) beechnut

buchen [′buxən] tr book, reserve; (com) enter

Bücher- [byçər] comb.fm. book

Bü′cherabschluß m balancing of books

Bücherausgabe f circulation desk

Bü′cherbrett n bookshelf

Bücherei [byçə′rɑɪ] f (-;-en) library

Bü′cherfreund m bibliophile

Bü′chergestell n bookrack, bookcase

Bü′cherregal n bookshelf; bookcase

Bü′cherrevision f audit

Bü′cherrevisor m auditor; accountant

Bü′cherschrank m bookcase

Bü′cherstütze f book end

Buch′führung f bookkeeping, accounting

Buch′halter –in §6 mf bookkeeper

Buch′haltung f bookkeeping; accounting department

Buch′händler –in §6 mf book dealer

Buch′handlung f bookstore

Büchlein [′byçlɑɪn] n (-s;-) booklet

Buch′macher m bookmaker

Buch′prüfer –in §6 mf auditor

Buchsbaum [′buksbɑum] m boxwood

Buchse [′buksə] f (-;-n) (mach) bushing

Büchse [′byksə] f (-;-n) box, case; (*Dose*) can; (*Gewhr*) rifle

Büch′senfleisch n canned meat

Büch′senöffner m can opener

Buchstabe [′buxʃtɑbə] m (-n;-n) letter

buchstabieren [buxʃtɑ′birən] tr & intr spell

buchstäblich [′buxʃteplɪç] adj literal

Bucht [buxt] f (-;-en) bay

Buch′umschlag m book jacket

Bu′chung f (-;-en) booking; (acct) entry

Buckel [′bukəl] m (-s;-) hump; (coll) back; **B. haben** be hunchback; **e-n B. machen** arch its back

buck(e)lig [′buk(ə)lɪç] adj hunchbacked || **Buck(e)lige** §5 mf hunchback

bücken [′bykən] tr & ref bow (down)

Bückling [′byklɪŋ] m (-s;-e) bow

Bude [′budə] f (-;-n) booth, stall; (coll) shanty; (coll) hole in the wall

Budget [by′dʒe] n (-s;-s) budget

Büfett [by′fe], [by′fet] n (-s;-s) buffet, sideboard; counter; (*Schanktisch*) bar; **kaltes B.** cold buffet

Büffel [′byfəl] m (-s;-) buffalo

Büffelei [byfə′lɑɪ] f (-;-en) cramming

büffeln [′byfəln] intr (für) cram (for)

Bug [buk] m (-[e]s;-e) (aer) nose; (naut) bow; (zool) shoulder, withers

Bügel [′bygəl] m (-s;-) handle; (*Kleider-*) coat hanger; (*Steig-*) stirrup; (e-r Säge) frame

Bü′gelbrett n ironing board

Bü′geleisen n iron, flatiron

Bü′gelfalte f crease

bü′gelfrei adj drip-dry

bügeln [′bygəln] tr iron, press

Bü′gelsäge f hacksaw

bugsieren [buk′sirən] tr tow

Buhldirne [′buldɪrnə] f (-;-n) bawd

buhlen [′bulən] intr have an affair; **um j-s Gunst b.** curry favor with s.o.

Bühne [′bynə] f (-;-n) stage; platform

Büh′nenanweisung f stage direction

Büh′nenaussprache f standard pronunciation

Büh′nenausstattung f, **Büh′nenbild** n set

Büh′nenbildner –in §6 mf stage designer

Büh′nendeutsch n standard German

Büh′nendichter –in §6 mf playwright

Büh′nendichtung f drama, play

Büh′nenkünstler m actor

Büh′nenkünstlerin f actress

Büh′nenleiter –in §6 mf stage manager

Büh′nenstück n play, stage play

buk [buk] pret of **backen**

Bukarest [′bukarest] n (-s;) Bucharest

Bulette [bu′letə] f (-;-n) meatball

Bulgarien [bul′garjən] n (-s;) Bulgaria

Bullauge [′bulaugə] n (-s;-en) porthole

Bulldogge [′buldɔgə] f (-;-n) bulldog

Bulle [′bulə] m (-n;-n) bull; brawny fellow; (sl) cop || f (-;-n) (eccl) bull

bullern [′bulərn] intr bubble, boil; (*Feuer*) roar; (*Sturm*) rage

Bummel [′buməl] m (-s;) stroll

Bummelei [bumə′lɑɪ] f (-;-en) dawdling; loafing; sloppiness

bummelig [′buməlɪç] adj slow; sloppy

bummeln [′buməln] intr loaf; dawdle; (*Autos*) crawl || intr (SEIN) stroll

Bum'melstreik m slowdown

Bum'melzug m (coll) slow train, local

Bummler ['bumlər] m (-s;-) loafer, bum; slowpoke; gadabout

Bums [bums] m (-es;-e) thud, thump, bang || *interj* boom!; bang!

bumsen ['bumsən] *intr* thud, thump, bump; (sl) have intercourse

Bums'lokal n (coll) dive, joint

Bund [bunt] m (-[e]s;ᵁⁱ) union, federation; (*Schlüssel*-) ring; (*Rand an Hose*) waistband; (*Ehe*-) bond; (mach) flange; (mus) fret; (pol) federal government; **im Bunde mit** with the cooperation of || n (-[e]s;- & -e) bunch, bundle

Bündel ['byndəl] n (-s;-) bunch, bundle; (phys) beam

Bundes- *comb.fm.* federal

Bun'desgenosse m ally, confederate

Bun'desgerichtshof m federal supreme court

Bun'deslade f ark of the covenant

bun'desstaatlich *adj* state; federal

Bun'destag m lower house

bündig ['byndıç] *adj* binding; (*überzeugend*) convincing; (*treffend*) succinct; **b. liegen** be flush

Bündnis ['byntnıs] n (-ses;-se) agreement, pact, alliance

Bunker ['buŋkər] m (-s;-) bin; (agr) silo; (aer) air-raid shelter; (mil) bunker; (nav) submarine pen

bunt [bunt] *adj* colored; (*mehrfarbig*) multicolored; (*gefleckt*) dappled; (*gemischt*) varied, motley; (*Farbe*) bright, gay; (*Wiese*) gay with flowers; **bunter Abend** variety show; **buntes Durcheinander** complete muddle

Bunt'metall n nonferrous metal

Bunt'stift m colored pencil, crayon

Bürde ['byrdə] f (-;-n) burden

Burg [burk] f (-;-en) fortress, stronghold; citadel; castle

Bürge ['byrgə] m (-;-n) bondsman, guarantor, surety; **B. sein für** (or **als B. haften für**) stand surety for (*s.o.*); vouch for (*s.th.*)

bürgen ['byrgən] *intr*—**b. für** put up bail for (*s.o.*); vouch for (*s.th.*)

Bürger -in ['byrgər(ın)] §6 *mf* citizen; member of the middle class; commoner

Bür'gerkrieg m civil war

bür'gerlich *adj* civic; civil; middle-class; (*nicht überfeinert*) plain

Bür'germeister m mayor

Bür'gerrecht n civil rights

Bür'gerschaft f (-;) citizens

Bür'gersteig m sidewalk

Bürgschaft ['byrk/aft] f (-;-en) security, guarantee; (jur) bail; **gegen B. freilassen** release on bail

Büro [by'ro] n (-s;-s) office

Büro'angestellte §5 *mf* clerk

Büro'bedarf m office supplies

Büro'klammer f paper clip

Büro'kraft f office worker; **Bürokräfte** office personnel

Bürokrat [byro'krat] m (-en;-en) bureaucrat

Bürokra·tie [byrokra'ti] f (-;-tien ['ti·ən]) bureaucracy; (fig) red tape

bürokratisch [byro'krati/] *adj* bureaucratic

Bursch(e) ['bur/(ə)] m (-[e]n;-[e]n) boy, fellow; (mil) orderly; **ein übler B.** a bad egg

burschikos [bur/ı'kos] *adj* tomboyish; devil-may-care

Bürste ['byrstə] f (-;-n) brush; (coll) crewcut

bürsten ['byrstən] *tr* brush

Bürzel ['byrtsəl] m (-s;-) rump (*of bird*)

Bus [bus] m (-ses;-se) bus

Busch [bu/] m (-es;ᵁⁱe) bush; forest

Büschel ['by/əl] m & n clump, bunch, cluster; (*Haar*-) tuft; (elec) brush

Busch'holz n brushwood

buschig ['bu/ıç] *adj* bushy; shaggy

Busch'klepper m bushwhacker

Busch'messer n machete

Busch'werk n bushes, brush

Busen ['buzən] m (-s;-) bosom, breast; (*Bucht*) bay, gulf; (fig) bosom

Bussard ['busart] m (-s;-e) buzzard

Buße ['busə] f (-n;-n) penance; (*Sühne*) atonement; (*Strafgeld*) fine

büßen ['bysən] *tr* atone for, pay for

Büßer -in ['bysər(ın)] §6 *mf* penitent

Busserl ['busərl] n (-s;-n) kiss

buß'fertig *adj* repentant

Bussole [bu'solə] f (-;-n) compass

Büste ['bystə] f (-;-n) bust

Bü'stenhalter m brassière, bra

Bütte ['bytə] f (-;-n) tub; vat

Butter ['butər] f (-;) butter

But'terbrot n bread and butter

But'terdose f butter dish

But'termilch f buttermilk

buttern ['butərn] *tr* butter || *intr* make butter

byzantinisch [bytsan'tini/] *adj* Byzantine

Byzanz [by'tsants] n (-';) Byzantium

bzw. *abbr* (**beziehungsweise**) respectively

C

C, c [tze] *invar* n C, c; (meteor) centigrade; (mus) C

Café [ka'fe] n (-s;-s) café; coffee shop

Camping ['kempıŋ] n (-s;-s) camping

Canaille [ka'nal)ə] f (-;-n) scoundrel

Cäsar ['tsezar] m (-s;) Caesar

Cellist -in [t/e'lıst(ın)] §7 *mf* cellist

Cello ['t/elo] n (-s;-s) cello

Cellophan [tselo'fan] n (-s;) cellophane

Celsius ['tselzjus] centigrade

Cembalo ['t/embalo] n (-s;-s) harpsichord

Ces [tses] n (-;-) (mus) C flat

Champagner [ʃamˈpanjər] m (-s;-) champagne

Champignon [ˈʃampɪnjɔ̃] m (-s;-s) mushroom

Chance [ˈʃɑ̃sə] f (-;-n) chance

Chaos [ˈkaːɔs] n (-;) chaos

chaotisch [kaˈoːtɪʃ] adj chaotic

Charak·ter [kaˈraktər] m (-s;-tere [ˈterə]) character; (mil) honorary rank

Charak'terbild n character sketch

Charak'tereigenschaft f trait

charak'terfest adj of a strong character

charakterisieren [karakteriˈziːrən] tr characterize

Charakteristik [karakteˈrɪstɪk] f (-;-en) characterization

Charakteristi·kum [karakteˈrɪstɪkum] n (-s;-ka [ka]) characteristic

charakteristisch [karakteˈrɪstɪʃ] adj (für) characteristic (of)

charak'terlich adj of character || adv in character

charak'terlos adj wishy-washy

Charak'terzug m characteristic, trait

Charge [ˈʃarʒə] f (-;-n) (metal) charge; (mil) rank; Chargen (mil) non-coms

charmant [ʃarˈmant] adj charming

Charme [ʃarm] m (-s;) charm, grace

Chas·sis [ʃaˈsi] n (-sis [ˈsi[s]]; -sis [ˈsis]) chassis

Chaus·see [ʃoˈse] f (-;-seen [ˈseːən]) highway

Chef [ʃef] m (-s;-s) chief, head; (com) boss; (culin) chef; C. des Generalstabs chief of staff; C. des Heeresjustizwesens judge advocate general

Chemie [çeˈmiː] f (-;) chemistry; technische C. chemical engineering

Chemie'faser f synthetic fiber

Chemikalien [çemiˈkaːljən] pl chemicals

Chemiker -in [ˈçemɪkər(ɪn)] §6 mf chemist; student of chemistry

chemisch [ˈçeːmɪʃ] adj chemical; chemische Reinigung dry cleaning

Chemotechniker -in [çemoˈtɛçnɪkər(ɪn)] §6 mf chemical engineer

Chiffre [ˈʃɪfər] f (-;-n) cipher; code; (in Anzeigen) box number

Chif'freschrift f code

chiffrieren [ʃɪˈfriːrən] tr code

China [ˈçiːna] n (-s;) China

Chinese [çiˈneːzə] m (-n;-n;), Chinesin [çiˈneːzɪn] f (-;-nen) Chinese

chinesisch [çiˈneːzɪʃ] adj Chinese

Chinin [çiˈniːn] n (-s;) quinine

Chirurg [çiˈrurk] m (-en;-en) surgeon

Chirurgie [çirurˈgiː] f (-s;) surgery

chirurgisch [çiˈrurgɪʃ] adj surgical

Chlor [kloːr] n (-s;) chlorine

chloren [ˈkloːrən] tr chlorinate

Chlorid [kloˈriːt] n (-[e]s;-e) chloride

Chloroform [kloroˈfɔrm] n (-s;) chloroform

chloroformieren [kloroforˈmiːrən] tr chloroform

Cholera [ˈkoːlera] f (-;) cholera

cholerisch [koˈleːrɪʃ] adj choleric

Chor [koːr] m (-s;⁻e) choir; chorus

Choral [koˈraːl] m (-s;⁻e) Gregorian chant; (Prot) hymn

Chor'altar m high altar

Chor'anlage f (archit) choir

Chor'bühne f choir loft

Choreograph -in [koreˈoˈgraf(ɪn)] §7 mf choreographer

Chor'hemd n surplice

Chor'stuhl m choir stall

Christ [krɪst] m (-s;) Christ || m (-en;-en) Christian

Christ'abend m Christmas Eve

Christ'baum m Christmas tree

Chri'stenheit f (-;) Christendom

Christentum [ˈkrɪstəntum] n (-s;) Christianity

Christin [ˈkrɪstɪn] f (-;-nen) Christian

Christ'kind m Christ child

christ'lich adj Christian

Christ'nacht f Holy Night

Chri·stus [ˈkrɪstus] m (-sti [sti];) Christ; nach Christi Geburt A.D.; vor Christus B.C.

Chri'stusbild n crucifix; picture of Christ

Chrom [krom] n (-s;) chromium, chrome

chromatisch [kroˈmatɪʃ] adj chromatic

Chromosom [kromoˈzom] n (-s;-en) chromosome

Chronik [ˈkroːnɪk] f (-;-en) chronicle

chronisch [ˈkroːnɪʃ] adj chronic

Chronist -in [kroˈnɪst(ɪn)] §7 mf chronicler

Chronolo·gie [kronoloˈgiː] f (-;-gien [ˈgiːən]) chronology

chronologisch [kronoˈloːgɪʃ] adj chronological

circa [ˈtsɪrka] adv approximately

Cis [tsɪs] n (-;-) (mus) C sharp

Clique [ˈklɪkə] f (-;-n) clique

Cocktail [ˈkɔktel] m (-s;-s) cocktail

Conferencier [kɔ̃feraˈsje] m (-s;-s) master of ceremony

Couch [kautʃ] f (-;-es) couch

Countdown [ˈkauntdaun] m (-s;-s) (rok) countdown

Couplet [kuˈple] n (-s;-s) song (in a musical)

Coupon [kuˈpɔ̃] m (-s;-s) coupon

Courage [kuˈraʒə] f (-;) courage

Courtage [kurˈtaʒə] f (-;-n) brokerage

Cousin [kuˈzɛ̃] m (-s;-s) cousin

Cousine [kuˈzinə] f (-;-n) cousin

Cowboy [ˈkaubɔr] m (-s;-s) cowboy

creme [krem] adj cream-colored || Creme [ˈkrem(ə)] f (-;) cream; custard

Crew [kru] f (-;) crew; (nav) cadets (of the same year)

Cut [kœt] m (-s;-s) cutaway

D

D, d [de] *invar n* D, d; (mus) D

da [da] *adv* there; then; in that case, **da und da** at such and such a place; **wieder da** back again ‖ *conj* since, because; when

dabei [da'baɪ] *adv* nearby; besides, moreover; at that; at the same time; (*trotzdem*) yet; **d. bleiben** stick to one's point; **d. sein** be present, take part; **d. sein zu** (*inf*) be on the point of (*ger*); **es ist nichts d.** there's nothing to it

da capo [da'kapo] *interj* encore!

Dach [dax] *n* (–[e]s;ⁿer) roof; (fig) shelter; **unter D. und Fach** under cover

Dach/boden *m* attic

Dach/decker *m* roofer

Dach/fenster *n* dormer window; skylight

Dach/first *m* ridge of a roof

Dach/geschoß *n* top floor

Dach/gesellschaft *f* holding company

Dach/kammer *f* attic room

Dach/luke *f* skylight

Dach/organisation *f* parent company

Dach/pappe *f* roofing paper

Dach/pfanne *f* roof tile

Dach/rinne *f* rain gutter; eaves

Dach/röhre *f* downspout

Dachs [daks] *m* (–es;–e) badger; **ein frecher D.** a young whippersnapper

Dachs/hund *m* dachshund

Dach/sparren *m* rafter

Dach/stube *f* attic, garret

Dach/stuhl *m* roof framework

dachte ['daxtə] *pret of* **denken**

Dach/traufe *f* rain gutter

Dach/werk *n* roof

Dach/ziegel *m* roof tile

dadurch [da'dʊrç] *adv* through it; thereby; by this means; **dadurch, daß** by (*ger*)

dafür [da'fyr] *adv* for it or them; in its place; that's why; therefore

Dafür/halten *n*—**nach meinem D.** in my opinion

dagegen [da'gegən] *adv* against it or them; in exchange for it or them; in comparison; on the other hand; **etw d. haben** have an objection; **ich bin d.** I'm against it

daheim [da'haɪm] *adv* at home

daher [da'her] *adv* from there; therefore; (bei Verben der Bewegung) along ‖ ['daher] *adv* that's why

dahin [da'hɪn] *adv* there, to that place; (*vergangen*) gone; (bei Verben der Bewegung) along; **bis d.** that far, up to there; until then; **es steht mir bis d.** I'm fed up with it

da/hinab *adv* up there

da/hinaus *adv* out there

dahin/geben §80 *tr* give away; give up

dahin/gehen §82 *intr* (SEIN) walk along; pass; (*sterben*) pass away; **dahingehend, daß** to the effect that

dahingestellt [da'hɪngəʃtɛlt] *adj*—**d.**

sein lassen, ob leave the question open whether

dahin/leben *intr* exist from day to day

dahin/raffen *tr* carry off

dahin/scheiden §112 *intr* (SEIN) pass on

dahin/schwinden *intr* (SEIN) dwindle away; fade away; pine away

dahin/stehen §146 *impers*—**es steht dahin** it is uncertain

dahin/ten *adv* back there

dahin/ter *adv* behind it or them

dahinterher' *adv*—**d. sein, daß** be insistent that

dahin/terkommen §99 *intr* (SEIN) find out about it; get behind the truth of it

dahin/tersetzen *tr* put (*s.o.*) to work on it

dahin/welken §113 *intr* (SEIN) fade away

dahin/ziehen §163 *intr* (SEIN) move along

Dakapo [da'kapo] *n* (–s;–s) encore

da/lassen §104 *tr* leave behind

dalli ['dalɪ] *interj*—**mach d.!** step on it!

damalig ['damalɪç] *adj* of that time

damals ['damals] *adv* then, at that time

Damast [da'mast] *m* (–es;–e) damask

Dame ['damə] *f* (–;–n) lady; (beim Tanz) partner; (cards, chess) queen; (checkers) king; **e–e D. machen** crown a checker; **meine D.!** madam!; **meine Damen und Herrn!** ladies and gentlemen!

Da/mebrett *n* checkerboard

Da/menbinde *f* sanitary napkin

Da/mendoppelspiel *n* (tennis) women's doubles

Da/meneinzelspiel *n* (tennis) women's singles

Da/mengesellschaft *f* hen party

da/menhaft *adj* ladylike

Da/menhemd *n* chemise

Da/menschneider –**in** §6 *mf* dressmaker

Da/menwäsche *f* lingerie

Da/mespiel *n* checkers

damisch ['damɪʃ] *adj* dopey

damit [da'mɪt] *adv* with it or them; by it; thereby; **d. hat's noch Zeit** that can wait; **es ist nichts d.** it is useless ‖ *conj* in order that, to

dämlich ['demlɪç] *adj* dopey

Damm [dam] *m* (–[e]s;ⁿe) dam; dike; embankment; causeway; breakwater; pier; (fig) barrier; (anat) perineum; **auf dem D. sein** feel up to it; **wieder auf dem D. sein** be on one's feet again

Dämmer ['demər] *m* (–s;) (poet) twilight

dammerig ['demərɪç] *adj* dusky, dim

Däm/merlicht *n* dusk, twilight

dämmern ['demərn] *intr* dawn, grow light; (*am Abend*) grow dark, become twilight

Däm′merung *f* (-;-en) (*Morgenrot*) dawn; (*am Abend*) dusk, twilight

Dämmplatte [′dɛmplatə] *f* acoustical tile

Dämmstoff [′dɛmʃtɔf] *m* insulation

Damm′weg *m* causeway

Dämon [′dɛmɔn] *m* (-s; **Dämonen** [de′monən] demon

dämonisch [de′monɪʃ] *adj* demoniacal

Dampf [dampf] *m* (-[e]s;≔e) steam; vapor; (*Angst*) (coll) fear; (*Hunger*) (coll) hunger; (vet) broken wind; **D. dahinter machen** (coll) step on it

dampfen [′dampfən] *intr* steam || *intr* (SEIN) steam along, steam away

dämpfen [′dɛmpfən] *tr* (*dünsten*) steam; (*Lärm*) muffle; (*Farben, Gefühle, Lichter*) subdue; (*Stoß*) absorb; (*Begeisterung*) dampen; **mit gedämpfter Stimme** under one's breath

Dampfer [′dampfər] *m* (-s;-) steamer

Dämpfer [′dɛmpfər] *m* (-s;-) (culin) steamer, boiler; (mach) baffle; (mus) mute; (*beim Klavier*) (mus) damper; **e-n D. aufsetzen** (*dat*) put a damper on

Dampf′heizung *f* steam heat

Dampf′kessel *m* steam boiler, boiler

Dampf′maschine *f* steam engine

Dampf′schiffahrtslinie *f* steamship line

Dämp′fungsfläche *f* (aer) stabilizer

Dampf′walze *f* steam roller

Damspiel [′dam/pil] *n* var of **Damespiel**

danach [da′nax] *adv* after it or them; accordingly; according to it or them; afterwards; **d. fragen** ask about it; **d. streben** strive for it; **d. sieht er auch aus** that's just what he looks like

Däne [′dɛnə] *m* (-n;-n) Dane

daneben [da′nebən] *adv* next to it or them || *adv* in addition

dane′bengehen §82 *intr* (SEIN) go amiss

dane′benhauen *intr* miss; (fig) be wrong

Dänemark [′dɛnəmark] *n* (-s;) Denmark

dang [daŋ] *pret* of **dingen**

daniederliegen [da′niderligən] §108 *intr* (fig) be down; **d. an** (*dat*) be laid up with

Dänin [′dɛnɪn] *f* (-;-nen) Dane

dänisch [′dɛnɪʃ] *adj* Danish

dank [daŋk] *prep* (*dat*) thanks to || **Dank** *m* (-[e]s;) thanks; gratitude; **Gott sei D.!** thank God!, thank heaven!

dankbar [′daŋkbar] *adj* thankful; (*lohnend*) rewarding, profitable

Dank′barkeit *f* (-;) gratitude

danken [′daŋkən] *intr* (*dat*) thank; **danke!** thanks!; (*bei Ablehnung*) no, thanks!; **danke schön!** thank you!; **nichts zu d.!** you are welcome!

dan′kenswert *adj* meritorious; rewarding

dank′sagen *intr* return thanks

Danksagung [′daŋkzaguŋ] *f* (-;) thanksgiving

Dank′sagungstag *m* Thanksgiving Day

Dank′schreiben *n* letter of thanks

dann [dan] *adv* then; **d. und wann** now and then

dannen [′danən] *adv*—**von d.** away

daran [da′ran] *adv* on, at, by, in, onto it or them; **das ist alles d.!** that's great!; **er ist gut d.** he's well off; **er tut gut d. zu** (*inf*) he does well to (*inf*); **es ist nichts d.** there's nothing to it; **ich will wissen, wie ich d. bin** I want to know where I stand; **jetzt bin ich d.** it's my turn; **nahe d. sein zu** (*inf*) be on the point of (*ger*); **was liegt d.?** what does it matter?

daran′gehen §82 *intr* (SEIN) go about it; **d. gehen zu** (*inf*) proceed to (*inf*)

daran′setzen *tr*—**alles d. zu** (*inf*) do one's level best to (*inf*)

darauf [da′rauf] *adv* on it or them; after that; **d. kommt es an** that's what matters; **gerade d. zu** straight towards; **gleich d.** immediately afterwards; **ich lasse es d. ankommen** I'll risk it

daraufhin [darauf′hɪn] *adv* thereupon

daraus [da′raus] *adv* of it, from it; from that; from them; hence; **d. wird nichts!** nothing doing!; **es wird nichts d.** nothing will come of it

darben [′darbən] *intr* live in poverty

darbieten [′darbitən] §58 *tr* present

Dar′bietung *f* (-;-en) presentation; (theat) performance

dar′bringen §65 *tr* present, offer

Dardanellen [darda′nɛlən] *pl* Dardanellen

darein [da′rain] *adv* into it or them

darein′reden *intr* interrupt; **er redet mir in alles d.** he interferes in all that I do

darin [da′rɪn] *adv* in it or them

dar′legen *tr* explain; state

Dar′legung *f* (-;-en) explanation

Darleh(e)n [′darle(ə)n] *n* (-s;-) loan

Dar′leh(e)nskasse *f* loan association

Darm [darm] *m* (-[e]s;≔e) intestine, gut; (*Wursthaut*) skin

Darm- *comb.fm.* intestinal

Darm′entzündung *f* enteritis

Darm′fäule *f* dysentery

dar′stellen *tr* describe; show, depict, portray; represent; mean; plot, chart; (indust) produce; (theat) play the part of

Dar′steller -in §6 *mf* performer

Dar′stellung *f* (-;-en) representation; portrayal; account; version; (indust) production; (theat) performance

dar′tun §154 *tr* prove; demonstrate

darüber [da′rybər] *adv* over it or them; (*querüber*) across it; (*betreffs*) about that; **d. hinaus** beyond it; moreover; **ich bin d. hinweg** I've gotten over it

darum [da′rum] *adv* around it or them; (*deshalb*) therefore; **er weiß d.** he's aware of it; **es ist mir nur d. zu tun, daß** all I ask is that

darunter [da′runtər] *adv* below it or them; among them; (*weniger*) less; **d. leiden** suffer from it; **zehn Jahre und d.** ten years and under

das [das] §1 *def art* the || §1 *dem adj & dem pron* this, that; **das und das**

such and such || §11 *rel pron* which, that, who

da′sein §139 *intr* (SEIN) be there; be present; exist; **es ist schon alles mal dagewesen** there's nothing new under the sun; **noch nie dagewesen** unprecedented || **Dasein** *n* (−s;) being, existence, life

Da′seinsberechtigung *f* raison d'être

daselbst [da′zelpst] *adv* just there; ibidem; **wohnhaft d.** address as above

dasjenige [′dasjenɪgə] §4,3 *dem adj* that || *dem pron* the one

daß [das] *conj* that; **daß du nicht vergißt!** be sure not to forget!; **daß er doch käme!** I wish he'd come; **es sei denn, daß** unless

dasselbe [das′zɛlbə] §4,3 *dem adj* & *dem pron* the same

da′stehen §146 *intr* stand there; **einzig d.** be unrivaled; **gut d.** be well-off; **wie stehe ich nun da!** how foolish I look now!

Daten [′datən] *pl* data

Da′tenverarbeitung *f* data processing

datieren [da′tirən] *tr* & *intr* date

Dativ [′datif] *m* (−s;−e) dative (case)

dato [′dato] *adv*—**bis d.** to date

Dattel [′datəl] *f* (−;−n) (bot) date

Da·tum [′datum] *n* (−s;−ten [tən]) date; **Daten** data, facts; **heutigen Datums** of today; **neueren Datums** of recent date; **welches D. haben wir heute?** what's today's date?

Daube [′daubə] *f* (−;−n) (barrel) stave

Dauer [′dau·ər] *f* (−;) length, duration; permanence; **auf die D.** in the long run; **für die D. von** for a period of; **von D. sein** last, endure

Dau′erauftrag *m* standing order

Dau′erbelastung *f* constant load

Dau′erertrag *m* constant yield

Dau′erfeuer *n* (mil) automatic fire

Dau′erflug *m* endurance flight

Dau′ergeschwindigkeit *f* cruising speed

dau′erhaft *adj* lasting, durable; (*Farbe*) fast

Dau′erkarte *f* season ticket; (rr) commutation ticket

Dau′erlauf *m* (long-distance) jogging

dauern [′dau·ərn] *tr*—**er dauert mich** I feel sorry for him || *intr* last, continue; **die Fahrt dauert fünf Stunden** the trip takes five hours; **es wird nicht lange d., dann** it won't be long before; **lange d.** take a long time

Dau′erplissee *n* permanent pleat

Dau′erprobe *f* endurance test

Dau′erschmierung *f* self-lubrication

Dau′erstellung *f* permanent job

Dau′erton *m* (telp) dial tone

Dau′erversuch *m* endurance test

Dau′erwelle *f* permanent wave

Dau′erwirkung *f* lasting effect

Dau′erwurst *f* hard salami

Dau′erzustand *m* permanent condition; **zum D. werden** get to be a regular thing

Daumen [′daumən] *m* (−s;−) thumb; **D. halten!** keep your fingers crossed!; **die D. drehen** twiddle one's thumbs; **über den D. peilen** (or **schätzen**) give a rough estimate of

Dau′menabdruck *m* thumb print

Dau′menindex *m* thumb index

Daune [′daunə] *f* (−;−n) downy feather; **Daunen** down

Dau′nenbett *n* feather bed

Davit [′devɪt] *m* (−s;−s) (naut) davit

davon [da′fɔn] *adv* of it or them; from it or them; about it or them; away

davon′kommen §99 *intr* (SEIN) escape

davon′laufen §105 *intr* (SEIN) run away; || **Davonlaufen** *n*—**es ist zum D.** (coll) it's enough to drive you insane

davon′machen *ref* take off, go away

davon′tragen §132 *tr* carry off; win

davor [da′for] *adv* in front of it or them; of it or them; from it or them

dawider [da′vidər] *adv* against it

dazu [da′tsu] *adv* thereto; to it or them; in addition to that; for that purpose; about it or them; with it or them

dazu′gehörig *adj* belonging to it; proper, appropriate

da′zumal *adv* at that time

dazu′tun §154 *tr* add || **Dazutun** *n*—**ohne sein D.** without any effort on his part

dazwischen [da′tsvɪʃən] *adv* in between; among them

dazwi′schenfahren §71 *intr* (SEIN) jump in to intervene

dazwi′schenfunken *intr* (coll) butt in

dazwi′schenkommen §99 *intr* (SEIN) intervene

Dazwischenkunft [da′tsvɪʃənkunft] *f* (−;) intervention

dazwi′schentreten §152 *intr* (SEIN) intervene

Debatte [de′batə] *f* (−;−n) debate, discussion; **zur D. stehen** be under discussion; **zur D. stellen** open to discussion

debattieren [deba′tirən] *tr* & *intr* debate, discuss

Debet [′debet] *n* (−s;) debit; **im D. stehen** be on the debit side

Debüt [de′by] *n* (−s;−s) debut

Debütantin [deby′tantɪn] *f* (−;−nen) debutante

debütieren [deby′tierən] *intr* make one's debut

Dechant [de′çant] *m* (−en;−en) (educ; R.C.) dean

dechiffrieren [deʃɪf′rirən] *tr* decipher

Deck [dek] *n* (−s;−s) deck

Deck′anstrich *m* final coat

Deck′bett *n* feather bed

Deck′blatt *n* overlay

Decke [′dekə] *f* (−;−n) cover, covering; (*Bett−*) blanket; (*Tisch−*) tablecloth; (*Zimmer−*) ceiling; (*Schicht*) layer; **mit j−m unter e−r D. stecken** be in cahoots with s.o.; **sich nach der D. strecken** make the best of it

Deckel [′dekəl] *m* (−s;−) lid, cap; (*Buch−*) cover; **j−m eins auf den D. geben** (coll) chew s.o. out

decken [′dekən] *tr* cover; (*Tisch*) set; **das Tor d.** guard the goal || *ref* coincide || *intr* cover

Deckenbeleuchtung (**Dek′kenbeleuchtung**) *f* (−;) ceiling lighting

Deckenlicht (Dek'kenlicht) n ceiling light; skylight; (aut) dome light

Deck'farbe f one-coat paint

Deck'konto n secret account

Deck'mantel m pretext, pretense

Deck'name m pseudonym; alias; (mil) code name, cover name

Deck'offizier m (nav) warrant officer

Deck'plane f awning; tarpaulin

Deckung (Dek'kung) f (–;-en) covering; protection; roofing; (box) defense; (com) security, surety; collateral

deckungsgleich (dek'kungsgleich) adj congruent

defekt [de'fekt] adj defective || **Defekt** m (–[e]s;-e) defect

defensiv [defen'zif] adj defensive || **Defensive** [defen'zivə] f (–;-n) defensive

definieren [defi'nirən] tr define

definitiv [defini'tif] adj (endgültig) definitive; (bestimmt) definite

Defizit ['defitsɪt] n (–s;-e) deficit

Degen ['degən] m (–s;-) sword; (poet) warrior; (typ) compositor

degradieren [degra'dirən] tr demote

Degradie'rung f (–;-en) demotion

dehnbar ['denbar] adj elastic; (Metall) ductile; (fig) vague, loose

dehnen ['denən] tr stretch; extend; expand; (Worte) drawl out; (Vokal) lengthen; (mus) sustain || ref stretch out; expand

Deh'nung f (–;-en) extension; expansion; dilation; (ling) lengthening

Deich [daɪç] m (–[e]s;-e) dike; (Damm) bank, embankment

Deichsel ['daɪksəl] f (–;-n) pole

deichseln ['daɪksəln] tr (coll) manage

dein [daɪn] §2 poss adj your, thy

deinerseits ['daɪnər'zaɪts] adv on your part

deinesgleichen ['daɪnəs'glaɪçən] invar pron your own kin, your equals, the likes of you

deinethalben ['daɪnət'halbən], **deinetwegen** ['daɪnət'vegən], **deinetwillen** ['daɪnət'vɪlən] adv for your sake; because of you, on your account

deinige ['daɪnɪgə] poss pron yours

Dekan [de'kan] m (–s;-e) dean

deklamieren [dekla'mirən] tr & intr declaim; recite

Deklination [deklɪna'tsjon] f (–;-en) declension

deklinieren [deklɪ'nirən] tr decline

dekolletiert [dekɔle'tirt] adj low-necked; (Dame) bare-necked

Dekorateur [dekɔra'tør] m (–s;-e) decorator, interior decorator

Dekoration [dekɔra'tsjon] f (–;-en) decoration; (theat) scenery

dekorieren [dekɔ'rirən] tr decorate

Dekret [de'kret] n (–[e]s;-e) decree

delikat [deli'kat] adj delicate; (lecker) delicious

Delikt [de'lɪkt] n (–[e]s;-e) offense

Delle ['delə] f (–;-n) dent; dip

Delphin [del'fin] m (–s;-e) dolphin

Delta ['delta] n (–s;-s) delta

dem [dem] §1 def art, dem adj & dem pron || §11 rel pron

Demagoge [dema'gogə] m (–n;-n) demagogue

Dementi [de'menti] n (–s;-s) official denial

dementieren [demen'tirən] tr deny (officially)

dem'entsprechend adj corresponding || adv correspondingly, accordingly

dem'gegenüber adv in contrast

dem'gemäß adv accordingly

dem'nach adv therefore; accordingly

dem'nächst adv soon, before long; (theat) (public sign) coming soon

demobilisieren [demobɪlɪ'zirən] tr & intr demobilize

Demokrat [demo'krat] m (–en;-en) democrat

Demokra·tie [demokra'ti] f (–;-tien ['ti·ən]) democracy

Demokratin [demo'kratɪn] f (–;-nen) democrat

demokratisch [demo'kratɪʃ] adj democratic

demolieren [demo'lirən] tr demolish

Demonstrant –in [demon'strant(ɪn)] §7 mf demonstrator

demonstrieren [demon'strirən] tr & intr demonstrate

Demontage [demon'taʒə] f (–;) dismantling

demontieren [demon'tirən] tr dismantle

demselben [dem'zelbən] §4,3 dem adj & dem pron

Demut ['demut] f (–;) humility

demütig ['demytɪç] adj humble

demütigen ['demytɪgən] tr humble; (beschämen) humiliate

De'mütigung f (–;-en) humiliation

de'mutsvoll adj submissive

dem'zufolge adv accordingly

den [den] §1 def art, dem adj & dem pron || §11 rel pron whom

denen ['denən] §11 rel pron to whom

Denkarbeit ['deŋkarbaɪt] f (–;) brainwork

Denkart ['deŋkart] f var of **Denkungsart**

Denkaufgabe ['deŋkaufgabə] f brain twister, problem

denkbar ['deŋkbar] adj conceivable; (vorstellbar) imaginable

denken ['deŋkən] §66 tr think, consider; **was d. Sie zu tun?** what do you intend to do? || ref—**bei sich** (or **für sich**) **d.** think to oneself; **denke dir e–e Zahl** think of a number; **d. Sie sich in ihre Lage** imagine yourself in her place; **sich** [dat] **etw d.** imagine s.th.; **was denkst du dir eigentlich?** what do you think you're doing? || intr think; **das gibt mir zu d.** that set me thinking; **d. an** (acc) think about

denk'faul adj mentally lazy

Denk'fehler m fallacy, false reasoning

Denk'mal n (–s;-e & ·er) monument

Denk'schrift f (pol) memorandum

Denkungsart ['deŋkuŋsart] f way of thinking, mentality

Denk'weise f way of thinking, mentality

denk'würdig adj memorable

Denk'zettel *m—j—m* e-n D. geben teach s.o. a lesson

denn [dɛn] *adv* then; es sei denn, daß unless ‖ *conj* for

dennoch ['dɛnɔx] *adv* nevertheless, all the same, (but) still

Dentist —in [dɛn'tɪst(ɪn)] §7 *mf* dentist

Denunziant —in [dɛnʊn'tsjant(ɪn)] §7 *mf* informer

denunzieren [dɛnʊn'tsirən] *tr* denounce

Depesche [dɛ'pɛʃə] *f* (-;-n) dispatch

De·ponens [dɛ'ponɛns] *n* (-;-ponenzien [pɔ'nɛntsjən]) (gram) deponent

deponieren [depo'nirən] *tr* (com) deposit

deportieren [depɔr'tirən] *tr* deport

Depot [dɛ'po] *n* (-s;-s) depot; warehouse; storage; safe; safe deposit

Depp [dɛp] *m* (-s;-e) (coll) dope

Depression [depre'sjon] *f* (-;-en) depression

der [der] §1 *def art* the ‖ §1 *dem adj & dem pron* this, that; der und der such and such, so and so ‖ §11 *rel pron* who, which, that; (to) whom

der'art *adv* so, in such a way; (coll) that

der'artig *adj* such, of that kind

derb [dɛrp] *adj* coarse; tough; rude

Derb'heit *f* (-;-en) coarseness; toughness; crude joke

dereinst' *adv* some day

deren ['dɛrən] §11 *rel pron* whose

derenthalben ['dɛrənt'halbən], **derentwegen** ['dɛrənt'vegən], **derentwillen** ['dɛrənt'vɪlən] *adv* for her sake, for their sake

dergestalt ['dɛrgə'ʃtalt] *adv* so

dergleichen ['dɛr'glaɪçən] *invar dem adj* such; similar; of that kind ‖ *invar dem pron* such a thing; und d. and the like; und d. mehr and so on

derjenige ['dɛrjenɪgə] §4,3 *dem adj* that ‖ *dem pron* the one; he

dermaßen [dɛr'masən] *adv* so, in such a way

derselbe [dɛr'zɛlbə] §4,3 *dem adj & dem pron* the same

derweilen ['dɛr'vaɪlən] *adv* meanwhile

derzeit ['dɛr'tsaɪt] *adv* at present

derzeitig ['dɛr'tsaɪtɪç] *adj* present; then, of that time

des [dɛs] *n* (-s;-) (mus) D flat

Desaster [dɛ'zastər] *n* (-s;-) disaster

Deserteur [dezɛr'tør] *m* (-s;-e) deserter

desertieren [dezɛr'tirən] *intr* (SEIN) desert

desgleichen ['dɛs'glaɪçən] *invar dem pron* such a thing ‖ *invar rel pron* the likes of which ‖ *adv* likewise

deshalb ['dɛshalp] *adv* therefore

Desinfektion [desɪnfɛk'tsjon] *f* (-;-en) disinfection

Desinfektions'mittel *n* disinfectant

desinfizieren [desɪnfi'tsirən] *tr* disinfect

Despot [dɛs'pot] *m* (-en;-en) despot

despotisch [dɛs'potɪʃ] *adj* despotic

Dessin [dɛ'sɛ̃] *n* (-s;-s) design

destillieren [dɛstɪ'lirən] *tr* distill

desto ['dɛsto] *adv* the; d. besser the better, all the better

deswegen ['dɛs'vegən] *adv* therefore

Detail [de'taɪ(l)] *n* (-s;-s) detail; (com) retail

Detail'geschäft *n* retail store

Detail'händler —in [de'taɪ] *m* §6 *mf* retail dealer

detaillieren [deta'jirən] *tr* relate in detail; specify; itemize

Detek·tiv [detɛk'tif] *m* (-s;-tive ['tivə]) private investigator; (coll) private eye

detonieren [deto'nirən] *intr* detonate; etw. d. lassen detonate s.th.

deuchte ['dɔɪçtə] *pret of* dünken

Deutelei [dɔɪtə'laɪ] *f* (-;-en) quibble

deuteln ['dɔɪtəln] *intr* (an dat) quibble (about), split hairs (over)

deuten ['dɔɪtən] *tr* interpret; falsch d. misinterpret ‖ *intr* (auf acc) (& fig) point (to)

deutlich ['dɔɪtlɪç] *adj* clear, distinct

deutsch [dɔɪtʃ] *adj* German ‖ **Deutsche** §5 *mf* German

Deu'tung *f* (-;-en) interpretation

Devise [de'vizə] *f* (-;-n) motto; **Devisen** foreign currency

Devi'senbestand *m* foreign-currency reserve

Devi'senbilanz *f* balance of payments

Devi'senkurs *m* rate of exchange

Dezember [de'tsɛmbər] *m* (-s;-) December

dezent [de'tsɛnt] *adj* unobtrusive; (Licht, Musik) soft; (anständig) decent

Dezernat [detsɛr'nat] *n* (-[e]s;-e) (administrative) department

dezimal [detsi'mal] *adj* decimal ‖ **Dezimale** [detsi'malə] *f* (-;-n) decimal

Dezimal'bruch *m* decimal fraction

Dezimal'zahl *f* decimal

dezimieren [detsi'mirən] *tr* decimate

Dia ['di·a] *n* (-s;-s) (coll) slide

Diadem [di·a'dem] *n* (-s;-e) diadem

Diagnose [di·a'gnozə] *f* (-;-n) diagnosis

diagnostizieren [di·agnɔsti'tsirən] *tr* diagnose

diagonal [di·ago'nal] *adj* diagonal ‖ **Diagonale** *f* (-;-n) diagonal

Diagramm [di·a'gram] *n* (-[e]s;-e) diagram; graph

Diakon [di·a'kon] *m* (-s;-e & -en;-en) deacon

Dialekt [di·a'lɛkt] *m* (-[e]s;-e) dialect

dialektisch [di·a'lɛktɪʃ] *adj* dialectical

Dialog [di·a'lok] *m* (-s;-e) dialogue

Diamant [di·a'mant] *m* (-en;-en) diamond

Diaposi·tiv [di·apozi'tif] *n* (-s;-tive ['tivə]) slide, transparency

Diät [di'ɛt] *f* (-;-en) diet (under medical supervision); **Diäten** daily allowance; diät leben be on a diet

Diät- *comb.fm.* dietary

diätetisch [diɛ'tetɪʃ] *adj* dietetic

dich [dɪç] §11 *pers pron* you, thee ‖ *reflex pron* yourself, thyself

dicht [dɪçt] *adj* dense; thick; heavy; leakproof; tight ‖ **Dichte** ['dɪçtə] *f* (-;-en) density

dichten ['dıçtən] *tr* tighten; caulk; compose, write || *intr* write poetry

Dichter ['dıçtər] *m* (–s;–) (important) writer; poet

Dichterin ['dıçtərın] *f* (–;-nen) poetess

dichterisch ['dıçtərıʃ] *adj* poetic(al)

dicht/gedrängt *adj* tightly packed

dicht/halten §90 *intr* keep mum

Dicht/heit *f* (–;), **Dich/tigkeit** *f* (–;) density; compactness; tightness

Dich/kunst *f* poetry

dicht/machen *tr* (coll) close up

Dich/tung *f* (–;-en) gasket; packing; imagination; fiction; poetry; poem;

Dich/tungsring *m*, **Dich/tungsscheibe** *f* washer; gasket

dick [dık] *adj* thick; fat; big; (*Luft, Freunde*) close; **dicke Luft!** (coll) cheese it!; **sich d. tun** talk big || **Dicke** *f* (–;) thickness, stoutness

Dick/darm *m* (anat) colon

dickfellig ['dıkfɛlıç] *adj* thick-skinned

dick/flüssig *adj* viscous

Dickicht ['dıkıçt] *n* (–[e]s;-e) thicket

Dick/kopf *m* thick head

dickköpfig ['dıkkœpfıç] *adj* thick-headed

dickleibig ['dıklaıbıç] *adj* stout, fat

Dick/schädel *m* thick head

dick/schädelig ['dıkʃedəlıç] *adj* thick-headed

die [di] §1 *def art* the || §1 *dem adj* & *dem pron* this, that; **die und die** such and such || §11 *rel pron* who, which, that

Dieb [dip] *m* (–[e]s;-e) thief

Dieberei [dibə'raı] *f* (–;-en) thievery; (*Diebstahl*) theft

Diebesbande ['dibəsbandə] *f* pack of thieves

Diebin ['dibın] *f* (–;-nen) thief

diebisch ['dibıʃ] *adj* thievish || *adv*—**sich d. freuen** be tickled pink

Diebstahl ['dip/tal] *m* (–[e]s;⸚) theft, larceny; **leichter D.** petty larceny; **schwerer D.** grand larceny

diejenige ['dijenıgə] §4,3 *dem adj* that || *dem pron* the one; she

Diele ['dilə] *f* (–;-n) floorboard; (*breiter Flur*) entrance hall; **Dielen** flooring

dienen ['dinən] *intr* (*dat*) serve; **damit ist mir nicht gedient** that doesn't help me any; **womit kann ich d.?** may I help you?

Diener **-in** ['dinər(ın)] §6 *mf* servant

die/nerhaft *adj* servile

dienern ['dinərn] *intr* bow and scrape

Die/nerschaft *f* (–;) domestics, help

dienlich ['dinlıç] *adj* useful

Dienst [dinst] *m* (–es;-e) service; job; employment; (adm, mil) grade; **außer D.** retired; **im. D.** on duty; **j-m e-n D. tun** do s.o. a favor

Dienstag ['dinstak] *m* (–[e]s;-e) Tuesday

Dienst/alter *n* seniority

dienstbar ['dinstbar] *adj* subservient

Dienst/barkeit *f* (–;) servitude, bondage; (jur) easement

dienst/beflissen *adj* eager to serve || *adv* eagerly

Dienst/bote *m* servant, domestic

Dienst/boteneingang *m* service entrance

Dienst/eid *m* oath of office

dienst/eifrig *adj* eager to serve || *adv* eagerly

Dienst/einteilung *f* work schedule; (mil) duty roster

Dienst/fahrt *f* official trip

dienst/frei *adj*—**d. haben** be off duty

Dienst/gebrauch *m*—**nur zum D.** for official use only

Dienst/gespräch *n* business call

Dienst/grad *m* (mil) rank, grade; (nav) rating

dienst/habend *adj* on duty

Dienst/herr *m* employer; (hist) lord

Dienst/leistung *f* service

dienst/lich *adj* official || *adv* officially; on official business

Dienst/mädchen *n* maid

Dienst/pflicht *f* official duty; compulsory military service

Dienst/plan *m* work schedule; (mil) duty roster

Dienst/sache *f* official business

dienst/tauglich *adj* fit for active service

diensttuend ['dinsttu‧ənt] *adj* on duty; active; in charge

Dienst/weg *m* official channels

Dienst/wohnung *f* official residence

dies [dis] *dem adj* & *dem pron* var of *dieses*

diese ['dizə] §3 *dem adj* this || *dem pron* this one

dieselbe [di'zɛlbə] §4,3 *dem adj* & *dem pron* the same

Dieselmotor ['dizəlmotər] *m* diesel engine

dieser ['dizər] §3 *dem adj* this || *dem pron* this one

dieses ['dizəs] §3 *dem adj* this || *dem pron* this one

diesig ['dizıç] *adj* hazy, misty

dies/jährig *adj* this year's

dies/mal *adv* this time

diesseits ['diszaıts] *prep* (*genit*) on this side of

Dietrich ['ditrıç] *m* (–s;-e) skeleton key; (*Einbrecherwerkzeug*) picklock

Differential [dıferən'tsjal] *n* (–s;-e) (aut, math) differential

Differential- *comb.fm.* (econ, elec, mach, math, phys) differential

Differenz [dıfe'rɛnts] *f* (–;-en) difference

Diktaphon [dıkta'fon] *n* (–[e]s;-e) dictaphone

Diktat [dık'tat] *n* (–s;-e) dictation; **nach D. schreiben** take dictation

Dik-tator [dık'tator] *m* (–s;-tatoren) [ta'torən]) dictator

diktatorisch [dıkta'torıʃ] *adj* dictatorial

Diktatur [dıkta'tur] *f* (–;-en) dictatorship

diktieren [dık'tirən] *tr* & *intr* dictate

Dilettant **-in** [dıle'tant(ın)] §7 *mf* dilettante, amateur

Diner [dı'ne] *n* (–s;-s) dinner

Ding [dıŋ] *n* (–[e]s;-e) thing; **ein D. drehen** (coll) pull a job

dingen ['dıŋən] §109 & §142 *tr* hire

ding'fest *adj*—j—n **d. machen** arrest s.o.
ding'lich *adj* real
Dings [dɪŋs] *n* (-s;) (coll) thing, doo-
dad, thingamajig
Dings'bums *m & n* (-;) var of **Dingsda**
Dings'da *mfn* (-s;) what-d'ye-call-it
Diözese [dɪ‧ø'tseːzə] *f* (-;-n) diocese
Diphtherie [dɪftε'riː] *f* (-;) diphtheria
Dipl.-Ing. *abbr* (**Diplom-Ingenieur**) en-
gineer holding a degree
Diplom [dɪ'ploːm] *n* (-s;-e) diploma
Diplom- *comb.fm.* holding a degree
Diplomat [dɪplə'maːt] *m* (-en;-en) diplomat
Diplomatie [dɪploma'tiː] *f* (-;) diplo-
macy
Diplomatin [dɪplə'maːtɪn] *f* (-;-nen)
diplomat
diplomatisch [dɪplə'maːtɪʃ] *adj* diplomatic
dir [diːr] §11 *pers pron* to or for you,
to or for thee || *reflex pron* to or for
yourself, to or for thyself
direkt [dɪ'rεkt] *adj* direct
Direktion [dɪrεk'tsjoːn] *f* (-;) direction; (*Verwaltung*) management
Direk·tor [dɪ'rεktor] *m* —s;-toren
['toːrən] director; (*e-r Bank*)· president; (*e-r Schule*) principal; (*e-s
Gefängnisses*) warden
Direktorat [dɪrεktə'raːt] *n* (-[e]s;-e)
directorship
Direktorin [dɪrεk'toːrɪn] *f* (-;-nen) director; (*educ*) principal
Direkto·rium [dɪrεk'toːri·um] *n* (-s;
-rien [ri·ən]) board of directors; executive committee
Direktrice [dɪrεk'triːsə] *f* (-;-n) direc-
tress, manager
Dirigent -in [dɪrɪ'gεnt(ɪn)] §7 *mf*
(mus) conductor
dirigieren [dɪrɪ'giːrən] *tr* direct, manage; (mus) conduct
Dirnd(e)l ['dɪrndəl] *n* (-s;-) girl;
(*Tracht*) dirndle
Dirne ['dɪrnə] *f* (-;-n) girl; (pej) prostitute
Dis [dɪs] *n* (-;-) D sharp
disharmonisch [dɪshar'moːnɪʃ] *adj* dis-
cordant
Diskont [dɪs'kɔnt] *m* (-[e]s;-e) discount
diskontieren [dɪskɔn'tiːrən] *tr* discount
Diskothek [dɪsko'teːk] *f* (-;-en) discotheque
diskret [dɪs'kreːt] *adj* discreet
Diskretion [dɪskre'tsjoːn] *f* (-;-en)
discretion
Diskussion [dɪsku'sjoːn] *f* (-;-en) discussion
diskutieren [dɪsku'tiːrən] *tr* discuss ||
intr—**d. über** (*acc*) discuss
disponieren [dɪspo'niːrən] *intr* (**über**
acc) dispose (of)
Disposition [dɪspozɪ'tsjoːn] *f* (-;-en)
disposition; arrangement; disposal
Distanz [dɪs'tants] *f* (-;-en) distance
distanzieren [dɪstan'tsiːrən] *tr* (**mit**)
beat (by, e.g., *one meter*) || *ref* (**von**)
dissociate oneself (from)
distanziert *adj* (fig) detached
Distel ['dɪstəl] *f* (-;-n) thistle
Dis'telfink *m* goldfinch

Distrikt [dɪs'trɪkt] *m* (-[e]s;-e) district
Disziplin [dɪstsɪ'pliːn] *f* (-;-en) discipline
disziplinarisch [dɪstsɪplɪ'naːrɪʃ] *adj*
disciplinary
dito ['diːto] *adv* ditto || **Dito** *n* (-s;-s)
ditto
Dividend [dɪvɪ'dεnt] *m* (-en;-en)‚
Dividende [dɪvɪ'dεndə] *f* (-;-n) dividend
dividieren [dɪvɪ'diːrən] *tr* divide
Division [dɪvɪ'zjoːn] *f* (-;-en) division
Diwan ['diːvan] *m* (-s;-e) divan
D-Mark ['deːmark] *f* (-;-) mark (*monetary unit of West Germany*)
doch [dɔx] *adv* yet; of course
Docht [dɔxt] *m* (-[e]s;-e) wick
Dock [dɔk] *n* (-[e]s;-s & -e) dock
docken ['dɔkən] *tr & intr* (naut, rok)
dock
Dogge ['dɔgə] *f* (-;-n) mastiff; **deut-
sche D.** Great Dane
Dog·ma ['dɔgma] *n* (-s;-men [mən])
dogma
Dohle ['doːlə] *f* (-;-n) jackdaw
Dok·tor ['dɔktor] *m* (-s;-toren
['toːrən]) doctor
Dok'torarbeit *f* dissertation
Dok'torvater *m* adviser (*for a doctoral
dissertation*)
Dokument [dɔku'mεnt] *n* (-[e]s;-e)
document; (jur) instrument, deed
Dokumentarfilm [dɔkumεn'tarfɪlm] *m*
documentary
dokumentarisch [dɔkumεn'tarɪʃ] *adj*
documentary
Dolch [dɔlç] *m* (-[e]s;-e) dagger
Dolch'stoß *m* (pol) stab in the back
Dollar ['dɔlar] *m* (-s;-) dollar
dolmetschen ['dɔlmεtʃən] *tr & intr* in-
terpret
Dol'metscher -in §6 *mf* interpreter
Dom [doːm] *m* (-[e]s;-e) cathedral;
dome
Domäne [dɔ'mεːnə] *f* (-;-n) domain
Domino ['dɔmino] *n* (-s;-s) domino
Donau ['doːnau] *f* (-;) Danube
Donner ['dɔnar] *m* (-s;-) thunder
Don'nerkeil *m* thunderbolt
donnern ['dɔnərn] *intr* thunder
Don'nerschlag *m* clap of thunder
Don'nerstag *m* (-[e]s;-e) Thursday
Don'nerwetter *n* thunderstorm; **zum
D.!** confound it! || *interj* geez!
doof [doːf] *adj* (coll) goofy
dopen ['doːpən] *tr* dope (*a racehorse*)
Doppel ['dɔpəl] *n* (-s;-) duplicate;
(tennis) doubles
Doppel- *comb.fm.* double, two, bi-,
twin
Dop'pelbelichtung *f* double exposure
Dop'pelbild *n* (telv) ghost
Dop'pelbruch *m* compound fracture
Dop'pelehe *f* bigamy
Dop'pelgänger *m* double; second self
Dop'pellaut *m* diphthong
doppeln ['dɔpəln] *tr* double
Dop'pelprogramm *n* double feature
Dop'pelpunkt *m* (typ) colon
doppelreihig ['dɔpəlraɪ·ɪç] *adj* double-
breasted
Dop'pelrendezvous *n* double date

dop'pelseitig *adj* reversible; (*Lungenentzündung*) double

Dop'pelsinn *m* double entendre

dop'pelsinnig *adj* ambiguous

Dop'pelspiel *n* (fig) double-dealing; (sport) double-header; (tennis) doubles

doppelt ['dɔpəlt] *adj* double; **doppelter Boden** false bottom; **ein doppeltes Spiel spielen mit** doublecross; **in doppelter Ausführung** in duplicate || *adv* twice; **ein Buch d. haben** have two copies of a book

Dop'pelverdiener **–in** §6 *mf* moonlighter

Dop'pelvokal *m* diphthong

doppelzüngig ['dɔpəltsynɪç] *adj* twofaced

Dorf [dɔrf] *n* (–[e]s;–er) village

Dorf'bewohner **–in** §6 *mf* villager

Dörfchen ['dœrfçən] *n* (–s;–) hamlet

Dorn [dɔrn] *m* (–[e]s;–en) thorn; tongue (*of a buckle*); (mach) pin; (sport) spike

Dorn'busch *m* briar, bramble

dornig ['dɔrnɪç] *adj* thorny

Dornröschen ['dɔrnrøsçən] *n* (–s;) Sleeping Beauty

Dörr- [dœr] *comb.fm.* dried

dorren ['dɔrən] *intr* (SEIN) dry (up)

dörren ['dœrən] *tr* dry

Dorschlebertran ['dɔrʃlebərtran] *m* (–[e]s;) cod-liver oil

dort [dɔrt] *adv* there, over there

dort'her *adv* from there

dort'hin *adv* there, to that place

dor'tig *adj* in that place, there

Dose ['dozə] *f* (–;–n) can; box

dösen ['døzən] *intr* doze

Do'senöffner *m* can opener

dosieren [do'zirən] *tr* prescribe (the correct dosage of)

Dosie'rung *f* (–;–en) dosage

Do·sis ['dozɪs] *f* (–;–sen [zən]) dose

dotieren [do'tirən] *tr* endow; **ein Preis mit 100 Mark dotiert** a prize worth 100 marks

Dotter ['dɔtər] *m & n* (–s;–) yolk

Double ['dubəl] *m & n* (–s;–s) (cin, theat) stand-in

Dozent **–in** [do'tsent(ɪn)] §7 (university) instructor, lecturer

Drache ['draxə] *m* (–n;–n) dragon; (*böses Weib*) battle-ax

Dra'chenfliegen *n* (–s;) hang gliding

Draht [drat] *m* (–[e]s;–e) wire; **auf D. sein** (coll) be on the beam

drahten ['dratən] *tr* telegraph, wire

draht'haarig *adj* wire-haired

Draht'hindernis *n* (mil) wire entanglement, barbed wire

drahtig ['dratɪç] *adj* wiry

draht'los *adj* wireless

Draht'seil *n* cable

Draht'seilbahn *f* cable car, funicular

Draht'zaun *m* wire fence

drall [dral] *adj* plump; (*Faden*) sturdy || **Drall** *m* (–s;–e) rifling

Dra·ma ['drama] *n* (–s;–men [mən]) drama

Dramatiker **–in** [dra'matɪkər(ɪn)] §6 *mf* dramatist, playwright

dramatisch [dra'matɪʃ] *adj* dramatic

dran [dran] *adv* var of **daran**

drang [draŋ] *pret* of **dringen** || **Drang** *m* (–[e]s;–e) pressure; urge

drängeln ['drɛŋəln] *tr & intr* shove

drängen ['drɛŋən] *tr & intr* push, shove; (*drücken*) press || *ref* crowd, crowd together; force one's way

Drangsal ['draŋzal] *f* (–;–e) distress, anguish; hardship

drangsalieren [draŋza'lirən] *tr* vex

drastisch ['drastɪʃ] *adj* drastic

drauf [drauf] *adv* var of **darauf**

Drauf'gänger *m* (–s;–) go-getter

drauf'gehen §82 *intr* (SEIN) (coll) go down the drain

drauflos' *adv*—**d. arbeiten an** (*dat*) work away at

drauflos'gehen §82 *intr* (SEIN)—**d. auf** (*acc*) make straight for

drauflos'reden *intr* ramble on

drauflos'schlagen §132 *intr* (**auf** *acc*) let fly (at)

draußen ['drausən] *adv* outside; out of doors; (*in der Fremde*) abroad

drechseln ['drɛksəln] *tr* work (*on a lathe*); (fig) embellish

Dreck [drɛk] *m* (–[e]s;) dirt; mud; excrement; (*Abfälle*) trash

dreckig ['drɛkɪç] *adj* dirty; muddy

Dreh- [dre] *comb.fm.* revolving, rotary

Dreh'arbeiten *pl* (cin) shooting

Dreh'aufzug *m* dumb waiter

Dreh'bank *f* (–;–e) lathe

drehbar ['drebar] *adj* revolving

Dreh'buch *n* (mov) script, scenario

drehen ['dre·ən] *tr* turn; (*Zigaretten*) roll; (coll) wangle; (cin) shoot || *ref* turn; rotate

Dreh'kreuz *n* turnstile

Dreh'orgel *f* hurdy-gurdy

Dreh'orgelspieler *m* organ grinder

Dreh'punkt *m* fulcrum; (fig) pivotal point

Dreh'scheibe *f* potter's wheel; (rr) turntable

Dreh'stuhl *m* swivel chair

Dre'hung *f* (–;–en) turn

Dreh'zahl *f* revolutions per minute

Dreh'zahlmesser *m* tachometer

drei [draɪ] *adj & pron* three || **Drei** *f* (–;–en) three; (educ) C

dreidimensional ['draɪdɪmɛnzjonal] *adj* three-dimensional

Dreieck ['draɪ·ɛk] *n* (–[e]s;–e) triangle

drei'eckig *adj* triangular

drei'fach *adj* threefold, triple

dreifältig ['draɪfɛltɪç] *adj* threefold, triple

Dreifaltigkeit [draɪ'faltɪçkaɪt] *f* (–;) Trinity

Drei'fuß *m* tripod

Dreikäsehoch [draɪ'kezəhoç] *m* (–s;–) (coll) shrimp, runt

drei'mal *adv* three times, thrice

Drei'rad *n* tricycle

Drei'sprung *m* hop, step, and jump

dreißig ['draɪsɪç] *adj & pron* thirty || **Dreißig** *f* (–;– & –en) thirty

dreißiger ['draɪsɪgər] *invar adj* of the thirties, in the thirties

dreißigste ['draɪsɪçstə] §9 *adj & pron* thirtieth

dreist [draɪst] *adj* brazen, bold
dreistimmig ['draɪ/tɪmɪç] *adj* for three voices
drei'zehn *adj* & *pron* thirteen || **Drei-zehn** *f* (-;-) thirteen
drei'zehnte §9 *adj* & *pron* thirteenth
dreschen ['drɛʃən] §67 *tr* thresh; (coll) thrash
Dresch'flegel *m* flail
Dresch'tenne *f* threshing floor
dressieren [drɛ'siːrən] *tr* train; (*Pferd*) break in
Dressur [drɛ'suːr] *f* (-;) training
dribbeln ['drɪbəln] *intr* (sport) dribble
drillen ['drɪlən] *tr* drill; train
Drillich ['drɪlɪç] *m* (-s;-e) denim
Dril'lichanzug *m* dungarees; (mil) fatigue uniform, fatigues
Dril'lichhosen *pl* dungarees, jeans
Drilling ['drɪlɪŋ] *m* (-s;-e) triplet
drin [drɪn] *adv* var of darin
dringen ['drɪŋən] §142 *intr* (auf *acc*) press (for), insist (on); (in *acc*) pressure, urge || *intr* (SEIN) (aus) break forth (from); (durch) penetrate, pierce; (durch) force one's way (through); (in *acc*) penetrate (into), get (into); **in die Öffentlichkeit d.** leak out; **in j-n d.** press the point with s.o.; **d. bis zu** get as far as
drin'gend *adj* urgent; (*Gefahr*) imminent; (*Verdacht*) strong
dring'lich *adj* urgent
Dring'lichkeit *f* (-;-en) urgency; priority
Drink [drɪŋk] *m* (-s;-s) alcoholic drink
drinnen ['drɪnən] *adv* inside
dritt [drɪt] *adv*—**zu d.** the three of
dritte ['drɪtə] §9 *adj* & *pron* third; **ein Dritter** a disinterested person; (com, jur) a third party
Drittel ['drɪtəl] *n* (-s;-) third (*part*)
drittens ['drɪtəns] *adv* thirdly
dritt'letzt *adj* third from last
droben ['droːbən] *adv* above; up there
Droge ['droːgə] *f* (-;-n) drug
Droge·rie [droːgə'riː] *f* (-;-rien ['riː·ən]) drugstore
Drogist -in [droː'gɪst(ɪn)] §7 *mf* druggist
Droh'brief *m* threatening letter
drohen ['droː·ən] *intr* (*dat*) threaten
dro'hend *adj* threatening; impending
Drohne ['droːnə] *f* (-;-n) drone
dröhnen ['drøːnən] *intr* boom, roar; (*Kopf, Motor*) throb
Dro'hung *f* (-;-en) threat
drollig ['drɔlɪç] *adj* amusing, funny
Dromedar [droːme'daːr] *n* (-s;-e) dromedary
drosch [drɔʃ] *pret* of dreschen
Droschke ['drɔʃkə] *f* (-;-n) cab, hackney; taxi
Drosch'kenkutscher *m* coachman
Drossel ['drɔsəl] *f* (-;-n) thrush; (aut) throttle
Dros'selhebel *m* (aut) throttle
drosseln ['drɔsəln] *tr* (coll) curb, cut; (aut) throttle; (elec) choke
drüben ['dryːbən] *adv* over there
Druck [drʊk] *m* (-s;-[e]s;ː‑e) (& fig) pressure; (*der Hand*) squeeze; (phys) compression, pressure || *m* (-[e]s;-e) printing; print, type; (tex) print
Druck'anzug *m* (aer) pressurized suit
Druck'bogen *m* (printed) sheet
druck'dicht *adj* pressurized
Drückeberger ['drʏkəbɛrgər] *m* (-s;-) shirker; absentee; (mil) goldbrick
drucken ['drʊkən] *tr* print
drücken ['drʏkən] *tr* press; squeeze; imprint; (*Preise*) lower; (cards) discard; **die Stimmung d.** be a kill-joy; **j-m die Hand d.** shake hands with s.o. || *intr* (*Schuh*) pinch
Druck'entlastung *f* decompression
Drucker ['drʊkər] *m* (-s;-) printer
Drücker ['drʏkər] *m* (-s;-) push button; (*e-s Schlosses*) latch, latch key; (*e-s Gewehrs*) trigger
Druckerei [drʊkə'raɪ] *f* (-;-en) print shop, press
Druckerschwärze (**Druk'kerschwärze**) *f* printer's ink
Druck'fehler *m* misprint
druck'fertig *adj* ready for the press
druck'fest *adj* pressurized
Druck'kabine *f* pressurized cabin
Druck'knopf *m* push button; (*am Kleid*) snap
Druck'knopfbetätigung *f* push-button control
Druck'luft *f* compressed air
Druckluft- *comb.fm.* pneumatic, air
Druck'luftbremse *f* air brake
Druck'lufthammer *m* jackhammer
Druck'messer *m* pressure gauge
Druck'sache *f* printed matter; **Druck-sachen** (com) literature
Druck'schrift *f* type; block letters; publication, printed work; leaflet
drucksen ['drʊksən] *intr* hem and haw
drum [drʊm] *adv* var of darum
Drüse ['dryːzə] *f* (-;-n) gland
Drüsen- *comb.fm.* glandular
Dschungel ['dʒʊŋəl] *m* (-s;-) jungle
du [duː] §11 *per pron* you, thou
Dübel ['dyːbəl] *m* (-s;-) dowel
Dublette [du'blɛtə] *f* (-;-n) duplicate; imitation stone
ducken ['dʊkən] *tr* (*den Kopf*) duck; (coll) take down a peg or two || *ref* duck
Duckmäuser ['dʊkmɔɪzər] *m* (-s;-) pussyfoot
dudeln ['duːdəln] *tr* hum || *intr* hum, drone; (mus) play the bagpipe
Dudelsack ['duːdəlzak] *m* bagpipe
Duell [du'ɛl] *n* (-s;-e) duel
duellieren [du·ə'liːrən] *recip* duel
Duett [du'ɛt] *n* (-[e]s;-e) duet
Duft [dʊft] *m* (-[e]s;ː‑e) fragrance
duften ['dʊftən] *intr* be fragrant
duf'tend *adj* fragrant
duftig ['dʊftɪç] *adj* flimsy, dainty
dulden ['dʊldən] *tr* (*ertragen*) bear; (*leiden*) suffer; (*zulassen*) tolerate || *intr* suffer
duldsam ['dʊldzam] *adj* tolerant
Duld'samkeit *f* (-;) tolerance
dumm [dʊm] *adj* stupid, dumb; foolish
Dumm'heit *f* (-;-en) stupidity; foolishness; (*Streich*) foolish prank
Dumm'kopf *m* dunderhead
dumpf [dʊmpf] *adj* dull, muffled;

(*schwül*) muggy; (*moderig*) musty, moldy; (*Ahnung*) vague

dumpfig ['dʊmpfɪç] *adj* musty, moldy; muggy

Düne ['dynə] *f* (-;-n) sand dune

Dung [dʊŋ] *m* (-[e]s;) dung; (*künstlicher*) fertilizer

düngen ['dyŋən] *tr* manure; fertilize

Dünger ['dyŋər] *m* (-s;) var of **Dung**

dunkel ['dʊŋkəl] *adj* dark; vague; obscure || **Dunkel** *n* (-s;) darkness

Dünkel ['dyŋkəl] *m* (-s;) conceit

dün'kelhaft *adj* conceited

Dun'kelheit *f* (-;) darkness; obscurity

Dun'kelkammer *f* (phot) darkroom

Dun'kelmann *m* (-[e]s;⁼er) shady character

dünn [dyn] *adj* thin

Dunst [dʊnst] *m* (-es;⁼e) vapor, mist, haze; (*Rauch*) smoke; (*Dampf*) steam; **in D. und Rauch aufgehen** (fig) go up in smoke; **sich in (blauen) D. auflösen** vanish in thin air

dünsten ['dynstən] *tr & intr* stew; steam

dunstig ['dʊnstɪç] *adj* steamy; (*Wetter*) misty, hazy

Duplikat [duplɪ'kat] *n* (-[e]s;-e) duplicate; copy

Dur [dur] *invar n* (mus) major

durch [dʊrç] *adv* throughout; **d. und d.** through and through || *prep* (*acc*) through, by, by means of

durch'arbeiten *tr* work through || *ref* (durch) work one's way (through); elbow one's way (through)

durchaus' *adv* throughout; entirely; quite, absolutely; **d. nicht** by no means

durch'backen §50 *tr* bake through and through

durch'blättern *tr* thumb through

durch'bleuen *tr* beat up

Durch'blick *m* vista

durch'blicken *intr* be apparent; (durch) look (through); **d. lassen** intimate

durchblutet [dʊrç'blutət] *adj* supplied with blood

durch'bohren *tr* bore through || **durchboh'ren** *tr* pierce

durch'braten §63 *tr* roast thoroughly

durchbre'chen §64 *tr* break through; (*Vorschriften*) violate; (mil) breach || **durch'brechen** *tr* cut (*a hole*); break in half || *intr* (SEIN) break through

durch'brennen §97 *tr* burn through; (*e-e Sicherung*) blow || *intr* (SEIN) run away; (*Sicherung*) blow

durch'bringen §65 *tr* get through; (*Gesetz*) pass; (*Geld*) spend; (med) pull (*a patient*) through || *ref* support oneself; **sich ehrlich d.** make an honest living

Durch'bruch *m* breakthrough; (*Öffnung*) breach, gap; (*der Zähne*) cutting

durch'denken §66 *tr* think through || **durchden'ken** *tr* think out, think over

durch'drängen *ref* push one's way through

durch'drehen *tr* grind; (*Wäsche*) put

through the wringer || *intr* (SEIN) (coll) go mad

durchdrin'gen §142 *tr* penetrate; pervade, imbue || **durch'dringen** *intr* (SEIN) get through; penetrate

durch'drucken (parl) push through

durchdrungen [dʊrç'drʊŋən] *adj* imbued

durchei'len *tr* rush through || **durch'eilen** *intr* (SEIN) (durch) rush through

durcheinan'der *adj & adv* in confusion || **Durcheinander** *n* (-s;-) mess, muddle

durcheinan'derbringen §65 *tr* muddle

durcheinan'dergeraten §63 *intr* (SEIN) get mixed up

durcheinan'derlaufen §105 *intr* (SEIN) mill about

durcheinan'derreden *intr* speak all at once

durcheinan'derwerfen §160 *tr* throw into confusion, turn upside down

durchfah'ren §71 *tr* travel through; (*Gedanke, Schreck*) strike || **durch'fahren** §71 *intr* (SEIN) go through without stopping

Durch'fahrt *f* passage; **keine D.!** no thoroughfare

Durch'fahrtshöhe *f* clearance

Durch'fall *m* diarrhea; (coll) flop; (educ) flunk, failure

durch'fallen §72 *intr* (SEIN) fall through; (educ) flunk; (theat) flop

durch'fechten §74 *tr* fight through

durch'finden §59 *ref* find one's way

durchflech'ten *tr* interweave

durchfor'schen *tr* examine, make an exhaustive study of

Durchfor'schung *f* exploration; search; thorough research

durch'fressen §70 *tr* eat through; corrode || *ref* (bei) sponge (on); (durch) work one's way (through)

Durchfuhr ['dʊrçfur] *f* (-;-en) transit

durchführbar ['dʊrçfyrbar] *adj* feasible

durch'führen *tr* lead through or across; (*Auftrag*) carry out; (*Gesetz*) enforce

Durch'gang *m* passage; aisle; (fig) transition; (astr, com) transit; **D. verboten!** no thoroughfare, no trespassing

Durch'gänger *m* (-s;-) runaway

Durch'gangslager *n* transit camp

Durch'gangsverkehr *m* through traffic

Durch'gangszug *m* through train

durch'geben §80 *tr* pass on

durch'gebraten *adj* (culin) well done

durch'gehen §82 *tr* (SEIN) go through; (*durchlesen*) go over || *intr* (SEIN) go through; (*Pferd*) bolt; (*heimlich davonlaufen*) run away; abscond; (*Vorschlag*) pass

durch'gehend(s) *adv* generally; (*durchaus*) throughout

durchgeistigt [dʊrç'gaɪstɪçt] *adj* highly intellectual

durch'greifen §88 *intr* reach through; (fig) take drastic measures

durch'greifend *adj* vigorous; drastic

durch'halten §90 *tr* keep up || *intr* hold out, stick it out

durch'hauen §93 *tr* chop through;

knock a hole through; (coll) thrash, beat

durch'hecheln tr (coll) run down

durch'helfen §96 intr (dat) (durch) help (through) ‖ ref get by, manage

durch'kämmen tr (& fig) comb through

durch'kochen tr boil thoroughly

durch'kommen §99 intr (SEIN) come through; (durch Krankheit) pull through; (sich durchhelfen) get by; (educ) pass

durchkreu'zen tr cross; (durchstreichen) cross out; (fig) frustrate

Durch'laß ['dʊrçlas] m (–lasses;–lässe) passage; outlet; culvert

durch'lassen §104 tr let through, let pass; (Licht) transmit; (educ) pass

durchlässig ['dʊrçlɛsɪç] adj permeable

Durch'laßschein m pass

durchlau'fen §105 tr run through; look through; (Schule) go through; seine Bahn d. run its course ‖ **durch'laufen** §105 ref—sich [dat] die Schuhe d. wear out one's shoes ‖ §105 intr (SEIN) run through

durchle'ben tr live through

durch'lesen §107 tr read over, peruse

durchleuch'ten tr illuminate; (Gesicht) light up; (Ei) test; X-ray

durch'liegen §108 ref develop bedsores ‖ **Durchliegen** n (–s;) bedsores

durchlo'chen tr punch

durch'löchern tr perforate; pierce; (mit Kugeln) riddle

durch'machen tr go through, undergo

Durch'marsch m marching through; (coll) diarrhea, runs

Durch'messer m diameter

durchnäs'sen tr soak, drench

durch'nehmen §116 tr (in der Klasse) do, have

durch'pausen tr trace

durch'peitschen tr whip soundly; (Gesetzentwurf) rush through

durchque'ren tr cross, traverse

durch'rechnen tr check, go over

Durch'reise f passage; auf seiner D. on his way through

durch'reisen intr (SEIN) travel through

Durch'reisende §5 mf transient, transit passenger

durch'reißen §53 tr tear in half ‖ intr (SEIN) tear, break, snap

Durch'sage f special announcement

durch'sagen tr announce

durchschau'en tr (fig) see through ‖ **durch'schauen** intr look through

durch'scheinen §128 intr shine through; show through; be seen

durch'scheuern tr rub through

durchschie'ßen §76 tr shoot through, riddle; (typ) lead ‖ **durch'schießen** §76 intr (durch) shoot (through) ‖ intr (SEIN) dash through

Durch'schlag m carbon copy; (Sieb) (large) strainer, separator; (elec) breakdown; (tech) punch

durchschla'gen §132 tr penetrate ‖ **durch'schlagen** §132 tr knock a hole through; (Holz) split; (Fensterscheibe) smash; (Nagel) drive through; (Kartoffeln, Früchte) strain; (mit Kohlepapier) make a carbon copy of

‖ ref fight one's way through; (sich durchhelfen) manage ‖ intr come through; penetrate; take effect; show up ‖ intr (SEIN) (Sicherung) blow

durch'schlagend adj effective; striking

Durch'schlagpapier n carbon paper

durch'schleichen §85 ref & intr (SEIN) creep through

durchschleu'sen tr pass (a ship) through a lock; (Passagiere, Rekruten, usw.) process; (fig) sneak (s.o.) through

durch'schneiden §106 tr cut through; cut in half ‖ **durchschnei'den** §106 tr cut through, cut across ‖ ref cross, intersect

Durch'schnitt m cutting through; average; cross section; der große D. der Menschen the majority of people; im D. on an average

durch'schnittlich adj average ‖ adv on the average

Durchschnitts— comb.fm. average; mean

Durch'schnittsmensch m average person

durch'schreiben §62 tr make a carbon copy of

durch'sehen §138 tr look over, examine; (flüchtig anschauen) scan; (Papiere, Post) check ‖ intr see through

durch'seihen tr filter; percolate

durchset'zen tr intersperse; penetrate ‖ **durch'setzen** tr carry through; d., daß bring it about that, succeed in (ger) ‖ ref get one's way

Durch'sicht f examination, inspection; (auf acc) view (of)

durch'sichtig adj transparent; clear

durch'sickern intr (SEIN) seep out; (Wahrheit, Gerücht) leak out

durch'sieben tr sift

durch'sprechen §64 tr talk over

durchste'chen §64 tr pierce ‖ **durch'stechen** §64 tr (Nadel) stick through

durch'stehen §146 tr go through

durchstö'bern tr rummage through

durch'stoßen §150 tr push (s.th.) through; (Tür) knock down; (Scheibe) smash in; (Ellbogen) wear through; (mil) penetrate ‖ **durchsto'ßen** §150 tr break through ‖ **durch'stoßen** §150 intr (SEIN), break through

durchstrei'chen §85 tr roam through ‖ **durch'streichen** §85 tr cross out

durchstrei'fen tr wander through

durchsu'chen tr go through, search

durch'treten §152 tr (Sohle) wear a hole in; (Gashebel) floor ‖ intr (SEIN) go through, pass through

durchtrieben [dʊrç'tribən] adj sly

durchwa'chen tr remain awake through

durchwach'sen adj gristly

durch'wählen tr & intr dial direct

durchwan'dern tr travel or walk through ‖ **durch'wandern** intr (SEIN) (durch) walk (through), hike (through)

durchwe'ben tr interweave

durch'weg adv throughout

durchwei'chen, **durch'weichen** tr soak

durchwüh'len tr burrow through; (Ge-

päck, Schränke) rummage through ‖
durch′wühlen *ref* burrow through;
(fig) work one's way through
durch′wursteln *ref* muddle through
durchzie′hen §163 *tr* pass through,
cross; *(Zimmer)* permeate, fill;
streak; (sew) interweave ‖ **durch′-**
ziehen §163 *tr* pull through ‖ *intr*
(SEIN) pass through; flow through
durchzucken (durchzuk′ken) *tr* flash
through the mind of
Durch′zug *m* passage; *(Luftzug)* draft
durch′zwängen *tr* force through ‖ *ref*
squeeze through
dürfen [′dʏrfən] §69 *aux* be allowed;
be likely; **darf ich?** may I?; **ich darf**
nicht I must not; **man darf wohl er-**
warten it is to be expected
durfte [′dʊrftə] *pret* of **dürfen**
dürftig [′dʏrftɪç] *adj* needy; poor,
wretched, miserable, scanty
dürr [dʏr] *adj* dry; *(Boden)* arid, barren; *(Holz)* dead, dry; *(Mensch)*
skinny ‖ **Dürre** [′dʏrə] *f* (-;) dryness; barrenness; leanness; drought
Durst [dʊrst] *m* (-[e]s;) **(nach)** thirst
(for); **D. haben** be thirsty

dursten [′dʊrstən], **dürsten** [′dʏr-
stən] *intr* be thirsty; **(nach)** thirst
(for)
durstig [′dʊrstɪç] *adj* thirsty
Dusche [′duʃə] *f* (-;-n) shower
duschen [′duʃən] *intr* take a shower
Düse [′dyzə] *f* (-;-n) nozzle, jet
Dusel [′duzəl] *m* (-s;-) (coll) fluke
Düsen- *comb.fm.* jet
Dü′senantrieb *m* jet propulsion
Dü′senjäger *m* jet fighter
düster [′dystər] *adj* gloomy; sad; dark
‖ **Düster** *n* (-s;) gloom; darkness
Dutzend [′dʊtsənt] *n* (-s;- & -e) dozen
dut′zendmal *adv* a dozen times
dut′zendweise *adv* by the dozen
Duzbruder [′dutsbrudər] *m* buddy
duzen [′dutsən] *tr* say **du** to, be on in-
timate terms with
Dynamik [dy′namɪk] *f* (-s;) dynamics
dynamisch [dy′namɪʃ] *adj* dynamic
Dynamit [dyna′mit] *n* (-s;-e) dyna-
mite
Dynamo [′dynamo] *m* (-s;-s) dynamo
Dyna·stie [dynas′ti] *f* (-;-stien
[′sti·ən] dynasty
D′-Zug *m* through train, express

E

E, e [e] *invar n* E, e; (mus) E
Ebbe [′ɛbə] *f* (-;-n) ebb tide
eben [′ebən] *adj* even, level, flat; **zu**
ebener Erde on the ground floor ‖
adv just; a moment ago; exactly
‖ *interj* exactly!; that's right!
E′benbild *n* image, exact likeness
ebenbürtig [′ebənbʏrtɪç] *adj* of equal
rank, equal
ebenda [eben′da] *adv* right there;
(beim Zitieren) ibidem
ebendersel′be §4,3 *adj* self-same
ebendes′wegen *adv* for that very reason
Ebene [′ebənə] *f* (-;-n) plain; (fig)
level; (geom) plane
e′benerdig *adj* ground-floor
e′benfalls *adv* likewise, too
E′benholz *n* ebony
E′benmaß *n* right proportions
e′benmäßig *adj* well-proportioned
e′benso *adv* just as; likewise
e′bensogut *adv* just as well
e′bensoviel *adv* just as much
e′bensowenig *adv* just as little
Eber [′ebər] *m* (-s;-) boar
E′beresche *f* mountain ash
ebnen [′ebnən] *tr* level, even; smooth
Echo [′ɛço] *n* (-s;-s) echo
echoen [′ɛçoən] *intr* echo
echt [ɛçt] *adj* genuine, real, true
Eck [ɛk] *n* (-[e]s;-e) corner; end
Eck- *comb.fm.* corner; end
Ecke [′ɛkə] *f* (-;-n) corner; edge
Ecker [′ɛkər] *f* (-;-n) beechnut
eckig [′ɛkɪç] *adj* angular; (fig) awkward; **eckige Klammer** bracket
Eck′stein *m* cornerstone; (cards) dia-
monds

Eck′stoß *m* (fb) corner kick
Eck′zahn *m* canine tooth
Eclair [e′klɛr] *n* (-s;-s) éclair
edel [′edəl] *adj* noble; *(Metall)* pre-
cious; *(Pferd)* thoroughbred; **edle**
Teile vital organs
e′deldenkend *adj* noble-minded
e′delgesinnt *adj* noble-minded
E′del-mann *m* (-[e]s;-leute) noble
e′delmütig *adj* noble-minded
E′delstahl *m* high-grade steel
E′delstein *m* precious stone, gem
E′delweiß *n* (-[e]s;-e) edelweiss
Edikt [ɛ′dɪkt] *n* (-[e]s;-e) edict
Edle [′edlə] §5 *mf* noble
Efeu [′efɔr] *m* (-s;-e) ivy
Effekt [ɛ′fɛkt] *m* (-[e]s;-e) effect
Effekten [ɛ′fɛktən] *pl* property; ef-
fects; (fin) securities, stocks
Effek′tenmakler -in §6 *mf* stock broker
Effekthascherei [ɛfɛktha/ə′raɪ] *f* (-;)
showiness
effektiv [ɛfɛk′tif] *adj* effective; *(wirk-*
lich) actual
Effektiv′lohn *m* take-home pay
Effet [ɛ′fe] *n* (-s;) spin, English
egal [ɛ′gal] *adj* equal; all the same
Egge [′ɛgə] *f* (-;-n) harrow
eggen [′ɛgən] *tr* harrow
Ego [′ego] *n* (-s;) ego
Egoismus [ego′ɪsmus] *m* (-;) egoism
Egoist -in [ego′ɪst(ɪn)] §7 *mf* egoist
egoistisch [ego′ɪstɪʃ] *adj* egoistic
Egotist -in [ego′tɪst(ɪn)] §7 *mf* egotist
eh [e] *adv* (Aust) anyhow, anyway
ehe [′e·ə] *conj* before ‖ **Ehe** *f* (-;-n)
marriage; matrimony
E′hebrecher *m* (-s;-) adulterer

E'hebrecherin f (-;-nen) adulteress
e'hebrecherisch adj adulterous
E'hebruch m adultery, infidelity
ehedem ['e·ə'dem] adv formerly
E'hefrau f wife
E'hegatte m spouse
E'hegattin f spouse
E'hegelöbnis n marriage vow
E'hehälfte f (coll) better half
E'heleute pl married couple
e'helich adj marital; (Kind) legitimate
e'helos adj unmarried, single
E'helosigkeit f (-;) celibacy
ehemalig ['e·əmalıç] adj former; ex-; (verstorben) late
ehemals ['e·əmals] adv formerly
E'hemann m husband
E'hepaar n married couple
eher ['e·ər] adv sooner; rather
E'hering m wedding band
ehern ['e·ərn] adj brass; (fig) unshakable
E'hescheidung f divorce
E'hescheidungsklage f divorce suit
E'heschließung f marriage
E'hestand m married state, wedlock
ehestens ['e·əstəns] adv at the earliest; as soon as possible
E'hestifter m §6 mf matchmaker
E'heversprechen n promise of marriage
Ehrabschneider –in ['erap/naɪdər(ın)] §6 mf slanderer
ehrbar ['erbar] adj honorable, respectable
Ehr'barkeit f (-;) respectability
Ehre ['erə] f (-;-n) honor; glory
ehren ['erən] tr honor; **Sehr geehrter Herr** Dear Sir
eh'renamtlich adj honorary
Eh'rendoktor m honorary doctor
Eh'renerklärung f apology
eh'renhaft adj honorable
ehrenhalber ['erənhalbar] invar adj— **Doktor e.** Doctor honoris causa
Eh'renmitglied n honorary member
Eh'renrechte pl—bürgerliche E. civil rights
Eh'rensache f point of honor
eh'renvoll adj honorable, respectable
eh'renwert adj honorable
Eh'renwort n word of honor; **auf E. entlassen** put on parole
ehrerbietig ['ererbitıç] adj respectful, reverent, deferential
Ehrerbietung ['ererbituŋ] f (-;), **Ehrfurcht** ['erfurçt] f (-;) respect, reverence; (vor dat) awe (of)
ehrfürchtig ['erfyrçtıç], **ehrfurchtsvoll** ['erfurçtsfol] adj respectful
Ehr'gefühl n sense of honor
Ehr'geiz m ambition
ehr'geizig adj ambitious
ehrlich ['erlıç] adj honest; sincere; fair; **j-n e. machen** restore s.o.'s good name
Ehr'lichkeit f (-;) honesty; candor
ehr'los adj dishonorable; (Frau) of easy virtue; infamous
Ehr'losigkeit f (-;) dishonesty; infamy
ehrsam ['erzam] adj respectable
Ehr'sucht f (-;) ambition
ehr'süchtig adj ambitious

Ehr'verlust m loss of civil rights
ehr'würdig adj venerable; (eccl) reverend
ei [aɪ] interj oh!; ah!; **ei,ei!** oh!; **ei je!** oh dear!; **ei was!** nonsense! ‖ **Ei** n (-[e]s;-er) egg
Eiche ['aɪçə] f (-;-n) oak
Eichel ['aɪçəl] f (-;-n) acorn; (cards) club
eichen ['aɪçən] adj oak ‖ tr gauge
Ei'chenlaub n oak leaf cluster
Eichhörnchen ['aɪçhœrnçən] n (-s;-), **Eichkätzchen** ['aɪçketsçən] n (-s;-) squirrel
Eichmaß ['aɪçmas] n gauge; standard
Eid [aɪt] m (-[e]s;-e) oath
Eid'bruch m perjury
eid'brüchig adj perjured
Eidechse ['aɪdeksə] f (-;-n) lizard
Eiderdaunen ['aɪdərdaʊnən] pl eider down
eidesstattlich ['aɪdəs/tatlıç] adj in lieu of an oath, solemn
eid'lich adj sworn ‖ adv under oath
Ei'dotter m egg yolk
Ei'erkrem f custard
Ei'erkuchen m omelet; pancake
Ei'erlandung f three-point landing
Ei'erlikör m eggnog
Ei'erschale f eggshell
Ei'erstock m ovary
Eifer ['aɪfər] m (-;) zeal, eagerness
Eiferer –in ['aɪfərər(ın)] §6 mf zealot
Ei'fersucht f jealousy
ei'fersüchtig adj (auf acc) jealous (of)
eifrig ['aɪfrıç] adj zealous; ardent
Ei'gelb n (-[e]s;-e) egg yolk
eigen ['aɪgən] adj own; of (my, your, etc.) own; (dat) peculiar (to), characteristic (of) ‖ invar pron—**etw mein e. nennen** call s.th. my own
ei'genartig adj peculiar; odd, queer
Eigenbrötler ['aɪgənbrøtlər] m (-s;-) (coll) lone wolf, loner; crank
Ei'gengewicht n dead weight
eigenhändig ['aɪgənhendıç] adj & adv with or in one's own hand
Ei'genheit f (-;-en) peculiarity
Ei'genliebe f self-love, egotism
Ei'genlob n self-praise
ei'genmächtig adj arbitrary, high-handed
Ei'genname m proper name
Ei'gennutz m self-interest
ei'gennützig adj selfish
eigens ['aɪgəns] adv expressly
Ei'genschaft f (-;-en) quality, property; **in seiner E. als** in his capacity as
Ei'genschaftswort n (-[e]s;⸚er) adjective
Ei'gensinn m stubbornness
ei'gensinnig adj stubborn
eigentlich ['aɪgəntlıç] adj actual ‖ adv actually, really
Eigentum ['aɪgəntum] n (-[e]s;⸚er) property, possession; ownership
Eigentümer –in ['aɪgəntymər(ın)] §6 mf (legal) owner ‖ m proprietor ‖ f proprietress
eigentümlich ['aɪgəntymlıç] adj odd; (dat) peculiar (to)
Ei'gentümlichkeit f (-;-en) peculiarity

Ei'gentumsrecht n ownership, title

Ei'genwechsel m promissory note

ei'genwillig adj independent; (Stil) original

eignen ['aɪgnən] ref (für) be suited (to); (als) be suitable (as); (zu) be cut out (for)

Eig'nung f (-ʒ;-en) qualification, aptitude

Ei'gnungsprüfung f aptitude test

Eilbrief ['aɪlbrif] m special delivery

Eile ['aɪlə] f (-ʒ) hurry; E. haben or in E. sein be in a hurry

eilen ['aɪlən] ref hurry (up) || intr be urgent || intr (SEIN) hurry; eilt! (Briefaufschrift) urgent! || impers—es eilt mir nicht damit I'm in no hurry about it

eilends ['aɪlənts] adv hurriedly

Eilgut ['aɪlgut] n express freight

eilig ['aɪlɪç] adj quick, hurried; urgent || adv hurriedly; es e. haben be in a hurry

Eilpost ['aɪlpɔst] f special delivery

Eilzug ['aɪltsuk] m (rr) limited

Eimer ['aɪmər] m (-sʒ-) bucket, pail

ein [aɪn] §2,1 indef art a, an || §2,1 num adj one || adv in; ein und aus in and out; nicht ein und aus wissen not know which way to turn || einer indef pron & num pron see einer

ein-, Ein- comb.fm. one-, single

einan'der invar recip pron each other; (unter mehreren) one another

ein'arbeiten tr train (for a job); (in acc) work (into) || ref in (acc) become familiar (with), get the hang (of)

einarmig ['aɪnarmɪç] adj one-armed

einäschern ['aɪneʃərn] tr reduce to ashes, incinerate; (Leiche) cremate

ein'atmen tr & intr inhale

ein'äugig adj one-eyed

einbahnig ['aɪnbanɪç] adj single-lane; single-line; one-way

Ein'bahnstraße f one-way street

ein'balsamieren tr embalm

Ein'band m (-[e]sʒ⸚e) binding; cover

ein'bauen tr build in, install

einbegriffen ['aɪnbəgrɪfən] adj included, inclusive

ein'behalten §90 tr retain; (Lohn) withhold

ein'berufen §122 tr call, convene; (mil) call up, draft || Einberufene §5 mf draftee

Ein'berufung f (-ʒ;-en) (mil) induction

ein'betten tr embed

ein'beziehen §163 tr include

ein'bilden ref—sich [dat] etw e. imagine s.th.

ein'binden §59 tr (bb) bind

ein'blenden tr (cin) fade in

Ein'blick m view; (fig) insight

ein'brechen §64 tr break in || intr (SEIN) collapse; (Nacht) fall; (Kälte) set in; (Dieb) break in

Ein'brecher -in §6 mf burglar

ein'bringen §65 tr bring in; earn; yield

Ein'bruch m break-in, burglary; invasion; E. der Nacht nightfall

Ein'bruchsdiebstahl m burglary

ein'bruchssicher adj burglarproof

einbürgern ['aɪnbyrgərn] tr naturalize || ref (fig) take root, become accepted

Ein'bürgerung f (-ʒ) naturalization

Ein'buße f loss, forfeiture

ein'büßen tr lose, forfeit

ein'dämmen tr check, contain

ein'decken tr cover || ref (mit) stock up (on)

Eindecker ['aɪndekər] m (-sʒ-) monoplane

ein'deutig adj unequivocal, clear

eindeutschen ['aɪndɔɪtʃən] tr Germanize

ein'drängen ref squeeze in; interfere

ein'dringen §142 intr (SEIN) penetrate, come in; e. auf (acc) crowd in on; e. in (acc) rush into; penetrate; infiltrate; (mil) invade

ein'dringlich adj urgent

Eindringling ['aɪndrɪŋlɪŋ] m (-sʒ-e) intruder, interloper; gate-crasher

Ein'druck m imprint; impression

ein'drücken tr press in; crash, flatten; imprint; (Fenster) smash in

Ein'druckskunst f impressionism

ein'drucksvoll adj impressive

ein'engen tr narrow; (fig) limit

einer ['aɪnər] §2,4 indef pron & num pron one || Einer m (-sʒ-) (math) unit

einerlei ['aɪnərlaɪ] invar adj (nur attributiv) one kind of; (nur prädikativ) all the same || Einerlei n (-ʒ) monotony

einerseits ['aɪnərzaɪts], einesteils ['aɪnəstaɪls] adv on the one hand

ein'fach adj single; simple || adv simply

einfädeln ['aɪnfedəln] tr thread; (fig) engineer

ein'fahren §71 tr (Auto) break in; (Ernte) bring in; (aer) retract || ref get driving experience; die Sache hat sich gut eingefahren it's off to a good start || intr (SEIN) drive in; (rr) arrive

Ein'fahrt f entrance; gateway

Ein'fall m inroad; (fig) idea; (mil) invasion

ein'fallen §72 intr (SEIN) fall in; cave in, collapse; (in die Rede) butt in; join in; e. in (acc) invade; j—m e. occur to s.o.; sich [dat] etw e. lassen take s.th. into one's head; think up s.th.; sich [dat] nicht e. lassen not dream of; was fällt dir ein? what's the idea?

ein'fallslos adj unimaginative

ein'fallsreich adj imaginative

Ein'falt f simplicity; simple-mindedness

einfältig ['aɪnfeltɪç] adj (pej) simple

Ein'faltspinsel m sucker, simpleton

ein'farbig adj one-colored; plain

ein'fassen tr edge, trim; (einschließen) enclose; (Edelstein) set

Ein'fassung f (-ʒ;-en) border; mounting

ein'fetten tr grease

ein'finden §59 ref show up

ein'flechten tr plait; (Haar) braid; (fig) insert

ein'fliegen §57 tr (Truppen) fly in;

(*Flugzeug*) flight-test || *intr* (SEIN) fly in

ein'fließen §76 *intr* (SEIN) flow in; **e. in** (*acc*) flow into; **einige Bemerkungen e. lassen** slip in a few remarks

ein'flößen *tr* infuse, instill

Ein'fluß *m* influx; (fig) influence

ein'flußreich *adj* influential

ein'förmig *adj* monotonous

einfried(ig)en ['aɪnfriːd(ɪg)ən] *tr* enclose, fence in

ein'frieren §77 *tr* (& fin) freeze || *intr* (SEIN) freeze (up) || **Einfrieren** *n* (-s;) (fin) freeze

ein'fügen *tr* insert, fit || *ref* fit in; (in *acc*) adapt oneself (to)

ein'fühlen *ref* (in *acc*) relate (to)

Einfuhr ['aɪnfuːr] *f* (-;-en) importation; **Einfuhren** imports

ein'führen *tr* import; introduce; (in *ein Amt*) install

Ein'führung *f* (-;-en) introduction

Ein'fuhrwaren *pl* imports

Ein'fuhrzoll *m* import duty

ein'füllen *tr*—**e. in** (*acc*) pour into

Ein'gabe *f* petition; application

Ein'gang *m* entrance; entry; beginning; introduction; (*von Waren*) arrival; **Eingänge** (com) incoming goods; incoming mail; (fin) receipts

ein'geben §80 *tr* suggest, prompt; (med) administer, give

eingebildet ['aɪngəbɪldət] *adj* imaginary; self-conceited

eingeboren ['aɪngəboːrən] *adj* native; only-begotten; (*Eigenschaft*) innate || **Eingeborene** §5 *mf* native

Ein'gebung *f* (-;-en) suggestion; (*höhere*) inspiration

eingedenk ['aɪngədɛŋk] *adj* (genit) mindful (of)

ein'gefallen *adj* (*Backen, Augen*) sunken

eingefleischt ['aɪngəflaɪʃt] *adj* inveterate

ein'gefroren *adj* icebound

ein'gehen §82 *tr* (HABEN & SEIN) enter into; (*Verpflichtungen*) incur; (*Wette, Geschäft*) make; (*Chance*) take; (*Versicherung*) take out; **e-n Vergleich e.** come to an agreement || *intr* (SEIN) come in; arrive; (*aufhören*) come to an end; fizzle out; (*Stoff*) shrink; (bot, zool) die off; (com) close down; **e. auf** (*acc*) go into, consider; consent to; **e. lassen** drop, discontinue; **es geht mir nicht ein, daß I** can't accept the fact that

ein'gehend *adj* thorough

eingelegt ['aɪngəleːkt] *adj* inlaid

Eingemachte ['aɪngəmaxtə] §5 *n* (-n;) preserves

eingemeinden ['aɪngəmaɪndən] *tr* (*Vorort*) incorporate

eingenommen ['aɪngənɔmən] *adj* prejudiced; **von sich e.** self-conceited

eingeschnappt ['aɪngəʃnapt] *adj* (coll) peeved

eingeschneit ['aɪngəʃnaɪt] *adj* snowed in

Eingesessene ['aɪngəzɛsənə] §5 *mf* resident

Ein'geständis *n* (-ses;-se) confession

ein'gestehen §146 *tr* confess, admit

Eingeweide ['aɪngəvaɪdə] *pl* viscera; intestines; (*von Vieh*) entrails

Eingeweihte ['aɪngəvaɪtə] §5 *mf* insider

ein'gewöhnen *tr* (in *acc*) accustom (to) || *ref* (in *acc*) become accustomed (to)

eingewurzelt ['aɪngəvurtsəlt] *adj* deep-rooted

ein'gießen §76 *tr* pour in, pour out

eingleisig ['aɪnglaɪzɪç] *adj* single-track

ein'gliedern *tr* integrate; annex

ein'graben §87 *tr* bury; engrave || *ref* burrow; (mil) dig in

ein'greifen §88 *intr* take action; interfere; (in *j-s Rechte*) encroach; (mach) mesh, be in gear || **Eingreifen** *n* (-s;) interference; (mach) meshing

Ein'griff *m* interference; encroachment; (mach) meshing; (surg) operation

ein'hacken *tr*—**e. auf** (*acc*) peck at; (fig) pick at

ein'haken *tr* (in *acc*) hook (into) || *ref* —**sich bei j-m e.** link arms with s.o. || *intr* (fig) cut in

Ein'halt *m* (-[e]s;) stop, halt; **E. gebieten** (*dat*) put a stop to

ein'halten §90 *tr* stick to; (*Verabredung*) keep; (*Zahlungen*) keep up; **die Zeit e.** be punctual || *intr* stop

ein'händigen *tr* hand over

ein'hängen §92 *tr* (*Türe*) hang; (in *acc*) hook (into); (telp) hang up || *ref*—**sich bei j-m e.** link arms with s.o. || *intr* (telp) hang up

ein'heften *tr* sew in; baste on

ein'heimisch *adj* domestic; local; homegrown; **e. in** (*dat*) native to

einheimsen ['aɪnhaɪmzən] *tr* reap

Einheit ['aɪnhaɪt] *f* (-;-en) oneness, unity; (math, mil) unit

Einheits- *comb.fm.* standard, uniform; unit; united

ein'heizen *intr* start a fire; **j-m tüchtig e.** (fig) burn s.o. up

einhellig ['aɪnhɛlɪç] *adj* unanimous

ein'holen *tr* bring in; (*Flagge*) hawl down; (*Segel*) hawl down; (*im Wettlauf*) catch up with; (*Erkundigungen*) lauf catch up with; (*Erkundigungen*) make; (*Rat, Nachricht, Erlaubnis*) get; (*Verlust*) make good; (*abholen und geleiten*) escort; (*Schiff, Tau*) tow in || *intr* shop

Ein'horn *n* (myth) unicorn

ein'hüllen *tr* wrap up; enclose

einig ['aɪnɪç] *adj* united; of one mind; **sich** [*dat*] **e. sein be in** agreement

einige ['aɪnɪgə] §9 *indef adj & indef pron* some

einigen ['aɪnɪgən] *tr* unite || *ref* come to terms, agree

einigermaßen ['aɪnɪgərmaːsən] *adv* to some extent; (*ziemlich*) somewhat

ein'niggehen §82 *intr* (SEIN) concur

Ei'nigkeit *f* (-;) unity; harmony; agreement

Ei'nigung f (-;-en) unification; agreement, understanding

ein'impfen tr—j-m Impfstoff e. inoculate s.o. with vaccine; j-m e., daß (fig) drive it into s.o. that

ein'jagen tr (dat) put (e.g., a scare) into

ein'jährig adj one-year-old; (bot) annual

ein'kassieren tr collect

Ein'kauf m purchase; **Einkäufe machen** go shopping

ein'kaufen tr purchase; **e. gehen** go shopping

Ein'käufer –in §6 mf shopper

Ein'kaufspreis m purchase price

Ein'kehr f—E. bei sich halten search one's conscience; E. halten stop off

ein'kehren intr (SEIN) stay overnight; (im Gasthaus) stop off, stay

ein'keilen tr wedge in

ein'kerben tr notch, cut a notch in

einkerkern ['aınkɛrkərn] tr imprison

einkesseln ['aınkɛsəln] tr encircle

ein'klagen tr sue for (a bad debt)

ein'klammern tr bracket, put in parentheses

Ein'klang m unison; accord

Ein'klebebuch n scrap book

ein'kleben tr (in acc) paste (into)

ein'kleiden tr clothe; vest; (mil) issue uniforms to

ein'klemmen tr jam in, squeeze in

ein'klinken tr & intr engage, catch

ein'knicken tr fold

ein'kochen tr thicken (by boiling); can || intr thicken

ein'kommen §99 intr (SEIN)—bei j-m um etw e. apply to s.o. for s.th. || Einkommen n (-s;) income, revenue

Ein'kommensteuer f income tax

Ein'kommensteuererklärung f income-tax return

Ein'kommensstufe f income bracket

ein'kreisen tr encircle

Einkünfte ['aınkynftə] pl revenue

ein'kuppeln tr let out the clutch

ein'laden §103 tr load; invite

Ein'ladung f (-;-en) invitation

Ein'lage f (-;-n) (im Brief) enclosure; (im Schuh) insole; arch support; (Zwischenfutter) padding; (Kapital–) investment; (Sparkassen–) deposit; (beim Spiel) bet; (culin) solids (in soup); (dent) temporary filling; (mus) musical extra

ein'lagern tr store, store up

Ein-laß ['aınlas] m (-lasses;) admission; admittance; (tech) intake

ein'lassen §104 tr let, admit; (tech) (in acc) sink (into) || ref (auf acc, in acc) let oneself get involved (in)

Ein'laßkarte f admission ticket

Ein'lauf m incoming mail; (e–s Schiffes) arrival; j–m e–n E. machen give s.o. an enema

ein'laufen §105 intr (SEIN) come in, arrive; (Stoff) shrink; das Badewasser e. lassen run the bath; j–m das Haus e. keep running to s.o.'s house || ref warm up (by running)

ein'leben ref (in acc) accustom oneself (to)

Ein'legearbeit f inlaid work

Ein'legebrett n (e–s Tisches) leaf

ein'legen tr put in; (Fleisch, Gurken) pickle; (Geld) deposit; (in e–n Brief) enclose; (Film, Kassette) insert; (Veto) interpose; (Beschwerde) lodge; (Protest) enter; (Berufung) (jur) file; Busse e. put on extra buses

ein'leiten tr introduce; (Buch) write a preface to; (beginnen, eröffnen) start, open; ein Verfahren e. gegen institute proceedings against s.o.

Ein'leitung f (-;-en) introduction; initiation

ein'lenken intr (fig) give in

ein'leuchten intr be evident; (coll) sink in

ein'liefern tr deliver; (ins Gefängnis) put, commit; ins Krankenhaus e. take to the hospital

ein'lösen tr ransom; redeem; (Scheck) cash

ein'machen tr can, preserve

ein'mal adv once; (künftig) one day; auf e. suddenly; all at the same time; einmal...einmal now...now; nicht e. (unstressed) not even; (stressed) not even once

Ein'maleins' n multiplication table

ein'malig adj unique

Einmann– comb.fm. one-man

Ein'marsch m entry

ein'marschieren intr (SEIN) march in

ein'mauern tr wall in

ein'mengen ref, **ein'mischen** ref (in acc) meddle (with), interfere (with)

Ein'mischung f (-;-en) interference

einmotorig ['aınmoˑtoriç] adj single-engine

einmummen ['aınmumən] ref bundle up

ein'münden intr (in acc) empty (into); (Straßen) run (into)

Ein'mündung f (-;-en) (e–s Flusses) mouth; (e–r Straße) junction

ein'mütig adj unanimous

ein'nähen tr sew in; (Kleid) take in

Ein'nahme f (-;-n) taking; capture; (fin) receipts; **Einnahmen** income

ein'nehmen §116 tr take; capture; (Essen) eat; (Geld) earn; (Steuern) collect; (Stellung) fill; (sew) take in; e–e Haltung e. assume an attitude; e–e hervorragende Stelle e. rank high; j–n für sich e. captivate s.o.; j–n gegen sich e. prejudice s.o. against oneself; seinen Platz e. take one's seat

ein'nicken intr (SEIN) doze off

ein'nisten ref (in dat) settle (in); (fig) find a home (at)

Ein'öde f desert, wilderness

ein'ordnen tr put in its place; file; classify || ref fit into place; (sich anstellen) get in line; links nach rechts (or links) e. get into the right (or left) lane

ein'packen tr pack up

ein'passen tr (in acc) fit (into)

ein'pauken tr—j–m etw e. drum s.th. into s.o.'s head

ein'pferchen tr pen up; (fig) crowd together

ein'pflanzen tr plant; implant
ein'pökeln tr pickle; salt
ein'prägen tr imprint, impress
ein'quartieren tr billet, quarter
ein'rahmen tr frame
ein'rammen tr ram in, drive in
ein'räumen tr (Recht, Kredit) grant; (zugeben) concede, admit; **e. in** (acc) put into
ein'rechnen tr include, comprise
Ein'rede f objection; (jur) plea
ein'reden tr—j-m etw e. talk s.o. into s.th; **das lasse ich mir nicht e.** I can't believe that || intr—**auf j-n e.** badger s.o.
ein'reiben §62 tr rub
ein'reichen tr hand in, file; (Rechnung) present; (Abschied) tender; (Gesuch) submit; (Beschwerde, Klage) file
ein'reihen tr file; rank; enroll; (Bücher) shelve || ref fall into place; fall in line
ein'reihig adj single-breasted
Ein'reise f entry
ein'reißen §53 tr tear; demolish || intr (SEIN) tear; (fig) spread
ein'renken tr (Knochen) set; (fig) set right
ein'richten tr arrange; establish; (Wohnung) furnish; (surg) set || ref settle down; economize, make ends meet; (auf acc) make arrangements (for); (nach) adapt oneself (to)
Ein'richtung f (-;-en) setup; establishment; furniture; equipment
Ein'richtungsgegenstand m piece of furniture, piece of equipment
ein'rosten intr (SEIN) get rusty
ein'rücken tr (Zeile) indent; (Anzeige) put in || intr (SEIN) march in; **in j-s Stelle e.** succeed s.o.; **zum Militär e.** enter military service
Ein'rückung f (-;-en) indentation
ein'rühren tr (in acc) stir (into)
eins [aɪns] pron one; one o'clock; **es ist mir eins** it's all the same to me || **Eins** f (-;-en) one; (auf Würfeln) ace; (educ) A
einsam ['aɪnzam] adj lonely, lonesome
ein'sammeln tr gather; (Geld) collect
Ein'satz m insert, insertion; (Wette) bet; (Risiko) risk; (Verwendung) use; (für Flaschen) deposit; (mil) sortie; (mil) action; (mus) starting in, entry; **im E. stehen** be in action; **im vollen E.** in full operation; **unter E. seines Lebens** at the risk of one's life; **zum E. bringen** employ, use; (Maschinen) put into operation; (Polizei) call out; (mil) throw into action
ein'satzbereit adj combat-ready
Ein'satzstück n insert
ein'saugen tr suck in; (fig) imbibe
ein'säumen tr (sew) hem
ein'schalten tr insert; (elec) switch on, turn on || ref intervene
ein'schärfen tr—j-m etw e. impress s.th. on s.o.
ein'schätzen tr appraise, value
ein'schenken tr pour
ein'schicken tr send in
ein'schieben §130 tr push in; insert

ein'schießen §76 tr (Gewehr) test; (Geld) contribute; (Brot in den Ofen) shove; (fb) score || ref (auf acc) zero in (on)
ein'schiffen tr & intr embark
Ein'schiffung f (-;-en) embarkation
ein'schlafen §131 intr (SEIN) fall asleep; (Glied) go to sleep
ein'schläf(e)rig adj single (bed)
einschläfern ['aɪnʃlɛfərn] tr lull to sleep; (vet) put to sleep
Ein'schlag m striking; impact; explosion; (Umschlag) wrapper; (fig) admixture, element; (golf) putt; (sew) tuck; (tex) weft, woof
ein'schlagen §132 tr (Nagel) drive in; (zerbrechen) smash, bash in; (einwickeln) wrap; (Weg) take; (Laufbahn) enter upon; (Pflanzen) stick in the ground; (golf) putt; **die Richtung e. nach** go in the direction of || intr (Blitz) strike; (Erfolg haben) be a success; **nicht e.** fail
einschlägig ['aɪnʃlɛgɪç] adj relevant
Ein'schlagpapier n wrapping paper
ein'schleichen §85 ref (in acc) creep (into), slip (into); (in j-s Gunst) worm one's way
ein'schleppen tr tow in; (e-e Krankheit) bring in (from abroad)
ein'schleusen tr (Schmuggelwaren) sneak in; (Spionen) plant
ein'schließen §76 tr lock up; (in e-m Brief) enclose; (fig) include; (mil) encircle, surround
ein'schließlich adv inclusive(ly) || prep (genit) inclusive of
ein'schlummern intr (SEIN) doze off
Ein'schluß m encirclement; **mit E.** (genit) including
ein'schmeicheln ref (bei) ingratiate oneself (with)
ein'schmeichelnd adj ingratiating
ein'schmuggeln tr smuggle in
ein'schnappen intr (SEIN) snap shut; (fig) take offense
ein'schneidend adj (fig) incisive
Ein'schnitt m cut, incision; (Kerbe) notch; (geol) gorge; (pros) caesura
ein'schnüren tr tie up; pinch
ein'schränken tr (auf acc) restrict (to), confine (to); (Ausgaben) cut; (Behauptung) qualify || ref economize
Ein'schränkung f (-;-en) restriction; **ohne jede E.** without reservation
Ein'schreibebrief m registered letter
ein'schreiben §62 tr enroll; (Brief) register; (eintragen) enter; **e-n Brief e. lassen** send a letter by registered mail || ref register
ein'schreiten §86 intr (SEIN) step in, intervene; (gegen) take action (against)
ein'schrumpfen intr (SEIN) shrivel up
ein'schüchtern tr intimidate, overawe
Ein'schüchterung f (-;) intimidation
ein'schulen tr enroll in school
Ein'schuß m hit (of a bullet)
ein'schütten tr pour in
ein'segnen tr (neues Gebäude) consecrate; (konfirmieren) confirm
ein'sehen §138 tr inspect; (Akten) consult; (fig) realize; (mil) observe ||

Einsehen *n*—**ein E. haben** show (some) consideration
ein'seifen *tr* soap; (coll) softsoap
ein'seitig *adj* one-sided
ein'senden §140 *tr* send in, submit
Ein'sender –in §6 *mf* sender
ein'senken *tr* (im acc) sink (into)
ein'setzen *tr* insert, put in; (Geld) bet; (Leben) risk; (Polizei) call out; (Truppen) commit; (Kräfte) muster; (Einfluß) use; (Beamten) install; (ernennen) appoint; (einpflanzen) plant; (Artillerie, Tanks, Bomber) employ; (Edelsteine) mount || ref (für) stand up (for) || intr set in, begin; (mus) come in
Ein'sicht *f* inspection; (fig) insight
ein'sichtig *adj* understanding
ein'sichtsvoll *adj* understanding
ein'sickern *intr* (SEIN) seep in; (mil) infiltrate
Einsiedelei [aɪnziːdəˈlaɪ] *f* (-;-en) hermitage
Einsiedler –in [ˈaɪnziːdlər(ɪn)] §6 *mf* hermit, recluse
einsilbig [ˈaɪnzɪlbɪç] *adj* monosyllabic; (fig) taciturn
ein'sinken §143 *intr* (SEIN) sink in; (Erdboden) subside
ein'sparen *tr* economize on, save
ein'sperren *tr* lock up
ein'springen §142 *intr* (SEIN) jump in; (für) substitute (for); (tech) catch
ein'spritzen *tr* inject
Ein'spritzung *f* (-;-en) injection
Ein'spruch *m* objection; (jur) appeal
einspurig [ˈaɪnʃpuːrɪç] *adj* single-track
einst [aɪnst] *adv* once; (künftig) someday; **e. wie jezt** (now) as ever
Ein'stand *m* (tennis) deuce
ein'stecken *tr* insert, put in; stick in, pocket; (Schwert) sheathe; (hinnehmen) take; (coll) lock up, jail
ein'stehen §146 *intr* (SEIN) (für) vouch (for), stand up (for); **für die Folgen e.** take the responsibility
ein'steigen §148 *intr* (SEIN) get in; **alle e.!** all aboard!
Ein'steigkarte *f* (aer) boarding pass
Ein'steigloch *n* manhole
einstellbar [ˈaɪnʃtɛlbɑːr] *adj* adjustable
ein'stellen *tr* put in; (Arbeiter) hire; (Gerät) set, adjust; (beenden) stop, quit; (Sender) tune in on; (Fernglas, Kamera) focus; **die Arbeit e.** go on strike; **etw bei j-m e.** leave s.th. at s.o.'s house; **in die Garage e.** put into the garage; **zum Heeresdienst e.** induct || ref show up, turn up; sich **e. auf** (acc) attune oneself to
Ein'stellung *f* (-;-en) adjustment; setting; focusing; stoppage; (der Feindseligkeiten, Zahlungen) suspension; hiring; (aut) timing; (mil) induction; **E. des Feuers** cease-fire; **geistige E.** mental attitude
einstig [ˈaɪnstɪç] *adj* former; (verstorben) late; (künftig) future
ein'stimmen *intr* join in; **e. in** (acc) agree to, consent to
einstimmig [ˈaɪnʃtɪmɪç] *adj* unanimous
ein'studieren *tr* study; rehearse
ein'stufen *tr* classify

ein'stürmen *intr* (SEIN) (auf acc) rush (at); (mil) charge
Ein'sturz *m* (-es;) collapse
ein'stürzen *intr* (SEIN) collapse; **e. auf** (acc) (fig) overwhelm
einstweilen [ˈaɪnstvaɪlən] *adv* for the present; temporarily
einstweilig [ˈaɪnstvaɪlɪç] *adj* temporary
Ein'tänzer *m* gigolo
ein'tauschen *tr* trade in; **e. gegen** exchange for
ein'teilen *tr* divide; (austeilen) distribute; (einstufen) classify; (Geld, Zeit) budget; (Arbeit) plan
eintönig [ˈaɪntøːnɪç] *adj* monotonous
Ein'tönigkeit *f* (-;) monotony
Ein'topf *m*, **Ein'topfgericht** *n* one-dish meal
Ein'tracht *f* (-;) harmony, unity
einträchtig [ˈaɪntrɛçtɪç] *adj* harmonious
Eintrag [ˈaɪntrɑːk] *m* (-[e]s;ꞋꞋe) entry; **E. tun** (dat) hurt
ein'tragen §132 *tr* enter, register; (Gewinn) bring in, yield; **j-m etw e.** bring down s.th. on s.o. || ref register
einträglich [ˈaɪntrɛklɪç] *adj* profitable, lucrative
Ein'tragung *f* (-;-en) entry
ein'treffen §151 *intr* (SEIN) arrive; (in Erfüllung gehen) come true
ein'treiben §62 *tr* drive in; (Geld) collect || *intr* (SEIN) drift in, sail in
ein'treten §152 *tr* smash in || ref—sich [dat] **e-n Nagel e.** step on a nail || *intr* (SEIN) enter; (geschehen) occur; (Fieber) develop; (Fall, Not) arise; (Dunkelheit) fall; **e. für** stand up for, champion; **e. in** (acc) join, enter
Ein'tritt *m* (-s;) entry; (Einlaß) admittance; (Anfang) beginning, onset; (rok) re-entry; **E. frei** free admission; **E. verboten** no admittance
Ein'trittsgeld *n* admission fee
Ein'trittskarte *f* admission ticket
ein'trocknen *intr* (SEIN) dry up
ein'trüben ref become overcast
ein'tunken *tr* (im acc) dip (into)
ein'üben *tr* practice; train, coach
ein'verleiben *tr* incorporate
Einvernahme [ˈaɪnfɛrnɑːmə] *f* (-;-n) interrogation
Ein'vernehmen *n* (-s;) agreement; **sich mit j-m ins E. setzen** try to come to an understanding with s.o.
einverstanden [ˈaɪnfɛrˌʃtɑndən] *adj* in agreement || *interj* agreed!
Ein'verständnis *n* agreement; approval
ein'wachsen *tr* wax || *intr* (SEIN) (in acc) grow (into)
Ein'wand *m* (-s;ꞋꞋe) objection
Ein'wanderer –in §6 *mf* immigrant
ein'wandern *intr* (SEIN) immigrate
Ein'wanderung *f* (-;) immigration
ein'wandfrei *adj* unobjectionable; (tadellos) flawless; (Alibi, Zustand) perfect; (Quelle) unimpeachable
einwärts [ˈaɪnvɛrts] *adv* inward(s)
Einweg- comb.fm. disposable
ein'weichen *tr* soak
ein'weihen *tr* consecrate, dedicate; **e. in** (acc) initiate into; let in on

Ein′weihung f (-;-en) dedication; initiation

ein′weisen §118 tr install; (*Verkehr*) direct; **e. in** (*acc*) assign to; **j-n in seine Pflichten e.** brief s.o. in his duties; **j-n ins Krankenhaus e.** have s.o. admitted to the hospital

ein′wenden §140 tr—**etw e. gegen** raise an objection to; **nichts einzuwenden haben gegen** have no objections to

Ein′wendung f (-;-en) objection

ein′werfen §160 tr throw in; (*Fenster*) smash; (*Brief*) mail; (*Münze*) insert; (fig) interject

ein′wickeln tr wrap (up); (fig) trick

ein′willigen intr (in acc) agree (to)

ein′wirken intr (auf acc) have an effect (on), exercise infuence (on)

Ein′wirkung f (-;-en) effect, influence

Ein′wohner -in §6 mf inhabitant

Ein′wurf m (*Schlitz*) slot; (e-r Münze) insertion; (*Einwand*) objection

ein′wurzeln intr take root

Ein′zahl f (-;) singular

ein′zahlen tr pay in; (in e-e Kasse) deposit

Ein′zahlung f (-;-en) payment; deposit

Ein′zahlungsschein m deposit slip

einzäunen [′aɪntsɔɪnən] tr fence in

Einzel [′aɪntsəl] n (-s;-) singles

Einzel- comb.fm. individual; single; isolated; detailed; retail

Ein′zelbild n (cin) frame; (phot) still

Ein′zelfall m individual case

Ein′zelgänger m (coll) lone wolf

Ein′zelhaft f solitary confinement

Ein′zelhandel m retail trade

Ein′zelheit f (-;-en) item; detail, particular; **wegen näherer Einzelheiten** for further particulars

einzellig [′aɪntselɪç] adj single-cell

einzeln [′aɪntsəln] adj single; particular, individual; separate

Ein′zelperson f individual

Ein′zelspiel n singles (match)

Ein′zelwesen n individual

Ein′zelzimmer n single room; (im Krankenhaus) private room

ein′ziehen §109 tr draw in; retract; (*Flagge*) hawl down; (*Segel*) take in; (*Münzen*) call in; (*eintreiben*) collect; (mil) draft || intr (SEIN) move in; **e. in** (acc) enter; penetrate

einzig [′aɪntsɪç] adj & adv only; **e. darstellen** be unique || indef pron—**ein einziger** one only; **kein einziger** not a single one

ein′zigartig adj unique; extraordinary

Ein′zug m entry; moving in; (*Beginn*) start; (typ) indentation; **seinen E. halten** make one's entry

ein′zwängen tr (in acc) squeeze (into)

Eis [aɪs] n (-es;) ice; (*Speise-*) ice cream || [′e-ɪs] n (-;-s) (mus) E sharp

Eis′bahn f ice-skating rink

Eis′bär m polar bear

Eis′bein n (culin) pigs feet

Eis′berg m iceberg

Eis′beutel m (med) ice pack

Eis′blume f window frost

Eis′creme f ice cream

Eis′diehle f ice cream parlor

Eisen [′aɪzən] n (-s;-) iron; **altes E.** scrap iron; **heißes E.** (fig) hot potato; **zum alten E. werfen** (fig) scrap

Ei′senbahn f railroad; **mit der E.** by train, by rail

Ei′senbahndamm m railroad embankment

Ei′senbahner m (-s;-) railroader

Ei′senbahnknotenpunkt m railroad junction

Ei′senblech n sheet iron

Ei′senerz n iron ore

Ei′senhütte f ironworks

Ei′senwaren pl hardware, ironware

Ei′senwarenhandlung f hardware store

Ei′senzeit f iron age

eisern [′aɪzərn] adj iron; (*Fleiß*) unflagging; (*Rationen*) emergency

Eis′glätte f icy road conditions

eis′grau adj hoary

eisig [′aɪsɪç] adj icy; icy-cold

Eis′kappe f ice cap

Eis′kunstlauf m figure skating

Eis′lauf m ice skating

Eis′laufbahn f ice-skating rink

eis′laufen §105 intr (SEIN) ice-skate

Eis′läufer -in §6 mf skater

Eis′meer n—**Nördliches E.** Arctic Ocean; **Südliches E.** Antarctic Ocean

Eis′pickel m ice axe

Eis′schnellauf m speed skating

Eis′scholle f ice floe

Eis′schrank m icebox

Eis′vogel m kingfisher

Eis′würfel m ice cube

Eis′würfelschale f ice-cube tray

Eis′zapfen m icicle

Eis′zeit f ice age, glacial period

eitel [′aɪtəl] adj (nutzlos) vain, empty; (selbstgefällig) vain; || invar adj pure || adv merely

Ei′telkeit f (-;) vanity

Eiter [′aɪtər] m (-s;) pus

Ei′terbeule f boil, abscess

eitern [′aɪtərn] intr fester, suppurate

Ei′terung f (-;-en) festering

eitrig [′aɪtrɪç] adj pussy

Ei′weiß n (-es;-e) egg white; albumen

Ekel [′ekəl] m (-s;) (vor dat) disgust (at) || n (-s;) (coll) pest

ekelerregend [′ekələreɡənt] adj sickening, nauseating

e′kelhaft adj disgusting

ekeln [′ekəln] impers—**es eket mir** or **mich I** am disgusted || ref (vor dat) feel disgusted (at)

eklig [′eklɪç] adj disgusting, revolting; nasty, beastly

Ekzem [ek′tsem] n (-s;-e) eczema

elastisch [e′lastɪʃ] adj elastic

Elch [elç] m (-[e]s;-e) elk, moose

Elefant [ele′fant] m (-en;-en) elephant

Elefan′tentreiber m mahout

Elefan′tenzahn m elephant's tusk

elegant [ele′ɡant] adj elegant

Eleganz [ele′ɡants] f (-;) elegance

Elektriker [e′lektrɪkər] m (-s;-) electrician

elektrisch [e′lektrɪʃ] adj electric(al)

elektrisieren [elektri′zirən] tr electrify

Elektrolyse [elektro′lyzə] f (-;-) electricity

Elektrizitäts– *comb.fm.* electric, electro–

Elektro– [elɛktrə] *comb.fm.* electrical, electro–

Elektrode [ɛlɛk'troːdə] *f* (–;–n) electrode

Elek'trogerät *n* electrical appliance

Elektrizität [elɛktrɪtsɪ'tɛt] *f* (–;) electricity

Elek·tron [e'lɛktrən] *n* (–s;–tronen ['troːnən]) electron

Elektronen– [elɛktroːnən–] *comb.fm.* electronic

Elektronik [elɛk'troːnɪk] *f* (–;) electronics

Elektrotechnik *f* (–;) electrical engineering

Elektrotech'niker *m* (–s;–) electrical engineer

Element [ele'mɛnt] *n* (–[e]s;–e) element; (elec) cell

elementar [elemɛn'taːr] *adj* elementary

Elementar'buch *n* primer

Elen ['eːlen] *m & n* (–s;–) elk

elend ['eːlənt] *adj* miserable ‖ **Elend** *n* (–[e]s;) misery; extreme poverty; **das graue E.** the blues

E'lendsviertel *n* slums

elf [ɛlf] *adj & pron* eleven ‖ **Elf** *f* (–;–en) eleven

Elfe ['ɛlfə] *m* (–n;–n), *f* (–;–n) elf

Elfenbein ['ɛlfənbaɪn] *n* (–s;) ivory

elfte ['ɛlftə] §9 *adj & pron* eleventh

Elftel ['ɛlftəl] *n* (–s;–) eleventh (*part*)

Elite [e'liːtə] *f* (–;) elite, flower

Ellbogen ['ɛlboːgən] *m* (–s;) elbow

Ell'bogenfreiheit *f* elbowroom

Elsaß ['ɛlzas] *n* (–;) Elsace

elsässisch ['ɛlzɛsɪʃ] *adj* Alsatian

Elster ['ɛlstər] *f* (–;–n) magpie

elterlich ['ɛltərlɪç] *adj* parental

Eltern ['ɛltərn] *pl* parents; **nicht von schlechtern E.** (coll) terrific

El'ternbeirat *m* Parent-Teacher Association

El'ternhaus *n* home

el'ternlos *adj* orphaned; **elternlose Zeugung** spontaneous generation

El'ternschaft *f* parenthood

El'ternteil *m* parent

Email [e'maj] *n* (–s;), **Emaille** [e'maljə] *f* (–;) enamel

Email'geschirr *n* enamelware

Email'lack *m* enamel paint

emaillieren [ema(l)'jiːrən] *tr* enamel

Email'waren *pl* enamelware

emanzipieren [emantsi'piːrən] *tr* emancipate

Embargo [em'bargo] *n* (–s;–s) embargo

Embo·lie [embə'liː] *f* (–;–lien ['liːən]) embolism

Embry·o ['ɛmbryo] *m* (–s;–onen ['onən]) embryo

Emigrant –in [emi'grant(ɪn)] §7 *mf* emigrant

Emission [emɪ'sjoːn] *f* (–;–en) emission; (fin) issuance; (rad) broadcasting

empfahl [em'pfaːl] *pret of* empfehlen

Empfang [em'pfaŋ] *m* (–[e]s;͘e) reception; (*Erhalten*) receipt; (*im Hotel*) reception desk

empfangen [em'pfaŋən] §73 *tr* receive; (*Kind*) conceive

Empfänger –in (em'pfɛŋər(ɪn)) §6 *mf* receiver, recipient; addressee

empfänglich [em'pfɛŋlɪç] *adj* (**für**) susceptible (to)

Empfängnis [em'pfɛŋnɪs] *f* (–;) conception

empfäng'nisverhütend *adj* contraceptive; **empfängnisverhütendes Mittel** contraceptive

Empfäng'nisverhütung *f* contraception

Empfangs'chef *m* desk clerk

Empfangs'dame *f* receptionist; (*im Restaurant*) hostess

Empfangs'schein *m* (com) receipt

empfehlen [em'pfeːlən] §147 *tr* recommend; **e. Sie mich** (*dat*) remember me to ‖ *ref* say goodbye

empfeh'lenswert *adj* commendable

Empfeh'lung *f* (–;–en) recommendation; (*Gruß*) compliments

empfinden [em'pfɪndən] §59 *tr* feel

empfindlich [em'pfɪntlɪç] *adj* sensitive; delicate, touchy; (*Kälte*) bitter; (gegen) susceptible (to)

Empfind'lichkeit *f* (–;–en) sensitivity, touchiness; susceptibility

empfindsam [em'pfɪntzam] *adj* sensitive, touchy; sentimental

Empfind'samkeit *f* (–;) sensibility; sentimentality

Empfin'dung *f* (–;–en) sensation; feeling, sentiment

empfin'dunglos *adj* numb; (fig) callous

Empfin'dungswort *n* (gram) interjection

Emphysem [emfy'zem] *n* (–s;) emphysema

empor [em'por] *adv* up, upwards

empören [em'pøːrən] *tr* anger, shock ‖ *ref* rebel, revolt; (mil) mutiny

empor'fahren §71 *intr* (SEIN) jump up

empor'kommen §99 *intr* (SEIN) rise up; (*in der Welt*) get ahead

Emporkömmling [em'pørkœmlɪŋ] *m* (–s;–e) upstart, parvenu

empor'ragen *intr* tower, rise

empor'steigen §148 *intr* (SEIN) rise

empor'streben *intr* (SEIN) rise, soar; (fig) aspire

Empö'rung *f* (–;–en) revolt; (**über** *acc*) indignation (at)

emsig ['emzɪç] *adj* industrious, busy

Em'sigkeit *f* (–;) industry; activity

End– [ɛnt] *comb.fm.* final, ultimate

Ende ['ɛndə] *n* (–s;–n) end; ending; outcome; **letzten Endes** in the final analysis; **zu E. gehen** end; **zu E. sein** be over

enden ['ɛndən] *tr & intr* end; **nicht e. wollend** unending

End'ergebnis *n* final result, upshot

End'gerade *f* (–;) home stretch

end'gültig *adj* final, definitive

endigen ['ɛndɪgən] *tr & intr* end; **e. auf** (*acc*) (gram) terminate in

Endivie [ɛn'diːvjə] *f* (–;–n) endive

End'lauf *m* (sport) final heat

end'lich *adj* final; limited, finite ‖ *adv* finally, at last

end'los *adj* endless

End'runde *f* final round, finals

End'station *f* final stop, terminus

End'summe *f* sum total

End'termin *m* final date; closing date

En'dung *f* (-;-en) ending

Ener·gie [ener'gi] *f* (-;-gien ['gi-ən]) energy

energisch [e'nergɪʃ] *adj* energetic

eng [ɛŋ] *adj* narrow; tight; (*Freunde*) close; (*innig*) intimate; **im engeren Sinne** strictly speaking

engagieren [ãga'ziːrən] *tr* engage, hire ‖ *ref* commit oneself

Enge ['ɛŋə] *f* (-;-n) narrowness; tightness; (*Meer*-) strait; (fig) tight spot

Engel ['ɛŋəl] *m* (-s;-) angel

en'gelhaft *adj* angelic

eng'herzig *adj* stingy; petty

England ['ɛŋlant] *n* (-s;) England

Engländer ['ɛŋlɛndər] *m* (-s;-) Englishman; **die E.** the English

Engländerin ['ɛŋlɛndərɪn] *f* (-;-nen) Englishwoman

englisch ['ɛŋlɪʃ] *adj* English

Eng'paß *m* pass, defile; (fig) bottleneck

engros [ã'gro] *adv* wholesale

engstirnig ['ɛŋʃtɪrnɪç] *adj* narrow-minded

Enkel ['ɛŋkəl] *m* (-s;-) grandson

Enkelin ['ɛŋkəlɪn] *f* (-;-nen) granddaughter

En'kelkind *n* grandchild

enorm [e'nɔrm] *adj* enormous

Ensemble [ã'sãbl(ə)] *n* (-s;-s) (mus) ensemble; (theat) company, cast

ent- [ɛnt] *insep pref*

entarten [ɛnt'artən] *intr* (SEIN) degenerate

entartet [ɛnt'artət] *adj* degenerate; (fig) decadent

entäu'ßern *ref* (*genit*) divest oneself of

entbehren [ɛnt'beːrən] *tr* lack, miss; do without; spare; dispense with

entbehr'lich *adj* dispensable; needless, superfluous

Entbeh'rung *f* (-;-en) privation, need

entbin'den §59 *tr* release, absolve; (*Frau*) deliver ‖ *intr* give birth

Entbin'dung *f* (-;-en) dispensation; (*Niederkunft*) delivery, childbirth

Entbin'dungsanstalt *f* maternity hospital

entblät'tern *tr* defoliate ‖ *ref* defoliate; (coll) strip

entblößen [ɛnt'bløsən] *tr* bare; uncover; (mil) expose ‖ *ref* strip; remove one's hat

entbren'nen §97 *intr* (SEIN) flare up

entdecken (entdek'ken) *tr* discover ‖ *ref*—**sich** j-m **e.** confide in s.o.

Entdeckung (Entdek'kung) *f* (-;-en) discovery

Ente ['ɛntə] *f* (-;-n) duck; (coll) hoax

enteh'ren *tr* dishonor; (*Mädchen*) violate, deflower

enteh'rend *adj* disgraceful

Enteh'rung *f* (-;-en) disgrace; rape

enteig'nen *tr* dispossess

enteisen [ɛnt'aɪzən] *tr* defrost; deice

enter'ben *tr* disinherit

Enterich ['ɛntərɪç] *m* (-s;-e) drake

entern ['ɛntərn] *tr* (naut) board

entfachen [ɛnt'faxən] *tr* kindle; (fig) provoke

entfah'ren §71 *intr* (SEIN) (*dat*) slip out (on)

entfal'len §72 *intr* (SEIN) (*dat*) slip (from); **auf** j—**n e.** fall to s.o.'s share; **entfällt** not applicable

entfal'ten *tr* unfold; display; (mil) deploy ‖ *ref* unfold; develop

entfernen [ɛnt'fɛrnən] *tr* remove ‖ *ref* withdraw, move away; deviate

entfernt [ɛnt'fɛrnt] *adj* distant; **nicht weit davon e. zu** (*inf*) far from (*ger*)

Entfer'nung *f* (-;-en) removal; range; distance; absence

Entfer'nungsmesser *m* (phot) range finder

entfes'seln *tr* unleash

entflam'men *tr* inflame ‖ *intr* (SEIN) ignite; flash; (fig) flare up

entflech'ten *tr* disentangle; (*Kartell*) break up; (mil) disengage

entflie'hen §75 *intr* (SEIN) flee, escape; (*Zeit*) fly

entfremden [ɛnt'frɛmdən] *tr* alienate

entfrosten [ɛnt'frɔstən] *tr* defrost

entfüh'ren *tr* abduct; kidnap; (*Flugzeug*) hijack; (hum) steal

Entführer -in §6 *mf* abductor, kidnaper; (aer) hijacker

Entführung *f* (-;-en) abduction; kidnaping; (aer) hijacking

entge'gen *prep* (*dat*) contrary to; in the direction of, towards

entge'gengehen §82 *intr* (SEIN) (*dat*) go to meet; (*dat*) face, confront

entge'gengesetzt *adj* contrary, opposite

entge'gengehalten §90 *tr* hold out; point out, say in answer

entge'genkommen §99 *intr* (SEIN) (*dat*) approach; (*dat*) come to meet; (*dat*) meet halfway ‖ **Entgegenkommen** *n* (-s;) courtesy

entge'genkommend *adj* on-coming; (fig) accommodating

entge'genlaufen §105 *intr* (SEIN) (*dat*) run towards; (*dat*) run counter to

entge'gennehmen §116 *tr* accept, receive

entge'gensehen §138 *intr* (*dat*) look forward to; (*dat*) await; (*dat*) face

entge'gensetzen *tr* put up, offer

entge'genstehen §146 *intr* (*dat*) oppose

entge'genstellen *tr* set in opposition ‖ *ref* (*dat*) oppose, resist

entge'genstrecken *tr* (*dat*) stretch out (toward)

entge'gentreten §152 *intr* (SEIN) (*dat*) walk toward; (fig) (*dat*) confront

entgegnen [ɛnt'gegnən] *tr* & *intr* reply

Entgeg'nung *f* (-;-en) reply

entge'hen §82 *intr* (SEIN) (*dat*) escape, elude; **sich** [*dat*] **etw e. lassen** let s.th. slip by

Entgelt [ɛnt'gelt] *n* (-[e]s;) compensation, payment

entgel'ten §83 *tr* pay for

entgeistert [ɛnt'gaɪstərt] *adj* aghast

entgleisen [ɛnt'glaɪzən] *intr* (SEIN) jump the track; (fig) make a slip

Entglei'sung *f* (-;-en) derailment; (fig) slip

entglei'ten §86 *intr* (SEIN) (*dat*) slip away (from)

entgräten [ɛnt'gretən] *tr* bone (*a fish*)

enthaaren [ɛnt'hɑːrən] *tr* remove the hair from

Enthaa'rungsmittel *n* hair remover

enthal'ten §90 *tr* contain; comprise ‖ *ref* (*genit*) refrain (from); **sich der Stimme e.** (parl) abstain

enthaltsam [ɛnt'haltzɑm] *adj* abstinent

Enthalt'samkeit *f* (–;) abstinence

Enthal'tung *f* (–;–en) abstention

enthär'ten *tr* (*Wasser*) soften

enthaupten [ɛnt'haʊptən] *tr* behead

enthäuten [ɛnt'hɔɪtən] *tr* skin

enthe'ben §94 *tr* (*genit*) exempt (from), relieve (of); (*e–s Amtes*) remove (*from office*)

enthei'ligen *tr* desecrate, profane

enthül'len *tr* unveil; reveal, expose

Enthül'lung *f* (–;–en) unveiling; (fig) exposé

enthül'sen *tr* shell; (*Mais*) husk

Enthusiasmus [ɛntuzi'asmʊs] *m* (–;) enthusiasm

enthusiastisch [ɛntuzi'astɪʃ] *adj* enthusiastic

entjungfern [ɛnt'jʊŋfərn] *tr* deflower

entkei'men *tr* sterilize; (*Milch*) pasteurize ‖ *intr* (SEIN) sprout

entkernen [ɛnt'kɛrnən] *tr* (*Obst*) pit

entklei'den *tr* undress; (*genit*) strip (of), divest (of) ‖ *ref* undress

Entklei'dungsnummer *f* striptease act

Entklei'dungsrevue *f* striptease show

entkom'men §99 *intr* (SEIN) (*dat*) escape (from) ‖ **Entkommen** *n* (–s;) escape

entkor'ken *tr* uncork, open

entkräften [ɛnt'krɛftən] *tr* weaken; (*Argument*) refute

entla'den §103 *tr* unload; (*Batterie*) discharge ‖ *ref* (*Gewehr*) go off; (*Sturm*) break; (elec) discharge; **sein Zorn entlud sich** he vented his anger

Entla'dung *f* (–;–en) unloading; discharge; explosion; **zur E. bringen** detonate

entlang' *adv* along ‖ *prep* (*dat* or *acc* or *an dat*; or after *genit* or *dat*) along

entlarven [ɛnt'larfən] *tr* expose

entlas'sen §104 *tr* dismiss, fire; set free; (mil) discharge

Entlas'sungspapiere *pl* discharge papers

entla'sten *tr* unburden; (**von**) relieve (of); (jur) exonerate

Entla'stungsstraße *f* bypass

Entla'stungszeuge *m* witness for the defense

entlauben [ɛnt'laʊbən] *tr* defoliate

entlaubt' *adj* leafless

entlau'fen §105 *intr* (SEIN) (*dat*) run away (from); (*mit e–m Liebhaber*) elope

entlausen [ɛnt'laʊzən] *tr* delouse

entledigen [ɛnt'leːdɪɡən] *tr* (*genit*) release (from) ‖ *ref* (*genit*) get rid (of), rid oneself (of)

entlee'ren *tr* empty; drain

entle'gen *adj* distant, remote

entleh'nen *tr* borrow

entlei'hen §81 *tr* borrow

entlo'ben *ref* break the engagement

entlocken [ɛnt'lɔkən] *tr* elicit

entloh'nen *tr* pay, pay off

entlüf'ten *tr* ventilate

entmannen [ɛnt'manən] *tr* castrate

entmilitarisieren [ɛntmɪlɪtarɪ'ziːrən] *tr* demilitarize

entmutigen [ɛnt'muːtɪɡən] *tr* discourage

entneh'men §116 *tr* (*dat*) take (from); (*Geld*) (**aus**) withdraw (from); (*dat* or **aus**) infer (from), gather (from)

entnerven [ɛnt'nɛrfən] *tr* enervate

entpuppen [ɛnt'pʊpən] *ref* emerge from the cocoon; **sich e. als** (fig) turn out to be

enträtseln [ɛnt'rɛtsəln] *tr* solve; (*Schriftzeichen*) decipher

entrei'ßen §53 *tr* (*dat*) wrest (from)

entrich'ten *tr* pay

entrin'nen §121 *intr* (SEIN) escape (from)

entrol'len *tr* unroll; unfurl ‖ *ref* unroll ‖ *intr* (SEIN) roll down

entrüsten [ɛnt'rʏstən] *tr* anger ‖ *ref*— **sich e. über** (*acc*) become incensed at; be shocked at

Entrü'stung *f* (–;) anger, indignation

entsa'gen *intr* (*dat*) renounce, forego; **dem Thron e.** abdicate

Entsatz' *m* (–es;) (mil) relief

entschä'digen *tr* compensate; reimburse

Entschä'digung *f* (–;) compensation

Entschä'digungsanspruch *m* damage claim

entschär'fen *tr* defuse

Entscheid [ɛnt'ʃaɪt] *m* (–[e]s;–e) (jur) decision

entschei'den §112 *tr*, *ref* & *intr* decide

entschei'dend *adj* decisive

Entschei'dung *f* (–;–en) decision

Entschei'dungsbefugnis *f* jurisdiction

Entschei'dungskampf *m* (sport) finals

Entschei'dungsspiel *n* (cards) rubber game; (sport) finals

Entschei'dungsstunde *f* moment of truth

entschei'dungsvoll *adj* critical

entschieden [ɛnt'ʃiːdən] *adj* decided; decisive; firm, resolute

entschla'fen §131 *intr* (SEIN) fall asleep; (*sterben*) pass away, die

entschlei'ern *tr* unveil; (fig) reveal

entschlie'ßen §76 *ref* (zu) decide (on)

Entschlie'ßung *f* (–;–en) (parl) resolution

entschlossen [ɛnt'lɔsən] *adj* resolute

entschlüp'fen *intr* (SEIN) (*dat*) slip away (from); (*dat*) slip out (on)

Entschluß' *m* resolve, decision

entschlüs'seln *tr* decipher

Entschluß'kraft *f* will power

entschulden [ɛnt'ʃʊldən] *tr* free of debt

entschuldigen [ɛnt'ʃʊldɪɡən] *tr* excuse; exculpate ‖ *ref* apologize; **es läßt sich e.** it's excusable; **sich e. lassen** beg to be excused; **sich mit Unwissenheit e.** plead ignorance

entschul'digend *adj* apologetic

Entschul'digung *f* (–;–en) excuse; apology; **ich bitte um E.** I beg your pardon

Entschul'digungsgrund *m* excuse

entseelt [ɛnt'zeːlt] *adj* lifeless, dead

entsen'den §140 *tr* send off

entset'zen *tr* horrify; (mil) relieve ‖

ref (über *acc*) be horrified (at) || **Ent-setzen** *n* (-s;) horror

entsetz'lich *adj* horrible, appalling || *adv* (coll) awfully

Entset'zung *f* (-;) dismissal; (mil) relief

entsi'chern *tr* take (*a gun*) off safety

entsie'geln *tr* unseal

entsin'nen §121 *ref* (*genit*) recall

entspan'nen *tr & ref* relax

Entspan'nung *f* (-;) relaxation; (pol) detente

entspre'chen §64 *intr* (*dat*) correspond (to); (*dat*) meet, suit; (*dat*) be equivalent (to); (*dat*) answer (*a description*)

entspre'chend *adj* corresponding; adequate; equivalent || *adv* accordingly || *prep* (*dat*) according to

entsprin'gen §142 *intr* (SEIN) rise, originate; (*entlaufen*) escape

entstaatlichen [ɛnt'ʃtɑːtliçən] *tr* free from state control, denationalize

entstam'men *intr* (SEIN) (*dat*) descend (from), originate (from)

entste'hen §146 *intr* (SEIN) originate

Entste'hung *f* (-;) origin

entstel'len *tr* disfigure; deface; (*Tatsachen*) distort

enttäu'schen *tr* disappoint

entthronen [ɛnt'troːnən] *tr* dethrone

entvölkern [ɛnt'fœlkərn] *tr* depopulate

entwach'sen §155 *intr* (SEIN) (*dat*) outgrow

entwaff'nen *tr* disarm

entwar'nen *intr* sound the all-clear

entwäs'sern *tr* drain; dehydrate

entweder [ɛnt'veːdər] *conj*—**entweder ... oder** either ... or

entwei'chen §85 *intr* (SEIN) escape

entwei'hen *tr* desecrate, profane

entwen'den *tr* steal

entwer'fen §160 *tr* sketch; draft

entwer'ten *tr* (*Geld*) depreciate; (*Briefmarke*) cancel; (*Karten*) punch

entwickeln (entwik'keln) *tr* develop; evolve; (mil) deploy || *ref* develop

Entwick'lung *f* (-;-en) development; evolution; (mil) deployment

Entwick'lungsland *n* developing country

Entwick'lungslehre *f* theory of evolution

entwin'den §59 *tr* (*dat*) wrest (from) || *ref* extricate oneself

entwirren [ɛnt'vɪrən] *tr & ref* unravel

entwi'schen *intr* (SEIN) escape; (*dat* or *aus*) slip away (from)

entwöhnen [ɛnt'vøːnən] *tr* wean; **j—n e.** (*genit*) break s.o. of || *ref* (*genit*) give up

Entwurf' *m* (-s;⁼e) sketch; draft

entwur'zeln *tr* uproot

entzau'bern *tr* disenchant

entzie'hen §163 *tr* (*dat*) withdraw (from), take away (from); (chem) extract; **j—m das Wort e.** (parl) rule s.o. out of order || *ref* (*dat*) shirk, elude

Entzie'hungsanstalt *f* rehabilitation center

entziffern [ɛnt'tsɪfərn] *tr* decipher

entzücken (entzük'ken) *tr* delight

Entzückung (Entzük'kung) *f* (-;-en) delight, rapture

Entzug' *m* (-[e]s;) deprivation

entzündbar [ɛnt'tsʏntbɑr] *adj* inflammable

entzün'den *tr* set on fire; (fig) inflame || *ref* catch fire; (pathol) become inflamed

Entzün'dung *f* (-;) kindling; (pathol) inflammation

entzwei' *adv* in two, apart

entzwei'brechen §64 *tr & intr* break in two, snap

entzweien [ɛnt'tsvaɪən] *tr* divide

Enzykli·ka [ɛn'tsyklɪkɑ] *f* (-;-ken [kən]) encyclicle

Enzyklopä·die [ɛntsyklɔpe'diː] *f* (-; -dien ['diːən]) encyclopedia

Enzym [ɛn'tsyːm] *n* (-[e]s;-e) enzyme

Epaulette [epɔ'letə] *f* (-;-n) epaulet

ephemer [efe'meːr] *adj* ephemeral

Epide·mie [epɪde'miː] *f* (-;-mien ['miːən]) epidemic

epidemisch [epɪ'deːmɪʃ] *adj* epidemic

Epigramm [epɪ'gram] *n* (-s;-e) epigram

Epik ['epɪk] *f* (-;) epic poetry

Epilog [epɪ'loːk] *m* (-s;-e) epilogue

episch ['epɪʃ] *adj* epic

Episode [epɪ'zoːdə] *f* (-;-n) episode

Epoche [e'pɔxə] *f* (-;-n) epoch

Epos ['epɔs] *n* (-; **Epen** ['epən]) epic

Equipage [ek(v)ɪ'paːʒə] *f* (-;-n) carriage; (naut) crew; (sport) team

Equipe [e'k(v)ɪp(ə)] *f* (-;-n) team; group

er [eːr] §11 *pers pron* he; it

er- [eːr] *insep pref*

erach'ten *tr* think || **Erachten** *n* (-s;) opinion; **meines Erachtens** in my opinion

erar'beiten *tr* acquire (*by working*)

Erb- [ɛrp] *comb.fm.* hereditary

Erb'anfall *m* inheritance

Erb'anlage *f* (biol) gene

erbarmen [ɛr'barmən] *tr* move to pity || *ref* (*genit*) pity; **erbarme Dich unser** have mercy on us || **Erbarmen** *n* (-s;) pity, mercy

erbar'menswert, erbar'menswürdig *adj* pitiable

erbärmlich [ɛr'bɛrmlɪç] *adj* pitiful; wretched, miserable || *adv* awfully

erbar'mungslos *adj* pitiless

erbau'en *tr* erect; (fig) edify || *ref* (an *dat*) be edified (by)

Erbau'er *m* (-s;-) builder

erbau'lich *adj* edifying

Erbau'ung *f* (-;) building; edification

Erbau'ungsbuch *n* book of devotions

erb'berechtigt *adj* eligible as heir

Erbe ['ɛrbə] *m* (-n;-n) heir; **ohne Leibliche Erben** without issue || *n* (-s;) inheritance, heritage; **väterliches E.** patrimony

erbe'ben *intr* (SEIN) tremble

erb'eigen *adj* hereditary

erben ['ɛrbən] *tr* inherit

erbet'teln *tr* get (by begging)

erbeuten [ɛr'bɔɪtən] *tr* capture

Erb'feind *m* traditional enemy

Erb'folge *f* succession

erbie'ten §58 *ref* volunteer

Erbin ['ɛrbɪn] f (-;-nen) heiress
erbit'ten §60 ref—sich [dat] etw e. ask for s.th., request s.th.
erbittern [ɛr'bɪtərn] tr embitter
Erb'krankheit f hereditary disease
erblassen [ɛr'blasən] intr (SEIN) turn pale
Erblasser –in ['ɛrplasər(ɪn)] §6 mf testator
erbleichen [ɛr'blaɪçən] §85 & §109 intr (SEIN) turn pale; (poet) die
erb'lich adj hereditary
Erb'lichkeit f (-;) heredity
erblicken (erblik'ken) tr spot, see
erblinden [ɛr'blɪndən] intr (SEIN) go blind
Erblin'dung f (-;) loss of sight
Erb'onkel m (coll) rich uncle
erbre'chen §64 tr break open || ref vomit
erbrin'gen §65 tr produce
Erb'schaft f (-;-en) inheritance
Erbse ['ɛrpsə] f (-;-en) pea
Erb'stück n heirloom
Erb'sünde f original sin
Erb'tante f (coll) rich aunt
Erb'teil m share (in an inheritance)
Erd– [ɛrt] comb.fm. earth, of the earth; geo–; ground
Erd'anschluß m (elec) ground
Erd'arbeiten pl excavation work
Erd'bahn f orbit of the earth
Erd'ball m globe
Erd'beben n (-s;-) earthquake
Erd'bebenmesser m seismograph
Erd'beere f strawberry
Erd'boden m ground, earth; dem E. gleichmachen raze (to the ground)
Erde ['ɛrdə] f (-;-n) earth; ground, soil, land; (elec) ground wire; zu ebener E. on the ground floor
erden ['ɛrdən] tr (elec) ground
erden'ken §66 tr think up
erdenk'lich adj imaginable
Erd'gas n natural gas
Erd'geschoß n ground floor
erdich'ten tr fabricate, think up
Erdich'tung f (-;-en) fabrication
erdig ['ɛrdɪç] adj earthy
Erd'innere §5 n interior of the earth
Erd'klumpen m clod
Erd'kreis m earth, world
Erd'kugel f globe, sphere; world
Erd'kunde f geography
Erd'leitung f (elec) ground wire
Erd'nuß f peanut
Erd'nußbutter f peanut butter
Erd'öl n petroleum, oil; auf E. stoßen strike oil
erdolchen [ɛr'dɔlçən] tr stab
Erd'reich n soil
erdreisten [ɛr'draɪstən] ref have the nerve, have the audacity
Erd'rinde f crust of the earth
erdros'seln tr strangle
erdrücken (erdrük'ken) tr crush to death
erdrückend (erdrük'kend) adj overwhelming
Erd'rutsch m land slide
Erd'schicht f stratum
Erd'spalte f fissure; chasm
Erd'teil m continent

erdul'den tr suffer
ereifern [ɛr'aɪfərn] ref get excited
ereignen [ɛr'aɪgnən] ref happen, occur
Ereignis [ɛr'aɪgnɪs] n (-ses;-se) event, occurrence
ereig'nislos adj uneventful
ereig'nisvoll adj eventful
Erektion [erek'tsjon] f (-;-en) erection
Eremit [ere'mɪt] m (-en;-en) hermit
erer'ben tr inherit
erfah'ren adj experienced || §71 tr find out; (erleben) experience; (Pflege) receive
Erfah'rung f (-;-en) experience
erfas'sen tr grasp; understand; include; register, list
erfin'den §59 tr invent
Erfin'der –in §6 mf inventor
erfinderisch [ɛr'fɪndərɪʃ] adj inventive
Erfin'dung f (-;-en) invention
Erfin'dungsgabe f inventiveness
erfle'hen tr obtain (by entreaty)
Erfolg [ɛr'fɔlk] m (-[e]s;-e) success; (Wirkung) result
erfol'gen intr (SEIN) ensue; occur
erfolg'los adj unsuccessful || adv in vain
erfolg'reich adj successful
Erfolgs'mensch m go-getter
erfolg'versprechend adj promising
erforderlich [ɛr'fɔrdərlɪç] adj required, necessary
erfor'derlichenfalls adv if need be
erfordern [ɛr'fɔrdərn] tr require
Erfordernis [ɛr'fɔrdərnɪs] n (-ses;-se) requirement; exigency
erfor'schen tr investigate; (Land) explore
Erfor'scher –in §6 mf explorer
Erfor'schung f (-;-en) investigation; exploration
erfra'gen tr ask for; find out
erfreu'en tr delight || ref (an dat) be delighted (at); sich e. (genit) enjoy
erfreulich [ɛr'frɔɪlɪç] adj delightful; (Nachricht) welcome, good
erfreut [ɛr'frɔɪt] adj (über acc) glad (about); e. zu (inf) pleased to (inf)
erfrie'ren §77 intr (SEIN) freeze to death; (Pflanzen) freeze
Erfrie'rung f (-;-en) frostbite
erfrischen [ɛr'frɪʃən] tr refresh
Erfri'schung f (-;-en) refreshment
erfül'len tr fill; fulfill; (Aufgabe) perform; (Bitte) comply with; (Hoffnungen) live up to || ref materialize
Erfül'lung f (-;) fulfillment; accomplishment; in E. gehen come true
erfunden [ɛr'fundən] adj made-up
ergänzen [ɛr'gɛntsən] tr complete; complement; (Statue) restore
ergän'zend adj complementary
ergattern [ɛr'gatərn] tr (coll) dig up
ergau'nern tr—etw von j–m e. cheat s.o. out of s.th.
erge'ben adj devoted || §80 tr yield; amount to; show || ref surrender; (dat) devote oneself (to); (aus) result (from); sich dem Trunk e. take to drinking; sich e. in (acc) resign oneself to
Erge'benheit f (-;) devotion; resignation

ergebenst [er'ge:bənst] *adv* respectfully

Ergebnis [er'ge:pnɪs] *n* (-ses;-se) result, outcome; (*Punktzahl*) score

Erge'bung *f* (-;) submission, resignation; (mil) surrender

erge'hen §82 *intr* (SEIN) come out, be published; e. lassen issue, publish; etw über sich e. lassen put up with s.th.; Gnade vor Recht e. lassen show leniency || *ref* take a stroll; sich e. in (*acc*) indulge in; sich e. über (*acc*) expatiate on || *impers*—es ist ihm gut ergangen things went well for him || Ergehen *n* (-s;) state of health

ergiebig [er'gi:bɪç] *adj* productive, fertile; rich, abundant

ergie'ßen §76 *ref* flow; pour out

ergötzen [er'gœtsən] *tr* amuse || *ref* (an *dat*) take delight (in)

ergötz'lich *adj* delightful

ergrau'en *intr* (SEIN) turn gray

ergrei'fen §88 *tr* seize; (*Verbrecher*) apprehend; (*Gemüt*) move; (*Beruf, Waffen*) take up; (*Maßnahmen*) take

Ergrei'fung *f* (-;) seizure

ergriffen [er'grɪfən] *adj* moved; e. von seized with

Ergrif'fenheit *f* (-;) emotion

ergrün'den *tr* get to the bottom of

Erguß' *m* discharge; (fig) flood of words

erha'ben *adj* elevated, lofty; erhabene Arbeit relief work; e. sein über (*acc*) be above

Erhalt' *m* (-es;) receipt

erhal'ten §90 *tr* get, receive; keep, keep up, maintain; conserve; (*Familie*) support; (*Gesundheit*) preserve; Betrag dankend e. (stamped on bills) paid; gut e. well preserved; noch e. sein survive || *ref* survive; (von) subsist (on)

erhältlich [er'hɛltlɪç] *adj* obtainable

Erhal'tung *f* (-;) preservation; maintenance; support; (*der Energie, usw.*) conservation

erhän'gen *tr* hang

erhär'ten *tr* harden; (fig) substantiate || *intr* (SEIN) harden

erha'schen *tr* catch; e-n Blick von ihr e. catch her eye

erhe'ben §94 *tr* raise; (*erhöhen*) elevate; (*preisen*) exalt; (*Steuern*) collect; (*Anklage*) bring; (math) raise || *ref* get up, rise, start; arise

erheblich [er'he:plɪç] *adj* considerable

Erhe'bung *f* (-;-en) elevation; promotion; uprising, revolt; Erhebungen machen make inquiries

erheitern [er'haɪtərn] *tr* amuse || *ref* cheer up

erhellen [er'hɛlən] *tr* light up; (fig) shed light on || *ref* grow light(er); light up || *impers*—es erhellt it appears

erhitzen [er'hɪtsən] *tr* heat; (fig) inflame || *ref* grow hot; get angry

erhöhen [er'hø:ən] *tr* raise; (fig) heighten || *ref* increase; be enhanced

Erhö'hung *f* (-;-en) rise

erho'len *ref* recover; relax

Erho'lung *f* (-;-en) recovery; relaxation; recreation

erho'lungsbedürftig *adj* in need of rest

Erho'lungsheim *n* convalescent home

erhö'ren *tr* (*Gebet*) hear; (*Bitte*) grant

erinnerlich [er'ɪnərlɪç] *adj*—das ist mir nicht e. it slipped my mind; soviel mir e. ist as far as I can remember

erinnern [er'ɪnərn] *tr* (an *acc*) remind (of) || *ref* (an *acc*) remember

Erin'nerung *f* (-;-en) recollection, remembrance; (*Mahnung*) reminder; zur E. an (*acc*) in memory of

Erin'nerungsvermögen *n* memory

erkalten [er'kaltən] *intr* (SEIN) cool off; (fig) grow cool

erkälten [er'kɛltən] *ref* catch cold

Erkäl'tung *f* (-;-en) cold

erkennbar [er'kɛnbar] *adj* recognizable

erkennen [er'kɛnən] §97 *tr* make out; recognize; detect; realize; j-n e. für (com) credit so. with; sich zu e. geben disclose one's identity; zu e. geben, daß indicate that || *intr*—auf e-e Geldstrafe e. impose a fine; gegen j-n e. judge against s.o.

erkenntlich [er'kɛntlɪç] *adj* grateful

Erkennt'lichkeit *f* (-;) gratitude

Erkenntnis [er'kɛntnɪs] *f* (-;-se) insight, judgment, realization, knowledge; (philos) cognition || *n* (-ses; -se) decision, finding

Erker ['ɛrkər] *m* (-s;-) (archit) oriel

Er'kerfenster *n* bay window

erklären [er'klɛːrən] *tr* explain, account for; (*aussprechen*) state

Erklä'rer -in §6 *mf* commentator

erklär'lich *adj* explicable

Erklä'rung *f* (-;-en) explanation; statement; commentary; (jur) deposition

erklin'gen §142 *intr* (SEIN) sound; (*widerhallen*) resound

erkor (er'kor) *pret of* erkiesen

erkoren [er'korən] *adj* chosen

erkranken [er'kraŋkən] *intr* (SEIN) get sick; (*Pflanzen*) become diseased

erkühnen [er'ky:nən] *ref* dare, venture

erkunden [er'kundən] *tr & intr* reconnoiter

erkundigen [er'kundɪgən] *ref* inquire

Erkun'digung *f* (-;-en) inquiry

Erkun'dung *f* (-;) reconnaissance

erlahmen [er'laːmən] *intr* (SEIN) tire; (*Kraft*) give out

erlangen [er'laŋən] *tr* reach; (*sich verschaffen*) get; wieder e. recover

Er·laß' [er'las] *m* (-lasses;-lässe) remission; exemption; edict, order

erlas'sen §142 *tr* release; (*Schulden*) cancel; (*Strafe*) remit; (*Sünden*) pardon; (*Verordnung*) issue; e. Sie es mir zu (*inf*) allow me not to (*inf*), don't ask me to (*inf*)

erläßlich [er'lɛslɪç] *adj* pardonable

erlauben [er'laubən] *tr* allow || *ref*—sich [*dat*] e. zu (*inf*) take the liberty to (*inf*); sich [*dat*] nicht e. not be able to afford

Erlaubnis [er'laupnɪs] *f* (-;-se) permission

Erlaub'nisschein *m* permit, license

erlaucht [er'lauxt] *adj* illustrious

erläutern [er'lɔɪtərn] *tr* explain

Erläu'terung *f* (-;-en) explanation

Erle **85** Erschaffung

Erle ['ɛrlə] f (-;-n) (bot) alder
erle'ben tr live to see; experience
Erlebnis [er'leːpnɪs] n (-ses;-se) experience, adventure; occurrence
erledigen [er'leːdɪgən] tr settle; (Post, Einkäufe, Gesuch) attend to, take care of; **j—n e.** (coll) do s.o. in
erledigt [er'leːdɪçt] adj (& fig) finished; (Stellung) open; (coll) bushed
erle'gen tr pay down; (töten) kill
erleichtern [er'laɪçtərn] tr lighten; make easy; (Not) relieve, ease
Erleich'terung f (-;) alleviation
erlei'den §106 tr suffer
erler'nen tr learn
erle'sen adj choice || §107 tr choose
erleuch'ten tr light up; enlighten
erlie'gen §108 intr (SEIN) (dat) succumb (to), fall victim to
erlogen [er'loːgən] adj false
Erlös [er'løːs] m (-es) proceeds
erlosch [er'lɔʃ] pret of erlöschen
erloschen [er'lɔʃən] pp of erlöschen
erlöschen [er'lœʃən] §110 intr (SEIN) go out; (Vertrag) expire; (fig) become extinct
erlö'sen tr redeem; free; get (by sale)
Erlö'ser m (-s;-) deliverer; (relig) Redeemer
Erlö'sung f (-;) redemption
ermächtigen [er'mɛçtɪgən] tr authorize
Ermäch'tigung f (-;-en) authorization
ermah'nen tr admonish
Ermah'nung f (-;-en) admonition
ermangeln [er'maŋəln] intr (genit) lack; **es an nichts e. lassen** spare no pains; **nicht e. zu** (inf) not fail to (inf)
Erman'gelung f—**in E.** (genit) in default of
ermä'ßigen tr reduce
ermatten [er'matən] tr tire || (SEIN) tire; grow weak; slacken
Ermat'tung f (-;) fatigue
ermes'sen §70 tr judge, estimate; realize; **e. aus** infer from || **Ermessen** n (-s;) judgment, decision; **nach freiem E.** at one's discretion
ermitteln [er'mɪtəln] tr ascertain || intr conduct an investigation
Ermitt'lung f (-;-en) ascertainment; **Ermittlungen** investigation
Ermitt'lungsausschuß m fact-finding committee
Ermitt'lungsbeamte m investigator
Ermitt'lungsverfahren n judicial inquiry
ermöglichen [er'møːklɪçən] tr enable, make possible
ermorden [er'mɔrdən] tr murder
ermüden [er'myːdən] tr tire || intr (SEIN) tire, get tired
Ermü'dung f (-;) fatigue
ermuntern [er'muntərn] tr cheer up; encourage || ref cheer up
Ermun'terung f (-;) encouragement
ermutigen [er'muːtɪgən] tr encourage
ernäh'ren tr nourish; (fig) support
Ernäh'rer m §6 mf supporter
Ernäh'rung f (-;) nourishment; support; (physiol) nutrition
ernen'nen §97 tr nominate, appoint
erneuern [er'nɔɪ-ərn] tr renew; reno-

vate; (Gemälde) restore; (Öl) change; (Reifen) retread; (mach) replace
erneu'ert adj repeated || adv anew
Erneu'erung f (-;-en) renewal; renovation; restoration; replacement
erniedrigen [er'niːdrɪgən] tr lower; (demütigen) humble; (im Rang) degrade || ref humble oneself; debase oneself
ernst [ɛrnst] adj earnest; serious || **Ernst** m (-[e]s;) seriousness; **im E.** in earnest
Ernst'fall m—**im E.** in case of emergency; (mil) in case of war
ernst'haft adj earnest, serious
ernst'lich adj earnest; serious
Ernte ['ɛrntə] f (-;-n) harvest; crop
ernten ['ɛrntən] tr reap, harvest
ernüch'tern tr sober; disallusion || ref sober up; be disallusioned
Ero'berer m §6 mf conqueror
erobern [er'oːbərn] tr conquer
Ero'berung f (-;-en) conquest
eröff'nen tr open; (feierlich) inaugurate; disclose || ref open; present itself; **sich j—m e.** unburden oneself to s.o.
Eröff'nung f (-;-en) (grand) opening; inauguration; announcement
erörtern [er'œrtərn] tr discuss
erotisch [e'roːtɪʃ] adj erotic
Erpel ['ɛrpəl] m (-s;-) drake
erpicht [er'pɪçt] adj—**e. auf** (acc) keen on, dead set on, hell bent on
erpres'sen tr extort; (Person) blackmail
Erpres'sung f (-;-en) extortion; blackmail
erpro'ben tr test, try out
erquicken [er'kvɪkən] tr refresh
erquick'lich adj refreshing; agreeable
erra'ten §63 tr guess
errech'nen tr calculate
erregbar [er'reːkbar] adj excitable; irritable
erregen [er'reːgən] tr excite; cause || ref get excited, get worked up
Erre'gung f (-;) excitation; agitation; excitement; **E. öffentlichen Ärgernisses** disorderly conduct
erreichbar [er'raɪçbar] adj reachable; available
errei'chen tr reach, attain; get to; (Zug, Bus) catch; **e., daß** bring it about that
erret'ten tr save, rescue
Erret'tung f (-;-en) rescue; (relig) Salvation
errich'ten tr erect; found
errin'gen §142 tr get; attain, achieve
errö'ten intr (SEIN) redden; blush
Errungenschaft [er'ruŋən/aft] f (-;-en) achievement; acquisition
Ersatz' m (-es;) substitute; replacement; compensation; (mil) recruitment
Ersatz- comb.fm. substitute, replacement; spare; alternative; recruiting
Ersatz'mann m substitute; alternate
Ersatz'stück n, **Ersatz'teil** n spare part, spare
erschaf'fen §126 tr create
Erschaf'fer m §6 mf creator
Erschaf'fung f (-;-en) creation

erschal′len §127 *intr* (SEIN) begin to sound; ring out; resound

erschau′ern *intr* shudder

erschei′nen §128 *intr* (SEIN) appear; (*Buch*) come out, be published

Erschei′nung *f* (-;-en) appearance; apparition; phenomenon

erschie′ßen §76 *tr* shoot (dead)

Erschie′ßung *f* (-;-en) shooting, execution

Erschie′ßungskommando *n* firing squad

erschlaffen [er′∫lafən] *tr* relax; enervate ∥ *intr* (SEIN) relax; weaken

erschla′gen §132 *tr* slay; wie e. dead tired

erschlie′ßen §76 *tr* open up; develop; e. aus infer from; derive from ∥ *ref* —sich j–m e. unburden oneself to s.o.

erschöp′fen *tr* exhaust; (fig) deplete

erschrak [er′∫rak] *pret* of erschrecken

erschrecken (erschrek′ken) *tr* startle; shock ∥ *ref* get scared ∥ §134 *intr* (SEIN) be startled

erschreckend (erschrek′kend) *adj* terrifying; alarming; dreadful

erschüt′ten *tr* shake; upset; move deeply

Erschüt′terung *f* (-;-en) tremor; vibration; deep feeling; concussion

erschweren [er′∫verən] *tr* make more difficult; hamper, impede

erschwin′deln *tr*—etw von j–m e. cheat s.o. out of s.th.

erschwin′gen §142 *tr* afford

erschwing′lich *adj* within one's means

erse′hen §138 *tr* (aus) gather (from)

erseh′nen *tr* long for

ersetzbar [er′zetsbar] *adj* replaceable

erset′zen *tr* replace; (*Schaden*) compensate for; (*Kräfte*) renew; j–m etw e. reimburse s.o. for s.th.; sie ersetzte ihm die Eltern she was mother and father to him

ersetz′lich *adj* replaceable

ersicht′lich *adj* evident

ersin′nen §121 *tr* think up

erspa′ren *tr* save

Ersparnis [er′sparnıs] *f* (-;-se) (an dat) saving (in)

erprießlich [er′prıslıç] *adj* useful

erst [erst] *adv* first; at first; just; only; not until; e. recht really; e. recht nicht most certainly not

erstar′ren *intr* (SEIN) grow stiff; (*Finger*) grow numb; (*Blut*) congeal; (*Zement*) set; (fig) run cold; vor Schreck e. be paralyzed with fear

erstatten [er′∫tatən] *tr* refund, repay; (*Bericht*) file; Meldung e. report

Erstat′tung *f* (-;-en) refund; reimbursement; compensation

Erst′aufführung *f* première

erstau′nen *tr* astonish ∥ *intr* (SEIN) (über *acc*) be astonished (at) ∥ Erstaunen *n* (-s;) astonishment; in E. setzen astonish

erstaun′lich *adj* astonishing

Erst′ausfertigung *f* original

erste [′erstə] §9 *adj* first; der erste beste the first that comes along; fürs e. for the time being; zum ersten, zum zweiten, zum dritten going, going, gone

erste′chen §64 *tr* stab

erste′hen §146 *tr* buy, get ∥ *intr* (SEIN) rise; (*Städte*) spring up

erstei′gen §148 *tr* climb

erstel′len *tr* provide, supply; erect

erstens [′erstəns] *adv* first; in the first place

erst′geboren *adj* first-born

ersticken [er′∫tıkən] *tr* choke, stifle, smother; im Keim e. nip in the bud ∥ *intr* (SEIN) choke; in Arbeit e. be snowed under

erstklassig [′erstklasıç] *adj* first-class

Erstling [′erstlıŋ] *m* (-s;-e) first-born child; (fig) first fruits

Erstlings– *comb.fm.* first

Erst′lingsausstattung *f* layette

erstmalig ∣ ′erstmalıç] *adj* first

erstre′ben *tr* strive for

erstrecken (erstrek′ken) *ref* extend

ersu′chen *tr* request, ask

ertappen [er′tapən] *tr* surprise, catch

ertel′len *tr* give; confer; (*Auftrag*) place; (*Audienz, Patent*) grant

ertö′nen *intr* (SEIN) sound; resound

ertö′ten *tr* (fig) stifle

Ertrag [er′trak] *m* (-[e]s;≐e) yield; proceeds; produce

erträg′lich ∣ er′treklıç] *adj* bearable

ertränken [er′treŋkən] *tr* drown

erträu′men *tr* dream of

ertrin′ken §143 *intr* (SEIN) drown

ertüchtigen [er′tyçtıgən] *tr* train

erübrigen [er′ybrıgən] *tr* save; (*Zeit*) spare ∥ *ref* be superfluous

erwa′chen *intr* (SEIN) wake up

erwach′sen *adj* adult ∥ §155 *intr* (SEIN) grow, grow up; arise ∥ Erwachsene §5 *mf* adult, grown-up

erwä′gen §156 *tr* weigh, consider

Erwä′gung *f* (-;-en) consideration

erwäh′len *tr* choose

erwäh′nen *tr* mention

erwäh′nenswert *adj* worth mentioning

Erwäh′nung *f* (-;-) mention

erwär′men *tr* warm, warm up

erwar′ten *tr* expect, await; etw zu e. haben be in for s.th.

Erwar′tung *f* (-;-en) expectation

erwar′tungsvoll *adj* expectant

erwecken (erwek′ken) *tr* wake; (*Hoffnungen*) raise; (*Gefühle*) awaken; den Anschein e. give the impression

erweh′ren (*genit*) *ref* ward off; (*genit*) refrain from; (*der Tränen*) hold back

erwei′chen *tr* soften; (fig) move, touch; sich e. lassen relent

erwei′sen §118 *tr* prove; show; (*Achtung*) show; (*Dienst*) render; (*Ehre, Gunst*) do ∥ *ref*—sich e. als prove

erweitern [er′vaıtərn] *tr* & *ref* widen; (*vermehren*) increase; extend, expand

Erwerb [er′verp] *m* (-[e]s;-e) acquisition; (*Verdienst*) earnings; (*Unterhalt*) living

erwer′ben §149 *tr* acquire; gain; (*verdienen*) earn; (*kaufen*) purchase

erwerbs′behindert *adj* disabled

Erwerbs′betrieb *m* business enterprise

erwerbs′fähig *adj* capable of earning a living

erwerbs′los *adj* unemployed

Erwerbs'quelle f source of income

Erwerbs'sinn m acquisitiveness

erwerbs'tätig adj gainfully employed

erwerbs'unfähig adj unable to earn a living

Erwerbs'zweig m line of business

Erwer'bung f (-;-en) acquisition

erwidern [ɛr'viːdərn] tr reply; reciprocate, return

Erwi'derung f (-;-en) reply; return; retaliation

erwir'ken tr secure, obtain

erwi'schen tr catch; **ihn hat's erwischt!** (coll) he's had it!

erwünscht [ɛr'vynʃt] adj desired; welcome; (wünschenswert) desirable

erwür'gen tr strangle

Erz [ɛrts] n (-es;-e) ore; brass; bronze

Erz-, erz- comb.fm. ore; bronze; utterly; (fig) arch–

erzäh'len [ɛr'tsɛlən] tr tell, narrate

Erzäh'lung f (-;-en) story, narrative

Erz'bischof m archbishop

Erz'engel m archangel

erzeu'gen tr beget; manufacture; produce; generate

Erzeugnis [ɛr'tsɔɪknɪs] n (-ses;-se) product; produce

Erzeu'gung f (-;-en) production; manufacture

erzie'hen §163 tr bring up, rear; (geistig) educate

Erzieher [ɛr'tsiːər] m (-s;-) educator; private tutor

Erzieherin [ɛr'tsi-ərɪn] f (-;-nen) educator; governess

erzieherisch [ɛr'tsi-ərɪʃ] adj educational, pedagogical

Erzie'hung f (-;) upbringing; education; (Lebensart) breeding

Erzie'hungslehre f (educ) education

Erzie'hungswesen n educational system

erzie'len tr achieve, reach; (Gewinn) realize; (sport) score

Erz'lager n ore deposit

Erz'probe f assay

erzür'nen tr anger ‖ ref get angry

erzwin'gen §142 tr force; wring, obtain by force; (Gehorsam) exact

es [ɛs] adv (as expletive) there; **es gibt** there is, there are ‖ §11 pers pron it; he; she ‖ **Es** n (-;-) (mus) E flat; (psychol) id

Esche ['ɛʃə] f (-;-n) ash tree

Esel ['eːzəl] m (-s;-) donkey, ass

Eselei [eːzə'laɪ] f (-;-en) foolish act, foolish remark

E'selsbrücke f (educ) pony

E'selsohr n dog's-ear

eskalieren [ɛska'liːrən] tr & intr escalate

Eskimo ['ɛskimoː] m (-s;-s) Eskimo

Espe ['ɛspə] f (-;-n) (bot) aspen

eßbar ['ɛsbar] adj edible, eatable

Eßbesteck ['ɛsbəʃtek] n knife, fork, and spoon

Esse ['ɛsə] f (-;-n) chimney; forge

essen ['ɛsən] §70 tr & intr eat; **zu Mittag e.** eat lunch ‖ **Essen** n (-s;) eating; food, meal

Essenz [ɛ'sɛnts] f (-;-en) essence

Eßgeschirr ['ɛsgəʃɪr] n (-s;-e) tableware; table service; (mil) mess kit

Eßgier ['ɛsgiːr] f (-;) gluttony

Essig ['ɛsɪç] m (-s;-e) vinegar

Es'siggurke f pickle, gherkin

Es'sigsäure f acetic acid

Eßlöffel ['ɛslœfəl] m (-s;-) tablespoon

Eßnapf ['ɛsnapf] m dinner pail

Eßsaal ['ɛszɑl] m dining room

Eßstäbchen ['ɛsʃtɛpçən] n chopstick

Eßwaren ['ɛsvɑrən] pl food, victuals

Eßzimmer ['ɛstsɪmər] n (-s;-) dining room

Estland ['ɛstlant] n (-s;) Estonia

Estrade [ɛs'trɑːdə] f (-;-n) dais

etablieren [eta'bliːrən] tr establish

Etablissement [etablɪs(ə)'mã] n (-s;-s) establishment

Etage [ɛ'tɑʒə] f (-;-n) floor, story

Eta'genbett n bunk bed

Eta'genwohnung f apartment

Etappe [ɛ'tapə] f (-;-n) (Teilstrecke) leg, stage; (mil) rear echelon, rear

Etat [ɛ'tɑ] m (-s;-s) budget

Etats'jahr n fiscal year

etepetete [etəpe'teːtə] adj overly particular

Ethik ['eːtɪk] f (-;) ethics

ethisch ['eːtɪʃ] adj ethical

ethnisch ['ɛtnɪʃ] adj ethnic

Ethnologie [ɛtnoloː'giː] f (-;) ethnology

Etikett [ɛti'ket] n (-s;-e) tab, label

Etikette [ɛti'ketə] f (-;) etiquette

etikettieren [ɛtɪke'tiːrən] tr label

etliche ['ɛtlɪçə] adj & pron a few

Etui [ɛ'tviː] n (-s;-s) case (for spectacles, cigarettes, etc.)

etwa ['ɛtvɑ] adv about, around; perhaps; by chance; for example

etwaig [ɛt'vɑ-ɪç] adj eventual

etwas ['ɛtvas] adj some, a little ‖ adv somewhat ‖ pron something; anything ‖ **Etwas** n—**ein gewißes E. a** certain something

euch [ɔɪç] pers pron you; to you ‖ reflex pron yourselves

euer ['ɔɪ-ər] adj your

Eukalyptus [ɔɪka'lyptus] m (-s- & -ten [tən]) eucalyptus

Eule ['ɔɪlə] f (-;-n) owl

Euphorie [ɔɪfoː'riː] f (-;) euphoria

euphorisch [ɔɪ'foːrɪʃ] adj euphoric

eurige ['ɔɪrɪgə] §2,5 pron yours

Europa [ɔɪ'roːpa] n (-s;) Europe

Europäer -in [ɔɪroː'pe-ər(ɪn)] §6 mf European

europäisch [ɔɪroː'pe-ɪʃ] adj European

Euter ['ɔɪtər] n (-s;-) udder

evakuieren [evaku'iːrən] tr evacuate

evangelisch [evan'geːlɪʃ] adj evangelical; Protestant

Evangelist [evange'lɪst] m (-en;-en) Evangelist

Evangelium [evan'geːljum] n (-s;-lien [ljən]) gospel

eventuell [eventu'el] adj eventual ‖ adv possibly

ewig ['eːvɪç] adj eternal; perpetual

E'wigkeit f (-;-en) eternity

e'wiglich adv forever

exakt [ɛ'ksakt] adj exact

Examen [ɛ'ksɑmən] n (-s;-s & -mina [mɪna]) examination

examinieren [ɛksamɪ'niːrən] tr examine

exekutiv [ɛkseku'tiːf] adj executive

Exempel [ε'ksempəl] n (-s;-) example; **ein E. statuieren an** (dat) make an example of

Exemplar [eksem'plɑr] n (-s;-e) sample, specimen; (e-s Buches) copy

exerzieren [ekser'tsirən] tr & intr exercise

Exil [e'ksil] n (-s;-e) exile

Existenz [eksi'stents] f (-;-en) existence; livelihood; personality

Existenz/minimum n living wage

existieren [eksis'tirən] intr exist

exklusiv [ekslu'zif] adj exclusive

Exkommunikation [ekskomunika'tsjon] f (-;-en) excommunication

exkommunizieren [ekskomuni'tsirən] tr excommunicate

Exkrement [ekskre'ment] n (-[e]s;-e) excrement

exmittieren [eksmi'tirən] tr evict

exotisch [e'ksoti ʃ] adj exotic

expedieren [ekspe'dirən] tr send, ship

Expedition [ekspedi'tsjon] f (-;-en) forwarding; (mil) expedition

Experiment [eksperi'ment] n (-[e]s; -e) experiment

experimentieren [eksperimen'tirən] intr experiment

explodieren [eksplo'dirən] intr (SEIN) explode; blow up

Explosion [eksplo'zjon] f (-;-en) explosion

exponieren [ekspo'nirən] tr expose; (darlegen) expound, set forth

Export [eks'port] m (-[e]s;-e) export

exportieren [ekspor'tirən] tr export

Ex·preß [eks'pres] m (-presses; -presse) express

Expreß/zug m express train

extra ['ekstrɑ] adv extra; (coll) on purpose, for spite

Ex'trablatt n (journ) extra

extrahieren [ekstra'hirən] tr extract

Extrakt [eks'trakt] m (-[e]s;-e) extract; (aus Büchern) excerpt

extravagant [ekstrava'gant] adj luxurious; wild, fantastic

Extravaganz [ekstrava'gants] f (-;-en) luxury

extrem [eks'trem] adj extreme || **Extrem** n (-s;-e) extreme

Exzellenz [ekstse'lents] f (-;-en) Excellency

exzentrisch [eks'tsentri ʃ] adj eccentric

Ex·zeß [eks'tses] m (-zesses;-zesse) excess

F

F, f [ef] invar n F, f; (mus) F

Fabel ['fɑbəl] f (-;-n) fable; story; (e-s Dramas) plot

fa'belhaft adj fabulous

fabeln ['fɑbəln] intr tell stories

Fabrik [fa'brik] f (-;-en) factory, mill

Fabrik'anlage f manufacturing plant

Fabrikant -in [fabri'kant(in)] §7 mf manufacturer, maker

Fabrikat [fabri'kɑt] n (-[e]s;-e) product; brand, make

Fabrikation [fabrikɑ'tsjon] f (-;) manufacture, manufacturing

Fabrikations/fehler m flaw, defect

Fabrikations/nummer f serial number

Fabrik/marke f trademark

fabrik/mäßig adj mass

Fabrik/nummer f serial number

Fabrik/waren pl manufactured goods

Fabrik/zeichen n trademark

fabrizieren [fabri'tsirən] tr manufacture

fabulieren [fabu'lirən] tr make up || intr tell yarns

fabulös [fabu'løs] adj fabulous

Facette [fa'setə] f (-;-n) facet

Fach [fax] n (-[e]s;⁻er) compartment; (im Schreibtisch) pigeonhole; (Bücherbrett) shelf; (fig) field, department; line, business; (educ) subject; **vom F. sein** be an expert

Fach'arbeiter -in §6 mf specialist

Fach'arzt m, **Fach'ärztin** f (med) specialist

Fach'ausbildung f professional training

Fach'ausdruck m technical term

fächeln ['feçəln] tr fan

Fächer ['feçər] m (-s;-) fan

Fä'cherpalme f palmetto

Fach'gebiet n field, line; department

Fach'gelehrte §5 mf expert

fach'gemäß adj expert, professional

Fach'genosse m colleague

Fach'kenntnisse pl specialized knowledge

Fach'kreis m experts, specialists

fach'kundig adj expert, experienced

fach'lich adj professional; technical, specialized

Fach'mann m (-es;⁻er & -leute) expert, specialist

fachmännisch ['faxmeni ʃ] adj expert

Fach'schule f vocational school

Fachsimpelei [faxzimpə'lai] f (-;-en) shoptalk

fachsimpeln ['faxzimpəln] intr talk shop

Fach'werk n framework; specialized book

Fach'zeitschrift f technical journal

Fackel ['fakəl] f (-;-n) torch

fackeln ['fakəln] intr flare; (fig) hesitate, dilly-dally

Fackelschein (**Fak'kelschein**) m torchlight

Fackelzug (**Fak'kelzug**) m torchlight procession

fade ['fɑdə] adj stale; (fig) dull

Faden ['fɑdən] m (-s;⁻) (& fig) thread; filament; (naut) fathom; **keinen guten F. lassen an** (dat) tear apart

Fa'denkreuz n crosshairs

Fa'dennudeln pl vermicelli

fadenscheinig ['fadən/faɪnɪç] *adj* threadbare

Fagott [fa'gɔt] *n* (-[e]s;-e) bassoon

fähig ['fɛ-ɪç] *adj* capable, able

Fä'higkeit *f* (-;-en) ability; talent

fahl [fal] *adj* pale; faded, washed-out

fahnden ['fandən] *intr* (**nach**) search (for), hunt (for)

Fahn'dung *f* (-;-en) search, hunt

Fahne ['fanə] *f* (-;-n) flag; pennant; (mil) colors; (typ) galley proof

Fah'nenabzug *m* galley proof

Fah'neneid *m* (mil) swearing in

Fah'nenflucht *f* desertion

fah'nenflüchtig *adj*—**f. werden** desert || **Fahnenflüchtige** §5 *mf* deserter

Fah'nenmast *m* flagpole

Fah'nenträger **-in** §6 *mf* standard bearer

Fähnrich ['fenrɪç] *m* (-s;-e) officer cadet; **F. zur See** midshipman

Fahrbahn ['farban] *f* (traffic) lane

fahrbar ['farbar] *adj* passable; navigable; mobile

fahrbereit ['farbəraɪt] *adj* in running order

Fahr'bereitschaft *f* (-;-en) motor pool

Fähre ['ferə] *f* (-;-n) ferry

fahren ['farən] §71 *tr* haul; (lenken) drive; (*Boot*) sail || *intr* (SEIN) go; travel, drive; ride; **es fuhr mir durch den Sinn** it flashed across my mind; **f. lassen** run (*a boat, train*); let go; (fig) abandon, renounce; **gut f. bei** do well in; **mit der Hand f. über** (*acc*) run one's hand over; **rechts f.** (public sign) keep right; **was ist in ihn gefahren?** what's gotten into him?

fah'renlassen §104 *tr* let go of

Fah'rer **-in** §6 *mf* driver

Fah'rerflucht *f* hit-and-run case

Fahrgast ['fargast] *m* passenger

Fahrgeld ['fargelt] *n* fare

Fahrgelegenheit ['fargelegənhaɪt] *f* transportation (facilities)

Fahrgestell ['fargə/tel] *n* (-[e]s;-e) (aer) landing gear; (aut) chassis

fahrig ['farɪç] *adj* fidgety

Fahrkarte ['farkartə] *f* ticket

Fahr'kartenausgabe *f*, **Fahr'kartenschalter** *m* ticket window

fahrlässig ['farlesɪç] *adj* negligent; **fahrlässige Tötung** involuntary manslaughter

Fahr'lässigkeit *f* (-;) negligence

Fahrlehrer **-in** ['farlerər(ɪn)] §6 *mf* driving instructor

Fahrnis ['farnɪs] *f* (-;-se) movables

Fährnis ['fernɪs] *f* (-;-se) (poet) danger

Fahrplan ['farplan] *m* schedule

fahr'planmäßig *adj* scheduled || *adv* on schedule, on time

Fahrpreis ['farpraɪs] *m* fare

Fahrprüfung ['farpryfuŋ] *f* driver's test

Fahrrad ['farrad] *n* bicycle

Fahrrinne ['farrɪnə] *f* channel

Fahrschein ['far/aɪn] *m* ticket

Fahrstuhl ['far/tul] *m* elevator; (med) wheel chair

Fahr'stuhlführer **-in** §6 *mf* elevator operator

Fahr'stuhlschacht *m* elevator shaft

Fahrstunde ['far/tundə] *f* driving lesson

Fahrt [fart] *f* (-;-en) ride, drive; trip; **auf F. gehen** go hiking; **F. verlieren** lose speed; **freie F. haben** have the green light; **in F. kommen** pick up speed; (fig) swing into action; **in F. sein** (coll) be keyed up; (coll) be on the warpath; (naut) be under way

Fährte ['fertə] *f* (-;-n) track, scent

Fahrt'unterbrechung *f* (-;-en) stopover

Fahrwasser ['farvasər] *n* navigable water; (& fig) wake

Fahrwerk ['farverk] *n* see **Fahrgestell**

Fahrzeug ['fartsɔɪk] *n* vehicle; vessel, craft

Fahr'zeugpark *m* (aut) fleet; (rr) rolling stock

fair [fer] *adj* fair

Fairneß ['fernes] *f* (-;) fairness

Fäkalien [fe'kaljən] *pl* feces

faktisch ['faktɪ/] *adj* actual, factual

Fak·tor ['faktɔr] *m* (-s;-toren ['torən]) factor; foreman; (com) agent

Faktu·ra [fak'tura] *f* (-;-ren [rən]) invoice

Fakultät [fakul'tet] *f* (-;-en) (educ) department, school

falb [falp] *adj* claybank (*horse*)

Falke ['falkə] *m* (-;-n) falcon; (pol) hawk

Fal'kenjagd *f* falconry

Falkner ['falknər] *m* (-s;-) falconer

Fall [fal] *m* (-[e]s;-e) fall, drop; downfall; case; **auf alle Fälle** in any case; **auf keinen F.** in no case; **auf jeden F.** in any case; **gesetzt den F.** supposing; **im besten F.** at best; **im schlimmsten F.** if worst comes to worst; **von F. zu F.** according to circumstances; **zu F. bringen;** (fig) ruin; (parl) defeat; **zu F. kommen** (fig) collapse

Fall'brücke *f* drawbridge

Falle ['falə] *f* (-;-n) (& fig) trap; (fig) pitfall; (*Bett*) (coll) sack

fallen ['falən] §72 *intr* (SEIN) fall, drop; (*Schuß*) be heard; (mil) fall in battle; **j—m ins Wort f.** interrupt s.o. || **Fallen** *n* (-s;) fall, drop; downfall

fällen ['felən] *tr* (*Bäume*) fell; (*Urteil*) pass; (chem) precipitate

Fallensteller ['falən/telər] *m* (-s;-) trapper

Fall'grube *f* trap, pit; (fig) pitfall

fällig ['felɪç] *adj* due; payable

Fäl'ligkeit *f* (-;) due date

Fall'obst *n* windfall

Fall'rohr *n* soil pipe; (e-r *Dachrinne*) down spout

falls [fals] *conj* in case, if

Fall'schirm *m* parachute

Fall'schirmabsprung *m* parachute jump

Fall'schirmjäger *m* paratrooper

Fall'schirmspringer **-in** §6 *mf* parachutist, sky diver

Fall'strick *m* snare

Fall'sucht *f* (pathol) epilepsy

fall'süchtig *adj* (pathol) epileptic

Fall'tür *f* trapdoor

falsch [falʃ] *adj* false; *(verkehrt)* wrong; *(unecht)* counterfeit; **falsches Spiel** double-dealing ‖ *adv* wrongly; **f. gehen** (horol) be off; **f. schreiben** misspell; **f. schwören** perjure oneself; **f. singen** sing off key; **f. spielen** cheat; **f. verbunden** wrong number ‖ **Falsch** *m*—**ohne F.** without guile

fälschen ['fɛlʃən] *tr* falsify; *(Geld)* counterfeit; *(Urkunde)* forge

Fäl'scher –in §6 *mf* forger; counterfeiter

Falsch'geld *n* counterfeit money

Falsch'heit *f* (–;-en) falsity; deceitfulness

fälschlich ['fɛlʃlɪç] *adv* falsely

Falsch'münzer *m* counterfeiter

Falsch'spieler –in §6 *mf* card sharp

Fäl'schung *f* (–;-en) falsification; forgery; fake

Faltboot ['faltbot] *n* collapsible boat

Falte ['faltə] *f* (–;-n) fold; *(Plissee)* pleat, crease; *(Runzel)* wrinkle

fälteln ['fɛltəln] *tr* pleat

falten ['faltən] *tr* fold; wrinkle

Fal'tenrock *m* pleated skirt

Falter ['faltər] *m* (–s;-) butterfly; *(Nacht-)* moth

faltig ['faltɪç] *adj* creased; wrinkled

Falz [falts] *m* (–es;-e) fold; *(Kerbe)* notch; (carp) rabbet

familiär [fami'ljɛr] *adj* intimate; familiar

Familie [fa'miljə] *f* (–;-n) family

Fami'lienangehörige §5 *mf* member of the family

Fami'lienanschluß *m*—**F. haben** live as one of the family

Fami'lienname *m* last name

Fami'lienstand *m* marital status

Fami'lienstück *n* family heirloom

Fami'lienzuwachs *m* addition to the family

famos [fa'mos] *adj* excellent, swell

Fan [fɛn] *m* (–s;-s) (sport) fan

Fanatiker –in [fa'natɪkər(ɪn)] §6 *mf* fanatic; (sport) fan

fanatisch [fa'natɪʃ] *adj* fanatic

fand [fant] *pret of* **finden**

Fanfare [fan'farə] *f* (–;-n) (mus) fanfare

Fang [faŋ] *m* (–[e]s;⸚e) capture; *(Fisch-)* haul, catch; *(Falle)* trap; *(Kralle)* claw

Fang'arm *m* tentacle

Fang'eisen *n* steel trap

fangen ['faŋən] §73 *tr* catch; trap; *(Ohrfeige)* get ‖ *ref* get caught ‖ **Fangen** *n*—**F. spielen** play catch

Fang'frage *f* loaded question

Fang'messer *n* hunting knife

Fang'zahn *m* fang; tusk

Farb– [farp] *comb.fm.* color

Farb'abzug *m* (phot) color print

Farb'aufnahme *f* color photograph

Farb'band *n* (–[e]s;⸚er) typewriter ribbon

Farbe ['farbə] *f* (–;-n) color; dye; *(zum Malen)* paint; *(Gesichts-)* complexion; (cards) suit; **F. bekennen** folow suit; (fig) lay one's cards on the table

färben ['fɛrbən] *tr* color, dye, tint ‖

ref take on color; change color; **sich rot f.** turn red; blush

far'benprächtig *adj* colorful

Fär'ber –in §6 *mf* dyer

Farb'fernsehen *n* color television

Farb'film *m* color film

farbig ['farbɪç] *adj* colored; colorful

Farb'kissen *n* ink pad

Farb'körper *m* pigment

farb'los *adj* colorless

Farb'spritzpistole *f* paint sprayer

Farb'stift *m* colored pencil; crayon

Farb'stoff *m* dye

Farb'ton *m* tone, hue, shade

Fär'bung *f* (–;-en) coloring; hue

Farm [farm] *f* (–;-en) farm

Farmer –in ['farmər(ɪn)] §6 *mf* farmer

Farn [farn] *m* (–[e]s;-e) fern

Farn'kraut *n* fern

Fasan [fa'zan] *m* (–s;-e & -en) pheasant

Fasching ['faʃɪŋ] *m* (–s;) carnival

Faschismus [fa'ʃɪsmus] *m* (–;) fascism

Faschist –in [fa'ʃɪst(ɪn)] §7 *mf* fascist

Faselei [fazə'laɪ] *f* (–;-en) drivel

Faselhans ['fazəlhans] *m* (–'-e & ⸚e) blabberer; scatterbrain

faseln ['fazəln] *intr* talk nonsense

Faser ['fazər] *f* (–;-n) fiber; *(im Holz)* grain; *(Fädchen)* thread, string

Fa'serholzplatte *f* fiberboard

fasern ['fazərn] *tr* unravel ‖ *ref* fray ‖ *intr* unravel

Fa'serschreiber *m* felt pen

Faß [fas] *n* (Fasses;Fässer) barrel, keg; *(Bütte)* vat, tub

Fassade [fa'sadə] *f* (–;-n) façade

faßbar ['fasbar] *adj* comprehensible

Faß'bier *n* draft beer

fassen ['fasən] *tr* (packen) seize; *(erwischen)* apprehend; *(begreifen)* grasp; *(Edelstein)* mount; *(enthalten können)* hold, seat; *(Essen)* (mil) draw; **e-n Gedanken f.** form an idea; **in Worte f.** put into words; **j-n bei der Ehre f.** appeal to s.o.'s honor; **Tritt fassen** fall in step ‖ *ref* get hold of oneself; **in sich f.** include; **sich f. an** *(acc)* put one's hand to, touch; **sich in Geduld f.** exercise patience; **sich kurz f.** be brief ‖ *intr* take hold; **(nach)** grab (for); **es ist nicht zu f.** it is incomprehensible

Faß'hahn *m* tap, faucet

faß'lich *adj* conceivable

Fasson [fa'sõ] *f* (–;-en) style, cut

Fas'sung *f* (–;-en) composure; *(schriftlich)* draft; *(für Edelsteine)* setting, mounting; *(Brillenrand)* frame; *(Wortlaut)* wording; *(Lesart)* version; (elec) socket; **aus der F. bringen** upset; **außer F. sein** be beside oneself

Fas'sungskraft *f* comprehension

fas'sungslos *adj* disconcerted, shaken

Fas'sungsvermögen *n* capacity; *(geistliches)* (powers of) comprehension

fast [fast] *adv* almost, nearly

fasten ['fastən] *intr* fast ‖ **Fasten** *n* (–s;) fasting

Fa'stenzeit *f* Lent, Lenten season

Fast'nacht *f* carnival

Fast'tag *m* day of fasting, fast day

faszinieren [fasts'ni:rən] *tr* fascinate

fatal [fa'ta:l] *adj* disastrous; (*unangenehm*) unpleasant

fauchen ['fauxən] *intr* hiss; (*Person*) snarl; (*Katze*) spit

faul [faul] *adj* rotten; lazy; bad, nasty; (*verdächtig*) fishy; (*Ausrede, Witz*) lame, poor; (*sport*) foul ‖ **Faul** *n* (-s;-s) (sport) foul

Fäule ['fɔɪlə] *f* (-;) rot, decay

faulen ['faulən] *intr* rot, decay

faulenzen ['faulentsən] *intr* loaf

Faulenzer ['faulentsər] *m* (-s;-) loafer; (*Liegestuhl*) chaise longue; (*Linienblatt*) ruled sheet of paper

Faul′heit *f* (-;) laziness

faulig ['fauliç] *adj* rotten, putrid

Fäulnis ['fɔɪlnɪs] *f* (-;) rot; **in F. übergehen** begin to rot

Faul′pelz *m* (coll) loafer

Faust [faust] *f* (-;ⁱ⁻e) fist; **auf eigene F.** on one's own

faust′dick′ *adj* (coll) whopping

Faust′handschuh *m* mitten

Faust′kampf *m* boxing match

Fäustling ['fɔɪstlɪŋ] *m* (-[e]s;-e) mitten

Faust′schlag *m* punch, blow

Favorit –in [favo'ri:t(ɪn)] §7 *mf* favorite

Faxen ['faksən] *pl* antics; faces; **F. machen** fool around; make a fuss; **F. schneiden** make faces

Fazit ['fa:tsɪt] *n* (-s;-e & -s) result; **das F. ziehen** sum it up

Feber ['fe:bər] *m* (-[s];-) (Aust) February

Februar ['fe:bru·ar] *m* (-[s];-e) February

fechten ['fɛçtən] §74 *intr* fence; fight; (*betteln*) beg

Feder ['fe:dər] *f* (-;-n) feather; pen; quill; (mach) spring; **F. und Nut** (carp) tongue and groove

Fe′derball *m* shuttlecock

Fe′derballspiel *n* badminton

Fe′derbett *n* feather bed

Fe′derbusch *m* plume

Fe′derdecke *f* feather quilt

Federfuchser ['fe:dərfuksər] *m* (-s;-) scribbler; hack writer

fe′derführend *adj* in charge

Fe′dergewicht *n* featherweight division

Federgewichtler ['fe:dərgʋɪçtlər] *m* (-s;-) featherweight (boxer)

Fe′derhubtor *n* overhead door

Fe′derkernmatratze *f* innerspring mattress

Fe′derkiel *m* quill

Fe′derkraft *f* springiness; tension

Fe′derkrieg *m* paper war, war of words

fe′derleicht′ *adj* light as a feather

Fe′derlesen *n*—**ohne viel Federlesen(s)** without much ado

Fe′dermesser *n* penknife

federn ['fe:dərn] *tr* fit with springs ‖ *intr* be springy; (*Vogel*) moult; (gym) bounce

Fe′derring *m* lock washer

Fe′derstrich *m* stroke of the pen

Fe′derung *f* (-;) (aut) suspension

Fe′derzug *m* stroke of the pen

Fee [fe:] *f* (-;Feen ['fe·ən]) fairy

Feg(e)feuer ['fe:g(ə)fɔɪ·ər] *n* (-s;) purgatory

fegen ['fe:gən] *tr* sweep; (*Laub*) tear off ‖ *intr* (SEIN) tear along

Fehde ['fe:də] *f* (-;-n) feud

Feh′dehandschuh *m* gauntlet

fehl [fe:l] *adj*—**f. am Ort** out of place ‖ **Fehl** *m* (-[e]s;-e) blemish; fault

fehl– *comb.fm.* wide of the mark; mis-, incorrectly, wrongly ‖ **Fehl–** *comb. fm.* missing; vain, unsuccessful; incorrect, wrong; faulty; negative

Fehl′anzeige *f* negative report

Fehl′ball *m* (tennis) fault

fehlbar ['fe:lbar] *adj* fallible

Fehl′betrag *m* shortage, deficit

Fehl′bitte *f* vain request; **e–e F. tun** meet with a refusal

fehlen ['fe:lən] *tr* miss ‖ *intr* be absent; be missing; be lacking; fail, be unsuccessful; sin, err; (*dat*) miss, e.g., **er fehlt mir sehr** I miss him very much; (*dat*) lack, e.g., **ihm fehlt die Zeit** he lacks the time; **was fehlt Ihnen?** what's wrong with you? ‖ *impers*—**es fehlte nicht viel, und ich wäre gefallen** I came close to falling

Fehler ['fe:lər] *m* (-s;-) mistake, error; flaw, imperfection; blunder

feh′lerfrei *adj* faultless, flawless

feh′lerhaft *adj* faulty

feh′lerlos *adj* faultless, flawless

Fehl′geburt *f* miscarriage

fehl′gehen §82 *intr* (SEIN) go wrong; (*Schuß*) miss

Fehl′gewicht *n* short weight

fehl′greifen §88 *intr* miss one's hold; (fig) make a mistake

Fehl′griff *m* mistake, blunder

Fehl′leistung *f* (Freudian) slip

fehl′leiten *tr* (& fig) misdirect

Fehl′schlag *m* miss; failure, disappointment; (baseball) foul

Fehl′schluß *m* false inference; fallacy

Fehl′spruch *m* miscarriage of justice

Fehl′start *m* false start

Fehl′tritt *m* false step; (fig) slip

Fehl′wurf *m* (*beim Würfeln*) crap

fehl′zünden *intr* backfire

feien ['fai·ən] *tr*—**gefeit sein gegen** be immune to; **j–n f. gegen** make s.o. immune to

Feier ['fai·ər] *f* (-;-n) celebration; ceremony

Fei′erabend *m* closing time

fei′erlich *adj* solemn

Fei′erlichkeit *f* (-;-en) solemnity; **Feierlichkeiten** festivities; ceremonies

feiern ['fai·ərn] *tr* celebrate, observe; honor ‖ *intr* rest from work

Fei′erstunde *f* commemorative ceremony

Fei′ertag *m* holiday; holy day

feig [faik] *adj* cowardly

feig′herzig *adj* faint-hearted

feige ['faigə] *adj* cowardly ‖ **Feige** *f* (-;-n) fig

Feig′heit *f* (-;) cowardice

Feigling ['faiklɪŋ] *m* (-s;-e) coward

feil [fail] *adj* for sale

feil′bieten §58 *tr* offer for sale

Feile ['failə] *f* (-;-n) file

feilen [ˈfaɪlən] *tr* file
feilschen [ˈfaɪlʃən] *intr* (**um**) haggle (over), dicker (about)
Feilspäne [ˈfaɪlʃpɛnə] *pl* filings
fein [faɪn] *adj* fine; delicate; fancy
feind [faɪnt] *adj* hostile || **Feind** *m* (-[e]s;-e) enemy, foe
Feind– *comb.fm.* enemy, hostile; against the enemy
Feind'fahrt *f* (nav) operation against the enemy
Feind'flug *m* (aer) combat mission
Feindin [ˈfaɪndɪn] *f* (-;-nen) enemy
feind'lich *adj* hostile
Feind'schaft *f* (-;-en) enmity
feind'selig *adj* hostile
Feind'seligkeit *f* (-;-en) hostility, animosity; hostile action
fein'fühlend, fein'fühlig *adj* sensitive
Fein'gefühl *n* sensitivity
Fein'heit *f* (-;-en) fineness, fine quality; delicacy; subtlety
Fein'mechanik *f* precision engineering
Feinschmecker [ˈfaɪnˌmɛkər] *m* (-s;-) gourmet, epicure
fein'sinnig *adj* sensitive; subtle
feist [faɪst] *adj* fat, plump
Feld [fɛlt] *n* (-[e]s;-er) field; panel, compartment; (checkers, chess) square; **auf dem Felde** in the field(s); **auf freiem Felde** in the open; **aufs F. gehen** go to (work in) the fields; **das F. behaupten** stand one's ground; **ins F. ziehen** take the field
Feld'bau *m* agriculture
Feld'becher *m* collapsible drinking cup
Feld'bett *n* army cot; camping cot
Feld'blume *f* wild flower
Feld'bluse *f* army jacket
feld'dienstfähig *adj* fit for active duty
Feld'flasche *f* canteen
Feld'geistliche *m* (-n;-n) army chaplain
Feld'gendarm *m* military police
Feld'gendarmerie *f* military police
Feld'geschrei *n* battle cry
Feld'geschütz *n* field gun, field piece
Feld'herr *m* general; commander in chief
Feld'lager *n* bivouac, camp
Feld'lazarett *n* evacuation hospital
Feld'lerche *f* skylark
Feld'marschall *m* field marshal
feld'marschmäßig *adj* with full field pack
Feld'messer *m* surveyor
Feld'meßkunst *f* (-;) surveying
Feld'mütze *f* (mil) overseas cap
Feld'postamt *n* army post office
Feld'schlacht *f* battle
Feld'stecher *m* field glasses
Feldwebel [ˈfɛltvebəl] *m* (-s;-) sergeant
Feld'zeichen *n* ensign, standard
Feld'zug *m* campaign
Felge [ˈfɛlgə] *f* (-;-n) rim
Fell [fɛl] *n* (-[e]s;-e) pelt, skin; fur; **ein dickes F. haben** be thick-skinned
Fels [fɛls] *m* (-es & -en;-en) rock; cliff; **zackige Felsen** crags
Fels'block *m* boulder
Felsen [ˈfɛlzən] *m* (-s;-) rock; cliff
fel'senfest *adj* firm as a rock

Fel'sengebirge *n* Rocky Mountains
Fel'senklippe *f* cliff
Fel'senriff *n* reef
felsig [ˈfɛlzɪç] *adj* rocky
Fenster [ˈfɛnstar] *n* (-s;-) window
Fen'sterbrett *n* window sill
Fen'sterflügel *m* casement
Fen'sterladen *m* window shutter
Fen'sterleder *n* chamois
Fen'sterplatz *m* (rr) window seat
Fen'sterrahmen *m* window frame; sash
Fen'sterrosette *f* rose window
Fen'sterscheibe *f* windowpane
Ferien [ˈferjən] *pl* vacation; (parl) recess
Fe'rienreisende §5 *mf* vacationer
Fe'rienstimmung *f* holiday spirit
Ferkel [ˈferkəl] *n* (-s;-) piglet
Ferkelei [ferkəˈlaɪ] *f* (-;-en) obscenity
fern [fern] *adj* far, distant; (*entlegen*) remote; (*weit fort*) far away
Fern'amt *n* long-distance exchange
Fern'anruf *m* long-distance call
Fern'aufklärung *f* long-range reconnaissance
Fern'bedienung *f* remote control
fern'bleiben §62 *intr* (SEIN) (dat) stay away (from) || **Fernbleiben** *n* (-s;) absence; absenteeism
Fern'blick *m* distant view, vista
Ferne [ˈfernə] *f* (-;-n) distance
ferner [ˈfernər] *adj* remote, distant || *adv* further; moreover
Fern'fahrer *m* long-distance trucker
Fern'fahrt *f* long-distance trip
Fern'gang *m* (aut) overdrive
Fern'geschoß *n* long-range missile
Fern'geschütz *n* long-range gun
Fern'gespräch *n* long-distance call; toll call
Fern'glas *n* binoculars
fern'halten §90 *tr & ref* keep away
Fern'heizung *f* heating from a central heating plant
Fern'kursus *m* correspondence course
Fern'laster *m* long-distance truck
fern'lenken *tr* guide by remote control
Fern'lenkrakete *f* guided missile
Fern'lenkung *f* (-;-en) remote control
Fern'lenkwaffe *f* guided missile
Fern'licht *n* (aut) high beam
fern'liegen §108 *impers*—**es liegt mir fern zu** (*inf*) I'm far from (*ger*)
Fernmelde– [fernmɛldə] *comb.fm.* communications, signal
Fern'meldetruppen *pl* signal corps
Fern'meldewesen *n* telecommunications system
fern'mündlich *adj & adv* by telephone
Fern'objektiv *n* telephoto lens
Fernost– *comb.fm.* Far Eastern
fern'östlich *adj* Far Eastern
Fern'rohr *n* telescope
Fern'rohraufsatz *m* telescopic gun sight
Fern'ruf *m* telephone call; telephone number
Fern'schnellzug *m* long-distance express
Fern'schreiber *m* teletype, telex
Fernseh– [fernze] *comb.fm.* television
Fern'sehansager –in §6 *mf* television announcer
Fern'sehapparat *m* television set

Fern′sehbildröhre f picture tube
fern′sehen §138 intr watch television
|| **Fernsehen** n (-s;) television
Fern′seher m (-s;-) television set;
television viewer
Fern′sehgerät n television set
Fern′sehkanal m television channel
Fern′sehschau f television show
Fern′sehsendung f telecast
Fern′sehteilnehmer –in §6 mf tele-
viewer
Fern′sehübertragung f telecast
Fern′sicht f view, vista; panorama
fern′sichtig adj far-sighted
Fernsprech– [fɛrn′ʃprɛç] comb.fm. tele-
phone
Fern′sprechauftragsdienst m answering
service
Fern′sprechautomat m pay phone
Fern′sprecher m telephone
Fern′sprechzelle f telephone booth
fern′stehen §146 intr (dat) have no
personal contact (with); (dat) not be
close (to)
Fern′stehende §5 mf outsider; disinterested observer
fern′steuern tr guide by remote control
Fern′studium n correspondence course
Ferse [′fɛrzə] f (-;-n) heel
Fer′sengeld n—**F.** geben take to one's
heels
fertig [′fɛrtıç] adj finished; ready;
(kaputt) ruined, done for
fertig–, **Fertig–** comb.fm. final; finished; finishing; prefabricated
fer′tigbringen §65 tr finish, get done;
bring about; **es glatt f. zu** (inf) be
capable of (ger); **es nicht f., ihm das
zu sagen** not have the heart to tell
him that
fertigen [′fɛrtıgən] tr manufacture
Fer′tigkeit f (-;-en) skill
Fer′tigrasen m sod
fer′tigstellen tr complete; get ready
Fer′tigung f (-;-en) manufacture, production; copy, draft
Fes [fɛs] n (mus) F flat
fesch [fɛʃ] adj smart, chic
Fessel [′fɛsəl] f (-;-n) fetter, bond;
(anat) ankle; (vet) fetlock
Fes′selballon m captive balloon
fesseln [′fɛsəln] tr chain, tie; (bezaubern) captivate, arrest; (mil) contain;
ans Bett gefesselt confined to bed,
bedridden
fes′selnd adj fascinating, gripping;
(Personalität) magnetic
fest [fɛst] adj firm; solid; tight; stationary; steady; (Preis, Kost, Einkommen, Gehalt) fixed; (Schlaf)
sound; (mil) fortified; **feste Straße**
improved road || **Fest** n (-es;-e)
feast; festival
fest′backen intr (SEIN) cake (on)
fest′besoldet adj with a fixed salary
fest′binden §59 tr (an dat) tie (to)
Fest′essen n banquet
fest′fahren §71 tr run aground || ref
come to a standstill
fest′halten §90 tr hold on to || ref (an
dat) cling (to), hold on (to)
festigen [′fɛstıgən] tr strengthen; con-
solidate || ref grow stronger

Fe′stigkeit f (-;-en) firmness; steadi-
ness; strength
Fe′stigung f (-;) strengthening; con-
solidation; stabilization
Fest′land n continent
fest′legen tr fix, determine, set; (Anordnung) lay down; (fin, naut) tie
up; **j–n f. auf** (acc) pin s.o. down on
|| ref (auf acc) commit oneself (to)
fest′lich adj festive
Fest′lichkeit f (-;-en) festivity
fest′liegen §108 intr be stranded
fest′machen tr fix; (fig) settle || intr
(naut) moor
Fest′mahl n feast
Fest′nahme f (-;-n) arrest
fest′nehmen §116 tr arrest, apprehend
Fest′rede f ceremonial speech
Fest′saal m grand hall, banquet hall
fest′schnallen tr buckle up || ref fasten
one's seat belt
Fest′schrift f homage volume
fest′setzen tr fix, set || ref settle down
(in a town, etc.)
fest′sitzen intr fit tight; be stuck
Fest′spiel n play for a festive occasion;
Festspiele (mus, theat) festival
fest′stehen §146 intr stand firm; (Tat-
sache) be certain || impers—**es steht
fest** it is a fact
fest′stehend adj stationary; (Achse)
fixed; (Tatsache) established
feststellbar [′fɛst′tɛlbar] adj ascertainable
Fest′stellbremse f hand brake
fest′stellen tr ascertain; (unbeweglich
machen) lock, secure; (Tatbestand)
find out, establish; (angeben) state;
(Schaden) assess; (Kurs) (fin) set, fix
Fest′stellschraube f set screw
Fest′tag m feastday; holiday
Fe′stung f (-;-en) fortress
Fe′stungsgraben m moat
Fest′wagen m float
Fest′wert m standard value; (math,
phys) constant
Fest′wiese f fairground
fest′ziehen §163 tr pull tight
Fest′zug m procession
Fetisch [′fetıʃ] m (-[e]s;-e) fetish
fett [fɛt] adj fat; (Boden, Milch, Ge-
misch) rich; (Zeiten, Leben) of
plenty || **Fett** n (-[e]s;-e) fat;
(Schmalz) lard; (Pflanzen-) shorten-
ing; (Schmier-) grease
Fett′auge n speck of fat
Fett′druck m boldface type
fetten [′fɛtən] tr grease, lubricate
Fett′fleck m grease spot
fettig [′fɛtıç] adj fatty, greasy, oily
Fett′kloß m (coll) fatso
Fett′kohle f bituminous coal
fettleibig [′fɛtlaıbıç] adj stout
Fettnäpfchen [′fɛtnɛpfçən] n—**bei j–m
ins F. treten** hurt s.o.'s feelings; **ins
F. treten** put one's foot in it
Fett′presse f (aut) grease gun
Fett′spritze f (aut) grease gun
Fett′sucht f obesity
Fett′wanst m (sl) fatso
Fetzen [′fɛtsən] m (-s;-) rag; bit,
scrap; (Aust) dishcloth; **daß die F.
fliegen** violently
feucht [fɔıçt] adj moist, damp, humid

feuchten ['fɔɪçtən] tr moisten, dampen
Feuch'tigkeit f (-;) moisture, damp-
  ness, humidity
feudal [fɔɪ'dɑl] adj feudal; (fig) mag-
  nificent
Feudalismus [fɔɪdɑ'lɪsmʊs] m (-;)
  feudalism
Feuer ['fɔɪ-ər] n (-s;-) fire
Feu'eralarm m fire alarm
Feu'eralarmübung f fire drill
feu'erbeständig adj fireproof
Feu'erbestattung f cremation
Feu'erbrand m firebrand
Feu'ereifer m enthusiasm, zeal
Feu'ereinstellung f cease-fire
feu'erfest adj fireproof
Feu'erfliege f firefly
feu'erflüssig adj molten
feu'ergefährlich adj inflammable
Feu'erhahn m hydrant, fireplug
Feu'erhaken m poker
Feu'erherd m fireplace
Feu'erkampf m fire fight, gun battle
Feu'erkraft f (mil) fire power
Feu'erleiter f fire ladder; (Nottreppe)
  fire escape
Feu'erlinie f firing line
Feu'erlöscher m fire extinguisher
Feu'ermelder m fire alarm
Feu'ermeldung f fire alarm
feuern ['fɔɪ-ərn] tr fire; (coll) fire,
  sack || intr fire, shoot
Feu'erprobe f ordeal by fire; acid test
Feu'ersalve f fusillade
Feu'erschneise f firebreak
Feu'erspritze f fire engine
Feu'erstein m flint
Feu'ertaufe f baptism of fire
Feu'erversicherung f fire insurance
Feu'erwache f firehouse
Feu'erwalze f (mil) creeping barrage
Feu'erwehr f fire department
Feu'erwehrmann m (-[e]s;-er &
  -leute) fireman
Feu'erwerk n fireworks
Feu'erwerkskörper m firecracker
Feu'erzange f fire tongs
Feu'erzeug n cigarette lighter
Feu'erzeugbenzin n lighter fluid
feurig ['fɔɪrɪç] adj fiery; ardent
Fiasko [fɪ'asko] n (-s;-s) fiasco
Fibel ['fibəl] f (-;-n) primer; (archeol)
  fibula
Fiber ['fibər] f (-;-n) fiber
Fichte ['fɪçtə] f (-;-n) spruce; pine
Fich'tennadel f pine needle
fidel [fɪ'del] adj jolly, cheerful
Fieber ['fibər] n (-s;-) fever; das F.
  messen take the temperature
fie'berhaft adj feverish
fieberig ['fibərɪç] adj feverish
fie'berkrank adj running a fever
fiebern ['fibərn] intr be feverish
Fie'berphantasie f delirium
Fie'bertabelle f temperature chart
Fiedel ['fidəl] f (-;-n) fiddle
Fie'delbogen m fiddlestick
fiel [fil] pret of fallen
Figur [fɪ'gur] f (-;-en) figure; (cards)
  face card
figürlich [fɪ'gyrlɪç] adj figurative
fiktiv [fɪk'tif] adj fictitious
Filet [fɪ'le] n (-s;-s) (culin) fillet

Filiale [fɪl'jɑlə] f (-;-n) branch
Filia'lengeschäft n chain store
Filigran [fɪlɪ'grɑn] n (-s;-e), Fili-
  gran'arbeit f filigree
Film [fɪlm] m (-s;-e) film; (cin) movie
Film'atelier n motion-picture studio
Film'empfindlichkeit f film speed
Film'kulisse f (cin) movie set
Film'leinwand f movie screen
Film'probe f screen test
Film'regisseur m (cin) director
Film'wesen n motion-picture industry
Filter ['fɪltər] m & n (-s;-) filter
Fil'teranlage f filtration plant
Fil'terkaffee m drip-grind coffee
Fil'termundstück n filter tip
filtern ['fɪltərn] tr filter, strain
filtrieren [fɪl'trirən] tr filter
Filz [fɪlts] m (-es;-e) felt; (coll)
  miser, skinflint
Filz'schreiber m felt pen
Fimmel ['fɪməl] m (-s;-) craze, fad
-fimmel m comb.fm. mania for
Finanz [fɪ'nants] f (-;-en) finance
Finanz- comb.fm. financial, fiscal
Finanz'amt n internal revenue service
Finanz'ausschuß m (adm) ways and
  means committee
Finanzen [fɪ'nantsən] pl finances
finanziell [fɪnan'tsjel] adj financial
finanzieren [fɪnan'tsirən] tr finance
Finanz'minister m secretary of the
  treasury
Finanz'ministerium n treasury department
Finanz'wesen n finances
Finanz'wirtschaft f public finances
Findelkind ['fɪndəlkɪnt] n foundling
finden ['fɪndən] §59 tr find; f. Sie
  nicht? don't you think so? || ref be
  found; ach, das wird sich schon f.
  oh, we'll see about that; es fanden
  sich there were; es findet sich it
  happens, it turns out; sich f. in (acc)
  resign oneself to; sie haben sich ge-
  funden they were united || intr find
  one's way
findig ['fɪndɪç] adj resourceful
Findling ['fɪntlɪŋ] m (-s;-e) foundling;
  (geol) boulder
fing [fɪŋ] pret of fangen
Finger ['fɪŋər] m (-s;-) finger
Fin'gerabdruck m fingerprint
fin'gerfertig adj deft
Fin'gerhut m thimble; (bot) foxglove
fingern ['fɪŋərn] tr finger
Fin'gerspitze f finger tip; bis in die
  Fingerspitzen through and through
Fin'gerspitzengefühl n sensitivity
Fin'gersprache f sign language
Fingerzeig ['fɪŋərtsaɪk] m (-s;-e) hint
fingieren [fɪŋ'girən] tr feign
fingiert [fɪŋ'girt] adj fictitious
Fink [fɪŋk] m (-en;-en) finch
Finne ['fɪnə] m (-n;-n) Finn || f (-;
  -n) fin; (Ausschlag) pimple
Fin'nenausschlag m acne
Finnin ['fɪnɪn] f (-;-nen) Finn
finnisch ['fɪnɪʃ] adj Finnish
Finnland ['fɪnlant] n (-s;) Finland
finster ['fɪnstər] adj dark; gloomy
Finsternis ['fɪnstərnɪs] f (-;) dark-
  ness; gloom

Finte ['fɪntə] *f* (-;-n) feint; trick

Firlefanz ['fɪrləfants] *m* (-es;) junk; F. treiben fool around

Fir·ma ['fɪrma] *f* (-;-men [mən]) firm

Firmament [fɪrma'mɛnt] *n* (-[e]s;-e) firmament

firmen ['fɪrmən] *tr* (Cath) confirm

Fir'menschild *n* (com) name plate

Fir'menwert *m* (com) good will

Firmling ['fɪrmlɪŋ] *m* (-s;-e) (Cath) person to be confirmed

Fir'mung *f* (-;-en) (Cath) confirmation

Fir·nis ['fɪrnɪs] *m* (-ses;-se) varnish; mit F. streichen varnish

firnissen ['fɪrnɪsən] *tr* varnish

First [fɪrst] *m* (-es;-e) (archit) ridge (of roof); (poet) mountain ridge

Fis [fɪs] *n* (-;-) (mus) F sharp

Fisch [fɪʃ] *m* (-es;-e) fish

fischen ['fɪʃən] *tr* fish for, catch ‖ *intr* (nach) fish (for)

Fi'scher *m* (-s;-) fisherman

Fischerei [fɪʃə'raɪ] *f* (-;-en) fishing; fishery; fishing trade

Fi'schergerät *n* fishing tackle

Fisch'fang *m* catch, haul

Fisch'gräte *f* fishbone

Fisch'grätenmuster *n* (tex) herringbone

Fisch'händler –in §6 *mf* fishmonger

fischig ['fɪʃɪç] *adj* fishy

Fisch'kunde *f* ichthyology

Fisch'laich *m* spawn, fish eggs

Fisch'otter *m & f* otter

Fisch'rogen *m* roe

Fisch'schuppe *f* scale (of a fish)

Fisch'zug *m* (& fig) catch

fiskalisch [fɪs'kalɪʃ] *adj* fiscal

Fis·kus ['fɪskʊs] *m* (-;-kusse & -ken [kən]) treasury

Fistelstimme ['fɪstəl͜ʃtɪmə] *f* falsetto

Fittich ['fɪtɪç] *m* (-es;-e) (poet) wing

fix [fɪks] *adj* (Idee, Preis) fixed; (flink) smart, sharp; fix und fertig all set; all in; done for; fix und fertig mit through with; mach fix! make it snappy!

fixen ['fɪksən] *intr* sell short

fixieren [fɪ'ksirən] *tr* fix, decide upon; stare fixedly at; (phot) fix

Fixier'mittel *n* (phot) fixer

flach [flax] *adj* flat, level; shallow; (Relief) low; (fig) dull

Fläche ['flɛçə] *f* (-;-n) surface; plain; expanse; facet; (geom) area

Flä'cheninhalt *m* (geom) area

Flä'chenraum *m* surface area

flach'fallen §72 *intr* (SEIN) (coll) fall flat, flop

Flach'heit *f* (-;) flatness; shallowness

Flach'land *n* lowland

Flach'relief *n* low relief, bas-relief

Flach'rennen *n* flat racing

Flachs [flaks] *m* (-es;-e) flax

flachsen ['flaksən] *intr* (coll) kid

flächse(r)n ['flɛksə(r)n] *adj* flaxen

Flach'zange *f* pliers

flackern ['flakərn] *intr* flicker; (Stimme) quaver, shake

Flagge ['flagə] *f* (-;-n) flag (esp. for signaling or identification)

Flag'genmast *m* flagpole

Flag'genstange *f* flagstaff

Flagg'schiff *n* flagship

Flak [flak] *abbr* (Flugzeugabwehrkanone) anti-aircraft gun

Flak'feuer *n* flak

Flakon [fla'kõ] *m & n* (-s;-s) perfume bottle

Flamme ['flamə] *f* (-;-n) flame

flammen ['flamən] *intr* blaze; be in flames

flam'mend *adj* passionate

Fla'mmenwerfer *m* flame thrower

Flandern ['flandərn] *n* (-s;) Flanders

flandrisch ['flandrɪʃ] *adj* Flemish

Flanell [fla'nɛl] *m* (-s;-e) flannel

Flanke ['flaŋkə] *f* (-;-n) flank

Flan'kenfeuer *n* (mil) enfilade; mit F. bestreichen enfilade

flankieren [flaŋ'kirən] *tr* flank

Flansch [flanʃ] *m* (-es;-e) flange

Flasche ['flaʃə] *f* (-;-n) bottle; (coll) flop; (mach) pulley

Fla'schengranate *f* Molotov cocktail

Fla'schenzug *m* block and tackle; (coll) pulley

Flaschner ['flaʃnər] *m* (-s;-) plumber

flatterhaft ['flatərhaft] *adj* fickle

flattern ['flatərn] *intr* flutter, flap

flau [flaʊ] *adj* stale; (schwach) feeble, faint; (fade) dull, lifeless; (com) slack; (phot) overexposed; mir ist f. (im Magen) I feel queezy

Flaum [flaʊm] *m* (-[e]s;) down; (am Gesicht, am Pfirsich) fuzz

flaumig ['flaʊmɪç] *adj* downy, fluffy

Flause ['flaʊzə] *f* (-;-n) fib; Flausen funny ideas, nonsense

Flaute ['flaʊtə] *f* (-;-n) (com) slack period; (naut) dead calm

fläzen ['flɛtsən] *ref* sprawl out

Flechse ['flɛksə] *f* (-;-n) (dial) sinew, tendon

Flechte ['flɛçtə] *f* (-;-n) plait; (bot) lichen; (pathol) ringworm

flechten ['flɛçtən] §74 *tr* braid, plait; (Körbe) weave

Fleck [flɛk] *m* (-[e]s;-e & -en) spot; blemish; (Flicken, Landstück) patch

Flecken ['flɛkən] *m* (-s;-) spot; piece of land; (Markt-) market town

fleckenlos (flɛk/kenlos) *adj* spotless

Fleck'fieber *n* spotted fever

fleckig ['flɛkɪç] *adj* spotty; splotchy

Fledermaus ['fledərmaʊs] *f* bat

Flegel ['flegəl] *m* (-s;-) flail; (coll) lout, boor

Flegelei [flegə'laɪ] *f* (-;) rudeness

fle'gelhaft *adj* uncouth, boorish

Fle'geljahre *pl* awkward age

flehen ['fle·ən] *intr* plea; zu j-m f. implore s.o. ‖ Flehen *n* (-s;-) supplication

Fleisch [flaɪʃ] *n* (-es;) flesh; meat; sich ins eigene F. schneiden cut one's own throat; wildes F. proud flesh

Fleisch'bank *f* (-;⁻e) meat counter

Fleisch'beil *n* cleaver

Fleisch'beschau *f* meat inspection

Fleisch'brühe *f* broth

Flei'scher *m* (-s;-) butcher

Flei'scheslust *f* (-;) lust

Fleisch'farbe *f* flesh color

fleisch'fressend *adj* carnivorous

Fleisch'hacker (-s;-) *m*, Fleisch'hauer *m* (-s;-) butcher

fleischig ['flaɪʃɪç] *adj* fleshy; meaty

fleisch'lich *adj* carnal

Fleisch'markt *m* meat market

Fleisch'pastete *f* meat pie

Fleisch'saft *m* meat juice, gravy

Fleisch'salat *m* diced-meat salad

Fleisch'speise *f* meat course

Fleisch'spieß *m* skewer

Fleischwerdung ['flaɪʃverduŋ] *f* (-;) incarnation

Fleisch'wolf *m* meat grinder

Fleisch'wunde *f* flesh wound, laceration

Fleisch'wurst *f* pork sausage

Fleiß [flaɪs] *m* (-es;) diligence, industry; mit F. intentionally

fleißig ['flaɪsɪç] *adj* diligent, hard-working

flektieren [flɛk'tirən] *tr* inflect

fletschen ['flɛtʃən] *tr* bare (*teeth*)

Flexion [flɛk'sjon] *f* (-;-en) (gram) inflection

flicken ['flɪkən] *tr* patch, repair || Flicken *m* (-s;-) patch

Flick'schuster *m* cobbler

Flick'werk *n* patchwork; hotchpotch; (*Pfuscherei*) bungling job

Flick'zeug *n* repair kit

Flieder ['flidər] *m* (-s;-) lilac

Fliege ['fligə] *f* (-;-n) fly; (coll) bow tie

fliegen ['fligən] §57 *tr* fly, pilot || *intr* (SEIN) fly; (coll) get sacked; in die Luft f. blow up

Flie'genfenster *n* window screen

Flie'gengewicht *n* flyweight division

Fliegengewichtler ['fligəngəvɪçtlər] *m* (-s;-) flyweight (boxer)

Flie'gengitter *n* screen

Flie'genklappe *f*, Flie'genklatsche *f* fly swatter

Flie'genpilz *m* toadstool

Flie'ger *m* (-s;-) flyer

Flieger- *comb.fm.* air-force; air, aerial; flying; airman's

Flie'gerabwehr *f* anti-aircraft defense

Flie'geralarm *m* air-raid alarm

Flie'gerangriff *m* air raid

Flie'gerheld *m* (aer) ace

Flie'gerhorst *m* air base

Flie'gerin *f* (-;-nen) flyer

Flie'gerschaden *m* air-raid damage

fliehen ['fli·ən] §75 *tr* run away from; avoid || *intr* (SEIN) flee

Flieh'kraft *f* (-;) centrifugal force

Fliese ['flizə] *f* (-;-n) tile

Flie'senleger *m* tiler, tile man

Fließband ['flisbant] *n* (-[e]s;-er) assembly line

fließen ['flisən] §76 *intr* (SEIN) flow

flie'ßend *adj* (*Wasser*) running; (fig) fluent

Fließheck ['flishɛk] *n* (aut) fastback

Fließpapier ['flispapir] *n* blotting paper

flimmern ['flɪmərn] *intr* glimmer; glisten, shimmer; flicker

flink [flɪŋk] *adj* nimble, quick; mach mal f.! get a move on!

Flinte ['flɪntə] *f* (-;-n) shotgun; gun

Flin'tenlauf *m* gun barrel

flirren ['flɪrən] *intr* shimmer

Flirt [flɪrt] *m* (-s;-s) flirtation; boy-friend, girlfriend

flirten ['flɪrtən] *intr* flirt

Flitter ['flɪtər] *m* (-s;-) sequins; (*Scheinglanz*) flashiness

Flit'terglanz *m* flashiness

Flit'tergold *n* gold tinsel

Flit'terkram *m* trinkets

Flit'terstaat *m* flashy clothes

Flit'terwochen *pl* honeymoon

flitzen ['flɪtsən] *intr* (SEIN) flit

flocht [flɔxt] *pret* of flechten

Flocke ['flɔkə] *f* (-;-n) flake; tuft

flog [flok] *pret* of fliegen

floh [flo] *pret* of fliehen || Floh *m* (-s;-e) flea; j-m e-n F. ins Ohr setzen put a bug in s.o.'s ear

Floh'hüpfspiel *n* tiddlywinks

Flor [flor] *m* (-s;-e) bloom || *m* (-s;-e & -e) gauze; (tex) nap, pile

Flor'band *n* (-[e]s;-e) crepe; mourning band

Florett [flo'rɛt] *n* (-s;-e) foil

florieren [flo'rirən] *intr* flourish

Floskel ['flɔskəl] *f* (-;-n) rhetorical ornament, flowery phrase

Floß [flos] *n* (-es;-e) raft

Flosse ['flɔsə] *f* (-;-n) fin; (aer) stabilizer

flößen ['fløsən] *tr* float

Flöte ['fløtə] *f* (-;-n) flute; (cards) flush

flöten ['fløtən] *tr* play on the flute || *intr* play the flute; f. gehen (fig) go to the dogs

flott [flɔt] *adj* afloat; brisk, lively; gay; chic, dashing

Flotte ['flɔtə] *f* (-;-n) fleet

Flot'tenstützpunkt *m* naval base

flott'gehend *adj* (com) brisk, lively

Flottille [flo'tɪljə] *f* (-;-n) flotilla

flott'machen *tr* set afloat; (fig) get going again

Flöz [fløts] *n* (-es;-e) (min) seam

Fluch [flux] *m* (-[e]s;-e) curse

fluchen ['fluxən] *intr* curse

Flucht [fluxt] *f* (-;-en) flight; escape; straight line, alignment; (*Häuser-*) row; (*Spielraum*) space, leeway; (*Zimmer-*) suite; außerhalb der F. out of line; in die F. schlagen put to flight

flüchten ['flʏçtən] *ref* (an *acc*, in *acc*) take refuge (in), have recourse (to) || *intr* (SEIN) flee; escape; (vor *dat*) run away (from)

flüchtig ['flʏçtɪç] *adj* fugitive; fleeting; cursory, superficial; hurried; (chem) volatile; f. sein be on the run; f. werden escape, flee

Flüch'tigkeitsfehler *m* oversight, slip

Flüchtling ['flʏçtlɪŋ] *m* (-s;-) fugitive; refugee

Flücht'lingslager *n* refugee camp

Flug [fluk] *m* (-[e]s;-e) flight

Flug'abwehr *f* anti-aircraft defense

Flugabwehr- *comb.fm.* anti-aircraft

Flug'anschluß *m* plane connection

Flug'aufgabe *f*, Flug'auftrag *m* (aer) mission

Flug'bahn *f* line of flight; trajectory

Flug'blatt *n* leaflet, flyer

Flügel ['flyːɡəl] *m* (-s;-) wing; (*e-r Doppeltür*) leaf; (*mus*) grand piano
Flü'geladjutant *m* aide-de-camp
Flü'gelfenster *n* casement window
Flü'gelmutter *f* wing nut
Flü'gelschlag *m* flap of the wings
Flü'gelschraube *f* thumb screw
Flü'gelschraubenmutter *f* wing nut
Flü'geltür *f* folding door
Flug'gast *m* (aer) passenger
flügge ['flyːɡə] *adj* (*Vogel*) fledged; (fig) ready to go on one's own
Flug'gesellschaft *f* airline company
Flug'hafen *m* airport
Flug'hafenbefeuerung *f* airport lights
Flug'kapitän *m* captain, pilot
Flug'karte *f* plane ticket; aeronautical chart
flug'klar *adj* ready for take-off
Flug'körper *m* missile; space vehicle
Flug'leitung *f* air-traffic control
Flug'linie *f* air route; airline
Flug'meldesystem *n* air-raid warning system
Flug'motor *m* aircraft engine
Flug'ortung *f* (aer) navigation
Flug'plan *m* flight schedule
Flug'platz *m* airfield, airport
Flug'post *f* air mail
Flug'preis *m* air fare
flugs [fluks] *adv* quickly; at once
Flug'schein *m* plane ticket
Flug'schneise *f* air lane
Flug'schrift *f* pamphlet
Flug'strecke *f* flying distance
Flug'stützpunkt *m* air base
flug'tauglich, **flug'tüchtig** *adj* airworthy
Flug'techniker –in §6 *mf* aeronautical engineer
Flug'verbot *n* (aer) grounding
Flug'verkehr *m* air traffic
Flug'wesen *n* aviation; aeronautics
Flug'wetter *n* flying weather
Flug'zeug *n* airplane, aircraft
Flug'zeugabwehrgeschütz *n*, **Flug'zeugabwehrkanone** *f* anti-aircraft gun
Flug'zeugführer *m* pilot; **zweiter F.** co-pilot, second officer
Flug'zeugführerschein *m* pilot's license
Flug'zeuggeschwader *n* wing (*consisting of 3 squadrons of 9 planes each*)
Flug'zeugkreuzer *m*, **Flug'zeugmutterschiff** *n* seaplane tender, seaplane carrier
Flug'zeugrumpf *m* fuselage
Flug'zeugstaffel *f* squadron (*consisting of 9 planes*)
Flug'zeugträger *m* aircraft carrier
Flug'zeugwerk *n* aircraft factory
Flunder ['flundər] *f* (-;-n) flounder
Flunkerer ['fluŋkərər] *m* (-s;-) fibber
flunkern ['fluŋkərn] *intr* fib
Flunsch [fluny] *m* (-es;-e) face; **e-n F. ziehen** (*od* **machen**) make a face
Fluor ['fluːər] *n* (-s;) fluorine
Fluoreszenz [fluːɔresˈtsɛnts] *f* (-;) fluorescence; fluorescent light
Fluorid [fluːɔˈriːt] *n* (-[e]s;-e) fluoride
Flur [fluːr] *m* (-[e]s;-e) entrance hall; hallway || *f* (-;-en) open farmland; meadow; community farmland

Flur'garderobe *f* hallway closet
Fluß [flus] *m* (**Flusses**; **Flüsse**) river; flow; (metal) fusion; (phys) flux
flußab'wärts *adv* downstream
flußauf'wärts *adv* upstream
Fluß'bett *n* riverbed, channel
Flüßchen ['flysçən] *n* (-s;-) rivulet
flüssig ['flysɪç] *adj* liquid; fluid; (*Gelder*) ready; **f. machen** convert into cash || *adv* fluently
Flüs'sigkeit *f* (-;-en) liquid, fluid; (fig) fluency; (fin) liquidity
Flüs'sigkeitsmaß *n* liquid measure
Fluß'pferd *n* hypopotamus
flüstern ['flystərn] *tr* & *intr* whisper
Flü'sterparole *f* rumor
Flut [fluːt] *f* (-;-en) flood; waters; high tide
fluten ['fluːtən] *tr* flood || *intr* (SEIN) flow, pour
Flut'grenze *f* high-water mark
Flut'licht *n* floodlight
Flut'linie *f* high-water mark
Flut'wasser *n* tidewater
Flut'welle *f* tidal wave
Flut'zeit *f* flood tide, high tide
focht [fɔxt] *pret of* **fechten**
Focksegel ['fɔkzeːɡəl] *n* (-s;-) foresail
fohlen ['foːlən] *intr* foal || **Fohlen** *n* (-s;-) foal
Folge ['fɔlɡə] *f* (-;-n) sequence; consequence; succession; series; (*e-s Romans*) continuation; (*e-r Zeitschrift*) number; **die Folgen tragen** take the consequences; **in der F.** subsequently
folgen ['fɔlɡən] *intr* (*dat*) obey || *intr* (SEIN) (*dat*) follow; (*dat*) succeed; (*aus*) ensue (from)
folgendermaßen ['fɔlɡəndərmaːsən] *adv* in the following manner, as follows
folgenschwer *adj* momentous, grave
folgerichtig *adj* logical, consistent
folgern ['fɔlɡərn] *tr* infer, conclude
Fol'gerung *f* (-;-en) inference, conclusion
Fol'gesatz *m* (gram) result clause
folgewidrig *adj* inconsistent
Fol'gezeit *f* —**in der F.** in subsequent times
folglich ['fɔlklɪç] *adv* consequently
folgsam ['fɔlkzaːm] *adj* obedient
Foliant [folˈjant] *m* (-en;-en) folio
Folie ['foːljə] *f* (-;-n) (metal) foil
Folter ['fɔltər] *f* (-;-n) torture; rack; **auf die F. spannen** put to the rack; (fig) keep in suspense
Fol'terbank *f* (-;⁻e) rack
foltern ['fɔltərn] *tr* torture
Fol'terqual *f* torture
Fol'terverhör *n* third degree
Fön [føn] *m* (-[e]s;-e) hand hairdryer
Fond [fõ] *m* (-s;-s) background; rear, back; (culin) gravy
Fonds [fõ] *m* (-s [fõs];-s [fõs]) fund
Fontäne [fɔnˈtɛːnə] *f* (-;-n) fountain
foppen ['fɔpən] *tr* tease; bamboozle
Fopperei [fɔpəˈraɪ] *f* (-;-en) teasing
forcieren [fɔrˈsiːrən] *tr* force; speed up
Förderband ['fœdərbant] *n* (-;⁻er) conveyor belt

För'derer *m* (-s;-) promoter; patron

för'derlich *adj* useful; (*dat*) conducive (to)

fordern ['fɔrdərn] *tr* demand; (*Recht*) claim; (*zum Zweikampf*) challenge; (*vor Gericht*) summon

fördern ['fœrdərn] *tr* promote, back; (*Kohle*) produce; **förderndes Mitglied** social member; **zutage f.** bring to light

For'derung *f* (-;-en) demand, claim; debt; (*zum Zweikampf*) challenge

För'derung *f* (-;-en) promotion; support; encouragement; (min) output

Forelle [fo'rɛlə] *f* (-;-n) trout

Forke ['fɔrkə] *f* (-;-n) pitchfork

Form [fɔrm] *f* (-;-en) form; shape; mold; condition; (gram) voice; **die F. wahren** keep up appearances

formal [fɔr'mɑl] *adj* formal

Formalität [fɔrmalɪ'tɛt] *f* (-;-en) formality

Format [fɔr'mɑt] *n* (-[e]s;-e) size, format; distinction, stature

Formel ['fɔrməl] *f* (-;-n) formula

for'melhaft *adj* (*Wendung, Gebet*) set

formell [fɔr'mɛl] *adj* formal

formen ['fɔrmən] *tr* form, shape, mold

For'menlehre *f* morphology

Form'fehler *m* defect; flaw; (jur) irregularity

formieren [fɔr'mirən] *tr & ref* line up

-förmig [fœrmɪç] *comb.fm.* -shaped

förmlich ['fœrmlɪç] *adj* formal ‖ *adv* virtually; literally; formally

form'los *adj* shapeless; informal; unconventional; rude; (chem) amorphous

form'schön *adj* well-shaped, beautiful

Formular [fɔrmu'lɑr] *n* (-s;-e) form, blank

formulieren [fɔrmu'lirən] *tr* formulate; word, phrase

Formulie'rung *f* (-;-en) formulation; wording

form'vollendet *adj* perfectly shaped

forsch [fɔrʃ] *adj* dashing ‖ *adv* briskly

forschen ['fɔrʃən] *intr* do research; (nach) search (for)

For'scher -in §6 *mf* researcher; scholar; explorer

For'schung *f* (-;-en) research

For'schungsanstalt *f* research center

Forst [fɔrst] *m* (-[e]s;-e) forest

Förster ['fœrstər] *m* (-s;-) forester; forest ranger

Forst'fach *n* forestry

Forst'mann *m* (-es;-leute) forester

Forst'revier *n* forest range

Forst'wesen *n*, Forst'wirtschaft *f* forestry

fort [fɔrt] *adv* away; gone, lost; (*weiter*) on; (*vorwärts*) forward; **ich muß f.** I must be off; **in e-m f.** continuously; **und so f.** and so forth ‖ Fort [fɔr] *n* (-s;-s) (mil) fort

fortan' *adv* from now on, henceforth

Fort'bestand *m* continued existence

fort'bestehen §146 *intr* continue

fort'bewegen §56 *tr* move along ‖ *ref* get about

fort'bilden *ref* continue one's studies

Fort'bildung *f* continuing education

fort'bleiben §62 *intr* (SEIN) stay away

Fort'dauer *f* continuance

fort'dauern *intr* continue; last

fort'fahren §71 *tr* hawl away; continue (*to say*); f. zu (*inf*) continue to (*inf*), go on (*ger*) ‖ *intr* continue, go on ‖ *intr* (SEIN) drive off, leave

Fort'fall *m* omission; discontinuation; **in F. kommen** be discontinued

fort'fallen §72 *intr* (SEIN) drop out; be omitted; be discontinued

fort'führen *tr* lead away; continue; (*Geschäft*) carry on; (*Linie*) extend

Fort'gang *m* departure; continuation; progress

fort'gehen §82 *intr* (SEIN) go away

fort'geschritten *adj* advanced; late

fort'gesetzt *adj* incessant

fort'kommen §99 *intr* (SEIN) go on, make progress; get away; **in der Welt f.** get ahead in the world ‖ Fortkommen *n* (-s;) progress

fort'lassen §104 *tr* allow to go; omit

fort'laufen §105 *intr* (SEIN) run away

fort'laufend *adj* continuing; (*Nummer*) consecutive

fort'leben *intr* live on

fort'pflanzen *tr* propagate; spread ‖ *ref* reproduce; propagate; spread

Fort'pflanzung *f* (-;) propagation

fort'reißen §53 *tr* tear away; **j-n mit sich f.** sweep s.o. off his feet; **sich f. lassen** be caried away

fort'schaffen *tr* remove

fort'scheren *ref* (coll) scram

fort'schreiten §86 *intr* (SEIN) progress, advance

Fort'schritt *m* progress; improvement

fort'schrittlich *adj* progressive

fort'setzen *tr* continue; resume

Fort'setzung *f* (-;-en) continuation; sequel; installment; **F. folgt** to be continued

fort'während *adj* continual; lasting, permanent ‖ *adv* all the time, always

Fossil [fɔ'sil] *n* (-s;-len [jən]) fossil

foul [faul] *adj* foul, dirty ‖ Foul *n* (-s;-) (sport) foul; **ein F. begehen an** (*dat*) commit a foul against

foulen ['faulən] *tr* (sport) foul

Foyer [fwa'je] *n* (-s;-s) foyer; (*im Hotel*) lobby

Fracht [fraxt] *f* (-;-en) freight, cargo

Fracht'brief *m* bill of lading

Frachter ['fraxtər] *m* (-s;-) freighter

Fracht'gut *n* freight, goods

Fracht'raum *m* cargo compartment; cargo capacity

Fracht'stück *n* package

Frack [frak] *m* (-[e]s;⸚e & -s) tails

Frack'schoß *m* coattail

Frage ['frɑgə] *f* (-;-n) question; **außer F. stehen** be out of the question; **e-e F. stellen** ask a question; **in F. stellen** call in question; **kommt nicht in F.!** nothing doing!

Fra'gebogen *m* questionnaire

fragen ['frɑgən] *tr* ask; **j-n f. nach** ask s.o. about; **j-n nach der Zeit f.** ask s.o. the time; **j-n f. um** ask s.o. for ‖ *ref* wonder ‖ *impers ref*—**es fragt sich, ob** the question is whether ‖ *intr* ask

Fra'gesatz *m* interrogative sentence; **abhängiger F.** indirect question

Fragesteller ['frogə/tɛlər] *m* (-s;-) questioner

Fra'gewort *n* (-es;⁼er) interrogative

Fra'gezeichen *n* question mark

fraglich ['fraklıç] *adj* questionable

fraglos ['fraklos] *adv* unquestionably

Fragment [frag'ment] *n* (-[e]s;-e) fragment

frag'würdig *adj* questionable

Fraktion [frak'tsjon] *f* (-;-en) (chem) fraction; (pol) faction

fraktionell [fraktsjo'nel] *adj* factional

Fraktur [frak'tur] *f* (-;-en) fracture; Gothic type, Gothic lettering; **mit j-m F. reden** talk turkey with s.o.

frank [fraŋk] *adv*—**f. und frei** quite frankly

Franke ['fraŋkə] *m* (-n;-n) Franconian; (hist) Frank

Franken ['fraŋkən] *m* (-[e]s;-) (Swiss) franc || *n* (-s;) Franconia

frankieren [fraŋ'kirən] *tr* frank, put postage on

Fränkin ['freŋkın] *f* (-;-nen) Frank

franko ['fraŋko] *adv* postage paid; **f. Berlin** freight paid to Berlin; **f. verzollt** free of freight and duty

Frank'reich *n* (-s;) France

Franse ['franzə] *f* (-;-n) fringe

fransen ['franzən] *intr* fray

Franzband ['frantsbant] *m* (-[e]s;⁼e) leather binding

Franz'branntwein *m* rubbing alcohol

Franzose [fran'tsozə] *m* (-;-n) Frenchman; **die Franzosen** the French

Französin [fran'tsøzın] *f* (-;-nen) Frenchwoman

französisch [fran'tsøzıʃ] *adj* French

frappant [fra'pant] *adj* striking

frappieren [fra'pirən] *tr* strike, astonish; (*Wein*) put on ice

fräsen ['frezən] *tr* mill

fraß [fros] *pret* of **fressen** || **Fraß** *m* (-es;) fodder, food; (pel) garbage

Fratz [frats] *m* (-es;-e) brat

Fratze ['fratsə] *f* (-;-n) grimace; (coll) face; **e–e F. schneiden** make a face

frat'zenhaft *adj* grotesque

Frau [frau] *f* (-;-en) woman; lady; wife; (*vor Namen*) Mrs; **zur F. geben** give in marriage

Frauen– *comb.fm.* of women

Frau'enarzt *m*, **Frau'enärztin** *f* gynecologist

Frau'enheld *m* ladykiller

Frau'enkirche *f* Church of Our Lady

Frau'enkleidung *f* women's wear

Frau'enklinik *f* women's hospital

Frau'enleiden *n* gynecological disorder

Frau'enzimmer *n* (pej) woman, female

Fräulein ['frɔılaın] *n* (-s;-) young lady; (*vor Namen*) Miss

frau'lich *adj* womanly

frech [freç] *adj* brazen; fresh, smart

Frech'dachs *m* smart aleck

Frech'heit *f* (-;-en) impudence

Fregatte [fre'gatə] *f* (-;-n) frigate

frei [fraı] *adj* free; (*Feld*) open; (*offen*) frank; **auf freien Fuß setzen** release; **auf freier Strecke** (rr) outside the station; **die freien Berufe** the professions; **freie Fahrt** (public sign) resume speed; **freies Spiel haben** have a free hand; **frei werden** (chem) be released; **ich bin so frei** thank you, I will have some; **sich frei machen** take off one's clothes || **Freie §5** *n*—**im Freien** out of doors; **ins Freie** out of doors, into the open

Frei'bad *n* outdoor swimming pool

Frei'bank *f* (-;⁼e) cheap-meat counter

frei'beruflich *adj* freelance

Frei'betrag *m* allowable deduction

Frei'brief *m* charter; (fig) license

Freier ['fraı·ər] *m* (-s;-) suitor

Frei'frau *f* baroness

Frei'gabe *f* release

frei'geben §80 *tr* release; **für den Verkehr f.** open to traffic || *intr*—**j-m f.** give s.o. (*time*) off

freigebig ['fraıgebıç] *adj* generous

Frei'gebigkeit *f* (-;) generosity

Frei'geist *m* freethinker

frei'geistig *adj* open-minded

frei'gestellt *adj* optional

frei'haben *intr* be off

Frei'hafen *m* free port

frei'halten §90 *tr* keep open; **j-n f.** pay the tab for s.o.

Frei'heit *f* (-;-en) freedom; **dichterische F.** poetic license

Frei'heitskrieg *m* war of liberation

Frei'heitsstrafe *f* imprisonment

Frei'herr *m* baron

Frei'karte *f* free ticket; (theat) complimentary ticket

Frei'korps *n* volunteer corps

frei'lassen §104 *tr* release, set free

Frei'lauf *m* coasting

frei'legen *tr* lay open, expose

frei'lich *adv* of course

Freilicht– *comb.fm.* open-air

frei'machen *tr* (*Platz*) vacate; (*Straße*) clear; (*Brief*) stamp; **den Arm f.** roll up one's sleeves || *ref* undress

Frei'marke *f* postage stamp

Frei'maurer *m* Freemason

Frei'maurerei *f* freemasonry

Frei'mut *m* frankness

frei'mütig *adj* frank, outspoken

frei'schaffend *adj* freelance

Frei'sinn *m* (pol) liberalism

frei'sinnig *adj* (pol) liberal

frei'sprechen §64 *tr* acquit

Frei'spruch *m* acquittal

frei'stehen §146 *intr*—**es steht Ihnen frei zu** (*inf*) you are free to (*inf*)

frei'stehend *adj* free-standing; (*Gebäude*) detached

Frei'stelle *f* scholarship

frei'stellen *tr* exempt; **j-m etw f.** leave it to s.o.'s discretion

Frei'stoß *m* (fb) free kick

Frei'tag *m* Friday

Frei'tod *m* suicide

Frei'treppe *f* outdoor stairway

Frei'wild *n* (& fig) fair game

frei'willig *adj* voluntary || **Freiwillige §5** *mf* (& mil) volunteer

Frei'zeichen *n* (telp) dial tone

Frei'zeit *f* spare time, leisure

Frei'zeitgestaltung *f* planning one's leisure time

freizügig ['fraıtsygıç] *adj* unhampered

fremd [fremt] *adj* foreign; strange; someone else's; (*Name*) assumed

fremd'artig *adj* strange, odd

Fremde ['fremdə] §5 *mf* foreigner; stranger || *f—aus der* F. from abroad; **in der F.** far from home; **in die F. gehen** go far from home; go abroad

Frem'denbuch *n* visitors' book

Frem'denführer –in §6 *mf* tour guide; (*Buch*) guidebook

Frem'denheim *n* boarding house

Frem'denlegion *f* foreign legion

Frem'denverkehr *m* tourism

Frem'denzimmer *n* guest room; spare room

Fremd'herrschaft *f* foreign domination

Fremd'körper *m* foreign body; (pol) alien element

fremdländisch ['fremtlendɪʃ] *adj* foreign

Fremdling ['fremtlɪŋ] *m* (**-s;-**) stranger

Fremd'sprache *f* foreign language

Fremd'wort *n* (**-es;-̈er**) foreign word

frequentieren [frekven'tirən] *tr* frequent

Frequenz [fre'kvents] *f* (**-;-en**) frequency; (*Besucherzahl*) attendance

Freske ['freskə] *f* (**-;-n**), **Fres·ko** ['fresko] *n* (**-s;-ken** [kən]) fresco

Freßbeutel ['fresbɔɪtəl] *m* feed bag

Fresse ['fresə] *f* (**-;-n**) (sl) puss

fressen ['fresən] §70 *tr* (*von Tieren*) eat; feed on; (sl) devour; (*ätzen*) corrode, pit; (tech) freeze || *ref—sich satt* f. stuff oneself || *intr* (sl) eat; (**an** *dat*) gnaw (at)

Fresserei [fresə'raɪ] *f* (**-;**) gluttony

Freude ['frɔɪdə] *f* (**-;-n**) joy, pleasure

Freu'denbotschaft *f* glad tidings

Freu'denfeier *f*, **Freu'denfest** *n* celebration, happy occasion

Freu'denhaus *n* brothel

Freu'denmädchen *n* prostitute

freudig ['frɔɪdɪç] *adj* joyful, happy

freud'los *adj* joyless, sad

freuen ['frɔɪ·ən] *tr* please || *ref* be happy; (**an** *dat*) be delighted (by); (**auf** *acc*) look forward (to); (**über** *acc*) be glad (about) || *impers—es* freut mich I am glad

Freund [frɔɪnt] *m* (**-[e]s;-e**) friend; boyfriend; **F. der Musik** music lover

Freundin ['frɔɪndɪn] *f* (**-;-nen**) friend; girlfriend

freund'lich *adj* friendly; cheerful

Freund'lichkeit *f* (**-;**) friendliness

Freund'schaft *f* (**-;-en**) friendship

Frevel ['frefəl] *m* (**-s;-**) outrage; crime; sacrilege

fre'velhaft *adj* wicked

freveln ['frefəln] *intr* commit an outrage; **am Gesetz f.** violate the law

Fre'veltat *f* outrage

Friede ['fridə] *m* (**-ns;**), **Frieden** ['fridən] *m* (**-s;**) peace

Frie'densrichter *m* justice of the peace

Frie'densschluß *m* conclusion of peace

Frie'densstifter –in §6 *mf* peacemaker

Frie'densverhandlungen *pl* peace negotiations

Frie'densvertrag *m* peace treaty

friedfertig ['fritfertɪç] *adj* peaceable

Friedhof ['frithof] *m* cemetery

friedlich ['fritlɪç] *adj* peaceful

friedliebend ['fritlibənt] *adj* peaceloving

frieren ['frirən] §77 *intr* be cold; freeze || *impers—es* friert mich I'm freezing

Fries [fris] *m* (**-es;-e**) frieze

Frikadelle [frɪka'delə] *f* (**-;-n**) meatball

frisch [frɪʃ] *adj* fresh; (*kühl*) cool; (*munter*) brisk || *adv* freshly; **f. gestrichen** (public sign) wet paint; **f. zu!** on with it! || **Frische** *f* (**-;**) freshness; coolness; briskness

Frisch'haltepackung *f* vacuum package

Friseur [frɪ'zør] *m* (**-s;-e**) barber

Friseur'laden *m* barbershop

Friseur'sessel *m* barber chair

Friseuse [frɪ'zøzə] *f* (**-;-n**) hairdresser

frisieren [frɪ'zirən] *tr* (*Dokumente*) doctor; (aut) soup up; **j–m die Haare f.** do s.o.'s hair

Frisier'haube *f* hair dryer; hair net

Frisier'kommode *f*, **Frisier'tisch** *m* dresser

Frist [frɪst] *f* (**-;-en**) time, period, term; (com, jur) grace; **die F. einhalten** meet the deadline

fristen ['frɪstən] *tr—das Leben* f. eke out a living

Frisur [frɪ'zur] *f* (**-;-en**) hairstyle

frivol [frɪ'vol] *adj* frivolous

froh [fro] *adj* glad, happy, joyful

froh'gelaunt *adj* cheerful

fröhlich ['frølɪç] *adj* gay, merry

froh'locken *intr* rejoice

Froh'sinn *m* good humor

fromm [from] *adj* pious, devout

Frömmelei [frœmə'laɪ] *f* (**-;-en**) sanctimoniousness; sanctimonious act

frommen ['frɔmən] *intr* (dat) profit

Frömmigkeit ['frœmɪçkaɪt] *f* (**-;**) piety

Frömmler –in ['frœmlər–ɪn] §6 *mf* hypocrite

Fron [fron] *f* (**-;**) drudgery; (hist) forced labor

frönen ['frønən] *intr* (dat) gratify

Fron'leichnam *m* Corpus Christi

Front [front] *f* (**-;-en**) (& mil) front

Front'abschnitt *m* (mil) sector

fror [fror] *pret* of **frieren**

Frosch [frɔʃ] *m* (**-es;-̈e**) frog; (*Feuerwerkkörper*) firecracker; **sei kein F.!** don't be a party pooper

Frost [frɔst] *m* (**-es;-̈e**) frost

Frost'beule *f* chilblain

frösteln ['frœstəln] *intr* feel chilly

Frosterfach ['frɔstərfax] *n* freezer compartment (*of refrigerator*)

frostig ['frɔstɪç] *adj* frosty; chilly

Frost'schutzmittel *n* antifreeze

Frottee [fro'te] *m* & *n* (**-s;-s**) terry cloth

frottieren [fro'tirən] *tr* rub down

Frottier'tuch *n* Turkish towel

Frucht [fruxt] *f* (**-;-̈e**) fruit; foetus

fruchtbar ['fruxtbar] *adj* fruitful

frucht'bringend *adj* productive

Früch'tebecher *m* fruit cup (*as dessert*)

fruchten ['fruxtən] *intr* bear fruit; have effect; be of use

Frucht′folge *f* rotation of crops
Frucht′knoten *m* (bot) pistil
frucht′los *adj* fruitless
Frucht′saft *m* fruit juice
Frucht′wechsel *m* rotation of crops
frugal [fru′gɑl] *adj* frugal
früh [fry] *adj* early ‖ *adv* early; in the morning; **von f. bis spät** from morning till night ‖ **Frühe** *f* (-;) early morning; **in aller F.** very early
früher [′fry·ər] *adj* earlier; former ‖ *adv* earlier; sooner; formerly
frühestens [′fry·əstəns] *adv* at the earliest
Früh′geburt *f* premature birth
Früh′jahr *n*, **Frühling** [′fryliŋ] *m* (-s; -e) spring
Früh′lingsmüdigkeit *f* spring fever
früh′reif *adj* precocious
Früh′schoppen *m* eye opener (*beer, wine*)
Früh′stück *n* breakfast; **zweites F.** lunch
frühstücken [′fry∫tykən] *intr* eat breakfast
früh′zeitig *adj & adv* (too) early
Fuchs [fuks] *m* (-es;–e) fox; (*Pferd*) sorrel, chestnut; (educ) freshman
Fuchsie [′fuksjə] *f* (-;-n) fuchsia
fuchsig [′fuksiç] *adj* red; (fig) furious, wild
Fuchs′jagd *f* fox hunt(ing)
fuchs′rot *adj* sorrel
Fuchs′schwanz *m* foxtail; (bot) amaranth; (carp) hand saw (*with tapered blade*)
fuchs′teufelswild′ *adj* hopping mad
Fuge [′fugə] *f* (-;-n) joint; (mus) fugue; **aus allen Fugen gehen** come apart; go to pieces, go to pot
fügen [′fygən] *tr* join; (*verhängen*) decree; (carp) joint ‖ *ref* give in; **es fügte sich** it so happened
fügsam [′fykzam] *adj* compliant; (*Haar*) manageable
Fü′gung *f* (-;-en) (gram) construction; **F. des Himmels, F. Gottes** divine providence; **F. des Schicksals** stroke of fate; **göttliche F.** divine providence
fühlbar [′fylbar] *adj* tangible; noticeable; **sich f. machen** make itself felt
fühlen [′fylən] *tr* feel, touch; sense ‖ *ref* feel; feel big ‖ *intr*—**f. mit** feel for (*s.o.*); **f. nach** feel for, grope for
–fühlig [fyliç] *comb.fm.* –feeling
Füh′lung *f* (-;) touch, contact; **F. nehmen mit** get in touch with
fuhr [fur] *pret* of **fahren**
Fuhre [′furə] *f* (-;-n) wagon load
führen [′fyrən] *tr* lead; guide; (*Artikel*) carry, sell; (*Besprechungen*) hold, conduct; (*Bücher*) keep; (*Geschäft*) run, manage; (*Krieg*) carry on; (*Sprache*) use; (*Titel*) bear; (*Truppen*) command; (*Waffe*) wield; (*Fahrzeug*) drive; (aer) pilot; **den Beweis f.** prove; **die Aufsicht f. über** (*acc*) superintend; **j–m den Haushalt f.** keep house for s.o. ‖ *ref* conduct oneself ‖ *intr* lead; (sport) be in the lead
Füh′rer –in §6 *mf* leader, guide; (aer)

pilot; (aut) driver; (com) manager; (sport) captain
Füh′rerschaft *f* (-;) leadership
Füh′rerschein *m* driver's license
Füh′rerscheinentzug *m* suspension of driver's license
Führhund [′fyrhunt] *m* Seeing Eye dog
Fuhr′park *m* (aut) fleet
Füh′rung *f* (-;-en) guidance; leadership; management; guided tour; behavior; (mil) command; (sport) lead
Füh′rungskraft *f* executive; **die Führungskräfte** management; (pol) authorities; **untere F.** junior executive
Füh′rungsschicht *f* (com) management
Füh′rungsspitze *f* top echelon
Fuhr′unternehmen *n* trucking
Fuhr′werk *n* cart, wagon; vehicle
Füllbleistift [′fylblai/tift] *m* mechanical pencil
Fülle [′fylə] *f* (-;) fullness; abundance, wealth; (*Körper*–) plumpness
füllen [′fylən] *tr* fill ‖ *ref* fill up ‖ **Füllen** *n* (-s;–) foal, colt, filly
Fül′ler *m* (-s;–) fountain pen
Füll′federhalter *m* fountain pen
Füll′horn *n* cornucopia
Füllsel [′fylzəl] *n* (-s;–) stopgap; (*beim Schreiben*) padding; (culin) stuffing
Fül′lung *f* (-;-en) (*Zahn*–) filling; (*Tür*–) panel; (culin) stuffing
Fund [funt] *m* (-[e]s;-e) find; discovery
Fundament [funda′ment] *n* (-[e]s;-e) foundation
fundamental [fundamen′tɑl] *adj* fundamental
Fund′büro *n* lost-and-found department
Fund′grube *f* (fig) mine, storehouse
fundieren [fun′dirən] *tr* lay the foundations of; found; establish; (*Schuld*) fund; **fundiertes Einkommen** unearned income; **gut fundiert** well-established
fünf [fynf] *adj & pron* five ‖ **Fünf** *f* (-;-en) five
Fünf′eck *n* pentagon
fünfte [′fynftə] §9 *adj & pron* fifth
Fünftel [′fynftəl] *n* (-s;–) fifth (*part*)
fünf′zehn *adj & pron* fifteen ‖ **Fünfzehn** *f* (-;-en) fifteen
fünf′zehnte §9 *adj & pron* fifteenth
Fünf′zehntel *n* (-s;–) fifteenth (*part*)
fünfzig [′fynftsiç] *adj* fifty
fünf′ziger *invar adj* of the fifties; **die f. Jahre** the fifties
fünfzigste [′fynftsiçstə] §9 *adj & pron* fiftieth
fungieren [fuŋ′girən] *intr* function; **f. als** function as, act as
Funk [fuŋk] *m* (-s;) radio
Funk′amateur *m* (rad) ham
Funk′bastler –in §6 *mf* (rad) ham
Fünkchen [′fyŋkçən] *n* (-s;–) small spark; **kein F.** (fig) not an ounce
Funke [′fuŋkə] *m* (-ns;-n), **Funken** [′fuŋkən] *m* (-s;–) spark
funkeln [′fuŋkəln] *intr* sparkle; (*Sterne*) twinkle
fun′kelnagelneu′ *adj* brand-new

funken ['funkən] *tr* radio, broadcast || *intr* spark
Fun'ker *m* (-s;-) radio operator
Funk'feuer *n* (aer) radio beacon
Funk'leitstrahl *m* radio beam
Funk'meßanlage *f* radar installation
Funk'meßgerät *n* radar
Funk'netz *n* radio network
Funk'peilung *f* radio direction finding
Funk'spruch *m* radiogram
Funk'streifenwagen *m* squad car
Funktionär –in [funktsjə'ner(ın)] §8 *mf* functionary
für [fyr] *prep* (*acc*) for || **Für** *n*—das Für und Wider the pros and cons
Für'bitte *f* intercession
Furche ['furçə] *f* (-;-n) furrow; (*Runzel*) wrinkle; (*Wagenspur*) rut
furchen ['furçən] *tr* furrow; wrinkle
Furcht [furçt] *f* (-;) fear, dread
furchtbar ['furçtbar] *adj* terrible
fürchten ['fyrçtən] *tr* fear, be afraid of || *ref* (**vor** *dat*) be afraid (of)
fürchterlich ['fyrçtərlıç] *adj* terrible, awful
furcht'erregend *adj* awe-inspiring
furcht'los *adj* fearless
furchtsam ['furçtzam] *adj* timid, shy
Furie ['furjə] *f* (-;-n) (myth) Fury
Furnier [fur'nir] *n* (-s;-e) veneer
Furore [fu'rorə] *f* (-;) & *n* (-s;) stir; **F. machen** cause a stir, be a big hit
Für'sorge *f* care; welfare
Für'sorgeamt *n* welfare department
Fürsorger –in ['fyrzorgər(ın)] §6 *mf* social worker; welfare officer
fürsorglich ['fyrzorklıç] *adj* thoughtful
Für'sprache *f* intercession; **F. einlegen** intercede
Für'sprecher –in §6 *mf* intercessor
Fürst [fyrst] *m* (-en;-en) prince
Fürstentum ['fyrstəntum] *n* (-s;"er) principality
Fürstin ['fyrstın] *f* (-;-nen) princess
fürst'lich *adj* princely
Furt [furt] *f* (-;-en) ford
Furunkel [fu'runkəl] *m* (-s;-) boil
Für'wort *n* (-[e]s;"er) pronoun

Furz [furts] *m* (-es;"e) (vulg) fart
Fusel ['fuzəl] *m* (-s;) (coll) booze
Fusion [fu'sjon] *f* (-;-en) (com) merger
Fuß [fus] *m* (-es;"e) foot; **auf freien Fuß setzen** set free; **zu Fuß** on foot; **zu Fuß gehen** walk
Fuß'abdruck *m* footprint
Fuß'ball *m* soccer; football
Fuß'bank *f* (-;"e) footstool
Fuß'bekleidung *f* footwear
Fuß'boden *m* floor; flooring
Fussel ['fusəl] *f* (-;-n) fuzz
fußen ['fusən] *intr*—**f. auf** (*dat*) be based on; rely on
Fuß'fall *m* prostration
fuß'fällig *adv* on one's knees
fuß'frei *adj* ankle-length
Fuß'freiheit *f* leg room
Fuß'gänger *m* (-s;-) pedestrian
Fuß'gelenk *n* ankle joint
Fuß'gestell *n* pedestal
–füßig [fysıç] *comb.fm.* –footed
Fuß'knöchel *m* ankle
Fuß'leiste *f* baseboard, washboard
Füßling ['fyslın] *m* (-s;-e) foot (*of stocking, sock, etc.*)
Fuß'note *f* footnote
Fuß'pfad *m* footpath
Fuß'pilz *m* athlete's foot
Fuß'spur *f* footprint(s)
Fuß'stapfe *f* footstep
Fuß'steg *m* footbridge; footpath
Fuß'steig *m* footpath; sidewalk
Fuß'tritt *m* step; (*Stoß*) kick
futsch [fut∫] *adj* (coll) gone; (coll) ruined
Futter ['futər] *n* (-s;) fodder, feed; (*e–s Mantels*) lining
Futteral [futə'ral] *n* (-s;-e) case
Fut'terkrippe *f* crib; (sl) gravy train
Fut'terkrippensystem *n* (pol) spoils system
futtern ['futərn] *intr* (coll) eat heartily
füttern ['fytərn] *tr* feed; (*Kleid, Mantel, Pelz*) line
Fut'terneid *m* jealousy
Fut'terstoff *m* lining
Fut'tertrog *m* feed trough

G

G, g [ge] *invar n* G, g; (mus) G
gab [gap] *pret* of **geben**
Gabardine [gabar'dinə] *m* (-s;-) (tex) gabardine
Gabe ['gabə] *f* (-;-n) gift; donation; talent; (med) dose; **milde G.** alms
Gabel ['gabəl] *f* (-;-n) fork; (arti) bracket; (telp) cradle
Ga'belbein *n* wishbone
Ga'belbissen *m* tidbit
Ga'belfrühstück *n* brunch
gabelig ['gabəlıç] *adj* forked
gabeln ['gabəln] *tr* pick up with a fork || *ref* divide, branch off
Ga'belstapler *m* forklift
Ga'belung *f* (-;-en) fork (*in the road*)

gackeln ['gakəln], **gackern** ['gakərn], **gacksen** ['gaksən] *intr* cackle, cluck
Gage ['gaʒə] *f* (-;-n) salary, pay
gähnen ['genən] *intr* yawn
gaffen ['gafən] *intr* gape; stare
Gala ['gala] *invar f* gala, Sunday best
galant [ga'lant] *adj* courteous; **galantes Abenteuer** love affair
Galante·rie [galantə'ri] *f* (-;-rien ['ri·ən]) courtesy; flattering word
Gala·xis [ga'laksıs] *f* (-;-xien [ksjən]) galaxy
Galeere [ga'lerə] *f* (-;-n) galley
Gale·rie [galə'ri] *f* (-;-rien ['ri·ən]) gallery
Galgen ['galgən] *m* (-s;-) gallows

Gal′genfrist *f* (coll) brief respite

Gal′genhumor *m* grim humor

Gal′genstrick *m*, **Gal′genvogel** *m* (coll) good-for-nothing

gälisch [ˈgɛlɪʃ] *adj* Gaelic

Galle [ˈgalə] *f* (-;) gall, bile; (fig) bitterness

Gal′lenblase *f* gall bladder

Gal′lenstein *m* gallstone

Gallert [ˈgalərt] *n* (-[e]s;-e), **Gallerte** [gaˈlɛrtə] *f* (-;-n) gelatine; jelly

gallig [ˈgalɪç] *adj* bitter; grouchy

Gallone [gaˈlonə] *f* (-;-n) gallon

Galopp [gaˈlɔp] *m* (-[e]s;-s & -e) gallop; **im G. reiten** gallop; **in gestrecktem G.** at full gallop; **in kurzem G.** at a canter

galoppieren [galɔˈpirən] *intr* (SEIN) gallop

galt [galt] *pret of* **gelten**

galvanisieren [galvaniˈzirən] *tr* galvanize; electroplate

Gambe [ˈgambə] *f* (-;-n) bass viol

gammeln [ˈgaməln] *intr* bum around

Gammler [ˈgamlər] *m* (-s;-) hippie

Gamsbart [ˈgamsbart] *m* goatee

gang [gaŋ] *adj*—**g. und gäbe** customary ‖ **Gang** *m* (-[e]s;=) walk, gait; (*e-r Maschine*) running, operation; (*im Hause*) hallway; (*zwischen Reihen*) aisle; (*Botengang*) errand; (*Röhre*) conduit; (*e-r Schraube*) thread; (anat) duct, canal; (aut) gear; (box) round; (culin) course; (min) vein, lode; (min) gallery; (mus) run; **außer G. setzen** stop; (aut) put in neutral; **erster G.** low gear; **es ist etw im G.** there is s.th. afoot; **im G. sein** in operation; be in progress; **in G. bringen** (or **setzen**) set in motion; **in vollem G.** in full swing

Gang′art *f* gait

gangbar [ˈgaŋbar] *adj* passable; (*Münze*) current; (com) marketable

Gängelband [ˈgɛŋəlbant] *n*—**am G. führen** (fig) lead by the nose, dominate

-gänger [gɛŋər] *comb.f.m.*, e.g., **Fußgänger** pedestrian

gängig [ˈgɛŋɪç] *adj see* **gangbar**

Gang′schaltung *f* (aut) gear shift

Gangster [ˈgɛŋstər] *m* (-s;-s) gangster

Ganove [gaˈnovə] *m* (-;-n) crook

Gans [gans] *f* (-;=e) goose

Gänseblümchen [ˈgɛnzəblymçən] *n* (-s;-) daisy

Gänsehaut [ˈgɛnzəhaut] *f* (coll) goose flesh, goose pimples

Gänseklein [ˈgɛnzəklaɪn] *n* (-s;) (culin) giblets

Gänsemarsch [ˈgɛnzəmarʃ] *m* single file

Gänserich [ˈgɛnzərɪç] *m* (-s;-e) gander

ganz [gants] *adj* whole; all; total; intact; **im ganzen in all** ‖ *adv* entirely, quite; **g. und gar** completely; **g. und gar nicht** not at all ‖ **Ganze §5** *n* whole; **aufs G. gehen** go all the way

Ganz′aufnahme *f* full-length photograph

Gänze [ˈgɛntsə] *f* (-;)—**in G. in** its entirety; **zur G.** entirely

Ganz′fabrikat *n* finished product

Ganz′leinenband *m* (-[e]s;=e) cloth-bound volume

gänzlich [ˈgɛntslɪç] *adj* entire, total

ganz′seitig *adj* full-page

ganz′tägig *adj* full-time

gar [gar] *adj* (culin) well done; (metal) refined ‖ *adv* quite, very; (*sogar*) even; **gar nicht** not at all

Garage [gaˈraʒə] *f* (-;-n) garage

Garan·tie [garanˈti] *f* (-;-tien [ˈti-ən] guarantee

garantieren [garanˈtirən] *tr* guarantee ‖ *intr*—**g. dafür, daß** guarantee that

Garaus [ˈgaraus] *m* (-;) finishing blow

Garbe [ˈgarbə] *f* (-;-n) sheaf, shock

Garde [ˈgardə] *f* (-;-n) guard

Gardenie [garˈdenjə] *f* (-;-n) gardenia

Garderobe [gardəˈrobə] *f* (-;-n) wardrobe; (*Kleiderablage*) cloakroom; (theat) dressing room

Gardero′benmarke *f* hat or coat check

Gardero′benständer *m* coatrack, hatrack

Garderobiere [gardəroˈbjerə] *f* (-;-n) cloakroom attendant

Gardine [garˈdinə] *f* (-;-n) curtain

Gardi′nenhalter *m* tieback

Gardi′nenpredigt *f* (coll) dressing down

Gardi′nenstange *f* curtain rod

gären [ˈgerən] §78 *intr* ferment; bubble; (fig) ferment

Gärmittel [ˈgermɪtəl] *n* ferment; leaven

Garn [garn] *n* (-[e]s;-e) yarn; thread; snare; (fig) trap; (fig) yarn

Garnele [garˈnelə] *f* (-;-n) shrimp

garnieren [garˈnirən] *tr* garnish; trim

Garnison [garniˈzon] *f* (-;-en) garrison

Garnitur [garniˈtur] *f* (-;-en) trimming; set (*of matching objects*); (mach) fittings, mountings; (mil) uniform

garstig [ˈgarstɪç] *adj* ugly; nasty

Garten [ˈgartən] *m* (-s;=) garden

Gar′tenanlage *f* gardens, grounds

Gar′tenarbeit *f* gardening

Gar′tenarchitekt *m* landscape gardener

Gar′tenbau *m* gardening; horticulture

Gar′tenlaube *f* arbor

Gar′tenmesser *n* pruning knife

Gärtner [ˈgertnər] *m* (-s;-) gardener

Gärtnerei [gertnəˈraɪ] *f* (-;-en) gardening; truck farm; nursery

Gä′rung *f* (-;-n) fermentation

Gas [gas] *n* (-es;-e) gas; **Gas geben** step on the gas

Gas′anstalt *f* gasworks

gas′artig *adj* gaseous

Gas′behälter *m* gas tank

gas′förmig *adj* gaseous

Gas′hebel *m* (aut) accelerator

Gas′heizung *f* gas heat(ing)

Gas′herd *m* gas range

Gas′krieg *m* chemical warfare

Gas′leitung *f* gas main

Gas′messer *m* gas meter

Gasse [ˈgasə] *f* (-;-n) side street; **über die G. verkaufen** sell takeouts

Gas′sendirne *f* streetwalker

Gas′senhauer *m* popular song

Gas′senjunge *m* urchin

Gast [gast] m (-[e]s;≃e) guest; boarder; (com) customer; (theat) guest performer; **zu Gast bitten** invite

Gästebuch ['gestəbux] n guest book; visitors' book

Gast′freund m guest

gast′freundlich adj hospitable

Gast′freundschaft f hospitality

Gast′geber m host

Gast′geberin f hostess

Gast′haus n, **Gast′hof** m inn

Gast′hörer –in §6 mf (educ) auditor

gastieren [gas′tirən] intr (telv, theat) appear as a guest

gast′lich adj hospitable

Gast′mahl n feast; banquet

Gast′professor m visiting professor

Gast′rolle f guest performance; **e-e G. geben** pay a flying visit

Gast′spiel n (theat) guest performance

Gast′stätte f restaurant

Gast′stube f dining room

Gast′wirt m innkeeper

Gast′wirtschaft f restaurant

Gas′uhr f gas meter

Gas′werk n gas works

Gas′zähler m gas meter

Gatte ['gatə] m (-n;-n) husband; **Gatten** married couple

Gatter ['gatər] n (-s;-) grating; latticework; iron gate

Gattin ['gatin] f (-;-nen) wife

Gattung ['gatuŋ] f (-;-en) kind, type, species; family; (biol) genus

Gat′tungsname m generic name; (gram) common noun

Gau [gau] m (-[e]s;-e) district

Gaukelbild ['gaukəlbilt] n illusion

gaukeln ['gaukəln] intr flit, flutter; perform hocus-pocus

Gau′kelspiel n, **Gau′kelwerk** n sleight of hand; delusion

Gaul [gaul] m (-[e]s;≃e) horse; nag

Gaumen ['gaumən] m (-s;-) palate

Gauner ['gaunər] m (-s;-) rogue; swindler

Gaunerei [gaunə′rai] f (-;-en) swindling, cheating

gaunern ['gaunərn] intr swindle

Gau′nersprache f thieves' slang

Gaze ['gazə] f (-;-n) gauze; cheesecloth

Gazelle [ga′tselə] f (-;-n) gazelle

Geächtete [gə′eçtətə] §5 mf outlaw

Geächze [gə′eçtsə] n (-s;) moaning

geartet [gə′artət] adj—**anders g. sein** be of a different disposition

Gebäck [gə′bɛk] n (-s;) baked goods, cookies

geballt [gə′balt] adj concentrated; dense; (Schnee) hardened; (Faust) clenched; (Stil) succinct

gebannt [gə′bant] adj spellbound

gebar [gə′bar] pret of gebären

Gebärde [gə′berdə] f (-;-n) gesture

gebärden [gə′berdən] ref behave

Gebär′denspiel n gesticulation

gebaren [gə′barən] ref behave, act ‖ **Gebaren** n (-s;) behavior

gebären [gə′berən] §79 tr bear ‖ **Gebären** n (-;) childbirth; labor

Gebär′mutter f (anat) uterus

Gebär′mutterkappe f diaphragm

Gebäude [gə′bɔidə] n (-s;-) building

gebefreudig ['gebəfrɔidiç] adj openhanded

Gebein [gə′bain] n (-[e]s;-e) bones; **Gebeine** bones; mortal remains

Gebell [gə′bel] n (-[e]s;), **Gebelle** [gə′belə] n (-s;) barking

geben ['gebən] §80 tr give; yield; (Gelegenheit) afford; (Laut) utter; (Karten) deal; **Feuer g.** give (s.o.) a light; (mil) open fire; **viel g. auf** (acc) set great store by; **von sich g.** utter; throw up; (Rede) deliver; (chem) give off ‖ ref give; (Kopfweh, usw.) get better; **sich g. als** pretend to be; **sich gefangen g.** surrender ‖ impers—**es gibt there is, there are; es wird Regen geben** it's going to rain

Ge′ber –in §6 mf giver, donor

Gebet [gə′bet] n (-[e]s;-e) prayer

gebeten [gə′betən] pp of bitten

Gebiet [gə′bit] n (-[e]s;-e) district, territory; (Fläche) area; (Fach) line; (Bereich) field, sphere

gebieten [gə′bitən] §58 tr (Stillschweigen) impose; (Ehrfurcht) command; (verlangen) demand; **j–m g., etw zu tun** order s.o. to do s.th. ‖ intr (über acc) have control (over); (dat) control

Gebieter [gə′bitər] m (-s;-) master; ruler; commander; governor

Gebieterin [gə′bitərin] f (-;-nen) mistress; (des Hauses) lady

gebieterisch [gə′bitəriʃ] adj imperious

Gebilde [gə′bildə] n (-s;-) shape, form; structure; (geol) formation

gebildet [gə′bildət] adj educated

Gebirge [gə′birgə] n (-s;-) mountain range, mountains; **festes G.** bedrock

gebirgig [gə′birgiç] adj mountainous

Gebirgs– [gəbirks] comb.fm. mountain

Gebirgs′bewohner –in §6 mf mountaineer

Gebirgs′kamm m, **Gebirgs′rücken** m mountain ridge

Gebirgs′zug m mountain range

Ge-biß [gə′bis] n (-bisses;-bisse) teeth; false teeth; (am Zaum) bit

gebissen [gə′bisən] pp of beißen

Gebläse [gə′blezə] n (-s;-) bellows; blower; (aut) supercharger

geblieben [gə′blibən] pp of bleiben

Geblök [gə′bløk] n (-[e]s;) bleating

geblümt [gə′blymt] adj flowered

Geblüt [gə′blyt] n (-[e]s;) (& fig) blood

geboren [gə′borən] pp of gebären ‖ adj born; native; **geborene** nee

geborgen [gə′bɔrgən] pp of bergen ‖ adj safe

Gebor′genheit f (-;) safety, security

geborsten [gə′bɔrstən] pp of bersten

Gebot [gə′bot] n (-[e]s;-e) order, command; commandment; (Angebot) bid

geboten [gə′botən] pp of bieten ‖ adj requisite; **dringend g.** imperative

Gebr. abbr. (Gebrüder) Brothers

gebracht [gə′braxt] pp of bringen

gebrannt [gə′brant] pp of brennen

Gebräu [gə'brɔɪ] *n* (-[e]s;-e) brew
Gebrauch [gə'braux] *m* (-s;-e) use; usage; (*Sitte*) custom
gebrauchen [gə'brauxən] *tr* use, employ
gebräuchlich [gə'brɔɪçlɪç] *adj* usual, in use; (*gemein*) common
Gebrauchs'anweisung *f* directions
gebrauchs'fertig *adj* ready for use; (*Kaffee, usw.*) instant
Gebrauchs'graphik *f* commercial art
Gebrauchs'gut *n* commodity
Gebrauchs'muster *n* registered pattern
gebraucht [gə'brauxt] *adj* second-hand
Gebraucht'wagen *m* used car
Gebrechen [gə'breçən] *n* (-s;-) physical disability, infirmity
gebrech'lich *adj* frail, weak; rickety
gebrochen [gə'brɔxən] *pp* of **brechen**
Gebrüder [gə'brydər] *pl* brothers
Gebrüll [gə'bryl] *n* (-[e]s) roaring; bellowing; lowing
Gebühr [gə'byr] *f* (-;-en) charge, fee; due, what is due; **nach G.** deservedly; **über G.** excessively; **zu ermäßigter G.** at a reduced rate
gebühren [gə'byrən] *intr* (*dat*) be due to || *impers ref*—**es gebührt sich** it is proper
gebüh'rend *adj* due; (*entsprechend*) appropriate || *adv* duly
gebüh'renfrei *adj* free of charge
gebüh'renpflichtig *adj* chargeable
gebunden [gə'bundən] *pp* of **binden** || *adj* bound; (*Hitze*) latent; (*Preise*) controlled; (*Kapital*) tied-up; **g. an** (*acc*) (chem) combined with; **gebundene Rede** verse
Geburt [gə'burt] *f* (-;-en) birth
Gebur'tenbeschränkung *f* birth control
Gebur'tenregelung *f* birth control
Gebur'tenrückgang *m* decline in births
gebürtig [gə'byrtɪç] *adj* native
Geburts'anzeige *f* announcement of birth; registration of birth
Geburts'fehler *n* congenital defect
Geburts'helfer **-in** §6 *mf* obstetrician || *f* midwife
Geburts'hilfe *f* obstetrics
Geburts'mal *n* birth mark
Geburts'recht *n* birthright
Geburts'schein *m* birth certificate
Geburts'tag *m* birthday
Geburts'tagskind *n* person celebrating his or her birthday
Geburts'wehen *pl* labor pains
Geburts'zange *f* forceps
Gebüsch [gə'by] *n* (-es;-e) thicket, underbrush; clump of bushes
Geck [gek] *m* (-en;-en) dude
geckenhaft [gek'kenhaft] *adj* flashy
gedacht [gə'daxt] *pp* of **denken**
Gedächtnis [gə'dɛçtnɪs] *n* (-ses;) memory; **aus dem G.** by heart; **im G. behalten** bear in mind; **zum G.** (*genit* or an *acc*) in memory of
Gedächt'nisfehler *m* lapse of memory
Gedächt'nisrede *f* memorial address
gedämpft [gə'dɛmpft] *adj* muffled; hushed, quiet; (*Licht, Stimme*) subdued; (culin) stewed
Gedanke [gə'daŋkə] *m* (-ns;-n) thought; notion, idea; **etw in Ge-**

danken tun do s.th. absent-mindedly; **in Gedanken sein** be preoccupied; **sich** |*dat*| **Gedanken machen über** (*acc*) worry about
Gedan'kenblitz *m* (iron) brain wave
Gedan'kenfolge *f*, **Gedan'kengang** *m* train of thought
gedan'kenlos *adj* thoughtless; absentminded; irresponsible
Gedan'kenpunkt *m* suspension point
Gedan'kenstrich *m* (typ) dash
Gedan'kenübertragung *f* telepathy
gedank'lich *adj* mental; intellectual
Gedärme [gə'dermə] *pl* intestines
Gedeck |gə'dek| *n* (-[e]s;-e) cover; table setting; menu
gedeihen [gə'daɪən] §81 *intr* (SEIN) thrive; succeed || **Gedeihen** *n* (-s) prosperity; success
Gedenk- |gədeŋk| *comb.fm.* memorial; commemorative
gedenken [gə'deŋkən] §66 *intr* (*genit*) think of, be mindful of; remember; mention; **g. zu** (*inf*) intend to (*inf*) || **Gedenken** *n* (-s;) memory
gedeucht [gə'dɔɪçt] *pp* of **dünken**
Gedicht |gə'dɪçt| *n* (-[e]s;-e) poem; (fig) dream
gediegen [gə'digən] *adj* (*Gold*) solid; (*Silber*) sterling; (*Arbeit*) excellent; (*Kenntnisse*) thorough; (*Möbel*) solidly made; (*Charakter*) sterling; (coll) very funny
gedieh |gə'di| *pret* of **gedeihen**
gediehen [gə'di-ən] *pp* of **gedeihen**
Gedränge [gə'dreŋə] *n* (-s;-) pushing; crowd; difficulties; (fb) scrimmage
gedrängt |gə'dreŋt| *adj* crowded, packed; (*Sprache*) concise
gedroschen [gə'drɔʃən] *pp* of **dreschen**
gedrückt |gə'drykt| *adj* depressed
gedrungen [gə'druŋən] *pp* of **dringen** || *adj* compact; stocky; squat; (*Sprache*) concise
Geduld [gə'dult] *f* (-;) patience
gedulden [gə'duldən] *ref* wait (patiently)
geduldig [gə'duldɪç] *adj* patient
Geduld'spiel *n* puzzle
gedungen [gə'duŋən] *pp* of **dingen**
gedunsen [gə'dunzən] *adj* bloated
gedurft |gə'durft| *pp* of **dürfen**
geehrt |gə'ert| *adj*—**Sehr geehrte Herren!** Dear Sirs; **Sehr geehrter Herr X!** Dear Mr. X
geeignet [gə'aɪgnət] *adj* suitable, right; qualified; appropriate
Gefahr [gə'far] *f* (-;-en) danger; (*Wagnis*) risk; **G. laufen zu** (*inf*) run the risk of (*ger*)
gefährden [gə'ferdən] *tr* jeopardize
gefährlich [gə'ferlɪç] *adj* dangerous
gefahr'los *adj* safe
Gefährt |gə'fert| *n* (-[e]s;-e) carriage
Gefährte [gə'fertə] *m* (-n;-n), **Gefährtin** [gə'fertɪn] *f* (-;-nen) companion; spouse
Gefälle [gə'felə] *n* (-s;-) pitch; slope
gefallen [gə'falən] *adj* fallen; (mil) killed in action; §72 *ref*—**sich g. in** (*dat*) take pleasure in || *intr* please; **das gefällt mir** I like this; **das lasse ich mir nicht g.** I won't stand for

this ‖ **Gefallen** m (-;-) favor ‖ n (-s;) (an dat) pleasure (in); j-m etw zu G. tun do s.th. to please s.o.; nach G. as one pleases; at one's descretion

gefällig [gə'fɛlɪç] adj pleasing; obliging; kind; j-m g. sein do s.o. a favor; Kaffee g.? would you care for coffee?; was ist g.? what can I do for you?; würden Sie so g. sein zu (inf)? would you be so kind as to (inf)?

Gefäl'ligkeit f (-;-en) favor

gefälligst [gə'fɛlɪçst] adv if you please; please

gefangen [gə'faŋən] pp of **fangen** ‖ adj captive; g. nehmen take prisoner ‖ **Gefangene** §5 mf captive, prisoner

Gefan'genenlager n prison camp; (mil) prisoner-of-war camp

Gefan'gennahme f (-;) capture; arrest

gefan'gennehmen §116 tr take prisoner

Gefan'genschaft f (-;) captivity; imprisonment; in G. geraten be taken prisoner

gefan'gensetzen tr imprison

Gefängnis [gə'fɛŋnɪs] n (-ses;-se) prison, jail; imprisonment

Gefäng'nisdirektor m warden

Gefäng'nisstrafe f prison term

Gefäng'niswärter –in §6 mf guard

Gefäß [gə'fɛs] n (-es;-e) vessel; jar

gefaßt [gə'fast] adj calm, composed; g. auf (acc) ready for

Gefecht [gə'fɛçt] n (-[e]s;-e) fight, battle, action

Gefechts'auftrag m (mil) objective

Gefechts'kopf m warhead

Gefechts'lage f tactical situation

Gefechts'stand m command post

gefeit [gə'fart] adj (gegen) immune (from), proof (against)

Gefieder [gə'fidər] n (-s;-) plumage

gefleckt [gə'flɛkt] adj spotted

geflissentlich [gə'flɪsəntlɪç] adj intentional, willful

geflochten [gə'flɔxtən] pp of **flechten**

geflogen [gə'flogən] pp of **fliegen**

geflohen [gə'flo-ən] pp of **fliehen**

geflossen [gə'flɔsən] pp of **fließen**

Geflügel [gə'flygəl] n (-s;) fowl; (Federvieh) poultry

Geflü'gelmagen m gizzard

Geflunker [gə'fluŋkər] m (-s;) (coll) fibbing

Geflüster [gə'flystər] n (-s;) whisper

Gefolge [gə'fɔlgə] n (-s;) retinue; in seinem G. in its wake

Gefolgschaft [gə'fɔlk/aft] f (-;-en) allegiance; followers

gefräßig [gə'frɛsɪç] adj gluttonous

Gefrä'ßigkeit f (-;) gluttony

Gefreite [gə'frartə] §5 m private first class; lance corporal (Brit)

gefressen [gə'frɛsən] pp of **fressen**

Gefrieranlage [gə'frirənlagə] f **Gefrierapparat** [gə'friraparat] m freezer

gefrieren [gə'frirən] §77 intr (SEIN) freeze

Gefrie'rer m (-s;-) freezer; deepfreeze

Gefrier'fach n freezing compartment

Gefrier'punkt m freezing point

Gefrier'schutz m, **Gefrier'schutzmittel** n antifreeze

gefroren [gə'frorən] pp of **frieren** ‖ **Gefrorene** §5 n ice cream

Gefüge [gə'fygə] n (-s;-) structure, make-up; arrangement; texture

gefügig [gə'fygɪç] adj pliant, pliable

Gefühl [gə'fyl] n (-[e]s;-e) feeling; feel; touch; sense; sensation

gefühl'los adj numb; callous

gefühls-, Gefühls- [gəfyls] comb.fm. of the emotions; emotional; sentimental; (anat) sensory

gefühls'betont adj emotional

Gefühlsduselei [gə'fylsduzəlar] f (-;) sentimentalism, mawkishness

gefühls'selig adj mawkish

gefühl'voll adj sensitive; tender-hearted ‖ adv with feeling

gefunden [gə'fundən] pp of **finden**

gefurcht [gə'furçt] adj furrowed

gegangen [gə'gaŋən] pp of **gehen**

gegeben [gə'gebən] pp of **geben** ‖ adj given; (Umstände) existing; gegebene Methode best approach; zu gegebener Zeit at the proper time

gege'benfalls adv if necessary

gegen ['gegən] prep (acc) towards; against; about, approximately; compared with; contrary to; in exchange for

gegen-, Gegen- comb.fm. anti-; counter-; contrary; opposite; back; in return

Ge'genantwort f rejoinder

Ge'genbeschuldigung f countercharge

Ge'genbild n counterpart

Gegend ['gegənt] f (-;-en) neighborhood, vicinity; region, district

gegeneinan'der adv against one another; towards one another

Ge'gengerade f back stretch

Ge'gengewicht n counterbalance; (am Rad) (aut) weight; das G. halten (dat) counterbalance

Ge'gengift n antidote

Ge'genkandidat –in §7 mf rival candidate

Ge'genklage f countercharge; counterclaim

Ge'genmittel n (gegen) remedy (for), antidote (against)

Ge'genrede f reply, rejoinder

Ge'gensatz m contrast; opposite, antithesis; (Widerspruch) opposition

gegensätzlich ['gegənzɛtslɪç] adj contrary, opposite, antithetical

Ge'genschlag m counterplot

ge'genseitig adj mutual, reciprocal

Ge'genstand m object, thing; subject

gegenständlich ['gegən/tentlɪç] adj objective; (fa) representational; (log) concrete

ge'genstandslos adj baseless; without purpose; irrelevant; (fa) non-representational

Ge'genstoß m (box) counterpunch; (mil) counterthrust

Ge'genstück n counterpart

Ge'genteil n contrary, opposite; im G. on the contrary

ge'genteilig adj contrary, opposite

gegenü'ber prep (dat) opposite to; across from; with regard to; compared with

gegenü'berstellen tr (dat) place opposite to; (dat) confront with; (dat) contrast with

Gegenü'berstellung f confrontation; comparison; (auf e–r Wache) line-up

Gegenwart ['gegənvart] f (–;) present; present time; (gram) present tense

gegenwärtig ['gegənvertiç] adj present, current ‖ adv at present; nowadays

Ge'genwehr f defense, resistance

Ge'genwind m head wind

Ge'genwirkung f (auf acc) reaction (to)

ge'genzeichnen tr countersign

Ge'genzug m countermove

geglichen [gə'gliçən] pp of gleichen

geglitten [gə'glitən] pp of gleiten

Gegner –in ['gegnər(in)] §6 mf opponent, rival ‖ m (mil) enemy

gegnerisch ['gegnərɪʃ] adj adverse; antagonistic; opposing; (mil) enemy

gegolten [gə'gɔltən] pp of gelten

gegoren [gə'gorən] pp of gären

gegossen [gə'gɔsən] pp of gießen

gegriffen [gə'grɪfən] pp of greifen

Gehabe [gə'habə] n (–s;) affectation

gehaben [gə'habən] ref fare; **gehab dich nicht so!** stop putting on!; **gehab dich wohl!** farewell!

Gehackte [gə'haktə] §5 n hamburger

Gehalt [gə'halt] m (–[e]s;–e) contents; capacity; standard; **G. an** (dat) percentage of ‖ n (–[e]s;¨er) salary

Gehalts'stufe f salary bracket

Gehalts'zulage f increment, raise

gehalt'voll adj substantial; profound

Gehänge [gə'hɛŋə] n (–s;–) slope; pendant; festoon; (e–s Degens) belt

gehangen [gə'haŋən] pp of hängen

gehässig [gə'hɛsɪç] adj spiteful, nasty

Gehäuse [gə'hɔizə] n (–s;–) case, box; housing; (e–r Schnecke) shell; (e–s Apfels) core

Gehege [gə'hegə] n (–s;–) enclosure

geheim [gə'haim] adj secret; **streng g.** top-secret

geheim'halten §90 tr keep secret

Geheimnis [gə'haimnis] n (–ses;–se) secret, mystery

geheim'nisvoll adj mysterious

Geheim'schrift f code; coded message

Geheim'tinte f invisible ink

Geheim'vorbehalt m mental reservation

Geheiß [gə'hais] n (–es;) bidding

gehen ['ge·ən] §82 intr (SEIN) go; walk; leave; (Teig) rise; (Maschine) work; (Uhr) go; (Ware) sell; (Wind) blow; **das geht nicht** that will not do; **das geht schon** it will be all right; **sich g. lassen** take it easy; **wieviel Zoll g. auf einen Fuß?** how many inches make a foot? ‖ impers—**es geht mir gut** I am doing well; **es geht nichts über** (acc) there is nothing like; **es geht um...** is at stake; **wie geht es Ihnen?** how are you?

geheuer [gə'hɔi·ər] adj—**mir war nicht recht g. zumute** I didn't feel quite at ease; **nicht g.** spooky; suspicious; risky

Geheul [gə'hɔil] n (–s;) howling; loud sobbing

Gehilfe [gə'hilfə] m (–n;–n), **Gehilfin** [gə'hilfin] f (–;–nen) assistant

Gehirn [gə'hirn] n (–[e]s;–e) brains; mind; (anat) brain; **sein G. anstrengen** rack one's brain

Gehirn– comb.fm. brain; cerebral

Gehirn'erschütterung f concussion

Gehirn'schlag m (pathol) stroke

Gehirn'wäsche f brainwashing

gehoben [gə'hobən] pp of **heben** ‖ adj (Stellung) high; (Stil) lofty; **gehobene Stimmung** high spirits

Gehöft [gə'hœft] n (–[e]s;–e) farm

geholfen [gə'hɔlfən] pp of helfen

Gehölz [gə'hœlts] n (–es;–e) grove; thicket

Gehör [gə'hør] n (–s;) hearing; ear

Gehör– comb.fm. of hearing; auditory

gehorchen [gə'hɔrçən] intr (dat) obey

gehören [gə'hørən] ref be proper, be right ‖ intr (dat or zu) belong to; (in acc) go into, belong in

gehörig [gə'høriç] adj proper, due; (dat or zu) belonging to ‖ adv properly; duly; thoroughly

Gehörn [gə'hørn] n (–s;–e) horns; **Gehörne** sets of horns

gehorsam [gə'horzam] adj obedient ‖ adv obediently; **gehorsamst** respectfully ‖ **Gehorsam** m (–s;) obedience

Gehor'samsverweigerung f disobedience

gehren ['gerən] tr (carp) miter

Gehrlade ['gerladə] f (–;–n) miter box

Gehrock ['gerɔk] m Prince Albert

Geh'rung f—**auf G., nach der G.** on the slant; **auf G. verbinden** miter

Geh'rungslade f (–;–n) miter box

Gehsteig ['geʃtaik] m sidewalk

Gehweg ['gevek] m sidewalk; footpath

Gehwerk ['geverk] n clockwork, works

Geier ['gai·ər] m (–s;–) vulture; **zum Geier!** what the devil!

Geifer ['gaifər] m (–s;) drivel; froth; slaver, foam; (fig) venom

geifern ['gaifərn] intr slaver

Geige ['gaigə] f (–;–n) violin, fiddle

Gei'genbogen m bow, fiddlestick

Gei'genharz n rosin

Gei'ger –in §6 mf violinist

geil [gail] adj lustful; in heat; (Boden) rich; (üppig) luxuriant

Geisel ['gaizəl] f (–;–n) hostage

Geiser ['gaizər] m (–s;) geyser

Geiß [gais] f (–;–en) she-goat

Geißel ['gaisəl] f (–;–n) scourge

geißeln ['gaisəln] tr scourge; (fig) castigate

Geist [gaist] m (–es;–er) spirit; (Gespenst) ghost; (Verstand) mind, intellect; **im Geiste** in one's imagination; **in spirit**

Gei'sterbeschwörung f (–;) necromancy

Gei'sterstadt f ghost town

Gei'sterstunde f witching hour

geistes– [gaistəs] comb.fm. spiritually; mentally, intellectually ‖ **Geistes–** comb.fm. spiritual; mental, intellectual

gei'stesabwesend adj absent-minded

Gei'stesanlagen pl natural gift

Gei'stesarbeit f brainwork

Gei'stesarmut f dullness, stupidity

Gei'stesblitz *m* brain wave; aphorism

Gei'stesflug *m* flight of the imagination

Gei'stesfreiheit *f* intellectual freedom

Gei'stesfrucht *f* brainchild

Gei'stesgegenwart *f* presence of mind

gei'stesgegenwärtig *adj* mentally alert

geistesgestört [ˈgaɪstəsgə/tørt] *adj* mentally disturbed

Gei'steshaltung *f* mentality

gei'steskrank *adj* insane

gei'stesschwach *adj* feeble-minded

Gei'stesstörung *f* mental disorder

Gei'stes- und Natur'wissenschaften *pl* arts and sciences

Gei'stesverfassung *f* frame of mind

gei'stesverwandt *adj* (mit) spiritually akin (to); (mit) congenial (with)

Gei'stesverwirrung *f* derangement

Gei'steswissenschaften *pl* humanities

gei'steswissenschaftlich *adj* humanistic

Gei'steszustand *m* state of mind

geistig [ˈgaɪstɪç] *adj* mental, intellectual; spiritual

geist'lich *adj* spiritual; (*Orden*) religious; (*kirchlich*) sacred, ecclesiastical; **der geistliche Stand** holy orders; **the clergy** || **Geistliche §5** *m* clergyman

Geist'lichkeit *f* (-;) clergy

geist'los *adj* spiritless; dull; stupid

geist'reich *adj* witty; ingenious

Geiz [gaɪts] *m* (-es;) stinginess; avarice

geizen [ˈgaɪtsən] *intr*—g. mit be sparing with; **nicht g. mit** show freely

Geiz'hals *m* (coll) tightwad

geizig [ˈgaɪtsɪç] *adj* stingy, miserly

Geiz'kragen *m* (coll) tightwad

Gejammer [gəˈjamər] *n* (-s;) wailing

gekannt [gəˈkant] *pp* of **kennen**

Geklapper [gəˈklapər] *n* (-s;) rattling

Geklatsche [gəˈklatʃə] *n* (-s;) clapping; gossiping

Geklirr [gəˈklɪr] *n* (-[e]s;) rattling

geklommen [gəˈkləmən] *pp* of **klimmen**

geklungen [gəˈkluŋən] *pp* of **klingen**

gekniffen [gəˈknɪfən] *pp* of **kneifen**

gekonnt [gəˈkɔnt] *pp* of **können**

Gekreisch [gəˈkraɪʃ] *n* (-es;) screaming; screeching

Gekritzel [gəˈkrɪtsəl] *n* (-s;) scribbling

gekrochen [gəˈkrɔxən] *pp* of **kriechen**

Gekröse [gəˈkrøzə] *n* (-s;) tripe

gekünstelt [gəˈkʏnstəlt] *adj* affected

Gelächter [gəˈlɛçtər] *n* (-s;) laughter

Gelage [gəˈlɑːgə] *n* (-s;) carousing

Gelände [gəˈlɛndə] *n* (-s;-) terrain; site, lot; (educ) campus; (golf) fairway

Gelän'delauf *m* crosscountry running

Gelän'depunkt *m* landmark

Geländer [gəˈlɛndər] *n* (-s;-) railing; guardrail; banister; parapet

gelang [gəˈlaŋ] *pret* of **gelingen**

gelangen [gəˈlaŋən] *intr* (SEIN) (an *acc*, **in** *acc*, **zu**) attain, reach

gelassen [gəˈlasən] *pp* of **lassen** || *adj* composed, calm

Gelatine [ʒelaˈtinə] *f* (-;) gelatin

geläufig [gəˈlɔɪfɪç] *adj* fluent; (*gemein*) common; (*Zunge*) glib

gelaunt [gəˈlaunt] *adj*—**gut gelaunt in good humor; zu etw g. sein** be in the mood for s.th.

Geläut [gəˈlɔɪt] *n* (-es;), **Geläute** [gəˈlɔɪtə] *n* (-s;) ringing; chimes

gelb [gɛlp] *adj* yellow || **Gelb** *n* (-s;) yellow

gelb'lich *adj* yellowish

Gelb'sucht *f* jaundice

Geld [gɛlt] *n* (-[e]s;) money; **bares G.** cash

Geld- *comb.fm.* money, financial

-geld *n* *comb.fm.* money; fee(s); tax, toll; allowance

Geld'anlage *f* investment

Geld'anleihe *f* loan

Geld'anweisung *f* money order; draft

Geld'ausgabe *f* expense; expenditure

Geld'beutel *m* pocketbook

Geld'bewilligung *f* (parl) appropriation

Geld'buße *f* fine

Geld'einlage *f* deposit

Geld'einwurf *m* coin slot

Geld'entwertung *f* inflation

Geld'erwerb *m* moneymaking

Geld'geber *m* investor; mortgagee

Geld'gier *f* avarice

Geld'mittel *pl* funds, resources

Geld'onkel *m* sugar daddy

Geld'schein *m* bank note, bill

Geld'schrank *m* safe

Geld'schublade *f* till (*of cash register*)

Geld'sendung *f* remittance

Geld'sorte *f* (fin) denomination

Geld'spende *f* contribution, donation

Geld'strafe *f* fine

Geld'stück *n* coin

Geld'überhang *m* surplus (of money)

Geld'währung *f* currency; monetary standard

Geld'wechsel *m* money exchange

Geld'wesen *n* financial system, finance

Gelee [ʒeˈle] *m & n* (-s;-s) jelly

gelegen [gəˈleːgən] *pp* of **liegen** || *adj* located; convenient; opportune; **du kommst mir gerade g.** you're just the person I wanted to see; **es kommt mir gerade gelegen** that suits me just fine; **mir ist daran g. zu** (*inf*) I'm anxious to (*inf*); **was ist daran g.?** what of it?

Gele'genheit *f* (-;-en) occasion; opportunity, chance; (com) bargain

Gelegenheits- *comb.fm.* occasional

Gele'genheitsarbeit *f* odd job

Gele'genheitskauf *m* good bargain

gele'gentlich *adj* occasional; casual; chance || *adv* occasionally || *prep* (*genit*) on the occasion of

gelehrig [gəˈleːrɪç] *adj* teachable; intelligent

gelehrsam [gəˈleːrzam] *adj* erudite

gelehrt [gəˈleːrt] *adj* learned, erudite || **Gelehrte §5** *mf* scholar

Geleise [gəˈlaɪzə] *n* (-s;-) rut; (rr) track; **totes G.** blind alley, deadlock

Geleit [gəˈlaɪt] *n* (-[e]s;) escort; **freies** (or **sicheres**) **G.** safe-conduct; **j-m das G. geben** escort s.o., accompany s.o.; **zum G.** forward

geleiten [gəˈlaɪtən] *tr* escort, accompany; **j-n zur Tür g.** see s.o. to the door

Geleit′zug m convoy
Geleit′zugsicherung f convoy escort
Gelenk [gə'leŋk] n (-[e]s;-e) joint
Gelenk′entzündung f arthritis
gelenkig [gə'leŋkıç] adj jointed; flexible; agile
gelernt [gə'lernt] adj skilled
Gelichter [gə'lıçtər] n (-s;) riffraff
Geliebte [gə'liptə] §6 mf beloved, sweetheart
geliehen [gə'li-ən] pp of **leihen**
gelieren [ʒe'lirən] intr jell, gel
gelinde [gə'lındə] adj soft; gentle, mild ‖ adv gently, mildly; **g. gesagt** to put it mildly
gelingen [gə'lıŋən] §142 intr (SEIN) succeed ‖ impers (SEIN)—es gelingt mir I succeed ‖ **Gelingen** n (-s;) success
gelitten [gə'lıtən] pp of **leiden**
gell [gel] adj shrill ‖ interj say!
gellen ['gelən] intr ring out; yell
gel′lend adj shrill, piercing
geloben [gə'lobən] tr solemnly promise, vow; take the vow of ‖ **ref—sich** [dat] g. vow to oneself
gelogen [gə'logən] pp of **lügen**
gelt [gelt] interj say!
gelten ['geltən] §83 tr be worth; **wenig g.** mean little ‖ intr be valid; (Münze) be legal tender; (Gesetz) be in force; (Grund) hold true; (Regel) apply; (Mittel) be allowable; (beim Spiel) count; **g. als** or **für** have the force of; be ranked as; pass for, be considered; **g. lassen** acknowledge as correct; **j—m g.** be aimed at s.o. ‖ impers—**es gilt** be at stake; be a matter of; be worth (s.th.); **es gilt mir gleich, ob** it's all the same to me whether; **es gilt zu** (inf) it is necessary to (inf); **jetzt gilt′s!** here goes!
Gel′tung f (-;) validity; value, importance; **zur G. bringen** make the most of; **zur G. kommen** show off well
Gel′tungsbedürfnis n need for recognition
Gelübde [gə'lYpdə] n (-s;-) vow
gelungen [gə'luŋən] pp of **gelingen** ‖ adj successful; (Wendung) well-turned; funny
Gelüst [gə'lYst] n (-[e]s;-e) desire
gelüsten [gə'lYstən] impers—es gelüstet mich nach I could go for
gemach [gə'max] adv slowly, by degrees ‖ **Gemach** n (-[e]s;⁺er) room; apartment; chamber
gemächlich [gə'meçlıç] adj leisurely; comfortable
Gemahl [gə'mal] m (-[e]s;-e) husband
Gemahlin [gə'malın] f (-;-nen) wife
Gemälde [gə'meldə] n (-s;-) painting
gemäß [gə'mes] prep (dat) according to
gemäßigt [gə'mesıçt] adj moderate
gemein [gə'main] adj common; mean, vile; **sich g. machen mit** associate with ‖ **Gemeine** §5 m (mil) private
Gemeinde [gə'maində] f (-;-n) community; municipality; (eccl) parish
Gemein′deabgaben pl local taxes
Gemein′deanleihen pl municipal bonds

Gemein′dehaus n town hall
gemein′frei adj in the public domain
gemein′gefährlich adj constituting a public danger, dangerous
gemein′gültig adj generally accepted
Gemein′heit f (-;-en) meanness; dirty trick; vulgarity
gemein′hin adv commonly, usually
Gemein′kosten pl overhead
Gemein′nutz m public interest
gemein′nützig adj non-profit
Gemein′platz m platitude
gemeinsam [gə'mainzam] adj common, joint; mutual
Gemein′schaft f (-;-en) community; close association
gemein′schaftlich adj common, joint; mutual
Gemein′schaftsanschluß m (telp) party line
Gemein′schaftsarbeit f teamwork
Gemein′schaftsgeist m esprit de corps
Gemein′sinn m public spirit
gemein′verständlich adj popular; **g. darstellen** popularize
Gemein′wesen n community
Gemein′wohl n commonweal
Gemenge [gə'meŋə] n (-s;-) mixture; (Kampfgewühl) scuffle, melee
gemessen [gə'mesən] pp of **messen** ‖ adj deliberate; precise; dignified; **g. an** (dat) compared with
Gemetzel [gə'metsəl] n (-s;-) massacre
gemieden [gə'midən] pp of **meiden**
Gemisch [gə'mıʃ] n (-es;-e) mixture
Gemischt′warenhandlung f general store
Gemme ['gemə] f (-;-n) gem
gemocht [gə'mɔxt] pp of **mögen**
gemolken [gə'mɔlkən] pp of **melken**
Gemse ['gemzə] f (-;-n) chamois
Gemunkel [gə'muŋkəl] n (-s;-) gossip, whispering
Gemurmel [gə'murməl] n (-s;) murmur
Gemüse [gə'myzə] n (-s;-) vegetable; vegetables
Gemü′sebau m (-[e]s;) vegetable gardening
Gemü′sekonserven pl canned vegetables
gemüßigt [gə'mysıçt] adj—**sich g. fühlen** feel compelled
gemußt [gə'must] pp of **müssen**
Gemüt [gə'myt] n (-[e]s;-er) mind; disposition; person, soul; warmth of feeling; **j—m etw zu Gemüte führen** bring s.th. home to s.o.
gemütlich [gə'mytlıç] adj good-natured, easy-going; (Wohnung) cosy
Gemüt′lichkeit f (-;) easy-going nature; cosiness
Gemüts′art f disposition, nature
Gemüts′bewegung f emotion
gemüts′krank adj melancholy
Gemüts′mensch m warm-hearted person
Gemüts′ruhe f—**in (aller) G.** in peace and quiet
Gemüts′stimmung f mood
Gemüts′verfassung f state of mind
Gemüts′zustand m frame of mind

gemüt'voll *adj* emotional

gen [gen] *prep* (*acc*) (poet) towards ‖ Gen [gen] *n* (-s;-e) (biol) gene

genannt [gə'nant] *pp* of nennen

genau [gə'nau] *adj* exact; fussy

genau'genommen *adv* strictly speaking

Genau'igkeit *f* (-;) exactness, accuracy; meticulousness

Gendarm [3a'darm] *m* (-en;-en) policeman

Gendarme-rie [3ădarmə'ri] *f* (-;-rien ['ri-ən]) rural police; rural police station

Genealo-gie [gene-alə'gi] *f* (-;-gien ['gi-ən]) genealogy

genehm [gə'nem] *adj* agreeable; acceptable; (*dat*) convenient (for)

genehmigen [gə'nemigən] *tr* grant; approve; **sich** [*dat*] etw g. (coll) treat oneself to s.th.; **genehmigt** O.K.

Geneh'migung *f* (-;-en) grant; approval; permission; permit

geneigt [gə'naıkt] *adj* sloping; (zu) inclined (to); (*dat*) well-disposed (towards)

Geneigt'heit *f* inclination; good will

General [gene'ral] *m* (-[e]s;-e & ⁼e) general

General'feldmarschall *m* field marshal

General'inspekteur *m* chief of the joint chiefs of staff

Generalität [generalı'tet] *f* (-;) body of generals

General'konsul *m* consul general

General'leutnant *m* lieutenant general; (aer) air marshal

General'major *m* major general

General'nenner *m* common denominator

General'probe *f* dress rehearsal

General'stabskarte *f* strategic map

General'vollmacht *f* full power of attorney

Generation [genera'tsjon] *f* (-;-en) generation

generell [gene'rel] *adj* general, blanket

genesen [gə'nezən] §84 *intr* (SEIN) convalesce; (von) recover (from)

Gene'sung *f* (-;-en) convalescence

Gene'sungsheim *n* convalescent home

genetisch [gə'netıʃ] *adj* genetic

Genf [genf] *n* (-s;) Geneva

Gen'forscher -in §6 *mf* genetic engineer

Gen'forschung *f* (-;) genetic engineering

genial [ge'njal] *adj* brilliant, gifted

Genick [gə'nık] *n* (-s;-e) nape of the neck

Genick'bruch *m* broken neck

Genick'schlag *m* (box) rabbit punch

Genie [3e'ni] *n* (-s;-s) (man of) genius

genieren [ge'nirən] *tr* bother; embarrass ‖ *ref* feel embarrassed

genieß'bar [gə'nisbar] *adj* edible; drinkable; (fig) agreeable

genießen [gə'nisən] §76 *tr* enjoy; eat; drink

Genie'streich *m* stroke of genius

Genitalien [genı'taljən] *pl* genitals

Geni-tiv ['genıtif] *m* (-s;-tive ['tivə]) genitive

genommen [gə'nəmən] *pp* of nehmen

genoß [gə'nəs] *pret* of genießen

Genosse [gə'nəsə] *m* (-n;-n) companion, buddy; (pol) comrade

-genosse *m comb.fm.* fellow-, -mate

Genos'senschaft *f* (-;-en) association; coöperative

Genossin [gə'nəsın] *f* (-;-nen) companion, buddy; (pol) comrade

genug [gə'nuk] *invar adj* & *adv* enough

Genüge [gə'nygə] *f*—;-m G. tun give s.o. satisfaction; **zur G.** enough; only too well

genügen [gə'nygən] *intr* suffice, do ‖ *ref*—**sich** [*dat*] g. lassen an (*dat*) be content with

genü'gend *adj* sufficient

genügsam [gə'nykzam] *adj* easily satisfied; frugal

genug'tun §154 *intr* (*dat*) satisfy

Genugtuung [gə'nuktu-uŋ] *f* (-;) satisfaction

Ge-nuß [gə'nus] *m* (-nusses;-nüsse) enjoyment; pleasure; (*Nutznießung*) use; (*von Speisen*) consumption

Genuß'mittel *n* semi-luxury (*as coffee, tobacco, etc.*)

genuß'reich *adj* thoroughly enjoyable

genuß'süchtig *adj* pleasure-seeking

Geographie [ge-ogra'fi] *f* (-;) geography

geographisch [ge-o'grafıʃ] *adj* geographical

Geologe [ge-o'logə] *m* (-n;-n) geologist

Geologie [ge-olo'gi] *f* (-;) geology

Geometer [ge-o'metər] *m* (-s;-) surveyor

Geometrie [ge-ome'tri] *f* (-;) geometry

Geophysik [ge-ofy'zik] *f* (-;) geophysics

Geopolitik [ge-opolı'tik] *f* (-;) geopolitics

Georgine [ge-or'ginə] *f* (-;-n) dahlia

Gepäck [gə'pek] *n* (-[e]s;) luggage

Gepäck'abfertigung *f* luggage check-in; luggage counter

Gepäck'ablage *f* luggage rack

Gepäck'anhänger *m* tag; luggage trailer

Gepäck'aufbewahrung *f* baggage room

Gepäck'netz *n* baggage rack (*net type*)

Gepäck'raum *m* luggage compartment

Gepäck'schein *m* luggage check

Gepäck'träger *m* porter; (aut) roof rack

Gepäck'wagen *m* (rr) baggage car

gepanzert [gə'pantsart] *adj* armored

gepfeffert [gə'pfefart] *adj* peppered; (*Worte*) sharp; (*Preis*) exorbitant

Gepfeife [gə'pfaıfə] *n* (-s;) whistling

gepfiffen [gə'pfıfən] *pp* of pfeifen

gepflogen [gə'pflogən] *pp* of pflegen

Gepflo'genheit *f* (-;-en) custom, practice

Geplänkel [gə'pleŋkəl] *n* (-s;) skirmish; (fig) exchange of words

Geplapper [gə'plapar] *n* (-s;) jabber

Geplärr [gə'pler] *n* (-s;) bawling

Geplauder [gə'plaudar] *n* (-s;) small talk, chat

Gepolter [gə'pəltar] *n* (-s;) rumbling

Gepräge [gə'pregə] *n* (-s;) impression; stamp, character

Gepränge [gə'preŋə] *n* (-s;) pomp

gepriesen [gə'pri:zən] *pp* of **preisen**

gequollen [gə'kvɔlən] *pp* of **quellen**

gerade [gə'ra:də] *adj* straight; even; direct; (*Haltung*) erect; (*aufrichtig*) straightforward ‖ *adv* straight; exactly; just; just now ‖ **Gerade** *f* (−n; −n) straight line; straightaway; (box) straight; **rechte G.** straight right

gerade(n)wegs [gə'ra:də(n)veks] *adv* immediately, straightaway

geradezu' *adv* downright

Geranie [ge'ra:njə] *f* (−;−n) geranium

gerannt [gə'rant] *pp* of **rennen**

Gerassel [gə'rasəl] *n* (−s;) clanking

Gerät [gə'rɛt] *n* (−[e]s;−e) device, instrument; tool; (rad, telv) set

geraten [gə'ra:tən] *pp* of **raten** ‖ *adj* successful; (*ratsam*) advisable ‖ §63 *intr* (SEIN) (*gut, schlecht, usw.*) turn out; **außer sich g.** be beside oneself; **g. an** (*acc*) come by; **g. auf** (*acc*) get into; get on to; **g. hinter** (*acc*) get behind; find out about; **g. in** (*acc*) get into, fall into; **g. nach** take after; **g. über** (*acc*) come across; **in Bewegung g.** begin to move; **in Brand g.** catch fire; **ins Schleudern g.** begin to skid; **ins Stocken g.** come to a standstill

Gerä'teschuppen *m* tool shed

Geratewohl [gə'ra:təvo:l] *n* (−s;)—**aufs G.** at random

geraum [gə'raum] *adj* considerable

geräumig [gə'rɔɪmɪç] *adj* spacious

Geräusch [gə'rɔɪʃ] *n* (−[e]s;−e) noise

gerben ['gɛrbən] *tr* tan

Gerberei [gɛrbə'raɪ] *f* (−;−en) tannery

gerecht [gə'rɛçt] *adj* just, fair; justified; **g. werden** (*dat*) do justice to

Gerech'tigkeit *f* (−;) justice; fairness

Gerede [gə're:də] *n* (−s;) talk; hearsay

gereichen [gə'raɪçən] *intr*—**es gereicht ihm zur Ehre** it does him justice; **es gereicht ihm zum Vorteil** it is to his advantage; **es gereicht mir zur Freude** it gives me pleasure

gereizt [gə'raɪtst] *adj* irritable; irritated

gereuen [gə'rɔɪ·ən] *tr* cause (*s.o.*) regret ‖ *ref*—**sich keine Mühe g. lassen** spare no trouble ‖ *impers*—**es gereut mich** I regret

Geriatrie [geri·a'tri] *f* (−;) geriatrics

Gericht [gə'rɪçt] *n* (−[e]s;−e) court; courthouse; judgment; (culin) dish; **das Jüngste G.** the Last Judgment

gericht'lich *adj* legal, judicial, court

Gerichtsbarkeit [gə'rɪçtsbarkaɪt] *f* (−;) jurisdiction

Gerichts'bote *m* (jur) bailiff

Gerichts'hof *m* law court; **Oberster G.** Supreme Court

Gerichts'medizin *f* forensic medicine

Gerichts'saal *m* courtroom

Gerichts'schreiber *m* in §6 *mf* (jur) clerk

Gerichts'stand *m* (jur) venue

Gerichts'verhandlung *f* hearing; trial

Gerichts'vollzieher *m* (jur) marshal

Gerichts'wesen *n* judicial system

gerieben [gə'ri:bən] *pp* of **reiben** ‖ *adj* cunning, smart

Geriesel [gə'ri:zəl] *n* (−s;) purling

gering [gə'rɪŋ] *adj* slight, trifling; small; (*niedrig*) low; (*ärmlich*) poor; (*minderwertig*) inferior; **nicht im geringsten** not in the least

gering'achten *tr* think little of

gering'fügig *adj* insignificant

gering'schätzen *tr* look down on

Gering'schätzung *f* contempt, disdain

gerinnen [gə'rɪnən] §121 *intr* coagulate, clot; (*Milch*) curdle

Gerinnsel [gə'rɪnzəl] *n* (−s;−) clot

Gerippe [gə'rɪpə] *n* (−s;−) skeleton; (*Gerüst*) framework

gerippt [gə'rɪpt] *adj* ribbed; (*Säule*) fluted; (*Stoff*) corded

gerissen [gə'rɪsən] *pp* of **reißen** ‖ *adj* sly

geritten [gə'rɪtən] *pp* of **reiten**

gern(e) ['gɛrn(ə)] *adv* gladly; **g. haben** or **mögen** like; **ich rauche g.** I like to smoke

gerochen [gə'rɔxən] *pp* of **riechen**

Geröll [gə'rœl] *n* (−s;) pebbles

geronnen [gə'rɔnən] *pp* of **gerinnen & rinnen**

Gerste ['gɛrstə] *f* (−;−n) barley

Ger'stenkorn *n* grain of barley; (pathol) sty

Gerte ['gɛrtə] *f* (−;−n) switch, rod

Geruch [gə'rux] *m* (−[e]s;ᵘe) smell

geruch'los *adj* odorless

Gerücht [gə'rʏçt] *m* (−[e]s;−e) rumor

geruhen [gə'ru:ən] *intr* deign

geruhsam [gə'ru:zam] *adj* quiet; relaxed

Gerümpel [gə'rʏmpəl] *n* (−s;) junk

gerungen [gə'ruŋən] *pp* of **ringen**

Gerüst [gə'rʏst] *n* (−s;−e) scaffold; (*Tragewerk*) frame; (fig) outline

Ges [gɛs] *n* (−;−) (mus) G flat

gesamt [gə'zamt] *adj* entire, total

gesamt-, Gesamt- *comb.fm.* total, overall; all-; joint; collective

gesandt [gə'zant] *pp* of **senden**

Gesand'te §5 *mf* envoy

Gesandt'schaft *f* (−;−en) legation

Gesang [gə'zaŋ] *m* (−[e]s;ᵘe) singing; song; (lit) canto

Gesang'verein *m* glee club

Gesäß [gə'zɛs] *n* (−es;−e) buttocks; (coll) behind

Geschäft [gə'ʃɛft] *n* (−[e]s;−e) business; deal, bargain; shop, store

Geschäftemacherei [gə'ʃɛftəmaxərai] *f* (−;) commercialism

geschäftig [gə'ʃɛtɪç] *adj* busy

Geschäf'tigkeit *f* (−;) hustle, bustle

geschäft'lich *adj* business ‖ *adv* on business

Geschäfts'abschluß *m* contract; deal

Geschäfts'aufsicht *f* receivership

Geschäfts'bedingungen *pl* terms

geschäfts'führend *adj* managing; executive; **geschäftsführende Regierung** caretaker government

Geschäfts'führer *m* in §6 *mf* manager

Geschäfts'haus *n* firm; office building

Geschäfts'inhaber *m* in §6 *mf* proprietor

geschäfts'kundig *adj* with business experience

Geschäfts'lokal *n* business premises; (*Laden*) shop; (*Büro*) office

Geschäfts'mann *m* (−[e]s;−leute) businessman

geschäfts'mäßig adj business-like

Geschäfts'ordnung f rules of procedure; **zur G.!** point of order!

Geschäfts'reise f business trip

Geschäfts'schluß m closing time

Geschäfts'stelle f office; branch

Geschäfts'träger m agent, representative; (pol) chargé d'affaires

geschäfts'tüchtig adj sharp

Geschäfts'verbindung f business connections

Geschäfts'verkehr m business transactions

Geschäfts'viertel n business district

Geschäfts'wert m (com) good will

Geschäfts'zweig m line of business

geschah |gə'ʃa] pret of **geschehen**

geschehen [gə'e·ən] §138 intr (SEIN) happen; take place; bring; **das geschieht dir recht!** serves you right! || **Geschehen** n (-s;) events

Geschehnis [gə'enɪs] n (-ses;-se) event

gescheit [gə'ʃart] adj clever; bright; sensible; **er ist wohl nicht ganz g.** he's not all there

Geschenk [gə'eŋk] n (-[e]s;-e) gift

Geschichte [gə'ɪçtə] f (-;-n) story; history; (coll) affair, thing

geschicht'lich adj historical

Geschichts'forscher –in §6 mf, **Geschichts'schreiber** –in §6 mf historian

Geschick [gə'ʃɪk] n (-[e]s;-e) fate, destiny; dexterity; skill

Geschick'lichkeit f (-;) skillfulness

geschickt [gə'ʃɪkt] adj skillful

geschieden [gə'idən] pp of **scheiden**

geschienen [gə'inən] pp of **scheinen**

Geschirr [gə'ɪr] n (-[e]s;-e) dishes; china; pot; (e–s Pferdes) harness

Geschirr'schrank m kitchen cabinet

Geschirrspülmaschine [gə'ɪr/pylma-/inə] f dishwasher

Geschirr'tuch n dishtowel

geschissen [ge'ɪsən] pp of **scheißen**

Geschlecht [gə'leçt] n (-[e]s;-er) sex; race; family; line; (generation; (gram) gender

geschlecht'lich adj sexual

Geschlechts'krankheit f venereal disease

Geschlechts'teile pl genitals

Geschlechts'trieb m sexual instinct

Geschlechts'verkehr m intercourse

Geschlechts'wort n (-[e]s;ˮ) (gram) article

geschlichen [gə'lɪçən] pp of **schleichen**

geschliffen [gə'lɪfən] pp of **schleifen** || adj (Glas) cut; (fig) polished

geschlissen [gə'lɪsən] pp of **schleißen**

geschlossen [gə'losən] pp of **schließen** || adj closed; enclosed; (Front) united; (Gesellschaft) private; (ling) close; (telv) closed-circuit || adv unanimously; **g. hinter j–m stehen** be solidly behind s.o.

geschlungen [gə'luŋən] pp of **schlingen**

Geschmack [gə'mak] m (-s;ˮe & ˮer) taste

Geschmacks'richtung f vogue

geschmeidig [ge'maɪdɪç] adj pliant; flexible; lithe; (Haar) manageable

Geschmeiß [gə'maɪs] n (-es;) vermin; rabble

geschmissen [gə'mɪsən] pp of **schmeißen**

geschmolzen [gə'moltsən] pp of **schmelzen**

Geschnatter [gə'natər] n (-s;) cackle

geschniegelt [gə'nigəlt] adj spruce

geschnitten [gə'nɪtən] pp of **schneiden**

geschnoben [gə'nobən] pp of **schnauben**

geschoben [gə'obən] pp of **schieben**

gescholten [gə'oltən] pp of **schelten**

Geschöpf [gə'œpf] n (-[e]s;-e) creature

geschoren [gə'orən] pp of **scheren**

Ge·schoß [gə'os] n (-schosses;-schosse) shot; missile; shell; floor, story

Geschoß'bahn f trajectory

geschossen [gə'osən] pp of **schießen**

geschraubt [gə'raubt] adj affected; (Stil) stilted

Geschrei [gə'rar] n (-[e]s;) shouting

Geschreibsel [gə'rarpsəl] n (-s;) scribbling, scrawl

geschrieben [gə'ribən] pp of **schreiben**

geschrieen [gə'rɪ·ən] pp of **schreien**

geschritten [gə'rɪtən] pp of **schreiten**

geschunden [gə'undən] pp of **schinden**

Geschütz [gə'yts] n (-es;-e) gun

Geschütz'bedienung f gun crew

Geschütz'legierung f gun metal

Geschütz'stand m gun emplacement

Geschwader [gə'vadər] n (-s;-) (aer) group (consisting of 27 aircraft); (nav) squadron

Geschwätz [gə'vets] n (-es;) chatter

geschweige [gə'vaɪgə]—**g. denn** let alone, much less

geschwiegen [gə'vigən] pp of **schweigen**

geschwind [gə'vɪnt] adj quick

Geschwin'digkeit f (-;-en) speed; velocity; **mit der G. von** at the rate of

Geschwin'digkeitsbegrenzung f speed limit

Geschwin'digkeitsmesser m speedometer

Geschwind'schritt m (mil) double time

Geschwister [gə'vɪstər] pl brother and sister, brothers, sisters, brothers and sisters; siblings

geschwollen [gə'volən] pp of **schwellen** || adj turgid

geschwommen [gə'vomən] pp of **schwimmen**

geschworen [gə'vorən] pp of **schwören** || **Geschworene** §5 mf juror; **die Geschworenen** the jury

Geschwo'renengericht n jury

Geschwulst [gə'vulst] f (-;ˮe) swelling; tumor

geschwunden [gə'vundən] pp of **schwinden**

geschwungen [gə'vuŋən] pp of **schwingen**

Geschwür [gə'vyr] n (-s;-e) ulcer

Geselle [gə'zɛlə] *m* (-n; -n) journeyman; companion; lad, fellow

gesellen [gə'zɛlən] *ref*—**sich zu j—m** g. join s.o.

gesellig [gə'zɛlɪç] *adj* gregarious, sociable

Gesell'schaft *f* (-; -en) society; company; (pej) bunch; (com) company; **j—m G. leisten** keep s.o. company

Gesell'schafter **-in** §6 *mf* companion; shareholder; (com) partner

gesell'schaftlich *adj* social

Gesell'schaftsspiel *n* party game

Gesell'schaftswissenschaft *f* social science; sociology

gesessen [gə'zɛsən] *pp* of **sitzen**

Gesetz [gə'zɛts] *n* (-es; -e) law

Gesetz'buch *n* legal code

Gesetz'entwurf *m* (parl) bill

Gesetzes- [gazɛtsəs] *comb.fm.* legal, of law, of the law

Geset'zesantrag *m*, **Geset'zesvorlage** *f* (parl) bill

gesetz'gebend *adj* legislative

Gesetz'geber **-in** §6 *mf* legislator

Gesetz'gebung *f* (-;) legislation

gesetz'lich *adj* legal

gesetz'los *adj* lawless

gesetz'mäßig *adj* legal; legitimate

Gesetz'sammlung *f* code of laws

gesetzt [gə'zɛtst] *adj* sedate; (*Alter*) mature; **g. den Fall, daß** assuming that ǁ *adv* in a dignified manner

gesetz'widrig *adj* illegal, unlawful

Gesicht [gə'zɪçt] *n* (-[e]s; -er) face; sight; eyesight; (*Aussehen*) look

Gesichts'farbe *f* complexion

Gesichts'kreis *m* horizon; outlook

Gesichts'punkt *m* point of view, angle

Gesichts'spannung *f* face lift

Gesichts'zug *m* feature

Gesims [gə'zɪms] *n* (-es; -e) molding

Gesindel [gə'zɪndəl] *n* (-s;) rabble; **lichtscheues G.** shady characters

gesinnt [gə'zɪnt] *adj* disposed; -minded

Gesinnung [gə'zɪnʊŋ] *f* (-; -en) mind; character; convictions

gesin'nungslos *adj* without definite convictions

gesin'nungsmäßig *adv* according to one's convictions

gesin'nungstreu, gesin'nungstüchtig *adj* staunch

gesittet [gə'zɪtət] *adj* polite; civilized

gesoffen [gə'zɔfən] *pp* of **saufen**

gesogen [gə'zogən] *pp* of **saugen**

gesonnen [gə'zɔnən] *pp* of **sinnen** ǁ *adj*—**g. sein zu** (*inf*) have a mind to (*inf*), be inclined to (*inf*)

gesotten [gə'zɔtən] *pp* of **sieden**

Gespann [gə'ʃpan] *n* (-[e]s; -e) team; pair, combination

gespannt [gə'ʃpant] *adj* stretched; tense; (*Aufmerksamkeit*) close; (*Beziehungen*) strained; **ich bin g.** (coll) I wonder, I am anxious to know

Gespenst [gə'ʃpɛnst] *n* (-[e]s; -er) ghost, specter

gespen'sterhaft *adj* ghostly; spooky

gespenstisch [gə'ʃpɛnstɪʃ] *adj* ghostly

gespie(e)n [gə'ʃpi(ə)n] *pp* of **speien**

Gespiele [gə'ʃpilə] *m* (-n; -n), **Gespielin** [gə'ʃpilɪn] *f* (-; -nen) playmate

Gespinst [gə'ʃpɪnst] *n* (-es; -e) yarn, (*Gewebe*) web

gesponnen [gə'ʃpɔnən] *pp* of **spinnen**

Gespött [gə'ʃpœt] *n* (-[e]s;) ridicule; laughing stock

Gespräch [gə'ʃprɛç] *n* (-[e]s; -e) conversation; (telp) call; **Gespräche** (pol) talks; **G. mit Voranmeldung** person-to-person call

gesprächig [gə'ʃprɛçɪç] *adj* talkative

gespreizt [gə'ʃpraɪtst] *adj* outspread; affected ǁ *adv*—**g. tun** act big

gesprenkelt [gə'ʃprɛŋkəlt] *adj* spotted

gesprochen [gə'ʃprɔçən] *pp* of **sprechen**

gesprossen [gə'ʃprɔsən] *pp* of **sprießen**

gesprungen [gə'ʃprʊŋən] *pp* of **springen**

Gestade [gə'ʃtadə] *n* (-s;-) (river) bank; (sea)shore

Gestalt [gə'ʃtalt] *f* (-; -en) shape; figure; (*Wuchs*) stature

gestalten [gə'ʃtaltən] *tr* shape; form; arrange ǁ *ref* take shape; turn out

Gestal'tung *f* (-; -en) formation; development; arrangement; design

gestanden [gə'ʃtandən] *pp* of **stehen**

geständig [gə'ʃtɛndɪç] *adj*—**g. sein** admit one's guilt

Geständnis [gə'ʃtɛntnɪs] *n* (-ses;-se) confession, admission

Gestank [gə'ʃtaŋk] *m* (-[e]s;) stench

Gestapo [gə'ʃtapo] *f* (-;) (Geheime Staatspolizei) secret state police

gestatten [gə'ʃtatən] *tr* permit, allow

Geste ['gɛstə] *f* (-;-n) gesture

gestehen [gə'ʃte-ən] §146 *tr* admit

Gestein [gə'ʃtaɪn] *n* (-[e]s;-e) rock

Gestell [gə'ʃtɛl] *n* (-[e]s;-e) frame; rack; mounting; (coll) beanpole

Gestel'lungsbefehl *m* (mil) induction orders

gestern ['gɛstərn] *adv* yesterday; **g. abend** last evening, last night

gestiefelt [gə'ʃtifəlt] *adj* in boots

gestiegen [gə'ʃtigən] *pp* of **steigen**

gestikulieren [gɛstiku'lirən] *intr* gesticulate

Gestirn [gə'ʃtɪrn] *n* (-[e]s;-e) star; (*Sternbild*) constellation

gestirnt [gə'ʃtɪrnt] *adj* starry

gestoben [gə'ʃtobən] *pp* of **stieben**

Gestöber [gə'ʃtøbər] *n* (-s;-) snow flurry

gestochen [gə'ʃtɔxən] *pp* of **stechen**

gestohlen [gə'ʃtolən] *pp* of **stehlen**

gestorben [gə'ʃtɔrbən] *pp* of **sterben**

gestoßen [gə'ʃtosən] *pp* of **stoßen**

Gesträuch [gə'ʃtrɔɪç] *n* (-[e]s;) bushes, shrubbery

gestreift [gə'ʃtraɪft] *adj* striped

gestrichen [gə'ʃtrɪçən] *pp* of **streichen**

gestrig ['gɛstrɪç] *adj* yesterday's

gestritten [gə'ʃtrɪtən] *pp* of **streiten**

Gestrüpp [gə'ʃtrʏp] *n* (-[e]s;) underbrush

gestunken [gə'ʃtʊŋkən] *pp* of **stinken**

Gestüt [gə'ʃtyt] *n* (-[e]s;-e) stud farm

Gestüt'hengst *m* stallion, studhorse

Gesuch [gə'zux] *n* (-[e]s;-e) request; application; (jur) petition

gesucht [gə'zuxt] *adj* wanted; in demand; studied; (*Vergleich*) farfetched

Gesudel [gə'zudəl] *n* (-s;) messy job

Gesumme [gə'zumə] n (-s;) humming
gesund [gə'zunt] adj healthy; sound; wholesome; **g. werden** get well
Gesund'beter –in §6 mf faith healer
Gesund'brunnen m mineral spring
gesunden [gə'zundən] intr (SEIN) get well again, recover
Gesund'heit f (-;) health; **auf Ihre G.!** to your health!; **G.!** (God) bless you!
Gesund'heitslehre f hygiene
Gesund'heitspflege f hygiene
Gesund'heitsrücksichten pl—**aus G.** for reasons of health
Gesund'heitswesen n public health
gesungen [gə'zuŋən] pp of **singen**
gesunken [gə'zuŋkən] pp of **sinken**
Getäfel [gə'tefəl] n (-s;) wainscoting
getä'felt adj inlaid
getan [gə'tɑn] pp of **tun**
Getöse [gə'tøzə] n (-s;) din, noise
getragen [gə'trɑgən] pp of **tragen** || adj solemn
Getrampel [gə'trampəl] n (-s;) trample
Getränk [gə'treŋk] n (-[e]s;-e) drink
getrauen [gə'trau-ən] ref dare
Getreide [gə'traidə] n (-s;-) grain
Getrei'deboden m granary
Getrei'despeicher m grain elevator
getreu [gə'trɔi] adj faithful, true
getreu'lich adv faithfully
Getriebe [gə'tribə] n (-s;-) hustle and bustle; (adm) machinery; (aut) transmission
getrieben [gə'tribən] pp of **treiben**
getroffen [gə'trɔmən] pp of **treffen**
getrogen [gə'trɔgən] pp of **trügen**
getrost [gə'trost] adj confident
getrunken [gə'truŋkən] pp of **trinken**
Getto ['geto] n (-s;-s) ghetto
Getue [gə'tu-ə] n (-s;) fuss
Getümmel [gə'tYməl] n (-s;) turmoil
getupft [gə'tupft] adj polka-dot
Geviert [gə'firt] n (-[e]s;-e) square
Gewächs [gə'veks] n (-es;-e) growth; plant
gewachsen [gə'vaksən] adj—**g. sein** (dat) be equal to, be up to
Gewächs'haus n greenhouse, hothouse
gewagt [gə'vakt] adj risky; off-color
gewählt [gə'velt] adj choice; refined
gewahr [gə'var] adj—**g. werden** (genit) become aware of
Gewähr [gə'ver] f (-;) guarantee
gewahren [gə'varən] tr notice
gewähren [gə'verən] tr grant
gewähr'leisten tr guarantee, ensure
Gewähr'leistung f (-;-en) guarantee
Gewahrsam [gə'varzam] m (-[e]s;) safekeeping, custody || n (-[e]s;-e) prison
Gewährs'mann m (-[e]s;-er & -leute) informant, source
Gewährs'pflicht f warranty
Gewalt [gə'valt] f (-;-en) force; violence; authority; (Aufsicht) control
Gewalt'haber m (-s;-) ruler; tyrant
Gewalt'herrschaft f tyranny
Gewalt'herrscher m tyrant
gewal'tig adj powerful; huge; (coll) awful || adv terribly
Gewalt'kur f drastic measure; (coll) crash program
gewalt'los adj nonviolent

Gewalt'marsch m forced march
Gewalt'mensch m brute, tyrant
gewaltsam [gə'valtzam] adj violent; forcible; drastic || adv by force
Gewalt'samkeit f (-;) violence
Gewalt'streich m bold stroke
Gewalt'tat f act of violence
gewalt'tätig adj violent, brutal
Gewalt'verbrechen n felony
Gewalt'verbrecher –in §6 mf felon
Gewand [gə'vant] n (-[e]s;-er) robe; appearance, guise; (eccl) vestment
gewandt [gə'vant] pp of **wenden** || adj agile; clever
gewann [gə'van] pret of **gewinnen**
gewärtig [gə'vertiç] adj—**g. sein** (genit) be prepared for
Gewäsch [gə'veʃ] n (-es;) nonsense
Gewässer [gə'vesər] n (-s;-) body of water; waters
Gewebe [gə'vebə] n (-s;-) tissue; (tex) fabric
geweckt [gə'vekt] adj bright, sharp
Gewehr [gə'ver] n (-[e]s;-e) rifle
Geweih [gə'vai] n (-[e]s;-e) antlers
Gewerbe [gə'verbə] n (-s;-) trade, business; calling, profession; industry
Gewer'bebetrieb m business enterprise
Gewer'beschule f trade school
gewerblich [gə'verpliç] adj industrial; commercial, business
gebwerbs'mäßig adj professional
Gewerkschaft [gə'verk/aft] f (-;-en) labor union
gewerk'schaftlich adj union || adv— **sich g. organisieren** unionize
Gewerk'schaftsbeitrag m union dues
gewesen [gə'vezən] pp of **sein**
gewichen [gə'viçən] pp of **weichen**
Gewicht [gə'viçt] n (-[e]s;-e) (& fig) weight
gewichtig [gə'viçtiç] adj weighty
gewiegt [gə'vigt] adj experienced, smart, shrewd
gewiesen [gə'vizən] pp of **weisen**
gewillt [gə'vilt] adj willing
Gewimmel [gə'viməl] n (-s;) swarm; (Menschen–) throng
Gewimmer [gə'vimər] n (-s;) whimpering; whining
Gewinde [gə'vində] n (-s;-) thread (of a screw); (Kranz) garland; skein
Gewinn [gə'vin] m (-[e]s;-e) winnings; profit; (Vorteil) advantage
Gewinn'anteil m dividend
Gewinn'aufschlag m (com) markup
Gewinn'beteiligung f profit sharing
gewinn'bringend adj profitable
gewinnen [gə'vinən] §121 tr win, gain; reach || intr win; make a profit; improve; **g. an** (dat) gain in; **g. von** or **durch** profit by
gewin'nend adj engaging
Gewinn'spanne f margin of profit
Gewinn'sucht f greed; profiteering
Gewinsel [gə'vinzəl] n (-s;) whimpering
Gewirr [gə'vir] n (-[e]s;-e) tangle; entanglement; maze
gewiß [gə'vis] adj sure, certain || adv certainly; **aber g.!** of course!
Gewissen [gə'visən] n (-s;-) conscience

gewis'senhaft *adj* conscientious
gewis'senlos *adj* unscrupulous
Gewis'sensbisse *pl* pangs of conscience
Gewis'sensnot *f* moral dilemma
gewis'sermaßen *adv* to some extent; so to speak
Gewiß'heit *f* (-;-en) certainty
gewiß'lich *adv* certainly
Gewitter [gə'vɪtər] *n* (-s;-) thunderstorm
gewittern [gə'vɪtərn] *impers*—es gewittert a storm is brewing
Gewit'terregen *m* thundershower
gewitzigt [gə'vɪtsɪçt] *adj*—g. sein to have learned from experience
gewitzt [gə'vɪtst] *adj* bright, smart
gewoben [gə'vobən] *pp* of weben
gewogen [gə'vogən] *pp* of wägen & wiegen || *adj* well disposed
Gewo'genheit *f* (-;) favorable attitude
gewöhnen [gə'vønən] *tr* (an *acc*) accustom (to) || *ref* (an *acc*) get used (to)
Gewohnheit [gə'vonhaɪt] *f* (-;-en) habit, custom
gewohn'heitsmäßig *adj* habitual
Gewohn'heitsmensch *m* creature of habit
gewöhnlich [gə'vønlɪç] *adj* usual; normal; common, ordinary
gewohnt [gə'vont] *adj* usual; g. sein (*acc*) be used to
Gewölbe [gə'vœlbə] *n* (-s;-) vault; arch
gewölbt [gə'vœlpt] *adj* vaulted
Gewölk [gə'vœlk] *n* (-[e]s;) clouds
gewonnen [gə'vonən] *pp* of gewinnen
geworben [gə'vorbən] *pp* of werben
geworden [gə'vordən] *pp* of werden
geworfen [gə'vorfən] *pp* of werfen
gewrungen [gə'vruŋən] *pp* of wringen
Gewühl [gə'vyl] *n* (-[e]s;) milling crowd
gewunden [gə'vundən] *pp* of winden
gewürfelt [gə'vyrfəlt] *adj* checkered
Gewürm [gə'vyrm] *n* (-[e]s;) vermin
Gewürz [gə'vyrts] *n* (-[e]s;-e) spice
Gewürz'nelke *f* clove
gewußt [gə'vust] *pp* of wissen
Geysir ['gaɪzɪr] *m* (-s;-) geyser
gezackt [gə'tsakt] *adj* jagged; (bot) serrated
gezähnt [gə'tsent] *adj* toothed; (*Rand*) perforated; (bot) dentated
Gezänk [gə'tsɛŋk] *n* (-[e]s;) squabbling
Gezeiten [gə'tsaɪtən] *pl* tides
Gezeiten- *comb.fm.* tidal
Gezeter [gə'tsetər] *n* (-s;) yelling
geziehen [gə'tsi·ən] *pp* of zeihen
geziemen [gə'tsimən] *intr* (dat) be proper for || *impers ref*—es geziemt sich für j-n it is right for s.o.
geziert [gə'tsirt] *adj* affected, phoney
Gezisch [gə'tsɪʃ] *n* (-es;) hissing
gezogen [gə'tsogən] *pp* of ziehen
Gezücht [gə'tsyçt] *n* (-[e]s;-e) riffraff
Gezwitscher [gə'tsvɪtʃər] *n* (-s;) chirping
gezwungen [gə'tsvuŋən] *pp* of zwingen || *adj* forced; (*Stil*) labored || *adv* stiffly
Gicht [gɪçt] *f* (-;-en) gout

Giebel ['gibəl] *m* (-s;-) gable
Gier [gir] *f* (-;) greed
gierig ['girɪç] *adj* (nach) greedy (for)
Gießbach ['gisbax] *m* torrent
gießen ['gisən] §76 *tr* pour; (*Blumen, usw.*) water; (metal) cast, found || *impers*—es gießt it is pouring
Gießer ['gisər] *m* (-s;-) foundryman
Gießerei [gisə'raɪ] *f* (-;-en) foundry
Gieß'form *f* casting mold; (typ) matrix
Gieß'kanne *f* sprinkling can
Gift [gɪft] *n* (-[e]s;-e) poison
giftig ['gɪftɪç] *adj* poisonous; malicious
Gigant [gi'gant] *m* (-en;-en) giant
Gilde ['gɪldə] *f* (-;-n) guild
Gimpel ['gɪmpəl] *m* (-s;-) (coll) sucker
ging [gɪŋ] *pret* of gehen
Gipfel ['gɪpfəl] *m* (-s;-) top; peak
Gip'felkonferenz *f* summit meeting
Gips [gɪps] *m* (-es;-e) gypsum; plaster of Paris; (surg) cast
Gips'arbeit *f* plastering
Gips'diele *f* plasterboard
gipsen ['gɪpsən] *tr* plaster
Gips'verband *m* (surg) cast
Giraffe [gi'rafə] *f* (-;-n) giraffe
girieren [ʒi'rirən] *tr* endorse
Girlande [gɪr'landə] *f* (-;-n) garland
Giro ['ʒiro] *n* (-s;-s) endorsement
girren ['gɪrən] *intr* coo
Gis [gɪs] *n* (-;-) (mus) G sharp
Gischt [gɪʃt] *m* (-es;) foam; spray
Gitarre [gi'tarə] *f* (-;-n) guitar
Gitter ['gɪtər] *n* (-s;-) grating, grille; bars; lattice; railing; trellis; (electron) grid
Git'terbett *n* baby crib
Git'ternetz *n* grid (on map)
Git'tertor *n* wrought-iron gate
Git'terwerk *n* latticework
Glacéhandschuhe [gla'sehant/u·ə] *pl* (& fig) kid gloves
Gladi·ator [gladɪ'atər] *m* (-s;-atoren [a'torən]) gladiator
Glanz [glants] *m* (-es;) shine; polish; luster; brilliance
glänzen ['glentsən] *tr* polish || *intr* shine; durch Abwesenheit g. be conspicuous by one's absence
glän'zend *adj* bright; glossy; polished; (fig) splendid, brilliant
Glanz'leder *n* patent leather
Glanz'licht *n* (paint) highlight
glanz'los *adj* dull; lackluster
Glanz'punkt *m* highlight
Glanz'stück *n* master stroke
glanz'voll *adj* brilliant, splendid
Glanz'zeit *f* heyday, golden age
Glas [glas] *n* (-es;-er) glass
Glaser ['glazər] *m* (-s;-) glazier
gläsern ['glezərn] *adj* glass; glassy
Glas'hütte *f* glassworks
glasieren [gla'zirən] *tr* glaze; (*Kuchen*) frost, ice
glasig ['glazɪç] *adj* glassy; vitreous
Glas'jalousie *f* jalousie window
Glas'scheibe *f* pane of glass
Glasur [gla'zur] *f* (-;-en) enamel (on pots); glaze; (culin) icing
glatt [glat] *adj* smooth; (*eben*) even; (*poliert*) glossy; (*schlüpfrig*) slippery; (*Absage*) flat; (*Lüge*) downright || *adv* smoothly; directly; entirely

Glätte ['glɛtə] f (-;) smoothness; slipperiness; (*Politur*) polish

Glatt/eis n sheet of ice; **bei G. fahren** drive in icy conditions

glätten ['glɛtən] tr smooth; smooth out || ref smooth out; become calm

glatt/streichen §85 tr smooth out

glatt/weg adv outright, point-blank

glattzüngig ['glattsʏŋɪç] adj smooth-talking

Glatze ['glatsə] f (-;-n) bald head

glatz/köpfig adj baldheaded

Glaube ['glaubə] m (-ns;), **Glauben** ['glaubən] m (-s;) belief; faith

glauben ['glaubən] tr believe; (*annehmen*) suppose || intr (dat) believe; **g. an** (acc) believe in; **j-m aufs Wort glauben** take s.o.'s word

Glau/bensbekenntnis n profession of faith; creed

Glau/benslehre f Christian doctrine

Glau/benssatz m dogma

gläubig ['glɔɪbɪç] adj believing || **Gläubige** §5 mf believer || **Gläubiger** -in §6 mf creditor

glaublich ['glauplɪç] adj credible

glaub/würdig adj credible; reliable; plausible

Glaukom [glau'kom] n (-s;-e) glaucoma

gleich [glaɪç] adj (dat) like; (an dat) equal (in); **es ist mir ganz g.** it's all the same to me || adv equally; immediately

gleichaltrig ['glaɪçaltrɪç] adj of the same age

gleich/artig adj similar, homogeneous

gleich/bedeutend adj synonymous

Gleich/berechtigung f (pol) equality

gleichen ['glaɪçən] §85 intr (dat) resemble, look like, be like

glei/chermaßen adv equally, likewise

gleich/falls adv likewise; as well

gleich/förmig adj uniform; regular; monotonous

gleich/gesinnt adj like-minded

Gleich/gewicht n equilibrium

gleich/gültig adj indifferent; **es ist mir g.** it's all the same to me

Gleich/heit f (-;-en) equality; (*Ähnlichkeit*) likeness

Gleich/klang m consonance; unison

gleich/kommen §99 intr (SEIN) (dat) equal; (dat) be tantamount to

gleich/laufend adj (mit) parallel (to)

gleich/machen tr make equal; standardize; **dem Erdboden g.** raze

Gleich/maß n regularity; evenness; balance, equilibrium; proportion

gleich/mäßig adj symmetrical; regular

Gleich/mut m equanimity, calmness

gleich/mütig adj calm

gleichnamig ['glaɪçnamɪç] adj of the same name; (phys) like

Gleichnis ['glaɪçnɪs] n (-ses;-se) parable; figure of speech; simile

Gleich/richter m (elec) rectifier

gleichsam ['glaɪçzam] adv so to speak; more or less, practically

gleichschenklig ['glaɪçʃɛŋklɪç] adj isosceles

Gleich/schritt m—**im G.** in cadence; **im G. marsch!** forward, march!

---

gleich/seitig adj equilateral

gleich/setzen tr (dat or mit) equate (with)

Gleich/setzung f (-;), **Gleich/stellung** f (-;) equalization

Gleich/strom m direct current

gleich/tun §154 tr—**es j-m g.** emulate s.o.

Glei/chung f (-;-en) (math) equation

gleichviel/ adv—**g.** wer no matter who

gleich/wertig adj evenly matched

gleichwohl/ adv nevertheless

gleich/zeitig adj simultaneous

gleich/ziehen §163 intr (mit) catch up (with or to)

Gleis [glaɪs] n (-es;-e) (rr) track

Gleitboot ['glaɪtbot] n hydrofoil

gleiten ['glaɪtən] §86 intr (SEIN) glide; slip, slide

Gleitfläche ['glaɪtflɛçə] f (aer) hydroplane

Gleitflugzeug ['glaɪtfluktsɔɪk] n (aer) glider

Gleitschutz- comb.fm. skid-proof

Gleit/zeit f flexitime

Gletscher ['glɛtʃər] m (-s;-) glacier

glich [glɪç] pret of gleichen

Glied [glit] n (-[e]s;-er) limb; member; joint; link; (anat) penis; (log, math) term; (mil) rank, file

glie/derlahm adj paralyzed

gliedern ['glidərn] tr arrange; plan; divide, break down || ref (in acc) consist of

Glie/derung f (-;-en) arrangement; construction; division; organization

Gliedmaßen ['glitmasən] pl limbs

glimmen ['glɪmən] intr §136 & §109 intr glimmer; glow

Glim/mer m (-s;) glimmer; (min) mica

glimpflich ['glɪmpflɪç] adj gentle; (*Strafe*) light, lenient

glitschen ['glɪtʃən] intr (SEIN) slip

glitschig ['glɪtʃɪç] adj slippery

glitt [glɪt] pret of gleiten

glitzern ['glɪtsərn] intr glitter

global [glo'bal] adj global

Globus ['globus] m (-bus & -busses; -busse & -ben [bən]) globe

Glöckchen ['glœkçən] n (-s;-) small bell

Glocke ['glɔkə] f (-;-n) bell; (e-s Rocks) flare

Glockenspiel (**Glok/kenspiel**) n carillon

Glockenstube (**Glok/kenstube**) f, **Glockenturm** (**Glok/kenturm**) m belfry

Glockenzug (**Glok/kenzug**) m bell rope

Glöckner ['glœknər] m (-s;-) bell ringer; sexton

glomm [glom] pret of glimmen

Glorie ['gloriə] f (-;-n) glory

Glo/rienschein m halo

glorreich ['glorraɪç] adj glorious

glotzäugig ['glɔtsɔɪgɪç] adj popeyed

glotzen ['glɔtsən] intr stare, goggle

Glück [glyk] n (-[e]s;) luck; fortune; happiness; **auf gut G.** at random; **zum G.** luckily

glucken ['glukən] intr cluck

glücken ['glykən] intr (SEIN) succeed || impers—**es glückt mir** I succeed

gluckern ['glukərn] intr gurgle

glück′lich adj lucky, fortunate; happy; (günstig) auspicious
glück′licherweise adv fortunately
glück′selig adj blissful; blessed; joyful
Glück′seligkeit f (–;) bliss; joy
glucksen [′gluksən] intr gurgle; chuckle
Glücks′fall m stroke of luck; windfall
Glücks′güter pl earthly possessions
Glücks′hafen m raffle drum
Glücks′pilz m (coll) lucky dog
Glücks′spiel n game of chance
Glücks′topf m grab bag
glück′verheißend adj auspicious
Glück′wunsch m good wishes, congratulations
Glück′wunschkarte f greeting card
Glühbirne [′glybɪrnə] f light bulb
glühen [′gly·ən] tr make red-hot; (metal) anneal || intr glow
glü′hendheiß′ adj red-hot
Glühfaden [′glyfadən] m filament
Glühwurm [′glyvurm] m firefly
Glut [glut] f (–;) embers; fire; scorching heat; (fig) ardor
Glyzerin [glytsə′rin] n (–s;) glycerine
GmbH abbr **(Gesellschaft mit beschränkter Haftung)** Inc.; Ltd. (Brit)
Gnade [′gnɑdə] f (–;-n) grace; favor; mercy; **von eigenen Gnaden** self-styled
Gna′denbeweis m token of favor
Gna′denbrot n—bei j–m das G. essen to live on s.o.'s charity
Gna′denfrist f grace, e.g., e–e G. von zwei Monaten two months' grace
Gna′dengesuch n plea for mercy
Gna′denstoß m coup de grâce, deathblow
gnädig [′gnɛdɪç] adj gracious, kind; merciful; **gnädige Frau** madam; **Sehr verehrte gnädige Frau** Dear Madam
Gold [gɔlt] n (–[e]s;) gold
Gold′blech n gold foil
Gold′fink m (orn) goldfinch
goldig [′gɔldɪç] adj (coll) cute
Gold′plombe f (dent) gold filling
Gold′schmied m goldsmith
Gold′schnitt m gilt edging
Golf [gɔlf] m (–[e]s;-e) gulf; bay || n (–s;) golf
Golf′platz m golf course
Golf′schläger m golf club
Gondel [′gɔndəl] f (–;-n) gondola
Gon′delführer m gondolier
gönnen [′gœnən] tr not begrudge; allow; j–m etw nicht g. begrudge s.o. s.th.
Gön′ner –in §6 mf patron
gön′nerhaft adj patronizing
Gön′nerschaft f (–;) patronage
gor [gor] pret of gären
Gorilla [go′rɪla] m (–s;-s) gorilla
goß [gɔs] pret of gießen
Gosse [′gɔsə] f (–;-n) gutter
Gote [′gotə] m (–n;-n) Goth
gotisch [′gotɪʃ] adj Gothic
Gott [gɔt] m (–[e]s;ℵer) god; God
gottbegnadet [′gɔtbəgnadət] adj gifted
gott′ergeben adj resigned to God's will
Got′tesdienst m divine service; Mass
got′tesfürchtig adj God-fearing
Got′tesgabe f godsend

got′teslästerlich adj blasphemous
Got′teslästerung f blasphemy
Got′tesurteil n ordeal
gott′gefällig adj pleasing to God
Gott′heit f (–;-en) deity, divinity
Göttin [′gœtɪn] f (–;-nen) goddess
göttlich [′gœtlɪç] adj godlike, divine; (fig) heavenly
gottlob′ interj thank goodness!
Gott′mensch m God incarnate
gott′selig adj godly
gott′verlassen adj godforsaken
Götze [′gœtsə] m (–n;-n) idol
Göt′zenbild n idol
Göt′zendiener –in §6 mf idolater
Göt′zendienst m idolatry
Gouvernante [guver′nantə] f (–;-n) governess
Gouverneur [guver′nør] m (–s;-e) governor
Grab [grap] n (–[e]s;ℵer) grave; tomb
graben [′grabən] §87 tr dig; burrow || **Graben** m (–s;ℵ) ditch; trench; moat
Grab′geläute n death knell
Grab′gesang m funeral dirge
Grab′hügel m burial mound
Grab′inschrift f epitaph
Grab′mal n tombstone; tomb, sepulcher
Grab′stätte f burial place
Grab′stelle f burial plot
Grad [grat] m (–[e]s;-e) degree; grade; (mil) rank
grade [′gradə] adv var of gerade
Grad′einteilung f gradation
Grad′messer m graduated scale; (fig) yardstick
grad′weise adv by degrees
Graf [graf] m (–en;-en) count; earl (Brit)
Gräfin [′grefɪn] f (–;-nen) countess
gräflich [′greflɪç] adj count's; earl's
Graf′schaft f (–;-en) county
gram [gram] adj—j–m g. sein be cross with s.o. || **Gram** m (–[e]s;) grief
grämen [′gremən] tr sadden, distress || ref (über acc) grieve (over)
grämlich [′gremlɪç] adj glum; crabby
Gramm [gram] n (–s;- & -e) gram
Grammatik [gra′matɪk] f (–;-en) grammar
grammatisch [gra′matɪʃ] adj grammatical
Gran [gran] n (–[e]s;) (fig) bit, jot
Granat [gra′nat] m (–[e]s;-e) garnet
Granat′apfel m pomegranate
Granate [gra′natə] f (–;-n) (arti) shell; (mil) grenade
Granat′feuer n shelling
Granat′hülse f shell case
Granat′splitter m shrapnel
Granat′werfer m (mil) mortar
grandios [grandɪ′os] adj grandiose
Granit [gra′nit] m (–[e]s;-e) granite
Graphik [′grafɪk] f (–;-en) graphic arts; print; engraving; woodcut
graphisch [′grafɪʃ] adj graphic
Graphit [gra′fit] m (–[e]s;) graphite
Gras [gras] n (–es;ℵer) grass
grasen [′grazən] intr graze
Gras′halm m blade of grass
Grashüpfer [′grashypfer] m (–s;-) grasshopper

grasig ['grɑzɪç] *adj* grassy

Gras'mäher *m* lawn mower; grass cutter

Gras'mähmaschine *f* lawn mower

Gras'narbe *f* sod, turf

grassieren [gra'sirən] *intr* rage

gräßlich ['grɛslɪç] *adj* grisly

Gras'weide *f* pasture

Grat [grɑt] *m* (-[e]s;-e) ridge; edge

Gräte ['grɛtə] *f* (-;-n) fishbone

Gratifikation [gratɪfɪka'tsjon] *f* (-; -en) bonus

grätig ['grɛtɪç] *adj* full of fishbones; (*mürrisch*) crabby

gratis ['grɑtɪs] *adv* gratis; g. und franko (coll) for free

Gratulation [gratula'tsjon] *f* (-;-en) congratulations

gratulieren [gratu'lirən] *intr—j—m* g. zu congratulate s.o. on

grau [grau] *adj* gray; (*Vorzeit*) remote || Grau *n* (- & -s;-s) gray

Grau'bär *m* grizzly bear

grauen ['grau·ən] *intr* dawn || *impers* —es graut day is breaking; es graut mir vor (*dat*) I shudder at || Grauen *n* (-s;) (vor *dat*) horror (of)

grau'enhaft, grau'envoll *adj* horrible

gräulich ['grɔɪlɪç] *adj* grayish

Graupe ['graupə] *f* (-;-n) peeled barley

graupeln ['graupəln] *impers*—es graupelt it is sleeting || Graupeln *pl* sleet

Graus [graus] *m* (-es;) dread, horror

grausam ['grauzam] *adj* cruel; (coll) awful

Grau'schimmel *m* gray horse

grausen ['grauzən] *impers*—es graust mir vor (*dat*) I shudder at

grausig ['grauzɪç] *adj* gruesome

Graveur [gra'vør] *m* (-s;-e) engraver

gravieren [gra'virən] *tr* engrave

gravie'rend *adj* aggravating

gravitätisch [gravɪ'tɛtɪʃ] *adj* stately

Grazie ['grɑtsjə] *f* (-;-n) grace, charm

graziös [gra'tsjøs] *adj* graceful

Greif [graɪf] *m* (-[e]s;-e) griffin

greifbar ['graɪfbar] *adj* tangible; at hand

greifen ['graɪfən] §88 *tr* grasp; seize; (*Note*) strike || *intr* (*Anker*) catch; (*Zahnrad*) engage; ans Herz g. touch deeply; an j-s Ehre g. attack s.o.'s honor; g. in (*acc*) reach into; g. nach reach for; try to seize; g. zu reach for; (fig) resort to; um sich g. grope about; (*Feuer*) spread; zu den Waffen g. take up arms

Greis [grɑɪs] *m* (-es;-e) old man

Grei'senalter *n* old age

grei'senhaft *adj* aged; senile

Greisin ['graɪzɪn] *f* (-;-nen) old lady

grell [grɛl] *adj* (*Ton*) shrill; (*Farbe, Kleider*) flashy; (*Licht*) glaring

Gre·mium ['gremjum] *n* (-s;-mien [mjən]) group, body; committee; corporation

Grenze ['grɛntsə] *f* (-;-n) boundary; frontier; borderline; limit

grenzen ['grɛntsən] *intr* (an *acc*) adjoin, border (on); (fig) verge (on)

gren'zenlos *adj* limitless

Grenz'fall *m* borderline case

Grenz'linie *f* boundary line

Grenz'sperre *f* ban on border traffic; frontier barricade

Grenz'stein *m* boundary stone

Greuel ['grɔɪ·əl] *m* (-s;-) abhorrence; horror, abomination

Greu'eltat *f* atrocity

greulich ['grɔɪlɪç] *adj* horrible

Griebs ['grips] *m* (-es;-e) core

Grieche ['griçə] *m* (-n;-n) Greek

Grie'chenland *n* (-s;) Greece

Griechin ['griçɪn] *f* (-;-nen) Greek

griechisch ['griçɪʃ] *adj* Greek

Griesgram ['grisgram] *m* (-[e]s;-e) (coll) grouch

Grieß [gris] *m* (-es;-e) grit; gravel

Grieß'mehl *n* farina

griff [grɪf] *pret* of greifen || Griff *m* (-[e]s;-e) grip; handle; hilt; (mus) touch

Grill [grɪl] *m* (-s;-s) grill; broiler

Grille ['grɪlə] *f* (-;-n) cricket; (fig) whim

grillen ['grɪlən] *tr* grill; broil

gril'lenhaft *adj* whimsical

Grimasse [grɪ'masə] *f* (-;-n) grimace

Grimm [grɪm] *m* (-[e]s;) anger, fury

grimmig ['grɪmɪç] *adj* furious

Grind [grɪnt] *m* (-[e]s;-e) scab

grinsen ['grɪnzən] *intr* grin

Grippe ['grɪpə] *f* (-;) grippe

grob [grop] *adj* coarse, rough; crude

Grobian ['grobjan] *m* (-s;-e) boor

gröblich ['grøplɪç] *adj* gross

grölen ['grølən] *intr* shout raucously

Groll [grɔl] *m* (-[e]s;) resentment

grollen ['grɔlən] *intr* rumble; (über *acc*) be resentful (about); j—m g. have a grudge against s.o.

Grönland ['grønlant] *n* (-s;) Greenland

Gros [gros] *n* (-ses;-) gross || [gro] *n* (-;-) bulk; (mil) main forces

Groschen ['grɔʃən] *m* (-s;-) (Aust) penny (*one hundredth of a shilling*)

groß [gros] *adj* big, large; tall; great

groß'artig *adj* grand; magnificent

Groß'aufnahme *f* (phot) close-up

groß'äugig *adj* wide-eyed

Groß'betrieb *m* big company

Großbritan'nien *n* Great Britain

Größe ['grøsə] *f* (-;-n) size, greatness; celebrity; (astr) magnitude; (math) quantity

Groß'eltern *pl* grandparents

Groß'enkel *m* great-grandson

Groß'enkelin *f* great-granddaughter

großenteils ['grosəntaɪls] *adv* largely

Größenwahn ['grøsənvan] *f* megalomania

Groß'grundbesitz *m* large estate

Groß'handel *m* wholesale trade; im G. kaufen buy wholesale

Großhandels- *comb.fm.* wholesale

Groß'händler -in §6 *mf* wholesaler

Groß'handlung *f* (-;-en) wholesale business

groß'herzig *adj* big-hearted

Grossist [grɔ'sɪst] *m* (-en;-en) wholesaler

groß'jährig *adj* of legal age

Groß'maul *n* bigmouth

Groß'mut *m* magnanimity

groß′mütig adj big-hearted
Groß′mutter f grandmother
Groß′onkel m great-uncle
Groß′schreibung f capitalization
Groß′segel n main sail
Groß′sprecher m braggart
großspurig [′gros/puriç] adj pompous
Groß′stadt f large city (with over 100,000 inhabitants)
Großstädter [′gros/tetər] m (-s;-) (coll) city slicker
Groß′tat f achievement
Groß′teil m major part
größtenteils [′grøstəntaıls] adv mainly
groß′tun §154 intr brag; put on the dog
Groß′vater m grandfather
Groß′wild n big game
groß′ziehen §163 tr bring up, raise
großzügig [′grostsygıç] adj broad-minded, liberal; generous; large-scale
grotesk [grɔ′tesk] adj grotesque
Grotte [′grɔtə] f (-;-n) grotto
grub [grup] pret of graben
Grübchen [′grypçən] n (-s;-) dimple
Grube [′grubə] f (-;-n) pit; mine
Grübelei [grybə′laı] f (-;-en) brooding
grübeln [′grybəln] intr brood
Gruben- [grubən] comb.fm. mine, miner's
Gruft [gruft] f (-;ᵉe) tomb, vault
grün [gryn] adj green; **Grüne Minna** (sl) paddy wagon || **Grün** n (-s;) green
Grün′anlage f public park
Grund [grunt] m (-[e]s;ᵉe) ground; land; bottom; foundation, basis; cause, ground; **auf G. von** on the strength of; **G. und Boden** property; **im Grunde genommen** after all; **in G. und Boden** outright
-grund m comb.fm. bottom of; -ground; grounds for, reasons for
Grund′anstrich m first coat
Grund′ausbildung f (mil) basic training
Grund′bedeutung f primary meaning
Grund′begriff m fundamental principle
Grund′besitz m real estate
Grund′buch n land register
grund′ehr′lich adj thoroughly honest
gründen [′gryndən] tr found; g. auf (acc) base on || ref (auf acc) be based (on)
Gründer -in [′gryndər(ın)] §6 mf founder
grund′falsch′ adj absolutely false
Grund′farbe f primary color
Grund′fläche f area; (geom) base
grundieren [grun′dirən] tr prime; size
Grundier′farbe f primer coat
Grundier′schicht f primer coat
Grund′kapital n capital stock
Grund′lage f basis, foundation
grund′legend adj basic, fundamental
Grund′legung f founding, foundation
gründlich [′gryntlıç] adj thorough
Grund′linie f (geom) base; **Grundlinien** basic features, outlines
Gründon′nerstag m Holy Thursday
Grund′riß m floor plan; outline

Grund′satz m principle
grundsätzlich [′gruntzetslıç] adj basic || adv as a matter of principle
Grund′schule f primary school
Grund′stein m cornerstone
Grund′stellung f position of attention; **die G. einnehmen** come to attention
Grund′steuer f real-estate tax
Grund′stoff m raw material; (chem) element
Grund′strich m downstroke
Grund′stück n lot, property
Grund′ton m (fig) prevailing mood; (mus) keynote; (paint) ground shade
Grün′dung f (-;-en) foundation
grund′verschie′den adj entirely different
Grund′wasserspiegel m water table
Grund′zahl f cardinal number
Grund′zug m main feature; **Grundzüge** fundamentals, essentials
Grüne [′grynə] n—**ins G.** into the country
grün′lich adj greenish
Grün′schnabel m know-it-all
Grünspan [′gryn/pan] m (-[e]s;) verdigris
Grün′streifen m grass strip; (auf der Autobahn) median strip
grunzen [′gruntsən] tr & intr grunt
Gruppe [′grupə] f (-;-n) group; (mil) squad
Grup′penführer m group leader; (hist) lieutenant general (of S.S. troops); (mil) squad leader
gruppieren [gru′pirən] tr & ref group
Gruppie′rung f (-;-en) grouping
gruselig [′gruzəlıç] adj creepy
gruseln [′gruzəln] intr—**j—n g. machen** give s.o. the creeps || ref have a creepy feeling || impers—**es gruselt mir** (or **mich**) it gives me the creeps
Gruß [grus] m (-es;ᵉe) greeting; salute; greetings, regards; **mit freundlichem Gruß, Ihr** ... Sincerely yours
grüßen [′grysən] tr greet; salute; **grüß Gott!** hello!; **j—n g. lassen** send best regards to s.o.
Grütze [′grytsə] f (-;-n) groats; (coll) brains
gucken [′gukən] intr look; peep
Guck′loch n peephole
Guerilla [ge′rılja] m (-s;-s) guerilla
Gulasch [′gula/] n (-[e]s;) goulash
gültig [′gyltıç] adj valid; legal
Gummi [′gumi] m & n (-s;-s) gum; rubber
gum′miartig adj gummy; rubbery
Gum′miband n (-[e]s;ᵉer) rubber band; elastic
Gum′mibaum m rubber plant
Gum′mibonbon m & n gumdrop
gummieren [gu′mirən] tr gum; rubberize
Gum′miknüppel m truncheon; billy club
Gummilinse f (phot) zoom lens
Gum′mimantel m mackintosh
Gum′mireifen m tire
Gum′mischuhe pl rubbers
Gum′mizelle f padded cell
Gunst [gunst] f (-;) favor, goodwill; kindness, good turn

Gunst′bezeigung f expression of good-will

günstig ['gʏnstɪç] adj favorable; (Bedingungen) easy

Günstling ['gʏnstlɪŋ] m (-s;-e) favorite; (pej) minion

Gurgel ['gurgəl] f (-;-n) gullet

gurgeln ['gurgəln] intr gurgle; gargle

Gurke ['gurkə] f (-;-n) cucumber

Gurt [gurt] m (-[e]s;-e) belt, strap

Gürtel ['gʏrtəl] m (-s;-) girdle; belt; (geog) zone

gürten ['gʏrtən] tr gird

Guß [gus] m (Gusses; Güsse) gush; (Regen) downpour; (Gießen) casting; (culin) icing; (typ) font

gut [gut] adj good; **es ist schon gut** it's all right; **mach's gut!** so long! || adv well || **Gut** n (-[e]s;̈er) good; possessions; estate; (com) commodity; **Güter** goods; assets

Gut′achten n (-s;-) expert opinion

gut′artig adj good-natured; (pathol) benign

gut′aussehend adj good-looking

Gut′dünken n (-s;) judgment; discretion; **nach G.** at will, as one pleases; (culin) to taste

Gute ['gutə] §5 n good; **alles G!** best of everything; **sein Gutes haben** have its good points

Güte ['gytə] f (-;) goodness

Güter- [gytər] comb.fm. freight; property; (com) of goods

Gü′terabfertigung f freight office

Gü′terbahnhof m (rr) freight yard

gut′erhalten adj in good condition

Gü′terwagen m freight car; **geschlossener G.** boxcar; **offener G.** gondola car

Gü′terzug m freight train

gut′gelaunt adj good-humored

gut′gesinnt adj well-disposed

gut′haben §89 tr have to one's credit || **Guthaben** n (-s;-) credit balance

gut′heißen §95 tr approve of

gut′herzig adj good-hearted

gütig ['gytɪç] adj kind, good

gütlich ['gytlɪç] adj amicable

gut′machen tr—**wieder g.** make good for

gut′mütig adj good-natured

gut′sagen intr—**für j-n g.** vouch for s.o.

Gut′schein m coupon; credit note

gut′schreiben §62 tr—**j-m e-n Betrag g.** credit s.o. with a sum

Gut′schrift f credit entry; credit item

Gut′schriftsanzeige f credit note

Guts′herr m landowner

gut′tun §154 intr do good; behave

gut′willig adj willing, obliging

Gymnasiast **-in** [gʏm′nazjast(ɪn)] §7 mf high school student

Gymna·sium [gʏm′nazjum] n (-s;-sien [zjən]) high school (with academic course)

Gymnastik [gʏm′nastɪk] f (-;) gymnastics

Gynäkologe [gʏnɛko′logə] m (-n;-n), **Gynakologin** [gʏnɛko′login] f (-; nen) gynecologist

Gynäkologie [gʏnɛkolo′gi] f (-;) gynecology

H

H, h [ha] invar n H, h; (mus) B

Haar [har] n (-[e]s;-e) hair; (tex) nap, pile; **aufs H.** exactly; **um ein H.** by a hair's breadth

Haar′büschel n tuft of hair

haaren ['harən] intr lose hair

Haarfärbmittel ['harferpmɪtəl] n hair dye

Haar′feder f hairspring

haar′genau adj exact, precise

haarig ['harɪç] adj hairy

haar′klein adj (coll) in detail

Haar′locke f lock of hair

Haar′nadel f hairpin

haar′scharf adj razor-sharp

Haar′schneider m barber

Haar′schnitt m haircut

Haar′spange f barrette

Haarspray ['harspre] m (-s;-s) hair spray

haar′sträubend adj hair-raising

Haar′teil m hair piece

Haar′tolle f loose curl

Haar′tracht f hairdo

Haar′trockner m, **Haar′trockenhaube** f hair dryer

Haar′wäsche f shampoo

Haar′wasser n hair tonic

Haar′wickler m curler; hair roller

Haar′zwange f tweezers

Hab [hap] invar n—**Hab und Gut** possessions

Habe ['habə] f (-;) possessions

haben ['habən] §89 tr & aux have || **Haben** n (-s;) credit side

Habe′nichts m (-es;-e) have-not

Hab′gier f greed, avarice

hab′haft adj—**h. werden** (genit) get hold of; (Diebes) apprehend

Habicht ['habɪçt] m (-[e]s;-e) hawk

Ha′bichtsnase f aquiline nose

Habilitation [habɪlɪta′tsjon] f (-;-en) accreditation as a university lecturer

habilitieren [habɪlɪ′tirən] ref be accredited as a university lecturer

Hab′seligkeiten pl belongings

Hab′sucht f greed, avarice

hab′süchtig adj greedy, avaricious

Hackbeil ['hakbaɪl] n cleaver

Hacke ['hakə] f (-;-n) heel; hoe; pick; pickax; hatchet; mattock

hacken ['hakən] tr hack, chop; peck || intr (nach) peck (at)

Häckerling ['hekərlɪŋ] m (-s;) chaff

Hackfleisch ['hakflaɪʃ] n ground meat

Häcksel ['heksəl] n (-s;) chaff

Hader ['haːdər] *m* (-s;) strife || *m* (-s; -n) rag

hadern ['haːdərn] *intr* quarrel

Hafen ['haːfən] *m* (-s;⁼) harbor; port; (fig) haven

Ha'fenamt *n* port authority

Ha'fenanlagen *pl* docks

Ha'fenarbeiter *m* longshoreman

Ha'fendamm *m* jetty, mole

Ha'fensperre *f* blockade

Ha'fenstadt *f* seaport

Ha'fenviertel *n* dock area, waterfront

Hafer ['haːfər] *m* (-s;-) oats; **ihn sticht der H.** he's feeling his oats

Ha'fergrütze *f*, **Ha'fermehl** *n* oatmeal

Hafner ['haːfnər] *m* (-s;-) potter

Haft [haft] *f* (-;) arrest; custody; imprisonment; **in H.** under arrest; in custody; in prison

haftbar ['haftbaːr] *adj* (jur) liable

Haft'befehl *m* warrant for arrest

haften ['haftən] *intr* (an *dat*) cling (to), stick (to); **h. für** vouch for; (jur) be held liable for; (jur) put up bail for

Haft'fähigkeit *f*, **Haft'festigkeit** *f* adhesion

Häftling ['heftlɪŋ] *m* (-s;-e) prisoner

Haft'lokal *n* (mil) guardhouse

Haft'pflicht *f* liability

haft'pflichtig *adj* (für) liable (for)

Haft'pflichtversicherung *f* liability insurance

Haft'richter *m* (jur) magistrate

Haft'schale *f* contact lens

Haf'tung *f* (-;-en) liability

Hag [haːk] *m* (-[e]s;-e) enclosure; (Hain) grove; (Buschwerk) bushes

Hagedorn ['haːgədɔrn] *m* hawthorn

Hagel ['haːgəl] *m* (-s;) hail

Ha'gelkorn *n* hailstone

hageln ['haːgəln] *intr* (SEIN) (fig) rain down || *impers*—**es hagelt** it is hailing

Ha'gelschauer *m* hailstorm

hager ['haːgər] *adj* gaunt, haggard

Hagestolz ['haːgəʃtɔlts] *m* (-es;-e) confirmed bachelor

Häher ['heːər] *m* (-s;-) (orn) jay

Hahn [haːn] *m* (-[e]s;⁼e) rooster; (Wasser-) faucet; **den H. spannen** cock the gun; **H. im Korbe sein** rule the roost

Hähnchen ['heːnçən] *n* (-s;-) young rooster

Hah'nenkamm *m* cockscomb

Hah'nenkampf *m* cock fight

Hah'nenschrei *m* crow of the cock

Hahnrei ['haːnraɪ] *m* (-s;-e) cuckold

Hai [haɪ] *m* (-[e]s;-e), **Hai'fisch** *m* shark

Hain [haɪn] *m* (-[e]s;-e) grove

Haiti ['haɪti] *n* (-s) Haiti

Häkelarbeit ['heːkəlarbaɪt] *f* crocheting

häkeln ['heːkəln] *tr & intr* crochet || **Häkeln** *n* (-s;) crocheting

Haken ['haːkən] *m* (-s;-) hook; (Spange) clasp; (fig) snag, hitch

Ha'kenkreuz *n* swastika

Ha'kennase *f* hooknose

halb [halp] *adj & adv* half

halb-, **Halb-** *comb.fm.* half-, semi-

Halb'blut *n* half-breed

-halber [halbər] *comb.fm.* for the sake of; owing to

halb'fett *adj* (typ) bold

Halb'franzband *m* (bb) half leather

halb'gar *adj* (culin) (medium) rare

Halb'gott *m* demigod

Halbheit ['halphaɪt] *f* (-;) half-

Halb'kugel *f* hemisphere

halbieren [hal'biːrən] *tr* halve, bisect

Halb'insel *f* peninsula

Halb'kettenfahrzeug *n* half-track

Halb'kugel *f* hemisphere

halb'lang *adj* half-length; **halblange Ärmel** half sleeves

halb'laut *adj* low || *adv* in a low voice

Halb'leiter *m* (elec) semiconductor

halb'mast *adv* at half-mast; **auf h.** at half-mast

Halb'messer *m* radius

halbpart ['halppart] *adv*—**mit j-m h. machen** go fifty-fifty with s.o.

Halb'schuh *m* low shoe

Halb'schwergewicht *n* light-heavyweight division

Halb'schwergewichtler *m* light-heavyweight

halb'stündig *adj* half-hour

halb'stündlich *adj* half-hourly || *adv* every half hour

Halb'vers *m* hemistich

halbwegs ['halbveks] *adv* halfway

Halb'welt *f* demimonde

halbwüchsig ['halpvyksɪç] *adj* teenage || **Halbwüchsige** §5 *mf* teenager

Halb'zug *m* (mil) section

Halde ['haldə] *f* (-;-n) slope; (Schutt-) slag pile

half [half] *pret* of **helfen**

Hälfte ['helftə] *f* (-;-n) half

Halfter ['halftər] *f* (-;-n) holster || *n* (-s;-) halter

Hall [hal] *m* (-[e]s;-e) sound; clang

Halle ['halə] *f* (-;-n) hall; (e-s Hotels) lobby; (aer) hangar; (rr) concourse

hallen ['halən] *intr* sound, resound

Hal'lenbad *n* indoor pool

Hallo [ha'loː] *n* (-s;) hullabaloo || *interj* (to attract attention) hey!; (telp) hello

Halm [halm] *m* (-[e]s;-e) stem, stalk; blade (of grass)

Hals [hals] *m* (-es;⁼e) neck; throat; **H. über Kopf** head over heels

Hals'abschneider *m* cutthroat

hals'abschneiderisch *adj* cutthroat

Hals'ader *f* jugular vein

Hals'ausschnitt *m* neckline, neck

Hals'band *n* (-[e]s;⁼er) necklace, choker; (e-s Hundes) collar

halsbrecherisch ['halsbreçərɪʃ] *adj* breakneck

Hals'entzündung *f* sore throat

Hals'kette *f* necklace, chain

Hals'kragen *m* collar

Hals'krause *f* frilled collar

hals'starrig *adj* stubborn

Hals'weh *n* sore throat

halt [halt] *adv* just, simply || *interj* stop!; (mil) halt! || **Halt** *m* (-[e]s; -e) hold; foothold; support; stability; stop, halt

haltbar ['haltbaːr] *adj* durable; tenable

halten ['haltən] §90 *tr* hold; keep; detain; (*Rede*) deliver; (*Vorlesung*) give; (*feiern*) celebrate; **es h. mit** do with; **have an affair with; etw auf sich h.** have self-respect; **j-n h. für** take s.o. for; **viel h. von** think highly of || *ref* keep, last; hold ones own; **an sich h.** restrain oneself; **auf sich h.** be particular about one's appearance; **sich an etw h.** (fig) stick to s.th.; **sich an j-n h.** hold s.o. liable; **sich gesund h.** keep healthy; **sich links h.** keep to the left || *intr* stop; last; **h. auf** (*acc*) pay attention to; **h. nach** head for; **h. zu** stick by; **was das Zeug hält** with might and main
Hal'ter *m* (-s;-) holder; rack; owner
Hal'teriemen *m* strap (*on bus or trolley*)
Hal'testelle *f* bus stop, trolley stop; (rr) stop
Hal'teverbot *n* (public sign) no stopping
-haltig [haltıç] *comb.fm.* containing
halt'los *adj* without support; helpless; unprincipled
halt'machen *intr* stop, halt
Hal'tung *f* (-;-en) pose, posture; attitude
Halte'zeichen *n* stop sign
Halunke [ha'luŋkə] *m* (-;-n) rascal
hämisch ['hemıʃ] *adj* spiteful, malicious
Hammel ['haməl] *m* (-s;-e & -) wether; (coll) mutton-head; (culin) mutton
Ham'melkeule *f* leg of mutton
Hammer ['hamər] *m* (-s;-) hammer; gavel; **unter den H. kommen** be auctioned off
hämmern ['hemərn] *tr & intr* hammer
Hämorrhoiden [hemərɔ'idən] *pl* hemorroids, piles
Hampelmann ['hampəlman] *m* (-[e]s; -er) jumping jack
hamstern ['hamstərn] *tr* hoard
Hand [hant] *f* (-;-e) hand; **an H. von** with the help of; **auf eigene H.** of one's own accord; **aus erster H.** (*bei Verkauf*) one-owner; **aus erster H. haben** have first-hand; **aus erster H. kaufen** buy directly; **bei der H.** at hand, handy; **die letzte H.** finishing touches; **die öffentliche H.** the state, public authorities; **es liegt auf der H.** it is obvious; **H. ans Werk legen** get down to work; **H. aufs Herz!** cross my heart; **Hände hoch!** hands up!; **H. und Fuß haben** make sense; **in die H.** (*or* **Hände**) **bekommen** get one's hands on; **j-m an die H. gehen** lend s.o. a hand; **j-m die H. drücken** shake hands with s.o.; **j-m etw an (die) H. geben** quote s.o. a price on s.th.; **j-m zur H. gehen** lend s.o. a hand; **unter der H.** underhandedly, unofficially; **von der H. weisen** reject; **zu Händen Herrn X** Attention Mr. X; **zur H.** at hand, handy
Hand'arbeit *f* manual labor; needlework
Hand'aufheben *n*, **Hand'aufhebung** *f* show of hands

Hand'ausgabe *f* abridged edition
Hand'bedienung *f* manual control
Hand'betrieb *m*—**mit** (or **für**) **H.** hand-operated
Hand'bibliothek *f* reference library
hand'breit *adj* wide as a hand || **Hand-breit** *f* (-;-) hand's breadth
Hand'bremse *f* (aut) hand brake
Hand'buch *n* handbook, manual
Händedruck ['hendədruk] *m* handshake
Händeklatschen ['hendəklatʃən] *n* clapping
Handel ['handəl] *m* (-s;-) trade; deal, bargain; business; affair; **e-n H. eingehen** conclude a deal; **e-n H. treiben** carry on business; **H. und Gewerbe** trade and industry; **Händel suchen** pick a quarrel; **im H. sein** be on the market; **in den H. bringen** put on the market
-handel *m comb.fm.* -trade, -business
handeln ['handəln] *intr* act; take action; proceed; **gegen das Gesetz h.** go against the law; **gut an j-m h.** treat s.o. well; **h. über** (*acc*) or **von** deal with; **h. mit** do business with; **im großen h.** do wholesale business || *impers ref*—**es handelt sich um** it is a matter of; **darum handelt es sich nicht** that's not the point
Han'delsabkommen *n* trade agreement
Han'delsartikel *m* commodity
Han'delsbetrieb *m* commercial enterprise; business; firm
Han'delsbilanz *f* balance of trade; **aktive H.** favorable balance of trade
Han'delsdampfer *m* (naut) merchant-man
han'delseinig *adj*—**h. werden mit** come to terms with
Han'delsgärtner *m* truck farmer
Han'delskammer *f* chamber of commerce
Han'delsmarine *f* merchant marine
Han'delsmarke *f* trademark
Han'delsminister *m* secretary of commerce
Han'delsministerium *n* department of commerce
Han'delsplatz *m* trade center
Han'delsschiff *n* merchantman
Han'delssperre *f* trade embargo
händelsüchtig ['hendəlzyçtıç] *adj* quarrelsome
Han'delsvertrag *m* commercial treaty
Han'delswert *m* trade-in value
Han'delszeichen *n* trademark
Hand'exemplar *n* desk copy
Hand'fertigkeit *f* manual dexterity
Hand'fessel *f* handcuff
hand'fest *adj* sturdy; well-founded
Hand'fläche *f* palm of the hand
Hand'geld *n* advance payment; deposit
Hand'gelenk *n* wrist; **aus** (or **mit**) **dem H.** (coll) easy as pie
hand'gemein *adj*—**h. werden** come to blows
Hand'gemenge *n* scuffle
Hand'gepäck *n* hand luggage
Hand'gepäckschließfach *n* locker
Hand'granate *f* hand grenade
hand'greiflich *adj* tangible; obvious;

j-m etw h. **machen** make s.th. clear to s.o.; **h. werden** come to blows

Hand/habe f (-;-n) handle; pretext; occasion; **er hat keine H. gegen mich** he has nothing on me

hand/haben tr handle; (*Maschine*) operate; (*Rechtspflege*) administer; (fig) manage

-händig [hendıç] *comb.fm.* -handed

Hand/karren m hand cart, push cart

Hand/koffer m suitcase; attaché case

Handlanger ['hantlaŋər] m (-s;-) handyman; (pej) underling

Händler -in ['hendlər(ın)] §6 mf dealer, merchant; storekeeper

Hand/lesekunst f palmistry

Hand/leserin f (-;-nen) palm reader

hand/lich adj handy

Hand/lung f (-;-en) shop; act, action

-handlung f *comb.fm.* business; shop

Hand/lungsgehilfe m clerk, salesman

Hand/lungsweise f conduct

Hand/pflege f manicure

Hand/pflegerin f (-;-nen) manicurist

Hand/rücken m back of the hand

Hand/schaltung f manual shift

Hand/schelle f handcuff

Hand/schlag m handshake

Hand/schreiben n hand-written letter

Hand/schrift f handwriting; manuscript; (sl) slap, box on the ear

Hand/schriftenkunde f paleography

hand/schriftlich adj hand-written

Hand/schuh m glove

Hand/schuhfach n (aut) glove compartment

Hand/streich m (mil) raid

Hand/tasche f handbag, purse

Hand/tuch n towel; **schmales H.** (sl) beanpole

Hand/tuchhalter m towel rack

Hand/umdrehen n—**im. H.** in a jiffy

Hand/voll f (-;-) handful

Hand/werk n craft, trade; **j-m ins H. pfuschen** (sl) stick one's nose in s.o. else's business

Hand/werker m craftsman

Hand/werkszeug n tool kit

Hand/wörterbuch n pocket dictionary

Hand/wurzel f wrist

Hand/zettel m handbill

hanebüchen ['hanəbyçən] adj (coll) incredible; (coll) monstrous

Hanf [hanf] m (-[e]s;) hemp

Hang [haŋ] m (-[e]s;ﬞe) slope; hillside; (fig) inclination, tendency

Hangar ['haŋgar] m (-s;-s) hangar

Hängebacken ['heŋəbakən] pl jowls

Hängebauch ['heŋəbaux] m potbelly

Hängebrücke ['heŋəbrykə] f suspension bridge

Hängematte ['heŋəmatə] f hammock

hängen ['heŋən] tr hang || ref—**sich an j-n** h. hang on to s.o.; **sich ans Telephon** h. be on the telephone || §92 intr hang; cling, stick

hän/genbleiben §62 intr (SEIN) stick; be detained, get stuck; (an dat) get caught (on); (educ) stay behind

Hans [hans] m (-' & -ens;) Johnny, Jack

Hans/dampf m (-[e]s;-e) busybody; **H. in allen Gassen** jack-of-all trades

Hänselei [henzə'laı] f (-;-en) teasing

hänseln ['henzəln] tr tease

Hans/narr m fool

Hans/wurst m (-es;-e & ﬞe) clown

Hantel ['hantəl] f (-;-n) dumbell

hantieren [han'tirən] intr (an acc) be busy (with); **mit etw h.** handle s.th.

hapern ['hapərn] impers—**bei mir hapert es an** (dat) (or **mit**) I am short of; **bei mir hapert es in** (dat) (or **mit**) I am weak in; **damit hapert's** that's the hitch

Happen ['hapən] m (-s;-) morsel; mouthful; (fig) good opportunity; **fetter H.** (coll) big hawl

happig ['hapıç] adj greedy; (*Preis*) steep

Härchen ['herçən] n (-s;-) tiny hair

Harem ['harem] m (-s;-s) harem

Häre·sie [here'zi] f (-;-sien ['zi·ən]) heresy

Häretiker [he'retıkər] m (-s;-) heretic

Harfe ['harfə] f (-;-n) harp

Harke ['harkə] f (-;-n) rake

harken ['harkən] tr & intr rake

Harm [harm] m (-[e]s;) harm; grief

härmen ['hermən] ref (**um**) grieve (over)

harm/los adj harmless

Harmo·nie [harmo'ni] f (-;-nien ['ni·ən]) harmony

harmonieren [harmo'nirən] intr harmonize

Harmoni·ka [har'monıka] f (-;-kas & -ken [kən]) accordion; harmonica

harmonisch [har'monıʃ] adj harmonious

Harn [harn] m (-[e]s;-e) urine; **H. lassen** pass water

Harn/blase f (anat) bladder

harnen ['harnən] intr urinate

Harn/glas n urinal

Harn/grieß m (pathol) gravel

Harnisch ['harnıʃ] m (-es;-e) armor; **in H. geraten über** (acc) fly into a rage over; **j-n in H. bringen** get s.o. hopping mad

Harn/leiter m (anat) ureter; (surg) catheter

Harn/röhre f urethra

harn/treibend adj diuretic

Harpune [har'punə] f (-;-n) harpoon

harpunieren [harpu'nirən] tr harpoon

harren ['harən] intr tarry; hope; (genit or auf acc) wait (for)

harsch [harʃ] adj harsh || **Harsch** m (-es;), **Harsch/schnee** m crushed snow

hart [hart] adj hard; severe || adv— **h. an** (dat) close to, hard by

Härte ['hertə] f (-;) hardness; severity

härten ['hertən] tr, ref & intr harden

Hart/faserplatte f fiber board

Hart/geld n coins

hartgesotten ['hartgəzotən] adj hard-boiled; (*Verbrecher*) hardened

hart/herzig adj hard-hearted

hart/köpfig adj thick-headed

hart/leibig adj constipated

Hart/leibigkeit f (-;) constipation

hart/löten tr braze

hartnäckig ['hartnɛkɪç] *adj* stubborn
Hart'platz *m* (tennis) hard court
Harz [harts] *n* (-es;-e) resin; rosin
harzig [hartsɪç] *adj* resinous
Hasardspiel [ha'zart/pil] *n* gambling game; gamble
haschen ['haʃən] *tr* snatch, grab ‖ *intr* (nach) try to catch, snatch (at)
Hase ['hazə] *m* (-n;-n) hare; **alter H.** old-timer, veteran
Ha'selnuß ['hazəlnus] *f* hazelnut
Hasenfuß *m* (coll) coward
Ha'senherz *n* (coll) yellow belly
Ha'senmaus *f* chinchilla
Hasenpanier ['hazənpanir] *n—das* **H. ergreifen** take to ones heels
ha'senrein *adj—nicht ganz* **h.** (fig) a bit fishy, rather shady
Ha'senscharte *f* harelip
Haspe ['haspə] *f* (-;-n) hasp
Haspel ['haspəl] *f* (-;-n) & *m* (-s;-) reel, spool; winch, windlass
haspeln ['haspəln] *tr* reel, spool
Haß *m* (Hasses) hatred
hassen ['hasən] *tr* hate
has'senswert, has'senswürdig *adj* hateful
häßlich ['hɛslɪç] *adj* ugly; nasty
Hast [hast] *f* (-;) haste
hasten ['hastən] *intr* be in a hurry, act quickly ‖ *intr* (SEIN) hasten, rush
hastig ['hastɪç] *adj* hasty
hätscheln ['hɛtʃəln] *tr* caress, cuddle; *(verzärteln)* coddle, spoil
hatte ['hatə] *pret* of **haben**
Haube ['haubə] *f* (-;-n) cap; (aer) cowling; (aut) hood; (orn) crest
Haubitze [hau'bɪtsə] *f* (-;-n) howitzer
Hauch [haux] *m* (-[e]s;-e) breath; breeze; *(Schicht)* thin layer; *(Spur)* trace
hauch'dünn' *adj* paper-thin
hauchen ['hauxən] *tr* whisper; (ling) aspirate ‖ *intr* breathe
Hauch'laut *m* (ling) aspirate
Haue ['hau·ə] *f* (-;-n) hoe; adze; **H. kriegen** get a spanking
hauen ['hau·ən] §93 *tr* hack, cut; strike; *(Baum)* fell; *(Stein)* hew ‖ §109 *tr* beat (up) ‖ *intr—***h. nach** lash out at; **um sich h.** flail
Hauer ['hau·ər] *m* (-s;-) tusk
häufeln ['hɔɪfəln] *tr* hill
häufen ['hɔɪfən] *tr & ref* pile up
Haufen ['haufən] *m* (-s;-) pile, heap
Hau'fenwolke *f* cumulus cloud
häufig ['hɔɪfɪç] *adj* frequent ‖ *adv* frequently
Häu'figkeit *f* (-;) frequency
Häu'fung *f* (-;-en) accumulation
Haupt [haupt] *n* (-[e]s;⸚er) head; top; chief, leader **aufs H. schlagen** vanquish
Haupt- *comb.fm.* head; chief; major; most important; prime, primary, leading
Haupt'altar *m* high altar
haupt'amtlich *adj* full-time
Haupt'bahnhof *m* main train station
Haupt'darsteller *m* leading man
Haupt'darstellerin *f* leading lady
Häuptel ['hɔɪptəl] *n* (-s;-) head
Haupt'fach *n* (educ) major

Haupt'farbe *f* primary color
Haupt'feldwebel *m* first sergeant
Haupt'film *m* (cin) feature
Haupt'gefreite §5 *m* private first class; lance corporal (Brit); seaman; airman second class
Haupt'geschäftsstelle *f* head office
Haupt'gewinn *m* first price
Haupt'haar *n* hair (on the head)
Häuptling ['hɔɪptlɪŋ] *m* (-s;-e) chief
häuptlings ['hɔɪptlɪŋs] *adv* head first
Haupt'linie *f* (rr) trunk line
Haupt'mann *m* (-[e]s;-leute) captain
Haupt'masse *f* bulk
Haupt'mast *m* mainmast
Hauptnenner ['hauptnenər] *m* (-s;-) (math) common denominator
Haupt'probe *f* dress rehearsal
Haupt'quartier *n* headquarters; **Großes H.** general headquarters
Haupt'rolle *f* leading role, lead
Haupt'sache *f* main thing; (jur) point at issue
haupt'sächlich *adj* main, principal
Haupt'satz *m* (gram) main clause; (phys) principle, law
Haupt'schalter *m* master switch
Haupt'schiff *n* (archit) nave
Haupt'schlagader *f* aorta
Haupt'schlüssel *m* master key, pass key
Haupt'schriftleiter *m* editor in chief
Haupt'spaß *m* great fun; great joke
Haupt'stadt *f* capital
Haupt'straße *f* main street; highway
Haupt'strecke *f* (rr) main line
Haupt'stütze *f* mainstay
Haupt'ton *m* primary accent
Haupt'treffer *m* first prize; jackpot
Haupt'verkehr *m* peak-hour traffic
Haupt'verkehrsstraße *f* main artery
Haupt'verkehrszeit *f* rush hour
Haupt'wort *n* (-[e]s;⸚er) noun
Haus [haus] *n* (-es;⸚er) house; **ein großes H. führen** do a lot of entertaining; **H. und Hof** house and home; **öffentliches H.** brothel; **nach Hause** home; **sich zu Hause fühlen** feel at home; **von zu Hause** from home
Haus'angestellte §5 *mf* domestic
Haus'apotheke *f* medicine cabinet
Haus'arbeit *f* housework; (educ) homework
Haus'arzt *m* family doctor
Haus'aufgabe *f* homework
haus'backen *adj* homemade; *(Frau)* plain; (fig) provincial
Haus'bedarf *m* household needs; **für den H.** for the home
Haus'brand *m* domestic fuel
Haus'bursche *m* porter
Haus'diener *m* porter
hausen ['hauzən] *intr* reside; (coll) make a mess; **schlimm h.** wreak havoc
Häuserblock ['hɔɪzərblɔk] *m* block of houses
Häusermakler **-in** ['hɔɪzərmaklər(ɪn)] §6 *mf* realtor
Haus'flur *m* entrance hall; hallway
Haus'frau *f* housewife; landlady
Haus'freund *m* friend of the family; (coll) wife's lover

Haus'gebrauch *m* family custom; household use
Haus'gehilfin *f* domestic
Haus'genosse *m*, **Haus'genossin** *f* occupant of the same house
Haus'gesinde *n* domestics
Haus'glocke *f* doorbell
Haus'halt *m* household; budget; **den H. führen** keep house
haus'halten §90 *intr* keep house; economize
Haushälter –in ['haʊʃɛltər(ɪn)] §6 *mf* housekeeper
haushälterisch ['haʊʃɛltərɪʃ] *adj* economical
Haus'haltsausschuß *m* ways and means committee
Haus'haltsgerät *n* household utensil
Haus'haltsjahr *n* fiscal year
Haus'haltsplan *m* budget
Haus'haltung *f* housekeeping; household; family budget; management
Haus'haltungslehre *f* home economics
Haus'herr *m* master of the house; landlord
Haus'herrin *f* lady of the house; landlady
haus'hoch' *adj* very high; vast
Haus'hofmeister *m* steward
hausieren [haʊ'zirən] *intr*—**mit etw h.** peddle s.th.; go around telling everyone about s.th.
Hausierer [haʊ'zirər] *m* (-s;-) door-to-door salesman
Haus'lehrer –in §6 *mf* private tutor
häuslich ['hɔɪslɪç] *adj* home, domestic; homey; thrifty
Häus'lichkeit *f* (-;) family life; home
Haus'mädchen *n* maid
Haus'meister *m* caretaker, janitor
Haus'mittel *n* home remedy
Haus'mutter *f* mother of the family
Haus'pflege *f* home nursing
Haus'schlüssel *m* front-door key
Haus'schuh *m* slipper
Hausse ['hosə] *f* (-;-n) (econ, st. exch.) boom
Haus'sespekulant *m* (st. exch.) bull
Haussier [hos'je] *m* (-s;-) (st. exch.) bull
haussieren [ho'sirən] *tr* (fin) raise ∥ *intr* (fin) go up, rise
Haus'stand *m* household
Haus'suchungsbefehl *m* search warrant
Haus'tier *n* domestic animal; pet
Haus'vater *m* father of the family
Haus'verwalter *m* superintendent
Haus'wesen *n* household
Haus'wirt *m* landlord
Haus'wirtin *f* landlady
Haus'wirtschaft *f* housekeeping
haus'wirtschaftlich *adj* domestic; household
Haus'wirtschaftslehre *f* home economics
Haus'zins *m* house rent
Haut [haʊt] *f* (-;̈e) skin; hide; **aus der H. fahren** fly off the handle
Haut'abschürfung *f* skin abrasion
Haut'arzt *m* dermatologist
Haut'ausschlag *m* rash
Häutchen ['hɔɪtçən] (-s;-) membrane; pellicle; film

häuten ['hɔɪtən] *tr* skin ∥ *ref* slough the skin
haut'eng *adj* skin-tight
Haut'farbe *f* complexion
Haut'plastik *f* skin graft
Haut'reizung *f* skin irritation
Haut'transplantation *f*, **Haut'verpflanzung** *f* skin grafting
havariert [hava'rirt] *adj* damaged
H'-Bombe *f* H-bomb
Hebamme ['hepamə] *f* (-;-n) midwife
Hebebaum ['hebəbaum] *m* lever
Hebebühne ['hebəbynə] *f* car lift
Hebeeisen ['hebə-aɪzən] *n* crowbar
Hebel ['hebəl] *m* (-s;-) lever
heben ['hebən] §94 *tr* lift, raise; (*steigern*) increase; (*fördern*) further; (aut) jack up ∥ *ref* rise
Heber ['hebər] *m* (-s;-) siphon; (aut) jack
Hebeschiff ['hebə/ʃɪf] *n* salvage ship
Hebräer –in [he'brɛ-ər(ɪn)] §6 *mf* Hebrew
hebräisch [he'brɛ-ɪʃ] *adj* Hebrew
He'bung *f* (-;-en) lifting; increase; improvement; (mus, pros) stress
Hecht [hɛçt] *m* (-[e]s;-e) (ichth) pike
hechten ['hɛçtən] *intr* dive
Hecht'sprung *m* flying leap; jacknife dive
Heck [hɛk] *n* (-[e]s;-e & -s) stern; (aer) tail; (aut) rear
Heck'antrieb *m* (aut) rear drive
Hecke ['hɛkə] *f* (-;-n) hedge; brood, hatch
hecken ['hɛkən] *tr & intr* breed
Heckenhüpfen (Heck'kenhüpfen) *n* (-s;) (aer) hedgehopping
Heckenschütze (Heck'kenschütze) *m* sniper
Heck'fenster *n* (aut) rear window
Heck'licht *n* (-s, aut) tail light
Heck'motor *m* rear engine
Heck'pfennig *m* lucky penny
Heck'schütze *m* (aer) tail gunner
heda ['hedɑ] *interj* hey there!
Heer [her] *n* (-[e]s;-e) army; host
Heeres– [herəs] *comb.fm.* army
Hee'resbericht *m* official army communiqué
Hee'resdienst *m* military service
Hee'resdienstvorschriften *pl* army regulations
Hee'resgeistliche §5 *m* army chaplain
Hee'resmacht *f* armed forces; army
Hee'reszug *m* (mil) campaign
Heer'lager *n* army camp; (pol) faction
Heer'schar *f* host, legion
Heer'zug *m* (mil) campaign
Hefe ['hefə] *f* (-;-n) yeast; dregs
He'feteig *m* leavened dough
Heft [hɛft] *n* (-[e]s;-e) haft, handle; notebook; (e—r *Zeitschrift*) issue
heften ['hɛftən] *tr* fasten together; sew, stitch; tack, baste; (*Blick*) fix ∥ *ref* (an *acc*) stick close (to)
heftig ['hɛftɪç] *adj* violent; (*Regen*) heavy; (*Fieber*) high; **h. werden** lose one's temper
Heft'klammer *f* paper clip; staple
Heft'maschine *f* stapler
Heft'stich *m* (sew) tack
Heft'zwecke *f* thumbtack

hegen ['heːgən] *tr* (*Wild*) preserve; (*Zweifel, Gedanken*) have; **h. und pflegen** lavish care on

Hehl [heːl] *n* (-[e]s;) secret

hehlen ['heːlən] *intr* receive stolen goods

Heh′ler –in §6 *mf* fence

hehr [heːr] *adj* sublime, noble

Heide ['haɪdə] *m* (-n;-n) heathen; (Bib) gentile || *f* (-;-n) heath

Hei′dekraut *n* heather

Heidelbeere ['haɪdəlbeːrə] *f* blueberry

Hei′denangst *f* (coll) jitters

Hei′dengeld *n* (coll) piles of money

Hei′denlärm *m* hullabaloo

hei′denmäßig *adv*—**h. viel** tremendous amount of

Hei′denspaß *m* (coll) great fun

Heidentum ['haɪdəntum] *n* (-s;) heathendom

heidi [haɪ′di] *adj* gone; lost; **h. gehen** get lost; be all gone || *interj* quick!

Heidin ['haɪdɪn] *f* (-;-nen) heathen

heidnisch ['haɪdnɪʃ] *adj* heathen

heikel ['haɪkəl] *adj* particular, fastidious; (*Sache*) ticklish

heil [haɪl] *adj* safe, sound; undamaged || **Heil** *n* (-[e]s;) welfare, benefit; salvation || **Heil** *interj* hail!

Heiland ['haɪlant] *m* (-[e]s;) Saviour

Heil′anstalt *f* sanitarium

Heil′bad *n* spa

heilbar ['haɪlbar] *adj* curable

heil′bringend *adj* beneficial, healthful

Heilbutt ['haɪlbut] *m* (-[e]s;-e) (ichth) halibut

heilen ['haɪlən] *tr* heal || *intr* (HABEN & SEIN) heal

Heil′gehilfe *m* male nurse

Heil′gymnastik *f* physical therapy

heilig ['haɪlɪç] *adj* holy, sacred || **Heilige** §5 *mf* saint

Hei′ligabend *m* Christmas Eve

heiligen ['haɪlɪgən] *tr* hallow

Hei′ligenschein *m* halo

Hei′ligkeit *f* (-;) holiness, sanctity

hei′ligsprechen §64 *tr* canonize

Heiligtum ['haɪlɪçtum] *n* (-[e]s;⁻er) sanctuary; shrine; sacred relic

Hei′ligung *f* (-;) sanctification

Heil′kraft *f* healing power

Heil′kraut *n* medicinal herb

Heil′kunde *f* medical science

heil′los *adj* wicked; (coll) awful

Heil′mittel *n* remedy; medicine

Heil′mittellehre *f* pharmacology

heilsam ['haɪlzam] *adj* healthful

Heils′armee *f* Salvation Army

Heil′stätte *f* sanitarium

Hei′lung *f* (-;-en) cure

heim [haɪm] *adv* home || **Heim** *n* (-[e]s;-e) home; (*Alters*-) old-age home

Heimat ['haɪmat] *f* (-;-en) home; hometown; homeland

hei′matlich *adj* native

hei′matlos *adj* homeless

Hei′matort *m* hometown, home village

Hei′matstadt *f* hometown, native city

heim′begeben §80 *ref* head home

Heimchen ['haɪmçən] *n* (-s;-) cricket

Heim′computer *m* home computer

Heim′fahrt *f* homeward journey

heim′finden §59 *intr* find one's way home

Heim′gang *m* going home; passing on

heimisch ['haɪmɪʃ] *adj* local; locally-produced; domestic; **heimische Sprache** vernacular; **h. werden** settle down; become established; **sich h. fühlen** feel at home

Heimkehr ['haɪmkeːr] *f* (-;) homecoming

heim′kehren *intr* (SEIN) return home

Heim′kunft *f* homecoming

heim′leuchten *intr* (sl) (*dat*) tell (*s.o.*) where to get off

heim′lich *adj* secret

Heim′lichkeit *f* (-;-en) secrecy; (*Geheimnis*) secret

Heim′reise *f* homeward journey

heim′suchen *tr* afflict, plague

Heim′tücke *f* treachery

heim′tückisch *adj* treacherous

heimwärts ['haɪmverts] *adv* homeward

Heim′weh *n* homesickness; nostalgia

heim′zahlen *tr*—j–m etw **h.** (coll) pay s.o. back for s.th.

Heinl ['haɪni] *m* (-s;) Harry; guy

Heinzelmännchen ['haɪntsəlmɛnçən] *pl* (myth) little people

Heirat ['haɪrat] *f* (-;-en) marriage

heiraten ['haɪratən] *tr & intr* marry

Hei′ratsantrag *m* marriage proposal

hei′ratsfähig *adj* marriageable

Hei′ratsgut *n* dowry

Hei′ratskandidat *m* eligible bachelor

Hei′ratsurkunde *f* marriage certificate

Hei′ratsvermittler –in §6 *mf* marriage broker

heischen ['haɪʃən] *tr* demand; beg

heiser ['haɪzər] *adj* hoarse

heiß [haɪs] *adj* hot; (fig) ardent

heißen ['haɪsən] §95 *tr* call; ask, bid; mean || *intr* be called; **das heißt** that is, i.e.; **wie h. Sie?** what is your name?

heiß′geliebt *adj* beloved

heiter ['haɪtər] *adj* cheerful; hilarious; serene; (*Wetter*) clear

Heiz– [haɪts] *comb.fm.* heating

Heiz′anlage *f* heating system

Heiz′apparat *m* heater

heizen ['haɪtsən] *tr* heat; **den Ofen mit Kohle h.** burn coal in the stove || *intr* give off heat; heat; turn on the heating; light the fire (or stove)

Hei′zer *m* (-s;) boilerman; (naut) stoker; (rr) fireman

Heiz′faden *m* (elec) filament

Heiz′kissen *n* heating pad

Heiz′körper *m* radiator; heater

Heiz′material *n* fuel

Heiz′platte *f* hot plate

Heiz′raum *m* boiler room

Heiz′schlange *f* heating coil

Heiz′ung *f* (-;) heating; (coll) central heating; radiator

Hei′zungskessel *m* boiler

Hei′zungsrohr *n* radiator pipe

Held [hɛlt] *m* (-en;-en) hero

Hel′denalter *n* heroic age

Hel′dengedicht *n* epic

Hel′dengeist *m* heroism

hel′denhaft *adj* heroic

Hel′denmut *m* heroism

hel′denmütig *adj* heroic
Hel′dentat *f* heroic deed, exploit
Heldentum [′hɛldəntum] *n* (-[e]s;) heroism
Heldin [′hɛldɪn] *f* (-;-nen) heroine
helfen [′hɛlfən] *intr* (*dat*) help; **es hilft nichts** it's of no use
Hel′fer –in §6 *mf* helper
Hel′fershelfer *m* accomplice
Helikopter [helɪ′kɔptər] *m* (-s;-) helicopter
hell [hɛl] *adj* clear; bright; lucid; (*Haar*) fair; (*Bier*) light; (*Wahnsinn, usw.*) sheer || **Helle** §5 *f* brightness; lightness; clarity || *n* light; **ein Helles** a glass of light beer
hellenisch [hɛ′leniʃ] *adj* Hellenic
Heller [′hɛlər] *m* (-s;-) penny
hellhörig [′hɛlhøːrɪç] *adj* having sharp ears; **h. werden** prick up one's ears
hellicht [′hɛlɪçt] *adj*—**hellichter Tag** broad daylight
Hel′ligkeit *f* (-;-en) brightness; (astr) magnitude
hell′sehen §138 *intr* be clairvoyant || **Hellsehen** *n* (-s;) clairvoyance
Hell′seher –in §6 *mf* clairvoyant; (coll) mind reader
hell′sichtig *adj* clear-sighted
hell′wach *adj* wide awake
Helm [hɛlm] *m* (-[e]s;-e) helmet; (archit) dome, spire; (naut) helm
Helm′busch *m* crest, plume
Hemd [hɛmt] *n* (-[e]s;-en) shirt
Hemd′brust *f* dickey, shirt front
Hemd′hose *f* union suit
hemmen [′hɛmən] *tr* slow up; stop; **gehemmt** inhibited
Hemmnis [′hɛmnɪs] *n* (-ses;-se) hindrance
Hemmschuh [′hɛmʃu] *m* (fig) hindrance; (rr) brake
Hem′mung *f* (-;-en) inhibition
hem′mungslos *adj* uninhibited
Hengst [hɛŋst] *m* (-es;-e) stallion
Henkel [′hɛŋkəl] *m* (-s;-) handle
henken [′hɛŋkən] *tr* hang (*s.o.*)
Henker [′hɛŋkər] *m* (-s;-) hangman
Henne [′hɛnə] *f* (-;-n) hen
her [her] *adv* hither, here; ago
herab [he′rap] *adv* down, downwards
herab- *comb.fm.* down; down here
herab′drücken *tr* press down; force down; **die Kurse h.** bear the market
herab′lassen §104 *ref* condescend
Herab′lassung *f* (-;) condescension
herab′sehen §138 *intr* (**auf** *acc*) look down (on)
herab′setzen *tr* put down; reduce; belittle, disparage
herab′steigen §148 *intr* (SEIN) climb down; (*vom Pferd*) dismount
herab′würdigen *tr* demean
Heraldik [he′raldɪk] *f* (-;) heraldry
heran [he′ran] *adv* near; up
heran′arbeiten *ref* (**an** *acc*) work one's way (towards)
heran′bilden *tr* (**zu**) train (as)
heran′brechen §64 *intr* (SEIN) (*Tag*) dawn, break; (*Nacht*) fall, come on
heran′gehen §82 *intr* (SEIN) go close; **h. an** (*acc*) approach, go up to
heran′kommen §99 *intr* (SEIN) come

near; **h. an** (*acc*) approach; get at; **h. bis an** (*acc*) reach as far as
heran′machen *ref*—**h. an** (*acc*) apply oneself to; approach
heran′nahen *intr* (SEIN) approach
heran′wachsen §155 *intr* (SEIN) (**zu**) grow up (to be)
heran′wagen *ref* (**an** *acc*) dare to approach
heran′ziehen §163 *tr* pull closer; call on for help; (*Quellen*) consult; (*zur Beratung*) call in; (*Pflanzen*) grow; (*Nachwuchs*) train || *intr* (SEIN) approach
herauf [he′rauf] *adv* up, up here; upstairs
herauf′arbeiten *ref* work one's way up
herauf′bemühen *ref* take the trouble to come up (or upstairs)
herauf′beschwören §137 *tr* conjure up; (*verursachen*) bring on, provoke
herauf′kommen §99 *intr* (SEIN) come up
herauf′setzen *tr* raise, increase
herauf′steigen §148 *intr* (SEIN) climb up; (*Tag*) dawn
herauf′ziehen §163 *tr* pull up || *intr* (SEIN) move upstairs; (*Sturm*) come up
heraus [he′raus] *adv* out, out here
heraus′bekommen §99 *intr* (aus) get out (of); (*Wort*) utter; (*Geld*) get back in change; (*Problem*) figure out
heraus′bringen §65 *tr* bring out; (*Wort*) utter; (*Lösung*) work out; (*Buch*) publish; (*Fabrikat*) bring out
heraus′drücken *tr* squeeze out; (*die Brust*) throw out
heraus′fahren §71 *intr* (SEIN) drive out; (*aus dem Bett*) jump out; (*Bemerkung*) slip out
heraus′finden §59 *tr* find out || *ref* (aus) find one's way out (of)
heraus′fordern *tr* challenge, call on
heraus′fordernd *adj* defiant || *adv* defiantly; **sich h. anziehen** dress provocatively
Heraus′forderung *f* (-;-en) challenge
heraus′fühlen *tr* sense
Heraus′gabe *f* surrender; (*e-s Buches*) publication; (jur) restitution
heraus′geben §80 *tr* surrender; give back; (*Buch*) publish || *intr* (dat) give (*s.o.*) his change; **h. auf** (*acc*) give change for
Heraus′geber *m* publisher; (*Redakteur*) editor
heraus′greifen §88 *tr* single out
heraus′haben §89 *tr* have (*s.th.*) figured out; **er hat den Bogen heraus** (coll) he has the knack of it
heraus′halten §90 *tr* hold out || *ref* (aus) keep out (of)
heraus′hängen §92 *tr* & *intr* hang out
heraus′kommen §99 *intr* (SEIN) come out
heraus′lesen §107 *tr* pick out; deduce; **zu viel aus e-m Gedicht h.** read too much into a poem
heraus′machen *tr* (*Fleck*) get out || *ref* (*Kinder*) turn out well; (*Geschäft*) make out well
heraus′nehmen §116 *tr* take out || *ref*

—sich [*dat*] **zu viel** (or **Freiheiten**) **h.** take liberties

heraus′platzen *intr* (SEIN)—**mit etw h.** blurt out s.th.

heraus′putzen *ref* dress up

heraus′reden *ref* (**aus**) talk one's way out (of)

heraus′rücken *tr* move out (here); (coil) (*Geld*) shell out ‖ *intr* (SEIN) —**mit dem Geld h.** shell out money; **mit der Sprache h.** reveal it, admit it

heraus′schälen *ref* become apparent

heraus′stehen §146 *intr* protrude

heraus′steigen §148 *intr* (SEIN) (**aus**) climb out (of), step out (of)

heraus′stellen *tr* put out; **groß h.** give a big build-up to; **klar h.** present clearly ‖ *ref* emerge, come to light; **sich h. als** prove to be

heraus′streichen §85 *tr* delete; (fig) praise

heraus′suchen *tr* pick out

heraus′treten §152 *intr* (SEIN) come out, step out; bulge, protrude

heraus′winden §59 *ref* extricate oneself

heraus′wirtschaften *tr* manage to save; (*Profit*) manage to make

heraus′ziehen §163 *tr* pull out

herb [herp] *adj* harsh; (*sauer*) sour; (*zusammenziehend*) tangy; (*Wein*) dry; (*Worte*) bitter; (*Schönheit*) austere ‖ **Herbe** *f* (–;) harshness; tang; bitterness; austerity

herbei′ *adv* here (*toward the speaker*)

herbei– *comb.fm.* up, along, here (*toward the speaker*)

herbei′bringen §65 *tr* bring along

herbei′eilen *intr* (SEIN) hurry here

herbei′führen *tr* bring here; cause

herbei′kommen §99 *intr* (SEIN) come up

herbei′lassen §104 *ref* condescend

herbei′rufen §122 *tr* call over; summon

herbei′schaffen *tr* bring here; procure; (*Geld*) raise

herbei′sehnen *tr* long for

herbei′strömen *intr* (SEIN) come flocking, flock

herbei′winken *tr* beckon (*s.o.*) to come over

herbei′wünschen *tr* long for, wish for

Herberge [′herbɛrgə] *f* (–;–n) lodging, shelter; hostel; (obs) inn

her′beten *tr* say mechanically

Herb′heit *f* (–;), **Herb′bigkeit** *f* (–;) harshness; tang; bitterness; austerity

her′bringen §65 *tr* bring here

Herbst [herpst] *m* (–es;–e) autumn

herbst′lich *adj* autumn, fall

Herd [hert] *m* (–[e]s;–e) hearth, fireplace; home; kitchen range; center

Herde [′herdə] *f* (–;–n) herd, flock

herein [he′raɪn] *adv* in, in here; **h.!** come in!

herein– *comb.fm.* in, in here (*toward the speaker*)

herein′bemühen *tr* ask (*s.o.*) to come in ‖ *ref* trouble oneself to come in

herein′bitten §60 *tr* invite in

Herein′fall *m* disappointment, letdown

herein′fallen §72 *intr* (SEIN) fall in; **h. auf** (*acc*) fall for; **h. in** (*acc*) fall into

herein′legen *tr* fool, take in

herein′platzen *intr* (SEIN) burst in

her′fallen §72 *intr* (SEIN)—**h. über** (*acc*) fall upon, attack

her′finden §59 *ref* & *intr* find one's way here

Her′gang *m* background details

her′geben §80 *tr* hand over; give up ‖ *ref*—**sich h. zu** be a party to

her′halten §90 *tr* hold out, extend ‖ *intr*—**h. müssen** (*Person*) be the victim; (*Sache*) have to do (*as a make-shift*)

Hering [′herɪŋ] *m* (–s;–e) herring; **sitzen wie die Heringe** be packed in like sardines

her′kommen §99 *intr* (SEIN) come here; (*Wort*) originate; **wo kommst du denn her?** where have you come from? ‖ **Herkommen** *n* (–s;–) origin; custom, tradition, convention

herkömmlich [′herkœmlɪç] *adj* customary, usual; traditional, conventional

Herkunft [′herkunft] *f* (–;) origin; birth, family

her′laufen §105 *intr* (SEIN) walk here; **hinter j–m h.** follow s.o.

her′leiten *tr* derive; deduce, infer

Her′leitung *f* (–;–en) derivation

her′machen *tr*—**viel h. von** make a fuss over ‖ *ref*—**sich h. über** (*acc*) attack; (fig) tackle

Hermelin [hermə′lin] *m* (–s;–e) ermine ‖ *n* (–s;–e) (zool) ermine

hermetisch [her′metɪʃ] *adj* hermetic

hernach′ *adv* afterwards

her′nehmen §116 *tr* get; **j–n scharf h.** give s.o. a good talking-to

hernie′der *adv* down, down here

Heroin [hero′in] *n* (–s;) (pharm) heroin

Heroine [hero′inə] *f* (–;–n) heroine

heroisch [he′ro·ɪʃ] *adj* heroic

Heroismus [hero′ɪsmus] *m* (–;) heroism

Herold [′herɔlt] *m* (–[e]s;–e) herald

Heros [′herɔs] *m* (–; **Heroen** [he′ro·ən] *hero*

Herr [her] *m* (–n;–en) lord; master; gentleman; (*als Anrede*) Sir; (*vor Eigennamen*) Mr.; (*Gott*) Lord; **meine Herren!** gentlemen!

her′reichen *tr* hand, pass

Herren– [′herən] *comb.fm.* man's, men's; gentlemen's

Her′renabend *m* stag party

Her′renbegleitung *f*—**in H.** accompanied by a gentleman

Her′rendoppel(spiel) *n* (tennis) men's doubles

Her′reneinzel(spiel) *n* (tennis) men's singles

Her′renfahrer *m* (aut) owner-driver

Her′renfriseur *m* barber

Her′rengesellschaft *f* male company; stag party

Her′rengröße *f* men's size

Her′rengut *n* domain, manor

Her′renhaus *n* mansion; House of Lords

Her′renhof *m* manor

Her′renleben *n* life of Riley**

her'renlos *adj* ownerless

Her'renmensch *m* born leader

Her'renschnitt *m* woman's very short hairstyle

Her'renzimmer *n* study

Herr'gott *m* Lord, Lord God

her'richten *tr* arrange; get ready

Herrin ['hɛrɪn] *f* (-;-nen) lady

herrisch ['hɛrɪ] *adj* masterful

herr'lich *adj* splendid

Herr'lichkeit *f* (-;-en) splendor

Herr'schaft *f* (-;-en) rule, domination; mastery; control; lord, master; estate; **meine Herrschaften!** ladies and gentlemen!

herr'schaftlich *adj* ruler's; gentleman's; high-class

herrschen ['hɛrʃən] *intr* rule; prevail; exist

Herr'scher -in §6 *mf* ruler

Herrschsucht ['hɛrʃzʊçt] *f* (-;) thirst for power; bossiness

herrsch'süchtig *adj* power-hungry; autocratic; domineering

her'rühren *intr*—**h. von** come from, originate with

her'sagen *tr* recite, say

her'schaffen *tr* get (here)

her'stammen *intr*—**h. von** come from, be descended from; (gram) be derived from

her'stellen *tr* put here; (*erzeugen*) produce; **fabrikmäßig h.** mass-produce; **Verbindung h.** establish contact; (telp) put a call through

Her'steller *m* (-s;-) manufacturer

Her'stellung *f* (-;-en) production

Her'stellungsbetrieb *m* factory

Her'stellungsverfahren *n* manufacturing process

herüber [hɛ'rybər] *adv* over, over here, in this direction (*toward the speaker*)

herum [hɛ'rʊm] *adv* around; about

herum'bringen §65 *tr* bring around; (*Zeit*) pass

herum'drehen *tr, ref & intr* turn around

herum'fragen *intr* make inquiries

herumfuchteln [hɛ'rʊmfʊxtəln] *intr*—**mit den Händen h.** wave one's hands about

herum'führen *tr* show around

herum'greifen §88 *intr*—**h. um** reach around

herum'hacken *intr*—**h. auf** (*dat*) pick on, criticize

herum'kauen *intr* (**an** *dat*, **auf** *dat*) chew away (on)

herum'kommen §99 *intr* (SEIN) get around; **h. um** get around; evade

herum'lungern *intr* loaf around

herum'reiten §86 *intr* (SEIN) ride around; **h. auf** (*dat*) harp on (*s.th.*); pick on (*s.o.*)

herum'schnüffeln *intr* snoop around

herum'streichen §85 *intr* (SEIN) prowl about

herum'streiten §86 *ref* squabble

herum'treiben §62 *tr* drive around ‖ *ref* roam around, knock about

Herum'treiber *m* (-s;-) loafer, tramp

herum'ziehen §163 *tr* pull around; **h. um** draw (*s.th.*) around ‖ *ref*—**sich h. um** surround ‖ *intr* (SEIN) wander

around; run around; **h. um** march around

herunter [hɛ'rʊntər] *adv* down, down here (*towards the speaker*); downstairs; **den Berg h.** down the mountain; **ins Tal h.** down into the valley

herun'terbringen §65 *tr* bring down; (fig) lower, reduce

herun'tergehen §82 *intr* (SEIN) go down; (*Preis, Temperatur*) fall, drop

herun'terhandeln *tr* (*Preis*) beat down

herun'terhauen §93 *tr* chop off; (*Brief*) dash off; **j—m eins h.** clout s.o.

herun'terkommen §99 *intr* (SEIN) come down; come downstairs; deteriorate

herun'terlassen §104 *tr* let down, lower

herun'terleiern *tr* drone

herun'terlesen §107 *tr* (*Liste*) read down; rattle off

herun'termachen *tr* take down; turn down; (coll) chew out; (coll) pan

herun'terschießen §76 *tr* shoot down

herun'tersein §139 *intr* (SEIN) be run-down

herun'terwirtschaften *tr* ruin (*through mismanagement*)

herun'terwürgen *tr* choke down

hervor [hɛr'for] *adv* out; forth

hervor'bringen §65 *tr* bring out; engender, produce; (*Wort*) utter

hervor'dringen §142 *intr* (SEIN) emerge

hervor'gehen §82 *intr* (SEIN)—**h. aus** come from; emerge from; to have been trained at

hervor'heben §94 *tr* highlight

hervor'holen *tr* produce

hervor'kommen §99 *intr* (SEIN) come out

hervor'lugen *intr* peep out

hervor'ragen *intr* jut out; be prominent; **h. über** (*acc*) tower over

hervor'ragend *adj* prominent

hervor'rufen §122 *tr* evoke, cause; (*Schauspieler*) recall

hervor'stechen §64 *intr* stick out; be conspicuous; be prominent

hervor'treten §152 *intr* (SEIN) emerge; come to the fore; become apparent; (*Augen*) bulge; (*Ader*) protrude

hervor'tun §154 *ref* distinguish oneself

hervor'wagen *ref* dare to come out; **sich mit e-r Antwort h.** venture an answer

hervor'zaubern *tr* produce by magic; **ein Essen h.** whip up a meal

Herweg ['hɛrvek] *m* way here; way home

Herz [hɛrts] *n* (-ens;-en) heart; (*als Anrede*) darling; (cards) heart(s); **ich bringe es nicht übers H. zu** (*inf*) I haven't the heart to (*inf*); **sich** [*dat*] **ein H. fassen** get up the courage; **seinem Herzen Luft machen** give vent to one's feelings

Herz- *comb.fm.* heart, cardiac

Herz'anfall *m* heart attack

Herz'beschwerden *pl* heart trouble

Herz'blume *f* (bot) bleeding heart

herzen ['hɛrtsən] *tr* hug, embrace

Her'zensgrund *m* bottom of one's heart

her'zensgut *adj* good-hearted

Her'zenslust *f*—nach **H.** to one's heart's content

herz'ergreifend *adj* moving, touching

Herz'geräusch *n* heart murmur

herz'haft *adj* hearty

herzig ['hertsɪç] *adj* sweet, cute –herzig *comb.fm.* –hearted

Herzinfarkt ['hertsɪnfarkt] *m* (–[e]s; –e) cardiac infarction

herz'innig *adj* heartfelt

herz'inniglich *adv* sincerely

Herz'klappe *f* cardiac valve

Herz'klopfen *n* palpitations

Herz'kollaps *m* heart failure

herz'lich *adj* cordial; sincere || *adv* very; **h. wenige** precious few

herz'los *adj* heartless

Herzog ['hertsok] *m* (–[e]s;–̈e) duke

Herzogin ['hertsɔgɪn] *f* (–;-nen) duchess

Herzogtum ['hertsɔktum] *n* (–[e]s;–̈er) dukedom; duchy

Herz'schlag *m* heartbeat; heart failure

Herz'stück *n* heart, central point

Herz'verpflanzung *f* heart transplant

Herz'weh *n* (& fig) heartache

Hetzblatt ['hetsblat] *n* scandal sheet

Hetze ['hetsə] *f* (–;-n) hunting; hurry, rush; vicious campaign; baiting

hetzen ['hetsən] *tr* hunt; bait; rush; (fig) hound; **e-n Hund auf j-n h. sic** a dog on s.o. || *ref* rush || *intr* stir up trouble; **h. gegen** conduct a vicious campaign against || *intr* (SEIN) race, dash

Het'zer –in §6 *mf* agitator

Hetz'hund *m* hound, hunting dog

Hetz'jagd *f* hunt; baiting; hurry

Hetz'rede *f* inflammatory speech

Heu [hɔɪ] *n* (–[e]s;) hay

Heu'boden *m* hayloft

Heuchelei [hɔɪçə'laɪ] *f* (–;-en) hypocrisy; piece of hypocrisy

heucheln ['hɔɪçəln] *tr* feign || *intr* be hypocritical

Heuch'ler –in §6 *mf* hypocrite

heuchlerisch ['hɔɪçlərɪʃ] *adj* hypocritical

heuen ['hɔɪ·ən] *intr* make hay

heuer ['hɔɪ·ər] *adv* this year

heuern ['hɔɪ·ərn] *tr* hire

Heu'fieber *n* hayfever

Heu'gabel *f* pitchfork

heulen ['hɔɪlən] *intr* bawl; (*Wind*) howl

heurig ['hɔɪrɪç] *adj* this year's || **Heurige** §5 *m* new wine

Heu'schnupfen *m* (–s;) hayfever

Heuschober ['hɔɪ/ʃobər] *m* (–s;-) haystack

Heu'schrecke *f* (–;-n) locust

heute ['hɔɪtə] *adv* today; **h. abend** this evening; **h. früh** (or **h. morgen**) this morning; **h. vor acht Tagen** a week ago today; **h. in acht Tagen** today a week

heutig ['hɔɪtɪç] *adj* today's; present-day; **am heutigen Tage** (or **der heutige Tag** or **mit dem heutigen Tag**) today

heutzutage ['hɔɪttsutagə] *adv* nowadays

Hexe ['heksə] *f* (–;-n) witch; hag

hexen ['heksən] *intr* practice witchcraft

He'xenkessel *m* chaos, inferno

He'xenmeister *m* wizard; sorcerer

He'xenschuß *m* lumbago

Hexerei [heksə'raɪ] *f* (–;) witchcraft

Hiatus [hɪ'ɑtus] *m* (–;-) (& pros) hiatus

Hibis·kus [hɪ'bɪskus] *m* (–;-ken [kən]) hibiscus

hieb [hip] *pret* of **hauen** || **Hieb** *m* (–[e]s;-e) blow, stroke; **Hiebe** thrashing

hieb'–undstich'fest *adj* (fig) watertight

Hieb'wunde *f* gash

hielt [hilt] *pret* of **halten**

hier [hir] *adv* here

hieran' *adv* at (by, in, on, to) it or them

Hierar·chie [hɪ·erar'çi] *f* (–;-chien ['çi·ən]) hierarchy

hierauf' *adv* on it, on them; then

hieraus' *adv* out of it (or them); from this (or these)

hierbei' *adv* near here; here; in this case; in connection with this

hierdurch' *adv* through it (or them); through here; hereby

hierfür' *adv* for it (or them)

hierge'gen *adv* against it

hierher' *adv* hither, here

hier'herum *adv* around here

hierhin' *adv* here; **bis h.** up to here

hierin' *adv* herein, in this

hiermit' *adv* herewith, with it

hiernach' *adv* after this, then; about this; according to this

Hieroglyphe [hɪ·erɔ'glyfə] *f* (–;-n) hieroglyph

hierorts ['hirɔrts] *adv* in this town

hierü'ber *adv* over it (or them); about it (or this)

hierzu' *adv* to it; in addition to it; concerning this

hiesig ['hizɪç] *adj* local

hieß [his] *pret* of **heißen**

Hilfe ['hɪlfə] *f* (–;-n) help, aid; **zu H. nehmen** make use of

Hil'feleistung *f* assistance

Hil'feruf *m* cry for help

hilf'los *adj* helpless

hilf'reich *adj* helpful

Hilfs– [hɪlfs] *comb.fm.* auxiliary

Hilfs'arbeiter –in §6 *mf* unskilled laborer

Hilfs'arzt *m*, **Hilf'ärztin** *f* intern

hilfs'bedürftig *adj* needy

hilfs'bereit *adj* ready to help

Hilfs'dienst *m* help, assistance

Hilfs'gerät *n* labor-saving device

Hilfs'kraft *f* assistant, helper; (mach) auxiliary power

Hilfs'kraftbremse *f* power brake

Hilfs'kraftlenkung *f* power steering

Hilfs'lehrer –in §6 *mf* student teacher

Hilfs'maschine *f* auxiliary engine

Hilfs'mittel *n* aid, device; remedy; financial aid

Hilfs'quellen *pl* material; sources

Hilfs'rakete *f* booster rocket

Hilfs'schule *f* school for the mentally slow

Hilfs'truppen pl auxiliaries

Hilfs'werk n welfare organization

Hilfs'zeitwort n (-[e]s;-er) (gram) auxiliary (verb)

Himbeere ['hɪmberə] f (-;-n) raspberry

Himmel ['hɪməl] m (-s;-) sky, skies; heaven(s); firmament; (eccl) baldachin; **ach du lieber H.!** good heavens!; **aus heiterem H.** out of the blue; **in den H. heben** praise to the skies

himmelan' adv skywards; heavenwards

him'melangst invar adj—**mir wird h. I** feel frightened to death

Him'melbett n canopy bed

him'melblau adj sky-blue

Him'melfahrt f ascension; assumption

Him'melfahrtstag m Ascension Day

Him'melreich n kingdom of heaven

Himmels– comb.fm. celestial

Him'melschreiend adj atrocious

Him'melsgegend f region of the sky; point of the compass

Him'melskörper m celestial body

Him'melsrichtung f point of the compass; direction

Him'melsschrift f skywriting

Him'melswagen m (astr) Great Bear

Him'melszelt n canopy of heaven

himmelwärts ['hɪməlverts] adv skywards; heavenwards

himmlisch ['hɪmlɪʃ] adj heavenly, celestial; divine; (coll) gorgeous

hin [hɪn] adv there (away from the speaker); **ganz hin** (coll) bushed; (coll) quite carried away; **hin ist hin** what's done is done; **hin und her** up and down, back and forth; **hin und wieder** now and then; **vor sich hin** to oneself

hinab' adv down

hinan' adv up; **bis an etw h.** up to s.th., as far as s.th.

hinauf' adv up, up there; upstairs; **den Fluß h.** up the river

hinauf'reichen tr hand (s.th.) up ‖ intr reach up

hinauf'schrauben tr (Preis) jack up

hinauf'setzen tr raise, increase

hinauf'steigen §148 tr (SEIN) (Treppe, Berg) climb ‖ intr (SEIN) climb up; (Temperatur) rise

hinaus' adv out, out there; **auf viele Jahre h.** for many years to come

hinaus'beißen §53 tr (coll) edge out

hinaus'gehen §82 intr (SEIN) go out; **h. auf** (acc) look out over; lead to; drive at, imply; **h. über** (acc) exceed

hinaus'kommen §99 intr (SEIN) come out; **es kommt auf eins** (or **aufs gleiche**) **hinaus** it amounts to the same thing; **h. über** (acc) get beyond

hinaus'laufen §105 intr (SEIN) run out; **es läuft aufs eins** (or **aufs gleiche**) **hinaus** it amounts to the same thing

hinaus'schieben §130 tr push out; (Termin, usw.) postpone

hinaus'werfen §160 tr throw out; fire

hinaus'wollen §162 intr want to go out; **h. auf** (acc) be driving at; **hoch h.** aim high, be ambitious

hinaus'ziehen §163 tr prolong ‖ ref

take longer than expected ‖ intr (SEIN) go out; move out

Hin'blick m—**im H. auf** (acc) in view of

hin'bringen §65 tr bring (there); take (there); (Zeit) pass

hinderlich ['hɪndərlɪç] adj in the way

hindern ['hɪndərn] tr block; **h. an** (dat) prevent from (ger)

Hindernis ['hɪndərnɪs] n (-ses;-se) hindrance; obstacle

Hin'dernisbahn f obstacle course

Hin'dernislauf m (sport) hurdles

Hin'dernisrennen n steeplechase; hurdles

hin'deuten intr (auf acc) point (to)

hindurch' adv through; **den ganzen Sommer h.** throughout the summer

hinein' adv in, in there

hinein'arbeiten ref—**sich h. in** (acc) work one's way into

hinein'denken §66 ref—**sich h. in** (acc) imagine oneself in

hinein'geraten §63 intr (SEIN)—**h. in** (acc) get into, fall into

hinein'leben intr—**in den Tag h.** live for the moment

hinein'tun §154 tr put in

Hin'fahrt f journey there, out-bound passage

hin'fallen §72 intr (SEIN) fall down

hinfällig ['hɪnfɛlɪç] adj frail; (Gesetz) invalid

hinfort' adv henceforth

hing [hɪŋ] pret of **hängen**

Hin'gabe f (an acc) devotion (to)

hin'geben §80 tr give up ‖ ref (dat) abandon oneself (to)

Hin'gebung f (-;) devotion

hinge'gen adv on the other hand

hin'gehen §82 intr (SEIN) go there; pass

hin'halten §90 tr hold out; (Person) keep waiting, string along; **den Kopf h.** (fig) take the rap

hinken ['hɪŋkən] intr limp; **der Vergleich hinkt** that's a poor comparison ‖ intr (SEIN) limp

hin'länglich adj sufficient

hin'legen tr put down ‖ ref lie down

hin'nehmen §116 tr accept; take, put up with

hin'raffen tr snatch away

hin'reichen tr (dat) pass to, hand to ‖ intr reach; suffice

hin'reißen §53 tr enchant, carry away

hin'richten tr execute; **h. auf** (acc) direct towards

Hin'richtung f (-;-en) execution

Hin'richtungsbefehl m death warrant

hin'setzen tr put down ‖ ref sit down

Hin'sicht f respect, way: **in H. auf** (acc) regarding, in regard to

hin'sichtlich prep (genit) regarding

hin'stellen tr put there; put down

hintan'setzen, hintan'stellen tr put last, consider last

hinten ['hɪntən] adv at the back, in the rear; **h. im Zimmer** at the back of the room; **nach h.** to the rear; backwards; **von h.** from the rear

hinter ['hɪntər] prep (dat) behind; **h. j-m her sein** be after s.o. ‖ prep (acc) behind; **h. etw kommen** find out about s.th., get to the bottom of s.th.

Hin′terachse *f* rear axle
Hin′terbacke *f* buttock
Hin′terbein *n* hind leg; **sich auf die Hinterbeine setzen** strain oneself
Hinterbliebene [ˈhɪntɐbliːbənə] §5 *mf* survivor (*of a deceased*); **H.** *pl* next-of-kin
hinterbrin′gen §65 *tr*—j-m etw h. let s.o. in on s.th.
Hin′terdeck *n* quarter deck
hinterdrein [hɪntɐˈdraɪn] *adv* after; subsequently, afterwards
hin′tere §9 *adj* back, rear ‖ **Hintere** §5 *m* (coll) behind
hintereinan′der *adv* one behind the other; in succession; one after the other
Hin′terfuß *m* hind foot
Hin′tergaumen *m* soft palate, velum
Hin′tergedanke *m* ulterior motive
hinterge′hen §82 *tr* deceive
Hin′tergrund *m* background
Hin′terhalt *m* ambush
hinterhältig [ˈhɪntɐhɛltɪç] *adj* underhanded
Hin′terhand *f* hind quarters (*of horse*)
Hin′terhaus *n* rear building
hinterher′ *adv* behind; afterwards
Hin′terhof *m* backyard
Hin′terkopf *m* back of the head
Hin′terland *n* hinterland
hinterlas′sen §104 *tr* leave behind
Hinterlas′senschaft *f* (–;–en) inheritance
Hin′terlauf *m* hind leg
hinterle′gen *tr* deposit
Hinterle′gung *f* (–;–en) deposit
Hin′terlist *f* deceit; trick, ruse
Hin′termann *m* (–[e]s;–er) instigator; wheeler-dealer; (pol) backer
Hintern [ˈhɪntɐn] *m* (–s;–) (coll) behind
Hin′terradantrieb *m* rear-wheel drive
hinterrücks [ˈhɪntɐryks] *adv* from behind; (fig) behind one's back
Hin′tertreffen *n*—ins H. geraten fall behind; **im H. sein** be at a disadvantage
hintertrei′ben §62 *tr* frustrate
Hintertrei′bung *f* (–;–en) frustration
Hin′tertreppe *f* backstairs
Hin′tertür *f* backdoor
Hinterwäldler [ˈhɪntɐvɛltlɐ] *m* (–s;–) hillbilly
hin′terwäldlerisch *adj* hillbilly
hinterzie′hen §163 *tr* evade
Hinterzie′hung *f* (–;) tax evasion
hinü′ber *adv* over, over there; across
hinun′ter *adv* down
hinun′tergehen §82 *tr* (SEIN) (*Treppe*) go down ‖ *intr* (SEIN) go down
hinweg [hɪnˈvɛk] *adv* away; **über etw h.** over s.th., across s.th. ‖ **Hinweg** [ˈhɪnvɛk] *m* way there
hinweg′kommen §99 *intr* (SEIN)—h. über (*acc*) get over
hinweg′sehen §138 *intr*—h. über (*acc*) look over; overlook, ignore
hinweg′setzen *ref*—sich h. über (*acc*) ignore, disregard
hinweg′täuschen *tr* mislead, blind

Hinweis [ˈhɪnvaɪs] *m* (–es;–e) reference; hint; announcement
hin′weisen §118 *tr*—j-n h. auf (*acc*) point s.th. out to s.o. ‖ *intr*—h. auf (*acc*) point to; point out
hin′werfen §160 *tr* throw down; (coll) dash off, jot down
hin′wirken *intr*—h. auf (*acc*) work toward(s)
hin′ziehen §163 *tr* attract protract ‖ *ref* drag on; **sich h. an** (*dat*) run along; **sich h. bis zu** extend to
hin′zielen *intr*—h. auf (*acc*) aim at
hinzu′ *adv* there, thither; in addition
hinzu′fügen *tr* add
hinzu′kommen §99 *intr* (SEIN) come (upon the scene); be added; **es kamen noch andere Gründe hinzu** besides, there were more reasons
hinzu′setzen *tr* add
hinzu′treten §152 *intr* (SEIN) (**zu**) walk up (to); **es traten noch andere Gründe hinzu** besides, there were other reasons
hinzu′tun §154 *tr* add
hinzu′ziehen §163 *tr* (*Arzt*) call in
Hirn [hɪrn] *n* (–[es];–e) brain; brains; **sein H. anstrengen** rack one's brains
Hirn- *comb.fm.* brain; cerebral; intellectual
Hirn′anhang *m* pituitary gland
Hirn′gespinst *n* figment of the imagination
Hirn′hautentzündung *f* meningitis
hirn′los *adj* brainless
Hirn′rinde *f* (anat) cortex
Hirn′schale *f* cranium
hirn′verbrannt *adj* (coll) crazy
Hirsch [hɪrʃ] *m* (–es;–e) deer, stag
Hirsch′fänger *m* hunting knife
Hirsch′kalb *n* fawn, doe
Hirsch′kuh *f* hind
Hirsch′leder *n* deerskin, buckskin
Hirt [hɪrt] *m* (–en;–en) shepherd **–hirte** [hɪrtə] *m* (–;–n)—herd
Hir′tenbrief *m* (eccl) pastoral letter
Hirtin [ˈhɪrtɪn] *f* (–;–nen) shepherdess
His [hɪs] *n* (–;) (mus) B sharp
hissen [ˈhɪsən] *tr* hoist
Historie [hɪsˈtoːrjə] *f* (–;–n) history; story
Historiker –in [hɪsˈtoːrɪkɐr(ɪn)] §6 *mf* historian
historisch [hɪsˈtoːrɪʃ] *adj* historical
Hitze [ˈhɪtsə] *f* (–;–n) heat
hit′zebeständig *adj* heat-resistant
Hit′zeferien *pl* school holiday (*because of hot weather*)
Hit′zeschild *m* (rok) heat shield
Hit′zewelle *f* heat wave
hitzig [ˈhɪtsɪç] *adj* hot-tempered
Hitz′kopf *m* hothead
hitz′köpfig *adj* hot-headed
Hitz′schlag *m* heatstroke
hob [hoːp] *pret of* heben
Hobel [ˈhoːbəl] *m* (–s;–) (carp) plane
Ho′belbank *f* carpenter's bench
hobeln [ˈhoːbəln] *tr* (carp) plane
hoch [hox], (**hohe** [ˈhoːə] §9) *adj* (**höher** [ˈhøːər]); **höchste** [ˈhøçstə] §9) high; noble; (*Alter*) advanced; **das ist mir zu h.** that's beyond me; **hohes Gericht!** your honor!; mem-

bers of the jury!; **in höchster Not** in dire need ‖ *adv* high; highly, very; (math) to the ... power ‖ **Hoch** *n* (-s;-s) (*Trinkspruch, Heilruf*) cheer; (meteor) high
hoch– *comb.fm.* up; upwards; highly, very; high, as high as
hoch′achten *tr* esteem
Hoch′achtung *f* (-;) esteem; **mit vorzüglicher H., Ihr ... or Ihre ...** Very truly yours, Respectfully yours
hoch′achtungsvoll *adj* respectful ‖ *adv* —**h., Ihr ... or Ihre ...** Very truly yours, Respectfully yours
Hoch′amt *n* (eccl) High Mass
Hoch′antenne *f* outdoor antenna
hoch′arbeiten *ref* work one's way up
hoch′aufgeschossen *adj* tall, lanky
Hoch′bahn *f* el, elevated train
Hoch′bauingenieur *m* structural engineer
hoch′bäumen *ref* rear up
Hoch′behälter *m* water tower; reservoir
Hochbeiner [′hoxbaɪnər] *m* (-s;-) (ent) daddy-long-legs
hoch′beinig *adj* long-legged
hoch′betagt *adj* advanced in years
Hoch′betrieb *m* bustle, big rush
Hoch′blüte *f* high bloom; (fig) heyday
hoch′bringen §65 *tr* restore to health; (*Geschäft*) put on its feet; **es h.** (sport) get a high score
Hoch′burg *f* fortress, citadel
hoch′denkend *adj* noble-minded
hoch′deutsch *adj* High German
Hoch′druck *m* high pressure; (fig) great pressure; (meteor) high; **mit H.** (fig) full blast
Hoch′druckgebiet *n* (meteor) high, high-pressure area
Hoch′ebene *f* plateau
hoch′fahrend *adj* high-handed
hoch′fein *adj* very refined; high-grade
Hoch′flut *f* high tide; (fig) deluge
Hoch′form *f* top form
hochfrequent [′hoxfrekvɛnt] *adj* high-frequency
Hoch′frequenz *f* high-frequency
Hoch′frisur *f* upsweep
Hoch′gefühl *n* elation
hoch′gemut *adj* cheerful
Hoch′genuß *m* great pleasure
Hoch′gericht *n* place of execution
hoch′gesinnt *adj* noble-minded
hoch′gespannt *adj* (*Hoffnungen*) high; (elec) high-voltage
hoch′gestellt *adj* high-ranking
Hoch′glanz *m* high polish, high gloss
Hoch′haus *n* high-rise (building)
hoch′herzig *adj* generous
hoch′jagen *tr* (*Wild*) ferret out; (*Motor*) race; (coll) blow up
hochkant [′hoxkant] *adv* on end
Hoch′konjunktur *f* (econ) boom
Hoch′land *n* highlands; plateau
Hoch′leistung *f* (-;-en) high output; (sport) first-class performance
Hochleistungs– *comb.fm.* high-powered; high-capacity; high-speed; heavy-duty
Hoch′mut *m* haughtiness, pride
hoch′mütig *adj* haughty, proud

hoch′näsig [′hoxnezɪç] *adj* snooty
Hoch′ofen *m* blast furnace
hoch′ragend *adj* towering
hoch′rappeln *ref* (coll) get on one's feet again, pick up again
hoch′rollen *tr* roll up
Hoch′ruf *m* cheer
Hoch′saison *f* height of the season
Hoch′schule *f* university, academy
Hoch′schüler **–in** §6 *mf* university student
Hoch′seefischerei *f* deep-sea fishing
hoch′selig *adj* late, of blessed memory
Hoch′spannung *f* high voltage
Hoch′spannungsleitung *f* high-tension line
hoch′spielen *tr* play up; put into the limelight
Hoch′sprache *f* standard language; (**die) deutsche H.** standard German
höchst *adv* see hoch
Höchst– *comb.fm.* maximum, top
Hochstapelei [hox′tɑpə′laɪ] *f* (-;) false pretenses; fraud
Hochstapler [′hox′tɑplər] *m* (-s;) confidence man; imposter, swindler
Hoch′start *m* (sport) standing start
Höchst′belastung *f* (-;-en) maximum load; (elec) peak load
höchstens [′høçstəns] *adv* at best, at the very most
Höchst′form *f* (sport) top form
Höchst′frequenz *f* ultrahigh frequency
Höchst′geschwindigkeit *f* top speed; **zulässige H.** speed limit
Höchst′leistung *f* (-;-en) maximum output; highest achievement; (sport) record
Hoch′straße *f* overpass
Hoch′ton *m* (ling) primary stress
hoch′tönend *adj* bombastic
hochtourig [′hoxturɪç] *adj* high-revving
hoch′trabend *adj* pompous
Hoch′-und Tief′bau *m* (-[e]s;) civil engineering
hoch′verdient *adj* of great merit
Hoch′verrat *m* high treason
Hoch′verräter **–in** §6 *mf* traitor
Hoch′wasser *n* flood(s); **der Fluß führt H.** the river is swollen
hoch′wertig *adj* high-quality
Hoch′wild *n* big game
Hoch′würden *pl* (*als Anrede*) Reverend; **Seine H. ...** the Reverend ...
Hoch′zeit *f* wedding
hoch′zeitlich *adj* bridal; nuptial
Hoch′zeitsfeier *f* wedding ceremony; wedding reception
Hoch′zeitspaar *n* newly-weds
Hoch′zeitsreise *f* honeymoon
Hocke [′hɔkə] *f* (-;-n) crouch
hocken [′hɔkən] *ref & intr* squat; (coll) sit down
Hocker [′hɔkər] *m* (-s;-) stool
Höcker [′hœkər] *m* (-s;-) hump; bump
höckerig [′hœkərɪç] *adj* hunchbacked; (*Weg*) bumpy
Hockey [′hɔki] *n* (-s;) hockey
Ho′ckeyschläger *m* hockey stick
Hode [′hodə] *f* (-;-n) testicle
Ho′densack *m* (anat) scrotum
Hof [hof] *m* (-[e]s;ꞏe) courtyard;

yard; barnyard; (*e-s Königs*) court; (astr) halo; corona; **e-m Mädchen den Hof machen** court a girl

Hoffart ['hɔfart] *f* (-;) haughtiness

hoffärtig ['hɔfertɪç] *adj* haughty

hoffen ['hɔfən] *tr*—**das Beste h.** hope for the best ‖ *intr* (auf *acc*) hope (for); **auf j-n h.** put one's hopes in s.o

hoffentlich ['hɔfəntlɪç] *adv* as I hope; **h. kommt er bald** I hope he comes soon

Hoffnung ['hɔfnʊŋ] *f* (-;-en) hope

hoff′nungslos *adj* hopeless

hoff′nungsvoll *adj* hopeful; promising

Hof′hund *m* watchdog

hofieren [ho'firən] *tr* court

höfisch ['høfɪʃ] *adj* court, courtly

höflich ['høflɪç] *adj* polite, courteous

Höf′lichkeit *f* (-;-en) politeness, courtesy

Höf′lichkeitsformel *f* complimentary close (*in a letter*)

Höfling ['høflɪŋ] *m* (-[e]s;-e) courtier

Hof′meister *m* steward; tutor

Hof′narr *m* court jester

Hof′staat *m* royal household; retinue

hohe ['ho·ə] *adj* see **hoch**

Höhe ['hø·ə] *f* (-;-en) height; altitude; (*Anhöhe*) hill; (mus) pitch; **auf der H.** in good shape; **das ist die H.!** that's the limit!; **in der H. von** in the amount of; **in die H.** up; **in die H. fahren** jump up; **wieder in die H. bringen** (com) put back on its feet

Hoheit ['hohart] *f* (-;-en) sovereignty; (*als Titel*) Highness

Ho′heitsbereich *m* (pol), **Ho′heitsgebiet** *n* (pol) territory

Ho′heitsgewässer *pl* territorial waters

Ho′heitsrechte *pl* sovereign rights

ho′heitsvoll *adj* regal, majestic

Ho′heitszeichen *n* national emblem

Hö′henmesser *m* altimeter

Hö′henruder *n* (aer) elevator

Hö′hensonne *f* ultra-violet lamp

Hö′henstrahlen *pl* cosmic rays

Hö′henzug *m* mountain range

Ho′hepriester *m* high priest

Hö′hepunkt *m* climax; height, acme

höher ['hø·ər] *adj* see **hoch**

hohl [hol] *adj* hollow

Höhle ['hølə] *f* (-;-n) cave; grotto; lair, den; hollow, cavity; socket

Höh′lenmensch *m* caveman

hohl′geschliffen *adj* hollow-ground

Hohl′heit *f* (-;) hollowness

Hohl′maß *n* dry measure; liquid measure

Hohl′raum *m* hollow, cavity

Hohl′saum *m* hemstitch

Hohl′weg *m* defile, narrow pass

Hohn [hon] *m* (-[e]s;) scorn; sarcasm; **etw j-m Hohn tun** do s.th. in defiance of s.o.

höhnen ['hønən] *intr* jeer; sneer

höhnisch ['hønɪʃ] *adj* scornful

hohn′sprechen §64 *intr* (*dat*) treat with scorn; defy; make a mockery of

Höker -in ['hø·kər(ɪn)] §6 *mf* huckster

hold [hɔlt] *adj* kindly; lovely; sweet

hold′selig *adj* lovely, sweet

holen ['holən] *tr* fetch; get; (*Atem, Luft*) draw; **h. lassen** send for; **sich** [*dat*] **etw h.** (coll) catch s.th.

Holland ['hɔlant] *n* (-s;) Holland

Holländer ['hɔlendər] *m* (-s;-) Dutchman

Holländerin ['hɔlendərɪn] *f* (-;-nen) Dutch woman

holländisch ['hɔlendɪʃ] *adj* Dutch

Hölle ['hœlə] *f* (-;) hell

Höl′lenangst *f* mortal fear

höllisch ['hœlɪʃ] *adj* hellish

Holm [hɔlm] *m* (-[e]s;-e) islet; (*Stiel*) handle; (aer) spar; (gym) parallel bar

holp(e)rig ['hɔlp(ə)rɪç] *adj* bumpy

holpern ['hɔlpərn] *intr* jolt, bump along; (*beim Lesen*) stumble

Holunder [ho'lundər] *m* (-s;-) (bot) elder

Holz [hɔlts] *n* (-es;¨er) wood; lumber; timber, trees; **ins H. gehen** go into the woods

Holz′apfel *m* crab apple

Holz′arbeit *f* woodwork; lumbering

Holz′arbeiter *m* woodworker; lumberjack

holz′artig *adj* woody

Holz′blasinstrumente *pl* wood winds

Holz′brei *m* wood pulp

holzen ['hɔltsən] *tr* fell; deforest; (coll) spank ‖ *intr* cut wood

hölzern ['hœltsərn] *adj* wooden; (fig) clumsy

Holzfäller ['hɔltsfelər] *m* (-s;-) lumberjack, logger

Holz′faser *f* wood fiber; wood pulp; grain; **gegen die H.** against the grain

Holz′faserstoff *m* wood pulp

Holzhacker ['hɔltshakər] *m* (-s;-), **Holzhauer** ['hɔltshau·ər] *m* (-s;-) lumberjack; wood chopper

holzig ['hɔltsɪç] *adj* woody, wooded; (*Gemüse*) stringy

Holz′knecht *m* lumberjack

Holz′kohle *f* charcoal

Holz′nagel *m* wooden peg

Holz′platz *m* lumber yard

holz′reich *adj* wooded

Holz′schnitt *m* woodcut; wood engraving

Holz′schuh *m* wooden shoe

Holz′schuppen *m* woodshed

Holz′wolle *f* excelsior

Homilie [homi'li] *f* (-;-lien ['li·ən]) homily

homogen [homo'gen] *adj* homogeneous

Homosexualität [homozeksu·ali'tet] *f* (-;) homosexuality

homosexuell [homozeksu'el] *adj* homosexual ‖ **Homosexuelle** §5 *mf* homosexual

Honig ['honɪç] *m* (-s;) honey

Ho′nigkuchen *m* gingerbread

ho′nigsüß *adj* sweet as honey

Ho′nigwabe *f* honeycomb

Honorar [hono'rar] *n* (-s;-e) fee

Honoratioren [honoratsi'orən] *pl* dignitaries

honorieren [hono'rirən] *tr* give an honorarium to; pay royalties to; (*Scheck*) honor

Hopfen ['hɔpfən] *m* (-s;) hops

hopp [hɔp] *interj* up!; quick!; **hopp, los!** get going!

hoppla ['hɔpla] *interj* whoops!; **jetzt aber h.!** come on!; look sharp!

hops [hɔps] *adj*—**h. gehen** go to pot; **h. sein** be done for

hopsasa ['hɔpsasa] *interj* upsy-daisy

hopsen ['hɔpsən] *intr* (SEIN) hop

Hop'ser *m* (-s;-) hop

Hörapparat ['høraparat] *m* hearing aid

hörbar ['hørbar] *adj* audible

hörbehindert ['hørbəhɪndərt] *adj* hard of hearing

Hörbericht ['hørbərɪçt] *m* radio report; radio commentary

horchen ['hɔrçən] *intr* listen; eavesdrop

Hor'cher **–in** §6 *mf* eavesdropper

Horch'gerät *n* sound detector; (nav) hydrophone

Horch'posten *m* (mil) listening post

Horde ['hɔrdə] *f* (-;-n) horde

hören ['hørən] *tr* hear; listen to; (*Vorlesung*) attend ‖ *intr* hear; **h. auf** (acc) pay attention to, obey

Hö'rer *m* (-s;-) listener; member of an audience; student; (telp) receiver

Hö'rerbrief *m* letter from a listener

Hö'rerkreis *m* listeners

Hö'rerschaft *f* (-;-en) audience; (educ) enrollment

Hör'folge *f* radio serial

Hör'gerät *n* hearing aid

hörig ['hørɪç] *adj* in bondage ‖ **Hörige** §5 *mf* serf, thrall

Horizont [hɔrɪ'tsɔnt] *m* (-[e]s;-e) horizon

horizontal [hɔrɪtsɔn'tal] *adj* horizontal ‖ **Horizontale** §5 *f* horizontal line

Horn [hɔrn] *n* (-[e]s;ⁱⁱer) horn; (mil) bugle; (mus) horn, French horn

Hörnchen ['hœrnçən] *n* (-s;-) crescent roll

Horn'haut *f* (anat) cornea

Hornisse [hɔr'nɪsə] *f* (-;-n) hornet

Hornist [hɔr'nɪst] *m* (-en;-en) bugler

Horn'ochse *m* (coll) dumb ox

Horoskop [hɔrɔ'skɔp] *n* (-[e]s;-e) horoscope

horrend [hɔ'rɛnt] *adj* (coll) terrible

Hör'rohr *n* stethoscope

Hör'saal *m* lecture room

Hör'spiel *n* radio play

Horst [hɔrst] *m* (-[e]s;-e) (eagle's) nest

Hort [hɔrt] *m* (-[e]s;-e) hoard, treasure; (place of) refuge; protector

Hör'weite *f*—**in H.** within earshot

Hose ['hozə] *f* (-;-n), **Hosen** ['hozən] *pl* pants, trousers; (*Unterhose*) shorts; panties; **sich auf die Hosen setzen** buckle down

Ho'senboden *m* seat (of trousers)

Ho'senklappe *f*, **Ho'senlatz** *m* fly

Ho'senrolle *f* (theat) male role

Ho'senträger *pl* suspenders

Hospitant [hɔspi'tant] *m* (-en;-en) (educ) auditor

hospitieren [hɔspi'tirən] *intr* (educ) audit a course

Hospiz [hɔs'pits] *n* (-es;-e) hospice

Hostie ['hɔstjə] *f* (-;-n) host, wafer

Hotel [hɔ'tɛl] *n* (-s;-s) hotel

Hotel'boy *m* bellboy, bellhop

Hotel'diener *m* hotel porter

Hotel'fach *n*, **Hotel'gewerbe** *n* hotel business

Hub [hup] *m* (-[e]s;ⁱⁱe) (mach) stroke

hübsch [hypʃ] *adj* pretty; handsome; (coll) good-sized

Hubschrauber ['hup/raubər] *m* (-s;-) helicopter

huckepack ['hukəpak] *adv* piggyback

hudeln ['hudəln] *intr* be sloppy

Huf [huf] *m* (-[e]s;-e) hoof

Huf'eisen *n* horseshoe

Huf'schlag *m* hoofbeat

Hüfte ['hyftə] *f* (-;-n) hip; **die Arme in die Hüften gestemmt** with arms akimbo

Hüft'gelenk *n* hip joint

Hüft'gürtel *m*, **Hüft'halter** *m* garter belt

Hügel ['hygəl] *m* (-s;-) hill; mound

hügelab' *adv* downhill

hügelauf' *adv* uphill

hügelig ['hygəlɪç] *adj* hilly

Huhn [hun] *n* (-[e]s;ⁱⁱer) fowl; hen, chicken

Hühnchen ['hynçən] *n* (-s;-) young chicken; **ein H. zu rupfen haben mit** (fig) have a bone to pick with

Hüh'nerauge *n* (pathol) corn

Hüh'nerdraht *m* chicken wire

Hüh'nerhund *m* bird dog

Huld [hult] *f* (-;) grace, favor

huldigen ['huldɪgən] *intr* (dat) pay homage to

Hul'digung *f* (-;) homage

Hul'digungseid *m* oath of allegiance

huld'reich, huld'voll *adj* gracious

Hülle ['hylə] *f* (-;-n) cover; case; wrapper; envelope; (*e-s Buches*) jacket; (fig) cloak; **in H. und Fülle** in abundance; **sterbliche H.** mortal remains

hüllen ['hylən] *tr* cover; veil; wrap

Hülse ['hylzə] *f* (-;-n) pod, hull; cartridge case, shell case

Hül'senfrucht *f* legume

human [hu'man] *adj* humane

humanistisch [huma'nɪstɪʃ] *adj* humanistic; classical

humanitär [humani'ter] *adj* humanitarian

Humanität [humani'tet] *f* (-;) humanity; humaneness

Humanitäts'duselei *f* sentimental humanitarianism

Humanitäts'verbrechen *n* crime against humanity

Hummel ['huməl] *f* (-;-n) bumblebee

Hummer ['humər] *m* (-s;-) lobster

Humor [hu'mor] *m* (-s;) humor

humoristisch [humo'rɪstɪʃ] *adj* humorous

humpeln ['humpəln] *intr* (SEIN) hobble

Hund [hunt] *m* (-[e]s;-e) dog

Hündchen ['hyntçən] *n* (-s;-) small dog; puppy

Hun'deangst *f*—**e-e H. haben** (coll) be scared stiff

Hun'dearbeit *f* drudgery

Hun'dehütte *f* doghouse

Hun'dekälte *f* severe cold

Hun′demarke *f* dog tag

hun′demü′de *adj* (coll) dog-tired

hundert [ˈhʊndərt] *invar adj & pron* hundred || **Hundert** *n* (-s;-e) hundred; **drei von H.** three percent; **im H.** by the hundred || *f* (-;-en) hundred

hun′dertfach *adj* hundredfold

Hundertjahr′feier *f* centennial

Hun′dertsatz *m* percentage

hundertste [ˈhʊndərtstə] §9 *adj & pron* hundredth

Hun′deschau *f* dog show

Hun′dezwinger *m* dog kennel

Hündin [ˈhʏndɪn] *f* (-;-nen) bitch

hündisch [ˈhʏndɪʃ] *adj* (*Benehmen*) servile; (*Angst*) deadly

hunds′gemein *adj* beastly

hunds′miserabel *adj* (sl) lousy

Hunds′stern *m* Dog Star

Hunds′tage *pl* dog days

Hüne [ˈhynə] *m* (-n;-n) giant

hü′nenhaft *adj* gigantic

Hunger [ˈhʊŋər] *m* (-s;) hunger; **H. haben** be hungry

Hun′gerkur *f* starvation diet

Hun′gerlohn *m* starvation wages

hungern [ˈhʊŋərn] *intr* be hungry; go without food; **h. nach** yearn for || *impers*—**es hungert mich** I am hungry

Hun′gersnot *f* famine

Hun′gertod *m* death from starvation

Hun′gertuch *n*—**am H. nagen** go hungry; live in poverty

hungrig [ˈhʊŋrɪç] *adj* hungry; (*Jahre*) lean

Hunne [ˈhʊnə] *m* (-n;-n) (hist) Hun

Hupe [ˈhupə] *f* (-;-n) (aut) horn

hupen [ˈhupən] *intr* blow the horn

hüpfen [ˈhʏpfən], **hupfen** [ˈhupfən] *intr* (SEIN) hop, jump

Hürde [ˈhʏrdə] *f* (-;-n) hurdle

Hure [ˈhurə] *f* (-;-n) whore

huren [ˈhurən] *intr* whore around

hurtig [ˈhʊrtɪç] *adj* nimble, swift

huschen [ˈhʊʃən] *intr* (SEIN) scurry

hüsteln [ˈhystəln] *intr* clear the throat

husten [ˈhustən] *tr* cough up || *intr* cough; **h. auf** (*acc*) (coll) not give a rap about

Hut [hut] *m* (-[e]s;-̈e) hat || *f* (-;) protection, care; **auf der Hut sein** be on guard

hüten [ˈhytən] *tr* guard, protect; tend; **das Bett h.** be confined to bed; **das Haus h.** stay indoors; **Kinder h.** baby-sit || *ref* (**vor** *dat*) be on guard (against), beware (of); **ich werde mich schön h.** (coll) I'll do no such thing

Hü′ter –in §6 *mf* guardian

Hut′krempe *f* brim of a hat

hut′los *adj* hatless

Hütte [ˈhytə] *f* (-;-n) hut; cabin; doghouse; glassworks; (Bib) tabernacle; (metal) foundry

Hüt′tenkunde *f*, **Hüt′tenwesen** *n* metallurgy

Hyäne [hyˈɛnə] *f* (-;-n) hyena

Hyazinthe [hyaˈtsɪntə] *f* (-;-n) hyacinth

Hydrant [hyˈdrant] *m* (-en;-en) hydrant

Hydraulik [hyˈdraʊlɪk] *f* (-;) hydraulics; hydraulic system

hydraulisch [hyˈdraʊlɪʃ] *adj* hydraulic

hydrieren [hyˈdrirən] *tr* hydrogenate

Hygiene [hyˈgjɛnə] *f* (-;) hygiene

hygienisch [hyˈgjenɪʃ] *adj* hygienic

Hymne [ˈhʏmnə] *f* (-;-n) hymn; anthem

Hyperbel [hyˈperbəl] *f* (-;-n) (geom) hyperbola; (rhet) hyperbole

Hypnose [hypˈnozə] *f* (-;-n) hypnosis

hypnotisch [hypˈnotɪʃ] *adj* hypnotic

Hypothese [hfipoˈtezə] *f* (-;-n) hypothesis

Hypochonder [hypoˈxondər] *m* (-s;-) hypochondriac

Hypothek [hypoˈtek] *f* (-;-en) mortgage

Hypothe′kengläubiger *m* mortgagee

Hypothe′kenschuldner *m* mortgagor

Hypothese [hypoˈtezə] *f* (-;-n) hypothesis

hypothetisch [hypoˈtetɪʃ] *adj* hypothetical

Hysterektomie [hysterektoˈmi] *f* (-;) hysterectomy

Hysterie [hysteˈri] *f* (-;) hysteria

hysterisch [hysˈterɪʃ] *adj* hysterical

I

I, i [i] *invar n* I, i

iah [ˈi˙ˈɑ] *interj* heehaw!

iahen [ˈi˙ɑ-ən] *intr* heehaw, bray

iberisch [iˈberɪʃ] *adj* Iberian

ich [ɪç] §11 *pers pron* I

ichbezogen [ˈɪçbətsogən] *adj* self-centered, egocentric

Ich′sucht *f* egotism

ideal [ideˈal] *adj* ideal || **Ideal** *n* (-s;-e) deal

idealisieren [ideˌalɪˈzirən] *tr* idealize

Idealismus [ideˌaˈlɪsmus] *m* (-;) idealism

Idealist –in [ideˌaˈlɪst(ɪn)] §7 *mf* idealist

idealistisch [ideˌaˈlɪstɪʃ] *adj* idealistic

I·dee [ɪˈde] *f* (-;-deen) [deˈən]) idea

Iden [ˈidən] *pl* **Ides**

identifizieren [ɪdɛntɪfɪˈtsirən] *tr* identify || *ref*—**i. mit** identify with

identisch [ɪˈdɛntɪʃ] *adj* identical

Identität [ɪdɛntiˈtet] *f* (-;-en) identity

Ideolo·gie [ideˌolˈgi] *f* (-;-gien [ˈgiˌən]) ideology

Idiom [ɪˈdjom] *n* (-s;-e) idiom, dialect, language

idiomatisch [ɪdjoˈmatɪʃ] *adj* idiomatic

Idiosynkra·sie [ɪdjoˌzynkraˈzi] *f* (-;-sien [ˈzi˙ən]) idiosyncrasy

Idiot [ɪˈdjot] *m* (-en;-en) idiot

Idio·tie [ɪdjə'ti] *f* (-;-tien ['ti·ən]) idiocy

Idiotin [ɪdjotɪn] *f* (-;-nen) idiot

Idol [ɪ'dol] *n* (-s;-e) idol

idyllisch [ɪ'dylɪʃ] *adj* idyllic

Igel ['igəl] *m* (-s;-) hedgehog

Ignorant [ɪgnə'rant] *m* (-en;-en) ignoramus

ignorieren [ɪgnə'rirən] *tr* ignore

ihm [im] §11 *pers pron* (dative of **er** and **es**) (to) him; (to) it

ihn [in] §11 *pers pron* (accusative of **er**) him

ihnen ['inən] §11 *pers pron* (dative of **sie**) (to) them ‖ **Ihnen** §11 *pers pron* (dative of **Sie**) (to) you

ihr [ir] §2,2 *poss adj* her; their ‖ §11 *pers pron* (dative of **sie**) (to) her ‖ **Ihr** §2,2 *poss adj* your

ihrerseits ['irərzaits] *adv* on her (or their) part; **Ihrerseits** on your part

ihresgleichen ['irəs'glaiçən] *pron* the likes of her (or them); her (or their) equal(s); **Ihresgleichen** the likes of you; your equal(s)

ihrethalben ['irət'halbən] *adv* var of **ihretwegen**

ihretwegen ['irət'vegən] *adv* because of her (or them); for her (or their) sake; **Ihretwegen** because of you, for your sake

ihretwillen ['irət'vɪlən] *adv* var of **ihretwegen**

ihrige ['irɪgə] §2,5 *poss pron* hers; theirs; **Ihrige** yours

Ikone [ɪ'konə] *f* (-;-n) icon

illegal [ɪle'gal] *adj* illegal

illegitim [ɪlegɪ'tim] *adj* illegitimate

illuminieren [ɪlumɪ'nirən] *tr* illuminate

Illusion [ɪlu'zjon] *f* (-;-en) illusion

illustrieren [ɪlus'trirən] *tr* illustrate

Illustrierte [ɪlus'trirtə] §5 *f* (illustrated) magazine

Iltis ['ɪltɪs] *m* (-ses;-se) polecat

im [ɪm] *contr* in dem

Image ['ɪmɪdʒ] *n* (-s;-s) (fig) image

imaginär [ɪmagɪ'ner] *adj* imaginary

Im·biß ['ɪmbɪs] *m* (-bisses;-bisse) snack

Im'bißhalle *f* luncheonette

Im'bißstube *f* snack bar

Imi·tator [ɪmi'tator] *m* (-s;-tatoren [ta'torən]) imitator; impersonator

Imker ['ɪmkar] *m* (-s;-) beekeeper

immateriell [ɪmate'rjel] *adj* immaterial, spiritual

immatrikulieren [ɪmatrɪku'lirən] *tr* & *intr* register; **sich i. lassen** get registered

immens [ɪ'mens] *adj* immense

immer ['ɪmər] *adv* always; **auf i. und ewig** for ever and ever; **für i.** for good; **i. langsam!** steady now!; **i. mehr** more and more; **i. wieder** again and again; **noch i.** still; **nur i. zu!** keep trying!; **was auch i.** whatever

immerdar' *adv* (Lit) forever

immerfort' *adv* all the time

im'mergrün *adj* evergreen ‖ **Immergrün** *n* (-s;-e) evergreen

immerhin' *adv* after all, anyhow

immerwäh'rend *adj* perpetual

immerzu' *adv* all the time, constantly

Immobilien [ɪmə'biljən] *pl* real estate

Immobi'lienmakler **-in** §6 *mf* real-estate broker

immun [ɪ'mun] *adj* (gegen) immune (to)

immunisieren [ɪmunɪ'zirən] *tr* immunize

Imperativ [ɪmpera'tif] *m* (-s;-e) (gram) imperative

Imperfek·tum [ɪmper'fektum] *n* (-s; -ta [ta]) (gram) imperfect

Imperialismus [ɪmperɪ·a·'lɪsmus] *m* (-;) imperialism

impfen ['ɪmpfen] *tr* vaccinate; inoculate

Impfling ['ɪmpflɪŋ] *m* (-s;-e) person to be vaccinated or inoculated

Impf'schein *m* vaccination certificate

Impf'stoff *m* vaccine

Imp'fung *f* (-;-en) vaccination; inoculation

imponieren [ɪmpo'nirən] *intr* (dat) impress

Import [ɪm'port] *m* (-[e]s;-e) import

importieren [ɪmpor'tirən] *tr* import

imposant [ɪmpo'zant] *adj* imposing

imprägnieren [ɪmpreg'nirən] *tr* waterproof; creosote

Impresario [ɪmpre'zarjo] *m* (-s;-s) agent, business manager

Impres·sum [ɪm'presum] *n* (-s;-sen [sən]) (journ) masthead

imstande [ɪm·'tandə] *adv*—**i. sein zu** (inf) be in a position to (inf)

in [ɪn] *prep* (position) (dat) in, at; (direction) (acc) in, into

Inangriffnahme [ɪn'angrɪfnamə] *f* (-;) starting; putting into action

Inanspruchnahme [ɪn'an/pruxnamə] *f* (-;) laying claim; demands; utilization

In'begriff *m* essence; embodiment

in'begriffen *adj* included

Inbrunst ['ɪnbrunst] *f* (-;) ardor

inbrünstig ['ɪnbrynstɪç] *adj* ardent

indem [ɪn'dem] *conj* while, as; by (ger)

Inder **-in** ['ɪndər(ɪn)] §6 *mf* Indian (inhabitant of India)

indes [ɪn'des], **indessen** [ɪn'desən] *adv* meanwhile; however ‖ *conj* while; whereas

Indianer **-in** [ɪn'djanər(ɪn)] §6 *mf* Indian (of North America)

Indien ['ɪndjən] *n* (-s;) India

Indio ['ɪndi·o] *m* (-s;-s) Indian (of Central or South America)

indisch ['ɪndɪʃ] *adj* Indian

indiskret [ɪndɪs'kret] *adj* indiscreet

indiskutabel [ɪndɪsku'tabəl] *adj* out of the question

individuell [ɪndɪvɪdu'el] *adj* individual

Individu·um [ɪndɪ'vidu·um] *n* (-s;-en [ən]) individual; (pej) character

Indizienbeweis [ɪn'ditsjənbəvais] *m* (piece of) circumstantial evidence

Indossament [ɪndəsa'ment] *n* (-[e]s; -e) indorsement

Indossant [ɪndə'sant] *m* (-en;-en) indorser

indossieren [ɪndə'sirən] *tr* indorse

industrialisieren [ɪndustri·alɪ'zirən] *tr* industrialize

Indus·trie [ɪndus'triː] f (-;-trien ['triːən]) industry
Industrie'anlage f industrial plant
Industrie'betrieb m industrial establishment
Industrie'kapitän m tycoon
industriell [ɪndustri'ɛl] adj industrial || **Industrielle** §5 m industrialist
ineinan'der adv into one another; i. **übergehen** merge
ineinan'derfügen tr dovetail
ineinan'dergreifen §88 intr mesh
ineinan'derpassen intr dovetail
infam [ɪn'fam] adj (coll) frightfully
Infante·rie [ɪnfantə'riː] f (-;-rien ['riːən]) infantry
Infanterist [ɪnfantə'rɪst] m (-en;-en) infantryman
infantil [ɪnfan'tiːl] adj infantile
Infektion [ɪnfɛk'tsjoːn] f (-;-en) infection
Infini·tiv [ɪnfɪnɪ'tiːf] m (-s;-tive ['tiːvə]) infinitive
infizieren [ɪnfɪ'tsiːrən] tr infect
infolge [ɪn'fɔlgə] prep (genit) in consequence of, owing to; according to
infolgedes'sen adv consequently
Information [ɪnfɔrma'tsjoːn] f (-;-en) (piece of) information
informieren [ɪnfɔr'miːrən] tr inform
infrarot [ɪnfra'roːt] adj infrared || **Infrarot** n (-s;-) infrared
Ingenieur [ɪnʒen'jøːr] m (-s;-e) engineer
Ingenieur'bau m (-[e]s;) civil engineering
Ingenieur'wesen n engineering
ingeniös [ɪngen'jøːs] adj ingenious
Ingrimm ['ɪngrɪm] m inner rage
Ingwer ['ɪŋvər] m (-s;) ginger
Ing'werplätzchen n gingersnap
Inhaber –in ['ɪnhaːbər(ɪn)] §6 mf owner; bearer; occupant; holder
inhaftieren [ɪnhaf'tiːrən] tr arrest
Inhalierapparat [ɪnha'liːrapaˑrat] m (med) inhalator
inhalieren [ɪnha'liːrən] tr & intr inhale
Inhalt ['ɪnhalt] m (-[e]s;-e) contents; subject matter; (geom) area; volume
In'haltsangabe f summary; list of contents
in'haltsarm, **in'haltsleer** adj empty
in'haltsreich adj substantive; (Leben) full
in'haltsschwer adj pregnant with meaning; momentous
In'haltsverzeichnis n table of contents
in'haltsvoll adj full of meaning
inhibieren [ɪnhi'biːrən] tr inhibit
Initiative [ɪnɪtsja'tiːvə] f (-;-en) initiative
Injektion [ɪnjɛk'tsjoːn] f (-;-en) injection
Injektions'nadel f hypodermic needle
injizieren [ɪnjɪ'tsiːrən] tr inject
Inkasso [ɪn'kaso] n (-s;-s) bill collecting
Inkas'sobeamte m bill collector
inklusive [ɪnkluˈziːvə] adj inclusive || prep (genit) including
inkonsequent ['ɪnkɔnzekvɛnt] adj inconsistent; illogical
Inkraft'treten n going into effect

In'land n (-[e]s;) home country; interior
Inländer –in ['ɪnlɛndər(ɪn)] §6 mf native
inländisch ['ɪnlɛndɪʃ] adj home, domestic; inland
In'landspost f domestic mail
Inlett ['ɪnlɛt] n (-[e]s;-e) bedtick
in'liegend adj enclosed
inmit'ten prep (genit) in the middle of, among
innehaben ['ɪnəhaːbən] §89 tr (Amt) hold; (Wohnung) occupy, own
innehalten ['ɪnəhaltən] §90 intr stop
innen ['ɪnən] adv inside; indoors; nach i. inwards; tief i. deep down
Innen– comb.fm. inner, internal; inside, interior; home, domestic
In'nenarchitekt –in §7 mf interior decorator
In'nenaufnahme f (phot) indoor shot
In'nenhof m quadrangle
In'nenleben n inner life
In'nenminister m Secretary of the Interior; Secretary of State for Home Affairs (Brit)
In'nenpolitik f domestic policy
In'nenraum m interior (of building)
In'nenstadt f center of town, inner city
inner– [ɪnər] comb.fm. internal; intra–
innere ['ɪnərə] §9 adj inner, internal; inside; inward; domestic || **Innere** §5 n inside, interior
in'nerhalb adv on the inside; i. **von** within || prep (genit) inside, within
in'nerlich adj inner, inward || adv inwardly; mentally, emotionally
In'nerlichkeit f (-;-en) introspection; inner quality
innerste ['ɪnərstə] §9 adj innermost
innesein ['ɪnəzaɪn] §139 intr (SEIN) (genit) be aware of
innewerden ['ɪnəveːrdən] §159 intr (SEIN) (genit) become aware of
innig ['ɪnɪç] adj close; deep, heartfelt || adv deeply
In'nigkeit f (-;) intimacy; deep feeling; tender affection
Innung ['ɪnʊŋ] f (-;-en) guild
inoffiziell ['ɪnɔfitsjel] adj unofficial
ins contr in das
Insasse ['ɪnzasə] m (-n;-n), **Insassin** ['ɪnsasɪn] f (-;-nen) occupant; (e-s Gefängnisses) inmate; (e-s Autos) passenger
insbesondere [ɪnsbə'zɔndərə] adv in particular, especially
In'schrift f inscription
Insekt [ɪn'zɛkt] n (-[e]s;-en) insect
Insek'tenbekämpfungsmittel n insecticide
Insek'tenkunde f entomology
Insek'tenstich m insect bite
Insektizid [ɪnzɛkti'tsiːt] n (-[e]s;-e) insecticide
Insel ['ɪnzəl] f (-;-n) island
Inserat [ɪnzə'raːt] n (-es;-e) classified advertisement, ad
inserieren [ɪnzə'riːrən] tr insert || intr (in dat) advertise (in)
insgeheim [ɪnsgə'haɪm] adv secretly
insgemein [ɪnsgə'maɪn] adv as a whole; in general, generally

insgesamt [ɪnsgə'zamt] *adv* in a body, as a unit; in all, altogether

inso'fern *adv* to this extent || **insofern'** *conj* in so far as

insoweit' *adv & conj* var of **insofern**

Inspek·tor [ɪn'spɛktər] *m* (-s;-toren ['torən]) inspector

inspirieren [ɪnspi'rirən] *tr* inspire

inspizieren [ɪnspi'tsirən] *tr* inspect

Installation [ɪnstala'tsjon] *f* (-;-en) installation

installieren [ɪnsta'lirən] *tr* install

instand [ɪn'ʃtant] *adv*—**i. halten** keep in good condition; **i. setzen** repair

Instand'haltung *f* upkeep, maintenance

instandig [ɪn'ʃtɛndɪç] *adj* insistent

Instand'setzung *f* repair, renovation

Instanz [ɪn'ʃtants] *f* (-;-en) (adm) authority; **e-e höhere I. anrufen** appeal to a higher court; **Gericht der ersten I.** court of primary jurisdiction; **Gericht der zweiten I.** court of appeal; **höchste I.** court of final appeal

Institut [ɪnstɪ'tut] *n* (-[e]s;-e) institute

instruieren [ɪnstru'irən] *tr* instruct

Instruktion [ɪnstrʊk'tsjon] *f* (-;-en) instruction

Instrument [ɪnstru'mɛnt] *n* (-[e]s;-e) instrument

Instrumentalist –in [ɪnstrumenta'lɪst (ɪn)] §7 *mf* instrumentalist

Insulaner –in [ɪnzu'lanər(ɪn)] §6 *mf* islander

insular [ɪnzʊ'lar] *adj* insular

Insulin [ɪnzʊ'lin] *n* (-s;) insulin

inszenieren [ɪnstse'nirən] *tr* stage

Intellekt [ɪnte'lɛkt] *m* (-[e]s;) intellect

intellektuell [ɪntelektu'el] *adj* intellectual || **Intellektuelle** §5 *mf* intellectual

intelligent [ɪntelɪ'gɛnt] *adj* intelligent

Intelligenzler [ɪntelɪ'gɛntslər] *m* (-s;-) (pej) egghead

Intendant [ɪnten'dant] *m* (-en;-en) (theat) director

intensiv [ɪnten'zif] *adj* intense; intensive

-intensiv *comb.fm.*, e.g., **lohnintensive Güter** goods of which wages constitute a high proportion of the cost

interessant [ɪntere'sant] *adj* interesting

Interesse [ɪntere'resə] *n* (-s;-n) (an *dat*, für) interest (in)

interes'selos *adj* uninterested

Interes'sengemeinschaft *f* community of interest; (com) syndicate

Interessent –in [ɪntere'sɛnt(ɪn)] §7 *mf* interested party

interessieren [ɪntere'sirən] *tr* (für) interest (in) || *ref*—**sich i. für** be interested in

interimistisch [ɪnterɪ'mɪstɪʃ] *adj* provisional

intern [ɪn'tern] *adj* internal

Internat [ɪnter'nat] *n* (-[e]s;-e) boarding school

international [ɪnternatsjo'nal] *adj* international

Internat(s)'schüler –in §6 *mf*, **Interne** [ɪn'ternə] §5 *mf* boarding student

internieren [ɪnter'nirən] *tr* intern

Internist –in [ɪnter'nɪst(ɪn)] §7 *mf* (med) internist

Interpret [ɪnter'pret] *m* (-en;-en) interpreter; exponent

interpunktieren [ɪnterpuŋk'tirən] *tr* punctuate

Interpunktion [ɪnterpuŋk'tsjon] *f* (-; -en) punctuation

Interpunktions'zeichen *n* punctuation mark

Intervall [ɪnter'val] *n* (-s;-e) interval

intervenieren [ɪnterve'nirən] *intr* intervene

Interview ['ɪntervju] *n* (-s;-s) interview

interviewen [ɪnter'vju-ən] *tr* interview

intim [ɪn'tim] *adj* intimate

Intimität [ɪntimi'tet] *f* (-;-en) intimacy

intolerant [ɪntole'rant] *adj* intolerant

intonieren [ɪnto'nirən] *tr* intone

intransitiv ['ɪntransitif] *adj* intransitive

intravenös [ɪntrave'nøs] *adj* intravenous

intrigant [ɪntri'gant] *adj* intriguing, scheming || **Intragant** –in §7 *mf* intriguer, schemer

Intrige [ɪn'trigə] *f* (-;-n) intrigue

introspektiv [ɪntrɔspek'tif] *adj* introspective

Introvertierte [ɪntrɔver'tirtə] §5 *mf* introvert

invalide [ɪnva'lidə] *adj* disabled || **Invalide** §5 *mf* invalid

Invalidität [ɪnvalidi'tet] *f* (-;) disability

Invasion [ɪnva'zjon] *f* (-;-en) invasion

Inventar [ɪnven'tar] *n* (-s;-e) inventory

Inventur [ɪnven'tur] *f* (-;-en) stock taking; **I. machen** take stock

inwärts ['ɪnverts] *adv* inwards

inwendig ['ɪnvendɪç] *adj* inward, inner

inwiefern' *adv* how far; in what way

inwieweit' *adv* var of **inwiefern**

In'zucht *f* inbreeding

inzwi'schen *adv* meanwhile

Ion [ɪ'ɔn] *n* (-s;-en) (phys) ion

ionisieren [ɪ-ɔni'zirən] *tr* ionize

Irak [ɪ'rak] *m* (-s;) Iraq

Iraker –in [ɪ'rakər(ɪn)] §6 *mf* Iraqi

irakisch [ɪ'rakɪʃ] *adj* Iraqi

Iran [ɪ'ran] *m* (-s;) Iran

Iraner –in [ɪ'ranər(ɪn)] §6 *mf* Iranian

iranisch [ɪ'ranɪʃ] *adj* Iranian

irden ['ɪrdən] *adj* earthen

irdisch ['ɪrdɪʃ] *adj* earthly, worldly || **Irdische** §5 *n* earthly nature

Ire ['irə] *m* (-n;-n) Irishman; **die Iren** the Irish

irgend ['ɪrgənt] *adv*—**i. etwas** something, anything; **i. jemand** someone, anyone; **nur i.** possibly

ir'gendein *adj* some, any || **ingendeiner** *indef pron* someone, anyone

ir'gendeinmal *adv* at some time or other

ir'gendwann *adv* at some time or other

ir'gendwelcher *adj* any; any kind of

ir'gendwer *indef pron* someone

ir'gendwie *adv* somehow or other

ir'gendwo *adv* somewhere or other; anywhere

ir'gendwoher *adv* from somewhere or other

ir'gendwohin *adv* somewhere or other

Irin ['ɪrɪn] *f* (-;-nen) Irish woman

Iris ['iːrɪs] *f* (-;-) (anat, bot) iris

irisch ['iːrɪʃ] *adj* Irish

Irland ['ɪrlant] *n* (-s) Ireland

Iro·nie [iro'niː] *f* (-;-nien ['niːən]) irony

ironisch [ɪ'roːnɪʃ] *adj* ironic(al)

irre ['ɪrə] *adj* stray; confused; mad; **i. werden** go astray; get confused; **i. werden an** (*dat*) lose faith in ‖ **Irre** §5 *mf* lunatic ‖ *f* maze; wrong track; **in die I. führen** put on the wrong track; **in die I. gehen** go astray

ir'refahren §71 *intr* (SEIN) lose one's way, go wrong

ir'reführen *tr* mislead

ir'regehen §82 *intr* (SEIN) lose one's way; (fig) go wrong

ir'remachen *tr* confuse; **j-n i. an** (*dat*) make s.o. lose faith in

irren ['ɪrən] *intr* go astray; err ‖ *ref* (**in** *dat*) be mistaken (about); **sich in der Straße i.** take the wrong road; **sich in der Zeit i.** misjudge the time

Ir'renanstalt *f,* **Ir'renhaus** *n* insane asylum

Ir'renhäusler ['ɪrənhɔɪzlər] *m* (-s;-) inmate of an insane asylum

ir'rereden *intr* rave; talk deliriously

Irrfahrt ['ɪrfart] *f* odyssey

Irrgang ['ɪrgaŋ] *m* winding path

Irrgarten ['ɪrgartən] *m* labyrinth

Irrglaube ['ɪrglaubə] *m* heresy

irrgläubig ['ɪrglɔɪbɪç] *adj* heretical

irrig ['ɪrɪç] *adj* mistaken

Irri·gator [ɪrɪ'gaːtor] *m* (-s;-gatoren [ga·toːrən]) douche

irritieren [ɪrɪ'tiːrən] *tr* irritate; (coll) confuse

Irrlehre ['ɪrleːrə] *f* false doctrine

Irrlicht ['ɪrlɪçt] *n* jack-o'-lantern

Irrsinn ['ɪrzɪn] *m* insanity

irr'sinnig *adj* insane

Irrtum ['ɪrtum] *n* (-s;-̈er) error

irrtümlich ['ɪrtymlɪç] *adj* erroneous

Irrweg ['ɪrveːk] *m* wrong track

Irrwisch ['ɪrvɪʃ] *m* (-es;-e) jack-o'-lantern; (coll) fireball

Islam [ɪs'laːm] *m* (-s;) Islam

Island ['iːslant] *n* (-s;) Iceland

Iso·lator [izo'laːtor] *m* (-s;-latoren [la'toːrən]) (elec) insulator

Isolier— [izo'liːr] *comb.fm.* isolation; insulating; insulated

Isolier'band *n* (-[e]s;-̈er) friction tape

isolieren [izo'liːrən] *tr* (*Kranke*) isolate; (*abdichten*) insulate

Isolier'haft *f* solitary confinement

Isolier'station *f* isolation ward

Isolie'rung *f* (-;-en) isolation; (elec) insulation

Isotop [izo'toːp] *n* (-[e]s;-e) isotope

Israel ['ɪsraːel] *n* (- & -s;) Israel

Israeli [ɪsraːˈeli] *m* (-s;-s) Israeli

israelisch [ɪsraːˈeliʃ] *adj* Israeli

Israelit –in [ɪsraːeˈliːt(ɪn)] §7 *mf* Israelite

israelitisch [ɪsraːeˈliːtiʃ] *adj* Israelite

Ist— [ɪst] *comb.fm.* actual

Ist'Bestand *m* actual stock; (fin) actual balance; (mil) actual stockpile

Ist-'Stand *m,* **Ist-'Stärke** *f* (mil) effective strength

Italien [ɪ'taljən] *n* (-s;) Italy

Italiener –in [ɪtal'jeːnər(ɪn)] §6 *mf* Italian

italienisch [ɪtal'jeːnɪʃ] *adj* Italian

J

J, j [jɔt] *invar n* J, j

ja [jaː] *adv* yes; indeed, certainly; of course ‖ **Ja** *n* (-s;-s) yes

Jacht [jaxt] *f* (-;-en) yacht

Jacke ['jakə] *f* (-;-n) jacket, coat

Jackenkleid ['jak(ə)ˈklaɪt] *n* lady's two-piece suit

Jackett [ʒaˈkɛt] *n* (-s;-s) jacket

Jagd [jaːkt] *f* (-;-en) hunt(ing); **auf die J. gehen** go hunting; **J. machen auf** (*acc*) hunt for

Jagd'abschirmung *f* (aer) fighter screen

Jagd'aufseher *m* gamewarden

jagdbar ['jaːktbar] *adj* in season, fair (*game*)

Jagd'bomber *m* (aer) fighter-bomber

Jagd'flieger *m* fighter pilot

Jagd'flugzeug *n* (aer) fighter plane

Jagd'gehege *n* game preserve

Jagd'geleit *n* (aer) fighter escort

Jagd'hund *m* hunting dog, hound

Jagd'rennen *n* steeplechase

Jagd'revier *n* hunting ground

Jagd'schein *m* hunting license

Jagd'schutz *m* (aer) fighter protection

Jagd'verband *m* (aer) fighter unit

Jagd'wild *n* game; game bird

jagen ['jaːgən] *tr* hunt; pursue; chase; (fig) follow close on; **in die Luft j.** blow up ‖ *intr* go hunting; **j. nach** pursue ‖ *intr* (SEIN) rush

Jäger ['jeːgər] *m* (-s;-) hunter; (aer) fighter plane; (mil) rifleman

Jägerei [jeːgəˈraɪ] *f* (-;) hunting

Jä'gerlatein *n* (coll) fish story

Jaguar ['jaːguːar] *m* (-s;-s) jaguar

jäh [je] *adj* sudden; steep ‖ **Jähe** *f* (-;) suddenness; steepness

jählings ['jeːlɪŋs] *adv* suddenly; steeply

Jahr [jaːr] *n* (-[e]s;-e) year

jahraus' *adv—***j. jahrein** year in year out, year after year

Jahr'buch *n* almanac; yearbook; annual

jahrelang ['jaːrəlaŋ] *adj* long-standing ‖ *adv* for years

jähren ['jeːrən] *ref* be a year ago

Jahres— [jaːrəs] *comb.fm.* annual, yearly, of the year

Jah'resfeier f anniversary
Jah'resfrist f period of a year
Jah'resrente f annuity
Jah'restag m anniversary
Jah'reszahl f date, year
Jah'reszeit f season
jah'reszeitlich adj seasonal
Jahr'gang m age group; class, year; crop; vintage; **er gehört zu meinem J.** he was born in the same year as I
Jahrhun'dert n century
–jährig [jɛrɪç] comb.fm. –year-old
jährlich ['jɛrlɪç] adj yearly, annual
Jahr'markt m fair
Jahr'marktplatz m fairground
Jahrtau'send n millennium
Jahrzehnt [jɑr'tsent] n (–[e]s;–e) decade
Jäh'zorn m fit of anger; hot temper
jäh'zornig adj quick-tempered
Jalou·sie [ʒalu'zi] f (–;–sien ['zi·ən]) louvre; Venetian blind
Jammer ['jamər] m (–s;) misery; wailing; **es ist ein J.,** daß it's a pity that
Jam'merlappen m (pej) jellyfish
jämmerlich ['jɛmərlɪç] adj miserable; pitiful; (Anblick) sorry
jammern ['jamərn] tr move to pity ‖ intr (über acc, um) moan (about); **j. nach** (or um) whimper for
Jam'merschade adj deplorable
Jänner ['jɛnər] m (–s & –;–) (Aust) January
Januar ['janu·ɑr] m (–s & –;–e) January
Japan ['japan] n (–s;) Japan
Japaner –in [ja'pɑnər(ɪn)] §6 mf Japanese
japanisch [ja'pɑnɪʃ] adj Japanese
jappen ['japən] intr pant, gasp
Jasager ['jɑzagər] m (–s;–) yes-man
jäten ['jɛtən] tr weed; **das Unkraut j.** pull out weeds ‖ intr weed
Jauche ['jauxə] f (–;–n) liquid manure; (sl) slop
jauchen ['jauxən] tr manure
Jau'chegrube f cesspool
jauchzen ['jauxtsən] intr rejoice; **vor Freude j.** shout for joy ‖ **Jauchzen** n (–s;) jubilation
Jauch'zer m (–s;–) shout of joy
jawohl [ja'vol] interj yes, indeed!
Ja'wort n (–[e]s;) consent
Jazz [dʒɛz], [jats] m (–;) jazz
je [je] adv ever; **denn je** than ever; **je länger, je** (or **desto**) **besser je** longer the better; **je nach** according to, depending on; **je nachdem, ob** according to whether; **je Pfund** per pound; **je zwei** two each; two by two, in twos; **je** always
Jeans [dʒinz] pl jeans
jedenfalls ['jedənfals] adv at any rate; **ich j.** I for one
jeder ['jedər] §3 indef adj each, every ‖ indef pron each one, everyone
jederlei ['jedər'lai] invar adj every kind of
je'dermann indef pron everyone, everybody
je'derzeit adv at all times, at any time
je'desmal adv each time, every time
jedoch [je'dɔx] adv however

jeglicher ['jeklɪçər] §3 indef adj each, every ‖ indef pron each one, everyone
je'her adv—**von j.** since time immemorial
Jelän·gerjelie·ber m & n honeysuckle
jemals ['jemals] adv ever
jemand ['jemant] indef pron someone, somebody; anyone, anybody
jener ['jenər] §3 dem adj that ‖ dem pron that one
jenseitig ['jenzaitɪç] adj opposite, beyond, otherworldly
jenseits ['jenzaits] prep (genit) on the other side of; beyond ‖ **Jenseits** n (–;) beyond
jetzig ['jetsɪç] adj present, current
jetzt [jetst] adv now
jeweilig ['jevailɪç] adj at that time
jeweils ['jevails] adv at that time
jiddisch ['jɪdɪʃ] adj Yiddish
Joch [jɔx] n (–[e]s;–e) yoke; yoke of oxen; (e–r Brücke) span; (e–s Berges) saddleback
Joch'bein n cheekbone
Joch'brücke f pile bridge
Jockei ['dʒɔki] m (–s;–s) jockey
Jod [jot] n (–s;) iodine
jodeln ['jodəln] intr yodel
Jodler –in ['jodlər(ɪn)] §6 mf yodeler ‖ m yodel
Jodtinktur ['jottrŋktur] f (–;) (pharm) iodine
Johannisbeere [jo'hanɪsberə] f currant
johlen ['jolən] intr yell, boo
jonglieren [ʒɔŋ'(g)lirən] tr & intr juggle
Journalist –in [ʒurna'lɪst(ɪn)] §7 mf journalist
jovial [jo'vjal] adj jovial
Jubel ['jubəl] m (–s;) jubilation
Ju'belfeier f, **Ju'belfest** n jubilee
Ju'beljahr n jubilee year
jubeln ['jubəln] intr rejoice; shout for joy
Jubilä·um [jubɪ'le·um] n (–s;–en [ən]) jubilee
juche [jux'he] interj hurray!
juchei [jux'hai] interj hurray!
juchzen ['juxtsən] intr shout for joy
jucken ['jukən] tr itch; scratch ‖ ref scratch ‖ intr itch ‖ impers—**es juckt mich** I feel itchy; **es juckt mir** (or **mich**) **in den Fingern zu** (inf) I am itching to (inf); **es juckt sie in den Beinen** she is itching to dance
Jude ['judə] m (–n;–n) Jew
Ju'denschaft f (–;) Jewry
Ju'denstern m star of David
Judentum ['judəntum] n (–s;) Judaism; **das J.** the Jews
Jüdin ['jydɪn] f (–;–nen) Jewish woman
jüdisch ['jydɪʃ] adj Jewish
Jugend ['jugənt] f (–s;) youth
Ju'gendalter n youth; adolescence
Ju'gendgericht n juvenile court
Ju'gendherberge f youth hostel
Ju'gendkriminalität f juvenile delinquency
jugendlich ['jugəntlɪç] adj youthful ‖ **Jugendliche** §5 mf youth, teenager
Ju'gendliebe f puppy love
Ju'gendstrich m youthful prank

Jugoslawien [jugɔ'slavjən] n (-s;) Yugoslavia

jugoslawisch [jugɔ'slavɪʃ] adj Yugoslav

Juli ['juli] m (-[s];-s) July

jung [juŋ] adj (jünger ['jyŋər]; jüngste ['jyŋstə] §9) young; (Erbsen) green; (Wein) new ‖ Junge §5 m boy ‖ n newly born; young

jungen ['juŋən] intr produce young

jun'genhaft adj boyish

Jünger ['jyŋər] m (-s;-) disciple

Jungfer ['juŋfər] f (-;-n) maiden; virgin

jüngeferlich ['jyŋfərlɪç] adj maidenly

Jung'fernfahrt f maiden voyage

Jung'fernhäutchen n hymen

Jung'fernkranz m bridal wreath

Jung'fernschaft f virginity

Jung'frau f virgin

jungfräulich ['juŋfrɔɪlɪç] adj maidenly; virgin

Jung'fräulichkeit f virginity

Jung'geselle m bachelor

Jung'gesellenstand m bachelorhood

Jung'gesellin f single girl

Jüngling ['jyŋlɪŋ] m (-s;-e) young man

jüngst [jyŋst] adv recently

jüng'ste adj see jung

Juni ['juni] m (-[s];-s) June

Junker ['juŋkər] m (-s;-) young nobleman; nobleman

Jura ['jura] pl—J. studieren study law

Jurist –in [ju'rɪst(ɪn)] §7 mf lawyer; (educ) law student

Juristerei [jurɪstə'raɪ] f (-;) jurisprudence

juristisch [ju'rɪstɪʃ] adj legal, law; juristische Person legal entity, corporation

just [just] adv just, precisely

justieren [jus'tirən] tr adjust

Justiz [jus'tits] f (-;) justice; administration of justice

Justiz'irrtum m miscarriage of justice

Justiz'minister m minister of justice; attorney general; Lord Chancellor (Brit)

Jutesack ['jutəzak] m gunnysack

Juwel [ju'vel] n (-s;-en) jewel, gem; Juwelen jewelry

Juwe'lenkästchen n jewel box

Juwelier –in [juve'lir(ɪn)] §6 mf jeweler

Juwelier'waren pl jewelry

Jux [juks] m (-es;-e) spoof, joke; aus Jux as a joke; sich [dat] e-n Jux mit j–m machen play a joke on s.o.

K

K, k [ka] invar n K, k

Kabale [ka'balə] f (-;-n) intrigue

Kabarett [kaba'ret] n (-[e]s;-e) cabaret; floor show; (drehbare Platte) lazy Suzan

Kabel ['kabəl] n (-s;-) cable

Ka'belgramm n (-es;-e) cablegram

Kabeljau ['kabəljau] m (-s;-e) codfish

kabeln ['kabəln] tr cable

Kabine [ka'binə] f (-;-n) cabin; booth; (aer) cockpit

Kabinett [kabɪ'net] n (-s;-e) closet; small room; (& pol) cabinet

Kabriolett [kabriɔ'let] n (-[e]s;-e) (aut) convertible

Kachel ['kaxəl] f (-;-n) glazed tile

kacken ['kakən] intr (sl) defecate

Kadaver [ka'davər] m (-s;-) cadaver

Kada'vergehorsam m blind obedience

Kadenz [ka'dents] f (-;-en) cadence

Kader ['kadər] m (-s;-) cadre

Kadett [ka'det] m (-en;-en) cadet

Käfer ['kefər] m (-s;-) beetle

Kaffee ['kafe] m (-s;-s) coffee

Kaf'feebohne f coffee bean

Kaf'feeklatsch m coffee klatsch

Kaf'feemaschine f coffee maker

Kaf'feepflanzung f, Kaf'feeplantage f coffee plantation

Kaf'feesatz m coffee grounds

Kaf'feetante f coffee fiend

Käfig ['kefɪç] m (-[e]s;-e) cage

kahl [kal] adj bald; (Baum) bare; (Landschaft) bleak, barren

kahl'köpfig adj bald-headed

Kahm [kam] m (-[e]s;-e) mold; scum

kahmig ['kamɪç] adj moldy; scummy

Kahn [kan] m (-[e]s;-̈e) boat; barge

Kai [kaɪ], [ke] m (-s;-s) quay, wharf

Kaiser ['kaɪzər] m (-s;-) emperor

Kaiserin ['kaɪzərɪn] f (-;-nen) empress

kai'serlich adj imperial

Kai'serreich n, Kaisertum ['kaɪzərtum] n (-[e]s;-er) empire

Kai'serschnitt m Caesarian operation

Kai'serzeit f (hist) Empire

Kajüte [ka'jytə] f (-;-n) (naut) cabin

Kajü'tenjunge m cabin boy

Kajü'tentreppe f (naut) companionway

Kakao [ka'ka.ɔ] m (-s;-) cocoa; j–n durch den K. ziehen pull s.o.'s leg

Kaktee [kak'te.ə] f (-;-n), Kaktus ['kaktus] m (-;-se) cactus

Kalauer ['kalau-ər] m (-s;-) pun

Kalb [kalp] n (-[e]s;-̈er) calf

Kalbe ['kalbə] f (-;-n) heifer

kalbern ['kalbərn] intr be silly

Kalb'fell n calfskin

Kalb'fleisch n veal

Kalbs'braten m roast veal

Kalbs'kotelett n veal cutlet

Kalbs'schnitzel n veal cutlet

Kaleidoskop [kalaɪdɔ'skop] n (-s;-e) kaleidoscope

Kalender [ka'lendər] m (-s;-) calendar

Kali ['kali] n (-s;) potash

Kaliber [ka'libər] n (-s;-) caliber

kalibrieren [kalɪ'brirən] tr calibrate; gauge

Kaliko ['kaliko] m (-s;-s) calico

Kalium ['kaljum] n (-s;) potassium

Kalk [kalk] *m* (-[e]s;-e) lime; calcium
kalken ['kalkən] *tr* whitewash; lime
kalkig ['kalkıç] *adj* limy
Kalk'ofen *m* limekiln
Kalk'stein *m* limestone
Kalk'steinbruch *m* limestone quarry
Kalkül [kal'kyl] *m & n* (-s;-e) calculation; (math) calculus
kalkulieren [kalku'lirən] *tr* calculate
Kal·mar ['kalmar] *m* (-s;-mare ['marə]) squid
Kalo·rie [kalə'ri] *f* (-;-rien ['ri·ən]) calorie
Kalotte [ka'lɔtə] *f* (-;-n) skullcap
kalt [kalt] *adj* (kälter ['keltər]; kälteste ['keltəstə] §9) cold
kaltblütig ['kaltblytıç] *adj* cold-blooded
Kälte ['keltə] *f* (-;) cold, coldness
käl'tebeständig *adj* cold-resistant
Käl'tegrad *m* degree below freezing
kälten ['keltən] *tr* chill
Käl'tewelle *f* (meteor) cold wave
Kalt'front *f* cold front
kalt'herzig *adj* cold-hearted
kalt'machen *tr* (sl) bump off
kaltschnäuzig ['kalt'nɔıtsıç] *adj* (coll) callous; (coll) cool, unflappable
kalt'stellen *tr* render harmless
kam [kam] *pret of* **kommen**
Kambodscha [kam'bɔtʃa] *n* (-s;) Cambodia
kambodschanisch [kambo'dʒanı] *adj* Cambodian
Kamel [ka'mel] *n* (-[e]s;-e) camel
Kamel'garn *n* mohair
Kamera ['kamera] *f* (-;-s) camera
Kamerad [kamə'rat] *m* (-en;-en), **Kameradin** [kamə'radın] *f* (-;-nen) comrade
Kamerad'schaft ((-;-en) comradeship
Kamin [ka'min] *m* (-s;-e) chimney; fireplace
Kamin'platte *f* hearthstone
Kamin'sims *n* mantelpiece
Kamm [kam] *m* (-[e]s;-e) comb; (e-s Gebirges) ridge; (e-r Welle) crest
kämmen ['kemən] *tr* comb; (Wolle) card
Kammer ['kamər] *f* (-;-n) chamber; (adm) board; (anat) ventricle
Kämmerer ['kemərər] *m* (-s;-) chamberlain; (Schatzmeister) treasurer
Kam'mermusik *f* chamber music
Kamm'garn *n* (tex) worsted
Kamm'rad *n* cogwheel
Kampagne [kam'panjə] *f* (-;-n) campaign
Kämpe ['kempə] *m* (-n;-n) warrior
Kampf [kampf] *m* (-[e]s;-e) fight
Kampf'bahn *f* (sport) stadium, arena
kämpfen ['kempfən] *tr & intr* fight
Kampfer ['kampfər] *m* (-s;) camphor
Kämpfer -in ['kempfər(ın)] §6 *mf* fighter
kämpferisch ['kempfərı] *adj* fighting
kampf'erprobt *adj* battle-tested
kampf'fähig *adj* fit to fight; (mil) fit for active service
Kampf'hahn *m* gamecock; (fig) scrapper
Kampf'handlung *f* (mil) action

Kampf'müdigkeit *f* combat fatigue
Kampf'parole *f* (pol) campaign slogan
Kampf'platz *m* battleground
Kampf'raum *m* battle zone
Kampf'richter *m* referee, umpire
Kampf'schwimmer *m* (nav) frogman
Kampf'spiel *n* (sport) competition
Kampf'staffel *f* tactical squadron
kampf'unfähig *adj* disabled; **k. machen** put out of action
Kampf'veranstalter *m* (sport) promotor
Kampf'verband *m* combat unit
Kampf'wert *m* fighting efficiency
Kampf'ziel *n* (mil) objective
kampieren [kam'pirən] *intr* camp
Kanada ['kanada] *n* (-s;) Canada
Kanadier -in [ka'nadjər(ın)] §6 *mf* Canadian || *m* canoe
kanadisch [ka'nadı] *adj* Canadian
Kanaille [ka'naljə] *f* (-;-n) bum; (Pöbel) riffraff
Kanal [ka'nal] *m* (-s;-e) canal; (für Abwasser) drain, sewer; (agr) irrigation ditch; (anat, elec) duct; (geol, telv) channel
Kanalisation [kanaliza'tsjon] *f* (-;) drainage; sewerage system
Kanalräumer [ka'nalrɔımər] *m* (-s;-) sewer worker
Kanal'wähler *m* (telv) channel selector
Kanapee [ka'napə] *n* (-s;-s) sofa
Kanarienvogel [ka'narjənfogəl] *m* canary
Kandare [kan'darə] *f* (-;-n) bit, curb; **j-n an die K. nehmen** take s.o. in hand
Kanda'renkette *f* curb chain
Kandelaber [kande'labər] *m* (-s;-) candelabrum
Kandidat -in [kandı'dat(ın)] §7 *mf* candidate
Kandidatur [kandıda'tur] *f* (-;-en) candidacy
kandideln [kan'didəln] *ref* get drunk
kandidieren [kandı'dirən] *intr* be a candidate, run for office
Kandis ['kandıs] *m* (-;) rock candy
Kaneel [ka'nel] *m* (-s;-e) cinnamon
Känguruh ['kenguru] *n* (-s;-s) kangaroo
Kaninchen [ka'nınçən] *n* (-s;-) rabbit
Kanister [ka'nıstər] *m* (-s;-) canister
Kanne ['kanə] *f* (-;-n) can; pot; jug
Kannelüre [kanə'lyrə] *f* (-;-n) (archit) flute
Kannibale [kanı'balə] *m* (-n;-n), **Kannibalin** [kanı'balın] *f* (-;-nen) cannibal
kannte ['kantə] *pret of* **kennen**
Ka·non ['kanɔn] *m* (-s;-s) (Maßstab; Gebet bei der Messe) canon; (mus) round || *m* (-s;-nones ['nonəs] canon (of Canon Law)
Kanone [ka'nonə] *f* (-;-n) (arti) gun; (hist) canon; (coll) expert; **unter aller K.** indescribably bad
Kano'nenboot *n* gunboat
Kano'nenrohr *n* gun barrel; **heiliges K.!** holy smokes!
kanonisieren [kanonı'zirən] *tr* canonize
Kante ['kantə] *f* (-;-n) edge

kanten ['kantən] *tr* set on edge; (*beim Schifahren*) cant || **Kanten** *m* (-s;-) end of a loaf, crust
Kanthaken ['kanthɑkən] *m* grappling hook
kantig ['kantɪç] *adj* angular; squared
Kantine [kan'tinə] *f* (-;-n) canteen; (mil) post exchange
Kanton [kan'ton] *m* (-s;-e) canton
Kan·tor ['kantɔr] *m* (-s;-toren ['torən] choir master; organist
Kanu [ka'nu] *n* (-s;-s) canoe
Kanzel ['kantsəl] *f* (-;-n) pulpit; (aer) cockpit
Kanzlei [kants'laɪ] *f* (-;-en) office; chancellery
Kanzlei'papier *n* official foolscap
Kanzlei'sprache *f* legal jargon
Kanzler ['kantslər] *m* (-s;-) chancellor
Kap [kap] *n* (-s;-s) cape, headland
Kapaun [ka'paun] *m* (-s;-e) capon
Kapazität [kapatsɪ'tɛt] *f* (-;-en) capacity; (*Könner*) authority
Kapelle [ka'pelə] *f* (-;-n) chapel; (mus) band
Kapell'meister *m* band leader; orchestra conductor
kapern ['kapərn] *tr* capture; (coll) nab
kapieren [ka'pirən] *tr* get, understand || *intr* get it; **kapiert?** got it?
kapital [kapɪ'tal] *adj* excellent || **Kapital** *n* (-s;-e & -ien [jən]) (fin) capital; **K. schlagen aus** capitalize on; **K. und Zinsen** principal and interest
Kapital'anlage *f* investment
Kapital'ertragssteuer *f* tax on unearned income
kapitalisieren [kapɪtalɪ'zirən] *tr* (fin) capitalize
Kapitalismus [kapɪta'lɪsmus] *m* (-s) capitalism
Kapitalist -in [kapɪta'lɪst(ɪn)] *m* §7 capitalist
Kapital'verbrechen *n* capital offense
Kapitän [kapɪ'ten] *m* (-s;-e) captain, skipper; **K. zur See** (nav) captain
Kapitän'leutnant *m* (nav) lieutenant
Kapitel [ka'pɪtəl] *n* (-s;-) chapter
Kapitell [kapɪ'tel] *n* (-s;-e) (archit) capital
kapitulieren [kapɪtu'lirən] *intr* capitulate, surrender; reenlist
Kaplan [ka'plan] *m* (-s;⁻e) chaplain; (R.C.) assistant (pastor)
Kapo ['kapo] *m* (-s;-s) prisoner overseer; (mil) (coll) N.C.O.
Kappe ['kapə] *f* (-;-n) cap; hood, cover; **etw auf seine eigene K. nehmen** take the responsibility for s.th.
Käppi ['kepɪ] *n* (-s;-s) garrison cap
Kaprice [ka'prisə] *f* (-;-n) caprice
Kapriole [kapri'olə] *f* (-;-n) caper
kaprizieren [kaprɪ'tsirən] *ref*—**sich k. auf** (*acc*) be dead set on
kapriziös [kaprɪ'tsjøs] *adj* capricious
Kapsel ['kapsəl] *f* (-;-n) capsule; (*e-r Flasche*) cap; (*e-s Sprengkörpers*) detonator
kaputt [ka'put] *adj* (sl) broken; (sl) ruined; (sl) exhausted; (sl) dead
kaputt'gehen §82 *intr* (SEIN) get ruined
kaputt'machen *tr* ruin

Kapuze [ka'putsə] *f* (-;-n) hood; (eccl) cowl
Kapuziner [kapu'tsinər] *m* (-s;-) Capuchin
Kapuzi'nerkresse *f* Nasturtium
Karabiner [kara'binər] *m* (-s;-) carbine
Karabi'nerhaken *m* snap
Karaffe [ka'rafə] *f* (-;-n) carafe
Karambolage [karambo'lɑʒə] *f* (-;-n) (coll) collision
karambolieren [karambo'lirən] *intr* (coll) collide
Karamelle [kara'melə] *f* (-;-n) caramel
Karat [ka'rat] *n* (-[e]s;) carat
-karätig [karetɪç] *comb.fm.* —*carat*
Karawane [kara'vanə] *f* (-;-n) caravan
Karbid [kar'bit] *n* (-[e]s;-e) carbide
Karbolsäure [kar'bolzɔɪrə] *f* (-s) carbolic acid
Karbon [kar'bon] *n* (-s;) (geol) carbon
Karbunkel [kar'buŋkəl] *n* (-s;-) carbuncle
Kardinal- [kardɪnal] *comb.fm.* cardinal, principal || **Kardinal** *m* (-s;⁻e) (eccl, orn) cardinal
Karenzzeit [ka'rentstsaɪt] *f* (ins) waiting period
Karfreitag [kar'fraɪtak] *m* Good Friday
karg [kark] *adj* (karger & kärger ['kergər]; kargste & kärgste ['kerstə] §9) (*ärmlich*) meager; (*Boden*) poor; (*Landschaft*) bleak
kargen ['kargən] *intr* be sparing
Karg'heit *f* (-;) bleakness; meagerness; frugality
kärglich ['kerlɪç] *adj* meager, poor
kariert [ka'rirt] *adj* checked, squared
Karikatur [karɪka'tur] *f* (-;-en) caricature; cartoon
karikieren [karɪ'kirən] *tr* caricature
Karl [karl] *m* (-s;) Charles; **Karl der Große** Charlemagne
Karmeliter [karme'litər] *m* (-s;-) Carmelite Friar
Karmelitin [karme'litɪn] *f* (-;-nen) Carmelite nun
karmesinrot [karme'zinrot], **karminrot** [kar'minrot] *adj* crimson
Karneval ['karnəval] *m* (-s;-s & -e) carnival
Karnickel [kar'nɪkəl] *n* (-s;-) (coll) rabbit; (*Sündenbock*) (coll) scapegoat; (*Einfaltspinsel*) simpleton
Karo ['karo] *n* (-s;-s) diamond; check, square; (cards) diamond(s)
Karosse [ka'rosə] *f* (-;-n) state carriage
Karosse·rie [karosə'ri] *f* (-;-rien ['ri·ən] (aut) body
Karotte [ka'rotə] *f* (-;-n) carrot
Karpfen ['karpfən] *m* (-s;-) carp
Karre ['karə] *f* (-;-n), **Karren** ['karən] *m* (-s;-) cart; wheelbarrow; **die alte K.** the old rattletrap
Karriere [ka'rjerə] *f* (-;-n) career; gallop; **K. machen** get ahead
Karte ['kartə] *f* (-;-n) card; ticket; (*Landkarte*) map; (*Speise-*) menu
Kartei [kar'taɪ] *f* (-;-en) card file
Kartei'karte *f* index card

Kartell [kar'tɛl] n (-s;-e) cartel

Kar'tenkunststück n card trick

Kartenlegerin ['kartənlegərɪn] f (-; -nen) fortuneteller

Kar'tenstelle f ration board

Kartoffel [kar'tɔfəl] f (-;-n) potato

Kartof'felbrei m mashed potatoes

Kartof'felpuffer [kar'tɔfəlpufər] m (-s; -) potato pancake

Karton [kar'tɔn] m (-s;-s) cardboard; carton; (paint) cartoon

Kartonage [kartə'naʒə] f (-;-n) cardboard box

kartoniert [kartə'nirt] adj (bb) softcover

Karton'papier n (thin) cardboard

Kartothek [kartə'tek] f (-;-en) card index; card filing system

Kartothek'ausgabe f loose-leaf edition

Karussell [karu'sɛl] n (-s;-e) merry-go-round

Karwoche ['karvɔxə] f Holy Week

Karzer ['kartsər] m (-s;-) (educ) detention room; **K. bekommen** get a detention

Kaschmir ['kaʃmɪr] m (-s;-e) cashmere

Käse ['kezə] m (-s;-) cheese; (sl) baloney

Kaserne [ka'zɛrnə] f (-;-n) barracks

käsig ['kezɪç] adj cheesy; (Gesichtsfarbe) pasty

Kasino [ka'zino] n (-s;-s) casino; (mil) officer's mess

Kas'pisches Meer ['kaspɪʃəs] n Caspian Sea

Kassa ['kasa] f—per K. in cash

Kassa- comb.fm. cash, spot

Kasse ['kasə] f (-;-n) money box; till; cash register; cashiers desk; (Bargeld) cash; (adm) finance department; (educ) bursars office; (sport) ticket window; (theat) box office; **gegen** (or **per**) **K.** cash, for cash; **gut bei K. sein** (coll) be flush

Kas'senabschluß m balancing of accounts

Kas'senbeamte m cashier; teller

Kas'senbeleg m sales slip

Kas'senbestand m cash on hand

Kas'senerfolg m (theat) hit

Kas'senführer –in §6 mf cashier

Kas'senschalter m teller's window

Kas'senschrank m safe

Kas'senzettel m sales slip

Kasserolle [kasə'rɔlə] f (-;-n) casserole

Kassette [ka'sɛtə] f (-;-n) base, box; (cin, phot) cassette

kassieren [ka'sirən] tr (Geld) take in; get; (Urteil) annul; (coll) confiscate; (coll) arrest; (mil) break

Kassie'rer –in §6 mf cashier; teller

Kastagnette [kastan'jɛtə] f (-;-n) castanet

Kastanie [kas'tanjə] f (-;-n) chestnut

Kästchen ['kɛstçən] n (-s;-) case, box

Kaste ['kastə] f (-;-n) caste

kasteien [kas'taɪ-ən] tr & ref mortify; **sein Leib k.** mortify the flesh

Kastell [kas'tɛl] n (-s;-e) small fort

Kasten ['kastən] m (-s;·· & –) chest, case, box; cupboard, cabinet; (Auto)

(coll) crate; (Boot) (coll) tub; (Gefängnis) (coll) jug

Ka'stengeist m snobbishness

Ka'stenwagen m (aut) panel truck; (rr) boxcar

Ka'stenwesen n caste system

Kastrat [kas'trat] m (-en;-en) eunuch

kastrieren [kas'trirən] tr castrate

Katakomben [kata'kɔmbən] pl catacombs

Katalog [kata'lok] m (-[e]s;-e) catalogue

katalogisieren [katalɔgi'zirən] tr catalogue

Katapult [kata'pult] m & n (-[e]s;-e) catapult

katapultieren [katapul'tirən] tr catapult

Katarakt [kata'rakt] m (-[e]s;-e) cataract, rapids; (pathol) cataract

Katasteramt [ka'tastəramt] n landregistry office

katastrophal [katastro'fal] adj catastrophic, disastrous

Katastrophe [kata'strofə] f (-;-n) catastrophe, disaster

Katastro'phengebiet m disaster area

Katego-rie [katego'ri] f (-;-rien ['ri-ən] category

kategorisch [kate'gorɪʃ] adj categorical

Kater ['katər] m (-s;-) tomcat; (coll) hangover

Katheder [ka'tedər] n & m (-s;-) teacher's desk

Kathe'derblüte f teacher's blunder

Kathedrale [kate'dralə] f (-;-n) cathedral

Kathode [ka'todə] f (-;-n) cathode

Katholik –in [kato'lik(ɪn)] §7 mf Catholic

katholisch [ka'tolɪʃ] adj Catholic

Kattun [ka'tun] m (-s;-e) calico

Kätzchen ['kɛtsçən] n (-s;-) kitten

Katze ['katsə] f (-;-n) cat; **für die K.** (coll) for the birds

kat'zenartig adj cat-like, feline

Kat'zenauge n reflector

Kat'zenbuckel m cat's arched back; **vor j–m K. machen** lick s.o.'s boots

kat'zenfreundlich adj overfriendly

Kat'zenjammer m hangover; blues

Kat'zenkopf m (coll) cobblestone; (box) rabbit punch

Kat'zensprung m stone's throw

Kauderwelsch ['kaudərvelʃ] n (-es;) gibberish

kauen ['kau-ən] tr chew

kauern ['kau-ərn] ref & intr cower

Kauf [kauf] m (-[e]s;··e) purchase; **in K. nehmen** (fig) take, put up with; **leichten Kaufes davonkommen** get off cheaply; **zum K. stehen** be for sale

Kauf'auftrag m (com) order

kaufen ['kaufən] tr purchase, buy

Käufer –in ['kɔɪfər(ɪn)] §6 mf buyer

Kauf'haus n department store

Kauf'kraft f purchasing power

käuflich ['kɔɪflɪç] adj for sale; (bestechlich) open to bribes

Kauf'mann m (-[e]s;-leute) businessman; salesman

kaufmännisch ['kaufmenɪʃ] *adj* commercial, business
Kauf'mannsdeutsch *n* business German
Kauf'zwang *m* obligation to buy
Kaugummi ['kaugumɪ] *m* chewing gum
kaukasisch [kau'kazɪʃ] *adj* Caucasian
Kaulquappe ['kaulkvapə] *f* (-;-n) tadpole, polliwog
kaum [kaum] *adv* hardly, scarcely
Kautabak ['kautabak] *m* chewing tobacco
Kaution [kau'tsjon] *f* (-;-en) (jur) bond; (*Bürgschaft*) (jur) bail; **gegen K. on bail**
Kautschuk ['kautʃuk] *m* (-s;-e) rubber
Kauz [kauts] *m* (-es;-e) owl; (sl) crackpot
Kavalier [kava'lir] *m* (-s;-e) cavalier; gentleman; beau
Kavalkade [kaval'kadə] *f* (-;-n) cavalcade
Kavalle-rie [kavalə'ri] *f* (-;-rien ['ri-ən]) cavalry
Kavallerist [kavalə'rɪst] *m* (-en;-en) cavalryman, trooper
Kaviar ['kavjar] *m* (-[e]s;-e) caviar
keck [kek] *adj* bold; impudent; cheeky
Kegel ['kegəl] *m* (-s;-) tenpin; (geom) cone; **K. schieben** bowl
Ke'gelbahn *f* bowling alley
kegeln ['kegəln] *intr* bowl
Keg'ler *–in* §6 *mf* bowler
Kehle ['kelə] *f* (-;-n) throat
kehlig ['kelɪç] *adj* throaty
Kehlkopf ['kelkopf] *m* larynx
Kehl'kopfentzündung *f* laryngitis
Kehre ['kerə] *f* (-;-n) turn, bend
kehren ['kerən] *tr* sweep; (*wenden*) turn; **alles zum besten k.** make the best of it; **j-m den Rücken k.** turn one's back on s.o. || *ref* turn; **in sich gekehrt sein** be lost in thought; **sich an nichts k.** not care about anything; **sich k. an** (*acc*) heed || *intr* sweep
Kehricht ['kerɪçt] *m & n* (-[e]s;) sweepings; trash, rubbish
Keh'richteimer *m* trash can
Keh'richtschaufel *f* dustpan
Kehr'maschine *f* street cleaner
Kehr'reim *m* refrain, chorus
Kehr'seite *f* reverse; (fig) seamy side
kehrtmachen ['kertmaxən] *intr* turn around; (mil) about-face
Kehrt'wendung *f* about-face
keifen ['kaifən] *intr* nag
Keiferei [kaifə'rai] *f* (-;-en) nagging; squabble
Keil [kail] *m* (-[e]s;-e) wedge
keilen ['kailən] *tr* wedge; (coll) recruit || *recip* scrap
Keilerei [kailə'rai] *f* (-;-en) scrap
keil'förmig *adj* wedge-shaped; tapered
Keil'hammer *m* sledgehammer
Keil'hose *f* tapered trousers
Keil'schrift *f* cuneiform writing
Keim [kaim] *m* (-[e]s;-e) germ; embryo; (fig) seeds; (bot) bud, sprout; **im K. ersticken** nip in the bud; **im K. vorhanden** at an embryonic stage; **Keime treiben** germinate
keimen ['kaimən] *intr* germinate;

sprout || **Keimen** *n*—**zum K. bringen** cause to germinate
keim'frei *adj* germ-free, sterile
Keimling ['kaimlɪŋ] *m* (-s;-e) embryo; sprout; seedling
keimtötend ['kaimtøtənt] *adj* germicidal; antiseptic, sterilizing
Keim'zelle *f* germ cell, sex cell
kein [kain] §2,2 *adj* no, not any
keiner ['kainər] §2,4 *indef pron* none; no one, nobody, not one; **k. von beiden** neither of them
keinerlei ['kainər'lai] *invar adj* no... of any kind, no...whatsoever
keineswegs ['kainəs'veks] *adv* by no means, not at all
Keks [keks] *m & n* (-es;-e) biscuit, cracker; cookie
Kelch [kelç] *m* (-[e]s;-e) cup; (bot) calyx; (eccl) chalice
Kelch'blatt *n* (bot) sepal
Kelle ['kelə] *f* (-;-n) ladle; (hort, mas) trowel
Keller ['kelər] *m* (-s;-) cellar
Kel'lergeschoß *n* basement
Kel'lergewölbe *n* underground vault
Kellner ['kelnər] *m* (-s;-e) waiter
Kellnerin ['kelnərin] *f* (-;-nen) waitress
Kelte ['keltə] *m* (-n;-n) Celt
Kelter ['keltər] *f* (-;-n) wine press
keltern ['keltərn] *tr* press
Keltin ['keltin] *f* (-;-nen) Celt
keltisch ['keltɪʃ] *adj* Celtic
kennbar ['kenbar] *adj* recognizable
kennen ['kenən] §97 *tr* be acquainted with, know
ken'nenlernen *tr* get to know, meet
Ken'ner *–in* §6 *mf* expert
Ken'nerblick *m* knowing glance
Ken'ner *–in* §6 *mf* expert
Kennkarte ['kenkartə] *f* identity card
kenntlich ['kentlɪç] *adj* identifiable, recognizable; conspicuous
Kenntnis ['kentnis] *f* (-;-se) knowledge; **gute Kenntnisse haben in** (dat) be well versed in; **j-n von etw in K. setzen** apprise s.o. of s.th.; **Kenntnisse** knowledge; skills; know-how; **oberflächliche Kenntnisse** a smattering; **von etw K. nehmen** take note of s.th.; **zur K. nehmen** take note of s.th.
Kennwort ['kenvort] *n* (-[e]s;-er) code word; (mil) password
Kennzeichen ['kentsaiçən] *n* distinguishing mark; hallmark; criterion; (aer) marking; (aut) license number
kennzeichnen ['kentsaiçnən] *tr* characterize; identify; brand
Kennziffer ['kentsifər] *f* code number
kentern ['kentərn] *intr* (SEIN) capsize
Keramik [ke'ramɪk] *f* (-;) ceramics; pottery
keramisch [ke'ramɪʃ] *adj* ceramic
Kerbe ['kerbə] *f* (-;-n) notch, groove
kerben ['kerbən] *tr* notch, nick; make a groove in; serrate
Kerbholz ['kerpholts] *n*—**etw auf dem K. haben** have a crime chalked up against one
Kerbtier ['kerptir] *n* insect
Kerker ['kerkər] *m* (-s;-) jail

Kerl [kerl] *m* (–s;–e) fellow, guy; (*Mädchen*) lass

Kern [kern] *m* (–[e]s;–e) kernel; (*im Obst*) pit, stone, pip; hard core; (*e–s Problems*) crux; (phys) nucleus

Kern– *comb.fm.* core; central, basic; through and through; (phys) nuclear

Kern'aufbau *m* nuclear structure

kern'deutsch' *adj* German through and through

Kern'energie *f* nuclear energy

kern'fächer *pl* core curriculum

kern'gesund' *adj* perfectly sound

Kern'holz *n* heartwood

kernig ['kerniç] *adj* full of seeds; robust, vigorous

kern'los *adj* seedless

Kern'physik *f* nuclear physics

Kern'punkt *m* gist, crux; focal point

Kern'schußweite *f*—auf K. at pointblank range

Kern'spaltung *f* nuclear fission

Kern'truppen *pl* crack troops

Kern'verschmelzung *f* nuclear fusion

Kern'waffe *f* nuclear weapon

Kerosin [kero'zin] *n* (–s;) kerosene

Kerze ['kertsə] *f* (–;–n) candle; (aut) plug

ker'zengera'de *adj* straight as an arrow ‖ *adv* bolt upright

Kessel ['kesəl] *m* (–s;–) kettle; cauldron; boiler; (geog) basin-shaped valley; (mil) pocket

Kes'selpauke *f* kettledrum

Kes'selraum *m* boiler room

Kes'selschmied *m* boilermaker

Kes'selwagen *m* (aut) tank truck; (rr) tank car

Kette ['ketə] *f* (–;–n) chain; (e–s Panzers) track

ketten ['ketən] *tr* (**an** *acc*) chain (to)

Ket'tengeschäft *n* chain store

Ket'tenglied *n* chain link

Ket'tenhund *m* watch dog

Ket'tenrad *n* sprocket

Ket'tenraucher –in §6 *mf* chain smoker

Ket'tenstich *m* chain stitch, lock stitch

Ketzer –in ['ketsər(ɪn)] §6 *mf* heretic

Ketzerei [ketsə'raɪ] *f* (–;–en) heresy

ketzerisch ['ketsərɪʃ] *adj* heretical

keuchen ['kɔɪçən] *intr* pant, gasp

Keuch'husten *m* (–s;) whooping cough

Keule ['kɔɪlə] *f* (–;–n) club; (culin) leg, drumstick

keusch [kɔɪʃ] *adj* chaste

Keusch'heit *f* (–;) chastity

KG *abbr* (**Kommanditgesellschaft**) Ltd.

Khaki ['kaki] *m* (–;) (tex) khaki

kichern ['kɪçərn] *intr* giggle

kicken ['kɪkən] *tr* (fb) kick

Kicker ['kɪkər] *m* (–s;–) soccer player

Kiebitz ['kibɪts] *m* (–[e]s;–e) (orn) lapwing; (*Zugucker*) kibitzer

kiebitzen ['kibɪtsən] *intr* kibitz

Kiefer ['kifər] *m* (–s;–) jaw(bone) ‖ *f* (–;–n) pine; **gemeine K.** Scotch pine

Kiel [kil] *m* (–[e]s;–e) (*Feder*) quill; (naut) keel

Kiel'raum *m* hold

Kiel'wasser *n* wake

Kieme ['kimə] *f* (–;–n) gill

Kien ['kin] *m* (–[e]s;–e) pine cone

Kien'span *m* pine torch

Kiepe ['kipə] *f* (–;–n) basket (*carried on one's back*)

Kies [kis] *m* (–es;–e) gravel

Kiesel ['kizəl] *m* (–s;–) pebble

Kilo ['kilo] *n* (–s;–s & –) kilogram

Kilogramm [kilo'gram] *n* (–s;–e & –) kilogram

Kilometer [kilo'metər] *m* & *n* (–s;–) kilometer

Kilome'terfresser *m* (coll) speedster

Kilowatt ['kilo'vat] *n* (–s;–) kilowatt

Kimm [kɪm] *m* (–es;–e) horizon ‖ *f* (–;–e) (naut) bilge

Kimme ['kɪmə] *f* (–;–n) notch; groove; (e–s Gewehrs) sight

Kind [kɪnt] *n* (–[e]s;–er) child; baby

Kinder– [kɪndər] *comb.fm.* child's, children's

Kinderei [kɪndə'raɪ] *f* (–;–en) childish behavior, childish prank

Kin'derfrau *f* nursemaid

Kin'derfräulein *n* governess

Kin'derfürsorge *f* child welfare

Kin'dergarten *m* nursery school, playschool

Kin'dergärtnerin *f* nursery school attendant

Kin'dergeld *n* see **Kinderzulage**

Kin'derheilkunde *f* pediatrics

Kin'derheim *n* children's home

Kin'derhort *m* day nursery

Kin'derlähmung *f* polio

kin'derleicht *adj* easy as pie

Kin'derlied *n* nursery rhyme

kin'derlos *adj* childless

Kin'dermädchen *n* nursemaid

Kin'derpuder *m* baby powder

Kin'derreim *m* nursery rhyme

Kin'derschreck *m* bogeyman

Kin'dersportwagen *m* stroller

Kin'derstube *f* nursery; (*Erziehung*) upbringing

Kin'derstuhl *m* highchair

Kin'derwagen *m* baby carriage

Kin'derzulage *f* family allowance (*paid by the employer*)

Kin'desalter *n* childhood; infancy

Kin'desannahme *f* adoption

Kin'desbeine *pl*—von **Kindesbeinen an** from childhood on

Kin'desentführer –in §6 *mf* kidnaper

Kin'desentführung *f*, **Kin'desraub** *m* kidnaping

Kind'heit *f* (–;) childhood

kindisch ['kɪndɪʃ] *adj* childish

kindlich ['kɪntlɪç] *adj* childlike

Kinetik [kɪ'netɪk] *f* (–;) kinetics

kinetisch [kɪ'netɪʃ] *adj* kinetic

Kinkerlitzchen ['kɪŋkərlɪtsçən] *pl* trifles; gimmicks

Kinn [kɪn] *n* (–[e]s;–e) chin

Kinn'backen *m* jawbone

Kinn'haken *m* (box) uppercut

Kinn'kette *f* curb chain

Kino ['kino] *n* (–s;–s) movie theater

Ki'nobesucher –in §6 *mf* moviegoer

Ki'nokamera *f* movie camera

Ki'nokasse *f* box office

Kiosk [ki'osk] *m* (–[e]s;–e) stand

Kipfel ['kɪpfəl] *n* (–s;–) (Aust) (culin) crescent roll

Kippe ['kɪpə] f (-;-n) edge; (Zigarettenstummel) butt; auf der K. stehen stand on edge; (fig) be touch and go

kippen ['kɪpən] tr tilt, tip over; dump || intr (SEIN) tilt; overturn

Kipper ['kɪpər] m (-s;-) dump truck

Kirche ['kɪrçə] f (-;-n) church

Kirchen– [kɪrçən] comb.fm. church, ecclesiastical

Kir'chenbann m excommunication; in den K. tun excommunicate

Kir'chenbau m (-[e]s;) building of churches || m (-[e]s;-ten) church

Kir'chenbesuch m church attendance

Kir'chenbuch n parish register

Kir'chendiener m sacristan, sexton

Kir'chengut n church property

Kir'chenlied n hymn

Kir'chenschändung f desecration of a church

Kir'chenschiff n (archit) nave

Kir'chenspaltung f schism

Kir'chenstaat m Papal States

Kir'chenstuhl m pew

Kir'chentag m Church congress

Kirchgang ['kɪrçgaŋ] m going to church

Kirch'gänger –in §6 mf church-goer

Kirch'hof m churchyard

kirch'lich adj church, ecclesiastical

Kirch'spiel n parish

Kirch'turm m steeple

Kirch'turmpolitik f (pej) parochialism

Kirch'turmspitze f spire

Kirchweih ['kɪrçvaɪ] f (-;-en) church picnic

Kirch'weihe f dedication of a church

Kirch'weihfest n church picnic

Kirsch [kɪrʃ] m (-es;-) cherry brandy

Kirsche ['kɪrʃə] f (-;-n) cherry

Kirsch'wasser n cherry brandy

Kissen ['kɪsən] n (-s;-) cushion, pillow; (Polster) pad

Kis'senbezug m pillowcase

Kiste ['kɪstə] f (-;-n) box, crate, case; (aer) crate; (aut) rattletrap; (naut) tub

Kitsch [kɪtʃ] m (-es;) kitsch

kitschig ['kɪtʃɪç] adj trashy; mawkish

Kitt [kɪt] m (-[e]s;-e) putty; cement; der ganze Kitt the whole caboodle

Kittchen ['kɪtçən] n (-s;-) (coll) jail

Kittel ['kɪtəl] m (-s;-) smock, coat; (Aust) skirt

Kit'telkleid n house dress

kitten ['kɪtən] tr putty; cement, glue; (fig) patch up

Kitzel ['kɪtsəl] m (-s;) tickle; (fig) itch

kitzeln ['kɪtsəln] tr tickle

kitzlig ['kɪtslɪç] adj ticklish

Kladderadatsch [kladəra'datʃ] m (-es;) crash, bang; mess, muddle

klaffen ['klafən] intr gape, yawn

kläffen ['klɛfən] intr yelp

Klafter ['klaftər] f (-;- & -n), m & n (-s;-) fathom; (Holz–) cord

klagbar ['klakbar] adj (jur) actionable

Klage ['klagə] f (-;-n) complaint; (jur) (civil) suit

Kla'gelied n dirge, threnody

klagen ['klagən] tr—j-m seinen Kummer k. pour out one's troubles to s.o.

|| intr complain; auf Scheidung k. sue for divorce; k. über (acc) complain about; k. um lament

Kläger –in ['klɛgər(ɪn)] §6 mf (jur) plaintiff

Kla'geweib n hired mourner

kläglich ['klɛklɪç] adj plaintive, pitiful; (Zustand) sorry; (Ergebnis, Ende) miserable

klaglos ['klaklos] adv uncomplainingly

klamm [klam] adj (erstarrt) numb; (feuchtkalt) clammy; k. an Geld (coll) short of dough || **Klamm** f (-;-en) gorge

Klammer ['klamər] f (-;-n) clamp; clip; paper clip; (Schließe) clasp; clothespin; hair clip, bobby pin; eckige K. bracket; runde K. parenthesis

klammern ['klamərn] tr clamp; clasp || ref—sich k. an (acc) cling to

Klamotte [kla'motə] f (-;-n)—alte K. oldy; (aer, aut) old crate; **Klamotten** things, clothes

Klampfe ['klampfə] f (-;-n) guitar

klang [klaŋ] pret of klingen || **Klang** m (-[e]s;:e) tone, sound

Klang'farbe f timbre

klang'getreu adj high-fidelity

Klang'regler m (rad) tone-control knob

Klang'taste f tone-control push button

klang'voll adj sonorous

Klappe ['klapə] f (-;-n) flap; (Mund) (sl) trap; (anat, mach) valve; in die K. gehen (sl) hit the sack

klappen ['klapən] tr flip || intr flap, fold || impers—es klappt (coll) it clicks, it turns out well

Klapper ['klapər] f (-;-n) rattle

klap'perdürr adj skinny

Klap'pergestell n (coll) beanpole; (Kiste) (coll) rattletrap

klappern ['klapərn] intr rattle, clatter; (Zähne) chatter

Klap'perschlange f rattlesnake

Klap'perstorch m stork

Klappflügel ['klapflygəl] m (aer) folding wing (of carrier plane)

Klappmesser ['klapmesər] n jackknife

klapprig ['klaprɪç] adj rickety

Klappstuhl ['klapʃtul] m folding chair

Klapptisch ['klaptɪʃ] m drop-leaf table

Klapptür ['klaptyr] f trap door

Klaps [klaps] m (-es;-e) smack, slap; e-n K. kriegen (sl) go nuts

klapsen ['klapsən] tr smack, slap

Klaps'mühle f (coll) booby hatch

klar [klar] adj clear; klar zum Start ready for take-off

Kläranlage ['klɛranlagə] f sewage-disposal plant

klären ['klɛrən] tr clear; (Mißverständnis) clear up || ref become clear

Klar'heit f (-;) clearness, clarity

Klarinette [klari'nɛtə] f (-;-n) clarinet

klar'legen, klar'stellen tr clear up

Klärung ['klɛruŋ] f (-;) clarification

Klasse ['klasə] f (-;-n) class; (educ) grade, class

Klas'senarbeit f test

Klas'senaufsatz m composition (written in class)

klas'senbewußt adj class-conscious

Klas′seneinteilung *f* classification
Klas′senkamerad **-in** §7 *mf* classmate
Klas′sentreffen *n* (-s;-) class reunion
klassifizieren [klasɪfɪ′tsirən] *tr* classify
Klassifizie′rung *f* (-;-en) classification
-klassig [klasɪç] *comb.fm.* -class, -grade
Klassik [′klasɪk] *f* (-;) classical antiquity, classical period
Klas′siker **-in** §6 *mf* classical author
klassisch [′klasɪʃ] *adj* classic(al)
Klatsch [klatʃ] *m* (-es;) clap; gossip
Klatsch′base *f* gossipmonger; tattletale
Klatsch′blatt *n* scandal sheet
Klatsche [′klatʃə] *f* (-;-n) fly swatter; tattletale; (educ) pony
klatschen [′klatʃən] *tr* smack, slap; **dem Lehrer etw k.** tattletale to the teacher about s.th.; **j-m Beifall k.** applaud s.o. || *intr* clap; (*Regen*) patter; (fig) gossip; **in die Hände** (or **mit den Händen**) **k.** clap the hands
Klatscherei [klatʃə′raɪ] *f* (-;-en) gossip
klatsch′naß′ *adj* soaking wet
Klatsch′spalte *f* glossip column
klauben [′klaubən] *tr* pick
Klaue [′klau-ə] *f* (-;-n) claw, talon; (*Spalthuf*) hoof; (coll) scrawl
klauen [′klau-ən] *tr* (coll) snitch
Klause [′klauzə] *f* (-;-n) hermitage; (*Schlucht*) defile; (coll) den, pad
Klausel [′klauzəl] *f* (-;-n) clause; (*Abmachung*) stipulation
Klausner [′klauznər] *m* (-s;-) hermit
Klausur [klau′zur] *f* (-;-en) seclusion; (educ) final examination
Klausur′arbeit *f* final examination
Klaviatur [klavja′tur] *f* (-;-en) keyboard
Klavier [kla′vir] *n* (-[e]s;-e) piano
Klavier′auszug *m* piano score
Klebemittel [′klebəmɪtəl] *n* (-s;-) adhesive, glue
kleben [′klebən] *tr & intr* stick
Kleberolle [′klebərələ] *f* roll of gummed tape
Klebestreifen [′klebə/traɪfən] *m* adhesive tape; Scotch tape (*trademark*)
Klebezettel [′klebətsetəl] *m* label, sticker
klebrig [′klebrɪç] *adj* sticky
Klebstoff [′klep/tɔf] *m* adhesive
Klecks [kleks] *m* (-es;-e) stain; dab
klecksen [′kleksən] *tr* splash || *intr* make blotches
Kleckser **-in** [′kleksər(ɪn)] §6 *mf* scribbler; dauber
Klee [kle] *m* (-s;) clover
Klee′blatt *n* cloverleaf; (fig) trio
Kleid [klaɪt] *n* (-[e]s;-er) garment; dress; robe; **Kleider** clothes
kleiden [′klaɪdən] *tr* dress; **j-n gut k.** look good on s.o.
Klei′derablage *f* cloakroom; (*Kleiderständer*) clothes rack
Klei′derbestand *m* wardrobe
Klei′derbügel *m* coat hanger
Klei′dersack *m* (mil) duffle bag
Klei′derschrank *m* clothes closet
Klei′derständer *m* clothes rack
kleidsam [′klaɪtzam] *adj* well-fitting, becoming

Klei′dung *f* (-;) clothing
Kleie [′klaɪ-ə] *f* (-;-n) bran
klein [klaɪn] *adj* small, little; short; **ein k. wenig** a little bit || **Kleine** §5 *m* little boy || *f* little girl || *n* little one
Klein′anzeigen *pl* classified ads
Klein′arbeit *f* detailed work
Klein′asien *n* Asia Minor
Klein′bahn *f* narrow-gauge railroad
Klein′bauer *m* small farmer
Klein′betrieb *m* small business
Kleinbild- *comb.fm.* (phot) 35mm
klein′bürgerlich *adj* lower middle-class
Klein′geld *n* change
klein′gläubig *adj* of little faith
Klein′handel *m* retail business
Klein′händler **-in** §6 *mf* retailer
Klein′hirn *n* (anat) cerebellum
Klein′holz *n* kindling; **K. aus j-m machen** (coll) beat s.o. to a pulp
Klei′nigkeit *f* small object; trifle, minor detail; small matter
Klei′nigkeitskrämer *m* fusspot
kleinkalibrig [′klaɪnkalibrɪç] *adj* small-bore
Klein′kind *n* infant
Klein′kinderbewahranstalt *f* day care center
Klein′kram *m* odds and ends; details
klein′laut *adj* subdued
klein′lich *adj* stingy; (*Betrag*) paltry; (*engstirnig*) narrow-minded, pedantic
Klein′mut *m* despondency; faint-heartedness
klein′mütig *adj* despondent; faint-hearted
Klei′nod [′klaɪnot] *n* (-[e]s;-node & -nodien [′nodjən] jewel, gem
klein′schneiden §106 *tr* chop up
Klein′schreibmaschine *f* portable typewriter
Kleister [′klaɪstər] *m* (-s;-) paste
Klemme [′klemə] *f* (-;-n) clamp, clip; (coll) tight spot, fix; (elec) terminal; (surg) clamp
klemmen [′klemən] *tr* tuck, put; (*stehlen*) pinch, swipe || *ref*—**sich** [*dat*] **den Finger k.** smash one's finger; **sich hinter die Arbeit k.** get down to business; **sich k. hinter** (*acc*) get after || *intr* be stuck
Klempner [′klempnər] *m* (-s;-) tinsmith; plumber
Klempnerei [klempnə′raɪ] *f* (-;) plumbing
Kleptomane [klepto′manə] §5 *mf* kleptomaniac
klerikal [klerɪ′kal] *adj* clerical
Kleriker [′klerɪkər] *m* (-s;-) clergyman, priest
Klerus [′klerus] *m* (-;) clergy
Klette [′kletə] *f* (-;-n) (bot) burr; (coll) pain in the neck
Klet′tergarten *m* training area (*for mountain climbing*)
klettern [′kletərn] *intr* (SEIN) climb
Klet′terpflanze *f* (bot) creeper
Klet′terrose *f* rambler
Klet′tertour *f* climbing expedition
Klient [klɪ′ent] *m* (-en;-en) client
Klientel [klɪ-en′tel] *f* (-;-en) clientele (*of a lawyer*)

Klientin [klɪ'ɛntɪn] f (-;-nen) client

Klima ['klima] n (-s;-s) climate

Kli'maanlage f air conditioner

kli'magerecht adj air-conditioned

klimatisch [kli'matɪʃ] adj climatic

klimatisieren [klimati'zirən] tr air-condition

Klimatisie'rung f (-;) air conditioning

Klimbim [klɪm'bɪm] m (-s;) (coll) junk; (coll) racket; (coll) fuss

klimmen ['klɪmən] §164 intr (SEIN) climb

klimpern ['klɪmpərn] intr jingle; (auf der Gitarre) strum; mit den Wimpern k. flutter one's eyelashes

Klinge ['klɪŋə] f (-;-n) blade; sword, saber; über die K. springen lassen put to the sword

Klingel ['klɪŋəl] f (-;-n) bell

Klin'gelbeutel m collection basket

Klin'gelknopf m doorbell button

klingeln ['klɪŋəln] intr ring, tinkle; (Vers, Reim) jingle || impers—es klingelt the doorbell is ringing; there goes the (school) bell; the phone is ringing

kling'klang interj ding-dong!

Klinik ['klinɪk] f (-;-en) teaching hospital (of a university); private hospital; nursing home

klinisch ['klinɪʃ] adj clinical; hospital

Klinke ['klɪŋkə] f (-;-n) door handle; (telp) jack; Klinken putzen beg or peddle from door to door

Klippe ['klɪpə] f (-;-n) rock, reef

klirren ['klɪrən] intr rattle, clang; (Gläser) clink; (Waffen) clash

Klischee [klɪ'ʃe] n (-s;-s) cliché

Klistier [klɪs'tir] n (-s;-e) enema

klistieren [klɪs'tirən] tr give an enema to

klitschig ['klɪtʃɪç] adj doughy

Klo [klo] n (-s;-s) (coll) john

Kloake [klo'akə] f (-;-n) sewer

Kloben ['klobən] m (-s;-) pulley; (Holz) block; (Schraubenstock) vise

klobig ['klobɪç] adj clumsy; bulky

klomm [klɔm] pret of klimmen

klopfen ['klɔpfən] tr (Nagel) drive; (Teppich) beat; (Fleisch) pound || intr knock; (Herz) beat, pound; (Motor) ping; j—m auf die Schulter k. pat s.o. on the back || impers—es klopft s.o. is knocking

klopf'fest adj antiknock

Klöppel ['klœpəl] m (-s;-) bobbin; (e-r Glocke) clapper; (mus) mallet

klöppeln ['klœpəln] tr make (lace) with bobbins

Klops [klɔps] m (-es;-e) meatball

Klosett [klo'zɛt] n (-s;-e & -s) (flush) toilet

Klosett'becken n toilet bowl

Klosett'brille f toilet seat

Klosett'deckel m toilet-seat lid

Klosett'papier n toilet paper

Kloß [klos] m (-es;-̈e) dumpling; e-n K. im Hals haben have a lump in one's throat

Kloster ['klostər] n (-s;-̈) monastery; convent

Kloster- comb.fm. monastic

Klo'sterbruder m lay brother, friar

Klo'sterfrau f nun

klösterlich ['kløstərlɪç] adj monastic

Klotz [klɔts] m (-es;-̈e) block; toy building block; (coll) blockhead; ein K. am Bein (coll) a drag; wie ein K. schlafen sleep like a log

klotzig ['klɔtsɪç] adj clumsy; uncouth || adv—k. reich filthy rich

Klub [klup] m (-s;-s) club

Klub'jacke f blazer

Klub'sessel m easy chair

Kluft [kluft] f (-;-̈e) gorge, ravine; (fig) gulf; (poet) chasm || f (-;-en) outfit, uniform

klug [kluk] adj (klüger ['klygər]; klügste ['klygstə] §9) clever, bright; wise; aus Schaden k. werden learn the hard way; nicht k. werden können aus be unable to figure out

klügeln ['klygəln] intr quibble

Klug'heit f (-;) cleverness; intelligence; wisdom

klüglich ['klyklɪç] adv wisely

Klug'redner m wise guy, know-it-all

Klumpen ['klumpən] m (-s;-) lump, clod; (Haufen) heap; (min) nugget

Klumpfuß ['klumpfus] m clubfoot

klumpig ['klumpɪç] adj lumpy

Klüngel ['klyŋəl] m (-s;-) clique

knabbern ['knabərn] intr nibble

Knabe ['knabə] m (-n;-n) boy

Kna'benalter n boyhood

kna'benhaft adj boyish

knack [knak] interj crack!; snap!; click!

knacken ['knakən] tr crack || intr crack; (Schloß) click; (Feuer) crackle

Knacks [knaks] m (-es;-e) crack; snap; click; e-n K. kriegen get a crack; e-n K. weg haben be badly hit; sich [dat] e-n K. holen suffer a blow

Knack'wurst f pork sausage; smoked sausage

Knall [knal] m (-[e]s;-e) crack, bang; K. und Fall on the spot, at once

Knallblättchen ['knalblɛtçən] n (-s;-) cap (for a toy pistol)

Knall'bonbon m & n noise maker

Knall'büchse f popgun

Knall'dämpfer m silencer

Knall'effekt m big surprise

knall'rot adj fiery red

knapp [knap] adj (eng) close, tight; (Mehrheit) bare; (Zeit) short; (Stil) concise; k. werden run short, run low

Knappe ['knapə] m (-n;-n) (hist) squire; (min) miner

Knapp'heit f (-;-) closeness, tightness; shortage; conciseness

Knapp'schaft f (-;-en) miner's union

Knapp'schaftskasse f miner's insurance

knarren ['knarən] intr creek

Knaster ['knastər] m (-s;-) tobacco

knattern ['knatərn] intr crackle; (Maschinengewehr) rattle || intr (SEIN) put-put along

Knäuel ['knɔɪ-əl] m & n (-s;-) (Garn-) ball; (Menschen-) throng

Knauf [knauf] m (-[e]s;-̈e) knob

Knauser -in ['knauzər(ɪn)] §6 mf tightwad

Knauserei [knauzə'raɪ] *f* (-;) stinginess

knauserig ['knauzərɪç] *adj* stingy

knausern ['knauzərn] *intr* be stingy

knautschen ['knautʃən] *tr* crumple ‖ *intr* crumple; (coll) wimper

Knebel ['kneːbəl] *m* (-s;-) gag

Kne'belbart *m* handlebar moustache

knebeln ['kneːbəln] *tr* gag; (fig) muzzle

Kne'belpresse *f* tourniquet

Kne'belung *f*—K. der Presse muzzling of the press

Knecht [knɛçt] *m* (-[e]s;-e) servant; farmhand; serf; slave

knechten ['knɛçtən] *tr* enslave; oppress

knechtisch ['knɛçtɪʃ] *adj* servile

Knecht'schaft *f* (-;) servitude

kneifen ['knaɪfən] §88 & §109 *tr* pinch ‖ §88 *intr* (*Kleid*) be too tight; back out, back down; (fencing) retreat; **k. vor** (*dat*) shirk, dodge

Kneifzange ['knaɪftsaŋə] *f* (pair of) pincers

Kneipe ['knaɪpə] *f* (-;-n) saloon

kneipen ['knaɪpən] *intr* (coll) booze

Knei'penwirt *m* saloon keeper

Kneiperei [knaɪpə'raɪ] *f* (-;-en) drinking bout

kneten ['kneːtən] *tr* knead; massage

Knick [knɪk] *m* (-[e]s;-e) bend; (*Bruch*) break; (*Falte*) fold, crease

knicken ['knɪkən] *tr* bend; break; fold; (*Hoffnungen*) dash ‖ *intr* (SEIN) snap

Knicker ['knɪkər] *m* (-s;-) tightwad

Knicks [knɪks] *m* (-es;-e) curtsy

knicksen ['knɪksən] *intr* curtsy

Knie [kni] *n* (-s;- ['kni·ə]) knee

Knie'beuge *f* knee bend

Knie'beugung *f* genuflection

knie'fällig *adj* on one's knees

knie'frei *adj* above-the-knee

Knie'freiheit *f* legroom

Knie'kehle *f* hollow of the knee

knien ['kni·ən] *intr* kneel

Knie'scheibe *f* kneecap

Knie'schützer *m* (sport) kneepad

kniff [knɪf] *pret* of **kneifen** ‖ **Kniff** *m* (-[e]s;-e) crease, fold; (*Kunstgriff*) knack

kniff(e)lig ['knɪf(ə)lɪç] *adj* tricky

kniffen ['knɪfən] *tr* crease, fold

Knigge ['knɪgə] *m* (-;) (fig) Emily Post

knipsen ['knɪpsən] *tr* (*Karte*) punch; (phot) snap ‖ *intr* snap a picture; **mit den Fingern k.** snap one's fingers

Knirps [knɪrps] *m* (-es;-e) (coll) shrimp

knirschen ['knɪrʃən] *intr* crunch; **mit den Zähnen k.** gnash one's teeth

knistern ['knɪstərn] *intr* crackle; (*Seide*) rustle

knitterfest ['knɪtərfɛst] *adj* wrinkleproof

knittern ['knɪtərn] *tr* wrinkle; crumple

knobeln ['knoːbəln] *intr* play dice; **an e-m Problem k.** puzzle over a problem

Knoblauch ['knoːblaux] *m* (-[e]s;) garlic

Knöchel ['knœçəl] *m* (-s;-) knuckle, joint; ankle

Knochen ['knɔxən] *m* (-s;-) bone

Kno'chenbruch *m* fracture

Kno'chengerüst *n* skeleton

Kno'chenmark *n* marrow

Kno'chenmühle *f* (coll) sweat shop

knöchern ['knœçərn] *adj* bone; bony

knochig ['knɔxɪç] *adj* bony

Knödel ['knøːdəl] *m* (-s;-) dumpling; **e-n K. im Hals haben** have a lump in one's throat

Knolle ['knɔlə] *f* (coll) bulbous nose; (bot) tuber

Knollen ['knɔlən] *m* (-s;-) lump; (coll) bulbous nose

knollig ['knɔlɪç] *adj* bulbous

Knopf [knɔpf] *m* (-[e]s;⁓e) button; knob; (*e-r Stechnadel*) head; **alter K.** old fogey

knöpfen ['knœpfən] *tr* button

Knopf'loch *n* buttonhole

knorke ['knɔrkə] *adj* (coll) super

Knorpel ['knɔrpəl] *m* (-s;-) cartilage

Knorren ['knɔrən] *m* (-s;-) knot, gnarl

knorrig ['knɔrɪç] *adj* gnarled, knotty

Knospe ['knɔspə] *f* (-;-n) bud

knospen ['knɔspən] *intr* bud

knoten ['knoːtən] *tr* & *intr* knot ‖ **Knoten** *m* (-s;-) knot; (*Schwierigkeit*) snag; (*Haarfrisur*) chignon; (*Seemeile*) knot; (astr, med, phys) node; (theat) plot

Kno'tenpunkt *m* intersection, interchange; (rr) junction

knotig ['knoːtɪç] *adj* knotty

Knuff [knuf] *m* (-[e]s;⁓e) (coll) poke

knuffen ['knufən] *tr* (coll) poke

knüllen ['knylən] *tr* crumple

Knüller ['knylər] *m* (-s;-) (coll) hit

knüpfen ['knypfən] *tr* tie, knot; (*Teppich*) weave; (*Bündnis*) form; (*befestigen*) fasten; **k. an** (*acc*) tie in with ‖ *ref*—**sich k. an** (*acc*) be tied in with

Knüppel ['knypəl] *m* (-s;-) cudgel; (*e-s Polizisten*) blackjack; (aer) control stick

knurren ['knurən] *intr* growl, snarl; (*Magen*) rumble; (fig) grumble

knurrig ['knurɪç] *adj* grumpy

knusprig ['knusprɪç] *adj* crisp; (*Mädchen*) attractive

Knute ['knuːtə] *f* (-;-n) whip; (*Gewalt*) power; (*Gewaltherrschaft*) tyranny

knutschen ['knuːtʃən] *tr, recip* & *intr* (coll) neck, pet

Knüttel ['knytəl] *m* (-s;-) cudgel

Knüt'telvers *m* doggerel

k.o. ['ka'o] *adj* knocked out ‖ *adv*—**k.o. schlagen** knock out ‖ **K.O.** *m* (-[s];-s) knockout

Koalition [ko·alɪ'tsjon] *f* (-;-en) coalition

Kobalt ['koːbalt] *n* (-es;) cobalt

Koben ['koːbən] *m* (-s;-) pigsty

Kobold ['koːbɔlt] *m* (-[e]s;-e) goblin

Kobolz [ko'bɔlts] *m*—**e-n K. schließen** do a somersault

Koch [kɔx] *m* (-[e]s;⁓e) cook

Koch'buch *n* cookbook

kochen ['kɔxən] *tr* & *intr* cook; boil

Kocher ['kɔxər] *m* (-s;-) cooker; boiler

Köcher ['kœçər] *m* (-s;-) quiver; golf bag
Koch'fett *n* shortening
Koch'geschirr *n* (mil) mess kit
Koch'herd *m* kitchen range
Köchin ['kœçɪn] *f* (-;-nen) cook
Koch'löffel *m* wooden spoon
Koch'salz *n* table salt
Köder ['kødər] *m* (-s;-) bait; lure
ködern ['kødərn] *tr* bait; lure
Kodex ['kodɛks] *m* (-es;-e) codex; (jur) code
kodifizieren [kodifi'tsirən] *tr* codify
Koffein [kɔfe'in] *n* (-s;) caffeine
Koffer ['kɔfər] *m* (-s;-) suitcase; trunk; case (*for portable items*)
Kof'ferfernseher *m* portable television
Kof'fergerät *n* (rad, telv) portable set
Kof'ferraum *m* (aut) trunk
Kof'ferschreibmaschine *f* portable typewriter
Kognak ['kɔnjak] *m* (-s;-s) cognac
Kohl [kol] *m* (-s;) cabbage; nonsense
Kohle ['kolə] *f* (-;-n) coal; (*Holz-kohle*) charcoal
Kohlehydrat ['koləhydrat] *n* (-[e]s; -e) carbohydrate
kohlen ['kolən] *tr* & *intr* carbonize
Koh'lenbergbau *m* coal mining
Koh'lenbergwerk *n* coal mine
Koh'lendioxyd *n* carbon dioxide
Koh'lenoxyd *n* carbon monoxide
Koh'lenrevier *n* coal field
Koh'lensäure *f* carbonic acid
Koh'lenstoff *m* carbon
Koh'lenwagen *m* coal truck; (rr) coal car
Koh'lepapier *n* carbon paper
Koh'leskizze *f* charcoal sketch
kohl'ra'benschwarz *adj* jet black
Koitus ['ko·ɪtus] *m* (-;) coitus
Koje ['kojə] *f* (-;-n) bunk, berth
Kojote [ko'jotə] *m* (-s;-n) coyote
Kokain [koka'in] *n* (-s;) cocaine
Kokerei [kokə'raɪ] *f* (-;-en) coking plant
kokett [ko'kɛt] *adj* flirtatious || **Kokette** *f* (-;-n) flirt
kokettieren [kokɛ'tirən] *intr* flirt
Kokon [ko'kõ] *m* (-s;-s) cocoon
Kokosnuß ['kokosnus] *f* coconut
Kokospalme ['kokospalmə] *f* coconut palm, coconut tree
Koks [koks] *m* (-es;-e) coke; (coll) nonsense; (*Geld*) (coll) dough
Kolben ['kɔlbən] *m* (-s;-) butt; (*Keule*) mace; (*Löt-*) soldering iron; (aut) piston; (chem) flask; (culin) cob; (elec) bulb
Kol'benhub *m* piston stroke
Kol'benring *m* piston ring
Kol'benstange *f* piston rod
Kolchose [kɔl'çozə] *f* (-;-n) collective farm
Kolibri ['kolibri] *m* (-s;-s) humming bird
Kolik ['kolɪk] *f* (-;-en) colic
Kolkrabe ['kɔlkrabə] *m* (-n;-n) raven
Kollaborateur [kolabora'tør] *m* (-s;-) collaborator (*with the enemy*)
kollaborieren [kolabo'rirən] *intr* collaborate
Kollaps [ko'laps] *m* (-es;-e) collapse

kollationieren [kolatsjo'nirən] *tr* collate
Kol·leg [ko'lek] *n* (-s;-s & –legien ['legjən]) lecture; course of lectures; theological college
Kollege [ko'legə] *m* (-n;-n) colleague
Kolleg'heft *n* lecture notes
Kollegin [ko'legɪn] *f* (-;-nen) colleague
Kollekte [ko'lɛktə] *f* (-;-n) collection; (eccl) collect
Kollektion [kolɛk'tsjon] *f* (-;-en) collection
kollektiv [kolɛk'tif] *adj* collective || **Kollektiv** *n* (-s;-e) collective
Koller ['kɔlər] *m* (-s;) rage, temper
kollern ['kɔlərn] *ref* roll about; (*vor Lachen*) double over || *intr* (*Puter*) gobble; (*Magen*) rumble || *intr* (SEIN) roll
kollidieren [koli'dirən] *intr* (SEIN) collide
Kollier [ko'lir] *n* (-s;-s) necklace
Kollision [koli'zjon] *f* (-;-en) collision
Köln [kœln] *n* (-s;) Cologne
Kölnischwasser ['kœlnɪʃˌvasər] *n* cologne
kolonial [kolo'njal] *adj* colonial
Kolonial'waren *pl* groceries
Kolonial'warengeschäft *n* grocery store
Kolo·nie [kolo'ni] *f* (-;-nien ['ni·ən]) colony
Kolonnade [kolo'nadə] *f* (-;-n) colonnade
Kolonne [ko'lonə] *f* (-;-n) column; (mil) convoy (*of vehicles*)
kolorieren [kolo'rirən] *tr* color
Kolorit [kolo'rit] *n* (-[e]s;-e) coloring
Ko·loß [ko'los] *m* (-losses;-losse) colossus; giant
kolossal [kolo'sal] *adj* colossal
Kolportage [kɔlpor'taʒə] *f* (-;-n) trashy literature; spreading of rumors
kolportieren [kɔlpor'tirən] *tr* peddle; (*Gerüchte*) spread
Kolumnist **–in** [kolum'nɪst(ɪn)] §7 *mf* columnist
Kombi ['kombi] *m* (-s;-s) (coll) station wagon
Kombination [kombina'tsjon] *f* (-; -en) combination; (*Flieger-*) flying suit; (*e-s Monteurs*) coveralls; sport suit; reasoning, deduction; conjecture
kombinieren [kombi'nirən] *tr* combine || *intr* reason
Kom'biwagen *m* station wagon
Kombüse ['kom'byzə] *f* (-;-n) (naut) galley, kitchen
Komik ['komɪk] *f* (-;) humor
Komiker ['komɪkər] *m* (-s;-) comedian
Komikerin ['komɪkərɪn] *f* (-;-nen) comedienne
komisch ['komɪʃ] *adj* funny
Komitee [komi'te] *n* (-s;-s) committee
Komma ['koma] *n* (-s;-s) comma; (*Dezimalzeichen*) decimal point
Kommandant [koman'dant] *m* (-en; -en) commanding officer; commandant

Kommandantur [kɔmandan'tur] *f* (-; -en) headquarters

Kommandeur [kɔman'dør] *m* (-s;-e) commanding officer, commander

kommandieren [kɔman'dirən] *tr* command, order; be in command of; (mil) detail; (mil) detach ‖ *intr* command, be in command

Kommanditgesellschaft [kɔman'ditgəzel/aft] *f* limited partnership; **K. auf Aktien** partnership limited by shares

Kommando [kɔ'mando] *n* (-s;-s) command, order; (mil) command; (mil) detachment, detail; **K. zurück!** as you were!

Komman'dobrücke *f* (nav) bridge

Komman'doraum *m* control room

Komman'dostab *m* baton

Komman'dostand *m*, **Komman'dostelle** *f* command post; (nav) bridge

Komman'dotruppe *f* commando unit

Komman'doturm *m* conning tower; control tower (*of an aircraft carrier*)

kommen ['kɔmən] §99 *intr* (SEIN) come; (geschehen) happen; **auf etw** [*acc*] **k.** hit on s.th.; **auf jeden k. drei Mark** each one gets three marks; **das kommt bloß daher, daß** that's entirely due to; **dazu k.** get around to it; get hold of it; **hinter etw** [*acc*] **k.** find s.th. out; **j-m grob k.** be rude to s.o.; **k. lassen** send for; **nichts k. lassen auf** (*acc*) defend; **so weit k., daß** reach the point where; **ums Leben k.** lose one's life; **wenn Sie mir so k.** if you talk like that to me; **weit k.** get far; **wieder zu sich k.** come to, regain consciousness; **wie kam er denn dazu?** how come he did it? **wie komme ich zum Bahnhof?** how do I get to the train station?

Kommentar [kɔmen'tar] *m* (-s;-) commentary; **kein K.!** no comment!

Kommen·tator [kɔmen'tator] *m* (-s; -tatoren [ta'torən]) commentator

kommentieren [kɔmen'tirən] *tr* comment on

Kommers [kɔ'mers] *m* (-es;-e) drinking party

Kommers'buch *n* students' song book

kommerziell [kɔmer'tsjel] *adj* commercial

Kommilitone [kɔmɪlɪ'tonə] *m* (-n;-n) fellow student

Kom·mis [kɔ'mi] *m* (-mis ['mis]; -mis ['mis]) clerk

Kom·miß [kɔ'mɪs] *m* (-misses;) (coll) army; (coll) army life

Kommissar [kɔmɪ'sar] *m* (-s;-e) commissioner; (pol) commissar

kommissarisch [kɔmɪ'sarɪ/] *adj* provisional, temporary

Kommission [kɔmɪ'sjon] *f* (-;-en) commission, board; **in K.** (com) on consignment; on a commission basis

Kommissionär [kɔmɪsjo'ner] *m* (-s;-e) agent; wholesale bookseller

Kommissions'gebühr *f* (com) commission

kommissions'weise *adv* on a commission basis

Kommiß'stiefel *m* army boot

kommod [kɔ'mot] *adj* comfortable

Kommode [kɔ'modə] *f* (-;-n) bureau, chest of drawers

kommunal [kɔmu'nɑl] *adj* municipal, local

Kommunal'politik *f* local politics

Kommune [kɔ'munə] *f* (-;-n) municipality; **die K.** the Commies

Kommunikant -in [kɔmunɪ'kant(ɪn)] §7 *mf* communicant

Kommunion [kɔmu'njon] *f* (-;-en) Communion

Kommuniqué [kɔmynɪ'ke] *n* (-s;-s) communiqué

Kommunismus [kɔmu'nɪsmus] *m* (-;) communism

Kommunist -in [kɔmu'nɪst(ɪn)] §7 *mf* communist

kommunistisch [kɔmu'nɪstɪ/] *adj* communist(ic)

Komödiant [kɔmø'djant] *m* (-en;-en) comedian; (pej) ham

Komödie [kɔ'mødjə] *f* (-;-n) comedy; **K. spielen** (coll) put on an act

Kompagnon [kɔmpan'jõ] *m* (-s;-s) (business) partner; associate

kompakt [kɔm'pakt] *adj* compact

Kompa·nie [kɔmpa'ni] *f* (-;-nien ['ni·ən]) company

Kompanie'chef *m* company commander

komparativ [kɔmpara'tif] *adj* comparative ‖ **Komparativ** *m* (-s;-e) comparative

Komparse [kɔm'parzə] *m* (-n;-n) (theat) extra

Kom·paß ['kɔmpas] *m* (-passes; -passe) compass

Kompen·dium [kɔm'pendjum] *n* (-s; -dien [djən]) compendium

Kompensation [kɔmpenza'tsjon] *f* (-; -en) compensation

Kompensations'geschäft *n* fair-value exchange

kompensieren [kɔmpen'zirən] *tr* compensate for, offset

Kompetenz [kɔmpe'tents] *f* (-;-en) (jur) jurisdiction

komplementär [kɔmplemen'ter] *adj* complementary

Komplet [kõ'ple] *n* (-s;-s) dress with matching coat

komplett [kɔm'plet] *adj* complete; everything included

komplex [kɔm'pleks] *adj* complex ‖ **Komplex** *m* (-es;-e) complex

Komplice [kɔm'plitsə] *m* (-n;-n) accomplice

komplizieren [kɔmplɪ'tsirən] *tr* complicate

Komplott [kɔm'plɔt] *n* (-[e]s;-e) plot

Komponente [kɔmpə'nentə] *f* (-;-n) component

komponieren [kɔmpə'nirən] *tr* compose

Komponist -in [kɔmpə'nɪst(ɪn)] §7 *mf* composer

Komposition [kɔmpozɪ'tsjon] *f* (-;-en) composition

Komposi·tum [kɔm'pozitum] *n* (-s; -ta [ta] & -ten [tən]) compound (word)

Kompott [kɔm'pɔt] *n* (-[e]s;-e) stewed fruit

Kompres·sor [kɔm'presɔr] *m* (-s; -soren ['soːrən]) compressor; (aut) supercharger

komprimieren [kɔmprɪ'miːrən] *tr* compress

Kompro·miß [kɔmprɔ'mɪs] *m* (-misses; -misse) compromise

kompromittieren [kɔmprɔmɪ'tiːrən] *tr* compromise

kondensieren [kɔndɛn'ziːrən] *tr, ref & intr* (SEIN) condense

Kondensmilch [kɔn'dɛnsmɪlç] *f* evaporated milk

Kondens'streifen [kɔn'dɛns/traɪfən] *m* contrail

Konditorei [kɔndɪtɔ'raɪ] *f* (-;-en) pastry shop

Konfekt [kɔn'fɛkt] *n* (-[e]s;) candy, chocolates; fancy cookies

Konfektion [kɔnfɛk'tsjoːn] *f* (-;) ready-made clothes; manufacture of ready-made clothes

Konfektionär [kɔnfɛktsjɔ'nɛːr] *m* (-s; -e) clothing manufacturer; clothing retailer

konfektionieren [kɔnfɛktsjɔ'niːrən] *tr* manufacture (*clothes*)

Konferenz [kɔnfe'rɛnts] *f* (-;-en) conference

konferieren [kɔnfe'riːrən] *intr* confer, hold a conference

Konfession [kɔnfɛ'sjoːn] *f* (-;-en) religious denomination; (eccl) confession; confession of faith, creed

konfessionell [kɔnfɛsjɔ'nɛl] *adj* denominational

konfessions'los *adj* nondenominational

Konfessions'schule *f* denominational school, parochial school

konfirmieren [kɔnfɪr'miːrən] *tr* (eccl) (Prot) confirm

konfiszieren [kɔnfɪs'tsiːrən] *tr* confiscate

Konfitüre [kɔnfɪ'tyːrə] *f* (-;-n) jam

Konflikt [kɔn'flɪkt] *m* (-[e]s;-e) conflict

konform [kɔn'fɔrm] *adj* concurring; **mit j-m k. gehen** agree with s.o.

Konfrontation [kɔnfrɔnta'tsjoːn] *f* (-; -en) confrontation

konfrontieren [kɔnfrɔn'tiːrən] *tr* confront

konfus [kɔn'fuːs] *adj* confused, puzzled

Kongruenz [kɔngru'ɛnts] *f* (-;) (geom) congruence; (gram) agreement

König ['køːnɪç] *m* (-[e]s;-e) king

Königin ['køːnɪgɪn] *f* (-;-nen) queen

kö'niglich *adj* kingly, royal

Kö'nigreich *n* kingdom

Kö'nigsadler *m* golden eagle

Kö'nigsrose *f* (bot) peony

Kö'nigsschlange *f* boa constrictor

kö'nigstreu *adj* royalist

Kö'nigswürde *f* kingship

Königtum ['køːnɪçtum] *n* (-s;) royalty, kinship; monarchy

konisch ['koːnɪʃ] *adj* conical

konjugieren [kɔnju'giːrən] *tr* conjugate

Konjunktion [kɔnjuŋk'tsjoːn] *f* (-;-en) conjunction

Konjunktiv ['kɔnjuŋk'tiːf] *m* (-s;-e) subjunctive mood

Konjunktur [kɔnjuŋk'tuːr] *f* (-;-en)

economic situation; business trend; (*Hochstand*) boom

konkav [kɔn'kaːf] *adj* concave

konkret [kɔn'kreːt] *adj* concrete

Konkurrent -in [kɔnku'rɛnt(ɪn)] §7 *mf* competitor

Konkurrenz [kɔnku'rɛnts] *f* (-;-en) competition; **K. machen** (*dat*) compete with

konkurrenz'fähig *adj* competitive

konkurrieren [kɔnku'riːrən] *intr* compete

Konkurs [kɔn'kurs] *m* (-es;-e) bankruptcy; **in K. gehen** (or **geraten**) go bankrupt; **K. anmelden** declare bankruptcy

Konkurs'masse *f* bankrupt company's assets

können ['kœnən] §100 *tr* able to do; know; **ich kann nichts dafür** I can't help it || *intr*—**ich kann nicht hinein** I can't get in || *mod aux* be able to; know how to; be allowed; **das kann sein** that may be; **ich kann nicht sehen** I can't see || **Können** *n* (-s;) ability

Könner ['kœnər] *m* (-s;-) expert

konnte ['kɔntə] *pret* of **können**

konsequent [kɔnze'kvɛnt] *adj* consistent

Konsequenz [kɔnze'kvɛnts] *f* (-;-en) consistency; (*Folge*) consequence

konservativ [kɔnzerva'tiːf] *adj* conservative

Konservato·rium [kɔnzerva'toːrjum] *n* (-s;-rien [rjən]) conservatory

Konserve [kɔn'zɛrvə] *f* (-;-n) canned food

Konser'venbüchse *f*, **Konser'vendose** *f* can

Konser'venfabrik *f* cannery

Konser'venöffner *m* can opener

konservieren [kɔnzer'viːrən] *tr* preserve

Konservie'rung *f* (-;) preservation

Konsisto·rium [kɔnzɪs'toːrjum] *n* (-s; -rien [rjən]) (eccl) consistory

Konsole [kɔn'zoːlə] *f* (-;-n) bracket; (archit) console

konsolidieren [kɔnzɔlɪ'diːrən] *tr* consolidate

Konsonant [kɔnzo'nant] *m* (-en;-en) consonant

Konsorte [kɔn'zɔrtə] *m* (-n;-n) (pej) accomplice; (fin) member of a syndicate

Konsor·tium [kɔn'zɔrtjum] *n* (-s;-tien [tjən]) (fin) syndicate

konstant [kɔn'stant] *adj* constant || **Konstante** §5 *f* (math, phys) constant

konstatieren [kɔnsta'tiːrən] *tr* ascertain; state; (med) diagnose

konsterniert [kɔnster'niːrt] *adj* stunned

konstituieren [kɔnstitu'iːrən] *tr* constitute || *ref* be established; **sich als Ausschuß k.** form a committee of the whole

konstitutionell [kɔnstitutsjɔ'nɛl] *adj* constitutional

konstruieren [kɔnstru'iːrən] *tr* construct; (*entwerfen*) design; (gram) construe

Konsul ['kɔnzul] *m* (-s;-n) consul

konsularisch [kɔnzu'larɪʃ] *adj* consular

Konsulat [kɔnzu'lat] *n* (-[e]s;-e) consulate; (hist) consulship

Konsulent [kɔnzu'lɛnt(ɪn)] §7 *mf* (jur) counsel

konsultieren [kɔnzul'tirən] *tr* consult

Konsum [kɔn'zum] *m* (-s;-s) cooperative store; (com) consumption

Konsument -in [kɔnzu'mɛnt(ɪn)] §7 *mf* consumer

Konsum'güter *pl* consumer goods

konsumieren [kɔnzu'mirən] *tr* consume

Konsum'verein *m* cooperative society

Kontakt [kɔn'takt] *m* (-[e]s;-e) contact

Kontakt'glas *n*, **Kontakt'schale** *f* contact lens

Konteradmiral ['kɔntəratmiral] *m* rear admiral

Konterfei [kɔntər'faɪ] *n* (-s;-e) portrait, likeness

kontern ['kɔntərn] *tr* counter

Kontinent ['kɔntinɛnt] *m* (-[e]s;-e) continent

Kontingent [kɔntɪŋ'gɛnt] *n* (-[e]s;-e) quota; (mil) contingent

Kon-to ['kɔnto] *n* (-s;-s & -ten [tən]) account

Kon'toauszug *m* bank statement

Kontor [kɔn'tor] *n* (-s;-e) (com) office

Kontorist -in [kɔnto'rɪst(ɪn)] §7 *mf* clerk (*in an office*)

Kontrahent [kɔntra'hɛnt] *m* (-en;-en) contracting party; dueller

kontrahieren [kɔntra'hirən] *tr* & *intr* contract

Kontrakt [kɔn'trakt] *m* (-[e]s;-e) contract

Kontrapunkt ['kɔntrapuŋkt] *m* (mus) counterpoint

konträr [kɔn'trer] *adj* contrary

Kontrast [kɔn'trast] *m* (-[e]s;-e) contrast

konstrastieren [kɔntras'tirən] *intr* contrast

Kontrast'regelung *f* (telv) contrast button

Kontroll- [kɔntrɔl] *comb.fm.* checking; control

Kontroll'abschnitt *m* stub (*of ticket*)

Kontrolle [kɔn'trɔlə] *f* (-;-n) control; check, inspection

Kontrolleur [kɔntrɔ'lør] *m* (-s;-e) inspector, supervisor; (aer) air-traffic controller; (indust) timekeeper

kontrollieren [kɔntrɔ'lirən] *tr* control; check, inspect; (*Bücher*) audit

Kontroll'kasse *f* cash register

Kontroll'leuchte *f* (aut) warning light (*on dashboard*)

Kontroll'turm *m* (aer) control tower

Kontroverse [kɔntrə'vɛrzə] *f* (-;-n) controversy

Kontur [kɔn'tur] *f* (-;-en) contour

Konvent [kɔn'vɛnt] *m* (-[e]s;-e) convent; monastery; (*Versammlung*) convention

Konvention [kɔnvɛn'tsjon] *f* (-;-en) convention

konventionell [kɔnvɛntsjə'nɛl] *adj* conventional

Konversation [kɔnvɛrza'tsjon] *f* (-;-en) conversation

Konversations'lexikon *n* encyclopedia; **wandelndes K.** (coll) walking encyclopedia

konvertieren [kɔnvɛr'tirən] *tr* convert || *intr* be converted

Konvertit -in [kɔnvɛr'tit(ɪn)] §7 *mf* convert

konvex [kɔn'vɛks] *adj* convex

Konvikt [kɔn'vɪkt] *n* (-s;-e) minor seminary

Konvoi ['kɔnvɔɪ] *m* (-s;-s) convoy

Konvolut [kɔnvə'lut] *n* (-[e]s;-e) bundle, roll

Konzentration [kɔntsɛntra'tsjon] *f* (-; -en) concentration

Konzentrations'lager *n* concentration camp

konzentrieren [kɔntsɛn'trirən] *tr* & *ref* (auf *acc*) concentrate (*on*)

konzentrisch [kɔn'tsɛntrɪʃ] *adj* concentric

Konzept [kɔn'tsɛpt] *n* (-[e]s;-e) rough draft; **aus dem K. bringen** confuse, throw off; **aus dem K. kommen** lose one's train of thought

Konzept'papier *n* scribbling paper

Konzern [kɔn'tsɛrn] *m* (-[e]s;-e) (com) combine

Konzert [kɔn'tsɛrt] *n* (-[e]s;-e) concert

Konzert'flügel *m* grand piano

Konzession [kɔntse'sjon] *f* (-;-en) concession; license

konzessionieren [kɔntsɛsjə'nirən] *tr* (com) license

Kon-zil [kɔn'tsil] *n* (-[e]s;-e & -zilien ['tsiljən]) (eccl) council

konziliant [kɔntsi'ljant] *adj* conciliatory; understanding

konzipieren [kɔntsi'pirən] *tr* conceive

koordinieren [kɔ'ɔrdɪ'nirən] *tr* coordinate

Kopf [kɔpf] *m* (-es;⁻e) head; **aus dem Kopfe** by heart; **j-m über den K. wachsen** be taller than s.o.; (fig) be too much for s.o.; **mit dem K. voran** head first; **seinen eigenen K. haben** have a mind of one's own; **seinen K. lassen müssen** lose one's life

Kopf'bedeckung *f* headgear, head wear

Kopf'brett *n* headboard

köpfen ['kœpfən] *tr* behead; (*Baum*) top; (fb) head

Kopf'ende *n* head (*of bed, etc.*)

Kopf'geld *n* reward (*for capture of criminal*)

Kopf'haut *f* scalp

Kopf'hörer *m* headset, earphones

-köpfig [kœpfɪç] *comb.fm.* -headed; -man

Kopf'kissen *n* pillow

Kopf'kissenbezug *m* pillowcase

kopf'lastig *adj* top-heavy

Kopf'lehne *f* headrest

Kopf'rechnen *n* (-s;) mental arithmetic

Kopf'salat *m* head lettuce

kopf'scheu *adj* (*Pferd*) nervous; (*Person*) shy; **k. werden** become alarmed

Kopf'schmerzen *pl* headache

Kopf'schuppen *pl* dandruff

Kopf'sprung *m* dive; **e-n K. machen** dive

Kopf'stand *m* handstand; **e-n K. machen** (aer) nose over

Kopf'stärke *f* (mil) strength

kopf'stehen §146 *intr* stand on one's head; (fig) be upside down

Kopf'steinpflaster *n* cobblestones

Kopf'steuer *f* poll tax

Kopf'stimme *f* falsetto

Kopf'stoß *m* butt; (fb) header

Kopf'tuch *n* kerchief, babushka

kopfü'ber *adv* head over heels

kopfun'ter *adv*—**kopfüber k.** head over heels

Kopf'weh *n* headache

Kopf'wellenknall *m* sonic boom

Ko·pie [ko'piː] *f* (-;-pien ['piː·ən]) copy, duplicate; (phot) print

kopieren [ko'piːrən] *tr* copy; (phot) print

Kopier'maschine *f* copier, photocopying machine

Kopier'papier *n* tracing paper; carbon paper; (phot) printing paper

Kopier'stift *m* indelible pencil

Koppel ['kɔpəl] *f* (-;-n) leash; (*Gehege*) enclosure, paddock ‖ *n* (-s;-) (mil) belt

koppeln ['kɔpəln] *tr* tie together, yoke; (fig) tie in; (elec) connect; (rad, rr) couple; (rok) dock ‖ **Koppeln** *n* (-s;) (aer, naut) dead reckoning; (rok) docking

Kopplungsgeschäft ['kɔplʊŋsɡəʃeft] *n* package deal

Koralle [ko'ralə] *f* (-;-n) coral

Korb [kɔrp] *m* (-[e]s;∸e) basket; **j-m den K. geben** (fig) give s.o. the brush-off

Korb'ball *m* basketball

Körbchen ['kœrpçən] *n* (-s;-) little basket; (*e-s Büstenhalters*) cup

Korb'flasche *f* demijohn

Korb'geflecht *n* wickerwork

Korb'möbel *pl* wicker furniture

Korb'weide *f* (bot) osier

Kordel ['kɔrdəl] *f* (-;-n) cord

Kordon [kɔr'dõ] *m* (-s;-s) cordon; (*Ordensband*) ribbon

Korea [ko're·a] *n* (-s;) Korea

koreanisch [kore'aːnɪʃ] *adj* Korean

Korinthe [ko'rɪntə] *f* (-;-n) currant

Kork [kɔrk] *m* (-[e]s;-e) cork

Korken ['kɔrkən] *m* (-s;-) cork, stopper

Korkenzieher ['kɔrkəntsiː·ər] *m* (-s;-) corkscrew

Korn [kɔrn] *n* (-[e]s;∸er) grain; seed; (*am Gewehr*) bead; (*Getreide*) rye; (*e-r Münze*) fineness; (phot) graininess; **j-n aufs K. nehmen** draw a bead on s.o.

Korn'ähre *f* ear of grain

Korn'branntwein *m* whiskey

Kornett [kɔr'net] *n* (-[e]s;-e) (mus) cornet

körnig ['kœrnɪç] *adj* granular

Korn'kammer *f* granary; (fig) breadbasket

koronar [koro'naːr] *adj* coronary

Körper ['kœrpər] *m* (-s;-) body; (geom, phys) solid

Kör'perbau *m* (-[e]s;) build, physique

kör'perbehindert *adj* physically handicapped

Kör'perbeschaffenheit *f* constitution

Körperchen ['kœrpərçən] *n* (-s;-) corpuscle

Kör'perfülle *f* plumpness, corpulence

Kör'pergeruch *m* body odor

Kör'perhaltung *f* posture, bearing

Kör'perkraft *f* physical strength

kör'perlich *adj* physical; (*stofflich*) corporeal

Kör'perpflege *f* personal hygiene

Kör'perpuder *m* talcum powder

Kör'perschaft *f* (-;-en) body (*of persons*); corporation

Kör'perverletzung *f* bodily injury

Korporation [kɔrpora'tsjoːn] *f* (-;-en) corporation

Korps [kɔr] *n* (- [kɔrs];- [kɔrs]) corps

Korps'geist *m* esprit de corps

Korps'student *m* member of a fraternity

korrekt [kɔ'rekt] *adj* correct, proper

Korrek·tor [kɔ'rektor] *m* (-s;-toren ['toːrən]) proofreader

Korrektur [kɔrek'tuːr] *f* (-;-en) correction; proofreading

Korrektur'bogen *m* page proof

Korrektur'fahne *f* galley proof

Korrelat [kɔre'laːt] *n* (-[e]s;-e) correlative

Korrespondent –in [kɔrespɔn'dent(ɪn)] §7 *mf* correspondent

Korrespondenz [kɔrespɔn'dents] *f* (-;-en) correspondence

Korrespondenz'karte *f* (Aust) postcard

Korridor ['kɔridor] *m* (-s;-e) corridor

korrigieren [kɔri'giːrən] *tr* correct

korrodieren [kɔro'diːrən] *tr & intr* corrode

Korse ['kɔrzə] *m* (-n;-n) Corsican

Korsett [kɔr'zet] *n* (-[e]s;-e & -s) corset

Korsika ['kɔrzika] *n* (-s;) Corsica

Korvette [kɔr'vetə] *f* (-;-n) corvette

Kosak [ko'zak] *m* (-en;-en) Cossack

K.-o.-Schlag [ka'oʃlak] *m* knockout punch

kosen ['koːzən] *tr* fondle, caress

Kosename ['koːzanamə] *m* pet name

Kosmetik [kɔs'meːtɪk] *f* (-;) beauty treatment; **chirugische K.** cosmetic surgery, plastic surgery

Kosme'tikartikel *m* cosmetic

Kosme'ti·kum [kɔs'meːtɪkʊm] *n* (-s;-ka [ka]) cosmetic

kosmisch ['kɔzmɪʃ] *adj* cosmic

kosmopolitisch [kɔsmopo'liːtɪʃ] *adj* cosmopolitan

Kosmos ['kɔsmɔs] *m* (-;) cosmos

Kost [kɔst] *f* (-;) food, board

kostbar ['kɔstbar] *adj* valuable; costly

Kost'barkeit *f* (-;-en) costliness; (fig) precious thing

kosten ['kɔstən] *tr* cost; taste, sip ‖ **Kosten** *pl* costs; (*auf K. (genit) at the expense of; **auf seine K. kommen** get one's money's worth; **sich in K. stürzen** go to great expense

Ko'stenanschlag *m* estimate

Ko'stenaufwand *m* expenditure, outlay

Ko'stenberechnung *f* cost accounting

Ko'stenersatz m, **Ko'stenerstattung** f reimbursement of expenses
ko'stenlos adj free of charge
Ko'stenvoranschlag m estimate
Kost'gänger –in §6 mf boarder
köstlich ['kœstlɪç] adj delicious; delightful || adv—**sich k.** amüsieren have a grand time
Kost'probe f sample (to taste)
kostspielig ['kɔst/pilɪç] adj expensive
Kostüm [kɔs'tym] n (–s;–e) costume; woman's suit; fancy dress
kostümieren [kɔsty'mirən] tr & ref dress up
Kostüm'probe f dress rehearsal
Kot [kot] m (–[e]s;) mud, dirt; (tierischer) dirt, dung; excrement
Kotelett [kɔtə'lɛt] n (–[e]s;–e & –s) pork chop; cutlet
Köter ['køtər] m (–s;–) mut, mongrel
Kot'flügel m (aut) fender
kotig ['kotɪç] adj muddy, dirty
kotzen ['kɔtsən] intr (sl) puke || **Kotzen** n—**es ist zum K.** it's enough to make you throw up
Krabbe ['krabə] f (–;–n) crab; shrimp; (niedliches Kind) little darling
krabbeln ['krabəln] tr & intr tickle || intr (SEIN) crawl
Krach [krax] m (–[e]s;–s & –e) crash, bang; (Lärm) racket; (Streit) row; (fin) crash; **K. machen** kick up a row
krachen ['kraxən] intr crash, crack
krächzen ['krɛçtsən] intr croak, caw
kraft [kraft] prep (genit) by virtue of || **Kraft** f (–;̈e) strength, power, force; **außer K. setzen** repeal; **in K. sein** be in force; **in K. treten** come into force
Kraft'anlage f (elec) power plant
Kraft'anstrengung f strenuous effort
Kraft'aufwand m effort
Kraft'ausdruck m swear word; **Kraftausdrücke** strong language
Kraft'brühe f concentrated broth
Kraft'fahrer –in §6 mf motorist
Kraft'fahrzeug n motor vehicle
kräftig ['krɛftɪç] adj strong, powerful; (Speise) nutritious || adv hard; heartily
kräftigen ['krɛftɪgən] tr strengthen
Kraft'leistung f feat of strength
kraft'los adj powerless; weak
Kraft'meier m (coll) bully; (coll) muscle man
Kraft'probe f test of strength
Kraft'protz m (coll) powerhouse
Kraft'rad n motorcycle
Kraft'stoff m fuel
Kraft'stoffleitung f fuel line
kraftstrotzend ['kraft/trɔtsənt] adj strapping
Kraft'übertragung f (aut) transmission
Kraft'wagen m motor vehicle
Kraft'werk n generating plant
Kraft'wort n (–[e]s;̈er) swear word
Kragen ['kragən] m (–s;–) collar
Krähe ['krɛ·ə] f (–;–n) crow
krähen ['krɛ·ən] intr crow
Krähenfüße ['krɛ·ənfysə] pl crow's feet (wrinkles)
Krakeel [kra'kel] m (–s;–e) (coll) rumpus; (lauter Streit) brawl

krakeelen [kra'kelən] intr (coll) kick up a storm
Kralle ['kralə] f (–;–n) claw
Kram [kram] m (–[e]s;) (coll) things, stuff; (coll) business, affairs
kramen ['kramən] intr rummage
Krämer –in ['krɛmər(ɪn)] §6 mf shopkeeper || m (pej) philistine
Krä'merseele f philistine
Kram'laden m general store
Krampe ['krampə] f (–;–n) staple
Krampf [krampf] m (–[e]s;̈e) cramp, spasm; convulsion; (Unsinn) nonsense
Krampf'ader f varicose vein
krampf'artig adj spasmodic
krampf'haft adj convulsive
Kran [kran] m (–[e]s;̈e & –e) (mach) crane
Kranich ['kranɪç] m (–s;–e) (orn) crane
krank [krank] adj sick, ill || **Kranke** §5 mf patient
–krank comb.fm. suffering from
kränkeln ['krɛŋkəln] intr be sickly
kranken ['kraŋkən] intr—**k. an** (dat) suffer from
kränken ['krɛŋkən] tr hurt, offend || ref (über acc) feel hurt (at)
Kran'kenanstalt f hospital
Kran'kenbahre f stretcher
Kran'kenbett n sickbed
Kran'kenfahrstuhl m wheel chair
Kran'kengeld n sick benefit
Kran'kenhaus n hospital; **ins K. einweisen** hospitalize
Kran'kenkasse f medical insurance plan
Kran'kenlager n sickbed
Kran'kenpflege f nursing
Kran'kenpfleger –in §6 mf nurse
Kran'kenrevier n (mil) sick quarters; (nav) sick bay
Kran'kensaal m hospital ward
Kran'kenschwester f nurse
Kran'kenstube f infirmary
Kran'kenstuhl m wheel chair
Kran'kenurlaub m sick leave
Kran'kenversicherung f health insurance
Kran'kenwagen m ambulance
krank'feiern intr (coll) play sick
krank'haft adj morbid, pathological
Krank'heit f (–;–en) sickness, disease
Krank'heitsbericht m medical bulletin
Krank'heitserscheinung f symptom
kränklich ['krɛŋklɪç] adj sickly
Kränk'lichkeit f (–;) poor health
Kränkung ['krɛŋkuŋ] f (–;–en) offense
Kran'wagen m (aut) wrecker, tow truck
Kranz [krants] m (–[e]s;̈e) wreath
Kränzchen ['krɛntsçən] n (–s;–) small wreath; ladies' circle; informal dance
kränzen ['krɛntsən] tr wreathe
Krapfen ['krapfən] m (–s;–) doughnut
kraß [kras] adj crass, gross
Krater ['kratər] m (–s;–) crater
Kratzbürste ['kratsbyrstə] f wire brush; (fig) stand-offish woman
Krätze ['krɛtsə] f (–;) itch, scabies
kratzen ['kratsən] tr & intr scratch
Krat'zer m (–s;–) scratch; scraper

krauen ['krau·ən] *tr* scratch gently

kraus [kraus] *adj* (*Haar*) frizzy; (*Gedanken*) confused; **die Stirn k. ziehen** knit one's brows

Krause ['krauzə] *f* (-;-n) ruffle

kräuseln ['krɔɪzəln] *tr & ref* curl

Krau'seminze *f* (bot) spearmint

Kraus'haar *n* frizz

Kraut [kraut] *n* (-[e]s;⁼er) herb, plant; leafy top; (*Kohl*) cabbage; **ins K. schießen** run wild

Krawall [kra'val] *m* (-[e]s;-e) riot; (coll) rumpus

Krawatte [kra'vatə] *f* (-;-n) necktie

Krawat'tenhalter *m* tie clip

kraxeln ['kraksəln] *intr* (SEIN) climb

Kreatur [kre·a'tur] *f* (-;-en) creature

Krebs [kreps] *m* (-es;-e) crawfish, crab; (pathol) cancer

krebs'artig *adj* (pathol) cancerous

Kredenz [kre'dɛnts] *f* (-;-en) buffet, credenza, sideboard

kredenzen [kre'dɛntsən] *tr* (*Wein*) serve

Kredit [kre'dit] *m* (-[e]s;-e) credit

Kredit'bank *f* commercial bank

kreditieren [kredɪ'tirən] *tr* credit || *intr* give credit

Kredit'karte *f* credit card

Kredit'würdigkeit *f* trustworthiness; (com) credit rating

Kreide ['kraɪdə] *f* (-;-n) chalk, piece of chalk, crayon

kreieren [kre'irən] *tr* create

Kreis [kraɪs] *m* (-es;-e) circle; (*Bereich*) field; (*Bezirk*) district; (adm) county; (elec) circuit

Kreis'abschnitt *m* segment

Kreis'amt *n* district office

Kreis'ausschnitt *m* sector

Kreis'bahn *f* orbit

Kreis'bogen *m* (geom) arc

kreischen ['kraɪ/ən] *intr* shriek

Kreisel ['kraɪzəl] *m* (-s;-) gyroscope; top (*toy*)

Krei'selbewegung *f* gyration

Krei'selhorizont *m* artificial horizon

kreiseln ['kraɪzəln] *intr* spin, rotate, gyrate; spin the top

Krei'selpumpe *f* centrifugal pump

kreisen ['kraɪzən] *intr* circle; revolve; (*Blut*) circulate

kreis'förmig *adj* circular

Kreis'lauf *m* circulation; cycle

Kreis'laufsstörung *f* circulatory disorder

kreis'rund *adj* circular

Kreis'säge *f* circular saw, buzz saw

kreißen ['kraɪsən] *intr* be in labor

Kreißsaal ['kraɪszal] *m* delivery room

Kreis'stadt *f* (rural) county seat

Kreis'umfang *m* circumference

Kreis'verkehr *m* traffic circle

Krem [krem] *f* (-;-s) & *m* (-s;-s) cream

Kreml ['kreməl] *m* (-[e]s;) Kremlin

Krempe ['krɛmpə] *f* (-;-n) brim, rim

Krempel ['krɛmpəl] *m* (-s;) (coll) stuff, junk || *f* (-;-n) (tex) card

Kren [kren] *m* (-[e]s;) horseradish

krepieren [kre'pirən] *intr* (SEIN) (*Tiere*) die; (*Granate*) explode, burst; (sl) kick the bucket

Krepp [krep] *m* (-s;-s) crepe

Kreta ['kreta] *n* (-s;) Crete

Kretonne [kre'tɔnə] *f* (-;-n) cretonne

kreuz [krɔɪts] *adv*—**k. und quer** crisscross || **Kreuz** *n* (-es;-e) cross; small of the back; (cards) club(s)

Kreuz'abnahme *f* deposition

Kreuz'band *n* (-[e]s;⁼er) mailing wrapper (*for newspapers, etc.*)

kreuz'brav' *adj* (coll) very honest; (coll) very well-behaved

kreuzen ['krɔɪtsən] *tr* cross || *recip* cross; interbreed || *intr* cruise

Kreuzer ['krɔɪtsər] *m* (-s;-) penny; (nav) cruiser

Kreuz'fahrer *m* crusader

Kreuz'fahrt *f* cruise; (hist) crusade

Kreuz'feuer *n* crossfire

kreuz'fidel' *adj* very cheerful

Kreuz'gang *m* (archit) cloister(s)

kreuzigen ['krɔɪtsɪgən] *tr* crucify

Kreu'zigung *f* (-;-en) crucifixion

Kreuz'otter *f* adder

Kreuz'ritter *m* crusader; Knight of the Teutonic Order

Kreuz'schiff *m* transept (of church)

Kreuz'schlitzschraubenzieher *m* Phillips screwdriver

Kreu'zung *f* (-;-en) intersection; crossbreeding; hybrid; (rr) crossing

Kreuz'verhör *n* cross-examination; **j-n ins K. nehmen** cross-examine s.o.

Kreuz'verweis *m* cross reference

Kreuz'weg *m* crossroad; (eccl) stations of the cross

Kreuz'worträtsel *n* crossword puzzle

Kreuz'zeichen *n* (eccl) sign of the cross; (typ) dagger

Kreuz'zug *m* crusade

kribbelig ['krɪbəlɪç] *adj* irritable; (*nervös*) edgy, on edge

kribbeln ['krɪbəln] *intr* tickle

kriechen ['kriçən] §102 *intr* (SEIN) creep, crawl

kriecherisch ['kriçərɪ/] *adj* fawning

Kriechtier ['kriçtir] *n* reptile

Krieg [krik] *m* (-[e]s;-e) war

kriegen ['krigən] *tr* (coll) get, catch

Krie'ger *m* (-s;-) warrior

kriegerisch ['krigərɪ/] *adj* warlike; (*Person*) belligerent

krieg'führend *adj* warring

Kriegs'akademie *f* war college

Kriegs'bemalung *f* war paint

Kriegs'berichter *m*, **Kriegs'berichterstatter** *m* war correspondent

Kriegs'dienst *m* military service

Kriegs'dienstverweigerer *m* conscientious objector

Kriegs'einsatz *m* (mil) action

Kriegs'entschädigung *f* reparations

Kriegs'fall *m*—**im K.** in case of war

Kriegs'flotte *f* fleet; naval force

Kriegs'fuß *m*—**mit j-m auf K. stehen** be at loggerheads with s.o.

Kriegs'gebiet *n* war zone

Kriegs'gefangene §5 *mf* prisoner of war

Kriegs'gericht *n* court martial

Kriegsgewinner ['kriksgəvɪnlər] *m* (-s;-) war profiteer

Kriegs'hafen *m* naval base

Kriegs'hetzer *m* warmonger

Kriegs'kamerad m fellow soldier
Kriegs'lazarett n base hospital
Kriegs'list f stratagem
Kriegs'marine f navy
Kriegs'ministerium n war department
Kriegs'opfer n war victim
Kriegs'pfad m warpath
Kriegs'rat m council of war
Kriegs'recht n martial law
Kriegs'rüstung f arming for war; war production
Kriegs'schauplatz m theater of war
Kriegs'schuld f war debt; war guilt
Kriegs'teilnehmer m combatant; (*ehemaliger*) ex-serviceman, veteran
Kriegs'verbrechen n war crime
Kriegs'versehrte §5 m disabled veteran
kriegs'verwendungsfähig adj fit for active duty
Kriegs'wesen n warfare, war
Kriegs'zug m (mil) campaign
Kriegs'zustand m state of war
Krim [krɪm] f (-;) Crimea
Krimi ['krimi] m (-s;-s) & (-;-s) (coll) murder mystery; (telv) thriller
kriminal [krɪmɪ'nɑl] adj criminal
Kriminal– comb.fm. criminal, crime
Kriminal'beamte m criminal investigator
Kriminal'roman m detective novel
Kriminal'stück n (telv) thriller
kriminell [krɪmɪ'nɛl] adj criminal ||
Kriminelle §5 mf criminal
Krimskrams ['krɪmskrams] m (-es;) (coll) junk
Kripo ['kripo] abbr (**Kriminalpolizei**) crime squad
Krippe ['krɪpə] f (-;-n) crib, manger; day nursery (*for infants up to 3 years*)
Krise ['krizə] f (-;-n) crisis
kriseln ['krizəln] impers—es kriselt there's a crisis, trouble is brewing
Kristall [krɪs'tal] m (-s;-e) crystal
Kristalleuchter (**Kristall'leuchter**) m crystal chandelier
Kristall'glas n crystal glass
kristallisieren [krɪstalɪ'zirən] ref & intr crystallize
Kristall'zucker m granulated sugar
Krite-rium [krɪ'terjʊm] n (-s;-rien [rjən]) criterion
Kritik [krɪ'tik] f (-;-en) criticism; critique; **unter aller K.** abominable
Kritikaster [krɪtɪ'kaster] m (-s;-) (pej) faultfinder
Kritiker –in ['krɪtɪkər(ɪn)] §6 mf critic; reviewer
kritik'los adj uncritical
kritisch ['krɪtɪʃ] adj critical
kritisieren [krɪtɪ'zirən] tr criticize; (*werten*) review
Kri'telei [krɪtə'lai] f (-;-en) faultfinding; petty criticism
kritteln ['krɪtəln] intr (an dat) find fault (with), grumble (about)
Kritzelei [krɪtsə'lai] f (-;-en) scribbling, scrawling; scribble, scrawl
kritzeln ['krɪtsəln] tr & intr scribble
kroch [krɔx] pret of **kriechen**
Krokodil [krɔkə'dil] n (-[e]s;-e) crocodile
Krokus ['krokus] m (-;- & -se) crocus

Krone ['kronə] f (-;-n) crown
krönen ['krønən] tr crown
Kronerbe ['kronerbə] m, **Kronerbin** ['kronerbɪn] f heir apparent
Kronleuchter ['kronlɔiçtər] m chandelier
Kronprinz ['kronprɪnts] m crown prince
Kronprinzessin ['kronprɪntsesɪn] f crown princess
Krö'nung f (-;-en) coronation
Kropf [krɔpf] m (-[e]s;ᵘe) crop (*of bird*); (pathol) goiter
Kröte ['krøtə] f (-;-n) toad; **Kröten** (coll) coins, coppers
Krücke ['krykə] f (-;-n) crutch
Krückstock ['kryk/tɔk] m walking stick
Krug [kruk] m (-[e]s;ᵘe) jar, jug; mug; pitcher; (*Wirtshaus*) tavern
Krume ['krumə] f (-;-n) crumb; topsoil
Krümel ['krymal] m (-s;-) crumb
krümeln ['krymaln] tr & intr crumble
krumm [krum] adj (**krummer & krümmer** ['krymər]; **krummste & krümmste** ['krymstə] §9) bent, stooping; crooked
krumm'beinig adj bowlegged
krümmen ['krymən] tr bend, curve ||
ref (*vor Schmerzen*) writhe; (*vor Lachen*) double up; (*Wurm*) wriggle; (*Holz*) warp; (*Fluß, Straße*) wind
Krümmer ['krymər] m (-s;-) (tech) elbow
krumm'nehmen §116 tr (coll) take the wrong way, take amiss
Krumm'stab m (eccl) crozier
Krüm'mung f (-;-en) bend, curve; winding
krumpeln ['krumpəln] tr & intr (coll) crumple, crease
Krüppel ['krypəl] m (-s;-) cripple; **zum K. machen** cripple
krüp'pelhaft adj deformed
krüp'pelig adj crippled; stunted
Kruste ['krustə] f (-;-n) crust
Kru'stentier n crustacean
krustig ['krustɪç] adj crusty
Kruzifix [krutsɪ'fɪks] n (-es;-e) crucifix
Krypta ['krypta] f (-;-ten [tən]) crypt
Kübel ['kybəl] m (-s;-) tub; bucket
kubieren [ku'birən] tr (math) cube
Kubik– [kubik] comb.fm. cubic
Kubik'maß n cubic measure
kubisch ['kubɪʃ] adj cubic
Kubismus [ku'bɪsmus] m (-;) cubism
Küche ['kyçə] f (-;-n) kitchen; (culin) cuisine
Kuchen ['kuxən] m (-s;-) cake, pie
Ku'chenblech n cookie sheet
Küchenchef m chef
Kü'chendienst m (mil) K.P.
Ku'chenform f cake pan
Kü'chengerät n kitchen utensil
Kü'chengeschirr n kitchen utensils
Kü'chenherd m kitchen range, stove
Kü'chenmaschine f electric kitchen appliance
Kü'chenmeister m chef

Kü'chenzettel *m* menu

Küchlein ['kyçlaın] *n* (-s;-) chick; (culin) small cake

Kuckuck ['kukuk] *m* (-s;-e) cuckoo; zum K. gehen (coll) go to hell

Kufe ['kufə] *f* (-;-n) vat; (*Schlitten-*) runner

Küfer ['kyfər] *m* (-s;-) cooper

Kugel ['kugəl] *f* (-;-n) ball; sphere; (*Geschoß*) bullet; (sport) shot

ku'gelfest *adj* bulletproof

ku'gelförmig *adj* spherical

Ku'gelgelenk *n* (mach) ball-and-socket joint; (anat) socket joint

Ku'gellager *n* ball bearing

kugeln ['kugəln] *tr* roll ‖ *ref* roll around; sich vor Lachen k. double over with laughter ‖ *intr* (SEIN) roll

Ku'gelregen *m* hail of bullets

ku'gelrund' *adj* round; (coll) tubby

Ku'gelschreiber *m* ball-point pen

Ku'gelstoßen *n* (sport) shot put

Kuh [ku] *f* (-;–e) cow

Kuh'dorf *n* hick town

Kuh'fladen *m* cow dung

Kuh'handel *m* (pol) horse trading

Kuh'haut *f* cowhide; das geht auf keine K. but that's a long story

kühl [kyl] *adj* cool

Kühl'anlage *f* refrigerator; cooling system; cold storage (room)

Kühle ['kylə] *f* (-;) cool, coolness

kühlen ['kylən] *tr* cool; (*Wein*) chill

Küh'ler *m* (-s;-) cooler; (aut) radiator

Küh'lerverschluß *m* radiator cap

Kühl'mittel *n* coolant

Kühl'schrank *m* refrigerator

Kühl'truhe *f* freezer

Kühl'wagen *m* refrigerator truck; (rr) refrigerator car

Kuh'magd *f* milkmaid

Kuh'mist *m* cow dung

kühn [kyn] *adj* bold, daring

Kühn'heit *f* (-;) boldness, daring

Kuhpocken ['kupɔkən] *pl* cowpox

Kuh'stall *m* cowshed, cow barn

Kujon [ku'jon] *m* (-s;-e) (pej) louse

kujonieren [kujo'nirən] *tr* bully

Küken ['kykən] *n* (-s;-) chick

Kukuruz ['kukuruts] *m* (-es;) (Aust) corn

kulant [ku'lant] *adj* obliging; generous

Kuli ['kuli] *m* (-s;-s) coolie

kulinarisch [kuli'narıʃ] *adj* culinary

Kulisse [ku'lısə] *f* (-;-n) (theat) wing; hinter den Kulissen behind the scenes; Kulissen scenery

Kulis'senfieber *n* stage fright

kullern ['kulərn] *intr* (SEIN) roll

kulminieren [kulmı'nirən] *intr* culminate

Kult [kult] *m* (-[e]s;-e) cult

kultivieren [kultı'virən] *tr* cultivate

Kultur [kul'tur] *f* (-;-en) culture, civilization; (agr) cultivation; (bact, chem) culture

Kultur'austausch *m* cultural exchange

kulturell [kultu'rel] *adj* cultural

Kultur'erbe *n* cultural heritage

Kultur'film *m* educational film

Kultur'geschichte *f* history of civilization; cultural history

Kultur'volk *n* civilized people

Kul·tus ['kultus] *m* (-;-te [tə]) cult

Kümmel ['kyməl] *m* (-s;-) caraway seed; caraway brandy

Küm'melbrot *n* seeded rye bread

Kummer ['kumər] *m* (-s;) grief, sorrow; worry, concern, trouble; j-m großen K. bereiten cause s.o. a lot of worry; sich [*dat*] K. machen über (*acc*) worry about

kümmerlich ['kymərlıç] *adj* wretched; (*dürftig*) needy

Kümmerling ['kymərlıŋ] *m* (-s;-e) stunted animal; stunted plant

kümmern ['kymərn] *tr* trouble, worry; concern ‖ *ref*—sich k. um worry about; take care of; sich nicht k. um not bother about; neglect

Kümmernis ['kymərnıs] *f* (-;-se) worry, trouble

kum'mervoll *adj* grief-stricken

Kumpan [kum'pan] *m* (-s;-e) companion; buddy

Kumpel ['kumpəl] *m* (-s;-) buddy, sidekick; (min) miner

kund [kunt] *adj* known

kündbar ['kyntbar] *adj* (*Vertrag*) terminable; (fin) redeemable

Kunde ['kundə] *m* (-n;-n) customer; übler K. (fig) tough customer ‖ *f* (-;) news, information; lore

-kunde *f* comb.fm. -ology; -graphy; science of; guide to, study of

Kun'dendienst *m* customer service; warranty service

Kun'denkreis *m* clientele

kund'geben §80 *tr* make known, announce

Kundgebung ['kuntgebuŋ] *f* (-;-en) manifestation; (pol) rally

kundig ['kundıç] *adj* well-informed; k. sein (genit) know

-kundig *comb.fm.* well versed in; able to

kündigen ['kyndıgən] *tr* (*Vertrag*) give notice to terminate; (*Wohnung*) give notice to vacate; (*Stellung*) give notice of quitting; (*Kapital*) call in; (*Hypothek*) foreclose on; j-n fristlos k. (coll) sack s.o. ‖ *intr* (*dat*) given notice to, release

Kün'digung *f* (-;-en) (*seitens des Arbeitnehmers*) resignation; (*seitens des Arbeitgebers*) notice (*of termination*); mit monatlicher K. subject to a month's notice

Kün'digungsfrist *f* period of notice

kund'machen *tr* make known, announce

Kund'machung *f* (-;-en) announcement

Kund'schaft *f* (-;) clientele, customer(s); (mil) reconnaissance

kundschaften ['kuntʃaftən] *intr* go on reconnaissance, scout

Kund'schafter *m* (-s;-) scout, spy

kund'tun §154 *tr* make known, announce

kund'werden §159 *intr* (SEIN) become known

künftig ['kynftıç] *adj* future, to come, next ‖ *adv* in the future, from now on

künf'tighin' *adv* from now on, hereafter

Kunst [kunst] f (-;-̈e) art; skill; **das ist keine K.** it's easy

Kunstbanause ['kunstbanauzə] m (-n; -n) philistine

Kunst′dünger m chemical fertilizer

Künstelei [kynstə'laı] f (-;-en) affectation

Kunst′faser f synthetic fiber

Kunst′fehler m—ärztlicher K. malpractice

kunst′fertig adj skillful, skilled

Kunst′flieger m stunt pilot

Kunst′flug m stunt flying

Kunst′freund –in §8 mf art lover; patron of the arts

Kunst′gegenstand m objet d'art

kunst′gerecht adj skillful; expert

Kunst′gewerbe n arts and crafts

Kunst′glied n artificial limb

Kunst′griff m trick

Kunst′händler –in §6 mf art dealer

Kunst′kenner –in §6 mf art connoisseur

Kunst′laufen n figure skating

Künstler –in ['kynstlər(ın)] §6 mf artist; performer

künstlerisch ['kynstlərɪʃ] adj artistic

künstlich ['kynstlıç] adj artificial; (chem) synthetic

Kunst′liebhaber –in §8 mf art lover

kunst′los adj unaffected

Kunst′maler –in §6 mf painter, artist

Kunst′pause f pause for effect

kunst′reich adj ingenious

Kunst′reiter m equestrian

Kunst′seide f rayon

Kunst′springen n (sport) diving

Kunst′stoff m plastic material; synthetic material; (tex) synthetic fiber

Kunststoff– comb.fm. plastic; plastics

Kunst′stopfen n invisible mending

Kunst′stück n trick, feat

Kunst′tischler m cabinet maker

Kunstverständige ['kunstfer/tendıgə] §5 mf art expert

kunst′voll adj elaborate, ornate

Kunst′werk n work of art

kunterbunt ['kuntərbunt] adj chaotic

Kupfer ['kupfər] n (-s;) copper

kupfern ['kupfərn] adj copper

kupieren [ku'pirən] tr (Schwanz, Ohren) cut off; (Spielkarten) cut; (Fahrkarten) punch

Kuppe ['kupə] f (-;-n) top, summit

Kuppel ['kupəl] f (-;-n) cupola

Kuppelei [kupə'laı] f (-;) procuring

kuppeln ['kupəln] tr couple, connect ‖ intr be a pimp; be a procuress; (aut) operate the clutch

Kuppler ['kuplər] m (-s;-) pimp

Kupplerin ['kuplərın] f (-;-nen) procuress

Kupplung ['kuplʊŋ] f (-;-en) (aut) clutch; (rr) coupling

Kur [kur] f (-;-en) cure (at a spa); **j–n in die Kur nehmen** give s.o. a talking to

Kuratel [kura'tel] f (-;) guardianship; **j–n unter K. stellen** appoint a guardian for s.o.

Ku·rator [ku'ratər] m (-s;-ratoren [ra'torən]) (e-s Museums) curator; (educ) trustee; (jur) guardian

Kurato·rium [kura'torjum] n (-s;-rien [rjən]) (educ) board of trustees

Kurbel ['kurbəl] f (-;-n) crank, handle, winch

Kurbelei [kurbə'laı] f (-;-en) shooting a film; (aer) dogfight

Kur′belgehäuse n (aut) crankcase

kurbeln ['kurbəln] tr crank; (Film) shoot ‖ intr engage in a dogfight

Kur′belstange f (mach) connecting rod

Kur′belwelle f (mach) crankshaft

Kürbis ['kyrbis] m (-ses;-se) pumpkin; (Kopf) (sl) bean

küren ['kyrən] §165 & §109 tr elect

Kurfürst ['kurfyrst] m (-en;-en) elector (of the Holy Roman Empire)

Kur′haus n spa; hotel

Kurie ['kurjə] f (-;-n) (eccl) curia

Kurier [ku'rir] m (-s;-e) courier

kurieren [ku'rirən] tr cure

kurios [ku'rjos] adj odd, curious

Kuriosität [kurjozı'tet] f (-;-en) quaintness; curio, curiosity

Kur′ort m health resort, spa

Kurpfuscher ['kurpfuʃər] m (-s;-) quack

Kurrentschrift [ku'rent/rıft] f cursive script

Kurs [kurs] m (-es;-e) (educ) course; (fin) rate of exchange; (fin) circulation; (naut) course; (st. exch.) price; **außer K.** setzen take out of circulation; **hoch im K.** stehen be at a premium; (fig) rate high; **zum Kurse von** at the rate of

Kurs′bericht m (st. exch.) market report

Kurs′buch n (rr) timetable

Kürschner ['kyr/nər] m (-s;-) furrier

Kurs′entwicklung f price trend

Kurs′gewinn m (st. exch.) gain

kursieren [kur'zirən] intr circulate

Kursive [kur'zivə] f (-;), **Kursivschrift** [kur'zif/rıft] f (-;) italics

Kurs′stand m (st. exch.) price level

Kur·sus ['kurzus] m (-;-se [zə]) (educ) course

Kurs′veränderung f (fin) change in exchange rates; (naut) change of course; (pol) change of policy; (st. exch.) price change

Kurs′wert m (st. exch.) market value

Kurve ['kurvə] f (-;-n) curve; **in die K. gehen** (aer) bank

kurz [kurts] adj (kürzer ['kyrtsər]; kürzeste ['kyrtsəstə] §9) short, brief; **auf das kürzeste** very briefly; **binnen kurzem** within a short time; **in kurzem** before long; **k. und gut in a** word; **seit kurzem** for the last few days or weeks; **über k. oder lang** sooner or later; **zu k. kommen** (coll) get the short end of it ‖ adv shortly; briefly; curtly

kurzatmig ['kurtsatmıç] adj shortwinded; (Pferd) broken-winded

Kürze ['kyrtsə] f (-;) shortness; brevity; **in K.** shortly; briefly

kürzen ['kyrtsən] tr shorten; (Gehalt) cut; (math) reduce

kurzerhand adv offhand

Kurz′fassung f abridged version

Kurz′film m (cin) short

kurzfristig ['kʊrtsfrɪstɪç] *adj* short-term
Kurz'geschichte *f* short story
kurzlebig ['kʊrtslebɪç] *adj* short-lived
kürzlich ['kʏrtslɪç] *adj* lately, recently
Kurz'meldung *f* news flash
Kurz'nachrichten *pl* news summary
kurz'schließen §76 *tr* short-circuit
Kurz'schluß *m* short circuit
Kurz'schlußbrücke *f* (elec) jumper
Kurz'schrift *f* shorthand
kurz'sichtig *adj* near-sighted; (fig) short-sighted
Kurz'streckenlauf *m* sprint
Kurz'streckenläufer –in §6 *mf* sprinter
kurzum' *adv* in short, in a word
Kür'zung *f* (–;-en) reduction; curtailment; (*e-s Buches*) abridgment
Kurz'waren *pl* sewing supplies
kurz'weg *adv* bluntly, flatly
Kurzweil ['kʊrtsvaɪl] *f* (–;) pastime
kurzweilig ['kʊrtsvaɪlɪç] *adj* amusing
kusch [kʊʃ] *interj* lie down! (*to a dog*)
kuschen ['kʊʃən] *ref* lie down; crouch || *intr* lie down; crouch, cringe; (*Person*) knuckle under, submit
Kusine [kʊ'zinə] *f* (–;-n) female cousin
Kuß [kʊs] *m* (Kusses; Küsse) kiss; **kalter K.** popsicle

küssen ['kʏsən] *tr & intr* kiss
Kuß'hand *f*—j-m e–e **K. zuwerfen** throw s.o. a kiss; **mit K.** with pleasure
Küste ['kʏstə] *f* (–;-n) coast, shore
Kü'stenfahrer *m* coasting vessel
Kü'stenfischerei *f* inshore fishing
Kü'stengewässer *n* coastal waters
Kü'stenlinie *f* coastline, shoreline
kü'stennah *adj* offshore; coastal
Kü'stenschiffahrt *f* coastal shipping
Kü'stenstreife *f* shore patrol
Küster ['kʏstər] *m* (–s;–) sexton
Kustos ['kʊstɔs] *m* (–; Kustoden [kʊs-'todən]) custodian
Kutsche ['kʊtʃə] *f* (–;-n) coach
Kut'scher *m* (–s;–) coachman
kutschieren [kʊ't/irən] *intr* drive a coach || *intr* (SEIN) ride in a coach
Kutte ['kʊtə] *f* (–;-n) (eccl) cowl
Kutteln ['kʊtəln] *pl* tripe
Kutter ['kʊtər] *m* (–s;–) (naut) cutter
Kuvert [kʊ'vert] *n* (–s;–s) & (–[e]s;-e) envelope; table setting
kuvertieren [kʊvɛr'tirən] *tr* put into an envelope
Kux [kʊks] *m* (–es;-e) mining share
Kyklon [ky'klon] *m* (–s;-e) cyclone
Kyniker ['kynɪkər] *m* (–s;–) (philos) cynic

L

L, l [el] *invar n* L, l
laben ['labən] *tr* refresh
Labial [la'bjal] *m* (–s;-e) labial
labil [la'bil] *adj* unstable
Labor [la'bor] *n* (–s;-s) (coll) lab
Laborant [labo'rant] (in) §7 *mf* laboratory technician
Laborato·rium [labora'torjum] *n* (–s; rien [rjən]) laboratory
laborieren [labo'rirən] *intr* experiment; **l. an** (*dat*) suffer from
Labsal ['lapzal] *n* (–[e]s;-e) refreshment
La'bung *f* (–;-en) refreshment
Labyrinth [laby'rɪnt] *n* (–[e]s;-e) labyrinth
Lache ['laxə] *f* (–;-n) puddle, pool; laugh; **e-e gellende L. anschlagen** break out in laughter
lächeln ['leçəln] *intr* (über *acc*) smile (at) || **Lächeln** *n* (–s;) smile; höhnisches **L.** sneer
lachen ['laxən] *intr* laugh; **daß ich nicht lache!** don't make me laugh! || **Lachen** *n* (–s;) laugh, laughter; **du hast gut L.!** you can laugh!
lächerlich ['leçərlɪç] *adj* ridiculous; **l. machen** ridicule; **sich l. machen** make a fool of oneself
lachhaft ['laxhaft] *adj* ridiculous
Lachkrampf ['laxkrampf] *m* fit of laughter
Lachs [laks] *m* (–es;-e) salmon
Lachsalve ['laxzalvə] *f* (–;-n) peal of laughter

Lachs'schinken *m* raw, lightly smoked ham
Lack [lak] *m* (–[e]s;-e) lacquer, varnish
Lackel ['lakəl] *m* (–s;–) (coll) dope
lackieren [la'kirən] *tr* lacquer, varnish; (*Autos*) paint
Lack'leder *n* patent leather
Lackmuspapier ['lakmuspapir] *n* litmus paper
Lack'schuhe *pl* patent-leather shoes
Lade ['ladə] *f* (–;-n) box, case; (*Schublade*) drawer
La'dearbeiter *m* loader
La'debaum *m* derrick
La'defähigkeit *f* loading capacity
La'dehemmung *f* jamming (*of a gun*); **L. haben** jam
La'deklappe *f* tailgate
La'deluke *f* (naut) hatch
laden ['ladən] §103 *tr* load; (*Gast*) invite; (elec) charge; (jur) summon; **geladen sein** (coll) be burned up || **Laden** *m* (–s;⸗) store, shop; (*Fenster-*) shutter; **den L. schmeißen** pull it off, lick it
La'dendieb *m*, **La'dendiebin** *f* shoplifter
La'dendiebstahl *m* shoplifting
La'denhüter *m* drug on the market
La'deninhaber –in §6 *mf* shopkeeper
La'denkasse *f* till
Lä'denmädchen *n* salesgirl
La'denpreis *m* retail price
La'denschluß *m* closing time

La′denschwengel m (pej) stupid shop clerk

La′dentisch m counter

La′derampe f loading platform

La′deschein m bill of lading

La′destock m ramrod

La′destreifen m cartridge clip

La′dung f (-;-en) loading; load; (Güter) freight; (elec) charge; (jur) summons; (mil) charge; (naut) cargo

Lafette [la′fɛtə] f (-;-n) gun mount

Laffe [′lafə] m (-n;-n) jazzy dresser

lag [lɑk] pret of liegen

Lage [′lɑgə] f (-;-n) site, location; situation; (Zustand) condition, state; (Haltung) posture; (Schicht) layer, deposit; (Salve) volley; (Bier) round; (bb) quire; (mil) position; (mus) pitch; mißliche L. predicament; versetzen Sie sich in meine L. put yourself in my position

Lager [′lɑgər] n (-s;-) bed; (e-s Wildes) lair; (Stapelplatz) dump; (Partei) side, camp; (von Waffen) cache; (Vorrat) stock; (Warenlager) stockroom; (geol) stratum, vein; (mach) bearing; (mil) camp; auf L. in stock; (fig) up one's sleeve; ein L. halten von keep stock of

La′geraufnahme f inventory

La′gerbier n lager beer

La′gerfähigkeit f shelf life

La′gerfeuer n campfire

La′gergebühr f storage charges

La′gerhalter m stock clerk

La′gerhaus n warehouse

Lagerist –in [lɑgə′rɪst(ɪn)] §7 mf warehouse clerk

La′gerleben n camp life

lagern [′lɑgərn] tr lay down; (Waren) stock, store; (altern) season; (mach) mount on bearings ‖ ref lie down, rest ‖ intr lie down, rest; (Waren) be stored; (Wein) season; (geol) be deposited; (mil) camp

La′gerort m, La′gerplatz m resting place; (Stapelplatz) dump; (mil) camp site

La′gerraum m storeroom, stockroom

La′gerstand m stock on hand, inventory

La′gerstätte f, La′gerstelle f resting place; (geol) deposit; (mil) camp site

La′gerung f (-;-en) storage; (Alterung) seasoning; (geol) stratification

La′gervorrat m stock, supply

Lagune [la′gunə] f (-;-n) lagoon

lahm [lɑm] adj lame; paralyzed ‖ Lahme §5 mf paralytic

lahmen [′lɑmən] intr be lame, limp

lähmen [′lɛmən] tr paralyze; (Verkehr) tie up; (fig) cripple

lahm′legen tr cripple, paralyze; (mil) neutralize

Läh′mung f (-;-en) paralysis

Laib [laɪp] m (-[e]s;-e) loaf

Laich [laɪç] m (-[e]s;-e) spawn

laichen [′laɪçən] intr spawn

Laie [′laɪə] m (-n;-n) layman; Laien laity

Lai′enbruder m lay brother

lai′enhaft adj layman's

Lakai [la′kaɪ] m (-en;-en) lackey

Lake [′lɑkə] f (-;-n) brine, pickle

Laken [′lɑkən] n (-s;-) sheet

lakonisch [la′konɪʃ] adj laconic

Lakritze [la′krɪtsə] f (-;-n) licorice

Lakune [la′kunə] f (-;-n) lacuna

lallen [′lalən] tr & intr stammer

lamellenförmig [la′mɛlənfœrmɪç] adj laminate

lamentieren [lamen′tirən] intr wail

Lametta [la′mɛta] n (-s;) tinsel

Lamm [lam] n (-[e]s;⸚er) lamb

Lamm′braten m roast lamb

Lämmerwolke [′lɛmərvɔlkə] f cirrus

Lamm′fleisch n (culin) lamb

lamm′fromm′ adj meek as a lamb

Lampe [′lampə] f (-;-n) lamp; light

Lam′penfieber n stage fright

Lam′penschirm m lamp shade

Lampion [lam′pjõ] m (-s;-s) Chinese lantern

lancieren [lɑ̃′sirən] tr launch, promote; (Kandidaten) (pol) groom

Land [lant] n (-[e]s;⸚er & -e) land; (Ackerboden) ground, soil; (Staat) country; (Provinz) state; (Gegensatz: Stadt) country; ans L. ashore; auf dem Lande in the country; aufs L. into the country; aus aller Herren Ländern from everywhere; außer Landes gehen go abroad; zu Lande by land

Land′arbeiter m farm hand

Land′armee f land forces

Land′bau m farming, agriculture

Land′besitz m landed property

Land′besitzer –in §6 mf landowner

Landebahn [′landəban] f runway

Landedeck [′landədɛk] n flight deck

Land′edel·mann m (-es;-leute) country gentleman

Landefeuer [′landəfɔɪ·ər] n runway lights

land′einwärts adv inland

Landekopf [′landəkɔpf] m beachhead

landen [′landən] tr & intr (SEIN) land

Land′enge f isthmus, neck of land

Landeplatz [′landəplats] m wharf; (aer) landing field

Länderei [lɛndə′raɪ] f (-;-en) or Ländereien pl lands, estates

Länderkunde [′lɛndərkundə] f geography

Landes– [landəs] comb.fm. national, native, of the land

Lan′desaufnahme f land survey

Lan′desbank f national bank

Lan′desbeschreibung f topography

lan′deseigen adj state-owned

Lan′deserzeugnis n domestic product

Lan′desfarben pl national colors

Lan′desfürst m sovereign

·Lan′desgesetz n law of the land

Lan′desherr m sovereign

Lan′desherrschaft f, Lan′deshoheit f sovereignty

Lan′dessprache f vernacular

Lan′destracht f national costume

Lan′destrauer f public mourning

lan′desüblich adj customary

Lan′desvater m sovereign

Lan′desverrat m high treason

Lan′desverräter –in §6 mf traitor

Lan′desverteidigung f national defense

Land'flucht f rural exodus
land'flüchtig adj exiled, fugitive
Land'friedensbruch m disturbance of the peace
Land'gericht n district court, superior court
Land'gewinnung f land reclamation
Land'gut n country estate
Land'haus n country house
Land'jäger m rural policeman; (culin) sausage
Land'junker m country squire
Land'karte f map
Land'kreis m rural district
land'läufig adj customary
Ländler ['lentlər] m (-s;-) waltz
Land'leute pl country folk
ländlich ['lentlıç] adj rural, rustic
Land'luft f country air
Land'macht f land forces
Land'mann m (-[e]s;-leute) farmer
Land'marke f landmark (for travelers and sailors)
Land'maschinen pl farm machinery
Land'messer m surveyor
Land'partie f outing, picnic
Land'plage f nation-wide plague; (coll) big nuisance
Land'rat m regional governor
Land'ratte f (fig) landlubber
Land'recht n common law
Land'regen m steady rain
Land'rücken m ridge
Land'schaft f (-;-en) landscape, scenery; (Bezirk) district, region
land'schaftlich adj scenic; regional
Landser ['lantsər] m (-s;-) G.I.
Lands'knecht m mercenary
Lands'mann m (-[e]s;-leute) fellow countryman
Land'spitze f promontory
Land'straße f highway
Land'streicher m (-s;-) tramp, hobo
Land'strich m tract of land
Land'sturm m home guard
Land'tag m state assembly
landumschlossen ['lantum/lɔsən] adj landlocked
Lan'dung f (-;-en) landing
Lan'dungsboot n landing craft
Lan'dungsbrücke f jetty, pier
Lan'dungsgestell n landing gear
Lan'dungssteg m gangplank
Land'vermessung f surveying
Land'volk n country folk
Land'weg m overland route
Land'wehr f militia, home guard
Land'wirt m farmer
Land'wirtschaft f agriculture; **L. betreiben** farm
land'wirtschaftlich adj farm, agricultural
Land'zunge f spit of land
lang [laŋ] adj (länger ['leŋər]; längste ['leŋstə] §9) long; (Person) tall || adv—die ganze Woche l. all week; e-e Stunde l. for an hour
langatmig ['laŋatmıç] adj long-winded
lang'beinig adj long-legged
lange ['laŋə] adv long, a long time; es ist noch l. nicht fertig it is far from ready; schon l. her long ago; schon l. her, daß a long time since;

so l. bis until; so l. wie as long as; wie l.? how long?
Länge ['leŋə] f (-;-n) length; long syllable; (geog) longitude; (pros) quantity; **auf die L.** in the long run; **der L. nach** lengthwise; **in die L. ziehen** drag out
langen ['laŋən] tr reach, hand; **j—m eine l.** (coll) give s.o. a smack || intr be enough; **l. nach** reach for || impers—es langt mir I have enough; **jetzt langt's mir aber!** I've had it!
Län'gengrad m degree of longitude
Län'genkreis m meridian
Län'genmaß n linear measure
Lan'geweile f boredom; **sich** [dat] **die L. vertreiben** (coll) kill time
Lang'finger m pickpocket
langfingerig ['laŋfıŋərıç] adj (fig) thievish
langfristig ['laŋfrıstıç] adj long-term
lang'jährig adj long-standing
Lang'lauf m crosscountry skiing
langlebig ['laŋlebıç] adj long-lived
lang'legen ref lie down, stretch out
länglich ['leŋlıç] adj oblong
läng'lichrund adj oval, elliptical
Lang'mut f patience
lang'mütig adj patient
Lang'mütigkeit f patience
längs [leŋs] prep (genit or dat) along
langsam ['laŋzam] adj slow
Lang'spielplatte f long-playing record
längst [leŋst] adv long since, long ago
längstens ['leŋstəns] adv at the latest; (höchstens) at the most
Langstrecken— comb.fm. long-range; (sport) long-distance
langweilen ['laŋvaılən] tr bore || ref feel bored
Lang'weiler m (-s;-) slowpoke
langweilig ['laŋvaılıç] adj boring
langwierig ['laŋvirıç] adj lengthy
Lanolin [lano'lin] n (-s;) lanolin
Lanze ['lantsə] f (-;-n) lance, spear
Lan'zenstechen n (-s;) jousting
Lanzette [lan'tsetə] f (-;-n) lancet
Lappalie [la'paljə] f (-;-n) trifle
Lappen ['lapən] m (-s;-) rag; washrag; (Flicken) patch; (anat) lobe
läppisch ['lepıʃ] adj silly, trifling
Lappland ['laplant] n (-s;) Lapland
Lärche ['lerçə] f (-;-n) (bot) larch
Lärm ['lerm] m (-[e]s;) noise; **L. schlagen** (fig) make a fuss
lärmen ['lermən] intr make noise
lär'mend adj noisy
Larve ['larfə] f (-;-n) mask; larva
las [las] pret of lesen
lasch [laʃ] adj limp; (Speise) insipid
Lasche ['laʃə] f (-;-n) (Klappe) flap; (Schuh-) tongue; (rr) fishplate
lasieren [la'zirən] tr glaze
lassen ['lasən] §104 tr let; (erlauben) allow; (bewirken) have, make; leave (behind, undone, open, etc.); **den Film entwickeln l.** have the film developed; **etw fallen l.** drop s.th.; **ich kann es nicht l.** I can't help it; **j—n warten l.** keep s.o. waiting; **kommen l.** send for; **laß den Lärm!** stop

the noise!; **laß es!** cut it out!; **laßt uns gehen** let us go; **sein Leben l.** lose one's life; **sein Leben l. für** sacrifice one's life for || *ref*—**das läßt sich denken** I can imagine; **das läßt sich hören!** now you're talking!; **es läßt sich nicht beschreiben** it defies description; **es läßt sich nicht leugnen, daß** it cannot be denied that; **sich** [*dat*] **Zeit l.** take one's time

lässig ['lɛsɪç] *adj* (*faul*) lazy; (*träge*) sluggish; (*nachlässig*) remiss

Läs'sigkeit *f* (–;) laziness; negligence

läßlich ['lɛslɪç] *adj* venial

Last [last] *f* (–;-en) load, weight; (*Bürde*) burden; (*Hypotek*) encumbrance; (*aer, naut*) cargo, freight; **j-m etw zur L. legen** blame s.o. for s.th.; **L. der Beweise** weight of evidence; **ruhende L.** dead weight; **zur L. fallen** (*dat*) become a burden for

lasten ['lastən] *intr* (**auf** *dat*) weigh (**on**)

la'stenfrei *adj* unencumbered

La'stensegler *m* transport glider

Laster ['lastər] *m* (-s;-) (*coll*) truck || *n* (-s;-) vice

Lästerer –in ['lɛstərər(ɪn)] §6 *mf* slanderer; blasphemer

la'sterhaft *adj* vicious

La'sterleben *n* life of vice

lästerlich ['lɛstərlɪç] *adj* slanderous; blasphemous

Lästermaul ['lɛstərmaul] *n* scandalmonger

lästern ['lɛstərn] *tr* slander; blaspheme

Lä'sterung *f* (–;-en) slander; blasphemy

lästig ['lɛstɪç] *adj* troublesome; **j-m l. fallen** bother s.o.

Last'kahn *m* barge

Last'kraftwagen *m* truck

Last'schrift *f* (acct) debit

Last'tier *n* beast of burden

Last'träger *m* porter

Last'wagen *m* truck

Last'zug *m* tractor-trailer (*consisting of several trailers*)

Lasur [la'zur] *f* (–;) glaze

Latein [la'taɪn] *n* (-s;) Latin

lateinisch [la'taɪnɪʃ] *adj* Latin

Laterne [la'tɛrnə] *f* (–;-n) lantern; lamp

Latrine [la'trinə] *f* (–;-n) latrine

Latri'nenparole *f* scuttlebut

Latsche ['lat/ə] *f* (–;-n) (*coll*) slipper || ['lat/ə] *f* (–;-n) (bot) dwarf pine

latschen ['lat/ən] *intr* (SEIN) shuffle along

Latte ['latə] *f* (–;-n) lath

Lat'tenkiste *f* crate

Lat'tenzaun *m* picket fence

Lattich ['latɪç] *m* (-[e]s;-e) lettuce

Latz [lats] *m* (-es;⸚e) bib; (*Klappe*) flap; (*Schürzchen*) pinafore

Lätzchen ['lɛtsçən] *n* (-s;-) bib

lau [lau] *adj* lukewarm; (*Wetter*) mild; (fig) half-hearted

Laub [laup] *n* (-[e]s;) foliage

Laub'baum *m* deciduous tree

Laube ['laubə] *f* (–;-n) arbor; (*Säulen-*

gang) portico; (*Bogengang*) arcade; (theat) box

Lau'bengang *m* arcade

Laub'säge *f* fret saw

Laub'sägearbeit *f* fretwork

Laub'werk *n* foliage

Lauer ['lau-ər] *f* (–;) ambush; **auf der L. liegen** lie in wait

lauern ['lau-ərn] *intr* lurk; **l. auf** (*acc*) lie in wait for, watch for

lau'ernd *adj* (*Blick*) wary; (*Gefahr*) lurking

Lauf [lauf] *m* (-[e]s;⸚e) running; run; (*e-s Flusses*) course; (*Strömung*) current; (*Wettlauf*) race; (*e-s Gewehrs*) barrel; (astr) path, orbit; **den Dingen freien L. lassen** let things take their course; **im Laufe der Zeit** in the course of time; **im vollen Laufe** at full speed

Lauf'bahn *f* career; (astr) orbit; (sport) lane

Lauf'bursche *m* errand boy; office boy

laufen ['laufən] §105 *intr* (SEIN) run; (*zu Fuß gehen*) walk; (*leck sein*) leak; (*Zeit*) pass; **die Dinge l. lassen** let things slide; **j-n l. lassen** let s.o. go; (*straflos*) let s.o. off

lau'fend *adj* (*ständig*) steady; (*Jahr, Preis*) current; (*Nummern*) consecutive; (*Wartung, Geschäft*) routine; (*Meter, usw.*) running; **auf dem laufenden** up to date; **laufendes Band** conveyor belt; assembly line

Läufer ['lɔɪfər] *m* (-s;-) runner; (*Teppich*) runner; (chess) bishop; (fb) halfback; (mach) rotor; (mus) run

Lauferei [laufə'raɪ] *f* (–;-en) running around

Lauf'feuer *n* (-s;) wildfire

Lauf'fläche *f* tread (on tire)

Lauf'gewicht *n* sliding weight

Lauf'gitter *n* playpen

Lauf'graben *m* trench

läufig ['lɔɪfɪç] *adj* in heat

Läu'figkeit *f* (–;) heat

Lauf'junge *m* errand boy; office boy

Lauf'kran *m* (mach) traveling crane

Lauf'kunde *m* chance customer

Lauf'masche *f* run (*in stocking*)

lauf'maschenfrei *adj* runproof

Lauf'paß *m* (coll) walking papers; (coll) brush-off

Lauf'planke *f* gangplank

Lauf'rad *n* (*e-r Turbine*) rotor; (aer) landing wheel

Lauf'schritt *m* double-quick time

Lauf'steg *m* footbridge

Laufställchen ['lauf/tɛlçən] *n* (-s;-) playpen

Lauf'zeit *f* rutting season; (*e-s Vertrags*) term; (cin) running time; (mach) (service) life

Lauge ['laugə] *f* (–;-n) lye; (*Salzlauge*) brine; (*Seifenlauge*) suds

Lau'gensalz *n* alkali

lau'gensalzig *adj* alkaline

Laune ['launə] *f* (–;-n) mood, humor; (*Grille*) whim

lau'nenhaft *adj* capricious

launig ['launɪç] *adj* humorous, witty

lau'nisch *adj* moody

Laus [laus] *f* (–;⸚e) louse

Laus'bub m rascal

lauschen ['lauʃən] intr listen; eavesdrop; **l. auf** (acc) listen to

Lau'scher –in §6 mf eavesdropper

lauschig ['lauʃɪç] adj cosy, peaceful

Lau'sebengel m, **Lau'sejunge** m, **Lau'sekerl** m (coll) rascal, brat

lausen ['lauzən] tr pick lice from; **ich denke, mich laust die Affe** (coll) I couldn't believe my eyes

lausig ['lauzɪç] adj lousy

laut [laut] adj loud; (lärmend) noisy; **l. werden** become public; **l. werden lassen** divulge || prep (genit & dat) according to; (com) as per; **l. Bericht** according to the report || **Laut** m (–[e]s;–e) sound

Laute ['lautə] f (–;–n) lute

lauten ['lautən] intr sound; (Worte) read, go, say; **das Urteil lautet auf Tod** the sentence is death

läuten ['lɔɪtən] tr & intr ring, toll || impers—es läutet the bell is ringing || **Läuten** n (–s;) toll

lauter ['lautər] adj pure; (aufrecht) sincere || invar adj (nichts als) nothing but

Lau'terkeit f (–;) purity; sincerity

läutern ['lɔɪtərn] tr purify; (Metall, Zucker) refine; (veredeln) ennoble

Laut'gesetz n phonetic law

Laut'lehre f phonetics, phonology

laut'lich adj phonetic

laut'los adj soundless

Laut'malerei f onomatopoeia

Laut'schrift f phonetic spelling

Laut'sprecher m loudspeaker

Laut'sprecheranlage f public address system

Laut'sprecherwagen m sound truck

Laut'stärke f volume

Laut'stärkeregler m volume control

Laut'system n phonetic system

Laut'zeichen n phonetic symbol

lau'warm adj lukewarm

Lava ['lava] f (–;) lava

Lavendel [la'vendəl] m (–s;) (bot) lavender

laven'delfarben adj lavender

lavieren [la'virən] intr (fig) maneuver; (naut) tack

Lawine [la'vinə] f (–;–n) avalanche

lax [laks] adj lax

Lax'heit f (–;) laxity

Laxiermittel [la'ksirmɪtəl] n laxative

Layout ['le·aut] n (–s;–s) layout

Lazarett [latsa'ret] n (–[e]s;–e) (mil) hospital

Lebedame ['lebədamə] f woman of leisure

Lebehoch [lebə'hox] n (–s;–s) cheer; toast; **ein dreimaliges L.** three cheers

Lebemann ['lebəman] m playboy

leben ['lebən] tr & intr live || **Leben** n (–s;–) life; existence; **am L. bleiben** survive; **am L. erhalten** keep alive; **ins L. rufen** bring into being; **sein L. lang** all his life; **ums L. kommen** lose one's life

lebendig [le'bendɪç] adj living, alive; (lebhaft) lively; (Darstellung) vivid

Le'bensalter n age, period of life

Le'bensanschauung f outlook on life

Le'bensart f manners

Le'bensaufgabe f mission in life

Le'bensbaum m (bot) arbor vitae

Le'bensbedingungen pl living conditions

Le'bensbeschreibung f biography

Le'bensdauer f life span

le'bensfähig adj viable

Le'bensfrage f vital question

Le'bensgefahr f mortal danger

le'bensgefährlich adj perilous

Le'bensgefährte m, **Le'bensgefährtin** f life companion, spouse

le'bensgroß adj life-size

Le'benshaltung f standard of living

Le'benshaltungskosten pl cost of living

Le'bensinteressen pl vital interests

Le'benskraft f vitality

Le'benskünstler m—**er ist ein L.** nothing can get him down

lebenslänglich ['lebənsleŋlɪç] adj life

Le'benslauf m curriculum vitae

Le'bensmittel pl groceries

Le'bensmittelgeschäft n grocery store

Le'bensmittelkarte f food ration card

Le'bensmittellieferant m caterer

le'bensmüde adj weary of life

le'bensnotwendig adj vital, essential

Le'bensprozeß m vital function

Le'bensstandard m standard of living

Le'bensstellung f lifetime job; tenure

Le'bensstil m life style

Le'bensunterhalt m livelihood

le'bensuntüchtig adj impractical

Le'bensversicherung f life insurance

Le'benswandel m conduct; life

Le'bensweise f way of life

Le'bensweisheit f worldly wisdom

le'benswichtig adj vital, essential

Le'benszeichen n sign of life

Le'benszeit f lifetime; **auf L.** for life

Leber ['lebər] f (–;–n) liver; **frei von der L. weg reden** speak frankly

Le'berfleck m mole

Leberkäs ['lebərkes] m (–es;) meat loaf (made with liver)

Le'bertran m cod-liver oil

Lebewesen ['lebəvezən] n living being

Lebewohl [lebə'vol] n (–[e]s;–e) farewell

lebhaft ['lephaft] adj lively; full of life; (Farbe) bright; (Straße) busy; (Börse) brisk; (Interesse) keen

Lebkuchen ['lepkuxən] m gingerbread

leblos ['leplos] adj lifeless

Lebtag ['leptak] m—**mein L.** in all my life

Lebzeiten ['leptsaɪtən] pl—**zu meinen L.** in my lifetime

lechzen ['leçtsən] intr (nach) thirst (for)

leck [lek] adj leaky || **Leck** n (–[e]s;–e) leak; **ein L. bekommen** spring a leak

lecken ['lekən] tr lick || intr leak; (naut) have sprung a leak

lecker ['lekər] adj dainty; (köstlich) delicious

Leckerbissen (Lek'kerbissen) m delicacy, dainty

Leckerei [lekə'raɪ] f (–;–en) daintiness; sweets

leckerhaft (lek'kerhaft) adj dainty

Leckermaul (Lek′kermaul) n—ein L. sein have a sweet tooth

Leder [′ledər] n (-s;) leather

ledern [′ledərn] adj leather; (fig) dull, boring

ledig [′ledɪç] adj single; (Kind) illegitimate; l. (genit) free of; **lediger Stand** single state; celibacy

le′diglich adv merely, only

leer [ler] adj empty, void; (fig) vain ‖ **Leere** f (-;) emptiness, void; vacuum ‖ n—**der Schlag ging ins L.** the blow missed; **ins L. starren** stare into space

leeren [′lerən] tr empty

Leer′gut n empties (bottles, cases)

Leer′lauf m (aut) idling, idle; (Gang) (aut) neutral

leer′laufen §105 intr (SEIN) idle

leer′stehend adj unoccupied, vacant

Leer′taste f (typ) space bar

legal [le′gal] adj legal

legalisieren [legalɪ′zirən] tr legalize

Legat [le′gat] m (-en;-en) legate ‖ n (-[e]s;-e) legacy, bequest

legen [′legən] tr lay, put; **auf die Kette l.** chain, tie up; **j—m ans Herz l.** recommend warmly to s.o.; **Nachdruck l. auf** (acc) emphasize; **Wert l. auf** (acc) attach importance to ‖ ref lie down; go to bed; (Wind) die down; **die Krankheit hat sich ihm auf die Lungen gelegt** his sickness affected his lungs

legendär [legɛn′der] adj legendary

Legende [le′gɛndə] f (-;-n) legend

legieren [le′girən] tr alloy

Legie′rung f (-;-en) alloy

Legion [le′gjon] f (-;-en) legion

Legionär [legjo′ner] m (-s;-e) legionnaire, legionary

legislativ [legɪsla′tif] adj legislative ‖ **Legislative** [legɪsla′tivə] f (-;-n) legislature

Legis·lator [legɪs′lator] m (-s;-latoren [la′torən]) legislator

Legislatur [legɪsla′tur] f (-;-en) legislature

legitim [legɪ′tim] adj legitimate

Legitimation [legɪtɪma′tsjon] f (-;-en) proof of identity

legitimieren [legɪtɪ′mirən] tr legitimize; (berechtigen) authorize ‖ ref prove one's identity

Lehen [′le·ən] n (-s;-) (hist) fief

Le′hensherr m liege lord

Le′hens·mann m (-[e]s;-leute) vassal

Lehm [lem] m (-[e]s;-e) clay, loam

lehmig [′lemɪç] adj clayey, loamy

Lehne [′lenə] f (-;-n) support; (e-s Stuhls) arm, back; (Abhang) slope

lehnen [′lenən] tr, ref & intr lean

Lehnsessel [′lenzesəl] m, **Lehnstuhl** [′len/tul] m armchair, easy chair

Lehn′wort [′lenvort] n (-[e]s;-″er) loan word

Lehramt [′leramt] n teaching profession; professorship

Lehranstalt [′leran/talt] f educational institution

Lehrbrief [′lerbrif] m apprentice's diploma

Lehrbube [′lerbubə] m apprentice

Lehrbuch [′lerbux] n textbook

Lehrbursche [′lerburʃə] m apprentice

Lehre [′lerə] f (-;-n) doctrine, teaching; (Wissenschaft) science; (Theorie) theory; (Unterweisung) instruction; (Warnung) lesson; (e-r Fabel) moral; (Richtschnur) rule, precept; (e-s Lehrlings) apprenticeship; (tech) gauge; **in der L. sein** be serving one's apprenticeship

lehren [′lerən] tr teach, instruct

Lehrer -in [′lerər(ɪn)] §6 mf teacher

Leh′rerbildungsanstalt f teacher's college

Leh′rerkollegium n teaching staff

Lehrfach [′lerfax] n subject

Lehrfilm [′lerfɪlm] m educational film

Lehrgang [′lergaŋ] m (educ) course

Lehrgedicht [′lergədɪçt] n didactic poem

Lehrgegenstand [′lergegən/tant] m (educ) subject

Lehrgeld [′lergelt] n—**L. zahlen** (fig) learn the hard way

lehrhaft [′lerhaft] adj didactic

Lehrjunge [′lerjuŋə] m apprentice

Lehrkörper [′lerkörpər] m teaching staff; faculty (of a university)

Lehrling [′lerlɪŋ] m (-s;-e) apprentice

Lehrmädchen [′lermetçən] n girl apprentice

Lehrmeister [′lermaɪstər] m master, teacher, instructor

Lehrmittel [′lermɪtəl] n teaching aid

Lehrplan [′lerplan] m curriculum

lehrreich [′lerraɪç] adj instructive

Lehrsaal [′lerzal] m lecture hall

Lehrsatz [′lerzats] m (eccl) dogma; (math) theorem

Lehrspruch [′ler/prux] m maxim

Lehrstelle [′ler/telə] f position as an apprentice

Lehrstoff [′ler/tɔf] m subject matter

Lehrstuhl [′ler/tul] m (educ) chair

Lehrstunde [′ler/tundə] f lesson

Lehrzeit [′lertsaɪt] f apprenticeship

Leib [laɪp] m (-[e]s;-er) body; (Bauch) belly, abdomen; (Taille) waist; (Mutterleib) womb; **am ganzen L. zittern** tremble all over; **bleib mir nur damit vom Leibe!** (coll) don't bother me with that: **e-n harten L. haben** be constipated; **gesegneten Leibes** with child; **L. und Leben** life and limb; **mit L. und Seele** through and through; **sich** [dat] **j—n vom Leibe halten** keep s.o. at arm's length; **zu Leibe gehen** (dat) tackle (s.th.), attack (s.o.)

Leib′arzt m personal physician

Leib′binde f sash

Leibchen [′laɪpçən] n (-s;-) bodice; vest

leib′eigen adj in bondage ‖ **Leibeigene** §5 mf serf

Leib′eigenschaft f (-;) serfdom, bondage

Lei′besbeschaffenheit f (-;-en) constitution

Lei′beserbe m (-n;-n) offspring

Lei′beserziehung f physical education

Lei′besfrucht f fetus

Lei′beskräfte pl—aus **Leibeskräften**

schreien scream at the top of one's lungs
Lei′besübungen pl physical education
Lei′besvisitation f body search
Leib′garde f bodyguard
Leibgardist [′laɪpgardɪst] m (-en;-en) bodyguard
Leib′gericht n favorite dish
leibhaft(ig) [′laɪphaft(ɪç)] adj incarnate, real
leib′lich adj bodily, corporal; **leiblicher Vetter** first cousin; **sein leiblicher Sohn** his own son
Leib′rente f annuity for life
Leib′schmerzen pl, **Leib′schneiden** n abdominal pains
Leibstandarte [′laɪpʃtandartə] f (-;-n) (hist) SS bodyguard
Leib′wache f bodyguard
Leib′wäsche f underwear
Leiche [′laɪçə] f (-;-n) corpse, body; carcass; (dial) funeral
Leichenbegängnis [′laɪçənbəgɛŋnɪs] n (-ses;-se) funeral, interment
Leichenbeschauer [′laɪçənbəʃau‿ər] m (-s;-) coroner
Leichenbestatter [′laɪçənbəʃtatər] m (-s;-) undertaker
Leichenbittermiene f woe-begone look
Leichenfledderer [′laɪçənfledərər] m (-s;-) body stripper
Lei′chengift n ptomaine poison
lei′chenhaft adj corpse-like
Lei′chenhalle f mortuary
Lei′chenöffnung f autopsy
Lei′chenräuber m body snatcher
Lei′chenrede f eulogy
Lei′chenschau f post mortem
Lei′chenschauhaus n morgue
Lei′chenstarre f rigor mortis
Lei′chenträger m pallbearer
Lei′chentuch n shroud
Lei′chenverbrennung f cremation
Lei′chenwagen m hearse
Lei′chenzug m funeral cortege
Leichnam [′laɪçnam] m (-[e]s;-e) corpse
leicht [laɪçt] adj light; (nicht schwierig) easy; (gering) slight; **leichten Herzens** light-heartedly
Leicht′atletik f track and field
Leicht′bauweise f lightweight construction
Leicht′benzin n cleaning fluid
leichtbeschwingt [′laɪçtbəʃvɪŋt] adj gay
leicht′blütig adj light-hearted
leicht′entzündlich adj highly flammable
Leichter [′laɪçtər] m (-s;-) (naut) lighter
leicht′fertig adj frivolous, flippant; careless
leicht′flüchtig adj highly volatile
leicht′flüssig adj thin
Leicht′gewicht n lightweight division
Leichtgewichtler [′laɪçtgəvɪçtlər] m (-s;-) lightweight boxer
leicht′gläubig adj gullible
leicht′hin′ adv lightly, casually
Leich′tigkeit f (-;) ease
leichtlebig [′laɪçtlebɪç] adj easygoing
Leicht′sinn m frivolity, irresponsibility;

(Sorglosigkeit) carelessness; (Unbedachtsamkeit) imprudence
leicht′sinnig adj frivolous, irresponsible
leicht′verdaulich adj easy to digest
leicht′verderblich adj perishable
leid [laɪt] adj—**er tut mir l.** I feel sorry for him; **es tut mir l., daß I am sorry that; es ist (or tut) mir l. um I** feel sorry for, I regret; **ich bin es l.** I'm fed up with it ‖ **Leid** n (-[e]s;) (Betrübnis) sorrow; (Schaden) harm; (Unrecht) wrong; **j-m ein L. antun** harm s.o.
Leideform [′laɪdəform] f (gram) passive voice
leiden [′laɪdən] §106 tr suffer; (ertragen) stand ‖ intr (an dat) suffer (from) ‖ **Leiden** n (-s;-) suffering; (Krankheit) ailment
Lei′denschaft f (-;-en) passion
lei′denschaftlich adj passionate
lei′denschaftslos adj dispassionate
Lei′densgefährte m, **Lei′densgefährtin** f fellow sufferer
Lei′densgeschichte f tale of woe; (relig) Passion
Lei′densweg m way of the cross
leider [′laɪdər] adv unfortunately
leiderfüllt [′laɪterfʏlt] adj sorrowful
leidig [′laɪdɪç] adj tiresome
leidlich [′laɪtlɪç] adv tolerable; (halbwegs gut) passable ‖ adv so-so
leidtragend [′laɪttragənt] adj in mourning ‖ **Leidtragende** §5 mf mourner; **er ist der L. dabei** he is the one that suffers for it
Leid′wesen n—**zu meinem L.** to my regret
Leier [′laɪ‿ər] f (-;-n) (mus) lyre
Lei′erkasten m hand organ, hurdygurdy
Lei′ermann m (-[e]s;‥er) organ grinder
leiern [′laɪ‿ərn] tr (winden) crank; (Gebete, Verse) drone ‖ intr drone
Leih- [laɪ] comb.fm. loan, rental
Leih′amt n, **Leih′anstalt** f loan office
Leih′bibliothek f rental library
leihen [′laɪ‿ən] tr lend, loan out; (entleihen) (von) borrow (from)
Leih′gebühr f rental fee
Leih′haus n pawnshop
Leim [laɪm] m (-[e]s;-e) glue; birdlime; **aus dem L. gehen** fall apart; **j-m auf den L. gehen** be taken in by s.o.
leimen [′laɪmən] tr glue; (betrügen) take in, fool
Leim′farbe f distemper
leimig [′laɪmɪç] adj gluey
Lein [laɪn] m (-[e]s;-e) flax
Leine [′laɪnə] f (-;-n) line, cord; (Hunde-) leash
Leinen [′laɪnən] n (-s;-) linen
Lei′neneinband m (-[e]s;‥e) (bb) cloth binding
Lei′nenschuh m sneaker, canvas shoe
Lei′nenzeug n linen fabric
Lein′öl n linseed oil
Lein′tuch n sheet
Lein′wand f linen cloth; canvas; (cin) screen
leise [′laɪzə] adj soft, low; (sanft) gentle; (gering) faint; (Schlaf) light

lei′sestellen *tr* (rad) turn down

Lei′setreter *m* (-s;-) pussyfoot

Leiste ['laɪstə] *f* (-;-n) (*Rand*) border; (anat) groin; (carp) molding

leisten ['laɪstən] *tr* do, perform, accomplish; (*Dienst*) render; (*Eid*) take; (*Abbitte, Hilfe, Widerstand*) offer; **Bürgschaft l. für** put up bail for; **Folge l.** (*dat*), **Gehorsam l.** (*dat*) obey; **Genüge l.** (*dat*) satisfy; **j-m Gesellschaft l.** keep s.o. company; **sich** |*dat*| **etw l. können** be able to afford s.th. || **Leisten** *m* (-s;-) last; **alles über e-n L. schlagen** (fig) be undiscriminating

Lei′stenbruch *m* hernia, rupture

Lei′stung *f* (-;-en) performance; efficiency; ability; feat, achievement; (*Ergebnis*) result; (*Erzeugung*) production; (*Abgabe, Ausstoß*) output; (*Beitrag*) contribution; (*Dienstleistungen*) services rendered; (elec) power, wattage; (indust) output, production; (insur) benefits; (mach) capacity

Lei′stungsanreiz *m* incentive

lei′stungsfähig *adj* (*Person*) efficient; (*Motor*) powerful; (*Fabrik*) productive; (phys) efficient

Lei′stungsfähigkeit *f* efficiency; proficiency; (*e-s Autos*) performance; (*e-s Motors*) power; (mach) output

lei′stungsgerecht *adj* based on merit

Lei′stungsgrenze *f* peak of performance

Leis′tungslohn *m* pay based on performance

Lei′stungszulage *f* bonus

Leit- [laɪt] *comb.fm.* leading, dominant, guiding

Leit′artikel *m* editorial

Leit′bild *n* (good) example, ideal

leiten ['laɪtən] *tr* lead, guide; (*Verkehr*) route; (*Betrieb*) direct, run; (*Versammlung*) preside over; (arti) direct; (elec, mus, phys) conduct

Lei′ter *m* (-s;-) leader; director; (educ) principal; (elec, mus) conductor || *f* (-;-n) ladder

Lei′terin *f* (-;-nen) leader; director

Leit′faden *m* manual, guide

Leit′fähigkeit *f* conductivity

Leit′gedanke *m* main idea, main theme

Leit′hammel *m* (fig) boss, leader

Leit′motiv *n* keynote; (mus) leitmotiv

Leit′satz *m* basic point

Leit′spruch *m* motto

Leit′stelle *f* head office

Leit′stern *m* polestar, lodestar

Lei′tung *f* (-;-en) direction, guidance; (*Beaufsichtigung*) management; (*Rohr*) pipeline; (*für Gas, Wasser*) main; (elec) lead; (phys) conduction; (telp) line; **e-e lange L. haben** be rather dense; **L. besetzt!** line is busy!

Lei′tungsdraht *m* (elec) lead

Lei′tungsmast *m* telephone pole

Lei′tungsnetz *n* (elec) power lines

Lei′tungsrohr *n* pipe, main

Lei′tungsvermögen *n* conductivity

Lei′tungswasser *n* tap water

Leit′werk *n* (aer) tail assembly

Leit′zahl *f* code number

Lektion [lek′tsjon] *f* (-;-en) lesson; (fig) lecture, rebuke

Lek·tor ['lektor] *m* (-s;-toren** ['torən]) lecturer; (*e-s Verlags*) reader

Lektüre [lek′tyrə] *f* (-;) reading matter, literature

Lende ['lendə] *f* (-;-n) loin; (*Hüfte*) hip

Len′denbraten *m* roast loin, sirloin

len′denlahm *adj* stiff; (*Ausrede*) lame

Len′denschurz *m* loincloth

Len′denstück *n* tenderloin, sirloin

lenkbar ['leŋkbar] *adj* manageable; steerable, maneuverable; **lenkbares Luftschiff** dirigible

lenken ['leŋkən] *tr* guide, control; (*Wagen*) drive; (*wenden*) turn; (*steuern*) steer; **Aufmerksamkeit l. auf** (*acc*) call attention to

Len′ker –in §6 *mf* ruler; (aut) driver

Lenkrad ['leŋkrat] *n* steering wheel

Lenksäule ['leŋkzɔɪlə] *f* steering column

Lenkstange ['leŋk′taŋə] *f* handlebar; (aut) connecting rod

Len′kung *f* (-;-en) guidance, control; (aut) steering mechanism

Lenz [lents] *m* (-es;-e) (fig) prime of life; (poet) spring

Lenz′pumpe *f* bilge pump

Lepra ['lepra] *f* (-;) leprosy

Lerche ['lerçə] *f* (-;-n) (orn) lark

lernbegierig ['lernbəgiriç] *adj* eager to learn, studious

lernen [‚'lernən] *tr & intr* learn; study

Lesart *f* ['lezart] *f* version

lesbar ['lezbar] *adj* legible; readable

Lesbierin ['lesbiˑərɪn] *f* (-;-nen) lesbian

lesbisch ['lesbɪʃ] *adj* lesbian; **lesbische Liebe** lesbianism

Lese ['leza] *f* (-;-n) gathering, picking; (*Wein-*) vintage

Lese- [leza] *comb.fm.* reading; lecture

Le′sebrille *f* reading glasses

Le′sebuch *n* reader

Le′sehalle *f* reading room

lesen ['lezən] §107 *tr* read; gather; (*Messe*) say || *intr* read; lecture; **l. über** (*acc*) lecture on

le′senswert *adj* worth reading

Le′seprobe *f* specimen from a book; (theat) reading rehearsal

Le′ser –in §6 *mf* reader; picker

Le′seratte *f* (coll) bookworm

le′serlich *adj* legible

Le′serzuschrift *f* letter to the editor

Le′sestoff *m* reading matter

Le′sezeichen *n* bookmark

Le′sung *f* (-;-en) reading

Lette ['letə] *m* (-n;-n), **Lettin** ['letɪn] *f* (-;-nen) Latvian

lettisch ['letɪʃ] *adj* Latvian

Lettland ['letlant] *n* (-[e]s;) Latvia

letzte ['letstə] §9 *adj* last; (*endgültig*) final, ultimate; (*neueste*) latest; (*Ausweg*) last; **bis ins l.** to the last detail; **in den letzten Jahren** in recent years; **in der letzten Zeit** lately; **letzten Endes** in the final analysis || **Letzte §5** *pron* last, last one; **am Letzten** on the last of the month; **sein Letztes hergeben** do one's utmost; **zu guter Letzt** finally, last but not least

letztens ['lɛtstəns] adv lately

letztere ['lɛtstərə] §5 mfn latter

letzthin [lɛtst'hɪn] adv lately

letztlich ['lɛtstlɪç] adv lately, recently; in the final analysis

letztwillig ['lɛtstvɪlɪç] adj testamentary

Leucht– [lɔɪçt] comb.fm. luminous; illuminating

Leucht'bombe f flare bomb

Leuchte ['lɔɪçtə] f (–;–n) light, lamp; lantern; (fig) luminary

leuchten ['lɔɪçtən] intr shine

leuch'tend adj shining, bright; luminous

Leuchter ['lɔɪçtər] m (–s;–) candlestick; chandelier

Leucht'farbe f luminous paint

Leucht'feuer n (aer) flare; (naut) beacon

Leucht'käfer m lightning bug

Leucht'körper m light bulb; light fixture

Leucht'kugel n tracer bullet; flare

Leucht'pistole f Very pistol

Leucht'rakete f (aer) flare

Leucht'reklame f neon sign

Leucht'röhre f fluorescent lamp

Leucht'spurgeschoß n tracer bullet

Leucht'turm m lighthouse

Leucht'zifferblatt n luminous dial

leugnen ['lɔɪgnən] tr deny; disclaim

Leukoplast [lɔɪkə'plast] n (–[e]s;–e) adhesive tape

Leumund ['lɔɪmunt] m (–[e]s;) reputation

Leu'mundszeugnis n character reference

Leute ['lɔɪtə] pl people, persons, men; (Dienstleute) servants

Leu'teschinder m oppressor; slave driver

Leutnant ['lɔɪtnant] m (–s;–s) lieutenant

Leut'priester m secular priest

leut'selig adj affable

Lexikograph [lɛksɪko'graf] m (–en;–en) lexicographer

Lexikon ['lɛksɪkon] n (–s;–s) encyclopedia

Libanon ['libanon] n (–s;) Lebanon

Libelle [li'bɛlə] f (–;–n) dragonfly; (carp) level

liberal [libe'ral] adj liberal

Liberalismus [libera'lɪsmus] m (–s;) liberalism

Libyen ['liby·ən] n (–s;) Libya

licht [lɪçt] adj light, bright; (durchsichtig) clear || **Licht** n (–[e]s;–er) light; (Kerze) candle

licht'beständig adj non-fading

Licht'bild n photograph

Licht'bildervortrag m illustrated lecture

licht'blau adj light-blue

Licht'blick m (fig) bright spot

Licht'bogen m (elec) arc

Licht'bogenschweißung f arc welding

Licht'brechung f (–;–en) refraction of light

Licht'druck m phototype

licht'durchlässig adj translucent

licht'echt adj non-fading

licht'empfindlich adj sensitized; **l. machen** sensitize

Licht'empfindlichkeit f (phot) speed

lichten ['lɪçtən] tr clear; thin; (Anker) weigh

lichterloh ['lɪçtərlo] adv ablaze; **l. brennen** be ablaze

Licht'hof m (archit) light well, inner court; (phot) halo

Licht'kegel m beam of light

Licht'maschine f generator, dynamo

Licht'pause f blueprint

Licht'punkt m (fig) ray of hope

Licht'schacht m light well

Licht'schalter m light switch

licht'scheu adj—**lichtscheues Gesindel** shady characters

Licht'schirm m lamp shade

Licht'seite f (fig) bright side

Licht'spiele pl, **Licht'spielhaus** n, **Licht'spieltheater** n movie theater

licht'stark adj (Objektiv) high-powered; (phot) high-speed

Lich'tung f (–;–en) clearing

Lid [lit] n (–[e]s;–er) eyelid

Lid'schatten m eye shadow

lieb [lip] adj dear; (nett) nice; **der liebe Gott** the good Lord; **es ist mir l., daß** I am glad that; **seien Sie so l. und** please; **sich lieb Kind machen bei** ingratiate oneself with

lieb'äugeln intr—**l. mit** (& fig) flirt with

Liebchen ['lipçən] n (–s;–) darling

Liebe ['libə] f (–;) (zu) love (for, of)

liebedienerisch ['libədinərɪʃ] adj fawning

Liebelei [libə'laɪ] f (–;–en) flirtation

lieben ['libən] tr love, be fond of

lie'bend adj loving || adv—**l. gern** gladly || **Liebende** §5 mf lover

lie'benswert adj lovable

lie'benswürdig adj lovable; charming; **das ist sehr l. von Ihnen** that's very kind of you

lieber ['libər] adv rather, sooner; **l. haben** prefer

Liebes– [libəs] comb.fm. love, of love

Lie'besdienst m favor, good turn

Lie'beserlebnis n romance

Lie'besgabe f charitable gift

Lie'beshandel m love affair

Lie'besmahl n love feast

Lie'besmühe f—**verlorene L.** wasted effort

Lie'bespaar n couple (of lovers)

Lie'bespfand n token of love

Lie'bestrank m love potion

Lie'bewerben n advances

lie'bevoll adj loving, affectionate

Lieb'frauenkirche f Church of Our Lady

lieb'gewinnen §121 tr grow fond of

lieb'haben §89 tr love, be fond of

Liebhaber ['liphabər] m (–s;–) lover, beau; amateur; fan, buff; **erster L.** leading man

lieb'kosen tr caress, fondle

lieb'lich adj lovely, sweet; charming

Liebling ['liplɪŋ] m (–s;–e) darling; (Haustier) pet; (Günstling) favorite

Lieblings– comb.fm. favorite

Lieb'lingsgedanke *m* pet idea
Lieb'lingswunsch *m* dearest wish
lieb'los *adj* unkind
lieb'reich *adj* kind, affectionate
Lieb'reiz *m* charm, attractiveness
lieb'reizend *adj* charming
Lieb'schaft *f* (-;-en) love affair
liebste ['lipstə] §9 *adj* favorite; **am liebsten trinke ich Wein** I like wine best of all
Lied [lit] *n* (-[e]s;-er) song; **er weiß ein L. davon zu singen** he can tell you all about it; **geistliches L.** hymn
liederlich ['lidərlɪç] *adj* dissolute; (*unordentlich*) disorderly
lief [lif] *pret of* **laufen**
Lieferant –in [lifə'rant(ɪn)] §7 *mf* supplier; (*Verteiler*) distributor; (*von Lebensmitteln*) caterer
Lieferauto ['lifərauto] *n* delivery truck
lieferbar ['lifərbar] *adj* available, deliverable
Liefergebühr ['lifərgə'byr] *f* delivery charge
liefern ['lifərn] *tr* deliver; (*beschaffen*) supply, furnish; (*Ertrag*) yield; **ich bin geliefert** (coll) I'm done for
Lieferschein ['lifərʃain] *m* delivery receipt
Lie'ferung *f* (-;-en) delivery, shipment; supply; (*e-s Werkes*) installment, number; **zahlbar bei L.** cash on delivery
Lieferwagen ['lifərvagən] *m* delivery truck
Liege ['ligə] *f* (-;-n) couch
Lie'gekur *f* rest cure
liegen ['ligən] §108 *intr* lie, be situated; **gut auf der Straße l.** hug the road; **l. an** (*dat*) lie near; (fig) be due to; **wie die Sache jetzt liegt as matters now stand** ‖ *impers*—**es liegt an ihm zu** (*inf*) it's up to him to (*inf*); **es liegt auf der Hand** it is obvious; **es liegt mir nichts daran** it doesn't matter to me; **es liegt mir (sehr viel) daran** it matters (a great deal) to me
lie'genbleiben §62 *intr* (SEIN) stay in bed; (*Waren*) remain unsold; (*stekkenbleiben*) have a breakdown; (*Arbeit*) be left undone
lie'genlassen §104 *tr* let lie; leave alone; (*Arbeit*) leave undone
Lie'genschaft *f* (-;-en) real estate
Lie'gestuhl *m* deck chair
Lie'gestütz *m* (gym) pushup
lieh [li] *pret of* **leihen**
ließ [lis] *pret of* **lassen**
Li·ga ['liga] *f* (-;-gen [gən]) league
Liguster [li'gustər] *m* (-s;-) privet
liieren [li'irən] *ref*—**sich l. mit** ally oneself with
Likör [li'kør] *m* (-s;-e) liqueur
lila ['lila] *adj* lilac
Lilie ['liljə] *f* (-;-n) lily
Limonade [limo'nadə] *f* (-;-n) soft drink, soda
lind [lɪnt] *adj* mild, gentle
Linde ['lɪndə] *f* (-;-n) (bot) linden
lindern ['lɪndərn] *tr* alleviate; (*Übel*) mitigate; (*mildern*) soften

Lindwurm ['lɪntvurm] *m* dragon
Lineal [line'al] *n* (-s;-e) ruler
Linguist –in [lɪŋgu'ɪst(ɪn)] §7 *mf* linguist
Linie ['linjə] *f* (-;-n) line; **auf gleicher L. mit** on a level with; **in erster L.** in the first place
Li'nienpapier *n* lined paper
Li'nienrichter *m* (sport) linesman
Li'nienschiff *n* ship of the line
li'nientreu *adj*—**l. sein** follow the party line
linieren [li'nirən] *tr* line, rule
linke ['lɪŋkə] §9 *adj* left; (*Seite*) wrong, reverse ‖ §5 **Linke** *m* (box) left ‖ §5 *f* left side; left hand; **die L.** (pol) the left
linkisch ['lɪŋkɪʃ] *adj* clumsy, awkward
links [lɪŋks] *adv* left; to the left; on the left; (*verkehrt*) inside out; **l. liegenlassen** bypass, ignore; **links um!** left, face!
links'drehend *adj* counterclockwise
linksgängig ['lɪŋksgeŋɪç] *adj* counterclockwise
Linkshänder ['lɪŋkshendər] *m* (-s;-) left-hander
links'läufig *adj* counterclockwise
links'stehend *adj* (pol) leftist
Linnen ['lɪnən] *n* (-s;) linen
Linse ['lɪnzə] *f* (-;-n) (bot) lentil; (opt) lens
Lippe ['lɪpə] *f* (-;-n) lip; **e-e L. riskieren** (fig) speak out of turn
Lip'penbekenntnis *n* lip service
Lip'penlaut *m* labial
Lip'penstift *m* lipstick
liquid [li'kvit] *adj* (*Geldmittel*) liquid; (*Gesellschaft*) solvent
Liquidation [likvida'tsjon] *f* (-;-en) liquidation; (*Kostenrechnung*) bill
liquidieren [likvi'dirən] *tr* liquidate; (*Geschäft*) wind up; (*Honorar*) charge
lispeln ['lɪspəln] *tr & intr* lisp; (*flüstern*) whisper
Lissabon [lɪsa'bɔn] *n* (-s;) Lisbon
List [lɪst] *f* (-;-en) cunning; trick
Liste ['lɪstə] *f* (-;-n) list; **schwarze L.** blacklist
Li'stenwahl *f* block voting
listig ['lɪstɪç] *adj* cunning, sly
Litanei [lita'nai] *f* (-;-en) litany
Litauen ['litau-ən] *n* (-s;) Lithuania
litauisch ['litau·ɪʃ] *adj* Lithuanian
Liter ['litər] *m & n* (-s;-) liter
literarisch [lɪtə'rarɪʃ] *adj* literary
Literatur [lɪtera'tur] *f* (-;-en) literature
Litfaßsäule ['lɪtfaszɔɪlə] *f* advertising pillar
Liturgie [lɪtur'gi] *f* (-;-gien ['gi·ən]) liturgy
Litze ['lɪtsə] *f* (-;-n) cord; (elec) strand
Li·vree [li'vre] *f* (-;-vreen ['vre·ən]) uniform, livery
Lizenz [li'tsɛnts] *f* (-;-en) license
Lob [lop] *n* (-[e]s;) praise
loben ['lobən] §109 *tr* praise
lo'benswert *adj* praiseworthy
Lobhudelei [lophudə'lai] *f* (-;-en) flattery

lob′hudeln tr heap praise on
löblich [ˈløplɪç] adj commendable
lob′preisen tr extol, praise
Lob′rede f panegyric
Loch [lɔx] n (-es;⸚er) hole
Loch′bohrer m auger
lochen [ˈlɔxən] tr punch, perforate
Locher [ˈlɔxər] m (-s;-) punch
löcherig [ˈlœçərɪç] adj full of holes
Loch′karte f punch card
Lo′chung f (-;-en) perforation
Locke [ˈlɔkə] f (-;-n) lock, curl
locken [ˈlɔkən] tr allure, entice; decoy; (Hund) whistle to
locker [ˈlɔkər] adj loose; (nicht straff) slack; spongy; (moralisch) loose
lockern [ˈlɔkərn] tr loosen
lockig [ˈlɔkɪç] adj curly, curled
Lock′mittel n, **Lock′speise** f (& fig) bait
Lockspitzel [ˈlɔkʃpɪtsəl] m stool-pigeon
Lo′ckung f (-;-en) allurement
Lock′vogel m (& fig) decoy
Loden [ˈlodən] m (-s;-) coarse woolen cloth
lodern [ˈlodərn] intr blaze; (fig) glow
Löffel [ˈlœfəl] m (-s;-) spoon; (culin) spoonful; (coll & hunt) ear; **über den L. balbieren** hoodwink
Löf′felbagger m power shovel
löffeln [ˈlœfəln] tr spoon out
log [lok] pret of **lügen**
Logbuch [ˈlɔkbux] n logbook
Loge [ˈloʒə] f (-;-n) (der Freimaurer) lodge; (theat) box
Lo′genbruder m freemason
Logierbesuch [loˈʒirbəzux] m house-guest(s)
logieren [loˈʒirən] intr stay (bei) stay (with)
Logik [ˈlogɪk] f (-;) logic
Logis [loˈʒi] invar n lodgings
logisch [ˈlogɪ] adj logical
Lohe [ˈlo·ə] f (-;-n) blaze, flame
Lohgerber [ˈlogɛrbər] m (-s;-) tanner
Lohn [lon] m (-[e]s;⸚e) pay, wages; (fig) reward
Lohn′abbau m wage cut
lohnen [ˈlonən] tr compensate, reward; (Arbeiter) pay; **j-m etw l.** reward s.o. for s.th. ‖ ref pay, be worth-while
löhnen [ˈlønən] tr pay, pay wages to
Lohn′erhöhung f raise, wage increase
Lohn′gefälle n wage differential
Lohn′herr m employer
lohn′intensiv adj with high labor costs
Lohn′liste f payroll
Lohn′satz m pay rate
Lohn′stopp m wage freeze
Lohn′tag m payday
Lohn′tüte f pay envelope
Löh′nung f (-;-en) payment
lokal [loˈkal] adj local ‖ **Lokal** n (-[e]s;-e) locality, premises; (Wirtshaus) restaurant, pub, inn
lokalisieren [lokaliˈzirən] tr localize
Lokalität [lokaliˈtɛt] f (-;-en) locality
Lokomotive [lokomoˈtivə] f (-;-n) locomotive
Lokomotiv′führer m (rr) engineer
Lokus [ˈlokus] m (-;-se) (coll) john
Lorbeer [ˈlɔrbər] m (-s;-en) laurel

los [los] adj loose; **es ist etw los** there is s.th. going on; **es ist nichts los** there is nothing going on; **etw los haben** have s.th. on the ball; **j-n** (or **etw**) **los sein** be rid of s.o. (or s.th.); **los!** go on!, scram!; (sprich!) fire away!; (mach schnell!) let's go!; (sport) play ball!; **mit ihm ist nicht viel los** he's no great shakes; **was ist los?** what's the matter? ‖ **Los** n (-[e]s;-e) lot; (Lotterie-) ticket; (Anteil), lot, portion; (Schicksal) fate; **das Große Los** first prize; **das Los ziehen** draw lots; **die Lose sind gefallen** the die is cast
los- comb.fm. un-, e.g., **losmachen** undo
los′arbeiten tr extricate ‖ ref get loose, extricate oneself ‖ intr (auf acc) work away (at)
lösbar [ˈløsbar] adj solvable
los′binden §59 tr loosen, untie
los′brechen §64 tr break off ‖ intr (SEIN) break loose
Löschblatt [ˈlœʃblat] n blotter
Löscheimer [ˈlœʃaimər] m fire bucket
löschen [ˈlœʃən] tr put out; (Durst) quench; (Schuld) cancel; (Schrift) blot; (Bandaufnahme) erase; (Firma) liquidate; (Hypotek) pay off; (naut) unload
Lö′scher m (-s;-) blotter; (Feuer-) fire extinguisher
Löschgerät [ˈlœʃgərɛt] n fire extinguisher
Löschmannschaft [ˈlœʃmanʃaft] f fire brigade
Löschpapier [ˈlœʃpapir] n blotting paper
Lö′schung f (-;-en) extinction; (Tilgung) cancellation; (naut) unloading
los′drehen tr unscrew, twist off
los′drücken tr fire ‖ intr pull the trigger
lose [ˈlozə] §9 adj loose
Lösegeld [ˈløzəgɛlt] n ransom
loseisen [ˈlozaizən] tr—**Geld l. von** wangle money out of; **j-n l. aus** get s.o. out of; **j-n l. von** get s.o. away from ‖ ref (von) worm one's way (out of)
losen [ˈlozən] intr draw lots
lösen [ˈløzən] tr loosen, untie; (abtrennen) sever; (Bremse) release; (Fahrkarte) buy; (loskaufen) ransom; (lossprechen) absolve; (Rätsel) solve; (Schuß) fire; (Verlobung) break off ‖ ref come loose, come undone; dissolve; (sich befreien) free oneself
los′fahren §71 intr (SEIN) drive off; **l. auf** (acc) head for; rush at; attack (verbally)
los′gehen §82 intr (SEIN) (coll) begin; (Gewehr) go off; (sich lösen) come loose; **auf j-n l.** attack s.o.
los′haken tr unhook
los′kaufen tr ransom
los′ketten tr unchain
los′kommen §99 intr (SEIN) come loose, come off; **ich komme nicht davon los** I can't get over it; **l. von** get away from; get rid of
los′lachen intr burst out laughing

los'lassen §104 *tr* let go; release; **den Hund l. auf** (*acc*) sic the dog on

los'legen *intr* (coll) start up, let fly; (*reden*) (coll) open up; **leg los!** (*coll*) fire away!

löslich ['lø̈slɪç] *adj* soluble

los'lösen *tr* detach

los'machen *tr* undo, untie; (*freimachen*) free ‖ *ref* disengage onself

los'platzen *intr* (SEIN) burst out laughing; **l. mit** blurt out

los'reißen §53 *tr* & *ref* break loose

los'sagen *ref*—**sich l. von** renounce

los'schlagen §132 *tr* knock off; (*verkaufen*) dispose of, sell cheaply ‖ *intr* open the attack; **l. auf** (*acc*) let fly at

los'schnallen *tr* unbuckle

los'schrauben *tr* unscrew

los'sprechen §64 *tr* absolve

los'steuern *intr*—**l. auf** (*acc*) head for

Lo'sung *f* (–;-en) (*Kot*) dung; (mil) password; (pol) slogan

Lö'sung *f* (–;-en) solution

Lö'sungsmittel *n* solvent; thinner

los'werden §159 *tr* (SEIN) get rid of

los'ziehen §163 *intr* (SEIN) set out, march away; **l. auf** (*acc*) talk about, run down

Lot [lot] *n* (–[e]s;-e) plummet; plumb line; (*Lötmetall*) solder; (geom) perpendicular; **im Lot** perpendicular; (fig) in order; **ins Lot bringen** (fig) set right

Löteisen ['lø̈taɪzən] *n* soldering iron

loten ['lotən] *tr* (naut) plumb ‖ *intr* (naut) take soundings

löten ['lø̈tən] *tr* solder

Lötkolben ['lø̈tkɔlbən] *m* soldering iron

Lötlampe ['lø̈tlampə] *f* blowtorch

Lötmetall ['lø̈tmetal] *n* solder

lot'recht *adj* perpendicular

Lotse ['lotsə] *m* (–n;-n) (aer) air traffic controller; (naut) pilot

lotsen ['lotsən] *tr* (*Flugzeuge*) guide in; (naut) pilot

Lotte·rie [lɔtə'ri] *f* (–;-rien ['ri-ən]) lottery, sweepstakes

Lotterie'los *n* lottery ticket

lotterig ['lɔtərɪç] *adj* sloppy

Lotterleben ['lɔtərlebən] *n* dissolute life

Lotto ['lɔto] *n* (–;-s) state-owned numbers game

Löwe ['lø̈və] *m* (–n;-n) lion

Lö'wenanteil *m* lion's share

Lö'wenbändiger –*in* §6 *mf* lion tamer

Lö'wengrube *f* lion's den

Lö'wenmaul *n* (bot) snapdragon

Lö'wenzahn *m* (bot) dandelion

Löwin ['lø̈vɪn] *f* (–;-nen) lioness

loyal [lɔa'jal] *adj* loyal

Luchs [luks] *m* (–es;-e) lynx

Lücke ['lʏkə] *f* (–;-n) gap, hole; (*Mangel*) deficiency; (*im Gesetz*) loophole; (*Zwischenraum*) interval; **auf L. stehend** staggered

Lückenbüßer ['lʏkənbysər] *m* (–s;–) stop-gap

lückenhaft (lük'kenhaft) *adj* defective, fragmentary

Luder ['ludər] *n* (–s;–) carrion; (coll)

cad; (*Weibsbild*) slut; **das arme L.!** the poor thing!; **dummes L.!** fathead!

Lu'derleben *n* dissolute life

ludern ['ludərn] *intr* lead a dissolute life

Luft [luft] *f* (–;̈e) air; (*Atem*) breath; (*Brise*) breeze; **die L. ist rein** the coast is clear; **es ist dicke L.** there is trouble brewing; **es liegt etw in der L.** (fig) there's s.th. in the air; **frische L. schöpfen** get a breath of fresh air; **in die L. fliegen** be blown up; **in die L. gehen** blow one's top; **in die L. sprengen** blow up; **j–n an die L. setzen** give s.o. the air; **nach L. schnappen** gasp for breath; **seinem Zorn L. machen** give vent to one's anger; **tief L. holen** take a deep breath

Luft'alarm *m* air-raid alarm

Luft'angriff *m* air raid

Luft'ansicht *f* aerial view

Luft'aufklärung *f* air reconnaissance

Luft'bild *n* aerial photograph

Luft'bremse *f* air brake

Luft'brücke *f* airlift

Lüftchen ['lʏftçən] *n* (–s;–) gentle breeze

luft'dicht' *adj* airtight

Luft'druck *m* atmospheric pressure; (*e–r Explosion*) blast; (aut) air pressure

Luft'druckbremse *f* air brake

Luft'druckmesser *m* barometer

Luft'druckprüfer *m* tire gauge

Luft'düse *f* air nozzle, air jet

lüften ['lʏftən] *tr* air, ventilate; **den Hut l.** tip one's hat

Luft'fahrt *f* aviation

Luft'fahrzeug *n* aircraft

Luft'flotte *f* air force

luft'förmig *adj* gaseous

Luft'hafen *m* airport

Luft'heizung *f* hot-air heating

Luft'herrschaft *f* air supremacy

Luft'hülle *f* atmosphere

luftig ['luftɪç] *adj* airy; (*windig*) windy; (*Person*) flighty; (*Kleidung*) loosely woven, light

Luftikus ['luftɪkus] *m* (–;-se) lightheaded person

Luft'klappe *f* air valve

luft'krank *adj* airsick

Luft'kurort *m* mountain resort

Luft'landetruppen *pl* airborne troops

luft'leer *adj* vacuous; **luftleerer Raum** vacuum

Luft'linie *f* beeline; **fünfzig Kilometer L.** 50 kilometers as the crow flies

Luft'loch *n* vent; (aer) air pocket

Luft'parade *f* flyover

Luft'post *f* airmail

Luft'raum *m* atmosphere; air space

Luft'reifen *m* tire

Luft'reklame *f* sky writing

Luft'röhre *f* (anat) windpipe

Luft'schiff *n* airship

Luft'schiffahrt *f* aviation

Luft'schloß *n* castle in the air

Luft'schutz *m* air-raid protection

Luft'schutzkeller *m* air-raid shelter

Luft'schutzwart *m* air-raid warden

Luft'spiegelung *f* mirage

Luft′sprung m caper
Luft′streitkräfte pl air force
Luft′strom m air current
Luft′strudel m (aer) wash
Luft′stützpunkt m air base
luft′tüchtig adj air-worthy
Lüf′tung f (-;) airing, ventilation
Luft′veränderung f change of climate
Luft′verkehrsgesellschaft f, **Luft′ver-kehrslinie** f airline
Luft′vermessung f aerial survey
Luft′verpestung f (-;), **Luft′ver-schmutzung** f (-;), **Luft′verunreini-gung** f (-;) air pollution
Luft′waffe f air force
Luft′warnung f air-raid warning
Luft′weg m air route; **auf dem Luft-wege** by air
Luft′widerstand m (phys) air resistance
Luft′zug m draft
Lug [luk] m (-[e]s;) lie; **Lug und Trug** pack of lies
Lüge [′lygə] f (-;-n) lie; **fromme L.** white lie; **j-n Lügen strafen** prove s.o. a liar
lugen [′lugən] intr peep
lügen [′lygən] §111 tr—**das Blaue vom Himmel herunter l.** lie like mad ‖ intr lie, tell a lie
Lügendetek·tor [′lygəndetektɔr] m (-s; -toren** [′tɔrən]) lie detector
Lü′gengeschichte f cock-and-bull story
Lü′gengespinst n, **Lü′gengewebe** n tissue of lies
lü′genhaft adj (Person) dishonest, lying; (Nachricht) untrue
Lügner –in [′lygnər(ɪn)] §6 mf liar
lügnerisch [′lygnərɪʃ] adj dishonest
Luke [′lukə] f (-;-n) (am Dach) dormer window; (naut) hatch
Lümmel [′lyməl] m (-s;-) lout
Lump [lump] m (-en;-en) scoundrel
lumpen [′lumpən] intr lead a wild life; **sich nicht l. lassen** (coll) be generous ‖ **Lumpen** m (-s;-) rag
Lum′pengeld n measly sum; **für ein L.** dirtcheap
Lum′pengesindel n mob, rabble
Lum′penhändler m ragman
Lum′penkerl m (coll) bum
Lum′penpack n rabble, riffraff
Lumperei [lumpə′raɪ] f (-;-en) shady deal; dirty trick; (Kleinigkeit) trifle
lumpig [′lumpɪç] adj ragged; shabby

Lunge [′luŋə] f (-;-n) lung
Lungen– comb.fm. pulmonary
Lun′genentzündung f pneumonia
Lun′genflügel m lung
lun′genkrank adj consumptive ‖ **Lun-genkranke** §5 mf consumptive
Lun′genschwindsucht f tuberculosis
lungern [′luŋərn] intr (HABEN & SEIN) loiter about, lounge about
Lunte [′luntə] f (-;-n) fuse; **L. riechen** smell a rat
Lupe [′lupə] f (-;-n) magnifying glass; **unter die L. nehmen** examine closely
lüpfen [′lypfən] tr lift gently
Lust [lust] f (-;̈e) pleasure; (Verlangen) desire; (Wollust) lust; **L. haben zu** (inf) feel like (ger); **mit L. und Liebe** with heart and soul
Lust′barkeit f (-;-en) amusement, entertainment
Lüster [′lystər] m (-s;-) luster
lüstern [′lystərn] adj (nach) desirous (of); lustful; (Bilder, Späße) lewd
Lü′sternheit f (-;) greediness; lustfulness; lewdness
Lust′fahrt f pleasure ride
lustig [′lustɪç] adv gay, jolly; (belustigend) amusing; **du bist vielleicht l.!** you must be joking!; **l. sein** have a gay time; **sich l. machen über** (acc) poke fun at
Lüstling [′lystlɪŋ] m (-s;-e) lecher
lust′los adj listless; (Börse) inactive
Lustmolch [′lustmɔlç] m (-[e]s;-e) sex fiend
Lust′mord m sex murder
Lust′reise f pleasure trip
Lust′seuche f venereal disease
Lust′spiel n comedy
lust′wandeln intr (SEIN) stroll
Lutheraner –in [lutə′ranər(ɪn)] §6 mf Lutheran
lutherisch [′lutərɪʃ] adj Lutheran
lutschen [′lutʃən] tr & intr suck
Lut′scher m (-s;-) nipple, pacifier
Luxus [′luksus] m (-;) luxury
Lu′xusausgabe f deluxe edition
Luzerne [lu′tsernə] f (-;-n) alfalfa
Lymphe [′lymfə] f (-;-n) lymph
lynchen [′lynçən] tr lynch
Lyrik [′lyrɪk] f (-;) lyric poetry
lyrisch [′lyrɪʃ] adj lyric(al)
Lyze·um [ly′tse·um] n (-s;-en [ən]) girls' high school

M

M, m [ɛm] invar n M, m
M abbr (**Mark**) (fin) mark
Maar [mar] n (-[e]s;-e) crater lake
Maat [mat] m (-[e]s;-e) (naut) mate
Machart [′maxart] f make, type
Mache [′maxə] f (-;) (coll) make-believe; **er hat es schon in der M.** he is working on it
machen [′maxən] tr make; (tun) do; (bewirken) produce; (verursachen) cause; (Prüfung, Reise, Spaziergang)

take; (Begriff) form; (Besuch) pay; (Freude) give; (Holz) chop; (Konkurrenz) offer; **das macht mir zu schaffen** that causes me trouble; **das macht nichts** it doesn't matter; never mind; **das macht Spaß** that's fun; **Dummheiten m.** behave foolishly; **Ernst m.** be in earnest; **gemacht!** right!; O.K.!; **Geschäfte m.** do business; **Geschichten m.** make a fuss; **Hochzeit m.** get married; **ich mache**

Spaß I'm joking; **mach dir nichts daraus!** don't worry about it; **mach's gut!** so long!; **wieviel macht es?** how much is it? ‖ *ref* make progress, do all right; **sich auf den Weg m.** set out; **sich** [*dat*] **etw m. lassen** have s.th. made to order; **sich m. an** (*acc*) get down to; **sich** [*dat*] **nichts daraus m.** not care for (or about) ‖ *intr*— **laß mich nur m.!** just leave it to me; **mach, daß . . . !** see to it that . . . !; **m. in** (*dat*) deal in; dabble in; **mach schon** (or **zu**)! get going!; **nichts zu m!** (coll) nothing doing! no dice!

Machenschaften ['maxənʃaftən] *pl* intrigues

Macher ['maxər] *m* (-s;-) instigator; (coll) big shot

Macht [maxt] *f* (-;⁻e) might; power; (*Kraft*) force, strength; **aus eigener M.** on one's own responsibility; **an der Macht** in power; **an die M. kommen** come to power

Macht'ausgleich *m* balance of power

Macht'befugnis *f* authority

Machthaber ['maxthabər] *m* (-s;-) ruler; dictator

machthaberisch ['maxthabərɪʃ] *adj* dictatorial

mächtig ['mɛçtɪç] *adj* mighty, powerful; (*riesig*) huge

macht'los *adj* powerless

Macht'losigkeit *f* (-;) impotence

Macht'politik *f* power politics

Macht'vollkommenheit *f* absolute power; **aus eigener M.** on one's own authority

Macht'wort *n* (-[e]s;⁻e)—**ein M. sprechen** put one's foot down

Machwerk ['maxverk] *n* bad job

Mädchen ['mɛtçən] *n* (-s;-) maid; maid

mäd'chenhaft *adj* girlish; maidenly

Mäd'chenhandel *m* white slavery

Mäd'chenname *m* maiden name; girl's name

Made ['madə] *f* (-;-n) maggot

Mädel ['mɛdəl] *n* (-s;-) (coll) girl

madig ['madɪç] *adj* wormy

Magazin [maga'tsin] *n* (-s;-e) warehouse; (*Zeitschrift*; *Fernsehprogramm*; *am Gewehr*) magazine

Magd [makt] *f* (-;⁻e) maid; (poet) maiden

Magen ['magən] *m* (-s;⁻ & -) stomach; **auf nüchternen M.** on an empty stomach

Ma'genbeschwerden *pl* stomach trouble

Ma'gengrube *f* pit of the stomach

Ma'gensaft *m* gastric juice

Ma'genweh *n* stomach ache

mager ['magər] *adj* lean; (*Ernte*) poor

Magie [ma'gi] *f* (-;) magic

Magier -in ['magjər(ɪn)] §6 *mf* magician

magisch ['magɪʃ] *adj* magic(al)

Magister [ma'gɪstər] *m* (-s;-) school teacher; **M. der freien Künste** Master of Arts

Magistrat [magɪs'trat] *m* (-[e]s;-e) city council; (hist) magistracy

Magnat [mag'nat] *m* (-en;-en) magnate

Magnet [mag'net] *m* (-[e]s;-e) or (-en;-en) magnet

magnetisch [mag'netɪʃ] *adj* magnetic

magnetisieren [magnetɪ'zirən] *tr* magnetize

Magnetismus [magne'tɪsmus] *m* (-;) magnetism

Mahagoni [maha'goni] *n* (-s;) mahogony

Mahd [mat] *f* (-;-en) mowing

Mähdrescher ['medreʃər] *m* (agr) combine

mähen ['me.ən] *tr* mow; (*Getreide*) reap

Mä'her *m* (-s;-) mower; reaper

Mahl [mal] *n* (-[e]s;⁻er) meal

mahlen ['malən] (*pp* **gemahlen**) *tr* grind ‖ *intr* spin

Mahl'zahn *m* molar

Mahl'zeit *f* meal; **prost M.!** that's a nice mess!

Mähmaschine ['memaʃinə] *f* reaper; (*Rasen*-) lawn mower

Mähne ['menə] *f* (-;-n) mane

mahnen ['manən] *tr* (an *acc*) remind (of); (an *acc*) warn (about or of)

Mahnmal ['manmal] *n* (-s;-e) monument

Mah'nung *f* (-;-en) admonition; (com) reminder, notice

Mähre ['merə] *f* (-;-n) old nag

Mähren ['merən] *n* (-s;) Moravia

Mai [maɪ] *m* (-[e]s;-e) May

Mai'baum *m* maypole

Mai'blume *f* lily of the valley

Maid [maɪt] *f* (-;-en) (poet) maiden

Mai'glöckchen *n* lily of the valley

Mai'käfer *m* June bug

Mailand ['maɪlant] *n* (-[e]s;) Milan

Mais [maɪs] *m* (-es;) Indian corn

Maische ['maɪʃə] *f* (-;) mash

Mais'hülse *f* corn husk

Mais'kolben *m* corncob

Majestät [majes'tet] *f* (-;-en) majesty

majestätisch [majes'tetɪʃ] *adj* majestic

Major [ma'jor] *m* (-s;-e) major

Majoran [majo'ran] *m* (-s;-e) marjoram

majorenn [majo'ren] *adj* of age

Majorität [majorɪ'tet] *f* (-;-en) majority

Makel ['makəl] *m* (-s;-) spot, stain

Mäkelei [mekə'laɪ] *f* (-;-en) carping

mäkelig ['mekəlɪç] *adj* critical; (*im Essen*) picky

ma'kellos *adj* spotless; (fig) impeccable

mäkeln ['mekəln] *intr* (an *dat*) carp (at), find fault (with)

Makkaroni [maka'roni] *pl* macaroni

Makler -in ['maklər(ɪn)] §6 *mf* agent, broker

Mäkler -in ['meklər(ɪn)] §6 *mf* faultfinder

Mak'lergebühr *f* brokerage

Makrele [ma'krelə] *f* (-;-n) mackerel

Makrone [ma'kronə] *f* (-;-n) macaroon

Makulatur [makula'tur] *f* (-;) waste

mal [mal] *adv* (coll) once; (arith) times; **komm mal her!** come here once!; **zwei mal drei** two times three; **zwei mal Spinat** two (orders of)

spinach ‖ **Mal** n (-[e]s;-e) mark,
sign; (*Mutter-*) birthmark, mole;
(*Fleck*) stain; time; **dieses Mal** this
time; **manches liebe Mal** many a
time; **mit e-m Male** all at once
Malbuch ['malbux] n coloring book
malen ['malən] tr & intr paint
Ma'ler –in §6 mf painter
Malerei [malə'raɪ] f (-;-en) painting
malerisch ['malərɪʃ] adj picturesque
Ma'lerleinwand f canvas
Malkunst ['malkunst] f art of painting
Malstrom ['mal/trom] m maelstrom
malträtieren [maltrɛ'tirən] tr maltreat
Malve ['malvə] f (-;-n) mallow
Malz [malts] n (-es;) malt
Malz'bonbon m cough drop
Mal'zeichen n multiplication sign
Mama [ma'ma], ['mama] f (-;-s)
mom, ma
Mamsell [mam'zɛl] f (-;-en) miss;
(*Wirtschafterin*) housekeeper
man [man] indef pron one, they, people, you; **man hat mir gesagt** I have
been told
manch [manç] invar adj—**manch ein**
many a ‖ **mancher** §3 adj many a;
manche pl some, several ‖ pron
many a person; many a thing
mancherlei ['mançərlaɪ] invar adj all
sorts of, various
Manchester [man'/ɛstər] m (-s;) corduroy
manch'mal adv sometimes
Mandant –in [man'dant(ɪn)] §7 mf
client
Mandarine [manda'rinə] f (-;-n) tangerine
Mandat [man'dat] n (-[e]s;-e) mandate
mandatieren [manda'tirən] tr mandate
Mandel ['mandəl] f (-;-n) almond;
(*15 Stück*) fifteen; (anat) tonsil
Man'delentzündung f tonsilitis
Mandoline [mando'linə] f (-;-n) mandolin
Mandschurei [mantʃʊ'raɪ] f (-;) Manchuria
Mangan [maŋ'gan] n (-s;) manganese
Mangel ['maŋəl] m (-s;⸚) lack, deficiency; (*Knappheit*) shortage;
(*Fehler*) shortcoming; **aus M. an**
(dat) for lack of; **M. haben an** (dat)
be deficient in; **M. leiden an** (dat)
be short of ‖ f (-;-n) mangle
Mangel– comb.fm. in short supply
Man'gelberuf m undermanned profession
man'gelhaft adj defective; faulty; unsatisfactory, deficient
Man'gelkrankheit f nutritional deficiency
mangeln ['maŋəln] tr (*Wäsche*) mangle
‖ intr (**an** dat) be short of, lack ‖
impers—**es mangelt mir an** (dat) I
lack
Mängelrüge ['mɛŋəlrygə] f (-;-n)
(com) complaint (*about a shipment*)
mangels ['maŋəls] prep (*genit*) for
want of, for lack of
Ma·nie [ma'ni] f (-;-nien ['ni-ən])
mania
Manier [ma'nir] f (-;-en) manner

maniert [ma'nirt] adj affected
Manieriert'heit f (-;-en) mannerism
manier'lich adj mannerly, polite
Manifest [mani'fɛst] n (-es;-e) (aer,
naut) manifest; (pol) manifesto
Maniküre [mani'kyrə] f (-;-n) manicure; manicurist
maniküren [mani'kyrən] tr manicure
manipulieren [manipu'lirən] tr manipulate
manisch ['manɪʃ] adj maniacal
Manko ['maŋko] n (-s;-s) deficit;
(com) shortage
Mann [man] m (-[e]s;⸚er) man;
(*Gatte*) husband; **an den M. bringen**
manage to get rid of; **der M. aus
dem Volke** the man in the street;
seinen M. stehen hold one's own
mannbar ['manbar] adj marriageable
Mann'barkeit f (-;) puberty; marriageable age (*of girls*)
Männchen ['mɛnçən] n (-s;-) little
man; (*Ehemann*) hubby; (zool) male;
M. machen sit on its hind legs
Männerchor ['mɛnərkor] m men's
choir
Mannesalter ['manəsaltər] n manhood
Manneszucht ['manəstsuxt] f discipline
mann'haft adj manly, valiant
mannigfaltig ['manɪçfaltɪç] adj manifold
Man'nigfaltigkeit f (-;) diversity
männlich ['mɛnlɪç] adj male; (fig)
manly; (gram) masculine
Männ'lichkeit f (-;) manhood; virility
Mannsbild ['mansbɪlt] n (pej) man
Mann'schaft f (-;-en) crew; (sport)
team, squad; **Mannschaften** (mil) enlisted men
Mann'schaftsführer –in §6 mf (sport)
captain
Mann'schaftswagen m (mil) personnel
carrier
Mannsleute ['manslɔɪtə] pl menfolk
mannstoll ['manstɔl] adj man-crazy
Manns'tollheit f (-;) nymphomania
Mann'weib n mannish woman
Manometer [mano'metər] n pressure
gauge
Manöver [ma'nøvər] n (-s;-) maneuver
manövrieren [manø'vrirən] intr ma-
neuver
manövrier'fähig adj maneuverable
Mansarde [man'zardə] f (-;-n) attic
manschen ['manʃən] tr & intr splash
Manschette [man'ʃɛtə] f (-;-n) cuff
Manschet'tenknopf m cuff link
Mantel ['mantəl] m (-s;⸚) overcoat;
(*Fahrrad-*) tire; (*e-s Kabels*) sheath-
ing; (*Geschoß-*) jacket, case; (geol,
orn) mantle
manuell [manu'ɛl] adj manual
Manufaktur [manufak'tur] f (-;-en)
manufacture
Manufaktur'waren pl manufactured
goods
Manuskript [manu'skrɪpt] n (-[e]s;-e)
manuscript
Mappe ['mapə] f (-;-n) briefcase;
(*Aktendeckel*) folder
Märchen ['mɛrçən] n (-s;-) fairy tale
mär'chenhaft adj legendary; (fig) fabu-
lous

Mär′chenland n fairyland
Marchese [mar′keze] m (–;–n) marquis
Marder [′mardər] m (–s;–) marten; (fig) thief
Margarine [marga′rinə] ƒ (–;) margarine
Marienbild [ma′ri·ənbɪlt] n image of the Virgin
Marienfäden [ma′ri·ənfedən] pl gossamer(s)
Marienglas [ma′ri·ənglas] n mica
Marienkäfer [ma′ri·ənkefər] m ladybug
Marine [ma′rinə] ƒ (–;–n) (Kriegs–) navy; (Handels–) merchant marine
mari′neblau adj navy-blue
Mari′neflugzeug n seaplane
Mari′neinfanterie ƒ marines
Mari′neminister m secretary of the navy
Mari′neoffizier –in §6 mƒ naval officer
Mari′nesoldat m marine
marinieren [marɪ′nirən] tr marinate
Marionette [marɪ·ə′netə] ƒ (–;–n) puppet
Marionet′tentheater n puppet show
Mark [mark] ƒ (–;–) (fin) mark; (hist) borderland, march ‖ n (–[e]s;) marrow; (im Holz) pith; bis ins M. to the quick; er hat M. (fig) he has guts; j–m durch M. und Bein gehen (fig) go right through s.o.
markant [mar′kant] adj (einprägsam) marked; (außergewöhnlich) striking; (Geländepunkt) prominent
Marke [′markə] ƒ (–;–n) mark; (Brief–) stamp; (Handelszeichen) trademark; (Sorte) brand; (Fabrikat) make; (Spiel–) counter
mark′erschütternd adj piercing
Marketenderei [markətendə′raɪ] ƒ (–; –en) post exchange, PX
Marketing [′markɪtɪŋ] n (–s;) (com) marketing
markieren [mar′kirən] tr mark; (spielen) pretend to be
Markise [mar′kizə] ƒ (–;–n) awning
Mark′stein m landmark
Markt [markt] m (–[e]s;–̈e) market; (Jahrmarkt) fair
Markt′bude ƒ booth, stall
markten [′marktən] intr (um) bargain (for)
markt′fähig adj marketable
Markt′flecken m market town
marktgängig [′marktgɛŋɪç] adj marketable
Markt′platz m market place
Markt′schreier m quack
Marmelade [marmə′ladə] ƒ (–;–n) jam
Marmor [′marmɔr] m (–s;–e) marble
Mar′morbruch m marble quarry
marmorn [′marmɔrn] adj marble
marode [ma′rodə] adj (coll) tired out
Marodeur [marə′dør] m (–s;–e) marauder
marodieren [marə′dirən] intr maraud
Marone [ma′ronə] ƒ (–;–n) chestnut
Maroquin [marə′kɛ̃] m (–s;) morocco
Marotte [ma′rɔtə] ƒ (–;–n) whim
marsch [marʃ] interj march!; be off!; m., m.! on the double ‖ **Marsch** m (–es;–̈e) march; in M. setzen get

going; j–m den M. blasen (coll) chew s.o. out; (sich) in M. setzen set out
Marschall [′marʃal] m (–s;–̈e) marshal
Mar′schallstab m marshal's baton
Marsch′gepäck n full field pack
marschieren [mar′ʃirən] intr (SEIN) march
Marsch′kompanie ƒ replacement company
Marsch′lied n marching song
Marsch′verpflegung ƒ field rations
Marter [′martər] ƒ (–;–n) torture
martern [′martərn] tr torture, torment
Mar′terpfahl m stake
Märtyrer –in [′mertyrər(ɪn)] §6 mƒ martyr
Märtyrertum [′mertyrərtum] n (–s;) martyrdom
März [merts] m (–[es];–e) March
Masche [′maʃə] ƒ (–;–n) mesh; stitch; (fig) trick
Ma′schendraht m chicken wire; screen; wire mesh
ma′schenfest adj runproof
Maschine [ma′ʃinə] ƒ (–;–n) machine; (aer) airplane
maschinell [maʃɪ′nel] adj mechanical ‖ adv by machine
Maschi′nenantrieb m—mit M. machine-driven
Maschi′nenbau m (–[e]s;) mechanical engineering
Maschi′nengewehr n machine gun
Maschi′nengewehrschütze m machine gunner
maschi′nenmäßig adj mechanical
Maschi′nenpistole ƒ tommy gun
Maschi′nenschaden m engine trouble
Maschi′nenschlosser m machinist
maschi′nenschreiben tr type ‖ **Maschi′nenschreiben** n (–s;–) typing; typewritten letter
Maschi′nenschrift ƒ typescript
Maschi′nensprache ƒ computer language
Maschinerie [maʃɪnə′ri] ƒ (–;) (& fig) machinery
Maschinist –in [maʃɪ′nɪst(ɪn)] §7 mƒ machinist
Masern [′mazərn] pl measles
Maserung [′mazəruŋ] ƒ (–;) grain (in wood)
Maske [′maskə] ƒ (–;–n) mask; (fig) disguise; (theat) make-up
Ma′skenball m masquerade
Maskerade [maskə′radə] ƒ (–;–n) masquerade
maskieren [mas′kirən] tr mask
Maskotte [mas′kɔtə] ƒ (–;–n) mascot
maskulin [masku′lin] adj masculine
Maskuli·num [masku′linum] n (–s;–na [na]) masculine noun
maß [mas] pret of **messen** ‖ **Maß** n (–es;–e) measure; (Messung) measurement; (Ausdehnung) dimension; (Verhältnis) rate, proportion; (Grad) degree; (Mäßigung) moderation; das Maß ist voll! I've had it!; das Maß überschreiten go too far; er hat sein gerütteltes Maß an Kummer gehabt he had his full share of trouble; in gewissem Maße to a certain extent; in hohem Maße

highly; **j-m Maß nehmen zu** take s.o.'s measurements for; **Maß halten** observe moderation; **mit Maße in** moderation; **nach Maß angefertigt** custom-made; **ohne Maß und Ziel** without limit; **weder Maß noch Ziel kennen** know no bounds; **zweierlei Maß** double standard || *f* (-;- & -e) quart (*of beer*), stein

massakrieren [masa'kriːrən] *tr* massacre

Maß'anzug *m* tailor-made suit

Maß'arbeit *f* work made to order

Masse ['masə] *f* (-;-n) mass; bulk; (*Menge*) volume; (*Volk*) crowd; (*Hinterlassenschaft*) estate; (elec) ground; **die breite M.** the masses; the rank and file; **e-e Masse...** (coll) lots of

Maß'einheit *f* unit of measure

Masseleisen ['masəlaızən] *n* pigiron

Massen- *comb.fm.* mass, bulk, wholesale

Mas'senabsatz *m* wholesale selling

Mas'senangriff *m* mass attack

Mas'senanziehung *f* gravitation

mas'senhaft *adj* in large quantities

Maß'gabe *f*—**mit der M., daß** with the understanding that; **nach M.** (genit) in proportion to; according to; (jur) as provided in

maß'gebend, maßgeblich ['masgeplıç] *adj* standard; authoritative; (*Kreise*) leading, influential; **das ist nicht maßgebend für** that is no criterion for

maß'gerecht *adj* to scale

maß'halten §90 *intr* observe moderation

maß'haltig *adj* precise

massieren [ma'siːrən] *tr* massage; (*Truppen*) mass

massig ['masıç] *adj* bulky; solid; (*Person*) stout || *adv*—**m. viel** (coll) very much

mäßig ['mesıç] *adj* moderate; frugal; (*Leistung*) mediocre

mäßigen ['mesıgən] *tr* moderate, tone down || *ref* control oneself

Mä'ßigkeit *f* moderation; frugality; temperance

Mä'ßigung *f* (-;) moderation

massiv [ma'sif] *adj* massive; solid

Maß'krug *m* beer mug, stein

Maß'liebchen *n* daisy

maß'los *adj* immoderate || *adv* extremely

Maß'nahme *f* (-;-n), **Maß'regel** *f* (-;-n) measure, step, move

maß'regeln *tr* reprimand

Maß'schneider *m* custom tailor

Maß'stab *m* ruler; (fig) yardstick, standard; (*auf Landkarten*) scale; **jeden M. verlieren** lose all sense of proportion

maß'voll *adj* moderate; (*Benehmen*) discreet

Mast [mast] *m* (-es;-en & -e) pole; (naut) mast || *f* (-;) (*Schweinfutter*) mast

Mast'baum *m* (naut) mast

Mast'darm *m* rectum

mästen ['mestən] *tr* fatten

Mast'korb *m* masthead, crow's nest

Material [materi'al] *n* (-s;-ien [i·ən]) material

Materialismus [materi·a'lismus] *m* (-;) materialism

materialistisch [materi·a'listıʃ] *adj* materialistic

Material'waren *pl* (Aust) medical supplies

Materie [ma'teri·ə] *f* (-;-n) matter

materiell [materi'el] *adj* material; (*Schwierigkeiten*) financial; (*Recht*) substantive

Mathe ['matə] *f* (-;) (coll) math

Mathematik [matema'tik] *f* (-;) mathematics

Mathematiker **-in** [mate'matıkər(ın)] §6 *mf* mathematician

mathematisch [mate'matıʃ] *adj* mathematical

Matratze [ma'tratsə] *f* (-;-n) mattress

Mätresse [me'tresə] *f* (-;-n) mistress

Matrize [ma'tritsə] *f* (-;-n) stencil; (*Stempel*) die, matrix

Matrone [ma'tronə] *f* (-;-n) matron

matro'nenhaft *adj* matronly

Matrose [ma'trozə] *m* (-n;-n) sailor

Matro'senanzug *m* sailor's uniform

Matro'senjacke *f* (nav) peacoat

Matsch [matʃ] *m* (-es;) (*Brei*) mush; (*Schlamm*) mud; (*halbgetauter Schnee*) slush

matschig ['matʃıç] *adj* mushy; muddy; slushy

matt [mat] *adj* dull; weak; limp; (*Glas, Birne*) frosted; (*Börse*) slack; (*erschöpft*) exhausted; (*Kugel*) spent; (*Licht*) dim; (*Metall*) tarnished; (phot) matt; **m. machen** dull; tarnish; **m. setzen** checkmate

Matte ['matə] *f* (-;-n) mat; (*Wiese*) Alpine meadow; (poet) mead

Matt'glas *n* frosted glass

Matt'gold *n* dull gold

Matt'heit *f* dullness; fatigue

matt'herzig *adj* faint-hearted

Matt'igkeit *f* (-;) fatigue

Matura [ma'tura] *f* (-;) (Aust) final examination (*before graduation*)

Mätzchen ['metsçən] *n* (-s;-) trick; **M. machen** play tricks; put on airs

Mauer ['mau·ər] *f* (-;-n) wall

Mau'erblümchen *n* (fig) wallflower

Mau'erkalk *m* mortar

mauern ['mau·ərn] *tr* build (*in stone or brick*)

Mau'erstein *m* brick

Mau'erwerk *n* brickwork; masonry

Mau'erziegel *m* brick

Maul [maul] *n* (-[e]s;-er) mouth; maw; **halt's M.!** (sl) shut up!

Maul'affe *m* gaping fool

Maul'beerbaum *m* mulberry tree

Maul'beere *f* mulberry

maulen ['maulən] *intr* gripe

Maul'esel *m* mule

maul'faul *adj* too lazy to talk

Maul'held *m* braggart

Maul'korb *m* muzzle

Maul'schelle *f* slap in the face

Maul'sperre *f* lock jaw

Maul'tier *n* mule

Maul'trommel *f* Jew's-harp

Maul'– und Klau'enseuche f hoof and mouth disease

Maul'werk n—**ein großes M. haben** have the gift of gab

Maul'wurf m (zool) mole

Maul'wurfshaufen m, **Maul'wurfshügel** m molehill

Maure ['mauɾə] m (-n;-n) Moor

Maurer ['mauɾər] m (-s;-) mason; bricklayer

Mau'rerkelle f trowel

Mau'rerpolier m bricklayer foreman

Maus [maus] f (-;̈e) mouse

Mäuschen ['mɔisçən] n (-s;-) little mouse; (fig) pet, darling; wench

Mau'sefalle f mousetrap

mausen ['mauzən] tr pilfer, swipe || intr catch mice

Mauser ['mauzər] f (-;) molting season; **in der M. sein** be molting

mausern ['mauzərn] ref molt

mau'setot' adj dead as a doornail

mausig ['mauzɪç] adj—**sich m. machen** put on airs, be stuck-up

Mauso·leum [mauzo'le·um] n (-s; -leen) ['le·ən] mausoleum

Maxime [ma'ksimə] f (-;-n) maxim

Mayonnaise [majo'nezə] f (-;) mayonnaise

Mechanik [me'çanɪk] f (-;-en) mechanics; (Triebwerk) mechanism

Mechaniker [me'çanɪkər] m (-s;-) mechanic

mechanisch [me'çanɪʃ] adj mechanical; power-

mechanisieren [meçanɪ'zirən] tr mechanize

Mechanis·mus [meça'nɪsmus] m (-; -men] [mən]) mechanism; (Uhrwerk) works

Meckerer · ['mɛkərər] m (-s;-) (coll) grumbler

meckern ['mɛkərn] intr bleat; (coll) grumble

Medaille [me'daljə] f (-;-n) medal

Medaillon [medal'jõ] n (-s;-s) medallion; locket

Medikament [medɪka'mɛnt] n (-s;-e) medication

Meditation [medɪta'tsjon] f (-;-en) meditation

meditieren [medɪ'tirən] intr meditate

Medizin [medɪ'tsin] f (-;-en) medicine

Medizinalassistant [medɪtsɪ'nalasɪs-tant(ɪn)] §7 mf intern

Medizinalbeamte [medɪtsɪ'nalbə·amtə] m health officer

Medizinalbehörde [medɪtsɪ'nalbəhørdə] f board of health

Mediziner –in [medɪ'tsinər(ɪn)] §6 mf physician; medical student

medizinisch [medɪ'tsinɪʃ] adj medical, medicinal; medicated; **medizinische Fakultät** medical school

Meer [mer] n (-[e]s;-e) sea; **am Meere** at the seashore; **übers M.** overseas

Meer'busen m bay, gulf

Meer'enge f straits

Meeres– [meɾəs] comb.fm. sea, marine

Mee'resarm m inlet

Mee'resboden m bottom of the sea

Mee'resbucht f bay

Mee'resgrund m bottom of the sea

Mee'reshöhe f sea level

Mee'reskiste f seacoast

Mee'resleuchten n phosphorescence

Mee'resspiegel m sea level

meer'grün adj sea-green

Meer'rettich m horseradish

Meer'schaum m meerschaum

Meer'schwein n porpoise

Meer'schweinchen n guinea pig

Meer'ungeheuer n sea monster

Meer'weib n mermaid

Mehl [mel] n (-[e]s;) (grobes) meal; (feines) flour; (Staub) dust, powder

Mehl'kloß m dumpling

Mehl'speise f pastry; pudding

Mehl'suppe f gruel

Mehl'tau m mildew

mehr [mer] invar adj & adv more; **immer m.** more and more; **kein Wort m.!** not another word!; **m. oder weniger** more or less, give or take; **nicht m.** no more, no longer; **nie m.** never again || **Mehr** n (-s;) majority; (Zuwachs) increase; (Überschuß) surplus

Mehr'arbeit f extra work; (Überstunden) overtime

Mehr'aufwand m, **Mehr'ausgabe** f additional expenditure

Mehr'betrag m surplus; extra charge

mehr'deutig adj ambiguous

mehren [ˌ'merən] tr & ref increase

mehrere ['merərə] adj & pron several

mehr'fach adj manifold; repeated, multiple

mehr'farbig adj multicolored

Mehr'gebot n higher bid

Mehr'gepäck n excess luggage

Mehr'gewicht n excess weight

Mehr'heit f (-;-en) majority; (pol) plurality

Mehr'heitsbeschluß m, **Mehr'heitsentscheidung** f plurality vote

mehr'jährig adj (bot) perennial

Mehr'kosten pl extra charges

Mehr'ladegewehr n repeater

Mehr'leistung f increased performance; (ins) extended benefits

mehrmalig ['mermalɪç] adj repeated

mehrmals ['mermals] adv several times, on several occasions; repeatedly

Mehr'porto n additional postage

Mehr'preis m extra charge

mehr'seitig adj multilateral; many-sided; (Brief) of many pages

mehrsilbig ['merzɪlbɪç] adj polysyllabic

mehrsprachig ['merʃpraxɪç] adj polyglot

mehrstöckig ['merʃtœkɪç] adj multi-story

mehrstufig ['merʃtufɪç] adj multistage

Meh'rung f (-;) increase, multiplication

Mehr'verbrauch m increased consumption

Mehr'wertsteuer f added value tax

Mehr'zahl f majority; (gram) plural

meiden ['maɪdən] §112 tr avoid, shun

Meier ['maɪ·ər] m (-s;-) tenant farmer; dairy farmer

Meierei [maɪ·ə'raɪ] f (-;-en) dairy

Mei′ergut n, **Mei′erhof** m dairy farm
Meile [′maɪlə] f (–;–n) mile
mei′lenweit adj extending for miles, miles and miles of ‖ adv far away; **m. auseinander** miles apart
Mei′lenzahl f mileage
mein [maɪn] §2,2 poss adj my ‖ §2,4,5 pron mine; **das Meine** my share; my due; **die Meinen** my family
Meineid [′maɪnaɪt] m (–[e]s;) perjury; **e–n M. schwören** (or **leisten**) commit perjury
meineidig [′maɪnaɪdɪç] adj perjured; **m. werden** perjure oneself
meinen [′maɪnən] tr think; (im Sinne haben) mean, intend; **das will ich m.** I should think so; **die Sonne meint es heute gut** the sun is very warm today; **es ehrlich m.** have honorable intentions; **es gut m.** mean well; **ich meinte dich im Recht** I thought you were in the right; **m. Sie das ernst** (or **im Ernst**)? do you really mean it?; **was m. Sie damit**? what do you mean by that?; **was m. Sie dazu**? what do you think of that? ‖ intr think; **m. Sie**? do you think so?; **m. Sie nicht auch**? don't you agree?; **wie m. Sie**? I beg your pardon?
meinerseits [′maɪnər′zaɪts] adv for my part
meinesgleichen [′maɪnəs′glaɪçən] pron people like me, the likes of me
meinethlben [′maɪnət′halbən], **meinetwegen** [′maɪnət′vegən] adv for my sake, on my account; for all I care
meinetwillen [′maɪnət′vɪlən] adv—**um m.** for my sake, on my behalf
meinige [′maɪnɪgə] §2,5 pron mine
Mei′nung f (–;–en) opinion; **anderer M. mit j–m sein über** (acc) disagree with s.o. about; **der M. sein** be of the opinion; **geteilter M. sein** be of two minds; **j–m die** (or **seine**) **M. sagen** give s.o. a piece of one's mind; **meiner M. nach** in my opinion; **vorgefaßte M.** preconceived idea
Mei′nungsäußerung f expression of opinion
Mei′nungsaustausch m exchange of views
Mei′nungsbefragung f, **Mei′nungsforschung** f public opinion poll
Mei′nungsumfrage f public opinion poll
Mei′nungsverschiedenheit f difference of opinion, disagreement
Meise [′maɪzə] f (–;–n) titmouse
Meißel [′maɪsəl] m (–s;–) chisel
meißeln [′maɪsəln] tr & intr chisel
meist [maɪst] adj most; **am meisten** most; **das meiste** the most; **die meisten Menschen** most people; **die meiste Zeit** most of the time; **die meiste Zeit des Jahres** most of the year ‖ adv usually, generally
Meist′begünstigungsklausel f most-favored nation clause
Meist′bietende §5 mf highest bidder
meistens [′maɪstəns] adv mostly
Meister [′maɪstər] m (–s;–) master; boss; (im Betrieb) foreman; (sport) champion
mei′sterhaft adj masterly

Meisterin [′maɪstərɪn] f (–;–nen) master's wife; (sport) champion
mei′sterlich adj masterly
meistern [′maɪstərn] tr master
Mei′sterschaft f (–;–en) mastery; (sport) championship
Mei′sterstück n, **Mei′sterwerk** n masterpiece
Mei′sterzug m master stroke
Melancholie [melaŋko′li] f (–;) melancholy
melancholisch [melaŋ′kolɪʃ] adj melancholy
Melasse [me′lasə] f (–;–n) molasses
Meldeamt [′meldə-amt] n. **Meldebüro** [′meldəbyro] n registration office
Meldefahrer [′meldəfarər] m (mil) dispatch rider
Meldegänger [′meldəgɛŋər] m (mil) messenger, runner
melden [′meldən] tr report; (polizeilich) turn (s.o.) in; **den Empfang m.** (genit) acknowledge the receipt of; **er hat nichts zu m.** he has nothing to say in the matter; **gemeldet werden zu** (sport) be entered in; **j–m m. lassen, daß** send s.o. word that ‖ ref report; (Alter) begin to show; (Gläubiger) come forward; (Kind) cry; (Magen) growl; (polizeilich) register; (Winter) set in; (telp) answer; **sich auf e–e Anzeige m.** answer an ad; **sich krank m.** (mil) go on sick call; **sich m. zu** apply for; (freiwillig) volunteer for; (mil) enlist in; (sport) enter; **sich zum Dienst m.** (mil) report for duty; **sich zum Wort m.** ask to speak; (in der Schule) hold up the hand
Mel′der m (–s;–) (mil) runner
Meldezettel [′meldətsetəl] m registration form
Mel′dung f (–;–en) report; message, notification; (Bewerbung) application
Melkeimer [′melkaɪmər] m milk pail
melken [′melkən] §113 tr milk
Melo·die [melo′di] f (–;–dien [′di-ən]) melody
melodisch [me′lodɪʃ] adj melodious
Melone [me′lonə] f (–;–n) melon; (coll) derby
Meltau [′meltau] m (–[e]s;) honeydew
Membran [mem′bran] f (–;–en), **Membrane** [mem′branə] f (–;–n) membrane
Memme [′memə] f (–;–n) coward
Memoiren [memo′arən] pl memoirs
memorieren [memo′rirən] tr memorize
Menge [′mɛŋə] f (–;–n) quantity, amount; crowd; **e–e M.** a lot of
mengen [′mɛŋən] tr mix ‖ ref (unter acc) mingle (with); (in acc) meddle (in)
Men′genlehre f (math) theory of sets
men′genmäßig adj quantitative
Mengsel [′mɛŋzəl] n (–s;–) hodgepodge
Mennige [′mɛnɪgə] f (–;) rust-preventive paint
Mensch [mɛnʃ] m (–en;–en) human being, man; person, individual; **die Menschen** the people; **kein M.** no one ‖ n (–es; –er) hussy, slut

Menschen– [menʃən] *comb.fm.* man, of men; human
Men′schenalter *n* generation, age
Men′schenfeind –in §8 *mf* misanthropist
Men′schenfresser *m* cannibal
Men′schenfreund –in §8 *mf* philanthropist
men′schenfreundlich *adj* philanthropic, humanitarian
Men′schengedenken *n*—**seit M.** since time immemorial
Men′schengeschlecht *n* mankind
Men′schengewühl *n* milling crowd
Men′schenglück *n* human happiness
Men′schenhandel *m* slave trade
Men′schenhaß *m* misanthropy
Men′schenjagd *f* manhunt
Men′schenkenner –in §6 *mf* judge of human nature
Men′schenkind *n* human being; **armes M.** poor soul
men′schenleer *adj* deserted
Men′schenliebe *f* philanthropy
Men′schenmaterial *n* manpower
men′schenmöglich *adj* humanly possible
Men′schenraub *m* kidnaping
Men′schenräuber –in §6 *mf* kidnaper
Men′schenrechte *pl* human rights
men′schenscheu *adj* shy, unsociable
Men′schenschinder *m* oppressor, slave driver
Men′schenschlag *m* race
Men′schenseele *f* human soul; **keine M.** not a living soul
Men′schenskind *interj* man alive!
Men′schensohn *m* (Bib) Son of man
men′schenunwürdig *adj* degrading
Men′schenverächter –in §6 *mf* cynic
Men′schenverstand *m*—**guter M.** common sense
Men′schenwürde *f* human dignity
men′schenwürdig *adj* decent
Mensch′heit *f* (–;) mankind, humanity
mensch′lich *adj* human; *(human)* humane
Mensch′lichkeit *f* (–;) humanity
Menschwerdung [′menʃ/verduŋ] *f* (–;) incarnation
Menstruation [mentru·a′tsjon] *f* (–;–en) menstruation
Mensur [men′zur] *f* (–;–en) measure; *(Meßglas)* measuring glass; students' duel
Mentalität [mentalitet] *f* (–;) mentality
Menuett [menu′et] *n* (–[e]s;–e) minuet
Meridian [merr′djan] *m* (–s;–e) (astr) meridian
merkbar [′merkbar] *adj* noticeable
Merkblatt [′merkblat] *n* instruction sheet
Merkbuch [′merkbux] *n* notebook
merken [′merkən] *tr* notice; realize; **etw m. lassen** show s.th., betray s.th.; **man merkte es sofort an ihrem Ausdruck, daß** one noticed immediately by her expression that ‖ *ref*—**m. Sie sich** [*dat*]**, was ich sage!** mark my word!; **sich** [*dat*] **etw m.** bear s.th. in mind; **sich** [*dat*] **nichts m. lassen** not give oneself away ‖ *intr*—**m. auf** *(acc)* pay attention to, heed
merk′lich *adj* noticeable

Merkmal [′merkmal] *n* (–[e]s;–e) mark, feature, characteristic
Merkur [mer′kur] *m & n* (–s;) mercury
Merk′wort *n* (–[e]s;–er) catchword; (theat) cue
merk′würdig *adj* remarkable; *(seltsam)* curious, strange
merkwürdigerweise [′merkvyrdigərvaizə] *adv* strange to say
Merk′würdigkeit *f* (–;–en) strange thing
Merk′zeichen *n* mark
meschugge [me′ʃugə] *adj* (coll) nuts
Mesner [′mesnər] *m* (–s;–) sexton
Meß– [mes] *comb.fm.* measuring; (eccl) mass
Meß′band *n* (–[e]s;–er) measuring tape
meßbar [′mesbar] *adj* measurable
Meß′buch *n* (relig) missal
Meß′diener *m* acolyte
Messe [′mesə] *f* (–;–n) fair; (eccl) mass; (mil) mess; (nav) officers' mess
messen [′mesən] §70 *tr* measure; *(Zeit)* time, clock; *(mustern)* size up ‖ *ref*—**sich m. mit** cope with; *(geistig)* match wits with; **sich nicht m. können mit** be no match for ‖ *intr* measure
Messer [′mesər] *m* (–s;–) gauge; meter ‖ *n* (–s;–) knife; (surg) scalpel; **bis aufs M.** to the death
Mes′serheld *m* (coll) cutthroat
mes′serscharf *adj* razor-sharp
Mes′serschmied *m* cutler
Messerschmiedewaren [′mesər/midəvarən] *pl* cutlery
Mes′serschneide *f* knife edge
Meß′gewand *n* (eccl) vestment; chasuble
Meß′hemd *n* (eccl) alb
Messias [me′si·as] *invar m* Messiah
Messing [′mesiŋ] *n* (–s;) brass
messingen [′mesiŋən] *adj* brass
Meß′opfer *n* sacrifice of the mass
Mes′sung *f* (–;–en) measurement
Metall [me′tal] *n* (–s;–e) metal
Metall′baukasten *m* erector set
metallen [me′talən], **metallisch** [me′taliʃ] *adj* metallic
Metall′säge *f* hacksaw
Metallurgie [metalur′gi] *f* (–;) metallurgy
metall′verarbeitend *adj* metal-processing
Metall′waren *pl* hardware
Metapher [me′tafər] *f* (–;–n) metaphor
Meteor [mete′or] *n* (–s;–e) meteor
Meteorologe [mete·oro′logə] *m* (–n;–n) meteorologist
Meteorologie [mete·orolo′gi] *f* (–;) meteorology
Meteorologin [mete·oro′login] *f* (–;–nen) meteorologist
meteorologisch [mete·oro′logiʃ] *adj* meteorological
Meteor′stein *m* meteorite, aerolite
Meter [′metər] *m & n* (–s;–) meter
Me′termaß *n* tape measure
Methode [me′todə] *f* (–;–n) method
methodisch [me′todiʃ] *adj* methodical
Metrik [′metrik] *f* (–;) metrics
metrisch [′metriʃ] *adj* metrical

Metropole [metro'poləl] *f* (-;-n) metropolis

Mette ['metə] *f* (-;-n) matins

Mettwurst ['metvurst] *f* soft sausage

Metzelei [metsə'laɪ] *f* (-;-en) massacre, slaughter

metzeln ['metsəln] *tr* massacre

Metzger ['metsgər] *m* (-s;-) butcher

Metzgerei [metsgə'raɪ] *f* (-;-en) butcher shop

Meuchelmord ['mɔɪçəlmɔrt] *m* assassination

Meuchelmörder **-in** ['mɔɪçəlmœrdər (ɪn)] §6 *mf* assassin

meucheln ['mɔɪçəln] *tr* murder

meuchlerisch ['mɔɪçlərɪʃ] *adj* murderous

meuchlings ['mɔɪçlɪŋs] *adv* treacherously

Meute ['mɔɪtə] *f* (-;-n) pack (*of hounds*); (fig) horde, gang

Meuterei [mɔɪtə'raɪ] *f* (-;-en) mutiny

meuterisch ['mɔɪtərɪʃ] *adj* mutinous

meutern ['mɔɪtərn] *intr* mutiny

Mexikaner **-in** [meksɪ'kanər(ɪn)] §6 *mf* Mexican

mexikanisch [meksɪ'kanɪʃ] *adj* Mexican

Mexiko ['meksɪko] *n* (-s;) Mexico

miauen [mɪ'au-ən] *intr* meow

mich [mɪç] §11 *pers pron* me || §11 *reflex pron* myself

mied [mit] *pret of* **meiden**

Mieder ['midər] *n* (-s;-) bodice

Mie/derwaren *pl* foundation garments

Mief [mif] *m* (-s;) foul air

Miene ['minə] *f* (-;-n) mien; facial expression; **M. machen zu** (*inf*) make a move to (*inf*); **ohne die M. zu verziehen** without flinching

mies [mis] *adj* (coll) miserable, lousy

Mies/macher *m* (-s;-) alarmist

Miet- [mit] *comb.fm.* rental, rented; rent

Miet/auto *n* rented car

Miete ['mitə] *f* (-;-n) rent; (*Zins*) rental; (*Erd-*) pit (*for storing vegetables*); **in M. geben** rent out; **in M. nehmen** rent; **kalte M.** rent not including heat; **zur M. wohnen** live in a rented apartment (or home)

mieten ['mitən] *tr* rent, hire; (*Flugzeug*) charter

Miet/entschädigung *f* allowance for house rent

Mie/ter **-in** §6 *mf* tenant

Miet/ertrag *m* rent, rental

Miet/kontrakt *m* lease

Mietling ['mitlɪŋ] *m* (-s;-e) hireling

Miets/haus *n* apartment building

Miets/kaserne *f* tenement house

Miet/vertrag *m* lease

Miet/wagen *m* rented car

Miet/wohnung *f* apartment

Miet/zins *m* rent

Mieze ['mitsə] *f* (-;-n) pussy

Migräne [mɪ'grɛnə] *f* (-;-n) migraine

Mikrobe [mɪ'krobə] *f* (-;-n) microbe

Mikrofilm ['mikrɔfɪlm] *m* microfilm

Mikrophon [mɪkrɔ'fon] *n* (-s;-e) microphone

Mikroskop [mɪkrɔ'skop] *n* (-s;-e) microscope

mikroskopisch [mɪkro'skopɪʃ] *adj* microscopic

Milbe ['mɪlbə] *f* (-;-n) (ent) mite

Milch [mɪlç] *f* (-;) milk

Milch/bart *m* sissy

Milch/brot *n*, **Milch/brötchen** *n* French roll

Milch/bruder *m* foster brother

Milch/drüse *f* mammary gland

Milch/eimer *m* milk pail

Milch/geschäft *n* creamery, dairy

Milch/glas *n* milk glass

milchig ['mɪlçɪç] *adj* milky

Milch/mädchen *n* milkmaid

Milch/mädchenrechnung *f* oversimplification

Milch/mixgetränk *n* milkshake

Milch/pulver *n* powdered milk

Milch/reis *m* rice pudding

Milch/schwester *f* foster sister

Milch/straße *f* Milky Way

Milch/tüte *f* carton of milk

Milch/wirtschaft *f* dairy

Milchzähne ['mɪlçtsenə] *pl* baby teeth

mild [mɪlt] *adj* mild; (*nicht streng*) lenient; (*Stiftung*) charitable; (*Wein*) smooth; (*Lächeln*) faint || **Milde** *f* (-;) mildness; leniency; kindness

mildern ['mɪldərn] *tr* soften, alleviate; **mildernde Umstände** extenuating circumstances

Mil/derung *f* (-;) softening, alleviation, mitigation

mild/herzig, mild/tätig *adj* charitable

Militär [mɪlɪ'ter] *n* (-s;) military, army; **zum M. gehen** join the army || *m* (-s;-s) professional soldier

Militär/dienst *m* military service

Militär/geistliche §5 *m* chaplain

Militär/gericht *n* military court

militärisch [mɪlɪ'terɪʃ] *adj* military

Militarismus [mɪlɪta'rɪsmus] *m* (-;) militarism

Miliz [mɪ'lɪts] *f* (-;) militia

Miliz/soldat *m* militiaman

Milliardär **-in** [mɪljar'der(ɪn)] §8 *mf* multimillionaire

Milliarde [mɪl'jardə] *f* (-;-n) billion

Milligramm [mɪlɪ'gram] *n* milligram

Millimeter [mɪlɪ'metər] *n* & *m* millimeter

Millime/terpapier *n* graph paper

Million [mɪl'jon] *f* (-;-en) million

Millionär **-in** [mɪljo'ner(ɪn)] §8 *mf* millionaire

millionste [mɪl'jonstə] §9 *adj* & *pron* millionth

Milz [mɪlts] *f* (-;) spleen

Mime ['mimə] *m* (-n;-n) mime

Mimiker **-in** ['mimɪkər(ɪn)] §6 *mf* mimic

Mimose [mɪ'mozə] *f* (-;-n) mimosa

minder ['mɪndər] *adj* lesser, smaller; (*geringer*) minor, inferior || *adv* less; **m. gut** inferior; **nicht m.** likewise

min/derbedeutend *adj* less important

min/derbegabt *adj* less talented

min/derbemittelt *adj* of moderate means

Min/derbetrag *m* shortage, deficit

Min/derheit *f* (-;-en) minority

min/derjährig *adj* underage || **Minderjährige** §5 *mf* minor

mindern ['mɪndərn] *tr* lessen, diminish
Min'derung *f* (-;-en) diminution
min'derwertig *adj* inferior
Min'derwertigkeit *f* inferiority
Min'derwertigkeitskomplex *m* inferiority complex
Min'derzahl *f* minority
Mindest- [mɪndəst] *comb.fm.* minimum
mindeste ['mɪndəstə] §9 *adj* least; (*kleinste*) smallest; **nicht die mindesten Aussichten** not the slightest chance; **nicht im mindesten** not in the least; **zum mindesten** at the very least
mindestens ['mɪndəstəns] *adv* at least
Min'destgebot *n* lowest bid
Min'destlohn *m* minimum wage
Mine ['minə] *f* (-;-n) (*im Bleistift*) lead; (mil, min) mine; **alle Minen springen lassen** (fig) pull out all the stops
Minenleger ['minənlegər] *m* (-s;-) minelayer
Minenräumboot ['minənrɔɪmbot] *n* minesweeper
Mineral [minə'ral] *n* (-s;-e & -ien [jən]) mineral
mineralisch [minə'ralɪʃ] *adj* mineral
Mineralogie [minəralɔ'gi] *f* (-;) mineralogy
Miniatur [minja'tur] *f* (-;-en) miniature
minieren [mi'nirən] *tr* (fig) undermine; (mil) mine
minimal [mini'mal] *adj* minimal
Minirock ['minirɔk] *m* miniskirt
Minister [mi'nɪstər] *m* (-s;-) minister, secretary
Ministe·rium [minɪs'terjum] *n* (-s; -rien [rjən]) ministry, department
Mini'sterpräsident *m* prime minister
Mini'sterrat *m* (-[e]s;-̈e) cabinet
Ministrant [minɪs'trant] *m* (-en;-en) altar boy, acolyte
Minne ['minə] *f* (-;) (obs) love
Min'nesänger *m* minnesinger; troubadour
minorenn [mino'ren] *adj* underage
minus ['minus] *adv* minus ‖ **Minus** *n* (-;-) minus; (com) deficit
Minute [mi'nutə] *f* (-;-n) minute
Minu'tenzeiger *m* minute hand
-minutig [minutɪç] *comb.fm.* -minute
Minze ['mintsə] *f* (-;-n) (bot) mint
mir [mir] §11 *pers pron* me, to me, for me; **mir ist kalt** I am cold; **mir nichts, dir nichts** suddenly; **von mir aus** for all I care ‖ §11 *reflex pron* myself, to myself, for myself
Mirabelle [mira'belə] *f* (-;-n) yellow plum
Mirakel [mi'rakəl] *n* (-s;-) miracle
Mira'kelspiel *n* miracle play
Mischehe ['mɪʃ·e·ə] *f* mixed marriage
mischen ['mɪʃən] *tr* mix, blend; (cards) shuffle
Mischling ['mɪʃlɪŋ] *m* (-es;-e) half-breed; mongrel
Mischmasch ['mɪʃmaʃ] *m* (-es;-e) hodgepodge
Mischpult ['mɪʃpʊlt] *n* (rad, telv) master console

Mischrasse ['mɪʃrasə] *f* cross-breed
Mi'schung *f* (-;-en) mixture, blend
Misere [mi'zerə] *f* (-;-n) misery
Miß-, miß- [mɪs] *comb.fm.* mis-, dis-, amiss; bad, wrong, false
mißach'ten *tr* disregard; (*geringschätzen*) slight
mißartet [mɪs'artət] *adj* degenerate
miß'behagen *intr* (dat) displease ‖ **Mißbehagen** *n* (-s;) displeasure
miß'bilden *tr* misshape, deform
Miß'bildung *f* (-;-en) deformity
miß'billigen *tr* disapprove
Miß'billigung *f* (-;-en) disapproval
Miß'brauch *m* abuse; (*falsche Anwendung*) misuse
mißbrau'chen *tr* abuse; misuse
mißbräuchlich ['mɪsbrɔɪçlɪç] *adj* improper
mißdeu'ten *tr* misinterpret
missen ['mɪsən] *tr* miss; do without
Miß'erfolg *m* failure, flop
Miß'ernte *f* bad harvest
Missetat ['mɪsətat] *f* misdeed; (*Verstoß*) offense; (*Verbrechen*) felony; (*Sünde*) sin
Missetäter -in ['mɪsətetər(ɪn)] §6 *mf* wrongdoer; offender; felon; sinner
mißfal'len §72 *intr* (dat) displease ‖ **Mißfallen** *n* (-s;) displeasure
miß'fällig *adj* displeasing; (*anstößig*) shocking; (*verächtlich*) disparaging
miß'farben, miß'farbig *adj* discolored
Miß'geburt *f* freak
mißgelaunt ['mɪsgəlaunt] *adj* in bad humor, sour
Miß'geschick *n* (-s;) mishap; misfortune
Miß'gestalt *f* deformity; monster
mißgestaltet *adj* deformed, misshapen
mißgestimmt ['mɪsgəʃtɪmt] *adj* grumpy
mißglücken (mißglük'ken) *intr* (SEIN) fail, not succeed
mißgön'nen *tr* begrudge
Miß'griff *m* mistake
Miß'gunst *f* grudge, jealousy
mißhan'deln *tr* mistreat
Miß'heirat *f* mismarriage
Mißhelligkeit ['mɪshelɪçkaɪt] *f* (-;-en) friction, disagreement
Mission [mi'sjon] *f* (-;-en) mission
Missionar [mɪsjo'nar] *m*, **Missionär** [mɪsjo'ner] *m* (-s;-e) missionary
Miß'klang *m* dissonance; (fig) sour note
Miß'kredit *m* discredit, disrepute
mißlang [mɪs'laŋ] *pret* of **mißlingen**
miß'lich *adj* awkward; (*gefährlich*) dangerous; (*bedenklich*) critical
miß'liebig *adj* unpopular
mißlingen [mɪs'lɪŋən] §142 *intr* (SEIN) go wrong, misfire, prove a failure ‖ **Mißlingen** *n* (-s;) failure
Miß'mut *m* bad humor; discontent
miß'mutig *adj* sullen; discontented
mißra'ten §63 *intr* (SEIN) go wrong, misfire; **mißratene Kinder** spoiled children
Miß'stand *m* bad state of affairs; **Mißstände abschaffen** remedy abuses
Miß'stimmung *f* dissension; (*Mißmut*) bad humor
Miß'ton *m* dissonance; (fig) sour note

mißtrau'en *intr* (*dat*) mistrust, distrust || **Miß'trauen** *n* (–s₃) mistrust

mißtrauisch ['mɪstrau·ɪʃ] *adj* distrustful

Miß'vergnügen *n* displeasure

miß'vergnügt *adj* cross; discontented

Miß'verhältnis *n* disproportion

Miß'verständnis *n* misunderstanding

miß'verstehen §146 *tr & intr* misunderstand

Miß'wirtschaft *f* mismanagement

Mist [mɪst] *m* (–es) dung, manure; (*Schmutz*) dirt; (fig) mess, nonsense; **M. machen** (coll) blow the job; (*Spaß machen*) (coll) horse around; **viel M. verzapfen** talk a lot of nonsense

Mist'beet *n* hotbed

Mistel ['mɪstəl] *f* (–ȥ–n) mistletoe

misten ['mɪstən] *tr* (*Stall*) muck; (*Acker*) fertilize

Mist'fink *m* (coll) dirty brat

Mist'haufen *m* manure pile

mistig ['mɪstɪç] *adj* dirty; (*sehr unangenehm*) very unpleasant

mit [mɪt] *adv* along; also, likewise; simultaneously || *prep* (*dat*) with; **mit 18 Jahren** at the age of eighteen

Mit'angeklagte §5 *mf* codefendant

Mit'arbeit *f* cooperation, collaboration

mit'arbeiten *intr* cooperate, collaborate; **m. an** (*dat*) contribute to

Mit'arbeiter –in §6 *mf* co-worker

Mit'arbeiterstab *m* staff

mit'bekommen §99 *tr* receive when leaving; (*verstehen*) get, catch

mit'benutzen *tr* use jointly

Mit'bestimmung *f* share in decision making

mit'bewerben *ref* (**um**) compete (for)

Mit'bewerber –in §6 *mf* competitor

mit'bringen §65 *tr* bring along

Mitbringsel ['mɪtbrɪŋzəl] *n* (–s₃–) little present

Mit'bürger –in §6 *mf* fellow citizen

Mit'eigentümer –in §6 *mf* co-owner

miteinan'der *adv* together

mit'empfinden §59 *tr* sympathize with

Mit'erbe *m*, **Mit'erbin** *f* coheir

Mitesser ['mɪtesər] *m* (–s₃–) pimple, blackhead

mit'fahren §71 *intr* (SEIN) ride along; **j–n m. lassen** give s.o. a lift

mit'fühlen *tr* share, sympathize with

mit'fühlend *adj* sympathetic

mit'gehen §82 *intr* (SEIN) (**mit**) go along (with)

Mit'gift *f* dowry

Mit'giftjäger *m* fortune hunter

Mit'glied *n* member; **M. auf Lebenszeit** life member

Mit'gliederversammlung *f* general meeting

Mit'gliederzahl *f* membership

Mit'gliedsbeitrag *m* dues

Mit'gliedschaft *f* (–ȥ–en) membership

Mit'gliedskarte *f* membership card

Mit'gliedstaat *m* member nation

Mit'haftung *f* joint liability

mit'halten §90 *intr* be one of a party; **ich halte mit** I'll join you

mit'helfen §96 *intr* help along, pitch in

Mit'helfer –in §6 *mf* assistant

Mit'herausgeber –in §6 *mf* coeditor

Mit'hilfe *f* assistance

mithin' *adv* consequently

mit'hören *tr* listen in on; (*zufällig*) overhear; (rad, telp) monitor

Mit'inhaber –in §6 *mf* copartner

Mit'kämpfer –in §6 *mf* fellow fighter

mit'klingen §142 *intr* resonate

mit'kommen §99 *intr* (SEIN) come along; (fig) keep up

mit'kriegen *tr* (coll) see mitbekommen

Mit'läufer –in §6 *mf* (pol) fellow traveler

Mit'laut *m* consonant

Mit'leid *n* compassion, pity

Mit'leidenschaft *f*–**j–n in M. ziehen** affect s.o.

mit'leidig *adj* compassionate; pitiful

Mit'leidsbezeigung *f* condolences

mit'leidslos *adj* pitiless

mit'leidsvoll *adj* full of pity

mit'machen *tr* participate in, join in on; (*ertragen*) suffer, endure

Mit'mensch *m* fellow man

mit'nehmen §116 *tr* take along; (*erschöpfen*) wear out, exhaust; (*abholen*) pick up; (*Ort, Museum*) visit, take in; **j–n arg m.** treat s.o. roughly

mitnichten [mɪt'nɪçtən] *adv* by no means, not at all

mit'rechnen *tr* include || *intr* count

mit'reden *tr*–**ein Wort mitzureden haben bei** have a say in || *intr* join in a conversation

Mit'reisende §5 *mf* travel companion

mit'reißen §53 *tr* (& fig) carry away

mit'reißend *adj* stirring

mitsamt [mɪt'zamt] *prep* (*dat*) together with

mit'schreiben §62 *intr* take notes

Mit'schuld *f* (an *dat*) complicity in

mit'schuldig *adj* (an *dat*) accessory (to) || **Mitschuldige** §5 *mf* accomplice

Mit'schüler –in §6 *mf* schoolmate

mit'singen §142 *intr* sing along

mit'spielen *intr* play along; (fig) be involved; **j–m arg** (or **übel**) **m.** play s.o. dirty

Mit'spieler –in §6 *mf* partner

Mit'spracherecht *n* right to share in decision making

mit'sprechen §64 *tr* say with (*s.o.*) || *intr* be involved; (an *e–r Entscheidung beteiligt sein*) share in decision making

Mit'tag *m* noon; (poet) South; **M. machen** stop for lunch; **zu M. essen** eat lunch

Mittag– *comb.fm.* midday, noon; lunch

Mit'tagbrot *n*, **Mit'tagessen** *n* lunch

mit'täglich *adj* midday, noontime

mittags ['mɪtaks] *adv* at noon

Mit'tagskreis *m*, **Mit'tagslinie** *f* meridian

Mit'tagsruhe *f* siesta

Mit'tagsstunde *f* noon; lunch hour

Mit'tagstisch *m* lunch table; lunch; **gut bürgerlicher M.** good home cooking

Mit'tagszeit *f* noontime; lunch time

Mit'täter –in §6 *mf* accomplice

Mit'täterschaft *f* complicity

Mitte ['mɪtə] *f* (-;-n) middle, midst; (*Mittelpunkt*) center; **ab durch die M.!** (coll) scram!; **aus unserer M. from among us; die goldene M.** the golden mean; **die richtige M. treffen** hit a happy medium; **er ist M. Vierzig** he is in his mid-forties; **in die M. nehmen** take by both arms; (sport) sandwich in; **j—m um die M. fassen** put one's arms around s.o.'s waist

mit'teilbar *adj* communicable

mit'teilen *tr* tell; (*im Vertrauen*) intimate; **ich muß Ihnen leider m., daß** I regret to inform you that

mitteilsam ['mɪttaɪlzam] *adj* communicative

Mit'teilung *f* (-;-en) communication; information; (*amtliche*) communiqué; (*an die Presse*) release

mittel ['mɪtəl] *adj* medium, average || **Mittel** *n* (-s;-) middle; means; (*Heil—*) remedy; (*Maßnahme*) measure; (*Ausweg*) expedient; (*Durchschnitt*) average; (math) mean; (phys) medium; **im M.** on the average; **ins M. treten** (or **sich ins M. legen**) intervene, intercede; **letztes M.** last resort; **mit allen Mitteln** by every means; **Mittel** *pl* resources, means; funds; **M. und Wege** ways and means; **M. zum Zweck** means to an end; **sicheres M.** reliable method

Mit'telalter *n* Middle Ages

mittelalterlich ['mɪtəlaltərlɪç] *adj* medieval

Mit'telamerika *n* Central America

mittelbar ['mɪtəlbar] *adj* indirect

Mit'telgang *m* center aisle

Mit'telgebirge *n* highlands

Mit'telgewicht *n* (box) middleweight class

Mittelgewichtler ['mɪtəlgəvɪçtlər] *m* (-s;-) middleweight boxer

Mit'telgröße *f* medium size

mit'telhochdeutsch *adj* Middle High German || **Mittelhochdeutsch** *n* (-es;) Middle High German

Mit'tellage *f* central position; (mus) middle range

mittelländisch ['mɪtəllendɪʃ] *adj* Mediterranean

Mit'telläufer *m* (fb) center halfback

mit'tellos *adj* penniless, destitute

Mit'telmaß *n* medium; balance; average

mitt'telmäßig *adj* medium, mediocre; (*leidlich*) indifferent; so–so

Mit'telmäßigkeit *f* mediocrity

Mit'telmast *m* mainmast

Mit'telmeer *n* Mediterranean

Mit'telohr *n* middle ear

Mit'telpreis *m* average price

Mit'telpunkt *m* center

mittels ['mɪtəls] *prep* (genit) by means of

Mit'telschrift *f* (archit) nave

Mit'telschule *f* secondary school

Mit'tels-mann *m* (-[e]s;-er & -leute) go-between; (com) middleman

Mit'telsorte *f* medium quality

Mit'telsperson *f* see **Mittelsmann**

Mit'telstand *m* middle class

Mit'telstürmer *m* (fb) center forward

Mit'telweg *m* middle course; **der goldene M.** the golden mean; **e-n M. einschlagen** steer a middle course

Mit'telwort *n* (-[e]s;-er) (gram) participle

mitten ['mɪtən] *adv*—**m. am Tage** in broad daylight; **m. auf dem Wege** well on the way; **m. auf der Straße;** right in the middle of the street; **m. aus** from the midst of, from among; **m. darin** right in the very center (of it, of them); **m. entzwei brechen** break right in two; **m. im Winter** in the dead of winter; **m. in der Luft** in midair; **m. ins zwanzigste Jahrhundert** well into the twentieth century

Mitternacht ['mɪtərnaxt] *f* midnight

mitternächtig ['mɪtərneçtɪç], **mitternächtlich** ['mɪtərneçtlɪç] *adj* midnight

Mittler –in ['mɪtlər(ɪn)] §6 *mf* mediator; (com) middleman

mittlere ['mɪtlərə] §9 *adj* middle, central; (*durchschnittlich*) average; (*mittelmäßig*) medium; (math) mean; **der Mittlere Osten** the Middle East; **in mittleren Jahren sein** be middle-aged; **von mittlerer Größe** medium-sized

mitt'lerweile *adv* in the meantime

mittschiffs ['mɪtʃɪfs] *adv* amidships

Mittwoch ['mɪtvɔx] *m* (-[e]s;-e) Wednesday

mitun'ter *adv* now and then

mit'unterzeichnen *tr* & *intr* countersign

mit'verantwortlich *adj* jointly responsible

Mit'verantwortung *f* joint responsibility

Mit'verschworene §5 *mf* co-conspirator

Mit'welt *f* present generation; our (his, etc.) contemporaries

mit'wirken *intr* (an *dat* or **bei**) cooperate (in)

Mit'wirkung *f* cooperation

Mit'wissen *n*—**ohne mein M.** without my knowledge

Mitwisser –in ['mɪtvɪsər(ɪn)] §6 *mf* accessory; one in the know

mit'zählen *tr* include || *intr* count along

mixen ['mɪksən] *tr* mix

Mixgetränk ['mɪksgətrɛŋk] *n* mixed drink

Mixtur [mɪks'tur] *f* (-;-en) mixture

Möbel ['møbəl] *n* (-s;-) piece of furniture; **Möbel** *pl* furniture

Mö'belstück *n* piece of furniture

Möbeltransporteur ['møbəltranspɔrtør] *m* (-s;-e) mover

Mö'belwagen *m* moving van

mobil [mo'bil] *adj* movable; (*flink*) chipper; (mil) mobile

Mobiliar [mobi'ljar] *n* (-[e]s;) furniture

Mobilien [mo'biljən] *pl* movables

mobilisieren [mobili'zirən] *tr* mobilize

Mobilisierung [mobili'ziruŋ] *f* (-;) mobilization

mobil'machen tr mobilize
Mobilmachung [moˈbilmaxʊŋ] f (-;) mobilization
möblieren [møˈbliːrən] tr furnish; **möbliert wohnen** (coll) live in a furnished room; **neu m.** refurnish
mochte [ˈmɔxtə] pret of **mögen**
Mode [ˈmoːdə] f (-;-n) fashion, style
Mo'debild n fashion plate
Modell [moˈdɛl] n (-[e]s;-e) model; (Muster) pattern; (fig) prototype; **M. stehen zu** (dat) model for
modellieren [modɛˈliːrən] tr fashion, shape
Modell'puppe f mannequin
modeln [ˈmoːdəln] tr fashion, shape; **(nach)** model (on) || ref—**zu alt sein, um sich m. zu lassen** be too old to change
Mo'dengeschäft n dress shop
Mo'denschau f fashion show
Mo'denzeitung f fashion magazine
Moder [ˈmoːdər] m (-;) mold; mustiness; (Schlamm) mud
Mo'derduft m, **Mo'dergeruch** m musty smell
moderig [ˈmoːdərɪç] adj moldy, musty
modern [moˈdɛrn] adj modern || [ˈmoːdərn] intr rot, decay || **Modern** n (-s;) decay
modernisieren [modɛrnɪˈziːrən] tr modernize; bring up to date
Mo'deschmuck m costume jewelry
Mo'deschriftsteller –in §6 mf popular writer
Mo'dewaren pl (com) novelties
modifizieren [modifiˈtsiːrən] tr modify
modisch [ˈmoːdɪʃ] adj fashionable
Modistin [moˈdɪstɪn] f (-;-nen) milliner
modrig [ˈmoːdrɪç] adj moldy
modulieren [modʊˈliːrən] tr modulate; (Stimme) inflect
Mo·dus [ˈmoːdʊs] m (-;-di [diː]) mode, manner; (gram) mood
mogeln [ˈmoːgəln] intr cheat || **Mogeln** n (-s;) cheating
mögen [ˈmøːgən] §114 tr like, care for; **ich mag lieber I** prefer || **mod aux** may; can; care to; **er mag nicht nach Hause gehen** he doesn't care to go home; **ich möchte lieber bleiben** I'd rather stay; **ich möchte wissen** I should like to know; **mag kommen was da will** come what may; **wer mag das nur sein?** who can that be?; **wie mag das geschehen sein?** how could this have happened?
möglich [ˈmøːklɪç] adj possible; (ausführbar) feasible; **sein möglichstes tun** do one's utmost || **Mögliche** §5 n possibility; **er muß alles Mögliche bedenken** he must consider every possibility; **im Rahmen des Möglichen** within the realm of possibility
möglichenfalls [ˈmøːklɪçənfals], **möglicherweise** [ˈmøːklɪçərvaɪzə] adv possibly, if possible
Mög'lichkeit f (-;-en) possibility; potentiality; **ist es die M.!** well, I never!; **finanzielle Möglichkeiten** financial means; **nach M.** as far as possible

möglichst [ˈmøːklɪçst] adv as ... as possible
Mohn [moːn] m (-[e]s;-e) poppyseed; (bot) poppy
Mohn'samen m poppyseed
Mohr [moːr] m (-en;-en) Moor
Möhre [ˈmøːrə] f (-;-n) carrot
Mohr'rübe f carrot
Mokka [ˈmɔka] m (-s;-s) mocha (coffee)
Molch [mɔlç] m (-[e]s;-e) salamander
Mole [ˈmoːlə] f (-;-n) mole, breakwater
Molekül [moleˈkyːl] n (-s;-e) molecule
molekular [moleˈkuˈlaːr] adj molecular
Molke [ˈmɔlkə] f (-;) whey
Molkerei [mɔlkəˈraɪ] f (-;-en) dairy
Moll [mɔl] m invar n (mus) minor
mollig [ˈmɔlɪç] adj plump; (Frau) buxom; (behaglich) snug, cozy
Moll'tonart f (mus) minor key
Moment [moˈmɛnt] m (-[e]s;-e) moment || n (-[e]s;-e) momentum; (Antrieb) impulse, impetus; (Faktor) factor, point; (Beweggrund) motive
momentan [momɛnˈtaːn] adj momentary
Moment'aufnahme f snapshot; (Bewegungsaufnahme) action shot
Monarch [moˈnarç] m (-en;-en) monarch
Monar·chie [monarˈçiː] f (-;-chien [ˈçiːən]) monarchy
Monat [ˈmoːnat] m (-[e]s;-e) month
monatelang [ˈmoːnataˈlaŋ] adj lasting for months || adv for months
mo'natlich adj monthly
Mo'natsbinde f sanitary napkin
Mo'natsfluß m menstruation
mo'natsweise adv monthly
Mönch [mœnç] m (-[e]s;-e) monk, friar
Mönchs'kappe f monk's cowl
Mönchs'kloster n monastery
Mönchs'kutte f monk's habit
Mönchs'orden m monastic order
Mönchs'wesen n monasticism
Mond [moːnt] m (-[e]s;-e) moon; **abnehmender M.** waning moon; **zunehmender M.** waxing moon
mondän [mɔnˈdɛːn] adj sophisticated
Mond'fähre f (rok) lunar lander
Mond'finsternis f lunar eclipse
mond'hell adj moonlit
Mond'jahr n lunar year
Mond'kalb n (fig) born fool
Mond'schein m moonlight
Mond'sichel f crescent moon
Mond'sucht f lunacy; somnambulism
mond'süchtig adj moonstruck
Moneten [moˈneːtən] pl (coll) dough
monieren [moˈniːrən] tr criticize; remind
Monogramm [monoˈgram] n (-s;-e) monogram
Monolog [monoˈloːk] m (-s;-e) monologue
Monopol [monoˈpoːl] n (-s;-e) monopoly
monopolisieren [monopoliˈziːrən] tr monopolize
monoton [monoˈtoːn] adj monotonous
Monotonie [monotoˈniː] f (-;) monotony

Monsterfilm ['mɔnstərfɪlm] *m* (cin) spectacular

Monstranz [mɔn'strants] *f* (-;-en) monstrance

monströs [mɔn'strøs] *adj* monstrous

Monstrosität [mɔnstrozɪ'tet] *f* (-;-en) monstrosity

Mon∙strum ['mɔnstrum] *n* (-;-stra [stra]) monster

Monsun [mɔ'zun] *m* (-s;-e) monsoon

Montag ['mɔntak] *m* (-[e]s;-e) Monday

Montage [mɔn'taʒə] *f* (-;-n) mounting, fitting; (mach) assembly

Monta′gebahn *f*, **Monta′geband** *n* assembly line

Monta′gehalle *f* assembly room

montags ['mɔntaks] *adv* Mondays

Montan- [mɔntan] *comb.fm.* mining

Monteur [mɔn'tør] *m* (-s;-e) assemblyman, mechanic

Monteur′anzug *m* coveralls

montieren [mɔn'tirən] *tr* mount, fit; (*zusammenbauen*) assemble; (*einrichten*) install; (*aufstellen*) set up

Montur [mɔn'tur] *f* (-;-en) uniform

Moor [mor] *n* (-[e]s;-e) swamp

Moor′bad *n* mud bath

moorig ['morɪç] *adj* swampy

Moos [mos] *n* (-es;-e) moss; (*Geld*) (coll) dough

Mop [mɔp] *m* (-s;-s) mop

Moped ['moped] *n* (-s;-s) motor bike, moped

moppen ['mɔpən] *tr* mop

mopsen ['mɔpsən] *tr* (coll) swipe ‖ *ref* be bored stiff; be upset

Moral [mo'ral] *f* (-;) morality; (*Nutzwendung*) moral; (mil) morale

moralisch [mo'ralɪʃ] *adj* moral

moralisieren [moralɪ'zirən] *intr* moralize

Moralität [moralɪ'tet] *f* (-;) morality

Morast [mo'rast] *m* (-es;-e & ⸚e) mire; morass, quagmire

Mord [mɔrt] *m* (-[e]s;-e) murder

Mord′anschlag *m* murder attempt; (pol) assassination attempt

Mord′brennerei *f* arson and murder

Mord′bube *m* murderer, assassin

morden ['mɔrdən] *tr & intr* murder

Mörder -in ['mœrdər(ɪn)] §6 murderer

möderisch ['mœrdərɪʃ] *adj* murderous; (coll) awful, terrible

mord′gierig *adj* bloodthirsty

Mord′kommission *f* homicide squad

mord′lustig *adj* bloodthirsty

Mords- [mɔrts] *comb.fm.* huge; terrible, awful; fantastic, incredible

Mords′angst *f* mortal fear

Mords′geschichte *f* tall story

Mords′geschrei *n* loud shouting

Mords′kerl *m* (coll) great guy

mords′mäßig *adv* (coll) awfully

Mords′spektakel *n* awful din

Mord′tat *f* murder

Mord′waffe *f* murder weapon

Mores ['mores] *pl*—**j-n M. lehren** teach s.o. manners

morgen ['mɔrgən] *adv* tomorrow; **m. abend** tomorrow evening (or night); **m. früh** tomorrow morning; **m. in**

acht Tagen (or **über acht Tage**) a week from tomorrow; **m. mittag** tomorrow noon ‖ **Morgen** *m* (-s;-) morning; acre; **des Morgens in the morning** ‖ *n* (-;) tomorrow

Mor′genblatt *n* morning paper

Mor′gendämmerung *f* dawn, daybreak

mor′gendlich *adj* morning

Mor′gengabe *f* wedding present

Mor′gengrauen *n* dawn, daybreak

Mor′genland *n* Orient

Morgenländer -in ['mɔrgənlendər(ɪn)] §6 *mf* Oriental

Mor′genrock *m* house robe

Mor′genrot *n*, **Mor′genröte** *f* dawn, sunrise; (fig) dawn, beginning

morgens ['mɔrgəns] *adv* in the morning

Mor′genstern *m* morning star

Mor′genstunde *f* morning hour

Mor′genzeitung *f* morning paper

morgig ['mɔrgɪç] *adj* tomorrow's

Morphium ['mɔrfjum] *n* (-s;) morphine

morsch [mɔrʃ] *adj* rotten; (*baufällig*) dilapidated; (*brüchig*) brittle; (fig) decadent

Morsealphabet ['mɔrzə-alfabet] *n* Morse code

Mörser ['mœrzər] *m* (-s;-) (& mil) mortar

Mör′serkeule *f* pestle

Mörtel ['mœrtəl] *m* (-s;-) mortar; plaster; **mit M. bewerfen** roughcast

Mör′telkelle *f* trowel

Mör′teltrog *m* hod

Mosaik [moza'ik] *n* (-s;-en) mosaic

mosaisch [mo'za-ɪʃ] *adj* Mosaic

Moschee [mo'ʃe] *f* (-;-n) mosque

Moskau ['moskau] *n* (-s;) Moscow

Moslem ['mosləm] *m* (-s;-s) Moslem

moslemisch [mos'lemɪʃ] *adj* Moslem

Most [mɔst] *m* (-es;-e) must, grape juice; new wine

Mostrich ['mɔstrɪç] *m* (-[e]s;-e) mustard

Motel [mo'tel] *n* (-s;-s) motel

Motiv [mo'tif] *n* (-[e]s;-e) (*Beweggrund*) motive; (mus, paint) motif

motivieren [motɪ'virən] *tr* justify

Mo∙tor ['motor], [mo'tor] *m* (-s; -toren ['torən] & -tore ['torə]) motor

Mo′tordefekt *m* motor trouble

Mo′torhaube *f* (aer) cowl; (aut) hood

-motorig [motorɪç] *comb.fm.* -motor, -engine

Mo′torpanne *f* (aut) breakdown

Mo′torpflug *m* tractor plow

Mo′torrad *n* motorcycle

Mo′torradfahrer -in §6 *mf* motorcyclist

Mo′torrasenmäher *m* power mower

Mo′torroller *m* motor scooter

Mo′torsäge *f* power saw

Mo′torschaden *m* engine trouble

Motte ['mɔtə] *f* (-;-n) moth

mot′tenfest *adj* mothproof

Mot′tenkugel *f* mothball

Motto ['mɔto] *n* (-s;-s) motto

moussieren [mu'sirən] *intr* fizz; (*Wein*) sparkle

Möwe ['møvə] *f* (-;-n) sea gull

Mucke ['mukə] *f* (-;-n) whim; (dial) gnat; **Mucken haben** have moods

Mücke ['mʏkə] *f* (-;-n) gnat; mosquito; (dial) fly

Mucker ['mukər] *m* (-s;-) hypocrite; bigot; grouch; (coll) awkward guy

Muckerei [mukə'raɪ] *f* (-;) hypocrisy

muckerhaft ['mukərhaft] *adj* hypocritical, bigoted

Mucks [muks] *m* (-es;-e) faint sound; **keinen M. mehr!** not another sound!

mucksen ['muksən] *ref & intr* stir, say a word; **nicht gemuckst!** stay pat!

müde ['mydə] *adj* tired; **zum Umfallen m.** ready to drop

Mü'digkeit *f* (-;) weariness

Muff [muf] *m* (-[e]s;-e) (*Handwärmer*) muff; (*Schimmel*) mold; musty smell

Muffe ['mufə] *f* (-;-n) (mach) sleeve

muffeln ['mufəln] *intr* sulk, be grouchy; (*anhaltend kauen*) munch; mumble

muffig ['mufɪç] *adj* musty; (*Person*) sulky; (*Luft*) stale, frowzy

Mühe ['my.ə] *f* (-;-n) trouble, pains; (*Anstrengung*) effort; **geben Sie sich keine M.!** don't bother; **j–m M. machen** cause s.o. trouble; **mit M.** with difficulty; **mit M. und Not** barely; **nicht der M. wert** not worthwhile; **sich** [*dat*] **große M. machen** go to great pains; **verlorene M.** wasted effort

mü'helos *adj* easy, effortless

muhen ['mu.ən] *intr* moo, low

mühen ['my.ən] *ref* take pains

mü'hevoll *adj* hard, troublesome

Mühewaltung ['my.əvaltuŋ] *f* (-;) trouble, efforts; **für Ihre M. dankend, verbleiben wir** ... thanking you for your cooperation, we remain ...

Mühle ['mylə] *f* (-;-n) mill

Mühlrad ['mylraːt] *n* water wheel

Mühlstein ['mylʃtaɪn] *m* millstone

Muhme ['mumə] *f* (-;-n) aunt; cousin

Mühsal ['myzaːl] *f* (-;-e) trouble

mühsam ['myzaːm] *adj* wearisome; (*Leben*) hard; (*Arbeit*) painstaking || *adv* with effort, with difficulty

mühselig ['myzelɪç] *adj* (*Arbeit*) hard; (*Leben*) miserable, tough

Mulatte [mu'latə] *m* (-n;-n), **Mulattin** [mu'latɪn] *f* (-;-nen) mulatto

Mulde ['muldə] *f* (-;-n) trough; (geol) depression, basin

Mull [mul] *m* (-[e]s;) gauze

Müll [mʏl] *m* (-[e]s;) dust, ashes; (*Abfälle*) trash, garbage

Müll'abfuhr *f* garbage disposal

Müll'abfuhrwagen *m* garbage truck

Müll'eimer *m* trash can, garbage can

Müller ['mʏlər] *m* (-s;-) miller

Müllerin ['mʏlərɪn] *f* (-;-nen) miller's wife; miller's daughter

Müll'fahrer *m* garbage man

Müll'haufen *m* scrap heap

Müll'platz *m* garbage dump

Müll'schaufel *f* dustpan

Mulm [mulm] *m* (-[e]s;) rotten wood

mul'mig *adj* rotten; dusty; (*Luft*) sticky; (*Lage*) ticklish

Multiplikation [multiplika'tsjon] *f* (-;) multiplication

multiplizieren [multipli'tsirən] *tr* multiply

Mumie ['mumjə] *f* (-;-n) mummy

Mumm [mum] *m* (-s;) (coll) drive, grit

Mummelgreis ['muməlgraɪs] *m* (coll) old fogey

mummeln ['muməln] *tr & intr* mumble

Mund [munt] *m* (-[e]s;ˮer) mouth; **den M. aufreißen** brag; **den M. halten** shut up; **den M. vollnehmen** talk big; **e–n losen M. haben** answer back; **sich** [*dat*] **den Mund verbrennen** put one's foot into it; **wie auf den M. geschlagen** dumbfounded

Mund'art *f* dialect

Mündel ['mʏndəl] *m & n* (-s;-) & *f* (-;-n) ward

Mündelgelder ['mʏndəlgeldər] *pl* trustfund

mün'delsicher *adj* gilt-edged; absolutely safe

munden ['mundən] *intr* taste good

münden ['mʏndən] *intr*—**m. in** (*acc*) empty into, flow into

mund'faul *adj* too lazy to talk

mund'gerecht *adj* palatable

Mund'geruch *m* halitosis

Mund'harmonika *f* mouth organ

Mund'höhle *f* oral cavity

mündig ['mʏndɪç] *adj* of age

Mün'digkeit *f* (-;) majority, full age

mündlich ['mʏntlɪç] *adj* oral, verbal

Mund'pflege *f* oral hygiene

Mund'sperre *f* lockjaw

Mund'stück *n* mouthpiece; (*Zigaretten–*) tip; (*Düse*) nozzle

mund'tot *adj*—**j–n m. machen** (fig) silence s.o.

Mund'tuch *n* table napkin

Mün'dung *f* (-s *Flusses*) mouth; (*e–r Feuerwaffe*) muzzle

Mün'dungsfeuer *n* muzzle flash

Mün'dungsweite *f* (arti) bore

Mund'vorrat *m* provisions

Mund'wasser *n* mouthwash

Mund'werk *n* (fig) mouth, tongue

Mund'winkel *m* corner of the mouth

Munition [muni'tsjon] *f* (-;) ammunition

Munitions'lager *n* ammunition dump

munkeln ['muŋkəln] *tr & intr* whisper

Münster ['mʏnstər] *n* (-s;-) cathedral

munter ['muntər] *adj* awake; (*lebhaft*) lively; (*rüstig*) vigorous; gay

Münz– [mʏnts] *comb.fm.* monetary; of the mint; coin; coinage; coin-operated

Münz'anstalt *f* mint

Münze ['mʏntsə] *f* (-;-n) coin; change; (*Münzanstalt*) mint; (*Denkmünze*) medal; **bare M.** hard cash; **für bare Münze nehmen** take at face value

Münz'einheit *f* monetary unit

Münz'einwurf *m* coin slot

münzen ['mʏntsən] *tr* coin, mint; **das ist auf ihn gemünzt** that is meant for him || **Münzen** *n* (-s;) mintage, coinage

Münz'fälscher *m* counterfeiter

Münz'fernsprecher *m* public telephone

Münz'kunde f numismatics
Münz'wesen n monetary system
Münz'wissenschaft f numismatics
mürb [mүrp], **mürbe** ['mүrbə] adj (Fleisch) tender; (sehr reif) mellow; (gut durchgekocht) well done; (Gebäck) crisp and flaky; (brüchig) brittle; (erschöpft) worn out; (mil) demoralized; **j-n mürbe machen** (fig) break s.o. down; **mürbe werden** soften, give in
Murks [mʊrks] m (–es;) bungling job
murksen ['mʊrksən] intr bungle
Murmel ['mʊrməl] f (–;-n) marble
murmeln ['mʊrməln] tr & intr murmur
Mur'meltier n ground hog, woodchuck
murren ['mʊrən] intr grumble
mürrisch ['mүrɪʃ] adj grouchy, crabby
Mus [mus] n (–es;-e) purée; sauce
Muschel ['mʊʃəl] f (–;-n) mussel; (Schale) shell; (anat) concha
Muse ['muzə] f (–;-n) (myth) Muse
Muse·um [mu'ze·ʊm] n (–s;-en) museum
Musik [mu'zik] f (–;) music
Musikalien [muzi'kaljən] pl music book
musikalisch [muzi'kaliʃ] adj musical
Musikant [muzi'kant] m (–en;-en) musician
Musikan'tenknochen m funny bone
Musik'automat m, **Musikbox** ['mjuzɪkbɔks] f (–;-en) juke box
Musiker –in ['muzɪkər(ɪn)] §6 mf musician
Musik'hochschule f conservatory
Musik'kapelle f band
Musik'korps n military band
Musik'pavillon m bandstand
Musik'schrank m, **Musik'truhe** f radio-phonograph console
Musi·kus ['muzikus] m (–;-zi [tsi]) (hum) musician
Musik'wissenschaft f musicology
musisch ['muzɪʃ] adj artistic
musizieren [muzi'tsirən] intr play music
Muskat [mʊs'kat] m (–[e]s;-e) nutmeg
Muskateller [mʊska'telər] m (–s;) muscatel
Muskat'nuß f nutmeg
Muskel ['mʊskəl] m (–s;-n) muscle
Mus'kelkater m (coll) charley horse
Mus'kelkraft f brawn
Mus'kelriß m torn muscle
Mus'kelschwund m muscular distrophy
Mus'kelzerrung f pulled muscle
Muskete [mʊs'ketə] f (–;-n) musket
Muskulatur [mʊskula'tur] f (–;-en) muscles, muscular system
muskulös [mʊsku'lø̈s] adj muscular
Muß [mus] invar n must, necessity
Muße ['musə] f (–;) leisure; **mit M.** at leisure
Muß'ehe f shotgun wedding
Musselin [mʊsə'lin] m (–s;-e) muslin
müssen ['mүsən] intr—**ich muß nach Hause** I must go home || mod aux—**ich muß** (inf) I must (inf), I have to (inf); **ich muß nicht** I don't have to; **muß das wirklich sein?** is it really neecessary?; **sie hätten hier sein m.**

they ought to have been here; **sie müssen bald kommen** they are bound to come soon
müßig ['mүsɪç] adj idle; (unnütz) unprofitable; (zwecklos) useless; (überflüssig) superfluous
Mü'ßiggang m idleness
Müßiggänger m loafer
mußte ['mustə] pret of **müssen**
Muster ['mʊstər] n (–s;-) pattern; (Probestück) sample; (Vorbild) example, model; **das M. e-r Hausfrau** a model housewife; **nach dem M. von** along the lines of; **sich** [dat] **ein M. nehmen an** (dat) model oneself on
Mu'sterbeispiel n typical example
Mu'sterbild n ideal, paragon
Mu'stergatte m model husband
Mu'stergattin f model wife
mu'stergültig adj model, ideal
Mu'stergut n model farm
mu'sterhaft adj model, ideal
Mu'sterknabe m (pej) sissy
Mu'sterkollektion f (kit of) samples
mustern ['mʊstərn] tr examine, eye, size up; (mil) inspect, review
Mu'sterprozeß m test case
Mu'sterschüler –in §6 mf model pupil
Mu'sterstück n specimen, sample
Mu'sterstudent –in §7 mf model student
Mu'sterung f (–;-en) inspection; examination; (mil) review
Mu'sterungsbescheid m induction notice
Mu'sterungskommission f draft board
Mu'sterwerk n standard work
Mu'sterwort n (–[e]s;-̈er) (gram) paradigm
Mut [mut] m (–[e]s;) courage; **den Mut sinken lassen** lose heart; **guten Mutes sein** feel encouraged; **j-m den Mut nehmen** discourage s.o.; **nur Mut!** cheer up!
Mutation [muta'tsjon] f (–;-en) (biol) mutation, sport
Mütchen ['mүtçən] n—**sein M. kühlen an** (dat) take it out on
mutieren [mu'tirən] intr (Stimme) change
mutig ['mutɪç] adj courageous, brave
–mütig [mүtɪç] comb.fm. –minded, –feeling
mut'los adj discouraged
Mut'losigkeit f (–;) discouragement
mutmaßen ['mutmasən] tr suppose, conjecture
mutmaßlich ['mutmaslɪç] adj supposed, alleged; **mutmaßlicher Erbe** heir presumptive || adv presumably
Mut'maßung f (–;-en) conjecture, guesswork; **Mutmaßungen anstellen** conjecture
Mutter ['mutər] f (–;-̈) mother; **werdende M.** expectant mother || f (–;-n) nut
Mut'terboden m rich soil
Mütterchen ['mүtərçən] n (–s;-) mummy; little old lady
Mut'tererde f rich soil; native soil
Mut'terfürsorge f maternity welfare
Mut'terkuchen m (anat) placenta

Mut′terleib m womb

Mütterlich [ˈmʏtərlɪç] adj motherly, maternal; **m. verwandt** related on the mother's side

mut′terlos adj motherless

Mut′termal n birthmark

Mut′terpferd n mare

Mut′terschaf n ewe

Mut′terschaft f (–;) motherhood, maternity

Mut′terschlüssel m (mach) wrench

mut′terseelenallein′ adj all alone

Muttersöhnchen [ˈmutərzøːnçən] n (–s;–) mamma's boy

Mut′tersprache f mother tongue

Mut′terstelle f—**bei j–m die M. vertreten** be a mother to s.o.

Mut′terstute f mare

Mut′tertier n (zool) dam

Mut′terwitz m common sense

Mutti [ˈmuti] f (–;–s) (coll) mom

mut′voll adj courageous

Mut′wille m mischievousness

mut′willig adj mischievous, wiliful

Mütze [ˈmʏtsə] f (–;–n) cap

Myriade [myriˈaːdə] f (–;–n) myriad

Myrrhe [ˈmʏrə] f (–;–n) myrrh

Myrte [ˈmʏrtə] f (–;–n) myrtle

Mysterienspiel [mysˈteːrjən/piːl] n (theat) mystery play

mysteriös [mysteˈrjøːs] adj mysterious

Myste·rium [mysˈteːrjum] n (–s;–rien [rjən]) mystery

mystifizieren [mystifiˈtsiːrən] tr mystify; (täuschen) hoax

Mystik [ˈmʏstɪk] f (–;) mysticism

My′stiker –in §6 mf mystic

mystisch [ˈmʏstɪʃ] adj mystic(al)

Mythe [ˈmyːtə] f (–;–n) myth

mythisch [ˈmyːtɪʃ] adj mythical

Mytholo·gie [mytoloˈgiː] f (–;–gien [ˈgiːən]) mythology

mythologisch [mytoˈloːgɪʃ] adj mythological

My·thus [ˈmyːtus] m (–;–then [tən]) myth

N

N, n [ɛn] invar n N, n

na [na] interj well!; **na also!** there you are!; **na, so was!** don't tell me!; **na, und ob!** I'll say!; **na, warte!** just you wait!

Nabe [ˈnaːbə] f (–;–n) hub

Nabel [ˈnaːbəl] m (–s;–) navel

Na′belschnur f umbilical cord

nach [nax] adv after; **n. und n.** little by little; **n. wie vor** now as ever ‖ prep (dat) (Zeit) after; (Reihenfolge) after, behind; (Ziel, Richtung) to, towards, for; (Art, Maß, Vorbild, Richtschnur) according to, after

Nach-, nach- comb.fm. subsequent, additional, supplementary; post-; over, over again, re–; after

nach′äffen tr ape, imitate

nachahmen [ˈnaxaːmən] tr imitate, copy

Nach′ahmer –in §6 mf imitator

Nach′ahmung f (–;–en) imitation, copy

nach′arbeiten tr copy; (ausbessern) touch up; (Versäumtes) make up for

nach′arten intr (SEIN) (dat) take after

Nachbar [ˈnaxbar] m (–s & –n;–n), **Nachbarin** [ˈnaxbarɪn] f (–;–nen) neighbor

nach′barlich adj neighborly; neighboring

Nach′barschaft f (–;–en) neighborhood; **gute N. halten** be on friendly terms with neighbors

Nach′bau m (–s;) imitation, duplication; licensed manufacture; **unerlaubter N.** illegal manufacture

Nach′behandlung f (med) follow-up treatment

nach′bestellen tr reorder, order more of

Nach′bestellung f (–;–en) repeat order

nach′beten tr & intr repeat mechanically

nach′bezahlen tr pay afterwards; pay the rest of ‖ intr pay afterwards

Nach′bild n copy

nach′bilden tr copy

Nach′bildung f (–;–en) copying; (Kopie) copy, reproduction; (Modell) mock-up; (Attrappe) dummy

nach′bleiben §62 intr (SEIN) remain behind; (educ) stay in; **hinter j–m n.** lag behind s.o.

nach′blicken intr (dat) look after

nach′brennen §97 intr smolder ‖ **Nachbrennen** n (–s;) (rok) afterburn

Nach′brenner m (aer) afterburner

nach′datieren tr postdate

nachdem [naxˈdem] adv afterwards; **je n.** as the case may be, it all depends ‖ conj after, when; **je n.** according to how, depending on how

nach′denken §66 intr think it over; **n. über** (acc) think over, reflect on ‖ **Nachdenken** n (–s;) reflection; **bei weiterem N.** on second thought

nach′denklich adj reflective, thoughtful; (Buch) thought-provoking; (abwesend) lost in thought

Nach′dichtung f (–;–en) free poetical rendering

nach′drängen intr (SEIN) (dat) crowd after; pursue

nach′dringen §142 intr be in hot pursuit; (dat) pursue

Nach′druck m (Betonung) stress, emphasis; energy; (Raubdruck) pirated edition; (typ) reprint; **mit N.** emphatically; **N. verboten** all rights reserved

nach′drucken tr reprint

nach′drücklich adj emphatic; **n. betonen** emphasize

nach′dunkeln intr get darker

nach′eifern intr (dat) emulate

nach/eilen *intr* (SEIN) (*dat*) hasten after, rush after

nacheinan/der *adv* one after another

nach/empfinden §59 *tr* have a feeling for; **j-m etw n.** sympathize with s.o. about s.th.

Nachen ['naxən] *m* (-s;-) (poet) boat

nach/erzählen *tr* repeat, retell

Nachfahr ['naxfɑr] *m* (-s;-en) descendant

nach/fahren §71 *intr* (SEIN) (*dat*) drive after, follow

nach/fassen *tr* (mil) get a second helping of ‖ *intr* (econ) do a follow-up

Nach/folge *f* succession

nach/folgen *intr* (*dat*) succeed, follow; follow in the footsteps of

nach/folgend *adj* following, subsequent

Nach/folger -in §6 *mf* follower; successor

nach/fordern *tr* charge extra; claim subsequently

nach/forschen *intr* (*dat*) investigate

Nach/frage *f* inquiry; (com) demand

nach/fragen *intr* (nach) ask (about)

Nach/frist *f* time extension

nach/fühlen *tr*—**j-m etw n.** sympathize with s.o. about s.th.

nach/füllen *tr* refill, fill up

nach/geben §80 *tr* give later; (*beim Essen*) give another helping of; **j-m nichts an Eifer n.** not be outdone by s.o. in zeal ‖ *intr* give way, give; (*schlaff werden*) slacken, give; (*dat*) give in to, yield to

nach/geboren *adj* younger; posthumous

Nach/gebühr *f* postage due

nach/gehen §82 *intr* (SEIN) (*dat*) follow; (*Geschäften*) attend to; (*untersuchen*) investigate, check on

nachgemacht ['naxgəmaxt] *adj* false, imitation; (*künstlich*) artificial

nachgeordnet ['naxgə-ɔrdnət] *adj* subordinate

nach/gerade *adv* by now; (*allmählich*) gradually; (*wirklich*) really

Nach/geschmack *m* aftertaste, bad taste

nachgewiesenermaßen ['naxgəvizənərmɑsən] *adv* as has been shown (or proved)

nachgiebig ['naxgibɪç] *adj* elastic, yielding, compliant; (*nachsichtig*) indulgent; (st. exch.) declining

nach/gießen §76 *tr* fill up, refill ‖ *intr* add more

nach/glühen *tr* (tech) temper ‖ *intr* smolder

nach/grübeln *intr* (*dat* or *über acc*) mull (over), ponder (on)

Nach/hall *m* echo, reverberation

nach/hallen *intr* echo, reverberate

nachhaltig ['naxhaltɪç] *adj* lasting

nach/hängen §92 *intr* (*dat*) give free rein to ‖ *impers*—**es hängt mir nach** I still feel the effects of it

nach/helfen §96 *intr* (*dat*) help along

nach/her *adv* afterwards, later, then; **bis n.!** so long!

nachherig ['naxherɪç] *adj* later

Nach/hilfe *f* assistance, help

Nach/hilfelehrer -in §6 *mf* tutor

Nach/hilfestunde *f* tutoring lesson

Nach/hilfeunterricht *m* tutoring

nach/hinken *intr* (*dat*) lag behind

Nachholbedarf ['naxholbədarf] *m* backlog of unsatisfied demands

nach/holen *tr* make up for

Nach/hut *f* (mil) rear guard

nach/jagen *tr*—**j-m etw n.** send words after s.o. ‖ *intr* (SEIN) (*dat*) pursue

Nach/klang *m* echo; (fig) reminiscence

nach/klingen §142 *intr* reecho, resound

Nachkomme ['naxkomə] *m* (-n;-n) offspring, descendant

nach/kommen §99 *intr* (SEIN) (*dat*) follow; join (*s.o.*) later; (*Vorschriften, e-m Gesetz*) obey; (*e-m Versprechen*) keep; (*e-r Pflicht*) live up to

Nach/kommenschaft *f* (-;) posterity

Nachkömmling ['naxkœmlɪŋ] *m* (-s; -e) offspring, descendant

Nach•laß ['naxlas] *m* (-lasses;-lässe) remission; (*am Preis*) reduction; (*Erbschaft*) estate; **literarischer N.** unpublished works

nach/lassen §104 *tr* leave behind; (*lockern*) slacken; **j-m 15% vom Preise n.** give s.o. a fifteen percent reduction in price ‖ *intr* (*sich lockern*) slacken; (*sich vermindern*) diminish; (*milder werden*) relent; (*Regen*) let up; (*Kräfte*) give out; (*Wind, Sturm*) die down; (*schlechter werden*) get worse

Nach/laßgericht *n* probate court

nach/lässig *adj* careless, negligent

Nach/lässigkeit *f* carelessness, negligence

nach/laufen §105 *intr* (SEIN) (*dat*) run after, pursue

nach/leben *intr* (*dat*) live up to ‖ **Nachleben** *n* afterlife

Nach/lese *f* gleanings

nach/lesen §107 *tr* glean; (*Stelle im Buch*) reread, look up

nach/liefern *tr* deliver subsequently

nach/machen *tr* imitate; (*fälschen*) counterfeit; **j-m alles n.** imitate s.o. in everything

nach/malen *tr* copy

nachmalig ['naxmalɪç] *adj* later

nachmals ['naxmals] *adv* afterwards

nach/messen §70 *tr* measure again

Nach/mittag *m* afternoon

nach/mittags *adv* in the afternoon

Nach/mittagsvorstellung *f* matinée

Nach/nahme *f* (-;) C.O.D.

Nach/name *m* last name, family name

nach/plappern *tr* repeat mechanically

Nach/porto *n* postage due

nachprüfbar ['naxpryfbɑr] *adj* verifiable

nach/prüfen *tr* verify, check out

nach/rechnen *tr* (acct) check

Nach/rede *f* epilogue; **j-n in üble N. bringen** bring s.o. into bad repute; **üble N.** slander; **üble N. verbreiten** spread nasty rumors

nach/reden *tr*—**j-m etw n.** say s.th. behind s.o.'s back

Nachricht ['naxrɪçt] *f* (-;-en) news; (*Bericht*) report; (*kurzer Bericht*) notice; (*Auskunft*) information; **e-e N. verbreiten** spread the news; **geben Sie mir von Zeit zu Zeit N.!** keep me advised; **Nachrichten** (rad, telv) news, news report; **Nachrichten ein-holen** make inquiries; **Nachrichten einziehen** gather information; **zur N.!** for your information

Nach'richtenabteilung f (mil) intelligence section

Nach'richtenagentur f news agency

Nach'richtenbüro n news room; news agency

Nach'richtendienst m news service; (mil) army intelligence

Nach'richtensatellit m communications satellite

Nach'richtensendung f newscast

Nach'richtenwesen n communications

nach'rücken intr (SEIN) (im Rang) move up; (mil) (dat) follow up; **j-m n.** move up into s.o.'s position

Nach'ruf m obituary

nach'rufen §122 tr (dat) call after

Nach'ruhm m posthumous fame

nach'rühmen tr—j-m etw n. say s.th. nice about s.o.

nach'sagen tr—j-m etw n. repeat s.th. after s.o.; say s.th behind s.o.'s back; **das lasse ich mir nicht n.** I won't let that be said of me

Nach'satz m concluding clause

nach'schaffen tr replace

nach'schauen intr (dat) gaze after

nach'schicken tr forward

Nachschlagebuch ['naxʃlagəbux] n reference book

nach'schlagen §132 tr look up; (Buch) consult || intr (box) counter

Nachschlagewerk ['naxʃlagəverk] n reference work

Nach'schlüssel m skeleton key

nach'schreiben §62 tr copy; take down from dictation

Nach'schrift f postscript

Nach'schub m (mil) supply, fresh supplies; (mil) supply lines

Nach'schublinie f (mil) supply line

Nach'schubstützpunkt m (mil) supply base

Nach'schubweg m supply line

nach'sehen §138 tr (nachschlagen) look up; (nachprüfen) check; (acct) audit; (mach) overhaul; **j-m vieles n.** overlook much in s.o. || intr (dat) gaze after || **Nachsehen** n—**das N. haben** get the short end

nach'senden §140 tr send after, forward

nach'setzen intr (dat) run after

Nach'sicht f patience; **mit j-m N. üben** have patience with s.o.

nach'sichtig, nach'sichtsvoll adj lenient, considerate

Nach'silbe f suffix

nach'sinnen §121 intr (über acc) reflect (on), muse (over)

nach'sitzen intr be kept in after school

Nach'sommer m Indian summer

Nach'speise f dessert

Nach'spiel n (fig) sequel

nach'spüren intr (dat) track down

nächst [neçst] prep (dat) next to

nächst'beste §9 adj second-best

nächstdem' adv thereupon

nächste ['neçstə] §9 adj (super of

nahe) next; (Weg) shortest; (Beziehungen) closest || **Nächste** §5 mf neighbor, fellow man, fellow creature

nach'stehen §146 intr (dat) be inferior to

nach'stehend adj following || adv (mentioned) below

nach'stellen tr (Schraube) reset, adjust; (Uhr) set back || intr (dat) be after; (e-m Mädchen) run after

Nach'stellung f (-;-en) persecution; ambush; (gram) postposition

nächsten ['neçstən] adv one of these days, before long; next time

Näch'stenliebe f charity

nächst'liegend adj nearest

nach'stöbern intr rummage about

nach'stoßen §150 intr (SEIN) (dat) (mil) follow up

nach'streben intr (dat) strive after; (e-r Person) emulate

nach'strömen, nach'strümen, nach'-stürzen intr (SEIN) (dat) crowd after

nach'suchen tr search for || intr—n. um apply for

Nach'suchung f (-;-en) search, inquiry; petition

Nacht [naxt] f (-;̈e) night; **bei N. und Nebel** under cover of night

Nacht'ausgabe f final (edition)

Nacht'teil m disadvantage

nach'teilig disadvantageous

Nacht'essen n supper

Nacht'eule f night owl

Nacht'falter m (ent) moth

Nacht'geschirr n chamber pot

Nacht'gleiche f equinox

Nacht'hemd n nightgown

Nachtigall ['naxtigal] f (-;-n) nightingale

nächtigen ['neçtigən] intr pass the night

Nach'tisch m dessert

Nacht'klub m, **Nacht'lokal** n nightclub

Nacht'lager n accommodations for the night

nächtlich ['neçtlɪç] adj night, nightly

Nacht'mal n supper

Nacht'musik f serenade

nach'tönen intr resound; (Note) linger

Nacht'quartier n accommodations for the night

Nachtrag ['naxtrak] m (-[e]s;̈e) supplement, addition

nach'tragen §132 tr add; **j-m etw n.** carry s.th. after s.o.; (fig) hold s.th. against s.o.

nachträgerisch ['naxtregərɪʃ] adj resentful, vindictive

nachträglich ['naxtreklɪç] adj supplementary; (später) subsequent

Nachtrags- comb.fm. supplementary

Nach'trupp m (-s;) rear guard

nachts [naxts] adv at night

Nacht'schicht f night shift

nacht'schlafend adj—**bei** (or **zu**) **nachtschlafender Zeit** late at night

Nacht'schwärmer -in §6 mf reveler

Nacht'tisch m night table

Nacht'topf m chamber pot

nach'tun §154 tr—j-m etw n. imitate s.o. in s.th.

Nacht'wache f night watch, vigil

Nacht'wächter m night watchman

Nachtwandler -in [ˈnaxtvandlər(ɪn)]
§6 *mf* sleepwalker, somnambulist
Nacht/zeug *n* overnight things
Nach/urlaub *m* extended leave
nach/wachsen §155 *intr* (SEIN) grow
again
Nach/wahl *f* special election
Nachwehen [ˈnaxve·ən] *pl* afterpains;
(fig) painful consequences
nach/weinen *tr*—**keine Tränen n.** (*dat*)
waste no tears over ‖ *intr* (*dat*) cry
over
Nachweis [ˈnaxvaɪs] *m* (-es;-e) proof;
den N. bringen (or führen) furnish
proof
nach/weisbar *adj* demonstrable
nach/weisen §118 *tr* point, show; (*beweisen*) prove; (*begründen*) substantiate; (*verweisen*) refer to
nach/weislich *adj* demonstrable
Nach/welt *f* posterity
nach/wiegen §57 *tr* verify the weight of
nach/wirken *intr* have an aftereffect
Nach/wirkung *f* (-;-en) aftereffect
Nach/wort *n* (-[e]s;-e) epilogue
Nach/wuchs *m* younger generation;
younger set; children
nach/zahlen *tr & intr* pay extra
nach/zählen *tr* count over, check
nach/zeichnen *tr* draw a copy of ‖ *intr*
copy
nach/ziehen §163 *tr* drag; tow; (*Linien*)
trace; (*Schraube*) tighten ‖ *intr*
(SEIN) (*dat*) follow after
nach/zoteln *intr* (SEIN) (coll) trot after
Nachzügler -in [ˈnaxtsyklər(ɪn)] §6
mf straggler; latecomer
Nackedei [ˈnakədaɪ] *m* (-[e]s;-e)
naked child; nude
Nacken [ˈnakən] *m* (-s;-) nape of the
neck
nackend [ˈnakənt] *adj* var of **nackt**
Nackenschlag (Nak/kenschlag) *m* rabbit punch; (fig) hard blow
-nackig [nakɪç] *comb.fm.* -necked
nackt [nakt] *adj* nude, bare; (*Tatsache*)
hard; **sich n. ausziehen** strip bare
Nackt/heit *f* (-;) nudity, nakedness
Nadel [ˈnadəl] *f* (-;-n) needle; pin;
wie auf Nadeln sitzen be on pins and
needles
Na/delbaum *m* coniferous tree
Na/delkissen *n* pin cushion
Nadelöhr [ˈnadəlør] *n* (-s;-e) eye of a
needle
Na/delstich *m* pinprick; (sew) stitch
Nagel [ˈnagəl] *m* (-s;⁼) nail; **an den
N. hängen** (fig) shelve; **an den Nägeln kauen** bite one's nails
Na/gelhaut *f* cuticle
nageln [ˈnagəln] *tr & intr* nail
na/gelneu *adj* brand-new
nagen [ˈnagən] *tr* gnaw; **das Fleisch
vom Knochen n.** pick the meat off
the bone ‖ *intr* (**an** *dat*) gnaw (at),
nibble (at); (fig) (**an** *dat*) rankle
Nagetier [ˈnagətir] *n* rodent
Nah- [na] *comb.fm.* close-range,
short-range
Näh- [ne] *comb.fm.* sewing, needlework
Näh/arbeit *f* sewing, needlework
Näh/aufnahme *f* (phot) close-up

nahe [ˈna·ə] *adj* (**näher** [ˈne·ər]; **nächste** [ˈneçstə] §9) near, close; nearby;
(*bevorstehend*) forthcoming; (*Gefahr*) imminent ‖ *adv*—**j-m zu n.
treten** hurt s.o.'s feelings; **n. an.** (*dat*
or *acc*), **n. bei** close to; **n. daran sein
zu** (*inf*) be on the point of (*ger*)
Nähe [ˈne·ə] *f* (-;-n) nearness; vicinity; **in der N.** close by
na/hebei *adv* nearby
na/hebringen §65 *tr* drive home
na/hegehen §82 *intr* (SEIN) (*dat*) affect,
touch, grieve
na/hekommen §99 *intr* (SEIN) approach; (*dat*) come near to; **der
Wahrheit n.** get at the truth
na/helegen *tr* suggest
na/heliegen §108 *intr* be close by; be
obvious; be easy
na/heliegend *adj* obvious
nahen [ˈna·ən] *ref & intr* (SEIN) approach; (*dat*) draw near to
nähen [ˈne·ən] *tr & intr* sew, stitch
näher [ˈne·ər] *adj* (*comp* of **nahe**)
nearer; **bei näherer Betrachtung**
upon further consideration ‖ *adv*
closer; **immer n. kommen** close in; **n.
treten Sie n.!** this way, please! ‖
Nähere §5 *n* details, particulars; **das
N. auseinandersetzen** explain fully;
Näheres erfahren learn further particulars; **sich des Näheren entsinnen**
remember all particulars; **wenn Sie
Näheres wissen wollen** if you want
details
Näherin [ˈne·ərɪn] *f* (-;-nen) seamstress
nähern [ˈne·ərn] *ref* approach; (*dat*)
draw near to, approach
Nä/herungswert *m* approximate value
na/hestehen §146 *intr* (*dat*) share the
view of
na/hetreten §152 *intr* (SEIN) (*dat*) come
into close contact with
na/hezu *adv* almost, nearly
Näh/garn *n* thread
Näh/kampf *m* hand-to-hand fighting;
(box) in-fighting
nahm [nam] *pret* of **nehmen**
Näh/maschine *f* sewing machine
-nahme [namə] *f* (-;-n) *comb.fm.* taking
Nähr- [ner] *comb.fm.* nutritive
Nähr/boden *m* rich soil; (fig) breeding
ground; (biol) culture medium
nähren [ˈnerən] *tr* nourish, feed;
(*Kind*) nurse ‖ *ref* make a living;
sich n. von subsist on ‖ *intr* be nutritious
nahrhaft [ˈnarhaft] *adj* nourishing, nutritious, nutritive
Nähr/mittel *pl* (*Teigwaren*) noodles;
(*Hülsenfrüchte*) beans and peas
Nahrung [ˈnarʊŋ] *f* (-;) nourishment;
(*Kost*) diet; (*Unterhalt*) livelihood
Nah/rungsmittel *pl* food
Nah/rungsmittelvergiftung *f* food poisoning
Nah/rungssorgen *pl* difficulty in making ends meet
Nähr/wert *m* nutritive value
Näh/stube *f* sewing room
Naht [nat] *f* (-;⁼e) seam

Nah'verkehr *m* local traffic

Näh'zeug *n* sewing kit

naiv [na'if] *adj* naive

Name ['namə] *m* (-ns;-n), **Namen** ['namən] *m* (-s;-) name

na'menlos *adj* nameless; (*unsäglich*) indescribable

namens ['naməns] *adv* named, called || *prep* (*genit*) in the name of, on behalf of

Na'mensschild *n* nameplate

Na'menstag *m* name day

Na'mensvetter *m* namesake

namentlich ['naməntliç] *adj*—**namentliche Abstimmung** roll-call vote || *adv* by name, individually; (*besonders*) especially

Na'menverzeichnis *n* index of names; nomenclature

namhaft ['namhaft] *adj* distinguished; (*beträchtlich*) considerable; **n. machen** name, specify

nämlich ['nemliç] *adv* namely, that is; (*coll*) you know, you see

nannte ['nantə] *pret* of **nennen**

nanu [na'nu] *interj* gee!

Napf [napf] *m* (-es;⁔e) bowl

Narbe ['narbə] *f* (-;-n) scar; (*des Leders*) grain; (agr) topsoil

narbig ['narbiç] *adj* scarred

Narkose [nar'kozə] *f* (-;-n) anesthesia

Narkoti-kum [nar'kotikum] *n* (-s;-ka [ka]) narcotic, dope

narkotisch [nar'koti] *adj* narcotic

Narr [nar] *m* (-en;-en) fool; (hist) jester; **j-n zum Narren halten** make a fool of s.o.

Närrchen ['nerçən] *n* (-s;-) silly little goose

narren ['narən] *tr* make a fool of

Narrenfest ['narənfest] *n* masquerade

Narrenhaus ['narənhaus] *n* madhouse

Narrenkappe ['narənkapə] *f* cap and bells

narrensicher ['narənziçər] *adj* (coll) foolproof

Narren(s)possen ['narən(s)pɔsən] *pl* horseplay; **laß die N.!** stop horsing around!

Narr'heit *f* (-;-en) folly

närrisch ['neri] *adj* foolish; (*verrückt*) crazy; (*Kauz*) eccentric; **n. sein auf** (*acc*) be crazy about

Narzisse [nar'tsisə] *f* (-;-n) (bot) narcissus; **gelbe N.** daffodil

naschen ['na/ən] *tr* nibble at || *intr* (**an** *dat*, **von**) nibble (on); **gern n. haben** have a sweet tooth

Näscher -in ['ne/ər(in)] §6 *mf* nibbler

Näscherei [ne/ə'rai] *f* (-;-en) snack

naschhaft ['na/haft] *adj* sweet-toothed

Naschkatze ['na/katsə] *f* nibbler

Naschmaul ['na/maul] *n* nibbler

Naschwerk ['na/verk] *n* sweets, tidbits

Nase ['nazə] *f* (-;-n) nose; **auf der N. liegen** be laid up in bed; **aufgeworfene N.** turned-up nose; **das sticht ihm in die N.** it annoys him; he's itching to have it; **daß du die N. im Gesicht behältst!** keep your shirt on!; **dem Kind die N. putzen** wipe the child's nose; **die N. läuft ihm blau an** his nose is getting red; **die N. rüm-**

pfen über (*acc*) turn up one's nose at; **die N. voll haben** von be fed up with; **e-e tüchtige N. voll bekommen** (or **einstecken müssen**) get chewed out; **faß dich an deine eigene N.!** mind your own business!; **feine N. für** flair for; **immer der N. nach!** follow your nose!; **in der N. bohren** poke one's nose; **j-m e-e lange N. machen** thumb one's nose at s.o.; **j-m e-e N. drehen** outwit s.o.; **j-m die Würmer aus der N. ziehen** worm it out of s.o.; **j-m etw auf die N. binden** divulge s.th. to s.o.; **j-m in die N. fahren** (or **steigen**) annoy s.o.; **j-n an der N. herumführen** lead s.o. by the nose; **man kann es ihm an der N. ansehen** it's written all over his face; **mit langer N. abziehen** be the loser; **pro N.** per head; **sich** [*dat*] **die N. begießen** wet one's whistle

näseln ['nezəln] *intr* speak through the nose || **Näseln** *n* (-s;) nasal twang

nä'selnd *adj* nasal

Na'senbein *n* nasal bone

Na'senbluten *n* (-s;) nosebleed

na'senlang *adv*—**alle n.** constantly

Na'senlänge *f*—**um e-e N.** by a nose

Na'senlaut *m* (phonet) nasal

Na'senloch *n* nostril

Na'senrücken *m* bridge of the nose

Na'senschleim *m* mucus

Na'senschleimhaut *f* mucous membrane

Nasenspray ['nazənspre] *m* (-s;-s) nose spray

Na'sentropfen *m* nose drop

na'seweis *adj* fresh, wise || **Naseweis** *m* (-es;-e) wise guy

Na'seweisheit *f* freshness

nasführen ['nasfyrən] *tr* lead by the nose; (*foppen*) fool

Nashorn ['nashɔrn] *n* (-[e]s;⁔er) rhinoceros

naß [nas] *adj* (**nasser** ['nasər] or **nässer** ['nesər]; **nasseste** ['nasəstə] or **nässeste** ['nesəstə] §9) wet; (*feucht*) moist || **Naß** *n* (Nasses) (poet) liquid

Nassauer ['nasau.ər] *m* (-s;-) sponger, chiseler

nassauern ['nasau.ərn] *intr* (coll) sponge

Nässe ['nesə] *f* (-;) wetness; moisture

nässen ['nesən] *tr* wet; moisten || *intr* ooze

naß'forsch *adj* rash, bold

naß'kalt *adj* raw, cold and damp

Nation [na'tsjon] *f* (-;-en) nation

national [natsjo'nal] *adj* national

National'hymne *f* national anthem

nationalisieren [natsjonali'zirən] *tr* nationalize

Nationalismus [natsjona'lismus] *m* (-;) nationalism

Nationalität [natsjonali'tet] *f* (-;-en) nationality; ethnic minority

National'sozialismus *m* national socialism, Nazism

National'sozialist -in §7 *mf* national socialist, Nazi

National'tracht *f* national costume

Nativität [nativi'tet] *f* (-;-en) horoscope

Natrium ['nɑtrɪ·um] *n* (-s;) sodium

Natter ['natər] *f* (-;-n) adder, viper

Natur [na'tur] *f* (-;-en) nature; (*Körperbeschaffenheit*) constitution; (*Gemütsart*) disposition; (*Art*) character; (*Person*) creature; **von N.** by nature

Natura [na'tura] *f*—**in N.** in kind

Naturalien [natu'raljən] *pl* produce

naturalisieren [naturalɪ'zirən] *tr* naturalize ‖ *ref*—**sich n. lassen** become naturalized

Natur'anlage *f* disposition

Natur'arzt *m* naturopath

Naturell [natu'rɛl] *n* (-[e]s;-e) nature, temperament

Natur'erscheinung *f* phenomenon

Natur'forscher –in §6 *mf* naturalist

Natur'gabe *f* natural gift, talent

natur'gemäß *adv* naturally

Natur'geschichte *f* natural history

Natur'gesetz *n* natural law

natur'getreu *adj* life-like

Natur'kunde *f*, **Natur'lehre** *f* natural science

natürlich [na'tyrlɪç] *adj* natural; (*echt*) real; (*ungezwungen*) natural; **das geht aber nicht mit natürlichen Dingen zu** there is s.th. fishy about it; **das geht ganz n. zu** there is nothing strange about it ‖ *adv* naturally, of course

Natur'mensch *m* primitive man; nature enthusiast

Natur'philosoph *m* natural philosopher

Natur'recht *n* natural right

Natur'schutz *m* preservation of natural beauty

Natur'schutzgebiet *n* wildlife preserve

Natur'schutzpark *m* national park

Natur'spiel *n* freak of nature

Natur'theater *n* outdoor theater

Natur'trieb *m* instinct

Natur'verehrung *f* natural religion

Natur'volk *n* primitive people

natur'widrig *adj* contrary to nature

Natur'wissenschaft *f* natural science

Natur'wissenschaftler –in §6 *mf* scientist

naturwüchsig [na'turvyksɪç] *adj* unspoiled by civilization

Natur'zustand *m* natural state

nautisch ['nautɪʃ] *adj* nautical

Navigation [navɪga'tsjon] *f* (-;) navigation

navigieren [navɪ'girən] *intr* navigate

Nazi ['nɑtsi] *m* (-s;-s) Nazi

Nazismus [na'tsɪmus] *m* (-;) Nazism

nazistisch [na'tsɪstɪʃ] *adj* Nazi

Nebel ['nebəl] *m* (-s;-) fog, mist; (*Dunst*) haze

Ne'belbank *f* (-;-ͤe) fog bank

Ne'belfeld *n* patch of fog

Ne'belferne *f* hazy distance; (fig) dim future

Ne'belfleck *m* (astr) nebula

ne'belhaft *adj* foggy, hazy; (*Ferne*) dim

Ne'belhorn *n* foghorn

nebeln ['nebəln] *intr* be foggy

Ne'belscheinwerfer *m* (aut) fog light

Ne'belscheid *f* fog bank

Ne'belschirm *m* smoke screen

Ne'belvorhang *m* smoke screen

neben ['nebən] *prep* (dat & acc) by, beside; side by side with, alongside, close to, next to; (*verglichen mit*) compared with; (*außer*) besides, aside from; in addition to; extra

Neben– *comb.fm.* secondary, accessory, by-, side-, subordinate

Ne'benabsicht *f* ulterior motive

Ne'benaltar *m* side altar

Ne'benamt *n* additional duties

nebenan' *adv* close by; next-door

Ne'benanschluß *m* (telp) extension; (telp) party line

Ne'benarbeit *f* extra work

Ne'benarm *m* tributary, branch

Ne'benausgaben *pl* incidentals, extras

Ne'benausgang *m* side exit

Ne'benbahn *f* (rr) branch line

Ne'benbedeutung *f* (-;-en) secondary meaning

nebenbei' *adv* close by; (*außerdem*) besides, on the side; (*beiläufig*) incidentally

Ne'benberuf *m* sideline, side job

ne'benberuflich *adj* sideline, spare-time

Ne'benbeschäftigung *f* sideline

Nebenbuhler –in ['nebənbulər(ɪn)] §6 *mf* competitor, rival

ne'benbuhlerisch *adj* rival

Ne'benbending *n* secondary matter

nebeneinan'der *adv* side by side; neck and neck; (*gleichzeitig*) simultaneously; **n. bestehen** coexist

Nebeneinan'derleben *n* coexistence

nebeneinan'derstellen *tr* juxtapose

Ne'beneingang *m* side entrance

Ne'beneinkünfte *pl*, **Ne'beneinnahmen** *pl* extra income

Ne'benerzeugnis *n* by-product

Ne'benfach *n* (educ) minor; **als N. studieren** minor in

Ne'benflügel *m* (archit) wing

Ne'benfluß *m* tributary

Ne'benfrage *f* side issue

Ne'benfrau *f* concubine

Ne'bengang *m* side aisle

Ne'bengasse *f* side street, alley

Ne'bengebäude *n* annex, wing

Ne'bengedanke *m* ulterior motive

Ne'bengericht *n* side dish

Ne'bengeschäft *n* (com) branch

Ne'bengleis *n* (rr) siding, sidetrack

Ne'benhandlung *f* (-;-en) subplot

nebenher' *adv* on the side; besides; along

nebenhin' *adv* incidentally, by the way

Ne'benkosten *pl* incidentals, extras

Ne'benlinie *f* (rr) branch line

Ne'benmann *m* (-[e]s;-ͤer) neighbor

Ne'benprodukt *n* by-product

Ne'benpunkt *m* minor point

Ne'benrolle *f* supporting role

Ne'bensache *f* side issue

ne'bensächlich *adj* subordinate; incidental; (*unwesentlich*) unimportant

Ne'bensächlichkeit *f* unimportance; triviality

Ne'bensatz *m* subordinate clause

Ne'benschaltung *f* (-;-en) (elec) shunt

Ne'benschluß *m* (elec) shunt

Ne'benspesen *pl* additional charges

Ne'benstehend *adj* marginal, in the margin ‖ **Nebenstehende** §5 *mf* bystander

Ne'benstelle *f* branch; (telp) extension
Ne'benstraße *f* side street
Ne'bentisch *m* next table
Ne'bentür *f* side door
Ne'benverdienst *m* extra pay; side job
Ne'benvorstellung *f* side show
Ne'benweg *m* side road
Ne'benwirkung *f* (-;-en) side effect
Ne'benzimmer *n* adjoining room
Ne'benzweck *m* secondary aim
neblig ['neblɪç] *adj* foggy, misty
nebst [nepst] *prep* (*dat*) including
necken ['nekən] *tr & recip* tease, kid
Neckerei [nekə'raɪ] *f* (-;-en) teasing
neckisch ['nekɪʃ] *adj* fond of teasing; (coll) cute
nee [ne] *adv* (dial) no
Neffe ['nefə] *m* (-n;-n) nephew
Negation [nega'tsjon] *f* (-;-en) negation
negativ [nega'tif] *adj* negative ‖ **Negativ** *n* (-s;-e) negative
Neger –in ['negər(ɪn)] §6 *mf* black, Negro
Negligé [neglɪ'ʒe] *n* (-s;-s) negligee
nehmen ['nemən] §116 *tr* take; (*weg*–) take away; (*anstellen*) take on, hire; (*Anwalt*) retain; (*Hindernis*) clear, take; (*Kurve*) negotiate; (*Schaden*) suffer; **Anfang n.** begin; **Anstand n.** hesitate; **an sich n.** pocket, misappropriate; collect; retrieve; **Anstoß n. an** (*dat*) take offense at; **auf sich n.** assume, take upon oneself; **das Wort n.** begin to speak; **den Mund voll n.** (coll) talk big; **die Folgen auf sich n.** bear the consequences; **ein Ende n.** come to an end; **ein gutes Ende n.** turn out all right; **er versteht es, die Kunden richtig zu n.** he knows how to handle customers; **etw genau n.** take s.th. literally; **ich lasse es mir nicht n. zu** (*inf*) I insist on (*ger*); **im Grunde genommen** basically; **in Angriff n.** begin; **in Arbeit n.** start making; **in die Hand n.** pick up; (fig) take in hand; **j–m etw n.** take s.th. away from s.o.; deprive s.o. of s.th.; **kein Ende n.** go on endlessly; **man nehme zwei Eier, usw.** (*im Kochbuch*) take two eggs, etc.; **n. Sie bitte Platz!** please sit down; **n. wir den Fall, daß** let's suppose that; **Rücksicht n. auf** (*acc*) show consideration for; **sich** [*dat*] **das Leben n.** take one's life; **sich** [*dat*] **nichts von seinen Rechten n. lassen** insist on one's rights; **streng genommen** strictly speaking; **Stunden n.** take lessons; **Urlaub n.** take a vacation; (mil) go on furlough; **wie man's nimmt** it all depends; **zu Hilfe n.** use; **zur Ehe n.** marry; **zu sich** [*dat*] **n.** put into one's pocket; (*Speise*) eat; (*Kind*) take charge of
Neid [naɪt] *m* (-es;) envy; **blasser** (or **gelber**) **N.** pure envy; **vor N. vergehen** die of envy
neiden ['naɪdən] *tr*—**j–m etw n.** envy s.o. for s.th.
Neid'hammel *m* envious person
nei'dig *adj* (dial) var of **neidisch**
neidisch ['naɪdɪʃ] *adj* (**auf** *acc*) envious (of)

neid'los *adj* free of envy
Neid'nagel *m* hangnail
Neige ['naɪgə] *f* (-;-n) slope; (*Abnahme*) decline; (*Überbleibsel*) sediment, dregs; **zur N. gehen** (*Geld, Vorräte*) run low; (*Sonne*) go down; (*Tag, Jahr*) draw to a close
neigen ['naɪgən] *tr* incline, bend; **geneigt** sloping; (fig) friendly, favorable ‖ *ref* (**vor** *dat*) bow (to); (*Abhang*) slope; **sich zum Ende n.** draw to a close ‖ *intr*—**n. zu** be inclined to
Nei'gung *f* (-;-en) slope, incline; (*des Hauptes*) bowing; (*e-s Schiffes*) list; (*in der Straße*) dip; (*Gefälle*) gradient; (*Hang*) inclination; (*Anlage*) tendency; (*Vorliebe*) taste, liking; (*Zuneigung*) affection; **e–e N. nach rechts haben** lean towards the right; **N. fassen zu** take (a fancy) to
nein [naɪn] *adv* no ‖ **Nein** *n* (-s;) no
Nein'stimme *f* (parl) nay
Nekrolog [nekrə'lok] *m* (-[e]s;-e) obituary
Nektar ['nektɑr] *m* (-s;) nectar
Nelke ['nelkə] *f* (-;-n) carnation; (*Gewürz*) clove
Nel'kenöl *n* oil of cloves
Nel'kenpfeffer *m* allspice
Nemesis ['nemezɪs] *f* (-;) Nemesis
nennbar ['nenbar] *adj* mentionable
nennen ['nenən] §97 *tr* name, call; (*erwähnen*) mention; (*benennen*) term ‖ *ref* be called, be named
nen'nenswert *adj* worth mentioning
Nenner ['nenər] *m* (-s;-) (math) denominator; **auf e–n gemeinsamen N. bringen** reduce to a common denominator
Nennform ['nenfɔrm] *f* (gram) infinitive
Nenngeld ['nengelt] *n* entry fee
Nen'nung *f* (-s;) naming; mentioning
Nennwert ['nenvert] *m* face value
Neologis·mus [ne·olo'gɪsmus] *m* (-;-men) [mən]) neologism
Neon ['ne·ɔn] *n* (-s;) neon
Ne'onlicht *n* neon light
Nepotismus [nepo'tɪsmus] *m* (-;) nepotism
neppen ['nepən] *tr* (coll) gyp, clip
Nepplokal ['neplɔkal] *n* (sl) clip joint
Neptun [nep'tun] *m* (-s;) Neptune
Nerv [nerf] *m* (-s;-en) nerve; **die Nerven behalten** keep cool; **die Nerven verlieren** lose one's head; **j–m auf die Nerven gehen** get on s.o.'s nerves; **mit den Nerven herunter sein** be a nervous wreck
Nerven–, nerven– [nerfən] *comb.fm.* nervous, neuro–, of nerves
Ner'venarzt *m*, **Ner'venärztin** *f* neurologist
ner'venaufreibend *adj* nerve-racking
Ner'venberuhigungsmittel *n* sedative
Ner'venbündel *n* (fig) bundle of nerves
Ner'venentzündung *f* neuritis
Ner'venfaser *f* nerve fiber
Ner'venheilanstalt *f* mental institution
Ner'venheilkunde *f* neurology
Ner'venkitzel *m* thrill, suspense
Ner'venknoten *m* ganglion
ner'venkrank *adj* neurotic

Ner'venkrieg *m* war of nerves
Ner'venlehre *f* neurology
Ner'vensäge *f* (coll) pain in the neck
Ner'venschmerz *m* neuralgia
Ner'venschwäche *f* nervousness
Ner'venzentrum *n* (fig) nerve center
Ner'venzusammenbruch *m* nervous breakdown
nervig ['nervɪç], ['nerfɪç] *adj* sinewy
nervös [ner'vøs] *adj* nervous
Nervosität [nervozɪ'tet] *f* (-;) nervousness
Nerz [nerts] *m* (-es;-e) (zool) mink
Nerz'mantel *m* mink coat
Nessel ['nɛsəl] *f* (-;-n) nettle; **sich in die Nesseln setzen** (fig) get oneself into hot water
Nest [nest] *n*. (-es;-er) nest; (*Schlupfwinkel*) hideout; small town; dead town; (*Bett*) (coll) bed
nesteln ['nestəln] *tr* lace, tie ‖ *intr* —n. an (*dat*) fiddle with, fuss with
Nesthäkchen ['nesthekçən] *n* (-s;-), Nestküken ['nestkykən] *n* (-s;-) baby (*of the family*)
nett [nɛt] *adj* nice; (*sauber*) neat; (*niedlich*) cute; **das kann ja n. werden!** (iron) that's going to be just dandy!
netto ['neto] *adv* net; clear
Net'togewicht *n* net weight
Net'togewinn *m* clear profit
Net'tolohn *m* take-home pay
Net'topreis *m* net price
Netz [nets] *n* (-es;-e) net; network; grid
netzen ['netsən] *tr* wet, moisten
Netz'haut *f* retina
Netz'werk *n* netting, webbing
neu [nɔɪ] *adj* new; (*frisch*) fresh; (*unlängst geschehen*) recent; **aufs neue** anew; **neuere Geschichte** modern history; **neuere Sprachen** modern languages; **von neuem** all over again ‖ *adv* newly; recently; anew; afresh ‖ **Neue** §5 *mf* newcomer ‖ §5 *n*— **was gibt es Neues?** what's new?
Neu-, neu- *comb.fm.* new-, newly; re-; neo-
Neu'anlage *f* new installation; (fin) reinvestment
Neu'anschaffung *f* recent acquisition
neu'artig *adj* novel; modern
Neu'aufführung *f* (-;-en) (theat) revival
Neu'ausgabe *f* new edition, republication; (*Neudruck*) reprint
Neu'bau *m* (-[e]s;-bauten) new building
neu'bearbeiten *tr* revise
Neubelebung ['nɔɪbələbuŋ] *f* (-;-en) revival
Neu'bildung *f* (-;-en) new growth; (gram) neologism
Neu'druck *m* reprint
neuerdings ['nɔɪ·ərdɪŋs] *adv* recently; (*vom neuem*) anew
Neuerer -in ['nɔɪ·ərər(ɪn)] §6 *mf* innovator
Neuerung ['nɔɪ·əruŋ] *f* (-;-en) innovation
neuestens ['nɔɪ·əstəns] *adv* recently
Neu'fassung *f* revision

Neufundland [nɔɪ'funtlant] *n* (-s;) Newfoundland
neu'gebacken *adj* fresh-baked; brand-new
neu'geboren *adj* new-born
neu'gestalten *tr* reorganize
Neu'gier *f*, Neugierde ['nɔɪgirdə] *f* (-;) curiosity, inquisitiveness
neu'gierig *adj* curious, nosey
Neu'gründung *f* (-;-en) reestablishment
Neu'gruppierung *f* (-;-en) regrouping; reshuffling
Neu'heit *f* (-;-en) novelty
neu'hochdeutsch *adj* modern High German
Neu'igkeit *f* (-;-en) news, piece of news
Neu'jahr *n* New Year
Neu'land *n* virgin soil; (fig) new ground
neu'lich *adv* lately
Neuling ['nɔɪlɪŋ] *m* (-[e]s;-e) beginner
neu'modisch *adj* fashionable; new-fangled
neun [nɔɪn] *invar adj & pron* nine ‖ Neun *f* (-;-en) nine
Neunmalkluge ['nɔɪnmalklugə] §5 *mf* wiseacre
neunte ['nɔɪntə] §9 *adj & pron* ninth
Neuntel ['nɔɪntəl] *n* (-s;-) ninth
neun'zehn *invar adj & pron* nineteen ‖ Neunzehn *f* (-;-en) nineteen
neun'zehnte §9 *adj & pron* nineteenth
neunzig ['nɔɪntsɪç] *invar adj & pron* ninety ‖ Neunzig *f* (-;-en) ninety
neunziger ['nɔɪntsɪgər] *invar adj of* the nineties; **die n. Jahre** the nineties ‖ Neunziger -in §6 *mf* nonagenarian
neunzigste ['nɔɪntsɪçstə] §9 *adj & pron* ninetieth
Neu'ordnung *f* (-;-en) reorganization
Neural·gie [nɔɪral'gi] *f* (-;-gien ['gi·ən]) neuralgia
Neu'regelung *f* (-;-en) rearrangement
Neu·ron ['nɔɪron] *n* (-s;-ronen ['ro·nən]) neuron
Neurose [nɔɪ'rozə] *f* (-;-n) neurosis
Neurotiker -in [nɔɪ'rotikər(ɪn)] §6 *mf* neurotic
neurotisch [nɔɪ'rotɪʃ] *adj* neurotic
Neusee'land *n* (-s;) New Zealand
Neu'silber *n* German silver
Neusprachler -in ['nɔɪʃpraxlər(ɪn)] §6 *mf* modern-language teacher
Neu'stadt *f* new section of town
Neu'steinzeit *f* neolithic age
neu'steinzeitlich *adj* neolithic
neutral [nɔɪ'tral] *adj* neutral
neutralisieren [nɔɪtralɪ'zirən] *tr* neutralize
Neutralität [nɔɪtralɪ'tet] *f* (-;) neutrality
Neu·tron ['nɔɪtron] *n* (-;-tronen ['tronən]) neutron
Neu·trum ['nɔɪtrum] *n* (-s;-tra [tra] & -tren [trən]) (gram) neuter
neuvermählt [nɔɪ'fermelt] *adj* newly married ‖ Neuvermählte §5 *pl* newlyweds
Neu'zeit *f* recent times
Nibelung ['nibəluŋ] *m* (-s;) (myth)

(King) Nibelung ‖ *m* (**-en;-en**) Nibelung

nicht [nɪçt] *adv* not; **auch...nicht** not ...either; **n. doch!** please don't; **n. einmal** not even, not so much as; **n. mehr** no longer, no more; **n. um die Welt** not for the world; **n. wahr?** isn't it so?, no?, right?

Nicht-, nicht- *comb.fm.* in-, im-, un-, non-

Nicht'achtung *f* disregard, disrespect; **N. des Gerichts** contempt of court

nicht'amtlich *adj* unofficial

Nicht'angriffspakt *m* nonaggression pact

Nicht'annahme *f* nonacceptance

Nichte ['nɪçtə] *f* (**-;-n**) niece

Nicht'einmischung *f* noninterference

Nicht'eisenmetall *n* nonferrous metal

nichtig ['nɪçtɪç] *adj* invalid; void; (*eitel*) vain; (*vergänglich*) transitory; **für n. erklären** annul

Nich'tigkeit *f* (**-;-en**) invalidity; futility; (*Kleinigkeit*) trifle; **Nichtigkeiten** trivia

Nich'tigkeitserklärung *f* annulment

Nicht'kämpfer *m* noncombatant

nicht'öffentlich *adj* private; (*Sitzung*) closed

nichts [nɪçts] *indef pron* nothing; **gar n.** nothing at all; **n. als** nothing but; **n. mehr davon!** not another word about it!; **n. und wieder n.** absolutely nothing; **soviel wie n.** next to nothing; **um n.** for nothing, to no avail; **weiter n.?** is that all?; **wenn es weiter n. ist!** if it's nothing worse than that ‖ **Nichts** *n* (**-s;**) nothingness; nonentity; (*Leere*) void; (*Kleinigkeit*) trifle; **vor dem N. stehen** be faced with utter ruin

nichtsdesto'weniger *adv* nevertheless

Nichts'könner *m* incompetent person; ignoramus

Nichts'nutz *m* good-for-nothing

nichts'nutzig *adj* good-for-nothing

nichts'sagend *adj* insignificant; (*Antwort*) vague; noncommittal; (*Gesicht*) vacuous; (*Redensart*) trite

Nichts'tuer -in §6 *mf* loafer

Nichts'wisser -in §6 *mf* ignoramus

nichts'würdig *adj* contemptible

Nicht'zutreffende §5 *n*—**Nichtzutreffendes streichen** §5 delete if not applicable

Nickel ['nɪkəl] *n* (**-s;-**) (metal) nickel

nicken ['nɪkən] *intr* nod; (*schlummern*) nap

Nickerchen ['nɪkərçən] *n* (**-s;-**) nap

nie [ni] *adv* never, at no time

nieder ['nidər] *adj* low; (*gemein*) base ‖ *adv* down

nie'derbrechen §64 *tr & intr* (SEIN) break down

nie'derbrennen §97 *tr & intr* (SEIN) burn down

nie'derdeutsch *adj* Low German ‖ **Niederdeutsch** *n* Low German ‖ **Niederdeutsche** §5 *mf* North German

nie'derdonnern *tr* (coll) shout down ‖ *intr* go (or come) crashing down

Nie'derdruck *m* low pressure

nie'derdrücken *tr* press down (fig) weigh down; (*unterdrücken*) oppress; (*entmutigen*) depress

Nie'derfallen §72 *intr* (SEIN) fall down

Nie'derfrequenz *f* low frequency; audio frequency

Nie'dergang *m* descent; (*der Sonne*) setting; (fig) decline, fall

nie'dergehen §82 *intr* (SEIN) go down; (*Flugzeug*) land; (*Regen*) fall; (*Vorhang*) drop

nie'dergeschlagen *adj* dejected

nie'derhalten §90 *tr* hold down, keep down

nie'derholen *tr* lower, haul down

Nie'derholz *n* underbrush

nie'derkämpfen *tr* (& fig) overcome

nie'derkommen §99 *intr* (SEIN) (**mit**) give birth (to)

Niederkunft ['nidərkunft] *f* (**-;**) confinement, childbirth

Nie'derlage *f* defeat; (*Lager*) warehouse; (*Filiale*) branch

Niederlande, die ['nidərlandə] *pl* The Netherlands, Holland

Niederländer ['nidərlendər] *m* (**-s;-**) Dutchman

niederländisch ['nidərlendɪʃ] *adj* Dutch

nie'derlassen §104 *tr* let down ‖ *ref* sit down, recline; (*Wohnsitz nehmen*) settle; (*ein Geschäft eröffnen*) set oneself up in business; (*Vogel, Flugzeug*) land

Nie'derlassung *f* (**-;-en**) settlement, colony; establishment; (*e-r Bank*) branch; (com) plant

nie'derlegen *tr* lay down, put down; (*Amt*) resign; (*Geschäft*) give up; (*Krone*) abdicate; (*schriftlich*) set down in writing; **die Arbeit n.** go on strike ‖ *ref* lie down; go to bed

nie'dermachen *tr* butcher, massacre

nie'dermähen *tr* mow down

nie'dermetzeln *tr* butcher, massacre

Nie'derschlag *m* (*Bodensatz*) sediment; (box) knockdown; (chem) precipitate; (meteor) precipitation; **radioaktiver N.** fallout

nie'derschlagen §132 *tr* knock down; (*Augen*) cast down; (*Aufstand*) put down; (*vertuschen*) hush up; (*Verfahren*) quash; (*Forderung*) waive; (*Hoffnungen*) dash; (chem) precipitate

nie'derschmettern *tr* knock to the ground; (fig) crush

nie'derschreiben §62 *tr* write down

nie'dersetzen *tr* set down ‖ *ref* sit down

nie'dersinken §143 *intr* (SEIN) sink down

nie'derstimmen *tr* vote down

Nie'dertracht *f* nastiness, meanness

nie'derträchtig *adj* nasty; underhand

Nie'derung *f* (**-;-en**) low ground, depression

niederwärts ['nidərverts] *adv* downward

nie'derwerfen §160 *tr* knock down; (*Aufstand*) put down ‖ *ref* fall down

Nie'derwild *n* small game

niedlich ['nitlɪç] *adj* nice, cute

Niednagel ['nitnagəl] *m* hangnail

niedrig ['niːdrɪç] *adj* low; (*Herkunft*) humble; (*gemein*) mean, base

niemals ['niːmals] *adv* never

niemand ['niːmant] *indef pron* no one, nobody

Nie′mandsland *n* no man's land

Niere ['niːrə] *f* (-;-n) kidney; **das geht mir an die Nieren** (fig) that cuts me deep

nieseln ['niːzəln] *impers*—**es nieselt** it is drizzling

Nie′selregen *m* drizzle

niesen ['niːzən] *intr* sneeze

Niet [niːt] *m* (-[e]s;-e) rivet

Niete ['niːtə] *f* (-;-n) rivet; (*in der Lotterie*) blank; (*Versager*) flop

nieten ['niːtən] *tr* rivet

niet-′ und na′gelfest *adj* nailed down

Nihilismus [nihi'lɪsmɪs] *m* (-;) nihilism

Nikotin [nɪkɔ'tiːn] *n* (-s;) nicotine

nikotin′arm *adj* low in nicotine

Nil [niːl] *m* (-s;) Nile

Nil′pferd *n* hippopotamus

Nimbus ['nɪmbus] *m* (-;-se) halo; aura; (*Ansehen*) prestige; (meteor) nimbus

nimmer ['nɪmər] *adv* never; (dial) no more

nim′mermehr *adv* never more; by no means

Nippel ['nɪpəl] *m* (-s;-) (mach) nipple

nippen ['nɪpən] *tr & intr* sip

Nippsachen ['nɪpzaxən] *pl* knicknacks

nirgends ['nɪrgɛnts] *adv* nowhere

nirgendwo ['nɪrgɛntvoː] *adv* nowhere

Nische ['niːʃə] *f* (-;-n) niche

nisten ['nɪstən] *intr* nest

Nitrat [nɪ'traːt] *n* (-[e]s;-e) nitrate

Nitrid [nɪ'triːt] *n* (-[e]s;-e) nitride

Nitroglyzerin [nɪtrɔglyːtsə'riːn] *n* (-s;) nitroglycerin

Niveau [nɪ'voː] *n* (-s;-s) level; **N. haben** have class; **unter dem N. sein** be substandard

Niveau′übergang *m* (rr) grade crossing

nivellieren [nɪveˈliːrən] *tr* level

nix [nɪks] *indef pron* (dial) nothing ‖ **Nix** *m* (-[e]s;-e) water sprite

Nixe ['nɪksə] *f* (-;-n) water nymph

nobel ['noːbəl] *adj* noble; elegant; (*freigebig*) generous

noch [nɔx] *adv* still, yet; even; else; **heute n.** this very day; **n. besser** even bettter; **n. dazu** over and above that; **n. einer** one more, still another; **n. einmal** once more; **n. einmal so viel** twice as much; **n. etwas** one more thing; **n. etwas?** anything else?; **n. heute** even today; **n. immer** still; **n. nicht** not yet; **n. nie** never before; **n. und n.** (coll) over and over; **sei es n. so klein** no matter how small it is; **was denn n. alles?** what next?; **wer kommt n.?** who else is coming?

noch′mal *adv* once more

nochmalig ['nɔxmaːlɪç] *adj* repeated

nochmals ['nɔxmals] *adv* once more

Nocke ['nɔkə] *f* (-;-n) (mach) cam

Nockenwelle (**Nok′kenwelle**) *f* camshaft

Nockerl ['nɔkərl] *n* (-s;- & -n) (Aust) dumpling

Nomade [nɔ'maːdə] *m* (-n;-n) nomad

nominell [nɔmɪ'nɛl] *adj* nominal

nominieren [nɔmɪ'niːrən] *tr* nominate

Nonne ['nɔnə] *f* (-;-n) nun

Non′nenkloster *n* convent

Noppe ['nɔpə] *f* (-;-n) (tex) nap

Nord [nɔrt] *m* (-[e]s;) North; (poet) north wind

Norden ['nɔrdən] *m* (-s;) North; **im N. von** north of

nordisch ['nɔrdɪʃ] *adj* northern; (*Rasse*) Nordic; (*skandinavisch*) Norse

nördlich ['nœrtlɪç] *adj* northern

Nord′licht *n* northern lights

nordwärts ['nɔrtverts] *adv* northward

Nörgelei [nœrgə'laɪ] *f* (-;-en) griping

nörgelig ['nœrgəlɪç] *adj* nagging

nörgeln ['nœrgəln] *intr*—**n. an** (dat) gripe about, kick about

Norm [nɔrm] *f* (-;-en) norm, standard

normal [nɔr'maːl] *adj* normal, standard

normalisieren [nɔrmalɪ'ziːrən] *tr* normalize

Normal′zeit *f* standard time

Normanne [nɔr'manə] *m* (-n;-n) Norman

normen ['nɔrmən], **normieren** [nɔr'miːrən] *tr* normalize, standardize

Norwegen ['nɔrveːgən] *n* (-s;) Norway

Norweger -in ['nɔrveːgər(ɪn)] §6 *mf* Norwegian

norwegisch ['nɔrveːgɪʃ] *adj* Norwegian

Not [noːt] *f* (-;-̈e) need, want; (*Notlage*) necessity; (*Gefahr*) distress; (*Dringlichkeit*) emergency; **es hat keine Not** there's no hurry about it; **es tut not** it is necessary; **in der Not** in a pinch; **im Not geraten** fall upon hard times; **j-m große Not machen** give s.o. a lot of trouble; **j-m seine Not klagen** cry on s.o.'s shoulders; **mit knapper Not** narrowly; **mit Not** scarcely; **Not haben zu** (inf) be scarcely able to (inf); **Not leiden** suffer want; **ohne Not** needlessly; **seine liebe Not haben mit** have a lot of trouble with; **sie haben Not auszukommen** they have difficulty making ends meet; **zur Not** if need be, in a pinch

Nota ['noːta] *f* (-;-s) note; **etw in N. geben** place an order for s.th.; **etw in N. nehmen** make a note of s.th.

Notar -in [nɔ'taːr(ɪn)] §8 *mf* notary public

Notariat [nɔta'rjaːt] *n* (-[e]s;-e) notary office

notariell [nɔta'rjɛl] *adv*—**n. beglaubigen** notarize

Not′ausgang *m* emergency exit

Not′ausstieg *m* escape hatch

Not′behelf *m* makeshift, stopgap

Not′bremse *f* (rr) emergency brake

Not′durft ['noːtdurft] *f* (-;) want; necessities of life; **seine N. verrichten** relieve oneself

not′dürftig *adj* scanty, poor; hard up; (*behelfsmäßig*) temporary

Note ['noːtə] *f* (-;-n) note; (*Banknote*) bill; (*Eigenart*) trait; (educ) mark; (mus) note; **in Noten setzen** set to music; **nach Noten** (fig) thoroughly; **persönliche Note** personal touch; **wie nach Noten** like clock-work

No'tenblatt n sheet music

No'tenbuch n, **No'tenheft** n music book

No'tenlinie f (mus) line

No'tenschlüssel m (mus) clef

No'tenständer m music stand

No'tensystem n (mus) staff

Not'fall m emergency

notfalls ['notfals] adv if necessary

notgedrungen ['notgədruŋən] adj compulsory ‖ adv of necessity

notieren [no'tirən] tr note down; jot down; (Preise) quote

Notie'rung f (-;-en) noting; (st. exch.) quotation

nötig ['nøtɪç] adj necessary; **das habe ich nicht n.!** I don't have to stand for that!; **n. haben** need

nötigen ['nøtɪgən] tr urge; (zwingen) force ‖ ref—**lassen Sie sich nicht n.!** don't wait to be asked; **sich genötigt sehen zu** (inf) feel compelled to (inf)

nö'tigenfalls adv in case of need

Nö'tigung f (-;) compulsion; urgent request; (jur) duress

Notiz [no'tits] f (-;-en) notice; (Vermerk) note, memorandum; **keine N. nehmen von** take no notice of; **sich** [dat] **Notizen machen** jot down notes

Notiz'block m scratch pad

Not'lage f predicament; emergency

Not'landung f emergency landing

Not'lüge f white lie

Not'maßnahme f emergency measure

Not'nagel m (fig) stopgap

notorisch [no'torɪʃ] adj notorious

Not'pfennig m savings; **sich e-n N. aufsparen** save up for a rainy day

Not'ruf m (telp) emergency

Not'signal n distress signal

Not'stand m state of emergency

Not'standsgebiet n disaster area

Not'treppe f fire escape

Not'wehr f—**aus N.** in self-defense

notwendig ['notvendɪç] adj necessary

Not'wendigkeit f (-;-en) necessity

Not'zeichen n distress signal

Not'zucht f rape

not'züchtigen tr rape, ravish

Nougat ['nugat] m & n (-s;-s) nougat

Novelle [no'vɛlə] f (-;-n) short story; (parl) amendment, rider

November [no'vɛmbər] m (-s;-) November

Novität [novi'tet] f (-;-en) novelty

Novize [no'vitsə] m (-n;-n), **Novizin** [no'vitsɪn] f (-;-nen) novice

Noviziat [novi'tsjat] n (-[e]s;-e) novitiate

Nu [nu] invar m—**im Nu** in a jiffy

Nuance [ny'ãsə] f (-;-n) nuance

nüchtern ['nɣçtərn] adj fasting; not having had breakfast; (Magen) empty; (nicht betrunken) sober; (leidenschaftslos) cool; (geistlos) dry, dull; (unsentimental) matter-of-fact

Nudel ['nudəl] f (-;-n) noodle; **e-e komische N.** (coll) a funny person

Nu'delholz n rolling pin

nudeln ['nudəln] tr force-feed

Nugat ['nugat] m (-s;-s) nougat

nuklear [nukle'ar] adj nuclear

Nukle·on ['nukle.ɔn] n (-s;-onen [-'onən]) nucleon

null [nul] adj null; **n. und nichtig** null and void; **n. und nichtig machen** annul ‖ **Null** f (-;-en) naught; zero; (fig) nobody; **in N. Komma nichts** in less than no time, in no time

Null'punkt m zero; freezing point; **auf dem N. angekommen sein** hit bottom

Numera·le [nume'ralə] n (-s;-lien [ljən] & -lia [lja]) numeral

numerieren [nume'rirən] tr number; **numerierten Platz** reserved seat

numerisch [nu'merɪʃ] adj numerical

Nummer ['numər] f (-;-n) number; (Größe) size; (e-r Zeitung) issue; **auf N. Sicher sitzen** (sl) be in jail; **bei j-m e-e gute N. haben** (coll) be in good with s.o.; **e-e bloße N.** a mere figurehead; **er ist e-e N.** he's quite a character; **laufende N.** serial number; **N. besetzt!** line is busy!

Num'mernfolge f numerical order

Num'mernscheibe f (telp) dial

Num'mernschild n (aut) license plate

nun [nun] adv now; **nun?** well?; **nun aber** now; **nun also!** well now!; **nun gut!** all right then!; **nun und nimmer(mehr)** never more; **von nun ab** from now on; **wenn er nun käme?** what if he came?

nun'mehr' adv now; from now on

nur [nur] adv only, merely, but; (lauter) nothing but; **nicht nur ... sondern auch** not only ... but also; **nur daß** except that; **nur eben** scarcely; (zeitlich) a moment ago; **nur zu!** go to it!; **wenn nur** if only, provided that

Nürnberg ['nɣrnberk] n (-s;) Nuremberg

nuscheln ['nuʃəln] intr (coll) mumble

Nuß [nus] f (-; Nüsse) nut

nuß'braun adj nut-brown; (Augen) hazel

Nuß'kern m kernel

Nußknacker ['nusknakər] m (-s;-) nutcracker

Nuß'schale f nutshell

Nüster ['nɣstər] f (-;-n) nostril

Nut [nut] f (-;-en), **Nute** ['nutə] f (-;-n) groove, rabbet

Nutte ['nutə] f (-;-n) whore

nutz [nuts] adj useful; **zu nichts n. sein** be good for nothing ‖ **Nutz** m (-es;) use; benefit; profit; **zu j-s N. und Frommen** for s.o.'s benefit

Nutz'anwendung f utilization

nutzbar ['nutsbar] adj useful; **sich** [dat] **etw n. machen** utilize s.th.

nutz'bringend adj useful, profitable

nütze ['nɣtsə] adj useful; **nichts n.** of no use; **zu nichts n. sein** be good for nothing

Nutz'effekt m efficiency

nutzen ['nutsən], **nützen** ['nɣtsən] tr make use of; **das kann mir viel (wenig, nichts) n.** this can do me much (little, no) good; **was nützt das**

alles? what's the good of all this? ‖
intr do good ‖ *impers*—es nützt
nichts it's no use ‖ **Nutzen** *m* (-s;-)
use; benefit; (*Gewinn*) profit; (*Vorteil*) advantage; **von N. sein** be of use
Nutz′fahrzeug *n* commercial vehicle
Nutz′garten *m* vegetable garden
Nutz′holz *n* lumber
Nutz′leistung *f* (mech) output

nützlich ['nʏtslɪç] *adj* useful
nutz′los *adj* useless
Nutz′losigkeit *f* (-;) uselessness
Nutz′schwelle *f* break-even point
Nutz′ung *f* (-;) use
Nylon ['naɪlɔn] *n* (-s;) nylon
Nymphe ['nʏmfə] *f* (-;-n) nymph
Nymphomanin [nʏmfo′manɪn] *f* (-;
-nen) nymphomaniac

O

O, o [o] *invar n* O, o
Oase [o′azə] *f* (-;-n) oasis
ob [ɔp] *prep* (*dat*) above; (*genit*) on
account of ‖ *conj* whether; **als ob**
as if; **na ob!** rather!; **und ob!** and
how!
Obacht ['obaxt] *f* (-;)—**in O. nehmen**
take care of; **O.!** watch out!; **O.
geben auf** (*acc*) pay attention to;
take care of
Obdach ['ɔpdax] *n* (-[e]s;) shelter
ob′dachlos *adj* homeless
Obduktion [ɔpdʊk′tsjon] *f* (-;-en)
autopsy
obduzieren [ɔpdʊ′tsirən] *tr* perform
an autopsy on
O-Beine ['obaɪnə] *pl* bow legs
O′-beinig *adj* bowlegged
Obelisk [obe′lɪsk] *m* (-en;-en) obelisk
oben ['obən] *adv* above; (*in der Höhe*)
up; (*im Himmelsraum*) on high; (*im
Hause*) upstairs; (*auf der Spitze*) at
the top; (*auf der Oberfläche*) on the
surface; (*Aufschrift auf Kisten*) this
side up; **da o.** up there; **nach o.
gehen** go up, go upstairs; **o. am
Tische sitzen** sit at the head of the
table; **o. auf** (*dat*) at the top of, on
the top of; **von o.** from above; **von
o. bis unten** from top to bottom;
from head to foot; **von o. herab** (fig)
condescendingly; **wie o. angegeben**
as stated above
obenan′ *adv* at the top, at the head
obenauf′ *adv* on top; **immer o. sein**
be always in top spirits
obendrein [obən′draɪn] *adv* on top of
it, into the bargain
o′benerwähnt, o′bengennant *adj* above-
mentioned
o′bengesteuert *adj* (aut) overhead
obenhin′ *adv* superficially; perfunctorily
obenhinaus′ *adv*—**o. wollen** have big
ideas
o′ben-oh′ne *adj* (coll) topless
o′benstehend *adj* given above
Ober ['obər] *m* (-s;-) (coll) waiter;
Herr O.! waiter!
Ober- *comb.fm.* upper, higher; superior; chief, supreme, head; southern
O′berägypten *n* Upper Egypt
O′berarm *m* upper arm
O′beraufseher *m* inspector general;
superintendent
O′beraufsicht *f* superintendence

O′berbau *m* (-[e]s;-ten) superstructure
O′berbefehl *m* supreme command; **O.
führen** have supreme command
O′berbefehlshaber *m* commander in
chief
O′berbegriff *m* wider concept
O′berdeck *n* upper deck
O′berdeckomnibus *m* double-decker
bus
o′berdeutsch *adj* of southern Germany
obere ['obərə] §9 *adj* higher, upper;
chief, superior; supreme ‖ **Obere** §5
m (eccl) father superior ‖ *n* top
o′berfaul *adj* (fig) fishy
O′berfeldwebel *m* sergeant first class
O′berfläche *f* surface
o′berflächlich *adj* superficial
O′bergefreite §5 *m* corporal
O′bergeschoß *n* upper floor
O′bergewalt *f* supreme authority
o′berhalb *prep* (*genit*) above
O′berhand *f* (fig) upper hand; **die O.
gewinnen über** (*acc*) get the better
of
O′berhaupt *n* head, chief
O′berhaus *n* upper house
O′berhaut *f* epidermis
O′berhemd *n* shirt, dress shirt
O′berherr *m* sovereign
O′berherrschaft *f* sovereignty; suprem-
acy
O′berhirte *m* prelate
O′berhofmeister *m* Lord Chamberlain
O′berhoheit *f* supreme authority
Oberin ['obərɪn] *f* (-;-nen) mother
superior; (med) head nurse
o′beringenieur *m* chief engineer
o′berirdisch *adj* above-ground; over-
head
O′berkellner *m* head waiter
O′berkiefer *m* upper jaw
O′berkleidung *f* outer wear
O′berkommando *n* general headquar-
ters
O′berkörper *m* upper part of the body
O′berland *n* highlands
Oberländer -in ['obərlɛndər(ɪn)] §6
mf highlander
o′berlastig *adj* top heavy
O′berleder *n* uppers
O′berlehrer -in §6 *mf* secondary school
teacher, high school teacher
O′berleitung *f* supervision; (elec) over-
head line (*of trolley, etc.*)
O′berleutnant *m* first lieutenant

O'berlicht n skylight
O'berliga f (sport) upper division
O'berlippe f upper lip
O'berpostamt n general post office
O'berprima f senior class
Obers ['obərs] m (–;) (Aust) cream
O'berschenkel m thigh
O'berschicht f upper layer; (der Bevölkerung) upper classes; **geistige O.** intelligentsia
O'berschule f high school
O'berschwester f (med) head nurse
O'berseite f topside, right side
Oberst ['obərst] m (–en;–en) colonel
O'berstaatsanwalt m attorney general
oberste ['obərstə] §9 adj (super of obere) uppermost, highest, top ‖ **Oberste** §5 mf senior, chief
O'berstimme f treble, soprano
O'berstleutnant m lieutenant colonel
O'berstock m upper floor
O'berwasser n—**O. haben** (fig) have the upper hand
O'berwelt f upper world
O'berwerk n upper manual (of organ)
obgleich' conj though, although
Ob'hut f (–;) care, protection
obig ['obɪç] adj above, above-mentioned
Objekt [ɔp'jɛkt] n (–[e]s;–e) object
objektiv [ɔpjɛk'tif] adj objective; (unparteiisch) impartial ‖ **Objektiv** n (–s;–e) objective lens
Objektivität [ɔpjɛktivi'tet] f (–;) objectivity; impartiality
Objekt'träger m slide (of microscope)
Oblate [ɔ'blatə] f (–;–n) wafer; (eccl) host
obliegen [ɔp'ligən] §108 intr (dat) apply oneself to, devote oneself to; (dat) be incumbent upon ‖ impers—**es obliegt mir zu** (inf) it's up to me to (inf)
Ob'liegenheit f (–;–en) obligation
obligat [ɔblɪ'gat] adj obligatory; (unerläßlich) indispensable; (unvermeidlich) inevitable
Obligation [ɔblɪga'tsjon] f (–;–en) bond; obligation
obligatorisch [ɔblɪga'torɪʃ] adj obligatory
Ob·mann ['ɔpman] m (–[e]s;–er & –leute) chairman; (jur) foreman
Oboe [ɔ'bo·ə] f (–;–n) oboe
Obrigkeit ['obrɪçkaɪt] f (–;–en) authority; (coll) authorities
o'brigkeitlich adj government(al)
obschon' conj though, although
Observato·rium [ɔpzɛrva'torjum] n (–s;–rien) [rjən] observatory
obsiegen ['ɔpzigən] intr be victorious; (dat) triumph over
obskur [ɔps'kur] adj obscure
Obst [opst] n (–es;) (certain kinds of) fruit (mainly central-European, e.g., apples, plums; but not bananas, oranges); **O. und Südfrüchte** European and (sub)tropical fruit
Obst'garten m orchard
Obst'kern m stone; seed, pip
Obstruktion [ɔpstruk'tsjon] f (–;–en) obstruction; (pol) filibuster; **O. treiben** filibuster

obszön [ɔps'tsøn] adj obscene
Obszönität [ɔpstsøni'tet] f (–;–en) obscenity
ob'walten, obwal'ten intr exist; prevail; hold sway
obwohl' conj though, although
Ochse ['ɔksə] m (–n;–n) ox
ochsen ['ɔksən] intr (educ) cram
O'chsenfleisch n beef
O'chsenfrosch m bullfrog
öde ['ødə] adj bleak ‖ **Öde** f (–;–n) wasteland; (fig) bleakness
Ödem [ø'dem] n (–s;–e) edema
oder ['odər] conj or
Öd·land ['øtlant] n (–[e]s;–ländereien [lendə'rai·ən]) wasteland
Ofen ['ofən] m (–s;") stove; (Back–) oven; (Hoch–) furnace; (Brenn–, Dürr–) kiln
O'fenklappe f damper
O'fenrohr n stovepipe
O'fenröhre f warming oven
offen ['ɔfən] adj open; (öffentlich) public; (fig) frank, open
offenbar ['ɔfənbar] adj obvious, manifest
offenbaren [ɔfən'barən] tr reveal
Offenba'rung f (–;–en) revelation
Of'fenheit f (–;) openness
of'fenherzig adj forthright; (Kleid) (hum) low-cut
of'fenkundig adj well-known; (offensichtlich) obvious; (Beweis) clear
of'fensichtlich adj obvious
offensiv [ɔfɛn'zif] adj offensive ‖ **Offensive** [ɔfɛn'zivə] f (–;–n) offensive
öffentlich ['œfəntlɪç] adj public; (Dienst) civil; **öffentliches Haus** brothel
Öf'fentlichkeit f (–;) public; publicity; **an die Ö. treten** appear in public; **im Licht der Ö.** in the limelight; **in aller Ö.** in public; **sich in die Ö. flüchten** rush into print
offerieren [ɔfə'rirən] tr offer
Offerte [ɔ'fɛrtə] f (–;–n) offer
Offerto·rium [ɔfɛr'torjum] n (–s;–rien [rjən]) offertory
Offiziant [ɔfɪ'tsjant] m (–en;–en) officiating priest
offiziell [ɔfɪ'tsjɛl] adj official
Offizier –in [ɔfɪ'tsir(ɪn)] §6 mf officer
Offiziers'anwärter –in §6 mf officer candidate
Offiziers'bursche m orderly
Offiziers'deck n quarter deck
Offiziers'kasino n officers' club
Offiziers'patent n officer's commission
Offizin [ɔfɪ'tsin] f (–;–en) drugstore; (Druckerei) print shop, press
offiziös [ɔfɪ'tsjøs] adj semiofficial
öffnen ['œfnən] tr & ref open
Öff'ner m (–s;–) opener
Öff'nung f (–;–en) opening
oft [ɔft], **öfter(s)** ['œftər(s)] adv often
oftmals ['ɔftmals] adv often(times)
oh [o] interj oh!, O!
Oheim ['ohaɪm] m (–s;–e) uncle
Ohm [om] m (–s;–e) (poet) uncle ‖ n (–s;–) (elec) ohm
ohne ['onə] prep (acc) without; **o. daß** (ind) without (ger); **o. mich!** count

me out!; **o. weiteres** right off; **o. zu** (*inf*) without (*ger*)

ohnedies' *adv* anyhow, in any case

ohneglei'chen *adj* unequaled

ohnehin' *adv* anyhow, as it is

Ohnmacht ['onmaxt] *f* (-;) faint, unconsciousness; helplessness; **in O. fallen** (or **sinken**) faint, pass out

ohnmächtig ['onmɛçtɪç] *adj* unconscious; helpless; **o. werden** faint

Ohr [or] *n* (-[e]s;-en) ear; (*im Buch*) dog-ear; **die Ohren spitzen** prick up the ears; **es dick hinter den Ohren haben** be sly; **ganz Ohr sein** be all ears; **j—m in den Ohren liegen** keep dinning it into s.o.'s ears; **j—n hinter die Ohren hauen** box s.o.'s ears; **j—n übers Ohr hauen** cheat s.o.; **sich aufs Ohr legen** take a nap; **zum e—n Ohr hinein, zum anderen wieder hinaus** in one ear and out the other

Öhr [ør] *n* (-[e]s;-e) eye (*of needle*); **ax hole, hammer hole**

ohrenbetäubend *adj* earsplitting

Oh'renklingen *n* ringing in the ears

Oh'rensausen *n* buzzing in the ear

Oh'renschmalz *n* earwax

Oh'renschmaus *m* treat for the ears

Ohrenschützer *m* earmuff

Ohr'feige *f* (-;-n) box on the ear

ohrfeigen ['orfaɪgən] *tr* box on the ear

Ohrläppchen ['orlɛpçən] *n* (-s;-) earlobe

Ohr'muschel *f* auricle

okkult [ɔ'kult] *adj* occult

Ökologie [økɔlɔ'gi] *f* (-;) ecology

ökologisch [økɔ'logiʃ] *adj* ecological

Ökonom [økɔ'nom] *m* (-en;-en) economist

Ökono•mie [økɔnɔ'mi] (-;-mien ['mi-ən]) economy; economics

ökonomisch [økɔ'nomiʃ] *adj* economical

Oktav [ɔk'taf] *n* (-s;-e) octavo

Oktave [ɔk'tavə] *f* (-;-n) octave

Oktober [ɔk'tobər] *m* (-s;-) October

oktroyieren [ɔktrwa'jirən] *tr* impose

Okular [ɔku'lar] *n* (-s;-e) eyepiece

okulieren [ɔku'lirən] *tr* inoculate

Ökumene [øku'menə] *f* (-;) ecumenism

ökumenisch [øku'meniʃ] *adj* ecumenical

Okzident ['ɔktsident] *m* (-s;) Occident

Öl [øl] *n* (-[e]s;-e) oil; **Öl ins Feuer gießen** (fig) add fuel to the fire

Öl'baum *m* olive tree

Öl'berg *m* Mount of Olives

Oleander [ole'andər] *m* (-s;-) oleander

ölen ['ølən] *tr* oil; (mach) lubricate

Öl'heizung *f* oil heat

ölig ['øliç] *adj* oily

Oligar•chie [ɔligar'çi] *f* (-;-chien ['çi-ən]) oligarchy

Olive [ɔ'livə] *f* (-;-n) olive

Oli'venöl *n* olive oil

Öl'leitung *f* pipeline

Öl'quelle *f* oil well

Öl'schlick *m* oil slick

Öl'stand *m* (aut) oil level

Öl'standanzeiger *m* oil gauge

Öl'standmesser *m* (aut) oil gauge; dipstick

Ö'lung *f* (-;-en) oiling; anointing; **die Letzte Ö.** extreme unction

Olymp [o'lymp] *m* (-s;) Mt. Olympus

Olmypiade [olym'pjadə] *f* (-;-n) olympiad

olympisch [o'lympiʃ] *adj* Olympian; Olympic; **die Olympischen Spiele** the Olympics

Öl'zweig *m* olive branch

Oma ['oma] *f* (-s;-s) (coll) grandma

Omelett [om(ə)'let] *n* (-[e]s;-e & -s) omelette

O•men ['omen] *n* (-s;-mina [mɪna]) omen

ominös [omɪ'nøs] *adj* ominous

Omnibus ['ɔmnibus] *m* (ses;-se) bus

Onanie [ona'ni] *f* (-;) masturbation

ondulieren [ondu'lirən] *tr* (Haar) wave

Onkel ['ɔŋkəl] *m* (-s;- & -s) uncle; **der große O.** (coll) the big toe

Opa ['opa] *m* (-s;-s) (coll) grandpa

Oper ['opər] *f* (-;-n) opera

Operateur [opera'tør] *m* (-s;-s) operator; (cin) projectionist; (surg) operating surgeon

Operation [opera'tsjon] *f* (-;-en) operation

Operations'gebiet *n* theater of operations

Operations'saal *m* operating room

operativ [opera'tif] *adj* surgical; operational, strategic

operieren [ope'rirən] *tr* operate on; **sich o. lassen** undergo an operation

O'pernglas *n*, **O'perngucker** *m* opera glasses

O'pernhaus *n* opera house, opera

Opfer ['opfər] *n* (-s;-) sacrifice; victim; **zum O. fallen** (dat) fall victim to

op'ferfreudig *adj* self-sacrificing

Op'fergabe *f* offering

Op'ferkasten *m* poor box

Op'ferlamm *n* sacrificial lamb; **Lamb of God;** (fig) victim

Op'fermut *m* spirit of sacrifice

opfern ['opfərn] *tr* sacrifice, offer up

Op'ferstock *m* poor box

Op'fertier *n* victim

Op'fertod *m* sacrifice of one's life

Op'fertrank *m* libation

Op'ferung *f* (-;-en) offering, sacrifice

op'ferwillig *adj* willing to make sacrifices

opponieren [opo'nirən] *intr* (dat) oppose

opportun [opor'tun] *adj* opportune

optieren [op'tirən] *intr—o. für** opt for

Optik ['optɪk] *f* (-;) optics

Optiker -in ['optɪkər(ɪn)] §6 *mf* optician

optimistisch [opti'mɪstɪʃ] *adj* optimistic

optisch ['optɪʃ] *adj* optic(al)

Orakel [o'rakəl] *n* (-s;-) oracle

ora'kelhaft *adj* oracular

orange [o'rãʒə] *adj* orange || **Orange** *f* (-;-n) orange

oran'genfarben, oran'genfarbig *adj* orange-colored

oratorisch [ora'toriʃ] *adj* oratorical

Orchester [ɔr'kɛstər] n (-s;-) orchestra
orchestral [ɔrçɛs'traːl] adj orchestral
orchestrieren [ɔrkɛs'triːrən] tr orchestrate
Orchidee [ɔrçi'deːə] f (-;-n) orchid
Orden ['ɔrdən] m (-s;-) medal, decoration; (eccl) order
Or'densband n (-[e]s;⸚er) ribbon
Or'densbruder m monk, friar
Or'denskleid n (eccl) habit
Or'densschwester f nun, sister
ordentlich ['ɔrdəntlɪç] adj orderly;
(aufgeräumt) tidy; (anständig) decent, respectable; (regelrecht) regular; (tüchtig) sound; (Frühstück)
solid; (Mitglied) active; (Professor)
full; **e-e ordentliche Leistung** a
pretty good job; **in ordentlichem
Zustand** in good condition || adv
thoroughly, properly; (sehr) (coll)
awfully, very; really
Order ['ɔrdər] f (-;-n) (com, mil) order
ordinär [ɔrdɪ'nɛr] adj ordinary; vulgar; rude
Ordina·rius [ɔrdɪ'narjʊs] m (-;-rien
[rjən]) professor; (eccl) ordinary
Ordinär'preis m retail price
ordinieren [ɔrdɪ'niːrən] tr ordain ||
intr (med) have office hours
ordnen ['ɔrdnən] tr arrange; (regeln)
put in order; (säubern) tidy up
Ord'nung f (-;-en) order, arrangement;
classification; system; class; rank;
regulation; (mil) formation; **aus der
O. bringen** disturb; **in bester O.** in
tiptop shape; **in O. bringen** set in
order; **in O. sein** be all right; **nicht
in O. sein** be out of order; be wrong;
be out of sorts
ord'nungsgemäß adv duly
Ord'nungsliebe f tidiness, orderliness
ord'nungsmäßig adj orderly, regular ||
adv duly
Ord'nungsruf m (parl) call to order
Ord'nungssinn m sense of order
Ord'nungsstrafe f fine
ord'nungswidrig adj irregular, illegal
Ord'nungszahl f ordinal number
Ordonnanz [ɔrdɔ'nants] f (-;-en) (mil)
orderly
Organ [ɔr'gaːn] n (-s;-e) organ
Organisation [ɔrganiza'tsjoːn] f (-;-en)
organization
organisch [ɔr'gaːnɪʃ] adj organic; (Ge-
webe) structural || adv organically
organisieren [ɔrgani'ziːrən] tr organize;
(mil) scrounge || ref unionize; **or-
ganisierter Arbeiter** union worker
Organis·mus [ɔrga'nɪsmʊs] m (-;-men
[mən]) organism
Organist **–in** [ɔrga'nɪst(ɪn)] §7 mf
organist
Orgas·mus [ɔr'gasmʊs] m (-;-men
[mən]) orgasm
Orgel ['ɔrgəl] f (-;-n) organ
Or'gelzug m organ stop
Orgie ['ɔrgjə] f (-;-n) orgy
Orient ['ɔrjɛnt] m (-s;) Orient
Orientale [ɔrjɛn'taːlə] m (-n;-n) **Ori-
entalin** [ɔrjɛn'taːlɪn] f (-;-nen) Oriental
orientalisch [ɔrjɛn'taːlɪʃ] adj oriental

orientieren [ɔrjɛn'tiːrən] tr orient; (fig)
inform, instruct; (mil) brief
Orientie'rung f (-;-en) orientation; in-
formation, instruction; **die O. ver-
lieren** lose one's bearings
Orientie'rungssinn m sense of direction
original [ɔrigi'naːl] adj original ||
Original n (-s;-e) original; (typ)
copy
Original'ausgabe f first edition
Originalität [ɔriginalɪ'tɛt] f (-;) originality
Original'sendung f live broadcast
originell [ɔrigi'nɛl] adj original
Orkan [ɔr'kaːn] m (-[e]s;-e) hurricane
Ornament [ɔrna'mɛnt] n (-[e]s;-e)
ornament
Ornat [ɔr'naːt] m (-[e]s;-e) robes
Ort [ɔrt] m (-[e]s;-e) place, spot;
(Örtlichkeit) locality; (Dorf) village;
am Ort sein be appropriate; **an
allen Orten** everywhere; **an Ort und
Stelle** on the spot; **an Ort und Stelle
gelangen** reach one's destination;
höheren Ortes at higher levels; **Ort
der Handlung** scene of action; **vor
Ort** on location; **vor Ort arbeiten**
(min) work at the face || n (-[e]s;
⸚er) position, locus
Örtchen ['œrtçən] n (-s;-) toilet
orten ['ɔrtən] tr get the bearing on,
locate || intr take a bearing
orthodox [ɔrto'dɔks] adj orthodox
Orthographie [ɔrtogra'fiː] f (-;) orthography
Orthopäde [ɔrto'pɛdə] m (-n;-n),
Orthopädin [ɔrto'pɛdɪn] f (-;-nen)
orthopedist
orthopädisch [ɔrto'pɛdɪʃ] adj ortho-
pedic
örtlich ['œrtlɪç] adj local, topical
Ört'lichkeit f (-;-en) locality
Orts-, orts- [ɔrts] comb.fm. local
Orts'amt n (telp) local exchange
Orts'angabe f address
orts'ansässig adj resident || **Ortsan-
sässige** §5 mf resident
Orts'behörde f local authorities
Orts'beschreibung f topography
Ort'schaft f (-;-en) place; (Dorf) vil-
lage
orts'fremd adj nonlocal, out-of-town
Orts'gespräch n (telp) local call
Orts'kenntnis f familiarity with a place
orts'kundig adj familiar with the lo-
cality
Orts'name m place name
Orts'sinn m sense of direction
Orts'veränderung f change of scenery
Orts'verkehr m local traffic
Orts'zeit f local time
Orts'zustellung f local delivery
Or'tung f (-;-en) (aer, naut) taking of
bearings, navigation
Öse ['øːzə] f (-;-n) loop, eye; (des
Schuhes) eyelet
Ost [ɔst] m (-es;-e) East; (poet) east
wind
Ost- comb.fm. eastern, East
Osten ['ɔstən] m (-s;) East; **der Ferne
O.** the Far East; **der Nahe O.** the
Near East; **nach O.** eastward
ostentativ [ɔstenta'tiːf] adj ostentatious

Oster– [ostər] *comb.fm.* Easter
O'sterei *n* Easter egg
O'sterfest *n* Easter
O'sterhase *m* Easter bunny
O'sterlamm *m* paschal lamb
Ostern ['ostərn] *n* (–;–) & *pl* Easter
österreich ['østəraıç] *n* (–s;) Austria
Österreicher –in ['østəraıçər(ın)] §6 *mf* Austrian
österreichisch ['østəraıçıʃ] *adj* Austrian
O'sterzeit *f* Eastertide
Ost'front *f* eastern front
Ost'gote *m* Ostrogoth
östlich ['œstlıç] *adj* eastern, easterly; Oriental; ö. von east of
Ost'mark *f* East-German mark
Ost'see *f* Baltic Sea
ostwärts ['ostverts] *adv* eastward

Otter ['otər] *m* (–s;–) otter ‖ *f* (–;–n) (*Schlange*) adder
Ouvertüre [uver'tyrə] *f* (–;–n) (mus) overture
oval [o'val] *adj* oval ‖ Oval *n* (–s;–e) oval
Ovar [o'var] *n* (–s;–e & –ien [jən]) ovary
Overall ['ovərol] *m* (–s;–s) overalls
Oxyd [o'ksyt] *n* (–[e]s;–e) oxide
Oxydation [oksyda'tsjon] *f* (–;) oxidation
oxydieren [oksy'dirən] *tr* & *intr* (SEIN) oxidize
Ozean ['otse·an] *m* (–s;–e) ocean; der Große (or Stille) O. the Pacific
Ozeanographie [otse·anogra'fi] *f* (–;) oceanography
Ozon [o'tson] *n* (–s;) ozone

P

P, p [pe] *invar n* P, p
paar [par] *adj* even ‖ *invar adj*—ein p. a couple of, a few ‖ Paar *n* (–[e]s; –e) pair, couple; zu Paaren treiben rout
paaren ['parən] *tr* match, mate ‖ *ref* mate
paarig ['parıç] *adj* in pairs
paar'laufen §105 *intr* (SEIN) skate as a couple
paar'mal *adv*—ein p. a couple of times
Paa'rung *f* (–;) pairing, matching; (*Begattung*) mating
Paa'rungszeit *f* mating season
paar'weise *adv* in pairs, two by two
Pacht [paxt] *f* (–;–en) lease; (*Geld*) rent; in P. geben lease out; in P. nehmen lease, rent
Pacht'brief *m* lease
pachten ['paxtən] *tr* take a lease on
Pächter –in ['pɛçtər(ın)] §6 *mf* tenant
Pacht'ertrag *m*, Pacht'geld *n* rent
Pacht'gut *n*, Pacht'hof *m* leased farm
Pacht'kontrakt *m* lease
Pacht'tung *f* (–;–en) leasing; leasehold
Pacht'vertrag *m* lease
Pacht'zeit *f* term of lease
Pacht'zins *m* rent
Pack [pak] *m* (–[e]s;–e & ⁼e) pack; (*Paket*) parcel; (*Ballen*) bale; ein P. Spielkarten a pack of cards ‖ *n* (–[e]s;) rabble; ein P. von Lügnern a pack of liars
Päckchen ['pɛkçən] *n* (–s;–) small package; (*Zigaretten*–) pack
packen ['pakən] *tr* pack, pack up; (*fassen*) seize, grab; (fig) grip, thrill; pack dich! scram! ‖ Packen *m* (–s;–) pack; (*Ballen*) bale ‖ *n* (–s;) packing
Pack'esel *m* (fig) drudge
Pack'papier *n* wrapping paper
Pack'pferd *n* packhorse
Pack'tier *n* pack animal
Packung (Pak'kung) *f* (–;–en) packing; (*Paket*) packet; P. Zigaretten pack of cigarettes

Pack'wagen *m* (rr) baggage car
Pädadoge [peda'gogə] *m* (–n;–n) pedagogue
Pädagogik [peda'gogık] *f* (–;) pedagogy
pädagogisch [peda'gogıʃ] *adj* pedagogical, educational
Paddel ['padəl] *n* (–s;–) paddle
Pad'delboot *n* canoe
paddeln ['padəln] *intr* paddle, canoe
Pädiatrie [pedı·a'tri] *f* (–;) pediatrics
paff [paf] *interj* bang!
paffen ['pafən] *tr* & *intr* puff
Page ['paʒə] *m* (–n;–n) page
Pa'genfrisur *f*, Pa'genkopf *m* pageboy
Pagode [pa'godə] *f* (–;–n) pagoda
Pair [per] *m* (–s;–s) peer
Pak [pak] *f* (–;– & –s) (Panzerabwehr-kanone) antitank gun
Paket [pa'ket] *n* (–[e]s;–e) parcel; (*Bücher*–, *Post*–) bundle
Paket'adresse *f* gummed label
Paket'post *f* parcel post
Pakt [pakt] *m* (–[e]s;–e) pact
paktieren [pak'tirən] *intr* make a pact
Paläontologie [pale·ontolo'gi] *f* (–;) paleontology
Palast [pa'last] *m* (–es;⁼e) palace
palast'artig *adj* palatial
Palästina [palɛ'stina] *n* (–s;) Palestine
Palette [pa'letə] *f* (–;–n) palette
Palisade [palı'zadə] *f* (–;–n) palisade
Palme ['palmə] *f* (–;–n) palm tree; palm branch; j–n auf die P. bringen (coll) drive s.o. up the wall
Palm'wedel *m*, Palm'zweig *m* palm branch
Pampelmuse ['pampəlmuzə] *f* (–;–n) grapefruit
Pamphlet [pam'flet] *n* (–[e]s;–e) lampoon
Panama ['panama] *n* (–s;) Panama
Paneel [pa'nel] *n* (–s;–e) panel
paneelieren [pane·'lirən] *tr* panel
Panier [pa'nir] *n* (–s;–e) slogan
panieren [pa'nirən] *tr* (culin) bread

Panik ['pɑnɪk] f (-;) panic
panisch ['pɑnɪʃ] adj panic-stricken
Panne ['panə] f (-;-n) breakdown;
(*Reifenpanne*) blowout; (fig) mishap
Panora·ma [pano'rɑma] n (-s;-men
[mən]) panorama
panschen ['pan/ən] tr adulterate, water
down || intr splash about; mix
Panther ['pantər] m (-s;-) panther
Pantine [pan'tinə] f (-;-n) clog
Pantoffel [pan'tofəl] m (-s;-n) slipper;
unter dem P. stehen be henpecked
Pantof'felheld m henpecked husband
Panzer ['pantsər] m (-s;-) armor; ar-
mor plating; (mil) tank; (zool) shell
Pan'zerabwehrkanone f antitank gun
Pan'zerbrechend adj armor-piercing
Pan'zerfalle f tank trap
Pan'zerfaust f bazooka
Pan'zergeschoß n, **Pan'zergranate** f
armor-piercing shell
Pan'zerhandschuh m gauntlet
Pan'zerhemd n coat of mail
Pan'zerkreuzer m battle cruiser
panzern ['pantsərn] tr armor || ref
arm oneself
Pan'zerschrank m safe
Panzerspähwagen ['pantsər/pevagən]
m (mil) armored car
Pan'zersperre f antitank obstacle
Pan'zerung f (-;-en) armor plating
Pan'zerwagen m armored car
Papagei [papa'gaɪ] m (-en;-en) &
(-[e]s;-en) parrot
Papier [pa'pir] n (-[e]s;-e) paper
Papier'bogen m sheet of paper
Papier'brei m paper pulp
papieren [pa'pirən] adj paper
Papier'fabrik f paper mill
Papier'format n size of paper
Papier'korb m wastebasket
Papier'krieg m (fig) red tape
Papier'mühle f paper mill
Papier'schlange f paper streamer
Papier'tüte f paper bag
Papier'waren pl stationery
Papp [pap] m (-[e]s;-e) (*Brei*) pap;
(*Kleister*) paste
Papp- [pap] comb.fm. sticky; card-
board
Papp'band m (-[e]s;-̈e) paperback
Papp'deckel m piece of cardboard
Pappe ['papə] f (-;-) cardboard
Pappel ['papəl] f (-;-n) poplar
päppeln ['pepəln] tr feed lovingly
pappen ['papən] tr paste, glue || intr
stick
Pap'penstiel m (coll) trifle; **das ist
keinen P. wert** (coll) this isn't worth
a thing
papperlapapp [papərla'pap] interj non-
sense!
pap'pig adj sticky
Papp'karton m, **Papp'schachtel** f card-
board box, cardboard carton
Papp'schnee m sticky snow (*for skiing*)
Paprika ['paprika] m (-s) paprika
Pap'rikaschote f (green) pepper
Papst [papst] m (-es;-̈e) pope
päpstlich ['pepstlɪç] adj papal
Papsttum ['papsttum] n (-s;) papacy
Papy·rus [pa'pyrus] m (-;-ri [ri])
papyrus

Parabel [pa'rabəl] f (-;-n) parable;
(geom) parabola
Parade [pa'radə] f (-;-n) parade;
(fencing) parry; (mil) review; (fb)
save
Para'deanzug m (mil) dress uniform
Paradeiser [para'daɪzər] m (-s;-)
(Aust) tomato
Para'depferd n (fig) show-off
Para'deplatz m parade ground
Para'deschritt m goose step
paradieren [para'dirən] intr parade;
(fig) show off
Paradies [para'dis] n (-es;-e) paradise
Paradies'apfel m tomato
paradox [para'dɔks] adj paradoxical ||
Paradox n (-es;-e) paradox
Paraffin [para'fin] n (-s;-e) paraffin
Paragraph [para'graf] m (-en & -s;
-en) paragraph; (jur) section
parallel [para'lel] adj parallel || **Paral-
lele** f (-;-n) parallel
Paralyse [para'lyzə] f (-;-n) paralysis
paralysieren [paraly'zirən] tr paralyze
Paralytiker -in [para'lytɪkər(ɪn)] §6
mf paralytic
Paranuß ['paranus] f Brazil nut
Parasit [para'zit] m (-en;-en) parasite
parat [pa'rat] adj ready
Pardon [par'dɔ̃] m (-s) pardon; **kei-
nen P. geben** (mil) given no quarter
Parenthese [paren'tezə] f (-;-n) parenthesis
Parfüm [par'fym] n (-[e]s;-e) perfume
Parfüme·rie [parfymə'ri] f (-;-rien
['ri·ən]) perfume shop
parfümieren [parfy'mirən] tr perfume
pari ['pari] adv at par || **Pari** m (-
[s];) par; **auf P.** at par
Paria ['parja] m (-s;-s) pariah
parieren [pa'rirən] tr (*Pferd*) rein in;
(*Hieb*) parry || intr (dat) obey
Pa'rikurs m (com) parity
Paris [pa'ris] n (-;) Paris
Pariser -in [pa'rizər(ɪn)] §6 mf Pari-
sian
Parität [parɪ'tet] f (-;) equality; (fin,
st. exch.) parity
paritätisch [parɪ'tetɪʃ] adj on a footing of equality
Park [park] m (-s;-s & -e) park
Park'anlage f park; **Parkanlagen**
grounds
parken ['parkən] tr & intr park
Parkett [par'ket] n (-[e]s;-e) (*Fußboden*) parquet; (theat) parquet
Parkett'fußboden m parquet flooring
Park'licht n parking light
Park'platz m parking lot
Park'platzwärter m parking lot attendant
Park'uhr f parking meter
Parlament [parla'ment] n (-[e]s;-e)
parliament
Parlamentär [parlamen'ter] m (-s;-e)
truce negotiator
parlamentarisch [parlamen'tarɪʃ] adj
parliamentary
parlamentieren [parlamen'tirən] intr
(coll) parley
Paro·die [paro'di] f (-;-dien ['di·ən])
parody
parodieren [parə'dirən] tr parody

Parole [pa'rolə] *f* (–;-n) (mil) password; (pol) slogan

Partei [par'tai] *f* (–;-en) party; (Mieter) tenant(s); (jur, pol) party; (sport) side; **j–s P. ergreifen or P. nehmen für j–n** side with s.o.

Partei'bonze *m* (pol) party boss

Partei'gänger –in §6 *mf* (pol) party sympathizer

Partei'genosse *m*, **Partei'genossin** *f* party member

Partei'grundsatz *m* party plank

parteiisch [par'tai.ıʃ] *adj* partial, biased; (pol) partisan

partei'lich *adj* partisan

Partei'lichkeit *f* (–;) partiality

partei'los *adj* (pol) independent || **Parteilose** §5 *mf* independent

Partei'losigkeit *f* (–;) impartiality; political independence

Partei'nahme *f* (–;) taking sides

Partei'programm *n* party platform

Partei'tag *m* party rally

Partei'zugehörigkeit *f* party affiliation

Parterre [par'ter] *n* (–s;-s) ground floor; (theat) parterre

Par-tie [par'ti] *f* (–;-tien ['ti-ən]) part; (Gesellschaft) party; (Spiel) game; (Ausflug) outing; (com) lot; (theat) role; **e–e gute P. machen** (coll) marry rich; **ich bin mit von der P.!** count me in!

partiell [par'tsjel] *adj* partial || *adv* partly, partially

Partikel [par'tikəl] *f* (–;-n) particle

Partisan –in [parti'zan(ın)] §7 *mf* partisan

Partitur [parti'tur] *f* (–;-en) (mus) score

Partizip [parti'tsip] *n* (–s;-ien [jən]) participle

Partner –in ['partnər(ın)] §6 *mf* partner

Part'nerschaft *f* (–;-en) partnership

Parzelle [par'tselə] *f* (–;-n) lot

parzellieren [partse'lirən] *tr* parcel out, allot

paschen ['paʃən] *tr* smuggle || *intr* smuggle; (würfeln) play dice

Paß [pas] *m* (Passes; Pässe) pass; passport; (geog) mountain pass

passabel [pa'sabəl] *adj* tolerable

Passage [pa'saʒə] *f* (–;-n) passage; (mus) run

Passagier [pasa'ʒir] *m* (–s;-e) passenger; **blinder P.** stowaway

Passagier'dampfer *m* passenger liner

Passagier'gut *n* luggage

Passah ['pasa] *n* (–s;), **Pas'sahfest** *n* Passover

Paß'amt *n* passport office

Passant –in [pa'sant(ın)] §7 *mf* passerby

Paß'ball *m* (sport) pass

Paß'bild *n* passport photograph

passen ['pasən] *ref* be proper || *intr* fit; (dat) suit; (cards, fb) pass; **p. auf** (acc) watch for, wait for; **p. zu** suit, fit; **sie p. zueinander** they are a good match

pas'send *adj* suitable; convenient; (Kleidungsstück) matching; **für p. halten** think it proper

Paß'form *f*—e–e gute P. haben be form-fitting

passierbar [pa'sirbar] *adj* passable

passieren [pa'sirən] *tr* pass, cross; (culin) sift, sieve || *intr* (SEIN) happen

Passier'schein *m* pass, permit

Passion [pa'sjon] *f* (–;-en) passion

passioniert [pasjo'nirt] *adj* ardent

Passions'spiel *n* passion play

passiv [pa'sif] *adj* passive; (Handelsbilanz) unfavorable; **passives Wahlrecht** eligibility || **Passiv** *n* (–s;-e) (gram) passive

Passiva [pa'siva] *pl*, **Passiven** [pa'sivən] *pl* debts, liabilities

Paß'kontrolle *f* passport inspection

Paste ['pastə] *f* (–;-n) paste

Pastell [pas'tel] *n* (–s;-e) pastel; crayon

pastell'farben *adj* pastel

Pastell'stift *m* crayon

Pastete [pas'tetə] *f* (–;-n) meat pie, fish pie

pasteurisieren [pastœri'zirən] *tr* pasteurize

Pastille [pas'tilə] *f* (–;-n) lozenge

Pa-stor ['pastor] *m* (–s;-storen ['torən]) pastor, minister, vicar

Pate ['patə] *m* (–n;-n) godfather || *f* (–;-n) godmother

Pa'tenkind *n* godchild

patent [pa'tent] *adj* neat; smart; **ein patenter Kerl** quite a fellow || **Patent** *n* (–[e]s;-e) patent; (mil) commission; **P. angemeldet** patent pending

Patent'amt *n* patent office

patentieren [paten'tirən] *tr* patent

Pater ['patər] *m* (–s; **Patres** ['patres]) (eccl) Father

pathetisch [pa'tetıʃ] *adj* impassioned; solemn

Pathologe [pato'logə] *m* (–n;-n) pathologist

Pathologie [patolo'gi] *f* (–;) pathology

Pathologin [pato'login] *f* (–;-nen) pathologist

Patient –in [pa'tsjent(ın)] §7 *mf* patient

Patin ['patın] *f* (–;-nen) godmother

Patriarch [patri'arç] *m* (–en;-en) patriarch

Patriot –in [patri'ot(ın)] §7 *mf* patriot

patriotisch [patri'otıʃ] *adj* patriotic

Patrize [pa'tritsə] *f* (–;-n) die, stamp

Patrizier –in [pa'tritsjər(ın)] §6 *mf* patrician

Patron [pa'tron] *m* (–s;-e) patron; (pej) guy

Patronat [patro'nat] *n* (–[e]s;-e) patronage

Patrone [pa'tronə] *f* (–;-n) cartridge

Patro'nengurt *m* cartridge belt

Patro'nenhülse *f* cartridge case

Patronin [pa'tronın] *f* (–;-nen) patroness

Patrouille [pa'truljə] *f* (–;-n) patrol

patrouillieren [patru'jirən] *tr & intr* patrol

Patsche ['patʃə] *f* (–;-n) (Pfütze) puddle; (coll) jam, scrape; **in der P. lassen** leave in a lurch; **in e–e P. geraten** get into a jam

patschen ['patʃən] *tr* slap ‖ *intr* splash; **in die Hände p.** clap hands
patsch'naß' *adj* soaking wet
patzig ['patsɪç] *adj* snappy, sassy
Pauke ['paukə] *f* (-;-n) kettledrum; **j–m e–e P. halten** give s.o. a lecture
pauken ['paukən] *tr* (educ) cram ‖ *intr* beat the kettledrum; (educ) cram
Pau'ker *m* (-s;-) (coll) martinet
pausbackig ['pausbakɪç], **pausbäckig** ['pausbɛkɪç] *adj* chubby-faced
pauschal [pau'ʃal] *adj* (*Summe*) flat
Pauschal'betrag *m* flat rate
Pauscha·le [pau'ʃalə] *n* (-s;-lien [ljən]) lump sum
Pauschal'preis *m* package price
Pauschal'reise *f* all-inclusive tour
Pauschal'summe *f* flat sum
Pause ['pauzə] *f* (-;-n) pause; (*Pauszeichnung*) tracing; (educ) recess, break; (mus) rest; (theat) intermission; **e–e P. machen** take a break
pausen ['pauzən] *tr* trace
pau'senlos *adj* continuous
Pau'senzeichen *n* (rad) station identification
pausieren [pau'zirən] *intr* pause; rest
Pauspapier ['pauzpapir] *n* tracing paper
Pavian ['pavjan] *m* (-s;-e) baboon
Pavillon ['pavɪljõ] *m* (-s;-s) pavilion
Pazifik [pa'tsifik] *m* (-s;) Pacific
pazifisch [pa'tsifiʃ] *adj* Pacific
Pazifist –in [patsi'fist(ɪn)] §7 *mf* pacifist
Pech [peç] *n* (-[e]s;-e) pitch; **P. haben** (coll) have tough luck
Pech'fackel *f* torch
Pech'kohle *f* bituminous coal
pech'ra'benschwarz' *adj* pitch-black
pech'schwarz' *adj* pitch-dark
Pech'strähne *f* streak of bad luck
Pech'vogel *m* (coll) unlucky fellow
Pedal [pe'dal] *n* (-s;-e) pedal
Pedant [pe'dant] *m* (-en;-en) pedant
pedantisch [pe'dantiʃ] *adj* pedantic
Pegel ['pegəl] *m* (-s;-) water gauge
Pe'gelstand *m* water level
Peil– [pail] *comb.fm.* direction-finding, sounding
peilen ['pailən] *tr* take the bearings of; (*Tiefe*) sound; **über den Daumen p.** (coll) estimate roughly ‖ *intr* take bearings
Pei'lung *f* (-;-en) bearings; taking of bearings; sounding
Pein [pain] *f* (-;) pain, torment
peinigen ['painigən] *tr* torment
pein'lich *adj* painful; embarrassing; (*genau*) painstaking; (*sorgfältig*) scrupulous ‖ *adv* scrupulously; carefully
Peitsche ['paitʃə] *f* (-;-n) whip; **mit der P. knallen** crack the whip
peitschen ['paitʃən] *tr* whip
Peit'schenhieb *m* whiplash
Peit'schenknall *m* crack of the whip
Pelerine [pelə'rinə] *f* (-;-n) cape
Pelikan ['pelikan] *m* (-s;-e) pelican
Pelle ['pelə] *f* (-;-n) peel, skin
pellen ['pelən] *tr* peel, skin
Pellkartoffeln ['pelkartɔfəln] *pl* potatoes in their jackets

Pelz [pelts] *m* (-es;-e) fur; (*Fell*) pelt; fur coat
Pelz'besatz *m* fur trimming
Pelz'futter *n* fur lining
Pelz'händler –in §6 *mf* furrier
pel'zig *adj* furry; (*Gefühl im Mund*) cottony
Pelz'tier *n* fur-bearing animal
Pelz'tierjäger *m* trapper
Pelz'werk *n* furs
Pendel ['pendəl] *n* (-s;-) pendulum
pendeln ['pendəln] *intr* swing, oscillate; (*zwischen zwei Orten*) commute
Pen'deltür *f* swinging door
Pen'delverkehr *m* commuter traffic; shuttle service
Pen'delzug *m* shuttle train
Pendler ['pentlər] *m* (-s;-) commuter
Penizillin [penitsɪ'lin] *n* (-s;) penicillin
Pension [pen'zjon] *f* (-;-en) pension, retirement pay; (*Fremdenhaus*) boarding house; (*Unterkunft und Verpflegung*) room and board; (*Pensionat*) girls' boarding school; **in P. gehen** go on pension
Pensionär [penzjo'ner] *m* (-s;-e) pensioner; boarder
Pensionat [penzjo'nat] *n* (-[e]s;-e) girls boarding school
pensionieren [penzjo'nirən] *tr* put on pension; (mil) retire on half pay; **sich p. lassen** retire
Pensions'kasse *f* pension fund
Pensions'preis *m* price of room and board
Pen·sum ['penzum] *n* (-s;-sen [zən] & -sa [za]) task, assignment; quota
per [per] *prep* (acc) per, by, with; (*zeitlich*) by, until; **per Adresse** care of, c/o; **per sofort** at once
perfekt [per'fekt] *adj* perfect; concluded ‖ **Perfekt** *n* (-[e]s;-e) perfect
Pergament [perga'ment] *n* (-[e]s;-e) parchment
Periode [per'jodə] *f* (-;-n) period
periodisch [per'jodiʃ] *adj* periodic
Periphe·rie [perife'ri] *f* (-;-rien ['ri·ən]) periphery
Periskop [peri'skop] *n* (-s;-e) periscope
Perle ['perlə] *f* (-;-n) pearl; (*aus Glas*) bead; (*Tropfen*) drop, bead; (*Bläschen*) bubble; (fig) gem
perlen ['perlən] *intr* sparkle
Per'lenauster *f* pearl oyster
Per'lenkette *f*, **Per'lenschnur** *f* pearl necklace, string of pearls
Perlhuhn ['perlhun] *n* guinea fowl
perlig ['perlɪç] *adj* pearly
Perl'muschel *f* pearl oyster
Perlmutt ['perlmut] *n* (-s;), **Perl'mutter** *f* mother of pearl
perplex [per'pleks] *adj* perplexed
Persenning [per'zenɪŋ] *f* (-;-en) tarpaulin
Persien ['perzjən] *n* (-s;) Persia
persisch [perziʃ] *adj* Persian
Person [per'zon] *f* (-;-en) person; (theat) character; **ich für meine P. I** for one; **klein von P.** small of stature
Personal [perzo'nal] *n* (-s;) personnel
Personal'akte *f* personal file, dossier

Personal'angaben pl personal data
Personal'aufzug m passenger elevator
Personal'ausweis m identity card
Personal'chef m personnel manager
Personalien [perzo'nɑljən] pl personal data, particulars
Personal'pronomen n personal pronoun
Perso'nengedächtnis n good memory for names
Perso'nenkraftwagen m passenger car
Perso'nenschaden m personal injury
Perso'nenverzeichnis n list of persons; (theat) dramatis personae, cast
Perso'nenwagen m passenger car
Perso'nenzug m passenger train; (rr) local
personifizieren [perzonɪfɪ'tsirən] tr personify
persönlich [per'zønlɪç] adj personal || adv personally, in person
Persön'lichkeit f (-;-en) personality
Perspektiv [perspek'tif] n (-s;-e) telescope
Perücke [pe'rʏkə] f (-;-n) wig
pervers [per'vers] adj perverse
pessimistisch [pesɪ'mɪstɪʃ] adj pessimistic
Pest [pest] f (-;) plague
pest'artig adj pestilential
Pestilenz [pestɪ'lents] f (-;-en) pestilence
Petersilie [petər'ziljə] f (-;) parsley
Petroleum [pe'trole·um] n (-s;) petroleum
Petschaft ['pet/aft] n (-s;-e) seal
Petting ['petɪŋ] n (-s;) petting
petto ['peto]—in p. haben have in reserve; (coll) have up one's sleeve
Petunie [pe'tunjə] f (-;-n) petunia
Petze ['petsə] f (-;-n) tattletale
petzen ['petsən] intr tattle, squeal
Pfad [pfɑt] m (-[e]s;-e) path, track
Pfadfinder ['pfɑtfɪndər] m (-s;-) boy scout
Pfadfinderin ['pfɑtfɪndərɪn] f (-;-nen) girl scout
Pfaffe ['pfɑfə] m (-n;-n) (pej) priest
Pfahl [pfɑl] m (-[e]s;ːer) stake; post
Pfahl'bau m (-[e]s;-bauten) lake dwelling
Pfahl'werk n palisade, stockade
Pfahl'wurzel f taproot
Pfahl'zaun n palisade, stockade
Pfälzer -in ['pfeltsər(ɪn)] §6 mf inhabitant of the Palatinate
Pfand [pfɑnt] n (-[e]s;ːer) pledge; deposit; (Bürgschaft) security, pawn; (auf Immobilien) mortgage; zum Pfande geben (or setzen) pawn, mortgage
pfändbar ['pfentbɑr] adj (jur) attachable
Pfand'brief m mortgage papers
pfänden ['pfendən] tr attach, impound
Pfand'geber m mortgagor
Pfand'gläubiger m mortgagee
Pfand'haus n, **Pfand'leihe** f pawnshop
Pfand'leiher -in §6 mf pawnbroker
Pfand'recht n lien
Pfand'schein m pawn ticket
Pfand'schuldner m mortgagor
Pfän'dung f (-;-en) attachment, confiscation

Pfanne ['pfɑnə] f (-;-n) pan; (anat) socket; etw auf der P. haben (fig) have s.th. up one's sleeve; in die P. hauen (fig) make mincemeat of
Pfan'nenstiel m panhandle
Pfann'kuchen m pancake; Berliner P. doughnut
Pfarr- [pfar] comb.fm. parish, parochial
Pfarr'amt n rectory
Pfarr'bezirk m parish
Pfarr'dorf n parish seat
Pfarre ['pfarə] f (-;-n) parish; (Pfarrhaus) rectory
Pfarrei [pfa'raɪ] f (-;-en) parish; (Pfarrhaus) rectory
Pfarrer ['pfarər] m (-s;-) pastor
Pfarr'gemeinde f parish
Pfarr'haus n rectory
Pfarr'kind n parishioner
Pfarr'kirche f parish church
Pfarr'schule f parochial school
Pfau [pfau] m (-[e]s;-en) peacock
Pfau'enhenne f peahen
Pfeffer ['pfefər] m (-s;) pepper
pfefferig ['pfefərɪç] adj peppery
Pfef'ferkorn n peppercorn
Pfef'ferkuchen m gingerbread
Pfef'ferminze f (bot) peppermint
Pfef'ferminzplätzchen n peppermint cookie
pfeffern ['pfefərn] tr pepper
Pfef'fernuß f ginger nut
Pfeife ['pfaɪfə] f (-;-n) whistle; (Orgel-) pipe; (zum Rauchen) (tobacco) pipe
pfeifen ['pfaɪfən] tr whistle; ich pfeife ihm was he can whistle for it || intr whistle; (Schiedsrichter) blow the whistle; (Maus) squeak; (Vogel) sing; (dat) whistle for or to; auf dem letzten Loche p. be on one's last legs; ich pfeife darauf! I couldn't care less!
Pfei'fenkopf m pipe bowl
Pfei'fenrohr n pipestem
Pfei'fer -in §6 mf whistler; (mus) piper, fife player
Pfeif'kessel m, **Pfeif'topf** m whistling kettle
Pfeil [pfaɪl] m (-[e]s;-e) arrow, dart; P. und Bogen bow and arrow
Pfei'ler m (-s;-) (& fig) pillar; (e-r Brücke) pier
pfeil'gera'de adj straight as an arrow
pfeil'schnell' adj swift as an arrow || adv like a shot
Pfeil'schütze m archer
Pfeil'spitze f arrowhead
Pfennig ['pfenɪç] m (-[e]s;-e & -) pfennig, penny (one hundredth of a mark)
Pfennigfuchser ['pfenɪçfuksər] m (-s; -) penny pincher
Pferch [pferç] m (-[e]s;-e) fold, pen
pferchen ['pferçən] tr herd together, pen in
Pferd [pfert] n (-[e]s;-e) horse; zu Pferde on horseback
Pferde- [pferdə] comb.fm. horse
Pfer'deapfel m horse manure
Pfer'debremse f horsefly
Pfer'dedecke f horse blanket

Pfer'defuß m (*Kennzeichen des Teufels*) cloven hoof; (pathol) clubfoot

Pfer'degeschirr n harness

Pfer'degespann n team of horses

Pfer'deknecht m groom

Pfer'dekoppel f corral

Pfer'delänge f (*beim Rennen*) length

Pfer'derennbahn f race track

Pfer'derennen n horse racing

Pfer'destärke f horsepower

Pfer'dezucht f horse breeding

pfiff [pfɪf] pret of **pfeifen** || **Pfiff** m (-[e]s;-e) whistle; **den P. heraushaben** (fig) know the ropes

Pfifferling ['pfɪfərlɪŋ] m (-s;-e) (bot) chanterelle; **keinen P. wert** not worth a thing

pfiffig ['pfɪfɪç] adj shrewd, sharp

Pfiffikus ['pfɪfɪkus] m (-;-), (-ses;-se) (coll) sly fox

Pfingsten ['pfɪŋstən] n (-s) Pentecost

Pfingst'rose f (bot) peony

Pfingst'sonn'ntag m Whitsunday

Pfirsich ['pfɪrzɪç] m (-[e]s;-e) peach

Pflanze ['pflantsə] f (-;-n) plant

pflanzen ['pflantsən] tr plant

Pflan'zenfaser f vegetable fiber

Pflan'zenfett n vegetable shortening

pflan'zenfressend adj herbivorous

Pflan'zenkost f vegetable diet

Pflan'zenkunde f botany

Pflan'zenleben n plant life, vegetation

Pflan'zenlehre f botany

Pflan'zenöl n vegetable oil

Pflan'zenreich n vegetable kingdom

Pflan'zensaft m sap, juice

Pflan'zenschutzmittel n pesticide

Pflan'zenwelt f flora

Pflan'zer -in §6 mf planter

pflanz'lich adj vegetable

Pflanz'schule f, **Pflanz'stätte** f nursery; (fig) hotbed

Pflan'zung f (-;-en) plantation

Pflaster ['pflastər] n (-s;-) pavement; (*Fleck*) patch; (med) Band-Aid; **als P.** (fig) in compensation; **ein teueres P.** (fig) an expensive place; **P. treten** (fig) pound the sidewalks

Pflasterer ['pflastərər] m (-s;-) paver

pfla'stermüde adj tired of walking the streets

pflastern ['pflastərn] tr pave

Pfla'sterstein m paving stone; (*Kopfstein*) cobblestone

Pfla'stertreter m (-s;-) loafer

Pfla'sterung f (-;-) paving

Pflaume ['pflaumə] f (-;-n) plum; (*spitze Bemerkung*) dig

pflaumen ['pflaumən] intr (coll) tease

pflau'menweich adj (fig) spineless

Pflege ['pfle:gə] f (-;-n) care; (*e-s Kranken*) nursing; (*Wartung*) tending; (*e-s Gartens, der Künste*) cultivation; **gute P. haben** be well cared for; **in P. nehmen** take charge of

Pflegebefohlene ['pfle:gəbəfo:lənə] §5 mf charge; fosterchild

Pfle'geeltern pl foster parents

Pfle'geheim n nursing home

Pfle'gekind n foster child

pflegen ['pfle:gən] tr take care of, look after; (*Kranken*) nurse; (*Garten, Kunst*) cultivate; (*Freundschaft*) fos-

ter; **Gesellligkeit p.** lead an active social life; **Umgang p. mit** associate with || *intr*—**p. zu** (*inf*) be wont to (*inf*), be in the habit of (*ger*); **sein Vater pflegte zu sagen** his father used to say; **sie pflegt morgens zeitig aufzustehen** she usually gets up early in the morning || *intr* (*pp gepflegt & gepflogen*) (*genit*) carry on; **der Liebe p.** enjoy the pleasures of love; **der Ruhe p.** take a rest; **Rats p. mit** consult with

Pfle'ger -in §6 mf nurse; (jur) guardian

Pfle'gesohn m foster son

Pfle'gestelle f foster home

Pfle'getochter f foster daughter

Pfle'gevater m foster father

pfleglich ['pfle:klɪç] adj careful

Pflegling ['pfle:klɪŋ] m (-s;-e) foster child; (*Pflegebefohlener*) charge

Pflegschaft ['pfle:kʃaft] f (-;-en) (jur) guardianship

Pflicht [pflɪçt] f (-;-en) duty; **sich seiner P. entziehen** evade one's duty

pflicht'bewußt adj conscientious

Pflicht'bewußtsein n conscientiousness

Pflicht'eifer m zeal

pflicht'eifrig adj zealous

Pflicht'erfüllung f performance of duty

Pflicht'fach n (educ) required course

Pflicht'gefühl n sense of duty

pflicht'gemäß adj dutiful

-pflichtig [pflɪçtɪç] comb.fm. obligated, e.g., **schulpflichtig** obligated to attend school

pflicht'schuldig adj duty-bound

pflicht'treu adj dutiful, loyal

pflicht'vergessen adj forgetful of one's duty; (*untreu*) disloyal

Pflicht'vergessenheit f dereliction of duty; disloyalty

Pflicht'verletzung f, **Pflicht'versäumnis** n neglect of duty

Pflock [pflɔk] m (-[e]s;⁻e) peg; **e-n P. zurückstecken** (fig) come down a peg

pflog [pflo:k] pret of **pflegen**

pflücken ['pflʏkən] tr pluck, pick

Pflug [pflu:k] m (-[e]s;⁻e) plow

pflügen ['pfly:gən] tr & intr plow

Pflug'schar f plowshare

Pforte ['pfɔrtə] f (-;-n) gate

Pförtner -in ['pfœrtnər(ɪn)] §6 mf gatekeeper || m doorman; (anat) pylorus

Pfosten ['pfɔstən] m (-s;-) post; (carp) jamb

Pfote ['pfo:tə] f (-;-n) paw; **j-m eins auf die Pfoten geben** rap s.o.'s knuckles

Pfriem [pfri:m] m (-[e]s;-e) awl

Pfropf [pfrɔpf] m (-[e]s;-e) stopper, plug, cork

pfropfen ['pfrɔpfən] tr cork, plug; (*stopfen*) cram; (hort) graft || **Pfropfen** m (-s;-) stopper, plug, cork

Pfropf'fenzieher m corkscrew

Pfropf'reis n (hort) graft

Pfründe ['pfrʏndə] f (-;-n) benefice; (*ohne Seelsorge*) sinecure; **fette P.** (fig) cushy, well-paying job

Pfuhl [pfu:l] m (-[e]s;-e) pool, puddle; (fig) pit

Pfühl [pfyl] m (-[e]s;-e) (poet) cushion
pfui ['pfu·ɪ] interj phooey!; **p. über dich!** shame on you!
Pfund [pfunt] n (-[e]s;-e) pound
pfundig ['pfundɪç] adj (coll) great
-pfündig [pfyndɪç] comb.fm. -pound
Pfundskerl ['pfuntskerl] m (coll) great guy
pfund'weise adv by the pound
Pfuscharbeit ['pfu·arbaɪt] f bungling
pfuschen ['pfu·ən] tr & intr bungle; **j-m ins Handwerk p.** meddle in s.o.'s business
Pfuscherei [pfu·ə'raɪ] f (-;-en) bungling
Pfütze ['pfytsə] f (-;-n) puddle
Phänomen [feno'men] n (-s;-e) phenomenon
phänomenal [fenome'nɑl] adj phenomenal
Phanta·sie [fanta'zi] f (-;-sien ['ziən]) imagination
Phantasie'gebilde n daydream
phantasieren [fanta'zirən] intr daydream; (mus) improvise; (pathol) be delirious
phantasie'voll adj imaginative
Phantast –in [fan'tast(ɪn)] §7 mf visionary
phantastisch [fan'tastɪ] adj fantastic
Phantom [fan'tom] n (-s;-e) phantom
Pharisäer [farɪ'ze·ər] m (-s;-) Pharisee; (fig) pharisee
pharmazeutisch [farma'tsɔɪtɪ] adj pharmaceutical
Pharmazie [farma'tsi] f (-;) pharmacy
Phase ['fazə] f (-;-n) phase
Philantrop –in [filan'trop(ɪn)] §7 mf philanthropist
philantropisch [filan'tropɪ] adj philanthropic
Philister [fɪ'lɪstər] m (-s;-) Philistine
Phiole [fɪ'olə] f (-;-n) vial, phial
Philologe [filo'logə] m (-n;-n) philologist
Philologie [filolo'gi] f (-;) philology
Philologin [filo'login] f (-;-nen) philologist
Philosoph [filo'zof] m (-en;-en) philosopher
Philoso·phie [filozo'fi] f (-;-fien ['fi·ən]) philosophy
philosophieren [filozo'firən] intr philosophize
philosophisch [filo'zofɪ] adj philosophic(al)
Phlegma ['flegma] n (-s;) indolence
Phonetik [fo'netɪk] f (-;) phonetics
phonetisch [fo'netɪ] adj phonetic
Phönix ['fønɪks] m (-[e]s;-e) phoenix
Phönizien [fø'nitsjən] n (-s;) Phoenicia
Phönizier –in [fø'nitsjər(ɪn)] §6 mf Phoenician
Phosphor ['fosfor] m (-s;) phosphorus
phos'phorig adj phosphorous
Photo ['foto] n (-s;-) photo
Pho'toapparat m camera
photogen [foto'gen] adj photogenic
Photograph [foto'grɑf] m (-en;-en) photographer
Photogra·phie [fotogra'fi] f (-;-fien ['fi·ən]) photography

photographieren [fotogra'firən] tr & intr photograph; **sich p. lassen** have one's photograph taken
Photographin [foto'grɑfin] f (-;-nen) photographer
photographisch [foto'grɑfɪ] adj photographic
Photokopie f photocopy
photokopie'ren tr photocopy
Pho'tozelle f photoelectric cell
Phrase ['frazə] f (-;-n) phrase; (fig) platitude; **das sind nur Phrasen** that's just talk
phra'senhaft adj empty, trite; windy
Physik [fy'zik] f (-;) physics
physikalisch [fyzɪ'kɑlɪʃ] adj physical
Physiker –in ['fysɪkər(ɪn)] §6 mf physicist
Physiogno·mie [fyzjogno'mi] f (-;-mien ['mi·ən]) physiognomy
Physiologie [fyzjolo'gi] f (-;) physiology
physiologisch [fyzjo'logɪ] adj physiological
physisch ['fyzɪ] adj physical
Pianino [pi·a'nino] n (-s;-s) small upright piano
Pianist –in [pi·a'nɪst(ɪn)] §7 mf pianist
picheln ['pɪçəln] tr & intr tipple
pichen ['pɪçən] tr pitch, cover with pitch
Pichler –in ['pɪçlər(ɪn)] §6 mf tippler
Picke ['pɪkə] f (-;-n) pickax
Pickel ['pɪkəl] m (-s;-) pimple; (Picke) pickax; (Eispicke) ice ax
Pickelhaube (Pik'kelhaube) f spiked helmet
Pickelhering (Pik'kelhering) m pickled herring
pickelig (pik'kelig) adj pimply
picken ['pɪkən] tr & intr peck
picklig ['pɪklɪç] adj var of **pickelig**
Picknick ['pɪknɪk] n (-s;-s) picnic
pieken ['pikən] tr sting; (coll) prick
piekfein ['pik'faɪn] adj tiptop
pieksauber ['pik'zaubər] adj spick and span
piepen ['pipən] intr chirp; (Maus) squeal; **bist dir piept's wohl?** are you quite all there? ‖ **Piepen n—das ist zum P.!** that's ridiculous
Pier [pir] m (-s;-e) pier
piesacken ['pizakən] tr (coll) pester
Pietät [pi·e'tet] f (-;) piety
pietät'los adj irreverent
pietät'voll adj reverent(ial)
Pigment [pɪg'ment] n (-[e]s;-e) pigment
Pik [pik], [pɪk] m (-s;-s & -e) (Bergspitze) peak ‖ m (-s;-e) (coll) grudge; **e-n Pik auf j-n haben** hold a grudge against s.o. ‖ n (-s;-e) (cards) spade(s)
pikant [pi'kant] adj piquant, pungent; (Bemerkung) suggestive
Pikante·rie [pikantə'ri] f (-;-rien ['ri·ən]) piquancy; spicy story, suggestive remark
Pike ['pikə] f (-;-n) pike, spear; **von der P. auf dienen** (fig) rise through the ranks
pikiert [pi'kirt] adj (über acc) piqued (at)

Pikkolo ['pɪkɔlo] *m* (-s;-s) apprentice waiter; (mus) piccolo

Pik'kolflöte *f* (mus) piccolo

Pilger ['pɪlgər] *m* (-s;-) pilgrim

Pil'gerfahrt *f* pilgrimage

Pilgerin ['pɪlgərɪn] *f* (-;-nen) pilgrim

pilgern ['pɪlgərn] *intr* (SEIN) go on a pilgrimage, make a pilgrimage

Pille ['pɪlə] *f* (-;-n) pill; **P. danach** morning-after pill

Pilot –in [pɪ'lot(ɪn)] §7 *mf* pilot

Pilz [pɪlts] *m* (-es;-e) fungus; mushroom

pimp(e)lig ['pɪmp(ə)lɪç] *adj* sickly, delicate; (*verweichlicht*) effeminate

Pinguin ['pɪŋgu'in] *m* (-s;-e) penguin

Pinie ['pinjə] *f* (-;-n) umbrella pine

Pinke ['pɪŋkə] *f* (-;) (coll) dough

Pinkel ['pɪŋkəl] *m* (-s;-) (coll) dude

pinkeln ['pɪŋkəln] *intr* (sl) pee

Pinne ['pɪnə] *f* (-;-n) pin; tack; (naut) tiller

Pinscher ['pɪnʃər] *m* (-s;-) terrier

Pinsel ['pɪnzəl] *m* (-s;-) brush; (fig) simpleton, dope

Pinselei [pɪnzə'laɪ] *f* (-;-en) daubing; (*schlechte Malerei*) daub

pinseln ['pɪnzəln] *tr & intr* paint

Pinzette [pɪn'tsetə] *f* (-;-n) pair of tweezers, tweezers

Pionier [pi.ɔ'nir] *m* (-s;-e) (fig) pioneer; (mil) engineer

Pionier'arbeit *f* (fig) spadework

Pionier'truppe *f* (mil) engineers

Pirat [pɪ'rat] *m* (-en;-en) pirate

Piraterie [pɪratə'ri] *f* (-;) piracy

Pirol [pɪ'rol] *m* (-s;-e) oriole

Pirsch [pɪr/ʃ] *f* (-;) hunt

pirschen ['pɪr/ʃən] *intr* stalk game

Pirsch'jagd *f* hunt

Pistazie [pɪs'tatsjə] *f* (-;-n) pistachio

Piste ['pɪstə] *f* (-;-n) beaten track; ski run; toboggan run; (aer) runway

Pistole [pɪs'tolə] *f* (-;-n) pistol

Pisto'lentasche *f* holster

pitsch(e)naß ['pɪtʃ(ə)'nas] *adj* soaked to the skin

pittoresk [pɪtɔ'resk] *adj* picturesque

Pkw., PKW *abbr* (**Personenkraftwagen**) passenger car

placieren [pla'sirən] *tr* place

placken ['plakən] *tr* pester, plague || *ref* toil, drudge

Plackerei [plakə'raɪ] *f* (-;) drudgery

plädieren [plɛ'dirən] *intr* plead

Plädoyer [pledwa'je] *n* (-s;-s) plea

Plage ['plagə] *f* (-;-n) trouble, bother; torment; (*Seuche*) plague

Pla'gegeist *m* pest, pain in the neck

plagen ['plagən] *tr* trouble, bother; (*mit Fragen, usw.*) pester

Plagiat [pla'gjat] *n* (-[e]s;-e) plagiarism

Pla'giator [pla'gjatɔr] *m* (-s;-giatoren [gja'torən]) plagiarist

Plakat [pla'kat] *n* (-[e]s;-e) poster

Plakat'träger *m* sandwich man

Plakette [pla'ketə] *f* (-;-n) plaque

plan [plan] *adj* plain, clear; (*eben*) level || **Plan** *m* (-[e]s;-e) plan; (*Stadt–*) map; (poet) battlefield; **auf den P. treten** appear on the scene

Plane ['planə] *f* (-;-n) tarpaulin

Plänemacher ['plɛnəmaxər] *m* (-s;-) schemer

planen ['planən] *tr* plan

Pläneschmied ['plɛnə/mit] *m* schemer

Planet [pla'net] *m* (-en;-en) planet

Planeta·rium [plane'tarjum] *n* (-s; -rien [rjən]) planetarium

Planeten– [planetən] *comb.fm.* planetary

Plane'tenbahn *f* planetary orbit

plan'gemäß *adv* according to plan

planieren [pla'nirən] *tr* level, grade

Planier'raupe *f* bulldozer

Planimetrie [planime'tri] *f* (-;) plane geometry

Planke ['plaŋkə] *f* (-;-n) plank

Plänkelei [plɛŋkə'laɪ] *f* (-;-en) skirmish, skirmishing

plänkeln ['plɛŋkəln] *intr* skirmish

plan'los *adj* aimless; indiscriminate

plan'mäßig *adj* systematic; fixed, regular; (*Verkehr*) scheduled || *adv* according to plan

planschen ['plan/ʃən] *intr* splash

Plantage [plan'taʒə] *f* (-;-n) plantation

Pla'nung *f* (-;) planning

plan'voll *adj* systematic, methodical

Plan'wagen *m* covered wagon

Plan'wirtschaft *f* planned economy

Plapperei [plapə'raɪ] *f* (-;) chatter

Plappermaul ['plapərmaul] *n* chatterbox

plappern ['plapərn] *intr* chatter; prattle

plärren ['plɛrən] *intr* (coll) bawl

Plas·ma ['plasma] *n* (-s;-men [mən]) plasma

Plastik ['plastɪk] *f* (-;-en) (*Bildwerk*) sculpture; (surg) plastic surgery || *n* (-s;) plastic

plastisch ['plasti/ʃ] *adj* plastic; (*anschaulich*) graphic

Platane [pla'tanə] *f* (-;-n) sycamore

Plateau [pla'to] *n* (-s;-s) plateau

Plateau'schuhe *pl* platform shoes

Platin [pla'tin] *n* (-s;) platinum

platin'blond *adj* platinum-blonde

Platoniker [pla'tonikər] *m* (-s;-) Platonist

platonisch [pla'toni/ʃ] *adj* Platonic

plätschern ['plet/ʃərn] *intr* splash; (*Bach*) babble

platt [plat] *adj* flat; (*nichtssagend*) trite; (coll) flabbergasted

Plättbrett ['pletbret] *n* ironing board

platt'deutsch *adj* Low German

Platte ['platə] *f* (-;-n) plate; top, surface; slab; (*Präsentierteller*) tray; (*Speise*) dish; (fig) pate, bean; (mus) record; (phot) plate

Plätteisen ['pletaɪzən] *n* flatiron

plätten ['pletən] *tr & intr* iron

Platt'enjockey *m* disc jockey

Platt'enspieler *m* record player

Platt'enteller *m* turntable

Platt'enwechsler *m* record changer

Platt'form *f* platform

Platt'fuß *m* (aut) flat; **Plattfüße** flat feet

platt'füßig *adj* flat-footed

Platt'heit *f* (-;-en) flatness; (fig) banality

plattieren [pla'tirən] *tr* plate
Plättwäsche ['pletvɛʃə] *f* ironing
Platz [plats] *m* (-es;⸚e) place; spot;
locality; square; (*Sitz*) seat; (*Raum*)
room, space; (*Stellung*) position;
(sport) ground, field; (tennis) court;
auf die Plätze, fertig, los! on your
marks, get set, go! **fester P.** (mil)
fortified position; **freier P.** open
space; **immer auf dem Platze sein**
be always on the alert; **nicht am P.
sein** be out of place; be irrelevant;
P. da! make way; **P. greifen** (fig)
take effect, gain ground; **P. machen**
make room; **P. nehmen** sit down;
seinen P. behaupten stand one's
ground
Platz'anweiser –in §6 *mf* usher
Plätzchen ['pletsçən] *n* (-s;-) little
place; little square; (*Süßware*) candy
wafer; (*Gebäck*) cookie, cracker
platzen ['platsən] *intr* (SEIN) burst;
split; crack; (*Granate*) explode;
(*Luftreifen*) blow out; (fig) come to
nothing; **da platzte ihm endlich der
Kragen** he finally blew his top; **der
Wechsel ist geplatzt** the check
bounced
Platz'karte *f* reserved-seat ticket
Platz'kommandant *m* commandant
Platz'konzert *n* open-air concert
Platz'patrone *f* blank cartridge; **mit
Platzpatronen schießen** fire blanks
Platz'regen *m* cloudburst
Platz'runde *f* (aer) circuit of a field
Platz'wechsel *m* change of place;
(sport) change in lineup
Platz'wette *f* betting on a horse to
finish in first, second, or third place,
bet to place
Plauderei [plaudə'raɪ] *f* (-;-en) chat;
small talk
Plau'derer –in §6 *mf* talker, chatterer
plaudern ['plaudərn] *intr* chat, chatter; **aus der Schule p.** tell tales out
of school
Plaudertasche ['plaudərtaʃə] *f* chatterbox
Plauderton ['plaudərton] *m* conversational tone
plausibel [plau'zibəl] *adj* plausible
plauz [plauts] *interj* crash!
pleite ['plaɪtə] *adj* (coll) broke ||
—p. gehen go broke || **Pleite** *f* (-;)
(coll) bankruptcy; **P. machen** (coll)
go broke
Plenarsitzung [plə'narzɪtsuŋ] *f* (-;-en)
plenary session
Plenum ['plenum] *n* (-s;) plenary session
Pleuelstange ['plɔɪəlʃtaŋə] *f* (mach)
connecting rod
Plexiglas ['pleksɪglas] *n* (-es;) plexiglass
Plinse ['plɪnzə] *f* (-;-n) pancake;
fritter
Plissee [plɪ'se] *n* (-s;-s) pleat
Plissee'rock *m* pleated skirt
plissieren [plɪ'sirən] *tr* pleat
Plombe ['plɔmbə] *f* (-;-n) lead seal;
(dent) filling
plombieren [plɔm'birən] *tr* seal with
lead; (dent) fill

plötzlich ['plœtslɪç] *adj* sudden || *adv*
suddenly, all of a sudden
plump [plump] *adj* (*unförmig*) shapeless; (*schwerfällig*) heavy, slow;
(*derb*) coarse; (*unbeholfen*) ungainly; (*taktlos*) tactless, blunt
plumps [plumps] *interj* plop! thump!
plumpsen ['plumpsən] *intr* (HABEN &
SEIN) plop, flop
Plunder ['plundər] *m* (-s;) junk
plündern ['plyndərn] *tr & intr* plunder
Plural ['plural] *m* (-s;-e) plural
plus [plus] *adv* plus || **Plus** *n* (-;-)
plus; (*Überschuß*) surplus; (*Vorteil*)
advantage, edge
Plus'pol *m* (elec) positive pole
Plutokrat [pluto'krat] *m* (-en;-en)
plutocrat
Plutonium [plu'tonjum] *n* (-s;) plutonium
pneumatisch [pnɔɪ'matɪʃ] *adj* pneumatic
Pöbel ['pøbəl] *m* (-s;) mob, rabble
pö'belhaft *adj* rude, rowdy
Pö'belherrschaft *f* mob rule
pochen ['pɔxən] *tr* (min) crush || *intr*
knock; (*Herz*) throb; **p. an** (*dat*)
knock on; **p. auf** (*acc*) pound on;
(fig) insist on
Pochmühle ['pɔxmylə] *f*, **Pochwerk**
['pɔxverk] *n* crushing mill
Pocke ['pɔkə] *f* (-;-n) pockmark; **Pok-
ken** (pathol) smallpox
Pockennarbe [Pok'kennarbe] *f* pockmark
pockennarbig (pok'kennarbig) *adj*
pockmarked
Podest [po'dest] *m & n* (-es;-e) pedes-
tal; (*Treppenabsatz*) landing; podium
Po·dium ['podjum] *n* (-s;-dien [djən])
podium, platform
Poesie [po·e'zi] *f* (-;) poetry
Poet [po'et] *m* (-en;-en) poet
Poetik [po'etɪk] *f* (-;) poetics
poetisch [po'etɪʃ] *adj* poetic
Pointe [po'ɛ̃tə] *f* (-;) point (*of joke*)
Pokal [po'kal] *m* (-s;-e) goblet;
(sport) cup
Pökel ['pøkəl] *m* (-s;) brine
Pö'kelfleisch *n* salted meat
Pö'kelhering *m* pickled herring
pökeln ['pøkəln] *tr* pickle, salt
Poker ['pokar] *n* (-s;) poker
Pol [pol] *m* (-s;-e) pole
Polar- [polar] *comb.fm.* polar
polarisieren [polari'zirən] *tr* polarize
Polarität [polari'tet] *f* (-;-en) polarity
Polar'kreis *m* polar circle; **nördlicher
P.** Arctic Circle; **südlicher P.** Ant-
arctic Circle
Polar'licht *n* polar lights
Polar'stern *m* polestar
Polar'zone *f* frigid zone
Pole ['polə] *m* (-n;-n) Pole
Polemik [po'lemɪk] *f* (-;) polemics
polemisch [po'lemɪʃ] *adj* polemical
Polen ['polən] *n* (-s;) Poland
Police [po'lisə] *f* (-;-n) (ins) policy
Polier [po'lir] *m* (-s;-e) foreman
polieren [po'lirən] *tr* polish
Polin ['polɪn] *f* (-;-nen) Pole
Politik [poli'tik] *f* (-;-en) policy;
(*Staatsangelegenheiten*) politics

Politiker –in [pɔ'litɪkər(ɪn)] §6 *mf* politician

Politi·kum [pɔ'litɪkʊm] *n* (–s;–ka [ka]) political issue, political matter

politisch [pɔ'litɪʃ] *adj* political

politisieren [pɔlɪtɪ'zirən] *intr* talk politics

Politur [pɔlɪ'tur] *f* (–;–en) polish

Polizei [pɔlɪ'tsaɪ] *f* (–;) police

Polizei′aufgebot *n* posse

Polizei′aufsicht *f*—unter P. stehen have to report periodically to the police

Polizei′beamte §5 *m* police officer

Polizei′büro *n*, **Polizei′dienststelle** *f* police station

Polizei′knüppel *m* billy club

Polizei′kommissar *m* police commissioner

polizei′lich *adj* police

Polizei′präsident *m* chief of police

Polizei′revier *n* police station

Polizei′spion *m*, **Polizei′spitzel** *m* stoolpigeon

Polizei′streife *f* raid; police patrol

Polizei′streifenwagen *m* squad car

Polizei′stunde *f* closing time; curfew

Polizei′wache *f* police station

polizei′widrig *adj* against police regulations

Polizist [pɔlɪ'tsɪst] *m* (–en;–en) policeman

Polizistin [pɔlɪ'tsɪstɪn] *f* (–;–nen) policewoman

Polizze [pɔ'lɪtsə] *f* (–;–n) (Aust) insurance policy

Polka ['pɔlka] *f* (–;–s) polka

polnisch ['pɔlnɪʃ] *adj* Polish

Polo ['polo] *n* (–s;) (sport) polo

Polster ['pɔlstər] *m & n* (–s;–) cushion

Pol′stergarnitur *f* living-room suite

Pol′stermöbel *pl* upholstered furniture

polstern ['pɔlstərn] *tr* upholster

Pol′stersessel *m* upholstered chair

Pol′sterstuhl *m* padded chair

Pol′sterung *f* (–;) padding, stuffing

Polterabend ['pɔltərabənt] *m* eve of the wedding day

Poltergeist ['pɔltərgaɪst] *m* poltergeist

poltern ['pɔltərn] *intr* make noise; (*rumpeln*) rumble; (*zanken*) bluster

Polyp [po'lyp] *m* (–en;–en) (pathol, zool) polyp; (*Polizist*) (sl) cop

Polytechni·kum [poly'teçnɪkʊm] *n* (–s; –ka [ka]) polytechnic institute

Pomade [po'madə] *f* (–;–n) pomade

Pomeranze [pomə'rantsə] *f* (–;–n) bitter orange

Pommern ['pɔmərn] *n* (–s;) Pomerania

Pommes frites [pɔm'frit] *pl* French fries

Pomp [pɔmp] *m* (–es;) pomp

Pompadour ['pɔmpadur] *m* (–s;–e & –s) lady's string-drawn bag

pomp′haft, pompös [pɔm'pøs] *adj* pompous

pontifikal [pɔntifi'kal] *adj* pontifical

Pontifikat [pɔntifi'kat] *n* (–[e]s;–e) pontificate

Pontius ['pɔntsjʊs] *m*—von P. zu Pilatus geschickt werden (coll) get the run-around

Pony ['pɔni] *m* (–s;–s) (*Damenfrisur*) pony ‖ *n* (–s;–s) (*Pferd*) pony

Popo [pɔ'po] *m* (–s;–s) (coll) backside

populär [pɔpu'ler] *adj* popular

Popularität [pɔpularɪ'tet] *f* (–;) popularity

Pore ['porə] *f* (–;–n) pore

porig ['porɪç] *adj* porous

Pornofilm ['pɔrnofɪlm] *m* (coll) smoker, pornographic movie

Pornoladen ['pɔrnoladən] *m* (coll) porn shop

Pornographie [pɔrnogra'fi] *f* (–;) pornography

poros [pɔ'ros] *adj* porous

Porphyr ['pɔrfyr] *m* (–s;) porphyry

Porree ['pɔre] *m* (–s;–s) (bot) leek

Portal [pɔr'tal] *n* (–s;–e) portal

Portemonnaie [pɔrtmo'ne] *n* (–s;–s) wallet

Portier [pɔr'tje] *m* (–s;–s) doorman

Portion [pɔr'tsjon] *f* (–;–en) portion; (culin) serving, helping; **halbe P.** (coll) half pint; **zwei Portionen Kaffee** two cups of coffee

Por·to ['pɔrto] *n* (–s;–ti [ti]) postage

Por′togebühren *pl* postage

Por′tokasse *f* petty cash

Porträt [pɔr'tret] *n* (–s;–s), (–[e]s;–e) portrait

porträtieren [pɔrtre'tirən] *tr* portray

Portugal ['pɔrtugal] *n* (–s;) Portugal

Portugiese [pɔrtu'gizə] *m* (–n;–n), **Portugiesin** [pɔrtu'gizɪn] *f* (–;–nen) Portuguese

portugiesisch [pɔrtu'gizɪʃ] *adj* Portuguese

Porzellan [pɔrtsə'lan] *n* (–s;–e) porcelain; china; **Meißener Porzellan** Dresden china

Porzellan′brennerei *f* porcelain factory

Posament [poza'ment] *n* (–[e]s;–en) trimming, lace

Posaune [po'zaunə] *f* (–;–n) trombone

posaunen [po'zaunən] *intr* play the trombone

Pose ['pozə] *f* (–;–n) pose

posieren [po'zirən] *intr* pose

Position [pozɪ'tsjon] *f* (–;–en) position

Positions′lampe *f* **Positions′licht** *n* (aer, naut) navigation light

positiv [pozɪ'tif] *adj* (*bejahend*) affirmative; (*Kritik*) favorable; (elec, math, med) positive ‖ *adv* in the affirmative; (coll) for certain ‖ **Positiv** *m* (–s;–e) (gram) positive degree ‖ *n* (–s;–e) (mus) small organ; (phot) positive

Positur [pozɪ'tur] *f* (–;–en) posture, attitude; **sich in P. setzen** (or **stellen** or **werfen**) strike a pose

Posse ['posə] *f* (–;–n) (theat) farce

Possen ['posən] *m* (–s;–) trick, practical joke; **j-m e-n P. spielen** play a practical joke on s.o.; **laß die P.!** cut out the nonsense; **P. treiben** (or **reißen**) crack jokes

pos′senhaft *adj* farcical, comical

Possenreißer ['posənraɪsər] *m* (–s;–) joker

Pos′senspiel *n* farce, burlesque

possierlich [po'sirlɪç] *adj* funny

Post [pɔst] *f* (–;–en) mail; (*Postgebäude*) post office

postalisch [pɔs'talɪʃ] *adj* postal

Postament [posta'ment] n (-[e]s;-e) pedestal

Post'amt n post office

Post'anweisung f money order

Post'auto n mail truck

Post'beamte m postal clerk

Post'beutel m mailbag

Post'bote m mailman

Post'direktor m postmaster

Posten ['postən] m (-s;-) post; (Stellung) position; (acct) entry, item; (com) line, lot; (mil) guard, sentinel; **auf dem P. sein** (fig) be on guard; **auf verlorenem P. kämpfen** (coll) play a losing game; **nicht recht auf dem P. sein** be out of sorts; **P. aufstellen** post sentries; **P. stehen** stand guard; **ruhiger P.** (mil) soft job

Po'stenjäger –in §6 mf job hunter

Po'stenkette f line of outposts

Post'fach n post-office box

Post'gebühr f postage

posthum [post'hum] adj posthumous

postieren [pos'tirən] tr post, place

Postille [pos'tilə] f (-;-n) devotional book

Post'karte f post card

Post'kasten m mail box

Post'kutsche f stagecoach

post'lagernd adj general-delivery || adv general delivery

Postleitzahl ['postlaittsal] f zip code

Post'minister m postmaster general

Post'nachnahme f (-;-n) C.O.D.

Post'sack m mailbag

Post'schalter m post-office window

Post'scheck m postal check

Postschließfach ['post/lisfax] n post-office box

Postskript [post'skript] n (-[e]s;-e) postscript

Post'stempel m postmark

Post'überweisung f money order

post'wendend adj & adv by return mail

Post'wertzeichen n postage stamp

Post'wesen n postal system

potent [po'tent] adj potent

Potential [poten'tsjal] n (-s;-e) potential

Potenz [po'tents] f (-;-en) potency; (math) power; **dritte P.** (math) cube; **zweite P.** (math) square

potenzieren [poten'tsirən] tr raise to a higher power; (fig) intensify

Pottasche ['pota/ə] f (-;) potash

Pottwal ['potval] m sperm whale

potz [pots] interj—p. **Blitz!** holy smoke!

potztau'send interj holy smoke!

poussieren [pu'sirən] tr (coll) flirt with; (coll) butter up || intr flirt

Pracht [praxt] f (-;) splendor, magnificence

Pracht'ausgabe f deluxe edition

Pracht'exemplar n beauty, beaut

prächtig ['preçtiç] adj splendid

Pracht'kerl m (coll) great guy

Pracht'stück n (coll) beauty, beaut

pracht'voll adj gorgeous

Pracht'zimmer n stateroom (in palace)

Prädikat [predi'kat] n (-[e]s;-e) title; (educ) mark, grade; (gram) predicate

Prädikatsnomen [predi'katsnomən] n (-s;-s) (gram) complement

Präfix [pre'fiks] n (-es;-e) prefix

Prag [prak] n (-s;) Prague

Prägeanstalt ['prega-anstalt] f mint

prägen ['pregən] tr stamp, coin || ref —**das hat sich mir tief in das Gedächtnis geprägt** that made a lasting impression on me

Prä'gestempel m (mach) die

pragmatisch [prag'mati/] adj pragmatic

prägnant [pre'gnant] adj pithy, terse

Prä'gung f (-;-en) coining, minting; (fig) coinage

prahlen ['pralən] intr (mit) brag (about); (mit) show off (with)

Prah'ler m (-s;-) braggart; show-off

Prahlerei [pralə'rai] f (-;-en) bragging, boasting; (Prunken) showing off

Prah'lerin f (-;-nen) braggart; show-off

prahlerisch ['praləri/] adj bragging

Prahlhans ['pralhans] m (-es;-e) braggart

Prahm [pram] m (-[e]s;-e) flat-bottomed lighter

Praktik ['praktik] f (-;-en) practice; (Kniff) trick

Praktikant –in [prakti'kant(in)] §7 mf student in on-the-job training

Praktiker ['praktikər] m (-s;-) practical person

Prakti-kum ['praktikum] n (-s;-ka [ka]) practical training

Praktikus ['praktikus] m (-;-se) old hand

praktisch ['prakti/] adj practical; **praktischer Arzt** general practitioner

praktizieren [prakti'tsirən] tr practice; **etw in die Tasche p.** manage to slip s.th. into the pocket

Prälat [pre'lat] m (-en;-en) prelate

Praline [pra'linə] f (-;-n) chocolate

prall [pral] adj (straff) tight; (Brüste) full; (Backen) chubby; (Arme, Beine) shapely; (Sonne) blazing || **Prall** m (-[e]s;-e) impact; collision

prallen ['pralən] intr (SEIN) bounce, rebound; (Sonne) beat down

Prämie ['premjə] f (-;-n) award, prize; premium; bonus

prämieren [premi'irən] tr award a prize to

prangen ['praŋən] intr shine; look beautiful

Pranger ['praŋər] m (-s;-) pillory

Pranke ['praŋkə] f (-;-n) claw

pränumerando [prenumə'rando] adv in advance, beforehand

Präparat [prepa'rat] n (-[e]s;-e) preparation

präparieren [prepa'rirən] tr prepare

Präposition [prepozi'tsjon] f (-;-en) preposition

Prä-rie [pre'ri] f (-;-rien ['ri-ən]) prairie

Präsens ['prezens] n (-; Präsentia [pre'zentsi-a]) (gram) present

präsent [pre'zent] adj present || **Präsent** n (-[e]s;-e) present, gift

präsentieren [prezen'tirən] tr present

Präsentier'teller m tray

Präsenzstärke [prɛ'zɛnts/tɛrkə] *f* effective strength

Präservativ [prɛzɛrva'tif] *m* (-s;-e) prophylactic, condom

Präsident [prɛzi'dɛnt] *m* (-en;-en) president

Präsidenten- [prɛzidɛntən] *comb.fm.* presidential

Präsident'schaft *f* (-;-en) presidency

präsidieren [prɛzi'dirən] *intr* preside

Präsi'dium [prɛ'zidjum] *n* (-s;-dien [djən]) presidency; chairmanship

prasseln ['prasəln] *intr* crackle; (*Regen*) patter

prassen ['prasən] *intr* lead a dissipated life

Prasserei [prasə'raɪ] *f* (-;) luxurious living, high life

Prätendent [prɛtɛn'dɛnt] *m* (-en;-en) (*auf acc*) pretender (to)

Pra·xis ['praksɪs] *f* (-;-xen [ksən]) practice; experience; doctor's office; law office; (*jur*) clientele; (*med*) patients

Präzedenzfall [prɛtsɛ'dɛntsfal] *m* precedent

präzis [prɛ'tsis] *adj* precise

Präzision [prɛtsi'zjon] *f* (-;) precision

predigen ['predigən] *tr* & *intr* preach

Prediger ['predigər] *m* (-s;-) preacher

Predigt ['predɪçt] *f* (-;-en) sermon

Preis [praɪs] *m* (-es;-e) price, rate, cost; (*poet*) praise, glory; **äußerster P.** (coll) rock-bottom price; **um jeden P.** (coll) at all costs; **um keinen P.** (fig) on no account; **zum P. von** at the rate of

Preis'aufgabe *f* project in a competition

Preis'aufschlag *m* extra charge

Preis'ausschreiben *n* competition

Preisdrückerei ['praɪsdrʏkəraɪ] *f* (-;-en) price cutting

Preiselbeere ['praɪzəlberə] *f* cranberry

preisen ['praɪzən] *tr* praise

Preis'ermäßigung *f* price reduction

Preis'frage *f* question in a competition; question of price (coll) sixty-four-dollar question

Preis'gabe *f* abandonment, surrender

preis'geben §80 *tr* abandon, surrender; (*Geheimnis*) betray; **j-n dem Spott p.** hold s.o. up to ridicule

preisgekrönt ['praɪsgəkrønt] *adj* prize-winning

Preis'gericht *n* jury

Preis'grenze *f* price limit; **obere P.** ceiling; **untere P.** minimum price

preis'günstig *adj* worth the money

Preis'lage *f* price range

Preis'niveau *n* price level

Preis'notierung *f* rate of exchange

Preis'richter *m* judge (*in competition*)

Preis'schießen *n* shooting competition

Preis'schild *n* price tag

Preis'schlager *m* bargain price

Preis'schrift *f* prize-winning essay

Preis'stopp *m* price freezing

Preis'sturz *m* drop in prices

Preis'träger -in §6 *mf* prize winner

Preistreiberei [praɪstraɪbə'raɪ] *f* (-;) price rigging

Preis'überwachung *f* price control

Preis'verzeichnis *n* price list

preis'wert, preis'würdig *adj* worth the money, reasonable

Preis'zuschlag *m* markup

prekär [prɛ'kɛr] *adj* precarious

Prellbock ['prɛlbɔk] *m* (rr) buffer

prellen ['prɛlən] *tr* bump; bounce; toss up (*in a blanket*); (um) cheat (out of) ‖ *ref*—**sich** [*dat*] **den Arm p.** bruise one's arm

Prel'ler *m* (-s;-) bump; ricochet; bilker, cheat

Prellerei [prɛlə'raɪ] *f* (-;-en) (act of) cheating

Prell'schuß *m* ricochet

Prell'stein *m* curbstone

Prel'lung *f* (-;-en) bruise

Premier [prə'mje] *m* (-s;-s) premier

Premiere [prə'mjɛrə] *f* (-;-n) (theat) premiere, first night, opening

Premier'minister *m* prime minister

Presbyterianer -in [prɛsbytə'rjanər (ɪn)] §6 *mf* Presbyterian

presbyterianisch [prɛsbytə'rjanɪʃ] *adj* Presbyterian

preschen ['prɛʃən] *intr* charge

pressant [prɛ'sant] *adj* pressing

Presse ['prɛsə] *f* (-;-n) (& journ) press; (educ) cram class

Press'agentur *f* press agency

Press'seamt *n* public-relations office

Press'seausweis *m* press card

Press'sebericht *m* press report

Press'sechef *m* press secretary

Press'sekonferenz *f* press conference

Press'semeldung *f* news item

Press'sestelle *f* public-relations office

Press'severtreter *m* reporter; public-relations officer

Preßkohle ['prɛskolə] *f* briquette

Preßluft ['prɛsluft] *f* compressed air

Preß'lufthammer *m* jackhammer

Preuße ['prɔɪsə] *m* (-n;-n) Prussian

Preußen ['prɔɪsən] *n* (-s;) Prussia

Preußin ['prɔɪsɪn] *f* (-;-nen) Prussian

preußisch ['prɔɪsɪʃ] *adj* Prussian

prickeln ['prɪkəln] *intr* tingle

Priem [prim] *m* (-[e]s;-e) plug (*of tobacco*)

priemen ['primən] *intr* chew tobacco

pries [pris] *pret* of **preisen**

Priester ['pristər] *m* (-s;-) priest

Prie'steramt *n* priesthood

Priesterin ['pristərɪn] *f* (-;-nen) priestess

prie'sterlich *adj* priestly

Prie'sterrock *m* cassock

Priestertum ['pristərtum] *n* (-s;) priesthood

Prie'sterweihe *f* (eccl) ordination

prima ['prima] *invar adj* first-class; terrific, swell

primär [pri'mɛr] *adj* primary ‖ *adv* primarily

Primat [pri'mat] *m* & *n* (-[e]s;-e) primacy, priority ‖ *m* (-en;-en) primate

Primel ['priməl] *f* (-;-n) primrose

primitiv [primi'tif] *adj* primitive

Prinz [prɪnts] *m* (-en;-en) prince

Prinzessin [prɪn'tsesɪn] *f* (-;-nen) princess

Prinz'gemahl *m* prince consort

Prin·zip [prɪn'tsip] *n* (-s; -zipien ['tsipjən]) principle
prinzipiell [prɪntsi'pjel] *adj* in principle, fundamentally
Prinzi'pienreiter *m* (coll) pedant
prinz'lich *adj* princely
Pri·or ['pri·ər] *m* (-s; -oren ['orən]) (eccl) prior
Priorität [pri·ɔrɪ'tet] *f* (-; -en) priority
Prise ['prizə] *f* (-; -n) pinch (*of salt, etc.*); (nav) prize
Pris·ma ['prɪsma] *n* (-s; -men [men]) prism
privat [prɪ'vat] *adj* private; personal
Privat'adresse *f*, **Privat'anschrift** *f* home address
Privat'dozent **–in** §7 *mf* non-salaried university lecturer
Privat'druck *m* private printing
Privat'eigentum *n* private property
Privat'gespräch *n* (telp) personal call
privatim [prɪ'vatɪm] *adv* privately; confidentially
privatisieren [prɪvatɪ'zirən] *intr* be financially independent
Privat'lehrer **–in** §6 *mf* tutor
Privat'recht *n* civil law
privat'rechtlich *adj* (jur) civil
Privi·leg [prɪvi'lek] *n* (-[e]s; -legien ['legjən]) privilege
privilegiert [prɪvɪle'girt] *adj* privileged
probat [pro'bat] *adj* tried, tested
Probe ['probə] *f* (-; -n) (*Versuch*) trial, experiment; (*Prüfung*) test; (*Muster*) sample; (*Beweis*) proof; (theat) rehearsal; **auf die P. stellen** put to the test; **auf** (or **zur**) **P.** on approval
Pro'beabdruck *m*, **Pro'beabzug** *m* (typ) proof
Pro'bebild *n* (phot) proof
Pro'bebogen *m* proof sheet
Pro'bedruck *m* (typ) proof
Pro'befahrt *f* road test, trial run
Pro'beflug *m* test flight
Pro'belauf *m* trial run; dry run
Pro'besendung *f* sample sent on approval
Pro'bestück *n* sample, specimen
pro'beweise *adv* on trial; on approval
Pro'bezeit *f* probation period
probieren [pro'birən] *tr* try out, test; try, taste; (metal) assay
Probier'glas *n* test tube
Probier'stein *m* touch-stone
Problem [pro'blem] *n* (-s; -e) problem
Produkt [pro'dʊkt] *n* (-[e]s; -e) product; (*des Bodens*) produce
Produktion [prodʊk'tsjon] *f* (-; -en) production; (indust) output
produktiv [prodʊk'tif] *adj* productive
Produzent [prodʊ'tsent] *m* (-en; -en) (& cin) producer
produzieren [prodʊ'tsirən] *tr* produce || *ref* perform; (pej) show off
profan [pro'fan] *adj* profane
profanieren [profa'nirən] *tr* profane
Profession [profe'sjon] *f* (-; -en) profession
Professional [profesjə'nal] *m* (-s; -e) (sport) professional
professionell [profesjə'nel] *adj* professional
Profes·sor [pro'fesɔr] *m* (-s; -soren [pro'fesorən]), **Professorin** [profe'sorɪn] *f* (-; -nen) professor; **außerordentlicher P.** associate professor; **ordentlicher P.** full professor
Professur [profe'sur] *f* (-; -en) professorship
Profi ['profi] *m* (-s; -s) (coll) pro
Profil [pro'fil] *n* (-s; -e) profile; (aut) tread; **im P.** in profile
profiliert [profi'lirt] *adj* outstanding
Profit [pro'fit] *m* (-[e]s; -e) profit
profitabel [profi'tabəl] *adj* profitable
Profit'gier *f* profiteering
profitieren [profi'tirən] *tr & intr* profit
Prognose [pro'gnozə] *f* (-; -n) (med) prognosis; (meteor) forecast
Programm [pro'gram] *n* (-s; -e) program; (pol) platform
programmieren [progra'mirən] *tr* (data proc) program
Projekt [pro'jekt] *n* (-[e]s; -e) project
Projektil [projek'til] *n* (-s; -e) projectile
Projektion [projek'tsjon] *f* (-; -en) projection
Projektions'apparat *m*, **Projektions'gerät** *n*, **Projek·tor** [pro'jektor] *m* (-s; -toren ['torən]) projector
projizieren [proji'tsirən] *tr* project
proklamieren [prokla'mirən] *tr* proclaim
Prokura [pro'kura] *f* (-;) power of attorney; **per P.** by proxy
Prolet [pro'let] *m* (-en; -en) (pej) cad
Proletariat [proleta'rjat] *n* (-[e]s; -e) proletariat
Proletarier **–in** [prole'tarjər(ɪn)] §6 *mf* proletarian
proletarisch [prole'tarɪʃ] *adj* proletarian
Prolog [pro'lok] *m* (-[e]s; -e) prologue
prolongieren [prolɔŋ'girən] *tr* extend; (cin) hold over
Promenade [promə'nadə] *f* (-; -n) avenue; (*Spaziergang*) promenade
promenieren [promə'nirən] *intr* stroll
prominent [promɪ'nent] *adj* prominent
Promotion [promo'tsjon] *f* (-; -en) awarding of the doctor's degree
promovieren [promo'virən] *intr* attain a doctor's degree
prompt [prompt] *adj* prompt, quick
Prono·men [pro'nomən] *n* (-s; -mina [mina]) pronoun
Propaganda [propa'ganda] *f* (-;) propaganda
propagieren [propa'girən] *tr* propagate
Propeller [pro'pelər] *m* (-s; -) propeller
Prophet [pro'fet] *m* (-en; -en) prophet
Prophetin [pro'fetɪn] *f* (-; -nen) prophetess
prophetisch [pro'fetɪʃ] *adj* prophetic
prophezeien [profe'tsar·ən] *tr* prophesy
Prophezei'ung *f* (-; -en) prophecy
Proportion [propɔr'tsjon] *f* (-; -en) proportion
proportional [propɔrtsjo'nal] *adj* proportional
proportioniert [propɔrtsjo'nirt] *adj* proportionate
Propst [propst] *m* (-es; -̈e) provost

Prosa ['proza] f (-;) prose
prosaisch [pro'za·ɪʃ] adj prosaic
prosit ['prozɪt] interj to your health!
‖ **Prosit** n (-s;-s) toast
Prospekt [pro'spɛkt] m (-[e]s;-e)
prospect, view; brochure, folder
prostituieren [prɔstɪtu'irən] tr prostitute
Prostituierte [prɔstɪtu'irtə] §5 f prostitute
protegieren [prote'girən] tr patronize;
(schützen) protect
Protektion [protɛk'tsjon] f (-;) pull, connections
Protest [pro'tɛst] m (-es;-e) protest
Protestant –in [protɛs'tant(ɪn)] §7 mf Protestant
protestantisch [protɛs'tantɪʃ] adj Protestant
protestieren [protɛs'tirən] tr & intr protest
Protokoll [proto'kɔl] n (-s;-e) protocol; record, minutes; **P. führen** take the minutes; **zu P. nehmen** take down
Protokoll'führer –in §6 mf recording secretary; (jur) clerk
protokollieren [prɔtokɔ'lirən] tr record
Pro·ton ['proton] n (-s;-tonen ['tonən]) (phys) proton
Protz [prɔts] m (-en;-en) show-off
protzen ['prɔtsən] intr show off
prot'zenhaft, protzig ['prɔtsɪç] adj show-offish
Prozedur [protse'dur] f (-;-en) procedure; (jur) proceeding
Prozent [pro'tsɛnt] n (-[e]s;-e) percent
Prozent'satz m percentage
Pro·zeß [pro'tses] m (-zesses;-zesse) process; (jur) case, suit; (jur) proceedings; **e–en P. anstrengen** (or führen) gegen sue; **kurzen P. machen mit** make short work of
Prozeß'akten pl (jur) record
Prozeß'führer –in §6 mf litigant
prozessieren [protse'sirən] intr go to court; **p. gegen** sue
Prozession [protse'sjon] f (-;-en) procession
Prozeß'kosten pl (jur) court costs
Prozeß'vollmacht f power of attorney
prüde ['prydə] adj prudish
prüfen ['pryfən] tr test; (nachprüfen) check, verify; (untersuchen) examine; (kosten) taste; (acct) audit
Prüfer –in §6 mf examiner; (acct) auditor
Prüfling ['pryflɪŋ] m (-s;-e) examinee
Prüfstein ['pryftaɪn] m touchstone
Prü'fung f (-;-en) test; examination; check, verification; (acct) audit; (jur) review
Prü'fungsarbeit f test paper
Prü'fungsausschuß m, **Prü'fungskommission** f examining board
Prügel ['prygəl] m (-s;-) stick, cudgel; **Prügel** pl whipping
Prügelei [prygə'laɪ] f (-;-en) brawl; free-for-all
Prü'gelknabe m whipping boy, scapegoat
prügeln ['prygəln] tr beat, whip ‖ ref have a fight

Prü'gelstrafe f corporal punishment
Prunk [pruŋk] m (-[e]s;) pomp, show
prunken ['pruŋkən] intr show off
Prunk'gemach n stateroom
prunk'haft adj showy
Prunk'sucht f ostentatiousness
prunk'süchtig adj ostentatious
prunk'voll adj gorgeous
Prunk'zimmer n stateroom
prusten ['prustən] intr snort
Psalm [psalm] m (-s;-en) psalm
Psalter ['psaltər] m (-s;-) psalter
Pseudonym [psɔɪdo'nym] n (-s;-e) pseudonym
Psychiater [psʏçɪ'atər] m (-s;-) psychiatrist
Psychiatrie [psʏçɪ·a'tri] f (-;) psychiatry
psychiatrisch [psʏçɪ'atrɪʃ] adj psychiatric
psychisch ['psʏçɪʃ] adj psychic(al)
Psychoanalyse [psʏço·ana'lyzə] f (-;) psychoanalysis
Psychoanalytiker –in [psʏço·ana'lytɪkər(ɪn)] §6 mf psychoanalyst
Psychologe [psʏço'logə] m (-n;-n) psychologist
Psychologie [psʏçolo'gi] f (-;) psychology
Psychologin [psʏço'login] f (-;-nen) psychologist
psychologisch [psʏço'logɪʃ] adj psychological
Psychopath –in [psʏço'pat(ɪn)] §7 mf psychopath
Psychose [psʏ'çozə] f (-;-n) psychosis
Psychotherapie [psʏçotera'pi] f (-;) psychotherapy
Pubertät [puber'tɛt] f (-;) puberty
publik [pub'lik] adj public
Publi·kum ['publikum] n (-s;-ka [ka]) public; (theat) audience
publizieren [publɪ'tsirən] tr publish
Publizist –in [publɪ'tsɪst(ɪn)] §7 mf (journ) writer on public affairs; teacher or student of journalism
Publizität [publɪtsɪ'tɛt] f (-;) publicity
Pudel ['pudəl] m (-s;-) poodle; **des Pudels Kern** (fig) gist of the matter
Pu'delmütze f fur cap; woolen cap
pu'delnaß adj (coll) soaking wet
Puder ['pudər] m (-s;-) powder
Pu'derdose f powder box; compact
Pu'derquaste f powder puff
Pu'derzucker m powdered sugar
Puff [puf] m (-[e]s;⸚e & -e) (Stoß) poke; (Knall) pop; (Bausch) puff; ‖ m (-s;-e) (coll) brothel
Puff'ärmel m puffed sleeve
puffen ['pufən] tr poke; (coll) prod ‖ intr puff; (knallen) pop, bang away
Puffer ['pufər] m (-s;-) buffer; pop-gun; (culin) potato pancake
Puf'ferbatterie f booster battery
Puf'ferstaat m buffer state
Puff'mais m popcorn
Puff'reis m (-es;) puffed rice
Pulli ['puli] m (-s;-s) (coll) sweater
Pullover [pu'lovər] m (-s;-) sweater
Puls [puls] m (-es;-e) pulse
Puls'ader f artery
pulsieren [pul'zirən] intr pulsate
Puls'schlag m pulse beat

Pult [pult] *n* (-[e]s;-e) desk
Pulver ['pulfər] *n* (-s;-) powder; (*Schieß*-) gunpowder; (coll) dough
pul'verig *adj* powdery
pulverisieren [pulfərɪ'zirən] *tr* pulverize
Pul'verschnee *m* powdery snow
Pummel ['puməl] *m* (-s;-) butterball (*chubby child*)
pummelig ['puməlɪç] *adj* (coll) chubby
Pump [pump] *m*—**auf P.** (coll) on tick
Pumpe ['pumpə] *f* (-;-n) pump
pumpen ['pumpən] *tr* pump; (coll) give on tick; (coll) get on tick || *intr* pump
Pum'penschwengel *m* pump handle
Pumpernickel ['pumpərnɪkəl] *m* (-s; -) pumpernickel
Pump'hosen *f* pair of knickerbockers
Punkt [puŋkt] *m* (-[e]s;-e) point; (*Tüpfelchen*) dot; (*Stelle*) spot; (*Einzelheit*) item; (gram) period; **der tote P.** a deadlock; **dunkler P.** (fig) skeleton in the closet; **nach Punkten siegen** win on points; **P. sechs Uhr** at six o'clock sharp; **springender P.** crux; **strittiger P.** point at issue; **wunder P.** (fig) sore spot
Punkt'gleichheit *f* (sport) tie
punktieren [puŋk'tirən] *tr* dot, stipple; **punktierte Linie** dotted line
pünktlich ['pyŋktlɪç] *adj* punctual
Punkt'sieg *m* (box) winning on points
punktum ['puŋktum] *interj*—**und damit p.!** and that's it!; period!
Punkt'zahl *f* (sport) score
Punsch [punʃ] *m* (-es;-e) punch (*drink*)
Punze ['puntsə] *f* (-;-n) punch, stamp
punzen ['puntsən] *tr* punch, stamp
Pupille [pu'pɪlə] *f* (-;-n) (anat) pupil
Puppe ['pupə] *f* (-;-n) doll; puppet; (*Schneider*-) dummy; (zool) pupa
Pup'penspiel *n* puppet show
Pup'penwagen *m* doll carriage
pur [pur] *adj* pure, sheer

Püree [py're] *n* (-s;-s) mashed potatoes; puree
purgieren [pur'girən] *tr & intr* purge
Purpur ['purpur] *m* (-s;) purple
pur'purfarben *adj* purple
purpurn [purpurn] *adj* purple
Purzelbaum ['purtsəlbaum] *m* somersault; **e-en P. schlagen** do a somersault
purzeln ['purtsəln] *intr* (SEIN) tumble
pusselig ['pusəlɪç] *adj* fussy
Puste ['pustə] *f* (-s;) (coll) breath
Pustel ['pustəl] *f* (-;-n) pustule
pusten ['pustən] *tr*—**ich puste dir was!** (coll) you may whistle for it! || *intr* puff, pant
Pu'sterohr *n* peashooter
Pute ['putə] *f* (-;-n) turkey (hen)
Puter ['putər] *m* (-s;-) turkey (cock)
Putsch [putʃ] *m* (-es;-e) putsch, uprising
Putz [puts] *m* (-es;) finery; trimming; ornaments; plaster
putzen ['putsən] *tr* (*reinigen*) clean; (*Schuhe*) polish; (*Zähne*) brush; (*Person*) dress; (*schmücken*) adorn || *ref* dress; **sich** [*dat*] **die Nase p.** blow one's nose
Put'zer *m* (-s;-) cleaner; (mil) orderly
Putzerei [putsə'raɪ] *f* (-;-en) (Aust) dry cleaner's; (Aust) laundry
Putz'frau *f* cleaning woman
putzig ['putsɪç] *adj* funny
Putz'lappen *m* cleaning cloth
Putz'mittel *n* cleaning agent
Putz'wolle *f* cotton waste
Putz'zeug *n* cleaning things
Pygmäe [pyg'me·ə] *m* (-n;-n) pygmy
Pyjama [pɪ'dʒama] *m* (-s;-s) pajamas
Pyramide [pyra'midə] *f* (-;-n) pyramid; (mil) stack
Pyrenäen [pyrɛ'ne·ən] *pl* Pyrenees
Pyrotechnik [pyrɔ'teçnɪk] *f* (-;) pyrotechnics
Pythonschlange ['pytɔn/laŋə] *f* python

Q

Q, q [ku] *invar n* Q, q
quabbelig ['kvabəlɪç] *adj* flabby; quivering, jelly-like
quabbeln ['kvabəln] *intr* quiver
Quackelei [kvakə'laɪ] *f* (-;-en) silly talk; (*unnützes Zeug*) rubbish
Quacksalber ['kvakzalbər] *m* (-s;-) quack
Quader ['kvadər] *m* (-s;-) ashlar
Quadrant [kva'drant] *m* (-en;-en) quadrant
Quadrat [kva'drat] *n* (-[e]s;-e) square; **e-e Zahl ins Q. erheben** square a number; **zwei Fuß im Q.** two feet square
quadratisch [kva'dratɪʃ] *adj* square; quadratic
Quadrat'meter *n* square meter
Quadrat'wurzel *f* square root
quadrieren [kva'drirən] *tr* square

quaken ['kvakən] *intr* (*Ente*) quack; (*Frosch*) croak
quäken ['kvekən] *intr* bawl
Qual [kval] *f* (-;-en) torment, agony
quälen ['kvelən] *tr* torment; worry; (*ständig bedrängen*) pester || *ref*—**sich mit e-r Arbeit q.** slave at a job; **sich umsonst q.** labor in vain; **sich zu Tode q.** worry oneself to death
Quälgeist ['kvelgaɪst] *m* pest
Qualifikation [kvalɪfɪka'tsjon] *f* (-; -en) qualification
qualifizieren [kvalɪfɪ'tsirən] *tr & ref* (zu) qualify (for)
Qualität [kvalɪ'tet] *f* (-;-en) quality
Qualitäts- *comb.fm.* high-quality, high-grade, quality
Qualle ['kvalə] *f* (-;-n) jellyfish
Qualm [kvalm] *m* (-[e]s;) smoke; vapor

qualmen ['kvalmən] *tr* smoke || *intr* smoke; (coll) smoke like a chimney
qual'mig *adj* smoky
qual'voll *adj* agonizing
Quantentheorie ['kvantɛnte·ori] *f* quantum theory
Quantität [kvantɪ'tet] *f* (-;-en) quantity
Quan·tum ['kvantum] *n* (-s;-ten [tən]) quantum; quantity; (*Anteil*) portion
Quappe ['kvapə] *f* (-;-n) tadpole
Quarantäne [kvaran'tenə] *f* (-;-n) quarantine
Quark [kvark] *m* (-[e]s;) curds; cottage cheese; (fig) nonsense
Quark'käse *m* cottage cheese
quarren ['kvarən] *intr* (*Frosch*) croak; (fig) groan
Quart [kvart] *n* (-s;-e) quart; quarto || *f* (-;-en) (mus) fourth
Quartal [kvar'tal] *n* (-s;-e) quarter (*of a year*)
Quartals'abrechnung *f* (fin) quarterly statement
Quartals'säufer *m* periodic drunkard
Quart'band *m* (-[e]s;ːe) quarto volume
Quarte ['kvartə] *f* (-;-n) (mus) fourth
Quartett [kvar'tet] *n* (-[e]s;-e) quartet
Quart'format *n* quarto
Quartier [kvar'tir] *n* (-s;-e) (*Stadtviertel*) quarter; (*Unterkunft*) quarters; (mil) quarters, billet
Quartier'meister *m* (mil) quartermaster
Quarz [kvarts] *m* (-es;-e) quartz
quasseln ['kvasəln] *tr* (coll) talk || *intr* talk nonsense
Quast [kvast] *m* (-[e]s;-e) brush
Quaste ['kvastə] *f* (-;-n) tassel
Quatsch [kvatʃ] *m* (-es;) (coll) baloney
quatschen ['kvatʃən] *intr* chatter; talk nonsense; (*durch Schlamm*) slog
Quecksilber ['kvekzɪlbər] *n* mercury
queck'silbrig *adj* fidgety
Quell [kvel] *m* (-[e]s;-e) (poet) var of **Quelle**
Quelle ['kvelə] *f* (-;-n) fountainhead; source; spring
quellen ['kvelən] §119 *tr* cause to swell; soak || *intr* (SEIN) spring, gush; (*Tränen*) well up; (*anschwellen*) swell; **ihm quollen die Augen fast aus dem Kopf** his eyes almost popped out
Quel'lenangabe *f* citation; bibliography
quel'lenmäßig *adj* according to the best authorities, authentic
Quel'lenmaterial *n* source material
Quel'lenstudium *n* original research

Quell'fluß *m* source
Quell'gebiet *n* headwaters
Quell'wasser *n* spring water
Quengelei [kveŋə'laɪ] *f* (-;-en) nagging
quengeln ['kveŋəln] *intr* nag
quer [kver] *adj* cross, transverse || *adv* crosswise; **q. über** (*acc*) across
Quer'balken *m* crossbeam
Quere ['kverə] *f* (-;) diagonal direction; **j-m in die Q. kommen** run across s.o.; (fig) disturb s.o.
queren ['kverən] *tr* traverse, cross
Quer'feldein' *adv* cross-country
Quer'kopf *m* contrary person
quer'köpfig *adj* contrary
Quer'pfeife *f* (mus) fife
Quer'ruder *n* (aer) aileron
Quer'schiff *n* (archit) transept
Quer'schläger *m* ricochet
Quer'schnitt *m* cross section
Quer'treiber *m* schemer, plotter
querü'ber *adv* straight across
Querulant -in [kveru'lant(ɪn)] §7 *mf* grumbler, grouch
Quetsche ['kvetʃə] *f* (-;-n) squeezer; (pej) joint
quetschen ['kvetʃən] *tr* squeeze, pinch; bruise; (*zerquetschen*) crush, mash
Quetsch'kartoffeln *pl* mashed potatoes
Quet'schung *f* (-;-en) bruise, contusion
Quetsch'wunde *f* bruise
quick [kvɪk] *adj* brisk, lively
quick'lebendig *adj* (coll) very lively
quieken ['kvikən] *intr* squeal, squeak
quietschen ['kvitʃən] *intr* (*Tür*) creak; (*Ferkel*) squeal; (*Bremsen*) screetch
Quintessenz ['kvintesents] *f* (-;) quintessence
Quintett [kvɪn'tet] *n* (-[e]s;-e) quintet
Quirl [kvɪrl] *m* (-[e]s;-e) (fig) fidgeter; (culin) whisk, mixer
quirlen ['kvɪrlən] *tr* beat, mix
quitt [kvɪt] *adj* even, square
Quitte ['kvɪtə] *f* (-;-n) quince
quittieren [kvɪ'tirən] *tr* give a receipt for; (*aufgeben*) quit
Quit'tung *f* (-;-en) receipt
Quiz [kvɪs] *n* (-;-) quiz
quoll [kvɔl] *pret* of **quellen**
Quotation [kvota'tsjon] *f* (-;-en) (st. exch.) quotation
Quote ['kvotə] *f* (-;-en) quota
Quotient [kvo'tsjent] *m* (-en;-en) quotient
quotieren [kvo'tirən] *tr* quote

R

R, r [er] *invar n* R, r
Rabatt [ra'bat] *m* (-[e]s;-e) reduction, discount
Rabatt'marke *f* trading stamp
Rabatz [ra'bats] *m*—**R. machen** (coll) raise Cain
Rab·bi ['rabi] *m* (-[s];-s & -binen ['binən]), **Rabbiner** [ra'binər] *m* (-s;-) rabbi
Rabe ['rabə] *m* (-n;-n) raven; **weißer R.** (fig) rare bird
Ra'benaas *n* (coll) beast
Ra'benmutter *f* hard-hearted mother
ra'benschwarz' *adj* jet-black

rabiat [ra'bjɑt] *adj* rabid, raving
Rache ['raxə] *f* (−;) revenge
Rachen ['raxən] *m* (−s;−) throat; mouth; (fig) jaws
rächen ['rɛçən] *tr* avenge ‖ *ref* (**an** *dat*) avenge oneself (on)
Ra'chenhöhle *f* pharynx
Ra'chenkatarrh *m* sore throat
Rä'cher −**in** §6 *mf* avenger
Rachgier ['raxgir] *f* revengefulness
rach/gierig, rach/süchtig *adj* vengeful
Rad [rɑt] *n* (−[e]s;=er) wheel; bike; **ein Rad schlagen** turn a ca͟rtwheel; (*Pfau*) fan the tail
Radar ['radar], [ra'dar] *n* (−s;) radar
Ra'dargerät *n* radar
Ra'darschirm *m* radarscope
Radau [ra'dau] *m* (−s;−) (coll) row
Radau'macher *m* rowdy
Rädchen ['rɛtçən] *n* (−s;−) little wheel
Rad'dampfer *m* river boat
radebrechen ['radəbrɛçən] §64 *tr* murder (*a language*)
radeln ['radəln] *intr* (SEIN) (coll) ride a bike
Rädelsführer ['redəlsfyrər] *m* ringleader
rädern ['redərn] *tr* torture; **wie gerädert sein** (coll) be bushed
Räderwerk ['redərverk] *n* gears; (fig) clockwork
rad'fahren §71 *intr* (SEIN) ride a bicycle
radieren [ra'dirən] *tr* erase; etch
Radie'rer *m* (−s;−) eraser; etcher
Radier'gummi *m* eraser
Radier'kunst *f* art of etching
Radier'messer *n* scraper, eraser
Radie'rung *f* (−;−en) erasure; etching
Radieschen [ra'disçən] *n* (−s;−) radish
radikal [radɪ'kɑl] *adj* radical ‖ **Radikale** §5 *mf* radical, extremist
Radio ['radjo] *n* (−s;−s) radio; **im R.** on the radio; **R. hören** listen to the radio
Ra'dioamateur *m* (rad) ham
Ra'dioapparat *m*, **Ra'diogerät** *n* radio set
Radiologe [radjo'logə] *m* (−n;−n) radiologist
Radiologie [radjolo'gi] *f* (−;) radiology
Ra'dioröhre *f* radio tube
Ra'diosender *m* radio transmitter
Radium ['radjum] *n* (−s;) radium
Ra·dius ['radjus] *m* (−;−dien [djən]) radius
Rad'kappe *f* hubcap
Rad'kranz *m* rim
Radler −**in** ['radlər(ɪn)] §6 *mf* cyclist
Rad'nabe *f* hub
Rad'rennen *n* bicycle race
−**rüdrig** [redrɪç] *comb.fm.* −wheeled
rad'schlagen §132 *intr* turn a cartwheel
Rad'spur *f* rut, track
Rad'stand *m* wheelbase
Rad'zahn *m* cog
raffen ['rafən] *tr* snatch up, gather up, (sew) take up
Raffgier ['rafgir] *f* rapacity
raffgierig ['rafgirɪç] *adj* rapacious
Raffine-rie [rafɪnə'ri] *f* (−;−rien ['ri·ən]) refinery
raffinieren [rafɪ'nirən] *tr* refine

raffiniert [rafɪ'nirt] *adj* refined; (fig) shrewd, cunning
Raffzahn ['raftsan] *m* canine tooth
ragen ['ragən] *intr* tower, loom
Ragout [ra'gu] *n* (−s;−s) (culin) stew
Rahe ['ra·ə] *f* (−;−n) (naut) yard
Rahm [ram] *m* (−[e]s;) cream
Rahmen ['ramən] *m* (−s;−) frame; (*Gefüge*) framework; (*Bereich*) scope, limits; (fig) setting; (aut) chassis; **aus dem R. fallen** be out of place; **e−n R. abgeben für** form a setting for; **im R.** (*genit*) in the course of; **im R. von** (or *genit*) within the scope of; within the framework of
Rah'menerzählung *f* story within a story
rahmig ['ramɪç] *adj* creamy
Rakete [ra'ketə] *f* (−;−n) rocket
Rake'tenabschußrampe *f* launch pad
Rake'tenbunker *m* silo
Rake'tenstart *m* rocket launch
Rake'tenwerfer *m* rocket launcher
Rake'tenwesen *n* rocketry
Rakett [ra'ket] *n* (−[e]s;−e & −s) (tennis) racket
Rammbär ['ramber] *m*, **Rammbock** ['rambɔk] *m*, **Ramme** ['ramə] *f* (−;−n) rammer; pile driver
rammeln ['raməln] *tr* shove; (*zusammenpressen*) pack; (*belegen*) copulate with ‖ *intr* copulate
rammen ['ramən] *tr* ram; (*Beton*) tamp
Rampe ['rampə] *f* (−;−n) ramp; (rok) launch pad; (rr) platform; (theat) apron
Ram'penlicht *n* footlights; (fig) limelight
Ramsch [ramʃ] *m* (−es;) odds and ends; junk; (com) rummage
Ramsch'verkauf *m* rummage sale
Ramsch'waren *pl* junk
Rand [rant] *m* (−[e]s;=er) edge, border; (*e−s Druckseite*) margin; **am Rande bemerken** note in passing; **außer R. und Band** completely out of control; **bis zum Rande** to the brim; **e−n R. hinterlassen** leave a ring (*e.g., from a wet glass*); **Ränder unter den Augen** circles under the eyes
Rand'auslöser *m* (typ) margin release
Rand'bemerkung *f* marginal note; (fig) snide remark
rändeln ['rendəln], **rändern** ['rendərn] *tr* border, edge; (*Münzen*) mill
Rand'gebiet *n* borderland; (*e−r Stadt*) outskirts
rand'los *adj* rimless
Rand'staat *m* border state
Ranft [ranft] *m* (−[e]s;=e) crust
rang [raŋ] *pret of* **ringen** ‖ **Rang** *m* (−[e]s;=e) rank; (theat) balcony; **j−m den R. ablaufen** (fig) run rings around s.o.
Rang'abzeichen *n* insignia of rank
Rang'älteste §5 *mf* ranking officer
Range ['raŋə] *m* (−n;−n) & *f* (−;−n) brat
Rangier'bahnhof *m* (rr) marshaling yard
rangieren [rã'ʒirən] *tr* rank; (rr) shunt, switch ‖ *intr* rank

Rang'ordnung f order of precedence

Rang'stufe f rank

rank [raŋk] adj slender

Ranke ['raŋkə] f (-;-n) tendril

Ränke ['rɛŋkə] pl schemes; **R. schmieden** scheme

ranken ['raŋkən] ref & intr creep, climb; **sich r. um** wind around

rän'kevoll adj scheming

rann [ran] pret of **rinnen**

rannte ['rantə] pret of **rennen**

Ranzen ['rantsən] m (-s;-) knapsack; school bag; (Bauch) belly; (mil) field pack

ranzig ['rantsɪç] adj rancid

rapid [ra'pit], **rapide** [ra'pidə] adj rapid

Rappe ['rapə] m (-n;-n) black horse

rar [rɑr] adj rare, scarce

Rarität [rari'tɛt] f (-;-en) rarity

rasant [ra'zant] adj grazing, point-blank (fire); (fig) impetuous

Rasanz [ra'zants] f (-;) flat trajectory; (fig) impetuosity

rasch [raʃ] adj quick; (hastig) hasty

rascheln ['raʃəln] intr rustle

Rasch'heit f (-;) haste, speed

rasen ['razən] intr rage, rave || intr (SEIN) rush; (aut) speed || **Rasen** m (-s;-) lawn, grass

ra'send adj raging, raving; wild, mad; (Hunger) ravenous; (Wut) towering; (Tempo) break-neck; **r. werden** see red

Ra'sendecke f turf

Ra'senmäher m lawn mower

Ra'senplatz m lawn

Ra'sensprenger m lawn sprinkler

Raserei [razə'rai] f (-;) rage, madness; (aut) reckless driving

Rasier- [ra'zir] comb.fm. shaving, razor

Rasier'apparat m safety razor

rasieren [ra'zirən] tr & ref shave

Rasier'klinge f razor blade

Rasier'messer n straight razor

Rasier'napf m shaving mug

Rasier'pinsel m shaving brush

Rasier'wasser n after-shave lotion

Rasier'zeug n shaving outfit

Raspel ['raspəl] f (-;-n) rasp; (culin) grater

raspeln ['raspəln] tr rasp; grate

Rasse ['rasə] f (-;-n) race; (Zucht) breed, blood, stock; (fig) good breeding

Rassel ['rasəl] f (-;-n) rattle

rasseln ['rasəln] intr rattle; **durchs Examen r.** (coll) flunk the exam

Rassen- [rasən] comb.fm. racial

Ras'senfrage f racial problem

Ras'senhaß m racism, race hatred

Ras'senkreuzung f miscegenation; crossbreeding

Ras'senkunde f ethnology

ras'senmäßig adj racial

Ras'senmerkmal n racial characteristic

Ras'sentrennung f segregation

Ras'senunruhen pl racial disorders

Ras'sepferd n thoroughbred (horse)

ras'serein adj racially pure; thoroughbred

Ras'sevieh n purebred cattle

rassig ['rasɪç] adj racy; thoroughbred

rassisch ['rasɪ] adj racial

Rast [rast] f (-;-en) rest; station, stage; (mach) notch, groove; (mil) halt; **e-e R. machen** take a rest

rasten ['rastən] intr rest; (mil) halt

rast'los adj restless

Rast'losigkeit f (-;) restlessness

Rast'platz m, **Rast'stätte** f resting place

Rast'tag m day of rest

Rasur [ra'zur] f (-;-en) shave

Rat [rɑt] m (-[e]s; **Ratschläge** ['rɑtʃlɛgə]) advice, piece of advice, counsel; (Beratung) deliberation; (Ausweg) means, solution; **auf e-n Rat hören** listen to reason; **sich** [dat] **keinen Rat mehr wissen** be at one's wits' end; **zu Rate ziehen** consult (a person, dictionary, etc.) || m (-[e]s; -̈e) council, board; (Person) councilor, alderman; advisor; (jur) counsel

Rate ['rɑtə] f (-;-n) installment; **auf Raten** on the installment plan

raten ['rɑtən] §63 tr guess; (Rätsel) solve; **das will ich dir nicht geraten haben!** you had better not!; **geraten!** you guessed it!; **j-m etw r.** advise s.o. about s.th.; **komm nicht wieder. das rate ich dir!** take my advice and don't come back! || intr guess; give advice; (dat) advise; **gut r.** take a good guess; **hin und her r.** make random guesses; **j-m gut r.** give s.o. good advice; **j-m zu etw r.** recommend s.th. to s.o. || **Raten** n (-s;) guesswork; advice

ra'tenweise adv by installments

Ra'tenzahlung f payment in installments; **auf R.** on the installment plan

Räterepublik ['rɛtərepublik] f Soviet Union, Soviet Republic

Rat'geber –in §6 mf adviser, counselor

Rat'haus n city hall

ratifizieren [ratɪfɪ'tsirən] tr ratify

Ratifizie'rung f (-;-en) ratification

Ration [ra'tsjon] f (-;-en) ration

rational [ratsjo'nɑl] adj rational

rationalisieren [ratsjonalɪ'zirən] tr streamline (operations in industry)

rationell [ratsjo'nɛl] adj rational

rationieren [ratsjo'nirən] tr ration

rätlich ['rɛtlɪç] adj advisable

rat'los adj helpless, perplexed

ratsam ['rɑtzam] adj advisable

Ratsche ['rɑtʃə] f (-;-n) rattle; (coll) chatterbox; (tech) ratchet

ratschen ['rɑtʃən] intr make noise with a rattle; (coll) chat

Rat'schlag m advice, piece of advice

rat'schlagen §132 intr deliberate, consult

Rat'schluß m decision, decree, resolution

Rätsel ['rɛtsəl] n (-s;-) puzzle; (fig) riddle, enigma, mystery

rät'selhaft adj puzzling; mysterious

Ratte ['rɑtə] f (-;-n) rat

Rat'tenschwanz m rat tail; (fig) tangle; (coll) whole string (of questions, etc.); (Haarzopf) (coll) pigtail

rattern ['rɑtərn] intr rattle

ratzekahl ['rɑtsə'kɑl] adj (Person)

completely bald; (*Landschaft*) completely barren ‖ *adv* completely

Raub [raup] *m* (-[e]s;) robbery; plunder; (*Beute*) prey, spoils; **zum Raube fallen** fall prey, fall victim

Raub- *comb.fm.* predatory, rapacious

Raub'bau *m* (-[e]s;) excessive exploitation (*of natural resources*)

rauben ['raubən] *tr—j-m etw* r. rob s.o. of s.th.; **e-m Mädchen die Unschuld r.** seduce a girl; **e-n Kuß r.** steal a kiss ‖ *intr* rob

Räuber ['rɔibər] *m* (-s;-) robber; **R. und Gendarm spielen** play cops and robbers

Räu'berbande *f* gang of robbers

Räu'berhauptmann *m* gang leader

räuberisch ['rɔibəriʃ] *adj* predatory

Raub'fisch *m* predatory fish

Raub'gesindel *n* gang of robbers

Raub'lust *f* rapacity

raub'gierig *adj* rapacious

Raub'lust *f* rapacity

Raub'mord *m* murder with robbery

Raub'mörder *m* robber and murderer

Raub'schiff *n* corsair, pirate ship

Raub'tier *n* beast of prey

Raub'überfall *m* holdup, robbery

Raub'vogel *m* bird of prey

Raub'zug *m* plundering raid

Rauch [raux] *m* (-[e]s;) smoke

rauchen ['rauxən] *tr & intr* smoke

Raucher ['rauxər] *m* (-s;-) smoker

Räucher- [rɔixər] *comb.fm.* smoked

Rau'cherabteil *n* smoking section

Räu'cherfaß *n* (eccl) censer

Räu'cherhering *m* smoked herring

Rau'cherhusten *m* cigarette cough

Räu'cherkammer *f* smokehouse

räuchern ['rɔixərn] *tr* smoke, cure; (*desinzieren*) fumigate

Räu'cherschinken *m* smoked ham

Räu'cherung *f* (-;) smoking; fumigation

Rau'cherwagen *m* (rr) smoker

Rauch'fahne *f* trail of smoke

Rauch'fang *m* (*über dem Herd*) hood; (*im Schornstein*) flue

Rauch'fleisch *n* smoked meat

rauchig ['rauxɪç] *adj* smoky

rauch'los *adj* smokeless

Rauch'schleier *m* (mil) smoke screen

Rauch'waren *pl* (*Pelze*) furs; (*Tabakwaren*) tobacco supplies

Räude ['rɔidə] *f* (-;) mange

räudig ['rɔidɪç] *adj* mangy; **räudiges Schaf** (fig) black sheep

Raufbold ['raufbɔlt] *m* (-[e]s;-e) roughneck, bully

Raufe ['raufə] *f* (-;-n) hayrack

raufen ['raufən] *tr* tear, pull out ‖ *recip & intr* fight, brawl, scuffle

Rauferei [raufə'rai] *f* (-;-en) fight, scuffle

Rauf'handel *m* fight, scuffle

rauf'lustig *adj* scrappy, belligerent

rauh [rau] *adj* rough; (*Hals*) hoarse; (*Behandlung*) harsh; **rauhe Wirklichkeit** hard facts

Rauh'bein *n* (fig) roughneck, churl

rauh'beinig *adj* tough, churlish

Rauh'heit *f* (-;) roughness; hoarseness

rauhen ['rau·ən] *tr* roughen

Rauh'futter *n* roughage

rauh'haarig *adj* shaggy, hirsute

Rauh'reif *m* hoarfrost

Raum [raum] *m* (-[e]s;ⁿe) room, space; (*Zimmer*) room; (*Bereich*) area; (*e-s Schiffes*) hold; **am Rande R. lassen** (typ) leave a margin; **freier R.** open space; **gebt R.!** make way! **luftleerer R.** vacuum; **R. bieten für** accommodate; **R. einnehmen** take up space; **R. geben** (dat) give way to; comply with

Raum'anzug *m* space suit

Räumboot ['rɔimbot] *n* minesweeper

Raum'dichte *f* (phys) density by volume

räumen ['rɔimən] *tr* clear; (*Wohnung*) vacate; (*Minen*) sweep; (mil) evacuate; **den Saal r.** clear the room; **das Lager r.** (com) clear out the stock; **j-n aus dem Wege r.** (fig) finish s.o. off

Raum'ersparnis *f* economy of space; **der R. wegen** to save space

Raum'fahrer *m* spaceman

Raum'fahrt *f* space travel

Raum'flug *m* space flight

Raum'gestaltung *f* interior decorating

Raum'inhalt *m* volume, capacity

Raum'kunst *f* interior decorating

Raum'lehre *f* geometry

räumlich ['rɔimlɪç] *adj* spatial

Räum'lichkeit *f* (-;-en) room

Raum'mangel *m* lack of space

Raum'medizin *f* space medicine

Raum'meter *m* cubic meter

Raum'schiff *n* space ship

Raum'schiffart *f* space travel

Raum'schiffkapsel *f* space capsule

Raum'sonde *f* unmanned space explorer

Raum'ton *m* stereophonic sound

Räu'mung *f* (-;-en) clearing, removal; (com) clearance; (mil) evacuation

Räu'mungsausverkauf *m* clearance sale

Räu'mungsbefehl *m* eviction notice; (mil) evacuation order

raunen ['raunən] *tr & intr* whisper

raunzen ['rauntsən] *intr* grumble

Raupe ['raupə] *f* (-;-n) (ent, mach) caterpillar

Rau'penfahrzeug *n* full-track vehicle

Rau'penkette *f* caterpillar track

Rau'penschlepper *m* caterpillar tractor

Rausch [rauʃ] *m* (-es;-e) drunkenness; (fig) intoxication, ecstasy; **e-n R. haben** be drunk; **sich** [dat] **e-n R. antrinken** get drunk

rauschen ['rauʃən] *intr* (*Blätter, Seide*) rustle; (*Bach*) murmur; (*Brandung, Sturm*) roar ‖ *intr* (SEIN) strut; rush

rau'schend *adj* rustling; (*Fest*) uproarious; (*Beifall*) thunderous

Rausch'gift *n* drug, dope

Rausch'gifthandel *m* drug traffic

Rausch'giftschieber –in §6 *mf* pusher

Rausch'giftsucht *f* drug addiction

Rausch'giftsüchtige §5 *mf* dope addict

Rausch'gold *n* tinsel

räuspern ['rɔispərn] *ref* clear one's throat

Rausschmeißer ['rausʃmaisər] *m* (-s;-) (coll) bouncer

Raute ['rautə] *f* (-;-n) (cards) diamond; (geom) rhombus

Rayon [rɛ'jõ] *m* (-s;-s) (*Bezirk*) district, region; (*im Warenhaus*) department

Raz·zia ['ratsja] *f* (-;-zien [tsjən]) police raid

Reagenzglas [re·a'gɛntsglas] *n* test tube

reagieren [re·a'girən] *intr* (auf *acc*) react (to)

Reaktion [re·ak'tsjon] *f* (-;-en) reaction

reaktionär [re·aktsjə'ner] *adj* reactionary ‖ **Reaktionär** *m* (-s;-e) reactionary

Reak·tor [re'aktər] *m* (-s;-toren ['torən]) (phys) reactor

real [re'al] *adj* real

Real'gymnasium *n* high school (*where modern languages, mathematics, or sciences are stressed*)

Realien [re'aljən] *pl* real facts, realities; exact sciences

realisieren [re·alı'zirən] *tr* realize

Realist **-in** [re·a'lıst(ın)] §7 *mf* realist

realistisch [re·a'lıstɪʃ] *adj* realistic

Realität [re·alı'tet] *f* (-;-en) reality; **Realitäten** real property

Real'lexikon *n* encyclopedia

Real'lohn *m* purchasing power of wages

Real'schule *f* non-classical secondary school

Rebe ['rebə] *f* (-;-n) vine; tendril

Rebell [re'bɛl] *m* (-en;-en) rebel

rebellieren [rebɛ'lirən] *intr* rebel

Rebellin [re'bɛlın] *f* (-;-nen) rebel

Rebellion [rebɛl'jon] *f* (-;-en) rebellion

rebellisch [re'bɛlıʃ] *adj* rebellious

Re'bensaft *m* (poet) juice of the grape

Rebhuhn ['rephun] *n* partridge

Rebstock ['rɛpʃtək] *m* vine

rechen ['reçən] *tr* rake ‖ **Rechen** *m* (-s;-) rake; grate

Re'chenaufgabe *f* arithmetic problem

Re'chenautomat *m* computer

Re'chenbrett *n* abacus

Re'chenbuch *n* arithmetic book

Re'chenexemplar *n* arithmetic problem

Re'chenkunst *f* arithmetic

Re'chenmaschine *f* calculator

Re'chenpfennig *m* counter

Re'chenschaft *f* (-;) account; **j-n zur R. ziehen** call s.o. to account

Re'chenschaftsbericht *m* report

Re'chenschieber *m* slide rule

rechnen ['reçnən] *tr* reckon, calculate, figure out ‖ *intr* reckon; calculate; **falsch r.** miscalculate; **r. auf** (*acc*) count on; **r. mit** be prepared for; expect; take into account; **r. zu** be counted among ‖ **Rechnen** *n* (-s;) arithmetic; calculation

Rech'ner *m* (-s;-) calculator, computer; **er ist ein guter R.** he is good at numbers

rechnerisch ['reçnərıʃ] *adj* arithmetical

Rech'nung *f* (-;-en) calculation; account; bill; (*Warenrechnung*) invoice; (*im Restaurant*) check; **auf j-s R. setzen** (or **stellen**) charge to s.o.'s

account; **auf R. kaufen** buy on credit; **auf seine R. kaufen** get one's money's worth; **außer R. lassen** overlook; **das geht auf meine R.** this is on me; **die R. begleichen** settle an account (or bill); **j-m in R. stellen** charge to s.o.'s account; **in R. ziehen** take into account; **R. tragen** (*dat*) make allowance for

Rech'nungsabschluß *m* closing of accounts

Rech'nungsauszug *m* (com) statement

Rech'nungsführer **-in** §6 *mf* accountant

Rech'nungsführung *f* accounting

Rech'nungsjahr *n* fiscal year

Rech'nungsprüfer **-in** §6 *mf* auditor

Rech'nungswesen *n* accounting

recht [reçt] *adj* right; (*richtig*) correct; (*echt*) real; (*gerecht*) all right, right; (*geziemend*) suitable, proper; **es ist mir nicht r.** I don't like it; **es ist schon r.** that's all right; **mir soll's r. sein** I don't mind; **zur rechten Zeit** at the right moment ‖ *adv* right; quite; (*sehr*) very; **das kommt mir gerade r.** that comes in handy; **erst r.** all the more; **es j-m r. machen** please s.o.; **es geschieht ihm r.** it serves him right; **j-m r. geben** agree with s.o.; **nun erst r.** nicht now less than ever; **r. daran tun zu** (*inf*) do right to (*inf*); **r. haben** be right ‖ **Recht** *n* (-[e]s;-e) right; (*Vorrecht*) privilege; (jur) law; **alle Rechte vorbehalten** all rights reserved; **die Rechte studieren** study law; **mit R.** with good reason; **R. sprechen** dispense justice; **sich** [*dat*] **selbst verschaffen** take the law into one's hands; **von Rechts wegen** by rights; **wieder zu seinem Rechte kommen** come into one's own again; **zu R. bestehen** be justified ‖ **Rechte** §5 *mf* right person; **an den Rechten kommen** meet one's match; **du bist der R.!** you're a fine fellow! ‖ *f* right hand; (box) right; **die R.** (pol) the right ‖ *n* right; **er dünkt sich** [*dat*] **was Rechtes** he thinks he's somebody; **nach dem Rechten sehen** look after things

Recht'eck *n* rectangle, oblong

recht'eckig *adj* rectangular

recht'fertigen *tr* justify, vindicate

Recht'fertigung *f* (-;-en) justification

recht'gläubig *adj* orthodox

rechthaberisch ['reçthabərıʃ] *adj* dogmatic

recht'lich *adj* legal, lawful; (*ehrlich*) honest, honorable

Recht'lichkeit *f* (-;) legality; (*Redlichkeit*) honesty

recht'los *adj* without rights

recht'mäßig *adj* legal; legitimate

Recht'mäßigkeit *f* (-;) legality; legitimacy

rechts [reçts] *adv* on the right; right, to the right

Rechts– *comb.fm.* legal

Rechts'angelegenheit *f* legal matter

Rechts'anspruch *m* legal claim

Rechts'anwalt *m* lawyer, attorney

Rechts'ausdruck m legal term
Rechts'auskunft f legal advice
Rechts'außen m (-;-) (fb) right wing
recht'schaffen adj honest
Recht'schaffenheit f (-;) honesty
Recht'schreibung f orthography
Rechts'fall m case, legal case
Rechts'gang m legal procedure
Rechts'gefühl n sense of justice
Rechts'gelehrsamkeit f jurisprudence
Rechts'grund m legal grounds; (An-spruch) title, claim
rechts'gültig adj legal, valid
Rechts'gültigkeit f legality
Rechts'gutachten n legal opinion
Rechts'handel m lawsuit
rechtshändig ['reçtshendɪç] adj right-handed
rechts'herum adv clockwise
Rechts'kraft f legal force
rechts'kräftig adj valid
Rechts'lage f legal status
Rechts'lehre f jurisprudence
Rechts'mittel n legal remedy
Rechts'pflege f administration of justice
Recht'sprechung f (-;) administration of justice; die R. (coll) the judiciary
Rechts'schutz m legal protection
Rechts'spruch m verdict
Rechts'streit m legal dispute; pending case; difference of opinion in the interpretation of the law
rechtsum' interj (mil) right face!
rechts'ungültig adj illegal, invalid
rechts'verbindlich adj legally binding
Rechtsverdreher -in ['reçtsferdre-ər(ɪn)] §6 mf pettifogger
Rechts'verletzung f (-;-en) violation of the law; infringement of another's rights
Rechts'weg m recourse to the law; auf dem Rechtswege by the courts; den R. beschreiten take legal action
Rechts'wissenschaft f jurisprudence
Reck [rek] n (-[e]s;-e) horizontal bar
recken ['rekən] tr stretch; den Hals r. crane one's neck
Redakteur [redak'tør] m (-s;-e) editor
Redaktion [redak'tsjon] f (-;-en) editorship; (Arbeitskräfte) editorial staff; (Arbeitsraum) editorial office
redaktionell [redaktsjo'nel] adj editorial
Redaktions'schluß m press time, deadline
Rede ['redə] f (-;-n) speech; (Ge-spräch) conversation; (Gerücht) rumor; das ist nicht der R. wert that is not worth mentioning; davon kann keine R. sein that's out of the question; die in R. stehende Person the person in question; e-e R. halten give a speech; es geht die R., daß it is rumored that; gebundene R. verse; gehobene R. lofty language; j-m in die R. fallen interrupt s.o.; j-m R. und Antwort stehen explain oneself to s.o.; j-n zur R. stellen take s.o. to task; keine R.! absolutely not!; lose Reden führen engage in loose talk; ungebundene R. prose

Re'defigur f figure of speech
Re'defluß m flow of words
Re'defreiheit f freedom of speech
Re'degabe f eloquence, fluency
re'degewandt adj fluent; (iron) glib
Re'degewandtheit f fluency, eloquence
Re'dekunst f eloquence
reden ['redən] tr speak, talk ‖ ref—mit sich r. lassen listen to reason; sich heiser r. talk oneself hoarse; von sich r. machen cause a lot of talk ‖ intr speak, talk; converse; du hast gut r.! it's easy for you to talk; j-m ins Gewissen r. appeal to s.o.'s conscience; j-m nach dem Munde r. humor s.o.; mit j-m deutsch r. (fig) talk turkey to s.o.
Re'densart f phrase, expression; idiom
Rederei [redə'raɪ] f (-;-en) empty talk
Re'deschwall m verbosity
Re'deteil m part of speech
Re'deweise f style of speaking
Re'dewendung f phrase, expression
redigieren [redi'girən] tr edit
redlich ['retlɪç] adj upright, honest ‖ adv—es r. meinen mean well; sich r. bemühen make an honest effort
Red'lichkeit f (-;) honesty, integrity
Redner -in ['rednər(ɪn)] §6 mf speaker
Red'nerbühne f podium, platform
Red'nergabe f (gift of) eloquence
rednerisch ['rednərɪʃ] adj rhetorical
Redoute [re'dutə] f (-;-n) masquerade; (mil) redoubt
redselig ['retzelɪç] adj talkative
Reduktion [reduk'tsjon] f (-;-en) reduction
reduplizieren [redupli'tsirən] tr reduplicate
reduzieren [redu'tsirən] tr (auf acc) reduce (to)
Reede ['redə] f (-;-n) (naut) roadstead
Reeder ['redər] m (-s;-) shipowner
Reederei [redə'raɪ] f (-;-en) shipping company; shipping business
reell [re'el] adj honest; (Preis) fair; (Geschäft) sound ‖ adv—r. bedient werden get one's money's worth
Reep [rep] n (-[e]s;-e) (naut) rope
Referat [refə'rat] n (-[e]s;-e) report; (Vortrag) paper; ein R. halten give a paper
Referendar [referen'dar] m (-s;-e) junior lawyer; in-service teacher
Referent -in [refe'rent(ɪn)] §7 mf reader of a paper; (Berichterstatter) reporter; (Gutachter) official adviser
Referenz [refe'rents] f (-;-en) reference; j-n als R. angeben give s.o. as a reference; über gute Referenzen verfügen have good references
referieren [refe'rirən] intr (über acc) give a report (on); (über acc) read a paper (on)
reffen ['refən] tr (naut) reef
reflektieren [reflek'tirən] tr reflect ‖ intr reflect; r. auf (acc) reflect on; (com) think of buying
Reflek-tor [re'flektor] m (-s;-toren ['torən]) reflector
Reflex [re'fleks] m (-es;-e) reflex
Reflex'bewegung f reflex action

Reflexion [refle'ksjon] *f* (-;-en) re-
flection
reflexiv [refle'ksif] *adj* reflexive
Reform [re'fɔrm] *f* (-;-en) reform
Reformation [refɔrma'tsjon] *f* (-;-en)
reformation
Refor·mator [refɔr'matɔr] *m* (-s;
[ma'torən]) reformer
Reform'haus *n* health-food store
reformieren [refɔr'mirən] *tr* reform
Reform'kost *f* health food
Refrain [rə'frɛ̃] *m* (-s;-s) refrain; **den
R. mitsingen** join in the refrain
Regal [re'gal] *n* (-s;-e) shelf
Regat·ta [re'gata] *f* (-;-ten [tən])
regatta
rege ['regə] *adj* brisk, lively
Regel ['regəl] *f* (-;-n) rule, regulation; (pathol) menstruation; **in der
R. as a rule**
re'gellos *adj* irregular; disorderly
Re'gellosigkeit *f* (-;-en) irregularity
re'gelmäßig *adj* regular
Re'gelmäßigkeit *f* regularity
regeln ['regəln] *tr* regulate; arrange;
control
re'gelrecht *adj* regular; downright
Re'gelung *f* (-;-en) regulation; control
re'gelwidrig *adj* against the rules;
(sport) foul
regen ['regən] *tr* & *ref* move, stir ‖
Regen *m* (-s;-) rain; **vom R. unter
die Traufe kommen** jump out of the
frying pan into the fire
re'genarm *adj* rainless, dry
Re'genbö *f* rain squall
Re'genbogen *m* rainbow
Re'genbogenhaut *f* (anat) iris
re'gendicht *adj* rainproof
Re'genfall *m* rainfall
re'genfest *adj* rainproof
Re'genguß *m* downpour
Re'genhaut *f* oilskin coat
Re'genmantel *m* raincoat
Re'genmenge *f* amount of rainfall
Re'genmesser *m* rain gauge
Re'genpfeifer *m* (orn) plover
Re'genschauer *m* shower
Re'genschirm *m* umbrella
Regent -in [re'gent(ɪn)] §7 *mf* regent
Re'gentag *m* rainy day
Re'gentropfen *m* raindrop
Re'genumhang *m* cape
Re'genwetter *n* rainy weather
Re'genwurm *m* earthworm
Re'genzeit *f* rainy season
Re·gie [re'ʒi] *f* (-;-gien ['ʒi·ən]) man-
agement, administration; (com) state
monopoly; (cin, theat) direction
Regie'assistent -in §7 *mf* (cin, theat)
assistant director
Regie'pult *n* (rad) control console
Regie'raum *m* (rad) control room
regieren [re'girən] *tr* govern, rule;
(gram) govern, take ‖ *intr* reign;
(fig) predominate
Regie'rung *f* (-;-en) government, rule;
administration; reign
Regie'rungsanleihe *f* government loan
Regie'rungsantritt *m* accession
Regie'rungsbeamte §5 *m* government
official
Regie'rungssitz *m* seat of government

Regie'rungszeit *f* reign; administration
Regime [re'ʒim] *n* (-s;-s) regime
Regiment [regi'mɛnt] *n* (-[e]s;-e)
rule, government ‖ *n* (-[e]s;-er)
(mil) regiment
Regiments- *comb.fm.* regimental
Regiments'kommandeur *m* regimental
commander
Region [re'gjon] *f* (-;-en) region
regional [regjo'nal] *adj* regional
Regisseur [reʒɪ'sør] *m* (-s;-e) (cin,
theat) director
Register [re'gɪstər] *n* (-s;-) file clerk;
(Inhaltsverzeichnis) index; (Orgel-)
stop
Regi·strator [regɪs'tratɔr] *m* (-s;
-stratoren [stra'torən]) registrar
Registratur [regɪstra'tur] *f* (-;-en)
filing; filing cabinet
registrieren [regɪs'trirən] *tr* register;
(Betrag) ring up
Registrier'kasse *f* cash register
Registrie'rung *f* (-;-en) registration
Reglement [reglə'mã] *n* (-s;-s) regu-
lation(s), rule(s)
Regler ['reglər] *m* (-s;-) regulator;
(mach) governor
reglos ['reklos] *adj* motionless
regnen ['regnən] *impers*—**es regnet** it
is raining; **es regnet Bindfäden** it's
raining cats and dogs; **es regnete
Püffe** blows came thick and fast
regnerisch ['regnərɪʃ] *adj* rainy
Re·greß [re'gres] *m* (-gresses;-gresse)
recourse, remedy; **R. nehmen zu**
have recourse to
regsam ['rekzam] *adj* lively; quick
regulär [regu'ler] *adj* regular
regulierbar [regu'lirbar] *adj* adjustable
regulieren [regu'lirən] *tr* regulate; adjust
Regung ['regun] *f* (-;-en) motion,
stirring; emotion; impulse
Reh [re] *n* (-[e]s;-e) deer
rehabilitieren [rehabɪlɪ'tirən] *tr* rehabilitate
Rehabilitie'rung *f* (-;-en) rehabilitation
Reh'bock *m* roebuck
Reh'braten *m* roast venison
Reh'kalb *n* fawn
Reh'keule *f* leg of venison
Rehkitz ['rekɪts] *n* (-es;-e) fawn
Reh'leder *n* doeskin
Reibahle ['raɪpalə] *f* (-;-n) reamer
Reibe ['raɪbə] *f* (-;-n) (coll) grater
Reibeisen ['raɪpaɪzən] *n* (culin) grater
reiben ['raɪbən] §62 *tr* rub; grate;
grind ‖ *ref*—**sich r. an** (*dat*) take
offense at ‖ *intr* rub
Reiberei [raɪbə'raɪ] *f* (-;-en) (coll)
friction, squabble
Rei'bung *f* (-;-en) friction
rei'bungslos *adj* frictionless; (fig)
smooth
reich [raɪç] *adj* wealthy; (**an** *dat*) rich
(in); (Fang) big; (Phantasie) fertile;
(Mahlzeit) lavish ‖ **Reich** *n* (-[e]s;
-e) empire, realm; kingdom
reichen ['raɪçən] *tr* reach; hand, pass
‖ *intr* reach, extend; do, manage;
das reicht! that will do!
reich'haltig *adj* rich; abundant

reich'lich adj plentiful, abundant || adv pretty, fairly
Reichs'kanzlei f chancellery
Reichs'kanzler m chancellor
Reichs'mark f reichsmark
Reichs'tag m (hist) diet; (hist) Reichstag (lower house)
Reichtum ['raiçtum] n (-s;⸗er) riches
Reich'weite f reach, range
reif [raif] adj ripe; (fig) mature || **Reif** m (-[e]s;) frost
Reife ['raifə] f (-;-) ripeness; (fig) maturity
reifen ['raifən] intr (SEIN) ripen; mature || impers—es reift there is frost || **Reifen** m (-s;-) tire; hoop
Rei'fendruckmesser m tire gauge
Rei'fenpanne f, **Rei'fenschaden** m flat tire, blowout
Rei'feprüfung f final examination (as prerequisite for entering university)
Rei'fezeugnis n high school diploma
reif'lich adj careful
Reigen ['raigən] m (-s;-) square dance
Reihe ['rai-ə] f (-;-n) row, string; set, series; rank, file; turn; **an der R. sein** be next; **an die R. kommen** get one's turn; **aus der R. tanzen** (fig) go one's own way; **die R. ist an mir** it's my turn; **nach der R.** in succession
reihen ['rai-ən] tr range, rank; (Perlen) string
Rei'hendorf n one-street village
Rei'henfabrikation f assembly-line production
Rei'henfolge f succession, sequence
Rei'henhaus n row house
Rei'henschaltung f (elec) series connection
reih'enweise adv in rows
Reiher ['rai-ər] m (-s;-) heron
Reim [raim] m (-[e]s;-e) rhyme
reimen ['raimən] tr (auf acc) make rhyme (with) || ref rhyme; (fig) make sense; (auf acc) rhyme (with) || intr rhyme
reim'los adj unrhymed, blank
rein [rain] adj pure; (sauber) clean; (klar) clear; (Gewinn) net; (Wahrheit) simple; (Wahnsinn) sheer, absolute; **etw ins reine bringen** clear up s.th.; **etw ins reine schreiben** write (or type) a final copy of s.th.; **mit j-m ins reine kommen** come to an understanding with s.o. || adv quite, downright; **r. alles** almost everything || **Rein** f (-;-en) pan
Reindl ['raindəl] n (-s; & -n) pan
Rei'nemachen n (-s;) housecleaning
Rein'ertrag m clear profit
Rein'fall m flop, disappointment
Rein'gewicht n net weight
Rein'gewinn m net profit
reinigen ['rainigən] tr clean, cleanse; (fig) purify, refine
Rei'nigung f (-;-en) cleaning; purification; dry cleaning
Rei'nigungsanstalt f dry cleaner's
Rei'nigungsmittel n cleaning agent
Reinmachefrau ['rainmaxəfrau] f cleaning woman
Rein'schrift f final copy

reinweg ['rain'vɛk] adv (coll) flatly, absolutely
rein'wollen adj all-wool
Reis [rais] m (-es;) rice || n (-es;-er) twig; (fig) scion
Reis'brei m rice pudding
Reise ['raizə] f (-;-n) trip, tour; (aer) flight; (naut) voyage; **auf der R.** while traveling; **auf Reisen sein** be traveling
Rei'sebericht m travelogue
Rei'sebeschreibung f travel book
rei'sefertig adj ready to leave
Rei'sebüro n travel agency
Rei'seführer m guidebook
Rei'segefährte m, **Rei'segefährtin** f travel companion
Rei'segenehmigung f travel permit
Rei'segepäck n luggage; (rr) baggage
Rei'segesellschaft f tour operator(s); travel group
Rei'sehandbuch n guidebook
Rei'seleiter –in §6 mf courier, guide
rei'selustig adj fond of traveling
reisen ['raizən] intr (SEIN) travel
Reisende ['raizəndə] §5 mf traveler
Rei'sepaß m passport
Rei'seplan m itinerary
Rei'seprospekt m travel folder
Rei'seroute f itinerary
Rei'sescheck m traveler's check
Rei'seschreibmaschine f portable typewriter
Rei'sespesen pl travel expenses
Rei'setasche f overnight bag, flight bag
Rei'seziel n destination
Reisig ['raiziç] n (-s;) brushwood
Rei'sigbündel n faggot
Reisige ['raizigə] §5 m cavalryman
Reißaus [rais'aus] n—**R. nehmen** (coll) take to one's heels
Reißbrett ['raisbret] n drawing board
reißen ['raisən] §53 tr tear, rip; (ziehen) pull, yank; (wegschnappen) wrest, snatch || intr tear; pull, tug; break, snap; (sich spalten) split, burst; **das reißt ins Geld** this is running into money; **mir reißt die Geduld** I am losing all patience || ref—**an sich r.** seize; (com) monopolize; **die Führung an sich r.** take the lead; **sich an e-m Nagel r.** scratch oneself on a nail; **sich um etw r.** scramble for s.th. || **Reißen** n (-s;) tearing; bursting; sharp pains; rheumatism
rei'ßend adj rapid; (Schmerz) sharp; (Tier) rapacious; **reißenden Absatz finden** (coll) sell like hotcakes
Reißer ['raisər] m (-s;-) bestseller; (cin) box-office hit; (com) good seller
Reißfeder ['raisfedər] f drawing pen
Reißleine ['raislainə] f rip cord
Reißnagel ['raisnagəl] m thumbtack
Reißschiene ['rais'inə] f T-square
Reißverschluß ['raisfer/lus] m zipper
Reißzahn ['raistsan] m canine tooth
Reißzeug ['raistsɔrk] n mechanical-drawing tools
Reißzwecke ['raistsvekə] f thumbtack
Reit- [rait] comb.fm. riding
Reit'anzug m riding habit

Reit′bahn f riding ring

reiten [′raɪtən] §86 tr ride; **e–n Weg r.** ride along a road; **ihn reitet der Teufel** (coll) he is full of the devil; **krumme Touren r.** (coll) pull shady deals; **Prinzipien r.** (fig) stick rigidly to principles; **über den Haufen r.** knock down || intr (SEIN) go horseback riding; **geritten kommen** come on horseback; **vor Anker r.** ride at anchor

Rei′ter –in §6 mf rider

Rei′terstandbild n equestrian statue

Reit′gerte f riding crop

Reit′hose f riding breeches

Reit′knecht m groom

Reit′kunst f horsemanship

Reit′peitsche f riding crop

Reit′pferd n saddle horse

Reit′schule f riding academy

Reit′stiefel m riding boot

Reit′weg m bridle path

Reiz [raɪts] m (–es;–e) charm, appeal; (Erregung) irritation; (physiol, psychol) stimulus; **e–n R. ausüben auf** (acc) attract; **sie läßt ihre Reize spielen** she turns on the charm

reizbar [′raɪtsbɑr] adj irritable; (empfindlich) sensitive, touchy

reizen [′raɪtsən] tr (entzünden, ärgern) irritate; (locken) allure; (anziehen) attract; (anregen) excite, stimulate; (aufreizen) provoke; (Appetit) whet || intr (cards) bid || impers—**es reizt mich zu** (inf) I'm itching to (inf)

rei′zend adj charming; cute, sweet; (pathol) irritating

Reiz′entzug m sensory deprivation

Reiz′husten m (–s;) constant cough

reiz′los adj unattractive; (Kost) bland

Reiz′mittel n stimulant; (fig) incentive

Reiz′stoff m irritant

Rei′zung f (–;–en) irritation; (Lockung) allurement; (Anregung) stimulation; (Aufreizung) provocation

reiz′voll adj charming, attractive; fascinating; (verlockend) tempting

rekeln [′rekəln] ref (coll) lounge

Reklamation [reklama′tsjon] f (–;–en) complaint, protest

Reklame [re′klamə] f (–;–n) advertisement, ad; publicity; **R. machen für** advertise

Rekla′mebüro n advertising agency

Rekla′mefeldzug m advertising campaign

reklamieren [rekla′mirən] tr claim || intr (gegen) protest (against); (wegen) complain (about)

rekognoszieren [rekɔs′tsirən] tr & intr reconnoiter

Rekonvaleszent –in [rekɔnvales′tsent (ɪn)] §7 mf convalescent

Rekonvaleszenz [rekɔnvales′tsents] f (–;) convalescence

Rekord [re′kɔrt] m (–[e]s;–e) record

Rekord′ernte f bumper crop, record crop

Rekordler –in [re′kɔrtlər(ɪn)] §6 mf (coll) record holder

Rekord′versuch m attempt to break the record

Rekrut [re′krut] m (–en;–en) recruit

Rekru′tenausbildung f basic training

Rekru′tenaushebung f recruitment

rekrutieren [rekru′tirən] tr recruit || ref—**sich r. aus** be recruited from

Rek·tor [′rektɔr] m (–s;–toren [′torən]) principal; (e–r Universität) president

Relais [rə′le] n (–lais [′le(s)];–lais [′les]) relay

relativ [rela′tif] adj relative

Relegation [relega′tsjon] f (–;–en) expulsion

relegieren [rele′girən] tr expel

Relief [re′ljef] n (–s;–s & –e) relief

Religion [reli′gjon] f (–;–en) religion

Religions′ausübung f practice of religion

Religions′bekenntnis n religious denomination

religiös [reli′gjøs] adj religious

Reling [′relɪŋ] f (–s;–s) (naut) rail

Reliquie [re′likvjə] f (–;–n) relic

Reli′quienschrein m reliquary

remis [rə′mi] adj (cards) tied || **Remis** n (–;–) (chess) tie, draw

remittieren [remi′tirən] tr (Geld) remit; (Waren) return || intr (Fieber) go down

rempeln [′rempəln] tr bump, jostle || intr (fb) block

Remter [′remtər] m (–s;–) refectory; assembly hall

Ren [ren] n (–s;–e) reindeer

Renaissance [rənɛ′sɑ̃s] f (–;–n) renaissance

Rendite [ren′ditə] f (–;–n) return

Renn– [ren] comb.fm. race, racing

Renn′bahn f race track; (aut) speedway

Renn′boot n racing boat

rennen [′renən] §97 tr run; **j–m den Degen durch den Leib r.** run s.o. through with a sword; **über den Haufen r.** run over; **zu Boden r.** knock down || intr (SEIN) run; race || **Rennen** n (–s;–) running; race; (Einzelrennen) heat; **das R. machen** win the race; **totes R.** dead heat, tie

Ren′ner m (–s;–) (good) race horse

Renn′fahrer m (aut) race driver

Renn′pferd n race horse

Renn′platz m race track; (aut) speedway

Renn′rad n racing bicycle, racer

Renn′sport m racing

Renn′strecke f race track; distance (to be raced); (aut) speedway

Renn′wagen m racing car, racer

Renommee [renɔ′me] n (–s;–s) reputation

renommieren [renɔ′mirən] intr (mit) brag (about), boast (about)

renommiert′ adj (wegen) renowned (for)

Renommist [renɔ′mɪst] m (–en;–en) braggart

renovieren [renɔ′virən] tr renovate; redecorate

rentabel [ren′tɑbəl] adj profitable

Rentabilität [rentabɪlɪ′tet] f (–;–en) (e–r Investition) return; (fin) productiveness

Rente ['rentə] _f_ (-;-n) income, revenue; pension; annuity
Ren'tenbrief _m_ annuity bond
Ren'tenempfänger **–in** §6 _mf_ pensioner
Rentier [ren'tje] _m_ (-s;-s) person of independent means ‖ ['rentir] _n_ (-s; -s;) reindeer
rentieren [ren'tirən] _ref_ pay
Rentner **–in** ['rentnər(ɪn)] §6 _mf_ person on pension
Reparatur [repara'tur] _f_ (-;-en) repair
Reparatur'werkstatt _f_ repair shop; (aut) garage
reparieren [repa'rirən] _tr_ repair, fix
Reportage [repor'taʒə] _f_ (-;-n) report; coverage
Reporter **–in** [re'portər(ɪn)] §6 _mf_ reporter
Repräsentant **–in** [reprezen'tant(ɪn)] §7 _mf_ representative
repräsentieren [reprezen'tirən] _tr_ represent ‖ _intr_ be a socialite
Repressalie [repre'saljə] _f_ (-;-n) reprisal
Reprise [re'prizə] _f_ (-;-n) (cin) rerun; (mus) repeat; (theat) revival
reproduzieren [reprodu'tsirən] _tr_ reproduce
Reptil [rep'til] _n_ (-s;-ien [jən] & –e) reptile
Republik [repu'blik] _f_ (-;-en) republic
Republikaner **–in** [republi'kanər(ɪn)] §6 _mf_ republican
republikanisch [republi'kanɪʃ] _adj_ republican
Requisit [rekvi'zit] _n_ (-[e]s;-en) requisite; **Requisiten** (theat) props
Reservat [rezer'vat] _n_ (-[e]s;-e) reservation
Reserve [re'zervə] _f_ (-;-n) reserve
Reser'vebank _f_ (-;-e) (sport) bench
Reser'vereifen _m_ spare tire
Reser'veteil _n_ spare part
Reser'vetruppen _pl_ (mil) reserves
reservieren [rezer'virən] _tr_ reserve
Reservie'rung _f_ (-;-en) reservation
Residenz [rezi'dents] _f_ (-;-en) residence
Residenz'stadt _f_ capital
residieren [rezi'dirən] _intr_ reside
resignieren [rezig'nirən] _intr_ resign
Respekt [re'spekt] _m_ (-[e]s;) respect
respektabel [respek'tabəl] _adj_ respectable
respektieren [respek'tirən] _tr_ respect
respekt'los _adj_ disrespectful
respekt'voll _adj_ respectful
Ressort [re'sor] _n_ (-s;-s) department
Rest [rest] _m_ (-es;-e & -er) rest; (Stoff-) remnant; (Zahlungs-) balance; (Bodensatz) residue; (math) remainder; **irdische** (or **sterbliche**) **Reste** earthly (or mortal) remains; **j–m den R. geben** (coll) finish s.o. off
Rest'auflage _f_ remainders
Restaurant [resto'rã] _n_ (-s;-s) restaurant
Restauration [restaura'tsjon] _f_ (-;-en) restoration; (Aust) restaurant
Rest'bestand _m_ remainder
Rest'betrag _m_ balance, remainder
Re'steverkauf _m_ remnant sale

rest'lich _adj_ remaining
rest'los _adj_ complete
Resultat [rezul'tat] _n_ (-[e]s;-e) result; upshot; (sport) score
retten ['retən] _tr_ save, rescue
Ret'ter _m_ (-s;-) rescuer; (Heiland) Savior
Rettich ['retɪç] _m_ (-s;-e) radish
Ret'tung _f_ (-;-en) rescue; salvation
Ret'tungsaktion _f_ rescue operation
Ret'tungsboot _n_ lifeboat
Ret'tungsfloß _n_ life raft
Ret'tungsgürtel _m_ life preserver
Ret'tungsleine _f_ life line
ret'tungslos _adj_ irretrievable
Ret'tungsmannschaft _f_ rescue party
Ret'tungsring _m_ life preserver
Ret'tungsstation _f_ first-aid station
retuschieren [retu'ʃirən] _tr_ retouch
Reue ['rɔiə] _f_ (-;) remorse
reu'elos _adj_ remorseless, impenitent
reuen ['rɔiən] _tr_—**die Tat reut mich** I regret having done it; **die Zeit reut mich** I regret wasting the time ‖ _impers_—**es reut mich, daß** I regret that, I am sorry that
reu'evoll _adj_ repentant, contrite
Reugeld ['rɔigelt] _n_ forfeit
reumütig ['rɔimytɪç] _adj_ repentant
Revanche [re'vã/ə] _f_ (-;) revenge
Revan'chekrieg _m_ punitive war
revan'chelustig _adj_ vengeful
Revan'chepartie _f_ (sport) return game
revanchieren [revã'ʃirən] _ref_ (an dat) take revenge (on); **sich für e–en Dienst r.** return a favor
Revers [re'vers] _m_ (-es;-e) (e–r Münze) reverse; (Erklärung) statement ‖ [re'ver] _m_ (Aust) & _n_ (-;-) lapel; cuff
revidieren [revi'dirən] _tr_ revise; (nachprüfen) check; (com) audit
Revier [re'vir] _n_ (-s;-e) district; quarter; hunting ground; police station; (mil) sick quarters
Revier'stube _f_ (mil) sickroom
Revision [revi'zjon] _f_ (-;-en) revision; (com) audit; (jur) appeal
Re'visor [re'vizor] _m_ (-s;-visoren [vi'zorən]) reviser; (com) auditor
Revolte [re'voltə] _f_ (-;-n) revolt
revoltieren [revol'tirən] _intr_ revolt
Revolution [revolu'tsjon] _f_ (-;-en) revolution
revolutionär [revolutsjo'ner] _adj_ revolutionary ‖ **Revolutionär** **–in** §8 _mf_ revolutionary
Revolver [re'volvər] _m_ (-s;-) revolver
Revol'verblatt _n_ (coll) scandal sheet
Revol'verschnauze _f_ (coll) lip, sass
Re-vue [re'vy] _f_ (-;-vuen ['vy·ən]) review; (theat) revue
Rezensent **–in** [retsen'zent(ɪn)] §7 _mf_ reviewer, critic
rezensieren [retsen'zirən] _tr_ review
Rezension [retsen'zjon] _f_ (-;-en) review
Rezept [re'tsept] _n_ (-[e]s;-e) (culin) recipe; (med) prescription
rezitieren [retsi'tirən] _tr_ recite
Rhabarber [ra'barbər] _m_ (-s;) rhubarb
Rhapso·die [rapso'di] _f_ (-;-dien ['di·ən]) rhapsody

Rhein [raɪn] *m* (-[e]s;) Rhine
Rhesusfaktor [ˈrezusfaktɔr] *m* (-s;) Rh factor
Rhetorik [reˈtoːrɪk] *f* (-;) rhetoric
rhetorisch [reˈtoːrɪʃ] *adj* rhetorical
rheumatisch [rɔɪˈmaːtɪʃ] *adj* rheumatic
Rheumatismus [rɔɪmaˈtɪsmus] *m* (-;) rheumatism
rhythmisch [ˈrʏtmɪʃ] *adj* rhythmical
Rhyth·mus [ˈrʏtmus] *m* (-;-men [mən]) rhythm
Richtbeil [ˈrɪçtbaɪl] *n* executioner's ax
Richtblei [ˈrɪçtblaɪ] *n* plummet
richten [ˈrɪçtən] *tr* arrange, adjust; put in order; (*lenken*) direct; (*Waffe, Fernrohr*) (*auf acc*) point (at), aim (at); (*Bitte, Brief, Frage, Rede*) (*an acc*) address (to); (*Augenmerk, Streben*) (*auf acc*) concentrate (on), focus (on); (*Bett*) make; (*Essen*) prepare; (*ausbessern*) fix; (*gerade biegen*) straighten; (*jur*) judge, sentence; (*mil*) dress; **zugrunde r.** ruin || *ref* (*auf acc, gegen*) be directed (at); **das richtet sich ganz danach, ob** it all depends on whether; **sich** [*dat*] **die Haare r.** do one's hair; **sich r. nach** follow the example of; **sich selbst r.** commit suicide || *intr* judge, sit in judgment
Rich'ter *m* (-s;-) judge
Rich'teramt *n* judgeship
Rich'terin *f* (-;-nen) judge
Rich'terkollegium *n* (jur) bench
rich'terlich *adj* judicial
Rich'terspruch *m* judgment; sentence
Rich'terstand *m* judiciary
Rich'terstuhl *m* tribunal, bench
richtig [ˈrɪçtɪç] *adj* right, correct; (*echt*) real, genuine; (*genau*) exact; (*Zeit*) proper || *adv* right, really, downright; **die Uhr geht r.** the clock keeps good time; **und r., da kam sie!** and sure enough, there she was!
rich'tiggehend *adj* (*Uhr*) keeping good time; (fig) regular
Rich'tigkeit *f* (-;) correctness; accuracy
rich'tigstellen *tr* rectify
Richtlinien [ˈrɪçtliːniən] *pl* guidelines
Richtlot [ˈrɪçtloːt] *n* plumbline
Richtmaß [ˈrɪçtmaːs] *n* standard, gauge
Richtplatz [ˈrɪçtplats] *m* place of execution
Richtpreis [ˈrɪçtpraɪs] *m* standard price
Richtschnur [ˈrɪçtʃnuːr] *f* plumbline; (fig) guiding principle
Richtschwert [ˈrɪçtveːrt] *n* executioner's sword
Richtstätte [ˈrɪçtʃtɛtə] *f* place of execution
Rich'tung *f* (-;-en) direction; (*Weg*) course; (*Entwicklung*) trend; (*Einstellung*) slant, view
Rich'tungszeiger *m* (aut) direction signal
Richtwaage [ˈrɪçtvaːgə] *f* level
rieb [riːp] *pret* of **reiben**
riechen [ˈriːçən] §102 *tr* smell; (fig) stand; **kein Pulver r. können** have no guts || *intr* smell; **r. an** (*dat*) sniff at; **r. nach** smell of
Riechsalz [ˈriːçzalts] *n* smelling salts

rief [riːf] *pret* of **rufen**
Riefe [ˈriːfə] *f* (-;-n) groove; (archit) flute
Riege [ˈriːgə] *f* (-;-n) (gym) squad
Riegel [ˈriːgəl] *m* (-s;-) bolt; (*Seife*) cake; (*Schokolade*) bar
riegeln [ˈriːgəln] *tr* bolt, bar
Riemen [ˈriːmən] *m* (-s;-) strap; (*Leib-, Trieb-*) belt; (*Ruder*) oar; (*e-s Gewehrs*) sling
Rie'menscheibe *f* pulley
Ries [riːs] *n* (-es;-e) ream (*of one thousand sheets*)
Riese [ˈriːzə] *m* (-;-n) giant
rieseln [ˈriːzəln] *intr* (HABEN & SEIN) trickle; (*Bach*) purl || *impers*—**es rieselt** it is drizzling
Rie'selregen *m* drizzle
Rie'senbomber *m* superbomber
Rie'senerfolg *m* smash hit
rie'sengroß *adj* gigantic
rie'senhaft *adj* gigantic
Rie'senrad *n* Ferris wheel
Rie'senschlange *f* boa constrictor
Rie'sentanne *f* (bot) sequoia
riesig [ˈriːzɪç] *adj* gigantic, huge || *adv* (coll) awfully
Riesin [ˈriːzɪn] *f* (-;-nen) giant
riet [riːt] *pret* of **raten**
Riff [rɪf] *n* (-[e]s;-e) reef
Rille [ˈrɪlə] *f* (-;-n) groove; small furtow; (archit) flute
Rimesse [rɪˈmɛsə] *f* (-;-n) (com) remittance
Rind [rɪnt] *n* (-[e]s;-er) head of cattle; **Rinder** cattle
Rinde [ˈrɪndə] *f* (-;-n) rind; (*Baum-*) bark; (*Brot-*) crust; (anat) cortex
Rin'derbraten *m* roast beef
Rin'derbremse *f* horsefly
Rin'derherde *f* herd of cattle
Rin'derhirt *m* cowboy
Rind'fleisch *n* beef
Rinds'leder *n* cowhide
Rinds'lendenstück *n* rump steak, tenderloin
Rinds'rückenstück *n* sirloin of beef
Rind'vieh *n* cattle; (sl) idiot
Ring [rɪŋ] *m* (-[e]s;-e) ring; (*Kreis*) circle; (*Kettenglied*) link; (*Kartell*) combine; (astr) halo
Ringel [ˈrɪŋəl] *m* (-s;) small ring; (*Locke*) ringlet, curl
Rin'gelblume *f* marigold
ringeln [ˈrɪŋəln] *tr* & *ref* curl
Rin'gelreihen *m* ring-around-the-rosy
Rin'gelspiel *n* merry-go-round
ringen [ˈrɪŋən] §142 *tr* wrestle; (*Wäsche, Hände*) wring; (*herauswinden*) wrest || *intr* wrestle; (fig) struggle
Rin'ger -in §6 *mf* wrestler
Ring'kampf *m* wrestling match
Ring'mauer *f* town wall, city wall
Ring'richter *m* (box) referee
rings [rɪŋs] *adv* around; **r. um all** around
Ring'schlüssel *m* socket wrench
rings'herum', **rings'um'**, **rings'umher'** *adv* all around
Rinne [ˈrɪnə] *f* (-;-n) groove; (*Strombett*) channel; (*Leitung*) duct; (*Gosse*) gutter; (*Erdfurche*) furrow

rinnen ['rınən] §121 *intr* (SEIN) run, flow; trickle ‖ *intr* (HABEN) leak

Rinnsal ['rɪnzal] *n* (-[e]s;-e) little stream

Rinn'stein *m* gutter; (*Ausgußbecken*) sink; (*unterirdisch*) culvert

Rippchen ['rɪpçən] *n* (-s;-) cutlet

Rippe ['rɪpə] *f* (-;-n) rib; (*Schokolade*) bar; (archit) groin

rippen ['rɪpən] *tr* rib, flute

Rip'penfellentzündung *f* pleurisy

Rip'penstoß *m* nudge (in the ribs)

Rip'penstück *n* loin end

Risi·ko ['rɪziko] *n* (-s;-s & -ken [kən]) risk; **ein R. eingehen** take a risk

riskant [rɪs'kant] *adj* risky

riskieren [rɪs'kirən] *tr* risk

riß [rɪs] *pret of* **reißen** ‖ **Riß** *m* (Risses; Risse) tear, rip; (*Bruch*) fracture; (*Lücke*) gap; (*Kratzer*) scratch; (*Spalt*) split, cleft; (*Spaltung*) fissure; (*Sprung*) crack; (*Zeichnung*) sketch; (eccl) schism; (geol) crevasse

rissig ['rɪsɪç] *adj* torn; cracked; split; (*Haut*) chapped

Rist [rɪst] *m* (-es;-e) wrist; (*des Fußes*) instep

ritt [rɪt] *pret of* **reiten** ‖ **Ritt** *m* (-[e]s; -e) ride

Ritter ['rɪtər] *m* (-s;-) knight; cavalier; **zum R. schlagen** knight

Rit'tergut *n* manor

Rit'terkreuz *n* (mil) Knight's Cross (*of the Iron Cross*)

rit'terlich *adj* knightly; (fig) chivalrous

Rit'terlichkeit *f* (-;) chivalry

Rit'terzeit *f* age of chivalry

rittlings ['rɪtlɪŋs] *adv*-**r. auf** (*dat or acc*) astride

Ritual [rɪtu'al] *n* (-s;-e & -ien [jən]) ritual

rituell [rɪtu'el] *adj* ritual

Ri·tus ['ritus] *m* (-;-ten [tən]) rite

Ritz [rɪts] *m* (-es;-e), **Ritze** ['rɪtsə] *f* (-;-en) crack, crevice; (*Schlitz*) slit; (*Schramme*) scratch

ritzen ['rɪtsən] *tr* scratch; (*Glas*) cut

Rivale [rɪ'valə] *m* (-n;-n), **Rivalin** [rɪ'valɪn] *f* (-;-nen) rival

rivalisieren [rɪvalɪ'zirən] *intr* be in rivalry; **r. mit** rival

Rivalität [rɪvalɪ'tet] *f* (-;-en) rivalry

Rizinusöl ['ritsinusøl] *n* castor oil

Robbe ['robə] *f* (-;-n) seal

robben ['robən] *intr* (HABEN & SEIN) (mil) crawl (*using one's elbows*)

Rob'benfang *m* seal hunt

Robe ['robə] *f* (-;-n) robe, gown

Roboter ['robotər] *m* (-s;-) robot

robust [ro'bust] *adj* robust

roch [rɔx] *pret of* **riechen**

röcheln ['rœçəln] *tr* gasp out ‖ *intr* rattle (*in one's throat*)

rochieren [ro'ʃirən] *intr* (chess) castle

Rock [rɔk] *m* (-[e]s;ᵉe) skirt; jacket

Rock'schoß *m* coattail

Rodel ['rodəl] *m* (-s;-) & *f* (-;-n) toboggan; (*mit Steuerung*) bobsled

Ro'delbahn *f* toboggan slide

rodeln ['rodəln] *intr* (HABEN & SEIN) toboggan

Ro'delschlitten *m* toboggan; bobsled

roden ['rodən] *tr* root out; (*Wald*) clear; (*Land*) make arable

Rogen ['rogən] *m* (-s;-) roe, spawn

Roggen ['rogən] *m* (-s;) rye

roh [ro] *adj* raw; crude; (*Steine*) unhewn; (*Dielen*) bare; (fig) uncouth, brutal

Roh'bau *m* (-[e]s;-ten) rough brickwork

Roh'diamant *m* uncut diamond

Roh'einnahme *f* gross receipts

Roh'eisen *n* pig iron

Roh'heit *f* (-;) rawness, raw state; crudeness; brutality

Roh'entwurf *m* rough sketch

Roh'gewicht *n* gross weight

Roh'gewinn *m* gross profit

Roh'gummi *m* crude rubber

Roh'haut *f* rawhide

Roh'kost *f* uncooked vegetarian food

Rohling ['rolɪŋ] *m* (-s;-e) blank; slug; (fig) thug, hoodlum

Roh'material *n* raw material

Roh'öl *n* crude oil

Rohr [ror] *n* (-[e]s;-e) reed, cane; (*Röhre*) pipe, tube; (*Kanal*) duct, channel; (*Gewehrlauf*) barrel

Rohr'anschluß *m* pipe joint

Rohr'bogen *m* elbow

Röhre ['rørə] *f* (-;-n) tube, pipe; (electron) tube

Röh'renblitz *m* electronic flash

Röh'renblitzgerät *n* electronic flash unit

Rohr'leger *m* pipe fitter

Rohr'leitung *f* pipeline, main

Rohr'schäftung *f* sleeve joint

Rohr'schelle *f* pipe clamp

Rohr'zange *f* pipe wrench

Rohr'zucker *m* cane sugar

Roh'stoff *m* raw material

Rolladen (**Roll'laden**) *m* sliding shutter; sliding cover

Rollbahn ['rolban] *f* (aer) runway; (mil) road leading up to the front

Röllchen ['rœlçən] *n* (-s;-) caster

Rolldach ['roldax] *n* (aut) sun roof

Rolle ['rolə] *f* (-;-n) roll; (*Walze*) roller; (*Flaschenzug*) pulley; (*Spule*) spool, reel; (*unter Möbeln*) caster; (*Mangel*) mangle; (*Liste*) list, register; (theat) role; **aus der R. fallen** (fig) misbehave; **spielt keine R.!** never mind!, forget it!

rollen ['rolən] *tr* roll; (*auf Rädern*) wheel; (*Wäsche*) mangle; ‖ *ref* curl up ‖ *intr* (HABEN & SEIN) roll; (*Flugzeug*) taxi; (*Geschütze*) roar ‖ **Rollen** *n*—**ins. R. kommen** get going

Rol'lenbesetzung *f* (theat) cast

Rol'lenlager *n* roller bearing

Rol'lenzug *m* block and tackle

Rol'ler *m* (-s;-) scooter; motor scooter

Roll'feld *n* (aer) runway

Roll'kragen *m* turtleneck

Roll'mops *m* pickled herring

Rollo ['rolo] *n* (-s;-s) (coll) blind, shade

Roll'schuh *m* roller skate; **R. laufen** roller-skate

Roll'schuhbahn *f* roller-skating rink

Roll'stuhl *m* wheelchair

Roll'treppe *f* escalator

Roll'wagen m truck
Rom [rom] n (-s;) Rome
Roman [rə'man] m (-s;-e) novel
Roman'folge f serial
roman'haft adj fictional
romanisch [ro'manɪʃ] adj (Sprache) Romance; (archit) Romanesque
Romanist –in [roma'nɪst(ɪn)] §7 mf scholar of Romance languages
Roman'schriftsteller –in §6 mf novelist
Romantik [ro'mantɪk] f (-;) Romanticism
romantisch [ro'mantɪʃ] adj romantic
Romanze [ro'mantsə] (-;-n) romance
Römer –in ['rømor(ɪn)] §6 mf Roman
römisch ['rømɪʃ] adj Roman
rö'misch-katho'lisch adj Roman Catholic
röntgen ['rœntgən] tr x-ray
Rönt'genapparat m x-ray machine
Rönt'genarzt m, **Rönt'genärztin** f radiologist
Rönt'genaufnahme f, **Rönt'genbild** n x-ray
Rönt'genstrahlen pl x-rays
rosa ['roza] adj pink || **Rosa** n (-s; & -s) pink
Rose ['rozə] f (-;-n) rose
Ro'senkohl m Brussels sprouts
Ro'senkranz m (eccl) rosary
ro'senrot adj rosy, rose-colored
Ro'senstock m rosebush
rosig ['rozɪç] adj (& fig) rosy; (Laune) happy
Rosine [ro'zinə] f (-;-n) raisin
Roß [rɔs] n (Rosses; Rosse) horse; (sl) jerk; (poet) steed
Rost [rɔst] m (-es;) rust; mildew || m (-es;-e) grate; grill; **auf dem R. braten** grill
Rost'braten m roast beef
Röstbrot ['røstbrot] n toast
rosten ['rɔstən] intr rust
rösten ['røstən] tr (auf dem Rost) grill; (in der Pfanne) roast; (Brot) toast; (Mais) pop; (Kaffee) roast
Rö'ster m (-s;-) roaster; toaster
Rost'fleck m rust stain
rost'frei adj rust-proof; (Stahl) stainless
rostig ['rɔstɪç] adj rusty, corroded
rot [rot] adj (röter ['røtər]; röteste ['røtəstə] §9) red || **Rot** n (-es;) red; (Schminke) rouge
Rotation [rota'tsjon] f (-;-en) rotation
Rotations'maschine f rotary press
rotbäckig ['rotbɛkɪç] adj red-cheeked
Rot'dorn m (bot) pink hawthorn
Röte ['røtə] f (-;) red(ness); blush
Röteln ['røtəln] pl German measles
rotieren [ro'tirən] intr rotate
Rotkäppchen ['rotkɛpçən] n (-s;) Little Red Riding Hood
Rotkehlchen ['rotkelçən] n (-s;-) robin
rötlich ['røtlɪç] adj reddish
Ro-tor ['rotor] m (-s;-toren ['torən]) (aer) rotor; (elec) armature
Rot'schimmel m roan (horse)
Rot'tanne f spruce
Rotte ['rɔtə] f (-;-n) gang, mob
Rotz [rɔts] m (-es;-e) (sl) snot
rot'zig adj (sl) snotty

Rouleau [ru'lo] n (-s;-s) window shade
Route ['rutə] f (-;-n) route
Routine [ru'tinə] f (-;) routine; practice, experience
routiniert [rutɪ'nirt] adj experienced
Rübe ['rybə] f (-;-n) beet; **gelbe R.** carrot; **weiße R.** turnip
Rubin [ru'bin] m (-s;-e) ruby
Rubrik [ru'brik] f (-;-en) rubric; heading; (Spalte) column
ruchbar ['ruxbar] adj known, public
ruchlos ['ruxlos] adj wicked
Ruck [ruk] m (-[e]s;-e) jerk; yank; jolt; **auf e-n R.** at once; **mit e-m R.** in one quick move
Rück-, rück- [ryk] comb.fm. re-, back, rear; return
Rück'ansicht f rear view
Rück'antwort f reply; **Postkarte mit R.** prepaid reply postcard
rück'bezüglich adj (gram) reflexive
Rück'bleibsel n remainder
rücken ['rykən] tr move, shove || intr (SEIN) move; (Platz machen) move over; (marschieren) march; **höher r.** be promoted; **näher r.** approach || **Rücken** m (-s;-) back; (Rückseite) rear; (der Nase) bridge
Rückendeckung (**Rük'kendeckung**) f (fig) backing, support
Rückenlehne (**Rük'kenlehne**) f back rest
Rückenmark (**Rük'kenmark**) n spinal cord
Rückenschwimmen (**Rük'kenschwimmen**) n backstroke
Rückenwind (**Rük'kenwind**) m tail wind
Rückenwirbel (**Rük'kenwirbel**) m (anat) vertebra
rück'erstatten tr reimburse, refund
Rück'fahrkarte f, **Rück'fahrschein** m round-trip ticket
Rück'fahrt f return trip
Rück'fall m relapse
rück'fällig adj habitual, relapsing
rück'federnd adj resilient
Rück'flug m return flight
Rück'frage f further question
Rück'führung f repatriation
Rück'gabe f return, restitution
Rück'gang m return; regression; (der Preise) drop; (econ) recession
rückgängig ['rykgɛnɪç] adj retrogressive; dropping; **r. machen** cancel
Rück'gewinnen §121 tr recover
Rück'grat n backbone, spine
Rück'griff m (auf acc) recourse (to)
Rück'halt m backing; (mil) reserves; **e-n R. an j-m haben** have s.o.'s backing; **ohne R.** without reservation
rück'haltlos adj frank, unreserved || adv without reserve
Rück'handschlag m (tennis) back-hand stroke
Rück'kauf m repurchase
Rück'kehr f return; (fig) comeback
Rück'kopplung f (electron) feedback
Rück'lage f reserves, savings
Rück'lauf m reverse; (mil) recoil
Rück'läufer m letter returned to sender
rückläufig ['ryklɔɪfɪç] adj retrograde

Rück'licht n (aut) taillight
rücklings ['rʏklɪŋs] adv backwards
Rück'nahme f withdrawal, taking back
Rück'porto n return postage
Rück'prall m bounce, rebound, recoil
Rück'reise f return trip
Ruck'sack m knapsack
Rück'schau f—**m—R. halten auf** (acc) look back on
Rück'schlag m back stroke; (e-s Balles) bounce; (fig) setback
Rück'schluß m conclusion, inference
Rück'schritt m backward step; (fig) falling off, retrogression
Rück'seite f back; reverse; wrong side
Rück'sicht f regard, respect, consideration; **aus R. auf** (acc) out of consideration for; **in** (or **mit**) **R. auf** (acc) in regard to; **ohne R. auf** (acc) irrespective of; **R. nehmen auf** (acc) take into account, show consideration for
rück'sichtlich prep (genit) considering
rück'sichtslos adj inconsiderate; reckless; ruthless
rück'sichtsvoll adj considerate
Rück'sitz m (aut) rear seat
Rück'spiegel m (aut) rear-view mirror
Rück'spiel n return match
Rück'sprache f discussion; conference; **R. nehmen mit** consult with
Rück'stand m arrears; (Satz) sediment; (Rest) remainder; (von Aufträgen, usw.) backlog; (chem) residue
rück'ständig adj behind, in arrears; (Geld) outstanding; (Raten) delinquent; (altmodisch) backward
Rück'stau m back-up water
Rück'stelltaste f backspace key
Rück'stoß m repulsion; recoil, kick
Rückstrahler ['rʏkʃtraːlər] m (-s;-) reflector
Rück'strahlung f reflection
Rück'tritt m resignation
Rück'trittbremse f coaster brake
Rück'umschlag m return envelope
rückwärts ['rʏkverts] adv backward(s)
Rück'wärtsgang m (aut) reverse
Rück'weg m way back, return
ruck'weise adv by fits and starts
rück'wirkend adj retroactive
Rück'wirkung f (-;-en) reaction; repercussion
rück'zahlen tr repay, refund
Rück'zug m withdrawal; retreat; **zum R. blasen** sound the retreat
Rück'zugsgefecht n running fight
rüde ['ryːdə] adj rude, coarse || **Rüde** m (-n;-n) male (wolf, fox, etc.)
Rudel ['ruːdəl] n (-s;-) herd; flock; (von Wölfen, U-Booten) wolf pack
Ruder ['ruːdər] n (-s;-) (aer, naut) rudder; (naut) oar
Ru'derblatt n blade of an oar
Ru'derboot n rowboat
Ru'derer —**in** §6 mf rower
Ru'derklampe f oarlock
rudern ['ruːdərn] tr & intr row
Ru'derschlag m stroke of the oar
Ru'dersport m (sport) crew
Ruf [ruːf] m (-[e]s;-e) call; shout, yell; (Berufung) vocation; (Nach-

rede) reputation; appointment; (com) credit
rufen ['ruːfən] §122 tr call; shout; **r. lassen** send for || intr call; shout
Ruf'mord m character assassination
Ruf'name m first name
Ruf'nummer f telephone number
Ruf'weite f—**in R.** within earshot
Ruf'zeichen n (rad) station identification; (telp) call sign
Rüge ['ryːgə] f (-;-n) reprimand
rügen ['ryːgən] tr reprimand
Ruhe ['ruːə] f (-;) rest; quiet, calm; (Frieden) peace; (Stille) silence; **immer mit der R.!** (coll) take it easy!
ru'hebedürftig adj in need of rest
Ru'hegehalt n pension
Ru'hekur f rest cure
ru'helos adj restless
ruhen ['ruːən] intr rest; sleep
Ru'hepause f pause, break
Ru'heplatz m resting place
Ru'hestand m retirement
Ru'hestätte f resting place
Ru'hestörer —**in** §6 mf disturber of the peace
Ru'hetag m day of rest, day off
Ru'hezeit f leisure
ruhig ['ruːɪç] adj still, quiet; calm
Ruhm [ruːm] m (-[e]s;) glory, fame
rühmen ['ryːmən] tr praise || ref (genit) boast (about)
rühmlich ['ryːmlɪç] adj praiseworthy
ruhm'los adj inglorious
ruhmredig ['ruːmreːdɪç] adj vainglorious
ruhm'reich adj glorious
ruhm'voll adj famous, glorious
ruhm'würdig adj praiseworthy
Ruhr [ruːr] f (-;) dysentery; **Ruhr** (river)
Rührei ['ryːraɪ] n scrambled egg
rühren ['ryːrən] tr stir; touch, move; (Trommel) beat; **alle Kräfte r.** exert every effort || ref stir, move; get a move on; **rührt euch!** (mil) at ease! || intr stir, move; **r. an** (acc) touch; (fig) mention; **r. von** originate in
rührig ['ryːrɪç] adj active; agile
Rührlöffel ['ryːrlœfəl] m ladle
rührselig ['ryːrzeːlɪç] adj sentimental
Rührstück ['ryːrʃtʏk] n soap opera
Rüh'rung f (-;-en) emotion
Ruin [ruˈiːn] m (-s;) ruin; decay
Ruine [ruˈiːnə] f (-;-n) ruins; (fig) wreck
rui'nenhaft adj ruinous
ruinieren [ruˈiːnirən] tr ruin
Rülps [rʏlps] m (-es;-e) belch
rülpsen ['rʏlpsən] intr belch
Rülp'ser m (-s;-) belch
Rum [rum] m (-s;-s) rum
Rumäne [ruˈmɛːnə] m (-n;-n) Rumanian
Rumänien [ruˈmɛːnjən] n (-s;) Rumania
Rumänin [ruˈmɛːnɪn] f (-;-nen) Rumanian
rumänisch [ruˈmɛːnɪʃ] adj Rumanian
Rummel ['ruməl] m (-s;) junk; racket; hustle and bustle; **auf den R. gehen** go to the fair; **den ganzen R. kaufen** (coll) buy the works
Rum'melplatz m amusement park, fair
Rumor [ruˈmoːr] m (-s;) noise, racket

Rumpel ['rumpəl] *f* (-;-n) scrub board
Rum'pelkammer *f* storage room, junk room
Rum'pelkasten *m* (aut) jalopy
rumpeln ['rumpəln] *tr* (*Wäsche*) scrub || *intr* rumble, rattle
Rumpf [rumpf] *m* (-[e]s;ːe) trunk, body; torso; (aer) fuselage; (naut) hull
rümpfen ['rympfən] *tr*—**die Nase r. über** (*acc*) turn up one's nose at
rund [runt] *adj* round; (*Absage*) flat || *adv* around; about, approximately; **r. um** around
Rund'blick *m* panorama
Rund'brief *m* circular letter
Runde ['rundə] *f* (-;-n) round; (box) round; (*beim Rennsport*) lap
runden ['rundən] *tr* make round; round off || *ref* become round
Rund'erlaß *m* circular
rund'erneuern *tr* (aut) retread; **runderneuerter Reifen** *m* retread
Rund'fahrt *f* sightseeing tour
Rund'flug *m* (aer) circuit
Rund'frage *f* questionnaire, poll
Rund'funk *m* radio; **im R.** on the radio
Rund'funkansage *f* radio announcement
Rund'funkansager –in §6 *mf* radio announcer
Rund'funkgerät *n* radio set
Rund'funkgesellschaft *f* broadcasting company
Rund'funkhörer –in §6 *mf* listener
Rund'funknetz *n* radio network
Rund'funksender *m* broadcasting station
Rund'funksendung *f* radio broadcast
Rund'funksprecher –in §6 *mf* announcer
Rund'funkwerbung *f* (rad) commercial
Rund'gang *m* tour; stroll
rund'heraus *adv* plainly, flatly
rundherum' *adv* all around
rund'lich *adj* round; (*dick*) plump
Rund'reise *f* sightseeing tour
Rund'schau *f* panorama; (journ) news in brief
Rund'schreiben *n* circular letter
rundweg ['runt'vek] *adv* bluntly, flatly

Runzel ['runtsəl] *f* (-;-n) wrinkle
runzelig ['runtsəliç] *adj* wrinkled
runzeln ['runtsəln] *tr* wrinkle; **die Brauen r.** knit one's brows; **die Stirn r.** frown || *ref* wrinkle
Rüpel ['rypəl] *m* (-s;-) boor
rü'pelhaft *adj* rude, boorish
rupfen ['rupfən] *tr* pluck; (fig) fleece
ruppig ['rupiç] *adj* shabby; (fig) rude
Ruprecht ['ruprɛçt] *m* (-s;-)—**Knecht R.** Santa Claus
Ruß [rus] *m* (-es;) soot
Russe ['rusə] *m* (-n;-n) Russian
Rüssel ['rysəl] *m* (-s;-) snout; (*Elephanten-*) trunk; (coll) snoot; (ent) proboscis
rußig ['rusiç] *adj* sooty
Russin ['rusin] *f* (-;-nen) Russian
russisch ['rusiʃ] *adj* Russian
Rußland ['ruslant] *n* (-s;) Russia
Rüst- [ryst] *comb.fm.* scaffolding; armament, munition
rüsten ['rystən] *tr* arm, equip; prepare || *ref* get ready || *intr* (zu) get ready (for); **zum Krieg r.** mobilize
Rüster ['rystər] *f* (-;-n) elm
rüstig ['rystiç] *adj* vigorous; alert
Rüst'kammer *f* armory, arsenal
Rü'stung *f* (-;-en) preparation; equipment; armament; mobilization; armor; implements; (archit) scaffolding
Rü'stungsbetrieb *m* munitions factory
Rü'stungsfertigung *f* war production
Rü'stungsindustrie *f* war industry
Rü'stungskontrolle *f* arms control
Rü'stungsmaterial *n* war materiel
Rü'stungsstand *m* state of preparedness
Rüst'zeug *n* kit; (fig) knowledge
Rute ['rutə] *f* (-;-n) rod; twig; tail; (anat) penis
Rutsch [rutʃ] *m* (-es;-e) slip, slide
Rutsch'bahn *f* slide; chute
Rutsche ['rutʃə] *f* (-;-n) slide; chute
rutschen ['rutʃən] *intr* (SEIN) slip, slide; (aut) skid
rutschig ['rutʃiç] *adj* slippery
rütteln ['rytəln] *tr* shake; jolt; (*Getreide*) winnow; (*aus dem Schlafe*) rouse || *intr*—**r. an** (*acc*) cause to rattle; (fig) try to undermine

S

S, s [es] *invar n* S, s
SA *abbr* (mil) (*Sturmabteilung*) storm troopers
Saal [zal] *m* (-[e]s; **Säle** ['zelə]) hall
Saat [zat] *f* (-;-en) seed; (*Säen*) sowing; (*Getreide auf dem Halm*) crop(s); **die S. bestellen** sow
Saat'bestellung *f* sowing
Saat'kartoffel *f* seed potato
Sabbat ['zabat] *m* (-s;-e) Sabbath
Sabberei [zabə'raɪ] *f* (-;-en) drooling; (*Geschwätz*) drivel
sabbern ['zabərn] *intr* drool, drivel

Säbel ['zebəl] *m* (-s;) saber; **mit dem S. rasseln** (pol) rattle the saber
sä'belbeinig *adj* bowlegged
säbeln ['zebəln] *tr* (coll) hack
Sä'belrasseln *n* (pol) saber rattling
Sabotage [zabo'taʒə] *f* (-;-n) sabotage
Saboteur [zabo'tør] *m* (-s;-e) saboteur
sabotieren [zabo'tirən] *tr* sabotage
Saccharin [zaxa'rin] *n* (-s;) saccharin
Sach- [zax] *comb.fm.* of facts, factual
Sach'anlagevermögen *n* tangible fixed assets
Sach'bearbeiter –in §6 *mf* specialist

Sach'beschädigung f property damage
Sach'bezüge pl compensation in kind
Sach'buch n nonfiction (work)
Sach'darstellung f statement of facts
sach'dienlich adj relevant, pertinent
Sache ['zaxə] f (-;-n) thing, matter;
cause; (jur) case; **bei der S.** sein be
on the ball; **beschlossene S.** foregone
conclusion; **die S. der Freiheit** the
cause of freedom; **große S.** big affair; **gute S.** good cause; **heikle S.**
delicate point; **in eigner S.** on one's
own behalf; **in Sachen X gegen Y**
(jur) in the case of X versus Y;
meine sieben Sachen all my belongings; **nicht bei der S. sein** not be with
it; **nicht zur S. gehörig** irrelevant;
von der S. abkommen get off the
subject; **zur S.!** come to the point!
(parl) question!
sach'gemäß adj proper, pertinent || adv
in a suitable manner
Sach'kenner –in §6 mf expert
Sach'kenntnis f, **Sach'kunde** f expertise
sach'kundig adj expert || **Sach'kundige**
§5 mf expert
Sach'lage f state of affairs, circumstances
Sach'leistung f payment in kind
sach'lich adj (treffend) to the point;
(gegenständlich) objective; (tatsächlich) factual; (unparteilisch) impar-
tial; (nüchtern) matter-of-fact || adv
to the point
sächlich ['zeçlɪç] adj (gram) neuter
Sach'lichkeit f (-;) objectivity; reality;
impartiality; matter-of-factness
Sach'register n index
Sach'schaden m property damage
Sach'schadenersatz m indemnity (for
property damage)
Sachse ['zaksə] m (-n;-n) Saxon
Sachsen ['zaksən] n (-s;) Saxony
sächsisch ['zeksɪʃ] adj Saxon
sacht(e) ['zaxt(ə)] adj soft, gentle;
(langsam) slow || adv gingerly; im-
mer sacht! easy does it!
Sach'verhalt m facts of the case
Sach'vermögen n real property
sach'verständig adj experienced ||
Sachverständige §5 mf expert
Sach'wert m actual value; **Sachwerte**
material assets
Sach'wörterbuch n encyclopedia
Sack [zak] m (-[e]s;¨e) sack, bag;
pocket; **j–n in den S. stecken** (coll)
be way above s.o.; **mit S. und Pack**
bag and baggage
Säckel ['zekəl] m (-s;–) little bag;
pocket; purse
sacken ['zakən] tr bag || ref be baggy
|| intr (SEIN) sag; (archit) settle;
(naut) founder
Sack'gasse f blind alley, dead end;
(fig) stalemate, dead end
Sack'leinwand f burlap
Sack'pfeife f bagpipe
Sack'tuch n handkerchief
Sadist –in [za'dɪst(ɪn)] §7 mf sadist
sadistisch [za'dɪstɪʃ] adj sadistic
säen ['zɛ·ən] tr & intr sow
Saffian ['zafjan] m (-s;) morocco

Safran ['zafran] m (-s;-e) saffron
Saft [zaft] m (-[e]s;¨e) juice; sap;
(culin) gravy
saftig ['zaftɪç] adj juicy; (Witze) spicy
saft'los adj juiceless; (fig) wishy-washy
saft'reich adj juicy, succulent
Sage ['zagə] f (-;-n) legend, saga
Säge ['zegə] f (-;-n) saw
Sä'geblatt n saw blade
Sä'gebock m sawhorse, sawbuck
Sä'gefisch m sawfish
Sä'gemehl n sawdust
sagen ['zagən] tr say; (mitteilen) tell;
das hat nichts zu s. that's neither
here nor there; **das will nicht s.** that
is not to say; **gesagt, getan** no sooner
said than done; **j–m s. lassen** send
s.o. word; **laß dir gesagt sein** let it
be a warning to you; **sich** [dat]
nichts s. lassen not listen to reason
sägen ['zegən] tr saw || intr saw; (coll)
snore, cut wood
sa'genhaft adj legendary
Sägespäne ['zegəʃpenə] pl sawdust
Sä'gewerk n sawmill
sah [za] pret of **sehen**
Sahne ['zanə] f (-;) cream
Saison [se'zõ] f (-;-s) season
Saison– comb.fm. seasonal
saison'bedingt, saison'mäßig adj sea-
sonal
Saite ['zaitə] f (-;-n) string, chord
Sal'teninstrument n string instrument
Sakko ['zako] m & n (-s;-s) suit coat
Sak'koanzug m sport suit
Sakrament [zakra'ment] n (-[e]s;-e)
sacrament; **das S. des Altars** the
Eucharist || interj (sl) dammit!
Sakrileg [zakri'lek] n (-s;-e) sacrilege
Sakristan [zakrɪs'tan] m (-s;-e) sac-
ristan
Sakristei [zakrɪs'tai] f (-;-en) sacristy
Säkular– [zekular] comb.fm. secular;
centennial
säkularisieren [zekularɪ'zirən] tr secu-
larize
Salami [za'lami] f (-;) salami
Salat [za'lat] m (-[e]s;-e) salad; lettuce; **gemischter S.** tossed salad
Salat'soße f salad dressing
salbadern [zal'badərn] intr talk hypo-
critically, put on the dog
Salbe ['zalbə] f (-;-n) salve
salben ['zalbən] tr put salve on; anoint
Sal'bung f (-;-en) anointing
sal'bungsvoll adj unctuous
saldieren [zal'dirən] tr (com) balance
Sal-do ['zaldo] m (-s;-s & di [di])
(acct) balance; **e–n S. aufstellen** (or
ziehen) strike a balance; **e–n S. ausweisen** show a balance
Saline [za'linə] f (-;-n) saltworks
Salmiak [zal'mjak] m (-s;) ammonium
chloride, sal ammoniac
Salmiak'geist m ammonia
Salon [za'lõ] m (-s;-s) salon; parlor,
living room
salon'fähig adj (Aussehen) presentable;
(Ausdruck) fit for polite company
Salon'held m, **Salon'löwe** m ladies' man
salopp [za'ləp] adj sloppy; (ungezwungen) casual
Salpeter [zal'petər] m (-s;) saltpeter

salpeterig [zal'petərɪç] *adj* nitrous

Salpe'tersäure *f* nitric acid

Salto ['zalto] *m* (-s;-s) somersault

Salut [za'lut] *m* (-[e]s;-e) salute; **S. schießen** fire a salute

salutieren [zalu'tirən] *tr & intr* salute

Salve ['zalvə] *f* (-;-n) volley, salvo

Salz [zalts] *n* (-es;-e) salt

Salz'bergwerk *n* salt mine

Salz'brühe *f* brine

salzen ['zaltsən] *tr* salt

Salz'faß *n* salt shaker

Salz'fleisch *n* salted meat

Salz'gurke *f* pickle

salz'haltig *adj* saline

Salz'hering *m* pickled herring

salzig ['zaltsɪç] *adj* salty; saline

Salz'kartoffeln *pl* boiled potatoes

Salz'lake *f* brine

Salz'säure *f* hydrochloric acid, muriatic acid

Salz'sole *f* brine

Salz'werk *n* salt works

Samariter –in [zama'ritər(ɪn)] §6 *mf* Samaritan

Same ['zamə] *m* (-ns;-n), **Samen** ['zamən] *m* (-s;-) seed; (biol) semen

Sa'menkorn *n* grain of seed

Sa'menstaub *m* pollen

Samentierchen ['zaməntɪrçən] *n* (-s;-) spermatozoon

sämig ['zemɪç] *adj* (culin) thick, creamy

Sämischleder ['zemɪʃledər] *n* chamois

Sämling ['zemlɪŋ] *m* (-s;-e) seedling

Sammel– [zaməl] *comb.fm.* collecting, collective

Sam'melbatterie *f* storage battery

Sam'melbecken *n* reservoir; storage tank

Sam'melbegriff *m* collective noun

Sam'melbüchse *f* poor box

Sam'mellinse *f* convex lens

sammeln ['zaməln] *tr* gather; collect; (*Aufmerksamkeit, Truppen*) concentrate || *ref* gather; compose oneself; sich wieder s. (mil) reassemble

Sam'melname *m* collective noun

Sam'melplatz *m* collecting point; meeting place; (mil) rendezvous

Sam'melverbindung *f* conference call

Sam'melwerk *n* compilation

Sammler ['zamlər] *m* (-s;-) collector; compiler; (elec) storage cell

Samm'lung *f* (-;-en) collection; (*Zusammenstellung*) compilation; (*Fassung*) composure; concentration

Samstag ['zamstak] *m* (-[e]s;-e) Saturday

samt [zamt] *adv—*s. und sonders each and everyone, without exception || *prep* (*dat*) together with || **Samt** *m* (-[e]s;-e) velvet

samt'artig *adj* velvety

sämtlich ['zemtlɪç] *adj* all, complete || *adv* all together

Sanato·rium [zana'torjʊm] *n* (-s;-rien [rjən]) sanitarium

Sand [zant] *m* (-[e]s;-e) sand; **im Sande verlaufen** (fig) peter out

Sandale [zan'dalə] *f* (-;-n) sandal

Sand'bahn *f* (sport) dirt track

Sand'bank *f* (-;ᵘe) sandbank

Sand'boden *m* sandy soil

Sand'düne *f* sand dune

Sand'grube *f* sand pit

sandig ['zandɪç] *adj* sandy

Sand'kasten *m* sand box

Sand'korn *n* grain of sand

Sand'mann *m* (-[e]s;) (*fig*) sandman

Sand'papier *n* sandpaper; **mit S. abschleifen** sand, sandpaper

Sand'sack *m* sandbag

Sand'stein *m* sandstone

Sand'steingebäude *n* brownstone

sand'strahlen *tr* sandblast

Sand'sturmgebiet *n* dust bowl

sandte ['zantə] *pret* of **senden**

Sand'torte *f* sponge cake

Sand'uhr *f* hour glass

Sand'wüste *f* sandy desert

sanft [zanft] *adj* soft, gentle

Sänfte ['zenftə] *f* (-;-n) sedan chair

Sanft'mut *f* gentleness, meekness

sanft'mütig *adj* gentle, meek, mild

sang [zaŋ] *pret* of **singen** || **Sang** *m* (-[e]s;ᵘe) song; **mit S. und Klang** (fig) with great fanfare

sang–'und klang'los *adv* unceremoniously

Sänger ['zeŋər] *m* (-s;-) singer

Sän'gerchor *m* glee club

Sängerin ['zeŋərɪn] *f* (-;-nen) singer

Sanguiniker [zaŋ'gwinɪkər] *m* (-s;-) optimist

sanguinisch [zaŋ'gwinɪʃ] *adj* sanguine

sanieren [za'nirən] *tr* cure; improve the sanitary conditions of; disinfect; (fin) put on a firm basis

Sanie'rung *f* (-;-en) restoration; reorganization

sanitär [zanɪ'ter] *adj* sanitary

Sanitäter [zanɪ'tetər] *m* (-s;-) first-aid-man; (mil) medic

Sanitäts– [zanɪtets] *comb.fm.* first-aid, medical

Sanitäts'korps *n* army medical corps

Sanitäts'soldat *m* medic

Sanitäts'wache *f* first-aid station

Sanitäts'wagen *m* ambulance

Sanitäts'zug *m* hospital train

sank [zaŋk] *pret* of **sinken**

Sanka ['zaŋka] *m* (-s;-s) (**Sanitätskraftwagen**) field ambulance

Sankt [zaŋkt] *invar* *m* Saint

Sanktion [zaŋk'tsjon] *f* (-;-en) sanction

sanktionieren [zaŋktsjo'nirən] *tr* sanction

sann [zan] *pret* of **sinnen**

Saphir ['zafir] *m* (-s;-e) sapphire

sapperment [zapər'ment] *interj* the deuce!

Sardelle [zar'dɛlə] *f* (-;-n) anchovy

Sardine [zar'dinə] *f* (-;-n) sardine

Sardinien [zar'dinjən] *n* (-s;) Sardinia

sardinisch [zar'dinɪʃ] *adj* Sardinian

Sarg [zark] *m* (-[e]s;ᵘe) coffin

Sarg'tuch *n* pall

Sarkasmus [zar'kasmʊs] *m* (-;) sarcasm

sarkastisch [zar'kastɪʃ] *adj* sarcastic

Sarkophag [zarko'fak] *m* (-s;-e) sarcophagus

saß [zas] *pret* of **sitzen**

Satan ['zatan] *m* (-s;-e) Satan

satanisch [za'tanɪʃ] *adj* satanic(al)
Satellit [zate'lit] *m* (-en;-en) satellite
Satin [sa'tɛ̃] *m* (-s;-s) satin
Satire [za'tirə] *f* (-;-n) satire
Satiriker -in [za'tirɪkər(ɪn)] §6 *mf* satirist
satirisch [za'tirɪʃ] *adj* satirical
satt [zat] *adj* satisfied; satiated; (*Farben*) deep, rich; (chem) saturated; **etw s. bekommen** (or **haben**) be fed up with s.th.; **ich bin s.** I've had enough; **sich s. essen** eat one's fill
Sattel ['zatəl] *m* (-s;⸚) saddle
sat'telfest *adj* (fig) well-versed
Sat'telgurt *m* girth
satteln ['zatəln] *tr* saddle
Sat'telschlepper *m* semi-trailer
Sat'teltasche *f* saddlebag
Satt'heit *f* (-;) saturation; (*der Farben*) richness
sättigen ['zɛtɪgən] *tr* satisfy, satiate; saturate
Sät'tigung *f* (-;) satiation; saturation
Sattler ['zatlər] *m* (-s;-) harness maker
sattsam ['zatzam] *adv* sufficiently
saturieren [zatu'rirən] *tr* saturate
Satz [zats] *m* (-es;⸚e) sentence; clause; phrase; (*Behauptung*) proposition; (*Bodensatz*) grounds; sediment; (*Betrag*) amount; (*Tarif*) rate; (*Gebühr*) fee; (*Garnitur*) set; (*Sprung*) leap; (*Wette*) stake; (*Menge*) batch; (math) theorem; (mus) movement; (tennis) set; (typ) typesetting, composition; **e-n S. machen** jump; **e-n S. aufstellen** set down an article of faith; **einfacher S.** simple sentence; **hauptwörtlicher S.** substantive clause; **in S. gehen** go to press; **verkürzter S.** phrase; **zum S. von** at the rate of; **zusammengesetzter S.** compound sentence
Satz'aussage *f* (gram) predicate
Satz'bau *m* (-[e]s;) (gram) construction
Satz'gefüge *n* complex sentence
Satz'gegenstand *m* (gram) subject
Satz'lehre *f* syntax
Satz'teil *m* (gram) part of speech
Sat'zung *f* (-;-en) rule, regulation; (*Vereins-*) bylaw; statute
sat'zungsgemäß, sat'zungsmäßig *adj* statutory, according to the bylaws
Satz'zeichen *n* punctuation mark
Sau [zau] *f* (-;⸚e) sow; (pej) pig; **wie e-e gesengte Sau fahren** drive like a maniac
Sau'arbeit *f* (coll) sloppy work; (coll) tough job; (coll) dirty job
sauber ['zaubər] *adj* clean; exact
säuberlich ['zɔɪbərlɪç] *adj* clean, neat; (*anständig*) decent
sau'bermachen *tr* clean, clean up
säubern ['zɔɪbərn] *tr* clean; (*freimachen*) clear; (*Buch*) expurgate; (mil) mop up; (pol) purge
Säu'berungsaktion *f* (mil) mopping-up operation; (pol) purge
Sau'borste *f* hog bristle
Sauce ['zosə] *f* (-;-n) sauce; gravy; (*Salat-*) dressing
sau'dumm *adj* (coll) awfully dumb
sauer ['zau·ər] *adj* sour

Sau'erbraten *m* braised beef soaked in vinegar
Sauerei [zau·ə'raɪ] *f* (-;-en) filth, filthy joke
Sau'erkohl *m*, **Sau'erkraut** *n* sauerkraut
säuerlich ['zɔɪ-ərlɪç] *adj* sourish, acidulous; (*Lächeln*) forced
säuern ['zɔɪ-ərn] *tr* sour; (*Teig*) leaven || *intr* turn sour, acidify
Sau'erstoff *m* (-[e]s;) oxygen
Sau'erstoffasche *f* oxygen tank
Sau'erteig *m* leaven
Sau'ertopf *m* (coll) sourpuss
Sau'erwasser *n* sparkling water
Saufaus ['zaufaus] *m* (-;-), **Saufbold** ['zaufbɔlt] *m* (-[e]s;-e), **Saufbruder** ['zaufbrudər] *m* (coll) booze hound
saufen ['zaufən] §124 *tr* drink, guzzle || *intr* drink; (sl) booze
Säufer -in ['zɔɪfər(ɪn)] §6 *mf* drunkard
Saufgelage ['zaufgəlagə] *n* booze party
Sau'fraß *m* terrible food, slop
Säugamme ['zɔɪkamə] *f* wet nurse
saugen ['zaugən] §109 & §125 *tr* suck || *ref—sich* [*dat*] **etw aus den Fingern s.** invent s.th., make up s.th.
säugen ['zɔɪgən] *tr* suckle, nurse
Sauger ['zaugər] *m* (-s;-) sucker; nipple; pacifier
Säuger ['zɔɪgər] *m* (-s;-), **Säugetier** ['zɔɪgətir] *n* mammal
Saug'flasche *f* baby bottle
Säugling ['zɔɪklɪŋ] *m* (-s;-e) baby
Säug'lingsausstattung *f* layette
Säug'lingsheim *n* nursery
Sau'glück *n* (coll) dumb luck
Saug'napf *m* suction cup
Saug'pumpe *f* suction pump
Saug'watte *f* absorbent cotton
Saug'wirkung *f* suction
Sau'hund *m* (sl) louse, dirty dog
Sau'igel *m* (sl) dirty guy
sauigeln ['zau·igəln] *intr* (sl) tell dirty jokes
Sau'kerl *m* (sl) cad, skunk
Säule ['zɔɪlə] *f* (-;-n) column; (& fig) pillar; (elec) dry battery; (phys) pile
Säu'lenfuß *m* base of a column
Säu'lengang *m* colonnade, peristyle
Säu'lenhalle *f* portico, gallery
Säu'lenkapitell *n*, **Säu'lenknauf** *m*, **Säu'lenknopf** *m* (archit) capital
Säu'lenschaft *m* shaft of a column
Säu'lenvorbau *m* portico, (front) porch
Saum [zaum] *m* (-[e]s;⸚e) seam, hem; (*Rand*) border; (*e-r Stadt*) outskirts
säumen ['zɔɪmən] *tr* hem; border; (*Straßen*) line || *intr* tarry
Sau'mensch *n* (vulg) slut
säumig ['zɔɪmɪç] *adj* tardy
Säumnis ['zɔɪmnɪs] *f* (-;-nisse) dilatoriness; (*Verzug*) delay; (*Nichterfüllung*) default
Saum'pfad *m* mule track
Saum'tier *n* beast of burden
Sau'pech *n* (coll) rotten luck
Säure ['zɔɪrə] *f* (-;-n) sourness; acidity; tartness; (chem) acid
Sauregur'kenzeit *f* slack season
Säu'remesser *m* (aut) battery tester
Saures ['zaurəs] *n—***gib ihm S.** (coll) give it to 'im!

Saus [zaus] *m*—in S. und Braus leben live high

säuseln ['zɔɪzəln] *intr* rustle; **mit säuselnder Stimme** in whispers

sausen ['zauzən] *intr* (*Wind, Kugel*) whistle; (*Wasser*) gush || *intr* (SEIN) rush, whiz || *impers*—**mir saust es in den Ohren** my ears are ringing || **Sausen** *n* (−s;) rush and roar; humming, ringing (*in the ears*)

Sau'stall *m* pigsty; (fig) terrible mess

Sau'wetter *n* (coll) nasty weather

Sau'wirtschaft *f* (coll) helluva mess

sau'wohl' *adj* (coll) in great shape

Saxophon [zakso'fon] *n* (−s;−e) saxophone

Schabe ['ʃabə] *f* (−;−n) cockroach

Schabeisen ['ʃapaɪzən] *n* scraper

schaben ['ʃabən] *tr* scrape; grate, rasp

Scha'ber *m* (−s;−) scraper

Schabernack ['ʃabərnak] *m* (−[e]s;−e) practical joke

schäbig ['ʃebɪç] *adj* shabby; (fig) mean

Schablone [ʃa'blonə] *f* (−;−n) (*Muster*) pattern, model; (*Matrize*) stencil; (*mechanische Arbeit*) routine; **nach der S.** mechanically

schablo'nenhaft, schablo'nenmäßig *adj* mechanical; (*Arbeit*) routine

Schach [ʃax] *n* (−[e]s;) chess; **in S. halten** (fig) keep in check; **S. bieten** (or geben) check; (fig) defy; **S. dem König!** check!

Schach'brett *n* chessboard

Schacher ['ʃaxər] *m* (−s;) haggling; **S. treiben** haggle, huckster

Schach'feld *n* (chess) square

Schach'figur *f* chessman; (fig) pawn

schach'matt' *adj* checkmated; (fig) beat

Schach'partie *f*, **Schach'spiel** *n* game of chess

Schacht [ʃaxt] *m* (−[e]s;−̈e) shaft; manhole

Schacht'deckel *m* manhole cover

Schachtel ['ʃaxtəl] *f* (−;−n) box; (*von Zigaretten*) pack; (fig) frump

Schach'zug *m* (chess & fig) move

schade ['ʃadə] *adj* too bad

Schädel ['ʃedəl] *m* (−s;−) skull; **mir brummt** (or **dröhnt**) **der S.** my head is throbbing

Schä'delbruch *m*, **Schä'delfraktur** *f* skull fracture

Schä'delhaut *f* scalp

Schä'delknochen *m* cranium

Schä'dellehre *f* phrenology

schaden ['ʃadən] *intr* do harm; (*dat*) harm, damage; **das wird ihr nichts s.** it serves her right; **ein Versuch kann nichts s.** there's no harm in trying || *impers*—**es schadet nichts** it doesn't matter || **Schaden** *m* (−s;−̈) damage, injury; (*Verlust*) loss; (*Nachteil*) disadvantage; **er will deinen S. nicht** he means you no harm; **j—m S. zufügen** inflict loss on s.o.; (coll) give s.o. a black eye; **mit S. verkaufen** sell at a loss; **S. nehmen** come to grief; **zu meinem S.** to my detriment

Scha'denersatz *m* compensation, damages; (*Wiedergutmachung*) reparation; **S. leisten** pay damages; make amends

Scha'denersatzklage *f* damage suit

Scha'denfreude *f* gloating

scha'denfroh *adj* gloating, malicious

Scha'denversicherung *f* comprehensive insurance

schadhaft ['ʃathaft] *adj* damaged; (*Material*) faulty; (*Zähne*) decayed; (*baufällig*) dilapidated

schädigen ['ʃedɪgən] *tr* inflict financial damage on; (*benachteiligen*) wrong; (*Ruf*) damage; (*Rechte*) infringe on

Schä'digung *f* (−;) damage

schädlich ['ʃetlɪç] *adj* harmful; (*nachteilig*) detrimental; (*verderblich*) noxious; (*Speise*) unwholesome

Schädling ['ʃetlɪŋ] *m* (−s;−e) (*Person*) parasite; (ent) pest; **Schädlinge** vermin

Schäd'lingsbekämpfung *f* pest control

schadlos ['ʃatlos] *adj*—**sich an j—n s. halten** make s.o. pay (*for an injury done to oneself*); **sich für etw s. halten** compensate oneself for s.th., make up for s.th.

Schaf [ʃaf] *n* (−[e]s;−e) sheep; (fig) blockhead, dope

Schaf'bock *m* ram

Schäfchen ['ʃefçən] *n* (−s;−) lamb; (*Wolken*) fleecy clouds

Schäf'chenwolke *f* fleecy cloud

Schäfer ['ʃefər] *m* (−s;−) shepherd

Schä'ferhund *m* sheep dog; **deutscher S.** German shepherd

Schaf'fell *n* sheepskin

schaffen ['ʃafən] §109 *tr* do; get; put; manage, manage to do; (*erreichen*) accomplish; (*liefern*) supply; (*erschaffen*) bring, cause; (*beibringen*) take; **auf die Seite s.** put aside; (*betrügerisch*) embezzle; **ich schaffe es noch, daß** I'll see to it that; **Rat s.** know what to do; **vom Halse s.** get off one's neck || §126 *tr* create; produce; **wie geschaffen sein für** cut out for || §109 *intr* do; (*arbeiten*) work; **j—m viel zu s. machen** cause s.o. a lot of trouble; **sich zu s. machen** be busy, putter around

schaf'fend *adj* working; (*schöpferisch*) creative; (*produktiv*) productive

Schaf'fensdrang *m* creative urge

Schaf'fenskraft *f* creative power

Schaffner ['ʃafnər] *m* (−s;−) (rr) conductor

Schaf'fung *f* (−;−en) creation

Schaf'hirt *m* shepherd

Schaf'pelz *m* sheepskin coat

Schaf'pferch *m* sheepfold

Schafs'kopf *m* (sl) mutton-head

Schaf'stall *m* sheepfold

Schaft [ʃaft] *m* (−[e]s;−̈e) shaft; (*e—r Feder*) stem; (*e—s Gewehrs*) stock; (*e—s Ankers*) shank; (bot) stem, stalk

Schaft'stiefel *m* high boot

Schaf'zucht *f* sheep raising

Schakal [ʃa'kal] *m* (−s;−e) jackal

schäkern ['ʃekərn] *intr* joke around; flirt

schal [ʃal] *adj* stale; insipid; (fig) flat || **Schal** *m* (−s;−e & −s) scarf; shawl

Schale ['ʃalə] *f* (−;−n) bowl; (*Tasse*) cup; (*von Obst*) peel, skin; (*Hülse*) shell; (*Schote*) pod; (*Rinde*) bark;

(*Waagschale*) scale; (zool) shell; **sich in S. werfen** (coll) doll up

schälen ['ʃɛlən] *tr* peel; (*Mais*) husk; (*Baumrinde*) bark || *ref* peel off

Scha'lentier *n* (zool) crustacean

Schalk [ʃalk] *m* (-[e]s;-e & ⸚e) rogue

schalk'haft *adj* roguish

Schall [ʃal] *m* (-[e]s;-e & ⸚e) sound; (*Klang*) ring; (*Lärm*) noise

Schall'boden *m* sounding board

Schall'dämpfer *m* (*an Schußwaffen*) silencer; (aut) muffler; (mus) soft pedal

schall'dicht *adj* soundproof

Schall'dose *f* (electron) pickup

Schall'druck *m* sonic boom

Schallehre (**Schall'lehre**) *f* acoustics

schallen ['ʃalən] *intr* sound, resound

Schall'grenze *f* sound barrier

Schall'mauer *f* sound barrier

Schall'meßgerät *n* sonar

Schall'pegel *m* sound level

Schall'platte *f* phonograph record

Schall'plattenaufnahme *f* recording

Schall'wand *f* baffle

Schall'welle *f* sound wave

Schalotte [ʃa'lɔtə] *f* (-;-n) (bot) scallion

schalt [ʃalt] *pret of* **schelten**

Schalt- *comb.fm.* switch; connecting; breaking; shifting

Schalt'bild *n* circuit diagram

Schalt'brett *n* switchboard; control panel; (aut) dashboard

Schalt'dose *f* switch box

schalten ['ʃaltən] *tr* switch; (*anlassen*) start; (*Gang*) (aut) shift || *intr* switch; (*regieren*) be in command; (aut) shift gears; **s. und walten mit** do as one pleases with

Schal'ter *m* (-s;-) switch; (*für Kundenverkehr*) window, ticket window

Schal'terdeckel *m* switch plate

Schalt'hebel *m* (aut) gearshift; (elec) switch lever

Schalt'jahr *n* leap year

Schalt'kasten *m* switch box

Schalt'pult *n* (rad, telv) control desk

Schalt'tafel *f* switchboard, instrument panel; (aut) dashboard

Schalt'uhr *f* timer

Schal'tung *f* (-;-en) switching; (elec) connection; (elec) circuit

Schaluppe [ʃa'lupə] *f* (-;-n) sloop

Scham [ʃam] *f* (-;) shame; (anat) genitals

Scham'bein *n* (anat) pubis

schämen ['ʃɛmən] *ref* (**über** *acc*) feel ashamed (of)

Scham'gefühl *n* sense of shame

Scham'haar *n* pubic hair

scham'haft *adj* modest, bashful

scham'los *adj* shameless

Schampun [ʃam'pun] *n* (-s;-s) shampoo

schampunieren [ʃampu'nirən] *tr* shampoo

scham'rot *adj* blushing; **s. werden** blush

Scham'teile *pl* genitals

Schand- [ʃant] *comb.fm.* of shame

schandbar ['ʃantbar] *adj* shameful; infamous

Schande ['ʃandə] *f* (-;) shame, disgrace

schänden ['ʃɛndən] *tr* disgrace; (*entweihen*) desecrate; (*Mädchen*) rape

Schän'der *m* (-s;-) violator; rapist

Schand'fleck *m* stain; (fig) blemish; (fig) good-for-nothing; **der S. der Familie** the disgrace of the family

schändlich ['ʃɛntlɪç] *adj* shameful, disgraceful; scandalous || *adv* (coll) awfully

Schand'mal *n* stigma

Schand'tat *f* shameful deed, crime

Schän'dung *f* (-;-en) desecration; disfigurement; rape

Schank [ʃaŋk] *m* (-[e]s;⸚e) bar, saloon

Schank'bier *n* draft beer

Schank'erlaubnis *f*, **Schank'gerechtigkeit** *f*, **Schank'konzession** *f* liquor license

Schank'stätte *f* bar, tavern

Schank'tisch *m* bar

Schank'wirt *m* bartender

Schank'wirtschaft *f* bar, saloon

Schanzarbeit ['ʃantsarbait] *f* earthwork; **Schanzarbeiten** entrenchments

Schanze ['ʃantsə] *f* (-;-n) entrenchments, trenches; (naut) quarter-deck; (sport) take-off ramp (*of ski jump*)

Schanz'gerät *n* entrenching tool

Schar [ʃar] *f* (-;-en) group, bunch; crowd; (*von Vögeln*) flock, flight

Scharade [ʃa'radə] *f* (-;-n) charade

scharen ['ʃarən] *ref* (**um**) gather (around)

scharf [ʃarf] *adj* (**schärfer** ['ʃɛrfər]; **schärfste** ['ʃɛrfstə] §9) sharp; (*Tempo*) fast; (*Bemerkung*) cutting; (*Blick*) hard; (*Brille*) strong; (*Fernrohr*) powerful; (*Geruch*) pungent; (*Munition*) live; (*Pfeffer, Senf*) hot; (*streng*) severe; (*genau*) exact; (*Ton*) shrill; (*wahrnehmend*) keen; **s. machen** sharpen; **s. sein auf** (acc) be keen on || *adv* hard; fast; **j-n s. nehmen** be very strict with s.o.; **s. ansehen** look hard at; **s. geladen** loaded; **s. schießen** shoot with live ammunition; **s. umreißen** define clearly

Scharf'blick *m* (fig) sharp eye

Schärfe ['ʃɛrfə] *f* (-;-n) sharpness; keenness; pungency; severity; accuracy

Scharf'einstellung *f* (phot) focusing

schärfen ['ʃɛrfən] *tr* sharpen, whet; make pointy; (fig) intensify

scharf'kantig *adj* sharp-edged

scharf'machen *tr* stir up; (*Bomben*) arm; (*Zünder*) activate

Scharf'macher *m* demagogue, agitator

Scharf'richter *m* executioner

Scharf'schütze *m* (mil) sharpshooter

scharf'sichtig *adj* sharp-eyed; (fig) clear-sighted

Scharf'sinn *m* sagacity, acumen

scharf'sinnig *adj* sharp, sagacious

Scharlach ['ʃarlax] *m* (-s;-e) scarlet; (pathol) scarlet fever

scharf'lachfarben *adj* scarlet

schar'lachrot *adj* scarlet

Scharlatan ['ʃarlatan] *m* (-s;-e) charlatan, quack

scharmant [ʃar'mant] *adj* charming

Scharmützel [ʃar'mʏtsəl] *n* (-s;-) skirmish

Scharnier [ʃar'niːr] *n* (-s;-e) hinge; joint

Schärpe ['ʃɛrpə] *f* (-;-n) sash

Scharre ['ʃarə] *f* (-;-n) scraper

Scharreisen ['ʃaraɪzən] *n* scraper

scharren ['ʃarən] *tr* scrape, paw || *intr* scrape; (**an** *acc*) scratch (on); **auf den Boden s.** paw the ground; **mit den Füßen** scrape the feet (*in disapproval*)

Scharte ['ʃartə] *f* (-;-n) nick, dent; (*Kerbe*) notch; (*Kratzer*) scratch; (*Riß*) crack; (*Bergsattel*) gap; (*fig*) mistake; **e-e S. auswetzen** (fig) make amends

Scharteke [ʃar'teːkə] *f* (-;-n) worthless old book; (fig) frump

schartig ['ʃartɪç] *adj* jagged; notched

Schatten ['ʃatən] *m* (-s;-) shade; shadow; **in den S. stellen** throw into the shade

Schat'tenbild *n* silhouette; (fig) phantom

Schat'tendasein *n* shadowy existence

Schat'tengestalt *f* shadowy figure

schat'tenhaft *adj* shadowy

Schat'tenriß *m* silhouette

Schat'tenseite *f* shady side; dark side; (fig) seamy side

schattieren [ʃa'tiːrən] *tr* shade; (*schraffieren*) hatch; (*abtönen*) tint

Schattie'rung *f* (-;-en) shading; (*Farbton*) shade, tint

schattig ['ʃatɪç] *adj* shadowy; shady

Schatulle [ʃa'tulə] *f* (-;-n) cash box; (*für Schmuck*) jewelry box; (hist) private funds (*of a prince*)

Schatz [ʃats] *m* (-es;⁻e) treasure; (*Vorrat*) store; (fig) sweetheart

Schatz'amt *n* treasury department

Schatz'anweisung *f* treasury bond

schätzbar ['ʃɛtsbaːr] *adj* valuable

schätzen ['ʃɛtsən] *tr* (*Grundstücke, Häuser, Schaden*) estimate, appraise; (*urteilen, vermuten*) guess; (*achten*) esteem, value; (*würdigen*) appreciate; **er schätzte mich auf 20 Jahre** he took me for 20 years old; **zu hoch s.** overestimate, overrate; **zu s. wissen** appreciate || *ref*—**sich** [*dat*] **es zu Ehre s.** consider it an honor; **sich glücklich s.** consider oneself lucky || *recip*—**sie s. sich nicht** there's no love lost between them

schät'zenswert *adj* valuable

Schät'zer -in §6 *mf* appraiser; (*zur Besteuerung*) assessor

Schatz'kammer *f* treasury; (fig) storehouse

Schatz'meister -in §6 *mf* treasurer

Schät'zung *f* (-;-en) estimate; (*Meinung*) estimation; (*Hochachtung*) esteem; (*Hochschätzung*) appreciation; (*zur Besteuerung*) assessment

schät'zungsweise *adv* approximately

Schät'zungswert *m* estimated value; assessed value; (*des Schadens*) appraisal

Schatz'wechsel *m* treasury bill

Schau [ʃaʊ] *f* (-;-en) view; (*Ausstel-*

lung) exhibition, show; (mil) review; (telv) show; **zur S. stehen** be on display; **zur S. stellen** put on display; **zur S. tragen** feign

Schau'bild *n* diagram, chart

Schauder ['ʃaʊdər] *m* (-s;-) shudder, shiver; (*Schrecken*) horror, terror

schauderbar ['ʃaʊdərbaːr] *adj* terrible

schau'dererregend *adj* horrifying

schau'derhaft *adj* horrible, awful

schaudern ['ʃaʊdərn] *intr* (**vor** *dat*) shudder (at) || *impers*—**es schaudert mich** I shudder

schauen ['ʃaʊ.ən] *tr* look at; (*beobachten*) observe || *intr* look

Schauer ['ʃaʊ.ər] *m* (-s;-) shower, downpour; (*Schauder*) shudder, chill; thrill; (*Anfall*) fit, attack; **einzelne S.** scattered showers

Schau'erdrama *n* (theat) thriller

schau'erlich *adj* dreadful, horrible

schauern ['ʃaʊ.ərn] *intr* shudder || *impers*—**es schauert** it is pouring; **es schauert mich** (or **mir**) **vor** (*dat*) I shudder at; I shiver with

Schau'erroman *m* thriller

Schaufel ['ʃaʊfəl] *f* (-;-n) shovel; scoop; (*Rad*—) paddle; (*Turbinen*—) blade, vane

schaufeln ['ʃaʊfəln] *tr* shovel; (*Grab*) dig || *intr* shovel

Schau'felrad *n* paddle wheel

Schau'fenster *n* display window; **die S. ansehen** go window-shopping

Schau'fensterauslage *f* window display

Schau'fensterbummel *m* window-shopping

Schau'fensterdekoration *f* window dressing

Schau'fliegen *n* stunt flying

Schau'flug *m* air show

Schau'gepränge *n* pageantry

Schau'gerüst *n* grandstand

Schau'kampf *m* (box) exhibition fight

Schau'kasten *n* showcase

Schaukel ['ʃaʊkəl] *f* (-;-n) swing

Schau'kelbrett *n* seesaw

schaukeln ['ʃaʊkəln] *tr* swing; rock || *intr* swing; rock; sway

Schau'kelpferd *n* rocking horse

Schau'kelreck *n* trapeze

Schau'kelstuhl *m* rocking chair

Schau'loch *n* peephole

Schaum [ʃaʊm] *m* (-[e]s;⁻e) foam, froth; (*Abschaum*) scum; (*Geifer*) slaver; **zu S. schlagen** whip; **zu S. werden** (fig) come to nothing

Schaum'bad *n* bubble bath

schäumen ['ʃɔɪmən] *intr* foam; (*Wein*) sparkle; (*aus Wut*) fume, boil

Schaum'gummi *n* & *m* foam rubber

Schaum'haube *f* head (*on beer*)

schaumig ['ʃaʊmɪç] *adj* foamy

Schaum'krone *f* whitecap (*on wave*)

Schau'modell *n* mock-up

Schaum'wein *m* sparkling wine

Schau'platz *m* scene, theater

Schau'prozeß *m* mock trial

schaurig ['ʃaʊrɪç] *adj* horrible

Schau'spiel *n* play, drama; spectacle

Schau'spieler *m* actor

Schau'spielerin *f* actress

schau'spielerisch *adj* theatrical

schauspielern ['ʃauʃpilərn] *intr* act; (*schwindeln*) act, make believe
Schau'spielhaus *n* theater
Schau'spielkunst *f* dramatic art
Schau'stück *n* show piece; (*Muster*) sample
Scheck [ʃɛk] *m* (-s;- & -e) check; **e-n S. ausstellen an** (*acc*) **über** (*acc*) write out a check to (*s.o.*) in the amount of; **e-n S. einlösen** cash a check; **e-n S. sperren lassen** stop payment on a check; **offener S.** blank check
Scheck'abschnitt *m* check stub
Scheck'formular *n* blank check
Scheck'heft *n* check book
scheckig ['ʃɛkɪç] *adj* dappled
Scheck'konto *n* checking account
scheel [ʃel] *adj* squinting; squint-eyed; (fig) envious, jealous
Scheffel ['ʃɛfəl] *m* (-s;-) bushel
scheffeln ['ʃɛfəln] *tr* amass
Scheibe ['ʃaibə] *f* (-;-n) disk; sheet; plate; (*Glas-*) pane; (*Honig-*) honeycomb; (*Ziel*) target; (*Schnitte*) slice; (astr) orb, disk; (mach) washer; (telp) dial
Schei'benbremse *f* disk brake
Schei'benkönig *m* top marksman
Schei'benschießen *n* target practice
Schei'benwäscher *m* windshield washer
Schei'benwischer *m* windshield wiper
Scheide ['ʃaidə] *f* (-;-n) sheath; border, boundary; (anat) vagina
Schei'debrief *m* farewell letter
Schei'degruß *m* goodbye
scheiden ['ʃaidən] §112 *tr* separate, divide; (*zerlegen*) decompose; (*Ehe*) dissolve; (*Eheleute*) divorce; (chem) analyze; (chem) refine ‖ *ref* part; **sich s. lassen** get a divorce ‖ *intr* (SEIN) part; depart; (*aus dem Amt*) resign, retire
schei'dend *adj* (*Tag*) closing; (*Sonne*) setting
Schei'dewand *f* partition
Schei'deweg *m* fork, crossroad; (fig) moment of decision
Schei'dung *f* (-;-en) separation; (*Ehe-*) divorce
Schein [ʃain] *m* (-[e]s;-e) shine; (*Licht*) (*Schimmer*) gleam, glitter; (*Strahl*) flash; (*Erscheinung*) appearance; (*Anschein*) pretense, show; (*Urkunde*) certificate, papers, license, ticket; (*Geldschein*) bill; (*Quittung*) receipt; **dem Scheine nach** apparently; **den äußeren S. wahren** save face; **sich** [*dat*] **den S. geben** make believe; **zum S.** pro forma
Schein– *comb.fm.* sham, mock, make-believe
scheinbar ['ʃainbar] *adj* seeming, apparent; likely; (*vorgeblich*) make-believe
Schein'bild *n* illusion; phantom
scheinen ['ʃainən] §128 *intr* shine; seem, appear ‖ *impers*—**es scheint** it seems
Schein'grund *n* pretext
schein'heilig *adj* sanctimonious, hypocritical
Schein'tod *m* suspended animation

Schein'werfer *m* flashlight; (aer) beacon; (aut) headlight
Scheit [ʃait] *n* (-[e]s;-e) piece of chopped wood; **Holz in Scheite hakken** chop wood
Scheitel ['ʃaitəl] *m* (-s;-) apex, top; top of the head; (*des Haares*) part; **e-n S. ziehen** make a part
scheiteln ['ʃaitəln] *tr & ref* part
Schei'telpunkt *m* (fig) summit; (astr) zenith; (math) vertex
Schei'telwinkel *m* opposite angle
Scheiterhaufen ['ʃaitərhaufən] *m* funeral pile; **auf dem S. sterben** die at the stake
scheitern ['ʃaitərn] *intr* (SEIN) run aground, be wrecked; (*Plan*) miscarry ‖ **Scheitern** *n* (-s;) shipwreck; (fig) failure
Schelle ['ʃɛlə] *f* (-;-n) bell; (*Fessel*) handcuff; (*Ohrfeige*) box on the ear
schellen ['ʃɛlən] *tr & intr* ring
Schel'lenkappe *f* cap and bells
Schellfisch ['ʃɛlfɪʃ] *m* haddock
Schelm [ʃɛlm] *m* (-[e]s;-e) rogue; (Lit) knave; **armer S.** poor devil
Schel'menstreich *m* prank
schelmisch ['ʃɛlmɪʃ] *adj* roguish, impish
Schelte ['ʃɛltə] *f* (-;-n) scolding
schelten ['ʃɛltən] *tr & intr* scold
Scheltwort ['ʃɛltvɔrt] *n* (-[e]s;-e & ⸚er) abusive word; word of reproof
Sche–ma ['ʃema] *n* (-s;-s & -mata [mata] & -men [mən]) scheme; diagram; (*Muster*) pattern, design
Schemel ['ʃeməl] *m* (-s;-) stool
Schemen ['ʃemən] *m* (-s;-) phantom, shadow
sche'menhaft *adj* shadowy
Schenk [ʃɛŋk] *m* (-en;-en) bartender
Schenke ['ʃɛŋkə] *f* (-;-n) bar, tavern
Schenkel ['ʃɛŋkəl] *m* (-s;-) thigh; (*e-s Winkels*) side; (*e-r Schere*) blade; (*e-s Zirkels*) leg
schenken ['ʃɛŋkən] *tr* give, offer; pour (out); (*Aufmerksamkeit*) pay; (*Schuld*) remit; **das ist geschenkt** that's dirt cheap; **das kann ich mir s.** I can pass that up; **das kannst du dir s.!** keep it to yourself! **j-m Beifall s.** applaud s.o.; **j-m das Leben s.** grant s.o. pardon
Schenk'stube *f* taproom, barroom
Schenk'tisch *m* bar
Schen'kung *f* (-;-en) donation
Schenk'wirt *m* bartender
scheppern ['ʃɛpərn] *intr* (coll) rattle
Scherbe ['ʃɛrbə] *f* (-;-n), **Scherben** ['ʃɛrbən] *m* (-s;-) broken piece; potsherd; **in Scherben gehen** go to pieces
Scher'bengericht *n* ostracism
Scherbett [ʃɛr'bɛt] *m* (-[e]s;-e) sherbe(r)t
Schere ['ʃerə] *f* (-;-n) (pair of) scissors; shears; (*Draht-*) cutter; (zool) claw
scheren ['ʃerən] *tr* bother; **was schert dich das?** what's that to you? ‖ §129 *tr* cut, clip, trim; (*Schafe*) shear; ‖ §109 *ref*—**scher dich ins Bett!** off to bed with you!; **scher dich zum Teu-**

fel! the devil with you!; **sich um etw s.** trouble oneself about s.th.

Schererei [ʃerə'raɪ] f (-;-en) trouble

Scherflein ['ʃerflaɪn] n (-s;-) bit; **sein S. beitragen** contribute one's bit

Scherz [ʃerts] m (-es;-e) joke; **im** (or **zum**) **S.** for fun; **S. treiben mit** make fun of

scherzen ['ʃertsən] intr joke, kid

scherz'haft adj joking, humorous

Scherz'name m nickname

scherz'weise adv in jest, as a joke

scheu [ʃɔɪ] adj shy; **s. machen** frighten; startle || **Scheu** f (-;) shyness

Scheuche ['ʃɔɪçə] f (-;-n) scarecrow

scheuchen ['ʃɔɪçən] tr scare (away)

scheuen ['ʃɔɪən] tr shun; shrink from; fear; (Mühen, Kosten) spare; **ohne die Kosten zu s.** regardless of expenses || ref be afraid (of); **ich s. mich zu** (inf) I am reluctant to (inf) || intr—**s. vor** (dat) shy at

Scheuer ['ʃɔɪ.ər] f (-;-n) barn

Scheu'erbürste f scrub brush

Scheu'erfrau f scrubwoman

Scheu'erlappen m scrub rag

scheuern ['ʃɔɪ.ərn] tr scrub, scour; (reiben) rub

Scheu'erpulver n scouring powder

Scheu'klappe f blinder (for horses)

Scheune ['ʃɔɪnə] f (-;-n) barn

Scheu'nendrescher m—**er ißt wie ein S.** (coll) he eats like a horse

Scheusal ['ʃɔɪzal] n (-s;-e) monster

scheußlich ['ʃɔɪslɪç] adj dreadful, atrocious; (coll) awful, rotten

Scheuß'lichkeit f (-;-en) hideousness; (Tat) atrocity

Schi [ʃi] m (-s;- & -er) ski; **Schi fahren** (or **laufen**) ski

Schicht [ʃɪçt] f (-;-en) layer, film; (Farb-) coat; (Arbeiter-) shift; (Gesellschafts-) class; (geol) stratum; (phot) emulsion; **Leute aus allen Schichten** people from all walks of life; **S. machen** (coll) knock off from work

Schicht'arbeit f shift work

schichten ['ʃɪçtən] tr arrange in layers; laminate; (Holz) stack (up); (in Klassen einteilen) classify; (geol) stratify; (Ladung) (naut) stow

Schich'tenaufbau m, **Schich'tenbildung** f (geol) stratification

-schichtig [ʃɪçtɪç] comb.fm. -layer, -ply

Schicht'linie f contour

Schicht'linienplan m contour map

Schicht'meister m shift foreman

schicht'weise adv in layers; in shifts

schick [ʃɪk] adj chic, swank || **Schick** m (-[e]s;) stylishness; (Geschick) skill; (Geschmack) tact, taste; **S. haben für** have a knack for

schicken ['ʃɪkən] tr send || ref—**sich s. für** (or **zu**) be suitable for; **sich s. in** (acc) adapt oneself to; resign oneself to || intr—**nach j—m s.** send for s.o. || impers—**es schickt sich** it is proper; (sich ereignen) come to pass

schick'lich adj proper; decent

Schick'lichkeit f (-;) propriety

Schick'lichkeitsgefühl n sense of propriety

Schicksal ['ʃɪkzal] n (-[e]s;-e) destiny, fate

Schick'salsgefährte m fellow sufferer

Schick'salsglaube m fatalism

Schick'salsgöttinnen pl (myth) Fates

Schick'salsschlag m stroke of fate

Schickung (Schik'kung) f (-;-en) (divine) dispensation

Schiebe- [ʃibə] comb.fm. sliding, push

Schie'beleiter f extension ladder

schieben ['ʃibən] §130 tr push, shove; traffic in; **bei die lange Bank s.** put off; **e-e ruhige Kugel s.** have a cushy job; **Kegel s.** bowl; **Wache s.** (mil) pull guard duty || ref move, shuffle || intr shuffle along; profiteer

Schieber ['ʃibər] m (-s;-) slide valve; (Riegel) bolt; (am Schornstein) damper; (fig) racketeer

Schie'bergeschäft f (com) racket

Schiebertum ['ʃibərtum] n (-s;) (com) racketeering

Schie'betür f sliding door

schied [ʃit] pret of **scheiden**

Schieds- [ʃits] comb.fm. of arbitration

Schieds'gericht n board of arbitration; **an ein S. verweisen** refer to arbitration

Schieds'mann m (-[e]s;"-er) arbitrator

Schieds'richter m arbitrator; (sport) referee, umpire

schieds'richterlich adj of an arbitration board || adv by arbitration

Schieds'spruch m decision; **e-n S. fällen** render a decision

schief [ʃif] adj (abfallend) slanting; (krumm) crooked; (einseitig) lopsided; (geneigt) inclined; (Winkel) oblique; (falsch) false, wrong; **auf die schiefe Ebene geraten** (fig) go downhill; **schiefe Lage** (fig) tight spot; **schiefes Licht** (fig) bad light || adv at an angle; awry; obliquely; wrong; **s. ansehen** look askance at; **s. halten** tip, tilt; **s. nehmen** take amiss

Schiefer ['ʃifər] m (-s;-) slate; (Splitter) splinter

Schie'ferbruch m slate quarry

Schie'feröl n shale oil

Schie'fertafel f (educ) slate

schief'gehen §82 intr (SEIN) go wrong

schief'treten §152 tr—**die Abstätze s.** wear down the heels

schieläugig ['ʃiloygɪç] adj squint-eyed; cross-eyed

schielen ['ʃilən] intr squint; **s. nach** squint at; leer at

schie'lend adj squinting; cross-eyed; furtive

schien [ʃin] pret of **scheinen**

Schienbein ['ʃinbaɪn] n shinbone, tibia

Schien'beinschützer m shinguard

Schiene ['ʃinə] f (-;-n) (rr) rail, track; (surg) splint; **aus den Schienen springen** jump the track

schienen ['ʃinən] tr put in splints

Schie'nenbahn f track, rails; streetcar; railroad

Schie'nenfahrzeug n rail car

Schie'nengleis n track

schier [ʃir] *adj* sheer || *adv* almost

Schierling [ˈʃirlɪŋ] *m* (-s;-e) (bot) hemlock

Schieß- [ʃis] *comb.fm.* shooting

Schieß'baumwolle *f* guncotton

Schieß'bedarf *m* ammunition

Schieß'bude *f* shooting gallery

Schieß'eisen *n* (hum) shooting iron

schießen [ˈʃisən] §76 *tr* shoot, fire; **e-n Bock s.** (coll) pull a boner; **ein Tor s.** make a goal || *intr* (**auf** *acc*) shoot (at); **aus dem Hinterhalt s.** snipe; **gut s.** be a good shot; **scharf s.** shoot with live ammunition || *intr* (SEIN) shoot up; spurt; zig, fly; **das Blut schoß ihm ins Gesicht** his face got red; **in Samen s.** go to seed; **ins Kraut s.** sprout || **Schießen** *n* (-s;) shooting; **das ist ja zum s.!** (coll) that's a riot!

Schießerei [ʃisəˈraɪ] *f* (-;-en) gun fight; pointless firing

Schieß'gewehr *n* firearm

Schieß'hund *m* (hunt) pointer

Schieß'lehre *f* ballistics

Schieß'platz *m* firing range

Schieß'prügel *m* (hum) shooting iron

Schieß'pulver *n* gunpowder

Schieß'scharte *f* loophole

Schieß'scheibe *f* target

Schieß'stand *m* shooting gallery; (mil) firing range, rifle range

Schieß'übung *f* firing practice

Schi'fahrer -in §6 *mf* skier

Schiff [ʃɪf] *n* (-[e]s;-e) ship; (archit) nave; (typ) galley

Schiffahrt (**Schiff'fahrt**) *f* navigation

Schiffahrtslinie (**Schiff'fahrtslinie**) *f* steamship line

Schiffahrtsweg (**Schiff'fahrtsweg**) *m* shipping lane

schiffbar [ˈʃɪfbar] *adj* navigable

Schiff'bau *m* (-[e]s;) shipbuilding

Schiff'bruch *m* shipwreck

schiff'brüchig *adj* shipwrecked

Schiff'brücke *f* pontoon bridge; (naut) bridge

Schiffchen [ˈʃɪfçən] *n* (-s;-) little ship; (mil) overseas cap; (tex) shuttle

schiffen [ˈʃɪfən] *intr* (vulg) pee || *impers*—**es schifft** (vulg) it's pouring

Schiffer [ˈʃɪfər] *m* (-s;-) seaman; skipper; (*Schiffsführer*) navigator

Schif'ferklavier *n* (coll) concertina

Schiffs'journal *n* log, logbook

Schiffs'junge *m* cabin boy

Schiffs'küche *f* galley

Schiffs'ladung *f* cargo

Schiffs'luke *f* hatch

Schiffs'mannschaft *f* crew

Schiffs'ortung *f* dead reckoning

Schiffs'raum *m* hold; tonnage

Schiffs'rumpf *m* hull

Schiffs'schraube *f* propeller

Schiffs'tau *n* hawser

Schiffs'taufe *f* christening of a ship

Schiffs'werft *f* shipyard, dockyard

Schiffs'winde *f* winch, capstan

Schiffs'zimmermann *m* ship's carpenter; (*bei e-r Werft*) shipwright

Schikane [ʃɪˈkanə] *f* (-;-n) chicanery; **mit allen Schikanen** with all the frills; (aut) fully loaded

schikanieren [ʃɪkaˈnirən] *tr* harass

schikanös [ʃɪkaˈnøs] *adj* annoying

Schi'langlauf *m* cross-country skiing

Schi'lauf *m* skiing

schi'laufen §105 *intr* (SEIN) ski || **Schilaufen** *n* (-s;) skiing

Schi'läufer -in §6 *mf* skier

Schild [ʃɪlt] *m* (-[e]s;-e) shield; (heral) coat of arms; **etw im Schilde führen** have s.th. up one's sleeve || *n* (-[e]s;-er) sign; road sign; nameplate; (*e-s Arztes, usw.*) shingle; (*Etikett*) label; (*Mützenschirm*) visor, shade

Schild'bürger *m* (fig) dunce

Schild'bürgerstreich *m* boner

Schild'drüse *f* thyroid gland

Schilderhaus [ˈʃɪldərhaus] *n* sentry box

Schil'dermaler *m* sign painter

schildern [ˈʃɪldərn] *tr* depict, describe

Schil'derung *f* (-;-en) description

Schild'kröte *f* tortoise, turtle

Schildpatt [ˈʃɪltpat] *n* (-[e]s;) tortoise shell, turtle shell

Schilf [ʃɪlf] *n* (-[e]s;-e) reed

Schilf'rohr *n* reed

Schi'lift *m* ski lift

Schiller [ˈʃɪlər] *m* (-s;) luster; iridescence

schillern [ˈʃɪlərn] *intr* be iridescent

Schil'lerwein *m* bright-red wine

Schilling [ˈʃɪlɪŋ] *m* (-s;- & -e) shilling; (Aust) schilling

Schimäre [ʃɪˈmerə] *f* (-;-n) chimera

Schimmel [ˈʃɪməl] *m* (-s;-) white horse; mildew, mould

schimmelig [ˈʃɪməlɪç] *adj* moldy

schimmeln [ˈʃɪməln] *intr* (HABEN & SEIN) get moldy

Schimmer [ˈʃɪmər] *m* (-s;) glimmer

schimmern [ˈʃɪmərn] *intr* glimmer

schimmlig [ˈʃɪmlɪç] *adj* moldy

Schimpanse [ʃɪmˈpanzə] *m* (-n;-n) chimpanzee

Schimpf [ʃɪmpf] *m* (-[e]s;-e) insult, abuse

schimpfen [ˈʃɪmpfən] *tr* scold, abuse || *intr* be abusive; (**über** *acc* or **auf** *acc*) curse (at), swear (at)

schimpf'lich *adj* disgraceful

Schimpf'name *m* nickname; **j-m Schimpfnamen geben** call s.o. names

Schimpf'wort *n* (-[e]s;-e & *⁻*er) swear word

Schindaas [ˈʃɪntas] *n* carrion

Schindel [ˈʃɪndəl] *f* (-;-n) shingle

schindeln [ˈʃɪndəln] *tr* shingle

schinden [ˈʃɪndən] §167 *tr* torment; oppress; exploit; **Eindruck s.** try to make an impression; **Eintrittsgeld s.** crash the gate; **Zeilen s.** pad the writing; **Zigaretten s.** bum cigarettes || *ref* break one's back

Schin'der *m* (-s;-) slave driver

Schinderei [ʃɪndəˈraɪ] *f* (-;-en) drudgery, grind

Schindluder [ˈʃɪntludər] *n* carrion; **mit j-m S. treiben** treat s.o. outrageously

Schindmähre [ˈʃɪntmerə] *f* old nag

Schinken [ˈʃɪŋkən] *m* (-s;-) ham; (hum) tome; (hum) huge painting

Schinnen [ˈʃɪnən] *pl* dandruff

Schippe ['ʃɪpə] f (-;-n) shovel, scoop; (cards) spade(s); **e-e S. machen** (or **ziehen**) pout; **j-n auf die S. nehmen** (coll) pull s.o.'s leg

schippen ['ʃɪpən] tr & intr shovel

Schirm [ʃɪrm] m (-[e]s;-e) screen; umbrella; x-ray screen; lampshade; visor; (fig) protection, shelter; (hunt) blind

Schirm′bild n x-ray

Schirm′bildaufnahme f x-ray

Schirm′dach n lean-to

schirmen ['ʃɪrmən] tr protect

Schirm′futteral n umbrella case

Schirm′herr m protector, patron

Schirm′herrin f protectress, patroness

Schirm′herrschaft f protectorate; patronage

Schirm′ständer m umbrella stand

Schir′mung f (-;-en) (elec) shielding

schirren ['ʃɪrən] tr harness

Schis·ma ['ʃɪsma] n (-;-mata [mata] & -men [mən] schism

Schi′sprung m ski jump

Schi′stock m ski pole

schizophren [sçɪtso′fren] adj schizophrenic

Schizophrenie [sçɪtsofre′ni] f (-;) schizophrenia

schlabbern ['ʃlabərn] tr lap up ‖ intr (geifern) slobber; (fig) babble

Schlacht [ʃlaxt] f (-;-en) battle; **die S. bei** the battle of

schlachten ['ʃlaxtən] tr slaughter

Schlach′tenbummler m camp follower; (sport) fan

Schlächter ['ʃlɛçtər] m (-s;-) butcher

Schlacht′feld n battlefield

Schlacht′flieger m combat pilot; close-support fighter

Schlacht′geschrei n battle cry

Schlacht′haus n slaughterhouse

Schlacht′kreuzer m heavy cruiser

Schlacht′opfer n sacrifice; (fig) victim

Schlacht′ordnung f battle array

Schlacht′roß n (hist) charger

Schlacht′ruf m battle cry

Schlacht′schiff n battleship

Schlach′tung f (-;-en) slaughter

Schlacke ['ʃlakə] f (-;-n) cinder; lava; (metal) slag, dross

schlackig ['ʃlakɪç] adj sloppy (weather)

Schlaf [ʃlaf] m (-[e]s;) sleep

Schlaf′abteil n sleeping compartment

Schlaf′anzug m pajamas

Schläfchen ['ʃlɛfçən] n (-s;-) nap; **ein S. machen** take a nap

Schläfe ['ʃlɛfə] f (-;-n) temple

schlafen ['ʃlafən] §131 tr sleep ‖ intr sleep; **sich s. legen** go to bed

Schla′fenszeit f bedtime

Schläfer -in ['ʃlɛfər(ɪn)] §6 mf sleeper

schläfern ['ʃlɛfərn] impers—**es schläfert mich** I'm sleepy

schlaff [ʃlaf] adj slack; limp; flabby; (locker) loose

Schlaf′gelegenheit f sleeping accommodations

Schlaf′kammer f bedroom

Schlaf′krankheit f sleeping sickness

schlaf′los adj sleepless

Schlaf′losigkeit f (-;) sleeplessness

Schlaf′mittel n sleeping pill

Schlaf′mütze f nightcap; (fig) sleepy-head

schläfrig ['ʃlɛfrɪç] adj sleepy, drowsy

Schläf′rigkeit f (-;) sleepiness, drowsiness

Schlaf′rock m housecoat

Schlaf′saal m dormitory

Schlaf′sack m sleeping bag

Schlaf′stätte f, **Schlaf′stelle** f place to sleep

Schlaf′stube f bedroom

Schlaf′trunk m (hum) nightcap

schlaf′trunken adj still half-asleep

Schlaf′wagen m (rr) sleeping car

schlaf′wandeln intr (SEIN) walk in one's sleep

Schlafwandler -in ['ʃlafvandlər(ɪn)] §6 mf sleepwalker

Schlaf′zimmer n bedroom

Schlag [ʃlak] m (-[e]s;-̈e) blow; stroke; (Puls-) beat; (Faust-) punch; (Hand-) slap; (Donner-) clap; (Tauben-) loft; (Art, Sorte) kind, sort, breed; (e-s Taues) coil; (der Vögel) song; (vom Pferd) kick; (e-r Kutsche) door; (Holz-) cut; (Pendel-) swing; (agr) field; (elec) shock; (mil) scoop, ladleful; (pathol) stroke; **ein S. ins Wasser** a vain attempt; **Leute seines Schlages** the likes of him; **S. zwölf Uhr** at the stroke of twelve; **von gutem S.** of the right sort

Schlag′ader f artery

Schlag′anfall m (pathol) stroke

schlag′artig adj sudden, surprise; (heftig) violent ‖ adv all of a sudden; with a bang

Schlag′baum m barrier

Schlag′besen m eggbeater

Schlag′bolzen m firing pin

Schlägel ['ʃlegəl] m (-s;-) sledge hammer

schlagen ['ʃlagən] §132 tr hit; strike; beat; (besiegen) defeat; (strafen) spank; (Alarm) sound; (Brücke) build; (Eier) beat; (Geld) coin; (Holz) fell; (Saiten) strike; (Schlacht) fight; **die Augen zu Boden s.** cast down the eyes; **durch ein Sieb s.** strain, sift; **e-e geschlagene Stunde** (coll) a solid hour; **in die Flucht s.** put to flight; **in Fesseln s.** put in chains; **in Papier s.** wrap in paper; **Wurzel s.** take root; **zu Boden s.** knock down ‖ ref come to blows; fight a duel; fence; **sich gut s.** stand one's ground; **sich s. zu** side with; **um sich s.** flail about ‖ intr strike; beat; (Pferd) kick; (Vogel) sing; **mit den Flügeln s.** flap the wings; **nach j-m s.** take a swing at s.o.; (fig) be like s.o., take after s.o.

schla′gend adj striking, impressive; convincing; **schlagende Verbindung** dueling fraternity; **schlagende Wetter** firedamp

Schla′ger m (-s;-) (tolle Sache) hot item; (mus, theat) hit

Schläger ['ʃlegər] m (-s;-) beater; hitter; batter; baseball bat; golf club; tennis racket; eggbeater; mallet; (Singvogel) warbler; (Raufbold) bully

Schlägerei [ʃlɛgəˈraɪ] *f* (-;-en) fight, fighting; brawl

Schla'gerpreis *m* rock-bottom price

Schla'gersänger –in §6 *mf* pop singer

schlag'fertig *adj* quick with an answer; (*Antwort*) ready

Schlag'holz *n* club, bat

Schlag'instrument *n* percussion instrument

Schlag'kraft *f* striking power

schlag'kräftig *adj* (*Armee*) powerful; (*Beweis*) conclusive

Schlag'licht *n* strong light; glare

Schlag'loch *n* pothole

Schlag'mal *n* (baseball) home plate

Schlag'ring *m* brass knuckles

Schlag'sahne *f* whipped cream

Schlag'schatten *m* deep shadow

Schlag'seite *f* (naut) list; **S. haben** have a list; (hum) be drunk

Schlag'uhr *f* striking clock

Schlag'weite *f* striking distance

Schlag'welle *f* breaker, comber

Schlag'wetter *pl* (min) firedamp

Schlag'wort *n* (-[e]s;-̈er & -e) slogan; key word, subject (*in cataloguing*); (*Phrasendrescherei*) claptrap

Schlag'wörterkatalog *m* (libr) subject index

Schlag'zeile *f* headline

Schlag'zeug *n* percussion instruments

Schlaks [ʃlaks] *m* (-es;-e) lanky person

schlaksig [ʃlaksɪç] *adj* lanky

Schlamassel [ʃlaˈmasəl] *m* & *n* (-s;-) (coll) jam, pickle, mess

Schlamm [ʃlam] *m* (-[e]s;-e) mud, slime; (*im Motor*) sludge; (fig) mire

Schlamm'bad *n* mud bath

schlämmen [ˈʃlɛmən] *tr* dredge; (metal) wash

schlammig [ˈʃlamɪç] *adj* muddy

Schlampe [ˈʃlampə] *f* (-;-n) frump; (sl) slut

Schlamperei [ʃlampəˈraɪ] *f* (-;-en) slovenliness; untidiness, mess

schlampig [ˈʃlampɪç] *adj* sloppy

schlang [ʃlaŋ] *pret* of **schlingen**

Schlange [ˈʃlaŋə] *f* (-;-n) snake; queue, waiting line; (*Wasserschlauch*) hose; **Schlange stehen nach** line up for

schlängeln [ˈʃlɛŋəln] *ref* wind; (*Fluß*) meander; (*sich krümmen*) squirm; wriggle; (fig) worm one's way

Schlan'genbeschwörer –in §6 *mf* snake charmer

Schlan'genlinie *f* wavy line

schlank [ʃlaŋk] *adj* slender, slim; **im schlanken Trabe** at a fast clip

Schlank'heit *f* (-;) slenderness

Schlank'heitskur *f*—e—e **S. machen** diet

schlankweg [ˈʃlaŋkvɛk] *adv* flatly; downright

schlapp [ʃlap] *adj* slack, limp; flabby; (*müde*) washed out ‖ **Schlappe** *f* (-;-n) setback; (*Verlust*) loss

schlappen [ˈʃlapən] *intr* flap; shuffle along ‖ **Schlappen** *m* (-s;-) slipper

schlappern [ˈʃlapərn] *tr* lap up

schlapp'machen *intr* (*zusammenbrechen*) collapse; (*ohnmächtig werden*) faint; (*nicht durchhalten*) call it quits

Schlapp'schwanz *m* (coll) weakling, sissy; (*Feigling*) coward

Schlaraffenland [ʃlaˈrafənlant] *n* paradise

Schlaraffenleben [ʃlaˈrafənlebən] *n* life of Riley

schlau [ʃlaʊ] *adj* sly; clever

Schlauch [ʃlaʊx] *m* (-[e]s;-̈e) hose; tube; (fig) souse; (aut) inner tube; (educ) pony

Schlauch'boot *n* rubber dinghy

schlauchen [ˈʃlaʊxən] *tr* drive hard; (mil) drill mercilessly

Schlauch'ventil *n* (aut) valve

Schläue [ˈʃlɔɪə] *f* (-;) slyness

schlau'erweise *adv* prudently

Schlaufe [ˈʃlaʊfə] *f* (-;-n) loop

Schlau'kopf *m*, **Schlau'meier** *m* sly fox

schlecht [ʃlɛçt] *adj* bad, poor; **mir wird s.** I'm getting sick; **schlechter werden** get worse; **s. werden** go bad ‖ *adv* poorly; **die Uhr geht s.** the clock is off; **s. daran sein** be badly off; **s. und recht** somehow; **s. zu sprechen sein auf** (acc) have it in for

schlechterdings [ˈʃlɛçtərdɪŋs] *adv* utterly, absolutely

schlecht'gelaunt *adj* in a bad mood

schlecht'hin *adv* simply, downright

schlecht'machen *tr* talk behind the back of

schlechtweg [ˈʃlɛçtvɛk] *adv* simply, downright

schlecken [ˈʃlɛkən] *tr* lick ‖ *intr* eat sweets, nibble

Schleckerei [ʃlɛkəˈraɪ] *f* (-;-en) sweets

schleckern [ˈʃlɛkərn] *intr* have a sweet tooth ‖ *impers*—**mich schleckert es nach** I have a yen for

Schlegel [ˈʃlegəl] *m* (-s;-) sledge hammer; (*Holz-*) mallet; (culin) leg; (mus) drumstick

schleichen [ˈʃlaɪçən] §85 *ref* & *intr* (SEIN) sneak

schlei'chend *adj* creeping; furtive; (*Krankheit*) lingering; (*Gift*) slow

Schlei'cher *m* (-s;-) sneak, hypocrite

Schleicherei [ʃlaɪçəˈraɪ] *f* (-;-en) sneaking; underhand dealing

Schleich'gut *n* contraband

Schleich'handel *m* underhand dealing; smuggling; black-marketing

Schleich'weg *m* secret path; **auf Schleichwegen** in a roundabout way

Schleier [ˈʃlaɪ.ər] *m* (-s;-) veil; haze; gauze

schlei'erhaft *adj* hazy; mysterious; (fig) veiled; **das ist mir s.** I don't know what to make of it

Schleif- [ʃlaɪf] *comb.fm.* sliding; grinding, abrasive

Schleif'bürste *f* (elec) brush

Schleife [ˈʃlaɪfə] *f* (-;-n) (*am Kleid, im Haar*) bow; (*in Schnüren*) slipknot; (*e-r Straße*) hairpin curve; (*e-s Flusses*) bend; (*Wende-*) loop; (*mit langen Bändern*) streamer; (*Rutschbahn*) slide, chute; (aer) loop

schleifen [ˈʃlaɪfən] *tr* drag; (*Kleid*) trail along; demolish; raze; (mus) slur ‖ §88 *tr* grind; whet; polish; (*Glas, Edelstein*) cut; (mil) drill hard ‖ §109 *intr* drag, trail

Schleif'mit'tel n abrasive
Schleif'papier n sandpaper
Schleif'rad n emery wheel
Schleif'stein m whetstone
Schleim [ʃlaim] m (-[e]s;-e) slime; mucus, phlegm
Schleim'haut f mucous membrane
schleimig ['ʃlaimiç] adj slimy; mucous
schleißen ['ʃlaisən] §53 tr split; slit; (Federkiele) strip || intr wear out
Schlemm [ʃlem] m (-s;-e) (cards) slam
schlemmen ['ʃlemən] intr carouse; gorge oneself; live high
Schlem'mer –in §6 mf glutton, guzzler; gourmet
schlem'merhaft adj gluttonous; (üppig) plentiful, luxurious
Schlem'merlokal n gourmet restaurant
Schlempe ['ʃlempə] f (-;-n) slop
schlendern ['ʃlendərn] intr (SEIN) stroll
Schlendrian ['ʃlendri·an] m (-s;) routine
schlenkern ['ʃleŋkərn] tr dangle, swing || intr dangle; **mit den Armen s.** swing the arms
Schlepp– ['ʃlep] comb.fm. towing, drag
Schlepp'dampfer m tugboat
Schlepp'dienst m towing service
Schleppe ['ʃlepə] f (-;-n) train
schleppen ['ʃlepən] tr drag; lug, tote; (aer, naut) tow || ref drag along; **sich mit etw s.** be burdened with s.th.
Schlep'penkleid n dress with a train
Schlep'per m (-s;-) hauler; tractor; tugboat; tender, tipper
Schlepp'fischerei f trawling
Schlepp'netz n dragnet, dredge; trawling net
Schlepp'netzboot n trawler
Schlepp'schiff n tugboat
Schlepp'tau n towline; **ins S. nehmen** take in tow
Schleuder ['ʃloidər] f (-;-n) sling; slingshot; (aer) catapult; (mach) centrifuge
schleudern ['ʃloidərn] tr fling; sling; (aer) catapult || intr (aut) skid; (com) undersell
Schleu'derpreis m cutrate price
Schleu'dersitz m (aer) ejection seat
schleunig ['ʃloiniç] adj speedy || adv in all haste; (sofort) at once
schleunigst ['ʃloiniçst] adv as soon as possible; right away
Schleuse ['ʃloizə] f (-;-n) lock, sluice, sluice way; drain, sewer
schleusen ['ʃloizən] tr (fig) maneuver
schlich [ʃliç] pret of **schleichen** || **Schlich** [ʃliç] m (-[e]s;-e) trick; **alle Schliche kennen** know all the ropes; **j-m auf die Schliche (or hinter j-s Schliche) kommen** be on to s.o.
schlicht [ʃliçt] adj smooth; plain
schlichten ['ʃliçtən] tr smooth; (fig) settle, arbitrate
Schlich'ter –in §6 mf arbitrator
Schlich'tung f (-;-en) arbitration; settlement
schlief [ʃlif] pret of **schlafen**
Schließe ['ʃlisə] f (-;-n) clasp; pin
schließen ['ʃlisən] §76 tr shut, close; lock; end, conclude; (Betrieb) shut

down; (Bücher) balance; (Konto; Klammer) close; (Bündnis) form; (Frieden; Rede) conclude; (Kompromiß) reach; (Heirat) form; (Geschäft, Handel) strike; (Versammlung) adjourn; (Wette) make; (Reihen) (mil) close; **ans Herz s.** press to one's heart; **aus etw. s., daß** conclude from s.th. that; **den Zug s.** (mil) bring up the rear; **e-n Vergleich s.** come to an agreement; **ins Herz s.** take a liking to; **kurz s.** (elec) short || ref shut, close; **in sich s.** comprise, include; (bedeuten) imply; (umfassen) involve; **von sich auf andere s.** judge others by oneself || intr shut, close; end
Schließ'fach n post office box; safe-deposit box
schließlich ['ʃlisliç] adj final, eventual || adv finally
schliff [ʃlif] pp of **schleifen** || **Schliff** m (-[e]s;-e) polish; (-s Diamanten) cut; (fig) polish; (mil) rigorous training
schlimm [ʃlim] adj bad; (bedenklich) serious; (traurig) sad; (wund) sore; (eklig) nasty; **am schlimmsten** worst; **immer schlimmer** worse and worse; **s. daran sein** be badly off
schlimmstenfalls ['ʃlimstənfals] adv at worst
Schlinge ['ʃliŋə] f (-;-n) loop; coil; (fig) trap, difficulty; (bot) tendril; (hunt) snare; (surg) sling; **in die S. gehen** (fig) fall into a trap
Schlingel ['ʃliŋəl] m (-s;-) rascal; **fauler S.** lazybones
schlingen ['ʃliŋən] §142 tr tie; twist; wind; wrap; gulp || ref wind, coil; climb, creep || intr gulp down food
Schlingerbewegung ['ʃliŋərbəveguŋ] f (naut) roll
schlingern ['ʃliŋərn] intr (naut) roll
Schlinggewächs ['ʃliŋgəveks] n,
Schlingpflanze ['ʃliŋpflantsə] f climber
Schlips [ʃlips] m (-es;-e) necktie
Schlitten ['ʃlitən] m (-s;-) sled; (an der Schreibmaschine) carriage
schlit'tenfahren §71 intr go sleigh riding; **mit j–m s.** make life miserable for s.o.
schlittern ['ʃlitərn] intr (HABEN & SEIN) slide; (Wagen) skid
Schlittschuh ['ʃlitʃu] m ice skate; **S. laufen** skate, go ice-skating
Schlitt'schuhläufer –in §6 mf ice skater
Schlitz [ʃlits] m (-es;-e) slit, slot; (Hosen–) fly
schlitz'äugig adj slit-eyed, sloe-eyed
schlitzen ['ʃlitsən] tr slit; rip
Schloß [ʃlos] n (Schlosses; Schlösser) castle; country mansion; lock; snap, clasp; **hinter S. und Riegel** behind bars; **unter S. und Riegel** under lock and key
Schloße ['ʃlosə] f (-;-n) hailstone
Schlosser ['ʃlosər] m (-s;-) mechanic; locksmith
Schloß'graben m moat
Schlot [ʃlot] m (-[e]s;-e & ≈e) chimney, smokestack; (fig) louse

Schlot'baron m (coll) tycoon

Schlot'feger m chimney sweep

schlotterig [ˈʃlɔtərɪç] adj loose, dangling; wobbly; (liederlich) slovenly

schlottern [ˈʃlɔtərn] intr fit loosely; (baumeln) dangle; (zittern) tremble; (wackeln) wobble

Schlucht [ʃlʊçt] f (-;-en) gorge; ravine

schluchzen [ˈʃlʊxtsən] intr sob

Schluck [ʃlʊk] m (-[e]s;-e) gulp; sip

Schluck'auf m (-s;) hiccups

schlucken [ˈʃlʊkən] tr & intr gulp

Schlucker [ˈʃlʊkər] m (-s;-)—armer S. (coll) poor devil

schlucksen [ˈʃlʊksən] intr have the hiccups

schluderig [ˈʃludərɪç] adj slipshod

schludern [ˈʃludərn] intr do slipshod work

Schlummer [ˈʃlumər] m (-s;) slumber

Schlum'merlied n lullaby

schlummern [ˈʃlumərn] intr slumber

schlum'mernd adj latent

Schlum'merrolle f cushion

Schlund [ʃlunt] m (-[e]s;-e) gullet; pharynx; (e-s Vulcans) crater; (fig) abyss

Schlund'röhre f esophagus

Schlupf [ʃlupf] m (-[e]s;-e) hole; (elec, mach) slip

schlüpfen [ˈʃlypfən] intr (SEIN) slip; sneak

Schlüp'fer m (-s;-) (pair of) panties; (pair of) bloomers

Schlupf'jacke f sweater

Schlupf'loch n hiding place; loophole

schlüpfrig [ˈʃlypfrɪç] adj slippery; (obszön) off-color

Schlupf'winkel m hiding place; haunt

schlurfen [ˈʃlurfən] intr (SEIN) shuffle

schlürfen [ˈʃlyrfən] tr slurp; lap up

Schluß [ʃlus] m (Schlusses; Schlüsse) end, close; (Ablauf) expiration; (Folgerung) conclusion; **S. damit!** time!; cut it out!; **S. folgt** to be concluded; **S. machen mit** put an end to; knock off from (work); break up with (s.o.); **zum S.** in conclusion

Schluß'effekt m upshot

Schlüssel [ˈʃlysəl] m (-s;-) key; wrench; quota; code key; (fig) key, clue

Schlüs'selbein n collarbone, clavicle

Schlüs'selblume f cowslip; **helle S.** primrose

Schlüs'selbrett n keyboard

Schlüs'selbund m bunch of keys

schlüs'selfertig adj ready for occupancy

Schlüs'selloch n keyhole

Schluß'ergebnis n final result

Schluß'folge f, **Schluß'folgerung** f conclusion, deduction

Schluß'formel f complimentary close

schlüssig [ˈʃlysɪç] adj determined; logical; (Beweis) conclusive; **sich** [dat] **noch nicht s. sein, ob** be undecided whether

Schluß'licht n (aut) taillight

Schluß'linie f (typ) dash

Schluß'rennen n (sport) final heat

Schluß'runde f (sport) finals

Schluß'schein m sales agreement

Schluß'verkauf m clearance sale

Schmach [ʃmax] f (-;) disgrace, shame; insult; humiliation

schmachten [ˈʃmaxtən] intr (vor dat) languish (with); **s. nach** long for

Schmachtfetzen [ˈʃmaxtfetsən] m sentimental song or book; melodrama

schmächtig [ˈʃmeçtɪç] adj scrawny

Schmachtriemen [ˈʃmaxtrimən] m—**den S. enger schnallen** (fig) tighten one's belt

schmach'voll adj disgraceful; humiliating

schmackhaft [ˈʃmakhaft] adj tasty

schmähen [ˈʃme·ən] tr revile, abuse; speak ill of

schmählich [ˈʃmeliç] adj disgraceful, scandalous; humiliating

Schmährede [ˈʃmeredə] f abuse; diatribe

Schmähschrift [ˈʃmeʃrɪft] f libel

schmähsüchtig [ˈʃmezyçtɪç] adj abusive

Schmäh'hung f (-;-en) abuse; slander

schmal [ʃmal] adj narrow; slim; meager

schmälern [ˈʃmelərn] tr curtail; belittle

Schmal'spurbahn f narrow-gauge railroad

Schmalz [ʃmalts] n (-[e]s;) lard, grease; (fig) schmaltz

schmalzen [ˈʃmaltsən] tr lard, grease

schmalzig [ˈʃmaltsɪç] adj greasy; fatty; (fig) schmaltzy

schmarotzen [ʃmaˈrɔtsən] intr (bei) sponge (on)

Schmarot'zer m (-s;-) sponger; (zool) parasite

schmarotzerisch [ʃmaˈrɔtsərɪʃ] adj sponging; (zool) parasitic(al)

Schmarre [ˈʃmarə] f (-;-n) scar; scratch

schmarrig [ˈʃmarɪç] adj scary

Schmatz [ʃmats] m (-es;-e) hearty kiss

schmatzen [ˈʃmatsən] tr (coll) kiss loudly ‖ intr smack one's lips

Schmaus [ʃmaus] m (-es;-e) feast; treat

schmausen [ˈʃmauzən] intr (von) feast (on)

schmecken [ˈʃmekən] tr taste, sample; (fig) stand ‖ intr taste good; **s. nach** taste like

Schmeichelei [ʃmaɪçəˈlaɪ] f (-;-en) flattery; coaxing

schmeichelhaft [ˈʃmaɪçəlhaft] adj flattering

schmeicheln [ˈʃmaɪçəln] ref—**sich** [dat] **s. zu** (inf) pride oneself on (ger) ‖ intr be flattering; (dat) flatter

Schmeich'ler –in §6 mf flatterer

schmeichlerisch [ˈʃmaɪçlərɪʃ] adj flattering; complimentary; fawning

schmeißen [ˈʃmaɪsən] §53 tr (coll) throw; (coll) manage; **e-e Runde Bier s.** set up a round of beer ‖ ref—**mit Geld um sich s.** throw money around

Schmelz [ʃmelts] m (-es;-e) enamel; glaze; melodious ring; (fig) bloom

schmelzen [ˈʃmeltsən] §133 tr melt; smelt ‖ intr (SEIN) melt; (fig) soften

schmel′zend adj mellow; melodious

Schmelzerei [ˌmɛltsə′raɪ] f (-;-en) foundry

schmelz′flüssig adj molten

Schmelz′hütte f foundry

Schmelz′käse m soft cheese

Schmelz′ofen m smelting furnace

Schmelz′punkt m melting point

Schmelz′tiegel m crucible, melting pot

Schmer [ʃmer] m & n (-s;) fat, grease

Schmer′bauch m (coll) potbelly

Schmerz [ʃmɛrts] m (-es;-en) pain, ache; **mit Schmerzen** (coll) anxiously, impatiently

schmerzen [′ʃmɛrtsən] tr & intr hurt

schmer′zend adj aching, sore

Schmer′zensgeld n damages (for pain or anguish)

Schmer′zenskind n problem child

schmerz′haft adj painful, aching

schmerz′lich adj painful, severe

schmerz′lindernd adj soothing

schmerz′los adj painless

Schmerz′schwelle f threshold of pain

Schmetterling [′ʃmɛtərlɪŋ] m (-s;-e) butterfly

Schmet′terlingsstil m (sport) butterfly

schmettern [′ʃmɛtərn] tr smash; **zu Boden s.** knock down || intr (Trompete) blare; (Vogel) warble

Schmied [ʃmit] m (-[e]s;-e) smith

Schmiede [′ʃmidə] f (-;-n) forge; blacksmith shop

Schmie′deeisen n wrought iron

Schmie′dehammer m sledge hammer

schmieden [′ʃmidən] tr forge; hammer; (Pläne, usw.) devise, concoct

schmiegen [′ʃmigən] tr—**das Kinn** (or **die Wange**) **in die Hand s.** prop one's chin (or cheek) in ône's hand || ref (an acc) snuggle up (to); **sich s. und biegen vor** (dat) bow and scrape before

schmiegsam [′ʃmikzam] adj flexible

Schmier− [ʃmir] comb.fm. grease, lubricating; smearing

Schmiere [′ʃmirə] f (-;-n) grease; lubricant; salve; (Schmutz) muck; (fig) mess; (fig) spanking; (theat) barnstormers; **S. stehen** be the lookout man

schmieren [′ʃmirən] tr grease, lubricate; smear; (Butter) spread; (Brot) butter; (bestechen) bribe; **j-m e-e s.** (coll) paste s.o.; **wie geschmiert** like greased lightning || ref—**sich** [dat] **die Kehle s.** (coll) wet one's whistle || intr scribble

Schmie′renkomödiant −in §7 mf (theat) barnstormer, ham

Schmiererei [ˌʃmirə′raɪ] f (-;-en) greasing; smearing; scribbling

Schmier′fink m scrawler; (Schmutzkerl) dirty fellow

Schmier′geld n (coll) bribe; (coll) hush money; (pol) slush fund

schmierig [′ʃmirɪç] adj smeary, greasy; oily; (Geschäfte) dirty

Schmier′käse m cheese spread

Schmier′mittel n lubricant

Schmier′pistole f, **Schmier′presse** f grease gun

Schmie′rung f (-;-en) lubrication

Schminke [′ʃmɪŋkə] f (-;-n) rouge; make-up

schminken [′ʃmɪŋkən] tr apply make-up to; rouge; **die Lippen s.** put on lipstick || ref put on make-up

Schminkunterlage [′ʃmɪŋkʊntərlagə] f base

Schmirgel [′ʃmɪrgəl] m (-s;) emery

Schmir′gelleinen n, **Schmir′gelleinwand** f emery cloth

Schmir′gelpapier n emery paper

Schmir′gelscheibe f emery wheel

Schmiß [ʃmɪs] m (Schmisses; Schmisse) (coll) stroke, blow; (coll) gash; (coll) dueling scar; (coll) zip

schmissig [′ʃmɪsɪç] adj (coll) snazzy

schmollen [′ʃmɔlən] intr pout, sulk

schmolz [ʃmɔlts] pret of **schmelzen**

Schmorbraten [′ʃmorbratən] m braised meat

schmoren [′ʃmorən] tr braise, stew || intr (fig) swelter; **laß ihn s.!** let him stew!

schmuck [ʃmʊk] adj nice, cute; smart, dapper; (sauber) neat || **Schmuck** m (-[e]s;) ornament; decoration; trimmings; trinket(s); jewelry

schmücken [′ʃmʏkən] tr adorn; decorate, trim; (Aufsatz) embellish || ref spruce up, dress up

Schmuck′kästchen n jewel box

schmuck′los adj unadorned, plain

Schmuck′waren pl jewelry

Schmuddel [′ʃmʊdəl] m (-s;-) slob

schmuddelig [′ʃmʊdəlɪç] adj dirty

Schmuggel [′ʃmʊgəl] m (-s;), **Schmuggelei** [ˌʃmʊgə′laɪ] f (-;-en) smuggling

schmuggeln [′ʃmʊgəln] tr & intr smuggle

Schmug′gelware f contraband

Schmuggler −in [′ʃmʊglər(ɪn)] §6 mf smuggler

schmunzeln [′ʃmʊntsəln] intr grin || **Schmunzeln** n (-s;) big grin

Schmutz [ʃmʊts] m (-es;) dirt, filth; (Zote) smut

schmutzen [′ʃmʊtsən] tr & intr soil

Schmutz′fink m (coll) slob

Schmutz′fleck m stain, smudge, blotch

schmutz′zig adj dirty

Schnabel [′ʃnabəl] m (-s;⁼) beak, bill; **halt den S.!** (sl) shut up!

Schna′belhieb m peck

schnäbeln [′ʃnebəln] tr & intr peck; (fig) kiss

Schnalle [′ʃnalə] f (-;-n) buckle; (vulg) whore

schnallen [′ʃnalən] tr buckle, fasten

schnalzen [′ʃnaltsən] intr—**mit den Fingern s.** snap one's fingers; **mit der Zunge s.** click one's tongue

schnapp [ʃnap] interj snap!

schnappen [′ʃnapən] tr grab; (Dieb) nab || intr snap; **ins Schloß s.** snap shut; **mit den Fingern s.** snap one's fingers; **nach Luft s.** gasp for air; **s. nach** snap at

Schnapp′messer n jackknife

Schnapp′schuß m (phot) snapshot

Schnaps [ʃnaps] m (-es;⁼e) hard liquor

Schnaps′brennerei f distillery

Schnaps′bruder m (coll) booze hound

Schnaps'idee f (coll) crazy idea
schnarchen ['∫narçən] intr snore
Schnarre ['∫narə] f (-;-n) rattle
schnarren ['∫narən] intr rattle; (Säge) buzz; (Insekten) drone, buzz
schnattern ['∫natərn] intr (Enten) cackle; (Zähne) chatter; (fig) gab
schnauben ['∫naubən] intr pant, puff; (Pferd) snort; **nach Rache s.** breathe revenge; **vor Wut s.** fume with rage || ref blow one's nose
schnaufen ['∫naufən] intr pant; wheeze
Schnau'fer m (-s;-) (coll) deep breath
Schnauzbart ['∫nautsbart] m mustache
Schnauze ['∫nautsə] f (-;-n) snout, muzzle; spout; (sl) snoot; (sl) big mouth
Schnauzer ['∫nautsər] m (-s;-) schnauzer
schnauzig ['∫nautsıç] adj rude
Schnecke ['∫nekə] f (-;-n) snail; (Nacht-) slug; (e-r Säule) volute; spiral; (anat) cochlea; (mach) worm; (e-r Violine) (mus) scroll
Schneckenhaus (Schnek'kenhaus) n snail shell
Schneckentempo (Schnek'kentempo) n (fig) snail's pace
Schnee [∫ne] m (-s;) snow; whipped egg white
Schnee'besen m eggbeater
Schnee'brett n snow slide, avalanche
Schnee'brille f snow goggles
Schnee'decke f blanket of snow
Schnee'flocke f snowflake
Schnee'gestöber n snow flurry
schneeig ['∫ne-ıç] adj snowy
Schnee'matsch m slush
Schnee'pflug m snowplow
Schnee'schaufel f, **Schnee'schippe** f snow shovel
Schnee'schläger m eggbeater
Schnee'schmelze f thaw
Schnee'treiben n blizzard
schneeverweht ['∫nefervet] adj snowbound
Schnee'verwehung f snowdrift
Schnee'wehe f snowdrift
Schneewittchen ['∫nevıtçən] n (-s;) Snow White
Schneid [∫naıt] m (-[e]s;) (coll) pluck; (Mut) (coll) guts
Schneid'brenner m cutting torch
Schneide ['∫naıdə] f (-;-n) (cutting) edge; (e-s Hobels) blade; **auf des Messers S.** (fig) on the razor's edge
Schnei'debrett n cutting board
Schnei'demaschine f cutter, slicer
Schnei'demühle f sawmill
schneiden ['∫naıdən] §106 tr cut; (Baum) prune; (Fingernägel) pare; (Hecke) trim; (nicht grüßen) snub; (surg) operate on; (tennis) slice; **Gesichter s.** make faces; **klein s.** cut up || ref (fig) be mistaken; (fig) be disappointed; (math) intersect; **sich in den Finger s.** cut one's finger || intr cut
Schnei'der (-s;-) m cutter; tailor
Schneiderei [∫naıdə'raı] f (-;-en) tailoring; (Werkstatt) tailorshop
Schnei'derin f (-;-nen) dressmaker

schneidern ['∫naıdərn] tr make || intr do tailoring; be a dressmaker
Schnei'derpuppe f dummy
Schnei'dezahn m incisor
schneidig ['∫naıdıç] adj sharp-edged; energetic; smart, sharp
schneien ['∫naı·ən] impers—**es schneit** it is snowing
Schneise ['∫naızə] f (-;-n) lane (between rows of trees)
schnell [∫nel] adj fast, quick
Schnellauf (Schnell'lauf) m race; sprint; speed skating
Schnell'bahn f high-speed railroad
Schnelle ['∫nelə] f (-;-n) speed; (Strom-) rapids; **auf die S.** (coll) in a hurry, very briefly
schnellen ['∫nelən] tr let fly || intr (SEIN) spring, jump up; (Preise) shoot up; **mit dem Finger s.** snap one's fingers
Schnell'gang m (aut) overdrive
Schnellhefter ['∫nelheftər] m (-s;-) folder, file
Schnell'imbiß m snack
Schnell'kraft f elasticity
schnellstens ['∫nelstəns] adv as fast as possible
Schnell'verfahren n quick process; (jur) summary proceeding
Schnell'zug m express train
Schneppe ['∫nepə] f (-;-n) spout; (sl) prostitute
schneuzen ['∫nɔıtsən] ref blow one's nose
schniegeln ['∫nigəln] ref dress up; **geschniegelt und gebügelt** dressed to kill
schnipfeln ['∫nıpfəln] tr & intr snip
Schnippchen ['∫nıpçən] n—**j-m ein S. schlagen** (coll) pull a fast one on s.o.; outwit s.o.
Schnippel ['∫nıpəl] m & n (-s;-) chip
schnippeln ['∫nıpəln] tr & intr snip
schnippen ['∫nıpən] intr—**mit den Fingern s.** (coll) snap one's fingers
schnippisch ['∫nıpı∫] adj fresh || adv pertly; **s. erwidern** snap back
schnitt [∫nıt] pret of **schneiden** ||
Schnitt m (-[e]s;-e) cut, incision; (Kerbe) notch; (Schnitte) slice; (Quer-) profile, cross section; (Durch-) average; (e-s Anzuges) cut, style; (Gewinn) cut; (agr) reaping; (bb) edge; (cin) editing; (geom) intersection; **weicher Schnitt** (cin) dissolve
Schnitt'ansicht f sectional view
Schnitt'ball m (tennis) slice
Schnitt'blumen pl cut flowers
Schnitt'bohnen pl string beans
Schnittchen ['∫nıtçən] n (-s;-) thin slice; sandwich
Schnitte ['∫nıtə] f (-;-n) slice
Schnit'ter –in §6 mf reaper, mower
Schnitt'fläche f (geom) plane
Schnitt'holz n lumber
schnittig ['∫nıtıç] adj smart-looking; (aut) streamlined
Schnitt'lauch ['∫nıtlaux] m (-[e]s;) (bot) chive
Schnitt'linie f (geom) secant
Schnitt'meister m (cin) editor

Schnitt′muster n pattern (of dress, etc.)

Schnitt′punkt m intersection

Schnitt′waren pl dry goods

Schnitt′wunde f cut, gash

Schnitz [ʃnɪts] m (-es;-e) cut; slice; chop; chip

Schnitzel [′ʃnɪtsəl] n (-s;-) chip; slice; shred; (Abfälle) parings; (culin) cutlet

schnitzeln [′ʃnɪtsəln] tr cut up; shred; (Holz) whittle

schnitzen [′ʃnɪtsən] tr carve

Schnit′zer m (-s;-) carver; (Fehler) blunder; **grober S.** boner

Schnitzerei [ʃnɪtsə′raɪ] f (-;-en) wood carving, carved work

schnob [ʃnop] pret of **schnauben**

schnodderig [′ʃnɔdərɪç] adj brash

schnöde [′ʃnødə] adj vile; disdainful; (Gewinn) filthy

Schnorchel [′ʃnɔrçəl] m (-s;-) snorkel

Schnörkel [′ʃnœrkəl] m (-s;-) (beim Schreiben) flourish; (fig) frills; (archit) scroll

schnorren [′ʃnɔrən] tr (coll) chisel, bum ‖ intr (coll) sponge, chisel

Schnösel [′ʃnøzəl] m (-s;-) wise guy

schnüffeln [′ʃnʏfəln] intr snoop around; (an dat) sniff (at)

Schnüff′ler –in §6 mf (coll) snoop

Schnuller [′ʃnʊlər] m (-s;-) pacifier

Schnultze [′ʃnʊltsə] f (-;-n) (coll) tear-jerker

schnultzig [′ʃnʊltsɪç] adj (coll) corny, mawkish

schnupfen [′ʃnʊpfən] tr snuff ‖ intr take snuff ‖ **Schnupfen** m (-s;-) cold; **den S. bekommen** catch a cold

Schnupftabak [′ʃnʊpftabak] m snuff

schnuppe [′ʃnʊpə] adj—**das ist mir s.** it′s all the same to me ‖ **Schnuppe** f (-;-n) shooting star; (e-r Kerze) snuff

Schnur [ʃnur] f (-;ˮe & -en) string; (Band) braid; (elec) flexible cord; **nach der S.** regularly

Schnürband [′ʃnyrbant] n (-[e]s;ˮer) shoestring; corset lace

Schnürchen [′ʃnyrçən] n (-s;-) string; **etw am S. haben** have at one′s fingertips; **wie am S.** like clockwork

schnüren [′ʃnyrən] tr tie; lace; (Perlen) string ‖ ref put on a corset

schnur′gerade adj straight ‖ adv straight, as the crow flies

schnurr [ʃnur] interj purr!; buzz!

Schnurrbart [′ʃnurbart] m mustache

schnurren [′ʃnurən] intr (Katze) purr; (Rad) whirr; (Maschine) hum; (schnorren) sponge, chisel

schnurrig [′ʃnurɪç] adj funny; queer

Schnürschuh [′ʃnyrʃu] m oxford shoe

Schnürsenkel [′ʃnyrzɛŋkəl] m shoe-string

schnurstracks [′ʃnurʃtraks] adv right away; directly; **s. entgegengesetzt** diametrically opposite; **s. losgehen auf** (acc) make a beeline for

schob [ʃop] pret of **schieben**

Schober [′ʃobər] m (-s;-) stack

Schock [ʃɔk] m (-[e]s;-s) shock ‖ n (-[e]s;-e) threescore

schockant [ʃɔ′kant] adj shocking

schockieren [ʃɔ′kirən] tr shock

schofel [′ʃofəl] adj mean; miserable; (schäbig) shabby; (geizig) stingy

Schöffe [′ʃœfə] m (-n;-n) juror

Schokolade [ʃɔkɔ′ladə] f (-;-n) chocolate

schokoladen [ʃɔkɔ′ladən] adj chocolate

Schokola′dentafel f chocolate bar

scholl [ʃɔl] pret of **schallen**

Scholle [′ʃɔlə] f (-;-n) clod; sod; stratum; ice floe; (ichth) sole; **heimatliche S.** native soil

schon [ʃon] adv already; as early as; yet, as yet; (sogar) even; (bloß) the bare, the mere; **ich komme s.!** all right, I′m coming!; **s. am folgenden Tage** on the very next day; **s. der Gedanke** the mere thought; **s. früher** before now; **s. gut!** all right!; **s. immer** always; **s. lange** long since, for a long time; **s. wieder** again

schön [ʃøn] adj beautiful; nice; (Künste) fine; (Mann) handsome; (Summe) nice round; (Geschlecht) fair; **schönen Dank!** many thanks!; **schönen Gruß an** (acc) best regards to ‖ adv nicely; **der Hund macht s.** the dog sits up and begs; **s. warm** nice and warm

schonen [′ʃonən] tr spare; take it easy on; treat with consideration ‖ ref take care of oneself

scho′nend adj careful; considerate

schön′färben tr gloss over

Schon′frist f period of grace

Schon′gang m (aut) overdrive

Schön′heit f (-;-en) beauty

Schön′heitsfehler m flaw

Schön′heitskönigin f beauty queen

Schön′heitspflege f beauty treatment

schön′tun §154 intr (dat) flatter; (dat) flirt (with)

Scho′nung f (-;-en) care, careful treatment; mercy; consideration; tree nursery; wild-game preserve

scho′nungslos adj unsparing; merciless; relentless

scho′nungsvoll adj considerate

Schon′zeit f (hunt) closed season

Schopf [ʃɔpf] m (-[e]s;ˮe) tuft of hair; (orn) crest

schöpfen [′ʃœpfən] tr draw; bail; scoop, ladle; (frische Luft) breathe; (Mut) take; **Verdacht s.** become suspicious; **wieder Atem (or Luft) s.** (fig) breathe freely again

Schöp′fer m (-s;-) creator; author; composer; painter; sculptor; dipper, ladle

schöpferisch [′ʃœpfərɪʃ] adj creative

Schöp′ferkraft f creative power

Schöpf′kelle f scoop

Schöpf′löffel m ladle

Schöp′fung f (-;-en) creation

Schoppen [′ʃɔpən] m (-s;-) pint; glass of beer, glass of wine

schor [ʃor] pret of **scheren**

Schorf [ʃɔrf] m (-[e]s;-e) scab

Schornstein [′ʃɔrnʃtaɪn] m chimney; smokestack

Schorn′steinfeger m chimney sweeper

Schoß [ʃos] m (Schosses; Schosse)

sprout || [ʃos] m (-es;ːe) lap; womb;
(fig) bosom; **die Hände in den S.
legen** cross one's arms; (fig) be idle

Schößling [ˈʃœslɪŋ] m (-s;-e) shoot

Schote [ˈʃotə] f (-;-n) pod, shell

Schotte [ˈʃotə] m (-n;-n) Scotchman
|| f (-;-n) (naut) bulkhead

Schotter [ˈʃotər] m (-s;-) gravel; macadam, crushed stone; (rr) ballast

Schottin [ˈʃotɪn] f (-;-nen) Scotch-
woman

schottisch [ˈʃotɪʃ] adj Scotch

schraffieren [ʃraˈfirən] tr hatch

schräg [ʃrɛk] adj oblique; (abfallend)
slanting, sloping; diagonal || adv
obliquely; **s. gegenüber von** diagonally across from; **s. geneigt** sloping

Schräg′linie f diagonal

schrak [ʃrak] pret of schrecken

Schramme [ˈʃramə] f (-;-n) scratch,
abrasion; scar

schrammen [ˈʃramən] tr scratch; skin

Schrank [ʃraŋk] m (-[e]s;ːe) closet

Schranke [ˈʃraŋkə] f (-;-n) barrier;
(fig) bounds, limit; (jur) bar; (rr)
gate; (sport) starting gate

schran′kenlos adj boundless; exagger-
ated

Schran′kenwärter m (rr) signalman

Schrank′fach n compartment

Schrank′koffer m wardrobe trunk

Schrapnell [ʃrapˈnɛl] n (-s;-e & -s)
shrapnel, piece of shrapnel

Schraubdeckel [ˈʃraupdɛkəl] m screw-
on cap

Schraube [ˈʃraubə] f (-;-n) screw;
bolt; (aer, naut) propeller

schrauben [ˈʃraubən] tr screw; **in die
Höhe s.** raise || ref—**sich in die
Höhe s.** circle higher and higher

Schrau′benflügel m propeller blade

Schrau′bengang m, **Schrau′bengewinde**
n thread (of a screw)

Schrau′benmutter f (-;-n) nut

Schrau′benschlüssel m wrench; **ver-
stellbarer S.** monkey wrench

Schrau′benstrahl m, **Schrau′benstrom**
m (aer) slipstream

Schraubenzieher [ˈʃraubəntsiːər] m
(-s;-) screwdriver

Schraubstock [ˈʃraupʃtok] m vice

Schrebergarten [ˈʃrebərgartən] m garden plot (at edge of town)

Schreck [ʃrɛk] m (-[e]s;-e) var of
Schrecken

Schreck′bild n frightful sight; boogey-
man

schrecken [ˈʃrekən] tr frighten, scare
|| **Schrecken** m (-s;-) fright, fear

Schreckensbotschaft (**Schreck′kensbot-
schaft**) f alarming news

Schreckensherrschaft (**Schrek′kensherr-
schaft**) f reign of terror

Schreckenskammer (**Schrek′kenskam-
mer**) f chamber of horrors

Schreckensregiment (**Schrek′kensregi-
ment**) n reign of teror, terrorism

Schreckenstat (**Schrek′kenstat**) f atrocity

schreck′haft adj timid

schreck′lich adj frightful, terrible

Schrecknis [ˈʃreknɪs] n (-ses;-se) horror

Schreck′schuß m warning shot

Schreck′sekunde f reaction time

Schrei [ʃrai] m (-[e]s;-e) cry, shout;
letzter S. latest fashion

Schreib- [ʃraip] comb.fm. writing

Schreib′art f style; spelling

Schreib′bedarf m stationery

Schreib′block m writing pad, note pad

schreiben [ˈʃraibən] §62 tr write; spell;
type; **ins Konzept s.** make a rough
draft of; **ins reine s.** make a clean
copy; **Noten s.** copy music || ref
spell one's name || intr write; spell;
type || **Schreiben** n (-s;-) writing;
(com) letter

Schrei′ber m (-s;-) writer; clerk; recording instrument, recorder

schreib′faul adj too lazy to write

Schreib′feder f pen

Schreib′fehler m slip of the pen

Schreib′heft n copybook, exercise book

Schreib′mappe f portfolio

Schreib′maschine f typewriter; **mit der
S. geschrieben** typed; **S. schreiben**
type

Schreib′maschinenfarbband n (-[e]s;
ːer) typewriter ribbon

Schreib′maschinenschreiber -**in** §6 mf
typist

Schreib′maschinenschrift f typescript

Schreib′materialien pl, **Schreib′papier**
n stationery

Schreib′schrift f (typ) script

Schreib′stube f (mil) orderly room

Schreib′tisch m desk

Schrei′bung f (-;-en) spelling

Schreib′unterlage f desk pad

Schreib′waren pl stationery

Schreib′warenhandlung f stationery
store

Schreibweise f style; spelling

Schreib′zeug n writing materials

schreien [ˈʃraiˈən] §135 tr cry, shout,
scream, howl || ref—**sich heiser s.**
shout oneself hoarse; **sich tot s.** yell
one's lungs out || intr cry, shout,
scream, howl; (Esel) bray; (Eule)
screech; (Schwein) squeal; **s. nach**
clamor for; **s. über** (acc) cry out
against; **s. vor** (dat) shout for (joy);
cry out in (pain); roar with (laugh-
ter) || **Schreien** n (-s) shouting; **das
ist zum S.!** that's a scream!

schrei′end adj shrill; (Farbe) loud;
(Unrecht) flagrant

Schrei′hals m (coll) crybaby

Schrei′krampf m crying fit

Schrein [ʃrain] m (-[e]s;-e) reliquary

Schreiner [ˈʃrainər] m (-s;-) carpenter; cabinetmaker

schreiten [ˈʃraitən] §86 intr (SEIN)
step; stride; **zur Abstimmung s.** proceed to vote; **zur Tat s.** proceed to
act

schrie [ʃri] pret of schreien

schrieb [ʃrip] pret of schreiben

Schrift [ʃrift] f (-;-en) writing; handwriting; letter, character; document;
book; publication; periodical; (auf
Münzen) legend; (typ) type, font;
die Heilige S. Holy Scripture; **nach
der S. sprechen** speak standard German

Schrift'art *f* type, font
Schrift'auslegung *f* exegesis
Schrift'bild *n* type face
Schrift'deutsch *n* literary German
Schrift'führer –in §6 *mf* secretary
Schrift'leiter –in §6 *mf* editor
schrift'lich *adj* written || *adv* in writing; **s. wiedergeben** transcribe
Schrift'satz *m* (jur) brief; (typ) composition
Schrift'setzer *m* typesetter
Schrift'sprache *f* literary language
Schriftsteller –in ['ʃrɪftʃtɛlər(ɪn)] §6 *mf* writer, author
Schrift'stück, *n* piece of writing; document
Schrifttum ['ʃrɪfttum] *n* (–s;) literature
Schrift'verkehr *m,* **Schrift'wechsel** *m* correspondence
Schrift'zeichen *n* letter, character
schrill [ʃrɪl] *adj* shrill
schrillen ['ʃrɪlən] *intr* ring loudly
schritt [ʃrɪt] *pret of* **schreiten** || **Schritt** *m* (–[e]s;–e) pace; stride; (*e–r Hose*) crotch; (fig) step
Schritt'macher *m* pacemaker
schritt'weise *adv* gradually; step by step
schroff [ʃrɔf] *adj* steep; rugged; rude, uncouth; rough, harsh; (*Ablehnung, Widerspruch*) flat
schröpfen ['ʃrœpfən] *tr* (fig) milk, fleece; (med) bleed, cup
Schrot [ʃrot] *m & n* (–[e]s;–e) scrap; (*Getreide*) crushed grain, grits; (*zum Schießen*) buckshot
Schrot'brot *n* whole grain bread
Schrot'flinte *f* shotgun
Schrot'korn *n,* **Schrot'kugel** *f* pellet
Schrott [ʃrɔt] *m* (–[e]s;) scrap metal
Schrott'platz *m* junk yard
schrubben ['ʃrubən] *tr* scrub
Schrulle ['ʃrulə] *f* (–;–n) (coll) nutty idea
schrul'lenhaft, schrullig ['ʃrulɪç] *adj* whimsical
schrumpelig ['ʃrumpəlɪç] *adj* crumpled; wrinkled, shriveled
schrumpeln ['ʃrumpəln] *intr* shrivel
schrumpfen ['ʃrumpfən] *intr* (SEIN) shrink; shrivel; (pathol) atrophy
Schub [ʃup] *m* (–[e]s;⁻e) shove, push; batch; (phys) thrust
Schub'fach *n* drawer
Schub'karre *f,* **Schub'karren** *m* wheelbarrow
Schub'kasten *m* drawer
Schub'kraft *f* thrust
Schub'lade *f* drawer
Schub'leistung *f* thrust
Schubs [ʃups] *m* (–es;–e) (coll) shove
schubsen ['ʃupsən] *tr & intr* shove
Schub'stange *f* (aut) connecting rod
schüchtern ['ʃʏçtərn] *adj* shy, bashful
schuf [ʃuf] *pret of* **schaffen**
Schuft [ʃuft] *m* (–[e]s;–e) cad
schuften ['ʃuftən] *intr* drudge, slave
Schufterei [ʃuftə'raɪ] *f* (–;) drudgery; (*Schuftigkeit*) meanness
schuftig ['ʃuftɪç] *adj* (fig) rotten
Schuh [ʃu] *m* (–[e]s;–e) shoe; boot
Schuh'band *n* (–[e]s;⁻er) shoestring

Schuhflicker ['ʃuflɪkər] *m* (–s;–) shoe repairman, shoemaker
Schuh'krem *m* shoe polish
Schuh'laden *m* shoe store
Schuh'leisten *m* last
Schuh'löffel *m* shoehorn
Schuh'macher *m* shoemaker
Schuhplattler ['ʃuplatlər] *m* (–s;–) Bavarian folk dance
Schuh'putzer *m* shoeshine boy
Schuh'sohle *f* sole
Schuhspanner ['ʃuʃpanər] *m* (–s;–) shoetree
Schuh'werk *n* footwear
Schuh'wichse *f* shoe polish
Schuh'zeug *n* footwear
Schul– [ʃul] *comb.fm.* school
Schul'amt *n* school board
Schul'arbeit *f* homework; (Aust) classroom work
Schul'aufsicht *f* school board
Schul'bank *f* (–;⁻e) school desk
Schul'behörde *f* school board; board of education
Schul'beispiel *n* (fig) test case
Schul'besuch *m* attendance at school
Schul'bildung *f* schooling, education
schuld [ʃult] *adj* at fault, to blame || **Schuld** *f* (–;–en) debt; fault; guilt
schuld'bewußt *adj* conscious of one's guilt
schulden ['ʃuldən] *tr* owe
schuld'haft *adj* culpable || **Schuld'haft** *f* imprisonment for debt
Schul'diener *m* school janitor
schuldig ['ʃuldɪç] *adj* guilty; responsible; **j–m etw s. sein** owe s.o. s.th. || **Schuldige** §5 *mf* culprit; guilty party
Schul'digkeit *f* (–;–en) duty, obligation; **seine S. tun** do one's duty
Schul'direktor *m* (school) §7 *m* principal
schuld'los *adj* innocent
Schuld'losigkeit *f* (–;) innocence
Schuldner –in ['ʃuldnər(ɪn)] §6 *mf* debtor
Schuld'schein *m* promissory note, IOU
Schuld'spruch *m* verdict of guilty
Schuld'verschreibung *f* promissory note, IOU; (*Obligation*) bond
Schule ['ʃulə] *f* (–;–n) school; **auf der S. in school; S. machen** (fig) set a precedent; **von der S. abgehen** quit school
schulen ['ʃulən] *tr* train; (pol) indoctrinate
Schüler ['ʃylər] *m* (–s;–) pupil (*in grammar school or high school*); trainee; (*Jünger*) disciple
Schü'leraustausch *m* student exchange
Schülerin ['ʃylərɪn] *f* (–;–nen) pupil
Schul'film *m* educational film
Schul'flug *m* training flight
schul'frei *adj*—**schulfreier Tag** holiday; **s. haben** have off
Schul'gelände *n* school grounds; campus
Schul'geld *n* tuition
Schul'gelehrsamkeit *f* book learning
Schul'hof *m* schoolyard, playground
Schul'kamerad *m* school chum
Schul'lehrer –in §6 *mf* schoolteacher
Schul'mappe *f* schoolbag
Schul'meister *m* schoolmaster; pedant
schul'meistern *intr* criticize

Schul'ordnung f school regulation

Schul'pflicht f compulsory school attendance

schul'pflichtig adj of school age; **schulpflichtiges Alter** school age

Schul'plan m curriculum

Schul'ranzen m schoolbag

Schul'rat m (**-[e]s;-̈e**) (educ) superintendent

Schul'reise f field trip

Schul'schiff n training ship

Schul'schluß m close of school

Schul'schwester f teaching nun

Schul'stunde f lesson, period

Schul'tasche f schoolbag

Schulter ['ʃultər] f (**-;-n**) shoulder

Schul'terblatt n shoulder blade

schul'terfrei adj off-the-shoulder; (**trägerfrei**) strapless

schultern ['ʃultərn] tr shoulder

Schul'terstück n epaulet

Schul'unterricht m instruction; schooling; **im S.** in school

Schul'wesen n school system

Schul'zeugnis n report card

Schul'zimmer n classroom

Schul'zwang m compulsory education

schummeln ['ʃuməln] intr (coll) cheat

schund [ʃunt] pret of **schinden** ‖ **Schund** m (**-[e]s;**) junk, trash

Schund'literatur f trashy literature

Schund'roman m dime novel

Schupo ['ʃupo] m (**-s;-s**) (Schutzpolizist) policeman, copy ‖ f (**-;**) (Schutzpolizei) police

Schuppe ['ʃupə] f (**-;-n**) scale; **Schuppen** dandruff

schuppen ['ʃupən] tr scale; scrape ‖ **Schuppen** m (**-s;-**) shed; (aer) hangar; (aut) garage

schuppig ['ʃupɪç] adj scaly, flaky

Schups [ʃups] m (**-es;-e**) shove

schupsen ['ʃupsən] tr shove

Schüreisen ['ʃyraɪzən] n poker

schüren ['ʃyrən] tr poke, stir; (fig) stir up, foment

schürfen ['ʃyrfən] tr scratch, scrape; dig for ‖ intr (nach) prospect (for)

schurigeln ['ʃurigəln] tr (coll) bully

Schurke ['ʃurkə] m (**-n;-n**) bum, punk

Schur'kenstreich m, **Schur'kentat** f, **Schurkerei** [ʃurkə'raɪ] f (**-;-en**) mean trick

schurkisch ['ʃurkiʃ] adj mean, lowdown

Schürze ['ʃyrtsə] f (**-;-n**) apron

schürzen ['ʃyrtsən] tr tuck up; tie

Schür'zenband n (**-[e]s;-̈er**) apron

Schür'zenjäger m skirt chaser, wolf

Schuß [ʃus] m (**Schusses; Schüsse**) shot; (Ladung) round; (Schußwunde) gunshot wound; (rasche Bewegung) rush; (Brot) batch; (bot) shoot; (culin) dash; (sport) shot; **blinder S.** blank; **e-n S. abgeben** fire a shot; **ein S. ins Blaue** a wild shot; **ein S. ins Schwarze** a bull's-eye; **im S. haben** have under control; **im vollen S.** in full swing; **in S. bekommen** get going; **in S. bringen** get (s.th.) going; **j-m vor den S. kommen** come within s.o.'s range; (fig) come across s.o.; **scharfer S.**

live round; **weit vom S.** out of harm's way

Schüssel ['ʃysəl] f (**-;-n**) bowl; (fig) dish

schuß'fest, schuß'sicher adj bulletproof

Schuß'waffe f firearm

Schuß'weite f range

Schuster ['ʃustər] m (**-s;-**) shoemaker; (fig) bungler

schustern ['ʃustərn] intr bungle

Schutt [ʃut] m (**-es;**) rubbish; rubble

Schutt'abladeplatz m dump

Schüttboden ['ʃytbodən] m granary

Schüttelfrost ['ʃytəlfrɔst] m shivers

schütteln ['ʃytəln] tr shake; **j-m die Hand s.** shake hands with s.o.

schütten ['ʃytən] tr pour, spill ‖ impers —**es schüttet** it is pouring

Schutz [ʃuts] m (**-es;**) protection, defense; (Obdach) shelter; (Deckung) cover; (Schirm) screen; (Schutzgeleit) safeguard; **zu S. und Trutz** defensive and offensive

Schutz'brille f safety goggles

Schütze ['ʃytsə] m (**-n;-n**) marksman, shot; (astr) Sagittarius; (mil) rifleman ‖ f (**-;**) sluice gate

schützen ['ʃytsən] tr (gegen) protect (against), defend (against); (vor dat) preserve (from) ‖ **Schützen** m (**-s;-**) (tex) shuttle

schüt'zend adj protective; tutelary

Schutz'engel m guardian angle

Schütz'engraben m (mil) foxhole

Schüt'zenkompanie f rifle company

Schüt'zenkönig m crack shot

Schüt'zenloch n (mil) foxhole

Schüt'zenmine f anti-personnel mine

Schutz'geleit n escort; safe conduct; (aer) air cover; (nav) convoy

Schutz'glocke f (aer) umbrella

Schutz'gott m, **Schutz'göttin** f tutelary deity

Schutz'haft f protective custody

Schutzheilige §5 mf patron saint

Schutz'herr m protector; patron

Schutz'herrin f protectress; patroness

Schutz'impfung f immunization

Schutz'insel f traffic island

Schützling ['ʃytslɪŋ] m (**-s;-e**) ward

schutz'los adj defenseless

Schutz'mann m (**-[e]s;-̈er & -leute**) policeman

Schutz'marke f trademark

Schutz'mittel n preservative; preventive

Schutz'patron -**in** §8 mf patron saint

Schutz'polizei f police

Schutz'polizist m policeman, cop

Schutz'scheibe f (aut) windshield

Schutz'staffel f SS troops

Schutz'umschlag m dust jacket

Schutz-'und-Trutz-'Bündnis f defensive and offensive alliance

Schutz'waffe f defensive weapon

Schutz'zoll m protective tariff

Schwabe ['ʃvabə] m (**-n;-n**) Swabian

Schwaben ['ʃvabən] n (**-s;**) Swabia

Schwäbin ['ʃvɛbɪn] f (**-;-nen**) Swabian

schwäbisch ['ʃvɛbɪʃ] adj Swabian; **das Schwäbische Meer** Lake Constance

schwach [ʃvax] adj (**schwächer** ['ʃvɛçər]; **schwächste** ['ʃvɛçstə] §9) weak; (*Hoffnung, Ton, Licht*) faint; (*unzureichend*) scanty; sparse; (*armselig*) poor

Schwäche [ˈʃvɛçə] *f* (-;-n) weakness

Schwach'kopf *m* dunce; sap, dope

schwächlich [ˈʃvɛçlɪç] *adj* feeble, delicate

Schwächling [ˈʃvɛçlɪŋ] *m* (-s;-e) weakling

schwach'sinnig *adj* feeble-minded ‖ **Schwachsinnige** §5 *mf* dimwit, moron

Schwach'strom *m* low-voltage current

Schwaden [ˈʃvaːdən] *m* (-s;-) swath; cloud (*of smoke, etc.*)

Schwadron [ʃvaˈdroːn] *f* (-;-en) squadron

schwadronieren [ʃvadroˈniːrən] *intr* (coll) brag

schwafeln [ˈʃvaːfəln] *intr* talk nonsense

Schwager [ˈʃvaːgər] *m* (-s;̈-) brother-in-law

Schwägerin [ˈʃvɛːgərɪn] *f* (-;-nen) sister-in-law

Schwalbe [ˈʃvalbə] *f* (-;-n) swallow

Schwal'bennest *n* (aer) gun turret

Schwal'benschwanz *m* (*Frack*) tails; (carp) dovetail

Schwall [ʃval] *m* (-[e]s;-e) flood; (*von Worten*) torrent

schwamm [ʃvam] *pret of* **schwimmen** ‖ **Schwamm** *m* (-[e]s;̈-e) sponge; mushroom; fungus; dry rot; **S. darüber!** skip it!

schwammig [ˈʃvamɪç] *adj* spongy

Schwan [ʃvaːn] *m* (-[e]s;̈-e) swan

schwand [ʃvant] *pret of* **schwinden**

schwang [ʃvaŋ] *pret of* **schwingen**

schwanger [ˈʃvaŋər] *adj* pregnant

schwängern [ˈʃvɛŋərn] *tr* make pregnant; (fig) impregnate

Schwan'gerschaft *f* (-;-en) pregnancy

Schwan'gerschaftsverhütung *f* contraception

schwank [ʃvaŋk] *adj* flexible; unsteady ‖ **Schwank** *m* (-[e]s;̈-e) prank; joke; funny story; (theat) farce

schwanken [ˈʃvaŋkən] *intr* stagger; (*schaukeln*) rock; (*schlingern*) roll; (*stampfen*) pitch; (*Flamme*) flicker; (*pendeln*) oscillate; (*vibrieren*) vibrate; (*wellenartig*) undulate; (*zittern*) shake; (*Preise*) fluctuate; (*zögern*) vacillate, hesitate

Schwanz [ʃvants] *m* (-es;̈-e) tail; (*Gefolge*) train; (vulg) pecker; **kein S.** not a living soul; **mit dem S. wedeln** (or **wippen**) wag its tail

schwänzeln [ˈʃvɛntsəln] *intr* wag its tail; **s. um** fawn on

schwänzen [ˈʃvɛntsən] *tr*—**die Schule s.** play hooky from school; **e-e Stunde s.** cut a class ‖ *intr* play hooky

schwappen [ˈʃvapən] *intr* slosh around; **s. über** (*acc*) spill over

schwapps [ʃvaps] *interj* slap!; splash!

Schwäre [ˈʃvɛːrə] *f* (-;-n) abscess

schwären [ˈʃvɛːrən] *intr* fester

Schwarm [ʃvarm] *m* (-[e]s;̈-e) swarm; flock, herd; (*von Fischen*) school; (fig) idol; (fig) craze; (aer) flight of five aircraft; **sie ist mein S.** (coll) I have a crush on her

schwärmen [ˈʃvɛrmən] *intr* swarm; stray; daydream; go out on the town; **s. für** (or **über** *acc* or **von**) rave about

Schwär'mer *m* (-s;-) enthusiast; reveler; daydreamer; firecracker; (religious) fanatic; (ent) hawk moth

Schwärmerei [ʃvɛrmaˈraɪ] *f* (-;-en) enthusiasm; daydreaming; revelry; fanaticism

schwärmerisch [ˈʃvɛrmərɪʃ] *adj* enthusiastic; gushy; fanatic; fanciful

Schwarte [ˈʃvartə] *f* (-;-n) rind, skin; (coll) old book

schwarz [ʃvarts] *adj* black; dark; (*ungesetzlich*) illegal; (*schmutzig*) dirty; (*düster*) gloomy; (*von der Sonne*) tanned; **schwarze Kunst** black magic; **schwarzes Brett** bulletin board ‖ *adv* illegally

Schwarz'arbeit *f* moonlighting; nonunion work; illicit work

Schwarz'brenner *m* moonshiner

Schwärze [ˈʃvɛrtsə] *f* (-;-n) blackness; darkness; printer's ink

schwärzen [ˈʃvɛrtsən] *tr* darken; blacken

schwarz'fahren §71 *intr* (SEIN) drive without a license; ride without a ticket

Schwarz'fahrer **-in** §6 *mf* unlicensed driver; rider without a ticket

Schwarz'fahrt *f* joy ride; ride without a ticket

Schwarz'handel *m* black-marketing

Schwarz'händler **-in** §6 *mf* black marketeer; (*mit Eintrittskarten*) scalper

schwärzlich [ˈʃvɛrtslɪç] *adj* blackish

Schwarz'markt *m* black market

Schwarz'seher **-in** §6 *mf* pessimist

Schwarz'sender *m* illegal transmitter

schwatzen [ˈʃvatsən], **schwätzen** [ˈʃvɛtsən] *tr* (coll) talk ‖ *intr* (coll) yap, talk nonsense; (coll) gossip

Schwät'zer **-in** §6 *mf* windbag; gossip

schwatz'haft *adj* talkative

Schwatz'maul *n* blabber mouth

Schwebe [ˈʃveːbə] *f* (-;) suspense; **in der S. sein** be undecided; be pending

Schwe'bebahn *f* cablecar

Schwe'beflug *m* hovering, soaring

schweben [ˈʃveːbən] *intr* (HABEN & SEIN) be suspended, hang; float; (*Hubschrauber*) hover; (*Segelflugzeug*) soar; glide; (fig) waver, be undecided; **in Gefahr s.** be in danger; **in Ungewißheit s.** be in suspense

Schwede [ˈʃveːdə] *m* (-n;-n) Swede

Schweden [ˈʃveːdən] *n* (-s;) Sweden

Schwedin [ˈʃveːdɪn] *f* (-;-nen) Swede

schwedisch [ˈʃveːdɪʃ] *adj* Swedish

Schwefel [ˈʃveːfəl] *m* (-s;) sulfur

Schwe'felsäure *f* sulfuric acid

Schweif [ʃvaɪf] *m* (-[e]s;-e) tail; (fig) train

schweifen [ˈʃvaɪfən] *tr* curve; (*spülen*) rinse ‖ *intr* (SEIN) roam, wander

Schweigegeld [ˈʃvaɪgəgɛlt] *n* hush money

schweigen [ˈʃvaɪgən] §148 *intr* be silent, keep silent; (*aufhören*) stop; **ganz zu s. von** to say nothing of; **s. zu** make no reply to

schwei'gend adj silent ‖ adv in silence
schweigsam ['ʃvaɪkzam] adj taciturn
Schwein [ʃvaɪn] n (-[e]s;-e) pig, hog; **S. haben** be lucky, have luck
Schwei'nebraten m roast pork
Schwei'nefleisch n pork
Schwei'nehund m (pej) filthy swine
Schwei'nekoben m pigsty, pig pen
Schweinerei [ʃvaɪnə'raɪ] f (-;-en) mess; dirty business
Schwei'nerippchen pl pork chops
Schwei'newirtschaft f dirty mess
Schweins'kotelett n pork chop
Schweiß [ʃvaɪs] m (-es;) perspiration
schweißen ['ʃvaɪsən] tr weld ‖ intr begin to melt, fuse; (hunt) bleed
Schwei'ßer –in §6 mf welder
Schweißfüße ['ʃvaɪsfysə] pl sweaty feet
schweißig ['ʃvaɪsɪç] adj sweaty; (hunt) bloody
Schweiß'perle f bead of sweat
Schweiz [ʃvaɪts] f (-;)—**die S.** Switzerland
Schwei'zer m Swiss; dairyman
schweizerisch ['ʃvaɪtsərɪʃ] adj Swiss
schwelen ['ʃveːlən] intr smolder
schwelgen ['ʃvɛlɡən] intr feast; **s. in** (dat) revel in; wallow in
Schwelgerei [ʃvɛlɡə'raɪ] f (-;-en) feasting, carousing
schwelgerisch ['ʃvɛlɡərɪʃ] adj riotous; luxurious
Schwelle ['ʃvɛlə] f (-;-n) sill; doorstep; (fig) verge; (psychol) threshold; (rr) railroad tie
schwellen ['ʃvɛlən] §119 tr swell ‖ intr (SEIN) swell; (Wasser) rise; (anwachsen) increase
Schwel'lung f (-;-en) swelling
Schwemme ['ʃvɛmə] f (-;-n) watering place; (coll) taproom; (com) glut
schwemmen ['ʃvɛmən] tr wash off, rinse; (Vieh) water; (Holz) float
Schwengel ['ʃvɛŋəl] m (-s;-) pump handle; (e-r Glocke) hammer
schwenkbar ['ʃvɛŋkbaːr] adj rotating
schwenken ['ʃvɛŋkən] tr swing; shake; (drohend) brandish; (Hut) wave; (spülen) rinse ‖ intr (SEIN) turn; swivel, pivot; (Geschütz) traverse; (mil) wheel; (pol) change sides
Schwen'kung f (-;-en) turn; wheeling; traversing; (fig) change of mind
schwer [ʃveːr] adj heavy; difficult, hard; serious; (schwerfällig) ponderous; (Strafe) severe; (Wein) strong; (Speise) rich; (unbeholfen) clumsy; (Kompanie) heavy-weapons; **drei Pfund s. sein** weigh three pounds; **schweres Geld bezahlen** pay a stiff price ‖ adv hard; with difficulty; (coll) very
Schwere ['ʃveːrə] f (-;) weight; seriousness; (des Weines) body; difficulty; significance; (phys) gravity
schwe'relos adj weightless
schwer'fällig adj heavy; clumsy, slow
Schwer'gewicht n heavyweight class; (Nachdruck) emphasis
Schwergewichtler –in [ʃveːrɡəvɪçtlər (ɪn)] §6 mf (sport) heavyweight
schwer'hörig adj hard of hearing

Schwer'industrie f heavy industry
Schwer'kraft f gravity
schwer'lich adv hardly
Schwer'mut f melancholy, depression
schwer'mütig adj melancholy, depressed
schwer'nehmen §116 tr take hard
Schwer'punkt m center of gravity; crucial point, focal point
Schwert [ʃveːrt] n (-[e]s;-er) sword
Schwer'verbrecher –in §6 mf felon
schwer'verdient adj hard-earned
schwer'wiegend adj weighty
Schwester ['ʃvɛstər] f (-;-n) sister; nurse; nun
Schwe'sterhelferin f nurse's aide
schwieg [ʃviːk] pret of **schweigen**
Schwieger– [ʃviːɡər] comb.fm. -in-law
Schwie'germutter f mother-in-law
Schwie'gersohn m son-in-law
Schwie'gertochter f daughter-in-law
Schwie'gervater m father-in-law
Schwiele ['ʃviːlə] f (-;-n) callus
schwielig ['ʃviːlɪç] adj callous
schwierig ['ʃviːrɪç] adj hard, difficult
Schwie'rigkeit f (-;-en) difficulty
Schwimm– [ʃvɪm] comb.fm. swimming
Schwimm'anstalt f, **Schwimm'bad** n, **Schwimm'bassin** n, **Schwimm'becken** n swimming pool
schwimmen ['ʃvɪmən] §136 intr (HABEN & SEIN) swim; float
Schwimm'gürtel m life belt
Schwimm'haut f web
Schwimm'hose f bathing trunks
Schwimm'kraft f buoyancy
Schwimm'panzer m amphibious tank
Schwimm'weste f life jacket
Schwindel ['ʃvɪndəl] m (-s;-) dizziness; swindle, gyp; (Unsinn) bunk; (pathol) vertigo; **der ganze S.** the whole caboodle
Schwin'delanfall m dizzy spell
Schwin'delfirma f fly-by-night
schwin'delhaft adj fraudulent, bogus
schwindelig ['ʃvɪndəlɪç] adj dizzy
schwindeln ['ʃvɪndəln] tr swindle ‖ intr fib ‖ impers—**mir schwindelt** I feel dizzy
Schwin'delunternehmen n fly-by-night
schwinden ['ʃvɪndən] §59 intr (SEIN) dwindle; decline; (Farbe) fade
Schwind'ler –in §6 mf swindler; fibber
schwindlig ['ʃvɪntlɪç] adj dizzy
Schwindsucht ['ʃvɪntzuçt] f tuberculosis
Schwinge ['ʃvɪŋə] f (-;-n) wing; fan; winnow; (poet) pinion
schwingen ['ʃvɪŋən] §142 tr swing; wave; brandish; (agr) winnow; (tex) swingle ‖ ref vault; soar ‖ intr swing; sway, oscillate; vibrate
Schwin'ger m (-s;-) oscillator; (box) haymaker
Schwin'gung f (-;-en) oscillation; vibration; swinging
Schwips [ʃvɪps] m—**e-n S. haben** (coll) be tipsy, be tipsy
schwirren ['ʃvɪrən] intr (HABEN & SEIN) whiz, whirr; buzz; (Gerüchte) fly
Schwitzbad ['ʃvɪtsbaːt] n Turkish bath
schwitzen ['ʃvɪtsən] tr & intr sweat

schwoll [ʃvɔl] *pret of* **schwellen**

schwor [ʃvoːr] *pret of* **schwören**

schwören [ˈʃvøːrən] §137 *tr & intr* swear; **auf j-n** (or **etw**) **s.** swear by s.o. (or s.th.)

schwul [ʃvuːl] *adj* (vulg) homosexual

schwül [ʃvyːl] *adj* sultry, muggy

Schwulität [ʃvulɪˈtɛt] *f* (-;-en) trouble

Schwulst [ʃvulst] *m* (-es;⁻e) bombast

schwülstig [ˈʃvylstɪç] *adj* bombastic

schwummerig [ˈʃvuməriç] *adj* (coll) shaky

Schwund [ʃvunt] *m* (-[e]s;) dwindling; shrinkage; loss; leakage; (*des Haares*) falling out; (rad) fading; (pathol) atrophy

Schwung [ʃvuŋ] *m* (-[e]s;⁻e) swing; vault; (*Tatkraft*) zip, go; (*der Phantasie*) flight; **in S. bringen** start; **S. bekommen** gather momentum

schwung'haft *adj* brisk, lively

Schwung'kraft *f* centrifugal force; (fig) zip, pep; (phys) momentum

Schwung'rad *n* (mach) flywheel

schwung'voll *adj* enthusiastic, lively

schwur [ʃvuːr] *pret of* **schwören** ‖

Schwur *m* (-[e]s;⁻e) oath

Schwur'gericht *n* jury

sechs [zɛks] *invar adj & pron* six ‖ **Sechs** *f* (-;-en) six

Sechs'eck *n* hexagon

Sechser [ˈzɛksər] *m* (-s;-) six; (*in der Lotterie*) jackpot

Sechsta'gerennen *n* six-day bicycle race

sechste [ˈzɛkstə] §9 *adj & pron* sixth

Sechstel [ˈzɛkstəl] *n* (-s;-) sixth

sech'zehn *invar adj & pron* sixteen ‖ **Sech'zehn** *f* (-;-en) sixteen

sech'zehnte §9 *adj & pron* sixteenth

Sech'zehntel *n* (-s;-) sixteenth

sechzig [ˈzɛçtsɪç] *invar adj & pron* sixty ‖ **Sechzig** *f* (-;-en) sixty

sechziger [ˈzɛçtsɪgər] *invar adj* of the sixties; **die s. Jahre** the sixties ‖ **Sechziger** *m* (-s;-) sexagenarian

sechzigste [ˈzɛçtsɪçstə] §9 *adj & pron* sixtieth

See [zeː] *m* (Sees; Seen [ˈzeː-ən] lake ‖ *f* (See; Seen [ˈzeː-ən]) sea; ocean; **an der See** at the seashore; **an die See gehen** go to the seashore; **auf See** at sea; **in See gehen** (or **stechen**) put out to sea; **in See sein** be in open water; **Kapitän zur See** navy captain; **zur See gehen** go to sea

See'bad *n* seashore resort

See'bär *m* (fig) sea dog

see'fähig *adj* seaworthy

See'fahrer *m* seafarer

See'fahrt *f* seafaring; voyage

see'fest *adj* seaworthy; **s. werden** get one's sea legs

See'gang *m*—**hoher** (or **schwerer** or **starker**) **S.** heavy seas

See'hafen *m* seaport

See'handel *m* maritime trade

See'hund *m* (zool) seal

See'jungfer *f*, **See'jungfrau** *f* mermaid

See'kadett *m* naval cadet

See'karte *f* (naut) chart

see'krank *adj* seasick

See'krebs *m* lobster

Seele [ˈzeːlə] *f* (-;-n) soul; mind; (*Ein-*

wohner) inhabitant, soul; (*e-s Geschützes*) bore; (*e-s Kabels*) core

See'lenangst *f* mortal fear

See'lenfriede *m* peace of mind

See'lenheil *n* salvation

See'lennot *f* mental distress

See'lenpein *f*, **See'lenqual** *f* mental anguish

See'lenruhe *f* peace of mind; composure

see'lensgut *adj* good-hearted

seelisch [ˈzeːlɪʃ] *adj* mental, psychic

Seel'sorge *f* (-;) ministry

Seel'sorger *m* (-s;-) minister, pastor

See'macht *f* sea power

See'mann *m* (-[e]s;-leute) seaman

See'meile *f* nautical mile

See'möwe *f* sea gull

See'not *f* (naut) distress

See'ratte *f* (fig) old salt

See'raub *m* piracy

See'räuber *m* pirate; corsair

See'räuberei *f* piracy

See'recht *n* maritime law

See'reise *f* voyage; cruise

See'sperre *f* naval blockade

See'stadt *f* seaport town; coastal town

See'straße *f* shipping lane

See'streitkräfte *pl* naval forces

See'tang *m* seaweed

see'tüchtig *adj* seaworthy

See'warte *f* oceanographic institute

See'weg *m* sea route; **auf dem S. by sea**

See'wesen *n* naval affairs

Segel [ˈzeːgəl] *n* (-s;-) sail

Se'gelboot *n* sailboat; (sport) yacht

Se'gelfliegen *n* gliding

Se'gelflieger *-in* §6 *mf* glider pilot

Se'gelflug *m* glide, gliding

Se'gelflugzeug *n* glider

Se'gelleinwand *f* sailcloth, canvas

segeln [ˈzeːgəln] *intr* (HABEN & SEIN) sail; (aer) glide

Se'gelschiff *n* sailing vessel

Se'gelsport *m* sailing

Se'geltuch *n* sailcloth, canvas

Se'geltuchhülle *f*, **Se'geltuchplane** *f* tarpaulin

Segen [ˈzeːgən] *m* (-s;-) blessing

se'gensreich *adj* blessed, blissful

Segler [ˈzeːglər] *m* (-s;-) yachtsma…, (aer) glider; (naut) sailing vessel

segnen [ˈzeːgnən] *tr* bless

Seh- [zeː] *comb.fm.* visual, of vision

sehen [ˈzeː-ən] §138 *tr see* ‖ *intr* see; look; **s. auf** (acc) look at; take care of; face (*a direction*); **s. nach** look for, look around for; **schlecht s.** have poor eyes ‖ **Sehen** *n* (-s;) sight; eyesight, vision; **vom S.** by sight

se'henswert *adj* worth seeing

Se'henswürdigkeit *f* object of interest; **Sehenswürdigkeiten** sights

Seher [ˈzeː-ər] *m* (-s;-) seer, prophet

Se'hergabe *f* gift of prophecy

Seh'feld *n* field of vision

Seh'kraft *f* eyesight

Sehne [ˈzeːnə] *f* (-;-n) tendon, sinew; (*Bogen-*) string; (geom) secant

sehnen [ˈzeːnən] *ref*—**sich s. nach** long for, crave ‖ **Sehnen** *n* (-s;) longing

Seh'nerv *m* optic nerve

sehnig ['zeniç] *adj* sinewy; *(Fleisch)* stringy
sehnlich ['zenliç] *adj* longing; ardent
Sehnsucht ['zenzuçt] *f* (-;) yearning
sehr [zer] *adv* very; very much
Seh'rohr *n* periscope
Seh'vermögen *n* sight, vision
Seh'weite *f* visual range; **in S.** within sight
seicht [zaiçt] *adj* (& fig) shallow
Seide ['zaidə] *f* (-;-n) silk
seiden ['zaidən] *adj* silk, silky
Sei'denatlas *m* satin
Sei'denpapier *n* tissue paper
Sei'denraupe *f* silkworm
Sei'denspinnerei *f* silk mill
Sei'denstoff *m* silk cloth
seidig ['zaidiç] *adj* silky
Seife ['zaifə] *f* (-;-n) soap
Sei'fenblase *f* soap bubble
Sei'fenbrühe *f* soapsuds
Sei'fenflocken *pl* soap flakes
Sei'fenlauge *f* soapsuds
Sei'fenpulver *n* soap powder
Sei'fenschale *f* soap dish
Sei'fenschaum *m* lather
seifig ['zaifiç] *adj* soapy
seihen ['zai·ən] *tr* strain, filter
Sei'her *m* (-s;-) strainer, filter
Seil [zail] *n* (-[e]s;-e) rope; cable
Seil'bahn *f* cable railway; cable car
seil'springen *intr* jump rope
Seil'tänzer **-in** §6 *mf* ropewalker
sein [zain] §139 *intr* (SEIN) be; exist; **es ist mir, als wenn** I feel as if; **es sei denn, daß** unless; **lassen Sie das s.!** stop it!; **wenn dem so ist** if that is the case; **wie dem auch sein mag** however that may be || *aux* (to form compound past tenses of intransitive verbs of motion, change of condition, etc.) have, e.g., **ich bin gegangen** I have gone, I went || §2,2 *poss adj* his; its; one's; her || §2,4,5 *poss pron* his; hers; **die Seinen** his family; **er hat das Seine getan** he did his share; **jedem das Seine** to each his own ||
Sein *n* (-s;) being; existence; reality
seinerseits ['zainər'zaits] *adv* for his part
seinerzeit ['zainər'tsait] *adv* in its time; in those days; in due time
seinesgleichen ['zainəs'glaiçən] *pron* people like him, the likes of him
seinethalben ['zainət'halbən], **seinetwegen** ['zainət'vegən] *adv* for his sake; on his account; *(von ihm aus)* for all he cares
seinetwillen ['zainət'vilən] *adv*—**um s.** for his sake, on his behalf
Seinige ['zainigə] §2,5 *pron* his; **das S.** his property, his own; his due; his share; **die Seinigen** his family
seit [zait] *prep* (dat) since, for; **s. e-m Jahr** for one year; **s. einiger Zeit** for some time past; **s. kurzem** lately; **s. langem** for a long time; **s. wann** since when || *conj* since
seitdem [zait'dem] *adv* since that time || *conj* since
Seite ['zaitə] *f* (-;-n) side; page; direction; *(Quelle)* source; (mil) flank
Sei'tenansicht *f* side view, profile

Sei'tenbau *m* (-[e]s;-ten) annex
Sei'tenblick *m* side glance
Sei'tenflosse *f* (aer) horizontal stabilizer
Sei'tenflügel *m* (archit) wing
Sei'tengang *m* side aisle
Sei'tengeleise *n* sidetrack
Sei'tenhieb *m* snide remark, dig
sei'tenlang *adj* pages of
Sei'tenriß *m* profile
sei'tens *prep* (genit) on the part of
Sei'tenschiff *n* (archit) aisle
Sei'tenschwimmen *n* sidestroke
Sei'tensprung *m* (fig) escapade
Sei'tenstück *n* (fig) counterpart
Sei'tenwind *m* cross wind
seither [zait'her] *adv* since then
-seitig [zaitiç] *comb.fm.* -sided
seit'lich *adj* lateral
seitwärts ['zaitverts] *adv* sideways, sidewards; aside
Sekretär **-in** [zekre'ter(in)] §8 *mf* secretary
Sekt [zekt] *m* (-[e]s;-e) champagne
Sekte ['zektə] *f* (-;-n) sect
Sek·tor ['zektor] *m* (-s;-toren ['torən]) sector; (fig) field
Sekundant [zekun'dant] *m* (-en;-en) (box) second
sekundär [zekun'der] *adj* secondary
Sekunde [ze'kundə] *f* (-;-n) second
Sekun'denbruchteil *m* split second
Sekun'denzeiger *m* second hand
Sekurit [zeku'rit] *n* (-s;) safety glass
selber ['zelbər] *invar pron* (coll) var of **selbst**
selbst [zelpst] *invar pron* self; in person, personally; *(sogar)* even; by oneself; **ich s.** I myself; **von s.** voluntarily; spontaneously; automatically || *adv* even; **s. ich** even I; **s. wenn** even if, even when
Selbst'achtung *f* self-respect
selbständig ['zelp/tendiç] *adj* independent
Selbst'bedienung *f* self-service
Selbst'beherrschung *f* self-control
Selbst'beobachtung *f* introspection
Selbst'bestimmung *f* self-determination
Selbst'betrug *m* self-deception
selbst'bewußt *adj* self-confident
Selbst'binder *m* necktie; (agr) combine
Selbst'erhaltung *f* self-preservation
selbst'gebacken *adj* homemade
selbst'gefällig *adj* complacent, smug
Selbst'gefühl *n* self-confidence
selbst'gemacht *adj* homemade
selbst'gerecht *adj* self-righteous
Selbst'gespräch *n* soliloquy
selbst'gezogen *adj* home-grown
selbst'herrlich *adj* high-handed
Selbst'herrschaft *f* autocracy
Selbst'herrscher *m* autocrat
Selbst'kosten *pl* production costs
Selbst'kostenpreis *m* factory price; **zum S. abgeben** sell at cost
Selbstlader ['zelpstladər] *m* (-s;-) automatic (weapon)
Selbst'laut *m* vowel
selbst'los *adj* unselfish
Selbst'mord *m* suicide
selbst'sicher *adj* self-confident
Selbst'steuer *n* automatic pilot

Selbst'sucht f egotism, selfishness
selbst'süchtig adj egotistical
selbst'tätig adj automatic
Selbst'täuschung f self-deception
Selbstüberhebung [ˈzɛlpstybərhebʊŋ] f (-;) self-conceit, presumption
Selbst'verbrennung f spontaneous combustion; self-immolation
Selbst'verlag m—**im S.** printed privately
Selbst'verleugnung f self-denial
Selbst'versorger m (-s;-) self-supporter
selbst'verständlich adj obvious; natural || adv of course
Selbst'verständlichkeit f foregone conclusion, matter of course
Selbst'verteidigung f self-defense
Selbst'vertrauen n self-confidence
Selbst'verwaltung f autonomy
Selbst'wähler m (-s;-) dial telephone
Selbst'zucht f self-discipline
selbst'zufrieden adj self-satisfied
Selbst'zufriedenheit f self-satisfaction
Selbst'zweck m end in itself
selig [ˈzeliç] adj blessed; (verstorben) late; (fig) ecstatic; (fig) tipsy; **seligen Angedenkens** of blessed memory; **s. werden** attain salvation, be saved
Se'ligkeit f (-;) happiness; salvation
Se'ligpreisung f (Bib) beatitude
se'ligsprechen §64 tr beatify
Sellerie [ˈzeləri] m (-s;) & f (-;) celery (bulb)
selten [ˈzɛltən] adj rare, scarce || adv seldom, rarely
Selterswasser [ˈzɛltərsvasər] n seltzer, soda water
seltsam [ˈzɛltzam] adj odd, strange
Semester [zeˈmɛstər] n (-s;-) semester
Semikolon [ˈzemɪkɔlɔn] n semicolon
Seminar [zemɪˈnar] n (-s;-e) seminary; (educ) seminar
Seminarist [zemɪnaˈrɪst] m (-en;-en) seminarian
semitisch [zeˈmɪtɪʃ] adj Semitic
Semmel [ˈzeməl] f (-;-n) roll
Senat [zeˈnat] m (-[e]s;-e) senate
Se-nator [zeˈnator] m (-s;-natoren [naˈtorən]) senator
Sende- [zɛndə] comb.fm. transmitting, transmitter, broadcasting
senden [ˈzɛndən] tr & intr transmit, broadcast; telecast || §120 & §140 tr send || intr—**s. nach** send for
Sen'der m (-s;-) (rad, telv) transmitter; (rad) broadcasting station
Sen'deraum m broadcasting studio
Sen'dezeichen n station identification
Sen'dezeit f air time
Sen'dung f (-;-en) sending; (fig) mission; (com) shipment; (rad) broadcast; (telv) telecast
Senf [zenf] m (-[e]s;-e) mustard
sengen [ˈzɛŋən] tr singe, scorch
seng(e)rig [ˈzɛŋ(ə)rɪç] adj burnt; (fig) suspicious, fishy
senil [zeˈnil] adj senile
Senilität [zenɪliˈtet] f (-;) senility
senior [ˈzenjor] adj senior
Senkblei [ˈzɛŋkblaɪ] n plummet; (naut) sounding lead
Senke [ˈzɛŋkə] f (-;-n) depression
senken [ˈzɛŋkən] tr lower; sink; (Kopf)

bow || ref sink, settle; dip, slope; (Mauer) sag
Senkfüße [ˈzɛŋkfysə] pl flat feet, fallen arches
Senk'fußeinlage f arch support
Senkgrube [ˈzɛŋkgrubə] f cesspool
Senkkasten [ˈzɛŋkkastən] m caisson
senkrecht [ˈzɛŋkreçt] adj vertical; (geom) perpendicular
Sen'kung f (-;-en) sinking; depression; dip, slope; sag; (der Preise) lowering
Sensation [zɛnzaˈtsjon] f (-;-en) sensation
sensationell [zɛnzatsjoˈnel] adj sensational
Sensations'blatt n (pej) scandal sheet
Sensations'lust f sensationalism
Sensations'meldung f, **Sensations'nachricht** f (journ) scoop
Sensations'presse f yellow journalism
Sense [ˈzɛnzə] f (-;-n) scythe
sensibel [zɛnˈzibəl] adj sensitive; (Nerven) sensory
Sensibilität [zɛnzɪbɪliˈtet] f (-;) sensitivity, sensitiveness
sentimental [zɛntɪmenˈtal] adj sentimental
separat [zepaˈrat] adj separate
September [zɛpˈtembər] m (-[s];) September
Serenade [zereˈnadə] f (-;-n) serenade
Serie [ˈzerjə] f (-;-n) series; line
Se'rienanfertigung f, **Se'rienbau** m, **Se'rienfabrikation** f, **Se'rienherstellung** f mass production
se'rienmäßig adj—**serienmäßige Herstellung** mass production || adv—**s. herstellen** mass-produce
Se'riennummer f serial number
Se'rienproduktion f mass production
seriös [zeˈrjøs] adj serious; reliable
Se-rum [ˈzerum] n (-s;-ren [rən] & -ra [ra]) serum
Service [ˈzørvɪs] m (Services [ˈzørvɪs(əs)];) (Kundendienst) service || [zerˈvis] n (Services [zerˈvis]; **Ser-vice** [zerˈvis(ə)]) (Tafelgeschirr) service
Servierbrett [zerˈvirbret] n tray
servieren [zerˈvirən] tr serve; **es ist serviert!** dinner is ready! || intr wait at table
Serviertisch [zerˈvirtɪʃ] m sideboard
Servierwagen [zerˈvirvagən] m serving cart
Serviette [zerˈvjetə] f (-;-n) napkin
Servo- [zervə] comb.fm. booster, auxiliary, servo, power, automatic
Ser'vobremsen pl power brakes
Ser'vokupplung f automatic transmission
Ser'volenkung f power steering
Servus [ˈzervus] interj (Aust) hello!; (coll) so long!
Sessel [ˈzesəl] m (-s;-) easy chair
Ses'sellift m chair lift
seßhaft [ˈzeshaft] adj settled; **sich s. machen** settle down
Setzei [ˈzetsaɪ] n fried egg
setzen [ˈzɛtsən] tr set, put, place; seat; (beim Spiel) bet; (Denkmal) erect; (Frist) fix; (Junge) breed; (Fische) stock; (Pflanzen) plant; (mus) com-

pose; (typ) set ‖ *ref* sit down; (*Kaffee*) settle ‖ *intr* set type; **s. auf** (*acc*) bet on ‖ *intr* (SEIN)—**s. über** (*acc*) jump over

Setz′zer *m* (-s;-) typesetter, compositor

Setz′fehler *m* typographical error

Seuche [′zɔɪçə] *f* (-;-n) epidemic

seufzen [′zɔɪftsən] *intr* sigh

Seuf′zer *m* (-s;-) sigh

Sex [zɛks] *m* (-es;) sex

Sex-Appeal [′zɛks ə′pil] *m* (-s;) sex appeal

Sex′-Bombe *f* (coll) sex pot

Sexual– [zɛksuɑl] *comb.fm.* sex

sexuell [zɛksu′ɛl] *adj* sexual

Sexus [′zɛksʊs] *m* (-;-) sex

sezieren [ze′tsirən] *tr* dissect

Shampoo [ʃam′pu] *n* (-s;-s) shampoo

Sibirien [zɪ′birjən] *n* (-s;) Siberia

sich [zɪç] §11 *reflex pron* oneself; himself; herself; itself; themselves; an (**und für**) **s.** in itself; **außer s. sein** be beside oneself ‖ *recip pron* each other, one another

Sichel [′zɪçəl] *f* (-;-n) sickle

sicher [′zɪçər] *adj* sure; positive; reliable; (**vor** *dat*) safe (from), secure (from) ‖ *adv* surely, certainly

Si′cherheit *f* (-;-en) safety, security; (*Gewißheit*) certainty; (*Zuverlässigkeit*) reliability; (*im Auftreten*) assurance; (com) security; (jur) bail

Si′cherheitsgurt *m*, **Si′cherheitsgürtel** *m* (aer, aut) seat belt

Si′cherheitsnadel *f* safety pin

Si′cherheitspolizei *f* security police

Si′cherheitsspielraum *m* margin of safety, leeway

si′cherlich *adv* surely, certainly

sichern [′zɪçərn] *tr* secure; fasten; guarantee; (*Gewehr*) put on safety

Si′cherstellung *f* safekeeping; guarantee

Si′cherung *f* (-;-en) protection; guarantee; (*an Schußwaffe*) safety catch; (elec) fuse; **durchgebrannte S.** blown fuse

Si′cherungskasten *m* fuse box

Sicht [zɪçt] *f* (-;) sight; (*Aussicht*) view; (*Sichtigkeit*) visibility; **auf kurze S.** short-range; **auf S.** at sight

sichtbar [′zɪçtbar] *adj* visible

sichten [′zɪçtən] *tr* sight; (fig) sift

sichtig [′zɪçtɪç] *adj* clear

sicht′lich *adj* visible

Sicht′vermerk *m* visa

sickern [′zɪkərn] *intr* (HABEN & SEIN) trickle, seep, leak

sie [zi] §11 *pers pron* she, her; it; they, them ‖ §11 **Sie** *pers pron* you

Sieb [zip] *n* (-[e]s;-e) sieve, colander; screen; (rad) filter

sieben [′ziban] *invar adj & pron* seven ‖ *tr* sift, strain; (fig) screen; (rad) filter ‖ **Sieben** *f* (-;-en) seven

siebente [′zibəntə] §9 *adj & pron* seventh

Siebentel [′zibəntəl] *n* (-s;-) seventh

siebte [′zipta] §9 *adj & pron* seventh

Siebtel [′ziptəl] *n* (-s;-) seventh

siebzehn [′ziptsen] *invar adj & pron* seventeen ‖ **Siebenzehn** *f* (-;-en) seventeen

siebzehnte [′ziptsentə] §9 *adj & pron* seventeenth

Siebzehntel [′ziptsentəl] *n* (-s;-) seventeenth

siebzig [′ziptsɪç] *invar adj & pron* seventy ‖ **Siebzig** *f* (-;-en) seventy

siebziger [′ziptsɪgər] *invar adj* of the seventies; **die s. Jahre** the seventies ‖ **Siebziger** *m* (-s;-) septuagenarian

siebzigste [′ziptsɪçstə] §9 *adj & pron* seventieth

siech [ziç] *adj* sickly

siechen [′ziçən] *intr* be sickly

Siechtum [′ziçtum] *n* (-s;) lingering illness

siedeheiß [′zidə′haɪs] *adj* piping hot

siedeln [′zidəln] *intr* settle

sieden [′zidən] §141 *tr & intr* boil

Siedepunkt [′zidəpʊŋkt] *m* boiling point

Siedler –in [′zidlər(ɪn)] §6 *mf* settler

Sied′lerstelle *f* homestead

Sied′lung *f* (-;-en) settlement; colony; housing development

Sieg [zik] *m* (-[e]s;-e) victory

Siegel [′zigəl] *n* (-s;-) seal

siegeln [′zigəln] *tr* seal

Sie′gelring *m* signet ring

siegen [′zigən] *intr* win, be victorious

Sie′ger –in §6 *mf* winner, victor; **zweiter Sieger** runner-up

Sieges– [zigəs] *comb.fm.* victory, of victory, triumphal

Sie′gesbogen *m* triumphal arch

sieg′reich *adj* victorious

Signal [zɪg′nal] *n* (-s;-e) signal

signalisieren [zɪgnalɪ′zirən] *tr* signal

Silbe [′zɪlbə] *f* (-;-n) syllable

Sil′bentrennung *f* syllabification

Silber [′zɪlbər] *n* (-s;) silver

silbern [′zɪlbərn] *adj* silver, silvery

Sil′berzeug *n* silver, silverware

Silhouette [zilu′ɛtə] *f* (-;-n) silhouette

Silo [′zilo] *m* (-s;-s) silo

Silvester [zɪl′vɛstər] *m* (-s;-), **Silve′sterabend** *m* New Year's Eve

simpel [′zɪmpəl] *adj* simple ‖ **Simpel** *m* (-s;-) simpleton

Sims [zɪms] *m & n* (-es;-e) ledge; (*Fenster–*) sill; (*Kamin–*) mantelpiece

Simulant –in [zimu′lant(ɪn)] §7 *mf* faker; (mil) goldbrick

simulieren [zimu′lirən] *tr* simulate, fake ‖ *intr* loaf

simultan [zimul′tan] *adj* simultaneous

Sinfo·nie [zɪnfo′ni] *f* (-;-nien [′ni-ən]) symphony

singen [′zɪŋən] §142 *tr & intr* sing

Singsang [′zɪŋzaŋ] *m* (-[e]s;) singsong

Sing′spiel *n* musical comedy, musical

Sing′stimme *f* vocal part

Singular [′zɪŋgular] *m* (-s;-e) singular

sinken [′zɪŋkən] §143 *intr* (SEIN) sink; slump, sag; (*Preise*) drop; **s. lassen** lower; (*Mut*) lose

Sinn [zɪn] *m* (-[e]s;-e) sense; mind; meaning; liking, taste

Sinn′bild *n* emblem, symbol

sinn′bildlich *adj* symbolic(al) ‖ *adv* symbolically; **s. darstellen** symbolize

sinnen [′zɪnən] §121 *tr* plan; plot ‖ *intr* (**auf** *acc*) plan, plot; (**über** *acc*) think (about) ‖ **Sinnen** *n* (-s;) reflection, meditation, reverie

sin'nend *adj* pensive, reflective

Sin'nenlust *f* sensuality

Sin'nenmensch *m* sensualist

Sin'nenwelt *f* material world

Sin'nesänderung *f* change of mind

Sin'nesart *f* character, disposition

Sin'nestäuschung *f* illusion, hallucination, mirage

sinn'lich *adj* sensual; material

sinn'los *adj* senseless

sinn'reich *adj* ingenious, bright

sinn'verwandt *adj* synonymous

sinn'voll *adj* meaningful; sensible

Sintflut ['zɪntflut] *f* deluge, flood

Sippe ['zɪpə] *f* (-;-n) kin; clan

Sipp'schaft *f* (-;-en) clique, set

Sirup ['zirup] *m* (-s;-e) syrup

Sitte ['zɪtə] *f* (-;-n) custom; habit; usage; **die Sitten** the morals

Sit'tenbild *n*, **Sit'tengemälde** *n* description of the manners (*of an age*)

Sit'tengesetz *n* moral law

Sit'tenlehre *f* ethics

sit'tenlos *adj* immoral

Sit'tenpolizei *f* vice squad

sit'tenrein *adj* chaste

Sit'tenrichter *m* censor

sit'tenstreng *adj* puritanical, prudish

Sittich ['zɪtɪç] *m* (-s;-e) parakeet

sittlich ['zɪtlɪç] *adj* moral, ethical

Sittlichkeit *f* (-;) morality

Sitt'lichkeitsverbrechen *n* indecent assault

sittsam ['zɪtzam] *adj* modest, decent

Situation [zɪtu·a'tsjon] *f* (-;-en) situation

situiert [zɪtu'irt] *adj*—**gut s.** well-to-do

Sitz [zɪts] *m* (-es;-e) seat; residence; (*e-s Kleides*) fit; (eccl) see

sitzen ['zɪtsən] §144 *intr* sit; dwell; (*Vögel*) perch; (*Kleider*) fit; (*Hieb*) hit home; (coll) be in jail

sit'zenbleiben §62 *intr* (SEIN) remain seated; (*beim Tanzen*) be a wallflower; (*bei der Heirat*) remain unmarried; (educ) stay behind, flunk

sit'zenlassen §104 *tr* leave, abandon; (*Mädchen*) jilt

Sitz'gelegenheit *f* seating accommodation

Sitz'ordnung *f* seating arrangement

Sitz'platz *m* seat

Sitz'streik *m* sit-down strike

Sit'zung *f* (-;-en) session

Sit'zungsbericht *m* minutes

Sit'zungsperiode *f* session; (jur) term

Sizilien [zi'tsiljən] *n* (-s;) Sicily

Ska·la ['skala] *f* (-;-len [lən]) scale

Skandal [skan'dal] *m* (-s;-e) scandal

skandalös [skanda'løs] *adj* scandalous

Skandinavien [skandi'navjən] *n* (-s;) Scandinavia

Skelett [ske'let] *n* (-[e]s;-e) skeleton

Skepsis ['skepsɪs] *f* (-;) skepticism

Skeptiker **-in** ['skeptɪkər(ɪn)] §6 *mf* skeptic

skeptisch ['skeptɪʃ] *adj* skeptical

Ski [ʃi] *m* (-s; **Skier** ['ʃi·ər]) ski

Skizze ['skɪtsə] *f* (-;-n) sketch

skizzieren [skɪ'tsirən] *tr & intr* sketch

Sklave ['sklavə] *m* (-n;-n) slave

Sklaverei [sklavə'raɪ] *f* (-;) slavery

sklavisch ['sklavɪʃ] *adj* slavish

Skonto ['skɔnto] *m & n* (-s;-s) discount

Skrupel ['skrupəl] *m* (-s;-) scruple

skru'pellos *adj* unscrupulous

skrupulös [skrupu'løs] *adj* scrupulous

Skulptur [skʊlp'tur] *f* (-;-en) sculpture

Slalom ['slalom] *m & n* (-s;-s) slalom

Slawe ['slavə] *m* (-n;-n), **Slawin** ['slavɪn] *f* (-;-nen) Slav

slawisch ['slavɪʃ] *adj* Slavic

Smaragd [sma'rakt] *m* (-[e]s;-e) emerald

Smoking ['smokɪŋ] *m* (-s;-s) tuxedo

so [zo] *adv* so; this way, thus; **so ein** such a; **so oder so** by hook or by crook; **so...wie** as...as

sobald' *conj* as soon as

Socke ['zɔkə] *f* (-;-n) sock

Sockenhalter (Sok'kenhalter) *m* garter

Soda ['zoda] *f* (-;) *& n* (-s;) soda

sodann' *adv* then

Sodbrennen ['zotbrenən] *n* (-s;) heartburn

soeben [zo'ebən] *adv* just now, just

Sofa ['zofa] *n* (-s;-s) sofa

sofern' *conj* provided, if

soff [zɔf] *pret of* saufen

sofort' *adv* at once, right away

sofortig [zo'fɔrtɪç] *adj* immediate

sog [zok] *pret of* saugen ‖ **Sog** *m* (-[e]s;) suction; undertow; (aer) wash

sogar' *adv* even

so'genannt *adj* so-called; would-be

sogleich' *adv* at once, right away

Sohle ['zolə] *f* (-;-n) sole; bottom

Sohn [zon] *m* (-[e]s;-e) son

solan'ge *conj* as long as

solch [zɔlç] *adj* such

Sold [zɔlt] *m* (-[e]s;-e) pay

Soldat [zɔl'dat] *m* (-en;-en) soldier

Söldner ['zœldnər] *m* (-s;-) mercenary

Sole ['zolə] *f* (-;-n) brine

solid [zo'lit] *adj* solid; sound; reliable; steady; respectable; (*Preis*) reasonable; (com) sound, solvent

solide [zo'lidə] *adj* var of **solid**

Solist **-in** [zo'lɪst(ɪn)] §7 *mf* soloist

Soll [zɔl] *n* (-s;-e) quota; (acct) debit side; **S. und Haben** debit and credit

Soll– *comb.fm.* estimated; debit

sollen ['zɔlən] §145 *mod* (*inf*) be obliged to (*inf*), have to (*inf*); (*inf*) be supposed to (*inf*); (*inf*) be said to (*inf*)

Soll'wert *m* face value

solo ['zolo] *adv* (mus) solo ‖ **So·lo** *n* (-s;-s & -li [li]) solo

somit' *adv* so, consequently

Sommer ['zɔmər] *m* (-s;-) summer

Som'merfrische *f* health resort; **in die S. fahren** go to the country

Sommerfrischler ['zɔmərfrɪʃlər] *m* (-s;-) vacationer

som'merlich *adj* summery

Som'mersprosse *f* freckle

sonach' *adv* consequently, so

Sonate [zo'natə] *f* (-;-n) sonata

Sonde ['zɔndə] *f* (-;-n) probe

Sonder– [zɔndər] *comb.fm.* special, extra; separate

sonderbar ['zɔndərbɑr] *adj* strange, odd; peculiar

son'derlich *adj* special, particular

Sonderling ['zɔndərlɪŋ] *m* (-s;-e) odd person, strange character

sondern ['zɔndərn] *tr* separate; sever; part; sort out; classify ‖ *conj* but

Son'derrecht *n* privilege

Son'derung *f* (-;-en) separation; sorting, sifting; classifying

Son'derverband *m* (mil) task force

Son'derzug *m* (rr) special

sondieren [zɔn'dirən] *tr* probe; (fig) sound out; (naut) sound

Sonnabend ['zɔnɑbənt] *m* (-s;-e) Saturday

Sonne ['zɔnə] *f* (-;-n) sun

sonnen ['zɔnən] *tr* sun ‖ *ref* sun oneself

Son'nenaufgang *m* sunrise

Son'nenbad *n* sun bath

Son'nenblende *f* (aut) sun visor; (phot) lens shade

Sonnenbrand *m* sunburn

Son'nenbräune *f* suntan

Son'nenbrille *f* (pair of) sun glasses

Son'nendach *n* awning

Son'nenenergie *f* solar energy

Son'nenfinsternis *f* eclipse of the sun

Son'nenfleck *m* sunspot

Son'nenjahr *n* solar year

son'nenklar *adj* sunny; (fig) clear as day

Son'nenlicht *n* sunlight

Son'nenschein *m* sunshine

Son'nenschirm *m* parasol

Son'nensegel *n* awning

Son'nenseite *f* sunny side

Son'nenstich *m* sunstroke

Son'nenstrahl *m* sunbeam

Son'nensystem *n* solar system

Son'nenuhr *f* sundial

Son'nenuntergang *m* sunset

son'nenverbrannt *adj* sunburnt, tanned

Son'nenwende *f* solstice

sonnig ['zɔnɪç] *adj* sunny

Sonntag ['zɔntɑk] *m* (-s;-e) Sunday

sonn'tags *adv* on Sundays

Sonn'tagsfahrer –in §6 *mf* Sunday driver

Sonn'tagskind *n* person born under a lucky star

Sonn'tagsstaat *m* Sunday clothes

sonor [zo'nor] *adj* sonorous

sonst [zɔnst] *adv* otherwise; else; (*ehemals*) formerly; **s. etw** something else; **s. keiner** no one else; **s. nichts** nothing else; **s. noch was?** anything else?; **wie s.** as usual; **wie s. was** (coll) like anything

sonstig ['zɔnstɪç] *adj* other

sonst'wer *pron* someone else

sonst'wie *adv* in some other way

sonst'wo *adv* somewhere else

Sopran [zo'prɑn] *m* (-s;-e) soprano; treble

Sopranist –in [zoprɑ'nɪst(ɪn)] §7 *mf* soprano

Sorge ['zɔrgə] *f* (-;-n) care; worry; **außer S. sein** be at ease; **keine S.!** don't worry; **sich** [*dat*] **Sorgen machen über** (*acc*) or **um** be worried about

sorgen ['zɔrgən] *intr*—**dafür s., daß** take care that, see to it that; **s. für** take care of ‖ *ref* be uneasy; **sich s. über** (*acc*) grieve over; **sich s. um** be worried about

sor'genfrei *adj* carefree; untroubled

Sor'genkind *n* problem child

sor'genlos *adj* carefree

sor'genvoll *adj* uneasy, anxious

Sor'gerecht *n* (für) custody (of)

Sorgfalt ['zɔrkfɑlt] *f* (-;) care, carefulness; accuracy

sorgfältig ['zɔrkfɛltɪç] *adj* careful

sorglich ['zɔrklɪç] *adj* careful

sorglos ['zɔrklos] *adj* careless; thoughtless; carefree

sorgsam ['zɔrkzɑm] *adj* careful; cautious

Sorte ['zɔrtə] *f* (-;-n) sort, kind

sortieren [zɔr'tirən] *tr* sort out

Sortiment [zɔrti'ment] *n* (-[e]s;-e) assortment

Soße ['zosə] *f* (-;-n) sauce; gravy

sott [zɔt] *pret of* **sieden**

Souffleur [zu'flør] *m* (-s;-s), **Souffleuse** [zu'fløzə] *f* (-;-n) prompter

soufflieren [zu'flirən] *intr* (*dat*) prompt

Soutane [zu'tɑnə] *f* (-;-n) cassock

Souvenir [zuvə'nir] *n* (-s;-s) souvenir

souverän [zuvə'ren] *adj* sovereign ‖ **Souverän** *m* (-s;-e) sovereign

Souveränität [zuvərenɪ'tet] *f* (-;) sovereignty

soviel' *adv* so much; **noch einmal s.** twice as much ‖ *conj* as far as

soweit' *conj* as far as

sowie' *conj* as well as

sowieso' *adv* in any case, anyhow

Sowjet [zɔv'jet] *m* (-s;-s) Soviet

sowjetisch [zɔv'jetɪʃ] *adj* Soviet

sowohl' *conj*—**sowohl...als auch** as well as, both...and

sozial [zo'tsjɑl] *adj* social

Sozial'fürsorge *f* social welfare

sozialisieren [zotsjɑlɪ'zirən] *tr* nationalize

Sozialismus [zotsjɑ'lɪsmʊs] *m* (-;) socialism

Sozialist –in [zotsjɑ'lɪst(ɪn)] §7 *mf* socialist

sozialistisch [zotsjɑ'lɪstɪʃ] *adj* socialistic

Sozial'wissenschaft *f* social science

Soziologie [zotsjolo'gi] *f* (-;) sociology

Sozius ['zotsjʊs] *m* (-;-se) associate, partner; (*auf dem Motorrad*) rider

sozusa'gen *adv* so to speak, as it were

Spachtel ['ʃpaxtəl] *m* (-s;-) & *f* (-;-n) spatula; putty knife

Spach'telmesser *n* putty knife

Spagat [ʃpa'gɑt] *m* (-[e]s;-e) (gym) split; (dial) string

spähen ['ʃpe-ən] *intr* peer; spy

Spä'her *m* (-s;-) lookout; (mil) scout

Spä'herblick *m* searching glance

Spähtrupp ['ʃpetrʊp] *m* reconnaissance squad

Späh'wagen *m* reconnaissance car

Spalier [ʃpa'lir] *n* (-s;-e) trellis; double line (*of people*)

Spalt [ʃpalt] *m* (-[e]s;-e) split; crack; slit; (geol) cleft

Spalte ['ʃpaltə] f (-;-n) split; crack; slit; (typ) column

spalten ['ʃpaltən] tr (pp **gespaltet** or **gespalten**) split; slit; crack; (Holz) chop

Spal′tung f (-;-en) split; (der Meinungen) division; (chem) decomposition; (eccl) schism; (phys) fission

Span [ʃpan] m (-[e]s;⸚e) chip; splinter; **Späne** shavings

Span′ferkel n suckling pig

Spange ['ʃpaŋə] f (-;-n) clasp; hair clip; (Schnalle) buckle

Spanien ['ʃpanjən] n (-s;) Spain

Spanier –in ['ʃpanjər(ɪn)] §6 mf Spaniard

spanisch ['ʃpanɪʃ] adj Spanish; **das kommt mir s. vor** (coll) that's Greek to me; **spanischer Pfeffer** paprika; **spanische Wand** folding screen

spann [ʃpan] pret of **spinnen** || **Spann** m (-s;-e) instep

Spanne ['ʃpanə] f (-;-n) span; (com) margin

spannen ['ʃpanən] tr stretch; strain; make tense; (Bogen) bend; (Feder) tighten; (Flinte) cock; (Erwartungen) raise; (Pferde) hitch; **straff s.** tighten; || intr be (too) tight; **s. auf** (acc) wait eagerly for; listen closely to

span′nend adj tight; exciting

Spann′kraft f tension; elasticity; (fig) resiliency

spann′kräftig adj elastic

Span′nung f (-;-en) stress; strain; pressure; close attention; suspense; excitement; strained relations; (elec) voltage

Spar- [ʃpar] comb.fm. savings

Spar′buch n bank book, pass book

Spar′büchse f piggy bank

sparen ['ʃparən] tr & intr save

Spar′flamme f pilot light

Spargel ['ʃpargəl] m (-s;-) asparagus

Spar′kasse f savings bank

Spar′konto n savings account

spärlich ['ʃperlɪç] adj scanty; scarce; sparse; frugal; (Haar) thin || adv poorly; scantily; sparsely

Sparren ['ʃparən] m (-s;-) rafter

sparsam ['ʃparzam] adj thrifty

Spaß [ʃpas] m (-es;⸚e) joke; fun; **aus S. in fun**; **S. beiseite!** all joking aside; **S. haben an** (dat) enjoy; **S. machen** be joking; be fun; **viel S.!** have fun!; **zum S.** for fun

spaß′haft, spaßig ['ʃpasɪç] adj funny, facetious

Spaß′macher m joker

Spaßverderber ['ʃpasverderbər] m (-s;-) (coll) kill-joy

Spaß′vogel m joker

spät [ʃpet] adj late; **wie s. ist es?** what time is it? || adv late

Spaten ['ʃpatən] m (-s;-) spade

später ['ʃpetər] adv later

späterhin′ adv later on

spätestens ['ʃpetəstəns] adv at the latest

Spät′jahr n autumn, fall

Spatz [ʃpats] m (-es & -en;-en) sparrow

spazieren [ʃpa'tsirən] intr (SEIN) stroll, take a walk

spazie′renfahren §71 intr (SEIN) go for a drive

spazie′renführen tr walk (e.g., a dog)

spazie′rengehen §82 intr (SEIN) go for a walk

Spazier′fahrt f drive

Spazier′gang m stroll, walk; **e-n S. machen** take a walk

Spazier′gänger –in §6 mf stroller

Spazier′weg m walk

Specht [ʃpeçt] m (-[e]s;-e) woodpecker

Speck [ʃpek] m (-[e]s;) fat; bacon; (beim Wal) blubber

Speck′bauch m (coll) potbelly

speckig ['ʃpekɪç] adj greasy, dirty

spedieren [ʃpe'dirən] tr dispatch, ship

Spediteur [ʃpedi'tør] m (-s;-e) shipper; furniture mover

Spedition [ʃpedi'tsjon] f (-;-en) shipment; moving company, movers

Speer [ʃper] m (-[e]s;-e) spear; (sport) javelin

Speiche ['ʃpaiçə] f (-;-n) spoke

Speichel ['ʃpaiçəl] m (-s;) saliva

Spei′chellecker m brown-noser

speicheln ['ʃpaiçəln] intr drool

Speicher ['ʃpaiçər] m (-s;-) warehouse; grain elevator; attic, loft

speichern ['ʃpaiçərn] tr store

speien ['ʃpai·ən] §135 tr vomit; spit; (Feuer) belch; (Wasser) spurt || intr vomit, throw up; spit

Speise ['ʃpaizə] f (-;-n) food; meal; (Gericht) dish

Spei′seeis n ice cream

Spei′sekammer f pantry

Spei′sekarte f menu

speisen ['ʃpaizən] tr feed; (fig) supply || intr eat; **auswärts s.** dine out

Spei′senfolge f menu

Spei′senreste pl leftovers

Spei′serohr n (mach) feed pipe

Spei′seröhre f esophagus

Spei′sesaal m dining room

Spei′seschrank m cupboard

Spei′sewagen m (rr) diner

Spei′sezimmer n dining room

Spektakel [ʃpek'takəl] m (-s;-) noise, racket

Spekulant –in [ʃpeku'lant(ɪn)] §7 mf speculator

Spekulation [ʃpekula'tsjon] f (-;-en) speculation; venture

spekulieren [ʃpeku'lirən] intr speculate, reflect; (fin) speculate

Spelunke [ʃpe'luŋkə] f (-;-n) (coll) drive, joint

Spende ['ʃpendə] f (-;-n) donation

spenden ['ʃpendən] tr give; donate; (Sakramente) administer; (Lob) bestow; **j-m Trost s.** comfort s.o.

spendieren [ʃpen'dirən] tr—**j-m etw s.** treat s.o. to s.th.

Sperling ['ʃperlɪŋ] m (-s;-e) sparrow

Sperr- [ʃper] comb.fm. barrage; barred

Sperr′baum m barrier, bar

Sperre ['ʃperə] f (-;-n) shutting; close; blockade; embargo; barricade; catch; lock; (rr) gate

sperren ['ʃperən] tr shut; (Gas, Licht) cut off; (Straße) block off; cordon off; *(blockieren)* blockade; *(mit Schloß)* lock; *(verriegeln)* bolt; *(Konto, Gelder)* freeze; *(Scheck)* stop payment on; *(verbieten)* stop; (sport) block; (sport) suspend; (typ) space ‖ *intr* jam, be stuck

Sperr'feuer *n* barrage

Sperr'gebiet *n* restricted area

Sperr'holz *n* plywood

sperrig [ˈʃpɛrɪç] *adj* bulky

Sperr'sitz *m* *(im Kino)* rear seat; *(im Zirkus)* front seat

Sperr'stunde *f* closing time; curfew

Sper'rung *f* (-;-en) stoppage; blocking; blockade; embargo; suspension *(of telephone service, etc.)*

Spesen [ˈʃpeːzən] *pl* costs, expenses

Spezi [ˈʃpeːtsi] *m* (-s;-s) (coll) buddy

spezial [ʃpeˈtsjaːl] *adj* special

Spezial'arzt *m*, **Spezial'ärztin** *f* specialist

Spezial'fach *n* specialty

Spezial'geschäft *n* specialty shop

spezialisieren [ʃpetsjaliˈziːrən] *ref (auf acc)* specialize (in)

Spezialist –in [ʃpetsjaˈlɪst(ɪn)] §7 *mf* specialist

Spezialität [ʃpetsjaliˈtɛt] *f* (-;-en) specialty

speziell [ʃpeˈtsjɛl] *adj* special

spezifisch [ʃpeˈtsiːfɪʃ] *adj* specific

Sphäre [ˈsfeːrə] *f* (-;-n) sphere

sphärisch [ˈsfeːrɪʃ] *adj* spherical

Spickaal [ˈʃpɪkaːl] *m* smoked eel

spicken [ˈʃpɪkən] *tr* lard; (fig) bribe

spie [ʃpiː] *pret* of **speien**

Spiegel [ˈʃpiːgəl] *m* (-s;-) mirror

Spie'gelbild *n* reflection *(in mirror)*

spie'gelblank' *adj* spick and span

Spie'gelei *n* fried egg

spie'gelglatt' *adj* glassy

spiegeln [ˈʃpiːgəln] *tr* reflect; mirror ‖ *ref* be reflected ‖ *intr* shine

Spiel [ʃpiːl] *n* (-[e]s;-e) game; play; set *(of chessmen or checkers)*; (cards) deck; (mach) play; (mus) playing; (sport) match; (theat) acting, performance; **auf dem S. stehen** be at stake; **aufs S. setzen** risk; **bei etw im S. sein** be at the bottom of s.th.; **leichtes S. haben mit** have an easy time with; **S. der Natur** freak of nature

Spiel'art *f* (biol) variety

Spiel'automat *m* slot machine

Spiel'bank *f* (-;-en) gambling table; gambling casino

Spiel'dose *f* music box

spielen [ˈʃpiːlən] *tr & intr* play

Spielerei [ʃpiːləˈraɪ] *f* (-;-en) fooling around; child's play

Spiel'ergebnis *n* (sport) score

spielerisch [ˈʃpiːlərɪʃ] *adj* playful

Spiel'feld *n* (sport) playing field

Spiel'film *m* feature film

Spiel'folge *f* program

Spiel'gefährte *m*, **Spiel'gefährtin** *f* playmate

Spiel'karten *pl* (playing) cards

Spiel'leiter *m* (cin, theat) director

Spiel'marke *f* chip, counter

Spiel'plan *m* program

Spiel'platz *m* playground; playing field

Spiel'raum *m* (fig) elbowroom; (mach) play

Spiel'sachen *pl* toys

Spiel'tisch *m* gambling table

Spiel'verderber *m* kill-joy

Spiel'verlängerung *f* overtime

Spiel'waren *pl* toys

Spiel'zeug *n* toy(s)

Spieß [ʃpiːs] *m* (-es;-e) spear, pike; (sl) top kick; (culin) spit; **den S. umdrehen gegen** turn the tables on

Spieß'bürger *m* Philistine, lowbrow

spieß'bürgerlich *adj* narrow-minded

spießen [ˈʃpiːsən] *tr* spear; spit

Spie'ßer *m* (-s;-) Philistine, lowbrow

Spieß'gesell *m* accomplice

Spießruten [ˈʃpiːsruːtən] *pl*—**S. laufen** run the gauntlet

spinal [ʃpiˈnaːl] *adj* spinal; **spinale Kinderlähmung** infantile paralysis

Spinat [ʃpiˈnaːt] *m* (-[e]s;-e) spinach

Spind [ʃpɪnt] *m & n* (-[e]s;-e) wardrobe; (mil) locker

Spindel [ˈʃpɪndəl] *f* (-;-n) spindle; *(Spinnrocken)* distaff

spin'deldürr' *adj* skinny, scrawny

Spinne [ˈʃpɪnə] *f* (-;-n) spider

spinnen [ˈʃpɪnən] *tr* spin; **Ränke s.** hatch plots ‖ *intr* purr; *(im Gefängnis sitzen)* do time; (sl) be looney

Spin'nengewebe *n* spider web

Spin'ner *m* (-s;-) spinner; (sl) nut

Spinnerei [ʃpɪnəˈraɪ] *f* (-;-en) spinning; spinning mill

Spinn'faden *m* spider thread; **Spinnfäden** gossamer

Spinn'gewebe *n* (-s;-) cobweb

Spinn'rad *n* spinning wheel

Spinn'webe *f* (-;-n) (Aust) cobweb

Spion [ʃpiˈoːn] *m* (-s;-e) spy

Spionage [ʃpiɔˈnaːʒə] *f* (-;) spying, espionage

Spiona'geabwehr *f* counterintelligence

spionieren [ʃpiɔˈniːrən] *intr* spy

Spirale [ʃpiˈraːlə] *f* (-;-n) spiral

Spirituosen [ʃpirituˈoːzən] *pl* liquor

Spiritus [ˈʃpiːritʊs] *m* (-;-se) alcohol

Spital [ʃpiˈtaːl] *n* (-s;-er) hospital

spitz [ʃpɪts] *adj* pointed; sharp; *(Winkel)* acute

Spitz'bart *m* goatee

Spitz'bube *m* rascal; thief; swindler

Spitze [ˈʃpɪtsə] *f* (-;-n) point; tip; top, summit; (tex) lace; **an der S. liegen** be in the lead; **auf die S. treiben** carry to extremes

Spitzel [ˈʃpɪtsəl] *m* (-s;-) spy; stool pigeon; plain-clothes man

spitzen [ˈʃpɪtsən] *tr* point; sharpen; *(Ohren)* prick up; **den Mund s.** purse the lips ‖ *ref*—**sich s. auf** *(acc)* look forward to ‖ *intr* be on one's toes

Spitzen– *comb.fm.* top; peak; leading; topnotch; maximum; (tex) lace

Spit'zenform *f* (sport) top form

Spit'zenleistung *f* top performance

Spit'zenmarke *f* (com) top brand

Spit'zer *m* (-s;-) pencil sharpener

spitz'findig *adj* subtle; sharp

Spitz'hacke *f*, **Spitz'haue** *f* pickax

spitzig [ˈʃpɪtsɪç] *adj* pointed; (& fig) sharp

Spitz'marke f (typ) heading
Spitz'name m nickname; pet name
Spitz'nase f pointed nose
spleißen ['ʃplaɪsən] §53 tr splice
spliß [ʃplɪs] pret of **spleißen**
Splitter ['ʃplɪtər] m (-s;-) splinter; chip; fragment
split'ternackt' adj stark-naked
Split'terpartei f splinter party
split'tersicher adj shatterproof
spontan [ʃpɔn'tan] adj spontaneous
Spore ['ʃporə] f (-;-n) spore
Sporn [ʃpɔrn] m (-[e]s; **Sporen** ['ʃporən]) spur; (fig) stimulus; (aer) tail skid; (naut) ram
spornen ['ʃpɔrnən] tr spur
Sport [ʃpɔrt] m (-[e]s;-e) sport(s); **S. ausüben** (or **treiben**) play sports
Sport'freund –in §8 mf sports fan
Sport'hose f shorts, trunks
Sport'jacke f sport jacket, blazer
Sport'kleidung f sportswear
Sportler –in ['ʃpɔrtlər(ɪn)] §6 mf athlete
sport'lich adj sportsmanlike; (Figur) athletic; (Kleidung) sport
Sport'wagen m sports car; (Kinderwagen) stroller
Sport'wart m trainer
Spott [ʃpɔt] m (-[e]s;) mockery; scorn
Spott'bild n caricature
spott'bil'lig adj dirt-cheap
Spott'drossel f mockingbird
Spöttelei [ʃpœtə'laɪ] f (-;-en) mockery
spotten ['ʃpɔtən] intr (über acc) scoff (at), ridicule; **das spottet jeder Beschreibung** that defies description
Spötterei [ʃpœtə'raɪ] f (-;-en) mockery
Spott'gebot n (com) ridiculous offer
spöttisch ['ʃpœtɪʃ] adj mocking, satirical; sneering
Spott'name m nickname
Spott'schrift f satire
sprach [ʃprax] pret of **sprechen**
Sprach– comb.fm. speech; grammatical; linguistic; philological
Sprache ['ʃpraxə] f (-;-n) language, tongue; speech; diction; style; idiom
Sprach'eigenheit f, **Sprach'eigentümlichkeit** f idiom, idiomatic expression
Sprach'fehler m speech defect
Sprach'forschung f linguistics
Sprach'führer m phrase book
Sprach'gebrauch m usage
Sprach'gefühl n feeling for a language
sprach'gewandt adj fluent
sprach'kundig adj proficient in languages
Sprach'lehre f grammar
Sprach'lehrer –in §6 mf language teacher
sprach'lich adj grammatical; linguistic
sprach'los adj speechless
Sprach'rohr n megaphone; (fig) mouthpiece
Sprach'schatz m vocabulary
Sprach'störung f speech defect
Sprach'wissenschaft f philology; linguistics
sprang [ʃpraŋ] pret of **springen**
Sprech– [ʃprɛç] comb.fm. speaking
Sprech'art f way of speaking

Sprech'bühne f legitimate theater
sprechen ['ʃprɛçən] §64 tr speak; talk; (Gebet) say; (Urteil) pronounce; speak to, see || intr (über acc, von) speak (about), talk (about); **er ist nicht zu s.** he's not available
Spre'cher –in §6 mf speaker, talker
Sprech'fehler m slip of the tongue
Sprech'funkgerät n walkie-talkie
Sprech'probe f audition
Sprech'sprache f spoken language
Sprech'stunde f office hours
Sprech'stundenhilfe f receptionist
Sprech'zimmer n office (of doctor, etc.)
Spreize ['ʃpraɪtsə] f (-;-n) prop, strut; (gym) split
spreizen ['ʃpraɪtsən] tr spread, stretch out || ref sprawl out; (fig) (mit) boast (of); **sich s. gegen** resist
Spreng– [ʃprɛŋ] comb.fm. high-explosive
Sprengel ['ʃprɛŋəl] m (-s;-) diocese; parish
sprengen ['ʃprɛŋən] tr break, burst; (mit Sprengstoff) blow up; (Tür) force; (Versammlung) break up; (Mine) set off; (bespritzen) sprinkle; (Garten) water || intr (SEIN) gallop
Spreng'kommando n bomb disposal unit
Spreng'kopf m warhead
Spreng'körper m, **Spreng'stoff** m explosive
Spreng'wagen m sprinkling truck
Sprenkel ['ʃprɛŋkəl] m (-s;-) speck
sprenkeln ['ʃprɛŋkəln] tr speckle
Spreu [ʃprɔɪ] f (-;) chaff
Sprichwort ['ʃprɪçvɔrt] n (-[e]s;ᵘer) proverb, saying
sprichwörtlich ['ʃprɪçvœrtlɪç] adj proverbial
sprießen ['ʃprisən] §76 intr (SEIN) sprout
Springbrunnen ['ʃprɪŋbrunən] m (-s;-) fountain
springen ['ʃprɪŋən] §142 intr (SEIN) jump; dive; burst; (Eis) crack; (coll) rush, hurry
Sprin'ger m (-s;-) jumper; (chess) knight; (sport) diver
Spring'insfeld m (-[e]s;-e) (coll) live wire
Spring'kraft f (& fig) resiliency
Spring'seil n jumping rope
Sprint [ʃprɪnt] m (-s;-s) sprint
Sprit [ʃprɪt] m (-[e]s;-e) alcohol; (coll) gasoline
Spritze ['ʃprɪtsə] f (-;-n) squirt; (Feuerwehr) fire engine; (med) injection, shot; (med) syringe
spritzen ['ʃprɪtsən] tr squirt; splash; (sprühen) spray; (sprengen) sprinkle; (Wein) mix with soda water; (med) inject || intr spurt, spout || impers— **es spritzt** it is drizzling || intr (SEIN) dash, flit
Spritz'tour f (coll) side trip
spröde ['ʃprødə] adj brittle; (Haut) chapped; (fig) prudish, coy
sproß [ʃprɔs] pret of **sprießen** || **Sproß** m (Sprosses; Sprosse) offspring, descendant; (bot) shoot

Sprosse ['ʃprɔsə] f (-;-n) rung; prong
sprossen ['ʃprɔsən] intr (HABEN & SEIN) sprout
Sprößling ['ʃprœslɪŋ] m (-s;-e) offspring, descendant; (bot) sprout
Spruch [ʃprux] m (-[e]s;ˮe) saying; motto; text, passage; (jur) sentence; (jur) verdict; e-n S. fällen give the verdict
Spruch'band n (-[e]s;ˮer) banderole
Sprudel ['ʃpruːdəl] m (-s;-) mineral water
sprudeln ['ʃpruːdəln] intr bubble
sprühen ['ʃpryː.ən] tr emit ‖ intr spray; sparkle; (fig) flash ‖ impers—es sprüht it is drizzling
Sprüh'regen m drizzle
Sprüh'teufel m (coll) spitfire
Sprung [ʃpruŋ] m (-[e]s;ˮe) jump; crack; (sport) dive
Sprung'brett n diving board; (fig) stepping stone
Spucke ['ʃpukə] f (-;) (coll) spit
spucken ['ʃpukən] tr spit ‖ intr spit; (Motor) sputter
Spuk [ʃpuk] m (-[e]s;-e) ghost, spook; (Lärm) racket; (Alptraum) nightmare
spuken ['ʃpuːkən] intr linger on ‖ impers—es spukt hier this place is haunted
spuk'haft adj spooky
Spülabort ['ʃpyːlabɔrt] m flush toilet
Spül'becken n sink
Spule ['ʃpuːlə] f (-;-n) spool, reel; (elec) coil
Spüle ['ʃpyːlə] f (-;-n) wash basin
spulen ['ʃpuːlən] tr reel, wind
spülen ['ʃpyːlən] tr wash, rinse; (Abort) flush; an Land s. wash ashore ‖ intr flush the toilet; undulate
Spü'ler m (-s;-) dishwasher
Spülicht ['ʃpyːlɪçt] n (-[e]s;-e) dishwater; swill, slop
Spül'maschine f dishwasher
Spül'mittel n detergent
Spülwasser n dishwater
Spund [ʃpunt] m (-[e]s;ˮe) bung, plug; (carp) feather, tongue
Spur [ʃpuːr] f (-;-en) trace; track, rut; (hunt) scent; S. Salz pinch of salt
spürbar ['ʃpyːrbar] adj perceptible
spüren ['ʃpyːrən] tr trace; track, trail; (fühlen) feel; (wahrnehmen) perceive
spur'los adj trackless ‖ adv without a trace
Spür'nase f (coll) good nose
Spür'sinn m flair
Spur'weite f (aut) tread; (rr) gauge
sputen ['ʃpuːtən] ref hurry up
SS ['ɛs'ɛs] f (-;) (Schutzstaffel) S.S.
Staat [ʃtat] m (-[e]s;-en) state; government; (Aufwand) show; (Putz) finery
Staats- comb.fm. state; government; national; public; political
Staatsangehörigkeit ['ʃtatsangəhøːrɪç-kaɪt] f (-;) nationality
Staats'anwalt m district attorney
Staats'bauten pl public works
Staats'beamte m civil servant

Staats'bürger -in §6 mf citizen
Staats'bürgerkunde f civics
Staats'bürgerschaft f citizenship
Staats'dienst m civil service
staats'eigen adj state-owned
Staats'feind m public enemy
staats'feindlich adj subversive
Staats'form f form of government
Staats'gewalt f supreme power
Staats'hoheit f sovereignty
staats'klug adj politic, diplomatic
Staats'klugheit f statecraft
Staats'kunst f statesmanship
Staats'mann m (-[e]s;ˮer) statesman
staats'männisch adj statesmanlike
Staats'oberhaupt n head of state
Staats'papiere pl government bonds
Staats'recht n public law
Staats'streich m coup d'état
Staats'wirtschaft f political economy
Staats'wissenschaft f political science
Stab [ʃtap] m (-[e]s;ˮe) staff; rod; bar; (e-r Jalousie) slat; (eccl) crozier; (mil) staff; (mil) headquarters; (mus, sport) baton
stab'hochspringen §142 intr (SEIN) pole-vault
stabil [ʃta'bil] adj stable, steady
stabilisieren [ʃtabili'ziːrən] tr stabilize
stach [ʃtax] pret of stechen
Stachel ['ʃtaxəl] m (-s;-n) prick; quill; (bot) thorn; (ent) sting
Sta'chelbeere f gooseberry
Sta'cheldraht m barbed wire
stachelig ['ʃtaxəlɪç] adj prickly; (& fig) thorny
Sta'chelschwein n porcupine
Sta·dion ['ʃtadjɔn] n (-s;-dien [djən]) stadium
Sta·dium ['ʃtadjʊm] n (-s;-dien [djən]) stage
Stadt [ʃtat] f (-;ˮe) city, town
Städtchen ['ʃtɛtçən] n (-s;-) town
Städtebau ['ʃtɛtəbau] m (-[e]s;) city planning
Stadt'gemeinde f township
Stadt'gespräch n talk of the town
städtisch ['ʃtɛtɪʃ] adj municipal
Stadt'plan m map of the city
Stadt'rand m outskirts
Stadt'rat m (-[e]s;ˮe) city council; (Person) city councilor
Stadt'teil m Stadt'viertel n quarter (of the city)
Stafette [ʃta'fetə] f (-;-n) courier; (sport) relay
Staffel ['ʃtafəl] f (-;-n) step, rung; (Stufe) degree; (aer) squadron (of nine aircraft); (sport) relay team
Staffelei [ʃtafə'lai] f (-;-en) easel
Staf'felkeil m (aer) V-formation
Staf'fellauf m relay race
staffeln ['ʃtafəln] tr graduate; (Arbeitszeit, usw.) stagger
stahl [ʃtal] pret of stehlen ‖ **Stahl** m (-[e]s;ˮe) steel
Stahl'beton m reinforced concrete
stählen ['ʃtɛlən] tr temper; (fig) steel
Stahl'kammer f steel vault
Stahlspäne ['ʃtal/pena] pl steel wool
stak [ʃtak] pret of stecken
Stalag ['ʃtalak] n (-s;-s) (Stammlager) main camp (for P.O.W.'s)

Stall [ʃtal] *m* (-[e]s;⸚e) stable; shed
Stall'knecht *m* groom
Stamm [ʃtam] *m* (-[e]s;⸚e) stem; stalk; trunk; stock, race; tribe; breed
Stamm'aktie *f* common stock
Stamm'baum *m* family tree; pedigree
stammeln [ˈʃtaməln] *tr & intr* stammer
Stamm'eltern *pl* ancestors
stammen [ˈʃtamən] *intr* (SEIN) (aus, von) come (from); (von) date (from); (gram) (von) be derived (from)
Stamm'gast *m* regular customer
stämmig [ˈʃtemɪç] *adj* stocky; husky
Stamm'kneipe *f* favorite bar
Stamm'kunde *m*, **Stamm'kundin** *f* regular customer
Stamm'personal *n* skeleton staff
Stamm'tisch *m* reserved table
Stammutter (Stamm'mutter) *f* ancestress
Stamm'vater *m* ancestor
stampfen [ˈʃtampfən] *tr* tamp, pound; (Kartoffeln) mash; (Boden) paw ‖ *intr* stamp the ground; (durch Schnee) trudge; (naut) pitch
stand [ʃtant] *pret of* stehen ‖ **Stand** *m* (-[e]s;⸚e) stand; footing, foothold; level, height; condition; status, rank; class, caste; booth; profession; trade; (sport) score; **seinen S. behaupten** hold one's ground
Standard [ˈʃtandart] *m* (-s;-s) standard
Standarte [ʃtanˈdartə] *f* (-;-n) banner; standard
Stand'bild *n* statue
Ständchen [ˈʃtentçən] *n* (-s;-) serenade; **j-m ein S. bringen** serenade s.o.
Ständer [ˈʃtendər] *m* (-s;-) stand, rack; pillar; stud; (mach) column
Stan'desamt *n* bureau of vital statistics
stan'desamtlich *adj & adv* before a civil magistrate
stan'desgemäß *adj* according to rank
Stan'desperson *f* dignitary
stand'fest *adj* stable, steady, sturdy
stand'haft *adj* steadfast
stand'halten §90 *intr* hold out; (dat) withstand
ständig [ˈʃtendɪç] *adj* permanent; steady, constant
Stand'licht *n* parking light
Stand'ort *m* position; station; (mil) base; (mil) garrison
Stand'pauke *f* (coll) lecture
Stand'punkt *m* standpoint
Stand'recht *n* martial law
Stand'uhr *f* grandfather's clock
Stange [ˈʃtaŋə] *f* (-;-n) pole; rod, bar; perch, roost; **e-e S. Zigaretten** a carton of cigarettes; **von der S.** ready-made (clothes)
stank [ʃtaŋk] *pret of* stinken
stänkern [ˈʃteŋkərn] *intr* (coll) stink; (coll) make trouble
Stanniol [ʃtaˈnjol] *n* (-s;-e), **Stanniol'papier** *n* tinfoil
Stanze [ˈʃtantsə] *f* (-;-n) stanza; punch, die, stamp
stanzen [ˈʃtantsən] *tr* (mach) punch
Stapel [ˈʃtapəl] *m* (-s;-) stack; depot;

stock; (naut) slip; (tex) staple; **auf S. liegen** be in drydock; **vom S. laufen lassen** launch
Sta'pellauf *m* launching
stapeln [ˈʃtapəln] *tr* stack, pile up
Sta'pelplatz *m* lumberyard; depot
stapfen [ˈʃtapfən] *intr* (SEIN) slog
Star [ʃtar] *m* (-[e]s;-e) (orn) starling; (pathol) cataract; **grauer S.** cataract; **grüner S.** glaucoma ‖ *m* (-s;-s) (cin, theat) star
starb [ʃtarp] *pret of* sterben
stark [ʃtark] *adj* (stärker [ˈʃterkər]; stärkste [ˈʃterkstə] §9) strong; stout; (Erkältung) bad; (Familie) big; (Kälte) severe; (Frost, Verkehr) heavy; (Wind) high; (Stunde) full ‖ *adv* much; hard; very
Stärke [ˈʃterkə] *f* (-;-n) strength; force; stoutness; thickness; might; violence; intensity; (Anzahl) number; (fig) forte; (chem) starch
stärken [ˈʃterkən] *tr* strengthen; (Wäsche) starch ‖ *ref* take some refreshment
Stark'strom *m* high-voltage current
Stär'kung *f* (-;-en) strengthening; refreshment; (Imbiß) snack
starr [ʃtar] *adj* stiff, rigid; fixed; inflexible; obstinate; dumbfounded; numb ‖ *adv*—**s. ansehen** stare at
starren [ˈʃtarən] *intr* (auf acc) stare (at); **s. von** be covered with
Starr'kopf *m* stubborn fellow
starr'köpfig *adj* stubborn
Starr'krampf *m* (-es;) tetanus
Starr'sinn *m* (-[e]s;) stubbornness
Start [ʃtart] *m* (-[e]s;-s & -e) start; (aer) take-off; (rok) launching
Start'bahn *f* (aer) runway
starten [ˈʃtartən] *tr* start; launch ‖ *intr* (SEIN) start; (aer) take off; (rok) lift off, be launched
Start'rampe *f* (rok) launch pad
Station [ʃtaˈtsjon] *f* (-;-en) station; (med) ward; **freie S.** free room and board
statisch [ˈʃtatɪʃ] *adj* static
Statist -in [ʃtaˈtɪst(ɪn)] §7 *mf* (cin) extra; (theat) supernumerary
Statistik [ʃtaˈtɪstɪk] *f* (-;-en) statistic; (Wissenschaft) statistics
statistisch [ʃtaˈtɪstɪʃ] *adj* statistical
Stativ [ʃtaˈtif] *n* (-s;-e) stand; (phot) tripod
statt [ʃtat] *prep* (genit) instead of; **s. zu** (inf) instead of (ger) ‖ **Statt** *f* (-;) place, stead; **an Kindes S. annehmen** adopt
Stätte [ˈʃtetə] *f* (-;-n) place, spot; (Wohnung) abode; home
statt'finden §59 *intr* take place
statt'haft *adj* admissible; legal
Statthalter [ˈʃtathaltər] *m* (-s;-) governor
statt'lich *adj* stately; imposing
Statue [ˈʃtatuˑə] *f* (-;-n) statue
statuieren [ʃtatuˈiran] *tr* establish; **ein Exempel s. an** (dat) make an example of
Statur [ʃtaˈtur] *f* (-;-en) stature
Statut [ʃtaˈtut] *n* (-[e]s;-en) statute; **Statuten** bylaws

Stau [ʃtau] *m* (-[e]s;-e) dammed-up water; updraft; (aut) tie-up

Staub [ʃtaup] *m* (-[e]s;) dust

Stau′becken *n* reservoir

stauben [′ʃtaubən] *intr* make dust

stäuben [′ʃtɔɪbən] *tr* dust; sprinkle, powder; (*Flüssigkeit*) spray || *intr* make dust; throw off spray

staubig [′ʃtaubɪç] *adj* dusty

staub′saugen *tr* & *intr* vacuum

Staub′sauger *m* vacuum cleaner

Staub′wedel *m* feather duster

Staub′zucker *m* powdered sugar

stauchen [′ʃtauçən] *tr* knock, jolt; compress; (sl) chew out

Stau′damm *m* dam

Staude [′ʃtaudə] *f* (-;-n) perennial

stauen [′ʃtau·ən] *tr* dam up; (*Waren*) stow away; (*Blut*) stanch || *ref* be blocked, jam up

Stau′er *m* (-s;-) stevedore

staunen [′ʃtaunən] *intr* (über *acc*) be astonished (at) || **Staunen** *n* (-s;) astonishment

stau′nenswert *adj* astonishing

Staupe [′ʃtaupə] *f* (-;) (vet) distemper

Stau′see *m* reservoir

Stau′ung *f* (-;-en) damming up; blockage; (*Engpaß*) bottleneck; (*Verkehrs-*) jam-up; (pathol) congestion

stechen [′ʃteçən] §64 prick; sting, bite; (*mit e-r Waffe*) stab; (*Torf*) cut; (*Star*) remove; (*Kontrolluhr*) punch; (*Wein*) draw; (*Näherei*) stitch; (*gravieren*) engrave; (cards) trump; (cards) take (*a trick*) || *intr* sting, bite; (*Sonne*) be hot; (cards) be trump; **j-m in die Augen s.** catch s.o.'s eye || *impers*—**es sticht mich in der Brust** I have a sharp pain in my chest

ste′chend *adj* (*Blick*) piercing; (*Geruch*) strong; (*Schmerz*) sharp, stabbing

Stech′karte *f* timecard

Stech′schritt *m* goosestep

Stech′uhr *f* time clock

Steckbrief [′ʃtɛkbrif] *m* warrant for arrest

steck′brieflich *adv*—**s. verfolgen** put out a "wanted" notice for

Steckdose [′ʃtɛkdozə] *f* (elec) outlet

stecken [′ʃtɛkən] *tr* & *intr* stick || **Stecken** *m* (-s;-) stick

steckenbleiben (stek′kenbleiben) §62 *intr* (SEIN) get stuck

Steckenpferd (Stek′kenpferd) hobbyhorse; (fig) hobby

Stecker (Stek′ker) *m* (-s;-) (elec) plug

Steck′kontakt *m* (elec) plug

Steck′nadel *f* pin

Steg [ʃtek] *m* (-[e]s;-e) footpath; footbridge; (*e-r Brille, Geige*) bridge; (*Landungs-*) jetty; (naut) gangplank

Steg′reif *m*—**aus dem S.** extempore

stehen [′ʃte·ən] §146 *tr*—**e-m Maler Modell s.** sit for a painter; **Schlange s.** stand in line; **Schmiere s.** (coll) be a lookout; **Wache s.** stand guard || *intr* (HABEN & SEIN) stand; stop; be; (gram) occur, be used; (*Kleider*) fit; **das steht bei Ihnen** that depends

on you; **gut s.** (*dat*) fit, suit; **gut s. mit** be on good terms with; **wie steht's?** (coll) how is it going?

ste′henbleiben §62 *intr* (SEIN) stop

ste′henlassen §104 *tr* leave standing; (*nicht anrühren*) leave alone; (*Fehler*) leave uncorrected; (*vergessen*) forget; (culin) allow to stand or cool

Ste′her *m* (-s;-) long-distance cyclist

Stehlampe [′ʃtelampə] *f* floor lamp

Stehleiter [′ʃtelaɪtər] *f* stepladder

stehlen [′ʃtelən] §147 *tr* & *intr* steal

Stehplatz [′ʃteplats] *m* standing room

steif [ʃtaif] *adj* stiff; rigid; (*Lächeln*) forced; (*förmlich*) formal; (*starr*) numb

steifen [′ʃtaifən] *tr* stiffen; (*Wäsche*) starch

Steig [ʃtaik] *m* (-[e]s;-e) path

Steig′bügel *m* stirrup

steigen [′ʃtaigən] §148 *tr* (*Treppen*) climb || *intr* (SEIN) climb; rise; go up; (*Nebel*) lift; (*Blut in den Kopf*) rush || **Steigen** *n* (-s;) rise; increase

steigern [′ʃtaigərn] *tr* raise, increase; (*verstärken*) enhance; (gram) compare || *ref* increase, go up

Stei′gerung *f* (-;-en) rising; increase; intensification; (gram) comparison

Stei′gerungsgrad *m* (gram) degree of comparison

Stei′gung *f* (-;-en) rise; (*Hang*) slope; (*e-s Propellers*) pitch

steil [ʃtail] *adj* steep

Stein [ʃtain] *m* (-[e]s;-e) stone; rock; (*horol*) jewel; (pathol) stone

stein′alt *adj* old as the hills

Stein′bruch *m* quarry

Stein′druck *m* lithography; (*Bild*) lithograph

steinern [′ʃtainərn] *adj* stone

Stein′gut *n* earthenware

steinig [′ʃtainɪç] *adj* stony, rocky

steinigen [′ʃtainɪgən] *tr* stone

Stein′kohle *f* hard coal

Stein′metz *m* stonemason

stein′reich *adj* (coll) filthy rich

Stein′salz *n* rock salt

Stein′schlag *m* (public sign) falling rocks

Stein′wurf *m* stone's throw

Stein′zeit *f* stone age

Steiß [ʃtais] *m* (-es;-e) buttocks

Stelldichein [′ʃtɛldɪçain] *n* (-[s]; -[s]) (coll) date

Stelle [′ʃtɛlə] *f* (-;-n) place, spot; position; job; agency, department; quotation; (math) digit; **an S. von** in place of; **auf der S.** on the spot; **auf der S. treten** (fig & mil) mark time; **freie (or offene) S.** opening; **zur S. sein** be on hand

stellen [′ʃtɛlən] *tr* put, place; set; stand; (*ein-*) regulate, adjust; (*anordnen*) fix, arrange; (*Frage*) ask; (*Horoskop*) cast; (*Diagnose*) give; (*Falle, Wecker*) set; (*Kaution*) put up; (*Zeugen*) produce; **e-n Antrag s.** make a motion; **in Dienst s.** appoint; put into service || *ref* place oneself, stand; give oneself up; **der Preis stellt sich auf…** the price is…; **sich s., als ob** act as if

Stel′lenangebot n help wanted
Stel′lenbewerber –in §6 mf applicant
Stel′lengesuch n situation wanted
Stel′lenjagd f job hunting
Stel′lennachweis m, **Stel′lenvermittlungsbüro** n employment agency
stel′lenweise adv here and there
–stellig [ˈʃtɛlɪç] comb.fm. –digit
Stell′schraube f set screw
Stel′lung f (–;–en) position; situation; job; standing; status; rank; posture; (mil) line, position; (mil) emplacement; **S. nehmen zu** express one's opinion on; (erklären) explain; (beantworten) answer
Stel′lungnahme f (–;–n) attitude, point of view; (Erklärung) comment; (Gutachten) opinion; (Bericht) report; (Beantwortung) answer; (Entscheid) decision; **sich** [dat] **e–e S. vorbehalten** not commit oneself
Stel′lungsgesuch n (job) application
stel′lungslos adj jobless
stell′vertretend adj acting
Stell′vertreter –in §6 mf representative; deputy; proxy; substitute
Stell′vertretung f (–;–en) representation; substitution; **in S. by proxy**
Stelzbein [ˈʃtɛltsbaɪn] n wooden leg
Stelze [ˈʃtɛltsə] f (–;–n) stilt
stelzen [ˈʃtɛltsən] intr (SEIN) stride
Stemmeisen [ˈʃtɛmaɪzən] n crowbar
stemmen [ˈʃtɛmən] tr support; (Gewicht) lift; (Loch) chisel ‖ ref—**sich s. gegen** oppose
Stempel [ˈʃtɛmpəl] m (–s;–) stamp; prop; (Kolben) piston; (bot) pistil
Stem′pelkissen n ink pad, stamp pad
stempeln [ˈʃtɛmpəln] tr stamp ‖ intr— **s. gehen** (coll) collect unemployment insurance
Stengel [ˈʃtɛŋəl] m (–s;–) stalk
Steno [ˈʃteno] f (–;) stenography
Stenograph [ʃtenoˈgraf] m (–en;–en) stenographer
Stenographie [ʃtenograˈfi] f (–;) stenography, shorthand
stenographieren [ʃtenoɡrˈfirən] tr take down in shorthand ‖ intr do shorthand
Stenographin [ʃtenoˈɡrafɪn] f (–;–nen) stenographer
Stenotypistin [ʃtenoˈtʏpɪstɪn] f (–; –nen) stenographer
Step [ʃtɛp] m (–s;–) tap dance; **S. tanzen** tap-dance
Steppdecke [ˈʃtɛpdɛkə] f comforter
Steppe [ˈʃtɛpə] f (–;–n) steppe
steppen [ˈʃtɛpən] tr quilt ‖ intr tap-dance ‖ **Steppen** n (–s;) tap-dancing
Sterbe– [ˈʃtɛrbə] comb.fm. dying, death
Ster′befall m death
Ster′begeld n death benefit
Ster′behilfe f euthanasia
sterben [ˈʃtɛrbən] §149 intr (SEIN) (an dat) die (of)
sterb′lich adj mortal ‖ adv—**s. verliebt in** (acc) head over heals in love with
Sterb′lichkeit f (–;) mortality
Sterb′lichkeitsziffer f death rate
stereotyp [stereoˈtyp] adj stereotyped
steril [ʃteˈril] adj sterile
sterilisieren [ʃteriliˈzirən] tr sterilize

Stern [ʃtɛrn] m (–[e]s;–e) star; (typ) asterisk
Stern′bild n constellation
Stern′blume f aster
Sterndeuter [ˈʃtɛrndɔɪtər] m (–s;–) astrologer
Sterndeuterei [ʃtɛrndɔɪtəˈraɪ] f (–;) astrology
Ster′nenbanner n Stars and Stripes
stern′ha′gelvoll adj (sl) dead drunk
stern′hell adj starlit
Stern′himmel m starry sky
Stern′kunde f astronomy
Stern′schuppe f shooting star
Stern′warte f observatory
stet [ʃtet], **stetig** [ˈʃtetɪç] adj steady
stets [ʃtets] adv constantly, always
Steuer [ˈʃtɔɪ.ər] f (–;–n) tax; duty ‖ n (–s;–) rudder, helm; (aer) controls; (aut) steering wheel; **am S. at the** helm; (aut) behind the wheel
Steu′eramt n tax office
Steu′erbord n (naut) starboard
Steu′ererhebung f levy of taxes
Steu′ererklärung f tax return
Steu′erflosse f vertical stabilizer
Steu′erhinterziehung f tax evasion
Steu′erjahr n fiscal year
Steu′erknüppel m control stick
Steu′er·mann m (–[e]s;–er & –leute) helmsman
steuern [ˈʃtɔɪ.ərn] tr steer; control; regulate; (aer, naut) pilot; (aut) drive ‖ intr (dat) curb, check
steu′erpflichtig adj taxable; dutiable
Steu′errad n steering wheel
Steu′erruder n rudder, helm
Steu′ersatz m tax rate
Steu′ersäule f (aer) control column; (aut) steering column
Steu′erstufe f tax bracket
Steu′erung f (–;–en) steering; (Bekämpfung) control; (Verhinderung) prevention; (aer) piloting; (aut) steering mechanism
Steu′erveranlagung f tax assessment
Steu′erwerk n (aer) controls
Steu′erzahler –in §6 mf tax payer
Steu′erzuschlag m surtax
Steven [ˈʃtevən] m (–s;–) (naut) stem
Stewar·deß [ˈst(j)u·ərdɛs] f (–;–dessen [dɛsən]) (aer) stewardess
stibitzen [ʃtɪˈbɪtsən] tr snitch
Stich [ʃtɪç] m (–[e]s;–e) prick; (Messer–) stab; (Insekten–) sting, bite; (Stoß) thrust; (Seitenstechen) sharp pain; (Kupfer–) engraving; (cards) trick; (naut) knot; (sew) stitch; **im S. lassen** abandon
Stichelei [ʃtɪçəˈlaɪ] f (–;–en) taunt
sticheln [ˈʃtɪçəln] intr—**gegen j–n s.** (fig) needle s.o.
Stich′flamme f flash
stich′haltig adj valid, sound
Stich′probe f spot check
Stich′tag m effective date; due date
Stich′wahl f run-off election
Stich′wort n (–[e]s;–er) key word; dictionary entry ‖ n (–[e]s;–e) (theat) cue
Stich′wunde f stab wound
sticken [ˈʃtɪkən] tr embroider ‖ intr embroider

Stickerei [ʃtɪkəˈraɪ] f (-;-en) embroidery
Stick'husten m whooping cough
stickig [ˈʃtɪkɪç] adj stuffy, close
Stick'stoff m nitrogen
stieben [ˈʃtibən] §130 intr (HABEN & SEIN) fly; (Menge) disperse
Stief [ʃtif] comb.fm. step-
Stief'bruder m stepbrother
Stiefel [ˈʃtifəl] m (-s;-) boot
Stie'felknecht m bootjack
Stief'mutter f stepmother
Stief'mütterchen n (bot) pansy
Stief'vater m stepfather
stieg [ʃtik] pret of **steigen**
Stiege [ˈʃtigə] f (-;-n) staircase
Stiel [ʃtil] m (-[e]s;-e) handle; (bot) stalk
stier [ʃtir] adj staring, glassy ‖ **Stier** m (-[e]s;-e) bull; (astr) Taurus
stieren [ˈʃtirən] intr (auf acc) stare (at)
Stier'kampf m bullfight
stieß [ʃtis] pret of **stoßen**
Stift [ʃtɪft] m (-[e]s;-e) pin; peg; pencil; crayon; (Zwecke) tack; (coll) apprentice ‖ n (-[e]s;-e & -er) charitable foundation or institution
stiften [ˈʃtɪftən] tr (gründen) found; (spenden) donate; (verursachen) cause; (Unruhe) stir up; (Frieden) make; (Brand) start; (e-e Runde Bier) set up
Stif'ter –in §6 mf founder; donor; (fig) author, cause
Stif'tung f (-;-en) foundation; donation; grant; **fromme S.** religious establishment; **milde S.** charitable institution
Stif'tungsfest n founder's day
Stil [ʃtil] m (-[e]s;-e) style
stil'gerecht adj in good taste
stilisieren [ʃtili'zirən] tr word
stilistisch [ʃtɪ'lɪstɪʃ] adj stylistic
still [ʃtɪl] adj still; calm; silent; (com) slack; **im stillen** in secret; **Stiller Ozean** Pacific Ocean ‖ **Stille** f (-;) stillness; silence
still'bleiben §62 intr (SEIN) keep still
Stilleben (Still'leben) n still life
stillegen (still'legen) tr (Betrieb) shut down; (Verkehr) stop; (Schiff) put into mothballs
stillen [ˈʃtɪlən] tr still; (Hunger) appease; (Durst) quench; (Blut) stanch; (Begierde) gratify
stilliegen (still'liegen) §108 intr lie still; (Betrieb) lie idle; (Verkehr) be at a standstill
still'schweigen §148 intr be silent; **s. zu** acquiesce in ‖ **Stillschweigen** n (-s;) silence; secrecy
still'schweigend adj silent; (fig) tacit
Still'stand m standstill; (Sackgasse) stalemate, deadlock
still'stehen §146 intr stand still; (Betrieb) be idle; (mil) stand at attention; **stillgestanden!** (mil) attention!
Stil'möbel pl period furniture
stil'voll adj stylish
Stimm- [ʃtɪm] comb.fm. vocal; voting
Stimm'abgabe f vote, voting
Stimm'band n (-[e]s;⁻er) vocal cord

Stimm'block m (parl) bloc
Stimm'bruch m change of voice
Stimme [ˈʃtɪmə] f (-;-n) voice; vote
stimmen [ˈʃtɪmən] tr make feel (happy, etc.); (mus) tune ‖ intr be right; vote; (mus) be in tune
Stim'menrusch m (pol) landslide
Stimm'enthaltung f abstention
Stimm'gabel f tuning fork
Stimm'recht n right to vote, suffrage
Stim'mung f (-;-en) tone; (Laune) mood; (mil) morale; (mus) tuning; (st.exch.) trend
stim'mungsvoll adj cheerful
Stimm'zettel m ballot
stinken [ˈʃtɪŋkən] §143 intr stink
Stink'tier n skunk
Stipen·dium [ʃtɪ'pɛndjum] n (-s;-dien [djən]) scholarship, grant
stippen [ˈʃtɪpən] tr (coll) dunk
Stippvisite [ˈʃtɪpvizitə] f (-;-n) short visit
Stirn [ʃtɪrn] f (-;-en), **Stirne** [ˈʃtɪrnə] f (-;-n) forehead, brow; (fig) insolence, gall; **die S. runzeln** frown
Stirn'runzeln n (-s;) frown(ing)
stob [ʃtop] pret of **stieben**
stöbern [ˈʃtøbərn] tr (Wild) flush; (aus dem Bett) yank ‖ intr poke around; browse; (Schnee) drift
stochern [ˈʃtɔxərn] intr poke around; **im Essen s.** pick at one's food; **im Feuer s.** stoke the fire; **in den Zähnen s.** pick one's teeth
Stock [ʃtɔk] m (-[e]s;⁻e) stick; cane; wand; baton; stem; vine; tree stump; cleaning rod; beehive; massif; story, floor; **im ersten S.** on the second floor
Stock-, stock- comb.fm. thoroughly
stock'blind adj stone-blind
stock'dun'kel adj pitch-dark
Stöckel [ˈʃtœkəl] m (-s;-) high heel
stocken [ˈʃtɔkən] intr stop; (Geschäft) slack off; (Blut) coagulate; (in der Rede) get stuck; (Milch) curdle; (Stimme) falter; (schimmeln) get moldy; (Unterhandlungen) become deadlocked; (Verkehr) get tied up; (zögern) hesitate ‖ **Stocken** n (-s;) stopping; hesitation; **ins S. bringen** tie up
stock'fin'ster adj pitch-black
Stock'fleck m mildew
stock'fleckig adj mildewy
stockig [ˈʃtokɪç] adj moldy
–stöckig [ˈʃtœkɪç] comb.fm. –story
stock'nüch'tern adj dead-sober
stock'steif adj stiff as a board
stock'taub adj stone-deaf
Stockung [ˈʃtokuŋ] f (-;-en) stoppage; (des Verkehrs) tie-up; (des Blutes) congestion; (Unterbrechung) interruption; (Verlangsamung) slowdown; (Zeitverlust) delay; (Pause) pause; (Zögern) hesitation; (der Unterhandlungen) deadlock
Stock'werk n story, floor
Stoff [ʃtɔf] m (-[e]s;-e) stuff, matter; fabric; material; cloth; subject; topic; (chem) substance
stoff'lich adj material
Stoff'rest m (tex) remnant

Stoff'wechsel m metabolism

stöhnen ['ʃtønən] intr groan, moan

Stolle ['ʃtɔlə] f (-;-n) fruit cake

Stollen ['ʃtɔlən] m (-s;-) fruit cake; tunnel; (Pfosten) post; (Stütze) prop

stolpern ['ʃtɔlpərn] intr (SEIN) stumble, trip

stolz [ʃtɔlts] adj (auf acc) proud (of) || **Stolz** m (-es;) pride

stolzieren [ʃtɔl'tsiːrən] intr (SEIN) strut; (Pferd) prance

stopfen ['ʃtɔpfən] tr stuff, cram; (Pfeife) fill; (Strumpf) darn; (mus) mute; **j-m den Mund s.** shut s.o. up || intr be filling; cause constipation

Stopf'garn n darning yarn

Stoppel ['ʃtɔpəl] f (-;-n) stubble

stoppelig ['ʃtɔpəlɪç] adj stubbly

stoppeln ['ʃtɔpəln] tr glean; (fig) patch

stoppen ['ʃtɔpən] tr stop; clock, time || intr stop

Stopp'licht n tail light; stoplight

Stopp'uhr f stopwatch

Stöpsel ['ʃtœsəl] m (-s;-) stopper, cork; (coll) squirt; (elec) plug

stöpseln ['ʃtœpsəln] tr plug; cork

Storch [ʃtɔrç] m (-[e]s;ˈe) stork

stören ['ʃtøːrən] tr disturb, bother; (Pläne) cross; (Vergnügen) spoil; (mil) harass; (rad) jam

Störenfried ['ʃtøːrənfriːt] m (-[e]s;-e) pain in the neck

störrig ['ʃtœrɪç], **störrisch** ['ʃtœrɪʃ] adj stubborn

Stö'rung f (-;-en) disturbance, trouble; breakdown; interruption; annoyance; intrusion; (rad) static; (rad) jamming

Stoß [ʃtoːs] m (-es;ˈe) push, shove; hit, blow; nudge, poke; (Einschlag) impact; (Erschütterung) shock; (Fecht-) pass; (Feuer-) burst of fire); (Fuß-) kick; (Haufen) pile, bundle; (Rück-) recoil; (Saum) seam, hem; (Schwimm-) stroke; (Trompeten-) blast; (Wind-) gust; (mil) thrust; (orn) tail

Stoß'dämpfer m shock absorber

Stößel ['ʃtøːsəl] m (-s;-) pestle

stoßen ['ʃtoːsən] §150 tr push, shove; hit, knock; kick; punch; jab, nudge, poke; ram; pound; pulverize; oust || ref bump oneself; **sich s. an** (dat) take offense at; take exception to || intr kick; (mit den Hörnen) butt; (Gewehr) recoil, kick; (Wagen) jolt; (Schiff) toss; **in die Trompete s.** blow the trumpet; **s. auf** (acc) swoop down on || intr (SEIN) come across; **s. an** (acc) bump against; adjoin; be next-door to; **s. auf** (acc) run into; come across; (naut) dash against; **s. durch** (mil) smash through; **vom Lande s.** shove off; **zu j-m s.** side with s.o.

Stoß'stange f (aut) bumper

Stoß'trupp m assault party; **Stoßtruppen** shock troops; commandos, rangers

Stoß'zahn m tusk

stottern ['ʃtɔtərn] tr stutter, stammer || intr stutter, stammer; (aut) sputter

stracks [ʃtraks] adv immediately; (geradeaus) straight ahead

Straf- [ʃtraːf] comb.fm. penal; criminal

Straf'anstalt f penal institution

Straf'arbeit f (educ) extra work

Straf'aufschub m reprieve

strafbar ['ʃtraːfbar] adj punishable

Strafe ['ʃtraːfə] f (-;-n) punishment; penalty; (Geld-) fine; **bei S. von** under pain of; **zur S.** as punishment

strafen ['ʃtraːfən] tr punish

straff [ʃtraf] adj tight; (Seil) taut; (gespannt) tense; (aufrecht) erect; (fig) strict; **s. spannen** tighten

straf'fällig adj punishable; culpable

Straf'geld n fine

Straf'gesetzbuch n penal code

sträflich ['ʃtreːflɪç] adj culpable

Sträfling ['ʃtreːflɪŋ] m (-s;-e) convict

straf'los adj unpunished

Straf'porto n postage due

Straf'predigt f talking-to, lecture

Straf'raum m (sport) penalty box

Straf'recht n criminal law

Straf'stoß m (sport) penalty kick

Straf'umwandlung f (jur) commutation

Straf'verfahren n criminal proceedings

Strahl [ʃtraːl] m (-[e]s;-en) ray; beam; flash; jet; (geom) radius

Strahl'antrieb m jet propulsion

strahlen ['ʃtraːlən] intr beam, shine

Strahl'motor m, **Strahl'triebwerk** n jet engine

Strah'lung f (-;-en) radiation

Strähne ['ʃtreːnə] f (-;-n) strand; lock; hank, skein

strähnig ['ʃtreːnɪç] adj wispy

stramm [ʃtram] adj tight; (kräftig) strapping; (Zucht) strict; (Arbeit) hard; (Soldat) smart; (Mädel) buxom || adv—**s. stehen** stand at attention

stramm'ziehen §163 tr draw tight

strampeln ['ʃtrampəln] intr kick

Strand [ʃtrant] m (-[e]s;ˈe) beach, seashore, shore

stranden ['ʃtrandən] intr (SEIN) be beached, run aground, be stranded

Strand'gut n flotsam, jetsam

Strand'gutjäger -in §6 mf beachcomber

Strand'korb m hooded beach chair

Strand'schirm m beach umbrella

Strang [ʃtraŋ] m (-[e]s;ˈe) rope; (Strähne) hank; (Zugseil) trace; (rr) track; **wenn alle Stränge reißen** (fig) if worse comes to worst

Strapaze [ʃtra'paːtsə] f (-;-n) fatigue; exertion, strain

strapazieren [ʃtrapa'tsiːrən] tr tire out; (Kleider) wear hard

strapazier'fähig adj heavy-duty

strapaziös [ʃtrapa'tsjøːs] adj tiring

Straße ['ʃtraːsə] f (-;-n) street; road; highway; (Meerenge) strait

Stra'ßenanzug m business suit

Stra'ßenbahn f streetcar, trolley; trolley line

Stra'ßenbahnwagen m streetcar

Stra'ßendirne f streetwalker

Stra'ßengraben m ditch, gutter

Stra'ßenhändler -in §6 mf street vendor

Stra'ßenjunge m urchin

Stra'ßenkarte f street map

Stra'ßenkreuzung f intersection

Stra'ßenlage f (aut) roadability

Stra'ßenrennen n drag race

Stra′ßenrinne f gutter
Stra′ßenschild n street sign
Stra′ßensperrung f (public sign) road closed
Stra′ßenstreife f highway patrol
strategisch [ʃtraˈteːgɪʃ] adj strategic
sträuben [ˈʃtrɔɪbən] tr ruffle ‖ ref bristle, stand on end; **sich s. gegen** resist, struggle against
Strauch [ʃtraux] m (-[e]s;-"er) shrub
straucheln [ˈʃtrauxəln] intr (SEIN) stumble, trip; (fig) go wrong
Strauß [ʃtraus] m (-[e]s;-"e) bouquet ‖ m (-[e]s;-e) ostrich
Strebe [ˈʃtreːbə] f (-;-n) prop, strut
Stre′bebogen m flying buttress
streben [ˈʃtreːbən] intr (nach) strive (after); (nach) tend (toward) ‖ **Streben** n (-s;-) striving; pursuit; (Hang) tendency; (Anstrengung) endeavor
Stre′ber m (-s;-) go-getter, eager beaver; social climber; (in der Schule) grind
strebsam [ˈʃtreːpzam] adj zealous
Streb′samkeit f (-;) zeal; industry
Strecke [ˈʃtrɛkə] f (-;-n) stretch; extent; distance; stage, leg; (geom) straight line; (hunt) bag; (rr) section; **zur S. bringen** catch up with; (box) defeat; (hunt) bag
strecken [ˈʃtrɛkən] tr stretch; (Metalle) laminate; (Wein) dilute; (fig) make last; **die Waffen s.** lay down one's arms ‖ ref stretch (oneself)
Streich [ʃtraɪç] m (-[e]s;-e) blow; (fig) trick, prank
streicheln [ˈʃtraɪçəln] tr stroke; pat
streichen [ˈʃtraɪçən] §85 tr stroke; (Butter, usw.) spread; (an-) paint; (Geige) play; (Messer) whet; (Rasiermesser) strop; (Streichholz) strike; (Flagge, Segel) lower; (Ärmel) roll down; (Ziegel) make; (mit Ruten) flog; delete; (sport) scratch ‖ intr—**mit der Hand s. über** (acc) pass one's hand over ‖ intr (SEIN) stretch, extend; wander; pass, move; rush
Streich′holz n match
Streich′holzbrief m matchbook
Streich′instrument n stringed instrument
Streich′orchester n string band
Streich′riemen m razor strop
Streif [ʃtraɪf] m (-[e]s;-e) streak, stripe; strip
Streif′band n (-[e]s;-"er) wrapper
Streife [ˈʃtraɪfə] f (-;-n) raid; (Runde) beat; (mil) patrol
streifen [ˈʃtraɪfən] tr stripe; streak; graze; skim over; (abziehen) strip; (grenzen an) verge on; (Thema) touch on ‖ intr (SEIN) roam; (mil) patrol; **s. an** (acc) brush against; (fig) verge on; **s. über** (acc) scan ‖ **Streifen** m (-s;-) stripe; streak; strip; slip; (cin) movie
Strei′fendienst m patrol duty
Strei′fenwagen m patrol car, squad car
streifig [ˈʃtraɪfɪç] adj striped
Streif′licht n flash, streak of light; **S. werfen auf** (acc) shed light on
Streif′wunde f scratch

Streif′zug m exploratory trip, look-see
Streik [ʃtraɪk] m (-[e]s;-s) strike, walkout; **wilder S.** wildcat strike
streiken [ˈʃtraɪkən] intr go on strike
Strei′kende §5 mf striker
Streik′posten m picket; **S. stehen** picket
Streit [ʃtraɪt] m (-[e]s;-e) fight; argument, quarrel; (jur) litigation
Streit′axt f battle-ax; **die S. begraben** (fig) bury the hatchet
streitbar [ˈʃtraɪtbar] adj belligerent
streiten [ˈʃtraɪtən] §86 recip & intr quarrel
Streit′frage f point at issue
streitig [ˈʃtraɪtɪç] adj controversial; at issue
Streit′kräfte pl (mil) forces, troops
streitlustig adj belligerent, scrappy
Streit′objekt n bone of contention
Streit′punkt m issue, point at issue
streit′süchtig adj quarrelsome
streng [ʃtrɛŋ] adj severe, stern; austere; strict; (Geschmack) sharp ‖ **Strenge** f (-;) severity, sternness; austerity; strictness; sharpness
streng′genommen adv strictly speaking
streng′gläubig adj orthodox
Streu [ʃtrɔɪ] f (-;-en) straw bed
Streu′büchse f shaker
streuen [ˈʃtrɔɪ-ən] tr strew, sprinkle; (ausbreiten) spread; (verbreiten) scatter ‖ intr spread, scatter
strich [ʃtrɪç]—pret of **streichen** ‖ **Strich** m (-[e]s;-e) stroke; line; (Streif) stripe; (Landstrich) tract; (carp) grain; (tex) nap; (typ) dash; **auf den S. gehen** walk the streets (as prostitute); **gegen den S. gehen** go against the grain; (fig) rub the wrong way
Strich′mädchen n streetwalker
Strich′punkt m semicolon
Strich′regen m local shower
strich′weise adv here and there
Strick [ʃtrɪk] m (-[e]s;-e) rope, cord; (fig) rogue, good-for-nothing
stricken [ˈʃtrɪkən] tr & intr knit
Strick′garn n knitting yarn
Strick′jacke f cardigan
Strick′kleid n knitted dress
Strick′leiter f rope ladder
Strick′waren pl knitwear
Strick′zeug n knitting things
Striemen [ˈʃtriːmən] m (-s;-) stripe, streak; (in der Haut) weal
Strippe [ˈʃtrɪpə] f (-;-n) string; strap; shoestring; (telp) line
stritt [ʃtrɪt] pret of **streiten**
strittig [ˈʃtrɪtɪç] adj controversial
Stroh [ʃtroː] n (-[e]s;) straw
Stroh′dach n thatched roof
Stroh′halm m straw; drinking straw
Stroh′mann m (-[e]s;-"er) scarecrow; (cards) dummy
Stroh′puppe f scarecrow
Stroh′sack m straw mattress; **heiliger S.!** holy smokes!
Strolch [ʃtrɔlç] m (-[e]s;-e) bum
strolchen [ˈʃtrɔlçən] intr bum around
Strom [ʃtroːm] m (-[e]s;-"e) river; stream; (von Worten) torrent; (& elec) current

stromab'wärts adv downstream
stromauf'wärts adv upstream
Strom'ausfall m (elec) power failure
strömen ['ʃtrømən] intr (HABEN & SEIN) stream; (Regen) pour (down)
Stro'mer m (-s;-) (coll) tramp
Strom'kreis m (elec) circuit
strom'linienförmig adj streamlined
Strom'richter m (elec) converter
Strom'schnelle f rapids
Strom'spannung f voltage
Strom'stärke f (elec) amperage
Strö'mung f (-;-en) current; trend
Strom'unterbrecher m (elec) circuit breaker
Strom'wandler m (elec) transformer
Strom'zähler m electric meter
Strophe ['ʃtrofə] f (-;-n) stanza
strotzen ['ʃtrɔtsən] intr—s. von or vor (dat) abound in, teem with
Strudel ['ʃtrudəl] m (-s;-) eddy, whirlpool; (fig) maelstrom; (culin) strudel
strudeln ['ʃtrudəln] intr eddy, whirl
Struktur [ʃtrʊk'tur] f (-;-en) structure; (tex) texture
Strumpf [ʃtrʊmpf] m (-[e]s;ːe) stocking
Strumpf'band n (-[e]s;ːer), **Strumpf'halter** m garter
Strumpf'waren pl hosiery
struppig ['ʃtrʊpɪç] adj shaggy, unkempt
Stube ['ʃtubə] f (-;-n) room
Stu'benmädchen n chambermaid
stu'benrein adj housebroken
Stuck [ʃtʊk] m (-[e]s;) stucco
Stück [ʃtyk] n (-[e]s;-e) piece; lot; plot; stretch distance; (Butter) pat; (Zucker) lump; (Seife) cake; (Vieh) head; (mus) piece, number; (theat) play, show; **pro S.** apiece
stückeln ['ʃtykəln] tr cut or break into small pieces; piece together
stück'weise adv piecemeal
Stück'werk n patchwork
Student [ʃtu'dent] m (-en;-en) college student
Studen'tenheim n dormitory
Studen'tenverbindung f fraternity
Studentin [ʃtu'dentɪn] f (-;-nen) college student, coed
Studie ['ʃtudjə] f (-;-n) (Lit) essay; (paint) study, sketch
Stu'diengang m (educ) course
Stu'dienplan m curriculum
Stu'dienrat m (-[e]s;ːe) high school teacher
Stu'dienreferendar –in §8 mf practice teacher
Stu'dienreise f (educ) field trip
studieren [ʃtu'dirən] tr & intr study (at college); examine
studiert [ʃtu'dirt] adj college-educated; (gekünstelt) affected
Studier'zimmer n study
Stu-dium ['ʃtudjʊm] n (-s;-dien [djən]) study (at college); studies
Stufe ['ʃtufə] f (-;-n) step, stair; (e-r Leiter) rung; (Grad) degree; (Niveau) level; stage; (mus) interval
Stu'fenfolge f graduation; succession
Stu'fenleiter f stepladder; (fig) gamut
stu'fenweise adv by degrees

Stuhl [ʃtul] m (-[e]s;ːe) chair; (Stuhlgang) stool, feces; **der Heilige S.** the Holy See
Stuhl'bein n leg of a chair
Stuhl'drang m urgent call of nature
Stuhl'gang m stool, feces; **S. haben** have a bowel movement
Stuhl'lehne f back of a chair
Stulpe ['ʃtʊlpə] f (-;-n) cuff
Stülpnase ['ʃtylpnazə] f snub nose
stumm [ʃtum] adj dumb, mute; (schweigend) silent; (gram) mute
Stummel ['ʃtuməl] m (-s;-) (e-s Armes, Baumes, e-r Zigarette) stump
Stümper ['ʃtympər] m (-s;-) bungler
Stümperei [ʃtympə'raɪ] f (-;-en) bungling
stüm'perhaft adj bungling
stümpern ['ʃtympərn] tr & intr bungle
stumpf [ʃtumpf] adj blunt; (& fig) obtuse || **Stumpf** m (-[e]s;ːe) stump
Stumpf'sinn m apathy, dullness
stumpf'sinnig adj dull, stupid
Stunde ['ʃtundə] f (-;-n) hour; (educ) class, lesson, period
stunden ['ʃtundən] tr grant postponement of
Stun'dengeld n tutoring fee
Stun'dengeschwindigkeit f miles per hour
Stun'denkilometer pl kilometers per hour
stun'denlang adv for hours
Stun'denlohn m hourly wage(s)
Stun'denplan m roster, schedule
stun'denweise adv by the hour
Stun'denzeiger m hour hand
-stündig [ʃtyndɪç] comb.fm. –hour
stündlich ['ʃtyntlɪç] adj hourly
Stun'dung f (-;-en) period of grace
Stunk [ʃtʊŋk] m (-[e]s;) stink; **S. machen** (sl) raise a stink
Stups [ʃtups] m (-es;-e) nudge
stupsen ['ʃtupsən] tr nudge
Stups'nase f snub nose
stur [ʃtur] adj stubborn; (Blick) fixed
Sturm [ʃturm] m (-[e]s;ːe) storm; gale
Sturm'abteilung f storm troopers
stürmen ['ʃtyrmən] tr storm || intr rage, roar || intr (SEIN) rush || impers—es stürmt it is stormy
Stürmer ['ʃtyrmər] m (-s;-) (fb) forward
stürmisch ['ʃtyrmɪʃ] adj stormy; impetuous || adv—nicht so s.! not so fast!
Sturm'schritt m (mil) double time
Sturm'trupp m assault party
Sturm'welle f (mil) assault wave
Sturm'wind m gale, hurricane
Sturz [ʃturts] m (-es;-e) fall, sudden drop; overthrow; collapse; (archit) lintel; (aut) camber; (com) slump
Sturz'bach m torrent
Sturz'bomber m dive bomber
Stürze ['ʃtyrtsə] f (-;-n) lid
stürzen ['ʃtyrtsən] tr throw down; upset, overturn; overthrow; (tauchen) plunge; **nicht s.!** this side up! || ref rush; plunge || intr (SEIN) fall, tumble; rush; (Tränen) pour; (aer) dive
Sturz'flug m (aer) dive
Sturz'helm m crash helmet

Sturz'regen *m* downpour
Sturz'see *f* heavy seas
Stute ['ʃtuːtə] *f* (-;-n) mare
Stütze ['ʃtʏtsə] *f* (-;-n) support, prop; (fig) help, support
stutzen ['ʃtutsən] *tr* cut short; (*Flügel*) clip; (*Bäume*) prune; (*Ohren*) crop; (*Bart*) trim ‖ *intr* stop short; be startled; (*Pferd*) shy
stützen ['ʃtʏtsən] *tr* support; prop; shore up; (fig) support ‖ *ref*—**sich s. auf** (*acc*) lean on; (fig) depend on
Stutzer ['ʃtutsər] *m* (-s;-) car coat; (coll) snazzy dresser
Stutz'flügel *m* baby grand piano
stutzig ['ʃtutsɪç] *adj* suspicious
Stütz'pfeiler *m* abutment
Stütz'punkt *m* footing; (mil) base; (phys) fulcrum
Subjekt [zup'jɛkt] *n* (-[e]s;-e) (coll) guy, character; (gram) subject
subjektiv [zupjɛk'tiːf] *adj* subjective
Substantiv [zupstan'tiːf] *n* (-[e]s;-e) (gram) substantive, noun
Substanz [zup'stants] *f* (-;-en) substance
subtil [zup'tiːl] *adj* subtle
subtrahieren [zuptra'hiːrən] *tr* subtract
Subtraktion [zuptrak'tsjoːn] *f* (-;-en) subtraction
Subvention [zupvɛn'tsjoːn] *f* (-;-en) subsidy
Such- [zuːx] *comb.fm.* search
Such'anzeige *f* want ad
Such'büro *n*, **Such'dienst** *m* missing-persons bureau
Suche ['zuːxə] *f* (-;-en) search; **auf der S. nach** in search of, in quest of
suchen ['zuːxən] *tr* search for, look for; (*erstreben*) seek; want, desire; (*in der Zeitung*) advertise for; (*Gefahr*) court; **das Weite s.** run away ‖ *intr* search; **nach etw s.** look for s.th.
Sucht [zuxt] *f* (-;-ːe) passion, mania; (*nach*) addition (to)
süchtig ['zʏçtɪç] *adj* addicted ‖ **Süchtige §5** *mf* addict
Sud [zuːt] *m* (-[e]s;-e) brewing; brew
Süd [zyːt] *m* (-[e]s;) south
sudelhaft ['zuːdəlhaft], **sudelig** ['zuːdəlɪç] *adj* slovenly, sloppy
sudeln ['zuːdəln] *tr* & *intr* mess up
Süden ['zyːdən] *m* (-s;) south
Sudeten [zu'deːtən] *pl* Sudeten mountains (*along northern border of Czechoslovakia*)
Süd'früchte *pl* (tropical and subtropical) fruit (*e.g., bananas, oranges*)
süd'lich *adj* south, southern, southerly; **s. von** south of ‖ *adv* south
Südost' *m*, **Südo'sten** *m* southeast
südöst'lich *adj* southeast(ern)
Süd'pol *m* (-s;) South Pole
südwärts ['zyːtvɛrts] *adv* southward
Südwest' *m*, **Südwe'sten** *m* southwest
süffig ['zʏfɪç] *adj* tasty
suggerieren [zuge'riːrən] *tr* suggest
suggestiv [zuges'tiːf] *adj* suggestive
Suggestiv'frage *f* leading question
suhlen ['zuːlən] *ref* wallow
Sühne ['zyːnə] *f* (-;) atonement
sühnen ['zyːnən] *tr* atone for, expiate
Sülze ['zʏltsə] *f* (-;-n) jellied meat

summarisch [zu'maːrɪʃ] *adj* summary
Summe ['zumə] *f* (-;-n) sum, total
summen ['zumən] *tr* hum ‖ *intr* hum; buzz
Sum'mer *m* (-s;-) buzzer
summieren [zu'miːrən] *tr* sum up, total ‖ *ref* run up, pile up
Summton ['zumtoːn] *m* (telp) dial tone
Sumpf [zumpf] *m* (-[e]s;-ːe) swamp
sumpfig ['zumpfɪç] *adj* swampy, marshy
Sünde ['zʏndə] *f* (-;-n) sin
Sün'denbock *m* scapegoat
Sün'denerlaß *m* absolution
Sün'denfall *m* original sin
Sün'der *m* (-s;-) sinner
Sünd'flut ['zʏntfluːt] *f* Deluge
sünd'haft, sündig ['zʏndɪç] *adj* sinful
sündigen ['zʏndɪgən] *intr* sin
Superlativ ['zuːpɛrlatiːf] *m* (-s;-e) (gram) superlative
Su'permarkt *m* supermarket
Suppe ['zupə] *f* (-;-n) soup
Sup'penschüssel *f* tureen
surren ['zurən] *intr* buzz
Surrogat [zuro'gaːt] *n* (-[e]s;-e) substitute
suspendieren [zuspen'diːrən] *tr* suspend
süß [zyːs] *adj* sweet ‖ **Süße** *f* (-;) sweetness
süßen ['zyːsən] *tr* sweeten
Sü'ßigkeit *f* (-;-en) sweetness; **Süßigkeiten** sweets, candy
Süß'kartoffel *f* sweet potato
süß'lich *adj* sweetish; (fig) mawkish
Süß'stoff *m* artificial sweetener
Süß'waren *pl* sweets, candy
Süß'wasser *n* fresh water
Symbol [zʏm'boːl] *n* (-s;-e) symbol
Symbolik [zʏm'boːlɪk] *f* (-;) symbolism
symbolisch [zʏm'boːlɪʃ] *adj* symbolic(al)
Symme-trie [zʏme'triː] *f* (-;-trien) ['tri-ən]) symmetry
symmetrisch [zʏ'meːtrɪʃ] *adj* symmetrical
Sympa-thie [zʏmpa'tiː] *f* (-;-thien ['ti-ən]) liking
sympathisch [zʏm'paːtɪʃ] *adj* likeable; **er ist mir s.** I like him
sympathisieren [zʏmpati'ziːrən] *intr*—**s. mit** sympathize with; like
Sympho-nie [zʏmfo'niː] *f* (-;-nien ['ni-ən]) symphony
Symptom [zʏmp'toːm] *n* (-s;-e) symptom
symptomatisch [zʏmptə'maːtɪʃ] *adj* (**für**) symptomatic (of)
Synagoge [zyna'goːgə] *f* (-;-n) synagogue
synchronisieren [zʏnkroni'ziːrən] *tr* synchronize
Syndikat [zʏndɪ'kaːt] *n* (-[e]s;-e) syndicate
Syndi-kus ['zʏndɪkus] *m* (-;-kusse & -ki [ki]) corporation lawyer
synonym [zyno'nyːm] *adj* synonymous ‖ **Synonym** *n* (-s;-e) synonym
Syntax ['zʏntaks] *f* (-;) syntax
synthetisch [zʏn'teːtɪʃ] *adj* synthetic
Syrien ['zyːrjən] *n* (-s;) Syria

System [zYs'tem] *n* (–s;–e) system
systematisch [zyste'mɑtɪʃ] *adj* systematic
Szene ['stsenə] *f* (–;–n) scene; **in S.**
setzen stage; **sich in S. setzen** put on
an act
Sze'nenaufnahme *f* (cin) take
Szenerie [stenə'ri] *f* (–;) scenery

T

T, t [te] *invar n* T, t
Tabak [ta'bak], ['tabak] *m* (–[e]s;–e)
tobacco
Tabaks'beutel *m* tobacco pouch
Tabak'trafik *f* (Aust) cigar store
Tabak'waren *pl* tobacco products
tabellarisch [tabe'lɑrɪʃ] *adj* tabular
tabellarisieren [tabelarɪ'zirən] *tr* tabu-
late
Tabelle [ta'belə] *f* (–;–n) table, chart;
graph
Tabernakel [taber'nakəl] *m & n* (–s;–)
tabernacle
Tablett [ta'blet] *n* (–[e]s;–e) tray
Tablette [ta'bletə] *f* (–;–n) tablet, pill
tabu [ta'bu] *adj* taboo || **Tabu** *n* (–s;
–s) taboo
Tachometer [taxo'metər] *n* speedometer
Tadel ['tadəl] *m* (–s;–) scolding;
(*Schuld*) blame; (educ) demerit
ta'dellos *adj* blameless; flawless
tadeln ['tadəln] *tr* scold, reprimand;
blame, find fault with
Tafel ['tafəl] *f* (–;–n) (*Tisch, Diagramm*) table; (*Anschlag–*) billboard;
(*Glas–*) pane; (*Holz–, Schalt–*) panel;
(*Mahlzeit*) meal, dinner; (*Metall–*)
sheet, plate; (*Platte*) slab; (*Schiefer–*)
slate; (*Schreib–*) tablet; (*Schokolade*)
bar; (*Wand–*) blackboard; **bei T.** at
dinner; **die T. decken** set the table;
offene T. halten have open house
Ta'felaufsatz *m* centerpiece
Ta'felbesteck *n* knife, fork, and spoon
ta'felförmig *adj* tabular
Ta'felgeschirr *n* table service
Ta'felland *n* tableland, plateau
Ta'felmusik *f* dinner music
tafeln ['tafəln] *intr* dine, feast
täfeln ['tefəln] *tr* (*Wand*) wainscot,
panel; (*Fußboden*) parquet
Ta'felöl *n* salad oil
Ta'felservice *n* tableware
Tä'felung *f* (–;–en) inlay; paneling
Taft [taft] *m* (–[e]s;–e) taffeta
Tag [tak] *m* (–[e]s;–e) day; daylight;
am Tage by day; **am Tage nach** the
day after; **an den Tag bringen** bring
to light; **bei Tage** by day, in the daytime; **den ganzen Tag** all day long;
e–n Tag um den andern every other
day; **e–s Tages** someday; **es wird Tag**
day is breaking; **guten Tag!** hello!;
how do you do?; (*bei Verabschiedung*) good day!; goodby!; **Tag der
offenen Tür** open house; **unter Tage**
(min) underground, below the surface
tagaus', tagein' *adv* day in and day out
Tage– ['tagə] *comb.fm.* day–, daily

Ta'geblatt *n* daily, daily paper
Ta'gebuch *n* diary, journal
Ta'gegeld *n* per diem allowance
ta'gelang *adv* for days
Ta'gelohn *m* daily wage
Tagelöhner –in ['tagəlønər(ɪn)] §6 *mf*
day laborer
tagen ['tagən] *intr* dawn; (*beraten*)
meet; (jur) be in session
Ta'gesanbruch *m* daybreak
Ta'gesangriff *m* (aer) daylight raid
Ta'gesbefehl *m* (mil) order of the day
Ta'gesbericht *m* daily report
Ta'geseinnahme *f* daily receipts
Ta'gesgespräch *n* topic of the day
ta'geshell' *adj* as light as day
Ta'geskasse *f* (theat) box office
Ta'gesleistung *f* daily output
Ta'geslicht *n* daylight
Ta'geslichtaufnahme *f* (phot) daylight
shot
Ta'gesordnung *f* agenda; (coll) order
of the day
Ta'gespreis *m* market price
Ta'gespresse *f* daily press
Ta'gesschau *f* (telv) news
Ta'geszeit *f* time of day; daytime; **zu
jeder T.** at any hour
Ta'geszeitung *f* daily paper
ta'geweise *adv* by the day
Ta'gewerk *n* day's work
–tägig [tegɪç] *comb.fm.* –day
täglich ['teklɪç] *adj* daily
tags [taks] *adv*–**t. darauf** the follow-
ing day; **t. zuvor** the day before
Tag'schicht *f* day shift
tags'über *adv* during the day, in the
daytime
Tagung ['taguŋ] *f* (–;–en) convention,
conference, meeting
Ta'gungsort *m* meeting place
Taifun [taɪ'fun] *m* (–s;–e) typhoon
Taille ['taljə] *f* (–;–n) waist; (*Mieder*) bodice
Takel ['takəl] *n* (–s;–) tackle
Takelage [takə'laʒə] *f* (–;–n) rigging
takeln ['takəln] *tr* rig
Ta'kelwerk *n* var of **Takelage**
Takt [takt] *m* (–[e]s;–e) tact; (mach)
stroke; (mus) time, beat; (mus) bar;
den T. schlagen mark time; **im T.** in
time; in step; **T. halten** mark time
takt'fest *adj* keeping good time; (fig)
reliable
Taktik ['taktɪk] *f* (–;–en) (& fig)
tactics
Tak'tiker *m* (–s;–) tactician
taktisch ['taktɪʃ] *adj* tactical
takt'los *adj* tactless
Takt'messer *m* metronome
Takt'stock *m* baton

Takt′strich *m* (mus) bar
takt′voll *adj* tactful
Tal [tɑl] *n* (–[e]s;⸗er) valley
Talar [ta'lɑr] *m* (–s;–e) robe, gown
Tal′boden *m* valley floor
Talent [ta'lɛnt] *n* (–[e]s;–e) talent
talentiert [talɛn'tirt] *adj* talented
Tal′fahrt *f* descent
Talg [talk] *m* (–[e]s;–e) suet; tallow
Talg′kerze *f*, **Talg′licht** *n* tallow candle
Talisman ['tɑlɪsman] *m* (–s;–e) talisman
Talk(um)puder ['talk(ʊm)pudər] *m* talcum powder
Talmi ['talmi] *n* (–s;) (fig) imitation
Tal′sperre *f* dam
Tamburin [tambʊ'rin] *n* (–s;–e) tambourine
Tampon [tã'põ] *m* (–s;–s) (med) tampon
Tamtam [tam'tam] *n* (–s;–s) gong; (fig) fanfare, drum beating
Tand [tant] *m* (–[e]s;) trifle; bauble
tändeln ['tɛndəln] *intr* trifle; flirt
Tang [taŋ] *m* (–[e]s;–e) seaweed
Tangente [taŋ'gɛntə] *f* (–;–n) (geom) tangent
tangieren [taŋ'girən] *tr* concern
Tango ['taŋgo] *m* (–s;–s) tango
Tank [taŋk] *m* (–[e]s;–e & –s) tank
tanken ['taŋkən] *intr* get gas; refuel
Tan′ker *m*, **Tank′schiff** *n* tanker
Tank′stelle *f* gas (or service) station
Tank′wagen *m* tank truck; (rr) tank car
Tankwart ['taŋkvart] *m* (–[e]s;–e) gas station attendant
Tanne ['tanə] *f* (–;–n) fir (tree)
Tan′nenbaum *m* fir tree
Tan′nenzapfen *m* fir cone
Tante ['tantə] *f* (–;–n) aunt; **T. Meyer** (coll) john
Tantieme [tã'tjemə] *f* (–;–n) dividend; (com) royalty
Tanz [tants] *m* (–es;⸗e) dance
Tanz′bein *n*—**das T. schwingen** (coll) cut a rug
Tanz′diele *f* dance hall
tänzeln ['tɛntsəln] *intr* (HABEN & SEIN) skip about; (*Pferd*) prance
tanzen ['tantsən] *tr & intr* dance
Tänzer –in ['tɛntsər(ɪn)] §6 *mf* dancer
Tanz′fläche *f* dance floor
Tanz′kapelle *f* dance band
Tanz′lokal *n* dance hall
Tanz′saal *m* ballroom
Tanz′schritt *m* dance step
Tanz′stunde *f* dancing lesson
Tapete [ta'petə] *f* (–;–n) wallpaper
Tape′tenpapier *n* wallpaper (*in rolls*)
Tape′tentür *f* wallpapered door
Tapezierarbeit [tapɛ'tsirarbaɪt] *f* paperhanging
tapezieren [tapɛ'tsirən] *tr* wallpaper
Tapezie′rer *m* (–s;–) paperhanger
tapfer ['tapfər] *adj* brave, valiant
Ta′pferkeit *f* (–;) bravery, valor
tappen ['tapən] *intr* (HABEN & SEIN) grope about; **t. nach** grope for
täppisch ['tɛpɪʃ] *adj* clumsy
tapsen ['tapsən] *intr* (SEIN) clump along

Tara ['tɑra] *f* (–;) (com) tare
Tarif [ta'rif] *m* (–s;–e) tariff; price list; wage scale; postal rates
Tarif′lohn *m* standard wages
Tarif′verhandlung *f* collective bargaining
Tarif′vertrag *m* wage agreement
Tarn– [tarn] *comb.fm.* camouflage
tarnen ['tarnən] *tr* camouflage
Tarn′kappe *f* (myth) magic cap (*rendering wearer invisible*)
Tar′nung *f* (–;) camouflage
Tasche ['taʃə] *f* (–;–n) pocket; handbag; pocketbook; schoolbag; flight bag; pouch; briefcase
Ta′schenausgabe *f* pocket edition
Ta′schenbuch *n* paperback
Ta′schendieb *m* pickpocket
Ta′schendiebstahl *m* pickpocketing
Ta′schengeld *n* pocket money
Ta′schenlampe *f* flashlight
Ta′schenmesser *n* pocketknife
Ta′schenrechner *m* pocket calculator
Ta′schenspieler –in §6 *mf* magician
Ta′schenspielerei *f* sleight of hand
Ta′schentuch *n* handkerchief
Ta′schenuhr *f* pocket watch
Ta′schenwörterbuch *n* pocket dictionary
Tasse ['tasə] *f* (–;–n) cup
Tastatur [tasta'tur] *f* (–;–en) keyboard
Taste ['tastə] *f* (–;–n) key
tasten ['tastən] *tr* feel, touch; (telg) send ‖ *ref* feel one's way ‖ *intr* (**nach**) grope (for)
Tastsinn ['tastzɪn] *m* sense of touch
tat [tɑt] *pret* of **tun** ‖ **Tat** *f* (–;–en) deed, act; (*Verbrechen*) crime; **auf frischer Tat ertappen** catch redhanded; **in der Tat** in fact; **in die Tat umsetzen** implement
Tat′bestand *m* facts of the case
Tat′bestandsaufnahme *f* factual statement
tatenlos ['tɑtənlos] *adj* inactive
Ta′tenlosigkeit *f* (–;) inactivity
Täter –in ['tetər(ɪn)] §6 *mf* doer, perpetrator; culprit
Tat′form *f* (gram) active voice
tätig ['tetɪç] *adj* active; busy; **t. sein bei** be employed by
tätigen ['tetɪgən] *tr* conclude
Tä′tigkeit *f* (–;–en) activity; occupation, job, profession
Tä′tigkeitsbericht *m* progress report
Tä′tigkeitsfeld *n* field, line
Tä′tigung *f* (–;–en) transaction
Tat′kraft *f* energy, strength; vigor
tat′kräftig *adj* energetic; vigorous
tätlich ['tetlɪç] *adj* violent; **tätliche Beleidigung** (jur) assault and battery; **t. werden gegen** assault ‖ *adv* —**t. beleidigen** (jur) assault
Tät′lichkeit *f* (–;–en) (act of) violence; **es kam zu Tätlichkeiten** it came to blows
Tat′ort *m* scene of the crime
tätowieren [tɛto'virən] *tr* tattoo
Tätowie′rung *f* (–;–en) tattoo
Tat′sache *f* fact
Tat′sachenbericht *m* factual report
tat′sächlich *adj* actual, real, factual
tätscheln ['tetʃəln] *tr* pet, stroke

Tatterich ['tatəriç] *m* (-s;) shakes
Tatze ['tatsə] *f* (-;-n) paw
Tau [tau] *m* (-[e]s;) dew ‖ *n* (-[e]s; -e) rope; (naut) hawser
taub [taup] *adj* deaf; (*betäubt*) numb; (*unfruchtbar*) barren; (*Gestein*) not containing ore; (*Nuß*) hollow; (*Ei*) unfertile; (*Hafer*) wild; **t. gegen** deaf to; **t. vor Kälte** numb with cold
Taube ['taubə] *f* (-;-n) pigeon; (pol) dove
Tau′benhaus *n*, **Tau′benschlag** *m* dovecote
Taub′heit *f* (-;) deafness; numbness
taub′stumm *adj* deaf and dumb ‖ **Taubstumme** §5 *mf* deaf-mute
Tauchboot ['tauxbot] *n* submarine
tauchen ['tauxən] *tr* dip, duck, immerse ‖ *intr* (HABEN & SEIN) dive, plunge; (naut) submerge, dive
Tau′cher –in §6 *mf* (& orn) diver
Tau′cheranzug *m* diving suit
Tau′chergerät *n* aqualung
Tau′cherglocke *f* diving bell
Tauch′krankheit *f* bends
Tauch′schwimmer *m* (nav) frogman
tauen ['tau‑ən] *tr* thaw, melt; (*schleppen*) tow ‖ *intr* (HABEN & SEIN) thaw ‖ *impers*—**es taut** dew is falling ‖ *impers* (HABEN & SEIN)—**es taut** it is thawing ‖ **Tauen** *n* (-s;) thaw
Tauf– [tauf] *comb.fm.* baptismal
Tauf′becken *n* baptismal font
Tauf′buch *n* parish register
Taufe ['taufə] *f* (-;-n) baptism, christening
taufen ['taufən] *tr* baptize, christen
Täufer ['tɔɪfər] *m*—**Johannes der T.** John the Baptizer
Täufling ['tɔɪflɪŋ] *m* (-s;-e) child (or person) to be baptized
Tauf′name *m* Christian name
Tauf′pate *m* godfather
Tauf′patin *f* godmother
Tauf′schein *m* baptismal certificate
taugen ['taugən] *intr* be of use; **zu etw t.** be good for s.th.
Taugenichts ['taugənɪçts] *m* (-es;-e) good-for-nothing
tauglich ['tauklɪç] *adj* (für, zu) good (for), fit (for), suitable (for); (mil) able-bodied; **t. zu** (*inf*) able to (*inf*)
Taumel ['tauməl] *m* (-s;) giddiness; (*Überschwang*) ecstasy
taumelig ['tauməlɪç] *adj* giddy; reeling
taumeln ['tauməln] *intr* (SEIN) reel, stagger; be giddy; be ecstatic
Tausch [tauʃ] *m* (-es;-e) exchange
tauschen ['tauʃən] *tr* (gegen) exchange (for) ‖ *intr*—**mit j-m t.** exchange places with s.o.
täuschen ['tɔɪʃən] *tr* deceive, fool; (*betrügen*) cheat; (*Erwartungen*) disappoint ‖ *ref* be mistaken
täu′schend *adj* deceptive, illusory; (*Ähnlichkeit*) striking
Tausch′geschäft *n* exchange, swap
Tausch′handel *m* barter; **T. treiben** barter
Täu′schung *f* (-;-en) deception, deceit; fraud; **optische T.** optical illusion
Täu′schungsangriff *m* (mil) feint attack
Täu′schungsmanöver *n* feint

Tausch′wert *m* trade-in value
tausend ['tauzənt] *invar adj & pron* thousand ‖ **Tausend** *m*—**ei der T.!** (or **potz T.!**) holy smokes! ‖ *f* (-; -en) thousand ‖ *n* (-s;-e) thousand
Tau′sendfuß *m*, **Tausendfüß(l)er** ['tauzəntfys(l)ər] *m* (-s;-) centipede
tausendste ['tauzəntstə] §9 *adj & pron* thousandth
Tausendstel ['tauzəntstəl] *n* (-s;-) thousandth
Tau′tropfen *m* dewdrop
Tau′werk *n* (naut) rigging
Tau′wetter *n* thaw
Tau′ziehen *n* tug of war
Taxameter [taksa′metər] *m* taxi meter
Taxe ['taksə] *f* (-;-n) tax; (*Schätzung*) appraisal; (*Gebühr*) fee; (*Taxi*) taxi
Taxi ['taksi] *n* (-s;-s) taxi, cab
taxieren [ta′ksirən] *tr* appraise; rate
Taxifahrer –in §6 *mf* taxi driver
Ta′xistand *m* taxi stand
Taxus ['taksus] *m* (-;-) (bot) yew
Team [tim] *n* (-s;-s) team
Technik ['tɛçnɪk] *f* (-;-en) technique; workmanship; technology
Tech′niker –in §6 *mf* technician; engineer
Techni-kum ['tɛçnikum] *n* (-s;-ka [ka] & –ken [kən]) technical school; school of engineering
technisch ['tɛçnɪʃ] *adj* technical; **technische Angelegenheit** technicality; **technische Hochschule** technical institute
Technologie [tɛçnolo′gi] *f* (-;) technology
technologisch [tɛçno′logɪʃ] *adj* technological
Tee [te] *m* (-s;-s) tea
Tee′gebäck *n* tea biscuit, cookie
Tee′kanne *f* teapot
Tee′kessel *m* teakettle
Tee′löffel *m* teaspoon; teaspoonful
Teenager ['tinedʒər] *m* (-s;-) teenager
Teer [ter] *m* (-[e]s;-e) tar
Teer′decke *f* tar surface, blacktop
teeren ['terən] *tr* tar
Teer′pappe *f* tar paper
Tee′satz *m* tealeaves
Teich [taɪç] *m* (-[e]s;-e) pond, pool
Teig [taɪk] *m* (-[e]s;-e) dough
teigig ['taɪgɪç] *adj* doughy
Teig′mulde *f* kneading trough
Teig′waren *pl* noodles; pastries
Teil [taɪl] *m & n* (-[e]s;-e) part; piece; portion; (*Abschnitt*) section; (jur) party; **der dritte T.** von one third of; **edle Teile des Körpers** vital parts; **zu gleichen Teilen** fifty-fifty; **zum größten T.** for the most part; **zum T.** partly, in part
Teil– *comb.fm.* partial
teilbar ['taɪlbar] *adj* divisible
Teilchen ['taɪlçən] *n* (-s;-) particle
teilen ['taɪlən] *tr* divide; (mit) share (with) ‖ *ref* (Weg) divide; (*Ansichten*) differ; **sich t. in** (acc) share
teil′haben §89 *intr* (an *dat*) participate (in), share (in)
Teilhaber –in ['taɪlhabər(ɪn)] §6 *mf* participant; (com) partner
Teil′haberschaft *f* (-;-en) partnership

–teilig [taɪlɪç] *comb.fm.* –piece
Teil'nahme *f* (–;) participation; sympathy; interest
teilnahmslos ['taɪlnɑmslos] *adj* indifferent; apathetic
Teil'nahmslosigkeit *f* (–;) indifference; apathy
teilnahmsvoll ['taɪlnɑmsfɔl] *adj* sympathetic; (*besorgt*) solicitous
teil'nehmen §116 *intr* (an *dat*) participate (in), take part (in); (**an** *dat*) attend; (fig) (**an** *dat*) sympathize (with)
Teil'nehmer –in §6 *mf* participant; (*Mitglied*) member; (sport) competitor; (telp) customer, party
teils [taɪls] *adv* partly
Teil'strecke *f* section, stage
Tei'lung *f* (–;-en) division; partition; separation; (*Grade*) graduation, scale; (*Anteile*) sharing
teil'weise *adv* partly
Teil'zahlung *f* partial payment; **auf T. kaufen** buy on the installment plan
Teint [tɛ̃] *m* (–s;-s) complexion
Telefon [tele'fon] *n* (–s;-e) telephone
Telegramm [tele'gram] *n* (–s;-e) telegram
Telegraph [tele'grɑf] *m* (–en;-en) telegraph
Telegra'phenstange *f* telegraph pole
telegraphieren [telegra'firən] *tr & intr* telegraph; (*nach Übersee*) cable
Teleobjektiv ['tele‧ɔbjektif] *n* telephoto lens
Telephon [tele'fon] *n* (–s;-e) telephone, phone; **ans T. gehen** answer the phone
Telephon'anruf *m* telephone call
Telephon'anschluß *m* telephone connection
Telephon'gespräch *n* telephone call
Telephon'hörer *m* receiver
telephonieren [telefo'nirən] *intr* telephone; **mit j-m t.** phone s.o.
telephonisch [tele'foniʃ] *adj* telephone || *adv* by telephone
Telephonist –in [telefo'nɪst(ɪn)] §7 *mf* telephone operator
Telephon'vermittlung *f* telephone exchange
Telephon'zelle *f* telephone booth
Telephon'zentrale *f* telephone exchange
Teleskop [tele'skop] *n* (–s;-e) telescope
Television [televɪ'zjon] *f* (–;) television
Teller ['telər] *m* (–s;–) plate
Tel'lereisen *n* trap
Tel'lermine *f* antitank mine
Tel'lertuch *n* dishtowel
Tempel ['tempəl] *m* (–s;–) temple
Temperament [tempəra'ment] *n* (–[e]s;-e) temperament; enthusiasm; **er hat kein T.** he has no life in him; **hitziges T.** hot temper
temperament'los *adj* lifeless, boring
temperament'voll *adj* lively, vivacious
Temperatur [tempera'tur] *f* (–;-en) temperature
Temperenzler [tempe'rentslər] *m* (–s; –) teetotaler
temperieren [tempe'rirən] *tr* temper; cool; air-condition; (mus) temper

Tem·po ['tempo] *n* (–s;-s & pi [pi]) tempo; speed; (mus) movement
Tem·pus ['tempus] *n* (–; –pora [pɔra]) (gram) tense
Tendenz [ten'dents] *f* (–;-en) tendency
Tender ['tendər] *m* (–s;–) (nav, rr) tender
Tenne ['tenə] *f* (–;-n) threshing floor
Tennis ['tenɪs] *n* (–;) tennis
Ten'nisplatz *m* tennis court
Ten'nisschläger *m* tennis racket
Ten'nisturnier *n* tennis tournament
Tenor ['tenɔr] *m* (–s;) (*Wortlaut*) tenor, purport || [te'nor] *m* (–[e]s; ≃e) tenor
Teppich ['tepɪç] *m* (–s;-e) rug, carpet
Teppichkehrmaschine ['tepɪçkerma‧ɪnə] *f* carpet sweeper
Termin [ter'min] *m* (–s;-e) date, time, day; deadline; (com) due date; **er hat heute T.** he is to appear in court today; **äußerster T.** deadline
termin'gemäß *adv* on time, punctually
Termin'geschäft *n* futures
Termin'kalender *m* appointment book; (jur) court calendar
Terminolo·gie [termɪnɔlɔ'gi] *f* (–; –gien ['gi‧ən]) terminology
termin'weise *adv* (com) on time
Terpentin [terpen'tin] *m* (–s;) terpentine
Terrain [te'rɛ̃] *n* (–s;-s) ground; (*Grundstück*) lot; (mil) terrain; **T. gewinnen** (fig & mil) gain ground
Terrasse [te'rasə] *f* (–;-n) terrace
terras'senförmig *adj* terraced
Terrine [te'rinə] *f* (–;-n) tureen
Territo·rium [terɪ'torjum] *n* (–s;-rien [rjən]) territory
Terror ['terɔr] *m* (–s;) terror
terrorisieren [terɔrɪ'zirən] *tr* terrorize
Terrorist –in [terɔ'rɪst(ɪn)] §7 *mf* terrorist
Terz [terts] *f* (–;-en) (mus) third
Terzett [ter'tset] *n* (–[e]s;-e) trio
Test [test] *m* (–[e]s;-e & –s) test
Testament [testa'ment] *n* (–[e]s;-e) will; (eccl) Testament
testamentarisch [testamen'tarɪʃ] *adj* testamentary || *adv* by will; **t. bestimmen** will
Testaments'vollstrecker –in §6 *mf* executor
testen ['testən] *tr* test
teuer ['tɔɪ‧ər] *adj* dear, expensive; (*Preis*) high
Teu'erung *f* (–;-en) rise in price
Teu'erungswelle *f* rise in prices
Teu'erungszulage *f* cost-of-living increase
Teufel ['tɔɪfəl] *m* (–s;–) devil; **des Teufels sein** be mad; **wer zum T.?** who the devil?
Teufelei [tɔɪfə'lar] *f* (–;-en) deviltry
Teufelsbanner ['tɔɪfəlsbanər] *m* (–s;–) exorcist
Teu'felskerl *m* helluva fellow
teuflisch ['tɔɪflɪʃ] *adj* devilish
Teutone [tɔɪ'tonə] *m* (–n;-n) Teuton
teutonisch [tɔɪ'tonɪʃ] *adj* Teutonic
Text [tekst] *m* (–[e]s;-e) text, words; (cin) script; (mus) libretto; (typ) double pica; **aus dem T. kommen**

lose the train of thought; **j—m den T. lesen** give s.o. a lecture
Text'buch *n* (mus) libretto
Texter -in ['tekstər(ın)] §6 *mf* ad writer, ad man; (mus) lyricist
Textil- [tekstil] *comb.fm.* textile
Textilien [teks'tiljən] *pl*, **Textil'waren** *pl* textiles
text'lich *adj* textual
Theater [te'atər] *n* (-s;-) theater; **T. machen** (fig) make a fuss; **T. spielen** (fig) make believe, put on
Thea'terbesucher -in §6 *mf* theater-goer
Thea'terdichter -in §6 *mf* playwright
Thea'terkarte *f* theater ticket
Thea'terkasse *f* box office
Thea'terprobe *f* rehearsal
Thea'terstück *n* play
Thea'terzettel *m* program
theatralisch [te·a'traːlıʃ] *adj* theater; (fig) theatrical
Theke ['teka] *f* (-;-n) counter; bar
The·ma ['tema] *n* (-s;-men [mən] & -mata [mata]) theme, subject
Theologe [te·ɔ'loga] *m* (-n;-n) theologian
Theologie [te·olɔ'gi] *f* (-;) theology
theologisch [te·ɔ'loɡıʃ] *adj* theological
theoretisch [te·ɔ'retıʃ] *adj* theoretic(al)
Theo·rie [te·ɔ'ri] *f* (-;-rien ['ri·ən]) theory
Thera·pie [tera'pi] *f* (-;-pien ['pi·ən]) therapy
Thermalbad [ter'malbat] *n* thermal bath
Thermometer [termɔ'metər] *n* thermometer
Thermome'terstand *m* thermometer reading
Thermosflasche ['termɔsflaʃə] *f* thermos bottle
Thermostat [termɔ'stat] *m* (-[e]s;-e) & (-en;-en) thermostat
These ['tezə] *f* (-;-n) thesis
Thrombose [trɔm'bozə] *f* (-;-n) thrombosis
Thron [tron] *m* (-[e]s;-e) throne
Thron'besteigung *f* accession to the throne
Thron'bewerber *m* pretender to the throne
Thron'folge *f* succession to the throne
Thron'folger *m* successor to the throne
Thron'himmel *m* canopy, baldachin
Thron'räuber *m* usurper
Thunfisch ['tunfıʃ] *m* tuna
Tick [tık] *m* (-[e]s;-s & -e) tic; (fig) eccentricity; **e-n T. auf j—n haben** have a grudge against s.o.; **e-n T. haben** (coll) be balmy
ticken ['tıkən] *intr* tick
ticktack ['tık'tak] *adv* ticktock || **Ticktack** *n* (-s;) ticktock
tief [tif] *adj* deep; profound; (niedrig) low; (Schlaf) sound; (Farbe) dark; (äußerst) extreme; **aus tiefstem Herzen** from the bottom of one's heart; **im tiefsten Winter** in the dead of winter || *adv* deeply; **zu t. singen** be flat || **Tief** *n* (-[e]s;-e) (meteor) low
Tief'angriff *m* low-level attack

Tief'bau *m* (-[e]s;) underground engineering; underground work
tief'betrübt *adj* deeply grieved
Tief'druckgebiet *n* (meteor) low
Tiefe ['tifə] *f* (-;-n) depth; profundity
Tief'ebene *f* lowlands, plain
teif'empfunden *adj* heartfelt
Tie'fenanzeiger *m* (naut) depth gauge
Tie'fenschärfe *f* (phot) depth of field
Tief'flug *m* low-level flight
Tief'gang *m* (fig) depth; (naut) draft
tief'gekühlt *adj* deep-freeze
tief'greifend *adj* far-reaching; radical; deep-seated
Tief'kühlschrank *m* deep freeze
Tief'land *n* lowlands
tief'liegend *adj* low-lying; deep-seated; (Augen) sunken
Tief'punkt *m* (& fig) low point
Tief'schlag *m* (box) low blow
Tiefsee- [tifze] *comb.fm.* deep-sea
tief'sinnig *adj* pensive; melancholy
Tief'stand *m* low level
Tiegel ['tigəl] *m* (-s;-) saucepan; (zum Schmelzen) crucible; (typ) platen
Tier [tir] *n* (-[e]s;-e) animal; (& fig) beast; **großes** (or **hohes**) **T.** (coll) big shot, big wheel
Tier'art *f* species (of animal)
Tier'arzt *m* veterinarian
Tier'bändiger -in §6 *mf* wild-animal tamer
Tier'garten *m* zoo
Tier'heilkunde *f* veterinary medicine
tierisch ['tirıʃ] *adj* animal (fig) brutish, bestial
Tier'kreis *m* zodiac
Tier'kreiszeichen *n* sign of the zodiac
Tier'quälerei *f* cruelty to animals
Tier'reich *n* animal kingdom
Tier'schutzverein *m* society for the prevention of cruelty to animals
Tier'wärter *m* keeper (at zoo)
Tier'welt *f* animal kingdom
Tiger ['tigər] *m* (-s;-) tiger
Tigerin ['tigərın] *f* (-;-nen) tigress
tilgen ['tılgən] *tr* wipe out; (ausrotten) eradicate; (Schuld) pay off; (Sünden) expiate; (streichen) delete
Til'gung *f* (-;-en) eradication, extinction; payment; deletion
Til'gungsfonds *m* sinking fund
Tingeltangel ['tıŋəltaŋəl] *m* & *n* (-s;-) honky-tonk
Tinktur [tıŋk'tur] *f* (-;-en) tincture
Tinte ['tıntə] *f* (-;-n) ink; **in der T. sitzen** (coll) be in a pickle
Tin'tenfaß *n* inkwell
Tin'tenfisch *m* cuttlefish
Tin'tenfleck *m*, **Tin'tenklecks** *m* ink spot
Tin'tenstift *m* indelible pencil
Tip [tıp] *m* (-s;-s) tip, hint
Tippelbruder ['tıpəlbrudər] *m* tramp
tippeln ['tıpəl] *intr* (SEIN) (coll) tramp; (coll) toddle
tippen ['tıpən] *tr* type || *intr* type; tap; (wetten) bet; **an j—n nicht t. können** not be able to come near s.o. (in performance); **daran kannst du nicht t.** that's beyond your reach; **t. auf** (acc) predict || *ref*—**sich an die Stirn t.** tap one's forehead

Tippfehler ['tɪpfelər] *m* typographical error

Tippfräulein ['tɪpfrɔɪlaɪn] *n* (coll) typist

tipptopp ['tɪp'tɔp] *adj* tiptop

Tirol [tɪ'rol] *n* (-s;) Tyrol

Tiroler –in [tɪ'rolər(ɪn)] §6 *mf* Tyrolean

tirolerisch [tɪ'rolərɪʃ] *adj* Tyrolean

Tisch [tɪʃ] *m* (-es;-e) table; (*Mahlzeit*) meal, dinner, supper; **bei T.** during the meal; **nach T.** after the meal; **reinen T. machen** make a clean sweep of it; **unter den T. fallen** be ignored; **vom grünen T.** arm-chair; bureaucratic; **vor T.** before the meal; **zu T., bitte!** dinner is ready

Tisch'aufsatz *m* centerpiece

Tisch'besen *m* crumb brush

Tisch'besteck *n* knife, fork, and spoon

Tisch'blatt *n* leaf of a table

Tisch'decke *f* tablecloth

Tisch'gast *m* dinner guest

Tisch'gebet *n*—**T. sprechen** say grace

Tisch'gesellschaft *f* dinner party

Tisch'glocke *f* dinner bell

Tisch'karte *f* name plate

Tisch'lampe *f* table lamp; desk lamp

Tischler ['tɪʃlər] *m* (-s;-) cabinet maker

Tisch'platte *f* table top

Tisch'rede *f* after-dinner speech

Tisch'tennis *n* Ping-Pong

Tisch'tuch *n* tablecloth

Tisch'zeit *f* mealtime, dinner time

Tisch'zeug *n* table linen and tableware

Titan [tɪ'tan] *m* (-en;-en) Titan ‖ *n* (-s;) (chem) titanium

titanisch [tɪ'tanɪʃ] *adj* titanic

Titel ['tɪtəl] *m* (-s;-) title; (*Anspruch*) claim; **e-n T. innehaben** (sport) hold a title

Ti'telbild *n* frontispiece; (*e-r Illustrierten*) cover picture

Ti'telblatt *n* title page

Ti'telkampf *m* (box) title bout

Ti'telrolle *f* title role

titulieren [tɪtu'lirən] *tr* title

Toast [tost] *m* (-es;-e & -s) toast

toasten ['tostən] *tr* (*Brot*) toast ‖ *intr* propose a toast, drink a toast; **auf j-n t.** toast s.o.

toben ['tobən] *intr* rage; (*Kinder*) raise a racket ‖ **Toben** *n* (-s;) rage, raging; racket, noise

Tob'sucht *f* frenzy, madness

tob'süchtig *adj* raving, mad; frantic

Tochter ['tɔxtər] *f* (-;̈) daughter

Toch'terfirma *f*, **Toch'tergesellschaft** *f* (com) subsidiary, affiliate

Tod [tot] *m* (-es;-e) death; (jur) decease; **des Todes sein** be a dead man; **sich** [*dat*] **den Tod holen** catch a death of a cold

tod'ernst' *adj* dead serious

Todes– [todəs] *comb.fm.* of death; deadly

To'desanzeige *f* obituary

To'desfall *m* death

To'desgefahr *f* mortal danger

To'deskampf *m* death struggle

To'deskandidat *m* one at death's door

To'desstoß *m* coup de grâce

To'desstrafe *f* death penalty; **bei T.** on pain of death

To'destag *m* anniversary of death

To'desursache *f* cause of death

To'desurteil *n* death sentence

todgeweiht ['totgəvaɪt] *adj* doomed

tödlich ['tøtlɪç] *adj* deadly, fatal

tod'mü'de *adj* dead tired

tod'schick' *adj* (coll) very chic

tod'si'cher *adj* (coll) dead sure

Tod'sünde *f* mortal sin

Toilette [twa'lɛtə] *f* (-;-n) toilet

Toilet'tentisch *m* dressing table

tolerant [tole'rant] *adj* (gegen) tolerant (toward)

Toleranz [tole'rants] *f* (-;-en) toleration; (mach) tolerance

tolerieren [tole'rirən] *tr* tolerate

toll [tɔl] *adj* mad, crazy; fantastic, terrific; **das wird noch toller kommen** the worst is yet to come; **er ist nicht so t.** (coll) he's not so hot; **es zu t. treiben** carry it a bit too far; **t. nach** crazy about

tollen ['tɔlən] *intr* (HABEN & SEIN) romp about

Toll'haus *n* (fig) bedlam

Toll'heit *f* (-;) madness

Toll'kopf *m* (coll) crackpot

toll'kühn *adj* foolhardy, rash

Toll'wut *f* rabies

Tolpatsch ['tɔlpatʃ] *m* (-es;-e), **Tölpel** ['tœlpəl] *m* (-s;-) (coll) clumsy ox

töl'pelhaft *adj* clumsy

Tomate [to'matə] *f* (-;-n) tomato

Ton [ton] *m* (-[e]s;̈e) tone; sound; tint, shade; (*Betonung*) accent, stress; (fig) fashion; **den Ton angeben** (fig) set the tone; (mus) give the keynote; **e-n anderen Ton anschlagen** change one's tune; **große Töne reden** talk big; **guter Ton** (fig) good taste; **hast du Töne!** can you beat that! ‖ *m* (-s;-e) clay

Ton'abnehmer *m* (electron) pickup

ton'angebend *adj* leading

Ton'arm *m* pickup arm

Ton'art *f* type of clay; (mus) key

Ton'atelier *n* (cin) sound studio

Ton'band *n* (-[e]s;̈er) (cin) sound track; (electron) tape

Ton'bandgerät *n* tape recorder

tönen ['tønən] *tr* tint, shade ‖ *intr* sound; (*läuten*) ring

tönern ['tønərn] *adj* clay, of clay

Ton'fall *m* intonation, accent

Ton'farbe *f* timbre

Ton'film *m* sound film

Ton'folge *f* melody

Ton'frequenz *f* audio frequency

Ton'geschirr *n* earthenware

Ton'höhe *f*, **Ton'lage** *f* pitch

Ton'leiter *f* (mus) scale

ton'los *adj* voiceless; unstressed

Ton'malerei *f* onomotopoeia

Ton'meister *m* sound engineer

Tonnage [to'naʒə] *f* (-;-n) (naut) tonnage

Tonne ['tonə] *f* (-;-n) barrel; ton

Ton'silbe *f* accented syllable

Ton'spur *f* groove (*of record*)

Ton'streifen *m* (cin) sound track

Tonsur [tɔn'zur] f (-;-en) tonsure
Ton'taube f clay-pigeon
Ton'taubenschießen n trapshooting
Tö'nung f (-;-en) tint; (phot) tone
Ton'verstärker m amplifier
Ton'waren pl earthenware
Topas [to'pas] m (-es;-e) topaz
Topf [tɔpf] m (-[e]s;ⁱe) pot
Topf'blume f potted flower
Töpfer ['tœpfər] m (-s;-) potter
Töpferei [tœpfə'raɪ] f (-;-en) potter's shop
Töp'ferscheibe f potter's wheel
Töp'ferwaren pl pottery
Topf'lappen m potholder
Topf'pflanze f potted plant
Topp [tɔp] m (-s;-e) (naut) masthead ‖ **topp** interj it's a deal
Tor [tor] m (-en;-en) fool ‖ n (-[e]s; -e) gate; gateway; (sport) goal
Torbogen m archway
Torf [tɔrf] m (-[e]s) peat
Tor'flügel m door (of double door)
Torf'moos n peat moss
Tor'heit f (-;-en) foolishness, folly
Tor'hüter m gatekeeper; (sport) goalie
töricht ['tørɪçt] adj foolish, silly
Törin ['tørɪn] f (-;-nen) fool
torkeln ['tɔrkəln] intr (HABEN & SEIN) (coll) stagger
Tor'latte f (sport) crossbar
Tor'lauf m slalom
Tor'linie f sport goal line
Tornister [tɔr'nɪstər] m (-s;-) knapsack; school bag; (mil) field pack
torpedieren [tɔrpe'dirən] tr torpedo
Torpedo [tɔr'pedo] m (-s;-s) torpedo
Tor'pfosten m doorpost; (fb) goal post
Tor'schluß m—kurz vor T. (fig) at the eleventh hour
Torte ['tɔrtə] f (-;-n) cake; pie
Tortur [tɔr'tur] f (-;-en) torture
Tor'wächter m, **Torwart** ['torvart] m (-[e]s;-e) (sport) goalie
Tor'weg m gateway
tosen ['tozən] intr (HABEN & SEIN) rage, roar ‖ **Tosen** n (-s) rage, roar
tot [tot] adj dead; (Kapital) idle; (Wasser) stagnant; **toter Punkt** dead center; (fig) snag; **totes Rennen** dead heat; **tote Zeit** dead season
total [to'tal] adj total; all-out
totalitär [totali'ter] adj totalitarian
tot'arbeiten ref work oneself to death
Tote ['totə] §5 mf dead person
töten ['tøtən] tr kill; (Nerv) deaden
To'tenacker m churchyard
To'tenbett n deathbed
to'tenblaß' adj deathly pale
To'tenblässe f deathly pallor
to'tenbleich' adj deathly pale
To'tengräber m gravedigger
To'tengruft f crypt
To'tenhemd n shroud, winding sheet
To'tenklage f lament
To'tenkopf m skull
To'tenkranz m funeral wreath
To'tenmaske f death mask
To'tenmesse f requiem
To'tenreich n (myth) underworld
To'tenschau f coroner's inquest
To'tenschein m death certificate
To'tenstadt f necropolis

To'tenstarre f rigor mortis
To'tenstille f dead silence
To'tenwache f wake
tot'geboren adj stillborn
Tot'geburt f stillbirth
tot'lachen ref die laughing
Toto ['toto] m (-s;-s) football pool
tot'schießen §76 tr shoot dead
Tot'schlag m manslaughter
tot'schlagen §132 tr strike dead; (Zeit) kill
tot'schweigen §148 tr hush up; keep under wraps ‖ intr hush up
tot'stellen ref feign death, play dead
tot'treten §152 tr trample to death
Tö'tung f (-;-en) killing
Tour [tur] f (-;-en) tour; turn; (Umdrehung) revolution; **auf die krumme T.** by hook or by crook; **auf die langsame T.** very leisurely; **auf höchsten Touren** at full speed; (fig) full blast; **auf Touren bringen** (aut) rev up; **auf Touren kommen** pick up speed; (fig) get worked up; **auf Touren sein** (coll) be in good shape
Tou'renzahl f revolutions per minute
Tourismus [tu'rɪsmus] m (-;) tourism
Tourist [tu'rɪst] m (-en;-en) tourist
Touri'stenverkehr m, **Touristik** [tu'rɪstɪk] f (-;) tourism
Touristin [tu'rɪstɪn] f (-;-nen) tourist
Tour·nee [tur'ne] f (-;-neen ['ne·ən]) (mus, theat) tour
Trab [trap] m (-[e]s;) trot; **im T.** at a trot
Trabant [tra'bant] m (-en;-en) satellite
traben ['trabən] intr (HABEN & SEIN) trot
Tra'ber m (-s;-) trotter
Tra'berwagen m sulky
Trab'rennen n harness racing
Tracht [traxt] f (-;-en) costume; (Last) load; (Ertrag) yield
trachten ['traxtən] intr—t. nach strive for; **t. zu** (inf) endeavor to (inf)
trächtig ['treçtɪç] adj pregnant
Tradition [tradɪ'tsjon] f (-;-en) tradition
traditionell [tradɪtsjo'nel] adj traditional
traf [traf] pret of **treffen**
Trafik [tra'fɪk] f (-;-en) (Aust) cigar store
träg [trek] adj var of **träge**
Tragbahre ['trakbarə] f (-;-n) stretcher, litter
Trag'balken ['trakbalkən] m supporting beam; girder; joist
Tragband ['trakbant] n (-[e]s;ⁱer) strap; shoulder strap
tragbar ['trakbar] adj portable; (Kleid) wearable; (fig) bearable
Trage ['tragə] f (-;-n) litter
träge ['tregə] adj lazy; slow; inert
tragen ['tragən] §132 tr carry; bear; endure; support; (Kleider) wear, have on; (hervorbringen) produce, yield; (Bedenken) have; (Folgen) take; (Risiko) run; (Zinsen) yield; **bei sich t.** have on one's person; **getragen sein von** de based on; **zur Schau t.** show off ‖ ref dress; **sich**

gut t. wear well ‖ *intr* (*Stimme*) carry; (*Schußwaffe*) have a range; (*Baum, Feld*) bear, yield; (*Eis*) be thick enough

Träger ['trɛːgər] *m* (-s;-) carrier; porter; (*Inhaber*) bearer; shoulder strap; (*archit*) girder, beam

Trä'gerflugzeug *n* carrier plane

trä'gerlos *adj* strapless

tragfähig ['trɑːkfeːɪç] *adj* strong enough, capable of carrying; **tragfähige Grundlage** (fig) sound basis

Trag'fähigkeit *f* (-;-en) capacity, load limit; (naut) tonnage

Tragfläche ['trɑːkflɛːçə] *f*, **Tragflügel** ['trɑːkflyːgəl] *m* airfoil

Träg'heit ['trɛːkhart] *f* (-;) laziness; (phys) inertia

Traghimmel ['trɑːkhɪməl] *m* canopy

Tragik ['trɑːgɪk] *f* (-;) tragedy

tragisch ['trɑːgɪʃ] *adj* tragic

Tragödie [traˈgøːdjə] *f* (-;-n) tragedy

Tragriemen ['trɑːkriːmən] *m* strap

Tragsessel ['trɑːkzɛsəl] *m* sedan chair

Tragtasche ['trɑːktaʃə] *f* shopping bag

Tragtier ['trɑːktiːr] *n* pack animal

Tragweite ['trɑːkvartə] *f* range; (*Bedeutung*) significance, moment

Tragwerk ['trɑːkvɛrk] *n* (aer) airfoil

Trainer ['trɛːnər] *m* (-s;-) coach

trainieren [trɛˈniːrən] *tr & intr* train; coach

Training ['trɛːnɪŋ] *n* (-s;) training

Trai'ningsanzug *m* sweat suit

traktieren [trakˈtiːrən] *tr* treat; treat roughly

Trak·tor ['traktər] *m* (-s;-toren ['toːrən]) tractor

trällern ['trɛlərn] *tr & intr* hum

trampeln ['trampəln] *tr* trample

Tram'pelpfad *m* beaten path

Tran [trɑːn] *m* (-[e]s;-e) whale oil; **im T. sein** to be drowsy; be under the influence of alcohol

tranchieren [trɑ̃ˈʃiːrən] *tr* carve

Träne ['trɛːnə] *f* (-;-n) tear

tränen ['trɛːnən] *intr* water

Trä'nengas *n* tear gas

trank [traŋk] *pret* of **trinken** ‖ **Trank** *m* (-[e]s;-e) drink, beverage; potion

Tränke ['trɛŋkə] *f* (-;-n) watering hole

tränken ['trɛŋkən] *tr* give (s.o.) a drink; (*Tiere*) water; soak

Transfor·mator [transfɔrˈmaːtər] *m* (-s; -matoren [maˈtoːrən]) transformer

transformieren [transfɔrˈmiːrən] *tr* transform; step up; step down

Transfusion [transfuˈzjoːn] *f* (-;-en) transfusion

Tran·sistor [tranˈzɪstər] *m* (-s;-sistoren [zɪsˈtoːrən]) transistor

transitiv [tranziˈtiːf] *adj* transitive

Transmission [transmɪˈsjoːn] *f* (-;-en) transmission

transparent [transpaˈrɛnt] *adj* transparent ‖ **Transparent** *n* (-[e]s;-e) transparency; (*Spruchband*) banderol

transpirieren [transpiˈriːrən] *intr* perspire

Transplantation [transplantaˈtsjoːn] *f* (-;-en) (surg) transplant

Transport [transˈpɔrt] *m* (-[e]s;-e) transportation

---

transportabel [transpɔrˈtaːbəl] *adj* transportable

Transporter [transˈpɔrtər] *m* (-s;-) troopship; transport plane

transport'fähig *adj* transportable

transportieren [transpɔrˈtiːrən] *tr* transport, ship

Transport'unternehmen *n* carrier

Trapez [traˈpeːts] *n* (-es;-e) trapeze; (geom) trapezoid

trappeln ['trapəln] *intr* (SEIN) clatter; (*Kinder*) patter

Trassant [traˈsant] *m* (-en;-en) (fin) drawer

Trassat [traˈsɑːt] *m* (-en;-en) drawee

trassieren [traˈsiːrən] *tr* trace, lay out; **e-n Wechsel t. auf** (acc) write out a check to

trat [trɑːt] *pret* of **treten**

Tratsch [trɑːtʃ] *m* (-es;) gossip

tratschen ['trɑːtʃən] *intr* gossip

Tratte ['tratə] *f* (-;-n) (fin) draft

Trau- [trau] *comb.fm.* wedding, marriage

Traube ['traubə] *f* (-;-n) grape; bunch of grapes; (fig) bunch

Trau'bensaft *m* grape juice

Trau'benzucker *m* glucose

trauen ['trauən] *tr* (*Brautpaar*) marry; **sich t. lassen** get married ‖ *ref* dare ‖ *intr* (dat) trust (in), have confidence (in)

Trauer ['trauər] *f* (-;) grief, sorrow; mourning; (*Trauerkleidung*) mourning clothes; **T. anlegen** put on mourning clothes; **T. haben** be in mourning

Trau'eranzeige *f* obituary

Trau'erbotschaft *f* sad news

Trau'erfall *m* death

Trau'erfeier *f* funeral ceremony

Trau'erflor *m* mourning crepe

Trau'ergefolge *n*, **Trau'ergeleit** *n* funeral procession

Trau'ergottesdienst *m* funeral service

Trau'erkloß *m* (coll) sad sack

Trau'ermarsch *m* funeral march

trauern ['trauərn] *intr* (um) mourn (for); (um) wear mourning (for)

Trau'erspiel *n* tragedy

Trau'erweide *f* weeping willow

Trau'erzug *m* funeral cortege

Traufe ['traufə] *f* (-;-n) eaves

träufeln ['trɔɪfəln] *tr & intr* drip

Trauf'rinne *f* rain gutter

Trauf'röhre *f* rain pipe

traulich ['traulɪç] *adj* intimate; cozy

Traum [traum] *m* (-[e]s;-e) dream; (fig) daydream, reverie

Traum'bild *n* vision, phantom

Traum'deuter -in §6 *mf* interpreter of dreams

träumen ['trɔɪmən] *tr & intr* dream

Träu'mer *m* (-s;-) dreamer

Träumerei [trɔɪməˈraɪ] *f* (-;-en) dreaming; daydream

Träumerin ['trɔɪmərɪn] *f* (-;-nen) dreamer

träumerisch ['trɔɪmərɪʃ] *adj* dreamy; absent-minded

Traum'gesicht *n* vision, phantom

traum'haft *adj* dream-like

traurig ['traurɪç] *adj* sad

Trau'ring *m* wedding ring (or band)

Trau'schein m marriage certificate
traut [traut] adj dear; cozy; intimate
Trau'ung f (-;-en) marriage ceremony; **kirchliche T.** church wedding; **standesamtliche T.** civil ceremony
Trau'zeuge m best man
Trecker ['trɛkər] m (-s;-) tractor
Treff [trɛf] n (-s;-s) (cards) club(s)
treffen ['trɛfən] §151 tr hit; (begegnen) meet; (betreffen) concern || ref meet; assemble; **sich t. mit** meet with || intr hit home; (box) land, connect || **Treffen** n (-s;-) meeting; (mil) encounter; (sport) meet
tref'fend adj pertinent; to the point; (Ähnlichkeit) striking
Tref'fer m (-s;-) hit; winner; prize
treff'lich adj excellent
Treff'punkt m rendezvous, meeting place
Treib- [traɪp] comb.fm. moving; driving
treiben ['traɪbən] §62 tr drive; propel; chase, expel; (Beruf) pursue; (Blätter, Blüten) put forth; (Geschäft) run, carry on; (Metall) work; (Musik, Sport) go in for; (Sprachen) study; (Pflanzen) force; **es zu weit t.** go too far; **was treibst du denn?** (coll) what are you doing? || intr blossom; sprout; (Teig) ferment || intr (SEIN) drift, float || **Treiben** n (-s;) doings, activity; drifting, floating
Treib'haus n hothouse
Treib'holz n driftwood
Treib'kraft f driving force
Treib'mine f floating mine
Treib'rakete f booster rocket
Treib'riemen m drive belt
Treib'sand m drifting sand; quicksand
Treib'stange f connecting rod
Treib'stoff m fuel; propellant
Treib'stoffbehälter m fuel tank
trennbar ['trɛnbar] adj separable
trennen ['trɛnən] tr separate; sever; (Naht) undo; (Ehe) dissolve; (elec, telp) cut off || ref part; separate; (Weg) branch off
Tren'nung f (-;-en) separation; parting; dissolution
Tren'nungsstrich m dividing line; hyphen
Trense ['trɛnzə] f (-;-n) snaffle
Treppe ['trɛpə] f (-;-n) stairs, stairway; flight of stairs; **die T. hinauffallen** (coll) be kicked upstairs; **zwei Treppen hoch wohnen** live two flights up
Trep'penabsatz m landing
Trep'penflucht f flight of stairs
Trep'pengeländer n banister
Trep'penhaus n staircase
Trep'penläufer m stair carpet
Trep'penstufe f step, stair
Tresor [tre'zor] m (-s;-e) safe; vault
Tresse ['trɛsə] f (-;-n) (mil) stripe
treten ['tretən] §152 tr tread; tread on; trample; (Fußhebel) work; (Orgel) pump; mit Füßen t. (fig) trample under foot || intr (SEIN) step, walk; tread; **an j-s Stelle t.** succeed s.o.; **auf der Stelle t.** (mil) mark time; **in**

Kraft t. go into effect; **j-m zu nahe t.** offend s.o.; **t. in** (acc) enter (into)
Tretmühle ['tretmylə] f treadmill
treu [trɔɪ] adj loyal, faithful, true
Treu'bruch m breach of faith
Treue ['trɔɪə] f (-;) loyalty, fidelity; allegiance; **j-m die T. halten** remain loyal to s.o.
Treu'eid m oath of allegiance
Treu'hand f (jur) trust
Treuhänder –in ['trɔɪhɛndər(ɪn)] §6 mf trustee
Treu'handfonds m trust fund
treu'herzig adj trusting; sincere
treu'los adj unfaithful; (gegen) disloyal (to)
Tribüne [tri'bynə] f (-;-n) rostrum; (mil) reviewing stand; (sport) grandstand
Tribut [tri'but] m (-[e]s;-e) tribute
Trichter ['trɪçtər] m (-s;-) funnel; (Bomben-) crater, pothole; (mus) bell (of wind instrument); **auf den T. kommen** (coll) catch on
Trick [trɪk] m (-s;-s & -e) trick
Trick'film m animated cartoon
trieb [trip] pret of **treiben** || **Trieb** m (-[e]s;-e) sprout, shoot; urge, drive; instinct
Trieb'feder f (horol) mainspring
Trieb'kraft f motive power
trieb'mäßig adj instinctive
Trieb'werk n motor, engine
triefäugig ['trifɔɪgɪç] adj bleary-eyed
triefen ['trifən] §153 intr drip; (Augen) water; (Nase) run
triezen ['tritsən] tr (coll) tease
Trift [trɪft] f (-;-en) pasture land; cattle track; log-running
triftig ['trɪftɪç] adj cogent; valid
Trigonometrie [trɪgonome'tri] f (-;) trigonometry
Trikot [tri'ko] m & n (-s;-s) knitted cloth; (sport) trunks, tights
Triller ['trɪlər] m (-s;-) trill; (mus) quaver
trillern ['trɪlərn] intr trill; (Vogel) warble
Tril'lerpfeife f whistle
Trink- [trɪŋk] comb.fm. drinking
trinkbar ['trɪŋkbar] adj drinkable
Trink'becher m drinking cup
trinken ['trɪŋkən] §143 tr & intr drink
Trin'ker –in §6 mf drinker
trink'fest adj able to hold one's liquor
Trink'gelage n drinking party
Trink'geld n tip, gratuity
Trink'glas n drinking glass
Trink'halm m straw
Trink'spruch m toast
Trink'wasser n drinking water
Trio ['tri-o] n (-s;-s) trio
trippeln ['trɪpəln] intr (SEIN) patter
Tripper ['trɪpər] m (-s;) gonorrhea
trist [trɪst] adj dreary
tritt [trɪt] pret of **treten** || m (-[e]s;-e) step; kick; pace; footstep; footprint; small stepladder; pedal; **j-m e-n T. versetzen** give s.o. a kick
Tritt'brett n running board
Tritt'leiter f stepladder
Triumph [tri'umf] m (-[e]s;-e) triumph

Triumph'bogen *m* triumphal arch

triumphieren [trɪ·ʊm'fi:rən] *intr* triumph

Triumph'zug *m* triumphal procession

trocken ['trɔkən] *adj* dry; arid; **trokkenes Brot** plain bread

Trockenbagger (**Trok'kenbagger**) *m* (mach) excavator

Trockendock (**Trok'kendock**) *n* dry-dock

Trockenei (**Trok'kenei**) *n* dehydrated eggs

Trockeneis (**Trok'keneis**) *n* dry ice

Trockenhaube (**Trok'kenhaube**) *f* hair drier

Trockenheit (**Trok'kenheit**) *f* (–;) dryness, aridity

trockenlegen (**trok'kenlegen**) *tr* (*Sumpf*) drain; (*Säugling*) change (the diapers of)

Trockenmaß (**Trok'kenmaß**) *n* dry measure

Trockenmilch (**Trok'kenmilch**) *f* powdered milk

Trockenschleuder (**Trok'kenschleuder**) *f* spin-drier, clothes drier

Trockenübung (**Trok'kenübung**) *f* dry run

trocknen ['trɔknən] *tr* dry || *intr* (SEIN) dry, dry up

Troddel ['trɔdəl] *f* (–;–n) tassel

Trödel ['trø:dəl] *m* (–s;) secondhand goods; old clothes; junk; (fig) nuisance, waste of time

Trö'delkram *m* junk

trödeln ['trø:dəln] *intr* waste time

Tröd'ler –in §6 *mf* secondhand dealer

troff [trɔf] *pret* of **triefen**

trog [tro:k] *pret* of **trügen   Trog** *m* (–[e]s;⸚e) trough

Trommel ['trɔməl] *f* (–;–n) drum

Trom'melfell *n* drumhead; (anat) eardrum

trommeln ['trɔməln] *tr & intr* drum

Trom'melschlag *m* drumbeat

Trom'melschlegel *m*, **Trom'melstock** *m* drumstick

Trom'melwirbel *m* drum roll

Trommler ['trɔmlər] *m* (–s;–) drummer

Trompete [trɔm'pe:tə] *f* (–;–n) trumpet

trompeten [trɔm'pe:tən] *intr* blow the trumpet; (*Elefant*) trumpet

Trompe'ter –in §6 *mf* trumpeter

Tropen ['tro:pən] *pl* tropics

Tropf [trɔpf] *m* (–[e]s;⸚e) simpleton; **armer T.** poor devil

tröpfeln ['trœpfəln] *tr & intr* drip || *intr* (SEIN) trickle || *impers*—**es tröpfelt** it is sprinkling

tropfen ['trɔpfən] *tr & intr* drip || *intr* (SEIN) trickle || **Tropfen** *m* (–s;–) drop; **ein T. auf den heißen Stein** a drop in the bucket

trop'fenweise *adv* drop by drop

Trophäe [tro'fɛ·ə] *f* (–;–n) trophy

tropisch ['tro:pɪʃ] *adj* tropical

Troß [trɔs] *m* (Trosses; Trosse) (coll) load, baggage; (coll) hangers-on

Trosse ['trɔsə] *f* (–;–n) cable; (naut) hawser

Trost [tro:st] *m* (–es;) consolation, comfort; **geringer T.** cold comfort;

wohl nicht bei T. sein not be all there

trösten ['trø:stən] *tr* console, comfort || *ref* cheer up; feel consoled

tröstlich ['trø:stlɪç] *adj* comforting

trost'los *adj* disconsolate; bleak

Trost'preis *m* consolation prize

trost'reich *adj* comforting

Trö'stung *f* (–;–en) consolation

Trott [trɔt] *m* (–[e]s;–e) trot; (coll) routine

Trottel ['trɔtəl] *m* (–s;–) (coll) dope

trotten ['trɔtən] *intr* (SEIN) trot

Trottoir [trɔ'twa:r] *n* (–s;–e & –s) sidewalk

trotz [trɔts] *prep* (*genit*) in spite of; **t. alledem** for all that || **Trotz** *m* (–es;) defiance; **j–m T. bieten** defy s.o.

trotz'dem *adv* nevertheless || *conj* although

trotzen ['trɔtsən] *intr* be stubborn; (*schmollen*) sulk; (*dat*) defy

trotzig ['trɔtsɪç] *adj* defiant; sulky; obstinate

Trotz'kopf *m* defiant child (or adult)

trüb [try:p], **trübe** ['try:bə] *adj* turbid, muddy; (*Wetter*) dreary; (*glanzlos*) dull; (*Erfahrung*) sad

Trubel ['tru:bəl] *m* (–s;) bustle

trüben ['try:bən] *tr* make turbid, muddy; dim; dull; disturb, trouble (*Freude, Stimmung*) spoil || *ref* grow cloudy; become muddy; become strained

Trübsal ['try:pza:l] *f* (–;–en) distress, misery; **T. blasen** be in the dumps

trüb'selig *adj* gloomy, sad

Trüb'sinn *m* (–[e]s;) gloom

trüb'sinnig *adj* gloomy

Trü'bung *f* (–;) muddiness; blurring

trudeln ['tru:dəln] *intr* go into a spin || **Trudeln** *n* (–s;) spin; **ins T. kommen** (aer) go into a spin

trug [tru:k] *pret* of **tragen** || **Trug** *m* (–[e]s;) deceit, fraud; delusion

Trug'bild *n* phantom; illusion

trügen ['try:gən] §111 *tr & intr* deceive

trügerisch ['try:gərɪʃ] *adj* deceptive, illusory; (*verräterisch*) treacherous

Trug'schluß *m* fallacy

Truhe ['tru:·ə] *f* (–;–n) trunk, chest

Trulle ['trʊlə] *f* (–;–n) slut

Trümmer ['trʏmər] *pl* ruins; rubble

Trumpf [trʊmpf] *m* (–[e]s;⸚e) trump

Trunk [trʊŋk] *m* (–[e]s;⸚e) drinking; **im T. when drunk

trunken ['trʊŋkən] *adj* drunk; **t. vor** (*dat*) elated with

Trunkenbold ['trʊŋkənbɔlt] *m* (–[e]s; –e) drunkard

Trun'kenheit *f* (–;) drunkenness; **T. am Steuer** (jur) drunken driving

trunk'süchtig *adj* alcoholic || **Trunksüchtige** §5 *mf* alcoholic

Trupp [trʊp] *m* (–s;–s) troop, gang; (mil) detail, detachment

Truppe ['trʊpə] *f* (–;–n) (mil) troop; (theat) troupe; **Truppen** (mil) troops

Trup'peneinheit *f* unit

Trup'penersatz *m* reserves

Trup'pengattung *f* branch of service

Trup'penschau *f* (mil) review, parade

Trup′pentransporter m (aer) troop carrier; (nav) troopship
Trüp′penübung f field exercise
Trup′penverband m unit; task force
Trup′penverbandplatz m (mil) first-aid station
Trust [trust] m (-[e]s;-e & -s) (com) trust
Truthahn [′truthɑn] m turkey (cock)
Truthenne [′truthenə] f turkey (hen)
trutzig [′trutsɪç] adj defiant
Tscheche [′tʃeçə] m (-n;-n), **Tschechin** [′tʃeçɪn] f (-;-nen) Czech
tschechisch [′tʃeçɪʃ] adj Czech
Tschechoslowakei [tʃeçoslovaˈkaɪ] f (-;)—**die T.** Czechoslovakia
Tube [′tubə] f (-;-n) tube; **auf die T. drücken** (aut) step on it
Tuberkulose [tuberkuˈlozə] f (-;) tuberculosis
Tuch [tux] n (-[e]s;-e) cloth; fabric || n (-[e]s;⸚er) kerchief; shawl; scarf
tuchen [′tuxən] adj cloth, fabric
Tuch′fühlung f—**T. haben mit** (mil) stand shoulder to shoulder with; **T. halten mit** keep in close touch with
Tuch′seite f right side (of cloth)
tüchtig [′tʏçtɪç] adj able, capable, efficient; sound, thorough; excellent; good; (Trinker) hard; **t. in** (dat) good at; **t. zu** qualified for || adv very much; hard; soundly, thoroughly; (sl) awfully
Tüch′tigkeit f (-;) ability, efficiency; soundness, thoroughness; excellency
Tuch′waren pl dry goods
Tücke [′tʏkə] f (-;-n) malice; **mit List und T.** by cleverness
tückisch [′tʏkɪʃ] adj insidious
tüfteln [′tʏftəln] intr—**t. an** (dat) (coll) puzzle over
Tugend [′tugənt] f (-;-en) virtue
Tugendbold [′tugəntbɔlt] m (-[e]s;-e) (pej) paragon of virtue
tu′gendhaft adj virtuous
Tulpe [′tulpə] f (-;-n) tulip
tummeln [′tuməln] tr (Pferd) exercise || ref hurry; (Kinder) romp about
Tum′melplatz m playground; (fig) arena
Tümmler [′tʏmlər] m (-s;-) dolphin; (Taube) tumbler
Tumor [′tumor] m (-s; **Tumoren** [tuˈmorən]) tumor
Tümpel [′tʏmpəl] m (-s;-) pond
Tumult [tuˈmult] m (-[e]s;-e) uproar; uprising
tun [tun] §154 tr do; make; take; **dazu tun** add to it; **e–n Zug tun** take a swig; **es zu tun bekommen mit** have trouble with; **j–n in ein Internat tun** send s.o. to a boarding school || intr do; be busy; **alle Hände voll zu tun haben** have one's hands full; **es ist mir darum zu tun** I am anxious about it; **groß tun** talk big; **mir ist sehr darum zu tun zu** (inf) it is very important for me to (inf); **als ob** pretend that; **spröde tun** be prudish; **stolz tun** be proud; **weh tun** hurt; **zu t. haben** be busy; have one's work cut out; **zu tun haben mit** have trouble with || impers—**es tut mir**

leid I am sorry; **es tut nichts** it doesn't matter || **Tun** n (-s;) doings; action; **Tun und Treiben** doings
Tünche [′tʏnçə] f (-;-n) whitewash
tünchen [′tʏnçən] tr whitewash
Tunichtgut [′tunɪçtgut] m (- & -[e]s; -e) good-for-nothing
Tunke [′tuŋkə] f (-;-n) sauce; gravy
tunken [′tuŋkən] tr dip, dunk
tunlichst [′tunlɪçst] adv—**das wirst du t. bleiben lassen** you had better leave it alone
Tunnel [′tunəl] m (-s;- & -s) tunnel
Tüpfchen [′tʏpfçən] n (-s;-) dot
Tüpfel [′tʏpfəl] m & n (-s;-) dot
tupfen [′tupfən] tr dab; dot || **Tupfen** m (-s;-) dot, spot
Tür [tyr] f (-;-en) door
Tür′angel f door hinge
Tür′anschlag m doorstop
Turbine [tur′binə] f (-;-n) turbine
Turboprop [′turbɔprɔp] m (-s;-s) turboprop
Tür′drücker m latch
Tür′flügel m door (of double door)
Tür′griff m door handle; door knob
Türke [′tʏrkə] m (-n;-n) Turk
Türkei [tyr′kaɪ] f (-;)—**die T.** Turkey
Türkin [′tʏrkɪn] f (-;-nen) Turk
Türkis [tyr′kis] m (-es;-e) turquoise
türkisch [′tʏrkɪʃ] adj Turkish
türkisen [tyr′kizən] adj turquoise
Tür′klingel f doorbell
Tür′klinke f door handle
Turm [turm] m (-[e]s;⸚e) tower; steeple; turret; (chess) castle
Türmchen [′tʏrmçən] n (-s;-) turret
türmen [′tʏrmən] tr & ref pile up || intr (SEIN) run away, bolt
turm′hoch adj towering || adv (by) far
Turm′spitze f spire
Turm′springen n high diving
Turn- [turn] comb.fm. gymnastic, gym, athletic
turnen [′turnən] intr do exercises || **Turnen** n (-s;) gymnastics
Tur′ner –in §6 mf gymnast
turnerisch [′turnərɪʃ] adj gymnastic
Turn′gerät n gymnastic apparatus
Turn′halle f gymnasium, gym
Turn′hemd n gym shirt
Turn′hose f trunks
Turnier [tur′nir] n (-s;-e) tournament
Turn′schuhe pl sneakers
Tür′pfosten m doorpost
Tür′rahmen m doorframe
Tür′schild n doorplate
Tür′schwelle f threshold
Tusche [′tuʃə] f (-;-n) (paint) wash; **chinesische T.** India ink
tuscheln [′tuʃəln] intr whisper
Tute [′tutə] f (-;-n) (aut) horn
Tüte [′tytə] f (-;-n) paper bag; paper cone; ice cream cone
tuten [′tutən] intr blow the horn; (coll) blare away
Twen [tvɛn] m (-s;-s) young man (in his twenties)
Typ [typ] m (-s;-en) type; (Bauart) model
Type [′typə] f (-;-n) type; (coll) strange character
Ty′pennummer f model number

Typhus ['tyfus] *m* (–;) typhoid
typisch ['typɪʃ] *adj* (für) typical (of)
Tyrann [tɪ'ran] *m* (–en;–en) tyrant
Tyrannei [tɪra'naɪ] *f* (–;–en) tyranny

tyrannisch [tɪ'ranɪʃ] *adj* tyrannical
tyrannisieren [tɪranɪ'ziːrən] *tr* tyrannize, oppress
Tz ['tɛtsɛt] *n*—**bis ins Tz** thoroughly

U

U, u [u] *invar n* U, u
u.A.w.g. (um Antwort wird gebeten) R.S.V.P.
U-Bahn ['uban] *f* (Untergrundbahn) subway
übel ['yˈbəl] *adj* evil; (*schlecht*) bad; (*unwohl*) queasy, sick; (*Geruch, usw.*) nasty, foul; **er ist ein übler Geselle** he's a bad egg; **mir ist ü.** I feel sick; **ü. daran sein** have it rough || *adv* badly; **est steht ü. mit** things don't look good for; **ü. auslegen** misconstrue; **ü. deuten** misinterpret; **ü. ergehen** fare badly; **ü. gelaunt** in bad humor || **Übel** *n* (–s;–) evil; ailment
ü'belgelaunt *adj* ill-humored
ü'belgesinnt *adj* evil-minded
Ü'belkeit *f* (–;) nausea
ü'belnehmen §116 *tr* take amiss; take offense at, resent
ü'belnehmend *adj* resentful
ü'belriechend *adj* foul-smelling
Ü'belstand *m* evil; bad state of affairs
Ü'beltat *f* misdeed, crime, offense
Ü'beltäter –in §6 *mf* wrongdoer; criminal
ü'belwollen §162 *intr* (dat) be ill-disposed towards || **Übelwollen** *n* (–s;) ill will, malevolence
ü'belwollend *adj* malevolent
üben ['ybən] *tr* practice, exercise; (*e–e Kunst*) cultivate; (*Handwerk*) pursue; (*Gewalt*) use; (*Verrat*) commit; (*mil*) drill; (*sport*) train; **Barmherzigkeit ü. an** (dat) have mercy on; **Gerechtigkeit ü. gegen** be just to; **Nachsicht ü. gegen** be lenient towards; **Rache ü. an** (dat) take revenge on || *ref*—**sich im Schifahren ü.** practice skiing
über ['ybər] *adv*—**j–m ü. sein in** (dat) be superior to s.o. in; **ü. und ü.** over and over || *prep* (dat) over; above, on top of || *prep* (acc) by way of, via; (*bei, während*) during; (*nach*) past; over; across; (*betreffend*) about, concerning; **Briefe ü. Briefe** letter after letter; **ein Scheck ü. 10 DM** a check for 10 marks; **es geht nichts ü.** there is nothing better than; **heute übers Jahr** a year from today; **ü. Gebühr** more than was due; **ü. kurz oder lang** sooner or later; **ü. Land** crosscountry
überall' *adv* everywhere, all over
überallher' *adv* from all sides
überallhin' *adv* in every direction
Ü'berangebot *n* over-supply
überan'strengen *tr* overexert, strain || *ref* overexert oneself, strain oneself

überar'beiten *tr* revise, touch up || *ref*—**sich ü.** overwork oneself
Überar'beitung *f* (–;–en) revision, touching up; revised text
ü/beraus *adv* extremely, very
überbacken (überbak'ken) §50 *tr* bake lightly
Ü/berbau *m* (–[e]s; –e & –ten [tən]) superstructure
ü/berbeanspruchen *tr* overwork
ü/berbelasten *tr* overload
ü/berbelegt *adj* overcrowded
ü/berbelichten *tr* (phot) overexpose
ü/berbetonen *tr* overemphasize
überbie'ten §58 *tr* outbid; (fig) outdo
Ü/berbleibsel ['ybərblaɪpsəl] *n* (–s;–) remains; leftovers
Ü/berblen'dung *f* (cin) dissolve
Ü'berblick *m* survey; (fig) synopsis
überblicken (überblik'ken) *tr* survey
überbrin'gen §65 *tr* deliver; convey
Überbrin'ger –in §6 *mf* bearer
überbrücken (überbrük'ken) *tr* (& fig) bridge
Überbrückung (Überbrük'kung) *f* (–; –en) bridging; (rr) overpass
Überbrückungs– *comb.fm.* emergency, stop-gap
überdachen [ybər'daxən] *tr* roof over
überdau'ern *tr* outlast
überdecken (überdek'ken) *tr* cover
überden'ken §66 *tr* think over
überdies' *adv* moreover, besides
überdre'hen *tr* (Uhr) overwind
Ü'berdruck *m* excess pressure
Ü'berdruckanzug *m* space suit
Ü'berdruckkabine *f* pressurized cabin
Über·druß ['ybərdrus] *m* (–drusses;) boredom; (*Übersättigung*) satiety; (*Ekel*) disgust; **bis zum Ü.** ad nauseam
überdrüssig ['ybərdrysɪç] *adj* (genit) sick of, disgusted with
ü/berdurchschnittlich *adj* above the average
Ü'bereifer *m* excessive zeal
ü/bereifrig *adj* overzealous
überei'len *tr* precipitate; rush || *ref* be in too big a hurry; act rashly
übereilt [ybər'aɪlt] *adj* hasty, rash
übereinan'der *adv* one on top of the other
übereinan'derschlagen §132 *tr* cross
überein'kommen §99 *intr* (SEIN) come to an agreement || **Übereinkommen** *n* (–s;–) agreement
Überein'kunft *f* agreement
überein'stimmen *intr* be in agreement; concur; (Farben, usw.) harmonize
Überein'stimmung *f* agreement; accord; (*Gleichförmigkeit*) conformity;

(*Einklang*) harmony; **in Ü. mit** in line with

ü'berempfindlich *adj* oversensitive

überfah'ren §71 *tr* run over, run down; (*Fluß, usw.*) cross; **ein Signal ü.** go through a traffic light; **ü. werden** (coll) be taken in || **ü'berfahren** §71 *tr* (*über e-n Fluß, usw.*) take across || *intr* (SEIN) drive over, cross

Ü'berfahrt *f* crossing

Ü'berfall *m* surprise attack, assault; (*Raubüberfall*) holdup; (*Einfall*) raid

überfal'len §72 *tr* (*räuberisch*) hold up; assault; (mil) surprise; (mil) invade, raid; **ü. werden** be overcome (*by sleep*); be seized (*with fear*)

ü'berfällig *adj* overdue

Ü'berfallkommando *n* riot squad

überflie'gen §57 *tr* fly over; (*Buch*) skim through

ü'berfließen §76 *intr* (SEIN) overflow

überflügeln [ybər'flygəln] *tr* outflank; (fig) outstrip

Ü'berfluß *m* abundance; excess; **im Ü. vorhanden sein** be plentiful

ü'berflüssig *adj* superfluous

überflu'ten *tr* overflow, flood, swamp || **ü'berfluten** *intr* (SEIN) overflow

überfor'dern *tr* demand too much of; overwork

Ü'berfracht *f* excess luggage

ü'berführen *tr* carry across; (*Leiche*) transport in state || **überführ'en** *tr* (genit) convince of; (genit) convict of

Überführ'ung *f* (-;-en) overpass; (*e-s Verbrechers*) conviction

ü'berfülle *f* superabundance

überfül'len *tr* stuff, jam, pack

Ü'bergabe *f* delivery; (& mil) surrender

Ü'bergang *m* passage; crossing; transition; (jur) transfer; (mil) desertion; (paint) blending; (rr) crossing

Ü'bergangsbeihilfe *f* severance pay

Ü'bergangsstadium *n* transition stage

Ü'bergangszeit *f* transitional period

überge'ben §80 *tr* hand over; give up; (*einreichen*) submit; (& mil) surrender; **dem Verkehr ü.** open to traffic || *ref* vomit, throw up

überge'hen §82 *tr* omit; overlook; **mit Stillschweigen ü.** pass over in silence || **ü'bergehen** §82 *intr* (SEIN) go over, cross; (*sich verändern*) change (into); **auf j—n ü.** devolve upon s.o.; **in andere Hände ü.** change hands; **in Fäulnis ü.** become rotten

Ü'bergewicht *n* overweight; (fig) preponderance; **das Ü. bekommen** become top-heavy; (fig) get the upper hand

ü'bergießen §76 *tr* spill || **übergie'ßen** §76 *tr* pour over, pour on; (*Braten*) baste; **mit Zuckerguß ü.** (culin) ice

ü'bergreifen §88 *intr* (auf acc) spread (to); (auf acc) encroach (on)

Ü'bergriff *m* encroachment

ü'bergroß *adj* huge, colossal; oversize

ü'berhaben §89 *tr* have left; (*Kleider*) have on; (fig) be fed up with

überhand'nehmen §116 *intr* get the upper hand; run riot

ü'berhängen §92 *tr* (*Mantel*) put on;

(*Gewehr*) sling over the shoulders || *intr* overhang, project

überhäu'fen *tr* overwhelm, swamp

überhaupt' *adv* really; anyhow; (*besonders*) especially; (*überdies*) besides; at all; **ü. kein** no...whatever; **ü. nicht** not at all; **wenn ü.** if...at all; **if...really**

überheblich [ybər'hepliç] *adj* arrogant

überhei'zen, übzerhit'zen *tr* overheat

überhöhen [ybər'hø-ən] *tr* (*Kurve*) bank; (*Preise*) raise too high

ü'berholen *tr* take across; **die Segel ü.** shift sails || *intr* (naut) heel || **überho'len** *tr* outdistance, outrun; (*ausbessern*) overhaul; (*Fahrzeug*) pass; (fig) outstrip

überholt [ybər'hɔlt] *adj* obsolete, out of date; (*repariert*) reconditioned

überhö'ren *tr* not hear, miss; ignore; misunderstand

ü'berirdisch *adj* supernatural

überkandidelt ['ybərkandidəlt] *adj* (coll) nutty, wacky

ü'berkippen *intr* (SEIN) tilt over

überkle'ben *tr* paper over; **ü. mit** cover with

Ü'berkleid *n* outer garment; overalls

ü'berklug *adj* (pej) wise, smart

ü'berkochen *intr* (SEIN) boil over

überkom'men *adj* traditional || §99 *tr* overcome || *intr* (SEIN) be handed down to

überla'den *adj* overdone || §103 *tr* overload

Ü'berlandbahn *f* interurban trolley line

Ü'berlandleitung *f* (elec) high-tension line; (telp) long-distance line

überlas'sen §104 *tr* yield, leave, relinquish; entrust; (com) sell; **das bleibt ihm ü.** he is free to do as he pleases || *ref* (dat) give way to

Ü'berlast *f* overload; overweight

überla'sten *tr* overload

überlau'fen *adj* overcrowded; (fig) swamped || §105 *tr* overrun; (*belästigen*) pester; **Angst überlief ihn** fear came over him || **ü'berlaufen** §105 *intr* (SEIN) run over, overflow; boil over; (fig & mil) desert; **die Galle läuft mir über** (fig) my blood boils || *impers*—**mich überläuft es kalt** I shudder

Ü'berläufer -in §6 *mf* (mil) deserter; (pol) turncoat

ü'berlaut *adj* too noisy

überle'ben *tr* outlive, survive || *ref* go out of style

überle'bend *adj* surviving || **Überlebende** §5 *mf* survivor

ü'berlebensgroß *adj* bigger than life

überlebt [ybər'lept] *adj* antiquated

überle'gen *adj* (dat) superior (to); (an dat) superior (in) || *tr* consider, think over || *ref*—**sich** [dat] **anders ü.** change one's mind; **sich** [dat] **ü.** consider, think over || *intr* think it over || **ü'berlegen** *tr* lay across; (*Mantel*) put on

Überle'genheit *f* (-;) superiority

überlegt' *adj* well considered; (jur) willful

Überle′gung f (–;–en) consideration

überle′sen §107 tr read over, peruse

überlie′fern tr deliver; hand down, transmit; (mil) surrender

Überlie′ferung f (–;–en) delivery; (fig) tradition; (mil) surrender

überli′sten tr outwit, outsmart

überma′chen tr bequeath

U′bermacht f superiority; (fig) predominance

ü′bermächtig adj overwhelming; predominant

überma′len tr paint over

übermannen [ybər′manən] tr overpower

U′bermaß n excess; **bis zum Ü.** to excess

ü′bermäßig adj excessive ‖ adv excessively; overly

U′bermensch m superman

ü′bermenschlich adj superhuman

übermitteln [ybər′mɪtəln] tr transmit, convey, forward

Übermitt′lung f (–;–en) transmission, conveyance, forwarding

ü′bermorgen adv the day after tomorrow

übermüdet [ybər′mydət] adj overtired

U′bermut m exuberance, mischievousness

ü′bermütig adj exuberant; haughty

ü′bernächste §9 adj next but one; **am übernächsten Tag** the day after tomorrow; **ü. Woche** week after next

übernach′ten intr spend the night

Übernach′tung f (–;–en) accommodations for the night; spending the night

U′bernahme f taking over, takeover

ü′bernatürlich adj supernatural

überneh′men §116 tr take over; assume; undertake; take upon oneself; accept, receive ‖ **ü′bernehmen** §116 tr (Mantel, Schal) put on; (Gewehr) shoulder ‖ **überneh′men** §116 ref overreach oneself; **sich beim Essen ü.** overeat

ü′berordnen tr place over, set over

ü′berparteilich adj nonpartisan

U′berproduktion f overproduction

überprü′fen tr examine again, check; verify; (Personen) screen

Überprü′fung f (–;–en) checking; checkup

ü′berquellen §119 intr (SEIN) (Teig) run over; **überquellende Freude** irrepressible joy

überqueren [ybər′kverən] tr cross

überra′gen tr tower over; (fig) surpass

überraschen [ybər′raʃən] tr surprise

Überra′schung f (–;–en) surprise

überrech′nen tr count over

überre′den tr persuade; **j–n zu etw ü.** talk a person into s.th.

Überre′dung f (–;) persuasion

ü′berreich adj (an dat) abounding (in) ‖ adv—**ü. ausgestattet** well equipped

überrei′chen tr hand over, present

ü′berreichlich adj superabundant

überreif adj overripe

überrei′zen tr overexcite; (Augen, Nerven) strain

überreizt′ adj overwrought

überren′nen §97 tr overrun; (fig) overwhelm

U′berrest m rest, remainder; **irdische Überreste** mortal remains

ü′berrock m topcoat, overcoat

überrum′peln tr take by surprise

Überrum′pelung f (–;–en) surprise

überrun′den tr (sport) lap

übersät [ybər′zet] adj (fig) strewn, dotted

übersät′tigen tr stuff; cloy; (chem) saturate, supersaturate

Übersät′tigung f (chem) supersaturation

Überschall– comb.fm. supersonic

überschat′ten tr overshadow

überschät′zen tr overestimate

U′berschau f survey

überschau′en tr look over, survey; overlook (a scene)

überschla′fen §131 tr (fig) sleep on

U′berschlag m rough estimate; (aer) loop; (gym) somersault

überschla′gen adj lukewarm ‖ §132 tr skip, omit; estimate roughly; consider ‖ ref go head over heels; do a somersault; (Auto) overturn; (Boot) capsize; (Flugzeug) do a loop; (beim Landen) nose over; (Stimme) break; (fig) (vor dat) outdo oneself (in) ‖ **ü′berschlagen** §132 tr (Beine) cross; flip over; **ü. in** (acc) (fig) change suddenly to

ü′berschnappen intr (SEIN) (Stimme) squeak; (coll) flip one's lid

überschnei′den §106 ref (Linien) intersect; (& fig) overlap

überschrei′ben §62 tr sign over

überschrei′en §135 tr shout down ‖ ref strain one's voice

überschrei′ten §86 tr cross, step over; (Kredit) overdraw; (Gesetz) violate, transgress; (fig) exceed, overstep

U′berschrift f heading, title

U′berschuh m overshoe

U′berschuß m surplus, excess; profit

ü′berschüssig adj surplus, excess

überschüt′ten tr shower; (& fig) overwhelm, flood

U′berschwang m (–[e]s;) rapture

überschwem′men tr flood, inundate

Überschwem′mung f (–;–en) flood, inundation

überschwenglich [′ybərʃvɛŋlɪç] adj effusive, gushing

U′bersee f (–;) overseas

U′berseedampfer m ocean liner

U′berseehandel m overseas trade

übersehbar [ybər′zebar] adj visible at a glance

überse′hen §138 tr survey, look over; (nicht bemerken) overlook; (absichtlich) ignore; (erkennen) realize

übersen′den §140 tr send, forward; transmit; (Geld) remit

Übersen′dung f (–;–en) forwarding; transmission; consignment

ü′bersetzen tr ferry across ‖ **überset′zen** tr translate

Überset′zung f (–;–en) translation; (mach) gear, transmission

U′bersicht f survey, review; (Abriß) abstract; (Zusammenfassung) summary; (*Umriß*) outline; (*Ausblick*) perspective; **jede Ü. verlieren** lose all perspective

ü'bersichtlich *adj* clear; (*Gelände*) open

Ü'bersichtsplan *m* general plan

ü'bersiedeln *intr* (SEIN) move; emigrate

ü'bersinnlich *adj* transcendental

überspan'nen *tr* span; cover; overstrain; (*fig*) exaggerate

überspannt [ybər'∫pant] *adj* eccentric; extravagant

Überspannt'heit *f* (-;-en) eccentricity

Überspan'nung *f* (-;-en) overstraining; (*fig*) exaggeration; (*elec*) excess voltage

überspie'len *tr* outplay; outwit; (*Tonbandaufnahme*) transcribe; (*Schüchternheit*) hide

überspitzt [ybər'∫pɪtst] *adj* oversubtle

übersprin'gen §142 *tr* jump; (*auslassen*) omit, skip ‖ **ü'berspringen** §142 *intr* (SEIN) jump

ü'bersprudeln *intr* (SEIN) bubble over

ü'berständig *adj* leftover; (*Bier*) flat; (*Obst*) overripe

überste'hen §146 *tr* stand, endure; (*Krankheit, usw.*) get over; (*Operation*) pull through; (*überleben*) survive ‖ **ü'berstehen** §146 *intr* jut out

überstei'gen §148 *tr* climb over; (*Hindernisse*) overcome; (*Erwartungen*) exceed ‖ **ü'bersteigen** §148 *intr* (SEIN) step over

überstim'men *tr* vote down, defeat

überstrah'len *tr* shine upon; (*verdunkeln*) outshine, eclipse

überstrei'chen §85 *tr* paint over

ü'berstreifen *tr* slip on

überströ'men *tr* flood, inundate ‖ **ü'berströmen** *intr* (SEIN) overflow

Ü'berstunde *f* hour of overtime; **Überstunden machen** work overtime

überstür'zen *tr* rush, hurry ‖ *ref* be in too big a hurry; act rashly; (*Ereignisse*) follow one another rapidly

überstürzt [ybər'∫tʏrtst] *adj* hasty

überteuern [ybər'tɔɪ-ərn] *tr* overcharge

übertölpeln [ybər'tœpəln] *tr* dupe

übertö'nen *tr* drown out

Übertrag ['ybərtrak] *m* (-[e]s;⸗e) (acct) carryover, balance

übertragbar [ybər'trakbər] *adj* transferable; (pathol) contagious

übertra'gen *adj* figurative, metaphorical ‖ §132 *tr* carry over, transfer; (*Amt, Titel*) confer; (*Aufgabe*) assign; (*Vollmacht*) delegate; (*Kurzschrift*) transcribe; (**in** *acc*) translate (into); (acct) transfer; (pathol) spread, communicate; (rad) broadcast, transmit; (*mit Relais*) relay; (telv) televise

Übertra'gung *f* (-;-en) carrying over; transfer; assignment; delegation; conferring; transcription; translation; copy; (pathol) spread; (rad) broadcast; relay; (telv) televising

übertref'fen §151 *tr* surpass, outdo

übertrei'ben §62 *tr* overdo; exaggerate; (theat) overact

Übertrei'bung *f* (-;-en) overdoing; exaggeration; (theat) overacting

übertre'ten §152 *tr* (*Gesetz*) transgress, break ‖ *ref*—**sich** [*dat*] **den Fuß ü.** sprain one's ankle ‖ **ü'bertreten** §152 *intr* (SEIN) (sport) go off sides; **ü. zu** (fig) go over to; (relig) be converted to

Übertre'tung *f* (-;-en) violation

Ü'bertritt *m* change, going over; (relig) conversion

übervölkern [ybər'fœlkərn] *tr* overpopulate

Übervöl'kerung *f* (-;) overpopulation

ü'bervoll *adj* brimful; crowded

übervorteilen [ybər'fortaɪlən] *tr* take advantage of, get the better of

überwa'chen *tr* watch over; supervise; (*kontrollieren*) inspect, check; (polizeilich) shadow; (rad, telv) monitor

Überwa'chung *f* (-;-en) supervision; inspection; control; surveillance

Überwa'chungsausschuß *m* watchdog committee

überwäl'tigen [ybər'vɛltɪgən] *tr* overpower (fig) overwhelm

überwei'sen §118 *tr* (*Geld*) send; (*zu e-m Spezialisten*) refer

Überwei'sung *f* (-;-en) sending, remittance; referral

ü'berweltlich *adj* otherworldly

ü'berwerfen §160 *tr* throw over ‖ **überwer'fen** §160 *ref* (**mit**) have a run-in (with)

überwie'gen §57 *tr* outweigh ‖ *intr* prevail, preponderate ‖ **Überwiegen** *n* (-s;) prevalence, preponderance

überwie'gend *adj* prevailing; (*Mehrheit*) vast ‖ *adv* predominantly

überwin'den §59 *tr* conquer, overcome ‖ *ref*—**sich ü. zu** (*inf*) bring oneself to (*inf*)

überwintern [ybər'vɪntərn] *intr* pass the winter; (bot) survive the winter

überwu'chern *tr* overrun; (fig) stifle

Ü'berwurf *m* wrap; shawl

Ü'berzahl *f* numerical superiority; majority

überzah'len *tr* & *intr* overpay

überzäh'len *tr* count over, recount

überzählig ['ybərtsɛlɪç] *adj* surplus

überzeu'gen *tr* convince ‖ *ref*—**sich selbst davon!** go and see for yourself!

Überzeu'gung *f* (-;-en) conviction

überzie'hen §163 *tr* cover; (*mit Farbe*) coat; (*Bett*) put fresh linen on; (*Konto*) overdraw; **ein Land mit Krieg ü.** invade a country ‖ **überziehen** §163 *tr* (*Mantel, usw.*) slip on; **j-m eins ü.** (coll) give s.o. a whack

Ü'berzieher *m* (-s;-) overcoat

überzuckern (**überzuk'kern**) *tr* (& fig) sugarcoat

Ü'berzug *m* coat, film; (*Decke*) cover; (*Hülle*) case; pillow case; (*Kruste*) crust; (*Schale, Rinde*) skin

üblich ['yplɪç] *adj* usual, customary

U'-Boot *n* (**Unterseeboot**) submarine

U'-Bootbunker *m* submarine pen

U'-Bootjäger *m* (aer) antisubmarine aircraft; (nav) subchaser

U'-Bootortungsgerät *n* sonar

U'-Bootrudel *n* (nav) wolf pack

übrig ['ybrɪç] *adj* left (over), remaining, rest (of); **die übrigen** the others, the rest; **ein übriges tun** do more than is necessary; **etw ü. haben für** have a soft spot for; **im übrigen** for the rest, otherwise

ü'brigbehalten §90 *tr* keep, spare

ü'brigbleiben §62 *intr* (SEIN) be left (over) ‖ *impers*—**es blieb mir nichts anderes ü. als zu** (*inf*) I had no choice but to (*inf*)

übrigens ['ybrɪgəns] *adv* moreover; after all; by the way

ü'briglassen §104 *tr* leave, spare

Übung ['ybʊŋ] *f* (–;–en) exercise; practice; (*Gewohnheit*) use; (*Ausbildung*) training; (mil) drill

Ü'bungsbeispiel *n* practical example

Ü'bungsbuch *n* composition book; workbook

Ü'bungsgelände *n* training ground; (*für Bomben*) target area

Ü'bungshang *m* (sport) training slope

Ü'bungsheft *n* composition book; workbook

Ufer ['ufər] *n* (–s;–) (*e–s Flusses*) bank; (*e–s Meers*) shore

U'ferdamm *m* embankment, levee

u'ferlos *adj* fruitless

Uhr [ur] *f* (–;–en) clock; watch; o'clock; **um wieviel Uhr?** at what time; **um zwölf Uhr** at twelve o'clock; **wieviel Uhr ist es?** what time is it?

Uhr'armband *n* (–[e]s;–er) watchband

Uhr'feder *f* watch spring

Uhr'glas *n* watch crystal

Uhr'macher *m* watchmaker

Uhr'werk *n* works, clockwork

Uhr'zeiger *m* hand

Uhr'zeigerrichtung *f*—**entgegen der U.** counterclockwise; **in der U.** clockwise

Uhr'zeigersinn *m*—**im U.** clockwise

Uhu ['uhu] *m* (–s;–s) owl

Ukraine [u'kraɪnə] *f* (–;)—**die U.** the Ukraine

ukrainisch [u'kraɪnɪʃ] *adj* Ukrainian

UK-Stellung [u'ka;telʊŋ] *f* (–;–en) military deferment

Ulk [ʊlk] *m* (–[e]s;–e) joke, fun

ulken ['ʊlkən] *intr* (coll) make fun

ulkig ['ʊlkɪç] *adj* funny

Ulme ['ʊlmə] *f* (–;–n) elm

Ultima·tum [ʊltɪ'matʊm] *n* (–s;–ten [tən] & –ta [ta]) ultimatum

Ultra-, ultra– [ʊltra] *comb.fm.* ultra–

Ul'trakurzfrequenz *f* ultrashort frequency

ultramontan [ʊltramɔn'tan] *adj* strict Catholic

ul'trarot *adj* infrared

Ultraschall– *comb.fm.* supersonic

ul'traviolett *adj* ultraviolet

um [ʊm] *adv*—**deine Zeit ist um** your time is up; **je…um so** the…the; **um so besser** all the better; **um so weniger** all the less; **um und um** round and round ‖ *prep* (*acc*) around, about; for; at; **um die Hälfte mehr** half as much again; **um die Wette laufen** race; **um ein Jahr älter** one year older; **um etw eintauschen** exchange for s.th.; **um jeden Preis** at

any price; **um…Uhr** at…o'clock; **um…zu** (*inf*) in order to (*inf*)

um'ackern *tr* plow up, turn over

um'adressieren *tr* readdress

um'ändern *tr* change (around)

Um'änderung *f* (–;–en) change, alteration

um'arbeiten *tr* rework; (*Metall*) recast; (*Buch*) revise; (*Haus*) remodel; (*berichtigen*) emend, correct; (*verbessern*) improve

umar'men *tr* embrace, hug

Umar'mung *f* (–;–en) embrace, hug

Um'bau *m* (–[e]s;–e & –ten) rebuilding; alterations, remodeling; reorganization

um'bauen *tr* remodel; reorganize ‖ **umbau'en** *tr* build around; **umbauter Raum** floor space

um'besetzen *tr* (*Stellungen*) switch around; (pol) reshuffle; (theat) recast

um'biegen §47 *tr* bend (over); bend up, bend down

um'bilden *tr* remodel; reconstruct; (adm) reorganize, (pol) reshuffle

Um'bildung *f* (–;–en) remodeling; reconstruction; reorganization; reshuffling

um'binden §59 *tr* (*Schürze, usw.*) put on ‖ **umbin'den** §59 *tr* (*verletztes Glied, usw.*) bandage

um'blättern *tr* turn ‖ *intr* turn the page(s)

um'brechen §64 *tr* (*Bäume, usw.*) knock down; (*Acker*) plow up ‖ **umbre'chen** *tr* make into page proof

um'bringen §65 *tr* kill

Um'bruch *m* upheaval; (typ) page proof

um'buchen *tr* transfer to another account; book for another date

um'denken §66 *tr* rethink

um'dirigieren *tr* redirect

um'disponieren *tr* rearrange

um'drängen *tr* crowd around

um'drehen *tr* turn around; (*Hals*) wring; (*j–s Worte*) twist ‖ *ref* turn around ‖ *intr* turn around

Umdre'hung *f* (–;–en) turn; revolution

Um'druck *m* reprint; (typ) transfer

umeinan'der *adv* around each other

um'erziehen §163 *tr* reeducate

um'fahren §71 *tr* run down ‖ **umfah'ren** §71 *tr* drive around; sail around

um'fallen §72 *intr* (SEIN) fall over, fall down; collapse; give in

Um'fang *m* circumference; perimeter; (*Bereich*) range; (*Ausdehnung*) extent; (*des Leibes*) girth; (fig) scope; (mus) range; **im großen U.** on a large scale

umfan'gen §73 *tr* surround; embrace

um'fangreich *adj* extensive; (*körperlich*) bulky; (*geräumig*) spacious

umfas'sen *tr* embrace; clasp; comprise, cover; include; contain; (mil) envelop

umfas'send *adj* comprehensive; extensive

Umfas'sung *f* (–;–en) embrace; clasp; enclosure, fence; (mil) envelopment

Umfas′sungsmauer f enclosure
umflat′tern tr flutter around
umflech′ten §74 tr braid
umflie′gen §57 tr fly around ‖ **um′flie-
gen** §57 intr (SEIN) (coll) fall down
umflie′ßen §76 tr flow around
um′formen tr reshape; (elec) convert
Um′former m (-s;-) (elec) converter
Um′frage f inquiry, poll; **öffentliche
U.** public opinion poll
umfrieden [umˈfridən] tr enclose
Um′gang m round, circuit; revolution,
rotation; (Zug) procession; association, company; (archit) gallery; **ge-
schlechtlicher U.** sexual intercourse;
schlechter U. bad company; **U. mit
j-m haben** (or **pflegen**) associate
with s.o.
umgänglich [ˈʊmgɛŋlɪç] adj sociable
Um′gangsformen pl social manners
Um′gangssprache f colloquial speech
um′gangssprachlich adj colloquial
umgar′nen tr (fig) trap
umge′ben §80 tr surround
Umgebung [umˈgebʊŋ] f (-;-en) surroundings, environs, neighborhood;
company, associates; background,
environment
Umgegend [ˈʊmgegənt] f (-;) (coll)
neighborhood
umgehen §82 tr go around; evade; bypass; (mil) outflank ‖ **um′gehen** §82
intr (SEIN) go around; (Gerücht) circulate; **an** (or **in**) **e-m Ort u.** haunt
a place; **mit dem Gedanken** (or
Plan) **u. zu** (inf) be thinking of (ger);
u. mit deal with, handle; manage; be
occupied with; hang around with
um′gehend adj immediate; **mit umge-
hender Post** by return mail; **umge-
hende Antwort erbeten!** please answer at your earliest convenience ‖
adv immediately
Umge′hung f (-;-en) going around;
bypassing; (fig) evasion; (mil) flank-
ing movement
Umge′hungsstraße f bypass
umgekehrt [ˈʊmgəkeɐt] adj reverse;
contrary ‖ adv on the contrary; vice
versa; upside down; inside out
um′gestalten tr alter; remodel
um′graben §87 tr dig up
umgren′zen tr fence in; (fig) limit
Umgren′zung f (-;-en) enclosure; (fig)
limit, boundary
um′gruppieren tr regroup; (pol) reshuffle
um′gucken ref look around
um′haben §89 tr have on, be wearing
Um′hang m wrap; cape; shawl
um′hängen tr put on; (Gewehr) sling;
(Bild) hang elsewhere
Um′hängetasche f shoulder bag
um′hauen §93 tr cut down; (coll) bowl
over
umher′ adv around, about
umher′blicken tr look around
umher′fuchteln intr gesticulate
umher′schweifen, umher′streifen intr
(SEIN) rove, roam about
umhin′ adv—**ich kann nicht u.** I can't
do otherwise; **ich kann nicht u. zu**
(inf) I can't help (ger)

umhül′len tr wrap up, cover; envelop
Umhül′lung f (-;-en) wrapping
Umkehr [ˈumkeɐ] f (-;) return;
change; conversion; (elec) reversal
um′kehren tr turn around; overturn;
(Tasche) turn out; (elec) reverse;
(gram, math, mus) invert ‖ intr
(SEIN) turn back, return
Um′kehrung f (-;-en) overturning; reversal; conversion; inversion
um′kippen tr upset ‖ intr (SEIN) tilt
over
umklam′mern tr clasp; cling to; (mil)
envelop; **einander u.** (box) clinch
Umklam′merung f (-;-en) embrace;
(box) clinch; (mil) envelopment
umklei′den tr clothe ‖ ref change
around ‖ **um′kleiden** tr change the
clothes of
Um′kleideraum m dressing room
um′kommen §99 intr (SEIN) perish;
(Essen) spoil
Um′kreis m circuit; vicinity; (geom)
circumference; **5 km im U.** within a
radius of 5 km
umkrei′sen tr circle, revolve around
um′krempeln tr (Ärmel) roll up; **völlig u.** (coll) change completely
um′laden §103 tr reload; transship
Um′lauf m circulation; (Umdrehung)
revolution, rotation; (Flugblatt) circular; (Rundschreiben) circular letter; **in U. setzen** circulate
Um′laufbahn f orbit
um′laufen §105 tr run down ‖ intr
(SEIN) circulate ‖ **umlau′fen** §105 tr
walk around
Um′laut m (-es;-e) umlaut, vowel mutation; mutated vowel
umlegbar [ˈʊmlekbar] adj reversible
um′legen tr lay down; turn down; (anders legen) shift; (Kragen) put on;
(gleichmäßig verteilen) apportion;
(coll) knock down; (vulg) lay
um′leiten tr detour, divert
Um′leitung f (-;-en) detour
um′lenken tr turn back
um′lernen tr relearn, learn anew
um′liegend adj surrounding
umau′ern tr wall in
um′modeln tr remodel
umnachtet [umˈnaxtət] adj deranged
Umnach′tung f (-;)—**geistige U.** mental derangement
um′nähen tr hem
umne′beln tr fog; (fig) dull; **umnebelter
Blick** glassy eyes
um′nehmen §116 tr put on
um′packen tr repack
um′pflanzen tr transplant ‖ **umpflan′-
zen** tr—**etw mit Blumen u.** plant
flowers around s.th.
um′pflügen tr plow up, turn over
umrah′men tr frame
umranden [umˈrandən] tr edge, border
Umran′dung f (-;-en) edging, edge
umran′ken tr twine around; **mit Efeu
umrankt** ivy-clad
um′rechnen tr convert; **umgerechnet
auf** (acc) expressed in
Um′rechnungskurs m rate of exchange
Um′rechnungstabelle f conversion table
Um′rechnungswert m exchange value

um′reißen §53 *tr* pull down; knock down ‖ **umrei′ßen** §53 *tr* outline

umrin′gen *tr* surround

Um′riß *m* outline

Um′rißzeichnung *f* sketch

um′rühren *tr* stir, stir up

um′satteln *tr* resaddle ‖ *intr* change jobs; (*educ*) change one's course or major; (*pol*) switch parties

Um′satz *m* turnover, sales

Um′satzsteuer *f* sales tax

umsäu′men *tr* enclose, hem in

um′schalten *tr* switch; (*Strom*) convert ‖ *intr* (**auf** *acc*) switch back (to)

Um′schalter *m* (elec) switch; (typ) shift key

Um′schaltung *f* (—;-en) switching; shifting

Um′schau *f* look around; **U. halten** have a look around

um′schauen *ref* look around

um′schichten *tr* regroup, reshuffle

umschichtig [′ʊmʃɪçtɪç] *adv* alternately

umschif′fen *tr* circumnavigate; (*ein Kap*) double

Um′schlag *m* (sudden) change, shift; envelope; (*e-s Buches*) cover, jacket; cuff; hem; transshipment; (med) compress

um′schlagen §132 *tr* knock down; (*Ärmel*) roll up; (*Bäume*) fell; (*Saum*) turn up; (*Seite*) turn; (*umladen*) transship ‖ *intr* (SEIN) (*Laune, Wetter*) change; (*Wind*) shift; (*kentern*) capsize

Um′schlagpapier *n* wrapping paper

umschlie′ßen §76 *tr* surround, enclose

umschlin′gen §142 *tr* clasp; embrace; wind around

um′schmeißen §53 *tr* (coll) throw over

um′schnallen *tr* buckle on

um′schreiben §62 *tr* rewrite; (*abschreiben*) transcribe; (*Wechsel*) re-endorse; **u. auf** (*acc*) transfer to ‖ **umschrei′ben** §62 *tr* circumscribe; paraphrase

Um′schreibung *f* (—;-en) transcription; transfer ‖ **Umschrei′bung** *f* (—;-en) paraphrase

Um′schrift *f* transcription; (*e-r Münze*) legend

um′schulen *tr* retrain

um′schütteln *tr* shake (up)

um′schütten *tr* spill; pour into another container

umschwär′men *tr* swarm around; (fig) idolize

Um′schweif *m* digression; **ohne Umschweife** point-blank; **Umschweife machen** beat around the bush

umschweifig [ʊm′ʃvaɪfɪç] *adj* roundabout

um′schwenken *intr* wheel around; (fig) change one's mind

Um′schwung *m* change; (*Drehung*) revolution; (*Umkehrung*) reversal; (*der Gesinnung*) revulsion

umse′geln *tr* sail around; (*Kap*) double

Umse′gelung *f* (—;-en) circumnavigation

um′sehen §138 *ref* (**nach**) look around (for); (fig) (**nach**) look out (for)

um′sein §139 *intr* (SEIN) (*Zeit*) be up; (*Ferien*) be over

um′setzen *tr* shift; transplant; (*Nährstoffe*) assimilate; (*Schüler*) switch around; (*Ware*) sell; (*verwandeln*) convert; (mus) transpose; **Geld u. in** (*acc*) spend money on; **in die Tat u.** translate into action ‖ *ref*—**sich u. in** (*acc*) (biochem) be converted into

Um′sicht *f* (—;) circumspection

umsichtig [′ʊmzɪçtɪç] *adj* circumspect

um′siedeln *tr* & *intr* (SEIN) resettle

Um′siedlung *f* (—;-en) resettlement

umsonst′ *adv* for nothing, gratis; (*vergebens*) in vain

um′spannen *tr* (*Wagenpferde*) change; (elec) transform ‖ **umspan′nen** *tr* span; encompass; include

Um′spanner *m* (—s;-) (elec) transformer

um′springen §142 *intr* (SEIN) (*Wind*) shift; **mit j-m rücksichtslos u.** (coll) treat s.o. thoughtlessly

Um′stand *m* circumstance; factor; fact; (*Einzelheit*) detail; (*Aufheben*) fuss; **in anderen Umständen** (coll) pregnant; **sich** [*dat*] **Umstände machen** go to the trouble; **Umstände machen** be formal; **unter Umständen** under certain conditions

umständehalber [′ʊmʃtɛndəhalbər] *adv* owing to circumstances

umständlich [′ʊmʃtɛntlɪç] *adj* detailed; (*förmlich*) formal; (*zu genau*) fussy; (*verwickelt*) complicated; (*Erzählung*) long-winded, round-about

Um′standskleid *n* maternity dress

Um′standskrämer *m* fusspot

Um′standswort *n* (—[e]s;—″er) adverb

um′stehend *adj* (*Seite*) next ‖ **Umstehende** §5 *mf* bystander

Um′steige(fahr)karte *f* transfer

um′steigen §148 *intr* (SEIN) transfer

um′stellen *tr* put into a different place, shift; (*Möbel*) rearrange; (**auf** *acc*) convert (to) ‖ *ref* (**auf** *acc*) adjust (to) ‖ **umstel′len** *tr* surround

Um′stellung *f* (—;-en) change of position, shift; conversion; readjustment

um′stimmen *tr* tune to another pitch; make (*s.o.*) change his mind

um′stoßen §150 *tr* knock down; (*Pläne*) upset; (*Vertrag*) annul; (*Urteil*) reverse

umstricken (umstrik′ken) *tr* ensnare

umstritten [ʊm′ʃtrɪtən] *adj* contested; controversial

Um′sturz *m* overthrow

um′stürzen *tr* overturn; overthrow; (*Mauer*) tear down; (*Plan*) change, throw out ‖ *intr* (SEIN) fall down

Umstürzler -in [′ʊmʃtʏrtslər(ɪn)] §6 *mf* revolutionary, subversive

umstürzlerisch [′ʊmʃtʏrtslərɪʃ] *adj* revolutionary; subversive

Um′tausch *m* exchange

um′tauschen *tr* (**gegen**) exchange (for)

um′tun §154 *tr* (*Kleider*) put on ‖ *ref*—**sich u. nach** look around for

um′wälzen *tr* roll around; (fig) revolutionize ‖ *ref* roll around

umwäl′zend *adj* revolutionary

Umwäl′zung *f* (—;-en) revolution

umwandelbar ['ʊmvandəlbɑr] *adj* (com) convertible

um'wandeln *tr* change; (elec, fin) convert; (jur) commute

Um'wandlung *f* (–;–en) change; (elec, fin) conversion; (jur) commutation

um'wechseln *tr* exchange; (fin) convert

Um'weg *m* detour; **auf Umwegen** indirectly

um'wehen *tr* knock down || **umwe'hen** *tr* blow around

Um'welt *f* environment

Um'weltverschmutzung *f* ecological pollution

um'wenden §140 *tr* turn over || *ref & intr* turn around

umwer'ben §149 *tr* court, go with

um'werfen §160 *tr* throw down; upset; *(Plan)* ruin; *(Kleider)* throw about one's shoulders

umwickeln (umwik'keln) *tr (mit Band)* tape

umwin'den *tr* wreathe

umwölken [ʊm'vœlkən] *ref & intr* cloud over

umzäunen [ʊm'tsɔɪnən] *tr* fence in

um'ziehen §163 *tr* change one's clothes || *intr* (SEIN) move || **umzie'hen** §163 *ref*—**der Himmel hat sich umzogen** the sky has become overcast

umzingeln [ʊm'tsɪŋəln] *tr* encircle

Um'zug *m* procession, parade; *(Wohnungswechsel)* moving; (pol) march

un- [ʊn] *comb.fm.* un–, in–, ir–, non–

unab'änderlich *adj* unalterable

un'abhängig *adj* (von) independent (of) || **Unabhängige** §5 *mf* (pol) independent

Un'abhängigkeit *f* independence

unabkömm'lich *adj* unavailable; indispensable; (mil) essential *(on the homefront)*; **ich bin augenblicklich u. I** can't get away at the moment

unablässig ['ʊnaplɛsɪç] *adj* incessant

unablösbar [ʊnap'løsbɑr], **unablöslich** [ʊnap'løslɪç] *adj* unpayable

unabseh'bar *adj* unforeseeable; immense

unabsetz'bar *adj* irremovable

unabsicht'lich *adj* unintentional

unabwendbar [ʊnap'vɛntbɑr] *adj* inevitable

un'achtsam *adj* careless, inattentive

um'ähnlich *adj* dissimilar, unlike

unanfecht'bar *adj* indisputable

un'angebracht *adj* out of place

un'angefochten *adj* undisputed

un'angemessen *adj* improper; inadequate; unsuitable

un'angenehm *adj* unpleasant, disagreeable; awkward

un'annehmbar *adj* unacceptable

Un'annehmlichkeit *f* unpleasantness; annoyance, inconvenience; **Unannehmlichkeiten** trouble

un'ansehnlich *adj* unsightly; *(unscheinbar)* plain, inconspicuous

un'anständig *adj* indecent; obscene

un'antastbar *adj* unassailable

un'appetitlich *adj* unappetizing; *(ekelhaft)* unsavory

Un'art *f* bad habit; *(Ungezogenheit)*

naughtiness; *(schlechte Manieren)* bad manners

un'artig *adj* ill-behaved, naughty

un'aufdringlich *adj* unostentatious; unobtrusive

un'auffällig *adj* inconspicuous

unauffindbar ['ʊnaʊffɪntbɑr] *adj* not to be found

unaufgefordert ['ʊnaʊfgəfordərt] *adj* unasked, uncalled for || *adv* spontaneously

unaufhaltbar ['ʊnaʊfhaltbɑr], **unaufhaltsam** ['ʊnaʊfhaltzam] *adj* irresistible; relentless

unaufhörlich ['ʊnaʊfhørlɪç] *adj* incessant

un'aufmerksam *adj* inattentive

un'aufrichtig *adj* insincere

unaufschiebbar ['ʊnaʊf'ʃɪpbɑr] *adj* not to be postponed, urgent

unausbleiblich ['ʊnaʊsblaɪplɪç] *adj* inevitable

unausführbar ['ʊnaʊsfyrbɑr] *adj* unfeasible, impracticable

unausgeglichen ['ʊnaʊsgəglɪçən] *adj* uneven; (fig) unbalanced

unauslöschbar ['ʊnaʊslœʃbɑr], **unauslöschlich** ['ʊnaʊslœʃlɪç] *adj* inextinguishable; *(Tinte)* indelible

unaussprechlich ['ʊnaʊs'preçlɪç] *adj* unspeakable, ineffable

unausstehlich ['ʊnaʊsʃtelɪç] *adj* intolerable, insufferable

unbändig ['ʊnbɛndɪç] *adj* wild

un'barmherzig *adj* unmerciful

un'beabsichtigt *adj* unintentional

un'beachtet *adj* unobserved, unnoticed

unbeanstandet ['ʊnbə-anʃtandət] *adj* unopposed, unhampered

unbearbeitet ['ʊnbə-arbaɪtət] *adj* unworked; *(roh)* raw; *(Land)* untilled; (mach) unfinished

unbebaut ['ʊnbəbaʊt] *adj* uncultivated; *(Gelände)* undeveloped

unbedacht ['ʊnbədaxt] *adj* thoughtless

un'bedenklich *adj* unhesitating; unswerving; unobjectionable, harmless || *adv* without hesitation

un'bedeutend *adj* unimportant; slight

un'bedingt *adj* unconditional, unqualified; implicit

un'befahrbar *adj* impassable

un'befangen *adj* unembarrassed; *(unparteiisch)* impartial; natural, unaffected

unbefleckt ['ʊnbəflɛkt] *adj* immaculate

un'befriedigend *adj* unsatisfactory

un'befriedigt *adj* unsatisfied

un'befugt *adj* unauthorized; (jur) incompetent || **Unbefugte** §5 *mf* unauthorized person

un'begabt *adj* untalented

unbegreif'lich *adj* incomprehensible

un'begrenzt *adj* unlimited

un'begründet *adj* unfounded

Un'behagen *n* discomfort, uneasiness

un'behaglich *adj* uncomfortable

unbehelligt ['ʊnbəhɛlɪçt] *adj* undisturbed, unmolested

unbehindert ['ʊnbəhɪndərt] *adj* unhindered; unrestrained

unbeholfen ['ʊnbəhɔlfən] *adj* clumsy

unbeirrbar ['ʊnbə·ɪrbar] *adj* unwavering

unbeirrt ['ʊnbə·ɪrt] *adj* unswerving

un'bekannt *adj* unknown; unfamiliar; unacquainted; (*Ursache*) unexplained || **Unbekannte** §5 *m/f* stranger || *f* (math) unknown quantity

unbekümmert ['ʊnbəkymərt] *adj* (**um**) unconcerned (about)

un'beladen *adj* unloaded

unbelastet ['ʊnbəlastət] *adj* unencumbered; (*Wagen*) unloaded; carefree

un'belebt *adj* inanimate; (*Straße*) quiet; (com) slack

unbelichtet ['ʊnbəlɪçtət] *adj* (*Film*) unexposed

un'beliebt *adj* unpopular, disliked

unbemannt ['ʊnbəmant] *adj* unmanned

un'bemerkbar *adj* imperceptible

un'bemittelt *adj* poor

un'benommen *adj*—**es bleibt Ihnen u. zu** (*inf*) you are free to (*inf*); **es ist mir u., ob** it's up to me whether

unbenutzbar ['ʊnbənʊtsbar] *adj* unusable

unbenutzt ['ʊnbənʊtst] *adj* unused

un'bequem *adj* inconvenient; uncomfortable

unberechenbar ['ʊnbəreçənbar] *adj* incalculable; unpredictable

un'berechtigt *adj* unauthorized; unjustified

unbeschadet ['ʊnbəʃadət] *prep* (*genit*) without prejudice to

unbeschädigt ['ʊnbəʃedɪçt] *adj* unhurt; undamaged

un'bescheiden *adj* pushy

unbescholten ['ʊnbəʃɔltən] *adj* of good reputation

un'beschränkt *adj* unlimited; absolute

unbeschreiblich ['ʊnbəʃraɪplɪç] *adj* indescribable

unbesehen ['ʊnbəze·ən] *adv* sight unseen

un'besetzt *adj* unoccupied, vacant

unbesiegbar ['ʊnbəzikbar] *adj* invincible

unbesoldet ['ʊnbəzɔldət] *adj* unsalaried

un'besonnen *adj* thoughtless; careless; rash

un'besorgt *adj* unconcerned; carefree

un'beständig *adj* unsteady, inconstant; (*Preise*) fluctuating; (*Wetter*) changeable; (*Person*) fickle, unstable

unbestätigt ['ʊnbəʃtetɪçt] *adj* unconfirmed

un'bestechlich *adj* incorruptible

un'bestimmt *adj* indeterminate; vague; (*unsicher*) uncertain; (*unentschieden*) undecided; (gram) indefinite

unbestraft ['ʊnbəʃtraft] *adj* unpunished

unbestreit'bar *adj* indisputable

unbestritten ['ʊnbəʃtrɪtən] *adj* undisputed, uncontested

unbeteiligt ['ʊnbətaɪlɪçt] *adj* uninterested; indifferent; impartial

un'beträchtlich *adj* trifling, slight

unbeugsam ['ʊnbɔɪkzam] *adj* inflexible

unbewacht ['ʊnbəvaxt] *adj* unguarded

unbewaffnet ['ʊnbəvafnət] *adj* unarmed; (*Auge*) naked

un'beweglich *adj* immovable; motionless

unbewiesen ['ʊnbəvizən] *adj* unproved

unbewohnt ['ʊnbəvont] *adj* uninhabited

un'bewußt *adj* unconscious; involuntary

unbezähmbar [ʊnbə'tsembar] *adj* untamable; (fig) uncontrollable

Un'bilden *pl*—**U. der Witterung** inclement weather

Un'bildung *f* lack of education

un'billig *adj* unfair

unbotmäßig ['ʊnbotmesɪç] *adj* unruly; insubordinate

unbrauch'bar *adj* useless, of no use

un'bußfertig *adj* unrepentant

un'christlich *adj* unchristian

und [ʊnt] *conj* and; **und? so what?** **und wenn even if**

Un'dank *m* ingratitude

un'dankbar *adj* ungrateful; thankless

Un'dankbarkeit *f* ingratitude

undatiert ['ʊndatirt] *adj* undated

undenk'bar *adj* unthinkable

undenklich [ʊn'deŋklɪç] *adj*—**seit undenklichen Zeiten** from time immemorial

un'deutlich *adj* unclear, indistinct

un'deutsch *adj* un-German

un'dicht *adj* not tight; leaky

Un'ding *n* nonsense, absurdity

un'duldsam *adj* intolerant

undurchdring'lich *adj* (**für**) impervious (to); **undurchdringliche Miene** poker face

undurchführ'bar *adj* not feasible

un'durchlässig *adj* (**für**) impervious (to)

un'durchsichtig *adj* opaque; (*Beweggründe*) hidden; (*Machenschaften*) shady

un'eben *adj* uneven; bumpy; **nicht u.!** (coll) not bad!

un'echt *adj* false, spurious; artificial; imitation; (*Farbe*) fading

un'edel *adj* ignoble; (*Metall*) base

un'ehelich *adj* illegitimate

Un'ehre *f* dishonor

un'ehrenhaft *adj* dishonorable

un'ehrerbietig *adj* disrespectful

un'ehrlich *adj* dishonest; underhand

un'eigennützig *adj* unselfish

un'einig *adj* disunited; at odds

Un'einigkeit *f* disagreement

uneinnehm'bar *adj* impregnable

un'eins *adj* at odds, at variance

un'empfänglich *adj* (**für**) insusceptible (to)

un'empfindlich *adj* (**gegen**) insensitive (to); (**gegen**) insensible (to)

unend'lich *adj* endless; infinite; **auf u. einstellen** (phot) set at infinity || *adv* endlessly; infinitely; **u. viele** an endless number of

unentbehr'lich *adj* indispensible

unentrinnbar [ʊnent'rɪnbar] *adj* inescapable

un'entschieden *adj* undecided; (*schwankend*) indecisive; (sport) tie || **Unentschieden** *n* (—s;—) (sport) tie

Un'entschiedenheit *f* indecision

un'entschlossen *adj* irresolute

Un'entschlossenheit *f* indecision
unentschuld'bar *adj* inexcusable
unentwegt ['unɛntvekt] *adj* staunch; unswerving || *adv* continuously; untiringly || **Unentwegte** §5 *mf* die-hard
unentwirrbar ['unɛntvɪrbar] *adj* inextricable
unerbittlich [unɛr'bɪtlɪç] *adj* inexorable; (*Tatsache*) hard
un'erfahren *adj* inexperienced
unerfindlich [unɛr'fɪntlɪç] *adj* incomprehensible, mysterious
unerforschlich [unɛr'fɔr/lɪç] *adj* inscrutable
unerfreulich ['unɛrfrɔilɪç] *adj* unpleasant
unerfüllbar [unɛr'fylbar] *adj* unattainable
un'ergiebig *adj* unproductive
un'ergründlich *adj* unfathomable
un'erheblich *adj* insignificant; **(für)** irrelevant (to)
unerhört [unɛr'hørt] *adj* unheard-of, unprecedented; outrageous || **un'erhört** *adj* (*Bitte*) unanswered
un'erkannt *adj* unrecognized || *adv* incognito
unerklär'lich *adj* inexplicable
unerläßlich [unɛr'lɛslɪç] *adj* indispensable
un'erlaubt *adj* illicit, unauthorized
un'erledigt *adj* unsettled, unfinished
unermeßlich [unɛr'mɛslɪç] *adj* immense
unermüdlich [unɛr'mydlɪç] *adj* untiring; (*Person*) indefatigable
unerquicklich [unɛr'kvɪklɪç] *adj* unpleasant
unerreich'bar *adj* unattainable, out of reach
unerreicht ['unɛrraɪçt] *adj* unrivaled
unersättlich [unɛr'zɛtlɪç] *adj* insatiable
unerschlossen ['unɛr/lɔsən] *adj* undeveloped; (*Boden*) unexploited
unerschöpflich [unɛr'/øpflɪç] *adj* inexhaustible
unerschrocken ['unɛr/rɔkən] *adj* intrepid, fearless
unerschütterlich [unɛr'/ytərlɪç] *adj* unshakable; imperturbable
unerschwing'lich *adj* unattainable; beyond one's means; exorbitant
unersetz'bar, unersetz'lich *adj* irreplaceable; (*Schaden*) irreparable
unerträg'lich *adj* intolerable
unerwähnt ['unɛrvent] *adj* unmentioned; **u. lassen** pass over in silence
unerwartet ['unɛrvartət] *adj* unexpected, sudden
unerweis'lich *adj* unprovable
un'erwünscht *adj* undesired; unwelcome
unerzogen ['unɛrtsogən] *adj* ill-bred
un'fähig *adj* incapable, unable; unqualified, inefficient
Un'fähigkeit *f* inability; inefficiency
Un'fall *m* accident, mishap
Un'fallflucht *f* hit-and-run offense
Un'fallstation *f* first-aid station
Un'falltod *m* accidental death
Un'fallversicherung *f* accident insurance
Un'fallziffer *m* accident rate

unfaß'bar, unfaß'lich *adj* incomprehensible; inconceivable
unfehl'bar *adj* infallible; unfailing
Unfehl'barkeit *f* infallibility
un'fein *adj* coarse; indelicate
un'fern *adj* near; **u. von** not far from || *prep* (*genit*) not far from
un'fertig *adj* not ready; not finished; immature
Unflat ['unflat] *m* (-s;) dirt, filth
unflätig ['unfletɪç] *adj* dirty, filthy
un'folgsam *adj* disobedient
Un'folgsamkeit *f* disobedience
unförmig ['unfœrmɪç] *adj* shapeless
un'förmlich *adj* informal
unfrankiert ['unfraŋkirt] *adj* unfranked, unstamped
un'frei *adj* not free; unstamped || *adv* —**u. schicken** send c.o.d.
un'freiwillig *adj* involuntary
un'freundlich *adj* unfriendly, unkind
Un'friede *m* dissension, discord
un'fruchtbar *adj* unfruitful, sterile; (fig) fruitless
Unfug ['unfuk] *m* (-[e]s;) nuisance, disturbance; mischief; misdemeanor; **U. treiben** cause mischief
ungang'bar *adj* impassable; unsalable
Ungar ['ungar] *m* (-;-n), **Ungarin** ['ungarin] *f* (-;-nen) Hungarian
ungarisch ['ungarɪ/] *adj* Hungarian
Ungarn ['ungarn] *n* (-s;) Hungary
un'gastlich *adj* inhospitable
ungeachtet ['ungə-axtət] *adj* not esteemed || *prep* (*genit*) regardless of
ungeahnt ['ungə-ant] *adj* unexpected
ungebärdig ['ungəberdɪç] *adj* unruly
ungebeten ['ungəbetən] *adj* unbidden
ungebeugt ['ungəbɔikt] *adj* unbowed; (gram) uninflected
un'gebildet *adj* uneducated
un'gebräuchlich *adj* unusual; (*veraltet*) obsolete
un'gebraucht *adj* unused
Un'gebühr *f* indecency, impropriety
un'gebührlich *adj* indecent, improper
ungebunden ['ungəbundən] *adj* unbound; (*ausschweifend*) loose, dissolute; (*frei*) unrestrained; **ungebundene Rede** prose
ungedeckt ['ungədekt] *adj* uncovered; (*Tisch*) unset; (*Haus*) roofless; (*Kosten*) unpaid; (*Scheck*) overdrawn
Un'geduld *f* impatience
un'geduldig *adj* impatient
un'geeignet *adj* unfit, unsuitable; unqualified
ungefähr ['ungəfer] *adj* approximate || *adv* approximately, about; **nicht von u.** on purpose
ungefährdet ['ungəferdət] *adj* safe, unendangered
un'gefährlich *adj* not dangerous
un'gefällig *adj* discourteous
un'gefüge *adj* monstrous; clumsy
un'gefügig *adj* unyielding, inflexible
ungefüttert ['ungəfytərt] *adj* unlined
un'gehalten *adj* (*Versprechen*) unkept, broken; **(über** *acc*) indignant (at)
ungeheißen ['ungəhaɪsən] *adv* of one's own accord
ungehemmt ['ungəhemt] *adj* unchecked

ungeheuer ['ʊngəhɔɪ.ər] *adj* huge; monstrous ‖ *adv* tremendously ‖ **Ungeheuer** *n* (-s;-) monster

un'geheuerlich *adj* monstrous ‖ *adv* (coll) tremendously

ungehobelt ['ʊngəhobəlt] *adj* unplaned; (fig) uncouth

un'gehörig *adj* improper; (*Stunde*) ungodly

Un'gehörigkeit *f* (-;-en) impropriety

un'gehorsam *adj* disobedient ‖ **Ungehorsam** *m* (-s;) disobedience

un'gekünstelt *adj* unaffected, natural

un'gekürzt *adj* unabridged

un'gelegen *adj* inconvenient

Un'gelegenheiten *pl* inconvenience

un'gelehrig *adj* unteachable

un'gelenk *adj* clumsy; stiff

un'gelernt *adj* (coll) unskilled

Un'gemach *n* discomfort; trouble

un'gemein *adj* uncommon

un'gemütlich *adj* uncomfortable; (*Zimmer*) dreary; (*Person*) disagreeable

un'genannt *adj* anonymous

un'genau *adj* inaccurate, inexact

ungeniert ['ʊnʒenirt] *adj* informal ‖ *adv* freely

ungenieß'bar *adj* inedible; undrinkable; (& fig) unpalatable

un'genügend *adj* insufficient; **u. bekommen** get a failing grade

ungepflastert ['ʊngəpflastərt] *adj* unpaved, dirt

un'gerade *adj* uneven; crooked; (*Zahl*) odd

un'geraten *adj* spoiled

un'gerecht *adj* unjust, unfair

Un'gerechtigkeit *f* injustice

ungereimt ['ʊngəraɪmt] *adj* unrhymed; (*unvernünft*) absurd; **ungereimtes Zeug reden** talk nonsense

un'gern *adv* unwillingly, reluctantly

ungerührt ['ʊngəryrt] *adj* (fig) unmoved

un'geschehen *adj* undone; **u. machen** undo

ungescheut ['ʊngəʃɔɪt] *adv* without fear

Un'geschick *n*, **Un'geschicklichkkeit** *f* awkwardness

un'geschickt *adj* awkward, clumsy

ungeschlacht ['ʊngəʃlaxt] *adj* uncouth

ungeschliffen ['ʊngəʃlɪfən] *adj* unpolished; (*Messer*) blunt; (*Edelstein*) uncut; (fig) rude

ungeschminkt ['ʊngəʃmɪŋkt] *adj* without makeup; (*Wahrheit*) unvarnished

un'gesellig *adj* unsociable

un'gesetzlich *adj* illegal

ungesittet ['ʊngəzɪtət] *adj* unmannerly; uncivilized

ungestört ['ʊngəʃtørt] *adj* undisturbed

ungestraft ['ʊngəʃtraft] *adj* unpunished ‖ *adv* scot-free

ungestüm ['ʊngəʃtym] *adj* impetuous, violent ‖ **Ungestüm** *n* (-[e]s;) impetuosity, violence

un'gesund *adj* unhealthy; unwholesome

ungeteilt ['ʊngətaɪlt] *adj* undivided

un'getreu *adj* disloyal, untrue

ungetrübt ['ʊngətrypt] *adj* cloudless; clear; (fig) untroubled

Ungetüm ['ʊngətym] *n* (-[e]s;-e) monster

ungeübt ['ʊngə.ypt] *adj* untrained; (*Arbeiter*) inexperienced

un'gewandt *adj* unskillful; clumsy

un'gewiß *adj* uncertain; **j-n im ungewissen lassen** keep s.o. in suspense

Un'gewißheit *f* uncertainty

Un'gewitter *n* storm

un'gewöhnlich *adj* unusual

un'gewohnt *adj* unusual; (*genit*) unaccustomed (to)

ungezählt ['ʊngətsɛlt] *adj* countless

Ungeziefer ['ʊngətsifər] *n* (-s;) vermin, bugs

ungeziemend ['ʊngətsimənt] *adj* improper; (*frech*) impudent

un'gezogen *adj* rude; naughty

ungezügelt ['ʊngətsygəlt] *adj* unbridled

un'gezwungen *adj* unforced; natural, easy-going

Un'glaube *m* disbelief, unbelief

un'gläubig *adj* incredulous; (*heidnisch*) infidel ‖ **Ungläubige** §5 *mf* infidel

unglaub'lich *adj* incredible

un'glaubwürdig *adj* untrustworthy; incredible

un'gleich *adj* uneven, unequal; (*ähnlich*) unlike, dissimilar; (*Zahl*) odd ‖ *adv* much, far, by far

un'gleichartig *adj* heterogeneous

un'gleichförmig *adj* unequal; irregular

Un'gleichheit *f* inequality; difference, dissimilarity; unevenness

un'gleichmäßig *adj* disproportionate

Unglimpf ['ʊnglɪmpf] *m* (-[e]s;-e) harshness; wrong, insult

un'glimpflich *adj* harsh

Un'glück *n* (-s;) bad luck; (*Unfall*) accident; disaster, calamity

un'glücklich *adj* unlucky; unfortunate; unhappy

un'glücklicherweise *adv* unfortunately

Un'glücksbote *m* bearer of bad news

Un'glücksbringer *m* (-s;-) jinx

un'glückselig *adj* miserable; disastrous

Un'glücksfall *m* accident, misfortune

Un'glücksmensch *m* unlucky person

Un'glücksrabe *m*, **Un'glücksvogel** *m* unlucky fellow

Un'gnade *f* (-;) disfavor, displeasure

un'gnädig *adj* ungracious; **etw u. aufnehmen** take s.th. amiss

un'gültig *adj* null and void, invalid; **für u. erklären** nullify, void

Un'gültigkeit *f* invalidity

Un'gültigkeitserklärung *f* annulment

Un'gunst *f* disfavor; **zu meinen Ungunsten** to my disadvantage

un'günstig *adj* unfavorable, bad, adverse

un'gut *adj* unkind; **nichts für u.!** no offense!; **ungutes Gefühl** misgivings

un'haltbar *adj* not durable; untenable

un'handlich *adj* unwieldy, unhandy

Un'heil *n* disaster; mischief; **U. anrichten** cause mischief; **U. heraufbeschwören** ask for trouble

unheil'bar *adj* incurable; irreparable

un'heilvoll *adj* ominous; disastrous

un'heimlich *adj* uncanny; sinister

un'höflich *adj* impolite, uncivil

Un'höflichkeit f impoliteness
un'hold adj unkind || **Unhold** m (-[e]s; -e) fiend
un'hörbar adj inaudible
un'hygienisch adj unsanitary
Uni ['uni] f (-;-s) (Universität) (coll) university
uniform [uni'form] adj uniform || **Uniform** f (-;-en) uniform
Uni·kum ['unikum] n (-s;-s & -ka [ka]) unique example; (coll) queer duck
un'interessant adj uninteresting
un'interessiert adj (an dat) uninterested (in)
Union [un'jon] f (-;-en) union
universal [univer'zal] adj universal
Universal'mittel n panacea, cure-all
Universal'schlüssel m monkey wrench
Universität [universi'tet] f (-;-en) university
Universitäts'auswahlmannschaft f varsity (team)
Universum [uni'verzum] n (-s;) universe
Unke ['uŋkə] f (-;-n) toad
unken ['uŋkən] intr (coll) be a prophet of doom
un'kenntlich adj unrecognizable; **u. machen** disguise
Un'kenntnis f (-;) ignorance
Un'kenruf m croak
un'keusch adj unchaste
un'kindlich adj precocious; (Verhalten) disrespectful
un'kirchlich adj secular, worldly
un'klar adj unclear; muddy; misty; **im unklaren sein über** (acc) be in the dark about
Un'klarheit f obscurity
un'kleidsam adj unbecoming
un'klug adj unwise, imprudent
Un'klugheit f imprudence; foolish act
un'kontrollierbar adj unverifiable
un'körperlich adj incorporeal
Un'kosten pl expenses, costs; overhead; **sich in U. stürzen** go to great expense
Un'kraut n weed, weeds; **U. jäten** pull weeds
Un'krautvertilgungsmittel n weed killer
un'kündbar adj binding; (Darlehen) irredeemable; (Stellung) permanent
un'kundig adj (genit) ignorant (of), unacquainted (with)
unlängst ['unleŋst] adv recently, the other day
un'lauter adj unfair
un'leidlich adj intolerable
un'lenksam adj unruly
unles'bar, unle'serlich adj illegible
unleugbar ['unloikbar] adj indisputable, undeniable
un'lieb adj disagreeable; **es ist mir u. I am sorry**
un'logisch adj illogical
unlös'bar adj (Problem) unsolvable; (untrennbar) inseparable; (chem) insoluble
unlös'lich adj (chem) insoluble
Un'lust f reluctance; listlessness
un'lustig adj reluctant; listless

un'manierlich adj impolite
un'männlich adj unmanly
Un'maß n excess; **im U.** to excess
Un'masse f (coll) vast amount, lots
un'maßgeblich adj unauthoritative; irrelevant; **nach meiner unmaßgeblichen Meinung** in my humble opinion
un'mäßig adj immoderate; excessive
Un'menge f (coll)—e-e U. von lots of
Un'mensch m brute, monster
un'menschlich adj inhuman, brutal
Un'menschlichkeit f brutality
un'merklich adj imperceptible
un'methodisch adj unmethodical
un'mißverständlich adj unmistakable
un'mittelbar adj direct, immediate
un'möbliert adj unfurnished
un'modern adj outmoded
un'möglich, unmög'lich adj impossible
Un'möglichkeit f impossibility
Un'moral f immorality
un'moralisch adj immoral
un'mündig adj underage
un'musikalisch adj unmusical
Un'mut m (über acc) displeasure (at)
un'mutig adj displeased, annoyed
unnachahmlich ['unnaxamliç] adj inimitable
un'nachgiebig adj unyielding
un'nachsichtig adj unrelenting, inexorable; strict
unnahbar [un'nabar] adj inaccessible
un'natürlich adj unnatural
un'nennbar adj inexpressible
un'nötig adj unnecessary
unnütz ['unnyts] adj useless; vain
un'ordentlich adj disorderly; untidy
Un'ordnung f disorder; mess; **in U. bringen** throw into disorder
un'organisch adj inorganic
un'paar, un'paarig adj unpaired, odd
un'parteiisch, un'parteilich adj impartial, disinterested
Un'parteilichkeit f impartiality
un'passend adj unsuitable; (unschicklich) improper; (unzeitgemäß) untimely
un'passierbar adj impassable
unpäßlich ['unpesliç] adj indisposed, ill
un'patriotisch adj unpatriotic
un'persönlich adj impersonal
un'politisch adj nonpolitical
un'populär adj unpopular
un'praktisch adj impractical; (unerfahren) unskillful
Un'rast f restlessness
Un'rat m (-[e]s;) garbage; dirt; **U. wittern** (coll) smell a rat
un'rätlich, un'ratsam adj inadvisable
un'recht adj wrong || **Unrecht** n (-[e]s;) —**im U. sein** be in the wrong; **j-m U. geben** decide against s.o.; **mit** (or **zu**) **U. wrongly; unjustly; illegally**
un'redlich adj dishonest
Un'redlichkeit f dishonesty
un'reell adj unfair
un'regelmäßig adj irregular
Un'regelmäßigkeit f irregularity
un'reif adj unripe, green; (fig) immature
Un'reife f unripeness; immaturity
un'rein adj unclean; (& fig) impure;

ins u. schreiben make a rough copy of
Un′reinheit f uncleanness; (& fig) impurity
un′reinlich adj dirty
un′rentabel adj unprofitable
un′rettbar adj irrecoverable
un′richtig adj incorrect, wrong
un′ritterlich adj unchivalrous
Un′ruh f (-;-en) (horol) balance wheel
Un′ruhe f restlessness; uneasiness; (Aufruhr) commotion, riot; (Störung) disturbance; (Besorgnis) anxiety
un′ruhig adj restless; uneasy; (laut) noisy; (Pferd) restive; (Meer) choppy; (nervös) jumpy
un′rühmlich adj inglorious
Un′ruhstifter **-in** §6 mf agitator, troublemaker; (Wirrkopf) screwball
uns [ʊns] pers pron us; to us || reflx pron ourselves; **wir sind doch unter uns** we are by ourselves || recip pron each other, one another; **wir sehen uns später** we′ll meet later
un′sachgemäß adj inexpert
un′sachlich adj subjective; personal
unsagbar [ʊn′zɑːkbɑr], **unsäglich** [ʊn′zɛːkliç] adj unspeakable; (fig) immense
un′sauber adj unclean; (unlauter) unfair, dirty
un′schädlich adj harmless
un′scharf adj (Apparat) out of focus; (Bild) blurred; (Begriff) poorly defined
un′schätzbar adj inestimable, invaluable
un′scheinbar adj inconspicuous, insignificant
un′schicklich adj unbecoming; indecent
Un′schicklichkeit f impropriety
un′schlüssig adj indecisive
Un′schlüssigkeit f indecision, hesitation
un′schmackhaft adj insipid, unpalatable
un′schön adj unlovely; plain, homely; (Angelegenheit) unpleasant
Un′schuld f innocence; **ich wasche meine Hände in U.** I wash my hands of it
un′schuldig adj innocent; (keusch) chaste; harmless; **sich für u. erklären** (jur) plead not guilty
un′schwer adj not difficult
Un′segen m adversity; (Fluch) curse
un′selbständig adj dependent, helpless
un′selig adj unfortunate; (Ereignis) fatal
unser [′ʊnzər] §2,3 poss adj our || §2,4 poss pron ours || pers pron us; of us; **erinnerst du dich unser noch?** do you still remember us?; **es waren unser vier** there were four of us
unseresgleichen [′ʊnzərəs′glaɪçən] pron people like us; the likes of us
unserige [′ʊnzərɪgə] §2,5 pron ours
unserthalben [′ʊnzərt′halbən], **unsert-wegen** [′ʊnzərt′veːgən] adv for our sake, on our behalf, on our account
un′sicher adj unsafe; shaky; precarious

Un′sicherheit f unsafeness; shakiness; insecurity; precariousness
un′sichtbar adj invisible
Un′sinn m (-[e]s;) nonsense, rubbish; **U. machen** fool around
un′sinnig adj nonsensical
Un′sitte f bad habit
un′sittlich adj immoral, indecent
Un′sittlichkeit f immorality
unsolid(e) adj unsolid; (Person) loose; (Firma) unreliable, shaky
unsortiert [′ʊnzɔrtirt] adj unsorted
un′sozial adj antisocial
un′sportlich adj unsportsmanlike
unsrerseits [′ʊnzrər′zaɪts] adv as for us, for our part
unsrige [′ʊnzrɪgə] §2,5 poss pron ours
un′ständig adj impermanent, temporary
un′statthaft adj inadmissible; forbidden
unsterb′lich adj immortal
Unsterb′lichkeit f immortality
Un′stern m unlucky star; (fig) disaster
un′stet adj unsteady; restless; changeable
un′stillbar adj unappeasable; (Durst) unquenchable; (Hunger) unsatiable
unstimmig [′ʊn′tɪmɪç] adj discrepant; inconsistent
Un′stimmigkeit f (-;-en) discrepancy; inconsistency; (Widerspruch) disagreement
un′sträflich adj blameless; guileless
un′streitig adj indisputable
Un′summe f enormous sum
un′symmetrisch adj asymmetrical
un′sympathisch adj unpleasant; **er ist mir u.** I don′t like him
un′tadelhaft adj blameless; flawless
Un′tat f crime
un′tätig adj inactive
un′tauglich adj unfit, unsuitable; useless; (Person) incompetent; **u. machen** disqualify
un′teilbar adj indivisible
unten [′ʊntən] adv below, beneath; downstairs; **da u.** down there; **er ist bei ihnen u. durch** they are through with him; **nach u.** downstairs; downwards; **tief u.** far below; **u. am Berge** at the foot of the mountain; **u. an der Seite** at the bottom of the page; **von u. her** from underneath
unter [′ʊntər] prep (dat) under, below; beneath, underneath; (zwischen) among; (während) during; **ganz u. uns gesagt** just between you and me; **u. aller Kritik** beneath contempt; **u. anderem** among other things; **u. diesem Gesichtspunkt** from this point of view; **u. Null** below zero; **was versteht man unter...?** what is meant by...? || prep (acc) under, below; beneath, underneath; among || **Unter** m (-s;-) (cards) jack
Unter-, unter- comb.fm. under-, sub-; lower
Un′terabteilung f subdivision
Un′terarm m forearm
Un′terart f subspecies
Un′terausschuß m subcommittee
Un′terbau m (-[e]s;-ten) foundation

un'terbelichten *tr* underexpose
un'terbewußt *adj* subconscious
Un'terbewußtsein *n* subconscious
unterbie'ten §58 *tr* undercut, undersell; underbid
un'terbinden §59 *tr* tie underneath || unterbin'den §59 *tr* (*Verkehr*) tie up; (*Blutgefäß*) tie off; (*verhindern*) prevent; (*Angriff*) neutralize
Unterbin'dung *f* stoppage; (surg) ligature
unterblei'ben §62 *intr* (SEIN) remain undone; not take place; be discontinued; **das muß u.** that must be stopped
unterbre'chen §64 *tr* interrupt; (*einstellen*) suspend; (*Schweigen, Stille, Kontakt*) break; (*Verkehr*) hold up; (telp) disconnect; **die Reise in München u.** have a stopover in Munich || *ref* stop short
Unterbre'cher *m* (elec) circuit breaker
Unterbre'chung *f* interruption; disconnection; (*e–r Fahrt*) stopover
unterbrei'ten *tr* submit
un'terbringen §65 *tr* provide a place for; find room for; (*Gäste*) accommodate, put up; (*Stapeln*) store; (*Anleihe*) place; (*Geld*) invest; (*Pferde*) stable; (*Wagen*) park; (*Truppe*) billet; **e–n Artikel bei e–r Zeitung u.** have an article published in a newspaper; **j–n auf e–m Posten** (or **in e–r Stellung**) **u.** find s.o. a job, place s.o.
Un'terbringung *f* (–;–en) accommodations, housing; billet; storage; investment; placement
Un'terbringungsmöglichkeiten *pl* accommodations
unterdes [untər'des], unterdessen [untər'desən] *adv* meanwhile
Un'terdruck *m* low pressure
unterdrücken (unterdrük'ken) *tr* suppress; (*Aufstand*) quell; (*bedrücken*) oppress; (*ersticken*) stifle; (*Seufzer*) repress
Un'terdruckgebiet *n* low-pressure area
Unterdrückung (Unterdrük'kung) *f* (–;) oppression; suppression
untere ['untərə] §9 *adj* lower, inferior
untereinan'der *adv* among one another; mutually; reciprocally
unterentwickelt ['untərentvikəlt] *adj* underdeveloped
unterernährt ['untərernert] *adj* undernourished
Un'terernährung *f* (–;) undernourishment
Un'terfamilie *f* subfamily
unterfer'tigen *tr* sign
Unterfüh'rung *f* (–;–en) underpass
unterfüt'tern *tr* line
Un'tergang *m* setting; (fig) decline, fall; (naut) sinking
unterge'ben *adj* (*dat*) subject (to), inferior (to) || **Untergebene** §5 *mf* subordinate
un'tergehen §82 *intr* (SEIN) go down, sink; (fig) perish; (astr) set
untergeordnet ['untərgə·ərdnət] *adj* subordinate || **Untergeordnete** §5 *mf* subordinate

Un'tergeschoß *n* ground floor; (*Kellergeschoß*) basement
Un'tergestell *n* undercarriage
Un'tergewand *n* underwear
un'tergliedern *tr* subdivide
untergra'ben §87 *tr* undermine
Un'tergrund *m* subsoil
Un'tergrundbahn *f* subway
Un'tergrundbewegung *f* underground movement
un'terhalb *prep* (*genit*) below
Un'terhalt *m* (–[e]s) support; maintenance, upkeep; livelihood
un'terhalten §90 *tr* hold under || unterhal'ten §90 *tr* maintain; support; (*Briefwechsel*) keep up; (*Feuer*) feed; entertain, amuse || *ref* enjoy oneself, have a good time; amuse oneself; **sich u. mit** talk with
unterhaltsam [untər'haltzam] *adj* entertaining, amusing, enjoyable
Un'terhaltsbeitrag *m* alimony; (*für Kinder*) support
Unterhaltsberechtigte ['untərhaltsbə·reçtigtə] §5 *mf* dependent
Un'terhaltskosten *pl* living expenses
Unterhal'tung *f* (–;–en) entertainment, amusement; (*Gespräch*) conversation; (*Aufrechterhaltung*) upkeep; (*Unterstützung*) support
Unterhal'tungskosten *pl* maintenance cost, maintenance
Unterhal'tungslektüre *f* light reading
unterhan'deln *intr* negotiate
Un'terhändler **–in** §6 *mf* negotiator; (*Vermittler*) mediator
Unterhand'lung *f* (–;–en) negotiation
Un'terhaus *n* (parl) lower house
Un'terhemd *n* undershirt
unterhöh'len *tr* undermine
Un'terholz *n* undergrowth, underbrush
Un'terhose *f* shorts; panties; **in Unterhosen zeigen** (coll) debunk
un'terirdisch *adj* underground, subterranean; (myth) of the underworld
Un'terjacke *f* vest
unterjo'chen *tr* subjugate
Unterjo'chung *f* (–;) subjugation
Un'terkiefer *m* lower jaw
Un'terkinn *n* double chin
Un'terkleid *n* slip
Un'terkleidung *f* (–;) underwear
un'terkommen §99 *intr* (SEIN) find accommodations; find employment || **Unterkommen** *n* (–s;) accommodations; (*Stellung*) job
Un'terkörper *m* lower part of the body
un'terkriegen *tr* (coll) get the better of; **er läßt sich nicht u.** he won't knuckle under
Unterkunft ['untərkunft] *f* (–;–ᵉe) accommodations; apartment; (*Obdach*) shelter, place to stay; (mil) quarters; **U. und Verpflegung** room and board
Un'terlage *f* foundation; base; pad; desk pad; rubber pad (*for a bed*); (*Teppich–*) underpad; (*Beleg*) voucher; (*Urkunde*) document; (archit) support; (geol) substratum; **keine Unterlagen haben** have nothing to go on; **Unterlagen** documentation; data
Un'terland *n* lowland

Unterlaß ['untərlas] *m*—**ohne U.** without letup

unterlas'sen §104 *tr* omit; neglect; skip; stop, cut out

Unterlas'sung *f* (–;–en) omission; neglect; failure

Unterlas'sungssünde *f* sin of omission

unterlau'fen *adj*—**blau u.** black-and-blue; **mit Blut u.** bloodshot ‖ **un'terlaufen** §105 *intr* (SEIN) (*Fehler*) slip in

un'terlegen *tr* lay under, put under; (*Bedeutung, Sinn*) attach; **der Musik Worte u.** set words to music ‖ **unterle'gen** *adj* defeated; (*dat*) inferior (to) ‖ **Unterlegene** §5 *mf* loser

Unterle'genheit *f* (–;) inferiority

Unterlegring ['untərlekrɪŋ] *m*, **Unterlegscheibe** ['untərlek/aɪbə] *f* washer

Un'terleib *m* abdomen

Unterleibs– *comb.fm.* abdominal

unterlie'gen §108 *intr* (SEIN) (*dat*) be beaten (by), lose (to); **e-m Rabatt u.** be subject to discount ‖ *impers* (SEIN)—**es unterliegt keinem Zweifel, daß** there is no doubt that

Un'terlippe *f* lower lip

unterma'len *tr* put the primer on; **mit Musik u.** accompany with music

untermau'ern *tr* support

Un'termiete *f* (–;) subletting; **in U. abgeben** sublet; **in U. wohnen bei** sublet from

Un'termieter *m* §6 *mf* subtenant

unterminie'ren *tr* (fig) undermine

unterneh'men §116 *tr* undertake; (*versuchen*) attempt; **Schritte u.** (fig) take steps ‖ **Unternehmen** *n* (–s;–) undertaking; venture; enterprise; (mil) operation

unterneh'mend *adj* enterprising

Unterneh'mensberater *m* management consultant

Unterneh'mer **–in** §6 *mf* entrepreneur; (*Arbeitgeber*) employer; (*Bau–*) contractor

Unterneh'mung *f* (–;–en) undertaking; enterprise, business; (mil) operation

Unterneh'mungsgeist *m* initiative

unterneh'mungslustig *adj* enterprising

Un'teroffizier *m* noncommissioned officer, N.C.O.

un'terordnen *tr* (*dat*) subordinate (to) ‖ *ref* (*dat*) submit (to)

unterre'den *ref* (*mit*) confer (with)

Unterre'dung *f* (–;–en) conference

Unterricht ['untərɪçt] *m* (–[e]s;–e) instruction, lessons

unterrich'ten *tr* instruct; **u. von** (or **über** *acc*) inform (of, about)

Un'terrichtsfach *n* subject, course

Un'terrichtsfilm *m* educational film; (mil) training film

Un'terrichtsministerium *n* department of public instruction

Un'terrichtsstunde *f* (educ) period

Un'terrichtswesen *n* education; teaching

Un'terrock *m* slip

untersa'gen *tr* forbid, prohibit

Un'tersatz *m* saucer; support; (*Gestell*) stand; (archit) socle; (log) minor premise

unterschät'zen *tr* underrate, underestimate; undervalue

unterschei'den §112 *tr* distinguish ‖ *ref* (**von**) differ (from)

Unterschei'dung *f* (–;–en) difference, distinction

Un'terschenkel *m* shank

un'terschieben §130 *tr* shove under; (**statt** *genit*) substitute (for); (*dat*) impute (to), foist (on)

Unterschied ['untər/it] *m* (–[e]s;–e) difference, distinction; **zum U. von** as distinct from, unlike

un'terschiedlich *adj* different; varying

un'terschiedslos *adj* indiscriminate

unterschla'gen §132 *tr* embezzle; (*Nachricht*) suppress; (*Brief*) intercept

Unterschla'gung *f* (–;–en) embezzlement; suppression; interception

Unterschlupf ['untər/lupf] *m* (–[e]s;) shelter; hide-out

unterschrei'ben §62 *tr* sign; (fig) subscribe to, agree to

Un'terschrift *f* signature

Un'terseeboot *n* submarine

unterseeisch ['untərze-ɪʃ] *adj* submarine

Un'terseekabel *n* transoceanic cable

Un'terseite *f* underside

untersetzt [untər'zetst] *adj* stocky

Un'tersetzung *f* (–;–en) (mech) reduction

un'tersinken §143 *intr* (SEIN) go down

Un'terstand *m* (mil) dugout

unterste ['untərstə] §9 *adj* lowest, bottom

unterste'hen §146 *ref* dare; **untersteh dich!** don't you dare! ‖ *intr* (*dat*) be under (*s.o.*) ‖ **un'terstehen** §146 *intr* take shelter

un'terstellen *tr* place under; (*Auto*) put into the garage ‖ *ref* take cover ‖ **unterstel'len** *tr* assume, suppose; (*dat*) impute (to); (mil) (*dat*) put under the command (of)

Unterstel'lung *f* (–;–en) assumption; imputation

unterstrei'chen §85 *tr* underline

unterstüt'zen *tr* support, back; help

Unterstüt'zung *f* (–;–en) support, backing; assistance; (*Beihilfe durch Geld*) relief; (ins) benefit

untersu'chen *tr* examine, inspect; investigate; study, do research on; (chem) analyze

Untersu'chung *f* (–;–en) examination; inspection; investigation; study, research; (chem) analysis

Untersu'chungsausschuß *m* fact-finding committee

Untersu'chungsgericht *n* court of inquiry

Untersu'chungshaft *f* (jur) detention

Untersu'chungsrichter *m* examining judge

Untertagebau [untər'tagəbau] *m* (–[e]s;) mine

Untertan ['untərtan] *m* (–s & –en;–en) subject

untertänig [untər'tenɪç] *adj* submissive

Un'tertasse *f* saucer; **fliegende U.** flying saucer

un'tertauchen *tr* submerge; duck || *intr* (SEIN) dive; (fig) disappear || **Unter-tauchen** *n* (-s;) dive; disappearance

Un'terteil *m & n* lower part, bottom

untertei'len *tr* subdivide

Untertei'lung *f* (-;-en) subdivision

Un'tertitel *m* subtitle; caption

Un'terton *m* undertone

un'tertreten §152 *intr* (SEIN) take cover

un'tervermieten *tr* sublet

Un'tervertrag *m* subcontract

unterwan'dern *tr* infiltrate

Un'terwäsche *f* underwear

Unterwasser– *comb.fm.* underwater, submarine

Un'terwasserbombe *f* depth charge

Un'terwasserhorchgerät *n* hydrophone

Un'terwasserortungsgerät *n* sonar

unterwegs [ʊntər'veks] *adv* on the way; (com) in transit

unterwei'sen §118 *tr* instruct

Unterwei'sung *f* (-;-en) instruction

Un'terwelt *f* underworld; (myth) lower world

unterwer'fen §160 *tr* subjugate; (*dat*) subject (to) || *ref* (*dat*) submit to, subject oneself to; **sich** [*dat*] **ein Volk u.** subjugate a people

Unterwer'fung *f* (-;) subjugation; submission

unterworfen [ʊntər'vɔrfən] *adj* subject

unterwürfig [ʊntərvʏrfɪç] *adj* submissive, subservient

unterzeich'nen *tr* sign

Unterzeich'ner –in §6 *mf* signer; signatory

Unterzeichnete [ʊntər'tsaɪçnətə] §5 *mf* undersigned

Unterzeich'nung *f* (-;-en) signing; signature

un'terziehen §163 *tr* put on underneath || **unterzie'hen** §163 *tr* (*dat*) subject (to) || *ref*—**sich der Mühe u. zu** (*inf*) take the trouble to (*inf*); **sich e-r Operation u.** have an operation; **sich e-r Prüfung u.** take an examination

un'tief *adj* shallow || **Untiefe** *f* (-;-n) shoal

Un'tier *n* (& fig) monster

untilg'bar *adj* inextinguishable; (*Tinte*) indelible; (*Anleihe*) irredeemable

untrag'bar *adj* unbearable; (*Kleidung*) unwearable; (*Kosten*) prohibitive

untrenn'bar *adj* inseparable

un'treu *adj* unfaithful || **Untreue** *f* unfaithfulness; infidelity

untröst'lich *adj* inconsolable

untrüg'lich *adj* unerring, infallible

un'tüchtig *adj* incapable; inefficient

Un'tugend *f* bad habit, vice

un'überlegt *adj* thoughtless; rash

unüberseh'bar *adj* vast, huge; incalculable || *adv* very

unübersetz'bar *adj* untranslatable

un'übersichtlich *adj* unclear; (*Kurve*) blind

unübersteig'bar, unübersteig'lich *adj* insurmountable

unübertreff'lich *adj* unsurpassable

unübertroffen [ʊnybər'trɔfən] *adj* unsurpassed

unüberwind'lich *adj* invincible; (*Schwierigkeiten*) insurmountable

unumgäng'lich *adj* indispensable

unumschränkt [ʊnʊm'reŋkt] *adj* unlimited; (pol) absolute

unumstößlich [ʊnʊm'tøslɪç] *adj* irrefutable; (*unwiderruflich*) irrevocable

unumwunden [ʊnʊmvʊndən] *adj* blunt

un'unterbrochen *adj* continuous

unverän'derlich *adj* unchangeable, invariable

unverant'wortlich *adj* irresponsible

unveräu'ßerlich *adj* inalienable

unverbesserlich [ʊnfer'besərlɪç] *adj* incorrigible

unverbind'lich *adj* without obligation; (*Verhalten*) proper, formal; (*Antwort*) noncommittal

un'verblümt *adj* blunt, plain

unverbürgt [ʊnfer'byrkt] *adj* unwarranted; (*Nachricht*) unconfirmed

un'verdächtig *adj* unsuspected

un'verdaulich *adj* indigestible

unverderbt [ʊnferderpt], **unverdorben** [ʊnferdɔrbən] *adj* unspoiled

unverdient [ʊnferdint] *adj* undeserved

un'verdrossen *adj* indefatigable

unverdünnt [ʊnferdʏnt] *adj* undiluted

unverehelicht [ʊnfere-əlɪçt] *adj* unmarried, single

un'vereinbar *adj* incompatible; contradictory

unverfälscht [ʊnferfɛlʃt] *adj* genuine; (*Wein*) undiluted

un'verfänglich *adj* innocent

un'verfroren *adj* brash

un'vergänglich *adj* imperishable

un'vergeßlich *adj* unforgettable

unvergleich'bar *adj* incomparable

unvergleichlich [ʊnferglaɪçlɪç] *adj* incomparable

un'verhältnismäßig *adj* disproportionate

un'verheiratet *adj* unmarried

unvergolten [ʊnfergɔltən] *adj* unrewarded

unverhofft [ʊnferhɔft] *adj* unhoped-for

unverhohlen [ʊnferholən] *adj* unconcealed; (fig) open

un'verkäuflich *adj* unsalable

unverkennbar [ʊnferkenbər] *adj* unmistakable

unverkürzt [ʊnferkʏrtst] *adj* unabridged

unverlangt [ʊnferlaŋt] *adj* unsolicited

un'verletzbar, un'verletzlich *adj* undamageable; (fig) inviolable

unverletzt [ʊnferletst] *adj* safe and sound, unharmed; (*Sache*) undamaged

unvermeid'lich *adj* inevitable

unvermindert [ʊnfermɪndərt] *adj* undiminished

unvermittelt [ʊnfermɪtəlt] *adj* sudden

Un'vermögen *n* inability; impotence

un'vermögend *adj* poor; impotent

unvermutet [ʊnfermutət] *adj* unexpected

un'vernehmlich *adj* imperceptible

Un'vernunft *f* unreasonableness; folly

un'vernünftig *adj* unreasonable; foolish

un'verschämt *adj* brazen, shameless

unverschuldet [ˈʊnfɛrˌʃʊldət] adj unencumbered; (unverdient) undeserved
un'versehens adv unawares, suddenly
unversehrt [ˈʊnfɛrzeːrt] adj undamaged
(Person) unharmed
unversichert [ˈʊnfɛrzɪçɛrt] adj unin-
sured
unversiegbar [ʊnfɛrˈziːkbaːr] unversieg-
lich [ʊnfɛrˈziːklɪç] adj inexhaustible
unversiegelt [ˈʊnfɛrziːgəlt] adj unsealed
un'versöhnlich adj irreconcilable
unversorgt [ˈʊnfɛrzɔrkt] adj unpro-
vided for
Un'verstand m lack of judgment
un'verständig adj foolish
un'verständlich adj incomprehensible
unversucht [ˈʊnfɛrzuːxt] adj untried
un'verträglich adj unsociable; quarrelsome; incompatible, contradictory
un'verwandt adj steady, unflinching
unverwelklich [ʊnfɛrˈvɛlklɪç] adj unfading
un'verwendbar adj unusable
unverweslich [ˈʊnfɛrveːzlɪç] adj incorruptible
unverwindbar [ʊnfɛrˈvɪntbaːr] adj irreparable; (Enttäuschung) lasting
un'verwundbar adj invulnerable
unverwüstlich [ˈʊnfɛrvyːstlɪç] adj indestructible; (Stoff) durable; (fig)
irrepressible
unverzagt [ˈʊnfɛrtsaːkt] adj undaunted
un'verzeihlich adj unpardonable
unverzerrt [ˈʊnfɛrtsɛrt] adj undistorted
unverzinslich [ˈʊnfɛrtsɪnslɪç] adj (fin)
without interest
unverzüglich [ˈʊnfɛrtsyːklɪç] adj
prompt, immediate ‖ adv without
delay
unvollendet [ˈʊnfɔlɛndət] adj unfinished
un'vollkommen adj imperfect
Un'vollkommenheit f imperfection
un'vollständig adj incomplete; (gram)
defective
un'vorbereitet adj unprepared; (Rede)
extemporaneous ‖ adv extempore
un'voreingenommen adj unbiased
un'vorhergesehen adj unforeseen
un'vorsätzlich adj unintentional
un'vorsichtig adj incautious; careless
un'vorteilhaft adj disadvantageous;
unprofitable; (Kleid) unflattering
un'wahr adj untrue
un'wahrhaftig adj untruthful
Un'wahrheit f untruth, falsehood
un'wahrnehmbar adj imperceptible
un'wahrscheinlich adj unlikely, improbable
unwan'delbar adj unchangeable
unwegsam [ˈʊnveːkzaːm] adj impassable
unweigerlich [ʊnˈvaɪgɛrlɪç] adj unhesitating; (Folge) necessary ‖ adv
without fail
un'weit adj—u. von not far from ‖
prep (genit) not far from
Un'wesen n mischief; sein U. treiben
be up to one's old tricks
un'wesentlich adj unessential; unimportant; (für) immaterial (to)
Un'wetter n storm

un'wichtig adj unimportant
unwiederbringlich [ʊnviːdɛrˈbrɪŋlɪç]
adj irretrievable, irreparable
unwiderleg'bar adj irrefutable
unwiderruf'lich adj irrevocable
unwidersteh'lich adj irresistible
Un'wille m, Un'willen m indignation,
displeasure; reluctance
un'willig adj (über acc) indignant (at),
displeased (at); u. zu (inf) reluctant
to (inf)
un'willkommen adj unwelcome
un'willkürlich adj involuntary
un'wirklich adj unreal
un'wirksam adj ineffective; inefficient;
(chem) inactive; (jur) null and void
Un'wirksamkeit f ineffectiveness; inefficiency; (chem) inactivity
unwirsch [ˈʊnvɪrʃ] adj surly
un'wirtlich adj inhospitable
un'wirtschaftlich adj uneconomical
unwissend [ˈʊnvɪsənt] adj ignorant
Unwissenheit [ˈʊnvɪsənhaɪt] f (–;) ignorance
un'wissenschaftlich adj unscientific
un'wissentlich adv unwittingly
un'wohl adj sickish; ich fühle mich u.
I don't feel well
un'wohnlich adj uninhabitable; (unbehaglich) uncomfortable
un'würdig adj unworthy
Un'zahl f (von) huge number (of)
unzähl'bar, unzählig [ʊnˈtseːlɪç] adj
countless, innumerable
un'zart adj indelicate
Unze [ˈʊntsə] f (–;–n) ounce
Un'zeit f wrong time
un'zeitgemäß adj out-of-date
un'zeitig adj untimely; (Obst) unripe
unzerbrech'lich adj unbreakable
unzerstör'bar adj indestructible
unzertrennlich [ʊntsɛrˈtrɛnlɪç] adj inseparable
unziemend [ˈʊntsiːmənt], un'ziemlich
adj unbecoming, unseemly
Un'zucht f unchastity; lewdness
un'züchtig adj unchaste; lewd
un'zufrieden adj dissatisfied
un'zugänglich adj inaccessible; aloof
un'zulänglich adj inadequate
un'zulässig adj inadmissible; (Beeinflussung, Einmischung) undue
un'zurechnungsfähig adj unaccountable
un'zureichend adj inadequate
un'zusammenhängend adj incoherent
un'zuträglich adj (dat) bad (for)
un'zutreffend adj not applicable
un'zuverlässig adj unreliable
un'zweckmäßig adj inappropriate; unsuitable; impractical
un'zweideutig adj unambiguous
un'zweifelhaft adj undoubted
üppig [ˈʏpɪç] adj luxurious, plush;
(Mahl) sumptuous; (Pflanzenwuchs)
luxuriant; (sinnlich) voluptuous
Ur-, ur- [uːr] comb.fm. original; very
ur'alt adj very old, ancient
Uran [uˈraːn] n (–s;) uranium
Ur'aufführung f world première
urbar [ˈuːrbaːr] adj arable; u. machen
reclaim
Urbarmachung [ˈuːrbaːrmaxʊŋ] f (–;)
reclamation

Ur'bewohner pl aborigines
Ur'bild n prototype; original
ur'deutsch adj hundred-percent German
ur'eigen adj one's very own; original
Ur'einwohner pl aborigines
Ur'eltern pl ancestors
Ur'enkel m great-grandson
Ur'geschichte f prehistory
Ur'großmutter f great-grandmother
Ur'großvater m great-grandfather
Urheber –in ['urhebər(ɪn)] §6 mf originator, author
Ur'heberrecht n copyright
Ur'heberschaft f (–;-e) authorship
Urin [u'rin] m (–s;) urine
urinieren [urɪ'nirən] intr urinate
ur'ko'misch adj very funny
Urkunde ['urkundə] f (–;-n) document; deed; (Vertrag) instrument
Ur'kundenmaterial n documentation
urkundlich ['urkʊntlɪç] adj documentary; (verbürgt) authentic
Urlaub ['urlaup] m (–[e]s;-e) vacation; (mil) furlough
Ur'lauber –in §6 mf vacationer
Ur'laubsschein m (mil) pass
Ur'laubstag m day off
Urne ['urnə] f (–;-n) urn; ballot box; **zur U. gehen** go to the polls
Ur'nengang m balloting

ur'plötz'lich adj sudden ‖ adv all of a sudden
Ur'sache f cause, reason; **keine U.!** don't mention it!
ur'sächlich adj causal
Ur'schleim m (–es;) protoplasm
Ur'schrift f original text, original
Ur'sprung m origin, source; beginning; (Ursache) cause
ursprünglich ['ur(ʃ)prʏŋlɪç] adj original
Ur'stoff m primary matter; (chem) element
Ur'teil n judgment; (Ansicht) view, opinion; (jur) verdict; (Strafmaß) (jur) sentence
urteilen ['urtaɪlən] intr judge; **u. nach** judge by
Ur'teilskraft f discernment
Ur'teilsspruch m verdict; sentence
Ur'text m original text
Ur'tier n protozoon
Ur'volk n aborigines
Ur'wald m virgin forest; jungle
ur'weltlich adj primeval
urwüchsig ['urvyksɪç] adj original; (fig) rough
Ur'zeit f remote antiquity
Utensilien [uten'ziljən] pl utensils
Uto·pie [uto'pi] f (–;-pien ['pi-ən]) utopia; pipe dream
uzen ['utsən] tr tease, kid

V, v [fau] invar n V, v
vag [vak] adj vague
Vagabund [vaga'bunt] m (–en;-en) vagabond, tramp, bum
vagabundieren [vagabun'dirən] intr (HABEN & SEIN) bum around
vage ['vagə] adj vague
vakant [va'kant] adj vacant
Vakanz [va'kants] f (–;-en) vacancy
Vaku·um ['vakʊ-ʊm] n (–s;-ua [u-a]) vacuum
Vakzine [vak'tsinə] f (–;-n) vaccine
vakzinieren [vaktsi'nirən] tr vaccinate
Valet [va'let] n (–s;-s) farewell
Valu·ta [va'luta] f (–;-ten [tən]) value; (foreign) currency
Vampir ['vampir] m (–s;-e) vampire
Vandale [van'dalə] m (–n;-n) Vandal; (fig) vandal
Vanille [va'nɪljə] f (–;) vanilla
Variante [varɪ'antə] f (–;-n) variant
Varietät [varɪ-ɛ'tɛt] f (–;-en) variety
Varieté [varɪ-ɛ'te] n (–s;-s) vaudeville; vaudeville stage
variieren [varɪ'irən] tr & intr vary
Vase ['vazə] f (–;-n) vase
Vaselin [vazɛ'lin] n (–s;-e), **Vaseline** [vazɛ'linə] f (–;-n) vaseline
Vater ['fatər] m (–s;⸚) father
Va'terland n (native) country
vaterländisch ['fatərlendɪʃ] adj national ‖ adv–v. gesinnt patriotic
Va'terlandsliebe f patriotism
väterlich ['fetərlɪç] adj fatherly

väterlicherseits ['fetərlɪçər'zaɪts] adv on the father's side
Va'terliebe f paternal love
Va'terschaft f (–;) fatherhood
Va'terschaftsklage f paternity suit
Va'tersname m family name, last name
Va'terstadt f home town
Va'terstelle f—**bei j–m V. vertreten** be a father to s.o.
Vatern'ser n (–s;–) Lord's Prayer
Vati ['fati] m (–s;-s) dad, daddy
Vatikan [vati'kan] m (–s) Vatican
v. Chr. abbr (vor Christus) B.C.
Vegetarier –in [vege'tarjər(ɪn)] §6 mf vegetarian
Vegetation [vegeta'tsjon] f (–;) vegetation
vegetieren [vege'tirən] intr vegetate
Veilchen ['faɪlçən] n (–s;–) (bot) violet
Vene ['venə] f (–;-n) (anat) vein
Venedig [ve'nedɪç] n (–s;) Venice
venerisch [ve'nerɪʃ] adj venereal; **venerisches Leiden** venereal disease
Ventil [ven'til] n (–s;-e) valve; (bei der Orgel) stop; (fig) outlet
Ventilation [ventɪla'tsjon] f (–;) ventilation
Venti·lator [ventɪ'lator] m (–s;-latoren [la'torən]) ventilator; fan
ver– [fer] pref up, e.g., **verbrauchen** use up; away, e.g., **verjagen** chase away; mis–, wrongly, e.g., **verstellen** misplace, **verdrehen** turn the wrong

way; (to form verbs from other parts of speech) **verwirklichen** realize, **vergöttern** deify; (to express a sense opposite that of the simple verb) **verlernen** forget, **verkaufen** sell; (to indicate consumption or waste through the action of the verb) **verschreiben** use up in writing; (to indicate intensification or completion) **verhungern** die of hunger; (to indicate cessation of action) **vergären** cease to ferment; (to indicate conversion to another state) **verflüssigen** liquify

verabfolgen [fɛr'ʔpfɔlgən] *tr* hand over; deliver; (*Arznei*) give, administer

verabreden [fɛr'apredən] *tr* agree upon; **schon anderweitig verabredet sein** have a prior engagement ‖ *ref* make an appointment

Verab'redung *f* (–;-en) agreement; appointment

verabreichen [fɛr'apraiçən] *tr* give

verabsäumen [fɛr'apzɔɪmən] *tr* var of **versäumen**

verabscheuen [fɛr'apʃɔɪən] *tr* detest, loath, abhor

verab'scheuenswert, **verab'scheuenswürdig** detestable

verabschieden [fɛr'apʃidən] *tr* dismiss; (*Beamte*) put on pension; (*Gesetz*) pass; (mil) disband ‖ *ref* (von) take leave of, say goodbye (to)

Verab'schiedung *f* (–;-en) dismissal; pensioning; (mil) disbanding; (parl) passing, enactment

verach'ten *tr* despise; **nicht zu v.** not to be sneezed at

verächtlich [fɛr'ɛçtlɪç] *adj* contemptuous; (*verachtungswert*) contemptible

Verach'tung *f* (–;) contempt

veralbern [fɛr'albərn] *tr* tease

verallgemeinern [fɛralgə'maɪnərn] *tr & intr* generalize

Verallgemei'nerung *f* (–;-en) generalization

veralten [fɛr'altən] *intr* become obsolete; (*Kleider*) go out of style

veraltet [fɛr'altət] *adj* obsolete; out of date, old-fashioned

Veran·da [ve'randa] *f* (–;-den [dən]) veranda, porch

veränderlich [fɛr'endərlɪç] *adj* changeable; (math) variable

Verän'derlichkeit *f* (–;-en) changeableness; fluctuation; instability

verän'dern [fɛr'endərn] *tr* change; vary ‖ *ref* change; look for a new job

Verän'derung *f* (–;-en) change

verängstigt [fɛr'ɛŋstɪçt] *adj* intimidated

verankern [fɛr'aŋkərn] *tr* anchor, moor

Veran'kerung *f* (–;-en) anchorage, mooring

veranlagen [fɛr'anlagən] *tr* (*zu e-r Steuer*) assess; **gut veranlagt** highly talented; **künstlerisch veranlagt** artificially inclined; **schlecht veranlagt** poorly endowed

Veran'lagung *f* (–;-en) talents; disposition; (fin) assessment

veran'lassen *tr* cause, occasion, make; (*bereden*) induce

Veran'lassung *f* (–;-en) cause, occasion; **auf V. von** at the suggestion of; **ohne jede V.** without provocation; **V. geben zu** give rise to

veranschaulichen [fɛr'anʃaulɪçən] *tr* make clear, illustrate

veran'schlagen §132 *tr* rate, value; (*im voraus berechnen*) estimate; **zu hoch v.** overrate

Veran'schlagung *f* (–;) estimate

veranstalten [fɛr'anʃtaltən] *tr* organize, arrange; (*Empfang*) give; (*Sammlung*) take up; (*Versammlung*) hold

Veran'stalter –in §6 *mf* organizer

Veran'staltung *f* (–;-en) organization, arrangement; affair; performance, show; meeting; (sport) event, meet

veran'tworten *tr* answer for, account for; (*verteidigen*) defend ‖ *ref* defend oneself, justify oneself

verantwortlich [fɛr'antvɔrtlɪç] *adj* responsible, answerable; **für etw v. zeichnen** sign for s.th.

Verant'wortlichkeit *f* (–;) responsibility; (jur) liability

Verant'wortung *f* (–;-en) responsibility; (*Rechtfertigung*) justification; **auf eigene V.** at one's own risk; **die V. abwälzen auf** (*acc*) pass the buck to; **zur V. ziehen** call to account

Verant'wortungsbewußtsein *n* sense of responsibility

verant'wortungsfreudig *adj* willing to assume responsibility

verant'wortungsvoll *adj* responsible

veräppeln [fɛr'ɛpəln] *tr* (coll) tease

verar'beiten *tr* manufacture, process; (zu) make (into); (*verdauen*) digest; (fig) assimilate

verar'beitend *adj* manufacturing

Verar'beitung *f* (–;-en) manufacturing; digestion; (fig) assimilation

verargen [fɛr'argən] *tr—j—m etw v.* blame s.o. for s.th.

verär'gern *tr* annoy

verarmen [fɛr'armən] *intr* (SEIN) grow poor

verästeln [fɛr'estəln] *ref* branch out

verausgaben [fɛr'ausgabən] *tr* pay out ‖ *ref* run short of money

veräußern [fɛr'ɔɪsərn] *tr* sell

Verb [vɛrp] *n* (–s;-en) verb

verbal [vɛr'bal] *adj* verbal

Verband [fɛr'bant] *m* (–[e]s;ᵉe) association, union, federation; (aer, nav) formation; (mil) unit; (surg) bandage, dressing; **sich aus dem V. lösen** (aer) peel off

Verband'kasten *m* first-aid kit

Verband'päckchen *n* first-aid pack

Verband'platz *m* first-aid station

Verband'stoff *m* bandage, dressing

verbannen [fɛr'banən] *tr* banish, exile

Verbannte [fɛr'bantə] §5 *mf* exile

Verban'nung *f* (–;-en) banishment; place of exile

verbarrikadie'ren *tr* barricade

verbau'en *tr* (*Gelände*) build up; use up (*in building*); (*Geld*) spend (*in building*); build poorly; **j—m den Weg v. zu** bar s.o.'s way to

verbei′ßen §53 *tr* swallow, suppress ‖ *ref* (in *acc*) stick (to)

verber′gen §54 *tr* & *ref* hide

verbes′sern *tr* improve; correct; (*Aufsatz*) grade; (*Gesetz*) amend; (*Tatsache*) rectify ‖ *ref* improve; better oneself

Verbes′serung *f* (–;–en) improvement; correction; amendment

verbeu′gen *ref* bow

Verbeu′gung *f* (–;–en) bow; curtsy

verbeulen [fɛr′bɔilən] *tr* dent; batter

verbie′gen §57 *tr* bend ‖ *ref* warp

verbie′ten §58 *tr* forbid

verbil′den *tr* spoil; educate badly

verbil′ligen *tr* reduce the price of

Verbil′ligung *f* (–;–en) reduction

verbin′den §59 *tr* tie, tie up; join, unite; (*verketten*) link; (*zu Dank verpflichten*) obligate; (*chem*) combine; (*med*) bandage; (*telp*) (**mit**) connect (with), put through (to); **j-m die Augen v.** blindfold s.o. ‖ *ref* unite

verbindlich [fɛr′bɪntlɪç] *adj* obliging; binding; **verbindlichsten Dank!** thank you ever so much!

Verbind′lichkeit *f* (–;–en) obligation; commitment; polite way; (*e-s Vertrags*) binding force

Verbin′dung *f* (–;–en) union; association; alliance; combination; contact; touch; (*Fuge, Gelenk*) joint; (*chem*) compound; (*educ*) fraternity; (*mach, rr, telp*) connection; (*mil*) liaison; **die V. verlieren mit** lose touch with; **e-e V. eingehen** (*chem*) form a compound; **er hat gute Verbindungen** he has good connections; **in V. mit** in conjunction with; **sich in V. setzen mit** get in touch with; **unmittelbare V.** (*telp*) direct call

Verbin′dungsbahn *f* connecting train

Verbin′dungsleitung *f* (telp) trunk line

Verbin′dungslinie *f* line of communication

Verbin′dungsoffizier *m* liaison officer

Verbin′dungspunkt *m*, **Verbin′dungsstelle** *f* joint, juncture

Verbin′dungsstück *n* joint, coupling

verbissen [fɛr′bɪsən] *adj* dogged, grim; (*Zorn*) suppressed; **v. sein in** (*dat*) stick doggedly to

Verbis′senheit *f* (–;) doggedness, grimness

verbitten [fɛr′bɪtən] §60 *ref*—**sich** [*dat*] **etw v.** not stand for s.th.

verbittern [fɛr′bɪtərn] *tr* embitter

Verbit′terung *f* (–;) bitterness

verblassen [fɛr′blasən] *intr* (SEIN) grow pale; (fig) fade

verblättern [fɛr′blɛtərn] *tr*—**die Seite v.** lose the page

Verbleib [fɛr′blaip] *m* (–[e]s;) whereabouts

verblei′ben §62 *intr* (SEIN) remain, be left; (**bei**) persist (in); **wir sind so verblieben, daß** we finally agreed that

verblei′chen §85 *intr* (SEIN) fade

verblen′den *tr* blind; dazzle; (*Mauer*) face; (*Fenster*) wall up

Verblen′dung *f* (–;–en) blindness, infatuation; (archit) facing

verblichen [fɛr′blɪçən] *adj* faded

verblödet [fɛr′bi̇ødət] *adj* idiotic

verblüffen [fɛr′blʏfən] *tr* dumbfound, flabbergast; bewilder, perplex

Verblüf′fung *f* (–;) bewilderment

verblü′hen *intr* (SEIN) wither; fade

verblümt [fɛr′blymt] *adj* euphemistic

verblu′ten *ref* & *intr* (SEIN) bleed to death

verbocken [fɛr′bɔkən] *tr* bungle

verboh′ren *ref*—**sich v. in** (*acc*) stick stubbornly to

verbohrt [fɛr′bort] *adj* stubborn; odd

verbolzen [fɛr′bɔltsən] *tr* bolt

verbor′gen *adj* secret; latent; hidden ‖ *tr* lend out ‖ **Verborgene** §5 *n*—**im Verborgenen** in secret, on the sly

Verbor′genheit *f* (–;) secrecy; concealment; seclusion

Verbot [fɛr′bot] *n* (–[e]s;–e) prohibition; (jur) injunction

verboten [fɛr′botən] *adj* forbidden; **Eintritt v.!** no admittance; **Plakatankleben v.!** post no bills!; **Stehenbleiben v.!** no loitering

verbrämen [fɛr′brɛmən] *tr* trim, edge; (fig) sugar-coat

verbrannt [fɛr′brant] *adj* burnt; torrid; **Politik der verbrannten Erde** scorched-earth policy

Verbrauch′ *m* (–[e]s;) use, consumption

verbrau′chen *tr* use up, consume; waste; (*abnutzen*) wear out

Verbrau′cher *m* (–s;–) consumer; (*Benützer*) user; (*Kunde*) customer

Verbrau′chergenossenschaft *f* co-op

Verbrauchs′güter *pl* consumer goods

verbraucht′ *adj* used up, consumed; worn out; (*Geld*) spent; (*Luft*) stale

verbre′chen §64 *tr* commit, do ‖ **Verbrechen** *n* (–s;–) crime

Verbre′cher *m* (–s;–) criminal

Verbre′cheralbum *n* rogues′ gallery

Verbre′cherin *f* (–;–nen) criminal

verbrecherisch [fɛr′brɛçərɪʃ] *adj* criminal

Verbre′cherkolonie *f* penal colony

verbreiten [fɛr′braitən] *tr* spread; (*Frieden, Licht*) shed ‖ *ref* spread; **sich v. über** (*acc*) expatiate on

verbreitern [fɛr′braitərn] *tr* & *ref* widen, broaden

Verbrei′terung *f* (–;) widening, broadening

Verbrei′tung *f* (–;) spreading; dissemination; diffusion

verbren′nen §97 *tr* burn; scorch; (*bräunen*) tan; (*Leichen*) cremate ‖ *ref* burn oneself; **sich** [*dat*] **die Finger v.** (& fig) burn one′s fingers

Verbren′nung *f* (–;–en) burning, combustion; cremation; (*Brandwunde*) burn

Verbren′nungskraftmaschine *f*, **Verbren′nungsmotor** *m* internal combustion engine

Verbren′nungsraum *m* combustion chamber

verbrin′gen §65 *tr* spend, pass; (*wegbringen*) take away

verbrüdern [fɛr′brydərn] *ref* (**mit**) fraternize (with)

Verbrü'derung f (-;) fraternizing
verbrü'hen tr scald
verbu'chen tr book; **etw als Erfolg v.** chalk s.th. up as a success
Ver·bum ['vɛrbum] n (-s;-ba [ba]) verb
verbunden [fɛr'bundən] adj connected; **falsch v.!** sorry, wrong number!; **untereinander v.** interconnected; **zu Dank v.** obligated
verbünden [fɛr'byndən] ref—**sich mit j–m v.** ally oneself with s.o.
Verbun'denheit f (-;) connection, ties; solidarity, union
Verbündete [fɛr'byndətə] §5 mf ally
verbür'gen tr guarantee, vouch for || ref—**sich v. für** vouch for
verbürgt [fɛr'byrkt] adj authenticated
verbüßen [fɛr'bysən] tr atone for, pay for; **seine Strafe v.** serve one's time
verchromen [fɛr'kromən] tr chromeplate
Verchro'mung f (-;-en) chromeplating
Verdacht [fɛr'daxt] m (-[e]s;) suspicion; **in V. kommen** come under suspicion; **V. hegen gegen** have suspicions about; **V. schöpfen** get suspicious
verdächtig [fɛr'dɛçtɪç] adj suspicious; (genit) suspected (of)
verdächtigen [fɛr'dɛçtɪgən] tr cast suspicion on; (genit) suspect (of)
Verdäch'tigung f (-;-en) insinuation
verdammen [fɛr'damən] tr condemn; damn
Verdammnis [fɛr'damnɪs] f (-;) damnation, perdition
verdammt' adj (sl) damn || interj (sl) damn it!
verdamp'fen tr & intr (SEIN) evaporate
Verdamp'fung f (-;) evaporation
verdan'ken tr—**j–m etw v.** be indebted to s.o. for s.th.
verdarb [fɛr'darp] pret of **verderben**
verdattert [fɛr'datərt] adj (coll) shook up
verdauen [fɛr'dau·ən] tr digest
verdaulich [fɛr'daulɪç] adj digestible
Verdau'ung f (-;) digestion
Verdau'ungsbeschwerden pl **Verdau'ungsstörung** f indigestion
Verdau'ungswerkzeug n digestive track
Verdeck [fɛr'dɛk] n (-[e]s;-e) hood (of baby carriage); (aut) convertible top; (naut) deck
verdecken (verdek'ken) tr cover; hide
verden'ken §66 tr—**j–m etw v.** blame s.o. for s.th.
Verderb [fɛr'dɛrp] m (-[e]s;) ruin; decay
verderben [fɛr'dɛrbən] §149 tr spoil; ruin; (Magen) upset; (verführen) corrupt || intr (SEIN) spoil, go bad; (fig) go to pot || **Verderben** (-s;) ruin; **j–n ins V. stürzen** ruin s.o.
verderblich [fɛr'dɛrplɪç] adj ruinous; (Lebensmittel) perishable
Verderbnis [fɛr'dɛrpnɪs] f (-;) depravity
verderbt [fɛr'dɛrpt] adj depraved
Verderbt'heit f (-;) depravity
verdeutlichen [fɛr'dɔɪtlɪçən] tr make plain, explain

verdeutschen [fɛr'dɔɪtʃən] tr translate into (or express in) German
verdich'ten tr condense, thicken || ref condense; solidify; thicken; (Nebel, Rauch) grow thicker; (Verdacht) become stronger, grow
verdicken [fɛr'dɪkən] tr & ref thicken
verdie'nen tr deserve; (Geld) earn
Verdienst [fɛr'dinst] m (-es;-e) earnings; gain, profit || n (-es;-e) merit; deserts; **es ist dein V., daß** it is owing to you that; **nach V.** deservedly; **nach V. behandelt werden** get one's due; **sich [dat] als (or zum) V. anrechnen** take credit for it; **V. um** services to
Verdienst'ausfall m loss of wages
verdienst'lich adj meritorious
Verdienst'spanne f margin of profit
verdienst'voll adj meritorious
verdient [fɛr'dint] adj—**sich um j–n v. machen** serve s.o. well
verdol'metschen tr translate orally; interpret
Verdol'metschung f (-;) oral translation; interpretation
verdonnern [fɛr'dɔnərn] tr (coll) condemn
verdop'peln tr & ref double
verdorben [fɛr'dɔrbən] adj spoiled; (Luft) foul; (Magen) upset; (moralisch) depraved
verdorren [fɛr'dɔrən] intr (SEIN) dry up, wither
verdrän'gen tr push aside, crowd out; dislodge; (phys) displace; (psychol) repress, inhibit
Verdrän'gung f (-;-en) (phys) displacement; (psychol) repression, inhibition
verdre'hen tr twist; (Augen) roll; (Glied) sprain; (fig) distort; **j–m den Kopf v.** make s.o. fall in love with one
verdreht' adj twisted; (fig) distorted; (fig) (verrückt) cracked
verdreifachen [fɛr'draɪfaxən] tr triple
verdre'schen §67 tr (coll) spank
verdrießen [fɛr'drisən] §76 tr bother, annoy, get down; **laß es dich nicht v.!** don't let it get you down; **sich keine Mühe v. lassen** spare no pains || impers—**es verdrießt mich, daß** it bothers me that
verdrießlich [fɛr'drislɪç] adj glum; tiresome, depressing; annoyed
verdroß [fɛr'drɔs] pret of **verdrießen**
verdro'ßen adj cross; (mürrisch) surly; (lustlos) listless
verdrucken (verdruk'ken) tr misprint
verdrücken (verdrük'ken) tr wrinkle; (coll) eat up, polish off || ref (coll) sneak away
Ver·druß [fɛr'drus] m (-drusses; -drusse) annoyance, vexation; **j–m etw zum V. tun** do s.th. to spite s.o.
verduften [fɛr'duftən] intr (SEIN) lose its aroma; (coll) take off, scram
verdummen [fɛr'dumən] tr make stupid || intr (SEIN) become stupid
verdunkeln [fɛr'duŋkəln] tr darken; obscure; (Glanz) dull; (fig) cloud; (astr) eclipse; (mil) black out || ref darken; (Himmel) cloud over

Verdun′kelung *f* (–;–en) darkening; (astr) eclipse; (mil) blackout

verdünnen [fer′dynən] *tr* thin; dilute; (*Gase*) rarefy

verdun′sten *intr* (SEIN) evaporate

Verdun′stung *f* (–;) evaporation

verdur′sten *intr* (SEIN) die of thirst

verdutzen [fer′dutsən] *tr* bewilder

veredeln [fer′edəln] *tr* ennoble; (*verfeinen*) refine; (*Rohstoff*) process; (*Boden*) enrich; (*Pflanze*, *Tier*) improve

Vere′delung *f* (–;) refinement; processing; enrichment; improvement

verehelichen [fer′e·əliçən] *ref* get married

verehren [fer′erən] *tr* revere; worship; (fig) adore; **j–m etw v.** present s.o. with s.th.

Vereh′rer –in §6 *mf* worshiper; (*Liebhaber*) admirer

verehrt [fer′ert] *adj*—**Sehr verehrte gnädige Frau!** Dear Madam; **Sehr verehrter Herr!** Dear Sir; **Verehrte Anwesende** (or **Gäste**)! Ladies and Gentlemen!

Vereh′rung *f* (–;) reverence, veneration; worship; adoration

vereiden [fer′aidən], **vereidigen** [fer′aidɪgən] *tr* swear in

Verein [fer′ain] *m* (–[e]s–e) society

vereinbar [fer′ainbar] *adj* compatible

vereinbaren [fer′ainbarən] *tr* agree to, agree upon ‖ *ref*—**das läßt sich mit meinen Grundsätzen nicht v.** that is inconsistent with my principles

Verein′barkeit *f* (–;) compatibility

Verein′barung *f* (–;) agreement, arrangement; terms; **nur nach V.** by appointment only

vereinen [fer′ainən] *tr* unite, join

vereinfachen [fer′ainfaxən] *tr* simplify

Verein′fachung *f* (–;–en) simplification

vereinheitlichen [fer′ainhaitliçən] *tr* standardize

vereinigen [fer′ainɪgən] *tr* unite, join; (*verbinden*) combine; (*verschmelzen*) merge; (*versammeln*) assemble ‖ *ref* unite, join; (*Flüsse*) meet; **sich v. mit** team up with; **sich v. lassen mit** be compatible with, square with

Verei′nigten Staa′ten *pl* United States

Verein′igung *f* (–;–en) union; combination; society, association

vereinnahmen [fer′ainnamən] *tr* take in

vereinsamen [fer′ainzamən] *intr* (SEIN) become lonely; become isolated

Verein′samung *f* (–;) loneliness; isolation

Vereins′meier –in §6 *mf* (coll) joiner

vereinzeln [fer′aintsəln] *tr* isolate

verein′zelt *adj* isolated; sporadic

vereisen [fer′aizən] *tr* (surg) freeze ‖ *intr* (SEIN) become covered with ice; (aer) ice up

vereiteln [fer′aitəln] *tr* frustrate; baffle

verekeln [fer′ekəln] *tr*—**j–m etw v.** spoil s.th. for s.o.

veren′den *intr* (SEIN) die

verengen [fer′eŋən] *tr & ref* narrow

vererr′ben *tr* bequeath; leave; (*über-*

mitteln) hand down; (*Krankheit*) transmit ‖ *ref* run in the family

Verer′bung *f* (–;–en) inheritance; transmission; heredity

Verer′bungslehre *f* genetics

verewigen [fer′evɪgən] *tr* perpetuate

verewigt [fer′eviçt] *adj* late, deceased

verfah′ren *adj* bungled, messed up ‖ §71 *tr* bungle; (*Geld*, *Zeit*) spend (*on travel*) ‖ *ref* lose one's way, take a track ‖ *intr* (SEIN) proceed; act ‖ **wrong turn**; (fig) be on the wrong

Verfahren *n* (–s;–) procedure, method; system; (chem) process; (jur) proceedings, case

Verfall *m* (–[e]s;) deterioration, decay; decline, downfall; (*Fristablauf*) expiration; (*von Wechseln*) maturity; **in V. geraten** become delapidated

verfal′len *adj* delapidated; **e–m Rauschgift v. sein** be addicted to a drug ‖ §72 *intr* (SEIN) decay, go to ruin, decline; (*ablaufen*) expire; (*Kranker*) waste away; (*Recht*) lapse; (*Pfand*) be forfeited; (*Wechsel*) mature

Verfall′tag *m* due date; date of maturity

verfäl′schen *tr* falsify; (*Geld*) counterfeit; (*Wein*) adulterate; (*Urkunde*) forge

Verfäl′schung *f* (–;–en) falsification; forging; adulteration

verfan′gen §73 *ref* become entangled ‖ *intr* (**bei**) have an effect (on)

verfänglich [fer′fɛŋlɪç] *adj* (*Frage*) loaded; (*Situation*) awkward

verfär′ben *ref* change color

verfas′sen *tr* compose, write

Verfas′ser –in §6 *mf* author

Verfas′sung *f* (–;–en) constitution; (*Zustand*) condition; frame of mind, mood

verfas′sungsgemäß, **verfas′sungsmäßig** *adj* constitutional

verfas′sungswidrig *adj* unconstitutional

verfau′len *intr* (SEIN) rot

verfech′ten §74 *tr* defend, stand up for

Verfech′ter *m* (–s;–) champion

verfeh′len *tr* (*Abzweigung*, *Ziel*, *Zug*) miss; (*Wirkung*) fail to achieve, not have; **ich werde nicht v. zu** (*inf*) I will not fail to (*inf*) ‖ *recip*—**wir haben uns verfehlt** we missed each other

verfehlt [fer′felt] *adj* wrong

Verfeh′lung *f* (–;–en) offense; mistake

verfeinden [fer′faindən] *recip* become enemies

verfeinern [fer′fainərn] *tr* refine, improve ‖ *ref* become refined, improve

verfertigen [fer′fertɪgən] *tr* manufacture, make

Verfer′tigung *f* (–;) manufacture

verfilmen [fer′filmən] *tr* adapt to the screen, make into a movie

Verfil′mung *f* (–;–en) film version

verfilzen [fer′filtsən] *ref* get tangled

verfinstern [fer′finstərn] *ref* get dark

verflachen [fer′flaxən] *tr* flatten ‖ *ref & intr* (SEIN) flatten out

verflech′ten §74 *tr* interweave; (fig) implicate, involve

verflie′gen §57 *ref* (aer) lose one's

bearings ‖ *intr* (SEIN) fly away; (*Zeit*) fly; evaporate; (fig) vanish

verflie′ßen §76 *intr* (SEIN) flow off; (*Frist*) run out, expire; (*Farben*) blend; (*Begriffe, Grenzen*) overlap

verflixt [fɛr′flɪkst] *adj* (sl) darn

verflossen [fɛr′flɔsən] *adj* past; former

verflu′chen *tr* curse, damn

verflucht′ *adj* (sl) damn ‖ *interj* (sl) damn it!

verflüchtigen [fɛr′flʏçtɪgən] *tr* volatilize ‖ *ref* evaporate; (fig) disappear

verflüssigen [fɛr′flʏsɪgən] *tr* & *ref* liquefy

Verfolg [fɛr′fɔlk] *m* (-s;) course; **im V.** (*genit*) in pursuance of

verfol′gen *tr* pursue; follow up; persecute; haunt; (hunt) track; (jur) prosecute; **j-n steckbrieflich v.** send out a warrant for the arrest of s.o.

Verfol′ger –in §6 *mf* pursuer; persecutor

Verfol′gung *f* (-;-en) pursuit; persecution; (jur) prosecution

Verfol′gungswahn *m*, **Verfol′gungswahnsinn** *m* persecution complex

verfrachten [fɛr′fraxtən] *tr* ship; (coll) bundle off

Verfrach′ter –in §6 *mf* shipper

verfrühen [fɛr′fry·ən] *ref* be too early

verfügbar [fɛr′fykbar] *adj* available, at one's disposal

verfü′gen *tr* decree, order ‖ *ref*—**sich v. nach** betake oneself to ‖ *intr*—**v. über** (*acc*) have at one's disposal, have control over

Verfü′gung *f* (-;-en) decree, order; disposal; **einstweilige V.** (jur) injunction; **j-m zur V. stehen be at** s.o.'s disposal; **j-m zur V. stellen put** at s.o.'s disposal; **letztwillige V.** last will and testament

verfüh′ren *tr* mislead; (*zum Irrtum*) lead; (*verlocken*) seduce

Verfüh′rer –in §6 *mf* seducer

verführerisch [fɛr′fyrərɪʃ] *adj* seductive, tempting

Verfüh′rung *f* (-;-en) seduction

vergaffen [fɛr′gafən] *ref* (coll) (**in** *acc*) fall in love (with)

vergammeln [fɛr′gaməln] *intr* (SEIN) (coll) go to the dogs

vergangen [fɛr′gaŋən] *adj* past; (*Schönheit*) faded

Vergan′genheit *f* (-;) past; background; (gram) past tense

vergänglich [fɛr′gɛŋlɪç] *adj* transitory

vergasen [fɛr′gazən] *tr* gas

Verga′ser *m* (-s;-) carburetor

vergaß [fɛr′gas] *pret* of **vergessen**

verge′ben §80 *tr* forgive (*s.th.*); give away; (*Chance*) miss, pass up; (*Amt, freie Stelle*) fill; (*Auftrag*) place; (*Karten*) misdeal; (*verleihen*) confer; **v. sein** have a previous engagement; be engaged (*to a man*) ‖ *ref*—**sich** [*dat*] **etw v.** compromise on s.th. ‖ *intr* (*dat*) forgive (*s.o.*)

verge′bens [fɛr′gebəns] *adv* in vain

vergeb′lich [fɛr′geplɪç] *adj* vain, futile

Verge′bung *f* (-;) forgiveness; bestowal

vergegenwärtigen [fɛr′gegənvɛrtɪgən] *ref*—**sich** [*dat*] **etw. v.** visualize s.th.

verge′hen §82 *ref*—**sich an j-m v.** offend s.o.; (*sexuell*) violate s.o. ‖ *intr* (SEIN) pass, go away; fade ‖ **Verge-hen** *n* (-s;-) offense, misdemeanor

vergel′ten §83 *tr* requite; **vergelt's Gott!** (coll) thank you!

Vergel′tung *f* (-;) repayment; retaliation, reprisal

Vergel′tungswaffe *f* V-1 or V-2

vergesellschaften [fɛrgə′zɛlʃaftən] *tr* socialize; nationalize

vergessen [fɛr′gesən] §70 *tr* forget

Verges′senheit *f* (-;)—**in V. geraten** fall (or sink) into oblivion

vergeßlich [fɛr′geslɪç] *adj* forceful

Vergeß′lichkeit *f* (-;) forgetfulness

vergeuden [fɛr′gɔidən] *tr* waste

Vergeu′dung *f* (-;) waste, squandering

vergewaltigen [fɛrgə′valtɪgən] *tr* do violence to; (*Mädchen*) rape

Vergewal′tigung *f* (-;-en) rape

vergewissern [fɛrgə′vɪsərn] *ref* (*genit*) make sure of, ascertain

vergie′ßen §76 *tr* spill; (*Tränen*) shed

vergiften [fɛr′gɪftən] *tr* (& fig) poison; (*verseuchen*) contaminate ‖ *ref* take poison

Vergif′tung *f* (-;-en) poisoning; contamination

vergipsen [fɛr′gɪpsən] *tr* plaster

Vergißmeinnicht [fɛr′gɪsmaɪnnɪçt] *n* (-[e]s;-e) forget-me-not

vergittern [fɛr′gɪtərn] *tr* bar up

Vergleich [fɛr′glaɪç] *m* (-[e]s;-e) comparison; (*Verständigung*) agreement; (*Ausgleich*) settlement; **e-n V. anstellen zwischen** make a comparison between; **e-n V. treffen** reach a settlement, come to an agreement

vergleichbar [fɛr′glaɪçbar] *adj* comparable

verglei′chen [fɛr′glaɪçən] §85 *tr* (**mit**) compare (with, to) ‖ *ref* (**mit**) come to an agreement (with)

Vergleichs′grundlage *f* basis for comparison

vergleichs′weise *adv* by way of comparison

Verglei′chung *f* (-;-en) comparison; matching; contrasting

verglü′hen *intr* (SEIN) cease to glow

vergnügen [fɛr′gnygən] *tr* amuse, delight ‖ *ref* enjoy oneself, amuse oneself ‖ **Vergnügen** *n* (-s;-) delight, pleasure; **mit V.** with pleasure; **V. finden an** (*dat*) take delight in; **viel V.!** (coll) have fun!; **zum V.** for fun

vergnügt [fɛr′gnykt] *adj* cheerful, gay; (**über** *acc*) delighted (with)

Vergnü′gung *f* (-;-en) pleasure, amusement

Vergnü′gungspark *m* amusement park

Vergnü′gungsreise *f* pleasure trip

Vergnü′gungssteuer *f* entertainment tax

vergnü′gungssüchtig *adj* pleasure-loving

vergolden [fɛr′gɔldən] *tr* gild

Vergol′dung *f* (-;-en) gilding

vergönnen [fɛr′gœnən] *tr* not begrudge

vergöttern [fɛr′gœtərn] *tr* deify; (fig) idolize

vergra′ben §87 *tr* (& fig) bury

vergrämen [fer'grɛmən] *tr* annoy, anger

vergrämt [fer'grɛmt] *adj* haggard

vergrei'fen §88 *ref* (mus) hit the wrong note; **sich v. an** (*dat*) lay violent hands on; (*fremdem Gut*) encroach on; (*Geld*) misappropriate; (*Mädchen*) assault; **sich im Ausdruck v.** express oneself poorly

vergreisen [fer'graizən] *intr* (SEIN) age; become senile

vergriffen [fer'grɪfən] *adj* sold out; (*Buch*) out of print

vergröbern [fer'grøbərn] *tr* roughen || *ref* become coarser

vergrößern [fer'grøsərn] *tr* enlarge; increase; (*ausdehnen*) expand; (opt) magnify || *ref* become larger

Vergrö'ßerung *f* (-;-en) enlargement; increase; expansion; (opt) magnification

Vergrö'ßerungsapparat *m* (phot) enlarger

Vergrö'ßerungsglas *m* magnifying glass

Vergünstigung [fer'gynstɪguŋ] *f* (-; -en) privilege; (*bevorzugte Behandlung*) preferential treatment

vergüten [fer'gytən] *tr* make good; (*Stahl*) temper; **j-m etw v.** reimburse (or compensate) s.o. for s.th.

Vergü'tung *f* (-;-en) reimbursement, compensation; tempering

verhaften [fer'haftən] *tr* apprehend

Verhaf'tung *f* (-;-en) apprehension

verhal'ten *adj* (*Atem*) bated; (*Stimme*) low || §90 *tr* hold back; (*Atem*) hold; (*Lachen*) suppress; (*Stimme*) keep down; **den Schritt v.** slow down; (*stehenbleiben*) stop || *ref* behave, act; be; **A verhält sich zu B wie X zu Y** A is to B as X is to Y; **sich anders v.** be different; **sich ruhig v.** keep quiet || *impers ref*—**wenn es sich so verhält** if that's the case || **Verhalten** *n* (-s;) conduct, behavior; attitude

Verhältnis [fer'hɛltnɪs] *n* (-ses;-se) proportion, ratio; (*Beziehung*) relation; (*Liebes-*) love affair; **aus kleinen Verhältnissen** of humble birth; **bei sonst gleichen Verhältnissen** other things being equal; **das steht in keinem V. zu** that is all out of proportion to; **Verhältnisse** circumstances, conditions; matters; means

verhält'nismäßig *adj* proportionate || *adv* relatively, comparatively

Verhält'nismaßregeln *pl* instructions

Verhält'niswahl *f* proportional representation

verhält'niswidrig *adj* disproportionate

Verhält'niswort *n* (-[e]s;⁼er) preposition

verhan'deln *tr* discuss; (*Waren*) sell || *intr* negotiate; argue; (*beraten*) confer; (jur) plead a case; **gegen j-n wegen etw v.** (jur) try s.o. for s.th.

Verhand'lung *f* (-;-en) negotiation; discussion; proceedings, trial

verhangen [fer'haŋən] *adj* overcast

verhän'gen *tr* (*Fenster*) put curtains on; (*Strafe*) impose; (*Untersuchung*) order; (*Belagerungszustand*) pro-

claim; **mit verhängtem Zügel** at full speed

Verhängnis [fer'hɛŋnɪs] *n* (-ses;-se) destiny, fate; (*Unglück*) disaster

verhäng'nisvoll *adj* fateful; disastrous

verhärmt [fer'hɛrmt] *adj* haggard

verharren [fer'harən] *intr* (HABEN & SEIN) remain; (**auf** *dat*, **in** *dat*, **bei**) stick (to)

verhärten [fer'hɛrtən] *tr* & *ref* harden

verhaßt [fer'hast] *adj* hated, hateful

verhätscheln [fer'hɛtʃəln] *tr* pamper

Verhau [fer'hau] *m* (-[e]s;-e) barbwire entanglement

verhau'en §93 *tr* lick, beat up; (*Kind*) spank; (*Auftrag, Ball, usw.*) muff || *ref* make a blunder

verheddern [fer'hɛdərn] *ref* get tangled up

verheeren [fer'herən] *tr* devastate

verhee'rend *adj* terrible; (coll) awful

Verhee'rung *f* (-;) devastation

verhehlen [fer'helən] *tr* conceal

verhei'len *intr* (SEIN) heal up

verheimlichen [fer'haimlɪçən] *tr* keep secret, conceal

Verheim'lichung *f* (-;) concealment

verhei'raten *tr* marry; (*Tochter*) give away || *ref* (**mit**) get married (to)

Verhei'ratung *f* (-;) marriage

verhei'ßen §95 *tr* promise

Verhei'ßung *f* (-;-en) promise

verhei'ßungsvoll *adj* promising

verhel'fen §96 *intr*—**j-m zu etw v.** help s.o. to acquire s.th.

verherrlichen [fer'hɛrlɪçən] *tr* glorify

Verherr'lichung *f* (-;) glorification

verhet'zen *tr* instigate

verhexen [fer'hɛksən] *tr* bewitch, hex

verhimmeln [fer'hɪməln] *tr* praise to the skies; (*Schauspieler*) idolize

verhin'dern *tr* prevent

Verhin'derung *f* (-;) prevention; **im Falle seiner V.** in case he's unavailable

verhohlen [fer'holən] *adj* hidden

verhöh'nen *tr* jeer at; make fun of

Verhöh'nung *f* (-;) jeering; ridicule

Verhör [fer'hør] *n* (-[e]s;-e) interrogation, questioning, hearing

verhö'ren *tr* interrogate, question || *ref* hear wrong

verhudeln [fer'hudəln] *tr* (coll) bungle

verhüllen [fer'hylən] *tr* cover, veil; wrap up; disguise

Verhüll'lung *f* (-;-en) cover; disguise

verhun'gern *intr* (SEIN) starve to death

verhunzen [fer'huntsən] *tr* (coll) botch

verhü'ten *tr* prevent, avert

verinnerlicht [fer'ɪnərlɪçt] *adj* introspective

verir'ren *ref* lose one's way; (*Augen, Blick*) wander; (fig) make a mistake

verirrt [fer'ɪrt] *adj* stray

verja'gen *tr* chase away

verjähren [fer'jerən] *intr* (SEIN) fall under the statute of limitations

verjubeln [fer'jubəln] *tr* squander

verjüngen [fer'jyŋən] *tr* rejuvenate; reduce in scale; taper || *ref* be rejuvenated; taper, narrow

Verjün'gung *f* (-;) rejuvenation; tapering; scaling down

verkatert [fer'katərt] *adj* suffering from a hangover

Verkauf' *m* (-[e]s;-̈e) sale

verkau'fen *tr* sell

Verkäu'fer –in §6 *mf* seller; salesclerk; vendor || *m* salesman || *f* salesgirl, saleswoman

verkäuf'lich *adj* salable

Verkaufs'anzeige *f* for-sale ad

Verkaufs'automat *m* vending machine

Verkaufs'leiter –in §6 *mf* sales manager

Verkaufs'schlager *m* good seller

Verkaufs'steigerung *f* sales promotion

Verkaufs'vertrag *m* agreement of sale

Verkehr [fer'ker] *m* (-s;) traffic; commerce; company, association; (*sexuell*) intercourse; (aer, rr) service; (fin) circulation

verkeh'ren *tr* reverse, invert; turn upside down; convert, change; (*Sinn, Worte*) twist || *intr* (*Fahrzeug*) run, run regularly; **mit j–m geschlechtlich v.** have intercourse with s.o.; **mit j–m v.** associate with s.o.

Verkehrs'ader *f* main artery

Verkehrs'ampel *f* traffic light

Verkehrs'andrang *m* heavy traffic

Verkehrs'betrieb *m* public transportation company

Verkehrs'delikt *n* traffic violation

Verkehrs'flugzeug *n* airliner

Verkehrs'insel *f* traffic island

Verkehrs'mittel *n* means of transportation

Verkehrs'ordnungen *pl* traffic regulations

Verkehrs'polizist –in §7 *mf* traffic cop

verkehrs'reich *adj* crowded, congested

verkehrs'stark *adj* busy

Verkehrs'stockung *f*, **Verkehrs'störung** *f* traffic jam

Verkehrs'unfall *m* traffic accident

Verkehrs'unternehmen *n* transportation company

Verkehrs'vorschrift *f* traffic regulation

Verkehrs'wesen *n* traffic, transportation

Verkehrs'zeichen *n* traffic sign

verkehrt [fer'kert] *adj* reversed; upside down; inside out; wrong

verken'nen §97 *tr* misunderstand; (*Person*) misjudge, mistake

verketten [fer'ketən] *tr* chain together; (fig) link

Verket'tung *f* (-;) chaining; (fig) concatenation; (fig) coincidence

verkit'ten *tr* cement; putty; seal, bond

verkla'gen *tr* accuse; (jur) sue

Verklagte [fer'klɑktə] §5 *mf* defendant

verklat'schen *tr* (coll) slander; (educ) squeal on

verkle'ben *tr* glue, cement; **v. mit** cover with

verklei'den *tr* disguise, dress up; (*täfeln*) panel; line, face; (mil) camouflage

Verklei'dung *f* (-;-en) disguise; paneling; lining, facing; (mil) camouflage

verkleinern [fer'klainərn] *tr* lessen, diminish; (fig) disparage; (math) reduce; **maßstäblich v.** scale down

Verklei'nerung *f* (-;-en) diminution, reduction; (fig) detraction

Verklei'nerungsform *f* diminutive

verklin'gen §142 *intr* (SEIN) die away

verkloppen [fer'klɔpən] *tr* (coll) beat up

verknacken [fer'knakən] *tr* (coll) sentence

verknallt [fer'knalt] *adj*—**in j–n v. sein** (coll) have a crush on s.o.

verknappen [fer'knapən] *intr* (SEIN) run short, run low

Verknap'pung *f* (-;) shortage

verkneifen §88 *ref*—**sich** [*dat*] **etw v.** deny oneself s.th.

verkniffen [fer'knifən] *adj* wry

verknip'sen *tr* (*Film*) waste

verknöchern [fer'knœçərn] *intr* (SEIN) ossify; (*Glieder*) become stiff

verknöchert [fer'knœçərt] *adj* pedantic; (*Junggeselle*) inveterate

verknoten [fer'knotən] *tr* snarl, tie up

verknüp'fen *tr* tie together; (fig) connect, combine, relate

verknusen [fer'knuzən] *tr* (coll) stand

verkohlen [fer'kolən] *tr* carbonize; char; **j–n v.** (coll) pull s.o.'s leg

verkom'men *adj* decayed; degenerate; (*Gebäude*) squalid || §99 *intr* (SEIN) decay, spoil; (fig) go to the dogs; **v. zu** degenerate into

Verkom'menheit *f* (-;) depravity

verkop'peln *tr* couple; (*Interessen*) (com) consolidate

verkorken [fer'korkən] *tr* cork up

verkorksen [fer'korksən] *tr* (coll) bungle || *ref*—**sich** [*dat*] **den Magen v.** (coll) upset one's stomach

verkörpern [fer'kœrpərn] *tr* embody, personify; (*Rolle*) play

Verkör'perung *f* (-;-en) embodiment, incarnation

verkra'chen *ref*—**sich mit j–m v.** have an argument with s.o. || *intr* (SEIN) (coll) go bankrupt

verkrampft [fer'krampft] *adj* cramped

verkrie'chen §102 *ref* hide; (& fig) crawl into a hole; **neben ihm kannst du dich v.!** you're no match for him!

verkrümeln [fer'kryməln] *tr* crumble || *ref* (fig) disappear

verkrüm'men *tr & ref* bend

Verkrüm'mung *f* (-;) bend, crookedness; curvature

verkrüppeln [fer'krypəln] *tr* cripple || *intr* (SEIN) become crippled; (*verkümmern*) become stunted

verkrustet [fer'krustət] *adj* caked

verküh'len *ref* catch a cold

verküm'mern *intr* (SEIN) become stunted; (pathol) atrophy

Verküm'merung *f* (-;) atrophy

verkünden [fer'kyndən], **verkündigen** [fer'kyndigən] *tr* announce, proclaim; (*Urteil*) pronounce

Verkün'digung *f* (-;-en), **Verkün'dung** *f* (-;-en) announcement, proclamation; pronouncement; **Mariä Verkündigung** (feast of the) Annunciation

verkup'peln *tr* couple; (*Mädchen, Mann*) procure; (*Tochter*) sell into prostitution

verkür'zen *tr* shorten; abridge; (*be-schränken*) curtail; (*Zeit*) pass

Verkür'zung *f* (–;-en) shortening; abridgement; curtailment

verla'chen *tr* laugh at

verla'den §103 *tr* load, ship

Verlag [fer'lɑk] *m* (–[e]s;-e) publisher; **im V. von** published by

verla'gern *tr* shift; (*aus Sicherheitsgründen*) evacuate ‖ *ref* shift

Verla'gerung *f* (–;-en) shift, shifting; evacuation

Verlags'anstalt *f* publisher

Verlags'buchhandlung *f* publisher and dealer

Verlags'recht *n* copyright

verlangen [fer'laŋən] *tr* demand, require; want, ask ‖ *intr*—**v. nach** ask for; long for ‖ **Verlangen** *n* (–s;) demand; request; wish; claim; (*Sehnsucht*) longing, yearning; **auf V.** upon demand, upon request

verlängern [fer'lɛŋərn] *tr* lengthen; prolong, extend; **seinen Paß v. lassen** have one's passport renewed

Verlän'gerung *f* (–;-en) lengthening; prolongation, extension; (sport) overtime

Verlän'gerungsschnur *f* extension cord

verlangsamen [fer'laŋzamən] *tr* slow down

verläppern [fer'lɛpərn] *tr* (coll) fritter away

Ver·laß [fer'las] *m* (–lasses;) reliance; **es ist kein V. auf ihn** you can't rely on him

verlas'sen *adj* abandoned, deserted; lonesome ‖ §104 *tr* leave; forsake, desert ‖ *ref*—**sich v. auf** (*acc*) rely on

Verlas'senheit *f* (–;) loneliness

verläßlich [fer'lɛslɪç] *adj* reliable

verlästern [fer'lɛstərn] *tr* slander

Verlä'sterung *f* (–;-en) slander

Verlaub [fer'laup] *m*—**mit V.** with your permission; **mit V. zu sagen** if I may say so

Verlauf' *m* (–[e]s;) course; **e–n guten V. haben** turn out well; **nach V.** von after a lapse of

verlau'fen §105 *intr* (SEIN) (*Zeit*) pass, lapse; (*ablaufen*) turn out, come off; (*vorgehen*) proceed, run ‖ *ref* lose one's way; (*Wasser*) run off; (*Menschenmenge*) disperse

verlau'ten *intr* (SEIN) become known, be reported; **kein Wort davon v. lassen** not breathe a word about it; **wie verlautet** as reported ‖ *impers*—**es verlautet** it is reported

verle'ben *tr* spend, pass

verlebt [fer'lept] *adj* haggard

verle'gen *adj* embarrassed; confused; **v. um** (*e–e Antwort*) at a loss for; (*Geld*) short of ‖ *tr* move, shift; transfer; misplace; (*Buch*) publish; (*Geleise, Kabel, Rohre*) lay; (*sperren*) block; (*vertagen*) postpone ‖ *ref*—**sich v. auf** (*acc*) apply onself to; devote oneself to; resort to

Verle'genheit *f* (–;) embarrassment; difficulties; predicament; **in V. bringen** embarrass

Verle'ger *m* (–s;–) publisher

Verle'gung *f* (–;-en) move, shift; transfer; postponement; (*von Kabeln, usw.*) laying

verlei'den *tr* spoil, take the joy out of

Verleih [fer'laɪ] *m* (–s;-e) rental service

verlei'hen §81 *tr* lend out, loan; rent out; (*Gunst*) grant; (*Titel*) confer; (*Auszeichnung*) award

Verlei'her –in §6 *mf* lender; grantor; (*von Filmen*) distributor

Verlei'hung *f* (–;-en) lending out; rental; grant; bestowal

verlei'ten *tr* mislead; (*zur Sünde, zum Trunk*) lead; (jur) suborn

verler'nen *tr* unlearn, forget

verle'sen §107 *tr* read out; (*Namen*) read off; (*Salat*) clean; (*Gemüse*) sort out ‖ *ref* misread

verletzen [fer'lɛtsən] *tr* (& fig) injure, hurt; (*kränken*) offend; (*Gesetz*) break; (*Recht*) violate

verlet'zend *adj* offensive

Verletzte [fer'lɛtstə] §5 *mf* injured party

Verlet'zung *f* (–;-en) injury; offense; (*e–s Gesetzes*) breaking; (*e–s Rechtes*) violation

verleug'nen *tr* deny; (*Kind*) disown; (*Glauben*) renounce ‖ *ref*—**sich selbst v.** act contrary to one's nature; **sich vor Besuchern v. lassen** refuse to see visitors

Verleug'nung *f* (–;-en) denial; renunciation; disavowal

verleumden [fer'lɔɪmdən] *tr* slander

verleumderisch [fer'lɔɪmdərɪʃ] *adj* slanderous, libelous

Verleum'dung *f* (–;-en) slander

verlie'ben *ref*—**sich in j–n v.** fall in love with s.o.

verliebt [fer'lipt] *adj* in love

verlieren [fer'lirən] §77 *tr* lose ‖ *ref* lose one's way; disappear; disperse

Verlies [fer'lis] *n* (–es;-e) dungeon

verlo'ben *ref* (mit) become engaged (to)

Verlöbnis [fer'løpnɪs] *n* (–ses;-se) engagement

Verlobte [fer'loptə] §5 *m* fiancé; **die Verlobten** the engaged couple ‖ *f* fiancée

Verlo'bung *f* (–;-en) engagement

verlocken (verlok'ken) *tr* lure, tempt; (*verführen*) seduce

verlockend (verlok'kend) *adj* tempting

Verlockung (Verlok'kung) *f* (–;-en) allurement, temptation

verlogen [fer'logən] *adj* dishonest

verlohn'nen *impers ref*—**es verlohnt sich nicht** it doesn't pay ‖ *impers*—**es verlohnt der Mühe nicht** it is not worth the trouble

verlor [fer'lor] *pret* of **verlieren**

verloren [fer'lorən] *pp* of **verlieren** ‖ *adj* lost; (*hilflos*) forlorn; (*Ei*) poached; **der verlorene Sohn** the prodigal son

verlo'rengeben §80 *tr* give up for lost

verlo'rengehen §82 *intr* (SEIN) be lost

verlö'schen §110 *tr* extinguish; (*Schrift*) erase ‖ *intr* (SEIN) (*Licht, Kerze*) go out; (*Zorn*) cease

verlo'sen *tr* raffle off, draw lots for

verlö'ten *tr* solder; **e-n v.** (coll) belt one down

verlottern [fɛr'lɔtərn] *intr* (coll) go to the dogs

verlumpen [fɛr'lumpən] *tr* (coll) blow, squander || *intr* (coll) go to the dogs

Verlust [fɛr'lust] *m* (-[e]s;-e) loss; **in V. geraten** get lost; **Verluste** (mil) casualties

Verlust'liste *f* (mil) casualty list

verma'chen *tr* bequeath, leave

Vermächtnis [fɛr'mɛçtnɪs] *n* (-ses;-se) bequest, legacy

vermählen [fɛr'mɛlən] *tr* marry || *ref* (mit) get married (to)

Vermäh'lung *f* (-;-en) marriage, wedding

vermah'nen *tr* admonish, warn

Vermah'nung *f* (-;-en) admonition

vermaledeien [fɛrmale'dai-ən] *tr* curse

vermanschen [fɛr'manʃən] *tr* (coll) make a mess of

vermasseln [fɛr'masəln] *tr* (coll) bungle, muff

vermassen [fɛr'masən] *intr* (SEIN) lose one's individuality

vermauern [fɛr'mau-ərn] *tr* wall up

vermehren [fɛr'merən] *tr & ref* increase; *(an Zahl)* multiply; **vermehrte Auflage** enlarged edition

vermei'den *tr* avoid

vermeidlich [fɛr'martlɪç] *adj* avoidable

Vermei'dung *f* (-;) avoidance

vermei'nen *tr* suppose; presume, allege

vermeintlich [fɛr'marntlɪç] *adj* supposed, alleged; *(erdacht)* imaginary

vermel'den *tr* (poet) announce

vermen'gen *tr* mix, mingle; confound || *ref* (mit) meddle (with)

Vermerk [fɛr'mɛrk] *m* (-[e]s;-e) note

vermer'ken *tr* note, record

vermes'sen *adj* daring, bold || §70 *tr* measure; *(Land)* survey || *ref* measure wrong; **sich v. zu** *(inf)* have the nerve to *(inf)*

Vermes'sung *f* (-;-en) surveying

vermie'ten *tr* rent out; lease out

Vermie'ter -in §6 *mf* (jur) lessor || *m* landlord || *f* landlady

vermindern [fɛr'mɪndərn] *tr* diminish, lessen; *(beschränken)* reduce, cut || *ref* diminish, decrease

Vermin'derung *f* (-;-en) diminution, decrease; reduction, cut

verminen [fɛr'minən] *tr* (mil) mine

vermi'schen *tr & ref* mix

Vermi'schung *f* (-;-en) mixture

vermissen [fɛr'mɪsən] *tr* miss

vermißt [fɛr'mɪst] *adj* (mil) missing in action || **Vermißte** §5 *mf* missing person

vermitteln [fɛr'mɪtəln] *tr* negotiate; arrange, bring about; *(beschaffen)* get, procure || *intr* mediate; intercede

vermittels [fɛr'mɪtəls] *prep* (genit) by means of, through

Vermitt'ler -in §6 *mf* mediator, go-between; (com) agent

Vermitt'lung *f* (-;-en) negotiation; mediation; procuring, providing; intercession; *(Mittel)* means; agency;

brokerage; (telp) exchange; **durch gütige V.** *(genit)* through the good offices of

Vermitt'lungsamt *n* (telp) exchange

Vermitt'lungsgebühr *f*, Vermitt'lungsprovision *f* commission; brokerage

vermo'dern *intr* (SEIN) rot, decay

vermöge [fɛr'møgə] *prep* (genit) by virtue of

vermö'gen §114 *tr* be able to do; **j-n v. zu** *(inf)* induce s.o. to *(inf)*; **sie vermag bei ihm viel** (or **wenig**) she has great (or little) influence with him; **v. zu** *(inf)* be able to *(inf)*, have the power to *(inf)* || **Vermögen** *n* (-s;-) ability; capacity; power; fortune, means; property; (fin) capital, assets; **nach bestem V.** to the best of one's ability

vermö'gend *adj* well-to-do, well-off

Vermö'genslage *f* financial situation

Vermö'genssteuer *f* property tax

vermorscht [fɛr'mɔrʃt] *adj* rotten

vermottet [fɛr'mɔtət] *adj* moth-eaten

vermummen [fɛr'mumən] *tr* disguise || *ref* disguise oneself

vermuten [fɛr'mutən] *tr* suppose, presume

vermutlich [fɛr'mutlɪç] *adj* presumable || *adv* presumably, I suppose

Vermu'tung *f* (-;-en) guess, conjecture

vernachlässigen [fɛr'nɑxlɛsɪgən] *tr* neglect

Vernach'lässigung *f* (-;) neglect

verna'geln *tr* nail up; board up

vernä'hen *tr* sew up

vernarben [fɛr'narbən] *intr* (SEIN) heal up

vernarren *ref*—**sich v. in** *(acc)* be crazy about, be stuck on

verna'schen *tr* spend on sweets; *(Mädchen)* make love to

vernebeln [fɛr'nebəln] *tr* (mil) screen with smoke; (fig) hide, cover over

vernehmbar [fɛr'nembar] *adj* perceptible

verneh'men §116 *tr* perceive; *(erfahren)* hear, learn; (jur) question; **sich v. lassen** be heard, express an opinion || **Vernehmen** *n* (-s;-)—**dem V. nach** reportedly, according to the report

vernehmlich [fɛr'nemlɪç] *adj* perceptible, audible; distinct

Verneh'mung *f* (-;-en) interrogation

vernei'gen *ref* bow; curtsy

Vernei'gung *f* (-;-en) bow; curtsy

verneinen [fɛr'namən] *tr* say no to; reject, refuse; disavow

vernei'nend *adj* negative

Vernei'nung *f* (-;-en) negation; denial

vernichten [fɛr'nɪçtən] *tr* destroy, annihilate; *(Hoffnung)* dash

vernich'tend *adj* *(Kritik)* scathing; *(Niederlage)* crushing

Vernich'tung *f* (-;) destruction

vernickeln [fɛr'nɪkəln] *tr* nickel-plate

vernie'ten *tr* rivet

Vernunft [fɛr'nunft] *f* (-;) reason; good sense; senses; **die gesunde V.** common sense; **V. annehmen** listen to reason; **zur V. bringen** bring to one's senses

Vernunft′ehe *f* marriage of convenience

vernunft′gemäß *adj* reasonable

vernünftig [fer′nүnftɪç] *adj* rational; reasonable; sensible, level-headed

vernunft′los *adj* senseless

vernunft′mäßig *adj* rational; reasonable

veröden [fer′ødən] *intr* (SEIN) become desolate

veröffentlichen [fer′œfəntlɪçən] *tr* publish; announce

Veröf′fentlichung *f* (–;-en) publication; announcement

verord′nen *tr* decree; (med) prescribe

Verord′nung *f* (–;-en) decree, order; (med) prescription

verpach′ten *tr* farm out; lease, rent out

Verpäch′ter –in §6 *mf* lessor

verpacken (verpak′ken) *tr* pack up

Verpackung (Verpak′kung) *f* (–;-en) packing (material); wrapping

verpas′sen *tr* (*Gelegenheit, Anschluß, usw.*) miss; **j–m e–n Anzug v.** fit s.o. with a suit; **j–m e–e v.** (coll) give s.o. a smack

verpatzen [fer′patsən] *tr* (coll) make a mess of

verpesten [fer′pestən] *tr* infect, contaminate

verpet′zen *tr* (coll) squeal on

verpfän′den *tr* pawn; mortgage; **sein Wort v.** give one's word of honor

verpflan′zen *tr* (bot, surg) transplant

Verpflan′zung *f* (–;-en) (bot, surg) transplant

verpfle′gen *tr* feed; (mil) supply

Verpfle′gung *f* (–;) feeding; board; (mil) rations, supplies

verpflichten [fer′pflɪçtən] *tr* obligate, bind; **zu Dank v.** put under obligation

Verpflich′tung *f* (–;-en) obligation; commitment; (jur) liability

verpfuschen [fer′pfu/ən] *tr* (coll) botch, bungle, muff

verplap′pern *ref* blab out a secret

verplau′dern *tr* waste in chatting

verpönt [fer′pønt] *adj* taboo

verprü′geln *tr* (coll) wallop, thrash

verpuf′fen *intr* (SEIN) fizzle; (fig) fizzle out

verpulvern [fer′pulfərn] *tr* (coll) waste, fritter away

verpum′pen *tr* (coll) loan

verpusten [fer′pustən] *ref* (coll) catch one's breath

Verputz [fer′puts] *m* (–es;-e) finishing coat (of plaster)

verput′zen *tr* plaster; (*aufessen*) polish off; (coll) stand

verquicken [fer′kvɪkən] *tr* interrelate

verquollen [fer′kvɔlən] *adj* (*Augen*) swollen; (*Gesicht*) puffy; (*Holz*) warped

verrammeln [fer′raməln] *tr* barricade

verramschen [fer′ram/ən] *tr* (coll) sell dirt-cheap

verrannt [fer′rant] *adj*—**v. sein in** (*acc*) be stuck on

Verrat′ *m* (–[e]s;) betrayal; treason

verra′ten §63 *tr* betray

Verräter –in [fer′retər(ɪn)] §6 *mf* traitor; betrayer

verräterisch [fer′retərɪ/] *adj* treacherous; (*Spur, usw.*) telltale

verrau′chen *tr* spend on smokes

verräu′chern *tr* fill with smoke

verrech′nen *tr* (*ausgleichen*) balance; (*Scheck*) deposit; (fin) clear ‖ *ref* miscalculate; (fig) be mistaken

Verrech′nung *f* (–;-en) miscalculation; (fin) clearing; **nur zur V.** for deposit only

Verrech′nungsbank *f*, **Verrech′nungskasse** *f* clearing house

verrecken [fer′rekən] *intr* (SEIN) die; (sl) croak; **verrecke!** drop dead!

verreg′nen *tr* spoil with too much rain

verrei′sen *intr* (SEIN) go on a trip; **v. nach** depart for

verreist [fer′raɪst] *adj* out of town

verren′ken *tr* wrench, dislocate ‖ *ref—sich* [*dat*] **den Arm v.** wrench one's arm; **sich** [*dat*] **den Hals v.** (coll) crane one's neck

Verren′kung *f* (–;-en) dislocation

verrich′ten *tr* do; (*Gebet*) say; **seine Notdurft v.** ease oneself

Verrich′tung *f* (–;-en) performance; task, duty

verrie′geln *tr* bolt, bar

verringern [fer′rɪɳərn] *tr* diminish, reduce ‖ *ref* diminish; be reduced

Verrin′gerung *f* (–;-en) diminution; reduction

verrin′nen §121 *intr* (SEIN) run off; (*Zeit*) pass

verro′sten *intr* (SEIN) rust

verrotten [fer′rɔtən] *intr* (SEIN) rot

verrucht [fer′ruxt] *adj* wicked

verrücken (verrük′ken) *tr* move, shift

verrückt [fer′rykt] *adj* crazy; **v. auf** *etw* crazy about s.th.; **v. nach** j–m crazy about s.o. ‖ **Verrückte** §5 *mf* lunatic

Verrückt′heit *f* (–;-en) craziness, madness; crazy action or act

Verruf′ *m* (–[e]s;) discredit, disrepute

verru′fen *adj* disreputable

verrüh′ren *tr* stir thoroughly

verrut′schen *intr* (SEIN) slip

Vers [fers] *m* (–es;-e) verse

versa′gen *tr* refuse; **versagt sein** have a previous engagement ‖ *ref—sich* [*dat*] *etw* **v.** deny oneself s.th.; **ich kann es mir nicht v. zu** (*inf*) I can't refrain from (*ger*) ‖ *intr* fail; (*Beine, Stimme, usw.*) give out; (*Gewehr*) misfire; (*Motor*) fail to start; **bei e–r Prüfung v.** flunk a test ‖ **Versagen** *n* (–s;) failure, flop; misfire

Versa′ger *m* (–s;-) failure, flop; (*Patrone*) dud

versal′zen *tr* oversalt; (fig) spoil

versam′meln *tr* gather together, assemble; convoke ‖ *ref* gather, assemble

Versamm′lung *f* (–;-en) assembly, meeting

Versand [fer′zant] *m* (–[e]s;) shipment; mailing

Versand′abteilung *f* shipping department

versanden [fer′zandən] *intr* (SEIN) silt up; (fig) bog down

Versand'geschäft n, **Versand'haus** n mail-order house

versäu'men tr (Gelegenheit, Schule, Zug) miss; (Geschäft, Pflicht) neglect; **v. zu** (inf) fail to (inf)

Versäumnis [fɛr'zɔɪmnɪs] f (-ʒ-se), n (-ses;-se) omission, neglect; (educ) absence; (jur) default

verschaf'fen tr get, obtain || ref—**sich** [dat] etw **v.** get; **sich** [dat] **Geld v.** raise money; **sich** [dat] **Respekt v.** gain respect

verschämt [fɛr'ʃɛmt] adj bashful, coy

Verschämt'heit f (-ʒ) bashfulness

verschandeln [fɛr'ʃandəln] tr deface

verschan'zen tr fortify || ref entrench oneself; **sich v. hinter** (dat) (fig) hide behind

Verschan'zung f (-ʒ-en) entrenchment

verschär'fen tr intensify; aggravate; **verschärfter Arrest** detention on a bread-and-water diet || ref get worse

verschei'den §112 intr (SEIN) pass away

verschen'ken tr give away

verscher'zen ref—**sich** [dat] etw **v.** throw away, lose (frivolously)

verscheu'chen tr scare away

verschicken (verschik'ken) tr send away; (deportieren) deport

Verschie'bebahnhof m marshaling yard

verschie'ben §130 tr postpone; shift; displace; black-market; (rr) shunt, switch || ref shift

Verschie'bung f (-ʒ-en) postponement; shift, shifting

verschieden [fɛr'ʃiːdən] adj different, various; distinct

verschie'denartig adj of a different kind

verschiedenerlei [fɛr'ʃiːdənərlaɪ] invar adj different kinds of

Verschie'denheit f (-ʒ-en) difference; variety, diversity

verschiedentlich [fɛr'ʃiːdəntlɪç] adv repeatedly; at times, occasionally

verschie'ßen §76 tr (Schießvorrat) use up, expend || intr (SEIN) (Farbe) fade

verschif'fen tr ship

Verschif'fung f (-ʒ) shipment

verschim'meln intr (SEIN) get moldy

verschla'fen adj sleepy, drowsy || §131 tr miss by sleeping; (Zeit) sleep away || intr oversleep

Verschla'fenheit f (-ʒ) sleepiness

Verschlag' m partition; crate

verschla'gen adj sly; (lau) lukewarm || §132 tr partition off; board up; (Kisten) nail shut; (Seite im Buch) lose; (naut) drive off course; (tennis) misserve; **j-m den Atem v.** take s.o.'s breath away; **j-m die Sprache** (or Rede, Stimme) **v.** make s.o. speechless; **v. werden auf** (acc) (or **in** acc) be driven to || impers—**es verschlägt nichts** it doesn't matter

verschlammen [fɛr'ʃlamən] intr (SEIN) silt up

verschlampen [fɛr'ʃlampən] tr ruin (through neglect); (verlegen) misplace || intr get slovenly

verschlechtern [fɛr'ʃlɛçtərn] tr make worse || ref get worse, deteriorate

Verschlech'terung f (-ʒ) deterioration

verschleiern [fɛr'ʃlaɪ-ərn] tr veil; (Tatsachen) cover up; (Stimme) disguise; (mil) screen; **die Bilanz v.** juggle the books || ref cloud up

verschleiert [fɛr'ʃlaɪ-ərt] adj hazy; (Stimme) husky; (Augen) misty

Verschlei'erung f (-ʒ) coverup; camouflaging; (jur) suppression of evidence

verschlei'fen §88 tr slur, slur over

Verschleiß [fɛr'ʃlaɪs] m (-es;) wear and tear; (Aust) retail trade

verschlei'ßen §53 tr wear out; (Aust) retail || ref wear out

verschleiß'fest adj durable

verschlep'pen tr drag off; abduct; (im Krieg) displace; (Verhandlungen) drag out; (Seuche) spread; (verzögern) delay

verschleu'dern tr waste, squander; (Waren) sell dirt-cheap

verschlie'ßen §76 tr shut; lock; put under lock and key || ref (dat) close one's mind to

verschlimmern [fɛr'ʃlɪmərn] tr make worse; (fig) aggravate || ref get worse

verschlin'gen §142 tr devour, wolf down; (verflechten) intertwine

verschlissen [fɛr'ʃlɪsən] adj frayed

verschlossen [fɛr'ʃlɔsən] adj shut; (fig) reserved, tight-lipped

verschlucken (verschluk'ken) tr swallow || ref swallow the wrong way

verschlungen [fɛr'ʃlʊŋən] adj (Weg) winding; (fig) intricate

Ver·schluß' m (-schlusses;-schlüsse) fastener; (Schnapp-) catch; (Schloß-) lock; (e-r Flasche) stopper; (Stöpsel) plug; (Plombe) seal; (e-s Gewehrs) breechlock; (phot) shutter; **unter V.** under lock and key

verschlüsseln [fɛr'ʃlʏsəln] tr code

Verschluß'laut m (ling) stop, plosive

verschmach'ten intr (SEIN) pine away; **vor Durst v.** be dying of thirst

verschmä'hen tr disdain

verschmel'zen §133 tr & intr (SEIN) fuse, merge; blend

Verschmel'zung f (-ʒ-en) fusion; (com) merger

verschmer'zen tr get over

verschmie'ren tr smear; soil, dirty; (verwischen) blur

verschmitzt [fɛr'ʃmɪtst] adj crafty

verschmut'zen tr dirty || intr (SEIN) get dirty

verschnap'pen ref give oneself away

verschnau'fen ref & intr stop for breath

verschnei'den §106 tr clip, trim; cut wrong; castrate; (Branntwein, Wein) blend

verschneit [fɛr'ʃnaɪt] adj snow-covered

Verschnitt' m (-[e]s;) blend

verschnup'fen tr annoy; **verschnupft sein** have a cold; (coll) be annoyed

verschnü'ren tr tie up

verschollen [fɛr'ʃɔlən] adj missing, never heard of again; (jur) presumed dead

verscho'nen tr spare; **j-n mit etw v.** spare s.o. s.th.

verschönern [fɛr'ʃønərn] tr beautify

verschossen [fer'ʃɔsən] *adj* faded, discolored; (**in** *acc*) (coll) be madly in love (with)

verschränken [fer'ʃreŋkən] *tr* fold (one's arms)

verschrau'ben *tr* screw tight

verschrei'ben §62 *tr* use up (*in writing*); (jur) make over; (med) prescribe ‖ *ref* make a mistake (*in writing*)

Verschrei'bung *f* (–;-en) prescription

verschrei'en §135 *tr* decry

verschrien [fer'ʃri·ən] *adj*—v. **sein als** have the reputation of being

verschroben [fer'ʃrobən] *adj* eccentric

Verschro'benheit *f* (–;-en) eccentricity

verschrotten [fer'ʃrɔtən] *tr* scrap

verschüch'tern *tr* intimidate

verschul'den *tr* encumber with debts; **etw v.** be guilty of s.th.; be the cause of s.th. ‖ **Verschulden** *n* (–s;) fault

verschuldet [fer'ʃʊldət] *adj* in debt

Verschul'dung *f* (–;-en) indebtedness; encumbrance

verschüt'ten *tr* spill; (*ausfüllen*) fill up; (*Person*) bury alive

verschwägert [fer'ʃvegərt] *adj* related by marriage

verschwei'gen §148 *tr* keep secret; **j-m etw v.** keep s.th. from s.o.

Verschwei'gung *f* (–;) concealment

verschwei'ßen *tr* weld (together)

verschwenden [fer'ʃvendən] *tr* (**an** *acc*) waste (on), squander (on)

Verschwen'der **–in** §6 *mf* spendthrift

verschwenderisch [fer'ʃvendərɪʃ] *adj* wasteful; lavish, extravagant

Verschwen'dung *f* (–;) waste; extravagance

verschwiegen [fer'ʃvigən] *adj* discreet; reserved, reticent

Verschwie'genheit *f* (–;) discretion; reticence; secrecy

verschwim'men §136 *intr* (SEIN) become blurred; (fig) fade

verschwin'den §59 *intr* (SEIN) disappear; **ich muß mal v.** (coll) I have to go (to the toilet); **v. lassen** put out of the way; spirit off ‖ **Verschwinden** *n* (–s;) disappearance

verschwistert [fer'ʃvɪstərt] *adj* closely related

verschwit'zen *tr* sweat up; (coll) forget

verschwollen [fer'ʃvɔlən] *adj* swollen

verschwommen [fer'ʃvɔmən] *adj* hazy, indistinct; (*Bild*) blurred

Verschwom'menheit *f* (–;) haziness

verschwö'ren §137 *tr* forswear ‖ *ref* (**gegen**) plot (against); **sich zu etw v.** plot s.th.

Verschwö'rer **–in** §6 *mf* conspirator

Verschwö'rung *f* (–;-en) conspiracy

verse'hen §138 *tr* (*Amt, Stellung*) hold; (*Dienst, Pflicht*) perform; (*Haushalt, usw.*) look after; (**mit**) provide (with); (eccl) administer the last rites to; **j–s Dienst v.** fill in for s.o.; **mit e–m Saum v.** hem; **mit Giro v.** endorse; **mit Unterschrift v.** sign ‖ *ref* make a mistake; **ehe man es sich versieht** before you know it; **sich v.** (*genit*) expect ‖ **Versehen** *n* (–s;–) mistake, slip; oversight; **aus V.** by mistake

versehentlich [fer'ze·əntlɪç] *adv* by mistake, erroneously, inadvertently

versehren [fer'zerən] *tr* injure

Versehrte [fer'zertə] §5 *mf* disabled person

versen'den §140 *tr* send, ship; **ins Ausland v.** export

versen'gen *tr* scorch; (*Haar*) singe

versen'ken *tr* sink; submerge; lower; (*Kabel*) lay; (*Schraube*) countersink; (naut) scuttle ‖ *ref*—**sich v. in** (*acc*) become engrossed in

Versen'kung *f* (–;-en) sinking; (theat) trapdoor; **in der V. verschwinden** (fig) vanish into thin air

versessen [fer'zesən] *adj*—v. **auf** (*acc*) crazy about, obsessed with

verset'zen *tr* move, shift; (*Pflanze*) transplant; (*Schulkind*) promote; (*Beamte*) transfer; (*Schlag*) deal, give; (*verpfänden*) pawn; (*vermischen*) mix; (*Metall*) alloy; (*erwidern*) reply; (*vergeblich warten lassen*) (coll) stand up; (mus) transpose; **in Angst v.** terrify; **in Erstaunen v.** amaze; **in den Ruhestand v.** retire; **in Zorn v.** anger ‖ *ref*—v. **Sie sich in meine Lage** put yourself in my place

Verset'zung *f* (–;-en) moving, shifting; transplanting; transfer; mixing; alloying; (educ) promotion

Verset'zungszeichen *n* (mus) accidental

verseuchen [fer'zɔɪçən] *tr* infect, contaminate

Verseu'chung *f* (–;) infection; contamination

Vers'fuß *m* (pros) foot

versicherbar [fer'zɪçərbər] *adj* insurable

versichern [fer'zɪçərn] *tr* assure; assert, affirm; insure ‖ *ref* (*genit*) assure oneself of

Versicherte [fer'zɪçərtə] §5 *mf* insured

Versi'cherung *f* (–;-en) assurance; affirmation; insurance

Versi'cherungsanstalt *f* insurance company

Versi'cherungsbeitrag *m* premium

versi'cherungsfähig *adj* insurable

Versi'cherungsgesellschaft *f* insurance company

Versi'cherungsleistung *f* insurance benefit

Versi'cherungsmathematiker **–in** §6 *mf* actuary

Versi'cherungsnehmer **–in** §6 *mf* insured

versi'cherungspflichtig *adj* subject to mandatory insurance

Versi'cherungspolice *f*, **Versi'cherungsschein** *m* insurance policy

Versi'cherungsträger *m* underwriter

Versi'cherungszwang *m* compulsory insurance

versickern (**versik'kern**) *intr* (SEIN) seep out, trickle away

versie'geln *tr* seal (up); (jur) seal off

Versie'gelung *f* (–;) sealing (off)

versie'gen *intr* (SEIN) dry up

versil'bern *tr* silver-plate; (coll) sell

Versil'berung *f* (–;) silver-plating

versin'ken §143 intr (SEIN) (in acc) sink (into); (fig) (in acc) lapse (into)
versinnbildlichen [fɛr'zɪnbɪltlɪçən] tr symbolize
Version [ver'zjon] ƒ (-ʒ-en) version
versippt [fɛr'zɪpt] adj (mit) related (to)
versklaven [fɛr'sklavən] tr enslave
Vers'kunst ƒ versification
Vers'macher –in §6 mƒ versifier
Vers'maß n meter
versoffen [fɛr'zɔfən] adj (coll) drunk
versohlen [fɛr'zolən] tr (coll) give (s.o.) a good licking
versöhnen [fɛr'zønən] tr (mit) reconcile (with) || ref become reconciled
versöhnlich [fɛr'zønlɪç] adj conciliatory
Versöh'nung ƒ (-ʒ) reconciliation
Versöh'nungstag m Day of Atonement
versonnen [fɛr'zɔnən] adj wistful
versor'gen tr look after; provide for; (mit) supply (with), provide (with)
Versor'ger –in §6 mƒ provider, breadwinner
Versor'gung ƒ (-ʒ) providing, supplying; (Unterhalt) maintenance; (Alters- und Validen-) social security
Versor'gungsbetrieb m public utility
Versor'gungstruppen pl service troops
Versor'gungswege pl supply lines
verspan'nen tr guy, brace
verspäten [fɛr'pɛtən] ref come late; (rr) be behind schedule
verspätet [fɛr'pɛtət] adj belated, late
Verspä'tung ƒ (-ʒ-en) lateness, delay; mit e-r Stunde V. one hour behind schedule; V. haben be late
verspei'sen tr eat up
verspekulie'ren tr lose on a gamble || ref lose all through speculation
versper'ren tr bar, block, obstruct; (Tür) lock
verspie'len tr lose, gamble away || intr —bei j—m v. lose favor with s.o.
verspielt [fɛr'pilt] adj playful, frivolous
versponnen [fɛr'pɔnən] adj—in Gedanken versponnen lost in thought
verspot'ten tr mock, deride
Verspot'tung ƒ (-ʒ) mockery, derision
verspre'chen §64 tr promise || ref make a mistake in speaking; ich verspreche mir viel davon I expect a lot from that || Versprechen n (-ʒ-) promise; slip of the tongue
Verspre'chung ƒ (-ʒ-en) promise
verspren'gen tr scatter, disperse
Versprengte [fɛr'prɛntə] §5 mƒ (mil) straggler
verspritz'zen tr squirt, spatter
versprü'hen tr spray
verspü'ren tr feel, sense
verstaatlichen [fɛr'tatlɪçən] tr nationalize
Verstaat'lichung ƒ (-ʒ) nationalization
verstädtern [fɛr'tɛtərn] tr urbanize
Verstäd'terung ƒ (-ʒ) urbanization
Verstand' m (-[e]ʒ) understanding; intellect; intelligence, brains; (Vernunft) reason; (Geist) mind; senses; sense; den V. verlieren lose one's

mind; gesunder V. common sense; klarer V. clear head; nicht bei V. sein be out of one's mind
Verstan'deskraft ƒ intellectual power
verstan'desmäßig adj rational
Verstan'desmensch m matter-of-fact person
verstän'dig adj intelligent; sensible, reasonable; wise
verständigen [fɛr'tɛndɪgən] tr (von) inform (about), notify (of) || ref— sich v. mit make oneself understood to; come to an understanding with
Verstän'digung ƒ (-ʒ) understanding; information; communication; (telp) quality of reception
verständlich [fɛr'tɛntlɪç] adj understandable, intelligible; sich v. machen make oneself understood
Verständnis [fɛr'tɛntnɪs] n (-ses;-se) (für) understanding (of), appreciation (for)
verständ'nislos adj uncomprehending
verständ'nisinnig adj with deep mutual understanding; (Blick) knowing
verständ'nisvoll adj understanding, appreciative; (Blick) knowing
verstän'kern tr stink up
verstär'ken tr strengthen; (steigern) intensify; (elec) boost; (mil) reinforce; (rad) amplify
Verstär'ker m (-ʒ;-) (rad) amplifier
Verstär'kung ƒ (-ʒ-en) strengthening; intensification; (mil) reinforcement; (rad) amplification
verstatten [fɛr'tatən] tr permit
verstau'ben intr (SEIN) get dusty
verstäu'ben intr atomize
verstaubt [fɛr'taupt] adj dusty; (fig) antiquated
verstau'chen tr sprain
Verstau'chung ƒ (-ʒ-en) sprain
verstau'en tr stow away
Versteck [fɛr'tɛk] m (-[e]ʒ;-e) hiding place; hideout; V. spielen play hide-and-seek
verstecken (verstek'ken) tr & ref hide
versteckt [fɛr'tɛkt] adj hidden, veiled; (Absicht) ulterior
verste'hen §146 tr understand, see; make out; realize; (Sprache) know; e–n Spaß v. take a joke; ich verstehe es zu (inf) I know how to (inf); falsch v. misunderstand; verstanden? get it?; v. Sie mich recht! don't get me wrong!; was v. Sie unter (dat)? what do you mean by? || ref—(das) versteht sich! that's understood! das versteht sich von selbst! that goes without saying; sich gut v. mit get along well with; sich v. auf (acc) be skilled in; sich zu etw v. (sich zu etw entschließen) bring oneself to do s.th.; (in etw einwilligen) agree to s.th. || recip understand each other
verstei'fen tr stiffen; strut, brace, reinforce || ref stiffen; sich v. auf (acc) insist on
verstei'gen §148 ref lose one's way in the mountain; sich dazu v., daß go so far as to (inf)
Verstei'gerer m (-ʒ;-) auctioneer
verstei'gern tr auction off

Verstei'gerung f (–;-en) auction
verstei'nern intr (SEIN) become petrified; (fig) be petrified
verstell'bar adj adjustable
verstel'len tr (regulieren) adjust; (versperren) block; (Stimme, usw.) disguise; (Weiche) throw; (Verkehrsampel) switch; (Zeiger e-r Uhr) move; misplace; **j-m den Weg v.** block s.o.'s way || ref put on an act
Verstel'lung f (–;-en) adjusting; disguise
versteu'ern tr pay taxes on
Versteu'erung f (–;) paying of taxes
verstiegen [fer'ʃtigən] adj (Idee, Plan) extravagant, fantastic
verstim'men tr put out of tune; (fig) put out of humor
verstimmt [fer'ʃtɪmt] adj out of tune; (Magen) upset; **v. über** (acc) upset over
Verstim'mung f (–;) bad humor; (zwischen zweien) bad feeling, bad blood
verstockt [fer'ʃtɔkt] adj stubborn; (Verbrecher) hardened; (eccl) impenitent
Verstockt'heit f (–;) stubbornness; (eccl) impenitence
verstohlen [fer'ʃtolən] adj furtive
verstop'fen tr stop up, clog; (Straße) block, jam; (Leib) constipate
Verstop'fung f (–;) stopping up, clogging; congestion; (pathol) constipation
verstorben [fer'ʃtɔrbən] adj late, deceased || **Verstorbene** §5 mf deceased
verstört [fer'ʃtørt] adj shaken, bewildered, distracted
Verstört'heit f (–;) bewilderment
Verstoß' m (gegen) violation (of), offense (against)
versto'ßen §150 tr disown || intr—v. gegen violate, break
verstre'ben tr prop, brace
verstrei'chen §85 tr (Butter) spread; (Risse) plaster up || intr (SEIN) pass, elapse; (Gelegenheit) slip by; (Frist) expire
verstreu'en tr scatter, disperse, strew
verstricken (verstrik'ken) tr use up in knitting; (fig) involve, entangle || ref get entangled
verstümmeln [fer'ʃtymbln] tr mutilate; (Funkspruch) garble
Verstüm'melung f (–;-en) mutilation; (rad) garbling
verstummen [fer'ʃtumən] intr (SEIN) become silent; (vor Erstaunen) be dumbstruck; (Geräusch) cease
Versuch [fer'zux] m (–[e]s;-e) try, attempt; (Probe) test, trial; (wissenschaftlich) experiment; **e-n V. machen mit** have a try at
versu'chen tr try; tempt; (kosten) taste
Versuchs'anstalt f research institute
Versuchs'ballon m (& fig) trial balloon
Versuchs'flieger m test pilot
Versuchs'flug m test flight
Versuchs'kaninchen n (fig) guinea pig
Versuchs'reihe f series of tests
versuchs'weise adv by way of a test; on approval
Versu'chung f (–;-en) temptation

versumpfen [fer'zumpfən] intr (SEIN) become marshy; (coll) go to the dogs
versün'digen ref (an dat) sin (against)
versunken [fer'zuŋkən] adj sunk; **v. in** (acc) (fig) lost in
versü'ßen tr sweeten
verta'gen tr & ref (auf acc) adjourn (till), recess (till)
Verta'gung f (–;-en) adjournment
vertändeln [fer'tendln] tr trifle away
vertäuen [fer'tɔɪ-ən] tr (naut) moor
vertau'schen tr (gegen) exchange (for)
Vertau'schung f (–;-en) exchange
verteidigen [fer'taɪdɪgən] tr defend
Vertei'diger –in §6 mf defender; (Befürworter) advocate; (jur) counsel for the defense || m (fb) back
Vertei'digung f (–;-en) defense
Vertei'digungsbündnis n defensive alliance
Vertei'digungsminister m secretary of defense
Vertei'digungsministerium n department of defense
Vertei'digungsschrift f written defense
Vertei'digungsstellung f defensive position
vertei'len tr distribute; (zuteilen) allot; (über e-e große Fläche) scatter; (steuerlich) spread out; (Rollen) (theat) cast || ref spread out
Vertei'ler m (–s;–) distributer; (Anschriftenliste) mailing list; (von Durchschlägen) distribution; (aut) distributor
Vertei'lung f (–;-en) distribution; allotment; (theat) casting
verteuern [fer'tɔɪ-ərn] tr raise the price of
verteufelt [fer'tɔɪfəlt] adj devilish; a devil of a
vertiefen [fer'tifən] tr make deeper; (fig) deepen || ref—sich v. in (acc) become absorbed in
Vertie'fung f (–;-en) deepening; (Höhlung) hollow, depression; (Nische) niche; (Loch) hole; (fig) absorption
vertiert [fer'tirt] adj bestial
vertikal [verti'kal] adj vertical || **Vertikale** f (–;-n) vertical
vertil'gen tr exterminate, eradicate; (aufessen) (coll) eat, polish off
Vertil'gung f (–;) extermination
vertip'pen tr type incorrectly || ref make a typing error
verto'nen tr set to music
Verto'nung f (–;-en) musical arrangement
vertrackt [fer'trakt] adj (coll) odd, strange; (coll) blooming
Vertrag [fer'trak] m (–[e]s;-̈e) contract, agreement; (pol) treaty
vertra'gen §132 tr stand, take; tolerate || recip agree, be compatible; (Farben) harmonize; (Personen) get along
vertrag'lich adj contractual || adv by contract, as stipulated; **sich v. verpflichten zu** (inf) contract to (inf)
verträglich [fer'treklıç] adj sociable, personable; (Speise) digestible
Vertrags'bruch m breach of contract
vertragsbrüchig [fer'traksbryçıç] adj —**v. werden** break a contract

vertrags'gemäß *adj* contractual
vertrags'widrig *adj* contrary to the terms of a contract or treaty
vertrau'en *intr* (*dat*) trust; **v. auf** (*acc*) trust in, have confidence in ‖ **Vertrauen** *n* (**-s**;) trust, confidence; **ganz im V.** just between you and me; **im V.** confidentially
vertrau'enerweckend *adj* inspiring confidence
Vertrau'ensbruch *m* breach of trust
Vertrau'ens·mann *m* (**-[e]s**;**ʺer & -leute**) confidential agent; (*Vertrauter*) confidant; (*Sprecher*) spokesman; (*Gewährsmann*) informant
Vertrau'ensposten *m,* **Vertrau'ensstellung** *f* position of trust
vertrau'ensvoll *adj* confident; trusting
Vertrau'ensvotum *n* vote of confidence
vertrau'enswürdig *adj* trustworthy
vertrauern [fɛr'trau·ərn] *tr* spend in mourning
vertraulich [fɛr'traulɪç] *adj* confidential; intimate
Vertrau'lichkeit *f* (**-;-en**) intimacy, familiarity; **sich** [*dat*] **Vertraulichkeiten herausnehmen** take liberties
verträu'men *tr* dream away
verträumt [fɛr'trɔɪmt] *adj* dreamy
vertraut [fɛr'traut]*adj* familiar; friendly, intimate ‖ **Vertraute** §5 *mf* intimate friend ‖ *m* confidant ‖ *f* confidante
Vertraut'heit *f* (**-;**) familiarity
vertrei'ben §62 *tr* drive away, expel; (*aus dem Hause*) chase out; (*aus dem Lande*) banish; (*Ware*) sell, market; (*Zeit*) pass, kill
Vertrei'bung *f* (**-;**) expulsion
vertre'ten §152 *tr* represent; substitute for; (*Ansicht, usw.*) advocate ‖ *ref* **—sich** [*dat*] **den Fuß v.** sprain one's ankle; **sich** [*dat*] **die Beine v.** (coll) stretch one's legs
Vertre'ter **-in** §6 *mf* representative; substitute; (*Bevollmächtigte*) proxy; (*im Amt*) deputy; (*Fürsprecher*) advocate; (com) agent
Vertre'tung *f* (**-;-en**) representation; substitution; (com) agency; (pol) mission; **in V.** by proxy; **in V.** (*genit*) signed for
Vertrieb' *m* (**-[e]s;-e**) sale, turnover; retail trade; sales department
Vertriebs'abkommen *n* franchise agreement
Vertriebs'abteilung *f* sales department
Vertriebs'kosten *pl* distribution costs
Vertriebs'leiter **-in** §6 *mf* sales manager
Vertriebs'recht *n* franchise
vertrin'ken §143 *tr* drink up
vertrock'nen *intr* (SEIN) dry up
vertrödeln [fɛr'trødəln] *tr* fritter away
vertrö'sten *tr* string along; **auf später v.** put off till later
vertun' §154 *tr* waste ‖ *ref* (coll) make a mistake
vertu'schen *tr* hush up
verübeln [fɛr'ybəln] *tr* take (*s.th.*) the wrong way; **j-m etw v.** blame s.o. for s.th.
verü'ben *tr* commit, perpetrate

verul'ken *tr* (coll) kid
verunehren [fɛr'uneːrən] *tr* dishonor
veruneinigen [fɛr'unaɪnɪgən] *tr* disunite ‖ *recip* fall out, quarrel
verunglimpfen [fɛr'unglɪmpfən] *tr* slander, defame
verunglücken [fɛr'unglykən] *intr* (SEIN) have an accident; (coll) fail
Verunglückte [fɛr'unglyktə] §5 *mf* victim, casualty
verunreinigen [fɛr'unraɪnɪgən] *tr* soil, dirty; (*Luft, Wasser*) pollute
Verun'reinigung *f* (**-;**) pollution
verunstalten [fɛr'unʃtaltən] *tr* disfigure, deface
veruntreuen [fɛr'untrɔɪ·ən] *tr* embezzle
Verun'treuung *f* (**-;**) embezzlement
verunzieren [fɛr'untsiːrən] *tr* mar
verursachen [fɛr'uːrzaxən] *tr* cause
verur'teilen *tr* condemn; sentence
Verur'teilung *f* (**-;-en**) condemnation; sentence
vervielfachen [fɛr'fiːlfaxən] *tr* multiply ‖ *ref* increase considerably
vervielfältigen [fɛr'fiːlfɛltɪgən] *tr* multiply; duplicate; mimeograph; (*nachbilden*) reproduce
Verviel'fältigung *f* (**-;-en**) duplication; mimeographing; reproduction; (phot) printing
Verviel'fältigungsapparat *m* duplicator
vervollkommnen [fɛr'fɔlkɔmnən] *tr* improve on, perfect
Vervoll'kommnung *f* (**-;**) improvement, perfection
vervollständigen [fɛr'fɔl/tɛndɪgən] *tr* complete
Vervoll'ständigung *f* (**-;**) completion
verwach'sen *adj* overgrown; deformed; hunchbacked; **mit etw v. sein** (fig) be attached to s.th. ‖ *intr* (SEIN) grow together; become deformed; (*Wunde*) heal up; **zu e-r Einheit v.** form a whole
Verwach'sung *f* (**-;-en**) deformity
verwackelt [fɛr'vakəlt] *adj* (phot) blurred
verwah'ren *tr* keep; **v. vor** (*dat*) protect against ‖ *ref* **—sich v. gegen** protest against
verwahrlosen [fɛr'vaːrloːzən] *tr* neglect ‖ *intr* (SEIN) (*Gebäude*) deteriorate; (*Kinder*) run wild; (*Personen*) go to the dogs
verwahrlost [fɛr'vaːrloːst] *adj* uncared-for; (*Person*) unkempt; (*sittlich*) degenerate; (*Garten*) overgrown with weeds
Verwahr'losung *f* (**-;**) neglect
Verwah'rung *f* (**-;**) care, safekeeping, custody; (fig) protest; **etw in V. nehmen** take care of s.th.; **j-m in V. geben** entrust to s.o.'s care
verwaisen [fɛr'vaɪzən] *intr* (SEIN) become an orphan, be orphaned
verwaist [fɛr'vaɪst] *adj* orphaned; (fig) deserted
verwalten [fɛr'valtən] *tr* administer, manage
Verwal'ter **-in** §6 *mf* administrator, manager
Verwal'tung *f* (**-;-en**) administration, management

Verwal'tungsapparat *m* administrative machinery

Verwal'tungsbeamte *m* civil service worker; administrative official

Verwal'tungsdienst *m* civil service

Verwal'tungsrat *m* advisory board; (*e-r Aktiengesellschaft*) board of directors; (*e-s Instituts*) board of trustees

verwan'deln *tr* change, turn, convert; (*Strafe*) commute || *ref* change, turn

Verwand'lung *f* (–;-en) change, transformation; (jur) commutation

verwandt [fer'vant] *adj* (mit) related (to); (*Wissenschaften*) allied; (*Wörter*) cognate; (*Seelen*) kindred || **Verwandte** §5 *mf* relative, relation

Verwandt'schaft *f* (–;-en) relationship; relatives; (chem) affinity

verwandt'schaftlich *adj* kindred

Verwandt'schaftsgrad *m* degree of relationship

verwanzt [fer'vantst] *adj* (coll) full of bugs, lousy

verwar'nen *tr* warn, caution

Verwar'nung *f* (–;-en) warning, caution

verwa'schen *adj* washed out, faded; (*verschwommen*) vague, fuzzy

verwäs'sern *tr* dilute; (fig) water down

verwe'ben §94 *tr* interweave

verwe'chseln *tr* confuse, get (*various items*) mixed up; (*Hüte, Mäntel*) take by mistake || **Verwechseln** *n* (–$;$)—**sie sehen sich zum V. ähnlich** they are as alike as two peas

Verwechs'lung *f* (–;-en) mix-up

verwegen [fer'vegən] *adj* bold, daring

verwe'hen (*Blätter*) blow away; (*Spur*) cover up (with snow) || *intr* (SEIN) be blown in all directions; (*Spur*) be covered up; (*Worte*) drift away

verweh'ren *tr*—**j-m etw v.** refuse s.o. s.th.; prevent s.o. from getting s.th.

Verwe'hung *f* (–;-en) (snow)drift

verweichlichen [fer'vaiçliçən] *tr* make effeminate; (*Kind*) coddle || *ref* & *intr* become effeminate; grow soft

verweichlicht [fer'vaiçliçt] *adj* effeminate; soft, flabby

Verweich'lichung *f* (–$;$) effeminacy

verwei'gern *tr* refuse, deny, turn down

Verwei'gerung *f* (–;-en) refusal

verweilen [fer'vailən] *intr* linger, tarry; (fig) dwell

verweint [fer'vaint] *adj* red with tears

Verweis [fer'vais] *m* (–es;-e) reprimand, rebuke; (*Hinweis*) reference

verwei'sen §118 *tr* banish; (*Schüler*) expel; **j-m etw v.** reprimand s.o. for s.th.; **j-n an j-n v.** refer s.o. to s.o.; **j-n auf etw v.** refer s.o. to s.th.

Verwei'sung *f* (–;-en) banishment; expulsion; (*an acc*) referral (to); (*auf acc*) reference (to)

verwel'ken *intr* (SEIN) wither, wilt

verweltlichen [fer'veltliçən] *tr* secularize

verwendbar [fer'ventbar] *adj* applicable; available; usable

Verwend'barkeit *f* (–$;$) availability; usefulness

verwen'den §140 *tr* use, employ; (*auf acc*, *für*) apply (to); **Zeit und Mühe v. auf** (*acc*) spend time and effort on || *ref*—**sich bei j-m v. für** intercede with s.o. for

Verwen'dung *f* (–;-en) use, employment; application; **keine V. haben für** have no use for; **vielseitige V.** versatility

verwen'dungsfähig *adj* usable

verwer'fen §160 *tr* reject; (*Plan*) discard; (*Berufung*) turn down; (*Klage*) dismiss; (*Urteil*) overrule || *ref* (*Holz*) warp; (geol) fault

verwerf'lich *adj* objectionable

Verwer'fung *f* (–;-en) rejection; warping; (geol) fault

verwer'ten *tr* utilize

Verwer'tung *f* (–;-en) utilization

verwesen [fer'vezən] *intr* (SEIN) rot

verwes'lich [fer'vesliç] *adj* perishable

Verwe'sung *f* (–$;$) decay

verwet'ten *tr* lose (*in betting*)

verwich'sen *tr* (coll) clobber

verwickeln (verwik'keln) *tr* snarl, entangle; complicate; (fig) involve || *ref*—**sich v. in** (*acc*) get entangled in; (fig) get involved in

Verwick'lung *f* (–;-en) snarl, tangle; involvement; complexity; complication

verwil'dern *intr* become overgrown; (*Person*) become depraved; (*Kind*) run wild, go wild

verwil'dert [fer'vildərt] *adj* wild, savage; weed-grown

verwin'den §59 *tr* get over; (*Verlust*) recover from

verwir'ken *tr* forfeit; (*Strafe*) incur || *ref*—**sich** [*dat*] **j-s Gunst v.** lose favor with s.o.

verwirklichen [fer'virkliçən] *tr* realize, make come true || *ref* come true

Verwirk'lichung *f* (–$;$) realization

Verwir'kung *f* (–;-en) forfeiture

verwirren [fer'virən] *tr* throw into disorder; (*Haar*) muss up; confuse

verwirrt [fer'virt] *adj* confused

Verwir'rung *f* (–;-en) confusion; **in V. geraten** become confused

verwirt'schaften *tr* squander

verwi'schen *tr* wipe out; (teilweise) blur; (*verschmieren*) smear; (*Spuren*) cover || *ref* become blurred

verwit'tern *intr* (SEIN) become weather-beaten; (*zerfallen*) crumble away

verwittert [fer'vitərt] *adj* weather-beaten

verwitwet [fer'vitvət] *adj* widowed

verwöhnen [fer'vønən] *tr* pamper, spoil

verworfen [fer'vorfən] *adj* depraved

Verwor'fenheit *f* (–$;$) depravity

verworren [fer'vorən] *adj* confused

verwundbar [fer'vuntbar] *adj* vulnerable

verwun'den *tr* wound

verwunderlich [fer'vundərliç] *adj* remarkable, astonishing

verwun'dern *tr* astonish || *ref* (**über** *acc*) be astonished (at), wonder (at)

Verwun'derung *f* (–$;$) astonishment; **j-n in V. setzen** astonish s.o.

verwundet [fer'vundət] *adj* wounded

‖ **Verwundete** §5 *mf* wounded person

verwunschen [fer'vunʃən] *adj* enchanted

verwün'schen *tr* damn, curse; (*in Märchen*) bewitch, put a curse on

verwünscht [fer'vynʃt] *adj* confounded, darn ‖ *interj* darn it!

Verwün'schung *f* (–;–en) curse

verwurzelt [fer'vurtsəlt] *adj* deeply rooted

verwüsten [fer'vystən] *tr* devastate

Verwü'stung *f* (–;–en) devastation

verzagen [fer'tsagən] *intr* (SEIN) lose heart, despair; **v. an** (*dat*) give up on

verzagt [fer'tsakt] *adj* despondent

Verzagt'heit *f* (–;) despondency

verzäh'len *ref* miscount

verzärteln [fer'tsertəln] *tr* pamper

verzau'bern *tr* bewitch, charm; **v. in** (*acc*) change into

Verzehr [fer'tser] *m* (–[e]s;) consumption

verzeh'ren *tr* consume; (*Geld*) spend; (*Mahlzeit*) eat ‖ *ref* (**in** *dat*, **vor** *dat*) pine away (with); (**nach**) yearn (for)

verzeh'rend *adj* (*Blick*) longing; (*Fieber*) wasting; (*Leidenschaft*) burning

Verzeh'rung *f* (–;) consumption

verzeich'nen *tr* draw wrong; make a list of; register; catalogue; (opt) distort

Verzeichnis [fer'tsaiçnıs] *n* (–ses;–se) list; catalogue; (*im Buch*) index; (*Inventar*) inventory; (*Tabelle*) table; (telp) directory

verzeihen [fer'tsaiən] §81 *tr* forgive, pardon (*s.th.*); condone ‖ *intr* (*dat*) forgive, pardon (*s.o.*)

verzeihlich [fer'tsailıç] *adj* pardonable

Verzei'hung *f* (–;) pardon

verzer'ren *tr* distort; contort

Verzer'rung *f* (–;–en) distortion; contortion; grimace

verzetteln [fer'tsetəln] *tr* fritter away; catalogue ‖ *ref* spread oneself too thin

Verzicht [fer'tsıçt] *m* (–[e]s;) renunciation; **V. leisten auf** (*acc*) waive

verzichten [fer'tsıçtən] *intr*—**v. auf** (*acc*) do without; (*verabsäumen*) pass up; (*aufgeben*) give up, renounce; (*Rechte*) waive

verzieh [fer'tsi] *pret* of **verzeihen**

verzie'hen §163 *tr* distort; (*Kind*) spoil; **den Mund v.** make a face; **ohne e–e Miene zu v.** without batting an eye ‖ *ref* disappear; (*Schmerz*) go away; (*Menge, Wolken*) disperse; (*Holz*) warp; (*durch Druck*) buckle; (coll) sneak off

verzie'ren *tr* decorate

Verzie'rung *f* (–;–en) decoration; (*Schmuck*) ornament

verzinsen [fer'tsınzən] *tr* pay interest on; **e–e Summe zu 6% v.** pay 6% interest on a sum ‖ *ref* yield interest; **sich mit 6% v.** yield 6% interest

verzinslich [fer'tsınslıç] *adj* bearing interest ‖ *adv*—**v. anlegen** put out at interest

Verzin'sung *f* (–;) interest

verzog [fer'tsok] *pret* of **verziehen**

verzogen [fer'tsogən] *adj* distorted; (*Kind*) spoiled; (*Holz*) warped

verzö'gern *tr* delay; put off, postpone ‖ *ref* be late

Verzö'gerung *f* (–;–en) delay; postponement

verzollen [fer'tsɔlən] *tr* pay duty on; (naut) clear; **haben Sie etw zu v.?** do you have anything to declare?

verzückt [fer'tsykt] *adj* ecstatic

Ver.ückung [fer'tsykuŋ] *f* (–;) ecstasy

Verzug' *m* (–[e]s;) delay; (*in der Leistung*) default; **in V. geraten mit** fall behind in; **ohne V.** without delay

verzwei'feln *intr* (HABEN & SEIN) (**an** *dat*) despair (of) ‖ **Verzweifeln** *n*—**es ist zum V.** it's enough to drive one to despair

verzweifelt [fer'tsvaifəlt] *adj* desperate

Verzweif'lung *f* (–;) despair

verzweigen [fer'tsvaigən] *ref* branch out

verzweigt [fer'tsvaikt] *adj* having many branches; (fig) complex

verzwickt [fer'tsvıkt] *adj* (coll) tricky, ticklish

Vestibül [vestı'byl] *n* (–s;–e) vestibule; (theat) lobby

Veteran [vete'ran] *m* (–en;–en) veteran, ex-serviceman

Veterinär –in [veterı'ner(ın)] §8 *mf* veterinarian

Veto ['veto] *n* (–s;–s) veto

Vetter ['fetər] *m* (–s;–) cousin

Vet'ternwirtschaft *f* nepotism

Vexierbild [ve'ksirbılt] *n* picture puzzle

vexieren [ve'ksirən] *tr* tease; pester

V-förmig ['faufœrmıç] *adj* V-shaped

vibrieren [vı'brirən] *intr* vibrate

Vieh [fi] *n* (–[e]s;) livestock; cattle; animal, beast

Vieh'bestand *m* livestock

Vieh'bremse *f* horsefly

viehisch ['fi·ıʃ] *adj* brutal

Vieh'tränke *f* water hole

Vieh'wagen *m* (rr) cattle car

Vieh'weide *f* cow pasture

Vieh'zucht *f* cattle breeding

Vieh'züchter –in §6 *mf* rancher

viel [fil] *adj* much; many; a lot of ‖ *adv* much; a lot ‖ *pron* much; many

viel'beschäftigt *adj* very busy

viel'eck *n* polygon

Viel'eck *n* polygon

vielerlei ['filər'lai] *invar adj* many kinds of

viel'fach *adj* multiple; manifold ‖ *adv* (coll) often

Vielfach– *comb.fm.* multiple

viel'fältig *adj* manifold, various

Viel'fältigkeit *f* (–;–en) multiplicity; variety

vielleicht' *adv* maybe, perhaps

vielmalig ['filmalıç] *adj* oft repeated

vielmals ['filmals] *adv* frequently; **danke v.!** many thanks!

vielmehr' *adv* rather, on the contrary

viel'sagend *adj* suggestive

viel'seitig *adj* many-sided, versatile

vielstufig ['fil'tufıç] *adj* multistage

viel'teilig *adj* of many parts

viel'versprechend *adj* very promising

vier [fir] *adj* four; **unter vier Augen** confidentially || *pron* four; **auf allen vieren** on all fours || **Vier** *f* (-;-en) four

vier'beinig *adj* four-legged

Vier'eck *n* quadrangle

vier'eckig *adj* quadrangular

viererlei ['firər'laɪ] *invar adj* four different kinds of

vier'fach, vier'fältig *adv* fourfold, quadruple

Vierfüßer ['fɪrfysər] *m* (-s;-) quadruped

vierhändig ['fɪrhendɪç] *adv*—**v. spielen** (mus) play a duet

Vierlinge ['fɪrlɪŋə] *pl* quadruplets

vier'mal *adv* four times

vierschrötig ['fɪr'røtɪç] *adj* stocky

vierstrahlig ['fɪr'ʃtraɪlɪç] *adj* four-engine (jet)

viert [fɪrt] *pron*—**zu v.** in fours; **wir gehen zu v.** the four of us are going

Viertakter ['fɪrtaktər] *m* (-s;-), **Viertaktmotor** ['fɪrtaktmotər] *m* four-cycle engine

Vierte ['fɪrtə] §9 *adj & pron* fourth

vier'teilen *tr* quarter

Viertel ['fɪrtəl] *n* (-s;-) quarter; fourth (*part*); (*Stadtteil*) quarter, section

Vierteljahr *n* quarter (*of a year*)

vierteljäh'rig, vierteljähr'lich *adj* quarterly

vierteln ['fɪrtəln] *tr* quarter

Vier'telnote *f* (*mus*) quarter note

Viertelpfund *n* quarter of a pound

Viertelstun'de *f* quarter of an hour

viertens ['fɪrtəns] *adv* fourthly

vier'zehn *invar adj & pron* fourteen || **Vierzehn** *f* (-;-en) fourteen

vier'zehnte §9 *adj & pron* fourteenth

Vier'zehntel *n* (-s;-) fourteenth (*part*)

vierzig ['fɪrtsɪç] *invar adj & pron* forty || **Vierzig** *f* (-;-en) forty

vierziger ['fɪrtsɪgər] *invar adj* of the forties; **die v. Jahre** the forties

vierzigste ['fɪrtsɪçstə] §9 *adj & pron* fortieth

Vikar [vɪ'kɑr] *m* (-s;-e) vicar

Vil-la ['vɪla] *f* (-;-len [lən]) villa

violett [vɪ·o'lɛt] *adj* violet

Violine [vɪ·o'linə] *f* (-;-n) violin

Violin'schlüssel *m* treble clef

Viper ['vɪpər] *f* (-;-n) viper

viril [vɪ'ril] *adj* virile

virtuos [vɪrtu'os] *adj* masterly || **Virtuose** [vɪrtu'ozə] *m* (-n;-n), **Virtuosin** [vɪrtu'ozɪn] *f* (-;-nen) virtuoso

Vi-rus ['vɪrus] *n* (-;-ren [rən]) virus

Visage [vɪ'zaʒə] *f* (-;-n) (coll) mug

Visier [vɪ'zir] *n* (-s;-e) visor; (*am Gewehr*) sight

visieren [vɪ'zirən] *tr* (*eichen*) gauge; (*Paß*) visa

Vision [vɪ'zjon] *f* (-;-en) vision

visionär [vɪzjo'ner] *adj* visionary || **Visionär** *m* (-s;-e) visionary

Visitation [vɪzɪta'tsjon] *f* (-;-en) inspection; search

Visite [vɪ'zitə] *f* (-;-n) formal call; **Visiten machen** (med) make the rounds

Visi'tenkarte *f* calling card

visuell [vɪzu'ɛl] *adj* visual

Vi·sum ['vizum] *n* (-s;-sa [za]) visa

vital [vɪ'tal] *adj* energetic

Vitalität [vɪtalɪ'tet] *f* (-;) vitality

Vitamin [vɪta'min] *n* (-s;-e) vitamin

Vitamin'mangel *m* vitamin deficiency

Vitrine [vɪ'trinə] *f* (-;-n) showcase

Vize- [fitsə], **Vize-** *comb.fm.* vice-

Vi'zekönig *m* viceroy

Vlies [flis] *n* (-es;-e) fleece

Vogel ['fogəl] *m* (-s;-̈) bird; (coll) chap, bird; **den V. abschießen** (coll) bring down the house; **du hast e-n V.!** (coll) you're cuckoo!

Vo'gelbauer *n* birdcage

Vogelbeerbaum ['fogəlberbaum] *m* mountain ash

vo'gelfrei *adj* outlawed

Vo'gelfutter *n* birdseed

Vo'gelkunde *f* ornithology

Vo'gelmist *m* bird droppings

vögeln ['føgəln] *tr & intr* (vulg) screw

Vo'gelperspektive *f*, **Vo'gelschau** *f* bird's-eye view

Vo'gelpfeife *f* bird call

Vo'gelscheuche *f* scarecrow

Vo'gelstange *f* perch

Vogel-Strauß'-Politik *f* burying one's head in the sand; **V. betreiben** bury one's head in the sand

Vo'gelstrich *m*, **Vo'gelzug** *m* migration of birds

Vöglein ['føglaɪn] *n* (-s;-) little bird

Vogt [fokt] *m* (-[e]s;-̈e) (obs) steward; (obs) governor, prefect, magistrate

Vokabel [vo'kabəl] *f* (-;-n) vocabulary word

Vokal [vo'kal] *m* (-s;-e) vowel

Volk [folk] *n* (-[e]s;-̈er) people, nation; lower classes; (von Bienen) swarm; (von Rebhühnern) covey

Völker- [fœlkər] *comb.fm.* international

Völ'kerbund *m* League of Nations

Völ'kerfriede *m* international peace

Völ'kerkunde *f* ethnology

Völ'kermord *m* genocide

Völ'kerrecht *n* international law

Völ'kerschaft *f* (-;-en) tribe

Völ'kerwanderung *f* barbarian invasions

volk'reich *adj* populous

Volks'abstimmung *f* plebiscite

Volks'aufwiegler *m* rabble rouser

Volks'ausdruck *m* household expression

Volks'befragung *f* public opinion poll

Volks'begehren *n* national referendum

Volks'bibliotek *f* free library

Volks'charakter *m* national character

Volks'deutsche §5 *mf* German national

Volks'dichter *m* popular poet

volks'eigen *adj* state-owned

Volks'entscheid *m* referendum

Volks'feind *m* public enemy

Volks'gunst *f* popularity

Volks'haufen *m* crowd, mob

Volks'herrschaft *f* democracy

Volks'hochschule *f* adult evening school

Volks'justiz *f* lynch law

Volks′küche f soup kitchen
Volks′kunde f folklore
Volks′lied n folksong
volks′mäßig adj popular
Volks′meinung f popular opinion
Volks′menge f populace, crowd of people
Volks′musik f popular music
Volks′partei f people's party
Volks′republik f people's republic
Volks′schule f grade school
Volks′sitte f national custom
Volks′sprache f vernacular
Volks′stamm m tribe; race
Volks′stimme f popular opinion
Volks′stimmung f mood of the people
Volks′tracht f national costume
Volkstum [′fɔlkstum] n (-s;) nationality
volkstümlich [′fɔlkstymlıç] adj national; popular
Volks′verführer –in §6 mf demagogue
Volks′versammlung f public meeting
Volks′vertreter –in §6 mf representative
Volks′wirt m political economist
Volks′wirtschaft f national economy
Volks′wirtschaftslehre f (educ) political economy
Volks′wohl n public good
Volks′wohlfahrt f public welfare
Volks′zählung f census
voll [fɔl] adj full, filled; whole, entire; (Tagespreis) broad; (coll) drunk; **aus dem vollen schöpfen** have unlimited resources; **j–n für v. ansehen** (or **nehmen**) take s.o. seriously || adv fully, in full; **v. und ganz** fully
vollauf′ adv—**das genügt v.** that's quite enough; **v. beschäftigt** plenty busy; **v. zu tun haben** have plenty to do
Voll′beschäftigung f full employment
Voll′besitz m full possession
Voll′blut n, **Voll′blutpferd** n thoroughbred
vollblütig [′fɔlblytıç] adj full-blooded
vollbrin′gen §65 tr achieve
vollbusig [′vɔlbuzıç] adj big-breasted
Voll′dampf m full steam; **mit V.** (fig) at full blast, full speed
vollenden [fɔl′ɛndən] tr bring to a close, finish, complete; (vervollkommnen) perfect; **er hat sein Leben vollendet** (poet) he died
vollendet [fɔl′ɛndət] adj perfect
vollends [′fɔlɛnts] adv completely
Vollen′dung f (-;) finishing, completing; (Vollkommenheit) perfection
Völlerei [fœlə′raı] f (-;) gluttony
voll′führen tr carry out, execute
voll′füllen tr fill up
Voll′gas n full throttle
Voll′gefühl n—**im V.** (genit) fully conscious of
Voll′genuß m full enjoyment
vollgepfropft [′fɔlgəpfrɔpft] adj jammed, packed
voll′gießen §76 tr fill up
völlig [′fœlıç] adj full, complete
voll′jährig adj of age
Voll′jährigkeit f legal age, majority
vollkom′men, voll′kommen adj perfect || adv (coll) absolutely

Vollkom′menheit f (-;) perfection
Voll′kornbrot n whole-grain bread
Voll′kraft f full vigor, prime
voll machen tr fill up; (coll) dirty
Voll′macht f full authority; (jur) power of attorney; **in V.** for...(prefixed to the signature of another at end of letter)
Voll′matrose m able-bodied seaman
Voll′milch f whole milk
Voll′mond m full moon
Voll′pension f full board and lodging
voll′saftig adj juicy, succulent
voll′schenken tr fill up
voll′schlagen §132 ref—**sich** [dat] **den Bauch v.** (coll) stuff oneself
voll′schlank adj well filled out
Voll′sit:ung f plenary session
Voll′spur f (rr) standard-gauge track
voll′ständig adj full; complete, entire || adv completely, quite
Voll′ständigkeit f (-;) completeness
voll′stopfen tr stuff, cram
vollstrecken (vollstrek′ken) tr (Urteil) carry out; (Testament) execute; **ein Todesurteil an j–m v.** execute s.o.
Vollstreckung (Vollstrek′kung) f. (-;) exe ′ution
voll′tanken tr (aut) fill up || intr (aut) fill it up
volltönend [′fɔltønənt] adj (Stimme) rich; (Satz) well-rounded
Voll′treffer m direct hit
Voll′versammlung f plenary session
Voll′waise f (full) orphan
voll′wertig adj of full value; complete, perfect
vollzählig [′fɔltseltç] adj complete; **sind wir v.?** are we all here? || adv in full force
vollzie′hen §163 tr execute, carry out, effect; (Vertrag) ratify; (Ehe) consummate || ref take place
vollzie′hend adj executive
Vollzi:′hung f. **Vollzug′** m execution, carrying out
Vollzugs′ausschuß m executive committee
Volontär –in [vɔlɔn′ter(ın)] §8 mf volunteer; trainee
volontieren [vɔlɔn′tirən] intr work as a trainee
Volt [vɔlt] n (–[e]s;–) (elec) volt
Volu∙men [vo′lumən] n (–s;– & –mina [mınə]) (Band; Rauminhalt) volume
vom [fɔm] abbr von dem
von [fɔn] prep (dat) (beim Passiv) by; **für den Genitiv** of; (räumlich, zeitlich) from; (über) about, of; **von... an** from...on; **von Holz** (made) of wood; **von Kindheit auf** from earliest childhood; **von mir aus** as far as I am concerned; **von selbst** automatically
voneinan′der adv from each other; of each other; apart
vonnöten [fɔn′nøtən] invar adj—**v. sein** be necessary
vonstatten [fɔn′/tatən] adv—**gut v. gehen** go well; **v. gehen** take place
vor [for] prep (dat) (örtlich) in front of, before; (zeitlich) before, prior to; (Abwehr) against, from; (wegen) of,

with, for; **etw vor sich haben** face s.th.; **heute vor acht Tagen** today a week ago; **vor sich gehen** take place, occur; **vor sich hin** to oneself || *prep (acc)* in front of

vorab' *adv* in advance

Vor'abend *m—am* **V.** *(genit)* on the eve of

Vor'ahnung *f* (coll) hunch, idea

voran' *adv* in front, out ahead || *interj* go ahead!, go on!

voran'gehen §82 *intr* (SEIN) go on ahead, take the lead; (fig) set an example; **die Arbeit geht gut voran** the work is coming along well

voran'kommen §99 *intr* (SEIN) make progress; **gut v.** come along well

Vor'anschlag *m* rough estimate

Vor'anzeige *f* preliminary announcement; (cin) preview of coming attractions

Vor'arbeit *f* preliminary work

vor'arbeiten *intr* do the work in advance; do the preliminary work

vorauf' *adv* ahead, in front

voraus' *adv* in front; *(dat)* ahead (of) || **vor'aus** *adv—im* **v.** in advance

Voraus'abteilung *f* (mil) vanguard

voraus'bedingen §142 *tr* stipulate beforehand

voraus'bestellen *tr* reserve

voraus'bestimmen *tr* predetermine

voraus'bezahlen *tr* pay in advance

voraus'eilen *intr* (SEIN) rush ahead

vorausgesetzt [fo'rausgəzetst] *adj—* **v., daß** provided that

Voraus'sage *f* prediction; prophecy; *(des Wetters)* forecast; *(Wink)* tip

voraus'sagen *tr* predict; prophesy; *(Wetter)* forecast

Voraus'sagung *f* var of **Voraussage**

voraus'schauen *intr* look ahead

voraus'schicken *tr* send ahead; (fig) mention beforehand

voraus'sehen §138 *tr* foresee

voraus'setzen *tr* presume, presuppose

Voraus'setzung *f* assumption; prerequisite; premise

Voraus'sicht *f* foresight

voraus'sichtlich *adj* probable, presumable || *adv* probably, presumably, the way it looks

Voraus'zahlung *f* advance payment

Vor'bau *m* (-[e]s;-ten) projection; balcony, porch

vor'bauen *tr* build out || *intr (dat)* take precautions against

vor'bedacht *adj* premeditated || **Vorbedacht** *m* (-[e]s;) —**mit V.** on purpose; **ohne V.** unintentionally

vor'bedeuten *tr* forebode

Vor'bedeutung *f* (-;-en) foreboding; omen, portent

Vor'bedingung *f* (-;-en) precondition

Vorbehalt ['forbəhalt] *m* (-[e]s;-e) reservation; proviso; **mit allem V. hinnehmen!** take it for what it's worth!; **mit** *(or* **unter) dem V., daß** with the proviso that; **stiller** *(or* **innerer) V.** mental reservation; **unter V. aller Rechte** all rights reserved

vor'behalten §90 *tr* reserve; **Änderungen v.!** subject to change without

notice || *ref—sich [dat]* **etw v. re-serve** s.th. for oneself

vor'behaltlich *prep (genit)* subject to

vor'behaltlos *adj* unreserved, unconditional

vorbei' *adv* over, past, gone; **es ist drei Uhr v.** it's past three o'clock; **v. an** *(dat)* past, by; **v. ist v.** done is done; **v. können** be able to pass

vorbei'eilen *intr* (SEIN) —**an j—m v.** rush past s.o.

vorbei'fahren §71 *intr* (SEIN) drive by

vorbei'fliegen §57 *intr* (SEIN) fly past

vorbei'fließen §76 *intr* (SEIN) flow by

vorbei'gehen §82 *intr* (SEIN) pass; **an j—m v.** pass by s.o. || **Vorbeigehen** *n* —**im V.** in passing

vorbei'gelingen §142 *intr* (SEIN) fail

vorbei'kommen §99 *intr* (SEIN) pass by; (coll) stop in

vorbei'lassen §104 *tr* let pass

Vorbei'marsch *m* parade

vorbei'marschieren *intr* (SEIN) march by

Vor'bemerkung *f* (-;-en) preliminary remark; (parl) preamble

vorbenannt ['forbənant] *adj* aforementioned

vor'bereiten *tr* prepare || *ref (auf acc, für)* get ready (for)

vor'bereitend *adj* preparatory

Vor'bereitung *f* (-;-en) preparation

Vor'bericht *m* preliminary report

Vor'besprechung *f* (-;-en) preliminary discussion

vor'bestellen *tr* order in advance; *(Zimmer, usw.)* reserve

Vor'bestellung *f* (-;-en) advance order; reservation

vor'bestraft *adj* previously convicted

vor'beten *tr* keep repeating || *intr* lead in prayer

vor'beugen *ref* bend forward || *intr (dat)* prevent

vor'beugend *adj* preventive

Vor'beugung *f* (-;-en) prevention

Vor'beugungsmittel *n* preventive

Vor'bild *n* model; *(Beispiel)* example

vor'bildlich *adj* exemplary, model

Vor'bildung *f* (-;-en) educational background

Vor'bote *m* forerunner; (fig) harbinger

vor'bringen §65 *tr* bring forward, produce; *(Gründe)* give; *(Plan)* propose; *(Klagen)* prefer; *(Wunsch)* express

vor'buchstabieren *tr* spell out

Vor'bühne *f* apron, proscenium

vor'datieren *tr* antedate

vordem [for'dem] *adv* formerly

Vorder- [fordər] *comb.fm.* front, fore-

Vor'derachse *f* front axle

Vor'derarm *m* forearm

Vor'derbein *n* foreleg

vordere ['fordərə] §9 *adj* front

Vor'derfront *f* front; (fig) forefront

Vor'derfuß *m* front foot

Vor'dergrund *m* foreground

vor'derhand *adv* for the time being

vor'derlastig *adj* (aer) nose-heavy

Vor'derlauf *m* (hunt) foreleg

Vor'dermann *m* (-[e]s;-er) man in front; **j—n auf V. bringen** (coll) put s.o. straight; **V. halten** keep in line

Vor′derpfote f front paw
Vor′derrad n front wheel
Vor′derradantrieb m front-wheel drive
Vor′derreihe f front row; front rank
Vor′dersicht f front view
Vor′derseite f front side, front; (e-r Münze) obverse, heads
Vor′dersitz m front seat
vorderste [′fɔrdərstə] §9 adj farthest front
Vor′dersteven m (naut) stem
Vor′derteil m & n front section; (naut) prow
Vor′dertür f front door
Vor′derzahn m front tooth
Vor′derzimmer n front room
vor drängen tr & ref press forward
vor drängen §142 intr (SEIN) forge ahead, advance
vor′dringlich adj urgent
Vor′druck m printed form, blank
vor′ehelich adj premarital
vor′eilig adj hasty, rash
Vor′eiligkeit f (–;) haste, rashness
vor′eingenommen adj biased, prejudiced
Vor′eingenommenheit f (–;–en) bias, prejudice
Vor′eltern pl ancestors, forefathers
vor′enthalten §90 tr—j-m etw v. withhold s.th. from s.o.
Vor′entscheidung f (–;–en) preliminary decision
vor′erst adv first of all; for the time being, for the present
vor′erwähnt [′fɔrervent] adj aforesaid
Vor′fahr [′fɔrfar] m (–en;–en) forebear
vor′fahren §71 intr (SEIN) (bei) drive up (to)
Vor′fahrt f, **Vor′fahrt(s)recht** n right of way
Vor′fall m incident; event
vor′fallen §72 intr (SEIN) happen
Vor′feld n (aer) apron (of airport); (mil) approaches
vor finden §59 tr find there
Vor′freude f anticipation
Vor′frühling m early spring
vor fühlen intr—bei j-m v. feel s.o. out, put out feelers to s.o.
Vor′führdame [′fɔrfyrdəmə] f mannequin
vor führen tr bring forward produce; display, demonstrate; (Kleider) model; (Film, show); (Stück) (theat) present
Vor′führung f (–;–en) production; demonstration; showing; show, performance
Vor′gabe f points, handicap
Vor′gaberennen n handicap (race)
Vor′gabespiel n handicap
Vor′gang m event, incident, phenomenon; (Verfahren) process, procedure; (Präzedenzfall) precedent; (in den Akten) previous correspondence
Vor′gänger –in §6 mf predecessor
Vor′garten m front yard
vor′geben §80 tr pretend; give as an excuse; **j-m zehn Punkte v.** give s.o. ten points odds ‖ intr—j-m v. give

s.o. odds ‖ **Vorgeben** n (–s;–) pretext
vor′gebirge n foothills; (Kap) cape
vorgeblich [′fɔrgeplɪç] adj ostensible
vorgefaßt [′fɔrgəfast] adj preconceived
Vor′gefühl n inkling; banges V. misgivings; **im V. von** or genit in anticipation of
vor′gehen §82 intr (SEIN) advance; go first; act; take action, proceed; (sich ereignen) go on, happen; (Uhr) be fast; (dat) take precedence (over); **die Arbeit geht vor** work comes first; **was geht hier vor?** what's going on here? ‖ **Vorgehen** n (–s;) advance; action, proceeding; **gemeinschaftliches V.** concerted action
vorgelagert [′fɔrgəlagərt] adj offshore
Vor′gelände n foreground
vorgenannt [′fɔrgənant] adj aforementioned
Vor′gericht n appetizer
Vor′geschichte f previous history; (Urgeschichte) prehistory
vor′geschichtlich adj prehistoric
Vor′geschmack m foretaste
Vorgesetzte [′fɔrgəzetstə] §5 mf superior; boss; (mil) senior officer
vor′gestern adv day before yesterday
vor′gestrig adj of the day before yesterday
vorgetäuscht [′fɔrgətɔɪʃt] adj make-believe
vor′greifen §88 intr (dat) anticipate
Vor′griff m anticipation
vor′gucken intr (Unterkleid) show
vor′haben §89 tr have in mind, plan; intend to do; (ausfragen) question; (schelten) scold; (Schürze) (coll) have on ‖ **Vorhaben** n (–s;–) intention, plan; project
Vor′halle f entrance hall; lobby
vor′halten §90 tr—j-m etw v. hold s.th. in front of s.o.; (fig) reproach s.o. with s.th. ‖ intr last
Vor′haltung f (–;–en) reproach; j-m Vorhaltungen machen über (acc) reproach s.o. for
Vor′hand f (cards) forehand; (tennis) forehand stroke; **die V. haben** (cards) lead off
vorhanden [fɔr′handən] adj present, at hand, available; (com) in stock; **v. sein** exist
Vorhan′densein n existence; presence
Vor′hang m (–[e]s;–e) curtain; (theat) (coll) curtain call; **Eiserner V.** iron curtain
Vorhängeschloß [′fɔrhenəʃlɔs] n padlock
Vor′hangstange f curtain rod
Vor′hangstoff m drapery material
Vor′haut f foreskin
Vor′hemd n dicky, shirt front
vor′her adv before, previously; (im voraus) in advance
vorher′bestellen tr reserve
vorher′bestimmen tr predetermine; (eccl) predestine
Vorher′bestimmung f predestination
vorher′gehend, vorherig [fɔr′herɪç] adj preceding, previous; prior
Vor′herrschaft f predominance

vor'herrschen *intr* predominate, prevail

vor'herrschend *adj* predominant, prevailing

Vorher'sage *f* prediction; forecast

vorher'sagen *tr* predict, foretell; (*Wetter*) forecast

vorhin' *adv* a little while ago

vor'historisch *adj* prehistoric

Vor'hof *m* front yard; (anat) auricle

Vor'hut *f* (mil) vanguard

vorige [ˈforɪgə] §9 *adj* previous, former; **voriges Jahr** last year

Vor'jahr *n* preceding year

vor'jährig *adj* last year's

Vor'kammer *f* (anat) auricle; (aut) precombustion chamber

Vor'kampf *m* (box) preliminary bout; (sport) heat

Vor'kämpfer –in §6 *mf* pioneer

Vorkehrung [ˈforkeruŋ] *f* (–;-en) precaution; **Vorkehrungen treffen** take precautions

Vor'kenntnis *f* (von) basic knowledge (of); **Vorkenntnisse** rudiments, basics; **Vorkenntnisse nicht erforderlich** no previous experience necessary

vor'knöpfen *ref*—**sich** [*dat*] **j–n** v. (coll) chew s.o. out

Vor'kommando *n* (mil) advance party

vor'kommen §99 *intr* (SEIN) happen; (*Fall*) come up; (*als Besucher*) be admitted; (*scheinen*) seem, look; (*sich finden*) be found; (*zu Besuch*) call on || *ref*—**er kam sich** [*dat*] **dumm vor** he felt silly || *impers*—**es kommt dir nur so vor** you are just imagining it; **es kommt mir vor** it seems to me || **Vorkommen** *n* (–s;-) occurrence; (min) deposit

Vorkommnis [ˈforkɔmnɪs] *n* (–ses;-se) event, occurrence

Vorkriegs– *comb.fm.* prewar

vor'laden §103 *tr* (jur) summon; (*unter Strafandrohung*) (jur) subpoena

Vor'ladung *f* (–;-en) (jur) summons; (*unter Strafandrohung*) (jur) subpoena

Vor'lage *f* submission, presentation; proposal; (*Muster*) pattern; bedside carpet; (fb) forward pass; (parl) bill

vor'lassen §104 *tr* let go ahead; (*Auto*) let pass; (*zulassen*) admit

Vor'lauf *m* (sport) qualifying heat

Vor'läufer –in §6 *mf* forerunner

vor'läufig *adj* preliminary; temporary || *adv* provisionally; temporarily, for the time being

vor'laut *adj* forward, fresh

Vor'leben *n* past life, former life

Vorlegebesteck [ˈforlegəbəˌtek] *n* carving set

Vorlegegabel [ˈforlegəgabəl] *f* carving fork

Vor'legelöffel [ˈforlegəlœfəl] *m* serving spoon

Vorlegemesser [ˈforlegəmesər] *n* carving knife

vor'legen *tr* put forward; propose; (*Ausweis, Paß*) show; (*Essen*) serve; (*zur Prüfung, usw.*) submit, present; **den Ball** v. (fb) pass the ball; **ein scharfes Tempo** v. (coll) speed it up;

j–m e–e Frage v. ask s.o. a question || *ref* lean forward

Ver'leger *m* (–s;–) throw rug

Vorlegeschloß [ˈforlegəʃlɔs] *n* padlock

vor'lesen §107 *tr*—**j–m etw** v. read s.th. to s.o.

Vor'lesung *f* (–;-en) reading; lecture; **e–e V. halten über** (*acc*) give a lecture on

Vor'lesungsverzeichnis *n* university catalogue

vor'letzte §9 *adj* second last; (gram) penultimate

Vor'liebe *f* preference

vorliebnehmen [forˈlipnemən] §116 *intr* take pot luck; **v. mit** put up with

vor'liegen §108 *intr* be present; exist; be under consideration; **dem Richter v.** be up before the judge; **heute liegt nichts vor** there's nothing doing today; **mir liegt e–e Beschwerde vor** I have a complaint here; **was liegt gegen ihn vor?** what is the charge against him?

vor'liegend *adj* present, at hand

vor'lügen §111 *tr*—**j–m etw** v. **über** (*acc*) tell s.o. lies about

vor'machen *tr*—**du kannst mir doch nichts** v. you can't put anything over on me; **j–m etw** v. show s.o. how to do s.th. || *ref*—**er läßt sich** [*dat*] **nichts** v. he's nobody's fool; **sich** [*dat*] **selbst etw** v. fool oneself

Vor'macht *f* leading power; supremacy

Vor'machtstellung *f* (position of) supremacy

vormalig | ˈformalɪç] *adj* former

vormals | ˈformals] *adv* formerly

Vor'marsch *m* advance

vor'merken *tr* note down; reserve; **sich v. lassen für** put in for

Vor'mittag *m* forenoon, morning

vor'mittags *adv* in the forenoon

Vor'mund *m* guardian

Vor'mundschaft *f* (–;-en) guardianship

vor'mundschaftlich *adj* guardian's

Vor'mundschaftsgericht *n* orphans' court

vorn [forn] *adv* in front; ahead; **ganz v.** all the way up front; **nach v.** forward; **nach v. heraus wohnen** live in the front part of the house; **nach v. liegen** face the front; **von v. from** the front; **von v. anfangen** begin at the beginning

Vor'nahme *f* undertaking

Vor'name *m* first name

vorne | ˈfornə] *adv* (coll) var of **vorn**

vornehm | ˈformem] *adj* distinguished, high-class; **vornehme Welt** high society; **vornehmste Aufgabe** principal task || *adv*—**v. tun** put on airs

vor'nehmen §116 *tr* (*umbinden*) put on; undertake, take up; (*Änderungen*) make; **wieder v.** resume || *ref*—**sich** |*dat*] **ein Buch** v. take up a book; **sich** |*dat*] **etw** v. decide upon s.th.; **j–n** v. take s.o. to task; **sich** |*dat*] **v. zu** (*inf*) make up one's mind to (*inf*); **sich** |*dat*] **zuviel** v. bite off more than one can chew

Vor'nehmheit *f* (–;) distinction, high rank; distinguished bearing

vor'nehmlich *adv* especially
vor'neigen *ref* bend forward
vorn'herein *adv*—**von v.** from the first
vornweg ['fornvɛk], (forn'vɛk] *adv*—
er ist weit v. he is way out in front;
mit dem Kopf v. head first; **mit dem
Mund v. sein** be fresh
Vor ort *m* suburb
Vorort- *comb.fm.* suburban
Vor'ortbahn *f* (rr) suburban line
Vor'ortzug *m* commuter train
Vor'platz *m* front yard; (*Diele*) entrance hall; (*Vorfeld*) (aer) apron
Vor'posten *m* (mil) outpost
Vor'rang *m* precedence; priority; pre-
eminence; **den V. vor j-m haben**
have precedence over s.o.
Vor'rat *m* (-[e]s;ᵉe) (an *dat*) stock
(of), supply (of); **auf V. kaufen** buy
in quantity; **e-n V. anlegen an** (*dat*)
stock
vorrätig ['fɔrretiç] *adj* in stock
Vor'ratskammer *f* pantry, storeroom
Vor'ratsraum *m* storeroom
Vor'ratsschrank *m* pantry
Vor'raum *m* anteroom
vor'rechnen *tr*—**j-m etw v.** figure out
s.th. for s.o.; **j-m seine Fehler v.**
enumerate s.o.'s mistakes to s.o.
Vor'recht *n* privilege, prerogative
Vor'rede *f* preface, introduction
vor'reden *tr*—**j-m etw v.** try to make
s.o. believe s.th.
Vor'redner -in §6 *mf* previous speaker
Vor'richtung *f* (-;-en) preparation;
(*Gerät*) device, appliance, mechanism; (mach) fixture
vor'rücken *tr* move forward ‖ *intr*
(SEIN) (*Truppen*) advance; (*Polizei*)
move in; (*im Dienst*) be promoted
Vor'runde *f* (sport) play-offs
vors [fɔrs] *abbr* **vor das**
vor'sagen *tr*—**j-m etw v.** recite s.th.
to s.o. ‖ *intr* (*dat*) prompt
Vor'sager -in §6 *mf* prompter
Vor'satz *m* purpose, intention; (jur)
premeditation; **den V. fassen zu** (*inf*)
make up one's mind to (*inf*); **mit V.**
on purpose; **seinen V. ausführen**
gain one's ends
Vor'satzblatt *n* (bb) end paper
Vor'satzgerät *n* adapter
vorsätz'lich ['fɔrzetslɪç] *adj* deliberate;
(*Mord*) premeditated
Vor'schau *f* (cin) preview
vor'schieben §130 *tr* push forward;
offer as an excuse; (fig) plead; **den
Riegel v.** (*dat*) (fig) prevent; **Truppen v.** move troops forward
vor'schießen §76 *tr* (*Geld*) (coll) advance ‖ *intr* (SEIN) dart ahead
Vor'schiff *n* (naut) forecastle
Vor'schlag *m* proposal; (*Angebot*)
offer, (*Anregung*) suggestion; (*Empfehlung*) recommendation; (mus)
grace note; (parl) motion; **in V. bringen** propose; (parl) move
vor'schlagen §132 *tr* propose; suggest;
recommend; **zur Wahl v.** nominate
Vor'schlagsliste *f* slate of candidates
Vor'schlußrunde *f* (sport) semifinal
vor'schnell *adj* rash, hasty
vor'schreiben §62 *tr* prescribe, order;

specify; write out; **ich lasse mir
nichts v.** I take orders from no one
vor'schreiten §86 *intr* (SEIN) step forward; advance
Vor'schrift *f* order, direction; regulation; (med) prescription
vor'schriftsmäßig *adj & adv* according
to regulations
vor'schriftswidrig *adj & adv* against
regulations
Vor'schub *m* assistance; (mach) feed;
V. leisten (*dat*) encourage; (jur) aid
and abet
Vor'schule *f* prep school; (*Elementar-
schule*) elementary school
Vor'schuß *m* (*Geld-*) advance; (jur)
retainer
vor'schützen *tr* pretend, plead
Vor'schützung *f* (-;) pretense
vor'schweben *intr*—**mir schwebte etw
anderes vor** I had s.th. else in mind;
das schwebt mir dunkel vor I have a
dim recollection of it
vor'schwindeln *tr*—**j-m etw v.** fool s.o.
about s.th.
vor'sehen §138 *tr* schedule, plan; provide; (fin) earmark; **das Gesetz sieht
vor, daß** the law provides that ‖ *ref*
be careful, take care; **sich mit etw
v.** provide oneself with s.th.; **sich v.
vor** (*dat*) be on one's guard against
Vor'sehung *f* (-;) Providence
vor'setzen *tr* put forward; (*Silbe*) prefix; **j-m etw v.** set s.th. before s.o.
(*to eat*); **j-m j-n v.** set s.o. over s.o.
Vor'sicht *f* caution, care; (*Umsicht*)
prudence; **V.!** watch out! (*auf
Kisten*) handle with care!; **V., Stufe!**
watch your step!
vor'sichtig *adj* cautious, careful
Vor'sichtigkeit *f* (-;) caution
vorsichtshalber ['fɔrziçtshalbər] *adv*
to be on the safe side, as a precaution
Vor'sichtsmaßnahme *f*, **Vor'sichts-
maßregel** *f* precaution
Vor'silbe *f* prefix
vor'singen §142 *tr*—**j-m etw v.** sing
s.th. to s.o. ‖ *intr* lead the choir
Vor'sitz *m* chairmanship, chair; presidency; **den V. haben** (or **führen**) **bei**
preside over; **unter V. von** presided
over by
Vorsitzende ['fɔrzɪtsəndə] §5 *mf*
chairperson; president
Vor'sorge *f* provision; **V. tragen** (or
treffen) **für** make provision for, provide for
vor'sorgen *intr* (**für**) provide (for)
vorsorglich ['fɔrzɔrklɪç] *adv* as a precaution, just in case
Vor'spann *m* (cin) credits; (*Kurzfilm*)
(cin) short
Vor'speise *f* appetizer
vor'spiegeln *tr*—**j-m etw v.** delude s.o.
with s.th.; **j-m falsche Tatsachen v.**
misrepresent facts to s.o.
Vor'spiegelung *f* (-;) sham; pretense;
V. falscher Tatsachen misrepresenta-
tion of facts
Vor'spiel *n* prelude; (*beim Geschlechtsverkehr*) foreplay; (mus)
overture; (theat) curtain raiser; **das**

war nur das V.! (fig) that was only the beginning!

vor'spielen *tr—j—m etw v.* play s.th. for s.o.

vor'sprechen §64 *tr—j—m etw v.* pronounce s.th. for s.o.; teach s.o. how to pronounce s.th. || *intr—bei j—m v.* drop in on s.o.; *j—m v.* audition before s.o.

vor'springen §142 *intr* (SEIN) leap forward; *(aus dem Versteck)* jump out; *(vorstehen)* stick out, protrude

Vor'sprung *m* projection; *(Sims)* ledge; *(Vorteil)* advantage; *(sport)* head start; *(sport)* lead

Vor'stadt *f* suburb

vor'städtisch *adj* suburban

Vor'stand *m* board of directors; executive committee, executive board; *(Person)* chairman of the board

vor'stehen §146 *intr* protrude; *(dat)* be at the head of, direct, manage

Vor'steher *m* (-s;-) head, director, manager; *(educ)* principal

Vor'steherdrüse *f* prostate gland

Vor'steherin *f* (-;-nen) head, director, manager; *(educ)* principal

vor'stellen *tr* place in front, put ahead; *(Uhr)* set ahead; *(einführen)* introduce, present; *(darstellen)* represent; *(bedeuten)* mean; *(hinweisen auf)* point out || *ref—sich [dat] etw v.* imagine s.th., picture s.th.

Vor'stellung *f* (-;-en) introduction, presentation; *(Begriff)* idea; *(Einspruch)* remonstrance, protest; *(cin)* show; *(theat)* performance

Vor'stellungsvermögen *n* imagination

Vor'stoß *m* (fig & mil) thrust, drive

vor'stoßen §150 *tr* push forward || *intr* (SEIN) push forward, advance

Vor'strafe *f* previous conviction

Vor'strafenregister *n* previous record

vor'strecken *tr* stretch out; *(Geld)* advance

Vor'stufe *f* preliminary stage

Vor'tag *m* previous day

vor'täuschen *tr* pretend, put on

Vor'teil *m* advantage; profit; *(tennis)* advantage

vor'teilhaft *adj* advantageous; profitable

Vortrag ['fortrak] *m* (-[e]s;⸗e) performance; *(Bericht)* report; *(e-s Gedichtes)* recitation; *(e-r Rede)* delivery; *(Vorlesung)* lecture; *(acct)* balance (carried over); *(mus)* recital; **e-n V. halten über** *(acc)* give a lecture on

vor'tragen §132 *tr* perform; present

Vortragende ['fortraganda] §5 *mf* performer; speaker; lecturer

Vor'tragsfolge *f* program

vortrefflich ['fortrɛfliç] *adj* excellent

vor'treten §152 *intr* (SEIN) step forward; *(fig)* stick out, protrude

Vor'tritt *m* (-[e]s;) precedence

vorü'ber *adv* past, by, along; *(zeitlich)* over, gone by

vorü'bergehen §82 *intr* (SEIN) pass; *(an dat)* pass by; *(fig)* disregard

vorü'bergehend *adj* passing, transitory || **Vorübergehende** §5 *mf* passer-by

vorü'berziehen §163 *intr* (SEIN) march by; *(Gewitter)* blow over

Vor'übung *f* warmup

Vor'untersuchung *f* preliminary investigation

Vor'urteil *n* prejudice

vor'urteilsfrei, vor'urteilslos *adj* unprejudiced

Vor'vergangenheit *f* (gram) past perfect

Vor'verkauf *m* advance sale; *(theat)* advance reservation

vor'verlegen *tr* advance, move up

Vor'wahl *f* (pol) primary

vor'wählen *tr* dial the area code

Vor'wählnummer *f* (telp) area code

Vor'wand *m* (-[e]s;⸗e) pretext; excuse

vorwärts ['forverts] *adv* forward, on, ahead || *interj* go on!

vor'wärtsbringen §65 *tr* bring forward; (fig) advance

vor'wärtsgehen §82 *intr* (SEIN) progress

vor'wärtskommen §99 *intr* (SEIN) go ahead; progress, make headway

vorweg ['for'vek] *adv* beforehand; out in front

Vorweg'nahme *f* anticipation

vorweg'nehmen §116 *tr* anticipate; presuppose, assume

vor'weisen §118 *tr* produce, show

Vor'welt *f* prehistoric world

vor'weltlich *adj* primeval

vor'werfen §160 *tr—j—m etw v.* throw s.th. to s.o.; *(fig)* throw s.th. up to s.o.

vorwiegend ['forvigant] *adj* predominant || *adv* predominantly, chiefly

Vor'wissen *n* foreknowledge

vor'witzig *adj* inquisitive; brash

Vor'wort *n* (-[e]s;⸗e) foreword

Vor'wurf *m* reproach, blame; *(e-s Dramas)* subject; **j—m Vorwürfe machen** blame s.o.

vor'wurfslos *adj* irreproachable

vor'wurfsvoll *adj* reproachful

vor'zählen *tr* enumerate

Vor'zeichen *n* omen; (math) sign; (mus) accidental; **negatives V.** minus sign

vor'zeichnen *tr—j—m etw v.* draw or sketch s.th. for s.o.

Vor'zeichnung *f* (-;-en) drawing; (mus) signature

vor'zeigen *tr* produce, show; *(Wechsel)* present

Vor'zeiger -in §6 *mf* bearer

Vor'zeigung *f* (-;-en) producing, showing; presentation

Vor'zeit *f* remote antiquity

vor'zeiten *adv* in days of old

vor'zeitig *adj* premature

vor'ziehen §163 *tr* draw forth; pull out; prefer; (mil) move up

Vor'zimmer *n.* anteroom; entrance hall

Vor'zug *m* preference; *(Vorteil)* advantage; *(Überlegenheit)* superiority; *(Vorrang)* priority; *(Vorrecht)* privilege; *(Vorzüglichkeit)* excellence; **e-r Sache den V. geben** prefer s.th.

vorzüglich ['fortsyklɩç] *adj* excellent, first-rate || *adv* especially

Vor'züglichkeit *f* (-;) excellence

Vor'zugsaktie *f* preferred stock

Vor'zugsbehandlung *f* preferential treatment
Vor'zugspreis *m* special price
Vor'zugsrecht *n* priority; privilege
vor'zugsweise *adv* preferably
votieren [vo'tirən] *intr* vote
Votiv- [votif] *comb.fm.* votive
Vo•tum ['votum] *n* (–s;–ten [tən] & –ta [ta]) vote

vulgär [vul'ger] *adj* vulgar
Vulkan [vul'kan] *m* (–s;–e) volcano
Vulkan'ausbruch *m* eruption
vulkanisch [vul'kanɪʃ] *adj* volcanic
vulkanisieren [vulkanɪ'zirən] *tr* vulcanize
Vulkan'schlot *m* volcanic vent
VW *abbr* (Volkswagen) VW
V-Waffe *f* (Vergeltungswaffe) V-1, V-2

W

W, w [ve] *invar n* W, w
Waage ['vagə] *f* (–;–n) (pair of) scales; (astr) Libra; (gym) horizontal position; **die beiden Dinge halten sich** [dat] **die W.** the two things balance each other; **die W. halten** (*dat*) counterbalance; **j—m die W. halten** be a match for s.o.
waa'gerecht, waagrecht ['vakreçt] *adj* horizontal, level
Waagschale [ˈvak/alə] *f* scale(s); **in die W. fallen** carry weight; **in die W. werfen** bring to bear
wabbelig ['vabəlɪç] *adj* (coll) flabby
Wabe ['vabə] *f* (–;–n) honeycomb
wach [vax] *adj* awake; (*lebhaft*) lively; (*Geist*) alert; **ganz w.** wide awake
Wach'ablösung *f* changing of the guard
Wach'dienst *m* guard duty
Wache ['vaxə] *f* (–;–n) guard, watch; (*Wachstube*) guardroom; (*Wachlokal*) guardhouse; (*Polizei-*) police station; (*Wachdienst*) guard duty; (*Posten*) guard, sentinel; **auf W. on guard; auf W. ziehen** mount guard; **W. schieben** (coll) pull guard duty
wachen ['vaxən] *intr* be awake; **bei j—m w.** sit up with s.o.; **w. über** (*acc*) watch over, guard
wach'habend *adj* on guard duty
wach'halten §90 *tr* keep awake; (fig) keep alive
Wach'hund *m* watchdog
Wach'lokal *n* guardroom; police station
Wach'mann *m* (–[e]s;–leute) (Aust) policeman
Wach'mannschaft *f* (mil) guard detail
Wacholder [va'xɔldər] *m* (–s;–) juniper
Wachol'derbranntwein *m* gin
Wach'posten *m* sentry
wach'rufen §122 *tr* wake up; (*Erinnerung*) bring back
Wachs [vaks] *n* (–es;–e) wax
wachsam ['vaxzam] *adj* vigilant
Wach'samkeit *f* (–;) vigilance
Wachs'bohne *f* wax bean
wachsen ['vaksən] *tr* wax || §155 *intr* (SEIN) grow; (an *dat*) increase (in)
wächsern ['veksərn] *adj* wax; (fig) waxy
Wachs'figurenkabinett *n* wax museum
Wachs'kerze *f*, **Wachs'licht** *n* wax candle
Wachs'leinwand *f* oilcloth

Wach'stube *f* guardroom
Wachs'tuch *n* oilcloth
Wachstum ['vaxstum] *n* (–s;) growth; increase
Wacht |vaxt] *f* (–;–en) guard, watch
Wächte | 'veçta] *f* (–;–n) snow cornice
Wachtel ['vaxtəl] *f* (–;–n) quail
Wach'telhund *m* spaniel
Wächter | 'veçtər] *m* (–s;–) guard
Wacht'meister *m* police sergeant
Wach'traum *m* daydream
Wacht'turm *m* watchtower
wackelig ['vakəlɪç] *adj* wobbly; (*Zahn*) loose; (fig) shaky
Wackelkontakt ['vakəlkɔntakt] *m* (elec) loose connection, poor contact
wackeln |'vakəln] *intr* wobble; shake; (*locker sein*) be loose
wacker |'vakər] *adj* decent, honest; (*tapfer*) brave || *adv* heartily
wacklig ['vaklɪç] *adj* var of **wackelig**
Wade | 'vadə] *f* (–;–n) (anat) calf
Wa'denbein *n* (anat) fibula
Wa'denkrampf *m* leg cramp
Wa'denstrumpf *m* calf-length stocking
Waffe | 'vafə] *f* (–;–n) weapon; branch of service; **die Waffen strecken** surrender; (fig) give up; **zu den Waffen greifen** take up arms
Waffel | 'vafəl] *f* (–;–n) waffle
Waf'fenbruder *m* comrade in arms
waf'fenfähig *adj* capable of bearing arms
Waf'fengang *m* armed conflict
Waf'fengattung *f* branch of service
Waf'fengewalt *f* force of arms
Waf'fenkammer *f* armory
Waf'fenlager *n* ordnance depot; **heimliches W.** cache of arms
waf'fenlos *adj* unarmed
Waf'fenruhe *f* truce
Waf'fenschein *m* gun permit
Waf'fenschmied *m* gunsmith
Waf'fenschmuggel *m* gunrunning
Waf'fen-SS *f* (–s) SS combat unit
Waf'fenstillstand *m* armistice
Wagehals |'vagəhals] *m* daredevil
Wagemut | 'vagəmut] *m* daring
wagen |'vagən] *tr* dare; risk || *ref* venture, dare || **Wagen** *m* (–s;–) wagon; (*Fahrzeug; Teil e–r Schreibmaschine*) carriage; (aut, rr) car; **der Große Wagen** the Big Dipper; **j—m an den W. fahren** (fig) step on s.o.'s toes
wägen ['vegən] *tr* (& fig) weigh
Wa'genabteil *n* (rr) compartment

Wa'genburg f barricade of wagons
Wa'genheber m (aut) jack
Wa'genpark m fleet of cars
Wa'genpflege f (aut) maintenance
Wa'genschlag m car door, carriage door
Wa'genschmiere f (aut) grease
Wa'genspur f wheel track, rut
Wa'genwäsche f car wash
Wagestück ['vagə/tyk] n hazardous venture, daring deed
Waggon [va'gõ] m (-s;-s) railroad car
waghalsig ['vakhalzɪç] adj foolhardy
Wagnis ['vaknɪs] n (-ses;-se) risk
Wahl |val] f (-;-en) choice, option; (Auswahl) selection; (Alternative) alternative; (pol) election; **e-e W. treffen** make a choice; **vor der W. stehen** have the choice
wähl'bar ['velbar] adj eligible
Wähl barkeit f (-;) eligibility
Wahl beeinflussung f interference with the election process
wahl berechtigt adj eligible to vote
Wahl beteiligung f election turnout
Wahl bezirk m ward
wählen ['velən] tr choose; select; (pol) elect; (telp) dial || intr vote
Wäh l: r m (-s;-) voter
Wahl'ergebnis n election returns
Wäh lerin f (-;-nen) voter
wähl: risch ['verlərɪʃ] adj choosy, particular
Wäh lerschaft f (-;-en) constituency
Wäh lerscheibe f (telp) dial
Wahl'fach n (educ) elective
wahl'fähig adj eligible for election; having a vote
wahl'frei adj (educ) elective
Wahl gang m ballot
Wahl kampf m election campaign
Wahl kreis m constituency; district
Wahl leiter m campaign manager
Wah l list f (pol) slate, ticket
Wahl'lokal n polling place
Wah l'lokomotive f (coll) vote getter
wa'l los adj indiscriminate
Wa'l parole f campaign slogan
Wa'l programm n (pol) platform
Wa'l recht n right to vote, suffrage
Wah l rede f campaign speech
Wah l'spruch m motto; (com, pol) slogan
Wahl'urne f ballot box
Wahl'versammlung f campaign rally
wahl'verwandt adj congenial
Wahl'zelle f voting booth
Wahl'zettel m ballot
Wahn [van] m (-[e]s;) delusion; error; folly; madness
Wahn'bild n phantom, delusion
wähnen ['venən] tr fancy, imagine
Wahn'idee f delusion; (coll) crazy idea
Wahn'sinn m (& fig) madness
wahn'sinnig adj (vor dat) mad (with); (coll) terrible || adv madly; (coll) awfully || **Wahnsinnige** §5 mf lunatic
Wahn'vorstellung f hallucination
Wahn'witz m (& fig) madness
wahn'witzig adj mad; (unverantwortlich) irresponsible
wahr [var] adj true; (wirklich) real; (echt) genuine; **nicht w.?** right?

wahren ['varən] tr keep; (Anschein) keep up; (vor dat) protect (against)
währen ['verən] intr last
während ['verənt] prep (genit) during; (jur) pending || conj while; whereas
wahr'haben §89 tr admit
wahr'haft, wahr haftig adj true, truthful; (wirklich) real || adv actually
Wahr haftigkeit f (-;) truthfulness
Wahr'heit f (-;-en) truth; **j-m die W. sagen** give s.o. a piece of one's mind
wahr'heitsgemäß, wahr'heitsgetreu adj true, faithful; truthful
Wahr'heitsliebe f truthfulness
wahr'heitsliebend adj truthful
wahr'lich adv truly; (Bib) verily
wahrnehmbar ['varnembar] adj noticeable
wahr'nehmen §116 tr notice; (benutzen) make use of; (Interesse) protect; (Recht) assert
Wahr'nehmung f (-;) observation, perception; (der Interessen) safeguarding
wahr'sagen ref—**sich** [dat] **w. lassen** have one's fortune told || intr prophesy; tell fortunes
Wahr'sagerin f (-;-nen) fortuneteller
wahrscheinlich [var'ʃaɪnlɪç] adj probable, likely || adv probably
Wahrschein'lichkeit f (-;) probability
Wahr spruch m verdict
Wah'rung f (-;) safeguarding
Wäh'rung f (-;-en) currency; standard
Wäh'rungsabwertung f devaluation
Wäh'rungseinheit f monetary unit
Wahr'zeichen n landmark
Waise ['vaizə] f (-;-n) orphan
Wai'senhaus n orphanage
Wal [val] m (-[e]s;-e) whale
Wald [valt] m (-[e]s;ˮer) forest, woods
Wald- comb.fm. forest; sylvan; wild
Wald'aufseher m forest ranger
Wald'brand m forest fire
waldig ['valdɪç] adj wooded
Waldung ['valdun] f (-;-en) forest
Wald'wirtschaft f forestry
Wal'fang m whaling
Wal'fänger m (-s;-) whaler
walken ['valkən] tr full
Wal'ker m (-s;-) fuller
Wall [val] m (-[e]s;ˮe) mound; embankment; (mil) rampart
Wallach ['valax] m (-[e]s;-e) gelding
wallen ['valən] intr (sieden) boil; (sprudeln) bubble; (Gewand, Haar) flow, fall in waves || intr (SEIN) go on a pilgrimage; travel, wander
wall'fahren insep intr (SEIN) go on a pilgrimage
Wall'fahrer -in §6 mf pilgrim
Wall'fahrt f pilgrimage
Wall graben m moat
Wal lung f (-;) simmering, boiling; bubbling; flow; flutter; (Blutandrang) congestion; **in W. bringen** enrage; **in W. geraten** fly into a rage; **Wallungen** hot flashes
Walnuß ['valnus] f walnut
Walroß ['valrɔs] n walrus
Wal'speck m blubber
walten ['valtən] intr rule; hold sway;

Gnade w. lassen show mercy; **seines Amtes w.** attend to one's duties

Wal'tran m whale oil

Walze ['valtsə] f (-;-n) cylinder, drum; roll, roller; (der Schreibmaschine) platen

walzen ['valtsən] tr roll

wälzen ['vɛltsən] tr roll; (Bücher) pore over; (Gedanken) turn over in one's mind; **die Schuld auf j-n w.** shift the blame to s.o. else || ref roll, toss; (im Kot) wallow; (im Blut) welter

Wal'zer m (-s;-) waltz

Wäl'zer m (-s;-) (coll) thick tome

Walz'werk n rolling mill

Wamme ['vamə] f (-;-n) dewlap; (coll) potbelly

Wampe ['vampə] f (-;-n) (coll) potbelly

wand [vant] pret of **winden** || **Wand** f (-;-e) wall; partition; (Fels-) cliff; **spanische W.** folding screen

Wand'apparat m (telp) wall phone

Wand'bekleidung f wainscot

Wandel ['vandəl] m (-s;) change

wandelbar ['vandəlbar] adj changeable

Wan'delgang m, **Wan'delhalle** f lobby

wandeln ['vandəln] tr change || ref (in acc) change (into) || intr (SEIN) walk

Wan'derer -in §6 mf wanderer; hiker

Wan'derlust f wanderlust, itch to travel

wandern ['vandərn] intr (SEIN) wander; hike; (Vögel) migrate

Wan'derniere f floating kidney

Wan'derpreis m challenge trophy

Wan'derschaft f (-;) travels, wanderings

Wan'derstab m walking stick

Wan'derung f (-;-en) hike; migration

Wan'dervogel m migratory bird; (coll) rover

Wand'gemälde n mural

Wand'karte f wall map

Wand'leuchter m sconce

Wand'lung f (-;-en) change, transformation; (eccl) consecration

Wand'malerei f wall painting

Wand'pfeiler m pilaster

Wand'schirm m folding screen

Wand'schrank m wall shelves

Wand'spiegel m wall mirror

Wand'steckdose f, **Wand'stecker** m (elec) wall outlet

Wand'tafel f blackboard

wandte ['vantə] pret of **wenden**

Wand'teppich m tapestry

Wange ['vaŋə] f (-;-n) cheek

-wangig [vaŋɪç] comb.fm. -cheeked

Wan'kelmut m fickleness

wan'kelmütig adj fickle

wanken ['vaŋkən] intr stagger; sway, rock; (fig) waver

wann [van] adv & conj when; **w. immer** anytime, whenever

Wanne ['vanə] f (-;-n) tub

Wanst [vanst] m (-es;-e) belly, paunch

-wanstig [vanstɪç] comb.fm. -bellied

Wanze ['vantsə] f (-;-n) bedbug

Wappen ['vapən] n (-s;-) coat of arms

Wap'penkunde f heraldry

Wap'penschild m escutcheon

wappnen ['vapnən] ref arm oneself; **sich mit Geduld w.** have patience

war [var] pret of **sein**

warb [varp] pret of **werben**

ward [vart] pret of **werden**

Ware ['varə] f (-;-n) ware; article; commodity; **Waren** goods, merchandise

-waren [varən] pl comb.fm. -ware

Wa'renaufzug m freight elevator

Wa'renausgabe f wrapping department

Wa'renbestand m stock

Wa'renbörse f commodity market

Wa'renhaus n department store

Wa'renlager n warehouse; stockroom

Wa'renmarkt m commodity market

Wa'renmuster n, **Wa'renprobe** f sample

Wa'renrechnung f invoice

Wa'renzeichen n trademark

warf [varf] pret of **werfen**

warm [varm] adj (wärmer ['vɛrmər]; wärmste ['vɛrmstə] §9) warm

Warmblüter ['varmblytər] m (-s;-) warm-blooded animal

warmblütig ['varmblytɪç] adj warm-blooded

Wärme ['vɛrmə] f (-;) warmth, heat

wär'mebeständig adj heatproof

Wär'meeinheit f thermal unit; calory

Wär'megrad m degree of heat, temperature

wärmen ['vɛrmən] tr warm, heat

Wär'meplatte f—**elektrische W.** hotplate

Wärm'flasche f hot-water bottle

warm'halten §90 tr keep warm

warm'herzig adj warm-hearted

warm'laufen §105 intr—**den Motor w. lassen** let the motor warm up

Warmluft'heizung f hot-air heating

Warmwas'serbehälter m hot-water tank

Warmwas'serheizung f hot-water heating

Warmwas'serspeicher m hot-water tank

Warn- [varn] comb.fm. warning

Warn'anlage f warning system

warnen ['varnən] tr (vor dat) warn (of), caution (against)

Warn'gebiet n danger zone

Warn'schuß m warning shot

Warn'signal n warning signal

War'nung f (-;-en) warning, caution; **zur W. as a** warning

War'nungsschild n, **Warn'zeichen** n danger sign

Warschau ['varʃau] n (-s;) Warsaw

Warte ['vartə] f (-;-n) watchtower, lookout

War'tefrau f attendant; nurse

War'tefrist f waiting period

warten ['vartən] tr tend, attend to; (pflegen) nurse || intr (auf acc) wait (for)

Wärter ['vɛrtər] m (-s;-) attendant; (Pfleger) male nurse; (Aufseher) caretaker; (Gefängnis-) guard; (rr) signalman

War'teraum m waiting room

Wärterin ['vɛrtərɪn] f (-;-nen) attendant; nurse

War′tesaal *m*, **War′tezimmer** *n* waiting room

War′tung *f* (–;) maintenance

warum [va′rum] *adv* why

Warze [′vartsə] *f* (–;-n) wart; (*Brust–*) n.pple

was [vas] *indef pron* something; na, so was! well, 1 never! || *interr pron* what; ach was! go on! was für ein what kind of, what sort of; was haben wir gelacht! how we laughed! || *rel pron* what; which; that; was auch immer no matter what; was immer whatever

Wasch– [vaʃ] *comb.fm.* wash, washing

waschbar [′vaʃbar] *adj* washable

Wasch′bär *m* racoon

Wasch′becken *n* sink

Wasch′benzin *n* cleaning fluid

Wasch′blau *n* bluing

Wasch′bütte *f* washtub

Wäsche [′veʃə] *f* (–;-n) wash, laundry; linen; underwear

Wä′schebeutel *m* laundry bag

wasch′echt *adj* washable; (fig) genuine

Wä′scheklammer *f* clothespin

Wä′schekorb *m* clothesbasket

Wä′scheleine *f* clothesline

waschen [′vaʃən] §158 *tr* wash; launder; (*Gold*) pan; (*Haar*) shampoo; (*reinigen*) purify || *ref* wash; sich [*dat*] die Hände w. wash one's hands || *intr* wash

Wä′scher [′veʃər] *m* (–s;–) washer; laundryman

Wäscherei [veʃə′raɪ] *f* (–;-en) laundry

Wäscherin [′veʃərɪn] *f* (–;-nen) washerwoman, laundress

Wä′scherolle *f* mangle

Wä′scheschleuder *f* spin-drier

Wä′scheschrank *m* linen closet

Wä′schezeichen *n* laundry mark

Wasch′frau *f* laundress

Wasch′haus *n* laundry

Wasch′korb *m* clothesbasket

Wasch′küche *f* laundry

Wasch′lappen *m* washcloth; (fig) wishy washy person

Wasch′maschine *f* washmachine, washer

Wasch′mittel *n* detergent

Wasch′raum *m* washroom, lavatory

Wasch′schüssel *f* wash basin

Wasch′tisch *m* washstand

Wasch′trog *m* washtub

Wa′schung *f* (–;-en) washing; ablution

Wasch′weib *n* (coll) gossip (*woman*)

Wasch′zettel *m* laundry list; (*am Schutzumschlag*) blurb

Wasser [′vasər] *n* (–s;–) water: das W. läuft mir im Mund zusammen my mouth is watering; j-m das W. abgraben pull the rug out from under s.o.; mit allen Wassern gewaschen sharp as a needle

was′serabstoßend *adj* water-repellent

was′serarm *adj* arid

Was′serball *m* water polo

Was′serbau *m* (–[e]s;) harbor and canal construction

Was′serbehälter *m* water tank; reservoir; cistern

Was′serblase *f* bubble; (*auf der Haut*) blister

Was′serbombe *f* depth charge

Was′serbüffel *m* water buffalo

Was′serdampf *m* steam

was′serdicht *adj* watertight, waterproof

Was′sereimer *m* bucket

Was′serfall *m* waterfall, cascade

Was′serfarbe *f* water color

Was′serflasche *f* water bottle

Was′serflugzeug *n* seaplane

Was′sergeflügel *n* waterfowl

Was′sergraben *m* drain; moat

Was′serhahn *m* faucet, spigot

Was′serhose *f* waterspout

wässerig [′vesərɪç] *adj* watery

Was′serjungfer *f* dragonfly

Was′serkessel *m* cauldron

Was′serklosett *n* toilet

Was′serkraftwerk *n* hydroelectric plant

Was′serkrug *m* water jug, water pitcher

Was′serkur *f* spa

Was′serland′flugzeug *n* amphibian plane

Was′serland′panzerwagen *m* amphibian tank

Was′serlauf *m* watercourse

Was′serleitung *f* water main; aqueduct

Was′sermangel *m* water shortage

Was′sermann *m* (–[e]s;) (astr) Aquarius

Was′sermelone *f* watermelon

wassern [′vasərn] *intr* land on water; (rok) splash down

wässern [′vesərn] *tr* water; irrigate; (phot) wash || *intr* (*Augen, Mund*) water

Was′serratte *f* water rat; (fig) old salt

Was′serrinne *f* gutter

Was′serrohr *n* water pipe

Was′serscheide *f* watershed, divide

was′serscheu *adj* afraid of water

Was′serschi *m* water ski

Was′serschlauch *m* hose

Was′serspeier [′vasərʃpaɪər] *m* (–s;–) gargoyle

Was′serspiegel *m* surface; water level

Was′sersport *m* aquatics

Was′serstand *m* water level

Was′serstiefel *m* rubber boots

Was′serstoff *m* hydrogen

was′serstoffblond *adj* peroxide-blond

Was′serstoffbombe *f* hydrogen bomb

Was′serstrahl *m* jet of water

Was′serstraß *f* waterway

Was′sersucht *f* dropsy

Was′serung *f* (–;-en) (aer) landing on water; (rok) splashdown

Wäs′serung *f* (–;) watering; irrigation

Was′serverdrängung *f* displacement

Was′serversorgung *f* water supply

Was′servogel *m* waterfowl

Was′serwaage *f* (carp) level

Was′serweg *m* waterway; auf dem W. by water

Was′serwerk *n* waterworks

Was′serzähler *m* water meter

Was′serzeichen *n* watermark

wässrig [′vesrɪç] *adj* watery

waten [′vatən] *intr* (SEIN) wade

Watsche [′vatʃə] *f* (–;-n) slap

watscheln [′vatʃəln] *intr* (SEIN) waddle

watschen [′vatʃən] *tr* slap

Watt [vat] n (-s;-) (elec) watt

Watte [ˈvatə] f (-;-en) absorbent cotton; wadding

Wat′tebausch m swab

Wat′tekugel f cotton ball

Wat′tenmeer n shallow coastal waters

Wat′testäbchen n Q-tip, cotton swab

wattieren [vaˈtirən] tr pad, wad

Wattie′rung f (-;-en) padding, wadding

wauwau [ˈvauˈvau] interj bow-wow! ‖ **Wauwau** m (-s;-s) bow-wow, doggy

weben [ˈvebən] §109 & §94 tr & intr weave

We′ber m (-s;-) weaver

Weberei [vebəˈraɪ] f (-;-en) weaving

We′berin f (-;-nen) weaver

We′berknecht m daddy-long-legs

Webstuhl [ˈvepʃtul] m loom

Webwaren [ˈvepvarən] pl textiles

Wechsel [ˈvɛksəl] m (-s;-) change, shift; (für Studenten) allowance; (agr) rotation (of crops); (fin) bill of exchange; (hunt) run, beaten track; gezogener W. draft; offener W. letter of credit; trockener (or eigener) W. promissory note

Wech′selbeziehung f correlation

Wechselfälle [ˈvɛksəlfɛlə] pl ups and downs, vicissitudes

Wech′selfieber n intermittent fever; malaria

Wech′selfrist f period of grace (before bill of exchange falls due)

Wech′selgeld n change, small change

Wech′selgesang m antiphony

Wech′selgespräch n dialogue

wech′selhaft adj changeable

Wech′selkurs m rate of exchange

Wech′selmakler -in §6 mf bill-broker

wechseln [ˈvɛksəln] tr change; vary; (austauschen) exchange; den Besitzer w. change hands; die Zähne w. get one's second set of teeth; seinen Wohnsitz w. move ‖ intr change; vary

Wech′selnehmer m (fin) payee

Wech′selnotierung f foreign exchange rate

Wech′selrichter m (elec) vibrator (producing a.c.)

wech′selseitig adj mutual, reciprocal

Wech′selseitigkeit f (-;) reciprocity

Wech′selspiel n interplay

Wech′selsprechanlage f intercom

Wech′selstrom m alternating current

Wech′selstube f money-exchange office

Wech′seltierchen n amoeba

wech′selvoll adj (Landschaft) changing; (Leben) checkered; (Wetter) changeable

wech′selweise adv mutually; alternately

Wech′selwirkung f interaction

Wech′selwirtschaft f crop rotation

wecken [ˈvɛkən] tr wake, awaken, rouse

Wecker (**Wek′ker**) m (-s;-) alarm clock

Weck′ruf m (mil) reveille

Wedel [ˈvedəl] m (-s;-) brush, whisk; (Schwanz) tail; (eccl) sprinkler

wedeln [ˈvedəln] tr brush away ‖ intr —mit dem Fächer w. fan oneself; mit dem Schwanz w. wag its tail

weder [ˈvedər] conj—weder...noch neither...nor

weg [vɛk] adv away, off; gone; lost ‖ **Weg** [vek] m (-[e]s;-e) way, path; road; route, course; (Art und Weise) way; (Mittel) means; am Wege by the roadside; auf dem besten Wege sein be well on the way; auf gütlichem Wege amicably; auf halbem Wege halfway; aus dem Weg räumen remove; (fig) bump off; etw in die Wege leiten prepare the way for s.th.; introduce s.th.; j-m aus dem Wege gehen make way for s.o.; steer clear of s.o.; Weg und Steg kennen know every turn in the road

weg′bekommen §99 tr (Fleck) get out; (Krankheit) catch; (verstehen) get the hang of; e-e w. (coll) get a crack

weg′bleiben §62 intr (SEIN) stay away; be omitted

weg′blicken intr glance away

weg′bringen §65 tr take away; (Fleck) get out

Wegebau [ˈvegəbau] m (-[e]s;) road building

Wegegeld [ˈvegəgɛlt] n mileage allowance; turnpike toll

wegen [ˈvegən] prep (genit) because of, on account of; for the sake of; (mit Rücksicht auf) in consideration of; (infolge) in consequence of; (jur) on (the charge of); von Amts w. officially; von Rechts w. by right

Wegerecht [ˈvegərɛçt] n right of way

weg′essen §70 tr eat up

weg′fahren §71 tr remove ‖ intr (SEIN) drive away, leave

weg′fallen §72 intr (SEIN) fall away, fall off; (ausgelassen werden) be omitted; (aufhören) cease; (abgeschafft werden) be abolished

weg′fangen §73 tr snap away, snatch

weg′fliegen §57 intr (SEIN) fly away

weg′fressen §70 tr devour

weg′führen tr lead away

Weggang [ˈvɛkgaŋ] m departure

weg′geben §80 tr give away

weg′gehen §82 intr (SEIN) go away; w. über (acc) pass over; wie warme Semmeln w. go like hotcakes

weg′haben §89 tr get rid of; (Schläge, usw.) have gotten one's share of; (verstehen) catch on to; der hat eins weg (sl) he has a screw loose; (sl) he's loaded

weg′jagen tr chase away

weg′kehren tr sweep away; (Gesicht) avert ‖ ref turn away

weg′kommen §99 intr (SEIN) come away; get away (verlorengehen) get lost; nicht w. über (acc) not get over

weg′können §100 intr—nicht w. not be able to get away

Wegkreuzung [ˈvɛkkrɔtsuŋ] f (-;-en) crossing, intersection

weg′kriegen tr get; (Fleck) get out

weg′lassen §104 tr leave out; let go; cross out; (gram) elide; (math) cancel

weg′legen tr put aside

weg'machen *tr* take away; (*Fleck*) take out

wegmüde ['vekmy:də] *adj* travel-weary

weg'müssen §115 *intr* have to go

Wegnahme ['ve:kna:mə] *f* (–;-n) taking away; confiscation; (mil) capture

weg'nehmen §116 *tr* take away; (*Raum, Zeit*) take up; (*beschlagnahmen*) confiscate; (mil) capture

weg'packen *tr* pack away || *ref* pack off

weg'raffen *tr* snatch away

Wegrand ['ve:krant] *m* wayside

weg'räumen *tr* clear away

weg'reißen §53 *tr* tear off, tear away

weg'rücken *tr* move away

weg'schaffen *tr* remove; get rid of

weg'scheren §129 *tr* clip || *ref* scram

weg'scheuchen *tr* scare away

weg'schicken *tr* send away

weg'schleichen §85 *ref & intr* (SEIN) sneak away, steal away

weg'schmeißen §53 *tr* (coll) throw away

weg'schneiden §106 *tr* cut away

weg'sehen §138 *intr* look away; **w. über** (*acc*) shut one's eyes to

weg'setzen *tr* put away || *ref*—**sich w. über** (*acc*) not mind; feel superior to || *intr* (SEIN)—**w. über** (*acc*) jump over

weg'spülen *tr* wash away; (geol) erode

weg'stehlen §147 *ref* slip away

weg'stellen *tr* put aside

weg'stoßen §150 *tr* shove aside

weg'streichen §85 *tr* cross out

weg'treten §152 *intr* (SEIN) step aside; (mil) break ranks; **weggetreten!** (mil) dismissed!; **w. lassen** (mil) dismiss

weg'tun §154 *tr* put away

Wegweiser ['ve:kvaizər] *m* (–s;–) roadsign; (*Buch, Reiseführer*) guide

weg'wenden §120 & §140 *tr & ref* turn away

weg'werfen §160 *tr* throw away || *ref* degrade oneself

weg'werfend *adj* disparaging

weg'wischen *tr* wipe away

weg'zaubern *tr* spirit away

weg'ziehen §163 *tr* pull away || *intr* (SEIN) move; (mil) pull out

weh [ve] *adj* painful. sore; **mir ist weh ums Herz** I am sick at heart || *adv*—**sich** |*dat*| **weh tun** hurt oneself; **weh tun** ache || *interj* woe! **weh mir!** woe is me! || **Weh** *n* (–[e]s;-e) pain, ache

wehe ['ve·ə] *adj, adv, & interj* var of **weh** || **Wehe** *f* (–;-n) drift

wehen ['ve·ən] *tr* blow; (*Schnee*) drift || *intr* (*Wind*) blow; (*Fahne, Kerzenflamme*) flutter || **Wehen** *pl* labor, labor pains; (fig) travail

Weh'geschrei *n* wails, wailing

Weh'klage *f* wail

weh'klagen *intr* (über *acc*) wail (over); **w. um** lament for

weh'leidig *adj* complaining, whining; **W. tun** whine

Weh'mut *f* (–;) melancholy; nostalgia

weh'mütig *adj* melancholy; nostalgic

Wehr [ver] *f* (–;-en) weapon; (*Abwehr*) defense, resistance; (*Brüstung*)

---

parapet; **sich zur W. setzen** offer resistance || **Wehr** *n* (–[e]s;-e) dam

Wehr'dienst *m* military service

wehr'dienstpflichtig *adj* subject to military service

Wehr'dienstverweigerer *m* (–s;–) conscientious objector

wehren ['ve:rən] *tr*—**j-m etw w.** keep s.o. (away) from s.th. || *ref* defend oneself; resist, put up a fight; **sich seiner Haut w.** save one's skin || *intr* (*dat*) resist; (*dat*) check

wehr'fähig *adj* fit for military service

wehr'haft *adj* (*Person*) full of fight; (*Burg*) strong

wehr'los *adj* defenseless

Wehr'macht *f* (hist) German armed forces

Wehr'meldeamt *n* draft board

Wehr'paß *m* service record

Wehr'pflicht *f* compulsory military service; **allgemeine W.** universal military training

wehr'pflichtig *adj* subject to military service

Weib [vaip] *n* (–[e]s;-er) woman; wife; **ein tolles W.** a luscious doll

Weibchen ['vaipçən] *n* (–s;–) (*Tier*) female; (*Ehefrau*) little woman

Weiberfeind ['vaibərfaint] *m* womanhater

Weiberheld ['vaibərhelt] *m* ladies' man

Weibervolk ['vaibərfolk] *n* womenfolk

weibisch ['vaibiʃ] *adj* womanish, effeminate

weib'lich *adj* female; womanly; (& gram) feminine

Weib'lichkeit *f* (–;) womanhood; feminine nature; **die holde W.** (hum) the fair sex

Weibs'bild *n* female; (pej) wench

Weibs'stück *n* (sl) woman

weich [vaiç] *adj* soft; (*Ei*) soft-boiled; (*zart*) tender; (*schwach*) weak; **w. machen** soften up; **w. werden** (& fig) soften; relent

Weich'bild *n* urban area, outskirts

Weiche ['vaiçə] *f* (–;-n) (anat) side, flank; (rr) switch; **Weichen stellen** throw the switch

weichen ['vaiçən] *tr & intr* soften; soak || §85 *intr* (SEIN) yield; give ground; (*Boden*) give way; (*dat*) give in to; **j-m nicht von der Seite w.** not leave s.o.'s side; **nicht von der Stelle w.** not budge from the spot; **von j-m w.** leave s.o.

Weichensteller ['vaiçənstelər] *m* (–s; –) (rr) switchman

Weich'heit *f* (–;) softness; tenderness

weich'herzig *adj* soft-hearted

Weich'käse *m* soft cheese

weich'lich *adj* soft; tender; flabby; insipid; (*weibisch*) effeminate; (*lässig*) indolent

Weichling ['vaiçliŋ] *m* (–s;-e) weakling

Weich'tier *n* mollusk

Weide ['vaidə] *f* (–;-n) pasture; (bot) willow

Wei'deland *n* pasture land

weiden ['vaidən] *tr* graze; (*Augen*)

feast || *ref*—**sich w. an** (*dat*) feast one's eyes on || *intr* graze

Wei′denkorb *m* wicker basket

weidlich [ˈvaitliç] *adv* heartily

weidmännisch [ˈvaitmɛniʃ] *adj* (hunt) sportsmanlike

weigern [ˈvaigərn] *ref*—**sich w. zu** (*inf*) refuse to (*inf*)

Wei′gerung *f* (-;-en) refusal

Weihe [ˈvaiə] *f* (-;-n) consecration; (*e-s Priesters*) ordination

weihen [ˈvaiən] *tr* consecrate; (*zum Priester*) ordain; (*widmen*) dedicate; **dem Tode geweiht** doomed to death || *ref* devote oneself

Wei′her *m* (-s;-) pond

wei′hevoll *adj* solemn

Weihnachten [ˈvainaxtən] *n* (-s;) & *pl* Christmas; **zu W.** for or at Christmas

Weih′nachtsabend *m* Christmas Eve

Weih′nachtsbaum *m* Christmas tree; (coll) bombing markers

Weih′nachtsbescherung *f* exchange of Christmas presents

Weih′nachtsfeier *f* Christmas celebration; (*in Betrieben*) Christmas party

Weih′nachtsfest *n* feast of Christmas

Weih′nachtsgeschenk *n* Christmas present

Weih′nachtsgratifikation *f* Christmas bonus

Weih′nachtslied *n* Christmas carol

Weih′nachtsmann *m* (-[e]s;) Santa Claus

Weih′nachtsmarkt *m* Christmas fair (*at which Christmas decorations are sold*)

Weih′nachtstag *m* Christmas day

Weih′rauch *m* incense

Weih′rauchfaß *n* censer

Weih′wasser *n* holy water

Weih′wedel *m* (eccl) sprinkler

weil [vail] *conj* because, since

weiland [ˈvailant] *adv* formerly

Weilchen [ˈvailçən] *n* (-s;) little while

Weile [ˈvailə] *f* (-;) while

weilen [ˈvailən] *intr* stay, linger

Wein [vain] *m* (-[e]s;-e) wine; (*Pflanze*) vine

Wein′bau *m* (-[e]s;) winegrowing

Wein′bauer *-in* §6 *mf* winegrower

Wein′beere *f* grape

Wein′berg *m* vineyard

Wein′blatt *n* vine leaf

Wein′brand *m* brandy

weinen [ˈvainən] *tr* (*Tränen*) shed || *intr* cry, weep; **vor Freude w.** weep for joy; **w. um** cry over

weinerlich [ˈvainərliç] *adj* tearful; (*Stimme*)) whining

Wein′ernte *f* vintage

Wein′essig *m* wine vinegar

Wein′faß *n* wine barrel

Wein′händler *m* wine merchant

Wein′jahr *n* vintage year

Wein′karte *f* wine list

Wein′keller *m* wine cellar

Wein′kelter *f* wine press

Wein′kenner *m* connoisseur of wine

Wein′krampf *m* crying fit

Wein′laub *n* vine leaves

Wein′lese *f* grape picking

Wein′presse *f* wine press

Wein′ranke *f* vine tendril

Wein′rebe *f* grapevine

wein′selig *adj* tipsy, tight

Wein′stock *m* vine

Wein′traube *f* grape; bunch of grapes

weise [ˈvaizə] *adj* wise || **Weise** §5 *m* wise man, sage || *f* (-;-n) way; (*Melodie*) tune; **auf diese W. in** this way

-weise *comb.fm.* -wise; by, e.g., **dutzendweise** by the dozen; -ly, e.g., **glücklicherweise** luckily

weisen [ˈvaizən] §118 *tr* point out, show; (*aus dem Lande*) banish; (*aus der Schule*) expel; **j–n w. an** (*acc*) refer s.o. to; **j–n w. nach** direct s.o. to; **j–n w. von** order s.o. off (*premises, etc.*); **von der Hand w.** refuse; **j–n w. von** || *ref*—**von sich w.** refuse || *intr*—**w. auf** (*acc*) point to

Weis′heit *f* (-;-en) wisdom; wise saying; **Weisheiten** words of wisdom

Weis′heitszahn *m* wisdom tooth

weis′lich *adv* wisely, prudently

weismachen [ˈvaismaxən] *tr*—**j–m etw w.** put s.th. over on s.o.; **mach das anderen weis!** tell it to the marines!

weiß [vais] *adj* white

weissagen [ˈvaiszagən] *tr* foretell

Weiß′blech *n* tin plate, tin

Weiß′blechdose *f* tincan

weiß′bluten *tr* bleed white

Weiß′brot *n* white bread

Weiß′dorn *m* (bot) hawthorn

Weiße [ˈvaisə] *f* (-;-n) whiteness; (Berlin) ale || §5 *m* white man || *f* white woman || *n* (*im Auge, im Ei*) white

weißen [ˈvaisən] *tr* whiten; (*tünchen*) whitewash

weiß′glühend *adj* white-hot

Weiß′glut *f* white heat, incandescence

Weiß′kohl *m*, **Weiß′kraut** *n* cabbage

weiß′lich *adj* whitish

Weiß′metall *n* pewter; Babbitt metal

Weiß′waren *pl* linens

Weiß′wein *m* white wine

Wei′sung *f* (-;-en) directions, instructions; directive

weit [vait] *adj* far, distant; (*ausgedehnt*) extensive; (*breit*) wide, broad; (*geräumig*) large; (*Gewissen*) elastic; (*Herz*) big; (*Kleid*) full, big; (*Meer*) broad; (*Reise, Weg*) long; (*Welt*) wide; **bei weitem besser** better by far; **von weitem** from afar || *adv* far, way; widely; greatly; **w. besser** far better

weit′ab′ *adv* (von) far away (from)

weit′aus′ *adv* by far

Weit′blick *m* farsightedness

weit′blickend *adj* farsighted

Weite [ˈvaitə] *f* (-;-n) width, breadth; (*Ferne*) distance; (*Umfang*) size; (*Ausdehnung*) extent; (*Durchmesser*) diameter; (fig) range; **in die W. ziehen** go out into the world

weiten [ˈvaitən] *tr* widen; (*Loch*) enlarge; (*Schuh*) stretch || *ref* widen

weiter [ˈvaitər] *adj* farther; further; wider; **bis auf weiteres** until further notice; **des weiteren** furthermore;

ohne weiteres without further ado ‖ *adv* farther; further; furthermore; (*voran*) on; **er kann nicht w.** he can't go on; **nur s. w.!** keep it up!; **und so w.** and so forth, and so on

weiter– *comb.fm.* on; keep on, continue to

wei′terbefördern *tr* forward

Wei′terbestand *m* continued existence

wei′terbestehen §146 *intr* survive

wei′terbilden *tr* develop ‖ *ref* continue one's studies

wei′tererzählen *tr* spread (*rumors*)

wei′terfahren §71 *intr* (SEIN) drive on

wei′tergeben §80 *tr* pass on, relay

wei′tergehen §82 *intr* (SEIN) go on

wei′terhin′ *adv* furthermore; again

wei′terkommen §99 *intr* (SEIN) get ahead, make progress

wei′terkönnen §100 *intr* be able to go on; **ich kann nicht weiter** I'm stuck

wei′terleben *intr* live on, survive

wei′termachen *tr & intr* continue ‖ *interj* (mil) as you were!, carry on!

weit′gehend *adj* far-reaching

weit′gereist *adj* widely traveled

weit′greifend *adj* far-reaching

weit′her′ *adv*—**von w.** from afar

weit′her′geholt *adj* far-fetched

weit′herzig *adj* broad-minded

weit′hin′ *adv* far off

weitläufig [′vaɪtlɔɪfɪç] *adj* lengthy, detailed; complicated; (*Verwandte*) distant; (*geräumig*) roomy ‖ *adv* at length, in detail

weit′reichend *adj* far-reaching

weitschweifig [′vaɪt∫vaɪfɪç] *adj* detailed, lengthy; long-winded

weit′sichtig *adj* (& fig) far-sighted

Weit′sprung *m* (sport) long jump

Weit′streckenflug *m* long-distance flight

weit′tragend *adj* long-range; (fig) far-reaching

Weit′winkelobjektiv *n* wide-angle lens

Weizen [′vaɪtsən] *m* (-s;-) wheat

Wei′zenmehl *n* wheat flour

welch [vɛlç] *interr adj* which ‖ *interr pron* which one; (*in Ausrufen*) what . . .!; **mit welcher** (or **mit welch einer**) **Begeisterung arbeitet er!** with what enthusiasm he works! ‖ *indef pron* any; some ‖ *rel pron* who, which, that

welcherlei [′vɛlçər′laɪ] *invar adj* what kind of; whatever

welk [vɛlk] *adj* withered; (*Haut, Lippen*) wrinkled; (fig) faded

welken [′vɛlkən] *intr* (SEIN) wither; (fig) fade

Wellblech [′vɛlblɛç] *n* corrugated iron

Well′blechhütte *f* Quonset hut

Welle [′vɛlə] *f* (-s;-n) wave; (*Wellbaum*) shaft; (gym) circle (*around horizontal bar*); (mach) shaft

wellen [′vɛlən] *tr & ref* wave

Wel′lenbereich *m* wave band

Wel′lenberg *m* crest (of wave)

Wel′lenbewegung *f* undulation

Wel′lenbrecher *m* breakwater

wel′lenförmig *adj* wavy

Wel′lenlänge *f* wavelength

Wel′lenlinie *f* wavy line

wel′lenreiten §86 *intr* surf; waterski ‖ **Wellenreiten** *n* (-s;) surfing, surfboard riding; waterskiing

Wel′lenreiter –in §6 *mf* surfer; waterskier

Wel′lenreiterbrett *n* surfboard; water ski

Wel′lental *n* trough (of wave)

wellig [′vɛlɪç] *adj* wavy

Well′pappe *f* corrugated cardboard

Welt [vɛlt] *f* (-;-en) world

Welt′all *n* universe; outer space

Welt′anschauung *f* outlook on life; ideology

Welt′ausmaß *m*—**im W.** on a global scale

Welt′ausstellung *f* world's fair

welt′bekannt, welt′berühmt *adj* world-renowned

Welt′enbummler *m* globetrotter

welt′erfahren *adj* sophisticated

Weltergewicht [′vɛltərɡəvɪçt] *n* welterweight class

Weltergewichtler [′vɛltərɡəvɪçtlər] *m* (-s;-) welterweight boxer

welt′erschüt′ternd *adj* earth-shaking

welt′fremd *adj* secluded; innocent

Welt′friede *m* world peace

Welt′geistlicher *m* secular priest

welt′gewandt *adj* worldly-wise

Welt′karte *f* map of the world

welt′klug *adj* worldly-wise

Welt′körper *m* heavenly body

Welt′krieg *m* world war

Welt′kugel *f* globe

Welt′lage *f* international situation

welt′lich *adj* worldly; secular

Welt′macht *f* world power

Welt′mann *m* (-[e]s;⁼er) man of the world

welt′männisch *adj* sophisticated

Welt′meer *n* ocean

Welt′meinung *f* world opinion

Welt′meister –in §6 *mf* world champion

Welt′meisterschaft *f* world championship

Welt′ordnung *f* cosmic order

Welt′postverein *m* postal union

Welt′priester *m* secular priest

Welt′raum *m* (-[e]s;) outer space

Welt′raumfahrer *m* spaceman

Welt′raumfahrt *f* space travel

Welt′raumfahrzeug *n* spacecraft

Welt′raumforschung *f* exploration of outer space

Welt′raumgeschoß *n* space shot

Welt′raumkapsel *f* space capsule

Welt′raumstation *f* space station

Welt′raumstrahlen *pl* cosmic rays

Welt′reich *n* world empire

Welt′reise *f* trip around the world

Welt′rekord *m* world record

Welt′ruf *m* world-wide renown

Welt′ruhm *m* world-wide fame

Welt′schmerz *m* world-weariness

Welt′sicherheitsrat *m* U.N. Security Council

Welt′stadt *f* metropolis (city with more than one million inhabitants)

Welt′teil *m* continent

welt′umfassend *adj* world-wide

Welt′weisheit *f* philosophy

wem [vem] *interr & rel pron* to whom
Wem'fall *m* dative case
wen [ven] *interr & rel pron* whom
Wende ['vendə] *f* (–;–n) turn; turning point; (gym) face vault, front vault
Wen'dekreis *m* (geog) tropic
Wendeltreppe ['vendəltrepə] *f* spiral staircase
Wen'demarke *f* (aer) pylon; (sport) turn post
wenden ['vendən] §**140** *tr* turn; turn around; turn over; (*Geld, Mühe*) spend || *ref* turn; (*Wind, Wetter*) change || *intr* turn, turn around
Wen'depunkt *m* turning point
wendig ['vendıç] *adj* maneuverable; (*Person*) versatile, resourceful
Wen'dung *f* (–;–en) turn; change; (*Redensart*) idiomatic expression
Wen'fall *m* accusative case
wenig ['venıç] *adj* little; **ein w.** a little, a bit of; **wenige** few, a few, some || *adv* little; not very; seldom || *indef pron* little; **wenige** few, a few
weniger ['venıgər] *adj* fewer; less; (arith) minus
We'nigkeit *f* (–;) fewness; smallness; pittance; trifle; **meine W.** (coll) poor little me
wenigste ['venıçstə] §**9** *adj* least; very few, fewest; **am wenigsten** least of all
wenigstens ['venıçstəns] *adv* at least
wenn [ven] *conj* if, in case; (*zeitlich*) when, whenever; **auch w.** even if; **außer w.** except when, except if, unless; **w. anders** provided that; **w. auch** although, even if; **w. schon, denn schon** go all the way || **Wenn** *n* (–;–) if
wenngleich', wennschon' *conj* although
Wenzel ['ventsəl] *m* (–s;–) (cards) jack
wer [ver] *interr pron* who, which one; **wer auch immer** whoever; **wer da?** who goes there? || *rel pron* he who, whoever || *indef pron* somebody, anybody
Werbe– [verbə] *comb.fm.* advertising; publicity; commercial
Wer'befernsehen *n* commercial television
Wer'befilm *m* commercial
Wer'befläche *f* advertising space
Wer'begraphik *f* commercial art
Wer'begraphiker –in §**6** *mf* commercial artist
werben ['verbən] §**149** *tr* (*neue Kunden*) try to get; (mil) recruit || *intr* advertise; **für e–n neuen Handelsartikel w.** advertise a new product; **um ein Mädchen w.** court a girl
Wer'beschrift *f* folder
Wer'bestelle *f* advertising agency
Wer'bung *f* (–;–en) advertising; publicity; courting; recruiting
Werdegang ['verdəgaŋ] *m* career, background; (*Entwicklung*) development; (*Wachstum*) growth; (*Ablauf der Herstellung*) process of production
werden ['verdən] §**159** *intr* (SEIN) become, grow, get, turn; **w. zu** change into; **zu nichts w.** come to nought || *aux* (SEIN) (to form the future) **er wird gehen** he will go; (to form the passive) **er wird geehrt** he is being honored || **Werden** *n* (–s;) becoming, growing; (*Entstehung*) evolution; (*Wachstum*) growth; **im W. sein** be in the process of development; be in the making
wer'dend *adj* nascent; (*Mutter*) expectant; (*Arzt*) future
Werder ['verdər] *m* (–s;–) islet
Wer'fall *m* subjective case
werfen ['verfən] §**160** *tr* throw, cast; (*Junge*) produce; (*Blasen*) form, blow; **Falten w.** wrinkle || *ref* (*Holz*) warp; **sich hin und her w.** toss; **sich in die Brust w.** throw out one's chest || *intr* throw; (*Tieren*) produce young
Werft [verft] *f* (–;–e) shipyard
Werft'halle *f* (aer) repair hangar
Werg [verk] *n* (–[e]s;) oakum, tow
Werk [verk] *n* (–[e]s;–e) work; (*Tat*) deed; (*Erzeugnis*) production; (*Leistung*) performance; (*Unternehmen*) undertaking; (*Fabrik*) works plant, mill; (horol) clockwork; **das ist dein W.** that's your doing; **gutes W.** good deed; **im Werke sein** be in the works; **zu Werke gehen** go to it
Werk'anlage *f* plant, works
Werk'bank *f* (–;¨e) workbench
werk'fremd *adj* (*Personen*) unauthorized
Werk'meister *m* foreman
Werk'nummer *f* factory serial number
Werks'angehörige §**5** *mf* employee
Werk'schutz *m* security force
Werks'kantine *f* factory cafeteria
Werk'statt *f*, **Werk'stätte** *f* workshop
Werk'stattwagen *m* maintenance truck
Werk'stoff *m* manufacturing material
Werk'stück *n* (indust) piece
Werk'tag *m* weekday; working day
werk'tägig *adj* workaday, ordinary
werk'tags *adv* (on) weekdays
werk'tätig *adj* working; practical
Werk'zeug *n* tool
Werk'zeugmaschine *f* machine tool
Wermut ['vermut] *m* (–[e]s;) vermouth; (bot) wormwood
wert [vert] *adj* worth; worthy; esteemed; **etw** [*genit* or *acc*] **w. sein** be worth s.th.; **nicht der Rede w. sein** not worth mentioning; **nichts w.** good for nothing; **Werter Herr X** Dear Mr. X || **Wert** *m* (–[e]s;–e) worth, value; price, rate; (*Wichtigkeit*) importance; (chem) valence; **äußerer W.** face value; **im W. von** valued at; **innerer W.** intrinsic value; **Werte** (com) assets; (phys) data
Wert'angabe *f* valuation
wert'beständig *adj* of lasting value; (*Währung*) stable
Wert'bestimmung *f* appraisal
Wert'brief *m* insured letter
werten ['vertən] *tr* (*bewerten*) value; (*nach Leistung*) rate; (*auswerten*) evaluate
Wert'gegenstand *m* valuable article; **Wertgegenstände** valuables
–wertig [vertıç] *comb.fm.* –value, –quality, e.g., **geringwertig** low-qual-

ity; (chem) –valent, e.g., **zweiwertig** bivalent

Wer'tigkeit f (–;–en) (chem) valence

wert'los adj worthless

Wert'papiere pl securities

Wert'sachen pl valuables

wert'voll adj valuable

Wert'zeichen n stamp; (Briefmarke) postage stamp; (Banknote) bill

Wesen | 'vezən] n (–s;–) being, creature; entity; (inneres Sein, Kern) essence; (Betragen) conduct, way; (Getue) fuss; (Natur) nature, character; **einnehmendes W.** pleasing personality; **höchtes W.** Supreme Being

-wesen n comb.fm. system

we'senhaft adj real; characteristic

we'senlos adj unreal; incorporeal

wesentlich | 'vezentliç] adj essential; (beträchtlich) substantial

Weser ['vezər] f (–) Weser (River)

Wes'fall m genitive case

weshalb [ves'halp] adv why; wherefore

Wespe ['vespə] f (–;–n) wasp

wessen ['vesən] interr pron whose

West [vest] m (–s;) west; (poet) west wind

Weste ['vestə] f (–;–n) vest; e–e reine **W.** a clean slate

Westen ['vestən] m (–s;) west; im **W.** von west of; **nach W.** westward

Westfalen [vest'falən] n (–s;) Westphalia

westfälisch [vest'feliʃ] adj Westphalian

West'gote m (–n;–n) Visigoth

Westindien [vest'ɪndjən] n (–s;) the West Indies

west'lich adj west, western; westerly

Westmächte ['vestmεçtə] pl Western Powers

westwärts ['vestverts] adv westward

weswegen [ves'vegən] adv why; wherefore

wett [vet] adj even, quits

Wett– comb.fm. competitive

Wett'bewerb m (–s;–e) competition, contest; (Treffen) meet

Wett'bewerber –in §6 mf competitor

Wette ['vetə] f (–;–n) bet, wager; e–e **W. abschließen** (or **eingehen**) make a bet; **mit j–m um die W. laufen** race s.o.; **was gilt die W.?** what do you bet?

Wett'eifer m competitiveness, rivalry

wetteifern ['vetaifərn] insep intr compete; **w. um** compete for

Wetter ['vetər] n (–s;) weather; (min) ventilation; **alle W.!** holy smokes!

wet'terbeständig, **wet'terfest** adj weatherproof

Wet'terglas n barometer

wet'terhart adj hardy

Wet'terkunde f meteorology

Wet'terlage f weather conditions

wet'terleuchten insep impers—es wetterleuchtet there is summer lightning || **Wetterleuchten** n (–s;) summer lightning, heat lightning

Wet'terverhältnisse pl weather conditions

Wet'tervorhersage f weather forecast

Wet'terwarte f meteorological station

Wet'terwechsel m change in the weather

wetterwendisch ['vetərvendɪʃ] adj moody

Wett'fahrer –in §6 mf racer

Wett'fahrt f race

Wett'kampf m competition, contest

Wett'kämpfer –in §6 mf competitor, contestant

Wett'lauf m race, foot race

Wett'läufer –in §6 mf runner

wett'machen tr make up for

Wett'rennen n race

Wett'rudern n boat race

Wett'rüsten n armaments race

Wett'schwimmen n swimming meet

Wett'segeln n regatta

Wett'spiel n game, match

Wett'streit m contest, match, game

Wett'zettel m betting ticket

wetzen ['vetsən] tr whet, sharpen

Wetzstein ['vets/tain] m whetstone

Whisky ['vɪski] m (–s;–s) whiskey

wich |vɪç] pret of **weichen**

Wichs |vɪks] m (es–;–e) gala; **in vollem W.** in full dress; **sich in W. werfen** dress up

Wichse ['vɪksə] f (–;–n) shoepolish || f (–;) (coll) spanking

wichsen ['vɪksən] tr polish; (coll) spank, beat up

Wicht |vɪçt] m (–[e]s;–e) elf; dwarf

Wichtel | 'vɪçtəl] m (–s;–) dwarf

wichtig | 'vɪçtɪç] adj important || adv —**w. tun** act important

Wich'tigkeit f (–;) importance

Wichtigtuer | 'vɪçtɪçtu‧ər] m (–s;–) busybody

wichtigtuerisch ['vɪçtɪçtu‧ərɪʃ] adj officious

Wicke | 'vɪkə] f (–;–n) (bot) vetch

Wickel | 'vɪkəl] m (–s;–) wrapper; curler, roller; (von Garn) ball; (med) compress

wickeln ['vɪkəln] tr wrap; wind (Haar) curl; (Kind) diaper; (Zigaretten) roll

Widder ['vɪdər] m (–s;–) ram; (astr) Ram

wider ['vidər] prep (acc) against, contrary to

wider– comb.fm. re–, con–, un–, counter–, contra–, anti–, with–

wi'derborstig adj stubborn, contrary

widerfah'ren §71 intr (SEIN) (dat) befall, happen to

Wi'derhaken m barb

Wi'derhall m echo, reverberation; (fig) response, reaction

wi'derhallen intr echo, resound

Wi'derlager n abutment

widerle'gen tr refute

wi'derlich adj repulsive

wi'dernatürlich adj unnatural

widerra'ten §63 tr—j–m etw w. dissuade s.o. from s.th.

wi'derrechtlich adj illegal

Wi'derrede f contradiction

Wi'derruf m recall; cancellation; retraction; denial; **bis auf W.** until further notice

widerru'fen §122 tr revoke; (Auftrag)

cancel; (*Befehl*) countermand; (*Behauptung*) retract
Widersacher **-in** [ˈvidərzaxər(ɪn)] §6 *mf* adversary
Wi′derschein *m* reflection
widerset′zen *ref* (*dat*) oppose, resist
widersetz′lich *adj* insubordinate
wi′dersinning *adj* absurd, nonsensical
widerspenstig [ˈvidərʃpɛnstɪç] *adj* refractory, contrary; (*Haar*) stubborn
wi′derspiegeln *tr* reflect ‖ *ref* (in *dat*) be reflected (in)
Wi′derspiel *n* contrary, reverse
widerspre′chen §64 *intr* (*dat*) contradict; (*dat*) oppose
widerspre′chend *adj* contradictory
Wi′derspruch *m* contradiction; opposition; **auf heftigen W. stoßen bei** meet with strong opposition from
widersprüchlich [ˈvidərˌpryçlɪç] *adj* contradictory
wi′derspruchsvoll *adj* full of contradictions
Wi′derstand *m* resistance; opposition; (elec) resistance; (elec) resistor
Wi′derstandsnest *n* pocket of resistance
widerste′hen §146 *intr* (*dat*) withstand, resist; (*dat*) be repugnant to
widerstre′ben *intr* (*dat*) oppose, resist; (*dat*) be repugnant to ‖ *impers*—**es widerstrebt mir zu** (*inf*) I hate to (*inf*)
widerstre′bend *adj* reluctant
Wi′derstreit *m* opposition, antagonism; (fig) conflict, clash
widerstrei′ten §86 *intr* (*dat*) clash with
widerwärtig [ˈvidərvɛrtɪç] *adj* nasty
Wi′derwille *m* (**gegen**) dislike (of, for), aversion (to); (*Widerstreben*) reluctance; **mit W.** reluctantly
wi′derwillig *adj* reluctant, unwilling
widmen [ˈvɪtmən] *tr* dedicate, devote ‖ *ref* (*dat*) devote oneself to
Wid′mung *f* (**-;-en**) dedication
widrig [ˈvidrɪç] *adj* contrary; (*ungünstig*) unfavorable, adverse
wid′rigenfalls *adv* otherwise, or else
wie [vi] *adv* how; (*vergleichend*) as, such as, like; **so…wie as…as; und wie!** and how!; **wie, bitte?** what did you say?; **wie dem auch sei** be that as it may; **wie wäre es mit…?** how about…?
wieder [ˈvidər] *adv* again; anew; (*zurück*) back; (*als Vergeltung*) in return
wieder– *comb.fm.* re–
Wie′derabdruck *m* reprint
wiederan′knüpfen *tr* resume
Wiederauf′bau *m* (**-ˈeˈs;**) rebuilding
wiederauf′bauen *tr* rebuild, reconstruct
wiederauf′erstehen §146 *intr* (SEIN) rise from the dead
Wiederauf′erstehung *f* resurrection
Wiederauf′führung *f* (theat) revival
wiederauf′kommen §99 *intr* (SEIN) (*Kranker*) recover; (*Mode*) come in again
Wiederauf′nahme *f* resumption; (jur) reopening
Wiederauf′nahmeverfahren *n* retrial
Wiederauf′rüstung *f* rearmament

Wie′derbeginn *m* reopening
wie′derbekommen §99 *tr* recover
wie′derbeleben *tr* revive, resuscitate
wie′derbeschaffen *tr* replace
wie′derbringen §65 *tr* bring back; restore, give back
wiederein′bringen §65 *tr* make up for
wiederein′setzen *tr* (in *acc*) reinstate (in); **in Rechte w.** restore to former rights
wiederein′stellen *tr* rehire; (mil) reenlist
Wie′dereintritt *m* (rok) reentry
wie′derergreifen §88 *tr* recapture
wie′dererhalten §90 *tr* get back
wie′dererkennen §97 *tr* recognize
wie′dererlangen *tr* recover, retrieve
wie′dererstatten *tr* restore; (*Geld*) refund
Wie′dergabe *f* return; reproduction; rendering
wie′dergeben §80 *tr* give back; (*Ton*) reproduce; (*spielen, übersetzen*) render; (*Ehre, Gesundheit*) restore
Wie′dergeburt *f* rebirth
wie′dergenesen §84 *intr* (SEIN) recover
wie′dergewinnen §52 *tr* regain
wiedergut′machen *tr* make good
Wiedergut′machung *f* (**-;-en**) reparation
wiederher′stellen *tr* restore
wie′derholen *tr* bring back; take back ‖ **wiederho′len** *tr* repeat
wiederholt [vidərˈhɔlt] *adv* repeatedly
Wiederho′lung *f* (**-;-en**) repetition
Wiederho′lungszeichen *n* dittomarks; (mus) repeat
Wie′derhören *n*—**auf W.!** (telp) goodbye!
wie′derimpfen *tr* give (*s.o.*) a booster shot
wiederinstand′setzen *tr* repair
wiederkäuen [ˈvidərkɔɪ-ən] *tr* ruminate; (fig) repeat over and over ‖ *intr* chew the cud
Wiederkehr [ˈvidərker] *f* (**-;**) return; recurrence; anniversary
wie′derkehren *intr* (SEIN) return; recur
wie′derkommen §99 *intr* (SEIN) come back
Wiederkunft [ˈvidərkunft] *f* (**-;**) return
wie′dersehen §138 *tr* see again ‖ *recip* meet again ‖ **Widersehen** *n* (**-s;-**) meeting again; **auf W.!** see you!
Wie′dertäufer *m* Baptist
wie′dertun §154 *tr* do again, repeat
wie′derum *adv* again; on the other hand
wie′dervereinigen *tr* reunite; reunify
Wie′dervereinigung *f* reunion; (pol) reunification
wie′derverheiraten *tr* & *recip* remarry
Wie′derverkäufer **-in** §6 *mf* retailer
Wie′derwahl *f* reelection
wie′derwählen *tr* reelect
wiederzu′lassen §104 *tr* readmit
Wiege [ˈvigə] *f* (**-;-n**) cradle
wiegen [ˈvigən] *tr* (*schaukeln*) rock ‖ *ref*—**sich in den Hüften w.** sway one′s hips; **sich w. in** (*acc*) lull oneself into ‖ §57 *tr* & *intr* weigh
Wie′gendruck *m* incunabulum
Wie′genlied *n* lullaby

wiehern ['vi·ərn] *intr* neigh; **wieherndes Gelächter** horselaugh

Wien [vin] *n* (–s;) Vienna

Wiener –in ['vinər(ɪn)] §6 *mf* Viennese

wienerisch ['vinərɪʃ] *adj* Viennese

wies [vis] *pret of* weisen

Wiese ['vizə] *f* (–;–n) meadow

Wiesel ['vizəl] *n* (–s;–) weasel

Wie'senland *n* meadowland

wieso' *adv* why, how come

wieviel' *adj* how much; **w. Uhr ist es?** what time is it? || *adv & pron* how much || **vieviele** *adj & pron* how many

wievielte [vi'filtə] §9 *adj* which, what; **den wievielten haben wir?** (or **der w. ist heute?**) what day of the month is it?

wiewohl' *conj* although

wild [vɪlt] *adj* wild; savage; (*grausam*) ferocious; (*Flucht*) headlong; (*auf acc*) wild (about); **wilde Ehe** concubinage; **wilder Streik** wildcat strike || **Wild** *n* (–es;) game

Wild'bach *m* torrent

Wild'braten *m* roast venison

Wildbret ['vɪltbret] *n* (–s;) game; venison

Wild'dieb *m* poacher

Wilde ['vɪldə] §5 *mf* savage; **wie ein Wilder** like a madman

Wild'ente *f* wild duck

Wilderer ['vɪldərər] *m* (–s;–) poacher

wildern ['vɪldərn] *intr* poach

Wild'fleisch *n* game; venison

wild'fremd' *adj* completely strange

Wild'hüter *m* game warden

Wild'leder *n* doeskin, buckskin; chamois; suede

Wildnis ['vɪltnɪs] *f* (–;) wilderness

Wild'schwein *n* wild boar

Wild'wasser *n* rapids

Wildwest'film *m* western

wildwüchsig ['vɪltvyksɪç] *adj* wild

Wille ['vɪlə] *m* (–ns;–n), **Willen** ['vɪlən] *m* (–s;–) will; (*Absicht*) intention; **mit W.** on purpose; **um j–s willen** for s.o.'s sake; **wider Willen** unwillingly; unintentionally; **willens sein zu** (*inf*) be willing to (*inf*)

wil'lenlos *adj* irresolute; unstable

Wil'lensfreiheit *f* free will

Wil'lenskraft *f* will power

wil'lensschwach *adj* weak-willed

wil'lensstark *adj* strong-willed

willfah'ren *intr* (*dat*) comply with

willig ['vɪlɪç] *adj* willing, ready

Wil'ligkeit *f* (–;) willingness

willkom'men *adj* welcome; **j–n w. heißen** welcome s.o. || **Willkommen** *m & n* (–s;) welcome

Willkür ['vɪlkyr] *f* (–;) arbitrariness

will'kürlich *adj* arbitrary

wimmeln ['vɪməln] *intr* (**von**) team (with)

wimmern ['vɪmərn] *intr* whimper

Wimpel ['vɪmpəl] *m* (–s;–) streamer; pennant

Wimper ['vɪmpər] *f* (–;–n) eyelash; **ohne mit der W. zu zucken** without batting an eye

Wim'perntusche *f* mascara

Wind [vɪnt] *m* (–[e]s;–e) wind; flatulence; (hunt) scent

Wind'beutel *m* (fig) windbag; (aer) windsock; (culin) cream puff

Winde ['vɪndə] *f* (–;–n) winch, windlass; reel; (naut) capstan

Windel ['vɪndəl] *f* (–;–n) diaper

win'delweich *adj*—**w. schlagen** (coll) beat to a pulp

winden ['vɪndən] §59 *tr* wind; twist, coil; (*Kranz*) weave, make | **ref** wriggle; (*Fluß*) wind; (*vor Schmerzen*) writhe

Wind'fang *m* storm porch

Wind'hose *f* tornado

Wind'hund *m* greyhound; (coll) windbag

windig ['vɪndɪç] *adj* windy; (fig) flighty

Wind'kanal *m* wind tunnel

Wind'licht *n* hurricane lamp

Wind'mühle *f* windmill

Wind'pocken *pl* chicken pox

Wind'sack *m* windsock

Wind'schatten *m* lee

Wind'schutzscheibe *f* windshield

Wind'stärke *f* wind velocity

wind'still *adj* calm || **Windstille** *f* calm

Wind'stoß *m* gust

Wind'strömung *f* air current

Win'dung *f* (–;–en) winding, twisting; (*Kurve*) bend; (*e–r Schlange*) coil; (*e–r Schraube*) thread, worm; (*e–r Muschel*) whorl

Wind'zug *m* air current, draft

Wink [vɪŋk] *m* (–[e]s;–e) sign; (*Zwinkern*) wink; (*mit der Hand*) wave; (*mit dem Kopfe*) nod; (*Hinweis*) hint, tip; **W. mit dem Zaunpfahl** broad hint

Winkel ['vɪŋkəl] *m* (–s;–) corner; (carp) square; (geom) angle; (mil) chevron

winkelig ['vɪŋkəlɪç] *adj* angular; (*Straße*) crooked

Win'kellinie *f* diagonal

Win'kelmaß *n* (carp) square

Win'kelzug *m* subterfuge; evasion

winken ['vɪŋkən] *intr* signal; **mit der Hand** wave; (*mit dem Kopfe*) nod; (*mit dem Auge*) wink; **mit dem Taschentuch w.** wave the handkerchief

Win'ker *m* (–s;–) signalman; (aut) direction signal

winseln ['vɪnzəln] *intr* whimper, whine

Winter ['vɪntər] *m* (–s;–) winter

win'terfest *adj* winterized; (*Pflanzen*) hardy

win'terlich *adj* wintry

Win'terschlaf *m* hibernation; **W. halten** hibernate

Win'tersonnenwende *f* winter solstice

Winzer ['vɪntsər] *m* (–s;–) vinedresser; (*Traubenleser*) grape picker

winzig ['vɪntsɪç] *adj* tiny

Wipfel ['vɪpfəl] *m* (–s;–) treetop

Wippe ['vɪpə] *f* (–;–n) seesaw

wippen ['vɪpən] *intr* seesaw; rock; balance oneself

wir [vir] §11 *pers pron* we

Wirbel ['vɪrbəl] *m* (–s;–) whirl; eddy; whirlpool; (*Trommel*-) roll; (*Violin*-)

peg; (anat) vertebra; **e-n W. machen** (coll) raise Cain

wirbelig ['vɪrbəlɪç] adj whirling; giddy

Wir'belknochen m (anat) vertebra

wir'bellos adj spineless, invertebrate

wirbeln ['vɪrbəln] tr warble || intr whirl; (Wasser) eddy; (Trommel) roll; (Lerche) warble; **mir wirbelt der Kopf** my head is spinning

Wir'belsäule f spinal column, spine

Wir'belsturm m hurricane, typhoon

Wir'beltier n vertebrate

Wir'belwind m whirlwind

wirken ['vɪrkən] tr work, bring about, effect; (Teig) knead; (Teppich) weave; (Pullover) knit; **Gutes w.** do good; **Wunder w.** work wonders || intr work; be active; function; look, appear; (Worte) tell, hit home; **als Arzt w.** be a doctor; **an e-r Schule (als Lehrer) w.** teach school; **anregend w.** act as a stimulant; **berauschend w. auf** (acc) intoxicate; **beruhigend w. auf** (acc) have a soothing effect on; **gut w.** work well; **lächerlich w.** look ridiculous; **stark w. auf** (acc) touch deeply; **w. auf** (acc) affect, have an effect on; **w. bei** have an effect on; **w. für** work for; **w. gegen** work against, counteract || **Wirken** n (-s;) action, performance; operation

wirk'lich adj real, actual; true || adv really, actually; truly

Wirk'lichkeit f (-;-en) reality; actual fact

Wirk'lichkeitsform f indicative mood

wirksam ['vɪrkzam] adj active; effective; (Hieb) telling; **w. für** good for

Wirk'samkeit f (-;) effectiveness

Wirk'stoff m metabolic substance (vitamin, hormone, or enzyme)

Wir'kung f (-;-en) effect; result; operation, action; influence, impression

Wir'kungsbereich m scope; effective range; (mil) zone of fire

wir'kungsfähig adj active; effective; efficient

Wir'kungskreis m domain, province

wir'kungslos adj ineffective; inefficient

wir'kungsvoll adj effective; efficacious

Wirk'waren pl knitware

wirr [vɪr] adj confused; (verworren) chaotic; (Haar) disheveled

Wirren ['vɪrən] pl disorders, troubles

Wirr'kopf m scatterbrain

Wirrwarr ['vɪrvar] m (-s;) mix-up, mess

Wirt [vɪrt] m (-[e]s;-e) host; innkeeper; landlord; (biol) host

Wirtin ['vɪrtɪn] f (-;-nen) hostess; innkeeper, innkeeper's wife; landlady

wirt'lich adj hospitable

Wirt'schaft f (-;-en) economy; business; industry and trade; (Haushaltung) housekeeping; (Hauswesen) household; (Gasthaus) inn; (Treiben) goings-on; (Durcheinander) mess; (Umstände) fuss, trouble; **die W. besorgen** (or **führen**) keep house; **gelenkte W.** planned economy

wirtschaften ['vɪrtʃaftən] intr keep

house; economize; (herumhantieren) bustle about; **gut w.** manage well

Wirt'schafter **-in** §6 mf manager || f housekeeper

Wirt'schaftler **-in** §6 m economist; economics teacher

wirt'schaftlich adj economical, thrifty; economic, industrial; (vorteilhaft) profitable

Wirt'schaftsgeld n housekeeping money

Wirt'schaftshilfe f economic aid

Wirt'schaftsjahr n fiscal year

Wirt'schaftslehre f economics

Wirt'schaftspolitik f economic policy

Wirt'schaftsprüfer **-in** §6 mf certified public accountant, CPA

Wirts'haus n inn, restaurant; bar

wischen ['vɪʃən] tr wipe

Wisch'lappen m dustcloth

Wisch'tuch n dishtowel

wispern ['vɪspərn] tr & intr whisper

Wißbegierde ['vɪsbəgirdə] f (-;) craving for knowledge; curiosity

wissen ['vɪsən] §161 tr & intr know || **Wissen** n (-s;) knowledge; learning; know-how; **meines Wissens** as far as I know

Wis'senschaft f (-;-en) knowledge; science

Wis'senschaftler **-in** §6 mf scientist

wis'senschaftlich adj scientific; scholarly; learned

Wis'sensdrang m, **Wis'sensdurst** m thirst for knowledge

Wis'sensgebiet n field of knowledge

wis'senswert adj worth knowing

wis'sentlich adj conscious; willful || adv knowingly; on purpose

wittern ['vɪtərn] tr scent, smell

Wit'terung f (-;-en) weather; (hunt) scent; **bei günstiger W.** weather permitting; **e-e feine W. haben** have a good nose

Wit'terungsverhältnisse pl weather conditions

Witwe ['vɪtvə] f (-;-n) widow

Witwer ['vɪtvər] m (-s;-) widower

Witz [vɪts] m (-es;-e) joke; wisecrack; wit; wittiness; **das ist der ganze W.** that's all; **Witze machen** (or **reißen**) crack jokes

Witz'blatt n comics

Witzbold ['vɪtsbɔlt] m (-[e]s;-e) joker

witzig ['vɪtsɪç] adj witty; funny

wo [vo] adv where; **wo auch** (or **wo immer**) wherever; **wo nicht** if not; **wo nur** wherever

woan'ders adv somewhere else

wob [vop] pret of **weben**

wobei' adv whereby; whereat; whereto; at which; in the course of which

Woche ['vɔxə] f (-;-n) week; **heute in e-r W.** a week from today; **in den Wochen sein** be in labor; **in die Wochen kommen** go into labor; **unter der W.** (coll) during the week

Wo'chenbeihilfe f maternity benefits

Wo'chenbett n post-natal period

Wo'chenblatt n weekly (newspaper)

Wo'chenende n weekend

Wo'chengeld n weekly allowance; (für Mütter) maternity benefits

wo'chenlang adj lasting many weeks || adv for weeks

Wo'chenlohn m weekly wages

Wo'chenschau f (cin) newsreel

wöchentlich ['vœçəntlıç] adj weekly || adv every week; **einmal w.** once a week

-wöchig [vœçıç] comb.fm. -week

Wöchnerin ['vœçnərın] f (-;-nen) recent mother

Wodka ['vɔtka] m (-s;) vodka

wodurch' adv whereby, by which; how

wofern' conj provided that; **w. nicht** unless

wofür' adv wherefore, for which; what for; **w. halten Sie mich?** what do you take me for?

wog [vok] pret of wägen & wiegen

Woge ['voga] f (-;-n) billow; **Wogen der Erregung** waves of excitement

woge'gen adv against what; against which; in exchange for what

wogen ['vogan] intr billow, surge, heave; (Getreide) wave; **hin und her w.** fluctuate

woher' adv from where; **w. wissen Sie das?** how do you know this?

wohin' adv whereto, where

wohinge'gen conj whereas

wohl [vol] adj well || adv well; (freilich) to be sure, all right; I guess; possibly, probably; perhaps; **es sich [dat] w. sein lassen** have a good time; **nun w.! well!; w. daran tun zu** (inf) do well to (inf); **w. dem, der** happy he who; **w. kaum hardly; w. oder übel** willy-nilly || **Wohl** n (-[e]s;) good health, well-being; (Wohlfahrt) welfare; (Gedeihen) prosperity; **auf Ihr W.!** to your health! **gemeines W.** common good

wohlan' interj all right then!

wohlauf' adj in good health, well || interj all right then!

wohlbedacht ['volbədaxt] adj well-thought-out

Wohl'befinden n (-s;) well-being

Wohl'behagen n comfort, contentment

wohl'behalten adj safe and sound

wohl'bekannt adj well-known

wohl'beschaffen adj in good condition

Wohl'ergehen n well-being

wohl'erzogen adj well-bred

Wohl'fahrt f (-;) welfare

Wohl'fahrtsarbeit f social work

wohl'feil adj cheap

Wohl'gefallen n (-s;) pleasure, satisfaction

wohl'gefällig adj pleasant, agreeable

wohl'gemeint adj well-meant

wohlgemut ['volgəmut] adj cheerful

wohl'genährt adj well-fed

wohl'geneigt adj affectionate

Wohl'geruch m fragrance, perfume

wohl'gesinnt adj well-disposed

wohl'habend adj well-to-do

wohlig ['volıç] adj comfortable

Wohl'klang m melodious sound

wohl'klingend adj melodious

Wohl'leben n good living, luxury

wohl'riechend adj fragrant

wohl'schmeckend adj tasty

Wohl'sein n good health, well-being

Wohl'stand m prosperity, wealth

Wohl'tat f benefit; (Gunst) kindness, good deed; **e-e W. sein** hit the spot

Wohl'täter -in §6 mf benefactor

wohl'tätig adj charitable; beneficent

Wohl'tätigkeit f charity

wohltuend ['voltu-ənt] adj pleasant

wohl'tun §154 intr do good; (dat) be pleasant (to)

wohl'unterrichtet adj well-informed

wohl'verdient adj well-deserved

wohl'verstanden interj mark my words!

wohl'weislich adv very wisely

wohl'wollen §162 intr (dat) be well-disposed towards || **Wollwollen** n (-s;) good will; (Gunst) favor

Wohn- [von] comb.fm. residential; dwelling, living

Wohn'anhänger m house trailer

Wohn'block m block of apartments

wohnen ['vonən] intr live, reside; (als Mieter) room

wohn'haft adj residing, living

Wohn'haus n dwelling; apartment house

Wohn'küche f efficiency apartment

Wohn'laube f garden house

wohn'lich adj livable; cozy

Wohn'möglichkeit f living accommodations

Wohn'ort m place of residence; (jur) domicile; **ständiger W.** permanent address

Wohn'raum m living space; room (of a house)

Wohn'sitz m place of residence

Woh'nung f (-;-en) dwelling, home; apartment; room; accommodations

Woh'nungsamt n housing authority

Woh'nungsbau m (-[e]s;) housing construction

Woh'nungsfrage f housing problem

Woh'nungsinhaber -in §6 mf occupant

Woh'nungsmangel m, **Woh'nungsnot** f housing shortage

Wohn'viertel n residential district

Wohn'wagen m mobile home

Wohn'wagenparkplatz m trailer camp

Wohn'zimmer n living room

wölben ['vœlbən] tr vault, arch || ref (über dat or acc) arch (over)

Wöl'bung f (-;-en) curvature; vault

Wolf [vɔlf] m (-[e]s;²e) wolf; (Fleisch-) meat grinder; (astr) Lupus; (pathol) lupus

Wolfram ['vɔlfram] n (-s;) tungsten

Wolke ['vɔlkə] f (-;-n) cloud

Wol'kenbildung f cloud formation

Wol'kenbruch m cloudburst

Wol'kendecke f cloudcover

Wol'kenfetzen m wispy cloud

Wol'kenhöhe f (meteor) ceiling

Wol'kenkratzer m (-s;-) skyscraper

Wol'kenwand f cloud bank

wolkig ['vɔlkıç] adj cloudy, clouded

Wolldecke ['vɔldekə] f woolen blanket

Wolle ['vɔlə] f (-;-n) wool

wollen ['vɔlən] adj woolen, wool || §162 tr want, wish; mean, intend; (gern haben) like || intr wish, like; **dem sei, wie ihm wolle** be that as it may; **wie Sie w.** as you please || mod aux want (to), wish (to), intend (to);

be going (to) ‖ **Wollen** *n* (-s;) will; volition

Wollfett ['vɔlfɛt] *n* lanolin

Wollgarn ['vɔlgarn] *n* worsted

wollig ['vɔlɪç] *adj* woolly

Wolljacke ['vɔljakə] *f* cardigan

Wollsachen ['vɔlzaxən] *pl* woolens

Wollstoff ['vɔlʃtɔf] *m* woolen fabric

Wollust ['vɔlʊst] *f* (-;⸚e) lust

wollüstig ['vɔlʏstɪç] *adj* voluptuous; (geil) lewd, lecherous

Wollüstling ['vɔlʏstlɪŋ] *m* (-s;-e) voluptuary

Wollwaren ['vɔlvarən] *pl* woolens

womit' *adv* with which; with what; wherewith; **w. kann ich dienen?** (com) can I help you?

womög'lich *adv* possibly, if possible

wonach' *adv* after which, whereupon; according to which

Wonne ['vɔnə] *f* (-;-n) delight; bliss

Won'negefühl *n* blissful feeling

Won'neschauer *m* thrill of delight

won'netrunken *adj* enraptured

won'nevoll, wonnig ['vɔnɪç] *adj* blissful

woran' *adv* at which; at what; **ich weiß nicht, w. ich bin** I don't know where I stand

worauf' *adv* on which; on what; whereupon; **w. warten Sie?** what are you waiting for?

woraus' *adv* out of what, from which; out of which, from which; **w. ist das gemacht?** what is this made of?

worden ['vɔrdən] *pp* of **werden**

worin' *adv* in what; in which

Wort [vɔrt] *n* (-[e]s;⸚er) word (individual; literal) ‖ *n* (-[e]s;-e) word (expression; figurative); (Ausspruch) saying; (Ehrenwort) word (of honor); **auf ein W.!** may I have a word with you!; **auf mein W.!** word of honor!; **aufs W.** implicitly, to the letter; **das W. ergreifen** begin to speak; (parl) take the floor; **das W. erhalten** (or **haben**) be allowed to speak; (parl) have the floor; **das W. führen** be the spokesman; **hast du Worte!** (coll) can you beat that!; **in Worten** in writing; **j—m das W. erteilen** allow s.o. to speak; **j—m ins W. fallen** cut s.o. short

Wort'art *f* (gram) part of speech

Wort'bedeutungslehre *f* semantics

Wort'beugung *f* declension

Wort'bildung *f* word formation

wort'brüchig *adj*—**w. werden** break one's word

Wörterbuch ['vœrtərbux] *n* dictionary

Wörterverzeichnis ['vœrtərfɛrtsaɪçnɪs] *n* word index; vocabulary; glossary

Wort'folge *f* word order

Wort'führer –in §6 *mf* spokesman

Wort'gefecht *n* dispute

wort'getreu *adj* literal; verbatim

wort'karg *adj* taciturn

Wortklauber –in ['vɔrtklaubər(ɪn)] §6 *mf* quibbler, hairsplitter

Wort'laut *m* wording; (fig) letter

wörtlich ['vœrtlɪç] *adj* word-for-word; literal; (Rede) direct

wort'los *adv* without saying a word

Wort'register *n* word index

Wort'schatz *m* vocabulary

Wort'schwall *m* flood of words, verbiage

Wort'spiel *n* pun

Wort'stamm *m* stem

Wort'stellung *f* word order

Wort'streit *m*, **Wort'wechsel** *m* argument

worüber' [vo'rybər] *adv* over what, over which

worum' [vo'rum] *adv* about what, about which

worunter' [vo'runtər] *adv* under what, under which; among which

wovon' *adv* from what, of what, from which, of which; **w. ist die Rede?** what are they talking about?

wovor' *adv* of what; before which

wozu' *adv* for what; why; to which

Wrack [vrak] *n* (-[e]s;-e & -s) (& fig wreck)

Wrack'gut *n* wreckage

wrang [vraŋ] *pret* of **wringen**

wringen ['vrɪŋən] §142 *tr* wring

Wringmaschine ['vrɪŋmaʃinə] *f* wringer

Wucher ['vuxər] *m* (-s;) profiteering; **das ist ja W.!** (coll) that's highway robbery!; **W. treiben** profiteer

Wu'cherer –in §6 *mf* profiteer; loan shark

Wu'chergewinn *m* excess profit

wu'cherhaft, wucherisch ['vuxərɪʃ] *adj* profiteering, exorbitant

Wu'chermiete *f* excessive rent

wuchern ['vuxərn] *intr* grow luxuriantly; (Wucher treiben) profiteer

Wu'cherung *f* (-;-en) (bot) rank growth; (pathol) growth

Wu'cherzinsen *pl* excessive interest

wuchs [vuks] *pret* of **wachsen** ‖ **Wuchs** *m* (-es;) growth; **groß von W.** tall

–wüchsig [vyksɪç] *comb.fm.* –growing, –grown

Wucht [vuxt] *f* (-;-en) weight, force

wuchten ['vuxtən] *tr* lift with effort

wuchtig ['vuxtɪç] *adj* heavy; massive

Wühlarbeit ['vylarbaɪt] *f* subversive activity

wühlen ['vylən] *intr* dig, burrow; (Schwein) root about; (suchend) rummage about; (pol) engage in subversive activities; **im Geld w.** be rolling in money; **in Schmutz w.** wallow in filth

Wüh'ler –in §6 *mf* subversive, agitator

Wulst [vulst] *m* (-es;⸚e) & *f* (-;⸚e) bulge; (aut) rim (of tire)

wulstig ['vulstɪç] *adj* bulging; (Lippen) thick

wund [vunt] *adj* sore; (poet) wounded

Wunde ['vundə] *f* (-;-n) wound; sore

Wunder ['vundər] *n* (-s;-) wonder; miracle; **W. wirken** work wonders

wunderbar ['vundərbar] *adj* wonderful; (& fig) miraculous

Wun'derding *n* marvel

Wun'derdoktor *m* faith healer

Wun'derkind *n* child prodigy

Wun'derkraft *f* miraculous power

wun'derlich *adj* queer, odd

wundern ['vundərn] *tr* amaze ‖ *ref*

(über *acc)* be amazed (at) ‖ *impers*
—es sollte mich w., wenn I'd be surprised if; **es wundert mich, daß** I am
surprised that
wun'derschön' *adv* lovely, gorgeous
Wun'dertat *f* miracle
Wun'dertäter –in §6 *mf* wonder worker
wundertätig *adj* miraculous
wun'dervoll *adj* wonderful, marvelous
Wun'derwerk *n* (& fig) miracle
Wun'derzeichen *n* omen, prodigy
Wund'klammer *f* (surg) clamp
wund'liegen §108 *ref* get bedsores
Wund'mal *n* scar, sore; (relig) wound
wund'reiten §86 *ref* become saddlesore
Wunsch [vunʃ] *m* (–es;¨e) wish;
(nach) desire (for); **auf W.** upon request; **ein frommer W.** wishful thinking; **nach W.** as desired
Wünschelrute ['vynʃəlrutə] *f* divining
rod
Wün'schelrutengänger *m* dowser
wünschen ['vynʃən] *tr* wish; wish for,
desire; **was w. Sie?** (com) may I help
you? ‖ *intr* wish, please
wün'schenswert *adj* desirable
Wunsch'form *f* (gram) optative
Wunsch'konzert *n* (rad) request program
wunsch'los *adj* contented ‖ *adv*—w.
glücklich perfectly happy
wuppdich ['vupdɪç] *interj* zip!, in a
flash!; all of a sudden!
wurde ['vurdə] *pret of* **werden**
Würde ['vyrdə] *f* (–;–n) honor; title;
dignity; post, office; **akademische
W.** academic degree; **unter aller W.**
beneath contempt
wür'delos *adj* undignified
Wür'denträger –in §6 *mf* dignitary
wür'devoll *adj* dignified
würdig ['vyrdɪç] *adj* dignified; (genit)
worthy (of), deserving (of)
würdigen ['vyrdɪgən] *tr* appreciate,
value; (genit) deem worthy (of)
Wurf [vurf] *m* (–[e]s;¨e) throw, cast,
pitch; (fig) hit, success; (zool) litter,
brood
Wurf'anker *m* grapnel
Würfel ['vyrfəl] *m* (–s;–) die; cube,

square; (geom) cube; **W. spielen**
play dice
Wür'felbecher *m* dice box
würfelig ['vyrfəlɪç] *adj* cube-shaped;
(Muster) checkered
würfeln ['vyrfəln] *intr* play dice
Wür'felzucker *m* cube sugar
Wurf'geschoß *n* projectile, missile
Wurf'pfeil *m* dart
würgen ['vyrgən] *tr* choke; strangle ‖
intr choke; **am Essen w.** gag on food
Wurm [vurm] *m* (–s;¨er) (& mach)
worm
wurmen ['vurmən] *tr* (coll) bug
wurmig ['vurmɪç] *adj* wormy; worm-
eaten
wurmstichig ['vurm/tɪçɪç] *adj* worm-
eaten
Wurst [vurst] *f* (–;¨e) sausage; **es geht
um die W.** now or never; **es ist mir
W.** I couldn't care less
Würstchen ['vyrstçən] *n* (–s;–), **Würstel** ['vyrstəl] *n* (–s;–n) hotdog
wursteln ['vurstəln] *intr* muddle along
Würze ['vyrtsə] *f* (–;–n) spice, seasoning; (fig) zest
Wurzel ['vurtsəl] *f* (–;–n) root; **W.
fassen** (or **schlagen**) take root
wurzeln ['vurtsəln] *intr* (HABEN & SEIN)
take root; **w. in** (dat) be rooted in
würzen ['vyrtsən] *tr* spice, season
würzig ['vyrtsɪç] *adj* spicy; aromatic
Würz'stoff *m* seasoning
wusch ['vuʃ] *pret of* **waschen**
wußte ['vustə] *pret of* **wissen**
Wust [vust] *m* (–es;) jumble, mess
wüst [vyst] *adj* desert, waste; (roh)
coarse; (wirr) confused
Wüste ['vystə] *f* (–;–en) desert
Wüstling ['vystlɪŋ] *m* (–s;–e) debauchee
Wut [vut] *f* (–;) rage, fury; madness
Wut'anfall *m* fit of rage
wüten ['vytən] *intr* rage
wü'tend *adj* furious (at) (auf acc)
Wüterich ['vytərɪç] *m* (–s;–e) madman; bloodthirsty villain
wut'schäumend *adj* foaming with rage
wut'schnaubend *adj* in a towering rage
Wut'schrei *m* shout of anger

X

X, x [ɪks] *invar n* X, x
X'-Beine *pl* knock-knees
x'-beinig *adj* knock-kneed
x'-beliebig *adj* any, whatever ‖ **X-
beliebige** §5 *m*—**jeder X.** every Tom,
Dick, and Harry
x'-fach *adj* (coll) hundredfold

x'-mal *adv* umpteen times
X'-Strahlen *pl* x-rays
X'-Tag *m* D-day
x-te [ˈɪkstə] §9 *adj* umpteenth; **die
x-te Potenz** (math) the nth power
Xylophon [ksylo'fon] *n* (–s;–e) xylophone

Y

Y, y [ypsilən] *invar n* Y, y
Yacht [jaxt] *f* (–;–en) yacht
Yamswurzel ['jamsvurtsəl] *f* (–;–n)
(bot) yam

Yankee ['jɛnki] *m* (–s;–s) Yankee
Yoghurt ['jogurt] *m & n* (–s;) yogurt
Yo-Yo ['jo'jo] *n* (–s;–s) yo-yo
Ypsilon ['ypsilən] *n* (–[s];–s) y

Z

Z, z [tset] *invar n* Z, z
Zacke ['tsakə] *f* (-;-n) sharp point; (*Zinke*) prong; (*Fels–*) crag; (*e-s Kamms, e-r Säge*) tooth; (*am Kleid*) scallop
zacken ['tsakən] *tr* notch; scallop ‖ **Zacken** *m* (-s;-) var of **Zacke**
zackig ['tsakɪç] *adj* toothed; notched; (*Felsen*) jagged; (*spitz*) pointed; (*Kleid*) scalloped; (fig) sharp
zagen ['tsagən] *intr* be faint-hearted
zaghaft ['tsakhaft] *adj* timid
zäh [tse] *adj* tough; (*klebig*) viscous; (*beharrlich*) persistent; (*Gedächtnis*) tenacious; (*halsstarrig*) dogged
zäh'flüssig *adj* viscous
Zäh'flüssigkeit *f* (-;) viscosity
Zä'higkeit *f* (-;) toughness; tenacity; viscosity; doggedness
Zahl [tsal] *f* (-;-en) number; (*Betrag, Ziffer*) figure; **an Z. übertreffen** outnumber; **arabische Z.** Arabic numeral; **der Z. nach** in number; **ganze Z.** integer; **gebrochene Z.** fraction; **gerade Z.** even number; **in roten Zahlen stecken** be in the red; **ungerade Z.** odd number; **wenig an der Z.** few in number
zahlbar ['tsalbar] *adj* payable; **z. bei Lieferung** cash on delivery
zählebig ['tselebɪç] *adj* hardy
zahlen ['tsalən] *tr* pay; (*Schuld*) pay off ‖ *intr* pay
zählen ['tselən] *tr* count; number, amount to ‖ *intr* count; be of importance, count; **nach Tausenden z.** number in the thousands; **z. auf** (*dat*) count on; **z. zu** be numbered among, belong to
Zah'lenangaben *pl* figures
Zah'lenfolge *f* numerical order
zah'lenmäßig *adj* numerical
Zah'ler –in *§6 mf* payer
Zäh'ler –in (-s;–) counter; recorder; (*für Gas, Elektrizität*) meter; (math) numerator; (parl) teller; (sport) scorekeeper
Zählerableser ['tseləraplezər] *m* (-s;–) meter man
Zahl'karte *f* money-order form
zahl'los *adj* countless, innumerable
Zahl'meister *m* paymaster; (mil) pay officer; (nav) purser
zahl'reich *adj* numerous
Zähl'rohr *n* Geiger counter
Zahl'stelle *f* cashier's window; (*e-r Bank*) branch office
Zahl'tag *m* payday
Zah'lung *f* (-;-en) payment; (*e-r Schuld*) settlement
Zäh'lung *f* (-;-en) counting; computation
Zah'lungsanweisung *f* draft; check; postal money order
Zah'lungsausgleich *m* balance of payments
Zah'lungsbedingungen *pl* (fin) terms
Zah'lungsbestätigung *f* receipt

Zah'lungsbilanz *f* balance of payments; **aktive** (or **passive**) **Z.** favorable (or unfavorable) balance of payments
zah'lungsfähig *adj* solvent
Zah'lungsfähigkeit *f* (-;) solvency
Zah'lungsfrist *f* due date
Zah'lungsmittel *n* medium of exchange; **gesetzliches Z.** legal tender; **bargeldloses Z.** instrument of credit
Zah'lungsschwierigkeiten *pl* financial embarrassment
Zah'lungssperre *f* stoppage of payments
Zah'lungstermin *m* date of payment; (fin) date of maturity
Zah'lungsverzug *m* (fin) default
Zähl'werk *n* meter
Zahl'wort *n* (-[e]s;⸚er) numeral
Zahl'zeichen *n* figure, cipher
zahm [tsam] *adj* tame; domesticated
zähmen ['tsemən] *tr* tame; domesticate; (fig) control ‖ *ref* control oneself
Zäh'mung *f* (-;) taming; domestication
Zahn [tsan] *m* (-[e]s;⸚e) tooth; (mach) tooth, cog; **j–m auf den Z. fühlen** sound s.o. out; **mit den Zähnen knirschen** grind one's teeth
Zahn'arzt *m*, **Zahn'ärztin** *f* dentist
Zahn'bürste *f* toothbrush
Zahn'creme *f* toothpaste
zahnen ['tsanən] *intr* cut one's teeth
Zahn'ersatz *m* denture
Zahn'fäule *f* tooth decay, caries
Zahn'fleisch *n* gum
Zahn'füllung *f* (dent) filling
Zahn'heilkunde *f* dentistry
Zahn'klammer *f* (-;-n) (dent) brace
Zahn'krem *f* toothpaste
Zahn'krone *f* (dent) crown
Zahn'laut *m* (phonet) dental
Zahn'lücke *f* gap between the teeth
Zahn'paste *f* toothpaste
Zahn'pflege *f* dental hygiene
Zahn'pulver *n* tooth powder
Zahn'rad *n* cog wheel; (*Kettenrad*) sprocket
Zahn'radbahn *f* cog railway
Zahn'schmerz *m* toothache
Zahn'spange *f* (-;-n) (dent) brace
Zahn'stein *m* (dent) tartar
Zahnstocher ['tsanʃtoxər] *m* (-s;–) toothpick
Zahn'techniker –in *§6 mf* dental technician
Zahn'weh *n* toothache
Zange ['tsaŋə] *f* (-;-en) (pair of) pliers; (pair of) tongs; (*Pinzette*) (pair of) tweezers; (dent, surg, zool) forceps; **j–n in die Z. nehmen** corner s.o. (*with tough questioning*)
Zank ['tsaŋk] *m* (-[e]s;) quarrel, fight
Zank'apfel *m* apple of discord
zanken ['tsaŋkən] *tr* scold ‖ *recip & intr* quarrel, fight
zank'haft, zänkisch ['tseŋkɪʃ], **zank'süchtig** *adj* quarrelsome

Zäpfchen ['tsepfçən] *n* (-s;-) little peg; (anat) uvula; (med) suppository

zapfen ['tsapfən] *tr* (*Bier, Wein*) tap || **Zapfen** *m* (-s;-) plug, bung; (*Stift*) stud; (*Drehpunkt*) pivot; (*Eis-*) icicle; (*Tannen-*) cone; (carp) tenon; (mach) pin; (mach) journal

Zap'fenstreich *m* (mil) taps

Zapfhahn ['tsapfhan] *m* tap, spigot

Zapfsäule ['tsapfzɔɪlə] *f* (-;-n) (aut) gasoline pump

Zapfstelle ['tsapf/telə] *f* (-;-n) (aut) service station, gas station

Zapfwart ['tsapfvart] *m* (-[e]s;-e) (aut) service station attendant

zappelig ['tsapəlɪç] *adj* fidgety

zappeln ['tsapəln] *intr* fidget; squirm; (*im Wasser*) flounder

Zar [tsar] *m* (-en;-en) czar

Zarge ['tsargə] *f* (-;-n) border; frame

zart [tsart] *adj* tender; (*Farbe, Haut*) soft; (*Gesundheit*) delicate

zart'fühlend *adj* tender; sensitive

Zart'gefühl *n* sensitivity; tact

Zart'heit *f* (-;) tenderness

zärtlich ['tsertlɪç] *adj* tender, affectionate

Zärt'lichkeit *f* (-;-en) tenderness; (*Liebkosung*) caress

Zaster ['tsastər] *m* (-s;) (coll) dough

Zauber ['tsaubər] *m* (-s;-) spell; magic; (fig) charm, glamor

Zauber– *comb.fm.* magic

Zauberei [tsaubə'raɪ] *f* (-;-en) magic; witchcraft, sorcery

Zau'berer *m* (-s;-) magician; sorcerer

Zau'berformel *f* incantation, spell

zau'berhaft *adj* magic; enchanting

Zau'berin *f* (-;-nen) sorceress, witch; enchantress

zauberisch ['tsaubərɪ/] *adj* magic

Zau'berkraft *f* magic power

Zau'berkunst *f* magic

Zau'berkünstler –in §6 *mf* magician

Zau'berkunststück *n* magic trick

Zau'berland *n* fairyland

zaubern ['tsaubərn] *tr* produce by magic || *intr* practice magic; do magic tricks

Zau'berspruch *m* incantation, spell

Zau'berstab *m* magic wand

Zau'bertrank *m* magic potion

Zau'berwerk *n* witchcraft

Zau'berwort *n* (-[e]s;-e) magic word

zaudern ['tsaudərn] *intr* procrastinate; hesitate; linger

Zaum [tsaum] *m* (-[e]s;⸚e) bridle; **im Z. halten** keep in check

zäumen ['tsɔɪmən] *tr* bridle

Zaun [tsaun] *m* (-[e]s;⸚e) fence; **e-n Streit vom Z. brechen** pick a quarrel

Zaun'gast *m* non-paying spectator

Zaun'könig *m* (orn) wren

Zaun'pfahl *m* fence post

zausen ['tsauzən] *tr* tug at; tousle, ruffle || *recip* tug at each other

Zebra ['tsebra] *n* (-s;-s) zebra

Ze'brastreifen *m* zebra stripe; (*auf der Fahrbahn*) passenger crossing

Zech– [tseç] *comb.fm.* drinking

Zech'bruder *m* boozehound

Zeche ['tseçə] *f* (-;-n) (*Wirtshausrechnung*) check; (min) mine **die Z.**

prellen (coll) sneak out without paying the bill

zechen ['tseçən] *intr* booze

Ze'cher –in §6 *mf* heavy drinker

Zech'gelage *n* drinking party

Zechpreller ['tseçprelər] *m* (-s;-) cheat, bilker

Zech'tour *f* binge; **e-e Z. machen** go on a binge

Zecke ['tsekə] *f* (-;-n) (ent) tick

Zeder ['tsedər] *f* (-;-n) cedar

Zehe ['tse.ə] *f* (-;-n) toe; (*Knoblauch-*) clove

Ze'hennagel *m* toenail

Ze'henspitze *f* tip of the toe; **auf den Zehenspitzen** (on) tiptoe

zehn [tsen] *invar adj & pron* ten || **Zehn** *f* (-;-en) ten

Zehner ['tsenər] *m* (-s;-) ten; ten-mark bill

zehn'fach, zehn'fältig *adj* tenfold

Zehnfin'gersystem *n* touch-type system

Zehn'kampf *m* decathlon

zehn'mal *adv* ten times

zehnte ['tsentə] §9 *adj & pron* tenth || **Zehnte** §5 *mfn* tenth

Zehntel ['tsentəl] *n* (-s;-) tenth (*part*)

zehren ['tserən] *intr* be debilitating; **an den Kräften z.** drain one's strength; **an der Gesundheit z.** undermine one's health; **z. an** (*dat*) (fig) gnaw at; **z. von** live on, live off

Zeh'rung *f* (-;) provisions; expenses

Zeichen ['tsaɪçən] *n* (-s;-) sign; signal; token; (*Merkmal*) distinguishing mark; (*Beweis*) proof; symbol; (astr) sign; (com) brand; (med) symptom; (rad) call sign; **er ist seines Zeichens Anwalt** he is a lawyer by profession; **zum Z., daß** as proof that

Zei'chenbrett *n* drawing board

Zei'chenbuch *n* sketchbook

Zei'chengerät *n* drafting equipment

Zei'chenheft *n* sketchbook

Zei'chenlehrer –in §6 *mf* art teacher

Zei'chenpapier *n* drawing paper

Zei'chensetzung *f* punctuation

Zei'chensprache *f* sign language

Zei'chentisch *m* drawing board

Zei'chentrickfilm *m* animated cartoon

Zei'chenunterricht *m* drawing lesson

zeichnen ['tsaɪçnən] *tr* draw; sketch; (*entwerfen*) design; (*brandmarken*) brand; (*Anleihe*) take out; (*Aktien*) buy; (*Geld*) pledge; (*Wäsche*) mark; (*Brief*) sign || *intr* draw; sketch; (hunt) leave a trail of blood; **z. für** sign for

Zeich'ner –in §6 *mf* draftsman; (*Mode-*) designer; (*e-r Anleihe*) subscriber

zeichnerisch ['tsaɪçnərɪ/] *adj* (*Begabung*) for drawing; (*Darstellung*) graphic

Zeich'nung *f* (-;-en) drawing; sketch; design; picture, illustration; diagram; signature; (*e-r Anleihe*) subscription; (*des Holzes*) grain

zeich'nungsberechtigt *adj* authorized to sign

Zeigefinger ['tsaɪgəfɪŋər] *m* index finger

zeigen ['tsaɪgən] *tr* show, indicate;

(*in e–r Rede*) point out; (*zur Schau stellen*) display; (*beweisen*) prove; (*dartun*) demonstrate || *ref* appear, show up; prove to be || *intr* point; **z. auf** (*acc*) point to; **z. nach** point toward || *impers ref*—**es zeigt sich, daß** it turns out that; **es wird sich ja z., ob** we shall see whether

Zei′ger *m* (-s;-) pointer; indicator; (*e–r Uhr*) hand

Zeigestock [′tsaɪgə/tɔk] *m* pointer

Zeile [′tsaɪlə] *f* (-;-n) line; (*Reihe*) row

Zeit [tsaɪt] *f* (-;-en) time; **auf Z.** (com) on credit, on time; **in der letzten Z.** lately; **in jüngster Z.** quite recently; **mit der Z.** in time, in the course of time; **vor Zeiten** in former times; **zu meiner Z.** in my time; **zu rechter Z.** in the nick of time; on time; **zur Z.** at present; **zur Z.** (*genit*) at the time of

Zeit′abschnitt *m* period, epoch

Zeit′abstand *m* interval of time

Zeit′alter *n* age

Zeit′angabe *f* time; date; exact date and hour; **ohne Z.** undated

Zeit′ansage *f* (rad) (giving of) time

Zeit′aufnahme *f* (phot) time exposure

Zeit′aufwand *m* loss of time; (**für**) time spent (on)

Zeit′dauer *f* term, period of time

Zeit′einteilung *f* timetable; timing

Zei′tenfolge *f* sequence of tenses

Zei′tenwende *f* beginning of the Christian era

Zeit′folge *f* chronological order

Zeit′form *f* tense

Zeit′geist *m* spirit of the times

zeit′gemäß *adj* timely; up-to-date

Zeit′genosse *m*, **Zeit′genossin** *f* contemporary

zeitgenössisch [′tsaɪtgənœsɪʃ] *adj* contemporary

Zeit′geschichte *f* contemporary history

zeitig [′tsaɪtɪç] *adj* early; (*reif*) mature, ripe

zeitigen [′tsaɪtɪgən] *tr* ripen

Zeit′karte *f* commuter ticket

Zeit′lage *f* state of affairs

Zeit′lang *f*—**e–e Z.** for some time

Zeit′lauf *m* course of time

zeit′lebens *adv* during my (his, your, etc.) life

zeit′lich *adj* temporal; chronological || *adv* in time || **Zeitliche** §5 *n*—**das Z. segnen** depart this world

zeit′los *adj* timeless

Zeit′lupe *f* (cin) slow motion

Zeit′mangel *m* lack of time

Zeit′maß *n* (mus) tempo; (pros) quantity

Zeit′nehmer –in §6 *mf* timekeeper

Zeit′ordnung *f* chronological order

Zeit′punkt *m* point of time, moment

Zeitraffer [′tsaɪtrafər] *m* (-s;) time-lapse photography

zeit′raubend *adj* time-consuming

Zeit′raum *m* space of time, period

Zeit′rechnung *f* era

Zeit′schaltgerät *n* timer

Zeit′schrift *f* periodical, magazine

Zeit′spanne *f* span (of time)

Zeit′tafel *f* chronological table

Zei′tung *f* (-;-en) newspaper; journal

Zei′tungsarchiv *n* (journ) morgue

Zei′tungsartikel *m* newspaper article

Zei′tungsausschnitt *m* newspaper clipping

Zei′tungsbeilage *f* supplement

Zei′tungsdeutsch *n* journalese

Zei′tungsente *f* (journ) hoax, spoof

Zei′tungskiosk *m* newsstand

Zei′tungsmeldung *f*, **Zei′tungsnotiz** *f* newspaper item

Zei′tungspapier *n* newsprint

Zei′tungsverkäufer –in §6 *mf* newsvendor

Zei′tungswesen *n*—**das Z.** the press

Zeit′vergeudung *f* waste of time

zeit′verkürzend *adj* entertaining

Zeit′verlust *m* loss of time

Zeit′vermerk *m* date

Zeit′verschwendung *f* waste of time

Zeit′vertreib *m* pastime

zeitweilig [′tsaɪtvaɪlɪç] *adj* temporary; periodic || *adv* temporarily; at times, from time to time

Zeit′wende *f* beginning of a new era

Zeit′wert *m* current value

Zeit′wort *n* (-[e]s;⸗er) verb

Zeit′zeichen *n* time signal

Zeit′zünder *m* time fuse

Zelle [′tselə] *f* (-;-n) cell; (aer) fuselage; (telp) booth

Zel′lenlehre *f* cytology

Zellophan [tselo′fan] *n* (-s;) cellophane

Zellstoff [′tsel/tɔf] *m* cellulose

Zelluloid [tselu′lɔɪt] *n* (-s;) celluloid

Zellulose [tselu′lozə] *f* (-;) cellulose

Zelt [′tselt] *n* (-[e]s;-e) tent

zelten [′tseltən] *intr* camp out

Zelt′leinwand *f* canvas

Zelt′pfahl *m* tent pole

Zelt′pflock *m* tent peg, tent stake

Zelt′stange *f*, **Zelt′stock** *m* tent pole

Zement [tse′ment] *m* (-[e]s;) cement

zementieren [tsemen′tirən] *tr* cement

Zenit [tse′nit] *m* (-[e]s;) zenith

zensieren [tsen′zirən] *tr* censor; (educ) mark, grade

Zen·sor [′tsenzor] *m* (-s;-soren [′zorən]) censor

Zensur [tsen′zur] *f* (-;-en) censorship; (educ) grade, mark

Zentimeter [tsentɪ′metər] *m & n* centimeter

Zentner [′tsentnər] *m* (-s;-) hundredweight

Zent′nerlast *f* (fig) heavy load

zentral [tsen′tral] *adj* central

Zentral′behörde *f* central authority

Zentrale [tsen′tralə] *f* (-;-n) central office; telephone exchange, switchboard; (elec) power station

Zentral′heizung *f* central heating

Zen·trum [′tsentrum] *m* (-s;-tren [trən]) center

Zephir [′tsefɪr] *m* (-s;-e) zephyr

Zepter [′tsepter] *n* (-s;-) scepter

zer– [tser] *pref* up, to pieces, apart

zerbei′ßen §53 *tr* bite to pieces

zerber′sten §55 *intr* (SEIN) split apart

zerbre′chen §64 *tr* break to pieces, shatter, smash || *ref*—**sich** [*dat*] **den**

Kopf z. über (acc) rack one's brains over || intr (SEIN) shatter

zerbrech′lich adj fragile, brittle

zerbröckeln (zerbrök′keln) tr & intr (SEIN) crumble

zerdrücken (zerdrük′ken) tr crush; (Kleid) wrinkle; (Kartoffeln) mash

Zeremonie [tseremo′ni] f (–;-nien [′ni-ən]) ceremony

zeremoniell [tseremo′njel] adj ceremonial || **Zeremoniell** n (–s;-e) ceremonial

Zeremo′nienmeister m master of ceremonies

zerfah′ren adj (Weg) rutted; (zerstreut) absent-minded; (konfus) scatterbrained

Zerfall′ m (–s;) decay, ruin; disintegration; (geistig) decadence

zerfal′len adj—z. sein mit be at variance with || §72 intr (SEIN) fall into ruin; decay; disintegrate; z. in (acc) divide into; z. mit fall out with

zerfa′sern tr unravel || intr fray

zerfet′zen tr tear to shreds

zerflei′schen tr mangle; lacerate

zerflie′ßen §76 intr (SEIN) melt; (Farben) run

zerfres′sen §70 tr eat away, chew up; erode, eat a hole in; corrode

zerge′hen §82 intr (SEIN) melt

zerglie′dern tr dissect; analyze

zerhacken (zerhak′ken) tr chop up

zerkau′en tr chew well

zerkleinern [tser′klaınərn] tr cut into small pieces; chop up

zerklop′fen tr pound

zerklüftet [tser′klyftət] adj jagged

zerknirscht [tser′knır/t] adj contrite

Zerknir′schung f (–;) contrition

zerknit′tern tr (Papier) crumple; (Kleider) rumple

zerknül′len tr crumple up

zerko′chen tr overcook

zerkrat′zen tr scratch up

zerkrü′meln tr & intr (SEIN) crumble

zerlas′sen §104 tr melt, dissolve

zerlegbar [tser′lekbar] adj collapsible; (chem) decomposable; (math) divisible

zerle′gen tr take apart; (zerstückeln) cut up; (Braten) carve; (Licht) disperse; (anat) dissect; (chem) break down; (geom, mus) resolve; (gram & fig) analyze; (mach) tear down

zerle′sen adj well-thumbed

zerlö′chern tr riddle with holes

zerlumpt [tser′lumpt] adj tattered

zermah′len tr grind

zermal′men tr crush

zermür′ben tr wear down

Zermür′bung f (–;) attrition, wear

zerna′gen tr gnaw, chew up; (chem) corrode

zerplat′zen intr (SEIN) burst; explode

zerquet′schen tr crush; (culin) mash

Zerrbild [′tserbılt] n distorted picture; caricature

zerren′nen tr sever

zerrei′ßen §95 tr tear; tear up; (zerfleischen) mangle; (fig) split; (pathol) rupture; j-m das Herz z. break s.o.'s heart || ref—sich z. für

(fig) knock oneself out for || intr (SEIN) tear

zerren [′tserən] tr drag; (Sehne) pull || intr (an dat) tug (at)

zerrin′nen §121 intr (SEIN) melt away

zerrissen [tser′rısən] adj torn

Zer′rung f (–;-en) strain, muscle pull

zerrütten [tser′rytən] tr disorganize; (Geist) unhinge; (Gesundheit) undermine; (Nerven) shatter; (Ehe) wreck

zersä′gen tr saw up

zerschel′len intr (SEIN) be wrecked; (Schiff) break up

zerschie′ßen §76 tr shoot up

zerschla′gen adj battered, broken; exhausted, beat || §132 tr beat up; break to pieces; smash; batter

zerschmel′zen tr & intr (SEIN) melt

zerschmet′tern tr smash, crush

zerschnei′den §106 tr cut up; mince

zerset′zen tr decompose; electrolyze; (fig) undermine || ref decompose, disintegrate

zerspal′ten tr split

zersplit′tern tr split up; splinter; (Menge) disperse; (Kraft, Zeit) fritter away || ref spread oneself thin

zerspren′gen tr blow up; (Kette) break; (mil) rout

zersprin′gen §142 intr (SEIN) break, burst; (Glas) crack; (Saite) snap; (Kopf) split; (vor Wut) explode; (vor Freude) burst

zerstamp′fen tr crush, pound; trample

zerstäu′ben tr pulverize, spray

Zerstäu′ber m (–s;–) sprayer; (für Parfüm) atomizer

zerste′chen §64 tr sting; bite

zerstie′ben intr §130 intr (SEIN) scatter

zerstö′ren tr destroy; (Fernsprechleitung) disrupt; (Leben, Ehe, usw.) ruin; (Illusionen) shatter

Zerstö′rer m (–s;–) (& nav) destroyer

Zerstö′rung f (–;-en) destruction; ruin; disruption

Zerstö′rungswerk n work of destruction

Zerstö′rungswut f vandalism

zersto′ßen §150 tr pound, crush

zerstreu′en tr scatter, disperse; (Bedenken, Zweifel) dispel; (ablenken) distract; (Licht) diffuse || ref scatter; amuse oneself

zerstreut′ adj dispersed; (Licht) diffused; (fig) absent-minded

Zerstreut′heit f (–;) absent-mindedness

Zerstreu′ung f (–;) scattering; diffusion; diversion; absent-mindedness

zerstückeln [tser′/tykəln] tr chop up; (Körper) dismember; (Land) parcel out

Zertifikat [tsertıfı′kat] n (–[e]s;-e) certificate

zertren′nen tr sever

zertre′ten §152 tr trample, squash; (Feuer) stamp out

zertrümmern [tser′trymərn] tr smash, demolish; (Atome) split

zerwüh′len tr root up; (Haar) dishevel; (Bett, Kissen) rumple

Zerwürfnis [tser'vʏrfnɪs] n (-ses;-se) disagreement, quarrel

zerzau'sen tr (Haar) muss; (Federn) ruffle

Zeter ['tsetər] n (-s;)—**Z. und Mordio schreien** (coll) cry bloody murder

zetern ['tsetərn] intr cry out, raise an outcry

Zettel ['tsetəl] m (-s;-) slip of paper; note; (Anschlag) poster; (zum Ankleben) sticker; (zum Anhängen) tag

Zet'telkartei f, **Zet'telkasten** m, **Zet'telkatalog** m card file

Zeug [tsɔɪk] n (-[e]s;-e) stuff, material; (Stoff) cloth, fabric; (Sachen) things; (Waren) goods; (Geräte) tools; (Plunder) junk; **dummes Z.** silly nonsense; **er hat das Z.** he has what it takes

-zeug n comb.fm. stuff; tools; equipment; tackle; instrument; things; -wear

Zeuge ['tsɔɪgə] m (-n;-n) witness; **als Z. aussagen** testify

zeugen ['tsɔɪgən] tr beget; (fig) produce, generate || intr produce offspring; testify; **z. für** testify in favor of; **z. von** bear witness to

Zeu'genaussage f deposition

Zeu'genbank f witness stand

Zeu'genbeeinflussung f suborning of witnesses

Zeu'genstand m witness stand

Zeugin ['tsɔɪgɪn] f (-;-nen) witness

Zeugnis ['tsɔɪknɪs] n (-ses;-se) evidence, testimony; proof; (Schein) certificate; (educ) report card; **j-m ein Z. ausstellen** (or **schreiben**) write s.o. a letter of recommendation; **Z. ablegen** testify; **zum Z. dessen** in witness whereof

Zeu'gung f (-;) procreation; breeding

Zeu'gungstrieb m sexual drive

zeu'gungsunfähig adj impotent

Zicke ['tsɪkə] f (-;-n) (pej) old nanny goat; **Zicken machen** (coll) play tricks

Zicklein ['tsɪklaɪn] n (-s;-) kid

Zickzack ['tsɪktsak] m (-[e]s;-e) zigzag; **im Z. laufen** run zigzag

Zick'zackkurs m—**im Z. fahren** zigzag

Ziege ['tsigə] f (-;-n) she-goat

Ziegel ['tsigəl] m (-s;-) brick; (Dach-) tile

Zie'gelbrenner m brickmaker; tilemaker

Zie'gelbrennerei f brickyard; tileworks

Zie'geldach n tiled roof

Zie'gelstein m brick

Zie'genbart m goatee

Zie'genbock m billy goat

Zie'genhirt m goatherd

Zie'genpeter m (pathol) mumps

Zieh- [tsi] comb.fm. draw; tow-; foster

Zieh'brunnen m well

ziehen ['tsiən] §163 tr pull; (Folgerung, Kreis, Linie, Los, Schwert, Seitengewehr, Vorhang, Wechsel) draw; (Glocke) ring; aus der Tasche) pull out; (Zahn) extract, pull; (züchten) grow, breed; (Kinder) raise; (beim Schach) move; (den Hut) tip; (Graben) dig; (Mauer) build; (Schiff) tow; (Blasen) raise; (Vergleich) make; (Gewehrlauf) rifle; (math) extract; **auf Fäden z.** string (pearls); **auf Flaschen z.** bottle; **auf seine Seite z.** win over to one's side; **den kürzeren z.** get the short end of it; **die Bilanz z.** balance accounts; **die Stirn kraus z.** knit the brows; **Grimassen z.** make faces; **ins Vertrauen z.** take into confidence; **j-n auf die Seite z.** take s.o. aside; **Nutzen z.** derive benefit; **Wasser z.** leak || ref (Holz) warp; (Stoff) stretch; (geog) extend, run; **an sich** (or **auf sich**) z. attract; **sich in die Länge z.** drag on || intr ache; (an dat) pull (on); (theat) (coll) pull them in; **an e-r Zigarette z.** puff on a cigarette || intr (SEIN) go; march; (Vögel) migrate; (Wohnung wechseln) move || impers: **es zieht** there is a draft; **es zieht mich nach** I feel drawn to || **Ziehen** n (-s;) drawing; cultivation; growing; raising; breeding; migration

Zieh'harmonika f accordion

Zieh'kind n foster child

Zie'hung f (-;-en) drawing (of lots)

Ziel [tsil] n (-[e]s;-e) aim; mark; goal; (beim Rennsport) finish line; (e-r Reise) destination; (beim Schießen) target; (Grenze) limit, boundary; (Zweck) end, object; (des Spottes) butt; (Frist) term; (mil) objective; **auf Z.** (com) on credit; **durchs Z. gehen** pass the finish line; **gegen zwei Jahre Z.** (or **mit zwei Jahren Z.**) with two years to pay; **j-m zwei Jahre Z. gewähren** give s.o. two years to pay; **seinem Ehrgeiz ein Z. setzen** set a limit to one's ambition

Ziel'anflug m (aer) bomb run

Ziel'band n (-[e]s;-er) (sport) tape

ziel'bewußt adj purposeful; single-minded

zielen ['tsilən] intr take aim; **z. auf** (acc) or **nach** aim at

Ziel'fernrohr n telescopic sight

Ziel'gerade f homestretch

Ziel'gerät n gunsight; (aer) bombsight

Ziel'landung f pinpoint landing

Ziel'linie f (sport) finish line

ziel'los adj aimless

Ziel'photographie f photo finish

Ziel'punkt m objective; bull's-eye

Ziel'scheibe f target; (fig) butt

Ziel'setzung f objective, target

ziel'sicher adj steady, unerring

Ziel'sprache f target language

zielstrebig ['tsil/trebɪç] adj single-minded, determined

Ziel'sucher m (rok) homing device

Ziel'vorrichtung f gunsight; bombsight

ziemen ['tsimən] ref be proper; **sich für j-n z.** become s.o. || intr (dat) be becoming to

ziemlich ['tsimlɪç] adj fit, suitable; (leidlich) middling; (mäßig) fair; (beträchtlich) considerable || adv pretty, rather, fairly; (fast) almost, practically

Zier [tsir] f (–;), **Zierat** ['tsirɑt] m (–s;) ornament, decoration

Zierde ['tsirdə] f (–;–n) ornament decoration; (fig) credit, honor

zieren ['tsirən] tr decorate, adorn || ref be affected, be coy; (beim Essen) need to be coaxed; **zier dich doch nicht so!** don't be coy!

Zier'leiste f trim(ming)

zier'lich adj delicate; (nett) nice

Zier'pflanze f ornamental plant

Zier'puppe f glamour girl

Ziffer ['tsɪfər] f (–;–n) digit, figure

Zif'ferblatt n face (of a clock)

zig [tsɪç] invar adj (coll) umpteen

Zigarette [tsɪga'retə] f (–;–n) cigarette

Zigaret'tenautomat m cigarette machine

Zigaret'tenetui n cigarette case

Zigaret'tenspitze f cigarette holder

Zigaret'tenstummel m cigarette butt

Zigarre [tsɪ'garə] f (–;–n) cigar

Zigeuner –**in** [tsɪ'gɔɪnər(ɪn)] §6 mf gipsy

Zimbel ['tsɪmbəl] f (–;–n) cymbal

Zimmer ['tsɪmər] n (–s;–) room

Zim'merantenne f indoor antenna

Zim'merarbeit f carpentry

Zim'merdienst m room service

Zim'mereinrichtung f furniture

Zim'merer m (–s;–) carpenter

Zim'merflucht f suite

Zim'mermädchen n chambermaid

Zim'mer·mann m (–[e]s;–leute) carpenter

zimmern ['tsɪmərn] tr carpenter, build || intr carpenter

Zim'mervermieter m landlord

–**zimmrig** [tsɪmrɪç] comb.fm. –room

zimperlich ['tsɪmpərlɪç] adj prudish; fastidious; (gegen Kälte) oversensitive

Zimt [tsɪmt] m (–[e]s;–) cinnamon

Zink [tsɪŋk] m & n (–[e]s;) zinc

Zinke ['tsɪŋkə] f (–;–n) prong; (e–s Kammes) tooth; (carp) dovetail

zinken ['tsɪŋkən] tr dovetail; (Karten) mark || **Zinken** m (–s;–) (sl) schnozzle

–**zinkig** [tsɪŋkɪç] comb.fm. –pronged

Zinn [tsɪn] n (–[e]s;) tin

Zinne ['tsɪnə] f (–;–n) pinnacle; battlement

zinnoberrot [tsɪ'nobərrot] adj vermilion

Zins [tsɪns] m (–es;–en) interest; (Miete) rent; **auf Zinsen anlegen** put out at interest; **j–m mit Zinsen (und Zinseszinsen) heimzahlen** (coll) pay s.o. back in full; **Zinsen berechnen** charge interest

zins'bringend adj interest-bearing

Zin'senbelastung f interest charge

Zinseszinsen ['tsɪnzəstsɪnzən] pl compound interest

zins'frei adj rent-free; interest-free

Zins'fuß m, **Zins'satz** m rate of interest

Zins'schein m (interest) coupon; dividend warrant

Zionismus [tsɪ·o'nɪsmʊs] m (–;) Zionism

Zipfel ['tsɪpfəl] m (–s;–) tip, point;

edge; (Ecke) corner; (e–r Wurst) end piece

Zip'felmütze f nightcap, tasseled cap

zirka ['tsɪrka] adv approximately

Zirkel ['tsɪrkəl] m (–s;–) circle; (Reißzeug) compass; (fig) circle

Zir'kelschluß m vicious circle

Zirkon [tsɪr'kon] m (–s;–e) zircon

zirkulieren [tsɪrku'lirən] intr (SEIN) circulate; **z. lassen** circulate

Zirkus ['tsɪrkʊs] m (–;–se) circus

zirpen ['tsɪrpən] intr chirp

zischeln ['tsɪʃəln] tr & intr whisper

zischen ['tsɪʃən] intr hiss; sizzle; (schwirren) whiz || **Zischen** n (–s;) hissing; sizzle; whiz

Zisch'laut m hissing sound; (phonet) sibilant

ziselieren [tsɪze'lirən] tr chase

Zisterne [tsɪs'tɛrnə] f (–;–n) cistern

Zitadelle [tsɪta'dɛlə] f (–;–n) citadel

Zitat [tsɪ'tɑt] n (–[e]s;–e) quotation

Zither ['tsɪtər] f (–;–n) zither

zitieren [tsɪ'tirən] tr quote; **j–n vor Gericht z.** issue s.o. a summons

Zitronat [tsɪtro'nɑt] n (–[e]s;–e) candied lemon peel

Zitrone [tsɪ'tronə] f (–;–n) lemon

Zitro'nenlimonade f lemonade; (mit Sodawasser) lemon soda

Zitro'nenpresse f lemon squeezer

Zitro'nensaft m lemon juice

Zitro'nensäure f citric acid

zitterig ['tsɪtərɪç] adj shaky

zittern ['tsɪtərn] intr quake, tremble; quiver; (flimmern) dance; (vor dat) shake (with), shiver (with); **beim dem Gedanken an etw** [acc] **z.** shudder at the thought of s.th.

Zit'terpappel ['tsɪtərpapəl] f aspen

Zitze ['tsɪtsə] f (–;–n) teat

zivil [tsɪ'vil] adj civil; civilian; (Preise) reasonable || **Zivil** n (–s;) civilians; **in Z.** in plain clothes

Zivil'courage f courage of one's convictions, moral courage

Zivil'ehe f civil marriage

Zivilisation [tsɪvɪlɪza'tsjon] f (–;–en) civilization

zivilisieren [tsɪvɪlɪ'zirən] tr civilize

Zivilist –**in** [tsɪvɪ'lɪst(ɪn)] §7 mf civilian

Zivil'klage f (jur) civil suit

Zivil'kleidung f civilian clothes

Zivil'person f civilian

Zobel ['tsobəl] m (–s;–) (zool) sable

Zofe ['tsofə] f (–;–n) lady-in-waiting

zog [tsok] pret of ziehen

zögern ['tsøgərn] intr hesitate; delay || **Zögern** n (–s;) hesitation; delay

Zögling ['tsøklɪŋ] m (–s;–e) pupil

Zölibat [tsølɪ'bɑt] m & n (–[e]s;) celibacy

Zoll [tsɔl] m (–[e]s;–e) duty, customs; (Brückenzoll) toll; (Maß) inch

Zoll'abfertigung f customs clearance

Zoll'amt n customs office

Zoll'beamte §5 m customs official

zollen ['tsɔlən] tr give, pay; **j–m Achtung z.** show s.o. respect; **j–m Beifall z.** applaud s.o.; **j–m Dank z.** thank s.o.; **j–m Lob z.** praise s.o.

Zoll'erklärung f customs declaration

zoll′frei adj duty-free
Zoll′grenze f customs frontier
–zöllig [tsœlɪç] comb.fm. –inch
Zoll′kontrolle f customs inspection
zoll′pflichtig adj dutiable
Zoll′schein m customs clearance
Zoll′schranke f customs barrier
Zoll′stab m, **Zoll′stock** m foot rule
Zoll′tarif m tariff
Zone [′tsonə] f (–;–n) zone; **blaue Z.** limited-parking area; **Z. der Windstille** doldrums
Zoo [tso] m (– & –s;–s) zoo
Zoologe [tso·ɔ′logə] m (–n;–n) zoologist
Zoologie [tso·olɔ′gi] f (–;) zoology
Zoologin [tso·ɔ′logɪn] f (–;–nen) zoologist
zoologisch [tso·ɔ′logɪʃ] adj zoological
Zopf [tsɔpf] m (–[e]s;⁼e) plait of hair; pigtail; twisted (bread) roll; **alter Z.** outdated custom
zopfig [′tsɔpfɪç] adj pedantic; old-fashioned
Zorn [tsɔrn] m (–[e]s;) anger, rage
Zorn′anfall m fit of anger
Zorn′ausbruch m outburst of anger
zornig [′tsɔrnɪç] adj (auf acc) angry (at)
zorn′mütig adj hotheaded
Zote [′tsotə] f (–;–n) obscenity; dirty joke; **Zoten reißen** crack dirty jokes; talk dirty
zo′tenhaft, zotig [′tsotɪç] adj obscene, dirty
Zotte [′tsotə] f (–;–n) tuft of hair; strand of hair
Zottel [′tsotəl] f (–;–n) strand of hair
Zot′telhaar n stringy hair
zottelig [′tsotəlɪç] adj stringy (hair)
zotteln [′tsotəln] intr (SEIN) (coll) saunter
zottig [′tsotɪç] adj shaggy; matted
zu [tsu] adj closed, shut || adv too; **immer zu!** (or **nur zu!**) go on! || prep (dat) at, in, on; to; along with; in addition to; beside, near; **zu Anfang** at the beginning; **zu dritt** in threes; **zu Wasser und zu Lande** by land and by sea
zuallererst [tsu·alər′erst] adv first of all
zuallerletzt [tsu·alər′letst] adv last of all
zubaiiern [′tsubalərn] tr (coll) slam
zu′bauen tr wall up, wall in
Zubehör [′tsubəhør] m & n (–s;) accessories; fittings; trimmings; **Wohnung mit allem Z.** apartment with all utilities
Zu′behörteil m accessory, attachment, component
zu′beißen §53 intr bite; snap at people
zu′bekommen §99 tr get in addition; (Tür, usw.) manage to close
zu′bereiten tr prepare; (Speise) cook; (Getränk) mix
Zu′bereitung f (–;–en) preparation
zu′billigen tr grant, allow, concede
zu′binden §59 tr tie up; **j–m die Augen z.** blindfold s.o.
zu′bleiben §62 intr (SEIN) remain closed

zu′blinzeln intr (dat) wink at
zu′bringen §65 tr (Zeit) spend; (coll) manage to shut; (tech) feed
Zu′bringer m (–s;–) (tech) feeder
Zu′bringerdienst m shuttle service
Zu′bringerstraße f access road
Zucht [tsuxt] f (–;) breeding; rearing; (Rasse) race, stock; (Pflanzen–) cultivation; (Schul–) education; discipline; training, drill; **Z. halten** maintain discipline
züchten [′tsyçtən] tr breed; rear, raise; (bot) grow, cultivate
Züch′ter m §6 mf breeder; grower
Zucht′haus n penitentiary, hard labor; **lebenslängliches Z.** life imprisonment
Zuchthäusler in [′tsuxthɔɪzlər(ɪn)] §6 mf convict, prisoner at hard labor
Zucht′hengst m studhorse
züchtig [′tsyçtɪç] adj modest, chaste
züchtigen [′tsyçtɪgən] tr chastise
zucht′los adj undisciplined
Zucht′losigkeit f (–;) lack of discipline
Zucht′meister m disciplinarian
Zucht′perle f cultured pearl
Züch′tung f (–;) breeding; rearing; growing, cultivation
zucken [′tsukən] tr (Achseln) shrug || intr twitch, jerk; (Blitz) flash; (vor Schmerzen) wince; **mit keiner Wimper z.** not bat an eye; **ohne zu z.** without wincing || impers—**es zuckte mir in den Fingern zu** (inf) my fingers were itching to (inf) || **Zucken** n (–s;) twitch
zücken [′tsykən] tr (Schwert) draw
Zucker [′tsukar] m (–s;) sugar
Zuckerdose (Zuk′kerdose) f sugar bowl
Zuckererbse (Zuk′kererbse) f sweet pea
Zuckerguß (Zuk′kerguß) m frosting
Zuckerharnruhr (Zuk′kerharnruhr) f diabetes
Zuckerhut (Zuk′kerhut) m sugar loaf
zuckerig [′tsukərɪç] adj sugary
zuckerkrank (zuk′kerkrank) adj diabetic || **Zuckerkranke** §5 mf diabetic
Zuckerkrankheit (Zuk′kerkrankheit) f diabetes
Zuckerlecken (Zuk′kerlecken) n (–s;) (fig) pushover, picnic
Zuckerrohr (Zuk′kerrohr) n sugar cane
Zuckerrübe (Zuk′kerrübe) f sugar beet
zuckersüß (zuk′kersüß) adj sweet as sugar
Zuckerwerk (Zuk′kerwerk) n, **Zuckerzeug** (Zuk′kerzeug) n candy
Zuckung (Zuk′kung) f (–;–en) twitch, spasm, convulsion
Zu′decke f (coll) bed covering
zu′decken tr cover up
zudem [tsu′dem] adv moreover, besides
zu′denken §66 tr—**j–m etw z.** intend s.th. as a present for s.o.
Zu′drang m crowding, rush
zu′drehen tr turn off; **j–m den Rücken z.** turn one's back on s.o.
zu′dringlich adj obtrusive; **z. werden** make a pass
zu′drücken tr close, shut
zu′eignen tr dedicate
Zu′eignung f (–;–en) dedication

zu'erkennen §97 *tr* confer, award; (jur) adjudge, award

zuerst' *adv* first; at first

zu'erteilen *tr* award; confer, bestow

zu'fahren §71 *intr* (SEIN) drive on; z. auf (acc) drive in the direction of (*s.th.*); rush at (*s.o.*)

Zu'fahrt *f* access

Zu'fahrtsrampe *f* on-ramp

Zu'fahrtsstraße *f* access road

Zu'fall *m* chance; coincidence; accident; **durch Z.** by chance

zu'fallen §72 *intr* (SEIN) close, shut; **j-m z.** fall to s.o.'s share

zufällig ['tsufelɪç] *adj* chance, fortuitous; accidental; casual ‖ *adv* by chance; accidentally

zu'fälligerweise *adv* by chance

Zufalls– *comb.fm.* chance

zu'fassen *intr* set to work; lend a hand; (e-e Gelegenheit wahrnehmen) seize the opportunity

Zu'flucht *f* refuge; (fig) recourse; **seine Z. nehmen zu** take refuge in; have recourse to

Zu'fluß *m* influx; (Nebenfluß) tributary; (mach) feed

zu'flüstern *intr* (dat) whisper to

zufolge [tsu'fɔlgə] *prep* (genit & dat) in consequence of; according to

zufrieden [tsu'fridən] *adj* satisfied; **j-m z. lassen** leave s.o. alone

zufrie'dengeben §80 *ref* (mit) be satisfied (with), acquiesce (in)

Zufrie'denheit *f* (–;) satisfaction

zufrie'denstellen *tr* satisfy

zufrie'denstellend *adj* satisfactory

Zufrie'denstellung *f* satisfaction

zu'frieren §77 *intr* (SEIN) freeze up

zu'fügen *tr* add; (Niederlage) inflict; (Kummer, Schaden, Schmerz) cause

Zufuhr ['tsufur] *f* (–;) supply; importation; supplies; (mach) feed

zu'führen *tr* convey, bring; (Waren) supply; (mach) feed

Zu'führung *f* (–;-en) conveyance; supply; importation; (elec) lead; (mach) feed

Zug [tsuk] *m* (–[e]s;⁻e) train; pull, tug; drawing, pulling; (Spannung) tension; strain; (beim Rauchen) puff; (beim Atmen) breath, gasp; (Schluck) drink, gulp, swig; (Luft–) draft; (Reihe) row, line; (Um–) procession, parade; (Kriegs–) campaign; (Geleit) escort; (von Vögeln) flock, flight, migration; (von Fischen) school; (Rudel) pack; (Trupp) platoon; (Gespann) team, yoke; (Gesichts–) feature; (Charakter–) trait; characteristic; (Neigung) trend, tendency; (im Gewehrlauf) groove, rifling; (Strich) stroke; (Schnörkel) flourish; (Umriß) outline; (beim Brettspiel) move; **auf dem Zuge** on the march; **auf e-n Zug** in one gulp; at one stroke; at a stretch; **du bist am Zug** (& fig) it's your move; **e-n guten Zug haben** drink like a fish; **e-n Zug tun** take a puff; make a move; take a drink; **gut im Zuge sein** (or **im besten Zuge sein**) be going strong; **in e-m Zuge** in one gulp; in one breath; at one stroke; at a stretch; **in großen Zügen** in broad outlines; **in vollen Zügen** thoroughly; **in Zug bringen** start; **nicht zum Zug kommen** not get a chance; **ohne rechten Zug** half-heartedly; **Zug um Zug** in rapid succession

Zu'gabe *f* addition; (theat) encore

Zu'gang *m* access; approach; entrance; (Zunahme) increase; (libr) accession

zugänglich ['tsugenlɪç] *adj* accessible; (Person) affable; (benutzbar) available; (dat, für) open (to); **nicht z. für** proof against

Zug'artikel *m* (com) popular article

Zug'brücke *f* drawbridge

zu'geben §80 *tr* add; (erlauben) allow; (anerkennen) admit, concede; (eingestehen) confess; (com) throw into the bargain

zugegen [tsu'gegən] *adj* (bei) present (at)

zu'gehen §82 *intr* (SEIN) go on; walk faster; (sich schließen) shut; **auf j-n z.** go up to s.o.; **j-m etw z. lassen** send s.th. to s.o.

zu'gehören *intr* (dat) belong to

zu'gehörig *adj* (dat) belonging to

Zu'gehörigkeit *f* (–;) (zu) membership (in)

Zügel ['tsygəl] *m* (–s;–) rein; bridle; (fig) curb

zü'gellos *adj* (& fig) unbridled; (ausschweifig) dissolute

Zü'gellosigkeit *f* (–;) licentiousness

zügeln ['tsygəln] *tr* bridle; (fig) curb

Zu'geständnis *n* admission, concession

zu'gestehen §146 *tr* admit, concede

zu'getan *adj* (dat) fond of

Zug'feder *f* tension spring

Zug'führer *m* (mil) platoon leader; (rr) chief conductor

zu'gießen §76 *tr* add

zugig ['tsugɪç] *adj* drafty

zügig ['tsygɪç] *adj* speedy, fast

Zug'klappe *f* damper

Zug'kraft *f* tensile force; (fig) drawing power

zug'kräftig *adj* attractive, popular

zugleich' *adv* at the same time; **z. mit** together with

Zug'luft *f* draft

Zug'maschine *f* tractor

Zug'mittel *n* (fig) attraction, draw

zu'graben §87 *tr* cover up

zu'greifen §88 *intr* grab hold; lend a hand; (fig) go into action; **greifen Sie zu!** (bei Tisch) help yourself!; (bei Reklamen) don't miss this opportunity!

Zu'griff *m* grip; (fig) clutches

zugrunde [tsu'grundə] *adv*—**z. gehen** go to ruin; **z. legen** (dat) take as a basis (for); **z. liegen** (dat) underlie

Zug'tier *n* draft animal

zu'gucken *intr* (coll) look on

zugunsten [tsu'gunstən] *prep* (genit) in favor of; for the benefit of

zugute [tsu'gutə] *adv*—**j-m etw z. halten** make allowance for s.o. for s.th.; **j-m z. kommen** stand s.o. in good stead

Zug'verkehr *m* train service

Zug'vogel *m* migratory bird
zu'haben §89 *tr* (*Augen*) have closed; (*Mantel*) have buttoned up || *intr* (*Geschäft*) be closed
zu'halten §90 *tr* keep closed; (*Ohren*) shut || *intr*—z. auf (*acc*) head for
Zuhälter ['tsuheltər] *m* (-s;-) pimp
Zuhälterei [tsuheltə'raɪ] *f* (-;) pimping
zuhanden [tsu'handən] *prep* (*genit*) (*auf Briefumschlägen*) Attn:
Zuhause [tsu'hauzə] *n* (-s;) home
zu'heilen *intr* (SEIN) heal up
zu'hören *intr* (*dat*) listen (to)
Zu'hörer -in §6 *mf* hearer, listener; **die Z.** the audience
Zu'hörerschaft *f* (-;) audience
zu'jauchzen, zu'jubeln *intr* cheer
zu'klappen *tr* shut, slam shut
zu'kleben *tr* glue up, paste up
zu'knallen *tr* bang, slam shut
zu'kneifen §88 *tr*—die Augen z. blink; **ein Auge z.** wink
zu'knöpfen *tr* button up
zu'kommen §99 *intr* (SEIN) (*dat*) reach; (*dat*) be due to; **auf j–n z.** come up to s.o.; **das kommt dir nicht zu** you're not entitled to it; **j–m etw z. lassen** let s.o. have s.th.; send s.th. to s.o. || *impers*—**mir kommt es nicht zu zu** (*inf*) it's not up to me to (*inf*)
zu'korken *tr* put the cork on
Zu'kost *f* vegetables; trimmings
Zukunft ['tsukunft] *f* (-;) future; (*gram*) future (tense)
zukünftig ['tsukynftɪç] *adj* future || *adv* in the future || **Zukünftige** §5 *m* (coll) fiancé || *f* (coll) fiancée
Zu'kunftsmusik *f* wishful thinking
Zu'kunftsroman *m* science fiction
zu'lächeln *intr* (*dat*) smile at; (*dat*) smile on
Zu'lage *f* extra pay; pay raise
zulande [tsu'landə] *adv*—**bei uns z.** in my (or our) country
zu'langen *intr* suffice, do; (*bei Tisch*) help oneself
zu'länglich *adj* adequate, sufficient
zu'lassen §104 *tr* admit; (*erlauben*) allow; (*Tür*) leave shut; (*Fahrzeug*) license; (*Zweifel*) admit of
zulässig ['tsulesɪç] *adj* permissible; **zulässige Abweichung** allowance, tolerance
Zu'lassung *f* (-;-en) admission; permission; approval; license
Zu'lassungsprüfung *f* college entrance examination
Zu'lassungsschein *m* registration card
Zu'lauf *m* crowd, rush; **Z. haben** be popular; (theat) have a long run
zu'laufen §105 *intr* (SEIN) run on; run faster; (*dat*) flock to; **auf j–n z.** run up to s.o.; **spitz z.** end in a point
zu'legen *tr* add; **etw z.** up one's offer || *ref*—**sich** [dat] etw. z. (coll) get oneself s.th.
zuleide [tsu'laɪdə] *adv*—**j–m etw z. tun** hurt s.o., do s.o. wrong
zu'leiten *tr* (*Wasser*) (*dat*) let in (to); (*dat*) direct (s.o.) (to); (*Schreiben*) (*dat*) pass on (to); **auf dem Amtsweg**) channel (to); (tech) feed

Zu'leitung *f* (-;-en) feed pipe; (elec) lead-in wire; (elec) conductor
zuletzt [tsu'letst] *adv* last; at last; finally; after all
zuliebe [tsu'libə] *prep* (*dat*) for (s.o.'s) sake
zum [tsum] *abbr* zu dem; **es ist zum** ...it's enough to make one...
zu'machen *tr* shut; (*Loch*) close up; (*zuknöpfen*) button up
zumal [tsu'mal] *adv* especially; **z. da** all the more because
zu'mauern *tr* wall up
zumindest [tsu'mɪndəst] *adv* at least
zumute [tsu'mutə] *adv*—**mir ist gut** (or **wohl**) z. I feel good; **mir ist nicht zum Lachen z.** I don't feel like laughing
zumuten ['tsumutən] *tr*—**j–m etw z.** expect s.th. of s.o. || *ref*—**sich** [dat] **zuviel z.** attempt too much
Zu'mutung *f* (-;-en) imposition
zunächst [tsu'neçst] *adv* first, at first, first of all; (*erstens*) to begin with; (*vorläufig*) for the time being || *prep* (*dat*) next to
zu'nageln *tr* nail up, nail shut
zu'nähen *tr* sew up
Zu'nahme *f* (-;-n) increase; growth; rise
Zu'name *m* last name, family name
Zünd– [tsynt] *comb.fm.* ignition
zünden ['tsyndən] *tr* ignite; kindle; (*Sprengstoff*) detonate || *intr* ignite, catch fire; (fig) catch on
Zün'der *m* (-s;-) fuse; detonator
Zünd'flamme *f* pilot light
Zünd'holz *n* match
Zünd'kerze *f* (aut) spark plug
Zünd'nadel *f* firing pin
Zünd'satz *m* primer
Zünd'schlüssel *m* ignition key
Zünd'schnur *f* fuse
Zünd'stein *m* flint
Zünd'stoff *m* fuel
Zün'dung *f* (-;-en) (aut) ignition
zu'nehmen §116 *intr* (an *dat*) increase (in); (*steigen*) rise; grow longer
zu'neigen *tr* (*dat*) tilt toward || *ref & intr* (*dat*) incline toward(s); **sich dem Ende z.** draw to a close
Zu'neigung *f* (-;) (für, zu) liking (for)
Zunft [tsunft] *f* (-;-en) guild
Zunge ['tsuŋə] *f* (-;-n) tongue
züngeln ['tsyŋəln] *intr* dart out the tongue; (*Flamme*) dart, leap up
Zun'genbrecher *m* tongue twister
zun'genfertig *adj* glib
Zun'genspitze *f* tip of the tongue
zunichte [tsu'nɪçtə] *adv*—**z. machen** destroy; (*Plan*) spoil; (*Theorie*) explode; **z. werden** come to nothing
zu'nicken *intr* (*dat*) nod to
zunutze [tsu'nutsə] *adv*—**sich etw z. machen** utilize s.th.
zuoberst [tsu'obərst] *adv* at the top
zupfen ['tsupfən] *tr* pull; pluck || *intr* (an *dat*) tug (at)
zu'prosten *intr* (*dat*) toast
zur [tsur] *abbr* zu der
zu'rechnen *tr* add; (*dat*) number among, classify with; (*dat*) attribute to

zu'rechnungsfähig *adj* accountable; responsible; of sound mind
Zu'rechnungsfähigkeit *f* responsibility; sound mind
zurecht– [tsʊ'rɛçt] *comb.fm.* right, in order; at the right time
zurecht'biegen §57 *tr* straighten out
zurecht'bringen §65 *tr* set right
zurecht'finden §59 *ref* find one's way; (fig) see one's way
zurecht'kommen §99 *intr* (SEIN) come on time; get on, manage; turn out all right; **mit etw nicht z.** make a mess of s.th.; **mit j–m z.** get along with s.o.
zurecht'legen *tr* lay out in order || *ref*—**sich** [*dat*] z. figure out
zurecht'machen *tr* & *ref* get ready
zurecht'schneiden §106 *tr* cut to size
zurecht'setzen *tr* set right, fix, adjust
zurecht'weisen §118 *tr* reprimand
zu'reden *intr* (*dat*) try to persuade; (*dat*) encourage
zu'reichen *tr* reach, pass || *intr* do
zu'reichend *adj* sufficient
zu'reiten §86 *tr* break in
zu'richten *tr* prepare; cook
zu'riegeln *tr* bolt
zürnen ['tsʏrnən] *intr* (*dat*) be angry (with)
zurren *tr* (naut) lash down
Zurschau'stellung *f* display
zurück [tsʊ'rʏk] *adv* back; backward; behind; **ein paar Jahre z.** a few years ago || *interj* back up!
zurück– *comb.fm.* back; behind; re–
zurück'behalten §90 *tr* keep back
zurück'bekommen §99 *tr* get back
zurück'bleiben §62 *intr* (SEIN) stay behind; fall behind; (*Uhr*) lose time; (hinter *dat*) fall short (of)
Zurück'blenden *n* (cin) flashback
zurück'blicken *intr* look back
zurück'bringen §65 *tr* bring back; **z. auf** (*acc*) (math) reduce to
zurück'datieren *tr* antedate
zurück'drängen *tr* force back; repress
zurück'dürfen §69 *intr* be allowed to return
zurück'erobern *tr* reconquer, win back
zurück'erstatten *tr* return; (*Ausgaben*) refund; (*Kosten*) reimburse
zurück'fahren §71 *tr* drive back || *intr* (SEIN) drive back, ride back; (*vor Schreck*) recoil, start
zurück'finden §59 *ref* find one's way back
zurück'fordern *tr* reclaim, demand back
zurück'führen *tr* lead back; trace back; **z. auf** (*acc*) refer to; attribute to
zurück'geben §80 *tr* give back, return
zurück'gehen §82 *intr* (SEIN) go back; (*Fieber, Preise*) drop; (*Geschwulst*) go down; (mil) fall back
zurück'gezogen *adj* secluded
zurück'greifen §88 *intr*—**z. auf** (*acc*) (fig) fall back on
zurück'halten §90 *tr* hold back; **j–n davon z. zu** (*inf*) keep s.o. from (*ger*) || **mit etw z.** conceal s.th.
zurück'haltend *adj* reserved; shy
Zurück'haltung *f* (–;–en) reserve

zurück'kehren *intr* (SEIN) return
zurück'kommen §99 *intr* (SEIN) return; **z. auf** (*acc*) come back to, revert to; (*hinweisen*) refer to
zurück'können §100 *intr* be able to return
zurück'lassen §104 *tr* leave behind; outstrip, outrun
zurück'legen *tr* (*Kopf*) lean back; (*Geld*) put aside; (*Jahre*) complete; (*Strecke*) cover; (*Ware*) lay away || *ref* lean back
zurück'lehnen *ref* lean back
zurück'liegen §108 *intr* belong to the past || *impers*—**es liegt jetzt zehn Jahre zurück, daß** it's ten years now that
zurück'müssen §115 *intr* have to return
zurück'nehmen §116 *tr* take back; (*widerrufen*) revoke; (*Auftrag*) cancel; (*Vorwurf*) retract; (*Klage*) withdraw; (*Versprechen*) go back on; (*Truppen*) pull back; **das Gas z.** slow down
zurück'prallen *intr* (SEIN) rebound; (*vor Schreck*) start, be startled
zurück'rufen §122 *tr* call back, recall
zurück'schauen *intr* look back
zurück'schicken *tr* send back
zurück'schlagen §132 *tr* beat back, throw back || *intr* strike back
zurück'schrecken *tr* frighten away; (*von*) deter (from) || §109 & §134 *intr* (SEIN) (**von, vor** *dat*) shrink back (from)
zurück'sehnen *ref* yearn to return
zurück'sein §139 *intr* (SEIN) be back; (**in** *dat*) be behind (in)
zurück'setzen *tr* put back; (*im Preis*) reduce; (fig) snub || *ref* sit back
zurück'stecken *tr* put back
zurück'stellen *tr* (*Uhr*) set back; (*Plan*) shelve; (mil) defer
zurück'stoßen §150 *tr* push back; repel
zurück'strahlen *tr* reflect
zurück'streifen *tr* (*Ärmel*) roll up
zurück'treten §152 *intr* (SEIN) step back; (**vom** *Amt*) resign; (*Wasser, Berge*) recede
zurück'tun §154 *tr* put back
zurück'verfolgen *tr* (*Schritte*) retrace; (fig) trace back
zurück'verweisen §118 *tr* (**an** *acc*) refer back (to); (parl) remand (to)
zurück'weichen §85 *intr* (SEIN) fall back, make way; (*Hochwasser*) recede; (*vor dem Feind*) give ground; **z. vor** (*dat*) shrink from
zurück'weisen §118 *tr* turn back; (*ablehnen*) turn down; (*Angriff*) repel || *intr*—**z. auf** (*acc*) refer to
Zurück'weisung *f* (–;–en) rejection
zurück'wenden §140 *tr* & *ref* turn back
zurück'werfen §160 *tr* throw back; (*e–n Patienten*) set back; (*Strahlen*) reflect; (*Feind*) hurl back
zurück'wirken *intr* (**auf** *acc*) react (on); (*Gesetz*) be retroactive
zurück'zahlen *tr* pay back; (fin) refund
zurück'ziehen §163 *tr* draw back; (*Antrag*) withdraw; (*Geld*) call in; (*Truppen*) pull back; (sport) scratch || *ref* withdraw; (*schlafengehen*) re-

tire; (mil) pull back ‖ *intr* (SEIN) move back; (mil) fall back, retreat

Zu'ruf *m* call; cheer; (parl) acclamation

zu'rufen §122 *tr*—j—m etw z. shout s.th. to s.o.

Zu'sage *f* (—;—n) assent; promise

zu'sagen *tr* promise ‖ *intr* accept an invitation; (*dat*) please; (*dat*) agree (with)

zusammen [tsu'zaman] *adv* together; in common; at the same time

Zusam'menarbeit *f* cooperation

zusam'menarbeiten *intr* cooperate

zusam'menballen *tr* (*Faust*) clench

zusam'menbeißen §53 *tr*—die Zähne z. grit one's teeth

zusam'menbinden §59 *tr* tie together

zusam'menbrauen *tr* concoct ‖ *ref* (*Sturm*) brew

zusam'menbrechen §64 *intr* (SEIN) break down; collapse

Zusam'menbruch *m* collapse; breakdown

zusam'mendrängen *tr* crowd together

zusam'mendrücken *tr* compress

zusam'menfahren §71 *intr* (SEIN) be startled; (mit) collide (with)

zusam'menfallen §72 *intr* (SEIN) fall in, collapse; (*Teig*) fall; (*Person*) lose weight; (mit) coincide (with)

Zusam'menfall *m* coincidence

zusam'menfalten *tr* fold

zusam'menfassen *tr* (*in sich fassen*) comprise; (*verbinden*) combine; (*Macht, Funktionen*) concentrate; (*Bericht*) summarize

zusam'menfassend *adj* comprehensive; summary

Zusam'menfassung *f* (—;—en) summary, résumé

zusam'menfinden §59 *ref* meet

zusam'menfügen *tr* join together; (*Scherben, Teile*) piece together

zusam'mengehen §82 *intr* (SEIN) go together; match; close; shrink

zusam'mengehören *intr* belong together

zusam'mengeraten §63 *intr* (SEIN) collide

zusammengewürfelt [tsu'zamangevyrfalt] *adj* mixed, motely

Zusam'menhalt *m* cohesion; consistency

zusam'menhalten §90 *tr* hold together; compare ‖ *intr* stick together

Zusam'menhang *m* connection, relation; context; coherence

zusam'menhängend *adj* coherent; allied

zusam'menklappen *tr* fold up; **die Hacken z.** click one's heels ‖ *intr* (SEIN) collapse

zusam'menkommen §99 *intr* (SEIN) come together

Zusammenkunft [tsu'zamankunft] *f* (—;ᵉe) meeting

zusam'menlaufen §105 *intr* (SEIN) run together; come together; flock; (*Milch*) curdle; (*Farben*) run; (*einschrumpfen*) shrink up; (geom) converge

zusammenlegbar [tsu'zamanlekbar] *adj* collapsible

zusam'menlegen *tr* put together; (*fal-*

ten) fold; (*Geld*) pool; (*vereinigen*) combine, consolidate ‖ *intr* pool money

zusam'mennehmen §116 *tr* gather up; (*Gedanken*) collect; (*Kräfte, Mut*) muster; **alles zusammengenommen** considering everything ‖ *ref* pull oneself together

zusam'menpacken *tr* pack up

zusam'menpassen *tr* & *intr* match

zusam'menpferchen *tr* crowd together

Zusam'menprall *m* collision; (fig) (mit) impact (on)

zusam'menprallen *intr* collide

zusam'menraffen *tr* collect in haste; (*ein Vermögen*) amass; (*Kräfte*) summon up, marshal ‖ *ref* pull oneself together

zusam'menreißen §53 *ref* (coll) pull oneself together

zusam'menrollen *tr* roll up

zusam'menrotten *ref* band together, form a gang; (*Aufrührer*) riot

zusam'menrücken *tr* push together ‖ *intr* (SEIN) move closer together

zusam'menschießen *tr* (*Stadt*) shoot up; (*Menschen*) shoot down; (*Geld*) pool

zusam'menschlagen §132 *tr* smash up; (*Absätze*) click; (*Beine, Zeitung*) fold; (*Hände*) clap; (*zerschlagen*) beat up; **die Hände über den Kopf z.** (fig) throw up one's hands ‖ *intr* (SEIN)—aneinander z. clash

zusam'menschließen §76 *tr* join; link together ‖ *ref* join together, unite

Zusam'menschluß *m* union; alliance

zusam'menschmelzen *intr* (SEIN) fuse; melt away; (fig) dwindle

zusam'menschnüren *tr* tie up

zusam'menschrumpfen *intr* (SEIN) shrivel; (*Geld*) (coll) dwindle away

zusam'mensetzen *tr* put together; (*mach*) assemble ‖ *ref* sit down together; **sich z. aus** consist of

Zusam'mensetzung *f* (—;—en) composition; (*Bestandteile*) ingredients; (*Struktur*) structure; (chem, gram) compound

Zusam'menspiel *n* teamwork

zusam'menstauchen *tr* browbeat, chew out

zusam'menstellen *tr* put together; (*Liste*) compile; (*Farben*) match; organize

Zusam'menstoß *m* collision; (*der Meinungen*) clash; (*Treffen*) encounter; (mil) engagement

zusam'menstoßen §150 *tr* knock together; (*Gläser*) touch ‖ *intr* adjoin; **mit den Gläsern z.** clink glasses ‖ *intr* (SEIN) collide; (*Gegner*) clash

zusam'menstückeln *tr* piece together

zusam'menstürzen *intr* (SEIN) collapse

zusam'mentragen §132 *tr* collect

zusam'mentreffen §151 *intr* (SEIN) meet; coincide ‖ **Zusammentreffen** *n* (—s;) encounter, meeting; coincidence

zusam'mentreiben §62 *tr* round up; (*Geld*) scrape up

zusam'mentreten §152 *intr* (SEIN) meet

zusam'menwirken *intr* cooperate; collaborate; interact ‖ **Zusammenwirken** n (-s;) cooperation; interaction

zusam'menzählen tr count up, add up

zusam'menziehen §163 tr draw together, contract; (*Lippen*) pucker; (*Brauen*) knit; (*Summe*) add up; (*kürzen*) shorten; (*Truppen*) concentrate ‖ ref contract; (*Gewitter*) brew ‖ intr (SEIN)—**mit j-m z.** move in with s.o.

Zu'satz m addition; (*Ergänzung*) supplement; (*Anhang*) appendix; (*Nachschrift*) postscript; (*Beimischung*) admixture; (*zu e-m Testament*) codicil; (parl) rider; **unter Z. von** with the addition of

Zu'satzgerät n attachment

zusätzlich ['tsuzetslɪç] adj additional, extra ‖ adv in addition

zuschanden [tsuˈʃandən] adv—**z. machen** ruin; **z. werden** go to ruin

zu'schauen intr look on; (dat) watch

Zu'schauer -in §6 mf spectator

Zu'schauerraum m auditorium

zu'schicken tr (dat) send (to)

zu'schieben §130 tr close, shut; (*Riegel*) push forward; **j-m die Schuld z.** push the blame on s.o.

Zu'schlag m extra charge; **den Z. erhalten** get the contract (*on a bid*)

zu'schlagen §132 tr (*Tür*) slam; (*Buch*) shut; (*auf Auktionen*) knock down; (*hinzurechnen*) add ‖ intr hit hard

zu'schließen §76 tr shut, lock

zu'schnallen tr buckle (up)

zu'schnappen intr snap shut; **z. lassen** snap shut

zu'schneiden §106 tr cut out; (*Anzug*) cut to size

Zu'schnitt m cut; (fig) style

zu'schnüren tr lace up

zu'schrauben tr screw tight

zu'schreiben §62 tr ascribe; (*Bedeutung*) attach; (*Grundstück, usw.*) transfer, sign over ‖ ref—**er hat es sich** [dat] **selbst zuzuschreiben** he has himself to thank for it

Zu'schrift f letter, communication

zuschulden [tsuˈʃuldən] adv—**sich** [dat] **etw. z. kommen lassen** take the blame for s.th.

Zu'schuß m subsidy; grant; allowance

zu'schütten tr add; (*Graben*) fill up

zu'sehen §138 intr look on; (dat) watch; **z., daß** see to it that

zusehends ['tsuze-ənts] adv visibly

zu'senden §120 & §140 tr (dat) send to

zu'setzen tr add; (*Geld*) lose ‖ intr (dat) pester; (dat) be hard on; (mil) (dat) put pressure on

zu'sichern tr—**j-m etw z.** assure s.o. of s.th.

Zu'sicherung f (-;-en) assurance

zu'siegeln tr seal up

Zu'speise f side dish

zu'sperren tr lock

zu'spielen tr—**j-m den Ball z.** pass the ball to s.o.; **j-m etw z.** slip s.th. to s.o.

zu'spitzen tr sharpen, make pointy ‖ ref (*Lage*) come to a head

zu'sprechen §64 tr (& jur) award

Zu'spruch m consolation, encouragement; (com) customers, clientele

zu'springen §142 intr (SEIN) snap shut

Zu'stand m state, condition; gegenwärtiger Z. status quo; **in gutem Z.** in good condition; **Zustände** state of affairs

zustande [tsuˈʃtandə] adv—**z. bringen** bring about; put across; get away with; **z. kommen** come about, come off; happen; be realized; (*Gesetz*) pass; (*Vertrag*) be reached

zu'ständig adj competent; (*Behörde*) proper; (*verantwortlich*) responsible

Zu'ständigkeit f (-;) jurisdiction

zustatten [tsuˈʃtatən] adv—**z. kommen** come in handy

zu'stehen §146 intr (dat) be due to

zu'stellen tr deliver; (jur) serve

Zu'stellung f (-;-en) delivery; (jur) serving

zu'steuern tr (*Geld*) contribute, kick in ‖ intr (dat, auf acc) head for

zu'stimmen intr (dat) agree to, approve of (*s.th.*); (dat) agree with (*s.o.*)

Zu'stimmung f (-;) consent, approval

zu'stopfen tr plug up

zu'stoßen §150 tr slam ‖ intr (SEIN) lunge; (dat) happen to

zu'streben intr (dat) strive for

zutage [tsuˈtagə] adv to light; **z. liegen** be evident

Zutaten ['tsutatən] pl ingredients

zuteil [tsuˈtaɪl] adv—**j-m z. werden** fall to s.o.'s share

zu'teilen tr allot; ration; award; (gewähren) grant; confer; (mil) assign

Zu'teilung f (-;-en) allotment, allocation; rationing; (mil) assignment

zu'tragen §132 tr carry; (*Neuigkeiten*) report ‖ ref happen

zuträglich ['tsutreklɪç] adj advantageous; (*Klima*) healthful; (*Nahrung*) wholesome; **j-m z. sein** agree with s.o.

zu'trauen tr—**j-m etw z.** give s.o. credit for s.th.; imagine s.o. capable of s.th. ‖ **Zutrauen** n (-s;) (zu) confidence (in)

zu'traulich adj trustful; (*zahm*) tame

zu'treffen §151 intr (SEIN) prove right; come true; hold true, be conclusive; **z. auf** (acc) apply to

zu'treffend adj correct; to the point; (*anwendbar*) applicable

zu'trinken §143 intr (dat) drink to

Zu'tritt m access; admission; entrance; **kein Z.!** no admittance!

zu'tun §154 tr close; (*hinzufügen*) add

zu'verlässig adj reliable; **von zuverlässiger Seite** on good authority

Zu'verlässigkeit f (-;) reliability

Zuversicht ['tsuferzɪçt] f (-;) confidence

zu'versichtlich adj confident

zuviel [tsuˈfil] adv & indef pron too much; **einer z.** one too many

zuvor [tsuˈfor] adv before, previously; first (of all); **kurz z.** shortly before

zuvor- comb.fm. beforehand

zuvor'kommen §99 intr (SEIN) (dat) anticipate; **j-m z.** get the jump on s.o.

zuvor'kommend adj obliging; polite

zuvor'tun §154 tr—es j—m z. outdo s.o.

Zu'wachs m increase; growth; **auf Z.** (big enough) to allow for growth

zu'wachsen §155 intr (SEIN) grow together; (Wunde) heal up; (dat) accrue (to)

Zu'wachsrate f rate of increase

zuwege [tsu'vegə] adv—**z. bringen** bring about; achieve; finish; **gut z. sein** be fit as a fiddle

zuweilen [tsu'vaɪlən] adv sometimes

zu'weisen §118 tr assign, allot

zu'wenden §120 & §140 tr (dat) turn (s.th.) towards; (dat) give (s.th.) to, devote (s.th.) to || ref (dat) devote oneself to, concentrate on

Zu'wendung f (—;—en) gift, donation

zuwenig [tsu'veniç] adv & pron too little

zu'werfen §160 tr (Tür) slam; (Blick) cast; (Grube) fill up; **j—m etw z.** throw s.o. s.th.

zuwider [tsu'vidər] adj (dat) distasteful (to) || prep (dat) contrary to

zuwi'derhandeln intr (dat) go against

Zuwi'derhandlung f (—;—en) violation

zu'winken intr (dat) wave to; beckon to

zu'zahlen tr pay extra

zu'zählen tr add

zuzeiten [tsu'tsaɪtən] adv at times

zu'ziehen §163 tr (Vorhang) draw; (Knoten) tighten; (Arzt, Experten) call in || ref—**sich** [dat] **etw z.** incur s.th.; contract s.th. || intr (SEIN) move in; move (to a city)

Zu'ziehung f—**unter Z.** (genit or von) in consultation with

zuzüglich ['tsutsykliç] prep (genit) plus; including

zwang [tsvaŋ] pret of **zwingen** || **Zwang** m (—[e]s) coercion, force; restraint; obligation; (Druck) pressure; (jur) duress; **auf j—n Z. ausüben** put pressure on s.o. || ref—**sich** [dat] **keinen Z. antun** (or auferlegen) relax

zwängen ['tsvεŋən] tr force, squeeze || ref (durch) squeeze (through)

zwang'los adj free and easy; informal

Zwang'losigkeit f (—;) ease; informality

Zwangs— [tsvaŋs] comb.fm. force, compulsory

Zwangs'arbeit f hard labor

Zwangs'arbeitslager n labor camp

Zwangs'jacke f strait jacket

Zwangs'lage f tight spot

zwangs'läufig adj inevitable

zwangs'mäßig adj forced; coercive

Zwangs'maßnahme f—**zu Zwangsmaßnahmen greifen** resort to force

Zwangs'verschleppte §5 mf displaced person

Zwangs'verwaltung f receivership

Zwangs'vorstellung f hallucination

zwangs'weise adv by force

Zwangs'wirtschaft f (econ) government control, controlled economy

zwanzig ['tsvantsiç] adj & pron twenty || **Zwanzig** f (—;—en) twenty

zwanziger ['tsvantsigər] invar adj of the twenties; **die z. Jahre** the twenties

zwanzigste ['tsvantsiçstə] §9 adj & pron twentieth

Zwanzigstel ['tsvantsiçstəl] n (—s;—) twentieth (part)

zwar [tsvar] adv indeed, no doubt, it is true; **und z.** namely, that is

Zweck [tsvεk] m (—[e]s;—e) purpose, aim, object, point; **es hat keinen Z.** there's no point to it

zweck'dienlich adj serviceable, useful

Zwecke ['tsvεkə] f (—;—n) tack; thumbtack

zweck'entfremden tr misuse

zweck'entsprechend adj appropriate

zweck'los adj pointless

zweck'mäßig adj serving its purpose; (Möbel) functional

zwecks [tsvεks] prep (genit) for the purpose of

zwei [tsvaɪ] adj & pron two; **alle z.** (coll) both; **zu zweien** in twos, two by two, in pairs; **zu zweien hintereinander** in double file || **Zwei** f (—;—en) two

zwei'beinig adj two-legged

Zwei'bettzimmer n double room

Zweidecker ['tsvaɪdekər] m (—s;—) biplane

zweideutig ['tsvaɪdɔɪtiç] adj ambiguous; (Witz) off-color; (schlüpfrig) suggestive

zweierlei ['tsvaɪ.ər'laɪ] invar adj two kinds of; **das ist z.** (coll) that's different

zwei'fach, zwei'fältig adj twofold, double; **in zweifacher Ausfertigung** in duplicate

Zweifami'lienhaus n duplex

zwei'farbig adj two-tone

Zweifel ['tsvaɪfəl] m (—s;—) doubt; **in Z. stellen** (or ziehen) call into question; **über allen Zweifeln erhaben** beyond reproach

zwei'felhaft adj doubtful; questionable; (Persönlichkeit) suspicious

zwei'fellos adj doubtless

zweifeln ['tsvaɪfəln] intr be in doubt; waver, hesitate; **z. an** (dat) doubt

Zwei'felsfall m—**im Z.** in case of doubt

Zweif'ler —in §6 mf skeptic

Zweig [tsvaɪk] m (—[e]s;—e) branch

Zweig'anstalt f, **Zweig'geschäft** n (com) branch

Zweig'gesellschaft f (com) affiliate

Zweig'niederlassung f, **Zweig'stelle** f (com) branch

Zwei'kampf m duel, single combat

zwei'mal adv twice

zweimalig ['tsvaɪmaliç] adj repeated

zweimotorig ['tsvaɪmotoriç] adj two-engine, twin-engine

zweireihig ['tsvaɪraɪ.iç] adj (Sakko) double-breasted

zwei'schneidig adj double-edged

zwei'seitig adj bilateral; reversible

zweisprachig ['tsvaɪpraxiç] adj bilingual

Zweistär'kenglas n bifocal lens; (Brille) bifocals

zwei'stimmig adj for two voices

zweistufig ['tsvaɪtufiç] adj (rok) two-stage

zwei'stündig adj two-hour

zwei'stündlich *adj & adv* every two hours

zweit [tsvaɪt] *adv*—**zu z.** by twos; **wir sind zu z.** there are two of us

Zwei'taktmotor *m* two-cycle engine

Zweit'ausfertigung *f* duplicate

zweit'beste §9 *adj* second-best

zweite ['tsvaɪtə] §9 *adj & pron* second; another; **aus zweiter Hand** second-hand; at second hand; **zum zweiten** secondly || **Zweite** §5 *mf* (sport) runner-up

zwei'teilig *adj* two-piece; two-part

zweitens ['tsvaɪtəns] *adv* secondly

zweit'klassig *adj* second-class

Zwerchfell ['tsvɛrçfɛl] *n* diaphragm

Zwerg [tsvɛrk] *m* (-[e]s;-e) dwarf

zwer'genhaft *adj* dwarfish

Zwetsche ['tsvɛt/ə] *f* (-;-n), **Zwetsch-ge** ['tsvɛt/gə] *f* (-;-n) plum

Zwetsch'genwasser *n* plum brandy

zwicken ['tsvɪkən] *tr* pinch

Zwicker [Zwik'ker] *m* (-s;-) pince-nez

Zwickmühle ['tsvɪkmylə] *f* (fig) fix

zwie- [tsvi] *comb.fm.* dis-, two-, double

Zwieback ['tsvibak] *m* (-s;ǝe & -e) zwieback

Zwiebel ['tsvibəl] *f* (-;-n) onion; (*Blumen-*) bulb

Zwie'gespräch *n* dialogue

Zwie'licht *n* twilight

Zwiesel ['tsvizəl] *f* (-;-n) fork (*of tree*)

Zwie'spalt *m* dissension; schism; discrepancy; **im Z. sein mit** be at variance with

zwiespältig ['tsvi/pɛltɪç] *adj* disunited, divided; divergent

Zwie'tracht *f* (-;) discord

Zwilling ['tsvɪlɪŋ] *m* (-s;-e) twin; **eineiige Zwillinge** identical twins

Zwil'lingsbruder *m* twin brother

Zwil'lingsschwester *f* twin sister

Zwinge ['tsvɪŋə] *f* (-;-n) ferrule; clamp; (*Schraubstock*) vise

zwingen ['tsvɪŋən] §142 *tr* force, compel; (*schaffen*) accomplish, swing

zwin'gend *adj* forceful, cogent

Zwin'ger *m* (-s;-) dungeon; cage; dog kennel; bear pit; lists

zwinkern ['tsvɪŋkərn] *intr* blink

Zwirn [tsvɪrn] *m* (-[e]s;-e) thread

Zwirns'faden *m* thread

zwischen ['tsvɪ/ən] *prep* (*dat & acc*) between, among

Zwi'schenbemerkung *f* interruption

Zwi'schendeck *n* steerage

Zwi'schending *n* cross, mixture

zwischendurch' *adv* in between; at times

Zwi'schenergebnis *n* incomplete result

Zwi'schenfall *m* (unexpected) incident

Zwi'schenhändler **–in** §6 *mf* middleman

Zwi'schenlandung *f* stopover

Zwi'schenlauf *m* (sport) quarterfinal; (sport) semifinal

Zwi'schenpause *f* break, intermission

Zwi'schenraum *m* space, interval

Zwi'schenruf *m* boo; interruption

Zwi'schenrunde *f* (sport) quarterfinal; (sport) semifinal

Zwi'schenspiel *n* interlude

zwi'schenstaatlich *adj* international; interstate

Zwi'schenstation *f* (rr) way station

Zwi'schenstecker *m* (elec) adapter

Zwi'schenstellung *f* (-;-en) intermediate position

Zwi'schenstück *n* insert; (*Verbindung*) connection; (elec) adapter

Zwi'schenstufe *f* intermediate stage

Zwi'schenträger **–in** §6 *mf* gossip

Zwi'schenwand *f* partition wall

Zwi'schenzeit *f* interval, meanwhile

Zwist [tsvɪst] *m* (-es;-e) discord; quarrel; (*Feindschaft*) enmity

Zwi'stigkeit *f* (-;-en) hostility

zwitschern ['tsvɪt/ərn] *tr*—**e–n z.** (coll) have a shot of liquor || *intr* chirp

Zwitter ['tsvɪtər] *m* (-s;-) hermaphrodite

Zwit'terfahrzeug *n* (mil) half-track

zwo [tsvo] *adj & pron* (coll) two

zwölf ['tsvœlf] *invar adj & pron* twelve || **Zwölf** *f* (-;-en) twelve

Zwölffin'gerdarm *m* duodenum

zwölfte ['tsvœlftə] §9 *adj & pron* twelfth

Zwölftel ['tsvœftəl] *n* (-s;-) twelfth (*part*)

Zyklon [tsy'klon] *m* (-s;-e), **Zyklone** [tsy'klonə] *f* (-;-n) cyclone

Zyk·lus ['tsyklʊs] *m* (-;-len [lən]) cycle; (*Reihe*) series, course

Zylinder [tsy'lɪndər] *m* (-s;-) cylinder (*e–r Lampe*) chimney; (*Hut*) top hat

zylindrisch [tsy'lɪndrɪ/] *adj* cylindrical

Zyniker ['tsynɪkər] *m* (-s;-) cynic; (philos) Cynic

zynisch ['tsynɪ/] *adj* cynical

Zypern ['tsypərn] *n* (-s;) Cyprus

Zypresse [tsy'prɛsə] *f* (-;-n) cypress

Zyste ['tsYstə] *f* (-;-n) cyst

GRAMMATICAL EXPLANATIONS

German Pronunciation

All the German letters and their variant spellings are listed below (in column 1) with their IPA symbols (in column 2), a description of their sounds (in column 3), and German examples with phonetic transcription (in column 4).

		VOWELS	
SPELLING	SYMBOL	APPROXIMATE SOUND	EXAMPLES
a	[a]	Like *a* in English *swat*	Apfel ['apfəl], lassen ['lasən], Stadt [ʃtat]
a	[ɑ]	Like *a* in English *father*	Vater ['fɑtər], laden ['lɑdən]
aa	[ɑ]	" "	Paar [pɑr], Staat [ʃtɑt]
ah	[ɑ]	" "	Hahn [hɑn], Zahl [tsɑl]
ä	[ɛ]	Like *e* in English *met*	Äpfel ['ɛpfəl], lässig ['lɛsɪç], Städte ['ʃtɛtə]
ä	[e]	Like *e* in English *they* (without the following sound of *y*)	mäßig ['mesɪç], Väter ['fetər]
äh	[e]	" "	ähnlich ['enlɪç], Zähne ['tsenə]
e	[ə]	Like *e* in English *system*	Bitte ['bɪtə], rufen ['rufən]
e	[ɛ]	Like *e* in English *met*	Kette ['kɛtə], messen ['mɛsən]
e	[e]	Like *e* in English *they* (without the following sound of *y*)	Feder ['fedər], regnen ['regnən]
ee	[e]	" "	Meer [mer], Seele ['zelə]
eh	[e]	" "	Ehre ['erə], zehn [tsen]
i	[ɪ]	Like *i* in English *sin*	bin [bɪn], Fisch [fɪʃ]
i	[i]	Like *i* in English *machine*	Maschine [ma'ʃinə], Lid [lit]
ih	[i]	" "	ihm [im], ihr [ir]
ie	[i]	" "	dieser ['dizər], tief [tif]
o	[ɔ]	Like *o* in English *often*	Gott [gɔt], offen ['ɔfən]
o	[o]	Like *o* in English *note*, but without the diphthongal glide	holen ['holən], Rose ['rozə]
oo	[o]	" "	Boot [bot], Moos [mos]
oh	[o]	" "	Bohne ['bonə], Kohle ['kolə]
ö	[œ]	The lips are rounded for [ɔ] and held without moving while the sound [ɛ] is pronounced.	Götter ['gœtər], öffnen ['œfnən]

3a

SPELLING	SYMBOL	APPROXIMATE SOUND	EXAMPLES
ö	[ø]	The lips are rounded for [o] and held without moving while the sound [e] is pronounced.	böse ['bøzə], Löwe ['løvə]
öh	[ø]	" "	Röhre ['rørə], Söhne ['zønə]
u	[ʊ]	Like u in English bush	Busch [bʊʃ], muß [mʊs], Hund [hʊnt]
u	[u]	Like u in English rule	Schule ['ʃulə], Gruß [grus]
uh	[u]	" "	Uhr [ur], Ruhm [rum]
ü	[ʏ]	The lips are rounded for [ʊ] and held without moving while the sound [ɪ] is pronounced.	Hütte ['hʏtə], müssen ['mʏsən]
ü	[y]	The lips are rounded for [u] and held without moving while the sound [i] is pronounced.	Schüler ['ʃylər], Grüße ['grysə]
üh	[y]	" "	Mühle ['mylə], kühn [kyn]
y	[ʏ]	Like ü [ʏ] above	Mystik ['mʏstɪk]
y	[y]	Like ü [y] above	Mythe ['mytə]

DIPHTHONGS

SPELLING	SYMBOL	APPROXIMATE SOUND	EXAMPLES
ai	[aɪ]	Like i in English night	Saite ['zaɪtə], Mais [maɪs]
au	[aʊ]	Like ou in English ouch	kaufen ['kaʊfən], Haus [haʊs]
äu	[ɔɪ]	Like oy in English toy	träumen ['trɔɪmən], Gebäude [gə'bɔɪdə]
ei	[aɪ]	Like i in English night	Zeit [tsaɪt], nein [naɪn]
eu	[ɔɪ]	Like oy in English toy	heute ['hɔɪtə], Eule ['ɔɪlə]

CONSONANTS

SPELLING	SYMBOL	APPROXIMATE SOUND	EXAMPLES
b	[b]	Like b in English boy	Buch [bux], haben ['haban]
b	[p]	Like p in English lap	gelb [gelp], lieblich ['liplɪç]
c	[k]	Like c in English car	Clown [klaun], Café [ka'fe]
c	[ts]	Like ts in English its	Cäsar ['tsezar], Centrale [tsen'tralə]
ch	[x]	This sound is made by breathing through a space between the back of the tongue and the soft palate.	auch [aux], Buche ['buxə]
ch	[ç]	This sound is made by breathing through a space left when the front of the tongue is pressed close to the hard palate with the tip of the tongue behind the lower teeth.	ich [ɪç], Bücher ['byçər], Chemie [çe'mi], durch [dʊrç]

4a

SPELLING	SYMBOL	APPROXIMATE SOUND	EXAMPLES
ch	[k]	Like *k* in English *key*	**Charakter** [ka'raktər], **Chor** [kor]
ch	[ʃ]	Like *sh* in English *shall*	**Chef** [ʃef], **Chassis** [ʃa'si]
chs	[ks]	Like *x* in English *box*	**sechs** [zɛks], **Wachs** [vaks]
ck	[k]	Like *k* in English *key* When *ck* in a vocabulary entry in this Dictionary has to be divided by an accent mark, the word is first spelled with *ck* and is then repeated in parentheses with the *ck* changed to *kk* in accordance with the principle which requires this change when the division comes at the end of the line, e.g., **Deckenlicht (Dek'ken-licht).**	**wecken** ['vɛkən], **Ruck** [rʊk]
d	[d]	Like *d* in English *door*	**laden** ['ladən], **deutsch** [dɔɪtʃ]
d	[t]	Like *t* in English *time*	**Freund** [frɔɪnt], **Hund** [hʊnt]
dt	[t]	" "	**verwandt** [fer'vant], **Stadt** [ʃtat]
f	[f]	Like *f* in English *five*	**Fall** [fal], **auf** [aʊf]
g	[g]	Like *g* in English *go*	**geben** ['gebən], **Regen** ['regən]
g	[k]	Like *k* in English *key*	**Krieg** [krik], **Weg** [vek]
g	[ç]	See **ch** [ç] above	**wenig** ['venɪç], **häufig** ['hɔɪfɪç]
h	[h]	Like *h* in English *hat*	**Haus** [haʊs], **Freiheit** ['fraɪhaɪt]
j	[j]	Like *y* in English *yet*	**Jahr** [jɑr], **jener** ['jenər]
k	[k]	Like *k* in English *key*	**Kaffee** [ka'fe], **kein** [kaɪn]
l	[l]	This sound is made with the tip of the tongue against the back of the upper teeth and the side edges of the tongue against the side teeth.	**laden** ['ladən], **fahl** [fɑl]
m	[m]	Like *m* in English *man*	**mehr** [mer], **Amt** [amt]
n	[n]	Like *n* in English *neck*	**Nase** ['nɑzə], **kaufen** ['kaʊfən]
n	[ŋ]	Like *n* in English *sink*	**sinken** ['zɪŋkən], **Funke** ['fʊŋkə]
ng	[ŋ]	" "	**Finger** ['fɪŋər], **Rang** [raŋ]
p	[p]	Like *p* in English *pond*	**Perle** ['perlə], **Opfer** ['ɔpfər]
ph	[f]	Like *f* in English *five*	**Phase** ['fazə], **Graphik** ['grafɪk]
qu	[kv]	Does not occur in English.	**Quelle** ['kvɛlə], **bequem** [bə'kvem]
r	[r]	This sound is a trilled sound made by vibrating the tip of the tongue against the upper gums or by vibrating the uvula.	**rufen** ['rufən], **Rede** ['redə]

5a

SPELLING	SYMBOL	APPROXIMATE SOUND	EXAMPLES
s	[s]	Like s in English sock	Glas [glɑs], erst [erst]
s	[z]	Like z in English zest	sind [zɪnt], Eisen ['aɪzən]
sch	[ʃ]	Like sh in English shall	Schuh [ʃu], Schnee [ʃne]
sp	[ʃp]	Does not occur in English in the initial position.	sparen ['ʃpɑrən], Spott [ʃpɔt]
ss	[s]	This spelling is used only in the intervocalic position and when the preceding vowel sound is one of the following: [a], [e], [ɪ], [ɔ], [œ], [ʊ], [ʏ]	Klasse ['klɑsə], essen ['esən], wissen ['vɪsən], Gosse ['gɔsə], Rössel ['rœsəl], Russe ['rʊsə], müssen ['mʏsən]
ß	[s]	This spelling is used instead of ss (a) when in the final position in a word or component, (b) when followed by a consonant, or (c) when intervocalic and preceded by a diphthong or one of the following vowel sounds: [ɑ], [e], [i], [o], [ø], [u], [y]	(a) Fluß [flʊs], Flußufer ['flusufər], (b) läßt [lest], (c) dreißig ['draɪsɪç], Straße ['ʃtrɑsə], mäßig ['mesɪç], schießen ['ʃisən], stoßen ['ʃtosən], Stößel ['ʃtøsəl], Muße ['musə], müßig ['mysɪç]
st	[ʃt]	Does not occur in English in the initial position.	Staub [ʃtaup], stehen ['ʃte·ən]
t	[t]	Like t in English time	Teller ['telər], Tau [tau]
th	[t]	" "	Theater [te'ɑtər], Thema ['tema]
ti+ vowel	[tsj]	Does not occur in English.	Station [sta'tsjon], Patient [pa'tsjent]
tz	[ts]	Like ts in English its	schätzen ['ʃetsən], jetzt [jetst]
v	[f]	Like f in English five	Vater ['fɑtər], brav [brɑf]
v	[v]	Like v in English vat	November [nɔ'vembər], Verb [verp]
w	[v]	" "	Wasser ['vasər], wissen ['vɪsən]
x	[ks]	Like x in English box	Export [eks'pɔrt], Taxe ['taksə]
z	[ts]	Like ts in English its	Zahn [tsan], reizen ['raɪtsən]

6a

German Grammar References

§1. Declension of the Definite Article

	SINGULAR			PLURAL
	MASC	FEM	NEUT	MASC, FEM, NEUT
NOM	der	die	das	die
ACC	den	die	das	die
DAT	dem	der	dem	den
GENIT	des	der	des	der

§2. Declension of the Indefinite Article and the Numeral Adjective

	SINGULAR			PLURAL
1.	MASC	FEM	NEUT	MASC, FEM, NEUT
NOM	ein	eine	ein	
ACC	einen	eine	ein	
DAT	einem	einer	einem	
GENIT	eines	einer	eines	

2. Other words that are declined like **ein** are: **kein** *no, not any* and the possessive adjectives **mein** *my;* **dein** *thy, your;* **sein** *his; her; its;* **ihr** *her; their;* **Ihr** *your;* **unser** *our;* **euer** *your.* Unlike **ein**, they have plural forms, as shown in the following paradigm.

	SINGULAR			PLURAL
	MASC	FEM	NEUT	MASC, FEM, NEUT
NOM	kein	keine	kein	keine
ACC	keinen	keine	kein	keine
DAT	keinem	keiner	keinem	keinen
GENIT	keines	keiner	keines	keiner

3. The **e** of **er** of **unser** and **euer** is generally dropped when followed by an ending, as shown in the following paradigm. And instead of the **e** of **er** dropping, the **e** of final **em** and **en** in these words may drop.

	SINGULAR			PLURAL
	MASC	FEM	NEUT	MASC, FEM, NEUT
NOM	unser	uns(e)re	unser	uns(e)re
ACC	uns(e)ren or unsern	uns(e)re	unser	uns(e)re
DAT	uns(e)rem or unserm	uns(e)rer	uns(e)rem or unserm	uns(e)ren or unsern
GENIT	uns(e)res	uns(e)rer	uns(e)res	uns(e)rer

All adjectives that follow these words are declined in the mixed declension.

4. The pronouns **einer** and **keiner**, as well as all the possessive pronouns, are declined according to the strong declension of adjectives. The neuter forms **eines** and **keines** have the variants **eins** and **keins.**

5. When the possessive adjectives are used as possessive pronouns, they are declined according to the strong declension of adjectives. When preceded by the definite article, they are declined according to the weak declension of adjectives. There are also possessive pronouns with the infix **ig** which are always preceded by the definite article and capitalized and are declined according to the declension of adjectives, e.g., **der, die, das Meinige** *mine.*

§3. Declension of the Demonstrative Pronoun

	SINGULAR			PLURAL
	MASC	FEM	NEUT	MASC, FEM, NEUT
NOM	dieser	diese	dieses or dies	diese
ACC	diesen	diese	dieses or dies	diese
DAT	diesem	dieser	diesem	diesen
GENIT	dieses	dieser	dieses	dieser

Other words that are declined like **dieser** are **jeder** *each;* **jener** *that;* **mancher** *many a;* **welcher** *which.* All adjectives that come after these words are declined in the weak declension.

§4. Declension of Adjectives.
Adjectives have three declensions: 1) the strong declension, 2) the weak declension, and 3) the mixed declension. On both sides of this Dictionary, adjectives occurring in the expressions consisting solely of an adjective and a noun are entered in their weak forms.

1. The strong declension of adjectives, whose endings are shown in the following table, is used when the adjective is not preceded by **der** or by **dieser** or any of the other words listed in §3 or by **ein** or any of the other words listed in §2.

	SINGULAR			PLURAL
	MASC	FEM	NEUT	MASC, FEM, NEUT
NOM	–er	–e	–es	–e
ACC	–en	–e	–es	–e
DAT	–em	–er	–em	–en
GENIT	–en	–er	–en	–er

2. The weak declension of adjectives, whose endings are shown in the following table, is used when the adjective is preceded by **der** or **dieser** or any of the other words listed in §3.

	SINGULAR			PLURAL
	MASC	FEM	NEUT	MASC, FEM, NEUT
NOM	–e	–e	–e	–en
ACC	–en	–e	–e	–en
DAT	–en	–en	–en	–en
GENIT	–en	–en	–en	–en

3. The **der** component of **derselbe** and **derjenige** is the article **der** and is declined like it, while the –**selbe** and –**jenige** components are declined according to the weak declension of adjectives.

4. The mixed declension of adjectives, whose endings are shown in the following table, is used when the adjective is preceded by **ein** or **kein** or any of the other words listed in §2.

	SINGULAR			PLURAL
	MASC	FEM	NEUT	MASC, FEM, NEUT
NOM	−er	−e	−es	−en
ACC	−en	−e	−es	−en
DAT	−en	−en	−en	−en
GENIT	−en	−en	−en	−en

§5. Adjectives Used as Nouns. When an adjective is used as a masculine, feminine, or neuter noun, it is spelled with an initial capital letter and is declined as an adjective in accordance with the principles set forth in §4. We have, for example, **der** or **die Fremde** the foreigner; **der** or **die Angestellte** *the employee;* **ein Angestellter** *a (male) employee,* **eine Angestellte** *a (female) employee;* **das Deutsche** *German* (i.e., *language*). These nouns are entered on both sides of this Dictionary in the weak form of the adjective and their genitives and plurals are not shown.

§6. Many masculine nouns ending in −er and −ier have feminine forms made by adding −in. The masculine forms have genitives made by adding s and remain unchanged in the plural, while the feminine forms remain unchanged in the singular and have plurals made by adding −nen. For example:

MASC	FEM
NOM SG	**Verkäufer** *salesperson (salesman)*	**Verkäuferin** *salesperson (saleslady)*
GENIT SG	**Verkäufers**	**Verkäuferin**
NOM PL	**Verkäufer**	**Verkäuferinnen**

§7. Many masculine nouns ending in −at (e.g., **Advokat**), or in −ant (e.g., **Musikant**), or in −ist (e.g., **Artist**), or in −ent (e.g., **Student**), or in −graph (e.g., **Choreograph**), or in −ot (e.g., **Pilot**), or in −et (e.g., **Analphabet**), or in −it (e.g., **Israelit**), or in −ast (e.g., **Phantast**), etc., have feminine forms made by adding −in. The masculine forms have genitives and plurals made by adding −en, while the femine forms remain unchanged in the singular and have plurals made by adding −nen. For example:

MASC	FEM
NOM SG	**Advokat** *attorney*	**Advokatin** *attorney*
GENIT SG	**Advokaten**	**Advokatin**
NOM PL	**Advokaten**	**Advokatinnen**

§8. Many masculine nouns ending in −ar (e.g., **Antiquar**) or in −är (e.g., **Milliardär**) have feminine forms made by adding −in. The masculine forms have genitives made by adding −(e)s and plurals made by adding −e, while the feminine forms remain unchanged in the singular and have plurals made by adding −nen. For example:

MASC	FEM
NOM SG	**Antiquar** *antique dealer*	**Antiquarin** *antique dealer*
GENIT SG	**Antiquar(e)s**	**Antiquarin**
NOM PL	**Antiquare**	**Antiquarinnen**

§9. Adjectives are generally given in their uninflected form, the form in which they appear in the predicate, e.g., **billig, reich, alt.** However, those adjectives which do not occur in an uninflected form are given with the weak ending −e, which in the nominative is the same for all genders, e.g., **andere, besondere, beste, hohe.**

9a

§10. Adjectives which denote languages may be used as adverbs. When so used with **sprechen, schreiben, können,** and a few others, they are translated in English by the corresponding noun, and actual and immediate action is implied, e.g., **deutsch sprechen** *to speak German* (i.e., to be speaking German right now). Adjectives which denote languages may be capitalized and used as invariable nouns, and when so used with **sprechen, schreiben, können,** and a few other verbs, general action is implied, e.g., **Deutsch sprechen** *to speak German* (i.e., to know how to speak German, to be a speaker of German).

With other verbs, these adjectives used as adverbs are translated by the corresponding noun preceded by "auf" or "in", e.g., **sich auf** (or **in**) **deutsch unterhalten** *to converse in German.*

811. Personal and Reflexive Pronouns

PERSONS	SUBJECT	PERSONAL DIRECT OBJECT	PERSONAL INDIRECT OBJECT	REFLEXIVE DIRECT OBJECT	REFLEXIVE INDIRECT OBJECT
SG					
1	ich *I*	mich *me*	mir *(to) me*	mich *myself*	mir *(to) myself*
2	du *you*	dich *you*	dir *(to) you*	dich *yourself*	dir *(to) yourself*
3 MASC	er *he; it*	ihn *him; it*	ihm *(to) him; (to) it*	sich *himself; itself*	sich *(to) himself; (to) itself*
3 FEM	sie *she; it*	sie *her; it*	ihr *(to) her; (to) it*	sich *herself; itself*	sich *(to) herself; (to) itself*
3 NEUT	es *it; she; he*	es *it; her; him*	ihm *(to) it; (to) her; (to) him*	sich *itself; herself; himself*	sich *(to) itself; (to) herself; (to) himself*
PL					
1	wir *we*	uns *us*	uns *(to) us*	uns *ourselves*	uns *(to) ourselves*
2	ihr *you*	euch *you*	euch *(to) you*	euch *yourselves*	euch *(to) yourselves*
3	sie *they*	sie *them*	ihnen *(to) them*	sich *themselves*	sich *(to) themselves*
2 FORMAL SG & PL	Sie *you*	Sie *you*	Ihnen *(to) you*	sich *yourself; yourselves*	sich *(to) yourself; (to) yourselves*

er means *it* when it stands for a masculine noun that is the name of an animal or a thing, as **Hund, Tisch.**
sie means *it* when it stands for a feminine noun that is the name of an animal or a thing, as **Hündin, Feder.**
es means *she* when it stands for a neuter noun that is the name of a female person, as **Fräulein, Mädchen, Weib;** it means *he* when it stands for a neuter noun that is the name of a male person, as **Söhnchen, Söhnlein.**
The dative means also *from me, from you,* etc., with certain verbs expressing separation such as **entnehmen.**

11a

§12. Separable and Inseparable Prefixes. Many verbs can be compounded either with a prefix, which is always inseparable and unstressed, or with a combining form (conventionally called also a prefix), which can be separable and stressed or inseparable and unstressed. Exceptions are indicated by the abbreviations *sep* and *insep.*

1. The inseparable prefixes are **be-, emp-, ent-, er-, ge-, ver-,** and **zer-,** e.g., **beglei′ten, erler′nen, verste′hen.** They are never stressed.

2. The separable prefixes (i.e., combining forms) are prepositions, e.g., **auf-** as in **auf′tragen,** adverbs, e.g., **vorwärts-** as in **vor′wärtsbringen,** adjectives, e.g., **tot-** as in **tot′schlagen,** nouns, e.g., **maschine-** as in **maschi′neschreiben,** or other verbs, e.g., **stehen-** as in **ste′henbleiben.** They are always stressed except as provided for those listed in the following section.

3. The prefixes (combining forms) **durch, hinter, über, um, unter, wider,** and **wieder,** when their meaning is literal, are separable and stressed, e.g. **durch′schneiden** *cut through, cut in two,* and, when their meaning is figurative or derived, are inseparable and unstressed, e.g., **durchschnei′den** *cut across, traverse.*

4. A compound prefix is (a) inseparable if it consists of an inseparable prefix plus a separable prefix, e.g., **beauf′tragen,** (b) separable if it consists of a separable prefix plus an inseparable prefix, e.g. **vor′bereiten—er bereitet etwas vor,** and (c) separable if it consists of two separable prefixes, e.g., **vorbei′laufen—sie lief vorbei.** Although verbs falling under (b) are separable, they do not take **-ge-** in the past participle, e.g., **vor′bereitet** (past participle of **vorbereiten**). But they do take the infix **-zu-** in the infinitive, e.g., **vor′zubereiten.** Note that compound prefixes falling under (c) are stressed on the second of the two separable components.

§13. German verbs are regarded as reflexive regardless of whether the reflexive pronoun is the direct or indirect object of the verb.

§14. The declension of German nouns is shown by giving the genitive singular followed by the nominative plural, in parentheses after the abbreviation indicating gender. This is done by presenting the whole noun by a hyphen with which the ending and/or the umlaut may or may not be shown according to the inflection; e.g., **Stadt** [ʃtat] *f* (-;⸚e) means *der* **Stadt** and *die* **Städte.** If the noun has no plural, the closing parenthesis comes immediately after the semicolon following the genitive singular, e.g., **Kleidung** [ˈklaɪduŋ] *f* (-;). In loan words in which the ending changes in the plural, the centered period is used to mark off the portion of the word that has to be detached before the portion showing the plural form is added, e.g., **Da·tum** [ˈdɑtʊm] *n* (-s;-ten [tən]).

When a vowel is added to a word ending in ß, the ß remains if it is preceded by a diphthong or one of the following vowel sounds: [ɑ], [e], [i], [o], [ø], [y], e.g., **Stoß** [ʃtos], plural: **Stöße; Strauß,** plural: **Sträuße,** but changes to **ss** if it is preceded by one of the following vowel sounds: [a], [e], [ɪ], [ɔ], [œ], [ʊ], [Y], e.g., **Roß** [rɔs], plural **Rosses.** In this Dictionary the inflection of words in which ß does not change is shown in the usual way, e.g., **Stoß** [ʃtos] *m* (-es;⸚e); **Strauß** [ʃtraʊs] *m* (-es;⸚e), while the inflection of words in which ß changes to **ss** is shown in monosyllables by repeating the full word in its inflected forms, e.g., **Roß** [rɔs] *n* (**Rosses; Rosse**) and in polysyllables by marking off with a centered dot the final syllable and then repeating it in its inflected forms, e.g., **Ver·laß** [ferˈlas] *m* (-lasses;).

§15. When a word ending in a double consonant is combined with a following word beginning with the same single consonant followed by a vowel, the resultant group of three identical consonants is shortened to two, e.g., **Schiff** combined with **Fahrt** makes **Schiffahrt** and **Schall** combined with **Lehre** makes

Schallehre.[1] However, when such a compound as a vocabulary entry has to be divided by an accent mark, the word is first spelled with two identical consonants and is then repeated in parentheses with three identical consonants, e.g., **Schiffahrt (Schiff'fahrt).** Furthermore, when such a compound has to be divided because the first component comes at the end of a line and is followed by a hyphen and the second component begins the following line, the three consonants are used, e.g., **Schiff–fahrt** and **Schall–lehre.**

When the medial group **ck** in a vocabulary entry has to be divided by an accent mark, the word is first spelled with **ck** and is then repeated in parentheses with the **ck** changed to **kk** in accordance with the orthographic principle which requires this change when the division comes at the end of the line, e.g., **Deckenlicht (Dek'kenlicht).**

[1] If the intial consonant of the following word is followed by a consonant instead of a vowel, the group of three identical consonants remains, e.g., **Fetttropfen, Rohstofffrage.**

13a

German Model Verbs

These verbs are models for all the verbs that appear as vocabulary entries in the German-English part of this Dictionary. If a section number referring to this table is not given with an entry, it is understood that the verb is a weak verb conjugated like **loben, reden, handeln,** or **warten.** If a section number is given, it is understood that the verb is a strong, mixed, or irregular verb and that it is identical in all forms with the model referred to in its radical vowel or diphthong and the consonants that follow the radical. Thus **schneiden** is numbered §106 to refer to the model **leiden.** Such words include the model itself, e.g., **denken,** numbered §66 to refer to the model **denken,** compounds of the model, e.g., **bekommen,** numbered §99 to refer to the model **kommen,** and verbs that have the same radical component, e.g., **empfehlen,** numbered §51 to refer to the model **befehlen.**

If a strong or mixed verb in a given function (transitive or intransitive) and/or meaning may be conjugated also as a weak verb, this is indicated by the insertion of the section number of the appropriate weak verb (**loben, handeln, reden,** or **warten**) after the section number of the model strong verb, e.g., **dingen** §142 & §109.

If a strong or mixed verb in a different function is conjugated as a weak verb, this is indicated by dividing the two functions by parallels and showing the conjugation of each by the insertion of the appropriate section numbers, e.g., **hängen** §92 *tr* . . . ‖ §109 *intr.*

If a strong or mixed verb in a different meaning is conjugated as a weak verb, this is indicated by dividing the two meanings by parallels and showing the conjugation of each by the insertion of the appropriate section numbers, e.g., **bewegen** *tr* move, set in motion . . . ‖ §56 *tr* move, induce.

It is understood that verbs with inseparable prefixes, verbs with compound separable prefixes of which the first component is separable and the second inseparable, and verbs ending in **–ieren** do not take **ge** in the past participle.

No account is taken here of the auxiliary used in forming compound tenses. The use of SEIN is indicated in the body of the Dictionary.

Alternate forms are listed in parentheses immediately below the corresponding principal part of the model verb.

	INFINITIVE	3D SG PRESENT INDICATIVE	IMPERFECT INDICATIVE	IMPERFECT SUBJUNCTIVE	PAST PARTICIPLE
§50	backen	bäckt	buk	büke	gebacken
§51	befehlen	befiehlt	befahl	beföhle	befohlen
§52	beginnen	beginnt	begann	begönne (begänne)	begonnen
§53	beißen	beißt	biß	bisse	gebissen
§54	bergen	birgt	barg	bärge (bürge)	geborgen
§55	bersten	birst (berstet)	barst	bärste (börste)	geborsten
§56	bewegen	bewegt	bewog	bewöge	bewogen
§57	biegen	biegt	bog	böge	gebogen
§58	bieten	bietet	bot	böte	geboten
§59	binden	bindet	band	bände	gebunden
§60	bitten	bittet	bat	bäte	gebeten
§61	blasen	bläst	blies	bliese	geblasen
§62	bleiben	bleibt	blieb	bliebe	geblieben
§63	braten	brät	briet	briete	gebraten
§64	brechen	bricht	brach	bräche	gebrochen
§65	bringen	bringt	brachte	brächte	gebracht
§66	denken	denkt	dachte	dächte	gedacht
§67	dreschen	drischt	drosch (drasch)	drösche (dräsche)	gedroschen
§68	dünken	dünkt (deucht)	dünkte (deuchte)	dünkte (deuchte)	gedünkt (gedeucht)

15a

	INFINITIVE	3D SG PRESENT INDICATIVE	IMPERFECT INDICATIVE	IMPERFECT SUBJUNCTIVE	PAST PARTICIPLE
§69	dürfen	darf	durfte	dürfte	gedurft (dürfen)
§70	essen	ißt	aß	äße	gegessen
§71	fahren	fährt	fuhr	führe	gefahren
§72	fallen	fällt	fiel	fiele	gefallen
§73	fangen	fängt	fing	finge	gefangen
§74	fechten	ficht	focht	föchte	gefochten
§75	fliehen	flieht	floh	flöhe	geflohen
§76	fließen	fließt	floß	flösse	geflossen
§77	frieren	friert	fror	fröre	gefroren
§78	gären	gärt	gor	göre	gegoren
§79	gebären	gebiert	gebar	gebäre	geboren
§80	geben	gibt	gab	gäbe	gegeben
§81	gedeihen	gedeiht	gedieh	gediehe	gediehen
§82	gehen	geht	ging	ginge	gegangen
§83	gelten	gilt	galt	gälte (gölte)	gegolten
§84	genesen	genest	genas	genäse	genesen
§85	gleichen	gleicht	glich	gliche	geglichen
§86	gleiten	gleitet	glitt	glitte	geglitten
§87	graben	gräbt	grub	grübe	gegraben
§88	greifen	greift	griff	griffe	gegriffen
§89	haben	hat	hatte	hätte	gehabt
§90	halten	hält	hielt	hielte	gehalten

	INFINITIVE	3D SG PRESENT INDICATIVE	IMPERFECT INDICATIVE	IMPERFECT SUBJUNCTIVE	PAST PARTICIPLE
§91	handeln	handelt	handelte	handelte	gehandelt
§92	hängen	hängt	hing	hinge	gehangen
§93	hauen	haut	hieb	hiebe	gehauen
§94	heben	hebt	hob	höbe	gehoben
§95	heißen	heißt	hieß	hieße	geheißen
§96	helfen	hilft	half	hälfe (hülfe)	geholfen
§97	kennen	kennt	kannte	kennte	gekannt
§98	kiesen	kiest	kor	köre	gekoren
§99	kommen	kommt	kam	käme	gekommen
§100	können	kann	konnte	könnte	gekonnt (können)
§101	kreischen	kreischt	kreischte (krisch)	kreischte (krische)	gekreischt (gekrischen)
§102	kriechen	kriecht	kroch	kröche	gekrochen
§103	laden	lädt	lud	lüde	geladen
§104	lassen	läßt	ließ	ließe	gelassen
§105	laufen	läuft	lief	liefe	gelaufen
§106	leiden	leidet	litt	litte	gelitten
§107	lesen	liest	las	läse	gelesen
§108	liegen	liegt	lag	läge	gelegen
§109	loben	lobt	lobte	lobte	gelobt
§110	löschen	lischt	losch	lösche	geloschen
§111	lügen	lügt	log	löge	gelogen

17a

§	INFINITIVE	3D SG PRESENT INDICATIVE	IMPERFECT INDICATIVE	IMPERFECT SUBJUNCTIVE	PAST PARTICIPLE
§112	meiden	meidet	mied	miede	gemieden
§113	melken	melkt	molk	mölke	gemolken
§114	mögen	mag	mochte	möchte	gemocht (mögen)
§115	müssen	muß	mußte	müßte	gemußt (müssen)
§116	nehmen	nimmt	nahm	nähme	genommen
§117	pflegen	pflegt	pflog	pflöge	gepflogen
§118	preisen	preist	pries	priese	gepriesen
§119	quellen	quillt	quoll	quölle	gequollen
§120	reden	redet	redete	redete	geredet
§121	rinnen	rinnt	rann	ränne (rönne)	geronnen
§122	rufen	ruft	rief	riefe	gerufen
§123	salzen	salzt	salzte	salzte	gesalzen
§124	saufen	säuft	soff	söffe	gesoffen
§125	saugen	saugt	sog	söge	gesogen
§126	schaffen	schafft	schuf	schüfe	geschaffen
§127	schallen	schallt	scholl	schölle	geschollen
§128	scheinen	scheint	schien	schiene	geschienen
§129	scheren	schert (schiert)	schor	schöre	geschoren
§130	schieben	schiebt	schob	schöbe	geschoben
§131	schlafen	schläft	schlief	schliefe	geschlafen

	INFINITIVE	3D SG PRESENT INDICATIVE	IMPERFECT INDICATIVE	IMPERFECT SUBJUNCTIVE	PAST PARTICIPLE
§132	schlagen	schlägt	schlug	schlüge	geschlagen
§133	schmelzen	schmilzt	schmolz	schmölze	geschmolzen
§134	schrecken	schrickt	schrak	schräke	geschrocken
§135	schreien	schreit	schrie	schriee	geschrie(e)n
§136	schwimmen	schwimmt	schwamm	schwämme (schwömme)	geschwommen
§137	schwören	schwört	schwur (schwor)	schwüre	geschworen
§138	sehen	sieht	sah	sähe	gesehen
§139	sein	ist	war	wäre	gewesen
§140	senden	sendet	sandte	sendete	gesandt
§141	sieden	siedet	sott	sötte	gesotten
§142	singen	singt	sang	sänge	gesungen
§143	sinken	sinkt	sank	sänke	gesunken
§144	sitzen	sitzt	saß	säße	gesessen
§145	sollen	soll	sollte	sollte	gesollt (sollen)
§146	stehen	steht	stand	stände (stünde)	gestanden
§147	stehlen	stiehlt	stahl	stähle (stöhle)	gestohlen
§148	steigen	steigt	stieg	stiege	gestiegen
§149	sterben	stirbt	starb	stürbe	gestorben
§150	stoßen	stößt	stieß	stieße	gestoßen

19a

	INFINITIVE	3D SG PRESENT INDICATIVE	IMPERFECT INDICATIVE	IMPERFECT SUBJUNCTIVE	PAST PARTICIPLE
§151	treffen	trifft	traf	träfe	getroffen
§152	treten	tritt	trat	träte	getreten
§153	triefen	trieft	troff	tröffe	getroffen
§154	tun	tut	tat	täte	getan
§155	wachsen	wächst	wuchs	wüchse	gewachsen
§156	wägen	wiegt	wog	wöge	gewogen
§157	warten	wartet	wartete	wartete	gewartet
§158	waschen	wäscht	wusch	wüsche	gewaschen
§159	werden	wird	wurde (ward)	würde	geworden (worden)
§160	werfen	wirft	warf	würfe	geworfen
§161	wissen	weiß	wußte	wüßte	gewußt
§162	wollen	will	wollte	wollte	gewollt (wollen)
§163	ziehen	zieht	zog	zöge	gezogen
§164	klimmen	klimmt	klomm	klömme	geklommen
§165	küren	kürt	kor	köre	gekoren
§166	schinden	schindet	schund	schünde	geschunden

20a

Die Aussprache des Englischen

Die nachstehenden Lautzeichen bezeichnen fast alle Laute der englischen Sprache:

VOKALE		
LAUTZEICHEN	**UNGEFÄHRER LAUT**	**BEISPIEL**
[æ]	Offener als ä in *hätte*	**hat** [hæt]
[ɑ]	Wie *a* in *Vater* Wie *a* in *Mann*	**father** [ˈfɑðər] **proper** [ˈprɑpər]
[ɛ]	Wie *e* in *Fett*	**met** [mɛt]
[e]	Offener als *eej* in *Seejungfrau*	**fate** [fet] **they** [ðe]
[ə]	Wie *e* in *finden*	**haven** [ˈhevən] **pardon** [ˈpɑrdən]
[i]	Wie *ie* in *sie*	**she** [ʃi] **machine** [məˈʃin]
[ɪ]	Offener als *i* in *bitte*	**fit** [fɪt] **beer** [bɪr]
[o]	Offenes *o* mit anschließendem kurzem (halbvokalischem) *u*	**nose** [noz] **road** [rod] **row** [ro]
[ɔ]	Wie *o* in *oft*	**bought** [bɔt] **law** [lɔ]
[ʌ]	Wie *er* in *jeder* (umgangssprachlich)	**cup** [kʌp] **come** [kʌm] **mother** [ˈmʌðər]
[ʊ]	Wie *u* in *Fluß*	**pull** [pʊl] **book** [bʊk] **wolf** [wʊlf]
[u]	Wie *u* in *Fluß*	**move** [muv] **tomb** [tum]

DIPHTHONGE		
LAUTZEICHEN	**UNGEFÄHRER LAUT**	**BEISPIEL**
[aɪ]	Wie *ei* in *nein*	**night** [naɪt] **eye** [aɪ]
[aʊ]	Wie *au* in *Haus*	**found** [faʊnd] **cow** [kaʊ]
[ɔɪ]	Wie *eu* in *heute*	**voice** [vɔɪs] **oil** [ɔɪl]

KONSONANTEN		
LAUTZEICHEN	**UNGEFÄHRER LAUT**	**BEISPIEL**
[b]	Wie *b* in *bin*	**bed** [bɛd] **robber** [ˈrɑbər]

21a

LAUTZEICHEN	UNGEFÄHRER LAUT	BEISPIEL
[d]	Wie *d* in *du*	dead [dɛd] add [æd]
[dʒ]	Wie *dsch* in *Dschungel*	gem [dʒɛm] jail [dʒel]
[ð]	*d* als Reibelaut ausgesprochen	this [ðɪs] Father ['fɑðər]
[f]	Wie *f* in *fett*	face [fes] phone [fon]
[g]	Wie *g* in *gehen*	go [go] get [gɛt]
[h]	Wie *h* in *Haus*	hot [hɑt] alcohol ['ælkə‚hɔl]
[j]	Wie *j* in *ja*	yes [jɛs] unit ['junɪt]
[k]	Wie *k* in *kann*	cat [kæt] chord [kɔrd] kill [kɪl]
[l]	Wie *l* in *lang*, aber mit angehobenem Zungenrücken	late [let] allow [ə'lau]
[m]	Wie *m* in *mehr*	more [mor] command [kə'mænd]
[n]	Wie *n* in *Nest*	nest [nɛst] manner ['mænər]
[ŋ]	Wie *ng* in *singen*	king [kɪŋ] conquer ['kɑŋkər]
[p]	Wie *p* in *Pech*	pen [pɛn] cap [kæp]
[r]	Im Gegensatz zum deutschen gerollten Zungenspitzen– oder Zäpfchen–r, ist das englische *r* mit retroflexer Zungenstellung und gerundeten Lippen zu artikulieren.	run [rʌn] far [far] art [ɑrt] carry ['kæri]
[s]	Wie *s* in *es*	send [sɛnd] cellar ['sɛlər]
[ʃ]	Wie *sch* in *Schule*	shall [ʃæl] machine [mə'ʃin] nation ['neʃən]
[t]	Wie *t* in *Tee*	ten [tɛn] dropped [drɑpt]
[tʃ]	Wie *tsch* in *deutsch*	child [tʃaɪld] much [mʌtʃ] nature ['netʃər]
[θ]	Ist als stimmloser linguadentaler Lispellaut zu artikulieren	think [θɪŋk] truth [truθ]
[v]	Wie *w* in *was*	vest [vɛst] over ['ovər] of [ɑv]
[w]	Ist als Halbvokal zu artikulieren	work [wʌrk] tweed [twid] queen [kwin]
[z]	Ist stimmhaft zu artikulieren wie *s* in *so*	zeal [zil] busy ['bɪzi] his [hɪz] winds [wɪndz]
[ʒ]	Wie *j* in *Jalousie*	azure ['ɛʒər] measure ['mɛʒər]

Aussprache der zusammengesetzten Wörter

Im englisch-deutschen Teil dieses Wörterbuches ist die Aussprache aller einfachen englischen Wörter in einer Neufassung der Lautzeichen des Internationalen Phonetischen Alphabets in eckigen Klammern angegeben.

Außer den mit Präfixen, Suffixen und Wortbildungselementen gebildeten Zusammensetzungen gibt es im Englischen drei Arten von zusammengesetzten Wörtern: (1) zusammengeschriebene, z.B. **bookcase** Bücherregal, (2) mit Bindestrich geschriebene, z.B. **short-circuit** kurzschließen, und (3) getrennt geschriebene, z.B. **post card** Postkarte. Die Aussprache der englischen zusammengesetzten Wörter ist nicht angegeben, sofern die Aussprache der Bestandteile an der Stelle angegeben ist, wo sie als selbständige Stichwörter erscheinen; angegeben ist jedoch die Betonung durch Haupt- und Nebentonakzent und zwar jeweils am Ende der betonten Silben, z.B. **book′case′**, **short′-cir′cuit**, **post′ card′**.

In Hauptwörtern, in denen der Nebenton auf den Bestandteilen –**man** und –**men** liegt, wird der Vokal dieser Bestandteile wie in den Wörtern **man** und **men** ausgesprochen, z.B. **mailman** [ˈmel͵mæn] und **mailmen** [ˈmel͵men]. In Hauptwörtern, in denen diese Bestandteile unbetont ausgesprochen werden, wird der Vokal beider Bestandteile als schwa ausgesprochen, z.B. **policeman** [pəˈlismən] und **policemen** [pəˈlismən]. Es gibt Hauptwörter, in denen diese Bestandteile entweder mit dem Nebenton oder unbetont ausgesprochen werden, z.B. **doorman** [ˈdor͵mæn] oder [ˈdormən] und **doormen** [ˈdor͵men] oder [ˈdormən]. In diesem Wörterbuch ist die Lautschrift für diese Wörter nicht angegeben, sofern sie für den ersten Bestandteil dort angeführt ist, wo er als Stichwort erscheint; angegeben sind jedoch Haupt- und Nebenton:

> **mail′man** s (–**men′**)
> **police′man** s (–**men**)
> **door′man′** & **door′man** s (–**men′** & –**men**)

Aussprache des Partizip Perfekt

Bei Wörtern, die auf –**ed** (oder –**d** nach stummem e) enden und nach den nachstehenden Regeln ausgesprochen werden, ist die Aussprache in diesem Wörterbuch nicht angegeben, sofern sie für die endungslose Form dort angegeben ist, wo diese als Stichwort erscheint. Die Doppelschreibung der Schlußkonsonanten nach einfachem betonten Vokal hat keinen Einfluß auf die Aussprache der Endung –**ed**.

Die Endung –**ed** (oder –**d** nach stummen e) der Vergangenheit, des Partizip Perfekt und gewisser Adjektive hat drei verschiedene Aussprachen je nach dem Klang des Konsonanten am Stammende.

1) Wenn der Stamm auf einen stimmhaften Konsonanten mit Ausnahme von [d] ausgeht, nämlich [b], [g], [l], [m], [n], [ŋ], [r], [v], [z], [ʒ], oder auf einen Vokal, wird –**ed** als [d] ausgesprochen.

KLANG DES STAMMENDES	INFINITIV	VERGANGENHEIT UND PARTIZIP PERFEKT
[b]	ebb [ɛb]	ebbed [ɛbd]
	rob [rɑb]	robbed [rɑbd]
	robe [rob]	robed [robd]
[g]	egg [ɛg]	egged [ɛgd]
	sag [sæg]	sagged [sægd]
[l]	mail [mel]	mailed [meld]
	scale [skel]	scaled [skeld]
[m]	storm [stɔrm]	stormed [stɔrmd]
	bomb [bɑm]	bombed [bɑmd]
	name [nem]	named [nemd]
[n]	tan [tæn]	tanned [tænd]
	sign [saɪn]	signed [saɪnd]
	mine [maɪn]	mined [maɪnd]
[ŋ]	hang [hæŋ]	hanged [hæŋd]
[r]	fear [fɪr]	feared [fɪrd]
	care [ker]	cared [kerd]
[v]	rev [rɛv]	revved [rɛvd]
	save [sev]	saved [sevd]
[z]	buzz [bʌz]	buzzed [bʌzd]
[ð]	smooth [smuð]	smoothed [smuðd]
	bathe [beð]	bathed [beðd]
[ʒ]	massage [məˈsɑʒ]	massaged [məˈsɑʒd]
[dʒ]	page [pedʒ]	paged [pedʒd]
Klang des Vokals	key [ki]	keyed [kid]
	sigh [saɪ]	sighed [saɪd]
	paw [pɔ]	pawed [pɔd]

23a

2) Wenn der Stamm auf einen stimmlosen Konsonanten mit Ausnahme von [t] ausgeht, nämlich: [f], [k], [p], [s], [θ], [ʃ] oder [tʃ], wird –ed als [t] ausgesprochen.

KLANG DES STAMMENDES	INFINITIV	VERGANGENHEIT UND PARTIZIP PERFEKT
[f]	loaf [lof] knife [naɪf]	loafed [loft] knifed [naɪft]
[k]	back [bæk] bake [bek]	backed [bækt] baked [bekt]
[p]	cap [kæp] wipe [waɪp]	capped [kæpt] wiped [waɪpt]
[s]	hiss [hɪs] mix [mɪks]	hissed [hɪst] mixed [mɪkst]
[θ]	lath [læθ]	lathed [læθt]
[ʃ]	mash [mæʃ]	mashed [mæʃt]
[tʃ]	match [mætʃ]	matched [mætʃt]

3) Wenn der Stamm auf einen Dentallaut ausgeht, nämlich: [t] oder [d], wird –ed als [ɪd] oder [əd] ausgesprochen.

KLANG DES STAMMENDES	INFINITIV	VERGANGENHEIT UND PARTIZIP PERFEKT
[t]	wait [wet] mate [met]	waited ['wetɪd] mated ['metɪd]
[d]	mend [mend] wade [wed]	mended ['mendɪd] waded ['wedɪd]

Es ist zu beachten, daß die Doppelschreibung des Schlußkonsonanten nach einem einfachen betonten Vokal die Aussprache der Endung –ed nicht beeinflußt: batted ['bætɪd], dropped [drɑpt], robbed [rɑbd].

Diese Regeln gelten auch für zusammengesetzte Adjektive, die auf –ed enden. Für diese Adjektive ist nur die Betonung angegeben, sofern die Aussprache der beiden Bestandteile ohne die Endung –ed dort angegeben ist, wo sie als Stichwörter erscheinen, z.B. o'pen-mind'ed.

Es ist jedoch zu beachten, daß bei manchen Adjektiven, deren Stamm auf einen anderen Konsonanten als [d] oder [t] ausgeht, das –ed als [ɪd] ausgesprochen wird; in diesem Fall ist die volle Aussprache in phonetischer Umschrift angegeben, z.B. blessed ['blesɪd], crabbed ['kræbɪd].

PART TWO

English-German

ENGLISH—GERMAN

A

A, a [e] *s* erster Buchstabe des englischen Alphabets; (mus) A *n*; **A flat** As *n*, **A sharp** Ais *n*

a [eɪ, ə] *indef art* ein ‖ *prep* pro; **once a year** einmal im Jahr

abandon [ə'bændən] *s*—**with a.** rückhaltlos ‖ *tr* (*forsake*) verlassen; (*give up*) aufgeben; (*a child*) aussetzen; (*a position*) (mil) überlassen; **a. oneself to** sich ergeben (*dat*)

abase [ə'bes] *tr* demütigen

abasement [ə'besmənt] *s* Demütigung *f*

abashed [ə'bæʃt] *adj* fassungslos

abate [ə'bet] *tr* mäßigen ‖ *intr* nachlassen

abbess ['æbɪs] *s* Äbtissin *f*

abbey ['æbi] *s* Abtei *f*

abbot ['æbət] *s* Abt *m*

abbreviate [ə'brivɪ,et] *tr* abkürzen

abbreviation [ə,brivɪ'eʃən] *s* Abkürzung *f*

ABC's [,e,bi'siz] *spl* Abc *n*

abdicate ['æbdɪ,ket] *tr* niederlegen; (*a right, claim*) verzichten auf (*acc*) ‖ *intr* abdanken

abdomen ['æbdəmən] *s* Unterleib *m*

abdominal [æb'dɑmɪnəl] *adj* Unterleibs-

abduct [æb'dʌkt] *tr* entführen

abet [ə'bet] *v* (*pret & pp* **abetted;** *ger* **abetting**) *tr* (*a person*) aufhetzen; (*a crime*) Vorschub leisten (*dat*)

abeyance [ə'be-əns] *s*—**in a.** in der Schwebe

ab·hor [æb'hɔr] *v* (*pret & pp* **-horred;** *ger* **-horring**) *tr* verabscheuen

abhorrent [æb'hɔrənt] *adj* verhaßt

abide [ə'baɪd] *v* (*pret & pp* **abode** [ə'bod] **& abided**) *intr*—**a. by** (*an agreement*) sich halten an (*acc*); (*a promise*) halten

ability [ə'bɪlɪti] *s* Fähigkeit *f*; **to the best of one's a.** nach bestem Vermögen

abject [æb'dʒekt] *adj* (*servile*) unterwürfig; (*poverty*) äußerst

ablative ['æblətɪv] *s* Ablativ *m*

ablaze [ə'blez] *adj* in Flammen; (**with**) glänzend (vor *dat*); (*excited*) (**with**) erregt (vor *dat*)

able ['ebəl] *adj* fähig, tüchtig; **be a. to** (*inf*) können (*inf*)

able-bodied ['ebəl'bɑdid] *adj* kräftig; (mil) wehrfähig; **a. seaman** Vollmatrose *m*

ably ['ebli] *adv* mit Geschick

abnormal [æb'nɔrməl] *adj* abnorm

abnormality [,æbnɔr'mælɪti] *s* Ungewöhnlichkeit *f*; (pathol) Mißbildung *f*

abnor'mal psychol'ogy *s* Psychopathologie *f*

aboard [ə'bord] *adv* an Bord; **all a.!** (*a ship*) alles an Bord! (*a bus, plane, train*) alles einsteigen! ‖ *prep* (*a ship*) an Bord (*genit*); (*a bus, train*) in (*dat*)

abode [ə'bod] *s* Wohnsitz *m*

abolish [ə'bɑlɪʃ] *tr* aufheben, abschaffen

abominable [ə'bɑmɪnəbəl] *adj* abscheulich

aborigines [,æbə'rɪdʒɪ,niz] *spl* Ureinwohner *pl*, Urvolk *n*

abort [ə'bɔrt] *tr* (rok) vorzeitig zur Explosion bringen ‖ *intr* fehlgebären; (fig) fehlschlagen

abortion [ə'bɔrʃən] *s* Abtreibung *f*

abortive [ə'bɔrtɪv] *adj* (fig) mißlungen; **prove a.** fehlschlagen

abound [ə'baund] *intr* reichlich vorhanden sein; **a. in** reich sein an (*dat*)

about [ə'baut] *adv* umher, herum; (*approximately*) ungefähr, etwa; **be a. to** (*inf*) im Begriff sein zu (*inf*) ‖ *prep* (*around*) um (*acc*); (*concerning*) über (*acc*); (*approximately at*) gegen (*acc*)

about' face' *interj* kehrt!

about'-face' *s*—**do an a.** (fig) umschwenken; **complete a.** (fig) völliger Umschwung *m*

above [ə'bʌv] *adj* obig ‖ *adv* oben, droben ‖ *prep* (*position*) über (*dat*); (*direction*) über (*acc*); (*physically*) oberhalb (*genit*); **a. all** vor allem

above'board' *adj & adv* ehrlich, redlich

above'-men'tioned *adj* obenerwähnt, obig

abrasion [ə'breʒən] *s* Abschleifen *n*; (*of the skin*) Abschürfung *f*

abrasive [ə'bresɪv] *adj* abschleifend; (*character*) auf die Nerven gehend ‖ *s* Schleifmittel *n*

abreast [ə'brest] *adj & adv* nebeneinander; **keep a. of** Schritt halten mit

abridge [ə'brɪdʒ] *tr* verkürzen

abridgement [ə'brɪdʒmənt] *s* Verkürzung *f*

abroad [ə'brɔd] *adv* im Ausland; (*direction*) ins Ausland; (*out of doors*) draußen

abrogate ['æbrə,get] *tr* abschaffen

abrupt [ə'brʌpt] *adj* (*sudden*) jäh; (*curt*) schroff; (*change*) unvermittelt; (*style*) abgerissen

abscess ['æbses] *s* Geschwür *n*, Abszeß *m*

abscond [æb'skɑnd] *intr* (**with**) durchgehen (mit)

absence ['æbsəns] *s* Abwesenheit *f*; (*lack*) Mangel *m*; **in the a. of** in Ermangelung von (or *genit*)

ab′sence without′ leave′ s unerlaubte Entfernung f von der Truppe

absent [′æbsənt] adj abwesend; **be a. fehlen** ‖ [æb′sent] tr—a. **oneself** (stay away) fernbleiben; (go away) sich entfernen

absentee [ˌæbsən′ti] s Abwesende mf

ab′sent-mind′ed adj geistesabwesend

absolute [′æbsəˌlut] adj absolut

absolutely [′æbsəˌlutlɪ] adv absolut, völlig ‖ [ˌæbsə′lutli] adv (coll) ganz bestimmt, jawohl; a. not! keine Rede!

absolve [æb′sɑlv] tr (from sin, an obligation) lossprechen; (sins) vergeben

absorb [æb′sɔrb] tr aufsaugen; (a shock) dämpfen; (engross) ganz in Anspruch nehmen; **be absorbed in** vertieft sein in (acc)

absorbent [æb′sɔrbənt] adj aufsaugend

absor′bent cot′ton s Verbandswatte f

absorb′ing adj (fig) packend

abstain [æb′sten] intr (from) sich enthalten (genit); (parl) sich der Stimme enthalten

abstention [æb′stenʃən] s (from) Enthaltung f (von); (parl) Stimmenthaltung f

abstinence [′æbstɪnəns] s Enthaltsamkeit f; (from) Enthaltung f (von)

abstinent [′æbstɪnənt] adj enthaltsam

abstract [′æbstrækt] adj abstrakt ‖ s (summary) Abriß m; in the a. an und für sich (betrachtet) ‖ [æb′strækt] tr (the general from the specific) abstrahieren; (summarize) kurz zusammenfassen; (purloin) entwenden

abstruse [æb′strus] adj dunkel

absurd [æb′sʌrd] adj unsinnig

absurdity [æb′sʌrdɪtɪ] s Unsinn m

abundance [ə′bʌndəns] s (of) Fülle f (von), Überfluß m (an dat, von)

abundant [ə′bʌndənt] adj reichlich; a. in reich an (dat)

abuse [ə′bjus] s (misuse) Mißbrauch m; (insult) Beschimpfung f; (physical ill-treatment) Mißhandlung f ‖ [ə′bjuz] tr mißbrauchen; (insult) beschimpfen; (ill-treat) mißhandeln; (a girl) schänden

abusive [ə′bjusɪv] adj mißbräuchlich; (treatment) beleidigend; a. language Schimpfworte pl; **become a.** ausfällig werden

abut [ə′bʌt] v (pret & pp abutted; ger abutting) intr—a. on grenzen an (acc)

abutment [ə′bʌtmənt] s (of arch) Strebepfeiler m; (of bridge) Widerlager n

abyss [ə′bɪs] s Abgrund m

academic [ˌækə′demɪk] adj akademisch

academ′ic gown′ s Talar m

academy [ə′kædəmi] s Akademie f

accede [æk′sid] intr beistimmen; a. to (s.o.'s wishes) gewähren; (an agreement) beitreten (dat); a. to the throne den Thron besteigen

accelerate [æk′seləˌret] tr & intr beschleunigen

accelerator [æk′seləˌretər] s Gashebel m

accent [′æksent] s (stress) Betonung f; (peculiar pronunciation) Akzent m ‖ [æk′sent] tr betonen

ac′cent mark′ s Tonzeichen n, Akzent m

accentuate [æk′sentʃuˌet] tr betonen

accept [æk′sept] tr annehmen; (one's fate, blame) auf sich [acc] nehmen; (put up with) hinnehmen; (recognize) anerkennen

acceptable [æk′septəbəl] adj annehmbar; (pleasing) angenehm; (welcome) willkommen

acceptance [æk′septəns] s Annahme f; (recognition) Anerkennung f

access [′ækses] s Zugang m; (to a person) Zutritt m; (data proc) Zugriff m

accessible [æk′sesɪbəl] adj (to) zugänglich (für)

accession [æk′seʃən] s (to an office) Antritt m; a. to the throne Thronbesteigung f

accessory [æk′sesəri] adj (subordinate) untergeordnet; (additional) zusätzlich ‖ s Zubehörteil n; (to a crime) Teilnehmer –in mf; (after the fact) Begünstiger –in mf; (before the fact) Anstifter –in mf

ac′cess road′ s Zufahrtsstraße f; (on a turnpike) Zubringerstraße f

accident [′æksɪdənt] s (mishap) Unfall m; (chance) Zufall m; **by a.** zufälligerweise; **have an a.** verunglücken

accidental [ˌæksɪ′dentəl] adj zufällig; a. death Unfalltod m ‖ s (mus) Versetzungszeichen n

acclaim [ə′klem] s Beifall m ‖ tr (e.g., as king) begrüßen, akklamieren

acclamation [ˌæklə′meʃən] s Beifall m

acclimate [′æklɪˌmet] tr akklimatisieren ‖ intr (to) sich gewöhnen (an acc)

accommodate [ə′kɑməˌdet] tr (oblige) aushelfen (dat); (have room for) Platz haben für

accom′modating adj gefällig

accommodation [əˌkɑmə′deʃən] s (convenience) Annehmlichkeit f; (adaptation, adjustment) Anpassung f; (willingness to please) Gefälligkeit f; (compromise) Übereinkommen n; **accommodations** (lodgings) Unterkunft f

accompaniment [ə′kʌmpənɪmənt] s Begleitung f

accompanist [ə′kʌmpənɪst] s Begleiter –in mf

accompa·ny [ə′kʌmpəni] v (pret & pp -nied) tr begleiten

accomplice [ə′kɑmplɪs] m Mitschuldige mf

accomplish [ə′kɑmplɪʃ] tr (a task) vollenden; (a goal) erreichen

accom′plished adj (skilled) ausgezeichnet

accomplishment [ə′kɑmplɪʃmənt] s (completion) Vollendung f; (achievement) Leistung f

accord [ə′kɔrd] s Übereinstimmung f; **in a. with** übereinstimmend mit; **of**

one's own a. aus eigenem Antriebe
|| tr gewähren || intr übereinstimmen
accordingly [ə'kɔrdɪŋli] adv demgemäß
accord'ing to' prep gemäß (dat), laut
(genit or dat), nach (dat)
accordion [ə'kɔrdɪ·ən] s Akkordeon n
accost [ə'kɔst] tr ansprechen
account [ə'kaunt] s Rechnung f; (narrative) Erzählung f; (report) Bericht
m; (importance) Bedeutung f; (com)
Konto n; **by all accounts** nach allem,
was man hört; **call to a.** zur Rechenschaft ziehen; **on a. of** wegen; **on no
a.** auf keinen Fall; **render an a. of
s.th. to s.o.** j-m Rechenschaft von
etw ablegen; **settle accounts with**
(coll) abrechnen mit; **take into a.** in
Betracht ziehen
accountable [ə'kauntəbəl] adj (explicable) erklärlich; (responsible) (for)
verantwortlich (für)
accountant [ə'kauntənt] s Rechnungsführer –in mf, Buchhalter –in mf
account'ing s Rechnungswesen n
accouterments [ə'kutərmənts] spl Ausrüstung f
accredit [ə'kredɪt] tr (e.g., an ambassador) beglaubigen; (a school) bestätigen; (a story) als wahr anerkennen; (give credit for) gutschreiben
accrue [ə'kru] v (pret & pp accrued;
ger accruing) tr freisprechen
of interest) auflaufen || intr sich
anhäufen
accumulation [ə,kjumjə'leʃən] s Anhäufung f
accuracy ['ækjərəsi] s Genauigkeit f
accurate ['ækjərɪt] adj genau
accursed [ə'kʌrsɪd], [ə'kʌrst] adj verwünscht
accusation [,ækjə'zeʃən] s Anschuldigung f; (jur) Anklage f
accusative [ə'kjuzətɪv] s Akkusativ m
accuse [ə'kjuz] tr (of) beschuldigen
(genit); (jur) (of) anklagen (wegen)
accustom [ə'kʌstəm] tr (to) gewöhnen
(an acc); **become accustomed to** sich
gewöhnen an (acc)
ace [es] s (aer, cards) As n
acetate ['æsɪ,tet] s Azetat n; (tex)
Azetatseide f
ace'tic ac'id [ə'sitɪk] s Essigsäure f
acetone ['æsɪ,ton] s Azeton n
acet'ylene torch' [ə'setɪ,lin] s Schweißbrenner m
ache [ek] s Schmerz m || intr schmerzen; **a. for** (coll) sich sehnen nach
achieve [ə't∫iv] tr erlangen; (success)
erzielen; (a goal) erreichen
achievement [ə't∫ivmənt] s (something
accomplished) Leistung f; (great
deed) Großtat f; (heroic deed)
Heldentat f; (of one's object) Erreichung f
achieve'ment test' s Leistungsprüfung f
Achil'les' ten'don [ə'kɪlis] s Achillessehne f
acid ['æsɪd] adj sauer || s Säure f
acidity [ə'sɪdɪti] s Säure f, Schärfe f;
(of the stomach) Magensäure f
ac'id test' s (fig) Feuerprobe f
acidy ['æsɪdi] adj säuerlich, säurig
acknowledge [æk'nɑlɪdʒ] tr anerken-

nen; (admit) zugeben; (receipt) bestätigen
acknowledgment [æk'nɑlɪdʒmənt] s
Anerkennung f; (e.g., of a letter)
Bestätigung f
acme ['ækmi] s Höhepunkt m
acne ['ækni] s (pathol) Akne f
acolyte ['ækə,laɪt] s Ministrant m
acorn ['ekɔrn] s Eichel f
acoustic(al) [ə'kustɪk(əl)] adj akustisch, Gehör–, Hör–
acous'tical tile' s Dämmplatte f
acoustics [ə'kustɪks] s & spl Akustik f
acquaint [ə'kwent] tr—a. s.o. with
s.th. j-n mit etw bekanntmachen,
j-m etw mitteilen; **be acquainted
with** kennen; **get acquainted with**
kennenlernen
acquaintance [ə'kwentəns] s Bekanntschaft f; (person) Bekannte mf
acquiesce [,ækwɪ'es] intr (in) einwilligen (in acc)
acquiescence [,ækwɪ'esəns] s (in) Einwilligung f (in acc)
acquire [ə'kwaɪr] tr erwerben, sich
[dat] anschaffen; **a. a taste for** Geschmack gewinnen an (dat)
acquisition [,ækwɪ'zɪʃən] s Anschaffung f
acquisitive [ə'kwɪzɪtɪv] adj gewinnsüchtig
acquit [ə'kwɪt] v (pret & pp acquitted;
ger acquitting) tr freisprechen
acquittal [ə'kwɪtəl] s Freispruch m
acre ['ekər] s Acre m
acreage ['ekərɪdʒ] s Fläche f
acrid ['ækrɪd] adj beißend, scharf
acrobat ['ækrə,bæt] s Akrobat –in mf
acrobatic [,ækrə'bætɪk] adj akrobatisch || **acrobatics** spl Akrobatik f;
(aer) Kunstflug m
acronym ['ækrənɪm] s Akronym n
across [ə'krɔs] adv herüber, hinüber;
a. from gegenüber (dat); **ten feet a.**
zehn Fuß im Durchmesser || prep
(quer) über (acc); (on the other side
of) jenseits (genit); **come a.** (a person) treffen; (a thing) stoßen auf
(acc); **come a. with it!** (say it!) heraus damit!; (give it!) her damit!
across'-the-board' adj allgemein
acrostic [ə'krɔstɪk] s Akrostichon n
act [ækt] s Tat f, Handlung f; (coll)
Theater n; (jur) Gesetz n; (telv)
Nummer f; (theat) Akt m, Aufzug
m; **catch in the act** auf frischer Tat
ertappen || tr spielen; || intr (take
action) handeln; (function) wirken;
(behave) (like) sich benehmen (wie);
(theat & fig) Theater spielen; **act as**
dienen als; **act as if** so tun, als ob;
act on (follow) befolgen; (affect)
(ein)wirken auf (acc)
act'ing adj stellvertretend; (theat)
Bühnen– || s (as an art) Schauspielkunst f
action ['ækʃən] s Tätigkeit f, Tat f;
(effect) Wirkung f; (jur) Klage f;
(mil) Gefecht n; (tech) Wirkungsweise f; **go into a.** eingreifen; **put
out of a.** (mil) außer Gefecht setzen;
(tech) außer Betrieb setzen; **see a.**
(mil) an der Front kämpfen

activate ['æktı‚vet] *tr* aktivieren; (mil) aufstellen

active ['æktıv] *adj* tätig; (*member*) ordentlich; (gram, mil) aktiv

ac'tive voice' *s* Tätigkeitsform *f*

activist ['æktıvıst] *s* Aktivist –in *mf*

activity [æk'tıvıtı] *s* Tätigkeit *f*

act' of God' *s* höhere Gewalt *f*

act' of war' *s* Angriffshandlung *f*

actor ['æktər] *s* Schauspieler *m*

actress ['æktrıs] *s* Schauspielerin *f*

actual ['ækt∫u-əl] *adj* wirklich

actually ['ækt∫u-əlı] *adv* (*really*) wirklich; (*as a matter of fact*) eigentlich

actuary ['ækt∫u‚erı] *s* Aktuar –in *mf*

actuate ['ækt∫u‚et] *tr* in Bewegung setzen; (*incite*) antreiben

acumen [ə'kjumən] *s* Scharfsinn *m*

acupuncture ['ækjə‚pʌŋkt∫ər] *s* Akupunktur *f*

acute [ə'kjut] *adj* (*stage, appendicitis*) akut; (*pain*) scharf; (*need*) vordringlich; (*vision*) scharf; (*hearing*) fein; (*problem*) brennend; (*shortage*) bedenklich; (*angle*) spitz

A.D. *abbr* n. Chr. (*nach Christus*)

ad [æd] *s* (coll) Anzeige *f*; **put an ad in the papers** inserieren

adage ['ædıdʒ] *s* Sprichwort *n*

adamant ['ædəmənt] *adj* unnachgiebig

Ad'am's ap'ple ['ædəmz] *s* Adamsapfel *m*

adapt [ə'dæpt] *tr* (**to**) anpassen (*dat* or an *acc*); **a. to the stage** für die Bühne bearbeiten; **a. to the screen** verfilmen ‖ *intr* sich anpassen

adaptation [‚ædæp'te∫ən] *s* (*adjustment*) (**to**) Anpassung *f* (an *acc*); (*reworking, rewriting*) (**for**) Bearbeitung *f* (für)

adapter [ə'dæptər] *s* Zwischenstück *n*; (elec) Zwischenstecker *m*

add [æd] *tr* hinzufügen; (math) addieren; **add** (*e.g.*, *10%*) **to the price** auf den Preis aufschlagen; **add up** zusammenrechnen ‖ *intr* (math) addieren; **add to** (*in number*) vermehren; (*in size*) vergrößern; **add up** (coll) stimmen; **add up to** betragen

adder ['ædər] *s* Natter *f*, Otter *f*

addict ['ædıkt] *s* Süchtige *mf* ‖ [ə'dıkt] *tr*—**a. oneself to** sich ergeben (*dat*)

addict'ed *adj* ergeben; **a. to drugs** rauschgiftsüchtig

addiction [ə'dık∫ən] *s* (**to**) Sucht *f* (nach)

add'ing machine' *s* Addiermaschine *f*

addition [ə'dı∫ən] *s* Hinzufügung *f*, Zusatz *m*; (*to a family, possessions*) Zuwachs *m*; (*to a building*) Anbau *m*; (math) Addition *f*; **in a.** außerdem; **in a. to** außer

additional [ə'dı∫ənəl] *adj* zusätzlich

additive ['ædıtıv] *s* Zusatz *m*

address [ə'dres], ['ædres] *s* Adresse *f*, Anschrift *f* ‖ [ə'dres] *s* Rede *f*; **deliver an a.** e-e Rede halten ‖ *tr* (*a letter*) (**to**) adressieren (an *acc*); (*words, a question*) (**to**) richten (an *acc*); (*an audience*) e-e Ansprache halten an (*acc*)

adduce [ə'd(j)us] *tr* anführen

adenoids ['ædə‚nɔıdz] *spl* Polypen *pl*

adept [ə'dept] *adj* (**in**) geschickt (in *dat*)

adequate ['ædıkwıt] *adj* angemessen; (**to**) ausreichend (für)

adhere [æd'hır] *intr* (**to**) haften (an *dat*); (fig) festhalten (an *dat*)

adherence [æd'hırəns] *s* (**to**) Festhaften *n* (an *dat*); (fig) Beharren *n* (bei)

adherent [æd'hırənt] *s* Anhänger –in *mf*

adhesion [æd'hiʒən] *s* (*sticking*) Ankleben *n*; (*loyalty*) Anhänglichkeit *f*; (pathol, phys) Adhäsion *f*

adhesive [æd'hisıv] *adj* anklebend ‖ *s* Klebemittel *n*, Klebstoff *m*

adhe'sive tape' *s* Heftpflaster *m*

adieu [ə'd(j)u] *s* (**adieus** & **adieux**) Lebewohl *n* ‖ *interj* lebe wohl!

adjacent [ə'dʒesənt] *adj* (**to**) angrenzend (an *acc*); (*angles*) Neben-

adjective ['ædʒıktıv] *s* Eigenschaftswort *n*, Adjektiv *n*

adjoin [ə'dʒɔın] *tr* angrenzen an (*acc*) ‖ *intr* angrenzen, naheliegen

adjoin'ing *adj* angrenzend; **a. rooms** Nebenzimmer *pl*

adjourn [ə'dʒʌrn] *tr* vertagen ‖ *intr* sich vertagen

adjournment [ə'dʒʌrnmənt] *s* Vertagung *f*

adjudge [ə'dʒʌdʒ] *tr* (*a prize*) zusprechen; **a. s.o. guilty** j-n für schuldig erklären

adjudicate [ə'dʒudı‚ket] *tr* gerichtlich entscheiden

adjunct ['ædʒʌŋkt] *s* (**to**) Zusatz *m* (zu)

adjust [ə'dʒʌst] *tr* (*to the right position*) einstellen; (*to an alternate position*) verstellen; (*fit*) (**to**) anpassen (*dat* or an *acc*); (*differences*) ausgleichen; (*an account*) bereinigen; (ins) berechnen ‖ *intr* (**to**) sich anpassen (*dat* or an *acc*)

adjustable [ə'dʒʌstəbəl] *adj* verstellbar

adjuster [ə'dʒʌstər] *s* (ins) Schadenssachverständiger –in *mf*

adjustment [ə'dʒʌstmənt] *s* (**to**) Anpassung *f* (*dat* or an *acc*); (*of an account*) Bereinigung *f*; (ins) Berechnung *f*; (mach) Einstellung *f*

adjutant ['ædʒətənt] *s* Adjutant *m*

ad-lib [‚æd'lıb] *v* (*pret* & *pp*) **–libbed;** *ger* **–libbing**) *tr* & *intr* improvisieren

ad-man ['æd‚mən] *s* (**–men**) Werbefachmann *m*; (*writer*) Werbetexter *m*

administer [æd'mınıstər] *tr* verwalten; (*help*) leisten; (*medicine*) eingeben; (*an oath*) abnehmen; (*punishment*) verhängen; (*a sacrament*) spenden; **a. justice** Recht sprechen ‖ *intr*— **a. to** dienen (*dat*)

administration [æd‚mınıs'tre∫ən] *s* (*of an institution*) Verwaltung *f*; (*of an official*) Amtsführung *f*; (*government*) Regierung *f*; (*period of government*) Regierungszeit *f*; (*of a president*) Amtszeit *f*; (*of tests*) Durchführung *f*; (*of an oath*) Abnahme *f*; (*of a sacrament*) Spendung *f*; **a. of justice** Rechtspflege *f*

administrator [æd'mɪnɪs,tretər] s Verwalter –in mf

admiral ['ædmɪrəl] s Admiral m

admiration [,ædmɪ'reʃən] s Bewunderung f

admire [æd'maɪr] tr (for) bewundern (wegen)

admirer [æd'maɪrər] s Bewunderer –in mf; (of a woman) Verehrer m

admissible [æd'mɪsɪbəl] adj (& jur) zulässig

admission [æd'mɪʃən] s (entry) Eintritt m; (permission to enter) Eintrittserlaubnis f; (entry fee) Eintrittsgebühr f; (of facts) Anerkennung f; (of guilt) Eingeständis n; (enrollment) (to, into) Aufnahme f (in acc); (to) (a profession) Zulassung f (zu)

ad•mit [æd'mɪt] v (pret & pp –mitted; ger –mitting) tr (hin)einlassen; (to) (a hospital, a society) aufnehmen (in acc); (to) (a profession) zulassen (zu); (accept) anerkennen; (concede) zugeben; (a crime, guilt) eingestehen || intr—a. of zulassen

admittance [æd'mɪtəns] s Eintritt m; **no a.** Eintritt verboten

admittedly [æd'mɪtɪdli] adv anerkanntermaßen

admixture [æd'mɪkstʃər] s Beimischung f

admonish [æd'mɑnɪʃ] tr ermahnen

admonition [,ædmə'nɪʃən] s Ermahnung f

ado [ə'du] s Getue n; **much ado about nothing** viel Lärm um nichts; **without further ado** ohne weiteres

adobe [ə'dobi] s Lehmstein m

adolescence [,ædə'lesəns] s Jugendalter n

adolescent [,ædə'lesənt] adj jugendlich || s Jugendliche mf

adopt [ə'dɑpt] tr (a child) adoptieren; (an idea) annehmen

adopt'ed child' s Adoptivkind n

adoption [ə'dɑpʃən] s (of a child) Adoption f; (of an idea) Annahme f

adorable [ə'dorəbəl] adj anbetungswürdig; (coll) entzückend

adore [ə'dor] tr anbeten; (coll) entzückend finden

adorn [ə'dɔrn] tr schmücken

adornment [ə'dɔrnmənt] s Schmuck m

adrenaline [ə'drenəlɪn] s Adrenalin n

adrift [ə'drɪft] adj—**be a.** treiben; (fig) weder aus noch ein wissen

adroit [ə'drɔɪt] adj geschickt, gewandt

adulation [,ædʒə'leʃən] s Schmeichelei f

adult [ə'dʌlt], ['ædʌlt] adj erwachsen || s Erwachsene mf

adult' educa'tion s Erwachsenenbildung f

adulterate [ə'dʌltə,ret] tr verfälschen; (e.g., wine) panschen

adulterer [ə'dʌltərər] s Ehebrecher m

adulteress [ə'dʌltərɪs] s Ehebrecherin f

adulterous [ə'dʌltərəs] adj ehebrecherisch

adultery [ə'dʌltəri] s Ehebruch m

advance [æd'væns] s Fortschritt m; (money) Vorschuß m; **in a. im vor-**aus; **make advances to** (e.g., a girl) Annäherungsversuche machen bei || tr vorrücken; (a clock) vorstellen; (money) vorschießen; (a date) aufschieben; (an opinion) vorbringen; (s.o.'s interests) fördern; (in rank) befördern || intr vorrücken

advancement [æd'vænsmənt] s Fortschritt m; (promotion) Beförderung f; (of a cause) Förderung f

advance' pay'ment s Voraus(be)zahlung f

advantage [æd'væntɪdʒ] s Vorteil m; **be of a.** nützlich sein; **take a. of** ausnutzen; **to a.** vorteilhaft

advantageous [,ædvən'tedʒəs] adj vorteilhaft

advent ['ædvent] s Ankunft f; **Advent** Advent m, Adventszeit f

adventure [æd'ventʃər] s Abenteuer n

adventurer [æd'ventʃərər] s Abenteurer m

adventuress [æd'ventʃərɪs] s Abenteurerin f

adventurous [æd'ventʃərəs] adj (person) abenteuerlustig; (undertaking) abenteuerlich

adverb ['ædvɑrb] s Umstandswort n

adverbial [æd'vɑrbɪəl] adj adverbial

adversary ['ædvər,seri] s Gegner –in mf

adverse [æd'vʌrs], ['ædvʌrs] adj ungünstig, nachteilig

adversity [æd'versɪti] s Unglück n, Not f

advertise ['ædvər,taɪz] tr Reklame machen für || intr Reklame machen; **a. for** durch Inserat suchen

advertisement [,ædvər'taɪzmənt], [æd'vertɪsmənt] s Anzeige f, Reklame f

ad'vertising a'gency s Reklamebüro n

ad'vertising campaign' s Werbefeldzug m

ad'vertising man' s (solicitor) Anzeigenvermittler m; (writer) Werbetexter m

advice [æd'vaɪs] s Rat m, Ratschlag m; **a piece of a.** ein Rat m; **get a. from** sich [dat] Rat holen bei; **give a. to** raten (dat)

advisable [æd'vaɪzəbəl] adj ratsam

advise [æd'vaɪz] tr raten (dat); (of) benachrichtigen (von); (on) beraten (über acc); **a. s.o. against s.th.** j-m von etw abraten

advisement [æd'vaɪzmənt] s—**take under a.** in Betracht ziehen

adviser [æd'vaɪzər] s Berater –in mf

advisory [æd'vaɪzəri] adj Beratungs-

advi'sory board' s Beirat m

advocate ['ædvə,ket] s Fürsprecher –in mf; (jur) Advokat –in mf || tr befürworten

aeon ['i·ən], ['i·ɑn] s Äon m

aerial ['erɪ·əl] adj Luft– || s Antenne f

aerodynamic [,erodaɪ'næmɪk] adj aerodynamisch || **aerodynamics** s Aerodynamik f

aeronautic(al) [,erə'nɔtɪk(əl)] adj aeronautisch || **aeronautics** s Aeronautik f, Luftfahrt f

aerosol ['erə,sɔl] s Sprühdose f

aerospace ['ɛrəspes] *adj* Raum—
aesthetic [ɛs'θɛtɪk] *adj* ästhetisch ||
aesthetics *s* Ästhetik *f*
afar [ə'fɑr] *adv*—a. off weit weg; **from a.** von weit her
affable ['æfəbəl] *adj* leutselig
affair [ə'fɛr] *s* Angelegenheit *f*; (*event, performance*) Veranstaltung *f*; (*romantic involvement*) Verhältnis *n*
affect [ə'fɛkt] *tr* (*influence*) berühren; (*injuriously*) angreifen; (*pretend*) vortäuschen
affectation [ˌæfɛk'teʃən] *s* Geziertheit *f*
affect'ed *adj* affektiert
affection [ə'fɛkʃən] *s* (**for**) Zuneigung *f* (**zu**); (*pathol*) Erkrankung *f*
affectionate [ə'fɛkʃənɪt] *adj* liebevoll
affidavit [ˌæfɪ'devɪt] *s* (schriftliche) eidesstattliche Erklärung *f*
affiliate [ə'fɪlɪˌet] *s* Zweiggesellschaft *f* || *tr* angliedern || *intr* sich angliedern
affinity [ə'fɪnɪti] *s* Verwandtschaft *f*
affirm [ə'fʌrm] *tr & intr* behaupten
affirmation [ˌæfər'meʃən] *s* Behauptung *f*
affirmative [ə'fʌrmətɪv] *adj* bejahend || *s* Bejahung *f*; **in the a.** bejahend, positiv
affix [ə'fɪks] *tr* (*a seal*) aufdrücken; (**to**) befestigen (**an** *dat*), anheften (**an** *acc*)
afflict [ə'flɪkt] *tr* plagen; **afflicted with** erkrankt an (*dat*)
affliction [ə'flɪkʃən] *s* Elend *n*, Leiden *n*; (*grief*) Betrübnis *f*
affluence ['æflu-əns] *s* Wohlstand *m*
affluent ['æflu-ənt] *adj* wohlhabend
af'fluent socie'ty *s* Wohlstandsgesellschaft *f*
afford [ə'fɔrd] *tr* (*confer*) gewähren; (*time*) erübrigen; (*be able to meet the expense of*) sich [*dat*] leisten
affront [ə'frʌnt] *s* Beleidigung *f* || *tr* beleidigen
afire [ə'faɪr] *adj & adv* in Flammen
aflame [ə'flem] *adj & adv* in Flammen
afloat [ə'flot] *adj* flott, schwimmend; (*awash*) überschwemmt; (*at sea*) auf dem Meer; (*in circulation*) im Umlauf; **keep a.** (& *fig*) über Wasser halten; **stay a.** (& *fig*) sich über Wasser halten
afoot [ə'fut] *adj & adv* (*on foot*) zu Fuß; (*in progress*) im Gange
aforesaid [ə'fɔrˌsɛd] *adj* vorerwähnt
afoul [ə'faul] *adj* (*entangled*) verwickelt || *adv*—**run a. of the law** mit dem Gesetz in Konflikt geraten
afraid [ə'fred] *adj* ängstlich; **be a. (of)** (*inf*) sich scheuen zu (*inf*)
afresh [ə'frɛʃ] *adv* aufs neue
Africa ['æfrɪkə] *s* Afrika *n*
African ['æfrɪkən] *adj* afrikanisch || *s* Afrikaner –in *mf*
aft [æft] *adv* (*nach*) achtern
after ['æftər] *adj* später; (*naut*) achter || *adv* nachher, darauf || *prep* nach (*dat*); **a. all** immerhin; **a. that** darauf; **be a. s.o.** hinter j—m her sein || *conj* nachdem
af'ter-din'ner speech' *s* Tischrede *f*

aftereffect' *s* Nachwirkung *f*; **have an a.** nachwirken
af'terlife' *s* (*later life*) zukünftiges Leben *n*; (*life after death*) Leben *n* nach dem Tode
aftermath ['æftərˌmæθ] *s* Nachwirkungen *pl*; (*agr*) Grummet *n*
af'ternoon' *s* Nachmittag *m*; **in the a.** am Nachmittag, nachmittags; **this a.** heute nachmittag
af'ter-shave' lo'tion *s* Rasierwasser *n*
af'tertaste' *s* Nachgeschmack *m*
af'terthought' *s* nachträglicher Einfall *m*
afterward(s) ['æftərwərd(z)] *adv* später
af'terworld' *s* Jenseits *n*
again [ə'gɛn] *adv* wieder, noch einmal; **half as much a.** anderthalbmal so viel; **what's his name a.?** wie heißt er doch schnell?
against [ə'gɛnst] *prep* gegen (*acc*); **a. it** dagegen; **a. the rules** regelwidrig; **be up a. it** (*coll*) in der Klemme sein
age [edʒ] *s* Alter *n*, Lebensalter *n*; (*period of history*) Zeitalter *n*; **at the age of** mit, im Alter von; **come of age** mündig werden; **for ages** e—e Ewigkeit; **of age** volljährig; **of the same age** gleichaltrig; **twenty years of age** zwanzig Jahre alt || *tr* machen; (*wine*) ablagern || *intr* altern; (*said of wine*) lagern
aged [edʒd] *adj* alt, e.g., **a. three** drei Jahre alt || ['edʒɪd] *adj* bejahrt
age' lim'it *s* Altersgrenze *f*
agency ['edʒənsi] *s* (*instrumentality*) Vermittlung *f*; (*activity*) Tätigkeit *f*; (*adm*) Behörde *f*; (*com*) Agentur *f*
agenda [ə'dʒɛndə] *s* Tagesordnung *f*
agent ['edʒənt] *s* Handelnde *mf*; (*biol, chem*) Agens *n*; (*com*) Agent –in *mf*
agglomeration [əˌgləmə'reʃən] *s* Anhäufung *f*
aggravate ['ægrəˌvet] *tr* erschweren, verschärfen; (*coll*) ärgern
aggravation [ˌægrə'veʃən] *s* Erschwerung *f*, Verschärfung *f*; (*coll*) Ärger *m*
aggregate ['ægrɪˌget] *adj* gesamt || *s* Aggregat *n*; **in the a.** im ganzen || *tr* anhäufen
aggression [ə'grɛʃən] *s* Agression *f*
aggressive [ə'grɛsɪv] *adj* aggressiv
aggressor [ə'grɛsər] *s* Aggressor *m*
aggrieved [ə'grivd] *adj* (*saddened*) betrübt; (*jur*) geschädigt
aghast [ə'gæst] *adj* entsetzt
agile ['ædʒɪl] *adj* flink; (*mind*) rege
agility [ə'dʒɪlɪti] *s* Flinkheit *f*; (*of the mind*) Regsamkeit *f*
agitate ['ædʒɪˌtet] *tr* hin und her bewegen; (*fig*) beunruhigen || *intr* agitieren
agitator ['ædʒɪˌtetər] *s* Unruhestifter –in *mf*; (*in a washer*) Rührapparat *m*
aglow [ə'glo] *adj & adv* (*of*) glühend
agnostic [æg'nɑstɪk] *adj* agnostisch || *s* Agnostiker –in *mf*
ago [ə'go] *adv* vor (*dat*), e.g., **a year ago** vor e—m Jahr; **long ago** vor langer Zeit
agog [ə'gɑg] *adv* gespannt, erpicht
agonize ['ægəˌnaɪz] *intr* sich quälen

ag′onizing adj qualvoll
agony [′ægənɪ] s Qual f; (death strug-gle) Todeskampf m
agrarian [ə′grɛrɪ-ən] adj landwirt-schaftlich, agrarisch
agree [ə′gri] intr übereinstimmen; **a. on** (or **upon**) sich einigen über (acc); **a. to** zustimmen (dat); **a. to** (inf) übereinkommen zu (inf); **a. with** (& gram) übereinstimmen mit; (affect one's health) bekommen (dat)
agreeable [ə′gri-əbəl] adj angenehm
agreed′ interj abgemacht!, einverstan-den!
agreement [ə′grimənt] s Abkommen n, Vereinbarung f; (contract) Ver-trag m; (& gram) Übereinstimmung f
agriculture [′ægrɪ‚kʌltʃər] s Landwirt-schaft f, Ackerbau m
aground [ə′graund] adv gestrandet; **run a.** stranden, auf Grund laufen
ahead [ə′hɛd] adj & adv (in the front) vorn; (to the front) nach vorn; (in advance) voraus; (forward) vorwärts; **a. of** vor (dat); **get a.** vorwärtskom-men; **go a.** vorangehen; **go a.!** los!; **go a. with** fortfahren mit; **look a. an** die Zukunft denken
ahoy [ə′hɔɪ] interj ahoi!
aid [ed] s Hilfe f, Beihilfe f ‖ tr helfen (dat); **aid and abet** Vorschub leisten (dat)
aide [ed] s Gehilfe m
aide-de-camp [′ɛddə′kæmp] s (aides-de-camp) Adjutant m
ail [el] tr schmerzen; **what ails you?** was fehlt Ihnen? ‖ intr (have pain) Schmerzen haben; (be ill) erkrankt sein
ail′ing adj leidend, kränklich
ailment [′elmənt] s Leiden n
aim [em] s Ziel n; (fig) Ziel n, Zweck m; **is your aim good?** zielen Sie gut?; **take aim** zielen ‖ tr (a gun, words) (at) richten auf (acc); **aim to** (inf) beabsichtigen zu (inf) ‖ intr zielen; **aim at** (& fig) zielen auf (acc); **aim for** streben nach
aimless [′emlɪs] adj ziellos, planlos
air [ɛr] s Luft f; (mus) Melodie f; **be on the air** (an announcer) senden; (a program) gesendet werden; **be up in the air** (fig) in der Luft hängen; **by air** per Flugzeug; **go off the air** die Sendung beenden; **go on the air** die Sendung beginnen; **in the open air** im Freien; **put on airs** groß tun; **walk on air** sich wie im Himmel fühlen ‖ tr lüften
air′base′ s Flugstützpunkt m
airborne [′ɛr‚bɔrn] adj aufgestiegen; **a. troops** Luftlandetruppen pl
air′brake′ s Druckluftbremse f
air′-condi′tion tr klimatisieren
air′ condi′tioner s Klimaanlage f
air′ cov′er s Luftsicherung f
air′craft′ s (pl aircraft) Flugzeug n
air′craft car′rier s Flugzeugträger m
air′ cur′rent s Luftströmung f
air′ fare′ s Flugpreis m
air′field′ s Flugplatz m
air′force′ s Luftstreitkräfte pl
air′ing s Lüftung f

air′ lane′ s Flugschneise f
air′lift′ s Luftbrücke f ‖ tr auf dem Luftwege transportieren
air′line(s)′ s Luftverkehrsgesellschaft f
air′line pi′lot s Flugkapitän m
air′lin′er s Verkehrsflugzeug n
air′mail′ s Luftpost f
air′-mail let′ter s Luftpostbrief m
air′-mail stamp′ s Luftpostmarke f
air′plane′ s Flugzeug n
air′ pock′et s Luftloch n
air′ pollu′tion s Luftverunreinigung f
air′port′ s Flughafen m, Flugplatz m
air′ raid′ s Fliegerangriff m
air′-raid drill′ s Luftschutzübung f
air′-raid shel′ter s Luftschutzraum m
air′-raid war′den s Luftschutzwart m
air′-raid warn′ing s Fliegeralarm m
air′ recon′naissance s Luftaufklärung f
air′show′ s Flugvorführung f
air′sick′ adj luftkrank
air′sleeve′, air′sock′ s Windsack m
air′strip′ s Start- und Landestreifen m
air′ suprem′acy s Luftherrschaft f
air′tight′ adj luftdicht
air′time′ s (rad, telv) Sendezeit f
air′-traffic control′ s Flugsicherung f
air′waves′ spl Rundfunk m; **on the a.** im Rundfunk
air′way′ s Luft(verkehrs)linie f
air′wor′thy adj lufttüchtig
airy [′ɛrɪ] adj (room) luftig; (lively) lebhaft; (flippant) leichtsinnig
aisle [aɪl] s Gang m; (archit) Seiten-schiff n
ajar [ə′dʒɑr] adj angelehnt
akimbo [ə′kɪmbo] adj—**with arms a.** die Arme in die Hüften gestemmt
akin [ə′kɪn] adj verwandt; **a. to** ähn-lich (dat)
alabaster [′ælə‚bæstər] s Alabaster m
alacrity [ə′lækrɪtɪ] s Bereitwilligkeit f
alarm [ə′lɑrm] s Alarm m; (sudden fear) Bestürzung f; (apprehension) Unruhe f ‖ tr alarmieren
alarm′ clock′ s Wecker m
alas [ə′læs] interj o weh!
Albania [æl′benɪ-ə] s Albanien n
Albanian [æl′benɪ-ən] adj albanisch ‖ s Alban(i)er –in mf
albatross [′ælbə‚trɔs] s Albatros m
album [′ælbəm] s Album n
albumen [æl′bjumən] s Eiweiß n
alchemy [′ælkɪmɪ] s Alchimie f
alcohol [′ælkə‚hɔl] s Alkohol m
alcoholic [‚ælkə′hɔlɪk] adj alkoholisch ‖ s Alkoholiker –in mf
alcove [′ælkov] s Alkoven m
alder [′ɔldər] s (bot) Erle f
al′der·man s (–men) Stadtrat m
ale [el] s Ale n, englisches Bier n
alert [ə′lʌrt] adj wachsam ‖ s (state of readiness) Alarmbereitschaft f; **on the a.** alarmbereit; (fig) auf der Hut ‖ tr alarmieren
alfalfa [æl′fælfə] s Luzerne f
algae [′ældʒi] spl Algen pl
algebra [′ældʒɪbrə] s Algebra f
Algeria [æl′dʒɪrɪ-ə] s Algerien n
Algerian [æl′dʒɪrɪ-ən] adj algerisch ‖ s Algerier –in mf
Algiers [æl′dʒɪrz] s Algier n

alias [ˈelɪ·əs] *adv* alias, sonst…genannt ‖ *s* Deckname *m*

ali·bi [ˈælɪ‚baɪ] *s* (*-bis*) Alibi *n*; (*excuse*) Ausrede *f*

alien [ˈeljən], [ˈelɪ·ən] *adj* fremd ‖ *s* Fremde *mf*, Ausländer *-in mf*

alienate [ˈeljə‚net], [ˈelɪ·ə‚net] *tr* entfremden; (*jur*) übertragen

alight [əˈlaɪt] *v* (*pret & pp* **alighted** & **alit** [əˈlɪt]) *intr* aussteigen; (*said of a bird*) (**on**) sich niederlassen (auf *dat* or *acc*); (*aer*) landen

align [əˈlaɪn] *tr* (**with**) ausrichten (nach); (*aut*) einstellen; **a. oneself with** sich anschließen an (*acc*) ‖ *intr* **—a. with** sich ausrichten nach

alignment [əˈlaɪnmənt] *s* Ausrichten *n*; (*pol*) Ausrichtung *f*; **bring into a.** gleichschalten; **out of a.** schlecht ausgerichtet

alike [əˈlaɪk] *adj* gleich, ähnlich; **look a.** sich [*dat*] ähnlich sehen; (*resemble completely*) gleich aussehen

alimony [ˈælɪ‚monɪ] *s* Unterhaltskosten *pl*

alive [əˈlaɪv] *adj* lebendig; (*vivacious*) lebhaft; **keep a.** am Leben bleiben; **keep s.o. a.** j-n am Leben erhalten

alka·li [ˈælkə‚laɪ] *s* (*-lis* & *-lies*) Laugensalz *n*, Alkali *n*

alkaline [ˈælkə‚laɪn] *adj* alkalisch

all [ɔl] *adj* all, ganz; **all day long** den ganzen Tag; **all kinds of** allerlei; **all the time** fortwährend; **for all that** trotzdem ‖ *adv* ganz, völlig; **all along** schon immer; **all at once** auf einmal; **all gone** alle; **all in** (*coll*) völlig erschöpft; **all over** (*everywhere*) überall; (*ended*) ganz vorbei; **all right** gut, schön; **all the better** um so besser; **all the same** dennoch; **not all there** (*coll*) nicht ganz richtig im Kopf sein ‖ *s*—**after all** schließlich; **all in all** im großen und ganzen; **and all** gesamt, e.g., **he went, family and all** er ging mit gesamter Familie; **in all** insgesamt; **not at all** überhaupt nicht, gar nicht ‖ *indef pron* alle; (*everything*) alles

all′-around′ *adj* vielseitig

allay [əˈle] *tr* beschwichtigen; (*hunger, thirst*) stillen

all′-clear′ *s* Entwarnung *f*

allege [əˈledʒ] *tr* behaupten; (*advance as an excuse*) vorgeben

alleged′ *adj* angeblich, mutmaßlich

allegiance [əˈlidʒəns] *s* Treue *f*

allegoric(al) [‚ælɪˈgɔrɪk(əl)] *adj* allegorisch

allegory [ˈælɪ‚gorɪ] *s* Allegorie *f*

allergic [əˈlʌrdʒɪk] *adj* allergisch

allergy [ˈælərdʒɪ] *s* Allergie *f*

alleviate [əˈlivɪ‚et] *tr* lindern

alley [ˈælɪ] *s* Gasse *f*; (*for bowling*) Kegelbahn *f*

alliance [əˈlaɪ·əns] *s* Bündnis *n*

allied′ *adj* (*field*) benachbart; (*science*) verwandt; (*mil, pol*) alliiert

alligator [ˈælɪ‚getər] *s* Alligator *m*

all′-inclu′sive *adj* Pauschal-

alliteration [ə‚lɪtəˈreʃən] *s* Stabreim *m*, Alliteration *f*

all′-know′ing *adj* allwissend

allocate [ˈælə‚ket] *tr* zuteilen

al·lot [əˈlɑt] (*pret & pp* **–lotted; ger –lotting**) *tr* zuteilen, austeilen

all′-out′ *adj* vollkommen, total

allow [əˈlaʊ] *tr* erlauben, gestatten; (*admit*) zugeben; (*e.g., a discount*) gewähren; **be allowed to** (*inf*) dürfen (*inf*) ‖ *intr*—**a. for** bedenken

allowable [əˈlaʊ·əbəl] *adj* zulässig

allowance [əˈlaʊ·əns] *s* (*tolerance*) Duldung *f*; (*permission*) Erlaubnis *f*; (*ration*) Zuteilung *f*, Ration *f*; (*pocket money*) Taschengeld *n*; (*discount*) Abzug *m*; (*salary for a particular expense*) Zuschuß *m*, Zulage *f*; (*for groceries*) Wirtschaftsgeld *n*; (*mach*) Toleranz *f*; **make a. for** berücksichtigen

alloy [ˈælɔɪ] *s* Legierung *f* ‖ [əˈlɔɪ] *tr* legieren

all′-pow′erful *adj* allmächtig

all′ right′ *adj*—**be a. in Ordnung sein** ‖ *interj* schon gut!

All′ Saints′ Day′ *s* Allerheiligen *n*

All′ Souls′ Day′ *s* Allerseelen *n*

all′spice′ *s* Nelkenpfeffer *m*

all′-star′ *adj* (*sport*) aus den besten Spielern bestehend

allude [əˈlud] *intr*—**a. to** anspielen auf (*acc*)

allure [əˈlʊr] *s* Charme *m* ‖ *tr* anlocken

allurement [əˈlʊrmənt] *s* Verlockung *f*

allur′ing *adj* verlockend

allusion [əˈluʒən] *s* (**to**) Anspielung *f* (auf *acc*)

al·ly [ˈælaɪ], [əˈlaɪ] *s* Alliierte *mf*, Verbündete *mf* ‖ [əˈlaɪ] *v* (*pret & pp* **–lied**) *tr*—**a. oneself with** sich verbünden mit

almanac [ˈɔlmə‚næk] *s* Almanach *m*

almighty [ɔlˈmaɪtɪ] *adj* allmächtig

almond [ˈɑmənd] *s* Mandel *f*

almost [ˈɔlmost], [ɔlˈmost] *adv* fast

alms [ɑmz] *s & spl* Almosen *n*

aloft [əˈlɔft] *adv* (*position*) oben; (*direction*) nach oben; **raise a.** emporheben

alone [əˈlon] *adj* allein; **let a.** (*not to mention*) geschweige denn; (*not bother*) in Ruhe lassen ‖ *adv* allein

along [əˈlɔŋ] *adv* vorwärts, weiter; **all a.** schon immer; **a. with** zusammen mit; **get a. with** sich gut vertragen mit; **go a. with** mitgehen mit; (*agree with*) sich einverstanden erklären mit ‖ *prep* (*direction*) entlang (*acc*); (*position*) an (*dat*), längs (*genit*)

along′side′ *adv* (*naut*) längsseits; **a. of** im Vergleich zu ‖ *prep* neben (*dat*); (*naut*) längsseits (*genit*)

aloof [əˈluf] *adj* zurückhaltend ‖ *adv*— **keep a.** (**from**) sich fernhalten (von); **stand a.** für sich bleiben

aloud [əˈlaʊd] *adv* laut

alphabet [ˈælfə‚bɛt] *s* Alphabet *n*

alphabetic(al) [‚ælfəˈbɛtɪk(əl)] *adj* alphabetisch

alpine [ˈælpaɪn] *adj* alpin, Alpen-**Alps** [ælps] *spl* Alpen *pl*

already [ɔlˈredɪ] *adv* schon, bereits

Alsace [ælˈses], [ˈælsæs] *s* Elsaß *n*

Alsatian [ælˈseʃən] *adj* elsässisch ‖ *s*

Elsässer –in *mf*; (*dog*) deutscher Schäferhund *m*

also ['ɔlso] *adv* auch

altar ['ɔltər] *s* Altar *m*

al'tar boy' *s* Ministrant *m*

alter ['ɔltər] *tr* ändern; (*castrate*) kastrieren || *intr* sich ändern

alteration [ˌɔltə're/ən] *s* Änderung *f*; **alterations** (*in construction*) Umbau *m*

alternate ['ɔltərnɪt] *adj* abwechselnd || *s* Ersatzmann *m* || ['ɔltər‚net] *tr* (ab)wechseln; (*e.g.*, *hot and cold compresses*) zwischen (*dat*) und (*dat*) abwechseln || *intr* miteinander abwechseln

al'ternating cur'rent *s* Wechselstrom *m*

alternative [ɔl'tʌrnətɪv] *adj* Ausweich-, Alternativ- || *s* Alternative *f*

although [ɔl'ðo] *conj* obgleich, obwohl

altimeter [æl'tɪmɪtər] *s* Höhenmesser *m*

altitude ['æltɪ‚t(j)ud] *s* Höhe *f*

al·to ['ælto] *s* (-tos) Alt *m*, Altstimme *f*; (*singer*) Altist *m*

altogether [ˌɔltə'geðər] *adv* durchaus; (*in all*) insgesamt

altruist ['æltru‚ɪst] *s* Altruist –in *mf*

alum ['æləm] *s* Alaun *m*

aluminum [ə'luminəm] *s* Aluminium *n*

alu'minum foil' *s* Aluminiumfolie *f*

alum·na [ə'lʌmnə] *s* (-nae [ni]) ehemalige Studentin *f*

alum·nus [ə'lʌmnəs] *s* (-ni [naɪ]) ehemaliger Student *m*

always ['ɔlwɪz], ['ɔlwez] *adv* immer

A.M. *abbr* (*ante meridiem*) vormittags; (*amplitude modulation*) Amplitudenmodulation *f*

amalgam [ə'mælgəm] *s* Amalgam *n*; (*fig*) Mischung *f*, Gemenge *n*

amalgamate [ə'mælgə‚met] *tr* amalgamieren || *intr* sich amalgamieren

amass [ə'mæs] *tr* aufhäufen, ansammeln

amateur ['æmət/ər] *adj* Amateur- || *s* Amateur *m*, Liebhaber *m*

amaze [ə'mez] *tr* erstaunen

amaz'ing *adj* erstaunlich

Amazon ['æmə‚zan] *s* (*river*) Amazonas *m*; (*fig*) Mannweib *n*; (*myth*) Amazone *f*

ambassador [æm'bæsədər] *s* Botschafter –in §6 *mf*; (*fig*) Bote *m*

ambassadorial [æm‚bæsə'dorɪ‚əl] *adj* Botschafts-

amber ['æmbər] *adj* Bernstein-; (*in color*) bernsteinfarben || *s* Bernstein *m*

ambiguity [ˌæmbɪ'gju‚ɪti] *s* Doppelsinn *m*, Zweideutigkeit *f*

ambiguous [æm'bɪgjʊ‚əs] *adj* doppelsinnig, zweideutig

ambit ['æmbɪt] *s* Bereich *m*

ambition [æm'brɪ/ən] *s* Ehrgeiz *m*; (*aim*, *object*) Ambition *f*

ambitious [æm'bɪ/əs] *adj* ehrgeizig

ambivalent [æm'bɪvələnt] *adj* (*chem*) ambivalent; (*psychol*) zwiespältig

amble ['æmbəl] *s* (*of a person*) gemächlicher Gang *m*; (*of a horse*) Paßgang *m* || *intr* schlendern; (*said of a horse*) im Paßgang gehen

ambulance ['æmbjələns] *s* Krankenwagen *m*

ambulatory ['æmbjələ‚torɪ] *adj* gehfähig

ambuscade [ˌæmbəs'ked] *s* Hinterhalt *m*

ambush ['æmbʊ/] *s* Hinterhalt *m* || *tr* aus dem Hinterhalt überfallen

ameliorate [ə'miljə‚ret] *tr* verbessern || *intr* besser werden

amen ['e'men], ['ɑ'men] *s* Amen *n* || *interj* amen!

amenable [ə'menəbəl] *adj* (*docile*) fügsam; **a. to** (*e.g.*, *flattery*) zugänglich (*dat*); (*e.g.*, *laws*) unterworfen (*dat*)

amend [ə'mend] *tr* (*a law*) (ver)bessern; (*one's ways*) (ab)ändern || *intr* sich bessern

amendment [ə'mendmənt] *s* Änderungsantrag *m*; (*by addition*) Zusatzantrag *m*; (*to the constitution*) Zusatzartikel *m*

amends [ə'mendz] *s & spl* Genugtuung *f*; **make a. for** wiedergutmachen

amenity [ə'menɪti] *s* (*pleasantness*) Annehmlichkeit *f*; **amenities** (*of life*) Annehmlichkeiten *pl*

America [ə'merɪkə] *s* Amerika *n*

American [ə'merɪkən] *adj* amerikanisch || *s* Amerikaner –in *mf*

Americanize [ə'merɪkə‚naɪz] *tr* amerikanisieren

amethyst ['æmɪθɪst] *s* Amethyst *m*

amiable ['emɪ‚əbəl] *adj* liebenswürdig

amicable ['æmɪkəbəl] *adj* freundschaftlich, gütlich

amid [ə'mɪd] *prep* inmitten (*genit*)

amidships [ə'mɪd/ɪps] *adv* mittschiffs

amiss [ə'mɪs] *adj* (*improper*) unpassend; (*wrong*) verkehrt; **there is s.th. a.** etwas stimmt nicht || *adv* verkehrt; **go a.** danebengehen; **take a.** übelnehmen

amity ['æmɪti] *s* Freundschaft *f*

ammo ['æmo] *s* (sl) Muni *m*

ammonia [ə'monɪ‚ə] *s* (*gas*) Ammoniak *n*; (*solution*) Salmiakgeist *m*

ammunition [ˌæmjə'nɪ/ən] *s* Munition *f*

amnesia [æm'nɪʒɪ‚ə] *s* Amnesie *f*

amnes·ty ['æmnɪsti] *s* Amnestie *f* || *v* (*pret & pp.* **-tied**) *tr* begnadigen

amoeba [ə'mibə] *s* Amöbe *f*

among [ə'mʌŋ] *prep* (*position*) unter (*dat*); (*direction*) unter (*acc*); **a. other things** unter anderem

amorous ['æmərəs] *adj* amourös

amortize ['æmər‚taɪz] *tr* tilgen

amount [ə'maunt] *s* (*sum*) Betrag *m*; (*quantity*) Menge *f* || *intr*—**a. to** betragen

ampere ['æmpɪr] *s* Ampere *n*

amphibian [æm'fɪbɪ‚ən] *s* Amphibie *f*

amphibious [æm'fɪbɪ‚əs] *adj* amphibisch

amphitheater ['æmfɪ‚θi‚ətər] *s* Amphitheater *n*

ample ['æmpəl] *adj* (*sufficient*) genügend; (*spacious*) geräumig

amplifier ['æmplɪ‚faɪ‚ər] *s* Verstärker *m*

ampli·fy ['æmplɪ‚faɪ] *v* (*pret & pp* **-fied**) *tr* (*a statement*) erweitern; (*electron*, *rad*, *phys*) verstärken

amplitude ['æmplı͵t(j)ud] s Weite f; (electron, rad, phys) Amplitude f

am'plitude modula'tion s Amplitudenmodulation f

amputate ['æmpjə͵tet] tr amputieren

amputee [͵æmpje'ti] s Amputierte mf

amuck [ə'mʌk] adv—**run a.** Amok laufen

amulet ['æmjəlıt] s Amulett n

amuse [ə'mjuz] tr amüsieren, belustigen

amusement [ə'mjuzmənt] s Vergnügen n

amuse'ment park' s Vergnügungspark m

amus'ing adj amüsant

an [æn], [ən] indef art ein

anachronism [ə'nækrə͵nızəm] s Anachronismus m

analogous [ə'næləgəs] adj (to) analog (dat), ähnlich (dat)

analogy [ə'nælədʒı] s Analogie f

analy·sis [ə'nælısıs] s (-ses [͵siz]) Analyse f; (of a literary work) Zergliederung f

analyst ['ænəlıst] s Analytiker –in mf

analytic(al) [͵ænə'lıtık(əl)] adj analytisch

analyze ['ænə͵laız] tr analysieren

anarchist ['ænərkıst] s Anarchist –in mf

anarchy ['ænərki] s Anarchie f

anatomic(al) [͵ænə'tɑmık(əl)] adj anatomisch

anatomy [ə'nætəmı] s Anatomie f

ancestor ['ænsestər] s Vorfahr m, Ahne m

ancestral [æn'sestrəl] adj angestammt, Ahnen–; (inherited) Erb–, ererbt

ancestry ['ænsestrı] s Abstammung f

anchor ['æŋkər] s Anker m; **cast a.** vor Anker gehen; **weigh a.** den Anker lichten || tr verankern || intr ankern

anchorage ['æŋkərıdʒ] s Ankerplatz m

anchovy ['æntʃovi] s Anschovis f

ancient ['entʃənt] adj (very old) uralt; (civilization) antik || **the ancients** spl die alten Griechen und Römer

an'cient his'tory s alte Geschichte f

and [ænd], [ənd] conj und; **and how!** und ob! **and so forth** und so weiter

andiron ['ænd͵aɪ·ən] s Kaminbock m

anecdote ['ænɪk͵dot] s Anekdote f

anemia [ə'nimɪ·ə] s Anämie f

anemic [ə'nimɪk] adj anämisch, blutarm

anesthesia [͵ænɪs'θiʒə] s Anästhesie f; **general a.** Vollnarkose f; **local a.** Lokalanästhesie f

anesthetic [͵ænɪs'θetɪk] adj betäubend || s Betäubungsmittel n; **local a.** örtliches Betäubungsmittel n

anesthetize [ə'nesθɪ͵taɪz] tr betäuben

anew [ə'n(j)u] adv von neuem, aufs neue

angel ['endʒəl] s Engel m; (financial backer) Hintermann m

angelic(al) [æn'dʒelɪk(əl)] adj engelgleich, engelhaft

anger ['æŋgər] s Zorn m || tr erzürnen

angina pectoris [æn'dʒaɪnə'pektərɪs] s Brustbeklemmung f, Herzbräune f

angle ['æŋgəl] s Winkel m; (point of view) Gesichtswinkel m; (ulterior motive) Hintergedanken m; (side) Seite f

angler ['æŋglər] s Angler –in mf

angry ['æŋgri] adj zornig, böse; (wound) entzündet; **a. at** (s.th.) zornig über (acc); **a. with** (s.o.) zornig auf (acc)

anguish ['æŋgwɪʃ] s Qual f, Pein f

angular ['æŋgjələr] adj kantig

animal ['ænɪməl] adj tierisch, Tier— || s Tier n

animate ['ænɪmɪt] adj belebt; (lively) lebhaft || ['ænɪ͵met] tr beleben, beseelen; (make lively) aufmuntern

an'imated cartoon' s Zeichentrickfilm m

animation [͵ænɪ'meʃən] s Lebhaftigkeit f; (cin) Herstellung f von Zeichentrickfilm

animosity [͵ænɪ'mɑsɪtɪ] s Feindseligkeit f

anion ['æn͵aɪ·ən] s Anion n

anise ['ænɪs] s Anis m

anisette [͵ænɪ'set] s Anisett m

ankle ['æŋkəl] s Fußknöchel m

an'kle support' s Knöchelstütze f

anklet ['æŋklɪt] s (ornament) Fußring m; (sock) Söckchen n

annals ['ænəlz] spl Annalen pl

anneal [ə'nil] tr ausglühen; (the mind) stählen

annex ['æneks] s (building) Anbau m, Nebengebäude n; (supplement) Zusatz m || [ə'neks] tr annektieren

annexation [͵æneks'eʃən] s Einverleibung f; (pol) Annexion f

annihilate [ə'naɪ·ɪ͵let] tr vernichten; (fig) zunichte machen

annihilation [ə͵naɪ·ɪ'leʃən] s Vernichtung f

anniversary [͵ænɪ'vʌrsərɪ] s Jahrestag m

annotate ['ænə͵tet] tr mit Anmerkungen versehen

annotation [͵ænə'teʃən] s Anmerkung f

announce [ə'naʊns] tr ankündigen, anmelden; (rad) ansagen, melden

announcement [ə'naʊnsmənt] s Ankündigung f; (rad) Durchsage f

announcer [ə'naʊnsər] s Ansager –in mf

annoy [ə'nɔɪ] tr ärgern; **be annoyed at** sich ärgern über (acc)

annoyance [ə'nɔɪ·əns] s Ärger m

annoy'ing adj ärgerlich

annual ['ænju·əl] adj jährlich, Jahres–; (plant) einjährig || s (book) Jahrbuch n; (bot) einjährige Pflanze f

annuity [ə'n(j)u·ɪtɪ] s Jahresrente f

an·nul [ə'nʌl] v (pret & pp -nulled; ger -nulling) tr annullieren

annulment [ə'nʌlmənt] s Annullierung f; (of marriage) Nichtigkeitserklärung f

anode ['ænod] s Anode f

anoint [ə'nɔɪnt] tr salben

anomaly [ə'nɑməlɪ] s Anomalie f

anonymous [ə'nɑnɪməs] adj anonym

another [ə'nʌðər] adj (a different) ein anderer; (an additional) noch ein; **a. Caesar** ein zweiter Cäsar || pron

(a different one) ein anderer; **(an additional one)** noch einer

answer ['ænsər] s Antwort f; **(to a problem)** Lösung f || tr **(a person)** antworten **(dat)**; **(a question, letter)** beantworten; **(need, description)** entsprechen **(dat)**; **(enemy fire)** antworten auf **(acc)**; **a. an ad** sich auf e-e Anzeige melden; **a. the door** die Tür öffnen; **a. the telephone** ans Telefon gehen || intr antworten; **(telp)** sich melden; **a. back** e-n losen Mund haben; **a. for** verantworten; **a. to** (a description) entsprechen **(dat)**

an'swering serv'ice s Fernsprechauftragsdienst m

ant [ænt] s Ameise f

antagonism [æn'tægə‚nɪzəm] s Feindseligkeit f

antagonize [æn'tægə‚naɪz] tr sich **[dat]** zum Gegner machen

antarctic [ænt'ɑrktɪk] adj antarktisch || **the Antarctic** s die Antarktis

Antarc'tic Cir'cle s südlicher Polarkreis m

Antarc'tic O'cean s südliches Eismeer n

ante ['æntɪ] s (cards) Einsatz m; (com) Scherflein n || tr (cards) einsetzen || intr **(in a joint venture)** sein Scherflein beitragen; **(pay up)** (coll) blechen; (cards) einsetzen

antecedent [‚æntɪ'sidənt] adj vorhergehend || s (gram) Beziehungswort n; **antecedents** Antezedenzien pl

antechamber ['æntɪ‚tʃembər] s Vorzimmer n

antelope ['æntɪ‚lop] s Antilope f

anten·na [æn'tenə] s (-nae [ni]) (ent) Fühler m || s (-nas) (rad) Antenne f

antepenult [‚æntɪ'pɪnʌlt] s drittletzte Silbe f

anthem ['ænθəm] s Hymne f

ant'hill' s Ameisenhaufen m

anthology [æn'θɑlədʒi] s Anthologie f

anthropology [‚ænθrə'pɑlədʒi] s Anthropologie f, Lehre f vom Menschen

antiaircraft [‚æntɪ'ær‚kræft] adj Flak-, Flugabwehr-- || s Flak f

antiair'craft gun' s Flak f

antibiotic [‚æntɪbaɪ'ɑtɪk] s Antibiotikum n

antibody ['æntɪ‚bɑdi] s Antikörper m

anticipate [æn'tɪsɪ‚pet] tr **(expect)** erwarten; **(remarks, criticism, etc.)** vorwegnehmen; **(trouble)** voraussahnen; **(pleasure)** vorausempfinden; **(s.o.'s wish or desire)** zuvorkommen **(dat)**

anticipation [æn‚tɪsɪ'peʃən] s Erwartung f, Vorfreude f

antics ['æntɪks] spl Possen pl

antidote ['æntɪ‚dot] s Gegengift n

antifreeze ['æntɪ‚friz] s Gefrierschutzmittel n

antiknock [‚æntɪ'nɑk] adj klopffest || s Antiklopfmittel n

antipathy [æn'tɪpəθi] s Abneigung f, Antipathie f

antiquarian [‚æntɪ'kwɛri‚ən] s Altertümlich || s Altertumsforscher –in mf

antiquated ['æntɪ‚kwetɪd] adj veraltet

antique [æn'tik] adj (ur)alt, antik || s Antiquität f

antique' deal'er s Antiquitätenhändler –in mf

antique' shop' s Antiquitätenladen m

antiquity [æn'tɪkwɪti] s Altertum n, Vorzeit f; **antiquities** Antiquitäten pl, Altertümer pl

antirust ['æntɪ'rʌst] adj Rostschutz-

anti-Semitic [‚æntɪsɪ'mɪtɪk] adj antisemitisch, judenfeindlich

antiseptic [‚æntɪ'sɛptɪk] adj antiseptisch || s Antiseptikum n

antitank ['æntɪ'tæŋk] adj Panzer-: **(unit)** Panzerjäger--

antithe·sis [æn'tɪθɪsɪs] s (-ses [‚siz]) Gegensatz m, Antithese f

antitoxin [‚æntɪ'tɑksɪn] s Gegengift n

antitrust ['æntɪ'trʌst] adj Antitrust-

antiwar ['æntɪ'wɔr] adj antimilitaristisch

antler ['æntlər] s Geweihsprosse f; **(pair of) antlers** Geweih n

antonym ['æntənɪm] s Antonym n

anus ['enəs] s After m

anvil ['ænvɪl] s Amboß m

anxiety [æŋ'zaɪ‚əti] s **(over)** Besorgnis f (um); (psychol) Beklemmung f

anxious ['æŋk/əs] adj **(about)** besorgt (um or wegen); **(for)** gespannt (auf acc), begierig (auf acc); **I am a. to (inf)** es liegt mir daran zu (inf)

any ['eni] indef adj irgendein, irgendwelch; **(a little)** etwas; **any (possible)** etwaig; **any (you wish)** jeder beliebige; **do you have any money on you?** haben Sie Geld bei sich?; **I do not have any money** ich habe kein Geld || adv—**any more** (e.g., coffee) noch etwas; **(e.g., apples)** noch ein paar; **not any better** keinswegs besser; **not ...any longer** nicht mehr; **not ...any more** nicht mehr

an'ybod'y indef pron var of **anyone**

an'yhow' adv sowieso, trotzdem; **(in any event)** jedenfalls

an'yone' indef pron **(irgend)jemand**, irgendeiner; **a. but** you jeder andere als du; **a. else** sonstnochwer; **ask a.** frag wen du willst; **I don't see a.** ich sehe niemand

an'yplace' adv (coll) var of **anywhere**

an'ything' indef pron (irgend)etwas, (irgend)was; **a. but** alles andere als; **a. else?** noch etwas?, sonst etwas?; **a. you want** was du willst; **not ...a.** nichts; **not for a. in the world** um keinen Preis

an'ytime' adv zu jeder (beliebigen) Zeit; **(at some unspecified time)** irgendwann

an'yway' adv sowieso, trotzdem

an'ywhere' adv **(position)** irgendwo; **(everywhere)** an jedem beliebigen Ort; **(direction)** irgendwohin; **(everywhere)** an jeden beliebigen Ort; **to any extent** einigermaßen, e.g., **a. near correct** einigermaßen richtig; **get a.** **(achieve success)** es zu etwas bringen

apace [ə'pes] adv schnell, rasch

apart [ə'pɑrt] adv **(to pieces)** auseinander; (*separately*) einzeln, für sich; **a. from** abgesehen von

apartment [ə'purtmənt] *s* Wohnung *f*

apart'ment house' *s* Apartmenthaus *n*

apathetic [,æpə'θetɪk] *adj* apathisch, teilnahmslos

apathy [ˈæpəθi] *s* Apathie *f*

ape [ep] *s* Affe *m* ‖ *tr* nachäffen

aperture [ˈæpərtʃər] *s* Öffnung *f*; (*phot*) Blende *f*

apex [ˈepeks] *s* (**apexes** & **apices** [ˈæpɪˌsiz]) Spitze *f*; (fig) Gipfel *m*

aphid [ˈæfɪd] *s* Blattlaus *f*

aphorism [ˈæfəˌrɪzəm] *s* Aphorismus *m*

apiary [ˈepɪˌeri] *s* Bienenhaus *n*

apiece [ə'pis] *adv* pro Stück; (*per person*) pro Person

aplomb [ə'plɑm] *s* sicheres Auftreten *n*

apogee [ˈæpəˌdʒi] *s* Erdferne *f*

apologetic [ə,pɑlə'dʒetɪk] *adj* (*remark*) entschuldigend; (*letter, speech*) Entschuldigungs–; **be a.** (*about*) Entschuldigungen vorbringen (für)

apologize [ə'pɑlə,dʒaɪz] *intr* sich entschuldigen; **a. to s.o. for s.th.** sich bei j–m wegen etw entschuldigen

apology [ə'pɑlədʒi] *s* (*excuse*) Entschuldigung *f*; (*apologia*) Verteidigung *f*

apoplec'tic stroke' [,æpə'plektɪk] *s* Schlaganfall *m*

apoplexy [ˈæpəˌpleksi] *s* Schlaganfall *m*

apostle [ə'pɑsəl] *s* Apostel *m*

apostolic [,æpəs'tɑlɪk] *adj* apostolisch

apostrophe [ə'pɑstrəfi] *s* (gram) Apostroph *m*; (rhet) Anrede *f*

apothecary [ə'pɑθɪˌkeri] *s* (*druggist*) Apotheker *m*; (*drugstore*) Apotheke *f*

appall [ə'pɔl] *tr* entsetzen

appall'ing *adj* entsetzlich

appara·tus [,æpə'retəs], [,æpə'rætəs] *s* (**-tus** & **-tuses**) Apparat *m*

apparel [ə'pærəl] *s* Kleidung *f*, Tracht *f*

apparent [ə'pærənt] *adj* (*visible*) sichtbar; (*obvious*) offenbar; (*seeming*) scheinbar

apparition [,æpə'rɪʃən] *s* Erscheinung *f*; (*ghost*) Gespenst *n*

appeal [ə'pil] *s* (*request*) Appell *m*, dringende Bitte *f*; (*to reason, etc.*) Appell *m*; (*charm*) Anziehungskraft *f*; (jur) (**to**) Berufung *f* (an *acc*) ‖ *tr*—**a. a case** Berufung einlegen in e–r Rechtssache ‖ *intr*—**a. to** (*entreat*) dringend bitten; (*be attractive to*) reizen; (jur) appellieren an (*acc*)

appear [ə'pir] *intr* erscheinen; (*seem*) scheinen; (*come before the public*) sich zeigen; (jur) sich stellen; (theat) auftreten; **a. as a guest** (telv) gastieren

appearance [ə'pirəns] *s* Erscheinen *n*; (*outward look*) Aussehen *n*; (*semblance*) Anschein *m*; (*on the stage*) Auftreten *n*; (jur) Erscheinen *n*; **for the sake of appearances** anstandshalber; **to all appearances** allem Anschein nach

appease [ə'piz] *tr* beruhigen; (*hunger*)

stillen; (*pain*) mildern; (dipl) beschwichtigen

appeasement [ə'pizmənt] *s* Beruhigung *f*; (*of hunger*) Stillung *f*; (dipl) Beschwichtigung *f*

appel'late court' [ə'pelɪt] *s* Berufungsgericht *n*

append [ə'pend] *tr* anhängen; (*a signature*) hinzufügen

appendage [ə'pendɪdʒ] *s* Anhang *m*

appendectomy [,æpən'dektəmi] *s* Blinddarmoperation *f*

appendicitis [ə,pendɪ'saɪtɪs] *s* Blinddarmentzündung *f*, Appendizitis *f*

appen·dix [ə'pendɪks] *s* (**-dixes** & **-dices** [dɪˌsiz]) Anhang *m*; (anat) Appendix *m*

appertain [,æpər'ten] *intr* (**to**) gehören (zu), gebühren (*dat*)

appetite [ˈæpɪˌtaɪt] *s* (**for**) Appetit *m* (auf *acc*)

appetizer [ˈæpɪˌtaɪzər] *s* Vorspeise *f*

ap'petizing *adj* appetitlich

applaud [ə'plɔd] *tr* Beifall klatschen (*dat*); (*praise*) billigen ‖ *intr* Beifall klatschen

applause [ə'plɔz] *s* Beifall *m*, Applaus *m*

apple [ˈæpəl] *s* Apfel *m*

ap'plecart' *s*—**upset the a.** die Pläne über den Haufen werfen

ap'ple of one's eye' *s* Augapfel *m*

ap'ple pie' *s* gedeckte Apfeltorte *f*

ap'ple-pol'isher *s* (coll) Speichellecker *m*

ap'plesauce' *s* Apfelmus *n*

ap'ple tree' *s* Apfelbaum *m*

appliance [ə'plaɪ·əns] *s* Gerät *n*, Vorrichtung *f*

applicable [ˈæplɪkəbəl] *adj* (**to**) anwendbar (auf *acc*); **not a.** nicht zutreffend

applicant [ˈæplɪkənt] *s* Bewerber –in *mf*

application [,æplɪ'keʃən] *s* (*use*) Anwendung *f*; (*for a job*) Bewerbung *f*; (*for a grant*) Antrag *m*; (*zeal*) Fleiß *m*; (med) Anlegen *n*

applica'tion blank' *s* (*for a job*) Bewerbungsformular *n*; (*for a grant*) Antragsformular *n*

applied' *adj* angewandt

apply [ə'plaɪ] *v* (*pret & pp* **-plied**) *tr* anwenden; (med) anlegen; **a. oneself to** sich befleißigen (*genit*); **a. the brakes** bremsen ‖ *intr* gelten; **a. for** (*a job*) sich bewerben um; (*a grant*) beantragen

appoint [ə'pɔɪnt] *tr* (*a person*) ernennen; (*a time, etc.*) festsetzen

appointment [ə'pɔɪntmənt] *s* Ernennung *f*; (*post*) Stelle *f*; (*engagement*) Verabredung *f*; **by a. only** nur nach Vereinbarung; **have an a. with** (*e.g., a dentist*) bestellt sein zu

appoint'ment book' *s* Terminkalender *m*

apportion [ə'pɔrʃən] *tr* zumessen

appraisal [ə'prezəl] *s* Abschätzung *f*

appraise [ə'prez] *tr* (ab)schätzen

appraiser [ə'prezər] *s* Schätzer –in *mf*

appreciable [ə'priʃɪ·əbəl] *adj* (*notice-*

able) merklich; (*considerable*) erheblich

appreciate [ə'priʃɪ,et] *tr* dankbar sein für; (*danger*) erkennen; (*regard highly*) hochschätzen || *intr* im (im Werte) steigen

appreciation [ə,priʃɪ'eʃən] *s* (*gratitude*) Dank *m.* Anerkennung *f*; (*for art*) Verständnis *n*; (*high regard*) Schätzung *f*; (*increase in value*) Wertzuwachs *m*

appreciative [ə'priʃɪ.ətɪv] *adj* (of) dankbar (für)

apprehend [,æprɪ'hɛnd] *tr* verhaften, ergreifen; (*understand*) begreifen

apprehension [,æprɪ'hɛnʃən] *s* (*arrest*) Verhaftung *f*; (*fear*) Befürchtung *f*; (*comprehending*) Begreifen *n*

apprehensive [,æprɪ'hɛnsɪv] *adj* (of) besorgt um

apprentice [ə'prɛntɪs] *s* Lehrling *m*

appren'ticeship' *s* Lehre *f*; **serve an a.** in der Lehre sein

apprise, apprize [ə'praɪz] *tr* (of) benachrichtigen (von)

approach [ə'protʃ] *s* Annäherung *f*; (*e.g., a road*) Zugang *m.* Zufahrt *f*; *e.g., to a problem*) Behandlung *f*; (*tentative sexual approach*) Annäherungsversuch *m*; (aer) Anflug *m* || *tr* sich nähern (*dat*); (*e.g., a problem*) behandeln; (*perfection*) nahekommen (*dat*); (aer) anfliegen || *intr* sich nähern

approachable [ə'protʃəbəl] *adj* zugänglich

approbation [,æprə'beʃən] *s* (*approval*) Beifall *m*; (*sanction*) Billigung *f*

appropriate [ə'proprɪ-ɪt] *adj* (**to**) angemessen (*dat*) || [ə'proprɪ,et] *tr* (*take possession of*) sich [*dat*] aneignen; (*authorize*) bewilligen

approval [ə'pruvəl] *s* (*approbation*) Beifall *m*; (*sanction*) Billigung *f*; **meet with s.o.'s a.** j-s Beifall finden; **on a.** auf Probe

approve [ə'pruv] *tr* (*sanction*) genehmigen; (*judge favorably*) billigen; (*a bill*) (parl) annehmen || *intr*—**a. of** billigen

approvingly [ə'pruvɪŋli] *adv* beifällig

approximate [ə'prɑksɪmɪt] *adj* annähernd || [ə'prɑksɪ,met] *tr* (*come close to*) nahekommen (*dat*); (*estimate*) schätzen; (*simulate closely*) täuschend nachahmen

approximately [ə'prɑksɪmɪtli] *adv* ungefähr, etwa

apricot ['epri,kɑt] *s* Aprikose *f*

ap'ricot tree' *s* Aprikosenbaum *m*

April ['eprɪl] *s* April *m*

A'pril fool' *interj* April, April!

A'pril Fools'' Day' *s* der erste April *m*

apron ['eprən] *s* Schürze *f*; (aer) Vorfeld *n*; (theat) Vorbühne *f*

apropos [,æprə'po] *adj* passend || *adv* —**a. of** in Bezug auf (*acc*)

apse [æps] *s* Apsis *f*

apt [æpt] *adj* (*suited to the occasion*) passend; (*suited to the purpose*) geeignet; (*metaphor*) zutreffend; **be apt to** (*inf*) (*be prone to*) dazu neigen zu

(*inf*); **he is apt to believe it** er wird es wahrscheinlich glauben

aptitude ['æptɪ,t(j)ud] *s* Eignung *f*

ap'titude test' *s* Eignungsprüfung *f*

aqualung ['ækwə,lʌŋ] *s* Tauchergerät *n*

aquamarine [,ækwəmə'rin] *adj* blaugrün || *s* Aquamarin *m*

aquari·um [ə'kwɛrɪ-əm] *s* (–**ums** & –**a** [ə]) Aquarium *n*

aquatic [ə'kwætɪk] *adj* Wasser- || **aquatics** *spl* Wassersport *m*

aqueduct ['ækwə,dʌkt] *s* Aquädukt *n*

aq'uiline nose' ['ækwɪ,laɪn] *s* Adlernase *f*

Arab ['ærəb] *adj* arabisch || *s* Araber –in *mf*

Arabia [ə'rebɪ-ə] *s* Arabien *n*

Arabic ['ærəbɪk] *adj* arabisch || *s* Arabisch *n*

arable ['ærəbəl] *adj* urbar, Acker–

arbiter ['ɑrbɪtər] *s* Schiedsrichter *m*

arbitrary ['ɑrbɪ,trɛri] *adj* (*act*) willkürlich; (*number*) beliebig; (*person, government*) tyrannisch

arbitrate ['ɑrbɪ,tret] *tr* schlichten || *intr* als Schiedsrichter fungieren

arbitration [,ɑrbɪ'treʃən] *s* Schlichtung *f*

arbitrator ['ɑrbɪ,tretər] *s* Schiedsrichter *m*

arbor ['ɑrbər] *s* Laube *f*; (mach) Achse *f*

arbore·tum [,ɑrbə'ritəm] *s* (–**tums** & –**ta** [tə]) Baumgarten *m*

arc [ɑrk] *s* (astr, geom, mach) Bogen *m*; (elec) Lichtbogen *m*

arcade [ɑr'ked] *s* Bogengang *m*, Arkade *f*

arcane [ɑr'ken] *adj* geheimnisvoll

arch [ɑrtʃ] *adj* (*liar, etc.*) abgefeimt || *s* Bogen *m* || *tr* wölben; (*span*) überwölben || *intr* sich wölben

archaeologist [,ɑrkɪ'alədʒɪst] *s* Archäolog(e) *m*, Archäologin *f*

archaeology [,ɑrkɪ'alədʒi] *s* Archäologie *f*

archaic [ɑr'ke-ɪk] *adj* (*word*) veraltet; (*manner, notion*) antiquiert

archangel ['ɑrk,endʒəl] *s* Erzengel *m*

archbishop ['ɑrtʃ'bɪʃəp] *s* Erzbischof *m*

archduke ['ɑrtʃ'd(j)uk] *s* Erzherzog *m*

archenemy ['ɑrtʃ,ɛnɪmi] *s* Erzfeind *m*

archer ['ɑrtʃər] *s* Bogenschütze *m*

archery ['ɑrtʃəri] *s* Bogenschießen *n*

archipela·go [,ɑrkɪ'peləgo] *s* (–**gos** & –**goes**) Inselmeer *n*; (*group of islands*) Inselgruppe *f*, Archipel *m*

architect ['ɑrkɪ,tɛkt] *s* Architekt –in *mf*

architecture ['ɑrkɪ,tɛktʃər] *s* Architektur *f*, Baukunst *f*

archives ['ɑrkaɪvz] *spl* Archiv *n*

arch'way' *s* Bogengang *m*, Torbogen *m*

arctic ['ɑrktɪk] *adj* arktisch, nördlich || **the Arctic** *s* die Arktis

Arc'tic Cir'cle *s* nördlicher Polarkreis *m*

arc' weld'ing *s* Lichtbogenschweißung *f*

ardent ['ɑrdənt] *adj* feurig, eifrig

ardor ['ɑrdər] *s* Eifer *m*, Inbrust *f*

arduous [ˈɑrdʒʊ·əs] adj mühsam

area [ˈɛrɪ·ə] s (surface) Fläche f; (district) Gegend f; (field of ent…rise) Bereich m, Gebiet n; (of danger) Zone f

arena [əˈrinə] s Arena f, Kampfbahn f

Argentina [ˌɑrdʒənˈtinə] s Argentinien n

argue [ˈɑrgjʊ] tr erörtern; (maintain) behaupten; **a. into** (ger) dazu überreden zu (inf) ǁ intr (**with**) streiten (mit); **a. for** (or **against**) s.th. für (or gegen) etw eintreten; **don't a.!** keine Widerrede!

argument [ˈɑrgjəmənt] s (discussion) Erörterung f; (point) Beweisgrund m; (disagreement) Auseinandersetzung f; (theme) Thema n

argumentative [ˌɑrgjəˈmɛntətɪv] adj streitsüchtig

aria [ˈɑrɪ·ə], [ˈɛrɪ·ə] s Arie f

arid [ˈærɪd] adj trocken, dürr

aridity [əˈrɪdɪtɪ] s Trockenheit f

arise [əˈraɪz] v (pret **arose** [əˈroz]; pp **arisen** [əˈrɪzən]) intr (come into being) (**from**) entstehen (aus); (get out of bed) aufstehen; (from a seat) sich erheben; (occur) aufkommen, auftauchen; (said of an opportunity) sich bieten; (stem) (**from**) stammen (von)

aristocracy [ˌærɪsˈtɑkrəsɪ] s Aristokratie f

aristocrat [əˈrɪstəˌkræt] s Aristokrat –in m f

aristocratic [ə ˌrɪstəˈkrætɪk] adj aristokratisch

arithmetic [əˈrɪθmətɪk] s Arithmetik f

arithmetical [ˌærɪθˈmɛtɪkəl] adj arithmetisch, rechnerisch

ark [ɑrk] s Arche f

ark′ of the cov′enant s Bundeslade f

arm [ɑrm] s Arm m; (of a chair) Seitenlehne f; (weapon) Waffe f; **keep s.o. at arm's length** sich j–n vom Leibe halten; **take up arms** zu den Waffen greifen; **up in arms** in Aufruhr ǁ tr bewaffnen; ǁ intr sich bewaffnen

armament [ˈɑrməmənt] s Kriegsausrüstung f, Bewaffnung f

ar′maments race′ s üstungswettlauf m

armature [ˈɑrmə ˌtʃər] s (of doorbell or magnet) Anker m; (of a motor or dynamo) Läufer m; (biol) Panzer m

arm′chair′ s Lehnsessel m; (unpadded) Lehnstuhl m

armed′ for′ces spl Streitkräfte pl

armed′ rob′bery s bewaffneter Raubüberfall m

Armenia [ɑrˈminɪ·ə] s Armenien n

armful [ˈɑrm ˌfʊl] s Armvoll m

armistice [ˈɑrmɪstɪs] s Waffenstillstand m

armor [ˈɑrmər] s Panzer m ǁ tr panzern

ar′mored car′ s Panzerwagen m

armor-piercing [ˈɑrmər ˌpɪrsɪŋ] adj panzerbrechend

ar′mor plat′ing [ˈpletɪŋ] s Panzerung f

armory [ˈɑrmərɪ] s (large arms storage) Arsenal n; (arms repair and storage room of a unit) Waffenkam-

mer f; (arms factory) Waffenfabrik f; (drill hall) Exerzierhalle f

arm′pit′ s Achselhöhle f

arm′ rest′ s Armlehne f

army [ˈɑrmɪ] adj Armes–, Heeres– ǁ s Armee f, Heer n; **join the a.** zum Militär gehen

aroma [əˈromə] s Aroma n, Duft m

aromatic [ˌærəˈmætɪk] adj aromatisch

around [əˈraʊnd] adv ringsherum; **be a. in der Nähe sein; get a.** viel herumkommen; **get a. to** (inf) dazukommen zu (inf) ǁ prep um (acc) herum; (approximately) etwa; (near) bei (dat); **a. town** in der Stadt

arouse [əˈraʊz] tr aufwecken; (fig) erwecken

arraign [əˈren] tr (accuse) anklagen; (jur) vor Gericht stellen

arrange [əˈrendʒ] tr arrangieren; (in a certain order) (an)ordnen; (a time) festsetzen; (mus) bearbeiten ǁ intr– **a. for** Vorkehrungen treffen für

arrangement [əˈrendʒmənt] s Anordnung f; (agreement) Vereinbarung f; (mus) Bearbeitung f; **make arrangements to** (inf) Vorbereitungen treffen, um zu (inf)

array [əˈre] s (of troops, facts) Ordnung f; (large number or quantity) Menge f; (apparel) Staat m ǁ tr ordnen; (dress up) putzen

arrears [əˈrɪrz] spl Rückstand m; **in a.** rückständig

arrest [əˈrɛst] s Verhaftung f; **make an a.** e–e Verhaftung vornehmen; **place under a.** in Haft nehmen; **under a.** verhaftet ǁ tr verhaften; (attention) fesseln; (a disease, progress) hemmen

arrival [əˈraɪvəl] s Ankunft f; (of merchandise) Eingang m; (a person) Ankömmling m

arrive [əˈraɪv] intr ankommen; (said of time, an event) kommen; **a. at** (a conclusion, decision) erlangen

arrogance [ˈærəgəns] s Anmaßung f

arrogant [ˈærəgənt] adj anmaßend

arrogate [ˈærə ˌget] tr sich (dat) anmaßen

arrow [ˈæro] s Pfeil m

ar′rowhead′ s Pfeilspitze f

arsenal [ˈɑrsənəl] s Arsenal n

arsenic [ˈɑrsɪnɪk] s Arsen n

arson [ˈɑrsən] s Brandstiftung f

arsonist [ˈɑrsənɪst] s Brandstifter –in m f

art [ɑrt] s Kunst f

artery [ˈɑrtərɪ] s Pulsader f; (highway) Verkehrsader f

artful [ˈɑrtfəl] adj (cunning) schlau, listig; (skillful) kunstvoll

arthritic [ɑrˈθrɪtɪk] adj arthritisch, gichtisch ǁ s Arthritiker –in m f

arthritis [ɑrˈθraɪtɪs] s Arthritis f

artichoke [ˈɑrtɪ ˌtʃok] s Artischocke f

article [ˈɑrtɪkəl] s (object) Gegenstand m; (com, gram, journ, jur) Artikel m

articulate [ɑrˈtɪkjəlɪt] adj deutlich ǁ [ɑrˈtɪkjə ˌlet] tr & intr deutlich aussprechen

artifact [ˈɑrtɪ ˌfækt] s Artefakt n

artifice [ˈɑrtɪfɪs] s Kunstgriff m

artificial [ˌɑrtɪˈfɪ/əl] adj Kunst–,

künstlich; (emotion, smile) gekünstelt

artillery [ɑr'tɪləri] s Artillerie f

artil'lery-man s (-men) Artillerist m

artisan ['ɑrtɪzən] s Handwerker –in mf

artist ['ɑrtɪst] s Künstler –in mf

artistic [ɑr'tɪstɪk] adj künstlerisch

artistry ['ɑrtɪstri] s Kunstfertigkeit f

artless ['ɑrtlɪs] adj (lacking art) unkünstlerisch; (made without skill) stümperhaft; (ingenuous) unbefangen

arts' and crafts' spl Kunstgewerbe n

arts' and sci'ences spl Geistes- und Naturwissenschaften pl

arty ['ɑrti] adj (coll) gekünstelt

Aryan ['ɛrɪ·ən], ['ɑrjən] adj arisch ‖ s Arier –in mf; (language) Arisch n

as [æz], [əz] adv wie; as…as (eben)so …wie; as far as Berlin bis nach Berlin; as far as I know soviel ich weiß; as far back as 1900 schon im Jahre 1900; as for me was mich betrifft; as if als ob; as long as solange; (with the proviso that) vorausgesetzt, daß; as soon as sobald wie; as though als ob; as well ebensogut, auch; as yet bis jetzt ‖ rel pron wie, was ‖ prep als; as a rule in der Regel ‖ conj wie; (while) als, während; (because) da, weil, indem; as it were sozusagen

asbestos [æs'bɛstəs] adj Asbest– ‖ s Asbest m

ascend [ə'sɛnd] tr (stairs) hinaufsteigen; (a throne, mountain) besteigen ‖ intr emporsteigen; (said of a balloon, plane) aufsteigen

ascendancy [ə'sɛndənsi] s Überlegenheit f

ascension [ə'sɛnʃən] s Aufsteigen n

Ascen'sion Day' s Himmelfahrtstag m

ascent [ə'sɛnt] s (on foot) Besteigung f; (by vehicle) Auffahrt f; (upward slope) Steigung f; (& fig) Aufstieg m

ascertain [ˌæsər'ten] tr feststellen

ascetic [ə'sɛtɪk] adj asketisch ‖ s Asket –in mf

ascribe [ə'skraɪb] tr—a. to zuschreiben (dat)

aseptic [ə'sɛptɪk] adj aseptisch

ash [æʃ] s Asche f; (tree) Esche f; ashes Asche f; (mortal remains) sterbliche Überreste pl

ashamed [ə'ʃemd] adj—be (or feel) a. (of) sich schämen (genit)

ash'can' s Ascheneimer m

ashen ['æʃən] adj aschgrau

ashore [ə'ʃor] adv (position) am Land; (direction) ans Land

ash'tray' s Aschenbecher m

Ash' Wednes'day s Aschermittwoch m

Asia ['eʒə], ['eʃə] s Asien n

A'sia Mi'nor s Kleinasien n

aside [ə'saɪd] adv zur Seite; a. from außer ‖ s (theat) Seitenbemerkung f

asinine ['æsɪˌnaɪn] adj eselhaft

ask [æsk] tr (request) bitten; (demand) auffordern; (a high price) fordern; (inquire of) fragen; ask a question (of s.o.) (j–m) e–e Frage stellen; ask in hereinbitten; that is asking too much das ist zuviel verlangt ‖ intr

fragen; **ask for** bitten um; **ask for trouble** sich [dat] selbst Schwierigkeiten machen

askance [əs'kæns] adv—look a. at schief ansehen

askew [ə'skju] adv schräg

ask'ing s—for the a. umsonst

asleep [ə'slip] adj schlafend; (numb) eingeschlafen; be a. schlafen; fall a. einschlafen

asp [æsp] s Natter f

asparagus [ə'spærəgəs] s Spargel m

aspect ['æspɛkt] s Gesichtspunkt m

aspen ['æspən] s Espe f

aspersion [ə'spɑrʒən] s (eccl) Besprengung f; cast aspersions on verleumden

asphalt ['æsfɔlt], ['æsfælt] s Asphalt m ‖ tr asphaltieren

asphyxiate [æs'fɪksɪˌet] tr & intr ersticken

aspirant [ə'spaɪrənt] s Bewerber –in mf

aspirate ['æspɪrɪt] s Hauchlaut m ‖ ['æspɪˌret] tr behauchen

aspire [ə'spaɪr] intr (after, to) streben (nach); a. to (inf) danach streben zu (inf)

aspirin ['æspɪrɪn] s Aspirin n

ass [æs] s Esel m; (vulg) Arsch m; make an ass of oneself (sl) sich lächerlich machen

assail [ə'sel] tr angreifen, anfallen; (with questions) bestürmen

assassin [ə'sæsɪn] s Meuchelmörder –in mf

assassinate [ə'sæsɪˌnet] tr ermorden

assassination [əˌsæsɪ'neʃən] s Meuchelmord m, Ermordung f

assault [ə'sɔlt] s Überfall m; (rape) Vergewaltigung f; (physical violence) (jur) tätlicher Angriff m; (threat of violence) (jur) unmittelbare Bedrohung f; (mil) Sturm m ‖ tr (er)stürmen, anfallen; (jur) tätlich beleidigen

assault' and bat'tery s schwere tätliche Beleidigung f

assay [ə'se], ['æse] s Prüfung f ‖ [ə'se] tr prüfen

assemble [ə'sɛmbəl] tr versammeln; (mach) montieren ‖ intr sich versammeln

assembly [ə'sɛmbli] s Versammlung f; (mach) Montage f; (pol) Unterhaus n

assem'bly line' s Fließband n

assent [ə'sɛnt] s Zustimmung f ‖ intr (to) zustimmen (dat)

assert [ə'sʌrt] tr behaupten; a. oneself sich behaupten

assertion [ə'sʌrʃən] s Behauptung f; (of rights) Geltendmachung f

assess [ə'sɛs] tr (damage) festsetzen; (property) (at) (ab)schätzen (auf acc); assessed value Schätzungswert m

assessment [ə'sɛsmənt] s (of damage) Festsetzung f; (valuation) Einschätzung f; (of real estate) Veranlagung f

assessor [ə'sɛsər] s Steuereinschätzer m

asset ['æset] *s* Vorzug *m*; (com) Aktivposten *m*; **assets** Vermögenswerte *pl*; **assets and liabilities** Aktiva und Passiva *pl*

assiduous [ə'sɪdʒu-əs] *adj* emsig

assign [ə'saɪn] *tr* zuweisen; *(homework)* aufgeben; *(transfer)* (jur) abtreten; (mil) zuteilen

assignment [ə'saɪnmənt] *s* Zuweisung *f*; *(homework)* Aufgabe *f*; *(task)* Auftrag *m*, Aufgabe *f*; *(transference)* (jur) Abtretung *f*; *(to a unit)* (mil) Zuteilung *f*

assimilate [ə'sɪmɪ‚let] *tr* angleichen || *intr* sich angleichen

assimilation [ə‚sɪmɪ'leʃən] *s* Assimilierung *f*, Angleichung *f*

assist [ə'sɪst] *s* (sport) Zuspiel *n* || *tr* beistehen *(dat)* || *intr*—**a. in** beistehen bei, behilflich sein bei

assistance [ə'sɪstəns] *s* Hilfe *f*

assistant [ə'sɪstənt] *adj* Hilfs-, Unter- || *s (helper)* Gehilfe *m*, Gehilfin *f*

associate [ə'soʃɪ‚ɪt] *adj* Mit-, beigeordnet; *(member)* außerordentlich || *s (companion)* Gefährte *m*, Gefährtin *f*; *(colleague)* Kollege *m*, Kollegin *f*; (com) Partner –in *mf* || [ə'soʃɪ‚et] *tr* verbinden || *intr* (**with**) verkehren (mit)

asso'ciate profes'sor *s* außerordentlicher Professor *m*

association [ə‚soʃɪ'eʃən] *s (connection)* Verbindung *f*; *(social intercourse)* Verkehr *m*; *(society)* Verband *m*; *(suggested ideas, feelings)* Assoziation *f*

assonance ['æsənəns] *s* Assonanz *f*

assorted [ə'sɔrtɪd] *adj* verschieden

assortment [ə'sɔrtmənt] *s* Sortiment *n*

assuage [ə'swedʒ] *tr (pain)* lindern; *(hunger)* befriedigen; *(thirst)* stillen

assume [ə's(j)um] *tr (a fact as true; a certain shape, property, habit)* annehmen; *(a duty)* auf sich nehmen; *(office)* antreten; *(power)* ergreifen; **assuming that** vorausgesetzt, daß

assumed' *adj (feigned)* erheuchelt; **a. name** Deckname *m*

assumption [ə'sʌmpʃən] *s (supposition)* Annahme *f*; *(e.g., of power)* Übernahme *f*

assurance [ə'ʃurəns] *s* Versicherung *f*

assure [ə'ʃur] *tr* versichern

aster ['æstər] *s* Aster *f*

asterisk ['æstə‚rɪsk] *s* Sternchen *s*

astern [ə'stʌrn] *adv* achtern, achteraus

asthma ['æzmə] *s* Asthma *n*

astonish [ə'stɑnɪʃ] *tr* in Erstaunen setzen; **be astonished at** staunen über *(acc)*, sich wundern über *(acc)*

aston'ishing *adj* erstaunlich

astonishment [ə'stɑnɪʃmənt] *s* Erstaunen *n*, Verwunderung *f*

astound [ə'staund] *tr* überraschen

astound'ing *adj* erstaunlich

astray [ə'stre] *adv*—**go a.** irregehen; **lead a.** irreführen

astride [ə'straɪd] *adv* rittlings || *prep (a road)* an beiden Seiten *(genit)*; *(a horse)* rittlings auf *(dat)*

astringent [əs'trɪndʒənt] *adj* stopfend || *s* Stopfmittel *n*

astrology [ə'strɑlədʒɪ] *s* Astrologie *f*

astronaut ['æstrə‚nɔt] *s* Astronaut *m*

astronautics [‚æstrə'nɔtɪks] *s* Raumfahrtwissenschaft *f*, Astronautik *f*

astronomer [ə'strɑnəmər] *s* Astronom –in *mf*

astronomic(al) [‚æstrə'nɑmɪk(əl)] *adj* astronomisch

astronomy [ə'strɑnəmɪ] *s* Astronomie *f*

astute [ə'st(j)ut] *adj* scharfsinnig; *(cunning)* schlau

asunder [ə'sʌndər] *adv* auseinander

asylum [ə'saɪləm] *s (refuge)* Asyl *n*; *(for the insane)* Irrenhaus *n*

at [æt], [ət] *prep (position)* an *(dat)*, auf *(dat)*, in *(dat)*, bei *(dat)*, zu *(dat)*; *(direction)* auf *(acc)*, gegen *(acc)*, nach *(dat)*, zu *(dat)*; *(manner, circumstance)* auf *(acc)*, in *(dat)*, unter *(dat)*, bei *(dat)*, zu *(dat)*; *(time)* um *(acc)*, bei *(dat)*, auf *(dat)* zu *(dat)*; **at all** *(in questions)* überhaupt; **at high prices** zu hohen Preisen; **even at that** so gar so

atheism ['eθɪ‚ɪzəm] *s* Atheismus *m*

atheist ['eθɪ-ɪst] *s* Atheist –in *mf*

Athens ['æθɪns] *s* Athen *n*

athlete ['æθlit] *s* Sportler –in *mf*

ath'lete's foot' *s* Fußflechte *f*

athletic [æθ'letɪk] *adj* athletisch, Sport-, Turn- || **athletics** *s* Athletik *f*

Atlantic [æt'læntɪk] *adj* atlantisch || *s* Atlantik *m*

atlas ['ætləs] *s* Atlas *m*

atmosphere ['ætməs‚fɪr] *s* (& fig) Atmosphäre *f*

atmospheric [‚ætməs'ferɪk] *adj* atmosphärisch

atom ['ætəm] *s* Atom *n*

atomic [ə'tɑmɪk] *adj* atomisch, atomar, Atom-

atom'ic age' *s* Atomzeitalter *n*

atom'ic bomb' *s* Atombombe *f*

atom'ic pow'er *s* Atomkraft *f*; **atomic powers** (pol) Atommächte *pl*

atomizer ['ætə‚maɪzər] *s* Zerstäuber *m*

atone [ə'ton] *intr*—**a. for** büßen

atonement [ə'tonmənt] *s* Buße *f*

atrocious [ə'troʃəs] *adj* gräßlich

atrocity [ə'trɑsɪtɪ] *s* Greueltat *f*

atro‧phy ['ætrəfɪ] *s* Verkümmerung *f*, Atrophie *f* || *v (pret & pp* **–phied)** *tr* auszehren || *intr* verkümmern

attach [ə'tæt] *tr (with glue, stitches, tacks)* **(to)** anheften (an *acc*); *(connect)* **(to)** befestigen (an *acc*); *(importance)* **(to)** beimessen *(dat)*; *(a person)* (jur) verhaften; *(a thing)* (jur) beschlagnahmen; (mil) **(to)** zuteilen *(dat)*; **a. oneself to** sich anschließen an *(acc)*; **be attached to** festhalten an *(dat)*; (fig) verwachsen sein mit

attaché [‚ætə'ʃe] *s* Attaché *m*

attaché' case' *s* Aktenköfferchen *n*

attachment [ə'tætʃmənt] *s* Befestigung *f*; *(regard)* **(to)** Zuneigung *f (zu)*; *(device)* Zusatzgerät *n*; *(of a person)* (jur) Verhaftung *f*; *(of a thing)* (jur) Beschlagnahme *f*

attack [ə'tæk] *s* Angriff *m*; (pathol)

Anfall *m* || *tr & intr* angreifen; (pathol) überfallen

attain [ə'ten] *tr* erreichen, erzielen || *intr*—a. to erreichen

attainment [ə'tenmənt] *s* Erreichen *n*; **attainments** Fertigkeiten *pl*

attempt [ə'tempt] *s* Versuch *m*; (*assault*) Attentat *n* || *tr* versuchen

attend [ə'tend] *tr* beiwohnen (*dat*); (*school, church*) besuchen; (*accompany*) begleiten; (*a patient*) behandeln || *intr*—a. to nachgehen (*dat*), erledigen

attendance [ə'tendəns] *s* Besuch *m*; (*number in attendance*) Besucherzahl *f*; (med) Behandlung *f*

attendant [ə'tendənt] *s* (*servant, waiter*) Diener –in *mf*; (*keeper*) Wärter –in *mf*; (*at a gas station*) Tankwart *m*; (*escort*) Begleiter –in *mf*

attention [ə'tenʃən] *s* Aufmerksamkeit *f*; Acht *f*; **a. Mr. X.** zu Händen von Herrn X; **call a. to** hinweisen auf (*acc*); **call s.o.'s a. to** j–n aufmerksam machen auf (*acc*); **pay a.** achtgeben; **pay a. to** achten auf (*acc*); **stand at a.** stillstehen || *interj* (mil) Achtung!

attentive [ə'tentɪv] *adj* aufmerksam

attenuate [ə'tenju‚et] *tr* (*dilute, thin*) verdünnen; (*weaken*) abschwächen

attest [ə'test] *tr* bezeugen || *intr*—a. to bezeugen

attic ['ætɪk] *s* Dachboden *m*; (*as living quarters*) Mansarde *f*

attire [ə'taɪr] *s* Putz *m* || *tr* kleiden

attitude ['ætɪ‚t(j)ud] *s* Haltung *f*; (aer, rok) Lage *f*

attorney [ə'tʌrni] *s* Rechtsanwalt *m*

attor'ney gen'eral *s* (**attorneys general**) Justizminister *m*

attract [ə'trækt] *tr* anziehen, reizen; (*attention*) erregen

attraction [ə'trækʃən] *s* Anziehungskraft *f*; (*that which attracts*) Anziehungspunkt *m*; (*in a circus, variety show*) Attraktion *f*; (theat) Zugstück *n*

attractive [ə'træktɪv] *adj* reizvoll; (*price, offer*) günstig

attribute ['ætrɪ‚bjut] *s* Attribut *n* || [ə'trɪbjut] *tr* (**to**) zuschreiben (*dat*)

attrition [ə'trɪʃən] *s* Abnutzung *f*, Verschleiß *m*

attune [ə't(j)un] *tr* (**to**) abstimmen (auf *acc*)

auburn ['ɔbərn] *adj* kastanienbraun

auction ['ɔkʃən] *s* Auktion *f* || *tr*—a. off versteigern; **be auctioned off** unter den Hammer kommen

auctioneer [‚ɔkʃən'ɪr] *s* Versteigerer –in *mf*

audacious [ə'deʃəs] *adj* (*daring*) kühn; (*brazen*) keck

audacity [ə'dæsɪti] *s* (*daring*) Kühnheit *f*; (*insolence*) Unverschämtheit *f*

audience ['ɔdɪ‚əns] *s* (*spectators*) Publikum *n*; (*formal hearing*) Audienz *f*; (rad) Zuhörerschaft *f*; (telv) Fernsehpublikum *n*

au'dio fre'quency ['ɔdɪ‚o] *s* Tonfrequenz *f*, Hörfrequenz *f*

au'dio-vis'ual *adj* audiovisuell; **a. aids** Lehrmittel *pl*

audit ['ɔdɪt] *s* Rechnungsprüfung *f* || *tr* prüfen, revidieren; (*a lecture*) als Gasthörer belegen

audition [ə'dɪʃən] *s* Hörprobe *f* || *tr* vorspielen (or vorsingen) lassen || *intr* vorspielen, vorsingen

auditor ['ɔdɪtər] *s* (com) Rechnungsprüfer –in *mf*; (educ) Gasthörer –in *mf*

auditorium [‚ɔdɪ'torɪ‚əm] *s* Hörsaal *m*

auger ['ɔgər] *s* Bohrer *m*

augment [ɔg'mɛnt] *tr* (*in size*) vergrößern; (*in number*) vermehren || *intr* sich vergrößern; sich vermehren

augur ['ɔgər] *s* Augur *m* || *intr* weissagen; **a. well for** Gutes versprechen für

augury ['ɔgərɪ] *s* Weissagung *f*

august [ə'gʌst] *adj* erhaben || **August** ['ɔgəst] *s* August *m*

aunt [ænt], [ɑnt] *s* Tante *f*

auricle ['ɔrɪkəl] *s* äußeres Ohr *n*; (*of the heart*) Herzohr *n*

auspices ['ɔspɪsɪz] *spl* Auspizien *pl*

auspicious [ɔs'pɪʃəs] *adj* glückverheißend

austere [ɔs'tɪr] *adj* (*stern*) streng; (*simple*) einfach; (*frugal*) genügsam; (*style*) schmucklos

Australia [ɔ'streljə] *s* Australien *n*

Australian [ɔ'streljən] *adj* australisch || *s* Australier –in *mf*

Austria ['ɔstrɪ‚ə] *s* Österreich *n*

Austrian ['ɔstrɪ‚ən] *adj* österreichisch || *s* Österreicher –in *mf*; (*dialect*) Österreichisch *n*

authentic [ɔ'θentɪk] *adj* authentisch

authenticate [ɔ'θentɪ‚ket] *tr* (*establish as genuine*) als echt erweisen; (*a document*) beglaubigen

author ['ɔθər] *s* (*of a book*) Autor –in *mf*; (*creator*) Urheber –in *mf*

authoritative [ɔ'θɔrɪ‚tetɪv] *adj* maßgebend

authority [ɔ'θɔrɪti] *s* (*power; expert*) Autorität *f*; (*right*) Recht *n*; (*approval*) Genehmigung *f*; (*source*) Quelle *f*; (*commanding influence*) Ansehen *n*; (*authoritative body*) Behörde *f*; **on one's own a.** auf eigene Verantwortung; **the authorities** die Behörden

authorize ['ɔθə‚raɪz] *tr* autorisieren

au'thorship' *s* Autorschaft *f*

au•to ['ɔto] *s* (**–tos**) Auto *n*

autobiography [‚ɔtobaɪ'ɑgrəfi] *s* Selbstbiographie *f*

autocratic [‚ɔtə'krætɪk] *adj* autokratisch

autograph ['ɔtə‚græf] *s* Autogramm *n* || *tr* autographieren

automat ['ɔtə‚mæt] *s* Automatenrestaurant *n*

automatic [‚ɔtə'mætɪk] *adj* automatisch || *s* Selbstladepistole *f*

automat'ic transmis'sion *s* Automatik *f*

automation [‚ɔtə'meʃən] *s* Automation *f*

automa•ton [ə'tɔmə‚tɑn] *s* (**–tons &** **–ta** [tə]) Automat *m*

automobile [ˌɔtəmoˈbil] *s* Automobil *n*

automotive [ˌɔtəˈmotɪv] *adj* Auto-

autonomous [ɔˈtʌnəməs] *adj* autonom

autonomy [ɔˈtʌnəmɪ] *s* Autonomie *f*

autopsy [ˈɔtɑpsɪ] *s* Obduktion *f*

autumn [ˈɔtəm] *adj* Herbst– || *s* Herbst *m*

autumnal [ɔˈtʌmnəl] *adj* herbstlich

auxiliary [ɔgˈzɪljərɪ] *adj* Hilfs– || *s* (*helper*) Helfer –in *mf*; (gram) Hilfszeitwort *n*; **auxiliaries** (mil) Hilfstruppen *pl*

avail [əˈvel] *s*—**to no a.** nutzlos; **without a.** vergeblich || *tr* nützen (*dat*); **a. oneself of** sich bedienen (*genit*) || *intr* nützen

available [əˈveləbəl] *adj* vorhanden, (*articles, products*) erhältlich; (*e.g., documents*) zugänglich; **be a.** (*for consultation, etc.*) zu sprechen sein; **make a.** (**to**) zur Verfügung stellen (*dat*)

avalanche [ˈævəˌlæntʃ] *s* Lawine *f*

avarice [ˈævərɪs] *s* Habsucht *f*, Geiz *m*

avaricious [ˌævəˈrɪ/əs] *adj* geizig

avenge [əˈvɛndʒ] *tr* (*a person*) rächen; (*a crime*) ahnden; **a. oneself on** sich rächen an (*dat*)

avenger [əˈvɛndʒər] *s* Rächer –in *mf*

avenue [ˈævəˌn(j)u] *s* (*wide street*) Straße *f*; (fig) Weg *m*

average [ˈævərɪdʒ] *adj* Durchschnitts– || *s* Durchschnitt *m*; (naut) Havarie *f*; **on the a.** im Durchschnitt || *tr* (*amount to, as a mean quantity*) durchschnittlich betragen; (*find the average of*) den Durchschnitt berechnen von; (*earn on the average*) durchschnittlich verdienen; (*travel on the average*) durchschnittlich zurücklegen

averse [əˈvʌrs] *adj* (**to**) abgeneigt (*dat*)

aversion [əˈvʌrʒən] *s* (**to**) Abneigung *f* (gegen)

avert [əˈvʌrt] *tr* abwenden

aviary [ˈevɪˌɛrɪ] *s* Vogelhaus *n*

aviation [ˌevɪˈe/ən] *s* Flugwesen *n*

aviator [ˈevɪˌetər] *s* Flieger –in *mf*

avid [ˈævɪd] *adj* gierig

avocation [ˌævəˈke/ən] *s* Nebenbeschäftigung *f*

avoid [əˈvɔɪd] *tr* (*a person*) meiden; (*a thing*) vermeiden

avoidable [əˈvɔɪdəbəl] *adj* vermeidbar

avoidance [əˈvɔɪdəns] *s* (*of a person*) Meidung *f*; (*of a thing*) Vermeidung *f*

avow [əˈvau] *tr* bekennen, gestehen

avowal [əˈvau‍əl] *s* Bekenntnis *n*

avowed′ *adj* (*declared*) erklärt; (*acknowledged*) offen anerkannt

await [əˈwet] *tr* erwarten

awake [əˈwek] *adj* wach, munter || *v* (*pret & pp* **awoke** [əˈwok] & **awaked**) *tr* wecken; (fig) erwecken || *intr* erwachen

awaken [əˈwekən] *tr* wecken; (fig) erwecken || *intr* erwachen

awak′ening *s* Erwachen *n*; **a rude a.** ein unsanftes Erwachen

award [əˈwɔrd] *s* Preis *m*, Prämie *f* || *tr* (**to**) zuerkennen (*dat*)

aware [əˈwɛr] *adj*—**be a. of** sich [*dat*] bewußt sein (*genit*)

awareness [əˈwɛrnɪs] *s* Bewußtsein *n*

awash [əˈwɑ/] *adj* überschwemmt

away [əˈwe] *adj* abwesend; (*on a trip*) verreist; (sport) Auswärts– || *adv* fort, (hin)weg; **do a. with** abschaffen; **make a. with** (*kill*) umbringen

awe [ɔ] *s* (*of*) Ehrfurcht *f* (*vor dat*); **stand in awe of s.o.** vor j–m Ehrfurcht haben

awesome [ˈɔsəm] *adj* ehrfurchtgebietend

awful [ˈɔfəl] *adj* ehrfurchtgebietend; (coll) furchtbar

awfully [ˈɔfəlɪ] *adv* (coll) furchtbar

awhile [əˈhwaɪl] *adv* eine Zeitlang

awkward [ˈɔkwərd] *adj* ungeschickt; (*situation*) peinlich

awl [ɔl] *s* Ahle *f*, Pfriem *m*

awning [ˈɔnɪŋ] *s* Markise *f*

awry [əˈraɪ] *adv*—**go a.** schiefgehen

ax [æks] *s* Axt *f*, Beil *n*

axiom [ˈæksɪˌəm] *s* Axiom *n*

axiomatic [ˌæksɪˌəˈmætɪk] *adj* axiomatisch

axis [ˈæksɪs] *s* (**axes** [ˈæksiz]) Achse *f*

axle [ˈæksəl] *s* Achse *f*

ay(e) [aɪ] *adv* (*yes*) ja; **aye, aye, sir!** zu Befehl, Herr (*Leutnant, etc.*) || *s* Ja *n*, Jastimme *f*; **the ayes have it** die Mehrheit ist dafür

azalea [əˈzeljə] *s* Azalee *f*

azure [ˈæʒər] *adj* azurblau || *s* Azur *m*

B

B, b [bi] zweiter Buchstabe des englischen Alphabets; (mus) H *n*; **B flat** B *n*; **B sharp** His *n*

babble [ˈbæbəl] *s* Geschwätz *n*; (*of brook*) Geplätscher *n* || *tr* schwätzen || *intr* schwätzen; (*said of a brook*) plätschern

babe [beb] *s* Kind *n*; (*naive person*) Kindskopf *m*; (*pretty girl*) Puppe *f*

baboon [bæˈbun] *s* (zool) Pavian *m*

ba·by [ˈbebɪ] *s* Baby *n*; (*youngest child*) Nesthäkchen *n* || *v* (*pret & pp* –bied) *tr* verzärteln

ba′by bot′tle *s* Saugflasche *f*

ba′by car′riage *s* Kinderwagen *m*

ba′by grand′ *s* Stutzflügel *m*

ba′by pow′der *s* Kinderpuder *m*

ba·by-sit′ *v* (*pret & pp* –sat; *ger* –sitting) *intr* Kinder hüten

ba′by-sit′ter *s* Babysitter *m*

ba′by talk′ s Babysprache f
ba′by teeth′ spl Milchzähne pl
baccalaureate [ˌbækəˈlɔrɪ·ɪt] s (bach-elor's degree) Bakkalaureat n; (serv-ice) Gottesdienst m bei der akade-mischen Promotion
bacchanal [ˈbækənəl] s (devotee) Bac-chantin f; (orgy) Bacchanal n
bachelor [ˈbætʃələr] s Junggeselle m
bach′elorhood′ s Junggesellenstand m
Bach′elor of Arts′ s Bakkalaureus m der Geisteswissenschaften
Bach′elor of Sci′ence s Bakkalaureus m der Naturwissenschaften
bacil·lus [bəˈsɪləs] s (–li [laɪ]) Ba-zillus m, Stäbchenbakterie f
back [bæk] adj Hinter-, Rück- || s (of a man, animal) Rücken m, Kreuz n; (of a hand, book, knife, mountain) Rücken m; (of a head, house, door, picture, sheet) Rückseite f; (of a fabric) linke Seite f; (of a seat) Rückenlehne f; (of a coin) Kehrseite f; (of clothing) Rückenteil m; (sport) Verteidiger m; **at the b. of** (e.g., a room) hinten in (dat); **b. to b.** (coll) nacheinander; **behind s.o.'s b.** hinter j-s Rücken; **have one's b. to the wall** an die Wand gedrückt sein; **turn one's b. on s.o.** (& fig) j-m den Rücken kehren || adv zurück; **b. and forth** hin und her; **b. home** bei uns (zulande); || tr (a person) den Rücken decken (dat); (a candidate, product) befürworten; (a horse) set-zen auf (acc); **b. up** (a car) rückwärts laufen lassen; **b. water** rückwärts rudern; das Schiff rückwärts fahren lassen; (fig) sich zurückziehen || intr —**b. down** klein beigeben; **b. down from** abstehen von; **b. out of** zurück-treten von; **b. up** zurückfahren, zurückgehen; (said of a sewer) zurückfließen
back′ache′ s Rückenschmerzen pl
back′bit′ing s Anschwärzerei f
back′bone′ s Rückgrat n; (fig) Willens-kraft f
back′break′ing adj mühsam
back′ door′ s Hintertür f
back′drop′ s (fig & theat) Hintergrund m
backer [ˈbækər] s Förderer m, Unter-stützer m; (com) Hintermann m
back′fire′ s Fehlzündung f || intr fehl-zünden; (fig) nach hinten losgehen
back′ground′ adj Hintergrund- || s (& fig) Hintergrund m; (e.g., of an ap-plicant) Vorbildung f, Erfahrung f
back′hand′ s (tennis) Ruckhandschlag m
back′hand′ed adj Rückhand–; (compli-ment) zweideutig
back′ing s Unterstützung f; (material) versteifende Ausfütterung f
back′lash′ s (& fig) Rückschlag m; (mach) toter Gang m
back′log′ s Rückstand m
back′ or′der s rückständiger Auftrag m
back′ pay′ s rückständiger Lohn m
back′ seat′ s Rücksitz m
back′side′ s Rückseite f; (coll) Gesäß n

back′space′ intr den Wagen zurück-schieben
back′space key′ s Rücktaste f
back′spin′ s Rückeffet n
back′stage′ adv hinten auf die Bühne
back′ stairs′ spl Hintertreppe f
back′stop′ s (baseball) Ballfang m
back′ stretch′ s Gegengerade f
back′stroke′ s Rückenschwimmen n
back′swept′ adj pfeilförmig
back′ talk′ s freche Antworten pl
back′track′ intr denselben Weg zurück-gehen; (fig) e–n Rückzieher machen
back′up s (stand-by) Beistand m; (in traffic) Verkehrsstauung f
back′up light′ s (aut) Rückfahrschein-werfer m
backward [ˈbækwərd] adj rückwärts gerichtet, Rück-; (country) rück-ständig; (in development) zurückge-blieben; (shy) zurückhaltend || adv rückwärts, zurück; (fig) verkehrt; **b. and forward** vor und zurück
backwardness [ˈbækwərdnɪs] s Rück-ständigkeit f; (shyness) Zurückhal-tung f
back′wash′ s zurücklaufende Strömung f
back′wa′ter s Rückstau m; (fig) Öde f
back′woods′ spl Hinterwälder pl
back′yard′ s Hinterhof m
bacon [ˈbekən] s Speck m; **bring home the b.** (sl) es schaffen
bacteria [bækˈtɪrɪ·ə] spl Bakterien pl
bacteriological [bækˌtɪrɪ·əˈladʒɪkəl] adj bakteriologisch
bacteriology [bækˌtɪrɪˈaɪədʒi] s Bak-teriologie f, Bakterienkunde f
bacteri·um [bækˈtɪrɪ·əm] s (–a [ə]) Bakterie f
bad [bæd] adj schlecht, schlimm; (un-favorable) ungünstig; (risk) zweifel-haft; (debt) uneinbringlich; (check) ungedeckt; (blood) böse; (breath) übelriechend; (language) anstößig; (pain) stark; **bad for** schädlich (dat); **from bad to worse** immer schlimmer; **I feel bad about it** es tut mir leid; **too bad!** schade!
bad′ egg′ s (sl) übler Kunde m
badge [bædʒ] s Abzeichen n
badger [ˈbædʒər] s Dachs m || tr quälen
bad′ luck′ s Unglück n, Pech n
badly [ˈbædli] adv schlecht, übel; (coll) dringend; **b. wounded** schwer-verwundet; **be b. off** übel dran sein
badminton [ˈbædmɪntən] s Federball-spiel n
bad′-tem′pered adj schlecht gelaunt
baffle [ˈbæfəl] s Sperre f; (on loud-speaker) Schallwand f || tr verwir-ren; (gas) drosseln
baf′fling adj verwirrend
bag [bæg] s Sack m; (for small items) Tüte f; (for travel) Reisetasche f; (sl) Frauenzimmer n; (hunt) Strecke f; **bag and baggage** mit Sack und Pack; **it's in the bag** das haben wir in der Tasche || v (pret & pp bagged; ger bagging) tr einsacken; (hunt) zur Strecke bringen || intr sich bauschen
baggage [ˈbægɪdʒ] s Gepäck n

bag′gage car′ s Gepäckwagen m

bag′gage check′ s Gepäckschein m

bag′gage count′er s Gepäckabfertigung f

bag′gage room′ s Gepäckaufbewahrung f

baggy [′bægi] adj bauschig

bag′pipe′ s Dudelsack m; **play the b.** dudeln

bail [bel] s Kaution f; **be out on b.** gegen Kaution auf freiem Fuß sein; **put up b. for** bürgen für ‖ tr—**b. out** (water) ausschöpfen; (fig) retten; (jur) durch Kaution aus der Haft befreien ‖ intr Wasser schöpfen; **b. out** (aer) abspringen

bailiff [′belɪf] s (agr) Gutsverwalter m; (jur) Gerichtsvollzieher m

bailiwick [′belɪwɪk] s (fig) Spezialgebiet n; (jur) Amtsbezirk m

bait [bet] s (& fig) Köder m ‖ tr (traps) mit Köder versehen; (lure) ködern; (harass) quälen

bake [bek] tr (bread) backen; (meat) braten; (in a kiln) brennen ‖ intr backen; (meat) braten

baked′ goods′ spl Gebäck n, Backwaren pl

baked′ pota′to s gebackene Pellkartoffel f

baker [′bekər] s Bäcker –in mf

bak′er′s doz′en s dreizehn Stück pl

bakery [′bekəri] s Bäckerei f

bak′ing pow′der s Backpulver n

bak′ing so′da s Backpulver n

balance [′bæləns] s (equilibrium) Gleichgewicht n; (remainder) Rest m; (scales) Waage f; (in a bank account) Bankguthaben n; (fig) Fassung f; (com) Bilanz f; ‖ tr balancieren; (offset) abgleichen; (make come out even) ausgleichen ‖ intr balancieren

bal′ance of pay′ments s Devisenbilanz f

bal′ance of pow′er s Gleichgewicht n der Kräfte

bal′ance sheet′ s Bilanz f

bal′ance wheel′ s (horol) Unruh f

balcony [′bælkəni] s Balkon m; (theat) Rang m

bald [bold] adj kahl; (eagle) weißköpfig; (fig) unverblümt

bald′head′ed adj kahlköpfig

baldness [′boldnɪs] s Kahlheit f

bald′ spot′ s Kahlstelle f

bale [bel] s Ballen m ‖ tr in Ballen verpacken

baleful [′belfəl] adj unheilvoll

balk [bok] intr (at) scheuen (vor dat)

Balkan [′bolkən] adj Balkan– ‖ s— **the Balkans** die Balkan

balky [′boki] adj störrisch

ball [bol] s Ball m; (dance) Ball m; (of yarn) Knäuel m & n; (of the foot) Ballen m; **be on the b.** (coll) bei der Sache sein; **have a lot on the b.** (coll) viel auf dem Kasten haben

ballad [′bæləd] s Ballade f

ball′-and-sock′et joint′ s Kugelgelenk n

ballast [′bæləst] s (aer, naut) Ballast m; (rr) Schotter m ‖ tr (aer, naut) mit Ballast beladen; (rr) beschottern

ball′ bear′ing s Kugellager n

ballerina [,bælə′rinə] s Ballerina f

ballet [bæ′le] s Ballett n

ball′ han′dling s (sport) Balltechnik f

ballistic [bə′lɪstɪk] adj ballistisch ‖ **ballistics** s Ballistik f

balloon [bə′lun] s Ballon m

ballot [′bælət] s Stimmzettel m ‖ intr abstimmen

bal′lot box′ s Wahlurne f

ball′-point pen′ s Kugelschreiber m

ball′room′ s Ballsaal m, Tanzsaal m

ballyhoo [′bælɪ,hu] s Tamtam n ‖ tr Tamtam machen um

balm [bam] s (& fig) Balsam m

balmy [′bami] adj mild, lind; **be b.** (coll) e-n Tick haben

baloney [bə′loni] s (sausage) (coll) Bolognawurst f; (sl) Quatsch m

balsam [′bolsəm] s Balsam m

Baltic [′boltɪk] adj baltisch ‖ s Ostsee f

baluster [′bæləstər] s Geländersäule f

balustrade [′bæləs,tred] s Brüstung f

bamboo [bæm′bu] s Bambus m, Bambusrohr n

bamboozle [bæm′buzəl] tr (cheat) anschmieren; (mislead) irreführen; (perplex) verwirren

ban [bæn] s Verbot n; (eccl) Bann m; ‖ v (pret & pp banned; ger banning) tr verbieten

banal [′benəl] adj banal

banana [bə′nænə] s Banane f; (tree) Bananenbaum m

band [bænd] s (e.g., of a hat) Band n; (stripe) Steifen m; (gang) Bande f; (mus) Musikkapelle f; (rad) Band n ‖ intr—**b. together** sich zusammenrotten

bandage [′bændɪdʒ] s Verband m ‖ tr verbinden

Band′-Aid′ s (trademark) Schnellverband m

bandit [′bændɪt] s Bandit m

band′lead′er s Kapellmeister m

band′ saw′ s Bandsäge f

band′stand′ s Musikpavillon m

band′wag′on s—**climb the b.** mitlaufen

bane [ben] s Ruin m

baneful [′benfəl] adj verderblich

bang [bæŋ] s Knall m; **bangs** Ponyfrisur f; **with a b.** mit Krach ‖ tr knallen lassen; (a door) zuschlagen; ‖ intr knallen; (said of a door) zuschlagen; ‖ interj bums! paff!

bang′-up′ adj (sl) tipptopp, prima

banish [′bænɪʃ] tr verbannen

banishment [′bænɪʃmənt] s Verbannung f

banister [′bænɪstər] s Geländer n

bank [bæŋk] s Bank f; (of a river) Ufer n; (in a road) Überhöhung f; (aer) Schräglage f; (rr) Böschung f; ‖ tr (money) in e-r Bank deponieren; (a road) überhöhen; (aer) in Schräglage bringen ‖ intr (at) ein Bankkonto haben (bei); (aer) in die Kurve gehen; **b. on** bauen auf (acc)

bank′ account′ s Bankkonto n

bank′ bal′ance s Bankguthaben n

bank′book′ s Sparbuch n, Bankbuch n

banker [′bæŋkər] s Bankier –in mf

bank'ing s Bankwesen n
bank' note' s Geldschein m
bank'roll' s Rolle f von Geldscheinen ‖ tr (sl) finanzieren
bankrupt ['bæŋkrʌpt] adj bankrott; go b. Pleite machen ‖ tr bankrott machen
bankruptcy ['bæŋkrʌptsɪ] s Bankrott m
bank' state'ment s Bankausweis m
bank' tell'er s Kassierer –in m
banner ['bænər] s Fahne f, Banner n
banquet ['bæŋkwɪt] s Bankett n ‖ intr tafeln
banter ['bæntər] s Neckerei f ‖ intr necken
baptism ['bæptɪzəm] s Taufe f
baptismal [bæp'tɪzməl] adj Tauf-
baptis'mal certi'ficate s Taufschein m
bap'tism of fire' s Feuertaufe f
Baptist ['bæptɪst] s Baptist –in mf, Wiedertäufer m
baptistery ['bæptɪstərɪ] s Taufkapelle f
baptize [bæp'taɪz] tr taufen
bar [bar] s Stange f; (of a door, window) Riegel m; (of gold, etc.) Barren m; (of chocolate, soap) Riegel m; (barroom) Bar f; (counter) Schanktisch m; (obstacle) (to) Schranke f (gegen); (jur) Gerichtshof m, Anwaltschaft f; (bar line) (mus) Taktstrich m; (measure) Takt m; (naut) Barre f; be admitted to the bar zur Advokatur zugelassen werden; behind bars hinter Gittern; ‖ prep—bar none ohne Ausnahme ‖ v (pret & pp barred; ger barring) tr (a door) verriegeln; (a window) vergittern; (the way) versperren; bar s.o. from j–n hindern an (dat)
barb [barb] s Widerhaken m; (fig) Stachelrede f; (bot) Bart m
barbarian [bar'berɪ.ən] s Barbar m
barbaric [bar'bærɪk] adj barbarisch
barbarism ['barbə‚rɪzəm] s Barbarei f; (gram) Barbarismus m
barbarity [bar'berɪtɪ] s Barbarei f
barbarous ['barbərəs] adj barbarisch
barbecue ['barbɪ‚kju] s am Spieß (or am Rost) gebratenes Fleisch n; (grill) Bratrost m; (outdoor meal) Gartengrillfest n ‖ tr am Spieß (or am Rost) braten
barbed' wire' s Stacheldraht m
barbed'-wire entan'glement s Drahtverhau m
barber ['barbər] s Friseur m
bar'ber chair' s Friseursessel m
bar'bershop' s Friseurladen m
bard [bard] s Barde m
bare [ber] adj nackt, bloß; (tree, wall) kahl; (facts) nackt; (majority) knapp ‖ tr entblößen; (heart, thoughts) offenbaren; (teeth) fletschen
bare'back' adj & adv sattellos
bare'faced' adj unverschämt
bare'foot' adj & adv barfuß
bare'head'ed adj & adv barhäuptig
barely ['berlɪ] adv kaum, bloß
bar'fly' s Kneipenhocker m
bargain ['bargɪn] s (deal) Geschäft n; (cheap purchase) Sonderangebot n; into the b.! obendrein; it's a b.! abge-

macht! ‖ tr—b. away mit Verlust verkaufen ‖ intr handeln; b. for verhandeln über (acc)
bar'gain price' s Preisschlager m
bar'gain sale' s Sonderverkauf m
barge [bardʒ] s Lastkahn m; ‖ intr—b. in hereinstürzen; b. into stürzen in (acc)
baritone ['bærɪ‚ton] s Bariton m
barium ['berɪ.əm] s Barium n
bark [bark] s (of a tree) Rinde f; (of a dog) Bellen n, Gebell n; (boat) Barke f; ‖ tr—b. out bellend hervorstoßen ‖ intr bellen; b. at anbellen
barker ['barkər] s Anreißer m
barley ['barlɪ] s Gerste f; grain of b. Graupe f
bar'maid' s Schankmädchen n, Bardame f
barn [barn] s Scheune f; (for animals) Stall m
barnacle ['barnəkəl] s Entenmuschel f
barn'storm' intr auf dem Lande Theateraufführungen veranstalten; (pol) auf dem Lande Wahlreden halten
barn'yard' s Scheunenhof m
barometer [bə'ramɪtər] s Barometer n
barometric [‚bærə'metrɪk] adj barometrisch
baron ['bærən] s Baron m
baroness ['bærənɪs] s Baronin f
baroque [bə'rok] adj barock ‖ s (style, period) Barock m & n
barracks ['bærəks] s (temporary wooden structure) Baracke f; (mil) Kaserne f
barrage [bə'raʒ] s Sperrfeuer n; moving b. Sperrfeuerwalze f
barrel ['bærəl] s Faß m, Tonne f; (of a gun) Lauf m; (of money, fun) große Menge f; have over the b. (sl) in der Gewalt haben ‖ intr (coll) rasen, sausen
barren ['bærən] adj dürr, unfruchtbar; (landscape) kahl
barricade ['bærɪ‚ked] s Barrikade f ‖ tr verbarrikadieren
barrier ['bærɪ.ər] s Schranke f, Schlagbaum m; (e.g., on a street) Sperre f
bar'room' s Schenkstube f, Bar f
bartend ['bar‚tend] intr Getränke ausschenken
bar'tend'er s Schankwirt m, Barmixer m
barter ['bartər] s Tauschhandel m ‖ tr tauschen ‖ intr Tauschhandel treiben
basalt ['bæsɔlt], [bæ'sɔlt] s Basalt m
base [bes] adj gemein, niedrig; (metal) unedel ‖ s (cosmetic) Schminkunterlage f; (fig) Grundlage f; (archit) Basis f, Fundament n; (baseball) Mal n; (chem) Base f; (geom) Grundlinie f, Grundfläche f; (math) Basis f; (mil) Stützpunkt m ‖ tr (mil) stationieren; b. on stützen auf (acc), gründen auf (acc)
base'ball' s Baseball m
base'board' s Wandleiste f
basement ['besmənt] s Kellergeschoß n
bash [bæʃ] s heftiger Schlag m
bashful ['bæʃfəl] adj schüchtern

basic [′besɪk] adj grundsätzlich; (e.g., salary) Grund-; (chem) basisch

basically [′besɪkəlɪ] adv grundsätzlich

ba′sic train′ing s Grundausbildung f

basilica [bə′sɪlɪkə] s Basilika f

basin [′besɪn] s Becken n; (geol) Mulde f; (naut) Bassin n

ba·sis [′besɪs] s (–ses [siz]) Basis f, Grundlage f; **b. of comparison** Vergleichsgrundlage f; **put on a firm b.** (fin) sanieren

bask [bæsk] intr (& fig) sich sonnen

basket [′bæskɪt] s (& sport) Korb m

bas′ketball′ s Basketball m, Korbball m

bas-relief [ˌbɑrɪ′lif] s Flachrelief n

bass [bes] adj Baß– || s (mus) Baß m || [bæs] s (ichth) Flußbarsch m, Seebarsch m

bass′ clef′ s Baßschlüssel m

bass′ drum′ s große Trommel f

bass′ fid′dle s Baßgeige f

bassoon [bə′sun] s Fagott n

bass viol [′bes′vaɪ-əl] s Gambe f

bastard [′bæstərd] adj Bastard–; (illegitimate in birth) unehelich || s Bastard m; (vulg) Schweinehund m

baste [best] tr (thrash) verprügeln; (scold) schelten; (culin) begießen; (sew) lose (an)heften

bastion [′bæstʃən] s Bastion f

bat [bæt] s (sport) Schläger m; (zool) Fledermaus f; **go to bat for s.o.** (fig) für j–n eintreten || v (pret & pp batted; ger batting) tr schlagen; **without batting an eye** ohne mit der Wimper zu zucken

batch [bætʃ] s Satz m, Haufen m; (of bread) Schub m; (of letters) Stoß m

bated [′betɪd] adj—**with b. breath** mit verhaltenem Atem

bath [bæθ] s Bad n; **take a b.** ein Bad nehmen

bathe [beð] tr & intr baden

bather [′beðər] s Badende mf

bath′house′ s Umkleideräume pl

bath′ing s Baden n, Bad n

bath′ing cap′ s Badehaube f

bath′ing suit′ s Badeanzug m

bath′ing trunks′ spl Badehose f

bath′robe′ s Bademantel m

bath′room′ s Badezimmer n

bath′room fix′tures spl Armaturen pl

bath′room scales spl Personenwaage f

bath′ tow′el s Badetuch n

bath′tub′ s Badewanne f

baton [bæ′tɑn] s (mil) Kommandostab m; (mus) Taktstock m

battalion [bə′tæljən] s Bataillon n

batter [′bætər] s Teig m; (baseball) Schläger –in mf || tr zerschlagen; (aer) bombardieren; **b. down** niederschlagen; **b. in** einschlagen

bat′tering ram′ s Sturmbock m

battery [′bætərɪ] s Batterie f; (secondary cell) Akkumulator m; (arti) Batterie f; (nav) Geschützgruppe f

battle [′bætəl] s Schlacht f; (& fig) Kampf m; **do b.** kämpfen; **in b.** im Felde || tr bekämpfen || intr kämpfen

bat′tle array′ s Schlachtordnung f

bat′tleax′ s Streitaxt f; (fig) Drachen m

bat′tle cruis′er s Schlachtkreuzer m

bat′tle cry′ s Schlachtruf m; (fig) Schlagwort n

bat′tle fatigue′ s Kriegsneurose f

bat′tlefield′ s Schlachtfeld n

bat′tlefront′ s Front f, Hauptkampflinie f

bat′tleground′ s Kampfplatz m

battlement [′bætəlmənt] s Zinne f

bat′tle scar′ s Kampfmal n

bat′tleship′ s Schlachtschiff n

bat′tle wag′on s (coll) Schlachtschiff n

batty [′bætɪ] adj (sl) doof

bauble [′bɔbəl] s Tand m; (jester's staff) Narrenstab m

Bavaria [bə′verɪ-ə] s Bayern f

Bavarian [bə′verɪ-ən] adj bayerisch || s Bayer –in mf

bawd [bɔd] s Dirne f

bawdy [′bɔdɪ] adj unzüchtig

bawl [bɔl] s Geplärr n || tr—**b. out** (names, etc.) ausschreien; (scold) anschnauzen || intr (coll) plärren

bay [be] adj kastanienbraun || s Bucht f; (horse) Rotfuchs m; (bot) Lorbeer m; **keep at bay** in Schach halten || intr laut bellen; **bay at** anbellen

bayo·net [′be-ənɪt] s Bajonett n, Seitengewehr n; **with fixed bayonets** mit aufgepflanztem Bajonett || v (pret & pp –net(t)ed; ger –net(t)ing) tr mit dem Bajonett erstechen

bay′ win′dow s Erkerfenster n

bazaar [bə′zɑr] s Basar m, Markt m

bazooka [bə′zukə] s Panzerfaust f

be [bi] v (pres am [æm], is [ɪz], are [ɑr]; pret was [wɑz], [wʌz], were [wʌr]; pp been [bɪn]) intr sein; **be about to** in der Nähe sein; **be about to** (inf) im Begriff sein zu (inf); **be after s.o.** hinter j–m her sein; **be along** hier sein; **be behind in** im Rückstand sein mit; **be behind s.o.** j–m den Rücken decken; **be from** (a country) stammen aus, sein aus; **be in** zu Hause sein; **be in for** zu erwarten haben; **be in for it** in der Patsche sitzen; **be in on** dabei sein bei; **be off** weggehen; **be on to s.o.** j–m auf die Schliche kommen; **be out** nicht zu Hause sein, aus sein; **be out for s.th.** auf der Suche nach etw sein; **be up** auf sein; **be up to s.th.** etw im Sinn haben; **how are you?** wie geht es Ihnen?, wie befinden Sie sich?; **how much is that?** wieviel kostet das?; **there are, there** is es gibt (acc) || aux—**he is studying** er studiert; **he is to go** er soll gehen; **he was hit** er ist getroffen worden || impers—**how is it that…?** wie kommt es, daß…?; **it is cold** es ist kalt; **it is to be seen that** es ist darauf zu sehen, daß

beach [bit/] s Strand m; **on the b.** am Strand, an der See || tr auf den Strand ziehen; **be beached** stranden

beach′comb′er s Strandgutjäger m; (wave) Strandwelle f

beach′head′ s Landekopf m

beach′ tow′el s Badetuch n

beach′ umbrel′la s Strandschirm m

beacon [′bikən] s Leuchtfeuer n, Bake f; (lighthouse) Leuchtturm m; (aer)

Scheinwerfer *m* ‖ *tr* lenken ‖ *intr* leuchten

bead [bid] (*of glass, wood, sweat*) Perle *f*; (*of a gun*) Korn *n*; **beads** (eccl) Rosenkranz *m*; **draw a b. on** zielen auf (*acc*)

beagle ['bigel] *s* Spürhund *m*

beak [bik] *s* Schnabel *m*; (*nose*) (sl) Rübe *f*

beam [bim] *s* (*of wood*) Balken *m*; (*of light, heat, etc.*) Strahl *m*; (*fig*) Glanz *m*; (*aer*) Leitstrahl *m*; (*width of a vessel*) (naut) größte Schiffsbreite *f*; (*horizontal structural member*) (naut) Deckbalken *m*; **b. of light** Lichtkegel *m*; **off the b.** (sl) auf dem Holzweg; **on the b.** (sl) auf Draht ‖ *intr* strahlen; **b. at** anstrahlen

bean [bin] *s* Bohne *f*; (*head*) (sl) Birne *f*; **spill the beans** (sl) alles ausquatschen

bean′pole′ *s* (& coll) Bohnenstange *f*

bear [ber] *adj* (market) flau, Baisse- ‖ *s* Bär *m*; (st. exch.) Baissier *m* ‖ *v* (*pret* **bore** [bor]; *pp* **borne** [born]) *tr* (*carry*) tragen; (*endure*) dulden, ertragen; (*children*) gebären; (*date*) tragen; (*a name, sword*) führen; (*a grudge, love*) hegen; (*a message*) überbringen; (*the consequences*) auf sich [*acc*] nehmen; **bear in mind** bedenken, beachten; **bear fruit** Früchte tragen; (fig) Frucht tragen; **bear out** bestätigen ‖ *intr*—**bear down on** losgehen auf (*acc*); (naut) zufahren auf (*acc*); **bear left** sich links halten; **bear on** sich beziehen auf (*acc*); **bear up (well) against** gut ertragen; **bear up with** Geduld haben mit

bearable ['berəbəl] *adj* erträglich

beard [bɪrd] *s* Bart *m*

beard′ed *adj* bärtig

beardless ['bɪrdlɪs] *adj* bartlos

bearer ['berər] *s* Träger –in *mf*; (*of a message*) Überbringer –in *mf*; (com) Inhaber –in *mf*

bear′ hug′ *s* (coll) Knutsch *m*

bear′ing *s* Körperhaltung *f*; (mach) Lager *n*; (on) Beziehung *f* (auf *acc*); **bearings** (aer, naut) Lage *f*, Richtung *f*, Peilung *f*; **lose one's bearings** die Richtung verlieren

bear′skin′ *s* Bärenfell *n*

beast [bist] *s* Tier *n*; (fig) Bestie *f*

beastly ['bistli] *adj* bestialisch; **b. weather** Hundewetter *n*

beast′ of bur′den *s* Lasttier *n*

beat [bit] *adj* (sl) erschöpft ‖ *s* (*of the heart*) Schlag *m*; (*of a policeman*) Runde *f*, Revier *n*; (mus) Takt *m* ‖ *v* (*pret* **beat**; *pp* **beat** & **beaten**) *tr* (*eggs, a child, record, team, etc.*) schlagen; (*a carpet*) ausklopfen; (metal) hämmern; (*a path*) treten; **b. it!** hau ab!; **b. one's brains out** sich [*dat*] den Kopf zerbrechen; **b. s.o. to it** j-m zuvorkommen; **b. up** verprügeln ‖ *intr* schlagen, klopfen; **b. against** peitschen gegen; **b. down** niederprallen

beati·fy [bɪ'ætɪ,faɪ] *v* (*pret* & *pp* **–fied**) *tr* seligsprechen

beat′ing *s* Prügel *pl*

beatitude [bɪ'ætɪ,t(j)ud] *s* Seligpreisung *f*

beau [bo] *s* (**beaus** & **beaux** [boz]) Liebhaber *m*

beautician [bju'tɪʃən] *s* Kosmetiker –in *mf*; (*hairdresser*) Friseuse *f*

beautiful ['bjutɪfəl] *adj* schön

beauti·fy ['bjutɪ,faɪ] *v* (*pret* & *pp* **–fied**) *tr* verschönern

beauty ['bjuti] *s* (*quality; woman*) Schönheit *f*; (coll) Prachtexemplar *n*

beau′ty queen′ *s* Schönheitskönigin *f*

beau′ty shop′ *s* Frisiersalon *m*

beau′ty sleep′ *s* Schönheitsschlaf *m*

beau′ty spot′ *s* Schönheitsmal *n*

beaver ['bivər] *s* Biber *m*

because [bɪ'kɔz] *conj* weil, da ‖ *interj* darum!

because′ of′ *prep* wegen (genit)

beck [bek] *s* Wink *m*; **be at s.o.'s b. and call** j-m ganz zu Diensten sein

beckon ['bekən] *tr* zuwinken (*dat*); (*summon*) heranwinken ‖ *intr* winken; **b. to s.o.** j-m zuwinken

become [bɪ'kʌm] *v* (*pret* **–came**; *pp* **–come**) *tr* (*said of clothes*) gut anstehen (*dat*); (*said of conduct*) sich schicken für ‖ *intr* werden; **what has b. of him?** was ist aus ihm geworden?

becom′ing *adj* (*said of clothes*) kleidsam; (*said of conduct*) schicklich

bed [bed] *s* (*for sleeping; of a river*) Bett *n*; (*of flowers*) Beet *n*; (*of straw*) Lager *n*; (geol) Lager *n*; (rr) Unterbau *m*; **put to bed** zu Bett bringen

bed′bug′ *s* Wanze *f*

bed′clothes′ *spl* Bettwäsche *f*

bed′ding *s* Bettzeug *n*; (*for animals*) Streu *f*

bed′fel′low *s*—**strange bedfellows** ein seltsames Paar *n*

bedlam ['bedləm] *s* (fig) Tollhaus *n*; **there was b.** es ging zu wie im Tollhaus

bed′ lin′en *s* Bettwäsche *f*

bed′pan′ *s* Bettschüssel *f*

bed′post′ *s* Bettpfosten *m*

bedraggled [bɪ'drægəld] *adj* beschmutzt

bedridden ['bed,rɪdən] *adj* bettlägerig

bed′rock′ *s* Grundgestein *n*; (fig) Grundlage *f*

bed′room′ *s* Schlafzimmer *n*

bed′side′ *s*—**at s.o.'s b.** an j-s Bett

bed′sore′ *s* wundgelegene Stelle *f*; **get bedsores** sich wundliegen

bed′spread′ *s* Bettdecke *f*, Tagesdecke *f*

bed′spring′ *s* (*one coil*) Sprungfeder *f*; (*framework of springs*) Sprungfedermatratze *f*

bed′stead′ *s* Bettgestell *n*

bed′time′ *s* Schlafenszeit *f*; **it's past b.** es ist höchste Zeit, zu Bett zu gehen

bee [bi] *s* Biene *f*

beech [bitʃ] *s* Buche *f*

beech′nut′ *s* Buchecker *f*

beef [bif] *s* Rindfleisch *n*; (*brawn*) (coll) Muskelkraft *f*; (*human flesh*) (coll) Fleisch *n*; (*complaint*) (sl) Gemecker *n* ‖ *tr*—**b. up** (coll) ver-

stärken || *intr* (*complain*) (sl)
meckern

beef′ broth′ *s* Kraftbrühe *f*

beef′ steak′ *s* Beefsteak *n*

beefy [′bifi] *adj* muskulös

bee′ hive′ *s* Bienenstock *m*, Bienenkorb *m*

bee′ line′ *s*—**make a b. for** schnurstracks losgehen auf (*acc*)

beer [bɪr] *s* Bier *n*

bee′ sting′ *s* Bienenstich *m*

beeswax [′biz‚wæks] *s* Bienenwachs *n*

beet [bit] *s* Rübe *f*

beetle [′bitəl] *s* Käfer *m*

be·fall [bɪ′fɔl] *v* (*pret* **-fell** [′fel]; *pp* **-fallen** [′fɔlən]) *tr* betreffen, zustoßen || *intr* sich ereignen

befit′ting *adj* passend

before [bɪ′fɔr] *adv* vorher, früher || *prep* (*position or time*) vor (*dat*); (*direction*) vor (*acc*); **b. long** binnen kurzem; **b. now** schon früher || *conj* bevor, ehe

before′ hand′ *adv* zuvor, vorher

befriend [bɪ′frɛnd] *tr* sich [*dat*] (*j-n*) zum Freund machen, sich anfreunden mit

befuddle [bɪ′fʌdəl] *tr* verwirren

beg [bɛg] *v* (*pret & pp* **begged**; *ger* **begging**) *tr* bitten um; (*a meal*) betteln um; **beg s.o. to** (*inf*) *j-n* bitten zu (*inf*); **I beg your pardon** (*ich bitte um*) Verzeihung! || *intr* betteln; (*said of a dog*) Männchen machen; **beg for** bitten um, flehen um; **beg off** absagen

be·get [bɪ′gɛt] *v* (*pret* **-got** [′gɑt]; *pp* **-gotten** & **-got**; *ger* **-getting**) *tr* erzeugen

beggar [′bɛgər] *s* Bettler *-in m f*

be·gin [bɪ′gɪn] *v* (*pret* **-gan** [′gæn]; *pp* **-gun** [′gʌn]; *ger* **-ginning** [′gɪnɪŋ]) *tr* beginnen, anfangen || *intr* beginnen, anfangen; **to b. with** zunächst

beginner [bɪ′gɪnər] *s* Anfänger *-in m f*

begin′ ning *s* Beginn *m*, Anfang *m*

begrudge [bɪ′grʌdʒ] *tr*—**b. s.o. s.th.** *j-m etw* mißgönnen

beguile [bɪ′gaɪl] *tr* (*mislead*) verleiten; (*charm*) betören

behalf [bɪ′hæf] *s*—**on b. of** zugunsten (*genit*), für; (*as a representative of*) im Namen (*genit*), im Auftrag von

behave [bɪ′hev] *intr* sich benehmen

behavior [bɪ′hevjər] *s* Benehmen *n*

behead [bɪ′hɛd] *tr* enthaupten

behind [bɪ′haɪnd] *adj* (*in arrears*) (**in**) im Rückstand (**mit**); **the clock is ten minutes b.** die Uhr geht zehn Minuten nach || *adv* (*in the rear*) hinten, hinterher; (*to the rear*) nach hinten, zurück; **from b.** von hinten || *s* (sl) Hintern *m*, Popo *m* || *prep* (*position*) hinter (*dat*); (*direction*) hinter (*acc*); **be b. schedule** sich verspäten; **b. time** zu spät; **b. the times** hinter dem Mond

be·hold [bɪ′hold] *v* (*pret & pp* **-held** [′hɛld]) *tr* betrachten || *interj* schau!

behoove [bɪ′huv] *impers*—**it behooves me** es geziemt mir

beige [beʒ] *adj* beige || *s* Beige *n*

be′ ing *adj*—**for the time b.** einstweilen

|| *s* Dasein *n*; (*creature*) Wesen *n*; **come into b.** entstehen

belabor [bɪ′lebər] *tr* herumreiten auf (*dat*)

belated [bɪ′letɪd] *adj* verspätet

belch [bɛltʃ] *s* Rülpser *m* || *tr* (*fire*) ausspeien || *intr* rülpsen

beleaguer [bɪ′ligər] *tr* belagern

belfry [′bɛlfri] *s* Glockenturm *m*

Belgian [′bɛldʒən] *adj* belgisch || *s* Belgier *-in m f*

Belgium [′bɛldʒəm] *s* Belgien *n*

belief [bɪ′lif] *s* (**in**) Glaube(n) *m* (an *acc*)

believable [bɪ′livəbəl] *adj* glaublich

believe [bɪ′liv] *tr* (*a thing*) glauben; (*a person*) glauben (*dat*) || *intr* glauben; **b. in** glauben an (*acc*); **I don't b. in war** ich halte nicht viel vom Kriege

believer [bɪ′livər] *s* Gläubige *m f*

belittle [bɪ′lɪtəl] *tr* herabsetzen

bell [bɛl] *s* Glocke *f*; (*small bell*) Klingel *f*; (*of a wind instrument*) Schalltrichter *m*; (*box*) Gong *m*

bell′ boy′ *s* Hotelboy *m*

bell′ hop′ *s* (sl) Hotelpage *m*

belligerent [bə′lɪdʒərənt] *adj* streitlustig || *s* kriegführender Staat *m*

bell′ jar′ *s* Glasglocke *f*

bellow [′belo] *s* Gebrüll *n*; **bellows** Blasebalg *m*; (phot) Balgen *m* || *tr & intr* brüllen

bell′ tow′ er *s* Glockenturm *m*

bel·ly [′bɛli] *s* Bauch *m*; (*of a sail*) Bausch *m* || *v* (*pret & pp* **-lied**) *intr* bauschen

bel′ lyache′ *s* (coll) Bauchweh *n* || *intr* (sl) jammern

bel′ ly but′ ton *s* Nabel *m*

bel′ ly danc′ er *s* Bauchtänzerin *f*

bel′ ly flop′ *s* Bauchklatscher *m*

bellyful [′bɛli‚ful] *s*—**have a b. of** die Nase voll haben von

bel′ ly-land′ ing *s* Bauchlandung *f*

belong [bɪ′lɔŋ] *intr* **b. to** (*designating ownership*) gehören (*dat*); (*designating membership*) gehören zu; **where does this table b.?** wohin gehört dieser Tisch?

belongings [bɪ′lɔŋɪŋz] *spl* Sachen *pl*

beloved [bɪ′lʌvɪd], [bɪ′lʌvd] *adj* geliebt || *s* Geliebte *m f*

below [bɪ′lo] *adv* (*position*) unten; (*direction*) nach unten, hinunter || *prep* (*position*) unter (*dat*), unterhalb (*genit*); (*direction*) unter (*acc*)

belt [bɛlt] *s* Riemen *m*, Gurt *m*, Gürtel *m*; (geol) Gebiet *n*; (mach) Treibriemen *m*; **tighten one's b.** den Riemen enger schnallen || *tr* (sl) e-n heftigen Schlag versetzen (*dat*)

belt′ buck′ le *s* Gürtelschnalle *f*

belt′ way′ *s* Verkehrsgürtel *m*

bemoan [bɪ′mon] *tr* betrauern, beklagen

bench [bɛntʃ] *s* Bank *f*; (jur) Gerichtshof *m*; (sport) Reservebank *f*, Bank *f*

bend [bɛnd] *s* Biegung *f*; (*in a road*) Kurve *f*; **bends** (pathol) Tauchkrankheit *f* || *v* (*pret & pp* **bent** [bɛnt]) *tr* biegen, beugen; (*a bow*) spannen ||

intr sich biegen, sich beugen; **b. down** sich bücken; **b. over backwards** (fig) sich [*dat*] übergroße Mühe geben

beneath [bɪ'niθ] *adv* unten || *prep* (*position*) unter (*dat*), unterhalb (*genit*); (*direction*) unter (*acc*); **b. me** unter meiner Würde

benediction [‚benɪ'dɪkʃən] *s* Segen *m*

benefactor ['benɪ‚fæktər] *s* Wohltäter –in *mf*

beneficence [bɪ'nefɪsəns] *s* Wohltätigkeit *f*

beneficent [bɪ'nefɪsənt] *adj* wohltätig

beneficial [‚benɪ'fɪʃəl] *adj* heilbringend, gesund; (**to**) nützlich (*dat*)

beneficiary [‚benɪ'fɪʃɪ‚eri] *s* Begünstigte *mf*; (ins) Bezugsberechtigte *mf*

benefit ['benɪfɪt] *s* Nutzen *m*; (*fundraising performance*) Benefiz *n*; (ins) Versicherungsleistung *f*

benevolence [bɪ'nevələns] *s* Wohlwollen *n*

benevolent [bɪ'nevələnt] *adj* wohlwollend

benign [bɪ'naɪn] *adj* gütig; (pathol) gutartig

bent [bent] *adj* krumm, verbogen; **b. on** versessen auf (*acc*) || *s* Hang *m*

benzene ['benzin] *s* Benzol *n*

bequeath [bɪ'kwið] *tr* vermachen

bequest [bɪ'kwest] *s* Vermächtnis *n*

berate [bɪ'ret] *tr* ausschelten, rügen

be·reave [bɪ'riv] *v* (*pret & pp* **-reaved** & **-reft** ['reft]) *tr* (**of**) berauben (*genit*)

bereavement [bɪ'rivmənt] *s* Trauerfall *m*

beret [bə're] *s* Baskenmütze *f*

Berlin [bər'lɪn] *adj* Berliner, berlinerisch || *s* Berlin *n*

Berliner [bər'lɪnər] *s* Berliner –in *mf*

berry ['beri] *s* Beere *f*

berserk [bər'sʌrk] *adj* wütend || *adv*— **go b.** wütend werden

berth [bʌrθ] *s* Schlafkoje *f*; (naut) Liegeplatz *m*; (rr) Bett *n*; **give s.o. wide b.** um j–n e–n weiten Bogen machen || *tr* am Kai festmachen

be·seech [bɪ'sitʃ] *v* (*pret & pp* **-sought** ['sot] & **-seeched**) *tr* anflehen

be·set [bɪ'set] *v* (*pret & pp* **-set**; *ger* **-setting**) *tr* bedrängen, umringen

beside [bɪ'saɪd] *prep* (*position*) neben (*dat*), bei (*dat*); (*direction*) neben (*acc*); **be b. oneself with** außer sich [*dat*] sein vor (*dat*)

besides [bɪ'saɪdz] *adv* überdies, außerdem || *prep* außer (*dat*)

besiege [bɪ'sidʒ] *tr* belagern

besmirch [bɪ'smʌrtʃ] *tr* beschmutzen

be·speak [bɪ'spik] *v* (*pret* **-spoke** ['spok]; *pp* **-spoken** ['spokən]) *tr* bezeigen

best [best] *adj* beste; **b. of all, very b.** allerbeste || *adv* am besten; **had b.** es wäre am besten, wenn || *s*—**at b.** bestenfalls; **be at one's b.** in bester Form sein; **for the b.** zum Besten; **make the b. of** sich abfinden mit; **to the b. of one's ability** nach bestem Vermögen

bestial ['bestʃəl] *adj* bestialisch

best' man' *s* Brautführer *m*

bestow [bɪ'sto] *tr* verleihen

bestowal [bɪ'sto·əl] *s* Verleihung *f*

best' sel'ler *s* (*book*) Bestseller *m*

bet [bet] *s* Wette *f*; **make a bet** e–e Wette abschließen (or eingehen) || *v* (*pret & pp* **bet** & **betted**; *ger* **betting**) *tr* (**on**) wetten (auf *acc*) || *intr* wetten; **you bet!** aber sicher!

betray [bɪ'tre] *tr* verraten; (*a secret*) preisgeben; (*ignorance*) offenbaren; (*a trust*) mißbrauchen

betrayal [bɪ'tre·əl] *s* Verrat *m*

betrayer [bɪ'tre·ər] *s* Verräter –in *mf*

better ['betər] *adj* besser; **the b. part of** der größere Teil (*genit*) || *s*—**change for the b.** sich zum Besseren wenden; **get the b. of** übervorteilen; **one's betters** die Höherstehenden *pl*; || *adv* besser; **all the b.** um so besser; **b. off** besser daran; (*financially*) wohlhabender; **so much the b.** desto besser; **you had b. do it at once** am besten tust du es sofort; **you had b. not** das will ich dir nicht geraten haben || *tr* verbessern; **b. oneself** sich verbessern

bet'ter half' *s* (coll) bessere Hälfte *f*

betterment ['betərmənt] *s* Besserung *f*

bettor ['betər] *s* Wettende *mf*

between [bɪ'twin] *adv*—**in b.** dazwischen || *prep* (*position*) zwischen (*dat*); (*direction*) zwischen (*acc*); **just b. you and me** ganz unter uns gesagt

bev·el ['bevəl] *adj* schräg || *s* schräge Kante *f* || *v* (*pret & pp* **-el(l)ed**; *ger* **-el(l)ing**) *tr* abschrägen

beverage ['bevərɪdʒ] *s* Getränk *n*

bevy ['bevi] *s* Schar *f*

bewail [bɪ'wel] *tr* beklagen

beware [bɪ'wer] *intr* sich hüten; **b.!** gib acht!; **b. of** sich hüten vor (*dat*); **b. of imitations** vor Nachahmungen wird gewarnt

bewilder [bɪ'wɪldər] *tr* verblüffen

bewilderment [bɪ'wɪldərmənt] *s* Verblüffung *f*

bewitch [bɪ'wɪtʃ] *tr* (fig) bezaubern

beyond [bɪ'jand] *adv* jenseits || *s*—**the b.** das Jenseits || *prep* jenseits (*genit*), über (*acc*) hinaus; (fig) über *acc*), außer (*dat*); **he is b. help** ihm ist nicht mehr zu helfen; **that's b. me** das geht über meinen Verstand

B'-girl' *s* (coll) Animiermädchen *n*

bias ['baɪ·əs] *s* Voreingenommenheit *f* || *tr* (**against**) einnehmen (gegen)

bi'ased *adj* voreingenommen

bib [bɪb] *s* Latz *m*, Lätzchen *n*

Bible ['baɪbəl] *s* Bibel *f*

Biblical ['bɪblɪkəl] *adj* biblisch

bibliographer [‚bɪblɪ'agrəfər] *s* Bibliograph –in *mf*

bibliography [‚bɪblɪ'agrəfi] *s* Bücherverzeichnis *n*; (*science*) Bücherkunde *f*

bi·ceps ['baɪseps] *s* (**-cepses** [sepsɪz] & **-ceps**) Bizeps *m*

bicker ['bɪkər] *intr* (sich) zanken

bick'ering *s* Gezänk *n*

bicuspid [baɪ'kʌspɪd] *s* kleiner Backenzahn *m*

bicycle ['baısıkəl] s Fahrrad n

bid [bıd] s Angebot n; (cards) Meldung f; (com) Kostenvoranschlag m || v (pret **bade** [bæd] & **bid**; pp **bidden** ['bıdən]) tr (ask) heißen; (at auction) bieten; (cards) melden, reizen || intr (cards) reizen; (com) ein Preisangebot machen; **bid for** sich bewerben um

bidder ['bıdər] s (at an auction) Bieter –in mf; **highest b.** Meistbietende m

bid'ding s (at an auction) Bieten n; (request) Geheiß n; (cards) Reizen n

bide [baıd] tr—**b. one's time** seine Gelegenheit abwarten

biennial [baı'enı-əl] adj zweijährig

bier [bır] s Totenbahre f

bifocals [baı'fokəlz] spl Zweistärkenbrille f

big [bıg] adj (bigger; biggest) groß

bigamist ['bıgəmıst] s Bigamist m

bigamous ['bıgəməs] adj bigamisch

bigamy ['bıgəmi] s Bigamie f

big'-boned' adj starkknochig

big' busi'ness s das große Geschäft; (collectively) Großunternehmertum n

Big' Dip'per s Großer Bär m

big' game' s Hochwild n

big'-heart'ed adj großherzig

big'mouth' s (sl) Großmaul n

bigot ['bıgət] s Fanatiker –in mf

bigoted ['bıgətıd] adj bigott, fanatisch

bigotry ['bıgətri] s Bigotterie f

big' shot' s (coll) hohes Tier n, Bonze m

big'-time' adj groß, erstklassig; **b. operator** Großschieber –in mf

big' toe' s große Zehe f

big' top' s (coll) großes Zirkuszelt n

big' wheel' s (coll) hohes Tier n

big'wig' s (coll) Bonze m

bike [baık] s (coll) Rad n

bikini [bı'kini] s Bikini m

bilateral [baı'lætərəl] adj beiderseitig verbindlich

bile [baıl] s Galle f

bilge [bıldʒ] s Bilge f, Kielraum m

bilge' wat'er s Bilgenwasser n

bilingual [baı'lıŋgwəl] adj zweisprachig

bilk [bılk] tr (out of) prellen (um)

bill [bıl] s Rechnung f; (paper money) Geldschein m, Schein m; (of a bird) Schnabel m; (parl) Gesetzvorlage f; **pass a b.** ein Gesetz verabschieden || tr in Rechnung stellen

bill'board' s Anschlagtafel f

bill' collec'tor s Einkassierer –in mf

billet ['bılıt] s (mil) Quartier n || tr (mil) einquartieren, unterbringen

bill'fold' s Brieftasche f

bil'liard ball' s Billardkugel f

billiards ['bıljərdz] s Billard n

bil'liard ta'ble s Billardtisch m

billion ['bıljən] s Milliarde f; (Brit) Billion f (million million)

bill' of exchange' s Tratte f, Wechsel m

bill' of fare' s Speisekarte f

bill' of health' s Gesundheitszeugnis n; **he gave me a clean b.** (fig) er hat mich für einwandfrei befunden

bill' of lad'ing ['ledıŋ] s Frachtbrief m

bill' of rights' s erste zehn Zusatzartikel pl zur Verfassung (der U.S.A.)

bill' of sale' s Kaufurkunde f

billow ['bılo] s Woge f || intr wogen

bil'ly club' ['brlɪ] s Polizeiknüppel m

bil'ly goat' s (coll) Ziegenbock m

bind [baınd] s—**in a b.** in der Klemme || v (pret & pp **bound** [baund]) tr binden; (obligate) verpflichten; (bb) einbinden

binder ['baındər] s Binder –in mf; (e.g., cement) Bindemittel n; (for loose papers) Aktendeckel m; (mach) Garbenbinder m

bindery ['baındəri] s Buchbinderei f

bind'ing adj (on) verbindlich (für) || s Binden n; (for skis) Bindung f; (bb) Einband v

binge [bındʒ] s (sl) Zechtour f; **go on a b.** (sl) e-e Zechtour machen

binoculars [baı'nakjələrz] spl Fernglas n

biochemistry [,baı-ə'kemıstri] s Biochemie f

biographer [baı'agrəfər] s Biograph –in mf

biographic(al) [,baı-ə'græfık(əl)] adj biographisch

biography [baı'agrəfi] s Biographie f

biologic(al) [,baı-ə'ladʒık(əl)] adj biologisch

biologist [baı'alədʒıst] s Biologe m, Biologin f

biology [baı'alədʒi] s Biologie f

biophysics [,baı-ə'fızıks] s Biophysik f

biopsy ['baı-apsi] s Biopsie f

bipartisan [baı'partızən] adj Zweiparteien–

biped ['baıped] s Zweifüßer m

bird [bırd] s Vogel m; **for the birds** für die Katz; **kill two birds with one stone** zwei Fliegen mit e-r Klappe schlagen

bird'cage' s Bauer n, Vogelkäfig m

bird' call' s Vogelruf m, Lockpfeife f

bird' dog' s Hühnerhund m

bird' of prey' s Raubvogel m

bird' seed' s Vogelfutter n

bird's'-eye view' s Vogelperspektive f

birth [bʌrθ] s Geburt f; (origin) Herkunft f; **give b. to** gebären

birth' certi'ficate s Geburtsurkunde f

birth' control' s Geburtenbeschränkung f

birth'day' s Geburtstag m

birth'day cake' s Geburtstagskuchen m

birth'day par'ty s Geburtstagsfeier f

birth'day pres'ent s Geburtstagsgeschenk n

birth'day suit' s (hum) Adamskostüm n

birth'mark' s Muttermal n

birth'place' s Geburtsort m

birth' rate' s Geburtenziffer f

birth'right' s Geburtsrecht n

biscuit ['bıskıt] s Keks m

bisect [baı'sekt] tr halbieren || intr sich teilen

bishop ['bı/əp] s Bischof m; (chess) Läufer m

bison ['baısən] s Bison m

bit [bıt] s Bißchen n; (of food) Stückchen *n*; (*of time*) Augenblick *m*; (*part of a bridle*) Gebiß *n*; (*drill*) Bohrer *m*; **a bit** (*somewhat*) ein wenig; **a little bit** ein klein wenig; **bit by bit** brockenweise; **bits and pieces** Brocken *pl*; **every bit as** ganz genauso

bitch [bɪtʃ] *s* Hündin *f*; (*vulg*) Weibsbild *n*

bite [baɪt] *s* Biß *m*; (*wound*) Bißwunde *f*; (*of an insect*) Stich *m*; (*a snake*) Biß *m*; (*snack*) Imbiß *m*; (*fig*) Bissigkeit *f*; **I have a b.** (*in fishing*) es beißt e-r an ‖ *v* (*pret* **bit** [bɪt] *pp* **bit & bitten** ['bɪtən]) *tr* beißen; (*said of insects*) stechen; (*said of snakes*) beißen; **b. one's nails** an den Nägeln kauen ‖ *intr* beißen; (*said of fish*) anbeißen; (*said of the wind*) schneiden; **b. into** anbeißen

bit'ing *adj* (*remark*) bissig; (*cold, wind*) schneidend

bit' part' *s* kleine Rolle *f*

bitter ['bɪtər] *adj* (& *fig*) bitter; (*Person, Blick*) bitterböse

bitterly ['bɪtərli] *adv* bitterlich

bitterness ['bɪtərnɪs] *s* Bitterkeit *f*

bitters ['bɪtərz] *spl* Magenbitter *m*

bitu'minous coal' [bɪ't(j)umɪnəs] *s* Fettkohle *f*

bivouac ['bɪvwæk] *s* Biwak *n* ‖ *intr* biwakieren

bizarre [bɪ'zɑr] *adj* bizarr

blab [blæb] *v* (*pret & pp* **blabbed;** *ger* **blabbing**) *tr* ausplaudern ‖ *intr* plaudern

blabber ['blæbər] *intr* schwatzen

blab'bermouth' *s* Schwatzmaul *n*

black [blæk] *adj* schwarz ‖ *s* Schwarz *n*; (*black person*) Neger –in *mf*, Schwarze *mf* ‖ *tr* schwärzen; **b. out** (*mil*) verdunkeln ‖ *intr*—**b. out** die Besinnung verlieren

black'-and-blue' *adj* blau unterlaufen; **beat s.o. b.** j-n grün und blau schlagen

black' and white' *s*—**in b.** schwarz auf weiß, schriftlich

black'-and-white' *adj* schwarzweiß

black'ball' *tr* (*ostracize*) ausschließen; (*vote against*) stimmen gegen

black'ber'ry *s* Brombeere *f*

black'berry bush' *s* Brombeerstrauch *m*

black'bird' *s* Amsel *f*

black'board' *s* Tafel *f*, Wandtafel *f*

blacken ['blækən] *tr* schwärzen; (*a name*) anschwärzen

black' eye' *s* blaues Auge *n*; **give s.o. a b.** (*fig*) j-m Schaden zufügen

black'head' *s* Mitesser *m*

blackish ['blækɪʃ] *adj* schwärzlich

black'jack' *s* (*club*) Totschläger *m*; (*cards*) Siebzehnundvier *n* ‖ *tr* niederknüppeln

black'list' *s* schwarze Liste *f* ‖ *tr* auf die schwarze Liste setzen

black' mag'ic *s* schwarze Kunst *f*

black'mail' *s* Erpressung *f* ‖ *tr* erpressen

blackmailer ['blæk,melər] *s* Erpresser –in *mf*

black' mar'ket *s* Schwarzmarkt *m*

black' marketeer' *s* Schwarzhändler –in *mf*

black'out' *s* (*fainting*) Bewußtlosigkeit *f*; (*of memory*) kurze Gedächtnisstörung *f*; (*of news*) Nachrichtensperre *f*; (*mil*) Verdunkelung *f*; (*telv*) Sperre *f*; (*theat*) Auslöschen *n* aller Rampenlichter

black' sheep' *s* (*fig*) schwarzes Schaf *n*

black'smith' *s* Grobschmied *m*; (*person who shoes horses*) Hufschmied *m*

bladder ['blædər] *s* Blase *f*

blade [bled] *s* (*of a sword, knife*) Klinge *f*; (*of grass*) Halm *m*; (*of a saw, ax, shovel, oar*) Blatt *n*; (*of a propeller*) Flügel *m*

blame [blem] *s* Schuld *f* ‖ *tr* die Schuld geben (*dat*); **b. s.o. for** j-m Vorwürfe machen wegen; **I don't b. you for laughing** ich nehme es Ihnen nicht übel, daß Sie lachen

blameless ['blemlɪs] *adj* schuldlos

blame'wor'thy *adj* tadelnswert, schuldig

blanch [blæntʃ] *tr* erbleichen lassen; (*celery*) bleichen; (*almonds*) blanchieren ‖ *intr* erbleichen

bland [blænd] *adj* sanft, mild

blandish ['blændɪʃ] *tr* schmeicheln (*dat*)

blank [blæŋk] *adj* blind; (*piece of paper, space, expression*) leer; (*form*) unausgefüllt; (*tape*) unbespielt; (*nonplussed*) verblüfft; **my mind went b.** ich konnte mich an nichts erinnern ‖ *s* (*cartridge*) Platzpatrone *f*; (*unwritten space*) leere Stelle *f*; (*form*) Formular *n*; (*unfinished piece of metal*) Rohling *m* ‖ *tr* (*sport*) auf Null halten

blank' check' *s* Blankoscheck *m*

blanket ['blæŋkɪt] *adj* generell, umfassend ‖ *s* Decke *f*

blank' verse' *s* Blankvers *m*

blare [bler] *s* Lärm *m*; (*of trumpets*) Geschmetter *n* ‖ *intr* schmettern; (*aut*) laut hupen

blasé [blɑ'ze] *adj* blasiert; **b. attitude** Blasiertheit *f*

blaspheme [blæs'fim] *tr & intr* lästern

blasphemous ['blæsfɪməs] *adj* lästerlich

blasphemy ['blæsfɪmi] *s* Lästerung *f*

blast [blæst] *s* (*of an explosion*) Luftdruck *m*; (*of a horn, trumpet, air*) Stoß *m*; (*of air*) Luftzug *m*; **at full b.** (*fig*) auf höchsten Touren ‖ *tr* (*e.g., a tunnel*) sprengen; (*ruin*) (fig) verderben; (*criticize*) wettern gegen; (*blight*) versengen; **b. it!** verdammt! ‖ *intr*—**b. off** (rok) starten

blast' fur'nace *s* Hochofen *m*

blast'-off' *s* (rok) Start *m*

blatant ['bletənt] *adj* (*lie, infraction*) eklatant; (*nonsense*) schreiend

blaze [blez] *s* Brand *m*; **b. of color** Farbenpracht *f*; **b. of glory** Ruhmesglanz *m*; **b. of light** Lichterglanz *m*; **go to blazes!** (sl) geh zum Teufel!; **like blazes** wie verrückt ‖ *tr*—**b. a trail** e-n Weg markieren; (fig) e-n Weg bahnen ‖ *intr* lodern; **b. away at** drauflosschießen auf (*acc*)

blazer ['blezər] s Sportjacke f
blaz'ing adj (sun) prall
bleach [blitʃ] s Bleichmittel n || tr bleichen; (hair) blondieren || intr bleichen
bleachers ['blitʃərs] spl Zuschauersitze pl im Freien
bleak [blik] adj öde, trostlos
bleary-eyed ['blɪri,aɪd] adj triefäugig
bleat [blit] s Blöken n || intr blöken; (said of a goat) meckern
bleed [blid] v (pret & pp bled [bled]) tr (brakes) entlüften; (med) zur Ader lassen; **b. white** (fig) zum Weißbluten bringen || intr bluten; **b. to death** verbluten
blemish ['blemɪʃ] s Fleck m, Makel m; (fig) Schandfleck m
blend [blend] s Mischung f; (liquor) Verschnitt m || v (pret & pp blended & blent [blent]) tr mischen; (wine, liquor) verschneiden || intr sich vermischen; (said of colors) zueinander passen, zusammenpassen
bless [bles] tr segnen; **God b. you!** (after a sneeze) Gesundheit!
blessed ['blesɪd] adj selig
bless'ing s Segen m, Gnade f; **b. in disguise** Glück n im Unglück
blight [blaɪt] s (fig) Gifthauch m; (agr) Brand m, Mehltau m || tr (fig) verderben; (agr) schädigen
blight'ed adj brandig
blimp [blɪmp] s unstarres Luftschiff n
blind [blaɪnd] adj blind; (curve) unübersichtlich; **go b.** erblinden || s Jalousie f; (hunt) Attrappe f || tr blenden; (fig) verblenden
blind' al'ley s (& fig) Sackgasse f
blind' date' s Verabredung f mit e-r (or e-m) Unbekannten
blinder ['blaɪndər] s Scheuklappe f
blind' fly'ing s Blindflug m
blind'fold adj mit verbundenen Augen || adv blindlings || tr die Augen verbinden (dat)
blind' man' s Blinder m
blind'man's' bluff' s Blindekuhspiel n
blindness ['blaɪndnɪs] s Blindheit f
blink [blɪŋk] s Blinken n; (with the eyes) blinzeln n; **on the b.** (sl) kaputt || tr—**b. one's eyes** mit den Augen zwinkern || intr (said of a light) blinken; (said of the eyes) blinzeln
blinker ['blɪŋkər] s (for horses) Scheuklappe f; (aut) Blinker m
blip [blɪp] s (radar) Leuchtfleck m
bliss [blɪs] s Wonne f
blissful ['blɪsfəl] adj glückselig
blister ['blɪstər] s Blase f; (from a burn) Brandblase f || intr (said of the skin) Blasen ziehen; (said of paint) Blasen werfen
blithe [blaɪð] adj fröhlich
blitzkrieg ['blɪts,krig] s Blitzkrieg m
blizzard ['blɪzərd] s Blizzard m
bloat [blot] tr aufblähen || intr anschwellen
bloc [blak] s (parl) Stimmblock m; (pol) Block m
block [blak] s (of wood) Klotz m; (toy) Bauklotz m; (for chopping) Hackklotz m; (of houses) Häuser-

block m; (of seats) Reihe f; (mach) Rolle f; (sport) Block m; **five blocks from here** fünf Straßen weiter || tr versperren; (traffic, a street, a player) blockieren; (a ball) abfangen; (a hat) aufdämpfen; **be blocked** sich stauen; **b. off** (a street) absperren; **b. up** verstopfen, versperren
blockade [bla'ked] s Blockade f, Sperre f || tr blockieren, sperren
blockade' run'ner s Blockadebrecher m
blockage ['blakɪdʒ] s Stockung f
block' and tac'kle s Flaschenzug m
block'head' s Klotz m, Dummkopf m
blond [bland] adj blond || s Blonde m
blonde [bland] s Blondine f
blood [blʌd] s Blut n; (lineage) Geblüt n; **in cold b.** kaltblütig
blood' circula'tion s Blutkreislauf m
blood' clot' s Blutgerinnsel m
bloodcurdling ['blʌd,kʌrdlɪŋ] adj haarsträubend
blood' do'nor s Blutspender –in mf
blood'hound' s (& fig) Bluthund m
bloodless ['blʌdlɪs] adj blutlos; (revolution) unblutig
blood' poi'soning s Blutvergiftung f
blood' pres'sure s Blutdruck m
blood' rela'tion s Blutsverwandte mf
blood'shed' s Blutvergießen n
blood'shot' adj blutunterlaufen
blood'stain' s Blutfleck m, Blutspur f
blood'stained' adj blutbefleckt
blood'stream' s Blutstrom m
blood'suck'er s (& fig) Blutsauger m
blood' test' s Blutprobe f
blood'thirst'y adj blutdürstig
blood' transfu'sion s Blutübertragung f
blood' type' s Blutgruppe f
blood' ves'sel s Blutgefäß n
blood-y ['blʌdɪ] adj blutig; (bloodstained) blutbefleckt || v (pret & pp –ied) tr mit Blut beflecken
bloom [blum] s Blüte f || intr blühen
blossom ['blasəm] s Blüte f || intr blühen
blot [blat] s Fleck m; (fig) Schandfleck m || v (pret & pp blotted; ger blotting) tr (smear) beschmieren; (with a blotter) (ab)löschen; **b. out** ausstreichen; (fig) auslöschen || intr (said of ink) klecksen
blotch [blatʃ] s Klecks m; (on the skin) Ausschlag m
blotter ['blatər] s Löscher m
blot'ting pa'per s Löschpapier n
blouse [blaus] s Bluse f
blow [blo] s Schlag m, Hieb m; (fig) Schlag m; **come to blows** handgemein werden || v (pret blew [blu]; pp blown) tr blasen; (money) (sl) verschwenden; (a fuse) durchbrennen; **b. a whistle** pfeifen; **b. off** steam sich austoben; **b. one's top** (coll) hochgehen; **b. out** (a candle) ausblasen; **b. up** (inflate) aufblasen; (with explosives) sprengen; (phot) vergrößern || intr blasen; **b. out** (said of a candle) auslöschen; (said of a tire) platzen; **blow over** vorüberziehen; **b. up** (& fig) in die Luft gehen
blower ['blo·ər] s Gebläse n, Bläser m

blow'out' s (sl) Gelage n; (aut) Reifen-panne f
blow'pipe' s Blasrohr n
blow'torch' s Lötlampe f
blubber ['blʌbər] s Tran m ‖ intr (cry noisily) jaulen
bludgeon ['blʌdʒən] s Knüppel m ‖ tr mit dem Knüppel bearbeiten
blue [blu] adj blau; (fig) bedrückt ‖ s Blau n; blues (mus) Blues m; have the blues trüb gestimmt sein; out of the b. aus heiterem Himmel
blue'ber'ry s Heidelbeere f
blue'bird' s Blaukehlchen n
blue' chip' s (cards) blaue Spielmarke f; (fin) sicheres Wertpapier n
blue'-col'lar work'er s Arbeiter m
blue' jeans' spl Jeans pl
blue' moon' s—once in a b. alle Jubeljahre einmal
blue'print' s Blaupause f
blue' streak' s—talk a b. (coll) in e-r Tour reden
bluff [blʌf] adj schroff; (person) derb ‖ s (coll) Bluff m; (geol) Steilküste f; call s.o.'s b. j—m beim Wort nehmen ‖ tr & intr bluffen
bluffer ['blʌfər] s Bluffer m
blu'ing s Waschblau n
bluish ['blu·ɪʃ] adj bläulich
blunder ['blʌndər] s Schnitzer m; ‖ intr e-n Schnitzer machen; b. into stolpern in (acc); b. upon zufällig geraten auf (acc)
blunt [blʌnt] adj stumpf; (fig) plump, unverblümt ‖ tr abstumpfen
bluntly ['blʌntli] adv unverblümt
blur [blʌr] s Verschwommenheit f ‖ v (pret & pp blurred; ger blurring) tr verwischen ‖ intr verschwommen werden
blurb [blʌrb] s Reklametext m
blurred adj verschwommen; (vision) unscharf
blurt [blʌrt] tr—b. out herausplatzen
blush [blʌʃ] s Röte f, Schamröte f ‖ intr (at) erröten (über acc)
bluster ['blʌstər] s Prahlerei f ‖ intr (said of a person) prahlen, poltern; (said of wind) toben
blustery ['blʌstəri] adj stürmisch
boa constrictor ['bo·ə kən'strɪktər] s Abgottschlange f, Königsschlange f
boar [bor] s Eber m; (wild boar) Wildschwein n
board [bord] s Brett n; (of administrators) Ausschuß m, Behörde f, Rat m; (meals) Kost f; (educ) Schultafel f; above b. offen; on b. an Bord ‖ tr (a ship) besteigen; (a plane, train) einsteigen in (acc); (paying guests) beköstigen; b. up mit Brettern vernageln ‖ intr (with) in Kost sein (bei)
boarder ['bordər] s Kostgänger –in mf
board'inghouse' s Pension f
board'ing pass' s Bordkarte f
board'ing school' s Internat n
board'ing stu'dent s Interne mf
board' of direc'tors s Verwaltungsrat m, Aufsichtsrat m
board' of educa'tion s Unterrichtsministerium n

board' of health' s Gesundheitsbehörde f
board' of trade' s Handelskammer f
board' of trustees' s Verwaltungsrat m
board'walk' s Strandpromenade f
boast [bost] s Prahlerei f; (cause of pride) Stolz m ‖ tr sich rühmen (genit) ‖ intr (about) prahlen (mit)
boastful ['bostfəl] adj prahlerisch
boat [bot] s Boot n; in the same b. (fig) in der gleichen Lage
boat'house' s Bootshaus n
boat'ing s Bootsfahrt f; go b. e-e Bootfahrt machen
boat'race' s Bootrennen n
boat' ride' s Bootsfahrt f
boatswain ['bosən] s Hochbootsmann m
bob [bab] s (jerky motion) Ruck m; (hairdo) Bubikopf m; (of a fishing line) Schwimmer m; (of a plumb line) Senkblei n ‖ v (pret & pp bobbed; ger bobbing) tr (hair) kurz schneiden ‖ intr sich hin und her bewegen; bob up and down sich auf und ab bewegen
bobbin ['babɪn] s Klöppel m
bobble ['babəl] tr (coll) ungeschickt handhaben
bob'by pin' ['babi] s Haarklammer f
bob'sled' s Bob m, Rennschlitten m
bode [bod] tr bedeuten
bodily ['badɪli] adj leiblich; b. injury Körperverletzung f ‖ adv leibhaftig
body ['badi] s Körper m; (of a person or animal) Körper m; (corpse) Leiche f; (collective group) Körperschaft f; (of a plane, ship) Rumpf m; (of a vehicle) Karosserie f; (of beer, wine) Schwere f; (of a letter) Text m; b. of water Gewässer n; in a b. geschlossen
bod'yguard' s Leibgarde f
bod'y o'dor s Körpergeruch m
bog [bag] s Sumpf m ‖ v (pret & pp bogged; ger bogging) intr—bog down steckenbleiben
bogey-man ['bogi‚mæn] s (-men) Kinderschreck m
bogus ['bogəs] adj schwindelhaft
Bohemia [bo'himi·ə] s Böhmen n
Bohemian [bo'himi·ən] adj böhmisch ‖ s (person) Böhme m, Böhmin f; (fig) Bohemien m; (language) Böhmisch n
boil [bɔɪl] s (pathol) Geschwür n; bring to a b. zum Sieden bringen ‖ tr kochen, sieden ‖ intr kochen, sieden; b. away verkochen; b. over überkochen
boiled' ham' s gekochter Schinken m
boiled' pota'toes spl Salzkartoffeln pl
boiler ['bɔɪlər] s (electrical water tank) Boiler m; (kettle) Kessel m
boil'ermak'er s Kesselschmied m
boil'er room' s Heizraum m
boil'ing adj siedend ‖ adv—be b. mad vor Zorn kochen; b. hot siedeheiß
boil'ing point' s Siedepunkt m
boisterous ['bɔɪstərəs] adj ausgelassen
bold [bold] adj kühn, gewagt; (outlines) deutlich
bold'face' s Fettdruck m

boldness ['bəʊldnɪs] s Kühnheit f
Bolshevik ['bɒlʃəvɪk] adj bolschewistisch ‖ s Bolschewik –in mf
bolster ['bəʊlstər] s Nackenrolle f ‖ tr unterstützen
bolt [bəʊlt] s Bolzen m; (door lock) Riegel m; (of cloth) Stoffballen m; (of lightning) Blitzstrahl m; **b. out of the blue** Blitz m aus heiterem Himmel ‖ tr (a door) verriegeln; (a political party) im Stich lassen; (food) hinunterschlingen ‖ intr davonstürzen; (said of a horse) durchgehen
bomb [bɒm] s (dropped from the air) Bombe f; (planted) Sprengladung f; (fiasco) (sl) Versager m ‖ tr (from the air) bombardieren; (blow up) sprengen ‖ intr (sl) versagen
bombard [bɒm'bɑrd] tr bombardieren, beschießen; (fig) bombardieren
bombardier [ˌbɒmbər'dɪr] s Bombenschütze m
bombardment [bɒm'bɑrdmənt] s Bombardement n, Beschießung f
bombast ['bɒmbæst] s Schwulst m
bombastic [bɒm'bæstɪk] adj schwülstig
bomb' bay' s Bombenschacht m
bomb' cra'ter s Bombentrichter m
bomber ['bɒmər] s Bomber m
bomb'ing s Bombenabwurf m
bomb'ing run' s Bomben(ziel)anflug m
bomb'proof' adj bombenfest, bombensicher
bomb'shell' s (& fig) Bombe f
bomb' shel'ter s Bombenkeller m
bomb'sight' s Bombenzielgerät n
bomb' squad' s Entschärfungskommando n
bona fide ['bɒnə ˌfaɪd] adj ehrlich, echt; (offer) solide
bonanza [bo'nænzə] s Goldgrube f
bond [bɒnd] s Fessel f; (fin) Obligation f
bondage ['bɒndɪdʒ] s Knechtschaft f
bond'hold'er s Inhaber –in mf e–r Obligation
bonds·man ['bɒndzmən] s (–men) Bürge m
bone [bɒn] s Knochen m, Bein n; (of fish) Gräte f; **bones** Gebein n; (mortal remains) Gebeine pl; **have a b. to pick with** ein Hühnchen zu rupfen haben mit; **make no bones about it** nicht viel Federlesens machen mit; **to the b.** bis ins Mark ‖ tr (meat) ausbeinen; (fish) ausgräten ‖ intr—**b. up for** (sl) büffeln für
bone'-dry' adj knochentrocken
bone'head' s Dummkopf m
boneless ['bɒnlɪs] adj ohne Knochen; (fish) ohne Gräten
boner ['bɒnər] s (sl) Schnitzer m; **pull a b.** (coll) e–n Schnitzer machen
bonfire ['bɒnˌfaɪr] s Freudenfeuer n
bonnet ['bɒnɪt] s Haube f
bonus ['bɒnəs] s Gratifikation f
bony ['bɒni] adj knochig; (fish) grätig
boo [bu] s Pfuiruf m ‖ tr niederbrüllen ‖ intr pfui rufen ‖ interj (to jeer) pfui!; (to scare someone) huh!
boob [bub] s (sl) Blödkopf m
booby ['bubi] s Blödkopf m
boo'by hatch' s (sl) Affenkasten m

boo'by prize' s Trostpreis m
boo'by trap' s Minenfalle f
boogey·man ['bugi ˌmæn], ['bogiˌmæn] s (–men) Schreckgespenst n
book [bʊk] s Buch n; (of stamps, tickets, matches) Heftchen n; **keep books** Bücher führen ‖ tr buchen; (e.g., seats) vorbestellen
book'bind'er s Buchbinder –in mf
book'bind'ery s Buchbinderei f
book'bind'ing s Buchbinderei f
book'case' s Bücherschrank m
book' end' s Bücherstütze f
bookie ['bʊki] s (coll) Buchmacher –in mf
book'ing s Buchung f
bookish ['bʊkɪʃ] adj lesefreudig
book'keep'er s Buchhalter –in mf
book'keep'ing s Buchhaltung f
book' learn'ing s Schulweisheit f
booklet ['bʊklɪt] s Büchlein n
book'mak'er s Buchmacher –in mf
book'mark' s Lesezeichen n
book'rack' s Büchergestell n
book' review' s Buchbesprechung f
book'sell'er s Buchhändler –in mf
book'shelf' s (–shelves) Bücherregal n
book'stand' s Bücher(verkaufs)stand m
book'store' s Buchhandlung f
book'worm' s (& fig) Bücherwurm m
boom [bum] s (noise) dumpfes Dröhnen n; (of a crane) Ausleger m; (cin, telv) Galgen m; (econ) Boom m, Hochkonjunktur f; (naut) Baum m, Spiere f; (st.exch.) Hausse f ‖ intr dröhnen; (said of an organ) brummen
boomerang ['buməˌræŋ] s Bumerang m
boon [bun] s Wohltat f, Segen m
boon' compan'ion s Zechkumpan m
boor [bʊr] s Rüpel m, Flegel m
boorish ['bʊrɪʃ] adj flegelhaft
boost [bust] s (push) Auftrieb m; (in pay) Gehaltserhöhung f ‖ tr fördern; (prices) in die Höhe treiben; (elec) verstärken; **b. business** die Wirtschaft ankurbeln
booster ['bustər] s (backer) Förderer m, Förderin f
boost'er rock'et s Hilfsrakete f
boost'er shot' s (med) Nachimpfung f
boot [but] s Stiefel m; (kick) Fußtritt m; **to b.** noch dazu; **you can bet your boots on that** (sl) darauf kannst du Gift nehmen ‖ tr (sl) stoßen; (fb) kicken; **b. out** (sl) 'rausschmeißen
booth [buθ] s (at a fair) Marktbude f; (for telephone, voting) Zelle f
boot'leg' adj geschmuggelt ‖ v (pret & pp –legged; ger –legging) tr (make illegally) illegal brennen; (smuggle) schmuggeln
bootlegger ['butˌlegər] s Alkoholschmuggler m, Bootlegger m
bootlicker ['butˌlɪkər] s (sl) Kriecher m
booty ['buti] s Beute f
booze [buz] s (coll) Schnaps m ‖ intr (coll) saufen
booze' hound' s Saufbold m, Saufaus m
border ['bɔrdər] s Rand m; (of a country) Grenze f; (of a dress, etc.) Saum

m, Borte f || tr umranden, begrenzen; **be bordered by** grenzen an (acc) || intr—b. **on** (& fig) grenzen an (acc)

bor'derline' s Grenzlinie f

bor'derline case' s Grenzfall m

bore [bor] s (drill hole) Bohrloch n; (of a gun) Bohrung f; (of a cylinder) innerer Zylinderdurchmesser m; (fig) langweiliger Mensch m || tr bohren; (fig) langweilen

boredom ['bordəm] s Langeweile f

bor'ing adj langweilig || s Bohren n

born [bɔrn] adj geboren; **he was b.** (said of a living person) er ist geboren; (said of a deceased person) er war geboren

borough ['bʌro] s Städtchen n

borrow ['baro] tr leihen

borrower ['boro·ər] s Entleiher –in mf; (fin) Kreditnehmer –in mf

bor'rowing s Borgen n; (fin) Kreditaufnahme f; (ling) Lehnwort n

bosom ['buzəm] s Busen m; (fig) Schoß m

bos'om friend' s Busenfreund m

boss [bas] s (coll) Chef m, Boß m; (of a shield) Buckel m; (pol) Bonze m || tr (around) herumkommandieren

bossy ['bɔsi] adj herrschsüchtig

botanical [bə'tænɪkəl] adj botanisch

botanist ['batənɪst] s Botaniker –in mf

botany ['batəni] s Botanik f

botch [bat∫] tr (coll) verpfuschen

both [boθ] adj & pron beide || conj— both...and sowohl... als auch

bother ['baðər] s Belästigung f, Mühe f || tr (annoy) belästigen, stören; (worry) bedrücken; (said of a conscience) quälen || intr sich bemühen; **b. about** sich bekümmern um; **b. with** (a thing) sich befassen mit; (a person) verkehren mit

bothersome ['baðərsəm] adj lästig

bottle ['batəl] s Flasche f || tr in Flaschen abfüllen; **bottled up** aufgestaut

bot'tleneck' s Flaschenhals m; (fig) Engpaß m, Stauung f

bot'tle o'pener s Flaschenöffner m

bottom ['batəm] adj niedrigste, unterste || s Boden m; (of a well, shaft, river, valley) Sohle f; (of a mountain) Fuß m; (of an affair) Grund m; (buttocks) Hintern m; at the b. of the page unten auf der Seite; **bottoms up!** prosit, ex!; **get to the b. of a problem** e–r Frage auf den Grund gehen; **reach b.** (fig) den Nullpunkt erreichen

bottomless ['batəmlɪs] adj bodenlos

bough [bau] s Ast m

bouillon ['buljan] s Kraftbrühe f

bouil'lon cube' s Bouillonwürfel m

boulder ['boldər] s Felsblock m

bounce [bauns] s Aufprall m; (fig) Schwung m || tr (a ball) aufprallen lassen; (throw out) (sl) 'rausschmeißen || intr aufprallen, aufspringen; (said of a check) (coll) platzen

bouncer ['baunsər] s (sl) Rausschmeißer m

bounc'ing adj (baby) stramm

bound [baund] adj gebunden, gefesselt; (book) gebunden; (in duty) verpflichtet; **be b. for** unterwegs sein nach; **be b. up with** eng verbunden sein mit; **I am b. to** (inf) ich muß (inf) || s Sprung m, Satz m; **bounds** (sport) in; **keep within bounds** in Schranken halten; **know no bounds** weder Maß noch Ziel kennen; **out of bounds** (sport) aus; **within the bounds of** im Bereich (genit) || tr begrenzen || intr aufprallen, aufspringen

boundary ['baundəri] s Grenze f; (fig) Umgrenzung f

boun'dary line' s Grenzlinie f

boun'dary stone' s Grenzstein m

boundless ['baundlɪs] adj grenzenlos

bountiful ['bauntɪfəl] adj (generous) freigebig; (ample) reichlich

bounty ['baunti] s (generosity) Freigebigkeit f; (gift) Geschenk n; (reward) Prämie f

bouquet [bu'ke] s Strauß m; (aroma) Blume f

bout [baut] s (box) Kampf m; (fencing) Gang m; (pathol) Anfall m

bow [bau] s Verbeugung f; (naut) Bug m || intr sich verbeugen; **bow and scrape before** sich schmiegen und biegen vor (dat); **bow down** sich bücken; **bow out** sich geschickt zurückziehen; **bow to** sich (ver)neigen vor (dat) || [bo] s (weapon) Bogen m; (of a violin) Geigenbogen m; (bowknot) Schleife f; **bow and arrow** Pfeil m und Bogen m || intr (mus) geigen

bowel ['bau·əl] s Darm m; **bowels** Eingeweide pl; **bowels of the earth** Erdinnere n

bow'el move'ment s Stuhlgang m

bowl [bol] s Napf m, Schüssel f; (of a pipe) Kopf m; (washbowl, toilet bowl) Becken n; (of a spoon) Höhlung f; (sport) Stadion n || tr umhauen; (fig) umwerfen || intr kegeln

bowlegged ['bo·leg(ɪ)d] adj O-beinig

bowler ['bolər] s Kegler –in mf

bowl'ing s Kegeln n

bowl'ing al'ley s Kegelbahn f

bowl'ing ball' s Kegelkugel f

bowl'ing pin' s Kegel m

bowstring ['bo·strɪŋ] s Bogensehne f

bow' tie' [bo] s Schleife f, Fliege f

bow' win'dow [bo] s Bogenfenster n

bowwow ['bau'wau] interj wauwau!

box [baks] s (small and generally of cardboard) Schachtel f; (larger and generally of cardboard) Karton m; (generally of wood) Kasten m; (larger and generally of wood) Kiste f; (of strips of wood) Spanschachtel f; (theat) Loge f; (typ) Kasten m; **box of candy** Bonbonniere f; **box on the ear** Ohrfeige f || tr (sport) boxen; **box in** einschließen; **box s.o.'s ears** j–n ohrfeigen || intr (sport) boxen

box'car' s geschlossener Güterwagen m

boxer ['baksər] s (sport, zool) Boxer m

box'ing s Boxen n, Boxsport m

box'ing glove' s Boxhandschuh m

box'ing match' s Boxkampf m
box' kite' s Kastendrachen m
box' of'fice s (cin, theat) Kasse f
box' seat' s Logenplatz m
box' wood' s Buchsbaum m
boy [bɔɪ] s Junge m; (servant) Boy m
boycott ['bɔɪkɑt] s Boykott m ‖ tr boykottieren
boy'friend' s Freund m
boy'hood' s Knabenalter n
boyish ['bɔɪ·ɪʃ] adj jungenhaft
boy' scout' s Pfadfinder m
bra [brɑ] s (coll) BH m
brace [bres] s (carp) Strebe f, Stütze f; (dent) Zahnklammer f, Zahnspange f; (hunt) Paar n; (med) Schiene f; (typ) geschweifte Klammer f ‖ tr verstreben; (fig) stärken; b. oneself sich zusammenreißen; b. oneself against sich stemmen gegen; b. oneself for seinen Mut zusammennehmen für; b. up (fig) aufpulvern
brace' and bit' s Bohrwinde f
bracelet ['breslɪt] s Armband n
brac'ing adj (invigorating) erfrischend
bracket ['brækɪt] s Winkelstütze f, Konsole f; (wall bracket) Wandarm m; (mounting clip) Befestigungsschelle f; (typ) eckige Klammer f ‖ tr einklammern; (arti) eingabeln
brackish ['brækɪʃ] adj brackig
brag [bræg] v (pret & pp bragged; ger bragging) intr (about) prahlen (mit)
braggart ['brægərt] s Prahler –in mf
brag'ging adj prahlerisch ‖ s Prahlerei f
braid [bred] s (of hair) Flechte f; (flat trimming) Tresse f, Litze f; (round trimming) Kordel f ‖ tr (hair, rope) flechten; (trim with braid) mit Tresse (or Borten) besetzen
braille [brel] s Blindenschrift f
brain [bren] s Hirn n; brains Hirn n; (fig) Grütze f ‖ tr (coll) den Schädel einschlagen (dat)
brain'child' s Geistesfrucht f
brainless ['brenlɪs] adj hirnlos
brain'storm' s (coll) Geistesblitz m
brain'wash' tr Gehirnwäsche vornehmen bei
brain'wash'ing s Gehirnwäsche f
brain' wave' s Hirnwelle f; (fig) Geistesblitz m
brain'work' s Gehirnarbeit f
brainy ['breni] adj geistreich
braise [brez] tr schmoren, dünsten
brake [brek] s Bremse f; put on the brakes bremsen ‖ intr bremsen
brake' drum' s Bremstrommel f
brake' light' s Bremslicht n
brake' lin'ing s Bremsbelag m
brake'man s (–men) Bremser m
brake'ped'al s (aut) Bremspedal n
brake' shoe' s Bremsbacke f
bramble ['bræmbəl] s Dornbusch m
bran [bræn] s Kleie f
branch [bræntʃ] s (of a tree) Ast m; (smaller branch; of lineage) Zweig m; (of river) Arm m; (of a road, railroad) Abzweigung f; (of science, work, a shop) Branche f, Unterabteilung f; (com) Filiale f, Nebenstelle

f ‖ intr—b. off abzweigen; b. out sich verzweigen
branch' line' s Seitenlinie f
branch' of'fice s Zweigstelle f
branch' of serv'ice s Truppengattung f
brand [brænd] s (kind) Marke f; (trademark) Handelsmarke f; (on cattle) Brandmal n; (branding iron) Brandeisen n; (dishonor) Schandfleck m ‖ tr (& fig) brandmarken
brand'ing i'ron s Brandeisen n
brandish ['brændɪʃ] tr schwingen; (threateningly) schwenken
brand'-new' adj nagelneu
brandy ['brændi] s Branntwein m
brash [bræʃ] adj schnodd(e)rig, frech
brass [bræs] adj Messing– ‖ s Messing n; (mil) hohe Offiziere pl; (mus) Blechinstrumente pl
brass' band' s Blechblaskapelle f
brassiere [brə'zɪr] s Büstenhalter m
brass' knuck'les spl Schlagring m
brass' tacks' spl—get down to b. (coll) zur Sache kommen
brat [bræt] s (coll) Balg m
bravado [brə'vɑdo] s Bravour f, Angabe f
brave [brev] adj tapfer, mutig ‖ s indianischer Krieger m ‖ tr trotzen (dat)
bravery ['brevəri] s Tapferkeit f
bra·vo ['brɑvo] s (–vos) Bravo n ‖ interj bravo!
brawl [brɔl] s Rauferei f ‖ intr raufen
brawler ['brɔlər] s Raufbold m
brawn [brɔn] s Muskelkraft f
brawny ['brɔni] adj muskulös, kräftig
bray [bre] s Eselsschrei m ‖ intr schreien, iahen
braze [brez] tr (brassplate) mit Messing überziehen; (solder) hartlöten
brazen ['brezən] adj Messing–, ehern; (fig) unverschämt ‖ tr—b. it out unverschämt durchsetzen
Brazil [brə'zɪl] s Brasilien n
Brazilian [brə'zɪljən] adj brasilianisch, brasilisch ‖ s Brasilier –in mf
Brazil' nut' s Paranuß f
breach [britʃ] s Bruch m; (mil) Bresche f ‖ tr (mil) durchbrechen
breach' of con'tract s Vertragsbruch m
breach' of prom'ise s Verlöbnisbruch m
breach' of the peace' s Friedensbruch m
breach' of trust' s Vertrauensbruch m
bread [bred] s Brot n; (money) (sl) Pinke f ‖ tr (culin) panieren
bread' and but'ter s Butterbrot n; (livelihood) Lebensunterhalt m
bread' box' s Brotkasten m
bread' crumb' s Brotkrume f
bread'ed adj paniert
bread'ed veal' cut'let s Wiener Schnitzel n
bread' knife' s Brotmesser n
breadth [brɛdθ] s Breite f
bread'win'ner s Brotverdiener –in mf
break [brek] s Bruch m; (split, tear) Riß m; (crack) Sprung m; (in relations) Bruch m; (in a forest) Lichtung f; (in the clouds) Lücke f; (recess) Pause f; (rest from work)

Arbeitspause *f*; (*luck*) Glück *n*; (*chance*) Chance *f*; (*box*) Lösen *n*; **bad b.** Pech *n*; **b. in the weather** Wetterumschlag *m*; **give s.o. a b. j—m e—e** Chance geben; **make a b. for** losstürzen auf (*acc*); **take a b. e—e** Pause machen; **tough b.** Pech *n*; **without a b.** ohne Unterbrechung ‖ *v* (*pret* **broke** [brok]; *pp* **broken** ['brokən]) *tr* (& fig) brechen; (*snap*) zerreißen; (*a string*) durchreißen; (*a dish*) zerbrechen; (*an appointment*) nicht einhalten; (*contact*) unterbrechen; (*an engagement*) auflösen; (*a law, limb*) verletzen; (*monotony*) auflockern; (*a record*) brechen; (*a seal*) erbrechen; (*a window*) einschlagen; (*one's word, promise*) nicht halten; **b. down** (*into constituents*) zerlegen; (*s.o.'s resistance*) überwinden; (*mach*) abmontieren; **b. in** (*a horse*) zureiten; (*a car*) einfahren; (*a person*) anlernen; **b. loose** losreißen; **b. off** abbrechen, losbrechen; (*an engagement*) auflösen; **b. open** aufbrechen; **b. s.o. from s.th. j**—m ihr abgewöhnen; **the news (to)** die Nachricht eröffnen (*dat*), die Nachricht beibringen (*dat*); **b. to pieces** zerbrechen; (*a meeting*) auflösen; (*forcibly*) sprengen; **break wind** e—n Darmwind abgehen lassen ‖ *intr* brechen; (*snap*) reißen; (*said of the voice*) mutieren; (*said of waves*) sich brechen; (*said of large waves*) sich überschlagen; (*said of the weather*) umschlagen; **b. down** zusammenbrechen; (*mach*) versagen; **b. even** gerade die Unkosten decken; **b. loose** losbrechen, sich losreißen; **b. out** (*said of fire, an epidemic, prisoner*) ausbrechen; **b. up** (*said of a meeting*) sich auflösen

breakable ['brekəbəl] *adj* zerbrechlich
breakage ['brekɪdʒ] *s* Bruch *m*; (*cost of broken articles*) Bruchschaden *m*
break'down' *s* (*of health, discipline, morals*) Zusammenbruch *m*; (*disintegration*) Zersetzung *f*; (*of costs, etc.*) Aufgliederung *f*; (*aut*) Panne *f*; (*chem*) Analyse *f*; (*elec*) Durchschlag *m*; (*of a piece of equipment*) (*mach*) Versagen *n*; (*e.g., of power supply, factory equipment*) Betriebsstörung *f*
breaker ['brekər] *s* Sturzwelle *f*; **breakers** Brandung *f*
breakfast ['brekfəst] *s* Frühstück *n* ‖ *intr* frühstücken
break'neck' *adj* halsbrecherisch
break' of day' *s* Tagesanbruch *m*
break'through' *s* Durchbruch *m*
break'up' *s* Aufbrechen *n*; (*of a meeting*) Auflösung *f*
break'wa'ter *s* Wellenbrecher *m*
breast [brest] *s* Brust *f*; (*of a woman*) Brust *f*, Busen *m*; **beat one's b.** sich an die Brust schlagen; **make a clean b.** of sich [*dat*] vom Herzen reden
breast'bone' *s* Brustbein *n*
breast' feed'ing *s* Stillen *n*
breast'plate' *s* Brustharnisch *m*
breast'stroke' *s* Brustschwimmen *n*

breath [breθ] *s* Atem *m*; (*single inhalation*) Atemzug *m*; (fig) Hauch *m*; **b. of air** Lüftchen *n*; **gasp for b.** nach Luft schnappen; **have bad b.** aus dem Mund riechen; **in the same b.** im gleichen Atemzug; **save one's b.** sich [*dat*] seine Worte ersparen; **take a deep b.** tief Luft holen; **take one's b. away j**—m den Atem verschlagen; **waste one's b.** in den Wind reden
breathe [brið] *tr* atmen, schöpfen; **b. a sigh of relief** aufatmen; **b. life into** beseelen; **b. one's last** die Seele aushauchen; **b. out** ausatmen; **not b. a word about it** kein Wort davon verlauten lassen ‖ *intr* atmen, hauchen; **b. again** aufatmen; **b. on** anhauchen
breath'ing space' *s* Atempause *f*
breathless ['brεθlɪs] *adj* atemlos
breath'-tak'ing *adj* atemberaubend
breech [britʃ] *s* Verschlußstück *n*
breed [brid] *s* Zucht *f*, Stamm *m*; (*sort, group*) Schlag *m*; (*of animals*) Rasse *f* ‖ *v* (*pret & pp* **bred** [brεd]) *tr* (*beget*) erzeugen; (*raise*) züchten; (fig) hervorrufen ‖ *intr* sich vermehren
breeder ['bridər] *s* Züchter –in *mf*
breed'ing *s* (*of animals*) Züchtung *f*, Aufzucht *f*; (fig) Erziehung *f*
breeze [briz] *s* Lüftchen *n*, Brise *f* ‖ *intr*—**b. by** vorbeiflitzen; **b. in** frisch und vergnügt hereinkommen
breezy ['brizi] *adj* luftig; (fig) keß
brevity ['brεvɪti] *s* Kürze *f*
brew [bru] *s* Brühe *f*; (*of beer*) Bräu *m* ‖ *tr* (*tea, coffee*) aufbrühen; (*beer*) brauen ‖ *intr* ziehen; (*said of a storm*) sich zusammenbrauen; **something is brewing** etwas ist im Anzuge
brewer ['bru‐ər] *s* Brauer –in *mf*
brewery ['bru‐əri] *s* Brauerei *f*
bribe [braɪb] *s* Bestechungsgeld *n* ‖ *tr* bestechen
bribery ['braɪbəri] *s* Bestechung *f*
brick [brɪk] *s* Ziegelstein *m*
bricklayer ['brɪk ‚le‐ər] *s* Maurer *m*
brick'work' *s* Mauerwerk *n*
brick'yard' *s* Ziegelei *f*
bridal ['braɪdəl] *adj* Braut–, Hochzeits–
brid'al gown' *s* Brautkleid *n*
brid'al veil' *s* Brautschleier *m*
bride [braɪd] *s* Braut *f*
bride'groom' *s* Bräutigam *m*
brides'maid' *s* Brautjungfer *f*
bridge [brɪdʒ] *s* (*over a river*) Brücke *f*; (*of eyeglasses*) Steg *m*; (*of a nose*) Nasenrücken *m*; (*cards*) Bridge *n*; (*dent*) Zahnbrücke *f*; (*naut*) Kommandobrücke *f* ‖ *tr* (& fig) überbrücken
bridge'head' *s* Brückenkopf *m*
bridge'work' *s* (*dent*) Brückenarbeit *f*
bridle ['braɪdəl] *s* Zaum *m*, Zügel *m* ‖ *tr* aufzäumen, zügeln
bri'dle path' *s* Reitweg *m*
brief [brif] *adj* kurz; **be b.** sich kurz fassen ‖ *s* (jur) Schriftsatz *m* ‖ *tr* einweisen, orientieren
brief' case' *s* Aktentasche *f*

brief′ing s Einsatzbesprechung f
brier ['braɪ·ər] s Dornbusch m
brig [brɪg] s (naut) Brigg f; (nav) Knast m
brigade [brɪ'ged] s Brigade f
brigadier′ gen′eral [,brɪgə'dɪr] s Brigadegeneral m
brigand ['brɪgənd] s Brigant m
bright [braɪt] adj hell; (color) lebhaft; (face) strahlend; (weather) heiter; (smart) gescheit, aufgeweckt || adv —**b. and early** in aller Frühe
brighten ['braɪtən] tr aufhellen || intr sich aufhellen
bright′-eyed adj helläugig
brightness ['braɪtnɪs] s Helle f
bright′ side s (fig) Lichtseite f
bright′ spot s (fig) Lichtblick m
brilliance ['brɪljəns], **brilliancy** ['brɪljənsi] s Glanz m
brilliant ['brɪljənt] adj (& fig) glänzend
brim [brɪm] s Rand m; (of a hat) Krempe f; **to the b.** bis zum Rande || v (pret & pp **brimmed**; ger **brimming**) intr—**b. over (with)** (fig) überschäumen (vor dat)
brimful ['brɪm,ful] adj übervoll
brim′stone′ s Schwefel m
brine [braɪn] s Salzwasser n, Sole f; (for pickling) Salzlake f
bring [brɪŋ] v (pret & pp **brought** [brɔt]) tr bringen; **b. about** zustande bringen; **b. back** zurückbringen; (memories) zurückrufen; **b. down** herunterbringen; (shoot down) abschießen; **b. down the house** (fig) Lachstürme entfesseln; **b. forth** (e.g., complaints) hervorbringen; **b. forward** vorbringen; **b. it about** that es durchsetzen, daß; **b. on** herbeiführen; **b. oneself to** (inf) sich überwinden zu (inf); **b. to** wieder zu sich bringen; **b. together** zusammenbringen; **b. up** (children) erziehen; (a topic) zur Sprache bringen
bring′ing-up′ s Erziehung f
brink [brɪŋk] s (& fig) Rand m
brisk [brɪsk] adj (pace, business) flott; (air) frisch, scharf
bristle ['brɪsəl] s Borste f || intr sich sträuben
bristly ['brɪsli] adj borstig
Britain ['brɪtən] s Britannien n
British ['brɪtɪʃ] adj britisch || **the B.** spl die Briten pl
Britisher ['brɪtɪʃər] s Brite m, Britin f
Briton ['brɪtən] s Brite m, Britin f
Brittany ['brɪtəni] s die Bretagne f
brittle ['brɪtəl] adj brüchig, spröde
broach [brotʃ] tr zur Sprache bringen
broad [brɔd] adj breit; (daylight) hellicht; (outline) grob; (sense) weit; (view) allgemein, umfassend
broad′cast′ s Sendung f, Übertragung f || v (pret & pp —cast) tr (rumors, etc.) ausposaunen || (pret & pp —cast & —casted) tr & intr senden, übertragen
broadcaster ['brɔd,kæstər] s Rundfunksprecher –in mf
broad′casting sta′tion s Sender m
broad′casting stu′dio s Senderaum m

broad′cloth′ s feiner Wäschestoff m
broaden ['brɔdən] tr verbreitern || intr sich verbreitern
broad′-gauge′ adj (rr) breitspurig
broad′-mind′ed adj großzügig
broad′-shoul′dered adj breitschultrig
broad′side′ s (guns on one side of ship) Breitseite f; (fig) Schimpfkanonade f
brocade [bro'ked] s Brokat m
broccoli ['brakəli] s Spargelkohl m
brochure [bro'ʃur] s Broschüre f
broil [brɔɪl] tr am Rost braten, grillen
broiler ['brɔɪlər] s Bratrost m
broke [brok] adj (coll) abgebrannt, pleite; **go b.** (coll) pleite gehen
broken ['brokən] adj zerbrochen; (limb, spirit, English) gebrochen; (home) zerrüttet; (line) gestrichelt
bro′ken-down′ adj erschöpft; (horse) abgearbeitet
bro′ken-heart′ed adj mit gebrochenem Herzen
broker ['brokər] s Makler –in mf
brokerage ['brokərɪdʒ] s Maklergeschäft n; (fee) Maklergebühr f
bromide ['bromaɪd] s Bromid n; (coll) Binsenweisheit f
bromine ['bromin] s Brom n
bronchial ['braŋki·əl] adj bronchial
bron′chial tube′ s Luftröhre f, Bronchie f
bronchitis [braŋ'kaɪtɪs] s Bronchitis f
bron·co ['braŋko] s (–cos) kleines halbwildes Pferd n
bronze [branz] adj Bronze– || s Bronze f || tr bronzieren || intr sich bräunen
brooch [brotʃ], [brutʃ] s Brosche f
brood [brud] s Brut f, Junge pl || tr ausbrüten || intr brüten; (coll) sinnieren; **b. over** grübeln über (acc)
brook [bruk] s Bach m || tr dulden
broom [brum] s Besen m
broom′stick′ s Besenstiel m
broth [brɔθ] s Brühe f
brothel ['braθəl] s Bordell n
brother ['brʌðər] s Bruder m; **brother(s) and sister(s)** Geschwister pl
broth′erhood′ s (& relig) Brüderschaft f
broth′er-in-law′ s (brothers-in-law) Schwager m
brotherly ['brʌðərli] adj brüderlich
brow [brau] s Stirn f
brow′beat′ v (pret —beat; pp —beaten) tr einschüchtern
brown [braun] adj braun || s Bräune f || tr & intr bräunen
brownish ['braunɪʃ] adj bräunlich
brown′-nose′ v (sl) kriechen (dat)
brown′ sug′ar s brauner Zucker m
browse [brauz] intr grasen, weiden; (through books) schmökern, stöbern; (through a store) herumsuchen
bruise [bruz] s Quetschung f || tr quetschen
brunette [bru'net] adj brünett || s Brünette f
brunt [brʌnt] s Anprall m; **bear the b.** die Hauptlast tragen
brush [brʌʃ] s Bürste f; (of an artist; for shaving) Pinsel m; (brief encoun-

ter) kurzer Zusammenstoß *m*; (*light touch*) leichte Berührung *f*; (*bot*) Gebüsch *n*; (*elec*) Bürste *f*; || *tr* bürsten; **b. aside** beiseite schieben; **b. off** abbürsten; (*devour*) verschlingen; (*make light of*) abwimmeln || *intr*—**b. against** streifen; **b. up on** auffrischen

brush'-off' *s* (coll) Laufpaß *m*

brush'wood' *s* Unterholz *n*, Niederwald *m*

brusque [brʌsk] *adj* brüsk

Brussels ['brʌsəlz] *s* Brüssel *n*

Brus'sels sprouts' *spl* Rosenkohl *m*

brutal ['brutəl] *adj* brutal

brutality [bru'tælɪti] *s* Brutalität *f*

brute [brut] *adj* viehisch; (*strength*) roh || *s* Tier *n*; (fig) Unmensch *m*

brutish ['brutɪʃ] *adj* tierisch, roh

bubble ['bʌbəl] *s* Blase *f*, Bläschen *n* || *intr* sprudeln; **b. over** (**with**) übersprudeln (*vor dat*)

bub'ble bath' *s* Schaumbad *n*

bub'ble gum' *s* Knallkaugummi *m*

bubbly ['bʌbli] *adj* sprudelnd; (*Person*) lebhaft

buck [bʌk] *s* Bock *m*; (sl) Dollar *m*; **pass the b.** (coll) die Verantwortung abschieben || *tr* (fig) kämpfen gegen; **b. off** abwerfen || *intr* bocken; **b. for** (*a promotion*) sich bemühen um

bucket ['bʌkɪt] *s* Eimer *m*

buck'et seat' *s* Schalensitz *m*

buckle ['bʌkəl] *s* Schnalle *f*; (*bend*) Ausbuchtung *f* || *tr* zuschnallen || *intr* (*from heat, etc.*) zusammensacken; **b. down** sich auf die Hosen setzen

buck' pri'vate *s* gemeiner Soldat *m*

buckram ['bʌkrəm] *s* Buckram *n*

buck'shot' *s* Rehposten *m*

buck'tooth' *s* (**-teeth**) vorstehender Zahn *m*

buck'wheat' *s* Buchweizen *m*

bud [bʌd] *s* Knospe *f*, Keim *m*; **nip in the bud** (fig) im Keime ersticken || *v* (*pret & pp* **budded;** *ger* **budding**) *intr* knospen, keimen, ausschlagen

buddy ['bʌdi] *s* (coll) Kumpel *m*

budge [bʌdʒ] *tr* (von der Stelle) bewegen || *intr* sich (von der Stelle) bewegen

budget ['bʌdʒɪt] *s* Budget *n*, Haushaltsplan *m*; (*of a state*) Staatshaushalt *m* || *tr* einteilen, vorausplanen

budgetary ['bʌdʒɪ ˌteri] *adj* Budget–

buff [bʌf] *adj* lederfarben || *s* Lederfarbe *f*; (coll) Schwärmer –in *mf* || *tr* polieren

buffa·lo ['bʌfə ˌlo] *s* (**-loes** & **-los**) Büffel *m*

buffer ['bʌfər] *s* Puffer *m*; (*polisher*) Polierer *m*; (rr) Prellbock *m*

buff'er state' *s* Pufferstaat *m*

buffet [bu'fe] *s* (*meal*) Büfett *n*; (*furniture*) Kredenz *f* || ['bʌfɪt] *tr* herumstoßen

buffoon [bə'fun] *s* Hanswurst *m*

bug [bʌg] *s* Insekt *n*, Käfer *m*; (*defect*) (coll) Defekt *m*; (electron) Abhörgerät *n*, Wanze *f*; **bugs** Ungeziefer *n* || *v* (*pret & pp* **bugged;** *ger* **bugging**) *tr* (*annoy*) (sl) ärgern;

(electron) (sl) Abhörgeräte einbauen in (*dat*)

bug'-eyed' *adj* (sl) mit großen Augen

buggy ['bʌgi] *adj* verwanzt; (*crazy*) (sl) verrückt || *s* Wagen *m*

bugle ['bjugəl] *s* Signalhorn *n*

bu'gle call' *s* Signal *n*

bugler ['bjuglər] *s* Hornist –in *mf*

build [bɪld] *s* Bauart *f*, Gestalt *f*; (*of a person*) Körperbau *m* || *v* (*pret & pp* **built** [bɪlt]) *tr* bauen; (*a bridge*) schlagen; (*with stone or brick*) mauern; (*a fire*) anmachen; **b. up** aufbauen; (*an area*) ausbauen; (*hopes*) erwecken

builder ['bɪldər] *s* Baumeister *m*

build'ing *s* Gebäude *n*

build'ing and loan' associa'tion *s* Bausparkasse *f*

build'ing block' *s* Zementblock *m*; (*for children*) Bauklötzchen *n*

build'ing con'tractor *s* Bauunternehmer *m*

build'ing in'dustry *s* Bauindustrie *f*

build'ing lot' *s* Bauplatz *m*, Grundstück *n*

build'ing mate'rial *s* Baustoff *m*

build'-up' *s* (coll) Propaganda *f*

built'-in' *adj* Einbau–

built'-up' *adj* bebaut

bulb [bʌlb] *s* (bot) Knolle *f*, Zwiebel *f*; (elec) Glühbirne *f*; (phot) Blitzlampe *f*

Bulgaria [bʌl'gɑrɪ-ə] *s* Bulgarien *n*

Bulgarian [bʌl'gɑrɪ-ən] *adj* bulgarisch || *s* Bulgare *m*, Bulgarin *f*; (*language*) Bulgarisch *n*

bulge [bʌldʒ] *s* Ausbauchung *f*, Beule *f*; (*of a sail*) Bausch *m*; (mil) Frontvorsprung *m* || *intr* sich bauschen; (*said of eyes*) hervortreten

bulg'ing *adj* (*belly, muscles*) hervorspringend; (*eyes*) hervorquellend; (*sails*) gebläht; **b. with** bis zum Platzen gefüllt mit

bulk [bʌlk] *adj* Massen–, unverpackt || *s* Masse *f*; (*main part*) Hauptteil *m*; **in b.** unverpackt || *intr*—**b. large** e–e große Rolle spielen

bulk'head' *s* (aer) Spant *m*; (naut) Schott *n*

bulky ['bʌlki] *adj* sperrig

bull [bʊl] *s* Bulle *m*, Stier *m*; (sl) Quatsch *m*; (eccl) Bulle *f*; (st. exch.) Haussier *m*; **like a b. in a china shop** wie ein Elefant im Porzellanladen; **shoot the b.** (sl) quatschen; **take the b. by the horns** den Stier an den Hörnern packen; **throw the b.** (sl) aufschneiden

bull'dog' *s* Bulldogge *f*

bull'doze' *tr* planieren; (fig) überfahren

bulldozer ['bʌl ˌdozər] *s* Planierraupe *f*

bullet ['bʊlɪt] *s* Kugel *f*

bul'let hole' *s* Schußöffnung *f*

bulletin ['bʊlətɪn] *s* (*report*) Bulletin *n*; (*flyer*) Flugschrift *f*

bul'letin board' *s* Anschlagbrett *n*

bul'letproof' *adj* kugelsicher

bull'fight' *s* Stierkampf *m*

bull'fight'er *s* Stierkämpfer –in *mf*

bull'frog' *s* Ochsenfrosch *m*

bull'-head'ed adj dickköpfig

bull' horn' s Richtungslautsprecher m

bullion ['buljən] s Barren m; (mil, nav) Kordel f

bull' mar'ket s Spekulationsmarkt m

bullock ['bulək] s Ochse m

bull'pen' s Stierpferch m; (baseball) Übungsplatz m für Reservewerfer

bull'ring' s Stierkampfarena f

bull' ses'sion s (sl) zwanglose Diskussion f

bull's'-eye' s (of a target) Schwarze m; (round window) Bullauge n; **hit the b.** ins Schwarze treffen

bul·ly ['buli] adj—**b. for you!** großartig! || s Raufbold m || v (pret & pp –lied) tr tyrannisieren

bulrush ['bul‚rʌʃ] s Binse f

bulwark ['bulwərk] s Bollwerk n

bum [bʌm] s Strolch m; **give s.o. the bum's rush** j-n auf den Schub bringen || v (pret & pp bummed; ger bumming) tr (sl) schinden, schnorren || intr—**bum around** bummeln

bumblebee ['bʌmbəl‚bi] s Hummel f

bump [bʌmp] s Stoß m, Bums m; (swelling) Beule f; (in the road) holp(e)rige Stelle f || tr (an)stoßen; **b. off** (sl) abknallen; **b. one's head against s.th.** mit dem Kopf gegen etw stoßen || intr zusammenstoßen; **b. against** stoßen an (acc); **b. into** stoßen gegen; (meet unexpectedly) in die Arme laufen (dat)

bumper ['bʌmpər] s Stoßstange f

bumpkin ['bʌmpkın] s Tölpel m

bumpy ['bʌmpi] adj holperig; (aer) böig

bum' steer' s—**give s.o. a b.** (coll) nasführen

bun [bʌn] s Kuchenbrötchen n; (of hair) Haarknoten m

bunch [bʌntʃ] s Bündel n; (of grapes) Traube f; (group) Schar f, Bande f; **b. of flowers** Blumenstrauß m; **b. of grapes** Weintraube f || tr—**b. together** zusammenfassen || intr—**b. together** sich zusammendrängen

bundle ['bʌndəl] s Bündel n; (heap) Stoß m; (of straw) Schütte f; **b. of nerves** Nervenbündel n || tr bündeln; **b. off** (coll) verfrachten; **b. up** sich warm anziehen

bung [bʌŋ] s Spund m || tr verspunden

bungalow ['bʌŋgə‚lo] s Bungalow m

bung'hole' s Spundloch n

bungle ['bʌŋgəl] s Pfuscherei f || tr verpfuschen || intr pfuschen

bungler ['bʌŋglər] s Pfuscher –in mf

bun'gling adj stümperhaft || s Stümperei f

bunk [bʌŋk] s Schlafkoje f; (sl) Unsinn m || intr (with) schlafen (mit)

bunk' bed' s Etagenbett n

bunker ['bʌŋkər] s Bunker m

bunny ['bʌni] s Kaninchen n

bunt'ing s (cloth) Fahnentuch n; (decoration) Fahnenschmuck m; (orn) Ammer f

buoy [bɔɪ], ['bu·i] s Boje f || tr—**b. up** flott erhalten; (fig) Auftrieb geben (dat)

buoyancy ['bɔɪ·ənsi] s Auftrieb m; (fig) Spannkraft f

buoyant ['bɔɪ·ənt] adj schwimmend; (fig) lebhaft

burden ['bʌrdən] s Bürde f, Last f; (fig) Belastung f || tr belasten

bur'den of proof' s Beweislast f

burdensome ['bʌrdənsəm] adj lästig

bureau ['bjuro] s Kommode f; (office) Büro n; (department) Amt n

bureaucracy [bju'rɑkrəsi] s Bürokratie f, Beamtenschaft f

bureaucrat ['bjurə‚kræt] s Bürokrat –in mf

bureaucratic [‚bjurə'krætık] adj bürokratisch

burglar ['bʌrglər] s Einbrecher –in mf

bur'glar alarm' s Einbruchssicherung f

burglarize ['bʌrglə‚raız] tr einbrechen in (acc)

bur'glarproof' adj einbruchssicher

burglary ['bʌrgləri] s Einbruchdiebstahl m

Burgundy ['bʌrgəndi] s Burgund n; (wine) Burgunder m

burial ['berı·əl] s Beerdigung f

bur'ial ground' s Begräbnisplatz m

burlap ['bʌrlæp] s Sackleinwand f

burlesque [bʌr'lesk] adj burlesk || s Burleske f || tr burlesk behandeln

burlesque' show' s Varieté n

burly ['bʌrli] adj stämmig, beleibt

Burma ['bʌrmə] s Birma n

Bur·mese [bʌr'miz] adj birmanisch || s (–mese) (person) Birmane m, Birmanin f; (language) Birmanisch n

burn [bʌrn] s Brandwunde f; || v (pret & pp burned & burnt [bʌrnt]) tr (ver)brennen; **be burned up** (coll) fauchen; **b. down** niederbrennen; **b. up** (coll) wütend machen || intr (ver)brennen; (said of food) anbrennen; **b. out** ausbrennen; (elec) durchbrennen; **b. up** ganz verbrennen; (during reentry) verglühen

burner ['bʌrnər] s Brenner m

burn'ing adj (& fig) brennend

burnish ['bʌrnıʃ] tr polieren

burn'out' s (rok) Brennschluß m

burnt adj verbrannt; (smell) brenzlig

burp [bʌrp] s Rülpser m || tr rülpsen lassen || intr rülpsen

burr [bʌr] s (growth on a tree) Auswuchs m; (in metal) Grat m; (bot) Klette f

burrow ['bʌro] s Bau m || tr graben || intr sich eingraben, wühlen

bursar ['bʌrsər] s Schatzmeister m

burst [bʌrst] s Bersten n; (split) Riß m; Bruch m; **b. of gunfire** Feuerstoß m || v (pret & pp burst) tr (auf)sprengen, zum Platzen bringen || intr bersten, platzen; (split) reißen; (said of a boil) aufgehen; **b. into** (acc); **b. into** tears in Tränen ausbrechen; **b. open** aufplatzen; **b. out laughing** loslachen

bur·y ['beri] v (pret & pp –ied) tr beerdigen, begraben; **be buried in thought** in Gedanken versunken sein; **b. alive** verschütten

bus [bʌs] s (busses & buses) Autobus m, Bus m || v (pret & pp) bussed &

bused; *ger* **bussing & busing**) *tr &
intr* mit dem Bus fahren
bus′ boy′ *s* Pikkolo *m*
bus′ driv′er *s* Autobusfahrer –in *mf*
bush [buʃ] *s* Busch *m;* **beat around
the b.** um die Sache herumreden
bushed *adj* (coll) abgeklappert
bushel [′buʃəl] *s* Scheffel *m;* **by the b.**
scheffelweise
bush′ing *s* Buchse *f*
bushy [′buʃi] *adj* strauchbewachsen;
(*brows*) buschig
business [′bɪznɪs] *s* Geschäfts– ‖ *s*
Geschäft *n;* (*company*) Firma *f,* Betrieb *m;* (*employment*) Beruf *m,* Gewerbe *m;* (*duty*) Pflicht *f;* (*right*)
Recht *n;* (coll) Sache *f;* **be in b.** ge-
schäftlich tätig sein; **do b. with** Geschäfte machen mit; **get down to b.**
(coll) zur Sache kommen; **go about
one's b.** seiner Arbeit nachgehen; **he
means b.** (coll) er meint es ernst;
know one's b. seine Sache verstehen;
make s.th. one's b. sich [*dat*] etw
angelegen sein lassen; **mind your
own b.** kümmere dich um deine
eigenen Sachen; **that's none of your
b.** das geht dich gar nichts an; **the
whole b.** die ganze Geschichte; **you
have no b. here** du hast hier nichts
zu suchen
busi′ness call′ *s* Dienstgespräch *n*
busi′ness card′ *s* Geschäftskarte *f*
busi′ness cen′ter *s* Geschäftszentrum *n*
busi′ness col′lege *s* Handelsschule *f*
busi′ness dis′trict *s* Geschäftsviertel *n*
busi′ness expens′es *spl* Geschäftsspesen
pl
busi′ness hours′ *s* Geschäftszeit *f*
busi′ness let′ter *s* Geschäftsbrief *m*
busi′nesslike *adj* sachlich; (pej) ge-
schäftsmäßig
busi′ness-man′ *s* (**–men′**) Geschäfts-
mann *m*
busi′ness reply′ card′ *s* Rückantwort-
karte *f*
busi′ness suit′ *s* Straßenanzug *m*
busi′ness-wom′an *s* (**–wom′en**) Ge-
schäftsfrau *f*
bus′ line′ *s* Autobuslinie *f*
bus′ stop′ *s* Autobushaltestelle *f*
bust [bʌst] *s* (*chest*) Busen *m;* (*measurement*) Oberweite *f;* (*statue*) Brustbild *n;* (*blow*) (sl) Faustschlag *m;*
(*failure*) (sl) Platzen *n;* (*binge*) (sl)
Sauftour *f* ‖ *tr* (sl) kaputtmachen;
(mil) degradieren ‖ *intr* (*break*) (sl)
kaputtgehen
bustle [′bʌsəl] *s* (*activity*) Hochbe-
trieb *m,* Trubel *m* ‖ *intr* umher-
hasten; **b. about** herumsausen
bus′tling *adj* geschäftig
bus·y [′bɪzi] *adj* tätig, beschäftigt;
(*day, life*) arbeitsreich; (*street*) lebhaft, verkehrsstark; (telp) belegt, besetzt; **be b.** (*be occupied*) zu tun
haben; (*be unavailable*) nicht zu
sprechen sein ‖ *v* (*pret & pp* **–ied**)
tr beschäftigen
bus′ybod′y *s* Wichtigtuer –in *mf*
bus′y sig′nal *s* (telp) Besetztzeichen *n*
but [bʌt] *adv* nur, lediglich, bloß;
(*just, only*) erst; **all but** beinahe ‖

prep außer (*dat*); (*after negatives*)
als; **all but one** alle bis auf einen ‖
conj aber; (*after negatives*) sondern
butcher [′butʃər] *s* Fleischer –in *mf,*
Metzger –in *mf;* (fig) Schlächter –in
mf ‖ *tr* schlachten; (fig) abschlachten
butch′er knife′ *s* Fleischermesser *n*
butch′er shop′ *s* Metzgerei *f*
butchery [′butʃəri] *s* (*slaughterhouse*)
Schlachthaus *n;* (fig) Gemetzel *n*
butler [′bʌtlər] *s* Haushofmeister *m*
butt [bʌt] *s* (*of a gun*) Kolben *m;* (*of
a cigarette*) Stummel *m;* (*with the
horns, head*) Stoß *m;* (*of ridicule*)
Zielscheibe *f* ‖ *tr* stoßen; **b. in** *intr*
stoßen; **b. in** (sl) sich einmischen,
dazwischentreten
butter [′bʌtər] *s* Butter *f* ‖ *tr* mit Butter bestreichen; (*bread*) schmieren;
b. s.o. up (coll) j–m Honig um den
Mund schmieren
but′terball′ *s* Butterkugel *f;* (*chubby
child*) Pummelchen *n*
but′tercup′ *s* Butterblume *f,* Hahnenfuß *m*
but′ter dish′ *s* Butterdose *f*
but′terfly′ *s* Schmetterling *m;* (sport)
Schmetterlingsstil *m*
but′ter knife′ *s* Buttermesser *n*
but′termilk′ *s* Buttermilch *f*
buttocks [′bʌtəks] *spl* Hinterbacken *pl*
button [′bʌtən] *s* Knopf *m* ‖ *tr* knöpfen; **button up** zuknöpfen
but′tonhole′ *s* Knopfloch *n* ‖ *tr* im
Gespräch festhalten
buttress [′bʌtrɪs] *s* Strebepfeiler *m;*
(fig) Stütze *f* ‖ *tr* (durch Strebepfeiler) stützen; (fig) (unter)stützen
butt′-weld′ *tr* stumpfschweißen
buxom [′bʌksəm] *adj* beleibt
buy [baɪ] *s* Kauf *m* ‖ *v* (*pret & pp*
bought [bɔt]) *tr* kaufen; (*bus ticket,
train ticket*) lösen; (*accept, believe*)
glauben; **buy off** (*bribe*) bestechen;
buy out auskaufen; **buy up** aufkaufen
buyer [′baɪər] *s* Käufer –in *mf*
buzz [bʌz] *s* Summen *n,* Surren *n;*
(telp) (coll) Anruf *m* ‖ *tr* (coll) (aer)
dicht vorbeisausen an (*dat*); (telp)
(coll) anrufen ‖ *intr* summen, surren; **b. around** herumsausen
buzzard [′bʌzərd] *s* Bussard *m*
buzz′ bomb′ *s* Roboterbombe *f,* V-
Waffe *f*
buzzer [′bʌzər] *s* Summer *m;* **did the
b. sound?** ist der Summer ertönt
buzz′ saw′ *s* Kreissäge *f,* Rundsäge *f*
by [baɪ] *adv* vorüber, vorbei; **by and
by** nach und nach; **by and large** im
großen und ganzen ‖ *prep* (*agency*)
von (*dat*), durch (*acc*); (*position*)
bei (*dat*), an (*dat*), neben (*dat*); (*no
later than*) bis spätestens; (*in division*) durch (*acc*); (*indicating mode
of transportation*) mit (*dat*); (*indicating authorship*) von (*dat*); (*according to*) nach (*dat*); (*past*) an
(*dat*) vorbei; (*by means of*) mit
(*dat*); **by** (*ger*) indem (*ind*); **by an
inch** um e–n Zoll; **by day** bei Tag;
by far bei weitem; **by heart** auswendig; **by itself** (*automatically*) von
selbst; **by land** zu Lande; **by mail**

per Post; **by myself** ganz allein; **by nature** von Natur aus; **by now** schon; **by the pound** per Pfund; **two by four** zwei mal vier

bye [baɪ] *s* (sport) Freilos *n*
bye/bye' *interj* Wiedersehen!
bygone ['baɪ ˌɡɔn] *adj* vergangen ‖ *s*—**let bygones be bygones** laß(t) das Vergangene ruhen
by/law' *s* Satzung *f*; **bylaws** (*of an organization*) Statuten *pl*, Satzungen *pl*
by/-line' *s* (journ) Verfasserangabe *f*

by/pass' *s* Umgehungsstraße *f*, Umleitung *f*; (elec) Nebenschluß *m* ‖ *tr* umgehen
by/prod/uct *s* Nebenprodukt *n*
bystander ['baɪ ˌstændər] *s* Umstehende *mf*
by/way' *s* Seitenweg *m*
by/word' *s* Sprichwort *n*
Byzantine ['bɪzən ˌtin], [bɪ'zæntin] *adj* byzantinisch ‖ *s* Byzantiner –in *mf*
Byzantium [bɪ'zænʃɪ-əm], [bɪ'zænti-əm] *s* Byzanz *n*

C

C, c [si] *s* dritter Buchstabe des englischen Alphabets; (mus) C *n*; **C flat** Ces *n*; **C sharp** Cis *n*
cab [kæb] *s* Taxi *n*; (*of a truck*) Fahrerkabine *f*
cabaret [ˌkæbə're] *s* Kabarett *n*
cabbage ['kæbɪdʒ] *s* Kohl *m*, Kraut *n*
cab/driv/er *s* Taxifahrer –in *mf*
cabin ['kæbɪn] *s* Hütte *f*; (aer) Kabine *f*; (naut) Kajüte *f*, Kabine *f*
cab/in boy/ *s* Schiffsjunge *m*
cabinet ['kæbɪnɪt] *adj* Kabinetts– ‖ *s* (*in a kitchen*) Küchenschrank *m*; (*for a radio*) Gehäuse *n*; (pol) Kabinett *n*, Ministerrat *m*
cab/inetmak/er *s* Tischler *m*
cable ['kebəl] *s* Kabel *n*, Seil *n*; (naut) Tau *m*; (telg) Kabelnachricht *f* ‖ *tr & intr* kabeln
ca/ble car/ *s* Seilbahn *f*, Schwebebahn *f*
ca/blegram/ *s* Kabelnachricht *f*
caboose [kə'bus] *s* (rr) Dienstwagen *m*
cab/stand/ *s* Taxistand *m*
cache [kæʃ] *s* Geheimlager *n*, Versteck *n*; **c. of arms** Waffenlager *n*
cachet [kæ'ʃe] *s* Siegel *n*; (fig) Stempel *m*; (pharm) Kapsel *f*
cackle ['kækəl] *s* (*of chickens*) Gegacker *n*; (*of geese*) Geschnatter *n* ‖ *intr* gackern, gackeln; schnattern
cac/tus ['kæktəs] *s* (–tuses & –ti [taɪ]) Kaktus *m*
cad [kæd] *s* (sl) Saukerl *m*, Schuft *m*
cadaver [kə'dævər] *s* Kadaver *m*, Leiche *f*
caddie ['kædi] *s* Golfjunge *m* ‖ *intr* die Schläger tragen
cadence ['kedəns] *s* (*rhythm*) Rhythmus *m*; (*flow of language*) Sprechrhythmus *m*; (mus) Kadenz *f*
cadet [kə'det] *s* Offizier(s)anwärter –in *mf*
cadre ['kædri] *s* Kader *m*
Caesar/ean opera/tion [sɪ'zerɪ-ən] *s* Kaiserschnitt *m*
café [kæ'fe] *s* Café *n*
cafeteria [ˌkæfə'tɪrɪ-ə] *s* Selbstbedienungsrestaurant *n*
caffeine [kæ'fin] *s* Koffein *n*
cage [kedʒ] *s* Käfig *m* ‖ *tr* in e–n Käfig sperren
cagey ['kedʒi] *adj* (coll) schlau

cahoots [kə'huts] *s*—**be in c.** (sl) unter e–r Decke stecken
Cain [ken] *s*—**raise C.** Krach schlagen
caisson ['kesən] *s* Senkkasten *m*
cajole [kə'dʒol] *tr* beschwatzen
cake [kek] *s* Kuchen *m*; (*round cake*) Torte *f*; (*of soap*) Riegel *m*; **he takes the c.** (coll) er schießt den Vogel ab; **that takes the c.** (coll) das ist die Höhe ‖ *intr* zusammenbacken; **c. on** anbacken
calamitous [kə'læmɪtəs] *adj* unheilvoll
calamity [kə'læmɪti] *s* Unheil *n*
calci·fy ['kælsɪ ˌfaɪ] *v* (*pret & pp* –fied) *tr & intr* verkalken
calcium ['kælsɪ-əm] *s* Kalzium *n*
calculate ['kælkjə ˌlet] *tr* berechnen ‖ *intr* rechnen
cal/culated risk/ *s*—**take a c.** ein bewußtes Risiko eingehen
cal/culating *adj* berechnend
calculation [ˌkælkjə'leʃən] *s* Berechnung *f*; **rough c.** Überschlagsrechnung *f*
calculator ['kælkjə ˌletər] *s* Rechenmaschine *f*; (data proc) Rechner *m*
calcu·lus ['kælkjələs] *s* (–luses & –li [ˌlaɪ]) (math) Differenzial– und Integralrechnung *f*; (pathol) Stein *m*
caldron ['kɔldrən] *s* Kessel *m*
calendar ['kæləndər] *s* Kalender *m*
calf [kæf] *s* (**calves** [kævz]) (*of a cow*) Kalb *n*; (*of certain other mammals*) Junge *n*; (anat) Wade *f*
calf/skin/ *s* Kalbleder *n*
caliber ['kælɪbər] *s* (& fig) Kaliber *n*
calibrate ['kælɪ ˌbret] *tr* kalibrieren
cali·co ['kælɪ ˌko] *s* (–coes & –cos) Kaliko *m*
calisthenics [ˌkælɪs'θenɪks] *spl* Leibesübungen *pl*
calk [kɔk] *tr* abdichten, kalfatern
calk/ing *s* Kalfaterung *f*
call [kɔl] *s* Ruf *m*; (*visit*) Besuch *m*; (*reason*) Grund *m*; (com) (for) Nachfrage *f* (nach); (naut) Anlaufen *n*; (telp) Anruf *m*; **on c.** auf Abruf ‖ *tr* rufen; (*name*) nennen; (*wake*) wecken; (*a meeting*) einberufen; (*a game*) absagen; (*a strike*) ausrufen; (*by phone*) anrufen; (*a witness*) vorladen; (*a doctor; taxi*) kommen las-

sen; **be called** heißen; **c. down** (coll) herunterputzen; **c. in** (*a doctor, specialist*) hinzuziehen; (*for advice*) zu Rate ziehen; (*currency*) einziehen; (*capital*) kündigen; **c. it a day** (coll) Schluß machen; **c. off** absagen; **c. out** ausrufen; (*the police*) einsetzen; **c. s.o. names** j-n beschimpfen; **c. up** (mil) einberufen; (telp) anrufen || *intr* rufen; (cards) ansagen; **c. for** (*require*) erfordern; (*fetch*) abholen; (*help*) rufen um; (*a person*) rufen nach; **c. on** (*a pupil*) aufrufen; (*visit*) e-n Besuch machen bei; **c. to s.o.** j-m zurufen; **c. upon** auffordern

call' bell' s Rufglocke f

call' boy' s Hotelpage m; (theat) Inspezientengehilfe m

caller ['kɔlər] s Besucher -in mf

call' girl' s Callgirl n

call'ing s Beruf m; (relig) Berufung f

call'ing card' s Visitenkarte f

call'ing-down' s (coll) Standpauke f

call' num'ber s (libr) Standortnummer f

callous ['kæləs] adj schwielig; (fig) gefühllos, abgestumpft

call'up' s (mil) Einberufung f

callus ['kæləs] s Schwiele f

calm [kɑm] adj ruhig || s Ruhe f; (naut) Flaute f || tr beruhigen; **c. down** beruhigen || intr—**c. down** sich beruhigen

calorie ['kælɔri] s Kalorie f

calumny ['kæləmni] s Verleumdung f

Calvary ['kælvəri] s Golgatha n

calve [kæv] intr kalben

cam [kæm] s Nocken m

camel ['kæməl] s Kamel n

camellia [kə'miljə] s Kamelie f

came·o ['kæmɪ‚o] s (-os) Kamee f

camera ['kæmərə] s Kamera f

cam'era-man' s (-men') Kameramann m

camouflage ['kæmə‚flɑʒ] s Tarnung f || tr tarnen

camp [kæmp] s (& fig) Lager n || intr kampieren, lagern, campen

campaign [kæm'pen] s (& fig) Feldzug m; (pol) Wahlfeldzug m || intr an e-m Feldzug teilnehmen; **c. for** (pol) Wahlpropaganda machen für

campaigner [kæm'penər] s (for a specific cause) Befürworter -in mf; (pol) Wahlredner -in mf

campaign' slo'gan s Wahlparole f

campaign' speech' s Wahlrede f

camper ['kæmpər] s Camper m

camp'fire' s Lagerfeuer n

camp'ground' s Campingplatz m

camphor ['kæmfər] s Kampfer m

camp'ing s Camping n

campus ['kæmpəs] s Universitätsgelände n

cam'shaft' s Nockenwelle f

can [kæn] s Dose f, Büchse f; (for gasoline, water) Kanister m || v (pret & pp **canned**; ger **canning**) tr einmachen; (sl) 'rausschmeißen || v (pret & cond) (**could**) aux—**I can come** ich kann kommen; **I cannot come** ich kann nicht kommen

Canada ['kænədə] s Kanada n

Canadian [kə'nedɪ‚ən] adj kanadisch || s Kanadier -in mf

canal [kə'næl] s Kanal m; (anat) Gang m

canary [kə'neri] s Kanarienvogel m || **the Canaries** spl die Kanarischen Inseln pl

can·cel ['kænsəl] v (pret & pp **-el(l)ed**; ger **-el(l)ing**) tr (an event) absagen; (an order) rückgängig machen; (something written) (aus)streichen, annulieren; (stamps) entwerten; (a debt) tilgen; (a newspaper) abbestellen; (math) streichen; **c. out** ausgleichen

cancellation [‚kænsə'leʃən] s (of an event) Absage f; (of an order) Annulierung f; (of something written) Streichung f; (of a debt) Tilgung f; (of a stamp) Entwertung f; (of a newspaper) Abbestellung f

cancer ['kænsər] s Krebs m

cancerous ['kænsərəs] adj krebsartig

candela·brum [‚kændə'labrəm] s (-bra [brə] & -brums) Armleuchter m

candid ['kændɪd] adj offen

candidacy ['kændɪdəsi] s Kandidatur f

candidate ['kændɪ‚det] s (for) Kandidat -in mf (für)

candied ['kændɪd] adj kandiert

candle ['kændəl] s Kerze f

can'dlelight' s Kerzenlicht n

can'dlepow'er s Kerzenstärke f

can'dlestick' s Kerzenhalter m

candor ['kændər] s Offenheit f

can·dy ['kændɪ] s Süßwaren pl; **piece of c.** Bonbon m & n || v (pret & pp -**died**) tr glacieren, kandieren

can'dy store' s Süßwarengeschäft n

cane [ken] s (plant; stem) Rohr n; (walking stick) Stock m || tr mit e-m Stock züchtigen

cane' sug'ar s Rohrzucker m

canine ['kenaɪn] adj Hunde– || s (tooth) Eckzahn m, Reißzahn m

canister ['kænɪstər] s Dose f

canker ['kæŋkər] s (bot) Brand m; (pathol) Mundgeschwür n

canned' goods' spl Dosenkonserven pl

canned' mu'sic s Konservenmusik f

canned' veg'etables spl Gemüsekonserven pl

cannery ['kænəri] s Konservenfabrik f

cannibal ['kænɪbəl] s Kannibale m

can'ning adj Konserven– || s Konservenfabrikation f

cannon ['kænən] s Kanone f

cannonade [‚kænə'ned] s Kanonade f, Beschießung f || tr beschießen

can'nonball' s Kanonenkugel f

can'non fod'der s Kanonenfutter n

canny ['kæni] adj (shrewd) schlau; (sagacious) klug

canoe [kə'nu] s Kanu n

canoe'ing s Kanufahren n

canoeist [kə'nu·ɪst] s Kanufahrer m

canon ['kænən] s Kanon m; (of a cathedral) Domherr m

canonical [kə'nɑnɪkəl] adj kanonisch || **canonicals** spl kirchliche Amtstracht f

canonize ['kænə,naɪz] tr heiligsprechen

can'on law' s kanonisches Recht n

can' o'pener s Dosenöffner m

canopy ['kænəpi] s Baldachin m; (above a king or pope) Thronhimmel m; (of a bed) Betthimmel m

cant [kænt] s (insincere statements) unaufrichtiges Gerede n; (jargon of thieves) Gaunersprache f; (technical phraseology) Jargon m

cantaloupe ['kæntə,lop] s Kantalupe f

cantankerous [kæn'tæŋkərəs] adj mürrisch, zänkisch

cantata [kən'tɑtə] s Kantate f

canteen [kæn'tin] s (service club, service store) Kantine f; (flask) Feldflasche f

canter ['kæntər] s kurzer Galopp m ‖ intr im kurzen Galopp reiten

canticle ['kæntɪkəl] s Lobgesang m

canton ['kæntən] s Kanton m

canvas ['kænvəs] s Leinwand f; (naut) Segeltuch n; (a painting) Gemälde n

canvass ['kænvəs] s (econ) Werbefeldzug m; (pol) Wahlfeldzug m ‖ tr (a district) (pol) bearbeiten; (votes) (pol) werben

canyon ['kænjən] s Schlucht f

cap [kæp] s Kappe f, Mütze f; (of a jar) Deckel m; (twist-off type) Kapsel f; (for a toy pistol) Knallblättchen n; (typ) großer Buchstabe m; **use caps** (typ) großschreiben ‖ v (pret & pp capped; ger capping) tr (a bottle) mit e-r Kapsel versehen; (e.g., with snow) bedecken; (outdo) übertreffen; (success) krönen

capability [,kepə'bɪlɪti] s Fähigkeit f

capable ['kepəbəl] adj tüchtig; **c. of** fähig (genit); (ger) fähig zu (inf)

capacious [kə'peʃəs] adj geräumig

capacity [kə'pæsɪti] adj maximal, Kapazitäts– ‖ s (ability) Fähigkeit f; (content) Fassungsvermögen n; (of a truck, bridge) Tragfähigkeit f; (tech) Kapazität f; **in my c.** as in meiner Eigenschaft als

cap' and gown' s Barett n und Talar m

cape [kep] s Umhang m; (geog) Kap n

Cape' of Good' Hope' s Kap n der Guten Hoffnung

caper ['kepər] s Luftsprung m; (prank) Schabernack m; (culin) Kaper f ‖ intr hüpfen

capita ['kæpɪtə] spl—**per c.** pro Kopf, pro Person

capital ['kæpɪtəl] adj (importance) äußerste, höchste; (city) Haupt–; (crime) Kapital– ‖ s (city) Hauptstadt f; (archit) Kapitell n; (fin) Kapital n; (typ) Großbuchstabe m

cap'ital gains' spl Kapitalzuwachs m

capitalism ['kæpɪtə,lɪzəm] s Kapitalismus m

capitalist ['kæpɪtəlɪst] s Kapitalist –in mf

capitalistic [,kæpɪtə'lɪstɪk] adj kapitalistisch

capitalize ['kæpɪtə,laɪz] tr (fin) kapitalisieren; (typ) groß schreiben (or drucken) ‖ intr—**c. on** Nutzen ziehen aus

cap'ital let'ter s Großbuchstabe m

cap'ital pun'ishment s Todesstrafe f

capitol ['kæpɪtəl] s Kapitol n

capitulate [kə'pɪtʃə,let] intr kapitulieren

capon ['kepən] s Kapaun m

caprice [kə'pris] s Grille f, Kaprice f

capricious [kə'prɪʃəs] adj kapriziös

capsize ['kæpsaɪz] tr zum Kentern bringen ‖ intr kentern

capsule ['kæpsəl] s Kapsel f

captain ['kæptən] s (of police, of firemen, in the army) Hauptmann m; (naut, sport) Kapitän m; (nav) Kapitän m zur See; (sport) Mannschaftsführer m

caption ['kæpʃən] s (heading of an article) Überschrift f; (wording under a picture) Bildunterschrift f; (cin) Untertitel m

captivate ['kæptɪ,vet] tr fesseln

captive ['kæptɪv] adj gefangen ‖ s Gefangene mf

captivity [kæp'tɪvɪti] s Gefangenschaft f

captor ['kæptər] s Fänger –in mf

capture ['kæptʃər] s Fangen n, Gefangennahme f; (naut) Kaperung f ‖ tr (animals) fangen; (soldiers) gefangennehmen; (a ship) kapern; (a town) erobern; (a prize) gewinnen

car [kɑr] s (aut, rr) Wagen m

carafe [kə'ræf] s Karaffe f

caramel ['kærəməl] s Karamelle f

carat ['kærət] s Karat n

caravan ['kærə,væn] s Karawane f

car'away seed' ['kærə,we] s Kümmelkorn n

carbide ['kɑrbaɪd] s Karbid n

carbine ['kɑrbaɪn] s Karabiner m

carbohydrate [,kɑrbo'haɪdret] s Kohlenhydrat n

carbol'ic ac'id [kɑr'bɑlɪk] s Karbolsäure f

carbon ['kɑrbən] s (chem) Kohlenstoff m; (elec) Kohlenstift m

carbonated ['kɑrbə,netɪd] adj kohlensäurehaltig, Brause–

car'bon cop'y s Durchschlag m; **make a c.** of durchschlagen

car'bon diox'ide s Kohlendioxid n

car'bon monox'ide s Kohlenoxyd n

car'bon pa'per s Kohlepapier n

carbuncle ['kɑrbʌŋkəl] s (stone) Karfunkel m; (pathol) Karbunkel m

carburetor ['kɑrb(j)ə,retər] s Vergaser m

carcass ['kɑrkəs] s Kadaver m, Aas n; (without offal) Rumpf m

car' coat' s Stutzer m

card [kɑrd] s Karte f; (coll) Kerl m; (text) Krempel f ‖ tr (text) kardätschen

card'board' s Kartonpapier n; (thick pasteboard) Pappe f; **piece of c.** Papp(en)deckel m

card'board box' s Pappkarton m, Pappschachtel f

card' cat'alogue s Kartothek f

card' file' s Kartei f
cardiac ['kɑrdɪˌæk] adj Herz– ‖ s (remedy) Herzmittel n; (patient) Herzkranke mf
cardinal ['kɑrdɪnəl] adj Kardinal– ‖ s (eccl, orn) Kardinal m
card' in'dex s Karthotek f, Kartei f
card'sharp' s Falschspieler –in mf
card' trick' s Kartenkunststück n
care [ker] s (accuracy) Sorgfalt f; (worry) Sorge f, Kummer m; (prudence) Vorsicht f; (upkeep) Pflege f; **be under a doctor's c.** unter der Aufsicht e–s Arztes stehen; **c. of** (on letters) bei; **take c.** aufpassen; **take c. not to** (inf) sich hüten zu (inf); **take c. of s.o.** (provide for s.o.) für j–n sorgen; (attend to) sich um j–n kümmern; **take c. of s.th.** etw besorgen; (e.g., one's clothes) schonen ‖ intr—c. about sich kümmern um; **c. for** (like) mögen, gern haben; (have concern for) sorgen für; (attend to) pflegen; **c. to** (inf) Lust haben zu (inf); **for all I c.** von mir aus
careen [kəˈrin] tr auf die Seite legen ‖ intr (aut) sich in die Kurve neigen
career [kəˈrɪr] adj Berufs– ‖ s Karriere f
career' wo'man s berufstätige Frau f
care'free' adj unbelastet, sorgenfrei
careful ['kerfəl] adj (cautious) vorsichtig; (accurate) sorgfältig; **b. c.!** gib acht!
careless ['kerlɪs] adj (incautious) unvorsichtig; (remark) unbedacht; (inaccurate) nachlässig
carelessness ['kerlɪsnɪs] s Unvorsichtigkeit f; Nachlässigkeit f
caress [kəˈrɛs] s Liebkosung f ‖ tr liebkosen
caret ['kærət] s Auslassungszeichen n
caretaker ['kerˌtekər] s Verwalter m
care'worn' adj abgehärmt, vergrämt
car'fare' s Fahrgeld n
car·go ['kɑrgo] s (–goes & –gos) Fracht f
car'go compart'ment s Frachtraum m
car'go plane' s Frachtflugzeug n
Caribbean [ˌkærɪˈbiˌən], [kəˈrɪbɪˌən] adj karibisch ‖ s Karibisches Meer n
caricature ['kærɪkətˌʃər] s Karikatur f ‖ tr karikieren
caries ['kɛriz] s (dent) Karies f
carillon ['kærɪˌlɑn] s Glockenspiel n
car' lift' s (aut) Hebebühne f
car'load' s Wagenladung f
carnage ['kɑrnɪdʒ] s Blutbad n
carnal ['kɑrnəl] adj fleischlich
car'nal know'ledge s Geschlechtsverkehr m
carnation [kɑrˈneʃən] s Nelke f
carnival ['kɑrnɪvəl] s Karneval m
carnivorous [kɑrˈnɪvərəs] adj fleischfressend
car·ol ['kærəl] s Weihnachtslied n ‖ v (pret & pp –ol(l)ed; ger –l(l)ing) intr Weihnachtslieder singen
carom ['kærəm] s (billiards) Karambolage f ‖ intr (fig) zusammenstoßen; (billiards) karambolieren
carouse [kəˈrauz] intr zechen

carp [kɑrp] s Karpfen m ‖ intr nörgeln
carpenter ['kɑrpəntər] s Zimmermann m
carpentry ['kɑrpəntri] s Zimmerei f
carpet ['kɑrpɪt] s Teppich m ‖ tr mit Teppichen belegen
car'pet sweep'er s Teppichkehrmaschine f
car'port' s Autoschuppen m
car'-ren'tal serv'ice s Autovermietung f
carriage ['kærɪdʒ] s Kutsche f; (of a typewriter) Wagen m; (bearing) Körperhaltung f; (econ) Transportkosten pl
car' ride' s Autofahrt f
carrier ['kærɪˌər] s Träger m; (company) Transportunternehmen m
car'rier pig'eon s Brieftaube f
carrion ['kærɪˌən] s Aas n
carrot ['kærət] s Karotte f, Mohrrübe f
carrousel [ˌkærəˈzɛl] s Karussell n
car·ry ['kæri] v (pret & pp –ried) tr tragen; (wares) führen; (a message) überbringen; (a tune) halten; (said of transportation) befördern; (insurance) haben; (math) übertragen; (parl) durchbringen; **be carried** (said of a motion, bill) angenommen werden; **be carried away by** (a & fig) mitgerissen werden von; **c. away** (an audience) mitreißen; **c. off** (a prize) davontragen; **c. on** weiterführen; (a business) betreiben, führen; **c. out** hinaustragen; (a duty) erfüllen; (measures) durchführen; (a sentence) vollstrecken; (an order) ausführen; **c. over** (acct) übertragen; **c. s.th. too far** etw übertreiben; **c. through** durchsetzen; ‖ intr (said of sounds) tragen; (parl) durchmachen; **c. on** (continue) weitermachen; (act up) (coll) toben; **c. on with** ein Verhältnis haben mit
car'rying char'ges spl Kreditgebühren pl
car'ry-o'ver s Überbleibsel n; (acct) Übertrag m
cart [kɑrt] s Karren m ‖ tr mit dem Handwagen befördern; **c. away** (or **c. off**) abfahren
cartel [kɑrˈtɛl] s Kartell n
cartilage ['kɑrtɪlɪdʒ] s Knorpel m
carton ['kɑrtən] s Karton m; **a c. of cigarettes** e–e Stange Zigaretten
cartoon [kɑrˈtun] s Karikatur f; (comic strip) Karikaturenreihe f; (cin) Zeichentrickfilm m; (paint) Entwurf m natürlicher Größe ‖ tr karikieren
cartoonist [kɑrˈtunɪst] s Karikaturenzeichner –in mf
cartridge ['kɑrtrɪdʒ] s Patrone f; (phot) Filmpatrone f
car'tridge belt' s Patronengurt m
cart'wheel' s Wagenrad n; **turn a c.** ein Rad schlagen
carve [kɑrv] tr (wood) schnitzen; (meat) tranchieren, vorschneiden; (stone) meißeln; **c. out** (e.g., a career) aufbauen

carver ['kɑrvər] s (at table) Vorschneider –in mf

carv'ing knife' s Tranchiermesser n

car' wash' s Wagenwäsche f

cascade [kæs'ked] s Kaskade f ‖ intr kaskadenartig herabstürzen

case [kes] s (instance) Fall m; (situation) Sache f; (box) Kiste f; (for a knife, etc.) Hülle f; (for cigarettes) Etui n; (for eyeglasses) Futteral n; (for shipping) Schutzkarton m; (of a watch) Gehäuse n; (of sickness) Krankheitsfall m; (sick person) Patient –in mf; (gram) Fall m; (jur) Fall m, Sache f, Prozeß m; (typ) Setzkasten m; **as the c. may be** je nachdem; **have a strong c.** schlüssige Beweise haben; **if that's the c.** wenn es sich so verhält; **in any c.** auf jeden Fall, jedenfalls; **in c.** falls; **in c. of** im Falle (genit); **in c. of emergency** im Notfall; **in no c.** keinesfalls ‖ (sl) genau ansehen; **the c. at issue** der vorliegende Fall

case' his'tory s Vorgeschichte f; (med) Krankengeschichte f

casement ['kesmənt] s Fensterflügel m

case'ment win'dow s Flügelfenster n

cash [kæʃ] adj Bar– ‖ s Bargeld n; (cash payment) Barzahlung f; **c. and carry** nur gegen Barzahlung und eigenen Transport; **in c.** per Kasse; **out of c.** nicht bei Kasse; **pay c. for** bar bezahlen ‖ tr einlösen ‖ intr—**c. in on** (coll) Nutzen ziehen aus

cash'box' s Schatulle f, Kasse f

cash' dis'count s Kassaskonto n

cashew' nut' [kə'ʃu], ['kæʃu] s Kaschunuß f

cashier [kæ'ʃɪr] s Kassierer –in mf

cashmere ['kæʃmɪr] s Kaschmir m

cash' on deliv'ery adv per Nachnahme

cash' reg'ister m Registrierkasse f

cas'ing s (wrapping) Verpackung f; (housing) Gehäuse n; (of a window or door) Futter n; (of a tire) Mantel m; (of a sausage) Wurstdarm m

casi·no [kə'sino] s (–nos) Kasino n

cask [kæsk] s Faß n, Tonne f

casket ['kæskɪt] s Sarg m

casserole ['kæsə,rol] s Kasserolle f

cassette [kæ'set] s Kassette f

cassock ['kæsək] s (eccl) Soutane f

cast [kæst] s (throw) Wurf m; (act of molding) Guß m; (mold) Gußform f; (object molded) Abguß m; (hue) Abtönung f; (surg) Gipsverband m; (theat) Rollenbesetzung f ‖ v (pret & pp cast) tr werfen; (a net, anchor) auswerfen; (a ballot) abgeben; (lots) ziehen; (skin, horns) abwerfen; (a shadow, glance) werfen; (metal) gießen; (a play or motion picture) die Rollen besetzen in (dat); **be c. down** niedergeschlagen sein; **c. aside** (reject) verwerfen; ‖ intr (angl) die Angel auswerfen; **c. off** (naut) loswerfen

castanet [,kæstə'net] s Kastagnette f

cast'away' adj verworfen; (naut) schiffbrüchig ‖ s (naut) Schiffbrüchige mf

caste [kæst] s Kaste f

caster ['kæstər] s (under furniture) Rolle f; (shaker) Streuer m

castigate ['kæstɪ,get] tr züchtigen; (fig) geißeln

cast'ing s Wurf m; (act of casting) (metal) Guß m; (the object cast) (metal) Gußstück n; (theat) Rollenverteilung f

cast'ing rod' s Wurfangel f

cast' i'ron s Gußeisen n

cast'-i'ron adj gußeisern; (fig) eisern

castle ['kæsəl] s Schloß n, Burg, f; (chess) Turm m ‖ intr (chess) rochieren

cast'off' adj abgelegt ‖ s (e.g., dress) abgelegtes Kleidungsstück n; (person) Verstoßene mf

cas'tor oil' ['kæstər] s Rizinusöl n

castrate ['kæstret] tr kastrieren

casual ['kæʒəəl] adj (cursory) beiläufig; (occasional) gelegentlich; (incidental) zufällig; (informal) zwanglos; (unconcerned) gleichgültig

casualty ['kæʒuəltı] s (victim) Opfer n; (accident) Unfall m; (person injured) Verunglückte mf; (person killed) (mil) Gefallene mf; (person wounded) (mil) Verwundete mf; **casualties** (in an accident) Verunglückte pl; (in war) Verluste pl

cas'ualty list' s Verlustliste f

cat [kæt] s Katze f; (guy) (sl) Typ m; (malicious woman) (sl) falsche Katze f

catacomb ['kætə,kom] s Katakombe f

catalog(ue) ['kætə,lɔg] s Katalog m; (list) Verzeichnis n; (of a university) Vorlesungsverzeichnis n ‖ tr katalogisieren

catalyst ['kætəlɪst] s Katalysator m

catapult ['kætə,pʌlt] s Katapult m & n ‖ tr katapultieren, abschleudern

cataract ['kætə,rækt] s Katarakt m; (pathol) grauer Star m; **remove s.o.'s c.** j–m den Star stechen

catastrophe [kə'tæstrəfi] s Katastrophe f

cat'call' s Auspfeifen n ‖ tr auspfeifen

catch [kætʃ] s Fang m; (of fish) Fischfang m; (device) Haken m, Klinke f; (desirable partner) Partie f; (fig) Haken m; ‖ v (pret & pp caught [kɔt]) tr fangen; (s.o. or s.th. falling) auffangen; (by pursuing) abfangen; (s.o. or s.th. that has escaped) einfangen; (by surprise) ertappen, erwischen; (in midair) aufschnappen; (take hold of) fassen; (said of a storm) überraschen; (e.g., a train) erreichen; **c. a cold** sich erkälten; **c. fire** in Brand geraten; **c. hold of** ergreifen; **c. it** (coll) sein Fett kriegen; **c. one's breath** wieder Atem schöpfen; **c. one's eye** j–m ins Auge fallen; **get caught on** hängenbleiben an (dat) ‖ intr (said of a bolt, etc.) einschnappen; **c. on** (said of an idea) Anklang finden; **c. on to** (fig) kapieren; **catch up** aufholen; **c. up on** nachholen; **c. up with** einholen

catch'ing adj (disease) ansteckend; (attractive) anziehend catch'word' s (*slogan*) Schlagwort n; (*actor's cue*) Stichwort n; (pol) Parteiparole f

catchy ['kætʃi] adj einschmeichelnd

catechism ['kætɪˌkɪzəm] s Katechismus m

category ['kætɪˌgori] s Kategorie f

cater ['ketər] tr Lebensmittel liefern für || intr—c. to schmeicheln (dat); (*deliver food to*) Lebensmittel liefern für

cater-corner ['kætərˌkɔrnər] adj & adv diagonal

caterer ['ketərər] s Lebensmittellieferant –in mf

caterpillar ['kætərˌpɪlər] s (ent, mach) Raupe f

cat'fish' s Katzenwels m, Katzenfisch m

cat'gut' s (mus) Darmseite f; (surg) Katgut m

cathedral [kə'θidrəl] s Dom m

catheter ['kæθɪtər] s Katheter n

cathode ['kæθod] s Kathode f

catholic ['kæθəlɪk] adj universal; Catholic katholisch || Catholic s Katholik –in mf

cat'nap' s Nickerchen n

catnip ['kætnɪp] s Baldrian m

catsup ['kætsəp], ['ketʃəp] s Ketschup m

cattle ['kætəl] spl Vieh n

cat'tle car' s (rr) Viehwagen m

cat'tle-man s (–men) Viehzüchter m

cat'tle ranch' s Viehfarm f

catty ['kæti] adj boshaft

cat'walk' s Steg m, Laufplanke f

Caucasian [kɔ'keʒən] adj kaukasisch || s Kaukasier –in mf

caucus ['kɔkəs] s Parteiführerversammlung f

cauliflower ['kɔlɪˌflau·ər] s Blumenkohl m

cause [kɔz] s (*origin*) Ursache f; (*reason*) Grund m; (*person*) Urheber –in mf; (*occasion*) Anlaß m; for a good c. für e–e gute Sache || tr verursachen; c. s.o. to (*inf*) j–n veranlassen zu (*inf*)

cause'way' s Dammweg m

caustic ['kɔstɪk] adj (& fig) ätzend

cauterize ['kɔtəˌraɪz] tr verätzen

caution ['kɔʃən] s (*carefulness*) Vorsicht f; (*warning*) Warnung f || tr (*against*) warnen (vor *dat*)

cautious ['kɔʃəs] adj vorsichtig

cavalcade ['kævəlˌked] s Kavalkade f

cavalier [ˌkævə'lɪr] adj hochmütig || s Kavalier m

cavalry ['kævəlri] s Kavallerie f

cav'alry-man s (–men) Kavallerist m

cave [kev] s Höhle f || intr—c. in (*collapse*) einstürzen

cave'-in' s Einsturz m

cave' man' s Höhlenmensch m

cavern ['kævərn] s (große) Höhle f

caviar ['kævɪˌɑr] s Kaviar m

cav-il ['kævɪl] v (*pret & pp* –l(l)ed; *ger* –l(l)ing) intr (at, about) herumnörgeln (an *dat*)

cavity ['kævɪti] s Hohlraum m; (anat) Höhle f; (dent) Loch n

cavort [kə'vɔrt] intr (coll) herumtollen

caw [kɔ] s Krächzen n || intr krächzen

cease [sis] s—without c. unaufhörlich || tr einstellen; (*ger*) aufhören (zu *inf*); c. fire das Feuer einstellen || intr aufhören

cease'fire' s Feuereinstellung f

ceaseless ['sislɪs] adj unaufhörlich

cedar ['sidər] s Zeder f

cede [sid] tr abtreten, überlassen

cedilla [sɪ'dɪlə] s Cedille f

ceiling ['silɪŋ] s Decke f; (fin) oberste Grenze f; hit the c. (coll) platzen

ceil'ing light' s Deckenlicht n

ceil'ing price' s Höchstpreis m

celebrant ['sɛlɪbrənt] s Zelebrant m

celebrate ['sɛlɪˌbret] tr (*a feast*) feiern; (*mass*) zelebrieren || intr feiern; (eccl) zelebrieren

cel'ebrat'ed adj (for) berühmt (wegen)

celebration [ˌsɛlɪ'breʃən] s Feier f; (eccl) Zelebrieren n; in c. of zur Feier (*genit*)

celebrity [sɪ'lɛbrɪti] s Berühmtheit f; (*person*) Prominente mf

celery ['sɛləri] s Selleriestengel m

celestial [sɪ'lɛstʃəl] adj himmlisch; (astr) Himmels-

celibacy ['sɛlɪbəsi] s Zölibat m & n

celibate ['sɛlɪbɪt] adj ehelos

cell [sɛl] s Zelle f

cellar ['sɛlər] s Keller m

cellist ['tʃɛlɪst] s Cellist –in mf

cel·lo ['tʃɛlo] s (–los) Cello n

cellophane ['sɛləˌfɛn] s Zellophan n

celluloid ['sɛljəˌlɔɪd] s Zelluloid n

Celt [sɛlt], [kɛlt] s Kelte m, Keltin f

Celtic ['sɛltɪk], ['kɛltɪk] adj keltisch

cement [sɪ'mɛnt] s (*glue*) Bindemittel n; (*used in building*) Zement m || tr zementieren; (*glue*) kitten; (fig) (be)festigen

cement' mix'er s Betonmischmaschine f

cemetery ['sɛmɪˌteri] s Friedhof m

censer ['sɛnsər] s Räucherfaß n

censor ['sɛnsər] s (*of printed matter, films*) Zensor m; (*of morals*) Sittenrichter m || tr zensieren

cen'sorship' s Zensur f

censure ['sɛnʃər] s Tadel m || tr tadeln

census ['sɛnsəs] s Volkszählung f

cent [sɛnt] s Cent m

centaur ['sɛntɔr] s Zentaur m

centennial [sɛn'tɛnɪ·əl] adj hundertjährig || s Hundertjahrfeier f

center ['sɛntər] s Zentrum n, Mittelpunkt m; (pol) Mitte f || tr in den Mittelpunkt stellen; (tech) zentrieren || intr—c. on sich konzentrieren auf (*acc*)

cen'ter aisle' s Mittelgang m

cen'ter cit'y s Stadtmitte f

cen'terpiece' s Tischaufsatz m

centigrade ['sɛntɪˌgred] s Celsius, e.g., one degree c. ein Grad Celsius

centimeter ['sɛntɪˌmitər] s Zentimeter m

centipede ['sɛntɪˌpid] s Hundertfüßler m

central ['sɛntrəl] adj zentral

Cen'tral Amer'ica s Mittelamerika n

centralize ['sɛntrəˌlaɪz] tr zentralisieren

centri'fugal force' [sɛn'trɪfjəgəl] s Fliehkraft f

centrifuge ['sɛntrɪ ‚fjudʒ] s Zentrifuge f

century ['sɛntʃəri] s Jahrhundert n

ceramic [sɪ'ræmɪk] adj keramisch || **ceramics** s (art) Keramik f; spl Töpferwaren pl

cereal ['sɪrɪ·əl] adj Getreide– || s (grain) Getreide n; (dish) Getreideflockengericht n

cerebral ['sɛrɪbrəl] adj Gehirn–

ceremonial [‚sɛrɪ'monɪ·əl] adj zeremoniell, feierlich

ceremonious [‚sɛrɪ'monɪ·əs] adj zeremoniös, umständlich

ceremony ['sɛrɪ ‚moni] s Zeremonie f

certain ['sʌrtən] adj (sure) sicher, bestimmt; (particular but unnamed) gewiß; **be c.** feststehen; **for c.** gewiß; **make c. of** sich vergewissern (genit); **make c. that** sich vergewissern, daß

certainly ['sʌrtənli] adv sicher(lich); (as a strong affirmative) allerdings

certainty ['sʌrtənti] s Sicherheit f

certificate [sər'tɪfɪkɪt] s Schein m; (educ) Abgangszeugnis n

certification [‚sʌrtɪfɪ'keʃən] s Bescheinigung f, Beglaubigung f

cer'tified adj beglaubigt

cer'tified check' s durch Bank bestätigter Scheck m

cer'tified pub'lic account'ant s amtlich zugelassener Wirtschaftsprüfer m

certi-fy ['sʌrtɪ ‚faɪ] v (pret & pp **–fied**) bescheinigen, beglaubigen

cervix ['sʌrvɪks] s (**cervices** [sər'vaɪsɪz]) Genick n

cessation [sɛ'seʃən] s (of territory) Abtretung f; (of activities) Einstellung f

cesspool ['sɛs ‚pul] s Senkgrube f

chafe [tʃef] tr (the skin) wundscheuern || intr (rub) scheuern; (become sore) sich wundreiben; (be irritated) (at) sich ärgern über (acc)

chaff [tʃæf] s Spreu f

chaf'ing dish' s Speisenwärmer m

chagrin [ʃə'grɪn] s Verdruß m || tr verdrießen

chain [tʃen] s Kette f || tr (to) anketten (an acc)

chain' gang' s Kettensträflinge pl

chain' reac'tion s Kettenreaktion f

chain' smok'er s Kettenraucher –in mf

chain' store' s Kettenladen m

chair [tʃɛr] s Stuhl m; (upholstered) Sessel m; (of the presiding officer) Vorsitz m; (presiding officer) Vorsitzende mf; (educ) Lehrstuhl m || tr den Vorsitz führen von

chair'la'dy s Vorsitzende f

chair' lift' s Sessellift m

chair'man s (**–men**) Vorsitzende m

chair'manship' s Vorsitz m

chalice ['tʃælɪs] s Kelch m

chalk [tʃɔk] s Kreide f || tr—**c. up** ankreiden; (coll) verbuchen

challenge ['tʃælɪndʒ] s Aufforderung f; (to a duel) Herausforderung f; (jur) Ablehnung f; (mil) Anruf m || tr auffordern; (to a duel) herausfor-

dern; (a statement, right) bestreiten; (jur) ablehnen; (mil) anrufen

chamber ['tʃembər] s Kammer f; (parl) Sitzungssaal m

chamberlain ['tʃembərlɪn] s Kammerherr m

cham'bermaid' s Stubenmädchen n

cham'ber of com'merce s Handelskammer f

chameleon [kə'milɪ·ən] s Chamäleon n

chamfer ['tʃæmfər] s Schrägkante f || tr abschrägen; (furrow) auskehlen

cham-ois ['ʃæmi] s (**–ois**) Sämischleder n; (zool) Gemse f

champ [tʃæmp] s (coll) Meister m || tr kauen; **champ the bit** am Gebiß kauen

champagne [ʃæm'pen] s Champagner m, Sekt m

champion ['tʃæmpɪ·ən] s (of a cause) Verfechter –in mf; (sport) Meister –in mf || tr eintreten für

cham'pionship' s Meisterschaft f

chance [tʃæns] adj zufällig || s (accident) Zufall m; (opportunity) Chance f, Gelegenheit f; (risk) Risiko n; (possibility) Möglichkeit f; (lottery ticket) Los n; **by c.** zufällig; **c. of a lifetime** einmalige Gelegenheit f; **chances are** (that) aller Wahrscheinlichkeit nach; **on the c. that** für den Fall, daß; **take a c.** ein Risiko eingehen; **take no chances** nichts riskieren; || tr riskieren || intr geschehen; **c. upon** stoßen auf (acc)

chancel ['tʃænsəl] s Altarraum m

chancellery ['tʃænsələri] s Kanzlei f

chancellor ['tʃænsələr] s Kanzler m; (hist) Reichskanzler m

chandelier [‚ʃændə'lɪr] s Kronleuchter m

change [tʃendʒ] s Veränderung f; (in times, styles, etc.) Wechsel m; (in attitude, relations, etc.) Wandel m; (small coins) Kleingeld n; (of weather) Umschlag m; **c. for the better** Verbesserung f; **c. for the worse** Verschlechterung f; **for a c.** zur Abwechslung; **give c. for a dollar** auf e–n Dollar herausgeben; **need a c.** Luftveränderung brauchen || tr verändern; (plans) ändern; (money, subject, oil) wechseln; (a baby) trockenlegen; (stations, channels) umschalten; **c. around** umändern; **c. hands** den Besitzer wechseln; **c. one's mind** sich anders besinnen; **c. trains** (or buses, streetcars) umsteigen || intr sich verändern; (said of a mood, wind, weather) umschlagen; (said of a voice) mutieren; (change clothes) sich umziehen **change into** sich wandeln in (acc)

changeable ['tʃendʒəbəl] adj veränderlich

changeless ['tʃendʒlɪs] adj unveränderlich

change' of heart' s Sinnesänderung f

change' of life' s Wechseljahre pl

change' of scen'ery s Ortsveränderung f

change'-o'ver s Umstellung f

chan·nel ['t∫ænəl] s (strait) Kanal m; (of a river) Fahrrinne f; (groove) Rinne f; (furrow) Furche f; (fig) Weg m; (telv) Kanal m; **through official channels** auf dem Amtswege || v (pret & pp **-nel(l)ed**; ger **-nel(l)ing**) tr lenken; (furrow) kanalisieren

chant [t∫ænt] s Gesang m; (singsong) Singsang m; (eccl) Kirchengesang m || tr singen

chanter ['t∫æntər] s Kantor m

chaos ['ke·as] s Chaos n

chaotic [ke'atɪk] adj chaotisch

chap [t∫æp] s (in the skin) Riß m; (coll) Kerl m || v (pret & pp **chapped**; ger **chapping**) tr (the skin) rissig machen || intr rissig werden, aufspringen

chapel ['t∫æpəl] s Kapelle f

chaperon ['∫æpə,ron] s Begleiter –in mf; (of a young couple) Anstandsdame f || tr als Anstandsdame begleiten

chaplain ['t∫æplɪn] s Kaplan m

chapter ['t∫æptər] s Kapitel n; (of an organization) Ortsgruppe f

char [t∫ar] v (pret & pp **charred**; ger **charring**) tr verkohlen

character ['kærɪktər] s Charakter m; (letter) Schriftzeichen n; (typewriter space) Anschlag m; (coll) Kauz m; (theat) handelnde Person f; **be out of c.** nicht passen

characteristic [,kærɪktə'rɪstɪk] adj (of) charakteristisch (für) || s Charakterzug m, Kennzeichen n

characterize ['kærɪktə,raɪz] tr charakterisieren, kennzeichnen

charade [∫ə'red] s Scharade f

charcoal ['t∫ar,kol] s Holzkohle f; (for sketching) Zeichenkohle f

charge [t∫ardʒ] s (accusation) Anklage f; (fee) Gebühr f; (custody) Obhut f; (responsibility) Pflicht f; (ward) Pflegebefohlene mf; (of an explosive or electricity) Ladung f; (assault) Ansturm m; (of a judge to the jury) Rechtsbelehrung f; **be in c. of** verantwortlich sein für; **charges** Spesen pl; **take c. of** die Verantwortung übernehmen für; **there is no c.** es kostet nichts; **under s.o.'s c.** unter j-s Aufsicht || tr (a battery) (auf)-laden; (with) anklagen (wegen); (a jury) belehren; (mil) stürmen; **c. s.o. ten marks for** j-m zehn Mark berechnen für; **c. s.o.'s account** auf j-s Rechnung setzen || intr (mil) anrechnen für; **c. to s.o.'s account** auf j-s Rechnung setzen || intr (mil) anstürmen

charge′ account′ s laufendes Konto n

charger ['t∫ardʒər] s (elec) Ladevorrichtung f; (hist) Schlachtroß n

chariot ['t∫ærɪ·ət] s Kampfwagen m

charitable ['t∫ærɪtəbəl] adj (generous) freigebig; (lenient) nachsichtig; **c. institution** wohltätige Stiftung f

charity ['t∫ærɪti] s (giving of alms) Wohltätigkeit f; (alms) Almosen n; (institution) Wohlfahrtsinstitut n; (love of neighbor) Nächstenliebe f

charlatan ['∫arlətən] s Scharlatan m

Charles [t∫arlz] s Karl m

char′ley horse′ ['t∫arli] s (coll) Muskelkater m

charm [t∫arm] s Charme m; (trinket) Amulett n || tr verzaubern; (fig) entzücken

charming adj scharmant, reizend

chart [t∫art] s Karte f; (table) Tabelle f; (naut) Seekarte f || tr entwerfen, auf e-r Karte graphisch darstellen

charter ['t∫artər] adj (plane, etc.) Charter– || s Freibrief m, Charter m; (of an organization) Gründungsurkunde f und Satzungen pl || tr chartern

char′ter mem′ber s gründendes Mitglied n

char·woman ['t∫ar ,wumən] s (–women [,wɪmɪn] Putzfrau f

chase [t∫es] s (pursuit) Verfolgung f; (hunt) Jagd f || tr jagen; (girls) nachsteigen (dat); **c. away** verjagen; **c. out** vertreiben || intr—**c. after** nachlaufen (dat)

chasm ['kæzəm] s (& fig) Abgrund m

chas·sis ['t∫æsi] s (–sis [siz]) Chassis n; (aut) Fahrgestell n

chaste [t∫est] adj keusch

chasten ['t∫esən] tr züchtigen

chastise [t∫æs'taɪz] tr züchtigen

chastity ['t∫æstrti] s Keuschheit f

chat [t∫æt] s Plauderei f || v (pret & pp **chatted**; ger **chatting**) intr plaudern

chattel ['t∫ætəl] s Sklave m; **chattels** Hab und Gut n

chatter ['t∫ætər] s (talk) Geplapper n; (of teeth) Klappern n || intr (talk) plappern; (said of teeth) klappern

chat′terbox′ s (coll) Plappermaul n

chauffeur ['∫ofər], [∫o'fʌr] s Chauffeur m || tr fahren

cheap [t∫ip] adj (inexpensive) billig; (shoddy) minderwertig; (base) gemein; (stingy) geizig; **feel c.** sich verlegen fühlen || adv billig; **get off c.** mit e-m blauen Auge davonkommen

cheapen ['t∫ipən] tr herabsetzen

cheat [t∫it] s Betrüger –in mf || tr (out of) betrügen (um) || intr schwindeln; (at cards) mogeln; **c. on** (e.g., a wife) betrügen

cheating s Betrügerei f; (at cards) Mogelei f

check [t∫ek] s (of a bank) Scheck m; (for luggage) Schein m; (in a restaurant) Rechnung f; (inspection) Kontrolle f; (test) Nachprüfung f; (repulse) Rückschlag m; (restraint) (on) Hemmnis n (für); (square) Karo n; (chess) Schach n; **hold in c.** in Schach halten || tr (restrain) hindern; (inspect) kontrollieren; (test) nachprüfen, überprüfen; (a hat, coat) abgeben, (luggage) aufgeben; (figures) nachrechnen; (chess) Schach bieten (dat); **c. off** abhaken || intr (agree) übereinstimmen; **c. out** (of a hotel) sich abmelden; **c. up on** überprüfen; (a person) sich erkundigen über (*acc*); **c. with** (*correspond to*) übereinstimmen mit; (*consult*) sich besprechen mit ‖ *interj* Schach!

check'book' *s* Scheckbuch *n*, Scheckheft *n*

checker ['tʃekər] *s* Kontrolleur *m*; (*in checkers*) Damestein *m*; **checkers** Damespiel *n*

check'erboard' *s* Damebrett *n*

check'ered *adj* kariert; (*life, career*) wechselvoll

check'ing account' *s* Scheckkonto *n*

check' list' *s* Kontrolliste *f*

check'mate' *s* Schachmatt *n*; (*fig*) Niederlage *f* ‖ *tr* (& *fig*) matt setzen ‖ *interj* schachmatt!

check'-out count'er *s* Kasse *f*

check'point' *s* Kontrollstelle *f*

check'room' *s* Garderobe *f*

check'up' *s* Überprüfung *f*; (*med*) ärztliche Untersuchung *f*

cheek [tʃik] *s* Backe *f*, Wange *f*; (coll) Frechheit *f*

cheek'bone' *s* Backenknochen *m*

cheek' by jowl' *adv* Seite an Seite

cheeky ['tʃiki] *adj* (coll) frech

cheer [tʃɪr] *s* (*applause*) Beifallsruf *m*; (*encouragement*) Ermunterung *f*; (sport) Ermunterungsruf *m*; **three cheers for** ein dreifaches Hoch auf (*acc*) ‖ *tr* zujubeln (*dat*); **c. on** anfeuern; **c. up** aufmuntern; **c. up!** nur Mut!

cheerful ['tʃɪrfəl] *adj* heiter; (*room, surroundings*) freundlich

cheer'lead'er *s* Anführer –in *mf* beim Beifallsrufen

cheerless ['tʃɪrlɪs] *adj* freudlos

cheese [tʃiz] *s* Käse *m*

cheeseburger ['tʃiz,bʌrɡər] *s* belegtes Brot *n* mit Frikadelle und überbackenem Käse

cheese' cake' *s* Käsekuchen *m*

cheese' cloth' *s* grobe Baumwollgaze *f*

cheesy ['tʃizi] *adj* (sl) minderwertig

chef [ʃef] *s* Küchenchef *m*

chemical ['kemɪkəl] *adj* chemisch; (*fertilizer*) Kunst– ‖ *s* Chemikalie *f*

chemist ['kemɪst] *s* Chemiker –in *mf*

chemistry ['kemɪstri] *s* Chemie *f*

cherish ['tʃerɪʃ] *tr* (*hold dear*) schätzen; (*hopes, thoughts*) hegen

cherry ['tʃeri] *s* Kirsche *f*

cher'ry tree' *s* Kirschbaum *m*

cher·ub ['tʃerəb] *s* (**–ubim** [əbɪm]) Cherub *m* ‖ *s* (**–ubs**) Engelskopf *m*

chess [tʃes] *s* Schach *n*

chess'board' *s* Schachbrett *n*

chess'man' *s* (**–men'**) Schachfigur *f*

chest [tʃest] *s* Truhe *f*; (anat) Brust *f*

chestnut ['tʃesnət] *adj* kastanienbraun ‖ *s* Kastanie *f*; (*tree*) Kastanienbaum *m*; (*horse*) Rotfuchs *m*

chest' of drawers' *s* Kommode *f*

chevron ['ʃevrən] *s* (mil) Winkel *m*

chew [tʃu] *s* Kauen *n*; (*stick of tobacco*) Priem *m* ‖ *tr* kauen; **c. the cud** wiederkäuen; **c. the rag** (sl) schwatzen

chew'ing gum' *s* Kaugummi *m*

chew'ing tobac'co *s* Kautabak *m*

chic [ʃik] *adj* schick ‖ *s* Schick *m*

chicanery [ʃɪ'kenəri] *s* Schikane *f*

chick [tʃɪk] *s* Küken *n*; (*girl*) (sl) kesse Biene *f*

chicken ['tʃɪkən] *adj* Hühner–; (sl) feig(e) ‖ *s* Huhn *n*, Hühnchen *n*

chick'en coop' *s* Hühnerstall *m*

chick'en-heart'ed *adj* feig(e)

chick'en pox' *s* Windpocken *pl*

chick'en wire' *s* Maschendraht *m*

chick'pea' *s* Kichererbse *f*

chicory ['tʃɪkəri] *s* Zichorie *f*

chide [tʃaɪd] *v* (*pret & pp* **chided** & **chid** [tʃɪd]; *pp* **chided**) *tr* tadeln

chief [tʃif] *adj* Haupt–, Ober–, oberste; (*leading*) leitend ‖ *s* Chef *m*, Oberhaupt *n*; (*of an Indian tribe*) Häuptling *m*

chief' exec'utive *s* Regierungsoberhaupt *n*

chief' jus'tice *s* Vorsitzender *m* des obersten Gerichtshofes

chiefly ['tʃifli] *adv* vorwiegend

chief' of police' *s* Polizeipräsident *m*

chief' of staff' *s* Generalstabschef *m*

chief' of state' *s* Staatschef *m*

chieftain ['tʃiftən] *s* Häuptling *m*

chiffon [ʃɪ'fɑn] *s* Chiffon *m*

child [tʃaɪld] *s* (**children** ['tʃɪldrən]) Kind *n*; **with c.** schwanger

child' abuse' *s* Kindermißhandlung *f*

child'birth' *s* Niederkunft *f*

child'hood' *s* Kindheit *f*

childish ['tʃaɪldɪʃ] *adj* kindisch

childless ['tʃaɪldlɪs] *adj* kinderlos

child'like' *adj* kindlich

child' prod'igy *s* Wunderkind *n*

child's' play' *s* (*fig*) Kinderspiel *n*

child' support' *s* Alimente *pl*

child' wel'fare *s* Jugendfürsorge *f*

Chile ['tʃɪli] *s* Chile *n*

chili ['tʃɪli] *s* Cayennepfeffer *m*

chil'i sauce' *s* Chillisoße *f*

chill [tʃɪl] *s* (*coldness*) Kälte *f*; (*sensation of cold or fear*) Schau(d)er *m*; **chills** Fieberschau(d)er *m* ‖ *tr* kühlen; (*hopes, etc.*) dämpfen; (*metals*) abschrecken; **be chilled to the bone** durchfrieren ‖ *intr* abkühlen

chilly ['tʃɪli] *adj* (& fig) frostig; **feel chilly** frösteln

chime [tʃaɪm] *s* Geläut *n*; **chimes** Glockenspiel *n* ‖ *intr* (*said of bells*) läuten; (*said of a doorbell*) ertönen; (*said of a clock*) schlagen; **c. in** (coll) beipflichten

chimera [kaɪ'mɪrə] *s* Hirngespinst *n*

chimney ['tʃɪmni] *s* Schornstein *m*; (*of a lamp*) Zylinder *m*

chimpanzee [tʃɪm'pænzi] *s* Schimpanse *m*

chin [tʃɪn] *s* Kinn *n*; **keep one's c. up** die Ohren steifhalten; **up to the c.** bis über die Ohren

china ['tʃaɪnə] *s* Porzellan *n* ‖ **China** *s* China *n*

chi'na clos'et *s* Porzellanschrank *m*

chi'na-man *s* (**–men**) (pej) Chinese *m*

chin'aware' *s* Porzellanwaren *pl*

Chi·nese [tʃaɪ'niz] *adj* chinesisch ‖ *s* (**–nese**) Chinese *m*, Chinesin *f*; (*language*) Chinesisch *n*

Chi'nese lan'tern *s* Lampion *m*

chink [tʃɪŋk] *s* Ritze *f*; (*of coins or*

glasses) Klang *m* ‖ *tr* (*glasses*) anstoßen

chin'-up' *s* Klimmzug *m*

chip [tʃɪp] *s* Span *m*, Splitter *m*; (*in china*) angestoßene Stelle *f*; (*in poker*) Spielmarke *f*; **a c. off the old block** (coll) ganz der Vater; **have a c. on one's shoulder** (coll) vor Zorn geladen sein ‖ *v* (*pret & pp* **chipped**; *ger* **chipping**) *tr* (*e.g., a cup*) anschlagen; **c. in** (coll) beitragen; **c. off** abbrechen ‖ *intr* (leicht) abbrechen; **c. in** (with) einspringen (mit); **c. off** (*said of paint*) abblättern

chipmunk ['tʃɪpˌmʌŋk] *s* Streifenhörnchen *n*

chipper ['tʃɪpər] *adj* (coll) munter

chiropodist [kaɪ'rɑpədɪst], [kɪ'rɑpədɪst] *s* Fußpfleger –in *mf*

chiropractor ['kaɪrəˌpræktər] *s* Chiropraktiker –in *mf*

chirp [tʃʌrp] *s* Gezwitscher *n* ‖ *intr* zwitschern

chis•el ['tʃɪzəl] *s* Meißel *m* ‖ *v* (*pret & pp* **-el[l]ed**; *ger* **-il[l]ing**) *tr* meißeln; (sl) bemogeln ‖ meißeln; (sl) mogeln

chiseler ['tʃɪzələr] *s* (sl) Mogler *m*

chitchat ['tʃɪtˌtʃæt] *s* Schnickschnack *m*

chivalrous ['ʃɪvəlrəs] *adj* ritterlich

chivalry ['ʃɪvəlri] *s* Rittertum *n*; (*politeness*) Ritterlichkeit *f*

chive [tʃaɪv] *s* Schnittlauch *m*

chloride ['klɔraɪd] *s* Chlorid *n*

chlorine ['klɔrin] *s* Chlor *n*

chloroform ['klɔrəˌfɔrm] *s* Chloroform *n* ‖ *tr* chloroformieren

chlorophyll ['klɔrəfɪl] *s* Chlorophyll *n*

chock-full ['tʃak'ful] *adj* zum Bersten voll

chocolate ['tʃɔkəlɪt] *adj* Schokoladen–; (*in color*) schokoladenfarben ‖ *s* Schokolade *f*; (*chocolate-covered candy*) Praline *f*

choc'olate bar' *s* Schokoladentafel *f*

choice [tʃɔɪs] *adj* (aus)erlesen ‖ *s* Wahl *f*; (*selection*) Auswahl *f*

choir [kwaɪr] *s* Chor *m*; (archit) Chor *m*

choir'boy' *s* Chorknabe *m*

choir' loft' *s* Chorgalerie *f*

choir'mas'ter *s* Chordirigent *m*

choke [tʃok] *s* (aut) Starterklappe *f* ‖ *tr* erwürgen, ersticken; **c. back** (*tears*) herunterschlucken; **c. down** herunterwürgen; **c. up** verstopfen ‖ *intr* ersticken; **c. on** ersticken an (*dat*)

choker ['tʃokər] *s* enges Halsband *n*

cholera ['kalərə] *s* Cholera *f*

cholesterol [kə'lɛstəˌrol] *s* Blutfett *n*

choose [tʃuz] *v* (*pret* **chose** [tʃoz]; *pp* **chosen** ['tʃozən]) *tr & intr* wählen

choosy ['tʃuzi] *adj* (coll) wählerisch

chop [tʃap] *s* Hieb *m*; (culin) Kotelett *n*, Schnitzel *n*; **chops** (sl) Maul *n* ‖ *v* (*pret & pp* **chopped**; *ger* **chopping**) *tr* hacken; **c. down** niederhauen; **c. off** abhacken; **c. up** zerhacken

chopper ['tʃapər] *s* (ax) Hackbeil *n*; (coll) Hubschrauber *m*

chop'ping block' *s* Hackklotz *m*

choppy ['tʃapi] *adj* (sea) bewegt

chop'stick' *s* Eßstäbchen *n*

choral ['kɔrəl] *adj* Chor–, Sänger–

chorale [ko'ral] *s* Choral *m*

chord [kɔrd] *s* (anat) Band *n*; (geom) Sehne *f*; (*combination of notes*) (mus) Akkord *m*; (mus & fig) Saite *f*

chore [tʃor] *s* Hausarbeit *f*

choreography [ˌkɔri'ɑgrəfi] *s* Choreographie *f*

chorus ['kɔrəs] *s* Chor *m*; (*refrain*) Kehrreim *m*

cho'rus girl' *s* Revuetänzerin *f*

chowder ['tʃaudər] *s* Fischsuppe *f*

Christ [kraɪst] *s* Christus *m*

Christ' child' *s* Christkind *n*

christen ['krɪsən] *tr* taufen

Christendom ['krɪsəndəm] *s* Christenheit *f*

chris'tening *s* Taufe *f*; **c. of a ship** Schiffstaufe *f*

Christian ['krɪstʃən] *adj* christlich ‖ Christ –in *mf*

Chris'tian E'ra *s* christliche Zeitrechnung *f*

Christianity [ˌkrɪstɪ'æniti] *s* (*faith*) Christentum *n*; (*all Christians*) Christenheit *f*

Chris'tian name' *s* Taufname *m*

Christmas ['krɪsməs] *adj* Weihnachts– ‖ *s* Weihnachten *pl*, Weihnachtsfest *n*

Christ'mas card' *s* Weihnachtskarte *f*

Christ'mas car'ol *s* Weihnachtslied *n*

Christ'mas Eve' *s* Heiliger Abend *m*

Christ'mas gift' *s* Weihnachtsgeschenk *n*

Christ'mas tree' *s* Christbaum *m*

Christ'mas tree' lights' *spl* Weihnachtskerzen *pl*

Christopher ['krɪstəfər] *s* Christoph *m*

chromatic [kro'mætɪk] *adj* chromatisch

chrome [krom] *adj* Chrom– ‖ *s* Chrom *n* ‖ *tr* verchromen

chrome'plate' *tr* verchromen

chromium ['kromɪ•əm] *s* Chrom *n*

chromosome ['kroməˌsom] *s* Chromosom *n*

chronic ['kranɪk] *adj* chronisch

chronicle ['kranɪkəl] *s* Chronik *f* ‖ *tr* aufzeichnen

chronicler ['kranɪklər] *s* Chronist –in *mf*

chronological [ˌkranə'ladʒɪkəl] *adj* chronologisch

chronology [krə'nalədʒi] *s* Chronologie *f*

chronometer [krə'namɪtər] *s* Chronometer *m*

chrysanthemum [krɪ'sænθɪməm] *s* Chrysantheme *f*

chubby ['tʃʌbi] *adj* pummelig

chuck [tʃʌk] *s* (culin) Schulterstück *n*; (mach) Klemmfutter *n* ‖ *tr* schmeißen

chuckle ['tʃʌkəl] *s* Glucksen *n* ‖ *intr* glucksen

chug [tʃʌg] *s* Tuckern *n* ‖ *v* (*pret & pp* **chugged**; *ger* **chugging**) *intr* tuckern; **c. along** tuckernd fahren

chum [tʃʌm] s (coll) Kumpel m ‖ v (pret & pp chummed; ger chumming) intr—c. around with sich eng anschließen an (acc)

chummy ['tʃʌmi] adj eng befreundet

chump [tʃʌmp] s (coll) Trottel m

chunk [tʃʌŋk] s Klotz m, Stück m

church [tʃʌrtʃ] adj Kirchen–, kirchlich ‖ s Kirche f

churchgoer ['tʃʌrtʃ,go·ər] s Kirchgänger –in mf

church' pic'nic s Kirchweih f

church' yard' s Kirchhof m

churl [tʃʌrl] s Flegel m

churlish ['tʃʌrlɪʃ] adj flegelhaft

churn [tʃʌrn] s Butterfaß n ‖ tr (cream) buttern; **c. up** aufwühlen ‖ intr sich heftig bewegen

chute [ʃut] s (for coal, etc.) Rutsche f; (for laundry, etc.) Abwurfschacht m; (sliding board) Rutschbahn f; (in a river) Stromschnelle f; (aer) Fallschirm m

cider ['saɪdər] s Apfelwein m

cigar [sɪ'gɑr] s Zigarre f

cigarette [,sɪgə'rɛt] s Zigarette f

cigarette' cough' s Raucherhusten m

cigarette' light'er s Feuerzeug n

cigar' store' s Rauchwarenladen m

cinch [sɪntʃ] s Sattelgurt m; (sure thing) totsichere Sache f; (snap) (sl) Kinderspiel n; (likely candidate) totsicherer Kandidat m ‖ tr (sl) sich [dat] sichern

cinder ['sɪndər] s (ember) glühende Kohle f; (slag) Schlacke f; **cinders** Asche f

Cinderella [,sɪndə'relə] s Aschenbrödel n

cin'der track' s (sport) Aschenbahn f

cinema ['sɪnəmə] s Kino n

cinematography [,sɪnəmə'tɑgrəfi] s Kinematographie f

cinnamon ['sɪnəmən] s Zimt m

cipher ['saɪfər] s Ziffer f; (zero) Null f; (code) Chiffre f ‖ tr chiffrieren

circle ['sʌrkəl] s Kreis m; **circles under the eyes** Ränder pl unter den Augen ‖ tr einkreisen; (go around) umkreisen ‖ intr kreisen

circuit ['sʌrkɪt] s (course) Kreislauf m; (elec) Stromkreis m; (jur) Bezirk m

cir'cuit break'er s Ausschalter m

cir'cuit court' s Bezirksgericht n

circuitous [sər'kju·ɪtəs] adj weitschweifig

circular ['sʌrkjələr] adj kreisförmig; (saw) Kreis– ‖ s Rundschreiben n

circulate ['sʌrkjə,let] tr in Umlauf setzen; (a rumor) verbreiten; (fin) girieren ‖ intr umlaufen; (said of blood) kreisen; (said of a rumor) umgehen

circulation [,sʌrkjə'leʃən] s (of blood) Kreislauf m; (of a newspaper) Auflage f; (of money) Umlauf m

circumcize ['sʌrkəm,saɪz] tr beschneiden

circumference [sər'kʌmfərəns] s Umfang m

circumflex ['sʌrkəm,flɛks] s Zirkumflex m

circumlocution [,sʌrkəmlo'kjuʃən] s Umschreibung f

circumscribe ['sʌrkəm,skraɪb] tr (geom) umschreiben; (fig) umgrenzen

circumspect ['sʌrkəm,spɛkt] adj umsichtig

circumstance ['sʌrkəm,stæns] s Umstand m; **circumstances** (financial situation) Verhältnisse pl

cir'cumstan'tial ev'idence [,sʌrkəm'stænʃəl] s Indizienbeweis m

circumvent [,sʌrkəm'vɛnt] tr umgehen

circus ['sʌrkəs] s Zirkus m

cistern ['sɪstərn] s Zisterne f

citadel ['sɪtədəl] s Burg f

citation [saɪ'teʃən] s Zitat n; (jur) Vorladung f; (mil) Belobung f

cite [saɪt] tr (quote) anführen; (jur) vorladen; (mil) belobigen

citizen ['sɪtɪzən] s Bürger –in mf

cit'izenship' s Staatsangehörigkeit f

cit'rus fruit' ['sɪtrəs] s Zitrusfrucht f

city ['sɪti] s Stadt f

cit'y coun'cil s Stadtrat m

cit'y fa'ther s Stadtrat m

cit'y hall' s Rathaus n

cit'y plan'ning s Stadtplanung f

civic ['sɪvɪk] adj bürgerlich, Bürger– ‖ **civics** s Staatsbürgerkunde f

civil ['sɪvɪl] adj (life, duty) bürgerlich; (service) öffentlich; (polite) höflich; (jur) privatrechtlich

civ'il cer'emony s standesamtliche Trauung f

civ'il defense' s zivile Verteidigung f

civ'il engineer'ing s Hoch– und Tiefbau m

civilian [sɪ'vɪljən] adj bürgerlich, Zivil– ‖ s Zivilist –in mf

civilization [,sɪvɪlɪ'zeʃən] s Zivilisation f, Kultur f

civilize ['sɪvɪ,laɪz] tr zivilisieren

civ'il rights' spl Bürgerrechte pl

civ'il serv'ant s Staatsbeamte m, Staatsbeamtin f

civ'il serv'ice s Staatsdienst m

civ'il war' s Bürgerkrieg m

claim [klem] s Anspruch m; (assertion) Behauptung f; (for public land) beanspruchtes Land n ‖ tr beanspruchen; (assert) behaupten; (attention) erfordern; **c. to be** sich ausgeben für

claim' check' s Aufgabeschein m

clairvoyance [kler'vɔɪ·əns] s Hellsehen n

clairvoyant [kler'vɔɪ·ənt] adj hellseherisch; **be c.** hellsehen ‖ s Hellseher –in mf

clam [klæm] s eßbare Meermuschel f

clamber ['klæmbər] intr klettern

clammy ['klæmi] adj feuchtkalt

clamor ['klæmər] s Geschrei n ‖ intr (for) schreien (nach)

clamorous ['klæmərəs] adj schreiend

clamp [klæmp] s Klammer f; (surg) Klemme f ‖ tr (ver)klammern ‖ intr—**c. down on** einschreiten gegen

clan [klæn] s Stamm m; (pej) Sippschaft f

clandestine [klæn'dɛstɪn] adj heimlich

clang [klæŋ] s Geklirr n ‖ intr klirren

clank [klæŋk] s Geklirr n, Gerassel n ‖ intr klirren, rasseln

clannish ['klænıʃ] adj stammesbewußt

clap [klæp] s (of the hands) Klatschen n; (of thunder) Schlag m ‖ v (pret & pp clapped; ger clapping) tr (a tax, fine, duty) (on) auferlegen (dat); clap hands in die Hände klatschen ‖ intr Beifall klatschen

clapper ['klæpər] s Klöppel m

clap'trap' s Phrasendrescherei f

claque [klæk] s Claque f

clari-fy ['klærı‚faı] v (pret & pp -fied) tr erklären

clarinet [‚klærı'net] s Klarinette f

clarity ['klærıtı] s Klarheit f

clash [klæʃ] s (sound) Geklirr n; (of interests, etc.) Widerstreit m ‖ intr (conflict) kollidieren; (said of persons) aufeinanderstoßen; (said of ideas) im Widerspruch stehen; (said of colors) nicht zusammenpassen

clasp [klæsp] s (fastener) Schließe f, Spange f; (on a necktie) Klammer f; (embrace) Umarmung f; (of hands) Händedruck m ‖ tr umklammern; c. s.o.'s hand j-m die Hand drücken

class [klæs] s (group) Klasse f; (period of instruction) Stunde f; (year) Jahrgang m; have c. (sl) Niveau haben ‖ tr einstufen

classic ['klæsık] adj klassisch ‖ s Klassiker m

classical ['klæsıkəl] adj klassisch; c. antiquity Klassik f; c. author Klassiker m

classicist ['klæsısıst] s Kenner -in mf der Klassik

classification [‚klæsıfı'keʃən] s Klassifikation f, Anordnung f

clas'sified adj geheimzuhaltend

clas'sified ad's kleine Anzeige f

classi-fy ['klæsı‚faı] v (pret & pp -fied) tr klassifizieren

class'mate' s Klassenkamerad m

class' reun'ion s Klassentreffen n

class'room' s Klassenzimmer n

classy ['klæsı] adj (sl) pfundig

clatter ['klætər] s Geklapper n ‖ intr klappern

clause [kləz] s Satzteil m; (jur) Klausel f

clavicle ['klævıkəl] s Schlüsselbein n

claw [klə] s Klaue f, Kralle f; (of a crab) Schere f ‖ tr zerkratzen; (a hole) scharren ‖ intr kratzen

clay [kle] adj tönern ‖ s Ton m, Lehm m

clay' pig'eon s Tontaube f

clean [klin] adj sauber, rein; (cut) glatt; (features) klar ‖ adv (coll) völlig ‖ tr reinigen, putzen; c. out (clear out by force) räumen; (empty) ausleeren; (sl) ausbeuten; c. up (a room) aufräumen ‖ intr putzen; c. up sich zurechtmachen; (in gambling sl) schwer einheimsen

clean'-cut' adj (person) ordentlich; (clearly outlined) klar umrissen

cleaner ['klinər] s (person, device) Reiniger m; cleaners (establishment) Reinigungsanstalt f

clean'ing flu'id s flüssiges Reinigungsmittel n

clean'ing wo'man s Reinemachefrau f

cleanliness ['klenlınıs] s Sauberkeit f

cleanse [klenz] tr reinigen

cleanser ['klenzər] s Reinigungsmittel n

clean'-shav'en adj glattrasiert

clean'up' s Reinemachen n; (e.g., of vice, graft) Säuberungsaktion f

clear [klır] adj klar; (sky, weather) heiter; (light) hell; (profit) netto; (conscience) rein; (proof) offenkundig ‖ adv (coll) völlig; (fin) netto ‖ tr klären; (streets) freimachen; (the table) abräumen; (a room) räumen; (a forest) roden; (the air) reinigen; (an obstacle without touching it) setzen über (acc); (a path) bahnen; (as profit) rein gewinnen; (at customs) zollamtlich abfertigen; (one's name) reinwaschen; c. away wegräumen; (doubts) beseitigen; c. up klarlegen ‖ intr sich klären; c. out (coll) sich davonmachen; c. up sich aufklären

clearance ['klırəns] s (approval) Genehmigung f; (at customs) Zollabfertigung f; (of a bridge) lichte Höhe f; (aer) Starterlaubnis f; (mach) Spielraum m

clear'ance sale' s Räumungsverkauf m

clear'-cut' adj klar, eindeutig

clear'-head'ed adj verständig

clear'ing s (in a woods) Lichtung f

clear'ing house' s Abstimmungszentrale f; (fin) Verrechnungsstelle f

clear'-sight'ed adj scharfsichtig

cleat [klit] s Stollen m

cleavage ['klivıdʒ] s Spaltung f

cleave [kliv] v (pret & pp cleft [kleft] & cleaved) tr zerspalten ‖ intr (split) sich spalten; (to) kleben (an dat)

cleaver ['klivər] s Hackbeil n

clef [klef] s Notenschlüssel m

cleft [kleft] s Riß m, Spalt m

clemency ['klemənsı] s Milde f; (jur) Begnadigung f

clement ['klemənt] adj mild

clench [klentʃ] tr (a fist) ballen; (the teeth) zusammenbeißen

clerestory ['klır‚storı] s Lichtgaden m

clergy ['klerdʒı] s Geistlichkeit f

cler'gy•man s (-men) Geistliche m

cleric ['klerık] s Kleriker m

clerical ['klerıkəl] adj Schreib-, Büro-; (eccl) geistlich

cler'ical er'ror s Schreibfehler m

cler'ical staff' s Schreibkräfte pl

cler'ical work' s Büroarbeit f

clerk [klʌrk] s (in a store) Verkäufer -in mf; (in an office) Büroangestellte mf; (in a post office) Schalterbeamte m; (jur) Gerichtsschreiber -in mf

clever ['klevər] adj (intelligent) klug; (adroit) geschickt; (witty) geistreich; (ingenious) findig

cleverness ['klevərnıs] s (intelligence) Klugheit f; (adroitness) Geschicklichkeit f; (ingeniousness) Findigkeit f

cliché [kli'ʃe] s Klischee n

click [klɪk] s Klicken n; (of the tongue) Schnalzen n; (of a lock) Einschnappen n || tr klicken lassen; **c. one's heels** die Hacken zusammenschlagen || intr klicken; (said of heels) knallen; (said of a lock) einschnappen || impers—**it clicks** (coll) es klappt

client ['klaɪ‑ənt] s (customer) Kunde m, Kundin f; (of a company) Auftraggeber –in mf; (jur) Klient –in mf

clientele [ˌklaɪ‑ən'tɛl] s Kundschaft f; (com, jur) Klientel f

cliff [klɪf] s Klippe f, Felsen m

climate ['klaɪmɪt] s Klima n

climax ['klaɪmæks] s Höhepunkt m

climb [klaɪm] s Aufstieg m, Besteigung f; (aer) Steigungsflug m || tr ersteigen, besteigen; (stairs) hinaufsteigen; **climb a tree** auf e-n Baum klettern; || intr steigen, klettern; (said of a street) ansteigen

climber ['klaɪmər] s Kletterer –in mf; (of a mountain) Bergsteiger –in mf; (bot) Kletterpflanze f

clinch [klɪntʃ] s (box) Clinch m || tr (settle) entscheiden || intr clinchen

clincher ['klɪntʃər] s (coll) Trumpf m

cling [klɪŋ] v (pret & pp **clung** [klʌŋ]) intr haften; **c. to** sich anklammern an (acc); (said of a dress) sich anschmiegen an (acc); (fig) festhalten an (dat)

clinic ['klɪnɪk] s Klinik f

clinical ['klɪnɪkəl] adj klinisch

clink [klɪŋk] s Klirren n; (prison) (sl) Kittchen n || tr—**c. glasses** mit den Gläsern anstoßen || intr klirren

clip [klɪp] s Klammer f; **go at a good c.** ein scharfes Tempo anlegen || v (pret & pp **clipped**; ger **clipping**) tr (a hedge) beschneiden; (hair) schneiden; (wings) stutzen; (sheep) scheren; (from newspapers, etc.) ausschneiden; (syllables) verschlucken; (sl) schröpfen; **c. together** zusammenklammern

clip′board′ s Manuskripthalter m

clip′ joint′ s (sl) Nepplokal n

clipper ['klɪpər] s (aer) Klipperflugzeug n; (naut) Klipper m; **clippers** Haarschneidemaschine f

clip′ping s (act) Stutzen n; (from newspapers) Ausschnitt m; (clippings) (of paper) Schnitzel pl; (scraps) Abfälle pl

clique [klik] s Sippschaft f

cliquish ['klikɪʃ] adj cliquenhaft

cloak [klok] s Umhang m; (fig) Deckmantel m; **under the c. of darkness** im Schutz der Dunkelheit || tr (fig) bemänteln

cloak′-and-dag′ger adj Spionage–

cloak′room′ s Garderobe f

clobber ['klɑbər] tr (coll) verwichsen

clock [klɑk] s Uhr f || tr (a runner) abstoppen

clock′mak′er s Uhrmacher –in mf

clock′ tow′er s Uhrturm m

clock′wise′ adv im Uhrzeigersinn

clock′work′ s Uhrwerk n; **like c.** wie am Schnürchen

clod [klɑd] s Klumpen m, Scholle f

clodhopper ['klɑdˌhɑpər] s Bauerntölpel m

clog [klɑg] s Verstopfung f; (shoe) Holzschuh m || v (pret & pp **clogged**; ger **clogging**) tr verstopfen || intr sich verstopfen

cloister ['klɔɪstər] s Kloster n; (covered walk) Kreuzgang m

close [klos] adj (near) nahe; (tight) knapp; (air) schwül; (ties, friend) eng; (attention) gespannt; (game) beinahe gleich; (observer) scharf; (surveillance) streng; (supervision) genau; (inspection) eingehend; (resemblance; competition) stark; (shave) glatt; (translation) wortgetreu; (stingy) geizig; (order) (mil) geschlossen; **c. to** (position) nahe an (dat), neben (dat); (direction) nahe an (acc), neben (acc) || adv dicht, eng; **from c. up** in der Nähe || [kloz] s Schluß m, Ende n; **bring to a c.** zu Ende bringen; **draw to a c.** zu Ende gehen || tr schließen; (an account, deal) abschließen; **c. down** stillegen; **c. off** abschließen; (a road) sperren; **c. out** (com) ausverkaufen; **c. up** zumachen || intr sich schließen; **c. in** immer näher kommen; **c. in on** umschließen

close-by ['klos'baɪ] adj nebenan

close-cropped ['klos'krɑpt] adj kurz geschoren

closed [klozd] adj geschlossen; **c. today** (public sign) heute Betriebsruhe

closed′ shop′ s Unternehmen n mit Gewerkschaftszwang

closefisted ['klos'fɪstəd] adj geizig

close-fitting ['klos'fɪtɪŋ] adj eng anliegend

close-mouthed ['klos'mauðd] adj verschwiegen

close′ or′der drill′ [klos] s (mil) geschlossenes Exerzieren n

closeout ['kloz‚aut] s Räumungsausverkauf m

close′ shave′ [klos] s glatte Rasure f; (fig) knappes Entkommen n; **have a c.** mit knapper Not davonkommen

closet ['klɑzɪt] s Schrank m

close-up ['klos‚ʌp] s Nahaufnahme f

clos′ing adj Schluß–; (day) scheidend || s Schließung f; (of an account) Abschluß m; (of a factory) Stillegung f; (of a road) Sperrung f

clos′ing price′ s Schlußkurs m

clos′ing time′ s (of a shop) Geschäftsschluß m; (of bars) Polizeistunde f

clot [klɑt] s Klumpen m; (of blood) Gerinnsel n || v (pret & pp **clotted**; ger **clotting**) intr gerinnen

cloth [klɔθ] s Stoff m, Tuch n; (for cleaning, etc.) Lappen m; **the c.** die Geistlichkeit

clothe [kloð] v (pret & pp **clothed** & **clad** [klæd]) tr ankleiden, (be)kleiden; (fig) (in) einhüllen in (acc)

clothes [kloz], [kloðz] spl Kleider pl; **change one's clothes** sich umziehen; **put on one's clothes** sich anziehen

clothes′bas′ket s Wäschekorb m

clothes′brush′ s Kleiderbürste f

clothes′ clos′et s Kleiderschrank m

clothes′ dri′er *s* Wäschetrockner *m*
clothes′ hang′er *s* Kleiderbügel *m*
clothes′line *s* Wäscheleine *f*
clothes′pin *s* Wäscheklammer *f*
clothier [′kloðjər] *s* Kleiderhändler *m*; (*cloth maker*) Tuchmacher *m*; (*cloth dealer*) Tuchhändler *m*
clothing [′kloðıŋ] *s* Kleidung *f*
cloud [klaud] *s* Wolke *f*; **be up in the clouds** (fig) in höheren Regionen schweben ‖ *tr* bewölken; (*a liquid*) trüben; (fig) verdunkeln ‖ *intr*—**c. over** (or **up**) sich bewölken
cloud′burst *s* Wolkenbruch *m*
cloud′-capped′ *adj* von Wolken bedeckt
cloudiness [′klaudınıs] *s* Bewölktheit *f*
cloudless [′klaudlıs] *adj* unbewölkt
cloudy [′klaudi] *adj* bewölkt; (*liquid*) trüb(e)
clout [klaut] *s* (*blow*) (coll) Hieb *m*; (*influence*) (coll) Einfluß *m* ‖ *tr*—**c. s.o.** (coll) j-m eins herunterhauen
clove [klov] *s* Gewürznelke *f*; **c. of garlic** Knoblauchzehe *f*
clo′ven hoof′ [′klovən] *s* (*as a sign of the devil*) Pferdefuß *m*
clover [′klovər] *s* Klee *m*
clo′ver-leaf′ *s* (**-leaves**) Kleeblatt *n*
clown [klaun] *s* Clown *m*, Hanswurst *m*
clownish [′klaunıʃ] *adj* närrisch
cloy [klɔı] *tr* übersättigen
club [klʌb] *s* (*weapon*) Keule *f*; (*organization*) Klub *m*; (cards) Kreuz *n*; (golf) Schläger *m* ‖ (*pret* & *pp* **clubbed**; *ger* **clubbing**) *tr* verprügeln
club′ car′ *s* (rr) Salonwagen *m*
club′house′ *s* Klubhaus *n*
cluck [klʌk] *s* Glucken *n* ‖ *intr* glucken
clue [klu] *s* Schlüssel *m*, Anhaltspunkt *m*
clump [klʌmp] *s* (*of earth*) Klumpen *m*; (*of hair, grass*) Büschel *n*; (*of trees*) Gruppe *f*; (*heavy tramping sound*) schwerer Tritt *m*; **c. of bushes** Gebüsch *n* ‖ *intr*—**c. along** trapsen
clumsy [′klʌmzi] *adj* ungeschickt, plump; **c. ox** Tölpel *m*
cluster [′klʌstər] *s* (*bunch growing together*) Büschel *n*; (*of grapes*) Traube *f*; (*group*) Gruppe *f* ‖ *intr*—**c. around** sich zusammendrängen um
clutch [klʌtʃ] *s* Griff *m*; (aut) Kupplung *f*; **fall into s.o.'s clutches** j-m in die Klauen geraten; **let out the c.** einkuppeln; **step on the c.** auskuppeln ‖ *tr* packen
clutter [′klʌtər] *s* Durcheinander *n* ‖ *tr*—**c. up** vollstopfen
Co. *abbr* (*Company*) Gesellschaft *f*
c/o *abbr* (*care of*) per Adresse, bei
coach [kotʃ] *s* Kutsche *f*; (rr) Personenwagen *m*; (sport) Trainer *m* ‖ *tr* Nachhilfeunterricht geben (*dat*); (sport) trainieren ‖ *intr* (sport) trainieren
coach′ing *s* Nachhilfeunterricht *m*; (sport) Training *m*
coach′man *s* (**-men**) Kutscher *m*

coagulate [ko′ægjə‚let] *tr* gerinnen lassen ‖ *intr* gerinnen
coal [kol] *s* Kohle *f*
coal′bin *s* Kohlenkasten *m*
coal′-black′ *adj* kohlrabenschwarz
coal′ car′ *s* (rr) Kohlenwagen *m*
coal′deal′er *s* Kohlenhändler *m*
coalesce [‚ko-ə′les] *intr* zusammenwachsen, sich vereinigen
coalition [‚ko-ə′lıʃən] *s* Koalition *f*
coal′ mine′ *s* Kohlenbergwerk *n*
coal′ min′ing *s* Kohlenbergbau *m*
coal′ oil′ *s* Petroleum *n*
coal′yard′ *s* Kohlenlager *n*
coarse [kors] *adj* (& fig) grob
coast [kost] *s* Küste *f*; **the c. is clear** (coll) die Luft ist rein ‖ *intr* im Leerlauf fahren; **c. along** (fig) sich mühelos fortbewegen
coastal [′kostəl] *adj* küstennah, Küsten-
coaster [′kostər] *s* (*for a glass*) Untersatz *m*; (naut) Küstenfahrer *m*
coast′guard′ *s* Küstenwachdienst *m*
coast′line′ *s* Küstenlinie *f*
coat [kot] *s* (*of a suit*) Jacke *f*, Rock *m*; (topcoat) Mantel *m*; (*of fur*) Fell *n*; (*of enamel, etc.*) Belag *m*; (*of paint*) Anstrich *m* ‖ *tr* (*e.g.*, *with teflon*) beschichten; (*e.g.*, *with chocolate*) überziehen; (*e.g.*, *with oil*) beschmieren
coat′ed *adj* überzogen; (*tongue*) belegt
coat′ hang′er *s* Kleiderbügel *m*
coat′ing *s* Belag *m*, Überzug *m*
coat′ of arms′ *s* Wappen *n*
coat′rack′ *s* Kleiderständer *m*
coat′room′ *s* Garderobe *f*
coat′tail′ *s* Rockschoß *m*; (*of formal wear*) Frackschoß *m*
coauthor [′ko‚ɔθər] *s* Mitautor *m*
coax [koks] *tr* schmeicheln (*dat*); **c. s.o. to** (*inf*) j-n überreden zu (*inf*)
cob [kab] *s* Kolben *m*
cobalt [′kobalt] *s* Kobalt *m*
cobbler [′kablər] *s* Flickschuster *m*
cobblestone [′kabəl‚ston] *s* Pflasterstein *m*, Kopfstein *m*
cobra [′kobrə] *s* Kobra *f*
cob′web′ *s* Spinn(en)gewebe *n*
cocaine [ko′ken] *s* Kokain *n*
cock [kak] *s* Hahn *m*; (faucet) Wasserhahn *m*; (*of a gun*) Gewehrhahn *m* ‖ *tr* (*one's ears*) spitzen; (*one's hat*) schief aufsetzen; (*the firing mechanism*) spannen
cock-a-doodle-doo [′kakə‚dudəl′du] *s* Kikeriki *n*
cock′-and-bull′ sto′ry *s* Lügengeschichte *f*
cockeyed [′kak‚aıd] *adj* (*cross-eyed*) nach innen schielend; (*slanted to one side*) (sl) schief; (*drunk*) (sl) blau; (*absurd*) (sl) verrückt
cock′fight′ *s* Hahnenkampf *m*
cock′pit′ *s* Hahnenkampfplatz *m*; (aer) Kabine *f*, Kanzel *f*
cock′roach′ *s* Schabe *f*
cock′sure′ *adj* todsicher
cock′tail′ *s* Cocktail *m*
cock′tail dress′ *s* Cocktailkleid *n*
cock′tail par′ty *s* Cocktailparty *f*

cock'tail shak'er s Cocktailmischgefäß n

cocky ['kɒkɪ] adj (coll) frech

cocoa ['koko] s Kakao m

coconut ['kokə‚nʌt] s Kokosnuß f

co'conut palm', **co'conut tree'** s Kokospalme f

cacoon [kə'kun] s Kokon m

C.O.D., c.o.d. abbr (**cash on delivery**) per Nachnahme

cod [kɒd] s Kabeljau m

coddle ['kɒdəl] tr hätscheln

code [kod] s Geheimschrift f; (jur) Kodex m || tr verschlüsseln, chiffrieren

codefendant [‚kodɪ'fendənt] s Mitangeklagte mf

code' name' s Deckname m

code' of hon'or s Ehrenkodex m

code' of laws' s Gesetzsammlung f

code' word' s Kennwort n

codex ['kodeks] s (**codices** ['kodɪ‚siz]) Kodex m

cod'fish' s Kabeljau m

codicil ['kadɪsɪl] s Kodizill n

codi-fy ['kodɪ‚faɪ] v (pret & pp **-fied**) tr kodifizieren

cod'-liver oil' s Lebertran m

coed, co-ed ['ko‚ed] s Studentin f

coeducation [‚ko‚edʒə'ke/ən] s Koedukation f

coeducational [‚ko‚edʒə'ke/ənəl] adj Koedukations-

coefficient [‚ko·ɪ'fɪ/ənt] s Koeffizient m

coerce [ko'ʌrs] tr zwingen

coercion [ko'ʌr/ən] s Zwang m

coexist [‚ko·ɪg'zɪst] intr koexistieren

coexistence [‚ko·ɪg'zɪstəns] s Koexistenz f

coffee ['kɔfɪ] s Kaffee m

cof'fee bean' s Kaffeebohne f

cof'fee break' s Kaffeepause f

cof'fee fiend' s Kaffeetante f

cof'fee grounds' spl Kaffeesatz m

cof'fee pot' s Kaffeekanne f

cof'fee shop' s Kaffeestube f

coffer ['kɔfər] s Truhe f; (archit) Deckenfeld n; **coffers** Schatzkammer f

cof'ferdam' s (caisson) Kastendamm m; (naut) Kofferdamm m

coffin ['kɔfɪn] s Sarg m

cog [kɑg] s Zahn m; (cogwheel) Zahnrad n

cogency ['kodʒənsɪ] s Beweiskraft f

cogent ['kodʒənt] adj triftig

cognac ['konjæk], ['kɑnjæk] s Kognak m

cognizance ['kɑgnɪzəns] s Kenntnis f; **take c. of s.th.** etw zur Kenntnis nehmen

cognizant ['kɑgnɪzənt] adj—**be c. of** Kenntnis haben von

cog'wheel' s Zahnrad n

cohabit [ko'hæbɪt] intr in wilder Ehe leben

coheir [ko'er] s Miterbe m, Miterbin f

cohere [ko'hɪr] intr zusammenhängen

cohesion [ko'hiʒən] s Kohäsion f

coiffeur [kwɑ'fʌr] s Friseur m

coiffure [kwɑ'fjʊr] s Frisur f

coil [kɔɪl] s (something wound in a

spiral) Spirale f, Rolle f; (of tubing) Schlange f; (single wind) Windung f; (elec) Spule f || tr aufrollen; (naut) aufschießen || intr—**c. up** sich zusammenrollen

coil' spring' s Spiralfeder f

coin [kɔɪn] s Münze f, Geldstück n || tr münzen, (& fig) prägen

coinage ['kɔɪnɪdʒ] s (minting) Prägen n; (coins collectively) Münzen pl; (fig) Prägung f

coincide [‚ko·ɪn'saɪd] intr (**with**) zusammentreffen (mit); (in time) (**with**) gleichzeitig geschehen (mit)

coincidence [ko'ɪnsɪdəns] s Zufall m; **by mere c.** rein zufällig

coin' machine' s Münzautomat m

coin' slot' s Münzeinwurf m

coition [ko'ɪ/ən], **coitus** ['ko·ɪtəs] s Koitus m, Beischlaf m

coke [kok] s Koks m; (coll) Coca-Cola n

colander ['kʌləndər] s Sieb n

cold [kold] adj kalt || s Kälte f; (indisposition) Erkältung f

cold' blood' s—**in c.** kaltblütig

cold'-blood'ed adj kaltblütig

cold' cream' s Cold Cream n

cold' com'fort s (fig) geringer Trost m

cold' chis'el s Kaltmeißel m

cold' cuts' spl kalter Aufschnitt m

cold' feet' spl—**have c.** (fig) Angst haben

cold' front' s Kaltfront f

cold'-heart'ed adj kaltherzig

coldness ['koldnɪs] s Kälte f

cold' should'er s—**give s.o. the c.** j-m die kalte Schulter zeigen

cold' snap' s plötzlicher Kälteeinbruch m

cold' stor'age s Lagerung f im Kühlraum

cold' war' s kalter Krieg m

cold' wave' s (meteor) Kältewelle f

coleslaw ['kol‚slɔ] s Krautsalat m

colic ['kɑlɪk] s Kolik f

coliseum [‚kɑlɪ'si·əm] s Kolosseum n

collaborate [kə'læbə‚ret] intr mitarbeiten; (pol) kollaborieren

collaboration [kə‚læbə're/ən] s Mitarbeit f; (pol) Kollaboration f

collaborator [kə'læbə‚retər] s Mitarbeiter -in mf; (pol) Kollaborateur m

collapse [kə'læps] s (of a bridge, etc.) Einsturz m; (com) Krach m; (pathol) Zusammenbruch m, Kollaps m || intr einstürzen; (fig) zusammenbrechen

collapsible [kə'læpsɪbəl] adj zusammenklappbar

collaps'ible boat' s Faltboot n

collar ['kɑlər] s Kragen m; (of a dog) Halsband n; (of a horse) Kummet n; (mach) Ring m, Kragen m

col'larbone' s Schlüsselbein n

collate [kə'let] tr kollationieren

collateral [kə'lætərəl] adj kollateral, Seiten- || s (fin) Deckung f

collation [kə'le/ən] s Kollation f

colleague ['kɑlig] s Kollege m, Kollegin f

collect ['kɑlekt] s (eccl) Kollekte f || [kə'lekt] adj—**make a c. call** ein R-

Gespräch führen || *adv*—**call c.** ein R-Gespräch führen; **send c.** gegen Nachnahme schicken || *tr* (*money*) (ein)kassieren; (*stamps, coins*) sammeln; (*e.g., examination papers*) einsammeln; (*taxes*) abheben; (*one's thoughts*) zusammennehmen; **c. oneself** sich fassen || *intr* sich (ver)sammeln; (*pile up*) sich anhäufen

collect'ed *adj* (*works*) gesammelt; (*self-possessed*) gefaßt

collection [kə'lekʃən] *s* (*of stamps, etc.*) Sammlung *f*; (*accumulation*) Ansammlung *f*; (*of money*) Einziehung *f*; (*in a church*) Kollekte *f*; (*of mail*) Leerung *f* des Briefkastens; (*com*) Kollektion *f*

collec'tion a'gency *s* Inkassobüro *n*

collec'tion bas'ket *s* Klingelbeutel *m*

collective [kə'lektɪv] *adj* kollektiv, Sammel-, Gesamt- || *s* (*pol*) Kollektiv *n*

collec'tive bar'gaining *s* Tarifverhandlungen *pl*

collec'tive farm' *s* Kolchose *f*

collector [kə'lektər] *s* (*e.g., of stamps*) Sammler –in *mf*; (*bill collector*) Einkassierer –in *mf*; (*of taxes*) Einnehmer –in *mf*; (*of tickets*) Fahrkartenabnehmer –in *mf*

college [kalɪdʒ] *s* College *n*; (*e.g., of cardinals*) Kollegium *m*

collide [kə'laɪd] *intr* zusammenstoßen

collie [kali] *s* Collie *m*

collision [kə'lɪʒən] *s* Zusammenstoß *m*

colloquial [kə'lokwɪ-əl] *adj* umgangssprachlich, Umgangs-

colloquialism [kə'lokwɪ-ə,lɪzəm] *s* Ausdruck *m* der Umgangssprache

colloquy [kaləkwi] *s* Gespräch *n*

collusion [kə'luʒən] *s* Kollusion *f*; **be in c.** kolludieren

colon [kolən] *s* (*anat*) Dickdarm *m*; (*gram*) Doppelpunkt *m*

colonel [kʌrnəl] *s* Oberst *m*

colonial [kə'lonɪ-əl] *adj* Kolonial- || *s* Einwohner –in *mf* e–r Kolonie

colonialism [kə'lonɪ-ə,lɪzəm] *s* Kolonialismus *m*

colonize [kalə,naɪz] *tr* besiedeln

colonnade [,kalə'ned] *s* Säulengang *m*

colony [kaləni] *s* Kolonie *f*

color [kʌlər] *adj* (*film, photo, photography, slide, television*) Farb- || *s* Farbe *f*; **lend c.** to beleben; **show one's colors** sein wahres Gesicht zeigen; **the colors** die Flagge; **with flying colors** glänzend || *tr* färben; (*fig*) (schön)färben || *intr* sich verfärben; (*become red*) erröten

col'or-blind' *adj* farbenblind

col'ored *adj* farbig

col'or-fast' *adj* farbecht

colorful [kʌlərfəl] *adj* bunt, farbenreich; (*fig*) farbig

col'oring *s* Kolorit *n*, Färbung *f*

col'oring book' *s* Malbuch *n*

colorless [kʌlərlɪs] *adj* farblos

col'or ser'geant *s* Fahnenträger *m*

colossal [kə'lasəl] *adj* kolossal

colossus [kə'lasəs] *s* Koloß *m*

colt [kolt] *s* Füllen *n*

Columbus [kə'lʌmbəs] *s* Kolumbus *m*

column [kaləm] *s* Säule *f*; (*syndicated article*) Kolumne *f*; (*mil*) Kolonne *f*; (*typ*) Spalte *f*, Rubrik *f*; **c. of smoke** Rauchsäule *f*

columnist [kaləmɪst] *s* Kolumnist –in *mf*

coma [komə] *s* Koma *n*

comb [kom] *s* Kamm *m*; (*honeycomb*) Wabe *f*; (*of a rooster*) Kamm *m* || *tr* kämmen; (*an area*) absuchen

com·bat [kambæt] (*e.g., pilot, strength, unit, zone*) Kampf- || *s* Kampf *m*, Streit *m* || [kambæt], [kəm'bæt] *v* (*pret & pp* –bat[t]ed; *ger* –bat[t]ing) *tr* bekämpfen || *intr* kämpfen

combatant [kambətənt] *s* Kämpfer –in *mf*

com'bat fatigue' *s* Kriegsneurose *f*

combative [kambətɪv] *adj* streitsüchtig

comber [komər] *s* Sturzwelle *f*

combination [,kambɪ'neʃən] *s* Verbindung *f*; (*com*) Konzern *m*

combine [kambaɪn] *s* (*agr*) Mähdrescher *m*; (*com*) Interessengemeinschaft *f* || [kəm'baɪn] *tr* kombinieren, verbinden

combustible [kəm'bʌstɪbəl] *adj* (*ver*)brennbar || *s* Brennstoff *m*

combustion [kəm'bʌstʃən] *s* Verbrennung *f*

combus'tion cham'ber *s* Brennkammer *f*

combus'tion en'gine *s* Verbrennungsmaschine *f*

come [kʌm] *v* (*pret* **came** [kem]; *pp* **come**) *intr* kommen; **c. about** geschehen, sich ereignen; **c. across** (*discover*) stoßen auf (*acc*); (*said of a speech, etc.*) ankommen; **c. across with** (*coll*) blechen; **c. after** folgen (*dat*); (*fetch*) holen kommen; **c. along** mitkommen; (*coll*) vorwärtskommen; **c. apart** auseinanderfallen; **c. around** herumkommen; (*said of a special day*) wiederkehren; (*improve*) wieder zu sich kommen; (*change one's view*) von e–r Ansicht abgehen; **c. back** zurückkehren; (*recur to the mind*) wieder einfallen; **c. between** treten zwischen (*acc*); **c. by** vorbeikommen; (*acquire*) geraten an (*acc*); **c. clean** (sl) mit der Wahrheit herausrücken; **c. down** (*said of prices*) sinken; (*& fig*) herunterkommen; **c. down with** erkranken an (*dat*); **c. first** (*have priority*) zuerst an die Reihe kommen; **c. for** abholen; **c. forward** vortreten; **c. from** herkommen; (*e.g., a rich family*) stammen aus; (*e.g., school*) kommen aus; **c. in** hereinkommen; **c. in for** (coll) erhalten; **c. in second** den zweiten Platz belegen; **c. off** (*said of a button*) abgehen; (*come loose*) losgehen; (*said of an event*) verlaufen; **c. on!** los!; **c. out** herauskommen; (*said of a spot*) herausgehen; (*said of a publication*) erscheinen; **c. out against** (*or* for) sich erklären gegen (*or* für); **c. over** (*said of fear, etc.*) überlaufen; **c. to** (*amount to*) betragen; *(after fainting)* wieder zu sich kommen; **c. together** zusammenkommen; **c. true** in Erfüllung gehen; **c. up** *(occur)* vorkommen; *(said of a number)* herauskommen; *(said of plants)* aufgehen; *(in conversation)* zur Sprache kommen; *(said of a storm)* heranziehen; **c. upon** kommen auf *(acc)*; **c. up to** entsprechen *(dat)*; **for years to c.** auf Jahre hinaus; **how c.?** (coll) wieso?; **it comes easy to me** es fällt mir leicht

come'back' s Comeback *n*

comedian [kə'midɪ.ən] s Komiker *m*; (pej) Komödiant –in *mf*

comedienne [kə‚midɪ'ɛn] s Komikerin *f*

come'down' s (coll) Abstieg *m*

comedy ['kɑmədɪ] s Komödie *f*

comely ['kʌmlɪ] *adj* anmutig

come'-on' s (sl) Lockmittel *n*

comet ['kɑmɪt] s Komet *m*

comfort ['kʌmfərt] s *(solace)* Trost *m*; *(of a room, etc.)* Behaglichkeit *f*; *(person or thing that comforts)* Tröster *m*; *(bed cover)* Steppdecke *f* ‖ *tr* trösten

comfortable ['kʌmfərtəbəl] *adj* behaglich, bequem; *(income)* ausreichend; **be (or feel) c.** sich wohl fühlen

comforter ['kʌmfərtər] s Tröster *m*; *(bed cover)* Steppdecke *f*

com'forting *adj* tröstlich

com'fort sta'tion s Bedürfnisanstalt *f*

comic ['kɑmɪk] *adj* komisch ‖ s Komiker *m*; **comics** Comics *pl*, Witzblatt *n*

comical ['kɑmɪkəl] *adj* komisch

com'ic op'era s Operette *f*

com'ic strip' s Bildstreifen *m*

com'ing *adj* künftig, kommend; **c. soon** *(notice at theater)* demnächst ‖ s Kommen *n*, Ankunft *f*; **c. of age** Mündigwerden *n*

comma ['kɑmə] s Komma *n*, Beistrich *m*

command [kə'mænd] s *(order)* Befehl *m*; *(of language)* Beherrschung *f*; (mil) Kommando *n*; *(jurisdiction)* (mil) Kommandobereich *m*; **at s.o.'s c.** auf j–s Befehl; **be in c. of** (mil) das Kommando führen über *(acc)*; **have a good c. of** gut beherrschen; **take c. of** (mil) das Kommando übernehmen über *(acc)* ‖ *tr* *(a person)* befehlen *(dat)*; *(respect, silence)* gebieten; *(troops)* führen; *(a high price)* erzielen ‖ *intr* (mil) kommandieren

commandant [‚kɑmən'dænt] s Kommandant *m*

commandeer [‚kɑmən'dɪr] *tr* (coll) organisieren; (mil) requirieren

commander [kə'mændər] s Truppenführer *m*; *(of a company)* Chef *m*; *(of a military unit from battalion to corps)* Kommandeur *m*; *(of an army)* Befehlshaber *m*; (nav) Fregattenkapitän *m*

comman'der in chief' s Oberbefehlshaber *m*

command'ing *adj* *(appearance)* eindrucksvoll; *(view)* weit; *(position)*

beherrschend; *(general)* kommandierend

command'ing of'ficer s Einheitsführer *m*

commandment [kə'mændmənt] s Gebot *n*

command' post' s Befehlsstand *m*

commemorate [kə'mɛmə‚ret] *tr* gedenken *(genit)*, feiern

commemoration [kə‚mɛmə're∫ən] s Gedenkfeier *f*; **in c. of** zum Gedächtnis von

commence [kə'mɛns] *tr* & *intr* anfangen

commencement [kə'mɛnsmənt] s Anfang *m*; (educ) Schulentlassungsfeier *f*

commend [kə'mɛnd] *tr* *(praise)* (& mil) belob(ig)en; *(entrust)* empfehlen

commendable [kə'mɛndəbəl] *adj* lobenswert

commendation [‚kɑmən'de∫ən] s Belobigung *f*

comment ['kɑmənt] s Bemerkung *f*, Stellungnahme *f*; **no c.!** kein Kommentar! ‖ *intr* Bemerkungen machen; **c. on** kommentieren

commentary ['kɑmən‚tɛri] s Kommentar *m*

commentator ['kɑmən‚tetər] s Kommentator –in *mf*; *(of a text)* Erklärer –in *mf*

commerce ['kɑmərs] s Handel *m*

commercial [kə'mʌr∫əl] *adj* Handels–, Geschäfts–, kommerziell ‖ s (rad, telv) Werbesendung *f*

commer'cial art' s Gebrauchsgraphik *f*

commercialism [kə'mʌr∫ə‚lɪzəm] s Handelsgeist *m*

commercialize [kə'mʌr∫ə‚laɪz] *tr* kommerzialisieren

commiserate [kə'mɪzə‚ret] *intr*—**c. with** bemitleiden

commissar ['kɑmɪ‚sɑr] s (pol) Kommissar *m*

commissary ['kɑmɪ‚sɛri] s *(deputy)* Kommissar *m*; *(store)* Militärversorgungsstelle *f*

commission [kə'mɪ∫ən] s *(order)* Auftrag *m*; *(of a crime)* Begehung *f*; *(committee)* Kommission *f*; *(percentage)* Provision *f*; (mil) Offizierspatent *n*; **out of c.** außer Betrieb; ‖ *tr* beauftragen; *(a work)* bestellen; *(a ship)* in Dienst stellen; (mil) ein Offizierspatent verleihen *(dat)*

commis'sioned of'ficer s Offizier –in *mf*

commissioner [kə'mɪ∫ənər] s Kommissar –in *mf*

com·mit [kə'mɪt] *v* (*pret* & *pp* **–mitted**; *ger* **–mitting**) *tr* *(a crime)* begehen; *(entrust)* anvertrauen; *(give over)* übergeben; *(to an institution)* einweisen; **c. oneself** to sich festlegen auf *(acc)*; **c. to memory** auswendig lernen; **c. to writing** zu Papier bringen

commitment [kə'mɪtmənt] s *(to)* Festlegung *f* (auf *acc*); *(to an asylum)* Anstaltsüberweisung *f*

committee [kə'mɪti] s Ausschuß *m*

commode [kə'mod] s Kommode *f*

commodious [kə'modɪ-əs] *adj* geräumig

commodity [kə'madɪtɪ] *s* Ware *f*

common ['kamən] *adj* (*language, property, interest*) gemeinsam; (*general*) allgemein; (*people*) einfach; (*soldier*) gemein; (*coarse, vulgar*) gemein; (*frequent*) häufig || *s*—in c. gemeinsam

com'mon denom'inator *s* gemeinsamer Nenner *m*; **reduce to a c.** auf e-n gemeinsamen Nenner bringen

commoner ['kamənər] *s* Bürger –in *mf*

com'mon-law mar'riage *s* wilde Ehe *f*

Com'mon Mar'ket *s* Gemeinsamer Markt *m*

com'mon noun' *s* Gattungsname *m*

com'monplace' *adj* alltäglich || *s* Gemeinplatz *m*

com'mon sense' *s* gesunder Menschenverstand *m*

com'mon stock' *s* Stammaktien *pl*

commonweal ['kamən,wil] *s* Gemeinwohl *n*

com'monwealth' *s* (*republic*) Republik *f*; (*state in U.S.A.*) Bundesstaat *m*

commotion [kə'moʃən] *s* Aufruhr *m*

commune ['kamjun] *s* Kommune *f* || [kə'mjun] *intr* sich vertraulich besprechen

communicable [kə'mjunɪkəbəl] *adj* übertragbar

communicant [kə'mjunɪkənt] *s* Kommunikant –in *mf*

communicate [kə'mjunɪ,ket] *tr* mitteilen; (*a disease*) (**to**) übertragen (auf *acc*) || *intr* sich besprechen

communication [kə,mjunɪ'keʃən] *s* Mitteilung *f*; (*message*) Nachricht *f*; **communications** Nachrichtenwesen *n*; (mil) Fernmeldewesen *n*

communicative [kə'mjunɪ,ketɪv] *adj* mitteilsam

communion [kə'mjunjən] *s* Gemeinschaft *f*; (Prot) Abendmahl *n*; (R. C.) Kommunion *f*

commun'ion rail' *s* Altargitter *n*

communiqué [kə,mjunɪ'ke] *s* Kommuniqué *n*

communism ['kamjə,nɪzəm] *s* Kommunismus *m*

communist ['kamjənɪst] *s* kommunistisch || *s* Kommunist –in *mf*

community [kə'mjunɪtɪ] *s* Gemeinschaft *f*; (*people living together*) Gemeinde *f*

communize ['kamjə,naɪz] *tr* kommunistisch machen

commutation [,kamjə'teʃən] *s* (jur) Umwandlung *f*

commuta'tion tick'et *s* Zeitkarte *f*

commutator ['kamjə,tetər] *s* (elec) Kommutator *m*, Kollektor *m*

commute [kə'mjut] *tr* (jur) umwandeln || *intr* pendeln

commuter [kə'mjutər] *s* Pendler –in *mf*

commut'er train' *s* Pendelzug *m*

compact [kəm'pækt] *adj* kompakt, dicht || ['kampækt] *s* (*for cosmetics*) Kompaktdose *f*; (*agreement*) Vertrag *m*; (aut) Kompaktwagen *m*

companion [kəm'pænjən] *s* Kumpan –in *mf*; (*one who accompanies*) Begleiter –in *mf*

companionable [kəm'pænjənəbəl] *adj* gesellig

compan'ionship' *s* Gesellschaft *f*

compan'ionway' *s* Kajütstreppe *f*

company ['kampənɪ] *s* (*companions*) Umgang *m*; (& com) Gesellschaft *f*; (mil) Kompanie *f*; (theat) Truppe *f*; **keep c. with** verkehren mit; **keep s.o. c.** j–m Gesellschaft leisten

com'pany command'er *s* Kompaniechef *m*

comparable ['kampərəbəl] *adj* vergleichbar

comparative [kəm'pærətɪv] *adv* vergleichend; (gram) komparativ || *s* (gram) Komparativ *m*

comparatively [kəm'pærətɪvlɪ] *adv* verhältnismäßig

compare [kəm'per] *s*—**beyond c.** unvergleichlich || *tr* (**with, to**) vergleichen (mit); (gram) steigern; **as compared with** im Vergleich zu

comparison [kəm'pærɪsən] *s* Vergleich *m*; (gram) Steigerung *f*

compartment [kəm'partmənt] *s* Fach *n*; (rr) Abteil *n*

compass ['kʌmpəs] *s* Kompaß *m*; (geom) Zirkel *m*; **within the c. of** innerhalb (*genit*)

com'pass card' *s* Kompaßrose *f*

compassion [kəm'pæʃən] *s* Mitleid *n*

compassionate [kəm'pæʃənɪt] *adj* mitleidig

compatible [kəm'pætɪbəl] *adj* vereinbar

compel [kəm'pel] *v* (*pret & pp* –**pelled**; *ger* –**pelling**) *tr* zwingen, nötigen

compendious [kəm'pendɪ-əs] *adj* gedrängt

compendium [kəm'pendɪ-əm] *s* (–**ums** & –**a** [ə]) Abriß *m*, Kompendium *n*

compensate ['kampən,set] *tr* entschädigen || *intr*—**c. for** Ersatz leisten (or bieten) für

compensation [,kampən'seʃən] *s* (*for damages*) Entschädigung *f*; (*remuneration*) Entgeld *n*

compete [kəm'pit] *intr* (**with**) konkurrieren (mit); (**for**) sich mitbewerben (um); (sport) am Wettkampf teilnehmen

competence ['kampɪtəns] *s* (*mental state*) Zurechnungsfähigkeit *f*; (*ability*) (**in**) Fähigkeit *f* (zu)

competent ['kampɪtənt] *adj* (*able*) fähig, tüchtig; (*witness*) zulässig

competition [,kampɪ'tɪʃən] *s* Wettbewerb *m*; (com) Konkurrenz *f*; (sport) Wettkampf *m*

competitive [kəm'petɪtɪv] *adj* (*bidding*) Konkurrenz–; (*prices*) konkurrenzfähig; (*person*) ehrgeizig; (*exam*) Auslese–

competitor [kəm'petɪtər] *s* Mitbewerber –in *mf*; (com) Konkurrent –in *mf*; (sport) Wettkämpfer –in *mf*

compilation [,kampɪ'leʃən] *s* Zusammenstellung *f*; (*book*) Sammelwerk *n*

compile [kəm'paɪl] *tr* zusammenstellen, kompilieren; (*Material*) zusammentragen

complacence [kəm'pleɪsəns], **complacency** [kəm'pleɪsns] *s* Selbstgefälligkeit *f*

complacent [kəm'pleɪsnt] *adj* selbstgefällig

complain [kəm'pleɪn] *intr* klagen; **c. to s.o. about** sich bei j-m beklagen über (*acc*)

complaint [kəm'pleɪnt] *s* Klage *f*; (*ailment*) Beschwerde *f*

complement ['kamplɪmənt] *s* (& *gram*) Ergänzung *f*; (*geom*) Komplement *n*; (nav) Bemannung *f* || ['kamplɪ,ment] *tr* ergänzen

complete [kəm'plit] *adj* ganz, vollkommen, vollständig; (*works*) sämtlich || *tr* (*make whole*) vervollständigen; (*make perfect*) vollenden; (*finish*) beenden; (*a job*) erledigen

completely [kəm'plitlɪ] *adv* völlig

completion [kəm'pliʃən] *s* Vollendung *f*

complex [kəm'pleks], ['kampleks] *adj* verwickelt || ['kampleks] *s* Komplex *m*

complexion [kəm'plekʃən] *s* Gesichtsfarbe *f*; (*appearance*) Aussehen *n*

complexity [kəm'pleksɪtɪ] *s* Kompliziertheit *f*

compliance [kəm'plaɪəns] *s* Einwilligung *f*; **in c. with your wishes** Ihren Wünschen gemäß

complicate ['kamplɪ,ket] *tr* komplizieren

com'plicat'ed *adj* kompliziert

complication [,kamplɪ'keʃən] *s* Verwicklung *f*; (& *pathol*) Komplikation *f*

complicity [kəm'plɪsɪtɪ] *s* (in) Mitschuld *f* (an *dat*)

compliment ['kamplɪmənt] *s* Kompliment *n*; (*praise*) Lob *n*; **compliments** Empfehlungen *pl*; **pay s.o. a (high) c.** j-m ein (großes) Lob spenden || *tr* (**on**) beglückwünschen (zu)

complimentary [,kamplɪ'mentərɪ] *adj* (*remark*) schmeichelhaft; (*free*) Frei-

com'ply [kəm'plaɪ] *v* (*pret* & *pp* **-plied**) *intr* sich fügen; **c. with** einwilligen in (*acc*); **c. with the rules** sich an die Vorschriften halten

component [kəm'ponənt] *adj* Teil- || *s* Bestandteil *m*; (math, phys) Komponente *f*

compose [kəm'poz] *tr* (*writings*) verfassen; (*a sentence*) bilden; (mus) komponieren; (typ) setzen; **be composed of** bestehen aus; **c. oneself** sich fassen

composed' *adj* ruhig, gefaßt

composer [kəm'pozər] *s* Verfasser –in *mf*; (mus) Komponist –in *mf*

composite [kəm'pazɪt] *adj* zusammengesetzt || *s* Zusammensetzung *f*

composition [,kampə'zɪʃən] *s* (chem) Zusammensetzung *f*; (*educ*) Aufsatz *m*; (mus, paint) Komposition *f*; (typ) Schriftsatz *m*

composi'tion book' *s* Übungsheft *n*

compositor [kəm'pazɪtər] *s* Setzer –in *mf*

composure [kəm'poʒər] *s* Fassung *f*

compote ['kampot] *s* (*stewed fruit*) Kompott *n*; (*dish*) Kompottschale *f*

compound ['kampaund] *adj* zusammengesetzt; (*fracture*) kompliziert || *s* Zusammensetzung *f*; (*enclosure*) umzäumtes Gelände *n*; (chem) Verbindung *f*; (gram) Kompositum *n*; (mil) Truppenlager *n* || [kam'paund] *tr* zusammensetzen

com'pound in'terest *s* Zinseszinsen *pl*

comprehend [,kamprɪ'hend] *tr* auffassen

comprehensible [,kamprɪ'hensɪbəl] *adj* faßlich, begreiflich

comprehension [,kamprɪ'henʃən] *s* Auffassung *f*; (*ability to understand*) Fassungskraft *f*

comprehensive [,kamprɪ'hensɪv] *adj* umfassend

compress ['kampres] *s* (med) Kompresse *f* || [kəm'pres] *tr* komprimieren

compressed' *adj* komprimiert; (*air*) Druck–; (fig) gedrängt

compression [kəm'preʃən] *s* Kompression *f*, Druck *m*

comprise [kəm'praɪz] *tr* umfassen; **be comprised of** bestehen aus

compromise ['kamprə,maɪz] *s* Kompromiß *m* || *tr* kompromittieren; (*principles*) preisgeben || *intr* (**on**) e–n Kompromiß schließen (über *acc*)

comptroller [kən'trolər] *s* Rechnungsprüfer *m*

compulsion [kəm'pʌlʃən] *s* Zwang *m*

compulsive [kəm'pʌlsɪv] *adj* triebhaft

compulsory [kəm'pʌlsərɪ] *adj* obligatorisch, Zwangs–; **c. military service** allgemeine Wehrpflicht *f*

compute [kəm'pjut] *tr* berechnen || *intr* rechnen

computer [kəm'pjutər] *s* Computer *m*

comput'er lan'guage *s* Maschinensprache *f*

comrade ['kamræd] *s* Kamerad *m*

con [kan] *v* (*pret* & *pp* **conned; ger conning**) *tr* beschwindeln

concave [kan'kev] *adj* konkav

conceal [kən'sil] *tr* verheimlichen

concealment [kən'silmənt] *s* Verheimlichung *f*; (*place*) Versteck *n*

concede [kən'sid] *tr* zugestehen, zubilligen; **c. victory** (pol) den Wahlsieg überlassen || *intr* nachgeben

conceit [kən'sit] *s* (*vanity*) Einbildung *f*, Dünkel *m*; (*witty expression*) Witz *m*

conceit'ed *adj* eingebildet

conceivable [kən'sivəbəl] *adj* denkbar

conceive [kən'siv] *tr* begreifen; (*a desire*) hegen; (*a child*) empfangen

concentrate ['kansən,tret] *tr* konzentrieren; (*troops*) zusammenziehen || *intr* (**on**) sich konzentrieren (auf *acc*); (*gather*) sich sammeln

concentration [,kansən'treʃən] *s* Konzentration *f*

concentric [kən'sentrɪk] *adj* konzentrisch

concept ['kansept] *s* Begriff *m*

conception [kən'sɛpʃən] s (*idea*) Vorstellung *f*; (*design*) Entwurf *m*; (biol) Empfängnis *f*

concern [kən'sʌrn] s (*worry*) Besorgnis *f*; (*matter*) Angelegenheit *f*; (com) Firma *f*; **that is no c. of mine** das geht mich nichts an || *tr* betreffen, angehen; **as far as I am concerned** von mir aus; **c. oneself about** sich bekümmern um; **c. oneself with** sich befassen mit; **to whom it may c.** Bescheinigung

concern'ing *prep* betreffend (*acc*), betreffs (*genit*), über (*acc*)

concert ['kɑnsərt] s (mus) Konzert *n*; **in c. (with)** im Einvernehmen (mit) || [kən'sʌrt] *tr* zusammenfassen

concession [kən'sɛʃən] s Konzession *f*

conciliate [kən'sɪlɪ,et] *tr* versöhnen

conciliatory [kən'sɪlɪ-ə,tori] *adj* versöhnlich

concise [kən'saɪs] *adj* kurz, bündig

conclude [kən'klud] *tr* schließen; **c. from s.th. that** aus etw schließen, daß; **to be concluded** Schluß folgt || *intr* (**with**) schließen (mit)

conclusion [kən'kluʒən] s Schluß *m*; **draw conclusions from** Schlüsse ziehen aus; **in c.** zum Schluß; **jump at conclusions** voreilige Schlüsse ziehen

conclusive [kən'klusɪv] *adj* (*decisive*) entscheidend; (*proof*) schlagkräftig

concoct [kən'kɑkt] *tr* (*brew*) zusammenbrauen; (*plans*) schmieden

concoction [kən'kɑkʃən] s Gebräu *n*

concomitant [kən'kɑmɪtənt] *adj* begleitend || s Begleitumstand *m*

concord ['kɑnkɔrd] s Eintracht *f*

concordance [kən'kɔrdəns] s Übereinstimmung *f*; (*book*) Konkordanz *f*

concourse ['kɑnkors] s (*of people*) Zusammenlaufen *n*, Anlauf *m*; (*of rivers*) Zusammenfluß *m*; (rr) Bahnhofshalle *f*

concrete ['kɑnkrit], [kɑn'krit] *adj* (*not abstract*) konkret; (*solid*) fest; (*evidence*) schlüssig; (*of concrete*) Beton–; (math) benannt || s Beton *m* || *tr* betonieren

con'crete block' s Betonblock *m*

con'crete noun' s Konkretum *n*

concubine ['kɑŋkjə,baɪn] s Nebenfrau *f*; (*mistress*) Konkubine *f*

con·cur [kən'kʌr] *v* (*pret & pp* **–curred;** *ger* **–curring**) *intr* (*agree*) übereinstimmen; (*coincide*) (**with**) zusammenfallen (mit); **c. in** (an *opinion*) beistimmen (*dat*)

concurrence [kən'kʌrəns] s (*agreement*) Einverständis *n*; (*coincidence*) Zusammentreffen *n*; (geom) Schnittpunkt *m*

condemn [kən'dɛm] *tr* verdammen; (& jur) verurteilen; (*a building*) für unbewohnlich erklären

condemnation [,kɑndɛm'neʃən] s Verurteilung *f*; (*of a building, ship, plane*) Untauglichkeitserklärung *f*

condense [kən'dɛns] *tr* (*make thicker*) verdichten; (*writing*) zusammendrängen; || *intr* kondensieren

condenser [kən'dɛnsər] s Kondensator *m*

condescend [,kɑndɪ'sɛnd] *intr* sich herablassen

condescend'ing *adj* herablassend

condescension [,kɑndɪ'sɛnʃən] s Herablassung *f*

condiment ['kɑndɪmənt] s Würze *f*

condition [kən'dɪʃən] s (*state*) Zustand *m*; (*state of health*) Verfassung *f*; (*stipulation*) Bedingung *f*; **conditions** (*e.g. for working; of the weather*) Verhältnisse *pl*; **on c. that** unter der Bedingung, daß || *tr* (*impose stipulations on*) bedingen; (*accustom*) (**to**) gewöhnen (an *acc*); (sport) in Form bringen

conditional [kən'dɪʃənəl] *adj* bedingt

condi'tional clause' s Bedingungssatz *m*

conditionally [kən'dɪʃənəli] *adv* bedingungsweise

condole [kən'dol] *intr* (**with**) kondolieren (*dat*)

condolence [kən'doləns] s Beileid *n*

condom ['kɑndəm] s Präservativ *n*

condominium [,kɑndə'mɪnɪ-əm] s Eigentumswohnung *f*

condone [kən'don] *tr* verzeihen

conducive [kən'd(j)usɪv] *adj*—**c. to** förderlich (*dat*)

conduct ['kɑndʌkt] s (*behavior*) Betragen *n*; (*guidance*) Führung *f* || [kən'dʌkt] *tr* (*business, a campaign, a tour*) führen; (elec, phys) leiten; (mus) dirigieren; **c. oneself** sich betragen || *intr* (mus) dirigieren

conductor [kən'dʌktər] s (elec, phys) Leiter *m*; (mus) Dirigent *m*; (rr) Schaffner *m*

conduit ['kɑnd(u)ɪt] s Röhre *f*; (elec) Isolierrohr *n*

cone [kon] s (*ice cream cone; paper cone*) Tüte *f*; (bot) Zapfen *m*; (geom) Kegel *m*, Konus *m*

confection [kən'fɛkʃən] s Konfekt *n*

confectioner [kən'fɛkʃənər] s Zuckerbäcker –*in mf*

confec'tioner's sug'ar s Puderzucker *m*

confectionery [kən'fɛkʃə,nɛri] s (*shop*) Konditorei *f*; (*sweets*) Zuckerwerk *n*

confederacy [kən'fɛdərəsi] s Bündnis *n*; (*conspiracy*) Verschwörung *f*

confederate [kən'fɛdərɪt] *adj* verbündet || s Bundesgenosse *m*, Bundesgenossin *f*; (*accomplice*) Helfershelfer –*in mf* || [kən'fɛdə,ret] *tr* verbünden || *intr* sich verbünden

confederation [kən,fɛdə'reʃən] s Bund *m*

con·fer [kən'fʌr] *v* (*pret & pp* **–ferred;** *ger* **–ferring**) *tr* (*on, upon*) verleihen (*dat*) || *intr* sich besprechen, konferieren

conference ['kɑnfərəns] s Konferenz *f*; (sport) Verband *m*

con'ference call' s Sammelverbindung *f*

confess [kən'fɛs] *tr* (ein)gestehen, bekennen; (*sins*) beichten || *intr* gestehen

confession [kən'fɛʃən] s Geständnis *n*, Bekenntnis *n*; (*of sins*) Beichte *f*; **go to c.** beichten

confessional [kən'fɛʃənəl] s Beicht-
stuhl m
confes'sion of faith' s Glaubensbekenntnis n
confessor [kən'fɛsər] s Beichtvater m
confidant [,kɑnfrɪ'dænt] s Vertraute
mf
confide [kən'faɪd] tr (to) anvertrauen
(dat) || intr—c. in vertrauen (dat)
confidence ['kɑnfɪdəns] s (trust) (in)
Vertrauen n (auf acc, zu); (assurance) Zuversicht f; in c. im Vertrauen
con'fidence man' s Bauernfänger m
confident ['kɑnfɪdənt] adj zuversichtlich; be c. of sich [dat] sicher sein
(genit)
confidential [,kɑnfɪ'dɛnʃəl] adj vertraulich
confine ['kɑnfaɪn] s—the confines die
Grenzen pl || tr [kən'faɪn] tr (limit)
(to) beschränken (auf acc); (shut in)
einsperren; be confined (in pregnancy) niederkommen; be confined
to bed bettlägerig sein
confinement [kən'faɪnmənt] s Beschränkung f; (arrest) Haft f; (childbirth) Niederkunft f
confirm [kən'fʌrm] tr bestätigen;
(Prot) konfirmieren; (R.C.) firmen;
confirm in writing verbriefen
confirmation [,kɑnfər'meʃən] s Bestätigung f; (Prot) Konfirmation f;
(R.C.) Firmung f
confirmed' adj (e.g., report) bestätigt;
(inveterate) unverbesserlich; c. bachelor Hagestolz m
confiscate ['kɑnfɪs,ket] tr beschlagnahmen, konfiszieren
confiscation [,kɑnfɪs'keʃən] s Beschlagnahme f
conflagration [,kɑnflə'greʃən] s Brand
m, Feuerbrunst f
conflict ['kɑnflɪkt] s (of interests, of
evidence) Konflikt m; (fight) Zu-
sammenstoß m || [kən'flɪkt] intr
(with) im Widerspruch stehen (zu)
conflict'ing adj einander widerspre-
chend
con'flict of in'terest s Interessenkon-
flikt m, Interessenkollision f
confluence ['kɑnflu·əns] s Zusammenfluß m
conform [kən'form] tr anpassen || intr
übereinstimmen; (to) sich anpassen
(dat)
conformity [kən'formɪti] s (adaptation) (to) Anpassung f (an acc);
(agreement) (with) Übereinstimmung
f (mit)
confound [kən'faʊnd] tr (perplex) verblüffen; (throw into confusion) verwirren; (erroneously identify) (with)
verwechseln (mit) || ['kɑn'faʊnd]
tr—c. it! zum Donnerwetter!
confound'ed adj (coll) verwünscht
confrere ['kɑnfrer] s Kollege m
confront [kən'frʌnt] tr (face) gegenüberstehen (dat); (a problem, an
enemy) entgegentreten (dat); be
confronted with gegenüberstehen
(dat); c. s.o. with j-n konfrontieren
mit

confrontation [,kɑnfrən'teʃən] s Konfrontation f; (of witnesses) Gegen-
überstellung f
confuse [kən'fjuz] tr (e.g., names)
verwechseln; (persons) verwirren
confused' adj konfus, verwirrt, wirr
confusion [kən'fjuʒən] s Verwechslung f; (disorder, chaos) Verwirrung
f
confute [kən'fjut] tr widerlegen
congeal [kən'dʒil] tr erstarren lassen
|| intr erstarren
congenial [kən'dʒinjəl] adj (person)
sympathisch; (surroundings) angenehm
congenital [kən'dʒenɪtəl] adj angeboren
congen'ital de'fect s Geburtsfehler m
congest [kən'dʒest] tr überfüllen
congest'ed adj überfüllt; (area) übervölkert; (with traffic) verkehrsreich
congestion [kən'dʒestʃən] s Über-
füllung f; (of traffic) Verkehrsstockung f; (of population) Übervölkerung f; (pathol) Blutandrang m
congratulate [kən'grætʃə,let] tr gratulieren (dat); c. s.o. on j-m gratulieren zu
congratulations [kən,grætʃə'leʃənz]
spl Glückwunsch m; c.! ich gratuliere!
congregate ['kɑŋgrɪ,get] intr sich
(ver)sammeln, zusammenkommen
congregation [,kɑŋgrɪ'geʃən] s Versammlung f; (eccl) Gemeinde f
congress ['kɑŋgres] s Kongreß m
congressional [kən'greʃənəl] adj Kon-
greß-
congress·man ['kɑŋgrɪsmən] s (-men)
Abgeordnete m
con'gress-wom'an s (-wom'en) Abgeordnete f
congruent ['kɑŋgru·ənt] adj kongruent
conical ['kɑnɪkəl] adj kegelförmig
conjecture [kən'dʒektʃər] s Vermutung
f, Mutmaßung f || tr & intr vermuten
conjugal ['kɑndʒəgəl] adj ehelich
conjugate ['kɑndʒə,get] tr abwandeln
conjugation [,kɑndʒə'geʃən] s Ab-
wandlung f
conjunction [kən'dʒʌŋkʃən] s Binde-
wort n; in c. with in Verbindung mit
conjure [kən'dʒur] tr (appeal solemn-
ly to) beschwören || ['kɑndʒər] tr—
c. away wegzaubern; c. up heraufbeschwören
conk [kɑŋk] tr (sl) hauen || intr—c.
out (sl) versagen
connect [kə'nekt] tr verbinden; (&
fig) verknüpfen; (elec) (to) anschließen (an acc); (telp) (with) verbinden
(mit) || intr verbunden sein; (said of
trains, etc.) (with) Anschluß haben
(an acc); (box) treffen
connect'ing adj Verbindungs-, Binde-
(trains, buses) Anschluß-; (rooms)
mit Zwischentür
connect'ing rod' s Schubstange f
connection [kə'nekʃən] s (e.g., of a
pipe) Verbindung f; (of ideas) Ver-
knüpfung f; (context) Zusammenhang m; (part that connects) Ver-
bindungsteil m; (elec) Schaltung f;

(mach, rr, telp) Verbindung *f*; **con-nections** Beziehungen *pl*; **in c. with** in Zusammenhang mit

con'ning tow'er [ˈkɑnɪŋ] *s* Kommandoturm *m*

connive [kəˈnaɪv] *intr*—**c. at** ein Auge zudrücken bei; **c. with** im geheimen Einverständnis stehen mit

connotation [ˌkɑnoˈteʃən] *s* Nebenbedeutung *f*

connote [kəˈnot] *tr* mitbezeichnen

conquer [ˈkɑŋkər] *tr* (*win in war*) erobern; (*overcome*) überwinden

conquerer [ˈkɑŋkərər] *s* Eroberer *m*

conquest [ˈkɑŋkwest] *s* Eroberung *f*

conscience [ˈkɑnʃəns] *s* Gewissen *n*

conscientious [ˌkɑnʃɪˈenʃəs] *adj* gewissenhaft, pflichtbewußt

conscien'tious objec'tor [əbˈdʒektər] *s* Wehrdienstverweigerer *m*

conscious [ˈkɑnʃəs] *adj* bei Bewußtsein; **c. of** bewußt (*genit*)

consciousness [ˈkɑnʃəsnɪs] *s* Bewußtsein *n*; (*awareness*) (**of**) Kenntnis *f* (*genit* or von); **regain c.** wieder zu sich kommen

conscript [ˈkɑnskrɪpt] *s* Dienstpflichtige *m*; (*mil*) Wehrdienstpflichtige *m* ‖ [kɑnˈskrɪpt] *tr* ausheben

conscription [kɑnˈskrɪpʃən] *s* Dienstpflicht *f*; (*draft*) Aushebung *f*

consecrate [ˈkɑnsɪˌkret] *tr* weihen

consecration [ˌkɑnsɪˈkreʃən] *s* Einweihung *f*; (*at Mass*) Wandlung *f*

consecutive [kɑnˈsekjətɪv] *adj* aufeinanderfolgend

consensus [kɑnˈsensəs] *s* allgemeine Übereinstimmung *f*; **the c. of opinion** die übereinstimmende Meinung

consent [kɑnˈsent] *s* Zustimmung *f*; **by common c.** mit allgemeiner Zustimmung ‖ *intr* zustimmen; **c. to** (*inf*) sich bereit erklären zu (*inf*)

consequence [ˈkɑnsɪˌkwens] *s* Folge *f*; (*influence*) Einfluß *m*; **in c. of** infolge (*genit*); **it is of no c.** es hat nichts auf sich; **suffer the consequences** die Folgen tragen

consequently [ˈkɑnsɪˌkwentli] *adv* folglich, infolgedessen, mithin

conservation [ˌkɑnsərˈveʃən] *s* Bewahrung *f*; (*of energy, etc.*) Erhaltung *f*; (*supervision of natural resources*) Naturschutz *m*; (*ecology*) Umweltschutz *m*

conservatism [kɑnˈsɑrvəˌtɪzəm] *s* Konservatismus *m*

conservative [kɑnˈsɑrvətɪv] *adj* konservativ; (*estimate*) vorsichtig ‖ *s* Konservative *mf*

conservatory [kɑnˈsɑrvəˌtori] *s* Treibhaus *n*; (*mus*) Konservatorium *n*

conserve [kɑnˈsɑrv] *tr* sparsam umgehen mit

consider [kɑnˈsɪdər] *tr* (*take into account*) berücksichtigen; (*show consideration for*) Rücksicht nehmen auf (*acc*); (*reflect on*) sich [*dat*] überlegen; (*regard as*) halten für, betrachten als; **all things considered** alles in allem

considerable [kɑnˈsɪdərəbəl] *adj* beträchtlich, erheblich

considerate [kɑnˈsɪdərɪt] *adj* (**towards**) rücksichtsvoll (**gegen**)

consideration [kɑnˌsɪdəˈreʃən] *s* (*taking into account*) Berücksichtigung *f*; (*regard*) (**for**) Rücksicht *f* (auf *acc*); **be an important c.** e-e wichtige Rolle spielen; **be under c.** in Betracht gezogen werden; **for a c.** entgeltlich; **in c. of** in Anbetracht (*genit*); **take into c.** in Betracht ziehen; **with c.** rücksichtsvoll

consid'ering *adv* (coll) den Umständen nach ‖ *prep* in Anbetracht (*genit*)

consign [kɑnˈsaɪn] *tr* (*ship*) versenden; (*address*) adressieren

consignee [ˌkɑnsaɪˈni] *s* Adressat –in *mf*

consignment [kɑnˈsaɪnmənt] *s* (*act of sending*) Versand *m*; (*merchandise sent*) Sendung *f*; **on c.** in Kommission

consist [kɑnˈsɪst] *intr*—**c. in** bestehen in (*dat*); **c. of** bestehen aus

consistency [kɑnˈsɪstənsi] *s* Konsequenz *f*; (*firmness*) Festigkeit *f*; (*viscosity*) Dickflüssigkeit *f*; (*agreement*) Übereinstimmung *f*; (*steadfastness*) (**in**) Beständigkeit *f* (in *dat*)

consistent [kɑnˈsɪstənt] *adj* (*performer*) stetig; (*performance*) gleichmäßig; (*free from contradiction*) konsequent; **c. with** in Übereinstimmung mit

consistory [kɑnˈsɪstəri] *s* Konsistorium *n*

consolation [ˌkɑnsəˈleʃən] *s* Trost *m*

console [ˈkɑnsol] *s* (*for radio or record player*) Musiktruhe *f*; (*of an organ*) Spieltisch *m*; (*television*) Fernsehtruhe *f* ‖ [kɑnˈsol] *tr* trösten

consolidate [kɑnˈsɑlɪˌdet] *tr* (*a position*) festigen; (*debts*) konsolidieren; (*combine*) zusammenlegen

consonant [ˈkɑnsənənt] *adj* (**with**) im Einklang (mit) ‖ *s* Mitlaut *m*

consort [ˈkɑnsort] *s* (*male*) Gemahl *m*; (*female*) Gemahlin *f* ‖ [kɑnˈsort] *intr* (**with**) Umgang haben (mit)

consorti·um [kɑnˈsortɪ·əm] *s* (**–a** [ə]) Konsortium *n*

conspicuous [kɑnˈspɪkju·əs] *adj* auffallend, auffällig; **c. for** bemerkenswert wegen

conspiracy [kɑnˈspɪrəsi] *s* Verschwörung *f*

conspirator [kɑnˈspɪrətər] *s* Verschwörer –in *mf*

conspire [kɑnˈspaɪr] *intr* sich verschwören

constable [ˈkɑnstəbəl] *s* Gendarm *m*

constancy [ˈkɑnstənsi] *s* Beständigkeit *f*

constant [ˈkɑnstənt] *adj* (*continuous*) dauernd, ständig; (*faithful*) treu; (*resolute*) standhaft; (*element, time element*) fest; (fig & tech) konstant ‖ *s* (math, phys) Konstante *f*

constantly [ˈkɑnstəntli] *adv* immerfort

constellation [ˌkɑnstəˈleʃən] *s* Sternbild *n*

consternation [ˌkɑnstərˈneʃən] *s* Bestürzung *f*

constipate ['kɑnstɪ,pet] *tr* verstopfen
constipation [,kɑnstɪ'peʃən] *s* Verstopfung *f*
constituency [kən'stɪt/ʊ·ənsi] *s* Wählerschaft *f*
constituent [kən'stɪt/ʊ·ənt] *adj* wesentlich; **c. part** Bestandteil *m* ‖ *s* Komponente *f*; (pol) Wähler –in *mf*
constitute ['kɑnstɪ,t(j)ut] *tr* (*make up*) ausmachen, bilden; (*found*) gründen
constitution [,kɑnstɪ't(j)uʃən] *s* (*of a country or organization*) Verfassung *f*; (*bodily condition*) Konstitution *f*; (*composition*) Zusammensetzung *f*
constitutional [,kɑnstɪ't(j)uʃənəl] *adj* (*according to a constitution*) konstitutionell; (*crisis, amendment, etc.*) Verfassungs-
constrain [kən'stren] *tr* zwingen
constraint [kən'strent] *s* Zwang *m*; (jur) Nötigung *f*
constrict [kən'strɪkt] *tr* zusammenziehen
construct [kən'strʌkt] *tr* errichten; (eng, geom, gram) konstruieren
construction [kən'strʌkʃən] *s* (*act of building*) Errichtung *f*; (*manner of building*) Bauweise *f*; (*interpretation*) Auslegung *f*; (eng, geom, gram) Konstruktion *f*; **under c.** im Bau
constructive [kən'strʌktɪv] *adj* konstruktiv
construe [kən'stru] *tr* (*interpret*) auslegen; (gram) konstruieren
consul ['kɑnsəl] *s* Konsul *m*
consular ['kɑns(j)ələr] *adj* konsularisch
consulate ['kɑns(j)əlɪt] *s* Konsulat *n*
con'sul gen'eral *s* Generalkonsul *m*
consult [kən'sʌlt] *tr* konsultieren, um Rat fragen; (*a book*) nachschlagen ‖ *intr*—**c. with** sich beraten mit
consultant [kən'sʌltənt] *s* Berater –in *mf*
consultation [,kɑnsəl'teʃən] *s* Beratung *f*; (& med) Konsultation *f*
consume [kən's(j)um] *tr* verzehren; (*use up*) verbrauchen; (*time*) beanspruchen
consumer [kən's(j)umər] *s* Konsument –in *mf*, Verbraucher –in *mf*
consum'er goods' *spl* Konsumgüter *pl*
consummate [kən'sʌmɪt] *adj* vollendet; (pej) abgefeimt ‖ ['kɑnsə,met] *tr* vollziehen
consumption [kən'sʌmpʃən] *s* (*of food*) Verzehr *m*; (econ) (**of**) Verbrauch *m* (**an** *dat*); (pathol) Schwindsucht *f*
consumptive [kə'sʌmptɪv] *adj* schwindsüchtig ‖ *s* Schwindsüchtige *mf*
contact ['kɑntækt] *s* Kontakt *m*, Berührung *f*; (fig) (**with**) Verbindung *f* (mit); (elec) Kontakt *m* ‖ *tr* (coll) sich in Verbindung setzen mit
con'tact lens' *s* Haftschale *f*
contagion [kən'tedʒən] *s* Ansteckung *f*
contagious [kən'tedʒəs] *adj* ansteckend
contain [kən'ten] *tr* enthalten; (*an*

enemy) aufhalten; (*one's feelings*) verhalten; **c. oneself** sich beherrschen
container [kən'tenər] *s* Behälter *m*
containment [kən'tenmənt] *s* (mil, pol) Eindämmung *f*
contaminate [kən'tæmɪ,net] *tr* verunreinigen; (fig) vergiften
contamination [kən,tæmɪ'neʃən] *s* Verunreinigung *f*; (fig) Vergiftung *f*
contemplate ['kɑntəm,plet] *tr* betrachten; (*intend*) beabsichtigen ‖ *intr* nachdenken
contemplation [,kɑntəm'pleʃən] *s* Betrachtung *f*; (*consideration*) Erwägung *f*
contemporaneous [kən,tempə'renɪ·əs] *adj* (**with**) gleichzeitig (mit)
contemporary [kən'tempə,reri] *adj* zeitgenössisch; (*modern*) modern ‖ *s* Zeitgenosse *m*, Zeitgenossin *f*
contempt [kən'tempt] *s* Verachtung *f*; **beneath c.** unter aller Kritik
contemptible [kən'temptɪbəl] *adj* verachtungswürdig
contempt' of court' *s* Mißachtung *f* des Gerichtes
contemptuous [kən'tempt/ʊ·əs] *adj* verachtungsvoll, verächtlich
contend [kən'tend] *tr* behaupten ‖ *intr* (**for**) sich bewerben (um); (**with**) kämpfen (mit)
contender [kən'tendər] *s* (**for**) Bewerber –in *mf* (um)
content [kən'tent] *adj* (**with**) zufrieden (mit); **c. to** (*inf*) bereit zu (*inf*) ‖ *s* Zufriedenheit *f*; **to one's heart's c.** nach Herzenslust ‖ ['kɑntənt] *s* Inhalt *m*; (chem) Gehalt *m*; **contents** Inhalt *m* ‖ [kən'tent] *tr* zufriedenstellen; **c. oneself with** sich begnügen mit
content'ed *adj* zufrieden
contention [kən'tenʃən] *s* (*strife*) Streit *m*; (*assertion*) Behauptung *f*
contest ['kɑntest] *s* (**for**) Wettkampf *m* (um); (*written competition*) Preisausschreiben *n* ‖ [kən'test] *tr* (*argue against*) bestreiten; (*a will*) anfechten; (mil) kämpfen um; **contested** umstritten
contestant [kən'testənt] *s* Bewerber –in *mf*; (sport) Wettkämpfer –in *mf*
context ['kɑntekst] *s* Zusammenhang *m*
contiguous [kən'tɪgjʊ·əs] *adj* einander berührend; (**to**) angrenzend (**an** *acc*)
continence ['kɑntɪnəns] *s* Enthaltsamkeit *f*
continent ['kɑntɪnənt] *adj* enthaltsam ‖ *s* Kontinent *m*
continental [,kɑntɪ'nentəl] *adj* kontinental, Kontinental-
contingency [kən'tɪndʒənsi] *s* Zufall *m*
contingent [kən'tɪndʒənt] *adj* (**upon**) abhängig (von) ‖ *s* (mil) Kontingent *n*
continual [kən'tɪnjʊ·əl] *adj* immer wiederkehrend
continuation [kən,tɪnju'eʃən] *s* Fortsetzung *f*; (*continued existence*) Fortdauer *f*
continue [kən'tɪnju] *tr* fortsetzen; **c.**

to (*inf*) fortfahren zu (*inf*); weiter-, e.g., **c. to read** weiterlesen; **to be continued** Fortsetzung folgt ‖ *intr* fortfahren; (*said of things*) anhalten

continuity [ˌkɑntɪ'n(j)u·ɪti] *s* Stetigkeit *f*

continuous [kən'tɪnju·əs] *adj* ununterbrochen, anhaltend

contortion [kən'tɔrʃən] *s* Verzerrung *f*

contour ['kɑntʊr] *s* Kontur *f*

con'tour line' *s* Schichtlinie *f*

con'tour map' *s* Landkarte *f* mit Schichtlinien

contraband ['kɑntrəˌbænd] *adj* Schmuggel- ‖ *s* Konterbande *f*, Schmuggelware *f*

contraceptive [ˌkɑntrə'sɛptɪv] *adj* empfängnisverhütend ‖ *s* Empfängnisverhütungsmittel *n*

contract ['kɑntrækt] *s* Vertrag *m*, Kontrakt *m*; (*order*) Auftrag *m* ‖ [kən'trækt] *tr* (*marriage*) (ab)schließen; (*a disease*) sich [*dat*] zuziehen; (e.g., *a muscle*) zusammenziehen; (*debts*) geraten in (*acc*); (ling) kontrahieren ‖ *intr* (*shrink*) sich zusammenziehen; **c. to** (*inf*) sich vertraglich verpflichten zu (*inf*)

contract'ing *adj* vertragsschließend

contraction [kən'trækʃən] *s* (& ling) Zusammenziehung *f*, Kontraktion *f*; (*contracted word*) Verkürzung *f*

contractor ['kɑntræktər] *s* (*supplier*) Lieferant *m*; (*builder*) Bauunternehmer *m*

contradict [ˌkɑntrə'dɪkt] *tr* widersprechen (*dat*)

contradiction [ˌkɑntrə'dɪkʃən] *s* Widerspruch *m*

contradictory [ˌkɑntrə'dɪktəri] *adj* widerspruchsvoll

contrail ['kɑnˌtrel] *s* Kondensstreifen *m*

contral·to [kən'trælto] *s* (**-tos**) (*person*) Altistin *f*; (*voice*) Alt *m*

contraption [kən'træpʃən] *s* (coll) Vorrichtung *f*; (*car*) (coll) Kiste *f*

contrary ['kɑntreri] *adj* konträr, gegensätzlich; (*person*) querköpfig; **c. to entgegen** (*dat*); **c. to nature** naturwidrig ‖ *s* Gegenteil *n*; **on the c.** im Gegenteil

contrast ['kɑntræst] *s* Gegensatz *m* ‖ [kən'træst] *tr* (**with**) gegenüberstellen (*dat*) ‖ *intr* (**with**) im Gegensatz stehen (zu)

contravene [ˌkɑntrə'vin] *tr* zuwiderhandeln (*dat*)

contribute [kən'trɪbjut] *tr* beitragen, spenden ‖ *intr*—**c. to** beitragen zu; (*with help*) mitwirken an (*dat*)

contribution [ˌkɑntrɪ'bjuʃən] *s* Beitrag *m*; (*of money*) Spende *f*

contributor [kən'trɪbjutər] *s* Spender -in *mf*; (*to a periodical*) Mitarbeiter -in *mf*

contrite [kən'traɪt] *adj* reuig

contrition [kən'trɪʃən] *s* Reue *f*

contrivance [kən'traɪvəns] *s* (*device*) Vorrichtung *f*; (*expedient*) Kunstgriff *m*; (*act of contriving*) Aushecken *n*

contrive [kən'traɪv] *tr* (*invent*) erfin-

den; (*devise*) ersinnen; **c. to** (*inf*) **es fertig bringen** zu (*inf*) ‖ *intr* Anschläge aushecken

con·trol [kən'trol] *s* Kontrolle *f*, Gewalt *f*; (mach) Steuerung *f*; (mach) (*devise*) Regler *m*; **be out of c.** nicht zu halten sein; **be under c.** in bester Ordnung sein; **controls** (aer) Steuerwerk *n*; **gain c. over** die Herrschaft gewinnen über (*acc*); **have c. over s.o.** über j-n Gewalt haben; **keep under c.** im Zaume halten ‖ *v* (*pret & pp* **-trolled**; *ger* **-trolling**) *tr* (*dominate*) beherrschen; (*verify*) kontrollieren; (*contain*) eindämmen; (*steer*) steuern; (*regulate*) regeln; **c. oneself** sich beherrschen

control' pan'el *s* Schaltbrett *n*

control' room' *s* Kommandoraum *m*; (rad) Regieraum *m*

control' stick' *s* (aer) Steuerknüppel *m*

control' tow'er *s* (*at an airport*) Kontrollturm *m*; (*on an aircraft carrier*) Kommandoturm *m*

controversial [ˌkɑntrə'vʌrʃəl] *adj* umstritten, strittig; **c. subject** Streitfrage *f*

controversy ['kɑntrəˌvʌrsi] *s* Kontroverse *f*, Auseinandersetzung *f*

controvert [ˌkɑntrə'vʌrt] *tr* (*argue against*) bestreiten; (*argue about*) streiten über (*acc*)

contusion [kən't(j)uʒən] *s* Quetschung *f*

convalesce [ˌkɑnvə'lɛs] *intr* genesen

convalescence [ˌkɑnvə'lɛsəns] *s* Genesung *f*

convalescent [ˌkɑnvə'lɛsənt] *s* Genesende *mf*

convales'cent home' *s* Genesungsheim *n*

convene [kən'vin] *tr* versammeln ‖ *intr* sich versammeln

convenience [kən'vinjəns] *s* Bequemlichkeit *f*; **at one's c.** nach Belieben; **at your earliest c.** möglichst bald; **modern conveniences** moderner Komfort *m*

convenient [kən'vinjənt] *adj* gelegen

convent ['kɑnvɛnt] *s* Nonnenkloster *n*

convention [kən'vɛnʃən] *s* (*professional meeting*) Tagung *f*; (*political meeting*) Konvent *m*; (*accepted usage*) Konvention *f*

conventional [kən'vɛnʃənəl] *adj* konventionell, herkömmlich

converge [kən'vʌrdʒ] *intr* zusammenlaufen; **c. on** sich stürzen auf (*acc*)

conversation [ˌkɑnvər'seʃən] *s* Gespräch *n*

conversational [ˌkɑnvər'seʃənəl] *adj* Gesprächs-

converse ['kɑnvʌrs] *adj* gegenteilig ‖ *s* (*of*) Gegenteil *n* (von) ‖ [kən'vʌrs] *intr* sich unterhalten

conversion [kən'vʌrʒən] *s* (*into*) Umwandlung *f* (in *acc*); (*of a factory*) (**to**) Umstellung *f* (auf *acc*); (*of a building*) (**into**) Umbau *m* (zu); (*of currency*) (**into**) Umwechslung *f* (in *acc*); (elec) (**to**) Umformung *f* (in *acc*); (math) Umrechnung *f*; (phys) Umsetzung *f*; (relig) Bekehrung *f*

convert ['kɔnvʌrt] *s* (**to**) Bekehrte *mf*
(zu) || [kən'vʌrt] *tr* (**into**) umwan-
deln (in *acc*); (*a factory*) (**to**) umstellen (auf *acc*); (*a building*) (**into**)
umbauen (zu); (*currency*) (**into**) um-
wechseln (in *acc*); (*biochem*) (**into**)
umsetzen (in *acc*); (*chem*) (**into**)
umwandeln (in *acc*), verwandeln (in
acc); (*elec*) (**to**) umformen (in *acc*);
(*math*) (**to**) umrechnen (in *acc*);
(*phys*) (**to**) umsetzen (in *acc*);
(*relig*) (**to**) bekehren (zu) || *intr* (**to**)
sich bekehren (zu)

converter [kən'vʌrtər] *s* (elec) Umfor-
mer *m*, Stromrichter *m*

convertible [kən'vʌrtɪbəl] *adj* umwan-
delbar; (fin) konvertierbar || *s* (aut)
Kabriolett *n*

convex ['kɔnveks], [kɑn'veks] *adj*
konvex

convey [kən've] *tr* (*transport*) befördern; (*greetings, message*) übermitteln; (*sound*) fortpflanzen; (*meaning*) ausdrücken; (*a property*) abtreten

conveyance [kən've-əns] *s* (*act*) Beförderung *f*; (*means*) Transportmit-
tel *n*; (jur) Abtretung *f*

conveyor [kən've-ər] *s* Beförderer –in
mf

convey'or belt' *s* Förderband *n*

convict ['kɔnvɪkt] *s* Sträfling *m* ||
[kən'vɪkt] *tr* (**of**) überführen (*genit*)

conviction [kən'vɪkʃən] *s* (*of a crime*)
Verurteilung *f*; (*certainty*) Überzeugung *f*; **convictions** Gesinnung *f*

convince [kən'vɪns] *tr* (**of**) überzeugen
(von)

convivial [kən'vɪvɪ·əl] *adj* gesellig

convocation [,kɑnvə'keʃən] *s* Zusam-
menberufung *f*; (educ) Eröffnungs-
feier *f*

convoke [kən'vok] *tr* zusammenberu-
fen

convoy ['kɑnvɔɪ] *s* (*of vehicles*) Kolonne *f*, Konvoi *m*; (nav) Geleitzug
m

convulse [kən'vʌls] *tr* erschüttern

convulsion [kən'vʌlʃən] *s* Krampf *m*;
go into convulsions Krämpfe bekommen

coo [ku] *intr* girren

cook [kʊk] *s* Koch *m*, Köchin *f* || *tr*
braten, backen; (*boil*) kochen; **c. up**
(fig) zusammenbrauen || *intr* braten,
backen; (*boil*) kochen

cook'book' *s* Kochbuch *n*

cookie ['kʊki] *s* Plätzchen *n*, Keks *m*
& *n*; **cookies** *pl* Gebäck *n*

cook'ing *s* Kochen *n*; **do one's own c.**
sich selbst beköstigen

cool [kul] *adj* (& fig) kühl; **keep c.!**
ruhig Blut!; **keep one's c.** (coll) ru-
hig Blut bewahren || *s* Kühle *f* || *tr*
kühlen; **c. down** (fig) beruhigen; **c.
off** abkühlen || *intr* (& fig) sich ab-
kühlen

cooler ['kulər] *s* Kühler *m*; (sl) Kittchen *n*

cool'-head'ed *adj* besonnen

coolie ['kuli] *s* Kuli *m*

coolness ['kulnɪs] *s* (& fig) Kühle *f*

coon [kun] *s* (zool) Waschbär *m*

coop [kup] *s* (*building*) Hühnerstall *m*;
(*enclosure*) Hühnerhof *m*; (*jail*) (sl)
Kittchen *n*; **fly the c.** (sl) auskneifen
|| *tr*—**c. up** einsperren

co-op ['ko·ɑp] *s* Konsumverein *m*

cooper ['kupər] *s* Küfer *m*, Böttcher *m*

cooperate [ko'ɑpə,ret] *intr* (**in**) mitwirken (an *dat*, bei); (**with**) mitarbeiten (mit)

cooperation [ko,ɑpə're·ən] *s* Mit-
wirkung *f*, Mitarbeit *f*

cooperative [ko'ɑpə,retɪv] *adj* hilfs-
bereit

coordinate [ko'ɔrdɪnɪt] *adj* gleichran-
gig; (gram) beigeordnet || *s* (math)
Koordinate *f* || [ko'ɔrdɪ,net] *tr*
koordinieren

coordination [ko,ɔrdɪ'neʃən] *s* Koor-
dination *f*; (gram) Beiordnung *f*

cootie ['kuti] *s* (sl) Laus *f*

co-owner ['ko,onər] *s* Miteigentümer
–in *mf*

cop [kɑp] *s* (sl) Bulle *m* || *v* (*pret &
pp* **copped**; *ger* **copped**) *tr* (*catch*)
(sl) erwischen; (*steal*) (sl) klauen ||
intr—**cop out** (coll) auskneifen

copartner [ko'pɑrtnər] *s* Mitinhaber
–in *mf*

cope [kop] *intr*—**c. with** sich messen
mit, aufkommen gegen

cope'stone' *s* Schlußstein *m*

copier ['kɑpɪ·ər] *s* Kopiermaschine *f*

copilot ['ko,paɪlət] *s* Kopilot *m*

coping ['kopɪŋ] *s* Mauerkappe *f*

copious ['kopɪ·əs] *adj* reichlich

cop'-out' *s* (*act*) Kneifen *n*; (*person*)
Drückeberger *m*

copper ['kɑpər] *adj* kupfern, Kupfer–;
(*color*) kupferrot || *s* Kupfer *n*;
(*coin*) Kupfermünze *f*; (sl) Schupo
m

cop'persmith' *s* Kupferschmied *m*

copter ['kɑptər] *s* (coll) Hubschrauber
m

copulate ['kɑpjə,let] *intr* sich paaren

cop-y ['kɑpi] *s* Kopie *f*; (*of a book*)
Exemplar *n*; (typ) druckfertiges
Manuskript *n* || *v* (*pret & pp* **-ied**)
tr kopieren; (*in school*) abschreiben

cop'ybook' *s* Schreibheft *n*, Heft *n*

cop'ycat' *s* (*imitator*) Nachäffer –in
mf

cop'yright' *s* Urheberrecht *n*, Verlags-
recht *n* || *tr* urheberrechtlich schüt-
zen, verlagsrechtlich schützen

cop'ywrit'er *s* Texter –in *mf*

coquette [ko'ket] *s* Kokette *f*

coquettish [ko'ketɪʃ] *adj* kokett

coral ['kɔrəl] *adj* Korallen– || *s* Ko-
ralle *f*

cor'al reef' *s* Korallenriff *n*

cord [kɔrd] *s* Schnur *f*, Strick *m*; (*of
wood*) Klafter *n*; (elec) Leitungs-
schnur *f*

cordial ['kɔrdʒəl] *adj* herzlich || *s* Li-
kör *m*; (med) Herzstärkung *f*

cordiality [kɔr'dʒælɪti] *s* Herzlichkeit
f

cordon ['kɔrdən] *s* Kordon *m*, Ab-
sperrkette *f* || *tr*—**c. off** absperren

corduroy ['kɔrdə,rɔɪ] *s* Kordsamt *m*;
corduroys Kordsamthose *f*

core [kor] *s* (*of fruit*) Kern *m*; (*of a*

cable) Seele *f;* (fig) Kern *m,* Mark *n;* (elec) Spulenkern *m*

cork [kɔrk] *s* Kork *m;* (*stopper*) Pfropfen *m,* Korken *m* ‖ *tr* verkorken

corker ['kɔrkər] *s* (sl) Schlager *m*

cork'ing *adj* (sl) fabelhaft

cork'oak', cork' tree' *s* Korkeiche *f*

cork'screw' *s* Korkenzieher *m*

corn [kɔrn] *s* (*Indian corn*) Mais *m;* (*on a foot*) Hühnerauge *n;* (*joke*) (sl) Kalauer *m*

corn'bread' *s* Maisbrot *n*

corn'cob' *s* Maiskolben *m*

corn'cob pipe' *s* Maiskolbenpfeife *f*

corn'crib' *s* Maisspeicher *m*

cornea ['kɔrnɪ-ə] *s* Hornhaut *f*

corned' beef' ['kɔrnd] *s* Pökelfleisch *n*

corner ['kɔrnər] *adj* Eck– ‖ *s* Ecke *f;* (*secluded spot*) Winkel *m;* (*curve*) Kurve *f;* **c. of the eye** Augenwinkel *m;* **from all corners of the world** von allen Ecken und Enden; **turn the c.** um die Ecke biegen ‖ *tr* (*a person*) in die Zange nehmen; (*the market*) aufkaufen

cor'nerstone' *s* Eckstein *m;* (*of a new building*) Grundstein *m*

cornet [kɔr'nɛt] *s* (mus) Kornett *n*

corn' exchange' *s* Getreidebörse *f*

corn'field' *s* Maisfeld *n;* (*grain field*) (Brit) Kornfeld *n*

corn'flakes' *spl* Maisflocken *pl*

corn' flour' *s* Maismehl *n*

corn'flow'er *s* Kornblume *f*

corn' frit'ter *s* Maispfannkuchen *m*

corn'husk' *s* Maishülse *f*

cornice ['kɔrnɪs] *s* Gesims *n*

corn' liq'uor *s* Maisschnaps *m*

corn' meal' *s* Maismehl *n*

corn' on the cob' *s* Mais *m* am Kolben

corn' silk' *s* Maisfasern *pl*

corn'stalk' *s* Maisstengel *m*

corn'starch' *s* Maisstärke *f*

cornucopia [,kɔrnə'kopɪ-ə] *s* Füllhorn *n*

corny ['kɔrni] *adj* (*sentimental*) rührselig; (*joke*) blöd

corollary ['kɔrə,lɛri] *s* (to) Folge *f* (von)

coron·a [kə'ronə] *s* (**-nas** & **-nae** [ni]) (astr) Hof *m,* Korona *f;* (archit) Kranzleiste *f*

coronary ['kɔrə,nɛri] *adj* koronar

coronation [,kɔrə'neʃən] *s* Krönung *f*

coroner ['kɔrənər] *s* Gerichtsmediziner *m*

cor'oner's in'quest *s* Totenschau *f*

coronet ['kɔrə,nɛt] *s* Krönchen *n;* (*worn by the nobility*) Adelskrone *f;* (*worn by women*) Diadem *n*

corporal ['kɔrpərəl] *adj* körperlich ‖ *s* (mil) Obergefreite *m*

corporate ['kɔrpərɪt] *adj* korporativ

corporation [,kɔrpə'reʃən] *s* (fin) Aktiengesellschaft *f;* (jur) Körperschaft *f*

corpora'tion law'yer *s* Syndikus *m*

corporeal [kɔr'porɪ-əl] *adj* körperlich

corps [kor] *s* (**corps** [korz]) Korps *n*

corpse [korps] *s* Leiche *f,* Leichnam *m*

corps'man *s* (**-men**) Sanitäter *m*

corpulent ['kɔrpjələnt] *adj* beleibt

corpuscle ['kɔrpəsəl] *s* Blutkörperchen *n*

cor·ral [kɛ'ræl] *s* Pferch *m* ‖ *v* (*pret* & *pp* **-ralled;** *ger* **-ralling**) *tr* zusammenpferchen

correct [kə'rɛkt] *adj* richtig; (*manners*) korrekt; (*time*) genau; **be c.** (*said of a thing*) stimmen; (*said of a person*) recht haben ‖ *tr* korrigieren; (*examination papers*) verbessern; (*beat*) züchtigen; (*scold*) zurechtweisen; (*an unjust situation*) ausgleichen

correction [kə'rɛkʃən] *s* Berichtigung *f;* (*of examination papers*) Verbesserung *f,* Korrektur *f;* (*punishment*) Bestrafung *f*

corrective [kə'rɛktɪv] *adj* (*measures*) Gegen–; (*lenses, shoes*) Ausgleichs–

correctness [kə'rɛktnɪs] *s* Richtigkeit *f;* (*in manners*) Korrektheit *f*

correlate ['kɔrə,let] *tr* in Wechselbeziehung bringen ‖ *intr* in Wechselbeziehung stehen

correlation [,kɔrə'leʃən] *s* Wechselbeziehung *f,* Korrelation *f*

correlative [kə'rɛlətɪv] *adj* korrelativ ‖ *s* Korrelat *n*

correspond [,kɔrɪ'spand] *intr* einander übereinstimmen; (**to, with**) entsprechen (*dat*); (*exchange letters*) (**with**) im Briefwechsel stehen (mit)

correspondence [,kɔrɪ'spandəns] *s* (*act of corresponding*) Übereinstimmung *f;* (*instance of correspondence*) Entsprechung *f;* (*exchange of letters; letters*) Korrespondenz *f*

correspon'dence course' *s* Fernkursus *m*

correspondent [,kɔrɪ'spandənt] *s* Briefpartner **–in** *mf;* (journ) Korrespondent **–in** *mf*

correspond'ing *adj* entsprechend

corridor ['kɔrɪdər] *s* Korridor *m*

corroborate [kə'rabə,ret] *tr* bestätigen

corrode [kə'rod] *tr & intr* korrodieren

corrosion [kə'roʒən] *s* Korrosion *f*

corrosive [kə'rosɪv] *adj* ätzend; (*influence*) schädigend ‖ *s* Ätzmittel *n*

cor'rugated card'board ['kɔrə,getɪd] *s* Wellpappe *f*

cor'rugated i'ron *s* Wellblech *n*

corrupt [kə'rʌpt] *adj* (*text*) verderbt; (*morally*) verdorben; (*open to bribes*) bestechlich ‖ *tr* verderben; (*bribe*) bestechen

corruption [kə'rʌpʃən] *s* Verderbtheit *f;* (*bribery*) Korruption *f*

corsage [kor'saʒ] *s* Blumensträußchen *n* zum Anstecken

corsair ['kɔrsɛr] *s* Korsar *m*

corset ['kɔrsɪt] *s* Korsett *n*

Corsica ['kɔrsɪkə] *s* Korsika *n*

Corsican ['kɔrsɪkən] *adj* korsisch

cortege [kor'tɛʒ] *s* Gefolge *n;* (*at a funeral*) Leichenzug *m*

cor·tex ['kɔr,tɛks] *s* (**-tices** [tɪ,siz]) Rinde *f,* Kortex *m*

cortisone ['kɔrtɪ,son] *s* Cortison *n*

corvette [kɔr'vɛt] *s* (naut) Korvette *f*

cosmetic [kaz'mɛtɪk] *adj* kosmetisch ‖ *s* Kosmetikum *n;* **cosmetics** Kosmetikartikel *pl*

cosmic ['kazmɪk] *adj* kosmisch
cosmonaut ['kazmə‚nɔt] *s* Kosmonaut –in *mf*
cosmopolitan [‚kazə'palɪtən] *adj* kosmopolitisch || *s* Kosmopolit –in *mf*
cosmos ['kazməs] *s* Kosmos *m*
cost [kɔst] *s* Preis *m*; **at all costs** (fig) um jeden Preis; **at c.** zum Selbstkostenpreis; **at the c. of** auf Kosten (genit); **costs** Kosten *pl*; (jur) Gerichtskosten *pl* || *v* (*pret & pp* cost) *intr* kosten
cost′ account′ing *s* Kostenrechnung *f*
costly ['kɔstlɪ] *adj* kostspielig; (*of great value*) kostbar
cost′ of liv′ing *s* Lebenshaltungskosten *pl*
costume ['kast(j)um] *s* Kostüm *n*; (*national dress*) Tracht *f*
cos′tume ball′ *s* Kostümball *m*
cos′tume jew′elry *s* Modeschmuck *m*
cot [kat] *s* Feldbett *n*
coterie ['kotəri] *s* Klüngel *m*, Koterie *f*
cottage ['katɪdʒ] *s* Hütte *f*; (*country house*) Landhaus *n*
cot′tage cheese′ *s* Quark *m*, Quarkkäse *m*
cot′ter pin′ ['katər] *s* Schließbolzen *m*
cotton ['katən] *s* (*fiber, yarn*) Baumwolle *f*; (*unspun cotton*) Watte *f*; (*sterilized cotton*) Verbandswatte *f*
cot′ton field′ *s* Baumwollfeld *n*
cot′ton gin′ *s* Entkörnungsmaschine *f*
cot′ton mill′ *s* Baumwollspinnerei *f*
cot′ton pick′er ['pɪkər] *s* Baumwollpflücker –in *mf*; (*machine*) Baumwollpflückmaschine *f*
cot′tonseed oil′ *s* Baumwollsamenöl *n*
cot′ton waste′ *s* Putzwolle *f*
couch [kaʊt͡ʃ] *s* Couch *f*, Liege *f* || *tr* (*words*) fassen; (*thoughts*) ausdrücken
cougar ['kugər] *s* Puma *m*
cough [kɔf] *s* Husten *m* || *tr*—**c. up** aushusten; (*money*) (sl) blechen || *intr* husten; (*in order to attract attention*) sich räuspern
cough′ drop′ *s* Hustenbonbon *m & n*
cough′ syr′up *s* Hustentropfen *pl*
could [kʊd] *aux*—**he c.** (*was able*) er konnte; **if he c.** (*were able*) wenn er könnte
council ['kaʊnsəl] *s* Rat *m*; (eccl) Konzil *n*
coun·cil·man *s* (–men) Stadtratsmitglied *n*
councilor ['kaʊnsələr] *s* Rat *m*
coun·sel ['kaʊnsəl] *s* Rat *m*; (*for the defense*) Verteidiger –in *mf*; (*for the prosecution*) Anklagevertreter –in *mf* || *v* (*pret & pp* -sel[l]ed) *ger* -sel[l]ing) *tr* raten (dat) || *intr* Rat geben
counselor ['kaʊnsələr] *s* Berater –in *mf*
count [kaʊnt] *s* Zahl *f*; (*nobleman*) Graf *m*; (jur) Anklagepunkt *m*; **lose c.** sich verzählen || *tr* zählen; (*the costs*) berechnen; **c. in** einschließen; **c. off** abzählen; **c. out** (*money, a boxer*) auszählen || *intr* zählen; **c. for little** (or **much**) wenig (or viel)

gelten; **c. off** (mil) abzählen; **c. on** zählen auf (*acc*)
count′down′ *s* Countdown *m & n*
countenance ['kaʊntɪnəns] *s* Antlitz *n* || *tr* (*tolerate*) zulassen; (*approve*) billigen
counter ['kaʊntər] *adj* Gegen– || *adv*—**c. to** wider; **run c. to** zuwiderlaufen (dat) || *s* Zähler *m*; (*in games*) Spielmarke *f*; (*in a store*) Ladentisch *m*, Theke *f*; (*in a restaurant*) Büffet *n*; (*in a bank*) Schalter *m*; **under the c.** (fig) heimlich || *tr* widerstreben (dat); (*in speech*) widersprechen (dat) || *intr* Gegenmaßnahmen treffen; (box) kontern, nachschlagen
coun′teract′ *tr* entgegenwirken (dat)
coun′terattack′ *s* Gegenangriff *m* || **coun′terattack′** *tr* e-n Gegenangriff machen auf (*acc*) || *intr* e-n Gegenangriff machen
coun′terbal′ance *s* Gegengewicht *n* || **coun′terbal′ance** *tr* das Gegengewicht halten (dat)
coun′terclock′wise *adj* linksläufig *adv* entgegen der Uhrzeigerrichtung
coun′teres′pionage *s* Gegenspionage *f*
counterfeit ['kaʊntərfɪt] *adj* gefälscht || *s* Fälschung *f*; (*money*) Falschgeld *n* || *tr* fälschen
counterfeiter ['kaʊntər‚fɪtər] *s* Falschmünzer –in *mf*
coun′terfeit mon′ey *s* Falschgeld *n*
coun′terintel′ligence *s* Spionageabwehr *f*
countermand ['kaʊntər‚mænd] *s* Gegenbefehl *m* || *tr* widerrufen
coun′termeas′ure *s* Gegenmaßnahme *f*
coun′teroffen′sive *s* Gegenoffensive *f*
coun′terpart′ *s* Gegenstück *n*; (*person*) Ebenbild *n*
coun′terpoint′ *s* (mus) Kontrapunkt *m*
coun′terrevolu′tion *s* Konterrevolution *f*
coun′tersign′ *s* Gegenzeichen *n* || *tr & intr* mitunterzeichnen
coun′tersink′ *v* (*pret & pp* -sunk) *tr* (*a screw*) versenken; (*a hole*) ausfräsen
coun′terspy′ *s* Gegenspion –in *mf*
coun′terstroke′ *s* Gegenstoß *m*
coun′terweight′ *s* Gegengewicht *n*
countess ['kaʊntɪs] *s* Gräfin *f*
countless ['kaʊntlɪs] *adj* zahllos
countrified ['kʌntrɪ‚faɪd] *adj* ländlich; (*boorish*) bäu(e)risch
country ['kʌntrɪ] *adj* (*air, house, life, road*) Land– || *s* (*state; rural area*) Land *n*; (*land of birth*) Heimatland *n*; **in the c.** auf dem Lande; **to the c.** aufs Land
coun′try club′ *s* exklusiver Klub *m* auf dem Lande
coun′tryfolk′ *spl* Landvolk *n*
coun′try gen′tleman *s* Landedelmann *m*
coun·try·man *s* (–men) Landsmann *m*
coun′tryside′ *s* Landschaft *f*, Land *n*
coun′try-wide′ *adj* über das ganze Land verbreitet (or ausgedehnt)
county ['kaʊntɪ] *s* Kreis *m*
coun′ty seat′ *s* Kreisstadt *f*

coup [ku] *s* Coup *m*

coup d'état [ku de 'ta] *s* Staatsstreich *m*

coupe [ku'pe], [kup] *s* Coupé *n*

couple ['kʌpəl] *s* Paar *n*; (*of lovers*) Liebespaar *n*; (*man and wife*) Ehepaar *n*; (*phys*) Kräftepaar *n*; **a c. of** ein paar, e.g., **a c. of days ago** vor ein paar Tagen || *tr* koppeln || *intr* sich paaren

couplet ['kʌplɪt] *s* Verspaar *n*

coupling ['kʌplɪŋ] *s* Verbindungsstück *n*; (rad) Kopplung *f*; (rr) Kupplung *f*

coupon ['k(j)upɑn] *s* Gutschein *m*

courage ['kʌrɪdʒ] *s* Mut *m*, Courage *f*; **get up the c. to** (*inf*) sich [*dat*] ein Herz fassen zu (*inf*)

courageous [kə'redʒəs] *adj* mutig

courier ['kʌrɪ-ər] *s* Eilbote *m*; (*tour guide*) Reiseleiter –in *mf*

course [kors] *s* (*direction*) Richtung *f*, Kurs *m*; (*of a river, of time*) Lauf *m*; (*method of procedure*) Weg *m*, Weise *f*, Kurs *m*; (*in racing*) Bahn *f*; (*archit*) Schicht *f*; (*culin*) Gang *m*; (*educ*) Kurs *m*; **c. of action** Handlungsweise *f*; **go off c.** (aer) sich verfliegen; **in due c.** zur rechten Zeit; **in the c. of** im Verlaufe von (or *genit*); (*with expressions of time*) im Laufe (*genit*); **of c.** natürlich; **run its c.** seinen Verlauf nehmen

court [kort] *s* (*of a king*) Hof *m*; (*of justice*) Gericht *n*; (*yard*) Hof *m*; (*tennis*) Platz *m*; **in c.** (or **into c.** or **to c.**) vor Gericht; **out of c.** außergerichtlich || *tr* (*a girl*) werben um; (*danger*) suchen; (*disaster*) heraufbeschwören

courteous ['kʌrtɪ-əs] *adj* höflich

courtesan ['kortɪʒən] *s* Kurtisane *f*

courtesy ['kʌrtɪsɪ] *s* Höflichkeit *f*; **by c. of** freundlicherweise zur Verfügung gestellt von

court′house′ *s* Gerichtsgebäude *n*

courtier ['kortɪ-ər] *s* Höfling *m*

court′ jest′er *s* Hofnarr *m*

courtly ['kortlɪ] *adj* höfisch

court′-mar′tial *s* (**courts-martial**) Kriegsgericht *n* || *v* (*pret & pp* –tial[l]ed; *ger* –tial[l]ing) *tr* vor ein Kriegsgericht stellen

court′room′ *s* Gerichtssaal *m*

court′ship′ *s* Werbung *f*

court′yard′ *s* Hof *m*

cousin ['kʌzɪn] *s* Vetter *m*; (*female*) Kusine *f*

cove [kov] *s* Bucht *f*

covenant ['kʌvənənt] *s* Vertrag *m*; (Bib) Bund *m*

cover ['kʌvər] *s* Decke *f*; (*lid*) Deckel *m*; (*wrapping*) Hülle *f*; (e.g., *of a bed*) Bezug *m*; (*of a book*) Einband *m*; (*protection*) Schutz *m*; (mil) Deckung *f*; **from c. to c.** von vorn bis hinten; **take c.** sich unterstellen; **under c.** im Geheimen; **under c. of night** im Schutz der Dunkelheit || *tr* bedecken, decken; (*conceal*) verdecken; (*distances*) zurücklegen; (*a sales territory*) bearbeiten; (*a bet*) die gleiche Summe setzen gegen; (*ex-*

penses, losses) decken; (*upholstered furniture*) beziehen; (*deal with*) behandeln; (*include*) umfassen; (*material in class*) durchnehmen; (*said of a reporter*) berichten über (*acc*); (*said of plants*) bewachsen; (*with insurance*) versichern, decken; (*protect with a gun*) sichern; (*threaten with a gun*) in Schach halten; (*have within range*) beherrschen; **c. up** zudecken; (*conceal*) verheimlichen || *intr*—**c. for** einspringen für

coverage ['kʌvərɪdʒ] *s* (*area covered*) Verbreitungsgebiet *n*; (*of news*) Berichterstattung *f*; (*ins*) Versicherungsschutz *m*; (rad, telv) Sendebereich *m*

coveralls ['kʌvər,ɔlz] *spl* Monteuranzug *m*

cov′ered wag′on *s* Planwagen *m*

cov′er girl′ *s* Covergirl *n*

cov′ering *s* Decke *f*, Bedeckung *f*

covert ['kovərt] *adj* verborgen

cov′erup′ *s* Beschönigung *f*, Bemäntelung *f*

covet ['kʌvɪt] *tr* begehren

covetous ['kʌvɪtəs] *adj* begehrlich

covetousness ['kʌvɪtəsnɪs] *s* Begehrlichkeit *f*

covey ['kʌvɪ] *s* (*brood*) Brut *f*; (*small flock*) Schwarm *m*; (*bevy*) Schar *f*

cow [kau] *s* Kuh *f* || *tr* einschüchtern

coward ['kau-ərd] *s* Feigling *m*, Memme *f*

cowardice ['kau-ərdɪs] *s* Feigheit *f*

cowardly ['kau-ərdlɪ] *adj* feig(e)

cow′bell′ *s* Kuhglocke *f*

cow′boy′ *s* Cowboy *m*

cower ['kau-ər] *intr* kauern

cow′herd′ *s* Kuhhirt *m*

cow′hide′ *s* Rindsleder *n*

cowl [kaul] *s* (*on a chimney*) Schornsteinkappe *f*; (aer) Motorhaube *f*; (eccl) Kapuze *f*

cowling ['kaulɪŋ] *s* (aer) Motorhaube *f*

co-worker ['ko,wʌrkər] *s* Mitarbeiter –in *mf*

cowpox ['kau,paks] *s* Kuhpocken *pl*

coxswain ['kaksən] *s* Steuermann *m*

coy [kɔɪ] *adj* spröde

coyote [kaɪ'otɪ], ['kaɪ-ot] *s* Kojote *m*, Präriewolf *m*, Steppenwolf *m*

cozy ['kozɪ] *adj* gemütlich

C.P.A. ['si'pi'e] *s* (**certified public accountant**) amtlich zugelassener Wirtschaftsprüfer *m*

crab [kræb] *s* Krabbe *f*; (*grouch*) Sauertopf *m*

crab′ ap′ple *s* Holzapfel *m*

crabbed ['kræbɪd] *adj* mürrisch; (*handwriting*) unleserlich; (*style*) schwer verständlich, verworren

crabby ['kræbɪ] *adj* mürrisch, grämlich

crack [kræk] *adj* erstklassig; (*troops*) Elite– || *s* Riß *m*, Sprung *m*; (*of a whip or rifle*) Knall *m*; (*blow*) (sl) Klaps *m*; (*opportunity*) (sl) Gelegenheit *f*; (*try*) (sl) Versuch *m*; (*cutting remark*) (sl) Seitenhieb *m*; **at the c. of dawn** bei Tagesanbruch; **take a c. at** (sl) versuchen || *tr* spalten; (*a nut, safe*) knacken; (*an egg*) aufschlagen;

(a code) entziffern; (hit) (sl) e-n Klaps geben (dat); (chem) spalten; **c. a joke** || intr Witz reißen; **c. a smile** lächeln || intr (make a cracking sound) knacken, krachen; (develop a crack) rissig werden; (said of a whip or rifle) knallen; (said of a voice) umschlagen; (said of ice) (zer)springen; **c. down on** scharf vorgehen gegen; **c. up** (coll) überschnappen; (aut) aufknallen

cracked adj (split) rissig; (crazy) (sl) übergeschnappt

cracker ['krækər] s Keks m & n

crack'er/jack' adj (coll) erstklassig || s (coll) Kanone f

crackle ['krækəl] s Krakelierung f || tr krakelieren || intr prasseln

crack'pot' adj (sl) verrückt || s (sl) Verrückte mf

crack' shot' s Meisterschütze m

crack'-up' s (aut) Zusammenstoß m

cradle ['kredəl] s Wiege f; (telp) Gabel f || tr in den Armen wiegen

craft [kræft] s Handwerk n, Gewerbe n; (naut) Fahrzeug n; **by c.** durch List || spl Fahrzeuge pl, Schiffe pl; **small c.** kleine Schiffe pl

craftiness ['kræftɪnɪs] s List f

crafts·man ['kræftsmən] s (-men) Handwerker m

crafts'manship' s Kunstfertigkeit f

crafty ['kræftɪ] adj arglistig

crag [kræg] s Felszacke f

cram [kræm] v (pret & pp crammed; ger cramming) tr vollstopfen; **c. into** hineinstopfen in (acc) || intr (educ) büffeln, ochsen; **c. into** sich hineinzwängen in (acc)

cram' course' s Presse f

cramp [kræmp] s Krampf m; (clamp) Klammer f || tr einschränken, beengen

cramped adj eng

cranberry ['kræn‚berɪ] s Preiselbeere f

crane [kren] s (mach) Kran m; (orn) Kranich m || **c. one's neck** den Hals recken

crani·um ['krenɪ·əm] s (-a [ə]) s Hirnschale f, Schädel m

crank [kræŋk] s Kurbel f; (grouch) (coll) Griesgram m; (eccentric) (coll) Sonderling m || tr kurbeln; **c. up** ankurbeln

crank'case' s Kurbelgehäuse n

crank'shaft' s Kurbelwelle f

cranky ['kræŋkɪ] adj launisch

cranny ['krænɪ] s Ritze f

crap [kræp] s (nonsense) (sl) Unsinn m; **craps** Würfel pl; **shoot craps** Würfel spielen

crash [kræʃ] s Krach m; (aer) Absturz m; (aut) Zusammenstoß m; (econ) Zusammenbruch m || tr zerschmettern; **(a party)** hineinplatzen in (acc); (aer) zum Absturz bringen || intr (produce a crashing sound) krachen; (shatter) zerbrechen; (collapse) zusammenstürzen; (aer) abstürzen; (aut) zusammenstoßen; **c. into** fahren gegen

crash' dive' s Schnelltauchen n

crash'-dive' intr schnelltauchen

crash' hel'met s Sturzhelm m

crash' land'ing s Bruchlandung f

crash' pro'gram s Gewaltkur f

crass [kræs] adj kraß

crate [kret] s Lattenkiste f; (old car, old plane) (coll) Kiste f || tr in e-r Lattenkiste verpacken

crater ['kretər] s Krater m; (of a bomb) Trichter m

crave [krev] tr ersehnen || intr—**c. for** verlangen nach

craven ['krevən] adj feige || s Feigling m

crav'ing s (for) Verlangen n (nach)

craw [krɔ] s Kropf m

crawl [krɔl] s Kriechen n || intr kriechen; (said of the skin) kribbeln; (said of a swimmer) kraulen; (said of cars) schleichen; **c. along** im Schneckentempo gehen (or fahren); **c. into a hole** (& fig) sich verkriechen; **c. with** wimmeln von

crayon ['kre·ən] s (wax crayon) Wachsmalkreide f; (colored pencil) Farbstift m; (artist's crayon) Zeichenkreide f

craze [krez] s Mode f, Verrücktheit f || tr verrückt machen

crazy ['krezɪ] adj verrückt; (senseless) sinnlos; **c. about** verrückt nach; **c. idea** Wahnidee f; **drive c.** verrückt machen

cra'zy bone' s Musikantenknochen m

creak [krik] s (high-pitched sound) Quietschen n; (low-pitched sound) Knarren n || intr quietschen; knarren

creaky ['krikɪ] adj quietschend; knarrend

cream [krim] adj Sahne-, Rahm-; (color) creme, cremefarben f; (color) creme, cremefarben f; Sahne f, Rahm m; (cosmetic) Creme f; (color) Cremefarbe f; (fig) Creme f || tr (milk) abrahmen; (trounce) (sl) schlagen

cream' cheese' s Rahmkäse m, Sahnekäse m

creamery ['krimərɪ] s Molkerei f

cream' pit'cher s Sahnekännchen n

cream' puff' s Windbeutel m

cream' sep'arator ['sepə‚retər] s Milchschleuder f, Milchzentrifuge f

creamy ['krimɪ] adj sahnig

crease [kris] s Falte f; (in trousers) Bügelfalte f || tr falten; (trousers) bügeln || intr knittern

create [kri'et] tr (er)schaffen; (excitement, an impression) hervorrufen; (noise) verursachen; (appoint) ernennen, machen zu; (a role, fashions) kreieren

creation [kri'eʃən] s Schaffung f; (of the world) Schöpfung f; (in fashions) Modeschöpfung f

creative [kri'etɪv] adj schöpferisch

creator [kri'etər] s Schöpfer m

creature ['kritʃər] s Kreatur f, Geschöpf n; **every living c.** jedes Lebewesen n

credence ['kridəns] s Glaube m

credentials [krɪ'denʃəlz] spl Beglaubigungsschreiben n, Akkreditiv n

credenza [krɪ'denzə] s Kredenz f

credibility [ˌkredɪˈbɪlɪti] s Glaubwürdigkeit f

credibil′ity gap′ s Vertrauenslücke f

credible [ˈkredɪbəl] adj glaubwürdig

credit [ˈkredɪt] s (credence) Glaube m; (honor) Ehre f; (recognition) Anerkennung f; (educ) Anrechnungspunkt m; (fin) Kredit m; (credit balance) (fin) Guthaben n; **be a c. to** Ehre machen (dat); **credits** (cin) Vorspann m; **give s.o. c. for s.th.** j-m etw hoch anrechnen; **on c.** auf Kredit; **on thirty days' c.** auf dreißig Tage Ziel; **take c. for** sich [dat] als Verdienst anrechnen; **to s.o.'s c.** zu j-s Ehre ‖ tr (believe) glauben (dat); (an account) gutschreiben (dat); **c. s.o. with s.th.** j-m etw hoch anrechnen

creditable [ˈkredɪtəbəl] adj ehrenwert

cre′dit card′ s Kreditkarte f

cre′dit hour′ s (educ) Anrechnungspunkt m

creditor [ˈkredɪtər] s Gläubiger –in f

cre′dit rat′ing s Bonität f

credulous [ˈkredʒələs] adj leichtgläubig

creed [krid] s (& fig) Glaubensbekenntnis n

creek [krik] s Bach m

creep [krip] s Kriechen n; (sl) Spinner m; **it gives me the creeps** mir gruselt ‖ v (pret & pp **crept** [krept]) intr kriechen, schleichen; (said of plants) kriechen; **c. along** dahinschleichen; **c. up on** heranschleichen an (acc); **it makes my flesh c.** es macht mich schaudern

creeper [ˈkripər] s Kletterpflanze f

creepy [ˈkripi] adj schauderregend; (sensation) gruselig; **have a c. feeling** gruseln

cremate [ˈkrimet] tr einäschern

cremation [krɪˈmeʃən] s Einäscherung f

crematory [ˈkrimɪˌtori] s Krematorium n

crepe [krep] s Krepp m; (mourning band) Trauerflor m

crepe′ pa′per s Kreppapier n

crescent [ˈkresənt] s Mondsichel f

cres′cent roll′ s Hörnchen n

cress [kres] s (bot) Kresse f

crest [krest] s (of a hill, wave, or rooster) Kamm m; (of a helmet) Helmbusch m; (of a bird) Federbüschel n

crestfallen [ˈkrestˌfɔlən] adj niedergeschlagen

Crete [krit] s Kreta n

crevice [ˈkrevɪs] s Riß m

crew [kru] s Gruppe f; (aer, nav) Besatzung f; (of a boat) (sport) Mannschaft f; (rowing) (sport) Rudersport m

crew′ cut′ s Bürstenschnitt m

crib [krɪb] s (manger) Krippe f; (for children) Kinderbettstelle f; (bin) Speicher m; (student's pony) Eselsbrücke f ‖ v (pret & pp **cribbed**; ger **cribbing**) tr & intr abbohren

cricket [ˈkrɪkɪt] s (ent) Grille f;

(sport) Kricketspiel n; **not c.** (coll) nicht fair

crime [kraɪm] s Verbrechen n

criminal [ˈkrɪmɪnəl] adj verbrecherisch; (act, case, code, court, law) Straf–; (investigation, trial, police) Kriminal– ‖ s Verbrecher –in mf

crim′inal charge′ s Strafanzeige f

crim′inal neg′ligence s grobe Fahrlässigkeit f

crim′inal offense′ s strafbare Handlung f

crim′inal rec′ord s Strafregister n

crimp [krɪmp] s Welle f; **put a c. in** (coll) e–n Dämpfer aufsetzen (dat) ‖ tr wellen, riffeln

crimson [ˈkrɪmzən] adj karmesinrot ‖ s Karmesin n

cringe [krɪndʒ] intr sich krümmen; (fawn) kriechen

crinkle [ˈkrɪŋkəl] s Runzel f ‖ tr runzeln; (one's nose) rümpfen

cripple [ˈkrɪpəl] s Krüppel m ‖ tr verkrüppeln; (fig) lähmen, lahmlegen

cri·sis [ˈkraɪsɪs] s (–ses [siz]) Krise f

crisp [krɪsp] adj (brittle) knusprig; (firm and fresh) mürb; (air, clothes) frisch; (manner) forsch

crisscross [ˈkrɪsˌkrɔs] adj & adv kreuz und quer ‖ tr kreuz und quer markieren ‖ intr sich kreuzen

criteri·on [kraɪˈtɪrɪ·ən] s (–a [ə] & –ons) Kennzeichen n, Kriterium n

critic [ˈkrɪtɪk] s Kritiker –in mf

critical [ˈkrɪtɪkəl] adj kritisch

criticism [ˈkrɪtɪˌsɪzəm] s Kritik f

criticize [ˈkrɪtɪˌsaɪz] tr kritisieren

critique [krɪˈtik] s (review) Rezension f; (critical discussion) Kritik f

croak [krok] s (of a frog) Quaken n; (of a raven) Krächzen n ‖ intr quaken; krächzen; (die) (sl) verrecken

cro·chet [kroˈʃe] s Häkelarbeit f ‖ v (pret & pp **–cheted** [ˈʃed]; ger **–cheting** [ˈʃe·ɪŋ]) tr & intr häkeln

crochet′ nee′dle s Häkelnadel f

crock [krɑk] s irdener Topf m, Krug m

crockery [ˈkrɑkəri] s irdenes Geschirr n

crocodile [ˈkrɑkəˌdaɪl] s Krokodil n

croc′odile tears′ spl Krokodilstränen pl

crocus [ˈkrokəs] s (bot) Krokus m

crone [kron] s altes Weib n

crony [ˈkroni] s alter Kamerad m

crook [kruk] s (of a shepherd) Hirtenstab m; (sl) Gauner m ‖ tr krümmen

crooked [ˈkrukɪd] adj krumm; (dishonest) unehrlich

croon [krun] tr & intr schmalzig singen

crooner [ˈkrunər] s Schnulzensänger m

crop [krɑp] s Ernte f; (whip) Peitsche f; (of a bird) Kropf m; (large number) Menge f; **the crops** die ganze Ernte ‖ v (pret & pp **cropped**; ger **cropping**) tr stutzen; (said of an animal) abfressen ‖ intr—**c. up** auftauchen

crop′ fail′ure s Mißerte f

croquet [kroˈke] s Krocket n

croquette [kro'ket] *s* (culin) Krokette *f*

crosier ['kroʒər] *s* Bischofsstab *m*

cross [krɔs] *adj* Quer-, Kreuz-; (biol) Kreuzungs-; (angry) (with) ärgerlich (auf *acc*, über *acc*) ‖ *s* (& fig) Kreuz *n*; (biol) Kreuzung *f* ‖ *tr* kreuzen; (a mountain) übersteigen; (oppose) in die Quere kommen (dat); **c. my heart!** Hand aufs Herz!; **c. oneself** sich bekreuzigen; **c. s.o.'s mind** j-m durch den Kopf gehen; **c. out** ausstreichen ‖ *intr* sich kreuzen; **c. over to** hinübergehen zu

cross′bones′ *spl* gekreuzte Skelettknochen *pl*

cross′bow′ *s* (hist) Armbrust *f*

cross′breed′ *v* (pret & pp –bred) *tr* kreuzen

cross′-coun′try *adj* (vehicle) geländegängig ‖ **cross′-coun′try** *s* (sport) Langlauf *m*

cross′cur′rent *s* Gegenströmung *f*

cross′-exam′ine *tr* ins Kreuzverhör nehmen

cross′-examina′tion *s* Kreuzverhör *n*

cross′-eyed′ *adj* schieläugig

cross′fire′ *s* Kreuzfeuer *n*

cross′ing *s* (of streets) Kreuzung *f*; (of the ocean) Überfahrt *f*, Überquerung *f*; (rr) Übergang *m*

cross′piece′ *s* Querstück *n*

cross′-pur′pose *s*—**be at cross-purposes** einander entgegenarbeiten

cross′ ref′erence *s* Querverweis *m*

cross′road′ *s* Querweg *m*; **crossroads** Straßenkreuzung *f*; (fig) Scheideweg *m*

cross′ sec′tion *s* Querschnitt *m*

cross′wind′ *s* Seitenwind *m*

cross′wise′ *adj & adv* quer, in die Quere

cross′word puz′zle *s* Kreuzworträtsel *n*

crotch [krɑtʃ] *s* (of a tree) Gabelung *f*; (of a body or trousers) Schritt *m*

crotchety ['krɑtʃɪti] *adj* verschroben

crouch [krautʃ] *s* Hocke *f* ‖ *intr* hocken

croup [krup] *s* (of a horse) Kruppe *f*; (pathol) Halsbräune *f*

croupier ['krupɪər] *s* Croupier –in *mf*

crouton ['krutɑn] *s* gerösteter Brotwürfel *m*

crow [kro] *s* (cry) Krähen *n*; (bird) Krähe *f*; **as the c. flies** schnurgrade; **eat c.** klein beigeben ‖ *intr* krähen

crow′bar′ *s* Stemmeisen *n*

crowd [kraud] *s* Menge *f*; (mob) Masse *f*; (set) Gesellschaft *f* ‖ *tr* vollstopfen; (push) stoßen; **c. out** verdrängen ‖ *intr* (around) sich drängen (um); **c. into** sich hineindrängen in (acc)

crowd′ed *adj* überfüllt; (street) belebt

crown [kraun] *s* Krone *f*; (dent) Zahnkrone *f* ‖ *tr* krönen, bekränzen; (checkers) zur Dame machen; (sl) eins aufs Dach geben; (dent) überkronen

crown′ jew′els *spl* Kronjuwelen *pl*

crown′ prince′ *s* Kronprinz *m*

crown′ prin′cess *s* Kronprinzessin *f*

crow′s′-feet′ *spl* (wrinkles) Krähenfüße *pl*

crow′s′-nest′ *s* (naut) Krähennest *n*

crucial ['kruʃəl] *adj* entscheidend; (point) springend; **c. question** Gretchenfrage *f*; **c. test** Feuerprobe *f*

crucible ['krusɪbəl] *s* Schmelztiegel *m*

crucifix ['krusɪfɪks] *s* Kruzifix *n*

crucifixion [,krusɪ'fɪkʃən] *s* Kreuzigung *f*

cruci·fy ['krusɪ,faɪ] *v* (pret & pp –fied) *tr* kreuzigen

crude [krud] *adj* (raw, unrefined) roh; (person) grob, ungeschliffen; **c. joke** plumper Scherz *m*

crudity ['krudɪti] *s* Roheit *f*

cruel ['kru·əl] *adj* (to) grausam (gegen)

cruelty ['kru·əlti] *s* Grausamkeit *f*; **c. to animals** Tierquälerei *f*

cruet ['kru·ɪt] *s* Fläschchen *n*; (relig) Meßkännchen *n*

cruise [kruz] *s* Kreuzfahrt *f* ‖ *intr* (aer) mit Reisegeschwindigkeit fliegen; (aut) herumfahren; (naut) kreuzen

cruiser ['kruzər] *s* (nav) Kreuzer *m*

cruise′ ship′ *s* Vergnügungsdampfer *m*

cruller ['krʌlər] *s* Krapfen *m*

crumb [krʌm] *s* Krümel *m*; (& fig) Bröckchen *n*; (sl) Schweinehund *m*

crumble ['krʌmbəl] *tr & intr* zerbröckeln

crumbly ['krʌmbli] *adj* bröcklig

crummy ['krʌmi] *adj* (sl) schäbig

crumple ['krʌmpəl] *tr* zerknittern ‖ *intr* (said of clothes) faltig werden; (collapse) zusammenbrechen

crunch [krʌntʃ] *s* Knacken *n*; (of snow) Knirschen *n*; (tight situation) Druck *m* ‖ *tr* knirschend kauen ‖ *intr* (said of snow) knirschen; **c. on** knirschend kauen

crusade [kru'sed] *s* Kreuzzug *m*

crusader [kru'sedər] *s* Kreuzfahrer *m*

crush [krʌʃ] *s* Gedränge *n*; **have a c. on s.o.** (coll) in j-n vernarrt sein ‖ *tr* (zer)quetschen, zerdrücken; (grain) schroten; (stone) zerkleinern; (suppress) unterdrücken; (oppress) bedrücken; (hopes) knicken; (overwhelm) zerschmettern; (min) pochen; **c. out** (a cigarette) ausdrücken ‖ *intr* zerdrückt werden

crush′ing *adj* (victory) entscheidend; (defeat) vernichtend; (experience) überwältigend

crust [krʌst] *s* Kruste *f*; (sl) Frechheit *f*

crustacean [krʌs'teʃən] *s* Krebstier *n*

crustaceous [krʌs'teʃəs] *adj* Krebs–

crusty ['krʌsti] *adj* krustig, rösch; (surly) mürrisch

crutch [krʌtʃ] *s* (& fig) Krücke *f*

crux [krʌks] *s* Kern *m*, Kernpunkt *m*

cry [kraɪ] *s* (cries) (shout) Schrei *m*, Ruf *m*; (weeping) Weinen *n*; **a far cry from** etw ganz anderes als; **cry for help** Hilferuf *m*; **have a good cry** sich ordentlich ausweinen ‖ *v* (pret & pp **cried**) *tr* schreien, rufen; **cry one's eyes out** sich [dat] die Augen aus dem Kopf weinen ‖ *intr* (weep) weinen; (shout) schreien; cry for help um Hilfe rufen; cry on s.o.'s shoulder j-m seine Not klagen; cry out against scharf verurteilen; cry out in (pain) schreien vor (dat); cry over nachweinen (dat)

cry'ba'by s (-bies) Schreihals m

cry'ing adj—c. jag Schreikrampf m; c. shame schreiende Ungerechtigkeit f ‖ s Weinen n; for c. out loud! um Himmels willen!

crypt [krɪpt] s Totengruft f, Krypta f

cryptic(al) ['krɪptɪk(əl)] adj (secret) geheim; (puzzling) rätselhaft; (coded) verschlüsselt

crystal ['krɪstəl] adj Kristall- ‖ s Kristall m; (cut glass) Kristallglas n; (of a watch) Uhrglas n

crys'tal ball' s Kristall m

crystalline ['krɪstəlɪn], ['krɪstə,laɪn] adj kristallinisch, kristallen

crystallize ['krɪstə,laɪz] tr kristallisieren ‖ intr kristallisieren; (fig) feste Form annehmen

cub [kʌb] s Junge n

Cuba ['kjubə] s Kuba n

Cuban ['kjubən] adj kubanisch ‖ s Kubaner –in m

cubbyhole ['kʌbɪ,hol] s gemütliches Zimmerchen n

cube [kjub] s Würfel m; (math) dritte Potenz f ‖ tr in Würfel schneiden; (math) kubieren

cubic ['kjubɪk] adj Raum-; (math) kubisch; c. foot Kubikfuß m

cub' report'er s unerfahrener Reporter m

cub' scout' s Wölfling m

cuckold ['kʌkəld] s Hahnrei m ‖ tr zum Hahnrei machen

cuckoo ['kuku] adj (sl) verrückt ‖ s Kuckuck m

cuck'oo clock' s Kuckucksuhr f

cucumber ['kjukʌmbər] s Gurke f

cud [kʌd] s—chew the cud wiederkäuen

cuddle ['kʌdəl] tr herzen ‖ intr sich kuscheln; c. up sich behaglich zusammenkuscheln

cudg·el ['kʌdʒəl] s Prügel m ‖ v (pret & pp -el[l]ed; ger -el[l]ing) tr verprügeln

cue [kju] s Hinweis m; (billiards) Billardstock m; (theat) Stichwort n; take the cue from s.o. sich nach j-m richten ‖ tr das Stichwort geben (dat)

cuff [kʌf] s (of a shirt) Manschette f; (of trousers) Aufschlag m; (blow) Ohrfeige f; off the c. aus dem Handgelenk

cuff' link' s Manschettenknopf m

cuisine [kwɪ'zin] s Küche f

culinary ['kjulɪ,neri] adj kulinarisch, Koch–; c. art Kochkunst f

cull [kʌl] tr (choose) auslesen; (pluck) pflücken

culminate ['kʌlmɪ,net] intr (in) kulminieren (in dat), gipfeln (in dat)

culmination [,kʌlmɪ'neʃən] s Gipfel m

culpable ['kʌlpəbəl] adj schuldhaft

culprit ['kʌlprɪt] s Schuldige mf

cult [kʌlt] s Kult m, Kultus m

cultivate ['kʌltɪ,vet] tr (soil) bearbeiten; (plants) ziehen; (activities) betreiben; (an art) pflegen; (friendship) hegen

cul'tivat'ed adj kultiviert

cultivation [,kʌltɪ'veʃən] s (of the soil) Bearbeitung f; (of the arts) Pflege f; (of friendship) Hegen n; under c. bebaut

cultivator ['kʌltɪ,vetər] s (mach) Kultivator m

cultural ['kʌltʃərəl] adj kulturell, Kultur-

culture ['kʌltʃər] s Kultur f

cul'tured adj kultiviert

cul'ture me'dium s Nährboden m

culvert ['kʌlvərt] s Rinnstein m

cumbersome ['kʌmbərsəm] adj (unwieldy) unhandlich; (slow-moving) schwerfällig; (burdensome) lästig

cunning ['kʌnɪŋ] adj (arg)listig ‖ s List f, Arglist f, Schlauheit f

cup [kʌp] s Tasse f; (of a bra) Körbchen n; (fig, bot, relig) Kelch m; (sport) Pokal m ‖ v (pret & pp cupped; ger cupping) tr (the hands) wölben; (med) schröpfen

cupboard ['kʌbərd] s Schrank m

cupidity [kju'pɪdɪti] s Habgier f

cupola ['kjupələ] s Kuppel f

cur [kʌr] s Köter m; (pej) Halunke m

curable ['kjurəbəl] adj heilbar

curate ['kjurɪt] s Kaplan m

curative ['kjurətɪv] adj heilend, Heil–

curator ['kju,retər] s Kustos m

curb [kʌrb] s (of a street) Randstein m; (of a horse) Kandare f ‖ tr (& fig) zügeln; (a person) an die Kandare nehmen

curb'stone' s Bordstein m

curd [kʌrd] s Quark m; curds Quark m

curdle ['kʌrdəl] tr gerinnen lassen; (fig) erstarren lassen ‖ intr gerinnen, stocken; (fig) erstarren

cure [kjur] s (restoration to health) Heilung f; (remedy) Heilmittel n; (treatment) Kur f ‖ tr (a disease, evil) heilen; (by smoking) räuchern; (by drying) trocknen; (by salting) einsalzen ‖ intr heilen

cure'-all' s Allheilmittel n

curfew ['kʌrfju] s Ausgehverbot n; (enforced closing time) Polizeistunde f

curi·o ['kjurɪ,o] s (-os) Kuriosität f

curiosity [,kjurɪ'ɑsɪti] s Neugier f; (strange article) Kuriosität f

curious ['kjurɪ·əs] adj neugierig; (odd) kurios, merkwürdig

curl [kʌrl] s (of hair) Locke f; (of smoke) Rauchkringel m ‖ tr locken; (lips) verächtlich schürzen ‖ intr sich kräuseln; c. up sich zusammenrollen; (said of an edge) sich umbiegen

curler ['kʌrlər] s Haarwickler m

curlicue ['kʌrlɪ,kju] s Schnörkel m

curly ['kʌrli] adj lockig; (leaves, etc.) gekräuselt

currant ['kʌrənt] s (raisin) Korinthe f; (genus Ribes) Johannisbeere f

currency [ˈkʌrənsi] s (*money*) Währung *f*; (*circulation*) Umlauf *m*; **foreign c.** Devisen *pl*; **gain c.** in Gebrauch kommen

current [ˈkʌrənt] *adj* (*year, prices, account*) laufend; (*events*) aktuell, Tages—; **be c.** Gültigkeit haben; (*said of money*) gelten ‖ *s* (& elec) Strom *m*

currently [ˈkʌrəntli] *adv* gegenwärtig

curricu·lum [kəˈrɪkjələm] *s* (**-lums &** **-la** [lə]) Lehrplan *m*

cur·ry [ˈkʌri] *s* Curry *m* ‖ *v* (*pret &* *pp* **–ried**) *tr* (*a horse*) striegeln; **c.** **favor with s.o.** sich bei j—m einzuschmeicheln suchen

cur′rycomb′ *s* Striegel *m*

cur′ry pow′der *s* Currypulver *n*

curse [kʌrs] *s* Fluch *m*; **put a c. on** verwünschen ‖ *tr* verfluchen ‖ *intr* (**at**) fluchen (**auf** *acc*)

cursed [ˈkʌrsɪd], [kʌrst] *adj* verflucht

curse′ word′ *s* Fluchwort *n*, Schimpfwort *n*

cursive [ˈkʌrsɪv] *adj* Kurrent—

cursory [ˈkʌrsəri] *adj* flüchtig

curt [kʌrt] *adj* barsch, schroff

curtail [kərˈtel] *tr* einschränken

curtain [ˈkʌrtɪn] *s* Gardine *f*; (*drape*) Vorhang *m*; (theat) Vorhang *m* ‖ *tr*—**c. off** mit Vorhängen abteilen

cur′tain call′ *s* Vorhang *m*, Hervorruf *m*

cur′tain rod′ *s* Gardinenstange *f*

curt·sy [ˈkʌrtsi] *s* Knicks *m* ‖ *v* (*pret* *& pp* **–sied**) *intr* (**to**) knicksen (**vor** *dat*)

curvaceous [kʌrˈveʃəs] *adj* kurvenreich

curvature [ˈkʌrvətʃər] *s* (*of the spine*) Verkrümmung *f*; (*of the earth*) Krümmung *f*

curved *adj* krumm

cushion [ˈkuʃən] *s* Kissen *n*, Polster *m & n*; (billiards) Bande *f* ‖ *tr* polstern; (*a shock*) abfedern

cuss [kʌs] *s* (sl) Kerl *m*; (*curse*) (sl) Fluch *m* ‖ *tr* (sl) verfluchen ‖ *intr* (sl) fluchen

cussed [ˈkʌsɪd] *adj* (sl) verflucht

cussedness [ˈkʌsɪdnɪs] *s* (sl) Bosheit *f*

custard [ˈkʌstərd] *s* Eierkrem *f*

custodian [kəsˈtodɪ·ən] *s* (*e.g., of records*) Verwalter *m*; (*of inmates*) Wärter *m*; (*caretaker*) Hausmeister *m*

custody [ˈkʌstədi] *s* Verwahrung *f*, Obhut *f*; (jur) Gewahrsam *m*; **c. of** (*children*) Sorgerecht für; **in the c.** **of** in der Obhut (*genit*); **take into c.** in Gewahrsam nehmen

custom [ˈkʌstəm] *s* Brauch *m*, Sitte *f*; (*habit*) Gewohnheit *f*; **customs** Zollkontrolle *f*; **pay customs on s.th.** für etw Zoll bezahlen

customary [ˈkʌstəˌmeri] *adj* gebräuchlich

cus′tom-built′ *adj* nach Wunsch gebaut

customer [ˈkʌstəmər] *s* Kunde *m*, Kundin *f*; (*in a restaurant*) Gast *m*; (telp) Teilnehmer *m* –in *mf*

cus′tom-made′ *adj* nach Maß angefertigt

cus′toms clear′ance *s* Zollabfertigung *f*

cus′toms declara′tion *s* Zollerklärung *f*; (*form*) Abfertigungsschein *m*

cus′toms inspec′tion *s* Zollkontrolle *f*

cus′toms of′fice *s* Zollamt *n*

customs of′ficer *s* Zollbeamte *m*, Zollbeamtin *f*

cus′tom tai′lor *s* Maßschneider *m*

cut [kʌt] *adj* (*glass*) geschliffen; **cut flowers** Schnittblumen *pl*; **cut out for** wie geschaffen für (**or** zu) ‖ *s* Schnitt *m*; (*piece cut off*) Abschnitt *m*; (*slice*) Schnitte *f*; (*wound*) Schnittwunde *f*; (*of a garment*) Schnitt *m*, Fasson *f*; (*of the profits*) Anteil *m*; (*in prices, pay*) Kürzung *f*, Senkung *f*; (*absence from school*) Schwänzen *n*; (*of meat*) Stück *n*; (cards) Abheben *n*; (tennis) Drehschlag *m*; **a cut above** e—e Stufe besser als ‖ *v* (*pret & pp* **cut**; *ger* **cutting**) *tr* schneiden; (*glass, precious stones*) schleifen; (*grass*) mähen; (*hedges*) stutzen; (*hay*) machen; (*a tunnel*) bohren; (*a motor*) abstellen; (*production*) drosseln; (*pay*) kürzen, vermindern; (*class*) (coll) schwänzen; (*prices*) herabsetzen, kürzen; (*whiskey*) (coll) panschen; (*cards*) abheben; (tennis) schneiden; **cut back** (*plants*) stutzen; (fig) abbauen; **cut down** fällen; **cut it out!** Schluß damit!; **cut off** abschneiden; (*a tail*) kupieren; (*gas, telephone, electricity*) absperren; (*troops*) absprengen; **cut one′s finger** sich in den Finger schneiden; **cut out the nonsense!** laß den Quatsch!; **cut short** (*e.g., a vacation*) abkürzen; (*a person*) dem Wort abschneiden (*dat*); **cut up** zerstückeln ‖ *intr* schneiden; **cut down on** einschränken, verringern; **cut in** sich einmischen; (*at a dance*) ablösen; **cut in ahead of s.o.** vor j—m einbiegen; **cut up** (sl) wild darauf losschießen

cut-and-dried [ˈkʌtənˈdraɪd] *adj* fix und fertig

cut′away′ *s* Cut *m*

cut′back′ *s* Einschränkung *f*

cute [kjut] *adj* (*pretty*) niedlich; (*shrewd*) (coll) klug

cut′ glass′ *s* geschliffenes Glas *n*

cuticle [ˈkjutɪkəl] *s* Nagelhaut *f*

cutie [ˈkjuti] *s* (sl) flotte Biene *f*

cutlass [ˈkʌtləs] *s* Entermesser *n*

cutlery [ˈkʌtləri] *s* Schneidwerkzeuge *pl*

cutlet [ˈkʌtlɪt] *s* Schnitzel *n*

cut′-off′ *s* (*turn-off*) Abzweigung *f*; (*cut-off point*) (acct) gemeinsamer Endpunkt *m*; (elec) Ausschaltvorrichtung *f*; (mach) Absperrvorrichtung *f*

cut′-off date′ *s* Abschlußtag *m*

cut′-out′ *s* Ausschnitt *m*; (*design to be cut out*) Ausschneidemuster *n*; (aut) Auspuffklappe *f*

cut′-rate′ *adj* (*price*) Schleuder—

cutter [ˈkʌtər] *s* (naut) Kutter *m*

cut′throat′ *adj* halsabschneiderisch ‖ *s* Halsabschneider *m* –in *mf*

cut′ting *adj* schneidend; (*tools*)

Schneide–; (*remark*) scharf ‖ *s* Abschnitt *m*; (*of prices*) Herabsetzung *f*; (*hort*) Steckling *m*; **cuttings** Abfälle *pl*

cut′ting board′ *s* Schneidebrett *n*

cut′ting edge′ *s* Schnittkante *f*

cut′ting room′ *s* (cin) Schneideraum *m*

cuttlefish [′kʌtəl,fɪʃ] *s* Tintenfisch *m*

cyanamide [saɪ′ænə,maɪd] *s* (chem) Zyanamid *n*; (com) Kalkstickstoff *m*

cycle [′saɪkəl] *s* Kreis *m*; (*of an internal combustion engine*) Takt *m*; (phys) Periode *f* ‖ *intr* radeln

cyclic(al) [′sɪklɪk(əl)] *adj* zyklisch, kreisförmig

cyclist [′saɪklɪst] *s* Radfahrer –in *mf*

cyclone [′saɪklon] *s* Zyklon *m*

cyclotron [′saɪklə,trɑn] *s* Zyklotron *n*, Beschleuniger *m*

cylinder [′sɪlɪndər] *s* Zylinder *m*

cyl′inder block′ *s* Zylinderblock *m*

cyl′inder bore′ *s* Zylinderbohrung *f*

cyl′inder head′ *s* Zylinderkopf *m*

cylindric(al) [sɪ′lɪndrɪk(əl)] *adj* zylindrisch

cymbal [′sɪmbəl] *s* Becken *n*

cynic [′sɪnɪk] *adj* (philos) zynisch ‖ *s* Menschenverächter –in *mf*; (philos) Zyniker *m*

cynical [′sɪnɪkəl] *adj* zynisch

cynicism [′sɪnɪ,sɪzəm] *s* Zynismus *m*; (*cynical remark*) zynische Bemerkung *f*

cypress [′saɪprəs] *s* Zypresse *f*

Cyprus [′saɪprəs] *s* Zypern *n*

Cyrillic [sɪ′rɪlɪk] *adj* kyrillisch

cyst [sɪst] *s* Zyste *f*

czar [zɑr] *s* Zar *m*

czarina [zɑ′hinə] *s* Zarin *f*

Czech [tʃɛk] *adj* tschechisch ‖ *s* Tscheche *m*, Tschechin *f*; (*language*) Tschechisch *n*

Czechoslovakia [,tʃɛkəslo′vækɪ-ə] *s* die Tschechoslowakei *f*

D

D, d [di] *s* vierter Buchstabe des englischen Alphabets; (mus) D; **D flat** Des *n*; **D sharp** Dis *n*

D.A. *abb* (**District Attorney**) Staatsanwalt *m*

dab [dæb] *s* (*of color*) Klecks *m*; (*e.g., of butter*) Stückchen *n* ‖ *v* (*pret & pp* **dabbed**) *ger* **dabbing**) *tr* betupfen ‖ *intr*—**dab at** betupfen

dabble [′dæbəl] *tr* bespritzen ‖ *intr* (*splash about*) plantschen; **d. in** herumstümpern in (*dat*)

dachshund [′dɑks,hʊnd] *s* Dachshund *m*

dad [dæd] *s* (coll) Vati *m*

daddy [′dædi] *s* (coll) Vati *m*

dad′dy-long′legs′ *s* (**–legs**) Weberknecht *m*

daffodil [′dæfədɪl] *s* gelbe Narzisse *f*

daffy [′dæfi] *adj* (coll) doof

dagger [′dægər] *s* Dolch *m*; (typ) Kreuzzeichen *n*; **look daggers at s.o.** j-n mit Blicken durchbohren

dahlia [′dæljə] *s* Georgine *f*, Dahlie *f*

daily [′deli] *adj* täglich, Tages– ‖ *adv* täglich ‖ *s* Tageszeitung *f*

dainty [′denti] *adj* zart; (*food*) lecker; (*finiky*) wählerisch

dairy [′deri] *s* Molkerei *f*

dair′y farm′ *s* Meierei *f*

dair′y farm′er *s* Meier –in *mf*

dais [′de·ɪs] *s* Tribüne *f*

daisy [′dezi] *s* Gänseblümchen *n*

dal-ly [′dæli] *v* (*pret & pp* **–lied**) *intr* (*delay*) herumtrödeln; (*play amorously*) liebäugeln

dam [dæm] *s* Damm *m*; (*female quadruped*) Muttertier *f* ‖ *v* (*pret & pp* **dammed**) *ger* **damming**) *tr* eindämmen; **dam up** anstauen

damage [′dæmɪdʒ] *s* Schaden *m*; **damages** (jur) Schadenersatz *m*; **do d.** Schaden anrichten; **sue for damages**

auf Schadenersatz klagen ‖ *tr* beschädigen; (*a reputation*) beeinträchtigen

dam′aging *adj* (*influence*) schädlich; (*evidence*) belastend

dame [dem] *s* Dame *f*; (sl) Weibsbild *n*

damn [dæm] *adj* (sl) verflucht ‖ *s*— **I don′t give a d. about it** (sl) ich mache mir e-n Dreck daraus; **not be worth a d.** (sl) keinen Pfifferling wert sein ‖ *tr* verdammen; (*curse*) verfluchen; **d. it!** (sl) verflucht!

damnation [dæm′neʃən] *s* Verdammnis *f*

damned *adj* verdammt; (sl) verflucht ‖ *adv* (sl) verdammt ‖ **the d.** *spl* die Verdammten *pl*

damp [dæmp] *adj* feucht ‖ *s* Feuchtigkeit *f* ‖ *tr* (be)feuchten; (*a fire; enthusiasm*) dämpfen; (elec, mus, phys) dämpfen

dampen [′dæmpən] *tr* befeuchten; (fig) dämpfen

damper [′dæmpər] *s* (*of a fireplace*) Schieber *m*; (*of a stove*) Ofenklappe *f*; (mus) Dämpfer *m*; **put a d. on** e-n Dämpfer aufsetzen (*dat*)

dampness [′dæmpnɪs] *s* Feuchtigkeit *f*

damsel [′dæmzəl] *s* Jungfrau *f*

dance [dæns] *s* Tanz *m* ‖ *tr & intr* tanzen

dance′ band′ *s* Tanzkapelle *f*

dance′ floor′ *s* Tanzfläche *f*

dance′ hall′ *s* Tanzsaal *m*, Tanzlokal *n*

dancer [′dænsər] *s* Tänzer –in *mf*

dance′ step′ *s* Tanzschritt *m*

danc′ing part′ner *s* Tanzpartner –in *mf*

dandelion [′dændɪ,laɪ-ən] *s* Löwenzahn *m*

dandruff [′dændrəf] *s* Schuppen *pl*

dandy ['dændi] *adj* (coll) pfundig, nett ‖ *s* Stutzer *m*
Dane [den] *s* Däne *m*, Dänin *f*
danger ['dendʒər] *s* (**to**) Gefahr *f* (für)
dan'ger list' *s*—**be on the d.** in Lebensgefahr sein
dangerous ['dendʒərəs] *adj* gefährlich
dangle ['dæŋgəl] *tr* schlenkern, baumeln lassen ‖ *intr* baumeln
Danish ['denɪʃ] *adj* dänisch ‖ *s* (*language*) Dänisch *n*
Dan'ish pas'try *s* feines Hefegebäck *n*
dank [dæŋk] *adj* feucht
Danube ['dænjub] *s* Donau *f*
dapper ['dæpər] *adj* schmuck
dappled ['dæpəld] *adj* scheckig, bunt
dare [dɛr] *s* Herausforderung *f* ‖ *tr* wagen; (*a person*) herausfordern; **d. to** (*inf*) es wagen zu (*inf*); **don't you d.** go unterstehen Sie sich, wegzugehen!; **I d. say** ich darf wohl behaupten ‖ *intr*—**don't you d.!** unterstehen Sie sich!
dare'dev'il *s* Waghals *m*, Draufgänger *m*
dar'ing *adj* (*deed*) verwegen; (*person*) wagemutig ‖ *s* Wagemut *m*
dark [dɑrk] *adj* finster; (*color, beer, complexion*) dunkel; (fig) düster ‖ *s* Finsternis *f*, Dunkel *n*; **be in the d. about** im unklaren sein über (*acc*)
Dark' A'ges *spl* frühes Mittelalter *n*
dark-complexioned ['dɑrkkəm'plekʃənd] *adj* dunkelhäutig
darken ['dɑrkən] *tr* (*a room*) verfinstern ‖ *intr* sich verfinstern; (fig) sich verdüstern
dark'-eyed' *adj* schwarzäugig
dark' horse' *s* Außenseiter *m*
darkly ['dɑrkli] *adv* geheimnisvoll
darkness ['dɑrknɪs] *s* Finsternis *f*
dark'room' *s* (phot) Dunkelkammer *f*
darling ['dɑrlɪŋ] *adj* lieb ‖ *s* Liebchen *n*
darn [dɑrn] *adj* (coll) verwünscht ‖ *adv* (coll) verdammt ‖ *s*—**I don't give a d. about** it ich pfeif drauf! ‖ *tr* (*stockings*) stopfen; **d. it!** (coll) verflixt!; **I'll be darned if** der Kuckuck soll mich holen, wenn
darn'ing nee'dle *s* Stopfnadel *f*
dart [dɑrt] *s* Wurfspieß *m*, Pfeil *m*; (sew) Abnäher *m*; **darts** (*game*) Pfeilwerfen *n*; **play darts** Pfeile werfen ‖ *intr* huschen; **d. ahead** vorschießen; **d. off** davonstürzen
dash [dæʃ] *s* (*rush*) Ansturm *m*; (*smartness*) Schneidigkeit *f*; (*spirit*) Schwung *m*; (*of solids*) Prise *f*; (*of liquids*) Schuß *m*; (sport) Kurzstreckenlauf *m*; (*typ*) Gedankenstrich *m*; **make a d. for** losstürzen auf (*acc*) ‖ *tr* (*throw*) schleudern; (*hopes*) niederschlagen, knicken; **d. off** (*a letter*) hinwerfen ‖ *intr* stürmen, stürzen
dash'board' *s* (aut) Armaturenbrett *n*
dash'ing *adj* schneidig, forsch
dastardly ['dæstərdli] *adj* feige
data ['detə] *s* or *spl* Daten *pl*, Angaben *pl*
da'ta proc'essing *s* Datenverarbeitung *f*

date [det] *s* Datum *n*; (*fixed time*) Termin *m*; (*period*) Zeitraum *m*; (*appointment*) (coll) Verabredung *f*; (*person on a date*) Freund –in *mf*; (bot) Dattel *f*; (jur) Termin *m*; **have a d. with** verabredet sein mit; **make a d. with** sich verabreden mit; **out of d.** veraltet; **to d.** bis heute; **what is the d. today?** der wievielte ist heute? ‖ *tr* datieren; (coll) ausgehen mit ‖ *intr*—**d. back to** zurückgehen auf (*acc*); **d. from** stammen aus
dat'ed *adj* (*provided with a date*) datiert; (*out-of-date*) zeitgebunden
date' line' *s* Datumsgrenze *f*
date'line' *s* (journ) Datumszeile *f*
date' palm' *s* Dattelpalme *f*
dative ['detɪv] *s* Dativ *m*, Wemfall *m*
daub [dɔb] *s* Bewurf *m* ‖ *tr* (*a canvas*) beschmieren; (*a wall*) bewerfen; (*e.g. mud, plaster*) (**on**) schmieren (auf *acc*) ‖ *intr* (paint) klecksen
daughter ['dɔtər] *s* Tochter *f*
daugh'ter-in-law' *s* (**daughters-in-law**) Schwiegertochter *f*
daunt [dɔnt] *tr* einschüchtern
dauntless ['dɔntlɪs] *adj* furchtlos
davenport ['dævən‚pɔrt] *s* Diwan *m*
davit ['dævɪt] *s* (naut) Bootskran *m*
daw [dɔ] *s* (orn) Dohle *f*
dawdle ['dɔdəl] *intr* trödeln, bummeln
dawn [dɔn] *s* Morgendämmerung *f*; (fig) Anbeginn *m* ‖ *intr* dämmern; **d. on s.o.** j–m zum Bewußtsein kommen
day [de] *adj* Tage–, Tages– ‖ *s* Tag *m*; (*specific date*) Termin *m*; **all day long** den ganzen Tag; **by day** am Tage, bei Tage; **by the day** tageweise; **call it a day** (coll) Feierabend machen; **day after day** Tag für Tag; **day by day** Tag für Tag; **day in, day out** tagaus, tagein; **day off** Urlaubstag *m*, Ruhetag *m*; **every other day** jeden zweiten Tag; **in days of old** in alten Zeiten; **in his day** zu seiner Zeit; **in those days** damals; **one day** e–s Tages; **one of these days** demnächst; **the day after** am folgenden Tag; **the day after tomorrow** übermorgen; **the day before** am Vortag; **the day before yesterday** vorgestern; **the other day** neulich, unlängst; **these days** heutzutage; **to this very day** bis auf den heutigen Tag; **what day of the week is it?** welchen Wochentag haben wir?
day' bed' *s* Ruhebett *n*, Liege *f*
day'break' *s* Tagesanbruch *m*
day'-by-day' *adj* tagtäglich, Tag für Tag
day'-care cen'ter *s* Kindertagesstätte *f*, Kindergarten *m*
day' coach' *s* (rr) Personenwagen *m*
day'dream' *s* Träumerei *f*, Wachtraum *m*; (*wild ideas*) Phantasterei *f* ‖ *intr* mit offenen Augen träumen
day'dream'er *s* Träumer –in *mf*
day' la'borer *s* Tagelöhner –in *mf*
day'light' *adj* Tageslicht– ‖ *s* Tageslicht *n*; **in broad d.** am hellichten Tag; **knock the daylights out of** (sl) zur Sau machen

day′light-sav′ing time′ *s* Sommerzeit *f*
day′ nurs′ery *s* Kleinkinderbewahran-
stalt *f*
day′ of reck′oning *s* Jüngster Tag *m*
day′ shift′ *s* Tagschicht *f*
day′time′ *s* Tageszeit *f*; **in the d.** bei
Tage, am Tage
daze [dez] *s* Benommenheit *f*; **be in a
d.** benommen sein ‖ *tr* betäuben
dazzle [′dæzəl] *s* Blenden *n* ‖ *tr* (&
fig) blenden
dazz′ling *adj* blendend
D-day [′di‚de] *s* X-Tag *m*; (hist) In-
vasionstag *m*
deacon [′dikən] *s* Diakon *m*
deaconess [′dikɪnɪs] *s* Diakonisse *f*
dead [ded] *adj* tot; (plant) abgestorben, dürr; (faint, sleep) tief; (numb)
gefühllos; (volcano, fire) erloschen;
(elec) stromlos; (sport) tot, nicht im
Spiel; **as a doornail** mausetot;
d. shot unfehlbarer Schütze *m*; **d.
stop** völliger Stillstand *m*; **d. silence**
Totenstille *f* ‖ *adv* völlig, tod– ‖ *s*—
in the d. of night mitten in der
Nacht; **in the d. of winter** im tief-
sten Winter
dead′ beat′ *s* (sl) Nichtstuer –in *mf*
dead′ bolt′ *s* Absteller *m*
dead′ calm′ *s* Windstille *f*
dead′ cen′ter *s* genaue Mitte *f*; (dead
point) (mach) toter Punkt *m*
deaden [′dedən] *tr* (pain) betäuben;
(a nerve) abtöten; (sound) dämpfen
dead′ end′ *s* (& fig) Sackgasse *f*
dead′head′ *s* Dummkopf *m*
dead′ heat′ *s* totes Rennen *n*
dead′-let′ter of′fice *s* Abteilung *f* für
unbestellbare Briefe
dead′line′ *s* (letzter) Termin *m*; (journ)
Redaktionsschluß *m*; **meet the d.**
den Termin einhalten; **set a d. for**
terminieren
dead′lock′ *s* Stillstand *m*; **break the d.**
den toten Punkt überwinden; **reach
a d.** steckenbleiben ‖ *tr* zum völligen
Stillstand bringen; **become deadlocked** stocken
deadly [′dedli] *adj* (fatal) tödlich; **d.
enemy** Todfeind –in *mf*; **d. fear**
Todesangst *f* ‖ *adv*—**d. dull** sterben-
langweilig; **d. pale** leichenblaß
dead′ly sins′ *spl* Todsünden *pl*
dead′pan′ *adj* (look) ausdruckslos;
(person) schafsgesichtig
dead′ pan′ *s* (coll) Schafsgesicht *n*
dead′ reck′oning *s* (naut) Koppelkurs
m
dead′ ring′er [′rɪŋər] *s* (coll) Doppelgänger *m*
dead′wood′ *s* (& fig) totes Holz *n*
deaf [def] *adj* taub; **d. and dumb** taubstumm; **d. to** (fig) taub gegen; **turn
a d. ear to** taube Ohren haben für
deafen [′defən] *tr* betäuben
deaf′ening *adj* ohrenbetäubend
deaf′-mute′ *adj* taubstumm ‖ *s* Taubstumme *mf*
deafness [′defnɪs] *s* Taubheit *f*
deal [dil] *s* (business transaction) Geschäft *n*; (underhanded agreement)
Schiebung *f*; (cards) Austeilen *n*,
Geben *n*; **a good d. of** (coll) ziemlich

viel; **a good d. worse** (coll) viel (or
weit) schlechter; **a great d. of** (coll)
sehr viel; **give s.o. a good d.** (be fair
to s.o.) j–n fair behandeln; (make
s.o. a good offer) j–m ein gutes Angebot machen; **give s.o. a raw d.** j–m
übel mitspielen; **it is my d.** (cards)
ich muß geben; **it's a d.!** abgemacht!; **make a d.** (coll) ein Abkommen treffen ‖ *v* (pret & pp **dealt**
[delt]) *tr* (a blow) versetzen; (cards)
austeilen, geben ‖ *intr* (cards) geben;
d. at (a store) kaufen bei; **d. in** handeln mit; **d. with** (settle) erledigen;
(occupy oneself or itself with) sich
befassen mit; (treat, e.g., fairly) behandeln; (patronize) kaufen bei; (do
business with) in Geschäftsbeziehun-
gen stehen mit; **I'll d. with you later**
mit Ihnen werde ich später abrechnen!
dealer [′dilər] *s* Geber –in *mf*; (com)
Händler –in *mf*
deal′ings *spl* (business dealings) Handel *m*; (relations) Umgang *m*; **I'll
have no d. with** ich will nichts zu
tun haben mit
dean [din] *s* (eccl, educ) Dekan *m*
dean′ship′ *s* (eccl, educ) Dekanat *n*
dear [dɪr] *adj* lieb, traut; (expensive)
teuer; **Dear Madam** Sehr verehrte
gnädige Frau!; **Dear Mrs. X** Sehr
geehrte Frau X; **Dear Mr. X** Sehr
geehrter Herr X!; **Dear Sir** Sehr
geehrter Herr! ‖ *s* Liebling *m*,
Schatz *m* ‖ *interj*—**oh d.!** ach herrje!
dearie [′dɪri] *s* (coll) Liebchen *n*
dearth [dʌrθ] *s* (of) Mangel *m* (an dat)
death [deθ] *s* Tod *m*; (in the family)
Todesfall *m*; **at death's door** lebens-
krank; **catch d. of a cold** sich
[dat] den Tod holen; **he'll be the d.
of me yet** er bringt mich noch ins
Grab; **put to d.** hinrichten; **to the d.**
bis aufs Messer; **work to d.** totarbeiten
death′bed′ *s* Totenbett *n*, Sterbebett *n*
death′blow′ *s* Gnadenstoß *m*; (fig)
Todesstoß *m*
death′ certif′icate *s* Totenschein *m*
death′ house′ *s* Todeshaus *n*
death′ knell′ *s* Grabgeläute *n*
deathless [′deθlɪs] *adj* unsterblich
deathly [′deθli] *adj* tödlich, Todes–,
Toten– ‖ *adv* toten–
death′ mask′ *s* Totenmaske *f*
death′ pen′alty *s* Todesstrafe *f*
death′ rate′ *s* Sterblichkeitsziffer *f*
death′ rat′tle *s* Todesröcheln *n*
death′ sen′tence *s* Todesurteil *n*
death′ strug′gle *s* Todeskampf *m*
death′ trap′ *s* (fig) Mausefalle *f*
death′ war′rant *s* Hinrichtungsbefehl
m
debacle [de′bakəl] *s* Zusammenbruch
m
de-bar [dɪ′bɑr] *v* (pret & pp **–barred**;
ger **–barring**) *tr* (from) ausschließen
(aus)
debark [dɪ′bɑrk] *tr* ausschiffen ‖ *intr*
sich ausschiffen, an Land gehen
debarkation [‚dibɑr′keʃən] *s* Ausschiffung *f*

debase [dɪ'bes] *tr* entwürdigen; (*currency*) entwerten

debatable [dɪ'betəbəl] *adj* strittig

debate [dɪ'bet] *s* Debatte *f* ‖ *tr & intr* debattieren

debauch [dɪ'bɔtʃ] *s* Schwelgerei *f* ‖ *tr* verderben; (*seduce*) verführen; **d. oneself** verkommen

debauched *adj* ausschweifend

debauchee [,debə'tʃi] *s* Wüstling *m*

debauchery [dɪ'bɔtʃəri] *s* Schwelgerei *f*

debenture [dɪ'bentʃər] *s* (*bond*) Obligation *f;* (*voucher*) Schuldschein *m*

debilitate [dɪ'bɪlɪ,tet] *tr* entkräften

debility [dɪ'bɪlɪti] *s* Schwäche *f*

debit [debɪt] *s* Debet *n*, Soll *n;* (*as entry*) Belastung *f*

de'bit bal'ance *s* Sollsaldo *m*

de'bit side' *s* Soll *n*, Sollseite *f*

debonair [,debə'ner] *adj* (*courteous*) höflich; (*carefree*) heiter und sorglos

debris [de'bri] *s* Trümmer *pl*

debt [det] *s* Schuld *f;* **be in s.o.'s d.** j-m verpflichtet sein; **run into d.** in Schulden geraten

debtor ['detər] *s* Schuldner –in *mf*

de-bug [dɪ'bʌg] *v pret & pp* **-bugged;** *ger* **-bugging**) *tr* (*remove defects from*) bereinigen; (*electron*) Abhörgeräte entfernen aus

debut [de'bju], [de'bju] *s* Debüt *n;* **make one's d.** debütieren

debutante ['debju,tant] *s* Debütantin *f*

decade ['deked] *s* Jahrzehnt *n*, Dekade *f*

decadence ['dekədəns] *s* Dekadenz *f*

decadent ['dekədənt] *adj* dekadent; (*art*) entartet

decal ['dikæl] *s* Abziehbild *n*

decanter [dɪ'kæntər] *s* Karaffe *f*

decapitate [dɪ'kæpɪ,tet] *tr* enthaupten

decathlon [dɪ'kæθlan] *s* Zehnkampf *m*

decay [dɪ'ke] *s* (*rotting*) Fäulnis *f;* (*fig*) Verfall *m;* (*dent*) Karies *f;* **fall into d.** (& *fig*) in Verfall geraten ‖ *intr* verfaulen; (*fig*) verfallen

decease [dɪ'sis] *s* Ableben *n*

deceased *adj* verstorben ‖ *s* Verstorbene *mf*

deceit [dɪ'sit] *s* Betrügerei *f*

deceitful [dɪ'sitfəl] *adj* betrügerisch

deceive [dɪ'siv] *tr* betrügen ‖ *intr* trügen

decelerate [dɪ'selə,ret] *tr* verlangsamen ‖ *intr* seine Geschwindigkeit verringern

December [dɪ'sembər] *s* Dezember *m*

decency ['disənsi] *s* Anstand *m;* **decencies** Anstandsformen *pl*

decent ['disənt] *adj* anständig

decentralize [dɪ'sentrə,laɪz] *tr* dezentralisieren

deception [dɪ'sepʃən] *s* (*act of deceiving*) Betrug *m;* (*state of being deceived*) Täuschung *f*

deceptive [dɪ'septɪv] *adj* trügerisch; (*misleading*) irreführend; (*similarity*) täuschend

decide [dɪ'saɪd] *tr* entscheiden ‖ *intr* (**on**) sich entscheiden, sich entschließen (über *acc*, für)

deciduous [dɪ'sɪdʒuˑəs] *adj* blattabwerfend; **d. tree** Laubbaum *m*

decimal ['desɪməl] *adj* dezimal ‖ *s* Dezimalzahl *f*

dec'imal place' *s* Dezimalstelle *f*

dec'imal point' *s* (in German the comma is used to separate the decimal fraction from the integer) Komma *n*

decimate ['desɪ,met] *tr* dezimieren

decipher [dɪ'saɪfər] *tr* entziffern

decision [dɪ'sɪʒən] *s* Entscheidung *f*, Entschluß *m;* (jur) Urteil *n*

decisive [dɪ'saɪsɪv] *adj* entscheidend

deck [dek] *s* (*of cards*) Spiel *n;* (data proc) Kartensatz *m;* (naut) Deck *n*, Verdeck *n* ‖ *tr* (coll) zu Boden schlagen; **d. out** ausschmücken

deck' chair' *s* Liegestuhl *m*

deck' hand' *s* gemeiner Matrose *m*

deck' land'ing *s* (aer) Trägerlandung *f*

declaim [dɪ'klem] *tr & intr* deklamieren

declaration [,deklə'reʃən] *s* Erklärung *f;* (*at customs*) Zollerklärung *f*

declarative [dɪ'klærətɪv] *adj*—**d. sentence** Aussagesatz *m*

declare [dɪ'kler] *tr* erklären; (*tourist's belongings*) verzollen; (*commercial products*) deklarieren; **d. oneself against** sich aussprechen gegen

declension [dɪ'klenʃən] *s* Deklination *f*

declinable [dɪ'klaɪnəbəl] *adj* deklinierbar

decline [dɪ'klaɪn] *s* (*decrease*) Abnahme *f;* (*in prices*) Rückgang *m;* (*deterioration*) Verschlechterung *f;* (*slope*) Abhang *m;* (fig) Niedergang *m;* **be on the d.** in Abnahme begriffen sein ‖ *tr* (*refuse*) ablehnen; (gram) deklinieren ‖ *intr* (*refuse*) ablehnen; (*descend*) sich senken; (*sink*) sinken; (*draw to a close*) zu Ende gehen

declivity [dɪ'klɪvɪti] *s* Abhang *m*

decode [di'kod] *tr* entschlüsseln

decompose [,dikam'poz] *tr* zerlegen ‖ *intr* sich zersetzen, verwesen

decomposition [,dikampə'zɪʃən] *s* Zersetzung *f*, Verwesung *f*

decompression [,dikəm'preʃən] *s* Dekompression *f*

decontamination [,dikən,tæmɪ'neʃən] *s* Entseuchung *f*

décor [de'kɔr] *s* Dekor *m*

decorate ['dekə,ret] *tr* dekorieren, (aus)schmücken; (*a new room*) einrichten; (*e.g., with a badge*) auszeichnen

decoration [,dekə'reʃən] *s* Schmuck *m;* (mil) Orden *m*, Ehrenzeichen *n*, Dekoration *f*

decorative ['dekərətɪv] *adj* dekorativ

decorator ['dekə,retər] *s* Dekorateur –in *mf*

decorous ['dekərəs] *adj* schicklich

decorum [dɪ'korəm] *s* Schicklichkeit *f*

decoy ['dikɔɪ] *s* (*bird or person*) Lockvogel *m;* (*anything used as a lure*) Lockmittel *n* ‖ [dɪ'kɔɪ] *tr* locken

decrease ['dikris] *s* Abnahme *f* ‖

[dɪ'kris] *tr* verringern || *intr* abnehmen

decree [dɪ'kri] *s* Dekret *n*, Verordnung *f* || *tr* dekretieren, verordnen

decrepit [dɪ'krepɪt] *adj* (*age-worn*) altersschwach; (*frail*) gebrechlich

de·cry [dɪ'kraɪ] *v* (*pret & pp* **-cried**) *tr* (*disparage*) herabsetzen; (*censure openly*) kritisieren

dedicate ['dedɪ,ket] *tr* (*a book, one's life*) (*to*) widmen (*dat*); (*a building*) einweihen

dedication [,dedɪ'keʃən] *s* Widmung *f*; (*of a building, etc.*) Einweihung *f*; (*to*) Hingabe *f* (*an acc*)

deduce [dɪ'd(j)us] *tr* (*from*) schließen (*aus*)

deduct [dɪ'dʌkt] *tr* abziehen, abrechnen

deduction [dɪ'dʌkʃən] *s* Abzug *m*; (*conclusion*) Schluß *m*, Folgerung *f*

deed [did] *s* (*act*) Tat *f*; (*jur*) Besitzurkunde *f*

deem [dim] *tr* halten für; **d. s.o. worthy of my confidence** j-n meines Vertrauens für würdig halten

deep [dip] *adj* tief; (*recondite*) dunkel; (*impression*) tiefgehend; (*color, sound*) tief, dunkel; **be d. in debt** tief in Schulden stecken; **four** (*ranks*) **d. in Viererreihen; in d. water** (fig) in Schwierigkeiten; **that's too d. for me** das ist mir zu hoch || *adv* tief; **d. down in** tief innen in (*dat*) || *s* Tiefe *f*, Meer *n*

deepen ['dipən] *tr* (& fig) vertiefen || *intr* sich vertiefen

deep'-freeze' *v* (*pret* **-freezed & -froze**; *pp* **-freezed & -frozen**) *tr* tiefkühlen

deep'-fry' *v* (*pret & pp* **-fried**) *tr* fritieren

deep'-laid' *adj* schlau angelegt

deep' mourn'ing *s* tiefe Trauer *f*

deep'-root'ed *adj* tiefsitzend

deep'-set' *adj* (*eyes*) tiefliegend

deer [dɪr] *s* Hirsch *m*, Reh *n*, Rotwild *n*

deer'skin' *s* Hirschleder *n*, Wildleder *n*

deface [dɪ'fes] *tr* (*disfigure*) verunstalten; (*make illegible*) unleserlich machen

defacement [di'fesmənt] *s* Verunstaltung *f*

de facto [di'fækto] *adj & adv* tatsächlich, de facto

defamation [,defə'meʃən] *s* Verleumdung *f*

defame [dɪ'fem] *tr* verleumden

default [dɪ'fɔlt] *s* (*in duties*) Unterlassung *f*; (fin) Verzug *m*; **by d.** (jur) durch Nichterscheinen; (sport) durch Nichtantreten; **in d. of** in Ermangelung (*genit*) || *tr* nicht erfüllen; (fin) nicht zahlen || *intr* seinen Verpflichtungen nicht nachkommen; (fin) in Verzug sein

defeat [dɪ'fit] *s* Niederlage *f*; (parl) Niederstimmen *n*; **admit d.** sich geschlagen geben || *tr* besiegen, schlagen; (*frustrate*) hilflos machen; (*plans*) zunichte machen; (*a bill*) niederstimmen; **d. the purpose** den Zweck verfehlen

defeatism [dɪ'fitɪzəm] *s* Defätismus *m*

defeatist [dɪ'fitɪst] *s* Defätist *-in mf*

defecate ['defɪ,ket] *intr* Stuhl haben

defect ['difekt] *s* Defekt *m*; (*physical or mental defect*) Gebrechen *n*; (*imperfection*) Mangel *m*; (*in manufacture*) Fabrikationsfehler *m* || [dɪ'fekt] *intr* (*from*) (*a religion*) abfallen (*von*); (*a party*) abtrünnig werden (*von*); (*to*) überlaufen (*zu*)

defection [dɪ'fekʃən] *s* Abfall *m*; (*to*) Übertritt *m* (*zu*)

defective [dɪ'fektɪv] *adj* fehlerhaft; (gram) unvollständig; (tech) defekt

defector [dɪ'fektər] *s* (pol) Abtrünnige *mf*, Überläufer *-in mf*

defend [dɪ'fend] *tr* verteidigen

defendant [dɪ'fendənt] *s* (*in civil suit*) Beklagte *mf*; (*in criminal suit*) Angeklagte *mf*

defender [dɪ'fendər] *s* Verteidiger *-in mf*; (sport) Titelverteidiger *-in mf*

defense [dɪ'fens] *s* (& jur, sport) Verteidigung *f*; (*tactical*) (mil) Abwehr *f*; **d. against** (*e.g., disease*) Schutz *m* vor (*dat*)

defenseless [dɪ'fenslɪs] *adj* schutzlos

defensible [dɪ'fensɪbəl] *adj* verteidigungsfähig; (*argument, claim*) verfechtbar

defensive [dɪ'fensɪv] *adj* defensiv; (mil) Verteidigungs-, Abwehr- || *s* Defensive *f*; (*tactical*) Abwehr *f*; **be on the d.**—sich in der Defensive befinden

de·fer [dɪ'fʌr] *v* (*pret & pp* **-ferred**; *ger* **-ferring**) *tr* verschieben; (mil) zurückschieben || *intr*—**d. to** nachgeben (*dat*)

deference ['defərəns] *s* (*courteous regard*) Ehrerbietung *f*; (*yielding*) Nachgiebigkeit *f*; **in d. to** aus Rücksicht gegen; **with all due d. to** bei aller Achtung vor (*dat*)

deferential [,defə'renʃəl] *adj* ehrerbietig, rücksichtsvoll

deferment [dɪ'fʌrmənt] *s* Aufschub *m*; (mil) Zurückstellung *f*

defiance [dɪ'faɪəns] *s* Trotz *m*; **in d. of s.o.** j-m zum Trotz

defiant [dɪ'faɪənt] *adj* trotzig

deficiency [dɪ'fɪʃənsi] *s* (*of*) Mangel *m* (*an dat*); (*shortcoming*) Defekt *m*; (*deficit*) Defizit *n*

deficient [dɪ'fɪʃənt] *adj* mangelhaft; **be d. in** Mangel haben an (*dat*); **mentally d.** schwachsinnig

deficit ['defɪsɪt] *s* Defizit *n*

defilade [,defi'led] *s* Deckung *f* || *tr* gegen Feuer sichern

defile [dɪ'faɪl], ['difaɪl] *s* Hohlweg *m* || [dɪ'faɪl] *tr* beflecken

defilement [dɪ'faɪlmənt] *s* Befleckung *f*

define [dɪ'faɪn] *tr* definieren, bestimmen; (*e.g., boundaries*) festlegen

definite ['defɪnɪt] *adj* bestimmt

definition [,defɪ'nɪʃən] *s* Definition *f*, Bestimmung *f*; (opt) Bildschärfe *f*

definitive [dɪ'fɪnɪtɪv] *adj* endgültig

deflate [dɪ'flet] *tr* Luft ablassen aus; (*prices*) herabsetzen; (*s.o.'s ego, hopes*) e-n Stoß versetzen (*dat*)

deflation [dɪˈfleʃən] s (fin) Deflation f

deflect [dɪˈflɛkt] tr ablenken ‖ intr (from) abweichen (von)

deflection [dɪˈflɛkʃən] s Ablenkung f; Abweichung f; (of an indicator) Ausschlag m; (of light rays) Beugung f; (radar, telv) Ablenkung f

deflower [dɪˈflaʊ-ər] tr entjungfern

defoliate [diˈfolɪˌet] tr entblättern

deforest [diˈfɔrest] tr abholzen

deform [dɪˈfɔrm] tr entstellen

deformed adj verwachsen, mißförmig

deformity [dɪˈfɔrmɪti] s (state of being deformed) Mißgestalt f; (deformed part) Verwachsung f; (ugliness) Häßlichkeit f

defraud [dɪˈfrɔd] tr (of) betrügen (um)

defray [dɪˈfre] tr tragen, bestreiten

defrock [diˈfrɑk] tr das Priesteramt entziehen (dat)

defrost [dɪˈfrɔst] tr entfrosten

defroster [dɪˈfrɔstər] s Entfroster m

deft [dɛft] adj flink, fingerfertig

defunct [dɪˈfʌŋkt] adj (person) verstorben; (no longer in operation) stillgelegt; (no longer in effect) außer Kraft (befindlich); (newspaper) eingegangen

de•fy [dɪˈfaɪ] v (pret & pp –fied) tr trotzen (dat); (challenge) herausfordern; **d. description** sich nicht beschreiben lassen

degeneracy [dɪˈdʒenərəsi] s Entartung f

degenerate [dɪˈdʒenərɪt] adj entartet, verkommen ‖ [dɪˈdʒenəˌret] intr entarten; (into) ausarten (in acc)

degrade [dɪˈgred] tr degradieren; (bring into low esteem) entwürdigen

degrading adj entwürdigend

degree [dɪˈgri] s Grad m; (gram) Steigerungsstufe f; **by degrees** gradweise; **d of latitude** Breitengrad m; **d. of longitude** Längengrad m; **take one's d.** promovieren; **to a d.** einigermaßen; **to a high d.** in hohem Maße

dehumanize [dɪˈhjuməˌnaɪz] tr entmenschlichen

dehumidifier [ˌdihjuˈmɪdɪˌfaɪ-ər] s Luftentfeuchter m

dehumidi•fy [ˌdihjuˈmɪdɪˌfaɪ] v (pret & pp –fied) tr entfeuchten

dehydrate [diˈhaɪdret] tr (vegetables) dörren, das Wasser entziehen (dat); (chem) dehydrieren ‖ intr das Wasser verlieren

dehydrated adj (vegetables) Trocken–; (body) dehydriert

deice [diˈaɪs] tr enteisen

dei•fy [ˈdiˌaɪ] v (pret & pp –fied) tr (a man) zum Gott erheben; (a woman) zur Göttin erheben

dejected adj niedergeschlagen

dejection [dɪˈdʒɛkʃən] s Niederschlagenheit f, Mutlosigkeit f

delay [dɪˈle] s Aufschub m, Verzögerung f; **without d.** unverzüglich ‖ tr (postpone) aufschieben; (detain) aufhalten ‖ intr zögern

delectable [dɪˈlɛktəbəl] adj ergötzlich

delegate [ˈdɛlɪˌget], [ˈdɛlɪgɪt] s De-

legierte mf ‖ [ˈdɛlɪˌget] tr delegieren; (authority) übertragen

delegation [ˌdɛlɪˈgeʃən] s (persons delegated) Delegation f; (e.g., of authority) Übertragung f

delete [dɪˈlit] tr tilgen

deletion [dɪˈliʃən] s Tilgung f

deliberate [dɪˈlɪbərɪt] adj (intentional) vorsätzlich, bewußt; (slow) gemessen, bedächtig ‖ [dɪˈlɪbəˌret] intr überlegen; (said of several persons) beratschlagen; **d. on** sich beraten über (acc)

deliberately [dɪˈlɪbərɪtli] adv mit Absicht

deliberation [dɪˌlɪbəˈreʃən] s Überlegung f; (by several persons) Beratung f; (slowness) Bedächtigkeit f

delicacy [ˈdɛlɪkəsi] s Zartheit f; (fine food) Delikatesse f

delicate [ˈdɛlɪkɪt] adj fein, delikat; (situation) heikel; (health) zart

delicatessen [ˌdɛlɪkəˈtɛsən] s (food) Delikatessen pl; (store) Delikatessengeschäft n

delicious [dɪˈlɪʃəs] adj köstlich

delight [dɪˈlaɪt] s Freude f; (high degree of pleasure) Entzücken n; **take d. in** Freude finden an (dat) ‖ tr entzücken, erfreuen; **be delighted by** sich freuen an (dat); **I'll be delighted to come** ich komme mit dem größten Vergnügen ‖ intr—**d. in** sich ergötzen an (dat)

delightful [dɪˈlaɪtfəl] adj entzückend

delimit [dɪˈlɪmɪt] tr abgrenzen

delineate [dɪˈlɪnɪˌet] tr zeichnen

delinquency [dɪˈlɪŋkwənsi] s Pflichtvergessenheit f; (misdeed) Vergehen n

delinquent [dɪˈlɪŋkwənt] adj pflichtvergessen; (guilty) straffällig; (overdue) rückständig; (in default) säumig ‖ s Straffällige mf

delirious [dɪˈlɪrɪ-əs] adj irre; (with) rasend (vor dat)

delirium [dɪˈlɪrɪ-əm] s Fieberwahn m; (fig) Rausch m

deliver [dɪˈlɪvər] tr liefern; (a message) überreichen; (free) befreien; (mail) zustellen; (a speech) halten; (a blow) versetzen; (a verdict) aussprechen; (a child) zur Welt bringen; (votes) bringen; (a ball) werfen; (relig) erlösen

deliverance [dɪˈlɪvərəns] s Erlösung f

delivery [dɪˈlɪvəri] s Lieferung f; (freeing) Befreiung f; (of mail) Zustellung f; (of a speaker, actor, singer) Vortragsweise f; (of a pitcher) Wurf m; (childbirth) Entbindung f

delivery-man s (–men) Austräger m

delivery room s Kreißsaal m

delivery truck s Lieferwagen m

dell [dɛl] s enges Tal n

delouse [diˈlaʊs] tr entlausen

delta [ˈdɛltə] s Delta n

delude [dɪˈlud] tr täuschen

deluge [ˈdɛljudʒ] s Überschwemmung f; (fig) Hochflut f; **Deluge** (Bib) Sintflut f ‖ tr überschwemmen; (with letters, etc.) überschütten

delusion [dɪˈluʒən] s (state of being deluded) Täuschung f; (misconcep-

tion) Wahnvorstellung *f;* (psychiatry) Wahn *m;* **delusions of grandeur** Größenwahn *m*

deluxe [dɪ'lʊks], [dɪ'lʌks] *adj* Luxus-

delve [delv] *intr*—**d. into** sich vertiefen in (*acc*)

demagogue ['demə͵gag] *s* Volksverführer –in *mf*

demand [dɪ'mænd] *s* Verlangen *n;* (com) (for) Nachfrage *f* (nach); **in (great) d.** (sehr) gefragt; **make demands on** Ansprüche erheben auf (*acc*); **on d.** auf Verlangen ‖ *tr* (**from** or **of**) verlangen (von), fordern (von)

demand'ing *adj* anspruchsvoll; (*strict*) streng

demarca'tion line' [͵dɪmar'keʃən] *s* Demarkationslinie *f*

demean [dɪ'min] *tr* erniedrigen

demeanor [dɪ'minər] *s* Benehmen *n*

demented [dɪ'mentɪd] *adj* wahnsinnig

demerit [dɪ'merɪt] *s* (*fault*) Fehler *m;* (*deficiency mark*) Minuspunkt *m*

demigod ['demɪ͵gad] *s* Halbgott *m*

demijohn ['demɪ͵dʒan] *s* Korbflasche *f*

demilitarize [di'mɪlɪtə͵raɪz] *tr* entmilitarisieren

demise [dɪ'maɪz] *s* Ableben *n*

demitasse ['demɪ͵tæs], ['demɪ͵tas] *s* Mokkatasse *f*

demobilize [di'mobɪ͵laɪz] *tr & intr* demobilisieren

democracy [dɪ'makrəsɪ] *s* Demokratie *f*

democrat ['demə͵kræt] *s* Demokrat –in *mf*

democratic [͵demə'krætɪk] *adj* demokratisch

demolish [dɪ'malɪʃ] *tr* (*raze*) niederreißen; (*destroy*) zertrümmern; (*an argument*) vernichten; (*devour*) (coll) verschlingen

demolition [͵demə'lɪʃən], [͵dimə-'lɪʃən] *s* (*act of razing*) Abbruch *m;* (*by explosives*) Sprengung *f;* **demolitions** Sprengstoff *m*

demoli'tion squad' *s* Sprengkommando *n*

demoli'tion work' *s* Sprengarbeiten *pl*

demon ['dimən] *s* Dämon *m,* böser Geist *m*

demonstrable [dɪ'manstrəbəl] *adj* beweisbar

demonstrate ['demən͵stret] *tr* (*prove*) beweisen; (*explain*) dartun; (*display*) zeigen; (*a product, process*) vorführen ‖ *intr* (pol) demonstrieren

demonstration [͵demən'streʃən] *s* (com) Vorführung *f;* (pol) Demonstration *f*

demonstrative [dɪ'manstrətɪv] *adj* (*showing emotions*) gefühlvoll; (*illustrative*) anschaulich; (gram) hinweisend

demonstrator ['demən͵stretər] *s* (*of products*) Vorführer –in *mf;* (*model used in demonstration*) Vorführmodell *n;* (pol) Demonstrant –in *mf*

demoralize [dɪ'mɔrə͵laɪz] *tr* demoralisieren

demote [dɪ'mot] *tr* (*an employee*) her-

abstufen; (*a student*) zurückversetzen; (mil) degradieren

demotion [dɪ'moʃən] *s* (*of an employee*) Herabstufung *f;* (*of a student*) Zurückversetzung *f;* (mil) Degradierung *f*

de·mur [dɪ'mʌr] *v* (*pret & pp* **–murred;** *ger* **–murring**) *intr* Einwände erheben

demure [dɪ'mjʊr] *adj* zimperlich

den [den] *s* (*of animals; of thieves*) Höhle *f;* (*comfortable room*) Freizeitraum *m*

denaturalize [di'nætʃərə͵laɪz] *tr* ausbürgern

denial [dɪ'naɪ·əl] *s* (*of an assertion*) Leugnung *f;* (*of guilt*) Leugnen *n;* (*of a request*) Ablehnung *f;* (*of faith*) Ableugnung *f;* (*of rights*) Verweigerung *f;* (*of a report*) Dementi *n*

denigrate ['denɪ͵gret] *tr* anschwärzen

denim ['denɪm] *s* Drillich *m*

denizen ['denɪzən] *s* Bewohner –in *mf*

Denmark ['denmark] *s* Dänemark *n*

denomination [dɪ͵namɪ'neʃən] *s* Bezeichnung *f;* (*class, kind*) Klasse *f;* (*of money*) Nennwert *m;* (*of shares*) Stückelung *f;* (relig) Konfession *f,* Bekenntnis *n;* **in denominations of five and ten dollars** in Fünf- und Zehndollarnoten

denotation [͵dino'teʃən] *s* Bedeutung *f*

denote [dɪ'not] *tr* (*mean*) bedeuten; (*indicate*) anzeigen

dénouement [͵denu'mã] *s* Auflösung *f*

denounce [dɪ'naʊns] *tr* (*inform against*) denunzieren; (*condemn openly*) brandmarken, anprangern; (*a treaty*) kündigen

dense [dens] *adj* dicht; (coll) beschränkt

density ['densɪtɪ] *s* Dichte *f*

dent [dent] *s* Beule *f* ‖ *tr* einbeulen

dental ['dentəl] *adj* Zahn–; (ling) dental ‖ *s* (ling) Zahnlaut *m*

den'tal hygiene' *s* Zahnpflege *f*

den'tal sur'geon *s* Zahnarzt *m,* Zahnärztin *f*

dentifrice ['dentɪfrɪs] *s* Zahnputzmittel *n*

dentist ['dentɪst] *s* Zahnarzt *m,* Zahnärztin *f*

dentistry ['dentɪstrɪ] *s* Zahnheilkunde *f*

denture ['dentʃər] *s* künstliches Gebiß *n*

denunciation [dɪ͵nʌnsɪ'eʃən] *s* (*informing against*) Denunzierung *f;* (*public condemnation*) Brandmarkung *f*

de·ny [dɪ'naɪ] *v* (*pret & pp* **–nied**) *tr* (*a statement*) leugnen; (*officially*) dementieren; (*a request*) ablehnen; (*one's faith*) ableugnen; (*rights*) verweigern; **d. oneself s.th.** sich [*dat*] etw versagen; **d. s.o. s.th.** j–m etw aberkennen

deodorant [di'odərənt] *s* Deodorant *n*

deodorize [di'odə͵raɪz] *tr* desodorieren

deoxidize [di'aksɪ͵daɪz] *tr* desoxydieren

depart [dɪ'pɑrt] *intr* (*on foot*) fortgehen; (*in a vehicle or boat*) abfahren; (*by plane*) abfliegen; (*on horseback*) abreiten; (*on a trip*) abreisen;
(*deviate*) abweichen
department [dɪ'pɑrtmənt] *s* (*subdivision*) Abteilung *f;* (*field*) Fach *n;*
(*principal branch of government*)
Ministerium *n;* (*government office*)
Amt *n;* (*educ*) Abteilung *f*
depart'ment head' *s* Abteilungsleiter
–in *mf*
depart'ment store' *s* Kaufhaus *n,*
Warenhaus *n*
departure [dɪ'pɑrtʃər] *s* (*on foot*)
Weggehen *n;* (*by car, boat, train*)
Abfahrt *f,* Abreise *f;* (*by plane*) Ab-
flug *m;* (*deviation*) Abweichung *f*
depend [dɪ'pend] *intr* (**on**) abhängen
(**von**); (*rely on*) sich verlassen (auf
acc); **depending on** je nach; **depending on how** je nachdem; **it all depends** (*coll*) es kommt darauf an
dependable [dɪ'pendəbəl] *adj* zuverlässig
dependence [dɪ'pendəns] *s* Abhängigkeit *f*
dependency [dɪ'pendənsi] *s* Schutzgebiet *n*
dependent [dɪ'pendənt] *adj* (**on**) abhängig (**von**) ‖ *s* Abhängige *mf;* (*for
tax purposes*) Unterhaltsberechtigte
mf
depict [dɪ'pɪkt] *tr* schildern
deplete [dɪ'plit] *tr* entleeren; (*fig*) erschöpfen
deplorable [dɪ'plorəbəl] *adj* (*situation*) beklagenswert; (*regrettable*) bedauerlich; (*bad*) schlecht
deplore [dɪ'plor] *tr* bedauern
deploy [dɪ'plɔɪ] *tr* entfalten ‖ *intr*
sich entfalten
deployment [dɪ'plɔɪmənt] *s* Entfaltung
f
depolarize [di'polə͵raɪz] *tr* depolari-
sieren
deponent [dɪ'ponənt] *s* (*gram*) De-
ponens *n;* (*jur*) Deponent –in *mf*
depopulate [di'pɑpjə͵let] *tr* entvölkern
deport [dɪ'port] *tr* deportieren; **d.
oneself** sich benehmen
deportation [͵dipor'teʃən] *s* Deportation *f*
deportment [dɪ'portmənt] *s* Benehmen
n
depose [dɪ'poz] *tr* (*from office*) absetzen; (*jur*) bezeugen ‖ *intr* (*jur*)
unter Eid aussagen; (*in writing*)
(*jur*) eidesstattlich versichern
deposit [dɪ'pɑzɪt] *s* (*partial payment*)
Anzahlung *f;* (*at a bank*) Einlage *f;*
(*for safekeeping*) Hinterlegung *f;*
(*geol*) Ablagerung *f;* (*min*) Vorkommen *n;* **for d. only** nur zur Verrech-
nung ‖ *tr* (*set down*) niederlegen;
(*money at a bank*) einlegen; (*a
check*) verrechnen; (*as part payment*) anzahlen; (*for safekeeping*)
deponieren; (*geol*) ablagern; (*a coin*)
(*telp*) einwerfen
depositor [dɪ'pɑzɪtər] *s* Einzahler –in
mf; (*of valuables*) Hinterleger –in *mf*
depos'it slip' *s* Einzahlungsbeleg *m*

depot ['dipo], ['depo] *s* (*bus station;
storage place*) Depot *n;* (*train station*) Bahnhof *m*
depraved [dɪ'prevd] *adj* verworfen
depravity [dɪ'prævɪti] *s* Verworfenheit
f
deprecate ['deprɪ͵ket] *tr* mißbilligen
depreciate [dɪ'priʃɪ͵et] *tr* (*money,
stocks*) abwerten; (*for tax purposes*)
abschreiben; (*value or price*) herabsetzen; (*disparage*) geringschätzen
‖ *intr* im Wert sinken
depreciation [dɪ͵priʃɪ'eʃən] *s* (*decrease in value*) Wertminderung *f;*
(*of currency or stocks*) Abwertung
f; (*for tax purposes*) Abschreibung *f*
depress [dɪ'pres] *tr* niederdrücken;
(*sadden*) deprimieren; (*cause to
sink*) herunterdrücken
depressed' *adj* (*saddened*) niedergeschlagen; (*market*) flau
depressed' ar'ea *s* Notstandsgebiet *n*
depress'ing *adj* deprimierend
depression [dɪ'preʃən] *s* (*mental state;
economic crisis*) Depression *f;* (*geol*)
Vertiefung *f*
deprive [dɪ'praɪv] *tr*—**d. s.o. of s.th.**
j–m etw entziehen; (*withhold*) j–m
etw vorenthalten
depth [depθ] *s* Tiefe *f;* **go beyond
one's d.** den Boden unter den Füßen
verlieren; **in d.** gründlich
depth' charge' *s* Wasserbombe *f*
depth' of field' *s* (*phot*) Tiefenschärfe
f
deputation [͵depjə'teʃən] *s* Abordnung
f
deputize ['depjə͵taɪz] *tr* abordnen
deputy ['depjəti] *s* Vertreter –in *mf;*
(*pol*) Abgeordnete *mf*
derail [dɪ'rel] *tr* zum Entgleisen bringen ‖ *intr* entgleisen
derailment [dɪ'relmənt] *s* Entgleisung
f
deranged [dɪ'rendʒd] *adj* geistesgestört
derangement [dɪ'rendʒmənt] *s* Geistes-
gestörtheit *f*
derby ['dʌrbi] *s* (*hat*) Melone *f;* (*race*)
Derbyrennen *n*
derelict ['derɪlɪkt] *adj* (*negligent*) (**in**)
nachlässig (**in** *dat*); (*abandoned*)
herrenlos ‖ *s* (*ship; bum*) Wrack *n*
dereliction [͵derɪ'lɪkʃən] *s* (*neglect*)
Vernachlässigung *f*
deride [dɪ'raɪd] *tr* verspotten
derision [dɪ'rɪʒən] *s* Spott *m*
derivation [͵derɪ'veʃən] *s* (*gram,
math*) Ableitung *f*
derivative [dɪ'rɪvətɪv] *adj* abgeleitet
‖ *s* (*chem*) Derivat *n;* (*gram, math*)
Ableitung *f*
derive [dɪ'raɪv] *tr* (*obtain*) gewinnen;
(*gram, math*) ableiten; **d. pleasure
from s.th.** Freude an etw finden ‖
intr (**from**) herstammen (**von**)
dermatologist [͵dʌrmə'tɑlədʒɪst] *s*
Hautarzt *m,* Hautärztin *f*
derogatory [dɪ'rɑgə͵tori] *adj* abfällig
derrick ['derɪk] *s* (*over an oil well*)
Bohrturm *m;* (*naut*) Ladebaum *m*
dervish ['dʌrvɪʃ] *s* Derwisch *m*
desalinization [di͵selɪnɪ'zeʃən] *s* Ent-
salzung *f*

desalt [di'sɔlt] *tr* entsalzen
descend [dɪ'send] *tr* hinuntergehen ‖ *intr* (*dismount, alight*) absteigen; (*said of a plane*) niedergehen; (*from a tree, from heaven*) herabsteigen; (*said of a road*) sich senken; (*pass by inheritance*) (**to**) übergehen (auf *acc*); **be descended from** abstammen von; **d. upon** hereinbrechen über (*acc*)
descendant [dɪ'sendənt] *s* Abkömmling *m*, Nachkomme *m*; **descendants** Nachkommenschaft *f*
descendent [dɪ'sendənt] *adj* absteigend
descent [dɪ'sent] *s* Abstieg *m*; (*lineage*) Herkunft *f*; (*of a plane or parachute*) Niedergehen *n*; (*slope*) Abhang *m*; (*hostile raid*) (**on**) Überfall *m* (auf *acc*)
describe [dɪ'skraɪb] *tr* beschreiben
description [dɪ'skrɪpʃən] *s* Beschreibung *f*; (*type*) Art *f*; **beyond d.** unbeschreiblich
descriptive [dɪ'skrɪptɪv] *adj* beschreibend
de·scry [dɪ'skraɪ] *v* (*pret & pp* **–scried**) *tr* erspähen, erblicken
desecrate ['desɪˌkret] *tr* entweihen
desecration [ˌdesɪ'kreʃən] *s* Entweihung *f*
desegregate [di'segrɪˌget] *tr* die Rassentrennung aufheben in (*dat*)
desegregation [diˌsegrɪ'geʃən] *s* Aufhebung *f* der Rassentrennung
desert ['dezərt] *adj* öde, wüst; (*sand, warfare, etc.*) Wüsten– ‖ *s* Wüste *f*; (*fig*) Öde *f* ‖ [dɪ'zʌrt] *s* Verdienst *m*; **get one's just deserts** seinen wohlverdienten Lohn empfangen ‖ *tr* verlassen ‖ *intr* (mil) desertieren; (**to**) überlaufen (zu)
deserter [dɪ'zʌrtər] *s* Deserteur *m*
desertion [dɪ'zʌrʃən] *s* Verlassen *n*; (*of a party*) Abfall *m*; (mil) Fahnenflucht *f*
deserve [dɪ'zʌrv] *tr* verdienen
deservedly [dɪ'zʌrvɪdli] *adv* mit Recht
deserv'ing *adj* (**of**) würdig (*genit*)
design [dɪ'zaɪn] *s* (*outline*) Entwurf *m*; (*pattern*) Muster *n*; (*plan*) Plan *m*; (*plot*) Anschlag *m*; (*of a building, etc.*) Bauart *f*; (*aim*) Absicht *f*; **designs on** böse Absichten auf (*acc*) ‖ *tr* (*make a preliminary sketch of*) entwerfen; (*draw up detailed plans for*) konstruieren; **designed for** gedacht für
designate ['dezɪɡˌnet] *tr* (**as**) bezeichnen (als); (**to**) ernennen (zu)
designation [ˌdezɪɡ'neʃən] *s* (*act of designating*) Kennzeichnung *f*; (*title*) Bezeichnung *f*; (*appointment*) Ernennung *f*
designer [dɪ'zaɪnər] *s* (*of patterns*) Musterzeichner –in *mf*; (*of fashions*) Modeschöpfer –in *mf*; (theat) Dekorateur –in *mf*
design'ing *adj* intrigant; (*calculating*) berechnend
desirable [dɪ'zaɪrəbəl] *adj* wünschenswert, begehrenswert
desire [dɪ'zaɪr] *s* (*wish*) Wunsch *m*; (*interest*) Lust *f*; (*craving*) Begierde

f; (*thing desired*) Gewünschte *n* ‖ *tr* wünschen
desirous [dɪ'zaɪrəs] *adj* (**of**) begierig (nach)
desist [dɪ'zɪst] *intr* (**from**) ablassen (von)
desk [desk] *s* Schreibtisch *m*; (*of a teacher*) Pult *n*; (*of a pupil*) Schulbank *f*; (*in a hotel*) Kasse *f*
desk' cop' *s* Freiexemplar *n*
desk' lamp' *s* Tischlampe *f*
desk' pad' *s* Schreibunterlage *f*
desolate ['desəlɪt] *adj* (*barren*) öde; (*joyless*) trostlos; (*deserted*) verlassen; (*dilapidated*) verfallen ‖ ['desəˌlet] *tr* verwüsten
desolation [ˌdesə'leʃən] *s* (*devastation*) Verwüstung *f*; (*dreariness*) Trostlosigkeit *f*
despair [dɪs'per] *s* Verzweiflung *f* ‖ *intr* (**of**) verzweifeln (an *dat*)
despair'ing *adj* verzweifelt
despera·do [ˌdespə'rado], [ˌdespə'redo] *s* (**–does & –dos**) Desperado *m*
desperate ['despərɪt] *adj* verzweifelt
desperation [ˌdespə'reʃən] *s* Verzweiflung *f*
despicable ['despɪkəbəl] *adj* verächtlich, verachtungswürdig
despise [dɪs'paɪz] *tr* verachten
despite [dɪs'paɪt] *prep* trotz (*genit*)
despondency [dɪs'pandənsi] *s* Kleinmut *m*
despondent [dɪs'pandənt] *adj* kleinmütig
despot ['despat] *s* Despot –in *mf*
despotic [des'patɪk] *adj* despotisch
despotism ['despəˌtɪzəm] *s* Despotie *f*; (*as a system*) Despotismus *m*
dessert [dɪ'zʌrt] *s* Nachtisch *m*
destination [ˌdestɪ'neʃən] *s* (*of a trip*) Bestimmungsort *m*, Reiseziel *n*; (*purpose*) Bestimmung *f*
destine ['destɪn] *tr* (**for**) bestimmen (zu or für)
destiny ['destɪni] *s* Schicksal *n*; (*doom*) Verhängnis *n*
destitute ['destɪˌt(j)ut] *adj* mittellos; **d. of** ohne
destitution [ˌdestɪ't(j)uʃən] *s* äußerste Armut *f*
destroy [dɪ'strɔɪ] *tr* vernichten, zerstören; (*animals, bacteria*) töten
destroyer [dɪ'strɔɪ·ər] *s* (nav) Zerstörer *m*
destroy'er es'cort *s* Zerstörergeleitschutz *m*
destruction [dɪ'strʌkʃən] *s* Zerstörung *f*; (*of species*) Ausrottung *f*
destructive [dɪ'strʌktɪv] *adj* zerstörend; (*criticism*) vernichtend; (*tendency*) destruktiv
desultory ['desəlˌtori] *adj* (*without plan*) planlos; (*fitful*) sprunghaft; (*remark*) deplaciert
detach [dɪ'tætʃ] *tr* ablösen; (*along a perforation*) abtrennen; (mil) abkommandieren
detachable [dɪ'tætʃəbəl] *tr* abnehmbar, ablösbar
detached' *adj* (*building*) alleinstehend; (*objective*) objektiv; (*aloof*) distanziert

detachment [dɪ'tæt∫mənt] s Objektivität f; (aloofness) Abstand m; (mil) Trupp m, Kommando n

detail [dɪ'tel], ['ditel] s Enzelheit f, Detail n; (mil) Kommando n, Trupp m; **details** (pej) Kleinkram m; **in d.** ausführlich ‖ [dɪ'tel] (relate in detail) ausführlich berichten; (list) einzeln aufzählen; (mil) abkommandieren

de'tail draw'ing s Detailzeichnung f

detailed/ adj ausführlich; **d. work** Kleinarbeit f

detain [dɪ'ten] tr zurückhalten; (jur) in Haft behalten

detect [dɪ'tekt] tr (discover) entdecken; (catch) ertappen

detection [dɪ'tek∫ən] s Entdeckung f

detective [dɪ'tektɪv] s Detektiv m

detec'tive sto'ry s Kriminalroman m

detector [dɪ'tektər] s (e.g., of smoke) Spürgerät n; (of objects) Suchgerät n; (rad) Detektor m

détente [de'tɑnt] s Entspannung f, Détente f

detention [dɪ'ten∫ən] s (jur) Haft f

deten'tion camp' s Internierungslager n

deten'tion home' s Haftanstalt f

de·ter [dɪ'tʌr] v (pret & pp –terred; ger–terring) tr (from) abschrecken (von), abhalten (von)

detergent [dɪ'tʌrdʒənt] s Reinigungsmittel n; (in a washer) Waschmittel n

deteriorate [dɪ'tɪrɪ·ə‚ret] tr verschlechtern ‖ intr sich verschlechtern

deterioration [dɪ‚tɪrɪ·ə're∫ən] s Verschlechterung f, Verfall m

determination [dɪ‚tʌrmɪ'ne∫ən] s Bestimmung f; (resoluteness) Entschlossenheit f; (of boundaries) Festlegung f

determine [dɪ'tʌrmɪn] tr (fix conclusively) bestimmen; (boundaries) festlegen; (decide) entscheiden

deter'mined adj entschlossen

deterrent [dɪ'tʌrənt] adj abschreckend ‖ s Abschreckungsmittel n

detest [dɪ'test] tr verabscheuen

detestable [dɪ'testəbəl] adj abscheulich

dethrone [dɪ'θron] tr entthronen

detonate ['detə‚net] tr explodieren lassen ‖ intr explodieren

detour [dɪ'tur] s (for cars) Umleitung f; (for pedestrians) Umweg m ‖ tr umleiten ‖ intr e–n Umweg machen

detract [dɪ'trækt] tr ablenken ‖ intr— **d. from** beeinträchtigen

detraction [dɪ'træk∫ən] s Beeinträchtigung f

detractor [dɪ'træktər] s Verleumder –in mf

detrain [dɪ'tren] tr ausladen ‖ intr aussteigen

detriment ['detrɪmənt] s Nachteil m

detrimental [‚detrɪ'mentəl] adj (to) nachteilig (für), schädlich (für)

deuce [d(j)us] s (in cards or dice) Zwei f; (in tennis) Einstand m; **what the d.?** was zum Teufel?

devaluate [di'vælju‚et] tr abwerten

devaluation [di‚vælju'e∫ən] s Abwertung f

devastate ['devəs‚tet] tr verheeren

develop [dɪ'veləp] tr entwickeln; (one's mind) (aus)bilden; (a habit) annehmen; (a disease) sich [dat] zuziehen; (cracks) bekommen; (land) nutzbar machen; (a mine) ausbeuten; (phot) entwickeln ‖ intr sich entwickeln; (said of habits) sich herausbilden; **d. into** sich entwicklen zu

developer [dɪ'veləpər] s (of land) Spekulant –in mf; (phot) Entwickler m

development [dɪ'veləpmənt] s Entwicklung f; (of relations, of a mine) Ausbau m; (of land) Nutzbarmachung f; (of housing) Siedlung f; (an event) Ereignis n; (educ) Ausbildung f; (phot) Entwicklung f

deviate ['divɪ‚et] intr abweichen

deviation [‚divɪ'e∫ən] s Abweichung f

device [dɪ'vaɪs] s Vorrichtung f, Gerät n; (means) Mittel n; (crafty scheme) Kniff m; (literary device) Kunstgriff m; (heral) Sinnbild n; **leave s.o. to his own devices** j–n sich [dat] selbst überlassen

dev·il ['devəl] s Teufel m; **a d. of a** (coll) verteufelt; **between the d. and the deep blue sea** zwischen zwei Feuern; **poor d.** armer Teufel; **the d. with you!** (coll) scher dich zum Teufel!; **what (who, etc.) the d.?** was (wer, etc.) zum Teufel? ‖ v (pret & pp –il[l]ed; ger –il[l]ing) tr (culin) mit viel Gewürz zubereiten

devilish ['devəlɪ∫] adj teuflisch

dev'il-may-care' adj (informal) wurstig; (reckless) verwegen

devilment ['devɪlmənt] s Unfug m

deviltry ['devɪltri] s Unfug m

devious ['divɪ·əs] adj abweichend; (tricky) unredlich; (reasoning) abwegig

devise [dɪ'vaɪz] tr ersinnen; (jur) vermachen

devoid [dɪ'vɔɪd] adj—**d. of** ohne

devolve [dɪ'vɑlv] intr—**d. on** zufallen (dat)

devote [dɪ'vot] tr widmen

devot'ed adj (dedicated) ergeben; (affectionate) liebevoll

devotee [‚devə'ti] s Anhänger –in mf

devotion [dɪ'vo∫ən] s Ergebenheit f; (devoutness) Frömmigkeit f; (special prayer) (to) Gebet n (zu); **devotions** Andacht f

devour [dɪ'vaur] tr verschlingen; (said of fire) verzehren

devout [dɪ'vaut] adj fromm; (e.g., hope) innig

dew [d(j)u] s Tau m; **dew is falling** es taut

dew'drop' s Tautropfen m

dew'lap' s Wamme f

dewy ['d(j)u·i] adj tauig

dexterity [deks'terɪti] s Geschicklichkeit f, Handfertigkeit f

dexterous ['dekstərəs] adj handfertig

dextrose ['dekstroz] s Traubenzucker m

diabetes [‚daɪ·ə'bitɪs] s Zuckerkrankheit f

diabetic [ˌdaɪ·ə'betɪk] *adj* zuckerkrank *mf*

diabolic(al) [ˌdaɪ·ə'bɑlɪk(ə)l] *adj* teuflisch

diacritical [ˌdaɪ·ə'krɪtɪkəl] *adj* diakritisch

diadem ['daɪ·əˌdem] *s* Diadem *n*

diaere·sis [daɪ'erɪsɪs] *s* (-ses [ˌsiz] Diäresis *f*; (*mark*) Trema *n*

diagnose [ˌdaɪ·əg'nos], [ˌdaɪ·əg'noz] *tr* diagnostizieren

diagno·sis [ˌdaɪ·əg'nosɪs] *s* (-ses [siz]) Diagnose *f*

diagonal [daɪ'æɡənəl] *adj* diagonal || *s* Diagonale *f*

diagonally [daɪ'æɡənəli] *adv*—**d. across from** schräg gegenüber von

diagram ['daɪ·əˌɡræm] *s* Diagramm *n*

di·al ['daɪ·əl] *s* Zifferblatt *n*; (tech) Skalenscheibe *f*; (telp) Wählscheibe *f* || *v* (*pret & pp* **-al[l]ed**; *ger* **-al[l]ing**) *tr & intr* (telp) wählen

di'aling *s* (telp) Wählen *n* der Nummer

dialogue ['daɪ·əˌlɔɡ] *s* Dialog *m*

di'al tel'ephone *s* Selbstanschlußtelefon *n*

di'al tone' *s* Summton *m*, Amtszeichen *n*

diameter [daɪ'æmɪtər] *s* Durchmesser *m*

diamond ['daɪmənd] *adj* diamanten; (*in shape*) rautenförmig || *s* Diamant *m*; (*cut diamond*) Brillant *m*; (*rhombus*) Raute *f*; (baseball) Spielfeld *n*; (cards) Karo *n*

dia'mond ring' *s* Brillantring *m*

diaper ['daɪpər] *s* Windel *f*; **change the diapers of** trockenlegen, wickeln

diaphanous [daɪ'æfənəs] *adj* durchsichtig, durchscheinend

diaphragm ['daɪ·əˌfræm] *s* (*for birth control*) Gebärmutterkappe *f*; (anat) Zwerchfell *n*; (phot) Blende *f*; (tech, telp) Membran *f*

diarrhea [ˌdaɪ·ə'ri·ə] *s* Durchfall *m*

diary ['daɪ·əri] *s* Tagebuch *n*

diastole [daɪ'æstəli] *s* Diastole *f*

diatribe ['daɪ·əˌtraɪb] *s* Schmährede *f*

dice [daɪs] *spl* Würfel *pl* || *tr* in Würfel schneiden

dice'box' *s* Würfelbecher *m*

dichotomy [daɪ'kɑtəmi] *s* Zweiteilung *f*; (bot) Gabelung *f*

dicker ['dɪkər] *intr* (about) feilschen (um)

dickey ['dɪki] *s* Hemdbrust *f*

dictaphone ['dɪktəˌfon] *s* Diktaphon *n*

dictate ['dɪktet] *s* Diktat *n*; **the dictates of conscience** das Gebot des Gewissens || *tr & intr* diktieren

dictation [dɪk'teʃən] *s* Diktat *n*

dictator ['dɪktetər] *s* Diktator *m*

dictatorial [ˌdɪktə'tori·əl] *adj* diktatorisch; (*power*) unumschränkt

dic'tatorship' *s* Diktatur *f*

diction ['dɪkʃən] *s* Ausdrucksweise *f*

dictionary ['dɪkʃəˌneri] *s* Wörterbuch *n*

dic·tum ['dɪktəm] *s* (-ta [tə]) (*saying*) Spruch *m*; (*pronouncement*) Ausspruch *m*

didactic [daɪ'dæktɪk] *adj* lehrhaft

die [daɪ] *s* (**dice** [daɪs]) Würfel *m*; **the die is cast** die Würfel sind gefallen || *s* (**dies**) (*coining die*) Prägestempel *m*; (*casting die*) Form *f*; (*forging die*) Gesenk *n*; (*threader*) Schneidkopf *m* || *v* (*pret & pp* **died**; *ger* **dying**) *tr*—**die a natural death** e–s natürlichen Todes sterben || *intr* sterben; (*said of plants and animals*) eingehen; **be dying for** (coll) sich sehnen nach; **die down** (*said of the wind*) sich legen; (*said of noise*) ersterben; **die from** sterben an (*dat*); **die laughing** sich totlachen; **die of hunger** verhungern; **die of thirst** verdursten; **die out** aussterben; (*said of fire*) erlöschen; **I am dying to** (*inf*) (coll) ich würde schrecklich gern (*inf*)

die'-hard' *s* Unentwegte *mf*

die'sel en'gine ['dizəl] *s* Dieselmotor *m*

die'sel oil' *s* Dieselöl *n*

die'stock' *s* Gewindeschneidkluppe *f*

diet ['daɪ·ət] *s* Kost *f*; (*special menu*) Diät *f*; (parl) Reichstag *m*; **be on a d.** diät leben; **put on a d.** auf Diät setzen || *intr* diät leben

dietary ['daɪ·əˌteri] *adj* Diät–; **d. laws** rituelle Diätvorschriften *pl*

dietetic [ˌdaɪ·ə'tetɪk] *adj* diätetisch || **dietetics** *spl* Diätetik *f*

dietitian [ˌdaɪ·ə'tɪʃən] *s* Diätspezialist –in *mf*

differ ['dɪfər] *intr* sich unterscheiden; (*said of opinions*) auseinandergehen; **d. from** abweichen von; **d.** in verschieden sein in (*dat*); **d. with** anderer Meinung sein als

difference ['dɪfərəns] *s* Unterschied *m*; (*argument*) Streit *m*; (math) Differenz *f*; **d. of opinion** Meinungsverschiedenheit *f*; **it makes no d. to me** es ist mir gleich; **split the d.** den Rest teilen

different ['dɪfərənt] *adj* verschieden; **a d. kind of** e–e andere Art von; **d. from** anders als, verschieden von; **d. kinds of** verschiedene

differential [ˌdɪfə'ren/əl] *adj* (econ, elec, mach, math, phys) Differential– || *s* (*difference*) Unterschied *m*; (mach) Differentialgetriebe *n*; (math) Differential *n*

dif'feren'tial cal'culus *s* Differentialrechnung *f*

differentiate [ˌdɪfə'ren/ɪˌet] *tr* unterscheiden; (math) differenzieren || *intr* —**d. between** unterscheiden zwischen (*dat*)

difficult ['dɪfɪˌkʌlt] *adj* schwierig, schwer

difficulty ['dɪfɪˌkʌlti] *s* Schwierigkeit *f*; **I have d. in** (*ger*) es fällt mir schwer zu (*inf*); **with d.** mit Mühe

diffuse [dɪ'fjus] *adj* (*weit*) zerstreut; (*style*) diffus || [dɪ'fjuz] *tr* (*spread*) verbreiten; (*pour out*) ausgießen; (phys) diffundieren || *intr* sich zerstreuen

diffusion [dɪ'fjuʃən] *s* (*spread*) Verbreitung *f*; (phys) Diffusion *f*

dig [dɪɡ] *s* (*jab*) Stoß *m*; (*sarcasm*)

Seitenhieb *m;* (archeol) Ausgrabung *f* ‖ *v* (*pret & pp* dug [dʌg] & digged; *ger* digging) *tr* graben; (*a ditch*) auswerfen; (*potatoes*) ausgraben; (*understand*) (sl) kapieren; (*look at*) (sl) anschauen; (*appreciate*) (sl) schwärmen für; dig up ausgraben; (*find*) auftreiben; (*information*) ausfindig machen; (*money*) aufbringen; ‖ *intr* graben, wühlen; dig in (*with the hands*) hineinfassen; (*work hard*) (coll) schuften; (mil) sich eingraben; dig for (*e.g., gold*) schürfen nach

digest ['daɪdʒɛst] *s* Zusammenfassung *f;* (jur) Gesetzessammlung *f* ‖ [daɪ'dʒɛst] *tr* verdauen; (*in the mind*) verarbeiten ‖ *intr* verdauen

digestible [daɪ'dʒɛstɪbəl] *adj* verdaulich, verträglich

digestion [daɪ'dʒɛstʃən] *s* Verdauung *f*

digestive [daɪ'dʒɛstɪv] *adj* Verdauungs–; d. tract Verdauungsapparat *m*

digit ['dɪdʒɪt] *s* (math) Ziffer *f* (unter zehn); (math) Stelle *f*

digital ['dɪdʒɪtəl] *adj* digital, Digital–

dig'ital comput'er *s* digitale Rechenanlage *f*

digitalis [dɪdʒɪ'tælɪs] *s* Digitalis *n*

dignified ['dɪgnɪ,faɪd] *adj* würdig

digni-fy ['dɪgnɪ,faɪ] *v* (*pret & pp* –fied) *tr* ehren

dignitary ['dɪgnɪ,teri] *s* Würdenträger –in *mf*

dignity ['dɪgnɪti] *s* Würde *f;* d. of man Menschenwürde *f;* stand on one's d. sich [*dat*] nichts vergeben

digress [daɪ'grɛs] *intr* (from) abschweifen (von)

digression [daɪ'grɛʃən] *s* Abschweifung *f*

dike [daɪk] *s* Deich *m*

dilapidated [dɪ'læpɪ,detɪd] *adj* baufällig

dilate [daɪ'let] *tr* ausdehnen ‖ *intr* sich ausdehnen

dilation [daɪ'leʃən] *s* Ausdehnung *f*

dilatory ['dɪlə,tori] *adj* saumselig; (*tending to cause delay*) hinhaltend

dilemma [dɪ'lɛmə] *s* Dilemma *n*

dilettan-te [,dɪlə'tænti], ['dɪlə,tɑnt] *s* (–tes & –ti [ti]) Dilettant –in *mf*

diligence ['dɪlɪdʒəns] *s* Fleiß *m*

diligent ['dɪlɪdʒənt] *adj* fleißig

dill [dɪl] *s* Dill *m*

dillydal·ly ['dɪlɪ,dæli] *v* (*pret & pp* –lied) *intr* herumtrödeln

dilute [dɪ'lut], [daɪ'lut] *adj* verdünnt ‖ [dɪ'lut] *tr* verdünnen; (*with water*) verwässern ‖ *intr* sich verdünnen

dilution [dɪ'luʃən] *s* Verdünnung *f;* (*with water*) Verwässerung *f*

dim [dɪm] *adj* (dimmer; dimmest) *adj* (*light, eyesight*) schwach; (*poorly lighted*) schwach beleuchtet; (*dull*) matt; (*chances, outlook*) schlecht; (*indistinct*) undeutlich; take a dim view of (*disapprove of*) mißbilligen; (*be pessimistic about*) sich [*dat*] etw schwarz ausmalen ‖ *v* (*pret & pp* dimmed; *ger* dimming) *tr* trüben; (*lights*) abblenden ‖ *intr* sich ver-

dunkeln; (*said of lights, hopes*) verblassen

dime [daɪm] *s* Zehncentstück *n*

dime' nov'el *s* Groschenroman *m*

dimension [dɪ'mɛnʃən] *s* Maß *n,* Ausdehnung *f;* dimensions Ausmaß *n*

diminish [dɪ'mɪnɪʃ] *tr* (ver)mindern, verringern ‖ *intr* sich vermindern

diminutive [dɪ'mɪnjətɪv] *adj* winzig; (gram) Verkleinerungs– ‖ *s* Verkleinerungsform *f*

dimmer ['dɪmər] *s* (aut) Abblendvorrichtung *f*

dimple ['dɪmpəl] *s* Grübchen *n*

dim'wit' *s* Schwachsinnige *mf*

din [dɪn] *s* Getöse *n* ‖ *v* (*pret & pp* dinned; *ger* dinning) *tr* betäuben; din s.th. into s.o. j-m etw einhämmern

dine [daɪn] *intr* speisen; d. out auswärts speisen

diner ['daɪnər] *s.* Tischgast *m;* (*small restaurant*) speisewagenähnliches Speiselokal *n;* (rr) Speisewagen *m*

dinette [daɪ'nɛt] *s* Speisenische *f*

dingbat ['dɪŋ,bæt] *s* (sl) (*person*) Dingsda *m;* (*thing*) Dingsda *n*

ding-dong ['dɪŋ,dɔŋ] *interj* bimbam!, klingklang!

dinghy ['dɪŋgɪ] *s* Beiboot *n;* rubber d. Schlauchboot *n*

dingy ['dɪndʒɪ] *adj* (*gloomy*) düster; (*shabby*) schäbig

din'ing car' *s* (rr) Speisewagen *m*

din'ing hall' *s* Speisesaal *m*

din'ing room' *s* Eßzimmer *n*

dinner ['dɪnər] *s* (supper) Abendessen *n;* (*main meal*) Hauptmahlzeit *f;* (*formal meal*) Diner *n;* after d. nach Tisch; at d. bei Tisch; before d. vor Tisch

din'ner guest' *s* Tischgast *m*

din'ner jac'ket *s* Smoking *m*

din'ner mu'sic *s* Tafelmusik *f*

din'ner par'ty *s* Tischgesellschaft *f*

din'ner time' *s* Tischzeit *f*

dinosaur ['daɪnə,sɔr] *s* Dinosaurier *m*

dint [dɪnt] *s*—by d. of kraft (*genit*)

diocesan [daɪ'ɑsɪsən] *adj* Diözesan–

diocese ['daɪə,sis] *s* Diözese *f*

diode ['daɪ·od] *s* (electron) Diode *f*

dioxide [daɪ'ɑksaɪd] *s* Dioxyd *n*

dip [dɪp] *s* (*in the road*) Neigung *f;* (*short swim*) kurzes Bad *n;* (*dunk*) Eintauchen *n;* (*sauce*) Tunke *f;* (*of ice cream*) Portion *f* ‖ *v* (*pret & pp* dipped; *ger* dipping) *tr* eintauchen; (*e.g., doughnuts*) eintunken; (*a flag*) senken ‖ *intr* sich senken; dip into (*e.g., reserves*) angreifen; dip into one's pockets (fig) in die Tasche greifen

diphtheria [dɪf'θɪrɪ·ə] *s* Diphtherie *f*

diphthong ['dɪfθɔŋ] *s* Doppelvokal *m*

diploma [dɪ'plomə] *s* Diplom *n*

diplomacy [dɪ'ploməsi] *s* Diplomatie *f*

diplomat ['dɪplə,mæt] *s* Diplomat –in *mf*

diplomatic [,dɪplə'mætɪk] *adj* (& fig) diplomatisch

dipper ['dɪpər] *s* Schöpflöffel *m*

dipsomania [,dɪpsə'meni·ə] *s* Trunksucht *f*

dip' stick' s (aut) Ölstandmesser m

dire [daɪr] adj (terrible) gräßlich; (need) äußerste

direct [dɪ'rɛkt] adj direkt, unmittelbar; (frank) unverblümt; (quotation) wörtlich ‖ tr (order) beauftragen; (a company) leiten; (traffic) regeln; (a movie, play) Regie führen bei; (an orchestra) dirigieren; (attention, glance) (to) richten (auf acc); (a person) (to) verweisen (an acc); (words, letter) (to) richten (an acc)

direct' call' s Selbstwählverbindung f

direct' cur'rent s Gleichstrom m

direct' dis'course s direkte Rede f

direct' hit' s Volltreffer m

direction [dɪ'rɛk/ən] s Richtung f; (order) Anweisung f; (leadership) Leitung f, Führung f; (cin, theat) Regie f; (mus) Stabführung f; **directions** Weisungen pl; (for use) Gebrauchsanweisung f; **in all directions** nach allen Richtungen

directional [dɪ'rɛk/ənəl] adj Richt-

direc'tion find'er s Peilgerät n

direc'tion sig'nal s (aut) Richtungsanzeiger m

directive [dɪ'rɛktɪv] s Anweisung f

direct' ob'ject s direktes Objekt n

direct' op'posite s genaues Gegenteil n

director [dɪ'rɛktər] s Leiter –in mf, Direktor –in mf; (cin, theat) Regisseur –in mf; (mus) Dirigent –in mf; (rad, telv) Sendeleiter –in mf

direc'torship' s Direktorat n

directory [dɪ'rɛktəri] s Verzeichnis n

dirge [dʌrdʒ] s Trauergesang m

dirigible [ˈdɪrɪdʒɪbəl] s lenkbares Luftschiff n

dirt [dʌrt] s Schmutz m, Dreck m; (moral filth) Schmutz m; (soil) Erde f

dirt'-cheap' adj spottbillig

dirt' farm'er s kleiner Farmer m

dirt' road' s unbefestigte Straße f

dirt·y [ˈdʌrti] adj schmutzig, dreckig; (morally) schmutzig; **d. business** Schweinerei f; **d. dog** Sauhund m; **d. joke** Zote f; **d. lie** gemeine Lüge f; **d. linen** schmutzige Wäsche f; **d. look** böser Blick m; **d. trick** übler Streich m; **that's a d. shame** das ist e–e Gemeinheit! ‖ v (pret & pp –ied) tr beschmutzen

disability [ˌdɪsəˈbɪlɪti] s Invalidität f

disable [dɪsˈebəl] tr (e.g., a worker) arbeitsunfähig machen; (make unsuited for combat) kampfunfähig machen; (jur) rechtsunfähig machen

disa'bled adj invalide; (mil) kampfunfähig; **d. veteran** Kriegsversehrte mf; **d. person** Invalide mf

disabuse [ˌdɪsəˈbjuz] tr—**d. of** befreien von

disadvantage [ˌdɪsədˈvæntɪdʒ] s Nachteil m; **place at a d.** benachteiligen

disadvantageous [dɪsˌædvənˈtedʒəs] adj nachteilig

disagree [ˌdɪsəˈgri] intr nicht übereinstimmen; (be contradictory) einander widersprechen; (quarrel) (sich) streiten; **d. with** (said of food) nicht bekommen (dat); **d. with s.o. on**

disagreeable [ˌdɪsəˈgriːəbəl] adj unangenehm

disagreement [ˌdɪsəˈgriːmənt] s (unlikeness) Verschiedenheit f; (dissention) Uneinigkeit f; (quarrel) Meinungsverschiedenheit f

disappear [ˌdɪsəˈpɪr] intr verschwinden

disappearance [ˌdɪsəˈpɪrəns] s Verschwinden n

disappoint [ˌdɪsəˈpɔɪnt] tr enttäuschen; **be disappointed at** (or **with**) enttäuscht sein über (acc)

disappointment [ˌdɪsəˈpɔɪntmənt] s Enttäuschung f

disapproval [ˌdɪsəˈpruvəl] s Mißbilligung f

disapprove [ˌdɪsəˈpruv] tr mißbilligen; (e.g., an application) nicht genehmigen ‖ intr—**d. of** mißbilligen

disarm [dɪsˈɑrm] tr (& fig) entwaffnen; (a bomb) entschärfen ‖ intr abrüsten

disarmament [dɪsˈɑrməmənt] s Abrüstung f

disarm'ing adj (fig) entwaffnend

disarray [ˌdɪsəˈre] s Unordnung f ‖ tr in Unordnung bringen, verwirren

disassemble [ˌdɪsəˈsɛmbəl] tr zerlegen

disaster [dɪˈzæstər] s Unheil n

disas'ter ar'ea s Katastrophengebiet n

disastrous [dɪˈzæstrəs] adj unheilvoll

disavow [ˌdɪsəˈvau] tr ableugnen

disavowal [ˌdɪsəˈvau·əl] s Ableugnung f

disband [dɪsˈbænd] tr auflösen ‖ intr sich auflösen

dis·bar [dɪsˈbɑr] v (pret & pp –barred; ger –barring) tr aus dem Anwaltsstand ausschließen

disbelief [ˌdɪsbɪˈlif] s Unglaube m

disbelieve [ˌdɪsbɪˈliv] tr & intr nicht glauben

disburse [dɪsˈbʌrs] tr auszahlen

disbursement [dɪsˈbʌrsmənt] s Auszahlung f

disc [dɪsk] s var of **disk**

discard [dɪsˈkɑrd] s Ablegen n ‖ tr (clothes, cards, habits) ablegen; (a plan) verwerfen

discern [dɪˈsʌrn] tr (perceive) wahrnehmen; **be able to d. right from wrong** zwischen Gut und Böse unterscheiden können

discern'ing adj scharfsinnig

discernment [dɪˈsʌrnmənt] s Scharfsinn m

discharge [dɪsˈtʃɑrdʒ] s (of a gun) Abfeuern n; (of a battery) Entladung f; (of water) Abfluß m; (of smoke) Ausströmen n; (of duties) Erfüllung f; (of debts) Tilgung f; (of employees, patients, soldiers) Entlassung f; (of a prisoner) Freilassung f; (pathol) Ausfluß m ‖ tr (a gun) abfeuern; (e.g., water) ergießen; (smoke) ausstoßen; (debts) tilgen; (duties) erfüllen; (an office) verwalten; (an employee, patient, soldier) entlassen ‖ intr (said of a gun) losgehen; (said of a battery) sich entladen; (*pour out*) abfließen; (*pathol*) eitern

disciple [dɪ'saɪpəl] *s* Jünger *m*

disciplinarian [ˌdɪsɪplɪ'nerɪ·ən] *s* Zuchtmeister *m*

disciplinary ['dɪsɪplɪˌneri] *adj* Disziplinar

discipline ['dɪsɪplɪn] *s* Disziplin *f*; (*punishment*) Züchtigung *f* ‖ *tr* disziplinieren; (*punish*) züchtigen

disclaim [dɪs'klem] *tr* leugnen; (*jur*) verzichten auf (*acc*)

disclose [dɪs'kloz] *tr* enthüllen

disclosure [dɪs'kloʒər] *s* Enthüllung *f*

discolor [dɪs'kʌlər] *tr* verfärben ‖ *intr* sich verfärben

discoloration [dɪsˌkʌlə'reʃən] *s* Verfärbung *f*

discomfiture [dɪs'kʌmfɪtʃər] *s* (*defeat*) Niederlage *f*; (*frustration*) Enttäuschung *f*; (*confusion*) Verwirrung *f*

discomfort [dɪs'kʌmfərt] *s* Unbehagen *n* ‖ *tr* Unbehagen verursachen (*dat*)

disconcert [ˌdɪskən'sʌrt] *tr* aus der Fassung bringen

dis'concert'ed *adj* fassungslos

disconnect [ˌdɪskə'nekt] *tr* trennen; (*elec*) ausschalten; (*mach*) auskuppeln; (*telp*) unterbrechen

disconsolate [dɪs'kɑnsəlɪt] *adj* trostlos

discontent [ˌdɪskən'tent] *s* Unzufriedenheit *f* ‖ *tr* unzufrieden machen

dis'content'ed *adj* (*with*) mißvergnügt (über *acc*)

discontinue [ˌdɪskən'tɪnju] *tr* (*permanently*) einstellen; (*temporarily*) aussetzen; (*a newspaper*) abbestellen; **d.** (*ger*) aufhören zu (*inf*)

discord ['dɪskord] *s* Mißklang *m*; (*dissention*) Zwietracht *f*

discordance [dɪs'kordəns] *s* Uneinigkeit *f*

discotheque [ˌdɪsko'tek] *s* Diskothek *f*

discount ['dɪskaunt] *s* (*in price*) Rabatt *m*; (*cash discount*) Kassaskonto *n*; (*deduction from nominal value*) Diskont *m*; **at a d.** mit Rabatt; (st. exch.) unter pari ‖ *tr* (*disregard*) außer acht lassen; (*minimize*) geringen Wert beimessen (*dat*); (*for cash payment*) e–n Abzug gewähren auf (*acc*); (*e.g., a promissory note*) diskontieren

dis'count store' *s* Rabattladen *m*

discourage [dɪs'kʌrɪdʒ] *tr* (*dishearten*) entmutigen; **d. s.o. from** (*ger*) (*deter*) j–n davon abschrecken zu (*inf*); (*dissuade*) j–m davon abraten zu (*inf*)

discour'aged *adj* mutlos

discouragement [dɪs'kʌrɪdʒmənt] *s* (*act*) Entmutigung *f*; (*state*) Mutlosigkeit *f*; (*deterrent*) Abschreckung *f*

discourse ['dɪskors] *s* (*conversation*) Gespräch *n*; (*formal treatment*) Abhandlung *f*; (*lecture*) Vortrag *m* ‖ [dɪs'kors] *intr* (**on**) sich unterhalten (über *acc*)

discourteous [dɪs'kʌrtɪ·əs] *adj* unhöflich

discourtesy [dɪs'kʌrtəsi] *s* Unhöflichkeit *f*

discover [dɪs'kʌvər] *tr* entdecken

discovery [dɪs'kʌvəri] *s* Entdeckung *f*

discredit [dɪs'kredɪt] *s* (*disrepute*) Mißkredit *m*; (*disbelief*) Zweifel *m* ‖ *tr* (*destroy confidence in*) in Mißkredit bringen; (*disbelieve*) anzweifeln; (*disgrace*) in Verruf bringen

discreditable [dɪs'kredɪtəbəl] *adj* schändlich

discreet [dɪs'krit] *adj* diskret

discrepancy [dɪs'krepənsi] *s* Unstimmigkeit *f*

discretion [dɪs'kreʃən] *s* Diskretion *f*, Besonnenheit *f*; **at one's d.** nach Belieben; **leave to s.o.'s d.** in j–s Belieben stellen

discriminate [dɪs'krɪmɪˌnet] *tr* voneinander unterscheiden ‖ *intr*—**d. against** diskriminieren

discrimination [dɪsˌkrɪmɪ'neʃən] *s* (*distinction*) Unterscheidung *f*; (*prejudicial treatment*) Diskriminierung *f*

discriminatory [dɪs'krɪmɪnəˌtori] *adj* diskriminierend

discus ['dɪskʌs] *s* Diskus *m*

discuss [dɪs'kʌs] *tr* besprechen, diskutieren; (*formally*) erörtern

discussion [dɪs'kʌʃən] *s* Diskussion *f*; (*formal consideration*) Erörterung *f*

disdain [dɪs'den] *s* Geringschätzung *f* ‖ *tr* geringschätzen

disdainful [dɪs'denfəl] *adj* geringschätzig; **be d. of** geringschätzen

disease [dɪ'ziz] *s* Krankheit *f*

diseased' *adj* krank, erkrankt

disembark [ˌdɪsem'bɑrk] *tr* ausschiffen, landen ‖ *intr* an Land gehen, landen

disembarkation [dɪsˌembɑr'keʃən] *s* Ausschiffung *f*

disembow·el [ˌdɪsem'bau·əl] *v* (*pret & pp* **-el[l]ed;** *ger* **-el[l]ing**) *tr* ausweiden

disenchant [ˌdɪsen'tʃænt] *tr* ernüchtern

disenchantment [ˌdɪsen'tʃæntmənt] *s* Ernüchterung *f*

disengage [ˌdɪsen'gedʒ] *tr* (*a clutch*) ausrücken; (*the enemy*) sich absetzen von; (*troops*) entflechten; **d. the clutch** auskuppeln ‖ *intr* loskommen; (mil) sich absetzen

disengagement [ˌdɪsen'gedʒmənt] *s* Lösung *f*; (mil) Truppenentflechtung *f*

disentangle [ˌdɪsen'tæŋgəl] *tr* entwirren

disentanglement [ˌdɪsen'tæŋgəlmənt] *s* Entwirrung *f*

disfavor [dɪs'fevər] *s* Ungunst *f*

disfigure [dɪs'fɪgjər] *tr* entstellen

disfigurement [dɪs'fɪgjərmənt] *s* Entstellung *f*

disfranchise [dɪs'fræntʃaɪz] *tr* die Bürgerrechte entziehen (*dat*)

disgorge [dɪs'gordʒ] *tr* ausspeien ‖ *intr* sich ergießen

disgrace [dɪs'gres] *s* Schande *f*; (*of a family*) Schandfleck *m* ‖ *tr* in Schande bringen; (*a girl*) schänden; **be disgraced** in Schande kommen

disgraceful [dɪs'gresfəl] *adj* schänd-lich, schimpflich

disgruntled [dɪs'grʌntəld] *adj* mürrisch

disguise [dɪs'gaɪz] *s* (*clothing*) Ver-kleidung *f*; (*insincere manner*) Ver-stellung *f* ‖ *tr* (*by dress*) verkleiden; (*e.g., the voice*) verstellen

disgust [dɪs'gʌst] *s* (*at*) Ekel *m* (vor *dat*) ‖ *tr* anekeln

disgust'ing *adj* ekelhaft

dish [dɪʃ] *s* Schüssel *f*, Platte *f*; (*food*) Gericht *n*; **do the dishes** das Ge-schirr spülen ‖ *tr*—**d. out** (coll) aus-teilen

dish'cloth' *s* Geschirrlappen *m*

dishearten [dɪs'hartən] *tr* entmutigen

disheveled [dɪ'ʃevəld] *adj* unordentlich

dishonest [dɪs'ɑnɪst] *adj* unehrlich

dishonesty [dɪs'ɑnɪsti] *s* Unehrlichkeit *f*

dishonor [dɪs'ɑnər] *s* Unehre *f* ‖ *tr* verunehren

dishonorable [dɪs'ɑnərəbəl] *adj* (*per-son*) ehrlos; (*action*) unehrenhaft

dishon'orable dis'charge *s* Entlassung *f* wegen Wehrunwürdigkeit

dish'pan' *s* Aufwaschschüssel *f*

dish'rack' *s* Abtropfkörbchen *n*

dish'rag' *s* Spüllappen *m*

dish'tow'el *s* Geschirrtuch *n*

dish'wash'er *s* (*person*) Aufwäscher –in *mf*; (*appliance*) Geschirrspül-maschine *f*

dish'wa'ter *s* Spülwasser *n*

disillusion [ˌdɪsɪ'luʒən] *s* Ernüchte-rung *f* ‖ *tr* ernüchtern

disillusionment [ˌdɪsɪ'luʒənmənt] *s* Er-nüchterung *f*

disinclination [ˌdɪsɪnklɪ'neʃən] *s* Ab-neigung *f*, Abgeneigtheit *f*

disinclined [ˌdɪsɪn'klaɪnd] *adj* abge-neigt

disinfect [ˌdɪsɪn'fɛkt] *tr* desinfizieren

disinfectant [ˌdɪsɪn'fɛktənt] *adj* des-infizierend ‖ *s* Desinfektionsmittel *n*

disinherit [ˌdɪsɪn'hɛrɪt] *tr* enterben

disintegrate [dɪs'ɪntɪˌgret] *tr* (& fig) zersetzen ‖ *intr* zerfallen

disintegration [dɪsˌɪntɪ'greʃən] *s* (& fig) Zerfall *m*

disin·ter [ˌdɪsɪn'tʌr] *v* (*pret & pp* –**terred**; *ger* –**terring**) *tr* ausgraben

disinterested [dɪs'ɪntəˌrɛstɪd] *adj* (*un-biased*) unparteiisch; (*uninterested*) desinteressiert

disjunctive [dɪs'dʒʌŋktɪv] *adj* disjunk-tiv

disk [dɪsk] *s* Scheibe *f*

disk' brake' *s* Scheibenbremse *f*

disk' jock'ey *s* Schallplattenjockei *m*

dislike [dɪs'laɪk] *s* (*of*) Abneigung *f* (gegen) ‖ *tr* nicht mögen

dislocate ['dɪsloˌket] *tr* verschieben; (*a shoulder*) verrenken; (fig) stören

dislocation [ˌdɪslo'keʃən] *s* Verschie-bung *f*; (*of a shoulder*) Verrenkung *f*; (fig) Störung *f*

dislodge [dɪs'lɑdʒ] *tr* losreißen; (mil) aus der Stellung werfen

disloyal [dɪs'lɔɪ·əl] *adj* untreu

disloyalty [dɪs'lɔɪ·əlti] *s* Untreue *f*

dismal ['dɪzməl] *adj* trübselig, düster

dismantle [dɪs'mæntəl] *tr* demontieren

dismay [dɪs'me] *s* Bestürzung *f* ‖ *tr* bestürzen

dismember [dɪs'mɛmbər] *tr* zerstük-keln

dismiss [dɪs'mɪs] *tr* verabschieden; (*an employee*) (**from**) entlassen (aus); (*a case*) (jur) abweisen; (mil) weg-treten lassen; **d. as** abtun als; **dis-missed!** (mil) wegtreten!

dismissal [dɪs'mɪsəl] *s* Entlassung *f*; (jur) Abweisung *f*

dismount [dɪs'maʊnt] *tr* (*throw down*) abwerfen; (*mach*) abmontieren ‖ *intr* (*from a carriage*) herabsteigen; (*from a horse*) absitzen

disobedience [ˌdɪsə'bidɪ·əns] *s* Unge-horsam *m*, Unfolgsamkeit *f*

disobedient [ˌdɪsə'bidɪ·ənt] *adj* unge-horsam, unfolgsam

disobey [ˌdɪsə'be] *tr* nicht gehorchen (*dat*) ‖ *intr* nicht gehorchen

disorder [dɪs'ɔrdər] *s* Unordnung *f*; (*public disturbance*) Unruhe *f*; (pathol) Erkrankung *f*; **throw into d.** in Unordnung bringen

disorderly [dɪs'ɔrdərli] *adj* unordent-lich, liederlich

disor'derly con'duct *s* ungebührliches Benehmen *n*

disor'derly house' *s* Bordell *n*; (*gam-bling house*) Spielhölle *f*

disorganize [dɪs'ɔrgəˌnaɪz] *tr* zerrüt-ten, desorganisieren

disown [dɪs'on] *tr* verleugnen

disparage [dɪ'spærɪdʒ] *tr* herabsetzen, geringschätzen

disparate ['dɪspərɪt] *adj* ungleichartig

disparity [dɪ'spærɪti] *s* (*inequality*) Ungleichheit *f*; (*difference*) Unter-schied *m*

dispassionate [dɪs'pæʃənɪt] *adj* leiden-schaftslos

dispatch [dɪ'spætʃ] *s* Abfertigung *f*; (*message*) Depesche *f*; **with d. in Eile** ‖ *tr* (*send off*) absenden; (*e.g., a truck*) abfertigen; (*e.g., a task*) schnell erledigen; (*kill*) töten; (*eat fast*) (coll) verputzen

dispatcher [dɪ'spætʃər] *s* (*of vehicles*) Fahrbereitschaftsleiter –in *mf*

dis·pel [dɪ'spɛl] *v* (*pret & pp* –**pelled**; *ger* –**pelling**) *tr* vertreiben; (*thoughts, doubts*) zerstreuen

dispensary [dɪ'spɛnsəri] *s* Arzneiaus-gabestelle *f*; (mil) Krankenrevier *n*

dispensation [ˌdɪspɛn'seʃən] *s* (eccl) (**from**) Dispens *m* (von); **by divine d.** durch göttliche Fügung

dispense [dɪ'spɛns] *tr* (*exempt*) (**from**) entbinden (von); (pharm) zubereiten und ausgeben; **d. justice** Recht sprechen ‖ *intr*—**d. with** verzichten auf (*acc*)

dispersal [dɪ'spʌrsəl] *s* Auflockerung *f*

disperse [dɪ'spʌrs] *tr* zerstreuen; (*a crowd*) zersprengen; (*one's troops*) auflockern; (*the enemy*) auseinander-sprengen ‖ *intr* (*said of clouds, etc.*) sich verziehen; (*said of crowds*) aus-einandergehen

dispirited [dɪ'spɪrɪtɪd] *adj* niederge-schlagen

displace [dɪs'pleɪs] *tr (people in war)* verschleppen; (phys) verdrängen

displacement [dɪs'pleɪsmənt] *s* Vertreibung *f*; (phys) Verdrängung *f*

display [dɪ'spleɪ] *s (of energy, wealth)* Entfaltung *f*; *(of goods)* Ausstellung *f*; *(pomp)* Aufwand *m*; **on d.** zur Schau || *tr (wares)* ausstellen; *(reveal)* entfalten; *(flaunt)* protzen mit

display' case' *s* Vitrine *f*

display' room' *s* Ausstellungsraum *m*

display' win'dow *s* Schaufenster *n*

displease [dɪs'pliz] *tr* mißfallen (dat); **be displeased with** Mißfallen finden an (dat) || *intr* mißfallen

displeas'ing *adj* mißfällig

displeasure [dɪs'plɛʒər] *s* Mißfallen *n*

disposable [dɪ'spozəbəl] *adj* Einwegdisposal

disposal [dɪ'spozəl] *s (riddance)* Beseitigung *f*; *(of a matter)* Erledigung *f*; *(distribution)* Anordnung *f*; **be at s.o.'s d.** j-m zur Verfügung stehen; **have at one's d.** verfügen über (acc); **put at s.o.'s d.** j-m zur Verfügung stellen

dispose [dɪ'spoz] *tr (incline)* **(to)** geneigt machen (zu); *(arrange)* anordnen || *intr*—**d. of** *(a matter)* erledigen; *(get rid of)* loswerden

disposed' *adj* gesinnt; **d. to** *(ger)* geneigt zu *(inf)*

disposition [ˌdɪspə'zɪʃən] *s (settlement)* Erledigung *f*; *(nature)* Gemütsart *f*; *(inclination)* Neigung *f*

dispossess [ˌdɪspə'zɛs] *tr*—**d. s.o. of s.th.** j-m etw enteignen

disproof [dɪs'pruf] *s* Widerlegung *f*

disproportionate [ˌdɪsprə'porʃənɪt] *adj* unverhältnismäßig; **be d. to** im Mißverhältnis stehen zu

disprove [dɪs'pruv] *tr* widerlegen

dispute [dɪs'pjut] *s (quarrel)* Streit *m*; *(debate)* Wortgefecht *n*; **beyond d.** unstreitig; **in d.** umstritten || *tr* bestreiten || *intr* disputieren

disqualification [dɪsˌkwɑlɪfɪ'keʃən] *s* Disqualifizierung *f*

disqual·ify [dɪs'kwɑlɪˌfaɪ] *v (pret & pp* **-fied)** *tr (make unfit)* **(for)** untauglich machen (für); *(declare ineligible)* disqualifizieren

disquiet [dɪs'kwaɪ·ət] *tr* beunruhigen

disqui'eting *adj* beunruhigend

disregard [ˌdɪsrɪ'gɑrd] *s (lack of attention)* Nichtbeachtung *f*; *(disrespect)* Mißachtung *f* || *tr (not pay attention to)* nicht beachten; *(treat without due respect)* mißachten

disrepair [ˌdɪsrɪ'pɛr] *s* Verfall *m*; **fall into d.** verfallen

disreputable [dɪs'rɛpjətəbəl] *adj* verrufen

disrepute [ˌdɪsrɪ'pjut] *s* Verruf *m*

disrespect [ˌdɪsrɪ'spɛkt] *s* Nichtachtung *f*, Mißachtung *f* || *tr* nicht achten

disrespectful [ˌdɪsrɪ'spɛktfəl] *adj* respektlos, unehrerbietig

disrobe [dɪs'rob] *tr* entkleiden || *intr* sich entkleiden

disrupt [dɪs'rʌpt] *tr (throw into confusion)* in Verwirrung bringen; *(interrupt)* unterbrechen; *(cause to*

break down) zum Zusammenbruch bringen

dissatisfaction [ˌdɪssætɪs'fækʃən] *s* Unzufriedenheit *f*

dissat'isfied' *adj* unzufrieden

dissatis·fy [dɪs'sætɪsˌfaɪ] *v (pret & pp* **-fied)** *tr* nicht befriedigen

dissect [dɪ'sɛkt] *tr (fig)* zergliedern; (anat) sezieren

dissection [dɪ'sɛkʃən] *s (fig)* Zergliederung *f*; (anat) Sektion *f*

dissemble [dɪ'sɛmbəl] *tr* verbergen || *intr* heucheln

disseminate [dɪ'sɛmɪˌnet] *tr* verbreiten

dissension [dɪ'sɛnʃən] *s* Uneinigkeit *f*

dissent [dɪ'sɛnt] *s* abweichende Meinung *f* || *intr* **(from)** anderer Meinung sein (als)

dissenter [dɪ'sɛntər] *s* Andersdenkende *mf*; (relig) Dissident *–in mf*

dissertation [ˌdɪsər'teʃən] *s* Dissertation *f*

disservice [dɪ'sʌrvɪs] *s* schlechter Dienst *m*; **do s.o. a d.** j-m e-n schlechten Dienst erweisen

dissidence ['dɪsɪdəns] *s* Meinungsverschiedenheit *f*

dissident ['dɪsɪdənt] *adj* andersdenkend || *s* Dissident *–in mf*

dissimilar [dɪ'sɪmɪlər] *adj* unähnlich

dissimilate [dɪ'sɪmɪˌlet] *tr* (phonet) dissimilieren

dissimulate [dɪ'sɪmjəˌlet] *tr* verheimlichen || *intr* heucheln

dissipate ['dɪsɪˌpet] *tr (squander)* vergeuden; *(scatter)* zerstreuen; *(dissolve)* auflösen || *intr (scatter)* sich zerstreuen; *(dissolve)* sich auflösen

dis'sipat'ed *adj* ausschweifend

dissipation [ˌdɪsɪ'peʃən] *s (squandering)* Vergeudung *f*; *(dissolute mode of life)* Ausschweifung *f*; (phys) Dissipation *f*

dissociate [dɪ'soʃɪˌet] *tr* trennen; **d. oneself from** abrücken von

dissolute ['dɪsəˌlut] *adj* ausschweifend

dissolution [ˌdɪsə'luʃən] *s* Auflösung *f*

dissolve [dɪ'zɑlv] *s* (cin) Überblendung *f* || *tr* auflösen; (cin) überblenden || *intr* sich auflösen; (cin) überblenden

dissonance ['dɪsənəns] *s* Mißklang *m*

dissuade [dɪ'swed] *tr* **(from)** abbringen (von); **d. s.o. from** *(ger)* j-n davon abbringen zu *(inf)*

dissyllabic [ˌdɪsɪ'læbɪk] *adj* zweisilbig

distaff ['dɪstæf] *s* Spinnrocken *m*; (fig) Frauen *pl*

dis'taff side' *s* weibliche Linie *f*

distance ['dɪstəns] *s* Entfernung *f*; *(between two points)* Abstand *m*; *(stretch)* Strecke *f*; *(of a race)* Rennstrecke *f*; **from a d.** aus einiger Entfernung; **go the d.** bis zum Ende aushalten; **in the d.** in der Ferne; **keep one's d.** zurückhaltend sein; **keep your d.** bleib mir vom Leib!; **within easy d. of** nicht weit weg von; **within walking d. of** zu Fuß erreichbar von

distant ['dɪstənt] *adj* entfernt; *(reserved)* zurückhaltend

distaste [dɪs'test] s (for) Abneigung f (gegen), Ekel m (vor dat)
distasteful [dɪs'testfəl] adj (unpleasant) (to) unangenehm (dat); (offensive) (to) ekelhaft (dat)
distemper [dɪs'tempər] s (of dogs) Staupe f; (paint) Temperafarbe f
distend [dɪs'tend] tr (swell) aufblähen; (extend) ausdehnen || intr (swell) anschwellen; (extend) (aus)dehnen
distension [dɪs'tenʃən] s Aufblähung f; Ausdehnung f
distill [dɪ'stɪl] tr destillieren; (e.g., whiskey) brennen
distillation [,dɪstɪ'leʃən] s Destillation f; (of whiskey) Brennen n
distiller [dɪs'tɪlər] s Brenner m
distillery [dɪs'tɪləri] s Brennerei f
distinct [dɪ'stɪŋkt] adj (clear) deutlich; (different) verschieden; as d. from zum Unterschied von; keep d. auseinanderhalten
distinction [dɪs'tɪŋkʃən] s (difference) Unterschied m; (differentiation) Unterscheidung f; (honor) Auszeichnung f; (eminence) Vornehmheit f; have the d. of (ger) den Vorzug haben zu (inf)
distinctive [dɪs'tɪŋktɪv] adj (distinguishing) unterscheidend; (characteristic) kennzeichnend
distinguish [dɪs'tɪŋgwɪʃ] tr (differentiate) unterscheiden; (classify) einteilen; (honor) auszeichnen; (characterize) kennzeichnen; (discern) erkennen || intr (between) unterscheiden (zwischen dat)
distin/guished adj (eminent) prominent; (for) berühmt (wegen)
distort [dɪs'tɔrt] tr verzerren; (the truth) entstellen; distorted picture Zerrbild n
distortion [dɪs'tɔrʃən] s Verzerrung f; (of the truth) Entstellung f
distract [dɪ'strækt] tr ablenken
distraction [dɪ'strækʃən] s (diversion of attention) Ablenkung f; (entertainment) Zerstreuung f; drive s.o. to d. j-n zum Wahnsinn treiben
distraught [dɪ'strɔt] adj (bewildered) verwirrt; (deeply agitated) (with) aufgewühlt (von); (crazed) (with) rasend (vor dat)
distress [dɪ'stres] s (anxiety) Kummer m; (mental pain) Betrübnis f; (danger) Notstand m, Bedrängnis f; (naut) Seenot f || tr betrüben
distress/ing adj betrüblich
distress/ sig/nal s Notzeichen n
distribute [dɪ'strɪbjut] tr verteilen; (divide) einteilen; (apportion) (jur) aufteilen
distribution [,dɪstrɪ'bjuʃən] s Verteilung f; (geographic range) Verbreitung f; (of films) Verleih m; (marketing) Vertrieb m; (of dividends) Ausschüttung f; (jur) Aufteilung f
distributor [dɪ'strɪbjətər] s Verteiler –in mf; (of films) Verleiher –in mf; (dealer) Lieferant –in mf; (aut) Verteiler m
distri/butorship/ s Vertrieb m

district ['dɪstrɪkt] s Bezirk m
dis/trict attor/ney s Staatsanwalt m
distrust [dɪs'trʌst] s Mißtrauen n || tr mißtrauen (dat)
distrustful [dɪs'trʌstfəl] adj (of) mißtrauisch (gegen)
disturb [dɪs'tʌrb] tr stören; (disquiet) beunruhigen; d. the peace die öffentliche Ruhe stören
disturbance [dɪs'tʌrbəns] s (interruption) Störung f; (breach of peace) Unruhe f
disunited [,dɪsju'naɪtɪd] adj uneinig
disunity [dɪs'junɪti] s Uneinigkeit f
disuse [dɪs'jus] s Nichtverwendung f; fall into d. außer Gebrauch kommen
ditch [dɪtʃ] s Graben m || tr (discard) (sl) wegschmeißen; (aer) (coll) auf dem Wasser notlanden mit || intr (aer) (coll) notwassern
dither ['dɪðər] s—be in a d. verdattert sein
dit•to ['dɪto] adj (coll) dito || s (–tos) Kopie f || tr vervielfältigen
dit/to mark/ s Wiederholungszeichen n
ditty ['dɪti] s Liedchen s
diva ['divə] s (mus) Diva f
divan ['daɪvæn], [dɪ'væn] s Diwan m
dive [daɪv] s Kopfsprung m; (coll) Spelunke f; (aer) Sturzflug m; (nav) Tauchen n; (sport) Kunstsprung m; make a d. for (fig) sich stürzen auf (acc) || v (pret & pp dived & dove [dov]) intr (submerge) tauchen; (plunge head first) e-n Kopfsprung machen; (aer) e-n Sturzflug machen; (nav) (unter)tauchen; (sport) e-n Kunstsprung machen
dive/-bomb/ tr & intr im Sturzflug mit Bomben angreifen
dive/ bomb/er s Sturzkampfbomber m
diver ['daɪvər] s Taucher –in mf; (orn) Taucher m; (sport) Kunstspringer –in mf
diverge [daɪ'vʌrdʒ] intr (said of roads, views) sich teilen; (from the norm) abweichen; (geom, phys) divergieren
diverse [daɪ'vʌrs] adj (different) verschieden; (of various kinds) vielförmig
diversi•fy [daɪ'vʌrsɪ,faɪ] v (pret & pp –fied) tr abwechslungsreich gestalten
diversion [daɪ'vʌrʒən] s Ablenkung f; (recreation) Zeitvertreib m; (mil) Ablenkungsmanöver n
diversity [daɪ'vʌrsɪti] s Mannigfaltigkeit f
divert [daɪ'vʌrt] tr (attention) ablenken; (traffic) umleiten; (a river) ableiten; (money) abzweigen; (entertain) zerstreuen
divest [daɪ'vest] tr—d. oneself of sich entäußern (genit); d. s.o. of (e.g., office, power) j-n entkleiden (genit); (e.g., rights, property) j-m (seine Rechte, etc.) entziehen
divide [dɪ'vaɪd] s (geol) Wasserscheide f || tr teilen; (cause to disagree) entzweien; (math) (by) teilen (durch); d. into einteilen in (acc); d. off (a room) abteilen; d. up (among) aufteilen (unter acc) || intr

(*said of a road*) sich teilen; **d. into** sich teilen in (*acc*)

dividend ['dɪvɪ‚dend] *s* Dividende *f*; (math) Dividend *m*; **pay dividends** Dividenden ausschütten; (fig) sich lohnen

divid'ing line' *s* Trennungsstrich *m*

divination [‚dɪvɪ'neʃən] *s* Weissagung *f*

divine [dɪ'vaɪn] *adj* göttlich || *s* Geistlicher *m* || *tr* (er)ahnen

divine' prov'idence *s* göttliche Vorsehung *f*

divine' right' of kings' *s* Königtum *n* von Gottes Gnaden

div'ing *s* Tauchen *n* (sport) Kunstspringen *n*

div'ing bell' *s* Taucherglocke *f*

div'ing board' *s* Sprungbrett *n*

div'ing suit' *s* Taucheranzug *m*

divin'ing rod' *s* Wünschelrute *f*

divinity [dɪ'vɪnɪti] *s* (*divine nature*) Göttlichkeit *f*; (*deity*) Gottheit *f*

divisible [dɪ'vɪzɪbəl] *adj* teilbar

division [dɪ'vɪʒən] *s* Teilung *f*; (*dissention*) Uneinigkeit *f*; (ädm) Abteilung *f*; (math, mil) Division *f*; (sport) Sportklasse *f*

divisor [dɪ'vaɪzər] *s* (math) Teiler *m*; Divisor *m*

divorce [dɪ'vors] *s* Scheidung *f*; **apply for a d.** die Scheidungsklage einreichen; **get a d.** sich scheiden lassen || *tr* (*said of a spouse*) sich scheiden lassen von; (*said of a judge*) scheiden; (*separate*) trennen

divorcee [dɪvor'si] *s* Geschiedene *f*

divulge [dɪ'vʌldʒ] *tr* ausplaudern

dizziness ['dɪzɪnɪs] *s* Schwindel *m*

dizzy ['dɪzɪ] *adj* schwindlig; (*causing dizziness*) schwindelerregend; (*mentally confused*) benommen; (*foolish*) damisch; (*feeling, spell*) Schwindel–

do [du] *v* (*3d pers* **does** [dʌz]; *pret* **did** [dɪd]; *pp* **done** [dʌn]; *ger* **doing** ['du‚ɪŋ] *tr* tun, machen; (*damage*) anrichten; (*one's hair*) frisieren; (*an injustice*) antun; (*a favor, disservice*) erweisen; (*time in jail*) absitzen; (*miles per hour*) fahren; (*tour*) (coll) besichtigen; (*Shakespeare, etc., in class*) durchnehmen; **do duty as** dienen als; **do in** (sl) umbringen; **do over** (*with paint*) neu anstreichen; (*with covering*) neu überziehen; **what can I do for you?** womit kann ich dienen? || *intr* tun machen; (*suffice*) genügen; **do away with** abschaffen; (*persons*) aus dem Wege räumen; **do away with oneself** sich [*dat*] das Leben nehmen; **do without** auskommen ohne; **I am doing well** es geht mir gut; (*financially*) ich verdiene gut; (*e.g., in history*) ich komme gut voran; **I'll make it do** ich werde schon damit auskommen; **nothing doing!** ausgeschlossen! **that will do!** genug davon!; **that won't do!** das geht nicht! || *aux* used in English but not specifically expressed in German: 1) in questions, e.g., **do you speak German?** sprechen Sie deutsch?; 2) in negative sentences,

e.g., **I do not live here** ich wohne hier nicht; 3) for emphasis, e.g., **I do feel better** ich fühle mich wirklich besser; 4) in imperative entreaties, e.g., **do come again** besuchen Sie mich doch wieder!; 5) in elliptical sentences, e.g., **I like Berlin. So do I** Mir gefällt Berlin. Mir auch.; **he drinks, doesn't he?** er trinkt, nicht wahr?; 6) in inversions after adverbs such as hardly, rarely, scarcely, little, e.g., **little did she realize that…** sie hatte keine Ahnung, daß… || *impers*—**it doesn't do to** (*inf*) es ist unklug zu (*inf*); **it won't do you any good to stay here** es wird Ihnen nicht viel nützen, hier zu bleiben

docile ['dɑsɪl] *adj* gelehrig; (*easy to handle*) fügsam, lenksam

dock [dɑk] *s* Anlegeplatz *m*; (jur) Anklagebank *f*; **docks** Hafenanlagen *pl*; **in the d.** (jur) auf der Anklagebank || *tr* (*a ship, space vehicle*) docken; (*a tail*) stutzen; (*pay*) kürzen; **d. an employee (for)** e–m Arbeitnehmer den Lohn kürzen (um) || *intr* (naut) (*am Kai*) anlegen; (rok) docken, koppeln

docket ['dɑkɪt] *s* (*agenda*) Tagesordnung *f*; (jur) Prozeßliste *f*

dock' hand' *s* Hafenarbeiter *m*

dock'ing *s* (naut) Anlegen *n*; (rok) Andocken *n*

dock' work'er *s* Dockarbeiter *m*

dock'yard' *s* Werft *f*

doctor ['dɑktər] *s* Doktor *m*; (*physician*) Arzt *m*, Ärztin *f* || *tr* (*records*) frisieren; (*adapt, e.g., a play*) zurechtmachen || *intr* (coll) in ärztlicher Behandlung stehen

doctorate ['dɑktərɪt] *s* Doktorwürde *f*

doctrine ['dɑktrɪn] *s* Doktrin *f*, Lehre *f*

document ['dɑkjəmənt] *s* Urkunde *f* || ['dɑkjə‚ment] *tr* dokumentieren

documentary [‚dɑkjə'mentərɪ] *adj* dokumentarisch || *s* Dokumentarfilm *m*

documentation [‚dɑkjəmən'teʃən] *s* Dokumentation *f*

doddering ['dɑdərɪŋ] *adj* zittrig

dodge [dɑdʒ] *s* Winkelzug *m* || *tr* (*e.g., a blow*) ausweichen (*dat*); (*e.g., a responsibility*) sich drücken vor (*dat*) || *intr* ausweichen

do-do ['dodo] *s* (**–does** & **–dos**) (coll) Depp *m*

doe [do] *s* Rehgeiß *f*, Damhirschkuh *f*

doer ['du‚ər] *s* Täter –in *mf*

doe'skin' *s* Rehleder *n*

doff [dɔf] *tr* (*a hat*) abnehmen; (*clothes*) ausziehen; (*habits*) ablegen

dog [dɔg] *s* Hund *m*; **dog eats dog** jeder für sich; **go to the dogs** (coll) vor die Hunde gehen; **lucky dog!** (coll) Glückspilz!; **put on the dog** (coll) großtun || *v* (*pret* & *pp* **dogged**; *ger* **dogging**) *tr* nachspüren (*dat*)

dog' bis'cuit *s* Hundekuchen *m*

dog' days' *spl* Hundstage *pl*

dog'-eared' *adj* mit Eselsohren

dog'face' *s* (mil) Landser *m*

dog'fight' s (aer) Kurbelei f
dogged ['dɔgɪd] adj verbissen
doggerel ['dɔgərəl] s Knittelvers m
doggone ['dɔg'gɔn] adj (sl) verflixt
dog'house' s Hundehütte f; **in the d.** (fig) in Ungnade
dog' ken'nel s Hundezwinger m
dogma ['dɔgmə] s Dogma n
dogmatic [dɔg'mætɪk] adj dogmatisch
do-gooder ['du'gudər] s Humanitäts-apostel m
dog' show' s Hundeschau f
dog's' life' s Hundeleben n
Dog' Star' s Hundestern m
dog' tag' s Hundemarke f; (mil) Erkennungsmarke f
dog'-tired' adj hundemüde
dog'wood' s Hartriegel m
doily ['dɔɪlɪ] s Zierdeckchen n
do'ing s Werk n; **doings** Tun und Treiben n; (events) Ereignisse pl
doldrums ['dɔldrəmz] spl Kalmengürtel m; **in the d.** (fig) deprimiert
dole [dol] s Spende f; **be on the d.** stempeln gehen || tr—**d. out** verteilen
doleful ['dolfəl] adj trübselig
doll [dɑl] s Puppe f || tr—**d. up** (coll) aufdonnern || intr (coll) sich aufdonnern
dollar ['dɑlər] s Dollar m
doll' car'riage s Puppenwagen m
dolly ['dɑlɪ] s Püppchen n; (cart) Schiebkarren m
dolphin ['dɑlfɪn] s Delphin m
dolt [dolt] s Tölpel m
domain [do'men] s (& fig) Domäne f
dome [dom] s Kuppel f
dome' light' s (aut) Deckenlicht n
domestic [də'mestɪk] adj (of the home) Haus-, häuslich, Haushalts-; (produced at home) einheimisch, inländisch, Landes-; (tame) Haus-; (e.g., policy) Innen-, innere || s Hausangestellte mf
domesticate [də'mestɪˌket] tr zähmen
domicile ['dɑmɪˌsaɪl] s Wohnsitz m
dominance ['dɑmɪnəns] s Vorherrschaft f
dominant ['dɑmɪnənt] adj vorherrschend; (factor) entscheidend
dominate ['dɑmɪˌnet] tr beherrschen || intr (over) herrschen (über acc)
domination [ˌdɑmɪ'neʃən] s Beherrschung f, Herrschaft f
domineer [ˌdɑmɪ'nɪr] tr & intr tyrannisieren
domineer'ing adj tyrannisch
dominion [də'mɪnjən] s (sovereignty) (over) Gewalt f (über acc); (domain) Domäne f; (of British Empire) Dominion n
domi·no ['dɑmɪˌno] s (–noes & nos) Dominostein m; **dominoes** ssg Dominospiel n
don [dɑn] s Universitätsprofessor m || v (pret & pp donned; ger donning) tr anlegen; (a hat) sich [dat] aufsetzen
donate ['donet] tr schenken, spenden
donation [do'neʃən] s Schenkung f; (small contribution) Spende f
done [dʌn] adj erledigt; (culin) gar, fertig; **d. for** kaputt; **d. with** (com-

pleted) fertig; **get** (*s.th.*) **d.** fertigbekommen; **well d.** (culin) durchgebraten
donkey ['dʌŋkɪ] s Esel m
donor ['donər] s Spender –in mf
doodad ['dudæd] s (gadget) Dings n; (decoration) Tand m
doodle ['dudəl] s Gekritzel n || tr bekritzeln || intr kritzeln
doom [dum] s Verhängnis n || tr verdammen, verurteilen
doomed adj todgeweiht
doomsday ['dumz ˌde] s der Jüngste Tag
door [dor] s Tür f; **from d. to d.** von Haus zu Haus; **out of doors** draußen, im Freien; **show s.o. the d.** j–m die Tür weisen; **two doors away** zwei Häuser weiter
door'bell' s Türklingel f; **the d. is ringing** es klingelt
door'bell but'ton s Klingelknopf m
door'frame' s Türrahmen m
door'han'dle s Türgriff m, Türklinke f
door'jamb' s Türpfosten m
door'knob' s Türknopf m
door'man' s (–men') Portier m
door'mat' s Abtreter m, Türmatte f
door'nail' s—**dead as a d.** mausetot
door'post' s Türpfosten m
door'sill' s Türschwelle f
door'step' s Türstufe f
door'stop' s Türanschlag m
door'-to-door' sales'man s Hausierer m
door'-to-door' sell'ing s Hausieren n
door'way' s Türöffnung f; (fig) Weg m
dope [dop] s (drug) (sl) Rauschgift n; (information) (sl) vertraulicher Tip m; (fool) (sl) Trottel m; (aer) Lack m || tr (a racehorse) (sl) dopen; (a person) (sl) betäuben, verdrogen; (aer) lackieren; **d. out** (sl) herausfinden, ausarbeiten; **d. up** (sl) verdrogen
dope' ad'dict s (sl) Rauschgiftsüchtige mf
dope' push'er s (sl) Rauschgiftschieber –in mf
dope'sheet' s (sl) vertraulicher Bericht m
dope' traf'fic s (sl) Rauschgifthandel m
dopey ['dopi] adj (dopier; dopiest) (sl) dämlich; (from sleep) (coll) schlaftrunken
dormant ['dɔrmənt] adj ruhend, untätig; (bot) in der Winterruhe
dormer ['dɔrmər] s Bodenfenster n; (the whole structure) Mansarde f
dor'mer win'dow s Bodenfenster n
dormitory ['dɔrmɪˌtori] s (building) Studentenheim n; (room) Schlafsaal m
dormouse ['dɔr ˌmaʊs] s (mice [ˌmaɪs]) Haselmaus f
dor'sal fin' ['dɔrsəl] s Rückenflosse f
dosage ['dosɪdʒ] s Dosierung f
dose [dos] s (& fig) Dosis f
dossier ['dɑsɪ ˌe] s Dossier m
dot [dɑt] s Punkt m, Tupfen m; **on the dot** auf die Sekunde; **three o'clock on the dot** Punkt drei Uhr || v (pret

& *pp* **dotted;** *ger* **dotting)** *tr* punktieren; tüpfeln; **dot one's i's** den Punkt aufs i setzen; (fig) übergenau sein

dotage ['dotɪdʒ] *s*—**be in one's d.** senil sein

dotard ['dotərd] *s* kindischer Greis *m*

dote [dot] *intr*—**d. on** vernarrt sein in (*acc*)

dot'ing *adj* (**on**) vernarrt (in *acc*)

dots' and dash'es *spl* (telg) Punkte und Striche *pl*

dot'ted *adj* (*pattern*) getüpfelt; (*with flowers, etc.*) übersät; (*line*) punktiert

double ['dʌbəl] *adj* doppelt ‖ *s* Doppelte *n*; (*person*) Doppelgänger *m* (cin, theat) Double *n*; **doubles** (tennis) Doppel *n*; **on the d.** im Geschwindschritt ‖ *tr* (ver)doppeln; (*the fist*) ballen; (cards) doppeln; (naut) umsegeln ‖ *intr* sich verdoppeln; (cards) doppeln; **d. back** umkehren; **d. up** mit sich biegen vor (*dat*)

dou'ble-bar'reled *adj* (*gun*) doppelläufig; (fig) mit zweifacher Wirkung

dou'ble bass' [bes] *s* Kontrabaß *m*

dou'ble bed' *s* Doppelbett *n*

dou'ble-breast'ed *adj* doppelreihig

dou'ble chin' *s* Doppelkinn *n*

dou'ble cross' *s* Schwindel *m*

dou'ble-cross' *tr* beschwindeln

dou'ble-cross'er *s* Schwindler –in *mf*

dou'ble date' *s* Doppelrendezvous *n*

dou'ble-deal'er *s* Betrüger –in *mf*

dou'ble-deal'ing *s* Doppelzüngigkeit *f*

dou'ble-deck'er *s* (*ship, bus*) Doppeldecker *m*; (*sandwich*) Doppelsandwich *n*; (*bed*) Etagenbett *n*

dou'ble-edged' *adj* (& fig) zweischneidig

double entendre ['dʌbələn'tandrə] *s* (*ambiguity*) Doppelsinn *m*; (*ambiguous term*) doppelsinniger Ausdruck *m*

dou'ble en'try *s* (com) doppelte Buchführung *f*

dou'ble expo'sure *s* Doppelbelichtung *f*

dou'ble fea'ture *s* Doppelprogramm *n*

dou'blehead'er *s* Doppelspiel *n*

dou'ble-joint'ed *adj* mit Gummigelenken

dou'blepark' *tr* & *intr* falsch parken

dou'ble-spaced' *adj* mit doppeltem Zeilenabstand

dou'ble stand'ard *s* zweierlei Maß *n*

doublet ['dʌblɪt] *s* (*duplicate; counterfeit stone*) Dublette *f*; (hist) Wams *m*; (ling) Doppelform *f*

dou'ble take' *s* (fig) Spätzündung *f*

dou'ble-talk' *s* zweideutige Rede *f*

dou'ble time' *s* (*wage rate*) doppelter Lohn *m*; (mil) Eilschritt *m*

dou'ble track' *s* (rr) doppelgleisige Bahnlinie *f*

doubly ['dʌbli] *adv* doppelt

doubt [daʊt] *s* Zweifel *m*; **be still in d.** (*said of things*) noch zweifelhaft sein; **beyond d.** ohne (jeden) Zweifel; **in case of d.** im Zweifelsfalle; **no d.** zweifellos; **raise doubts** Bedenken

erregen; **there is no d. that** es unterliegt keinem Zweifel, daß ‖ *tr* bezweifeln ‖ *intr* zweifeln

doubter ['daʊtər] *s* Zweifler –in *mf*

doubtful ['daʊtfəl] *adj* zweifelhaft

doubtless ['daʊtlɪs] *adj* & *adv* zweifellos

douche [duʃ] *s* (*device*) Irrigator *m*; (*act of cleansing*) Spülung *f* ‖ *tr* & *intr* spülen

dough [do] *s* Teig *m*; (sl) Pinke *f*

dough'boy' *s* (sl) Landser *m*

dough'nut' *s* Krapfen *m*

doughty ['daʊti] *adj* wacker

doughy ['do-i] *adj* teigig

dour [daʊr], [dʊr] *adj* mürrisch

douse [daʊs] *tr* eintauchen; (**with**) übergießen (mit); (*a fire*) auslöschen

dove [dʌv] *s* (& pol) Taube *f*

dovecote ['dʌv‚kot] *s* Taubenschlag *m*

dove'tail' *s* (carp) Schwalbenschwanz *m* ‖ *tr* verzinken; (fig) ineinanderfügen ‖ *intr* ineinanderpassen

dowager ['daʊ‚ədʒər] *s* Witwe *f* (von Stand); (coll) Matrone *f*

dowdy ['daʊdi] *adj* schlampig

dow•el ['daʊ‚əl] *s* Dübel *m* ‖ *v* (*pret* & *pp* **-el[l]ed;** *ger* **-el[l]ing)** *tr* (ein)dübeln

down [daʊn] *adj* (*prices*) gesunken; (*sun*) untergegangen; **be d. for** vorgemerkt sein für; **be d. on s.o.** auf j-m herumtrampeln; **be d. three points** (sport) drei Punkte zurück sein; **be d. with a cold** mit e-r Erkältung im Bett liegen; **d. and out** völlig erledigt; **d. in the mouth** niedergedrückt ‖ *adv* herunter, hinunter; **d. from now...herab;** **d. there** da unten; **d. to** bis hinunter zu; **d. to the last man** bis zum letzten Mann; **d. with...!** nieder mit...! ‖ *s* (*of fowl*) Daune *f*; (*fine hair*) Flaum *m*; **downs** grasbedecktes Hügelland *n* ‖ *prep* (postpositive) (*acc*) herunter, hinunter; **a little way d. the road** etwas weiter auf der Straße; **d. the river** flußabwärts ‖ *tr* niederschlagen; (*a glass of beer*) (coll) hinunterstürzen; (aer) abschießen

down'cast' *adj* niedergeschlagen

down'draft' *s* Abwind *m*, Fallwind *m*

down'fall' *s* Untergang *m*

down'grade' *s* Gefälle *n*; **on the d.** (fig) im Niedergang ‖ *tr* herabsetzen; niedriger einstufen

down'heart'ed *adj* niedergeschlagen

down'hill' *adj* bergabgehend; (*in skiing*) Abfahrts– ‖ *adv* bergab; **he's going d.** (coll) mit ihm geht es abwärts

down' pay'ment *s* Anzahlung *f*

down'pour' *s* Regenguß *m*, Sturzregen *m*

down'right' *adj* ausgesprochen; (*lie*) glatt; (*contradiction*) schroff ‖ *adv* ausgesprochen

down'spout' *s* Fallrohr *n*

down'stairs' *adj* unten befindlich ‖ *adv* (*position*) unten; (*direction*) nach unten

down'stream' *adv* stromabwärts

down′stroke′ s (in writing) Grund-
strich m; (of a piston) Abwärtshub
m
down′-the-line′ adj vorbehaltlos
down-to-earth′ adj nüchtern
down′town′ adj im Geschäftsviertel
gelegen ‖ adv (position) im Geschäftsviertel; (direction) ins Geschäftsviertel, in die Stadt ‖ s
Geschäftsviertel n
down′trend′ s Baissestimmung f
downtrodden [′daun͵trɑdən] adj un-
terdrückt
downward [′daunwərd] adj Abwärts–
‖ adv abwärts
downwards [′daunwərdz] adv abwärts
downy [′dauni] adj flaumig; (soft)
weich wie Flaum
dowry [′dauri] s Mitgift f
dowser [′dauzər] s (rod) Wünschelrute f; (person) Wünschelrutengän-
ger m
doze [doz] s Schläfchen n ‖ intr dösen
dozen [′dʌzən] s Dutzend n; a d. times
dutzendmal
Dr. abbr (**Doctor**) Dr.; (in addresses:
Drive) Str.
drab [dræb] adj (**drabber; drabbest**)
graubraun; (fig) trüb
drach·ma [′drækmə] s (**–mas & –mae**
[mi]) Drachme f
draft [dræft] s (of air; drink) Zug m;
(sketch) Entwurf m; (fin) Tratte f;
(mil) Einberufung f; on d. vom Faß
‖ tr (sketch) entwerfen, abfassen;
(mil) einberufen
draft′ age′ s wehrpflichtiges Alter n
draft′ beer′ s Schankbier n
draft′ board′ s Wehrmeldeamt n
draft′ dodg′er [′dɑdʒər] s Drückeberger m
draftee [͵dræf′ti] s Dienstpflichtige
mf
draft′ing s (of a document) Abfassung
f; (mechanical drawing) Zeichnen n;
(mil) Aushebung f
draft′ing board′ s Zeichenbrett n
draft′ing room′ n Zeichenbüro n
drafts·man [′dræftsmən] s (**–men**)
Zeichner m
drafty [′dræfti] adj zugig
drag [dræg] s (sledge) Lastschlitten
m; (in smoking) (coll) Zug m; (boring person) langweiliger Mensch m;
(s.th. tedious) etwas langweiliges;
(encumbrance) (on) Hemmschuh m
(für); (aer) Luftwiderstand m; (for
recovering objects) (naut) Schleppnetz n; (for retarding motion) (naut)
Schleppanker m ‖ v (pret & pp
dragged; ger dragging) tr schleppen,
schleifen; **d. one's feet** schlurfen;
(fig) sich [dat] Zeit lassen; **d. out**
dahinschleppen; (protract) verschleppen; **d. through the mud** (fig) in den
Schmutz zerren; **d. up** (fig) aufwärmen ‖ intr (said of a long dress,
etc.) schleifen; (said of time) dahinschleichen; **d. on** (be prolonged) sich
hinziehen
drag′net′ s Schleppnetz n
dragon [′drægən] s Drache m
drag′onfly′ s Libelle f

dragoon [drə′gun] s Dragoner m ‖ tr
(coerce) zwingen
drag′ race′ s Straßenrennen n; (sport)
Kurzstreckenrennen n
drain [dren] s (sewer) Kanal m; (under a sink) Abfluß m; (fig) (on)
Belastung f (genit); (surg) Drain m;
down the d. (fig) zum Fenster hinaus ‖ tr (land) entwässern; (water)
ableiten; (a cup, glass) austrinken;
(fig) verzehren ‖ intr ablaufen;
(culin) abtropfen
drainage [′drenidʒ] s Ableitung f;
(e.g., of land) Entwässerung f; (surg)
Drainage f
drain′age ditch′ s Abflußgraben m
drain′ cock′ s Entleerungshahn m
drain′ pipe′ s Abflußrohr n
drain′ plug′ s Abflußstöpsel m
drake [drek] s Enterich m
dram [dræm] s Dram n
drama [′drɑmə] s Drama n; (art and
genre) Dramatik f
dra′ma crit′ic s Theaterkritiker –in mf
dramatic [drə′mætɪk] adj dramatisch
‖ **dramatics** s Dramatik f; spl (pej)
Schauspielerei f
dramatist [′dræmətɪst] s Dramatiker
–in mf
dramatize [′dræmə͵taɪz] tr dramati-
sieren
drape [drep] s Vorhang m; (hang of a
drape or skirt) Faltenwurf m ‖ tr
drapieren
drapery [′drepəri] s Vorhänge pl
dra′pery mate′rial s Vorhangstoff m
drastic [′dræstɪk] adj drastisch
draught [dræft] s & tr var of **draft**
draw [drɔ] s (in a lottery) Ziehen n;
(that which attracts) Schlager m;
(power of attraction) Anziehungskraft f; **end in a d.** unentschieden
ausgehen ‖ v (pret **drew** [dru]; pp
drawn [drɔn]) tr (pictures) zeichnen;
(a line, comparison, parallel, conclusion, lots, winner, sword, wagon)
ziehen; (a crowd) anlocken; (a distinction) machen; (blood) vergießen; (curtains) zuziehen; (a check)
nehmen; (rations) (mil) in Empfang
nehmen; **d. a blank** (coll) e-e Niete
ziehen; **d. aside** beiseitezichen; **d. attention to** die Aufmerksamkeit lenken auf (acc); **d. into** (e.g., an argument) hineinziehen in (acc); **d. lots
for** losen um; **d. out** (protract) in
die Länge ziehen; (money from a
bank) abheben; **d. s.o. out** j–n aus-
holen; **d. the line** (fig) e-e Grenze
ziehen; **d. up** (a document) verfassen; (plans) entwerfen ‖ intr zeichnen; **d. away** sich entfernen; **d. back**
sich zurückziehen; **d. near** heran-
nahen; **d. on** zurückgreifen auf (acc);
d. to a close sich dem Ende zuneigen
draw′back′ s Nachteil m
draw′bridge′ s Zugbrücke f
drawee [͵drɔ′i] s Trassat –in mf
drawer [′drɔ·ər] s Zeichner –in mf;
(com) Trassant –in mf ‖ [drɔr] s
Schublade f; **drawers** Unterhose f
draw′ing s (of pictures) Zeichnen n;

(*picture*) Zeichnung *f*; (*in a lottery*) Ziehung *f*, Verlosung *f*
draw'ing board' *s* Reißbrett *n*
draw'ing card' *s* Zugnummer *f*
draw'ing room' *s* Empfangszimmer *n*
drawl [drɔl] *s* gedehntes Sprechen *n* ‖ *intr* gedehnt sprechen
drawn [drɔn] *adj* (*face*) (**with**) verzerrt (vor *dat*); (*sword*) blank
dray [dre] *s* niedriger Rollwagen *m*; (*sledge*) Schleife *f*
dread [drɛd] *adj* furchtbar ‖ *s* Furcht *f* ‖ *tr* fürchten
dreadful ['drɛdfəl] *adj* furchtbar
dream [drim] *s* Traum *m*; (*aspiration, ambition*) Wunschtraum *m*; (*ideal*) (*coll*) Gedicht *n* ‖ *v* (*pret & pp* **dreamed & dreamt** [drɛmt] *tr* träumen; **d. away** verträumen; **d. up** zusammenträumen ‖ *intr* träumen; **d. of** (*long for*) sich [*dat*] enträumen; **I dreamt of her** mir träumte von ihr
dreamer ['drimər] *s* Träumer –in *mf*
dream'land' *s* Traumland *n*
dream'-like' *adj* traumhaft
dream'world' *s* Traumwelt *f*
dreamy ['drimi] *adj* (*place*) verträumt; (*eyes*) träumerisch
dreary ['drɪri] *adj* trüb, trist
dredge [drɛdʒ] *s* Bagger *m* ‖ *tr* (aus)-baggern ‖ *intr* baggern
dredger ['drɛdʒər] *s* Bagger *m*
dredg'ing *s* Baggern *n*
dregs [drɛgz] *spl* Bodensatz *m*; (*of society*) Abschaum *m*, Auswurf *m*
drench [drɛnt/] *tr* durchnässen
Dres'den chi'na ['drɛzdən] *s* Meißner Porzellan *n*
dress [drɛs] *s* Kleidung *f*; (*woman's dress*) Kleid *n* ‖ *tr* anziehen; (*a store window*) dekorieren; (*skins*) gerben; (*a salad, goose, chicken*) zubereiten; (*vines*) beschneiden; (*stones*) behauen; (*ore*) aufbereiten; (*wounds*) verbinden; (*hair*) frisieren; (*tex*) appretieren; **d. down** (*coll*) ausschimpfen; **d. ranks** die Glieder ausrichten; **get dressed** sich anziehen ‖ *intr* sich anziehen; **d. up** sich fein machen
dress' affair' *s* Galaveranstaltung *f*
dresser ['drɛsər] *s* Frisierkommode *f*; **be a good d.** sich gut kleiden
dress'ing *s* (*stuffing for fowl*) Füllung *f*; (*for salad*) Soße *f*; (*surg*) Verband *m*
dress'ing down' *s* Gardinenpredigt *f*
dress'ing room' *s* Umkleideraum *m*; (*theat*) Garderobe *f*
dress'ing sta'tion *s* Verbandsplatz *m*
dress'ing ta'ble *s* Frisierkommode *f*
dress'mak'er *s* Schneiderin *f*
dress'mak'ing *s* Modenschneiderei *f*
dress' rehear'sal *s* Kostümprobe *f*
dress' shirt' *s* Frackhemd *n*
dress' shop' *s* Modenhaus *n*, Modengeschäft *n*
dress' suit' *s* Frackanzug *m*, Frack *m*
dress' un'iform *s* Paradeuniform *f*
dressy ['drɛsi] *adj* (*showy*) geschniegelt; (*stylish*) modisch; (*for formal affairs*) elegant
dribble ['drɪbəl] *s* (*trickle*) Getröpfel

n; (*sport*) Dribbeln *n* ‖ *tr & intr* tröpfeln; (*sport*) dribbeln
driblet ['drɪblɪt] *s* Bißchen *n*
dried [draɪd] *adj* Trocken–, Dörr–
dried' beef' *s* Dörrfleisch *n*
dried' fruit' *s* Dörrobst *n*
dried'-up' *adj* ausgetrocknet, verdorrt
drier ['draɪ-ər] *s* Trockner *m*; (*for the hair*) Haartrockenhaube *f*; (*hand model*) Fön *m*
drift [drɪft] *s* (*of sand, snow*) Wehe *f*; (*tendency*) Richtung *f*, Neigung *f*; (*intent*) Absicht *f*; (*meaning*) Sinn *m*; (*aer, naut, rad*) Abtrift *f*; (*flow of the ocean current*) (naut) Drift *f* ‖ *intr* (*said of sand, snow*) sich anhäufen; (*said of a boat*) treiben; **d. away** (*said of sounds*) verwehen; (*said of a crowd*) sich verlaufen; **d. shut** verweht werden
drifter ['drɪftər] *s* zielloser Mensch *m*
drift' ice' *s* Treibeis *n*
drift'wood' *s* Treibholz *n*
drill [drɪl] *s* (*tool*) Bohrer *m*; (*exercise*) Drill *m*; (*tex*) Drillich *m* ‖ *tr* bohren; (*exercise*) drillen; **d. s.th. into s.o.** j–m etw einpauken ‖ *intr* bohren; (*exercise*) drillen
drill'mas'ter *s* (mil) Ausbilder *m*
drill' press' *s* Bohrpresse *f*
drink [drɪŋk] *s* Trunk *m* ‖ *v* (*pret* **drank** [dræŋk]; *pp* **drunk** [drʌŋk] *tr* trinken; (*said of animals*) saufen; (pej) saufen; **d. away** (*money*) versaufen; **d. down** hinunterkippen; **d. in** (*air*) einschlürfen; (*s.o.'s words*) verschlingen ‖ *intr* trinken; (*excessively*) saufen; **d. to** trinken auf (*acc*); **d. up** austrinken
drinkable ['drɪŋkəbəl] *adj* trinkbar
drinker ['drɪŋkər] *s* Trinker –in *mf*; **heavy drinker** Zecher –in *mf*
drink'ing foun'tain *s* Trinkbrunnen *m*
drink'ing par'ty *s* Zechgelage *n*
drink'ing song' *s* Trinklied *n*
drink'ing straw' *s* Strohhalm *m*
drink'ing trough' *s* Viehtränke *f*
drink'ing wa'ter *s* Trinkwasser *n*
drip [drɪp] *s* Tröpfeln *n* ‖ *v* (*pret & pp* **dripped**; *ger* **dripping**) *tr & intr* tröpfeln
drip' cof'fee *s* Filterkaffee *m*
drip'-dry' *adj* bügelfrei
drip' pan' *s* Bratpfanne *f*
drip'pings *spl* Bratenfett *n*
drive [draɪv] *s* (*in a car*) Fahrt *f*; (*road*) Fahrweg *m*; (*energy*) Schwungkraft *f*; (*inner urge*) Antrieb *m*; (*campaign*) Aktion *f*; (*for raising money*) Spendeaktion *f*; (golf) Treibschlag *m*; (mach) Antrieb *m*; (mil) Vorstoß *m*; (tennis) Treibschlag *m*; **go for a d.** spazierenfahren ‖ *v* (*pret* **drove** [drov]; *pp* **driven** ['drɪvən] *tr* (*a car, etc.*) fahren; (*e.g., cattle*) treiben; (*a tunnel*) vortreiben; **d. a hard bargain** zäh um den Preis feilschen; **d. away** abtreiben; (*oneself, a horse*) nach abjagen; **d. home** nahebringen; **d. in** (*a nail*) einschlagen; **d. off course** (naut) verschlagen; **d. on** antreiben; **d. out** austreiben; **d. s.o. to** (*inf*) j–n

dazu bringen zu (inf); **d. to despair** zur Verzweiflung treiben || intr fahren; **d. along** mitfahren; **d. at** abzielen auf (acc); **d. away** wegfahren; **d. by** vorbeifahren an (dat); **d. in** einfahren; **d. on** weiterfahren; **d. out** herausfahren; **d. up** anfahren

drive' belt' s Treibriemen m

drive'-in' s Autorestaurant n; (cin) Autokino n

driv·el ['drɪvəl] s (slobber) Geifer m; (nonsense) Faselei f || v (pret & pp -el[l]ed; ger -el[l]ing) intr sabbern; (fig) faseln

driver ['draɪvər] s (of a car) Fahrer -in mf; (of a locomotive, streetcar) Führer m; (golf) Treibschläger m; (mach) Treibhammer m

driv'er's li'cense s Führerschein m

drive' shaft' s Antriebswelle f

drive'way' s Einfahrt f

drive'-yourself' serv'ice s Autovermietung f an Selbstfahrer

driv'ing adj (rain) stürmisch || s (aut) Steuerung f

driv'ing instruc'tor s Fahrlehrer -in mf

driv'ing les'son s Fahrstunde f

driv'ing school' s Autofahrschule f

drizzle ['drɪzəl] s Nieselregen m || impers—**it is drizzling** es nieselt

droll [drol] adj drollig

dromedary ['draməˌderɪ] s Dromedar n

drone [dron] s (bee; loafer) Drohne f; (buzz) Gesumme n; (monotonous speech) Geleier n || tr (e.g., prayers) leiern || intr summen; (fig) leiern

drool [drul] intr sabbern

droop [drup] s Herabhängen n; (stoop) gebeugte Haltung f || intr herabhängen; (said of flowers) zu welken beginnen; (fig) den Kopf hängen lassen

droopy ['drupɪ] adj (saggy) schlaff herabhängend; (dejected) mutlos; (shoulders) abfallend; (flowers) welkend

drop [drap] s (of liquid) Tropfen m; (candy) Fruchtbonbon m & n; (fall) Fall m; (height differential) Gefälle n; (reduction) Abnahme f; (in prices) Rückgang m; (in temperature) Sturz m; (of bombs or supplies) Abwurf m; (of paratroopers) Absprung m; **a fifty-meter d.** ein Fall m aus e-r Höhe von fünfzig Metern; **d. by d.** tropfenweise; **d. in the bucket** Tropfen m auf e-n heißen Stein || v (pret & pp **dropped**; ger **dropping**) tr (let fall) fallenlassen; (bombs, supplies) abwerfen; (a subject, remarks, hints) fallenlassen; (the eyes, voice) senken; (anchor; young of animals) werfen; (money in gambling) (sl) verlieren; (terminate) einstellen; (from membership roll) ausschließen; (paratroopers) absetzen; **d. it!** laß das!; **d. s.o. a line** j-m ein paar Zeilen schreiben || intr fallen; (drip) tropfen; (said of prices, temperature) sinken, fallen; (keel over) umfallen; (said of a curtain) niedergehen; **d. behind** zurück-

fallen; **d. dead!** (sl) laß dich begraben!; **d. in on s.o.** auf e-n Sprung bei j-m vorbeikommen; **d. off to sleep** einschlafen; (sport) ausscheiden; **d. out of school** von der Schule abgehen

drop' ar'ea s (aer) Abwurfraum m

drop' cur'tain s (bemalter) Vorhang m

drop' ham'mer s Fallhammer m

drop'-leaf ta'ble s Tisch m mit herunterklappbaren Flügeln

drop'light' s Hängelampe f

drop'out' s Gescheiterte mf; (educ) Abgänger -in mf

dropper ['drapər] s (med) Tropfer m

drop'ping adj (prices) rückgängig || s (of bombs, supplies) Abwurf m; **droppings** tierischer Kot m

dropsy ['drapsɪ] s Wassersucht f

drop' ta'ble s Klapptisch m

dross [drɔs] s (slag) Schlacke f; (waste) Abfall m

drought [draut] s Dürre f

drove [drov] s Herde f

drown [draun] tr (& fig) ertränken; **d. out** übertönen || intr ertrinken

drowse [drauz] intr dösen

drowsiness ['drauzɪnɪs] s Schläfrigkeit f

drowsy ['drauzɪ] adj schläfrig, dösig

drub [drʌb] v (pret & pp **drubbed**; ger **drubbing**) tr (flog) verprügeln; (sport) entscheidend schlagen

drudge [drʌdʒ] s Packesel m || intr sich placken, schuften

drudgery ['drʌdʒərɪ] s Plackerei f

drug [drʌg] s Droge f, Arznei f; (narcotic) Betäubungsmittel n; (addictive narcotic) Rauschgift n || v (pret & pp **drugged**; ger **drugging**) tr betäuben

drug' ad'dict s Rauschgiftsüchtige mf

drug' addic'tion s Rauschgiftsucht f

druggist ['drʌgɪst] s Apotheker -in mf

drug'store' s Apotheke f, Drogerie f

drug' traf'fic s Rauschgifthandel m

druid ['dru·ɪd] s Druide m

drum [drʌm] s (musical instrument; container) Trommel f || v (pret & pp **drummed**; ger **drumming**) tr trommeln; **d. s.th. into s.o.** j-m etw einpauken; **d. the table** auf den Tisch trommeln; **d. up** zusammentrommeln || intr trommeln

drum' and bu'gle corps' s Musikzug m

drum'beat' s Trommelschlag m

drum'fire' s (mil) Trommelfeuer n

drum'head' s Trommelfell n

drum' ma'jor s Tambourmajor m

drum' majorette' s Tambourmajorin f

drummer ['drʌmər] s Trommler -in mf

drum'stick' s Trommelschlegel m; (culin) Unterschenkel m

drunk [drʌŋk] adj betrunken || s Säufer -in mf

drunkard ['drʌŋkərd] s Trunkenbold m

drunken ['drʌŋkən] adj betrunken

dry [draɪ] adj trocken; (boring) trocken; (wine) herb; (thirsty) durstig; (rainless) regenarm; (wood) dürr || v (pret & pp **-dried**) tr (ab)trocknen;

(*e.g., fruit*) dörren; **dry off** abtrocknen; **dry out** austrocknen; **dry up** austrocknen; (fig) erschöpfen ‖ *intr* trocknen; **dry out** austrocknen; **dry up** vertrocknen; (*said of grass, flowers*) verdorren; (fig) versiegen; (*keep quiet*) (sl) die Klappe halten

dry' bat'tery *s* Trockenbatterie *f*

dry' cell' *s* Tockenelement *n*

dry'-clean' *tr* (*chemically*) reinigen

dry' clean'er's *s* Reinigungsanstalt *f*

dry' clean'ing *s* chemische Reinigung *f*

dry' dock' *s* Trockendock *n*

dry'-eyed' *adj* ungerührt

dry' goods' *spl* Schnittwaren *pl*

dry' ice' *s* Trockeneis *n*

dry' land' *s* fester Boden *m*

dry' meas'ure *s* Trockenmaß *n*

dryness ['draɪnɪs] *s* Trockenheit *f*, Dürre *f*; (fig) Nüchternheit *f*

dry' nurse' *s* Säuglingsschwester *f*

dry' rot' *s* Trockenfäule *f*

dry' run' *s* Vorübung *f*; (*test run*) Probelauf *m*; (*with blank ammunition*) Zielübung *f*

dry' sea'son *s* Trockenzeit *f*

dual ['d(j)u·əl] *adj* Zwei-, doppelt; (tech) Doppel-

dualism ['d(j)u·ə‚lɪzəm] *s* Dualismus *m*

du'al-pur'pose *adj* e—m doppelten Zweck dienend

dub [dʌb] *v* (*pret & pp* **dubbed**; *ger* **dubbing**) *tr* (*nickname*) betiteln; (cin) synchronisieren; (golf) schlecht treffen; (hist) zum Ritter schlagen

dub'bing *s* (cin) Synchronisierung *f*

dubious ['d(j)ubɪ·əs] *adj* zweifelhaft

ducal ['d(j)ukəl] *adj* herzoglich

duchess ['dʌtʃɪs] *s* Herzogin *f*

duchy ['dʌtʃi] *s* Herzogtum *n*

duck [dʌk] *s* Ente *f* ‖ *tr* (*the head*) ducken; (*in water*) (unter)tauchen; (*evade*) sich drücken vor (*dat*) ‖ *intr* ducken; (*go under the surface*) untertauchen

duck'ing *s*—**give s.o. a d.** j—n untertauchen

duck' pond' *s* Ententeich *m*

duck' soup' *s* (sl) Kinderspiel *n*

ducky ['dʌki] *adj* (coll) nett, lieb

duct [dʌkt] *s* Rohr *n*, Kanal *m*, Leitung *f*; (anat, elec) Kanal *m*

duct'less gland' *s* endokrine Drüse *f*

duct'work' *s* Rohrleitungen *pl*

dud [dʌd] *s* (sl & mil) Versager *m*, Blindgänger *m*; **duds** (coll) Klamotten *pl*

dude [d(j)ud] *s* (*dandy*) Geck *m*

dude' ranch' *s* Vergnügungsfarm *f*

due [d(j)u] *adj* (*payment; bus, train*) fällig; (*proper*) gehörig; (*consideration*) reiflich; **be due to** (*as a cause*) beruhen auf (*dat*); (*said of an honor*) gebühren (*dat*); (*said of money*) zustehen (*dat*); **be due to** (*inf*) sollen, müssen; **in due course** im gegebenen Moment; **in due time** zur rechten Zeit ‖ *adv* (naut) genau ‖ *s*—**dues** Beitrag *m*; **get one's due** nach Verdienst behandelt werden; **give every-**

one his due jedem geben, was ihm gebührt

due' date' *s* (*of a payment*) Termin *m*

duel ['d(j)u·əl] *s* Duell *n*; **fight a d.** sich duellieren ‖ *v* (*pret & pp* **duel[l]ed**; *ger* **duel[l]ing**) *intr* sich duellieren

dues-paying ['d(j)uz‚pe·ɪŋ] *adj* beitragzahlend

duet [d(j)u'ɛt] *s* Duett *n*

due' to' *prep* wegen (*genit*)

duf'fle bag' ['dʌfəl] *s* (mil) Kleidersack *m*

dug'out' *s* (*boat*) Einbaum *m*; (*baseball, mil*) Unterstand *m*

duke [d(j)uk] *s* Herzog *m*

dukedom ['d(j)ukdəm] *s* Herzogtum *n*

dull [dʌl] *adj* (*not sharp*) stumpf; (*pain*) dumpf; (*not shining*) glanzlos, matt; (*uninteresting*) nüchtern, geistlos; (*stupid*) stumpfsinnig; (com) flau ‖ *tr* stumpf machen; (fig) abstumpfen ‖ *intr* stumpf werden; (fig) abstumpfen

dullard ['dʌlərd] *s* Dummkopf *m*

dullness ['dʌlnɪs] *s* (*of a blade*) Stumpfheit *f*; (*of color*) Mattheit *f*; (*of a speech, etc.*) Stumpfsinn *m*

duly ['d(j)uli] *adv* ordnungsgemäß

dumb [dʌmb] *adj* stumm; (*stupid*) dumm ‖ *adv*—**play d.** sich unwissend stellen

dumb'bell' *s* Hantel *f*; (sl) Dummkopf *m*

dumbstruck ['dʌm‚strʌk] *adj* wie auf den Mund geschlagen

dumb' wait'er *s* (*elevator*) Speiseaufzug *m*; (*serving table*) Serviertisch *m*

dumdum ['dʌm‚dʌm] *s* Dumdumgeschoß *n*

dumfound [dʌm'faʊnd] *tr* verblüffen

dummy ['dʌmi] *adj* (*not real*) Schein-; (mil) blind, Übungs- ‖ *s* (*representation for display*) Attrappe *f*; (*clothes form*) Schneiderpuppe *f*; (*dolt*) Ölgötze *m*; (*cards*) Strohmann *m*; (mil) Übungspatrone *f*; (typ) Blindband *m*

dump [dʌmp] *s* (*trash heap*) Schuttabladeplatz *m*; (mil) Bude *f*; (mil) Lager *n*; **be down in the dumps** (coll) Trübsal blasen ‖ *tr* (aus)kippen; (*fling down*) hinplumpsen; (*garbage*) abladen; (com) verschleudern; **be dumped** (*be fired*) entlassen werden; **no dumping** (*public sign*) Schuttabladen verboten

dumpling ['dʌmplɪŋ] *s* Kloß *m*, Knödel *m*

dump' truck' *s* Kipper *m*

dumpy ['dʌmpi] *adj* rundlich

dun [dʌn] *adj* schwarzbraun ‖ *v* (*pret & pp* **dunned**; *ger* **dunning**) *tr* drängen

dunce [dʌns] *s* Schwachkopf *m*

dunce' cap' *s* Narrenkappe *f*

dune [d(j)un] *s* Düne *f*

dung [dʌŋ] *s* Dung *m*, Mist *m* ‖ *tr* düngen

dungarees [‚dʌŋgə'riz] *spl* Drillichhose *f*, Drillichanzug *m*

dungeon ['dʌndʒən] *s* Verlies *n*; (hist) Bergfried *m*

dung′hill′ s Düngerhaufen m
dunk [dʌŋk] tr eintunken
duo [′d(j)u·o] s (duet) Duett n; (a pair) Duo n
duode·num [ˌd(j)u·ə′dinəm] s (-na [nə]) Zwölffingerdarm m
dupe [d(j)up] s Düpierte mf ‖ tr düpieren, übertölpeln
duplex [′d(j)upleks] s Doppelhaus n
duplicate [′d(j)uplɪkɪt] adj Duplikat–; (parts) Ersatz–; **d. key** Nachschlüssel m ‖ s Duplikat n, Abschrift f; **in d.** abschriftlich ‖ [′d(j)uplɪˌket] tr (make a copy of) kopieren; (make many copies of) vervielfältigen; (reproduce by writing) abschreiben; (repeat) wiederholen; (perform again) nachmachen
duplication [ˌd(j)uplɪ′keʃən] s Vervielfältigung f
duplicator [′d(j)uplɪˌketər] s Vervielfältigungsapparat m
duplicity [d(j)u′plɪsɪti] s Duplizität f
durable [′d(j)ʊrəbəl] adj dauerhaft
duration [d(j)u′reʃən] s Dauer f
duress [d(j)ʊres] s (jur) Nötigung f
during [′d(j)ʊrɪŋ] prep während (genit), bei (dat); **d. the meal** bei Tisch; **d. the day** tagsüber
dusk [dʌsk] s Abenddämmerung f
dust [dʌst] s Staub m; **cover with d.** bestauben; **make d.** stauben ‖ tr (free of dust) abstauben; (sprinkle, spray with insecticides) bestäuben
dust′ bowl′ s Staubsturmgebiet n
dust′ cloth′ s Staubtuch n
dust′ collec′tor s Staubfänger m
duster [′dʌstər] s (feather duster) Staubwedel m; (for insecticides) Zerstäuber m
dust′ing pow′der s Streupulver n
dust′ jac′ket s Schutzumschlag m
dust′ mop′ s Mop m
dust′pan′ s Kehrichtschaufel f
dust′proof′ adj staubdicht
dust′ rag′ s Staublappen m
dusty [′dʌsti] adj staubig
Dutch [dʌtʃ] adj niederländisch; **go D.** (coll) getrennt bezahlen ‖ s (language) Niederländisch n; **in D.** (coll)

in der Patsche; **the D.** die Niederländer
Dutch′man s (-men) Niederländer m
Dutch′ treat′ s (coll) Beisammensein n bei getrennter Kasse
dutiable [′d(j)utɪ·əbəl] adj steuerpflichtig
dutiful [′d(j)utɪfəl] adj pflichtgetreu
duty [′d(j)uti] s (to) Pflicht f (gegenüber dat); (service) Dienst m; (task) Aufgabe f; (tax) Zoll m, Abgabe f; **be in d. bound to** (inf) pflichtgemäß müssen (inf); **do d. as** (said of a thing) dienen als; (said of a person) Dienst tun als; **off d.** außer Dienst, dienstfrei; **on. d.** im Dienst; **pay d. on** verzollen
du′ty-free′ adj zollfrei
du′ty ros′ter s (mil) Diensteinteilung f
dwarf [dwɔrf] adj zwergenhaft, Zwerg– ‖ s Zwerg m ‖ tr (stunt) in der Entwicklung behindern; (fig) in den Schatten stellen
dwell [dwel] v (pret & pp dwelled & dwelt [dwelt]) intr wohnen; **d. on** verweilen bei
dwell′ing s Wohnung f
dwell′ing house′ s Wohnhaus n
dwindle [′dwɪndəl] intr schwinden, abnehmen; **d. away** dahinschwinden
dye [daɪ] s Farbe f ‖ v (pret & pp dyed; ger dyeing) tr färben
dyed′-in-the-wool′ adj (fig) in der Wolle gefärbt
dye′ing s Färben n
dyer [′daɪ·ər] s Färber –in mf
dy′ing adj (person) sterbend; (words) letzte ‖ s Sterben n
dynamic [daɪ′næmɪk] adj dynamisch ‖ **dynamics** s Dynamik f; **dynamics** spl (fig) Triebkraft f
dynamite [′daɪnəˌmaɪt] s Dynamit n ‖ tr sprengen
dyna·mo [′daɪnəˌmo] s (-mos) Dynamo m
dynastic [daɪ′næstɪk] adj dynastisch
dynasty [′daɪnəsti] s Dynastie f
dysentery [′dɪsənˌteri] s Ruhr f
dyspepsia [dɪs′pepsɪ·ə] s Verdauungsstörung f

E

E, e [i] s fünfter Buchstabe des englischen Alphabets; (mus) E n; **E flat** Es n; **E sharp** Eis n
each [itʃ] indef adj jeder; **e. and every** jeder einzelne ‖ adv je, pro Person, pro Stück ‖ indef pron jeder; **e. other** einander, sich
eager [′igər] adj eifrig; **e. for** begierig nach; **e. to** (inf) begierig zu (inf)
ea′ger bea′ver s (coll) Streber –in mf
eagerness [′igərnɪs] s Eifer m
eagle [′igəl] s Adler m
ea′gle-eyed′ adj adleräugig
ear [ɪr] s Ohr n; (of corn, wheat) Ähre f; (fig) Gehör n; **be all ears**

ganz Ohr sein; **bend s.o.'s ears** (sl) j–m die Ohren vollreden; **be up to one's ears** in bis über die Ohren stecken in (dat); **by ear** nach Gehör; **ear for music** musikalisches Gehör n; **fall on deaf ears** kein Gehör finden; **in one ear and out the other** zu e–m Ohr hinein und zum anderen hinaus; **turn a deaf ear to** taub sein gegen
ear′ache′ s Ohrenschmerzen pl
ear′drops′ spl (med) Ohrentropfen pl
ear′drum′ s Trommelfell n
earl [ʌrl] s Graf m
ear′lobe′ s Ohrläppchen n

early ['ʌrli] *adj* früh; (*reply*) baldig; (*far back in time*) Früh–; **at the earliest possible moment** baldigst; **at your earliest convenience** bei erster Gelegenheit; **be too e.** sich verfrühen || *adv* früh, frühzeitig; (*too soon*) zu früh; **as e.** as schon

ear'ly bird' *s* Frühaufsteher –in *mf*

ear'ly ris'er *s* Frühaufsteher –in *mf*

ear'ly warn'ing sys'tem *s* Vorwarnungssystem *n*

ear'mark' *s* (fig) Kennzeichen *n* || *tr* (*mark out*) kennzeichnen; (*e.g., funds*) (**for**) bestimmen (für)

ear'muffs' *spl* Ohrenschützer *m*

earn [ʌrn] *tr* (*money*) verdienen; (*a reputation*) sich [*dat*] erwerben; (*interest*) einbringen

earnest ['ʌrnɪst] *adj* ernst, ernsthaft || *s*—**are you in e.?** ist das Ihr Ernst?; **be in e. about** es ernst meinen mit; **in e.** im Ernst

ear'phone' *s* Kopfhörer *m*

ear'piece' *s* (*earphone*) Hörer *m*; (*of eyeglasses*) Bügel *m*

ear'ring' *s* Ohrring *m*

ear'shot' *s*—**within e.** in Hörweite

ear'split'ting *adj* ohrenbetäubend

earth [ʌrθ] *s* Erde *f*; **come down to e.** auf den Boden der Wirklichkeit zurückkehren; **on e.** (coll) in aller Welt

earthen ['ʌrθən] *adj* irden

earth'enware' *s* Tonwaren *pl*

earthly ['ʌrθli] *adj* irdisch; **be of no e. use** völlig unnütz sein; **e. possessions** Glücksgüter *pl*

earth'quake' *s* Erdbeben *n*

earth'shak'ing *adj* welterschütternd

earth'work' *s* Schanze *f*

earth'worm' *s* Regenwurm *m*

earthy ['ʌrθi] *adj* erdig; (fig) deftig

ear'wax' *s* Ohrenschmalz *m*

ease [iz] *s* (*facility*) Leichtigkeit *f*; (*comfort*) Bequemlichkeit *f*; (*informality*) Zwanglosigkeit *f*; **at e.!** (mil) rührt euch!; **feel at e. with s.o.** sich in j-s Gegenwart wohl fühlen; **put at e.** beruhigen; **with e.** mühelos || *tr* (*work*) erleichtern; (*pain*) lindern; (*move carefully*) lavieren; **e. out** (*of a job*) hinausmanövrieren || *intr*—**e. up** nachlassen; **e. up on** (*work*) es sich [*dat*] leichter machen mit

easel ['izəl] *s* Staffelei *f*

easement ['izmənt] *s* (jur) Dienstbarkeit *f*

easily ['izəli] *adv* leicht, mühelos; **e. satisfied** genügsam

easiness ['izɪnɪs] *s* Leichtigkeit *f*

east [ist] *adj* Ost–, östlich || *adv* ostwärts, nach Osten; **e. of** östlich von || *s* Osten *m*; **the East** der Osten

east'bound' *adj* nach Osten fahrend

Easter ['istər] *adj* Oster– || *s* Ostern *n* & *pl*

easterly ['istərli] *adj* österlich

eastern ['istərn] *adj* Ost–

East'ertide' *s* Osterzeit *f*

East'-Ger'man mark' *s* Ostmark *f*

eastward ['istwərd] *adv* ostwärts

easy ['izi] *adj* leicht; (*terms*) günstig; (*virtue*) locker; (*pace*) gemächlich; **e. on the eye** knusprig; **e. to digest**

leichtverdaulich; **have an e. time of it** leichtes Spiel haben; **it's e. for you to talk** du hast gut reden!; **make e.** erleichtern || *adv*—**e. come, e. go** wie gewonnen, so zerronnen; **get off e.** gnädig davonkommen; **take it e.** (*relax*) es sich [*dat*] leicht machen; *take on'e time*) sich [*dat*] Zeit lassen; (*in parting*) mach's gut! (*remain calm*) reg dich nicht auf!; **take it e. on** (*a person*) schonend umgehen mit; (*a thing*) sparsam umgehen mit

eas'y chair' *s* Lehnsessel *m*

eas'ygo'ing *adj* ungeniert, ungezwungen

eas'y mark' *s* (coll) leichte Beute *f*

eat [it] *s*—**eats** *pl* (coll) Essen *n* || *v* (*pret* **ate** [et]; *pp* **eaten** ['itən]) *tr* essen; (*said of animals*) fressen; **eat away** zerfressen; **eat one's fill** sich satt essen; **eat one's heart out** sich in Kummer verzehren; **eat one's words** das Gesagte zurücknehmen; **eat up** aufessen; **what's eating him?** was hat er denn? || *intr* essen; **eat out** auswärts essen

eatable ['itəbəl] *adj* eßbar

eaves [ivz] *spl* Dachrinne *f*, Traufe *f*

eaves'drop' *v* (*pret & pp* **–dropped**; *ger* **–dropping**) *intr* horchen; **e. on** belauschen

eaves'drop'per *s* Horcher –in *mf*

ebb [eb] *s* Ebbe *f*; **at a low ebb** sehr heruntergekommen || *intr* ebben; (fig) nachlassen

ebb' and flow' *s* Ebbe und Flut *f*

ebb' tide' *s* Ebbe *f*

ebony ['ebəni] *s* Ebenholz *n*

ebullient [ɪ'bʌljənt] *adj* überschwenglich, hochbegeistert

eccentric [ek'sentrɪk] *adj* (& fig) exzentrisch || *s* Sonderling *m*, Kauz *m*; (mach) Exzenter *m*

eccentricity [,eksen'trɪsɪti] *s* Verschrobenheit *f*, Tick *f*

ecclesiastic [ɪ,klizi'æstɪk] *adj* kirchlich; (*law*) Kirchen– || *s* Geistlicher *m*

echelon ['eʃə,lan] *s* (*level*) Befehlsebene *f*; (*group occupying a particular level*) Stabsführung *f*; (*flight formation*) Staffel *f*; **in echelons** staffelförmig || *tr* staffeln

ech•o ['eko] *s* (**-oes**) Echo *n* || *tr* (*sounds*) zurückwerfen; (fig) nachsprechen || *intr* widerhallen, echoen

éclair [e'kler] *s* Eclair *n*

eclectic [ek'lektɪk] *adj* eklektisch || *s* Eklektiker –in *mf*

eclipse [ɪ'klɪps] *s* Verfinsterung *f*; **go into e.** sich verfinstern; **in e.** im Schwinden || *tr* verfinstern; (fig) in den Schatten stellen

eclogue ['eklɔg] *s* Ekloge *f*

ecological [,ekə'ladʒɪkəl] *adj* ökologisch

ecology [ɪ'kalədʒi] *s* Ökologie *f*

economic [,ikə'namɪk], [,ekə'namɪk] *adj* wirtschaftlich, Wirtschafts–

economical [,ikə'namɪkəl], [,ekə'namɪkəl] *adj* sparsam

economics [,ikə'namɪks], [,ekə'namɪks] *s* Wirtschaftswissenschaften *pl*

economist [ɪ'kɑnəmɪst] *s* Volkswirtschaftler –in *mf*

economize [ɪ'kɑnə‚maɪz] *intr* sparen

economy [ɪ'kɑnəmi] *s* Wirtschaft *f*; *(thriftiness)* Sparsamkeit *f*; *(a saving)* Ersparnis *f*

ecstasy ['ɛkstəsi] *s* Verzückung *f*; **go into e.** in Verzückung geraten

ecstatic [ɛk'stætɪk] *adj* verzückt

ecumenic(al) [‚ɛkjə'mɛnɪk(əl)] *adj* ökumenisch

eczema [ɛg'zimə] *s* Ausschlag *m*

ed·dy ['ɛdi] *s* Strudel *m* ‖ *v (pret & pp –died) intr* strudeln

edelweiss ['edəl‚vaɪs] *s* Edelweiß *n*

edge [ɛdʒ] *s (of a knife)* Schneide *f*; *(of a forest, town, water, road)* Rand *m*; *(e.g., of a table)* Kante *f*; *(keenness)* Schärfe *f*; (bb) Schnitt *m*; **have an e. on s.o.** den Vorteil gegenüber j–m haben; **on e.** *(said of a person or teeth)* kribbelig; *(said of nerves)* aufs äußerste gespannt; **take the e. off** abstumpfen; (fig) die Schärfe nehmen *(dat)* ‖ *tr (a lawn)* beschneiden; *(put a border on)* einfassen; **e. out** (sport) knapp schlagen ‖ *intr* —**e. forward** langsam vorrücken

edge′wise *adv*—**not get a word in e.** nicht zu Worte kommen können

edg′ing *s* Umrandung *f*, Besatz *m*

edgy ['ɛdʒi] *adj* kribbelig

edible ['ɛdɪbəl] *adj* eßbar, genießbar

edict ['idɪkt] *s* Edikt *n*, Erlaß *m*

edification [‚ɛdɪfɪ'keʃən] *s* Erbauung *f*

edifice ['ɛdɪfɪs] *s* Bauwerk *n*, Gebäude *n*

edi·fy ['ɛdɪ‚faɪ] *v (pret & pp –fied) tr* erbauen; **be edified by** sich erbauen an *(dat)*

ed′ifying *adj* erbaulich

edit ['ɛdɪt] *tr (a book)* herausgeben; *(a newspaper)* redigieren; (cin) schneiden

edition [ɛ'dɪʃən] *s* Ausgabe *f*

editor ['ɛdɪtər] *s (of a newspaper or magazine)* Redakteur –in *mf*; *(of a book)* Herausgeber –in *mf*; *(of editorials)* Leitartikler –in *mf*; (cin) Schnittmeister –in *mf*

editorial [‚ɛdɪ'torɪ-əl] *adj* redaktionell, Redaktions– ‖ *s* Leitartikel *m*

editorialize [‚ɛdɪ'torɪ-ə‚laɪz] *intr* (on) seine Meinung zum Ausdruck bringen *(über acc)*; *(report with a slant)* tendenziös berichten

edito′rial of′fice *s* Redaktion *f*

edito′rial staff′ *s* Redaktion *f*

ed′itor in chief′ *s* Chefredakteur –in *mf*

educate ['ɛdʒʊ‚ket] *tr* bilden, erziehen

education [‚ɛdʒʊ'keʃən] *s* Bildung *f*, Erziehung *f*; (educ) Pädagogik *f*

educational [‚ɛdʒʊ'keʃənəl] *adj* Bildungs–; **e. background** Vorbildung *f*; **e. film** Lehrfilm *m*; **e. institution** Lehranstalt *f*

educator ['ɛdʒʊ‚ketər] *s* Erzieher –in *mf*

educe [ɪ'd(j)us] *tr* hervorholen

eel [il] *s* Aal *m*

eerie, eery ['ɪri] *adj* unheimlich

efface [ɪ'fes] *tr* austilgen; **e. oneself** sich zurückhalten

effect [ɪ'fɛkt] *s* (on) Wirkung *f* (auf *acc*); *(consequence)* (on) Auswirkung *f* (auf *acc*); *(impression)* Eindruck *m*; **effects** *(movable property)* Habe *f*; **for e.** zum Effekt; **go into e.** in Kraft treten; **have an e. on** wirken auf *(acc)*; **in e.** praktisch; **put into e.** in Kraft setzen; **take e.** zur Geltung kommen; **to the e. that** des Inhalts, daß ‖ *tr* bewirken

effective [ɪ'fɛktɪv] *adj* wirkungsvoll; *(actual)* effektiv; **e. against** wirksam gegen; **e. date** Tag *m* des Inkrafttretens; **e. from** mit Wirkung von; **e. immediately** mit sofortiger Wirkung; **e. strength** (mil) Iststärke *f*

effectual [ɪ'fɛktʃʊ-əl] *adj* wirksam

effectuate [ɪ'fɛktʃʊ‚et] *tr* bewirken

effeminacy [ɪ'fɛmɪnəsi] *s* Verweichlichung *f*

effeminate [ɪ'fɛmɪnɪt] *adj* verweichlicht

effervesce [‚ɛfər'vɛs] *intr* aufbrausen

effervescence [‚ɛfər'vɛsəns] *s* Aufbrausen *n*, Moussieren *n*

effervescent [‚ɛfər'vɛsənt] *adj (liquid; personality)* aufbrausend

effete [ɪ'fit] *adj* entkräftet

efficacious [‚ɛfɪ'keʃəs] *adj* wirksam

efficacy ['ɛfɪkəsi] *s* Wirksamkeit *f*, Wirkungskraft *f*

efficiency [ɪ'fɪʃənsi] *s* Tüchtigkeit *f*; (phys) Nutzeffekt *m*; (tech) Leistungsfähigkeit *f*

efficient [ɪ'fɪʃənt] *adj* tüchtig; (tech) leistungsfähig

effigy ['ɛfɪdʒi] *s* Abbild *n*; **hang in e.** symbolisch hängen

effort ['ɛfərt] *s (exertion)* Mühe *f*; *(attempt)* Bestreben *n*; **efforts** Bemühungen *pl*; **make an honest e. to** *(inf)* sich redlich bemühen zu *(inf)*

effortless ['ɛfərtlɪs] *adj* mühelos

effrontery [ɪ'frʌntəri] *s* Frechheit *f*, Unverschämtheit *f*

effusion [ɪ'fjuʒən] *s* Erguß *m*

effusive [ɪ'fjusɪv] *adj* überschwenglich

egg [ɛg] *s* Ei *n*; **bad egg** (sl) übler Geselle *m*; **good egg** (sl) feiner Kerl *m*; **lay an egg** ein Ei legen; (fig) e–e völlige Niete sein ‖ *tr*—**egg on** anstacheln

egg′beat′er *s* Schneeschläger *m*

egg′cup′ *s* Eierbecher *m*

egg′head′ *s* (coll) Intelligenzler –in *mf*

eggnog ['ɛg‚nɑg] *s* Eierlikör *m*, Egg-Nog *m*

egg′plant′ *s* Eierfrucht *f*

egg′shell′ *s* Eierschale *f*

egg′ white′ *s* Eiweiß *n*

egg′ yolk′ *s* Eigelb *n*, Eidotter *m*

ego ['igo] *s* Ego *n*, Ich *n*; (coll) Ichsucht *f*

egocentric [‚igo'sɛntrɪk] *adj* egozentrisch

egoism ['igo‚ɪzəm] *s* Selbstsucht *f*

egoist ['igo-ɪst] *s* Egoist *m*

egotism ['igo‚tɪzəm] *s* Ichsucht *f*

egotistic(al) [‚igo'tɪstɪk(əl)] *adj* egotistisch, geltungsbedürftig

egregious [ɪ'griːdʒəs] *adj* unerhört

egress ['iːgres] *s* Ausgang *m*

Egypt ['iːdʒɪpt] *s* Ägypten *n*

Egyptian [ɪ'dʒɪp/ən] *adj* ägyptisch || *s* Ägypter –in *mf; (language)* Ägyptisch *n*

eiderdown ['aɪdər‚daʊn] *s* Eiderdaunen *pl; (cover)* Daunenbett *n*

eight [et] *adj & pron* acht || *s* Acht *f*

eight/ball' *s*—**be behind the e.** (sl) in der Klemme sitzen

eighteen ['et'tiːn] *adj & pron* achtzehn || *s* Achtzehn *f*

eighteenth ['et'tiːnθ] *adj* achtzehnte || *s (fraction)* Achtzehntel *n;* **the e.** *(in dates or in a series)* der Achzehnte

eighth [etθ] *adj* achte || *s (fraction)* Achtel *n;* **the e.** *(in dates or in a series)* der Achte

eighth' note' *s* (mus) Achtelnote *f*

eightieth ['etɪ‚ɪθ] *adj* achtzigste || *s (fraction)* Achtzigstel *n;* **the e.** der Achtzigste

eighty ['etɪ] *adj & pron* achtzig || *s* Achtzig *f;* **the eighties** die achtziger Jahre *pl*

eigh'ty-one' *adj & pron* einundachtzig

either ['iːðər], ['aɪðər] *adj—***e. one is correct** beides ist richtig; **e. way auf** die e–e oder andere Art; **in e. case** in jedem der beiden Fälle; **on e. side** auf beiden Seiten || *adv—***not...e.** auch nicht || *pron* einer von beiden; **e. of you** einer von euch beiden; **I didn't see e.** ich habe beide nicht gesehen || *conj—***e....or** entweder... oder

ejaculate [ɪ'dʒækjə‚let] *tr* ausstoßen; (physiol) ejakulieren

eject [ɪ'dʒekt] *tr* ausstoßen; *(from a property)* **(from)** hinauswerfen (aus)

ejection [ɪ'dʒek/ən] *s* Ausstoßung *f*

ejec'tion seat' *s* Schleudersitz *m*

eke [ik] *tr*—**eke out a living** das Leben fristen

el [el] *s* (coll) Hochbahn *f*

elaborate [ɪ'læbərɪt] *adj (detailed)* weitläufig; *(ornate)* kunstvoll; *(idea)* compliziert || [ɪ'læbə‚ret] *tr* ausarbeiten || *intr*—**e. on** sich verbreiten über *(acc)*

elaboration [ɪ‚læbə're/ən] *s* Ausarbeitung *f*

elapse [ɪ'læps] *intr* verrinnen

elastic [ɪ'læstɪk] *adj* elastisch; *(conscience)* weit || *s* Gummiband *n*

elasticity [‚ɪlæs'tɪsɪtɪ] *s* Elastizität *f*

elated [ɪ'letɪd] *adj* freudig erregt

elation [ɪ'le/ən] *s* Hochgefühl *n*

elbow ['elbo] *s* Ellbogen *m; (of a pipe)* Rohrknie *n;* **at one's e.** bei der Hand; **rub elbows with s.o.** mit j–m in nähere Berührung kommen || *tr*—**e. one's way** sich [*dat*] seinen Weg bahnen

el'bow grease' *s* (coll) Knochenschmalz *n*

el'bowroom' *s* Spielraum *m*

elder ['eldər] *adj* älter || *s* Ältere *mf;* (bot) Holunder *m;* (eccl) Kirchenälteste *mf*

el'derber'ry *s* Holunderbeere *f*

elderly ['eldərlɪ] *adj* ältlich

el'der states'man *s* profilierter Staatsmann *m*

eldest ['eldɪst] *adj* älteste

elect [ɪ'lekt] *adj* erlesen; *(elected but not yet installed)* zukünftig; (relig) auserwählt || **the e.** *spl* die Auserwählten *pl* || *tr* wählen; **e. s.o. president** j–n zum Präsidenten wählen

election [ɪ'lek/ən] *adj* Wahl– || *s* Wahl *f*

elec'tion campaign' *s* Wahlkampf *m*

elec'tion day' *s* Wahltag *m*

electioneer [ɪ‚lek/ə'nɪr] *intr* Stimmen werben

elective [ɪ'lektɪv] *adj* (educ) wahlfrei; (pol) Wahl– || *s* (educ) Wahlfach *n*

electoral [ɪ'lektərəl] *adj* Wahl–

elec'toral col'lege *s* Wahlmänner *pl*

electorate [ɪ'lektərɪt] *s* Wählerschaft *f*

electric(al) [ɪ'lektrɪk(əl)] *adj* elektrisch, Elektro–

elec'trical appli'ance *s* Elektrogerät *n*

elec'trical engineer' *s* Elektroingenieur *m*

elec'trical engineer'ing *s* Elektrotechnik *f*

elec'tric blan'ket *s* Heizdecke *f*

elec'tric bulb' *s* Glühbirne *f*

elec'tric chair' *s* elektrischer Stuhl *m;* (penalty) Hinrichtung *f* auf dem elektrischen Stuhl

elec'tric cir'cuit *s* Stromkreis *m*

elec'tric eel' *s* Zitteraal *m*

elec'tric eye' *s* Photozelle *f*

elec'tric fan' *s* Ventilator *m*

elec'tric fence' *s* elektrisch geladener Drahtzaun *m*

electrician [ɪ‚lek'trɪ/ən] *s* Elektriker –in *mf*

electricity [‚ɪlek'trɪsɪtɪ] *s* Elektrizität *f;* (current) Strom *m*

elec'tric light' *s* elektrisches Licht *n*

elec'tric me'ter *s* Stromzähler *m*

elec'tric saw' *s* Motorsäge *f*

elec'tric shav'er *s* elektrischer Rasierapparat *m*

elec'tric storm' *s* Gewittersturm *m*

elec'tric stove' *s* Elektroherd *m*

electri-fy [ɪ'lektrɪ‚faɪ] *v (pret & pp* **-fied)** *tr* (& fig) elektrisieren; *(a streetcar, railroad)* elektrifizieren

electrocute [ɪ'lektrə‚kjut] *tr* durch elektrischen Strom töten; (jur) auf dem elektrischen Stuhl hinrichten

electrode [ɪ'lektrod] *s* Elektrode *f*

electrolysis [ɪ‚lek'trɑlɪsɪs] *s* Elektrolyse *f*

electrolyte [ɪ'lektrə‚laɪt] *s* Elektrolyt *m*

electromagnet [ɪ‚lektrə'mægnət] *s* Elektromagnet *m*

electromagnetic [ɪ‚lektrəmæg'netɪk] *adj* elektromagnetisch

electron [ɪ'lektrɑn] *s* Elektron *n*

electronic [ɪ‚lek'trɑnɪk] *adj* elektronisch, Elektronen– || **electronics** *s* Elektronik *f*

electron'ic flash' *s* Röhrenblitz *m; (device)* Blitzgerät *n*

electronic [ɪ‚lek'trɑnɪk] *adj* elektroplattieren, galvanisieren

electrostatic [ɪ͵lektrə'stætɪk] *adj* elektrostatisch

electrotype [ɪ'lektrə͵taɪp] *s* Galvano *n* || *tr* galvanoplastisch vervielfältigen

elegance ['elɪgəns] *s* Eleganz *f*

elegant ['elə͵gɒnt] *adj* elegant

elegiac [͵elɪ'dʒaɪ-æk] *adj* elegisch

elegy ['elɪdʒɪ] *s* Elegie *f*

element ['elɪmənt] *s* (& fig) Element *n*; (e.g., of truth) Körnchen *n*

elementary [͵elɪ'mentərɪ] *adj* elementar, grundlegend

elemen'tary school *s* Grundschule *f*

elephant ['elɪfənt] *s* Elefant *m*

elevate ['elɪ͵vet] *tr* erheben, erhöhen

el'evated *adj* (eyes) erhoben; (style) erhaben || *s* (coll) Hochbahn *f*

elevation [͵elɪ've∫ən] *s* (height) Höhe *f*; (hill) Anhöhe *f*; (above sealevel) Seehöhe *f*; (to the throne) Erhebung *f*; (archit) Aufriß *m*; (arti) Richthöhe *f*; (astr, relig) Elevation *f*

elevator ['elɪ͵vetər] *s* Aufzug *m*, Fahrstuhl *m*; (aer) Höhenruder *n*; (agr) Getreidespeicher *m*

el'evator op'erator *s* Fahrstuhlführer –in *mf*

el'evator shaft' *s* Fahrstuhlschacht *m*

eleven [ɪ'levən] *adj & pron* elf || *s* Elf *f*

eleventh [ɪ'levənθ] *adj* elfte || *s* (fraction) Elftel *n*; **the e.** (in dates and in a series) der Elfte

elev'enth hour' *s*—**at the e.** (fig) kurz vor Torschluß

elf [elf] *s* (elves [elvz]) Elf *m*, Elfe *f*

elicit [ɪ'lɪsɪt] *tr* hervorlocken; (an answer) entlocken

elide [ɪ'laɪd] *tr* elidieren

eligible ['elɪdʒɪbəl] *adj* qualifiziert; (entitled) berechtigt; (for office) wählbar; (for marriage) heiratsfähig

el'igible bach'elor *s* Heiratskandidat *m*

eliminate [ɪ'lɪmɪ͵net] *tr* ausscheiden; (alg) eliminieren

elimination [ɪ͵lɪmɪ'ne∫ən] *s* Ausscheidung *f*

elimina'tion bout' *s* Ausscheidungskampf *m*

elision [ɪ'lɪʒən] *s* Auslassung *f*

elite [e'lit] *adj* Elite– || *s* Elite *f*

elixir [ɪ'lɪksər] *s* Elixier *n*

elk [elk] *s* Elch *m*

ellipse [ɪ'lɪps] *s* (geom) Ellipse *f*

ellip·sis [ɪ'lɪpsɪs] *s* (–ses [siz]) (gram) Ellipse *f*

elliptic(al) [ɪ'lɪptɪk(əl)] *adj* elliptisch

elm [elm] *s* Ulme *f*

elocution [͵elə'kju∫ən] *s* (art) Vortragskunst *f*; (style) Vortragsweise *f*

elope [ɪ'lop] *intr* ausreißen

elopement [ɪ'lopmənt] *s* Ausreißen *n*

eloquence ['eləkwəns] *s* Beredsamkeit *f*

eloquent ['eləkwənt] *adj* beredt

else [els] *adj* sonst; **someone else's house** das Haus e–s anderen; **what e.?** was sonst?; (in addition) was noch?; (in addition) was noch? || *adv* sonst, anders; **nowhere e.** sonst nirgends; **or e.** sonst, andernfalls; **where e.?** wo sonst?

else'where' *adv* (position) woanders;

(direction) sonstwohin; **from e.** anderswoher

elucidate [ɪ'lusɪ͵det] *tr* erläutern

elucidation [ɪ͵lusɪ'de∫ən] *s* Erläuterung *f*

elude [ɪ'lud] *tr* entgehen (dat)

elusive [ɪ'lusɪv] *adj* schwer zu fassen; (memory) unzuverlässig

emaciated [ɪ'me∫ɪ͵etɪd] *adj* abgezehrt

emanate ['emə͵net] *intr*—**e. from** (said of gases) ausströmen aus; (said of rays) ausstrahlen aus; (fig) ausgehen von

emancipate [ɪ'mænsɪ͵pet] *tr* emanzipieren

emasculate [ɪ'mæskjə͵let] *tr* (& fig) entmannen

embalm [em'bam] *tr* einbalsamieren

embankment [em'bæŋkmənt] *s* Damm *m*

embar·go [em'bargo] *s* (–goes) Sperre *f*, Embargo *n* || *tr* sperren

embark [em'bark] *intr* (for) sich einschiffen (nach); **e. upon** sich einlassen auf (acc)

embarkation [͵embar'ke∫ən] *s* Einschiffung *f*

embarrass [em'bærəs] *tr* in Verlegenheit bringen

embar'rassed *adj* verlegen; **feel e.** sich genieren

embar'rassing *adj* peinlich

embarrassment [em'bærəsmənt] *s* Verlegenheit *f*

embassy ['embəsɪ] *s* Botschaft *f*

em-bed [em'bed] *v* (pret & pp –bedded; ger –bedding) *tr* einbetten; **e. in concrete** einbetonieren

embellish [em'belɪ∫] *tr* verschönern

embellishment [em'belɪ∫mənt] *s* Verschönerung *f*

ember ['embər] *s* glühende Kohle *f*; **embers** Glut *f*

Em'ber day' *s* Quatember *m*

embezzle [em'bezəl] *tr* unterschlagen

embezzlement [em'bezəlmənt] *s* Unterschlagung *f*, Veruntreuung *f*

embezzler [em'bezlər] *s* Veruntreuer –in *mf*

embitter [em'bɪtər] *tr* verbittern

emblazon [em'blezən] *tr* (decorate) verzieren; (extol) verherrlichen; (heral) heraldisch darstellen

emblem ['embləm] *s* Sinnbild *n*

emblematic(al) [͵emblə'mætɪk(əl)] *adj* sinnbildlich

embodiment [em'badɪmənt] *s* Verkörperung *f*

embod·y [em'badɪ] *v* (pret & pp –ied) *tr* verkörpern

embolden [em'boldən] *tr* ermutigen

embolism ['embə͵lɪzəm] *s* Embolie *f*

emboss [em'bɔs] *tr* bossieren

embossed' *adj* getrieben

embrace [em'bres] *s* Umarmung *f* || *tr* umarmen; (include) umfassen; (a religion, idea) annehmen || *intr* sich umarmen

embrasure [em'breʒər] *s* Schießscharte *f*

embroider [em'brɔɪdər] *tr* sticken

embroidery [em'brɔɪdərɪ] *s* Stickerei *f*

embroi'dery nee'dle *s* Sticknadel *f*

embroil [em'brɔɪl] *tr* verwickeln

embroilment [em'brɔɪlmənt] *s* Verwicklung *f*

embry·o ['embrɪ‚o] *s* (**-os**) Embryo *m*

embryology [‚embrɪ'ɑlədʒi] *s* Embryologie *f*

embryonic [‚embrɪ'ɑnɪk] *adj* embryonal

emend [ɪ'mend] *tr* berichtigen

emendation [‚imen'deʃən] *s* Berichtigung *f*

emerald ['emərəld] *adj* smaragdgrün ‖ *s* Smaragd *m*

emerge [ɪ'mʌrdʒ] *intr* (*come forth*) hervortreten; (*surface*) auftauchen; (*result*) (**from**) herauskommen (bei)

emergence [ɪ'mʌrdʒəns] *s* Hervortreten *n*; (*surfacing*) Auftauchen *n*

emergency [ɪ'mʌrdʒənsi] *adj* Not– ‖ *s* Notlage *f*; **in case of e.** im Notfall

emeritus [ɪ'merɪtəs] *adj* emeritiert

emersion [ɪ'mʌrʒən] *s* Auftauchen *n*

emery ['eməri] *s* Schmirgel *m*

em'ery cloth' *s* Schmirgelleinwand *f*

em'ery wheel' *s* Schmirgelrad *n*

emetic [ɪ'metɪk] *adj* Brech– ‖ *s* Brechmittel *n*

emigrant ['emɪgrənt] *s* Auswanderer –in *mf*

emigrate ['emɪ‚gret] *intr* auswandern

emigration [‚emɪ'greʃən] *s* Auswanderung *f*

eminence ['emɪnəns] *s* (*height*) Anhöhe *f*; (*fame*) Berühmtheit *f*; **Eminence** (*title of a cardinal*) Eminenz *f*; **rise to e.** zu Ruhm und Würde gelangen

eminent ['emɪnənt] *adj* hervorragend

emissary ['emɪ‚seri] *s* Abgesandte *mf*

emission [ɪ'mɪʃən] *s* (*biol*) Erguß *m*; (*phys*) Austrahlung *f*, Ausströmung *f*

emis'sion control' *s* Abgasentgiftung *f*

emit [ɪ'mɪt] *v* (*pret & pp* **emitted;** *ger* **emitting**) *tr* von sich geben; (*rays*) ausstrahlen; (*gases*) ausströmen; (*sparks*) sprühen

emolument [ɛ'mɑljəmənt] *s* Vergütung *f*

emotion [ɪ'moʃən] *s* Gemütsbewegung *f*

emotional [ɪ'moʃənəl] *adj* (*e.g., disorder*) Gemüts–; (*person*) gefühlvoll; (*e.g., sermon*) ergreifend; (*mawkish*) rührselig

emperor ['empərər] *s* Kaiser *m*

empha·sis ['emfəsɪs] *s* (**-ses** [‚siz]) Betonung *f*

emphasize ['emfə‚saɪz] *tr* betonen

emphatic [em'fætɪk] *adj* nachdrücklich

emphysema [‚emfɪ'simə] *s* Emphysem *n*

empire ['empaɪr] *s* Reich *n*; (*Roman period*) Kaiserzeit *f*

Em'pire fur'niture *s* Empiremöbel *n*

empiric(al) [em'pɪrɪk(əl)] *adj* erfahrungsmäßig, empirisch

empiricist [em'pɪrɪsɪst] *s* Empiriker –in *mf*

emplacement [ɛm'plesmənt] *s* Stellung *f*

employ [em'plɔɪ] *s* Dienst *m* ‖ *tr* (*hire*) anstellen; (*keep in employ-*

ment) beschäftigen; (*use*) verwenden; (*troops, police*) einsetzen

employee [em'plɔɪ·i], [‚emplɔɪ'i] *s* Arbeitnehmer –in *mf*

employer [em'plɔɪ·ər] *s* Arbeitgeber –in *mf*

employment [em'plɔɪmənt] *s* (*work*) Beschäftigung *f*, Arbeit *f*; (*use*) Verwendung *f*; (*e.g., of troops*) Einsatz *m*; **out of e.** arbeitslos

employ'ment a'gency *s* Arbeitsvermittlung *f*

empower [em'pau·ər] *tr* ermächtigen

empress ['emprɪs] *s* Kaiserin *f*

emptiness ['emptɪnɪs] *s* Leere *f*; (*fig*) Nichtigkeit *f*

emp·ty ['empti] *adj* leer; **e. talk** leere Worte *pl*; **on an e. stomach** auf nüchternen Magen; **empties** *spl* Leergut *n* ‖ *v* (*pret & pp* **–tied**) *tr* (*aus*)leeren ‖ *intr*—**e. into** münden in (*acc*)

emp'ty-hand'ed *adj* mit leeren Händen

emp'ty-head'ed *adj* hohlköpfig

emulate ['emjə‚let] *tr* nacheifern (*dat*)

emulation [‚emjə'leʃən] *s* Nacheiferung *f*

emulator [‚emjə'letər] *s* Nacheiferer –in *mf*

emulsi·fy [ɪ'mʌlsɪ‚faɪ] *v* (*pret & pp* **–fied**) *tr* emulgieren

emulsion [ɪ'mʌlʃən] *s* Emulsion *f*; (*phot*) Schicht *f*

enable [en'ebəl] *tr* befähigen

enact [en'ækt] *tr* erlassen

enactment [en'æktmənt] *s* Erlassen *n*

enam·el [ɪ'næməl] *s* Email *n*; (*dent*) Zahnschmelz *m* ‖ *v* (*pret & pp* **–el[l]ed;** *ger* **–el[l]ing**) *tr* emaillieren

enam'el paint' *s* Emaillack *m*

enam'elware' *s* Emailwaren *pl*

enamored [ɛ'næmərd] *adj*—**be e. of** verliebt sein in (*acc*)

encamp [en'kæmp] *tr* in e–m Lager unterbringen ‖ *intr* lagern, sich lagern

encampment [en'kæmpmənt] *s* (*camping*) Lagern *n*; (*campsite*) Lager *n*

encase [en'kes] *tr* einschließen

enchant [en't'fænt] *tr* verzaubern; (*fig*) bezaubern

enchanter [en't'fæntər] *s* Zauberer –in *mf*

enchant'ing *adj* bezaubernd

enchantment [en't'fæntmənt] *s* (*state*) Verzauberung *f*; (*cause of enchantment*) Zauber *m*

enchantress [en't'fæntrɪs] *s* Zauberin *f*

encircle [en'sʌrkəl] *tr* umgeben; (*mil*) einschließen

encirclement [en'sʌrkəlmənt] *s* (*mil*) Einschließung *f*

enclave ['enklev] *s* Enklave *f*

enclitic [en'klɪtɪk] *adj* enklitisch ‖ *s* Enklitikon *n*

enclose [en'kloz] *tr* einschließen; (*land*) umzäunen; (*in a letter*) beilegen; **e. in parentheses** einklammern; **please find enclosed in der** Anlage erhalten Sie

enclosure [en'kloʒər] *s* Umzäunung *f*; (*in a letter*) Anlage *f*

encomi·um [ɛn'komɪ·əm] *s* (**–ums &** **–a** [ə]) Lobpreisung *f*, Enkomion *n*

encompass [ɛn'kʌmpəs] *tr* umfassen

encore ['aṇkor] *s* (*performance*) Zugabe *f*; (*recall*) Dakaporuf *m* ‖ *interj* da capo!; noch einmal!

encounter [ɛn'kauntər] *s* Begegnung *f*; (*hostile meeting*) Zusammenstoß *m*; (mil) Gefecht *n* ‖ *tr* begegnen (*dat*)

encourage [ɛn'kʌrɪdʒ] *tr* ermutigen

encouragement [ɛn'kʌrɪdʒmənt] *s* Ermutigung *f*

encroach [ɛn'krot/] *intr*—e. on übergreifen auf (*acc*); (*rights*) beeinträchtigen

encroachment [ɛn'krot/mənt] *s* Übergriff *m*

encrust [ɛn'krʌst] *tr* überkrusten

encumber [ɛn'kʌmbər] *tr* belasten; (*with debts*) verschulden

encumbrance [ɛn'krʌmbrəns] *s* Belastung *f*

encyclical [ɛn'sɪklɪkəl] *s* Enzyklika *f*

encyclopedia [ɛn ˌsaɪklə'pidɪ·ə] *s* Enzyklopädie *f*

encyclopedic [ɛn ˌsaɪklə'pidɪk] *adj* enzyklopädisch

end [ɛnd] *s* Ende *n*; (*purpose*) Zweck *m*; (*goal*) Ziel *n*; (*closing*) Schluß *m*; (*outcome*) Ausgang *m*, Ergebnis *n*; **at the end of one's strength** am Rande seiner Kraft; **come to a bad end** ein schlimmes Ende finden; **come to an end** zu Ende gehen; **end in itself** Selbstzweck *m*; **gain one's ends** seinen Vorsatz ausführen; **go off the deep end** sich unnötig aufregen; **in the end** schließlich; **make both ends meet** gerade auskommen; **no end of** unendlich viel(e); **on end** hochkant; (*without letup*) ununterbrochen; **put an end to** ein Ende machen (*dat*); **that will be the end of me** das überlebe ich nicht; **to no end** vergebens ‖ *tr* beenden ‖ *intr* enden; (gram) auslauten; **end in a point** spitz zulaufen; **end up (in)** (coll) landen (in *dat*); **end up with** beenden mit

end'-all' *s* Schluß *m* vom Ganzen

endanger [ɛn'dendʒər] *tr* gefährden

endear [ɛn'dɪr] *tr*—e. s.o. to j-n einschmeicheln bei

endear'ing *adj* gewinnend

endearment [ɛn'dɪrmənt] *s* Beliebtheit *f*

endeavor [ɛn'devər] *s* Bestreben *n* ‖ *intr*—e. to (*inf*) sich bestreben zu (*inf*), versuchen zu (*inf*)

endemic [ɛn'demɪk] *adj* endemisch ‖ *s* Endemie *f*, endemische Krankheit *f*

end'ing *s* Beendigung *f*, Abschluß *m*; (gram) Endung *f*

endive ['ɛndaɪv] *s* Endivie *f*

endless ['ɛndlɪs] *adj* endlos; **an e. number of** unendlich viele

end'most' *adj* entfernteste

endocrine ['ɛndo·kraɪn] *adj* endokrin

endorse [ɛn'dɔrs] *tr* (*confirm*) bestätigen; (*a check*) indossieren

endorsee [ˌɛndɔr'si] *s* Indossat –in *mf*

endorsement [ɛn'dɔrsmənt] *s* Indossament *n*; (*approval*) Bestätigung *f*

endorser [ɛn'dɔrsər] *s* Indossant –in *mf*; (*backer*) Hintermann *m*

endow [ɛn'dau] *tr* (*provide with income*) dotieren; (*with talent*) begaben

endowment [ɛn'daumənt] *s* Dotierung *f*; (*talent*) Begabung *f*

endow'ment fund' *s* Stiftungsvermögen *n*

endurance [ɛn'd(j)urəns] *s* Dauer *f*; (*ability to hold out*) Ausdauer *f*

endur'ance test' *s* Dauerprobe *f*

endure [ɛn'd(j)ur] *tr* aushalten ‖ *intr* fortdauern

endur'ing *adj* dauerhaft

enema ['ɛnəmə] *s* Einlauf *m*

enemy ['ɛnəmi] *adj* feindlich, Feind- ‖ *s* Feind *m*; **become enemies** sich verfeinden

energetic [ˌɛnər'dʒɛtɪk] *adj* energisch

energy ['ɛnərdʒi] *s* Energie *f*

enervate ['ɛnər ˌvet] *tr* entkräften

enfeeble [ɛn'fibəl] *tr* entkräften

enfilade ['ɛnfɪ ˌled] *s* (mil) Flankenfeuer *n* ‖ *tr* mit Flankenfeuer bestreichen

enfold [ɛn'fold] *tr* einhüllen

enforce [ɛn'fors] *tr* durchsetzen; (*obedience*) erzwingen

enforcement [ɛn'forsmənt] *s* Durchsetzung *f*

enfranchise [ɛn'frænt/aɪz] *tr* (*admit to citizenship*) einbürgern; (*give the right to vote to*) das Wahlrecht verleihen (*dat*)

engage [ɛn'gedʒ] *tr* (*hire*) anstellen; (*reserve*) vorbestellen; (*attention*) fesseln; (*gears*) einrücken; (*one's own troops*) einsetzen; (*the enemy*) angreifen; **be engaged in** beschäftigt sein mit; **e. in** verwickeln in (*acc*) ‖ *intr* (mach) (ein)greifen; **e. in** sich einlassen in (*acc*)

engaged' *adj* verlobt; **get e. (to)** sich verloben mit)

engaged' cou'ple *s* Brautleute *pl*

engagement [ɛn'gedʒmənt] *s* (*betrothal*) Verlobung *f*; (*appointment*) Verabredung *f*; (*obligation*) Verpflichtung *f*; (mil) Gefecht *n*; **have a previous e.** verabredet sein

engage'ment ring' *s* Verlobungsring *m*

engag'ing *adj* gewinnend

engender [ɛn'dʒɛndər] *tr* hervorbringen

engine ['ɛndʒɪn] *s* Maschine *f*; (aer, aut) Motor *m*; (rr) Lokomotive *f*

engineer [ˌɛndʒə'nɪr] *s* Ingenieur *m*, Techniker *m*; (mil) Pionier *m*; (rr) Lokomotivführer *m*; **engineers** (mil) Pioniertruppe *f* ‖ *tr* errichten; (fig) bewerkstelligen

engineer'ing *s* Ingenieurwesen *n*

engineer'ing school' *s* Technikum *n*

en'gine house' *s* Spritzenhaus *n*

en'gine room' *s* Maschinenraum *m*

England ['ɪŋglənd] *s* England *n*

English ['ɪŋglɪ/] *adj* englisch ‖ *s* (spin) Effet *n*; (*language*) Englisch *n*; **in plain E.** unverblümt; **the E.** die Engländer

Eng/lish Chan/nel s Ärmelkanal m

Eng/lish horn/ s Englischhorn n

Eng/lish·man s (**-men**) Engländer m

Eng/lish-speak/ing adj englischsprechend

Eng/lish·wom/an s (**-wom/en**) Engländerin f

engraft [en'græft] tr aufpropfen; (fig) einprägen

engrave [en'grev] tr gravieren

engraver [en'grevər] s Graveur m

engrav/ing s Kupferstich m

engross [en'gros] tr in Anspruch nehmen; (a document) mit großen Buchstaben schreiben; **become engrossed in** sich versenken in (acc)

engross/ing adj fesselnd

engulf [en'gʌlf] tr (fig) verschlingen

enhance [en'hæns] tr erhöhen; **be enhanced** sich erhöhen

enhancement [en'hænsmənt] s Erhöhung f

enigma [ɪ'nɪgmə] s Rätsel n

enigmatic(al) [ˌɪnɪg'mætɪk(əl)] adj rätselhaft

enjoin [en'dʒɔɪn] tr (forbid) (**from** ger) verbieten (dat) (zu inf); **e. s.o. to** (inf) j-m auferlegen zu (inf)

enjoy [en'dʒɔɪ] tr (take pleasure in) Gefallen finden an (dat); (have the advantage of) genießen, sich erfreuen (genit); **e. doing s.th.** gern etw tun; **e. oneself** sich gut unterhalten; **e. to the full** auskosten; **I e. the wine** mir schmeckt der Wein

enjoyable [en'dʒɔɪ·əbəl] adj erfreulich; **thoroughly e.** genußreich

enjoyment [en'dʒɔɪmənt] s Genuß m

enkindle [en'kɪndəl] tr entzünden

enlarge [en'lardʒ] tr vergrößern ‖ intr sich vergrößern; **e. upon** näher eingehen auf (acc)

enlargement [en'lardʒmənt] s Vergrößerung f

enlarger [en'lardʒər] s (phot) Vergrößerungsapparat m

enlighten [en'laɪtən] tr aufklären

enlightenment [en'laɪtənmənt] s (act) Aufklärung f; (state) Aufgeklärtheit f

enlist [en'lɪst] tr (services) in Anspruch nehmen; (mil) anwerben; **e. s.o. in a cause** j-n für e-e Sache gewinnen ‖ intr (**in**) sich freiwillig melden (zu)

enlist/ed man/ s Soldat m; **enlisted men** Mannschaften pl

enlistment [en'lɪstmənt] s Anwerbung f; (period of service) Militärdienstzeit f

enliven [en'laɪvən] tr beleben

enmesh [en'meʃ] tr verstricken

enmity ['enmɪti] s Feindschaft f

ennoble [en'nobəl] tr veredeln, adeln

ennui ['ɑnwi] s Langeweile f

enormity [ɪ'nɔrmɪti] s Ungeheuerlichkeit f

enormous [ɪ'nɔrməs] adj enorm, ungeheuer

enough [ɪ'nʌf] adj & adv genug, genügend; **be e.** genügen; **I have e. of it** ich bin es satt; **it's e. to drive one crazy** es ist zum Verrücktwerden

enounce [ɪ'nauns] tr (declare) verkünden; (pronounce) aussprechen

enrage [en'redʒ] tr wütend machen

enraged/ adj (**at**) wütend (über acc)

enrapture [en'ræptʃər] tr hinreißen

enrich [en'rɪtʃ] tr (a person with money; the mind, a program) bereichern; (soil) fruchtbarer machen; (food, metals, gases) anreichern

enrichment [en'rɪtʃmənt] s Bereicherung f; (of food, metals, gases) Anreicherung f

enroll [en'rol] tr als Mitglied aufnehmen ‖ intr (educ) sich immatrikulieren lassen

enrollment [en'rolmənt] s (in a course or school) Schülerzahl f; (of a society) Mitgliederzahl f

en route [ɑn 'rut] adv unterwegs

ensconce [en'skɑns] tr verbergen

ensemble [ɑn'sɑmbəl] s Ensemble n

ensign ['ensɪn] s (flag) (mil) Fahne f; (flag) (nav) Flagge f; (emblem) Abzeichen n; (nav) Leutnant m zur See

enslave [en'slev] tr versklaven

enslavement [en'slevmənt] s Versklavung f

ensnare [en'sner] tr (fig) umgarnen

ensue [en's(j)u] intr (**from**) (er)folgen (aus)

ensu/ing adj darauffolgend

ensure [en'ʃur] tr gewährleisten

entail [en'tel] tr mit sich bringen

entangle [en'tæŋgəl] tr verwickeln; **get entangled** sich verwickeln

entanglement [en'tæŋgəlmənt] s Verwicklung f; (mil) Drahtverhau m

enter ['entər] tr (a room) betreten, treten in (acc); (political office) antreten; (a university) beziehen; (a protest) erheben; (a career) einschlagen; (in the records) eintragen; **e. the army** Soldat werden ‖ intr eintreten, hereinkommen; (by car) einfahren; (sport) melden; (theat) auftreten; **e. into** (an agreement) treffen; (a contract) abschließen; **e. upon** anfangen; (a career) einschlagen; (an office, inheritance) antreten; (year of life) eintreten in (acc)

enterprise ['entər‚praɪz] s Unternehmen n; (spirit) Unternehmungsgeist m

en/terprising adj unternehmungslustig

entertain [‚entər'ten] tr unterhalten; (guests) bewirten; (doubts, hopes, suspicions) hegen ‖ intr Gäste haben

entertainer [‚entər'tenər] s Unterhaltungskünstler –in m f

entertain/ing adj unterhaltsam ‖ s—**do a lot of e.** ein großes Haus führen

entertainment [‚entər'tenmənt] s Unterhaltung f

entertain/ment tax/ s Vergnügungssteuer f

enthrall [en'θrɔl] tr bezaubern, fesseln

enthrone [en'θron] tr auf den Thron setzen; **be enthroned** thronen

enthuse [en'θ(j)uz] tr (coll) begeistern

enthusiasm [en'θ(j)uzɪ‚æzəm] s Begeisterung f, Schwärmerei f

enthusiast [en'θ(j)uzɪ‚æst] *s* Schwärmer –in *mf*
enthusiastic [en‚θ(j)uzɪ'æstɪk] *adj* (**about**) begeistert (über *acc* or von)
entice [en'taɪs] *tr* (ver)locken
enticement [en'taɪsmənt] *s* Verlockung *f*
entic/ing *adj* verlockend
entire [en'taɪr] *adj* ganz, gesamt; (*trust*) voll
entirely [en'taɪrli] *adv* ganz, gänzlich
entirety [en'taɪrti] *s*—**in its e.** in seiner Gesamtheit
entitle [en'taɪtəl] *tr* (*call*) betiteln; (**to**) berechtigen (zu); **be entitled to** Anspruch haben auf (*acc*); **be entitled to** (*inf*) berechtigt sein zu (*inf*)
entity ['entɪti] *s* Wesen *n*
entomb [en'tum] *tr* bestatten
entombment [en'tummənt] *s* Bestattung *f*
entomology [‚entə'malədʒi] *s* Entomologie *f*
entourage [‚antu'raʒ] *s* Begleitung *f*
entrails ['entrelz] *spl* Eingeweide *pl*
entrain [en'tren] *tr* verladen ‖ *intr* einsteigen
entrance ['entrəns] *s* Eingang *m*; (*drive*) Einfahrt *f*; (*of a home*) Flur *m*; (*upon office*) Antritt *m*; (*theat*) Auftritt *m*; **make one's e.** eintreten ‖ [en'træns] *tr* mitreißen
en/trance examina/tion *s* Aufnahmeprüfung *f*
en/trance fee/ *s* Eintrittspreis *m*
entrant ['entrənt] *s* (**in**) Teilnehmer –in *mf* (an *dat*)
en-trap [en'træp] *v* (*pret & pp* –**trapped;** *ger* –**trapping**) *tr* verleiten
entreat [en'trit] *tr* anflehen
entreaty [en'triti] *s* dringende Bitte *f*; **at his e.** auf seine Bitte
entrée ['antre] *s* (*access*) Zutritt *m*; (*before main course*) Vorspeise *f*; (*between courses*) Zwischengericht *n*; (*main course*) Hauptgericht *n*
entrench [en'trentʃ] *tr* verschanzen; **be entrenched in** (fig) eingewurzelt sein in (*dat*)
entrenchment [en'trentʃmənt] *s* (*activity*) Schanzbau *m*; (*the result*) Verschanzung *f*
entrepreneur [antrəprə'nʌr] *s* Unternehmer –in *mf*
entrust [en'trʌst] *tr* (**to**) anvertrauen (*dat*)
entry ['entri] *s* Eintritt *m*; (*by car*) Einfahrt *f*; (*door*) Eingang *m*, Eingangstür *f*; (*into a country*) Einreise *f*; (*into office*) Antritt *m*; (*in a dictionary*) Stichwort *n*; (*into a race*) Nennung *f*; (*contestant*) Bewerber –in *mf*; (com) Buchung *f*; (theat) Auftritt *m*; **unlawful e.** Hausfriedensbruch *m*
entwine [en'twain] *tr* umwinden
enumerate [ɪ'n(j)umə‚ret] *tr* aufzählen
enunciate [ɪ'nʌnsɪ‚et] *tr* aussprechen ‖ *intr* deutlich aussprechen
envelop [en'veləp] *tr* (*said of crowds, waves*) verschlingen; (*said of mist, clouds, darkness*) umhüllen; (mil) umfassen

envelope ['envə‚lop] *s* Umschlag *m*
envelopment [en'veləpmənt] *s* Umhüllung *f*; (mil) Umfassung *f*
envenom [en'venəm] *tr* vergiften
enviable ['envɪ-əbəl] *adj* beneidenswert
envious ['envɪ-əs] *adj* (**of**) neidisch (auf *acc*)
environment [en'vaɪrənmənt] *s* (*ecological condition*) Umwelt *f*; (*surroundings*) Umgebung *f*
environmental [en‚vaɪrən'mentəl] *adj* Umwelt–; umgebend, Umgebungs–
environmentalist [en‚vaɪrən'mentəlɪst] *s* Umweltschützer –in *mf*
environs [en'vaɪrənz] *spl* Umgebung *f*
envisage [en'vɪzɪdʒ] *tr* ins Auge fassen
envoy ['envɔɪ] *s* Gesandte *mf*
en-vy ['envɪ] *s* Neid *m* ‖ *v* (*pret & pp* –**vied**) *tr* (**for**) beneiden (um)
enzyme ['enzaɪm] *s* Enzym *n*
epaulet, epaulette ['epə‚let] *s* Epaulette *f*, Schulterstück *n*
ephemeral [ɪ'femərəl] *adj* flüchtig
epic ['epɪk] *adj* episch; **e. poetry** Epik *f* ‖ *s* Epos *n*, Heldengedicht *n*
epicure ['epɪ‚kjur] *s* Feinschmecker –in *mf*
epicurean [‚epɪkju'ri-ən] *adj* genußsüchtig; (philos) epikureisch ‖ *s* Genußmensch *m*; (philos) Epikureer *m*
epidemic [‚epɪ'demɪk] *adj* epidemisch ‖ *s* Epidemie *f*, Seuche *f*
epidermis [‚epɪ'dʌrmɪs] *s* Oberhaut *f*
epigram ['epɪ‚græm] *s* Epigramm *n*
epigraph ['epɪ‚græf] *s* Inschrift *f*
epigraphy [e'pɪgrəfi] *s* Inschriftenkunde *f*
epilepsy ['epɪ‚lepsi] *s* Epilepsie *f*
epileptic [‚epɪ'leptɪk] *adj* epileptisch ‖ *s* Epileptiker –in *mf*
epilogue ['epɪ‚log] *s* Nachwort *n*
Epiphany [ɪ'pɪfəni] *s* Dreikönigsfest *n*
Episcopal [ɪ'pɪskəpəl] *adj* bischöflich
Episcopalian [ɪ‚pɪskə'peli-ən] *adj* Episkopal– ‖ *s* Episkopale *m*, Episkopalin *f*
epis/copal see/ *s* Bischofssitz *m*
episcopate [ɪ'pɪskə‚pet] *s* Bischofsamt *n*
episode ['epɪ‚sod] *s* Episode *f*
epistemology [ɪ‚pɪstə'malədʒi] *s* Epistemologie *f*, Erkenntnistheorie *f*
epistle [ɪ'pɪsəl] *s* Epistel *f*
epitaph ['epɪtæf] *s* Grabinschrift *f*
epithet ['epɪ‚θet] *s* Beiwort *n*
epitome [ɪ'pɪtəmi] *s* Auszug *m*; (fig) Verkörperung *f*
epitomize [ɪ'pɪtə‚maɪz] *tr*—e–n Auszug machen von or aus; (fig) verkörpern
epoch ['epək], ['ipɑk] *s* Epoche *f*
epochal ['epəkəl] *adj* epochal
e/poch-mak/ing *adj* bahnbrechend
Ep/som salts/ ['epsəm] *spl* Bittersalz *n*
equable ['ekwəbəl] *adj* gleichmäßig; (*disposition*) gleichmütig
equal ['ikwəl] *adj* gleich; (*in birth or status*) ebenbürtig; (*in worth*) gleichwertig; (*in kind*) gleichartig; **be e. to** (*e.g., a task*) gewachsen sein (*dat*); **be on e. terms** (*be on the same level*) auf gleichem Fuß stehen; **other**

things being e. bei sonst gleichen Verhältnissen ‖ s Gleiche *mfn;* her or their e.(s) ihresgleichen; my (your, *etc.*) e.(s) meines– (deines–, *etc.*) gleichen ‖ v (*pret & pp* equal[l]ed; *ger* equal[l]ing *tr* gleichkommen (*dat*); (*a record*) erreichen; (*math*) ergeben

equality [ɪ'kwɑlɪti] s Gleichheit *f;* (*in standing*) Gleichberechtigung *f*

equalize ['ikwə‚laɪz] *tr* gleichmachen

equally ['ikwəli] *adv* gleich, ebenso

equanimity [‚ikwə'nɪmɪti] s Gleichmut *m*

equate [i'kwet] *tr* (**to** or **with**) gleichsetzen (*dat* or mit)

equation [ɪ'kweʒən] s Gleichung *f*

equator [i'kwetər] s Äquator *m*

equatorial [‚ikwə'tori‚əl] *adj* äquatorial

equestrian [ɪ'kwestri‚ən] *adj* Reiter–; e. statue Reiterstandbild *n* ‖ s Kunstreiter –in *mf*

equilateral [‚ikwɪ'lætərəl] *adj* gleichseitig

equilibrium [‚ikwɪ'lɪbrɪ‚əm] s Gleichgewicht *n;* (*fig*) Gleichmaß *n*

equinox ['ikwɪ‚naks] s Tagundnachtgleiche *f*

equip [ɪ'kwɪp] v (*pret & pp* equipped; *ger* equipping) *tr* ausrüsten, ausstatten

equipment [ɪ'kwɪpmənt] s Ausrüstung *f*, Ausstattung *f*

equipoise ['ikwɪ‚pɔɪz] s Gleichgewicht *n*

equitable ['ɛkwɪtəbəl] *adj* gerecht

equity ['ɛkwɪti] s (*fairness*) Unparteilichkeit *f;* (*fin*) Nettowert *m*

equivalent [ɪ'kwɪvələnt] *adj* gleichwertig; (**to**) gleichbedeutend (mit) ‖ s Gegenwert *m;* (*of*) Äquivalent *n* (für)

equivocal [ɪ'kwɪvəkəl] *adj* zweideutig

equivocate [ɪ'kwɪvə‚ket] *intr* zweideutig reden

equivocation [ɪ‚kwɪvə‚keʃən] s Zweideutigkeit *f*

era ['ɪrə], ['irə] s Zeitalter *n*

eradicate [ɪ'rædɪ‚ket] *tr* ausrotten

erase [ɪ'res] *tr* ausradieren; (*a tape recording*) löschen; (*a blackboard*) abwischen; (*fig*) auslöschen

eraser [ɪ'resər] s Radiergummi *m;* (*for a blackboard*) Tafelwischer *m*

erasure [ɪ'reʃər], [ɪ'reʒər] s (*action*) Ausradieren *n;* (*erased spot*) Rasur *f*

ere [ɛr] *prep* (poet) vor (*dat*) ‖ *conj* (poet) ehe, bevor

erect [ɪ'rɛkt] *adj* aufrecht, straff; (*hair*) gesträubt; **with head e.** erhobenen Hauptes ‖ *tr* errichten

erection [ɪ'rɛkʃən] s Errichtung *f;* (*of sexual organs*) Erektion *f*

erg [ʌrg] s Erg *n*

ermine ['ʌrmɪn] s Hermelinpelz *m*

erode [ɪ'rod] *tr* (*corrode*) zerfressen; (*fig*) unterhöhlen; (geol) erodieren ‖ *intr* zerfressen werden

erosion [ɪ'roʒən] s (*corrosion*) Zerfressen *n;* (*fig*) Unterhöhlung *f;* (geol) Erosion *f*

erotic [ɪ'rɑtɪk] *adj* erotisch

err [ʌr] *intr* irren, sich irren

errand ['ɛrənd] s Besorgung *f;* **run an e.** e–e Besorgung machen

er'rand boy' s Laufbursche *m*

erratic [ɪ'rætɪk] *adj* regellos, ziellos; (geol) erratisch

erroneous [ɪ'roni‚əs] *adj* irrtümlich

erroneously [ɪ'roni‚əsli] *adv* irrtümlicherweise, versehentlich

error ['ɛrər] s Fehler *m*, Irrtum *m*

erudite ['ɛr(j)u‚daɪt] *adj* gelehrt

erudition [‚ɛr(j)u'dɪʃən] s Gelehrsamkeit *f*

erupt [ɪ'rʌpt] *intr* ausbrechen

eruption [ɪ'rʌpʃən] s Ausbruch *m;* (pathol) Ausschlag *m*

escalate ['ɛskə‚let] *tr & intr* eskalieren

escalation [‚ɛskə'leʃən] s Eskalierung *f*

escalator ['ɛskə‚letər] s Rolltreppe *f*

es'calator clause' s Indexklausel *f*

escapade ['ɛskə‚ped] s Eskapade *f*

escape [ɛs'kep] s Flucht *f;* (*of gas or liquid*) Ausströmen *n;* **have a narrow e.** mit knapper Not davonkommen ‖ *intr* (*said of gas or liquid*) ausströmen; (**from**) flüchten (aus)

escape' clause' s Ausweichklausel *f*

escapee [‚ɛskə'pi] s Flüchtling *m*

escape' hatch' s Notausstieg *m*

escapement [ɛs'kepmənt] s (horol) Hemmung *f*

escape' wheel' s (horol) Hemmungsrad *n*

escapism [ɛs'kepɪzəm] s Wirklichkeitsflucht *f*

escarpment [ɛs'kɑrpmənt] s (geol) Steilabhang *m;* (mil) Abdachung *f*

eschew [ɛs't/u] *tr* (ver)meiden

escort ['ɛskɔrt] s Geleit *n*, Schutzgeleit *n;* (*person*) Begleiter *m;* (mil) Begleitmannschaft *f*, Bedeckung *f;* (nav) Geleitschutz *m* ‖ [ɛs'kɔrt] *tr* begleiten; (mil, nav) geleiten

es'cort ves'sel s Geleitschiff *n*

escutcheon [ɛs'kʌtʃən] s Wappenschild *m;* (*doorplate*) Schlüssellochschild *n*

Eskimo ['ɛskɪ‚mo] *adj* Eskimo– ‖ s (–mos & –mo) Eskimo *m*

esophagus [i'sɑfəgəs] s (–gi [‚dʒaɪ]) Speiseröhre *f*

esoteric [‚ɛso'tɛrɪk] *adj* esoterisch

especial [ɛs'pɛʃəl] *adj* besondere

especially [ɛs'pɛʃəli] *adv* besonders

espionage [‚ɛspi‚ə'naʒ] s Spionage *f*

espousal [ɛs'pauzəl] s (**of**) Annahme *f* (von)

espouse [ɛs'pauz] *tr* annehmen

esprit de corps [ɛs'pri də 'kɔr] s Korpsgeist *m*, Gemeinschaftsgeist *m*

espy [ɛs'paɪ] v (*pret & pp* espied) *tr* erspähen

essay ['ɛse] s Aufsatz *m*, Essay *n* ‖ [ɛ'se] *tr* probieren

essayist ['ɛse‚ɪst] s Essayist –in *mf*

essence ['ɛsəns] s Wesenheit *f;* (*scent*) Duft *m;* (*extract*) Essenz *f;* (philos) inneres Wesen *n;* **in e.** im wesentlichen

essential [ɛ'sɛnʃəl] *adj* (**to**) wesentlich (für) ‖ s Hauptsache *f;* **the essentials** die Grundzüge *pl*

establish [es'tæblɪʃ] *tr* (*found*) gründen; (*a business, an account*) eröffnen; (*relations, connections*) herstellen; (*order*) schaffen; (*a record*) aufstellen; (*a fact*) feststellen

establishment [es'tæblɪʃmənt] *s* (*act*) Gründung *f*; (*institution*) Anstalt *f*; (*business*) Unternehmen *n*; **the Establishment** das Establishment

estate [es'tet] *s* (*landed property*) Landgut *n*; (*possessions*) Vermögen *n*; (*property of deceased person*) Nachlaß *m*; (*social station*) Stand *m*

esteem [es'tim] *s* Hochachtung *f*; **hold in e.** achten || *tr* achten

esthete ['esθit] *s* Ästhetiker –in *mf*

esthetic [es'θetɪk] *adj* ästhetisch ||
esthetics *s* Ästhetik *f*

estimable ['estɪməbəl] *adj* schätzenswert

estimate ['estɪ‚met], ['estɪmɪt] *s* Kostenanschlag *m*; (*judgment of value*) Schätzung *f*; **rough e.** Überschlag *m* || ['estɪ‚met] *tr* (*costs*) veranschlagen; (*the value*) abschätzen; (*homes, damages*) schätzen; (*at*) beziffern (auf *acc*); **e. roughly** überschlagen

estimation [‚estɪ'meʃən] *s* Schätzung *f*; **in my e.** nach meiner Schätzung

Estonia [es'tonɪ‚ə] *s* Estland *n*

estrangement [es'trendʒmənt] *s* Entfremdung *f*

estuary ['estʃu‚erɪ] *s* (*of a river*) Mündung *f*; (*inlet*) Meeresarm *m*

etch [etʃ] *tr* radieren, ätzen

etcher ['etʃər] *s* Radierer –in *mf*

etch'ing *s* Radierung *f*; (*as an art*) Radierkunst *f*

eternal [ɪ'tʌrnəl] *adj* ewig

eternity [ɪ'tʌrnɪti] *s* Ewigkeit *f*

ether ['iθər] *s* Äther *m*

ethereal [ɪ'θɪrɪ‚əl] *adj* ätherisch

ethical ['eθɪkəl] *adj* ethisch, sittlich

ethics ['eθɪks] *s* Ethik *f*, Sittenlehre *f*

Ethiopia [‚iθɪ'opɪ‚ə] *s* Äthiopien *n*

Ethiopian [‚iθɪ'opɪ‚ən] *adj* äthiopisch || *s* Äthiopier –in *mf*; (*language*) Äthiopisch *n*

ethnic(al) ['eθnɪk(əl)] *adj* völkisch; **e. group** Volksgruppe *f*

ethnography [eθ'nagrəfɪ] *s* Ethnographie *f*

ethnology [eθ'nalədʒɪ] *s* Völkerkunde *f*

ethyl ['eθɪl] *s* Äthyl *m*

ethylene ['eθɪ‚lin] *s* Äthylen *n*

etiquette ['etɪ‚ket] *s* Etikette *f*

etymology [‚etɪ'malədʒɪ] *s* Etymologie *f*

ety·mon ['etɪ‚man] *s* (**-mons** & **-ma** [mə]) Etymon *n*

eucalyp·tus [‚jukə'lɪptəs] *s* (**-tuses** & **-ti** [taɪ]) Eukalyptus *m*

Eucharist ['jukərɪst] *s*—**the E.** das heilige Abendmahl, die Eucharistie *f*

eugenics [juˈdʒenɪks] *s* Rassenhygiene *f*

eulogize ['julə‚dʒaɪz] *tr* lobpreisen

eulogy ['julədʒɪ] *s* Lobrede *f*

eunuch ['junək] *s* Eunuch *m*

euphemism ['jufɪ‚mɪzəm] *s* Euphemismus *m*

euphemistic [‚jufə'mɪstɪk] *adj* euphemistisch, verblümt

euphonic [ju'fanɪk] *adj* wohlklingend

euphony ['jufənɪ] *s* Wohlklang *m*

euphoria [ju'forɪ‚ə] *s* Euphorie *f*

euphoric [ju'forɪk] *adj* euphorisch

euphuism ['jufju‚ɪzəm] *s* gezierte Ausdrucksweise *f*

Europe ['jurəp] *s* Europa *n*

European [‚jurə'pi‚ən] *adj* europäisch || *s* Europäer –in *mf*

Europe'an plan' *s* Hotelpreis *m* ohne Mahlzeiten

euthanasia [‚juθə'neʒə] *s* Euthanasie *f*

evacuate [ɪ'vækju‚et] *tr* evakuieren; (*med*) entleeren; (*an area*) räumen || *intr* sich zurückziehen

evacuation [ɪ‚vækju'eʃən] *s* Evakuierung *f*; (*med*) Entleerung *f*

evade [ɪ'ved] *tr* ausweichen (*dat*); (*duties*) vernachlässigen; (*laws*) umgehen; (*prosecution, responsibility*) sich entziehen (*dat*); (*taxes*) hinterziehen

evaluate [ɪ'vælju‚et] *tr* (*e.g., jewels*) (ab)schätzen; (*e.g., a performance*) beurteilen

evaluation [ɪ‚vælju'eʃən] *s* Abschätzung *f*; (*judgment*) Beurteilung *f*

evangelic(al) [‚iven'dʒelɪk(əl)], [‚evən'dʒelɪk(əl)] *adj* evangelisch

Evangelist [ɪ'vændʒəlɪst] *s* Evangelist *m*

evaporate [ɪ'væpə‚ret] *tr* eindampfen || *intr* (*above boiling point*) verdampfen; (*below boiling point*) verdunsten; (fig) sich verflüchtigen

eva'porated milk' *s* Kondensmilch *f*

evasion [ɪ'veʒən] *s* (*dodge*) Ausweichen *n*; (*of the law*) Umgehung *f*; (*of responsibility*) Vernachlässigung *f*; (*in speech*) Ausflucht *f*

evasive [ɪ'vesɪv] *adj* ausweichend

eve [iv] *s* Vorabend *m*

even ['ivən] *adj* (*smooth*) eben, gerade; (*number*) gerade; (*uniform*) gleichmäßig; (*chance*) gleich; (*temperament*) ruhig, ausgeglichen; **an e. dozen** genau ein Dutzend; **be e.** (coll) quitt sein; **e. with** auf gleicher Höhe mit; **get e. with** mit j-m abrechnen || *adv* selbst, sogar; (*before comparatives*) noch; (*as intensifier before nouns and pronouns*) selbst; **break** s. gerade auf seine Kosten kommen; **e. if** selbst wenn, wenn auch; **e. so** trotzdem; **e. though** obgleich; **e. today** noch heute; **e. when** selbst wenn || *tr* ebnen; **e. up** ausgleichen

e'ven-hand'ed *adj* unparteiisch

evening ['ivnɪŋ] *adj* Abend– || *s* Abend *m*; **in the e.** am Abend; **this e.** heute abend

eve'ning gown' *s* Abendkleid *n*

eve'ning pa'per *s* Abendblatt *n*

eve'ning school' *s* Abendschule *f*

evenly ['ivənlɪ] *adv* gleichmäßig; **e. matched** (sport) gleichwertig

ev'en-mind'ed *adj* gleichmütig

evenness ['ivənnɪs] *s* (*smoothness*)

Ebenheit *f;* (*uniformity*) Gleichmäßigkeit *f*

event [ɪ'vent] *s* Ereignis *n;* (sport) Veranstaltung *f;* **at all events, in any e.** auf jeden Fall; **in the e.** of im Falle (*genit*)

eventful [ɪ'ventfəl] *adj* ereignisvoll

eventual [ɪ'ventʃυ-əl] *adj* schließlich

eventuality [ɪ,ventʃυ'ælɪti] *s* Möglichkeit *f*

eventually [ɪ'ventʃυ ,əli] *adj* schließlich

ever ['evər] *adv* je, jemals; (*before comparatives*) immer; **did you e.!** hat man schon sowas gehört!; **e. after** die ganze Zeit danach; **e. so** noch so; **e. so much** (coll) sehr; **hardly e.** fast nie

ev'ergreen' *adj* immergrün ‖ *s* Immergrün *n*

ev'erlast'ing *adj* ewig; (*continual*) fortwährend; (iron) ewig

ev'ermore' *adv* immer; **for e.** in Ewigkeit

every ['evri] *adj* jeder; (*confidence*) voll; **e. bit** (coll) völlig; **e. now and then** ab und zu; **e. once in a while** dann und wann; **e. other day** alle zwei Tage; **e. time (that)** jedesmal (wenn)

ev'erybod'y *indef pron* jeder, jedermann

ev'eryday' *adj* alltäglich, Alltags–

ev'eryone', ev'ery one' *indef pron* (**of**) jeder (von); **e. else** alle anderen

ev'erything' *indef pron* alles

ev'erywhere' *adv* (*position*) überall; (*direction*) überallhin

evict [ɪ'vɪkt] *tr* delogieren

eviction [ɪ'vɪkʃən] *s* Delogierung *f*

evidence ['evidəns] *s* Beweismaterial *n,* Beweis pl; (*piece of evidence*) Beweis *m;* **as e.** of zum Beweis (*genit*); **for lack of e.** wegen Mangels an Beweisen; **give e.** aussagen; **in e.** sichtbar

evident ['evidənt] *adj* (*obvious*) offensichtlich; (*visible*) ersichtlich; **be e.** zutage treten

evidently ['evidəntli] *adv* offenbar

evil ['ivəl] *adj* übel, böse ‖ *s* Übel *n*

e'vildo'er *s* Übeltäter –in *mf*

e'vildo'ing *s* Missetat *f*

e'vil eye' *s* böser Blick *m*

e'vil-mind'ed *adj* übelgesinnt

E'vil One' *s* Böse *m*

evince [ɪ'vɪns] *tr* bekunden

evoke [ɪ'vok] *tr* hervorrufen

evolution [,evə'luʃən] *s* Evolution *f*

evolve [ɪ'valv] *tr* entwickeln, entfalten ‖ *intr* sich entwickeln, sich entfalten

ewe [ju] *s* Mutterschaf *n*

ewer ['ju-ər] *s* Wasserkanne *f*

exact [eg'zækt] *adj* genau ‖ *tr* (*e.g., money*) beitreiben; (*obedience*) erzwingen

exact'ing *adj* (*strict*) streng; (*task*) aufreibend; (*picky*) anspruchsvoll

exactly [eg'zæktli] *adv* genau

exactness [eg'zæktnɪs] *s* Genauigkeit *f*

exact' sci'ences *spl* Realien pl

exaggerate [eg'zædʒə,ret] *tr* übertreiben

exaggeration [eg,zædʒə'reʃən] *s* Übertreibung *f*

exalt [eg'zɔlt] *tr* erheben

exam [eg'zæm] *s* (coll) Prüfung *f*

examination [eg,zæmɪ'neʃən] *s* Prüfung *f,* Examen *n;* (jur) Verhör *n,* Vernehmung *f;* (med) Untersuchung *f;* **direct e.** (jur) direkte Befragung *f;* **fail an e.** bei e–r Prüfung durchfallen; **on closer e.** bei näherer Prüfung; **pass an e.** e–e Prüfung bestehen; **take an e.** e–e Prüfung ablegen

examine [eg'zæmɪn] *tr* prüfen; (jur) verhören, vernehmen; (med) untersuchen

examinee [eg,zæmɪ'ni] *s* Prüfling *m*

examiner [eg'zæmɪnər] *s* (educ) Prüfer –in *mf;* (med) Untersucher –in *mf*

example [eg'zæmpəl] *s* Beispiel *n;* **for e.** zum Beispiel; **make an e. of** ein Exempel statuieren an (*dat*); **set a good e.** mit gutem Beispiel vorangehen

exasperate [eg'zæspə,ret] *tr* reizen

excavate ['ekskə,vet] *tr* ausgraben

excavation [,ekskə've ʃən] *s* Ausgrabung *f*

excavator ['ekskə,vetər] *s* (archeol) Ausgräber –in *mf;* (mach) Trockenbagger *m*

exceed [ek'sid] *tr* überschreiten

exceedingly [ek'sidɪŋli] *adv* außerordentlich

ex-cel [ek'sel] *v* (*pret & pp* –**celled;** *ger* –**celling**) *tr* übertreffen ‖ *intr* (**in**) sich auszeichnen (in *dat*)

excellence ['eksələns] *s* Vorzüglichkeit *f*

excellency ['eksələnsi] *s* Vorzüglichkeit *f;* **Your Excellency** Eure Exzellenz

excellent ['eksələnt] *adj* ausgezeichnet

excelsior [ek'selsɪ-ər] *s* Holzwolle *f*

except [ek'sept] *adv–* **e. for** abgesehen von; **e. if** außer wenn; **e. that** außer daß; **e. when** außer wenn ‖ *prep* außer (*dat*), ausgenommen (*acc*) ‖ *tr* ausnehmen, ausschließen

exception [ek'sepʃən] *s* Ausnahme *f;* **by way of e.** ausnahmsweise; **take e. to** Anstoß nehmen an (*dat*); **without e.** ausnahmslos; **with the e. of** mit Ausnahme von

exceptional [ek'sepʃənəl] *adj* außergewöhnlich, Sonder–

excerpt ['eksʌrpt] *s* Auszug *m* ‖ [ek-'sʌrpt] *tr* exzerpieren

excess ['ekses], [ek'ses] *adj* überschüssig ‖ [ek'ses] *s* (*surplus*) Überschuß *m;* (*immoderate amount*) (**of**) Übermaß *n* (von or an *dat*); **carry to e.** übertreiben; **excesses** Ausschreitungen pl; **in e. of** mehr als; **to e.** übermäßig

ex'cess bag'gage *s* Überfracht *f*

excessive [ek'sesɪv] *adj* übermäßig

ex'cess-prof'its tax' *s* Mehrgewinnsteuer *f*

exchange [eks'tʃendʒ] *s* Austausch *m;* (*e.g., of purchases*) Umtausch *m;* (*of words*) Wechselgespräch *n;* (*of* *money)* Geldwechsel *m;* (fin) Börse *f;* (mil) Kantine *f;* (telp) Vermittlung *f;* **e. of letters** Briefwechsel *m;* **in e.** dafür; **in e. for** für ‖ *tr (trade)* tauschen; *(replace)* auswechseln; **e. for** umtauschen gegen; **e. places with** s.o. mit j-m tauschen

exchequer [eks'tʃekər] *s* Staatskasse *f; (department)* Schatzamt *n*

ex'cise tax' ['eksaɪz] *s* Verbrauchssteuer *f*

excitable [ek'saɪtəbəl] *adj* erregbar

excite [ek'saɪt] *tr* erregen, aufregen

excitement [ek'saɪtmənt] *s* Erregung *f,* Aufregung *f*

excit'ing *adj* erregend, aufregend

exclaim [eks'klem] *tr & intr* ausrufen

exclamation [ˌeksklə'meʃən] *s* Ausruf *m*

exclama'tion point' *s* Ausrufungszeichen *n*

exclude [eks'klud] *tr* ausschließen

exclusion [eks'kluʒən] *s* Ausschließung *f,* Ausschluß *m;* **to the e. of** unter Ausschluß *(genit)*

exclusive [eks'klusɪv] *adj (rights, etc.)* alleinig, ausschließlich; *(club)* exklusiv; *(shop)* teuer; **e. of** ausschließlich *(genit)*

excommunicate [ˌekskə'mjunɪˌket] *tr* exkommunizieren

excommunication [ˌekskəˌmjunɪ'keʃən] *s* Exkommunikation *f,* Kirchenbann *m*

excoriate [eks'korɪˌet] *tr* (fig) heruntermachen

excrement ['ekskrəmənt] *s* Exkremente *pl*

excrescence [eks'kresəns] *s* Auswuchs *m*

excruciating [eks'kruʃɪˌetɪŋ] *adj* qualvoll

exculpate ['ekskʌlˌpet] *tr* entschuldigen

excursion [eks'kʌrʒən] *s (side trip)* Abstecher *m; (short trip)* Ausflug *m*

excusable [eks'kjuzəbəl] *adj* entschuldbar, verzeihlich

excuse [eks'kjus] *s* Ausrede *f;* **give as an e.** vorgeben; **make excuses** sich ausreden ‖ [eks'kjuz] *tr* entschuldigen; **e. me!** entschuldigen Sie!; **you may be excused now** Sie können jetzt gehen

execute ['eksɪˌkjut] *tr (a condemned man)* hinrichten; *(by firing squad)* erschießen; *(perform)* durchführen, vollziehen; *(a will, a sentence)* vollstrecken; (mus) vortragen

execution [ˌeksɪ'kjuʃən] *s* Hinrichtung *f; (by firing squad)* Erschießung *f; (performance)* Durchführung *f,* Vollziehung *f;* (mus) Vortrag *m*

executioner [ˌeksɪ'kjuʃənər] *s* Scharfrichter *m*

executive [eg'zekjətɪv] *adj* vollziehend, exekutiv ‖ *s* (com) Manager *m,* leitender Angestellte *mf;* **the Executive** *(pol)* die Exekutive *f*

exec'utive commit'tee *s* Vollzugsausschuß *m,* Vorstand *m*

exec'utive or'der *s* Durchführungsverordnung *f*

executor [eg'zekjətər] *s* Vollstrecker *m*

executrix [eg'zekjətrɪks] *s* Vollstreckerin *f*

exemplary [eg'zempləri] *adj* vorbildlich, mustergültig

exempli·fy [eg'zemplɪˌfaɪ] *v (pret & pp* **–fied)** *tr (demonstrate)* an Beispielen erläutern; *(embody)* als Beispiel dienen für

exempt [eg'zempt] *adj (from)* befreit (von) ‖ *tr* befreien; (mil) freistellen

exemption [eg'zempʃən] *s* Befreiung *f;* (mil) Freistellung *f*

exercise ['eksər ˌsaɪz] *s* Übung *f; (of the body)* Bewegung *f; (of power)* Ausübung *f;* (mil) Exerzieren *n;* **take e.** sich *[dat]* Bewegung machen ‖ *tr* üben; *(the body, a horse)* bewegen; *(power, influence)* ausüben; (mil) exerzieren ‖ *intr* üben; (mil) exerzieren

exert [eg'zɜrt] *tr* ausüben; **e. every effort** alle Kräfte rühren; **e. oneself** sich anstrengen

exertion [eg'zʌrʃən] *s* Anstrengung *f; (e.g., of power)* Ausübung *f*

exhalation [ˌeks·hə'leʃən] *s* Ausatmung *f; (of gases)* Gasabgabe *f*

exhale [eks'hel] *tr & intr* ausatmen

exhaust [eg'zɔst] *s* (aut) Auspuff *m* ‖ *tr* erschöpfen

exhaust'ed *adj* erschöpft

exhaust' fan' *s* Absaugventilator *m*

exhaust' gas' *s* Abgas *m*

exhaust'ing *adj* anstrengend, mühselig

exhaustion [eg'zɔstʃən] *s* Erschöpfung *f*

exhaustive [eg'zɔstɪv] *adj* erschöpfend

exhaust' pipe' *s* Auspuffrohr *n*

exhaust' valve' *s* Auspuffventil *n*

exhibit [eg'zɪbɪt] *s (exhibition)* Ausstellung *f; (object exhibited)* Ausstellungsstück *n;* (jur) Beleg *m* ‖ *tr* zur Schau stellen; *(wares)* ausstellen; *(e.g., courage)* zeigen

exhibition [ˌeksɪ'bɪʃən] *s* Ausstellung *f*

exhilarating [eg'zɪlə ˌretɪŋ] *adj* erheiternd

exhort [eg'zɔrt] *tr* ermahnen

exhume [eks'hjum] *tr* exhumieren

exigency ['eksɪdʒənsi] *s (demand, need)* Erfordnis *n; (state of urgency)* Dringlichkeit *f*

exigent ['eksɪdʒənt] *adj* dringlich

exile ['egzaɪl] *s* Exil *n; (person)* Verbannte *mf* ‖ *tr* verbannen

exist [eg'zɪst] *intr* existieren; *(continue to be)* bestehen; **e. from day to day** dahinleben

existence [eg'zɪstəns] *s* Existenz *f,* Dasein *n;* **be in e.** bestehen; **come into e.** entstehen

existential [ˌegzɪs'tenʃəl] *adj* existentiell

existentialism [ˌegzɪs'tenʃə ˌlɪzəm] *s* Existentialismus *m*

exit ['egzɪt] *s* Ausgang *m; (by car)* Ausfahrt *f;* (theat) Abgang *m* ‖ *intr* (theat) abtreten

exodus ['eksədəs] *s* Abwanderung *f*

exonerate [eg'zɑnə ˌret] *tr* entlasten

exorbitant [ɛg'zɔrbɪtənt] *adj* schwindelhaft; **e. price** Wucherpreis *m*

exorcise ['ɛksɔr‚saɪz] *tr* exorzieren

exotic [ɛg'zɑtɪk] *adj* exotisch

expand [ɛks'pænd] *tr* (aus)dehnen; *(enlarge)* erweitern; *(math)* entwickeln ‖ *intr* sich ausdehnen

expanse [ɛks'pæns] *s* Weite *f*, Fläche *f*

expansion [ɛks'pænʃən] *s* Ausdehnung *f*; *(expanded part)* Erweiterung *f*

expansive [ɛks'pænsɪv] *adj* expansiv; (fig) mitteilsam

expatiate [ɛks'peʃɪ‚et] *intr* (on) sich verbreiten (über *acc*)

expatriate [ɛks'petrɪ‚ɪt] *adj* ausgebürgert ‖ *s* Ausgebürgerte *mf* ‖ [ɛks'petrɪ‚et] *tr* ausbürgern

expect [ɛks'pɛkt] *tr* erwarten ‖ *intr*—**she's expecting** (coll) sie ist in anderen Umständen

expectancy [ɛks'pɛktənsɪ] *s* Ewartung *f*

expectant [ɛks'pɛktənt] *adj* erwartungsvoll; *(mother)* werdende

expectation [‚ɛkspɛk'teʃən] *s* Erwartung *f*

expectorate [ɛks'pɛktə‚ret] *tr & intr* spucken

expediency [ɛks'pidɪ‚ənsɪ] *s* Zweckmäßigkeit *f*

expedient [ɛks'pidɪ‚ənt] *adj* zweckmäßig ‖ *s* Mittel *n*, Hilfsmittel *f*

expedite ['ɛkspɪ‚daɪt] *tr* beschleunigen; *(a document)* ausstellen

expedition [‚ɛkspɪ'dɪʃən] *s* Expedition *f*

expedi'tionary force' [‚ɛkspɪ'dɪʃə‚nerɪ] *s* (mil) Expeditionsstreitkräfte *pl*

expeditious [‚ɛkspɪ'dɪʃəs] *adj* schleunig

ex·pel [ɛks'pɛl] *v* *(pret & pp* **-pelled;** *ger* **-pelling)** *tr* (aus)treiben; *(a student)* (from) verweisen (von)

expend [ɛks'pɛnd] *tr* *(time, effort, etc.)* aufwenden; *(money)* ausgeben

expendable [ɛks'pɛndəbəl] *adj* entbehrlich

expenditure [ɛks'pɛndɪtʃər] *s* Aufwand *m*; *(of money)* Ausgabe *f*

expense [ɛks'pɛns] *s* Ausgabe *f*; **at s.o.'s e.** (& fig) auf j-s Kosten; **expenses** Unkosten *pl*; **go to great e.** sich in Unkosten stürzen

expense' account' *s* Spesenkonto *n*

expensive [ɛks'pɛnsɪv] *adj* kostspielig

experience [ɛks'pɪrɪ‚əns] *s* Erfahrung *f*; *(an event)* Erlebnis *n*; **no previous e. necessary** Vorkenntnisse nicht erforderlich ‖ *tr* erfahren; *(pain)* erdulden; *(loss)* erleiden

expe'rienced *adj* erfahren

experiment [ɛks'pɛrɪmənt] *s* Experiment *n*, Versuch *m* ‖ [ɛks'pɛrɪ‚mɛnt] *intr* experimentieren, Versuche anstellen

experimental [ɛks‚pɛrɪ'mɛntəl] *adj* experimentell, Versuchs-

expert ['ɛkspɔrt] *adj* fachmännisch, erfahren; **e. advice** Gutachten *n* ‖ *s* Fachmann *m;* (jur) Sachverständige *mf*

expertise [‚ɛkspɛr'tiz] *s* *(opinion)* Gutachten *n;* *(skill)* Sachkenntnis *f*

expiate ['ɛkspɪ‚et] *tr* sühnen, büßen

expiation [‚ɛkspɪ'eʃən] *s* Sühnung *f*

expiration [‚ɛkspɪ'reʃən] *s* Verfall *m*

expira'tion date' *s* Verfalltag *m*

expire [ɛks'paɪr] *tr* ausatmen ‖ *intr* verfallen; *(die)* verscheiden

explain [ɛks'plen] *tr* erklären, erläutern; *(justify)* rechtfertigen

explanation [‚ɛksplə'neʃən] *s* Erklärung *f*, Erläuterung *f*

explanatory [ɛks'plænə‚torɪ] *adj* erklärend, erläuternd

expletive [ɛks'plɪtɪv] *s* Füllwort *n*

explicit [ɛks'plɪsɪt] *adj* ausdrücklich

explode [ɛks'plod] *tr* explodieren lassen; *(a theory)* verwerfen ‖ *intr* explodieren; *(said of a grenade)* krepieren; *(with)* platzen (vor *dat*)

exploit ['ɛksplɔɪt] *s* Heldentat *f*, Großtat *f* ‖ [ɛks'plɔɪt] *tr* ausnutzen; *(pej)* ausbeuten; *(min)* abbauen

exploitation [‚ɛksplɔɪ'teʃən] *s* Ausnutzung *f*; *(pej)* Ausbeutung *f*; *(min)* Abbau *m*

exploration [‚ɛksplə'reʃən] *s* Erforschung *f*

explore [ɛks'plor] *tr* erforschen

explorer [ɛks'plorər] *s* Forscher –in *mf*

explosion [ɛks'ploʒən] *s* Explosion *f*

explosive [ɛks'plosɪv] *adj* explosiv, Spreng– ‖ *s* *(explosive substance)* Sprengstoff *m;* *(device)* Sprengkörper *m*

explo'sive charge' *s* Sprengladung *f*

exponent [ɛks'ponənt] *s* Exponent *m*

export ['ɛksport] *adj* Ausfuhr– ‖ *s* Ausfuhr *m*, Export *m;* **exports** Ausfuhrgüter *pl* ‖ [ɛks'port] *tr* ausführen

exportation [‚ɛkspor'teʃən] *s* Ausfuhr *m*

exporter ['ɛksportər], [ɛks'portər] *s* Ausfuhrhändler –in *mf*, Exporteur –in *mf*

expose [ɛks'poz] *tr* *(to danger, ridicule, sun)* aussetzen; *(bare)* entblößen; *(a person)* (as) bloßstellen (als), entlarven (als); *(phot)* belichten

exposition [‚ɛkspo'ze] *s* Enthüllung *f*

exposition [‚ɛkspo'zɪʃən] *s* Ausstellung *f;* (rhet) Exposition *f*

expostulate [ɛks'pɑstʃə‚let] *intr* protestieren; **e. with s.o. about** j–m ernste Vorhaltungen machen über *(acc)*

exposure [ɛks'poʒər] *s* *(of a child)* Aussetzung *f;* *(laying bare)* Entblößung *f;* *(unmasking)* Entlarvung *f;* *(of a building)* Lage *f;* (phot) Belichtung *f*

expo'sure me'ter *s* Belichtungsmesser *m*

expound [ɛks'paund] *tr* erklären

express [ɛks'prɛs] *adj* ausdrücklich ‖ *s* (rr) Expreß *m;* **by e.** als Eilgut *n* ‖ *tr* ausdrücken; *(feelings)* zeigen; **e. oneself** sich äußern

express' com'pany *s* Paketpostgesellschaft *f*

expression [ɛks'prɛʃən] *s* Ausdruck *m*

expressive [eks'presɪv] *adj* ausdrucks-voll

express' train' *s* Expreßzug *m*

express' way' *s* Schnellverkehrsstraße *f*

expropriate [eks'proprɪ,et] *tr* enteignen

expulsion [eks'pʌlʃən] *s* Austreibung *f*; (*from school or a game*) Verweisung *f*

expunge [eks'pʌndʒ] *tr* ausstreichen

expurgate ['ekspər,get] *tr* säubern

exquisite ['ekskwɪzɪt], [eks'kwɪzɪt] *adj* exquisit, vorzüglich

ex-service-man [,eks'sʌrvɪs,mæn] *s* (**-men'**) ehemaliger Soldat *m*

extant ['ekstənt] *adj* noch bestehend

extemporaneous [eks,tempə'renɪ·əs] *adj* aus dem Stegreif, unvorbereitet

extempore [eks'tempərɪ] *adj* unvorbereitet ‖ *adv* aus dem Stegreif

extemporize [eks'tempə,raɪz] *tr & intr* extemporieren

extend [eks'tend] *tr* (*expand*) ausdehnen; (*a line*) fortführen; (*time*) verlängern; (*congratulations, invitation*) aussprechen; (*one's hand*) ausstrecken; (*a building*) ausbauen ‖ *intr* (**to**) sich erstrecken (bis); **e. beyond** hinausgehen über (*acc*)

extension [eks'tenʃən] *s* Ausdehnung *f*; (*of time, credit*) Verlängerung *f*; (*archit*) Anbau *m*; (*telp*) Nebenanschluß *m*

exten'sion cord' *s* Verlängerungsschnur *f*

exten'sion lad'der *s* Ausziehleiter *f*

exten'sion ta'ble *s* Ausziehtisch *m*

extensive [eks'tensɪv] *adj* umfassend

extent [eks'tent] *s* Umfang *m*, Ausmaß *n*; **to some e.** eingermaßen; **to the full e.** in vollem Umfang; **to what e.** inwiefern

extenuating [eks'tenju,etɪŋ] *adj* mildernd

exterior [eks'tɪrɪ·ər] *adj* Außen-, äußere ‖ *s* Äußere *n*

exterminate [eks'tʌrmɪ,net] *tr* vertilgen, ausrotten

extermination [eks,tʌrmɪ'neʃən] *s* Vertilgung *f*; (*of vermin*) Raumentwesung *f*

exterminator [eks'tʌrmɪ,netər] *s* Raumentweser *m*

external [eks'tʌrnəl] *adj* Außen-, äußerlich ‖ **externals** *spl* Äußerlichkeiten *pl*

extinct [eks'tɪŋkt] *adj* (*volcano*) erloschen; (*animal*) ausgestorben; **become e.** aussterben

extinguish [eks'tɪŋgwɪʃ] *tr* auslöschen; **be extinguished** erlöschen

extinguisher [eks'tɪŋgwɪʃər] *s* Löschgerät *n*

extirpate ['ekstər,pet] *tr* ausrotten

ex·tol [eks'tol] *v* (*pret & pp* **-tolled**; *ger* **-tolling**) *tr* erheben, lobpreisen

extort [eks'tort] *tr* erpressen

extortion [eks'torʃən] *s* Erpressung *f*

extortionate [eks'torʃənɪt] *adj* überhöht

extra ['ekstrə] *adj* übrig; (*special*) Sonder-, Extra-; **meals are e.** Mahlzeiten werden zusätzlich berechnet

‖ *adv* extra, besonders ‖ *s* (cin) Statist **–in** *mf*; (journ) Sonderausgabe *f*; (theat) Komparse *m*; **extras** (*expenses*) Nebenausgaben *pl*; (*accessories*) Zubehör *n*

extract ['ekstrækt] *s* Extrakt *m*, Auszug *m*; (*excerpt*) Ausschnitt *m* ‖ [eks'trækt] *tr* extrahieren, ausziehen; (dent, math) ziehen

extraction [eks'trækʃən] *s* (*lineage*) Abstammung *f*; (dent) Zahnziehen *n*; (min) Gewinnung *f*

extracurricular [,ekstrəkə'rɪkjələr] *adj* außerplanmäßig

extradite ['ekstrə,daɪt] *tr* ausliefern

extradition [,ekstrə'dɪʃən] *s* Auslieferung *f*

ex'tra in'come *s* Nebeneinkünfte *pl*

ex'tra·mar'ital *adj* außerehelich

extramural [,ekstrə'mjurəl] *adj* außerhalb der Schule stattfindend

extraneous [eks'trenɪ·əs] *adj* unwesentlich

extraordinary [,eks'trordɪ,nerɪ] *adj* außerordentlich

ex'tra pay' *s* Zulage *f*

extrapolate [eks'træpə,let] *tr & intr* extrapolieren

extrasensory [,ekstrə'sensərɪ] *adj* übersinnlich

extravagance [eks'trævəgəns] *s* Verschwendung *f*

extravagant [eks'trævəgənt] *adj* verschwenderisch, extravagant; (*idea, plan*) überspannt

extreme [eks'trim] *adj* äußerst; (*radical*) extrem; (*old age*) höchst; (*necessity*) dringend ‖ *s* Äußerste *n*; **at the other e.** am entgegengesetzten Ende; **carry to extremes** auf die Spitze treiben; **in the e.** äußerst

extremely [eks'trimlɪ] *adj* äußerst

extreme' unc'tion *s* letzte Ölung *f*

extremist [eks'trimɪst] *s* Extremist **–in** *mf*

extremity [eks'tremɪtɪ] *s* Äußerste *n*, äußerstes Ende *n*; **be reduced to extremities** aus dem letzten Loch pfeifen; **extremities** (*hands and feet*) Extremitäten *pl*

extricate ['ekstrɪ,ket] *tr* befreien

extrinsic [eks'trɪnsɪk] *adj* äußerlich

extrovert ['ekstrə,vʌrt] *s* Extravertierte *mf*

extrude [eks'trud] *tr* ausstoßen

exuberant [eg'z(j)ubərənt] *adj* (*luxuriant*) üppig; (*lavish*) überschwenglich

exude [eg'zud] *tr* ausschwitzen; (fig) ausstrahlen

exult [eg'zʌlt] *intr* jauchzen

exultant [eg'zʌltənt] *adj* jauchzend

eye [aɪ] *s* Auge *n*; (*of a needle*) Öhr *n*; **an eye for an eye** Auge um Auge; **be all eyes** große Augen machen; **by eye** nach dem Augenmaß; **close one's eyes to** die Augen schließen vor (*dat*); **have an eye for** Sinn haben für; **have good eyes** gut sehen; **in my eyes** nach meiner Ansicht; **in the eyes of the law** vom Standpunkt des Gesetzes aus; **keep a close eye on** s.o. j–m auf die Finger sehen; **keep an eye on s.th.** ein wachsames Auge auf etw [*acc*] haben; **keep one's eyes peeled** scharf aufpassen; **lay eyes on** zu Gesicht bekommen; **makes eyes at** verliebte Blicke zuwerfen (*dat*); **see eye to eye with** völlig übereinstimmen mit; **with an eye to** mit Rücksicht auf (*acc*) ‖ *v* (*pret & pp* eyed; *ger* eying & eyeing) *tr* mustern, schielen nach

eye'ball' *s* Augapfel *m*

eye'brow' *s* Augenbraue *f*

eye'brow pen'cil *s* Augenbrauenstift *m*

eye' cat'cher *s* Blickfang *m*

eye'cup' *s* Augenspülglas *n*

eye' drops' *spl* Augentropfen *pl*

eyeful ['aɪfʊl] *s*—**get an e.** etw Hübsches sehen

eye'glass' *s* Augenglas *n*; **eyeglasses** Brille *f*

eye'lash' *s* Wimper *f*

eyelet ['aɪlɪt] *s* Öse *f*

eye'lid' *s* Lid *n*, Augenlid *n*

eye'o'pener *s* (*surprise*) Überraschung *f*; (*liquor*) Schnäpschen *n*

eye'piece' *s* Okular *n*

eye'shade' *s* Augenschirm *m*

eye' shad'ow *s* Lidschatten *m*

eye'shot' *s*—**within e.** in Sehweite

eye'sight' *s* Augenlicht *n*, Sehkraft *f*; (*range*) Sehweite *f*; **have bad (or good) e.** schlechte (or gute) Augen haben

eye' sock'et *s* Augenhöhle *f*

eye'sore' *s* (fig) Dorn *m* im Auge

eye'strain' *s* Überanstrengung *f* der Augen

eye'tooth' *s* (–teeth) Augenzahn *m*; **cut one's eyeteeth** (fig) erfahrener werden

eye'wash' *s* Augenwasser *n*; (sl) Schwindel *m*

eye'wit'ness *s* Augenzeuge *m*, Augenzeugin *f*

F

F, f [ef] *s* sechster Buchstabe des englischen Alphabets; (mus) F *n*; **F flat** *n*; **F sharp** Fis *n*

fable ['febəl] *s* Fabel *f*, Märchen *n*

fabric ['fæbrɪk] *s* Gewebe *n*; (*cloth*) Stoff *m*; (fig) Gefüge *n*

fabricate ['fæbrɪ‚ket] *tr* herstellen; (*lies*) erfinden

fabrication [‚fæbrɪ'ke/ən] *s* Herstellung *f*; (fig) Erfindung *f*

fabulous ['fæbjələs] *adj* fabelhaft

façade [fə'sɑd] *s* Fassade *f*

face [fes] *s* Gesicht *n*; (*dial*) Zifferblatt *n*; (tex) rechte Seite *f*; (typ) Satzspiegel *m*; **f. to f. with** Auge in Auge mit; **in the f. of** angesichts (*genit*); **lose f.** sich blamieren; **make faces at s.o.** j–m Gesichter schneiden; **on the f. of it** augenscheinlich; **save f.** das Gesicht wahren; **show one's f.** sich blicken lassen ‖ *tr* (& fig) ins Auge sehen (*dat*); (*said of a building*) liegen nach; (e.g., with brick) verkleiden; **be faced with** stehen vor (*dat*); **facing** gegenüber (*dat*); **have to f. the music** die Suppe löffeln müssen ‖ *intr* (*in some direction*) liegen; **about f.!** (mil) kehrt!; **he faced up to it like a man** er stellte seinen Mann

face' card' *s* Bildkarte *f*, Figur *f*

face' cream' *s* Gesichtskrem *f*

face' lift'ing *s* Gesichtsstraffung *f*; (of a building) Schönheitsreparatur *f*

face' pow'der *s* Gesichtspuder *m*

facet ['fæsɪt] *s* Facette *f*; (fig) Aspekt *m*

facetious [fə'si/əs] *adj* scherzhaft

face' val'ue *s* Nennwert *m*; **take at f.** (fig) für bare Münze nehmen

facial ['fe/əl] *adj* Gesichts–; **f. expression** Miene *f* ‖ *s* Gesichtspflege *f*

facilitate [fə'sɪlɪ‚tet] *tr* erleichtern

facility [fə'sɪlɪti] *s* (*ease*) Leichtigkeit

f; (*skill*) Geschicklichkeit *f*; **facilities** Einrichtungen *pl*

fac'ing *s* (archit) Verkleidung *f*; (sew) Besatz *m*

facsimile [fæk'sɪmɪli] *s* Faksimile *n*

fact [fækt] *s* Tatsache *f*; **apart from the f. that** abgesehen davon, daß; **facts of the case** Tatbestand *m*; **in f.** tatsächlich; **it is a f. that** es steht fest, daß

fact'-find'ing *adj* Untersuchungs–

faction ['fæk/ən] *s* Clique *f*

factional ['fæk/ənəl] *adj* klüngelhaft

factor ['fæktər] *s* (& math) Faktor *m*

factory ['fæktəri] *s* Fabrik *f*

factual ['fækt/ʊ‚əl] *adj* sachlich

faculty ['fækəlti] *s* Vermögen *n*; (educ) Lehrkörper *m*

fad [fæd] *s* Mode *f*; **latest fad** letzter Schrei *m*

fade [fed] *tr* verblassen lassen; **f. in** einblenden; **f. out** ausblenden ‖ *intr* (*said of colors, memories*) verblassen; (*said of cloth, wallpaper, etc.*) verschießen; (*said of flowers*) verwelken; **f. away** (*said of sounds*) abklingen; **f. in** (cin, rad, telv) einblenden; **f. out** (cin, rad, telv) ausblenden

fade'-in' *s* (cin, rad, telv) Einblenden *n*

fade'-out' *s* (cin, rad, telv) Ausblenden *n*

fag [fæg] *s* (*cigarette*) (sl) Glimmstengel *m*; (*homosexual*) (sl) Schwuler *m* ‖ *v* (*pret & pp* fagged; *ger* fagging) *tr*—**fag out** (sl) auspumpen

fagged *adj* (sl) erschöpft

fagot ['fægət] *s* Reisigbündel *n*

fail [fel] *s*—**without f.** ganz bestimmt ‖ *tr* (*an examination*) durchfallen bei; (*a student*) durchfallen lassen; (*friends*) im Stich lassen; (*a father*) enttäuschen; **failing this** widrigenfalls; **I f. to see** ich kann nicht einsehen; **words f. me** mir fehlen die

Worte || *intr* (*said of a person or device*) versagen; (*said of a project, attempt*) fehlschlagen; (*said of crops*) schlecht ausfallen; (*said of strength*) abnehmen; (*said of health*) sich verschlechtern; (*com*) in Konkurs geraten

failure ['feljər] *s* Versagen *n;* (*person*) Versager –in *mf;* (*lack of success, unsuccessful venture*) Mißerfolg *m;* (*omission*) Versäumnis *n;* (*deterioration*) Schwäche *f;* (*educ*) ungenügende Zensur *f;* (*com*) Konkurs *m*

faint [fent] *adj* schwach; (*slight*) leise; **feel f.** sich schwach fühlen || *s* Ohnmacht *f* || *intr* ohnmächtig werden

faint'-heart'ed *adj* kleinmütig

faint'ing spell' *s* Ohnmachtsanfall *m*

fair [fer] *adj* (*just*) gerecht, fair; (*blond*) blond; (*complexion*) hell; (*weather*) heiter; (*chance, knowledge*) mittelmäßig; (*warning*) rechtzeitig; **f. to middling** gut bis mäßig || *s* Jahrmarkt *m*, Messe *f*

fair' game' *s* (& *fig*) Freiwild *n*

fair'ground' *s* Jahrmarktplatz *m*

fairly ['ferli] *adv* ziemlich

fair'-mind'ed *adj* unparteiisch

fairness ['fernɪs] *s* Gerechtigkeit *f;* **in f. to s.o.** um j–m Gerechtigkeit widerfahren zu lassen

fair' play' *s* fair Play *n*

fair' sex', the *s* das schöne Geschlecht

fair'way' *s* (*golf*) Spielbahn *f;* (*naut*) Fahrwasser *n*

fair'-weath'er *adj* (*friend*) unzuverlässig

fairy ['feri] *adj* Feen– || *s* Fee *f;* (*sl*) Schwule *mf*

fair'y god'mother *s* gute Fee *f*

fair'yland' *s* Märchenland *n*

fair'ytale' *s* (& *fig*) Märchen *n*

faith [feθ] *s* Glaube(n) *m;* (*in*) Vertrauen *n* (auf *acc* or zu); **on the f. of** im Vertrauen auf (*acc*); **put one's f. in** Glauben schenken (*dat*)

faithful ['feθfəl] *adj* (**to**) (ge)treu (*dat*); (*exact*) genau, wahrheitsgemäß || **the f.** *spl* die Gläubigen

faith' heal'er *s* Gesundbeter –in *mf*

faithless ['feθlɪs] *adj* treulos

fake [fek] *adj* verfälscht || *s* Fälschung *f;* (*person*) Simulant –in *mf* || *tr* vortäuschen, simulieren; (*forge*) fälschen

faker ['fekər] *s* Simulant –in *mf*

falcon ['fɔ(l)kən] *s* Falke *m*

falconer ['fɔ(l)kənər] *s* Falkner *m*

fall [fɔl] *adj* Herbst– || *s* Fall *m;* (*of prices, of a government*) Sturz *m;* (*moral*) Verfall *m;* (*of water*) Fall *m;* (*autumn*) Herbst *m;* (*Bib*) Sündenfall *m;* || *v* (*pret* **fell** [fel]; *pp* **fallen** ['fɔlən]) *intr* (*said of a person, object, rain, snow, holiday, prices, temperature*) fallen; (*said of a town*) gestürzt werden; **f. apart** auseinanderfallen; **f. away** wegfallen; **f. back** zurückfallen; (*mil*) sich zurückziehen; **f. back on** zurückgreifen auf (*acc*); **f. behind** (**in**) zurückbleiben (**mit**); **f. below** unterschreiten; **f. down** umfallen; (*said only of per*-

sons) hinfallen; **f. down on the job** versagen; **f. due** fällig werden; **f. flat** (*coll*) flachfallen; **f. for** reinfallen auf (*acc*); **f. from** abfallen von; **f. from grace** in Ungnade fallen; **f. in** (*said of a roof*) einstürzen; (*mil*) antreten; **f. in love with** sich verlieben in (*acc*); **f. in step** Tritt fassen; **f. into** (*e.g., a hole*) hereinfallen in (*acc*); (*e.g., trouble*) geraten in (*acc*); **f. into ruin** zerfallen; **f. in with s.o.** j–n zufällig treffen; **f. off** abfallen; (*com*) zurückgehen; **f. out** (*said of hair*) ausfallen; **f. out with s.o.** sich verfeinden mit; **f. over** umfallen; **f. short** knapp werden; (*arti*) kurz gehen; **f. short of** zurückbleiben hinter (*dat*); **f. through** durchfallen; **f. to s.o.'s share** j–m zufallen; **f. under s.o.'s influence** unter j–s Einfluß geraten; **f. upon** herfallen über (*acc*)

fallacious [fə'leʃəs] *adj* trügerisch

fallacy ['fæləsi] *s* Trugschluß *m*, Fehlschluß *m*

fall' guy' *s* (*sl*) Sündenbock *m*

fallible ['fælɪbəl] *adj* fehlbar

fall'ing off' *s* Rückschritt *m*

fall'ing rocks' *spl* (*public sign*) Steinschlag *m*

fall'ing star' *s* Sternschnuppe *f*

fall'out' *s* radioaktiver Niederschlag *m*

fallow ['fælo] *adj* (*agr*) brach; **lie f.** (& *fig*) brachliegen

false [fɔls] *adj* falsch, Miß–; (*start, step*) Fehl–; (*bottom*) doppelt; (*ceiling*) Zwischen–

false' alarm' *s* blinder Alarm *m;* (*fig*) Schreckschuß *m*

false' face' *s* Maske *f*

false' front' *s* (*fig*) (*coll*) Mache *f*

false'-heart'ed *adj* treulos

false'hood' *s* Unwahrheit *f*

false' pretens'es *spl* Hochstapelei *f*

false' teeth' *spl* (künstliches) Gebiß *n*

falset·to [fɔl'seto] *s* (–*tos*) Falset *n*

falsi·fy ['fɔlsɪ,faɪ] *v* (*pret & pp* **–fied**) *tr* (ver)fälschen

falsity ['fɔlsɪti] *s* Falschheit *f*

falter ['fɔltər] *intr* schwanken; (*in speech*) stocken

fame [fem] *s* Ruf, *m,* Ruhm *m*

famed *adj* (**for**) berühmt (wegen, durch)

familiar [fə'mɪljər] *adj* bekannt; (*expression*) geläufig; (*e.g., sight*) gewohnt; (*close*) vertraut; **become f. with** sich bekannt machen mit

familiarity [fə,mɪlɪ'erɪti] *s* Vertrautheit *f;* (*closeness*) Vertraulichkeit *f*

familiarize [fə'mɪljə,raɪz] *tr* bekannt machen

family ['fæm(ɪ)li] *adj* Familien–; **in a f. way** in anderen Umständen || *s* Familie *f*

fam'ily doc'tor *s* Hausarzt *m*

fam'ily man' *s* häuslicher Mann *m*

fam'ily name' *s* Familienname *m*

fam'ily tree' *s* Stammbaum *m*

famine ['fæmɪn] *s* Hungersnot *f*

famish ['fæmɪʃ] *tr* (ver)hungern lassen || *intr* verhungern

fam'ished *adj* ausgehungert

famous ['feməs] *adj* (**for**) berühmt (wegen, durch)

fan [fæn] *s* Fächer *m*, Wedel *m*; (*electric*) Ventilator *m*; (*sl*) Fan *m* ‖ *v* (*pret & pp* **fanned**; *ger* **fanning**) *tr* fächeln; (*a fire*) anfachen; (*passions*) entfachen ‖ *intr*—**fan out** (*said of roads*) fächerförmig auseinandergehen; (*mil*) ausschwärmen

fanatic [fə'nætɪk] *adj* fanatisch ‖ *s* Fanatiker –in *mf*

fanatical [fə'nætɪkəl] *adj* fanatisch

fanaticism [fə'nætɪ͵sɪzəm] *s* Fanatismus *m*

fan′ belt′ *s* (aut) Keilriemen *m*

fan′cied *adj* eingebildet

fancier ['fænsɪ·ər] *s* Liebhaber –in *mf*

fanciful ['fænsɪfəl] *adj* phantastisch

fan·cy ['fænsi] *adj* (*extra*)fein; (*e.g., dress*) Luxus–; (*sport*) Kunst–; **f. price** Phantasiepreis *m* ‖ *s* Phantasie *f*; **passing f.** vorübergehender Spleen *m*; **take a f. to** Gefallen finden an (*dat*) ‖ *v* (*pret & pp* **–cied**) *tr* sich [*dat*] vorstellen

fan′cy foods′ *spl* Feinkost *f*

fan′cy-free′ *adj* ungebunden

fan′fare′ *s* Fanfare *f*; (*fuss*) Tamtam *n*

fang [fæŋ] *s* Fangzahn *m*; (*of a snake*) Giftzahn *m*

fan′ mail′ *s* Verehrerbriefe *pl*

fantastic(al) [fæn'tæstɪk(əl)] *adj* phantastisch, toll

fantasy ['fæntəsi] *s* Phantasie *f*

far [far] *adj* (& fig) weit; **at the far end** am anderen Ende; **far cry from** etw ganz anderes als; **far side** andere Seite *f*; **in the far future** in der fernen Zukunft ‖ *adv* weit; **as far as** soweit; (*up to*) bis zu, bis an (*acc*); **as far as I am concerned** was mich anbelangt; **as far as I know** soviel ich weiß; **as far as that goes** was das betrifft; **by far** weitaus, bei weitem; **far and away** weitaus; **far away** weit entfernt; **far below** tief unten; **far better** weit besser; **far from it!** weit gefehlt!; **far from ready** noch lange nicht fertig; **far into the night** tief in die Nacht hinein; **far out** (sl) ausgefallen; **from far** von weitem; (*from a distant place*) von weit her; **go far** es weit bringen; **go far towards** (*ger*) viel beitragen zu (*inf*); **go too far** das Maß überschreiten; **not far from** unweit von; **so far** soweit, bisher

far′away′ *adj* weit entfernt; (fig) träumerisch

farce [fars] *s* Possenspiel *n*, Farce *f*; (fig) Posse *f*, Schwank *m*

farcical ['farsɪkəl] *adj* possenhaft

fare [fer] *s* (*travel price*) Fahrpreis *m*; (*money for travel*) Fahrgeld *n*; (*passenger*) Fahrgast *m*; (*food*) Kost *f* ‖ *intr* (er)gehen; **how did you f., well or ill?** wie ist es Ihnen ergangen, gut oder schlecht?

Far′ East′, the *s* der Ferne Osten

Far′ East′ern *adj* fernöstlich

fare′well′ *s* Valet *n*, Lebewohl *n*; **bid s.o. f.** j–m Lebewohl sagen ‖ *interj* lebe wohl!; lebt wohl!

farewell′ din′ner *s* Abschiedsschmaus *m*

farewell′ par′ty *s* Abschiedsfeier *f*

far-fetched ['far'fet/t] *adj* gesucht

far-flung ['far'flʌŋ] *adj* weit ausgedehnt

farina [fə'rinə] *s* Grießmehl *n*

farm [farm] *adj* landwirtschaftlich ‖ *s* Farm *f*, Bauernhof *m* ‖ *tr* bebauen, bewirtschaften ‖ *intr* Landwirtschaft betreiben, Bauer sein

farm′ hand′ *s* Landarbeiter *m*

farm′house′ *s* Bauernhaus *n*

farm′ing *adj* landwirtschaftlich ‖ *s* Landwirtschaft *f*

farm′land′ *s* Ackerland *n*

farm′ machin′ery *s* Landmaschinen *pl*

farm′-off′ *adj* fernliegend

farm′yard′ *s* Bauernhof *m*

far′-reach′ing *adj* weitreichend; (*decision*) folgenschwer

far′-sight′ed *adj* weitsichtig; (fig) weitblickend

farther ['farðər] *adj & adv* weiter

farthest ['farðɪst] *adj* weiteste ‖ *adv* am weitesten

farthing ['farðɪŋ] *s*—**not worth a f.** keinen Pfifferling wert

fascinate ['fæsɪ͵net] *tr* faszinieren

fas′cinating *adj* faszinierend

fascination [͵fæsɪ'neʃən] *s* Faszination *f*

fascism ['fæʃɪzəm] *s* Faschismus *m*

fascist ['fæʃɪst] *s* Faschist –in *mf*

fashion ['fæʃən] *s* Mode *f*; (*manner*) Art *f*, Weise *f*; **after a f.** in gewisser Weise; **in f.** in Mode; **out of f.** aus der Mode ‖ *tr* gestalten, bilden

fashionable ['fæʃənəbəl] *adj* (*modern*) modisch; (*elegant*) elegant

fash′ion magazine′ *s* Modenzeitschrift *f*

fash′ion plate′ *s* Modedame *f*

fash′ion show′ *s* Mode(n)schau *f*

fast [fæst] *adj* schnell; (*dye*) dauerhaft; (*company*) flott; (*life*) locker; (phot) lichtstark; **be f.** (*said of a clock*) vorgehen; **f. train** Schnellzug *m*; **pull a f. one on s.o.** (coll) j–m ein Schnippchen schlagen ‖ *adv* schnell; (*firmly*) fest; **as f. as possible** schnellstens; **be f. asleep** im tiefen Schlaf liegen; **hold f.** festhalten; **not so f.!** nicht so stürmisch! ‖ *s* Fasten *n* ‖ *intr* fasten

fast′ day′ *s* Fasttag *m*

fasten ['fæsən] *tr* festmachen, sichern; (*a buckle*) schnallen; (**to**) befestigen (an *dat*); **f. one's seat belt** sich anschnallen; **f. the blame on** die Schuld zuschieben (*dat*) ‖ *intr*—**f. upon** sich heften an (*acc*)

fastener ['fæsənər] *s* Verschluß *m*

fastidious [fæs'tɪdɪ·əs] *adj* wählerisch

fast′ing *s* Fasten *n*

fat [fæt] *adj* (*fatter*; *fattest*) fett; (*plump*) dick, fett; (*profits*) reich ‖ *s* Fett *n*; **chew the fat** (sl) schwatzen

fatal ['fetəl] *adj* tödlich; (*mistake*) verhängnisvoll; **f. to** verhängnisvoll für

fatalism ['fetə͵lɪzəm] *s* Fatalismus *m*

fatalist ['fetəlɪst] *s* Fatalist –in *mf*

fatality [fə'tælɪtɪ] s Todesfall m; (accident victim) Todesopfer n; (disaster) Unglück n

fat' cat' s (sl) Geldgeber –in mf

fate [fet] s Schicksal n, Verhängnis n; **the Fates** die Parzen pl

fated ['fetɪd] adj vom Schicksal bestimmt

fateful ['fetfəl] adj verhängnisvoll

fat'head' s (coll) dummes Luder n

father ['fɑðər] s Vater m; (eccl) Pater m || tr (beget) erzeugen; (originate) hervorbringen

fa'therhood' s Vaterschaft f

fa'ther-in-law' s (fathers-in-law) Schwiegervater m

fa'therland' s Vaterland n

fatherless ['fɑðərlɪs] adj vaterlos

fatherly ['fɑðərlɪ] adj väterlich

Fa'ther's Day' s Vatertag m

fathom ['fæðəm] s Klafter f || tr sondieren; (fig) ergründen

fathomless ['fæðəmlɪs] adj unergründlich

fatigue [fə'tig] s Ermattung f; (mil) Arbeitsdienst m; **fatigues** (mil) Arbeitsanzug m || tr abmatten

fat·so ['fætso] s (-sos & -soes) (coll) Fettkloß m

fatten ['fætən] tr mästen || intr—f. up (coll) sich mästen

fatty ['fætɪ] adj fettig, fett; **f. tissue** Fettgewebe n || s (coll) Dicke mf

fatuous ['fæt/ʊ·əs] adj albern

faucet ['fɔsɪt] s Wasserhahn m

fault [fɔlt] s (blame) Schuld f; (misdeed) Vergehen n, Fehler m; (defect) Defekt m; (geol) Verwerfung f; (tennis) Fehlball m; **at f.** schuld; **find f. with** etw zu tadeln finden an (dat); **to a f.** allzusehr || intr (geol) sich verwerfen

fault'find'er s Krittler –in mf

fault'find'ing adj tadelsüchtig || s Krittelei f

faultless ['fɔltlɪs] adj fehlerfrei

faulty ['fɔltɪ] adj fehlerhaft

faun [fɔn] s (myth) Faun m

fauna ['fɔnə] s Fauna f

favor ['fevər] s (kind act) Gefallen m; (good will) Gunst f; **in f. of** zugunsten (genit), für; **in s.o.'s f.** zu j-s Gunsten; **lose f. with** s.o. sich (dat) j-s Gunst verwirken; **speak in f. of s.th.** für etw aussprechen || tr begünstigen; (prefer) bevorzugen; (a sore limb) schonen

favorable ['fevərəbəl] adj günstig; (criticism) positiv; (report) beifällig

favorite ['fevərɪt] adj Lieblings– || s Liebling m; (sport) Favorit –in mf

favoritism ['fevərɪ‚tɪzəm] s Günstlingswirtschaft f

fawn [fɔn] s Rehkalb n || intr—f. on schmeicheln (dat)

fawn'ing adj schmeichlerisch

faze [fez] tr (coll) auf die Palme bringen

FBI [‚ɛf‚bi'aɪ] s (Federal Bureau of Investigation) Bundessicherheitspolizei f

fear [fɪr] s (of) Furcht f (vor dat), Angst f (vor dat); **for f. of** aus Angst

vor (dat); **for f. of** (ger) um nicht zu (inf); **stand in f. of** sich fürchten vor (dat) || tr fürchten, sich fürchten vor (dat); **f. the worst** das Schlimmste befürchten || intr sich fürchten; **f. for** besorgt sein um

fearful ['fɪrfəl] adj (afraid) furchtsam; (terrible) furchtbar

fearless ['fɪrlɪs] adj furchtlos

feasible ['fizɪbəl] adj durchführbar

feast [fist] s Fest n; (sumptuous meal) Schmaus m || tr—f. one's eyes on seine Augen weiden an (dat) || intr schwelgen; **f. on** sich gütlich tun an (dat)

feast'day' s Festtag m

feast'ing s Schmauserei f

feat [fit] s Kunststück n; **f. of arms** Waffentat f

feather ['fɛðər] s Feder f; **a f. in his cap** ein Triumph für ihn || tr mit Federn versehen; (aer) auf Segelstellung fahren; (crew) flach drehen; **f. one's nest** sich warm betten

feath'er bed' s Federbett n

feath'erbed'ding s Anstellung f unnötiger Arbeitskräfte

feath'erbrain' s Schwachkopf m

feath'er dust'er s Staubwedel m

feath'eredge' s feine Kante f

feath'erweight' adj Federgewichts– || s (boxer) Federgewichtler m

feathery ['fɛðərɪ] adj federartig; (light as feathers) federleicht

feature ['fit/ər] s (of the face) Gesichtszug m; (characteristic) Merkmal n; **f. film** Spielfilm m; **main f.** Grundzug m; (cin) Hauptfilm m || tr als Hauptschlager herausbringen; (cin) in der Hauptrolle zeigen

fea'ture writ'er s Sonderberichterstatter –in mf

February ['febru‚ɛri] s Februar m

feces ['fisiz] spl Kot m, Stuhl m

feckless ['fɛklɪs] adj (incompetent) unfähig; (ineffective) unwirksam; (without spirit) geistlos

fecund ['fikənd] adj fruchtbar

federal ['fedərəl] adj Bundes–, bundesstaatlich; **f. government** Bundesregierung f

federate ['fedə‚ret] adj verbündet || tr zu e-m Bund vereinigen || intr sich verbünden

federation [‚fedə'refən] s Staatenbund m

fed' up' [fed] adj—be f. die Nase voll haben; **be f. with** s.th. etw satt haben

fee [fi] s Gebühr f; (of a doctor) Honorar n

feeble ['fibəl] adj schwächlich

fee'ble-mind'ed adj schwachsinnig

feed [fid] s Futter n; (mach) Zuführung f || v (pret & pp fed [fed]) tr (animals) füttern; (persons) zu Essen geben; (in a restaurant) verpflegen; (e.g., a nation) nähren; (a fire) unterhalten; (mach) zuführen || intr fressen; **f. on** sich ernähren von

feed'back' s Rückwirkung f; (electron) Rückkoppelung f

feed' bag' s Futtersack m; **put on the f.** (sl) futtern

feeder ['fidər] s (elec) Speiseleitung f; (mach) Zubringer m

feed'er line' s (aer, rr) Zubringerlinie f

feed'ing s (of animals) Fütterung f; (& mach) Speisung f

feed' trough' s Futtertrog m

feed' wire' s (elec) Zuleitungsdraht m

feel [fil] s Gefühl n; **get the f. of** sich gewöhnen an (acc) || v (pret & pp **felt** [fɛlt]) tr fühlen; (a pain) spüren; **f. one's way** sich vortasten; (fig) sondieren; **f. s.o. out** bei j-m vorfühlen || intr (sick, tired, well) sich fühlen; **f. about for** herumtasten nach; **f. for s.o.** mit j-m fühlen; **f. like** (ger) Lust haben zu (inf); **f. up to** sich gewachsen fühlen (dat); **his head feels hot** sein Kopf fühlt sich heiß an; **how do you f. about it?** was halten Sie davon?; **I don't quite f. myself** ich fühle mich nicht ganz wohl; **I f. as if** es ist mir, als wenn; **make itself felt** sich fühlbar machen

feeler ['filər] s (ent) Fühler m; **put out feelers to** vorfühlen bei

feel'ing s Gefühl n; **bad f.** Verstimmung f; **good f.** Wohlwollen n; **have a f. for** Sinn haben für; **have a f. that** das Gefühl haben, daß; **with f.** gefühlsvoll

feign [fen] tr vortäuschen; **f. death** sich totstellen

feint [fent] s Finte f, Scheinangriff m

feldspar ['fɛld,spɑr] s Feldspat m

feline ['filaɪn] adj katzenartig

fell [fɛl] adj grausam || tr fällen

fellow ['fɛlo] s (coll) Kerl m; (of a society) Mitglied n

fel'low be'ing s Mitmensch m

fel'low citizen s Mitbürger –in mf

fel'low coun'tryman s Landsmann m

fel'low crea'ture s Mitgeschöpf n

fel'lowman' s (–men') Mitmensch m

fel'low mem'ber s Mitglied n

fel'lowship' s Kameradschaft f; (educ) Stipendium n

fel'low stu'dent s Kommilitone m

fel'low trav'eler s Mitreisende mf; (pol) Mitläufer –in m

felon ['fɛlən] s Schwerverbrecher –in m

felony ['fɛləni] s Schwerverbrechen n

felt [fɛlt] adj Filz– || s Filz m

felt' pen' s Filzschreiber m, Faserstift m

female ['fimel] adj weiblich || s (of animals) Weibchen n; (pej) Weibsbild n

feminine ['fɛmɪnɪn] adj weiblich

feminism ['fɛmɪ,nɪzəm] s Feminismus m

fen [fɛn] s Bruch m & n

fence [fɛns] s Zaun m; (of stolen goods) Hehler m; **on the f.** (fig) unentschlossen || tr—f. in einzäunen; **f. off** abzäunen || intr (sport) fechten

fence' post' s Zaunpfahl m

fenc'ing s Fechten n

fend [fɛnd] tr—f. off abwehren || intr —f. for oneself für sich selbst sorgen

fender ['fɛndər] s (aut) Kotflügel m

fennel ['fɛnəl] s Fenchel m

ferment ['fʌrmənt] s Gärmittel n; (fig) Unruhe f || [fər'mɛnt] tr in Gärung bringen || intr gären

fermentation [,fʌrmən'teʃən] s Gärung f

fern [fʌrn] s Farn m

ferocious [fə'roʃəs] adj wild

ferocity [fə'rɑsɪti] s Wildheit f

ferret ['fɛrɪt] s Frettchen n || tr—f. out aufspüren

Fer'ris wheel' ['fɛrɪs] s Riesenrad n

ferrule ['fɛrul], ['fɛrəl] s Stockzwinge f, Zwinge f

fer·ry ['fɛri] s Fähre f || v (pret & pp –ried) tr übersetzen

fer'ryboat' s Fährboot n

fer'ry·man s (–men') Fährmann m

fertile ['fʌrtɪl] adj fruchtbar

fertility [fər'trlɪti] s Fruchtbarkeit f

fertilization [,fʌrtɪlɪ'zeʃən] s Befruchtung f; (of soil) Düngung f

fertilize ['fʌrtɪ,laɪz] tr (a field) düngen; (an egg) befruchten

fertilizer ['fʌrtɪ,laɪzər] s Kunstdünger m

fervent ['fʌrvənt] adj inbrünstig

fervid ['fʌrvɪd] adj brennend

fervor ['fʌrvər] s Inbrunst f

fester ['fɛstər] intr schwären, eitern; (fig) nagen

festival ['fɛstɪvəl] adj festlich, Fest– || s Fest n; (mus, theat) Festspiele pl

festive ['fɛstɪv] adj festlich

festivity [fɛs'tɪvɪti] s Feierlichkeit f

festoon [fɛs'tun] s Girlande f || tr mit Girlanden schmücken

fetch [fɛtʃ] tr holen, abholen

fetch'ing adj entzückend

fete [fet] s Fest n

fetid ['fɛtɪd], ['fitɪd] adj stinkend

fetish ['fɛtɪʃ], ['fitɪʃ] s Fetisch m

fetlock ['fɛtlɑk] s Köte f; (tuft of hair) Kötenzopf m

fetter ['fɛtər] s Fessel f || tr fesseln

fettle ['fɛtəl] s—in fine f. in Form

fetus ['fitəs] s Leibesfrucht f

feud [fjud] s Fehde f

feudal ['fjudəl] adj feudal

feudalism ['fjudə,lɪzəm] s Feudalismus m

fever ['fivər] s Fieber n

feverish ['fivərɪʃ] adj fieberig; **be f.** fiebern

few [fju] adj & pron wenige; **a few** ein paar

fiancé [,fi·ɑn'se] s Verlobte m

fiancée [,fi·ɑn'se] s Verlobte f

fias·co [fɪ'æsko] s (–cos & –coes) Fiasko n

fib [fɪb] s Flunkerei f || v (pret & pp **fibbed**; ger **fibbing**) intr flunkern

fibber ['fɪbər] s Flunkerer –in mf

fiber ['faɪbər] s Faser f

fibrous ['faɪbrəs] adj faserig

fickle ['fɪkəl] adj wankelmütig

fickleness ['fɪkəlnɪs] s Wankelmut m

fiction ['fɪkʃən] s Dichtung f, Romanliteratur f

fictional ['fɪkʃənəl] adj romanhaft

fic'tion writ'er s Romanschriftsteller –in mf

fictitious [fɪk'tɪʃəs] adj fingiert

fiddle ['fɪdəl] s Fiedel f, Geige f || tr fiedeln; **f. away** (time) vergeuden ||

intr fiedeln; **f. with** herumfingern an *(dat)*

fiddler ['fɪdlər] *s* Fiedler –in *mf*

fid'dlestick' *s* Fiedelbogen *m* ‖ **fiddlesticks** *interj* Quatsch!

fidelity [fɪ'delɪti] *s* Treue *f*

fidget ['fɪdʒɪt] *intr* zappeln; **f. with** nervös spielen mit

fidgety ['fɪdʒɪti] *adj* zappelig

fiduciary [fɪ'd(j)uʃɪ,eri] *adj* treuhänderisch; *(note)* ungedeckt ‖ *s* Treuhänder –in *mf*

fief [fif] *s* (hist) Lehen *n*

field [fild] *adj (artillery, jacket, hospital, kitchen)* Feld– ‖ *s* Feld *n; (under cultivation)* Acker *m; (contestants collectively)* Wettbewerbsteilnehmer *pl; (specialty)* Gebiet *n;* (aer) Flugplatz *m;* (elec) Feld *n; (of a motor)* (elec) Magnetfeld *n;* (sport) Spielfeld *n*

field' am'bulance *s* Sanitätskraftwagen *m*

field' day' *s* (fig) großer Tag *m*

fielder ['fildər] *s* Feldspieler *m*

field' ex'ercise *s* Truppenübung *f*

field' glass'es *spl* Feldstecher *m*

field' hock'ey *s* Rasenhockey *n*

field'mar'shal *s* Feldmarschall *m*

field' mouse' *s* Feldmaus *f*

field' of vi'sion *s* Blickfeld *n*

field' pack' *s* (mil) Tornister *m*

field' piece' *s* Feldgeschütz *n*

field' trip' *s* Studienfahrt *f*

field' work' *s* praktische Arbeit *f*

fiend [find] *s (devil)* Teufel *m; (wicked person)* Unhold *m; (addict)* Süchtige *mf*

fiendish ['findɪʃ] *adj* teuflisch

fierce [fɪrs] *adj* wild, wütend; *(vehement)* heftig; *(menacing)* drohend; *(heat)* glühend

fiery ['faɪri], *[-əri] adj* feurig

fife [faɪf] *s* Querpfeife *f*

fifteen ['fɪf'tin] *adj & pron* fünfzehn ‖ *s* Fünfzehn *f*

fifteenth ['fɪf'tinθ] *adj & pron* fünfzehnte ‖ *s (fraction)* Fünfzehntel *n;* **the f.** *(in dates or a series)* der Fünfzehnte

fifth [fɪfθ] *adj & pron* fünfte ‖ *s (fraction)* Fünftel *n;* **the f.** *(in dates or a series)* der Fünfte

fifth' col'umn *s* (pol) Fünfte Kolonne *f*

fiftieth ['fɪfti·ɪθ] *adj & pron* fünfzigste ‖ *s (fraction)* Fünfzigstel *n*

fifty ['fɪfti] *adj & pron* fünfzig ‖ *s* Fünfzig *f;* **the fifties** die fünfziger Jahre

fif'ty-fif'ty *adv* halbpart; **go f. with s.o.** mit j–m halbpart machen

fig [fɪg] *s* Feige *f;* (fig) Pfifferling *m*

fight [faɪt] *s* Kampf *m,* Gefecht *n; (quarrel)* Streit *m; (brawl)* Rauferei *f;* (box) Boxkampf *m;* **pick a f.** Zank suchen ‖ *tr* bekämpfen; *(a case)* durchkämpfen; **f. back** *(tears)* niederkämpfen; **f. it out** ausfechten; **f. one's way out** sich durchkämpfen ‖ *intr* kämpfen; *(quarrel)* streiten; *(brawl)* raufen

fighter ['faɪtər] *adj* (aer) Jagd– ‖ *s* Kämpfer –in *mf;* (aer) Jäger *m;* (box) Boxkämpfer *m*

fight'er pi'lot *s* Jagdflieger *m*

fight'ing *s* Schlägerei *f; (quarreling)* Streiten *n;* (mil) Kampfhandlungen *pl*

fig' leaf' *s* Feigenblatt *n*

figment ['fɪgmənt] *s*—**f. of the imagination** Hirngespinst *n*

fig' tree' *s* Feigenbaum *m*

figurative ['fɪgjərətɪv] *adj* bildlich; *(meaning)* übertragen

figure ['fɪgjər] *s* Figur *f; (personage)* Persönlichkeit *f; (number)* Zahl *f;* **be good at figures** ein guter Rechner sein; **cut a fine** *(or* **poor)** f. e–e gute *(or* schlechte) Figur abgeben; **run into three figures** in die Hunderte gehen ‖ *tr* (coll) glauben, meinen; **f. out** ausknobeln ‖ *intr*—**f. large** e–e große Rolle spielen; **f. on** rechnen mit

fig'urehead' *s* Strohmann *m;* (naut) Bugfigur *f;* **a mere f.** e–e bloße Nummer

fig'ure of speech' *s* Redewendung *f*

fig'ure skat'ing *s* Kunstlauf *m*

figurine [,fɪgjə'rin] *s* Figurine *f*

filament ['fɪləmənt] *s* Faser *f,* Faden *m;* (elec) Glühfaden *m*

filbert ['fɪlbərt] *s* Haselnuß *f*

filch [fɪltʃ] *tr* mausen

file [faɪl] *s (tool)* Feile *f; (record)* Akte *f;* (cards) Kartei *f;* (row) Reihe *f;* **put on f.** zu den Akten legen ‖ *tr (with a tool)* feilen; *(letters, etc.)* ablegen, abheften; *(a complaint)* erheben; *(a report)* erstatten; *(a claim)* anmelden; *(a petition)* einreichen; **f. suit** e–n Prozeß anstrengen ‖ *intr*—**f. for** sich bewerben um; **f. out in** Gänsemarsch herausmarschieren; **f. past** vorbeidefilieren (an *dat)*

file' cab'inet *s* Aktenschrank *m*

file' card' *s* Karteikarte *f*

filial ['fɪlɪ·əl] *adj* kindlich

filibuster ['fɪlɪ,bʌstər] *s* Obstruktion *f* ‖ *intr* Obstruktion treiben

filigree ['fɪlɪ,gri] *s* Filigran *n*

fil'ing *s* Feilen *n; (of records)* Ablegen *n* von Akten; *(of a claim)* Anmeldung *f; (of a complaint)* Erhebung *f; (of a petition)* Einreichung *f;* **filings** Feilspäne *pl*

Filipi•no [,fɪlɪ'pino] *adj* filipinisch ‖ *s* (**-nos**) Filipino *m*

fill [fɪl] *s (fullness)* Fülle *f; (land fill)* Aufschüttung *f;* **eat one's f.** sich satt essen; **I have had my f. of it** ich habe es satt ‖ *tr* füllen; *(an order)* ausführen; *(a pipe)* stopfen; *(a position)* besetzen; *(dent)* plombieren, füllen; **f. full** vollfüllen; **f. in** *(empty space)* ausfüllen; *(one's name)* einsetzen; *(a hole, grave)* zuwerfen; **f. it up** (aut) volltanken; **f. up** auffüllen; *(a tank)* nachfüllen; *(a bag)* anfüllen; *(a glass)* vollschenken; **f. with smoke** verräuchern ‖ *intr* sich füllen; *(said of sails)* sich blähen; **f. in for** einspringen für; **f. out** rund werden; **f. up** sich füllen

filler ['fɪlər] *s* Füller *m; (of a cigar)*

fillet 118 fire

Einlage *f;* (journ) Lückenbüßer *m;* (paint) Grundierfirnis *m*
fillet ['fɪlət] *s* (headband) Kopfbinde *f;* (archit) Leiste *f* ‖ [fɪ'le] *s* (culin) Filet *n* ‖ *tr* filetieren
fillet' of beef' *s* Rinderfilet *n*
fillet' of sole' *s* Seezungenfilet *n*
fill'ing *s* (culin, dent) Füllung *f*
fill'ing sta'tion *s* Tankstelle *f*
fillip ['fɪlɪp] *s* Schnippchen *n;* (on the nose) Nasenstüber *m*
filly ['fɪlɪ] *s* Stutenfüllen *n*
film [fɪlm] *s* (thin layer) Schicht *f;* (cin, phot) Film *m;* f. of grease Fettschicht *f*
film' fes'tival *s* Filmfestspiele *pl*
film' li'brary *s* Filmarchiv *n*
film' speed' *s* Filmempfindlichkeit *f*
film' star' *s* Filmstar *m*
film'strip' *s* Bildstreifen *m*
filmy ['fɪlmɪ] *adj* trüb
filter ['fɪltər] *s* Filter *m;* (rad) Sieb *n* ‖ *tr* filtern; (rad) sieben
fil'tering *s* Filtrierung *f*
fil'ter pa'per *s* Filterpapier *n*
fil'ter tip' *s* Filtermundstück *n;* (coll) Filterzigarette *f*
filth [fɪlθ] *s* Schmutz *m;* (fig) Unflätigkeit *f*, Zote *f*
filthy ['fɪlθɪ] *adj* schmutzig (talk) unflätig; (lucre) schnöd(e) ‖ *adv*—f. rich (sl) klotzig reich
filtrate ['fɪltret] *s* Filtrat *n* ‖ *tr & intr* filtrieren
filtration [fɪl'treʃən] *s* Filtrierung *f*
fin [fɪn] *s* Flosse *f;* (of a shark or whale) Finne *f;* (of a bomb) Steuerschwanz *m;* (aer) Flosse *f*
final ['faɪnəl] *adj* End—, Schluß—; (definitive) endgültig ‖ *s* (educ) Abschlußprüfung *f;* **finals** (sport) Endrunde *f*, Endspiel *n*
finale [fɪ'nɑlɪ] *s* Finale *n*
finalist ['faɪnəlɪst] *s* Finalist –in *mf*
finality [faɪ'nælɪtɪ] *s* Endgültigkeit *f*
finally ['faɪnəlɪ] *adv* schließlich
finance [faɪ'næns], [fɪ'næns] *s* Finanz *f;* **finances** Finanzwesen *n* ‖ *tr* finanzieren
financial [fɪ'nænʃəl], [faɪ'nænʃəl] *adj* (e.g., policy, situation, crisis, aid) Finanz—; (e.g., affairs, resources, embarrassment) Geld—
financier [,fɪnən'sɪr], [,faɪnən'sɪr] *s* Finanzmann *m*
financ'ing, fi'nancing *s* Finanzierung *f*
finch [fɪntʃ] *s* Fink *m*
find [faɪnd] *s* Fund *m;* (archeol) Bodenfund *m* ‖ *v* (pret & pp found [faʊnd]) *tr* finden; (math) bestimmen; f. one's way sich zurechtfinden; f. one's way back zurückfinden; f. out herausfinden; f. s.o. guilty *j-n* für schuldig erklären ‖ *intr*—f. out about s.th. hinter etw [acc] kommen
finder ['faɪndər] *s* Finder –in *mf*
find'ing *s* Finden *n;* **findings** Tatbestand *m*
fine [faɪn] *adj* fein; (excellent) hervorragend; (weather) schön; f.! gut! ‖ *s* Geldstrafe *f* ‖ *tr* mit e-r Geldstrafe belegen
fine' arts' *spl* schöne Künste *pl*

fineness ['faɪnnɪs] *s* Feinheit *f;* (of a coin or metal) Feingehalt *m*
fine' point' *s* Feinheit *f*
fine' print' *s* Kleindruck *m*
finery ['faɪnərɪ] *s* Putz *m*, Staat *m*
fine-spun ['faɪn,spʌn] *adj* feingesponnen
finesse [fɪ'nɛs] *s* Finesse *f;* (cards) Impaß *m* ‖ *tr & intr* impassieren
fine-toothed ['faɪn,tuθt] *adj* feingezahnt; go over with a f. comb unter die Lupe nehmen
fine' touch' *s* Feinheit *f*
fine' tun'ing *s* Feineinstellung *f*
finger ['fɪŋgər] *s* Finger *m;* have a f. in the pie die Hand im Spiel haben; keep your fingers crossed halten Sie mir den Daumen; not lift a f. keinen Finger rühren; put the f. on s.o. (sl) *j-n* verpetzen; snap one's fingers mit den Fingern schnellen; twist around one's little f. um den kleinen Finger wickeln ‖ *tr* befingern
fin'ger bowl' *s* Fingerschale *f*
fin'gering *s* (mus) Fingersatz *m*
fin'gernail' *s* Fingernagel *m*
fin'gernail pol'ish *s* Nagellack *m*
fin'gerprint' *s* Fingerabdruck *m* ‖ *tr*—f. s.o. *j-m* die Fingerabdrücke abnehmen
fin'gertip' *s* Fingerspitze *f;* have at one's fingertips parat haben
finicky ['fɪnɪkɪ] *adj* wählerisch
finish ['fɪnɪʃ] *s* Ende *n*, Abschluß *m;* (polish) Lack *m*, Politur *f;* put a f. on fertig bearbeiten ‖ *tr* beenden; (complete) vollenden; (put a finish on) fertig bearbeiten; (smooth) glätten; (polish) polieren; (ruin) kaputt machen; f. drinking austrinken; f. eating aufessen; f. off (supplies) aufbrauchen; (food) aufessen; (a drink) austrinken; (kill) sl) erledigen; f. reading (a book) auslesen
fin'ished *adj* beendet, fertig; be all f. fix und fertig sein
fin'ished prod'uct *s* Fertigprodukt *n*
fin'ishing coat' *s* Deckanstrich *m*
fin'ishing mill' *s* Nachwalzwerk *n*
fin'ishing school' *s* Mädchenpensionat *n*
fin'ishing touch'es *spl*—put the f. to die letzte Hand legen an (acc)
fin'ish line' *s* Ziel *n*, Ziellinie *f*
finite ['faɪnaɪt] *adj* endlich
fi'nite verb' *s* Verbum *n* finitum
fink [fɪŋk] *s* (informer) (sl) Verräter –in *mf;* (strikebreaker) (sl) Streikbrecher –in *mf*
Finland ['fɪnlənd] *s* Finnland *n*
Finn [fɪn] *s* Finne *m*, Finnin *f*
Finnish ['fɪnɪʃ] *adj* finnisch ‖ *s* (language) Finnisch *n*
fir [fʌr] *s* Tanne *f*
fir' cone' *s* Tannenzapfen *m*
fire [faɪr] *s* Feuer *n;* (conflagration) Brand *m;* (mil) Feuer *n;* come under f. unter Beschuß geraten; on f. in Brand; open f. Feuer eröffnen; set on f. in Brand stecken ‖ *tr* (a gun, pistol, shot) abfeuern; (bricks, ceramics) brennen; (an oven) befeuern; (an employee) entlassen; (throw

hard) feuern; **f. questions at s.o.** j-n mit Fragen bombardieren; **f. up** (& fig) anfeuern || *intr* feuern, schießen; **f. away!** schieß los!; **f. on** (mil) beschießen

fire′ alarm′ s Feuermeldung f; (box) Feuermelder m

fire′arm′ s Schußwaffe f

fire′ball′ s Feuerball m; (hustler) Draufgänger m

fire′bomb′ s Brandbombe f || tr mit Brandbomben belegen

fire′brand′ s (fig) Aufwiegler –in mf

fire′break′ s Feuerschneise f

fire′ brigade′ s Feuerwehr f

fire′bug′ m (coll) Brandstifter –in mf

fire′ chief′ s Branddirektor m

fire′ com′pany s Feuerwehr f

fire′crack′er s Knallfrosch m

fire′damp′ s Schlagwetter pl

fire′ depart′ment s Feuerwehr f

fire′ drill′ s Feueralarmübung f; (by a fire company) Feuerwehrübung f

fire′ en′gine s Spritze f

fire′ escape′ s Feuerleiter f

fire′ extin′guisher s Feuerlöscher m

fire′fly′ s Glühwurm m

fire′ hose′ s Spritzenschlauch m

fire′house′ s Feuerwache f

fire′ hy′drant s Hydrant m

fire′ insur′ance s Brandversicherung f

fire′ i′rons spl Kamingeräte pl

fire′lane′ s Feuer(schutz)schneise f

fire′man s (-men) Feuerwehrmann m; (stoker) Heizer m

fire′place′ s Kamin m, Herd m

fire′plug′ s Hydrant m

fire′ pow′er s (mil) Feuerkraft f

fire′proof′ adj feuerfest || tr feuerfest machen

fire′ sale′ s Ausverkauf m von feuerbeschädigten Waren

fire′ screen′ s Feuervorhang m

fire′side′ s Kamin m, Herd m

fire′trap′ s feuergefährdetes Gebäude n

fire′ wall′ s Brandmauer f

fire′wa′ter s (coll) Feuerwasser n

fire′wood′ s Brennholz n

fire′works′ spl Feuerwerk n

fir′ing s (of a weapon) Abfeuern n; (of an employee) Entlassung f

fir′ing line′ s Feuerlinie f

fir′ing range′ s Schießstand m

fir′ing squad′ s Erschießungskommando n; (for ceremonies) Ehrensalutkommando n; **put to the f.** an die Wand stellen

firm [fʌrm] adj fest || s (com) Firma f

firmament ['fʌrməmənt] s Firmament n

firmness ['fʌrmnɪs] s Festigkeit f

first [fʌrst] adj erste; **very f.** allererste || adv erst, erstens; **f. of all** zunächst || s (aut) erster Gang m; **at f.** zuerst; **f. come, f. served** wer zuerst kommt, mahlt zuerst; **from the f.** von vornherein; **the f.** (in dates or in a series) der Erste

first′ aid′ s Erste Hilfe f

first′-aid′ kit′ s Verbandpäckchen n

first′-aid′ sta′tion s Unfallstation f; (mil) Verbandsplatz m

first′-born′ adj erstgeboren

first′-class′ adj erstklassig || adv erster Klasse

first′-class′ mail′ s Briefpost f

first′-class′ tic′ket s Fahrkarte f (or Flugkarte f) erster Klasse

first′ cous′in s leiblicher Vetter m, leibliche Cousine f

first′-degree′ adj ersten Grades

first′ draft′ s Konzept n

first′ fin′ger s Zeigefinger m

first′ floor′ s Parterre n, Erdgeschoß n

first′ fruits′ spl Erstlinge pl

first′ lieuten′ant s Oberleutnant m

firstly ['fʌrstli] adv erstens

first′ mate′ s Obersteuermann m

first′ name′ s Vorname m

first′ night′ s (theat) Erstaufführung f

first-nighter ['fʌrst'naɪtər] s (theat) Premierenbesucher –in mf

first′ offend′er s noch nicht Vorbestrafte mf

first′ of′ficer s erster Offizier m

first′ prize′ s Hauptgewinn m, Haupttreffer m

first′-rate′ adj erstklassig

first′ ser′geant s Hauptfeldwebel m

fir′ tree′ s Tannenbaum m

fiscal ['fɪskəl] adj (period, year) Rechnungs–; (policy) Finanz–

fish [fɪʃ] s Fisch m; **drink like a f.** wie ein Bürstenbinder saufen; **like a f. out of water** nicht in seinem Element || tr fischen || intr fischen; **f. for** angeln nach

fish′bone′ s Gräte f, Fischgräte f

fish′ bowl′ s Fischglas n

fisher ['fɪʃər] s Fischer –in mf

fish′er·man s (-men) Angler m

fishery ['fɪʃəri] s Fischerei f

fish′hook′ s Angelhaken m

fish′ing adj Fisch–, Angel– || s Fischen n

fish′ing line′ s Angelschnur f

fish′ing reel′ s Angelschnurrolle f

fish′ing rod′ s Angelrute f

fish′ing tack′le s Fischgerät n

fish′ mar′ket s Fischmarkt m

fishmonger ['fɪʃ‚mʌŋgər] s Fischhändler –in mf

fish′pond′ s Fischteich m

fish′ sto′ry s Jägerlatein n

fish′tail′ s (aer) Abbremsen n || intr (aer) abbremsen

fishy ['fɪʃi] adj fischig; (eyes, look) ausdruckslos; (suspicious) anrüchig; **there's s.th. f. about it** das geht nicht mit rechten Dingen zu

fission ['fɪʃən] s (phys) Spaltung f

fissionable ['fɪʃənəbəl] adj spaltbar

fissure ['fɪʃər] s Riß m, Spalt m

fist [fɪst] s Faust f; **make a f.** die Faust ballen; **shake one's f. at s.o.** j-m mit der Faust drohen

fist′ fight′ s Handgemenge n

fisticuffs ['fɪstɪ‚kʌfs] spl Faustschläge pl

fit [fɪt] adj (fitter; fittest) gesund; (for) tauglich (für, zu); (sport) gut in Form; **be fit as a fiddle** kerngesund sein; **be fit to be tied** Gift und Galle spucken; **feel fit** auf der Höhe sein; **fit for military service**

diensttauglich; **fit to eat** genießbar; **fit to drink** trinkbar; **keep fit in Form bleiben; see fit to** (*inf*) es für richtig halten zu (*inf*) || *s* (*of clothes*) Sitz *m*; **by fits and starts** ruckweise; **fit of anger** Wutanfall *m*; **fit of laughter** Lachkrampf *m*; **give s.o. fits** j–n auf die Palme bringen; **it is a good** (or **a bad**) **fit** es sitzt gut (or schlecht); **throw a fit** e–n Wutanfall kriegen || *v* (*pret* & *pp* **fitted**; *ger* **fitting**) *tr* passen (*dat*); **fit in** (*for an appointment*) einschieben; **fit out** ausrüsten, ausstatten || *intr* passen; **fit into** sich einfügen in (*acc*); **fit in with** passen zu; **fit together** zusammenpassen

fitful ['fɪtfəl] *adj* unregelmäßig

fitness ['fɪtnɪs] *s* Tauglichkeit *f*; **physical f.** gute körperliche Verfassung *f*

fit'ting *adj* passend, angemessen || *s* (*of a garment*) Anprobe *f*; (*mach*) Montage *f*; **fittings** Armaturen *pl*

five [faɪv] *adj* & *pron* fünf || *s* Fünf *f*

five'-year plan' *s* Fünfjahresplan *m*

fix [fɪks] *s* (*determination of a position*) Standortbestimmung *f*; (*position*) Standort *m*; (*injection of heroin*) (sl) Schuß *m*; **be in a fix** (coll) in der Klemme sein || *tr* befestigen; (*a price, time*) festsetzen; (*repair*) reparieren, wieder in Ordnung bringen; (*get even with*) (sl) erledigen, das Handwerk legen (*dat*); (*one's glance*) (**on**) heften (auf *acc*); (*the blame*) (**on**) zuschreiben (*dat*); (*a game* sl) auf unehrliche Weise beeinflussen; (*bayonets*) aufpflanzen; (*phot*) fixieren

fixed *adj* (*unmovable*) unbeweglich; (*stare*) starr; (*income*) fest; (*idea, cost*) fix; **f. date** Termin *m*

fixer ['fɪksər] *s* (*phot*) Fixiermittel *n*

fix'ing *s* (*making fast*) Befestigung *f*; (*of a date, etc.*) Festsetzung *f*; **fixings** (culin) Zutaten *pl*

fix'ing bath' *s* (*phot*) Fixierbad *n*

fixture ['fɪkstʃər] *s* Installationsteil *m*; **he is a permanent f.** er gehört zum Inventar

fizz [fɪz] *s* Zischen *n* || *intr* zischen

fizzle ['fɪzəl] *s* (coll) Pleite *f* || *intr* aufzischen; **f. out** verpuffen

flabbergast ['flæbər,gæst] *tr* verblüffen

flabby ['flæbi] *adj* schlaff, schlapp

flag [flæg] *s* Fahne *f*, Flagge *f* || *v* (*pret* & *pp* **flagged**; *ger* **flagging**) *tr* signalisieren || *intr* nachlassen

flag'pole' *s* Fahnenmast *m*

flagrant ['flegrənt] *adj* schreiend

flag'ship' *s* Flaggschiff *n*

flag'staff' *s* Flaggenmast *m*

flag'stone' *s* Steinfliese *f*

flag' stop' *s* (rr) Bedarfshaltestelle *f*

flail [flel] *s* Dreschflegel *m* || *tr* dreschen || *intr—***f. about** um sich schlagen

flair [fler] *s* Spürsinn *m*, feine Nase *f*

flak [flæk] *s* Flak *f*, Flakfeuer *n*

flake [flek] *s* (*thin piece*) Schuppe *f*; (*of snow, soap*) Flocke *f* || *intr* Schuppen bilden; **f. off** abblättern

flaky ['fleki] *adj* (*skin*) schuppig; (*pastry*) blätterig; (sl) überspannt

flamboyant [flæm'bɔɪ-ənt] *adj* (*person*) angeberisch; (*style*) überladen

flame [flem] *s* Flamme *f*; **be in flames** in Flammen stehen; **burst into flames** in Flammen aufgehen || *intr* flammen

flamethrower ['flem,θro·ər] *s* Flammenwerfer *m*

flam'ing *adj* flammend

flamin·go [flə'mɪŋgo] *s* (**–gos** & **–goes**) (orn) Flamingo *m*

flammable ['flæməbəl] *adj* brennbar

Flanders ['flændərz] *s* Flandern *n*

flange [flændʒ] *s* (*of a pipe*) Flansch *m*; (*of a wheel*) (rr) Spurkranz *m*

flank [flæŋk] *s* (anat, mil, zool) Flanke *f* || *tr* flankieren

flank'ing move'ment *s* (mil) Umgehung *f*

flannel ['flænəl] *adj* flanellen || *s* Flanell *m*

flap [flæp] *s* Klappe *f*; **f. of the wing** Flügelschlag *m* || *v* (*pret* & *pp* **flapped**; *ger* **flapping**) *tr—***f. the wings** mit den Flügeln schlagen || *intr* flattern

flare [fler] *s* Leuchtsignal *n*; (*of anger, excitement*) Aufbrausen *n*; (*of a skirt*) Glocke *f*; (mil) Leuchtrakete *f*, Leuchtbombe *f* || *intr* flackern; (*said of a skirt*) glockenförmig abstehen; **f. up** auflodern; (fig) aufbrausen

flare'-up' *s* Auflodern *n*; (*of anger*) Aufbrausen *n*

flash [flæʃ] *s* Blitz *m*; (*of a gun*) Mündungsfeuer *n*; (phot) Blitzlicht *n*; **f. of genius** Geistesblitz *m*; **f. of light** Lichtstrahl *m*; **f. of lightning** Blitzstrahl *m*; **in a f.** im Nu || *tr* (*a glance*) zuwerfen; (*a message*) funkeln; **f. a light in s.o.'s face** j–m ins Gesicht leuchten || *intr* blitzen; (*said of eyes*) funkeln; **f. by** vorbeisausen; **f. on** aufleuchten; **f. through one's mind** j–m durch den Kopf schießen

flash'back' *s* (cin) Rückblende *f*

flash' bulb' *s* Blitzlichtbirne *f*

flash' cube' *s* Blitzlichtwürfel *m*

flash' flood' *s* plötzliche Überschwemmung *f*

flash' gun' *s* Blitzlichtgerät *n*

flash'light' *s* Taschenlampe *f*

flash' pic'ture, flash' shot' *s* Blitzlichtaufnahme *f*

flashy ['flæ/i] *adj* auffällig; (*clothes*) protzig; (*colors*) grell

flask [flæsk] *s* Taschenflasche *f*; (*for laboratory use*) Glaskolben *m*

flat [flæt] *adj* (**flatter**; **flattest**) platt, flach; (*food*) fad(e); (*rate*) Pauschal–; (*tire*) platt; (*color*) matt; (*beer, soda*) schal; (*lie*) glatt; (*denial*) entschieden; (mus) erniedrigt; **be f.** (mus) zu tief singen || *adv* (*e.g., in exactly ten minutes*) genau; **fall f.** (fig) flachfallen; **go f. schal** werden; **lie f.** flach liegen || *s* (*apartment*) Wohnung *f*; (*tire*) Reifenpanne *f*

flat'boat' *s* Flachboot *n*

flat-broke ['flæt'brok] *adj* (coll) völlig pleite
flat'car' *s* Plattformwagen *m*
flat' feet' *spl* Plattfüße *pl*
flat'-foot'ed *adj* plattfüßig; **catch f.** auf frischer Tat ertappen
flat'i'ron *s* Bügeleisen *n*
flatly ['flætli] *adv* rundweg, reinweg
flatten ['flætən] *tr* (*paper, cloth*) glattstreichen; (*raze*) einebnen; **f. out** abplatten; (aer) abfangen || *intr* sich verflachen; (aer) ausschweben
flatter ['flætər] *tr* schmeicheln (*dat*); **be flattered** sich geschmeichelt fühlen; **f. oneself** sich [dat] einbilden
flatterer ['flætərər] *s* Schmeichler –in *mf*
flat'tering *adj* schmeichelhaft
flattery ['flætəri] *s* Schmeichelei *f*
flat' tire' *s* Reifenpanne *f*
flat'top' *s* (coll) Flugzeugträger *m*
flat' trajec'tory *s* Rasanz *f*
flatulence ['flætʃələns] *s* Blähung *f*
flat'ware' *s* (silverware) Eßbestecke *pl*
flaunt [flɔnt] *tr* prunken mit
flavor ['flevər] *s* Aroma *n* || *tr* würzen
fla'voring *s* Würze *f*
flavorless ['flevərlɪs] *adj* fad(e)
flaw [flɔ] *s* Fehler *m*; (crack) Riß *m*; (in glass, precious stone) Blase *f*
flawless ['flɔlɪs] *adj* tadellos
flax [flæks] *s* Flachs *m*, Lein *m*
flaxen ['flæksən] *adj* flachsen
flax'seed' *s* Leinsamen *m*
flay [fle] *tr* ausbalgen
flea [fli] *s* Floh *m*
flea'bag' *s* (sleeping bag) (coll) Flohkiste *f*; (hotel) (coll) Penne *f*
flea'bite' *s* Flohbiß *m*
flea'mar'ket *s*, Flohmarkt *m*
fleck [flɛk] *s* Fleck *m*
fledgling ['fledʒlɪŋ] *s* eben flügge gewordener Vogel *m*; (fig) Grünschnabel *m*
flee [fli] *v* (*pret & pp* **fled** [fled]) *intr* fliehen
fleece [flis] *s* Vlies *n* || *tr* (coll) rupfen
fleecy ['flisi] *adj* wollig; **f. clouds** Schäfchenwolken *pl*
fleet [flit] *adj* flink || *s* Flotte *f*; (aer) Geschwader *n*; (nav) Kriegsflotte *f*; **f. of cars** Wagenpark *m*
fleet'ing *adj* flüchtig
Flemish ['flemɪʃ] *adj* flämisch || *s* Flämisch *n*
flesh [flɛʃ] *s* Fleisch *n*; **in the f.** leibhaftig
flesh'-col'ored *adj* fleischfarben
fleshiness ['fleʃɪnɪs] *s* Fleischigkeit *f*
flesh' wound' *s* Fleischwunde *f*
fleshy ['fleʃi] *adj* fleischig
flex [flɛks] *tr* biegen; (muscles) anspannen
flexible ['fleksɪbəl] *adj* biegsam
flex(i)time ['fleks(ɪ),taɪm] *s* Gleitzeit *f*
flick [flɪk] *s* Schnippen *n* || *tr* (away) wegschnippen
flicker ['flɪkər] *s* (of a flame) Flakkern *n*; (of eyelids) Zucken *n* || *intr* flackern
flier ['flaɪ·ər] *s* Flieger –in *mf*; (handbill) Flugblatt *n*

flight [flaɪt] *s* Flug *m*; (fleeing) Flucht *f*; (of birds, geese) Schar *f*; (of stairs) Treppe *f*; **f. of stairs** Treppenflucht *f*; **f. of the imagination** Geistesschwung *m*; **live two flights up** zwei Treppen hoch wohnen; **put to f.** in die Flucht schlagen; **take to f.** sich davonmachen
flight' bag' *s* (aer) Reisetasche *f*
flight' deck' *s* (nav) Landedeck *n*
flight' engineer' *s* Bordmechaniker *m*
flight' instruc'tor *s* Fluglehrer –in *mf*
flight' path' *s* Flugstrecke *f*
flighty ['flaɪti] *adj* leichtsinnig
flim-flam ['flɪm,flæm] *s* (nonsense) Unsinn *m*; (deception) Betrügerei *f* || *v* (*pret & pp* **-flammed**; *ger* **-flamming**) *tr* (coll) betrügen
flimsy ['flɪmzi] *adj* (material) hauchdünn; (excuse, construction) schwach
flinch [flɪntʃ] *intr* (at) zurückweichen (vor *dat*), zusammenfahren (vor *dat*)
flinch'ing *s*—**without f.** ohne mit der Wimper zu zucken
fling [flɪŋ] *s* Wurf *m*; **go on** (or **have**) **a f.** sich austoben; **have a f. at** versuchen || *v* (*pret & pp* **flung** [flʌŋ]) *tr* schleudern; **f. off** abschleudern; **f. open** aufreißen
flint [flɪnt] *s* Feuerstein *m*
flinty ['flɪnti] *adj* steinhart; (fig) hart
flip [flɪp] *adj* leichtfertig || *s* (of a coin) Hochwerfen *n*; (somersault) Purzelbaum *m* || *v* (*pret & pp* **flipped**; *ger* **flipping**) *tr* schnellen; (a coin) hochwerfen; **f. one's lid** (sl) rasend werden; **f. over** umdrehen
flippancy ['flɪpənsi] *s* Leichtfertigkeit *f*
flippant ['flɪpənt] *adj* leichtfertig
flipper ['flɪpər] *s* Flosse *f*
flirt [flɜrt] *s* Flirt *m* || *intr* kokettieren, flirten; (with an idea) liebäugeln
flirtation [flɜr'teʃən] *s* Liebelei *f*
flit [flɪt] *v* (*pret & pp* **flitted**; *ger* **flitting**) *intr* flitzen; **f. by** vorbeiflitzen; (said of time) verfliegen
float [flot] *s* Schwimmkörper *m*; (of a fishing line) Schwimmer *m*; (raft) Floß *n*; (in parades) Festwagen *m* || *tr* (logs) flößen; (a loan) auflegen || *intr* schwimmen; (in the air) schweben; **f. about** herumtreiben
float'ing kid'ney *s* Wanderniere *f*
float'ing mine' *s* Treibmine *f*
flock [flɑk] *s* (of sheep) Herde *f*; (of birds) Schar *f*, Schwarm *m*; (of people) Menge *f* || *intr* herbeiströmen; **come flocking** herbeigeströmt kommen; **f. around** sich scharen um; **f. into** strömen in (*acc*); **f. to** zulaufen (*dat*); **f. together** sich zusammenscharen
floe [flo] *s* Eisscholle *f*
flog [flɑg] *v* (*pret & pp* **flogged**; *ger* **flogging**) *tr* prügeln
flood [flʌd] *s* Flut *f*; (caused by heavy rains) Überschwemmung *f*; (sudden rise of a river) Hochwasser *n*; (fig) Schwall *m*; (Bib) Sintflut *f* || *tr* (& fig) überschwemmen; (e.g., with mail) überschütten

flood′gate′ *s* (& fig) Schleusentor *n*
flood′light′ *s* Flutlicht *n* ‖ *tr* anstrahlen
flood′ tide′ *s* Flut *f;* **at f.** zur Zeit der Flut
flood′ wa′ters *spl* Flutwasser *n*
floor [flor] *s* Fußboden *m; (story)* Stock *m;* (parl) Sitzungssaal *m;* **have the f.** das Wort haben; **may I have the f.?** ich bitte ums Wort; **on the third f.** im zweiten Stock ‖ *tr* zu Boden strecken; (coll) verblüffen
floor′board′ *s* Diele *f*
floor′ing *s* Fußbodenbelag *m*
floor′ lamp′ *s* Stehlampe *f*
floor′ plan′ *s* Grundriß *m*
floor′ pol′ish *s* Bohnermasse *f*
floor′ sam′ple *s* Vorführungsmuster *n*
floor′ show′ *s* Kabarett *n*
floor′ tile′ *s* Bodenfliese *f*
floor′walk′er *s* Abteilungsaufseher –in *mf*
floor′ wax′ *s* Bohnerwachs *n*
flop [flɑp] *s* (coll) Mißerfolg *m;* (person) Niete *f;* (fall) (coll) Plumps *m;* **take a f.** (coll) plumpsen *f* ‖ *v* (pret & pp flopped; ger flopping) *intr* (fall) (coll) plumpsen; (fail) (coll) versagen; (theat) (coll) durchfallen; **f. down** in (coll) sich plumpsen lassen in (acc)
flora [′florə] *s* Pflanzenwelt *f*
floral [′florəl] *adj* Blumen-
Florence [′flɑrəns] *s* Florenz *n*
florescence [flo′resəns] *s* Blüte *f*
florid [′flɑrɪd] *adj* (ornate) überladen; (complexion) blühend
florist [′flɑrɪst] *s* Blumenhändler –in *mf*
floss [flɔs] *s* Rohseide *f;* (of corn) Narbenfaden *pl*
floss′ silk′ *s* Florettseide *f*
flossy [′flɔsi] *adj* seidenweich
flotilla [flo′tɪlə] *s* Flotille *f*
flotsam [′flɑtsəm] *s* Wrackgut *n*
flot′sam and jet′sam *s* Treibgut *n;* (trifles) Kleinigkeiten *pl*
flounce [flauns] *s* Volant *m* ‖ *tr* mit Volants besetzen ‖ *intr* erregt stürmen
flounder [′flaundər] *s* Flunder *f* ‖ *intr* taumeln; (fig) ins Schwimmen kommen
flour [flaur] *s* Mehl *n*
flourish [′flʌrɪʃ] *s* (in writing) Schnörkel *m;* (in a speech) Floskel *f;* (gesture) große Geste *f;* (mus) Tusch *m;* **f. of trumpets** Trompetengeschmetter *n* ‖ *tr* (banners) schwenken; (swords) schwingen ‖ *intr* blühen, gedeihen
flour′ishing *adj* blühend; (business) schwunghaft
flour′ mill′ *s* Mühle *f*
floury [′flauri] *adj* mehlig
flout [flaut] *tr* verspotten ‖ *intr*—**f. at** spotten über (acc)
flow [flo] *s* Fluß *m* ‖ *intr* fließen, rinnen; (said of hair, clothes) wallen; **f. by** vorbeifließen; **f. into** zuströmen (dat)
flower [′flau·ər] *s* Blume *f;* **cut flowers** Schnittblumen *pl* ‖ *intr* blühen

flow′er bed′ *s* Blumenbeet *n*
flow′er gar′den *s* Blumengarten *m*
flow′er girl′ *s* Blumenmädchen *n*
flow′erpot′ *s* Blumentopf *m*
flow′er shop′ *s* Blumenladen *m*
flow′er show′ *s* Blumenausstellung *f*
flow′er stand′ *s* Blumenstand *m*
flowery [′flau·əri] *adj* blumig; (fig) geziert; **f. phrase** Floskel *f*
flu [flu] *s* (coll) Grippe *f*
flub [flʌb] *v* (pret & pp flubbed; ger flubbing) *tr* (coll) verkorksen
fluctuate [′flʌkt∫u‚et] *intr* schwanken
fluctuation [‚flʌkt∫u′e∫ən] *s* Schwankung *f*
flue [flu] *s* Rauchrohr *n*
fluency [′flu·ənsi] *s* Geläufigkeit *f*
fluent [′flu·ənt] *adj* (speaker) redegewandt; (speech) fließend
fluently [′flu·əntli] *adv* fließend
fluff [flʌf] *s* Staubflocke *f;* (blunder) Schnitzer *m* ‖ *tr* verpfuschen; **f. up** (a pillow) schütteln; (a rug) aufrauhen
fluffy [′flʌfi] *adj* flaumig
fluid [′flu·ɪd] *adj* flüssig ‖ *s* Flüssigkeit *f*
fluke [fluk] *s* Ankerflügel *m;* (coll) Dusel *m*
flunk [flʌŋk] *s* Durchfallen *n* ‖ *tr* (a test) (coll) durchfallen in (dat); (a student) (coll) durchfallen lassen ‖ *intr* (coll) durchfallen
flunky [′flʌŋki] *s* Schranze *mf*
fluorescent [flo′resənt] *adj* fluoreszierend
fluores′cent light′ *s* Leuchtstofflampe *f*
fluores′cent tube′ *s* Leuchtröhre *f*
fluoridate [′flɑrɪ‚det] *tr* mit e-m Fluorid versetzen
fluoride [′floraɪd] *s* Fluorid *n*
fluorine [′florin] *s* Fluor *n*
fluorite [′floraɪt] *s* Fluorkalzium *n*
fluoroscope [′florə‚skop] *s* Fluoroskop *n*
flurry [′flʌri] *s* (of snow) Schneegestöber *m;* (st. exch.) kurzes Aufflackern *n;* **f. of activity** fieberhafte Tätigkeit *f*
flush [flʌʃ] *adj* (even) eben, glatt; (well-supplied) gut bei Kasse; (full to overflowing) übervoll ‖ *adv* direkt ‖ *s* (on the cheeks) Erröten *n;* (of youth) Blüte *f;* (of a toilet) Spülung *f;* (cards) Flöte *f;* **f. of victory** Siegesrausch *m* ‖ *tr* (a toilet) spülen; (hunt) auftreiben; **f. down** hinunterspülen; **f. out** (animals) auftreiben ‖ *intr* erröten
flush′ switch′ *s* Unterputzschalter *m*
flush′ tank′ *s* Spülkasten *m*
flush′ toi′let *s* Spülklosett *n*
fluster [′flʌstər] *s* Verwirrung *f* ‖ *tr* verwirren
flute [flut] *s* (archit) Kannelüre *f;* (mus) Flöte *f* ‖ *tr* riffeln
flut′ing *s* (archit) Kannelierung *f*
flutist [′flutɪst] *s* Flötist –in *mf*
flutter [′flʌtər] *s* Flattern *n;* (excitement) Aufregung *f* ‖ *tr*—**f. one′s eyelashes** mit den Wimpern klimpern ‖ *intr* flattern

flux [flʌks] *s* (*flow*) Fließen *n*, Fluß *m*; (*for fusing metals*) Schmelzmittel *n*; **in f. im Fluß**

fly [flai] *s* Fliege *f*; (*of trousers*) Schlitz *m*; (angl) künstliche Fliege *f*; **flies** (theat) Soffitten *pl*; **fly in the ointment** Haar *n* in der Suppe ‖ *v* (*pret* **flew** [flu]; *pp* **flown** [flon]) *tr* fliegen ‖ *intr* fliegen; (*rush*) stürzen; (*said of rumors*) schwirren; (*said of time*) verfliegen; **fly around** umherfliegen; (*e.g., the globe*) umfliegen; **fly at s.o.** auf j-n losgehen; **fly away** abfliegen; **fly in all directions** nach allen Seiten zerstieben; **fly low** tief fliegen; **fly off the handle** (fig) aus der Haut fahren; **fly open** aufspringen; **fly over** überfliegen; **fly past** vorbeifliegen (an *dat*); **let fly** (*e.g., an arrow*) schnellen

fly′ ball′ *s* (baseball) Flugball *m*

fly′-by-night′ *adj* unverläßlich ‖ *s* (coll) Schwindelunternehmen *n*

fly′ cast′ing *s* Fischen *n* mit der Wurfangel

flyer [′flai·ər] *s var of* **flier**

fly′-fish′ *intr* mit künstlichen Fliegen angeln

fly′ing *adj* fliegend; (*boat, field, time*) Flug–; (*suit, club, school*) Flieger– ‖ *s* Fliegen *n*

fly′ing but′tress *s* Strebebogen *m*

fly′ing col′ors *spl*—**come through with f.** e-n glänzenden Sieg erringen

fly′ing sau′cer *s* fliegende Untertasse *f*

fly′leaf′ *s* (–leaves′) Vorsatzblatt *n*

fly′pa′per *s* Fliegenfänger *m*

fly′ rod′ *s* Angelrute *f*

fly′speck′ *s* Fliegendreck *m*

fly′ swat′ter [‚swatər] *s* Fliegenklappe *f*

fly′trap′ *s* Fliegenfalle *f*

fly′wheel′ *s* Schwungrad *n*

foal [fol] *s* Fohlen *n* ‖ *intr* fohlen

foam [fom] *s* Schaum *m*; (*of waves*) Gischt *m*; (*from the mouth*) Geifer *m* ‖ *intr* schäumen; (*said of waves*) branden

foam′ rub′ber *s* Schaumgummi *m*

foamy [′fomi] *adj* (*full of foam*) schaumig; (*beer*) schäumend; (*foamlike*) schaumartig

F.O.B., f.o.b. [‚ef‚o′bi] *adv* (free on board) frei an Bord

focal [′fokəl] *adj* fokal; **be the f. point** im Brennpunkt stehen; **f. point** (fig & opt) Brennpunkt *m*

fo·cus [′fokəs] *s* (–cuses & –ci [sai]) (math, opt) Brennpunkt *m*; (pathol) Herd *m*; **bring into f.** richtig (or scharf) einstellen; **in f.** scharf eingestellt; **out of f.** unscharf ‖ *v* (*pret & pp* –cus[s]ed; *ger* –cus[s]ing) *tr* (*a camera*) einstellen; (*attention, etc.*) (on) richten (auf *acc*) ‖ *intr* sich scharf einstellen

fo′cusing s Scharfeinstellung *f*

fodder [′fadər] *s* Futter *n*

foe [fo] *s* Feind –in *mf*

fog [fog] *s* Nebel *m*; (fig) Verwirrung *f*; (phot) Grauschleier *m* ‖ *v* (*pret & pp* fogged; *ger* fogging) *tr* ver-

nebeln; (fig) umnebeln ‖ *intr* (phot) verschleiern; **fog up** beschlagen

fog′ bank′ *s* Nebelbank *f*

fog′ bell′ *s* Nebelglocke *f*

fog′-bound′ *adj* durch Nebel festgehalten

fogey [′fogi] *s* Kauz *m*

foggy [′fogi] *adj* neblig, nebelhaft; (phot) verschleiert; **he hasn't the foggiest idea** er hat nicht die leiseste Ahnung

fog′horn′ *s* Nebelhorn *n*

fog′ light′ *s* (aut) Nebelscheinwerfer *m*

foible [′fɔibəl] *s* Schwäche *f*

foil [fɔil] *s* (*of metal*) Folie *f*; (*of a mirror*) Spiegelbelag *m*; (fig) (to) Hintergrund *m* (für); (fencing) Florett *n* ‖ *tr* (*a plan*) durchkreuzen; (*an attempt*) vereiteln

foist [fɔist] *tr*—**f. s.th. on s.o.** j-m etw anhängen

fold [fold] *s* Falte *f*; (*in stiff material*) Falz *m*; (*for sheep*) Pferch *m*; (*flock of sheep*) Schafherde *f*; (relig) Herde *f* ‖ *tr* falten; (*stiff material*) falzen; (*e.g., a chair*) zusammenklappen; (*the arms*) kreuzen; (*the wash*) zusammenlegen ‖ *intr* sich (zusammen) falten; (com) zusammenbrechen

folder [′folder] *s* (*loose-leaf binder*) Schnellhefter *m*; (*manila folder*) Mappe *f*; (*brochure*) Prospekt *m*

fold′ing *adj* (bed, chair, camera, wing) Klapp–

fold′ing door′ *s* Falttür *f*

fold′ing screen′ *s* spanische Wand *f*

foliage [′fɔli·idʒ] *s* Laubwerk *n*, Laub *n*

foli·o [′fɔli‚o] *adj* Folio–, in Folio ‖ *s* (–os) (*page*) Folioblatt *n*; (*book*) Foliant *m* ‖ *tr* paginieren

folk [fok] *adj* Volks– ‖ **folks** *spl* (*people*) Leute *pl*; (*family*) Angehörige *pl*

folk′ dance′ *s* Volkstanz *m*

folk′lore′ *s* Volkskunde *f*

folk′ mu′sic *s* Volksmusik *f*

folk′ song′ *s* Volkslied *n*

folksy [′foksi] *adj* (*person*) leutselig; (*speech, expression*) volkstümlich

folk′ tale′ *s* Volkssage *f*

folk′ways′ *spl* volkstümliche Lebensweise *f*

follicle [′falikəl] *s* Follikel *n*

follow [′falo] *tr* folgen (*dat*); (*instructions*) befolgen; (*a goal, events, news*) verfolgen; (*in office*) folgen auf (*acc*); (*a profession*) ausüben; (*understand*) folgen können (*dat*); **f. one another** aufeinanderfolgen; (*said of events*) sich überstürzen; **f. up** nachgehen (*dat*); **f. your nose!** immer der Nase nach! ‖ *intr* (nach)folgen; **as follows** folgendermaßen; **f. after** nachfolgen (*dat*); **f. through** (sport) ganz durchziehen; **f. upon** folgen auf (*acc*); **it follows that** daraus folgt, daß

follower [′falo·ər] *s* Anhänger –in *mf*

fol′lowing *adj* nachstehend, folgend ‖ *s* Gefolgschaft *f*

fol′low-up′ *adj* Nach– ‖ *s* weitere Verfolgung *f*

folly ['fɔli] s Torheit f; **follies** (theat) Revue f

foment [fo'ment] tr schüren, anstiften

fond [fɔnd] adj (hope, wish) sehnlich; **become f. of** lieb gewinnen; **be f. of** gern haben; **be f. of reading** gern lesen

fondle ['fɔndəl] tr liebkosen

fondness ['fɔndnɪs] s Verliebtheit f; **(for)** Hang m (zu), Vorliebe f (für)

font [fɑnt] s (for holy water) Weihwasserbecken n; (for baptism) Taufbecken n; (typ) Schriftart f

food [fud] adj Nähr-, Speise- ‖ s (on the table) Essen n; (in a store) Lebensmittel pl; (requirement for life) Nahrung f; (for animals) Futter n; (for plants) Nährstoff m; **f. and drink** Speis' und Trank; **f. for thought** Stoff m zum Nachdenken

food' poi'soning s Nahrungsmittelvergiftung f

food'stuffs' spl Nahrungsmittel pl

food' val'ue s Nährwert m

fool [ful] s Narr m; **born f.** Mondkalb n; **make a f. of oneself** sich blamieren ‖ tr täuschen, anführen ‖ intr— **f. around** herumtrödeln; **f. around with** herumspielen mit; (romantically) sich herumtreiben mit

fool'har'dy adj tollkühn

fool'ing s Späße pl; **f. around** Firlefanz m; **no f.!** na, so was!

foolish ['fulɪʃ] adj töricht, albern

foolishness ['fulɪnɪs] s Torheit f

fool'-proof' adj narrensicher

fools'cap' s Narrenkappe f; (paper size) Kanzleipapier n

foot [fut] s (feet [fit]) Fuß m; **be (back) on one's feet** (wieder) auf den Beinen sein; **f. of the bed** Fußende n des Bettes; **on f.** zu Fuß; **put one's best f. forward** sich ins rechte Licht setzen; **put one's f. down** (fig) ein Machtwort sprechen; **put one's f. in it** (coll) ins Fettnäpfchen treten; **stand on one's own two feet** auf eigenen Füßen stehen ‖ tr—**f. the bill** blechen

footage ['futɪdʒ] s Ausmaß n in Fuß

foot'-and-mouth' disease' s Maul- und Klauenseuche f

foot'ball' s Fußball m

foot'board' s (in a car) Trittbrett n; (of a bed) Fußbrett n

foot'bridge' s Steg m

foot'fall' s Schritt m

foot'hills' spl Vorgebirge n

foot'hold' s (& fig) Halt m; **gain a f.** festen Fuß fassen

foot'ing s Halt m; **lose one's f.** ausgleiten; **on an equal f. with** auf gleichem Fuße mit

foot'lights' spl Rampenlicht n

foot'man s (-men) Lakai m

foot'note' s Fußnote f

foot'path' s Fußpfad m, Fußsteig m

foot'print' s Fußstapfe f

foot' race' s Wettlauf m

foot'rest' s Fußraste f

foot' rule' s Zollstock m

foot' sol'dier s Infanterist m

foot'sore' adj fußkrank

foot'step' s Tritt m; **follow in s.o.'s footsteps** in j-s Fußstapfen treten

foot'stool' s Schemel m

foot'wear' s Schuhwerk n

foot'work' s (sl) Lauferei f; (sport) Beinarbeit f

foot'worn' adj abgetreten

fop [fɑp] s Geck m

for [fɔr] prep für; (a destination) nach (dat); (with an English present perfect tense) schon (acc), e.g., **I have been living here for a month** ich wohne hier schone e-n Monat (or seit e-m Monat; (with an English future tense) für or auf (acc); **for good** für immer; **for joy** vor Freude; **for years** jahrelang ‖ conj denn

forage ['fɔrɪdʒ] s Furage f ‖ intr furagieren

foray ['fore] s (raid) Raubzug m; (e.g., into politics) Streifzug m ‖ intr plündern

for-bear [fɔr'ber] v (pret –bore ['bor]; pp –borne ['born]) tr unterlassen ‖ intr ablassen

forbearance [fɔr'berəns] s (patience) Geduld f; (leniency) Nachsicht f

for-bid [fɔr'bɪd] v (pret –bade ['bæd] & –bad ['bæd]; pp –bidden ['bɪdən]) tr verbieten

forbid'ding adj abschreckend; (dangerous) gefährlich

force [fɔrs] s (strength) Kraft f; (compulsion) Gewalt f; (phys) Kraft f; **be in f.** in Kraft sein; **by f.** gewaltsam; **come into f.** in Kraft treten; **forces** (mil) Streitkräfte pl; **have the f. of** gelten als; **resort to f.** zu Zwangsmaßnahmen greifen; **with full f.** mit voller Wucht ‖ tr zwingen; (plants) treiben; (a door) aufsprengen; (e.g., an issue) forcieren; (into) zwängen (in acc); **f. down** hinunterdrücken; (aer) zur Landung zwingen; **f. one's way** sich durchdrängen; **f. s.th. on s.o.** j-m etw aufdrängen

forced' land'ing s Notlandung f

forced' march' s Gewaltsmarsch m

forceful ['fɔrsfəl] adj eindrucksvoll

for-ceps ['fɔrseps] s (-ceps & –cipes [sɪ‚piz]) (dent, surg, zool) Zange f

forcible ['fɔrsɪbəl] adj (strong) kräftig; (violent) gewaltsam

ford [fɔrd] s Furt f ‖ tr durchwaten

fore [fɔr] adj Vorder- ‖ adv (naut) vorn ‖ s—**come to the f.** hervortreten ‖ interj (golf) Achtung!

fore' and aft' adv längsschiffs

fore'arm' s Vorderarm m, Unterarm m

fore'bears' spl Vorfahren pl

forebode [fɔr'bod] tr vorbedeuten

forebod'ing s (omen) Vorzeichen n; (presentiment) Vorahnung f

fore'cast' s Voraussage f ‖ v (pret & pp –cast & –casted) tr voraussagen

forecastle ['foksəl] s Back f

foreclose tr (a mortgage) für verfallen erklären; (shut out) ausschließen

foredoom' tr im voraus verurteilen

fore'fa'thers spl Vorfahren pl

fore'fin'ger s Zeigefinger m

fore'front' s Spitze f

fore'go'ing adj vorhergehend

fore′gone′ conclu′sion s ausgemachte Sache f
fore′ground′ s Vordergrund m
forehead ['fɔrɪd] s Stirn(e) f
foreign ['fɔrɪn] adj (e.g., aid, product) Auslands-; (e.g., body, language, word, worker) Fremd–; (e.g., minister, office, policy, trade) Außen–; (e.g., affairs, service) auswärtig
foreigner ['fɔrɪnər] s Ausländer –in mf
for′eign exchange′ s Devisen pl
fore′leg′ s Vorderbein n
fore′lock′ s Stirnlocke f
fore′man s (–men) Vorarbeiter m; (jur) Obmann m; (min) Steiger m
foremast ['fɔr‚mæst] s Fockmast m
fore′most′ adj vorderste || adv zuerst
fore′noon′ s Vormittag m
fore′part′ s vorderster Teil m
fore′paw′ s Vorderpfote f
fore′quart′er s Vorderviertel n
fore′run′ner s Vorbote m
fore′sail′ s Focksegel n
fore•see′ v (pret –saw′; pp –seen′) tr voraussehen
foreseeable [for'si·əbəl] adj absehbar
foreshad′ow tr ahnen lassen
foreshort′en tr verkürzen
fore′sight′ s Voraussicht f
fore′sight′ed adj umsichtig
fore′skin′ s Vorhaut f
forest ['fɔrɪst] s Wald m, Forst m
forestall′ tr zuvorkommen (dat)
for′est fire′ s Waldbrand m
for′est rang′er s Forstbeamte m
forestry ['fɔrɪstri] s Forstwirtschaft f
fore′taste′ s Vorgeschmack m
fore•tell′ v (pret & pp –told′) tr vorhersagen, weissagen
fore′thought′ s Vorsorge f, Vorbedacht m
forev′er adv ewig, für immer; **f. and ever** auf immer und ewig
forewarn′ tr (of) vorher warnen (vor dat)
fore′word′ s Vorwort n
forfeit ['fɔrfɪt] s Einbuße f || tr einbüßen, verwirken
forfeiture ['fɔrfɪtʃər] s Verwirkung f
forgather [fɔr'gæðər] intr sich treffen
forge [fɔrdʒ] s Schmiede f || tr schmieden; (documents) fälschen || intr— **forge ahead** vordringen
forger ['fɔrdʒər] s Fälscher –in mf
forgery ['fɔrdʒəri] s Fälschung f; (coin) Falschgeld n
for•get [fɔr'gɛt] v (pret –got; pp –got & –gotten; ger –getting) tr vergessen; **f. it!** spielt keine Rolle!; **f. oneself** sich vergessen
forgetful [fɔr'gɛtfəl] adj vergeßlich
forgetfulness [fɔr'gɛtfəlnɪs] s Vergeßlichkeit f
forget′–me–not′ s Vergißmeinnicht n
forgivable [fɔr'gɪvəbəl] adj verzeihlich
for•give [fɔr'gɪv] v (pret –gave; pp –given) tr (a person) vergeben (dat); (a thing) vergeben
forgiveness [fɔr'gɪvnɪs] s Vergebung f
forgiv′ing adj versöhnlich
for•go [fɔr'go] v (pret –went; pp –gone) tr verzichten auf (acc)

fork [fɔrk] s Gabel f; (in the road) Gabelung f; (of a tree) Astgabelung f || tr gabeln; **f. over** (coll) übergeben
forked adj gabelförmig; (tongue) gespalten
fork′lift truck′ s Gabelstapler m
forlorn [fɔr'lɔrn] adj (forsaken) verlassen; (wretched) elend; (attempt) verzweifelt
forlorn′ hope′ s aussichtsloses Unternehmen n
form [fɔrm] s Form f, Gestalt f; (paper to be filled out) Formular n || tr formen, bilden; (a plan) fassen; (a circle, alliance) schließen; (suspicions) schöpfen; (a habit) annehmen; (blisters) werfen || intr sich bilden
formal ['fɔrməl] adj formell, förmlich
for′mal call′ s Höflichkeitsbesuch m
for′mal educa′tion s Schulbildung f
formality [fɔr'mælɪti] s Formalität f; **without f.** ohne Umstände
format ['fɔrmæt] s Format n
formation [fɔr'meʃən] s Bildung f; (aer) Verband m; (geol, mil) Formation f
former ['fɔrmər] adj ehemalig, früher; **the f.** jener
formerly ['fɔrmərli] adv ehemals, früher
form′–fit′ting adj—**be f.** e–e gute Paßform haben
formidable ['fɔrmɪdəbəl] adj (huge) gewaltig; (dreadful) schrecklich
formless ['fɔrmlɪs] adj formlos
form′ let′ter s Rundbrief m
formu•la ['fɔrmjələ] s (–las & –lae [‚li]) Formel f; (baby food) Kindermilch f
formulate ['fɔrmjə‚let] tr formulieren
formulation [‚fɔrmjə'leʃən] s Formulierung f
fornicate ['fɔrnɪ‚ket] intr Unzucht treiben
fornication [‚fɔrnɪ'keʃən] s Unzucht f
for•sake [fɔr'sek] v (pret –sook ['sʊk]; pp –saken ['sekən]) tr verlassen
fort [fɔrt] s Burg f; (mil) Fort n
forte [fɔrt] s Stärke f
forth [fɔrθ] adv hervor; **and so f.** und so fort; **from that day f.** von dem Tag an
forth′com′ing adj bevorstehend
forth′right′ adj ehrlich, offen
forth′with′ adv sofort
fortieth ['fɔrtɪ·ɪθ] adj & pron vierzigste; (in a series) Vierzigste mfn
fortification [‚fɔrtɪfɪ'keʃən] s Befestigung f
forti•fy ['fɔrtɪ‚faɪ] v (pret & pp –fied) tr (a place) befestigen; (e.g., with liquor) kräftigen; (encourage) ermutigen
fortitude ['fɔrtɪ‚t(j)ud] s Seelenstärke f
fortnight ['fɔrtnaɪt] s vierzehn Tage pl
fortress ['fɔrtrɪs] s Festung f
fortuitous [fɔr't(j)u·ɪtəs] adj zufällig
fortunate ['fɔrtʃənɪt] adj glücklich
fortunately ['fɔrtʃənɪtli] adv glücklicherweise

fortune ['fort∫ən] s Glück n; (money) Vermögen n; **make a f.** sich [dat] ein Vermögen erwerben; **have one's f. told** sich [dat] wahrsagen lassen; **tell fortunes** wahrsagen

for'tune hunt'er s Mitgiftjäger –in mf

for'tunetell'er s Wahrsagerin f

forty ['forti] adj & pron vierzig || s Vierzig f; **the forties** die vierziger Jahre

fo·rum ['forəm] s (–rums & –ra [rə]) (& fig) Forum n

forward ['forwərd] adj vordere, Vorwärts–; (person) keck; (mil) vorgeschoben || adv vorwärts, nach vorn; **bring f.** (an idea) vorschlagen; (a proposal) vorbringen; **come f.** sich melden; **look f. to** sich freuen auf (acc); **put f.** vorlegen || s (fb) Stürmer m || tr befördern; **please f.** bitte nachsenden || interj—f., march! im Gleichschritt, marsch!

fossil ['fasıl] adj versteinert || s Fossil n

foster ['fostər] adj (child, father, mother, home) Pflege–; (brother, sister) Milch– || tr pflegen

foul [faul] adj übel; (in smell) übelriechend; (air, weather) schlecht; (language) unflätig; (means) unfair || s (sport) Foul n || tr (make dirty) besudeln; (the lines) verwickeln; (sport) foulen; **f. up** durcheinanderbringen || intr (sport) foulen

foul' line' s (baseball) Grenzlinie f; (basketball) Freiwurflinie f

foul-mouthed ['faul,mauðd], ['faul,mauθt] adj zotige Reden führend

foul' play' s unfaires Spiel n; (crime) Verbrechen n, Mord m

found [faund] tr gründen; (cast) gießen

foundation [faun'de∫ən] s (act) Gründung f; (of a structure) Fundament n; (fund) Stiftung f; (fig) Grundlage f; **lay the foundation of** (& fig) den Grund legen zu

founda'tion gar'ments spl Miederwaren pl

founda'tion wall' s Grundmauer f

founder ['faundər] s Gründer –in mf; (metal) Gießer –in mf || intr (said of a ship) sinken; (fail) scheitern

foundling ['faundlıŋ] s Findling m

foundry ['faundri] s Gießerei f

fount [faunt] s Quelle f

fountain ['fauntən] s Springbrunnen m

foun'tainhead' s Urquell m

foun'tain pen' s Füller m

four [for] adj & pron vier || s Vier f; **on all fours** auf allen vieren

four'-cy'cle adj (mach) Viertakt–

four'-en'gine adj viermotorig

fourflusher ['for,fl∧∫ər] s Angeber m

four'foot'ed adj vierfüßig

four' hun'dred adj & pron vierhundert || spl—**the Four Hundred** die oberen Zehntausend

four'lane' adj Vierbahn–

four'-leaf' adj vierblätterig

four'-leg'ged adj vierbeinig

four'-let'ter word' s unanständiges Wort n

foursome ['forsəm] s Viererspiel n; (group of four) Quartet n

fourteenth [for'tinθ] adj & pron vierzehnte || s (fraction) Vierzehntel n; **the f.** (in dates and in a series) der Vierzehnte

fourth [forθ] adj & pron vierte || s (fraction) Viertel n; **the f.** (in dates and in a series) der Vierte

fourth' estate' s Presse f

fowl [faul] s Huhn n, Geflügel n

fox [faks] s (& fig) Fuchs m

fox'glove' s (bot) Fingerhut m

fox'hole' s (mil) Schützenloch n

fox' hound' s Hetzhund m

fox' hunt' s Fuchsjagd f

fox' ter'rier s Foxterrier m

fox' trot' s Foxtrott m

foyer ['foı·ər] s (of a theater) Foyer n; (of a house) Diele f

fracas ['frekəs] s Aufruhr m

fraction ['fræk∫ən] s Bruchteil m; **fractions** Bruchrechnung f

fractional ['fræk∫ənəl] adj Bruch–

fracture ['frækt∫ər] s Bruch m || tr sich [dat] brechen

fragile ['fræd3ıl] adj zerbrechlich

fragment ['frægmənt] s Bruchstück n; (of writing) Fragment n

fragmentary ['frægmən,teri] adj bruchstückhaft; (writing) fragmentarisch

fragmenta'tion bomb' [,frægmən'te∫ən] s Splitterbombe f

fragrance ['fregrəns] s Duft m

fragrant ['fregrənt] adj duftend; **be f.** duften

frail [frel] adj schwach, hinfällig; (fragile) zerbrechlich

frailty ['frelti] s Schwachheit f

frame [frem] s (e.g., of a picture, door) Rahmen m; (of glasses) Fassung f; (of a house) Balkenwerk n; (structure) Gestell n; (anat) Körperbau m; (cin, telv) Bild n; (naut) Spant n || tr (a picture) einrahmen; (a plan) ersinnen; (sl) reinhängen

frame' house' s Holzhaus n

frame' of mind' s Gemütsverfassung f

frame' of ref'erence s Bezugspunkte pl

frame'-up' s abgekartete Sache f

frame'work' s Gebälk n, Fachwerk n; (fig) Rahmen m; (aer) Aufbau m

franc [fræŋk] s Franc m; (Swiss) Franken m

France [fræns] s Frankreich n

Frances ['frænsıs] s Franziska f

franchise ['frænt∫aız] s Konzession f; (right to vote) Wahlrecht n

Francis ['frænsıs] s Franz m

Franciscan [fræn'sıskən] adj Franziskaner– || s Franziskaner m

frank [fræŋk] adj offen || s Freivermerk m; **Frank** (masculine name) Franz m; (medieval German person) Franke m, Frank f || tr franieren

frankfurter ['fræŋkfərtər] s Würstel n

frankincense ['fræŋkın,sens] s Weihrauch m

Frankish ['fræŋkı∫] adj fränkisch

frankness ['fræŋknıs] s Offenheit f; (bluntness) Freimut m

frantic ['fræntık] adj (with) außer sich (vor dat); (efforts) krampfhaft

fraternal [frə'tʌrnəl] *adj* brüderlich; *(twins)* zweieiig

fraternity [frə'tʌrnɪti] *s* Bruderschaft *f*; *(educ)* Studentenverbindung *f*

fraternize ['frætər‚naɪz] *intr* **(with)** sich anfreunden (mit)

fraud [frɔd] *s* Betrug *m*; *(person)* (coll) Betrüger –in *mf*

fraudulent ['frɔdjələnt] *adj* betrügerisch

fraught [frɔt] *adj*—**f. with** voll mit; **f. with danger** gefahrvoll

fray [fre] *s* Schlägerei *f*; *(battle)* Kampf *m* ‖ *tr* ausfranzen; *(the nerves)* aufreiben ‖ *intr (said of edges)* sich ausfranzen; *(become threadbare)* sich durchscheuern

freak [frik] *s* Mißbildung *f*; *(whimsy)* Laune *f*; *(enthusiast)* Enthusiast –in *mf*; *(abnormal person)* verrückter Kerl *m*; **f. of nature** Monstrum *n*

freakish ['frikɪʃ] *adj* grotesk; *(capricious)* launisch

freckle ['frekəl] *s* Sommersprosse *f*

freckled ['frekəld], **freckly** ['frekli] *adj* sommersprossig

Frederick ['fredərɪk] *s* Friedrich *m*

free [fri] *adj* **(freer** ['fri‑ər]; **freest** ['fri‑ɪst]) frei; *(off duty)* dienstfrei; **for f.** (coll) gratis; **f. with** *(e.g., money, praise)* freigebig mit; **go f.** frei ausgehen; **he is f. to** *(inf)* es steht ihm frei zu *(inf)*; **set f.** freilassen ‖ *adv* umsonst, kostenlos ‖ *v (pret & pp* **freed** [frid]; *ger* **freeing** ['fri‑ɪŋ]) *tr (liberate)* befreien; *(untie)* losmachen

free′ **and ea′sy** *adj* zwanglos

freebooter ['fri‚butər] *s* Freibeuter *m*

free′born′ *adj* freigeboren

freedom ['fridəm] *s* Freiheit *f*

free′dom of assem′bly *s* Versammlungsfreiheit *f*

free′dom of speech′ *s* Redefreiheit *f*

free′dom of the press′ *s* Pressefreiheit *f*

free′dom of wor′ship *s* Glaubensfreiheit *f*

free′ en′terprise *s* freie Wirtschaft *f*

free′-for-all′ *s* allgemeine Prügelei *f*

free′ hand′ *s* freie Hand *f*

free′-hand draw′ing *s (activity)* Freihandzeichnen *n*; *(product)* Freihandzeichnung *f*

free′hand′ed *adj* freigebig

free′hold′ *s* (jur) Freigut *n*

free′ kick′ *s* (fb) Freistoß *m*

free′-lance′ *adj* freiberuflich ‖ *intr* freiberuflich tätig sein

free-lancer ['fri‚lænsər] *s* Freiberufliche *mf*

free′ li′brary *s* Volksbibliothek *f*

free′man *s* (–men) Ehrenbürger *m*

Free′ma′son *s* Freimaurer *m*

Free′ma′sonry *s* Freimaurerei *f*

free′ of charge′ *adj* & *adv* kostenlos

free′ on board′ *adv* frei an Bord

free′ play′ *s* (fig & mach) Spielraum *m*

free′ port′ *s* Freihafen *m*

free′ sam′ple *s (of food)* Gratiskostprobe *f*; *(of products)* Gratismuster *n*

free′ speech′ *s* Redefreiheit *f*

free′-spo′ken *adj* freimütig

free′stone′ *adj* mit leicht auslösbarem Kern

free′think′er *s* Freigeist *m*

free′ thought′ *s* Freigeisterei *f*

free′ trade′ *s* Freihandel *m*

free′way′ *s* Autobahn *f*

free′ will′ *s* Willensfreiheit *f*; **of one's own f.** aus freien Stücken

freeze [friz] *s* Frieren *n* ‖ *v (pret* **froze** [froz]; *pp* **frozen** ['frozən]) *tr* frieren; *(assets)* einfrieren; *(prices)* stoppen; *(food)* tiefkühlen; *(surg)* vereisen ‖ *intr* (ge)frieren; *(e.g., with fear)* erstarren; **f. over** zufrieren; **f. to death** erfrieren; **f. up** vereisen

freeze′-dry′ *v (pret & pp* **–dried)** *tr* gefriertrocknen

freezer ['frizər] *s (chest)* Tiefkühltruhe *f*; *(cabinet)* Tiefkühlschrank *m*

freez′er compart′ment *s* Gefrierfach *n*

freez′ing *s* Einfrieren *n*; **below f.** unter dem Gefrierpunkt

freight [fret] *s (load)* Fracht *f*; *(cargo)* Frachtgut *n*; *(fee)* Frachtgebühr *f*; **by f. als** Frachtgut ‖ *tr* beladen

freight′ car′ *s* Güterwagen *m*

freight′ el′evator *s* Warenaufzug *m*

freighter ['fretər] *s* Frachter *m*

freight′ of′fice *s* Güterabfertigung *f*

freight′ train′ *s* Güterzug *m*

freight′ yard′ *s* Güterbahnhof *m*

French [frentʃ] *adj* französisch ‖ *s (language)* Französisch *n*; **the F.** die Franzosen

French′ doors′ *spl* Glastüre *pl*

French′ fries′ *spl* Pommes frites *pl*

French′ horn′ *s* (mus) Waldhorn *n*

French′ leave′ *s*—**take F.** sich französisch empfehlen

French′man *s* (–men) Franzose *m*

French′ roll′ *s* Schrippe *f*

French′ toast′ *s* arme Ritter *pl*

French′ win′dow *s* Flügelfenster *n*

French′ wom′an *s* (–wom′en) Französin *f*

frenzied ['frenzid] *adj* rasend

frenzy ['frenzi] *s* Raserei *f*

frequency ['frikwənsi] *s* Häufigkeit *f*; (phys) Frequenz *f*

fre′quency modula′tion *s* Frequenzmodulation *f*

frequent ['frikwənt] *adj* häufig ‖ [fri‑'kwənt] *tr* besuchen, frequentieren

frequently ['frikwəntli] *adv* häufig

fres·co ['fresko] *s* (**–coes** & **–cos**) Fresko *n*, Freskogemälde *n*

fresh [freʃ] *adj* frisch; (coll) frech ‖ *adv* neu, kürzlich

fresh′-baked′ *adj* neugebacken

freshen ['freʃən] *tr* erfrischen; **f. up** auffrischen ‖ *intr*—**f. up** sich auffrischen

freshet ['freʃɪt] *s* Hochwasser *n*; *(fresh-water stream)* Fluß *m*

fresh′man *s* (–men) Fuchs *m*

freshness ['freʃnɪs] *s* Frische *f*; (coll) Naseweisheit *f*

fresh′ wa′ter *s* Süßwasser *n*

fresh′-wa′ter *adj* Süßwasser-

fret [fret] *s* Verdruß *m*; (carp) Laubsägewerk *n*; (mus) Bund *m* ‖ *v (pret*

& *pp* **fretted;** *ger* **fretting**) *tr* gitter-
förmig verzieren ‖ *intr* sich ärgern
fretful ['fretfəl] *adj* verdrießlich
fret'work' *s* Laubsägewerk *n*
Freudian ['frɔidɪ·ən] *adj* Freudsch ‖
s Freudianer –in *mf*
friar ['fraɪ·ər] *s* Klosterbruder *m*
fricassee [,frɪkə'siː] *s* Frikassee *n*
friction ['frɪkʃən] *s* Reibung *f;* (fig)
Reiberei *f,* Mißhelligkeit *f*
fric'tion tape' *s* Isolierband *n*
Friday ['fraɪdɪ] *s* Freitag *m*
fried [fraɪd] *adj* gebraten, Brat–,
Back–
fried' chick'en *s* Backhuhn *n*
fried' egg' *s* Spiegelei *n*
fried' pota'toes *spl* Bratkartoffeln *pl*
friend [frend] *s* Freund –in *mf;* **be**
(close) friends (eng) befreundet sein;
make friends (with) sich anfreunden
(mit)
friendliness ['frendlɪnɪs] *s* Freundlichkeit *f*
friendly ['frendli] *adj* freundlich; **on f.**
terms with in freundschaftlichem
Verhältnis mit
friend'ship' *s* Freundschaft *f*
frieze [friːz] *s* Fries *m*
frigate ['frɪgɪt] *s* Fregatte *f*
fright [fraɪt] *s* Schrecken *m*
frighten ['fraɪtən] *tr* schrecken; **be**
frightened erschrecken; **f. away** ver-
scheuchen, vertreiben
frightful ['fraɪtfəl] *adj* schrecklich
frigid ['frɪdʒɪd] *adj* eiskalt; (pathol)
Frigid
frigidity [frɪ'dʒɪdɪtɪ] *s* Kälte *f;* (pathol)
Frigidität *f*
Frig'id Zone' *s* kalte Zone *f*
frill [frɪl] *s* (ruffle) Volant *m,* Krause
f; (frippery) Schnörkel *m;* **put on**
frills sich aufgeblasen benehmen;
with all the frills mit allen Schikanen
fringe [frɪndʒ] *s* Franse *f* ‖ *tr* mit
Fransen besetzen; (fig) einsäumen
fringe' ar'ea *s* Randgebiet *n*
fringe' ben'efit *s* zusätzliche Sozial-
leistung *f*
frippery ['frɪpərɪ] *s* (cheap finery, trifles) Flitterkram *m*
frisk [frɪsk] *tr* (sl) durchsuchen ‖ *intr*
—f. about herumtollen
frisky ['frɪskɪ] *adj* ausgelassen
fritter ['frɪtər] *s* Beignet *m* ‖ *tr*—**f.**
away vertrödeln, verzetteln
fritz [frɪts] *s*—**on the f.** kaputt
frivolous ['frɪvələs] *adj* leichtfertig;
(object) geringfügig
friz [frɪz] *s* (frizzes) Kraushaar *n* ‖
v (pret & pp **frizzed;** *ger* **frizzing**) *tr*
kräuseln ‖ *intr* sich kräuseln
frizzle ['frɪzəl] *s* Kraushaar *n* ‖ *tr*
(hair) kräuseln; (food) knusprig braten ‖ *intr* sich kräuseln; (sizzle)
zischen
frizzy ['frɪzɪ] *adj* kraus
fro [fro] *adv*—**to and fro** hin und her
frock [frak] *s* Kleid *n;* (eccl) Mönchs-
kutte *f*
frog [frɔg] *s* (animal; slight hoarseness) Frosch *m*
frog'man' *s* (**–men'**) Froschmann *m*
frol·ic ['frɑlɪk] *s* Spaß *m* ‖ *v* (pret &

pp **–icked;** *ger* **–icking**) *intr* Spaß
machen; (frisk about) herumtollen
frolicsome ['frɑlɪksəm] *adj* ausgelassen
from [frʌm] *prep* von (dat), aus (dat),
von (dat) aus; **f. afar** von weitem;
f. now on künftig; **f. ... on** von ...
an
front [frʌnt] *adj* Vorder–, vordere ‖
s (façade) Vorderseite *f;* (of a shirt,
dress) Einsatz *m;* (cover-up) Aushängeschild *n;* (meteor, mil) Front
f; **from the f.** von vorn; **in f. vorn;**
in f. of vor (dat or acc); **in the f.**
of the book vorn im Buch; **put on**
a bold f. Mut zeigen; **present on a**
big f. alles Fassade! ‖ *tr* gegenüber-
liegen (dat) ‖ *intr*—**f. for s.o.** j–m
als Strohmann dienen; **f. on mit der**
Front liegen nach
frontage ['frʌntɪdʒ] *s* Straßenfront *f*
frontal ['frʌntəl] *adj* Frontal–; (anat)
Stirn–
fron'tal view' *s* Vorderansicht *f*
front' door' *s* Haustür *f*
front' foot' *s* Vorderfuß *m*
frontier [frʌn'tɪr] *s* (border) Grenze
f; (area) Grenzland *n;* (fig) Grenz-
bereich *m*
frontiers'man *s* (**–men**) Pionier *m*
frontispiece ['frʌntɪs,piːs] *s* Titelbild
n
front' line' *s* Front *f,* Frontlinie *f*
front'-line' *adj* Front–, Gefechts–
front' page' *s* Titelseite *f*
front' porch' *s* Veranda *f*
front' rank' *s* (mil) vorderes Glied *n;*
be in the f. (fig) im Vordergrund
stehen
front' row' *s* erste Reihe *f*
front' run'ner *s* (pol) Spitzenkandidat
–in *mf*
front' seat' *s* Vordersitz *m*
front' steps' *spl* Vordertreppe *f*
front' yard' *s* Vorgarten *m,* Vorplatz *m*
frost [frɔst] *s* (freezing) Frost *m;*
(frozen dew) Reif *m* ‖ *tr* mit Reif
überziehen; (culin) glasieren
frost'bite' *s* Erfrierung *f*
frost'bit'ten *adj* erfroren
frost'ed glass' *s* Mattglas *n*
frost'ing *s* Glasur *f*
frost' line' *s* Frostgrenze *f*
frosty ['frɔstɪ] *adj* (& fig) frostig
froth [frɔθ] *s* (foam) Schaum *m;*
(slaver) Geifer *m* ‖ *intr* schäumen;
geifern
frothy ['frɔθɪ] *adj* schäumend
froward ['frowərd] *adj* eigensinnig
frown [fraun] *s* Stirnrunzeln *n* ‖ *intr*
die Stirn runzeln; **f. at** böse anschauen; **f. on** mißbilligen
frowsy, frowzy ['frauzɪ] *adj* (slovenly)
schlampig; (ill-smelling) muffig
froz'en as'sets *s* [frɔzən] *spl* eingefro-
rene Guthaben *pl*
froz'en foods' *spl* tiefgekühlte Lebensmittel *pl*
frugal ['frugəl] *adj* frugal
fruit [frut] *adj* (tree) Obst–, Süd-
frucht– ‖ *s* Frucht *f,* Obst *n,* Südfrüchte *pl;* (fig) Frucht *f*
fruit' cake' *s* Stolle *f,* Stollen *m*

fruit′ cup′ s gemischte Früchte pl
fruit′ fly′ s Obstfliege f
fruitful [′frutfəl] adj fruchtbar
fruition [fru′ɪʃən] s Reife f; **come to f.** zur Reife gelangen
fruit′ jar′ s Konservenglas n
fruit′ juice′ s Fruchtsaft m, Obstsaft m
fruitless [′frutlɪs] adj (& fig) fruchtlos
fruit′ sal′ad s Obstsalat m
fruit′ stand′ s Obststand m
frump [frʌmp] s Scharteke f
frumpish [′frʌmpɪ/] adj schlampig
frustrate [′frʌstret] tr (discourage) frustrieren; (an endeavor) vereiteln
frustration [frʌs′treʃən] s Frustration f; (of an endeavor) Vereitelung f
fry [fraɪ] s Gebratenes n || v (pret & pp **fried**) tr & intr braten
fry′ing pan′ s Bratpfanne f; **jump out of the f. into the fire** vom Regen unter die Traufe kommen
fuchsia [′fju/ə] s (bot) Fuchsie f
fudge [fʌdʒ] s weiches, milchhaltiges, mit Kakao versetztes Zuckerwerk n
fuel [′fjuəl] s Brennstoff m; (for engines) Treibstoff m; (fig) Nahrung f; **add f. to the flames** Öl ins Feuer gießen || v (pret & pp **fuel[l]ed**; ger **fuel[l]ing**) tr mit Brennstoff versorgen || intr tanken
fu′el dump′ s Treibstofflager n
fu′el gauge′ s Benzinuhr f
fu′el tank′ s Treibstoffbehälter m
fugitive [′fjudʒɪtɪv] adj flüchtig || s Flüchtling m
fugue [fjug] s (mus) Fuge f
ful·crum [′fʌlkrəm] s (–crums & –cra [krə]) Stützpunkt m, Drehpunkt m
fulfill [ful′fɪl] tr erfüllen
fulfillment [ful′fɪlmənt] s Erfüllung f
full [ful] adj voll; (with food) satt; (clothes) weit; (hour) ganz; (life) inhaltsreich; (voice) wohlklingend; (professor) ordentlich; **f. of** voller, voll von; **too f.** übervoll; **work f. time** ganztägig arbeiten || adv—**f. well** sehr gut || s—**in f.** voll, ganz || tr (tex) walken
full′back′ s (fb) Außenverteidiger m
full′-blood′ed adj vollblütig
full-blown [′ful′blon] adj (flower) voll aufgeblüht; (fig) voll erblüht
full′-bod′ied adj (wine) stark, schwer
full′ dress′ s Gesellschaftsanzug m; (mil) Paradeanzug m
full′-dress′ adj Gala–, formell
full′-faced′ adj pausbackig; (portrait) mit voll zugewandtem Gesicht
full-fledged [′ful′fledʒd] adj richtiggehend
full-grown [′ful′gron] adj voll ausgewachsen
full′ house′ s (cards) Full house n; (theat) volles Haus n
full′-length′ adj (dress) in voller Größe; (portrait) lebensgroß; (movie) abendfüllend
full′ moon′ s Vollmond m
full′-page′ adj ganzseitig
full′ pay′ s volles Gehalt n
full′ profes′sor s Ordinarius m
full′-scale′ adj in voller Größe
full′-sized′ adj in natürlicher Größe

full′ speed′ adv auf höchsten Touren
full′ stop′ s (gram) Punkt m; **come to a f.** völlig stillstehen
full′ swing′ s—**in f.** in vollem Gange
full′ throt′tle s Vollgas n
full′ tilt′ adv auf höchsten Touren
full′-time′ adj ganztägig
full′ view′ s—**in f.** direkt vor den Augen
fully [′ful(l)i] adj völlig; **be f. booked** ausverkauft sein
fulsome [′fulsəm] adj (excessive) übermäßig; (offensive) widerlich
fumble [′fʌmbəl] tr (a ball) fallen lassen || intr fummeln; **f. for** umherfühlen nach
fume [fjum] s Gas n, Dampf m || intr dampfen; (smoke) rauchen; **f. with rage** vor Wut schnauben
fumigate [′fjumɪˌget] tr ausräuchern
fun [fʌn] s Spaß m; **be (great) fun** (viel) Spaß machen; **for fun** zum Spaß; **for the fun of it** spaßeshalber; **have fun!** viel Spaß!; **make fun of** sich lustig machen über (acc); **poke fun at** witzeln über (acc)
function [′fʌŋkʃən] s Funktion f; (office) Amt n; (formal occasion) Feier f || intr funktionieren; (officiate) fungieren
functional [′fʌŋkʃənəl] adj (practical) Zweck–, zweckmäßig; (disorder) funktionell, Funktions–
functionary [′fʌŋkʃəˌneri] s Funktionär –in mf
fund [fʌnd] s Fonds m; (fig) Vorrat m **funds** Geldmittel pl || tr fundieren
fundamental [ˌfʌndə′mentəl] adj grundlegend, Grund– || s Grundbegriff m
fundamentalist [ˌfʌndə′mentəlɪst] s Fundamentalist –in mf
fundamentally [ˌfʌndə′mentəli] adv im Grunde, prinzipiell
funeral [′fjunərəl] adj Leichen–, Trauer–, Begräbnis– || s Begräbnis n
fu′neral direc′tor s Bestattungsunternehmer –in mf
fu′neral home′ s Aufbahrungshalle f
fu′neral proces′sion s Trauergefolge n
fu′neral serv′ice s Trauergottesdienst m
fu′neral wreath′ s Totenkranz m
funereal [fju′nɪrɪəl] adj düster
fungus [′fʌŋgəs] s (funguses & fungi [′fʌndʒaɪ]) Pilz m, Schwamm m
funicular [fju′nɪkjələr] s Drahtseilbahn f
funk [fʌŋk] s (fear) Mordsangst f; **be in a f.** niedergeschlagen sein
fun·nel [′fʌnəl] s Trichter m; (naut) Schornstein m || v (pret & pp –**nel[l]ed**; ger –**nel[l]ing**) tr durch e–n Trichter gießen; (fig) (into) konzentrieren (auf acc)
funnies [′fʌniz] spl Witzseite f
funny [′fʌni] adj komisch; (strange, suspicious) sonderbar; **don′t try anything f.** mach mir keine Dummheiten!
fun′ny bone′ s Musikantenknochen m
fun′ny bus′iness s dunkle Geschäfte pl
fun′ny ide′as spl Flausen pl

fun'ny pa'per s Witzblatt n
fur [fʌr] adj (coat, collar) Pelz– ‖ s Pelz m; (on the tongue) Belag m
furbish ['fʌrbiʃ] tr aufputzen
furious ['fjuri-əs] adj (at) wütend (auf acc); **be f.** wüten
furl [fʌrl] tr zusammenrollen
fur'-lined' adj pelzgefüttert
furlong ['fʌrlɔŋ] s Achtelmeile f
furlough ['fʌrlo] s (mil) Urlaub m; **go on f.** auf Urlaub kommen ‖ tr beurlauben
furnace ['fʌrnis] s Ofen m
furnish ['fʌrniʃ] tr (a room) möblieren; (e.g., an office) ausstatten; (proof) liefern; (supply) (with) versehen (mit)
fur'nished room' s möbliertes Zimmer n
furnishings ['fʌrniʃiŋz] spl Ausstattung f
furniture ['fʌrnitʃər] s Möbel pl; **piece of f.** Möbelstück n
fur'niture store' s Möbelhandlung f
furor ['fjuror] s (rage) Wut f; (uproar) Furore f; (vogue) Mode f; **cause a f.** Furore machen
furrier ['fʌri-ər] s Pelzhändler –in mf
furrow ['fʌro] s Furche f ‖ tr furchen
furry ['fʌri] adj pelzig
further ['fʌrðər] adj weiter; (particulars) näher ‖ adv weiter ‖ tr fördern
furtherance ['fʌrðərəns] s Förderung f
fur'thermore' adv überdies, außerdem
furthest ['fʌrðist] adj weiteste ‖ adv am weitesten
furtive ['fʌrtiv] adj verstohlen

fury ['fjuri] s Wut f; **Fury** (myth) Furie f
fuse [fjuz] s (of an explosive) Zünder m; (elec) Sicherung f; **blown f.** durchgebrannte Sicherung f ‖ tr verschmelzen ‖ intr verschmelzen; (fig) sich vereinigen
fuse' box' s Sicherungskasten m
fuselage ['fjuzəlɪdʒ] s (aer) Rumpf m
fusible ['fjuzibəl] adj schmelzbar
fusillade ['fjusə‚led] s Feuersalve f; (fig) Hagel m
fusion ['fjuʒən] s Verschmelzung f; (pol, phys) Fusion f
fuss [fʌs] s Getue n; **make a f. over** viel Aufhebens machen von ‖ intr sich aufregen; **f. around** herumwirtschaften; **f. over** viel Aufhebens machen von; **f. with** herumspielen mit
fuss' bud'get, fuss'pot' s Umstandskrämer m
fussy ['fʌsi] adj (given to detail) umständlich; (fastidious) heikel; (irritable) reizbar; **be f.** Umstände machen
fustian ['fʌstʃən] s (bombast) Schwulst m; (tex) Barchent m
fusty ['fʌsti] adj (musty) muffig; (old-fashioned) veraltet
futile ['fjutəl] adj vergeblich, nutzlos
futility [fju'tiliti] s Nutzlosigkeit f
future ['fjutʃər] adj (zu)künftig ‖ s Zukunft f; **futures** (econ) Termingeschäfte pl; **in the f.** künftig
fuzz [fʌz] s (from cloth) Fussel f; (on peaches) Flaum m
fuzzy ['fʌzi] adj flaumig; (unclear) unklar; (hair) kraus

G

G, g [dʒi] s siebenter Buchstabe des englischen Alphabets
gab [gæb] s (coll) Geschwätz n ‖ v (pret & pp **gabbed;** ger **gabbing**) intr schwatzen
gabardine ['gæbər‚din] s Gabardine m
gabble ['gæbəl] s Geschnatter n ‖ intr schnattern
gable ['gebəl] s Giebel m
ga'ble end' s Giebelwand f
ga'ble roof' s Giebeldach n
gad [gæd] v (pret & pp **gadded;** ger **gadding**) intr—**gad about** umherstreifen
gad'about' s Bummler –in mf
gad'fly' s Viehbremse f; (fig) Störenfried m
gadget ['gædʒit] s (coll) Gerät n
Gaelic ['gelik] adj gälisch ‖ s (language) Gälisch n
gaff [gæf] s Fischhaken m
gag [gæg] s (something put into the mouth) Knebel m; (joke) Witz m; (hoax, trick) amüsanter Trick m; v (pret & pp **gagged;** ger **gagging**) tr knebeln; (said of a tight collar) würgen; (fig) mundtot machen ‖ intr (on food) würgen

gage [gedʒ] s (challenge) Fehdehandschuh m; (pawn) Pfand m
gaiety ['ge-iti] s Fröhlichkeit f
gaily ['geli] adv fröhlich
gain [gen] s Gewinn m; (advantage) Vorteil m; **g. in weight** Gewichtszunahme f ‖ tr gewinnen; (pounds) zunehmen; (a living) verdienen; (a victory) erringen; **g. a footing** festen Fuß fassen; **g. ground** (mil & fig) Terrain gewinnen; **g. speed** schneller werden; **g. weight** an Gewicht zunehmen ‖ intr (said of a car) aufholen; (said of a clock) vorgehen; **g. from** Gewinn haben von; **g. in** gewinnen an (dat); **g. on s.o.** j–m den Vorteil abgewinnen
gainful ['genfəl] adj einträglich
gainfully ['genfəli] adv—**g. employed** erwerbstätig
gain'say' v (pret & pp **–said** [‚sed], [‚sed]) tr (a thing) verneinen; (a person) widersprechen (dat)
gait [get] s Gang m, Gangart f
gala ['gælə], ['gelə] adj festlich ‖ s (celebration) Feier f; (dress) Gala f
galaxy ['gæləksi] s Galaxis f; (fig) glänzende Versammlung f

gale [gel] s Sturm m, Sturmwind m; **gales of laughter** Lachensalven pl

gale' warn'ing s Sturmwarnung f

gall [gɔl] s Galle f; (audacity) Unverschämtheit f || tr (rub) wundreiben; (vex) ärgern, belästigen

gallant ['gælənt] adj (tapfer); (stately) stattlich || [gə'lænt] adj galant || s Galan m

gallantry ['gæləntri] s (bravery) Tapferkeit f; (courteous behavior) Ritterlichkeit f

gall' blad'der s Gallenblase f

galleon ['gæli·ən] s Galeone f

gallery ['gæləri] s (arcade) Säulenhalle f; (art, theat) Galerie f; (min) Stollen m; **play to the g.** (coll) Effekthascherei treiben

galley ['gæli] s (a ship) Galeere f; (a kitchen) Kombüse f; (typ) Setzschiff n

gal'ley proof' s (typ) Fahne f

gal'ley slave' s Galeerensklave m

Gallic ['gælɪk] adj gallisch

gall'ing adj verdrießlich

gallivant ['gælɪˌvænt] intr bummeln

gallon ['gælən] s Gallone f

galloon [gə'lun] s Tresse f

gallop ['gæləp] s Galopp m; **at full g.** in gestrecktem Galopp || tr in Galopp setzen || intr galoppieren

gal·lows ['gæloz] s (-lows & -lowses) Galgen m

gall'lows bird' s (coll) Galgenvogel m

gall'stone' s Gallenstein m

galore [gə'lor] adv im Überfluß

galosh [gə'lɑ/] s Galosche f

galvanize ['gælvəˌnaɪz] tr galvanisieren

gambit ['gæmbɪt] s (fig) Schachzug m; (chess) Gambit n

gamble ['gæmbəl] s Hasardspiel n; (risk) Risiko n; (com) Spekulationsgeschäft n || tr—g. **away** verspielen || intr spielen, hasardieren

gambler ['gæmblər] s Spieler -in mf; (fig) Hasardeur m, Hasardeuse f

gam'bling s Spielen n, Spiel n

gam'bling house' s Spielhölle f

gam'bling ta'ble s Spieltisch m

gam·bol ['gæmbəl] s Luftsprung m || v (pret & pp -bol[l]ed; ger -bol[l]ing) intr umhertollen

gambrel ['gæmbrəl] s (hock) Hachse f; (in a butcher shop) Spriegel m

gam'brel roof' s Mansardendach n

game [gem] adj bereit; (fight) tapfer; (leg) lahm; (hunt) Wild-, Jagd- || s Spiel n; (e.g., of chess) Partie f; (fig) Absicht f; (culin) Wildbret n; (hunt) Wild n, Jagdwild n; **have the g. in the bag** den Sieg in der Tasche haben; **play a losing g.** auf verlorenem Posten kämpfen; **the g. is up** das Spiel ist aus

game' bird' s Jagdvogel m

game' board' s Spielbrett n

game'cock' s Kampfhahn m

gameness ['gemnɪs] f Tapferkeit f

game' of chance' s Glücksspiel n

game' preserve' s Wildpark m

game' war'den s Jagdaufseher m

gamut ['gæmət] s Skala f

gamy ['gemi] adj nach Wild riechend; **g. flavor** Wildgeschmack m

gander ['gændər] s Gänserich m; **take a g. at** (coll) e-n Blick werfen auf (acc)

gang [gæŋ] s (group of friends) Gesellschaft f; (antisocial group) Bande f; (of workers) Kolonne f || intr—g. **up** (on) sich zusammenrotten (gegen)

gangling ['gæŋglɪŋ] adj schlaksig

gangli·on ['gæŋglɪ·ən] s (-ons & -a [ə]) (cystic tumor) Überbein n; (of nerves) Nervenknoten m

gangly ['gæŋgli] adj schlaksig

gang'plank' s Laufplanke f, Steg m

gangrene ['gæŋgrin] s Gangrän n, Brand m || intr brandig werden

gangrenous ['gæŋgrɪnəs] adj brandig

gangster ['gæŋstər] s Gangster m

gang'way' s (passageway) Durchgang m; (naut) Laufplanke f || interj aus dem Weg!

gantlet ['gɔntlət] s (rr) Gleisverschlingung f

gantry ['gæntri] s (rok) Portalkran m; (rr) Signalbrücke f

gan'try crane' s Portalkran m

gap [gæp] s Lücke f; (in the mountains) Schlucht f; (mil) Bresche f

gape [gep] s Riß m, Sprung m; (gaping) Gaffen n || intr gaffen; (said of wounds, etc.) klaffen; **g. at** angaffen

garage [gə'rɑʒ] s Garage f; (repair shop) Reparaturwerkstatt f; **put into the g.** unterstellen

garb [gɑrb] s Tracht f

garbage ['gɑrbɪdʒ] s Müll m; (nonsense) Unsinn m

gar'bage can' s Mülltonne f

gar'bage dispos'al s Müllabfuhr f

gar'bage dump' s Müllplatz m

gar'bage man' s Müllfahrer m

gar'bage truck' s Müllabfuhrwagen m

garble ['gɑrbəl] tr verstümmeln

garden ['gɑrdən] s Garten m; **gardens** Gartenanlage f

gardener ['gɑrdənər] s Gärtner -in mf

gar'den hose' s Gartenschlauch m

gardenia [gɑr'dini·ə] s Gardenie f

gar'dening s Gartenarbeit f

gar'den par'ty s Gartengesellschaft f

gargle ['gɑrgəl] s Mundwasser n || tr & intr gurgeln

gargoyle ['gɑrgɔɪl] s Wasserspeier m

garish ['gerɪʃ], ['gærɪʃ] adj grell

garland ['gɑrlənd] s Girlande f

garlic ['gɑrlɪk] s Knoblauch m

garment ['gɑrmənt] s Kleidungsstück n

garner ['gɑrnər] tr (grain) aufspeichern; (gather) ansammeln

garnet ['gɑrnɪt] s Granat m

garnish ['gɑrnɪʃ] s Verzierung f; (culin) Garnierung f || tr verzieren; (culin) garnieren

garret ['gerɪt] s Dachstube f

garrison ['gerɪsən] s (troops) Garnison f, Besatzung f; (fort) Festung f || tr mit e-r Garnison versehen; (troops) in Garnison stationieren

gar'rison cap' s Schiffchen n

garrote [gə'rɑt], [gə'rot] s Garrotte f || tr garrottieren

garrulous ['gær(j)ələs] *adj* schwatzhaft

garter ['gɑrtər] *s* Strumpfband *n*

gar'ter belt' *s* Strumpfhaltergürtel *m*

gas [gæs] *adj* (*e.g., generator, light, main, meter*) Gas– || *s* Gas *n;* (coll) Benzin *n*, Sprit *m;* (*empty talk*) (sl) leeres Geschwätz *n;* **get gas** (coll) tanken; **step on the gas** (coll) Gas geben || *v* (*pret & pp* **gassed;** *ger* **gassing**) *tr* vergasen || *intr* sl schwatzen; **gas up** (coll) volltanken

gas' attack' *s* Gasangriff *m*

gas' burn'er *s* Gasbrenner *m*

gas' en'gine *s* Gasmotor *m*

gaseous ['gæsɪ·əs], ['gæʃəs] *adj* gasförmig

gas' fit'ter *s* Gasinstallateur *m*

gash [gæʃ] *s* tiefe Schnittwunde *f* || e–e tiefe Schnittwunde beibringen (*dat*)

gas' heat' *s* Gasheizung *f*

gas'hold'er *s* Gasbehälter *m*

gasi•fy ['gæsɪ,faɪ] *v* (*pret & pp* **–fied**) *tr* in Gas verwandeln || *intr* zu Gas werden

gas' jet' *s* Gasflamme *f*

gasket ['gæskɪt] *s* Dichtung *f*

gas' mask' *s* Gasmaske *f*

gasoline ['gæsə'lin] *s* Benzin *n*

gas'oline' pump' *s* Benzinzapfsäule *f*

gasp [gæsp] *s* Keuchen *n* || *tr* (out) hervorstoßen || *intr* keuchen; **g. for air** nach Luft schnappen; **g. for breath** nach Atem ringen

gas' range' *s* Gasherd *m*

gas' sta'tion *s* Tankstelle *f*

gas' sta'tion attend'ant *s* Tankwart *m*

gas' stove' *s* Gasherd *m*

gas' tank' *s* Benzinbehälter *m*

gastric ['gæstrɪk] *adj* gastrisch

gas'tric juice' *s* Magensaft *m*

gastronomy [gæs'trɑnəmi] *s* Gastronomie *f*

gas'works' *spl* Gasanstalt *f*

gate [get] *s* Tor *n*, Pforte *f;* (rr) Sperre *f;* (sport) eingenommenes Eintrittsgeld *n;* **crash the g.** ohne Eintrittskarte durchschlupfen

gate' crash'er [ˌkræʃər] *s* unberechtigter Zuschauer *m*

gate'keep'er *s* Pförtner –in *mf*

gate'post' *s* Torpfosten *m*

gate'way' *s* Tor *n*, Torweg *m*

gather ['gæðər] *tr* (*things*) sammeln; (*people*) versammeln; (*flowers, fruit, peas*) pflücken; (*courage*) aufbringen; (*the impression*) gewinnen; (*information*) einziehen; (*strength, speed*) zunehmen an (*dat*); (*conclude*) (**from**) schließen (aus); **g. together** versammeln; **g. up** aufheben; (*curtains, dress*) raffen || *intr* sich (an)sammeln; (*said of clouds*) sich zusammenziehen; **g. around** sich scharen um

gath'ered *adj* (*skirt*) gerafft

gath'ering *s* Versammlung *f;* (sew) Kräuselfalten *pl*

gaudy ['gɔdi] *adj* (*overdone*) überladen; (*color*) grell

gauge [gedʒ] *s* (*instrument*) Messer *m*, Anzeiger *m;* (*measurement*) Eichmaß *n;* (*of wire*) Stärke *f;* (*of a shot-*

gun) Kaliber *n;* (fig) Maß *n;* (mach) Lehre *f;* (rr) Spurweite *f* || *tr* messen; (*check for accuracy*) eichen; (fig) abschätzen

Gaul [gɔl] *s* Gallien *n;* (*native*) Gallier –in *mf*

Gaulish ['gɔlɪʃ] *adj* gallisch

gaunt [gɔnt] *adj* hager

gauntlet ['gɔntlɪt] *s* Panzerhandschuh *m;* (fig) Fehdehandschuh *m;* **run the g.** Spießruten laufen

gauze [gɔz] *s* Gaze *f*

gavel ['gævəl] *s* Hammer *m*

gawk [gɔk] *s* (coll) Depp *m* || *intr*–**g. at** (coll) blöde anstarren

gawky ['gɔki] *adj* schlaksig

gay [ge] *adj* lustig; (*homosexual*) schwul

gay' blade' *s* lebenslustiger Kerl *m*

gaze [gez] *intr* starren; **g. at** anstarren; (*in astonishment*) anstaunen

gazelle [gə'zel] *s* Gazelle *f*

gazetteer [ˌgæzə'tɪr] *s* Ortslexikon *n*

gear [gɪr] *s* (*equipment*) Ausrüstung *f;* (aut) Schaltgetriebe *n*, Gang *m;* (mach) Zahnrad *n;* **gears** Räderwerk *n;* **in g.** eingeschaltet; **in high g.** im höchsten Gang; (fig) auf Touren; **shift gears** umschalten; **throw into g.** einschalten; **throw out of g.** (fig) aus dem Gleichgewicht bringen || *tr*–**g. to** anpassen (*dat*)

gear'box' *s* Schaltgetriebe *n*

gear'shift' *s* Gangschaltung *f;* (*lever*) Schalthebel *m*

gear'wheel' *s* Zahnrad *n*

gee [dʒi] *interj* nanu!

Geiger counter ['gaɪgər ˌkauntər] *s* Geigerzähler *m*

gel [dʒel] *s* Gel *n* || *v* (*pret & pp* **gelled;** *ger* **gelling**) *intr* gelieren; (coll) klappen

gelatin ['dʒelətɪn] *s* Gelatine *f*

geld [geld] *v* (*pret & pp* **gelded & gelt** [gelt]) *tr* kastrieren

geld'ing *s* Wallach *m*

gem [dʒem] *s* Edelstein *m;* (fig) Perle *f*

Gemini ['dʒemɪ,naɪ] *s* (astr) Zwillinge *pl*

gender ['dʒendər] *s* Geschlecht *n*

gene [dʒin] *s* Gen *n*, Erbanlage *f*

genealogical [ˌdʒinɪ·ə'lɑdʒɪkəl] *adj* genealogisch, Stamm–

genealog'ical ta'ble *s* Stammtafel *f*

genealog'ical tree' *s* Stammbaum *m*

genealogy [ˌdʒinɪ'ælədʒi] *s* Genealogie *f*

general ['dʒenərəl] *adj* allgemein, Gesamt– || *s* General *m;* **in g.** im allgemeinen

Gen'eral Assem'bly *s* Vollversammlung *f*

gen'eral deliv'ery *adv* postlagernd

gen'eral head'quarters *spl* Oberkommando *n*

generalissi•mo [ˌdʒenərə'lɪsɪmo] *s* (**–mos**) Generalissimus *m*

generality [ˌdʒenə'rælɪti] *s* Allgemeingültigkeit *f;* **generalities** Gemeinplätze *pl*

generalization [ˌdʒenərəlɪ'zeʃən] *s* Verallgemeinerung *f* generalize ['dʒenərə,laɪz] tr & intr verallgemeinern

generally ['dʒenərəli] adv im allgemeinen; (usually) gewöhnlich; (mostly) meistens

gen'eral man'ager s Generaldirektor –in mf

gen'eral plan' s Übersichtsplan m

gen'eral post' of'fice s Oberpostamt n

gen'eral practi'tioner s praktischer Arzt m

gen'eralship' s Führereigenschaften pl

gen'eral staff' s Generalstab m

gen'eral store' s Gemischtwarenhandlung f

gen'eral strike' s Generalstreik m

generate ['dʒenə,ret] tr (procreate) zeugen; (fig) verursachen; (elec) erzeugen; (geom) bilden

gen'erating sta'tion s Kraftwerk n

generation [,dʒenə're∫ən] s Generation f; present g. Mitwelt f; younger g. junge Generation f

genera'tion gap' s Generationsproblem n

generator ['dʒenə,retər] s Erzeuger m; (chem, elec) Generator m; (elec) Stromerzeuger m

generic [dʒɪ'nerɪk] adj generisch, Gattungs–; g. name Gattungsname m

generosity [,dʒenə'rɑsɪti] s Freigebigkeit f

generous ['dʒenərəs] adj freigebig

gene·sis ['dʒenɪsɪs] s (–ses [,sɪz]) Genese f, Entstehung f; Genesis (Bib) Genesis f

genetic [dʒɪ'netɪk] adj genetisch

genet'ic engineer' s Gen-Ingineur m

genet'ic engineer'ing s Gen-Manipulation f

genetics [dʒɪ'netɪks] s Genetik f, Vererbungslehre f

Geneva [dʒɪ'nivə] adj Genfer || s Genf n

Genevieve ['dʒenə,viv] s Genoveva f

genial ['dʒinɪ·əl] adj freundlich

genie ['dʒini] s Kobold m

genital ['dʒenɪtəl] adj Genital– || genitals spl Genitalien pl

genitive ['dʒenɪtɪv] s Genitiv m, Wesfall m

genius ['dʒinɪ·əs] s (geniuses) Genie n || s (genii ['dʒini,aɪ]) Genius m

Genoa ['dʒeno·ə] s Genua n

genocidal [,dʒenə'saɪdəl] adj rassenmörderisch

genocide ['dʒenə,saɪd] s Rassenmord m

genre ['ʒɑnrə] s Genre n

genteel [dʒen'til] adj vornehm

gentile ['dʒentaɪl] adj nichtjüdisch; (pagan) heidnisch || s Nichtjude m, Nichtjüdin f; (pagan) Heide m, Heidin f

gentility [dʒen'tɪlɪti] s Vornehmheit f

gentle ['dʒentəl] adj sanft, mild; (tame) zahm

gen'tle·man s (–men) Herr m, Gentleman m

gentlemanly ['dʒentəlmənli] adj weltmännisch

gen'tleman's agree'ment s Kavaliersab-

kommen n, Gentleman's Agreement n

gentleness ['dʒentəlnɪs] s Sanftmut f

gen'tle sex' s zartes Geschlecht n

gentry ['dʒentri] s feine Leute pl

genuflection [,dʒenju'flek∫ən] s Kniebeugung f

genuine ['dʒenjʊ·ɪn] adj echt

genus ['dʒinəs] s (genera ['dʒenərə] & genuses) (biol, log) Gattung f

geographer [dʒɪ'ɑgrəfər] s Geograph –in mf

geographic(al) [,dʒɪ·ə'græfɪk(əl)] adj geographisch

geography [dʒɪ'ɑgrəfi] s Geographie f

geologic(al) [,dʒɪ·ə'lɑdʒɪk(əl)] adj geologisch

geolog'ical e'ra s Erdalter n

geologist [dʒɪ'ɑlədʒɪst] s Geologe m, Geologin f

geology [dʒɪ'ɑlədʒi] s Geologie f

geometric(al) [,dʒi·ə'metrɪk(əl)] adj geometrisch

geometrician [dʒɪ,ɑmɪ'trɪ∫ən] s Geometer –in mf

geometry [dʒɪ'ɑmɪtri] s Geometrie f

geophysics [,dʒi·ə'fɪzɪks] s Geophysik f

geopolitics [,dʒi·ə'pɑlɪtɪks] s Geopolitik f

George [dʒordʒ] s Georg m

geranium [dʒɪ'renɪ·əm] s Geranie f

geriatrics [,dʒerɪ'ætrɪks] s Geriatrie f

germ [dʒʌrm] s Keim m

German ['dʒʌrmən] adj & adv deutsch || s Deutsche mf; (language) Deutsch n; in G. auf deutsch

germane [dʒer'men] adj (to) passend (zu)

Germanize ['dʒʌrmə,naɪz] tr eindeutschen

Ger'man mea'sles s & spl Röteln pl

Ger'man shep'herd s deutscher Schäferhund m

Ger'man sil'ver s Alpaka n, Neusilber n

Germany ['dʒʌrməni] s Deutschland n

germ' cell' s Keimzelle f

germicidal [,dʒʌrmɪ'saɪdəl] adj keimtötend

germicide ['dʒʌrmɪ,saɪd] s Keimtöter m

germinate ['dʒʌrmɪ,net] intr keimen

germ' war'fare s bakteriologische Kriegsführung f

gerontology [,dʒerən'tɑlədʒi] s Gerontologie f

gerund ['dʒerənd] s Gerundium n

gerundive [dʒɪ'rʌndɪv] s Gerundiv n

gestation [dʒes'te∫ən] s Schwangerschaft f; (in animals) Trächtigkeit f

gesticulate [dʒes'tɪkjə,let] intr gestikulieren, sich gebärden

gesticulation [dʒes,tɪkjə'le∫ən] s Gebärdenspiel n, Gestikulation f

gesture ['dʒest∫ər] s Geste f || intr Gesten machen

get [get] v (pret got [gat]; pp got & gotten ['gatən]; ger getting) tr (acquire) bekommen; (receive) erhalten; (procure) beschaffen, besorgen; (fetch) holen; (understand) (coll) kapieren; (s.o. to do s.th.) dazu bringen; (*reach by telephone*) erreichen; (*make, e.g., dirty*) machen; (*convey, e.g., a message*) übermitteln; **get across** klarmachen; **get back** zurückbekommen; **get down** (*depress*) verdrießen; (*swallow*) hinunterwürgen; **get going** in Gang setzen; **get hold of** (*a person*) erwischen; (*a thing*) erlangen; (*grip*) ergreifen; **get off** (*e.g., a lid*) abbekommen; **get one's way** sich durchsetzen; **get out** (*e.g., a spot*) herausbekommen; **get s.o. used to** j-n gewöhnen an (*acc*); **get s.th. into one's head** sich [*dat*] etw in den Kopf setzen; **get the hang of** (coll) wegbekommen; **get the jump on s.o.** j-m zuvorkommen; **get the worst of it** am schlechtesten dabei wegkommen; **get** (*s.th.*) **wrong** falsch verstehen; **you're going to get it!** (coll) du wirst es kriegen! || *intr* (*become*) werden; **get about** sich fortbewegen; **get ahead in the world** in der Welt fortkommen; **get along** auskommen; **get along with** zurechtkommen mit; **get around** herumkommen; **get around to it** dazu kommen; **get at** herankommen an (*acc*); (*e.g., the real reason*) herausfinden; **get away** (*run away*) entlaufen; (*escape*) entkommen; **get away from me!** geh weg von mir!; **get away with** davonkommen mit; **get back at s.o.** es j-m heimzahlen; **get by** (*e.g., the guards*) vorbeikommen an (*dat*); (*on little money*) durchkommen; **get down** (*step down*) absteigen; **get down to brass tacks** (*or business*) zur Sache kommen; **get going** sich auf den Weg machen; **get going!** mach, daß du weiter kommst!; **get into** (*a vehicle*) einsteigen in (*acc*); (*trouble, etc.*) geraten in (*acc*); **get loose** sich losmachen; **get lost** verloren gehen, abhanden kommen; (*lose one's way*) sich verirren; **get lost!** (sl) hau ab!; **get off** aussteigen; **get off with** (*a light sentence*) davonkommen mit; **get on** (*e.g., a train*) einsteigen (in *acc*); **get on one's feet again** sich hochrappeln; **get on with** (*s.o.*) zurechtkommen mit; **get out** aussteigen; **get out of a tight spot** sich aus der Schlinge ziehen; **get over** (*a hurdle*) nehmen; (*a misfortune*) überwinden; (*a sickness*) überstehen; **get ready** sich fertig machen; **get through** durchkommen; **get through to s.o.** sich verständlich machen (*dat*); (telp) erreichen; **get to be** werden; **get together** (*meet*) sich treffen; (*agree*) (*on*) sich einig werden (über *acc*); **get to the bottom of** ergründen; **get up** aufstehen; **get used to** sich gewöhnen an (*acc*); **get well** gesund werden; **get with it!** (coll) zur Sache!

get'away' s Entkommen *n*; (sport) Start *m*; **make one's g.** entkommen
get'away car' s Fluchtwagen *m*
get'-togeth'er s zwangloses Treffen *n*
get'up' s (coll) Aufzug *m*

get' up' and go' s Unternehmungsgeist *m*
gewgaw ['g(j)ugə] s Plunder *m*
geyser ['gaizər] s Geiser *m*
ghastly ['gæstli] adj (ghostly) gespenstisch; (*e.g., crime*) grausig; (*intensely unpleasant*) schrecklich
gherkin ['garkin] s Essiggurke *f*
ghet·to ['geto] s (-tos) Getto *n*
ghost [gost] s Gespenst *n*, Geist *m*; (telv) Doppelbild *n*; **give up the g.** den Geist aufgeben; **not a g. of a chance** nicht die geringsten Aussichten
ghostly ['gostli] adj gespenstisch
ghost' sto'ry s Spukgeschichte *f*
ghost' town' s Geisterstadt *f*
ghost' writ'er s Ghostwriter *m*
ghoul [gul] s (& fig) Unhold *m*
ghoulish ['gulɪʃ] adj teuflisch
GHQ ['dʒi'etʃ'kju] s (**General Headquarters**) Oberkommando *n*
GI ['dʒi'ai] s (**GI's**) (coll) Landser *m*
giant ['dʒai·ənt] adj riesig, Riesen- || s Riese *m*, Riesin *f*
giantess ['dʒai·əntis] s Riesin *f*
gibberish ['dʒibərɪʃ], ['gibərɪʃ] s Klauderwelsch *n*
gibbet ['dʒibit] s Galgen *m* || *intr* hängen
gibe [dʒaib] s Spott *m* || *intr* spotten; **g. at** verspotten
giblets ['dʒiblits] spl Gänseklein *n*
giddiness ['gidinis] s Schwindelgefühl *n*; (*frivolity*) Leichtsinn *m*
giddy ['gidi] adj (dizzy) schwindlig; (*height*) schwindelerregend; (*frivolous*) leichtsinnig
gift [gift] s Geschenk *n*; (*natural ability*) Begabung *f*
gift'ed adj begabt
gift' horse' s—**never look a g. in the mouth** e-m geschenkten Gaul schaut man nicht ins Maul
gift' of gab' s (coll) gutes Mundwerk *n*
gift' shop' s Geschenkartikelladen *m*
gift'-wrap' v (pret & pp -wrapped; ger -wrapping) tr als Geschenk verpacken
gift'wrap'ping s Geschenkverpackung *f*
gigantic [dʒai'gæntik] adj riesig
giggle ['gigəl] s Gekicher *n* || *intr* kichern
gigly ['gigli] adj allezeit kichernd
gigo·lo ['dʒigə‚lo] s (-los) Gigolo *m*
gild [gild] v (pret & pp gilded & gilt [gilt]) tr vergolden
gild'ing s Vergoldung *f*
gill [gil] s (of a fish) Kieme *f*; (of a cock) Kehllappen *m*
gilt [gilt] adj vergoldet || s Vergoldung *f*
gilt' edge' s Goldschnitt *m*
gilt'-edged' adj mit Goldschnitt versehen; (*first-class*) (coll) erstklassig
gimlet ['gimlit] s Handbohrer *m*
gimmick ['gimik] s (sl) Trick *m*
gin [dʒin] s Wacholderbranntwein *m*, Gin *m*; (snare) Schlinge *f* || v (pret & pp ginned; ger ginning) tr entkörnen
ginger ['dʒindʒər] s Ingwer *m*

gin'ger ale' s Ingwerlimonade f
gin'gerbread' s Pfefferkuchen m
gingerly ['dʒɪndʒərli] adv sacht(e)
gin'gersnap' s Ingwerplätzchen n
gingham ['gɪŋəm] s Gingham m
giraffe [dʒɪ'ræf] s Giraffe f
gird [gʌrd] v (pret & pp girt [gʌrt]
& girded) tr gürten; g. oneself with
a sword sich [dat] ein Schwert um-
gürten
girder ['gʌrdər] s Tragbalken m
girdle ['gʌrdəl] s Gürtel m
girl [gʌrl] s Mädchen n, Mädel n
girl' friend' s Freundin f, Geliebte f
girl'hood' s Mädchenzeit f
girlish ['gʌrlɪʃ] adj mädchenhaft
girl' scout' s Pfadfinderin f
girth [gʌrθ] s Umfang m; (for a horse)
Sattelgurt m
gist [dʒɪst] s Kernpunkt m; g. of the
matter des Pudels Kern
give [gɪv] s Elastizität f; (yielding)
Nachgeben n ‖ v (pret gave [gev];
pp given ['gɪvən]) tr geben; (a gift,
credence) schenken; (free of charge)
verschenken; (contribute) spenden;
(hand over) übergeben; (a report)
erstatten; (a reason, the time) angeben; (attention, recognition) zollen; (a lecture) halten; (an award)
zusprechen; (homework) aufgeben;
(a headache, etc.) verursachen; (joy)
machen; (a reception) veranstalten;
(a blow) versetzen; g. away weg-
geben; (divulge) verraten; g. away
the bride Brautvater sein; g. back
zurückgeben; g. ground zurückweichen; g. it to 'em! (coll) hau zu!;
g. off von sich geben; (steam) ausströmen lassen; g. oneself away sich
verplappern; g. oneself up sich stellen; g. or take mehr oder weniger;
g. out ausgeben; g. rise to Anlaß
geben zu; g. up aufgeben; (a business) schließen; g. up for lost ver-
lorengeben; g. way weichen; g. way
to sich überlassen (dat) ‖ intr (yield)
nachgeben; (collapse) einstürzen; g.
in to nachgeben (dat), weichen (dat);
g. out (said of the voice, legs) versagen; (said of strength) nachlassen;
g. up aufgeben; (mil) die Waffen
strecken; g. up on verzagen an (dat)
give'-and-take' s Kompromiß m & n;
(exchange of opinion) Meinungs-
austausch m
give'away' s (betrayal of a secret) unbeabsichtigte Preisgabe f; (promo-
tional article) Gratisprobe f
give'away show' s Preisrätselsendung f
given ['gɪvən] adj gegeben; (time)
festgesetzt; (math, philos) gegeben;
g. to drinking dem Trunk ergeben
giv'en name' s Vorname m
giver ['gɪvər] s Geber –in mf; (of a
contribution) Spender –in mf
gizzard ['gɪzərd] s Geflügelmagen m
gla'cial per'iod ['gle/əl] s Eiszeit f
glacier ['gle/ər] s Gletscher m
glad [glæd] adj (gladder; gladdest)
froh; be g. (about) sich freuen (über
acc); g. to (inf) erfreut zu (inf); g. to
meet you sehr erfreut!, sehr ange-

nehm!; I'll be g. to do it for you
ich werde das gern für Sie tun
gladden ['glædən] tr erfreuen
glade [gled] s Waldwiese f, Waldlich-
tung f
gladiator ['glædɪ‚etər] s Gladiator m
gladiola [‚glædɪ'olə] s Gladiole f
gladly ['glædli] adv gern(e)
gladness ['glædnɪs] s Freude f
glad' rags' spl (sl) Sonntagsstaat m
glad' tid'ings spl Freudenbotschaft f
glamorous ['glæmərəs] adj bezaubernd
glamour ['glæmər] s (of a girl) Zauber
m; (of an event) Glanz m
glam'our girl' s gefeierte Schönheit f;
(pej) Zierpuppe f
glance [glæns] s Blick m; at a g., at
first g. auf den ersten Blick; ‖ intr
(at) blicken (auf acc or nach); g.
around umherblicken; g. off abglei-
ten an (dat); g. through (or over)
flüchtig durchsehen; g. up auf-
blicken
gland [glænd] s Drüse f
glanders ['glændərz] spl Rotzkrank-
heit f
glare [gler] s grelles Licht n; (look)
böser Blick m ‖ tr blenden; (look)
böse starren; g. at böse anstarren
glar'ing adj (light) grell; (fig) schreiend, aufdringlich
glass [glæs] adj gläsern, Glas– ‖ s
Glas n; glasses Brille f
glass' bead' s Glasperle f
glass' blow'er ['blo‚ər] s Glasbläser
–in mf
glass' blow'ing s Glasbläserei f
glass' case' s Schaukasten m
glass' cut'ter s Glasschleifer –in mf;
(tool) Glasschneider m
glassful ['glæsful] s Glas n
glass'ware' s Glaswaren pl
glass' wool' s Glaswolle f
glass'works' s Glasfabrik f, Glashütte
f
glassy ['glæsi] adj (surface) spiegel-
glatt; (eyes) glasig
glaucoma [glau'komə] s Glaukom n,
grüner Star m
glaze [glez] s (on ceramics) Glasur f;
(on paintings) Lasur f; (of ice)
Glatteis n ‖ tr (ceramics, baked
goods) glasieren; (a window) ver-
glasen; (a painting) lasieren
glazed adj (ceramics, baked goods) gla-
siert; (eyes) glasig; g. tile Kachel f
glazier ['glezər] s Glaser –in mf
gleam [glim] s Lichtstrahl m; g. of
hope Hoffnungsschimmer m ‖ intr
strahlen
glean [glin] tr & intr auflesen; (fig)
zusammentragen
gleanings ['glinɪŋz] spl Nachlese f
glee [gli] s Frohsinn m
glee' club' s Gesangverein m
glen [glen] s Bergschlucht f
glib [glɪb] adj (glibber; glibbest)
(tongue) beweglich; (person) zungen-
fertig
glide [glaɪd] s Gleiten n; (aer) Gleit-
flug m; (with a glider) m Segel-
flug m; (ling) Gleitlaut m; (mus)
Glissando n ‖ intr gleiten

glider ['glaɪdər] *s* (*porch swing*) Schaukelbett *n*; (aer) Segelflugzeug *n*

glid′er pi′lot *s* Segelflieger –in *mf*

glid′ing *s* Segelfliegen *n*

glimmer ['glɪmər] *s* Schimmer *m*; **g. of hope** Hoffnungsschimmer *m* ‖ *intr* schimmern

glim′mering *adj* flimmernd ‖ *s* Flimmern *n*

glimpse [glɪmps] *s* flüchtiger Blick *m*; **catch a g.** of flüchtig zu sehen bekommen ‖ *tr* flüchtig erblicken ‖ *intr*—g. at e-n flüchtigen Blick werfen auf (*acc*)

glint [glɪnt] *s* Lichtschimmer *m* ‖ *intr* schimmern

glisten ['glɪsən] *s* Glanz *m* ‖ *intr* glänzen

glitter ['glɪtər] *s* Glitzern *n*, Glanz *m* ‖ *intr* glitzern, glänzen

gloat [glot] *intr* schadenfroh sein; **g. over** sich weiden an (*dat*)

gloat′ing *s* Schadenfreude *f*

global ['global] *adj* global, Welt-

globe [glob] *s* Erdkugel *f*, Globus *m*

globe′-trot′ter *s* Weltenbummler –in *mf*

globule ['glɑbjul] *s* Kügelchen *n*

glockenspiel ['glɑkən,ʃpil] *s* Glockenspiel *n*

gloom [glum] *s* Düsternis *f*; (fig) Trübsinn *m*

gloominess ['gluminɪs] *s* Düsterkeit *f*; (fig) Trübsinn *m*

gloomy ['glumi] *adj* düster; (*depressing*) bedrückend; (*depressed*) trübsinning

glorification ['glorɪfɪ,keʃən] *s* Verherrlichung *f*

glori·fy ['glorɪ,faɪ] *v* (*pret & pp* –**fied**) *tr* verherrlichen

glorious ['glorɪ-əs] *adj* (*full of glory*) glorreich; (*magnificent*) herrlich

glo·ry ['glori] *s* Ruhm *m*; (*magnificence*) Herrlichkeit *f*; **be in one′s g.** im seligsten Himmel sein ‖ *v* (*pret & pp* –**ried**) *intr*—**g.** in frohlocken über (*acc*)

gloss [glɔs] *s* (*shine*) Glanz *m*; (*notation*) Glosse *f* ‖ *tr* glossieren; **g. over** verschleiern

glossary ['glɔsəri] *s* Glossar *n*

glossy ['glɔsi] *adj* glänzend

glottis ['glɑtɪs] *s* Stimmritze *f*

glove [glʌv] *s* Handschuh *m*; **fit like a g.** wie angegossen passen

glove′ compart′ment *s* Handschuhfach *n*

glow [glo] *s* Glühen *n* ‖ *intr* glühen; **g. with** (fig) (er)glühen vor (*dat*)

glower ['glau-ər] *s* finsterer Blick *m* ‖ *intr* finster blicken; **g. at** finster anblicken

glow′ing *adj* glühend; (*account*) begeistert

glow′worm′ *s* Glühwurm *m*

glucose ['glukos] *s* Glukose *f*

glue [glu] *s* Leim *m*, Klebemittel *n* ‖ *tr* (*wood*) leimen; (*paper*) kleben

gluey ['glu-i] *adj* leimig

glum [glʌm] *adj* (**glummer; glummest**) verdrießlich

glut [glʌt] *s* Übersättigung *f*; **a g. on the market** e-e Überschwemmung des Marktes ‖ *v* (*pret & pp* **glutted**; *ger* **glutting**) *tr* übersättigen; (com) überschwemmen

glutton ['glʌtən] *s* Vielfraß *m*

gluttonous ['glʌtənəs] *adj* gefräßig

gluttony ['glʌtəni] *s* Gefräßigkeit *f*

glycerine ['glɪsərɪn] *s* Glyzerin *n*

gnarled [narld] *adj* knorrig

gnash [næʃ] *tr*—**g. one′s teeth** mit den Zähnen knirschen

gnat [næt] *s* Mücke *f*

gnaw [nɔ] *tr* zernagen; **g. off** abnagen ‖ *intr* (on) nagen (an *dat*)

gnome [nom] *s* Gnom *m*, Berggeist *m*

go [go] *s*—**be on the go** auf den Beinen sein; **have a lot of go** viel Mumm in den Knochen haben; **it′s no go** es geht nicht; **let′s have a go at it** probieren wir′s mal; **make a go of it** es zu e-m Erfolg machen ‖ *v* (*pret* **went** [wɛnt]; *pp* **gone** [gɔn]) *tr*—**go it alone** es ganz allein(e) machen ‖ *intr* gehen; (*depart*) weggehen; (*travel*) fahren, reisen; (*operate*) arbeiten; (*belong*) gehören; (*turn out*) verlaufen; (*collapse*) zusammenbrechen; (*fail, go out of order*) kaputtgehen; (*said of words*) lauten; (*said of bells*) läuten; (*said of a buzzer*) ertönen; (*said of awards*) zugeteilt werden; (*said of a road*) führen; **be going to,** e.g., **I am going to study** ich werde studieren; **go about** umhergehen; (*a task*) in Angriff nehmen; **go about it** darangehen; **go after** (*run after*) nachlaufen; (*strive for*) streben nach; **go against the grain** gegen den Strich gehen; **go ahead** vorausgehen; **go ahead!** voran!; **go along with** (*accompany*) mitgehen mit; (*agree with*) zustimmen mit; **go and see for yourself** überzeugen Sie sich selbst davon!; **go around** herumgehen; (*suffice*) (aus)reichen; (*an obstacle*) umgehen; **go at** (*a person*) losgehen auf (*acc*); (*a thing*) herangehen an (*acc*); **go away** weggehen; **go bad** schlecht werden; **go back** zurückkehren; (*ride back*) zurückfahren; **go back on** (*one′s word*) brechen; **go beyond** überschreiten; **go by** (*pass by*) vorbeigehen (an *dat*); (*said of time*) vergehen; (*act according to*) sich richten nach; **go down** niedergehen; (*said of the sun or a ship*) untergehen; (*said of a swelling*) zurückgehen; (*said of a fever or a price*) sinken; **go down in history** in die Geschichte eingehen; **go for** (*fetch*) holen; (*apply to*) gelten für; (*be enthusiastic about*) schwärmen für; (*have a crush on*) verknallt sein in (*acc*); (*be sold for*) verkauft werden für; (*attack*) losgehen auf (*acc*); **go in** hineingehen; (*said of the sun*) verschwinden; **go in for** schwärmen für; (sport) treiben; **go into** eintreten in (*acc*); (*arith*) enthalten sein in (*dat*); **go**

into detail ins Detail gehen; **go in with s.o. on** sich beteiligen mit j–m an (dat); **go off** (depart) weggehen; (said of a gun) losgehen; (said of a bomb) explodieren; **go on** (happen) vorgehen; (continue) weitergehen; (with) fortfahren (mit); (theat) auftreten; **go on!** (expressing encouragement) nur zu!; (expressing disbelief) ach was!; **go on reading** weiterlesen; **go on to** (another theme) übergehen auf (acc); **go over** (check) überprüfen; (review) noch einmal durchgehen; (figures) nachrechnen; (be a success) einschlagen; **go over to** hinübergehen zu; (the enemy) übergehen zu; **go out** (e.g., of the house) hinausgehen; (on an errand or socially; said of a light) ausgehen; **go out of one's way** sich besonders anstrengen; **go out to dinner** auswärts essen; **go through** (penetrate) durchdringen; (a traffic signal) überfahren; (endure) durchmachen; **go through with** zu Ende führen; **go to** (said of a prize) zugeteilt werden (dat); **go together** zueinanderpassen; **go to it!** los!; **go to show** ein Beweis sein für; **go with** (fit, match) passen zu; (associate with) verkehren mit; **go without** entbehren; **go under an assumed name** e–n angenommenen Namen führen; **go up to s.o.** auf j–n zugehen

goad [god] s Stachel m ∥ tr antreiben; **g. on** (fig) anstacheln

go'-ahead' sig'nal n freie Bahn f

goal [gol] s Ziel n; (sport) Tor n; **make a goal** (sport) ein Tor schießen

goalie ['goli] s Torwart m

goal'keep'er s Torwart m

goal' line' s Torlinie f

goal' post' s Torpfosten m

goat [got] s Ziege f, Geiß f; (male goat) Ziegenbock m; **get s.o.'s g.** (sl) j–n auf die Palme bringen

goatee [go'ti] s Ziegenbart m, Spitzbart m

goat' herd' s Ziegenhirt m

goat'skin' s Ziegenfell n

gob [gab] s (coll) Klumpen m; (sailor) (coll) Blaujacke f; **gobs of money** (coll) ein Haufen m Geld

gobble ['gabəl] s Kollern n ∥ tr verschlingen; **g. up** (food) herunterschlingen; (e.g., land) zusammenraffen ∥ intr (said of a turkey) kollern

gobbledegook ['gabəldi‚guk] s (coll) Amtssprache f

gobbler ['gablər] s (coll) Fresser –in mf; (orn) (coll) Puter m, Truthahn m

go'-between' s Vermittler –in mf, Unterhändler –in mf

goblet ['gablit] s Kelchglas n

goblin ['gablin] s Kobold m

go'cart' s (walker) Laufstuhl m; (stroller) Sportwagen m; (small racer) Go-Kart m; (handcart) Handwagen m

god [gad] s Gott m; **God forbid!** Gott bewahre!; **God knows** weiß Gott; **my God!** du lieber Gott!; **so help**

me God! so wahr mir Gott helfe!; **ye gods!** heiliger Strohsack!

god'child' s (–chil'dren) Patenkind n

goddess ['gadis] s Göttin f

god'fa'ther s Pate m; **be a g.** Pate stehen

God'-fear'ing adj gottesfürchtig

god'forsak'en adj gottverlassen

god'head' s Göttlichkeit f; **Godhead** Gott m

godless ['gadlis] adj gottlos

god'like' adj göttlich

godly ['gadli] adj gottselig

god'moth'er s Patin f; **be a g.** Patin stehen

god'send' s Segen m

God'speed' s—**wish s.o. G.** j–m Lebewohl sagen

go-getter ['go‚getər] s Draufgänger m

goggle ['gagəl] intr glotzen

gog'gle-eyed' adj glotzäugig

goggles ['gagəlz] spl Schutzbrille f

go'ing adj (rate) gültig, üblich; **g. on** (e.g., six o'clock) gegen; **I'm g. to do it** ich werde es tun

go'ing concern' s schwunghaftes Geschäft n

go'ing-o'ver s Überprüfung f; (beating) Prügel pl

go'ings on' spl Treiben n, Wirtschaft f

goiter ['gəitər] s Kropf m

gold [gold] adj Gold– ∥ s Gold n

gold' bar' s Goldbarren m

gold'brick' s (mil) Drückeberger m

gold'-brick' intr faulenzen

gold'-brick'ing s (mil) Drückebergerei f

gold'crest' s Goldhähnchen n

gold' dig'ger ['digər] s Goldgräber m; (sl) Vamp m

golden ['goldən] adj golden; (opportunity) günstig

gold'en age' s Glanzzeit f, Goldenes Zeitalter n

gold'en calf', **the** s das Goldene Kalb

gold'en ea'gle s Goldadler m

Gold'en Fleece', **the** (myth) das Goldene Vlies

gold'en mean' s goldene Mitte f

gold'en rule' s goldene Regel f

gold'en wed'ding s goldene Hochzeit f

gold'-filled' adj vergoldet

gold' fill'ing s (dent) Goldplombe f

gold'finch' s Goldfink m, Stieglitz m

gold'fish' s Goldfisch m

goldilocks ['goldi‚laks] s (bot) Hahnenfuß m

gold' leaf' s Blattgold n

gold'mine' s Goldbergwerk n

gold' nug'get s Goldklumpen m

gold' plate' s Goldgeschirr n

gold'-plate' tr vergolden

gold'smith' s Goldschmied –in mf

gold' stand'ard s Goldwährung f

golf [galf] s Golf n ∥ intr Golf spielen

golf' bag' s Köcher m

golf' club' s Golfschläger m; (organization) Golfklub m

golf' course' s Golfplatz m

golfer ['galfər] s Golfspieler –in mf

golf' links' spl Golfplatz m

gondola ['gandələ] s Gondel f

gon'dola car' s offener Güterwagen m

gondolier [‚gɑndə'lır] s Gondelführer m

gone [gɔn] adj hin, weg; (ruined) futsch; **all g.** ganz weg; (sold out) ausverkauft; **he is g.** er ist fort

goner ['gɔnər] s (coll) verlorener Mensch m

gong [gɔŋ] s Gong m, Tamtam n

gonorrhea [‚gɑnə'ri-ə] s Tripper m

goo [gu] s (sl) klebrige Masse f

good [gud] adj (better; best) gut; (well behaved) brav, artig; (in health) gesund; (valid) gültig; **as g.** as so gut wie; **be g. enough to** (inf) so gut sein und; **g. and** recht, e.g., **g. and cheap** recht billig; **g. at** gut in (dat); **g. for** (suited to) geeignet zu; (effective against) wirksam für; (valid for) gültig für; **g. for you!** (serves you right!) das geschieht dir recht!; (expressing congratulations) ich gratuliere!, bravo!; **make g.** wiedergutmachen; (losses) vergüten; (a promise) erfüllen; ‖ s Gut n; (welfare) Wohl n; (advantage) Nutzen m; (philos) Gut n, das Gute; **be up to no g.** nichts Gutes im Schilde führen; **catch with the goods** auf frischer Tat ertappen; **do g.** wohltun; **for g.** für immer; **goods** Waren pl; **to the g.** als Nettogewinn; **what g. is it?, what's the g. of it?** was nutzt es?

good'-by', **good'-bye'** s Lebewohl n; **say g.** (to) sich verabschieden (von) ‖ interj auf Wiedersehen!; (on the telephone) auf Wiederhören!

good' day' interj guten Tag!

good' deed' s Wohltat f

good' egg' s (sl) feiner Kerl m

good' eve'ning interj guten Abend!

good' fel'low s netter Kerl m

good'-fel'lowship s gute Kameradschaft f

good'-for-noth'ing adj nichtsnutzig ‖ s Taugenichts m, Nichtsnutz m

Good' Fri'day s Karfreitag m

good' grac'es spl—be in s.o.'s g. in j-s Gunst stehen

good'-heart'ed adj gutherzig

good'-hu'mored adj gutgelaunt, gutmütig

good'-look'ing adj gutaussehend, hübsch

goodly ['gudli] adj beträchtlich; **a g. number of** viele

good' morn'ing interj guten Morgen!

good'-na'tured adj gutmütig

goodness ['gudnıs] s Güte f; **for g. sake!** um Himmels willen!; **g. knows** weiß Gott; **thank g.** Gott sei Dank!

good' night' interj gute Nacht!

good' sense' s Sinn m; (common sense) gesunder Menschenverstand m; **make g. Sinn haben**

good'-sized' adj ziemlich groß

good'-tem'pered adj ausgeglichen

good' time' s—**have a g.** sich gut unterhalten; **keep g.** taktfest sein

good' turn' s Gefallen m; **one g. deserves another** e-e Hand wäscht die andere

good' will' s Wohlwollen n; (com) Geschäftswert m

goody ['gudi] s Näscherei f ‖ interj pfundig!

gooey ['gu·i] adj klebrig

goof [guf] s (person) (sl) Depp m; (mistake) (sl) Schnitzer m ‖ tr (sl) verpfuschen ‖ intr (sl) e-n Schnitzer machen; **g. off** (sl) faulenzen

goof'ball' s (pill) (sl) Beruhigungspille f; (eccentric person) (sl) Sonderling m

goofy ['gufi] adj (sl) dämlich; **g. about** (sl) vernarrt in (acc)

goon [gun] s (sl) Dummkopf m; (in strikes) bestellter Schläger m

goose [gus] s (geese [gis]) Gans f; (culin) Gänsebraten m; **cook s.o.'s g.** j-n erledigen

goose'ber'ry s Stachelbeere f

goose' egg' s Gänseei n; (sl) Null f

goose' flesh' s Gänsehaut f

goose'neck' s Schwanenhals m

goose' pim'ples spl Gänsehaut f

goose' step' s Stechschritt m

goose'-step' v (pret & pp –stepped; ger –stepping) intr im Stechschritt marschieren

gopher ['gofər] s Taschenratte f

gore [gor] s geronnenes Blut n ‖ tr aufspießen

gorge [gɔrdʒ] s Schlucht f ‖ tr vollstopfen ‖ intr schlingen

gorgeous ['gɔrdʒəs] adj prachtvoll

gorilla [gə'rılə] s Gorilla m

gorse [gɔrs] s Stechginster m

gory ['gori] adj blutig

gosh [gɑʃ] interj herrjeh!

Gospel ['gɑspəl] s Evangelium n

gos'pel truth' s reine Wahrheit f

gossamer ['gɑsəmər] s Sommerfäden pl

gossip ['gɑsıp] s Klatsch m; (woman) Klatschweib n; (man) Schwätzer m ‖ intr klatschen, tratschen

gos'sip col'umn s Klatschspalte f

gossipmonger ['gɑsıp ‚mʌŋgər] s Klatschbase f

gossipy ['gɑsıpi] adj tratschsüchtig

Goth [gɑθ] s Gote m, Gotin f

Gothic ['gɑθık] adj gotisch ‖ s (language) Gotisch n

Goth'ic arch' s Spitzbogen m

gouge [gaudʒ] s (tool) Hohlmeißel m; (hole made by a gouge) ausgemeißelte Vertiefung f ‖ tr aushöhlen; (overcharge) übervorteilen; **g. out** (eyes) herausdrücken

gouger ['gaudʒər] s Wucherer –in mf

goulash ['gula ʃ] s Gulasch n

gourd [gord], [gurd] s Kürbis m

gourmand ['gurmənd] s (glutton) Schlemmer –in mf; (gourmet) Feinschmecker m

gourmet ['gurme] s Feinschmecker m

gout [gaut] s Gicht f

govern ['gʌvərn] tr regieren; (fig) beherrschen; (gram) regieren ‖ intr regieren

governess ['gʌvərnıs] s Gouvernante f

government ['gʌvərnmənt] adj Regierungs–, Staats– ‖ s Regierung f

gov'ernment con'tract s Staatsauftrag m

gov'ernment control' s Zwangsbewirtschaftung f

gov'ernment employ'ee s Staatsbeamte m, Staatsbeamtin f

gov'ernment grant' s Staatszuschuß m

gov'ernment-in-ex'ile s Exilregierung f

governor ['gʌvərnər] s Statthalter m, Gouverneur m; (mach) Regler m

gov'ernorship' s Statthalterschaft f

gown [gaʊn] s Damenkleid n; (of a judge, professor) Robe f, Talar m

grab [græb] s—make a g. for grapschen nach || v (pret & pp grabbed; ger grabbing) tr schnappen; g. hold of anpacken || intr—g. for greifen nach

grab' bag' s Glückstopf m

grace [gres] s (mercy, divine favor) Gnade f; (charm) Grazie f; (table prayer) Tischgebet n; (charm) Grazie f; Graces (myth) Grazien pl

graceful ['gresfəl] adj graziös, anmutig

gracious ['greʃəs] adj gnädig; (living) angenehm || interj lieber Himmel!

gradation [gre'deʃən] s Stufenfolge f

grade [gred] s (level) Stufe f, Grad m; (quality) Qualität f; (class year) Schulklasse f; (mark in a course, test) Zensur f; (slope) Steigung f; (mil) Dienstgrad m || tr (sort) einstufen; (evaluate) bewerten; (make level) planieren; (educ) zensieren

grade' cross'ing s (rr) Schienenübergang m

grade' school' s Grundschule f

gradient ['gredɪ-ənt] s Neigung f

gradual ['grædʒʊ-əl] adj allmählich

graduate ['grædʒʊ-ɪt] adj (student) graduiert; (course) Graduierten– || s Promovierte mf; (from a junior college) Abiturient –in mf; (from a university) Absolvent –in mf || ['grædʒʊ,et] tr & intr graduieren, promovieren; g. from absolvieren

grad'uated adj (tax) abgestuft; (marked by divisions of measurement) graduiert; g. scale Gradmesser m

graduation [,grædʒʊ'eʃən] s Graduierung f, Promotion f; (marking on a vessel or instrument) Gradeinteilung f

gradua'tion ex'ercises spl Schlußfeier f

graft [græft] s (illegal gain) Schiebung f; (money involved in graft) Schmiergeld n; (twig) (hort) Pfropfreis n; (place where scion is inserted) (hort) Propfstelle f; (organ transplanted) (surg) verpflanztes Gewebe n; (transplanting) (surg) Gewebeverpflanzung f || tr (hort) pfropfen; (surg) verpflanzen

gra'ham bread' ['gre-əm] s Grahambrot n

gra'ham crack'er s Grahamplätzchen n

gra'ham flour' s Grahammehl n

grain [gren] s Korn n; (of leather) Narbe f; (in wood, marble) Maserung f; (unit of weight) Gran n; (cereals) Getreide n; (phot) Korn n; against the g. (& fig) gegen den Strich; g. of truth Körnchen n Wahrheit

grain' el'evator s Getreidesilo m

grain'field' s Saatfeld n, Kornfeld n

gram [græm] s Gramm n

grammar ['græmər] s Grammatik f

gram'mar school' s Grundschule f

grammatical [grə'mætɪkəl] adj grammatisch, grammatikalisch

gramophone ['græmə,fon] s Grammophon n

granary ['grenəri] s Getreidespeicher m

grand [grænd] adj großartig; (large and striking) grandios; (lofty) erhaben; (wonderful) (coll) herrlich

grand'aunt' s Großtante f

grand'child' s (–chil'dren) Enkelkind n

grand'daugh'ter s Enkelin f

grand' duch'ess s Großfürstin f, Großherzogin f

grand' duch'y s Großfürstentum n, Großherzogtum n

grand' duke' s Großfürst m, Großherzog m

grandee [græn'di] s Grande m

grandeur ['grændʒər], ['grændʒʊr] s Großartigkeit f, Erhabenheit f

grand'fath'er s Großvater m

grand'father's clock' s Standuhr f

grandiose ['grændɪ,os] adj grandios

grand' ju'ry s Anklagekammer f

grand' lar'ceny s schwerer Diebstahl m

grand' lodge' s Großloge f

grandma ['grænd(d),mɑ], ['græm,mɑ] s (coll) Oma f

grand'moth'er s Großmutter f

grand'neph'ew s Großneffe m

grand'niece' s Großnichte f

grandpa ['grænd(d),pɑ], ['græm,pɑ] s (coll) Opa m

grand'par'ents spl Großeltern pl

grand' pian'o s Konzertflügel m

grand' slam' s Schlemm m

grand'son' s Enkel m

grand'stand' s Tribüne f

grand' to'tal s Gesamtsumme f

grand'un'cle s Großonkel m

grand' vizier' s Großwesir m

grange [grendʒ] s Farm f; (organization) Farmervereinigung f

granite ['grænɪt] adj Granit– || s Granit m

granny ['græni] s (coll) Oma f

grant [grænt] s (of money) Beihilfe f; (of a pardon) Gewährung f; (of an award) Verleihung f || tr (permission) geben; (credit) bewilligen; (a favor) gewähren; (a request) erfüllen; (a privilege, award) verleihen; (admit) zugeben; granted that angenommen, daß; take for granted als selbstverständlich hinnehmen

grantee [græn'ti] s Empfänger –in mf

grant'-in-aid' s (grants-in-aid) (by the government) Subvention f; (educ) Stipendium n

grantor ['græntər] s Verleiher –in mf

granular ['grænjələr] adj körnig

granulate ['grænjə,let] tr körnen

gran′ulated sug′ar *s* Streuzucker *m*

granule ['grænjul] *s* Körnchen *n*

grape [grep] *s* Weintraube *f*

grape′ ar′bor *s* Weinlaube *f*

grape′fruit′ *s* Pampelmuse *f*

grape′ juice′ *s* Most *m*, Traubensaft *m*

grape′ pick′er *s* Weinleser –in *mf*

grape′vine′ *s* Weinstock *m;* **through the g.** gerüchteweise

graph [græf] *s* Diagramm *n*

graphic(al) ['græfɪk(əl)] *adj* graphisch; *(description)* anschaulich, bildhaft

graph′ic arts′ *spl* Graphik *f*

graphite ['græfaɪt] *s* Graphit *m*

graph′ pa′per *s* Millimeterpapier *n*

grapnel ['græpnəl] *s* Wurfanker *m*

grapple ['græpəl] *s* Enterhaken *m; (fight)* Handgemenge *n* ‖ *tr* packen ‖ *intr (use a grapple)* (naut) e–n Enterhaken gebrauchen; **g. with** (& fig) ringen mit

grap′pling hook′, grap′pling i′ron *s* Wurfanker *m;* (naut) Enterhaken *m*

grasp [græsp] *s* Griff *m;* (control) Gewalt *f;* (comprehension) Verständnis *n;* (reach) Reichweite *f;* **have a good g.** of gut beherrschen ‖ *tr* (& fig) fassen ‖ *intr*—**g. at** schnappen nach

grasp′ing *adj* habgierig, geldgierig

grass [græs] *s* Gras *n;* (lawn) Rasen *m;* (pasture land) Weide *f*

grass′ court′ *s* Rasenspielplatz *m*

grass′hop′per *s* Grashüpfer *m*

grass′ land′ *s* Weideland *n*, Grasland *n*

grass′-roots′ *adj* (coll) volkstümlich

grass′ seed′ *s* Grassamen *m*

grass′ wid′ow *s* Strohwitwe *f*

grassy ['græsi] *adj* grasig

grate [gret] *s* (on a window) Gitter *n;* (of a furnace) Rost *m* ‖ *tr* (e.g., cheese) reiben; **g. the teeth** mit den Zähnen knirschen ‖ *intr* knirschen; **g. on one's nerves** an den Nerven reißen

grateful ['gretfəl] *adj* dankbar

grater ['gretər] *s* (culin) Reibeisen *n*

grati-fy ['grætɪ‚faɪ] *v* (pret & pp –fied) *tr* befriedigen; **be gratified by** sich freuen über (acc)

grat′ifying *adj* erfreulich

grat′ing *adj* knirschend ‖ *s* Gitter *n*

gratis ['grætɪs], ['gretɪs] *adj & adv* unentgeltlich

gratitude ['grætɪ‚t(j)ud] *s* Dankbarkeit *f*

gratuitous [grə't(j)u·ɪtəs] *adj* unentgeltlich; (undeserving) unverdient

gratuity [grə't(j)u·ɪti] *s* Trinkgeld *n*

grave [grev] *adj* (face) ernst; (condition) besorgniserregend; (mistake) folgenschwer; (sound) tief ‖ *s* Grab *n;* (accent) Gravis *m*

gravedigger ['grev‚dɪgər] *s* Totengräber *m*

gravel ['grævəl] *s* (rounded stones) Kies *m;* (crushed stones) Schotter *m;* (pathol) Harngrieß *m* ‖ *tr* mit Kies (or Schotter) bestreuen

gravelly ['grævəli] *adj* heiser

grav′el pit′ *s* Kiesgrube *f*

grav′el road′ *s* Schotterstraße *f*

grave′stone′ *s* Grabstein *m*

grave′yard′ *s* Friedhof *m*

gravitate ['grævɪ‚tet] *intr* gravitieren; **g. towards** (fig) neigen zu

gravitation [‚grævɪ'teʃən] *s* Gravitation *f*, Massenanziehung *f*

gravitational [‚grævɪ'teʃənəl] *adj* Gravitations–, Schwer–

gravita′tional force′ *s* Schwerkraft *f*

gravita′tional pull′ *s* Anziehungskraft *f*

gravity ['grævɪti] *s* (seriousness) Ernst *m;* (of a situation) Schwere *f;* (phys) Schwerkraft *f*

gravy ['grevi] *s* Soße *f;* (coll) leichter Gewinn *m*

gra′vy boat′ *s* Soßenschüssel *f*

gra′vy train′ *s* (sl) Futterkrippe *f*

gray [gre] *adj* grau ‖ *s* Grau *n* ‖ *intr* ergrauen

gray′beard′ *s* Graubart *m*

gray′-haired′ *adj* grauhaarig

grayish ['gre·ɪʃ] *adj* gräulich

gray′ mat′ter *s* graue Substanz *f*

graze [grez] *tr* (said of a bullet) streifen; (cattle) weiden lassen ‖ *intr* weiden

graz′ing land′ *s* Weide *f*

grease [gris] *s* Fett *n*, Schmiere *f* ‖ [griz] *tr* (aut) schmieren

grease′ gun′ [gris] *s* Schmierpresse *f*

grease′ paint′ *s* Schminke *f*

grease′ pit′ *s* (aut) Schmiergrube *f*

grease′ spot′ *s* Fettfleck *m*

greasy ['grisi], ['grizi] *adj* fett(ig)

great [gret] *adj* groß; (wonderful) (coll) großartig; **a g. many (of)** e–e große Anzahl von; **g. fun** Heidenspaß *m;* **g. guy** Prachtkerl *m*

great′-aunt′ *s* Großtante *f*

Great′ Bear′ *s* Großer Bär *m*

Great′ Brit′ain *s* Großbritannien *n*

Great′ Dane′ *s* deutsche Dogge *f*

great′-grand′child′ *s* (–chil′dren) Urenkel *m*

great′-grand′daugh′ter *s* Urenkelin *f*

great′-grand′fa′ther *s* Urgroßvater *m*

great′-grand′moth′er *s* Urgroßmutter *f*

great′-grand′par′ents *spl* Urgroßeltern *pl*

great′-grand′son′ *s* Urenkel *m*

greatly ['gretli] *adv* sehr, stark

great′-neph′ew *s* Großneffe *m*

greatness ['gretnɪs] *s* Größe *f*

great′-niece′ *s* Großnichte *f*

great′-un′cle *s* Großonkel *m*

Grecian ['griʃən] *adj* griechisch

Greece [gris] *s* Griechenland *n*

greed [grid] *s* Habgier *f*, Gier *f*

greediness ['gridɪnɪs] *s* Gierigkeit *f*

greedy ['gridi] *adj* (for) gierig (nach)

Greek [grik] *adj* griechisch ‖ *s* (person) Grieche *m*, Griechin *f;* (language) Griechisch *n;* **that's G. to me** das kommt mir spanisch vor

green [grin] *adj* grün; (unripe) unreif; (inexperienced) unerfahren, neu; **become g.** grünen; **turn g. with envy** grün vor Neid werden ‖ *s* (& golf) Grün *n;* **greens** Blattgemüse *n*

green′back′ *s* (coll) Geldschein *m*

greenery ['grinəri] *s* Grün *n*

green'-eyed' adj grünäugig; (fig) neidisch

green'gro'cer s Obst- und Gemüsehändler –in mf

green'horn' s Ausländer –in mf

green'house' s Gewächshaus n

greenish ['grinɪʃ] adj grünlich

Green'land s Grönland n

green' light' s (fig) freie Fahrt f

greenness ['grɪnnɪs] s Grün n; (inexperience) Unerfahrenheit f

green' pep'per s Paprikaschote f

green'room' s (theat) Aufenthaltsraum m

greensward ['grin,swɔrd] s Rasen m

green' thumb' s—have a g. gärtnerisches Geschick besitzen

greet [grit] tr grüßen; (welcome) begrüßen

greet'ing s Gruß m; (welcoming) Begrüßung f; **greetings** Grüße pl

greet'ing card' s Glückwunschkarte f

gregarious [grɪ'gerɪ-əs] adj gesellig

Gregor'ian cal'endar [grɪ'gorɪ-ən] s Gregorianischer Kalender m

Gregor'ian chant' s Gregorianischer Gesang m

grenade [grɪ'ned] s Granate f

grenade' launch'er s Gewehrgranatgerät n

grey [gre] adj, s, & intr var of gray

grey'hound' s Windhund m

grid [grɪd] s (on a map) Gitternetz n; (culin) Bratrost m; (electron) Gitter n

griddle ['grɪdəl] s Bratpfanne f; (cookie sheet) Backblech n

grid'dlecake' s Pfannkuchen m

grid'i'ron s Bratrost m; (sport) Spielfeld n; (theat) Schnürboden m

grid' leak' s (electron) Gitterwiderstand m

grief [grif] s Kummer m; **come to g.** zu Fall (or Schaden) kommen, scheitern

grief'-strick'en adj gramgebeugt

grievance ['grivəns] s Beschwerde f

grieve [griv] tr bekümmern ǁ intr (over) sich grämen (über acc)

grievous ['grivəs] adj (causing grief) schmerzlich; (serious) schwerwiegend

griffin ['grɪfɪn] s Greif m

grill [grɪl] s Grill m ǁ tr grillen; (an accused person) scharf verhören

grille [grɪl] s Gitter n

grim [grɪm] adj (grimmer; grimmest) grimmig; **g. humor** Galgenhumor m

grimace ['grɪməs], [grɪ'mes] s Grimasse f ǁ intr Grimassen schneiden

grime [graɪm] s Schmutz m, Ruß m

grimness ['grɪmnɪs] s Grimmigkeit f

grimy ['graɪmi] adj schmutzig, rußig

grin [grɪn] s Grinsen n, Schmunzeln n ǁ v (pret & pp grinned; ger grinning) intr grinsen, schmunzeln; **I had to g. and bear it** ich mußte gute Miene zum bösen Spiel machen

grind [graɪnd] s (of coffee, grain) Mahlen n; (hard work) Schinderei f; (a student) (coll) Streber –in mf; **the daily g.** der graue Alltag ǁ v (pret & pp ground [graʊnd]) tr (coffee, grain) mahlen; (glass, tools) schleifen; (meat) zermahlen; (in a mortar) stampfen; **g. down** zerreiben; **g. one's teeth** mit den Zähnen knirschen; **g. out** (e.g., articles) ausstoßen; (tunes) leiern

grinder ['graɪndər] s (molar) (dent) Backenzahn m; (mach) Schleifmaschine f

grind'stone' s Schleifstein m

grip [grɪp] s Griff m; (handle) Handgriff m; (handbag) Reisetasche f; (power) Gewalt f; **come to grips with** in Angriff nehmen; **have a good g. on** (fig) sicher beherrschen; **lose one's g.** (fig) den Halt verlieren ǁ v (pret & pp gripped; ger gripping) tr (& fig) packen

gripe [graɪp] s Meckerei f ǁ intr (about) meckern (über acc)

grippe [grɪp] s (pathol) Grippe f

grip'ping adj fesselnd, packend

grisly ['grɪzli] adj gräßlich

grist [grɪst] s Mahlkorn n; **that's g. for his mill** das ist Wasser auf seine Mühle

gristle ['grɪsəl] s Knorpel m

gristly ['grɪsli] adj knorpelig

grist'mill' s Getreidemühle f

grit [grɪt] s (abrasive particles) Grieß m; (pluck) (coll) Mumm m; **grits** Schrotmehl n ǁ v (pret & pp gritted; ger gritting) tr (one's teeth) zusammenbeißen

gritty ['grɪti] adj grießig

grizzly ['grɪzli] adj gräulich

griz'zly bear' s Graubär m

groan [gron] s Stöhnen n; **groans** Geächze m ǁ intr stöhnen; (grumble) (coll) brumen

grocer ['grosər] s Lebensmittelhändler –in mf

grocery ['grosəri] s (store) Lebensmittelgeschäft n; **groceries** Lebensmittel pl

gro'cery store' s Lebensmittelgeschäft n

grog [grɑg] s Grog m

groggy ['grɑgi] adj benommen

groin [grɔɪn] s (anat) Leiste f, Leistengegend f; (archit) Rippe f

groom [grum] s Bräutigam m; (stableboy) Reitknecht m ǁ tr (a person, animal) pflegen; (for a position) heranziehen

groove [gruv] s Kerbe f; (for letting off water) Rinne f; (of a record) Rille f; (in a barrel) Zug m; **in the g.** (fig) im richtigen Fahrwasser

grope [grop] tr—**g. one's way** sich vorwärtstasten ǁ intr tappen; **g. about** herumtappen; **g. for** tappen nach, tasten nach

gropingly ['gropɪŋli] adv tastend

gross [gros] adj (coarse, vulgar) roh, derb; (mistake) grob; (crass, extreme) kraß; (without deductions) Brutto– ǁ s Gros n ǁ tr e–n Bruttogewinn haben von

grossly ['grosli] adv sehr, stark

gross' na'tional prod'uct s Bruttosozialprodukt n

gross' receipts' *spl* Bruttoeinnahmen *pl*

grotesque [gro'tɛsk] *adj* grotesk

grot·to ['grato] *s* (**-toes** & **-tos**) Grotte *f*, Höhle *f*

grouch [graut∫] *s* (coll) Brummbär *m*, Griesgram *m* ‖ *intr* brummen

grouchy ['graut∫i] *adj* (coll) brummig

ground [graund] *s* Grund *m*, Boden *m*; *(reason)* Grund *m*; (elec) Erde *f*; **every inch of g.** jeder Fußbreit Boden; **grounds** *(e.g., of an estate)* Anlagen *pl*; *(reasons)* Gründe *pl*; *(of coffee)* Satz *m*; **break g.** mit dem Bau beginnen; **gain g. (an)** Boden gewinnen; **hold one's g.** seinen Standpunkt behaupten; **level to the g.** dem Erdboden gleichmachen; **lose g. (an)** Boden verlieren; **low g.** Niederung *f*; **new g.** (fig) Neuland *n*; **on the grounds that** mit dem Begründung, daß; **run into the g.** (fig) bis zum Überdruß wiederholen; **stand one's g.** standhalten; **yield g.** (fig) nachgeben ‖ *tr (a pilot)* Startverbot erteilen *(dat)*; *(a ship)* auflaufen lassen; (elec) erden; **be grounded by bad weather** wegen schlechten Wetters am Starten gehindert werden

ground' connec'tion *s* (elec) Erdung *f*

ground' crew' *s* (aer) Bodenmannschaft *f*

ground' floor' *s* Parterre *n*, Erdgeschoß *n*

ground' glass' *s* Mattglas *n*

ground' hog' *s* Murmeltier *n*

groundless ['graundlɪs] *adj* grundlos

ground' meat' *s* Hackfleisch *n*

ground' plan' *s* Grundriß *m*; (fig) Entwurf *m*

ground' speed' *s* Geschwindigkeit *f* über Grund

ground' swell' *s* Dünung *f*; (fig) wogende Erregung *f*

ground'-to-air' *adj* Boden-Bord-

ground' wa'ter *s* Grundwasser *n*

ground' wire' *s* (elec) Erdleitung *f*

ground'work' *s* Grundlage *f*

group [grup] *adj* Gruppen- ‖ *s* Gruppe *f*; *(consisting of 18 aircraft)* Geschwader *n* ‖ *tr* gruppieren ‖ *intr* sich gruppieren

group'ing *s* Gruppierung *f*

group' insur'ance *s* Gruppenversicherung *f*

group' ther'apy *s* Gruppentherapie *f*

grouse [graus] *s* Waldhuhn *n* ‖ *intr* (sl) meckern

grout [graut] *s* dünner Mörtel *m* ‖ *tr* verstreichen

grove [grov] *s* Gehölz *n*, Hain *m*

grov·el ['grʌvəl], ['grɑvəl] *v* (*pret* & *pp* **-el[l]ed**; *ger* **-el[l]ing**) *intr* (& fig) kriechen; **g. in filth** in Schmutz wühlen

grow [gro] *v* (*pret* **grew** [gru]; *pp* **grown** [gron]) *tr (plants)* pflanzen, züchten; *(grain)* anbauen; *(a beard)* sich *[dat]* wachsen lassen; **the ram grows horns** dem Widder wachsen Hörner ‖ *intr* wachsen; *(become)* werden; *(become bigger)* größer werden; **g. fond of** liebgewinnen; **g. luxuriantly** wuchern; **g. older** an Jahren zunehmen; **g. on s.o.** j-m ans Herz wachsen; **g. out of** *(clothes)* herauswachsen aus; (fig) entstehen aus; **g. pale** erblassen; **g. together** zusammenwachsen; *(close)* zuwachsen; **g. up** aufwachsen; **g. wild** *(luxuriantly)* wuchern; *(in the wild)* wild wachsen

grower ['gro·ər] *s* Züchter –in *mf*

growl [graul] *s* *(of a dog, stomach)* Knurren *n*; *(of a bear)* Brummen *n* ‖ *tr (words)* brummen ‖ *intr* knurren; *(said of a bear)* brummen; **g. at** anknurren

grown [gron] *adj* erwachsen

grown'-up' *adj* erwachsen ‖ *s* (**grown-ups**) Erwachsene *mf*

growth [groθ] *s* Wachstum *n*; *(increase)* Zuwachs *m*; (pathol) Gewächs *n*; **full g.** volle Größe *f*

grub [grʌb] *s* Larve *f*, Made *f*; (sl) Fraß *m* ‖ *v* (*pret* & *pp* **grubbed**; *ger* **grubbing**) *tr* ausjäten ‖ *intr* wühlen; **g. for** graben nach

grubby ['grʌbi] *adj* *(dirty)* schmutzig

grudge [grʌdʒ] *s* Mißgunst *f*, Groll *m*; **bear (or have) a g. against s.o.** j-m grollen ‖ *tr* mißgönnen

grudg'ing *adj* mißgünstig

grudg'ingly *adv* (nur) ungern

gruel ['gru·əl] *s* Haferschleim *m*

gruel'ing *adj* strapaziös

gruesome ['grusəm] *adj* grausig

gruff [grʌf] *adj* barsch

grumble ['grʌmbəl] *s* Murren *n* ‖ *intr* *(over)* murren *(über acc)*

grumbler ['grʌmblər] *s* Brummbär *m*

grumpy ['grʌmpi] *adj* übellaunig

grunt [grʌnt] *s* Grunzen *n* ‖ *tr* & *intr* grunzen

G'-string' *s* *(of a dancer)* letzte Hülle *f*; *(of a native)* Lendenschurz *m*

guarantee [ˌgærən'ti] *s* Garantie *f* ‖ *tr* garantieren für

guarantor ['gærən͵tɔr] *s* Garant –in *mf*

guaranty ['gærənti] *s* Garantie *f* ‖ *v* (*pret* & *pp* **-tied**) *tr* garantieren

guard [gɑrd] *s* *(watch; watchman)* Wache *f*; *(person)* Wächter –in *mf*; (fb) Verteidiger *m*; (mach) Schutzvorrichtung *f*; *(soldier)* (mil) Posten *m*; *(soldiers)* (mil) Wachmannschaft *f*, Wache *f*; **be on g. against** sich hüten vor *(dat)*; **be on one's g.** auf der Hut sein; **keep under close g.** scharf bewachen; **mount g.** Wache beziehen; **relieve the g.** die Wache ablösen; **stand g.** Posten (or Wache) stehen; *(during a robbery)* Schmiere stehen ‖ *tr* bewachen; (fig) hüten; **g. one's tongue** seine Zunge im Zaum halten ‖ *intr*—**g. against** sich vorsehen gegen; **g. over** wachen über *(acc)*

guard' de'tail *s* Wachmannschaft *f*

guard' du'ty *s* Wachdienst *m*; **pull g.** Wache schieben

guard'house' *s* *(building used by guards)* Wache *f*; *(military jail)* Arrestlokal *n*

guardian ['gɑrdɪ·ən] *s* (*custodian*) Wächter –in *mf;* (jur) Vormund *m*

guard'ian an'gel *s* Schutzengel *m*

guard'ianship' *s* Obhut *f;* (jur) Vormundschaft *f*

guard'rail' *s* Geländer *n*

guard'room' *s* Wachstube *f,* Wachlokal *n*

guerrilla [gə'rɪlə] *s* Guerillakämpfer –in *mf*

gueril'la war'fare *s* Guerillakrieg *m*

guess [ges] *s* Vermutung *f;* **anybody's g.** reine Vermutung *f;* **take a good g.** gut raten || *tr* vermuten; **you guessed it!** geraten! || *intr* raten; **g. at** schätzen

guesser ['gesər] *s* Rater –in *mf*

guess'work' *s* Raten *n,* Mutmaßung *f*

guest [gest] *adj* Gast–, Gäste– || *s* Gast *m;* **be a g. of** zu Gaste sein bei

guest' book' *s* Gästebuch *n*

guest' perform'ance *s* Gastspiel *n;* **give a g.** (theat) gastieren

guest' perform'er *s* Gast *m*

guest' room' *s* Gästezimmer *n*

guest' speak'er *s* Gastredner –in *mf*

guffaw [gə'fɔ] *s* Gewieher *n* || *intr* wiehern

guidance ['gaɪdəns] *s* Leitung *f,* Führung *f;* (educ) Studienberatung *f;* **for your g.** zu Ihrer Orientierung

guid'ance coun'selor *s* Studienberater –in *mf*

guide [gaɪd] *s* Führer –in *mf;* (*book*) Reiseführer *m;* (*tourist escort*) Reiseführer –in *mf;* (*for gardening, etc.*) Leitfaden *m* || *tr* führen; (rok) lenken

guide'book' *s* Reiseführer *m,* Führer *m*

guid'ed mis'sile *s* Fernlenkkörper *m*

guid'ed tour' *s* Führung *f*

guide'line' *s* Richtlinie *f*

guide'post' *s* Wegweiser *m*

guide' word' *s* Stichwort *n*

guild [gɪld] *s* Zunft *f,* Gilde *f*

guile [gaɪl] *s* Arglist *f*

guileful ['gaɪfəl] *adj* arglistig

guileless ['gaɪllɪs] *adj* arglos

guillotine ['gɪlə‚tin] *s* Fallbeil *n,* Guillotine *f* || *tr* mit dem Fallbeil (or mit der Guillotine) hinrichten

guilt [gɪlt] *s* Schuld *f*

guilt'-rid'den *adj* schuldbeladen

guilty ['gɪlti] *adj* (of) schuldig (*genit*); (*conscience*) schlecht; **plead g.** sich schuldig bekennen; **plead not g.** sich für nicht schuldig erklären

guil'ty par'ty *s* Schuldige *mf*

guil'ty ver'dict *s* Schuldspruch *m*

guin'ea fowl' ['gɪni], **guin'ea hen'** *s* Perlhuhn *n*

guin'ea pig' *s* Meerschweinchen *n;* (fig) Versuchskaninchen *n*

guise [gaɪz] *s* Verkleidung *f;* **under the g. of** unter dem Schein (*genit*)

guitar [gɪ'tɑr] *s* Gitarre *f*

guitarist [gɪ'tɑrɪst] *s* Gitarrenspieler –in *mf*

gulch [gʌltʃ] *s* Bergschlucht *f*

gulf [gʌlf] *s* Golf *m;* (fig) Kluft *f*

Gulf' Stream' *s* Golfstrom *m*

gull [gʌl] *s* Möwe *f;* (coll) Tölpel *m* || *tr* übertölpeln

gullet ['gʌlɪt] *s* Gurgel *f,* Schlund *m*

gullible ['gʌlɪbəl] *adj* leichtgläubig

gully ['gʌli] *s* Wasserrinne *f*

gulp [gʌlp] *s* Schluck *m,* Zug *m;* **at one g.** in e–m Zuge || *tr* schlucken; **g. down** schlingen || *intr* schlucken

gum [gʌm] *s* Gummi *m & n;* (*chewing gum*) Kaugummi *m & n;* (anat) Zahnfleisch *n* || *v* (*pret & pp* **gummed;** *ger* **gumming**) *tr* (*e.g.,* labels) gummieren; **gum up the works** (coll) die Arbeit (or das Spiel) vermasseln

gum' ar'abic *s* Gummiarabikum *n*

gum'boil' *s* (pathol) Zahngeschwür *n*

gum'drop' *s* Gummibonbon *m & n*

gummy ['gʌmi] *adj* klebrig

gumption ['gʌmpʃən] *s* Unternehmungsgeist *m,* Mumm *m*

gun [gʌn] *s* Gewehr *n;* (*handgun*) Handfeuerwaffe *f;* (arti) Geschütz *n;* **stick to one's guns** bei der Stange bleiben || *v* (*pret & pp* **gunned;** *ger* **gunning**) *tr—***gun down** niederschießen; **gun the engine** Gas geben || *intr* auf die Jagd gehen; **be out gunning for** auf dem Korn haben; **gun for game** auf die Jagd gehen

gun' bar'rel *s* Gewehrlauf *m;* (arti) Geschützrohr *n*

gun' bat'tle *s* Feuerkampf *m*

gun' belt' *s* Wehrgehänge *n*

gun'boat' *s* Kanonenboot *n*

gun' car'riage *s* Lafette *f*

gun'cot'ton *s* Schießbaumwolle *f*

gun' crew' *s* Bedienungsmannschaft *f*

gun' emplace'ment *s* Geschützstand *m*

gun' fight' *s* Schießerei *f*

gun'fire' *s* Geschützfeuer *n*

gun'man *s* (–men) bewaffneter Bandit *m*

gun' met'al *s* Geschützlegierung *f*

gun' mount' *s* Lafette *f;* (*of swivel type*) Schwenklafette *f*

gunner ['gʌnər] *s* Kanonier *m;* (aer) Bordschütze *m*

gunnery ['gʌnəri] *s* Geschützwesen *n*

gun'nery prac'tice *s* Übungsschießen *n*

gunnysack ['gʌni‚sæk] *s* Jutesack *m*

gun' per'mit *s* Waffenschein *m*

gun'point' *s—***at g.** mit vorgehaltenem Gewehr

gun'pow'der *s* Schießpulver *n*

gun'run'ning *s* Waffenschmuggel *m*

gun'shot' *s* Schuß *m;* (*range*) Schußweite *f*

gun'shot wound' *s* Schußwunde *f*

gun'-shy' *adj* schußscheu

gun'sight' *s* Visier *n*

gun'smith' *s* Büchsenmacher *m*

gun'stock' *s* Gewehrschaft *m*

gun' tur'ret *s* Geschützturm *m;* (aer) Schwalbennest *n*

gunwale ['gʌnəl] *s* Schandeckel *m*

guppy ['gʌpi] *s* Millionenfisch *m*

gurgle ['gʌrgəl] *s* Glucksen *n,* Gurgeln *n* || *intr* glucksen, gurgeln

gush [gʌʃ] *s* Guß *m;* (fig) Erguß *m* || *intr* sich ergießen; **g. out** hervorströmen; **g. over** (fig) viel Aufhebens machen von

gusher ['gʌʃər] *s* Schwärmer –in *mf;* (*oil well*) sprudelnde Ölquelle *f*

gush'ing adj (fig) überschwenglich
gushy [ˈgʌʃi] adj schwärmerisch
gusset [ˈgʌsit] s Zwickel m
gust [gʌst] s Stoß m; (of wind) Windstoß m, Bö f
gusto [ˈgʌsto] s Gusto m
gusty [ˈgʌsti] adj böig
gut [gʌt] s Darm m; **guts** Eingeweide pl; (coll) Schneid m ‖ v (pret & pp **gutted;** ger **gutting**) tr ausbrennen; **be gutted** ausbrennen
gutter [ˈgʌtər] s Gosse f; (of a roof) Dachrinne f
gut'tersnipe' s (coll) Straßenjunge m
guttural [ˈgʌtərəl] adj kehlig; (ling) Kehl– ‖ s (ling) Kehllaut m
guy [gai] s Halteseil n; (of a tent) Spannschnur f; (coll) Kerl m; **dirty guy** (coll) Sauigel m; **great guy** Prachtkerl m ‖ tr verspannen
guy' wire' s Spanndraht m
guzzle [ˈgʌzəl] tr & intr saufen
guzzler [ˈgʌzlər] s Säufer –in mf
gym [dʒim] adj (coll) Turn– ‖ s (coll) Turnhalle f
gym' class' s (coll) Turnstunde f

gymnasi·um [dʒimˈnezi·əm] s (**–ums** & **–a** [ə]) Turnhalle f
gymnast [ˈdʒimnæst] s Turner –in mf
gymnastic [dʒimˈnæstik] adj Turn–, gymnastisch; **g. exercise** Turnübung f ‖ **gymnastics** spl Gymnastik f, Turnen n
gynecologist [ˌgainəˈkɑlədʒist] s Gynäkologe m, Gynäkologin f
gynecology [ˌgainəˈkɑlədʒi] s Gynäkologie f
gyp [dʒip] s (sl) Nepp m; (person) Nepper m; **that's a gyp** das ist Nepp! ‖ v (pret & pp **gypped;** ger **gypping**) tr neppen
gyp' joint' s Nepplokal n
gypper [ˈdʒipər] s Nepper m
gypsy [ˈdʒipsi] adj Zigeuner– ‖ s Zigeuner –in mf
gyp'sy moth' s Großer Schwammspinner m
gyrate [ˈdʒairet] intr sich drehen; kreiseln
gyration [dʒaiˈreʃən] s Kreiselbewegung f
gyroscope [ˈdʒairəˌskop] s Kreisel m

H

H, h [etʃ] s achter Buchstabe des englischen Alphabets
haberdasher [ˈhæbərˌdæʃər] s Inhaber –in mf e–s Herrenmodengeschäfts
haberdashery [ˈhæbərˌdæʃəri] s Herrenmodengeschäft n
habit [ˈhæbit] s Gewohnheit f; (eccl) Ordenskleid n; **be in the h. of** (ger) pflegen zu (inf); **break s.o. of that h. of smoking** j–m das Rauchen abgewöhnen; **from h. aus** Gewohnheit; **get into the h. of smoking** sich (dat) das Rauchen angewöhnen; **make a h. of it** es zur Gewohnheit werden lassen
habitat [ˈhæbiˌtæt] s Wohngebiet n
habitation [ˌhæbiˈteʃən] s Wohnort m
habitual [həˈbitʃu·əl] adj gewohnheitsmäßig, Gewohnheits–
hack [hæk] s (blow) Hieb m; (notch) Kerbe f; (rasping cough) trockener Husten m; (worn-out horse) Schindmähre f; (hackney) Droschke f; (taxi) (coll) Taxi n; (writer) (coll) Schreiberling m ‖ tr hacken, hauen; (basketball) auf den Arm schlagen ‖ intr Taxi fahren
hackney [ˈhækni] s (carriage) Droschke f; (horse) gewöhnliches Gebrauchspferd n
hackneyed [ˈhæknid] adj abgedroschen
hack'saw' s Metallsäge f, Bügelsäge f
haddock [ˈhædək] s Schellfisch m
haft [hæft] s Griff m
hag [hæg] s Vettel f; (witch) Hexe f
haggard [ˈhægərd] adj hager
haggle [ˈhægəl] intr (over) feilschen (um)

Hague, the [heg] s den Haag m
hail [hel] s Hagel m; **h. of bullets** Kugelhagel m ‖ tr (a taxi, ship) anrufen; (acclaim) preisen; (as) begrüßen (als) ‖ intr hageln; **h. from** stammen aus (or von) ‖ interj Heil!
Hail' Mar'y s Ave Maria n
hail'stone' s Hagelkorn n, Schloße f
hail'storm' s Hagelschauer m
hair |her| s (single hair) Haar n; (collectively) Haare pl; **by a h.** um ein Haar; **do s.o.'s h.** j–n frisieren; **get in s.o.'s h.** j–m auf die Nerven gehen lassen; **split hairs** Haarspalterei treiben
hair'breadth' s—**by a h.** um Haaresbreite
hair'brush' s Haarbürste f
hair' clip' s Spange f, Klammer f
hair'cloth' s Haartuch n
hair'curl'er s Lockenwickler m
hair'cut' s Haarschnitt m; **get a h.** sich (dat) die Haare schneiden lassen
hair'do' s (**–dos**) Frisur f
hair'dress'er s Friseur m, Friseuse f
hair'dri'er s Haartrockner m
hair' dye' s Haarfärbemittel n
hairiness [ˈheriniş] s Behaartheit f
hairless [ˈherliş] adj haarlos
hair'line' s Haaransatz m
hair' net' s Haarnetz n
hair' oil' s Haaröl n
hair'piece' s Haarteil m
hair'pin' s Haarnadel f
hair'–pin curve' s Haarnadelkurve f
hair'–rais'ing adj haarsträubend
hair' rinse' s Spülmittel n

hair'roll'er s Haarwickler m
hair' set' s Wasserwelle f
hair' shirt' s Büßerhemd n
hair'split'ting s Haarspalterei f
hair' spray' s Haarspray m
hair'spring' s Haarfeder f, Spirale f
hair'style' s Frisur f
hair' ton'ic s Haarwasser n
hairy ['heri] adj haarig, behaart
Haiti ['heti] s Haiti n
halberd ['hælbərd] s Hellebarde f
hal'cyon days' ['hælsɪ-ən] spl (fig) glückliche Zeit f
hale [hel] adj gesund; **h. and hearty** gesund und munter
half [hæf] adj halb; **at h. price** zum halben Preis; **have h. a mind to** (inf) halb und halb entschlossen sein zu (inf); **one and a h.** eineinhalb || adv halb; **h. as much as** nur halb so wie; **h. as much again** um die Hälfte mehr; **h. past three** halb vier; **not h.** durchaus nicht || s (halves [hævz]) Hälfte f; **cut in h.** in die Hälfte schneiden; **go halves with** halbpart machen mit
half'-and-half' adj & adv halb und halb || s Halb-und-halb-Mischung f
half'back' s (fb) Läufer m
half'-baked' adj halb gebacken; (plans, etc.) halbfertig; (person) unerfahren
half'-blood' s Halbblut n
half'-breed' s Halbblut n, Mischling m
half' broth'er s Halbbruder m
half'-cocked' adv (coll) nicht ganz vorbereitet
half'-day' adv halbtags
half'-full' adj halbvoll
half'-heart'ed adj zaghaft
half'-hour' adj halbstündig || s halbe Stunde f; **every h.** halbstündlich
half' leath'er s (bb) Halbleder n
half'-length' adj halblang; (portrait) in Halbfigur
half'-length por'trait s Brustbild n
half'-light' s Halbdunkel n
half-mast' s—**at h.** auf halbmast
half'-meas'ure s Halbheit f
half'-moon' s Halbmond m
half' note' s (mus) halbe Note f
half' pay' s Wartegeld n; **be on h.** Wartegeld beziehen
half' pint' s (sl) Zwerg m
half' sis'ter s Halbschwester f
half' sleeves' spl halblange Ärmel pl
half' sole' s Halbsohle f
half'-staff' s—**at h.** auf halbmast
half'-tim'bered adj Fachwerk-
half' time' s (sport) Halbzeit f
half'-time' adj Halbzeit-
half' ti'tle s Schmutztitel m
half'tone' s (mus, paint, typ) Halbton m
half'-track' s Halbkettenfahrzeug n
half'-truth' s halbe Wahrheit f
half'way' adj auf halbem Wege liegend || adv halbwegs, auf halbem Wege; **meet s.o. h.** j-m auf dem halbem Wege entgegenkommen
half'way meas'ure s Halbheit f
half'-wit' s Schwachkopf m
half'-wit'ted adj blöd
halibut ['hælɪbət] s Heilbutt m

halitosis [ˌhælɪ 'tosɪs] s Mundgeruch m
hall [hɔl] s (entranceway) Diele f, Flur m; (passageway) Gang m; (large meeting room) Saal m; (building) Gebäude n
hall'mark' s Kennzeichen n
hal·lo [hə'lo] s (-los) Hallo n || interj hallo!
hall' of fame' s Ruhmeshalle f
hallow ['hælo] tr heiligen
hallucination [həˌlusɪ'neʃən] s Sinnestäuschung f, Halluzination f
hall'way' s Flur m, Diele f; (passageway) Gang m
ha·lo ['helo] s (-los) Glorienschein m; (astr) Ring m, Hof m
halogen ['hælədʒən] s Halogen n
halt [hɔlt] s Halt m, Stillstand m; (rest) Rast f; **bring to a h.** zum Stillstand bringen; **call a h. to** halten lassen; **come to a h.** stehenbleiben || tr anhalten || intr halten; (rest) rasten || interj halt!
halter ['hɔltər] s (for a horse) Halfter m; (noose) Strick m
halt'ing adj (gait) hinkend; (voice) stockend
halve [hæv] tr halbieren
halyard ['hæljərd] s Fall n
ham [hæm] s (pork) Schinken m; (back of the knee) Kniekehle f; (actor) (sl) Schmierenschauspieler -in mf; (rad) (sl) Funkamateur m
hamburger ['hæmˌbʌrgər] s Hackfleisch n, deutsches Beefsteak n
hamlet ['hæmlɪt] s Dörfchen n
hammer ['hæmər] s Hammer m; (of a bell) Klöppel m; (sport) Wurfhammer m || tr hämmern; **h. in** (a nail) einschlagen; (e.g., rules) einhämmern; **h. out** aushämmern || intr hämmern; **h. away at** (fig) herumarbeiten an (dat)
hammock ['hæmək] s Hängematte f
hamper ['hæmpər] s Wäschebehälter m || tr behindern
hamster ['hæmstər] s Hamster m
ham'string' s Kniesehne f || v (pret & pp -strung) tr (fig) lähmen
hand [hænd] s Hand f; (applause) Beifall m; (handwriting) Handschrift f; (of a clock) Zeiger m; (help) Hilfe f; **all hands on deck!** (naut) alle Mann an Deck!; **at first h.** aus erster Hand; **at h.** vorhanden, zur Hand; **at the hands of** von seiten (genit); **be on h.** zur Stelle sein; **by h.** mit der Hand; **change hands** in andere Hände übergehen; **fall into s.o.'s hands** in j-s Hände fallen; **from h. to mouth** von der Hand in den Mund; **get one's hands on** in die Hände bekommen; **get the upper h.** die Oberhand gewinnen; **give s.o. a free h.** j-m freies Spiel lassen; **give s.o. a h.** (help s.o.) j-m helfen; (applaud s.o.) j-m Beifall spenden; **go h. in h. with** (fig) Hand in Hand gehen mit; **h. and foot** eifrig; **h. in h.** Hand in Hand; **hands off!** Hände weg!; **hands up!** Hände hoch!; **have a good h.** (cards) gute Karten haben; **have a h.**

in die Hand im Spiel haben bei; **have one's hands full** alle Hände voll zu tun haben; **have well in h.** gut in der Hand haben; **hold hands** sich bei den Händen halten; **in one's own h.** eigenhändig; **I wash my hands of it** ich wasche meine Hände in Unschuld; **join hands** (fig) sich zusammenschließen; **new h.** Neuling m; **on all hands** auf allen Seiten; **on h.** (com) vorrätig; **on one h. ... on the other** einerseits ... anderseits; **out of h.** außer Rand und Band; **play into s.o.'s hands** j-m in die Hände spielen; **put one's h. on** (fig) finden; **show one's h.** (fig) seine Karten aufdecken; **take a h. in** mitarbeiten in (dat); **throw up one's hands** verzweifelt die Hände hochwerfen; **try one's h.** at versuchen; **win hands down** spielend gewinnen; **with a heavy h.** streng || **tr** (zu)reichen; **h. down** (*to s.o. below*) herunterreichen; (*e.g., traditions*) überliefern; **h. in** (*e.g., homework*) abgeben; (*an application*) einreichen; **h. out** austeilen; **h. over** übergeben; (*relinquish*) aushändigen, hergeben; **I have to h. it to you** (coll) ich muß dir recht geben

hand'bag' *s* Handtasche *f*, Tasche *f*
hand'ball' *s* Handball *m*
hand'bill' *s* Handzettel *m*
hand'book' *s* Handbuch *n*
hand' brake' *s* (aut) Handbremse *f*
hand'breadth' *s* Handbreit *f*
hand' cart' *s* Handkarren *m*
hand'clasp' *s* Händedruck *m*
hand'cuff' *s* Handschelle *f* || *tr* Handschellen anlegen (*dat*)
-handed [ˈhændɪd] *suf* –händig
handful [ˈhændˌfʊl] *s* Handvoll *f*; (*a few*) ein paar; (fig) Nervensäge *f*
hand'glass' *s* Leselupe *f*
hand' grenade' *s* Handgranate *f*
handi·cap [ˈhændɪˌkæp] *s* Handikap *n*, Benachteiligung *f* || *v* (*pret & pp* –capped; *ger* –capping) *tr* handikapen, benachteiligen
hand'icap race' *s* Vorgaberennen *n*
handicraft [ˈhændɪˌkræft] *s* Handwerk *n*
handily [ˈhændɪli] *adv* (*dexterously*) geschickt; (*easily*) mit Leichtigkeit
handiwork [ˈhændɪˌwʌrk] *s* Handarbeit *f*; (fig) Werk *n*, Schöpfung *f*
handkerchief [ˈhæŋkərtʃɪf] *s* Taschentuch *n*
handle [ˈhændəl] *s* Griff *m*; (*of a pot*) Henkel *m*; (*of a frying pan, broom, etc.*) Stiel *m*; (*of a crank*) Handkurbel *f*; (*of a pump*) Schwengel *m*; (*of a door*) Drücker *m*; (*name*) (coll) Name *m*; (*title*) (coll) Titelkram *m*; **fly off the h.** vor Wut platzen || *tr* (*touch*) berühren; (*tools, etc.*) handhaben; (*operate*) bedienen; (fig) erledigen; (com) handeln mit; **h. with care!** Vorsicht!; **know how to h. customers** es verstehen, mit Kunden umzugehen || *intr*—**h. well** sich leicht lenken lassen

han'dlebars' *spl* Lenkstange *f*, (*mustache*) (coll) Schnauzbart *m*
handler [ˈhændlər] *s* (sport) Trainer *m*
han'dling *s* (*e.g., of a car*) Lenkbarkeit *f*; (*of merchandise, theme, ball*) Behandlung *f*; (*of a tool*) Handhabung *f*
han'dling charg'es *spl* Umschlagspesen *pl*
hand' lug'gage *s* Handgepäck *n*
hand'made' *adj* handgemacht
hand'-me-downs' *spl* getragene Kleider *pl*
hand' mir'ror *s* Handspiegel *m*
hand'-op'erated *adj* mit Handbetrieb
hand' or'gan *s* Drehorgel *f*
hand'out' *s* milde Gabe *f*; (*sheet*) Handzettel *m*
hand'-picked' *adj* handgepflückt; (fig) ausgesucht
hand'rail' *s* Geländer *n*
hand'saw' *s* Handsäge *f*
hand'shake' *s* Handschlag *m*, Händedruck *m*
handsome [ˈhænsəm] *adj* schön
hand'-to-hand' fight'ing *s* Nahkampf *m*
hand'-to-mouth' *adj* von der Hand in den Mund
hand'work' *s* Handarbeit *f*
hand'writ'ing *s* Handschrift *f*
handwritten [ˈhændˌrɪtən] *adj* handschriftlich; **h. letter** Handschreiben *n*
handy [ˈhændi] *adj* handlich; (*practical*) praktisch; (*person*) geschickt; **come in h.** gelegen kommen; **have h.** zur Hand haben
hand'y·man' *s* (*-men'*) Handlanger *m*
hang [hæŋ] *s* (*of curtains, clothes*) Fall *m*; **get the h. of** (coll) sich einarbeiten in (*acc*); **I don't give a h. about it** (coll) es ist mir Wurst || *v* (*pret & pp* hung [hʌŋ]) *tr* hängen; (*a door*) einhängen; (*wallpaper*) ankleben; **h. one's head** den Kopf hängen lassen; **h. out** heraushängen; **h. up** aufhängen; (*the receiver*) auflegen; **I'll be hanged if** ich will mich hängen lassen, wenn || *intr* hängen; (*float*) schweben; **h. around** herumlungern; **h. around the bar** sich in der Bar herumtreiben; **h. around with** umgehen mit; **h. back** sich zurückhalten; **h. by** (*a thread, rope*) hängen an (*dat*); **h. down** niederhängen; **h. in the balance** in der Schwebe sein; **h. on** durchhalten; **h. on s.o.'s words** an j-s Worten hängen; **h. on to** festhalten; (*retain*) behalten; **h. together** zusammenhalten; **h. up** (telp) einhängen || *v* (*pret & pp* hanged & hung) *tr* hängen
hangar [ˈhæŋər] *s* Hangar *m*
hang'-dog look' *s* Armesündergesicht *n*
hanger [ˈhæŋər] *s* Kleiderbügel *m*
hang'er-on' *s* (*hangers-on*) Mitläufer –in *mf*
hang'ing *adj* (herab)hängend || *s* Hängen *n*
hang'man *s* (*-men*) Henker *m*
hang'nail' *s* Niednagel *m*

hang'out' s Treffpunkt m
hang'o'ver s (coll) Kater m
hank [hæŋk] s Strähne f
hanker ['hæŋkər] intr (for) sich sehnen (nach)
hanky-panky ['hæŋki'pæŋki] s (coll) Schwindel m
haphazard [,hæp'hæzərd] adj wahllos
haphazardly [,hæp'hæzərdli] adv aufs Geratewohl
hapless ['hæplɪs] adj unglücklich
happen ['hæpən] intr geschehen; **h. to see** zufällig sehen; **h. upon** zufällig stoßen auf (acc); **what happens now?** was soll nun werden?
hap'pening s Ereignis n
happily ['hæplɪ] adv glücklich
happiness ['hæpɪnɪs] s Glück n
happy ['hæpi] adj glücklich; **be h. about s.th.** über etw erfreut sein; **be h. to** (inf) sich freuen zu (inf); **h. as a lark** quietschvergnügt
Hap'py Birth'day interj Herzlichen Glückwunsch zum Geburtstag!
hap'py-go-luck'y adj unbekümmert
hap'py me'dium s—strike a h. e-n glücklichen Ausgleich treffen
Hap'py New' Year' interj Glückliches Neujahr!
harangue [hə'ræŋ] s leidenschaftliche Rede f ‖ tr e-e leidenschaftliche Rede halten an (acc)
harass [hə'ræs], ['hærəs] tr schikanieren; (mil) stören
harass'ing fire' s (mil) Störungsfeuer n
harassment [hə'ræsmənt], ['hærəsmənt] s Schikane f; (mil) Störung f
harbinger ['harbɪndʒər] s Vorbote m ‖ tr anmelden
harbor ['harbər] adj Hafen– ‖ s Hafen m ‖ tr (give refuge to) beherbergen; (hide) verbergen; (thoughts) hegen
har'bor mas'ter s Hafenmeister m
hard [hard] adj (substance, water, words) hart; (problem) schwierig; (worker) fleißig; (blow, times, work) schwer; (life) mühsam; (fact) nackt; (rain) heftig; (winter) streng; (drinks) alkoholisch; **be h. on s.o.** j-m schwer zusetzen; **have a h. time** Schwierigkeiten haben; **h. to believe** kaum zu glauben; **h. to please** anspruchsvoll; **h. to understand** schwer zu verstehen ‖ adv hart; (energetically) fleißig; **he was h. put to** (inf) es fiel ihm schwer zu (inf); **rain h.** stark regnen; **take h.** schwer nehmen; **try h.** mit aller Kraft versuchen
hard'-and-fast' adj fest
hard-bitten ['hard ,bɪtən] adj verbissen
hard'-boiled' adj (egg) hartgekocht; (coll) hartgesotten
hard' can'dy s Bonbons pl
hard' cash' s bare Münze f
hard' ci'der s Apfelwein m
hard' coal' s Steinkohle f
hard'-earned' adj schwer verdient
harden ['hardən] tr & intr (er)härten
hard'ened adj (criminal) hartgesotten
hard'ening s Verhärtung f
hard'-head'ed adj nüchtern
hard'-heart'ed adj hartherzig

hardihood ['hardɪ ,hʊd] s Kühnheit f; (insolence) Frechheit f
hardiness ['hardɪnɪs] s Ausdauer f, Widerstandsfähigkeit f
hard' la'bor s Zwangsarbeit f
hard' luck' s Pech n
hardly ['hardli] adv kaum, schwerlich; **h. ever** fast gar nicht
hardness ['hardnɪs] s Härte f
hard'-of-hear'ing adj schwerhörig
hard'-pressed' adj schwer bedrängt
hard'-shell' adj hartschalig; (coll) unnachgiebig
hard'ship' s Mühsal f
hard'top' s (aut) Hardtop n
hard' up' adj (for money) schlecht bei Kasse; **h. for** in Verlegenheit um
hard'ware' s Eisenwaren pl; (e.g., on doors, windows) Beschläge pl; **military h.** militärische Ausrüstung f
hard'ware store' s Eisenwarenhandlung f
hard'wood' s Hartholz n
hard'wood floor' s Hartholzboden m
hard'-work'ing adj fleißig
hardy ['hardi] adj (plants) winterfest; (person) widerstandsfähig
hare [her] s Hase m
hare'brained' adj unbesonnen
hare'lip' s Hasenscharte f
harem ['herəm] s Harem m
hark [hark] intr horchen; **h. back to** zurückgehen auf (acc)
harlequin ['harləkwɪn] s Harlekin m
harlot ['harlət] s Hure f
harm [harm] s Schaden m; **do h.** Schaden anrichten; **I meant no h.** by **it** ich meinte es nicht böse; **out of harm's way** in Sicherheit; **there's no h. in trying** ein Versuch kann nicht schaden ‖ tr beschädigen; (e.g., a reputation, chances) schaden (dat); **h. s.o.** (physically) j-m etw zuleide tun; (fig) schaden (dat)
harmful ['harmfəl] adj schädlich
harmless ['harmlɪs] adj unschädlich
harmonic [har'manɪk] adj harmonisch ‖ s (mus) Oberton m
harmonica [har'manɪkə] s Harmonika f
harmonious [har'monɪ-əs] adj harmonisch
harmonize ['harmə ,naɪz] intr harmonieren
harmony ['harməni] s Harmonie f; **be in h. with** im Einklang stehen mit
harness ['harnɪs] s Geschirr n; **die in the h.** in den Sielen sterben ‖ tr anschirren; (e.g., a river, power) nutzbar machen
har'ness mak'er s Sattler m
har'ness rac'ing s Trabrennen n
harp [harp] s Harfe f ‖ intr—**h. on** herumreiten auf (dat)
harpist ['harpɪst] s Harfner –in mf
harpoon [har'pun] s Harpune f ‖ tr harpunieren
harpsichord ['harpsɪ ,kɔrd] s Cembalo n
harpy ['harpi] s (myth) Harpyie f
harrow ['hæro] s Egge f ‖ tr eggen
har'rowing adj schrecklich

har·ry [ˈhæri] *v* (*pret & pp* **–ried**) *tr* martern

Harry [ˈhæri] *s* Heinz *m*

harsh [haːʃ] *adj* (*conditions*) hart; (*tone*) schroff; (*light*) grell; (*treatment*) rauh

harshness [ˈhaːʃnɪs] *s* Härte *f*; Schroffheit *f*; Grelle *f*; Rauheit *f*

hart [haːt] *s* Hirsch *m*

harum-scarum [ˈhɛrəmˈskɛrəm] *adj* wild || *adv* wie ein Wilder

harvest [ˈhaːvɪst] *s* Ernte *f*; **bad h.** Mißernte *f* || *tr & intr* ernten

harvester [ˈhaːvɪstər] *s* Schnitter –in *mf*; (*mach*) Mähmaschine *f*

har′vest moon′ *s* Erntemond *m*

has-been [ˈhæz͵bɪn] *s* (coll) Gestrige *mf*

hash [hæʃ] *s* Gehacktes *n*; **make h. of** (coll) verwursteln || *tr* zerhacken

hashish [ˈhæʃiʃ] *s* Haschisch *n*

hasp [hæsp] *s* Haspe *f*

hassle [ˈhæsəl] *s* (coll) Streit *m*

hassock [ˈhæsək] *s* Hocker *m*

haste [hest] *s* Hast *f*, Eile *f*; **in (all) h.** in (aller) Eile; **make h.** sich beeilen

hasten [ˈhesən] *tr* beschleunigen || *intr* hasten, eilen

hasty [ˈhesti] *adj* eilig; (*rash*) hastig

hat [hæt] *s* Hut *m*; **keep under one's h.** für sich behalten

hat′band′ *s* Hutband *n*

hat′block′ *s* Hutform *f*

hat′box′ *s* Hutschachtel *f*

hatch [hæt̬] *s* (*opening*) (aer, naut) Luke *f*; (*cover*) (naut) Lukendeckel *m* || *tr* (*eggs*) ausbrüten; (*a scheme*) aushecken; (*mark with strokes*) schraffieren || *intr* Junge ausbrüten; (*said of chicks*) aus dem Ei kriechen

hat′check girl′ *s* Garderobe(n)fräulein *n*

hatchet [ˈhætʃɪt] *s* Beil *n*; **bury the h.** die Streitaxt begraben

hatch′ing *s* Schraffierung *f*

hatch′way′ *s* (naut) Luke *f*

hate [het] *s* Haß *m* || *tr* hassen; **I h. to** (*inf*) es widerstrebt mir zu (*inf*)

hateful [ˈhetfəl] *adj* verhaßt

hatless [ˈhætlɪs] *adj* hutlos

hat′pin′ *s* Hutnadel *f*

hat′rack′ *s* Hutständer *m*

hatred [ˈhetrɪd] *s* Haß *m*

haughtiness [ˈhɔtɪnɪs] *s* Hochmut *m*

haughty [ˈhɔti] *adj* hochmütig

haul [hɔl] *s* Schleppen *n*; (*hauling distance*) Transportstrecke *f*; (*amount caught*) Fang *m*; **make a big h.** (fig) reiche Beute machen; **over the long h.** auf die Dauer || *tr* (*tug*) schleppen; (*transport*) transportieren; **h. ashore** ans Land ziehen; **h. down** (*a flag*) einholen; **h. into court** vor Gericht schleppen; **h. out of bed** aus dem Bett herausholen || *intr*—**h. off** (naut) abdrehen; **h. off and hit** ausholen um zu schlagen

haulage [ˈhɔlɪdʒ] *s* Transport *m*; (*costs*) Transportkosten *pl*

haunch [hɔntʃ] *s* (hip) Hüfte *f*; (*hind quarter of an animal*) Keule *f*

haunt [hɔnt] *s* Aufenthaltsort *m* || *tr* verfolgen; **h. a place** an e–m Ort umgehen; **this place is haunted** es spukt hier

haunt′ed house′ *s* Haus *n* in dem es spukt

have [hæv] *s*—**the haves and the have-nots** die Besitzenden und die Besitzlosen || *v* (*pret & pp* **had** [hæd]) *tr* haben; (*a baby*) bekommen; (*a drink*) trinken; (*food*) essen; **h. back** zurückhaben; **h. in mind** vorhaben; **h. it in for s.o.** j–n auf dem Strich haben; **h. it out with s.o.** sich mit j–m aussprechen; **h. it your way** meinetwegen machen Sie es, wie Sie wollen; **h. left** übrig haben; **h. on** (*clothes*) anhaben; (*a hat*) aufhaben; (*e.g., a program*) vorhaben; **h. on one's person** bei sich tragen; **h. to do with s.o.** mit j–m zu tun haben; **h. what it takes** das Zeug dazu haben; **I've had it!** jetzt langt's mir aber!; **I will not h. it!** ich werde es nicht dulden!; **you had better** es wäre besser, wenn Sie; **what would you h. me do?** was soll ich machen? || *intr*—**h. done with it** fertig sein damit; **h. off** frei haben || *aux* (to form compound past tenses) haben, e.g., **he has paid the bill** er hat die Rechnung bezahlt; (to form compound past tenses of certain intransitive verbs of motion and change of condition, of the verb **bleiben**, and of the transitive verb **eingehen**) sein, e.g., **she has gone to the theater** sie ist ins Theater gegangen; **they h. become rich** sie sind reich geworden; **you h. stayed too long** Sie sind zu lange geblieben; **I h. assumed an obligation** ich bin e–e Verpflichtung eingegangen; (to express causation) lassen, e.g., **I am having a new suit made** ich lasse mir e–n neuen Anzug machen; (to express necessity) müssen, e.g., **I h. to study now** jetzt muß ich studieren; **that will h. to do** das wird genügen müssen

haven [ˈhevən] *s* Hafen *m*

haversack [ˈhævər͵sæk] *s* Brotbeutel *m*

havoc [ˈhævək] *s* Verwüstung *f*; **wreak h. on** verwüsten

haw [hɔ] *s* (bot) Mehlbeere *f*; (*in speech*) Äh *n* || *tr* nach links lenken || *intr* nach links gehen || *interj* (*to a horse*) hü!

Hawaii [həˈwaɪ·i] *s* Hawaii *n*

Hawaiian [həˈwarjən] *adj* hawaiisch

Hawai′ian Is′lands *spl* Hawaii-Inseln *pl*

hawk [hɔk] *s* Habicht *m* || *tr* (*wares*) verhökern; **h. up** aushusten || *intr* sich räuspern

hawker [ˈhɔkər] *s* Straßenhändler –in *mf*

hawse [hɔz] *s* (*hole*) (naut) Klüse *f*; (*prow*) (naut) Klüsenwand *f*

hawse′hole′ *s* (naut) Klüse *f*

hawser [ˈhɔzər] *s* (naut) Trosse *f*, Tau *n*

hawthorn [ˈhɔθɔrn] *s* Weißdorn *m*

hay [he] *s* Heu *n*; **hit the hay** (sl) sich

in die Falle hauen; **make hay** Heu machen

hay′ fe′ver s Heufieber n

hay′field′ s Kleefeld n

hay′fork′ s Heugabel f

hay′loft′ s Heuboden m

hay′mak′er s (box) Schwinger m

hay′rack′ s Heuraufe f

hayrick [′he‚rɪk] s Heuschober m

hay′ride′ s Ausflug m in e-m teilweise mit Heu gefüllten Wagen

hay′seed′ s (coll) Bauerntölpel m

hay′stack′ s Heuschober m

hay′wire′ adj (sl) übergeschnappt; **go h.** (go wrong) schiefgehen; (go insane) überschnappen

hazard [′hæzərd] s (danger) Gefahr f; (risk) Risiko n || tr riskieren

hazardous [′hæzərdəs] adj gefährlich

haze [hez] s Dunst m; (fig) Unklarheit f || tr (students) piesacken

hazel [′hezəl] adj (eyes) nußbraun || s (bush) Hasel f

ha′zelnut′ s Haselnuß f

haziness [′hezɪnɪs] s Dunstigkeit f; (fig) Verschwommenheit f

haz′ing s (of students) Piesacken n

hazy [′hezi] adj dunstig; (recollection) verschwommen

H-bomb [′et∫‚bam] s Wasserstoffbombe f

he [hi] pers pron er; **he who** wer || s Männchen n

head [hed] adj Kopf-; (chief) Haupt-, Ober-, Chef- || s (of a body, cabbage, nail, lettuce, pin) Kopf m; (of a gang, family) Haupt m; (of a firm) Chef m; (of a school) Direktor -in mf; (of a department) Leiter -in mf; (of a bed) Kopfende n; (of a coin) Bildseite f; (of a glass of beer) Blume f; (of cattle) Stück n; (of stairs) oberer Absatz m; (of a river) Quelle f; (of a parade, army) Spitze f; (toilet) Klo n; **a h.** pro Person, pro Kopf; **at the h. of** an der Spitze (genit); **be at the h. of** vorstehen (dat); **be h. and shoulders above s.o.** haushoch über j-m stehen; (be far superior to s.o.) j-m haushoch überlegen sein; **be over one's h.** über j-s Verstand gehen; **bring to a h.** zur Entscheidung bringen; **by a h.** um e-e Kopflänge; **from h. to foot** von Kopf bis Fuß; **go over s.o.'s h.** über j-s Verstand gehen; (adm) über j-s Kopf hinweg handeln; **go to s.o.'s h.** j-m zu Kopfe steigen; **have a good h. for** begabt sein für; **h. over heels** kopfüber; (in love) bis über die Ohren; (in debt) bis über den Hals; **heads or tails?** Kopf oder Wappen?; **heads up!** aufpassen!; **keep one's h.** kaltes Blut behalten; **keep one's h. above water** sich über Wasser halten; **lose one's h.** den Kopf verlieren; **my h. is spinning** es schwindelt mir; **not be able to make h. or tail of** nicht klug werden aus; **out of one's h.** nicht ganz richtig im Kopf; **per h.** pro Kopf; **put heads together** die Köpfe zusammenstecken; **talk over**

s.o.'s h. über j-s Kopf hinwegreden; **talk s.o.'s h. off** j-n dumm und dämlich reden; **take it into one's h.** es sich [dat] in den Kopf setzen || tr (be in charge of) leiten; (a parade, army, expedition) anführen; (steer, guide) lenken; **h. a list** als erster auf e-r Liste stehen; **h. off** abwehren; **h. up** (a committee) vorsitzen (dat) || intr—**h. back** zurückkehren; **h. for** auf dem Wege sein nach; (naut) ansteuern; **h. home** sich heimbegeben; **where are you heading?** wo wollen Sie hin?

head′ache′ s Kopfweh n, Kopfschmerzen pl

head′band′ s Kopfband n

head′board′ s Kopfbrett n

head′cold′ s Schnupfen m

head′ doc′tor s Chefarzt m, Chefärztin f

head′dress′ s Kopfputz m

-headed [‚hedɪd] suf -köpfig

head first adv kopfüber; (fig) Hals über Kopf

head′gear′ s Kopfbedeckung f

head′hunt′er s Kopfjäger m

head′ing s Überschrift f; (aer) Steuerkurs m

headland [′hedlənd] s Landspitze f

headless [′hedlɪs] adj kopflos; (without a leader) führerlos

head′light′ s (aut) Scheinwerfer m

head′line′ s (in a newspaper) Schlagzeile f; (at the top of a page) Überschrift f; **hit the headlines** (coll) Schlagzeilen liefern

head′lin′er s Hauptdarsteller -in mf

head′long′ adj stürmisch || adv kopfüber

head′man′ s (-men) Häuptling m, Chef m

head′mas′ter s Direktor m

head′mis′tress s Direktorin f

head′ nurse′ s Oberschwester f

head′ of′fice s Hauptgeschäftsstelle f

head′ of gov′ernment s Regierungschef m

head′ of hair′ s—**beautiful h.** schönes volles Haar n

head′ of the fam′ily s Familienoberhaupt n

head′-on′ adj Frontal- || adv frontal

head′phones spl Kopfhörer pl

head′piece′ s Kopfbedeckung f; (brains) (coll) Kopf m; (typ) Zierleiste f

head′quar′ters s Hauptquartier n; (of police) Polizeidirektion f; (mil) Hauptquartier n, Stabsquartier n

head′quarters com′pany s Stabskompanie f

head′rest′ s Kopflehne f; (aut) Kopfstütze f

head′ restrain′er s (aut) Kopfstütze f

head′set′ s Kopfhörer m

head′ shrink′er s (coll) Psychiater -in mf

head′stand′ s Kopfstand m

head′ start′ s Vorsprung m

head′stone′ s Grabstein m

head′strong′ adj starrköpfig

head′ wait′er s Oberkellner m
head′ wa′ters spl Quellflüsse pl
head′way′ s Vorwärtsbewegung f; (fig)
Fortschritte pl
head′wear′ s Kopfbedeckung f
head′wind′ s Gegenwind m
head′work′ s Kopfarbeit f
heady [′hɛdi] adj (wine) berauschend;
(news) spannend; (impetuous) unbesonnen

heal [hil] tr & intr heilen; **h. up** zu-
heilen
healer [′hilər] s Heilkundige mf
heal′ing s Heilung f
health [hɛlθ] s Gesundheit f; **drink to
s.o.'s h.** auf j-s Wohl trinken; **in
good h.** gesund; **in poor h.** kränklich; **to your h.!** auf Ihr Wohl!
health′ certi′ficate s Gesundheitspaß m
healthful [′hɛlθfəl] adj heilsam; (climate) bekömmlich
health′ insur′ance s Krankenversiche-
rung f
health′ resort′ s Kurort m
healthy [′hɛlθi] adj gesund; (respect)
gehörig; **keep h.** sich gesund halten
heap [hip] s Haufen m; **in heaps** hau-
fenweise || tr beladen; **h.** (e.g., praise)
on s.o. j-n überhäufen mit; **h. up**
anhäufen
hear [hɪr] v (pret & pp **heard** [hʌrd])
tr hören; (find out) erfahren; (get
word) Bescheid bekommen; **h. s.o.'s
lessons** j-n überhören; **h. s.o. out**
j-n ganz ausreden lassen || intr hö-
ren; **h. about** hören über (acc) or
von; **h. from** Nachricht bekommen
von; **h. of** hören von; **h. wrong** sich
verhören; **he wouldn't h. of it** er
wollte nichts davon hören
hearer [′hɪrər] s Hörer –in mf; **hearers**
Zuhörer pl
hear′ing s Hören n, Gehör n; (jur)
Verhör n; **within h.** in Hörweite
hear′ing aid′ s Hörgerät n, Hörapparat
m
hear′say′ s Hörensagen n; **know s.th.
by h.** etw nur vom Hörensagen kennen; **that's mere h.** das ist bloßes
Gerede
hearse [hʌrs] s Leichenwagen m
heart [hɑrt] s Herz n; **after my own h.**
nach meinem Herzen; **at h.** im
Grunde genommen; **be the h. and
soul of** die Seele sein (genit); **by h.**
auswendig; **cross my h.!** Hand aufs
Herz!; **cry one's h. out** sich ausweinen; **eat one's h. out** sich vor
Kummer verzehren; **get to the h. of**
auf den Grund kommen (dat); **have
a h.** (coll) ein Herz haben; **have
one's h. in s.th.** mit dem Herzen bei
etw sein; **have the h. to** (inf) es übers
Herz bringen zu (inf); **h. and soul**
mit Leib und Seele; **hearts** (cards)
Herz n; **lose h.** den Mut verlieren;
lose one's h. to sein Herz verlieren an
(acc); **set one's h. on** sein Herz hängen an (acc); **take h.** Mut fassen;
take to h. beherzigen; **to one's heart's
content** nach Herzenslust; **wear one's
h. on one's sleeve** das Herz auf der

Zunge tragen; **with all one's h.** mit
ganzem Herzen
heart′ache′ s Herzweh n
heart′ attack′ s Herzanfall m
heart′beat′ s Herzschlag m
heart′break′ s Herzeleid n
heart′break′er s Herzensbrecher –in
mf
heartbroken [′hɑrt‚brokən] adj trostlos
heart′burn′ s Sodbrennen n
heart′ disease′ s Herzleiden n
–hearted [‚hɑrtɪd] suf –herzig
hearten [′hɑrtən] tr ermutigen
heart′ fail′ure s Herzschlag m
heartfelt [′hɑrt‚fɛlt] adj herzinnig,
tiefempfunden; (wishes) herzlich
hearth [hɑrθ] s Herd m
hearth′stone′ s Kaminplatte f
heartily [′hɑrtɪli] adv (with zest) herzhaft; (sincerely) von Herzen
heartless [′hɑrtlɪs] adj herzlos
heart′ mur′mur s Herzgeräusch n
heart′-rend′ing adj herzzerreißend
heart′sick′ adj tief betrübt
heart′ strings′ spl—**pull at s.o.'s h.** j-m
ans Herz greifen
heart′ throb′ s Schwarm m
heart′ trans′plant s Herzverpflanzung f
heart′ trou′ble s Herzbeschwerden pl
heart′wood′ s Kernholz n
hearty [′hɑrti] adj herzhaft; (meal)
reichlich; (eater) stark; (appetite) gut
heat [hit] s Hitze f, Wärme f; (heating) Heizung f; (sexual) Brunst f; (in
the case of dogs) Läufigkeit f; (of
battle) Eifer m; (sport) Rennen n,
Einzelrennen n; **be in h.** brunsten;
(said of dogs) läufig sein; **final h.**
Schlußrennen n; **put the h. on** (sl)
unter Druck setzen; **qualifying h.**
Vorlauf m || tr (e.g., food) wärmen;
(fluids) erhitzen; (a house) heizen;
h. up aufwärmen || intr—**h.** (up)
warm (or heiß) werden
heat′ed adj erhitzt; (fig) erregt
heater [′hitər] s Heizkörper m; (oven)
Heizofen m
heath [hiθ] s Heide f
hea·then [′hiðən] adj heidnisch || s
(–then & –thens) Heide m, Heidin f
heathendom [′hiðəndəm] s Heidentum
n
heather [′hɛðər] s Heiderkraut n
heat′ing s Heizung f
heat′ing pad′ s Heizkissen n
heat′ing sys′tem s Heizanlage f
heat′ light′ning s Wetterleuchten n
heat′ prostra′tion s Hitzekollaps m
heat′-resis′tant adj hitzebeständig
heat′ shield′ s (rok) Hitzeschild m
heat′ stroke′ s Hitzschlag m
heat′ treat′ment s Wärmebehandlung f
heat′ wave′ s Hitzewelle f
heave [hiv] s Hub m; (throw) Wurf m;
heaves (vet) schweres Atmen n || v
(pret & pp **heaved** & **hove** [hov]) tr
heben; (throw) werfen; (a sigh) aus-
stoßen; (the anchor) lichten || intr
(said of the breast or sea) wogen;
(retch) sich übergeben; **h. in sight**
auftauchen; **h. to** (naut) stoppen

heaven ['hevən] *s* Himmel *m*; **for heaven's sake** um Himmels willen; **good heavens!** ach du lieber Himmel!; **the heavens** der Himmel

heavenly ['hevənli] *adj* himmlisch

hea'venly bod'y *s* Himmelskörper *m*

heavenwards ['hevənwərdz] *adv* himmelwärts

heavily ['hevrli] *adv* schwer; **h. in debt** überschuldet

heavy ['hevi] *adj* schwer; (*food*) schwer verdaulich; (*fine, price*) hoch; (*walk*) schwerfällig; (*heart*) bedrückt, schwer; (*traffic, frost, rain*) stark; (*fog*) dicht; (*role*) (*theat*) ernst, düster; **h. drinker** Gewohnheitstrinker –in *mf*; **h. seas** Sturzsee *f*; **h. with sleep** schlaftrunken

heavy'-armed' *adj* schwerbewaffnet

heav'y-du'ty *adj* Hochleistungs–, Schwerlast–

heav'y-du'ty truck' *s* Schwerlastwagen *m*

heav'y-heart'ed *adj* bedrückt

heav'y in'dustry *s* Schwerindustrie *f*

heav'y·set' *adj* untersetzt

heav'y weight' *adj* Schwergewicht– || *s* Schwergewichtler *m*

Hebrew ['hibru] *adj* hebräisch || Hebräer –in *mf*; (*language*) Hebräisch *n*

hecatomb ['hekə‚tom] *s* Hekatombe *f*

heck [hek] *s*—**give s.o. h.** (sl) j-n tüchtig einheizen; **what the h. are you doing?** (sl) was zum Teufel tust du? || *interj* (sl) verflixt!

heckle ['hekəl] *tr* durch Zwischenrufe belästigen

heckler ['heklər] *s* Zwischenrufer –in *mf*

hectic ['hektɪk] *adj* hektisch

hectograph ['hektə‚græf] *s* Hektograph *m* || *tr* hektographieren

hedge [hedʒ] *s* Hecke *f* || *tr*—**h. in** (or **h. off**) einhegen || *intr* sich den Rücken decken

hedge'hog' *s* Igel *m*

hedge'hop' *v* (*pret & pp* –hopped; *ger* hopping) *intr* (aer) heckenspringen

hedge'hop'ping *n* (aer) Heckenhüpfen *n*

hedge'row' *s* Hecke *f*

hedonism ['hidə‚nɪzəm] *s* Hedonismus *m*

hedonist ['hidənɪst] *s* Hedonist –in *mf*

heed [hid] *s* Acht *f*; **pay h. to** acht-geben auf (*acc*); **take h.** achtgeben || *tr* beachten || *intr* achtgeben

heedful ['hidfəl] *adj* (of) achtsam (auf *acc*)

heedless ['hidlɪs] *adj* achtlos; **h. of** ungeachtet (*genit*)

heehaw ['hi‚hɔ] *s* Iah *n* || *interj* iah!

heel [hil] *s* (*of the foot*) Ferse *f*; (*of a shoe*) Absatz *m*; (*of bread*) Brot-ende *n*; (sl) Schurke *m*; **down at the h.** abgerissen; **cool one's heels** sich [*dat*] die Beine in den Bauch stehen; **take to one's heels** Fersengeld geben || *intr* (said of a dog) auf den Fersen folgen

hefty ['hefti] *adj* (*heavy*) schwer; (*muscular*) stämmig; (*blow*) zünftig

heifer ['hefər] *s* Färse *f*

height [haɪt] *s* Höhe *f*; (*e.g., of power*) Gipfel *m*; **h. of the season** Hochsaison *f*

heighten ['haɪtən] *tr* erhöhen; (fig) verschärfen

heinous ['henəs] *adj* abscheulich

heir [er] *s* Erbe; *m*; **become h. to** er-ben; **become s.o.'s h.** j-n beerben

heir' appar'ent *s* (**heirs apparent**) Thronerbe *m*

heiress ['erɪs] *s* Erbin *f*

heir'loom' *s* Erbstück *n*

heir' presump'tive *s* (**heirs presumptive**) mutmaßlicher Erbe *m*

Helen ['helən] *s* Helene *f*

helicopter ['helɪ‚kaptər] *s* Hubschrauber *m*

heliport ['helɪ‚pɔrt] *s* Hubschrauber-landeplatz *m*

helium ['hilɪ‚əm] *s* Helium *n*

helix ['hilɪks] *s* (**helixes & helices** ['helɪ‚siz]) Spirale *f*; (archit) Schnecke *f*

hell [hel] *s* Hölle *f*

hell'bent' *adj*—**h. on** (sl) erpicht auf (*acc*)

hell'cat' *s* (*shrew*) Hexe *f*

Hellene ['helin] *s* Hellene *m*, Hellenin *f*

Hellenic [he'lenɪk] *adj* hellenisch

hell'fire' *s* Höllenfeuer *n*

hellish ['helɪʃ] *adj* höllisch

hel·lo [he'lo] *s* (–los) Hallo *n* || *interj* guten Tag!; (in southern Germany and Austria) Grüß Gott!; (to get s.o.'s attention and in answering the telephone) hallo!

helm [helm] *s* (& fig) Steuerruder *n*

helmet ['helmɪt] *s* Helm *m*

helms'man *s* (–men) Steuermann *m*

help [help] *s* Hilfe *f*; (*domestic*) Hilfe *f*, Hilfskraft *f*; (*temporary*) Aushilfe *f*; **h. wanted** (in newspapers) Stel-lenangebot *n*; **there's no h. for it** da ist nicht zu helfen; **with the h. of** mit Hilfe (*genit*) || *tr* helfen (*dat*); **can I h. you?** womit kann ich (Ihnen) dienen?; **h. along** nachhelfen (*dat*); **h. down from** herunterhelfen (*dat*) von (*dat*); **h. oneself** sich helfen; (at table) zugreifen; **h. oneself to** sich [*dat*] nehmen; **h. out** aushelfen (*dat*); **h. s.o. on** (or **off**) **with the coat** j-m in den (or aus dem) Mantel helfen; **I cannot h.** (ger), **I cannot h. but** (*inf*) ich kann nicht umhin zu (*inf*); **sorry, that can't be helped** es tut mir leid, aber es geht nicht anders || *intr* helfen || *interj* Hilfe!

helper ['helpər] *s* Gehilfe *m*, Gehilfin *f*

helpful ['helpfəl] *adj* (*person*) hilfs-bereit; (*e.g., suggestion*) nützlich

help'ing *s* Portion *f*

help'ing hand' *s* hilfreiche Hand *f*

helpless ['helplɪs] *adj* hilflos, ratlos

helter-skelter ['heltər'skeltər] *adj* wirr || *adv* holterdiepolter

hem [hem] *s* Saum *m* || *v* (*pret & pp* hemmed; *ger* hemming) *tr* säumen; **hem in** umringen || *intr* stocken; **hem**

and **haw** nicht mit der Sprache herauswollen || *interj* hm!

hemisphere ['hemɪ,sfɪr] *s* Halbkugel ||

hemistich ['hemɪ,stɪk] *s* Halbvers *m*

hem'line' *s* Rocklänge *f*

hem'lock' *s* (*conium*) Schierling *m*; (*poison*) Schierlingsgift *n*; (*Tsuga canadensis*) Kanadische Hemmlocktanne *f*

hemoglobin [,himə'globɪn] *s* Blutfarbstoff *m*, Hämoglobin *n*

hemophilia [,himə'fɪlɪ·ə] *s* Bluterkrankheit *f*, Hämophilie *f*

hemorrhage ['hemərɪdʒ] *s* Blutung *f*

hemorrhoids ['hemə,rɔɪdz] *spl* Hämorrhoiden *pl*

hemostat ['himə,stæt] *s* Unterbindungssklemme *f*

hemp [hemp] *s* Hanf *m*

hem'stitch' *s* Hohlsaum *m* || *tr* mit e-m Hohlsaum versehen

hen [hen] *s* Henne *f*, Huhn *n*

hence [hens] *adv* von hier; (*therefore*) daher, daraus; **a year h.** in e-m Jahr

hence'forth' *adv* hinfort, von nun an

hench·man ['hentʃmən] *s* (**-men**) Anhänger *m*; (*gang member*) Helfershelfer *m*

hen'house' *s* Hühnerstall *m*

henna ['henə] *s* Henna *f*

hen' par'ty *s* (coll) Damengesellschaft *f*

hen'peck' *tr* unter dem Pantoffel haben; **be henpecked** unter dem Pantoffel stehen; **henpecked husband** Pantoffelheld *m*

Henry ['henrɪ] *s* Heinrich *m*

hep [hep] *adj* (**to**) eingeweiht (in *acc*)

her [hʌr] *poss adj* ihr; (if the antecedent is neuter, e.g., Fräulein) sein || *pers pron* sie; (if the antecedent is neuter) es; (indirect object) ihr; (if the antecedent is neuter) ihm

herald ['herəld] *s* Herold *m*; (fig) Vorbote *m* || *tr* ankündigen; **h.** in einführen

heraldic [he'rældɪk] *adj* heraldisch; **h. figure** Wappenbild *n*; **h. motto** Wappenspruch *m*

heraldry ['herəldrɪ] *s* Wappenkunde *f*

herb [(h)ʌrb] *s* Kraut *n*, Gewürz *n*; (pharm) Arzneikraut *n*

herculean [hʌrkju'li·ən] *adj* herkulisch

herd [hʌrd] *s* Herde *f*; (of game) Rudel *n*; **the common h.** der Pöbel || *tr* hüten; **h. together** zusammenpferchen || *intr* in e-r Herde gehen (or leben)

herds'man *s* (**-men**) Hirt *m*

here [hɪr] *adv* (*position*) hier; (*direction*) hierher, her; **h. and there** hie(r) und da; **h. below** in diesem Leben; **h. goes!** jetzt gilt's!; **here's to you!** auf Ihr Wohl!; **neither h. nor there** belanglos || *interj* hier!

hereabouts ['hɪrə,bauts] *adv* hier in der Nähe

hereaf'ter *adv* hiernach || *s* Jenseits *n*

hereby' *adv* hierdurch

hereditary [hɪ'redɪ,terɪ] *adj* erblich, Erb–; **be h.** sich vererben

heredity [hɪ'redɪtɪ] *s* Vererbung *f*

herein' *adv* hierin

hereof' *adv* hiervon

hereon' *adv* hierauf

heresy ['herəsɪ] *s* Ketzerei *f*

heretic ['herətɪk] *s* Ketzer –in *mf*

heretical [hɪ'retɪkəl] *adj* ketzerisch

heretofore' [,hɪrtu'for] *adv* zuvor

here'upon' *adv* daraufhin

herewith' *adv* hiermit; (*in a letter*) anbei, in der Anlage

heritage ['herɪtɪdʒ] *s* Erbe *n*

hermet'ically sealed' [hʌr'metɪkəlɪ] *adj* hermetisch verschlossen

hermit ['hʌrmɪt] *s* Einsiedler –in *mf*; (eccl) Eremit *m*

hermitage ['hʌrmɪtɪdʒ] *s* Eremitage *f*

herni·a ['hʌrnɪ·ə] *s* (**-as** & **-ae** [,i]) Bruch *m*

he·ro ['hɪro] *s* (**-roes**) Held *n*

heroic [hɪ'ro·ɪk] *adj* heldenhaft, Helden–; (pros) heroisch || **heroics** *spl* Heldentaten *pl*

hero'ic age' *s* Helden(zeit)alter *n*

hero'ic coup'let *s* heroisches Reimpaar *n*

hero'ic verse' *s* heroisches Vermaß *n*

heroin ['hero·ɪn] *s* Heroin *n*

heroine ['hero·ɪn] *s* Heldin *f*

heroism ['hero·ɪzəm] *s* Heldenmut *m*

heron ['herən] *s* (orn) Fischreiher *m*

he'ro wor'ship *s* Heldenverehrung *f*

herring ['herɪŋ] *s* Hering *m*

her'ringbone' *s* (*pattern*) Grätenmuster *n*; (*parquetry*) Riemenparkett *n*

hers [hʌrz] *poss pron* der ihre (or ihrige), ihrer

herself' *reflex pron* sich; **she's not h. today** sie ist heute gar nicht wie sonst || *intens pron* selbst, selber

hesitancy ['herzɪtənsɪ] *s* Zaudern *n*

hesitant ['hezɪtənt] *adj* zögernd

hesitate ['hezɪ,tet] *intr* zögern

hesitation [,hezɪ'teʃən] *s* Zögern *n*

heterodox ['hetərə,daks] *adj* andersgläubig, heterodox

heterodyne ['hetərə,daɪn] *adj* Überlagerungs– || *tr & intr* überlagern

heterogeneous [,hetərə'dʒinɪ·əs] *adj* heterogen

hew [hju] *v* (*pret* **hewed**; *pp* **hewed** & **hewn**) *tr* (*stone*) hauen; (*trees*) fällen; **hew down** umhauen

hex [heks] *s* (*spell*) Zauber *m*; (*witch*) Hexe *f*; **put a hex on** (coll) behexen || *tr* (coll) behexen

hexagon ['heksəgən] *s* Hexagon *n*

hey [he] *interj* hei!; **hey there!** heda!

hey'day' *s* Hochblüte *f*, Glanzzeit *f*

H'-hour' *s* (mil) X-Zeit *f*

hi [haɪ] *interj* hei!; **hi there!** heda!

hia·tus [haɪ'etəs] *s* (**-tuses** & **-tus**) Lücke *f*; (ling) Hiatus *m*

hibernate ['haɪbər,net] *intr* (& fig) Winterschlaf halten

hibernation [,haɪbər'neʃən] *s* Winterschlaf *m*

hibiscus [haɪ'bɪskəs] *s* Hibiskus *m*

hiccough, hiccup ['hɪkəp] *s* Schluckauf *m*

hick [hɪk] *s* Tölpel *m*

hickory ['hɪkərɪ] *s* Hickorybaum *m*

hick' town' *s* Kuhdorf *n*

hidden ['hɪdən] *adj* verborgen, versteckt; (*secret*) geheim
hide [haɪd] *s* Haut *f*, Fell *n* || *v* (*pret* hid [hɪd]; *pp* hid & hidden ['hɪdən] *tr* verstecken; (*a view*) verdecken; (fig) verbergen; **h. from** verheimlichen vor (*dat*) || *intr* (**out**) sich verstecken
hide'-and-seek' *s* Versteckspiel *n*; **play h.** Verstecke spielen
hide'away' *s* Schlupfwinkel *m*
hide'bound' *adj* engherzig
hideous ['hɪdɪ-əs] *adj* gräßlich
hide'out' *s* (coll) Versteck *n*
hid'ing *s* Verstecken *n*; **be in h.** sich versteckt halten; **get a h.** (coll) Prügel bekommen
hid'ing place' *s* Versteck *n*
hierarchy ['haɪ-ə‚rɑrki] *s* Hierarchie *f*
hieroglyphic [‚haɪ-ərə'glɪfɪk] *adj* Hieroglphen– || *s* Hieroglyphe *f*
hi-fi ['haɪ'faɪ] *adj* Hif-fi– || *s* Hi-Fi *n*
high [haɪ] *adj* hoch; (*wind*) stark; (*hopes*) hochgespannt; (*fever*) heftig (*spirits*) gehoben; **h. and dry** auf dem Trockenen; **it is h. time** es ist höchste Zeit || *adv* hoch; **h. and low** weit und breit || *s* (*e.g., in prices*) Hochstand *m*; (aut) höchster Gang *m*; (meteor) Hoch *n*; **on h.** oben; **shift into h.** den höchsten Gang einschalten
high' al'tar *s* Hochaltar *m*
high'ball' *s* Highball *m*
high'born' *adj* hochgeboren
high'boy' *s* hochbeinige Kommode *f*
high'brow' *adj* intellektuell || *s* Intellektuelle *mf*
high' chair' *s* Kinderstuhl *m*
High' Church' *s* Hochkirche *f*
high'-class' *adj* vornehm, herrschaftlich
high' command' *s* Oberkommando *n*
high' cost' of liv'ing *s* hohe Lebenshaltungskosten *pl*
high' div'ing *s* Turmspringen *n*
high'er educa'tion *s* Hochschulbildung *f*
high'er-up' *s* (coll) hohes Tier *n*
high'est bid' ['haɪ-ɪst] *s* Meistgebot *n*
high'est bid'der *s* Meistbietende *mf*
high' explo'sive *s* hochexplosiver Sprengstoff *m*
highfalutin [‚haɪfə'lutən] *adj* hochtönend
high' fidel'ity *s* äußerst getreue Tonwiedergabe *f*, High Fidelity *f*
high'-fidel'ity *adj* klanggetreu
high' fre'quency *s* Hochfrequenz *f*
high'-fre'quency *adj* hochfrequent
high' gear' *s* höchster Gang *m*; **shift into h.** den höchsten Gang einschalten; (fig) auf Hochtouren gehen
High' Ger'man *s* Hochdeutsch *n*
high'-grade' *adj* hochfein, Qualitäts–
high'-grade steel' *s* Edelstahl *m*
high'-hand'ed *adj* anmaßend
high' heel' *s* Stöckel *m*
high'-heeled shoe' *s* Stöckelschuh *m*
high' horse' *s*—**come off one's h.** klein beigeben; **get up on one's h.** sich aufs hohe Roß setzen

high' jinks' [‚dʒɪŋks] *spl* Ausgelassenheit *f*
high' jump' *s* (sport) Hochsprung *m*
highland ['haɪlənd] *s* Hochland *n*; **highlands** Hochland *n*
highlander ['haɪləndər] *s* Hochländer –in *mf*
high' life' *s* Prasserei *f*, Highlife *n*
high'light' *s* (*big moment*) Höhepunkt *m*; (*in a picture*) Glanzlicht *n* || *tr* hervorheben; (*in a picture*) Glanzlichter aufsetzen (*dat*)
highly ['haɪli] *adv* hoch, hoch–, höchst; **h. sensitive** hochempfindlich; **speak h. of** in den höchsten Tönen sprechen von; **think h. of** große Stücke halten auf (*acc*)
High' Mass' *s* Hochamt *n*
high'-mind'ed *adj* hochgesinnt
high'-necked' *adj* hochgeschlossen
highness ['haɪnɪs] *s* Höhe *f*; **Highness** (*title*) Hoheit *f*
high' noon' *s*—**at h.** am hellen Mittag
high'-oc'tane *adj* mit hoher Oktanzahl
high'-pitched' *adj* (*voice*) hoch; (*roof*) steil
high'-pow'ered *adj* starkmotorig; **h. engine** Hochleistungsmotor *m*
high' pres'sure *s* Hochdruck *m*
high'-pres'sure *adj* Hochdruck–; **h. area** Hochdruckgebiet *n* || *tr* (com) bearbeiten
high'-priced' *adj* kostspielig
high' priest' *s* Hohe(r)priester *m*
high'-qual'ity *adj* Qualitäts–, hochwertig
high'-rank'ing *adj* hochgestellt
high' rise' *s* Hochbau *m*, Hochhaus *n*
high' road' *s* (fig) sicherer Weg *m*
high' school' *s* Oberschule *f*
high' sea' *s*—**on the high seas** auf offenem Meer
high' soci'ety *s* vornehme Welt *f*, High Society *f*
high'-sound'ing *adj* hochtönend
high'-speed' *adj* Schnell–; (phot) lichtstark
high'-speed steel' *s* Schnelldrehstahl *m*
high'-spir'ited *adj* hochgemut; (*horse*) feurig
high' spir'its *spl* gehobene Stimmung *f*
high-strung ['haɪ'strʌŋ] *adj* überempfindlich
high' ten'sion *s* Hochspannung *f*
high'-ten'sion *adj* Hochspannungs–
high'-test' gas'oline *s* Superbenzin *n*
high' tide' *s* Flut *f*
high' time' *s* höchste Zeit *f*; (sl) Heidenspaß *m*
high' trea'son *s* Hochverrat *m*
high' volt'age *s* Hochspannung *f*
high'-volt'age *adj* Hochspannungs–
high'-wa'ter mark' *s* Hochwassermarke *f*; (fig) Höhepunkt *m*
high'way' *s* Landstraße *f*, Chaussee *f*
high'way'man *s* (**-men**) Straßenräuber *m*
high'way patrol' *s* Straßenstreife *f*
high'way rob'bery *s* Straßenraub *m*
hijack ['haɪ‚dʒæk] *tr* (*a truck*) überfallen und rauben; (*a plane*) entführen

hijacker ['haɪˌdʒækər] s (of a truck) Straßenräuber –in mf; (of a plane) Entführer –in mf

hi'jack'ing s Entführung f

hike [haɪk] s Wanderung f; (in prices) Erhöhung f || tr (prices) erhöhen || intr wandern

hiker ['haɪkər] s Wanderer –in mf

hik'ing s Wandern n

hilarious [hɪ'lɛrɪ-əs] adj heiter

hill [hɪl] s Hügel m; **go over the h.** (mil) ausbüxen; **over the h.** (coll) auf dem absteigenden Ast || tr häufeln

hill'bil'ly adj hinterwäldlerisch || s Hinterwäldler –in mf

hill' coun'try s Hügelland n

hillock ['hɪlək] s Hügelchen n

hill'side s Hang m

hilly ['hɪli] adj hügelig

hilt [hɪlt] s Griff m; **armed to the h.** bis an die Zähne bewaffnet; **to the h.** (fig) gründlich

him [hɪm] pers pron (dative) ihm; (accusative) ihn

himself reflex pron sich; **he is not h. today** er ist heute gar nicht wie sonst || intens pron selbst, selber

hind [haɪnd] adj Hinter– || s Hirschkuh f

hinder ['hɪndər] tr (ver)hindern

hind'most adj hinterste

hind'quar'ter s Hinterviertel n; (of a horse) Hinterhand f; (of venison) Ziemer m

hindrance ['hɪndrəns] s (to) Hindernis n (für)

hind'sight s späte Einsicht f

Hindu ['hɪndu] adj Hindu– || s Hindu m

hinge [hɪndʒ] s Scharnier n; (of a door) Angel f || intr—**h. on** abhängen von

hint [hɪnt] s Wink m, Andeutung f; **give a broad h.** e-n Wink mit dem Zaunpfahl geben; **take the h.** den Wink verstehen || intr—**h. at** andeuten

hinterland ['hɪntərˌlænd] s Hinterland n

hip [hɪp] adj (sl) im Bild || s Hüfte f; (of a roof) Walm m

hip'bone' s Hüftbein n

hip'joint' s Hüftgelenk n

hipped adj—**h. on** (coll) erpicht auf (acc)

hippopota·mus [ˌhɪpə'pɑtəməs] s (–muses & –mi [ˌmaɪ]) Nilpferd n

hip' roof' s Walmdach n

hire [haɪr] s Miete f; (salary) Lohn m; **for h.** zu vermieten || tr (workers) anstellen; (rent) mieten; **h. oneself out to** sich verdingen bei; **h. out** vermieten

hired' hand' s Lohnarbeiter –in mf

hireling ['haɪrlɪŋ] s Mietling m

his [hɪz] poss adj sein || poss pron seiner, der seine (or seinige)

Hispanic [hɪs'pænɪk] adj hispanisch

hiss [hɪs] s Zischen n || tr auszischen || intr zischen

hiss'ing s Zischen n, Gezisch n

hiss'ing sound' s Zischlaut m

hist [hɪst] interj st!

historian [hɪs'tɔrɪ-ən] s Historiker –in mf

historic [hɪs'tɔrɪk] adj historisch bedeutsam

historical [hɪs'tɔrɪkəl] adj historisch, geschichtlich

history ['hɪstəri] s Geschichte f

historionic [ˌhɪstrɪ'ɑnɪk] adj schauspielerisch; (fig) übertrieben || **histrionics** spl theatralisches Benehmen n

hit [hɪt] s Schlag m, Stoß m; (a success) Schlager m; (sport) Treffer m; (theat) Zugstück n || v (pret & pp hit; ger hitting) tr (e.g., with the fist) schlagen; (a note, target) treffen; **hit bottom** (fig) auf dem Nullpunkt angekommen sein; **hit it off** gut miteinander auskommen; **hit one's head against** mit dem Kopf stoßen gegen; **hit s.o. hard** (said of misfortunes, etc.) schwer treffen; **hit the road** sich auf den Weg machen; **hit the sack** sich hinhauen || intr schlagen; **hit on** (or **upon**) kommen auf (acc)

hit'-and-run' adj (driver) flüchtig; **h. accident** Unfall m mit Fahrerflucht; **h. attack** Zerstörangriff m

hitch [hɪtʃ] s (difficulty) Haken m; (knot) Stich m; (term of service) Dienstzeit f; **that's the h.** das ist ja gerade der Haken; **without a h.** reibungslos || tr spannen; **h. a ride** (to) per Anhalter fahren (nach); **h. to the wagon** vor (or an) den Wagen spannen; **h. up** (horses) anspannen; (trousers) hochziehen

hitch'hike' intr per Anhalter fahren

hitch'ing post' s Pfosten m (zum Anbinden von Pferden)

hither ['hɪðər] adv her, hierher; **h. and thither** hierhin und dorthin

hitherto' adv bisher

hit' or miss' adv aufs Geratewohl

hit'-or-miss' adj planlos

hitter ['hɪtər] s Schläger m

hive [haɪv] s Bienenstock m; **hives** (pathol) Nesselausschlag m

hoard [hɔrd] s Hort m || tr & intr horten; (food) hamstern

hoarder ['hɔrdər] s Hamsterer –in mf

hoard'ing s Horten n; (of food) Hamstern n

hoarfrost ['hɔrˌfrɔst] s Rauhreif m

hoarse [hɔrs] adj heiser

hoarseness ['hɔrsnɪs] s Heiserkeit f

hoary ['hɔri] adj ergraut; (fig) altersgrau

hoax [hoks] s Schnabernack m || tr anführen

hob [hɑb] s Kamineinsatz m

hobble ['hɑbəl] s Humpeln n || intr humpeln

hobby ['hɑbi] s Hobby n

hob'byhorse' s (stick with horse's head) Steckenpferd n; (rocking horse) Schaukelpferd n

hob'gob'lin s Kobold m; (bogy) Schreckgespenst n

hob'nail' s grober Schuhnagel m

hob·nob ['hɑb,nɑb] v (pret & pp -nobbed; ger -nobbing) intr—h. with freundschaftlich verkehren mit

ho·bo ['hobo] s (-bos & -boes) Landstreicher m

hock [hɑk] s (of a horse) Sprunggelenk n; in h. verpfändet || tr (hamstring) lähmen; (pawn) (coll) verpfänden

hockey ['hɑki] s Hockey n

hoc'key stick' s Hockeystock m

hock'shop' s (coll) Leihhaus n

hocus-pocus ['hokəs'pokəs] s Hokuspokus m

hod [hɑd] s Mörteltrog m

hodgepodge ['hɑdʒ,pɑdʒ] s Mischmasch m

hoe [ho] s Hacke f, Haue f || tr hacken

hog [hɔg] s Schwein n || v (pret & pp hogged; ger hogging) tr (sl) gierig an sich reißen; **hog the road** rücksichtslos fahren

hog'back' s scharfer Gebirgskamm m

hog' bris'tle s Schweinsborste f

hoggish ['hɔgɪʃ] adj schweinisch, gefräßig

hog'wash' s (nonsense) Quatsch m

hoist [hɔɪst] s (apparatus for lifting) Hebezeug n; (act of lifting) Hochwinden n || tr hochwinden; (a flag, sail) hissen

hokum ['hokəm] s (nonsense) (coll) Quatsch m; (flimflam) (coll) Effekthascherei f

hold [hold] s Halt m, Griff m; (naut) Raum m; (sport) Griff m; **get h. of** (catch) erwischen; (acquire) erwerben; **get h. of oneself** sich fassen; **take h. of** anfassen || v (pret & pp held [held] tr halten; (contain) enthalten; (regard as) halten für; (one's breath) anhalten; (an audience) fesseln; (a meeting, election, court) abhalten; (an office, position) bekleiden, innehaben; (talks) führen; (a viewpoint) vertreten; (a meet) (sport) veranstalten; **able to h. one's liquor** trinkfest; **h. back** zurückhalten; (news) geheimhalten; **h. dear** werthalten; **h. down** niederhalten; **h. in contempt** verachten; **h. it!** halt!; **h. off** abhalten; **h. office** amtieren; **h. one's ground** die Stellung halten; **h. one's own** seinen Mann stehen; **h. one's own against** sich behaupten gegen; **h. one's tongue** den Mund halten; **h. open** (a door) aufhalten; **h. out** (a hand) hinhalten; (proffer) vorhalten; **h. over** (e.g., a play) verlängern; **h. s.th. against s.o.** j-m etw nachtragen; **h. sway** walten; **h. under** niederhalten; **h. up** (raise) hochhalten; (detain) aufhalten; (traffic) behindern; (rob) (räuberisch) überfallen; **h. up to ridicule** dem Spott preisgeben; **h. the line** (telp) am Apparat bleiben; **h. the road well** e-e gute Straßenlage haben; **h. together** zusammenhalten; **h. water** (fig) stichhaltig sein || intr (said of a knot) halten; **h. back** sich zurückhalten; **h. forth** (coll) dozieren; **h. on** warten; **h. on to** festhalten, sich

festhalten an (dat); **h. out** aushalten; **h. out for** abwarten; **h. true** gelten; **h. true for** zutreffen auf (acc); **h. up** (wear well) halten

holder ['holdər] s (device) Halter m; (e.g., of a title) Inhaber –in mf

hold'ing s (of a meeting) Abhaltung f; (of an office) Bekleidung f; **holdings** Besitz m, Bestand m

hold'ing com'pany s Holdinggesellschaft f

hold'ing pat'tern s (aer) Platzrunde f

hold'-o'ver s Überbleibsel n

hold'up' s (delay) Aufenthalt m; (robbery) Raubüberfall m; (in traffic) Verkehrsstauung f

hold'up man' s Räuber m

hole [hol] s Loch n; (of animals) Bau m; **h. in the wall** Loch n; **in a h.** in der Patsche; **in the h.** hängengeblieben, e.g., **I am ten dollars in the h.** ich bin mit zehn Dollar hängengeblieben; **pick holes in** (fig) herumkritisieren an (dat); **wear holes in** völlig abtragen || intr—**h. out** (golf) ins Loch spielen; **h. up** sich vergraben; (fig) sich verstecken

holiday ['hɑlɪ,de] s Feiertag m; (vacation) Ferien pl; **take a h.** e-n freien Tag machen, Urlaub nehmen

hol'iday mood' s Ferienstimmung f

holiness ['holɪnɪs] s Heiligkeit f; **His Holiness** Seine Heiligkeit

Holland ['hɑlənd] s Holland n

Hollander ['hɑləndər] s Holländer –in mf

hollow ['halo] adj hohl || s Höhle f, Höhlung f; (geol) Talmulde f || tr—h. out aushöhlen

hol'low-cheeked' adj hohlwangig

hol'low-eyed' adj hohläugig

holly ['hɑli] s Stechpalme f

holm' oak' [hom] s Steineiche f

holocaust ['hɑlə,kɔst] s Brandopfer n; (disaster) Brandkatastrophe f

holster ['holstər] s Pistolentasche f

holy ['holi] adj heilig; **h. smokes!** (coll) heiliger Strohsack!

Ho'ly Commun'ion s Kommunion f, das Heilige Abendmahl

ho'ly day' s Feiertag m

Ho'ly Ghost' s Heiliger Geist m

Ho'ly of Ho'lies s Allerheiligste n

ho'ly or'ders spl Priesterweihe f

Ho'ly Scrip'ture s die Heilige Schrift

Ho'ly See' s Heiliger Stuhl m

Ho'ly Sep'ulcher s Heiliges Grab n

Ho'ly Spir'it s Heiliger Geist m

ho'ly wa'ter s Weihwasser n

Ho'ly Week' s Karwoche f

Ho'ly Writ' s die Heilige Schrift

homage ['(h)ɑmɪdʒ] s Huldigung f; **pay h. to** huldigen (dat)

home [hom] adj inländisch, Innen– || adv nach Hause, heim; **bring h. to s.o.** j-m beibringen || s Heim n; (house) Haus n, Wohnung f; (place of residence) Wohnort m; (institution) Heim n; **at h.** zu Hause, daheim; **at h. and abroad** im In- und Ausland; **feel at h.** sich zu Hause fühlen; **for the h.** für den Hausbedarf; **from h.** von zu Hause; **h. for the aged** Altersheim *n*; **h. for the blind** Blindenheim *n*; **h. of one's own** Zuhause *n*

home′ address′ *s* Privatadresse *f*

home′-baked′ *adj* hausbacken

home′ base′ *s* (aer) Heimatflughafen *m*

home′bod′y *s* Stubenhocker –in *mf*

homebred [′hom ‚bred] *adj* einheimisch

home′-brew′ *s* selbstgebrautes Getränk *n*

home′-brewed′ *adj* selbstgebraut

home′com′ing *s* Heimkehr *f*

home′ comput′er *s* Heimcomputer *m*

home′ coun′try *s* Heimatstaat *m*

home′ econom′ics *s* Hauswirtschaftslehre *f*

home′-fried pota′toes *spl*, **home′ fries′** [‚fraɪz] *spl* Bratkartoffeln *pl*

home′ front′ *s* Heimatfront *f*

home′-grown′ *adj* selbstgezogen

home′ guard′ *s* Landsturm *m*

home′land′ *s* Heimatland *n*

homeless [′homlɪs] *adj* obdachlos ‖ *s* Obdachlose *mf*

home′like′ *adj* anheimelnd

homely [′homli] *adj* unschön

home′made′ *adj* selbstgemacht; (culin) selbstgebacken

home′mak′er *s* Hausfrau *f*

home′ of′fice *s* Hauptbüro *n*

home′ own′er *s* Hausbesitzer –in *mf*

home′ plate′ *s* Schlagmal *n*

home′ rem′edy *s* Hausmittel *n*

home′ rule′ *s* Selbstverwaltung *f*

home′ run′ *s* (baseball) Vier-Mal-Lauf *m*

home′sick′ *adj*—**be h.** Heimweh haben

home′sick′ness *s* Heimweh *n*

homespun [′hom ‚spʌn] *adj* selbstgemacht; (fig) einfach

home′stead′ *s* Siedlerstelle *f*

home′stretch′ *s* Zielgerade *f*

home′ team′ *s* Ortsmannschaft *f*

home′town′ *adj* Heimat- ‖ *s* Heimatstadt *f*

homeward [′homwərd] *adv* heimwärts

home′ward jour′ney *s* Heimreise *f*

home′work′ *s* Hausaufgabe *f*

homey [′homi] *adj* anheimelnd

homicidal [‚hɑmɪ′saɪdəl] *adj* mörderisch

homicide [′hɑmɪ ‚saɪd] *s* (act) Totschlag *m*; (person) Totschläger –in *mf*

hom′icide squad′ *s* Mordkommission *f*

homily [′hɑmɪli] *s* Homilie *f*

hom′ing device′ [′homɪŋ] *s* Zielsucher *m*

hom′ing pi′geon *s* Brieftaube *f*

homogeneous [‚homə′dʒɪnɪ·əs] *adj* homogen

homogenize [hə′mɑdʒə ‚naɪz] *tr* homogenisieren

homonym [′hɑmənɪm] *s* Homonym *n*

homosexual [‚homə′sɛk/ʊ·əl] *adj* homosexuell ‖ *s* Homosexuelle *mf*

hone [hon] *s* Wetzstein *m* ‖ *tr* honen

honest [′ɑnɪst] *adj* ehrlich, aufrecht

honestly [′ɑnɪstli] *adv* ehrlich; **to tell you h.** offengestanden ‖ *interj* auf mein Wort!

honesty [′ɑnɪsti] *s* Ehrlichkeit *f*

hon·ey [′hʌni] *s* Honig *m*; (as a term of endearment) Schatz *m*, Liebling *m* ‖ *v* (pret & pp **–eyed** & **–ied**) *tr* versüßen; (speak sweetly to) schmeicheln (dat)

hon′eybee′ *s* Honigbiene *f*

hon′eycomb′ *s* Honigwabe *f* ‖ *tr* (e.g., a hill) wabenartig durchlöchern

hon′eyed *adj* mit Honig gesüßt; (fig) honigsüß

hon′ey lo′cust *s* Honigdorn *m*

hon′eymoon′ *s* Flitterwochen *pl* ‖ *intr* die Flitterwochen verbringen

hon′eysuck′le *s* Geißblatt *n*

honk [hɔŋk] *s* (aut) Hupensignal *n* ‖ *tr—h. the horn* hupen ‖ *intr* hupen

honkytonk [′hɔŋki ‚tɔŋk] *s* (sl) Tingeltangel *m* & *n*

honor [′ɑnər] *s* Ehre *f*; (award) Auszeichnung *f*; (chastity) Ehre *f*; **be held in h.** in Ehren gehalten werden; **consider it an h.** es sich [dat] zur Ehre anrechnen; **do the honors** die Honneurs machen; **have the h. of** (ger) sich beehren zu (inf); **in s.o.'s h.** j–m zu Ehren; **your Honor** Euer Gnaden ‖ *tr* ehren; (favor) beehren; (a check) honorieren; **feel honored** sich geehrt fühlen

honorable [′ɑnərəbəl] *adj* (person) ehrbar; (intentions) ehrlich; (peace treaty) ehrenvoll

honorari·um [‚ɑnə′rɛrɪ·əm] *s* (**–ums** & **–a** [ə]) Honorar *n*; **give an h. to** honorieren

hon′orary degree′ *s* Ehrendoktorat *n*

honorific [‚ɑnə′rɪfɪk] *adj* ehrend, Ehren– ‖ *s* Ehrentitel *m*

hooch [hutʃ] *s* (sl) Fusel *m*, Schnaps *m*

hood [hʊd] *s* Haube *f*; (of a monk) Kapuze *f*; (of a baby carriage) Verdeck *n*; (sl) Gangster *m*; (aut) Motorhaube *f*; (culin) Rauchabzug *m*; (educ) Talarüberwurf *m* ‖ *tr* mit e–r Haube versehen; (fig) verhüllen

hoodlum [′hʊdləm] *s* Ganove *m*

hoodoo [′hudu] *s* Unglücksbringer *m* ‖ *tr* Unglück bringen (dat)

hood′wink′ *tr* täuschen

hooey [′hu·i] *s* (sl) Quatsch *m*

hoof [hʊf], [huf] *s* Huf *m* ‖ *tr—h. it* auf Schusters Rappen reiten

hoof′beat′ *s* Hufschlag *m*

hook [hʊk] *s* Haken *m*; (angl) Angelhaken *m*; (baseball) Kurvball *m*; (box) Haken *m*; (golf) Hook *m*; **by h. or by crook** so oder so; **h., line, and sinker** mit allem Drum und Dran; **off the h.** (coll) aus der Schlinge; **on one's own h.** (coll) auf eigene Faust ‖ *tr* festhaken, einhaken; (e.g., a boyfriend) angeln; (steal) schnappen; (box) e–n Haken versetzen (dat); (golf) nach links verziehen; **h. up** zuhaken; (elec) anschließen ‖ *intr* sich krümmen; **h. up with s.o.** sich j–m anschließen

hook′ and eye′ *s* Haken *m* und Öse *f*

hook′-and-lad′der truck′ *s* Feuerwehrfahrzeug *n* mit Drehleiter

hooked *adj* hakenförmig; **h. on drugs** rauschgiftsüchtig

hooker ['hukər] *s* (sl) Nutte *f*

hook/nose/ *s* Hakennase *f*

hook/up/ *s* (elec, electron) Schaltung *f*; (electron) Schaltbild *n*; (rad, telv) Gemeinschaftsschaltung *f*

hook/worm/ *s* Hakenwurm *m*

hooky ['huki] *s*—**play/h.** schwänzen

hooligan ['huligən] *s* Straßenlümmel *m*

hoop [hup] *s* Reifen *m* || *tr* binden

hoop/ skirt/ *s* Reifrock *m*

hoot [hut] *s* Geschrei *n*; **not give a h. about** keinen Pfifferling geben für || *intr* schreien; **h. at** anschreien

hoot/ owl/ *s* Waldkauz *m*

hop [hap] *s* Hopser *m*; (dance) Tanz *m*; **hops** (bot) Hopfen *m* || *v* (pret & pp **hopped**; ger **hopping**) *tr* (e.g., a train) aufspringen auf (acc); **hop a ride** (coll) mitfahren || *intr* hüpfen; **hop around** herumhüpfen

hope [hop] *s* (of) Hoffnung *f* (auf acc); **beyond h.** hoffnungslos; **not get up one's hopes** sich [dat] keine Hoffnungen machen || *tr* hoffen || *intr* hoffen; **h. for** hoffen auf (acc); **h. for the best** das Beste hoffen; **I h.** (parenthetical) hoffentlich

hope/ chest/ *s* Aussteuertruhe *f*

hopeful ['hopfəl] *adj* hoffnungsvoll || *s* (pol) Kandidat –in *mf*

hopefully ['hopfəli] *adv* hoffentlich

hopeless ['hoplɪs] *adj* hoffnungslos

hopper ['hapər] *s* Fülltrichter *m*; (in a toilet) Spülkasten *m*; (storage container) Vorratsbehälter *m*; (data proc) Kartenmagazin *n*

hop/per car/ *s* (rr) Selbstentladewagen *m*

hop/ping mad/ *adj* fuchsteufelswild

hop/scotch/ *s* Himmel und Hölle

horde [hord] *s* Horde *f*

horehound ['hor,haund] *s* (lozenge) Hustenbonbon *m*; (bot) Andorn *m*

horizon [hə'raizən] *s* Horizont *m*

horizontal [,harı'zantəl] *adj* horizontal, waagerecht || *s* Horizontale *f*

horizon/tal bar/ *s* (gym) Reck *n*

horizon/tal controls/ *spl* (aer) Seitenleitwerk *n*

horizon/tal sta/bilizer *s* (aer) Höhenflosse *f*

hormone ['hormon] *s* Hormon *n*

horn [horn] *s* (of an animal; wind instrument) Horn *n*; (aut) Hupe *f*; **blow one's own h.** (coll) ins eigene Horn stoßen; **blow the h.** (aut) hupen; **horns** (of an animal) Geweih *n* || *intr*—**h. in** (on) (coll) sich eindrängen (in acc)

hornet ['hornɪt] *s* Hornisse *f*

hor/net's nest/ *s*—**stir up a h. in** ein Wespennest stechen

horn/ of plen/ty *s* Füllhorn *n*

horn/-rimmed glass/es *spl* Hornbrille *f*

horny ['horni] *adj* (callous) schwielig; (having horn-like projections) verhornt; (sl) geil

horoscope ['hora,skop] *s* Horoskop *n*; **cast s.o.'s h.** j-m das Horoskop stellen

horrible ['horɪbəl] *adj* (& coll) schrecklich

horrid ['horɪd] *adj* abscheulich

horri·fy ['horɪ,faɪ] *v* (pret & pp –**fied**) *tr* erschrecken, entsetzen

horror ['horər] *s* Schrecken *m*, Entsetzen *n*

hor/ror sto/ry *s* Schauergeschichte *f*

hors d'oeuvre [ɔr'dʌrv] *s* (hors d'oeuvres** [ɔr'dʌrvz]) Vorspeise *f*

horse [hors] *s* Pferd *n*; (carp) Sägebock *m*; **back the wrong h.** (fig) auf's falsche Pferd setzen; **bet on a h.** auf ein Pferd setzen; **hold your horses** immer mit der Ruhe!; **h. of another color** e-e andere Sache; **mount a h.** zu Pferd steigen; **straight from the horse's mouth** direkt von der Quelle || *intr*—**h. around** (sl) herumalbern; **stop horsing around** laß den Unsinn!

horse/back/ *s*—**on h.** zu Pferd || *adv*—**ride h.** reiten

horse/back rid/ing *s* Reiten *n*

horse/ blan/ket *s* Pferdedecke *f*

horse/ chest/nut *s* Roßkastanie *f*

horse/ col/lar *s* Kummet *n*

horse/ doc/tor *s* (coll) Roßarzt *m*

horse/fly/ *s* Pferdebremse *f*

horse/hair/ *s* Roßhaar *n*, Pferdehaar *n*

horse/laugh/ *s* wieherndes Gelächter *n*

horse/man *s* (–men) Reiter *m*

horse/manship/ *s* Reitkunst *f*

horse/ meat/ *s* Pferdefleisch *n*

horse/ op/era *s* (coll) Wildwestfilm *m*

horse/play/ *s* grober Unfug *m*

horse/pow/er *s* Pferdestärke *f*

horse/ race/ *s* Pferderennen *n*

horse/rad/ish *s* Meerrettich *m*, Kren *m*

horse/ sense/ *s* gesunder Menschenverstand *m*

horse/shoe/ *s* Hufeisen *n* || *tr* beschlagen

horse/shoe mag/net *s* Hufeisenmagnet *m*

horse/ show/ *s* Pferdeschau *f*

horse/ tail/ *s* Pferdeschwanz *m*

horse/ trad/er *s* Pferdehändler *m*; (fig) Kuhhändler *m*

horse/ trad/ing *s* Pferdehandel *m*; (fig) Kuhhandel *m*

horse/whip/ *s* Reitpeitsche *f* || *v* (pret & pp –**whipped**; ger –**whipping**) *tr* mit der Reitpeitsche schlagen

horse/wom/an *s* (–wom/en) Reiterin *f*

horsy ['horsi] *adj* pferdeartig; (horse-loving) pferdeliebend

horticultural [,hortı'kʌltʃərəl] *adj* Gartenbau–

horticulture ['hortı,kʌltʃər] *s* Gartenbau *m*, Gärtnerei *f*

hose [hoz] *s* Schlauch *m* || *s* (hose) Strumpf *m*; (collectively) Strümpfe *pl*

hosiery ['hoʒəri] *s* Strumpfwaren *pl*; (mill) Strumpffabrik *f*

hospice ['haspɪs] *s* Hospiz *n*

hospitable ['haspɪtəbəl], [has'pɪtəbəl] *adj* gastlich, gastfreundlich

hospital ['haspɪtəl] *s* Hospital *n*, Krankenhaus *n*; (mil) Lazarett *n*

hospitality [,haspı'tælıti] *s* Gast-

freundschaft *f*; **show s.o. h.** j-m
Gastfreundschaft gewähren
hospitalize [ˈhɒspitə‚laiz] *tr* ins
Krankenhaus einweisen
hos'pital ship' *s* Lazarettschiff *f*
hos'pital train' *s* Sanitätszug *m*
hos'pital ward' *s* Kranken(haus)station
f
host [host] *s* Gastgeber *m*; (*at an inn*)
Wirt *m*; (*in a television show*) Leiter
m; (*multitude*) Heerschar *f*; (*army*)
Heer *n*; **Host** (*relig*) Hostie *f*
hostage [ˈhɒstidʒ] *s* Geisel *mf*
hostel [ˈhɒstəl] *s* Herberge *f*
hostelry [ˈhɒstəlri] *s* Gasthaus *n*
hostess [ˈhɒstis] *s* Gastgeberin *f*; (*at
an inn*) Wirtin *f*; (*on an airplane*)
Stewardeß *f*; (*in a restaurant*) Empfangsdame *f*; (*on a television show*)
Leiterin *f*
hostile [ˈhɒstil] *adj* feindlich; (**to**)
feindselig (gegen)
hostility [hɒsˈtiliti] *s* Feindseligkeit *f*;
hostilities Feindseligkeiten *pl*
hot [hɒt] *adj* heiß; (*spicy*) scharf;
(*meal*) warm; (*stolen, sought by the
police, radioactive; jazz, tip*) heiß;
(*trail, scent*) frisch; (*in heat*) geil;
be hot (*said of the sun*) stechen; **get
into hot water** in die Patsche geraten;
hot and bothered aufgeregt; **hot from
the press** frisch von der Presse; **hot
on s.o.'s trail** j-m dicht auf der Spur;
hot stuff (sl) toller Kerl *m*; **I am hot**
mir ist heiß; **I don't feel so hot** (coll)
ich fühle mich nicht besonders; **she's
not so hot** (coll) sie is nicht so toll
hot' air' *s* Heißluft *f*; (sl) blauer Dunst
m
hot'-air heat' *s* Heißluftheizung *f*
hot'bed' *s* Frühbeet *n*; (fig) Brutstätte
f
hot'-blood'ed *adj* heißblütig
hot' cake' *s* Pfannkuchen *m*; **sell like
hot cakes** wie warme Semmeln weggehen
hotchpotch [ˈhɒtʃ‚pɒtʃ] *s* (coll) Mischmasch *m*
hot' dog' *s* warmes Würstel *n*
hotel [hoˈtel] *adj* Hotel– || *s* Hotel *n*;
(*small hotel*) Gasthof *m*
hotel' busi'ness *s* Hotelgewerbe *n*
hotel'man *s* (–men) Hotelbesitzer *m*
hot'foot' *adv* in aller Eile || *tr*—**h. it**
schleunigst eilen; **h. it after s.o.** j-m
nacheilen
hot'head' *s* Hitzkopf *m*
hot'-head'ed *adj* hitzköpfig
hot'house' *s* Treibhaus *n*, Gewächshaus
f
hot' line' *s* (telp) heißer Draht *m*
hot' mon'ey *s* (sl) Fluchtkapital *n*
hot' pep'per *s* scharfe Paprikaschote *f*
hot' plate' *s* Heizplatte *f*
hot' pota'to *s* (coll) schwieriges Problem *n*
hot' rod' *s* (sl) frisiertes altes Auto *n*
hot' rod'der [‚rɑdər] *s* (sl) Fahrer *m*
e–s frisierten Autos
hot' seat' *s* (sl) elektrischer Stuhl *m*
hot' springs' *spl* Thermalquellen *pl*
hot' tem'per *s* hitziges Temperament *n*

hot'-tem'pered *adj* hitzig, hitzköpfig
hot' war' *s* Schießkrieg *m*
hot' wa'ter *s* Heißwasser *n*; **be in h.**
(fig) in der Tinte sitzen; **get into h.**
(fig) in die Patsche geraten
hot'-wa'ter bot'tle *s* Gummiwärm-
flasche *f*
hot'-wa'ter heat'er *s* Heißwasserberei-
ter *m*
hot'-wa'ter heat'ing *s* Heißwasserhei-
zung *f*
hot'-wa'ter tank' *s* Heißwasserspeicher
m
hound [haund] *s* Jagdhund *m* || *tr*
hetzen
hour [aur] *s* Stunde *f*; **after hours**
nach Arbeitsschluß; **at any h.** zu
jeder Tageszeit; **by the h.** stunden-
weise; **every h.** stündlich; **for an h.**
e–e Stunde lang; **for a solid h.** e–e
geschlagene Stunde lang; **for hours**
stundenlang; **h. of death** Todes-
stunde *f*; **h. overtime** Überstunde *f*;
in the small hours in den frühen
Morgenstunden; **keep late hours** spät
zu Bett gehen; **keep regular hours**
zur Zeit aufstehen und schlafengehen; **on the h.** zur vollen Stunde
–**hour** *suf* –stündig
hour'glass' *s* Stundenglas *n*
hour' hand' *s* Stundenzeiger *m*
hourly [ˈaurli] *adj* stündlich; **h. rate**
Stundensatz *m*; **h. wages** Stunden-
lohn *m* || *adv* stündlich
house [haus] *adj* (*boat, dress*) Haus–
|| *s* (**houses** [ˈhauziz]) Haus *n*; **h.
and home** Haus und Hof; **h. for rent**
Haus *n* zu vermieten; **keep h.** (for
s.o.) (j–m) den Haushalt führen; **on
the h.** auf Kosten des Wirts; **put
one's h. in order** (fig) seine Ange-
legenheiten in Ordnung bringen ||
[hauz] *tr* unterbringen
house' arrest' *s* Hausarrest *m*
house'boat' *s* Hausboot *n*
house'break'ing *s* Einbruchsdiebstahl
m
housebroken [ˈhaus‚brokən] *adj* stu-
benrein
house' clean'ing *s* Hausputz *m*; (fig)
Säuberungsaktion *f*
house'fly' *s* Stubenfliege *f*
houseful [ˈhaus‚ful] *s* Hausvoll *n*
house'guest' *s* Logierbesuch *m*
house'hold' *adj* Haushalts– || *s* Haus-
halt *m*
house'hold'er *s* Haushaltsvorstand *m*
house'hold fur'nishings *spl* Hausrat *m*
house'hold needs' *spl* Hausbedarf *m*
house'hold word' *s* Alltagswort *n*
house' hunt'ing *s* Wohnungssuche *f*
house'keep'er *s* Haushälterin *f*
house'keep'ing *s* Hauswirtschaft *f*
house'maid' *s* Dienstmädchen *n*
house'moth'er *s* Hausmutter *f*
house' of cards' *s* Kartenhaus *n*
House' of Com'mons *s* Unterhaus *n*
house' of corec'tion *s* Zuchthaus *n*,
Besserungsanstalt *f*
house' of ill' repute' *s* öffentliches
Haus *n*
House' of Lords' *s* Oberhaus *n*

house' physi'cian s Krankenhausarzt m; (in a hotel) Hausarzt m
house'-to-house' adv von Haus zu Haus; **sell h.** hausieren
house'warm'ing s Einzugsfest n
house'wife' s (wives') Hausfrau f
house'work' s Hausarbeit f
hous'ing s Unterbringung f, Wohnung f; (mach) Gehäuse n
hous'ing devel'opment s Siedlung f
hous'ing pro'ject s Sozialsiedlung f
hous'ing short'age s Wohnungsnot f
hous'ing un'it s Wohneinheit f
hovel ['hʌvəl], ['hɑvəl] s Hütte f
hover ['hʌvər] intr schweben; (fig) pendeln; **h. about** sich herumtreiben in der Nähe von
Hov'ercraft' s (trademark) Schwebefahrzeug n
how [haʊ] adv wie; **and how!** und wie!; **how about ...?** (would you care for ...?) wie wäre es mit ...?; (what's the progress of ...?) wie steht es mit ...?; (what do you think of ...?) was halten Sie von ...?; **how are you?** wie befinden Sie sich?; **how beautiful!** wie schön!; **how come?** wieso?, wie kommt es?; **how do you do?** (as a greeting) guten Tag!; (at an introduction) freut mich sehr!; **how many** wie viele; **how much** wieviel; **how on earth** wie in aller Welt; **how the devil** wie zum Teufel || s Wie n
how-do-you-do ['haʊdəjə'du] s—**that's a fine h.!** (coll) das ist e-e schöne Geschichte!
howev'er adv jedoch, aber; (with adjectives and adverbs) wie ... auch immer; **h. it may be** wie es auch sein mag
howitzer ['haʊ·ɪtsər] s Haubitze f
howl [haʊl] s Geheul n, Gebrüll n || tr heulen, brüllen; **h. down** (a speaker) niederschreien; **h. out** hinausbrüllen || intr (said of a dog, wolf, wind, etc.) heulen; (in pain, anger) brüllen; **h. with laughter** vor Lachen brüllen
howler ['haʊlər] s (coll) Schnitzer m
hub [hʌb] s Nabe, f, Radnabe f
hubbub ['hʌbʌb] s Rummel m
hubby ['hʌbi] s (coll) Mann m
hub'cap' s Radkappe f
huckleberry ['hʌkəl,beri] s Heidelbeere f
huckster ['hʌkstər] s (hawker) Straßenhändler m; (peddler) Hausierer m; (adman) Reklamefachmann m || tr verhökern
huddle ['hʌdəl] s (fb) Zusammendrängen n; **go into a h.** die Köpfe zusammenstecken || intr sich zusammendrängen; (fb) sich um den Mannschaftsführer drängen
hue [hju] s Farbton m
hue' and cry' s Zetergeschrei n
huff [hʌf] s Aufbrausen n; **in a h.** beleidigt
huffy ['hʌfi] adj übelnehmerisch
hug [hʌg] s Umarmung f; **give s.o. a hug** j–n an sich drücken || v (pret & pp hugged; ger hugging) tr umar-

men; **hug the road** gut auf der Straße liegen; **hug the shore** sich dicht an der Küste halten || intr einander herzen
huge [hjudʒ] adj riesig, ungeheuer; **h. success** (theat) Bombenerfolg m
hulk [hʌlk] s (body of an old ship) Schiffsrumpf m; (old ship used as a warehouse, etc.) Hulk m & f; **h. of a man** Koloß m
hulk'ing adj ungeschlacht
hull [hʌl] s (of seed) Schale f; (naut) Schiffsrumpf m || tr schälen
hullabaloo [,hʌləbə'lu] s Heidenlärm m
hum [hʌm] s Summen n || v (pret & pp hummed; ger humming) tr summen; **hum** (e.g., a tune) **to oneself** vor sich hin summen || intr summen; (fig) in lebhafter Bewegung sein
human ['hjumən] adj menschlich, Menschen–
hu'man be'ing s Mensch m, menschliches Wesen n
humane [hju'men] adj human
humaneness [hju'mennɪs] s Humanität f
humanistic [hjumə'nɪstɪk] adj humanistisch
humanitarian [hju,mænɪ'terɪ·ən] adj menschenfreundlich || s Menschenfreund –in mf
humanity [hju'mænɪti] s (mankind) Menschheit f; (humaneness) Humanität f, Menschlichkeit f; **humanities** Geisteswissenschaften pl; (Greek and Latin studies) klassische Philologie f
humanize ['hjumə,naɪz] tr zivilisieren
hu'mankind' s Menschengeschlecht n
humanly ['hjumənli] adv menschlich; **h. possible** menschenmöglich; **h. speaking** nach menschlichen Begriffen
hu'man na'ture s menschliche Natur f
hu'man race' s Menschengeschlecht n
humble ['(h)ʌmbəl] adj demütig; (origens) niedrig; **in my h. opinion** nach meiner unmaßgeblichen Meinung || tr demütigen
hum'ble pie' s—**eat h.** sich demütigen
hum'bug' s Humbug m
hum'drum' adj eintönig
humer·us ['hjumərəs] s (–i [,aɪ]) Oberarmknochen m
humid ['hjumɪd] adj feucht
humidifier [hju'mɪdɪ,faɪ·ər] s Verdunster m
humidity [hju'mɪdɪti] s Feuchtigkeit f
humiliate [hju'mɪlɪ,et] tr erniedrigen
humil'iating adj schmachvoll
humiliation [hju,mɪlɪ'eʃən] s Erniedrigung f
hum'mingbird' s Kolibri m
humor ['(h)jumər] s (comic quality) Komik f; (frame of mind) Laune f; **in bad** (or **good**) **h.** bei schlechter (or guter) Laune || tr bei guter Laune halten
humorist ['(h)jumərɪst] s Humorist –in mf
humorous ['(h)jumərəs] adj humorvoll
hump [hʌmp] s Buckel m; (of a camel)

Höcker *m; (slight elevation)* kleiner Hügel *m;* **over the h.** (fig) über den Berg ‖ *tr*—**h.** its back *(said of an animal)* e-n Buckel machen
hump'back' *s* Buckel *m; (person)* Bucklige *mf*

Hun [hʌn] *s* (hist) Hunne *m,* Hunnin *f*
hunch [hʌntʃ] *s (hump)* Buckel *m;* (coll) Ahnung *f* ‖ *intr*—**h. over** sich bücken über *(acc)*
hunch'back' *s* Bucklige *mf*
hunch'backed' *adj* bucklig
hunched *adj*—**h. up** zusammengekauert
hundred [ˈhʌndrəd] *adj & pron* hundert ‖ *s* Hundert *n;* **by the h.(s)** hundertweise; **hundreds (and hundreds) of** Hunderte (und aber Hunderte) von
hun'dredfold' *adj & adv* hundertfach
hundredth [ˈhʌndrədθ] *adj & pron* hundertste; **for the h. time** (fig) zum X-ten Male; **h. anniversary** Hundertjahrfeier *f* ‖ *s (fraction)* Hundertstel *n*
hun'dredweight' *s* Zentner *m*
Hungarian [hʌŋˈgɛri‐ən] *adj* ungarisch ‖ *s (person)* Ungar –in *mf; (language)* Ungarisch *n*
Hungary [ˈhʌŋgəri] *s* Ungarn *n*
hunger [ˈhʌŋgər] *s* Hunger *m* ‖ *intr* hungern; **h. for** hungern nach
hun'ger strike' *s* Hungerstreik *m*
hungry [ˈhʌŋgri] *adj* hungrig; **be h.** Hunger haben; **be h. for** (fig) begierig sein nach; **go h.** am Hungertuch nagen; **I feel h.** es hungert mich
hunk [hʌŋk] *s* großes Stück *m*
hunt [hʌnt] *s* Jagd *f; (search) (for)* Suche *f* (nach); **on the h. for** auf der Suche nach ‖ *tr* jagen; *(a horse)* jagen mit; *(look for)* suchen; **h. down** erjagen ‖ *intr* jagen; **h. for** suchen; *(game)* jagen; *(a criminal)* fahnden nach; **go hunting** auf die Jagd gehen
hunter [ˈhʌntər] *s* Jäger –in *mf; (horse)* Jagdpferd *n*
hunt'ing *adj (e.g., dog, knife, season)* Jagd– ‖ *s* Jägerei *f; (on horseback)* Parforcejagd *f*
hunt'ing ground' *s* Jagdrevier *n*
hunt'ing li'cense *s* Jagdschein *m*
hunt'ing lodge' *s* Jagdhütte *f*
huntress [ˈhʌntris] *s* Jägerin *f*
hunts'man *s* (–men) Weidmann *m*
hurdle [ˈhʌrdəl] *s* Hürde *f;* (fig) Hindernis *n;* **hurdles** (sport) Hürdenlauf *m* ‖ *tr* überspringen; (fig) überwinden
hurdygurdy [ˈhʌrdiˌgɑrdi] *s* Drehorgel *f*
hurl [hʌrl] *s* Wurf *m* ‖ *tr* scheudern; **h. abuse at s.o.** j–m Beleidigungen ins Gesicht schleudern; **h. down** zu Boden werfen
hurrah [həˈrɑ], **hurray** [həˈre] *s* Hurra *n* ‖ *interj* hurra!
hurricane [ˈhʌriˌken] *s* Orkan *m*
hur'ricane lamp' *s* Sturmlaterne *f*
hurried [ˈhʌrid] *adj* eilig, flüchtig
hurriedly [ˈhʌridli] *adv* eilig, eilends
hur·ry [ˈhʌri] *s* Eile *f;* **be in too much of a h.** sich übereilen; **in a h.** in Eile; **there's no h.** es hat keine Eile ‖ *v*

(pret & pp –ried) tr (prod) antreiben; *(expedite)* beschleunigen; *(an activity)* zu schnell tun; *(to overhasty action)* drängen ‖ *intr* eilen; **h. away** wegeilen; **h. over s.th.** etw flüchtig erledigen; **h. up** sich beeilen
hurt [hʌrt] *adj (injured, offended)* verletzt; **feel h. (about)** sich verletzt (or gekränkt) fühlen (durch) ‖ *s* Verletzung *f* ‖ *v (pret & pp* **hurt**) *tr (a person, animal, feelings)* verletzen; *(e.g., a business)* schaden (dat); **it hurts him to think of it** es schmerzt ihn, daran zu denken ‖ *intr* (& fig) weh tun, schmerzen; **my arm hurts** mir tut der Arm weh; **that won't h.** das schadet nichts; **will it h. if I'm late?** macht es etw aus, wenn ich zu spät komme?
hurtle [ˈhʌrtəl] *tr* schleudern ‖ *intr* stürzen
husband [ˈhʌzbənd] *s* Ehemann *m;* **my h.** mein Mann *m* ‖ *tr* haushalten mit
hus'bandman *s* (–men) Landwirt *m*
husbandry [ˈhʌzbəndri] *s* Landwirtschaft *f*
hush [hʌʃ] *s* Stille *f* ‖ *tr* zur Ruhe bringen; **h. up** *(suppress)* vertuschen ‖ *intr* schweigen ‖ *interj* still!
hush'-hush' *adj* streng vertraulich und geheim
hush' mon'ey *s* Schweigegeld *n*
husk [hʌsk] *s* Hülse *f; (of corn)* Maishülse *f* ‖ *tr* enthülsen
husky [ˈhʌski] *adj* stämmig; *(voice)* belegt ‖ *s* Eskimohund *m*
hussy [ˈhʌsi] *s (prostitute)* Dirne *f; (saucy girl)* Fratz *m*
hustle [ˈhʌsəl] *s* (coll) Betriebsamkeit *f;* **h. and bustle** Getriebe *n* ‖ *tr (jostle, rush)* drängen; *(wares, girls)* an den Mann bringen; *(customers)* bearbeiten; *(money)* betteln ‖ *intr* rührig sein; *(shove)* sich drängen; *(hasten)* hasten; *(make money by fraud)* Betrügereien verüben; *(engage in prostitution)* Prostitution betreiben
hustler [ˈhʌslər] *s* rühriger Mensch *m*
hut [hʌt] *s* Hütte *f;* (mil) Baracke *f*
hutch [hʌtʃ] *s* Stall *m*
hyacinth [ˈhaɪ‐əsɪnθ] *s* Hyazinthe *f*
hybrid [ˈhaɪbrɪd] *adj* hybrid ‖ *s* Kreuzung *f*
hydrant [ˈhaɪdrənt] *s* Hydrant *m*
hydrate [ˈhaɪdret] *s* Hydrat *n* ‖ *tr* hydratisieren, hydrieren
hydraulic [haɪˈdrɔlɪk] *adj* hydraulisch ‖ **hydraulics** *s* Hydraulik *f*
hydrau'lic brakes' *spl* Öldruckbremsen *pl*
hydrocarbon [ˌhaɪdrəˈkɑrbən] *s* Kohlenwasserstoff *m*
hydrochlor'ic ac'id [ˌhaɪdrəˈklorɪk] *s* Salzsäure *f*
hydroelectric [ˌhaɪdro‐ɪˈlɛktrɪk] *adj* hydroelektrisch
hydroelec'tric plant' *s* Wasserkraftwerk *n*
hydrofluo'ric ac'id [ˌhaɪdrəfluˈorɪk] *s* Flußsäure *f*
hydrofoil [ˈhaɪdrəˌfɔɪl] *s* Tragflügelboot *n*

hydrogen ['haɪdrədʒən] s Wasserstoff m

hy'drogen bomb' s Wasserstoffbombe f

hy'drogen perox'ide s Wasserstoffsuperoxyd n

hydrometer [haɪ'drɑmɪtər] s Hydrometer m

hydrophobia [,haɪdrə'fobɪ·ə] s Wasserscheu f; (rabies) Tollwut f

hydrophone ['haɪdrə ,fon] s Unterwasserhorchgerät n, Hydrophon n

hydroplane ['haɪdrə ,plen] s (aer) Wasserflugzeug n; (aer) Gleitfläche f; (naut) Gleitboot n; (in a submarine) (nav) Tiefenruder n

hydroxide [haɪ'drɑksaɪd] s Hydroxyd n

hyena [haɪ'inə] s Hyäne f

hygiene ['haɪdʒin] s Hygiene f; (educ) Gesundheitslehre f

hygienic [haɪ'dʒɪnɪk] adj hygienisch

hymn [hɪm] s Hymne f; (eccl) Kirchenlied n

hymnal ['hɪmnəl] s Gesangbuch n

hymn'book' s Gesangbuch n

hyperacidity [,haɪpərə'sɪdɪti] s Übersäuerung f

hyperbola [haɪ'pʌrbələ] s Hyperbel f

hyperbole [haɪ'pʌrbəli] s Hyperbel f

hypersensitive [,haɪpər'sɛnsɪtɪv] adj (to) überempfindlich (gegen)

hypertension [,haɪpər'tɛnʃən] s Hypertonie f

hyphen ['haɪfən] s Bindestrich m

hyphenate ['haɪfə ,net] tr mit Bindestrich schreiben

hypnosis [hɪp'nosɪs] s Hypnose f

hypnotic [hɪp'nɑtɪk] adj hypnotisch

hypnotism ['hɪpnə ,tɪzəm] s Hypnotismus m

hypnotist ['hɪpnətɪst] s Hypnotiseur m

hypnotize ['hɪpnə ,taɪz] tr hypnotisieren

hypochondriac [,haɪpə'kɑndrɪ ,æk] s Hypochonder m

hypocrisy [hɪ'pɑkrəsi] s Heuchelei f

hypocrite ['hɪpəkrɪt] s Heuchler –in mf; **be a h.** heucheln

hypocritical [,hɪpə'krɪtɪkəl] adj heuchlerisch

hypodermic [,haɪpə'dʌrmɪk] adj subkutan || s (injection) subkutane Spritze f

hypoderm'ic nee'dle s Injektionsnadel f

hypotenuse [haɪ'pɑtɪ ,n(j)us] s Hypotenuse f

hypothe·sis [haɪ'pɑθɪsɪs] s (–ses [,siz]) Hypothese f

hypothetic(al) [,haɪpə'θɛtɪk(əl)] adj hypothetisch

hysterectomy [,hɪstə'rɛktəmi] s Hysterektomie f

hysteria [hɪs'tɪrɪ·ə] s Hysterie f

hysteric [hɪs'tɛrɪk] adj hysterisch || **hysterics** spl Hysterie f; **go into hysterics** e–n hysterischen Anfall bekommen

hysterical [hɪs'tɛrɪkəl] adj hysterisch

I

I, i [aɪ] s elfter Buchstabe des englischen Alphabets

I pers pron ich

iambic [aɪ'æmbɪk] adj jambisch

Iberian [aɪ'bɪrɪ·ən] adj iberisch

ibex ['aɪbɛks] s (ibexes & ibices ['ɪbɪ ,siz]) Steinbock m

ice [aɪs] s Eis n; **break the ice** (coll) das Eis brechen; **cut no ice** (coll) nicht ziehen || tr (a cake) glasieren || intr—**ice up** vereisen

ice' age' s Eiszeit f

iceberg ['aɪs ,bʌrg] s Eisberg m

ice'boat' s (sport) Segelschlitten m

ice'bound' adj (boat) eingefroren; (port, river) zugefroren

ice'box' s Eisschrank m; (refrigerator) Kühlschrank m

ice'break'er s Eisbrecher m

ice' buck'et s Sektkübel m

ice'cap' s Eiskappe f

ice' cream' s Eis n, Eiskrem f

ice'-cream cone' s Tüte f Eis

ice' cube' s Eiswürfel m

ice'-cube tray' s Eiswürfelschale f

iced' tea' s Eistee m

ice' floe' s Eisscholle f

ice' hock'ey s Eishockey n

Iceland ['aɪslənd] s Island n

Icelander ['aɪs ,lændər] s Isländer –in mf

Icelandic [aɪs'lændɪk] adj isländisch || s (language) Isländisch n

ice'man' s (–men') Eismann m

ice' pack' s (geol) Packeis n; (med) Eisbeutel m

ice' pick' s Eispfriem m; (mount) Eispickel m

ice' skate' s Schlittschuh m

ice'-skate' intr eislaufen

ichthyology [,ɪkθɪ'ɑlədʒi] s Ichthyologie f, Fischkunde f

icicle ['aɪsɪkəl] s Eiszapfen m

icing ['aɪsɪŋ] s Glasur f, Zuckerguß m; (aer) Vereisung f

icon ['aɪkɑn] s Ikone f

iconoclast [aɪ'kɑnə ,klæst] s Bilderstürmer –in mf

icy ['aɪsi] adj (& fig) eisig

id [ɪd] s (psychol) Es n

I.D. card ['aɪ'di'kɑrd] s Ausweis m

idea [aɪ'di·ə] s Idee f, Vorstellung f; (intimation) Ahnung f; **crazy i.** Schnapsidee f; **have big ideas** große Rosinen im Kopf haben; **that's the i.!** so ist's richtig!; **the i.!** na so was!; **what's the i.?** wie kommen Sie darauf?

ideal [ar'dɪ·əl] *adj* ideal ‖ *s* Ideal *n*

idealism [ar'dɪ·ə‚lɪzəm] *s* Idealismus *m*

idealist [ar'dɪ·əlɪst] *s* Idealist –in *mf*

idealistic [ar‚dɪ·əl'ɪstɪk] *adj* idealistisch

idealize [ar'dɪ·ə‚laɪz] *tr* idealisieren

identical [ar'dentɪkəl] *adj* identisch

identification [ar‚dentɪfɪ'keʃən] *s* Identifizierung *f*

identifica'tion tag' *s* Erkennungsmarke *f*

identi·fy [ar'dentɪ‚faɪ] *v* (*pret & pp* **-fied**) *tr* identifizieren; **i. oneself** sich ausweisen ‖ *intr*—**i. with** sich einfühlen in (*acc*)

identity [ar'dentɪti] *s* Identität *f*; **prove one's i.** sich ausweisen

iden'tity card' *s* Ausweis *m*

ideological [‚aɪdɪ·ə'lɑdʒɪkəl] *adj* ideologisch

ideology [‚aɪdɪ·əl'ɑdʒi] *s* Ideologie *f*

idiocy ['ɪdɪ·əsi] *s* Idiotie *f*

idiom ['ɪdɪ·əm] *s* (*phrase*) Redewendung *f*; (*language, style*) Idiom *n*

idiomatic [‚ɪdɪ·ə'mætɪk] *adj* idiomatisch; **i. expression** (idiomatische) Redewendung *f*

idiosyncrasy [‚ɪdɪ·ə'sɪnkrəsi] *s* Idiosynkrasie *f*

idiot ['ɪdɪ·ət] *s* Idiot *m*, Trottel *m*

idiotic [‚ɪdɪ'ɑtɪk] *adj* idiotisch

idle ['aɪdəl] *adj* (*person, question, hours*) müßig; (*machine, factory*) stillstehend; (*capital*) tot; (*fears*) grundlos; (*talk, threats*) leer; **lie i.** stilliegen; **stand i.** stillstehen ‖ *s* (aut) Leerlauf *m* ‖ *tr* arbeitslos machen; **i. away** vertrödeln ‖ *intr* (aut) leerlaufen

idleness ['aɪdəlnɪs] *s* Müßiggang *m*

idler ['aɪdlər] *s* Müßiggänger *m*

i'dling *s* (aut) Leerlauf *m*

idol ['aɪdəl] *s* Abgott *m*; (fig) Idol *n*

idolatry [ar'dɑlətri] *s* Abgötterei *f*

idolize ['aɪdə‚laɪz] *tr* verhimmeln

idyll ['aɪdəl] *s* Idyll *n*, Idylle *f*

idyllic [ar'dɪlɪk] *adj* idyllisch

if [ɪf] *s* Wenn *n* ‖ *conj* wenn; (*whether*) ob

igloo ['ɪglu] *s* Schneehütte *f*, Iglu *m & n*

ignite [ɪg'naɪt] *tr & intr* zünden

ignition [ɪg'nɪʃən] *adj* Zünd– ‖ *s* Entzünden *n*; (aut) Zündung *f*

igni'tion key' *s* Zündschlüssel *m*

igni'tion switch' *s* Zündschloß *n*

ignoble [ɪg'nobəl] *adj* unedel

ignominious [‚ɪgnə'mɪnɪ·əs] *adj* schmachvoll, schändlich

ignoramus [‚ɪgnə'reməs] *s* Ignorant –in *mf*

ignorance ['ɪgnərəns] *s* Unwissenheit *f*; (of) Unkenntnis *f* (*genit*)

ignorant ['ɪgnərənt] *adj* unwissend; **be i. of** nicht wissen

ignore [ɪg'nor] *tr* ignorieren; (*words*) überhören; (*rules*) nicht beachten

ilk [ɪlk] *s*—**of that ilk** derselben Art

ill [ɪl] *adj* (*worse* [wʌrs], *worst* [wʌrst]) krank; (*repute*) schlecht; (*feelings*) feindselig; **fall** (*or* **take**)

ill krank werden ‖ *adv* schlecht; **he can ill afford to** (*inf*) er kann es sich [*dat*] kaum leisten zu (*inf*); **take s.th. ill** etw übelnehmen

ill'-advised' (*person*) schlecht beraten; (*action*) unbesonnen

ill'-at-ease' *adj* unbehaglich

ill'-bred' *adj* ungezogen

ill'-consid'ered *adj* unbesonnen

ill'-disposed' *adj*—**be i. towards** übelgesinnt sein (*dat*)

illegal [ɪ'ligəl] *adj* illegal

illegible [ɪ'ledʒɪbəl] *adj* unlesbar

illegitimate [‚ɪlɪ'dʒɪtɪmɪt] *adj* unrechtmäßig; (*child*) illegitim

ill'-fat'ed *adj* unglücklich

illgotten ['ɪl‚gɑtən] *adj* unrechtmäßig erworben

ill' health' *s* Kränklichkeit *f*

ill'-hu'mored *adj* übellaunt

illicit [ɪ'lɪsɪt] *adj* unerlaubt

illiteracy [ɪ'lɪtərəsi] *s* Analphabetentum *n*

illiterate [ɪ'lɪtərɪt] *adj* analphabetisch ‖ *s* Analphabet –in *mf*

ill'-man'nered *adj* ungehobelt

ill'-na'tured *adj* bösartig

illness ['ɪlnɪs] *s* (& fig) Krankheit *f*

illogical [ɪ'lɑdʒɪkəl] *adj* unlogisch

ill'-spent' *adj* verschwendet

ill'-starred' *adj* unglücklich

ill'-suit'ed *adj* (to) unpassend (*dat*)

ill'-tem'pered *adj* schlechtgelaunt

ill'-timed' *adj* unpassend

ill'-treat' *tr* mißhandeln

illuminate [ɪ'lumɪ‚net] *tr* beleuchten; (*public buildings, manuscripts*) illuminieren; (*enlighten*) erleuchten; (*explain*) erklären

illumination [ɪ‚lumɪ'neʃən] *s* Beleuchten *n*; Erleuchtung *f*; Illuminierung *f*

illusion [ɪ'luʒən] *s* Illusion *f*

illusive [ɪ'lusɪv] *adj* trügerisch

illusory [ɪ'lusəri] *adj* illusorisch

illustrate ['ɪləs‚tret] *tr* (*exemplify*) erläutern; (*a book*) illustrieren; **illustrated lecture** Lichtbildervortrag *m*; **richly illustrated** bilderreich

illustration [‚ɪləs'treʃən] *s* Erläuterung *f*; (*in a book*) Abbildung *f*

illustrative [ɪ'lʌstrətɪv] *adj* erläuternd; **i. material** Anschauungsmaterial *n*

illustrator ['ɪləs‚tretər] *s* Illustrator *m*

illustrious [ɪ'lʌstrɪ·əs] *adj* berühmt

ill' will' *s* Feindschaft *f*

image ['ɪmɪdʒ] *s* Bild *n*; (*reflection*) Spiegelbild *n*; (*statue*) Standbild *n*; (*before the public*) Image *n*; (opt, phot, telv) Bild *n*; **the spitting i. of his father** ganz der Vater

imagery ['ɪmɪdʒ(ə)ri] *s* Bildersprache *f*

imaginable [ɪ'mædʒɪnəbəl] *adj* erdenklich

imaginary [ɪ'mædʒɪ‚neri] *adj* imaginär

imagination [ɪ‚mædʒɪ'neʃən] *s* Phantasie *f*, Einbildungskraft *f*; **that's pure i.** das ist pure Einbildung

imaginative [ɪ'mædʒɪnətɪv] *adj* phantasievoll

imagine [ɪ'mædʒɪn] *tr* sich [*dat*] vorstellen, sich [*dat*] denken; **i. oneself**

in sich hineindenken in (acc); **you're only imagining things** das bilden Sie sich [dat] nur ein || **intr**—**I can i.** das läßt sich denken; **I i.** so ich glaube schon; **just i.** denken Sie nur mal!

imbecile ['ɪmbɪsɪl] adj geistesschwach || s Geistesschwache mf

imbecility [ˌɪmbɪ'sɪlɪti] s Geistesschwäche f, Blödheit f

imbibe [ɪm'baɪb] tr aufsaugen; (coll) trinken; (fig) (geistig) aufnehmen

imbue [ɪm'bju] tr durchfeuchten; (fig) **(with)** durchdringen (mit)

imitate ['ɪmɪˌtet] tr nachahmen, nachmachen; **i. s.o.** in everything j-m alles nachmachen

imitation [ˌɪmɪ'teʃən] adj unecht, nachgemacht || s Nachahmung f; **in i. of** nach dem Muster (genit)

imita'tion leath'er s Kunstleder n

imitator ['ɪmɪˌtetər] s Nachahmer –in mf

immaculate [ɪ'mækjəlɪt] adj makellos; (sinless) unbefleckt

immaterial [ˌɪmə'tɪrɪ-əl] adj immateriell, unkörperlich; (unimportant) unwesentlich; **it's i.** to me es ist mir gleichgültig

immature [ˌɪmə'tjʊr] adj unreif

immaturity [ˌɪmə'tjʊrɪti] s Unreife f

immeasurable [ɪ'meʒərəbəl] adj unermeßlich

immediacy [ɪ'midɪ-əsi] s Unmittelbarkeit f

immediate [ɪ'midɪ-ɪt] adj sofortig; (direct) unmittelbar

immediately [ɪ'midɪ-ɪtli] adv sofort; **i. afterwards** gleich darauf

immemorial [ˌɪmɪ'morɪ-əl] adj uralt; **since time i.** seit Menschengedenken

immense [ɪ'mens] adj unermeßlich

immensity [ɪ'mensɪti] s Unermeßlichkeit f

immerse [ɪ'mʌrs] tr (unter)tauchen; **immersed in** (books, thought, work) vertieft in (acc); **i. oneself in** sich vertiefen in (acc)

immersion [ɪ'mʌrʒən] s Untertauchen n; (fig) Versunkenheit f

immigrant ['ɪmɪgrənt] adj einwandernd || s Einwanderer –in mf

immigrate ['ɪmɪˌgret] intr einwandern

immigration [ˌɪmɪ'greʃən] s Einwanderung f

imminent ['ɪmɪnənt] adj drohend

immobile [ɪ'mobɪl] adj unbeweglich

immobilize [ɪ'mobɪˌlaɪz] tr unbeweglich machen; (tanks) bewegungsunfähig machen; (troops) fesseln; (med) ruhigstellen

immoderate [ɪ'madərɪt] adj unmäßig

immodest [ɪ'madɪst] adj unbescheiden

immolate ['ɪmoˌlet] tr opfern

immoral [ɪ'mɔrəl] adj unsittlich

immorality [ˌɪmə'rælɪti] s Unsittlichkeit f

immortal [ɪ'mɔrtəl] adj unsterblich

immortality [ˌɪmɔr'tælɪti] s Unsterblichkeit f

immortalize [ɪ'mɔrtəˌlaɪz] tr unsterblich machen

immovable [ɪ'muvəbəl] adj unbeweglich

immune [ɪ'mjun] adj (free, exempt) **(from)** immun (gegen); (not responsive) **(to)** gefeit (gegen); (med) **(to)** immun (gegen)

immunity [ɪ'mjunɪti] s Immunität f

immunization [ˌɪmjunɪ'zeʃən] s Schutzimpfung f, Immunisierung f

immunize ['ɪmjəˌnaɪz] tr (against) immunisieren (gegen)

immutable [ɪ'mjutəbəl] adj unwandelbar

imp [ɪmp] s Schlingel m

impact ['ɪmpækt] s Anprall m; (of a shell) Aufschlag m; (fig) Einwirkung f

impair [ɪm'per] tr beeinträchtigen

impale [ɪm'pel] tr pfählen

impanel [ɪm'pænəl] v (pret & pp -el[l]ed; ger -el[l]ing) tr in die Geschworenenliste eintragen

impart [ɪm'part] tr mitteilen

impartial [ɪm'parʃəl] adj unparteiisch

impassable [ɪm'pæsəbəl] adj (on foot) ungangbar; (by car) unbefahrbar

impasse ['ɪmpæs] s Sackgasse f; **reach an i.** in e-e Sackgasse geraten

impassible [ɪm'pæsɪbəl] adj **(to)** unempfindlich (für)

impassioned [ɪm'pæʃənd] adj leidenschaftlich

impassive [ɪm'pæsɪv] adj (person) teilnahmslos; (expression) ausdruckslos

impatience [ɪm'peʃəns] s Ungeduld f

impatient [ɪm'peʃənt] adj ungeduldig

impeach [ɪm'pitʃ] tr (an official) wegen Amtsmißbrauchs unter Anklage stellen; (a witness, motives) in Zweifel ziehen

impeachment [ɪm'pitʃmənt] s (of an official) öffentliche Anklage f; (of a witness, motives) Anzweiflung f

impeccable [ɪm'pekəbəl] adj makellos

impecunious [ˌɪmpɪ'kjunɪ-əs] adj mittellos

impede [ɪm'pid] tr behindern, erschweren

impediment [ɪm'pedɪmənt] s Behinderung f; (of speech) Sprachfehler m

impel [ɪm'pel] v (pret & pp -pelled; ger -pelling) tr antreiben

impending [ɪm'pendɪŋ] adj nahe bevorstehen; (threatening) drohend

impenetrable [ɪm'penɪtrəbəl] adj undurchdringlich; (fig) unergründlich

impenitent [ɪm'penɪtənt] adj unbußfertig

imperative [ɪm'perətɪv] adj dringend nötig || s Imperativ m

imper'ative mood' s Befehlsform f

imperceptible [ˌɪmpər'septɪbəl] adj nicht wahrnehmbar, unmerklich

imperfect [ɪm'pʌrfɪkt] adj unvollkommen || s (gram) Imperfekt(um) n

imperfection [ˌɪmpər'fekʃən] s Unvollkommenheit f; (flaw) Fehler m

imperial [ɪm'pɪrɪ-əl] adj kaiserlich

imperialism [ɪm'pɪrɪ-əˌlɪzəm] s Imperialismus m

imperialist [ɪm'pɪrɪ-əlɪst] adj imperialistisch || s Imperialist –in mf

imper·il [ɪm'perɪl] v (pret & pp –il[l]ed; ger –il[l]ing) tr gefährden
imperious [ɪm'perɪ·əs] adj herrisch, anmaßend
imperishable [ɪm'perɪʃəbəl] adj unvergänglich
impersonal [ɪm'pʌrsənəl] adj unpersönlich
impersonate [ɪm'pʌrsə‚net] tr (imitate) nachahmen; (e.g., an officer) sich ausgeben als; (theat) darstellen
impersonator [ɪm'pʌrsə‚netər] s Imitator –in mf
impertinence [ɪm'pʌrtɪnəns] s Ungezogenheit f
impertinent [ɪm'pʌrtɪnənt] adj ungezogen
imperturbable [‚ɪmpʌr'tʌrbəbəl] adj unerschütterlich
impetuous [ɪm'petʃʊ·əs] adj ungestüm
impetus ['ɪmpɪtəs] s (& fig) Antrieb m
impiety [ɪm'paɪ·əti] s Gottlosigkeit f
impinge [ɪm'pɪndʒ] intr—1. on (an) stoßen an (acc); (said of rays) fallen auf (acc); (fig) eingreifen in (acc)
impious ['ɪmpɪ·əs] adj gottlos
impish ['ɪmpɪʃ] adj spitzbübisch
implant [ɪm'plænt] tr einpflanzen
implement ['ɪmplɪmənt] s Werkzeug n, Gerät n || ['ɪmplɪ‚ment] tr durchführen
implicate ['ɪmplɪ‚ket] tr (in) verwickeln (in acc)
implication [‚ɪmplɪ'keʃən] s (involvement) Verwicklung f; (implying) Andeutung f; **implications** Folgerungen pl
implicit [ɪm'plɪsɪt] adj (approval) stillschweigend; (trust) unbedingt
implied [ɪm'plaɪd] adj stillschweigend
implore [ɪm'plor] tr anflehen
im·ply [ɪm'plaɪ] v (pret & pp –plied) tr (express indirectly) andeuten; (involve) in sich schließen; (said of words) besagen
impolite [‚ɪmpə'laɪt] adj unhöflich
import ['ɪmport] s Import m, Einfuhr f; (meaning) Bedeutung f; **imports** Einfuhrwaren pl || [ɪm'port], ['ɪmport] tr importieren, einführen
importance [ɪm'portəns] s Wichtigkeit f; a man of i. ein Mann m von Bedeutung; of no i. unwichtig
important [ɪm'portənt] adj wichtig
im'port du'ty s Einfuhrzoll m
importer [ɪm'portər] s Importeur m
importune [‚ɪmpor'tʃ(j)un] adj aufdringlich || tr bestürmen
impose [ɪm'poz] tr (on, upon) auferlegen (dat) || intr—i. on über Gebühr beanspruchen
impos'ing adj imposant
imposition [‚ɪmpə'zɪʃən] s (of hands, of an obligation) Auferlegung f; (taking unfair advantage) Zumutung f
impossible [ɪm'pasɪbəl] adj unmöglich
impostor [ɪm'pastər] s Hochstapler m
imposture [ɪm'pastjər] s Hochstapelei f
impotence ['ɪmpətəns] s Machtlosigkeit f; (pathol) Impotenz f

impotent ['ɪmpətənt] adj machtlos; (pathol) impotent
impound [ɪm'paund] tr beschlagnahmen
impoverish [ɪm'pavərɪʃ] tr arm machen; **become impoverished** verarmen
impracticable [ɪm'præktɪkəbəl] adj unausführbar
impractical [ɪm'præktɪkəl] adj unpraktisch
impregnable [ɪm'pregnəbəl] adj uneinnehmbar
impregnate [ɪm'pregnet] tr (saturate) imprägnieren; (& fig) schwängern
impresari·o [‚ɪmprɪ'sarɪ‚o] s (–os) Impresario m
impress [ɪm'pres] tr (affect) imponieren (dat), beeindrucken; (imprint, emphasize) einprägen; i. s.th. on s.o. j–m etw einprägen
impression [ɪm'preʃən] s Eindruck m; (stamp) Gepräge n; **try to make an i.** Eindruck schinden
impressive [ɪm'presɪv] adj eindrucksvoll
imprint ['ɪmprɪnt] s Aufdruck m; (fig) Eindruck m || [ɪm'prɪnt] tr (on) aufdrucken (auf acc); i. on s.o.'s memory j–m ins Gedächtnis einprägen
imprison [ɪm'prɪzən] tr einsperren
imprisonment [ɪm'prɪzənmənt] s Haft f; (penalty) Freiheitsstrafe f; (captivity) Gefangenschaft f
improbable [ɪm'prabəbəl] adj unwahrscheinlich
impromptu [ɪm'prampt(j)u] adj & adv aus dem Stegreif || s Stegreifstück n
improper [ɪm'prapər] adj ungehörig, unschicklich; (use) unzulässig
improve [ɪm'pruv] tr verbessern; (relations) ausbauen; (land) kultivieren; (a salary) aufbessern; i. oneself sich bessern; (financially) sich verbessern || intr bessern; (com) sich erholen; i. on Verbesserungen vornehmen an (dat)
improvement [ɪm'pruvmənt] s Verbesserung f; (reworking) Umarbeitung f; (of money value) Erholung f; (of a salary) Aufbesserung f; (in health) Besserung f; **be an i. on** ein Fortschritt sein gegenüber
improvident [ɪm'pravɪdənt] adj unbedacht
improvise ['ɪmprə‚vaɪz] tr improvisieren || intr improvisieren; (mus) phantasieren
imprudence [ɪm'prudəns] s Unklugheit f
imprudent [ɪm'prudənt] adj unklug
impudence ['ɪmpjədəns] s Unverschämtheit f
impudent ['ɪmpjədənt] adj unverschämt
impugn [ɪm'pjun] tr bestreiten
impulse ['ɪmpʌls] s Impuls m; **act on i.** impulsiv handeln
impulsive [ɪm'pʌlsɪv] adj impulsiv
impunity [ɪm'pjunɪti] s Straffreiheit f; **with i.** ungestraft
impure [ɪm'pjur] adj (& fig) unrein

impurity [ɪm'pjʊrɪtɪ] *s* (& fig) Unreinheit *f*

impute [ɪm'pjut] *tr* (**to**) unterstellen (*dat*)

in [ɪn] *adv* (*position*) drin, drinnen; (*direction away from the speaker*) hinein; (*direction toward the speaker*) herein; **be all in** ganz erschöpft sein; **be in** da sein; (*said of a political party*) an der Macht sein; (*be in style*) in Mode sein; **be in for** zu erwarten haben; **have it in** for einen Strich haben ‖ *s*—**the ins and outs of** die Einzelheiten (*genit*) ‖ *prep* (*position*) in (*dat*); (*direction*) in (*acc*); (*e.g., the morning, afternoon, evening*) am; (*a field, the country; one eye*) auf (*dat*); (*one's opinion; all probability*) nach (*dat*); (*circumstances; a reign*) unter (*dat*); (*ink; one stroke*) mit (*dat*); (*because of pain, joy, etc.*) vor (*dat*); **he doesn't have it in him to** (*inf*) er hat nicht das Zeug dazu zu (*inf*); **in German** auf deutsch

inability [,ɪnə'bɪlɪtɪ] *s* Unfähigkeit *f*; **i. to pay** Zahlungsunfähigkeit *f*

inaccessible [,ɪnæk'sɛsɪbəl] *adj* unzugänglich

inaccuracy [ɪn'ækjərəsɪ] *s* Ungenauigkeit *f*

inaccurate [ɪn'ækjərɪt] *adj* ungenau

inaction [ɪn'ækʃən] *s* Untätigkeit *f*

inactive [ɪn'æktɪv] *adj* untätig; (*chem*) unwirksam; (st. exch.) lustlos

inactivity [,ɪnæk'tɪvɪtɪ] *s* Untätigkeit *f*

inadequate [ɪn'ædɪkwɪt] *adj* unangemessen

inadmissible [,ɪnəd'mɪsɪbəl] *adj* unstatthaft, unzulässig

inadvertent [,ɪnəd'vʌrtənt] *adj* versehentlich

inadvisable [,ɪnəd'vaɪzəbəl] *adj* nicht ratsam

inalienable [ɪn'eljənəbəl] *adj* unveräußerlich

inane [ɪn'en] *adj* leer, unsinnig

inanimate [ɪn'ænɪmɪt] *adj* unbeseelt

inappropriate [,ɪnə'proprɪ·ɪt] *adj* unangemessen

inarticulate [,ɪnɑr'tɪkjəlɪt] *adj* unartikuliert, undeutlich

inartistic [,ɪnɑr'tɪstɪk] *adj* unkünstlerisch, kunstlos

inasmuch as [,ɪnəz'mʌtʃ /æz] *conj* da

inattentive [,ɪnə'tɛntɪv] *adj* adv (**to**) unaufmerksam (or unachtsam) (gegenüber)

inaudible [ɪn'ɔdɪbəl] *adj* unhörbar

inaugural [ɪn'ɔg(j)ərəl] *adj* Antritts–

inaugurate [ɪn'ɔg(j)ə,ret] *tr* feierlich eröffnen; (*a new policy*) einleiten

inauguration [ɪn,ɔg(j)ə're'ʃən] *s* Eröffnung *f*; (*of an official*) Amtsantritt *m*

inauspicious [,ɪnɔ'spɪʃəs] *adj* ungünstig

inborn ['ɪn,bɔrn] *adj* angeboren

inbred ['ɪn,brɛd] *adj* angeboren, ererbt

in'breed'ing *s* Inzucht *f*

incalculable [ɪn'kælkjələbəl] *adj* unberechenbar

incandescent [,ɪnkən'dɛsənt] *adj* Glüh–

incantation [,ɪnkæn'teʃən] *s* Beschwörung *f*

incapable [ɪn'kepəbəl] *adj* untüchtig; **i. of** (*ger*) nicht fähig zu (*inf*)

incapacitate [,ɪnkə'pæsɪ,tet] *tr* unfähig machen; (*jur*) für geschäftsunfähig erklären

incarcerate [ɪn'kɑrsə,ret] *tr* einkerkern

incarnate [ɪn'kɑrnet] *adj*—**God i.** Gottmensch *m*; **the devil i.** der Teufel in Menschengestalt

incarnation [,ɪnkɑr'neʃən] *s* (fig) Verkörperung *f*; (eccl) Fleischwerdung *f*

incendiary [ɪn'sɛndɪ,ɛrɪ] *adj* Brand–; (fig) aufhetzend ‖ *s* Brandstifter –in *mf*

incense ['ɪnsɛns] *s* Weihrauch *m* ‖ *tr* (eccl) beräuchern ‖ [ɪn'sɛns] *tr* erzürnen

in'cense burn'er *s* Räuchergefäß *n*

incentive [ɪn'sɛntɪv] *s* Anreiz *m*

inception [ɪn'sɛpʃən] *s* Anfang *m*

incessant [ɪn'sɛsənt] *adj* unaufhörlich

incest ['ɪnsɛst] *s* Blutschande *f*

incestuous [ɪn'sɛstʃu·əs] *adj* blutschänderisch

inch [ɪntʃ] *s* Zoll *m*; **beat within an i. of one's life** fast zu Tode prügeln; **by inches** nach und nach; **not yield an i.** keinen Fußbreit nachgeben ‖ *intr*—**i. along** dahinschleichen; **i. forward** langsam vorrücken

incidence ['ɪnsɪdəns] *s* Vorkommen *n*

incident ['ɪnsɪdənt] *s* Vorfall *m*; (*adverse event*) Zwischenfall *m*

incidental [,ɪnsɪ'dɛntəl] *adj* zufällig; **i. to** gehörig zu ‖ **incidentals** *spl* Nebenausgaben *pl*

incidentally [,ɪnsɪ'dɛntəlɪ] *adv* übrigens

incinerate [ɪn'sɪnə,ret] *tr* einäschern

incinerator [ɪn'sɪnə,retər] *s* Verbrennungsofen *m*

incipient [ɪn'sɪpɪ·ənt] *adj* beginnend

incision [ɪn'sɪʒən] *s* Schnitt *m*

incisive [ɪn'saɪsɪv] *adj* (*biting*) beißend; (*penetrating*) durchdringend; (*sharp*) scharf

incisor [ɪn'saɪzər] *s* Schneidezahn *m*

incite [ɪn'saɪt] *tr* aufreizen, aufhetzen

inclement [ɪn'klɛmənt] *adj* ungünstig

inclination [,ɪnklɪ'neʃən] *s* (& fig) Neigung *f*

incline ['ɪnklaɪn] *s* Abhang *m* ‖ [ɪn'klaɪn] *tr* neigen ‖ *intr* (**towards**) sich neigen (nach or zu); (fig) (**towards**) neigen (zu); **the roof inclines sharply** das Dach fällt steil ab

include [ɪn'klud] *tr* einschließen; **i. among** rechnen unter (*acc*); **i. in** einrechnen in (*acc*)

includ'ed *adj* (mit) inbegriffen

includ'ing *prep* einschließlich (*genit*)

inclusive [ɪn'klusɪv] *adj* umfassend, gesamt; **all i.** alles inbegriffen; **from ... to ... i.** von ... zu ... einschließlich (or inklusive); **i. of** einschließlich (*genit*)

incognito [ɪnˈkɑgnɪˌto] adv inkognito

incoherent [ˌɪnkoˈhɪrənt] adj unzusammenhängend; **be i.** (said of a person) nicht ganz bei sich sein

incombustible [ˌɪnkəmˈbʌstɪbəl] adj unverbrennbar

income [ˈɪnkʌm] s (from) Einkommen n (aus)

in'come tax' s Einkommensteuer f

in'come-tax return' s Einkommensteuererklärung f

in'com'ing adj (e.g., tide) hereinkommend; (bus, train) ankommend; (official) neu eintretend; **i. goods, i. mail** Eingänge pl

incomparable [ɪnˈkɑmpərəbəl] adj unvergleichlich

incompatible [ˌɪnkəmˈpætɪbəl] adj (with) unvereinbar (mit); (persons) unverträglich

incompetent [ɪnˈkɑmpɪtənt] adj untauglich; (not legally qualified) nicht zuständig; (not legally capable) geschäftsunfähig; (inadmissible) unzulässig ‖ s Nichtkönner –in mf

incomplete [ˌɪnkəmˈplit] adj unvollständig

incomprehensible [ˌɪnkɑmprɪˈhensɪbəl] adj unbegreiflich

inconceivable [ˌɪnkənˈsivəbəl] adj undenkbar

inconclusive [ˌɪnkənˈklusɪv] adj (not convincing) nicht überzeugend; (leading to no result) ergebnislos

incongruous [ɪnˈkɑŋgru·əs] adj nicht übereinstimmend

inconsequential [ɪnˌkɑnsɪˈkwenʃəl] adj belanglos

inconsiderate [ˌɪnkənˈsɪdərɪt] adj unüberlegt; (towards) rücksichtslos (gegen)

inconsistency [ˌɪnkənˈsɪstənsi] s (lack of logical connection) Inkonsequenz f; (contradiction) Unstimmigkeit f; (instability) Unbeständigkeit f

inconsistent [ˌɪnkənˈsɪstənt] adj inkonsequent; (uneven) unbeständig

inconspicuous [ˌɪnkənˈspɪkju·əs] adj unauffällig

inconstant [ɪnˈkɑnstənt] adj unbeständig

incontinent [ɪnˈkɑntɪnənt] adj zügellos

incontrovertible [ˌɪnkɑntrəˈvʌrtɪbəl] adj unwiderlegbar

inconvenience [ˌɪnkənˈvini·əns] s Ungelegenheit f ‖ tr bemühen, belästigen

inconvenient [ˌɪnkənˈvini·ənt] adj ungelegen

incorporate [ɪnˈkɔrpəˌret] tr einverleiben; (an organization) zu e–r Körperschaft machen ‖ intr e–e Körperschaft werden

incorporation [ɪnˌkɔrpəˈreʃən] s Einverleibung f; (jur) Körperschaftsbildung f

incorrect [ˌɪnkəˈrekt] adj unrichtig, falsch; (conduct) unschicklich

incorrigible [ɪnˈkɔrɪdʒɪbəl] adj unverbesserlich

increase [ˈɪnkris] s Zunahme f; **be on the i.** steigen; **i. in costs** Kostensteigerung f; **i. in pay** Gehaltserhöhung f; (mil) Solderhöhung f; **i. in population** Bevölkerungszunahme f; **i. in prices** Preiserhöhung f; **i. in rent** Mieterhöhung f; **i. in taxes** Steuererhöhung f; **i. in value** Wertsteigerung f; **i. in weight** Gewichtszunahme f ‖ [ɪnˈkris] tr (in size) vergrößern; (in height) erhöhen; (in quantity) vermehren; (in intensity) verstärken; (prices) heraufsetzen ‖ intr zunehmen, sich vergrößern; (rise) sich erhöhen; (in quantity) sich vermehren; (in intensity) sich verstärken; **i. in** zunehmen an (dat)

increasingly [ɪnˈkrisɪŋli] adv immer mehr; **i. more difficult** immer schwieriger

incredible [ɪnˈkredɪbəl] adj unglaublich

incredulous [ɪnˈkredʒələs] adj ungläubig

increment [ˈɪnkrɪmənt] s Zunahme f, Zuwachs m; (in pay) Gehaltszulage f

incriminate [ɪnˈkrɪmɪˌnet] tr belasten

incrust [ɪnˈkrʌst] tr überkrusten

incubate [ˈɪnkjəˌbet] tr & intr brüten

incubator [ˈɪnkjəˌbetər] s Brutapparat m

inculcate [ɪnˈkʌlket], [ˈɪnkʌlˌket] tr (in) einprägen (dat)

incumbency [ɪnˈkʌmbənsi] s (obligation) Obliegenheit f; (term of office) Amtszeit f

incumbent [ɪnˈkʌmbənt] adj—**be i. on** obliegen (dat) ‖ s Amtsinhaber –in mf

incunabula [ˌɪnkjuˈnæbjələ] spl (typ) Wiegendrucke pl

in-cur [ɪnˈkʌr] v (pret & pp –curred; ger –curring) tr sich [dat] zuziehen; (debts) machen; (a loss) erleiden; (a risk) eingehen

incurable [ɪnˈkjurəbəl] adj unheilbar ‖ s unheilbarer Kranke m

incursion [ɪnˈkʌrʒən] s Einfall m

indebted [ɪnˈdetɪd] adj (to) verschuldet (bei); **be i. to s.o. for s.th.** j–m etw zu verdanken haben

indecency [ɪnˈdisənsi] s Unsittlichkeit f

indecent [ɪnˈdisənt] adj unsittlich; **i. assault** Sittlichkeitsvergehen n

indecision [ˌɪndɪˈsɪʒən] s Unentschlossenheit f

indecisive [ˌɪndɪˈsaɪsɪv] adj (person) unentschlossen; (battle) nicht entscheidend

indeclinable [ˌɪndɪˈklaɪnəbəl] adj undeklinierbar

indeed [ɪnˈdid] adv ja, zwar ‖ interj jawohl!

indefatigable [ˌɪndɪˈfætɪgəbəl] adj unermüdlich

indefensible [ˌɪndɪˈfensɪbəl] adj nicht zu verteidigen(d); (argument) unhaltbar; (behavior) unentschuldbar

indefinable [ˌɪndɪˈfaɪnəbəl] adj undefinierbar

indefinite [ɪnˈdefɪnɪt] adj (unlimited) unbegrenzt; (not exact) unbestimmt; (answer) ausweichend; (vague) undeutlich; (gram) unbestimmt

indelible [ɪnˈdelɪbəl] *adj* (*ink, pencil*)
wasserfest; (fig) unauslöschlich
indelicate [ɪnˈdelɪkɪt] *adj* unzart
indemnification [ɪnˌdemnɪfɪˈkeʃən] *s*
Schadenersatzleistung *f*
indemni·fy [ɪnˈdemnɪˌfaɪ] *v* (*pret &*
pp **–fied**) *tr* entschädigen
indemnity [ɪnˈdemnɪtɪ] *s* Schadenersatz *m*
indent [ɪnˈdent] *tr* (*notch*) einkerben;
(*the coast*) tiefe Einschnitte bilden
in (*dat*); (typ) einrücken ‖ *intr* (typ)
einrücken
indentation [ˌɪndenˈteʃən] *s* Kerbe *f*;
(typ) Absatz *m*
indenture [ɪnˈdentʃər] *s* (*service con-*
tract) Arbeitsvertrag *m*; (*apprentice*
contract) Lehrvertrag *m* ‖ *tr* vertraglich binden
independence [ˌɪndɪˈpendəns] *s* Un-
abhängigkeit *f*
independent [ˌɪndɪˈpendənt] *adj* (*of*)
unabhängig (von) ‖ *s* Unabhängige
mf
indescribable [ˌɪndɪˈskraɪbəbəl] *adj*
unbeschreiblich
indestructible [ˌɪndɪˈstrʌktɪbəl] *adj*
unzerstörbar
index [ˈɪndeks] *s* (**indexes & indices**
[ˈɪndɪˌsiz]) (*in a book*) Register *n*;
(fig) (**to**) Hisweis *m* (auf *acc*); Index
Index *m* ‖ *tr* registrieren; (*a book*)
mit e–m Register versehen
in′dex card′ *s* Karteikarte *f*
in′dex fin′ger *s* Zeigefinger *m*
India [ˈɪndɪ·ə] *s* Indien *n*
In′dia ink′ *s* chinesische Tusche *f*
Indian [ˈɪndɪ·ən] *adj* indisch; (*e.g.,*
chief, tribe) Indianer– ‖ *s* (*of India*)
Inder –in *mf*; (*of North America*)
Indianer –in *mf*; (*of Central or South*
America) Indio *m*
In′dian corn′ *s* Mais *m*
In′dian file′ *adv* in Gänsemarsch
In′dian O′cean *s* Indischer Ozean *m*
In′dian sum′mer *s* Altweibersommer *m*
indicate [ˈɪndɪˌket] *tr* angeben, anzeigen
indication [ˌɪndɪˈkeʃən] *s* Angabe *f*;
(*of s.th. imminent*) (**of**) Anzeichen *n*
(für); **give i. of** anzeigen
indicative [ɪnˈdɪkətɪv] *adj* (gram) indikativ; **be i. of** hindeuten auf (*acc*)
‖ *s* (gram) Wirklichkeitsform *f*, Indikativ *m*
indicator [ˈɪndɪˌketər] *s* Zeiger *m*
indict [ɪnˈdaɪt] *tr* (**for**) anklagen (wegen)
indictment [ɪnˈdaɪtmənt] *s* Anklage *f*
indifference [ɪnˈdɪfərəns] *s* (**to**) Gleich-
gültigkeit *f* (gegen oder gegenüber)
indifferent [ɪnˈdɪfərənt] *adj* (*mediocre*)
mittelmäßig; (**to**) gleichgültig (gegen)
indigenous [ɪnˈdɪdʒɪnəs] *adj* (**to**) einheimisch (in *dat*)
indigent [ˈɪndɪdʒənt] *adj* bedürftig
indigestible [ˌɪndɪˈdʒestɪbəl] *adj* un-
verdaulich
indigestion [ˌɪndɪˈdʒestʃən] *s* Verdauungsstörung *f*, Magenverstimmung *f*
indignant [ɪnˈdɪgnənt] *adj* (**at**) empört
(über *acc*)

indignation [ˌɪndɪgˈneʃən] *s* (**at**) Em-
pörung *f* (über *acc*)
indignity [ɪnˈdɪgnɪtɪ] *s* Beleidigung *f*
indigo [ˈɪndɪˌgo] *adj* Indigo– ‖ *s* Indigo *m & n*
indirect [ˌɪndɪˈrekt] *adj* indirekt
in′direct dis′course *s* indirekte Rede *f*
in′direct ques′tion *s* indirekter Frage-
satz *m*
indiscreet [ˌɪndɪsˈkrit] *adj* indiskret
indiscretion [ˌɪndɪsˈkreʃən] *s* Indiskre-
tion *f*
indiscriminate [ˌɪndɪsˈkrɪmɪnɪt] *adj*
unterschiedslos
indispensable [ˌɪndɪsˈpensəbəl] *adj* un-
entbehrlich
indisposed *adj* (*ill*) unpäßlich; **i. to**
abgeneigt (*dat*)
indissoluble [ˌɪndɪˈsaljəbəl] *adj* unauf-
lösbar
indistinct [ˌɪndɪˈstɪŋkt] *adj* undeutlich
individual [ˌɪndɪˈvɪdʒʊ·əl] *adj* individuell, Einzel–, einzeln ‖ *s* Indi-
viduum *n*
individ′ual case′ *s* Einzelfall *m*
individuality [ˌɪndɪˌvɪdʒʊˈæltɪ] *s*
Individualität *f*
individually [ˌɪndɪˈvɪdʒʊ·əli] *adv* einzeln
indivisible [ˌɪndɪˈvɪzɪbəl] *adj* unteil-
bar
Indochina [ˈɪndoˈtʃaɪnə] *s* Indochina *n*
indoctrinate [ɪnˈdɑktrɪˌnet] *tr* (**in**)
schulen (in *dat*), unterweisen (in *dat*)
indoctrination [ˌɪndɑktrɪˈneʃən] *s*
Schulung *f*, Unterweisung *f*
Indo-European [ˈɪndoˌjʊrəˈpi·ən] *adj*
indogermanisch ‖ *s* (*language*) Indogermanisch *n*
indolence [ˈɪndələns] *s* Trägheit *f*
indolent [ˈɪndələnt] *adj* träge
Indonesia [ˌɪndoˈniʒə] *s* Indonesien *n*
Indonesian [ˌɪndoˈniʒən] *adj* indo-
nesisch ‖ *s* Indonesier –in *mf*
indoor [ˈɪnˌdor] *adj* Haus–, Zimmer,
Innen–; (sport) Hallen–
indoors [ɪnˈdorz] *adv* innen, drin(nen)
in′door shot′ *s* (phot) Innenaufnahme *f*
induce [ɪnˈd(j)us] *tr* veranlassen, bewegen; (*bring about*) verursachen;
(elec, phys) induzieren
inducement [ɪnˈd(j)usmənt] *s* Anreiz *m*
induct [ɪnˈdʌkt] *tr* (*into*) einführen (in
acc); (mil) (*into*) einberufen (zu)
inductee [ˌɪndʌkˈti] *s* Einberufene *mf*
induction [ɪnˈdʌkʃən] *s* Einführung *f*;
(elec, log) Induktion *f*; (mil) Einberufung *f*
induc′tion coil′ *s* Induktionsspule *f*
indulge [ɪnˈdʌldʒ] *tr* (*a desire*) frönen
(*dat*); (*a person*) befriedigen; (*chil-*
dren) verwöhnen; **i. oneself in**
schwelgen in (*dat*) ‖ *intr* (coll) trinken; **i. in s.th.** sich [*dat*] etw gestatten
indulgence [ɪnˈdʌldʒəns] *s* (*of a desire*)
Frönen *n*; (*tolerance*) Duldung *f*;
(relig) Ablaß *m*; **ask s.o.'s i.** j–n um
Nachsicht bitten
indulgent [ɪnˈdʌldʒənt] *adj* schonend;
(**toward**) nachsichtig (gegen)
industrial [ɪnˈdʌstri·əl] *adj* (*e.g., bank,*

center, alcohol, product, worker) Industrie–; *(e.g., accident, medicine)* Betriebs–; *(e.g., revolution)* industriell; *(e.g., school, engineering)* Gewerbe–

industrialist [ɪnˈdʌstrɪ-əlɪst] *s* Industrielle *mf*

industrialize [ɪnˈdʌstrɪ-əˌlaɪz] *tr* industrialisieren

indus/trial man/agement *s* Betriebswirtschaft *f*

industrious [ɪnˈdʌstrɪ-əs] *adj* fleißig

industry [ˈɪndəstri] *s* Industrie *f;* *(energy)* Fleiß *m*

inebriated [ɪnˈibrɪˌetɪd] *adj* betrunken

inedible [ɪnˈedɪbəl] *adj* ungenießbar

ineffable [ɪnˈefəbəl] *adj* unaussprechlich

ineffective [ˌɪnɪˈfektɪv] *adj* unwirksam; *(person)* untüchtig

ineffectual [ˌɪnɪˈfekt/ʊ-əl] *adj* unwirksam

inefficient [ˌɪnɪˈfɪʃənt] *adj* untüchig; *(process, procedure)* unrationell; *(mach)* nicht leistungsfähig

ineligible [ɪnˈelɪdʒɪbəl] *adj* nicht wählbar; *(not suitable)* ungeeignet

inept [ɪnˈept] *adj* ungeschickt

inequality [ˌɪnɪˈkwalɪti] *s* Ungleichheit *f*

inequity [ɪnˈekwɪti] *s* Ungerechtigkeit *f*

inertia [ɪnˈʌr/ə] *s* Trägheit *f*

inescapable [ˌɪnesˈkepəbəl] *adj* unentrinnbar, unabwendbar

inevitable [ɪnˈevɪtəbəl] *adj* unvermeidlich, unausweichlich

inexact [ˌɪnegˈzækt] *adj* ungenau

inexcusable [ˌɪneksˈkjuzəbəl] *adj* unentschuldbar

inexhaustible [ˌɪnegˈzɔstɪbəl] *adj* unerschöpflich

inexorable [ɪnˈeksərəbəl] *adj* unerbittlich

inexpensive [ˌɪnekˈspensɪv] *adj* billig

inexperience [ˌɪnekˈspɪrɪ-əns] *s* Unerfahrenheit *f*

inexpe/rienced *adj* unerfahren

inexplicable [ɪnˈeksplɪkəbəl] *adj* unerklärlich

inexpressible [ˌɪnekˈspresɪbəl] *adj* unaussprechlich

infallibility [ˌɪnfælɪˈbɪlɪti] *s* Unfehlbarkeit *f*

infallible [ɪnˈfælɪbəl] *adj* unfehlbar

infamous [ˈɪnfəməs] *adj* schändlich

infamy [ˈɪnfəmi] *s* Schändlichkeit *f*

infancy [ˈɪnfənsi] *s* Kindheit *f;* **be still in its i.** (fig) noch in den Kinderschuhen stecken

infant [ˈɪnfənt] *adj* Säuglings– ‖ *s* Kleinkind *n,* Säugling *m*

infantile [ˈɪnfənˌtaɪl] *adj* infantil

in/fantile paral/ysis *s* Kinderlähmung *f*

infantry [ˈɪnfəntri] *s* Infanterie *f*

in/fantry-man *s* (**–men**) Infanterist *m*

infatuated [ɪnˈfæt/ʊˌetɪd] *adj* betört

infatuation [ɪnˌfæt/ʊˈeʃən] *s* Betörung *f*

infect [ɪnˈfekt] *tr* anstecken, infizieren; **become infected** sich anstecken

infection [ɪnˈfekʃən] *s* Ansteckung *f*

infectious [ɪnˈfekʃəs] *adj* (& fig) ansteckend

in-fer [ɪnˈfʌr] *v* *(pret & pp* **–ferred;** *ger* **–ferring)** *tr* folgern

inference [ˈɪnfərəns] *s* Folgerung *f*

inferior [ɪnˈfɪrɪ-ər] *adj* *(in rank)* niedriger; *(in worth)* minderwertig; **(to)** unterlegen *(dat)*

inferiority [ɪnˌfɪrɪˈarɪti] *s* Unterlegenheit *f;* *(in worth)* Minderwertigkeit *f*

inferior/ity com/plex *s* Minderwertigkeitskomplex *m*

infernal [ɪnˈfʌrnəl] *adj* höllisch

infest [ɪnˈfest] *tr* in Schwärmen überfallen; **be infested with** wimmeln von

infidel [ˈɪnfɪdəl] *adj* ungläubig ‖ *s* Ungläubige *mf*

infidelity [ˌɪnfɪˈdelɪti] *s* Untreue *f*

in/field *s* (baseball) Innenfeld *n*

infiltrate [ɪnˈfɪltret], [ˈɪnfɪlˌtret] *tr* *(filter through)* infiltrieren; *(mil)* durchsickern durch; *(pol)* unterwandern ‖ *intr* infiltrieren

infinite [ˈɪnfɪnɪt] *adj* unendlich

infinitive [ɪnˈfɪnɪtɪv] *s* (gram) Nennform *f,* Infinitiv *m*

infinity [ɪnˈfɪnɪti] *s* Unendlichkeit *f;* **to i.** endlos

infirm [ɪnˈfʌrm] *adj* schwach; *(from age)* altersschwach

infirmary [ɪnˈfʌrməri] *s* Krankenstube *f;* (mil) Revier *n*

infirmity [ɪnˈfʌrmɪti] *s* Schwachheit *f*

inflame [ɪnˈflem] *tr* (fig & pathol) entzünden; **become inflamed** sich entzünden

inflammable [ɪnˈflæməbəl] *adj* entzündbar, feuergefährlich

inflammation [ˌɪnfləˈmeʃən] *s* Entzündung *f*

inflammatory [ɪnˈflæməˌtori] *adj* aufrührerisch; *(pathol)* Entzündungs-

inflate [ɪnˈflet] *tr* aufblasen; *(tires)* aufpumpen

inflation [ɪnˈfleʃən] *s* (econ) Inflation *f*

inflationary [ɪnˈfleʃəˌneri] *adj* inflationistisch

inflect [ɪnˈflekt] *tr* *(the voice)* modulieren; *(gram)* flektieren

inflection [ɪnˈflekʃən] *s* *(of the voice)* Tonfall *m;* *(gram)* Flexion *f*

inflexible [ɪnˈfleksɪbəl] *adj* unbiegsam; *(person)* unbeugsam; *(law)* unabänderlich

inflict [ɪnˈflɪkt] *tr* *(punishment)* **(on)** auferlegen *(dat);* *(a defeat)* **(on)** zufügen *(dat);* *(a wound)* **(on)** beibringen *(dat)*

influence [ˈɪnflu-əns] *s* **(on)** Einfluß *m* *(auf acc)* ‖ *tr* beeinflussen

influential [ˌɪnfluˈenʃəl] *adj* einflußreich, maßgebend

influenza [ˌɪnfluˈenzə] *s* Grippe *f*

influx [ˈɪnflʌks] *s* Zufluß *m*

inform [ɪnˈform] *tr* (of) benachrichtigen (von) ‖ *intr*—**i. against** anzeigen

informal [ɪnˈforməl] *adj* zwanglos

informant [ɪnˈformənt] *s* Gewährsmann *m*

information [ˌɪnfərˈmeʃən] *s* Nachricht *f,* Auskunft *f;* *(items of information)*

Informationen *pl;* **a piece of i.** e–e Auskunft *f;* **for your i.** zu Ihrer Information
informa'tion desk' *s* Auskunftsstelle *f*
informative [ɪn'fɔrmətɪv] *adj* belehrend
informed' *adj* unterrichtet
informer [ɪn'fɔrmər] *s* Denunziant –in *mf*
infraction [ɪn'frækʃən] *s* (of) Verstoß *m* (gegen)
infrared [‚ɪnfrə'red] *adj* infrarot
infrequent [ɪn'frikwənt] *adj* selten
infringe [ɪn'frɪndʒ] *tr* verletzen || *intr* —**i. on** eingreifen in (acc)
infringement [ɪn'frɪndʒmənt] *s* (of a law) Verletzung *f;* (of a right) Eingriff *m* (in acc)
infuriate [ɪn'fjʊrɪ‚et] *tr* wütend machen
infuse [ɪn'fjuz] *tr* (& fig) (into) einflößen (dat)
infusion [ɪn'fjuʒən] *s* (& fig) Einflößung *f;* (med) Infusion *f*
ingenious [ɪn'dʒinɪ‚əs] *adj* erfinderisch
ingenuity [‚ɪndʒɪ'n(j)u‚ɪti] *s* Erfindungsgabe *f,* Scharfsinn *m*
ingenuous [ɪn'dʒɛnju‚əs] *adj* aufrichtig; (naive) naiv
ingest [ɪn'dʒɛst] *tr* zu sich nehmen
inglorious [ɪn'glorɪ‚əs] *adj* (shameful) unrühmlich; (without honor) ruhmlos
ingot ['ɪŋgət] *s* Block *m;* (of gold or silver) Barren *m*
ingrained', in'grained *adj* eingewurzelt
ingrate ['ɪngret] *s* Undankbare *mf*
ingratiate [ɪn'greʃɪ‚et] *tr*—**i. oneself with** sich einschmeicheln bei
ingra'tiating *adj* einschmeichelnd
ingratitude [ɪn'grætɪ‚t(j)ud] *s* Undankbarkeit *f,* Undank *m*
ingredient [ɪn'gridɪ‚ənt] *s* Bestandteil *m;* (culin) Zutat *f*
in'grown' *adj* eingewachsen
inhabit [ɪn'hæbɪt] *tr* bewohnen
inhabitant [ɪn'hæbɪtənt] *s* Bewohner –in *mf,* Einwohner –in *mf*
inhale [ɪn'hel] *tr* & *intr* einatmen; inhalieren
inherent [ɪn'hɪrənt] *adj* innewohnend; (right) angeboren
inherit [ɪn'herɪt] *tr* (biol, jur) erben
inheritance [ɪn'herɪtəns] *s* Erbschaft *f*
inher'itance tax' *s* Erbschaftssteuer *f*
inheritor [ɪn'herɪtər] *s* Erbe *m,* Erbin *f*
inhibit [ɪn'hɪbɪt] *tr* hemmen, inhibieren
inhibition [‚ɪnɪ'bɪʃən] *s* Hemmung *f*
inhospitable [ɪn'hɑspɪtəbəl] *adj* ungastlich; (place) unwirtlich
inhuman [ɪn'hjumən] *adj* unmenschlich
inhumane [‚ɪnju'men] *adj* inhuman
inhumanity [‚ɪnhju'mænɪti] *s* Unmenschlichkeit *f*
inimical [ɪ'nɪmɪkəl] *adj* (to) abträglich (dat)
iniquity [ɪ'nɪkwɪti] *s* Niederträchtigkeit *f,* Ungerechtigkeit *f*
ini·tial [ɪn'ɪ/əl] *adj* anfänglich || *s* Anfangsbuchstabe *m,* Initiale *f* || *v*

(pret & pp –tial[l]ed; ger –tial[l]ing) *tr* mit den Initialen unterzeichnen
initially [ɪ'nɪ/əli] *adv* anfangs
initiate [ɪ'nɪʃɪ‚et] *tr* einführen; (reforms) einleiten; (into) aufnehmen in (acc)
initiation [ɪ‚nɪʃɪ'eʃən] *s* Einführung *f;* (into) Aufnahme *f* (in acc)
initiative [ɪ'nɪʃ(ɪ)ətɪv] *s* Unternehmungsgeist *m;* **take the i.** die Initiative ergreifen
inject [ɪn'dʒɛkt] *tr* (a needle) einführen; (a word) dazwischenwerfen; (e.g., bigotry into a campaign) einfließen lassen; (a liquid) (med) injizieren
injection [ɪn'dʒɛkʃən] *s* (mach) Einspritzung *f;* (med) Injektion *f*
injudicious [‚ɪndʒu'dɪʃəs] *adj* unverständig
injunction [ɪn'dʒʌŋkʃən] *s* Gebot *n;* (jur) gerichtliche Verfügung *f*
injure ['ɪndʒər] *tr* verletzen; (fig) schädigen
injurious [ɪn'dʒurɪ‚əs] *adj* schädlich
injury ['ɪndʒəri] *s* Verletzung *f;* (to) Schädigung *f* (genit)
injustice [ɪn'dʒʌstɪs] *s* Ungerechtigkeit *f*
ink [ɪŋk] *s* Tinte *f* || *tr* schwärzen
inkling ['ɪŋklɪŋ] *s* leise Ahnung *f*
ink' pad' *s* Stempelkissen *n*
ink' spot' *s* Tintenklecks *m*
inky ['ɪŋki] *adj* tiefschwarz
inlaid ['ɪn‚led] *adj* eingelegt
in'laid floor' *s* Parkettfußboden *m*
inland ['ɪnlənd] *adj* Binnen– || *adv* landeinwärts || *s* Binnenland *n*
in'-laws' *spl* angeheiratete Verwandte *pl*
inlay ['ɪn‚le] *s* Einlegearbeit *f;* (dent) gegossene Plombe *f*
in'let *s* Meeresarm *m;* (opening) Öffnung *f*
in'mate *s* Insasse *m,* Insassin *f*
inn [ɪn] *s* Gasthaus *n,* Wirtshaus *n*
innards ['ɪnərdʒ] *spl* (coll) Innere *n*
innate [ɪ'net] *adj* angeboren
inner ['ɪnər] *adj* innere, inwendig, Innen–
in'nermost' *adj* innerste
in'nerspring mat'tress *s* Federkernmatratze *f*
in'ner tube' *s* Schlauch *m*
inning ['ɪnɪŋ] *s* Runde *f*
inn'keep'er *s* Wirt *m,* Wirtin *f*
innocence ['ɪnəsəns] *s* Unschuld *f;* (of a crime) Schuldlosigkeit *f*
innocent ['ɪnəsənt] *adj* (of) unschuldig (an dat); (harmless) harmlos, (guileless) arglos || *s* Unschuldige *mf*
innocuous [ɪ'nɑkju‚əs] *adj* harmlos
innovation [‚ɪnə'veʃən] *s* Neuerung *f*
innovative ['ɪnə‚vetɪv] *adj* (person) neuerungssüchtig; (thing) Neuerungs–
innuen·do [‚ɪnju'endo] *s* (–does) Unterstellung *f*
innumerable [ɪ'n(j)umərəbəl] *adj* unzählbar, unzählig
inoculate [ɪn'ɑkjə‚let] *tr* impfen
inoculation [ɪn‚ɑkjə'leʃən] *s* Impfung *f*

inoffensive [ˌɪnə'fensɪv] *adj* unschädlich

inopportune [ɪn ˌapər 't(j)un] *adj* ungelegen

inordinate [ɪn'ɔrdɪnɪt] *adj* übermäßig

inorganic [ˌɪnɔr'gænɪk] *adj* unorganisch; (chem) anorganisch

in'put' *adj* (data proc) Eingabe– ‖ *s* (*in production*) Aufwand *m*; (data proc) Eingabe *f*, Eingangsinformation *f*; (elec) Stromzufuhr *f*

inquest ['ɪnkwest] *s* Untersuchung *f*

inquire [ɪn'kwaɪr] *intr* anfragen; **i. about** sich erkundigen nach; **i. into** untersuchen; **i. of** sich erkundigen bei

inquiry [ɪn'kwaɪri], ['ɪnkwɪri] *s* Anfrage *f*; (*investigation*) Untersuchung *f*; **make inquiries (about)** Erkundigungen einziehen (über *acc*)

inquisition [ˌɪnkwɪ'zɪʃən] *s* Inquisition *f*

inquisitive [ɪn'kwɪzɪtɪv] *adj* wißbegierig

in'road *s* (*raid*) Einfall *m*; (fig) Eingriff *m*

ins' and outs' *spl* alle Kniffe *pl*

insane [ɪn'sen] *adj* wahnsinnig; (*absurd*) unsinnig

insane' asy'lum *s* Irrenanstalt *f*

insanity [ɪn'sænɪti] *s* Wahnsinn *m*

insatiable [ɪn'seʃəbəl] *adj* unersättlich

inscribe [ɪn'skraɪb] *tr* (*a name*) einschreiben; (*a book*) widmen; (*a monument*) mit e–r Inschrift versehen

inscription [ɪn'skrɪpʃən] *s* Inschrift *f*; (*of a book*) Widmung *f*

inscrutable [ɪn'skrutəbəl] *adj* unerforschlich

insect ['ɪnsekt] *s* Insekt *n*, Kerbtier *n*

insecticide [ɪn'sektɪ saɪd] *s* Insektenvertilgungsmittel *n*, Insektizid *n*

insecure [ˌɪnsɪ'kjur] *adj* unsicher

insecurity [ˌɪnsɪ'kjurɪti] *s* Unsicherheit *f*

insensitive [ɪn'sensɪtɪv] *adj* (to) unempfindlich (gegen)

inseparable [ɪn'sepərəbəl] *adj* untrennbar; (*friends*) unzertrennlich

insert ['ɪnsʌrt] *s* Einsatzstück *n* ‖ [ɪn'sʌrt] *tr* einfügen; (*a coin*) einwerfen

insertion [ɪn'sʌrʃən] *s* Einfügung *f*; (*of a coin*) Einwurf *m*

in'set' (*of a map*) Nebenkarte *f*; (*inserted piece*) Einsatz *m*

in'shore' *adj* Küsten– ‖ *adv* auf die Küste zu

in'side' *adj* innere, Innen–; (*information*) vertraulich ‖ *adv* innen, drinnen; **come i.** hereinkommen; **i. of** innerhalb von; **i. out** verkehrt; **know i. out** in– und auswendig kennen; **turn i. out** umdrehen ‖ *s* Innenseite *f*, Innere *n*; **on the i.** innen ‖ *prep* innerhalb (*genit*)

insider [ɪn'saɪdər] *s* Eingeweihte *mf*

in'side track' *s* (sport) Innenbahn *f*; **have the i.** (fig) im Vorteil sein

insidious [ɪn'sɪdɪ·əs] *adj* hinterlistig

in'sight' *s* Einsicht *f*

insigni·a [ɪn'sɪgnɪ·ə] *s* (*-a & -as*) Abzeichen *n*; **i. of office** Amtsabzeichen *pl*; **i. of rank** Rangabzeichen *pl*

insignificant [ˌɪnsɪg'nɪfɪkənt] *adj* bedeutungslos, geringfügig

insincere [ˌɪnsɪn'sɪr] *adj* unaufrichtig

insincerity [ˌɪnsɪn'serɪti] *s* Unaufrichtigkeit *f*

insinuate [ɪn'sɪnju ˌet] *tr* andeuten

insipid [ɪn'sɪpɪd] *adj* (& fig) fad(e)

insist [ɪn'sɪst] *intr*—**i. on** bestehen auf (*dat*); **i. on** (*ger*) darauf bestehen zu (*inf*)

insistent [ɪn'sɪstənt] *adj* beharrlich

insofar as [ˌɪnso'far ˌæz] *conj* insoweit als

insolence ['ɪnsələns] *s* Unverschämtheit *f*

insolent ['ɪnsələnt] *adj* unverschämt

insoluble [ɪn'saljəbəl] *adj* unlösbar

insolvency [ɪn'salvənsi] *s* Zahlungsunfähigkeit *f*, Insolvenz *f*

insolvent [ɪn'salvənt] *adj* zahlungsunfähig

insomnia [ɪn'samnɪ·ə] *s* Schlaflosigkeit *f*

insomuch as [ˌɪnso'mʌtʃəz] *conj* insofern als

inspect [ɪn'spekt] *tr* (*view closely*) besichtigen; (*check*) kontrollieren; (aut) untersuchen; (mil) besichtigen

inspection [ɪn'spekʃən] *s* Besichtigung *f*; Kontrolle *f*; (aut) Untersuchung *f*; (mil) Truppenbesichtigung *f*

inspector [ɪn'spektər] *s* Kontrolleur *m*; (*of police*) Inspektor *m*

inspiration [ˌɪnspɪ'reʃən] *s* Begeisterung *f*

inspire [ɪn'spaɪr] *tr* begeistern; (*feelings*) erwecken

inspir'ing *adj* begeisternd

instability [ˌɪnstə'bɪlɪti] *s* Unbeständigkeit *f*

install [ɪn'stɔl] *tr* (*appliances*) installieren; (*in office*) einführen

installation [ˌɪnstə'leʃən] *s* (*of appliances*) Installation *f*; (mil) Anlage *f*

installment [ɪn'stɔlmənt] *s* Installation *f*; (*in a serialized story*) Fortsetzung *f*; (*partial payment*) Rate *f*; **in installments** ratenweise

install'ment plan' *s* Teilzahlungsplan *m*

instance ['ɪnstəns] *s* (*case*) Fall *m*; (*example*) Beispiel *n*; (jur) Instanz *f*; **for i.** zum Beispiel

instant ['ɪnstənt] *adj* augenblicklich; (*foods*) gebrauchsfertig ‖ *s* Augenblick *m*; **this i.** sofort

instantaneous [ˌɪnstən'tenɪ·əs] *adj* augenblicklich, sofortig

instead [ɪn'sted] *adv* statt dessen

instead' of *prep* (an)statt (*genit*); (*ger*) anstatt zu (*inf*)

in'step' *s* Rist *m*

instigate ['ɪnstɪ ˌget] *tr* anstiften

instigation [ˌɪnstɪ'geʃən] *s* Anstiftung *f*

instigator ['ɪnstɪ ˌgetər] *s* Anstifter –in *mf*

instill [ɪn'stɪl] *tr* einflößen

instinct ['ɪnstɪŋkt] *s* Trieb *m*, Instinkt *m*; **by i.** instinktiv

instinctive [ɪn'stɪŋktɪv] *adj* instinktiv

institute ['ɪnstɪ‚t(j)ut] s Institut n ||
  tr einleiten
institution [‚ɪnstɪ't(j)uʃən] s Anstalt f
instruct [ɪn'strʌkt] tr anweisen, beauftragen; (teach) unterrichten
instruction [ɪn'strʌkʃən] s (teaching)
  Unterricht m; **instructions** Anweisun-
  gen pl; **instructions for use** Gebrauchsanweisung f
instructive [ɪn'strʌktɪv] adj lehrreich
instructor [ɪn'strʌktər] s Lehrer –in
  mf; (at a university) Dozent –in mf
instrument ['ɪnstrəmənt] s Instrument
  n; (tool) Werkzeug n; (jur) Dokument n
instrumental [‚ɪnstrə'mentəl] adj (mus)
  instrumental; **he was i. in my getting
  an award** er war mir behilflich, e–n
  Preis zu erhalten
instrumentality [‚ɪnstrəmən'tælɪti] s
  Vermittlung f
in'strument land'ing s Instrumenten-
  landung f
in'strument pan'el s Armaturenbrett n
insubordinate [‚ɪnsə'bɔrdɪnɪt] adj wi-
  dersetzlich
insubordination [‚ɪnsəbɔrdɪ'neʃən] s
  Widersetzlichkeit f
insufferable [ɪn'sʌfərəbəl] adj unausstehlich
insufficient [‚ɪnsə'fɪʃənt] adj unge-
  nügend, unzureichend
insular ['ɪns(j)ələr] adj insular
insulate ['ɪnsə‚let] tr isolieren
insulation [‚ɪnsə'leʃən] s Isolierung f;
  (insulating material) Isolierstoff m
insulator ['ɪnsə‚letər] s Isolator m
insulin ['ɪnsəlɪn] s Insulin n
insult ['ɪnsʌlt] s Beleidigung f || [ɪn-
  'sʌlt] tr beleidigen, beschimpfen
insurance [ɪn'ʃurəns] adj Versiche-
  rungs– || s Versicherung f
insure [ɪn'ʃur] tr versichern
insured adj (letter, package) Wert– ||
  s Versicherungsnehmer –in mf
insurer [ɪn'ʃurər] s Versicherer –in mf
insurgent [ɪn'sʌrdʒənt] adj aufstän-
  disch || s Aufständische mf
insurmountable [‚ɪnsər'mauntəbəl] adj
  unübersteigbar; (fig) unüberwindlich
insurrection [‚ɪnsə'rekʃən] s Aufstand
  m
intact [ɪn'tækt] adj unversehrt
in'take s (aut) Einlaß m; **i. of food**
  Nahrungsaufnahme f
in'take valve' s Einlaßventil n
intangible [ɪn'tændʒɪbəl] adj immateriell
integer ['ɪntɪdʒər] s ganze Zahl f
integral ['ɪntɪgrəl] adj wesentlich;
  (math) Integral– || s Integral n
integrate ['ɪntɪ‚gret] tr eingliedern;
  (a school) die Rassentrennung aufheben in (dat); (& math) integrieren
integration [‚ɪntɪ'greʃən] s Integration f; (of schools) Aufhebung f der
  Rassentrennung
integrity [ɪn'tegrɪti] s Redlichkeit f
intellect ['ɪntə‚lekt] s Intellekt m
intellectual [‚ɪntə'lektʃʊ‚əl] adj intel-
  lektuell; (freedom, history) Geistes–
  || s Intellektuelle mf

intelligence [ɪn'telɪdʒəns] s Intelligenz
  f, Klugheit f; (information) Nachricht f; (department) Nachrichten-
  dienst m; **gather i.** Nachrichten einziehen
intel'ligence quo'tient s Intelligenz-
  Quotient m
intel'ligence test' s Begabungsprüfung f
intelligent [ɪn'telɪdʒənt] adj intelligent,
  klug
intelligentsia [ɪn‚telɪ'dʒentsɪ·ə] s Intelligenz f, geistige Oberschicht f
intelligible [ɪn'telɪdʒɪbəl] adj (to) verständlich (dat)
intemperate [ɪn'tempərɪt] adj unmäßig;
  (in drink) trunksüchtig
intend [ɪn'tend] tr beabsichtigen; **be
  intended for** bestimmt sein für, ge-
  münzt sein auf (acc) **i. by** bezwecken
  mit; **i. for s.o.** j–m zudenken
intend'ed s (coll) Verlobte mf
intense [ɪn'tens] adj intensiv, stark
intensi•fy [ɪn'tensɪ‚faɪ] v (pret & pp
  –fied) tr steigern, verstärken || intr
  sich steigern, stärker werden
intensity [ɪn'tensɪti] s Stärke f
intensive [ɪn'tensɪv] adj intensiv;
  (gram) verstärkend
inten'sive care' s Intensivstation f
intent [ɪn'tent] adj (on) erpicht (auf
  acc) || s Absicht f; **to all intents and
  purposes** praktisch genommen
intention [ɪn'tenʃən] s Absicht f; **good
  i.** guter Wille m; **have honorable intentions** es ehrlich meinen; **with the
  i. of** (ger) in der Absicht zu (inf)
intentional [ɪn'tenʃənəl] adj absichtlich
intently [ɪn'tentli] adv gespannt
in•ter [ɪn'tʌr] v (pret & pp –terred;
  ger –terring) tr beerdigen
interact [‚ɪntər'ækt] intr zusammenwirken, aufeinander wirken
interaction [‚ɪntər'ækʃən] s Wechsel-
  wirkung f
inter•breed [‚ɪntər'brid] v (pret & pp
  –bred) tr kreuzen || intr sich kreuzen
intercede [‚ɪntər'sid] intr Fürsprache
  einlegen; **i. for s.o. with** Fürsprache
  einlegen für j–n bei
intercept [‚ɪntər'sept] tr (a letter, aircraft) abfangen; (a radio message)
  abhören; (cut off, check) den Weg
  abschneiden (dat)
interceptor [‚ɪntər'septər] s (aer) Ab-
  fangjäger m
intercession [‚ɪntər'seʃən] s Fürsprache f; (relig) Fürbitte f
interchange ['ɪntər‚tʃendʒ] s Wechsel
  m; (on a highway) Anschlußstelle f
  || [‚ɪntər'tʃendʒ] tr auswechseln ||
  intr (with) abwechseln (mit)
interchangeable [‚ɪntər'tʃendʒəbəl] adj
  auswechselbar, austauschbar
intercom ['ɪntər‚kam] s Wechsel-
  sprachanlage f
intercourse ['ɪntər‚kors] s Verkehr m;
  (sexual) Geschlechtsverkehr m
interdependent [‚ɪntərdɪ'pendənt] adj
  voneinander abhängig
interdict ['ɪntər‚dɪkt] s Verbot n;
  (eccl) Interdikt n || [‚ɪntər'dɪkt] tr

verbieten; **i. s.o. from** (*ger*) j—m verbieten zu (*inf*)
interest [ˈɪnt(ə)rɪst] *s* (**in**) Interesse *n* (an *dat*, für); (fin) Zinsen *pl*; **at i.** gegen Zinsen; **be in s.o.'s i.** in j-s Interesse liegen; **have an i.** in beteiligt sein an (*dat*) or bei; **interests** Belange *pl*; **pay i.** (*bring in interest*) Zinsen abwerfen; (*pay out interest*) Zinsen zahlen; **take an i.** in sich interessieren für; **with i.** (& *fig*) mit Zinsen || *tr* (**in**) interessieren (für)
in'terested *adj*—**i. in** interessiert an (*dat*); **the i. parties** die Beteiligten *pl*
in'teresting *adj* interessant
in'terest rate' *s* Zinsfuß *m*, Zinssatz *m*
interfere [ˌɪntərˈfɪr] *intr* (*said of a thing*) dazwischenkommen; (*said of a person*) eingreifen; (**in** or **with**) sich (ein)mengen (in *acc*); **i. with** (rad, telv) stören; **i. with s.o.'s work** j-n bei seiner Arbeit stören
interference [ˌɪntərˈfɪrəns] *s* Einmischung *f*; (phys) Interferenz *f*; (rad, telv) Störung *f*
interim [ˈɪntərɪm] *adj* Zwischen- || *s* Zwischenzeit *f*
interior [ɪnˈtɪrɪ-ər] *adj* innere, Innen- || *s* Innere *n*; (*of a building*) Innenraum *m*; (*of a country*) Inland *n*
inte'rior dec'orator *s* Innenarchitekt –in *mf*
interject [ˌɪntərˈdʒɛkt] *tr* dazwischenwerfen
interjection [ˌɪntərˈdʒɛkʃən] *s* Zwischenwurf *m*; (gram) Interjektion *f*
interlard [ˌɪntərˈlɑrd] *tr* (& *fig*) spicken
interlinear [ˌɪntərˈlɪnɪ-ər] *adj* Interlinear-
interlock [ˌɪntərˈlɑk] *tr* miteinander verbinden || *intr* sich ineinanderschließen
interloper [ˌɪntərˈlopər] *s* Eindringling *m*
interlude [ˈɪntərˌlud] *s* (*interval*) Pause *f*; (fig, mus, theat) Zwischenspiel *n*
intermediary [ˌɪntərˈmidɪˌɛri] *adj* vermittelnd || *s* Vermittler –in *mf*
intermediate [ˌɪntərˈmidɪ-ɪt] *adj* zwischenliegend, Zwischen-
interment [ɪnˈtʌrmənt] *s* Beerdigung *f*
intermez·zo [ˌɪntərˈmɛtso] *s* (**-zos** & **zi** (tsi)) Intermezzo *n*
intermingle [ˌɪntərˈmɪŋgəl] *tr* vermischen || *intr* sich vermischen
intermission [ˌɪntərˈmɪʃən] *s* Unterbrechung *f*; (theat) Pause *f*
intermittent [ˌɪntərˈmɪtənt] *adj* intermittierend
intermix [ˌɪntərˈmɪks] *tr* vermischen || *intr* sich vermischen
intern [ˈɪntʌrn] *s* Assistenzarzt *m*, Assistenzärztin *f*
internal [ɪnˈtʌrnəl] *adj* innere, intern; (*domestic*) einheimisch; (*trade, rhyme*) Binnen-
inter'nal-combus'tion en'gine *s* Verbrennungsmotor *m*
inter'nal med'icine *s* innere Medizin *f*
inter'nal rev'enue *s* Steueraufkommen *n*

international [ˌɪntərˈnæʃənəl] *adj* international
interna'tional date' line' *s* internationale Datumsgrenze *f*
interna'tional law' *s* Völkerrecht *n*
interne'cine war' [ˌɪntərˈnisɪn] *s* gegenseitiger Vernichtungskrieg *m*
internee [ˌɪntərˈni] *s* Internierte *mf*
internment [ɪnˈtʌrnmənt] *s* Internierung *f*
in'ternship' *s* Pflichtzeit *f* als Assistenzarzt (or Assistenzärztin)
interoffice [ˌɪntərˈɔfɪs] *adj* Haus-
interplanetary [ˌɪntərˈplænɪˌtɛri] *adj* interplanetarisch
interplay [ˈɪntərˌple] *s* Wechselspiel *n*
interpolate [ɪnˈtʌrpəˌlet] *tr* interpolieren
interpose [ˌɪntərˈpoz] *tr* (*an obstacle*) dazwischensetzen; (*a remark*) einschieben
interpret [ɪnˈtʌrprɪt] *tr* (& *mus*) interpretieren; (*translate*) verdolmetschen || *intr* dolmetschen
interpretation [ɪnˌtʌrprɪˈteʃən] *s* (& *mus*) Interpretation *f*
interpreter [ɪnˈtʌrprɪtər] *s* Dolmetscher –in *mf*; **act as i.** dolmetschen
interrogate [ɪnˈtɛrəˌget] *tr* ausfragen; (jur) verhören, vernehmen
interrogation [ɪnˌtɛrəˈgeʃən] *s* Verhör *n*
interrogative [ˌɪntərˈrɑgətɪv] *adj* Frage-
interrupt [ˌɪntəˈrʌpt] *tr* unterbrechen
interruption [ˌɪntəˈrʌpʃən] *s* Unterbrechung *f*; (*in industry*) Betriebsstörung *f*
intersect [ˌɪntərˈsɛkt] *tr* durchschneiden || *ref* sich kreuzen
intersection [ˌɪntərˈsɛkʃən] *s* Straßenkreuzung *f*; (math) Schnittpunkt *m*
intersperse [ˌɪntərˈspʌrs] *tr* durchsetzen
interstate [ˈɪntərˌstet] *adj* zwischenstaatlich
interstellar [ˌɪntərˈstɛlər] *adj* interstellar
interstice [ɪnˈtʌrstɪs] *s* Zwischenraum *m*
intertwine [ˌɪntərˈtwaɪn] *tr* verflechten || *intr* sich verflechten
interval [ˈɪntərvəl] *s* Abstand *m*; (mus) Stufe *f*, Intervall *n*
intervene [ˌɪntərˈvin] *intr* dazwischenkommen; (*interfere*) eingreifen; (*intercede*) intervenieren
intervention [ˌɪntərˈvɛnʃən] *s* Dazwischenkommen *n*; Eingreifen *n*; Intervention *f*
interview [ˈɪntərˌvju] *s* Interview *n* || *tr* interviewen
inter·weave [ˌɪntərˈwiv] *v* (*pret* **–wove** & **–weaved**; *pp* **–woven**, **–woven** & **–weaved**) *tr* durchweben, durchflechten
intestate [ɪnˈtɛstet] *adj* ohne Testament
intestine [ɪnˈtɛstɪn] *s* Darm *m*; **intestines** Gedärme *pl*
intimacy [ˈɪntɪməsi] *s* Vertraulichkeit *f*; **intimacies** Intimitäten *pl*
intimate [ˈɪntɪmɪt] *adj* intim, vertraut

|| *s* Vertraute *mf* || ['ıntı‚met] *tr* andeuten

intimation [‚ıntı'meʃən] *s* Andeutung *f*

intimidate [ın'tımı‚det] *tr* einschüchtern

intimidation [‚ıntımı'deʃən] *s* Einschüchterung *f*

into ['ıntu], ['ıntʊ] *prep* in (*acc*)

intolerable [ın'talərəbəl] *adj* unerträglich

intolerance [ın'talərəns] *s* (of) Intoleranz *f* (gegen)

intolerant [ın'talərənt] *adj* (of) intolerant (gegen)

intonation [‚ınto'neʃən] *s* Tonfall *m*

intone [ın'ton] *tr* intonieren

intoxicate [ın'taksı‚ket] *tr* berauschen; (*poison*) vergiften

intoxication [ın‚taksı'keʃən] *s* (& fig) Rausch *m*; (*poisoning*) Vergiftung *f*

intractable [ın'træktəbəl] *adj* (*person*) störrisch; (*thing*) schwer zu bearbeiten(d)

intransigent [ın'trænsıdʒənt] *adj* unversöhnlich

intransitive [ın'trænsıtıv] *adj* intransitiv

intravenous [‚ıntrə'vinəs] *adj* intravenös

intrepid [ın'trepıd] *adj* unerschrocken

intricate ['ıntrıkıt] *adj* verwickelt

intrigue [ın'trig], ['ıntrig] *s* Intrige *f* || [ın'trig] *tr* fesseln || *intr* intrigieren

intrigu'ing *adj* fesselnd

intrinsic(al) [ın'trınsık(əl)] *adj* innere, innerlich; (*value*) wirklich

introduce [‚ıntrə'd(j)us] *tr* einführen; (*strangers*) vorstellen

introduction [‚ıntrə'dʌkʃən] *s* Einführung *f*; (of strangers) Vorstellung *f*; (in a book) Einleitung *f*

introductory [‚ıntrə'dʌktəri] *adj* (offer, price) Einführungs–; (remarks) einleitend

introspection [‚ıntrə'spekʃən] *s* Selbstbeobachtung *f*

introspective [‚ıntrə'spektıv] *adj* introspektiv

introvert ['ıntrə‚vʌrt] *s* Introvertierte *mf*

intrude [ın'trud] *intr* (on) sich aufdrängen (dat); **am I intruding?** störe ich?

intruder [ın'trudər] *s* Eindringling *m*

intrusion [ın'truʒən] *s* Eindrängen *n*, Stören *n*

intrusive [ın'trusıv] *adj* störend, lästig

intuition [‚ınt(j)u'ıʃən] *s* Intuition *f*

inundate ['ınən‚det] *tr* überschwemmen

inundation [‚ınən'deʃən] *s* Überschwemmung *f*

inure [ın'jur] *tr* (to) abhärten (gegen)

invade [ın'ved] *tr* (a country) eindringen in (*acc*); (rights) verletzen; (privacy) stören

invader [ın'vedər] *s* Eindringling *m*; (mil) Angreifer *m*

invalid [ın'vælıd] *adj* ungültig || ['ınvəlıd] *adj* kränklich || *s* Invalide *m*

invalidate [ın'vælı‚det] *tr* ungültig machen; (a law) außer Kraft setzen

invalidity [‚ınvə'lıdıtı] *s* Ungültigkeit *f*

invaluable [ın'væljʊ‚əbəl] *adj* unschätzbar

invariable [ın'verı‚əbəl] *adj* unveränderlich

invasion [ın've ʃən] *s* Invasion *f*

invective [ın'vektıv] *s* Schmähung *f*

inveigh [ın've] *intr*—i. against schimpfen über (*acc*) or auf (*acc*)

inveigle [ın'vigel] *tr* verleiten; **i. s.o. into** (ger) j–n verleiten zu (inf)

invent [ın'vent] *tr* erfinden; (a story) sich [dat] ausdenken

invention [ın'venʃən] *s* Erfindung *f*

inventive [ın'ventıv] *adj* erfinderisch

inventiveness [ın'ventıvnıs] *s* Erfindungsgabe *f*

inventor [ın'ventər] *s* Erfinder –in *mf*

invento·ry ['ınvən‚təri] *s* (stock) Inventar *n*; (act) Inventur *f*; (list) Bestandsverzeichnis *n*; **take i.** Inventur machen || *v* (pret & pp –ried) *tr* inventarisieren

inverse [ın'vʌrs] *adj* umgekehrt

inversion [ın'vʌrʒən] *s* Umkehrung *f*; (gram) Umstellung *f*

invert [ın'vʌrt] *tr* umkehren; (gram) umstellen

invertebrate [ın'vʌrtı‚bret] *adj* wirbellos || *s* wirbelloses Tier *n*

invest [ın'vest] *tr* (in) investieren (in *acc*); (mil) belagern; **i. with** ausstatten mit

investigate [ın'vestı‚get] *tr* untersuchen

investigation [ın‚vestı'geʃən] *s* Untersuchung *f*

investigator [ın'vestı‚getər] *s* Untersucher –in *mf*

investment [ın'vestmənt] *s* Anlage *f*, Investition *f*; (with an office) Amtseinführung *f*; (mil) Belagerung *f*

investor [ın'vestər] *s* Investor –in *mf*

inveterate [ın'vetərıt] *adj* (habitual) eingefleischt; (firmly established) eingewurzelt

invidious [ın'vıdı‚əs] *adj* haßerregend

invigorate [ın'vıgə‚ret] *tr* beleben

invig'orating *adj* belebend

invincible [ın'vınsıbəl] *adj* unbesiegbar

invisible [ın'vızıbəl] *adj* unsichtbar

invis'ible ink' *s* Geheimtinte *f*

invitation [‚ınvı'teʃən] *s* Einladung *f*

invite [ın'vaıt] *tr* einladen; **i. in** hereinbitten

invit'ing *adj* lockend

invocation [‚ınvə'keʃən] *s* Anrufung *f*; (relig) Bittgebet *n*

invoice ['ınvɔıs] *s* Faktura *f*, Warenrechnung *f*; **as per i.** laut Rechnung || *tr* fakturieren

invoke [ın'vok] *tr* anrufen; (cite) zitieren

involuntary [ın'vɑlən‚teri] *adj* (against one's will) unfreiwillig; (without one's will) unwillkürlich

invol'untary man'slaughter *s* unbeabsichtigte Tötung *f*

involve [ɪn'vɑlv] tr verwickeln; (*include*) einschließen; (*affect*) betreffen; (*entail*) zur Folge haben
involved' adj verwickelt, kompliziert; **be i. in** (*e.g.*, *construction*) beschäftigt sein bei; (*e.g.*, *a crime*) verwickelt sein in (*acc*); **be i. with** (*e.g.*, *a married person*) e–e Affäre haben mit
involvement [ɪn'vɑlʌmənt] s Verwicklung f
invulnerable [ɪn'vʌlnərəbəl] adj unverwundbar
inward ['ɪnwərd] adj inner(lich) ‖ adv nach innen
inwardly ['ɪnwərdli] adv innerlich
iodine ['aɪ·ə‚dɪn] s (chem) Jod n ‖ ['aɪ·ə‚daɪn] s (pharm) Jodtinktur f
ion ['aɪ·ən], ['aɪ·ɑn] s Ion n
ionize ['aɪ·ə‚naɪz] tr ionisieren
IOU ['aɪ‚o'ju] s (**I owe you**) Schuldschein m
I.Q. ['aɪ'kju] s (**intelligence quotient**) Intelligenz-Quotient m
Iran [ɪ'ran], [aɪ'ræn] s Iran m
Iranian [aɪ'renɪ·ən] adj iranisch ‖ s Iran(i)er –in mf
Iraq [ɪ'rak] s Irak m
Ira·qi [ɪ'raki] adj irakisch ‖ s –(qis) Iraker –in mf
irascible [ɪ'ræsɪbəl] adj jähzornig
irate ['aɪret], [aɪ'ret] adj zornig
ire [aɪr] s Zorn m
Ireland ['aɪrlənd] s Irland n
iris ['aɪrɪs] s (anat, bot) Iris f
Irish ['aɪrɪʃ] adj irisch ‖ s (*language*) Irisch n; **the I.** die Iren pl
I'rish·man s (**–men**) Ire m
I'rishwom'an s (**–wom'en**) Irin f
irk [ʌrk] tr ärgern
irksome ['ʌrksəm] adj ärgerlich
iron ['aɪ·ərn] adj (& fig) eisern ‖ s Eisen n; (*for pressing clothes*) Bügeleisen n ‖ tr bügeln; **i. out** ausbügeln; (fig) ins Reine bringen
ironclad ['aɪ·ərn‚klæd] adj (fig) unumstößlich
i'ron cur'tain s eiserner Vorhang m
ironic(al) [aɪ'ranɪk(əl)] adj ironisch
i'roning s (*act*) Bügeln n; (*clothes*) Bügelwäsche f
i'roning board' s Bügelbrett n
i'ron lung' s eiserne Lunge f
i'ron ore' s Eisenerz n
irony ['aɪrəni] s Ironie f
irradiate [ɪ'redɪ‚et] tr bestrahlen; (*light*) ausstrahlen; (*a face*) aufheitern
irrational [ɪ'ræʃənəl] adj irrational
irreconcilable [‚ɪrekən'saɪləbəl] adj unversöhnlich
irredeemable [‚ɪrɪ'dimɪbəl] adj (*loan*, *bond*) nicht einlösbar; (*hopeless*) hoffnungslos
irrefutable [‚ɪrɪ'fjutəbəl] adj unwiderlegbar
irregular [ɪ'regjələr] adj unregelmäßig
irregularity [ɪ‚regjə'lærɪti] s Unregelmäßigkeit f
irrelevant [ɪ'reləvənt] adj (**to**) nicht anwendbar (auf *acc*)
irreligious [‚ɪrɪ'lɪdʒəs] adj irreligiös

irreparable [ɪ'repərəbəl] adj unersetzlich
irreplaceable [‚ɪrɪ'plesɪbəl] adj unersetzlich
irrepressible [‚ɪrɪ'presɪbəl] adj unbezähmbar
irreproachable [‚ɪrɪ'protʃəbəl] adj untadelig
irresistible [‚ɪrɪ'zɪstɪbəl] adj unwiderstehlich
irresolute [ɪ'rezəlut] adj unentschlossen, unschlüßig
irrespective [‚ɪrɪ'spektɪv] adj—**i. of** ohne Rücksicht auf (*acc*)
irresponsible [‚ɪrɪ'spansɪbəl] adj unverantwortlich
irretrievable [‚ɪrɪ'trivəbəl] adj unwiederbringlich, unrettbar
irreverent [ɪ'revərənt] adj unehrerbietig
irrevocable [ɪ'revəkəbəl] adj unwiderruflich
irrigate ['ɪrɪ‚get] tr verwässern; (med) irrigieren
irrigation [‚ɪrɪ'geʃən] s Bewässerung f
irritable ['ɪrɪtəbəl] adj reizbar
irritant ['ɪrɪtənt] s Reizstoff m
irritate ['ɪrɪ‚tet] tr reizen, irritieren
irritating adj ärgerlich
irritation [‚ɪrɪ'teʃən] s Reizung f
irruption ['ɪrʌp/ʃən] s Einbruch m
isinglass ['aɪzɪŋ‚glæs] s Fischleim m; (*mica*) Glimmer m
Islam ['ɪsləm] s Islam m
island ['aɪlənd] s Insel f
islander ['aɪləndər] s Insulaner –in mf
isle [aɪl] s kleine Insel f
isolate ['aɪsə‚let] tr isolieren
isolation [‚aɪsə'leʃən] s Isolierung f
isolationist [‚aɪsə'leʃənɪst] s Isolationist –in mf
isola'tion ward' s Isolierstation f
isometric [‚aɪsə'metrɪk] adj isometrisch
isosceles [aɪ'sɑsə‚liz] adj gleichschenklig
isotope ['aɪsə‚top] s Isotop n
Israel ['ɪzrɪ·əl] s Israel n
Israe·li [ɪz'reli] adj israelisch ‖ s (**–li**) Israeli m
Israelite ['ɪzrɪ·ə‚laɪt] adj israelitisch ‖ s Israelit –in mf
issuance ['ɪ/ʊ·əns] s Ausgabe f
issue ['ɪ/ʊ] s (*of a magazine*) Nummer f; (*result*) Ausgang m; (*e.g.*, *of securities*) Ausgabe f, Emission f; (*under discussion*) Streitpunkt m; (*offspring*) Nachkommenschaft f; **avoid the i.** der Frage ausweichen; **be at i.** zur Debatte stehen; **make an i. of it** e–e Streitfrage daraus machen; **take i. with** anderer Meinung sein als ‖ tr (*orders*, *supplies*, *stamps*, *stocks*) ausgeben; (*a pass*) ausstellen ‖ intr (**from**) herauskommen (aus)
isthmus ['ɪsməs] s Landenge f
it [ɪt] pron es; **about it** darüber, davon; **it is I** ich bin es
Italian [ɪ'tælɪ·ən] adj italienisch ‖ s (*person*) Italiener –in mf; (*language*) Italienisch n
italicize [ɪ'tælɪ‚saɪz] tr kursiv drucken

italics [ɪ'tælɪks] *spl* Kursivschrift *f*

Italy ['ɪtəli] *s* Italien *n*

itch [ɪtʃ] *s* Jucken *n*; (pathol) Krätze *f* ‖ *intr* jucken; **I am itching to** (*inf*) es reizt mich zu (*inf*); **my nose itches me** es juckt mich in der Nase

itchy ['ɪtʃi] *adj* juckend; (pathol) krätzig

item ['aɪtəm] *s* Artikel *m*; (*in a list*) Punkt *m*; (com) Posten *m*; (journ) Nachricht *f*; **hot i.** (coll) Schlager *m*

itemize ['aɪtə‚maɪz] *tr* einzeln aufführen

itinerant [aɪ'tɪnərənt], [ɪ'tɪnərənt] *adj* Wander-, reisend ‖ *s* Reisende *mf*

itinerary [aɪ'tɪnə‚reri] *s* Reiseplan *m*

its [ɪts] *poss adj* sein

itself *reflex pron* sich; **in i.** an und für sich ‖ *intens pron* selbst, selber

ivied ['aɪvid] *adj* efeubewachsen

ivory ['aɪvəri] *adj* elfenbeinern, Elfenbein-; (*color*) kremfarben ‖ *s* Elfenbein *n*; **tickle the ivories** in die Tasten greifen

i'vory tow'er *s* (fig) Elfenbeinturm *m*

ivy ['aɪvi] *s* Efeu *m*

J

J, j [dʒe] *s* zehnter Buchstabe des englischen Alphabets

jab [dʒæb] *s* Stoß *m*; (box) Gerade *f* ‖ *v* (*pret & pp* **jabbed**; *ger* **jabbing**) *tr* stoßen; (box) mit der Gerade stoßen

jabber ['dʒæbər] *tr & intr* plappern

jack [dʒæk] *s* (*money*) (sl) Pinke *f*; (aut) Wagenheber *m*; (cards) Bube *m*; (telp) Klinke *f*; **Jack Hans** *m* ‖ *tr*—**j. up** (aut) heben; (*prices*) hinaufschrauben

jackal ['dʒækəl] *s* Schakal *m*

jack'ass' *s* Esel *m*

jacket ['dʒækɪt] *s* Jacke *f*; (*of a book*) Umschlag *m*; (*of a potato*) Schale *f*

Jack' Frost' *s* Herr Winter *m*

jack'ham'mer *s* Preßlufthammer *m*

jack'-in-the-box' *s* Kastenteufel *m*

jack'knife' *s* (-knives) Klappmesser *n*; (*dive*) Hechtbeuge *f* ‖ *intr* zusammenklappen

jack'-of-all'-trades' *s* Hansdampf *m* in allen Gassen

jack'pot' *s* Jackpot *m*; **hit the j.** das Große Los gewinnen

jack' rab'bit *s* Hase *m*

Jacob ['dʒekəb] *s* Jakob *m*

jade [dʒed] *adj* jadegrün ‖ *s* (*stone*) Jade *m*; (*color*) Jadegrün *n*; (*horse*) Schindmähre *f*

jad'ed *adj* ermattet

jag [dʒæg] *s* Zacke *f*; **have a jag on** (sl) e–n Schwips haben

jagged ['dʒægɪd] *adj* zackig, schartig

jaguar ['dʒægwər] *s* Jaguar *m*

jail [dʒel] *s* Gefängnis *n*, Untersuchungsgefängnis *n*; **be in j.** sitzen ‖ *tr* einsperren

jail'bird' *s* Knastbruder *m*

jailer ['dʒelər] *s* Gefängniswärter *m*

jalopy [dʒə'lɑpi] *s* Rumpelkasten *m*

jal'ousie win'dow ['dʒæləsi] *s* Glasjalousie *f*

jam [dʒæm] *s* Marmelade *f*; **be in a jam** (coll) in der Patsche sitzen ‖ *v* (*pret & pp* **jammed**; *ger* **jamming**) *tr* (*a room*) überfüllen; (*a street*) verstopfen; (*a finger*) quetschen; (rad) stören; **be jammed in** eingezwängt sein; **jam on the brakes** auf die Bremsen drücken; **jam s.th. into**

etw stopfen in (*acc*) ‖ *intr* (*said of a window*) klemmen; (*said of a gun*) sich verklemmen; (*said of gears*) Ladehemmung haben; **jam into** sich hineinquetschen in (*acc*)

jamb [dʒæm] *s* Pfosten *m*

jamboree [‚dʒæmbə'ri] *s* Trubel *m*; (*of scouts*) Pfadfindertreffen *n*

James [dʒemz] *s* Jakob *m*

jam'ming *s* (rad) Störung *f*

Jane [dʒen] *s* Johanna *f*

Janet ['dʒænɪt] *s* Hanna *f*

jangle ['dʒæŋgəl] *s* Rasseln *n* ‖ *tr* rasseln lassen; **j. s.o.'s nerves** j–m auf die Nerven gehen ‖ *intr* rasseln

janitor ['dʒænɪtər] *s* Hausmeister *m*

January ['dʒænju‚eri] *s* Januar *m*

Japan [dʒə'pæn] *s* Japan *n*

Japanese [‚dʒæpə'niz] *adj* japanisch ‖ *s* Japaner –in *mf*; (*language*) Japanisch *n*

Jap'anese bee'tle *s* Japankäfer *m*

jar [dʒɑr] *s* Krug *m*; (*e.g., of jam*) Glas *n*; (*jolt*) Stoß *m* ‖ *v* (*pret & pp* **jarred**; *ger* **jarring**) *tr* (*jolt*) anstoßen; (fig) erschüttern ‖ *intr* nicht harmonieren; **jar on the nerves** auf die Nerven gehen

jargon ['dʒɑrgən] *s* Jargon *m*

jasmine ['dʒæzmɪn] *s* Jasmin *m*

jaundice ['dʒɔndɪs] *s* Gelbsucht *f*

jaun'diced *adj* gelbsüchtig

jaunt [dʒɔnt] *s* Ausflug *m*

jaunty ['dʒɔnti] *adj* (*sprightly*) lebhaft; (*clothes*) fesch

javelin ['dʒæv(ə)lɪn] *s* Speer *m*

jaw [dʒɔ] *s* Kiefer *m*; **the jaws of death** die Klauen des Todes

jaw'bone' *s* Kiefer *m* ‖ *intr* (sl) sich stark machen

jay [dʒe] *s* (orn) Häher *m*

jay'walk' *intr* verkehrswidrig die Straße überqueren

jazz [dʒæz] *s* Jazz *m* ‖ *tr*—**j. up** (coll) aufmöbeln

jazz' band' *s* Jazzband *f*

jazzy ['dʒæzi] *adj* bunt, grell

jealous ['dʒeləs] *adj* (of) eifersüchtig (auf *acc*)

jealousy ['dʒeləsi] *s* Eifersucht *f*

jeans [dʒinz] *spl* Jeans *pl*

jeep [dʒip] s Jeep m
jeer [dʒɪr] s Hohn m || tr verhöhnen || intr höhnen; **j. at** verhöhnen
Jeffrey ['dʒɛfri] s Gottfried m
Jehovah [dʒɪ'hovə] s Jehova m
jell [dʒɛl] s Gelee n || intr gelieren; (fig) zum Klappen kommen
jellied ['dʒɛlɪd] adj geliert
jelly ['dʒɛli] s Gallerte f
jel'lyfish' s Qualle f; (pej) Waschlappen m
jeopardize ['dʒɛpər‚daɪz] tr gefährden
jeopardy ['dʒɛpərdi] s Gefahr f
jerk [dʒʌrk] s Ruck m; (sl) Knülch m || tr ruckweise ziehen || intr zucken
jerky ['dʒʌrki] adj ruckartig
jersey ['dʒʌrzi] s (material) Jersey m; (shirt) Jersey n; (sport) Trikot n
jest [dʒɛst] s Scherz m; **in j.** scherzweise || intr scherzen
jester ['dʒɛstər] s Hofnarr m; (joker) Spaßvogel m
Jesuit ['dʒɛʒʊ‚ɪt] adj Jesuiten- || s Jesuit m
Jesus ['dʒizəs] s Jesus m
jet [dʒɛt] adj Düsen- || s (stream) Strahl m; (nozzle) Düse f; (plane) Jet m, Düsenflugzeug n || v (pret & pp jetted; ger jetting) herausströmen; (aer) jetten
jet'-black' adj rabenschwarz
jet' propul'sion s Düsenantrieb m
jetsam ['dʒɛtsəm] s Seewurfgut n
jet' stream' s Strahlströmung f
jettison ['dʒɛtɪsən] s Seewurf m || tr (aer) abwerfen; (naut) über Bord werfen
jetty ['dʒɛti] s (warf) Landungsbrücke f; (breakwater) Hafendamm m
Jew [dʒu] s Jude m, Jüdin f
jewel ['dʒu·əl] s (& fig) Juwel n; (in a watch) Stein m
jew'el box' s Schmuckkästchen n
jewel(l)er ['dʒu·ələr] s Juwelier -in mf
jewelry ['dʒu·əlri] s Juwelen pl; **piece of j.** Schmuckstück n
jew'elry store' s Juweliergeschäft n
Jewish ['dʒu·ɪʃ] adj jüdisch
Jews'/ harp' s Maultrommel f
jib [dʒɪb] s Ausleger m; (naut) Klüver m
jibe [dʒaɪb] intr (coll) übereinstimmen
jiffy ['dʒɪfi] s—**in a j.** im Nu
jig [dʒɪg] s (dance) Gigue f; (tool) Spannvorrichtung f; **the jig is up** (sl) das Spiel ist aus
jigger ['dʒɪgər] s Schnapsglas n; (gadget) Dingsbums n; (naut) Besan f
jiggle ['dʒɪgəl] tr & intr rütteln
jig'saw' s Laubsäge f
jig'saw puz'zle s Puzzlespiel n
jilt [dʒɪlt] tr (a girl) sitzenlassen; (a boy) den Laufpaß geben (dat)
jim-my ['dʒɪmi] s Brecheisen n || v (pret & pp -mied) tr mit dem Brecheisen aufbrechen
jingle ['dʒɪŋgəl] s (of coins) Klimpern n; (bell) Schelle f; (verse) Verseklingel n || tr klimpern mit || intr klimpern; (said of verses) klingeln
jin-go ['dʒɪŋgo] s (-goes) Chauvinist -in mf; **by j.!** alle Wetter!

jinx [dʒɪŋks] s Unglücksrabe m || tr Pech bringen (dat); **be jinxed** vom Pech verfolgt sein
jitters ['dʒɪtərz] spl—**have the j.** wahnsinnig nervös sein; **give s.o. the j.** j-n wahnsinnig nervös machen
jittery ['dʒɪtəri] adj durchgedreht
Joan [dʒon] s Johanna f
job [dʒab] s (employment) Job m; (task, responsibility) Aufgabe f; **bad job** Machwerk n; **do a good job** gute Arbeit leisten; **fall down on the job** seine Pflicht nicht erfüllen; **know one's job** seine Sache verstehen; **on the job** bei der Arbeit; (fig) auf Draht; **out of a job** arbeitslos
jobber ['dʒabər] s (middleman) Zwischenhändler -in mf; (pieceworker) Akkordarbeiter -in mf
job'hold'er s Stelleninhaber -in mf
jobless ['dʒablɪs] adj stellungslos
jockey ['dʒaki] s Jockei m || tr manövrieren
jog [dʒag] s Dauerlauf m; (of a horse) Trott m || v (pret & pp jogged; ger jogging) tr (shake) rütteln; (the memory) auffrischen || intr trotten; (for exercise) langsam rennen, Dauerlauf machen
John [dʒan] s Johann m; **john** (sl) Klo n
Johnny ['dʒani] s Hans m
John'ny-come'-late'ly s Neuling m, Nachzügler m
join [dʒɔɪn] tr verbinden; (a club) beitreten (dat); (a person) sich anschließen (dat); (two parts) zusammenfügen; **j. the army** zum Militär gehen || intr sich verbinden; **j. in** sich beteiligen an (dat); **j. up** (mil) einrücken
joiner ['dʒɔɪnər] s (coll) Vereinsmeier m; (carp) Tischler m
joint [dʒɔɪnt] adj (account, venture) gemeinschaftlich; (return) gemeinsam; (committee) gemischt; (heir, owner) Mit- || s Verbindungspunkt m; (in plumbing) Naht f; (sl) Bumslokal n; (anat, bot, mach) Gelenk n; (carp) Fuge f; (culin) Bratenstück n; **throw out of j.** auskugeln
jointly ['dʒɔɪntli] adv gemeinsam
joint'-stock' com'pany s Aktiengesellschaft f
joist [dʒɔɪst] s Tragbalken m
joke [dʒok] s Witz m; **he can't take a j.** er versteht keinen Spaß; **make a j. of** ins Lächerliche ziehen; **play a j. on** e-n Streich spielen (dat) || intr Spaß machen; **j. about** witzeln über (acc); **j. around** schäkern; **joking aside** Spaß beiseite
joker ['dʒokər] s Spaßvogel m; (pej) Knülch m; (cards) Joker m
jolly ['dʒali] adj lustig
jolt [dʒolt] s Stoß m || tr stoßen || intr holpern; **j. along** dahinholpern
Jordan ['dʒɔrdən] s (country) Jordanien n; (river) Jordan m
josh [dʒaʃ] tr & intr hänseln
jostle ['dʒasəl] tr & intr drängeln
jot [dʒat] s—**not a jot** kein Jota || v

(pret & pp **jotted; ger jotting)** *tr—* **jot down** notieren

journal ['dʒʌrnəl] *s (daily record)* Tagebuch *n; (magazine)* Zeitschrift *f*

journalism ['dʒʌrnə ,lɪzəm] *s* Journalismus *m,* Zeitungswesen *n*

journalist ['dʒʌrnəlɪst] *s* Journalist –in *mf*

journey ['dʒʌrni] *s* Reise *f;* **go on a j.** verreisen || *intr* reisen

jour'ney-man *adj* tüchtig || *s* (–men) Geselle *m*

joust [dʒaʊst] *s* Tjost *f* || *intr* turnieren

jovial ['dʒovɪ-əl] *adj* jovial

jowls [dʒaʊlz] *spl* Hängebacken *pl*

joy [dʒɔɪ] *s* Freude *f*

joyful ['dʒɔɪfəl] *adj* froh, freudig

joyless ['dʒɔɪlɪs] *adj* freudlos

joy' ride' *s* (coll) Schwarzfahrt *f*

joy' stick' *s* (aer) Steuerknüppel *m*

Jr. *abbr* **(Junior)** jr., jun.

jubilant ['dʒubɪlənt] *adj* frohlockend

jubilation [,dʒubɪ'le/ən] *s* Jubel *m*

jubilee ['dʒubɪ ,li] *s* Jubiläum *n*

Judaea [dʒu'di-ə] *s* Judäa *f*

Judaic [dʒu'de-ɪk] *adj* jüdisch

Judaism ['dʒudə ,ɪzəm] *s* Judaismus *m*

judge [dʒʌdʒ] *s (in a competition)* Preisrichter –in *mf; (box)* Punktrichter –in *mf; (jur)* Richter –in *mf* || *tr* **(by)** beurteilen (nach); *(distances)* abschätzen; *(jur)* richten || *intr* urteilen; *(jur)* richten; **judging by his words** seinen Worten nach zu urteilen

judge' ad'vocate *s* Kriegsgerichtsrat *m*

judgment ['dʒʌdʒmənt] *s (& jur)* Urteil *n;* **in my j.** meines Erachtens; **show good j.** ein gutes Urteilsvermögen haben; **sit in j. over** zu Gericht sitzen über *(acc)*

Judg'ment Day' *s* Tag *m* des Gerichts

judicial [dʒu'dɪ/əl] *adj* Rechts-

judiciary [dʒu'dɪ/ɪ ,eri] *adj* richterlich || *s (branch)* richterliche Gewalt *f; (judges)* Richterstand *m*

judicious [dʒu'dɪ/əs] *adj* klug

judo ['dʒudo] *s* Judo *n*

jug [dʒʌg] *s* Krug *m; (jail)* Kittchen *n*

juggle ['dʒʌgəl] *tr* jonglieren; *(accounts)* frisieren || *intr* jonglieren

juggler ['dʒʌglər] *s* Gaukler –in *mf*

Jugoslav ['jugo ,slɑv] *adj* jugoslawisch || *s* Jugoslawe *m,* Jugoslawin *f*

Jugoslavia [,jugo'slɑvɪ-ə] *s* Jugoslawien *n*

jug'ular vein' ['dʒʌgjələr] *s* Halsader *f*

juice [dʒus] *s* Saft *m*

juicy ['dʒusi] *adj* saftig

jukebox ['dʒuk ,bɑks] *s* Musikautomat *m*

July [dʒu'laɪ] *s* Juli *m*

jumble ['dʒʌmbəl] *s* Wust *m* || *tr* durcheinanderwerfen

jumbo ['dʒʌmbo] *adj* Riesen-

jump [dʒʌmp] *s* Sprung *m; (aer)* Absprung *m;* **get the j. on** zuvorkommen *(dat)* || *tr* überspringen; *(attack)* überfallen; *(a hurdle)* nehmen; *(in*

checkers) schlagen; **j. bail** die Kaution verfallen lassen; **j. channels** den amtlichen Weg nicht einhalten; **j. rope** seilspringen; **j. ship** vom Schiff weglaufen; **j. the gun** übereilt handeln; *(sport)* zu früh starten; **j. the track** entgleisen || *intr* springen; *(be startled)* auffahren; **j. at** *(a chance)* stürzen auf *(acc);* **j. down s.o.'s throat** j–n anfahren

jump' ball' *s (basketball)* Sprungball *m*

jumper ['dʒʌmpər] *s (dress)* Jumper *m; (elec)* Kurzschlußbrücke *f*

jump'-off' *s* Beginn *m; (sport)* Start *m*

jump' rope' *s* Springseil *n*

jumpy ['dʒʌmpi] *adj* unruhig, nervös

junction ['dʒʌŋk/ən] *s* Verbindung *f; (of roads, rail lines)* Knotenpunkt *m*

juncture ['dʒʌŋkt/ər] *s* Verbindungsstelle *f;* **at this j.** in diesem Augenblick

June [dʒun] *s* Juni *m*

June' bug' *s* Maikäfer *m*

jungle ['dʒʌŋgəl] *s* Dschungel *m, n & f*

junior ['dʒunjər] *adj* jünger || *s* Student –in *mf* im dritten Studienjahr

juniper ['dʒunɪpər] *s* Wacholder *m*

junk [dʒʌŋk] *s* Altwaren *pl; (scrap iron)* Schrott *m; (useless stuff)* Plunder *m; (naut)* Dschunke *f*

junket ['dʒʌŋkɪt] *s* Vergnügungsreise *f* auf öffentliche Kosten

junk' mail' *s* Wurfsendung *f*

junk'yard' *s* Schrottplatz *m*

junta ['hʌntə], [dʒʌntə] *s* Junta *f*

jurisdiction [,dʒurɪs'dɪk/ən] *s* Zuständigkeit *f;* **have j. over** zuständig sein für

jurisprudence [,dʒurɪs'prudəns] *s* Rechtswissenschaft *f*

jurist ['dʒurɪst] *s* Jurist –in *mf*

juror ['dʒurər] *s* Geschworene *mf*

jury ['dʒuri] *s* Geschworene *pl*

ju'ry box' *s* Geschworenenbank *f*

ju'ry tri'al *s* Schwurgerichtsverfahren *n*

just [dʒʌst] *adj* gerecht || *adv* gerade; *(only)* nur; *(simply)* einfach

justice ['dʒʌstɪs] *s* Gerechtigkeit *f; (of a claim)* Berechtigung *f; (judge)* Richter *m;* **bring to j.** vor Gericht bringen; **do j. to** *(a meal)* wacker zusprechen *(dat); (said of a picture)* gerecht werden *(dat)*

jus'tice of the peace' *s* Friedensrichter *m*

justification [,dʒʌstɪfɪ'ke/ən] *s* Rechtfertigung *f*

justi-fy ['dʒʌstɪ ,faɪ] *v (pret & pp –fied) tr* rechtfertigen

justly ['dʒʌstli] *adv* mit Recht

jut [dʒʌt] *v (pret & pp* **jutted; ger jutting)** *intr—***jut out** hervorragen

juvenile ['dʒuvə ,naɪl] *adj (books, court)* Jugend–; *(childish)* unreif

ju'venile delin'quency *s* Jugendkriminalität *f*

ju'venile delin'quent *s* jugendlicher Verbrecher *m*

juxtapose [,dʒʌkstə'poz] *tr* nebeneinanderstellen

K

K, k [ke] *s* elfter Buchstabe des englischen Alphabets

kale [kel] *s* Grünkohl *m*

kaleidoscopic [kə͵laɪdə'skɑpɪk] *adj* (& fig) kaleidoskopisch

kangaroo [͵kæŋgə'ru] *s* Känguruh *n*

kangaroo court' *s* Scheingericht *n*

kashmir ['kae/mɪr] *s* (tex) Kaschmir *m*

kayo ['ke'o] *s* K.O. *m* ‖ *tr* k.o. schlagen

keel [kil] *s* Kiel *m*; **on an even k.** (fig) gleichmäßig ‖ *intr*—**k. over** umkippen; (naut) kentern

keen [kin] *adj* (*sharp*) scharf; (*interest*) lebhaft; **k. on** scharf auf (*acc*)

keenness ['kinnɪs] *s* Schärfe *f*

keep [kip] *s* Unterhalt *m*; (*of a castle*) Bergfried *m*; **for keeps** (*forever*) für immer; (*seriously*) im Ernst ‖ *v* (*pret & pp* **kept** [kɛpt]) *tr* (*retain*) behalten; (*detain*) aufhalten; (*save for s.o.*) aufbewahren; (*a secret*) bewahren; (*a promise*) (ein)halten; (*animals*) halten; (*books*) (acct) führen; **be kept in school** nachsitzen müssen; **k. at arm's length** vom Leibe halten; **k. at bay** sich erwehren (*genit*); **k. away** fernhalten; **k. back** zurückhalten; (*retain*) zurückbehalten; **k.** (*s.o.*) **company** Gesellschaft leisten (*dat*); **k. down** (*one's head*) niederhalten; (*one's voice*) verhalten; (*prices*) niedrig halten; **k. from** abhalten von; **k. from** (*ger*) daran hindern zu (*inf*); **k. going** im Gange halten; **k. good time** gut gehen; **k. guard** Wache halten; **k. house** den Haushalt führen; **k. in good condition** instand halten; **k. in mind** sich [*dat*] merken; **k. it up!** nur so weiter; **k. on** (*a garment*) anbehalten; (*a hat*) aufbehalten; **k. oneself from** (*ger*) es fertigbringen nicht zu (*inf*); **k. one's temper** sich beherrschen; **k. out** ausschließen; (*light*) nicht durchlassen; (*rain*) abhalten; **k. posted** auf dem laufenden halten; **k. score** die Punktliste führen; **k. secret** geheimhalten; **k. step** Tritt halten; **k. s.th. from s.o.** j-m etw verschweigen; **k. track of** sich [*dat*] merken; **k. under wraps** (coll) totschweigen; **k. up** instand halten; (*appearances*) wahren; (*correspondence*) unterhalten; **k. up the good work!** arbeiten Sie weiter so gut!; **k. waiting** warten lassen; **k. warm** warm halten; **k. your shirt on!** (coll) daß du die Nase im Gesicht behältst! ‖ *intr* (*said of food*) sich halten; **k. at** beharren bei; **k. at it!** bleib dabei!; **k. away** sich fernhalten; **k. cool** (fig) die Nerven behalten; **k. cool!** ruhig Blut!; **k. from** sich enthalten (*genit*); **k. from** (*ger*) es unterlassen zu (*inf*); **k. from** laughing sich das Lachen verkneifen;

k. going weitermachen; **k. moving** weitergehen; **k. on** (*ger*) weiter (*inf*), e.g., **k. on driving** weiterfahren; **k. out!** Eintritt verboten! **k. out of** sich fernhalten von; **k. quiet** sich ruhig verhalten; **k. quiet!** sei still!; **k. to the right** sich rechts halten; **k. up with** (*work*) nachkommen mit; **k. up with the Joneses** mit den Nachbarn Schritt halten; **k. within** bleiben innerhalb (*genit*)

keeper ['kipər] *s* (*of animals*) Halter –in *mf*; (*at a zoo*) Tierwärter –in *mf*; (*watchman*) Wächter *m*

keep'ing *s* Verwahrung *f*; **in k. with** in Einklang mit

keep'sake' *s* Andenken *n*

keg [kɛg] *s* Faß *n*

ken [kɛn] *s* Gesichtskreis *m*

kennel ['kɛnəl] *s* Hundezwinger *m*

kep·i ['kepi], ['kɛpi] *s* (–is) Kappi *n*

kerchief ['kʌrt/ɪf] *s* (*for the head*) Kopftuch *n*; (*for the neck*) Halstuch *n*

kernel ['kʌrnəl] *s* (*of fruit*) Kern *m*; (*of grain*) Korn *n*; (fig) Kern *m*

kerosene [͵kɛrə'sin] *s* Petroleum *n*

kerplunk [kər'plʌŋk] *interj* bums!

ketchup ['ket/əp] *s* Ketchup *m & n*

kettle ['kɛtəl] *s* Kessel *m*

ket'tledrum' *s* Kesselpauke *f*

key [ki] *adj* (*ring, hole, industry, position*) Schlüssel– ‖ *s* (& fig) Schlüssel *m*; (*of a map*) Zeichenerklärung *f*; (*of a typewriter, piano, organ*) Taste *f*; (*of windinstrument*) Klappe *f*; (*reef*) Riff *n*; (*low island*) Insel *f*; (mus) Tonart *f*; **key of C major** C-dur; **off key** falsch ‖ *tr* (mach) festkeilen

key'board' *s* Tastatur *f*

keyed *adj*—**k. to** gestimmt auf (*acc*); **k. up** in Hochspannung

key' man' *s* Schlüsselfigur *f*

key'note *s* Grundgedanke *m*; (mus) Tonika *f*

key'note address' *s* programmatische Rede *f*

keynoter ['kɪ ͵notər] *s* Programmatiker –in *mf*

keypuncher ['ki ͵pʌntf/ər] *s* Locher –in *mf*

key'stone' *s* Schlußstein *m*; (fig) Grundlage *f*

key' word' *s* Stichwort *n*

kha·ki ['kæki] *adj* Khaki– ‖ *s* (–kis) Khaki *m*; **khakis** Khakiuniform *f*

kibitz ['kɪbɪts] *intr* (coll) kiebitzen

kibitzer ['kɪbɪtsər] *s* (coll) Kiebitz *m*

kick [kɪk] *s* Fußtritt *m*; (*of a rifle*) Rückstoß *m*; (*of a horse*) Schlag *m*; (*final spurt*) (sport) Endspurt *m*; **give s.o. a k.** j-m e-n Fußtritt versetzen; **I get a** (**great**) **k. out of him** er macht mir (riesigen) Spaß ‖ *tr* treten, stoßen; (fb) kicken; **be kicked upstairs** (coll) die Treppe hinauffallen;

I could k. myself ich könnte mich ohrfeigen; k. a goal (fb) ein Tor schießen; k. (s.o.) around schlecht behandeln; (e.g., an idea) beschwatzen; k. in (money) beisteuern; k. open (a door) aufstoßen; k. out (coll) rausschmeißen; k. s.o. in the shins j-n gegen das Schienbein treten; k. the bucket (sl) krepieren; k. up a storm Krach schlagen ‖ intr (said of a gun) stoßen; (said of a horse) ausschlagen; (complain) (about) meckern (über acc); k. around Europe in Europa herumbummeln; k. off (fb) anspielen

kick′back′ s Schmiergeld n

kick′off′ s (commencement) Beginn m; (fb) Anstoß m

kid [kɪd] s Zicklein n; (coll) Kind n ‖ v (pret & pp kidded; ger kidding) tr necken ‖ intr scherzen; no kidding! mach keine Witze!

kid′ gloves′ spl Glacéhandschuhe pl; handle with k. (fig) mit Glacéhandschuhen anfassen

kid′nap′ v (pret & pp –nap(p)ed; ger –nap(p)ing) tr kidnappen, entführen

kidnap(p)er [′kɪd͵næpər] s Kidnapper m

kid′nap(p)ing s Entführung f

kidney [′kɪdni] s Niere f

kid′ney bean′ s rote Bohne f

kid′ney-shaped′ adj nierenförmig

kid′ney stone′ s Nierenstein m

kid′ney trans′plant s Nierenverpflanzung f; (transplanted kidney) verpflanzte Niere f

kid′ney trou′ble s Nierenleiden n

kid′ stuff′ s (coll) Kinderei f

kill [kɪl] s (aer) Abschuß m; (hunt) Jagdbeute f; (nav) Versenkung f ‖ tr töten; (murder) ermorden, killen; (plants) zum Absterben bringen; (time) totschlagen; (a proposal, plans, competition) zu Fall bringen; (the motor) abwürgen; (the ball) stark schlagen; (a bottle) austrinken; be killed in action (im Felde) fallen; it won′t k. you (coll) es wird dich nicht umbringen; k. off abschlachten; k. oneself sich umbringen; k. two birds with one stone zwei Fliegen mit e–r Klappe schlagen; she is dressed to k. sie ist totschick angezogen

killer [′kɪlər] s Totschläger –in mf, Killer m

kill′er whale′ s Schwertwal m

kill′ing s Tötung f; make a k. e–n unerhofften Gewinn erzielen

kill′joy′ s Spaßverderber m

kiln [′kɪl(n)] s Brennofen m

kil·o [′kɪlo], [′kilo] s (–os) Kilo n

kilocycle [′kɪlə͵sɑɪkəl] s Kilohertz n

kilogram [′kɪlə͵græm] s Kilogramm n

kilohertz [′kɪlə͵hɑrts] s Kilohertz n

kilometer [kɪ′lɑmɪtər] s Kilometer m; kilometers per hour Stundenkilometer pl

kilowatt [′kɪlə͵wɑt] s Kilowatt n

kil′owatt′-hour′ s Kilowattstunde f

kilt [kɪlt] s Kilt m

kilter [′kɪltər] s—out of k. nicht in Ordnung

kimo·no [kɪ′mono] s (–nos) Kimono m

kin [kɪn] s Sippe f; the next of kin die nächsten Angehörigen

kind [kaɪnd] adj liebenswürdig; (to) gütig (zu), freundlich (zu); would you be so k. as to (inf)? würden Sie so gefällig sein zu (inf)?; with k. regards mit freundlichen Grüßen ‖ s Art f, Sorte f; all kinds of allerlei; another k. of ein anderer; any k. of irgendwelcher; every k. of jede Art von; in. k. (fig) auf gleiche Weise; k. of (coll) etwas; nothing of the k. nichts dergleichen; that k. of derartig; two (three) kinds of zweierlei (dreierlei); what k. of was für ein

kindergarten [′kɪndər͵gɑrtən] s Vorschule f, Vorschuljahr n

kind′-heart′ed adj gütmütig

kindle [′kɪndəl] tr anzünden; (fig) erwecken ‖ intr sich entzünden

kindling [′kɪndlɪŋ] s Entzündung f; (wood) Kleinholz n

kindly [′kaɪndli] adj gütig, freundlich ‖ adv freundlich; (please) bitte

kindness [′kaɪndnɪs] s Freundlichkeit f; (deed) Gefälligkeit f

kindred [′kɪndrəd] adj verwandtschaftlich; (fig) verwandt ‖ s Verwandtschaft f

kinescope [′kɪnɪ͵skop] s (trademark) Fernsehempfangsröhre f

kinetic [kɪ′netɪk] adj kinetisch ‖ kinetics s Kinetik f

king [kɪŋ] s König m; (cards, chess) König m; (checkers) Dame f

kingdom [′kɪŋdəm] s Königreich n; (of animals, etc.) Reich n; k. of heaven Himmelreich n

king′fish′er s Königsfischer m

kingly [′kɪŋli] adj königlich

king′pin′ s (coll) Boß m; (bowling) König m

king′ship′ s Königtum n

king′-size′ adj übergroß

kink [kɪŋk] s (in a wire) Knick m; (in the hair) Kräuselung f; (in a muscle) Muskelkrampf m; (flaw) Fehler m

kinky [′kɪŋki] adj gekräuselt

kin′ship′ s Verwandtschaft f

kins′man s (–men) Blutsverwandte m

kins′wom′an s (–wom′en) Blutsverwandte f

kipper [′kɪpər] s Räucherhering m ‖ tr einsalzen und räuchern

kiss [kɪs] s Kuß m ‖ tr & intr küssen

kisser [′kɪsər] s (sl) Fresse f

kit [kɪt] s (equipment) Ausrüstung f; (tool kit) Werkzeugkasten m; (for models) Modellsatz m; (e.g., for a convention) Mappe f; the whole kit and caboodle (things) der ganze Kram; (persons) die ganze Sippschaft

kitchen [′kɪt/ən] s Küche f

kitchenette [͵kɪt/ə′net] s Kochnische f

kit′chen knife′ s Küchenmesser n

kit′chen police′ s (mil) Küchendienst m

kit′chen range′ s Herd m, Kochherd m

kit′chen sink′ s Ausguß m
kit′chenware′ s Küchengeschirr n
kite [kaɪt] s Drachen m; (orn) Weih m; **fly a k.** e-n Drachen steigen lassen; **go fly a k.!** (coll) scher dich zum Kuckuck!
kith′ and kin′ [kɪθ] spl Freunde and Verwandte pl
kitten [′kɪtən] s Kätzchen n
kitty [′kɪti] s Kätzchen n; (cards) gemeinsame Kasse f; **Kitty** Käthchen n
kleptomaniac [ˌkleptə′meni̩ˌæk] s Kleptomane m, Kleptomanin f
knack [næk] s—have a k. for Talent haben für; **have the k. of it** den Griff heraus haben
knapsack [′næpˌsæk] s Rucksack m
knave [nev] s Schelm m; (cards) Bube m
knavery [′nevəri] s Schelmenstreich m
knead [nid] tr kneten
knead′ing trough′ s Teigmulde f
knee [ni] s Knie n; **bring s.o. to his knees** j-n auf die Knie zwingen; **go down on one's knees** niederknien; **on bended knees** kniefällig
knee′ bend′ s Kniebeuge f
knee′ breech′es spl Kniehose f
knee′cap′ s Kniescheibe f
knee′-deep′ adj knietief
knee′-high′ adj kniehoch
knee′ jerk′ s Patellarreflex m
kneel [nil] v (pret & pp **knelt** [nelt] & **kneeled**) intr knien
knee′-length′ adj kniefreit
knee′pad′ s (sport) Knieschützer m
knee′pan′ s Kniescheibe f
knee′ swell′ s (of organ) Knieschweller m
knell [nel] s Totengeläute n
knickers [′nɪkərz] spl Knickerbockerhosen pl
knicknack [′nɪkˌnæk] s Nippsache f
knife [naɪf] s (knives [naɪvz]) Messer n ‖ tr erstechen
knife′ sharp′ener s Messerschleifer m
knife′ switch′ s (elec) Messerschalter m
knight [naɪt] s Ritter m; (chess) Springer m ‖ tr zum Ritter schlagen
knight′hood′ s Ritterschaft f
knightly [′naɪtli] adj ritterlich
knit [nɪt] v (pret & pp **knitted** & **knit**; ger **knitting**) tr stricken; **k. one's brows** die Brauen runzeln ‖ intr stricken; (said of bones) zusammenheilen
knit′ goods′ spl Trikotwaren pl
knit′ted dress′ s Strickkleid n
knit′ting s (act) Strickerei f; (materials) Strickzeug n
knit′ting machine′ s Strickmaschine f
knit′ting nee′dle s Stricknadel f
knit′ting yarn′ s Strickgarn n
knit′wear′ s Strickwaren pl
knob [nab] s (of a door) Drücker m; (lump) Auswuchs m; (in wood) Knorren m; (of a radio) Knopf m
knock [nak] s (& aut) Klopfen n ‖ tr (criticize) tadeln; **k. a hole through** durchbrechen; **k. around** herumstoßen; (mistreat) unsanft behandeln;

k. down niederschlagen; (with a car) umfahren; (trees) umbrechen; (at auctions) zuschlagen; **k. it off!** (sl) hör mal auf!; **k. oneself out over** sich [dat] die Zähne ausbeißen an (dat); **k. one's head against the wall** mit dem Kopf gegen die Wand rennen; **k. out** ausschlagen; (exhaust) (coll) strapazieren; (a tank) abschießen; (box) k.o. schlagen; **k. over** umwerfen; **k. together** (build hurriedly) schnell zusammenhauen; **k. to the ground** zu Boden schlagen; **k. up a girl** (sl) e-m Mädchen ein Kind anhängen ‖ intr (an)klopfen; (aut) klopfen; **k. about** herumbummeln; **k. against** stoßen an (acc); **k. off** (from) (coll) aufhören (mit)
knock′down′ s (box) Niederschlag m
knocker [′nakər] s Türklopfer m; **knockers** (sl) Brüste pl
knock-kneed [′nakˌnid] adj x-beinig
knock′-knees′ spl X-beine pl
knock′out′ s (woman) (coll) Blitzmädel n; (box) Knockout m
knock′out drops′ spl Betäubungsmittel n
knock′-out punch′ s K.o.-Schlag m
knoll [nol] s Hügel m
knot [nat] s Knoten m; (in wood) Knorren m; (of people) Gruppe f; (naut) Knoten m; **tie a k.** e-n Knoten machen; **tie the k.** (coll) sich verheiraten ‖ tr e-n Knoten machen in (acc); (two ends) zusammenknoten
knot′hole′ s Astloch n
knotty [′nati] adj knorrig; (problem) knifflig
know [no] s—be in the k. Bescheid wissen ‖ v (pret **knew** [n(j)u]; pp **known**) tr (facts) wissen; (be familiar with) kennen; (a language) können; **come to k.** erfahren; **get to k.** kennenlernen; **known** bekannt; **k. one's way around** sich auskennen; **k. the ropes** (coll) Bescheid wissen; **k. what's what** (coll) den Rummel kennen ‖ intr wissen; **he ought to k. better** er sollte mehr Verstand haben; **k. about** wissen über (acc); **k. of** wissen von; **not that I k. of** (coll) nicht, daß ich wüßte; **you k.** (coll) wissen Sie
knowable [′no·əbəl] adj kenntlich
know′-how′ s Sachkenntnis f
know′ing adj (glance) vielsagend
knowingly [′no·ɪŋli] adv wissentlich; (intentionally) absichtlich
know′-it-all′ s Naseweis m
knowledge [′nalɪdʒ] s Wissen n, Kenntnisse pl; (information) (of) Kenntnis f (von); **basic k. of** Grundkenntnisse pl in (dat); **come to s.o.'s k.** j-m zur Kenntnis kommen; **to my k.** soweit (or soviel) ich weiß; **to the best of my k.** nach bestem Wissen; **without my k.** ohne mein Mitwissen; **working k. of** praktisch verwertbare Kenntnisse pl (genit)
knowledgeable [′nalɪdʒəbəl] adj kenntnisreich
known [non] adj bekannt; **become k.**

kundwerden; **k. all over town** stadt-
bekannt; **make k.** bekanntgeben
know′-noth′ing s Nichtswisser m
knuckle [ˈnʌkəl] s Knöchel m, Finger-
knöchel m; (mach) Gelenkstück n;
k. of ham Eisbein n ‖ intr—**k. down
to work** sich ernsthaft an die Arbeit
machen; **k. under** klein beigeben
k.o. [ˈkeˈo] s K.o. m ‖ tr k.o.-schlagen
Koran [koˈræn] s Koran m
Korea [koˈri·ə] s Korea n

Korean [koˈri·ən] adj koreanisch ‖ s
Koreaner –in mf; (language) Koreanisch n
kosher [ˈkoʃər] adj (& coll) koscher
kowtow [ˈkauˈtau] intr e–n Kotau
machen; **k. to** kriechen vor (dat)
K.P. [ˈkeˈpi] s (**kitchen police**) (mil)
Küchendienst m
Kremlin [ˈkrɛmlɪn] s Kreml m
kudos [ˈk(i)udɑs] s (coll) Ruhm m,
Renommee n

L

L, l [el] s zwölfter Buchstabe des englischen Alphabets
lab [læb] s (coll) Labor n
la·bel [ˈlebəl] s Etikett n; (brand)
Marke f; (fig) Bezeichnung f ‖ v
(pret & pp **-bel[l]ed**; ger **-bel[l]ing**)
tr etikettieren; (fig) bezeichnen
labial [ˈlebɪ·əl] adj Lippen– ‖ s Lip-
penlaut m, Labial n
labor [ˈlebər] adj Arbeits–, Arbeiter–
‖ s Arbeit f; (toil) Mühe f; **be in
l.** in den Wehen liegen ‖ tr (a point)
ausführlich eingehen auf (acc) ‖ intr
sich abmühen; (at) arbeiten an (dat);
(exert oneself) sich anstrengen; (said
of a ship) stampfen; **l. under** zu leiden haben unter (dat)
la′bor and man′agement spl Arbeitnehmer und Arbeitgeber pl
laboratory [ˈlæbərəˌtori] s Laborato-
rium n
lab′oratory techni′cian s Laborant –in
mf
la′bor camp′ s Zwangsarbeitslager n
la′bor con′tract s Tarifvertrag m
la′bor dis′pute s Arbeitsstreitigkeit f
la′bored adj (e.g., breathing) mühsam;
(style) gezwungen
laborer [ˈlebərər] s Arbeiter –in mf;
(unskilled) Hilfsarbeiter –in mf
la′bor force′ s Arbeitskräfte pl
laborious [ləˈbori·əs] adj mühsam,
schwierig
la′bor law′ s Arbeitsrecht n
la′bor lead′er s Arbeiterführer –in mf
la′bor mar′ket s Arbeitsmarkt m
la′bor move′ment s Arbeiterbewegung
f
la′bor pains′ spl Geburtswehen pl
la′bor-sav′ing adj arbeitssparend; **l.
device** Hilfsgerät n
la′bor short′age s Mangel m an Arbeits-
kräften
la′bor supply′ s Arbeitsangebot n
la′bor un′ion s Gewerkschaft f
laburnum [ləˈbʌrnəm] s Goldregen m
labyrinth [ˈlæbɪrɪnθ] s Labyrinth n
lace [les] adj (collar, dress) Spitzen–
‖ s Spitze f; (shoestring) Schnürsenkel m ‖ tr (e.g., shoes) schnüren;
(braid) flechten; (drinks) (coll) mit
e–m Schuß Branntwein versetzen;
(beat) (coll) prügeln; **l. up** zuschnü-
ren

lacerate [ˈlæsəˌret] tr zerfleischen
laceration [ˌlæsəˈreʃən] s Fleischwunde f
lace′ trim′ming s Spitzenbesatz m
lace′work′ s Spitzenarbeit f
lachrymose [ˈlækrɪˌmos] adj tränen-
reich
lac′ing s Schnürung f; (coll) Prügel pl
lack [læk] s (of) Mangel m (an dat);
for l. of aus Mangel an (dat); **l. of
space** Raummangel m; **l. of time**
Zeitmangel m ‖ tr—**I l.** es mangelt
mir an (dat) ‖ intr—**be lacking** fehlen; **he is lacking in courage** ihm
fehlt der Mut
lackadaisical [ˌlækəˈdezɪkəl] adj teilnahmslos, gleichgültig
lackey [ˈlæki] s Lakai m
lack′ing prep mangels (genit)
lack′lus′ter adj glanzlos
laconic [ləˈkɑnɪk] adj lakonisch
lacquer [ˈlækər] s Lack m ‖ tr lackieren
lac′quer ware′ s Lackwaren pl
lacrosse [ləˈkrɔs] s Lacrosse n
lacu·na [ləˈkjunə] s (**-nas** & **-nae** [ni])
Lücke f, Lakune f
lacy [ˈlesi] adj spitzenartig
lad [læd] s Bube m
la′dies′ man′ s Weiberheld m, Salonlöwe m
la′dies′ room′ s Damentoilette f
ladle [ˈledəl] s Schöpflöffel m ‖ tr
ausschöpfen
lady [ˈledi] s Dame f; **ladies and gentlemen** meine Damen und Herren!
la′dybird′, la′dybug′ s Marienkäfer m
f
la′dy compan′ion s Gesellschaftsdame
f
la′dyfin′ger s Löffelbiskuit m & n
la′dy-in-wait′ing s (**ladies-in-waiting**)
Hofdame f
la′dy-kil′ler s Schwerenöter m
la′dylike′ adj damenhaft
la′dylove′ s Geliebte f
la′dy of the house′ s Hausherrin f
la′dy′s maid′ s Zofe f
la′dy′s man′ s var of **ladies′ man**
lag [læg] s Zurückbleiben n; (aer)
Rücktrift f; (phys) Verzögerung f ‖
v (pret & pp **lagged**; ger **lagging**) intr
(**behind**) zurückbleiben (hinter dat)
la′ger beer′ [ˈlagər] s Lagerbier n
laggard [ˈlægərd] s Nachzügler m

lagoon [lə'gun] s Lagune f
laid' up' adj (with) bettlägerig (infolge von); **be l. in bed** auf der Nase liegen
lair [ler] s Höhle f, Lager n
laity ['le·ɪti] s Laien pl
lake [lek] s See m
Lake' Con'stance ['kɑnstəns] s der Bodensee
lamb [læm] s Lamm n; (culin) Lammfleisch n
lambaste [læm'best] tr (berate) (coll) herunterputzen; (beat) (coll) verdreschen
lamb' chop' s Hammelrippchen n
lambkin ['læmkɪn] s Lammfell n
lame [lem] adj (person, leg; excuse) lahm; **be l. in one leg** auf e–m Bein lahm sein || tr lähmen
lament [lə'ment] s Jammer m; (dirge) Klagelied n || tr beklagen || intr wehklagen
lamentable ['læməntəbəl] adj beklagenswert; (pej) jämmerlich
lamentation [,læmə'teʃən] s Wehklage f
laminate ['læmɪ,net] tr schichten
lamp [læmp] s Lampe f
lamp' chim'ney s Lampenzylinder m
lamp'light' s Lampenlicht n
lamp'light'er s Laternenanzünder m
lampoon [læm'pun] s Schmähschrift f || tr mit e–r Schmähschrift verspotten
lamp'post' s Laternenpfahl m
lamp'shade' s Lampenschirm m
lance [læns] s Lanze f; (surg) Lanzette f || tr (surg) aufstechen
lance' cor'poral s (Brit) Hauptgefreite m
lancet ['lænsɪt] s Lanzette f
land [lænd] s (dry land; country) Land n; (ground) Boden m; **by l.** zu Lande || tr (a plane, troops, punch) landen; (a ship, fish) an Land bringen; (a job) (coll) kriegen; **l. s.o. in trouble** j–n in Schwierigkeiten bringen || intr (aer, naut, & fig) landen; (said of a blow) treffen; **l. on s.o.'s head** j–m auf den Kopf fallen; **l. on water** auf dem Wasser aufsetzen
land' breeze' s Landwind m
land'ed prop'erty s Landbesitz m
land'fall' s (sighting of land) Sichten n von Land; **make l.** landen
land' forc'es spl Landstreitkräfte pl
land'ing s Landung f; (of a staircase) Absatz m; **l. on the moon** Mondlandung f
land'ing craft' s Landungsboot n
land'ing field' s Landeplatz m
land'ing force' s Landekorps n
land'ing gear' s Fahrgestell n
land'ing par'ty s Landeabteilung f
land'ing stage' s Landungssteg m
land'ing strip' s Start– und Landestreifen m
land'la'dy s (of an apartment) Hauswirtin f; (of an inn) Gastwirtin f
land'locked' adj landumschlossen
land'lord' s (of an apartment) Hauswirt m; (of an inn) Gastwirt m
landlubber ['lænd ,lʌbər] s Landratte f

land'mark' s Landmarke f; (cardinal event) Markstein m
land' of'fice s Grundbuchamt n
land'-office bus'iness s (fig) Bombengeschäft n
land'own'er s Grundbesitzer –in mf
landscape ['lænd ,skep] s Landschaft f; (paint) Landschaftsbild n || tr landschaftlich gestalten
land'scape ar'chitect s Landschaftsarchitekt –in mf
land'scape paint'er s Landschaftsmaler –in mf
land'slide' s Bergrutsch m; (pol) Stimmenrutsch m
landward ['lændwərd] adv landwärts
land' wind' [wɪnd] s Landwind m
lane [len] s Bahn f; (country road) Feldweg m; (aer) Flugschneise f; (aut) Fahrbahn f; (naut) Fahrtroute f; (sport) Laufbahn f; (sport) Schwimmbahn f
language ['læŋgwɪdʒ] s Sprache f
lan'guage instruc'tion s Sprachunterricht m
lan'guage teach'er s Sprachlehrer –in mf
languid ['læŋgwɪd] adj schlaff
languish ['læŋgwɪʃ] intr schmachten
languor ['læŋgər] s Mattigkeit f
languorous ['læŋgərəs] adj matt
lank [læŋk] adj schlank; (hair) glatt
lanky ['læŋki] adj schlaksig
lanolin ['lænəlɪn] s Lanolin n
lantern ['læntərn] s Laterne f
lan'tern slide' s Diapositiv n
lanyard ['lænjərd] s (around the neck) Halsschnur f; (naut) Taljereep n
Laos ['le·ɑs] s Laos n
Laotian [le'oʃən] adj laotisch || s Laote m, Laotin f; (language) Laotisch n
lap [læp] s (of the body or clothing) Schoß m; (of the waves) Plätschern n; (sport) Runde f || v (pret & pp lapped; ger lapping) tr schlappen; (sport) überrunden; **lap up** auf(sch)lecken || intr—**lap against** (e.g., a boat, shore) plätschern gegen; **lap over** hinausragen über (acc)
lap' dog' s Schoßhund m
lapel [lə'pel] s Aufschlag m
Lap'land' s Lappland n
Laplander ['læp ,lændər] s Lappländer –in mf
Lapp [læp] s Lappe m, Lappin f; (language) Lappisch n
lapse [læps] s (error) Versehen n; (of time) Ablauf m; **after a l. of** nach Ablauf von; **l. of duty** Pflichtversäumnis f; **l. of memory** Gedächtnislücke f || intr (said of a right, an insurance policy) verfallen; (said of time) ablaufen; **l. into** verfallen in (acc); **l. into unconsciousness** das Bewußtsein verlieren
lap'wing' s Kiebitz m
larceny ['lɑrsəni] s Diebstahl m
larch [lɑrtʃ] s (bot) Lärche f
lard [lɑrd] s Schmalz n || tr spicken
larder ['lɑrdər] s Speisekammer f
large [lɑrdʒ] adj groß; **at l.** (as a whole) gesamt; (at liberty) auf freiem

Fuß; (said of an official) zur besonderen Verfügung; **become larger** sich vergrößern; **on a l. scale** in großem Umfang

large′ intes′tine s Dickdarm m

largely ['lɑrdʒli] adv größtenteils

largeness ['lɑrdʒɪns] s Größe f

large′-scale′ adj Groß–; (map) in großem Maßstab; (production) Serien–

largesse ['lɑrdʒes] s (generosity) Freigebigkeit f; (handout) Geldverteilung f

lariat ['lærɪ-ət] s Lasso m & n; (for grazing animals) Halteseil n

lark [lɑrk] s (orn) Lerche f; **for a l.** zum Spaß

lark′spur′ s (bot) Rittersporn m

lar·va ['lɑrvə] s (–vae [vi]) Larve f

laryngitis [,lærɪn'dʒaɪtɪs] s Kehlkopfentzündung f, Laryngitis f

larynx ['lærɪŋks] s (larynxes & larynges [lə'rɪndʒiz]) Kehlkopf m

lascivious [lə'sɪvɪ-əs] adj wollüstig

lasciviousness [lə'sɪvɪ-əsnɪs] s Wollüstigkeit f

laser ['lezər] s Laser m

lash [læʃ] s Peitsche f; (as a punishment) Peitschenhieb m; (of the eye) Wimper f || tr (whip) peitschen; (bind) (to) anbinden (an acc); (said of rain, storms) peitschen || intr— **l. out** (at) ausschlagen (nach)

lass [læs] s Mädel n

lassitude ['læsɪ,t(j)ud] s Mattigkeit f

last [læst] adj letzte; **very l.** allerletzte || adv zuletzt; **l. of all** zuallerletzt || s Leiste mfn; (of a cobbler) Schuhleisten m; **at l.** schließlich; **at long l.** zu guter Letzt; **look one's l.** on zum letzten Mal blicken auf (acc); **see the l. of s.o.** j–n nicht mehr wiedersehen; **to the l.** bis zum Letzten || intr (remain unchanged) anhalten; (for a specific time) dauern; (said of money, supplies) reichen; (said of a person) aushalten

last′ing adj dauerhaft, andauernd; **l. effect** Dauerwirkung f; **l. for months** monatelang

Last′ Judg′ment s Jüngstes Gericht n

lastly ['læstli] adv zuletzt

last′-min′ute adj in letzter Minute

last′-minute news′ s neueste Nachrichten pl

last′ night′ adv gestern abend

last′ quar′ter s (astr) abnehmendes Mondviertel n; (com) letztes Quartal n

last′ resort′ s letztes Mittel n

last′ sleep′ s Todesschlaf m

last′ straw′ s—that's the l. das schlägt dem Faß den Boden aus

Last′ Sup′per, the s das Letzte Abendmahl

last′ week′ adv vorige Woche

last′ will′ and test′ament s letztwillige Verfügung f

last′ word′ s letztes Wort n; **the l.** (fig) der letzte Schrei

latch [lætʃ] s Klinke f || tr zuklinken || intr einschnappen; **l. on to** (coll) spitzkriegen

latch′key′ s Hausschlüssel m

late [let] adj (after the usual time) spät; (at a late hour) zu später Stunde; (deceased) verstorben; **be l.** sich verspäten; (said of a train) Verspätung haben; **keep l. hours** spät aufbleiben || adv spät; **come l.** zu spät kommen; **of l.** kürzlich; **see you later** (coll) bis später!

latecomer ['let ,kʌmər] s Nachzügler m

lateen′ sail′ [læ'tin] s Lateinsegel n

lateen′ yard′ s Lateinrah f

lately ['letli] adv neulich, unlängst

lateness ['letnɪs] s Verspätung f

latent ['letənt] adj latent, verborgen

later ['letər] adj später || adv später, nachher; **l. on** späterhin

lateral ['lætərəl] adj seitlich, Seiten–

lath [læθ] s Latte f || tr belatten

lathe [leð] s Drehbank f; **turn on a l.** drechseln

lather ['læðər] s Seifenschaum m; (of a horse) schäumender Schweiß m || tr einseifen || intr schäumen

lathing ['læθɪŋ] s Lattenwerk n

Latin ['lætɪn] adj lateinisch || s (Romance-speaking person) Romane m, Romanin f; (language) Lateinisch n

La′tin Amer′ica s Lateinamerika n

La′tin-Amer′ican adj lateinamerikanisch || s Lateinamerikaner –in mf

latitude ['lætɪ ,t(j)ud] s Breite f; (fig) Spielraum m

latrine [lə'trin] s Latrine f

latter ['lætər] adj (later) später; (final) End–; (recent) letzte; **in the l. part of** (e.g., the year) in der zweiten Hälfte (genit); **the l.** dieser

lat′ter-day′ adj (later) später; (recent) letzte

Lat′ter-day Saint′ s Heilige mf der Jüngsten Tage

lattice ['lætɪs] s Gitter n || tr vergittern

lat′ticework′ s Gitterwerk n

Latvia ['lætvɪ-ə] s Lettland n

Latvian ['lætvɪ-ən] adj lettisch || s Lette m, Lettin f; (language) Lettisch n

laud [lɔd] tr loben, preisen

laudable ['lɔdəbəl] adj löblich

laudanum ['lɔd(ə)nəm] s Opiumtinktur f

laudatory ['lɔdə ,tɔri] adj Lob-

laugh [læf] s Lachen n, Gelächter n; **for laughs** zum Spaß; **have a good l.** sich auslachen || tr—**l. off** sich lachend hinwegsetzen über (acc) || intr lachen; **it's easy for you to l.** Sie haben leicht lachen; **l. about** lachen über (acc); **l. at** (deride) auslachen; (find amusement in) lachen über (acc)

laughable ['læfəbəl] adj lächerlich

laugh′ing adj lachend; **it's no l. matter** es ist nichts zum Lachen

laugh′ing gas′ s Lachgas n

laugh′ingstock′ s Gespött n

laughter ['læftər] s Gelächter n, Lachen n; **roar with l.** vor Lachen brüllen

launch [lɔntʃ] s (open boat) Barkasse

f ‖ *tr* (*a boat*) aussetzen; (*a ship*) vom Stapel laufen lassen; (*a plane*) katapultieren; (*a rocket*) starten; (*a torpedo*) abschießen; (*an offensive*) beginnen; **be launched** (naut) vom Stapel laufen; (rok) starten ‖ *intr—* **l. into** sich stürzen in (*acc*)

launch'ing *s* (*of a ship*) Stapellauf *m*; (*of a torpedo*) Ausstoß *m*; (*of a rocket*) Abschuß *m*, Start *m*

launch' pad' *s* (rok) Startrampe *f*

launder ['lɔndər] *tr* waschen

laundress ['lɔndrɪs] *s* Wäscherin *f*

laundry ['lɔndrɪ] *s* (*clothes*) Wäsche *f*; (*room*) Waschküche *f*; (*business*) Wäscherei *f*

laun'drybag' *s* Wäschebeutel *m*

laun'drybas'ket *s* Wäschekorb *m*

laun'dry list' *s* Waschzettel *m*

laun'dry-man' *s* (**-men'**) Wäscher *m*

laun'dry-wom'an *s* (**-wom'en**) Wäscherin *f*

laurel ['lɔrəl] *s* Lorbeer *m*

lau'rel tree' *s* Lorbeerbaum *m*

lava ['lɑvə] *s* Lava *f*

lavatory ['lævə‚torɪ] *s* Waschraum *m*; (*toilet*) Toilette *f*

lavender ['lævəndər] *adj* lavendelfarben ‖ *s* (bot) Lavendel *m*

lavish ['lævɪʃ] *adj* (*person*) verschwenderisch; (*dinner*) üppig ‖ *tr—***l.** care on hegen und pflegen; **l. s.th. on s.o.** j-n mit etw überhäufen

lavishness ['lævɪʃnɪs] *s* Üppigkeit *f*

law [lɔ] *s* Gesetz *n*; (*system*) Recht *n*; (*as a science*) Rechtswissenschaft *f*; (relig) Gebot *n*; **according to law** dem Recht entsprechend; **act within the law** sich ans Gesetz halten; **against the law** gesetzwidrig; **become law** Gesetzkraft erlangen; **by law** gesetzlich; **go against the law** gegen das Gesetz handeln; **lay down the law** gebieterisch auftreten; **practice law** den Anwaltsberuf ausüben; **study law** Jura studieren; **take the law into one's own hands** sich [*dat*] selbst sein Recht verschaffen; **under the law** nach dem Gesetz

law'-abid'ing *adj* friedlich

law' and or'der *s* Ruhe und Ordnung *pl*

law'-and-or'der *adj* für Ruhe und Ordnung

law'break'er *s* Rechtsbrecher –in *mf*

law'break'ing *s* Rechtsbruch *m*

law'court' *s* Gerichtshof *m*, Gericht *n*

lawful ['lɔfəl] *adj* gesetzmäßig

lawless ['lɔlɪs] *adj* gesetzlos

lawlessness ['lɔlɪsnɪs] *s* Gesetzlosigkeit *f*

law'mak'er *s* Gesetzgeber *m*

lawn [lɔn] *s* Rasen *m*; (tex) Batist *m*

lawn' mow'er *s* Rasenmäher *m*

lawn' par'ty *s* Gartenfest *n*

lawn' sprin'kler *s* Rasensprenger *m*

law' of dimin'ishing returns' *s* Gesetz *n* der abnehmenden Erträge

law' of'fice *s* Anwaltsbüro *n*

law' of na'tions *s* Völkerrecht *n*

law' of na'ture *s* Naturgesetz *n*

law' of probabil'ity *s* Wahrscheinlichkeitsgesetz *n*

law' of supply' and demand' *s* Gesetz *n* von Angebot und Nachfrage

law' of the land' *s* Landesgesetz *n*

law' school' *s* juristische Fakultät *f*

law' stu'dent *s* Student –in *mf* der Rechtswissenschaft

law'suit' *s* Klage *f*, Prozeß *m*

lawyer ['lɔjər] *s* Advokat –in *m*, Anwalt –in *mf*

lax [læks] *adj* lax, nachlässig

laxative ['læksətɪv] *s* Abführmittel *n*

laxity ['læksɪtɪ] *s* Laxheit *f*

lay [le] *adj* (*not of the clergy*) Laien–, weltlich; (*non-expert*) laienhaft ‖ *s* (*poem*) Lied *n* ‖ *v* (*pret & pp* laid [led]) *tr* legen; (*eggs*; *foundation*, *bricks*, *lineoleum*) legen; (*cables*, *pipes*, *tracks*) verlegen; (*vulg*) umlegen; **be laid up with** das Bett hüten müssen wegen (*genit*); **I'll lay you two to one** ich wette mit dir zwei zu eins; **lay aside** beiseite legen; (*save*) sparen; **lay bare** bloßlegen; **lay down** niederlegen; (*principles*) aufstellen; **lay claim to** Anspruch erheben auf (*acc*); **lay it on thick** dick auftragen; **lay low** (*said of an illness*) bettlägerig machen; **lay off** (*workers*) vorübergehend entlassen; **lay open** freilegen; **lay out** auslegen; (*a garden*) anlegen; (*money*) aufwenden; (*a corpse*) aufbahren; (surv) abstecken; **lay siege to** belagern; **lay waste** verwüsten ‖ *intr* (*said of hens*) legen; **lay for** auflauern (*dat*); **lay into** (*beat*) (coll) verdreschen; (*scold*) (coll) heruntermachen; **lay off** (*abstain from*) sich enthalten (*genit*); (*let alone*) in Ruhe lassen; **lay over** (*on a trip*) sich aufhalten; **lay to** (naut) stilliegen

lay' broth'er *s* Laienbruder *m*

layer ['le‚ər] *s* Schicht *f*; (bot) Ableger *m*; **in layers** schichtenweise; **l. of fat** Fettschicht *f*; **thin l.** Hauch *m*

lay'er cake' *s* Schichttorte *f*

layette [le'et] *s* Babyausstattung *f*

lay' fig'ure *s* Gliederpuppe *f*

lay'man *s* (**-men**) Laie *m*; **layman's** laienhaft

lay'off' *s* vorübergehende Entlassung *f*

lay' of the land' *s* Gestaltung *f* des Terrains; (fig) Gesichtspunkt *m* der Angelegenheit

lay'out' *s* Anlage *f*, Anordnung *f*; (typ) Layout *n*; **l. of rooms** Raumverteilung *f*

laziness ['lezɪnɪs] *s* Faulheit *f*

lazy ['lezɪ] *adj* faul

la'zybones' *s* (coll) Faulpelz *m*

la'zy Su'san *s* drehbares Tablett *n*

lea [li] *s* (poet) Aue *f*

lead [led] *adj* Blei– ‖ *s* Blei *n*; (*in a pencil*) Mine *f*; (*plumb line*) Bleilot *n* ‖ *v* (*pret & pp* leaded; *ger* leading) *tr* verbleien; (typ) durchschießen ‖ [lid] *s* Führung *f*; (cards) Vorhand *f*; (elec) Zuführung *f*; (sport) Vorsprung *m*; (theat) Hauptrolle *f*; **be in the l.** an der Spitze stehen; **have the l.** die Führung haben; **take the l.** die Führung übernehmen ‖ *v* (*pret & pp*

led [led]) *tr* führen, leiten; *(to error, drinking, etc.)* verleiten; *(a parade)* anführen; *(a life)* führen; **l. astray** verführen; **l. away** wegführen; *(e.g., a criminal)* abführen; **l. back** zurückführen; **l. by the nose** an der Nase herumführen; **l. on** weiterführen; *(deceive)* täuschen; **l. the way** vorangehen || *intr* führen; *(cards)* anspielen; **l. nowhere** zu nichts führen; **l. off** den Anfang machen; **l. to** hinausgehen auf *(acc)*; **l. up to** hinauswollen auf *(acc)* **where will all this l. to?** wo soll das alles hinführen?

leaden ['ledən] *adj* bleiern; *(in color)* bleifarbig; *(sluggish)* schwerfällig; **l. sky** bleierner Himmel *m*

leader ['lidər] *s* Führer –in *mf*; *(of a band)* Dirigent –in *mf*; *(of a film)* Vorspann *m*; *(lead article)* Leitartikel *m*

lead'ership *s* Führung *f*

leading ['lidɪŋ] *adj* *(person, position, power)* führend

lead'ing ide'a *s* Leitgedanke *m*

lead'ing la'dy *s* Hauptdarstellerin *f*

lead'ing man' *s* Hauptdarsteller *m*

leading' ques'tion *s* Suggestivfrage *f*

lead'ing role' *s* Hauptrolle *f*

lead'-in wire' *s* Zuleitungsdraht *m*

lead' pen'cil [led] *s* Bleistift *m*

lead' pipe' [led] *s* Bleirohr *n*

lead' poi'soning [led] *s* Bleivergiftung *f*

leaf [lif] *s* (**leaves** [livz]) Blatt *n*; *(of a folding door)* Flügel *m*; *(of a folding table)* Tischklappe *f*; *(insertable table board)* Einlegebrett *n*; **turn over a new l.** ein neues Leben anfangen || *intr*—**l. through** durchblättern

leafage ['lifɪdʒ] *s* Laubwerk *n*

leafless ['liflɪs] *adj* blattlos

leaflet ['liflɪt] *s* Werbeprospekt *m*, Flugblatt *n*; *(bot)* Blättchen *n*

leafy ['lifi] *adj* *(abounding in leaves)* belaubt; *(e.g., vegetables)* Blatt-

league [lig] *s* Bund *m*; *(unit of distance)* Meile *f*; *(sport)* Liga *f*; **in l. with** verbündet mit || *tr* verbünden || *intr* sich verbünden

League' of Na'tions *s* Völkerbund *m*

leak [lik] *s* Leck *n*; **spring a l.** ein Leck bekommen; **take a l.** (vulg) schiffen || *tr* *(e.g., a story to the press)* durchsickern lassen || *intr* *(said of a container)* leck sein; *(said of a boat)* lecken; *(said of a fluid)* auslaufen; *(said of a spigot)* tropfen; **l. out** (& fig) durchsickern

leakage ['likɪdʒ] *s* Lecken *n*; (& fig) Durchsickern *n*; (com) Schwund *m*; (elec) Streuung *f*

leaky ['liki] *adj* leck

lean [lin] *adj* mager || *v* (*pret & pp* **leaned** & **leant** [lent]) *tr* (*against*) lehnen (an *acc* or gegen) || *intr* lehnen; **l. against** sich anlehnen an *(acc)*; **l. back** sich zurücklehnen; **l. forward** sich vorbeugen; **l. on** sich stützen auf *(acc)*; **l. over** *(e.g., a railing)* sich neigen über *(acc)*; **l. toward** (fig) neigen zu

lean'ing *adj* sich neigend; *(tower)* schief || *s* (*toward*) Neigung *f* (zu)

leanness ['linnɪs] *s* Magerkeit *f*

lean'-to' *s* (**-tos**) Anbau *m* mit Pultdach

lean' years' *spl* magere Jahre *pl*

leap [lip] *s* Sprung *m*, Satz *m*; **by leaps and bounds** sprungweise; **l. in the dark** (fig) Sprung *m* ins Ungewisse || *v* (*pret & pp* **leaped** & **leapt** [lept]) *tr* überspringen || *intr* springen; **l. at** anspringen; **l. at an opportunity** e-e Gelegenheit beim Schopf ergreifen; **l. forward** vorspringen; **l. up** emporschnellen

leap'frog' *s* Bocksprung *m*; **play l.** Bocksprünge machen

leap' year' *s* Schaltjahr *n*

learn [lʌrn] *v* (*pret & pp* **learned** & **learnt** [lʌrnt]) *tr* lernen; *(find out)* erfahren; **l. s.th. from s.o.**

learned ['lʌrnɪd] *adj* *(person, word)* gelehrt; *(for or of scholars)* Gelehrten-

learn'ed jour'nal *s* Gelehrtenzeitschrift *f*

learn'ed soci'ety *s* Gelehrtenvereinigung *f*

learn'ed world' *s* Gelehrtenwelt *f*

learn'ing *s* *(act)* Lernen *n*; *(erudition)* Gelehrsamkeit *f*

lease [lis] *s* Mietvertrag *m*; *(of land)* Pachtvertrag *m* || *tr* *(in the role of landlord)* vermieten; *(land)* verpachten; *(in the role of tenant)* mieten; *(land)* pachten

lease'hold' *adj* Pacht– || *s* Pachtbesitz *m*

leash [liʃ] *s* Leine *f*, Hundeleine *f*; **keep on the l.** an der Leine führen; **strain at the l.** (fig) an der Leine zerren || *tr* an die Leine nehmen

leas'ing *s* Miete *f*; *(of land)* Pachtung *f*; **l. out** Vermietung *f*; *(of land)* Verpachtung *f*

least [list] *adj* mindeste, wenigste || *adv* am wenigsten; **l. of all** am wenigsten von allen || *s* Geringste *mfn*; **at l.** mindestens, wenigstens; **at the very l.** zum mindesten; **not in the l.** nicht im mindeste

leather ['lɛðər] *adj* ledern || *s* Leder *n*

leath'er bind'ing *s* Ledereinband *m*

leath'erbound' *adj* ledergebunden

leath'erneck' *s* (sl) Marineinfanterist *m*

leathery ['lɛðəri] *adj* *(e.g., steak)* (coll) lederartig

leave [liv] *s* *(permission)* Erlaubnis *f*; (mil) Urlaub *m*; **on l.** auf Urlaub; **take l.** (*from*) Abschied nehmen (von); **take l. of one's senses** (coll) den Verstand verlieren || *v* (*pret & pp* **left** [lɛft]) *tr* *(go away from)* verlassen; *(undone, open, etc.)* lassen; *(a message, bequest)* hinterlassen; *(a job)* aufgeben; *(a scar)* zurücklassen; *(forget)* liegenlassen, stehenlassen; *(e.g., some food for s.o.)* übriglassen; **be left** übrig sein; **l. alone** *(a thing)* bleibenlassen; *(a person)* in Frieden lassen; **l. behind** *(said of a deceased person)* hinterlassen; *(forget)* liegenlassen; **l. home** von zu Hause fortgehen; **l. it at that!** überlaß es mir!; **l. lying about** herumliegen lassen; **l. nothing to chance** nichts dem Zufall überlassen; **l. nothing undone** nichts unversucht lassen; **l. open** offen lassen; **l. out** auslassen; **l. standing** stehenlassen; **l.** *(e.g., work)* **undone** liegenlassen ‖ *intr* fortgehen; *(on travels)* abreisen; *(said of vehicles)* abfahren; *(aer)* abfliegen; **l. off** *(e.g., from reading)* aufhören

leaven ['levən] *s* Treibmittel *n* ‖ *tr* säuern

leav'ening *s* Treibstoff *m*

leave' of ab'sence *s* Urlaub *m*

leave'-tak'ing *s* Abschiednehmen *n*

leavings ['livɪŋz] *spl* Überbleibsel *pl*

Leba·nese [,lebə'niz] *adj* libanesisch ‖ *s* **(-nese)** Libanese *m*, Libanesin *f*

Lebanon ['lebənən] *s* Libanon *m*

lecher ['letʃər] *s* Lüstling *m*

lecherous ['letʃərəs] *adj* wollüstig

lechery ['letʃəri] *s* Wollust *f*

lectern ['lektərn] *s* Lesepult *n*

lector ['lektər] *s* *(eccl)* Lektor *m*

lecture ['lektʃər] *s* Vorlesung *f*, Vortrag *m*; *(coll)* Standpauke *f*; **give a l. on** e-n Vortrag halten über *(acc)*; **give s.o. a l.** j-m den Text lesen ‖ *tr* *(coll)* abkanzeln ‖ *intr* lesen

lecturer ['lektʃərər] *s* Vortragende *mf*; *(at a university)* Dozent –in *mf*

lec'ture room' *s* Hörsaal *m*

ledge [ledʒ] *s* Sims *m* & *n*; *(of a cliff)* Felsenriff *n*

ledger ['ledʒər] *s* *(acct)* Hauptbuch *n*

lee [li] *s* Lee *f*

leech [litʃ] *s* Blutegel *m*; *(fig)* Blutsauger –in *mf*

leek [lik] *s* *(bot)* Porree *m*, Lauch *m*

leer [lɪr] *s* lüsterner Seitenblick *m* ‖ *intr* *(at)* lüstern schielen *(nach)*

leery ['lɪri] *adj* mißtrauisch; **be l. of** mißtrauen *(dat)*

lees [liz] *spl* Hefe *f*

lee' side' *s* Leeseite *f*

leeward ['liwərd] *adv* leewärts ‖ *s* Leeseite *f*

Lee'ward Is'lands *spl* Inseln *pl* unter dem Winde

lee'way' *s* *(coll)* Spielraum *m*; *(aer, naut)* Abtrift *f*

left [left] *adj* linke; *(left over)* übrig ‖ *adv* links; **l. face!** *(mil)* links um! ‖ *s* *(left hand)* Linke *f*; **on our l.** zu unserer Linken; **the l.** *(pol)* die Linke; **the third street to the l.** die dritte Querstraße, die **l.** nach links; **to the l. of** links von

left' field' *s* *(baseball)* linkes Außenfeld *n*

left' field'er ['fildər] *s* Spieler *m* im linken Außenfeld

left'-hand driver' *s* Linkssteuerung *f*

left'-hand'ed *adj* linkshändig; *(compliment)* fragwürdig; *(counterclockwise)* linksgängig; *(clumsy)* linkisch

left-hander ['left'hændər] *s* Linkshänder –in *mf*

leftish ['leftɪʃ] *adj* linksgerichtet

leftist ['leftɪst] *s* Linksradikaler *m*; *(pol)* Linkspolitiker –in *mf*

left'o'ver *adj* übriggeblieben ‖ **leftovers** *spl* Überbleibsel *pl*

left'-wing' *adj* Links-

left' wing' *s* *(pol)* linker Flügel *m*; *(sport)* Linksaußen *m*

left-winger ['left'wɪŋər] *s* *(coll)* Linkspolitiker –in *mf*

lefty ['lefti] *adj* *(coll)* linkshändig ‖ *s* *(coll)* Linkshänder –in *mf*

leg [leg] *s* *(of a body, of furniture, of trousers)* Bein *n*; *(stretch)* Etappe *f*; *(of a compass)* Schenkel *m*; *(of a boot)* Schaft *m*; **be on one's last legs** auf dem letzten Loche pfeifen; **pull s.o.'s leg** *(coll)* j-n auf die Schippe nehmen; **run one's legs off** sich abrennen; **you don't have a leg to stand on** Sie haben keinerlei Beweise

legacy ['legəsi] *s* Vermächtnis *n*

legal ['ligəl] *adj* *(according to the law)* gesetzlich, legal; *(pertaining to or approved by law)* Rechts-, juristisch; **take l. action** den Rechtweg beschreiten; **take l. steps against s.o.** gerichtlich gegen j-n vorgehen

le'gal advice' *s* Rechtsberatung *f*

le'gal advis'er *s* Rechtsberater –in *mf*

le'gal age' *s* Volljährigkeit *f*; **of l.** großjährig

le'gal aid' *s* Rechtshilfe *f*

le'gal ba'sis *s* Rechtsgrundlage *f*

le'gal case' *s* Rechtsfall *m*

le'gal claim' *s* Rechtsanspruch *m*

le'gal en'tity *s* juristische Person *f*

le'gal force' *s* Rechtskraft *f*

le'gal grounds' *spl* Rechtsgrund *m*

le'gal hol'iday *s* gesetzlicher Feiertag *m*

legality [lɪ'gælɪti] *s* Gesetzlichkeit *f*, Rechtlichkeit *f*

legalize ['ligə,laɪz] *tr* legalisieren

le'gal jar'gon *s* Kanzleisprache *f*

le'gal profes'sion *s* Rechtsanwaltsberuf *m*

le'gal rem'edy *s* Rechtsmittel *n*

le'gal ten'der *s* gesetzliches Zahlungsmittel *n*; **be l.** gelten

le'gal ti'tle *s* Rechtsanspruch *m*

legate ['legɪt] *s* Legat –in *mf*

legatee [,legə'ti] *s* Legatar –in *mf*

legation [lɪ'geʃən] *s* Gesandtschaft *f*

legend ['ledʒənd] *s* Legende *f*

legendary ['ledʒən,deri] *adj* legendär

legerdemain [,ledʒərdɪ'men] *s* Taschenspielerei *f*

leggings ['legɪnz] *spl* hohe Gamaschen *pl*

leggy ['legi] *adj* langbeinig

Leg'horn' *s* *(chicken)* Leghorn *n*; *(town in Italy)* Livorno *n*

legibility [,ledʒɪ'bɪlɪti] *s* Lesbarkeit *f*

legible ['ledʒɪbəl] *adj* lesbar

legion ['lidʒən] *s* Legion *f*; *(fig)* Heerschar *f*

legionnaire [,lidʒə'ner] *s* Legionär *m*

legislate ['ledʒɪs,let] *tr* durch Gesetzgebung bewirken ‖ *intr* Gesetze geben

legislation [,ledʒɪs'leʃən] *s* Gesetzgebung *f*

legislative [ˈlɛdʒɪs ˌletɪv] *adj* gesetzgebend

legislator [ˈlɛdʒɪs ˌletər] *s* Gesetzgeber –in *mf*

legislature [ˈlɛdʒɪs ˌletʃər] *s* Legislatur *f*

legitimacy [lɪˈdʒɪtɪməsi] *s* Rechtmäßigkeit *f*

legitimate [lɪˈdʒɪtɪmɪt] *adj* gesetzmäßig, legitim; (*child*) ehelich || [lɪˈdʒɪtɪ ˌmet] *tr* legitimieren

legit′imate the′ater *s* literarisch wertvolles Theater *n*

legitimize [lɪˈdʒɪtɪ ˌmaɪz] *tr* legitimieren

leg′ of lamb′ *s* Lammkeule *f*

leg′ of mut′ton *s* Hammelkeule *f*

leg′ room′ *s* Beinfreiheit *f*

leg′work′ *s* Vorarbeiten *pl*

leisure [ˈliʒər] *s* Muße *f*; **at l.** mit Muße; **at s.o.'s l.** wenn es j–m paßt

lei′sure class′ *s* wohlhabende Klasse *f*

lei′sure hours′ *spl* Mußestunden *pl*

leisurely [ˈliʒərli] *adj & adv* gemächlich

lei′sure time′ *s* Freizeit *f*

lemon [ˈlɛmən] *adj* Zitronen– || *s* Zitrone *f*; (sl) Niete *f*

lemonade [ˌlɛmɪˈned] *s* Zitronenlimonade *f*

lem′on squeez′er *s* Zitronenpresse *f*

lend [lɛnd] *v* (*pret & pp* **lent** [lɛnt]) *tr* leihen, borgen; **l. at five percent interest** zu fünf Prozent Zinsen anlegen; **l. itself to** sich eignen zu or für; **l. oneself to** sich hergeben zu; **l. out** ausleihen, verborgen; **l. s.o. a hand** j–m zur Hand gehen

lender [ˈlɛndər] *s* Verleiher –in *mf*

lend′ing li′brary *s* Leihbücherei *f*

length [lɛŋθ] *s* Länge *f*; (*of time*) Dauer *f*; (*in horse racing*) Pferdelänge *f*; **at great l.** sehr ausführlich; **at l.** ausführlich; (*finally*) schließlich; **at some l.** ziemlich ausführlich; **go to any l.** alles Erdenkliche tun; **go to great lengths** sich sehr bemühen; **keep s.o. at arm′s l.** zu j–m Abstand wahren; **stretch out full l.** sich der Länge nach ausstrecken

lengthen [ˈlɛŋθən] *tr* verlängern; (*a vowel*) dehnen

length′ening *s* Verlängerung *f*; (ling) Dehnung *f*

length′wise′ *adj & adv* der Länge nach

lengthy [ˈlɛŋθi] *adj* langwierig

leniency [ˈlinɪ-ənsi] *s* Milde *f*

lens [lɛnz] *s* Linse *f*; (*combination of lenses*) Objektiv *n*

Lent [lɛnt] *s* Fastenzeit *f*

Lenten [ˈlɛntən] *adj* Fasten–

lentil [ˈlɛntɪl] *s* (bot) Linse *f*

leopard [ˈlɛpərd] *s* Leopard *m*

leper [ˈlɛpər] *s* Aussätzige *mf*

leprosy [ˈlɛprəsi] *s* Aussatz *m*, Lepra *f*

lesbian [ˈlɛzbɪ-ən] *adj* lesbisch || *s* Lesbierin *f*

lesbianism [ˈlɛzbɪ-ə ˌnɪzəm] *s* lesbische Liebe *f*

lesion [ˈliʒən] *s* Wunde *f*

less [lɛs] *comp adj* weniger, geringer;

l. and l. immer weniger || *adv* weniger, minder; **l. than** weniger als || *s—do with l.* mit weniger auskommen; **for l.** billiger; **in l. than no time** in Null Komma nichts || *prep* abzüglich (*genit* or *acc*); (arith) weniger (*acc*), minus (*acc*)

lessee [lɛˈsi] *s* Mieter –in *mf*; (*of land*) Pächter –in *mf*

lessen [ˈlɛsən] *tr* vermindern || *intr* sich vermindern, abnehmen

lesser [ˈlɛsər] *comp adj* minder, geringer

lesson [ˈlɛsən] *s* Unterrichtsstunde *f*, Stunde *f*; (*in a textbook*) Lektion *f*; (*warning*) Lehre *f*; **learn a l. from** e–e Lehre ziehen aus; **let that be l. to you!** lassen Sie sich das e–e Lehre sein

lessor [ˈlɛsər] *s* Vermieter –in *mf*; (*of land*) Verpächter –in *mf*

lest [lɛst] *conj* damit nicht; (*after expressions of fear*) daß

let [lɛt] *v* (*pret & pp* **let**; *ger* **letting**) *tr* lassen; **I really let him have it!** (coll) ich hab's ihm ordentlich gegeben!; **let alone** in Ruhe lassen; (*not to mention*) geschweige denn; **let down** herunterlassen; (*disappoint*) enttäuschen; **let drop** fallen lassen; **let fly** fliegen lassen; (coll) loslassen; **let go** fortlassen, loslassen; **let go ahead** vorlassen; **let in** hereinlassen; (*water*) zuleiten; **let in on** (*e.g., a secret*) einweihen in (*acc*); **let it go,** e.g., **I'll let it go this time** diesmal werde ich es noch hingehen lassen; **let lie** liegenlassen; **let know** wissen lassen, Bescheid geben (*dat*); **let off** (*e.g., at the next corner*) absetzen; **let off easy** noch so davonkommen lassen; **let off scot-free** straflos laufen lassen; **let one's hair down** (fig) sich gehenlassen; **let out** (*seams, air, water*) auslassen; (*e.g., a yell*) von sich geben; **let pass** durchlassen; **let s.o. have s.th.** j–m etw zukommen lassen; **let stand** (fig) gelten lassen; **let through** durchlassen; **let things slide** die Dinge laufen lassen; **let things take their course** den Dingen ihren Lauf lassen; **let's go!** los!; **let us** (or **let's**) (*inf*), e.g., **let's** (or **let us**) **sing** singen wir || *intr* (*be rented out*) für; vermietet werden (für); **let fly with** (coll) loslegen mit; **let go of** loslassen; **let on that** sich [dat] anmerken lassen, daß; **let up** nachlassen; **let up on** (coll) ablassen von

let′down′ *s* Hereinfall *m*

lethal [ˈliθəl] *adj* tödlich

lethargic [lɪˈθɑrdʒɪk] *adj* lethargisch

lethargy [ˈlɛθərdʒi] *s* Lethargie *f*

letter [ˈlɛtər] *s* Brief *m*, Schreiben *n*; (*of the alphabet*) Buchstabe *m*; **by l.** brieflich, schriftlich; **to the l.** aufs Wort || *tr* beschriften

let′ter box′ *s* Briefkasten *m*

let′ter car′rier *s* Briefträger –in *mf*

let′ter drop′ *s* Briefeinwurf *m*

let′tered *adj* gelehrt

let′ter file′ *s* Briefordner *m*

let'terhead' s Briefkopf m
let'tering s (act) Beschriften n; (inscription) Beschriftung f
let'ter of condol'ence s Beileidsbrief m
let'ter of cred'it s Kreditbrief m
let'ter of recommenda'tion s Empfehlungsbrief m
letter o'pener s Brieföffner m
let'terper'fect adj buchstabengetreu
let'terpress' s (typ) Hochdruck m
let'ter scales' spl Briefwaage f
let'ter to the ed'itor s Leserbrief m
lettuce ['lɛtɪs] s Salat m
let'up' s Nachlassen n; **without l.** ohne Unterlaß
leukemia [lu'kimɪ·ə] s Leukämie f
Levant [lɪ'vænt] s Levante f
Levantine [lɪ'væntɪn] adj levantinisch || s Levantiner –in mf
levee ['lɛvi] s Uferdamm m
lev·el ['lɛvəl] adj eben, gerade; (flat) flach; (spoonful) gestrichen; **be l. with** so hoch sein wie; (fig) **do one's l. best** sein Möglichstes tun; **have a l. head** ausgeglichen sein; **keep a l. head** e–n klaren Kopf behalten || s (& fig) Niveau n; (tool) Wasserwaage f; **at higher levels** höheren Ortes; **be up to the usual l.** (fig) auf der gewöhnlichen Höhe sein; **on a l. with** (& fig) auf gleicher Höhe mit; **on the l.** (fig) ehrlich || v (pret & pp –el[l]ed; ger –el[l]ing tr (a street, ground) planieren; **l.** (e.g., a rifle) **at** richten auf (acc); (e.g., complaints) richten gegen; **l. off** nivellieren; (aer) abfangen; **l. to the ground** dem Erdboden gleichmachen || intr—**l. off** sich verflachen; (said of prices) sich stabilisieren; (aer) in Horizontalflug übergehen; **l. with s.o.** mit j–m offen sein
lev'elhead'ed adj besonnen, vernünftig
lever ['lɪvər] s Hebel m, Brechstange f || tr mit e–r Brechstange fortbewegen
leverage ['lɪvərɪdʒ] s Hebelkraft f; (fig) Einfluß m
leviathan [lɪ'vaɪ·əθən] s Leviathan m
levitate ['lɛvɪ‚tet] tr schweben lassen || intr frei schweben
levitation [‚lɛvɪ'teʃən] s Schweben n
levity ['lɛvɪti] s Leichtsinn m
lev·y ['lɛvi] s Truppenaushebung f; (of taxes) Erhebung f; (tax) Steuer f || v (pret & pp –vied) tr (troops) ausheben; (taxes) erheben; **l. war on** Krieg führen gegen
lewd [lud] adj unzüchtig
lewdness ['ludnɪs] s Unzucht f
lexical ['lɛksɪkəl] adj lexikalisch
lexicographer [‚lɛksɪ'kagrəfər] s Lexikograph –in mf
lexicographic(al) [‚lɛksɪkə'græfɪk(əl)] adj lexikographisch
lexicography [‚lɛksɪ'kagrəfi] s Lexikographie f
lexicology [‚lɛksɪ'kalədʒi] s Wortforschung f, Lexikologie f
lexicon ['lɛksɪkən] s Wörterbuch n
liability [‚laɪ·ə'bɪlɪti] s (ins) Haftpflicht f; (jur) Haftung f; **liabilities** Schulden pl; (acct) Passiva pl

liabil'ity insur'ance s Haftpflichtversicherung f
liable ['laɪ·əbəl] adj (jur) (for) haftbar (für); **be l. to** (inf) (coll) leicht können (inf); **l. for damages** schadenersatzpflichtig
liaison [li'ɛzən] s Verbindung f; (illicit affair) Liaison f; (ling) Bindung f
liai'son of'ficer s Verbindungsoffizier m
liar ['laɪ·ər] s Lügner –in mf
libation [laɪ'beʃən] s Opfertrank m
li·bel ['laɪbəl] s Verleumdung f; (in writing) Schmähschrift f || v (pret & pp –bel[l]ed; ger –bel[l]ing) tr verleumden
libelous ['laɪbələs] adj verleumderisch
li'bel suit' s Verleumdungsklage f
liberal ['lɪbərəl] adj (views) liberal, freisinnig; (with money) freigebig; (gift) großzügig; (interpretation) weitherzig; (education) allgemeinbildend; (pol) liberal || s Liberale mf
lib'eral arts' spl Geisteswissenschaften pl
liberalism ['lɪbərə‚lɪzəm] s Liberalismus m
liberality [‚lɪbə'rælɪti] s Freigebigkeit f, Großzügigkeit f
liberate ['lɪbə‚ret] tr befreien; (chem) freimachen
liberation [‚lɪbə'reʃən] s Befreiung f; (chem) Freimachen n
liberator ['lɪbə‚retər] s Befreier –in mf
libertine ['lɪbər‚tin] s Wüstling m
liberty ['lɪbərti] s Freiheit f; **take liberties** sich [dat] Freiheiten herausnehmen; **you are at l. to** (inf) es steht Ihnen frei zu (inf)
libidinous [lɪ'bɪdɪnəs] adj wollüstig
libido [lɪ'bido] s Libido f
librarian [laɪ'brɛrɪ·ən] s Bibliothekar –in mf
library ['laɪ‚brɛri] s Bibliothek f
li'brary card' s Benutzerkarte f
libret·to [lɪ'brɛto] s (–tos) Operntext m, Libretto n
Libya ['lɪbɪ·ə] s Libyen n
Libyan ['lɪbɪ·ən] adj libysch || s Libyer –in mf
license ['laɪsəns] s Lizenz f, Genehmigung f; (document) Zulassungsschein m; (for a business, restaurant) Konzession f; (to drive) Führerschein m; (excessive liberty) Zügellosigkeit f || tr konzessionieren; (aut) zulassen
li'cense num'ber s (aut) Kennzeichen n
li'cense plate' or tag' s Nummernschild n
licentious [laɪ'sɛnʃəs] adj unzüchtig
lichen ['laɪkən] s (bot) Flechte f
lick [lɪk] s Lecken n || tr lecken; (thrash) (coll) wichsen; (defeat) (coll) schlagen; (said of a flame) züngeln an (dat); **l. clean** auslecken; **l. into shape** auf Hochglanz bringen; **l. off** ablecken; **l. one's chops** sich [dat] die Lippen lecken; **l. s.o.'s boots** vor j–m kriechen; **l. up** auflecken
lick'ing s Prügel pl; **give s.o. a good l.** j–n versohlen

licorice [ˈlɪkərɪs] s Lakritze f
lid [lɪd] s Deckel m
lie [laɪ] s Lüge f; **give the lie to s.o.**
(or **s.th.**) j-n (or etw) Lügen strafen;
tell a lie lügen ‖ v (pret & pp **lied**;
ger **lying**) tr—**lie one's way out of**
sich herauslügen aus ‖ intr lügen;
lie like mad das Blaue vom Himmel
herunter lügen; **lie to** belügen ‖ v
(pret **lay** [le]; pp **lain** [len]; ger
lying) intr liegen; **lie down** sich hin-
legen; **lie down!** (to a dog) leg dich!;
lie in wait auf der Lauer liegen; **lie
in wait for** auflauern (dat); **lie low**
sich versteckt halten; (bide one's
time) abwarten; **take s.th. lying down**
etw widerspruchslos hinnehmen
lie′ detec′tor s Lügendetektor m
lien [lin] s Pfandrecht n
lieu [lu] s—**in l. of** statt (genit)
lieutenant [luˈtɛnənt] s Leutnant m;
(nav) Kapitänleutnant m
lieuten′ant colo′nel s Oberstleutnant m
lieuten′ant comman′der s Korvetten-
kapitän m
lieuten′ant gen′eral s Generalleutnant
m
lieuten′ant gov′ernor s Vizegouverneur
m
lieuten′ant jun′ior grade′ s (nav) Oberleutnant m zur See
lieuten′ant sen′ior grade′ s (nav) Kapitänleutnant m
life [laɪf] adj (imprisonment) lebenslänglich ‖ s (lives [laɪvz]) Leben n;
(e.g., of a car) Lebensdauer f; **all
my l.** mein ganzes Leben lang; **as big
as l.** in voller Lebensgröße; **bring
back to l.** wieder zum Bewußtsein
bringen; **bring to l.** ins Leben bringen; **for dear l.** ums liebe Leben;
for l. auf Lebenszeit; **full of l.** voller
Leben; **I can't for the l.** of me ich
kann beim besten Willen nicht; **lives
lost** Menschenleben pl; **not on your
l.** auf keinen Fall; **put l. into** beleben; **such is l.!** so ist nun mal das
Leben; **take one's l.** sich [dat] das
Leben nehmen; **upon my l!** so wahr
ich lebe!; **you can bet your l.** on
that! darauf kannst du Gift nehmen!
life′-and-death′ adj auf Leben und Tod
life′ annu′ity s Lebensrente f
life′ belt′ s Schwimmgürtel m
life′blood′ s Lebensblut n
life′boat′ s Rettungsboot n
life′ buoy′ s Rettungsboje f
life′ expect′ancy s Lebenserwartung f
life′ guard′ s (at a pool) Bademeister
–in mf; (at the shore) Strandwärter
–in mf
life′ impris′onment s lebenslängliche
Haft f
life′ insur′ance s Lebensversicherung f
life′ jack′et s Schwimmweste f
lifeless [ˈlaɪflɪs] adj leblos, (fig)
schwunglos
life′-like′ adj naturgetreu, lebensecht
life′ line′ s Rettungsleine f; (for a
diver) Signalleine f; (supply line)
Lebensader f
life′long′ adj lebenslänglich

life′ mem′ber s Mitglied n auf Lebenszeit
life′ of lei′sure s Wohlleben n
life′ of plea′sure s Wohlleben n
life′ of Ri′ley [ˈraɪli] s Herrenleben n
life′ of the par′ty s—**be the l.** die ganze
Gesellschaft unterhalten
life′ preserv′er [prɪ ˌzʌrvər] s Rettungs-
ring m
lifer [ˈlaɪfər] s (sl) Lebenslängliche mf
life′ raft′ s Rettungsfloß n
lifesaver [ˈlaɪf ˌsevər] s Rettungs-
schwimmer –in mf; (fig) rettender
Engel m
life′ sen′tence s Verurteilung f zu le-
benslänglicher Haft
life′-size(d)′ adj lebensgroß
life′ span′ s Lebensdauer f
life′ style′ s Lebensweise f
life′time′ adj lebenslänglich ‖ s Leben
n; **for a l.** auf Lebenszeit; **once in a
l.** einmal im Leben
life′ vest′ s Schwimmweste f
life′work′ s Lebenswerk n
lift [lɪft] s (elevator) Aufzug m; (aer
& fig) Auftrieb m; **give s.o. a l.** j-n
im Wagen mitnehmen ‖ tr heben;
(gently) lüpfen; (with effort) wuchten; (weights) stemmen; (the receiver) abnehmen; (an embargo) aufheben; (steal) (sl) klauen; **l. up** aufheben; (the eyes) erheben; **not l. a
finger** keinen Finger rühren ‖ intr
(said of a mist) steigen; **l. off** (rok)
starten
lift′-off′ s (rok) Start m
lift′ truck′ s Lastkraftwagen m mit
Hebevorrichtung
ligament [ˈlɪgəmənt] s Band n
ligature [ˈlɪgətʃər] s (mus) Bindung f;
(act) (surg) Abbinden n; (filament)
(surg) Abbindungsschnur f; (typ)
Ligatur f
light [laɪt] adj (clothing, meal, music,
heart, wine, sleep, punishment,
weight) leicht; (day, beer, color,
complexion, hair) hell; **as l. as day**
tageshell; **l. as a feather** federleicht;
make l. of auf die leichte Schulter
nehmen; (belittle) als bedeutungslos
hinstellen ‖ s Licht n; **according to
his lights** nach dem Maß seiner Einsicht; **bring to l.** ans Licht bringen;
come to l. ans Licht kommen; **do
you have a l.?** haben Sie Feuer?;
in the l. of im Lichte (genit), angesichts (genit); **put in a false l.** in
falsches Licht stellen; **see the l. of
day** (be born) das Licht der Welt
erblicken; **shed l. on** Licht werfen
auf (acc); **throw quite a different l.
on** ein ganz anderes Licht werfen
auf (acc) ‖ v (pret & pp **lighted** &
lit [lɪt]) tr (a fire, cigarette) anzünden; (an oven) anheizen; (a
street) beleuchten; (a hall) erleuchten; (a face) aufleuchten lassen ‖
intr sich entzünden; **l. up** (said of a
face) aufleuchten; (light a cigarette)
sich [dat] e-e Zigarette anstecken
light′-blue′ adj lichtblau, hellblau
light′ bulb′ s Glühbirne f

light-complexioned [ˈlaɪtkəmˈplɛkʃənd] *adj* von heller Hautfarbe

lighten [ˈlaɪtən] *tr* (*in weight*) leichter machen; (*brighten*) erhellen; (fig) erleichtern || *intr* (*become brighter*) sich aufhellen; (*during a storm*) blitzen

lighter [ˈlaɪtər] *s* Feuerzeug *n*; (naut) Leichter *m*

ligh′ter flu′id *s* Feuerzeugbenzin *n*

light′-fin′gered *adj* geschickt; (*thievish*) langfingerig

light′-foot′ed *adj* leichtfüßig

light′-head′ed *adj* leichtsinnig; (*dizzy*) schwindlig

light′-heart′ed *adj* leichtherzig

light′-heav′y-weight′ *adj* (box) Halbschwergewichts– || *s* Halbschwergewichtler *m*

light′house′ *s* Leuchtturm *m*

light′ing *s* Beleuchtung *f*

light′ing effects′ *spl* Lichteffekte *pl*

light′ing fix′ture *s* Beleuchtungskörper *m*

lightly [ˈlaɪtli] *adv* leicht; (*without due consideration*) leichthin; (*disparagingly*) geringschätzig

light′ me′ter *s* Lichtmesser *m*

lightness [ˈlaɪtnɪs] *s* (*in weight*) Leichtigkeit *f*; (*in shade*) Helligkeit *f*

lightning [ˈlaɪtnɪŋ] *s* Blitz *m* || *impers* —it is l. es blitzt

light′ning arrest′er [əˌrɛstər] *s* Blitzableiter *m*

light′ning bug′ *s* Leuchtkäfer *m*

light′ning rod′ *s* Blitzableiter *m*

light′ning speed′ *s* Windeseile *f*

light′ op′era *s* Operette *f*

light′ read′ing *s* Unterhaltungslektüre *f*

light′ship′ *s* Leuchtschiff *n*

light′ sleep′ *s* Dämmerschlaf *m*

light′ switch′ *s* Lichtschalter *m*

light′ wave′ *s* Lichtwelle *f*

light′weight′ *adj* (box) Leichtgewichts– || *s* (*coll*) geistig Minderbemittelter *m*; (box) Leichtgewichtler *m*

light′-year′ *s* Lichtjahr *n*

likable [ˈlaɪkəbəl] *adj* sympathisch, lieb

like [laɪk] *adj* gleich, ähnlich; **be l.** gleichen (*dat*) || *adv*—l. **crazy** (coll) wie verrückt || *s*—**and the l.** und dergleichen; **likes and dislikes** Neigungen und Abneigungen *pl* || *tr* gern haben, mögen; **I l. him** er ist mir sympathisch; **I l. the picture** das Bild gefällt mir; **I l. the food** das Essen schmeckt mir; **l. to** (*inf*), e.g., **I l. to read** ich lese gern || *intr*—**as you l.** wie Sie wollen; **if you l.** wenn Sie wollen || *prep* wie; **feel l.** (*ger*) Lust haben zu (*inf*); **feel l. hell** (sl) sich elend fühlen; **it looks l.** es sieht nach … aus; **l. greased lightning** wie geschmiert; **that′s just l. him** das sieht ihm ähnlich; **there′s nothing l. traveling** es geht nichts übers Reisen

likelihood [ˈlaɪklɪˌhʊd] *s* Wahrscheinlichkeit *f*

likely [ˈlaɪkli] *adj* wahrscheinlich; **a l. story!** (iron) e–e glaubhafte Geschichte!; **it′s l. to rain** es wird wahrscheinlich regen

like′-mind′ed *adj* gleichgesinnt

liken [ˈlaɪkən] *tr* (**to**) vergleichen (mit)

likeness [ˈlaɪknɪs] *s* Ähnlichkeit *f*; **a good l. of** ein gutes Portrait (*genit*)

like′wise′ *adv* gleichfalls, ebenso

lik′ing *s* (**for**) Zuneigung *f* (*zu*); **not to my l.** nicht nach meinem Geschmack; **take a l. to** Zuneigung fassen zu

lilac [ˈlaɪlək] *adj* lila || *s* Flieder *m*

lilt [lɪlt] *s* rhythmischer Schwung *m*; (*lilting song*) lustiges Lied *n*

lily [ˈlɪli] *s* Lilie *f*

lil′y of the val′ley *s* Maiglöckchen *n*

lil′y pad′ *s* schwimmendes Seerosenblatt *n*

lil′y-white′ *adj* lilienweiß

li′ma bean′ [ˈlaɪmə] *s* Limabohne *f*

limb [lɪm] *s* Glied *n*; (*of a tree*) Ast *m*; **go out on a l.** (fig) sich exponieren; **limbs** Gliedmaßen *pl*

limber [ˈlɪmbər] *adj* geschmeidig || *tr* —**l. up** geschmeidig machen || *intr*— sich geschmeidig machen

lim-bo [ˈlɪmbo] *s* (**–bos**) Vorhölle *f*; (fig) Vergessenheit *f*

lime [laɪm] *s* Kalk *m*; (bot) Limonelle *f*

lime′kiln′ *s* Kalkofen *m*

lime′light′ *s* (& fig) Rampenlicht *n*

limerick [ˈlɪmərɪk] *s* Limerick *m*

lime′stone′ *adj* Kalkstein– || *s* Kalkstein *m*

limit [ˈlɪmɪt] *s* Grenze *f*; **go the l.** zum Äußersten gehen; **off limits** Zutritt verboten; **set a l. to** e-e Grenze ziehen (*dat*); **that′s the l.!** das ist denn doch die Höhe!; **there′s a l. to everything** alles hat seine Grenzen; **within limits** in Grenzen; **without l.** schrankenlos || *tr* begrenzen; (**to**) beschränken (auf *acc*)

limitation [ˌlɪmɪˈteʃən] *s* Begrenzung *f*, Beschränkung *f*

lim′ited *adj* (**to**) beschränkt (*auf* acc)

lim′ited-ac′cess high′way *s* Autobahn *f*

lim′ited mon′archy *s* konstitutionelle Monarchie *f*

limitless [ˈlɪmɪtlɪs] *adj* grenzenlos

limousine [ˈlɪməˌzin], [ˌlɪməˈzin] *s* Limousine *f*

limp [lɪmp] *adj* (& fig) schlaff || *s* Hinken *n*; **walk with a l.** hinken || *intr* (& fig) hinken

limpid [ˈlɪmpɪd] *adj* durchsichtig

linchpin [ˈlɪntʃˌpɪn] *s* Achsnagel *m*

linden [ˈlɪndən] *s* Linde *f*, Lindenbaum *m*

line [laɪn] *s* Linie *f*, Strich *m*; (*boundary*) Grenze *f*; (*of a page*) Zeile *f*; (*of verse*) Verszeile *f*; (*of a family*) Zweig *m*; (*sphere of activity*) Fach *n*; (*e.g., of a streetcar*) Linie *f*, Strecke *f*; (*wrinkle*) Furche *f*; (*of articles for sale*) Sortiment *n*; (*for wash*) Leine *f*; (*queue*) Schlange *f*; (sl) zungenfertiges Gerede *n*; (angl) Schnur *f*; (mil) Linie *f*, Front *f*; (telp) Leitung *f*; **all along the l.** (fig) auf der ganzen Linie; **along the lines**

of nach dem Muster von; **draw the l.
(at)** (fig) e–e Grenze ziehen (bei);
fall into l. sich einfügen; **forget one's
lines** (theat) steckenbleiben; **form a
l.** sich in e–r Reihe aufstellen; **get a
l. on** (coll) herausklamüsern; **give
s.o. a l.** (sl) j–m schöne Worte machen; **hold the l.** die Stellung halten;
(telp) am Apparat bleiben; **in l. of
duty** im Dienst; **in l. with** in Übereinstimmung mit; **keep in l.** in der
Reihe bleiben; **keep s.o. in l.** j–n im
Zaum halten; **stand in l.** Schlange
stehen; **the l. is busy** (telp) Leitung
besetzt! || tr linieren; (e.g., a coat)
füttern; (a face) furchen; (a drawer)
ausschlagen; (a wall) verkleiden; **l.
one's purse** sich [dat] den Beutel
spicken; **l. the streets** in den Straßen
Spalier bilden; **l. up** ausrichten; (mil)
aufstellen || intr—**l. up** Schlange ste-
hen; (mil) antreten; **l. up for** sich
anstellen nach

lineage ['lɪnɪ-ɪdʒ] s Abkunft f, Abstammung f

lineal ['lɪnɪ-əl] adj (descent) direkt;
(linear) geradlinig

lineaments ['lɪnɪ-əmənts] spl Gesichts-
züge pl

linear ['lɪnɪ-ər] adj (arranged in a line)
geradlinig; (involving a single dimension) Längen–; (using lines) Linien–;
(math) linear

lined' pa'per s Linienpapier n
line'man s (–men) (rr) Streckenwärter
m; (telp) Telephonarbeiter m
linen ['lɪnən] adj Leinen– || s Leinen
n; (in the household) Wäsche f; (of
the bed) Bettwäsche f; linens Weiß-
zeug n; **put fresh l. on the bed** das
Bett überziehen

lin'en clos'et s Wäscheschrank m
lin'en cloth' s Leinwand f
lin'en goods' spl Weißwaren pl
line' of approach' s (aer) Anflug-
schneise f
line' of bus'iness s Geschäftszweig m
line' of communica'tion s Verbindungs-
linie f
line' of fire' s Schußlinie f
line' of sight' s (of a gun) Visierlinie
f; (astr) Sichtlinie f
liner ['laɪnər] s Einsatz m; (naut)
Linienschiff n
lines'man s (–men) (sport) Linienrich-
ter m
line'up' s (at a police station) Gegen-
überstellung f; (sport) Aufstellung f
linger ['lɪŋɡər] intr (tarry) verweilen;
(said of memories) nachwirken; (said
of a melody) nachtönen; **l. over** verweilen bei
lingerie [,læⁿʒə'ri] s Damenunter-
wäsche f
lin'gering adj (disease) schleichend;
(tune) nachklingend; (memory, taste,
feeling) nachwirkend
lingo ['lɪŋɡo] s Kauderwelsch n
linguist ['lɪŋɡwɪst] s Sprachwissen-
schaftler –in mf
linguistic [lɪŋ'ɡwɪstɪk] adj (e.g., skill)
sprachlich; (of linguistics) sprach-

wissenschaftlich || **linguistics** s
Sprachwissenschaft f
liniment ['lɪnɪmənt] s Einreibemittel n
lin'ing s (of a coat) Futter n; (of a
brake) Bremsbelag m; (e.g., of a
wall) Verkleidung f
link [lɪŋk] s Glied n; (fig) Bindeglied
n || tr verbinden; (fig) verketten; **l.
to** verbinden mit; (fig) in Verbindung
bringen mit || intr—**l. up** (rok) dok-
ken; **l. up with** sich anschließen an
(acc)
linnet ['lɪnɪt] s (orn) Hänfling m
linoleum [lɪ'nolɪ-əm] s Linoleum n
linotype ['laɪnə,taɪp] s (trademark)
Linotype f
lin'seed oil' ['lɪn,sid] s Leinöl n
lint [lɪnt] s Fussel f
lintel ['lɪntəl] s Sturz m
lion ['laɪ-ən] s Löwe m
li'on cage' s Löwenzwinger m
lioness ['laɪ-ənɪs] s Löwin f
lionize ['laɪ-ə,naɪz] tr zum Helden des
Tages machen
li'ons' den' s Löwengrube f
li'on's share' s Löwenanteil m
li'on tam'er s Löwenbändiger –in mf
lip [lɪp] s Lippe f; (edge) Rand m; **bite
one's lips** sich auf die Lippen beißen;
smack one's lips sich [dat] die Lippen lecken
lip' read'ing s Lippenlesen n
lip' serv'ice s Lippenbekenntnis n; **pay
l. to** ein Lippenbekenntnis ablegen zu
lip'stick' s Lippenstift m
lique·fy ['lɪkwɪ,faɪ] v (pret & pp
–fied) tr verflüssigen || intr sich ver-
flüssigen
liqueur [lɪ'kɜr] s Likör m
liquid ['lɪkwɪd] adj flüssig; (clear)
klar || s Flüssigkeit f
liq'uid as'sets spl flüssige Mittel pl
liquidate ['lɪkwɪ,det] tr (a debt) tilgen; (an account) abrechnen; (a company) liquidieren
liquidation [,lɪkwɪ'deʃən] s (of a debt)
Tilgung f; (of an account) Abrechnung f; (of a company) Liquidation f
liquidity [lɪ'kwɪdɪti] s flüssiger Zustand m; (fin) Liquidität f
liq'uid meas'ure s Hohlmaß m
liquor ['lɪkər] s Spirituosen pl, Schnaps
m; **have a shot of l.** einen zwitschern
liquorice ['lɪkərɪs] s Lakritze f
li'quor li'cense s Schankerlaubnis f
Lisbon ['lɪzbən] s Lissabon n
lisp [lɪsp] s Lispeln n || tr & intr lis-
peln
lissome ['lɪsəm] adj biegsam, gelenkig
list [lɪst] s Liste f, Verzeichnis n; (naut)
Schlagseite f **enter the lists** (& fig)
in die Schranken treten; **make a l. of**
verzeichnen || tr verzeichnen || intr
(naut) Schlagseite haben
listen ['lɪsən] intr horchen, zuhören;
l. closely die Ohren aufsperren; **l.
for** achten auf (acc); **l. in** mithören;
l. to zuhören (dat); (a thing) horchen
auf (acc); (obey) gehorchen (dat);
(take advice from) hören auf (acc);
l. to reason auf e–n Rat hören; **l. to
the radio** Radio hören

listener ['lɪsənər] *s* Zuhörer –in *mf;* (rad) Rundfunkhörer –in *mf*

lis'tening post *s* Abhör-, Horch-

lis'tening post' *s* Horchposten *m*

listless ['lɪstlɪs] *adj* lustlos

list' price' *s* Listenpreis *m*

litany ['lɪtəni] *s* (& fig) Litanei *f*

liter ['litər] *s* Liter *m & n*

literacy ['lɪtərəsi] *s* Kenntnis *f* des Lesens und Schreibens

literal ['lɪtərəl] *adj* buchstäblich; (*person*) pedantisch; **l. sense** wörtlicher Sinn *m*

literally ['lɪtərəli] *adv* buchstäblich

literary ['lɪtə‚reri] *adj* literarisch; **l. language** Literatursprache *f*; **l. reference** Schrifttumsangabe *f*

literate ['lɪtərɪt] *adj* des Lesens und des Schreibens kundig; (*educated*) gebildet ‖ *s* Gebildete *mf*

literati [‚lɪtə'rati] *spl* Literaten *pl*

literature ['lɪtərətʃər] *s* Literatur *f;* (com) Drucksachen *pl*

lithe [laɪð] *adj* gelenkig

lithia ['lɪθɪə] *s* (chem) Lithiumoxyd *n*

lithium ['lɪθɪəm] *s* Lithium *n*

lithograph ['lɪθə‚græf] *s* Steindruck *m* ‖ *tr* lithographieren

lithographer [lɪ'θagrəfər] *s* Lithograph –in *mf*

lithography [lɪ'θagrəfi] *s* Steindruck *m*, Lithographie *f*

Lithuania [‚lɪθu'enɪ‚ə] *s* Litauen *f*

Lithuanian [‚lɪθu'enɪ‚ən] *adj* litauisch ‖ *s* Litauer –in *mf;* (*language*) Litauisch *n*

litigant ['lɪtɪgənt] *adj* prozessierend; **the l. parties** die streitenden Parteien ‖ *s* Prozeßführer –in *mf*

litigate ['lɪtɪ‚get] *tr* prozessieren gegen ‖ *intr* prozessieren

litigation [‚lɪtɪ'geʃən] *s* Rechtsstreit *m*

lit'mus pa'per ['lɪtməs] *s* Lackmuspapier *n*

litter ['lɪtər] *s* (*stretcher*) Tragbahre *f;* (*bedding for animals*) Streu *f;* (*of pigs, dogs*) Wurf *m;* (*trash*) herumliegender Abfall *m;* (hist) Sänfte *f* ‖ *tr* verunreinigen ‖ *intr* (*bear young*) werfen; (*strew litter*) Abfälle wegwerfen; **no littering!** das Wegwerfen von Abfällen ist verboten!

lit'terbug' *s*—**don't be a l.** wirf keine Abfälle weg

little ['lɪtəl] *adj* (*in size*) klein; (*in amount*) wenig ‖ *adv* wenig; **l. by l.** nach und nach ‖ *s*—**after a l.** nach kurzer Zeit; **l.** ein wenig, ein bißchen; **make l. of** wenig halten von

Lit'tle Bear' *s* Kleiner Bär *m*

Lit'tle Dip'per *s* Kleiner Wagen *m*, Kleiner Bär *m*

lit'tle fin'ger *s* kleiner Finger *m*

lit'tle peo'ple *s* kleine Leute *pl;* (myth) Heinzelmännchen *pl*

Lit'tle Red Rid'inghood' *s* Rotkäppchen *n*

lit'tle slam' *s* (cards) Klein-Schlemm *m*

liturgic(al) [lɪ'tʌrdʒɪk(əl)] *adj* liturgisch

liturgy ['lɪtərdʒi] *s* Liturgie *f*

livable ['lɪvəbəl] *adj* (*place*) wohnlich; (*life*) erträglich

live [laɪv] *adj* lebendig; (*coals*) glühend; (*ammunition*) scharf; (elec) stromführend; (rad, telv) live; **l. program** Originalsendung *f* ‖ *adv* (rad, telv) live ‖ [lɪv] *tr* leben; (*a life*) führen; **l. down** durch einwandfreien Lebenswandel vergessen machen; **l. it up** (coll) das Leben genießen; **l. out** (*survive*) überleben ‖ *intr* leben; (*reside*) wohnen; (*reside temporarily*) sich aufhalten; **l. and learn!** man lernt nie aus!; **l. for the moment** in den Tag hineinleben; **l. high off the hog** in Saus und Braus leben; **l. off s.o.** j–m auf der Tasche liegen; **l. on** (*subsist on*) sich nähren von; (*continue to live*) fortleben; **l. through** durchmachen; **l. to see** erleben; **l. up to** gerecht werden (*dat*)

livelihood ['laɪvlɪ‚hud] *s* Lebensunterhalt *m*

liveliness ['laɪvlɪnɪs] *s* Lebhaftigkeit *f*

livelong ['lɪv‚lɔŋ] *adj*—**all the l. day** den lieben langen Tag

lively ['laɪvli] *adj* lebhaft; (*street*) belebt

liven ['laɪvən] *tr* aufmuntern ‖ *intr* munter werden

liver ['lɪvər] *s* (anat) Leber *f*

liverwurst ['lɪvər‚wurst] *s* Leberwurst *f*

livery ['lɪvəri] *s* Livree *f*

liv'ery sta'ble *s* Mietstallung *f*

live' show' [laɪv] *s* Originalsendung *f*, Livesendung *f*

livestock ['laɪv‚stak] *s* Viehstand *m*

live' wire' [laɪv] *s* geladener Draht *m;* (coll) energiegeladener Mensch *m*

livid ['lɪvɪd] *adj* bleifarben; (*enraged*) wütend

living ['lɪvɪŋ] *adj* (*alive*) lebend, lebendig; (*for living*) Wohn–; **not a l. soul** keine Mutterseele ‖ *s* Unterhalt *n; good* **l.** Wohlleben *n;* **make a l.** (as) sein Auskommen haben (als); **what do you do for a l.?** wie verdienen Sie Ihren Lebensunterhalt?

liv'ing accommoda'tions *spl* Unterkunft *f*

liv'ing be'ing *s* Lebewesen *n*

liv'ing condi'tions *spl* Lebensbedingungen *pl*

liv'ing expens'es *spl* Unterhaltskosten *pl*

liv'ing quar'ters *spl* Unterkunft *f*

liv'ing room' *s* Wohnzimmer *n*

liv'ing-room set' (or *suite'*) *s* Polstergarnitur *f*

liv'ing space' *s* Lebensraum *m*

liv'ing wage' *s* Existenzminimum *n*

lizard ['lɪzərd] *s* Eidechse *f*

load [lod] *s* Last *f*, Belastung *f;* (*in a truck*) Fuhre *f;* **get a l. of that!** schau dir das mal an!; **have a l. on** (sl) einen sitzen haben; **loads of** (coll) Mengen von; **that's a l. off my mind** mir ist dabei ein Stein vom Herzen gefallen ‖ *tr* (*a truck, gun*) laden; (*cargo on a ship*) laden; (*with work*) überladen; (*with worries*) belasten; **l. down** belasten; **l. the cam-**

era den Film einlegen; **l. up** aufladen || *intr* das Gewehr laden

load'ed *adj* (*rifle*) scharf geladen; (*dice*) falsch; (*question*) verfänglich; (*very rich*) (sl) steinreich; (*drunk*) (sl) sternhagelvoll; **fully l.** (aut) mit allen Schikanen

loader [ˈlodər] *s* (*worker*) Ladearbeiter –in *mf*; (*device*) Verladevorrichtung *f*

load'ing *s* Ladung *f*, Verladung *f*

load'ing plat'form *s* Ladebühne *f*

load'ing ramp' *s* Laderampe *f*

load' lim'it *s* Tragfähigkeit *f*; (elec) Belastungsgrenze *f*

load'stone' *s* Magneteisenstein *m*

loaf [lof] *s* (**loaves** [lovz]) Laib *m* || *intr* faulenzen; **l. around** herumlungern

loafer [ˈlofər] *s* Faulenzer *m*

loaf'ing *s* Faulenzen *n*

loam [lom] *s* Lehm *m*

loamy [ˈlomi] *adj* lehmig

loan [lon] *s* Anleihe *f*, Darlehe(n) *n* || *tr* (ver)leihen, borgen; **l. out** leihen

loan' com'pany *s* Leihanstalt *f*

loan' shark' *s* (coll) Wucherer *m*

loan' word' *s* Lehnwort *n*

loath [loθ] *adj*—**be l. to** (*inf*) abgeneigt sein zu (*inf*)

loathe [loð] *tr* verabscheuen

loathing [ˈloðɪŋ] *s* (**for**) Abscheu *m* (vor *dat*)

loathsome [ˈloðsəm] *adj* abscheulich

lob [lɑb] *s* (tennis) Lobball *m* || *v* (*pret* & *pp* **lobbed**; *ger* **lobbing**) *tr* lobben, hochschlagen

lob·by [ˈlɑbi] *s* (*of a hotel or theater*) Vorhalle *f*, Foyer *n*; (pol) Interessengruppe *f* || *v* (*pret* & *pp* **–bied**) *intr* antichambrieren

lob'bying *s* Beeinflussung *f* von Abgeordneten, Lobbying *n*

lobbyist [ˈlɑbɪ·ɪst] *s* Lobbyist –in *mf*

lobe [lob] *s* (anat) Lappen *m*

lobster [ˈlɑbstər] *s* Hummer *m*; **red as a l.** (fig) krebsrot

local [ˈlokəl] *adj* örtlich, Orts–; (*produce*) heimisch || *s* (*group*) Ortsgruppe *f*; (rr) Personenzug *m*

lo'cal anesthe'sia *s* Lokalanästhese *f*

lo'cal call' *s* (telp) Ortsgespräch *n*

lo'cal col'or *s* Lokalkolorit *n*

lo'cal deliv'ery *s* Ortszustellung *f*

locale [loˈkæl] *s* Ort *m*

lo'cal gov'ernment *s* Gemeindeverwaltung *f*

locality [loˈkælɪti] *s* Örtlichkeit *f*

localize [ˈlokəˌlaɪz] *tr* lokalisieren

lo'cal news' *s* Lokalnachrichten *pl*

lo'cal pol'itics *s* Kommunalpolitik *f*

lo'cal show'er *s* Strichregen *m*

lo'cal tax' *s* Gemeindesteuer *f*

lo'cal time' *s* Ortszeit *f*

lo'cal traf'fic *s* Nahverkehr *m*, Ortsverkehr *m*

locate [loˈket], [ˈloket] *tr* (*find*) ausfindig machen; (*a ship, aircraft*) orten; (*the trouble*) feststellen; (*set up, e.g., an office*) errichten; **be located** liegen, gelegen sein || *intr* sich niederlassen

location [loˈkeʃən] *s* Lage *f*; **on l.** (cin) auf Außenaufnahme

lock [lɑk] *s* Schloß *n*; (*of hair*) Locke *f*; (*of a canal*) Schleuse *f*; **l., stock, and barrel** mit allem Drum und Dran; **under l. and key** unter Verschluß || *tr* zusperren; (*arms*) verschränken; **l.** in einsperren; **l. out** aussperren; **l. up** (*a house*) zusperren; (*imprison*) einsperren || *intr* (*said of a lock*) zuschnappen; (*said of brakes*) sperren; **l. together** (*said of bumpers*) sich ineinander verhaken

locker [ˈlɑkər] *s* (*as in a gym or barracks*) Spind *m* & *n*; (*for luggage*) Schließfach *n*

lock'er room' *s* Umkleideraum *m*

locket [ˈlɑkɪt] *s* Medaillon *n*

lock'jaw' *s* Maulsperre *f*

lock' nut' *s* Gegenmutter *f*

lock'out' *s* Aussperrung *f*

lock'smith' *s* Schlosser –in *mf*

lock'smith shop' *s* Schlosserei *f*

lock' step' *s* Marschieren *n* in dicht geschlossenen Gliedern

lock' stitch' *s* Kettenstich *m*

lock'up' *s* (coll) Gefängnis *n*

lock' wash'er *s* Sicherungsring *m*

locomotion [ˌlokəˈmoʃən] *s* (act) Fortbewegung *f*; (power) Fortbewegungsfähigkeit *f*

locomotive [ˌlokəˈmotɪv] *s* Lokomotive *f*

lo·cus [ˈlokəs] *s* (**–ci** [saɪ]) Ort *m*; (geom) geometrischer Ort *m*

locust [ˈlokəst] *s* (*black locust*) (bot) Robinie *f*; (*carob*) (bot) Johannisbrotbaum *m*; (*Cicada*) (ent) Zikade *f*

lode [lod] *s* (min) Gang *m*

lode'star' *s* Leitstern *m*

lodge [lɑdʒ] *s* (*of Masons*) Loge *f*; (*for hunting*) Jagdhütte *f*; (*for weekending*) Wochenendhäuschen *n*; (*summer house*) Sommerhäuschen *n* || *tr* unterbringen; **l. a complaint** e–e Beschwerde einreichen || *intr* wohnen; (*said of an arrow, etc.*) steckenbleiben

lodger [ˈlɑdʒər] *s* Untermieter –in *mf*

lodg'ing *s* Unterkunft *f*; **lodgings** Logis *n*

loft [lɔft] *s* Speicher *m*; (*for hay*) Heuboden *m*; (*of a church*) Chor *m*; (*of a golf club*) Hochschlaghaltung *f* || *tr* (*a golf club*) in Hochschlaghaltung bringen; (*a golf ball*) hochschlagen

loftiness [ˈlɔftɪnɪs] *s* Erhabenheit *f*

lofty [ˈlɔfti] *adj* (*style*) erhaben; (*high*) hochragend; (*elevated in rank*) gehoben; (*haughty*) anmaßend

log [lɔg] *s* (*trunk*) Baumstamm *m*; (*for the fireplace*) Holzklotz *m*; (*record book*) Tagebuch *n*; (aer, naut) Log *n*; **sleep like a log** wie ein Klotz schlafen || *v* (*pret* & *pp* **logged**; *ger* **logging**) *tr* (*trees*) fällen und abästen; (*cut into logs*) in Klötze schneiden; (*an area*) abholzen; (*enter into a logbook*) in das Logbuch eintragen; (*traverse*) zurücklegen

logarithm [ˈlɔgəˌrɪðəm] *s* Logarithmus *m*

log'book' *s* (aer, naut) Logbuch *n*
log' cab'in *s* Blockhaus *n*, Blockhütte *f*
logger ['lɔgər] *s* Holzfäller *m*
log'gerhead' *s*—**at loggerheads** auf Kriegsfuß
log'ging *s* Holzarbeit *f*
logic ['lɑdʒɪk] *s* Logik *f*
logical ['lɑdʒɪkəl] *adj* logisch
logician [lo'dʒɪʃən] *s* Logiker –in *mf*
logistic(al) [lo'dʒɪstɪk(əl)] *adj* logistisch
logistics [lo'dʒɪstɪks] *s* Logistik *f*
log'jam' *s* aufgestaute Baumstämme *pl*; (fig) völlige Stockung *f*
log'wood' *s* Kampescheholz *n*
loin [lɔɪn] *s* (*of beef*) Lendenstück *n*; (anat) Lende *f*; **gird up one's loins** (fig) sich rüsten
loin'cloth' *s* Lendentuch *n*
loin' end' *s* (*of pork*) Rippenstück *n*
loiter ['lɔɪtər] *tr*—**l. away** vertrödeln || *intr* trödeln; (*hang around*) herumlungern
loiterer ['lɔɪtərər] *s* Bummler –in *mf*
loi'tering *s* Trödelei *f*; **no l. Herumlungern verboten!**
loll [lɑl] *intr* sich bequem ausstrecken
lollipop ['lɑlɪ‚pɑp] *s* Lutschbonbon *m & n*
Lombardy ['lʌmbərdi] *s* die Lombardei
London ['lʌndən] *adj* Londoner || *s* London *n*
Londoner ['lʌndənər] *s* Londoner –in *mf*
lone [lon] *adj* (*sole*) alleinig; (*solitary*) einzelstehend
loneliness ['lonlɪnɪs] *s* Einsamkeit *f*
lonely ['lonli] *adj* einsam; **become l.** vereinsamen
loner ['lonər] *s* Einzelgänger *m*
lonesome ['lonsəm] *adj* einsam; **be l. for** sich sehnen nach
lone' wolf' *s* (fig) Einzelgänger *m*
long [lɔŋ] *adj* (**longer** ['lɔŋgər]; **longest** ['lɔŋgɪst]) lang; (*way, trip*) weit; (*detour*) groß; **a l. time** lange; **a l. time since** schon lange her, daß; **in the l. run** auf die Dauer || **as l. as** so lange wie; **but not for l.** aber nicht lange; **l. after** lange nach; **l. ago** vor langer Zeit; **l. live . . .!** es lebe . . .!; **l. since** längst; **so l.!** bis dann! || *intr*—**l. for** sich danach sehnen; **l. to** (*inf*) sich danach sehnen zu (*inf*)
long'boat' *s* Pinasse *f*
long' dis'tance *s* (telp) Ferngespräch *n*; **call l.** ein Ferngespräch anmelden
long'-dis'tance *adj* (sport) Langstrecken–
long'-dis'tance call' *s* Ferngespräch *n*
long'-dis'tance flight' *s* Langstreckenflug *m*
long'-drawn'-out' *adj* ausgedehnt; (*story*) langatmig
longevity [lɑn'dʒɛvɪti] *s* Langlebigkeit *f*
long' face' *s* langes Gesicht *n*
long'hair' *adj* (fig) intellektuell || *s* (fig) Intellektueller *m*; (mus) (coll) konservativer Musiker *m*
long'hand' *s* Langschrift *f*; **in l.** mit der Hand geschrieben

long'ing *adj* sehnsüchtig || *s* (**for**) Sehnsucht *f* (**nach**)
longitude ['lɑndʒɪ‚t(j)ud] *s* Länge *f*
longitudinal [‚lɑndʒɪ't(j)udɪnəl] *adj* Longitudinal–
long' jump' *s* Weitsprung *m*
long-lived ['lɔŋ'laɪvd] *adj* langlebig
long'-play'ing rec'ord *s* Langspielplatte *f*
long'-range' *adj* (plan) auf lange Sicht; (aer) Langstrecken–
long'shore'man *s* (–men) Hafenarbeiter *m*
long' shot' *s* (coll) riskante Wette *f*; **by a l.** bei weitem
long'stand'ing *adj* althergebracht, alt
long'-suf'fering *adj* langmütig
long' suit' *s* (fig) Stärke *f*; (cards) lange Farbe *f*
long'-term' *adj* langfristig
long-winded ['lɔŋ'wɪndɪd] *adj* langatmig
look [lʊk] *s* (*glance*) Blick *m*; (*appearance*) Aussehen *n*; (*expression*) Ausdruck *m*; **from the looks of things** wie die Sache aussieht; **give a second l.** sich [*dat*] genauer ansehen; **have a l. around** Umschau halten; **have a l. at s.th.** sich [*dat*] etw ansehen; **I don't like the looks of it** die Sache gefällt mir nicht; **looks** Ansehen *n*; **new l.** verändertes Aussehen *n*; (*latest style*) neueste Mode *f*; **take a l. at s.th.** sich [*dat*] etw ansehen || *tr*—**he looks his age** man sieht ihm sein Alter an; **l. one's best** sich in bester Verfassung zeigen; **l. one's last at** zum letzten Mal ansehen; **l. s.o. in the eye** j–m in die Augen sehen; **l. s.o. over** j–n mustern; **l. s.th. over** etw (über)prüfen (or durchsehen); **l. up** (*e.g., a word*) nachschlagen; (*e.g., a friend*) aufsuchen; **l. up and down** von oben bis unten mustern || *intr* schauen; (*appear, seem*) aussehen; **l. after** (*e.g., children*) betreuen; (*a household, business*) besorgen; (*a departing person*) nachblicken (*dat*); **l. ahead** vorausschauen; **l. around** (**for**) sich [*dat*] umsehen (**nach**); **l. at** anschauen; **l. back (on)** zurücksehen (auf *acc*); **l. down** herabsehen; (*cast the eyes down*) die Augen niederschlagen; **l. down on** herabsehen auf (*acc*); (*in contempt*) über die Achseln ansehen; **l. for** suchen; (*e.g., a criminal*) fahnden nach; **l. forward to** sich freuen auf (*acc*); **l. hard at** scharf ansehen; **l. into** (*a mirror, the future*) blicken in (*acc*); (*a matter*) nachgehen (*dat*); **l. like** gleichen (*dat*); (*e.g., rain*) aussehen nach; **l. on** zuschauen; **l. on s.o. as** j–n betrachten als; **l. out!** aufpassen!; **l. out for** aussehen nach; **l. out on** (*a view*) hinausgehen auf (*acc*); **l. over** hinwegsehen über (*acc*); **l. sharp!** jetzt aber hopplá!; **l. through** (*e.g., a window*) blicken durch; (*s.o. or s.o.'s motives*) durchschauen; **l. up** (*raise one's gaze*) aufschauen; **l. up to s.o.** zu j–m hinaufsehen; **things**

are beginning to l. up es wird langsam besser; **things don't l. so good for est** steht übel mit; **what does he l. like?** wie sieht er aus?

look'ing glass' s Spiegel m

look'out' s (watchman) Wachposten m; (observation point) Ausguck m; (matter of concern) Sache f; **be a l.** Schmiere stehen; **be on the l.** (for) Auschau halten (nach)

look'out man' s—**be the l.** Schmiere stehen

look'out tow'er s Aussichtsturm m

loom [lum] s Webstuhl m ‖ intr undeutlich und groß auftauchen; **l. large** von großer Bedeutung scheinen

loon [lun] s (orn) Taucher m

loony ['luni] adj verrückt; **be l.** spinnen

loop [lup] s Schleife f, Schlinge f; (e.g., on a dress for a hook) Öse f; (aer) Looping m; **do a l.** (aer) e-n Looping drehen ‖ tr schlingen ‖ intr Schlingen (or Schleifen) bilden

loop'hole' s Guckloch n; (in a fortification) Schießscharte f; (in a law) Lücke f

loose [lus] adj locker, los; (wobbly) wackelig; (morally) locker, unsolid; (unpacked) unverpackt; (translation) frei; (interpretation) dehnbar; (dress, tongue) lose; (skin) schlaff; **l. connection** (elec) Wackelkontakt m ‖ adv—**break l.** (from an enclosure) ausbrechen; (e.g., from a hitching) sich losmachen; (said of a storm, hell) losbrechen; **come l.** losgehen; **cut l.** (act up) (coll) außer Rand und Band geraten; **turn l.** befreien; **work l.** sich lockern; (said of a button) abgehen; (said of a brick, stone, shoestring) sich lösen ‖ **s—on the l.** ungehemmt, frei ‖ tr (a boat) losmachen; (a knot) lösen

loose' change' s Kleingeld n

loose' end' s (fig) unerledigte Kleinigkeit f; **at loose ends** im ungewissen

loose'-leaf note'book s Loseblattbuch n

loosen ['lusən] tr lockern, locker machen ‖ intr locker werden

looseness ['lusnɪs] s Lockerheit f

loot [lut] s Beute f ‖ tr erbeuten; (plunder) plündern; (e.g., art treasures) verschleppen

lop [lɑp] v (pret & pp **lopped;** ger **lopping**) tr—**lop off** abhacken

lope [lop] s Trab m ‖ intr—**l. along** in großen Schritten laufen

lop'sid'ed adj schief; (score) einseitig

loquacious [lo'kwe/əs] adj geschwätzig

lord [lɔrd] s Herr m; (Brit) Lord m; **Lord** Herrgott m ‖ tr—**l. it over** sich als Herr aufspielen über (acc)

lordly ['lɔrdli] adj würdig; (haughty) hochmütig

Lord's' Day' s Tag m des Herrn

lord'ship' s Herrschaft f

Lord's' Prayer' s Vaterunser n

Lord's' Sup'per s heiliges Abendmahl n

lore [lor] s Kunde f; (traditional wisdom) überlieferte Kunde f

lorry ['lɔri] s (Brit) Lastkraftwagen m

lose [luz] v (pret & pp **lost** [lɔst]) tr verlieren; (several minutes, as a clock does) zurückbleiben; (in betting) verwetten; (in gambling) verspielen; (the page in a book) verblättern; **l. one's way** sich verirren; (on foot) sich verlaufen; (by car) sich verfahren ‖ intr verlieren; (sport) geschlagen werden; **l. to** (sport) unterliegen (dat)

loser ['luzər] s Unterlegene mf; **be the l.** mit langer Nase abziehen

los'ing adj verlierend; (com) verlustbringend ‖ **losings** spl Verluste pl

los'ing game' s aussichtsloses Spiel n

loss [lɔs] s (in) Verlust m (an dat); **at a l.** in Verlegenheit; (com) mit Verlust; **be at a l. for words** nach Worten suchen; **inflict l. on s.o.** j-m Schaden zufügen; **l. of appetite** Appetitlosigkeit f; **l. of blood** Blutverlust m; **l. of face** Blamage f; **l. of life** Verluste pl an Menschenleben; **l. of memory** Gedächtnisverlust m; **l. of sight** Erblindung f; **l. of time** Zeitverlust m; **straight l.** Barverlust m

lost [lɔst] adj verloren; **be l.** (said of a thing) verlorengehen; (not know one's way) sich verirrt haben; **be l. on s.o.** auf j-n keinen Eindruck machen; **get l.** in Verlust geraten; **get l.!** hau ab!; **l. in thought** in Gedanken versunken

lost'-and-found' depart'ment s Fundbüro n

lost' cause' s aussichtslose Sache f

lot [lɑt] s (fate) Los n, Schicksal n; (in a drawing) Los n; (portion of land) Grundstück n; (cin) Filmgelände n; (com) Posten m, Partie f; **a lot** viel, sehr; **a lot of** (or **lots of**) viel(e); **the lot** das Ganze

lotion ['lo/ən] s Wasser n

lottery ['lɑtəri] s Lotterie f

lot'tery tick'et s Lotterielos n

lotto ['lɑto] s Lotto n

lotus ['lotəs] s Lotos m

loud [laud] adj laut; (colors) schreiend

loud-mouthed ['laud,mauðd] adj laut

loud'speak'er s Lautsprecher m

lounge [laundʒ] s Aufenthaltsraum m ‖ intr sich recken; **l. around** herumlungern

lounge' chair' s Klubsessel m

lounge' liz'ard s (sl) Salonlöwe m

louse [laus] s (lice [laɪs]) Laus f; (sl) Sauhund m ‖ tr—**l. up** (sl) versauen

lousy ['lauzi] adj verlaust; (sl) lausig; **l. with** (people) wimmelnd von; **l. with money** stinkreich

lout [laut] s Lümmel m

louver ['luvər] s Jalousie f

lovable ['lʌvəbəl] adj liebenswürdig

love [lʌv] adj Liebes— ‖ s (for, of) Liebe f (zu); **be in l. with** verliebt sein in (acc); **for the l. of God** um Gottes willen; **fall (madly) in l. with** sich (heftig) verlieben in (acc); **Love** (at the end of a letter) herzliche Grüße; **l. at first sight** Liebe f auf den ersten Blick; **make l. to** herzen;

(sl) geschlechtlich verkehren mit; **not for l. or money** nicht für Gold und gute Worte; **there's no l. lost between them** sie schätzen sich nicht ‖ *tr* lieben; (*like*) gern haben; **l. to dance** sehr gern tanzen

love′ affair′ *s* Liebeshandel *m*, Liebesverhältnis *n*

love′birds′ *spl* (coll) Unzertrennlichen *pl*

love′ child′ *s* Kind *n* der Liebe

love′ feast′ *s* (eccl) Liebesmahl *n*

love′ game′ *s* (tennis) Nullpartie *f*

love′ knot′ *s* Liebesschleife *f*

loveless [′lʌvlɪs] *adj* lieblos

love′ let′ter *s* Liebesbrief *m*

lovelorn [′lʌv‚lɔrn] *adj* vor Liebe vergehend

lovely [′lʌvli] *adj* lieblich

love′-mak′ing *s* Geschlechtsverkehr *m*

love′ match′ *s* Liebesheirat *f*

love′ po′em *s* Liebesgedicht *n*

love′ po′tion *s* Liebestrank *m*

lover [′lʌvər] *s* Liebhaber *m*; **lovers** Liebespaar *n*

love′ scene′ *s* Liebesszene *f*

love′ seat′ *s* Sofasessel *m*

love′sick′ *adj* liebeskrank

love′ song′ *s* Liebeslied *n*

love′ to′ken *s* Liebespfand *n*

lov′ing *adj* liebevoll; **Your l. ...** Dich liebender ...

lov′ing-kind′ness *s* Herzensgüte *f*

low [lo] *adj* (*building, mountain, forehead, birth, wages, estimate, prices, rent*) niedrig; (*number*) nieder; (*altitude, speed*) gering; (*not loud*) leise; (*vulgar*) gemein; (*grades, company*) schlecht; (*fever*) leicht; (*pulse, pressure*) schwach; (*ground*) tiefgelegen; (*bow, voice*) tief; (*almost empty*) fast leer; (*supplies, funds*) knapp; **be low** (*said of the sun, water*) niedrigstehen; **be low in funds** knapp bei Kasse sein; **feel low** niedergeschlagen sein; **have a low opinion of** e–e geringe Meinung haben von ‖ *adv* niedrig; **lay low** über den Haufen werfen; **lie low** sich versteckt halten; (*bide one's time*) abwarten; **run low** knapp werden; **sing low** tief singen; **sink low** tief sinken ‖ *s* (*low point*) (fig) Tiefstand *m*; (meteor) Tief *n* ‖ *intr* muhen, brüllen

low′ blow′ *s* (box) Tiefschlag *m*

low′born′ *adj* von niederer Herkunft

low′brow′ *s* Spießbürger *m*

low′-cost hous′ing *s* sozial geförderter Wohnungsbau *m*

Low′ Coun′tries, the *spl* die Niederlande

low′-cut′ *adj* tiefausgeschnitten

low′-down′ *adj* schurkisch ‖ *s* (*unadorned facts*) unverblümte Wahrheit *f*; (*inside information*) Geheimnachrichten *pl*

lower [′loər] *comp adj* untere; (*e.g., deck, house, jaw, lip*) Unter– ‖ *tr* herunterlassen; (*the eyes, voice, water level, temperature*) senken; (*prices*) herabsetzen; (*a flag, sail*) streichen; (*lifeboats*) aussetzen; **l.**

lower′self sich herablassen ‖ [′laʊ‑ər] *intr* finster blicken; **l. at** finster anblicken

low′er ab′domen [′lo‑ər] *s* Unterbauch *m*

low′er berth′ [′lo‑ər] *s* untere Koje *f*

low′er case′ [′lo‑ər] *s* Kleinbuchstaben *pl*

lower-case [′lo‑ər′kes] *adj* klein

low′er course′ [′lo‑ər] *s* (*of a river*) Unterlauf *m*

low′er mid′dle class′ [′lo‑ər] *s* Kleinbürgertum *n*

lowermost [′lo‑ər‚most] *adj* niedrigste

low′er world′ [′lo‑ər] *s* Unterwelt *f*

low′-fly′ing *adj* tieffliegend

low′ fre′quency *s* Niederfrequenz *f*

low′-fre′quency *adj* Niederfrequenz–

low′ gear′ *s* erster Gang *m*

low′-grade′ *adj* minderwertig

low′ing *s* Gebrüll *n*

lowland [′loland] *s* Flachland *n*; **Lowlands** (*in Scotland*) Unterland *n*

low′ lev′el *s* Tiefstand *m*

low′-lev′el attack′ *s* Tiefangriff *m*

low′-lev′el flight′ *s* Tiefflug *m*

lowly [′loli] *adj* bescheiden; (*humble in spirit*) niederträchtig

low′-ly′ing *adj* tiefliegend

Low′ Mass′ *s* stille Messe *f*

low′-mind′ed *adj* niedrig gesinnt

low′ neck′ *s* (*of a dress*) Ausschnitt *m*

low′-necked′ *adj* tief ausgeschnitten

low′-pitched′ *adj* (*sound*) tief; (*roof*) mit geringer Neigung

low′-pres′sure *adj* Tiefdruck–, Unterdruck–

low′-priced′ *adj* billig

low′ shoe′ *s* Halbschuh *m*

low′-speed′ *adj* mit geringer Geschwindigkeit; (*film*) unempfindlich

low′-spir′ited *adj* niedergeschlagen

low′ spir′its *spl* Niedergeschlagenheit *f*; **be in l.** niedergeschlagen sein

low′ tide′ *s* Ebbe *f*; (fig) Tiefstand *m*

low′ wa′ter *s* Niedrigwasser *n*

low′-wa′ter mark′ *s* (fig) Tiefpunkt *m*

loyal [′lɔɪ‑əl] *adj* treu, loyal

loyalist [′lɔɪ‑əlɪst] *s* Regierungstreue *mf*

loyalty [′lɔɪ‑əlti] *s* Treue *f*

lozenge [′lɑzɪndʒ] *s* Pastille *f*

LP [′el′pi] *s* (trademark) (**long-playing record**) Langspielplatte *f*

Ltd. *abbr* (Brit) (**Limited**) Gesellschaft *f* mit beschränkter Haftung

lubricant [′lubrɪkənt] *s* Schmiermittel *n*

lubricate [′lubrɪ‚ket] *tr* (ab)schmieren

lubrication [‚lubrɪ′keʃən] *s* Schmierung *f*

lucerne [lu′sʌrn] *s* (bot) Luzerne *f*; **Lucerne** Luzern *n*

lucid [′lusɪd] *adj* (*clear*) klar, deutlich; (*bright*) hell

luck [lʌk] *s* Glück *n*; (*chance*) Zufall *m*; **as l. would have it** wie es der Zufall wollte; **be down on one's l.** an seinem Glück verzagen; **be in l.** Glück haben; **be out of l.** Unglück haben; **dumb l.** (coll) Sauglück *n*; **have tough l.** (coll) Pech haben;

rotten l. (coll) Saupech *n*; **try one's l.** sein Glück versuchen; **with l. you should win** wenn Sie Glück haben, werden Sie gewinnen

luckily ['lʌkɪli] *adv* zum Glück

luckless ['lʌklɪs] *adj* glücklos

lucky ['lʌki] *adj* glücklich; **be l.** Glück haben; **l. dog** (coll) Glückspilz *m*; **l. penny** Glückspfennig *m*

luck'y shot' *s* Glückstreffer *m*

lucrative ['lukrətɪv] *adj* gewinnbringend

ludicrous ['ludɪkrəs] *adj* lächerlich

lug [lʌg] *s* (*pull, tug*) Ruck *m*; (*lout*) (sl) Lümmel *m*; (elec) Öse *f* || *v* (*pret & pp* lugged; *ger* lugging) *tr* schleppen

luggage ['lʌgɪdʒ] *s* Gepäck *n*; **excess l.** Mehrgepäck *n*; **piece of l.** Gepäckstück *n*

lug'gage car'rier *s* Gepäckträger *m*

lug'gage compart'ment *s* (aer) Frachtraum *m*

lug'gage rack' *s* Gepäckablage *f*; (*on the roof of a car*) Dachgepäckträger *m*

lug'gage receipt' *s* Aufgabeschein *m*

lugubrious [lu'g(j)ubrɪ-əs] *adj* tieftraurig

lukewarm ['luk,wɔrm] *adj* lau, lauwarm

lull [lʌl] *s* Windstille *f*; (com) Flaute *f* || *tr* einlullen; (*e.g., fears*) beschwichtigen; **l. to sleep** einschläfern || *intr* nachlassen

lullaby ['lʌlə,baɪ] *s* Wiegenlied *n*

lumbago [lʌm'bego] *s* Hexenschluß *m*

lumber ['lʌmbər] *s* Bauholz *n* || *intr* sich schwerfällig fortbewegen

lum'berjack' *s* Holzfäller *m*

lum'ber-man' *s* (–men') (*dealer*) Holzhändler *m*; (*lumberjack*) Holzfäller *m*

lum'beryard' *s* Holzplatz *m*

luminary ['lumɪ,neri] *s* Leuchtkörper *m*; (fig) Leuchte *f*

luminescent [,lumɪ'nesənt] *adj* lumineszierend

luminous ['lumɪnəs] *adj* leuchtend, Leucht–

lu'minous di'al *s* Leuchtzifferblatt *n*

lu'minous paint' *s* Leuchtfarbe *f*

lummox ['lʌmǝks] *s* Lümmel *m*

lump [lʌmp] *s* (*e.g., of clay*) Klumpen *m*; (*on the body*) Beule *f*; **have a l. in one's throat** e–n Kloß (or Knödel) im Hals haben; **l. of sugar** Würfel *m* Zucker || *tr*—**l. together** (fig) zusammenwerfen

lumpish ['lʌmpɪʃ] *adj* klumpig

lump' sug'ar *s* Würfelzucker *m*

lump' sum' *s* Pauschalbetrag *m*

lumpy ['lʌmpi] *adj* klumpig; (*sea*) bewegt

lunacy ['lunəsi] *s* Irrsinn *m*

lu'nar eclipse' ['lunər] *s* Mondfinsternis *f*

lu'nar land'ing *s* Mondlandung *f*

lu'nar mod'ule *s* (rok) Mondfähre *f*

lu'nar year' *s* Mondjahr *n*

lunatic ['lunətɪk] *s* Irre *mf*

lu'natic asy'lum *s* Irrenhaus *n*

lu'natic fringe' *s* Extremisten *pl*

lunch [lʌntʃ] *s* (*at noon*) Mittagessen *n*, Lunch *m*; (*light meal*) Zwischenmahlzeit *f*; **eat l.** zu Mittag essen; **have** (*s.th.*) **for l.** zum Mittagessen haben || *intr* zu Mittag essen, lunchen

lunch' coun'ter *s* Theke *f*

luncheon ['lʌntʃən] *s* gemeinsames Mittagessen *n*

luncheonette [,lʌntʃə'net] *s* Imbißstube *f*

lunch' hour' *s* Mittagsstunde *f*

lunch'room' *s* Imbißhalle *f*

lunch'time' *s* Mittagszeit *f*

lung [lʌŋ] *s* Lunge *f*; **at the top of one's lungs** aus voller Kehle

lunge ['lʌndʒ] *s* Sprung *m* vorwärts; (fencing) Ausfall *m* || *tr* (*a horse*) an der Longe laufen lassen || *intr*— e–n Sprung vorwärts machen; (*with a sword*) (at) e–n Ausfall machen (gegen); **l. at** losstürzen auf (*acc*)

lurch [lʌrtʃ] *s* Torkeln *n*, Taumeln *n*; **leave in a l.** im Stich lassen || *intr* torkeln; (*said of a ship*) zur Seite rollen

lure [lur] *s* Köder *m* || *tr* ködern; (fig) verlocken; **l. away** weglocken

lurid ['lurɪd] *adj* (*light*) gespenstisch; (*sunset*) düsterrot; (*gruesome*) grausig; (*pallid*) fahl

lurk [lʌrk] *intr* lauern

luscious ['lʌʃəs] *adj* köstlich; **a l. doll** (coll) ein tolles Weib

lush [lʌʃ] *adj* üppig

lust [lʌst] *s* Wollust *f*; (**for**) Begierde *f* (nach) || *intr* (**after, for**) gieren (nach)

luster ['lʌstər] *s* Glanz *m*; (*e.g., chandelier*) Lüster *m*

lusterless ['lʌstərlɪs] *adj* matt

lus'terware' *s* Tongeschirr *n* mit Lüster

lustful ['lʌstfəl] *adj* lüstern, geil

lustrous ['lʌstrəs] *adj* glänzend

lusty ['lʌsti] *adj* kräftig

lute [lut] *s* Laute *f*

Lutheran ['luθərən] *adj* lutherisch || *s* Lutheraner –in *mf*

luxuriance [lʌg'ʒurɪ-əns] *s* Üppigkeit *f*

luxuriant [lʌg'ʒurɪ-ənt] *adj* üppig

luxuriate [lʌg'ʒurɪ,et] *intr* (*thrive*) gedeihen; (*delight*) (**in**) schwelgen (in *dat*)

luxurious [lʌg'ʒurɪ-əs] *adj* luxuriös; **l. living** Prasserei *f*

luxury ['lʌgʒəri] *s* Extravaganz *f*, Luxus *m*; (*object of luxury*) Luxusartikel *m*; **live a life of l.** im vollen leben

lye [laɪ] *s* Lauge *f*

ly'ing *adj* lügenhaft || *s* Lügen *n*

ly'ing-in' hos'pital *s* Entbindungsanstalt *f*

lymph [lɪmf] *s* Lymphe *f*

lymphatic [lɪm'fætɪk] *adj* lymphatisch

lynch [lɪntʃ] *tr* lynchen

lynch'ing *s* Lynchen *n*

lynch' law' *s* Lynchjustiz *f*

lynx [lɪŋks] *s* Luchs *m*

lynx'-eyed' *adj* luchsäugig

lyre [laɪr] s (mus) Leier f
lyric ['lɪrɪk] adj lyrisch; **l. poetry** Lyrik f ‖ s lyrisches Gedicht n; (of a song) Text m

lyrical ['lɪrɪkəl] adj lyrisch
lyricism ['lɪrɪ,sɪzəm] s Lyrik f
lyricist ['lɪrɪsɪst] s (of a song) Texter –in mf; (poet) lyrischer Dichter m

M

M, m [ɛm] s dreizehnter Buchstabe des englischen Alphabets
ma [mɑ] s (coll) Mama f
ma'am [mæm] s (coll) gnädige Frau f
macadam [mə'kædəm] s Makadamdecke f
macadamize [mə'kædə,maɪz] tr makadamisieren
maca'dam road' s Straße f mit Makadamdecke
macaroni [,mækə'roni] spl Makkaroni pl
macaroon [,mækə'run] s Makrone f
macaw [mə'kɔ] s (orn) Ara m
mace [mes] s Stab m, Amtsstab m
mace'bear'er s Träger m des Amtsstabes
machination [,mækɪ'nɛʃən] s Intrige f; **machinations** Machenschaften pl
machine [mə'ʃin] s Maschine f; (pol) Apparat m; **by m.** maschinell ‖ tr spannabhebend formen
machine'-driv'en adj mit Maschinenantrieb
machine' gun' s Maschinengewehr n
machine'-gun' v (pret & pp -gunned; ger -gunning) tr unter Maschinengewehrfeuer nehmen
machine' gun'ner s Maschinengewehrschütze m
machine'-made' adj maschinell hergestellt
machinery [mə'ʃinəri] s (& fig) Maschinerie f
machine' screw' s Maschinenschraube f
machine' shop' s Maschinenhalle f
machine' tool' s Werkzeugmaschine f
machinist [mə'ʃinɪst] s (maker and repairer of machines) Maschinenbauer m; (machine operator) Maschinenschlosser –in mf
mackerel ['mækərəl] s Makrele f
mad [mæd] adj (madder; maddest) verrückt; (angry) böse; **be mad about** vernarrt sein in (acc); **be mad at** böse sein auf (acc); **drive mad** verrückt machen; **go mad** verrückt werden
madam ['mædəm] s gnädige Frau f; (of a brothel) (sl) Bordellmutter f
mad'cap' adj ausgelassen ‖ s Wildfang m
madden ['mædən] tr verrückt machen; (make angry) zornig machen
made'-to-or'der adj nach Maß angefertigt
made'-up' adj (story) erfunden; (artificial) künstlich; (with cosmetics) geschminkt

mad'house' s Irrenhaus n, Narrenhaus n
madly ['mædli] adv (coll) wahnsinnig
mad'man' s (-men') Verrückter m
madness ['mædnɪs] s Wahnsinn m
Madonna [mə'dɑnə] s Madonna f
maelstrom ['melstrəm] s (& fig) Strudel m
magazine [,mægə'zin] s (periodical) Zeitschrift f; (illustrated) Illustrierte f; (warehouse for munitions; cartridge container) Magazin n; (for a camera) Kassette f
magazine' rack' s Zeitschriftenständer m
Maggie ['mægi] s Gretchen n
maggot ['mægət] s Made f
Magi ['medʒaɪ] spl—**the three M.** (Bib) die drei Weisen pl aus dem Morgenland
magic ['mædʒɪk] adj (enchanting) zauberhaft; (trick, word, wand) Zauber- ‖ s Zauberkunst f
magician [mə'dʒɪʃən] s Zauberer –in mf
ma'gic lan'tern s Laterna magica f
magisterial [,mædʒɪs'tɪrɪ-əl] adj (of a magistrate) obrigkeitlich; (authoritative) autoritativ; (pompous) anmaßend
magistrate ['mædʒɪs,tret] s Polizeirichter m
magnanimous [mæg'nænɪməs] adj großmütig
magnate ['mægnet] s Magnat m
magnesium [mæg'nizɪ-əm] s Magnesium n
magnet ['mægnɪt] s Magnet m
magnetic [mæg'netɪk] adj magnetisch; (personality) fesselnd
magnetism ['mægnɪ,tɪzəm] s Magnetismus m; (fig) Anziehungskraft f
magnetize ['mægnɪ,taɪz] tr magnetisieren
magnificence [mæg'nɪfɪsəns] s Pracht f
magnificent [mæg'nɪfɪsənt] adj prächtig
magnifier ['mægnɪ,faɪ-ər] s (electron) Verstärker m
magni·fy ['mægnɪ,faɪ] v (pret & pp -fied) tr vergrößern; (fig) übertreiben
mag'nifying glass' s Lupe f
magnitude ['mægnɪ,t(j)ud] s (& astr) Größe f
magno'lia tree' [mæg'noli-ə] s Magnolia f
magpie ['mæg,paɪ] s (& fig) Elster f
mahlstick ['mɑl,stɪk] s Malerstock m

mahogany [mə'hɑgəni] s Mahagoni n
mahout [mə'haut] s Elefantentreiber m
maid [med] s Dienstmädchen n
maiden ['medən] s Jungfer f; (poet) Maid f
maid'enhair' s (bot) Jungfernhaar n
maid'enhead' s Jungfernhäutchen n
maid'enhood' s Jungfräulichkeit f
maidenly ['medənli] adj jungfräulich
maid'en name' s Mädchenname m
maid'en voy'age s Jungfernfahrt f
maid'-in-wait'ing s (maids-in-waiting) Hofdame f
maid' of hon'or s erste Brautjungfer f
maid'serv'ant s Dienstmädchen n
mail [mel] adj Post— || s Post f; (armor) Kettenpanzer m; by m. brieflich; by return m. postwendend || tr (put into the mail) aufgeben; (send) abschicken; m. to zuschicken (dat)
mail'bag' s Postsack m
mail'boat' s Postschiff n
mail'box' s Briefkasten m
mail' car'rier s Briefträger –in mf
mail' deliv'ery s Postzustellung f
mail' drop' s Briefeinwurf m
mailer ['melər] s (phot) Versandbeutel m
mail'ing s Absendung f
mail'ing list' s Postversandliste f
mail'ing per'mit s Zulassung f zum portofreien Versand
mail'man' s (-men') Briefträger m
mail' or'der s Bestellung f durch die Post
mail'-order house' s Versandhaus n
mail' plane' s Postflugzeug n
mail' train' s Postzug m
mail' truck' s Postauto n
maim [mem] tr verstümmeln
main [men] adj Haupt— || s Hauptleitung f; in the main hauptsächlich
main' clause' s (gram) Hauptsatz m
main' course' s Hauptgericht n
main' deck' s Hauptdeck n
main' floor' s Erdgeschoß n
mainland ['men‚lænd] s Festland n
main' line' s (rr) Hauptstrecke f
mainly ['menli] adv größtenteils
mainmast ['men‚mæst] s Großmast m
main' of'fice s Hauptbüro n, Zentrale f
main' point' s springender Punkt m
mainsail ['men‚sel] s Großsegel m
main'spring' s (horol & fig) Triebfeder f
main'stay' s (fig) Hauptstütze f; (naut) Großstag n
main' street' s Hauptstraße f
maintain [men'ten] tr aufrechterhalten; (e.g., a family) unterhalten; (assert) behaupten; (one's reputation) wahren; (e.g., in good condition) bewahren; (order, silence) halten; (a road) instand halten
maintenance ['mentɪnəns] s (upkeep) Instandhaltung f; (support) Unterhalt m; (e.g., of an automobile) Wardirektor m
maître d'hôtel [‚metərdo'tel] s (head waiter) Oberkellner m; (owner)

Hotelbesitzer m; (manager) Hoteltung f
majestic [mə'dʒestɪk] adj majestätisch
majesty ['mædʒɪsti] s Majestät f
major ['medʒər] adj Haupt—; (mus) –Dur || s (educ) Hauptfach n; (mil) Major m || intr—m. in als Hauptfach studieren
majordomo ['medʒər'domo] s Haushofmeister m
ma'jor gen'eral s Generalmajor m
majority [mə'dʒɔrɪti] adj Mehrheits- || s Mehrheit f; (full age) Mündigkeit f; (mil) Majorsrang m; (parl) Stimmenmehrheit f; be in the m. in der Mehrheit sein; in the m. of cases in der Mehrzahl der Fälle; the m. of people die meisten Menschen
major'ity vote' s Mehrheitsbeschluß m
ma'jor league' s Oberliga f
make [mek] s Fabrikat n, Marke f || tr machen; (in a factory) herstellen; (cause) lassen; (force) zwingen; (clothes) anfertigen; (money) verdienen; (a reputation, name) erwerben; (a choice) treffen; (a confession) ablegen; (a report) erstatten; (plans) schmieden; (changes) vornehmen; (a movie) drehen; (contact) herstellen; (a meal) (zu)bereiten; (conditions) stellen; (rules, assertions) aufstellen; (a bet, compromise, peace) schließen; (excuses, requests, objections) vorbringen; (a protest) erheben; (a goal) schießen (or erzielen); (a comparison) ziehen; (a speech) halten; (e.g., a good father) abgeben; (be able to) fit through, e.g., a window) gehen durch; (e.g., a train, bus, destination) erreichen; (e.g., ten miles) zurücklegen; (a girl) (sl) verführen; (arith) machen; m. (s.o.) believe weismachen (dat); m. into verarbeiten zu; m. of halten von; m. out (e.g., writing) entziffern; (e.g., a person at a distance) erkennen; (understand) kapieren; (a blank or form) ausfüllen; (a check, receipt) ausstellen; m. over to (jur) überschreiben auf (acc); m. s.o. out to be a liar j–n als Lügner hinstellen; m. s.th. of oneself es weit bringen; m. the most of ausnutzen; m. time Zeit gewinnen; m. time with (a woman) (coll) flirten mit; m. up (e.g., a list) zusammenstellen; (a bill) ausstellen; (a sentence) bilden; (a story) sich [dat] ausdenken; m. up one's mind (about) sich [dat] schlüssig werden (über acc); m. way! Platz da!; m. way for ausweichen vor (dat) || intr—m. believe schauspielern; m. believe that nur so tun, als ob; m. do with sich behelfen mit; m. for losteuern auf (acc); m. off with durchbrennen mit; m. out well gut auskommen; m. sure of sich vergewissern (genit); m. sure that vergewissern, daß; m. up (after a quarrel) sich versöhnen; m. up for (past mistakes) wieder gutmachen; (lost time) wieder einbringen

make'-believe' *adj* Schein-, vorgetäuscht || *s* Schein *m*, Mache *f*

maker ['mekər] *s* Hersteller –in *mf*; **Maker** Schöpfer *m*

make'shift' *adj* behelfsmäßig, Behelfs- || *s* Notbehelf *m*

make'-up' *s* Aufmachung *f*; *(cosmetic)* Make-up *n*, Schminke *f*; *(of a team)* Aufstellung *f*; *(theat)* Maske *f*; *(typ)* Umbruch *m*; **apply m.** sich schminken

make'weight' *s* Gewichtszugabe *f*

mak'ing *s* Herstellung *f*; **be in the m.** im Werden sein; **have the makings of** das Zeug haben zu; **this is of his own m.** dies ist sein eigenes Werk

maladjusted [ˌmælə'dʒʌstɪd] *adj* unausgeglichen

maladroit [ˌmælə'drɔɪt] *adj* ungeschickt

malady ['mælədi] *s* (& fig) Krankheit *f*

malaise [mæ'lez] *s* *(physical)* Unwohlsein *n*; *(mental)* Unbehagen *n*

malaria [mə'lɛrɪ·ə] *s* Malaria *f*

Malaya [mə'le·ə] *s* Malaya *f*

Malaysia [mə'leʒɪ·ə] *s* Malaysia *n*

malcontent ['mælkən‚tɛnt] *adj* unzufrieden || *s* Unzufriedene *mf*

male [mel] *adj* männlich || *s* Mann *m*; (bot) männliche Pflanze *f*; (zool) Männchen *n*

malediction [ˌmælɪ'dɪkʃən] *s* Verwünschung *f*

malefactor ['mælɪˌfæktər] *s* Übeltäter –in *mf*

male' nurse' *s* Pfleger *m*

malevolence [mæ'lɛvələns] *s* Böswilligkeit *f*

malevolent [mə'lɛvələnt] *adj* böswillig

malfeasance [ˌmæl'fizəns] *s* strafbare Handlung *f*; **m. in office** Amtsvergehen *n*

malfunction [mæl'fʌŋkʃən] *s* technische Störung *f*

malice ['mælɪs] *s* Bosheit *f*

malicious [mə'lɪʃəs] *adj* boshaft

malign [mə'laɪn] *adj* böswillig || *tr* verleumden

malignancy [mə'lɪgnənsi] *s* (pathol) Bösartigkeit *f*

malignant [mə'lɪgnənt] *adj* böswillig; (pathol) bösartig

malinger [mə'lɪŋgər] *intr* simulieren

malingerer [mə'lɪŋgərər] *s* Simulant –in *mf*

mall [mɔl] *s* *(promenade)* Laubenpromenade *f*; *(shopping center)* überdachtes Einkaufszentrum *n*, Mall *f*

mallard ['mælərd] *s* Stockente *f*

malleable ['mælɪ·əbəl] *adj* schmiedbar

mallet ['mælɪt] *s* Schlegel *m*

mallow ['mælo] *s* Malve *f*

malnutrition [ˌmæln(j)u'trɪʃən] *s* Unterernährung *f*

malodorous [mæl'odərəs] *adj* übelriechend

malpractice [mæl'præktɪs] *s* ärztlicher Kunstfehler *m*

malt [mɔlt] *s* Malz *n*

maltreat [mæl'trit] *tr* mißhandeln

mamma ['mɑmə] *s* Mama *f*, Mutti *f*

mammal ['mæməl] *s* Säugetier *n*

mammalian [mæ'melɪ·ən] *adj* Säugetier– || *s* Säugetier *n*

mam'mary gland' ['mæməri] *s* Milchdrüse *f*

mam'ma's boy' *s* Muttersöhnchen *n*

mammoth ['mæməθ] *adj* ungeheuer (groß) || *s* (zool) Mammut *n*

man [mæn] *s* (**men** [mɛn]) *(adult male)* Mann *m*; *(human being)* Mensch *m*; *(servant)* Diener *m*; *(worker)* Arbeiter *m*; *(mankind)* die Menschheit *f*; (checkers) Stein *m*; **man alive!** Menschenskind! || *v* (*pret* & *pp* **manned**; *ger* **manning**) *tr* besetzen; (nav, rok) bemannen

man' about town' *s* weltgewandter Mann *m*

manacle ['mænəkəl] *s* Handschelle *f* || *tr* fesseln

manage ['mænɪdʒ] *tr* (*a business, household*) leiten; (*an estate*) verwalten; (*tools, weapons*) handhaben; (*e.g., a boat, car*) völlig in der Gewalt haben; (*children*) fertig werden mit; **I'll m. it** ich werde es schon schaffen; **m. the situation** die Sache deichseln || *intr* zurechtkommen; (**with, on**) auskommen (mit); **m. to** (*inf*) es fertigbringen zu (*inf*)

manageable ['mænɪdʒəbəl] *adj* handlich; (*hair*) fügsam

management ['mænɪdʒmənt] *s* Unternehmensführung *f*; (*group which manages*) Direktion *f*; (*as opposed to labor*) Management *n*

man'agement consult'ant *s* Unternehmungsberater –in *mf*

manager ['mænɪdʒər] *s* Manager *m*, Geschäftsführer –in *mf*; (*of a bank or hotel*) Direktor –in *mf*; (*of an estate*) Verwalter –in *mf*; (*of a department*) Abteilungsleiter –in *mf*; (*of a star, theater, athlete*) Manager *m*

managerial [ˌmænə'dʒɪrɪ·əl] *adj* Leitungs–, Führungs–

man'aging *adj* geschäftsführend

man'aging direc'tor *s* Geschäftsführer –in *mf*

Manchuria [mæn't ʃʊrɪ·ə] *s* Mandschurei *f*

man'darin or'ange ['mændərɪn] *s* Mandarine *f*

mandate ['mændet] *s* Mandat *n* || *tr* (**to**) zuweisen (*dat*)

mandatory ['mændə‚tori] *adj* verbindlich

mandolin ['mændəlɪn] *s* Mandoline *f*

mandrake ['mændrek] *s* (bot) Alraune *f*

mane [men] *s* Mähne *f*

maneuver [mə'nuvər] *s* Manöver *n*; **go on maneuvers** (mil) ins Manöver ziehen || *tr* manövrieren; **m. s.o. into** (*ger*) j–n dazubringen zu (*inf*)

maneuverability [mə‚nuvərə'bɪlɪti] *s* Manövrierbarkeit *f*

maneuverable [mə'nuvərəbəl] *adj* manövrierfähig

manful ['mænfəl] *adj* mannhaft

manganese ['mæŋgə‚niz] *s* Mangan *n*

mange [mendʒ] *s* Räude *f*

manger ['mendʒər] *s* Krippe *f*

mangle ['mæŋgəl] *s* Mangel *f* ‖ *tr* (*tear apart*) zerfleischen; (*wash*) mangeln

mangy ['mendʒi] *adj* räudig; (fig) schäbig

man'han'dle *tr* grob behandeln

man'hole' *s* Kanalschacht *m*, Mannloch *n*

man'hole cov'er *s* Schachtdeckel *m*

man'hood' *s* (*virility*) Männlichkeit *f*; (*age*) Mannesalter *n*

man'-hour' *s* Arbeitsstunde *f* pro Mann

man'hunt' *s* Fahndung *f*

mania ['meni-ə] *s* Manie *f*

maniac ['meni‚æk] *s* Geisteskranke *mf*

maniacal [mə'nai-əkəl] *adj* manisch

manicure ['mæni‚kjur] *s* Maniküre *f*, Handpflege *f* ‖ *tr* maniküren

manicurist ['mæni‚kjurist] *s* Maniküre *f*

manifest ['mæni‚fest] *adj* offenkundig, offenbar ‖ *s* (aer, naut) Manifest *n* ‖ *tr* bekunden, bezeigen

manifestation [‚mænifes'te/ən] *s* (*manifesting*) Offenbarung *f*; (*indication*) Anzeichen *n*

manifes·to [‚mæni'festo] *s* (**-toes**) Manifest *n*

manifold ['mæni‚fold] *adj* mannigfaltig ‖ *s* (aut) Rohrverzweigung *f*

manikin ['mænikin] *s* Männchen *n*; (*for teaching anatomy*) anatomisches Modell *n*; (*mannequin*) Mannequin *n*

man' in the moon' *s* Mann *m* im Mond

man' in the streets' *s* Durchschnittsmensch *m*

manipulate [mə'nipjə‚let] *tr* manipulieren

man'kind' *s* Menschheit *f*

manliness ['mænlinis] *s* Männlichkeit *f*

manly ['mænli] *adj* mannhaft, männlich

man'-made' *adj* künstlich

manna ['mænə] *s* Manna *n*, Himmelsbrot *n*

manned' space'craft *s* bemanntes Raumfahrzeug *n*

mannequin ['mænikin] *s* (*clothes model*) Mannequin *n*; (*in a display window*) Schaufensterpuppe *f*

manner ['mænər] *s* Art *f*, Weise *f*; (*custom*) Sitte *f*; **after the m. of** nach der Art von; **by all m. of means** auf jeden Fall; **by no m. of means** auf keinen Fall; **in a m.** gewissermaßen; **in a m. of speaking** sozusagen; **in like m.** gleicherweise; **in the following m.** folgendermaßen; **in this m.** auf diese Weise; **it's bad manners to** (*inf*) es schickt sich nicht zu (*inf*); **m. of death** Todesart *f*; **manners** Manieren *pl*

mannerism ['mænə‚rizəm] *s* Manieriertheit *f*

mannerly ['mænərli] *adj* manierlich

mannish ['mæni/] *adj* männisch; (*woman*) unweiblich

man' of let'ters *s* Literat *m*

man' of the world' *s* Weltmann *m*

man' of war' *s* Kriegsschiff *n*

manor ['mænər] *s* Herrengut *n*

man'or house' *s* Herrenhaus *n*

man'pow'er *s* Arbeitskräfte *pl*; (mil) Kriegsstärke *f*

man'serv'ant *s* (**menservants**) Diener *m*

mansion ['mæn/ən] *s* Herrenhaus *n*

man'slaugh'ter *s* Totschlag *m*

mantel ['mæntəl] *s* Kaminsims *m* & *n*

man'telpiece' *s* Kaminsims *m* & *n*

mantilla [mæn'tilə] *s* Mantille *f*

mantle ['mæntəl] *s* (& fig) Mantel *m*; (*of a gaslight*) Glühstrumpf *m*; (geol) Mantel *m* ‖ *tr* verhüllen

manual ['mænju-əl] *adj* manuell, Hand- ‖ *s* (*book*) Handbuch *n*, Leitfaden *m*; (mus) Manual *n*

man'ual control' *s* Handbedienung *f*

man'ual dexter'ity *s* Handfertigkeit *f*

man'ual la'bor *s* Handarbeit *f*

man'ual of arms' *s* (mil) Dienstvorschrift *f*

man'ual train'ing *s* Werkunterricht *m*

manufacture [‚mænjə'fækt/ər] *s* Herstellung *f*; (*production*) Erzeugnis *n* ‖ *tr* herstellen; (*clothes*) konfektionieren

manufac'tured goods' *spl* Fertigwaren *pl*

manufacturer [‚mænjə'fækt/ərər] *s* Hersteller –in *mf*

manure [mə'n(j)ur] *s* Mist *m* ‖ *tr* misten

manuscript ['mænjə‚skript] *adj* handschriftlich ‖ *s* Manuskript *n*

many ['meni] *adj* viele; **a good** (or **great**) **m.** sehr viele; **how m.** wieviele; **in so m. words** ausdrücklich; **m. a** mancher, manch ein; **m. a person** manch einer; **m. a time** manchmal; **twice as m.** noch einmal so viele ‖ *pron* viele; **as m. as** ten nicht weniger als zehn; **how m.** wieviele

man'y-sid'ed *adj* vielseitig

map [mæp] *s* Karte *f*, Landkarte *f*; (*of a city*) Plan *m*; (*of a local area*) Spezialkarte *f*; **map of the world** Weltkarte *f*; **put on the map** (coll) ausposaunen ‖ *v* (*pret & pp* **mapped**; *ger* **mapping**) *tr* kartographisch aufnehmen; **map out** planen

maple ['mepəl] *s* Ahorn *m*

ma'ple sug'ar *s* Ahornzucker *m*

ma'ple syr'up *s* Ahornsirup *m*

mar [mar] *v* (*pret & pp* **marred;** *ger* **marring**) *tr* (*detract from the beauty of*) verunzieren; (*e.g., a reputation*) beeinträchtigen

marathon ['mærə‚θɑn] *s* Dauerwettbewerb *m*

mar'athon race' *s* Marathonlauf *m*

maraud [mə'rɔd] *tr* & *intr* plündern

marauder [mə'rɔdər] *s* Plünderer *m*

marble ['mɑrbəl] *adj* marmorn ‖ *s* Marmor *m*; (*little glass ball*) Murmel *f*; **marbles** (*game*) Murmelspiel *n* ‖ *tr* marmorieren

mar'ble quar'ry *s* Marmorbruch *m*

march [mɑrt/] *s* Marsch *m*; (*festive parade*) Umzug *m*; **March** März *m*; **on the m.** auf dem Marsch; **steal a**

m. on s.o. j-m den Rang ablaufen; **the m. of time** der Lauf der Zeit || *tr* marschieren || *intr* marschieren; **m. by** vorbeimarschieren (an *dat*); **m. off** abmarschieren || *interj* marsch!

marchioness ['marʃənɪs] *s* Marquise *f*

mare [mer] *s* Stute *f*

Margaret ['margərɪt] *s* Margarete *f*

margarine ['mardʒərɪn] *s* Margarine *f*

margin ['mardʒɪn] *s (of a page)* Rand *m; (leeway)* Spielraum *m; (fin)* Spanne *f;* **by a narrow m.** mit knappem Abstand; **leave a m.** am Rande Raum lassen; **m. of profit** Gewinnspanne *f;* **m. of safety** Sicherheitsfaktor *m;* **win by a ten-second m.** mit zehn Sekunden Abstand gewinnen; **write in the m.** an dem Rand schreiben

marginal ['mardʒɪnəl] *adj (costs, profits, case)* Grenz-; *(in the margin)* Rand-

mar′ginal note′ *s* Randbemerkung *f*

mar′gin release′ *s* Randauslöser *m*

mar′gin set′ter *s* Randsteller *m*

marigold ['mærɪ‚gold] *s* Ringelblume *f*

marijuana [‚marɪ'hwanə] *s* Marihuana *n*

marinate ['mærɪ‚net] *tr* marinieren

marine [mə'rin] *adj* See-, Meer(es)- || *s (fleet)* Marine *f; (fighter)* Marineinfanterist *m; marines* Marinetruppen *pl*

Marine′ Corps′ *s* Marineinfanteriekorps *n*

mariner ['mærɪnər] *s* Seemann *m*

marionette [‚mærɪ-ə'net] *s* Marionette *f*

marital ['mærɪtəl] *adj* ehelich, Gatten-

mar′ital sta′tus *s* Familienstand *m*

maritime ['mærɪ‚taɪm] *adj* See-

marjoram ['mardʒərəm] *s* Majoran *m*

mark [mark] *s (& fig)* Zeichen *n; (stain, bruise)* Fleck *m*, Mal *n; (German unit of currency)* Mark *f; (educ)* Zensur *f;* **be an easy m.** (coll) leicht reinzulegen sein; **hit the m.** ins Schwarze treffen; **make one's m.** sich durchsetzen; **m. of confidence** Vertrauensbeweis *m;* **m. of favor** Gunstbezeichnung *f;* **m. of respect** Zeichen *n* der Hochachtung; **on your marks!** auf die Plätze!; **wide of the m.** am Ziel vorbei || *tr (aus)zeichnen*, bezeichnen; *(student papers)* zensieren; *(cards)* zinken; *(labels)* beschriften; *(laundry)* zeichnen; *(the score)* anschreiben; **m. down** aufschreiben, niederschreiben; *(com)* im Preis herabsetzen; **m. my words!** merken Sie sich, was ich sage!; **m. off** abgrenzen; *(surv)* abstecken; **m. time** (mil & fig) auf der Stelle treten; *(mus)* den Takt schlagen; **m. up** *(e.g., a wall)* beschmieren; *(com)* im Preis heraufsetzen

mark′down′ *s* Preisnachlaß *m*

marked *adj (difference)* merklich; **a m. man** ein Gezeichneter *m*

marker ['markər] *s (of scores)* Anschreiber -in *mf; (commemorative*

marker) Gedenktafel *f; (on a firing range)* Anzeiger *m; (bombing marker)* Leuchtbombe *f; (felt pen)* Filzschreiber *m*

market ['markɪt] *s* Markt *m; (grocery store)* Lebensmittelgeschäft *n; (stock exchange)* Börse *f; (ready sale)* Absatz *m;* **be in the m. for** Bedarf haben an *(dat);* **be on the m.** zum Verkauf stehen; **put on the m.** auf den Markt bringen || *tr* verkaufen

marketable ['markɪtəbəl] *adj* marktfähig

mar′ket anal′ysis *s* Marktanalyse *f*

mar′keting *s (econ)* Marketing *n;* **do the m.** Einkäufe machen

mar′keting research′ *s* Absatzforschung *f*

mar′ketplace′ *s* Marktplatz *m*

mar′ket price′ *s* Marktpreis *m*

mar′ket town′ *s* Marktflecken *m*

mar′ket val′ue *s* Marktwert *m; (st. exch.)* Kurswert *m*

mark′ing *s* Kennzeichen *n*

marks·man ['marksmən] *s* (-men) Schütze *m*

marks′manship′ *s* Schießkunst *f*

mark′up′ *s* (com) Gewinnaufschlag *m*

marl [marl] *s* Mergel *m* || *tr* mergeln

marmalade ['marmə‚led] *s* Marmelade *f*

maroon [mə'run] *adj* rotbraun, kastanienbraun || *s* Kastanienbraun *n* || *tr* aussetzen; **be marooned** von der Außenwelt abgeschnitten sein

marquee [mar'ki] *s* Schutzdach *n*

marquess ['markwɪs] *s* Marquis *m*

marquis ['markwɪs] *s* Marquis *m*

marquise [mar'kiz] *s* Marquise *f*

marriage ['mærɪdʒ] *s* Heirat *f; (state)* Ehe *f*, Ehestand *m;* **by m.** angeheiratet, schwägerlich; **give in m.** verheiraten

marriageable ['mærɪdʒəbəl] *adj* heiratsfähig; **m. age** *(of a girl)* Mannbarkeit *f*

mar′riage brok′er *s* Heiratsvermittler -in *mf*

mar′riage cer′emony *s* Trauung *f*

mar′riage li′cense *s* Heiratsurkunde *f*

mar′riage por′tion *s* Mitgift *f*

mar′riage propos′al *s* Heiratsantrag *m*

mar′riage vow′ *s* Ehegelöbnis *n*

mar′ried cou′ple *s* Ehepaar *n*

mar′ried state′ *s* Ehestand *m*

marrow ['mæro] *s* Knochenmark *n; (fig)* Mark *n*

mar·ry ['mæri] *v (pret & pp -ried) tr* heiraten; *(said of a priest or minister)* trauen; **m. off** (to) verheiraten (mit) || *intr* heiraten; **m. rich** e-e gute Partie machen

Mars [marz] *s* Mars *m*

marsh [marʃ] *s* Sumpf *m*

mar·shal ['marʃəl] *s* Zeremonienmeister *m; (police officer)* Bezirkspolizeichef *m; (mil)* Marschall *m* || *v (pret & pp -shal[l]ed; ger -shal[l]ing) tr (troops)* ordnungsgemäß aufstellen; *(strength)* zusammenraffen

marsh'land' s Sumpfland n

marsh' mal'low s (bot) Eibisch m

marsh'mal'low s (candy) Konfekt n aus Stärkesirup, Zucker, Stärke, Gelatine, und geschlagenem Eiweiß

marshy ['mɑrʃi] adj sumpfig

mart [mɑrt] s Markt m

marten ['mɑrtən] s (zool) Marder m

Martha ['mɑrθə] s Martha f

martial ['mɑrʃəl] adj Kriegs-

mar'tial law' s Standrecht n; declare m. das Standrecht verhängen; under m. standrechtlich

martin ['mɑrtɪn] s Mauerschwalbe f; **Martin** Martin m

martinet [,mɑrtɪ'nɛt] s Pauker –in mf; (mil) Schleifer m

martyr ['mɑrtər] s Märtyrer –in mf || tr martern

martyrdom ['mɑrtərdəm] s Märtyrertum n

mar'vel ['mɑrvəl] s Wunder n || v (pret & pp -vel[l]ed; ger -vel[l]ing) intr (at) sich wundern (über acc)

marvelous ['mɑrvələs] adj wundervoll; (coll) pfundig

Marxist ['mɑrksɪst] adj marxistisch || Marxist –in mf

marzipan ['mɑrzɪ,pæn] s Marzipan n

mascara [mæs'kærə] s Lidtusche f

mascot ['mæskɑt] s Maskotte f

masculine ['mæskjəlɪn] adj männlich

mash [mæʃ] s Brei m; (in brewing) Maische f || tr zerquetschen; (potatoes) zerdrücken

mashed' pota'toes spl Kartoffelbrei m

mask [mæsk] s Maske f || tr maskieren

masked' ball' s Maskenball m

mason ['mesən] s Maurer m; **Mason** Freimaurer m

Masonic [mə'sɑnɪk] adj Freimaurer-

masonite ['mesə,naɪt] s Holzfaserplatte f

masonry ['mesənri] s Mauerwerk n; **Masonry** Freimaurerei f

masquerade [,mæskə'red] s (& fig) Maskerade f || intr (& fig) sich maskieren; m. as sich ausgeben als

mass [mæs] adj Massen- || s Masse f; (eccl) Messe; the masses die breite Masse f || tr massieren || intr sich ansammeln

massacre ['mæsəkər] s Massaker n || tr massakrieren, niedermetzeln

massage [mə'sɑʒ] s Massage f || tr massieren

masseur [mə'sʌr] s Masseur m

masseuse [mə'suz] s Masseuse f

massif ['mæsɪf] s Gebirgsstock m

massive ['mæsɪv] adj massiv

mass' me'dia ['midɪ-ə] spl Massenmedien pl

mass' meet'ing s Massenversammlung f

mass' mur'der s Massenmord m

mass'-produce' tr serienmäßig herstellen

mass' produc'tion s Serienherstellung f

mast [mæst] s Mast m; (food for swine) Mast f

master ['mæstər] adj (bedroom, key, switch, cylinder) Haupt- || s Herr m,

Meister m; (male head of a household) Hausherr m; (of a ship) Kapitän m || tr beherrschen

mas'ter build'er s Baumeister m

mas'ter car'penter s Zimmermeister m

mas'ter cop'y s Originalkopie f

masterful ['mæstərfəl] adj herrisch; (masterly) meisterhaft

masterly ['mæstərli] adj meisterhaft

mas'ter mechan'ic s Schlossermeister m

mas'termind' s führender Geist m || tr planen und überwachen

Mas'ter of Arts' s Magister m der freien Künste

mas'ter of cer'emonies s Zeremonienmeister m

mas'ter of the house' s Hausherr m

mas'terpiece' s Meisterstück n

mas'ter ser'geant s Oberfeldwebel m

mas'ter stroke' s Meisterstreich m

mas'terwork' s Meisterwerk n

mastery ['mæstəri] s (of) Beherrschung f (genit); gain m. over die Oberhand gewinnen über (acc)

mast'head' s (naut) Topp m; (typ) Impressum n

masticate ['mæstɪ,ket] tr zerkauen || intr kauen

mastiff ['mæstɪf] s Mastiff m

masturbate ['mæstər,bet] intr onanieren

masturbation [,mæstər'beʃən] s Onanie f

mat [mæt] s (for a floor) Matte f; (before the door) Türvorleger m; (under cups, vases, etc.) Zierdeckchen n || v (pret & pp matted; ger matting) tr (cover with matting) mit Matten belegen; (the hair) verfilzen || intr sich verfilzen

match [mætʃ] s Streichholz n; (for marriage) Partie f; (sport) Match n; be a good m. zueinanderpassen; be a m. for gewachsen sein (dat); be no m. for sich nicht messen können mit; meet one's m. seinen Mann finden || tr (fit together) zusammenstellen; (harmonize with) passen zu; (equal) (in) gleichkommen (in dat); (funds) in gleicher Höhe aufbringen; (adapt) in Übereinstimmung bringen mit; be well matched auf gleicher Höhe sein; m. up zusammenpassen; m. wits with sich geistig messen mit || intr zueinanderpassen

match'book' s Streichholzbrief m

match' box' s Streichholzschachtel f

match'ing adj (clothes) passend; (funds) in gleicher Höhe || s Paarung f

match'mak'er s Heiratsvermittler –in mf; (sport) Veranstalter m

mate [met] s Genosse m, Kamerad m; (in marriage) Ehepartner m; (one of a pair, e.g., of gloves) Gegenstück n; (especially of birds) Männchen n, Weibchen n; (naut) Maat m || tr paaren || intr sich paaren

material [mə'tɪrɪ,əl] adj materiell; (important) wesentlich || s Material n, Stoff m; (tex) Stoff m

materialist [mə'tɪrɪ·əlɪst] *s* Materialist –in *mf*

materialistic [mə‚tɪrɪ·ə'lɪstɪk] *adj* materialistisch

materialize [mə'tɪrɪ·ə‚laɪz] *intr* sich verwirklichen

materiel [mə‚tɪrɪ'el] *s* Material *n*; (mil) Kriegsmaterial *n*

maternal [mə'tʌrnəl] *adj* mütterlich; (*relatives*) mütterlicherseits

maternity [mə'tʌrnɪti] *s* Mutterschaft *f*

mater′nity dress′ *s* Umstandskleid *n*

mater′nity hos′pital *s* Wöchnerinnenheim *n*

mater′nity ward′ *s* Wöchnerinnenstation *f*

math [mæθ] *s* (coll) Mathe *f*

mathematical [‚mæθɪ'mætɪkəl] *adj* mathematisch

mathematician [‚mæθɪmə'tɪʃən] *s* Mathematiker –in *mf*

mathematics [‚mæθɪ'mætɪks] *s* Mathematik *f*

matinée [‚mætɪ'ne] *s* Nachmittagsvorstellung *f*

mat′ing sea′son *s* Paarungszeit *f*

matins ['mætɪnz] *spl* Frühmette *f*

matriarch ['metrɪ‚ark] *s* Stammesmutter *f*

matriarchal [‚metrɪ'arkəl] *adj* matriarchalisch

matriarchy ['metrɪ‚arki] *s* Matriarchat *n*

matricide ['mætrɪ‚saɪd] *s* (*act*) Muttermord *m*; (*person*) Muttermörder –in *mf*

matriculate [mə'trɪkjə‚let] *tr* immatrikulieren ‖ *intr* sich immatrikulieren

matriculation [mə‚trɪkjə'leʃən] *s* Immatrikulation *f*

matrimonial [‚mætrɪ'monɪ·əl] *adj* Ehe-

matrimony ['mætrɪ‚moni] *s* Ehestand *m*

ma·trix ['metrɪks] *s* (**–trices** [trɪ‚siz] & **–trixes**) (*mold*) Gießform *f*; (math) Matrix *f*; (typ) Matrize *f*

matron ['metrən] *s* Matrone *f*

matronly ['metrənli] *adj* matronenhaft, gesetzt

matt [mæt] *adj* (phot) matt

matter ['mætər] *s* Stoff *m*; (*affair*) Sache *f*, Angelegenheit *f*; (*pus*) Eiter *m*; (phys) Materie *f*; **as a m. of course** routinemäßig; **as matters now stand** wie die Sache jetzt liegt; **for that m.** was das betrifft; **it's a m. of** es handelt sich um; **it's a m. of life and death** es geht um Leben und Tod; **m. of opinion** Ansichtssache *f*; **m. of taste** Geschmackssache *f*; **something is the m. with his heart** er hat was am Herz; **no laughing m.** nichts zum Lachen; **no m.** ganz gleich; **what's the m. (with)?** was ist los (mit)? ‖ *intr* von Bedeutung sein; **it doesn't m.** es macht nichts (aus); **it doesn't m. to me** es liegt mir nichts daran; **it matters a great deal to me** es liegt mir sehr viel daran

mat′ter of fact′ *s* Tatsache *f*; **as a m.** tatsächlich

mat′ter-of-fact′ *adj* sachlich, nüchtern

Matthew ['mæθju] *s* Matthäus *m*

mattock ['mætək] *s* Breithacke *f*

mattress ['mætrɪs] *s* Matratze *f*

mature [mə'tʃur] *adj* (& fig) reif ‖ *tr* reifen lassen ‖ *intr* reifen; (fin) fällig werden

maturity [mə'tʃurɪti] *s* Reife *f*; (fin) Verfall *m*

maudlin ['mɔdlɪn] *adj* rührselig

maul [mɔl] *tr* schlimm zurichten

maulstick ['mɔl‚stɪk] *s* Mahlstock *m*

mausole·um [‚mɔsə'li·əm] *s* (**–ums** & **–a** [ə]) Mausoleum *n*

maw [mɔ] *s* (*mouth of an animal*) Rachen *m*; (*stomach of an animal*) Tiermagen *m*; (*of birds*) Kropf *m*

mawkish ['mɔkɪʃ] *adj* rührselig

maxim ['mæksɪm] *s* Maxime *f*, Lehrspruch *m*

maximum ['mæksɪməm] *adj* Höchst-; **m. load** Höchstbelastung *f* ‖ *s* Maximum *n*

May [me] *s* Mai *m* ‖ **may** *v* (*pret* **might** [maɪt]) *aux* (expressing possibility) mögen, können; (expressing permission) dürfen; (expressing a wish) mögen; **be that as it may** wie dem auch sei; **come what may** komme, was da wolle; **it may be too late** es ist vielleicht zu spät; **that may be** das kann (or mag) sein

maybe ['mebi] *adv* vielleicht

May′ Day′ *s* der erste Mai

mayhem ['mehəm] *s* Körperverletzung *f*

mayonnaise [‚me·ə'nez] *s* Mayonnaise *f*

mayor [mer] *s* Bürgermeister *m*; (*of a large city*) Oberbürgermeister *m*

May′pole′ *s* Maibaum *m*

May′ queen′ *s* Maikönigin *f*

maze [mez] *s* Irrgarten *m*; (fig) Gewirr *n*

me [mi] *pers pron* (*direct object*) mich; (*indirect object*) mir; **this one is on me** das geht auf meine Rechnung

mead [mid] *s* (hist) Met *m*; (poet) Aue *f*

meadow ['medo] *s* Wiese *f*

mead′owland′ *s* Wiesenland *n*

meager ['migər] *adj* karg, kärglich

meal [mil] *s* Mahl *n*, Mahlzeit *f*; (*grain*) grobes Mehl *n*

meal′ tick′et *s* Gutschein *m* für e-e Mahlzeit

meal′time′ *s* Essenszeit *f*

mealy ['mili] *adj* mehlig

mealy-mouthed ['mili‚mauðd] *adj* zurückhaltend

mean [min] *adj* (*nasty*) bösartig; (*lowly*) gemein, niedrig; (*shabby*) schäbig; (*in statistics*) mittlere; **no m.** kein schlechter ‖ *s* (log) Mittelbegriff *m*; (math) Mittel *n*; **by all means** unbedingt; **by every means** mit allen Mitteln; **by fair means or foul** ganz gleich wie; **by lawful means** auf dem Rechtswege; **by means of**

mittels (*genit*); **by no means** keineswegs; **live beyond one's means** über seine Verhältnisse leben; **live within one's means** seinen Verhältnissen entsprechend leben; **means** (*way*) Mittel *n*; (*resources*) Mittel *pl*, Vermögen *n*; **means of transportation** Verkehrsmittel *n*; **means to an end** Mittel *pl* zum Zweck; **of means** bemittelt || *v* (*pret & pp* **meant** [ment]) *tr* (*intend, intend to say*) meinen; (*signify*) bedeuten; **be meant for** (*said, e.g., of a remark*) gelten (*dat*); (*said, e.g., of a gift*) bestimmt sein für; **it means a lot to me to** (*inf*) mir liegt viel daran zu (*inf*); **m. business** es ernst meinen; **m. little** (or **much**) wenig (or viel) gelten; **m. no harm** es nicht böse meinen; **m. s.o. no harm** j-n nicht verletzen wollen; **m. the world to s.o.** j-m alles bedeuten; **what is meant by ...?** was versteht man unter ...? || *intr*—**m. well** es gut meinen

meander [mɪ'ændər] *intr* sich winden

mean'ing *s* Bedeutung *f*; **take on m.** e-n Sinn bekommen; **what's the m. of this?** was soll das heißen?

meaningful ['minɪŋfəl] *adj* sinnvoll

meaningless ['minɪŋlɪs] *adj* sinnlos

mean'-look'ing *adj* bösartig aussehend

meanness ['minnɪs] *s* Gemeinheit *f*; (*nastiness*) Bösartigkeit *f*

mean'time', mean'while' *adv* mittlerweile || *s*—**in the m.** mittlerweile, in der Zwischenzeit

measles ['mizəlz] *s* Masern *pl*; (*German measles*) Röteln *pl*

measly ['mizli] *adj* kümmerlich, lumpig

measurable ['meʒərəbəl] *adj* meßbar

measure ['meʒər] *s* Maß *n*; (*step*) Maßnahme *f*; (*law*) Gesetz *n*; (*mus*) Takt *m*; **beyond m.** übermäßig; **for good m.** obendrein; **in a great m. in** großem Maß; **to some m.** gewissermaßen; **take drastic measures** durchgreifen; **take measures to** (*inf*) Maßnahmen ergreifen um zu (*inf*); **take s.o.'s m.** (fig) j-n einschätzen || *tr* messen; **m. off** abmessen; **m. out** ausmessen || *intr* messen; **m. up to** gewachsen sein (*dat*)

measurement ['meʒərmənt] *s* (*measured dimension*) Maß *n*; (*measuring*) Messung *f*; **measurements** Maße *pl*; **take s.o.'s measurements for** j-m Maß nehmen zu

meas'uring cup' *s* Meßbecher *m*

meas'uring tape' *s* Meßband *n*

meat [mit] *s* Fleisch *n*; (*of a nut, of the matter*) Kern *m*

meat'ball' *m* Fleischklößchen *n*

meat' grind'er *s* Fleischwolf *m*

meat'hook' *s* Fleischhaken *m*

meat'mar'ket *s* Fleischmarkt *m*

meat' pie' *s* Fleischpastete *f*

meaty ['miti] *adj* fleischig; (fig) kernig

Mecca ['mekə] *s* Mekka *n*

mechanic [mə'kænɪk] *s* Mechaniker *m*, Schlosser *m*; (aut) Autoschlosser *m*; **mechanics** Mechanik *f*

mechanical [mə'kænɪkəl] *adj* mechanisch

mechan'ical engineer' *s* Maschinenbauingenieur *m*

mechan'ical engineer'ing *s* Maschinenbau *m*

mechanism ['mekə‚nɪzəm] *s* Mechanismus *m*

mechanize ['mekə‚naɪz] *tr* mechanisieren

medal ['medəl] *s* Medaille *f*, Orden *m*

medallion [mɪ'dæljən] *s* Medaillon *n*

meddle ['medəl] *intr* sich einmischen; **m. with** sich abgeben mit

meddler ['medlər] *s* zudringliche Person *f*

meddlesome ['medəlsəm] *adj* zudringlich

media ['midɪ‚ə] *spl* Medien *pl*

median ['midɪ‚ən] *adj* mittlere, Mittel- || *s* (arith) Mittelwert *m*; (geom) Mittellinie *f*

me'dian strip' *s* Mittelstreifen *m*

mediate ['midɪ‚et] *tr & intr* vermitteln

mediation [‚midɪ'eʃən] *s* Vermittlung *f*

mediator ['midɪ‚etər] *s* Vermittler –in *mf*

medic ['medɪk] *s* (mil) Sanitäter *m*

medical ['medɪkəl] *adj* (*of a doctor*) ärztlich; (*of medicine*) medizinisch; (*of the sick*) Kranken-

med'ical bul'letin *s* Krankheitsbericht *m*

med'ical corps' *s* Sanitätstruppe *f*

med'ical profes'sion *s* Arztberuf *m*

med'ical school' *s* medizinische Fakultät *f*

med'ical sci'ence *s* Heilkunde *f*

med'ical stu'dent *s* Medizinstudent –in *mf*

medication [‚medɪ'keʃən] *s* Medikament *n*

medicinal [mə'dɪsɪnəl] *adj* medizinisch

medicine ['medɪsɪn] *s* Medizin *f*, Arznei *f*; (*profession*) Medizin *f*; **practice m.** den Arztberuf ausüben

med'icine cab'inet *s* Hausapotheke *f*

med'icine kit' *s* Reiseapotheke *f*

med'icine man' *s* Medizinmann *m*

medic-o ['medɪ‚ko] *s* (–cos) (coll) Mediziner –in *mf*

medieval [‚midɪ'ivəl], [‚medɪ'ivəl] *adv* mittelalterlich

mediocre [‚midɪ'okər] *adj* mittelmäßig

mediocrity [‚midɪ'ɑkrɪti] *s* Mittelmäßigkeit *f*

meditate ['medɪ‚tet] *tr* vorhaben || *intr* (on) meditieren (über *acc*)

meditation [‚medɪ'teʃən] *s* Meditation *f*

Mediterranean [‚medɪtə'reni‚ən] *adj* Mittelmeer– || *s* Mittelmeer *n*

medi·um ['midɪ‚əm] *adj* Mittel-, mittlere || *s* (–ums & –a [ə]) Mittel *n*; (*culture*) Nährboden *m*; (*in spiritualism, communications*) Medium *n*; **through the m. of** vermittels (*genit*)

me'dium of exchange' *s* Tauschmittel *n*

me'dium-rare' *adj* halb durchgebraten

me'dium size' *s* Mittelgröße *f*

med'ium-sized' *adj* mittelgroß
medley ['medli] *s* Mischmasch *m*; (mus) Potpourri *n*
medul·la [mɪ'dʌlə] *s* (–las & –lae [li]) Knochenmark *n*, Mark *n*
meek [mik] *adj* sanftmütig; **m. as a lamb** lammfromm
meekness ['miknɪs] *s* Sanftmut *m*
meerschaum ['mɪr/əm] *s* Meerschaum *m*
meet [mit] *adj* passend ‖ *s* (sport) Treffen *n*, Veranstaltung *f* ‖ *v* (*pret & pp* **met** [met]) *tr* begegnen (*dat*), treffen; (*make the acquaintance of*) kennenlernen; (*demands*) befriedigen; (*obligations*) nachkommen (*dat*); (*wishes*) erfüllen; (*a deadline*) einhalten; **m. s.o. at the train** j–n von der Bahn abholen; **m. s.o. halfway** j–m auf halbem Wege entgegenkommen; **m. the train** zum Zug gehen; **pleased to m. you** freut mich sehr, sehr angenehm ‖ *intr* (*said of persons, of two ends*) zusammenkommen; (*said of persons*) sich treffen; (*in conference*) tagen; (*said of roads, rivers*) sich vereinigen; **make both ends m.** gerade mit dem Geld auskommen; **m. again** sich wiedersehen; **m. up with s.o.** j–n einholen; **m. with** zusammentreffen mit; **m. with an accident** verunglücken; **m. with a refusal** e–e Fehlbitte tun; **m. with approval** Beifall finden; **m. with success** Erfolg haben
meet'ing *s* (*of an organization*) Versammlung *f*; (*e.g., of a committee*) Sitzung *f*; (*of individuals*) Zusammenkunft *f*
meet'ing place' *s* Treffpunkt *m*
megacycle ['megə,sarkəl], **megahertz** ['megə,hʌrts] *s* (elec) Megahertz *n*
megalomania [,megəlo'menɪ·ə] *s* Größenwahn *m*
megaphone ['megə,fon] *s* Sprachrohr *n*
megohm ['meg,om] *s* Megohm *n*
melancholy ['melən,kɑli] *adj* schwermütig ‖ *s* Schwermut *f*
melee ['mele], ['mele] *s* Gemenge *n*
mellow ['melo] *adj* (*very ripe*) mürb(e); (*wine*) abgelagert; (*voice*) schmelzend; (*person*) gereift ‖ *tr* zur Reife bringen; (fig) mildern ‖ *intr* mürb(e) werden; (fig) mild werden
melodic [mɪ'lɑdɪk] *adj* melodisch
melodious [mɪ'lodɪ·əs] *adj* melodisch
melodrama ['melo,drɑmə] *s* (& fig) Melodrama *f*
melody ['melədi] *s* Melodie *f*
melon ['melən] *s* Melone *f*
melt [melt] *tr & intr* schmelzen
melt'ing point' *s* Schmelzpunkt *m*
melt'ing pot' *s* (& fig) Schmelztiegel *m*
member ['membər] *s* Glied *n*; (*person*) Mitglied *n*, Angehörige *mf*; **m. of the family** Familienangehörige *mf*
mem'bership *s* Mitgliedschaft *f*; (*collectively*) Mitglieder *pl*; (*number of members*) Mitgliederzahl *f*
mem'bership card' *s* Mitgliedskarte *f*

membrane ['membren] *s* Häutchen *n*, Membran(e) *f*
memen·to [mɪ'mento] *s* (–tos & –toes) Erinnerung *f*, Memento *n*
mem·o ['memo] *s* (–os) (coll) Notiz *f*
mem'o book' *s* Notizbuch *n*, Agenda *f*
memoirs ['memwɑrz] *spl* Memoiren *pl*
mem'o pad' *s* Notizblock *m*, Agenda *f*
memorable ['memərəbəl] *adj* denkwürdig
memoran·dum [,memə'rændəm] *s* (–dums & –da [də]) Notiz *f*, Vermerk *m*; (dipl) Memorandum *n*
memorial [mɪ'morɪ·əl] *adj* Gedächtnis–. Erinnerungs– ‖ *s* Denkmal *n*
Memor'ial Day' *s* Gefallenengedenktag *m*
memorialize [mɪ'morɪ·ə,laɪz] *tr* gedenken (*genit*)
memorize ['memə,raɪz] *tr* auswendig lernen
memory ['meməri] *s* (*faculty*) Gedächtnis *n*; (*of*) Gedenken *n* (an *acc*), Erinnerung *f* (an *acc*); **commit to m.** auswendig lernen; **escape one's m.** seinem Gedächtnis entfallen; **from m.** aus dem Gedächtnis; **in m. of** zur Erinnerung an (*acc*); **of blessed m.** seligen Angedenkens; **within the m. of** men seit Menschengedenken
menace ['menɪs] *s* (**to**) Drohung *f* (*genit*) ‖ *tr* bedrohen
menagerie [mə'nædʒəri] *s* Menagerie *f*
mend [mend] *s* Besserung *f*; **on the m.** auf dem Wege der Besserung ‖ *tr* (*clothes*) ausbessern; (*socks*) stopfen; (*repair*) reparieren
mendacious [men'deʃəs] *adj* lügnerisch
mendicant ['mendɪkənt] *adj* Bettel– ‖ *s* Bettelmönch *m*
menfolk ['men,fok] *spl* Mannsleute *pl*
menial ['minɪ·əl] *adj* niedrig ‖ *s* Diener –in *mf*
menopause ['menə,pɔz] *s* Wechseljahre *pl*
menses ['mensiz] *spl* Monatsfluß *m*
men's' room' *s* Herrentoilette *f*
men's' size' *s* Herrengröße *f*
men's' store' *s* Herrenbekleidungsgeschäft *n*
menstruate ['menstru,et] *intr* menstruieren
menstruation [,menstru'eʃən] *s* Menstruation *f*
men's' wear' *s* Herrenbekleidung *f*
mental ['mentəl] *adj* geistig, Geistes–
men'tal an'guish *s* Seelenpein *f*
men'tal arith'metic *s* Kopfrechnen *n*
men'tal capac'ity *s* Fassungskraft *f*
men'tal disor'der *s* Geistesstörung *f*
men'tal institu'tion *s* Nervenheilanstalt *f*
mentality [men'tælɪti] *s* Mentalität *f*
mentally ['mentəli] *adv* geistig, Geistes–; **m. alert** geistesgegenwärtig; **m. disturbed** geistesgestört; **m. lazy** denkfaul
men'tal reserva'tion *s* geistiger Vorbehalt *m*
men'tal telep'athy *s* Gedankenübertragung *f*
mention ['menʃən] *s* Erwähnung *f*;

make m. of erwähnen || *tr* erwähnen, nennen; **be mentioned** zur Sprache kommen; **don't m. it!** keine Ursache!; **not worth mentioning** nicht der Rede wert

menu ['menju] *s* Speisekarte *f*

meow [mi'aʊ] *s* Miauen *n* || *intr* miauen

mercantile ['mʌrkən‚til], ['mʌrkən‚taɪl] *adj* Handels-, kaufmännisch

mercenary ['mʌrsə‚neri] *adj* gewinnsüchtig || *s* Söldner *m*

merchandise ['mʌrt/ən‚daɪz] *s* Ware *f* || *tr* handeln

mer'chandising *s* Verkaufspolitik *f*

merchant ['mʌrt/ənt] *s* Händler, Kaufmann *m*

mer'chant-man *s* (-men) Handelsschiff *n*

mer'chant marine' *s* Handelsmarine *f*

mer'chant ves'sel *s* Handelsschiff *n*

merciful ['mʌrsɪfəl] *adj* barmherzig

merciless ['mʌrsɪlɪs] *adj* erbarmungslos

mercurial [mer'kjʊrɪ‚əl] *adj* quecksilbrig

mercury ['mʌrkjəri] *s* Quecksilber *n*

mercy ['mʌrsi] *s* Barmherzigkeit *f*; **be at s.o.'s m.** in j–s Gewalt sein; **be at the m. of** (*e.g.*, *the wind, waves*) preisgegeben sein (*dat*); **beg for m.** um Gnade flehen; **show no m.** keine Gnade walten lassen; **show s.o. m.** sich j–s erbarmen; **throw oneself on the m. of** sich auf Gnade und Ungnade ergeben (*dat*); **without m.** ohne Gnade

mere [mɪr] *adj* bloß, rein

merely ['mɪrli] *adv* nur, lediglich

meretricious [‚merɪ'trɪʃəs] *adj* (*tawdry*) flitterhaft; (*characteristic of a prostitute*) dirnenhaft

merge [mʌrdʒ] *tr* verschmelzen || *intr* sich verschmelzen

merger ['mʌrdʒər] *s* (com) Fusion *f*; (jur) Verschmelzung *f*

meridian [mə'rɪdɪ‚ən] *s* (astr) Meridian *m*; (geog) Meridian *m*, Längenkreis *m*

meringue [mə'ræŋ] *s* (*topping*) Eierschnee *m*; (*pastry*) Schaumgebäck *n*

merit ['merɪt] *s* Verdienst *n*; **of great m.** hochverdient || *tr* verdienen

meritorious [‚merə'torɪ‚əs] *adj* verdienstvoll

merlin ['mʌrlɪn] *s* (orn) Merlinfalke *m*

mermaid ['mʌr‚med] *s* Seejungfer *f*

merriment ['merɪmənt] *s* Fröhlichkeit *f*

merry ['meri] *adj* fröhlich, heiter

Mer'ry Christ'mas *s* fröhliche Weihnachten *pl*

mer'ry-go-round' *s* Karussell *n*

mer'rymak'er *s* Zecher –in *mf*

mesh [meʃ] *s* Masche *f*; (*network*) Netzwerk *n*; (mach) Ineinandergreifen *n*; **meshes** (fig) Schlingen *pl* || *intr* ineinandergreifen

mesmerize ['mesmə‚raɪz] *tr* hypnotisieren

mess [mes] *s* (*disorder*) Durcheinander *n*; (*dirty condition*) Schweinerei *f*; (*for officers*) Messe *f*; **a nice m.!** e–e schöne Wirtschaft!; **get into a m.** in die Klemme geraten; **make a m.** Schmutz machen; **make a m. of** verpfuschen; **what a m.!** nette Zustände! || *tr* — **m. up** (*dirty*) beschmutzen; (*put into disarray*) in Unordnung bringen || *intr* — **m. around** herumtrödeln; **m. around with** herummurksen an (*dat*)

message ['mesɪdʒ] *s* Botschaft *f*

messenger ['mesəndʒər] *s* Bote *m*, Botin *f*

mess' hall' *s* Messe *f*

Messiah [mə'saɪ‚ə] *s* Messias *m*

mess' kit' *s* Eßgeschirr *n*

messy ['mesi] *adj* (*disorderly*) unordentlich; (*dirty*) dreckig

metabolism [mə'tæbə‚lɪzəm] *s* Stoffwechsel *m*

metal ['metəl] *s* Metall *n*

metallic [mɪ'tælɪk] *adj* metallisch

metallurgy ['metə‚lʌrdʒi] *s* Hüttenwesen *n*, Metallurgie *f*

met'alwork' *s* Metallarbeit *f*

metamorpho‧sis [‚metə'mɔrfəsɪs] *s* (-ses [‚siz]) Verwandlung *f*

metaphor ['metə‚fɔr] *s* Metapher *f*

metaphorical [‚metə'fɔrɪkəl] *adj* bildlich

metaphysical [‚metə'fɪzɪkəl] *adj* metaphysisch

metaphysics [‚metə'fɪzɪks] *s* Metaphysik *f*

metathe‧sis [mɪ'tæθɪsɪs] *s* (-ses [‚siz]) Metathese *f*, Lautversetzung *f*

mete [mit] *tr* — **m. out** austeilen

meteor ['mitɪ‚ər] *s* Meteor *n*

meteoric [‚mitɪ'ɔrɪk] *adj* meteorisch; (fig) kometenhaft

meteorite ['mitɪ‚ə‚raɪt] *s* Meteorit *m*

meteorologist [‚mitɪ‚ə'ralədʒɪst] *s* Meteorologe *m*, Meteorologin *f*

meteorology [‚mitɪ‚ə'ralədʒi] *s* Meteorologie *f*, Wetterkunde *f*

meter ['mitər] *s* Meter *m* & *n*; (*instrument*) Messer *m*, Zähler *m*; (pros) Versmaß *n*

me'ter read'er *s* Zählerableser –in *mf*

methane ['meθen] *s* Methan *n*, Sumpfgas *n*

method ['meθəd] *s* Methode *f*

methodic(al) [mɪ'θadɪk(əl)] *adj* methodisch

Methodist ['meθədɪst] *s* Methodist –in *mf*

methodology [‚meθə'dalədʒi] *s* Methodenlehre *f*

Methuselah [mɪ'θuzələ] *s* Methusalem *m*

meticulous [mɪ'tɪkjələs] *adj* übergenau

metric(al) ['metrɪk(əl)] *adj* metrisch

metrics ['metrɪks] *s* Metrik *f*

metronome ['metrə‚nom] *s* Metronom *n*

metropolis [mɪ'trapəlɪs] *s* Metropole *f*

metropolitan [‚metrə'palɪtən] *adj* großstädtisch || *s* (eccl) Metropolit *m*

mettle ['metəl] *s* (*temperament*) Veranlagung *f*; (*courage*) Mut *m*

mettlesome ['metəlsəm] *adj* mutig

mew [mju] s Miau n || intr miauen

Mexican ['mɛksɪkən] adj mexikanisch || s Mexikaner –in mf

Mexico ['mɛksɪ,ko] s Mexiko n

mezzanine ['mɛzə,nin] s Zwischengeschoß n

mica ['maɪkə] s Glimmer m, Marienglas n

Michael ['maɪkəl] s Michel m

microbe ['maɪkrob] s Mikrobe f

microbiology [,maɪkrəbaɪ'alədʒi] s Mikrobiologie f

microcosm ['maɪkrə,kazəm] s Mikrokosmos m

microfilm ['maɪkrə,fɪlm] s Mikrofilm m || tr mikrofilmen

microgroove ['maɪkrə,gruv] s Mikrorille f

mic'rogroove rec'ord s Schallplatte f mit Mikrorillen

microphone ['maɪkrə,fon] s Mikrophon n

microscope ['maɪkrə,skop] s Mikroskop n

microscopic [,maɪkrə'skapɪk] adj mikroskopisch

microwave ['maɪkrə,wev] s Mikrowelle f

mid [mɪd] adj mittlere

midair' s—in m. mitten in der Luft

mid'day' adj mittäglich, Mittags– || s Mittag m

middle ['mɪdəl] adj mittlere || s Mitte f, Mittel n; in the m. of inmitten (genit), mitten in (dat)

mid'dle age' s mittleres Lebensalter n; **Middle Ages** Mittelalter n

middle-aged ['mɪdəl,edʒd] adj mittleren Alters

mid'dle class' s Mittelstand m

mid'dle-class' adj bürgerlich

mid'dle dis'tance s Mittelgrund m

mid'dle ear' s Mittelohr n

Mid'dle East', **the** s der Mittlere Osten

mid'dle fin'ger s Mittelfinger m

Mid'dle High' Ger'man s Mittelhochdeutsch n

Mid'dle Low' Ger'man s Mittelniederdeutsch n

mid'dle-man' s (-men') Mittelsmann m, Zwischenhändler m

mid'dleweight box'er s Mittelgewichtler m

mid'dleweight divi'sion s Mittelgewicht n

middling ['mɪdlɪŋ] adj mittelmäßig || adv leidlich, ziemlich

middy ['mɪdi] s (nav) Fähnrich m zur See

midget ['mɪdʒɪt] s Zwerg m

mid'get rail'road s Liliputbahn f

mid'get submarine' s Kleinst-U-Boot n

midland ['mɪdlənd] adj binnenländisch

mid'night' adj mitternächtlich; **burn the m. oil** bis in die tiefe Nacht arbeiten || s Mitternacht f; **at m.** um Mitternacht

midriff ['mɪdrɪf] s (of a dress) Mittelteil m; (diaphragm) Zwerchfell n; (middle part of the body) Magengrube f; **have a bare m.** die Taille frei lassen

mid'shipman' s (-men') Fähnrich m zur See

midst [mɪdst] s Mitte f; **from our m.** aus unserer Mitte; **in the m. of** mitten in (dat)

mid'stream' s—in m. in der Mitte des Stromes

mid'sum'mer s Mittsommer m

mid'-term' adj mitten im Semester || **midterms** spl Prüfungen pl mitten im Semester

mid'way' adj in der Mitte befindlich || adv auf halbem Weg || s Mitte f des Weges; (at a fair) Mittelstraße f

mid'week' s Wochenmitte f

mid'wife' s (-wives') Hebamme f

mid'win'ter s Mittwinter m

mid'year' adj in der Mitte des Studienjahres || **midyears** spl Prüfungen pl in der Mitte des Studienjahres

mien [min] s Miene f

miff [mɪf] s kleine Auseinandersetzung f || tr ärgern

might [maɪt] s Macht f, Kraft f; **with m. and main** mit aller Kraft || aux used to form the potential mood, e.g., **she m. lose her way** sie könnte sich verirren; **we m. as well go** es ist wohl besser, wenn wir gehen

mightily ['maɪtəli] adv gewaltig; (coll) enorm

mighty ['maɪti] adj mächtig || adv (coll) furchtbar

migraine ['maɪgren] s Migräne f

mi'grant work'er ['maɪgrənt] s Wanderarbeiter –in mf

migrate ['maɪgret] intr wandern, ziehen

migration [maɪ'grefən] s Wanderung f; (e.g., of birds) Zug m

migratory ['maɪgrə,tori] adj Wander–

mi'gratory bird' s Zugvogel m

Milan [mɪ'læn] s Mailand n

mild [maɪld] adj mild, lind

mildew ['mɪl,d(j)u] s Mehltau m

mildly ['maɪldli] adv leicht, schwach; **to put it m.** gelinde gesagt

mildness ['maɪldnɪs] s Milde f

mile [maɪl] s Meile f; **for miles** meilenweit; **miles apart** meilenweit auseinander; **miles per hour** Stundengeschwindigkeit

mileage ['maɪlɪdʒ] s Meilenzahl f; (charge) Meilengeld n

mile'post' s Wegweiser m mit Entfernungsangabe

mile'stone' s (& fig) Meilenstein m

militancy ['mɪlɪtənsi] s Kampfgeist m

militant ['mɪlɪtənt] adj militant || s Kämpfer –in mf

militarism ['mɪlɪtə,rɪzəm] s Militarismus m

militarize ['mɪlɪtə,raɪz] tr auf den Krieg vorbereiten

military ['mɪlə,teri] adj militärisch; (academy, band, government) Militär– || s Militär n

mil'itary campaign' s Feldzug m

mil'itary cem'etery s Soldatenfriedhof m

mil'itary obliga'tions spl Wehrpflicht f

mil'itary police' s Militärpolizei f

mil'itary police'man s (–men) Militär-
polizist m
mil'itary sci'ence s Kriegswissenschaft
f
militate ['mɪlɪ‚tet] intr (against) entgegenwirken (dat)
militia [mɪ'lɪʃə] s Miliz f
mili'tia-man s (–men) Milizsoldat m
milk [mɪlk] s Milch f || tr (& fig)
melken
milk' bar' s Milchbar f
milk' car'ton s Milchtüte f
milk'maid' s Milchmädchen n
milk'man' s (–men') Milchmann m
milk' pail' s Melkeimer m
milk'shake' s Milchmischgetränk n
milk'sop' s Milchbart m
milk' tooth' s Milchzahn m
milk'weed' s Wolfsmilch f, Seiden-
pflanze f
milky ['mɪlkɪ] adj milchig
Milk'y Way' s Milchstraße f
mill [mɪl] s Mühle f; (factory) Fabrik
f, Werk n; put through the m. (coll)
durch e-e harte Schule schicken || tr
(grain) mahlen; (coins) rändeln;
(with a milling machine) fräsern;
(chocolate) quirlen || intr—m. around
durcheinanderlaufen
millenial [mɪ'lɛnɪ‐əl] adj tausendjährig
millenni•um [mɪ'lɛnɪ‐əm] s (–ums &
–a [ə]) Jahrtausend n
miller ['mɪlər] s Müller m
millet ['mɪlɪt] s Hirse f
milligram ['mɪlɪ‚græm] s Milligramm
n
millimeter ['mɪlɪ‚mitər] s Millimeter
n
milliner ['mɪlɪnər] s Putzmacher –in
mf
mil'linery shop' ['mɪlɪ‚nɛrɪ] s Damen-
hutgeschäft n
mill'ing s (of grain) Mahlen n; (of
wood or metal) Fräsen n
mill'ing machine' s Fräsmaschine f
million ['mɪljən] adj—one m. people
e-e Million Menschen; two m. people
zwei Millionen Menschen || s Million
f
millionaire [‚mɪljən'ɛr] s Millionär –in
mf
millionth ['mɪljənθ] adj & pron mil-
lionste || s (fraction) Millionstel n
mill'pond' s Mühlteich m
mill'stone' s Mühlstein m
mill' wheel' s Mühlrad n
mime [maɪm] s Mime m, Mimin f || tr
mimen
mimeograph ['mɪmɪ‐ə‚græf] s Verviel-
fältigungsapparat m || tr vervielfäl-
tigen
mim•ic ['mɪmɪk] s Mimiker –in mf ||
v (pret & pp –icked; ger –icking) tr
nachäffen
mimicry ['mɪmɪkrɪ] s Nachäffen n;
(zool) Mimikry f
mimosa [mɪ'mosə] s Mimose f
minaret [‚mɪnə'rɛt] s Min₁rett n
mince [mɪns] tr (meat) zerhacken; not
m. words kein Blatt vor ₁en Mund
nehmen
mince'meat' s Pastetenfüllung f;

(chopped meat) Hackfleisch n; **make
m. of** (fig) in die Pfanne hauen
mind [maɪnd] s Geist m; **bear in m.**
denken an (acc); **be of one m.** ein
Herz und e-e Seele sein; **be of two
minds** geteilter Meinung sein; **be out
of one's m.** nicht bei Trost sein;
call to m. erinnern; (remember) sich
erinnern; **change one's m.** sich anders besinnen; **give s.o. a piece of
one's m.** j-m gründlich die Meinung
sagen; **have a good m. to** (inf) große
Lust haben zu (inf); **have in m.** im
Sinn haben zu (inf); **have one's m.
on s.th.** ständig an etw denken
müssen; **I can't get her out of my m.**
sie will mir nicht aus dem Sinn;
know one's own m. wissen, was man
will; **of sound m.** zurechnungsfähig;
put s.th. out of one's m. sich [dat]
etw aus dem Sinn schlagen; **set one's
m. on** sein Sinnen und Trachten
richten auf (acc); **slip s.o.'s m.** j-m
entfallen; **to my m.** meines Erach-
tens || tr (watch over) aufpassen auf
(acc); (obey) gehorchen (dat); (be
troubled by: take care of) sich kümmern um; **do you m. if I smoke?**
macht es Ihnen etw aus, wenn ich
rauche?; **do you m.the smoke?** macht
Ihnen der Rauch etw aus?; **I don't
m. your smoking** ich habe nichts dagegen, daß (or wenn) Sie rauchen;
m. your own business! kümmere dich
um deine Angelegenheit!; **m. you!**
wohlgemerkt! || intr—**I don't m.** es
macht mir nichts aus; **I don't m. if
I do** (coll) ja, recht gern; **never m.!**
schon gut!
-minded [‚maɪndɪd] suf –mütig. -ge-
sinnt, –sinnig
mindful ['maɪndfəl] adj (of) eingedenk
(genit); **be m. of** achten auf (acc)
mind' read'er s Gedankenleser –in mf
mind' read'ing s Gedankenlesen n
mine [maɪn] s Bergwerk n, Mine f;
(fig) Fundgrube f; (mil) Mine f ||
poss pron meiner || tr (e.g., coal)
abbauen; (mil) verminen || intr—**m.
for** graben nach
mine' detec'tor s Minensuchgerät n
mine'field' s Minenfeld n
minelayer ['maɪn‚le‐ər] s Minenleger
m
miner ['maɪnər] s Bergarbeiter m
mineral ['mɪnərəl] adj mineralisch,
Mineral– || s Mineral n
mineralogy [‚mɪnə'rɑlədʒɪ] s Mineralogie f
min'eral resour'ces spl Bodenschätze
pl
min'eral wa'ter s Mineralwasser n
mine'sweep'er s Minenräumboot n
mingle ['mɪŋgəl] tr vermengen || intr
(with) sich mischen (unter acc)
miniature ['mɪnɪ‐ət/ər] ['mɪnɪt/ər]
adj Miniatur-, Klein– || s Miniatur f
minimal ['mɪnɪməl] adj minimal, Mindest–
minimize ['mɪnə‚maɪz] tr auf das
Minimum herabsetzen; (fig) bagatellisieren

minimum ['mɪnɪməm] *adj* minimal, Mindest– ‖ *s* Minimum *n*; *(lowest price)* untere Preisgrenze *f*

min'imum wage' *s* Mindestlohn *m*

min'ing *adj* Bergbau– ‖ *s* Bergbau *m*, Berg˞sen *n*; (mil) Minenlegen *n*

minion ˞'mɪnjən] *s* Günstling *m*

miniskirt ['mɪnɪ‚skʌrt] *s* Minirock *m*

minister ['mɪnɪstər] *s* (eccl) Geistlicher *m*; (pol) Minister *m* ‖ *intr*—m. to dienen *(dat)*; *(aid)* Hilfe leisten *(dat)*

ministerial [‚mɪnɪs'tɪrɪ‑əl] *adj* (eccl) geistlich; (pol) ministeriell

ministry ['mɪnɪstri] *s* *(office)* (eccl) geistliches Amt *n*; *(the clergy)* (eccl) geistlicher Stand *m*; (pol) Ministerium *n*

mink [mɪŋk] *s* (zool) Nerz *m*; *(fur)* Nerzfell *n*

mink' coat' *s* Nerzmantel *m*

minnow ['mɪno] *s* Pfrille *f*, Elritze *f*

minor ['maɪnər] *adj* minder, geringer, Neben– ‖ *s* *(person)* Minderjährige *mf*; *(educ)* Nebenfach *n*; (log) Untersatz *m*; (mus) Moll *n* ‖ *intr*—m. in als Nebenfach studieren

minority [mɪ'nɔrɪti] *adj* Minderheits– ‖ *s* Minderheit *f*; *(of votes)* Stimmenminderheit *f*; *(ethnic group)* Minorität *f*

mi'nor key' *s* Molltonart *f*; **in a m.** in Moll

minstrel ['mɪnstrəl] *s* (hist) Spielmann *m*

mint [mɪnt] *s* Münzanstalt *f*; (bot) Minze *f* ‖ *tr* münzen

mintage ['mɪntɪdʒ] *s* Prägung *f*

minuet [‚mɪnju'et] *s* Menuett *n*

minus ['maɪnəs] *adj* negativ ‖ *prep* minus, weniger; *(without)* (coll) ohne *(acc)*

mi'nus sign' *s* Minuszeichen *n*

minute [maɪ'n(j)ut] *adj* winzig ‖ ['mɪnɪt] *s* Minute *f*; **minutes** Protokoll *n*; **take the minutes** das Protokoll führen

–minute [mɪnɪt] *suf* –minutig

min'ute hand' *s* Minutenzeiger *m*

minutiae [mɪ'n(j)u/ɪ‑i] *spl* Einzelheiten *pl*

minx [mɪŋks] *s* Range *f*

miracle ['mɪrəkəl] *s* Wunder *n*

mir'acle play' *s* Mirakelspiel *n*

miraculous [mɪ'rækjələs] *adj* wunderbar; *(e.g., power)* Wunder–

mirage [mɪ'rɑʒ] *s* Luftspiegelung *f*; (fig) Luftbild *n*, Täuschung *f*

mire [maɪr] *s* Morast *m*, Schlamm *m*

mirror ['mɪrər] *s* Spiegel *m* ‖ *tr* spiegeln

mirth [mʌrθ] *s* Fröhlichkeit *f*

miry ['maɪri] *adj* sumpfig, schlammig

misadventure [‚mɪsəd'ventʃər] *s* Mißgeschick *n*

misanthrope ['mɪsən‚θrop] *s* Menschenfeind *m*

misapprehension [‚mɪsæprɪ'hɛnʃən] *s* Mißverständnis *n*

misappropriate [‚mɪsə'propri‚et] *tr* sich *(dat)* widerrechtlich aneignen

misbehave [‚mɪsbɪ'hev] *intr* sich schlecht benehmen

misbehavior [‚mɪsbɪ'hevɪ‑ər] *s* schlechtes Benehmen *n*

miscalculate [mɪs'kælkjə‚let] *tr* falsch berechnen ‖ *intr* sich verrechnen

miscalculation [‚mɪskælkjə'leʃən] *s* Rechenfehler *m*

miscarriage [mɪs'kærɪdʒ] *s* Fehlgeburt *f*; (fig) Fehlschlag *m*

miscar'riage of jus'tice *s* Justizirrtum *m*

miscar‑ry [mɪs'kæri] *v* *(pret & pp –ried)* *intr* e–e Fehlgeburt haben; *(said of a plan)* scheitern, fehlschlagen

miscellaneous [‚mɪsə'leni‑əs] *adj* vermischt

miscellany ['mɪsə‚leni] *s* Gemisch *n*; *(of literary works)* Sammelband *m*

mischief ['mɪstʃɪf] *s* Unfug *m*; **be up to m.** e–n Unfug im Kopf haben; **cause m.** Unfug treiben; **get into m.** etw anstellen

mis'chief-mak'er *s* Störenfried *m*

mischievous ['mɪstʃɪvəs] *adj* mutwillig

misconception [‚mɪskən'sepʃən] *s* falsche Auffassung *f*

misconduct [mɪs'kɑndʌkt] *s* schlechtes Benehmen *n*; **m. in office** Amtsvergehen *n* ‖ [‚mɪskən'dʌkt] *tr* schlecht verwalten; **m. oneself** sich schlecht benehmen

misconstrue [‚mɪskən'stru] *tr* falsch auffassen

miscount [mɪs'kaunt] *s* Rechenfehler *m* ‖ *tr* falsch zählen ‖ *intr* sich verzählen

miscreant ['mɪskrɪ‑ənt] *s* Schurke *m*

miscue [mɪs'kju] *s* (fig) Fehler *m*; (billiards) Kicks *m* ‖ *intr* (billiards) kicksen; (theat) den Auftritt verpassen

mis-deal ['mɪs‚dil] *s* falsches Geben *n* ‖ [mɪs'dil] *v* *(pret & pp –delt* [delt]*)* *tr* falsch geben ‖ *intr* sich vergeben

misdeed [mɪs'did] *s* Missetat *f*

misdemeanor [‚mɪsdɪ'minər] *s* Vergehen *n*

misdirect [‚mɪsdɪ'rekt], [‚mɪsdaɪ'rekt] *tr* *(& fig)* fehlleiten

misdoing [mɪs'du‑ɪŋ] *s* Missetat *f*

miser ['maɪzər] *s* Geizhals *m*

miserable ['mɪzərəbəl] *adj* elend; **feel m.** sich elend fühlen; **make life m. for s.o.** j–m das Leben sauer machen

miserly ['maɪzərli] *adj* geizig

misery ['mɪzəri] *s* Elend *n*

misfeasance [mɪs'fizəns] *s* (jur) Amtsmißbrauch *m*

misfire [mɪs'faɪr] *s* Versagen *n* ‖ *intr* versagen

misfit ['mɪsfɪt] *s* *(clothing)* schlecht sitzendes Kleidungsstück *n*; *(person)* Gammler *m*

misfortune [mɪs'fɔrtʃən] *s* Unglück *n*

misgiving [mɪs'gɪvɪŋ] *s* böse Ahnung *f*; **full of misgivings** ahnungsvoll

misgovern [mɪs'gʌvərn] *tr* schlecht verwalten

misguidance [mɪs'gaɪdəns] *s* Irreführung *f*

misguide [mɪs'gaɪd] *tr* irreleiten

misguid'ed *adj* irregeleitet

mishap ['mɪshæp] s Unfall m

mishmash ['mɪʃ‚mæʃ] s Mischmasch m

misinform [‚mɪsɪn'fɔrm] tr falsch informieren, falsch unterrichten

misinterpret [‚mɪsɪn'tʌrprɪt] tr mißdeuten, falsch auffassen

misjudge [mɪs'dʒʌdʒ] tr (e.g., a person, situation) falsch beurteilen; (distance) falsch schätzen

mis·lay [mɪs'le] v (pret & pp –laid) tr verlegen, verkramen

mis·lead [mɪs'lid] v (pret & pp –led) tr irreführen

mislead'ing adj irreführend

mismanage [mɪs'mænɪdʒ] tr schlecht verwalten; (funds) verwirtschaften

mismanagement [mɪs'mænɪdʒmənt] s Mißwirtschaft f, schlechte Verwaltung f

mismarriage [mɪs'mærɪdʒ] s Mißheirat f

misnomer [mɪs'nomər] s Fehlbezeichnung f

misplace [mɪs'ples] tr verlegen

misprint ['mɪs‚prɪnt] s Druckfehler m || [mɪs'prɪnt] tr verdrucken

mispronounce [‚mɪsprə'nauns] tr falsch aussprechen

mispronunciation [‚mɪsprənʌnsɪ'eʃən] s falsche Aussprache f

misquote [mɪs'kwot] tr falsch zitieren

misread [mɪs'rid] v (pret & pp –read ['red]) tr falsch lesen || intr sich verlesen

misrepresent [‚mɪsrɛprɪ'zɛnt] tr falsch darstellen; m. the facts to s.o. j-m falsche Tatsachen vorspiegeln

miss [mɪs] s Fehlschlag m, Versager m; **Miss Fräulein** n; **Miss America** die Schönheitskönigin von Amerika || tr (a target; one's calling; a person, e.g., at the station; a town along the road; one's way) verfehlen; (feel the lack of) verpassen; (school, a train, an opportunity) versäumen; **m. one's step** fehltreten; **m. the mark** vorbeischießen; (fig) sein Ziel verfehlen; **m. the point** die Pointe nicht verstanden haben || intr fehlen; (in shooting) vorbeischießen

missal ['mɪsəl] s Meßbuch n

misshapen [mɪs'ʃepən] adj mißgestaltet

missile ['mɪsɪl] s Geschoß n; (rok) Rakete f

missing ['mɪsɪŋ] adj—be m. fehlen; (said, e.g., of a child) vermißt werden; **m. in action** vermißt

miss'ing per'son s Vermißte mf

miss'ing-per'sons bu'reau s Suchdienst m

mission ['mɪʃən] s Mission f; **m. in life** Lebensaufgabe f

missionary ['mɪʃən‚ɛri] adj Missions– || s Missionar –in mf

missis ['mɪsɪz] s—**the m.** (the wife) die Frau; (of the house) (coll) die Frau des Hauses

missive ['mɪsɪv] s Sendschreiben n

mis·spell [mɪs'spɛl] v (pret & pp –spelled & –spelt) tr & intr falsch schreiben

misspell'ing s Schreibfehler m

misspent [mɪs'spɛnt] adj vergeudet

misstate [mɪs'stet] tr falsch angeben

misstatement [mɪs'stetmənt] s falsche Angabe f

misstep [mɪs'stɛp] s (& fig) Fehltritt m

mist [mɪst] s feiner Nebel m || tr umnebeln || intr (said of the eyes) sich trüben; **mist over** nebeln

mis·take [mɪs'tek] s Fehler m; **by m.** aus Versehen || v (pret –took ['tuk], pp –taken) tr verkennen; **m. s.o. for s.o. else** j–n mit e–m anderen verwechseln

mistaken [mɪs'tekən] adj falsch, irrig; **be m. (about)** sich irren (in dat); **unless I'm m.** wenn ich mich nicht irre

mistak'en iden'tity s Personenverwechslung f

mistakenly [mɪs'tekənli] adv versehentlich

mister ['mɪstər] s Herr m || interj (pej) Herr!

mistletoe ['mɪsəl‚to] s Mistel f

mistreat [mɪs'trit] tr mißhandeln

mistreatment [mɪs'tritmənt] s Mißhandlung f

mistress ['mɪstrɪs] s Herrin f; (lover) Mätresse f, Geliebte f

mistrial [mɪs'traɪəl] s fehlerhaft geführter Prozeß m

mistrust [mɪs'trʌst] s Mißtrauen n || tr mißtrauen (dat)

misty ['mɪsti] adj neblig; (eyes) umflort; (fig) unklar

misunder·stand [‚mɪsʌndər'stænd] v (pret & pp –stood) tr & intr mißverstehen

misunderstanding [‚mɪsʌndər'stændɪŋ] s Mißverständnis n

misuse [mɪs'jus] s Mißbrauch m || [mɪs'juz] tr mißbrauchen; (mistreat) mißhandeln

misword [mɪs'wʌrd] tr in falsche Worte fassen

mite [maɪt] s (ent) Milbe f

miter ['maɪtər] s Bischofsmütze f || tr auf Gehrung verbinden

mi'ter box' s Gehrlade f

mitigate ['mɪtɪ‚get] tr lindern

mitigation [‚mɪtɪ'geʃən] s Linderung f

mitt [mɪt] s Fausthandschuh m; (sl) Flosse f; (baseball) Fängerhandschuh m

mitten ['mɪtən] s Fausthandschuh m

mix [mɪks] s Mischung f, Gemisch n || tr (ver)mischen; (a drink) mixen; (a cake) anrühren; **mix in** beimischen; **mix up** vermischen; (confuse) verwirren || intr sich (ver)mischen; **mix with** vekehren mit

mixed adj vermischt; (feelings, company, doubles) gemischt

mixed' drink' s Mixgetränk n

mixed' mar'riage s Mischehe f

mixer ['mɪksər] s Mischer –in mf; (of cocktails) Mixer –in mf; (mach) Mischmaschine f; **a good m.** ein guter Gesellschafter

mixture ['mɪkstʃər] s (e.g., of gases)

Gemisch n; (e.g., of tobacco, coffee) Mischung f; (pharm) Mixtur f

mix'-up' s Wirrwar m, Verwechslung f

mizzen ['mɪzən] s Besan m

mnemonic [nə'manɪk] s Gedächtnishilfe f

moan [mon] s Stöhnen n || intr stöhnen; **m. about** jammern über (acc) or um

moat [mot] s Schloßgraben m

mob [mab] s (populace) Pöbel m; (crush of people) Andrang m; (gang of criminals) Verbrecherbande f || v (pret & pp **mobbed**; ger **mobbing**) tr (crowd into) lärmend eindringen in (acc); (e.g., a consulate) angreifen; (a celebrity) umringen

mobile ['mobɪl] adj fahrbar; (mil) motorisiert

mo'bile home' s Wohnwagen m

mobility [mo'bɪlɪti] s (& mil) Beweglichkeit f

mobilization [,mobɪlɪ'zefən] s Mobilisierung f

mobilize ['mobɪ,laɪz] tr mobilisieren; (strength) aufbieten

mob' rule' s Pöbelherrschaft f

mobster ['mabstər] s Gangster m

moccasin ['makəsɪn] s Mokassin m; (snake) Mokassinschlange f

Mo'cha cof'fee ['mokə] s Mokka m

mock [mak] adj Schein– || tr verspotten; (imitate) nachäffen || intr spotten; **m. at** sich lustig machen über (acc); **m. up** improvisieren

mocker ['makər] s Spötter –in mf

mockery ['makəri] s Spott m, Spöttelei f; **make a m. of** hohnsprechen (dat)

mock'ing adj spöttisch

mock'ingbird' s Spottdrossel f

mock' tri'al s Schauprozeß m

mock' tur'tle soup' s falsche Schildkrötensuppe f

mock'-up' s Schaumodell n

modal ['modəl] adj modal, Modal–

mode [mod] s Modus m; (mus) Tonart f

mod-el ['madəl] adj vorbildlich; (student, husband) Muster– || s (e.g., of a building) Modell n; (at a fashion show) Vorführdame f; (for art or photography) Modell n; (example for imitation) Vorbild n, Muster n; (make) Typ m, Bauart f || v (pret & pp –el[l]ed; ger –el[l]ing) tr (clothes) vorführen; **m. oneself on** sich [dat] ein Muster nehmen an (dat); **m. s.th. on** etw formen nach; (fig) etw gestalten nach || intr (for) Modell stehen (zu dat)

mod'el air'plane s Flugzeugmodell n

mod'el num'ber s (aut) Typennummer f

moderate ['madərɪt] adj (climate) gemäßigt; (demand) maßvoll; (price) angemessen; (e.g., in drinking) mäßig; **of m. means** minderbemittelt || ['madə,ret] tr mäßigen; (a meeting) den Vorsitz führen über (acc) or bei; (a television show) moderieren || intr sich mäßigen

moderation [,madə're/ən] s Mäßigung

f, Maß n; **in m.** mit Maß; **observe m.** Maß halten

moderator ['madə,retər] s Moderator m

modern ['madərn] adj modern, zeitgemäß

mod'ern Eng'lish s Neuenglisch n

mod'ern his'tory s Neuere Geschichte f

modernize ['madər,naɪz] tr modernisieren

mod'ern lan'guages spl neuere Sprachen pl

mod'ern times' spl die Neuzeit f

modest ['madɪst] adj bescheiden

modesty ['madɪsti] s Bescheidenheit f

modicum ['madɪkəm] s bißchen; **a m. of truth** ein Körnchen Wahrheit

modification [,madɪfɪ'ke/ən] s Abänderung f

modifier ['madɪ,faɪ.ər] s (gram) nähere Bestimmung f

modi-fy ['madɪ,faɪ] v (pret & pp –fied) tr abändern; (gram) näher bestimmen

modish ['modɪ/] adj modisch

modulate ['madjə,let] tr & intr modulieren

modulation [,madjə'le/ən] s Modulation f

mohair ['mo,her] s Mohair m

Mohammedan [mo'hæmɪdən] adj mohammedanisch || s Mohammedaner –in mf

Mohammedanism [mo'hæmɪdə,nɪzəm] s Mohammedanismus m

moist [mɔɪst] adj feucht; (eyes) tränenfeucht

moisten ['mɔɪsən] tr anfeuchten; (lips) befeuchten || intr feucht werden

moisture ['mɔɪst/ər] s Feuchtigkeit f

molar ['molər] s Backenzahn m

molasses [mə'læsɪz] s Melasse f

mold [mold] s Form f; (mildew) Schimmel m; (typ) Matrize f || tr formen || intr (ver)schimmeln

molder ['moldər] s Former –in mf; (fig) Bildner –in mf || intr modern

mold'ing s Formen n; (carp) Gesims n

moldy ['moldi] adj mod(e)rig, schimmlig

mole [mol] s (breakwater) Hafendamm m; (blemish) Muttermal n; (zool) Maulwurf m

molecular [mə'lekjələr] adj molekular

molecule ['malɪ,kjul] s Molekül n

mole'skin' s (fur) Maulwurfsfell n; (tex) Englischleder n

molest [mə'lest] tr belästigen

molli-fy ['malɪ,faɪ] v (pret & pp –fied) tr besänftigen

mollusk ['maləsk] s Weichtier n

mollycoddle ['malɪ,kadəl] s Weichling m || tr verweichlichen

Mol'otov cock'tail ['malətəf] s Flaschengranate f

molt [molt] s intr sich mausern

molten ['moltən] adj schmelzflüssig

molybdenum [mə'lɪbdɪnəm] s Molybdän n

mom [mam] s (coll) Mama f, Mutti f

moment ['momənt] s Moment m, Au

genblick *m;* a m. ago nur eben; **at a moment's notice** jeden Augenblick; **at any m.** jederzeit; **at the m.** im Augenblick, zur Zeit; **of great m.** von großer Tragweite; **the very m.** I spotted her sobald ich sie erblickte

momentarily ['momǝn‚terɪli] *adv* momentan; (*in a moment*) gleich

momentary ['momǝn‚teri] *adj* vorübergehend

momentous [mo'mentǝs] *adj* folgenschwer

momen·tum [mo'mentǝm] *s* (**-tums** & **-ta** [tǝ]) (phys) Moment *n;* (fig) Schwung *m;* **gather m.** Schwung bekommen

monarch ['monǝrk] *s* Monarch *m*

monarchical [mǝ'narkɪkǝl] *adj* monarchisch

monarchy ['monǝr‚teri] *s* Monarchie *f*

monastery ['monǝs‚teri] *s* Kloster *n*

monastic [mǝ'næstɪk] *adj* Kloster-, Mönchs-

monasticism [mǝ'næstɪ‚sɪzǝm] *s* Mönchswesen *n*

Monday ['mʌndi], ['mʌnde] *s* Montag *m;* **on M. am** Montag

monetary ['monɪ‚teri] *adj* (e.g., *crisis, unit*) Währungs-; (e.g., *system, value*) Geld-

mon'etary stand'ard *s* Münzfuß *m*

money ['mʌni] *adj* Geld- ‖ *s* Geld *n;* **big m.** schweres Geld; **get one's money's worth** reell bedient werden; **make m. (on)** Geld verdienen (an *dat);* **put m. on** Geld setzen auf (*acc*)

mon'eybag' *s* Geldbeutel *m;* **moneybags** (coll) Geldsack *m*

mon'ey belt' *s* Geldgürtel *m*

moneychanger ['mʌni‚tʃendʒǝr] *s* Wechsler –in *mf*

moneyed ['mʌnid] *adj* vermögend

mon'ey exchange' *s* Geldwechsel *m*

mon'eylend'er *s* Geldverleiher –in *mf*

mon'eymak'er *s* (fig) Goldgrube *f*

mon'ey or'der *s* Postanweisung *f*

Mongol ['mongǝl] *adj* mongolid ‖ *s* Mongole *m,* Mongolin *f*

Mongolian [mʌn'golɪ·ǝn] *adj* mongolisch ‖ *s* (*language*) Mongolisch *n*

mon·goose ['mongus] *s* (**-gooses**) Mungo *m*

mongrel ['mʌngrǝl] *s* Bastard *m*

monitor ['monɪtǝr] *s* (*at school*) Klassenordner *m;* (rad, telv) Überwachungsgerät *n,* Monitor *m* ‖ *tr* überwachen

monk [mʌŋk] *s* Mönch *m*

monkey ['mʌŋki] *s* Affe *m;* (*female*) Äffin *f;* **make a m. of** zum Narren halten ‖ *intr*—**m. around** (*trifle idly*) herumlaufen; **m. around with s.o.** es mit j–m treiben; **m. around with s.th.** an etw [*dat*] herummurksen

mon'keybusi'ness *s* (*underhanded conduct*) Gaunerei *f;* (*frivolous behavior*) (sl) Unfug *m*

mon'keyshine' *s* (sl) Possen *m*

mon'key wrench' *s* Engländer *m*

monocle ['monǝkǝl] *s* Monokel *n*

monogamous [mǝ'nagǝmǝs] *adj* monogam

monogamy [mǝ'nagǝmi] *s* Einehe *f*

monogram ['monǝ‚græm] *s* Monogramm *n*

monograph ['monǝ‚græf] *s* Monographie *f*

monolithic [‚monǝ'lɪθɪk] *adj* (& fig) monolithisch

monologue ['monǝ‚log] *s* Monolog *m*

monomania [‚monǝ'meni·ǝ] *s* Monomanie *f*

monoplane ['monǝ‚plen] *s* Eindecker *m*

monopolize [mǝ'napǝ‚laɪz] *tr* monopolisieren

monorail ['monǝ‚rel] *s* Einschienenbahn *f*

monosyllable ['monǝ‚sɪlǝbǝl] *s* einsilbiges Wort *n*

monotheism [‚monǝ'θi·ɪzǝm] *s* Monotheismus *m*

monotonous [mǝ'natǝnǝs] *adj* eintönig

monotony [mǝ'natǝni] *s* Eintönigkeit *f*

monotype ['monǝ‚taɪp] *s* Monotype *f*

monoxide [mǝ'naksaɪd] *s* Monoxyd *n*

monsignor [man'sinjǝr] *s* (**monsignors** & **monsignori** [‚monsi'njori]) (eccl) Monsignore *m*

monsoon [man'sun] *s* Monsun *m*

monster ['monstǝr] *s* (& fig) Ungeheuer *n*

monstrance ['monstrǝns] *s* Monstranz *f*

monstrosity [mans'trasɪti] *s* Monstrosität *f,* Ungeheuerlichkeit *f*

monstrous ['monstrǝs] *adj* ungeheuer(lich)

month [mʌnθ] *s* Monat *m*

monthly ['mʌnθli] *adj* & *adv* monatlich ‖ *s* Monatszeitschrift *f*

monument ['monjǝmǝnt] *s* Denkmal *n*

monumental [‚monjǝ'mentǝl] *adj* monumental

moo [mu] *s* Muhen *n* ‖ *intr* muhen

mood [mud] *s* Laune *f,* Stimmung *f;* (gram) Aussageweise *f,* Modus *m;* **be in a bad m.** schlechtgelaunt sein; **be in the m. for s.th.** zu etw gelaunt sein

moody ['mudi] *adj* launisch

moon [mun] *s* Mond *m* ‖ *intr*—**m. about** herumlungern

moon'beam' *s* Mondstrahl *m*

moon'light' *s* Mondschein *m* ‖ *intr* schwarzarbeiten

moon'light'er *s* Doppelverdiener –in *mf*

moon'light'ing *s* Schwarzarbeit *f*

moon'lit' *adj* mondhell

moon'shine' *s* Mondschein *m;* (sl) schwarz gebrannter Whisky *m*

moonshiner ['mun‚ʃaɪnǝr] *s* Schwarzbrenner –in *mf*

moon'shot' *s* Mondgeschoß *n*

moor [mur] *s* Moor *n,* Heidemoor *n;* **Moor** Mohr *m* ‖ *tr* (naut) vertäuen ‖ *intr* (naut) festmachen

moor'ing *s* (act) Festmachen *n;* **moorings** (cables) Vertäuung *f;* (*place*) Liegeplatz *m*

Moorish ['murɪʃ] *adj* maurisch

moose [mus] *s* (**moose**) amerikanischer Elch *m*

moot [mut] *adj* umstritten

mop [mɑp] s Mop m; (of hair) Wust m ‖ v (pret & pp mopped; ger mopping) tr mit dem Mop wischen; **mop up** mit dem Mop aufwischen; (mil) säubern

mope [mop] intr Trübsal blasen

moped ['moped] s Moped n

mop'ping-up' opera'tion s (mil) Säuberungsaktion f

moral ['mɔrəl] adj moralisch ‖ s Moral f; **morals** Sitten pl

morale [mə'ræl] s Moral f

morality [mə'ræliti] s Sittlichkeit f

moralize ['mɔrə,laiz] intr moralisieren

morass [mə'ræs] s Morast m

moratori·um [,mɔrə'tori·əm] s (-ums & a- [ə]) Moratorium n

Moravia [mə'revi·ə] s Mähren n

morbid ['mɔrbid] adj krankhaft, morbid

mordacious [mɔr'deʃəs] adj bissig

mordant ['mɔrdənt] adj beißend

more [mɔr] comp adj mehr; **one m. minute** noch e-e Minute ‖ comp adv mehr; **all the m.** erst recht; **all the m. because** zumal, da; **m. and m.** immer mehr; **m. and m. expensive** immer teurer; **m. or less** gewissermaßen; **m. than anything** über alles; **no m.** nicht mehr; **not any m.** nicht mehr; **once m.** noch einmal; **the more ... the** (expressing quantity) je mehr ... desto; (expressing frequency) je öfter ... desto ‖ s mehr; **see m. of s.o.** j-n noch öfter sehen; **what's m.** außerdem ‖ pron mehr

more'o'ver adv außerdem, übrigens

morgue [mɔrg] s Leichenschauhaus n; (journ) Archiv n, Zeitungsarchiv n

morning ['mɔrnɪŋ] adj Morgen- ‖ s Morgen m; **from m. till night** von früh bis spät; **in the early m.** in früher Morgenstunde; **in the m.** am Morgen; **this m.** heute morgen; **tomorrow m.** morgen früh

morn'ing-af'ter pill' s Pille f danach

morn'ing-glo'ry s Trichterwinde f

morn'ing sick'ness s morgendliches Erbrechen n

morn'ing star' s Morgenstern m

Moroccan [mə'rakən] adj marokkanisch ‖ s Marokkaner –in mf

morocco [mə'rako] s (leather) Saffian m; **Morocco** Marokko n

moron ['mɔran] s Schwachsinnige mf

morose [mə'ros] adj mürrisch

morphine ['mɔrfin] s Morphium n

morphology [mɔr'faledʒi] s Morphologie f

morrow ['mɔro] s—**on the m.** am folgenden Tag

Morse' code' [mɔrs] s Morsealphabet n

morsel ['mɔrsəl] s Bröckchen n

mortal ['mɔrtəl] adj sterblich ‖ s Sterbliche mf

mor'tal dan'ger s Lebensgefahr f

mor'tal en'emy s Todfeind m

mor'tal fear' s Heidenangst f

mortality [mɔr'tæliti] s Sterblichkeit f

mortally ['mɔrtəli] adv tödlich

mor'tal remains' spl irdische Überreste pl

mor'tal sin' s Todsünde f

mor'tal wound' s Todeswunde f

mortar ['mɔrtər] s (vessel) Mörser m; (archit) Mörtel m; (mil) Granatwerfer m

mor'tarboard' s Mörtelbrett n

mor'tar fire' s Granatwerferfeuer n

mor'tar shell' s Granate f

mortgage ['mɔrgidʒ] s Hypothek f ‖ tr mit e-r Hypothek belasten

mortgagee [,mɔrgi'dʒi] s Hypothekengläubiger –in mf

mortgagor ['mɔrgidʒər] s Hypothekenschuldner –in mf

mortician [mɔr'tiʃən] s Leichenbestatter –in mf

morti·fy ['mɔrti,fai] v (pret & pp -fied) tr (the flesh) abtöten; (humiliate) demütigen; **m. oneself** sich kasteien

mortise ['mɔrtis] s (carp) Zapfenloch n ‖ tr (carp) verzapfen

mortuary ['mɔrtʃu,eri] s Leichenhalle f

mosaic [mo'ze·ik] adj mosaisch ‖ s Mosaik n

Moscow ['masko], ['maskau] s Moskau n

Moses ['moziz], ['mozis] s Moses m

mosey ['mozi] intr (coll) dahinschlürfen

Mos·lem ['mazləm] adj muselmanisch ‖ s (-lems & -lem) Moslem –in mf

mosque [mask] s Moschee f

mosqui·to [məs'kito] s (-toes & -tos) Moskito m, Mücke f

mosqui'to net' s Moskitonetz n

moss [mɔs] s Moos n

mossy ['mɔsi] adj bemoost

most [most] super adj meist ‖ super adv am meisten; (very) höchst; **m. of all** am allermeisten ‖ s—**at (the) m.** höchstens; **make the m. of** möglichst gut ausnützen; **m. of** die meisten; **m. of the day** der größte Teil des Tages; **the m.** das meiste, das Höchste ‖ pron die meisten

mostly ['mostli] adv meistens

motel [mo'tel] s Motel n

moth [mɔθ] s Nachtfalter m; (clothes moth) Motte f

moth'ball' s Mottenkugel f; **put into mothballs** (nav) stillegen, einmotten ‖ tr (& fig) einmotten

moth-eaten ['mɔθ,itən] adj mottenzerfressen

mother ['mʌðər] s Mutter f ‖ tr (produce) gebären; (take care of as a mother) bemuttern

moth'er coun'try s Mutterland n

moth'erhood' s Mutterschaft f

moth'er-in-law' s (mothers-in-law) Schwiegermutter f

motherless ['mʌðərlis] adj mutterlos

motherly ['mʌðərli] adj mütterlich

mother-of-pearl ['mʌðərəv'pʌrl] adj perlmuttern ‖ s Perlmutter f

Moth'er's Day' s Muttertag m

moth'er's help'er s Stütze f der Hausfrau

moth'er supe'rior s (Schwester) Oberin f

moth'er tongue' s Muttersprache f

moth' hole' s Mottenfraß m

mothy ['mɔθɪ] adj mottenzerfressen

motif [mo'tif] s (mus, paint) Motiv n

motion ['moʃən] s Bewegung f; (parl) Antrag m; **make a m.** e–n Antrag stellen; **set in m.** in Bewegung setzen || tr zuwinken (dat); **m. s.o. to** (inf) j–n durch e–n Wink auffordern zu (inf)

motionless ['moʃənlɪs] adj bewegungslos

mo'tion pic'ture s Film m; **be in motion pictures** beim Film sein

mo'tion-pic'ture adj Film-

mo'tion-pic'ture the'ater s Kino n

motivate ['motɪ,vet] tr begründen, motivieren

motive ['motɪv] s Anlaß m, Beweggrund m

mo'tive pow'er s Triebkraft f

motley ['mɑtlɪ] adj bunt zusammengewürfelt

motor ['motər] adj Motor- || s Motor m

motorcade ['motər,ked] s Wagenkolonne f

mo'torcy'cle s Motorrad n

mo'torcyc'list s Motorradfahrer –in mf

mo'toring s Autofahren n

motorist ['motərɪst] s Autofahrer –in mf

motorize ['motə,raɪz] tr motorisieren

mo'tor launch' s Motorbarkasse f

mo'tor-man s (–men) Straßenbahnführer m

mo'tor pool' s Fahrbereitschaft f

mo'tor scoot'er s Motorroller m

mo'tor ve'hicle s Kraftfahrzeug n

mottle ['mɑtəl] tr sprenkeln

mot·to ['mɑto] s (–toes & –tos) Motto n

mound [maund] s Wall m, Erdhügel m

mount [maunt] s (mountain) Berg m; (riding horse) Reittier n || tr (a horse, mountain) besteigen; (stairs) hinaufgehen; (e.g., a machinegun) in Position bringen; (a precious stone) fassen; (photographs in an album) einkleben; (photographs on a backing) aufkleben; **m.** (e.g., a gun) on montieren auf (acc)

mountain ['mauntən] s Berg m; **down the m.** bergab; **up the m.** bergauf

moun'tain climb'er s Bergsteiger –in mf

moun'tain climb'ing s Bergsteigen n

mountaineer [,mauntə'nɪr] s Bergbewohner –in mf

mountainous ['mauntənəs] adj gebirgig

moun'tain pass' s Gebirgspaß m, Paß m

moun'tain rail'road s Bergbahn f

moun'tain range' s Gebirge n

moun'tain scen'ery s Berglandschaft f

mountebank ['mauntə,bæŋk] s Quacksalber m; (charlatan) Scharlatan m

mount'ing s Montage f; (of a precious stone) Fassung f

mourn [morn] tr betrauern || intr trauern; **mourn for** betrauern, trauern um

mourner ['mornər] s Leidtragende mf

mournful ['mornfəl] adj traurig

mourn'ing s Trauer f; **be in m.** Trauer tragen

mourn'ing band' s Trauerflor m

mourn'ing clothes' spl Trauerkleidung f; **wear m.** Trauer tragen

mouse [maus] s (mice [maɪs]) Maus f

mouse'hole' s Mauseloch n

mouse'trap' s Mausefalle f

moustache [məs'tæʃ] s Schnurbart m

mouth [mauθ] s (mouths [mauðz]) Mund m; (of an animal) Maul n; (of a gun, bottle, river) Mündung f; (sl) Maul n; **keep one's m. shut** den Mund halten; **make s.o.'s m. water** j–m das Wasser im Munde zusammenlaufen lassen

mouthful ['mauθ,ful] s Mundvoll m; (sl) großes Wort n

mouth' or'gan s Mundharmonika f

mouth'piece' s (of an instrument) Ansatz m; (box) Mundstück n; (fig) Sprachrohr n

mouth'wash' s Mundwasser n

movable ['muvəbəl] adj beweglich, mobil || movables spl Mobilien pl

move [muv] s (movement) Bewegung f; (step, measure) Maßnahme f; (re-settlement) Umzug m; (checkers) Zug m; (parl) Vorschlag m; **be on the m.** unterwegs sein; **don't make a m.!** keinen Schritt!; **get a m. on** (coll) sich rühren; **it's your m.** (& fig) du bist am Zug; **she won't make a m. without him** sie macht keinen Schritt ohne ihn || tr bewegen; (emotionally) rühren; (shove) rücken; (checkers) e–n Zug machen mit; (parl) beantragen; **m. the bowels** abführen; **m. up** (mil) vorschieben || intr (stir) sich bewegen; (change residence) umziehen; (in society) verkehren; (checkers) ziehen; (com) Absatz haben; **m. away** wegziehen; **m. back** zurückziehen; **m. for** (e.g., a new trial) beantragen; **m. in** zuziehen; **m. into** (a home) beziehen; **m. on** fortziehen; **m. out (of)** ausziehen (aus); **m. over** (make room) zur Seite rücken; **m. up** (to a higher position) vorrücken; (into a vacated position) nachrücken; (said of a team) aufsteigen

movement ['muvmənt] s (& fig) Bewegung f; (mus) Satz m

mover ['muvər] s Möbeltransporteur m; (parl) Antragsteller –in mf

movie ['muvi] adj (actor, actress, camera, projector) Film- || s (coll) Film m; **movies** Kino n; **go to the movies** ins Kino gehen

mov'ie cam'era s Filmkamera f

moviegoer ['muvi,go·ər] s Kinobesucher –in mf

mov'ie house' s Kino n

mov'ie screen' s Filmleinwand f

mov'ie set' s Filmkulisse f

mov'ie the'ater s Kino n

mov'ing adj beweglich; (force) treibend; (fig) herzergreifend ‖ *s* (*change of residence*) Umzug *m*

mov'ing pic'ture *s* Lichtspiel *n*, Film *m*

mov'ing spir'it *s* führender Kopf *m*

mow [mo] *v* (*pret* **mowed;** *pp* **mowed & mown**) *tr* mähen; **mow down** (*enemies*) niedermähen

mower ['mo‧ər] *s* Mäher *m*

m.p.h. ['em'pi'et∫] *spl* (**miles per hour**) Stundenmeilen; **drive sixty m.p.h.** mit sechzig Stundenmeilen fahren

Mr. [ˈmɪstər] *s* Herr *m*

Mrs. [ˈmɪsɪz] *s* Frau *f*

Ms. [mɪz] *s* Fräulein *n*

much [mʌt∫] *adj*, *adv* & *pron* viel; **as m. again** noch einmal soviel; **how m.** wieviel; **m. less** (*not to mention*) geschweige denn; **not so m.** as nicht einmal; **so m. so so** sehr; **so m. the better** um so besser; **very m.** sehr

mucilage [ˈmjusɪlɪdʒ] *s* Klebstoff *m*

muck [mʌk] *s* (& fig) Schmutz *m*

muck'rake' *intr* (coll) Korruptionsfälle enthüllen

muckraker [ˈmʌkˌrekər] *s* (coll) Korruptionsschnüffler –in *mf*

mucky [ˈmʌki] *adj* schmutzig

mucous [ˈmjukəs] *adj* schleimig

muc'ous mem'brane *s* Schleimhaut *f*

mucus [ˈmjukəs] *s* Schleim *m*

mud [mʌd] *s* Schlamm *m*; **drag through the mud** (fig) in den Schmutz ziehen

mud' bath' *s* Schlammbad *n*, Moorbad *n*

muddle [ˈmʌdəl] *s* Durcheinander *n* ‖ *tr* durcheinanderbringen ‖ *intr*—**m. through** sich durchwursteln

mud'dlehead' *s* Wirrkopf *m*

mud·dy [ˈmʌdi] *adj* schlammig; (fig) trüb ‖ *v* (*pret* & *pp* **–died**) trüben

mud'hole' *s* Schlammloch *n*

mudslinging [ˈmʌdˌslɪŋɪŋ] *s* (fig) Verleumdung *f*

muff [mʌf] *s* Muff *m* ‖ *tr* (coll) verpfuschen

muffin [ˈmʌfɪn] *s* Teekuchen *m* aus Backpulverteig

muffle [ˈmʌfəl] *tr* (*sounds*) dämpfen; **m. up** (*wrap up*) einhüllen

muf'fled *adj* dumpf

muffler [ˈmʌflər] *s* (*scarf*) Halstuch *n*; (aut) Auspufftopf *m*

mufti [ˈmʌfti] *s* Zivil *n*

mug [mʌg] *s* Krug *m*; (*for beer*) Seidel *n*; (*thug*) (sl) Rocker *m*; (*face*) (sl) Fratze *f* ‖ *v* (*pret* & *pp* **mugged;** *ger* **mugging**) *tr* (sl) photographieren; (*assault*) (sl) überfallen ‖ *intr* (sl) Gesichter schneiden

muggy [ˈmʌgi] *adj* schwül

mug' shot' *s* (sl) Polizeiphoto *n*

mulat·to [məˈlæto] *s* (**-toes**) Mulatte *m*, Mulattin *f*

mulberry [ˈmʌlˌbɛri] *s* Maulbeere *f*

mul'berry tree' *s* Maulbeerbaum *m*

mulch [mʌlt∫] *s* Streu *n*

mulct [mʌlkt] *tr* (**of**) betrügen (um)

mule [mjul] *s* Maulesel *m*, Maultier *n*

mulish [ˈmjulɪ∫] *adj* störrisch

mull [mʌl] *intr*—**m. over** nachgrübeln über (*acc*)

mullion [ˈmʌljən] *s* Mittelpfosten *m*

multicolored [ˈmʌltɪˌkɒlərd] *adj* bunt

multigraph [ˈmʌltɪˌgræf] *s* (trademark) Vervielfältigungsmaschine *f* ‖ *tr* vervielfältigen

multilateral [ˌmʌltiˈlætərəl] *adj* mehrseitig

multimillionaire [ˈmʌltɪˌmɪljəˈnɛr] *s* vielfacher Millionär *m*

multiple [ˈmʌltɪpəl] *adj* mehrfach, Vielfach– ‖ *s* (math) Vielfaches *n*

multiplication [ˌmʌltɪplɪˈke∫ən] *s* Vermehrung *f*; (arith) Multiplikation *f*

multiplica'tion ta'ble *s* Einmaleins *n*

multiplicity [ˌmʌltɪˈplɪsɪti] *s* Vielfältigkeit *f*

multi·ply [ˈmʌltɪˌplaɪ] *v* (*pret* & *pp* **–plied**) *tr* vervielfältigen; (biol) vermehren; (math) multiplizieren ‖ *intr* sich vervielfachen; (biol) sich vermehren

multistage [ˈmʌltɪˌstedʒ] *adj* mehrstufig

multistory [ˈmʌltɪˌstori] *adj* mehrstöckig

multitude [ˈmʌltɪˌt(j)ud] *s* (*large number*) Vielheit *f*; (*of people*) Masse *f*

mum [mʌm] *adj* still; **keep mum about** Stillschweigen beobachten über (*acc*); **mum's the word!** Mund halten!

mumble [ˈmʌmbəl] *tr* & *intr* murmeln

mummery [ˈmʌməri] *s* Hokuspokus *m*

mummy [ˈmʌmi] *s* Mumie *f*

mumps [mʌmps] *s* Ziegenpeter *m*, Mumps *m*

munch [mʌnt∫] *tr* & *intr* geräuschvoll kauen

mundane [mʌnˈden] *adj* irdisch

municipal [mjuˈnɪsɪpəl] *adj* städtisch

muni'cipal bond' *s* Kommunalobligation *f*

municipality [mjuˌnɪsɪˈpælɪti] *s* Stadt *f*, Gemeinde *f*; (*governing body*) Stadtverwaltung *f*

munificent [mjuˈnɪfɪsənt] *adj* freigebig

munificence [mjuˈnɪfɪsəns] *s* Freigebigkeit *f*

munitions [mjuˈnɪ∫əns] *s* Kriegsmaterial *n*, Munition *f*

muni'tions dump' *s* Munitionsdepot *n*

muni'tions fac'tory *s* Rüstungsfabrik *f*

mural [ˈmjʊrəl] *s* Wandgemälde *n*

murder [ˈmʌrdər] *s* Mord *m* ‖ *tr* (er)morden; (*a language*) radebrechen

murderer [ˈmʌrdərər] *s* Mörder *m*

murderess [ˈmʌrdərɪs] *s* Mörderin *f*

mur'der mys'tery *s* Krimi *m*

murderous [ˈmʌrdərəs] *adj* mörderisch

mur'der plot' *s* Mordanschlag *m*

murky [ˈmʌrki] *adj* düster

murmur [ˈmʌrmər] *s* Gemurmel *n* ‖ *tr* & *intr* murmeln

muscle [ˈmʌsəl] *s* Muskel *m*; **muscles** Muskulatur *f*

muscular [ˈmʌskjələr] *adj* muskulös

Muse [mjuz] *s* Muse *f* ‖ **muse** *intr* (**over**) nachsinnen (über *acc*)

museum [mjuˈzi·əm] *s* Museum *n*

mush [mʌ∫] *s* (*corn meal*) Maismehlbrei *m*; (*soft mass*) Matsch *m*; (*sentimental talk*) Süßholzraspeln *n*

mush'room' *s* Pilz *m*, Champignon *m*

‖ *intr* wie Pilze aus dem Boden schießen

mushy ['mʌʃi] *adj* matschig; *(sentimental)* rührselig

music ['mjuːzɪk] *s* Musik *f*; *(score)* Noten *pl*; **face the m.** die Sache ausbaden; **set to m.** vertonen

musical ['mjuːzɪkəl] *adj* musikalisch ‖ *s* (cin) Singspielfilm *m*; (theat) Musical *n*, Singspiel *n*

mu'sical in'strument *s* Musikinstrument *n*

musicale [ˌmjuːzɪ'kæl] *s* Musikabend *n*

mu'sic box' *s* Spieldose *f*

musician [mjuː'zɪʃən] *s* Musikant –in *mf*; *(accomplished artist)* Musiker –in *mf*

musicology [ˌmjuːzɪ'kɑlədʒi] *s* Musikwissenschaft *f*

mu'sic stand' *s* Notenständer *m*

mus'ing *s* Grübelei *f*

musk [mʌsk] *s* Moschus *m*

musket ['mʌskɪt] *s* Muskete *f*

musk'rat' *s* Bisamratte *f*

muslin ['mʌzlɪn] *s* Musselin *m*

muss [mʌs] *tr (hair)* zerzausen; *(dirty)* schmutzig machen; *(rumple)* zerknittern

mussel ['mʌsəl] *s* Muschel *f*

mussy ['mʌsi] *adj (hair)* zerzaust; *(clothes)* zerknittert

must [mʌst] *s (a necessity)* Muß *n*; *(new wine)* Most *m*; *(mold)* Moder *m* ‖ *mod*—**I m.** *(inf)* ich muß *(inf)*

mustache [məs'tæʃ] *s* Schnurrbart *m*

mustard ['mʌstərd] *s* Senf *m*

mus'tard plas'ter *s* Senfpflaster *n*

muster ['mʌstər] *s* Appell *m*; **pass m.** die Prüfung bestehen ‖ *tr (troops)* antreten lassen; *(courage, strength)* aufbringen; **m. out** ausmustern

musty ['mʌsti] *adj* mod(e)rig

mutation [mjuː'teʃən] *s* (biol) Mutation *f*

mute [mjuːt] *adj (& ling)* stumm ‖ *s* (ling) stummer Buchstabe *m*; (mus) Dämpfer ‖ *tr* (mus) dämpfen

mutilate ['mjuːtɪˌlet] *tr* verstümmeln

mutineer [ˌmjuːtɪ'nɪr] *s* Meuterer *m*

mutinous ['mjuːtɪnəs] *adj* meuterisch

muti·ny ['mjuːtɪni] *s* Meuterei *f* ‖ *v (pret & pp* –nied) *intr* meutern

mutt [mʌt] *s* (coll) Köter *m*

mutter ['mʌtər] *s* Gemurmel *n* ‖ *tr & intr* murmeln

mutton ['mʌtən] *s* (culin) Hammel *m*

mut'ton-head' *s* (sl) Hammel *m*

mutual ['mjuːtʃu·əl] *adj* gegenseitig; *(friends)* gemeinsam

mu'tual fund' *s* Investmentfond *m*

mu'tual insur'ance com'pany *s* Versicherungsgesellschaft *f* auf Gegenseitigkeit

mutually ['mjuːtʃu·əli] *adv* gegenseitig

muzzle ['mʌzəl] *s* Maulkorb *m*; *(of a gun)* Rohrmündung *f*; *(snout)* Schnauze *f* ‖ *tr (an animal)* e-n Maulkorb anlegen *(dat)*; *(e.g., the press)* mundtot machen

muz'zle flash' *s* Mündungsfeuer *n*

my [maɪ] *poss adj* mein

myopic [maɪ'ɑpɪk] *adj* kurzsichtig

myriad ['mɪrɪ·əd] *adj* Myriade *f*

myrrh [mʌr] *s* Myrrhe *f*

myrtle ['mʌrtəl] *s* Myrte *f*

myself ['maɪ'self] *reflex pron* mich; *(indirect object)* mir ‖ *intens pron* selbst, selber

mysterious [mɪs'tɪrɪ·əs] *adj* mysteriös

mystery ['mɪstəri] *s* Geheimnis *n*; (fi) Rätsel *n*; (relig) Mysterium *n*

mys'tery nov'el *s* Kriminalroman *m*

mys'tery play' *s* Mysterienspiel *n*

mystic ['mɪstɪk] *adj* mystisch ‖ *s* Mystiker –in *mf*

mystical ['mɪstɪkəl] *adj* mystisch

mysticism ['mɪstɪˌsɪzəm] *s* Mystik *f*

mystification [ˌmɪstɪfɪ'keʃən] *s* Verwirrung *f*

mysti·fy ['mɪstɪˌfaɪ] *v (pret & pp* –fied) *tr* verwirren

myth [mɪθ] *s* Mythe *f*, Mythos *m*; *(ill-founded belief)* Märchen *n*

mythical ['mɪθɪkəl] *adj* mythisch

mythological [ˌmɪθə'lɑdʒɪkəl] *adj* mythologisch

mythology [mɪ'θɑlədʒi] *s* Mythologie *f*

N

N, n [ɛn] *s* vierzehnter Buchstabe des englischen Alphabets

nab [næb] *v (pret & pp* nabbed; *ger* –nabbing) *tr* (coll) schnappen

nadir ['nedɪr] *s* (fig) Tiefpunkt *m*; (astr) Nadir *m*

nag [næg] *s* Gaul *m*; **old nag** Schindmähre *f* ‖ *v (pret & pp* nagged; *ger* nagging) *tr* zusetzen *(dat)* ‖ *intr* nörgeln; **nag at** herumnörgeln an *(dat)*

nag'ging *adj* nörgelnd ‖ *s* Nörgelei *f*

naiad ['naɪ·æd] *s* Najade *f*

nail [nel] *s* Nagel *m*; **hit the n. on the head** den Nagel auf den Kopf treffen ‖ *tr* **(to)** annageln (an *acc*); *(catch)*

(coll) erwischen; (box) (coll) treffen; **n. down** (fig) festnageln; **n. shut** zunageln

nail' clip'pers *spl* Nagelzange *f*

nail' file' *s* Nagelfeile *f*

nail' pol'ish *s* Nagellack *m*

nail' scis'sors *s & spl* Nagelschere *f*

naïve [nɑ'iv] *adj* naiv

naked ['nekɪd] *adj* nackt; *(eye)* bloß

nakedness ['nekɪdnɪs] *s* Nacktheit *f*

name [nem] *s* Name *m*; *(reputation)* Name *m*, Ruf *m*; **by n.** dem Namen nach; **by the n. of** namens; **in n. only** nur dem Namen nach; **of the same n.** gleichnamig; **spell one's n.** sich

schreiben; **what is your n.?** wie heißen Sie? ‖ *tr* nennen; *(nominate)*
ernennen; **be named after** heißen
nach; **n. after** nennen nach; **named**
namens
name'-call'ng *s* Beschimpfung *f*
name' day' *s* Namenstag *m*
nameless ['nemlɪs] *adj* namenlos
namely ['nemli] *adv* nämlich, und
zwar
name'plate' *s* Namensschild *n*
name'sake' *s* Namensvetter *m*
nanny ['næni] *s* Kindermädchen *n*
nan'ny goat' *s* (coll) Ziege *f*
nap [næp] *s* Schläfchen *n*; (tex) Noppe
f; **take a nap** ein Schläfchen machen
‖ *v* (*pret & pp* **napped**; *ger* **napping**)
intr schlummern; **catch s.o. napping**
(fig) j–n überrumpeln
napalm ['nepɑm] *s* Napalm *n*
nape [nep] *s*—**n. of the neck** Nacken
m
naphtha ['næfθə] *s* Naphtha *f & n*
napkin ['næpkɪn] *s* Serviette *f*
nap'kin ring' *s* Serviettenring *m*
narcissism ['nɑrsɪ‚sɪzəm] *s* Narzißmus
m
narcissus [nɑr'sɪsəs] *s* (bot) Narzisse *f*
narcotic [nɑr'kɑtɪk] *adj* narkotisch ‖
s (med) Betäubungsmittel *n*, Narko-
tikum *n*; *(addictive drug)* Rauschgift
n; *(addict)* Rauschgiftsüchtige *mf*
narrate [næ'ret] *tr* erzählen
narration [næ'reʃən] *s* Erzählung *f*
narrative ['nærətɪv] *adj* erzählend ‖ *s*
Erzählung *f*
narrator [næ'retər] *s* Erzähler *m*; (telv)
Moderator *m*
narrow ['næro] *adj* eng, schmal; *(e.g.,
margin)* knapp ‖ **narrows** *spl*
Meerenge *f* ‖ *tr* verengen ‖ *intr* sich
verengen
nar'row escape' *s*—**have a n.** mit
knapper Not entkommen
nar'row-gauge rail'road *s* Schmalspur-
bahn *f*
narrowly ['næroli] *adv* mit knapper
Not
nar'row-mind'ed *adj* engstirnig
nasal ['nezəl] *adj* *(of the nose)* Nasen–;
(sound) näselnd ‖ *s* (phonet) Nasen-
laut *m*
nasalize ['nezə‚laɪz] *tr* nasalieren ‖
intr näseln
na'sal twang' *s* Näseln *n*
nascent ['nesənt] *adj* werdend
nastiness ['næstɪnɪs] *s* Ekligkeit *f*
nasturtium [nə'stʌr/əm] *s* Kapuziner-
kresse *f*
nasty ['næsti] *adj* *(person, smell, taste)*
ekelhaft; *(weather)* scheußlich; *(dog,
accident, tongue)* böse; **n. to** garstig
zu or gegen
nation ['neʃən] *s* Nation *f*, Volk *n*
national ['næʃənəl] *adj* national, Landes–
des– ‖ *s* Staatsangehörige *mf*
na'tional an'them *s* Nationalhymne *f*
na'tional defense' *s* Landesverteidigung
f
nationalism ['næʃənə‚lɪzəm] *s* Nationalismus *m*
nationality [‚næʃə'nælɪti] *s* *(citizen-*

ship) Staatsangehörigkeit *f*; *(ethnic
identity)* Nationalität *f*
nationalization [‚næʃənəlɪ'zeʃən] *s*
Verstaatlichung *f*
nationalize ['næʃənə‚laɪz] *tr* verstaatlichen
na'tional park' *s* Naturschutzpark *m*
na'tional so'cialism *s* Nationalsozialis-
mus *m*
na'tionwide' *adj* im ganzen Land
native ['netɪv] *adj* eingeboren; *(products)* heimisch, Landes– ‖ *s* Eingebo-
rene *mf*; **be a n. of** beheimatet sein
in *(dat)*
na'tive coun'try *s* Vaterland *n*
na'tive land' *s* Heimatland *n*
na'tive tongue' *s* Muttersprache *f*
nativity [nə'tɪvɪti] *s* Geburt *f*; (astrol)
Nativität *f*; **the Nativity** die Geburt
Christi
NATO ['neto] *(North Atlantic Treaty
Organization)* NATO *f*
natty ['næti] *adj* elegant
natural ['nætʃərəl] *adj* natürlich; *(behavior)* ungezwungen ‖ *s* (mus)
weiße Taste *f*; *(symbol)* (mus) Auf-
lösungszeichen *n*; **a n.** *(person)* (coll)
ein Naturtalent *n*; *(thing)* (coll) e–e
totsichere Sache *f*
na'tural his'tory *s* Naturgeschichte *f*
naturalism ['nætʃərə‚lɪzəm] *s* Natura-
lismus *m*
naturalist ['nætʃərəlɪst] *s* *(student of
natural history)* Naturforscher –in
mf; *(paint, philos)* Naturalist –in *mf*
naturalization [‚nætʃərəlɪ'zeʃən] *s* Ein-
bürgerung *f*
naturalize ['nætʃərə‚laɪz] *tr* einbürgern
na'tural law' *s* Naturgesetz *n*
na'tural phenom'enon *s* *(occurring in
nature)* Naturereignis *n*; *(not supernatural)* natürliche Erscheinung *f*
na'tural re'sources *spl* Bodenschätze *pl*
na'tural sci'ence *s* Naturwissenschaft *f*
na'tural state' *s* Naturzustand *m*
nature ['netʃər] *s* die Natur; *(quali-
ties)* Natur *f*, Beschaffenheit *f*; **by n.**
von Natur aus
naught [nɔt] *s* Null *f*; **all for n.** ganz
umsonst; **bring to n.** zuschanden machen; **come to n.** zunichte werden
naughty ['nɔti] *adj* unartig, ungezogen
nausea ['nɔʃɪə], ['nɔsɪə] *s* Übelkeit *f*
nauseate ['nɔʃɪ‚et], ['nɔsɪ‚et] *tr* Übelkeit erregen *(dat)*
naus'eating *adj* Übelkeit erregend
nauseous ['nɔʃɪəs], ['nɔsɪəs] *adj*
(causing nausea) Übelkeit erregend;
I feel n. mir ist übel
nautical ['nɔtɪkəl] *adj* See–, nautisch
nau'tical mile' ['nɔtɪkəl] *s* Seemeile *f*
nau'tical term' *s* Ausdruck *m* der See-
mannssprache *f*
naval ['nevəl] *adj* *(e.g., battle, blockade, cadet, victory)* See–; *(unit)*
Flotten–; *(academy, officer)* Marine–
na'val base' *s* Flottenstützpunkt *m*
na'val cap'tain *s* Kapitän *m* zur See
na'val engage'ment *s* Seegefecht *n*
na'val forc'es *s* Seestreitkräfte *pl*
na'val suprem'acy *s* Seeherrschaft *f*

nave [nev] s (of a church) Schiff n; (of a wheel) Nabe f

navel [ˈnevəl] s Nabel m

na'vel or'ange s Navelorange f

navigable [ˈnævɪgəbəl] adj schiffbar

navigate [ˈnævɪˌget] tr (traverse) befahren; (steer) steuern ‖ intr (aer, naut) navigieren

navigation [ˌnævɪˈgeʃən] s (plotting courses) Navigation f; (sailing) Schiffahrt f

naviga'tion chart' s Navigationskarte f

naviga'tion light' s (aer, naut) Positionslicht n

navigator [ˈnævɪˌgetər] s Seefahrer m; (aer) Navigator m

navy [ˈnevi] adj Marine– ‖ s Kriegsmarine f

na'vy bean' s Weiße Bohne f

na'vy blue' adj marineblau ‖ s Marineblau n

na'vy yard' s Marinewerft f

nay [ne] adv nein n; (parl) Neinstimme f; **the nays have it** die Mehrheit stimmt dagegen

Nazarene [ˌnæzəˈrin] adj aus Nazareth ‖ s Nazarener m

Nazi [ˈnɑtsi] adj Nazi– ‖ s Nazi m

Nazism [ˈnɑtsɪzəm] s Nazismus m

N.C.O. [ˈenˈsiˈo] s (noncommissioned officer) Unteroffizier m

neap' tide' [nip] s Nippflut f

near [nɪr] adj nahe(liegend); (escape) knapp; **n. at hand** zur Hand f ‖ adv nahe; **draw n. (to)** sich nähern (dat); **live n.** (e.g., a church) in der Nähe wohnen (genit) ‖ prep nahe (dat), nahe an (dat), bei (dat); **n. here** hier in der Nähe

near'by' adj nahe(gelegen) ‖ adv in der Nähe

Near' East', the s der Nahe Osten

nearly [ˈnɪrli] adv beinahe, fast

nearness [ˈnɪrnɪs] s Nähe f

near'-sight'ed adj kurzsichtig

near'-sight'edness s Kurzsichtigkeit f

neat [nit] adj sauber, ordentlich; (simple but tasteful) nett; (cute) niedlich; (tremendous) (coll) prima

neatness [ˈnitnɪs] s Sauberkeit f

nebu·la [ˈnebjələ] s (–lae [ˌli] & –las) (astr) Nebelfleck m

nebulous [ˈnebjələs] adj nebelhaft; (astr) Nebel–

necessarily [ˌnesɪˈserɪli] adv notwendigerweise, unbedingt

necessary [ˈnesɪˌseri] adj notwendig, nötig; (consequence) zwangsläufig; **if n.** notfalls

necessitate [nɪˈsesɪˌtet] tr notwendig machen, erfordern

necessity [nɪˈsesɪti] s (state of being necessary) Notwendigkeit f; (something necessary) Bedürfnis n; (poverty) Not f; **in case of n.** im Notfall; **necessities of life** Lebensbedürfnisse pl; **of n.** notwendigerweise

neck [nek] s Hals m; (of a dress) Halsausschnitt m; **break one's n.** (& fig) sich [dat] den Hals brechen; **get it in the n.** (sl) eins aufs Dach kriegen; **get s.o. off one's n.** sich [dat] j–n

vom Halse schaffen; **n. and n.** Seite an Seite ‖ intr (coll) sich knutschen

–necked [ˌnekt] suf –halsig, –nackig

neckerchief [ˈnekərtʃɪf] s Halstuch n

neck'ing s Abknutscherei f

necklace [ˈneklɪs] s Halsband n; (metal chain) Halskette f

neck'line' s Halsausschnitt m; **with a low n.** tief ausgeschnitten

neck'tie' s Krawatte f, Schlips m

necrology [neˈkrɑlədʒi] s (list of the dead) Totenliste f; (obituary) Nekrolog m

necromancer [ˈnekrəˌmænsər] s Geistesbeschwörer –in mf

necromancy [ˈnekrəˌmænsi] s Geistesbeschwörung f

necropolis [neˈkrɑpəlɪs] s Nekropolis f

nectar [ˈnektər] s (bot, myth) Nektar m

nectarine [ˌnektəˈrin] s Nektarine f

nee [ne] adj geborene, e.g., **Mrs. Mary Schmidt, nee Müller** Frau Maria Schmidt, geborene Müller

need [nid] s Bedarf m, Bedürfnis n; **be in n.** in Not sein; **be in n. of repair** reparaturbedürftig sein; **be in n. of s.th.** etw nötig haben; **if n. be** erforderlichenfalls; **meet s.o.'s needs** j–s Bedarf decken; **needs** Bedarfsartikel pl ‖ tr benötigen, brauchen; **as needed** nach Bedarf

needful [ˈnidfəl] adj nötig

needle [ˈnidəl] s Nadel f ‖ tr (prod) anstacheln; **n. s.o. about** gegen j–n stacheln, anstacheln; **n. s.o. about** gegen j–n stacheln wegen

nee'dlepoint', nee'dlepoint lace' s Nadelspitze f

needless [ˈnidlɪs] adj unnötig; **n. to say** es erübrigt sich zu sagen

nee'dlework' s Näharbeit f

needy [ˈnidi] adj bedürftig

ne'er [ner] adv nie

ne'er'-do-well' s Tunichtgut m

nefarious [nɪˈferɪəs] adj ruchlos

negate [nɪˈget] tr verneinen

negation [nɪˈgeʃən] s Verneinung f

negative [ˈnegətɪv] adj negativ ‖ s Verneinung f; (elec) negativer Pol m; (gram) Verneinungswort n; (phot) Negativ n

neglect [nɪˈglekt] s Vernachlässigung f ‖ tr vernachlässigen; **n. to** (inf) unterlassen zu (inf)

négligée, negligee [ˌneglɪˈʒe] s Negligé n

negligence [ˈneglɪdʒəns] s Fahrlässigkeit f

negligent [ˈneglɪdʒənt] adj fahrlässig

negligible [ˈneglɪdʒɪbəl] adj geringfügig

negotiable [nɪˈgoʃɪ·əbəl] adj diskutierbar; (fin) übertragbar, bankfähig

negotiate [nɪˈgoʃɪˌet] tr (a contract) abschließen; (a curve) nehmen ‖ intr verhandeln

negotiation [nɪˌgoʃɪˈeʃən] s Verhandlung f; **carry on negotiations with** in Verhandlungen stehen mit; **enter negotiations with** in Verhandlungen treten mit

negotiator [nɪˈgoʃɪ͵etər] s Unterhändler –in mf

Ne·gro [ˈnigro] s (–groes) Neger –in mf

neigh [ne] s Wiehern n ‖ intr wiehern

neighbor [ˈnebər] s Nachbar –in mf; (fellow man) Nächste m ‖ tr angrenzen an (acc) ‖ intr—**n. on** angrenzen an (acc)

neigh′borhood′ s Nachbarschaft f; (vicinity) Umgebung f; **in the n. of** (coll) etwa

neigh′boring adj benachbart, Nachbar-, angrenzend

neighborliness [ˈnebərlɪnɪs] s gutnachbarliche Beziehungen pl

neighborly [ˈnebərli] adj (gut)nachbarlich

neither [ˈniðər] indef adj keiner ‖ indef pron (**of**) keiner (von); **n. of them** keiner von beiden ‖ conj noch, ebensowenig; auch nicht, z.B., **n. do I** ich auch nicht; **neither ... nor** weder ... noch; **that's n. here nor there** das hat nichts zu sagen

neme·sis [ˈnemɪsɪs] s (–ses [͵sɪz]) Nemesis f

Neolith′ic Age′ [͵ni·əˈlɪθɪk] s Neusteinzeit f

neologism [niˈʊlə͵dʒɪzəm] s Neubildung f, Neologismus m

neon [ˈni·ɑn] s Neon n

ne′on light′ s Neonröhre f

ne′on sign′ s Neonreklame f

neophyte [ˈni·ə͵faɪt] s Neuling m; (relig) Neubekehrte mf

nephew [ˈnɛfju] s Neffe m

nepotism [ˈnɛpə͵tɪzəm] s Nepotismus m

Neptune [ˈnɛpt(j)un] s Neptun m

neptunium [nɛpˈt(j)unɪ·əm] s Neptunium n

nerve [nʌrv] adj Nerven- ‖ s Nerv m; (courage) Wagemut m; (coll) Unverfrorenheit f; **get on s.o.'s nerves** j–m auf die Nerven gehen; **lose one's n.** die Nerven verlieren; **nerves of steel** Nerven pl wie Drahtseile

nerve′ cen′ter s Nervenzentrum n

nerve′-rack′ing adj nervenaufreibend

nervous [ˈnʌrvəs] adj nervös; (system) Nerven-; (horse) kopfscheu; **be a n. wreck** mit den Nerven herunter sein

ner′vous break′down s Nervenzusammenbruch m

nervousness [ˈnʌrvəsnɪs] s Nervosität f

nervy [ˈnʌrvi] adj (brash) unverschämt; (courageous) mutig

nest [nɛst] s Nest n ‖ intr nisten

nest′ egg′ s (fig) Sparpfennig m

nestle [ˈnɛsəl] intr (**up to**) sich anschmiegen (an acc)

net [nɛt] adj Rein- ‖ adv netto, rein ‖ s Netz n; (for fire victims) Sprungtuch n ‖ v (pret & pp **netted**; ger **netting**) tr (e.g., fish, butterflies) mit dem Netz fangen; (said of an enterprise) netto einbringen; (said of a person) rein verdienen

net′ball′ s (tennis) Netzball m

Netherlander [ˈnɛðər͵lændər] s Niederländer –in mf

Netherlands, the [ˈnɛðərləndz] s & spl die Niederlande

net′ting s Netzwerk n

nettle [ˈnɛtəl] s Nessel f ‖ tr reizen

net′work′ s Netzwerk n; (rad, telv) Sendergruppe f

neuralgia [n(j)ʊˈrældʒə] s Neurologie f

neuritis [n(j)ʊˈraɪtɪs] s Nervenentzündung f

neurologist [n(j)ʊˈrɑlədʒɪst] s Nervenarzt m, Nervenärztin f

neurology [n(j)ʊˈrɑlədʒi] s Nervenheilkunde f, Neurologie f

neuron [ˈn(j)ʊrɑn] s Neuron n

neuro·sis [n(j)ʊˈrosɪs] s (–ses [siz]) Neurose f

neurotic [n(j)ʊˈrɑtɪk] adj neurotisch ‖ s Neurotiker –in mf

neuter [ˈn(j)utər] adj (gram) sächlich ‖ s (gram) Neutrum n

neutral [ˈn(j)utrəl] adj neutral ‖ s Neutrale mf; (aut) Leerlauf m

neutrality [n(j)ʊˈtrælɪti] s Neutralität f

neutralize [ˈn(j)utrə͵laɪz] tr (a bomb) entschärfen; (& chem) neutralisieren; (troops) lahmlegen; (an attack) unterbinden

neutron [ˈn(j)utrɑn] s Neutron n

never [ˈnɛvər] adv nie(mals); **n. again** nie wieder; **n. before** noch nie; **n. mind!** spielt keine Rolle!

ne′vermore′ adv nimmermehr

ne′vertheless′ adv nichtsdestoweniger

new [n(j)u] adj neu; (wine) jung; (inexperienced) unerfahren; **what's new?** was gibt's Neues?

new′ arriv′al s Neuankömmling m

new′born′ adj neugeboren

New′cas′tle s—**carry coals to N.** Eulen nach Athen tragen

newcomer [ˈn(j)u͵kʌmər] s. Neuankömmling m

newel [ˈn(j)u·əl] s Treppenspindel f

new′el post′ s Geländerpfosten m

newfangled [ˈn(j)u͵fæŋgəld] adj neumodisch

Newfoundland [ˈn(j)ufənd͵lænd] s Neufundland n ‖ [n(j)uˈfaundlənd] s (dog) Neufundländer m

newly [ˈn(j)uli] adv neu, Neu-

new′lyweds′ spl Neuvermählten pl

new′ moon′ s Neumond m

new-mown [ˈn(j)u͵mon] adj frischgemäht

newness [ˈn(j)unɪs] s Neuheit f

news [n(j)uz] s Nachricht f; (rad, telv) Nachrichten pl; **that's not n. to me** das ist mir nicht neu; **piece of n.** Neuigkeit f

news′ a′gency s Nachrichtenagentur f

news′boy′ s Zeitungsjunge m

news′ bul′letin s Kurznachricht f

news′cast′ s Nachrichtensendung f

news′cast′er s Nachrichtensprecher –in mf

news′deal′er s Zeitungshändler –in mf

news′ ed′itor s Nachrichtenredakteur –in mf

news′let′ter *s* Rundschreiben *n*

news′man′ *s* (**-men′**) Journalist *m*; (*dealer*) Zeitungshändler *m*

news′pa′per *adj* Zeitungs- ‖ *s* Zeitung *f*

news′paper clip′ping *s* Zeitungsausschnitt *m*

news′paper-man′ *s* (**-men′**) Journalist *m*; (*dealer*) Zeitungshändler *m*

news′paper se′rial *s* Zeitungsroman *m*

news′print′ *s* Zeitungspapier *n*

news′reel′ *s* Wochenschau *f*

news′ report′ *s* Nachrichtensendung *f*

news′ report′er *s* Zeitungsreporter –in *mf*

news′ room′ *s* Nachrichtenbüro *n*

news′stand′ *s* Zeitungskiosk *m*

news′wor′thy *adj* berichtenswert

New′ Tes′tament *s* Neues Testament *n*

New′ World′ *s* Neue Welt *f*

New′ Year′ *s* Neujahr *n*; **happy N.!** glückliches Neues Jahr!

New′ Year′s′ Eve′ *s* Silvesterabend *m*

New′ Zea′land [ˈzilənd] *s* Neuseeland *n*

next [nɛkst] *adj* nächste; **be n.** an der Reihe sein; **come n.** folgen; **in the n. place** (*dat*): **n. best** nächstbeste; **n. time** das nächste Mal; **n. to** (*locally*) gleich neben (*dat*); (*almost*) sogut wie; **the n. day** am nächsten Tag ‖ *adv* dann, danach; **what should I do n.?** was soll ich als Nächstes tun?

next′-door′ *adj*—**n.** neighbor unmittelbarer Nachbar *m* ‖ **next′-door′** *adv* nebenan; **n. to** direkt neben (*dat*)

next′ of kin′ *s* (*pl*: **next of kin**) nächster Angehöriger *m*

niacin [ˈnaɪ-əsɪn] *s* Niacin *n*

Niag′ara Falls′ [naɪˈægrə] *s* Niagarafall *m*

nib [nɪb] *s* Spitze *f*; (*of a pen*) Federspitze *f*

nibble [ˈnɪbəl] *tr* knabbern ‖ *intr* (**on**) knabbern (an *dat*)

Nibelung [ˈnibəluŋ] *s* (myth) Nibelung *m*

nice [naɪs] *adj* nett; (*pretty*) hübsch; (*food*) lecker; (*well-behaved*) artig; (*distinction*) fein; **have a n. time** sich gut unterhalten; **n. and warm** schön warm

nicely [ˈnaɪsli] *adv* nett; **he's doing n.** es geht ihm recht gut; **that will do n.** das paßt gut

nicety [ˈnaɪsəti] *s* Feinheit *f*; **niceties of life** Annehmlichkeiten *pl* des Lebens

niche [nɪtʃ] *s* Nische *f*; (fig) rechter Platz *m*

nick [nɪk] *s* Kerbe *f*, Scharte *f*; **in the n. of time** gerade im rechten Augenblick ‖ *tr* kerben

nickel [ˈnɪkəl] *s* Nickel *n*; (*coin*) Fünfcentstück *n* ‖ *tr* vernickeln

nick′el-plate′ *tr* vernickeln

nick′name′ *s* Spitzname *m* ‖ *tr* e-n Spitznamen geben (*dat*)

nicotine [ˈnɪkə‚tin] *s* Nikotin *n*; **low in n.** nikotinarm

niece [nis] *s* Nichte *f*

nifty [ˈnɪfti] *adj* (coll) fesch, prima

niggard [ˈnɪgərd] *s* Knauser –in *mf*

niggardly [ˈnɪgərdli] *adj* knauserig

night [naɪt] *adj* (*light, shift, train, watch*) Nacht- ‖ *s* Nacht *f*; **all n.** (*long*) die ganze Nacht (über); **at n.** nachts; **last n.** gestern abend; **n. after n.** Nacht für Nacht; **n. before last** vorgestern abend

night′ cap′ *s* Nachtmütze *f*; (*drink*) Schlummertrunk *m*

night′ club′ *s* Nachtklub *m*

night′fall′ *s* Anbruch *m* der Nacht; **at n.** bei Anbruch der Nacht

night′gown′ *s* Damennachthemd *n*

nightingale [ˈnaɪtən‚gel] *s* Nachtigall *f*

night′light′ *s* Nachtlicht *n*

night′long′ *adj* & *adv* die ganze Nacht dauernd

nightly [ˈnaɪtli] *adj* & *adv* allnächtlich

night′mare′ *s* Alptraum *m*

nightmarish [ˈnaɪt‚mɛrɪʃ] *adj* alpartig

night′ owl′ *s* (coll) Nachteule *f*

night′ school′ *s* Abendschule *f*

night′time′ *s* Nachtzeit *f*; **at n.** zur Nachtzeit

night′ watch′man *s* Nachtwächter *m*

nihilism [ˈnaɪ-ɪ‚lɪzəm] *s* Nihilismus *m*

nil [nɪl] *s* Nichts *n*, Null *f*

Nile [naɪl] *s* Nil *m*

nimble [ˈnɪmbəl] *adj* flink

nincompoop [ˈnɪnkəm‚pup] *s* Trottel *m*

nine [naɪn] *adj* & *pron* neun ‖ *s* Neun *f*

nineteen [ˈnaɪn′tin] *adj* & *pron* neunzehn ‖ *s* Neunzehn *f*

nineteenth [ˈnaɪn′tinθ] *adj* & *pron* neunzehnte ‖ *s* (*fraction*) Neunzehntel *n*; **the nineteenth** (*in dates or in a series*) der Neunzehnte

ninetieth [ˈnaɪnti-ɪθ] *adj* & *pron* neunzigste ‖ *s* (*fraction*) Neunzigstel *n*

ninety [ˈnaɪnti] *adj* & *pron* neunzig ‖ *s* Neunzig *f*; **the nineties** die neunziger Jahre

nine′ty-first′ *adj* & *pron* einundneunzigste

nine′ty-one′ *adj* & *pron* einundneunzig

ninny [ˈnɪni] *s* (coll) Trottel *m*

ninth [naɪnθ] *adj* & *pron* neunte ‖ *s* (*fraction*) Neuntel *n*; **the n.** (*in dates or in a series*) der Neunte

nip [nɪp] *s* (*pinch*) Kneifen *n*; (*of cold weather*) Schneiden *n*; (*of liquor*) Schluck *m* ‖ *v* (*pret* & *pp* **nipped**; *ger* **nipping**) *tr* (*pinch*) kneifen; (*alcohol*) nippen; **nip in the bud** im Keime ersticken

nippers [ˈnɪpərz] *spl* Zwickzange *f*

nipple [ˈnɪpəl] *s* (*of a nursing bottle*) Lutscher *m*; (anat) Brustwarze *f*; (mach) Schmiernippel *m*

nippy [ˈnɪpi] *adj* schneidend

nirvana [nɪrˈvɑnə] *s* Nirwana *n*

nit [nɪt] *s* (ent) Nisse *f*

niter [ˈnaɪtər] *s* Salpeter *m*

nit′pick′er *s* (coll) Pedant –in *mf*

nitrate [ˈnaɪtret] *s* Nitrat *n* ‖ *tr* nitrieren

ni′tric ac′id [ˈnaɪtrɪk] *s* Salpetersäure *f*

nitride ['naɪtraɪd] s Nitrid n
nitrogen ['naɪtrədʒən] s Stickstoff m
nitroglycerin [ˌnaɪtrə'glɪsərɪn] s Nitroglyzerin n
ni'trous ac'id ['naɪtrəs] s salpetrige Säure f
ni'trous ox'ide s Stickstoffoxydul n
nit'wit' s Trottel m
no [no] adj kein; **no admittance** Zutritt verboten; **no ... of any kind** keinerlei; **no offense!** nichts für ungut!; **no parking** Parkverbot; **no smoking** Rauchen verboten; **no thoroughfare** Durchgang verboten; **no ... whatever** überhaupt kein || adv nein; **no?** nicht wahr?; **no longer** (or no more) nicht mehr || s Nein n; **give no for an answer** mit (e-m) Nein antworten
No'ah's Ark' ['no·əz] s Arche f Noah(s)
nobility [no'bɪlɪti] s (nobleness; aristocracy) Adel m; (noble rank) Adelsstand m; **n. of mind** Seelenadel m
noble ['nobəl] adj (rank) ad(e)lig; (character, person) edel || s Adliger m; **nobles** Edelleute pl
no'ble·man s (-men) Edelmann m
no'blemind'ed adj edelgesinnt
nobleness ['nobəlnɪs] s Vornehmheit f
no'ble·wom'an s (-wom'en) Edelfrau f
nobody ['no,badi] s indef pron niemand, keiner; **n. else** sonst keiner || s (coll) Null f
nocturnal [nak'tʌrnəl] adj nächtlich
nod [nad] s Kopfnicken n || v (pret & pp **nodded**; ger **nodding**) tr—**nod one's head** mit dem Kopf nicken || intr nicken; **nod to** zunicken (dat)
node [nod] s (anat, astr, math, phys) Knoten m
nodule ['nadʒul] s Knötchen n; (bot) Knollen m
noise [nɔɪz] s Geräusch n; (disturbingly loud) Lärm m || tr—**n. abroad** ausposaunen
noiseless ['nɔɪzlɪs] adj geräuschlos
noisy ['nɔɪzi] adj lärmend, geräuschvoll
nomad ['nomæd] s Nomade m, Nomadin f
no' man's' land' s Niemandsland n
nomenclature ['nomən,kletʃər] s Nomenklatur f
nominal ['namɪnəl] adj nominell
nominate ['namɪ,net] tr ernennen; **n. as candidate** als Kandidaten aufstellen
nomination [ˌnamɪ'neʃən] s Ernennung f; (of a candidate) Aufstellung f
nominative ['namɪnətɪv] s Nominativ m
nominee [ˌnamɪ'ni] s Designierte mf
non- [nan] pref Nicht-, nicht-
non'accept'ance s Nichtannahme f
non'bel'ligerent adj nicht am Krieg teilnehmend
non'break'able adj unzerbrechlich
non'-Cath'olic adj nichtkatholisch || s Nichtkatholik –in mf
nonchalant [ˌnanʃə'lant] adj zwanglos

noncom ['nan,kam] s (coll) Kapo m
non'com'batant s Nichtkämpfer m
non'commis'sioned of'ficer s Unteroffizier m
noncommittal [ˌnankə'mɪtəl] adj nichtssagend; (person) zurückhaltend
nondescript ['nandɪ,skrɪpt] adj unbestimmbar
none [nʌn] adv—**n. too** keineswegs zu || indef pron keiner; **that's n. of your business** das geht dich nichts an
nonen'tity s (fig) Null f
non'exis'tent adj nichtexistent
nonfic'tion s Sachbücher pl
nonfulfill'ment s Nichterfüllung f
non'interven'tion s Nichteinmischung f
non'met'al s Nichtmetall n, Metalloid n
non'nego'tiable adj unübertragbar; (demands) unabdingbar
nonpar'tisan adj überparteilich
nonpay'ment s Nichtbezahlung f
non'polit'ical adj unpolitisch
non-plus [nan'plʌs] s Verlegenheit f || v (pret & pp **-plus[s]ed**; ger **-plus[s]ing**) tr verblüffen
nonprof'it adj gemeinnützig
nonres'ident adj nich ansässig || s Nichtansässige mf
non'return'able adj (bottles, etc.) Einweg–; (merchandise) nicht rücknehmbar
non'scien'tific adj nichtwissenschaftlich
non'sectar'ian adj keiner Sekte angehörend
nonsense ['nansəns] s Unsinn m
nonsen'sical adj unsinnig, widersinnig
non'skid' adj rutschsicher
nonsmok'er s Nichtraucher –in mf
non'stop' adj & adv ohne Zwischenlandung
nonvi'olence s Gewaltlosigkeit f
nonvi'olent adj gewaltlos
noodle ['nudəl] s Nudel f; (head) (coll) Birne f
noo'dle soup' s Nudelsuppe f
nook [nʊk] s Ecke f; (fig) Winkel m
noon [nun] s Mittag m; **at n.** zu Mittag
no' one', **no'-one'** indef pron niemand, keiner; **n. else** kein anderer
noon' hour' s Mittagsstunde f
noon'time' adj mittäglich || s Mittagszeit f
noose [nus] s Schlinge f
nor [nɔr] conj (after **neither**) noch; auch nicht, e.g., **nor do I** ich auch nicht
Nordic ['nɔrdɪk] adj nordisch
norm [nɔrm] s Norm f
normal ['nɔrməl] adj normal
normalcy ['nɔrməlsi] s Normalzustand m
normalize ['nɔrmə,laɪz] tr normalisieren
Norman ['nɔrmən] adj normannisch || s Normanne m, Normannin f
Normandy ['nɔrməndi] s die Normandie
Norse [nɔrs] adj altnordisch || s (language) Altnordisch n; **the N.** die Skandinavier pl
Norse'man s (-men) Nordländer m

north [nɔrθ] adj nördlich, Nord– || adv nach Norden || s Norden m; **to the n. of** im Norden von

North′ Amer′ica s Nordamerika n

North′ Amer′ican adj nordamerikanisch || s Nordamerikaner –in mf

north′east′ adj & adv nordöstlich || s Nordosten m

north′east′er s Nordostwind m

northerly [′nɔrðərli] adj nördlich

northern [′nɔrðərn] adj (direction) nördlich; (race) nordisch

north′ern expo′sure s Nordseite f

North′ern Hem′isphere s nördliche Halbkugel f

north′ern lights′ spl Nordlicht n

nor′thernmost′ adj nördlichst

North′ Pole′ s Nordpol m

North′ Sea′ s Nordsee f

northward [′nɔrθwərd] adv nach Norden

north′west′ adj & adv nordwestlich || s Nordwesten m

north′ wind′ s Nordwind m

Norway [′nɔrwe] s Norwegen n

Norwegian [nɔr′widʒən] adj norwegisch || s Norweger –in mf; (language) Norwegisch n

nose [noz] s Nase f; (aer) Nase f, Bug m; **by a n.** (sport) um e–e Nasenlänge; **blow one's n.** sich schneuzen; **lead around by the n.** an der Nase herumführen; **pay through the n.** e–n zu hohen Preis bezahlen; **turn one's n. up at** die Nase rümpfen über (acc) || tr—**n. out** (fig) mit knappem Vorsprung besiegen; (sport) um e–e Nasenlänge schlagen || intr—**n. about** herumschnüffeln; **n. over** (aer) sich überschlagen

nose′bleed′ s Nasenbluten n

nose′ cone′ s (rok) Raketenspitze f

nose′ dive′ s (aer) Sturzflug m

nose′-dive′ intr e–n Sturzflug machen

nose′ drops′ spl Nasentropfen pl

nose′gay′ s Blumenstrauß m

nose′-heav′y adj (aer) vorderlastig

nostalgia [nɑ′stældʒə] s Heimweh n

nostalgic [nɑ′stældʒɪk] adj wehmütig

nostril [′nɑstrɪl] s (anat) Nasenloch n; (zool) Nüster f

nostrum [′nɑstrəm] s Allheilmittel n

nosy [′nozi] adj neugierig

not [nɑt] adv nicht; **not at all** überhaupt nicht; **not even** nicht einmal; **not one** keiner; **not only ... but also** nicht nur ... sondern auch

notable [′notəbəl] adj bemerkenswert || s Standesperson f

notarial [no′tɛri·əl] adj notariell

notarize [′notə‚raɪz] tr notariell beglaubigen

no′tary pub′lic [′notəri] s (notaries public) Notar m, Notarin f

notation [no′teʃən] s (note) Aufzeichnung f; (system of symbols) Bezeichnung f; (method of noting) Schreibweise f

notch [nɑtʃ] s Kerbe f; (in a belt) Loch n; (degree, step) Grad m; (of a wheel) Zahn m || tr einkerben

note [not] s Notiz f; (to a text) Anmerkung f; (slip) Zettel m; (e.g., doubt) Ton m; (mus) Note f; **jot down notes** sich [dat] Notizen machen; **make a n. of** sich [dat] notieren; **take n. of** zur Kenntnis nehmen; **take notes** sich [dat] Notizen machen || tr beachten; **n. down** notieren; **n. in passing** am Rande bemerken

note′book′ s Heft n, Notizbuch n

note′ pad′ s Schreibblock m

note′wor′thy adj beachtenswert

nothing [′nʌθɪŋ] indef pron nichts; **be for n.** vergebens sein; **come to n.** platzen; **for n.** (gratis) umsonst; **have n. to go on** keine Unterlagen haben; **next to n.** soviel wie nichts; **n. at all** gar nichts; **n. but** lauter; **n. doing!** kommt nicht in Frage!; **n. else** sonst nichts; **n. new** nichts Neues; **there is n. like** es geht nichts über (acc)

nothingness [′nʌθɪŋnɪs] s (nonexistence) Nichts n; (utter insignificance) Nichtigkeit f

notice [′notɪs] s (placard) Anschlag m; (in the newspaper) Anzeige f; (attention) Beachtung f; (announcement) Ankündigung f; (notice of termination) Kündigung f; **at a moment's n.** jeden Moment; **escape s.o.'s n.** j–m entgehen; **give s.o. a week's n.** j–m acht Tage vorher kündigen; **take n. of** Notiz nehmen von; **until further n.** bis auf weiteres || tr (be)merken, wahrnehmen; **be noticed by s.o.** j–m auffallen; **n. s.th. about s.o.** j–m etw anmerken

noticeable [′notɪsəbəl] adj wahrnehmbar

notification [‚notɪfɪ′keʃən] s Benachrichtigung f

noti·fy [′notɪ‚faɪ] v (pret & pp –fied) tr (about) benachrichtigen (von)

notion [′noʃən] s (idea) Vorstellung f; **I have a good n. to** (inf) ich habe gute Lust zu (inf); **notions** Kurzwaren pl

notoriety [‚notə′raɪ·ɪti] s Verruf m

notorious [no′tori·əs] adj (for) notorisch (wegen)

no′-trump′ adj ohne Trumpf || s Ohne Trumpf-Ansage f

notwithstanding [‚nɑtwɪθ′stændɪŋ] adv trotzdem || prep trotz (genit)

noun [naʊn] s Hauptwort n

nourish [′nʌrɪʃ] tr (er)nähren

nour′ishing adj nahrhaft, Nähr–

nourishment [′nʌrɪʃmənt] s (feeding) Ernährung f; (food) Nahrung f

Nova Scotia [′novə′skoʃə] s Neuschottland n

novel [′nɑvəl] adj neuartig || s Roman m

novelist [′nɑvəlɪst] s Romanschriftsteller –in mf

novelty [′nɑvəlti] s Neuheit f

November [no′vembər] s November m

novena [no′vinə] s Novene f

novice [′nɑvɪs] s Neuling m; (eccl) Novize m, Novizin f

novitiate [no′vɪʃi·ɪt] s Noviziat n

novocaine [′novə‚ken] s Novokain n

now [naʊ] adv jetzt; (without tem-

poral force) nun; **before now** schon früher; **by now** nachgerade; **from now on** von nun ab, fortan; **now and then** dann und wann; **now ... now bald ... bald; now or never** jetzt oder nie

nowadays ['nɑʊ-ə ‚dez] *adv* heutzutage

no'way', **no'ways'** *adv* keineswegs

no'where' *adv* nirgends

noxious ['nɑk/əs] *adj* schädlich

nozzle ['nɑzəl] *s* Düse *f*; (*on a can*) Schnabel *m*

nth [enθ] *adj*—**nth times** zig mal; **to the nth degree** (fig) im höchsten Maße

nuance ['n(j)u‑ɑns] *s* Nuance *f*

nub [nʌb] *s* Knoten *m*; (*gist*) Kernpunkt *m*

nuclear ['n(j)uklɪ‑ər] *adj* nuklear; (*energy, fission, fusion, physics, reactor, weapon*) Kern—

nu'clear pow'er *s* Atomkraft *f*

nu'clear pow'er plant' *s* Atomkraftwerk *n*

nucleolus [n(j)u'kli‑ələs] *s* Nukleolus *m*

nucleon ['n(j)ukli‑ɑn] *s* Nukleon *n*

nucle·us ['n(j)uklɪ‑əs] *s* (**-uses** & **i-** [‚aɪ]) Kern *m*

nude [n(j)ud] *adj* nackt ‖ *s* (*nude figure*) Akt *m*; **in the n.** nackt

nudge [nʌdʒ] *s* Stups *m* ‖ *tr* stupsen

nudist ['n(j)udɪst] *s* Nudist –in *mf*

nudity ['n(j)udɪti] *s* Nacktheit *f*

nugget ['nʌgɪt] *s* Klumpen *m*

nuisance ['n(j)usəns] *s* Ärgernis *n*; **be a n.** lästig sein

nui'sance raid' *s* Störungsangriff *m*

null' and void' [nʌl] *adj* null und nichtig

nulli·fy ['nʌlɪ ‚faɪ] *v* (*pret & pp* **-fied**) *tr* (*e.g., a law*) für ungültig erklären; (*e.g., the effects*) aufheben

numb [nʌm] *adj* taub; (**with**) starr (vor *dat*); (fig) betäubt; **grow n.** erstarren ‖ *tr* (& fig) betäuben; (*said of cold*) starr machen

number ['nʌmbər] *s* Nummer *f*; (*count*) Zahl *f*, Anzahl *f*; (*article*) (com) Artikel *m*; (gram) Zahl *f*; (mus) Stück *n*; **in n.** der Zahl nach; **get s.o.'s n.** (coll) j–m auf die Schliche kommen ‖ *tr* (*e.g., pages*) numerieren; (*amount to*) zählen; **be numbered among** zählen zu; **n. among** zählen zu

numberless ['nʌmbərlɪs] *adj* zahllos

num'bers game' *s* Zahlenlotto *n*

numbness ['nʌmnɪs] *s* Taubheit *f*; (*from cold*) Starrheit *f*

numeral ['n(j)umərəl] *adj* Zahl– ‖ *s* Zahl *f*, Ziffer *f*; (gram) Zahlwort *n*

numerator ['n(j)umə ‚retər] *s* Zähler *m*

numerical [n(j)u'merɪkəl] *adj* numerisch; **n. order** Zahlenfolge *f*; **n. superiority** Überzahl *f*; **n. value** Zahlenwert *m*

numerous ['n(j)umərəs] *adj* zahlreich

numismatic [‚n(j)umɪz'mætɪk] *adj* numismatisch ‖ **numismatics** *s* Münzkunde *f*

numskull ['nʌm ‚skʌl] *s* Dummkopf *m*

nun [nʌn] *s* Nonne *f*

nunci·o ['nʌnʃi‑o] *s* (**-os**) Nuntius *m*

nuptial ['nʌp/əl] *adj* Braut–, Hochzeits– ‖ **nuptials** *spl* Trauung *f*

Nuremberg ['n(j)urəm ‚bʌrg] *s* Nürnberg *n*

nurse [nʌrs] *s* Krankenschwester *f*; (*male*) Krankenpfleger *m*; (*wet nurse*) Amme *f* ‖ *tr* (*the sick*) pflegen; (*a child*) stillen; (*hopes*) hegen; **n. a cold** e–e Erkältung kurieren

nurse'maid' *s* Kindermädschen *n*

nursery ['nʌrsəri] *s* Kinderstube *f*; (*for day care*) Kindertagesstätte *f*; (hort) Baumschule *f*, Pflanzschule *f*

nurs'ery·man *s* (**-men**) Kunstgärtner *m*

nurs'ery rhyme' *s* Kinderlied *n*

nurs'ery school' *s* Kindergarten *m*

nurse's aide' *s* Schwesternhelferin *f*

nurs'ing *s* (*as a profession*) Krankenpflege *f*; (*of a person*) Pflege *f*; (*of a baby*) Stillen *n*

nurs'ing home' *s* Pflegeheim *n*

nurture ['nʌrt/ər] *s* Nahrung *f* ‖ *tr* (er)nähren

nut [nʌt] *s* Nuß *f*; (sl) verrückter Kerl *m*; (mach) Mutter *f*, Schraubenmutter *f*; **be nuts** (sl) verrückt sein; **be nuts about** (sl) vernarrt sein in (*acc*); **go nuts** (sl) e–n Klaps kriegen

nut'crack'er *s* Nußknacker *m*

nutmeg ['nʌt ‚meg] *s* (*spice*) Muskatnuß *f*; (*tree*) Muskat *m*

nutrient ['nutri‑ənt] *s* Nährstoff *m*

nutriment ['n(j)utrimənt] *s* Nährstoff *m*

nutrition [n(j)u'trɪ/ən] *s* Ernährung *f*

nutritious [n(j)u'trɪ/əs] *adj* nahrhaft

nutritive ['n(j)utrɪtɪv] *adj* nahrhaft, Nähr–

nut'shell' *s* Nußschale *f*; **in a n.** mit wenigen Worten

nutty ['nʌti] *adj* nußartig; (sl) spleenig, verrückt

nuzzle ['nʌzəl] *tr* sich mit der Schnauze (or Nase) reiben an (*dat*) ‖ *intr* (*burrow*) mit der Schnauze wühlen; **n. up to** sich anschmiegen an (*acc*)

nylon ['naɪlɑn] *s* Nylon *n*

nymph [nɪmf] *s* Nymphe *f*

nymphomaniac [‚nɪmfə'meni‑æk] *s* Nymphomanin *f*

O

O, o [o] fünfzehnter Buchstabe des englischen Alphabets

oaf [of] *s* Tölpel *m*

oak [ok] *adj* eichen ‖ *s* Eiche *f*

oak' leaf' clus'ter *s* Eichenlaub *n*

oak' tree' *s* Eichbaum *m*

oakum ['okəm] *s* Werg *n*

oar [or], [ɔr] *s* Ruder *n*, Riemen *m*

oar'lock' s Ruderdolle f

oars'man' s (-men') Ruderer m

oa·sis [o'esɪs] s (-ses [siz] Oase f

oath [oθ] s (oaths [oðz]) Eid m; o. of allegiance Treueid m; o. of office Amtseid m; under o. eidlich

oat'meal' s Hafergrütze f, Hafermehl n

oats [ots] spl Hafer m; he's feeling his o. (coll) ihn sticht der Hafer; sow one's wild o. (coll) sich [dat] die Hörner ablaufen

obbligato [ˌɑblɪ'gɑto] adj hauptstimmig || s Obligato m

obdurate ['ɑbdjərɪt] adj verstockt

obedience [o'bidɪ·əns] s (to) Gehorsam m (gegenüber dat, gegen); blind o. Kadavergehorsam m

obedient [o'bidɪ·ənt] adj (to) gehorsam (dat)

obeisance [o'bisəns] s Ehrerbietung f

obelisk ['ɑbəlɪsk] s Obelisk m

obese [o'bis] adj fettleibig

obesity [o'bisɪti] s Fettleibigkeit f

obey [o'be] tr gehorchen (dat); (a law, order) befolgen || intr gehorchen

obfuscate [ɑb'fʌsket] tr verdunkeln

obituary [o'bɪtʃu̇ˌɛri] adj Todes– || s Todesanzeige f, Nachruf m

object ['ɑbdʒɪkt] s Gegenstand m; (aim) Ziel n, Zweck m; (gram) Ergänzung f, Objekt n; money is no o. Geld spielt keine Rolle || [ɑb'dʒɛkt] intr (to) Einwände erheben (gegen)

objection [ɑb'dʒɛkʃən] s Einwand m; I have no o. to his staying ich habe nichts dagegen (einzuwenden), daß er bleibe

objectionable [ɑb'dʒɛkʃənəbəl] adj nicht einwandfrei

objective [ɑb'dʒɛktɪv] adj sachlich, objektiv || s Ziel n

objec'tive case' s Objektsfall m

ob'ject les'son s Lehre f

obligate ['ɑblɪˌget] tr verpflichten; be obligated to s.o. j-m zu Dank verbunden sein

obligation [ˌɑblɪ'geʃən] s Verpflichtung f

obligatory ['ɑblɪgəˌtori], [ə'blɪgəˌtori] adj verpflichtend, obligatorisch

oblige [ə'blaɪdʒ] tr (bind) verpflichten; (do a favor to) gefällig sein (dat); be obliged to (inf) müssen (inf); feel obliged to (inf) sich bemüßigt fühlen zu (inf); I'm much obliged to you ich bin Ihnen sehr verbunden

oblig'ing adj gefällig

oblique [ə'blik] adj schief

obliterate [ə'blɪtəˌret] tr auslöschen; (traces) verwischen; (writing) unleserlich machen

oblivion [ə'blɪvɪ·ən] s Vergessenheit f

oblivious [ə'blɪvɪ·əs] adj—be o. of sich [dat] nicht bewußt sein (genit)

oblong ['ɑblɔŋ] adj länglich || s Rechteck n

obnoxious [ɑb'nɑkʃəs] adj widerlich

oboe ['obo] s Oboe f

oboist ['obo·ɪst] s Oboist –in mf

obscene [ɑb'sin] adj obszön

obscenity [ɑb'sɛnɪti] s Obszönität f

obscure [əb'skjur] adj dunkel, obskur || tr verdunkeln

obscurity [əb'skjurɪti] s Dunkelheit f

obsequies ['ɑbsɪkwiz] spl Totenfeier f

obsequious [əb'sikwɪ·əs] adj unterwürfig

observance [əb'zʌrvəns] s Beachtung f, Befolgung f; (celebration) Feier f

observant [əb'zʌrvənt] adj beobachtend

observation [ˌɑbzər've/ən] s Beobachtung f; keep under o. beobachten

observa'tion tow'er s Aussichtsturm m

observatory [əb'zʌrvəˌtori] s Sternwarte f, Observatorium n

observe [əb'zʌrv] tr (a person, rules) beobachten; (a holiday) feiern; o. silence Stillschweigen bewahren

obsess [əb'sɛs] tr verfolgen; obsessed (by) besessen (von)

obsession [əb'sɛ/ən] s Besessenheit f

obsolescent [ˌɑbsə'lɛsənt] adj veraltend

obsolete ['ɑbsəˌlit] adj veraltet; become o. veralten

obstacle ['ɑbstəkəl] s Hindernis n

ob'stacle course' s Hindernisbahn f

obstetrical [əb'stɛtrɪkəl] adj Geburtshilfe–, Entbindungs–

obstetrician [ˌɑbstə'trɪ/ən] s Geburtshelfer –in mf

obstetrics [əb'stɛtrɪks] s Geburtshilfe f

obstinacy ['ɑbstɪnəsi] s Starrheit f

obstinate ['ɑbstɪnɪt] adj starr

obstreperous [əb'strɛpərəs] adj (clamorous) lärmend; (unruly) widerspenstig

obstruct [əb'strʌkt] tr (e.g., a pipe) verstopfen; (a view, way) versperren; (traffic) behindern; o. justice die Rechtspflege behindern

obstruction [əb'strʌk/ən] s (of a view, way) Versperrung f; (of traffic) Behinderung f; (obstacle) Hindernis n; (parl, pathol) Obstruktion f

obtain [əb'ten] tr erhalten, erlangen || intr bestehen

obtrusive [əb'trusɪv] adj aufdringlich

obtuse [əb't(j)us] adj (& fig) stumpf

obviate ['ɑbvɪˌet] tr erübrigen

obvious ['ɑbvɪ·əs] adj naheliegend; it is o. es liegt auf der Hand

occasion [ə'keʒən] s Gelegenheit f; (reason) Anlaß m; on o. gelegentlich; on the o. of anläßlich (genit) || tr veranlassen

occasional [ə'keʒənəl] adj gelegentlich

occasionally [ə'keʒənəli] adv gelegentlich, zuweilen

occident ['ɑksɪdənt] s Abendland n

occidental [ˌɑksɪ'dɛntəl] adj abendländisch || s Abendländer –in mf

occlusion [ə'kluʒən] s Okklusion f

occult [ə'kʌlt] adj geheim, okkult

occupancy ['ɑkjəpənsi] s Besitz m, Besitzergreifung f; (of a home) Einzug m

occupant ['ɑkjəpənt] s Besitzer –in mf; (of a home) Inhaber –in mf; (of a car) Insasse m, Insassin f

occupation [ˌɑkjə'pe/ən] s (employ-

ment) Beruf *m*, Beschäftigung *f*;
(mil) Besetzung *f*, Besatzung *f*

occup'ational disease' [,akjə'peʃənəl]
s Berufskrankheit *f*

occupa'tional ther'apy *s* Beschäftigungstherapie *f*

occupa'tion troops' *spl* Besatzungstruppen *pl*

occu·py ['akjə ,paɪ] *v* (*pret & pp* **–pied**)
tr in Besitz nehmen; (*a house*) bewohnen; (*time*) in Anspruch nehmen;
(*keep busy*) beschäftigen; (mil) besetzen; **occupied** (*said of a seat or toilet*) besetzt; (*said of a person*)
beschäftigt; **o. oneself with** sich befassen mit

oc·cur [ə'kʌr] *v* (*pret & pp* **–curred**,
ger **–curring**) *intr* sich ereignen;
(*come to mind*) (*to*) einfallen (*dat*)

occurrence [ə'kʌrəns] *s* Ereignis *n*;
(*e.g., of a word*) Vorkommen *n*

ocean ['oʃən] *s* Ozean *m*

oceanic [,oʃɪ'ænɪk] *adj* Ozean-, ozeanisch

o'cean lin'er *s* Ozeandampfer *m*

oceanography [,oʃən'agrəfɪ] *s* Ozeanographie *f*

ocher ['okər] *s* Ocker *m & n*

o'clock [ə'klak] *adv* Uhr; **at ... o'clock**
um ... Uhr

octane num'ber *s* Oktanzahl *f*

oc'tane num'ber *s* Oktanzahl *f*

octave ['aktɪv], ['aktev] *s* Oktave *f*

October [ak'tobər] *s* Oktober *m*

octogenarian [,aktədʒɪ'nerɪ·ən] *s*
Achtzige *mf*

octo·pus ['aktəpəs] *s* (**–puses & –pi**
[,paɪ]) Seepolyp *m*

ocular ['akjələr] *adj* Augen-

oculist ['akjəlɪst] *s* Augenarzt *m*, Augenärztin *f*

odd [ad] *adj* (*strange*) seltsam, eigenartig; (*number*) ungerade; (*e.g.,
glove*) einzeln; **two hundred odd
pages** etwas über zweihundert Seiten
|| **odds** *spl* (*probability*) Wahrscheinlichkeit *f*; (*advantage*) Vorteil *m*;
(*in gambling*) Vorgabe *f*; **at odds**
uneinig; **lay** (*or* **give**) **odds** vorgeben;
the odds are two to one die Chancen
stehen zwei zu eins

odd' ball' *s* (sl) Sonderling *m*

oddity ['adɪtɪ] *s* Seltsamkeit *f*

odd' jobs' *spl* Gelegenheitsarbeit *f*;
(*chores*) kleine Aufgaben *pl*

odds' and ends' *spl* Kleinkram *m*

ode [od] *s* Ode *f*

odious ['odɪ·əs] *adj* verhaßt

odor ['odər] *s* Duft *m*, Geruch *m*; **be
in bad o.** in schlechtem Ruf stehen

odorless ['odərlɪs] *adj* geruchlos

odyssey ['adɪsɪ] *s* Irrfahrt *f*; **Odyssey**
Odyssee *f*

of [av], [əv] *prep* von (*dat*); *genit*,
e.g., **the name of the dog** der Name
des Hundes

off [ɔf] *adj* (*free from work*) dienstfrei; (*poor, bad*) schlecht; (*electric
current*) ausgeschaltet, abgeschaltet;
be badly off in schlechten Verhältnissen sein; **be off** (*said of a clock*)
nachgehen; (*said of a measurement*)

falsch sein; (*said of a person*) im
Irrtum sein; (*be crazy*) nicht ganz
richtig im Kopf sein; **be well off** in
guten Verhältnissen sein; **the deal**
(*or* **party**) **is off** es ist aus mit dem
Geschäft (or mit der Party) || *adv*
(*distant*) weg; **he was off in a flash**
er war im Nu weg; **I must be off**
ich muß fort || *prep* von (*dat*); **off
duty** außer Dienst; **off limits** Zutritt
verboten

offal ['ɔfəl] *s* (*refuse*) Abfall *m*; (*of
butchered meat*) Innereien *pl*

off' and on' *adv* ab und zu

off'beat' *adj* (sl) ungewöhnlich

off' chance' *s* geringe Chance *f*

off'-col'or *adj* schlüpfrig

off'-du'ty *adj* außerdienstlich

offend [ə'fɛnd] *tr* beleidigen || *intr*—
o. against verstoßen gegen

offender [ə'fɛndər] *s* Missetäter –in
mf; **first o.** nicht Vorbestrafte *mf*;
second o. Vorbestrafte *mf*

offense [ə'fɛns] *s* (*against*) Vergehen
n (gegen); **give o.** Anstoß geben;
no o.! nichts für ungut!; **take o.** (**at**)
Anstoß nehmen (an *dat*)

offensive [ə'fɛnsɪv] *adj* anstößig; (*odor*)
ekelhaft; (*action*) offensiv || *s* Offensive *f*; **take the o.** die Offensive ergreifen

offer ['ɔfər] *s* Angebot *n* || *tr* anbieten; (*a price*) bieten; (*help, resistance*) leisten; (*friendship*) schenken;
o. an excuse e-e Entschuldigung vorbringen; **o. as an excuse** als Entschuldigung vorbringen; **o. for sale** feilbieten; **o. one's services** sich anbieten; **o. up** aufopfern || *intr*—**o. to**
(*inf*) sich erbieten zu (*inf*)

of'fering *s* (*act*) Opferung *f*; (*gift*)
Opfergabe *f*

offertory ['ɔfər ,torɪ] *s* Offertorium *n*

off'hand' *adj* (*excuse*) unvorbereitet;
(*manner*) lässig || *adv* kurzerhand

office ['ɔfɪs] *s* (*room*) Büro *n*, Amt *n*;
(*position*) Amt *n*; (*of a doctor*)
Sprechzimmer *n*; **be in o.** amtieren;
through the good offices of durch die
freundliche Vermittlung (*genit*); **run
for o.** für ein Amt kandidieren

of'fice boy' *s* Bürojunge *m*

of'fice build'ing *s* Bürogebäude *n*

of'ficehold'er *s* Amtsträger –in *mf*

of'fice hours' *spl* Dienststunden *pl*; (*of
a doctor, lawyer*) Sprechstunde *f*

officer ['ɔfɪsər] *s* (adm) Beamte *m*,
Beamtin *f*; (com) Direktor –in *mf*;
(mil) Offizier –in *mf*

of'ficer can'didate *s* Offiziersanwärter
–in *mf*

of'ficers' mess' *s* Offizierskasino *n*;
(nav) Offiziersmesse *f*

of'fice seek'er *s* Amtsbewerber –in *mf*

of'fice supplies' *spl* Bürobedarf *m*

of'fice work' *s* Büroarbeit *f*

official [ə'fɪʃəl] *adj* amtlich; (*in line
of duty*) Dienst-; (*visit*) offiziell;
(*document*) öffentlich; **on o. business**
dienstlich || *s* Beamte *m*, Beamtin *f*;
top officials Spitzenkräfte *pl*

offi'cial busi'ness *s* Dienstsache *f*

offi'cial call' s (telp) Dienstgespräch n
officialdom [ə'fɪʃəldəm] s Beamtentum n
officialese [ə,fɪʃə'liz] s Amtssprache f
officially [ə'fɪʃəlɪ] adv offiziell
offi'cial use' s Dienstgebrauch m
officiate [ə'fɪʃɪ,et] intr amtieren; o. at a marriage e–n Traugottesdienst halten
officious [ə'fɪʃəs] adj dienstbeflissen
offing ['ɔfɪŋ] s—in the o. in Aussicht
off'-lim'its adj gesperrt
off'print' s Abdruck m, Sonderdruck m
off'-seas'on prices Preise pl während der Vor- und Nachsaison ‖ s Vor- und Nachsaison f
off'set' s (compensation) Ausgleich m; (typ) Offsetdruck m ‖ **off'set'** v (pret –set; ger –setting) tr ausgleichen
off'set press' s Offsetdruck m
off'shoot' s Ableger m
off'shore' adj küstennah
off'side' adv (sport) abseits
off'spring' s Sprößling m
off'stage' adj hinter der Bühne befindlich ‖ adv hinter der Bühne
off'-the-cuff' adj aus dem Stegreif
off'-the-rec'ord adj im Vertrauen
often ['ɔfən] adv oft, häufig; every so o. von Zeit zu Zeit; quite o. öfters
of'tentimes' adv oftmals
ogive ['odʒaɪv] s (diagonal vaulting rib) Gratrippe f; (pointed arch) Spitzbogen m
ogle ['ogəl] tr liebäugeln mit ‖ intr liebäugeln
ogre ['ogər] s Scheusal n; (myth) Menschenfresser m
oh [o] interj oh!; oh, dear! o weh!
ohm [om] s Ohm n
oil [ɔɪl] s Öl n; strike oil auf Öl stoßen ‖ tr ölen
oil' burn'er s Ölbrenner m
oil'can' s Ölkanne f
oil'cloth' s Wachsleinwand f
oil' col'or s Ölfarbe f
oil' drum' s Ölfaß n
oil' field' s Ölfeld n
oil' gauge' s Ölstandsanzeiger m
oil' heat' s Ölheizung f
oil' lev'el s Ölstand m
oil'man' s (–men') Ölhändler m
oil' paint'ing s Ölgemälde n
oil' pres'sure s Öldruck m
oil' rig' s Ölbohrinsel f
oil' shale' s Ölschiefer m
oil' slick' s Öllache f
oil' tank' s Ölbehälter m
oil' tank'er s Öltanker m
oil' well' s Ölquelle f
oily ['ɔɪlɪ] adj ölig; (unctious) salbungsvoll
ointment ['ɔɪntmənt] s Salbe f
O.K. ['o'ke] adj in Ordnung, okay ‖ s Billigung f ‖ v (pret & pp O.K.'d; ger O.K.'ing) tr billigen ‖ intr okay!
old [old] adj alt; as old as the hills uralt; (said of a person) steinalt
old' age' s Alter n, Greisenalter n
old'-age' home' s Altersheim n
old' coun'try s Heimatland n
olden ['oldən] adj alt

old'-fash'ioned adj altmodisch
old' fog'(e)y ['fogɪ] s alter Kauz m
Old' Glo'ry s Sternenbanner n
old' hand' s alter Hase m
old' hat' adj bärtig
old' la'dy s Greisin f; (wife) (pej) Alte f
old' maid' s alte Jungfer f
old' man' s Greis m; (mil) Alter m
old' mas'ter s (paint) alter Meister m
old' moon' s letztes Viertel n
old' salt' s alter Seebär m
oldster ['oldstər] s alter Knabe m
Old' Tes'tament s Altes Testament n
old'-time' adj altväterisch
old'-tim'er s (coll) alter Hase m
old' wives'' tale' s Altweibergeschichte f
Old' World' s alte Welt f
oleander [,olɪ'ændər] s Oleander m
olfactory [al'fæktorɪ] adj Geruchs-
oligarchy ['alɪ,garkɪ] s Oligarchie f
olive ['alɪv] s Olive f
ol'ive branch' s Ölzweig m
ol'ive grove' s Olivenhain m
ol'ive oil' s Olivenöl n
ol'ive tree' s Ölbaum m, Olivenbaum m
olympiad [o'lɪmpɪ,æd] s Olympiade f
Olympian [o'lɪmpɪ-ən] adj olympisch
Olympic [o'lɪmpɪk] adj olympisch ‖ the Olympics spl die Olympischen Spiele
omelet, omelette ['amə,let] s Eierkuchen m, Omelett n
omen ['omən] s Omen n, Vorzeichen n
ominous ['amɪnəs] adj ominös, unheilvoll
omission [o'mɪʃən] s Auslassung f; (of a deed) Unterlassung f
omit [o'mɪt] v (pret & pp omitted; ger omitting) tr (a word) auslassen; (a deed) unterlassen; be omitted ausfallen; o. (ger) es unterlassen zu (inf)
omnibus ['amnɪ,bʌs] adj Sammel-, Mantel- ‖ s Omnibus m, Autobus m
omnipotent [am'nɪpətənt] adj allmächtig
omnipresent [,amnɪ'prezənt] adj allgegenwärtig
omniscient [am'nɪʃənt] adj allwissend
on [ɔn] adj (in progress) im Gange; (light, gas, water) an; (radio, television) angestellt; (switch) eingeschaltet; (brakes) angezogen; be on to s.o. j–n durchschen; be on to s.th. über etw [acc] im Bilde sein ‖ adv weiter; on and off dann und wann; on and on in e–m fort ‖ prep auf (dat or acc), an (dat or acc); (concerning) über (acc)
once [wʌns] adv einmal; (formerly) einst; at o. auf einmal; (immediately) sofort; not o. nicht ein einziges Mal; o. and for all ein für allemal; o. before früher einmal; o. in a while ab und zu; o. more noch einmal; o. upon a time was es war einmal ‖ s—this o. dieses (eine) Mal ‖ conj sobald
once'-o'ver s—give (s.o. or s.th.) the o. rasch mustern
one [wʌn] adj ein; (one certain, e.g.,

Mr. Smith) ein gewisser; **for one thing** zunächst; **her one care** ihre einzige Sorge; **it's all one to me** es ist mir ganz gleich; **one and a half hours** anderthalb Stunden; **one day** e-s Tages; **one more** noch ein; **one more thing** noch etwas; **one o'clock** ein Uhr, eins; **on the one hand ... on the other** einerseits ... andererseits ‖ *s* Eins *f* ‖ *pron* einer; **I for one** was mich betrifft, ich jedenfalls; **one after another** einer nach dem anderen; **one after the other** nacheinander; **one another** einander, sich; **one at a time, please!** einer nach dem anderen, bittel; **one behind the other** hintereinander; **one by one** einer nach dem anderen; **one of these days** früher oder später; **one on top of the other** übereinander, aufeinander; **one to nothing** eins zu Null; **this one** dieser da, der da; **with one another** miteinander ‖ *indef pron* man; **one's** sein

one'-armed' *adj* einarmig
one'-eyed' *adj* einäugig
one'-horse town' s Kuhdorf *n*
one'-leg'ged *adj* einbeinig
onerous ['ɔnərəs] *adj* lästig
oneself *reflex pron* sich; **be o.** sein, wie man immer ist; **by o.** allein; **to o.** vor sich [*acc*] hin
one'-sid'ed *adj* (& *fig*) einseitig
one'-track' *adj* eingleisig; (*fig*) einseitig
one'-way street' s Einbahnstraße *f*
one'-way tick'et s einfache Fahrkarte *f*
one'-week' *adj* achttägig
onion ['ʌnjən] s Zwiebel *f*; **know one's onions** (*coll*) Bescheid wissen
on'ionskin' s Durchschlagpapier *n*
on'look'er s Zuschauer –in *mf*
only ['onli] *adj* (*son, hope*) einzig ‖ *adv* nur; **not only ... but** also nicht nur ... sondern auch; **o. too** nur (all)zu; **o. too well** zur Genüge; **o. yesterday** erst gestern ‖ *conj* aber; **o. that** nur daß
on'ly-begot'ten *adj* eingeboren
onomatopoeia [,ɑnə,mætə'pi·ə] s Lautmalerei *f*
on'-ramp' s Zufahrtsrampe *f*
on'rush' s Ansturm *m*
on'set' s Anfang *m*; (*attack*) Angriff *m*
onslaught ['ɔn,slɔt] s Angriff *m*
on'to *prep auf* (*acc*) hinauf; **be o. s.o.** hinter j-s Schliche kommen; **be o. s.th.** über etw [*acc*] im Bilde sein
onus ['onəs] s Last *f*; **o. of proof** Beweislast *f*
onward(s) ['ɑnwərd(z)] *adv* vorwärts
onyx ['ɑnɪks] s Onyx *m*
oodles ['udəlz] *spl* (*coll*) (**of**) Unmengen *pl* (von)
ooze [uz] s Sickern *n*; (*mud*) Schlamm *m* ‖ *tr* ausschwitzen ‖ *intr* sickern; **o. out** durchsickern
opal ['opəl] s Opal *m*
opaque [o'pek] *adj* undurchsichtig; (*stupid*) stumpf
open ['opən] *adj* (*window, position, sea, question, vowel*) offen; (*air, field, seat*) frei; (*business, office*)

geöffnet; (*seam*) geplatzt; (*account*) laufend; (*meeting*) öffentlich; **be o.** offenstehen; **get o.** aufbekommen; **have an o. mind about s.th.** sich noch nicht auf etw [*acc*] festgelegt haben; **keep o.** offenhalten; **lay oneself o. to** sich aussetzen (*dat*); **o. to** (*the public*) zugänglich (*dat*); (*criticism*) ausgesetzt (*dat*); (*doubt*) unterworfen (*dat*); **o. to bribery** bestechlich (*dat*); **o. to question** strittig ‖ *s*—**come out into the o.** (*fig*) mit seinen Gedanken herauskommen; **in the o.** im Freien ‖ *tr* öffnen, aufmachen; (*a business, account, meeting, hostilities, fire*) eröffnen; (*a book*) aufschlagen; (*eyes in surprise*) aufreißen; (*a box, bottle*) anbrechen; (*an umbrella*) aufspannen; **o. the attack** losschlagen; **o. to traffic** dem Verkehr übergeben; **o. wide** weit aufreißen ‖ *intr* sich öffnen, aufgehen; (*said of a school, speech, play*) beginnen; **o. onto** hinausgehen auf (*acc*); **o. up** sich auftun; **o. with hearts** (*cards*) Herz ausspielen
o'pen-air' *adj* Freiluft–; (*theat*) Freilicht–; **o. concert** Konzert *n* im Freien
opener ['opənər] s Öffner *m*, **for openers** (*coll*) für den Anfang
o'pen-eyed' *adj* mit offenen Augen
o'pen-hand'ed *adj* freigebig
o'pen-heart'ed *adj* offenherzig
o'pen house' s allgemeiner Besuchstag *m*
o'pening *adj* (*scene*) erste; (*remarks*) Eröffnungs– ‖ *s* Öffnung *f*; (*of a speech, play*) Anfang *m*; (*of a store, etc.*) Eröffnung *f*; (*vacant job*) freie (or offene) Stelle *f*; (*in the woods*) Lichtung *f*; (*good opportunity*) günstige Gelegenheit *f*; (*theat*) Erstaufführung *f*
o'pening night' s Eröffnungsvorstellung *f*, Premiere *f*
o'pening num'ber s erstes Stück *n*
o'pen-mind'ed *adj* aufgeschlossen
openness ['opənnɪs] s Offenheit *f*
o'pen sea'son s Jagdzeit *f*
o'pen se'cret s offenes Geheimnis *n*
o'pen shop' s offener Betrieb *m* (für den kein Gewerkschaftszwang besteht)
opera ['ɑpərə] s Oper *f*
op'era glass'es *spl* Opernglas *n*
op'era house' s Opernhaus *n*
operate ['ɑpə,ret] *tr* (*a machine, gun*) bedienen; (*a tool*) handhaben; (*a business*) betreiben; **be operated by electricity** elektrisch betrieben werden ‖ *intr* (*said of a device, machine*) funktionieren, laufen; (*surg*) operieren, on **o.** (*surg*) operieren
operatic [,ɑpə'rætɪk] *adj* opernhaft
op'erating costs' *spl* Betriebskosten *pl*
op'erating instruc'tions *spl* Bedienungsanweisung *f*
op'erating room' s Operationssaal *m*
op'erating ta'ble s Operationstisch *m*
operation [,ɑpə'reʃən] s (*process*) Verfahren *n*; (*of a machine*) Bedie-

nung *f; (of a business)* Leitung *f;* (mil) Operation *f,* Aktion *f;* (surg) Operation *f;* **be in o.** *(said of a machine)* in Betrieb sein; *(said of a law)* in Kraft sein; **have** (or **undergo**) **an o.** sich e-r Operation unterziehen; **in a single o.** in e-m einzigen Arbeitsgang; **put into o.** in Betrieb setzen

operational [ˌɑpəˈreʃənəl] *adj (ready to be used)* betriebsbereit; *(pertaining to operations)* Betriebs– Arbeits–; (mil) Einsatz-, Operations-

opera′tions room′ *s* (aer) Bereitschaftsraum *m*

operative [ˈɑpərətɪv] *adj* funktionsfähig, wirkend; **become o.** in Kraft treten || *s* Agent –in *mf*

operator [ˈɑpəˌretər] *s (of a machine)* Bedienende *mf; (of an automobile)* Fahrer –in *mf;* (sl) Schieber –in *mf;* (telp) Telephonist –in *mf;* **o.!** (telp) Zentrale!

op′erator's li′cense *s* Führerschein *m*

operetta [ˌɑpəˈretə] *s* Operette *f*

ophthalmologist [ˌɑfθəlˈmɑledʒɪst] *s* Augenarzt *m,* Augenärztin *f*

ophthalmology [ˌɑfθəlˈmɑledʒi] *s* Augenheilkunde *f,* Ophthalmologie *f*

opiate [ˈopɪˌet] *s* Opiat *n;* (fig) Betäubungsmittel *n*

opinion [əˈpɪnjən] *s* Meinung *f;* **be of the o.** der Meinung sein; **give an o. on** begutachten; **have a high o. of** große Stücke halten auf (*acc*); **in my o.** meiner Meinung nach, meines Erachtens

opinionated [əˈpɪnjəˌnetɪd] *adj* von sich eingenommen

opin′ion poll′ *s* Meinungsumfrage *f*

opium [ˈopɪ·əm] *s* Opium *n*

o′pium den′ *s* Opiumhöhle *f*

o′pium pop′py *s* Schlafmohn *m*

opossum [əˈpɑsəm] *s* Opossum *n*

opponent [əˈponənt] *s* Gegner –in *mf*

opportune [ˌɑpərˈt(j)un] *adj* gelegen

opportunist [ˌɑpərˈt(j)unɪst] *s* Opportunist –in *mf*

opportunity [ˌɑpərˈt(j)unɪti] *s* Gelegenheit *f*

oppose [əˈpoz] *tr* sich widersetzen (*dat*); *(for comparison)* gegenüberstellen; **be opposed to s.th.** gegen etw sein

oppos′ing *adj (team, forces)* gegnerisch; *(views)* entgegengesetzt

opposite [ˈɑpəsɪt] *adj (side, corner)* gegenüberliegend; *(meaning)* entgegengesetzt; *(view)* gegenteilig; **o. angle** (geom) Gegenwinkel *m;* **o. to** gegenüber (*dat*) || *s* Gegensatz *m,* Gegenteil *n* || *prep* gegenüber (*dat*)

op′posite num′ber *s* Gegenstück *n,* Gegenspieler –in *mf*

opposition [ˌɑpəˈzɪʃən] *s* Widerstand *m;* (pol) Opposition *f;* **meet with stiff o.** auf heftigen Widerstand stoßen; **offer o.** Widerstand leisten

oppress [əˈpres] *tr* unterdrücken

oppression [əˈpreʃən] *s* Unterdrückung *f*

oppressive [əˈpresɪv] *adj* bedrückend

oppressor [əˈpresər] *s* Unterdrücker –in *mf*

opprobrious [əˈprobrɪ·əs] *adj* schändlich

opprobrium [əˈprobrɪ·əm] *s* Schande *f*

opt [ɑpt] *intr*—**opt for** optieren für

optic [ˈɑptɪk] *adj* Augen– || **optics** *s* Optik *f*

optical [ˈɑptɪkəl] *adj* optisch

op′tical illus′ion *s* optische Täuschung *f*

optician [ɑpˈtɪʃən] *s* Optiker –in *mf*

op′tic nerve′ *s* Augennerv *m*

optimism [ˈɑptɪˌmɪzəm] *s* Optimismus *m*

optimist [ˈɑptɪmɪst] *s* Optimist –in *mf*

optimistic [ˌɑptɪˈmɪstɪk] *adj* optimistisch

option [ˈɑpʃən] *s (choice)* Wahl *f; (alternative)* Alternative *f;* (ins) Option *f*

optional [ˈɑpʃənəl] *adj* wahlfrei; **be o.** freistehen

optometrist [ɑpˈtɑmɪtrɪst] *s* Augenoptiker –in *mf*

optometry [ɑpˈtɑmɪtri] *s* Optometrie *f*

opulent [ˈɑpjələnt] *adj (wealthy)* reich; *(luxurious)* üppig

or [ər] *conj* oder

oracle [ˈɔrəkəl] *s* Orakel *n*

oracular [oˈrækjələr] *adj* orakelhaft

oral [ˈɔrəl] *adj* mündlich

o′ral hygiene′ *s* Mundpflege *f*

orange [ˈɔrɪndʒ] *adj* orange || *s* Orange *f,* Apfelsine *f*

orangeade [ˌɔrɪndʒˈed] *s* Orangeade *f*

or′ange blos′som *s* Orangenblüte *f*

or′ange grove′ *s* Orangenhain *m*

or′ange tree′ *s* Orangenbaum *m*

orang-outang [oˈræŋˌtæŋ] *s* Orang-Utan *m*

oration [oˈreʃən] *s* Rede *f*

orator [ˈɔrətər] *s* Redner –in *mf*

oratorical [ˌɔrəˈtɔrɪkəl] *adj* rednerisch

oratori·o [ˌɔrəˈtɔrɪˌo] *s* (–os) Oratorium *n*

oratory [ˈɔrəˌtɔri] *s* Redekunst *f*

orb [ɔrb] *s* Kugel *f; (of the moon or sun)* Scheibe *f*

orbit [ˈɔrbɪt] *s* Umlaufbahn *f;* **send into o.** in die Umlaufbahn schicken || *tr* umkreisen

orbital [ˈɔrbɪtəl] *adj* Kreisbahn–

orchard [ˈɔrtʃərd] *s* Obstgarten *m*

orchestra [ˈɔrkɪstrə] *s* Orchester *n*

or′chestra pit′ *s* Orchesterraum *m*

orchestrate [ˈɔrkɪˌstret] *tr* orchestrieren

orchid [ˈɔrkɪd] *s* Orchidee *f*

ordain [ɔrˈden] *tr* verordnen; (eccl) ordinieren, zum Priester weihen

ordeal [ɔrˈdil] *s* Qual *f;* (hist) Gottesurteil *n;* **o. by fire** Feuerprobe *f*

order [ˈɔrdər] *s (command)* Befehl *m; (decree)* Verordnung *f; (order, arrangement)* Ordnung *f; (medal)* Orden *m; (sequence)* Reihenfolge *f;* (archit, bot, zool) Ordnung *f;* (com) **(for)** Auftrag *m (auf acc),* Bestellung *f (auf acc);* (eccl) Orden *m;* (jur) Beschluß *m;* **according to orders** befehlsgemäß; **be in good o.** in gutem

Zustand sein; **be the o. of the day** (coll) an der Tagesordnung sein; **be under orders to** (inf) Befehl haben zu (inf); **by o. of** auf Befehl von (or genit); **call to o.** (a meeting) für eröffnet erklären; (reestablish order) zur Ordnung rufen; **in o.** (functioning) in Ordnung; (proper, in place) angebracht; **in o. of** geordnet nach; **in o. that** damit; **in o. to** (inf) um ... zu (inf); **make to o.** nach Maß machen; **of a high o.** von ausgezeichneter Art; **on o.** (com) in Auftrag; **o.!, o.!** zur Ordnung! **out of o.** (defective) außer Betrieb; (not functioning at all) nicht in Ordnung; (disarranged) in Unordnung; (parl) im Widerspruch zur Geschäftsordnung, unzulässig; **put in o.** in Ordnung bringen; **restore to o.** die Ordnung wiederherstellen; **you are out of o.** Sie haben nicht das Wort || tr (command) befehlen, anordnen; (decree) verordnen; (com) bestellen; **as ordered** auftragsgemäß; **o. around** herumkommandieren; **o. in advance** vor(her)bestellen; **o. more of** nachbestellen; **o. s.o off** (e.g., the premises) j-n weisen von

or'der blank' s Auftragsformular n
orderliness ['ɔrdərlɪnɪs] s (of a person) Ordnungsliebe f; (of a room, etc.) Ordnung f
orderly ['ɔrdərli] adj ordentlich || s (med) Krankenwärter m; (mil) Bursche m
or'derly room' s (mil) Schreibstube f
or'der slip' s Bestellzettel m
ordinal ['ɔrdɪnəl] adj Ordnungs– || s Ordnungszahl f
ordinance ['ɔrdɪnəns] s Verfügung f; (of a city) Verordnung f
ordinary ['ɔrdɪ‚neri] adj gewöhnlich; (member) ordentlich; **p. person** Alltagsmensch m || s Gewöhnliche n; (eccl) Ordinarius m; **nothing out of the o.** nichts Ungewöhnliches; **out of the o.** außerordentlich
ordination [‚ɔrdɪ'neʃən] s Priesterweihe f
ordnance ['ɔrdnəns] s Waffen und Munition pl; (arti) Geschützwesen n
ore [or] s Erz n
organ ['ɔrgən] s (means) Werkzeug n; (publication) Organ n; (adm, biol) Organ n; (mus) Orgel f
organdy ['ɔrgəndi] s Organdy m
or'gan grind'er s Drehorgelspieler m
organic [ɔr'gænɪk] adj organisch
organism ['ɔrgə‚nɪzəm] s Organismus m
organist ['ɔrgənɪst] s Organist –in mf
organization [‚ɔrgənɪ'zeʃən] s Organisation f
organizational [‚ɔrgənɪ'zeʃənəl] adj organisatorisch
organize ['ɔrgə‚naɪz] tr organisieren
organizer ['ɔrgə‚naɪzər] s Organisator –in mf
or'gan loft' s Orgelbühne f
orgasm ['ɔrgæzəm] s Orgasmus m
orgy ['ɔrdʒi] s Orgie f

Orient ['ɔrɪ‚ənt] s Orient m || **orient** ['ɔrɪ‚ent] tr orientieren
oriental [‚ɔrɪ'entəl] adj orientalisch || **Oriental** s Orientale m, Orientalin f
orientation [‚ɔrɪ‚ən'teʃən] s Orientierung f; (of new staff members) Einführung f
orifice ['ɔrɪfɪs] s Öffnung f
origin ['ɔrɪdʒɪn] s Ursprung m; (of a person or word) Herkunft f
original [ə'rɪdʒɪnəl] adj ursprünglich; (first) Ur–; (novel, play) originell; (person) erfinderisch || s Original n
originality [ə‚rɪdʒɪ'nælɪtɪ] s Originalität f
ori'ginal research' s Quellenstudium n
ori'ginal sin' s Erbsünde f, Sündenfall m
originate [ə'rɪdʒɪ‚net] tr hervorbringen || intr (from) entstehen (aus); **o. in** seinen Ursprung haben in (dat)
originator [ə'rɪdʒɪ‚netər] s Urheber –in mf
oriole ['ɔrɪ‚ol] s Goldamsel f, Pirol m
ormolu ['ɔrmə‚lu] s Malergold n
ornament ['ɔrnəmənt] s Verzierung f, Schmuck m || ['ɔrnə‚ment] tr verzieren
ornamental [‚ɔrnə'mentəl] adj Zier–
ornamentation [‚ɔrnəmən'teʃən] s Verzierung f
ornate [ɔr'net] adj überladen; (speech) bilderreich
ornery ['ɔrnəri] adj (cantankerous) mürrisch; (vile) gemein
ornithology [‚ɔrnɪ'θɑlədʒi] s Vogelkunde f, Ornithologie f
orphan ['ɔrfən] s Waise f; **become an o.** verwaisen
orphanage ['ɔrfənɪdʒ] s Waisenhaus n
or'phaned adj verwaist; **be o.** verwaisen
or'phans' court' s Vormundschaftsgericht n
orthodox ['ɔrθə‚dɑks] adj orthodox
orthography [ɔr'θɑgrəfi] s Orthographie f, Rechtschreibung f
orthopedist [‚ɔrθə'pidɪst] s Orthopäde m, Orthopädin f
oscillate ['ɑsɪ‚let] intr schwingen
oscillation [‚ɑsɪ'leʃən] s Schwingung f
oscillator ['ɑsɪ‚letər] s Oszillator m
osier ['oʒər] s Korbweide f
osmosis [ɑs'mosɪs] s Osmose f
osprey ['ɑspri] s Fischadler m
ossi·fy ['ɑsɪ‚faɪ] v (pret & pp –fied) tr verknöchern lassen || intr verknöchern
ostensible [ɑs'tensɪbəl] adj vorgeblich
ostentation [‚ɑstən'teʃən] s Zurschaustellung f, Prahlerei f
ostentatious [‚ɑstən'teʃəs] adj prahlerisch, prunksüchtig
osteopath ['ɑstɪ‚ə‚pæθ] s Osteopath –in mf
osteopathy [‚ɑstɪ'ɑpəθi] s Osteopathie f
ostracism ['ɑstrə‚sɪzəm] s Ächtung f; (hist) Scherbengericht n
ostracize ['ɑstrə‚saɪz] tr verfemen
ostrich ['ɑstrɪtʃ] s Strauß m
Ostrogoth ['ɑstrə‚gɑθ] s Ostgote m

other ['ʌðər] *adj* andere, sonstig; **among o. things** unter anderem; **every o. day** jeden zweiten Tag; **none o. than he** kein anderer als er; **on the o. hand** andererseits; **o. things being equal** unter gleichen Voraussetzungen; **someone or o.** irgend jemand; **some ... or o.** irgendein; **the o. day** unlängst || *adv*—**o. than** anders als || *indef pron* andere; **the others** die anderen

otherwise ['ʌðər‚waɪz] *adj* sonstig || *adv* sonst; **I can't do o.** ich kann nicht umhin; **o. engaged** anderweitig beschäftigt; **think o.** anders denken

otter ['ɑtər] *s* Otter *m*; (*snake*) Otter *f*

Ottoman ['ɑtəmən] *adj* osmanisch || **ottoman** *s* (*couch*) Ottomane *m*; (*cushioned stool*) Polsterschemel *m*; **O. Osmane** *m*

ouch [autʃ] *interj* au!

ought [ɔt] *aux* used to express obligation, e.g., **you o. to tell her** Sie sollten es ihr sagen; **they o. to have been here** sie hätten hier sein sollen

ounce [auns] *s* Unze *f*

our [aur] *poss adj* unser

ours [aurz] *poss pron* der uns(e)rige, der uns(e)re, uns(e)rer; **a friend of o.** ein Freund von uns; **this is o.** das gehört uns

ourselves [aur'selvz] *reflex pron* uns; **we are by o.** wir sind doch unter uns || *intens pron* selbst, selber

oust [aust] *tr* (**from**) verdrängen (aus); **o. from office** seines Amtes entheben

ouster ['austər] *s* Amtsenthebung *f*

out [aut] *adj*—**an evening out** ein Ausgehabend *m*; **be out** (*of the house*) ausgegangen sein; (*said of a light, fire*) aus sein; (*said of a new book*) erschienen sein; (*said of a secret*) enthüllt sein; (*said of flowers*) aufgeblüht sein; (*said of a dislocated limb*) verrenkt sein; (*be out of style*) aus der Mode sein; (*be at an end*) aus sein; (*be absent from work*) der Arbeit fernbleiben; (*be on strike*) streiken; **be out after s.o.** hinter j-m her sein; **be out for a good time** dem Vergnügen nachgehen; **be out on one's feet** (coll) erledigt sein; **be out ten marks** zehn Mark eingebüßt haben; **be out to** (*inf*) darauf ausgehen (or aus sein) zu (*inf*); **that's out** das kommt nicht in Frage; **the best thing out** das Beste, was es gibt || *adv* (*gone forth; ended, terminated*) aus; **out of** (*curiosity, pity, etc.*) aus (*dat*); (*fear*) vor (*dat*); (*a certain number*) von (*dat*); (*deprived of*) beraubt (*genit*); **out of breath** außer Atem; **out of money** ohne Geld; **out of place** verlegt; (*not appropriate or proper*) unpassend; **out of the window** zum Fenster hinaus || *s* (*pretext*) Ausweg *m*; **be on the outs with s.o.** mit j-m auf gespanntem Fuße sein || *prep* aus (*dat*) || *interj* (sport) aus!; **out with it!** heraus damit!

out' and away' *adv* bei weitem

out'-and-out' *adj* abgefeimt

out'-ar'gue *tr* in Grund und Boden argumentieren

out'bid' *v* (*pret* **–bid**; *pp* **–bid & –bidden**; *ger* **–bidding**) *tr* überbieten

out'board mo'tor *s* Außenbordmotor *m*

out'bound' *adj* nach auswärts bestimmt; (*traffic*) aus der Stadt fließend

out'break' *s* Ausbruch *m*

out'build'ing *s* Nebengebäude *n*

out'burst' *s* Ausbruch *m*; **o. of anger** Zornausbruch *m*

out'cast' *adj* ausgestoßen || *s* Ausgestoßene *mf*

out'come' *s* Ergebnis *n*

out'cry' *s* Ausruf *m*; **raise an o.** ein Zetergeschrei erheben

out-dat'ed *adj* zeitlich überholt

out'dis'tance *tr* hinter sich [*dat*] lassen

out'do' *v* (*pret* **–did**; *pp* **–done**) *tr* überbieten, übertreffen; **not to be outdone by s.o. in zeal** j-m nichts an Eifer nachgeben; **o. oneself** in sich überbieten in (*dat*)

out'door' *adj* Außen—

out'doors' *adv* draußen, im Freien || *s*—**in the outdoors** im Freien

out'door shot' *s* (phot) Außenaufnahme *f*

out'door swim'ming pool *s* Freibad *n*

out'door the'ater *s* Naturtheater *n*

out'door toil'et *s* Abtritt *m*

outer ['autər] *adj* äußere, Außen—

out'er ear' *s* Ohrmuschel *f*

out'er gar'ment *s* Überkleid *n*

out'ermost' *adj* äußerste

out'er space' *s* Weltall *n*, Weltraum *m*

out'field' *s* (baseball) Außenfeld *n*

out'fit' *s* (*equipment*) Ausrüstung *f*; (*set of clothes*) Ausstattung *f*; (*uniform*) Kluft *f*; (*business firm*) Gesellschaft *f*; (mil) Einheit *f* || *v* (*pret –fitted*; *ger –fitting*) *tr* (*with equipment*) ausrüsten; (*with clothes*) neu ausstaffieren

out'flank' *tr* überflügeln, umfassen

out'flow' *s* Ausfluß *m*

out'go'ing *adj* (*sociable*) gesellig; (*officer*) bisherig; (*tide*) zurückgehend; (*train, plane*) abgehend

out'grow' *v* (*pret* **–grew**; *pp* **–grown**) *tr* herauswachsen aus; (fig) entwachsen (*dat*)

out'growth' *s* Auswuchs *m*; (fig) Folge *f*

out'ing *s* Ausflug *m*

outlandish [aut'lændɪʃ] *adj* fremdartig; (*prices*) überhöht

out'last' *tr* überdauern

out'law' *s* Geächtete *mf* || *tr* ächten

out'lay' *s* Auslage *f*, Kostenaufwand *m* || **out'lay'** *v* (*pret & pp* **–laid**) *tr* auslegen

out'let' *s* (*for water*) Abfluß *m*, Ausfluß *m*; (fig) (**for**) Ventil *n* (für); (com) Absatzmarkt *m*; (elec) Steckdose *f*; **find an o. for** (fig) Luft machen (*dat*); **no o.** Sackgasse *f*

out'line' *s* (*profile*) Umriß *m*; (*sketch*) Umrißzeichnung *f*; (*summary*) Grundriß *m*; **rough o.** knapper Umriß *m* || *tr* umreißen

out'live' *tr* überleben

out'look' *s* (*place giving a view*) Ausguck *m*; (*view from a place*) Ausblick *m*; (*point of view*) Anschauung *f*; (*prospects*) Aussichten *pl*

out'ly'ing *adj* Außen–

out'maneu'ver *tr* ausmanövrieren; (fig) überlisten

outmoded [,aut'modɪd] *adj* unmodern

out'num'ber *tr* an Zahl übertreffen

out'-of-bounds' *adj* (fig) nicht in den Schranken; (sport) im Aus

out'-of-court' *set'tlement* *s* außergerichtlicher Vergleich *m*

out'-of-date' *adj* veraltet

out'-of-door' *adj* Außen–

out'-of-doors' *adj* Außen– ‖ *adv* im Freien, draußen ‖ *s*—**in the o.** im Freien

out'-of-pock'et *adj*—**o. expenses** Barauslagen *pl*

out' of print' *adj* vergriffen

out'-of-the-way' *adj* abgelegen

out' of tune' *adj* verstimmt

out' of work' *adj* arbeitslos, erwerbslos

out'pace' *tr* überholen

out'pa'tient *s* ambulant Behandelte *mf*

out'patient clin'ic *s* Ambulanz *f*

out'play' *tr* überspielen

out'point' *tr* (sport) nach Punkten schlagen

out'post' *s* (mil) Vorposten *m*

out'pour'ing *s* (& fig) Erguß *m*

out'put' *s* (*of a machine or factory*) Arbeitsleistung *f*; (*of a factory*) Produktion *f*; (mech) Nutzleistung *f*; (min) Förderung *f*

out'rage' *s* Unverschämtheit *f*; (against) Verletzung *f* (genit) ‖ *tr* gröblich beleidigen

outrageous [aut'redʒəs] *adj* unverschämt

out'rank' *tr* im Rang übertreffen

out'rid'er *s* Vorreiter *m*

outrigger [ˈaut͵rɪgər] *s* Ausleger *m*; (*of a racing boat*) Outrigger *m*

out'right' *adj* (*lie, refusal*) glatt; (*loss*) total; (*frank*) offen ‖ *adv* (*completely*) völlig; (*without reserve*) ohne Vorbehalt; (*at once*) auf der Stelle; **buy o.** per Kasse kaufen; **refuse o.** glatt ablehnen

out'run' *v* (*pret* **–ran**; *pp* **–run**; *ger* **–running**) *tr* hinter sich [*dat*] lassen

out'sell' *v* (*pret* & *pp* **–sold**) *tr* e-n größeren Umsatz haben als

out'set' *s* Anfang *m*

out'shine' *v* (*pret* & *pp* **–shone**) *tr* überstrahlen

out'side' *adj* (*help, interference*) von außen; (*world, influence, impressions*) äußere; (*lane, work*) Außen– ‖ *adv* draußen ‖ *s* Außenseite *f*, Äußere *n*; **at the** (*very*) **o.** (aller–) höchstens; **from the o.** von außen ‖ *prep* außerhalb (genit)

outsider [,aut'saɪdər] *s* Außenstehende *mf*; (sport) Außenseiter *m*

out'size' *adj* übergroß ‖ *s* Übergröße *f*

out'skirts' *spl* Randgebiet *n*, Stadtrand *m*

out'smart' *tr* überlisten

out'spo'ken *adj* freimütig

out'spread' *adj* (legs) gespreizt; (arms, wings) ausgebreitet

out'stand'ing *adj* hervorragend, profiliert; (*money, debts*) ausstehend

out'strip' *v* (*pret* & *pp* **–stripped**; *ger* **–stripping**) *tr* (& fig) hinter sich [*dat*] lassen

out'vote' *tr* überstimmen

outward [ˈautwərd] *adj* äußerlich, äußere ‖ *adv* auswärts, nach außen

outwardly [ˈautwərdlɪ] *adv* äußerlich

outwards [ˈautwərdz] *adv* auswärts

out'weigh' *tr* an Gewicht übertreffen; (fig) überwiegen

out'wit' *v* (*pret* & *pp* **–witted**; *ger* **–witting**) *tr* überlisten

oval [ˈovəl] *adj* oval ‖ *s* Oval *n*

ovary [ˈovərɪ] *s* Eierstock *m*

ovation [o'veʃən] *s* Huldigung *f*, Ovation *f*

oven [ˈʌvən] *s* Ofen *m*; (*for baking*) Backofen *m*

over [ˈovər] *adj* (*ended*) vorbei, aus; **it's all o. with him** es ist vorbei mit ihm; **o. and done with** total erledigt ‖ *adv*—**all o.** (*everywhere*) überall; (*on the body*) über und über; **children of twelve and o.** Kinder von zwölf Jahren und darüber; **come o.!** komm herüber!; **o.!** (*turn the page*) bitte wenden!; **o. again** noch einmal; **o. against** gegenüber (*dat*); **o. and above** obendrein; **o. and out!** (rad) Ende!; **o. and o. again** immer wieder; **o. in Europe** drüben in Europa; **o. there** dort, da drüben ‖ *prep* (*position*) über (*dat*); (*motion*) über (*acc*); (*because of*) wegen (*genit*); (*in the course of, e.g., a cup of tea*) bei (*dat*); (*during; more than*) über (*acc*); **all o. town** (*position*) in der ganzen Stadt; (*direction*) durch die ganze Stadt; **be o. s.o.** über j–m stehen; **b. o. s.o.'s head** j–m zu hoch sein; **from all o.** Germany aus ganz Deutschland; **o. and above** außer (*genit*); **o. the radio** im Radio

o'veract' *tr* & *intr* (theat) übertreiben

o'verac'tive *adj* übermäßig tätig

overage [ˈovəredʒ] *adj* über das vorgeschriebene Alter hinaus

o'verall' *adj* Gesamt– ‖ **o'veralls'** *spl* Monteuranzug *m*; (*trousers*) Überziehhose *f*

o'verambi'tious *adj* allzu ehrgeizig

o'veranx'ious *adj* überängstlich; (*overeager*) übereifrig

o'verawe' *tr* einschüchtern

o'verbear'ing *adj* überheblich

o'verboard' *adv* über Bord; **go o. about** sich übermäßig begeistern für

o'vercast' *adj* bewölkt, bedeckt; **become o.** sich bewölken ‖ *s* Bewölkung *f*

o'vercharge' *s* Überteuerung *f*; (elec) Überladung *f* ‖ **o'vercharge'** *tr* e-n Überpreis abverlangen (*dat*); (elec) überladen

o'vercoat' *s* Mantel *m*, Überrock *m*

o'ver·come' *v* (*pret* **–came**; *pp* **–come**)

tr überwältigen; **be o. with joy** vor Freude hingerissen sein

o'vercon'fidence *s* zu großes Selbstvertrauen *n*

o'vercon'fident *adj* zu vertrauensvoll

o'vercook' *tr* (*overboil*) zerkochen; (*overbake*) zu lange backen, zu lange braten

o'vercrowd' *tr* überfüllen; (*a room, hotel, hospital*) überbelegen

o'ver·do' *v* (*pret* –did; *pp* –done) *tr* übertreiben; **o. it** sich überanstrengen

o'verdone' *adj* (culin) übergar

o'verdose' *s* Überdosis *f*

o'verdraft' *s* Überziehung *f*

o'ver·draw' *v* (*pret* –drew; *pp* –drawn) *tr* überziehen

o'verdress' *intr* sich übertrieben kleiden

o'verdrive' *s* (aut) Schongang *m*

o'verdue' *adj* überfällig

o'ver·eat' *v* (*pret* –ate; *pp* –eaten) *intr* sich überessen

o'verem'phasis *s* Überbetonung *f*

o'verem'phasize *tr* überbetonen

o'veres'timate *tr* überschätzen

o'verexcite' *tr* überreizen

o'verexert' *tr* überanstrengen

o'verexer'tion *s* Überanstrengung *f*

o'verexpose' *tr* (phot) überbelichten

o'verexpo'sure *s* Überbelichtung *f*

o'verextend' *tr* übermäßig ausweiten

o'verflow' *s* (*inundation*) Überschwemmung *f*; (*surplus*) Überschuß *m*; (*outlet for surplus liquid*) Überlauf *m*; **filled to o.** bis zum Überfließen gefüllt || o'verflow' *tr* überfluten; **o. the banks** über die Ufer treten || *intr* überfließen

o'ver·fly' *v* (*pret* –flew; *pp* –flown) *tr* überfliegen

o'verfriend'ly *adj* katzenfreundlich

o'vergrown' *adj* überwachsen; (*child*) lang aufgeschossen; **become o.** (*said of a garden*) verwildern; **become o. with** überwuchert werden von

o'verhang' *s* Überhang *m* || o'ver·hang' *v* (*pret & pp* –hung) *tr* hervorragen über (*acc*); (*threaten*) bedrohen || *intr* überhängen

o'verhaul' *s* Überholung *f* || o'verhaul' *tr* (*repair; overtake*) überholen

o'verhead' *adj* (line) oberirdisch; (*valve*) obengesteuert || *adv* droben || *s* (econ) Gemeinkosten *pl*, laufende Unkosten *pl*

o'verhead door' *s* Federhubtor *n*

o'verhead line' *s* (of a trolley) Oberleitung *f*

o'ver·hear' *v* (*pret & pp* –heard) *tr* mithören; **be o.** belauscht werden

o'verheat' *tr* überhitzen; (*a room*) überheizen || *intr* heißlaufen

o'verindulge' *tr* verwöhnen || *intr* (**in**) sich allzusehr ergehen (in *dat*)

o'verkill' *s* Overkill *m*

overjoyed [‚ovər'dʒɔɪd] *adj* überglücklich

overland ['ovər‚lænd] *adj* Überland–; **o. route** Landweg *m* || *adv* über Land

o'verlap' *s* Überschneiden *n* || o'verlap' *v* (*pret & pp* –lapped; *ger* –lapping)

tr sich überschneiden mit || *intr* (& fig) sich überschneiden

o'verlap'ping *s* (& fig) Überschneidung *f*

o'verlay' *s* Auflage *f*; (*for a map*) Planpause *f*; **o. of gold** Goldauflage *f*

o'verload' *s* Überbelastung *f*; (elec) Überlast *f* || o'verload' *tr* überlasten; (*a truck*) überladen; (*in radio communications*) übersteuern; (elec) überlasten

o'verlook' *tr* (*by mistake*) übersehen; (*a mistake*) hinwegsehen über (*acc*); (*a view*) überblicken

overly ['ovərli] *adv* übermäßig

o'vernight' *adj*–o. stop Aufenthalt *m* von e–r Nacht; **o. things** Nachtzeug *n* || *adv* über Nacht; **stay o.** übernachten

o'vernight' bag' *s* Nachtzeugtasche *f*

o'verpass' *s* Überführung *f*

o'ver·pay' *v* (*pret & pp* –paid) *tr & intr* überbezahlen

o'verpay'ment *s* Überbezahlung *f*

o'verpop'ulat'ed *adj* übervölkert

o'verpop'ula'tion *s* Übervölkerung *f*

o'verpow'er *tr* (& fig) überwältigen

o'verproduc'tion *s* Überproduktion *f*

o'verrate' *tr* zu hoch schätzen

o'verreach' *tr* (*extend beyond*) hinausragen über (*acc*); (*an arm*) zu weit ausstrecken; **o. oneself** sich übernehmen

o'verrefined' *adj* überspitzt

o'verripe' *adj* überreif

o'verrule' *tr* (*an objection*) zurückweisen; (*a proposal*) verwerfen; (*a person*) überstimmen

o'verrun' *s* Überproduktion *f* || o'ver·run' *v* (*pret* –ran; *pp* –run; *ger* –running) *tr* überrennen; (*said of a flood*) überschwemmen; **o. with** (*weeds*) überwuchert von; (*tourists*) überlaufen von; (*vermin*) wimmeln von

o'versalt' *tr* versalzen

o'versea(s)' *adj* Übersee– || *adv* nach Übersee

o'ver·see' *v* (*pret & pp* –saw; *pp* –seen) *tr* beaufsichtigen

o'verse'er *s* Aufseher –in *mf*

o'versen'sitive *adj* überempfindlich

o'vershad'ow *tr* überschatten; (fig) in den Schatten stellen

o'vershoe' *s* Überschuh *m*

o'ver·shoot' *v* (*pret & pp* –shot) *tr* (& fig) hinausschießen über (*acc*)

o'versight' *s* Versehen *n*; **through an o.** aus Versehen

o'versimplifica'tion *s* allzu große Vereinfachung *f*

o'versize' *adj* übergroß || *s* Übergröße *f*

o'ver·sleep' *v* (*pret & pp* –slept) *tr & intr* verschlafen

o'verspe'cialized *adj* überspezialisiert

o'verstaffed' *adj* (mit Personal) übersetzt

o'verstay' *tr* überschreiten

o'ver·step' *v* (*pret & pp* –stepped; *ger* –stepping) *tr* überschreiten o'verstock' tr überbevorraten

o'verstrain' tr überanstrengen

o'verstuffed' adj überfüllt; (furniture) überpolstert

o'versupply' s zu großer Vorrat m; (com) Überangebot n || o'versup·ply' v (pret & pp -plied) tr überreichlich versehen; (com) überreichlich anbieten

overt ['ovərt], [o'vʌrt] adj offenkundig

o'ver·take' v (pret -took; pp -taken) tr (catch up to) einholen; (pass) überholen; (suddenly befall) überfallen

o'vertax' tr überbesteuern; (fig) überfordern, übermäßig in Anspruch nehmen

o'ver-the-coun'ter adj (pharm) rezeptfrei; (st. exch.) freihändig

o'verthrow' s Sturz m || o'ver·throw' (pret -threw; pp -thrown) tr stürzen

o'vertime' adj Überstunden- || adv—work o. Überstunden arbeiten; work five hours o. fünf Überstunden machen || s Überstunden pl; (sport) Spielverlängerung f

o'vertired' adj übermüdet

o'vertone' s (fig) Nebenbedeutung f; (mus) Oberton m

o'vertrump' tr überstechen

overture ['ovərt/ər] s Antrag m; (mus) Ouvertüre f

o'verturn' tr umstürzen || intr umkippen; (aut) sich überschlagen

overweening [,ovər'winɪŋ] adj hochmütig

o'verweight' adj zu schwer || s Übergewicht n; (of freight) Überfracht f

overwhelm [,ovər'whelm] tr (with some feeling) überwältigen; (e.g., with questions, gifts) überschütten; (with work) überbürden

o'verwhelm'ing adj überwältigend

overwind [,ovər'waɪnd] v (pret & pp -wound) tr überdrehen

o'verwork' s Überarbeitung f, Überanstrengung f || o'verwork' tr überfordern || intr sich überarbeiten

o'verwrought' adj überreizt

o'verzeal'ous adj übereifrig

ow [aʊ] interj au!

owe [o] tr schulden (dat), schuldig sein (dat); he owes her everything er verdankt ihr alles

ow'ing adj—it is o. to you that es ist dein Verdienst, daß; o. to infolge (genit)

owl [aʊl] s Eule f; (barn owl, screech owl) Schleiereule f

own [on] adj eigen || s—be left on one's own sich [dat] selbst überlassen sein; be on one's own auf eigenen Füßen stehen; come into one's own zu seinem Recht kommen; hold one's own sich behaupten; of one's own für sich allein; on one's own (initiative) aus eigener Initiative; (responsibility) auf eigene Faust || tr besitzen; (acknowledge) anerkennen; who owns this house? wem gehört dieses Haus? || intr—own to sich bekennen zu; own up to zugeben (dat)

owner ['onər] s Eigentümer –in m

own'ership' s Eigentum n; (legal right of possession) Eigentumsrecht n; under new o. unter neuer Leitung

ox [aks] s (oxen ['aksən]) Ochse m

ox'cart' s Ochsenkarren m

oxfords ['aksfordz] spl Halbschuhe pl

oxide ['aksaɪd] s Oxyd n

oxidize ['aksɪ,daɪz] tr & intr oxydieren

oxydation [,aksɪ'de/ən] s Oxydation f

oxygen ['aksɪdʒən] s Sauerstoff m

oxygenate ['aksɪdʒə,net] tr mit Sauerstoff anreichern

ox'ygen mask' s Sauerstoffmaske f

ox'ygen tank' s Sauerstofflasche f

ox'ygen tent' s Sauerstoffzelt n

oxytone ['aksɪ,ton] adj oxytoniert || s Oxytonon n

oyster ['ɔɪstər] s Auster f

oys'ter bed' s Austernbank f

oys'ter farm' s Austernpark m

oys'ter·man s (-men) Austernfischer m

oys'tershell' s Austernschale f

oys'ter stew' s Austernragout n

ozone ['ozon] s Ozon n

O'zone layer' s Ozonschicht f

P

P, p [pi] s sechzehnter Buchstabe des englischen Alphabets

pace [pes] s Schritt m; (speed) Tempo n; at a fast p. in schnellem Tempo; keep p. with Schritt halten mit; put s.o. through his paces j–n auf Herz und Nieren prüfen; set the p. das Tempo angeben; (sport) Schrittmacher sein || tr (the room, floor) abschreiten; p. off abschreiten || intr—p. up and down (in) auf und ab schreiten (in dat)

pace'mak'er s Schrittmacher m

pacific [pə'sɪfɪk] adj pazifisch; the

Pacific Ocean der Pazifische (or Stille) Ozean || s—the Pacific der Pazifik

pacifier ['pæsɪ,faɪ·ər] s Friedensvermittler –in mf; (for a baby) Schnuller m

pacifism ['pæsɪ,fɪzəm] s Pazifismus m

pacifist ['pæsɪfɪst] s Pazifist –in mf

paci·fy ['pæsɪ,faɪ] v (pret & pp -fied) tr (a country) befrieden; (a person) beruhigen

pack [pæk] s Pack m, Packen m; (of a soldier) Gepäck n; (of wolves, submarines) Rudel n; (of hounds) Meute

f; (*of cigarettes*) Päckchen *n,* Schachtel *f;* (*on pack animals*) Last *f;* (*med*) Packung *f;* **p. of cards** Spiel *n* Karten; **p. of lies** Lug und Trug ‖ *tr* (*a trunk*) packen; (*clothes*) einpacken; (*seal*) abdichten; **p. in** (*above normal capacity*) einpferchen; **p. up** zusammenpacken ‖ *intr* packen; **send s.o. packing** j–m Beine machen
package ['pækɪdʒ] *adj* (*price, tour, agreement*) Pauschal– ‖ *s* Paket *n* ‖ *tr* (*ver*)packen
pack'age deal' *s* Koppelgeschäft *n*
pack' an'imal *s* Packtier *n*
packet ['pækɪt] *s* Paket *n,* Päckchen *n;* (*naut*) Postschiff *n*
pack'ing *s* (*act*) Packen *n;* (*seal*) Dichtung *f;* (*wrapper*) Verpackung *f*
pack'ing case' *s* Packkiste *f*
pack'ing house' *s* Konservenfabrik *f*
pack'sad'dle *s* Packsattel *m*
pact [pækt] *s* Pakt *m;* **make a p.** paktieren
pad [pæd] *s* (*of writing paper*) Block *m;* (*ink pad*) Stempelkissen *n;* (*cushion*) Kissen *n;* (*of butter*) Stück *n;* (*under a rug*) Unterlage *f;* (*living quarters*) Bude *f;* (*rok*) Abschußrampe *f;* (*sport*) Schützer *m;* (*surg*) Bausch *m* ‖ *v* (*pret & pp* **padded**; *ger* **padding**) *tr* (*e.g., the shoulders*) wattieren; (*writing*) ausbauschen
pad'ded cell' *s* Gummizelle *f*
pad'ding *s* Wattierung *f;* (*coll*) Ballast *m*
paddle ['pædəl] *s* (*of a canoe*) Paddel *n;* (*for table tennis*) Schläger *m* ‖ *tr* paddeln; (*spank*) prügeln ‖ *intr* paddeln
pad'dle wheel' *s* Schaufelrad *n*
paddock ['pædək] *s* Pferdekoppel *f;* (*at the races*) Sattelplatz *m*
pad'dy wag'on ['pædi] *s* (*sl*) Grüne Minna *f*
pad'lock' *s* Vorhängeschloß *n* ‖ *tr* mit e–m Vorhängeschloß verschließen
paean ['pi·ən] *s* Siegeslied *n*
pagan ['pegən] *adj* heidnisch ‖ *s* Heide *m,* Heidin *f*
paganism ['pegə‚nɪzəm] *s* Heidentum *n*
page [pedʒ] *s* Seite *f;* (*in a hotel or club; at court*) Page *m* ‖ *tr* (*summon*) über den Lautsprecher (*or* durch Pagen*) holen lassen ‖ *intr*—**p. through** durchblättern
pageant ['pædʒənt] *s* Festspiel *n;* (*procession*) Festzug *m*
pageantry ['pædʒəntri] *s* Schaugepränge *n*
page'boy' *s* Pagenfrisur *f*
page' proof' *s* Umbruchabzug *m*
pagoda [pə'godə] *s* Pagode *f*
paid' in full' [ped] *adj* voll bezahlt
paid'-up' *adj* (*debts*) abgezahlt; (*policy, capital*) voll eingezahlt
pail [pel] *s* Eimer *m*
pain [pen] *s* Schmerz *m;* **on p. of death** bei Todesstrafe; **take pains** sich bemühen—**it** *tr & intr* schmerzen ‖ *impers*—**it pains me to** (*inf*) es fällt mir schwer zu (*inf*)

painful ['penfəl] *adj* schmerzhaft; (*fig*) peinlich
pain' in the neck' *s* (*coll*) Nervensäge *f*
pain'kill'er *s* schmerzstillendes Mittel *n*
painless ['penlɪs] *adj* schmerzlos
pains'tak'ing *adj* (*work*) mühsam; (*person*) sorgfältig
paint [pent] *s* Farbe *f;* (*for a car*) Lack *m* ‖ *tr* (*be*)malen; (*e.g., a house*) (*an*) streichen; (*a car*) lackieren; (*with watercolors*) aquarellieren; (*fig*) schildern; **p. the town red** tüchtig auf die Pauke hauen ‖ *intr* malen; (*with house paint*) überstreichen
paint'box' *s* Malkasten *m*
paint'brush' *s* Pinsel *m*
paint' can' *s* Farbendose *f*
painter ['pentər] *s* Maler –in *mf;* (*of houses, etc.*) Anstreicher –in *mf*
paint'ing *s* Malerei *f;* (*picture*) Gemälde *n*
paint' remov'er *s* Farbenabbeizmittel *n*
paint' spray'er *s* Farbspritzpistole *f*
pair [per] *s* Paar *n;* **a p. of glasses** e–e Brille *f;* **a p. of gloves** ein Paar *n* Handschule; **a p. of pants** e–e Hose *f;* **a p. of scissors** e–e Schere *f;* **a p. of twins** ein Zwillingspaar *n;* **in pairs** paarweise ‖ *tr* paaren; **p. off** paarweise ordnen; (*coll*) verheiraten ‖ *intr*—**p. off** sich paarweise absondern
pajamas [pə'dʒɑməz] *s* Pyjama *m*
Pakistan ['pækɪ‚stæn] *s* Pakistan *n*
Pakista·ni [‚pækɪ'stæni] *adj* pakistanisch ‖ *s* (*-nis*) Pakistaner –in *mf*
pal [pæl] *s* Kamerad *m* ‖ *v* (*pret & pp* **palled**; *ger* **palling**) *intr*—**pal around with** dick befreundet sein mit
palace ['pælɪs] *s* Palast *m*
palatable ['pælətəbəl] *adj* (*& fig*) mundgerecht
palatal ['pælətəl] *adj* Gaumen– ‖ *s* (*phonet*) Gaumenlaut *m*
palate ['pælɪt] *s* Gaumen *m*
palatial [pə'leʃəl] *adj* palastartig
Palatinate [pə'lætɪ‚net] *s* Rheinpfalz *f*
pale [pel] *adj* (*face, colors, recollection*) blaß; **turn pale** erblassen, erbleichen ‖ *s* Pfahl *m* ‖ *intr* erblassen; **pale beside** (*fig*) verblassen neben (*dat*)
pale'face' *s* Bleichgesicht *n*
Palestine ['pælɪs‚taɪn] *s* Palästina *n*
palette ['pælɪt] *s* Palette *f*
palisade [‚pælɪ'sed] *s* Palisade *f;* (*line of cliffs*) Flußklippen *pl*
pall [pɔl] *s* Bahrtuch *n;* (*of smoke, gloom*) Hülle *f* ‖ *intr* (*on*) zuviel werden (*dat*)
pall'bear'er *s* Sargträger *m*
pallet ['pælɪt] *s* Lager *n*
palliate ['pælɪ‚et] *tr* lindern; (*fig*) bemänteln
pallid ['pælɪd] *adj* blaß, bleich
pallor ['pælər] *s* Blässe *f*
palm [pɑm] *s* (*of the hand*) Handfläche *f;* (*tree*) Palme *f;* **grease s.o.'s palm** j–n schmieren; **palm of victory** Siegespalme *f* ‖ *tr* (*a card*) in der Hand verbergen; **palm s.th. off on s.o.** j–m etw andrehen

palmette [pæl'met] s Palmette f
palmet·to [pæl'meto] s (–tos & –toes) Fächerpalme f
palmist ['pɑmɪst] s Wahrsager –in mf
palmistry ['pɑmɪstri] s Handlesekunst f
palm' leaf' s Palmblatt n
Palm' Sun'day s Palmsonntag m
palm' tree' s Palme f
palpable ['pælpəbəl] adj greifbar
palpitate ['pælpɪ,tet] intr klopfen
palsied ['pɔlzid] adj lahm, gelähmt
palsy ['pɔlzi] s Lähmung f
paltry ['pɔltri] adj armselig
pamper ['pæmpər] tr verwöhnen
pamphlet ['pæmflɪt] s Flugschrift f
pan [pæn] s Pfanne f; (sl) Visage f || tr (gold) waschen; (a camera) schwenken; (criticize sharply) (coll) verreißen || intr (cin) panoramieren; **pan out** glücken, klappen
panacea [,pænə'si·ə] s Allheilmittel n
Panama ['pænəmɑ] s Panama n
Pan'ama Canal' s Panamakanal m
Pan-American [,pænə'merikən] adj panamerikanisch
pan'cake' s (flacher) Pfannkuchen m || intr (ae) absacken, bumslanden
pan'cake land'ing s Bumslandung f
panchromatic [,pænkro'mætɪk] adj panchromatisch
pancreas ['pænkrɪ·əs] s Bauchspeicheldrüse f
pandemic [pæn'demɪk] adj pandemisch
pandemonium [,pændə'moni·əm] s Höllenlärm m
pander ['pændər] s Kuppler m || intr kuppeln; **p. to** Vorschub leisten (dat)
pane [pen] s Scheibe f
panegyric [,pænɪ'dʒɪrɪk] s Lobrede f
pan·el ['pænəl] s Tafel f, Feld n; (in a door) Füllung f; (for instruments) Schlattafel f; (of experts) Diskussionsgruppe f; (archit) Paneel n; (jur) Geschworenenliste f || v (pret & pp –el[l]ed; ger –el[l]ing) tr täfeln
pan'el discus'sion s Podiumsdiskussion f
pan'eling s Täfelung f
panelist ['pænəlɪst] s Diskussionsteilnehmer –in mf
pang [pæŋ] s stechender Schmerz m; (fig) Angst f; **pangs of conscience** Gewissensbisse pl; **pangs of hunger** nagender Hunger m
pan'han'dle s Pfannenstiel m; (geog) Landzunge f || intr (sl) betteln
pan'han'dler s (sl) Bettler –in mf
pan·ic ['pænɪk] s Panik f || v (pret & pp –icked; ger –icking) tr in Panik versetzen || intr von panischer Angst erfüllt werden
pan'ic-strick'en adj von panischem Schrecken erfaßt
panicky ['pænɪki] adj übernervös
panoply ['pænəpli] s Pracht f; (full suit of armor) vollständige Rüstung f
panorama [,pænə'ræmə] s Panorama n
pansy ['pænzi] s Stiefmütterchen n
pant [pænt] s Keuchen n; **pants** Hose f, Hosen pl || intr keuchen; **p. for or after** gieren nach

pantheism ['pænθi,ɪzəm] s Pantheismus m
pantheon ['pænθɪ,ɑn] s Pantheon n
panther ['pænθər] s Panther m
panties ['pæntiz] spl Schlüpfer m
pantomime ['pæntə,maɪm] s Pantomime f
pantry ['pæntri] s Speisekammer f
pap [pæp] s Brei m, Kleister m
papa ['pɑpə] s Papa m, Vati m
papacy ['pepəsi] s Papsttum n
papal ['pepəl] adj päpstlich
Pa'pal State' s Kirchenstaat m
paper ['pepər] adj (money, plate, towel) Papier– || s Papier n; (before a learned society) Referat n; (newspaper) Zeitung f; **papers** (documents) Papiere pl || tr tapezieren
pa'perback' s Taschenbuch n, Pappband m
pa'per bag' s Papiertüte f, Tüte f
pa'perboy' s Zeitungsjunge m
pa'per clip' s Büroklammer f
pa'per cone' s Tüte f
pa'per cup' s Papierbecher m
pa'per cut'ter s Papierschneidemaschine f
pa'perhang'er s Tapezierer –in mf
pa'perhang'ing s Tapezierarbeit f
pa'pering s Tapezieren n
pa'per mill' s Papierfabrik f
pa'per nap'kin s Papierserviette f
pa'per weight' s Briefbeschwerer m
pa'perwork' s Schreibarbeit f
papier-mâché [,pepərmɑ'ʃe] s Papier-maché n, Pappmaché n
paprika ['pæprika] s Paprika m
papy·rus [pə'paɪrəs] s (–ri [raɪ]) Papyrus m
par [pɑr] s (fin) Pari n; (golf) festgesetzte Schlagzahl f; **at par** pari, auf Pari; **on a par with** auf gleicher Stufe mit; **up to par** (coll) auf der Höhe
parable ['pærəbəl] s Gleichnis n
parabola [pə'ræbələ] s Parabel f
parachute ['pærə,ʃut] s Fallschirm m || tr mit dem Fallschirm abwerfen || intr abspringen
par'achute jump' s Fallschirmabsprung m
parachutist ['pærə,ʃutɪst] s Fallschirmspringer –in mf
parade [pə'red] s Parade f || tr Schau stellen || intr paradieren; (mil) aufmarschieren
paradigm ['pærədɪm], ['pærə,daɪm] s Musterbeispiel n, Paradigma n
paradise ['pærə,daɪs] s Paradies n
paradox ['pærə,dɑks] s Paradox n
paradoxical [,pærə'dɑksɪkəl] adj paradox
paraffin ['pærəfɪn] s Paraffin n
paragon ['pærə,gɑn] s Musterbild n
paragraph ['pærə,græf] s Absatz m, Paragraph m
parakeet ['pærə,kit] s Sittich m
paral·lel ['pærə,lel] adj parallel; **be (or run) p. to** parallel verlaufen zu || s Parallele f; (of latitude) Breiten-

kreis *m;* (fig) Gegenstück *n;* **without p.** ohnegleichen ‖ *v* (*pret & pp* **-lel[l]ed;** *ger* **-lel[l]ing**) *tr* parallel verlaufen zu; (*match*) gleichkommen (*dat*); (*correspond to*) entsprechen (*dat*)

par'allel bars' *spl* Barren *m*

paraly·sis [pə'rælɪsɪs] *s* (**-ses** [ˌsɪz]) Lähmung *f*, Paralyse *f*

paralytic [ˌpærə'lɪtɪk] *adj* paralytisch ‖ *s* Paralytiker *–in mf*

paralyze ['pærəˌlaɪz] *tr* lähmen, paralysieren; (*traffic*) lahmlegen

parameter [pə'ræmɪtər] *s* Parameter *m*

paramilitary [ˌpærə'mɪlɪˌteri] *adj* halbmilitärisch

paramount ['pærəˌmaunt] *adj* oberste; **be p. an** erster Stelle stehen; **of p. importance** von äußerster Wichtigkeit

paranoia [ˌpærə'nɔɪ·ə] *s* Paranoia *f*

paranoiac [ˌpærə'nɔɪ·æk] *adj* paranoisch ‖ *s* Paranoiker *–in mf*

paranoid ['pærəˌnɔɪd] *adj* paranoid

parapet ['pærəˌpet] *s* (*of a wall*) Brustwehr *f;* (*of a balcony*) Geländer *n*

paraphernalia [ˌpærəfər'neli·ə] *s* Zubehör *n*, Ausrüstung *f*

paraphrase ['pærəˌfrez] *s* Umschreibung *f* ‖ *tr* umschreiben

parasite ['pærəˌsaɪt] *s* (& fig) Parasit *m*

parasitic(al) [ˌpærə'sɪtɪk(əl)] *adj* parasitisch

parasol ['pærəˌsɔl] *s* Sonnenschirm *m*

paratrooper ['pærəˌtrupər] *s* Fallschirmjäger *m*

par·cel ['pɑrsəl] *s* Paket *n;* (com) Posten *m* ‖ *v* (*pret & pp* **-cel[l]ed;** *ger* **-cel[l]ing**) *tr*—**p. out** aufteilen

par'cel post' *s* Paketpost *f*

parch [pɑrtʃ] *tr* ausdörren; **my throat is parched** mir klebt die Zunge am Gaumen

parchment ['pɑrtʃmənt] *s* Pergament *n*

pardon ['pɑrdən] *s* Verzeihung *f;* (jur) Begnadigung *f;* **I beg your p.** ich bitte um Entschuldigung; **p.?** wie, bitte? ‖ *tr* (*a person*) verzeihen (*dat*); (*an act*) verzeihen; (*officially*) begnadigen

pardonable ['pɑrdənəbəl] *adj* verzeihlich

pare [per] *tr* (*nails*) schneiden; (*e.g., potatoes*) (ab)schälen; (*costs*) beschneiden

parent ['perənt] *s* Elternteil *m;* **parents** Eltern *pl*

parentage ['perəntɪdʒ] *s* Abstammung *f*

parental [pə'rentəl] *adj* elterlich

parenthe·sis [pə'renθɪsɪs] *s* (**-ses** [ˌsɪz]) Klammer *f;* (*expression in parentheses*) Parenthese *f*

parenthetic(al) [ˌperən'θetɪk(əl)] *adj* parenthetisch

parenthood ['perəntˌhʊd] *s* Elternschaft *f*

pariah [pə'raɪ·ə] *s* Paria *m*

par'ing knife' *s* Schälmesser *n*

Paris ['pærɪs] *s* Paris *n*

parish ['pærɪʃ] *adv* Pfarr- ‖ *s* Pfarrgemeinde *f*

parishioner [pə'rɪʃənər] *s* Gemeindemitglied *n*, Pfarrkind *n*

Parisian [pə'rɪʒən] *adj* Pariser ‖ *s* Pariser *–in mf*

parity ['pærɪti] *s* Parität *f*

park [pɑrk] *s* Park *m* ‖ *tr* abstellen, parken ‖ *intr* parken

park'ing *s* Parken *n;* **no p.** (public sign) Parken verboten

park'ing light' *s* Parklicht *n*

park'ing lot' *s* Parkplatz *m*

park'ing lot' atten'dant' *s* Parkplatzwärter *–in mf*

park'ing me'ter *s* Parkuhr *f*

park'ing place', park'ing space *s* Parkplatz *m*, Parkstelle *f*

park'ing tick'et *s* gebührenpflichtige Verwarnung *f* (wegen falschen Parkens)

park'way *s* Aussichtsautobahn *f*

parley ['pɑrli] *s* Unterhandlung *f* ‖ *intr* unterhandeln

parliament ['pɑrləmənt] *s* Parlament *n*

parliamentary [ˌpɑrlə'mentəri] *adj* parlamentarisch

parlor ['pɑrlər] *s* Salon *m;* (*living room*) Wohnzimmer *n*

par'lor game' *s* Gesellschaftsspiel *n*

parochial [pə'roki·əl] *adj* Pfarr-; (fig) beschränkt

paro'chial school' *s* Pfarrschule *f*

paro·dy ['pærədi] *s* Parodie *f* ‖ *v* (*pret & pp* **-died**) *tr* parodieren

parole [pə'rol] *s* bedingte Strafaussetzung *f;* **be out on p.** bedingt entlassen sein ‖ *tr* bedingt entlassen

par·quet [pɑr'ke], [pɑr'ket] *v* (*pret & pp* **-queted** ['ked]; *ger* **-queting** ['ke·ɪŋ]) *tr* parkettieren

parquetry ['pɑrkɪtri] *s* Parkettfußboden *m*

parrot ['pærət] *s* Papagei *m* ‖ *tr* nachplappern

par·ry ['pæri] *s* Parade *f* ‖ *v* (*pret & pp* **-ried**) *tr* parieren

parse [pɑrs] *tr* zergliedern

parsimonious [ˌpɑrsɪ'moni·əs] *adj* sparsam

parsley ['pɑrsli] *s* Petersilie *f*

parsnip ['pɑrsnɪp] *s* Pastinak *m*

parson ['pɑrsən] *s* Pfarrer *m*

parsonage ['pɑrsənɪdʒ] *s* Pfarrhaus *n*

part [pɑrt] *adv*—**p. ... p.** zum Teil ... zum Teil ‖ *s* Teil *m & n;* (*section*) Abschnitt *m;* (*spare part*) Ersatzteil *m;* (*of a machine, etc.*) Bestandteil *m;* (*share*) Anteil *m;* (*of the hair*) Scheitel *m;* (mus) Partie *f;* (theat) Rolle *f;* **do one's p.** das Seinige tun; **for his p.** seinerseits; **for the most p.** größtenteils; **have a p. in** Anteil haben an (*dat*); **in p.** zum Teil, teilweise; **make a p.** (*in the hair*) e-n Scheitel ziehen; **on his p.** seinerseits; **p. and parcel** ein wesentlicher Bestandteil *m;* **take p.** (in) teilnehmen (an *dat*); **take s.o.'s p.** j-s Partei ergreifen ‖ *tr* (ab)scheiden; (*the hair*) scheiteln; **p. company** von einander scheiden ‖ *intr* sich trennen; **p. with** hergeben

par·take [par'tek] *v* (*pret* **–took**; *pp* **taken**) *intr*—**p. in** teilnehmen an (*dat*); **p. of** zu sich nehmen

partial ['parʃəl] *adj* Teil-, partiell; (*prejudiced*) parteiisch; **be p. to** bevorzugen

partiality [‚parʃɪ'ælɪtɪ] *s* Parteilichkeit *f*, Befangenheit *f*

partially ['parʃəlɪ] *adv* teilweise

participant [par'tɪsɪpənt] *s* Teilnehmer –in *mf*

participate [par'tɪsɪ‚pet] *intr* (**in**) teilnehmen (an *dat*)

participation [par‚tɪsɪ'peʃən] *s* (**in**) Teilnahme *f* (*an* dat)

participle ['partɪ‚sɪpəl] *s* Mittelwort *n*, Partizip *n*

particle ['partɪkəl] *s* Teilchen *n*; (gram, phys) Partikel *f*

particular [par'tɪkjələr] *adj* (*specific*) bestimmt; (*individual*) einzeln; (*meticulous*) peinlich genau; (*especial*) peinlich genau; (*choosy*) heikel ‖ *s* Einzelheit *f*; **in p.** insbesondere

partisan ['partɪzən] *adj* parteiisch ‖ *s* (mil) Partisan –in *mf*; (pol) Parteigänger –in *mf*

partition [par'tɪʃən] *s* Teilung *f*; (*wall*) Scheidewand *f* ‖ *tr* (auf)teilen; **p. off** abteilen

partly ['partlɪ] *adv* teils, teilweise

partner ['partnər] *s* Partner –in *mf*

part'nership' *s* Partnerschaft *f*

part' of speech' *s* Wortart *f*

partridge ['partrɪdʒ] *s* Rebhuhn *n*

part'-time' *adj* & *adv* nicht vollzeitlich

part'-time work' *s* Teilzeitarbeit *f*

party ['partɪ] *s* Gesellschaft *f*, Party *f*; (jur) Partei *f*; (mil) Kommando *n*; (pol) Partei *f*; (telp) Teilnehmer –in *mf*; **be a p.** to sich hergeben zu

par'ty affilia'tion *s* Parteizugehörigkeit *f*

par'ty line' *s* (pol) Parteilinie *f*; (telp) Gemeinschaftsanschluß *m*

par'ty mem'ber *s* Parteigenosse *m*, Parteigenossin *f*

par'ty pol'itics *s* Parteipolitik *f*

paschal ['pæskəl] *adj* Oster-

pass [pæs] *s* (*over a mountain*; *permit*) Paß *m*; (*erotic advance*) Annäherungsversuch *m*; (*fencing*) Stoß *m*; (fb) Paßball *m*; (mil) Urlaubsschein *m*; (theat) Freikarte *f*; **make a p. at** (*flirt with*) e–n Annäherungsversuch machen bei; (aer) vorbeifliegen an (*dat*) ‖ *tr* (*go by*) vorbeigehen an (*dat*), passieren; (*a test*) bestehen; (*a student in a test*) durchlassen; (*a bill*) verabschieden; (*hand over*) reichen; (*judgment*) abgeben; (*sentence*) sprechen; (*time*) verbringen; (*counterfeit money*) in Umlauf bringen; (*a car*) überholen; (*e.g., a kidney stone*) ausscheiden; (*a ball*) weitergeben; (**to**) zuspielen (*dat*); **p. around** herumgeben lassen; **p. away** (*time*) vertreiben; **p. in** einhändigen; **p. off as** ausgeben als; **p. on** weiterleiten; (*e.g., news*) weitersagen; **p.**

out ausgeben; **p. over in silence** unerwähnt lassen; **p. up** verzichten auf (*acc*) ‖ *intr* (by) vorbeikommen (an *dat*), vorbeigehen (an *dat*); (*in a car*) (by) vorbeifahren (an *dat*); (*in a test*) durchkommen; (*e.g., from father to son*) übergehen; (*cards*) passen; (parl) zustandekommen; **bring to p.** herbeiführen; **come to p.** geschehen; **p.!** (*cards*) passe!; **p. away** verscheiden; **p. for** gelten als; **p. on** abscheiden; **p. out** ohnmächtig werden; **p. over** (*disregard*) hinweggehen über (*acc*); **p. through** durchgehen (*durch*); (*said of an army*) durchziehen (*durch*); (*said of a train*) berühren

passable ['pæsəbəl] *adj* (*road*) gangbar; (*by car*) befahrbar; (*halfway good*) leidlich, passabel

passage ['pæsɪdʒ] *s* Korridor *m*, Gang *m*; (*crossing*) Überfahrt *f*; (*in a book*) Stelle *f*; (*of a law*) Annahme *f*; (*of time*) Ablauf *m*; **book p. for** e–e Schiffskarte bestellen nach

pas'sageway' *s* Durchgang *m*, Passage *f*

pass'book' *s* Sparbuch *n*

passenger ['pæsəndʒər] *s* Passagier –in *mf*; (*in public transportation*) Fahrgast *m*; (*in a car*) Insasse *m*, Insassin *f*

pas'senger car' *s* Personenkraftwagen *m*

pas'senger plane' *s* Passagierflugzeug *n*

pas'senger train' *s* Personenzug *m*

passer-by ['pæsər'baɪ] *s* (**passers-by**) Passant –in *mf*

pass'ing *adj* vorübergehend; **a p. grade** die Note „befriedigend" ‖ *s* (*act of passing*) Vorbeigehen *n*; (*of a law*) Verabschiedung *f*; (*of time*) Verstreichen *n*; (*dying*) Hinscheiden *n*; **in p.** im Vorbeigehen; (*as understatement*) beiläufig; **no p.** (*public sign*) Überholen verboten

passion ['pæʃən] *s* Leidenschaft *f*; (*of Christ*) Passion *f*; **fly into a p.** in Zorn geraten; **have a p. for** e–e Vorliebe haben für

passionate ['pæʃənɪt] *adj* leidenschaftlich

pas'sion play' *s* Passionsspiel *n*

passive ['pæsɪv] *adj* (& gram) passiv ‖ *s* Passiv(um) *n*

pass'key' *s* (*master key*) Hauptschlüssel *m*; (*skeleton key*) Nachschlüssel *m*

Pass'o'ver *s* Passah *n*

pass'port *s* Paß *m*, Reisepaß *m*

pass'port of'fice *s* Paßamt *n*

pass'word' *s* (mil) Kennwort *n*

past [pæst] *adj* (*e.g., week*) vergangen; (*e.g., president*) ehemalig, früher; (*gone*) vorbei; **for some time p.** seit einiger Zeit ‖ *s* Vergangenheit *f* ‖ *prep* (*e.g., one o'clock*) nach; (*beyond*) über (*acc*) hinaus; **get p.** (*an opponent*) (sport) umspielen; **go p.** vorbeigehen an (*dat*); **it's way p. bedtime** es ist schon längst Zeit zum Schlafengehen

paste [pest] *s* (*glue*) Kleister *m*; (*culin*) Brei *m*, Paste *f* ‖ *tr* (*e.g., a wall*) (**with**) bekleben (mit); **p. on** aufkleben auf (acc); **p. together** zusammenkleben

paste′board′ s Pappe f

pastel [pæsˈtel] adj pastellfarben ‖ s Pastell n

pastel′ col′or s Pastellfarbe f

pasteurize [ˈpæstəˌraɪz] tr pasteurisieren

pastime [ˈpæsˌtaɪm] s Zeitvertreib m

past′ mas′ter s Experte m

pastor [ˈpæstər] s Pastor m

pastoral [ˈpæstərəl] adj Schäfer-, Hirten-; (eccl) Hirten-, pastoral ‖ s Schäfergedicht n

pas′toral let′ter s Hirtenbrief m

pastorate [ˈpæstərɪt] s Pastorat n

pastry [ˈpestri] s Gebäck n; **pastries** Backwaren pl

pas′try shop′ s Konditorei f

past′ tense′ s Vergangenheit f

pasture [ˈpæstʃər] s Weide f ‖ tr & intr weiden

pas′ture land′ s Weideland n

pasty [ˈpesti] adj (sticky) klebrig; (complexion) bläßlich

pat [pæt] adj (answer) treffend; **have s.th. down pat** etw in- und auswendig wissen ‖ adv—**stand pat** bei der Stange bleiben ‖ s Klaps m; (of butter) Klümpchen n ‖ tr tätscheln; **pat s.o. on the back** j-m auf die Schulter klopfen; (fig) j-m beglückwünschen

patch [pætʃ] s (of clothing, land, color) Fleck m; (garden bed) Beet n; (for clothing, inner tube) Flicken m; (over the eye) Binde f; (for a wound) Pflaster n ‖ tr flicken; **p. together** (& fig) zusammenflicken; **p. up** (a friendship) kitten; (differences) beilegen

patch′work′ s Flickwerk n; (fig) Stückwerk n

patch′work quilt′ s Flickendecke f

pate [pet] s (coll) Schädel m

patent [ˈpetənt] adj öffentlich ‖ [ˈpætənt] adj Patent-, e.g., **p. lawyer** Patentanwalt m ‖ s Patent n; **p. pending** Patent angemeldet ‖ tr patentieren

pa′tent leath′er [ˈpætənt] s Lackleder n

pa′tent-leath′er shoe′ s Lackschuh m

pat′ent med′icine [ˈpætənt] s rezeptfreies Medikament n

pat′ent rights′ [ˈpætənt] spl Schutzrechte pl

paternal [pəˈtʌrnəl] adj väterlich

paternity [pəˈtʌrnɪti] s Vaterschaft f

path [pæθ] s Pfad m; (astr) Lauf m; **clear a p.** e-n Weg bahnen; **cross s.o.'s p.** j-s Weg kreuzen

pathetic [pəˈθɛtɪk] adj (moving) rührend; (evoking contemptuous pity) kläglich

path′find′er s Pfadfinder m; (aer) Beleuchter m

pathologist [pəˈθɑlədʒɪst] s Pathologe m, Pathologin f

pathology [pəˈθɑlədʒi] s Pathologie f

pathos [ˈpeθɑs] s Pathos n

path′way′ s Weg m, Pfad m

patience [ˈpeʃəns] s Geduld f

patient [ˈpeʃənt] adj geduldig ‖ s Patient –in mf

pati·o [ˈpætɪ·o] s (–os) Terasse f

patriarch [ˈpetrɪˌɑrk] s Patriarch m

patrician [pəˈtrɪʃən] adj patrizisch ‖ s Patrizier –in mf

patricide [ˈpætrɪˌsaɪd] s (act) Vatermord m; (person) Vatermörder –in mf

patrimony [ˈpætrɪˌmoni] s väterliches Erbe n

patriot [ˈpetrɪ·ət] s Patriot –in mf

patriotic [ˌpetrɪˈɑtɪk] adj patriotisch

patriotism [ˈpetrɪ·əˌtɪzəm] s Patriotismus m

pa·trol [pəˈtrol] s Patrouille f, Streife f ‖ v (pret & pp –trolled; ger –trolling) tr & intr patrouillieren

patrol′ car′ s Streifenwagen m

patrol′man s (–men) Polizeistreife f

patrol′ wag′on s Gefangenenwagen m

patron [ˈpetrən] s Schutzherr m; (com) Kunde m, Kundin f; (eccl) Schutzpatron m

patronage [ˈpetrənɪdʒ] s Patronat n

patroness [ˈpetrənɪs] s Schutzherrin f; (eccl) Schutzpatronin f

patronize [ˈpetrəˌnaɪz] tr beschützen, protegieren; (com) als Kunde besuchen; (theat) regelmäßig besuchen

pa′tronizing adj gönnerhaft

pa′tron saint′ s Schutzheilige mf

patter [ˈpætər] s (of rain) Prasseln n; (of feet) Getrappel n ‖ intr (said of rain) prasseln; (said of feet) trappeln

pattern [ˈpætərn] s Muster n; (sew) Schnittmuster n

patty [ˈpæti] s Pastetchen n

paucity [ˈpɔsɪti] s Knappheit f

paunch [pɔntʃ] s Wanst m

paunchy [ˈpɔnʃi] adj dickbäuchig

pauper [ˈpɔpər] s Arme m; (person on welfare) Unterstützte mf

pause [pɔz] s Pause f; (mus) Fermate f ‖ intr pausieren

pave [pev] tr pflastern; **p. the way for** (fig) anbahnen

pavement [ˈpevmənt] s Pflaster n; (sidewalk) Bürgersteig m, Trottoir m

pavilion [pəˈvɪljən] s Pavillon m

pav′ing s Pflasterung f

pav′ing stone′ s Pflasterstein m

paw [pɔ] s Pfote f ‖ tr (scratch) kratzen; (coll) befummeln; **paw the ground** auf dem Boden scharren ‖ intr (said of a horse) mit dem Huf scharren

pawl [pɔl] s Sperrklinke f

pawn [pɔn] s Pfand n; (fig) Schachfigur f; (chess) Bauer m ‖ tr verpfänden

pawn′brok′er s Pfandleiher –in mf

pawn′shop′ s Pfandhaus n

pawn′ tick′et s Pfandschein m

pay [pe] s Lohn m; (mil) Sold m ‖ v (pret & pp **paid** [ped]) tr bezahlen; (a visit) abstatten; (a dividend) ausschütten; (a compliment) machen; **pay back** zurückzahlen; **pay damages** Schadenersatz leisten; **pay down** anzahlen; **pay extra** nachzahlen; **pay in advance** vorausbezahlen; **pay in full**

begleichen; **pay interest on** verzinsen; **pay off** (*a debt*) abbezahlen; (*a person*) entlohnen; **pay one's way** ohne Verlust arbeiten; **pay out** auszahlen; **pay s.o. back for s.th.** j–m etw heimzahlen; **pay taxes on** versteuern; **pay up** (*a debt*) abbezahlen; (ins) voll einzahlen || *intr* zahlen; (*be worthwhile*) sich lohnen; **pay extra** zuzahlen; **pay for** (*a purchase*) (be)-zahlen für; (*suffer for*) büßen

payable ['pe·əbəl] *adj* fällig, zahlbar
pay′ check′ *s* Lohnscheck *m*
pay′day′ *s* Zahltag *m*
pay′ dirt′ *s*—**hit p.** sein Glück machen
payee [pe'i] *s* (*of a draft*) Zahlungsempfänger –in *mf*; (*of a check*) Wechselnehmer –in *mf*
pay′ en′velope Lohntüte *f*
payer ['pe·ər] *s* Zahler –in *mf*
pay′load′ *s* Nutzlast *f*; (*explosive energy*) Sprengladung *f*
pay′mas′ter *s* Zahlmeister *m*
payment ['pemənt] *s* Zahlung *f*; **in p.** **of** zur Bezahlung (*genit*)
pay′ phone′ *s* Münzfernsprecher *m*
pay′ raise′ *s* Gehaltserhöhung *f*
pay′ rate′ *s* Lohnsatz *m*
pay′roll′ *s* Lohnliste *f*; (*money paid*) gesamte Lohnsumme *f*
pay′ sta′tion *s* Telephonautomat *m*
pea [pi] *s* Erbse *f*
peace [pis] *s* Friede(n) *m*; (*quiet*) Ruhe *f*; **be at p. with** in Frieden leben mit; **keep the p.** die öffentliche Ruhe bewahren
peaceable ['pisəbəl] *adj* friedfertig
Peace′ Corps′ *s* Friedenskorps *n*
peace′-lov′ing *adj* friedliebend
peace′mak′er *s* Friedensstifter –in *mf*
peace′ nego′tia′tions *spl* Friedensverhandlungen *pl*
peace′ of mind′ *s* Seelenruhe *f*
peace′pipe′ *s* Friedenspfeife *f*
peace′time′ *adj* Friedens– || *s*—**in p.** in Friedenszeiten
peace′ trea′ty *s* Friedensvertrag *m*
peach [pitʃ] *s* Pfirsich *m*
peach′ tree′ *s* Pfirsichbaum *m*
peachy ['pitʃi] *adj* (coll) pfundig
pea′cock′ *s* Pfau *m*
pea′hen′ *s* Pfauenhenne *f*
pea′ jack′et *s* (nav) Matrosenjacke *f*
peak [pik] *adj* Spitzen– || *s* (& fig) Gipfel *m*; (*of a cap*) Mützenschirm *m*; (elec) Leistungsspitze *f*; (phys) Scheitelwert *m*
peak′ hours′ *spl* (*of traffic*) Hauptverkehrszeit *f*; (elec) Stoßzeit *f*
peak′ load′ *s* (elec) Spitzenlast *f*
peak′ vol′tage *s* Spitzenspannung *f*
peal [pil] *s* Geläute *n* || *intr* erschallen
peal′ of laugh′ter *s* Lachsalve *f*
peal′ of thun′der *s* Donnergetöse *n*
pea′nut′ *s* Erdnuß *f*; **peanuts** (coll) kleine Fische *pl*
pea′nut but′ter *s* Erdnußbutter *f*
pear [pɛr] *s* Birne *f*
pearl [pʌrl] *s* Perle *f*; **pearls** *spl* Perlen– || *s* Perle *f*
pearl′ neck′lace *s* Perlenkette *f*
pearl′ oys′ter *s* Perlenauster *f*
pearl′ tree′ *s* Birnbaum *m*

peasant ['pɛzənt] *adj* Bauern–, bäuerlich || *s* Bauer *m*, Bäuerin *f*
peasantry ['pɛzəntri] *s* Bauernstand *m*
pea′shoot′er *s* Blasrohr *n*
pea′ soup′ *s* Erbsensuppe *f*; (fig) Waschküche *f*
peat [pit] *s* Torf *m*
peat′ moss′ *s* Torfmull *m*
pebble ['pɛbəl] *s* Kiesel *m*; **pebbles** Geröll *n*
peck [pɛk] *s* (*measure*) Viertelscheffel *m*; (e.g., *of a bird*) Schnabelhieb *n*; (*kiss*) (coll) flüchtiger Kuß *m*; (*of trouble*) (coll) Menge *f* || *tr* hacken; (*food*) aufpicken || *intr* hacken, picken; (*eat food*) picken; **p. at** hacken nach; (*food*) (coll) herumstochern in (*dat*)
peculation [,pɛkjə'leʃən] *s* Geldunterschlagung *f*
peculiar [pɪ'kjuljər] *adj* eigenartig, absonderlich; **p. to** eigen (*dat*)
peculiarity [,pɪkjulɪ'ærɪti] *s* Eigenheit *f*, Absonderlichkeit *f*
pedagogic(al) [,pɛdə'gɑdʒɪk(əl)] *adj* pädagogisch, erzieherisch
pedagogue ['pɛdə,gɑg] *s* Pädagoge *m*, Erzieher *m*
pedagogy ['pɛdə,gɑdʒi] *s* Pädagogik *f*, Erziehungskunde *f*
ped·al ['pɛdəl] *s* Pedal *n* || *v* (*pret & pp* **-al[l]ed;** *ger* **-al[l]ing**) *tr* fahren || *intr* die Pedale treten
pedant ['pɛdənt] *s* Pedant –in *mf*
pedantic [pɪ'dæntɪk] *adj* pedantisch
pedantry ['pɛdəntri] *s* Pedanterie *f*
peddle ['pɛdəl] *tr* hausieren mit || *intr* hausieren
peddler ['pɛdlər] *s* Hausierer –in *mf*
pedestal ['pɛdɪstəl] *s* Sockel *m*, Postament *n*; **put s.o. on a p.** (fig) j–n aufs Podest erheben
pedestrian [pɪ'dɛstrɪən] *adj* Fußgänger–; (fig) schwunglos || *s* Fußgänger –in *mf*
pediatrician [,pidɪə'trɪʃən] *s* Kinderarzt *m*, Kinderärztin *f*
pediatrics [,pidɪ'ætrɪks] *s* Kinderheilkunde *f*
pediment ['pɛdɪmənt] *s* Giebelfeld *n*
peek [pik] *s* schneller Blick *m* || *intr* gucken; **p. at** angucken
peekaboo ['pikə,bu] *adj* durchsichtig || *interj* guck, guck!
peel [pil] *s* Schale *f* || *tr* schälen; **p. off** abschälen || *intr* sich schälen; (*said of paint*) abbröckeln; **p. off** (aer) sich aus dem Verband lösen
peep [pip] *s* schneller Blick *m*; heimlicher Blick *m*; **not another p.** **out of you!** kein Laut mehr aus dir! || *intr* gucken; (*look carefully*) lugen; **p. out** hervorlugen
peep′hole′ *s* Guckloch *n*
peep′ show′ *s* Fleischbeschau *f*
peer [pɪr] *s* Gleichgestellte *mf* || *intr* blicken; **p. at** mustern
peerless ['pɪrlɪs] *adj* unvergleichlich
peeve [piv] *s* (coll) Beschwerde *f* || *tr* (coll) ärgern
peeved *adj* verärgert
peevish ['pivɪʃ] *adj* sauertöpfisch

peg [peg] *s* Pflock *m;* *(for clothes)* Haken *m;* *(e.g., of a violin)* Wirbel *m;* **take down a peg or two** ducken ‖ *v* *(pret & pp* **pegged;** *ger* **pegging)** *tr* festpflocken; *(prices)* festlegen; *(throw)* (sl) schmeißen; *(identify)* (sl) erkennen

peg′board′ *s* Klammerplatte *f*

Peggy [′pegi] *s* Gretchen *n,* Gretl *f & n*

peg′ leg′ *s* Stelzbein *n*

Pekin·ese [‚piki′niz] *s* (—ese) Pekinese *m*

pelf [pelf] *s* (pej) Mammon *m*

pelican [′peliken] *s* Pelikan *m*

pellet [′pelit] *s* Kügelchen *n;* *(bullet)* Schrotkugel *f,* Schrotkorn *n*

pell-mell [′pel′mel] *adj* verworren ‖ *adv* durcheinander

pelt [pelt] *s* Fell *n,* Pelz *m;* *(whack)* Schlag *m* ‖ *tr* **(with)** bewerfen (mit); *(with questions)* bombardieren

pelvis [′pelvis] *s* Becken *n*

pen [pen] *s* Feder *f;* *(fountain pen)* Füllfederhalter *m;* *(enclosure)* Pferch *m;* *(prison)* (sl) Kittchen *n* ‖ *v* *(pret & pp* **penned;** *ger* **penning)** *tr (a letter)* verfassen ‖ *(pret & pp* **penned & pent;** *ger* **penning)** *tr*—**pen in** pferchen

penal [′pinəl] *adj* strafrechtlich, Straf-

pe′nal code′ *s* Strafgesetzbuch *n*

penalize [′pinə‚laiz] *tr* bestrafen; *(box)* mit Strafpunkten belegen

penalty [′penəlti] *s* Strafe *f;* *(point deducted)* (sport) Strafpunkt *m;* **under p. of death** bei Todesstrafe

pen′alty ar′ea *s* (sport) Strafraum *m*

pen′alty box′ *s* Strafbank *f*

pen′alty kick′ *s* Strafstoß *m*

penance [′penəns] *s* Buße *f*

penchant [′penʃənt] *s* **(for)** Hang *m* (zu)

pen·cil [′pensəl] *s* Bleistift *m* ‖ *v* *(pret & pp* **—cil[l]ed;** *ger* **—cil[l]ing)** *tr* mit Bleistift anzeichnen

pen′cil push′er *s* (coll) Schreiberling *m*

pen′cil sharp′ener *s* Bleistiftspitzer *m*

pendant [′pendənt] *s* Anhänger *m;* *(electrical fixture)* Hängeleuchter *m*

pendent [′pendənt] *adj* (herab)hängend

pend′ing *adj* schwebend; **he p.** in (der) Schwebe sein ‖ *prep (during)* während *(genit);* *(until)* bis zu *(dat)*

pendulum [′pendʒələm] *s* Pendel *n*

pen′dulum bob′ *s* Pendelgewicht *n*

penetrate [′peni‚tret] *tr* eindringen in *(acc)* ‖ *intr* eindringen

penetration [‚peni′treʃən] *s* Durchdringen *n;* *(of, e.g., a country)* Eindringen *n* (in *acc);* *(in ballistics)* Durchschlagskraft *f*

penguin [′peŋgwin] *s* Pinguin *m*

penicillin [‚peni′silin] *s* Penizillin *n*

peninsula [pə′ninsələ] *s* Halbinsel *f*

pe·nis [′pinis] *s* (—nes [niz] & —nises) Penis *m*

penitence [′penitəns] *s* Bußfertigkeit *f*

penitent [′penitənt] *adj* bußfertig ‖ *s* Büßer —in *mf;* (eccl) Beichtkind *n*

penitentiary [‚peni′tenʃəri] *s* Zuchthaus *n*

pen′knife′ *s* (—knives′) Federmesser *n*

penmanship [′penmən‚ʃip] *s* Schreibkunst *f*

pen′ name′ *s* Schriftstellername *m*

pennant [′penənt] *s* Wimpel *m;* (nav) Stander *m*

penniless [′peniləs] *adj* mittellos

penny [′peni] *s* Pfennig *m;* *(U.S.A.)* Cent *m*

pen′ny pinch′er [‚pintʃər] *s* Pfennigfuchser *m*

pen′ pal′ *s* Schreibfreund —in *mf*

pension [′penʃən] *s* Pension *f,* Rente *f;* **put on p.** pensionieren ‖ *tr* pensionieren

pensioner [′penʃənər] *s* Pensionär —in *mf;* (ins) Rentenempfänger —in *mf*

pen′sion fund′ *s* Pensionskasse *f*

pensive [′pensiv] *adj* sinnend

pentagon [′pentə‚gan] *s* Fünfeck *n;* **the Pentagon** das Pentagon

Pentecost [′penti‚kost] *s* Pfingsten *n*

penthouse [′pent‚haus] *s* Wetterdach *n;* *(exclusive apartment)* Penthouse *n*

pent-up [′pent′ʌp] *adj* verhalten

penult [′pinʌlt] *s* vorletzte Silbe *f*

penurious [pi′nuri·əs] *adj* karg

penury [′penjəri] *s* Kargheit *f*

peony [′pi·əni] *s* Pfingstrose *f*

people [′pipəl] *spl* Leute *pl,* Menschen *pl;* **his p.** die Seinen; **p. like him** seinesgleichen; **p. say** man sagt, die Leute sagen ‖ *s* **(peoples)** Volk *n* ‖ *tr* bevölkern

pep [pep] *s* (coll) Schwungkraft *f* ‖ *v* *(pret & pp* **pepped;** *ger* **pepping)** *tr*—**pep up** aufpulvern

pepper [′pepər] *s (spice)* Pfeffer *m;* *(plant)* Paprika *f;* *(vegetable)* Paprikaschote *f* ‖ *tr* pfeffern

pep′per mill′ *s* Pfeffermühle *f*

pep′permint′ *adj* Pfefferminz— ‖ *s* Pfefferminze *f*

pep′per shak′er *s* Pfefferstreuer *m*

peppery [′pepəri] *adj* pfefferig

per [pʌr] *prep* pro *(acc);* **as per** laut *(genit & dat)*

perambulator [pər′æmbjə‚letər] *s* Kinderwagen *m*

per capita [pər′kæpitə] pro Kopf

perceivable [pər′sivəbəl] *adj* wahrnehmbar

perceive [pər′siv] *tr* wahrnehmen

percent [pər′sent] *s* Prozent *n*

percentage [pər′sentidʒ] *s* Prozentsatz *m;* **p. of** *(e.g., the profit)* Anteil *m* an *(dat);* *(e.g., of a group)* Teil *m* *(genit)*

perceptible [pər′septəbəl] *adj* wahrnehmbar

perception [pər′sepʃən] *s* Wahrnehmung *f*

perch [pʌrtʃ] *s* Stange *f;* (ichth) Barsch *m* ‖ *tr* setzen ‖ *intr* sitzen

percolate [′pʌrkə‚let] *tr* durchseihen; *(coffee)* perkolieren ‖ *intr* durchsickern

percolator [′pʌrkə‚letər] *s* Perkolator *m*

percussion [pər′kʌʃən] *s* Schlag *m;* (med) Perkussion *f*

percus′sion in′strument *s* Schlaginstrument *n*

per di'em allow'ance [pər'daɪ·əm] s Tagegeld n

perdition [pər'dɪʃən] s Verdammnis f

perennial [pə'renɪ·əl] adj immerwährend; (bot) ausdauernd ‖ s ausdauernde Pflanze f

perfect ['pʌrfɪkt] adj perfekt, vollkommen; **he is a p. stranger to me** er ist mir völlig fremd ‖ s (gram) Perfekt(um) n ‖ [pər'fekt] tr vervollkommnen

perfection [pər'fekʃən] s Vollkommenheit f; **to p.** vollkommen

perfectionist [pər'fekʃənɪst] s Perfektionist –in mf

perfectly ['pʌrfɪktli] adv völlig, durchaus; **p. well** ganz genau

perfidious [pər'fɪdɪ·əs] adj treulos

perfidy ['pʌrfɪdi] s Treubruch m

perforate ['pʌrfə‚ret] tr durchlöchern

per'forated line' s durchlochte Linie f

perforation [‚pʌrfə're/ən] s gelochte Linie f

perforce [pər'fors] adv notgedrungen

perform [pər'fɔrm] tr ausführen; (an operation) vornehmen; (theat) aufführen ‖ intr (öffentlich) auftreten; (mach) funktionieren

performance [pər'fɔrməns] s Ausführung f; (mach) Leistung f; (theat) Aufführung f

performer [pər'fɔrmər] s Künstler –in mf

perform'ing arts' spl darstellende Künste pl

perfume [pər'fjum] s Parfüm n ‖ tr parfümieren

perfunctorily [pər'fʌŋktərɪli] adv oberflächlich

perfunctory [pər'fʌŋktəri] adj oberflächlich

perhaps [pər'hæps] adv vielleicht

per hour' pro Stunde, in der Stunde

peril ['perɪl] s Gefahr f; **at one's own p.** auf eigene Gefahr

perilous ['perɪləs] adj gefährlich

perimeter [pə'rɪmɪtər] s (math) Umfang m; (mil) Rand m

period ['pɪrɪ·əd] s Periode f, Zeitabschnitt m; (menstrual period) Periode f; (educ) Stunde f; (gram) Punkt m; (sport) Viertel n; **extra p.** (sport) Verlängerung f; **for a p. of** für die Dauer von; **p.!** und damit punktum!; **p. of grace** Frist f; **p. of life** Lebensalter n; **p. of time** Zeitdauer pl

pe'riod fur'niture s Stilmöbel pl

periodic [‚pɪrɪ'ɑdɪk] adj zeitweilig

periodical [‚pɪrɪ'ɑdɪkəl] s Zeitschrift f

peripheral [pə'rɪfərəl] adj peripher

periphery [pə'rɪfəri] s Peripherie f

periscope ['perɪ‚skop] s Periskop n

perish ['perɪʃ] intr umkommen; (said of wares) verderben

perishable ['perɪʃəbəl] adj vergänglich; (food) leicht verderblich

perjure ['pʌrdʒər] tr—**p. oneself** Meineid begehen

perjury ['pʌrdʒəri] s Meineid m; **commit p.** e–n Meineid leisten

perk [pʌrk] tr—**p. up** (the head) aufwerfen; (the ears) spitzen ‖ intr

(percolate) (coll) perkolieren; **p. up** lebhaft werden

permanence ['pʌrmənəns] s Dauer f

permanent ['pʌrmənənt] adj (fort)dauernd, bleibend ‖ s Dauerwelle f

per'manent address' s ständiger Wohnort m

per'manent job' s Dauerstellung f

per'manent wave' s Dauerwelle f

permeable ['pʌrmɪ·əbəl] adj durchlässig

permeate ['pʌrmɪ‚et] tr durchdringen ‖ intr durchsickern

permissible [pər'mɪsɪbəl] adj zulässig

permission [pər'mɪʃən] s Erlaubnis f; **with your p.** mit Verlaub

permissive [pər'mɪsɪv] adj nachsichtig

per-mit ['pʌrmɪt] s Erlaubnis f; (document) Erlaubnisschein m ‖ [pər'mɪt] v (pret & pp —mitted; ger —mitting) tr erlauben, gestatten; **be permitted to** (inf) dürfen (inf)

permute [pər'mjut] tr umsetzen; (math) permutieren

pernicious [pər'nɪʃəs] adj (to) schädlich (für)

perox'ide blonde' [pə'rɑksaɪd] s Wasserstoffblondine f

perpendicular [‚pʌrpən'dɪkjələr] adj senkrecht ‖ s Senkrechte f

perpetrate ['pʌrpɪ‚tret] tr verüben

perpetual [pər'petʃʊ·əl] adj (everlasting) ewig; (continual) unaufhörlich

perpetuate [pər'petʃʊ‚et] tr verewigen

perplex [pər'pleks] tr verblüffen

perplexed' adj verblüfft

perplexity [pər'pleksɪti] s Verblüffung f

persecute ['pʌrsɪ‚kjut] tr verfolgen

persecution [‚pʌrsɪ'kjuʃən] s Verfolgung f

persecutor ['pʌrsɪ‚kjutər] s Verfolger –in mf

perseverance [‚pʌrsɪ'vɪrəns] s Ausdauer f, Beharrlichkeit f

persevere [‚pʌrsɪ'vɪr] intr ausdauern; **p. in** (cling to) beharren auf (acc); (e.g., efforts, studies) fortfahren mit

Persia ['pʌrʒə] s Persien n

Persian ['pʌrʒən] adj persisch ‖ s Perser –in mf; (language) Persisch n

Per'sian rug' s Perserteppich m

persimmon [pər'sɪmən] s Persimone f

persist [pər'sɪst] intr andauern; **p. in** verbleiben bei

persistent [pər'sɪstənt] adj andauernd

person ['pʌrsən] s Person f; **in p.** persönlich; **per p.** pro Person

personable ['pʌrsənəbəl] adj (attractive) ansehnlich; (good-natured) verträglich

personage ['pʌrsənɪdʒ] s Persönlichkeit f

personal ['pʌrsənəl] adj persönlich; (private) Privat–; **become p.** anzüglich werden

per'sonal da'ta spl Personalien pl

per'sonal hygiene' s Körperpflege f

per'sonal in'jury s Personenschaden m

personality [‚pʌrsə'nælɪti] s Persönlichkeit f

personally ['pʌrsənəli] adv persönlich

per'sonal pro'noun s Personalprono-
men n
personi·fy [pər'sɑnɪˌfaɪ] v (pret & pp
–fied) tr personifizieren, verkörpern
personnel [ˌpʌrsə'nɛl] s Personal n
per'son-to-per'son call' s Gespräch n
mit Voranmeldung
f
perspective [pər'spɛktɪv] s Perspektive
f
perspicacious [ˌpʌrspɪ'keʃəs] adj
scharfsinnig
perspiration [ˌpʌrspɪ'reʃən] s Schweiß
m; (perspiring) Schwitzen n
perspire [pər'spaɪr] intr schwitzen
persuade [pər'swed] tr überreden
persuasion [pər'sweʒən] s Überredung
f
persuasive [pər'swesɪv] adj redegewandt
pert [pʌrt] adj keck; (sprightly) lebhaft
pertain [pər'ten] intr—p. to betreffen,
sich beziehen auf (acc)
pertinacious [ˌpʌrtɪ'neʃəs] adj behar-
lich
pertinent ['pʌrtɪnənt] adj einschlägig;
be p. to sich beziehen auf (acc)
perturb [pər'tʌrb] tr beunruhigen
peruse [pə'ruz] tr sorgfältig durch-
lesen
pervade [pər'ved] tr durchdringen
perverse [pər'vʌrs] adj (abnormal)
pervers; (obstinate) verstockt
perversion [pər'vʌrʒən] s Perversion f;
(of truth) Verdrehung f
perversity [pər'vʌrsɪti] s Perversität f
pervert ['pʌrvərt] s perverser Mensch
m || [pər'vʌrt] tr (corrupt) verder-
ben; (twist) verdrehen; (misapply)
mißbrauchen
pesky ['pɛski] adj (coll) lästig
pessimism ['pɛsɪˌmɪzəm] s Pessimis-
mus m
pessimist ['pɛsɪmɪst] s Pessimist –in
mf
pessimistic [ˌpɛsɪ'mɪstɪk] adj pessimistisch
pest [pɛst] s (insect) Schädling m; (annoying person) Plagegeist m; (pestilence) Pest f
pest' control' s Schädlingsbekämpfung
f
pester ['pɛstər] tr piesacken; (with
questions) belästigen
pesticide ['pɛstɪˌsaɪd] s Pestizid n
pestilence ['pɛstɪləns] s Pestilenz f
pestle ['pɛsəl] s Stößel m
pet [pɛt] adj Lieblings– || s (animal)
Haustier n; (person) Liebling m;
(favorite child) Schoßkind n || v
(pret & pp petted; ger petting) tr
streicheln || intr sich abknutschen
petal ['pɛtəl] s Blumenblatt n
Peter ['pitər] s Peter m || intr—peter
out im Sande verlaufen
pet' ide'a s Lieblingsgedanke m
petition [pɪ'tɪʃən] s Eingabe f; (jur)
Gesuch n || tr (s.o.) ersuchen
pet' name' s Kosename m
petri·fy ['pɛtrɪˌfaɪ] v (pret & pp –fied)
tr (& fig) versteinern; be petrified
versteinern; (fig) zu Stein werden

petroleum [pə'trolɪəm] s Petroleum n
pet' shop' s Tierhandlung f
petticoat ['pɛtɪˌkot] s Unterrock m
pet'ting s Petting n
petty ['pɛti] adj klein, geringfügig;
(narrow) engstirnig
pet'ty cash' s Handkasse f
pet'ty lar'ceny s geringer Diebstahl m
pet'ty of'ficer s (nav) Maat m
petulant ['pɛtʃələnt] adj verdrießlich
petunia [pə'tju̇nɪə] s Petunie f
pew [pju] s Bank f, Kirchenstuhl m
pewter ['pjutər] s Weißmetall n
Pfc. ['pi'ɛf'si] s (private first class)
Gefreiter m
phalanx ['fælæŋks] s Phalanx f
phantasm ['fæntæzəm] s Trugbild n
phantom ['fæntəm] s Phantom n
Pharaoh ['fɛro] s Pharao m
Pharisee ['færɪˌsi] s Pharisäer m
pharmaceutical [ˌfɑrmə'sutɪkəl] adj
pharmazeutisch
pharmacist ['fɑrməsɪst] s Apotheker
–in mf
pharmacy ['fɑrməsi] s Apotheke f;
(science) Pharmazie f
pharynx ['færɪŋks] s Rachenhöhle f
phase [fez] s Phase f || tr in Phasen
einteilen; p. out abwickeln
pheasant ['fɛzənt] s Fasan m
phenobarbital [ˌfino'bɑrbɪˌtæl] s
Phenobarbital n
phenomenal [fɪ'nɑmɪnəl] adj phänomenal
phenome·non [fɪ'nɑmɪˌnɑn] s (–na
[nə]) (& fig) Phänomen n, Erscheinung f
phial ['faɪəl] s Phiole f
philanderer [fɪ'lændərər] s Schürzen-
jäger m
philanthropist [fɪ'lænθrəpɪst] s Men-
schenfreund –in mf, Philanthrop –in
mf
philanthropy [fɪ'lænθrəpi] s Menschen-
liebe f, Philanthropie f
philately [fɪ'lætəli] s Briefmarken-
kunde f
Philippine ['fɪlɪˌpin] adj philippinisch
|| the Philippines spl die Philippinen
Philistine ['fɪlɪstɪn] adj (& fig) phi-
listerhaft || s (& fig) Philister m
philologist [fɪ'lɑlədʒɪst] s Philologe m,
Philologin f
philology [fɪ'lɑlədʒi] s Philologie f
philosopher [fɪ'lɑsəfər] s Philosoph m
philosophic(al) [ˌfɪlə'sɑfɪk(əl)] adj
philosophisch
philosophy [fɪ'lɑsəfi] s Philosophie f
phlebitis [flɪ'baɪtɪs] s Venenentzün-
dung f
phlegm [flɛm] s Schleim m
phlegmatic(al) [flɛg'mætɪk(əl)] adj
phlegmatisch
phobia ['fobɪə] s Phobie f
Phoenicia [fɪ'nɪʃə] s Phönizien n
Phoenician [fɪ'nɪʃən] adj phönizisch f
|| s Phönizier m
phoenix ['finɪks] s Phönix m
phone [fon] s (coll) Telephon n; on the
p. am Apparat || tr (coll) anrufen ||
intr telephonieren
phone' call' s (coll) Anruf m

phonetic [fo'nɛtɪk] *adj* phonetisch, Laut- || **phonetics** *s* Lautlehre *f*, Phonetik *f*

phonograph ['fonə‚græf] *s* Grammophon *n*

pho'nograph rec'ord *s* Schallplatte *f*

phonology [fə'nalədʒi] *s* Lautlehre *f*

phony ['foni] *adj* falsch, Schein- || *s* Schwindler –in *mf*

phosphate ['fasfet] *s* Phosphat *n*

phosphorescent [‚fasfə'resənt] *adj* phosphoreszierend

phospho·rus ['fasfərəs] *s* (**–ri** [‚raɪ]) Phosphor *m*

pho·to ['foto] *s* (**–tos**) (coll) Photo *n*

pho'tocop'y *s* Photokopie *f* || *v* (*pret & pp* **–ied**) *tr* photokopieren

pho'toengrav'ing *s* Lichtdruckverfahren *n*

pho'to fin'ish *s* Zielphotographie *f*

photogenic [‚foto'dʒɛnɪk] *adj* photogen

photograph ['fotə‚græf] *s* Photographie *f* || *tr & intr* photographieren

photographer [fə'tagrəfər] *s* Photograph –in *mf*

photography [fə'tagrəfi] *s* Photographie *f*

photostat ['fotə‚stæt] *s* (trademark) Photokopie *f* || *tr* photokopieren

phrase [frez] *s* Sinngruppe *f* || *tr* formulieren; (mus) phrasieren

phrenology [frə'nalədʒi] *s* Schädellehre *f*

physic ['fɪzɪk] *s* Abführmittel *n*; **physics** *s* Physik *f*

physical ['fɪzɪkəl] *adj* körperlich, physisch || *s* (*examination*) ärztliche Untersuchung *f*

phys'ical condi'tion *s* Gesundheitszustand *m*

phys'ical de'fect *s* körperliches Gebrechen *n*

phys'ical educa'tion *s* Leibeserziehung *f*

phys'ical ex'ercise *s* Leibesübungen *pl*; (*calisthenics*) Bewegung *f*

phys'ical hand'icap *s* Körperbehinderung *f*

physician [fɪ'zɪʃən] *s* Arzt *m*, Ärztin *f*

physicist ['fɪzɪsɪst] *s* Physiker –in *mf*

physics ['fɪzɪks] *s* Physik *f*

physiognomy [‚fɪzɪ'agnəmi] *s* Gesichtsbildung *f*, Physiognomie *f*

physiological [‚fɪzɪ-ə'ladʒɪkəl] *adj* physiologisch

physiology [‚fɪzɪ'alədʒi] *s* Physiologie *f*

physique [fɪ'zik] *s* Körperbau *m*

pi [paɪ] *s* (math) Pi *n* || *tr* (typ) zusammenwerfen

pianist ['pi·ənɪst] *s* Pianist –in *mf*

pian·o [pɪ'æno] *s* (**–os**) Klavier *n*

pian'o stool' *s* Klavierschemel *m*

picayune [‚pɪkə'jun] *adj* (*paltry*) geringfügig; (*person*) kleinlich

picco·lo ['pɪkəlo] *s* (**–los**) Pikkoloflöte *f*

pick [pɪk] *s* (*tool*) Spitzhacke *f*; (*choice*) Auslese *f*; **the p. of the crop** das Beste von allem || *tr* (*choose*) sich [*dat*] aussuchen; (e.g., *fruit*)

pflücken; (*one's teeth*) stochern in (*dat*); (*one's nose*) bohren in (*dat*); (*a lock*) mit e–m Dietrich öffnen; (*a quarrel*) suchen; (*a bone*) abnagen; **p. off** abpflücken; (*shoot*) (coll) abknallen; **p. out** auswählen; **p. s.o.'s brains** j–s Ideen klauen; **p. s.o.'s pocket** j–m die Tasche ausräumen; **p. up** (*lift up*) aufheben; (*a girl*) (coll) aufgabeln; (*a suspect*) aufgreifen; (*with a car*) abholen; (*passengers; the scent*) aufnehmen; (*a language; news*) aufschnappen; (*a habit*) annehmen; (*a visual object*) erkennen; (*strength*) wieder erlangen; (*weight*) zunehmen an (*dat*); **p. up speed** in Fahrt kommen || *intr*—**p. and choose** wählerisch suchen; **p. at** herumstochern in (*dat*); **p. on** herumreiten auf (*dat*); **p. up** (*improve in health or business*) sich (wieder) erholen

pick'ax' *s* Picke *f*, Pickel *m*

picket ['pɪkɪt] *s* Holzpfahl *m*; (*of strikers*) Streikposten *m* || *tr* durch Streikposten absperren, Streikposten stehen vor (*dat*) || *intr* Streikposten stehen

pick'et fence' *s* Lattenzaun *m*

pick'et line' *s* Streikkette *f*

pickle ['pɪkəl] *s* Essiggurke *f*; **be in a p.** (coll) im Schlamassel sitzen || *tr* (ein)pökeln

pick'led *adj* (sl) blau

pick'led her'ring *s* Rollmops *m*

pick'pock'et *s* Taschendieb *m*

pick'up' *s* (*of a car*) Beschleunigungsvermögen *n*; (*girl*) Straßenbekanntschaft *f*; (*restorative*) Stärkungsmittel *n*, Erfrischung *f*; (*a stop to pick up*) Abholung *f*; (*of a phonograph*) Schalldose *f*

pick'up truck' *s* offener Lieferwagen *m*

picky ['pɪki] *adj* wählerisch

pic·nic ['pɪknɪk] *s* Picknick *n* || *v* (*pret & pp* **–nicked**; *ger* **–nicking**) *intr* picknicken

pictorial [pɪk'torɪ-əl] *adj* illustriert || *s* Illustrierte *f*

picture ['pɪktʃər] *s* Bild *n*; (fig) Vorstellung *f*; **look the p. of health** kerngesund aussehen || *tr* sich [*dat*] vorstellen

pic'ture gal'lery *s* Gemäldegalerie *f*

pic'ture post'card *s* Ansichtspostkarte *f*

picturesque [‚pɪktʃə'resk] *adj* malerisch, pittoresk; (*language*) bilderreich

pic'ture tube' *s* Bildröhre *f*

pic'ture win'dow *s* Panoramafenster *n*

piddling ['pɪdlɪŋ] *adj* lumpig

pie [paɪ] *s* Torte *f*; (*meat-filled*) Pastete *f*; **pie in the sky** Luftschloß *n*

piece [pis] *s* Stück *n*; (checkers) Stein *m*; (chess) Figur *f*; (mil) Geschütz *n*; (mus, theat) Stück *n*; **a p. of advice** ein Rat *m*; **a p. of bad luck** ein unglücklicher Zufall *m*; **a p. of furniture** ein Möbelstück *n*; **a p. of luggage** ein Gepäckstück *n*; **a p. of**

news e–e Neuigkeit *f;* **a p. of paper** ein Blatt Papier; **a p. of toast** e–e geröstete Brotscheibe *f;* **say one's p.** seine Meinung sagen

piece′meal *adv* stückweise

piece′work′ *s* Akkordarbeit *f;* **do p.** in Akkord arbeiten

piece′work′er *s* Akkordarbeiter –in *mf*

pier [pɪr] *s* Landungsbrücke *f,* Pier *m* & *f; (of a bridge)* Pfeiler *m*

pierce [pɪrs] *tr* durchstechen, durchbohren

pierc′ing *adj (look, pain)* scharf, stechend; *(cry)* gellend; *(cold)* schneidend

piety [′paɪ.əti] *s* Frömmigkeit *f*

pig [pɪg] *s* Schwein *n*

pigeon [′pɪdʒən] *s* Taube *f*

pi′geonhole′ *s* Fach *n* ‖ *tr* auf die lange Bank schieben

pi′geon loft′ *s* Taubenschlag *m*

pi′geon-toed′ *adj* & *adv* mit einwärts gerichteten Zehen

piggish [′pɪgɪʃ] *adj* säuisch

piggyback [′pɪgɪ.bæk] *adv* huckepack

pig′gy bank′ *s* Sparschweinchen *n*

pig′head′ed *adj* dickköpfig

pig′ i′ron *s* Roheisen *n*

pigment [′pɪgmənt] *s* Pigment *n*

pig′pen′ *s* Schweinekoben *m*

pig′skin′ *s* Schweinsleder *n; (sport) (coll)* Fußball *m*

pig′sty′ *s* Schweinestall *m*

pig′tail′ *s (hair style)* Rattenschwanz *m*

pike [paɪk] *s* Pike *f,* Spieß *m; (highway)* Landstraße *f; (ichth)* Hecht *m*

piker [′paɪkər] *s (coll)* Knicker *m*

pilaster [pɪ′læstər] *s* Wandpfeiler *m*

pile [paɪl] *s (heap)* Haufen *m; (e.g., of papers)* Stoß *m; (stake)* Pfahl *m; (fortune) (coll)* Menge *f;* (atom. phys) Meiler *m,* Reaktor *m;* (elec, phys) Säule *f;* (tex) Flor *m;* **piles** (pathol) Hämorrhoiden *pl;* **piles of money** (coll) Heidengeld *n* ‖ *tr* anhäufen, aufhäufen; **p. it on** (coll) dick auftragen ‖ *intr—***p. into** sich drängen in *(acc);* **p. on** sich übereinander stürzen; **p. out of** sich hinausdrängen aus; **p. up** sich (an)häufen

pile′ driv′er *s* Pfahlramme *f,* Rammbär *m*

pilfer [′pɪlfər] *tr* mausen, stibitzen

pilgrim [′pɪlgrɪm] *s* Pilger –in *mf*

pilgrimage [′pɪlgrɪmɪdʒ] *s* Pilgerfahrt *f;* **go on a p.** pilgern

pill [pɪl] *s* (& fig) Pille *f*

pillar [′pɪlər] *s* Pfeiler *m,* Säule *f*

pill′box′ *s* Pillenschachtel *f;* (mil) Bunker *m*

pillo·ry [′pɪləri] *s* Pranger *m* ‖ *v (pret* & *pp* **–ried)** *tr* an den Pranger stellen; (fig) anprangern

pillow [′pɪlo] *s* Kopfkissen *n*

pil′lowcase′ *s* Kopfkissenbezug *m*

pilot [′paɪlət] *adj (experimental)* Versuchs– ‖ *s* (aer) Pilot *m,* Flugzeugführer –in *mf;* (naut) Lotse *m* ‖ *tr* (aer) steuern, führen; (naut) steuern, lotsen

pi′lothouse′ *s* (naut) Ruderhaus *n*

pi′lot light′ *s* Sparflamme *f*

pi′lot's li′cense *s* Flugzeugführerschein *m*

pimp [pɪmp] *s* Zuhälter *m* ‖ *intr* kuppeln

pimp′ing *s* Zuhälterei *f*

pimple [′pɪmpəl] *s* Pickel *m*

pimply [′pɪmpli] *adj* pickelig

pin [pɪn] *s* Stecknadel *f;* (ornament) Anstecknadel *f;* (bowling) Kegel *m;* (mach) Pinne *f,* Zapfen *m;* **be on pins and needles** wie auf Nadeln sitzen ‖ *v (pret* & *pp* **pinned;** *ger* **pinning)** *tr (fasten with a pin)* mit e–r Nadel befestigen; (e.g., a dress) abstecken; (e.g., under a car) einklemmen; (e.g., against the wall) drücken; (in wrestling) auf die Schultern legen; **pin down** (a person) festlegen; (troops) niederhalten; **pin one's hopes on** seine Hofnungen setzen auf (acc); **pin s.th. on** (coll) (fig) j–m etw anhängen; **pin up** (a sign) anschlagen; (the hair, a dress) aufstecken

pinafore [′pɪnə.for] *s* Latz *m*

pin′ball machine′ *s* Spielautomat *m*

pin′ boy′ *s* Kegeljunge *m*

pincers [′pɪnsərz] *s* & *spl* Kneifzange *f*

pinch [pɪntʃ] *s* Kneifen *n; (of salt)* Prise *f;* **give s.o. a p.** j–n kneifen; **in a p.** zur Not, in der Not ‖ *tr* kneifen, zwicken; *(steal)* (sl) klauen; *(arrest)* (coll) schnappen; **I got my finger pinched in the door** ich habe mir den Finger in der Tür geklemmt; **p. and scrape every penny** sich *[dat]* jeden Groschen vom Munde absparen; **p. off** abzwicken ‖ *intr (said of shoe)* (& fig) drücken

pinchers [′pɪntʃərz] *s* & *spl* Kneifzange *f*

pinch′-hit′ *v (pret* & *pp* **–hit;** *ger* **–hitting)** *intr* einspringen

pinch′ hit′ter *s* Ersatzmann *m*

pin′cush′ion *s* Nadelkissen *n*

pine [paɪn] *adj* Kiefern– ‖ *s* Kiefer *f* ‖ *intr—***p. away** sich abzehren; **p. for** sich sehnen nach

pine′ap′ple *s* Ananas *f*

pine′ cone′ *s* Kiefernzapfen *m*

pine′ nee′dle *s* Kiefernnadel *f*

ping [pɪŋ] *s* Päng *n; (of a motor)* Klopfen *n* ‖ *intr* (aut) klopfen

ping-pong [′pɪŋ.pɑŋ] *s* Ping-pong *n*

pin′head′ *s* (& fig) Stechnadelkopf *m*

pink [pɪŋk] *adj* rosa ‖ *s* Rosa *n*

pin′ mon′ey *s* Nadelgeld *n*

pinnacle [′pɪnəkəl] *s* Zinne *f*

pin′point′ *adj* haarscharf; **p. landing** Ziellandung *f* ‖ *tr* markieren

pin′prick′ *s* Nadelstich *m*

pint [paɪnt] *s* Schoppen *m,* Pinte *f*

pin′up girl′ *s* Pin-up-Girl *n*

pin′wheel′ *s (toy)* Windmühle *f; (fireworks)* Feuerrad *n*

pioneer [.paɪ.ə′nɪr] *s* Bahnbrecher –in *mf;* (fig & mil) Pionier *m* ‖ *tr* (fig) den Weg freimachen für ‖ *intr* (fig) Pionierarbeit leisten

pious [′paɪ.əs] *adj* fromm

pip [pɪp] *s* (in fruit) Kern *m; (on dice)* Punkt *m; (on a radarscope)* Leuchtpunkt *m; (of chickens)* Pips *m*

pipe [paɪp] *s* Rohr *n*; (*for smoking; of an organ*) Pfeife *f* ‖ *tr* durch ein Rohr (weiter)leiten ‖ *intr* pfeifen; **p. down** (sl) das Maul halten; **p. up** (coll) anfangen zu sprechen, loslegen

pipe′ clean′er *s* Pfeifenreiniger *m*

pipe′ dream′ *s* Wunschtraum *m*

pipe′ joint′ *s* Rohranschluß *m*

pipe′ line′ *s* Rohrleitung *f*, Pipeline *f*; (*of information*) Informationsquelle *f*

pipe′ or′gan *s* Orgel *f*

piper [′paɪpər] *s* Pfeifer –in *mf*

pipe′ wrench′ *s* Rohrzange *f*

piping [′paɪpɪŋ] *adv*—**p. hot** siedend heiß ‖ *s* Rohrleitung *f*; (*on uniforms*) Biese *f*; (sew) Paspel *f*

piquancy [′pikənsi] *s* Pikanterie *f*

piquant [′pikənt] *adj* pikant

pique [pik] *s* Pik *m* ‖ *tr* verärgern; **be piqued at** pikiert sein über (*acc*)

piracy [′paɪrəsi] *s* Seeräuberei *f*

pirate [′paɪrɪt] *s* Seeräuber *m* ‖ *tr* (*a book*) (ungesetzlich) nachdrucken

pirouette [ˌpiru′et] *s* Pirouette *f*

pista/chio nut′ [pɪs′tæʃɪɔ] *s* Pistaziennuß *f*

pistol [′pɪstəl] *s* Pistole *f*

pis′tol point′ *s*—**at p.** mit vorgehaltener Pistole

piston [′pɪstən] *s* Kolben *m*

pis′ton ring′ *s* Kolbenring *m*

pis′ton rod′ *s* Kolbenstange *f*

pis′ton stroke′ *s* Kolbenhub *m*

pit [pɪt] *s* Grube *f*; (*in fruit*) Kern *m*; (*trap*) Fallgrube *f*; (*in the skin*) Narbe *f*; (*from corrosion*) Rostgrübchen *n*; (*in auto racing*) Box *f*; (*for cockfights*) Kampfplatz *m*; (*for coal*) Schacht *m*; (theat) Parkett *n*; (mus) Orchester *n*; **pit of the stomach** Magengrube *f* ‖ *v* (*pret & pp* **pitted**) *ger* **pitting**) *tr* (*a face*) mit Narben bedecken; (*fruit*) entkernen; (*through corrosion*) anfressen; **pit A against B** A gegen B ausspielen; **pit one's strength against s.th.** seine Kraft mit etw messen

pitch [pɪtʃ] *s* Pech *n*; (*of a roof*) Dachschräge *f*; (*downward slope*) Gefälle *n*; (*of a ship*) Stampfen *n*; (*of a screw, thread*) Teilung *f*; (*of a propeller*) Steigung *f*; (*throw*) Wurf *m*; (*sales talk*) Verkaufsgespräch *n*; (mus) Tonhöhe *f* ‖ *tr* (*seal with pitch*) verpichen; (*a tent*) aufschlagen; (*a ball*) dem Schläger zuwerfen; (*hay*) mit der Heugabel werfen ‖ *intr* (naut) stampfen; **p. and toss** schlingern; **p. in** mithelfen

pitch′ ac′cent *s* musikalischer Tonakzent *m*

pitch′-black′ *adj* pechrabenschwarz

pitcher [′pɪtʃər] *s* (*jug*) Krug *m*

pitch′fork′ *s* Heugabel *f*

pitch′ing *s* (naut) Stampfen *n*

pit′fall′ *s* Fallgrube *f*; (fig) Falle *f*

pith [pɪθ] *s* (& fig) Mark *n*

pithy [′pɪθi] *adj* (& fig) markig

pitiable [′pɪtɪ·əbəl] *adj* erbarmenswert

pitiful [′pɪtɪfəl] *adj* erbärmlich

pitiless [′pɪtɪlɪs] *adj* erbarmungslos

pit′ted *adj* (*by corrosion*) angefressen; (*fruit*) entkernt

pit•y [′pɪti] *s* Erbarmen *n*, Mitleid *n*; **have p. on** Mitleid haben mit; **it's a p. that** (es ist) schade, daß; **move to p.** jammern; **what a p.!** wie schade! ‖ *v* (*pret & pp* **–ied**) *tr* sich erbarmen (*gent*), bemitleiden

pivot [′pɪvət] *s* Drehpunkt *m* ‖ *intr* (**on**) sich drehen (um); (mil) schwenken

placard [′plækərd] *s* Plakat *n*

placate [′pleket] *tr* begütigen

place [ples] *s* (*seat; room*) Platz *m*; (*area, town, etc.*) Ort *m*, Ortschaft *f*; (*in a book; in a room*) Stelle *f*; (*situation*) Lage *f*; (*spot to eat in, dance in, etc.*) Lokal *n*; **all over the p.** überall; **at your p.** (coll) bei Ihnen; **in my p.** an meiner Stelle; **in p. of** anstelle von (or *genit*); **in the first p.** erstens; **know one's p.** wissen, wohin man gehört; **out of p.** (& fig) nicht am Platz; **p. to stay** Unterkunft *f*; **put s.o. in his p.** j–n in seine Schranken verweisen; **take one's p.** antreten; **take p.** stattfinden; **take s.o.'s p.** an j–s Stelle treten ‖ *tr* setzen, stellen; (*an advertisement*) aufgeben; (*an order*) erteilen; (*find a job for*) unterbringen; **I can't p. him** ich weiß nicht, wo ich ihn hintun soll; **p. a call** (telp) ein Gespräch anmelden ‖ *intr* (*in horseracing*) sich als Zweiter placieren; (sport) sich placieren

place•bo [plə′sibo] *s* (**–bos** & **–boes**) Placebo *n*

place′ card′ *s* Tischkarte *f*

place′ mat′ *s* Tischmatte *f*

placement [′plesmənt] *s* Unterbringung *f*

place′-name′ *s* Ortsname *m*

place′ of birth′ *s* Geburtsort *m*

place′ of employ′ment *s* Arbeitsstätte *f*

place′ of res′idence *s* Wohnsitz *m*

placid [′plæsɪd] *adj* ruhig, sanftmütig

plagiarism [′pledʒəˌrɪzəm] *s* Plagiat *n*

plagiarist [′pledʒərɪst] *s* Plagiator –in *mf*

plagiarize [′pledʒəˌraɪz] *intr* ein Plagiat begehen

plague [pleg] *s* Seuche *f* ‖ *tr* heimsuchen

plaid [plæd] *adj* buntkariert ‖ *s* Schottenkaro *n*

plain [plen] *adj* (*simple*) einfach; (*clear*) klar; (*fabric*) einfarbig; (*homely*) unschön; (*truth*) rein; (*food*) bürgerlich; (*paper*) unlin(i)iert; (*speech*) unverblümt; (*alcohol*) unverdünnt ‖ *s* Ebene *f*

plain′ clothes′ *spl*—**in p.** in Zivil

plain′-clothes′ man′ *s* Geheimpolizist *m*

plaintiff [′plentɪf] *s* Kläger –in *mf*

plaintive [′plentɪv] *adj* Klage-, klagend

plait [plet] *s*, [plæt] *s* Flechte *f*; **p. of hair** Zopf *m* ‖ *tr* flechten

plan [plæn] *s* Plan *m*; (*intention*) Vorhaben *n*; **according to p.** planmäßig;

what are your plans for this evening?
was haben Sie für heute abend vor?
|| *v* (*pret & pp* **planned**; *ger* **planning**) *tr* planen; (*one's time*) einteilen; **p. to** (*inf*) vorhaben zu (*inf*) || *intr*—**p. for** Pläne machen für; **p. on** rechnen mit

plane [plen] *s* (*airplane*) Flugzeug *n*, Maschine *f*; (*airfoil*) Tragfläche *f*; (*carp*) Hobel *m*; (*geom*) Ebene *f*; **on a high p.** (fig) auf e-m hohen Niveau || *tr* hobeln; **p. down** abhobeln

plane′ connec′tion *s* Fluganschluß *m*
plane′ geom′etry *s* Planimetrie *f*
planet [′plænɪt] *s* Planet *m*
planetari·um [‚plænɪ′terɪ·əm] *s* (**-a** [ə] & **-ums**) Planetarium *n*
planetary [′plænə‚teri] *adj* Planeten-
plane′ tick′et *s* Flugkarte *f*
plane′ tree′ *s* Platane *f*
plank [plæŋk] *s* Brett *n*, Planke *f*; (pol) Programmpunkt *m*
planned′ par′enthood *s* Familienplanung *f*
plant [plænt] *s* (*factory*) Anlage *f*; (*spy*) Spion -in *mf*; (bot) Pflanze *f* || *tr* (an)pflanzen; (*a field*) bepflanzen; (*a colony*) gründen; (*as a spy*) als Falle einstellen; (*a bomb*) verstecken; **p. oneself** sich hinstellen
plantation [plæn′teʃən] *s* Plantage *f*
planter [′plæntər] *s* (*person who plants; plantation owner*) Pflanzer -in *mf*; (*decorative container*) Blumentrog *m*; (mach) Pflanzmaschine *f*
plasma [′plæzmə] *s* Plasma *n*
plaster [′plæstər] *s* Verputz *m*; (med) Pflaster *n* || *tr* verputzen; (*e.g., with posters*) bepflastern; **be plastered** (sl) besoffen sein
plas′terboard′ *s* Gipsdiele *f*
plas′ter cast′ *s* (med) Gipsverband *m*; (sculp) Gipsabguß *m*
plasterer [′plæstərər] *s* Stukkateur *m*
plas′tering *s* Verputz *m*
plas′ter of Par′is *s* Gips *m*
plastic [′plæstɪk] *adj* Plastik- || *s* Plastik *n*
plas′tic sur′gery *s* Plastik *f*
plas′tic wood′ *s* Holzpaste *f*
plate [plet] *s* (*dish*) Teller *m*; (*of metal*) Platte *f*; (*in a book*) Tafel *f*; (elec, phot, typ) Platte *f*; (electron) Plattenelektrode *f* || *tr* plattieren
plateau [plæ′to] *s* Plateau *n*
plate′ glass′ *s* Tafelglas *n*
platen [′plætən] *s* Schreibmaschinenwalze *f*
platform [′plæt‚fɔrm] *s* Plattform *f*; (*for a speaker*) Bühne *f*; (*for loading*) Rampe *f*; (pol) Programm *n*; (rr) Bahnsteig *m*
plat′form shoes′ *spl* Plateauschuhe *pl*
plat′ing *s* (*e.g., of gold*) Plattierung *f*; (*armor*) Panzerung *f*
platinum [′plætɪnəm] *s* Platin *n*
plat′inum blonde′ *s* Platinblondine *f*
platitude [′plætɪ‚t(j)ud] *s* Gemeinplatz *m*
Plato [′pleto] *s* Plato *m*

Platonic [plə′tɑnɪk] *adj* platonisch
platoon [plə′tun] *s* Zug *m*
platter [′plætər] *s* Platte *f*
plausible [′plɔzɪbəl] *adj* plausibel
play [ple] *s* Spiel *n*; (mach) Spielraum *m*; (sport) Spielzug *m*; (theat) Stück *n*; **in p.** im Spiel; **out of p.** aus dem Spiel || *tr* spielen; (*a card*) ausspielen; (*an opponent*) spielen gegen; **p. back** (*a tape, record*) abspielen; **p. down** bagatellisieren; **p. the horses** bei Pferderennen wetten || *intr* spielen; (*records, tapes*) abspielen; **p. about** (*the lips*) umspielen; **p. along** mitspielen; **p. around with** herumspielen mit; **p. for** (*stakes*) spielen um; (*a team*) spielen für; **p. into s.o.'s hands** j-m in die Hände spielen; **p. safe** auf Nummer Sicher gehen; **p. up to** schmeicheln (*dat*)
play′back′ *s* (*reproduction*) Wiedergabe *f*; (*device*) Abspielgerät *n*
play′boy′ *s* Playboy *m*
player [′ple·ər] *s* Spieler -in *mf*; (sport) Sportler -in *mf*; (theat) Schauspieler -in *mf*
playful [′plefəl] *adj* spielerisch
play′ground′ *s* Spielplatz *m*
play′house′ *s* Theater *n*; (*for children*) Spielhaus *n*
play′ing card′ *s* Spielkarte *f*
play′ing field′ *s* Spielfeld *n*
play′mate′ *s* Spielkamerad -in *mf*
play′-offs′ *spl* Vorrunde *f*
play′ on words′ *s* Wortspiel *n*
play′pen′ *s* Laufgitter *n*
play′room′ *s* Spielzimmer *n*
play′school′ *s* Kindergarten *m*
play′thing′ *s* (& fig) Spielzeug *n*
playwright [′ple‚raɪt] *s* Schauspieldichter -in *mf*
plea [pli] *s* Bitte *f*; (jur) Plädoyer *n*
plead [plid] *v* (*pret & pp* **pleaded** & **pled** [pled]) *tr* (*ignorance*) vorschützen || *intr* plädieren; **p. guilty** sich schuldig bekennen; **p. not guilty** sich als nichtschuldig erklären; **p. with s.o.** anflehen
pleasant [′plezənt] *adj* angenehm
pleasantry [′plezəntri] *s* Heiterkeit *f*; (*remark*) Witz *m*
please [pliz] *tr* gefallen (*dat*); **be pleased to** (*inf*) sich freuen zu (*inf*); **be pleased with** sich freuen über (*acc*); **pleased to meet you!** sehr angenehm || *intr* gefallen; **as one pleases** nach Gefallen; **do as you p.** tun Sie, wie Sie wollen; **if you p.** wenn ich bitten darf; (iron) gefälligst; **p.!** bitte!
pleasing *adj* angenehm, gefällig
pleasure [′pleʒər] *s* Vergnügen *n*
pleas′ure trip′ *s* Vergnügungsreise *f*
pleat [plit] *s* Plissee *n* || *tr* plissieren
pleat′ed skirt′ *s* Plisseerock *m*
plebeian [plɪ′bi·ən] *adj* plebejisch || *s* Plebejer -in *mf*
plectrum [′plektrəm] *s* (**-rums** & **-ra** [rə]) Plektron *n*; (*for zither*) Schlagring *m*
pledge [pledʒ] *s* (*solemn promise*) Gelübde *n*; (*security for a payment*)

Pfand *n;* (fig) Unterpfand *n* ‖ *tr* geloben; (*money*) zeichnen

plenary ['pli:nəri] *adj* Plenar–, Voll-
ple'nary indul'gence *s* vollkommener Ablaß *m*

ple'nary ses'sion *s* Plenum *n*

plenipotentiary [,plenɪpə'tenʃɪ ,erɪ] *adj* bevollmächtigt ‖ *s* Bevollmächtigte *mf*

plentiful ['plentɪfəl] *adj* reichlich

plenty ['plenti] *s* Fülle *f;* **have p. of** Überfluß haben an (*dat*); **have p. to do** vollauf zu tun haben ‖ *adv* (coll) reichlich

pleurisy ['plʊrɪsi] *s* Brustfellentzündung *f*

plexiglass ['plɛksɪ ,glæs] *s* Plexiglas *n*

pliant ['plaɪ-ənt] *adj* biegsam; (fig) gefügig

pliers ['plaɪ-ərz] *s &* spl Zange *f*

plight [plaɪt] *s* Notlage *f*

plod [plad] *v* (*pret & pp* **plodded;** *ger* **plodding**) *intr* stapfen; **p. along** mühsam weitermachen

plop [plap] *v* (*pret & pp* **plopped;** *ger* **plopping**) *tr* plumpsen lassen ‖ *intr* plumpsen ‖ *interj* plumps!

plot [plat] *s* (*conspiracy*) Komplott *n;* (*of a story*) Handlung *f;* (*of ground*) Grundstück *n* ‖ *v* (*pret & pp* **plotted;** *ger* **plotting**) *tr* (*a course*) abstecken; (*intrigues*) schmieden; (*e.g., murder*) planen ‖ *intr* sich verschwören

plough [plaʊ] *s, tr & intr* var of **plow**

plow [plaʊ] *s* Pflug *m* ‖ *tr* pflügen; **p. up** umpflügen; **p. under** unterpflügen ‖ *intr* pflügen; **p. through the waves** durch die Wellen streichen

plow'man *s* (**-men**) Pflüger *m*

plow'share *s* Pflugschar *f*

pluck [plʌk] *s* (*tug*) Ruck *m;* (fig) Schneid *m* ‖ *tr* (*e.g., a chicken*) rupfen; (*flowers, fruit*) pflücken; (*eyebrows*) auszupfen; (mus) zupfen ‖ *intr*—**p. up** Mut fassen

plug [plʌg] *s* (*for a sink*) Pfropfen *m;* (*of tobacco*) Priem *m;* (*old horse*) alter Klepper *m;* (*advertising*) Befürwortung *f;* (aut) Zündkerze *f;* (elec) Stecker *m* ‖ *v* (*pret & pp* **plugged;** *ger* **plugging**) *tr* (*a hole*) zustopfen; **p. in** an die Steckdose anschließen ‖ *intr*—**p. away** (*work hard*) schuften; (*study hard*) pauken

plum [plʌm] *s* Pflaume *f*

plumage ['plumɪdʒ] *s* Gefieder *n*

plumb [plʌm] *adj* lotrecht ‖ *adv* (coll) völlig ‖ *s* Lot *n;* **out of p.** aus dem Lot ‖ *tr* loten, sondieren

plumb' bob' *s* Lot *n*

plumber ['plʌmər] *s* Installateur *m*

plumb'ing *s* (*plumbing work*) Installateurarbeit *f;* (*pipes*) Rohrleitung *f*

plumb' line' *s* Lotschnur *f*

plume [plum] *s* Feder *f;* (*on a helmet*) Helmbusch *m;* **p. of smoke** Rauchfahne *f* ‖ *tr* (*adorn with plumes*) mit Federn schmücken; **p. itself** sich putzen

plummet ['plʌmɪt] *s* Lot *n* ‖ *intr* stürzen

plump [plʌmp] *adj* rundlich ‖ *tr* plumpsen; **p. oneself down** sich schwerfällig hinwerfen

plum' tree' *s* Pflaumenbaum *m*

plunder ['plʌndər] *s* (*act*) Plünderung *f;* (*booty*) Beute *f* ‖ *tr & intr* plündern

plunderer ['plʌndərər] *s* Plünderer *m*

plunge [plʌndʒ] *s* Sturz *m* ‖ *tr* stürzen ‖ *intr* (*fall*) stürzen; (*throw oneself*) sich stürzen

plunger ['plʌndʒər] *s* Saugglocke *f*

plunk [plʌŋk] *adv* (*squarely*) (coll) genau ‖ *tr* (*e.g., a guitar*) zupfen; **p. down** klirrend auf den Tisch legen

pluperfect [,plu'pʌrfɛkt] *s* Vorvergangenheit *f,* Plusquamperfekt(um) *n*

plural ['plʊrəl] *adj* Plural– ‖ *s* Mehrzahl *f,* Plural *m*

plurality [plʊ'rælɪti] *s* Mehrheit *f;* (pol) Stimmenmehrheit *f*

plus [plʌs] *adj* Plus–; (elec) positiv ‖ *s* Plus *n* ‖ *prep* plus (acc)

plush [plʌʃ] *adj* (coll) luxuriös

plus' sign' *s* Pluszeichen *n*

plutonium [plu'tonɪ-əm] *s* Plutonium *n*

ply [plaɪ] *s* (*of wood, etc.*) Schicht *f;* (*of yarn*) Strähne *f* ‖ *v* (*pret & pp* **plied**) *tr* (*e.g., a needle*) (eifrig) handhaben; (*a trade*) betreiben; (*with questions*) bestürmen; (*a waterway*) regelmäßig befahren ‖ *intr* (**between**) verkehren (zwischen *dat*)

ply'wood *s* Sperrholz *n*

pneumatic [n(j)u'mætɪk] *adj* pneumatisch

pneumat'ic drill' *s* Preßluftbohrer *m*

pneumonia [n(j)u'monɪ-ə] *s* Lungenentzündung *f*

poach [potʃ] *tr* (*eggs*) pochieren ‖ *intr* wildern

poached' egg' *s* verlorenes Ei *n*

poacher ['potʃər] *s* Wilderer *m*

pock [pak] *s* Pocke *f,* Pustel *f*

pocket ['pakɪt] *adj* (*comb, flap, knife, money, watch*) Taschen– ‖ *s* Tasche *f;* (billiards) Loch *n;* (mil) Kessel *m* ‖ *tr* in die Tasche stecken; (billiards) ins Loch spielen

pock'etbook' *s* Handtasche *f;* (*book*) Taschenbuch *n*

pock'et cal'culator *s* Taschenrechner *m*

pock'mark' *s* Pockennarbe *f*

pock'marked' *adj* pockennarbig

pod [pad] *s* Hülse *f*

podi-um ['podɪ-əm] *s* (**-ums** *& -***a** [ə]) Podium *n*

poem ['po-ɪm] *s* Gedicht *n*

poet ['po-ɪt] *s* Dichter *m,* Poet *m*

poetaster ['po-ɪt ,æstər] *s* Dichterling *m*

poetess ['po-ɪtɪs] *s* Dichterin *f*

poetic [po'ɛtɪk] *adj* dichterisch, poetisch ‖ **poetics** *s* Poetik *f*

poetry ['po-ɪtri] *s* Dichtung *f;* **write p.** dichten, Gedichte schreiben

poignant ['pɔɪn(j)ənt] *adj* (*touching*) ergreifend; (*pungent*) scharf; (*cutting*) beißend

point [pɔɪnt] *s* (*dot, score*) Punkt *m;*

(tip) Spitze *f;* *(of a joke)* Pointe *f;*
(of a statement) Hauptpunkt *m;* *(side of a character)* Seite *f;* *(purpose)* Sinn *m;* *(matter, subject)* Sache *f;* *(of a compass)* Kompaßstrich *m;* *(to show decimals)* Komma *n;* *(aut)* Zündkontakt *m;* *(geog)* Landspitze *f;* *(typ)* Punkt *m;* **at this p.** in diesem Augenblick; **be on the p. of** *(ger)* gerade im Begriff sein zu *(inf);* **come to the p.!** zur Sache!; **get the p.** verstehen; **in p. of fact** tatsächlich; **make a p. of** bestehen auf *(dat);* **make it a p. to** *(inf)* es sich *[dat]* zur Pflicht machen zu *(inf);* **not to the p.** nicht zur Sache gehörig; **off the p.** unzutreffend; **on points** *(sport)* nach Punkten; **p. at issue** strittiger Punkt *m;* **p. of order!** zur Tagesordnung!; **p. of time** Zeitpunkt *m;* **score a p.** *(fig)* e-n Punkt für sich buchen; **that's beside the p.** darum handelt es sich nicht; **there's no p. to it** es hat keinen Zweck; **to the p.** zutreffend; **up to a certain p.** bis zu e-m gewissen Grade ‖ *tr* *(e.g., a gun)* **(at)** richten (auf *acc);* **p. out** (auf)zeigen; **p. s.th. out to s.o.** j-n auf etw *[acc]* hinweisen; **p. the finger at** mit dem Finger zeigen auf *(acc)* ‖ *intr* mit dem Finger zeigen; **p. to** deuten auf *(acc);* *(fig)* hinweisen auf *(acc)*
point'-blank' *adj* *(refusal)* glatt; *(shot)* rasant, Kernschuß–; **at p. range** auf Kernschußweite ‖ *adv* *(at close range)* aus nächster Nähe; *(fig)* glatt; *(arti)* auf Kernschußweite
point'ed *adj* spitzig; *(remark)* anzüglich; *(gun)* gerichtet; *(arch, nose)* Spitz–
pointer ['pɔɪntər] *s* *(of a meter)* Zeiger *m;* *(stick)* Zeigestock *m;* *(advice)* Tip *m;* *(hunting dog)* Vorstehhund *m*
pointless ['pɔɪntlɪs] *adj* zwecklos
point' of hon'or *s* Ehrensache *f*
point' of law' *s* Rechtsfrage *f*
point' of view' *s* Gesichtspunkt *m*
poise [pɔɪz] *s* sicheres Auftreten *n* ‖ *tr* im Gleichgewicht halten ‖ *intr* schweben
poison ['pɔɪzən] *s* Gift *n* ‖ *tr* *(& fig)* vergiften
poi'son gas' *s* Giftgas *n*
poi'son i'vy *s* Giftsumach *m*
poisonous ['pɔɪzənəs] *adj* giftig
poke [pok] *s* Stoß *m,* Knuff *m* ‖ *tr* anstoßen, knuffen; *(the fire)* schüren; *(head, nose)* stecken; **p. fun at** sich lustig machen über *(acc);* **p. out** *(an eye)* ausstechen; **p. s.o. in the ribs** j-m e-n Rippenstoß geben ‖ *intr* bummeln; **p. around** herumstochern; *(be slow)* herumbummeln; *(in another's business)* herumstöbern
poker ['pokər] *s* Schürhaken *m;* *(cards)* Poker *n*
pok'er face' *s* Pokergesicht *n*
poky ['poki] *adj* bummelig
Poland ['polənd] *s* Polen *n*
polar ['polər] *adj* Polar–
po'lar bear' *s* Eisbär *m*

polarity [po'lærɪti] *s* Polarität *f*
polarize ['polə‚raɪz] *tr* polarisieren
pole [pol] *s* *(rod)* Stange *f;* *(for telephone lines, flags, etc.)* Mast *m;* *(astr, geog, phys)* Pol *m;* **Pole** Pole *m,* Polin *f* ‖ *tr* *(a raft, boat)* staken
pole'cat' *s* Iltis *m*
polemic(al) [pə'lemɪk(əl)] *adj* polemisch
polemics [pə'lemɪks] *s* Polemik *f*
pole'star' *s* Polarstern *m*
pole'-vault' *intr* stabhochspringen
pole' vault'ing *s* Stabhochsprung *m*
police [pə'lis] *adj* polizeilich ‖ *s* Polizei *f* ‖ *tr* polizeilich überwachen; *(clean up)* *(mil)* säubern
police' es'cort *s* Polozeibedeckung *f*
police'man *s* (**-men**) Polizist *m*
police' of'ficer *s* Polizeibeamte *m,* Polizeibeamtin *f*
police' pre'cinct *s* Polizeirevier *n*
police' state' *s* Polizeistaat *m*
police' sta'tion *s* Polizeiwache *f*
police'wom'an *s* (**-wom'en**) Polizistin *f*
policy ['palɪsi] *s* Politik *f;* *(ins)* Police *f*
polio ['polɪ‚o] *s* Polio *f*
polish ['palɪʃ] *s* *(material; shine)* Politur *f;* *(for shoes)* Schuhcreme *f;* *(fig)* Schliff *m* ‖ *tr* polieren; *(fingernails)* lackieren; *(shoes, silver, etc.)* putzen; *(floors)* bohnern; *(fig)* abschleifen; **p. off** *(eat)* *(sl)* verdrücken; *(an opponent)* *(sl)* erledigen; *(work)* *(sl)* hinhauen ‖ *intr*—**p. up on** aufpolieren ‖ **Polish** ['polɪʃ] *adj* polnisch ‖ *s* Polnisch *n*
polite [pə'laɪt] *adj* höflich
politeness [pə'laɪtnɪs] *s* Höflichkeit *f*
politic ['palɪtɪk] *adj* diplomatisch
political [pə'lɪtɪkəl] *adj* politisch
poli'tical econ'omy *s* Volkswirtschaft *f*
poli'tical sci'ence *s* Staatswissenschaften *pl*
politician [‚palɪ'tɪʃən] *s* Politiker *–in mf*
politics ['palɪtɪks] *s* Politik *f;* **be in p.** sich politisch betätigen; **talk p.** politisieren
polka ['po(l)kə] *s* Polka *f*
pol'ka-dot' *adj* getupft
poll [pol] *s* *(voting)* Abstimmung *f;* *(of public opinion)* Umfrage *f;* **be defeated at the polls** e-e Wahlniederlage erleiden; **go to the polls** zur Wahl gehen; **polls** *(voting place)* Wahllokal *n;* **take a p.** e-e Umfrage halten ‖ *tr* befragen
pollen ['palən] *s* Pollen *m*
poll'ing booth' *s* Wahlzelle *f*
pollster ['polstər] *s* Meinungsforscher *–in mf*
poll' tax' *s* Kopfsteuer *f*
pollute [pə'lut] *tr* verunreinigen
pollution [pə'luʃən] *s* Verunreinigung *f*
polo ['polo] *s* *(sport)* Polo *n*
po'lo shirt' *s* Polohemd *n*
polygamist [pə'lɪgəmɪst] *s* Polygamist *m*
polygamy [pə'lɪgəmi] *s* Polygamie *f*
polyglot ['palɪ‚glat] *s* Polyglott *m*

polygon ['palɪ ˌgan] *s* Vieleck *n*

polyp ['palɪp] *s* Polyp *m*

polytheism [ˌpalɪ'θi ˌɪzəm] *s* Vielgötterei *f*, Polytheismus *m*

polytheistic [ˌpalɪθi'ɪstɪk] *adj* polytheistisch

pomade [pə'med] *s* Pomade *f*

pomegranate ['pɑm ˌgrænɪt] *s* Granatapfel *m*; *(tree)* Granatapfelbaum *m*

Pomerania ['pɑmə'reni·ə] *s* Pommern *n*

pom·mel ['pʌməl] *s (of a sword)* Degenkopf *m*; *(of a saddle)* Sattelknopf *m* ‖ *v (pret & pp* **–mel[l]ed;** *ger* **–el[l]ing)** *tr* mit der Faust schlagen

pomp [pamp] *s* Pomp *m*, Prunk *m*

pompous ['pampəs] *adj* hochtrabend

pon·cho ['pant/o] *s* (**–chos**) Poncho *m*

pond [pand] *s* Teich *m*

ponder ['pandər] *tr* erwägen; *(words)* abwägen ‖ *intr* **(over)** nachsinnen *(über acc)*

ponderous ['pandərəs] *adj* schwerfällig

pontiff ['pantɪf] *s* (eccl) Papst *m*; (hist) Pontifex *m*

pontifical [pan'tɪfɪkəl] *adj* pontifikal

pontoon [pan'tun] *s* Ponton *m*; (aer) Schwimmer *m*

pony ['poni] *s (small horse; hair style)* Pony *n*; *(crib)* Eselbrücke *f*

poodle ['pudəl] *s* Pudel *m*

pool [pul] *s (small pond)* Tümpel *m*; *(of blood)* Lache *f*; *(swimming pool)* Schwimmbecken *n*; *(in betting)* Pool *m*; *(game)* Billiard *n*; *(fin)* Pool *m* ‖ *tr* zusammenlegen

pool′room′ *s* Billardsalon *m*

pool′ ta′ble *s* Billardtisch *m*

poop [pup] *s* Heck *n* ‖ *tr* (sl) erschöpfen; **be pooped (out)** erschöpft sein

poor [pur] *adj* arm; *(e.g., in spelling)* schwach; *(soil, harvest)* schlecht; *(miserable)* armselig; **p. in** arm an *(dat)*

poor′ box′ *s* Opferstock *m*

poor′house′ *s* Armenhaus *n*

poorly ['purli] *adv* schlecht

pop [pap] *s (concert, singer, music)* Pop– ‖ *s* Puff *m*, Knall *m*; *(dad)* Vati *m*; *(soda)* Brauselimonade *f*; *(mus)* Popmusik *f* ‖ *v (pret & pp* **popped;** *ger* **popping)** *tr (corn)* rösten; *(cause to pop)* knallen lassen; **pop the question** (coll) e–n Heiratsantrag machen ‖ *intr (make a popping noise)* knallen; *(said of popcorn)* aufplatzen; **pop in** *(visit unexpectedly)* (coll) hereinplatzen; **pop off** (sl) das Maul aufreißen; **pop up** *(appear)* (coll) auftauchen; *(jump up)* hochfahren

pop′corn′ *s* Puffmais *m*

pope [pop] *s* Papst *m*

pop′eyed′ *adj* glotzäugig

pop′gun′ *s* Knallbüchse *f*

poplar ['paplər] *s* Pappel *f*

poppy ['papi] *s* Mohnblume *f*, Mohn *m*

pop′pycock′ *s* (coll) Quatsch *m*

pop′pyseed′ *s* Mohn *m*

popsicle ['pap ˌsɪkəl] *s* Eis *n* am Stiel

populace ['papjələs] *s* Pöbel *m*

popular ['papjələr] *adj* populär; *(e.g., music, expression)* volkstümlich; **p. with** beliebt bei

popularity [ˌpapjə'lærɪti] *s* Popularität *f*, Beliebtheit *f*

popularize ['papjələ ˌraɪz] *tr* popularisieren

populate ['papjə ˌlet] *tr* bevölkern

population [ˌpapjə'le/ən] *s* Bevölkerung *f*

popula′tion explo′sion *s* Bevölkerungsexplosion *f*

populous ['papjələs] *adj* volkreich

porcelain ['pɔrs(ə)lɪn] *s* Porzellan *n*

porch [pɔrt/] *s* Vorbau *m*, Veranda *f*

porcupine ['pɔrkjə ˌpaɪn] *s* Stachelschwein *n*

pore [por] *s* Pore *f* ‖ *intr*—**p. over** eifrig studieren

pork [pork] *adj* Schweine– ‖ *s* Schweinefleisch *n*

pork′chop′ *s* Schweinekotelett *n*

pornography [pɔr'nagrəfi] *s* Pornographie *f*

porous ['porəs] *adj* porös

porphyry ['pɔrfɪri] *s* Porphyr *m*

porpoise ['pɔrpəs] *s* Tümmler *m*

porridge ['pɔrɪdʒ] *s* Brei *m*

port [port] *s* Hafen *m*; *(wine)* Portwein *m*; *(slit for shooting)* Schießscharte *f*; *(naut)* Backbord *m & n*; **to p.** (naut) backbord

portable ['portəbəl] *adj* tragbar; *(radio, television, typewriter)* Koffer–

portal ['portəl] *s* Portal *n*

portend [pɔr'tend] *tr* vorbedeuten

portent ['portənt] *s* schlimmes Vorzeichen *n*, böses Omen *n*

portentous [pɔr'tentəs] *adj* unheildrohend

porter ['portər] *s (in a hotel)* Hausdiener *m*; *(at a station)* Gepäckträger *m*; *(doorman)* Portier *m*

portfoli·o [port'foli ˌo] *s* (**–os**) Aktenmappe *f*; (fin) Portefeuille *f*; **without p.** ohne Geschäftsbereich

port′hole′ *s (for shooting)* Schießscharte *f*; (naut) Bullauge *n*

porti·co ['portɪ ˌko] *s* (**–coes &** **–cos**) Säulenvorbau *m*, Portikus *m*

portion ['por/ən] *s* Anteil *m*; *(serving)* Portion *f*; *(dowry)* Heiratsgut *n* ‖ *tr* **–p. out** austeilen, einteilen

portly ['portli] *adj* wohlbeleibt

port′ of call′ *s* Anlaufhafen *m*

port′ of en′try *s* Einfuhrhafen *m*

portrait ['portret] *s* Porträt *n*

portray [pɔr'tre] *tr* porträtieren; (fig) beschreiben; (theat) darstellen

portrayal [pɔr'tre·əl] *s* Porträtieren *n*; (fig) Beschreibung *f*; (theat) Darstellung *f*

port′side′ *s* Backbord *m & n*

Portugal ['port/əgəl] *s* Portugal *n*

Portuguese ['port/ə ˌgiz] *adj* portugiesisch ‖ *s* Portugiese *m*, Portugiesin *f*; *(language)* Portugiesisch *n*

port′ wine′ *s* Portwein *m*

pose [poz] *s* Haltung *f*, Pose *f* ‖ *tr (a question, problem)* stellen ‖ *intr* posieren; **p. as** sich ausgeben als; **p. for an artist** e–m Künstler Modell stehen; **p. for a picture** sich e-m Photographen stellen

posh [paʃ] *adj* (sl) großartig

position [pəˈziʃən] *s* Stellung *f*; (*situation, condition*) Lage *f*; (*job; place of defense*) Stellung *f*; (*point of view*) Standpunkt *m*; (aer, naut) Standort *m*; (astr, mil, naut) Position *f*; **be in a p. to** (*inf*) in der Lage sein zu (*inf*); **in p.** am rechten Platz; **p. wanted** (*as in an ad*) Stelle gesucht; **take a p. on** Stellung nehmen zu; **take one's p.** sich aufstellen

positive [ˈpazɪtɪv] *adj* (*reply, result, attitude*) positiv; (*answer*) zustimmend; (*sure*) sicher; (*offer*) fest; (elec, math, med, phot, phys) positiv ‖ *s* (gram) Positiv *m*; (phot) Positiv *n*

posse [ˈpasɪ] *s* Polizeiaufgebot *n*

possess [pəˈzes] *tr* besitzen; **be possessed by the devil** von dem Teufel besessen sein

possession [pəˈzeʃən] *s* Besitz *m*; (*property*) Eigentum *n*; **be in p. of s.th.** etw besitzen; **take p. of s.th.** etw in Besitz nehmen

possessive [pəˈzesɪv] *adj* eifersüchtig; (gram) besitzanzeigend, Besitz-

possibility [ˌpasɪˈbrlɪti] *s* Möglichkeit *f*

possible [ˈpasɪbəl] *adj* möglich; **make p.** ermöglichen

possibly [ˈpasɪbli] *adv* möglicherweise

possum [ˈpasəm] *s* Opossum *n*; **play p.** sich verstellen; (*play dead*) sich tot stellen

post [post] *s* (*pole*) Pfahl *m*; (*job; of a sentry*) Posten *m*; (*military camp*) Standort *m* ‖ *tr* (*a notice*) anschlagen; (*a guard*) aufstellen; **p. bond** Kaution stellen; **p. no bills** Plakatankleben verboten

postage [ˈpostɪdʒ] *s* Porto *n*

post′age due′ *s* Nachporto *n*

post′age stamp′ *s* Briefmarke *f*

postal [ˈpostəl] *adj* Post-

post′al mon′ey or′der *s* Postanweisung *f*

post′card′ *s* Ansichtskarte *f*

post′date′ *tr* nachdatieren

post′ed *adj*—**keep s.o. p.** j-n auf dem laufenden halten

poster [ˈpostər] *s* Plakat *n*

posterity [pasˈterɪti] *s* Nachkommenschaft *f*, Nachwelt *f*

postern [ˈpostərn] *s* Hintertür *f*

post′ exchange′ *s* Marketenderei *f*

post′haste′ *adv* schnellstens

posthumous [ˈpastʃuməs] *adj* posthum

post′man *s* (-men) Briefträger *m*

post′mark′ *s* Poststempel *m* ‖ *tr* abstempeln

post′mas′ter *s* Postmeister *m*

post′master gen′eral *s* Postminister *m*

post-mortem [ˌpostˈmortəm] *s* Obduktion *f*

post′ of′fice *s* Post *f*, Postamt *n*

post′-office box′ *s* Postschließfach *n*

post′paid′ *adv* frankiert

postpone [postˈpon] *tr* (**till, to**) aufschieben (auf *acc*)

postponement [postˈponmənt] *s* Aufschub *m*

post′script′ *s* Nachschrift *f*

posture [ˈpastʃər] *s* Haltung *f*

post′war′ *adj* Nachkriegs-

posy [ˈpozi] *s* Sträußchen *n*

pot [pat] *s* Topf *m*; (*for coffee, tea*) Kanne *f*; (*in gambling*) Einsatz *m*; **go to pot** (sl) hops gehen; **pots and pans** Kochgeschirr *n*

potash [ˈpatˌæʃ] *s* Pottasche *f*, Kali *n*

potassium [pəˈtæsɪəm] *s* Kalium *n*

pota·to [pəˈteto] *s* (-toes) Kartoffel *f*

pota′to chips′ *spl* Kartoffelchips *pl*

potbellied [ˈpatˌbelɪd] *adj* dickbäuchig

pot′bel′ly *s* Spitzbauch *m*

potency [ˈpotənsi] *s* Stärke *f*; (physiol) Potenz *f*

potent [ˈpotənt] *adj* (*powerful*) mächtig; (*persuasive*) überzeugend; (*e.g., drugs*) wirksam; (physiol) potent

potentate [ˈpotənˌtet] *s* Potentat *m*

potential [pəˈtenʃəl] *adj* möglich; (phys) potentiell ‖ *s* (& elec, math, phys) Potential *n*

pot′hold′er *s* Topflappen *m*

pot′hole′ *s* Schlagloch *n*

potion [ˈpoʃən] *s* Trank *m*

pot′luck′ *s*—**take p.** mit dem vorliebnehmen, was es gerade gibt

pot′ roast′ *s* Schmorbraten *m*

pot′sherd′ *s* Topfscherbe *f*

pot′ shot′ *s* müheloser Schuß *m*; **take a p. at** unfair bekritteln

pot′ted *adj* Topf-

potter [ˈpatər] *s* Töpfer *m*

pot′ter's clay′ *s* Töpferton *m*

pot′ter's wheel′ *s* Töpferscheibe *f*

pottery [ˈpatəri] *s* Tonwaren *pl*

potty [ˈpati] *s* (coll) Töpfchen *n*

pouch [pautʃ] *s* Beutel *m*

poultice [ˈpoltɪs] *s* Breiumschlag *m*

poultry [ˈpoltri] *s* Geflügel *n*

poul′try-man *s* (-men) Geflügelzüchter *m*; (*dealer*) Geflügelhändler *m*

pounce [pauns] *intr*—**p. on** sich stürzen auf (*acc*)

pound [paund] *s* Pfund *n*; (*for animals*) Pferch *m* ‖ *tr* (zer)stampfen; (*meat*) klopfen; **p. the sidewalks** Pflaster treten ‖ *intr* (*said of the heart*) klopfen; **p. on** (*e.g., a door*) hämmern an (*acc*)

-pound *suf* -pfündig

pound′ ster′ling *s* Pfund *n* Sterling

pour [por] *tr* gießen; (*e.g., coffee*) einschenken; **p. away** wegschütten ‖ *intr* (meteor) gießen; **p. out of** (*e.g., a theater*) strömen aus ‖ *impers*—**it's pouring** es gießt

pout [paut] *s* Schmollen *n* ‖ *intr* schmollen

pout′ing *adj* (*lips*) aufgeworfen ‖ *s* Schmollen *n*

poverty [ˈpavərti] *s* Armut *f*

pov′erty-strick′en *adj* verarmt

POW [ˈpiˈoˈdʌblju] *s* (**prisoner of war**) Kriegsgefangener *m*

powder [ˈpaudər] *s* Pulver *n*; (*cosmetic*) Puder *m* ‖ *tr* (*e.g., the face*) pudern; (*plants*) stäuben; (*a cake*) bestreuen ‖ *intr* zu Pulver werden

pow'der box' s Puderdose f
pow'dered milk' s Milchpulver n
pow'dered sug'ar s Staubzucker m
pow'der keg' s Pulverfaß n
pow'der puff' s Puderquaste f
pow'der room' s Damentoilette f
powdery ['paudəri] adj pulverig
power ['pau-ər] s Macht f; (personal control) Gewalt f; (electricity) Strom m; (math) Potenz f; (opt) Vergrößerungskraft f; (phys) Leistung f; (pol) Macht f; be in p. an der Macht sein; be in s.o.'s p. in j-s Gewalt sein; be within s.o.'s p. in j-s Macht liegen; come to p. an die Macht gelangen; have the p. to (inf) vermögen zu (inf); more p. to you! viel Erfolg!; the powers that be die Obrigkeit f || tr antreiben
pow'er brake' s (aut) Servobremse f
pow'er dive' s (aer) Vollgassturzflug m
pow'er drill' s Elektrobohrer m
pow'er-driv'en adj mit Motorantrieb
pow'er fail'ure s Stromausfall m
powerful ['pau-ərfəl] adj mächtig; (opt) stark
pow'erhouse' s Kraftwerk n; (coll) Kraftprotz m
pow'erhun'gry adj herrschsüchtig
powerless ['pau-ərlıs] adj machtlos
pow'er line' s Starkstromleitung f
pow'er mow'er s Motorrasenmäher m
pow'er of attor'ney s Vollmacht f
pow'er plant' s (powerhouse) Kraftwerk n; (aer, aut) Triebwerk n
pow'er shov'el s Löffelbagger m
pow'er sta'tion s Kraftwerk n
pow'er steer'ing s Servolenkung f
pow'er supply' s Stromversorgung f
practicable ['præktıkəbəl] adj praktikabel, durchführbar
practical ['præktıkəl] adj praktisch
prac'tical joke' s Streich m
practically ['præktıkəli] adv praktisch; (almost) fast, so gut wie
prac'tical nurse' s praktisch ausgebildete Krankenschwester f
practice ['præktıs] s (exercise) Übung f; (habit) Gewohnheit f; (of medicine, law) Praxis f; in p. (in training) in der Übung; (in reality) in der Praxis; make it a p. to (inf) es sich [dat] zur Gewohnheit machen zu (inf); out of p. aus der Übung || tr (a profession) tätig sein als; (patience, reading, dancing, etc.) sich üben in (dat); (music, gymnastics) treiben; (piano, etc.) üben || intr üben; (said of a doctor) praktizieren; p. on (e.g., the violin, piano, parallel bars) üben auf (dat)
prac'tice game' s Übungsspiel n
prac'tice teach'er s Studienreferendar –in mf
practitioner [præk'tıʃənər] s Praktiker –in mf
pragmatic [præg'mætık] adj pragmatisch
pragmatism ['prægmə‚tızəm] s Sachlichkeit f; (philos) Pragmatismus m
Prague [prog] s Prag n
prairie ['preri] s Steppe f, Prärie f

praise [prez] s Lob n || tr (for) loben (wegen); **p. to the skies** verhimmeln
praise'wor'thy adj lobenswert
prance [præns] intr tänzeln
prank [prænk] s Schelmenstreich m
prate [pret] intr schwätzen
prattle ['prætəl] s Geplapper n || intr plappern, schwätzen
prawn [prɔn] s Garnele f
pray [pre] tr & intr beten
prayer [prer] s Gebet n; **say a p.** ein Gebet sprechen
prayer' book' s Gebetbuch n
preach [pritʃ] tr & intr predigen
preacher ['pritʃər] s Prediger –in
preamble ['pri‚æmbəl] s Präambel f
precarious [prı'keri-əs] adj prekär
precaution [prı'kɔʃən] s Vorsichtsmaßnahme f; **as a p.** vorsichtshalber; **take precautions** Vorkehrungen treffen
precede [prı'sid] tr vorausgehen (dat) || intr vorangehen
precedence ['presıdəns] s Vorrang m; **take p. over** den Vorrang haben vor (dat)
precedent ['presıdənt] s Präzedenzfall m; **set a p.** e-n Präzedenzfall schaffen
preced'ing adj vorhergehend
precept ['prisept] s Vorschrift f
precinct ['prisınkt] s Bezirk m
precious ['preʃəs] adj (expensive) kostbar; (valuable) wertvoll; (excessively refined) geziert; (child) lieb || adv **p. few** (coll) herzlich wenige
pre'cious stone' s Edelstein m
precipice ['presıpıs] s Abgrund m
precipitate [prı'sıpı‚tet] adj steil abfallend || s (chem) Niederschlag m || tr (hurl) (into) stürzen (in acc); (bring about) heraufbeschwören; (vapor) (chem) niederschlagen; (from a solution) (chem) ausfällen || intr (chem, meteor) sich niederschlagen
precipitation [prı‚sıpı'teʃən] s (meteor) Niederschlag m
precipitous [prı'sıpıtəs] adj jäh
precise [prı'saıs] adj präzis, genau
precision [prı'sıʒən] s Präzision f
preclude [prı'klud] tr ausschließen
precocious [prı'koʃəs] adj frühreif
preconceived [‚prikən'sivd] adj vorgefaßt
predatory ['predə‚tori] adj Raub-
predecessor ['predı‚sesər] s Vorgänger –in mf
predestination [‚prıdestı'neʃən] s Prädestination f
predicament [prı'dıkəmənt] s Mißliche Lage f
predicate ['predıkıt] s (gram) Aussage f, Prädikat n || ['predı‚ket] tr (of) aussagen (über acc); (base) (on) gründen (auf acc)
predict [prı'dıkt] tr voraussagen
prediction [prı'dıkʃən] s Voraussage f
predispose [‚prıdıs'poz] tr (to) im voraus geneigt machen (zu); (pathol) empfänglich machen (für)
predominant [prı'dɑmınənt] adj vorwiegend

preeminent [prɪ'emɪnənt] adj hervorragend

preempt [prɪ'empt] tr (a program) ersetzen; (land) durch Vorkaufsrecht erwerben

preen [prin] tr putzen

prefabricated [pri'fæbrɪ‚ketɪd] adj Fertig-

preface ['prefɪs] s Vorwort n, Vorrede f || tr einleiten

prefer [prɪ'fʌr] v (pret & pp -ferred; ger -ferring) tr bevorzugen; (charges) vorbringen; **I p. to wait** ich warte lieber

preferable ['prefərəbəl] adj (to) vorzuziehen(d) (dat)

preferably ['prefərəbli] adv vorzugsweise

preferred' stock' s Vorzugsaktie f

prefix ['prifɪks] s Vorsilbe f, Präfix n || tr vorsetzen

pregnancy ['pregnənsi] s Schwangerschaft f; (of animals) Trächtigkeit f

pregnant ['pregnənt] adj schwanger; (animals) trächtig; (fig) inhaltsschwer

prehistoric [‚prihɪs'torɪk] adj vorgeschichtlich, prähistorisch

prejudice ['predʒədɪs] s Voreingenommenheit f; (detriment) Schaden m || tr beeinträchtigen; **p. s.o. against** j-n einnehmen gegen

pre'judiced adj voreingenommen

prejudicial [‚predʒə'dɪʃəl] adj (to) schädlich (für)

prelate ['prelɪt] s Prälat m

preliminary [prɪ'lɪmɪ‚neri] adj einleitend, Vor-- || s Vorbereitung f

prelude ['prel(j)ud] s (fig, mus, theat) Vorspiel n

premarital [pri'mærɪtəl] adj vorehelich

premature [‚primə't(j)ur] adj verfrüht; **p. birth** Frühgeburt f

premeditated [pri'medɪ‚tetɪd] adj vorbedacht; (murder) vorsätzlich

premier [prɪ'mɪr] s Premier m

premiere [prɪ'mɪr] s Erstaufführung f

premise ['premɪs] s Voraussetzung f; **on the premises** an Ort und Stelle; **the premises** das Lokal

premium ['primɪ‚əm] s Prämie f; **at a p.** (in demand) sehr gesucht; (at a high price) über pari

premonition [‚primə'nɪʃən] s Vorahnung f

preoccupation [pri‚ɑkjə'peʃən] s (with) Beschäftigtsein n (mit)

preoccupied [pri'ɑkjə‚paɪd] adj ausschließlich beschäftigt

preparation [‚prepə'reʃən] s Vorbereitung f; (med) Präparat n

preparatory [prɪ'pærə‚tori] adj vorbereitend; **p. to** vor (dat)

prepare [prɪ'per] tr vorbereiten; (a meal) zubereiten; (a prescription) anfertigen; (a document) abfassen

preparedness [prɪ'perɪdnɪs] s Bereitschaft f; (mil) Einsatzbereitschaft f

pre·pay [pri'pe] v (pret & pp -paid) tr im voraus bezahlen

preponderant [prɪ'pɑndərənt] adj überwiegend

preposition [‚prepə'zɪʃən] s Präposition f, Verhältniswort n

prepossessing [‚pripə'zesɪŋ] adj einnehmend

preposterous [prɪ'pɑstərəs] adj lächerlich

prep' school' [prep] s Vorbereitungsschule f

prerecorded [‚priri'kordɪd] adj vorher aufgenommen

prerequisite [pri'rekwɪzɪt] s Voraussetzung f, Vorbedingung f

prerogative [prɪ'rɑgətɪv] s Vorrecht n

presage ['presɪdʒ] s Vorzeichen n || [prɪ'sedʒ] tr ein Vorzeichen sein für

Presbyterian [‚prezbɪ'tɪrɪ‚ən] adj presbyterianisch || s Presbyterianer -in mf

prescribe [prɪ'skraɪb] tr vorschreiben; (med) verordnen

prescription [prɪ'skrɪpʃən] s Vorschrift f; (med) Rezept n, Verordnung f

presence ['prezəns] s Anwesenheit f

pres'ence of mind' s Geistesgegenwart f

present ['prezənt] adj (at this place) anwesend; (of the moment) gegenwärtig || s (gift) Geschenk n; (present time or tense) Gegenwart f; **at p.** zur Zeit; **for the p.** vorläufig || [prɪ'zent] tr bieten; (facts) darstellen; (introduce) vorstellen; (theat) vorführen; **p. s.o. with s.th.** j-m etw verehren

presentable [prɪ'zentəbəl] adj presentabel

presentation [‚prezən'teʃən] s Vorstellung f; (theat) Aufführung f

pres'ent-day' adj heutig, aktuell

presentiment [prɪ'zentɪmənt] s Ahnung f

presently ['prezəntli] adv gegenwärtig; (soon) alsbald

preservation [‚prezər've ʃən] s Erhaltung f; (from) Bewahrung f (vor dat)

preservative [prɪ'zʌrvətɪv] s Konservierungsmittel n

preserve [prɪ'zʌrv] s Revier n; **preserves** Konserven pl || tr konservieren; **p. from** schützen vor (dat)

preside [prɪ'zaɪd] intr (over) den Vorsitz führen (über acc or bei)

presidency ['prezɪdənsi] s Präsidentschaft f

president ['prezɪdənt] s Präsident -in mf; (of a university) Rektor -in mf; (of a board) Vorsitzende mf

presidential [‚prezɪ'dentʃəl] adj Präsidenten-

press [pres] adj (agency, agent, conference, gallery, report, secretary) Presse- || s (wine press; printing press; newspapers) Presse f; **go to p.** in Druck gehen || tr drucken; (a suit) (auf)bügeln; (a person) bedrängen; (fruit) ausdrücken; **be pressed for** knapp sein an (dat); **p. s.o. to** (inf) j-n dringend bitten zu (inf); **p. the button** auf den Knopf drücken || intr (said of time) drängen; **p. for** drängen auf (acc); **p. forward** sich vorwärtsdrängen

press′ box′ s Pressekabine f

press′ card′ s Presseausweis m

press′ing adj dringend, dringlich

press′ release′ s Pressemitteilung f

pressure [′preʃər] s Druck m; (of work) Andrang m; (aut) Reifendruck m; **put p. on** unter Druck setzen ‖ tr drängen

pres′sure cook′er s Schnellkochtopf m

pres′sure group′ s Interessengruppe f

pressurize [′preʃə‚raɪz] tr druckfest machen

prestige [pres′tiʒ] s Prestige n

presumably [prɪ′z(j)uməbli] adv vermutlich

presume [prɪ′z(j)um] tr vermuten ‖ intr vermuten; **p. on** pochen auf (acc)

presumption [prɪ′zʌmpʃən] s Vermutung f; (presumptuousness) Anmaßung f

presumptuous [prɪ′zʌmptʃʊ‑əs] adj anmaßend

presuppose [‚prisə′poz] tr voraussetzen

pretend [prɪ′tend] tr vorgeben; **he pretended that he was a captain** er gab sich für e‑n Hauptmann aus ‖ intr so tun, als ob

pretender [prɪ′tendər] s Quaksalber m; **p. to the throne** Thronbewerber m

pretense [prɪ′tens], [′pritəns] s Schein m; **under false pretenses** unter Vorspiegelung falscher Tatsachen; **under the p. of** unter dem Vorwand (genit)

pretentious [prɪ′tenʃəs] adj (person) anmaßend; (home) protzig

pretext [′pritekst] s Vorwand m

pretty [′priti] adj hübsch ‖ adv (coll) ziemlich

pretzel [′pretsəl] s Brezel f

prevail [prɪ′vel] intr (predominate) (vor)herrschen; (triumph) (against) sich behaupten (gegen); **p. on** überreden

prevail′ing adj (fashion, view) (vor)herrschend; (situation) obwaltend

prevalence [′prevələns] s Vorherrschen n

prevalent [′prevələnt] adj vorherrschend; **be p.** herrschen

prevaricate [prɪ′værɪ‚ket] intr Ausflüchte machen

prevent [prɪ′vent] tr verhindern; (war, danger) abwenden; **p. s.o. from** j‑n hindern an (dat); **p. s.o. from** (ger) j‑n daran hindern zu (inf)

prevention [prɪ′venʃən] s Verhütung f

preventive [prɪ′ventɪv] adj vorbeugend ‖ s Schutzmittel n

preview [′pri‚vju] s Vorschau f

previous [′privi‑əs] adj vorhergehend, vorig; Vor‑, e.g., **p. conviction** Vorstrafe f; **p. day** Vortag m; **p. record** Vorstrafenregister n

previously [′privi‑əsli] adv vorher

prewar [′pri‚wɔr] adj Vorkriegs‑

prey [pre] s Beute f, Raub m; (fig) Opfer n; **fall p. to** (& fig) zum Opfer fallen (dat) ‖ intr—**p. on** erbeuten; (exploit) ausbeuten; **p. on s.o.'s mind** an j‑s Gewissen nagen

price [praɪs] s Preis m; (st. exch.) Kurs m; **at any p.** um jeden Preis; **at the p. of** im Wert von ‖ tr mit Preisen versehen; (inquire about the price of) nach dem Preis fragen (genit)

price′ control′ s Preiskontrolle f

price′ fix′ing s Preisbindung f

price′ freeze′ s Preisstopp m

priceless [′praɪsləs] adj unbezahlbar; (coll) sehr komisch

price′ range′ s Preislage f

price′ rig′ging s Preistreiberei f

price′ tag′ s Preiszettel m, Preisschild n

price′-wage′ spi′ral s Preis-Lohn-Spirale f

price′ war′ s Preiskrieg m

prick [prɪk] s (& fig) Stich m ‖ tr stechen; **p. up** (ears) spitzen

prickly [′prɪkli] adj stachelig, Stech‑

prick′ly heat′ s Hitzepickel pl

pride [praɪd] s Stolz m; (pej) Hochmut m; **swallow one's p.** seinen Stolz in die Tasche stecken; **take p. in** stolz sein auf (acc) ‖ tr—**p. oneself on** sich viel einbilden auf (acc)

priest [prist] s Priester m

priestess [′pristɪs] s Priesterin f

priest′hood′ s Priestertum n

priestly [′pristli] adj priesterlich

prig [prɪg] s Tugendbold m

prim [prɪm] adj (primmer; primmest) spröde

primacy [′praɪməsi] s Primat m & n

primarily [praɪ′merɪli] adv vor allem

primary [′praɪ‚meri] adj primär, Haupt‑; (e.g., color, school) Grund‑ ‖ s (pol) Vorwahl f

primate [′praɪmet] s (zool) Primat m

prime [praɪm] adj (chief) Haupt‑; (best) erstklassig ‖ s Blüte f; (math) Primzahl f; **p. of life** Lenz m des Lebens ‖ tr (a pump) ansaugen lassen; (ammunition) scharfmachen; (a surface for painting) grundieren; (with information) vorher informieren

prime′ min′ister s Ministerpräsident m; (in England) Premierminister m

primer [′praɪmər] s Fibel f ‖ [′praɪmər] s (for painting) Grundierfarbe f; (of an explosive) Zündsatz m; (aut) Einspritzpumpe f

prime′ time′ s schönste Zeit f

primeval [praɪ′mivəl] adj urweltlich, Ur‑; **p. world** Urwelt f

primitive [′prɪmɪtɪv] adj primitiv ‖ s Primitive mf, Urmensch m

primp [prɪmp] tr aufputzen ‖ intr sich aufputzen, sich zieren

prim′rose′ s Himmelsschlüssel m

prince [prɪns] s Prinz m, Fürst m

Prince′ Al′bert s Gehrock m

princely [′prɪnsli] adj prinzlich

princess [′prɪnsɪs] s Prinzessin f, Fürstin f

principal [′prɪnsəpəl] adj Haupt‑ ‖ s (educ) Schuldirektor –in mf; (fin) Kapitalbetrag m, Kapital n

principality [‚prɪnsɪ′pælɪti] s Fürstentum n

principally [ˈprɪnsɪpəlɪ] *adv* größtenteils

principle [ˈprɪnsɪpəl] *s* Grundsatz *m*, Prinzip *n*; **in p.** im Prinzip

print [prɪnt] *s* (*lettering; design on cloth*) Druck *m*; (*printed dress*) bedrucktes Kleid *n*; (*phot*) Abzug *m*; **in cold p.** schwarz auf weiß; **out of p.** vergriffen ‖ *tr* drucken; (*e.g., one's name*) in Druckschrift schreiben; (*phot*) kopieren; (*tex*) bedrucken

print′ed mat′ter *s* Drucksache *f*

printer [ˈprɪntər] *s* Drucker *m*; (*phot*) Kopiermaschine *f*

prin′ter's ink′ *s* Druckerschwärze *f*

print′ing *s* Drucken *n*; (*of a book*) Buchdruck *m*; (*subsequent printing*) Abdruck *m*; (*phot*) Kopieren *n*, Abziehen *n*

print′ing press′ *s* Druckerpresse *f*

print′ shop′ *s* Druckerei *f*

prior [ˈpraɪ·ər] *adj* vorherig; **p. to** vor (*dat*) ‖ *s* (eccl) Prior *m*

priority [praɪˈɒrɪtɪ] *s* Priorität *f*

prism [ˈprɪzəm] *s* Prisma *n*

prison [ˈprɪzən] *s* Gefängnis *n*

pris′on camp′ *s* Gefangenenlager *n*

prisoner [ˈprɪz(ə)nər] *s* Gefangene *mf*; (*in a concentration camp*) Häftling *m*; **be taken p.** in Gefangenschaft geraten; **take p.** gefangennehmen

pris′oner of war′ *s* Kriegsgefangene *mf*

prissy [ˈprɪsɪ] *adj* zimperlich

privacy [ˈpraɪvəsɪ] *s* Zurückgezogenheit *f*; **disturb s.o.'s p.** j-s Ruhe stören

private [ˈpraɪvɪt] *adj* privat; (*personal*) persönlich; **keep p.** geheimhalten ‖ *s* (mil) Gemeine *mf*; **in p.** privat(im); **privates** Geschlechtsteile *pl*

pri′vate cit′izen *s* Privatperson *f*

pri′vate eye′ *s* (coll) Privatdetektiv *m*

pri′vate first′ class′ *s* Gefreite *mf*

privately [ˈpraɪvɪtlɪ] *adv* privat(im)

privet [ˈprɪvɪt] *s* Liguster *m*

privilege [ˈprɪvɪlɪdʒ] *s* Privileg *n*

privy [ˈprɪvɪ] *adj*—**p. to** eingeweiht in (*acc*) ‖ *s* Abtritt *m*

prize [praɪz] *s* Preis *m*, Prämie *f*; (*nav*) Prise *f* ‖ *tr* schätzen

prize′ fight′ *s* Preisboxkampf *m*

prize′ fight′er *s* Berufsboxer *m*

prize′ ring′ *s* Boxring *m*

pro [pro] *s* (**pros**) (coll) Profi *m*; **the pros and the cons** das Für und Wider ‖ *prep* für (*acc*)

probability [ˌprɒbəˈbɪlɪtɪ] *s* Wahrscheinlichkeit *f*; **in all p.** aller Wahrscheinlichkeit nach

probable [ˈprɒbəbəl] *adj* wahrscheinlich

probate [ˈprobet] *s* Testamentsbestätigung *f* ‖ *tr* bestätigen

pro′bate court′ *s* Nachlaßgericht *n*

probation [proˈbeʃən] *s* Probe *f*; (*jur*) Bewährungsfrist *f*; **on p.** auf Probe; (*jur*) mit Bewährung

proba′tion of′ficer *s* Bewährungshelfer –in *m*

probe [prob] *s* (jur) Untersuchung *f*;

(mil) Sondierungsangriff *m*; (rok) Versuchsrakete *f*; (surg) Sonde *f* ‖ *tr* (*with the hands*) abtasten; (fig & surg) sondieren

problem [ˈprɒbləm] *s* Problem *n*; (math) Aufgabe *f*

prob′lem child′ *s* Sorgenkind *n*

procedure [proˈsidʒər] *s* Verfahren *n*

proceed [proˈsid] *intr* (*go on*) fortfahren; (*act*) verfahren; **p. against** (jur) vorgehen gegen; **p. from** kommen von; **p. to** (*inf*) darangehen zu (*inf*)

proceed′ing *s* Vorgehen *n*; **proceedings** (*of a society*) Sitzungsberichte *pl*; (jur) Verfahren *n*

proceeds [ˈprosidz] *spl* Erlös *n*

process [ˈprɒsɛs] *s* Verfahren *n*, Prozeß *m*; **be in p.** im Gang sein; **in the p.** dabei ‖ *tr* (*raw materials*) verarbeiten; (*applications*) bearbeiten; (*persons*) abfertigen; (phot) entwickeln und vervielfältigen

procession [proˈsɛʃən] *s* Prozession *f*

proclaim [proˈklem] *tr* ankündigen; (*a law*) bekanntmachen; **p. (as) a holiday** zum Feiertag erklären

proclamation [ˌprɒkləˈmeʃən] *s* Aufruf *m*, Proklamation *f*

procrastinate [proˈkræstɪˌnet] *intr* zaudern

proctor [ˈprɒktər] *s* Aufsichtsführende *mf* ‖ *tr* beaufsichtigen

procure [proˈkjur] *tr* besorgen, verschaffen; (*said of a pimp*) verkuppeln

procurement [proˈkjurmənt] *s* Besorgung *f*

procurer [proˈkjurər] *s* Kuppler *m*

prod [prɒd] *s* Stoß *m*; (*stick*) Stachelstock *m* ‖ *v* (*pret & pp* **prodded**; *ger* **prodding**) *tr* stoßen; **prod s.o. into** (*ger*) j-n dazu anstacheln zu (*inf*)

prodigal [ˈprɒdɪgəl] *adj* verschwenderisch

prod′igal son′ *s* verlorener Sohn *m*

prodigious [proˈdɪdʒəs] *adj* großartig

prodigy [ˈprɒdɪdʒɪ] *s* Wunderzeichen *n*; (*talented child*) Wunderkind *n*

produce [ˈprɒd(j)us] *s* (*product*) Erzeugnis *n*; (*amount produced*) Ertrag *m*; (*fruits and vegetables*) Bodenprodukte *pl* ‖ [proˈd(j)us] *tr* produzieren; (*manufacture*) herstellen; (*said of plants, trees*) hervorbringen; (*interest, profit*) abwerfen; (*proof*) beibringen; (*papers*) vorlegen; (cin) produzieren; (theat) inszenieren ‖ *intr* (bot) tragen; (econ) Gewinne abwerfen

pro′duce depart′ment *s* Obst– und Gemüseabteilung *f*

producer [proˈd(j)usər] *s* Hersteller *m*; (cin, theat) Produzent –in *mf*

product [ˈprɒdʌkt] *s* Erzeugnis *n*, Produkt *n*

production [proˈdʌkʃən] *s* Erzeugung *f*, Produktion *f*; (fa, lit) Werk *n*

productive [proˈdʌktɪv] *adj* produktiv

profane [proˈfen] *adj* profan; **p. language** Fluchen *n* ‖ *tr* profanieren

profanity [proˈfænɪtɪ] *s* Fluchen *n*; **profanities** Flüche *pl*

profess [prə'fes] *tr* gestehen

profession [prə'feʃən] *s* Beruf *m*; *(of faith)* Bekenntnis *n*; **by p.** von Beruf

professional [prə'feʃənəl] *adj* berufsmäßig, professionell ‖ *s (expert)* Fachmann *m*; *(sport)* Profi *m*

profes'sional jea'lousy *s* Brotneid *m*

professor [prə'fesər] *s* Professor –in *mf*

profes'sorship' *s* Professur *f*

proffer ['prafər] *s* Angebot *n* ‖ *tr* anbieten

proficient [prə'fɪʃənt] *adj* tüchtig

profile ['profaɪl] *s* Profil *n*; *(biographical sketch)* Kurzbiographie *f*

profit ['prafɪt] *s* Gewinn *m*; **show a p.** e–n Gewinn abwerfen ‖ *tr* nutzen ‖ *intr (by)* Nutzen ziehen aus

profitable ['prafɪtəbəl] *adj* einträglich

profiteer [,prafɪ'tɪr] *s* Wucherer *m*, Schieber *m* ‖ *intr* wuchern, schieben

prof'it shar'ing *s* Gewinnbeteiligung *f*

profligate ['praflɪgɪt] *adj* verkommen; *(extravagant)* verschwenderisch ‖ *s* verkommener Mensch *m*; *(spendthrift)* Verschwender –in *mf*

profound [prə'faund] *adj (knowledge)* gründlich; *(change)* tiefgreifend

profuse [prə'fjus] *adj* überreichlich

progeny ['pradʒəni] *s (& bot)* Nachkommenschaft *f*; *(of animals)* Junge *pl*

progno·sis [prag'nosɪs] *s (–ses* [siz]) Prognose *f*

prognosticate [prag'nastɪ,ket] *tr* voraussagen

pro·gram ['program] *s* Programm *n*; *(radio or television show)* Sendung *f* ‖ *v (pret & pp* –grammed; *ger* –gramming) *tr* programmieren

progress ['pragres] *s* Fortschritt *m*; **be in progress** im Gang sein ‖ [prə'gres] *intr (make progress)* fortschreiten; *(develop)* sich fortentwickeln

progressive [prə'gresɪv] *adj* fortschrittlich; *(party)* Fortschritts– ‖ *s* Fortschrittler –in *mf*

prog'ress report' *s* Tätigkeitsbericht *m*

prohibit [pro'hɪbɪt] *tr* verbieten

prohibition [,pro·ə'bɪʃən] *s* Verbot *n*; *(hist)* Prohibition *f*

prohibitive [pro'hɪbɪtɪv] *adj (costs)* unertragbar; *(prices)* unerschwinglich

project ['pradʒekt] *s* Project *n*, Vorhaben *n* ‖ [prə'dʒekt] *tr (light, film)* projizieren; *(plan)* vorhaben ‖ *intr* vorspringen, vorragen

projectile [prə'dʒektɪl] *s (fired from a gun)* Projektil *n*; *(thrown object)* Wurfgeschoß *n*

projection [prə'dʒekʃən] *s (jutting out)* Vorsprung *m*, Vorbau *m*; *(cin)* Projektion *f*

projector [prə'dʒektər] *s* Projektor *m*

proletarian [,prolɪ'terɪ·ən] *adj* proletarisch ‖ *s* Proletarier –in *mf*

proletariat [,prolɪ'terɪ·ət] *s* Proletariat *n*

proliferate [prə'lɪfə,ret] *intr* sich stark vermehren

prolific [prə'lɪfɪk] *adj* fruchtbar

prolix [pro'lɪks] *adj* weitschweifig

prologue ['prolɔg] *s* Prolog *m*

prolong [pro'lɔŋ] *tr* verlängern

promenade [,pramɪ'ned] *s* Promenade *f* ‖ *intr* promenieren

promenade' deck' *s* Promenadendeck *n*

prominent ['pramɪnənt] *adj* hervorragend, prominent; *(chin)* vorstehend

promiscuity [,pramɪs'kju·ɪti] *s* Promiskuität *f*

promiscuous [pro'mɪskju·əs] *adj* unterschiedslos; *(sexually)* locker

promise ['pramɪs] *s* Versprechen *n* ‖ *tr* versprechen

prom'ising *adj (thing)* aussichtsreich; *(person)* vielversprechend

prom'issory note' *s* [,pramɪ,sori] *s* Eigenwechsel *m*

promontory ['pramən,tori] *s* Landspitze *f*

promote [prə'mot] *tr (in rank)* befördern; *(a cause)* fördern; *(a pupil)* versetzen; *(wares)* werben für

promoter [prə'motər] *s* Förderer –in *mf*; *(sport)* Veranstalter –in *mf*

promotion [prə'moʃən] *s (in rank)* Beförderung *f*; *(of a cause)* Förderung *f*; *(of a pupil)* Versetzung *f*

prompt [prampt] *adj* prompt ‖ *tr* veranlassen; *(theat)* soufflieren *(dat)*

prompter ['pramptər] *s* Souffleur *m*, Souffleuse *f*

promp'ter's box' *s* Souffleurkasten *m*

promptness ['pramptnɪs] *s* Pünktlichkeit *f*

promulgate [pro'mʌlget] *tr* bekanntmachen

prone [pron] *adj*—**be p. to** neigen zu; **in the p. position** auf Anschlag liegend

prong [prɔŋ] *s (of a fork)* Zinke *f*; *(of a deer)* Sprosse *f*

pronoun ['pronaun] *s* Fürwort *n*

pronounce [prə'nauns] *tr (enunciate)* aussprechen; **p. sentence** das Strafausmaß festsetzen; **p. s.o.** *(e.g. guilty, insane, man and wife)* erklären für

pronouncement [prə'naunsmənt] *s (announcement)* Erklärung *f*; *(of a sentence)* (jur) Verkündung *f*

pronunciation [prə,nʌnsɪ'eʃən] *s* Aussprache *f*

proof [pruf] *adj*—**p. against** (fig) gefeit gegen; **90 p.** 45 prozentig ‖ *s* Beweis *m*; *(phot)* Probebild *n*; *(typ)* Korrekturbogen *m*

proof'read'er *s* Korrektor –in *mf*

prop [prap] *s* Stütze *f*; **props** (coll) Beine *pl*; *(theat)* Requisiten *pl* ‖ *v (pret & pp* propped; *ger* propping) *tr* stützen; **p. oneself up** sich aufstemmen; **p. up** abstützen

propaganda [,prapə'gændə] *s* Propaganda *f*

propagate ['prapə,get] *tr* fortpflanzen; *(fig)* propagieren ‖ *intr* sich fortpflanzen

pro·pel [prə'pel] *v (pret & pp* –pelled; *ger* –pelling) *tr* antreiben

propeller [prə'pelər] *s* (aer) Propeller *m*; *(naut)* Schraube *f*

propensity [prə'pensɪti] *s* Neigung *f*

proper ['prɑpər] *adj* passend; *(way, time)* richtig; *(authority)* zuständig; *(strictly so-called)* selbst, e.g., **Germany p.** Deutschland selbst

properly ['prɑpərlɪ] *adj* gehörig

prop'er name' *s* Eigenname *m*

property ['prɑpərtɪ] *s* Eigentum *n*; *(land)* Grundstück *n*; *(quality)* Eigenschaft *f*

prop'erty dam'age *s* Sachschaden *m*

prop'erty tax' *s* Grundsteuer *f*

prophecy ['prɑfɪsɪ] *s* Prophezeiung *f*

prophe·sy ['prɑfɪ‚saɪ] *v* *(pret & pp -sied)* *tr* prophezeien

prophet ['prɑfɪt] *s* Prophet *m*

prophetess ['prɑfɪtɪs] *s* Prophetin *f*

prophylactic [‚prɑfɪ'læktɪk] *adj* prophylaktisch ‖ *s* Prophylaktikum *n*; *(condom)* Präservativ *n*

propitiate [prə'pɪʃɪ‚et] *tr* versöhnen

propitious [prə'pɪʃəs] *adj* günstig

prop'jet' *s* Flugzeug *n* mit Turboprop

proportion [prə'porʃən] *s* Verhältnis *n*; **in p. to** im Verhältnis zu; **out of p. to** in keinem Verhältnis zu; **proportions** Proportionen *pl* ‖ *tr* bemessen; **well proportioned** gut proportioniert

proposal [prə'pozəl] *s* Vorschlag *m*; *(of marriage)* Heiratsantrag *m*

propose [prə'poz] *tr* vorschlagen; *(intend)* beabsichtigen; **p. a toast** to e-n Toast ausbringen auf *(acc)* ‖ *intr* **(to)** e-n Heiratsantrag machen *(dat)*

proposition [‚prɑpə'zɪʃən] *s* Vorschlag *m*; *(log, math)* Lehrsatz *m* ‖ *tr* ansprechen

propound [prə'paʊnd] *tr* vortragen

proprietor [prə'praɪ·ətər] *s* Inhaber *m*

proprietress [prə'praɪ·ətrɪs] *s* Inhaberin *f*

propriety [prə'praɪ·ətɪ] *s* Anstand *m*; **proprieties** Anstandsformen *pl*

propulsion [prə'pʌlʃən] *s* Antrieb *m*

prorate [pro'ret] *tr* anteilmäßig verteilen

prosaic [pro'ze·ɪk] *adj* prosaisch

proscribe [pro'skraɪb] *tr* proskribieren

prose [proz] *adj* Prosa– ‖ *s* Prosa *f*

prosecute ['prɑsɪ‚kjut] *tr* verfolgen

prosecutor ['prɑsɪ‚kjutər] *s* Ankläger –in *mf*

proselytize ['prɑsɪlə‚taɪz] *intr* Anhänger gewinnen

prose' writ'er *s* Prosaiker –in *mf*

prosody ['prɑsədɪ] *s* Silbenmessung *f*

prospect ['prɑspekt] *s* Aussicht *f*; *(person)* Interessent –in *mf*; **hold out the p. of s.th.** etw in Aussicht stellen ‖ *intr* **(for)** schürfen (nach)

prospector ['prɑspektər] *s* Schürfer *m*

prospectus [prə'spektəs] *s* Prospekt *m*

prosper ['prɑspər] *intr* gedeihen

prosperity [prɑs'perɪtɪ] *s* Wohlstand *m*

prosperous ['prɑspərəs] *adj* wohlhabend

prostitute ['prɑstɪ‚t(j)ut] *s* Prostituierte *f* ‖ *tr* prostituieren

prostrate ['prɑstret] *adj* hingestreckt; *(exhausted)* erschöpft ‖ *tr* niederwerfen; *(fig)* niederzwingen

prostration [prɑs'treʃən] *s* Niederwerfen *n*; *(abasement)* Demütigung *f*

protagonist [pro'tægənɪst] *s* Protagonist *m*, Hauptfigur *f*

protect [prə'tekt] *tr* (be)schützen; *(interests)* wahrnehmen; **p. from** schützen vor *(dat)*

protection [prə'tekʃən] *s* **(from)** Schutz *m* (vor *dat)*

protector [prə'tektər] *s* Beschützer *m*

protein ['protin] *s* Protein *n*

protest ['protest] *s* Protest *m* ‖ [pro'test] *tr & intr* protestieren

Protestant ['prɑtɪstənt] *adj* protestantisch ‖ *s* Protestant –in *mf*

protocol ['protə‚kɑl] *s* Protokoll *n*

proton ['protɑn] *s* Proton *n*

protoplasm ['protə‚plæzəm] *s* Protoplasma *n*

prototype ['protə‚taɪp] *s* Prototyp *m*

protozo·an [‚protə'zo·ən] *s* **(–a** [ə]**)** Einzeller *m*

protract [pro'trækt] *tr* hinziehen

protrude [pro'trud] *intr* hervorstehen

proud [praʊd] *adj* **(of)** stolz (auf *acc)*

prove [pruv] *v* *(pret proved; pp proved & proven* ['pruvən]*)* *tr* beweisen; **p. a failure** sich nicht bewähren; **p. one's worth** sich bewähren ‖ *intr*—**p. right** zutreffen; **p. to be** sich erweisen als

proverb ['prɑvərb] *s* Sprichwort *n*

proverbial [prə'vʌrbɪ·əl] *adj* sprichwörtlich

provide [prə'vaɪd] *tr* *(s.th.)* besorgen; **p. s.o. with s.th.** j–n mit etw versorgen ‖ *intr*—**p. for** *(e.g., a family)* sorgen für; *(e.g., a special case)* vorsehen; *(the future)* voraussehen

provid'ed *adj* **(with)** versehen (mit) ‖ *conj* vorausgesetzt, daß

Providence ['prɑvɪdəns] *s* Vorsehung *f*

providential [‚prɑvɪ'dentʃəl] *adj* von der Vorsehung bestimmt

provid'ing *conj* vorausgesetzt, daß

province ['prɑvɪns] *s* *(district)* Provinz *f*; *(special field)* Ressort *n*

provision [prə'vɪʒən] *s* *(providing)* Versorgung *f*; *(stipulation)* Bestimmung *f*; **make p. for** Vorsorge treffen für; **provisions** Lebensmittelvorräte *pl* ‖ *tr* *(mil)* verpflegen

provisional [prə'vɪʒənəl] *adj* vorläufig

provi·so [prə'vaɪzo] *s* **(–sos & –soes)** Vorbehalt *m*

provocation [‚prɑvə'keʃən] *s* Provokation *f*

provocative [prə'vɑkətɪv] *adj* aufreizend

provoke [prə'vok] *tr* *(a person)* provozieren; *(e.g., laughter)* erregen

provok'ing *adj* ärgerlich

prow [praʊ] *s* Bug *m*

prowess ['praʊ·ɪs] *s* Tapferkeit *f*

prowl [praʊl] *intr* herumschleichen

prowl' car' *s* Streifenwagen *m*

prowler ['praʊlər] *s* mutmaßlicher Einbrecher *m*

proximity [prɑk'sɪmɪtɪ] *s* Nähe *f*

proxy ['prɑksɪ] *s* Stellvertreter –in *mf*; **by p.** in Vertretung

prude [prud] *s* prüde Person *f*

prudence ['prudəns] *s* Klugheit *f*; (*caution*) Vorsicht *f*

prudent ['prudənt] *adj* klug; (*cautious*) umsichtig

prudish ['prudɪʃ] *adj* prüde

prune [prun] *s* Zwetschge *f* || *tr* stuzen

Prussia ['prʌʃɪə] *s* Preußen *n*

Prussian ['prʌʃən] *adj* preußisch || *s* Preuße *m*, Preußin *f*

pry [praɪ] *v* (*pret & pp* pried) *tr*—**pry open** aufbrechen; **pry s.th. out of s.o.** etw aus j–m herauspressen || *intr* herumschnüffeln; **pry into** seine Nase stecken in (*acc*)

P.S. ['pi'es] *s* (**postscript**) NS

psalm [sɑm] *s* Psalm *m*

pseudo– ['sudo] *adj* Pseudo–, falsch

pseudonym ['sudənɪm] *s* Deckname *m*

psyche ['saɪkɪ] *s* Psyche *f*

psychiatrist [saɪ'kaɪətrɪst] *s* Psychiater –in *mf*

psychiatry [saɪ'kaɪətrɪ] *s* Psychiatrie *f*

psychic ['saɪkɪk] *adj* psychisch || *s* Medium *n*

psychoanalysis [ˌsaɪko·ə'næləsɪs] *s* Psychoanalyse *f*

psychoanalyze [ˌsaɪko'ænəˌlaɪz] *tr* psychoanalytisch behandeln

psychologic(al) [ˌsaɪko'lɑdʒɪk(əl)] *adj* psychologisch

psychologist [saɪ'kɑlədʒɪst] *s* Psychologe *m*, Psychologin *f*

psychology [saɪ'kɑlədʒɪ] *s* Psychologie *f*

psychopath ['saɪkəˌpæθ] *s* Psychopath –in *mf*

psycho-sis [saɪ'kosɪs] *s* (**-ses** [siz]) Psychose *f*

psychotic [saɪ'kɑtɪk] *adj* psychotisch || *s* Psychosekranke *mf*

pto'main poi'soning ['tomen] *s* Fleischvergiftung *f*

pub [pʌb] *s* Kneipe *f*

puberty ['pjubərtɪ] *s* Pubertät *f*

public ['pʌblɪk] *adj* öffentlich || *s* Öffentlichkeit *f*, Publikum *n*

pub'lic address' sys'tem *s* Lautsprecheranlage *f*

publication [ˌpʌblɪ'keʃən] *s* Veröffentlichung *f*

pub'lic domain' *n*—**in the p. d.** gemeinfrei

publicity [pʌb'lɪsɪtɪ] *s* Publizität *f*

publicize ['pʌblɪˌsaɪz] *tr* bekanntmachen

pub'lic opin'ion *s* öffentliche Meinung *f*

pub'lic-opin'ion poll' *s* öffentliche Meinungsumfrage *f*

pub'lic pros'ecutor *s* Staatsanwalt *m*

pub'lic rela'tions *spl* Kontaktpflege *f*

pub'lic serv'ant *s* Staatsangestellte *mf*

pub'lic util'ity *s* öffentlicher Versorgungsbetrieb *m*

publish ['pʌblɪʃ] *tr* veröffentlichen

publisher ['pʌblɪʃər] *s* Verleger –in *mf*

pub'lishing house' *s* Verlag *m*

puck [pʌk] *s* Puck *m*

pucker ['pʌkər] *tr* (*the lips*) spitzen || *intr*—**p. up** den Mund spitzen

pudding ['pudɪŋ] *s* Pudding *m*

puddle ['pʌdəl] *s* Pfütze *f*, Lache *f*

pudgy ['pʌdʒɪ] *adj* dicklich

puerile ['pjuˌərɪl] *adj* knabenhaft

puff [pʌf] *s* (*on a cigarette*) Zug *m*; (*of smoke*) Rauchwölkchen *n*; (*sleeves*) Puff *m* || *tr* (*e.g., a cigar*) paffen; **p. oneself up** sich aufblähen; **p. out** ausblasen || *intr* keuchen; **p. on** (*a pipe, cigar*) paffen an (*dat*)

pugilist ['pjudʒɪlɪst] *s* Faustkämpfer *m*

pugnacious [pʌg'neʃəs] *adj* kampflustig

pug-nosed ['pʌgˌnozd] *adj* stupsnasig

puke [pjuk] *s* (sl) Kotze *f* || *intr* (sl) kotzen

pull [pul] *s* Ruck *m*; (*influence*) Beziehungen *pl*; (*of gravity*) Anziehungskraft *f* || *tr* ziehen; (*a muscle*) zerren; (*proof*) (typ) abziehen; **p. down** (*e.g., a shade*) herunterziehen; (*a building*) niederreißen; **p. off** (coll) zuwegebringen; **p. oneself together** sich zusammennehmen; **p. out** (*weeds*) herausreißen; **p. up** (*e.g., a chair*) heranrücken || *intr* (on) ziehen (an *dat*); **p. back** sich zurückziehen; **p. in** (*arrive*) ankommen; **p. out** (*depart*) abfahren; **p. over to the side** an den Straßenrand heranfahren; **p. through** durchkommen; **p. up** (*e.g., in a car*) vorfahren

pullet ['pulɪt] *s* Hühnchen *n*

pulley ['pulɪ] *s* Rolle *f*; (*pulley block*) Flaschenzug *m*

pull'o'ver *s* Pullover *m*

pulmonary ['pʌlməˌnerɪ] *adj* Lungen–

pulp [pʌlp] *s* Brei *m*; (*to make paper*) Papierbrei *m*; **beat to a p.** windelweich schlagen

pulpit ['pulpɪt] *s* Kanzel *f*

pulsate ['pʌlset] *intr* pulsieren

pulsation [pʌl'seʃən] *s* Pulsieren *n*

pulse [pʌls] *s* Puls *m*; **take s.o.'s p.** j–m den Puls fühlen

pulverize ['pʌlvəˌraɪz] *tr* pulverisieren

pum'ice stone' ['pʌmɪs] *s* Bimsstein *m*

pum-mel ['pʌməl] *v* (*pret & pp* **-mel[l]-ed; ger -mel[l]ing**) *tr* mit der Faust schlagen

pump [pʌmp] *s* Pumpe *f*; (*shoe*) Pump *m* || *tr* pumpen; (*for information*) ausfragen; **p. up** (*a tire*) aufpumpen

pump'han'dle *s* Pumpenschwengel *m*

pumpkin ['pʌmpkɪn] *s* Kürbis *m*

pun [pʌn] *s* Wortspiel *n* || *v* (*pret & pp* punned; *ger* punning) *intr* ein Wortspiel machen

punch [pʌntʃ] *s* Faustschlag *m*; (*to make holes*) Locher *m*; (*drink*) Punsch *m* || *tr* mit der Faust schlagen; (*a card*) lochen; (*a punch clock*) stechen

punch' bowl' *s* Punschschüssel *f*

punch' card' *s* Lochkarte *f*

punch' clock' *s* Kontrolluhr *f*

punch'-drunk' *adj* von Faustschlägen betäubt

punch'ing bag' *s* Punchingball *m*

punch' line' *s* Pointe *f*

punctilious [pʌŋk'tɪlɪ·əs] *adj* förmlich

punctual ['pʌŋktʃu·əl] *adj* pünktlich

punctuate ['pʌŋktʃu,et] *tr* interpunktieren

punctuation [ˌpʌŋktʃuˈeʃən] *s* Interpunktion *f*

punctua′tion mark′ *s* Satzzeichen *n*

puncture [′pʌŋkt∫ər] *s* Loch *n* ‖ *tr* durchstechen; **p. a tire** e–e Reifenpanne haben

punc′ture-proof′ *adj* pannensicher

pundit [′pʌndɪt] *s* Pandit *m*

pungent [′pʌndʒənt] *adj* beißend, scharf

punish [′pʌnɪʃ] *tr* (be)strafen

punishment [′pʌnɪʃmənt] *s* Strafe *f*, Bestrafung *f*; (educ) Strafarbeit *f*

punk [pʌŋk] *adj* (sl) mies; **I feel p.** mir ist mies ‖ *s* (sl) Rocker *m*

punster [′pʌnstər] *s* Wortspielmacher *m*

puny [′pjuni] *adj* kümmerlich, winzig

pup [pʌp] *s* junger Hund *m*

pupil [′pjupəl] *s* Schüler –in *mf*; (of the eye) Pupille *f*

puppet [′pʌpɪt] *s* Marionette *f*

pup′pet gov′ernment *s* Marionettenregierung *f*

pup′pet show′ *s* Marionettentheater *n*

puppy [′pʌpi] *s* Hündchen *n*

pup′py love′ *s* Jugendliebe *f*

purchase [′pʌrt∫əs] *s* Kauf *m*; (leverage) Hebelwirkung *f* ‖ *tr* kaufen

pur′chasing pow′er *s* Kaufkraft *f*

pure [pjur] *adj* (& fig) rein

purgative [′pʌrgətɪv] *s* Abfuhrmittel *n*

purgatory [′pʌrgəˌtori] *s* Fegefeuer *n*

purge [pʌrdʒ] *s* (pol) Säuberungsaktion *f* ‖ *tr* reinigen; (pol) säubern

puri-fy [′pjurɪˌfaɪ] *v* (*pret & pp* –fied) *tr* reinigen, läutern

puritan [′pjurɪtən] *adj* puritanisch ‖ **Puritan** *s* Puritaner –in *mf*

purity [′pjurɪti] *s* Reinheit *f*

purloin [pʌr′lɔɪn] *tr* entwenden

purple [′pʌrpəl] *adj* purpurn ‖ *s* Purpur *m*

purport [′pʌrport] *s* Sinn *m* ‖ [pər′port] *tr* vorgeben; (imply) besagen

purpose [′pʌrpəs] *s* Absicht *f*; (goal) Zweck *m*; **on p.** absichtlich; **to no p.** ohne Erfolg

purposely [′pʌrpəsli] *adv* absichtlich

purr [pʌr] *s* Schnurren *n* ‖ *intr* schnurren

purse [pʌrs] *s* Beutel *m*; (handbag) Handtasche *f* ‖ *tr*—**p. one's lips** den Mund spitzen

purse′ strings′ *spl*—**hold the p.** über das Geld verfügen

pursue [pər′s(j)u] *tr* (a person; a plan, goal) verfolgen; (studies, profession) betreiben; (pleasures) suchen

pursuit [pər′s(j)ut] *s* Verfolgung *f*; **in hot p.** hart auf den Fersen

pursuit′ plane′ *s* Jäger *m*

purvey [pər′ve] *tr* liefern, versorgen

pus [pʌs] *s* Eiter *m*

push [pʊ] *s* Schub *m*; (mil) Offensive *f* ‖ *tr* (e.g., a cart) schieben; (jostle) stoßen; (a button) drücken auf (acc); **p. around** (coll) schlecht behandeln; **p. aside** beiseite schieben; (curtains) zurückschlagen; **p. one's way through** sich durchdrängen; **p. through** durchsetzen ‖ *intr* drängen

push′ but′ton *s* Druckknopf *m*

push′ cart′ *s* Verkaufskarren *m*

push′o′ver *s* (snap) (coll) Kinderspiel *n*; (sucker) Gimpel *m*; (easy opponent) leicht zu besiegender Gegner *m*

push′-up′ *s* (gym) Liegestütz *m*

pushy [′pʊʃi] *adj* zudringlich

puss [pʊs] *s* (cat) Mieze *f*; (face) (sl) Fresse *f*

pussy [′pʌsi] *adj* eit(e)rig ‖ [′pʊsi] *s* Mieze *f*

puss′y wil′low *s* Salweide *f*

put [pʊt] *v* (*pret & pp* **put**; *ger* putting) *tr* (stand) stellen; (lay) legen; (set) setzen; **feel put out** ungehalten sein; **put across to** beibringen (dat); **put aside** beiseite legen; **put down** (a load) abstellen; (a rebellion) niederschlagen; (in writing) aufschreiben; **put in** (e.g., a windowpane) einsetzen; (e.g., a good word) einlegen; (time) (on) verwenden (auf acc); **put off** (a person) hinhalten; (postpone) aufschieben; **put on** (clothing) anziehen; (a hat) aufsetzen; (a ring) anstecken; (an apron) umbinden; (the brakes) betätigen; (to cook) ansetzen; (a play) aufführen; **put on an act** sich in Szene setzen; **put oneself into** sich hineindenken in (acc); **put oneself out** sich [dat] Umstände machen; **put on its feet again** (com) auf die Beine stellen; **put s.o. on to s.th.** j–n auf etw [acc] bringen; **put out** (a fire) löschen; (lights) auslöschen; (throw out) herauswerfen; (a new book) herausbringen; **put out of action** kampfunfähig machen; **put over on s.o.** j–n übers Ohr hauen; **put through** durchsetzen; (a call) (telp) herstellen; **put (s.o.) through to** (telp) j–n verbinden mit; **put to good use** gut verwenden; **put up** (erect) errichten; (bail) stellen; (for the night) unterbringen; **put up a fight** sich zur Wehr setzen; **put up to** anstiften zu; **to put it mildly** gelinde gesagt ‖ *intr* —**put on** sich verstellen; **put out to sea** (said of a ship) in See gehen; **put up with** sich abfinden mit

put′-on′ *adj* vorgetäuscht ‖ *s* (affectation) Affektiertheit *f*; (parody) Jux *m*

put-put [′pʌt′pʌt] *s* Tacktack *n* ‖ *intr* —**p. along** knattern

putrid [′pjutrɪd] *adj* faul(ig)

putt [pʌt] *s* & *intr* (golf) putten

putter [′pʌtər] *s* (golf) Putter *m* ‖ *intr*—**p. around** herumwursteln

put-ty [′pʌti] *s* Kitt *m* ‖ *v* (*pret & pp* –tied) *tr* (ver)kitten

put′ty knife′ *s* Spachtel *m* & *f*

put′-up job′ *s* abgekartete Sache *f*

puzzle [′pʌzəl] *s* Rätsel *n*; (game) Geduldspiel *n* ‖ *tr* verwirren; **be puzzled** verwirrt sein; **p. out** enträtseln ‖ *intr*—**p. over** tüfteln an (dat)

puzzler [′pʌzlər] *s* Rätsel *n*

puz′zling *adj* rätselhaft

PW [′pi′dʌbəlˌju] *s* (**prisoner of war**) Kriegsgefangene *mf*

pygmy [´pɪgmi] s Pygmäe m, Pygmäin f

pylon [´paɪlɑn] s (entrance to Egyptian temple) Pylon m; (aer) Wendemarke f; (elec) Leitungsmast m

pyramid [´pɪrəmɪd] s Pyramide f

pyre [paɪr] s Scheiterhaufen m

Pyrenees [´pɪrɪ‚niz] spl Pyrenäen pl

pyrotechnics [‚paɪrə´teknɪks] spl Feuerwerkskunst f, Pyrotechnik f

python [´paɪθən] s Pythonschlange f

pyx [pɪks] s (eccl) Pyxis f

Q

Q, q [kju] s siebzehnter Buchstabe des englischen Alphabets

quack [kwæk] s Quacksalber m, Kurpfuscher m ‖ intr schnattern

quadrangle [´kwɑd‚ræŋgəl] s Viereck n; (inner yard) Innenhof m, Lichthof m

quadrant [´kwɑdrənt] s Quadrant m

quadratic [kwɑd´rætɪk] adj quadratisch

quadruped [´kwɑdru‚ped] s Vierfüßer m

quadruple [kwɑd´rupəl] adj vierfach ‖ s Vierfache n ‖ tr vervierfachen ‖ intr sich vervierfachen

quadruplets [kwɑd´ruplets] spl Vierlinge pl

quaff [kwɑf] tr in langen Zügen trinken

quagmire [´kwæg‚maɪr] s Morast m

quail [kwel] s Wachtel f ‖ intr verzagen

quaint [kwent] adj seltsam

quake [kwek] s Zittern n; (geol) Beben n ‖ intr zittern; (geol) beben

Quaker [´kwekər] s Quäker –in mf

qualification [‚kwɑlɪfɪ´keʃən] s (for) Qualifikation f (für)

quali·fy [´kwɑlɪ‚faɪ] v (pret & pp –fied) tr qualifizieren; (modify) einschränken ‖ intr sich qualifizieren

quality [´kwɑltti] s (characteristic) Eigenschaft f; (grade) Qualität f

qualm [kwɑm] s Bedenken n

quandary [´kwɑndərɪ] s Dilemma n

quantity [´kwɑntɪtɪ] s Menge f, Quantität f; (math) Größe f; (pros) Silbenmaß n; buy in q. auf Vorrat kaufen

quan'tum the'ory [´kwɑntəm] s Quantentheorie f

quarantine [´kwɔrən‚tin] s Quarantäne f ‖ tr unter Quarantäne stellen

quar·rel [´kwɔrəl] s Streit m; pick a q. Händel suchen ‖ v (pret & pp –rel[l]ed; ger –el[l]ing) intr (over) streiten (über acc or um)

quarrelsome [´kwɔrəlsəm] adj streitsüchtig, händelsüchtig

quar·ry [´kwɔrɪ] s Steinbruch m; (hunt) Jagdbeute f ‖ v (pret & pp –ried) tr brechen

quart [kwɔrt] s Quart n

quarter [´kwɔrtər] s Viertel n; (of a city) Stadtviertel n; (of the moon) Mondviertel n; (of the sky) Himmelsrichtung f; (coin) Vierteldollar m; (econ) Quartal n; (sport) Viertelzeit f; a q. after one (ein) Viertel nach

eins; a q. of an hour e–e Viertelstunde f; a q. to eight dreiviertel acht, (ein) viertel vor acht; at close quarters im Nahkampf; from all quarters von überall; give no q. keinen Pardon geben; quarters (& mil) Unterkunft f, Quartier n ‖ tr (lodge) einquartieren; (divide into four, tear into quarters) vierteilen ‖ intr im Quartier liegen

quar'ter-deck' s Quarterdeck n

quar'terfi'nal s Zwischenrunde f

quar'ter-hour' s Viertelstunde f

quarterly [´kwɔrtərlɪ] adj vierteljährig; (econ) Quartals– ‖ s Vierteljahresschrift f

quar'termas'ter s Quartiermeister m

Quar'termaster Corps' s Versorgungstruppen pl

quar'ter note' s (mus) Viertelnote f

quar'ter rest' s (mus) Viertelpause f

quartet [kwɔr´tet] s Quartett n

quartz [kwɔrts] s Quarz m

quash [kwɑʃ] tr niederschlagen

quatrain [´kwɑtren] s Vierzeiler m

quaver [´kwevər] s Zittern n; (mus) Triller m ‖ intr zittern; (mus) trillern, tremolieren

queasy [´kwizɪ] adj übel

queen [kwin] s Königin f; (cards) Dame f

queen' bee' s Bienenkönigin f

queen' dow'ager s Königinwitwe f

queenly [´kwinli] adj königlich

queen' moth'er s Königinmutter f

queer [kwɪr] adj sonderbar; (homosexual) schwul ‖ s (homosexual) Schwule mf

queer' duck' s (coll) Unikum n

quell [kwel] tr unterdrücken

quench [kwentʃ] tr (thirst) löschen; (a fire) (aus)löschen

que·ry [´kwɪrɪ] s Frage f ‖ v (pret & pp –ried) tr befragen; (cast doubt on) bezweifeln

quest [kwest] s Suche f; in q. of auf der Suche nach

question [´kwestʃən] s Frage f; ask (s.o.) a q. (j–m) e–e Frage stellen; be out of the q. außer Frage stehen; beyond q. außer Frage; call into q. in Frage stellen; call the q. (parl) um Abstimmung bitten; in q. betreffend; it is a q. of (ger) es handelt sich darum zu (inf); q. of time Zeitfrage f; that's an open q. darüber läßt sich streiten; there's no q. about it darüber besteht kein Zweifel ‖ tr be-

fragen; *(said of the police)* verhören; *(cast doubt on)* bezweifeln
questionable ['kwest/ənəbəl] *adj* fraglich, fragwürdig; *(doubtful)* zweifelhaft; *(character)* bedenklich
ques'tioning *s* Verhör *n*, Vernehmung *f*
ques'tion mark' *s* Fragezeichen *n*
questionnaire [,kwest/ə'ner] *s* Fragebogen *m*
queue [kju] *s* Schlange *f* ‖ *intr*—q. up sich anstellen
quibble ['kwɪbəl] *s* Deutelei *f* ‖ *intr* (about) deuteln (an *dat*)
quibbler ['kwɪblər] *s* Wortklauber *m*
quick [kwɪk] *adj* schnell, fix ‖ *s*—cut to the q. bis ins Mark treffen
quicken ['kwɪkən] *tr* beschleunigen ‖ *intr* sich beschleunigen
quick'lime' *s* gebrannter ungelöschter Kalk *m*
quick' lunch' *s* Schnellimbiß *m*
quick'sand' *s* Treibsand *m*
quick'sil'ver *s* Quecksilber *n*
quick'-tem'pered *adj* jähzornig
quick'-wit'ted *adj* scharfsinnig
quiet ['kwaɪ·ət] *adj* ruhig; *(person)* schweigsam; *(still)* still; *(street)* unbelebt; **be q.!** sei still!; **keep q.** schweigen ‖ *s* Stille *f* ‖ *tr* beruhigen ‖ *intr*—q. down sich beruhigen; *(said of excitement, etc.)* sich legen
quill [kwɪl] *s* Feder *f*, Federkiel *m*; *(of a porcupine)* Stachel *m*
quilt [kwɪlt] *s* Steppdecke *f* ‖ *tr* steppen
quince [kwɪns] *s* Quitte *f*
quince' tree' *s* Quittenbaum *m*
quinine ['kwaɪnaɪn] *s* Chinin *n*
quintessence [kwɪn'tesəns] *s* Inbegriff *m*
quintet [kwɪn'tet] *s* Quintett *n*
quintuplets [kwɪn'tʌplets] *spl* Fünflinge *pl*
quip [kwɪp] *s* witziger Seitenhieb *m* ‖ *v (pret & pp* quipped; *ger* quipping) *tr* witzig sagen ‖ *intr* witzeln

quire [kwaɪr] *s* (bb) Lage *f*
quirk [kwʌrk] *s* Eigenart *f*; *(subterfuge)* Ausflucht *f*; *(sudden change)* plötzliche Wendung *f*
quit [kwɪt] *adj* quitt; **let's call it quits!** (coll) Strich drunter! ‖ *v (pret & pp* quit & quitted; *ger* quitting) *tr* aufgeben; *(e.g., a gang)* abspringen von; **q. it!** hören Sie damit auf! ‖ *intr* aufhören; *(at work)* seine Stellung aufgeben
quite [kwaɪt] *adv* recht, ganz; **q. a disappointment** e–e ausgesprochene Enttäuschung *f*; **q. recently** in jüngster Zeit; **q. the reverse** genau das Gegenteil
quitter ['kwɪtər] *s* Schlappmacher *m*
quiver ['kwɪvər] *s* Zittern *n*; *(to hold arrows)* Köcher *m* ‖ *intr* zittern
quixotic [kwɪks'ɑtɪk] *adj* überspannt
quiz [kwɪz] *s* Prüfung *f*; *(game)* Quiz *n* ‖ *v (pret & pp* quizzed; *ger* quizzing) *tr* ausfragen; **q. s.o. on s.th.** j–n etw abfragen
quiz'mas'ter *s* Quizonkel *m*
quiz' show' *s* Quizshow *f*
quizzical ['kwɪzɪkəl] *adj* *(puzzled)* verwirrt; *(strange)* seltsam; *(mocking)* spöttisch
quoit [kwɔɪt] *s* Wurfring *m*
quondam ['kwɑndæm] *adj* ehemalig
Quon'set hut' ['kwɑnsət] *s* Nissenhütte *f*
quorum ['kworəm] *s* beschlußfähige Anzahl *f*
quota ['kwotə] *s* Quote *f*, Anteil *m*; *(work)* Arbeitsleistung *f*
quotation [kwo'te/ən] *s* Zitat *n*; *(price)* Notierung *f*
quota'tion marks' *spl* Anführungszeichen *pl*
quote [kwot] *s* Zitat *n*; *(of prices)* Notierung *f* ‖ *tr* zitieren; *(prices)* notieren ‖ *interj*—q. . . . unquote Beginn des Zitats! . . . Ende des Zitats!
quotient ['kwo/ənt] *s* Quotient *m*

R

R, r [ɑr] *s* achtzehnter Buchstabe des englischen Alphabets
rabbet ['ræbɪt] *s* Falz *m* ‖ *tr* falzen
rabbi ['ræbaɪ] *s* Rabbiner *m*
rabbit ['ræbɪt] *s* Kaninchen *n*
rabble ['ræbəl] *s* Pöbel *m*
rab'ble-rous'er *s* Volksaufwiegler –in *mf*
rabid ['ræbɪd] *adj* rabiat; *(dog)* tollwütig
rabies ['rebiz] *s* Tollwut *f*
raccoon [ræ'kun] *s* Waschbär *m*
race [res] *s* Rasse *f*; *(contest)* Wettrennen *n*; *(fig)* Wettlauf *m* ‖ *tr* um die Wette laufen mit; *(in a car)* um die Wette fahren mit; *(a horse)* rennen lassen; *(an engine)* hochjagen ‖ *intr*

rennen; *(on foot)* um die Wette laufen; *(in a car)* um die Wette fahren
race' driv'er *s* Rennfahrer –in *mf*
race' horse' *s* Rennpferd *n*
racer ['resər] *s* *(person)* Wettfahrer –in *mf*; *(car)* Rennwagen *m*; *(in speed skating)* Schnelläufer –in *mf*
race' ri'ot *s* Rassenaufruhr *m*
race' track' *s* Rennbahn *f*
racial ['re/əl] *adj* rassisch, Rassen–
rac'ing *s* Rennsport *m*
racism ['resɪzəm] *s* Rassenhaß *m*
rack [ræk] *s* *(shelf)* Regal *n*, Ablage *f*; *(for clothes, bicycles, hats)* Ständer *m*; *(for luggage)* Gepäcknetz *n*; *(for fodder)* Futterraufe *f*; *(for torture)* Folter *f*; *(toothed bar)* Zahnstange *f*;

go to r. and ruin völlig zugrunde gehen; put to the r. auf die Folter spannen || *tr* (*with pain*) quälen; r. one's brains (over) sich [*dat*] den Kopf zerbrechen (über *acc*)

racket ['rækɪt] *s* (*noise*) Krach *m*; (*illegal business*) Schiebergeschäft *n*; (*tennis*) Rakett *n*

racketeer [,rækɪ'tɪr] *s* Schieber –in *mf*

racketeer'ing *s* Schiebertum *n*

rack' rail'way *s* Zahnradbahn *f*

racy ['resɪ] *adj* (*off-color*) schlüpfrig; (*vivacious, pungent*) rassig

radar ['redɑr] *s* Radar *n*

ra'darscope *s* Radarschirm *m*

radial ['redɪəl] *adj* radial

radiance ['redɪəns] *s* Strahlung *f*

radiant ['redɪənt] *adj* (*with*) strahlend (vor *dat*); (*phys*) Strahlungs–

radiate ['redɪ,et] *tr & intr* ausstrahlen

radiation [,redɪ'eʃən] *s* Strahlung *f*

radia'tion belt' *s* Strahlungsgürtel *m*

radia'tion treat'ment *s* Bestrahlung *f*; give r. treatment to bestrahlen

radiator ['redɪ,etər] *s* Heizkörper *m*; (aut) Kühler *m*

ra'diator cap' *s* Kühlerverschluß *m*

radical ['rædɪkəl] *adj* radikal || *s* Radikale *mf*

radically ['rædɪkəli] *adv* von Grund auf

radi·o ['redɪ,o] *s* (–os) Radio *n*, Rundfunk *m*; go on the r. im Rundfunk sprechen || *tr* funken

ra'dioac'tive *adj* radioaktiv

ra'dio announc'er *s* Rundfunkansager –in *mf*

ra'dio bea'con *s* (aer) Funkfeuer *n*

ra'dio beam' *s* Funkleitstrahl *m*

ra'dio broad'cast *s* Rundfunksendung *f*

radiocar'bon dat'ing *s* Radiokarbonmethode *f*

ra'diofre'quency *s* Hochfrequenz *f*

radiogram ['redɪ·o,græm] *s* Radiogramm *n*

radiologist [,redɪ'ɑlədʒɪst] *s* Röntgenologe *m*, Röntgenologin *f*

radiology [redɪ'ɑlədʒɪ] *s* Röntgenologie *f*

ra'dio net'work *s* Rundfunknetz *n*

ra'dio op'erator *s* Funker –in *mf*

radioscopy [,redɪ'askəpɪ] *s* Durchleuchtung *f*

ra'dio set' *s* Radioapparat *m*

ra'dio sta'tion *s* Rundfunkstation *f*

radish ['rædɪʃ] *s* Radieschen *n*

radium ['redɪ·əm] *s* Radium *n*

radi·us ['redɪ·əs] *s* (–i [,aɪ] & –uses) Halbmesser *m*; (anat) Speiche *f*; within a r. of in e–m Umkreis von

raffish ['ræfɪʃ] *adj* gemein, niedrig

raffle ['ræfəl] *s* Tombola *f* || *tr*–r. off in e–r Tombola verlosen

raft [ræft] *s* Floß *n*; a r. of (coll) ein Haufen *m*

rafter ['ræftər] *s* Dachsparren *m*; rafters Sparrenwerk *n*

rag [ræg] *s* Lumpen *m*; chew the rag (sl) quasseln

ragamuffin ['rægə,mʌfɪn] *s* Lump *m*

rag' doll' *s* Stoffpuppe *f*

rage [redʒ] *s* Wut *f*; all the r. letzter

Schrei *m*; be the r. die große Mode sein; fly into a r. in Wut geraten || *intr* wüten, toben

ragged ['rægɪd] *adj* zerlumpt, lumpig

rag'man *s* (–men) Lumpenhändler *m*

ragout [ræ'gu] *s* Ragout *n*

rag'weed' *s* Ambrosiapflanze *f*

raid [red] *s* Beutezug *m*; (*by police*) Razzia *f*; (mil) Überfall *m* || *tr* überfallen; e–e Razzia machen auf (*acc*)

raider ['redər] *s* (naut) Kaperkreuzer *m*; raiders (mil) Kommandotruppe *f*

rail [rel] *s* Geländerstange *f*; (naut) Reling *f*; (rr) Schiene *f*; by r. per Bahn ||–r. at beschimpfen

rail'head' *s* Schienenkopf *m*

rail'ing *s* Geländer *n*; (naut) Reling *f*

rail'road' cross'ing *s* Bahnübergang *m*

rail'road embank'ment *s* Bahndamm *m*

rail'road sta'tion *s* Bahnhof *m*

rail'road tie' *s* Schwelle *f*

rail'way *adj* Eisenbahn– || *s* Eisenbahn *f*

raiment ['remənt] *s* Kleidung *f*

rain [ren] *s* Regen *m*; it looks like r. es sieht nach Regen aus; r. or shine bei jedem Wetter || *tr*—r. cats and dogs Bindfäden regnen; r. out verregnen || *intr* regnen

rainbow ['ren,bo] *s* Regenbogen *m*

rain'coat' *s* Regenmantel *m*

rain'drop' *s* Regentropfen *m*

rain'fall' *s* Regenfall *m*; (*amount of rain*) Regenmenge *f*

rain' gut'ter *s* Dachrinne *f*

rain' pipe' *s* Fallrohr *n*

rain'proof' *adj* regenfest, regendicht

rainy ['renɪ] *adj* regnerisch; (*e.g., day, weather*) Regen–; save money for a r. day sich [*dat*] e–n Notpfennig aufsparen

rain'y sea'son *s* Regenzeit *f*

raise [rez] *s* Lohnerhöhung *f*; (in poker) Steigerung *f* || *tr* (*lift*) heben, erheben; (*increase*) erhöhen, steigern; (*erect*) aufstellen; (*children*) großziehen; (*a family*) ernähren; (*grain, vegetables*) anbauen; (*animals*) züchten; (*dust*) aufwirbeln; (*money, troops*) aufbringen; (*blisters*) ziehen; (*a question*) aufwerfen; (*hopes*) erwecken; (*a laugh, smile*) hervorrufen; (*the ante*) steigern; (*a siege*) aufheben; (*from the dead*) auferwecken; r. Cain (or hell) Krach schlagen; r. the arm (*before striking*) mit dem Arm ausholen; r. the price of verteuern; r. to a higher power potenzieren || *intr* (*in poker*) höher wetten

raisin ['rezən] *s* Rosine *f*

rake [rek] *s* Rechen *m*; (*person*) Wüstling *m* || *tr* rechen; (*with gunfire*) bestreichen; r. in (*money*) kassieren; r. together (or up) zusammenrechen

rake'-off' *s* (coll) Gewinnanteil *m*

rakish ['rekɪʃ] *adj* (*dissolute*) liederlich; (*jaunty*) schmissig

ral·ly ['rælɪ] *s* (*meeting*) Massenversammlung *f*; (*recovery*) Erholung *f*;

(mil) Umgruppierung *f* ‖ *v* (*pret & pp* **–lied**) *tr* (wieder) sammeln ‖ *intr* sich (wieder) sammeln; (*recover*) sich erholen

ram [ræm] *s* Schafbock *m* ‖ *v* (*pret & pp* **rammed;** *ger* **ramming**) *tr* rammen; **ram s.th. down s.o.'s throat** j-m etw aufdrängen

ramble ['ræmbəl] *intr—r.* **about** herumwandern; **r. on** daherreden

ramification [ˌræmɪfɪ'keʃən] *s* Verzweigung *f*

ramp [ræmp] *s* Rampe *f*

rampage ['ræmpedʒ] *s* Toben *n*, Wüten *n*; **go on a r.** toben, wüten

rampant ['ræmpənt] *adj*—**be r.** grassieren

rampart ['ræmpɑrt] *s* Wall *m*, Ringwall *m*

ram'rod' *s* Ladestock *m*; (*cleaning rod*) Reinigungsstock *m*

ram'shack'le *adj* baufällig

ranch [rænt*ʃ*] *s* Ranch *f*

rancid ['rænsɪd] *adj* ranzig

random ['rændəm] *adj* zufällig, Zufalls–; **at r.** aufs Geratewohl

range [rendʒ] *s* (*row*) Reihe *f*; (*mountains*) Bergkette *f*; (*stove*) Herd *m*; (*for firing practice*) Schießplatz *m*; (*of a gun*) Schießweite *f*; (*distance*) Reichweite *f*; (*mus*) Umfang *m*; **at a r. of** in e-r Entfernung von; **at close r.** auf kurze Entfernung; **come within s.o.'s r.** j-m vor den Schuß kommen; **out of r.** außer Reichweite; (*in shooting*) außer Schußweite; **within r.** in Reichweite; (*in shooting*) in Schußweite ‖ *tr* reihen ‖ *intr—* **r. from ... to** sich bewegen zwischen (*dat*) ... und

range' find'er *s* Entfernungsmesser *m*

ranger ['rendʒər] *s* Förster *m*; **rangers** *pl* Stoßtruppen *pl*

rank [ræŋk] *adj* (*rancid*) ranzig; (*smelly*) stinkend; (*absolute*) kraß; (*excessive*) übermäßig; (*growth*) üppig ‖ *s* Rang *m*; **according to r.** standesgemäß; **person of r.** Standesperson *f* ‖ *tr* einreihen, rangieren; **be ranked as** gelten als ‖ *intr* rangieren; **r. above** stehen über (*dat*); **r. among** zählen zu; **r. below** stehen unter (*dat*); **r. with** mitzählen zu

rank' and file' *s* die breite Masse

rank'ing of'ficer *s* Rangälteste *mf*

rankle ['ræŋkəl] *tr* nagen an (*dat*) ‖ *intr* nagen

ransack ['rænsæk] *tr* durchstöbern

ransom ['rænsəm] *s* Lösegeld *n* ‖ *tr* auslösen

rant [rænt] *intr* schwadronieren

rap [ræp] *s* (*on the door*) Klopfen *n*; (*blow*) Klaps *m*; **not give a rap for** husten auf (*acc*); **take the rap** den Kopf hinhalten; **there was a rap on the door** es klopfte an der Tür ‖ *v* (*pret & pp* **rapped;** *ger* **rapping**) *tr* (*strike*) schlagen; (*criticize*) tadeln ‖ *intr* (*talk freely*) offen reden; (*on*) klopfen (an *dat*)

rapacious [rə'peʃəs] *adj* raffgierig; (*animal*) raubgierig

rape [rep] *s* Vergewaltigung *f* ‖ *tr* vergewaltigen

rapid ['ræpɪd] *adj* rapid(e); (*river*) reißend ‖ **rapids** *spl* Stromschnelle *f*

rap'id-fire' *adj* Schnell–; (mil) Schnellfeuer–

rap'id trans'it *s* Nahschnellverkehr *m*

rapier ['repɪ*·*ər] *s* Rapier *n*

rapist ['repɪst] *s* sexueller Gewaltverbrecher *m*

rap'ses'sion *s* zwanglose Diskussion *f*

rapt [ræpt] *adj* (*attention*) gespannt; (*in thought*) vertieft

rapture ['ræptʃər] *s* Entzückung *f*; **go into raptures** in Entzücken geraten

rare [rer] *adj* selten; (culin) halbgar

rare' bird' *s* (fig) weißer Rabe *m*

rare·fy ['rerɪˌfaɪ] *v* (*pret & pp* **–fied**) *tr* verdünnen

rarely ['rerli] *adv* selten

rarity ['rerɪti] *s* Rarität *f*

rascal ['ræskəl] *s* Bengel *m*

rash [ræʃ] *adj* vorschnell, unbesonnen ‖ *s* Ausschlag *m*

rasp [ræsp] *s* (*sound*) Kratzlaut *m*; (*tool*) Raspel *f* ‖ *tr* raspeln

raspberry ['ræzˌberi] *s* Himbeere *f*

rat [ræt] *s* Ratte *f*; (*deserter*) (sl) Überläufer –in *mf*; (*informer*) (sl) Spitzel *m*; (*scoundrel*) (sl) Gauner *m*; **smell a rat** (coll) den Braten riechen ‖ *intr—***rat on** (sl) verpetzen

ratchet ['rætʃɪt] *s* (*wheel*) Sperrad *n*; (*pawl*) Sperrklinke *f*

rate [ret] *s* Satz *m*; (*for mail, freight*) Tarif *m*; **at any r.** auf jeden Fall; **at the r. of** (*a certain speed*) mit der Geschwindigkeit von; (*a certain price*) zum Preis von; **at the r. of a dozen per week** ein Dutzend pro Woche; **at this** (or **that**) **r.** bei diesem Tempo ‖ *tr* bewerten ‖ *intr* (coll) hochgeschätzt sein

rate' of exchange' *s* Kurs *m*

rate' of in'terest *s* Zinssatz *m*

rather ['ræðər] *adv* ziemlich; **I would r. wait** ich würde lieber warten; **r. ... than** lieber ... als ‖ *interj* na ob!

rati·fy ['rætɪˌfaɪ] *v* (*pret & pp* **–fied**) *tr* ratifizieren, bestätigen

rat'ing *s* Beurteilung *f*; (mach) Leistung *f*; (mil) Dienstgrad *m*; (sport) Bewertung *f*

ra·tio ['reʃ(ɪ)ˌo] *s* (**–tios**) Verhältnis *n*

ration ['ræʃən], ['reʃən] *s* Ration *f*; **rations** (mil) Verpflegung *f* ‖ *tr* rationieren

ra'tion card' *s* Bezugsschein *m*

ra'tioning *s* Rationierung *f*

rational ['ræʃənəl] *adj* vernünftig

rationalize ['ræʃənəˌlaɪz] *tr & intr* rationalisieren

rat' poi'son *s* Rattengift *n*

rat' race' *s* (fig) Hetzjagd *f*

rattle ['rætəl] *s* Geklapper *n*; (*toy*) Klapper *f*, Schnarre *f* ‖ *tr* (*confuse*) verwirren; **get s.o. rattled** j-n aus dem Konzept bringen; **r. off** herunterschnarren; **r. the dishes** mit dem Geschirr klappern ‖ *intr* klappern; (*said of a machine gun*) knattern;

(said of windows) klirren; **r. on** daherplappern

rat'tlebrain' s Hohlkopf m
rat'tlesnake' s Klapperschlange f
rat'tletrap' s (coll) Kiste f, Karre f
rat'trap' s Rattenfalle f
raucous ['rɔkəs] adj heiser
ravage ['rævɪdʒ] s Verwüstung f, Verheerung f || tr verwüsten, verheeren
rave [rev] s (coll) Modeschrei m || intr irreoden; **r. about** schwärmen von
raven ['revən] adj *(black)* rabenschwarz || s Kolkrabe m, Rabe m
ravenous ['rævənəs] adj rasend
ravine [rə'vin] s Bergschlucht f
rav'ing adj (coll) toll || adv—**r. mad** tobsüchtig
ravish ['rævɪʃ] tr vergewaltigen
rav'ishing adv entzückend
raw [rɔ] adj roh; *(weather)* naßkalt; *(throat)* rauh; *(recruit)* unausgebildet; *(skin)* wundgerieben; *(leather)* ungegerbt; *(wool)* ungesponnen
raw'-boned' adj hager
raw' deal' s (sl) unfaire Behandlung f
raw'hide' s Rohhaut f
raw' mate'rial s Rohstoff m
ray [re] s Strahl m; (ichth) Rochen m; **ray of hope** Hoffnungsstrahl m
rayon ['re·ɑn] adj kunstseiden || s Kunstseide f, Rayon m
raze [rez] tr abtragen; **r. to the ground** dem Erdboden gleichmachen
razor ['rezər] s Rasiermesser n; *(safety razor)* Rasierapparat m
ra'zor blade' s Rasierklinge f
razz [ræz] tr (sl) aufziehen
re [ri] prep betreffs (gen)
reach [rit∫] s Reichweite f; **beyond the r. of s.o.** für j–n unerreichbar; **out of r.** unerreichbar; **within easy r.** leicht zu erreichen; **within r.** in Reichweite || tr *(a goal, person, city, advanced age, an understanding)* erreichen; *(a certain amount)* sich belaufen auf *(acc)*; *(a compromise)* schließen; *(an agreement)* treffen; *(e.g., the ceiling)* heranreichen an *(acc)*; **r. out** ausstrecken || intr *(extend)* reichen, sich erstrecken; **r. for** greifen nach; **into one's pocket** in die Tasche greifen
react [rɪ'ækt] intr (to) reagieren (auf acc); **r. upon** zurückwirken auf *(acc)*
reaction [rɪ'æk∫ən] s Reaktion f
reactionary [rɪ'æk∫ən‚erɪ] adj reaktionär || s Reaktionär –in mf
reac'tion time' s Reaktionszeit f
reactor [rɪ'æktər] s Reaktor m
read [rid] v *(pret & pp* read [red]) tr lesen; **r. a paper on** referieren über *(acc)*; **r. off** verlesen; **r. over** durchlesen; **r. to** vorlesen *(dat)* || intr lesen; *(said of a passage)* lauten; *(said of a thermometer)* zeigen; **r. up on** studieren
readable ['ridəbəl] adj lesbar
reader ['ridər] s *(person)* Leser –in mf; *(book)* Lesebuch n
readily ['redɪlɪ] adv gern(e)
readiness ['redɪnɪs] s Bereitwilligkeit f; *(preparedness)* Bereitschaft f

read'ing s *(act)* Lesen n; *(material)* Lektüre f; *(version)* Lesart f; (eccl, parl) Lesung f
read'ing glass'es spl Lesebrille f
read'ing lamp' s Leselampe f
read'ing room' s Lesesaal m
readjustment [‚ri·ə'dʒʌstmənt] s Umstellung f
read·y ['redɪ] adj *(done)* fertig; **be r.** *(stand in readiness)* in Bereitschaft stehen; **get r.** sich fertig (or bereit) machen; **get s.th. r.** etw fertigstellen; **r. for** bereit zu; **r. for take-off** startbereit; **r. for use** gebrauchsfertig; **r. to** *(inf)* bereit zu *(inf)* || v *(pret & pp* –ied) tr fertigmachen
read'y cash' s flüssiges Geld n
read'y-made' adj von der Stange
read'y-made' clothes' spl Konfektion f
reaffirm [‚ri·ə'fʌrm] tr nochmals beteuern
real ['ri·əl] adj wirklich; *(genuine)* echt; *(friend)* wahr
re'al estate' s Immobilien pl
re'al-estate' a'gent s Immobilienmakler –in mf
re'al-estate tax' s Grundsteuer f
realist ['ri·əlɪst] s Realist –in mf
realistic [ri·ə'lɪstɪk] adj wirklichkeitsnah, realistisch
reality [rɪ'ælɪtɪ] s Wirklichkeit f; **in r.** wirklich; **realities** *(facts)* Tatsachen pl
realize ['ri·ə‚laɪz] tr einsehen; *(a profit)* erzielen; *(a goal)* verwirklichen; *(a good)* realisieren
really ['ri·əlɪ] adv wirklich; **not r.** eigentlich nicht
realm [relm] s Königreich n; (fig) Reich n, Gebiet n; **within the r. of possibility** im Rahmen des Möglichen
Realtor² ['ri·əltər] s Immobilienmakler –in mf
ream [rim] s Ries n || tr ausbohren
reamer ['rimər] s Reibahle f
reap [rip] tr *(cut)* mähen; (& fig) ernten
reaper ['ripər] s Mäher –in mf; (mach) Mähmaschine f
reappear [‚ri·ə'pɪr] intr wiederauftauchen, wiedererscheinen
rearmament [ri'ɑrməmənt] s Wiederscheinen s
reappoint [‚ri·ə'pɔɪnt] tr wieder anstellen
rear [rɪr] adj hintere, rückwärtig || s Hinterseite f; *(of an army)* Nachhut f; (sl) Hintern m; **bring up the r.** den Schluß bilden; (mil) den Zug beschließen; **from the r.** von hinten; **to the r.** nach hinten; **to the r., march!** kehrt, marsch! || tr *(children)* aufziehen; *(animals)* züchten; *(a structure, one's head)* aufrichten || intr sich bäumen
rear' ad'miral s Konteradmiral m
rear' ax'le s Hinterachse f
rear' end' s (sl) Hintern m
rear' guard' s (mil) Nachhut f
rear' gun'ner s Heckschütze m

rearm [ri'arm] *tr* wieder aufrüsten

rearmament [ri'armemənt] *s* Wiederaufrüstung *f*

rearrange [ˌri·ə'rendʒ] *tr* umstellen

rear' seat' *s* Hintersitz *m*

rear'-view mir'ror *s* Rückspiegel *m*

rear'-wheel drive' *s* Hinterradantrieb *m*

rear' win'dow *s* (aut) Heckfenster *n*

reason ['rizən] *tr* Vernunft *f*; (cause) Grund *m*; **by r.** of auf Grund (genit); **for this r.** aus diesem Grund; **listen to r.** sich belehren lassen; **not listen to r.** sich [dat] nichts sagen lassen; **not without good r.** nicht umsonst || *tr*—r. **out** durchdenken || *intr*—r. **with** vernünftig reden mit

reasonable ['rizənəbəl] *adj* (person) vernünftig; (price) solid; (wares) preiswert

reassemble [ˌri·ə'sembəl] *tr* (people) wieder versammeln; (mach) wieder zusammenbauen || *intr* sich wieder sammeln

reassert [ˌri·ə'sert] *tr* wieder behaupten

reassurance [ˌri·ə'ʃurəns] *s* Beruhigung *f*

reassure [ˌri·ə'ʃur] *tr* beruhigen

reawaken [ˌri·ə'wekən] *tr* wieder erwecken || *intr* wieder erwachen

rebate ['ribet] *s* Rabatt *m*

re·bel ['rebəl] *adj* Rebellen- || *s* Rebell -in *mf* || [ri'bel] *v* (pret & pp -belled; ger -belling) *intr* rebellieren

rebellion [ri'beljən] *s* Aufstand *m*, Rebellion *f*

rebellious [ri'beljəs] *adj* aufständisch

rebirth ['ribʌrθ] *s* Wiedergeburt *f*

rebore [ri'bor] *tr* nachbohren

rebound ['ri,baund] *s* Rückprall *m* || [ri'baund] *intr* zurückprallen

rebroad·cast [ri'brɔd,kæst] *s* Wiederholungssendung *f* || *v* (pret & pp -cast & -casted) *tr* nochmals übertragen

rebuff [ri'bʌf] *s* Zurückweisung *f* || *tr* schroff abweisen

re·build [ri'bɪld] *v* (pret & pp -built) *tr* wiederaufbauen; (mach) überholen; (confidence) wiederherstellen

rebuke [ri'bjuk] *s* Verweis *m* || *tr* verweisen

re·but [ri'bʌt] *v* (pret & pp -butted; ger -butting) *tr* widerlegen

rebuttal [ri'bʌtəl] *s* Widerlegung *f*

recall [ri'kɔl], ['rikɔl] *s* (recollection) Erinnerungsvermögen *n*; (com) Zurücknahme *f*; (dipl, pol) Abberufung *f*; **beyond r.** unwiderruflich || [ri'kɔl] *tr* (remember) sich erinnern an (dat); (an ambassador) abberufen; (workers) zurückrufen; (mil) wiedereinberufen

recant [ri'kænt] *tr & intr* (öffentlich) widerrufen

re·cap ['ri,kæp] *s* Zusammenfassung *f* || *v* (pret & pp -capped; ger -capping) *tr* zusammenfassen; (a tire) runderneuern

recapitulate [ˌrikə'pɪtʃə,let] *tr* zusammenfassen

recapitulation [ˌrikə,pɪtʃə'leʃən] *s* Rekapitulation *f*, Zusammenfassung *f*

re·cast ['ri,kæst] *s* Umguß *m* || [ri'kæst] *v* (pret & pp -cast) *tr* umgießen; (a sentence) umarbeiten; (theat) neubesetzen

recede [ri'sid] *intr* zurückgehen; (become more distant) zurückweichen

reced'ing *adj* (forehead, chin) fliehend

receipt [ri'sit] *s* Quittung *f*; acknowledge r. of den Empfang bestätigen (genit); **receipts** Eingänge *pl* || *tr* quittieren

receive [ri'siv] *tr* bekommen, erhalten; (a guest) empfangen; (pay) beziehen; (rad) empfangen

receiver [ri'sivər] *s* Empfänger -in *mf*; (jur) Zwangsverwalter -in *mf*; (telp) Hörer *m*

receiv'ership' *s* Zwangsverwaltung *f*

recent ['risənt] *adj* neu, jung; **in r. years** in den letzten Jahren; **of r. date** neueren Datums

recently ['risəntli] *adv* kürzlich

receptacle [ri'septəkəl] *s* Behälter *m*; (elec) Steckdose *f*

reception [ri'sepʃən] *s* (& rad) Empfang *m*

recep'tion desk' *s* Empfang *m*

receptionist [ri'sepənɪst] *s* Empfangsdame *f*; (med) Sprechstundenhilfe *f*

receptive [ri'septɪv] *adj* (to) aufgeschlossen (für)

recess [ri'ses], ['rises] *s* (alcove) Nische *f*; (cleft) Einschnitt *m*; (at school) Pause *f*; (jur) Unterbrechung *f*; (parl) Ferien *pl* || [ri'ses] *tr* (place in a recess) versenken || *intr* (until) sich vertagen (auf acc)

recession [ri'seʃən] *s* Rezession *f*, Rückgang *m*

recharge [ri'tʃardʒ] *tr* wieder aufladen

recipe ['resɪ,pi] *s* Rezept *n*

recipient [ri'sɪpi·ənt] *s* Empfänger -in *mf*

reciprocal [ri'sɪprəkəl] *adj* gegenseitig

reciprocate [ri'sɪprə,ket] *tr* sich erkenntlich zeigen für || *intr* sich erkenntlich zeigen

reciprocity [ˌresɪ'prɑsɪti] *s* Gegenseitigkeit *f*

recital [ri'saɪtəl] *s* Vortrag *m*

recite [ri'saɪt] *tr* vortragen

reckless ['reklɪs] *adj* (careless of consequences) unbekümmert; (lacking caution) leichtsinnig; (negligent) fahrlässig

reck'less driv'ing *s* rücksichtsloses Fahren *n*

reckon ['rekən] *tr* (count) rechnen; (compute) (coll) schätzen || *intr* rechnen; (coll) schätzen; **r. on** rechnen auf (acc); **r. with** (deal with) abrechnen mit; (take into consideration) rechnen mit

reck'oning *s* (accounting) Abrechnung *f*; (computation) Berechnung *f*; (aer, naut) Besteck *n*

reclaim [ri'klem] *tr* (demand back) zurückfordern; (from wastes) rückgewinnen; (land) urbar machen

reclamation [ˌreklə'meʃən] s (of land) Urbarmachung f

recline [rɪ'klaɪn] intr ruhen; r. against sich lehnen an (acc); r. in (a chair) sich zurücklehnen in (dat)

recluse ['reklus] s Einsiedler –in mf

recognition [ˌrekəg'nɪʃən] s Wiedererkennung f; (acknowledgement) Anerkennung f; gain r. zur Geltung kommen

recognizable [ˌrekəg'naɪzəbəl] adj erkennbar

recognize ['rekəgˌnaɪz] tr (by) erkennen (an dat); r. as anerkennen als

recoil ['rɪkɔɪl] s (of a rifle) Rückstoß m; (arti) Rücklauf m || [rɪ'kɔɪl] intr (in fear) zurückfahren; (from, e.g., a challenge) zurückschrecken vor (dat); (said of a rifle) zurückstoßen; (arti) zurücklaufen

recoilless [rɪ'kɔɪllɪs] adj rückstoßfrei

recollect [ˌrekə'lekt] tr sich erinnern an (acc)

recollection [ˌrekə'lekʃən] s Erinnerung f

recommend [ˌrekə'mend] tr empfehlen

recommendation [ˌrekəmən'deʃən] s Empfehlung f

recompense ['rekəmˌpens] s (for) Vergütung f (für) || tr vergüten

reconcile ['rekənˌsaɪl] tr (with) versöhnen (mit); become reconciled sich versöhnen; r. oneself to sich abfinden mit

reconciliation [ˌrekənˌsɪlɪ'eʃən] s Versöhnung f, Aussöhnung f

recondite ['rekənˌdaɪt] adj (deep) tiefgründig; (obscure) dunkel

recondition [ˌrikən'dɪʃən] tr wiederinstandsetzen

reconnaissance [rɪ'kɑnɪsəns] s Aufklärung f

reconnoiter [ˌrekə'nɔɪtər] tr erkunden || intr aufklären

reconquer [rɪ'kɑŋkər] tr zurückerobern

reconquest [rɪ'kɑŋkwest] s Zurückeroberung f

reconsider [ˌrikən'sɪdər] tr noch einmal erwägen

reconstruct [ˌrikən'strʌkt] tr (rebuild) wiederaufbauen; (make over) umbauen; (e.g., events of a case) rekonstruieren

record ['rekərd] adj Rekord– || s (highest achievement) Rekord m; (document) Akte f, Protokoll n; (documentary evidence) Aufzeichnung f; (mus) Schallplatte f; have a criminal r. vorbestraft sein; keep a r. of Buch führen über (acc); make a r. of zu Protokoll nehmen; off the r. inoffiziell; on r. bisher registriert; set a r. e-n Rekord aufstellen || [rɪ'kɔrd] tr (in writing) aufzeichnen; (officially) protokollieren; (on tape or disk) aufnehmen || intr Schallplatten aufnehmen

rec′ord chang′er s Plattenwechsler m

recorder [rɪ'kɔrdər] s Protokollführer –in mf; (device) Zähler m; (on tape

or disk) Aufnahmegerät; (mus) Blockflöte f

rec′ord hold′er s Rekordler –in mf

record′ing adj aufzeichnend; (on tape or disk) Aufnahme– || s Aufzeichnung f; (on tape or disk) Tonaufnahme f

record′ing sec′retary s Protokollführer –in mf

rec′ord play′er s Plattenspieler m

recount ['rɪˌkaunt] s Nachzählung f || [rɪ'kaunt] tr (count again) nachzählen || [rɪ'kaunt] tr (relate) im einzelnen erzählen

recoup [rɪ'kup] tr (losses) wieder einbringen; (a fortune) wiedererlangen; (reimburse) entschädigen

recourse [rɪ'kors], ['rikors] s (to) Zuflucht f (zu); (jur) Regreß m; have r. to seine Zuflucht nehmen zu

recover [rɪ'kʌvər] tr (get back) wiedererlangen; (losses) wiedereinbringen; (e.g., a spent rocket) bergen; (one's balance) wiederfinden; (e.g., a chair) neu beziehen || intr (from) sich erholen (von)

recovery [rɪ'kʌvəri] s Wiedererlangung f, Rückgewinnung f; (of health) Genesung f; (of a rocket) Bergung f

recreation [ˌrekrɪ'eʃən] s Erholung f

recrea′tion room′ s Unterhaltungsraum m

recruit [rɪ'krut] s Rekrut m || (& mil) rekrutieren; be recruited from sich rekrutieren aus

recruit′ing of′ficer s Werbeoffizier m

recruitment [rɪ'krutmənt] s Rekrutierung f; (mil) Rekrutenaushebung f

rectangle ['rekˌtæŋgəl] s Rechteck n

rectangular [rek'tæŋgjələr] adj rechteckig

rectifier ['rektəˌfaɪ-ər] s Berichtiger m; (elec) Gleichrichter m

recti•fy ['rektɪˌfaɪ] v (pret & pp –fied) tr berichtigen; (elec) gleichrichten

rector ['rektər] s Rektor m

rectory ['rektəri] s Pfarrhaus n

rec•tum ['rektəm] s (–ta [tə]) Mastdarm m

recumbent [rɪ'kʌmbənt] adj liegend

recuperate [rɪ'k(j)upəˌret] intr sich (wieder) erholen

re•cur [rɪ'kʌr] v (pret & pp –curred; ger –curring) intr wiederkehren

recurrence [rɪ'kʌrəns] s Wiederkehr f

red [red] adj (redder; reddest) rot || s Rot n, Röte f; be in the red in den Roten Zahlen stecken; Red (pol) Rote mf; see red wild werden

red′ ant′ s rote Waldameise f

red′bird′ s Kardinal m

red′blood′ed adj lebensprühend

red′breast′ s Rotkehlchen n

red′ cab′bage s Rotkohl m

red′ car′pet s (fig) roter Teppich m

red′ cent′ s; not give a r. for keinen roten Heller geben für

red′-cheeked′ adj rotbäckig

Red′ Cross′, the s das Rote Kreuz

redden ['redən] tr röten, rot machen || intr erröten, rot werden

reddish ['redɪʃ] adj rötlich

redecorate [ri'dɛkə‚ret] *tr* neu dekorieren

redeem [ri'dim] *tr* zurückkaufen; (*a pawned article, promise*) einlösen; **r. oneself** seine Ehre wiederherstellen

redeemable [ri'diməbəl] *adj* (fin) ablösbar, kündbar

Redeemer [ri'dimər] *s* Erlöser *m*

redemption [ri'dɛmpʃən] *s* Rückkauf *m*, Wiedereinlösung *f*; (relig) Erlösung *f*

red'-haired' *adj* rothaarig

red'-hand'ed *adj*—**catch s.o. r.** j-n auf frischer Tat ertappen

red'head' *s* Rotkopf *m*

red' her'ring *s* Bückling *m*; (fig) Ablenkungsmanöver *n*

red'-hot' *adj* glühend heiß, rotglühend

redirect [‚ridɪ'rɛkt] *tr* umdirigieren

rediscover [‚ridɪs'kʌvər] *tr* wiederentdecken

red'-let'ter day' *s* Glückstag *m*

red' light' *s* rotes Licht *n*

red'-light' dis'trict *s* Bordellviertel *n*

red' man' *s* Rothaut *f*

redness ['rɛdnɪs] *s* Röte *f*

re·do ['ri'du] *v* (*pret* **–did**; *pp* **–done**) *tr* neu machen; (*redecorate*) renovieren

redolent ['rɛdələnt] *adj* (*with*) r. duftend (*nach*)

redoubt [ri'daut] *s* Redoute *f*

redound [ri'daund] *intr*—**r. to** gereichen zu

red' pep'per *s* spanischer Pfeffer *m*

redress [ri'drɛs] *s* Wiedergutmachung *f* ‖ *tr* wiedergutmachen

Red' Rid'inghood' *s* Rotkäppchen *n*

red'skin' *s* Rothaut *f*

red' tape' *s* Amtsschimmel *m*

reduce [ri'd(j)us] *tr* reduzieren, verringern; (*prices*) herabsetzen; (math) (ab)kürzen

reduction [ri'dʌkʃən] *s* Verminderung *f*; (*gradual reduction*) Abbau *m*; (*in prices*) Absetzung *f*; (*in weight*) Abnahme *f*

redundant [ri'dʌndənt] *adj* überflüssig

red' wine' *s* Rotwein *m*

red'wing' *s* Rotdrossel *f*

red'wood' *s* Rotholz *n*

reecho [ri'ɛko] *tr* wiederhallen lassen ‖ *intr* wiederhallen

reed [rid] *s* Schilf *n*; (*in mouthpiece*) Rohrblatt *n*; (*of metal*) Zunge *f*; (*pastoral pipe*) Hirtenflöte *f*

reedit [ri'ɛdɪt] *tr* neu herausgeben

reeducate [ri'ɛdʒu‚ket] *tr* umerziehen

reef [rif] *s* Riff *n*; (naut) Reff *n* ‖ *tr* (naut) reffen

reek [rik] *intr* (**of**) riechen (*nach*)

reel [ril] *s* (*sway*) Taumeln *n*; (*for cables*) Trommel *f*; (angl, cin) Spule *f*; (min, naut) Haspel *f* ‖ *tr* (angl, cin) spulen; (min, naut) haspeln; **r. in** (*a fish*) einholen; **r. off** abhaspeln; (fig) herunterrasseln ‖ *intr* taumeln

reelect [‚ri·ɪ'lɛkt] *tr* wiederwählen

reelection [‚ri·ɪ'lɛkʃən] *s* Wiederwahl *f*

reenlist [‚ri·ɛn'lɪst] *tr* wieder anwerben ‖ *intr* sich weiterverpflichten

reenlistment [‚ri·ɛn'lɪstmənt] *s* Weiterverpflichtung *f*

reentry [ri'ɛntri] *s* Wiedereintritt *m*

reexamination [‚ri·ɛg‚zæmɪ'neʃən] *s* Nachprüfung *f*

re·fer [ri'fʌr] *v* (*pret* & *pp* **–ferred**; *ger* **–ferring**) *tr*—**r. s.o. to** j-n verweisen an (*acc*) ‖ *intr*—**r. to** hinweisen auf (*acc*); (*e.g., to an earlier correspondence*) sich beziehen auf (*acc*)

referee [‚rɛfə'ri] *s* (box) Ringrichter *m*; (sport) Schiedsrichter *m* ‖ *tr* als Schiedsrichter fungieren bei ‖ *intr* als Schiedsrichter fungieren

reference ['rɛfərəns] *s* (**to**) Hinweis *m* (auf *acc*); (*person or document*) Referenz *f*; **in r. to** in Bezug auf (*acc*); **make r. to** hinweisen auf (*acc*)

ref'erence lib'rary *s* Handbibliothek *f*

ref'erence work' *s* Nachschlagewerk *n*

referen·dum [‚rɛfə'rɛndəm] *s* (**-da** [də]) Volksentscheid *m*

referral [ri'fʌrəl] *s* (**to**) Zuweisung *f* (an *acc*, auf *acc*); **by r.** auf Empfehlung

refill ['rifɪl] *s* Nachfüllung *f*; (*for a pencil, ball-point pen*) Ersatzmine *f* ‖ [ri'fɪl] *tr* nachfüllen

refine [ri'faɪn] *tr* (metal) läutern; (*oil, sugar*) raffinieren; (fig) verfeinern

refinement [ri'faɪnmənt] *s* Läuterung *f*; (*of oil, sugar*) Raffination *f*; (fig) Verfeinerung *f*

refinery [ri'faɪnəri] *s* Raffinerie *f*

reflect [ri'flɛkt] *tr* (& fig) widerspiegeln ‖ *intr* (*throw back rays*) reflektieren; (**on**) nachdenken (über *acc*); **r. on** (*comment on*) sich äußern über (*acc*); (*bring reproach on*) ein schlechtes Licht werfen auf (*acc*)

reflection [ri'flɛkʃən] *s* (*e.g., of light*) Reflexion *f*; (*reflected image*) Spiegelbild *n*; (*thought*) Überlegung *f*; **that's no r. on you** das färbt nicht auf Sie ab

reflector [ri'flɛktər] *s* Reflektor *m*

reflex ['riflɛks] *s* Reflex *m*

reflexive [ri'flɛksɪv] *adj* (gram) reflexiv ‖ *s* Reflexivform *f*

reforestation [‚rifɔrɪs'teʃən] *s* Aufforstung *f*

reform [ri'fɔrm] *s* Reform *f* ‖ *tr* reformieren, verbessern ‖ *intr* sich bessern

reformation [‚rɛfər'meʃən] *s* Besserung *f*; **Reformation** Reformation *f*

reformatory [ri'fɔrmə‚tori] *s* Besserungsanstalt *f*

reformer [ri'fɔrmər] *s* Reformator *-in* *mf*

reform' school' *s* Besserungsanstalt *f*

refraction [ri'frækʃən] *s* Ablenkung *f*

refrain [ri'fren] *s* Kehrreim *m* ‖ *intr*—**r. from** sich enthalten (*genit*); **r. from** (*ger*) es unterlassen zu (*inf*)

refresh [ri'frɛʃ] *tr* erfrischen; (*the memory*) auffrischen

refresh'er course' [ri'frɛʃər] *s* Auffrischungskurs *m*

refresh'ing *adj* erfrischend

refreshment [rɪ'freʃmənt] s Erfrischung f

refresh'ment stand' s Erfrischungsstand m

refrigerant [rɪ'frɪdʒərənt] s Kühlmittel n

refrigerate [rɪ'frɪdʒə,ret] tr kühlen

refrigerator [rɪ'frɪdʒə,retər] s Kühlschrank m; (walk-in type) Kühlraum m

refrig'erator car' s (rr) Kühlwagen m

re•fuel [ri'fjul] v (pret & pp –fuel[l]ed; ger –fuel[l]ing) tr auftanken || intr tanken

refuge ['refjudʒ] s Zuflucht f; take r. in (sich) flüchten in (acc)

refugee [,refju'dʒi] s Flüchtling m

refugee' camp' s Flüchtlingslager n

refund ['rifʌnd] s Zurückzahlung f || [rɪ'fʌnd] tr (pay back) zurückzahlen || [ri'fʌnd] tr (fund again) neu fundieren

refurnish [ri'fʌrnɪʃ] tr neu möblieren

refusal [rɪ'fjuzəl] s Ablehnung f

refuse ['refjus] s Abfall m || [rɪ'fjuz] tr ablehnen; r. to (inf) sich weigern zu (inf)

refutation [,refju'teʃən] s Widerlegung f

refute [rɪ'fjut] tr widerlegen

regain [rɪ'gen] tr zurückgewinnen

regal ['rigəl] adj königlich

regale [rɪ'gel] tr (delight) ergötzen; (entertain) reichlich bewirten

regalia [rɪ'gelɪ-ə] spl Insignien pl

regard [rɪ'gɑrd] s (for) Rücksicht f (auf acc); best regards to herzlichster Gruß an (acc); have little r. for wenig achten; in every r. in jeder Hinsicht; in (or with) r. to in Hinsicht auf (acc); in this r. in dieser Hinsicht; without r. for ohne Rücksicht auf (acc) || tr betrachten; as regards in Bezug auf (acc)

regard/ing prep hinsichtlich (genit)

regardless [rɪ'gɑrdlɪs] adv (coll) ungeniert; r. of ungeachtet (genit)

regatta [rɪ'gætə] s Regatta f

regency ['ridʒənsi] s Regentschaft f

regenerate [rɪ'dʒenə,ret] tr regenerieren

regent ['ridʒənt] s Regent –in mf

regicide ['redʒɪ,saɪd] s (act) Königsmord m; (person) Königsmörder –in mf

regime [re'ʒim] s Regime n

regiment ['redʒɪmənt] s (mil) Regiment n || ['redʒɪ,ment] tr reglementieren

regimental [,redʒɪ'mentəl] adj Regiments–

region ['ridʒən] s Gegend f, Region f

regional ['ridʒənəl] adj regional

register ['redʒɪstər] s Register n, Verzeichnis n || tr registrieren; (students) immatrikulieren; (feelings) erkennen lassen || intr sich einschreiben lassen; (at a hotel) sich eintragen lassen

reg/istered let/ter s eingeschriebener Brief m

reg/istered nurse/ s (staatlich) geprüfte Krankenschwester f

registrar ['redʒɪstrɑr] s Registrator –in mf

registration [,redʒɪs'treʃən] s (e.g., of firearms) Registrierung f; (for a course; at a hotel) Anmeldung f; (of a trademark) Eintragung f; (aut) Zulassung f; (educ) Einschreibung f

registra/tion blank/ s Meldeformular n

registra/tion fee/ s Anmeldegebühr f

registra/tion num/ber s Registriernummer f

regression [rɪ'greʃən] s Rückgang m

regret [rɪ'gret] s (over) Bedauern n (über acc) || v (pret & pp –gretted; ger regretting) tr bedauern; I r. to say es tut mir leid, sagen zu müssen

regrettable [rɪ'gretəbəl] adj bedauerlich

regroup [rɪ'grup] tr umgruppieren

regular ['regjələr] adj (usual) gewöhnlich; (pulse, breathing, features, intervals) regelmäßig; r. army stehendes Heer n; r. guy (coll) Pfundskerl m; r. officer Berufsoffizier –in mf

regularity [,regjə'lærɪti] s Regelmäßigkeit f

regulate ['regjə,let] tr regeln

regulation [,regjə'leʃən] s Regelung f; (rule) Vorschrift f, Bestimmung f; against regulations vorschriftswidrig

regulator ['regjə,letər] s Regler m

rehabilitate [,rihə'bɪlɪ,tet] tr rehabilitieren

rehash [ri'hæʃ] tr (coll) aufwärmen

rehearsal [rɪ'hʌrsəl] s Probe f

rehearse [rɪ'hʌrs] tr & intr proben

rehire [ri'haɪr] tr wiedereinstellen

reign [ren] s Regierung f; (period of rule) Regierungszeit f || intr regieren; r. over herrschen über (acc)

reimburse [ri-ɪm'bʌrs] tr (costs) rückerstatten; r. s.o. for s.th. j–m etw vergüten

rein [ren] s Zügel m; give free r. to die Zügel schießen lassen (dat) || tr —r. in (a horse) parieren

reincarnation [,ri-ɪnkɑr'neʃən] s Reinkarnation f, Wiedergeburt f

rein/deer/ s Rentier n

reinforce [,ri-ɪn'fors] tr verstärken

reinforced/ concrete/ s Stahlbeton m

reinforcement [,ri-ɪn'forsmənt] s Verstärkung f; reinforcements (mil) Verstärkungen pl

reinstate [,ri-ɪn'stet] tr (in) wiedereinsetzen (in acc)

reiterate [ri'ɪtə,ret] tr wiederholen

reject ['ridʒekt] s Ausschußware f || [rɪ'dʒekt] tr ablehnen, zurückweisen; (a request, appeal) abweisen

rejection [rɪ'dʒekʃən] s Ablehnung f; (of a request, appeal) Abweisung f

rejoice [rɪ'dʒɔɪs] intr frohlocken

rejoin [rɪ'dʒɔɪn] tr (answer) erwidern; (a group) sich wieder anschließen (dat)

rejoinder [rɪ'dʒɔɪndər] s Erwiderung f; (jur) Duplik f

rejuvenate [rɪ'dʒuvɪ,net] tr verjüngen

rekindle [ri'kɪndəl] tr wieder anzünden; (fig) wieder entzünden

relapse [rɪ'læps] s (& pathol) Rückfall

m ‖ *intr* (**into**) wieder verfallen (in *acc*)

relate [rɪ'let] *tr* (*a story*) erzählen; (*connect*) verknüpfen; **r. sth. to s.th.** etw auf etw [*acc*] beziehen ‖ *intr*—**r. to** in Beziehung stehen mit

relat'ed *adj* (*by blood*) verwandt; (*by marriage*) verschwägert; (*subjects*) benachbart

relation [rɪ'leʃən] *s* Beziehung *f*, Verhältnis *n*; (*relative*) Verwandte *mf*; **in r. to** in Bezug auf (*acc*); **relations** (*sex*) Verkehr *m*

rela'tionship' *s* (*connection*) Beziehung *f*; (*kinship*) Verwandschaft *f*

relative ['relətɪv] *adj* relativ, verhältnismäßig; **r. to** bezüglich (*genit*) ‖ *s* Verwandte *mf*

rel'ative clause' *s* Relativsatz *m*

rel'ative pro'noun *s* Relativpronomen *n*

relativity [‚relə'tɪvɪti] *s* Relativität *f*

relax [rɪ'læks] *tr* auflockern; (*muscles*) entspannen ‖ *intr* sich entspannen

relaxation [‚rilæk'seʃən] *s* Entspannung *f*; **r. of tension** Entspannung *f*

relay ['rile] *s* Relais *n*; (*sport*) Staffel *f* ‖ [ri'le] *v* (*pret & pp* **-layed**) *tr* übermitteln; (*through relay stations*) übertragen

re'lay race' *s* Staffellauf *m*

re'lay team' *s* Staffel *f*

release [rɪ'lis] *s* (*from*) Entlassung *f* (*aus*); (*of bombs*) Abwurf *m*; (*of news*) Mitteilung *f* ‖ *tr* entlassen; (*a film, book*) freigeben; (*bombs*) abwerfen; (*energy*) freisetzen; (*brakes*) lösen; **r. the clutch** auskuppeln

relegate ['reli‚get] *tr* (**to**) verweisen (*an acc*); **r. to second position** auf den zweiten Platz verweisen

relent [rɪ'lent] *intr* (*let up*) nachlassen; (*yield*) sich erweichen lassen

relentless [rɪ'lentlɪs] *adj* (*tireless*) unermüdlich; (*unappeasable*) unerbittlich; (*never-ending*) unaufhörlich

relevant ['relɪvənt] *adj* sachdienlich

reliable [rɪ'laɪ-əbəl] *adj* zuverlässig

reliance [rɪ'laɪ-əns] *s* Vertrauen *n*

relic ['relɪk] *s* Reliquie *f*; **r. of the past** Zeuge *m* der Vergangenheit

relief [rɪ'lif] *s* Erleichterung *f*; (*for the poor*) Armenunterstützung *f*; (*replacement*) Ablösung *f*; (*sculpture*) Relief *n*; **on r.** von Sozialhilfe lebend; **bring r.** Linderung schaffen; **go on r.** stempeln gehen

relief' map' *s* Reliefkarte *f*

relieve [rɪ'liv] *tr* erleichtern; (*from guard duty*) ablösen; **r. oneself** seine Notdurft verrichten

religion [rɪ'lɪdʒən] *s* Religion *f*

religious [rɪ'lɪdʒəs] *adj* religiös; (*order*) geistlich

relinquish [rɪ'lɪŋkwɪʃ] *tr* aufgeben; **r. the right to s.th. to s.o.** j-m das Recht auf etw [*acc*] überlassen

relish ['relɪ/] *s* (*for*) Genuß *m* (*an acc*); (*condiment*) Würze *f* ‖ *tr* genießen

reluctance [rɪ'lʌktəns] *s* Widerstreben *n*

reluctant [rɪ'lʌktənt] *adj* widerstrebend; **be r. to do s.th.** etw ungern tun

reluctantly [rɪ'lʌktntli] *adv* ungern

re-ly [rɪ'laɪ] *v* (*pret & pp* **-lied**) *intr*—**r. on** sich verlassen auf (*acc*)

remain [rɪ'men] *s*—**remains** Überreste *pl*; (*corpse*) sterbliche Reste *pl* ‖ *intr* bleiben; (*at end of letter*) verbleiben; **r. behind** zurückbleiben; **r. seated** sitzenbleiben; **r. steady** (*said of prices*) sich behaupten

remainder [rɪ'mendər] *s* Restbestand *m*, Rest *m* ‖ *tr* verramschen

remark [rɪ'mark] *s* Bemerkung *f* ‖ *tr* bemerken

remarkable [rɪ'markəbəl] *adj* markant, bemerkenswert

remar-ry [ri'mæri] *v* (*pret & pp* **-ried**) *tr* sich wiederverheiraten mit ‖ *intr* sich wiederverheiraten

reme-dy ['remɪdi] *s* (*for*) Heilmittel *n* (*für*); (*fig*) (*for*) Gegenmittel *n* (*gegen*) ‖ *v* (*pret & pp* **-died**) *tr* abhelfen (*dat*); (*damage, shortage*) abheben

remember [rɪ'membər] *tr* sich erinnern an (*acc*); **r. me** to empfehlen Sie mich (*dat*) ‖ *intr* sich erinnern

remembrance [rɪ'membrəns] *s* Erinnerung *f*; **in r. of** zum Andenken an (*acc*)

remind [rɪ'maɪnd] *tr* (**of**) erinnern (*an acc*); **r. s.o. to** (*inf*) j-n mahnen zu (*inf*)

reminder [rɪ'maɪndər] *s* (*note*) Zettel *m*; (*from a creditor*) Mahnung *f*

reminisce [‚remɪ'nɪs] *intr* in Erinnerungen schwelgen

remiss [rɪ'mɪs] *adj* nachlässig

remission [rɪ'mɪʃən] *s* Nachlaß *m*

re-mit [rɪ'mɪt] *v* (*pret & pp* **-mitted;** *ger* **-mitting**) *tr* (*in cash*) übersenden; (*by check*) überweisen; (*forgive*) vergeben

remittance [rɪ'mɪtəns] *s* (*in cash*) Übersendung *f*; (*by check*) Überweisung *f*

remnant ['remnənt] *s* Rest *m*; (*of cloth*) Stoffrest *m*

remod-el [ri'madəl] *v* (*pret & pp* **-el[l]ed;** *ger* **-el[l]ing**) *tr* umgestalten; (*a house*) umbauen

remonstrate [rɪ'manstret] *intr* protestieren; **r. with s.o.** j-m Vorwürfe machen

remorse [rɪ'mɔrs] *s* Gewissensbisse *pl*

remorseful [rɪ'mɔrsfəl] *adj* reumütig

remote [rɪ'mot] *adj* fern; (*possibility*) vage; (*idea*) blaß; (*resemblance*) entfernt; (*secluded*) abgelegen

remote' control' *s* Fernsteuerung *f*; (*telv*) Fernbedienung *f*; **guide by r.** fernlenken

removable [rɪ'muvəbəl] *adj* entfernbar

removal [rɪ'muvəl] *s* Entfernung *f*; (*by truck*) Abfuhr *f*; (*from office*) Absetzung *f*

remove [rɪ'muv] *tr* entfernen; (*clothes*) ablegen; (*one's hat*) abnehmen; (*e.g., dishes from the table*) abräumen; (*a stain*) entfernen; (*from office*) absetzen; (*furniture*) ausräumen

remuneration [rɪ‚mjunə'reʃən] s Vergütung f

renaissance [‚renə'sɑns] s Renaissance f

rend [rend] v (pret & pp **rent** [rent]) tr (& fig) zerreißen

render ['rendər] tr (give) geben; (a service) leisten; (honor) erweisen; (thanks) abstatten; (a verdict) fällen; (translate; play, e.g., on the piano) wiedergeben; **r. harmless** unschädlich machen

rendez·vous ['rɑndə‚vu] s (–vous [‚vuz]) Rendezvous n, Treffpunkt m; (mil) Sammelplatz m ‖ v (pret & pp –voused [‚vud]; ger –vousing [‚vu·ɪŋ]) intr sich treffen; (mil) sich versammeln

rendition [ren'dɪʃən] s Wiedergabe f

renegade ['renɪ‚ged] s Renegat –in mf

renege [rɪ'nɪg] s Renonce f ‖ intr (cards) nicht bedienen; **r. on** nicht einhalten

renew [rɪ'n(j)u] tr erneuern; (e.g., a passport) verlängern lassen

renewable [rɪ'n(j)u·əbəl] adj erneuerbar

renewal [rɪ'n(j)u·əl] s Erneuerung f; (e.g., of a passport) Verlängerung f

renounce [rɪ'nauns] tr verzichten auf (acc)

renovate ['renə‚vet] tr renovieren; (fig) erneuern

renovation [‚renə've‚ʃən] s Renovierung f

renown [rɪ'naun] s Ruhm m

renowned [rɪ'naund] adj (for) berühmt (wegen)

rent [rent] adj zerrissen ‖ s Miete f; (tear) Riß m ‖ tr mieten; **r. out** vermieten

rental ['rentəl] s Miete f

rent'al serv'ice s Verleih m

rent'ed car' s Mietwagen m, Mietauto n

renter ['rentər] s Mieter –in mf

renunciation [rɪ‚nʌnsɪ'eʃən] s (of) Verzicht m (auf acc)

reopen [ri'opən] tr wieder öffnen; (a business) wieder eröffnen; (an argument; school year) wieder beginnen ‖ intr (said of a shop or business) wieder geöffnet werden; (said of a school year) wieder beginnen

reopening [ri'opənɪŋ] s (of a business) Wiedereröffnung f; (of school) Wiederbeginn m; (jur) Wiederaufnahme f

reorder [ri'ɔrdər] tr nachbestellen

reorganization [‚ri·ɔrgənɪ'zeʃən] s Reorganisation f, Neuordnung f

reorganize [ri'ɔrgə‚naɪz] tr reorganisieren; (an administration) umbilden

repack [ri'pæk] tr umpacken

repair [rɪ'per] s Ausbesserung f, Reparatur f; **in bad r.** in schlechtem Zustand; **keep in good r.** in Stande halten ‖ tr ausbessern, reparieren ‖ intr (to) sich begeben (nach, zu)

repair' gang' s Störungstrupp m

repair' shop' s Reparaturwerkstatt f

repaper [ri'pepər] tr neu tapezieren

reparation [‚repə're/ən] s Wiedergutmachung f; **reparations** Reparationen pl, Kriegsentschädigung f

repartee [‚repar'ti] s schlagfertige Antwort f

repast [rɪ'pæst] s Mahl n

repatriate [ri'petrɪ‚et] tr repatriieren

re·pay [rɪ'pe] v (pret & pp –paid) tr (e.g., a loan) zurückzahlen; (a person) entschädigen; **r. a favor** e–n Gefallen erwidern

repayment [rɪ'pemənt] s Rückzahlung f; (reprisal) Vergeltung f

repeal [rɪ'pil] s Aufhebung f ‖ tr aufheben, außer Kraft setzen

repeat [rɪ'pit] tr wiederholen; (a story, gossip) weitererzählen; **r. s.th. after s.o.** j–m etw nachsagen

repeat'ed adj abermalig, mehrmalig

repeatedly [rɪ'pitɪdli] adv wiederholt

re·pel [rɪ'pel] v (pret & pp –pelled; ger –pelling) tr (an enemy, an attack) zurückschlagen; (e.g., water) abstoßen

repellent [rɪ'pelənt] s Bekämpfungsmittel n

repent [rɪ'pent] tr bereuen ‖ intr Reue empfinden; **r. of** bereuen

repentance [rɪ'pentəns] s Reue f

repentant [rɪ'pentənt] adj reuig

repercussion [‚ripər'kʌʃən] s Rückwirkung f

repertory ['repər‚tori] s Repertoire n

repetition [‚repɪ'tɪʃən] s Wiederholung f

replace [rɪ'ples] tr (with) ersetzen (durch)

replaceable [rɪ'plesəbəl] adj ersetzbar

replacement [rɪ'plesmənt] s (act) Ersetzen n; (substitute part) Ersatz m; (person) Ersatzmann m

replay ['riple] s (sport) Wiederholungsspiel n ‖ [ri'ple] tr nochmals spielen

replenish [rɪ'plenɪʃ] tr wieder auffüllen

replete [rɪ'plit] adj angefüllt

replica ['replɪkə] s Replik f

re·ply [rɪ'plaɪ] s Erwiderung f; (letter) Antwortschreiben n; **in r. to your letter** in Beantwortung Ihres Schreibens ‖ v (pret & pp –plied) tr & intr erwidern

report [rɪ'port] s Bericht m; (rumor) Gerücht n; (e.g., of a gun) Knall m ‖ tr (give an account of) berichten; (give notice of) melden; **r. s.o. to the police** j–n bei der Polizei anzeigen ‖ intr (to) sich melden (bei); **r. in** sich anmelden

report' card' s Zeugnis n

reportedly [rɪ'portɪdli] adv angeblich

reporter [rɪ'portər] s Reporter –in mf

repose [rɪ'poz] s Ruhe f ‖ intr ruhen

repository [rɪ'pazɪ‚tori] s Verwahrungsort m; (of information) Fundgrube f

represent [‚reprɪ'zent] tr vertreten; (depict) darstellen

representation [‚reprɪzen'teʃən] s Vertretung f; (depiction) Darstellung f

representative [‚reprɪ'zentətɪv] adj (function) stellvertretend; (government) parlamentarisch; (typical) (of)

typisch (für) ‖ s Vertreter –in mf;
(pol) Abgeordnete mf
repress [rɪˈpres] tr unterdrücken;
(psychoanal) verdrängen
repression [rɪˈpreʃən] s Unterdrückung
f; (psychoanal) Verdrängung f
reprieve [rɪˈpriːv] s Strafaufschub m;
(fig) Gnadenfrist f, Atempause f
reprimand [ˈreprɪˌmænd] s Verweis
m; give s.o. a r. j-m e-n Verweis
erteilen ‖ tr (for) zurechtweisen
(wegen, für), rügen (wegen, für)
reprint [ˈriprɪnt] s Nachdruck m ‖
[riˈprɪnt] tr nachdrucken
reprisal [rɪˈpraɪzəl] s Vergeltung f;
take reprisals against or on Repres-
salien ergreifen gegen
reproach [rɪˈproʧ] s Vorwurf m ‖ tr
(for) tadeln (wegen); r. s.o. with
s.th. j-m etw vorwerfen
reproduce [ˌriprəˈd(j)uːs] tr reproduzieren; (copies) vervielfältigen; (an
experiment) wiederholen; (a play)
neuaufführen; (a sound) wiedergeben; (a lost limb) regenerieren ‖ intr
sich fortpflanzen
reproduction [ˌriprəˈdʌkʃən] s Repro-
duktion f; (making copies) Vervielfältigung f; (of sound) Wiedergabe f;
(biol) Fortpflanzung f
reproductive [ˌriprəˈdʌktɪv] adj Fort-
pflanzungs-
reproof [rɪˈpruːf] s Rüge f
reprove [rɪˈpruːv] tr rügen
reptile [ˈreptaɪl] s Kriechtier n
republic [rɪˈpʌblɪk] s Republik f
republican [rɪˈpʌblɪkən] adj republikanisch ‖ s Republikaner –in mf
repudiate [rɪˈpjuːdɪˌet] tr (disown) verleugnen; (a charge) zurückweisen; (a
debt) nicht anerkennen; (a treaty)
für unverbindlich erklären; (a
woman) verstoßen
repugnant [rɪˈpʌgnənt] adj widerwärtig
repulse [rɪˈpʌls] s (refusal) Zurück-
weisung f; (setback) Rückschlag m ‖
tr zurückweisen; (mil) zurückschlagen
repulsive [rɪˈpʌlsɪv] adj abstoßend
reputable [ˈrepjətəbəl] adj anständig
reputation [ˌrepjəˈteʃən] s Ruf m, Ansehen n; have the r. of being in the
Rufe stehen zu sein
repute [rɪˈpjuːt] s—be held in high r.
hohes Ansehen genießen; bring into
bad r. in üble Nachrede bringen;
of r. von Ruf ‖ tr—she is reputed to
be a beauty sie soll e-e Schönheit
sein
reputedly [rɪˈpjutɪdli] adv angeblich
request [rɪˈkwest] s Bitte f, Gesuch n;
at his r. auf seine Bitte; on r. auf
Wunsch ‖ tr (a person) bitten; (a
thing) bitten um, ersuchen
Requiem [ˈrekwɪˌem] s (Mass) Seelen-
messe f; (chant, composition)
Requiem n
require [rɪˈkwaɪr] tr erfordern; if required erforderlichenfalls
requirement [rɪˈkwaɪrmənt] s Anfor-
derung f
requisite [ˈrekwɪzɪt] adj erforderlich ‖

s Erfordernis n; (required article)
Requisit n
requisition [ˌrekwɪˈzɪʃən] s Anforde-
rung f; (mil) Requisition f ‖ tr anfordern; (mil) beschlagnahmen
requital [rɪˈkwaɪtəl] s (retaliation)
Vergeltung f; (for a kindness) Belohnung f
requite [rɪˈkwaɪt] tr vergelten; r. s.o.
for a favor sich j-m für e-n Gefallen
erkenntlich zeigen
re-read [riˈrid] v (pret & pp –read
[red]) tr nachlesen
rerun [ˈriˌrʌn] s (cin) Reprise f
resale [ˈriˌsel] s Wiederverkauf m
rescind [rɪˈsɪnd] tr (an order) rückgängig machen; (a law) aufheben
rescue [ˈreskju] s Rettung f, Bergung
f ‖ tr retten, bergen
rescuer [ˈreskjuˌər] s Retter –in mf
research [rɪˈsʌrʧ, ˈrisʌrʧ] s Forschung f; do r. on Forschungen betreiben über (acc) ‖ intr forschen
researcher [ˈrisʌrʧər] s Forscher –in
mf
re-sell [riˈsel] v (pret & pp –sold) tr
wiederverkaufen, weiterverkaufen
resemblance [rɪˈzembləns] s (to) Ähnlichkeit f (mit); bear a close r. to s.o.
große Ähnlichkeit mit j-m haben
resemble [rɪˈzembəl] tr ähneln (dat)
resent [rɪˈzent] tr—I r. your remark
Ihre Bemerkung paßt mir nicht
resentful [rɪˈzentfəl] adj grollend
resentment [rɪˈzentmənt] s Groll m;
feel r. toward God Groll hegen gegen
reservation [ˌrezərˈveʃən] s Vorbestel-
lung f; (Indian land) Reservation f;
do you have a r.? haben Sie vorbe-
stellt?; make reservations vorbestellen
reserve [rɪˈzʌrv] s (discretion) Zurückhaltung f; (econ, mil) Reserve f;
without r. rückhaltlos ‖ tr (e.g.,
seats) reservieren, belegen; r. judgment mit seinem Urteil zurückhalten
reserved [rɪˈzʌrvd] adj (place) belegt; (person)
zurückhaltend
reserve' officer s Reserveoffizier m
reservist [rɪˈzʌrvɪst] s Reservist –in mf
reservoir [ˈrezərˌvwar] s Staubecken
m
re-set [riˈset] v (pret & pp –set; ger
–setting) tr (a gem) neu fassen;
(mach) nachstellen; (typ) neu setzen
resettle [riˈsetəl] tr & intr umsiedeln
reshape [riˈʃep] tr umformen
reshuffle [riˈʃʌfəl] tr (cards) neu
mischen; (pol) umgruppieren
reside [rɪˈzaɪd] intr wohnen
residence [ˈrezɪdəns] s Wohnsitz m;
(for students) Studentenheim n
resident [ˈrezɪdənt] adj wohnhaft ‖ s
Einwohner –in mf
residential [ˌrezɪˈdenʃəl] adj Wohn-
residue [ˈrezɪˌd(j)u] s Rest m; (chem)
Rückstand m
resign [rɪˈzaɪn] tr (an office) niederlegen; r. oneself to sich ergeben in
(acc) ‖ intr zurücktreten
resignation [ˌrezɪgˈneʃən] s (from an
office) Rücktritt m; (submissive

state) Ergebung *f;* **hand in one's r.** sein Entlassungsgesuch einreichen

resilience [rɪ'zɪlɪ·əns] *s* Elastizität *f;* (fig) Spannkraft *f*

resilient [rɪ'zɪlɪ·ənt] *adj* elastisch; (fig) unverwüstlich

resin ['rɛzɪn] *s* Harz *n*

resist [rɪ'zɪst] *tr* widerstehen (*dat*) ‖ *intr* Widerstand leisten

resistance [rɪ'zɪstəns] *s* (& elec) Widerstand *m*

resole [ri'sol] *tr* neu besohlen

resolute ['rɛzə‚lut] *adj* entschlossen

resolution [‚rɛzə'luʃən] *s* (*resoluteness*) Entschlossenheit *f;* (parl) Beschluß *m;* **make good resolutions** gute Vorsätze fassen

resolve [rɪ'zɑlv] *s* Vorsatz *m* ‖ *tr* auflösen; (*a question, problem*) lösen; **r. to** (*inf*) beschließen zu (*inf*) ‖ *intr* —**r. into** sich auflösen in (*acc*); **r. upon s.th.** sich [*dat*] etw vornehmen

resonance ['rɛzənəns] *s* Resonanz *f*

resort [rɪ'zɔrt] *s* (*refuge*) Zuflucht *f;* (*for health*) Kurort *m;* (*for vacation*) Ferienort *m,* Sommerfrische *f;* **as a last r.** als letztes Mittel ‖ *intr*—**r. to** greifen zu

resound [rɪ'zaund] *intr* widerhallen

resource ['risors] *s* Mittel *n;* **resources** (fin) Geldmittel *pl*

resourceful [rɪ'sorsfəl] *adj* findig

respect [rɪ'spɛkt] *s* (*esteem*) Achtung *f,* Respekt *m;* (*reference*) Hinsicht *f;* **in every r.** in jeder Hinsicht; **pay one's respects to s.o.** j-m seine Aufwartung machen; **with r. to** mit Bezug auf (*acc*) ‖ *tr* achten

respectable [rɪ'spɛktəbəl] *adj* achtbar; (*e.g., firm*) angesehen

respect'ed angesehen

respectful [rɪ'spɛktfəl] *adj* ehrerbietig

respectfully [rɪ'spɛktfəli] *adv*—**r. yours** hochachtungsvoll, Ihr ... or Ihre ...

respective [rɪ'spɛktɪv] *adj* jeweilig

respectively [rɪ'spɛktɪvli] *adv* beziehungsweise

respiration [‚rɛspɪ'reʃən] *s* Atmung *f*

respirator ['rɛspɪ‚retər] *s* Atemgerät *n*

respiratory ['rɛspɪrə‚tori] *adj* Atmungs-

respite ['rɛspɪt] *s* (*pause*) Atempause *f;* (*reprieve*) Aufschub *m;* **without r.** ohne Unterlaß

resplendent [rɪ'splɛndənt] *adj* glänzend

respond [rɪ'spɑnd] *tr* antworten ‖ *intr* (*reply*) (**to**) antworten (auf *acc*); (*react*) (**to**) ansprechen (auf *acc*)

response [rɪ'spɑns] *s* Antwort *f;* (*reaction*) Reaktion *f;* (fig) Widerhall *m;* **in r. to** als Antwort auf (*acc*)

responsibility [rɪ‚spɑnsɪ'bɪlɪti] *s* Verantwortung *f*

responsible [rɪ'spɑnsɪbəl] *adj* (*position*) verantwortlich; (*person*) verantwortungsbewußt; **be held r. for** verantwortlich gemacht werden für; **be r. for** (*be answerable for*) verantwortlich sein für; (*be to blame for*) schuld sein an (*dat*); (*be the cause of*) die Ursache sein (*genit*); (*be liable for*) haften für

responsive [rɪ'spɑnsɪv] *adj*—**be r. to** ansprechen auf (*acc*)

rest [rɛst] *s* (*repose*) Ruhe *f;* (*from work*) Ruhepause *f;* (*e.g., from walking*) Rast *f;* (*remainder*) Rest *m;* (*support*) Stütze *f;* (mus) Pause *f;* **all the r.** (*in number*) alle andern; (*in quantity*) alles übrige; **be at r.** (*be calm*) beruhigt sein; (*be dead*) ruhen; (*not be in motion*) sich in Ruhelage befinden; **come to r.** stehenbleiben; **put one's mind to r.** sich beruhigen; **take a r.** sich ausruhen; **the r. of the boys** die übrigen (or andern) Jungen ‖ *intr* ruhen lassen, ausruhen; (*support, e.g., one's elbow*) stützen ‖ *intr* sich ausruhen; **r. on** lasten auf (*dat*); (*be based on*) beruhen auf (*dat*); **r. with** liegen bei

restaurant ['rɛstərənt] *s* Restaurant *n*

restful ['rɛstfəl] *adj* ruhig

rest' home' *s* Erholungsheim *n*

rest'ing place' *s* Ruheplatz *m;* **final r.** letzte Ruhestätte *f*

restitution [‚rɛstɪ't(j)uʃən] *s* Wiedergutmachung *f;* **make r.** Genugtuung leisten

restive ['rɛstɪv] *adj* (*restless*) unruhig; (*balky*) störrisch

restless ['rɛstlɪs] *adj* ruhelos

restock [ri'stɑk] *tr* wieder auffüllen; (*waters*) wieder mit Fischen besetzen

restoration [‚rɛstə'reʃən] *s* (*of a work of art or building*) Restaurierung *f*

restore [rɪ'stor] *tr* (*order*) wiederherstellen; (*a painting, building*) restaurieren; (*stolen goods*) zurückerstatten; **r. to health** wiederherstellen

restrain [rɪ'stren] *tr* zurückhalten; (*feelings; a horse*) zügeln; (*trade*) einschränken; **r. s.o. from** (*ger*) j-n davon abhalten zu (*inf*)

restrain'ing or'der *s* Unterlassungsurteil *n*

restraint [rɪ'strent] *s* Zurückhaltung *f;* (*force*) Zwang *m*

restrict [rɪ'strɪkt] *tr* begrenzen; **r. to** beschränken auf (*acc*)

restrict'ed ar'ea *s* Sperrgebiet *n*

rest' room' *s* Abort *m,* Toilette *f*

result [rɪ'zʌlt] *s* Ergebnis *n,* Resultat *n;* (*consequence*) Folge *f;* **as a r. of** als Folge (*genit*); **without r.** ergebnislos ‖ *intr*—**r. from** sich ergeben aus; **r. in** führen zu

result' clause' *s* Folgesatz *m*

resume [rɪ'zum] *tr* wieder aufnehmen; (*a journey*) fortsetzen

résumé ['rɛzu‚me] *s* Zusammenfassung *f*

resumption [rɪ'zʌmpʃən] *s* Wiederaufnahme *f*

resurface [ri'sʌrfɪs] *tr*—**r. the road with** die Straßendecke erneuern von ‖ *intr* (naut & fig) wiederauftauchen

resurrect [‚rɛzə'rɛkt] *tr* (*the dead*) wieder zum Leben erwecken; (fig) wieder aufleben lassen

resurrection [‚rɛzə'rɛkʃən] *s* Auferstehung *f*

resuscitate [rɪ'sʌsɪ‚tet] *tr* wiederbeleben

retail ['ritel] *adj* Kleinhandels– || *adv* im Kleinhandel || *tr* im Kleinhandel verkaufen || *intr*—r. at two dollars im Kleinverkauf zwei Dollar kosten

re'tail busi'ness *s* Kleinhandel *m*

retailer ['riteler] *s* Kleinhändler –in *mf*

retain [rɪ'ten] *tr* (zurück)behalten; (*a lawyer*) sich [*dat*] nehmen

retainer [rɪ'tenər] *s* (hist) Gefolgsmann *m*; (jur) Honorarvorschuß *m*

retain'ing wall' *s* Stützmauer *f*

retake ['ritek] *s* (cin) Neuaufnahme *f* || [ri'tek] *tr* (*a town*) zurückerobern; (cin) nochmals aufnehmen

retaliate [rɪ'tælɪ͵et] *intr* (**against**) Vergeltung üben (an *dat*)

retaliation [rɪ͵tælɪ'eʃən] *s* Vergeltung *f*

retaliatory [rɪ'tælɪ‧ə͵torɪ] *adj* Vergeltungs–

retard [rɪ'tɑrd] *tr* verzögern

retard'ed *adj* zurückgeblieben

retch [retʃ] *intr* würgen

retch'ing *s* Würgen *n*

retell [ri'tel] *tr* wiedererzählen

retention [rɪ'tenʃən] *s* Beibehaltung *f*

re‑think [ri'θɪŋk] *v* (*pret & pp* –thought) *tr* umdenken

reticence ['retɪsəns] *s* Verschwiegenheit *f*

reticent ['retɪsənt] *adj* verschwiegen

retina ['retɪnə] *s* Netzhaut *f*, Retina *f*

retinue ['retɪ͵n(j)u] *s* Gefolge *n*

retire [rɪ'taɪr] *tr* pensionieren || *intr* (*from employment*) in den Ruhestand treten; (*withdraw*) sich zurückziehen; (*go to bed*) sich zur Ruhe begeben

retired' *adj* pensioniert

retirement [rɪ'taɪrmənt] *s* Ruhestand *m*; **go into r.** in den Ruhestand treten, sich pensionieren lassen

retire'ment pay' *s* Pension *f*

retire'ment plan' *s* Pensionsplan *m*

retir'ing *adj* zurückhaltend

retort [rɪ'tɔrt] *s* schlagfertige Erwiderung *f*; (chem) Retorte *f* || *tr & intr* erwidern

retouch [ri'tʌtʃ] *tr* retuschieren

retrace [ri'tres] *tr* zurückverfolgen

retract [rɪ'trækt] *tr* (*a statement*) widerrufen; (claws; landing gear) einziehen

retract'able land'ing gear' [rɪ'træktəbəl] *s* Verschwindfahrgestell *n*

retrain [ri'tren] *tr* umschulen

retread ['ri͵tred] *s* (aut) runderneuerter Reifen *m* || *tr* runderneuern

retreat [rɪ'trit] *s* (quiet place) Ruhesitz *m*; (mil) Rückzug *m*; (rel) Exerzitien *pl*; **beat a hasty r.** eilig den Rückzug antreten || *intr* sich zurückziehen

retrench [rɪ'trentʃ] *tr* einschränken || *intr* sich einschränken

retribution [͵retrɪ'bjuʃən] *s* Vergeltung *f*

retrieval [rɪ'trivəl] *s* Wiedererlangung *f*

retrieve [rɪ'triv] *tr* wiedererlangen; (*a loss*) wettmachen; (hunt) apportieren

retriever [rɪ'trivər] *s* Apportierhund *m*

retroactive [͵retro'æktɪv] *adj* (**from**) rückwirkend von ... an

retrogressive [͵retrə'gresɪv] *adj* rückläufig

retrorocket ['retro͵rɑkɪt] *s* Bremsrakete *f*

retrospect ['retrə͵spekt] *s*—**in r.** rückblickend

re‑try [ri'traɪ] *v* (*pret & pp* –tried) *tr* (jur) nochmals verhandeln

return [rɪ'tʌrn] *s* Rückkehr *f*; (giving back) Rückgabe *f*; (the way back) Rückweg *m*; (tax form) Steuererklärung *f*; (profit) Umsatz *m*; (tennis) Rückschlag *m*; **in r. dafür**; **in r. for** als Entgelt für; **returns** (profits) Ertrag *m*; (of an election) Ergebnisse *pl* || *tr* zurückgeben; (send back) zurücksenden; (put back) zurückstellen; (thanks) abstatten; (a verdict) fällen; (a favor, love, gun fire) erwidern; (tennis) zurückschlagen || *intr* zurückkehren; **r. to** (e.g., a topic) zurückkommen auf (acc)

return' address' *s* Rückadresse *f*

return' flight' *s* Rückflug *m*

return' match' *s* Revanchepartie *f*

return' tick'et *s* Rückfahrkarte *f*; (aer) Rückflugkarte *f*

reunification [͵ri͵junɪfɪ'keʃən] *s* (pol) Wiedervereinigung *f*

reunion [ri'junjən] *s* Treffen *n*

rev [rev] *v* (*pret & pp* revved; ger revving) *tr* (up) auf Touren bringen || *intr* auf Touren kommen

revamp [ri'væmp] *tr* umgestalten

reveal [rɪ'vil] *tr* offenbaren

reveille ['revəli] *s* Wecken *n*

rev‑el ['revəl] *s* Gelage *n* || *v* (*pret & pp* –el[l]ed; ger –el[l]ing) *intr* ein Gelage halten; **r. in** (fig) schwelgen in (dat)

revelation [͵revə'leʃən] *s* Offenbarung *f*; **Revelations** (Bib) Offenbarung *f*

reveler ['revələr] *s* Zecher –in *mf*

revelry ['revəlrɪ] *s* Zechgelage *n*

revenge [rɪ'vendʒ] *s* Rache *f*; **take r. on s.o. for s.th.** sich an j–m für etw rächen || *tr* rächen

revengeful [rɪ'vendʒfəl] *adj* rachsüchtig

revenue ['revə͵n(j)u] *s* (yield) Ertrag *m*; (internal revenue) Steueraufkommen *n*

rev'enue stamp' *s* Banderole *f*

reverberate [rɪ'vʌrbə͵ret] *intr* widerhallen

revere [rɪ'vɪr] *tr* verehren

reverence ['revərəns] *s* (respect given or received) Ehrerbietung *f*; (respect felt) Ehrfurcht *f*

reverend ['revərənd] *adj* ehrwürdig; **the Reverend ...** Hochwürden ...

reverie ['revərɪ] *s* Träumerei *f*; **be lost in r.** in Träumen versunken sein

reversal [rɪ'vʌrsəl] *s* Umkehrung *f*; (of opinion) Umschwung *m*

reverse [rɪ'vʌrs] *adj* umgekehrt; (side) linke *f*; (back side) Rückseite *f*; (opposite) Gegenteil *n*; (setback) Rückschlag *m*; (of a coin) Revers *m*;

(aut) Rückwärtsgang m ‖ tr umkehren, umdrehen; (a decision) umstoßen ‖ intr sich rückwärts bewegen

reverse' side' s Rückseite f, Kehrseite f

reversible [rɪ'vʌrsɪbəl] adj (decision) umstoßbar; (material) zweiseitig; (chem, phys) umkehrbar; (mach) umsteuerbar

revert [rɪ'vʌrt] intr—r. to zurückkommen auf (acc); (jur) zurückfallen an (acc)

review [rɪ'vju] s (of) Überblick m (über acc); (of a lesson) Wiederholung f; (of a book) Besprechung f; (periodical) Rundschau m; (mil) Besichtigung f; pass in r. mustern ‖ tr (a lesson) wiederholen; (a book) besprechen; (e.g., the events of the day) überblicken; (mil) besichtigen

reviewer [rɪ'vju·ər] s Besprecher –in mf

revile [rɪ'vaɪl] tr schmähen

revise [rɪ'vaɪz] tr (a book) umarbeiten; (one's opinion) revidieren

revised' edi'tion s verbesserte Auflage f

revision [rɪ'vɪʒən] s Neubearbeitung f

revival [rɪ'vaɪvəl] s Wiederbelebung f; (rel) Erweckung f; (theat) Reprise f

reviv'al meet'ing s Erweckungsversammlung f

revive [rɪ'vaɪv] tr wieder aufleben lassen; (memories) aufführen; (a victim) wieder zu Bewußtsein bringen ‖ intr wieder aufleben

revoke [rɪ'vok] tr widerrufen

revolt [rɪ'volt] s Aufstand m ‖ tr abstoßen ‖ intr revoltieren

revolt'ing adj abstoßend

revolution [ˌrevə'luʃən] s Revolution f; (turn) Umdrehung f; **revolutions per minute** Drehzahl f

revolutionary [ˌrevə'luʃəˌneri] adj revolutionär ‖ s Revolutionär –in mf

revolve [rɪ'vɑlv] intr (around) sich drehen (um)

revolver [rɪ'vɑlvər] s Revolver m

revolv'ing adj Dreh-

revue [rɪ'vju] s (theat) Revue f

revulsion [rɪ'vʌlʃən] s Abscheu m

reward [rɪ'wɔrd] s Belohnung f ‖ tr belohnen

reward'ing adj lohnend

re·wind [rɪ'waɪnd] v (pret & pp –wound) tr (a tape, film) umspulen; (a clock) wieder aufziehen

rewire [rɪ'waɪr] tr Leitungen neu legen in (dat)

rework [rɪ'wʌrk] tr umarbeiten

re·write [rɪ'raɪt] v (pret –wrote; pp –written) tr umschreiben

rhapsody ['ræpsədi] s Rhapsodie f

rheostat ['ri·əˌstæt] s Rheostat m

rhetoric ['retərɪk] s Redekunst f

rhetorical [rɪ'tɔrɪkəl] adj rhetorisch

rheumatic [ru'mætɪk] adj rheumatisch

rheumatism ['ruməˌtɪzəm] s Rheumatismus m

Rhine [raɪn] s Rhein m

Rhineland ['raɪnˌlænd] s Rheinland n

rhine'stone' s Rheinkiesel m

rhinoceros [raɪ'nɑsərəs] s Nashorn n

rhubarb ['rubɑrb] s Rhabarber m; (sl) Krach m

rhyme [raɪm] s Reim m ‖ tr & intr reimen

rhythm ['rɪðəm] s Rhythmus m

rhythmic(al) ['rɪðmɪk(əl)] adj rhythmisch

rib [rɪb] s Rippe f ‖ v (pret & pp ribbed; ger ribbing) tr (coll) sich lustig machen über (acc)

ribald ['rɪbəld] adj zotig

ribbon ['rɪbən] s Band n; (decoration) Ordensband n; (for a typewriter) Farbband n

rice [raɪs] s Reis m

rich [rɪtʃ] adj reich; (voice) volltönend; (soil) fruchtbar; (funny) (coll) köstlich; r. in reich an (dat) ‖ **riches** spl Reichtum m

rickets ['rɪkɪts] s Rachitis f

rickety ['rɪkɪti] adj (building) baufällig; (furniture) wackelig

rid [rɪd] v (pret & pp rid; ger ridding) tr (of) befreien (von); **get rid of** loswerden

riddance ['rɪdəns] s Befreiung f; good r.! den (or die or das) wäre ich glücklich los!

riddle ['rɪdəl] s Rätsel n

ride [raɪd] s Fahrt f; **give s.o. a r.** j–n im Auto mitnehmen; **take for a r.** (murder) entführen und umbringen; (dupe) hochnehmen ‖ v (pret rode [rod]; pp ridden ['rɪdən]) tr (a bicycle) fahren; (a horse) reiten; (a train, bus) fahren mit; (harass) hetzen; **r. out** (a storm) gut überstehen ‖ intr (e.g., in a car) fahren; (on a horse) reiten; **let s.th. r.** sich mit etw abfinden

rider ['raɪdər] s (on horseback) Reiter –in mf; (on a bicycle) Radfahrer –in mf; (in a vehicle) Fahrer –in mf; (to a document) Zusatzklausel f

ridge [rɪdʒ] s (of a hill; of the nose) Rücken m; (of a roof) Dachfirst m

ridge'pole' s Firstbalken m

ridicule ['rɪdɪˌkjul] s Spott m ‖ tr verspotten

ridiculous [rɪ'dɪkjələs] adj lächerlich; **look r.** lächerlich wirken

rid'ing acad'emy s Reitschule f

rid'ing boot' s Reitstiefel m

rid'ing breech'es spl Reithose f

rid'ing hab'it s Reitkostüm n

rife [raɪf] adj häufig; **r. with** voll von

riffraff ['rɪfˌræf] s Gesindel n

rifle ['raɪfəl] s Gewehr n ‖ tr ausplündern

rift [rɪft] s (& fig) Riß m

rig [rɪg] s (gear) Ausrüstung f; (horse and carriage) Gespann n; (truck) Laster m; (oil drill) Bohrturm m; (getup) (coll) Aufmachung f; (naut) Takelung f ‖ v (pret & pp rigged; ger rigging) tr (auf)takeln; (prices, elections, accounts) manipulieren

rig'ging s Takelung f

right [raɪt] adj (side, glove, angle) recht; (just) gerecht; (correct) richtig; (moment) richtig; **do you have the r. time?** können Sie mir die genaue Uhrzeit sagen?; **be in one's r. mind** bei klarem Verstand sein; **it is all r.** es ist schon gut; **r.?** nicht wahr?; **that's r.!** eben!; **the r. thing** das Richtige; **you are r.** Sie haben recht || *adv* direkt; *(to the right)* rechts; **r. along** durchaus; **r. away** sofort, gleich; **r. behind the door** gleich hinter der Tür; **r. glad** (coll) recht froh; **r. here** gleich hier; **r. now** *(at the moment)* momentan; *(immediately)* sofort; **r. through** durch und durch || *s* Recht *n*; (box) Rechte *f*; **all rights reserved** alle Rechte vorbehalten; **by rights** von Rechts wegen; **in the r.** im Recht; **on the r.** rechts, zur Rechten || *tr* aufrichten; *(an error)* berichtigen; *(a wrong)* wiedergutmachen || *interj* stimmt!

righteous [ˈraɪt/əs] *adj* gerecht, rechtschaffen; *(smug)* selbstgerecht

rightful [ˈraɪtfəl] *adj (owner)* rechtmäßig; *(claim, place)* berechtigt

right'-hand' *adj (for Rechten)*; *(glove)* recht

right'-hand'ed *adj* rechtshändig

right-hander [ˈraɪtˈhændər] *s* Rechtshänder –in *mf*

right'-hand man' *s* rechte Hand *f*

rightist [ˈraɪtɪst] *adj* rechtsstehend || *s* Rechtspolitiker –in *mf*

rightly [ˈraɪtli] *adv* richtig; *(rightfully)* rechtmäßig

right' of way' *s (in traffic)* Vorfahrtsrecht *n*; *(across another's land)* Grunddienstbarkeit *f*

right' wing' *s* rechter Flügel *m*

rigid [ˈrɪdʒɪd] *adj* steif, starr

rigmarole [ˈrɪgmə‚rol] *s (meaningless talk)* Geschwafel *n*; *(fuss)* Getue *n*

rigorous [ˈrɪgərəs] *adj* hart, streng

rile [raɪl] *tr* aufbringen

rill [rɪl] *s* Bächlein *n*

rim [rɪm] *s* Rand *m*; *(of eyeglasses)* Fassung *f*; *(of a wheel)* Felge *f*

rind [raɪnd] *s* Rinde *f*

ring [rɪŋ] *s (for the fingers; for boxing; of criminals or spies; of a circus; circle under the eyes)* Ring *m*; *(of a bell, voice, laughter)* Klang *m*; **give s.o. a r.** (telp) j–n anrufen; **run rings around s.o.** j–n in die Tasche stecken || *v (pret & pp ringed) tr* umringen; **r. in** einschließen || *v (pret rang* [ræŋ]; *pp rung* [rʌŋ]) *tr* läuten; **r. the bell** läuten, klingeln; **r. out** ausläuten; **r. up** anrufen || *intr* läuten, klingeln; **my ears are ringing** mir klingen die Ohren; **r. for s.o.** nach j–m klingeln; **r. out** laut schallen; **the bell is ringing** es läutet

ring'ing *adj* schallend || *s* Läuten *n*; *(in the ears)* Klingen *n*

ring'lead'er *s* Rädelsführer *m*

ring'mas'ter *s* Zirkusdirektor *m*

ring'side' *s* Ringplatz *m*

ring'worm' *s* Scherpilzflechte *f*

rink [rɪŋk] *s* Eisbahn *f*; *(for rollerskating)* Rollschuhbahn *f*

rinse [rɪns] *s* Spülen *n* || *tr* ausspülen

riot [ˈraɪ-ət] *s* Aufruhr *m*; **r. of colors**

Farbengemisch *n*; **run r.** sich austoben; *(said of plants)* wuchern || *intr* sich zusammenrotten

ri'ot act'—**read the r. to s.o.** j–m die Leviten lesen

rioter [ˈraɪ-ətər] *s* Aufrührer –in *mf*

rip [rɪp] *s* Riß *m* || *v (pret & pp ripped; ger ripping) tr* (zer)reißen; **rip off** abreißen; *(the skin)* abziehen; *(cheat)* betrügen || *intr* reißen

rip' cord' *s* Reißlinie *f*

ripe [raɪp] *adj* reif

ripen [ˈraɪpən] *tr (& fig)* reifen lassen || *intr (& fig)* reifen

rip' off' *s* (sl) Wucher *m*

ripple [ˈrɪpəl] *s* leichte Welle *f* || *intr* leichte Wellen schlagen

rise [raɪz] *s* Aufsteigen *n*; *(in prices)* Steigerung *f*; *(of heavenly bodies)* Aufgang *m*; *(increase, e.g., in population)* Zunahme *f*; *(in the ground)* Erhebung *f*; **get a r. out of s.o.** j–n zu e–r Reaktion veranlassen; **give r. to** veranlassen || *v (pret rose* [roz]; *pp risen* [ˈrɪzən]) *intr (said of the sun, of a cake)* aufgehen; *(said of a river, prices, temperature, barometer)* steigen; *(said of a road)* ansteigen; *(get out of bed)* aufstehen; *(stand up)* sich erheben; *(from the dead)* auferstehen; *(said of anger)* hochsteigen; **r. to the occasion** sich der Lage gewachsen zeigen; **r. up from the ranks** von der Pike auf dienen

riser [ˈraɪzər] *s (of a staircase)* Futterbrett *n*; **early r.** Frühaufsteher –in *mf*; **late r.** Langschläfer –in *mf*

risk [rɪsk] *s* Risiko *n*; **run the r. of** *(ger)* Gefahr laufen zu *(inf)* || *tr* wagen, aufs Spiel setzen

risky [ˈrɪski] *adj* riskant, gewagt

risque [rɪsˈke] *adj* schlüpfrig

rite [raɪt] *s* Ritus *m*; **last rites** Sterbesakramente *pl*

ritual [ˈrɪt/ʊ-əl] *adj* rituell || *s* Ritual *n*

ri-val [ˈraɪvəl] *adj* rivalisierend || *s* Rivale *m*, Rivalin *f* || *v (pret & pp -val[l]ed; ger -val[l]ing) tr* rivalisieren, wetteifern mit

rivalry [ˈraɪvəlri] *s* Rivalität *f*

river [ˈrɪvər] *adj* Fluß– || *s* Fluß *m*

riv'er ba'sin *s* Flußgebiet *n*

riv'erfront' *s* Flußufer *n*

riv'erside' *adj* am Flußufer gelegen || *s* Flußufer *n*

rivet [ˈrɪvɪt] *s* Niet *m* || *tr* nieten

riv'et gun' *s* Nietmaschine *f*

riv'eting *s (act)* Vernieten *n*; *(connection)* Nietnaht *f*

rivulet [ˈrɪvjəlɪt] *s* Flüßchen *n*

R.N. [ˈɑrˈen] *s (registered nurse)* staatlich geprüfte Krankenschwester *f*

roach [rotʃ] *s (ent)* Schabe *f*; (ichth) Plötze *f*

road [rod] *s (& fig)* Weg *m*; **be (much) on the r.** (viel) auf Reisen sein; **go on the r.** auf Tour gehen; (theat) auf Tournee gehen

road'bed' *s* Bahnkörper *m*

road'block' *s* Straßensperre *f*

road′ hog′ *s* rücksichtsloser Autofahrer *m*

road′ house′ *s* Wirtshaus *n*, Rasthaus *n*

road′ map′ *s* Straßenkarte *f*, Autokarte *f*

road/side′ *adj* Straßen– ‖ *s* Straßenrand *m*

road/side inn′ *s* Rasthaus *n*

road/sign′ *s* Wegweiser *m*

road/stead′ *s* Reede *f*

road′ test′ *s* (aut) Probefahrt *f*

road/way′ *s* Fahrweg *m*

roam [rom] *tr* durchstreifen ‖ *intr* herumstreifen

roar [ror] *s* Gebrüll *n*; (*of a waterfall, sea, wind*) Brausen *n*; (*of an engine*) Dröhnen *n*; (*laughter*) schallendes Gelächter *n* ‖ *intr* brüllen; (*said of a waterfall, sea, wind*) brausen; **r. at** anbrüllen; (*e.g., a joke*) schallend lachen über (*acc*); **r. by** vorbeibrausen; **r. with** brüllen vor (*dat*)

roast [rost] *adj* gebraten ‖ *s* Braten *m* ‖ *tr* (*meat, fish*) braten, rösten; (*coffee, chestnuts*) rösten; (*a person*) (coll) durch den Kakao ziehen ‖ *intr* braten

roast′ beef′ *s* Roastbeef *n*

roaster [′rostər] *s* (*appliance*) Röster *m*, Röstapparat *m*; (*fowl*) Brathuhn *n*

roast′ pork′ *s* Schweinsbraten *m*

rob [rɑb] *v* (*pret & pp* **robbed**; *ger* **robbing**) *tr* (*a thing*) rauben; (*a person*) (*of*) berauben (*genit*)

robber [′rɑbər] *s* Räuber –in *mf*

robbery [′rɑbəri] *s* Raubüberfall *m*

robe [rob] *s* Robe *f*; (*house robe*) Hausrock *m* ‖ *tr* feierlich ankleiden ‖ *intr* sich feierlich ankleiden

robin [′rɑbɪn] *s* Rotkehlchen *n*

robot [′robɑt] *s* Roboter *m*

robust [ro′bʌst] *adj* robust

rock [rɑk] *adj* (mus) Rock– ‖ *s* Fels *m*; (*one that is thrown*) Stein *m*; (mus) Rockmusik *f*; **on the rocks** mit Eiswürfeln; (*ruined*) kaputt ‖ *tr* schaukeln, wiegen; **r. the boat** (fig) die Sache ins Wanken bringen; **r. to sleep** in den Schlaf wiegen ‖ *intr* schwanken, wanken; (*said of a boat*) schaukeln

rock′-bot′tom *adj* äußerst niedrig ‖ *s* Tiefpunkt *m*

rock′ can′dy *s* Kandiszucker *m*

rock′ crys′tal *s* Bergkristall *m*

rocker [′rɑkər] *s* Schaukelstuhl *m*; **go off one's r.** (coll) den Verstand verlieren

rocket [′rɑkɪt] *s* Rakete *f*

rock′et launch′er *s* Raketenwerfer *m*

rocketry [′rɑkətri] *s* Raketentechnik *f*

rock′et ship′ *s* Rakentenflugkörper *m*

rock′ gar′den *s* Steingarten *m*

rock′ing chair′ *s* Schaukelstuhl *m*

rock′ing horse′ *s* Schaukelpferd *m*

rock-'n'-roll [′rɑkən′rol] *s* Rock 'n Roll *m*

rock′ salt′ *s* Steinsalz *n*

rocky [′rɑki] *adj* felsig; (*shaky*) wacklig

rod [rɑd] *s* Stab *m*, Stange *f*; (*whip*)

Zuchtrute *f*; (*of the retina; of a microorganism*) Stäbchen *n*; (*revolver*) (sl) Schießeisen *n*; (angl) Angelrute *f*; (Bib) Reis *n*; (mach) Pleuelstange *f*; (surg) Absteckpfahl *m*

rodent [′rodənt] *s* Nagetier *n*

roe [ro] *s* (*deer*) Reh *n*; (ichth) Rogen *m*

rogue [rog] *s* Schuft *m*, Schurke *m*

rogues′′ gal′lery *s* Verbrecheralbum *n*

roguish [′rogɪʃ] *adj* schurkisch

role, rôle [rol] *s* Rolle *f*

roll [rol] *s* Rolle *f*; (*bread*) Brötchen *n*; (*of thunder, of a ship*) Rollen *n*; (*of drums*) Wirbel *m*; (*of fat*) Wulst *m*; **call the r.** die Namen verlesen; (mil) Appell halten ‖ *tr* rollen; (*cigarettes*) drehen; (*metals, roads*) walzen; **r. over** überrollen; **r. up** zusammenrollen; (*sleeves*) zurückstreifen ‖ *intr* sich wälzen; **be rolling in money** im Geld wühlen

roll/back′ *s* (com) Senkung *f*

roll/call′ *s* Namensverlesung *f*; (mil) Appell *m*

roll′er bear′ing *s* Rollenlager *n*

roll′er coast′er *s* Berg-und-Tal-Bahn *f*

roll′er skate′ *s* Rollschuh *m*

roll′er-skate′ *intr* rollschuhlaufen

roll′er tow′el *s* Rollhandtuch *n*

roll′ing mill′ *s* Walzwerk *n*

roll′ing pin′ *s* Nudelholz *n*, Teigrolle *f*

roll′ing stock′ *s* (rr) rollendes Material *n*

roly-poly [′roli′poli] *adj* dick und rund

roman [′romən] *adj* (typ) Antiqua–; **Roman** römisch ‖ *s* (typ) Antiqua *f*; **Roman** Römer –in *mf*

Ro′man can′dle *s* Leuchtkugel *f*

Ro′man Cath′olic *adj* römisch-katholisch ‖ *s* Katholik –in *mf*

romance [ro′mæns] *adj* (ling) romanisch ‖ *s* Romanze *f*

Romanesque [,romə′nɛsk] *adj* romanisch ‖ *s* das Romanische

Ro′man nose′ *s* Römernase *f*

Ro′man nu′meral *s* römische Ziffer *f*

romantic [ro′mæntɪk] *adj* romantisch

romanticism [ro′mæntɪ,sɪzəm] *s* Romantik *f*

romp [rɑmp] *intr* umhertollen

rompers [′rɑmpərz] *spl* Spielanzug *m*

roof [ruf] *s* Dach *n*; (aut) Verdeck *n*; **raise the r.** (coll) Krach machen; **r. of the mouth** Gaumendach *n*

roofer [′rufər] *s* Dachdecker *m*

roof′ gar′den *s* Dachgarten *m*

roof′ tile′ *s* Dachziegel *m*

rook [ruk] *s* (chess) Turm *m*; (orn) Saatkrähe *f* ‖ *tr* (coll) (*out of*) beschwindeln (um)

rookie [′ruki] *s* (coll) Neuling *m*

room [rum] *s* Zimmer *n*; (*space*) Raum *m*, Platz *m*; **make r.** Platz machen; **r. for complaint** Anlaß *m* zur Klage; **take up too much r.** zu viel Platz in Anspruch nehmen ‖ *intr* wohnen

room′ and board′ *s* Kost und Quartier *m*

room′ clerk′ *s* Empfangschef *m*

roomer [′rumər] *s* Mieter –in *mf*

room'ing house' *s* Pension *f*
room'mate' *s* Zimmergenosse *m*
room' serv'ice *s* Bedienung *f* aufs Zimmer
roomy ['rumɪ] *adj* geräumig
roost [rust] *s* Hühnerstange *f*; **rule the r.** Hahn im Korb sein || *intr* auf der Stange sitzen
rooster ['rustər] *s* Hahn *m*
root [rut] *s* Wurzel *f*; **get to the r. of s.th.** etw [*dat*] auf den Grund gehen; **take r.** Wurzel schlagen; (fig) sich einbürgern || *tr*—**be rooted in** wurzeln in (*dat*); **rooted to the spot** festgewurzelt; **r. out** ausrotten || *intr* —**r. about** wühlen; **r. for** zujubeln (*dat*)
rope [rop] *s* Strick *m*, Seil *n*; **know the ropes** alle Kniffe kennen || *tr* mit e—m Seil festbinden; (*a steer*) mit e—m Lasso einfangen; **r. in** (coll) einwickeln; **r. off** absperren
rosary ['rozərɪ] *s* Rosenkranz *m*
rose [roz] *adj* rosenrot || *s* Rose *f*
rose'bud' *s* Rosenknospe *f*
rose'bush' *s* Rosenstock *m*
rose'-col'ored *adj* rosenfarbig; (fig) rosa(rot)
rosemary ['roz meri] *s* Rosmarin *m*
rosin ['rɑzɪn] *s* Harz *n*; (*for violin bow*) Kolophonium *n*
roster ['rɑstər] *s* Namensliste *f*; (educ) Stundenplan *m*; (mil, naut) Dienstplan *m*
rostrum ['rɑstrəm] *s* Rednerbühne *f*
rosy ['rozɪ] *adj* (& fig) rosig
rot [rɑt] *s* Fäulnis *f*; (sl) Quatsch *m* || *v* (*pret* & *pp* **rotted**; *ger* **rotting**) *tr* faulen lassen || *intr* verfaulen
rotate ['rotet] *tr* rotieren lassen; (*tires*) auswechseln; (agr) wechseln || *intr* rotieren; (*take turns*) sich abwechseln
rotation [ro'teʃən] *s* Rotation *f*; **in r.** wechselweise; **r. of crops** Wechselwirtschaft *f*
rote [rot] *s*—**by r.** mechanisch
rotisserie [ro'tɪsərɪ] *s* Fleischbraterei *f*
rotten ['rɑtən] *adj* faul; (*trick*) niederträchtig; **feel r.** (sl) sich elend fühlen
rotund [ro'tʌnd] *adj* rundlich
rotunda [ro'tʌndə] *s* Rotunde *f*
rouge [ruʒ] *s* Rouge *n* || *tr* schminken
rough [rʌf] *adj* (*hands, voice, person*) rauh; (*piece of wood*) roh; (*work, guess, treatment*) grob; (*water, weather*) stürmisch; (*road*) uneben; **have it r.** viel durchmachen || *tr*— **r. in** roh entwerfen; (carp) grob bearbeiten; **r. it** primitiv leben; **r. up** grob behandeln
rough' draft' *s* Konzept *n*
roughen ['rʌfən] *tr* aufrauhen
rough'house' *s* Radau *m* || *intr* Radau machen
roughly ['rʌflɪ] *adv* grob; (*about*) etwa
rough'neck' *s* (coll) Rauhbein *n*
roulette [ru'let] *s* Roulett *n*
round [raund] *adj* rund || *s* Runde *f*; (*of applause*) Salve *f*; (*shot*) Schuß *m*; (*of drinks*) Lage *f*; (*of a sentinel,*

---

policeman, inspector, mailman) Rundgang *m*; **daily r.** Alltag *m* || *prep* um (*acc*) herum || *tr* (*make round*) runden; (*a corner*) herumgehen (*or* herumfahren) um (*acc*); **r. off** abrunden; (*finish*) vollenden; **r. up** (*animals*) zusammentreiben; (*persons*) zusammenbringen; (*criminals*) ausheben
round'house' *s* (rr) Lokomotivschuppen *m*
round'-shoul'dered *adj* mit runden Schultern
round' steak' *s* Kugel *f*
round'-ta'ble *adj* am runden Tisch
round' trip' *s* Hin-und Rückfahrt *f*; (aer) Hin- und Rückflug *m*
round'-trip' *tick'et* *s* Rückfahrkarte *f*
round'up' *s* (*of cattle*) Zusammentreiben *n*; (*of criminals*) Aushebung *f*
rouse [rauz] *tr* (*from*) aufwecken (aus)
rout [raut] *s* völlige Niederlage *f*; (mil) wilde Flucht *f*; **put to r.** in die Flucht schlagen || *tr* (mil) zersprengen
route [rut], [raut] *s* Route *f*, Weg *m* || *tr* leiten
routine [ru'tin] *adj* routinemäßig || *s* Routine *f*; **be r.** die Regel sein
rove [rov] *intr* umherwandern
row [rau] *s* Krach *m*; **raise a row** (coll) Krach machen || [ro] Reihe *f*; **in a row** hintereinander || *tr* rudern
rowboat ['ro ,bot] *s* Ruderboot *n*
rowdy ['raudɪ] *adj* flegelhaft || *s* Flegel *m*
rower ['ro-ər] *s* Ruderer –in *mf*
rowing ['ro-ɪŋ] *s* Rudersport *m*
royal ['rɔɪ-əl] *adj* königlich
royalist ['rɔɪ-əlɪst] *adj* königstreu || *s* Königstreue *mf*
royalty ['rɔɪ-əltɪ] *s* (*royal status*) Königswürde *f*; (*personage*) fürstliche Persönlichkeit *f*; (*collectively*) fürstliche Persönlichkeiten *pl*; (*author's compensation*) Tantieme *f*; (*inventor's compensation*) Lizenzgebühr *f*
r.p.m. ['ɑr'pi'em] *spl* (**revolutions per minute**) Drehzahl *f*
R.S.V.P. *abbr* u.A.w.g. (um Antwort wird gebeten)
rub [rʌb] *s* Reiben *n*; **there's the rub** (coll) da sitzt der Haken || *v* (*pret* & *pp* **rubbed**; *ger* **rubbing**) *tr* reiben; **rub down** abreiben; **rub elbows with** verkehren mit; **rub in** einreiben; **rub it in** (sl) es (j—m) unter die Nase reiben; **rub out** ausradieren; (sl) umbringen; **rub s.o. the wrong way** j—m auf die Nerven gehen || *intr* reiben; **rub against** sich reiben an (*dat*); **rub off on** (fig) abfärben auf (*acc*)
rubber ['rʌbər] *adj* Gummi– || *s* Gummi *m* & *n*; (*cards*) Robber *m*; **rubbers** Gummischuhe *pl*
ru'ber band' *s* Gummiband *n*
rubberize ['rʌbə ,raɪz] *tr* gummieren
rub'ber plant' *s* Kautschukpflanze *f*
rub'ber stamp' *s* Gummistempel *m*
rub'ber-stamp' *tr* abstempeln; (coll) automatisch genehmigen
rubbery ['rʌbərɪ] *adj* gummiartig
rub'bing al'cohol *s* Franzbranntwein *m*

rubbish ['rʌbɪʃ] s (trash) Abfall m; (nonsense) dummes Zeug n
rubble ['rʌbəl] s Schutt m; (used in masonry) Bruchstein m
rub'down' s Abreibung f
rubric ['rubrɪk] s Rubrik f
ruby ['rubi] adj rubinrot ‖ s Rubin m
ruckus ['rʌkəs] s (coll) Krawall m
rudder ['rʌdər] s (aer) Seitenruder n; (naut) Steuerruder n
ruddy ['rʌdi] adj rosig
rude [rud] adj grob
rudeness ['rudnɪs] s Grobheit f
rudiments ['rudɪmənts] spl Grundlagen pl
rue [ru] tr bereuen
rueful ['rufəl] adj reuig; (pitiable) kläglich; (mournful) wehmütig
ruffian ['rʌfɪ-ən] s Raufbold m
ruffle ['rʌfəl] s Rüsche f; (in water) Kräuseln n; (of a drum) gedämpfter Trommelwirbel m ‖ tr kräuseln; (feathers, hair) sträuben
rug [rʌg] s Teppich m
rugged ['rʌgɪd] adj (country) wild; (robust) kräftig; (life) hart
ruin ['ru-ɪn] s Ruine f; (undoing) Ruin m; go to r. zugrunde gehen; lie in ruins in Trümmern liegen; ruins (debris) Trümmer pl ‖ tr ruinieren
rule [rul] s (reign) Herrschaft f; (regulation) Regel f; as a r. in der Regel; become the r. zur Regel werden ‖ tr beherrschen; (paper) linieren; r. out ausschließen ‖ intr (over) herrschen (über acc)
rule' of law' s Rechtsstaatlichkeit f
rule' of thumb' s Faustregel f; by r. über den Daumen gepeilt
ruler ['rulər] s Herrscher –in mf; (for measuring) Lineal n
rul'ing adj herrschend ‖ s Regelung f
rum [rʌm] s Rum m
Rumania [ru'menɪ-ə] s Rumänien n
Rumanian [ru'menɪ-ən] adj rumänisch ‖ s Rumäne m, Rumänin f; (language) Rumänisch n
rumble ['rʌmbəl] s (of thunder) Rollen n; (of a truck) Rumpeln n ‖ intr rollen; rumpeln
ruminate ['rumɪ‚net] tr & intr wiederkäuen
rummage ['rʌmɪdʒ] intr—r. through durchsuchen
rum'mage sale' s Ramschverkauf m
rumor ['rumər] s Gerücht n ‖ tr—it is rumored that es geht das Gerücht, daß
rump [rʌmp] s (of an animal) Hinterteil m & n; (buttocks) Gesäß n
rumple ['rʌmpəl] tr (clothes) zerknittern; (hair) zerzausen
rump' steak' s Rumpsteak n
rumpus ['rʌmpəs] s (coll) Krach m; raise a r. (coll) Krach machen
rum'pus room' s Spielzimmer n
run [rʌn] s Lauf m; (in stockings) Laufmasche f; (fin) Run m; (theat) Laufzeit f; be on the run auf der Flucht sein; in the long run auf die Dauer; run of bad luck Pechsträhne f; run of good luck Glückssträhne f ‖

v (pret ran [ræn]; pp run; ger running) tr (a machine) bedienen; (a business, household) führen; (a distance) laufen; (a blockade) brechen; (a cable) verlegen; run a race um die Wette laufen; run down (with a car) niederfahren; (clues) nachgehen (dat); (a citation) aufspüren; (through gossip) schlechtmachen; run off (typ) Abzüge machen von; run over (with a vehicle) überfahren; (rehearse) nochmal durchgehen; run through (with a sword) erstechen; run up (bills) auflaufen lassen; (prices) in die Höhe treiben; (a flag) hissen ‖ intr laufen, rennen; (flow) fließen; (said of buses, etc.) verkehren; (said of the nose) laufen, e.g., ihm läuft die Nase his nose is running; (said of colors) auslaufen; (said of a meeting) dauern; (said of a lease) gelten (auf acc); run across zufällig treffen; run after nachlaufen (dat); run around herumlaufen; run around with sich herumtreiben mit; run away weglaufen; (said of a spouse) durchgehen; run down (said of a clock) ablaufen; (said of a battery) dry austrocknen; run for kandidieren für; run high, e.g., feelings ran high die Gemüter waren erhitzt; run in the family in der Familie liegen; run into (e.g., a tree) fahren gegen; (e.g., trouble, debt) geraten in (acc); (e.g., a friend) unerwartet treffen; run into the thousands in die Tausende gehen; run low knapp werden; run out (said of liquids) ausgehen; (said of supplies, time) zu Ende gehen; run out of ausgehen, e.g., they ran out of supplies die Vorräte gingen ihnen aus; run over (said of a pot) überlaufen; run up against stoßen auf (acc); run up to s.o. j-m entgegenlaufen; run wild verwildern
run'-around' s—give s.o. the r. j-n von Pontius zu Pilatus schicken
run'away' adj flüchtig; (horse) durchgegangen ‖ s Ausreißer m; (horse) Durchgänger m
run'down' s kurze Zusammenfassung f
run'-down' adj (condition) heruntergekommen; (clock) abgelaufen; (battery) entladen
rung [rʌŋ] s (of a ladder) Sprosse f; (of a chair) Querleiste f
run-in' s (coll) Zusammenstoß m
runner ['rʌnər] s Läufer –in mf; (of a sled or skate) Kufe f; (of a sliding door) Laufschiene f; (rug) Läufer m; (bot) Ausläufer m; (mil) Meldegänger m
run'ner-up' s (runners-up) Zweitbeste mf; (sport) Zweite mf
run'ning adj (water) fließend; (debts, expenses, sore) laufend ‖ s Laufen n, Lauf m; be in the r. gut im Rennen liegen; be out of the r. (out of the race) aus dem Rennen ausgeschieden sein; (not among the front runners) keine Aussichten haben

run′ning board′ s Trittbrett n
run′ning start′ s fliegender Start m
run′off′ s (sport) Entscheidungslauf m
run′off′ elec′tion s entscheidende Vorwahl f
run′-of-the-mill′ adj Durchschnitts–
runt [rʌnt] s Dreikäsehoch m
run′way′ s Startbahn f
rupture [′rʌptʃər] s Bruch m ‖ tr (relations) abbrechen; **be ruptured** e–n
Bruch (or Riß) bekommen; **r. oneself** sich [dat] e–n Bruch zuziehen ‖
intr platzen
rural [′rʊrəl] adj ländlich
ruse [ruz] s List f
rush [rʌʃ] adj dringend ‖ s Eile f; (for)
Ansturm m (auf acc); (bot) Binse f;
be in a r. es eilig haben; **what′s your
r.?** wozu die Eile? ‖ tr (a person)
hetzen; (a defensive position) im
Sturm nehmen; (work) schnell erledigen; (goods) schleunigst schicken;
(e.g., to a hospital) schleunigst schaffen; **be rushed for time** sehr wenig
Zeit haben; **r. through** (a bill) durch-
peitschen; **r. up** (reinforcements)
schnell herbeischaffen ‖ intr eilen,
sich stürzen; **r. at** zustürzen auf

(acc); **r. forward** vorstürmen; **r. into**
stürzen in (acc); **r. up to** zuschießen
auf (acc); **the blood rushed to his
head** ihm stieg das Blut in den Kopf
rush′ hours′ spl Hauptverkehrszeit f
rush′ or′der s Eilauftrag m
russet [′rʌsɪt] adj rotbraun
Russia [′rʌʃə] s Russland n
Russian [′rʌʃən] adj russisch ‖ s Russe
m, Russin f; (language) Russisch n
rust [rʌst] s Rost m ‖ tr rostig machen
‖ intr (ver)rosten
rustic [′rʌstɪk] adj (rural) ländlich;
(countryish) bäuerlich ‖ s Bauer m
rustle [′rʌsəl] s Rauschen n; (of silk)
Knistern n ‖ tr rascheln mit; (cattle)
stehlen ‖ intr rauschen; (said of silk)
knistern
rust′proof′ adj rostfrei
rusty [′rʌsti] adj rostig; (fig) einge-
rostet
rut [rʌt] s Geleise n, Spur f; (fig) alter
Trott m
ruthless [′ruθlɪs] adj erbarmungslos
rye [raɪ] s (grain) Roggen m; (whiskey)
Roggenwhisky m
rye′ bread′ s Roggenbrot n
rye′ grass′ s Raigras n

S

S, s [ɛs] s neunzehnter Buchstabe des
englischen Alphabets
Sabbath [′sæbəθ] s Sabbat m
sabbat′ical year′ [sə′bætɪkəl] s ein-
jähriger Urlaub m (e–s Professors)
saber [′sebər] s Säbel m
sable [′sebəl] adj schwarz ‖ s (fur)
Zobelpelz m; (zool) Zobel m
sabotage [′sæbə ,tɑʒ] s Sabotage f ‖ tr
sabotieren
saboteur [,sæbə′tʌr] s Saboteur –in
mf
saccharin [′sækərɪn] s Saccharin n
sachet [sæ′ʃe] s Duftkissen n
sack [sæk] s Sack m; (bed) (coll) Falle
f; **hit the s.** (coll) in die Falle gehen
‖ tr einsacken; (dismiss) (coll) an
die Luft setzen; (mil) ausplündern
sack′cloth′ s Sacktuch n; **in s. and ashes**
in Sack und Asche
sacrament [′sækrəmənt] s Sakrament n
sacramental [,sækrə′mentəl] adj sakra-
mental
sacred [′sekrəd] adj heilig; **s. to** ge-
weiht (dat)
sacrifice [′sækrɪ ,faɪs] s Opfer n; **at a
s.** mit Verlust ‖ tr opfern
sacrilege [′sækrɪlɪdʒ] s Sakrileg n
sacrilegious [,sækrɪ′lɪdʒəs] adj frevel-
haft, gotteslästerlich
sacristan [′sækrɪstən] s Sakristan m
sacristy [′sækrɪsti] s Sakristei f
sad [sæd] adj traurig; (plight) schlimm
sadden [′sædən] tr traurig machen
saddle [′sædəl] s Sattel m ‖ tr satteln;
be saddled with auf dem Halse haben

sad′dlebag′ s Satteltasche f
sadism [′sedɪzəm] s Sadismus m
sadistic [se′dɪstɪk] adj sadistisch
sadness [′sædnɪs] s Traurigkeit f
sad′ sack′ s (sl) Trauerkloß m
safe [sef] adj (from) sicher (vor dat);
(arrival) glücklich; **s. and sound** heil
und gesund; (said of a thing) unversehrt; **to be on the s. side** vorsichtshalber ‖ s Geldschrank m
safe′-con′duct s sicheres Geleit n
safe′-depos′it box′ s Schließfach n
safe′ dis′tance s Sicherheitsabstand m
safe′guard′ s Schutz m ‖ tr schützen
safe′keep′ing s sicherer Gewahrsam m
safety [′sefti] adj Sicherheits– ‖ s
Sicherheit f
safe′ty belt′ s Sicherheitsgurt m
safe′ty pin′ s Sicherheitsnadel f
safe′ty ra′zor s Rasierapparat m
safe′ty valve′ s Sicherheitsventil n
saffron [′sæfrən] adj safrangelb ‖ s
Safran m
sag [sæg] s Senkung f ‖ v (pret & pp
sagged; ger sagging) intr sich senken;
(said of a cable) durchhängen; (fig)
sinken
sagacious [sə′geʃəs] adj scharfsinnig
sage [sedʒ] adj weise, klug ‖ s Weise
m; (plant) Salbei f
sage′brush′ s Beifuß m
sail [sel] s Segel n; **set s. for** in See
stechen nach ‖ tr (a boat) fahren;
(the sea) segeln über (acc) ‖ intr
segeln; (depart) abfahren; **s. across**
übersegeln; **s. along the coast** an der

Küste entlangsegeln; **s. into** (coll) herunterputzen

sail′boat′ *s* Segelboot *n*

sail′cloth′ *s* Segeltuch *n*

sail′ing *s* Segelfahrt *f*; (sport) Segelsport *m*; **it will be smooth s.** (fig) es wird alles glattgehen

sail′ing ves′sel *s* Segelschiff *n*

sailor [′selər] *s* Matrose *m*

Saint [sent] *s* Heilige *mf*; **S. George** der heilige Georg, Sankt Georg

Saint′ Bernard′ *s* (*dog*) Bernhardiner *m*

sake [sek] *s*—**for her s.** ihretwegen; **for his s.** seinetwegen; **for my s.** meinetwegen; **for our s.** unsertwegen; **for their s.** ihretwegen; **for the s. of** um (*genit*) willen; **for your s.** deinetwegen, Ihretwegen

salable [′seləbəl] *adj* verkäuflich

salacious [sə′le∫əs] *adj* (*person*) geil; (*writing, pictures*) obszön

salad [′sæləd] *s* Salat *m*

sal′ad bowl′ *s* Salatschüssel *f*

sal′ad dress′ing *s* Salatsoße *f*

sal′ad oil′ *s* Salatöl *n*

salami [sə′lɑmi] *s* Salami *f*

salary [′sæləri] *s* Gehalt *n*

sale [sel] *s* Verkauf *m*; (*special sale*) Ausverkauf *m*; **be up for s.** zum Kauf stehen; **for s.** zu verkaufen; **sales** (com) Absatz *m*, Umsatz *m*; **put up for s.** zum Verkauf anbieten

sales′ clerk′ *s* Verkäufer –in *mf*

sales′girl′ *s* Ladenmädchen *n*

sales′la′dy *s* Verkäuferin *f*

sales′man *s* (**–men**) Verkäufer *m*

sales′man′ship *s* Verkaufstüchtigkeit *f*

sales′ promo′tion *s* Verkaufsförderung *f*

sales′ slip′ *s* Kassenzettel *m*, Bon *m*

sales′ tax′ *s* Umsatzsteuer *f*

saliva [sə′laɪvə] *s* Speichel *m*

sallow [′sælo] *adj* bläßlich

sal·ly [′sæli] *s* (*side trip*) Abstecher *m*; (mil) Ausfall *m* ‖ *v* (*pret & pp* **–lied**) *intr* (mil) ausfallen; **s. forth** sich aufmachen

salmon [′sæmən] *adj* lachsfarben ‖ *s* Lachs *m*

saloon [sə′lun] *s* Kneipe *f*; (naut) Salon *m*

salt [sɔlt] *s* Salz *n* ‖ *tr* salzen; **s. away** (coll) auf die hohe Kante legen

salt′cel′lar *s* Salzfaß *n*

salt′ed meat′ *s* Salzfleisch *n*

salt′ mine′ *s* Salzbergwerk *n*; **back to the salt mines** zurück zur Tretmühle

salt′pe′ter *s* Salpeter *m*

salt′ shak′er *s* Salzfaß *n*

salty [′sɔlti] *adj* salzig

salutary [′sæljə‚teri] *adj* heilsam

salute [sə′lut] *s* Salut *m* ‖ *tr & intr* salutieren

salvage [′sælvɪdʒ] *s* (*saving by ship*) Bergung *n*; (*property saved by ship*) Bergungsgut *n*; (*discarded material*) Altmaterial *n* ‖ *tr* bergen; (*discarded material*) verwerten

salvation [sæl′ve∫ən] *s* Heil *n*

Salva′tion Ar′my *s* Heilsarmee *f*

salve [sæv] *s* Salbe *f* ‖ *tr* (*one's conscience*) beschwichtigen

sal·vo [′sælvo] *s* (**–vos & –voes**) Salve *f*

Samaritan [sə′mærɪtən] *s* Samariter –in *mf*; **good S.** barmherziger Samariter *m*

same [sem] *adj*—**at the s. time** gleichzeitig; **it's all the s. to me** es ist mir ganz gleich; **just the s.** trotzdem; **thanks, s. to you!** danke, gleichfalls!; **the s.** derselbe

sameness [′semnɪs] *s* Eintönigkeit *f*

sample [′sæmpəl] *s* Muster *n*, Probe *f* ‖ *tr* (aus)probieren

sancti·fy [′sæŋktɪ‚faɪ] *v* (*pret & pp* **–fied**) *tr* heiligen

sanctimonious [‚sæŋktɪ′moni‚əs] *adj* scheinheilig

sanction [′sæŋk∫ən] *s* Sanktion *f* ‖ *tr* sanktionieren

sanctity [′sæŋktɪti] *s* Heiligkeit *f*

sanctuary [′sæŋkt∫u‚eri] *s* (*shrine*) Heiligtum *n*; (*of a church*) Altarraum *m*; (*asylum*) Asyl *n*

sand [sænd] *s* Sand *m* ‖ *tr* mit Sandpapier abschleifen; (*a road, sidewalk*) mit Sand bestreuen

sandal [′sændəl] *s* Sandale *f*

san′dalwood′ *s* Sandelholz *n*

sand′bag′ *s* Sandsack *m*

sand′bank′ *s* Sandbank *f*

sand′ bar′ *s* Sandbank *f*

sand′blast′ *tr* sandstrahlen

sand′box′ *s* Sandkasten *m*

sand′ cas′tle *s* Strandburg *f*

sand′ dune′ *s* Sanddüne *f*

sand′glass′ *s* Sanduhr *f*

sand′man′ *s* (**–men**) (fig) Sandmann *m*

sand′pa′per *s* Sandpapier *n* ‖ *tr* mit Sandpapier abschleifen

sand′stone′ *s* Sandstein *m*

sand′storm′ *s* Sandsturm *m*

sandwich [′sændwɪt∫] *s* belegtes Brot *n*, Sandwich *n* ‖ *tr* (*in between*) einzwängen (zwischen *dat*)

sandy [′sændi] *adj* sandig; (*color*) sandfarben

sane [sen] *adj* geistig gesund; (*e.g., advice*) vernünftig

sanguine [′sæŋgwɪn] *adj* (*about*) zuversichtlich (in Bezug auf *acc*)

sanitarium [‚sænɪ′teri‚əm] *s* Heilanstalt *f*, Sanatorium *n*

sanitary [′sænɪ‚teri] *adj* sanitär

san′itary nap′kin *s* Damenbinde *f*

sanitation [‚sænɪ′te∫ən] *s* Gesundheitswesen *n*; (*in a building*) sanitäre Einrichtungen *pl*

sanity [′sænɪti] *s* geistige Gesundheit *f*

Santa Claus [′sæntə‚klɔz] *s* der Weihnachtsmann *m*, der Nikolaus

sap [sæp] *s* Saft *m*; (coll) Schwachkopf *m* ‖ *v* (*pret & pp* **sapped**; *ger* **sapping**) *tr* (*strength*) erschöpfen

sapling [′sæplɪŋ] *s* junger Baum *m*

sapphire [′sæfaɪr] *s* Saphir *m*

Saracen [′særəsən] *adj* sarazenisch ‖ *s* Sarazene *m*, Sarazenin *f*

sarcasm [′sɑrkæzm] *s* Sarkasmus *m*

sarcastic [sɑr′kæstɪk] *adj* sarkastisch

sarcophagus [sɑr′kɑfəgəs] *s* Sarkophag *m*

sardine [sɑr′din] *s* Sardine *f*; **packed**

in like **sardines** zusammengedrängt wie die Heringe

Sardinia [sɑr'dɪnɪ‧ə] s Sardinien n

Sardinian [sɑr'dɪnɪ‧ən] adj sardinisch ‖ s Sardinier –in mf; (language) Sardinisch n

sash [sæʃ] s Schärpe f; (of a window) Fensterrahmen m

sass [sæs] s (coll) Revolverschnauze f ‖ tr (coll) (off) patzig antworten (dat)

sassy ['sæsɪ] adj (coll) patzig

Satan ['setən] s Satan m

satanic(al) [sə'tænɪk(əl)] adj satanisch

satchel ['sætʃəl] s Handtasche f

sate [set] tr übersättigen

satellite ['sætə‚laɪt] s Satellit m

sat'ellite coun'try s Satellitenstaat m

satiate ['seʃɪ‚et] tr sättigen

satin ['sætɪn] s Seidenatlas m

satire ['sætaɪr] s Satire f

satiric(al) [sə'tɪrɪk(əl)] adj satirisch

satirize ['sætɪ‚raɪz] tr verspotten

satisfaction [‚sætɪs'fækʃən] s Befriedigung f, Genugtuung f

satisfactory [‚sætɪs'fæktərɪ] adj friedenstellend, genügend

satis•fy ['sætɪs‚faɪ] v (pret & pp –fied) tr (desires, needs) befriedigen; (requirements) genügen (dat); (a person) zufriedenstellen; **be satisfied with** zufrieden sein mit ‖ intr befriedigen

saturate ['sætʃə‚ret] tr (& chem) sättigen, saturieren

satura'tion bomb'ing s Bombenteppich m

satura'tion point' s Sättigungspunkt m

Saturday ['sætər‚de] s Samstag m; **on S.** am Samstag

sauce [sɔs] s Soße f; (coll) Frechheit f ‖ tr mit Soße zubereiten; (season) würzen

sauce'pan' s Stielkasserolle f

saucer ['sɔsər] s Untertasse f

saucy ['sɔsɪ] adj (impertinent) frech; (amusingly flippant) keß; (trim) flott

sauerkraut ['saʊr‚kraʊt] s Sauerkraut n

saunter ['sɔntər] s Schlendern n ‖ intr schlendern

sausage ['sɔsɪdʒ] s Wurst f

saute [so'te] v (pret & pp sauteed) tr sautieren

savage ['sævɪdʒ] adj wild ‖ s Wilde mf

savant ['sævənt] s Gelehrte m

save [sev] tr (rescue) retten; (money, fuel) sparen; (keep, preserve) aufheben; (trouble) ersparen; (time) gewinnen; (stamps) sammeln; **s. face** das Gesicht wahren; **s. from** bewahren vor (dat) ‖ prep außer (dat)

sav'ing adj (grace) seligmachend; (quality) ausgleichend ‖ s (of souls) Rettung f; (in) Ersparnis f (an dat); **savings** Ersparnisse pl

sav'ings account' s Sparkonto n

sav'ings bank' s Sparkasse f

sav'ings certi'ficate s Sparbon m

sav'ings depos'it s Spareinlage f

savior ['sevjər] s Retter –in mf; **Saviour** Heiland m

savor ['sevər] s Wohlgeschmack m ‖ tr auskosten ‖ intr—**s. of** (smell of) riechen nach; (taste of) schmecken nach

savory ['sevərɪ] adj wohlschmeckend

saw [sɔ] s Säge f; (saying) Sprichwort n ‖ tr sägen; **saw up** zersägen

saw'dust' s Sägespäne pl

saw'horse' s Sägebock m

saw'mill' s Sägemühle f

Saxon ['sæksən] adj sächsisch ‖ s Sachse m, Sachsin f

Saxony ['sæksənɪ] s Sachsen n

saxophone ['sæksə‚fon] s Saxophon n

say [se] v (pret & pp said) tr **have a** (or **no**) **say in etw** (or nichts) zu sagen haben bei; **have one's say** (about) seine Meinung äußern (über acc) ‖ v (pret & pp said [sed]) tr sagen; (Mass) lesen; (a prayer) sprechen; (one's prayers) verrichten; (said of a newspaper article, etc.) besagen; **it says in the papers** in der Zeitung steht; (let's) **say** sagen wir; **no sooner said than done** gesagt, getan; **say!** (to draw attention) sag mal!; (to elicit agreement) gelt!; **say s.th. behind s.o.'s back** j–m etw nachsagen; **she is said to be clever** sie soll klug sein; **that is not to say** das will nicht sagen; **that is to say** das heißt; **they say** man sagt; **to say nothing of** ganz zu schweigen von; **you don't say so!** tatsächlich!

say'ing s Sprichwort n; **as the s. goes** wie man zu sagen pflegt; **it goes without s.** das versteht sich von selbst

say'-so' s (assertion) Behauptung f; (order) Anweisung f; (final authority) letztes Wort n

scab [skæb] s Schorf m; (sl) Streikbrecher –in mf

scabbard ['skæbərd] s Schwertscheide f

scabby ['skæbɪ] adj schorfig

scads [skædz] spl (sl) e–e Menge f

scaffold ['skæfəld] s Gerüst n; (for executions) Schafott n

scaf'folding s Baugerüst n

scald [skɔld] tr verbrühen; (milk) aufkochen

scale [skel] s (on fish, reptiles) Schuppe f; (pan of a balance) Waagschale f; (of a thermometer, wages) Skala f; (mus) Tonleiter f; **on a grand s.** im großen Stil; **on a large** (or **small**) **s.** in großem (or kleinem) Maßstab; **s. 1:1000** Maßstab 1:1000; **scales** Waage f; **to s.** maßstabgerecht ‖ tr erklettern; **s. down** maßstäblich verkleinern; (prices) herabsetzen

scallop ['skæləp] s Kammuschel f; (sew) Zacke f ‖ tr auszacken; (culin) überbacken

scalp [skælp] s Kopfhaut f; (Indian trophy) Skalp m ‖ tr skalpieren

scalpel ['skælpəl] s Skalpell n

scaly ['skelɪ] adj schuppig

scamp [skæmp] s Fratz m, Wildfang m

scamper ['skæmpər] intr herumtollen; **s. away** davonlaufen

scan [skæn] v (pret & pp scanned; ger

scanning *tr* (*a page*) überfliegen; (*a verse*) skandieren; (*examine*) genau prüfen; (radar, telv) abtasten

scandal ['skændəl] *s* Skandal *m*

scandalize ['skændə‚laɪz] *tr* schockieren

scandalmonger ['skændəl‚mʌŋgər] *s* Lästermaul *n*

scandalous ['skændələs] *adj* skandalös

scan'dal sheet' *s* Sensationsblatt *n*

Scandinavia [‚skændɪ'nevɪ-ə] *s* Skandinavien *n*

Scandinavian [‚skændɪ'nevɪ-ən] *adj* skandinavisch || *s* Skandinavier –in *mf*; (*language*) Skandinavisch *n*

scansion ['skænʃən] *s* Skandieren *n*

scant [skænt] *adj* gering; **a s. two hours** knapp zwei Stunden

scantily ['skæntɪli] *adv*—**s. clad** leicht bekleidet

scanty ['skænti] *adj* kärglich, knapp

scapegoat ['skep‚got] *s* Sündenbock *m*

scar [skɑr] *s* Narbe *f*; (fig) Makel *m* || *v* (*pret & pp* **scarred**; *ger* **scarring**) *tr* (*e.g., a face*) entstellen; (*e.g., a tabletop*) verschrammen; (fig) beinträchtigen

scarce [skɛrs] *adj* knapp, rar; **make oneself s.** (coll) das Weite suchen

scarcely ['skɛrsli] *adv* kaum; **be s. able to** (*inf*) Not haben zu (*inf*)

scarcity ['skɛrsɪti] *s* (*of*) Knappheit *f* (an *dat*), Mangel *m* (an *dat*)

scare [skɛr] *s* Schrecken *m*; **be scared** erschrecken; **be scared stiff** e-e Hundeangst haben; **give s.o. a s.** j-m e-n Schrecken einjagen || *tr* erschrecken; **s. away** verscheuchen; **s. up** (*money*) auftreiben || *intr* erschrecken

scare'crow' *s* Vogelscheuche *f*

scarf [skɑrf] *s* (scarfs & scarves [skɑrvz]) Schal *m*

scarlet ['skɑrlɪt] *adj* scharlachrot || *s* Scharlachrot *n*

scar'let fe'ver *s* Scharlach *m*

scarred *adj* narbig, schrammig

scary ['skɛri] *adj* schreckenregend

scat [skæt] *interj* weg!

scathing ['skeðɪŋ] *adj* vernichtend

scatter ['skætər] *tr* zerstreuen || *intr* sich zerstreuen

scat'terbrain' *s* Wirrkopf *m*

scat'tered show'ers *spl* einzelne Schauer *pl*

scenari-o [sɪ'nɛrɪ-o] *s* (-os) Drehbuch *n*

scene [sin] *s* Szene *f*; **be on the s.** zur Stelle sein; **behind the scenes** hinter den Kulissen; **make a s.** e-e Szene machen; **s. of the crime** Tatort *m*

scenery ['sinəri] *s* Landschaft *f*; (theat) Bühnenausstattung *f*

scenic ['sinɪk] *adj* landschaftlich; (theat) szenisch

scent [sɛnt] *s* Duft *m*; (*of a dog*) Witterung *f*; (hunt) Spur *f*; **have a s.** duften || *tr* wittern

scepter ['sɛptər] *s* Zepter *n*

sceptic ['skɛptɪk] *s* Skeptiker –in *mf*

scepticism ['skɛptɪ‚sɪzəm] *s* (*doubt*) Skepsis *f*; (*doctrine*) Skeptizismus *m*

schedule ['skɛdjul] *s* Plan *m*; (*for work*) Arbeitsplan *m*; (*in travel*) Fahrplan *m*; (*at school*) Stundenplan *m*; (*appendix to a tax return*) Einkommensteuerformular *n*; (*table*) Einkommensteuertabelle *f*; **on s. fahrplanmäßig** || *tr* ansetzen; **the plane is scheduled to arrive at six** nach dem Flugplan soll die Maschine um sechs Uhr ankommen

scheme [skim] *s* (*schematic*) Schema *n*; (*plan, program*) Plan *m*; (*intrigue*) Intrige *f* || *tr* planen || *intr* Ränke schmieden

schemer ['skimər] *s* Ränkeschmied *m*

schilling ['ʃɪlɪŋ] *s* (Aust) Schilling *m*

schism ['sɪzəm] *s* (fig) Spaltung *f*; (eccl) Schisma *n*

schizophrenia [‚skɪtso'frini-ə] *s* Schizophrenie *f*, Bewußtseinsspaltung *f*

schizophrenic [‚skɪtso'frɛnɪk] *adj* schizophren

schmaltzy ['ʃmɒltsi] *adj* schmalzig

scholar ['skɒlər] *s* Gelehrte *mf*

scholarly ['skɒlərli] *adj* gelehrt

schol'arship' *s* Gelehrsamkeit *f*; (*award*) Stipendium *n*

scholastic [skə'læstɪk] *adj* Schul-, Bildungs-; (hist) scholastisch

school [skul] *adj* (*book, house, master, room, teacher, yard, year*) Schul- || *s* Schule *f*; (*of a university*) Fakultät *f*; (*of fish*) Schwarm *m*; **s. is over** die Schule ist aus || *tr* schulen

school' age' *s* schulpflichtiges Alter *n*; **of s.** schulpflichtig

school'bag' *s* Schulranzen *m*

school' board' *s* Schulausschuß *m*

school'boy' *s* Schüler *m*

school'girl' *s* Schülerin *f*

school'ing *s* (*formal education*) Schulbildung *f*; (*training*) Schulung *f*

school'mate' *s* Mitschüler –in *mf*

schooner ['skunər] *s* Schoner *m*

sciatica [saɪ'ætɪkə] *s* Hüftschmerz *m*

science ['saɪ-əns] *s* Wissenschaft *f*; **the sciences** die Naturwissenschaften *pl*

sci'ence fic'tion *s* Science-fiction *f*

scientific [‚saɪ-ən'tɪfɪk] *adj* wissenschaftlich

scientist ['saɪ-əntɪst] *s* Wissenschaftler –in *mf*

scimitar ['sɪmɪtər] *s* Türkensäbel *m*

scintillate ['sɪntɪ‚let] *intr* funkeln

scion ['saɪ-ən] *s* Sprößling *m*; (bot) Pfropfreis *n*

scissors ['sɪzərz] *s & spl* Schere *f*; (*in wrestling*) Zangengriff *m*

scoff [skɒf] *s* Spott *m* || *intr* (at) spotten (über *acc*)

scold [skold] *tr & intr* schelten

scold'ing *s* Schelte *f*; **get a s.** Schelte bekommen

sconce [skɑns] *s* Wandleuchter *m*

scoop [skup] *s* (*ladle*) Schöpfkelle *f*; (*for sugar, flour*) Schaufel *f*; (*amount scooped*) Schlag *m*; (journ) Knüller *m* || *tr* schöpfen; **s. out** ausschaufeln; **s. up** schöpfen

scoot [skut] *intr* (coll) flitzen

scooter ['skutər] *s* Roller *m*

scope [skop] *s* (*extent*) Umfang *m*;

(*range*) Reichweite *f*; **give free s. to the imagination** der Phatasie freien Lauf lassen; **give s.o. free s.** j-m freie Hand geben; **within the s. of** im Rahmen (*genit*) or von

scorch [skɔrtʃ] *tr* versengen

scorched′-earth′ pol′icy *s* Politik *f* der verbrannten Erde

scorch′ing *adj & adv* sengend

score [skor] *s* (*of a game*) Punktzahl *f*; (*final score*) Ergebnis *n*; (*notch*) Kerbe *f*; (*mus*) Partitur *f*; **a s. of** zwanzig; **have an old s. to settle with s.o.** mit j-m e-e alte Rechnung zu begleichen haben; **keep s.** die Punktzahl anschreiben; **know the s.** (coll) auf Draht sein; **on that s.** diesbezüglich; **what's the s.?** wie steht das Spiel? || *tr* (*points*) erzielen; (*goals*) schießen; (*notch*) einkerben; (*mus*) in Partitur setzen || *intr* e-n Punkt erzielen

score′board′ *s* Anzeigetafel *f*

score′card′ *s* Punktzettel *m*

score′keep′er *s* Anschreiber –in *mf*

score′sheet′ *s* Spielberichtsbogen *m*

scorn [skɔrn] *s* Verachtung *f*; **laugh to s.** auslachen || *tr* verachten

scornful [′skɔrnfəl] *adj* verächtlich

scorpion [′skɔrpɪ-ən] *s* Skorpion *m*

Scot [skat] *s* Schotte *m*, Schottin *f*

Scotch [skatʃ] *adj* schottisch; (sl) geizig || *s* schottischer Whisky *m*; (*dialect*) Schottisch *n* || *tr* (*a rumor*) ausrotten; (*with a chock*) blockieren; (*render harmless*) unschädlich machen

Scotch′man *s* (**–men**) Schotte *m*

Scotch′ pine′ *s* gemeine Kiefer *f*

Scotch′ tape′ *s* (trademark) durchsichtiger Klebstreifen *m*

scot′-free′ *adj* ungestraft

Scotland [′skatlənd] *s* Schottland *n*

Scottish [′skatɪʃ] *adj* schottisch || *s* (*dialect*) Schottisch *n*; **the S.** die Schotten *pl*

scoundrel [′skaundrəl] *s* Lump *m*

scour [skaur] *tr* scheuern; (*the city*) absuchen

scourge [skʌrdʒ] *s* Geißel *f* || *tr* geißeln

scout [skaut] *s* Pfadfinder *m*; (mil, sport) Kundschafter *m* || *tr* aufklären || *intr* kundschaften

scout′mas′ter *s* Pfadfinderführer *m*

scowl [skaul] *s* finsterer Blick *m* || *intr* finster blicken; **s. at** grollend ansehen

scram [skræm] *v* (*pret & pp* **scrammed**; *ger* **scramming**) *intr* (coll) abhauen

scramble [′skræmbəl] *s* (*for*) Balgerei *f* (um) || *tr* (*mix up*) durcheinandermischen; (*a message*) unverständlich machen; **s. eggs** Rührei machen || *intr* (*e.g., over rocks*) klettern; **s. for s.th.** sich um etw reißen; **s. to one's feet** sich aufrappeln

scram′bled eggs′ *spl* Rührei *n*

scrap [skræp] *s* (*of metal*) Schrott *m*; (*of paper*) Fetzen *m*; (*of food*) Rest *m*; (*refuse*) Abfall *m*; (*quarrel*) (coll) Zank *m*; (*fight*) (coll) Rauferei *f* || *v* (*pret & pp* **scrapped**; *ger*

scrapping) *tr* ausrangieren || *intr* (*quarrel*) (coll) zanken; (*fight*) (coll) raufen

scrap′book′ *s* Einklebebuch *n*

scrape [skrep] *s* Kratzer *m*; (coll) Patsche *f* || *tr* schaben; (*the skin*) abscheuern; **s. off** abschaben; **s. together** (or **up**) zusammenkratzen

scrap′ heap′ *s* Schrotthaufen *m*; (*refuse heap*) Abfallhaufen *m*

scrap′ i′ron *s* Schrott *m*, Alteisen *n*

scrapper [′skræpər] *s* Zänker –in *mf*

scrappy [′skræpi] *adj* (*made of scraps*) zusammengestoppelt; (coll) rauflustig

scratch [skrætʃ] *s* Kratzer *m*, Schramme *f*; **start from s.** wieder ganz von vorne anfangen || *tr* kratzen; (sport) streichen; **s. open** aufkratzen; **s. out** (*a line*) ausstreichen; (*eyes*) aushacken; **s. the surface of** nur streifen || *intr* kratzen; (*scratch oneself*) sich kratzen

scratch′ pad′ *s* Notizblock *m*

scratch′ pa′per *s* Schmierpapier *n*

scrawl [skrɔl] *s* Gekritzel *n* || *tr & intr* kritzeln

scrawny [′skrɔni] *adj* spindeldürr

scream [skrim] *s* Aufschrei *m*; **he's a s.!** er ist zum Schreien! || *tr & intr* schreien

screech [skritʃ] *s* Kreischen *n* || *intr* (*said of tires, brakes*) kreischen; (*said of an owl*) schreien

screech′ owl′ *s* Kauz *m*

screen [skrin] *s* Wandschirm *m*; (*for a window*) Fliegengitter *n*; (*camouflage*) Tarnung *f*; (aer) (of) Abschirmung *f* (durch); (cin) Leinwand *f*; (nav) Geleitschutz *m*; (radar, telv) Leinwand *f* || *tr* (*sand, gravel, coal; applications*) durchsieben; (*applicants*) überprüfen; (*a porch, windows*) mit Fliegengittern versehen; (mil) verschleiern; **s. off** abschirmen

screen′play′ *s* Filmdrama *n*; (*scenario*) Drehbuch *n*

screen′ test′ *s* Probeaufnahme *f*

screw [skru] *s* Schraube *f*; **he has a s. loose** (coll) bei ihm ist e-e Schraube locker || *tr* schrauben; (*cheat*) (sl) hereinlegen; (*vulg*) vögeln; **s. tight** festschrauben; **s. up** (*courage*) aufbringen; (*bungle*) (coll) verpfuschen

screw′ball′ *adj* (coll) verrückt || *s* (coll) Wirrkopf *m*

screw′driv′er *s* Schraubenzieher *m*

screw′-on cap′ *s* Schraubendeckel *m*

screwy [′skru-i] *adj* (sl) verrückt

scribble [′skrɪbəl] *s* Gekritzel *n* || *tr & intr* kritzeln

scribe [skraɪb] *s* Schreiber *m*; (Bib) Schriftgelehrte *m*

scrimmage [′skrɪmɪdʒ] *s* (fb) Übungsspiel *n*

scrimp [skrɪmp] *tr* knausern mit || *intr* (on) knausern (mit)

scrimpy [′skrɪmpi] *adj* knapp

script [skrɪpt] *s* (*handwriting*) Handschrift *f*; (cin) Drehbuch *n*; (rad) Textbuch *n*; (typ) Schreibschrift *f*

scriptural [′skrɪptʃərəl] *adj* biblisch; **s. passage** Bibelstelle *f*

Scripture ['skrɪptʃər] s die Heilige Schrift; (*Bible passage*) Bibelzitat n

script'writ'er s (cin) Drehbuchautor m

scrofula ['skrɑfjələ] s Skrofeln pl

scroll [skrol] s Schriftrolle f; (archit) Schnörkel m

scroll'work' s Schnörkelverzierung f

scro·tum ['skrotəm] s (**-ta** [tə] or **-tums**) Hodensack m

scrounge [skraundʒ] tr stibitzen || intr **—s.** around for herumstöbern nach

scrub [skrʌb] s Schrubben n; (shrubs) Buschwerk n; (sport) Ersatzmann m || v (pret & pp **scrubbed**; ger **scrubbing**) tr schrubben

scrub'bing brush' s Scheuerbürste f

scrub'wom'an s (**-wom'en**) Scheuerfrau f

scruff [skrʌf] s—**s. of the neck** Genick n

scruple ['skrupəl] s Skrupel m

scrupulous ['skrupjələs] adj skrupulös

scrutinize ['skrutɪ ˌnaɪz] tr genau prüfen; (a person) mustern

scrutiny ['skrutɪni] s genaue Prüfung f

scud [skʌd] s Wolkenfetzen m

scuff [skʌf] tr (a shoe, waxed floor) abschürfen || intr (shuffle) schurfen

scuffle ['skʌfəl] s Rauferei f || intr raufen

scuff' mark' s Schmutzfleck m

scull [skʌl] s (sport) Skull m || intr (sport) skullen

scullery ['skʌləri] s Spülküche f

scul'lery maid' s Spülerin f

sculptor ['skʌlptər] s Bildhauer m

sculptress ['skʌlptrɪs] s Bildhauerin f

sculptural ['skʌlptʃərəl] adj bildhauerisch

sculpture ['skʌlptʃər] s (art) Bildhauerei f; (work of art) Skulptur f || tr meißeln || intr bildhauern

scum [skʌm] s (& fig) Abschaum m

scummy ['skʌmi] adj schaumig; (fig) niederträchtig

scurrilous ['skʌrɪləs] adj skurril

scur·ry ['skʌri] v (pret & pp **-ried**) intr huschen

scurvy ['skʌrvi] adj gemein || s Skorbut m

scuttle ['skʌtəl] s (naut) Springluke f || tr (hopes, plans) vernichten; (naut) selbst versenken

scut'tlebutt' s (coll) Latrinenparole f

scut'tling s Selbstversenkung f

scythe [saɪð] s Sense f

sea [si] s See f, Meer n; **at sea** auf See; **go to sea** zur See gehen; **heavy seas** hoher (or schwerer) Seegang m

sea'board' s Küstenstrich m

sea' breeze' s Seebrise f

sea'coast' s Seeküste f, Meeresküste f

seafarer ['si ˌferər] s Seefahrer m

seafaring ['si ˌferɪŋ] s Seefahrt f

sea'food' s Fischgerichte pl

sea'go'ing adj seetüchtig

sea' gull' s Seemöwe f, Möwe f

seal [sil] s Siegel n; (zool) Seehund m || tr (a document) siegeln; (a deal, s.o.'s fate) besiegeln; (against leakage) verschließen, abdichten; **s. off** (mil) abriegeln; **s. up** abdichten

sea' legs' spl—**get one's s.** seefest werden

sea'lev'el s Meereshöhe f

seal'ing wax' s Siegellack m

seal'skin' s Seehundsfell n

seam [sim] s (groove) Fuge f; (geol) Lager n; (min) Flöz n; (sew) Naht f

sea'man s (**-men**) Seemann m; (nav) Matrose m

sea' mile' s Seemeile f

seamless ['simlɪs] adj nahtlos

sea' mon'ster s Meeresungeheuer n

seamstress ['simstrɪs] s Näherin f

seamy ['simi] adj verrufen; **s. side** (fig) Schattenseite f

séance ['se-ɑns] s Séance f

sea'plane' s Seeflugzeug n

sea'port' s Seehafen m

sea'port town' s Hafenstadt f

sea' pow'er s Seemacht f

sear [sɪr] tr versengen

search [sʌrtʃ] s Durchsuchung f; (for a person) (for) Fahndung f (nach); **in s. of** auf der Suche nach || tr durchsuchen || intr suchen; **s. for** suchen, fahnden nach

search'ing adj gründlich; (glance) forschend

search'light' s Scheinwerfer m

search' war'rant s Haussuchungsbefehl m

seascape ['si ˌskep] s Seegemälde n

sea'shell' s Muschel f

sea'shore' s Strand m

sea'shore resort' s Seebad n

sea'sick' adj seekrank

sea'sick'ness s Seekrankheit f

sea'side' adj Meeres–, See–

season ['sizən] s Jahreszeit f; (appropriate period) Saison f; **closed s.** (hunt) Schonzeit f; **dry s.** Trockenzeit f; **in and out of s.** jederzeit; **in s.** zur rechten Zeit; **out of s.** (game) außerhalb der Saison; (fruits, vegetables) nicht auf dem Markt; **peak s.** Hochsaison f || tr (food) würzen; (wine) lagern; (wood) austrocknen lassen; (tobacco) reifen lassen; (soldiers) abhärten || intr (e.g., said of wine) (ab)lagern

seasonal ['sizənəl] adj jahreszeitlich; (caused by seasons) saisonbedingt

sea'sonal work' s Saisonarbeit f

sea'soned adj erfahren; (troops) kampfgewohnt, fronterfahren

sea'soning s Würze f

sea'son's greet'ings spl Festgrüße pl

sea'son tick'et s Dauerkarte f

seat [sit] s Sitz m, Platz m; (of trousers) Gesäß n; **have a s.** Platz nehmen; **keep one's s.** sitzenbleiben || tr (a person) e-n Platz anweisen (dat); (said of a room) Sitzplätze bieten für; **be seated** sich hinsetzen

seat' belt' s (aer, aut) Sicherheitsgurt m; **fasten seat belts!** bitte anschnallen!

seat' cov'er s (aut) Auto-Schonbezug m

seat'ing capac'ity s (for) Sitzgelegenheit f (für); **have a s. of** fassen

seat' of gov'ernment s Regierungssitz m

sea'wall' s Strandmauer f

sea'way' s Seeweg m; (heavy sea) schwerer Seegang m

sea'weed' s Alge f, Seetang m

sea'wor'thy adj seetüchtig

secede [sɪ'sid] intr sich trennen

secession [sɪ'sɛʃən] s Sezession f

seclude [sɪ'klud] tr abschließen

seclud'ed adj abgeschieden; (life) zurückgezogen; (place) abgelegen

seclusion [sɪ'kluʒən] s Zurückgezogenheit f, Abgeschiedenheit f

second ['sɛkənd] adj zweite; be s. to none niemandem nachstehen; in the s. place zweitens; s. in command stellvertretender Kommandeur m || s (unit of time) Sekunde f; (moment) Augenblick m; (in boxing or dueling) Sekundant m; George the Second Georg der Zweite; the s. (of the month) der zweite || pron zweite || tr unterstützen

secondary ['sɛkən‚dɛrɪ] adj sekundär, Neben– || s (elec) Sekundärwicklung f; (fb) Spieler pl in der zweiten Reihe

sec'ondary school' s Oberschule

sec'ondary-school teach'er s Oberlehrer –in mf

sec'ondary sourc'es spl Sekundärliteratur f

sec'ondary tar'get s Ausweichziel n

sec'ond best' s Zweitbeste mfn

sec'ond-best' adj zweitbeste; come off s. den kürzeren ziehen

sec'ond-class' adj zweitklassig; s. ticket Fahrkarte f zweiter Klasse

sec'ond cous'in s Cousin m (or Kusine f) zweiten Grades

sec'ond fid'dle s—play s. die zweite Geige spielen

sec'ond hand' s (horol) Sekundenzeiger m

sec'ondhand' adj (car) gebraucht (information) aus zweiter Hand; (books) antiquarisch

sec'ondhand book'store s Antiquariat n

sec'ondhand deal'er s Altwarenhändler –in mf

sec'ond lieuten'ant s Leutnant m

secondly ['sɛkəndlɪ] adv zweitens

sec'ond mate' s (naut) zweiter Offizier m

sec'ond na'ture s zweite Natur f

sec'ond-rate' adj zweitklassig

sec'ond sight' s zweites Gesicht n

sec'ond thought' s—have second thoughts Bedenken hegen; on s. bei weiterem Nachdenken

sec'ond wind' s—get one's s. wieder zu Kräften kommen

secrecy ['sikrəsɪ] s Heimlichkeit f

secret ['sikrɪt] adj geheim || s Geheimnis n; in s. insgeheim; keep no secrets from keine Geheimnisse haben vor (dat); keep s. geheimhalten; make no s. of kein Hehl machen aus

secretary ['sɛkrə‚tɛrɪ] s (man, desk, bird) Sekretär m; (female) Sekretärin f; (in government) Minister m

sec'retary-gen'eral s Generalsekretär m

sec'retary of com'merce s Handelsminister m

sec'retary of defense' s Verteidigungsminister m

sec'retary of la'bor s Arbeitsminister m

sec'retary of state' s Außenminister m

sec'retary of the inter'ior s Innenminister m

sec'retary of the treas'ury s Finanzminister n

se'cret bal'lot s geheime Abstimmung f

secrete [sɪ'krit] tr (hide) verstecken; (physiol) absondern, ausscheiden

secretive ['sikrɪtɪv] adj verschwiegen

se'cret police' s Geheimpolizei f

se'cret serv'ice s Geheimdienst m

sect [sɛkt] s Sekte f

sectarian [sɛk'tɛrɪ·ən] adj sektiererisch; (school) Konfessions–

section ['sɛkʃən] s (segment, part) Teil m; (of a newspaper, chapter) Abschnitt m; (of a city) Viertel n; (group) Abteilung f; (cross section; thin slice, e.g., of tissue) Schnitt m; (jur) Paragraph m; (mil) Halbzug m; (rr) Strecke f; (surg) Sektion f || tr— s. off abteilen

sectional ['sɛkʃənəl] adj (view) Teil–; (pride) Lokal–

sec'tional fur'niture s Anbaumöbel n

sec'tion hand' s Schienenleger m

sector ['sɛktər] s Sektor m

secular ['sɛkjələr] adj weltlich || s Weltpriester m, Weltgeistlicher m

secularism ['sɛkjələ‚rɪzəm] s Weltlichkeit f, Säkularismus m

secure [sɪ'kjur] adj sicher || tr (make fast) sichern; (obtain) sich [dat] beschaffen

security [sɪ'kjurɪtɪ] s (& jur) Sicherheit f; securities Wertpapiere pl

sedan [sɪ'dæn] s Limousine f

sedan' chair' s Sänfte f

sedate [sɪ'det] adj gesetzt

sedation [sɪ'deʃən] s Beruhigung f

sedative ['sɛdətɪv] s Beruhigungsmittel n

sedentary ['sɛdən‚tɛrɪ] adj sitzend

sedge [sɛdʒ] s (bot) Segge f

sediment ['sɛdɪmənt] s Bodensatz m; (geol) Ablagerung f, Sediment n

sedition [sɪ'dɪʃən] s Aufruhr m

seditious [sɪ'dɪʃəs] adj aufrührerisch

seduce [sɪ'd(j)us] tr verführen

seducer [sɪ'd(j)usər] s Verführer –in mf

seduction [sɪ'dʌkʃən] s Verführung f

seductive [sɪ'dʌktɪv] adj verführerisch

sedulous ['sɛdʒələs] adj emsig

see [si] s (eccl) (erz)bischöflicher Stuhl m || v (pret saw [sɔ]; pp seen [sin]) tr sehen; (comprehend) verstehen; (realize) einsehen; (a doctor) gehen zu; see red rasend werden; see s.o. off j–n an den Zug (aus Flugzeug) bringen; see s.o. to the door j–n zur Tür geleiten; see s.th. through etw durchstehen; that remains to be seen das wird man erst sehen || intr sehen; see through (fig) durchschauen; see to sich kümmern um; see to it that sich darum kümmern, daß; **you see** (*parenthetical*) wissen Sie

seed [sid] s Samen m; (*collective & fig*) Saat f; (*in fruit*) Kern m; (*physiol*) Samen m; **go to s.** in Samen schießen; **seeds** (fig) Keim m || tr besäen

seed'bed' s Samenbeet n

seed'ed rye' bread' s Kümmelbrot n

seedless ['sidlɪs] adj kernlos

seedling ['sidlɪŋ] s Sämling m

seedy ['sidi] adj (*person*) heruntergekommen; (*thing*) schäbig

see'ing s Sehen n || conj—s. that in Anbetracht dessen, daß

See'ing Eye' dog' s Blindenhund m

seek [sik] v (pret & pp sought [sɔt]) tr suchen; **s. s.o.'s advice** j–s Rat erbitten; **s. to** (inf) versuchen zu (inf) || intr—s. after suchen nach

seem [sim] intr scheinen || impers—it seems to me es kommt mir vor

seemingly ['simɪŋli] adv anscheinend

seemly ['simli] adj schicklich

seep [sip] intr sickern

seepage ['sipɪdʒ] s Durchsickern n

seer [sɪr] s Seher m

seeress ['sɪrɪs] s Seherin f

see'saw' s Schaukelbrett n, Wippe f || intr wippen; (fig) schwanken

seethe [sið] intr sieden; **s. with** (fig) sieden vor (dat)

segment ['segmənt] s Abschnitt m

segregate ['segrɪˌget] tr trennen, absondern

segregation [ˌsegrɪ'geʃən] s Absonderung f; (*of races*) Rassentrennung f

seismograph ['saɪzməˌgræf] s Erdbebenmesser m, Seismograph m

seismology [saɪz'mɑlədʒi] s Erdbebenkunde f, Seismologie f

seize [siz] tr anfassen; (*a criminal*) festnehmen; (*a town, fortress*) einnehmen; (*an opportunity*) ergreifen; (*power*) an sich reißen; (*confiscate*) beschlagnahmen

seizure ['siʒər] s Besitzergreifung f; (*confiscation*) Beschlagnahme f; (*pathol*) plötzlicher Anfall m

seldom ['seldəm] adv selten

select [sɪ'lekt] adj erlesen || tr auslesen, auswählen

select'ed adj ausgesucht

selection [sɪ'lekʃən] s Auswahl f

selective [sɪ'lektɪv] adj Auswahl–; (rad) trennscharf

selec'tive serv'ice s allgemeine Wehrpflicht f

self [self] s (selves [selvz]) Selbst n, Ich n; **be one's old s. again** wieder der alte sein; **his better s.** sein besseres Ich || pron—payable to s. auf Selbst ausgestellt

self'-addressed' en'velope s mit Anschrift versehener Freiumschlag m

self'-assur'ance s Selbstbewußtsein n

self'-cen'tered adj ichbezogen

self'-conceit'ed adj eingebildet

self'-con'fident adj selbstsicher

self'-con'scious adj befangen

self'-control' s Selbstbeherrschung f

self'-decep'tion s Selbsttäuschung f

self'-defense' s Selbstverteidigung f; **in s.** aus Notwehr

self'-deni'al s Selbstverleugnung f

self'-destruc'tion s Selbstvernichtung f

self'-determina'tion s Selbstbestimmung f

self'-dis'cipline s Selbstzucht f

self'-ed'ucated per'son s Autodidakt –in mf

self'-employed' adj selbständig

self'-esteem' s Selbsteinschätzung f

self'-ev'ident adj selbstverständlich

self'-explan'ator'y adj keiner Erklärung bedürftig

self'-gov'ernment s Selbstverwaltung f

self'-impor'tant adj eingebildet

self'-indul'gence s Genußsucht f

self'-in'terest s Eigennutz m

selfish ['selfɪʃ] adj eigennützig

selfishness ['selfɪnɪs] s Eigennutz m

selfless ['selflɪs] adj selbstlos

self'-love' s Selbstliebe f

self'-made man' s Selfmademan m

self'-por'trait s Selbstbildnis n

self'-possessed' adj selbstbeherrscht

self'-praise' s Eigenlob n

self'-preserva'tion s Selbsterhaltung f

self'-reli'ant adj selbstsicher

self'-respect' s Selbstachtung f

self'-right'eous adj selbstgerecht

self'-sac'rifice s Selbstaufopferung f

self'same' adj ebenderselbe

self'-sat'isfied adj selbstzufrieden

self'-seek'ing adj selbstsüchtig

self'-serv'ice adj mit Selbstbedienung || s Selbstbedienung f

self'-styled' adj von eigenen Gnaden

self'-suffi'cient adj selbstgenügsam

self'-support'ing adj finanziell unabhängig

self'-taught' adj autodidaktisch

self'-willed' adj eigenwillig

self'-wind'ing adj automatisch

sell [sel] (pret & pp sold [sold]) tr verkaufen; (at auction) versteigern; (wares) führen; **be sold on** (coll) begeistert sein von; **s. dirt cheap** verramschen; **s. s.o. on s.th.** (coll) j–n zu etw überreden; **s. out** ausverkaufen; (betray) verraten; **s. short** (st. exch.) in blanko verkaufen || intr sich verkaufen; **s. for** verkauft werden für; **s. short** fixen

seller ['selər] s Verkäufer –in mf; **good s.** (com) Reißer m

Seltzer ['seltsər] s Selterswasser n

selvage ['selvɪdʒ] s (of fabric) Salleiste f; (of a lock) Eckplatte f

semantic [sɪ'mæntɪk] adj semantisch || **semantics** s Wortbedeutungslehre f

semaphore ['seməˌfor] s Winkzeichen n; (rr) Semaphor m || intr winken

semblance ['sembləns] s Anschein m

semen ['simən] s Samen m

semicircle ['semɪˌsʌrkəl] s Halbkreis m

semicolon ['semɪˌkolən] s Strichpunkt m

semiconductor [ˌsemɪkən'dʌktər] s Halbleiter m

semiconscious [ˌsemɪ'kanʃəs] adj halbbewußt

semifinal [ˌsemɪ'faɪnəl] *adj* Halb-finale- ‖ *s* Halbfinale *n*, Vorschluß-runde *f*

seminar ['semɪˌnɑr] *s* Seminar *n*

seminarian [ˌsemɪ'nerɪ-ən] *s* Seminarist *m*

seminary ['semɪˌnerɪ] *s* Seminar *n*

semiprecious [ˌsemɪ'preʃəs] *adj* halbedel

Semite ['semaɪt] *s* Semit –in *mf*

Semitic [sɪ'mɪtɪk] *adj* semitisch

semitrailer ['semɪˌtreɪlər] *s* Schleppanhänger *m*

senate ['senɪt] *s* Senat *m*

senator ['senətər] *s* Senator *m*

senatorial [ˌsenə'torɪ-əl] *adj* (*of one senator*) senatorisch; (*of the senate*) Senats-

send [send] *v* (*pret & pp* **sent** [sent]) *tr* schicken, senden; (*rad, telv*) senden; **s. back** zurückschicken; **s. back word** zurücksagen lassen; **s. down** (*box*) niederschlagen; **s. forth** (*leaves*) treiben; **s. off** absenden; **s. on** (*forward*) weiterbefördern; **s. word** that benachrichtigen, daß ‖ *intr*—**s. for** (*e.g., free samples*) bestellen; (*e.g., a doctor*) rufen lassen

sender ['sendər] *s* Absender –in *mf*; (*telg*) Geber –in *mf*

send'-off' *s* Abschiedsfeier *f*

senile ['sinaɪl] *adj* senil

senility [sɪ'nɪlɪtɪ] *s* Senilität *f*

senior ['sinjər] *adj* (*in age*) älter; (*in rank*) ranghöher; (*class*) oberste; **Mr. John Smith Senior** Herr John Smith senior ‖ *s* Älteste *mf*; (*student*) Student –in *mf* im letzten Studienjahr

sen'ior cit'izen *s* bejahrter Mitbürger *m*

seniority [sin'jɑrɪtɪ] *s* Dienstalter *n*

sen'ior of'ficer *s* Vorgesetzte *mf*

sen'ior part'ner *s* geschäftsführender Partner *m*

sen'ior year' *s* letztes Studienjahr *n*

sensation [sen'seʃən] *s* (*feeling*) Gefühl *n*; (*cause of interest*) Sensation *f*

sensational [sen'seʃənəl] *adj* sensationell

sensationalism [sen'seʃənəˌlɪzəm] *s* Sensationsgier *f*

sense [sens] *s* (*e.g., of sight; meaning*) Sinn *m*; (*feeling*) Gefühl *n*; (*common sense*) Verstand *m*; **be out of one's senses** von Sinnen sein; **bring s.o. to his senses** j–n zur Vernunft bringen; **in a s.** in gewissem Sinne; **in the broadest s.** im weitesten Sinne; **make s.** Sinn haben; **there's no s. to it** da steckt kein Sinn drin ‖ *tr* spüren, fühlen

senseless ['senslɪs] *adj* sinnlos; (*from a blow*) bewußtlos

sense' of direc'tion *s* Ortssinn *m*

sense' of du'ty *s* Pflichtgefühl *n*

sense' of guilt' *s* Schuldgefühl *n*

sense' of hear'ing *s* Gehör *n*

sense' of hon'or *s* Ehrgefühl *n*

sense' of hu'mor *s* Humor *m*

sense' of jus'tice *s* Gerechtigkeitsgefühl *n*

sense' of responsibil'ity *s* Verantwortungsbewußtsein *n*

sense' of sight' *s* Gesichtssinn *m*

sense' of smell' *s* Geruchssinn *m*

sense' of taste' *s* Geschmackssinn *m*

sense' of touch' *s* Tastsinn *m*

sense' or'gan *s* Sinnesorgan *n*

sensibility [ˌsensɪ'bɪlɪtɪ] *s* Empfindlichkeit *f*

sensible ['sensɪbəl] *adj* vernünftig

sensitive ['sensɪtɪv] *adj* (**to**, *e.g., cold*) empfindlich (gegen); (*touchy*) überempfindlich; **s. post** Vertrauensposten *m*; **very s.** überempfindlich

sensitize ['sensɪˌtaɪz] *tr* (phot) lichtempfindlich machen

sensory ['sensərɪ] *adj* Sinnes-sen'sory depriva'tion *s* Reizentzug *m*

sensual ['sensʊ-əl] *adj* sinnlich

sensuality [ˌsensʊ'ælɪtɪ] *s* Sinnlichkeit *f*, Sinnenlust *f*

sensuous ['sensʊ-əs] *adj* sinnlich

sentence ['sentəns] *s* (gram) Satz *m*; (jur) Urteil *n*; **pronounce s.** das Urteil verkünden ‖ *tr* verurteilen

sentiment ['sentɪmənt] *s* Empfindung *f*

sentimental [ˌsentɪ'mentəl] *adj* sentimental, rührselig

sentinel ['sentɪnəl] *s* Posten *m*; stand *s.* Wache halten

sentry ['sentrɪ] *s* Wachposten *m*

sen'try box' *s* Schilderhaus *n*

separable ['sepərəbəl] *adj* trennbar

separate ['sepərɪt] *adj* getrennt; **under s. cover** separat ‖ ['sepəˌret] *tr* trennen; (*segregate*) absondern; (*scatter*) zerstreuen; (*discharge*) entlassen; **s. into** teilen in (*acc*) ‖ *intr* sich trennen, sich scheiden

sep'arated *adj* (*couple*) getrennt

separation [ˌsepə're[ən] *s* Trennung *f*

September [sep'tembər] *s* September *m*

sep'tic tank' ['septɪk] *s* Kläranlage *f*

sepulcher ['sepəlkər] *s* Grabmal *n*

sequel ['sikwəl] *s* Fortsetzung *f*; (fig) Nachspiel *n*

sequence ['sikwəns] *s* Reihenfolge *f*

se'quence of tens'es *s* Zeitenfolge *f*

sequester [sɪ'kwestər] *tr* (*remove*) entfernen; (*separate*) absondern; (jur) sequestrieren

sequins ['sikwɪnz] *spl* Flitter *m*

seraph ['serəf] *s* (**-aphs & -aphim** [əfɪm]) Seraph *m*

Serb [sɑrb] *adj* serbisch ‖ *s* Serbe *m*, Serbin *f*

Serbia ['sʌrbɪ-ə] *s* Serbien *n*

serenade [ˌserə'ned] *s* Ständchen *n* ‖ *tr* ein Ständchen bringen (*dat*)

serene [sɪ'rin] *adj* heiter; (*sea*) ruhig

serenity [sɪ'renɪtɪ] *s* Heiterkeit *f*

serf [sʌrf] *s* Leibeigene *mf*

serfdom ['sʌrfdəm] *s* Leibeigenschaft *f*

serge [sʌrdʒ] *s* (tex) Serge *f*

sergeant ['sɑrdʒənt] *s* Feldwebel *m*

ser'geant-at-arms' *s* (**sergeants-at-arms**) Ordnungsbeamter *m*

ser'geant first' class' *s* Oberfeldwebel *m*

ser′geant ma′jor s (sergeant majors) Hauptfeldwebel m

serial ['sɪrɪ·əl] s Fortsetzungsroman m, Romanfolge f

serialize ['sɪrɪ·ə‚laɪz] tr in Fortsetzungen veröffentlichen

se′rial num′ber s laufende Nummer f; (of a product) Fabriknummer f

se·ries ['sɪriz] s (–ries) Serie f, Reihe f; **in s.** reihenweise; (elec) hintereinandergeschaltet

serious ['sɪrɪ·əs] adj ernst; (mistake) schwerwiegend; (illness) gefährlich

seriously ['sɪrɪ·əsli] adv ernstlich; **s. wounded** schwerverwundet; **take s.** ernst nehmen

seriousness ['sɪrɪ·əsnɪs] s Ernst m

sermon ['sɑrmən] s Predigt f

sermonize ['sɑrmə‚naɪz] intr e–e Moralpredigt halten

serpent ['sɑrpənt] s Schlange f

serrated ['seretɪd] adj sägeartig

se·rum ['sɪrəm] s (–rums & –ra [rə]) Serum n

servant ['sɑrvənt] s Diener –in mf; (domestic) Hausdiener –in mf

serv′ant girl′ s Dienstmädchen s

serve [sʌrv] s (tennis) Aufschlag m || tr (a master, God) dienen (dat); (food) servieren; (a meal) anrichten; (guests) bedienen; (time in jail) verbüßen; (one's term in the service) abdienen; (the purpose) erfüllen; (tennis) aufschlagen; **s. mass** (eccl) zur Messe dienen; **s. notice on s.o.** j–n vorladen; **s. up** (food) auftragen || intr (& mil) dienen; (at table) servieren; **s. as** dienen als; **s. on a committe** e–m Ausschuß angehören

server ['sʌrvər] s (eccl) Ministrant m; (tennis) Aufschläger m

service ['sʌrvɪs] s (diplomatic, secret, foreign, public, etc.) Dienst m; (in a restaurant) Bedienung f; (set of table utensils) Besteck n; (set of dishes) Service n; (assistance at a repair shop) Service m; (maintenance) Wartung f; (transportation) Verkehr m; (relig) Gottesdienst m; (tennis) Aufschlag m; **at your s.** zu Ihren Diensten; **be in s.** (mach) in Betrieb sein; **be in the s.** (mil) beim Militär sein; **be of s.** behilflich sein; **do s.o. a s.** j–m e–n Dienst erweisen; **essential services** lebenswichtige Betriebe pl; **fit for active s.** kriegsverwendungsfähig; **see s.** Kriegsdienst tun; **the services** die Waffengattungen pl || tr (mach) warten

serviceable ['sʌrvɪsəbəl] adj (usable) verwendungsfähig; (helpful) nützlich; (durable) haltbar

serv′ice club′ s (mil) Soldatenklub m

serv′ice en′trance s Diensboteneingang m

serv′ice-man′ s (–men′) Monteur m; (at a gas station) Tankwart m; (mil) Soldat m

serv′ice rec′ord s Wehrpaß m

serv′ice sta′tion s Tankstelle f

serv′ice-station atten′dant s Tankwart m

serv′ice troops′ spl Versorgungstruppen pl

servile ['sʌrvaɪl] adj kriecherisch

serv′ing s Portion f; (e.g., of a subpoena) Zustellung f

serv′ing cart′ s Servierwagen m

servitude ['sʌrvɪ‚t(j)ud] s Knechtschaft f

ses′ame seed′ ['sesəmi] s Sesamsamen m

session ['seʃən] s Sitzung f, Tagung f; (educ) Semester n; **be in session** tagen

set [set] adj (price, time) festgesetzt; (rule) festgelegt; (speech) wohlüberlegt; **be all set** fix und fertig sein; **be set in one's ways** festgefahren sein || s (group of things belonging together) Satz m, Garnitur f; (of chess or checkers) Spiel n; (clique) Sippschaft f; (rad, telv) Apparat m; (tennis) Satz m; (theat) Bühnenbild n; **younger set** Nachwuchs m || v (pret & pp set; ger setting) tr (put) setzen; (stand) stellen; (lay) legen; (a clock, a trap) stellen; (the hair) legen; (a record) aufstellen; (an example) geben; (a time, price) festsetzen; (the table) decken; (jewels) (ein)fassen; (a camera) einstellen; (surg) einrenken; (typ) setzen; **set ahead** (a clock) vorstellen; **set back** (a clock) nachstellen; (a patient) zurückwerfen; **set down** niedersetzen; **set down in writing** schriftlich niederlegen; **set foot in** (or on) betreten; **set forth** (explain) erklären; **set free** freilassen; **set in order** in Ordnung bringen; **set limits to** Schranken setzen (dat); **set off** (a bomb) sprengen lassen; **set (s.o.) over** (j–n) überordnen (dat); **set right** wieder in Ordnung bringen; **set store by** Gewicht beimessen (dat); **set straight (on)** aufklären (über acc); **set the meeting for two** die Versammlung auf zwei Uhr ansetzen; **set up** (at the bar) (coll) zu e–m Gläschen einladen; (mach) montieren; (typ) aufstellen; **set up housekeeping** Wirtschaft führen; **set up in business** etablieren || intr (said of cement) abbinden; (astr) untergehen; **set about** (ger) darangehen zu (inf); **set in** einsetzen; **set out (for)** sich auf den Weg machen (nach); **set out on** (a trip) antreten; **set to work** sich an die Arbeit machen

set′back′ s Rückschlag m, Schlappe f

set′screw′ s Stellschraube f

settee [sɛ′ti] s Polsterbank f

setter ['setər] s Vorstehhund m

set′ting s (of the sun) Niedergang m; (of a story) Ort m der Handlung; (of a gem) Fassung f; (theat) Bühnenbild m

settle ['setəl] tr (conclude) erledigen; (decide) entscheiden; (an argument) schlichten; (a problem) erledigen; (an account) begleichen; (one's affairs) in Ordnung bringen; (a creditor's claim) befriedigen; (a lawsuit) durch Vergleich beilegen; (a region) besiedeln; (*people*) ansiedeln ‖ *intr* (*in a region*) sich niederlassen; (*said of a building*) sich senken; (*said of a ship*) absacken; (*said of dust*) sich legen; (*said of a liquid*) sich klären; (*said of suspended particles*) sich setzen; (*said of a cold*) (**in**) sich festsetzen (in *dat*); **s. down** (*in a chair*) sich niederlassen; (*calm down*) sich beruhigen; **s. down to** (e.g., *work*) sich machen an (*acc*); **s. for** sich einigen auf (*acc*); **s. on** sich entscheiden für; **s. up** (fin) die Verbindlichkeit vergleichen

settlement ['setəlmənt] *s* (*colony*) Siedlung *f*; (*agreement*) Abkommen *n*; (*of an argument*) Beilegung *f*; (*of accounts*) Abrechnung *f*; (*of a debt*) Begleichung *f*; **reach a s.** e-n Vergleich schließen

settler ['setlər] *s* Ansiedler –in *mf*

set'up' *s* Aufbau *m*, Anlage *f*

seven ['sevən] *adj & pron* sieben ‖ *s* Sieben *f*

seventeen ['sevən'tin] *adj & pron* siebzehn ‖ *s* Siebzehn *f*

seventeenth ['sevən'tinθ] *adj & pron* siebzehnte ‖ *s* (*fraction*) Siebzehntel *n*; **the s.** (*in dates or a series*) der Siebzehnte

seventh ['sevənθ] *adj & pron* sieb(en)te ‖ *s* (*fraction*) Sieb(en)tel *n*; **the s.** (*in dates or a series*) der Sieb(en)te

seventieth ['sevəntɪ·ɪθ] *adj & pron* siebzigste ‖ *s* (*fraction*) Siebzigstel *n*

seventy ['sevənti] *adj & pron* siebzig ‖ *s* Siebzig *f*; **the seventies** die siebziger Jahre

sev'enty-first' *adj & pron* einundsiebzigste

sev'enty-one' *adj* einundsiebzig

sever ['sevər] *tr* (ab)trennen; (*relations*) abbrechen

several ['sevərəl] *adj & indef pron* mehrere; **s. times** mehrmals

severance ['sevərəns] *s* Trennung *f*; (*of relations*) Abbruch *m*

sev'erance pay' *s* (& mil) Abfindungsentschädigung *f*

severe [sɪ'vɪr] *adj* (*judge, winter, cold*) streng; (*blow, sentence, winter*) hart; (*illness, test*) schwer; (*criticism*) scharf

severity [sɪ'verɪti] *s* Strenge *f*; Härte *f*; Schärfe *f*

sew [so] *v* (*pret* **sewed**; *pp* **sewed & sewn**) *tr & intr* nähen

sewage ['su·ɪdʒ] *s* Abwässer *pl*

sew'age-dispos'al plant' *s* Kläranlage *f*

sewer ['su·ər] *s* Kanal *m* ‖ ['so·ər] *s* Näher –in *mf*

sewerage ['su·ərɪdʒ] *s* Kanalisation *f*

sew'er pipe' ['su·ər] *s* Abwasserleitung *f*

sew'ing *s* Näharbeit *f*

sew'ing bas'ket *s* Nähkasten *m*

sew'ing kit' *s* Nähzeug *n*

sew'ing machine' *s* Nähmaschine *f*

sex [seks] *adj* (*crime, education, harmone*) Sexual– ‖ *s* Geschlecht *n*; (*intercourse*) Sex *m*

sex appeal' *s* Sex-Appeal *m*

sex' pot' *s* (coll) Sexbombe *f*

sextent ['sekstənt] *s* Sextant *m*

sexton ['sekstən] *s* Küster *m*

sexual ['sek/u·əl] *adj* geschlechtlich, Geschlechts–, sexuell

sex'ual in'tercourse *s* Geschlechtsverkehr *m*

sexuality [sek/u'ælɪti] *s* Sexualität *f*

sexy ['seksi] *adj* sexy

shabbily ['ʃæbɪli] *adv* schäbig; (*in treatment*) stiefmütterlich

shabby ['ʃæbi] *adj* schäbig

shack [ʃæk] *s* Bretterbude *f*

shackle ['ʃækəl] *s* (naut) Schäkel *m*; **shackles** Fesseln *pl* ‖ *tr* fesseln

shad [ʃæd] *s* Shad *m*, Alse *f*

shade [ʃed] *s* Schatten *m*; (*for a window*) Rollo *n*; (*of a lamp*) Schirm *m*; (*hue*) Schattierung *f*; **throw into the s.** (fig) in den Schatten stellen ‖ *tr* beschatten; (paint) schattieren

shad'ing *s* Schattierung *f*

shadow ['ʃædo] *s* Schatten *m* ‖ *tr* (a *person*) beschatten

shad'ow box'ing *s* Schattenboxen *n*

shadowy ['ʃædo·i] *adj* (*like a shadow*) schattenhaft; (*indistinct*) verschwommen; (*shady*) schattig

shady ['ʃedi] *adj* schattig; (coll) dunkel; **s. character** Dunkelmann *m*; **s. side** (& fig) Schattenseite *f*

shaft [ʃæft] *s* Schaft *m*; (*of an elevator*) Schacht *m*; (*handle*) Stiel *m*; (*of a wagon*) Deichsel *f*; (*of a column*) Säulenschaft *m*; (*of a transmission*) Welle *f*

shaggy ['ʃægi] *adj* zottig, struppig

shake [ʃek] *s* Schütteln *n*; **he's no great shakes** mit ihm ist nicht viel los ‖ *v* (*pret* **shook** [ʃuk]; *pp* **shaken**) *tr* schütteln; **s. a leg!** (coll) rühr dich ein bißchen; **s. before using** vor Gebrauch schütteln; **s. down** (sl) erpressen; **s. hands** sich [*dat*] die Hand geben; **s. hands with** j–m die Hand drücken; **s. off** (& fig) abschütteln; **s. one's head** mit dem Kopf schütteln; **s. out** (a *rug*) ausschütteln; **s. up** aufschütteln; (fig) aufrütteln ‖ *intr* (**with**) zittern (vor *dat*), beben (vor *dat*)

shake'down' *s* (sl) Erpressung *f*

shake'down cruise' *s* Probefahrt *f*

shaker ['ʃekər] *s* (*for salt*) Streuer *m*; (*for cocktails*) Shaker *m*

shake'-up' *s* Umgruppierung *f*

shaky ['ʃeki] *adj* (& fig) wacklig

shale [ʃel] *s* Schiefer *m*

shale' oil' *s* Schieferöl *n*

shall [ʃæl] *v* (*pret* **should** [ʃʊd]) *aux* (*to express future tense*) werden, e.g., **I s.** go ich werde gehen; (*to express obligation*) sollen, e.g., **s. I stay?** soll ich bleiben?

shallow ['ʃælo] *adj* (*river, person*) seicht; (*water, bowl*) flach ‖ **shallows** *spl* Untiefe *f*

sham [ʃæm] *adj* Schein– ‖ *s* Schein *m* ‖ *v* (*pret & pp* **shammed**; *ger* **shamming**) *tr* vortäuschen

sham' bat'tle *s* Scheingefecht *n*

shambles ['ʃæmbəlz] *s* Trümmerhaufen *m*

shame [ʃem] *s* Schande *f*; (*feeling of shame*) Scham *f*; **put s.o. to s.** (*outdo s.o.*) j–n in den Schatten stellen; **s. on you!** schäm dich!; **what a s.!** wie schade! ‖ *tr* beschämen

shame'faced' *adj* verschämt

shameful ['ʃemfəl] *adj* schändlich

shameless ['ʃemlɪs] *adj* unverschämt

shampoo [ʃæm'pu] *s* Shampoo *n* ‖ *tr* shampoonieren

shamrock ['ʃæmrɑk] *s* Kleeblatt *n*

Shanghai [ʃæŋ'haɪ] *s* Shanghai *n* ‖ shanghai ['ʃæŋhaɪ] *tr* schanghaien

shank [ʃæŋk] *s* Unterschenkel *m*; (*of an anchor, column, golf club*) Schaft *m*; (*cut of meat*) Schenkel *m*

shanty ['ʃænti] *s* Bude *f*

shan'tytown' *s* Bretterbudensiedlung *f*

shape [ʃep] *s* Form *f*, Gestalt *f*; **in bad s.** (coll) in schlechter Form; **in good s.** in gutem Zustand; **out of s.** aus der Form; **take s.** sich gestalten ‖ *tr* formen, gestalten ‖ *intr*—**s. up** (coll) sich zusammenfassen

shapeless ['ʃeplɪs] *adj* formlos

shapely ['ʃepli] *adj* wohlgestaltet

share [ʃer] *s* Anteil *m*; (st. exch.) Aktie *f*; **do one's s.** das Seine tun ‖ *tr* teilen ‖ *intr*—**s. in** teilhaben an (*dat*)

share'hold'er *s* Aktionär –in *mf*

shark [ʃɑrk] *s* Hai *m*, Haifisch *m*

sharp [ʃɑrp] *adj* scharf; (*pointed*) spitzig; (*keen*) pfiffig ‖ *adv* pünktlich ‖ *s* (mus) Kreuz *n*

sharpen ['ʃɑrpən] *tr* schärfen; (*a pencil*) spitzen

sharply ['ʃɑrpli] *adv* scharf

sharp'shoot'er *s* Scharfschütze *m*

shatter ['ʃætər] *tr* zersplittern; (*the nerves*) zerrütten; (*dreams*) zerstören ‖ *intr* zersplittern

shat'terproof' *adj* splittersicher

shave [ʃev] *s*—**get a s.** sich rasieren lassen ‖ *tr* rasieren ‖ *intr* sich rasieren

shav'ing brush' *s* Rasierpinsel *m*

shav'ing cream' *s* Rasierkrem *m*

shav'ing mug' *s* Rasiernapf *m*

shawl [ʃɔl] *s* Schal *m*

she [ʃi] *s* Weibchen *n* ‖ *pers pron* sie

sheaf [ʃif] *s* (**sheaves** [ʃivz]) Garbe *f*

shear [ʃɪr] *s*—**shears** Schere *f* ‖ *v* (*pret sheared*; *pp sheared* & **shorn** [ʃɔrn]) *tr* scheren; **s. off** abschneiden

sheath [ʃiθ] *s* Scheide *f*

sheathe [ʃið] *tr* in die Scheide stecken

shed [ʃed] *s* Schuppen *m* ‖ *v* (*pret* & *pp shed*; *ger shedding*) *tr* (*leaves*) abwerfen; (*tears*) vergießen; (*hair, leaves*) verlieren; (*peace*) verbreiten; **s. light on** (fig) Licht werfen auf (*acc*)

sheen [ʃin] *s* Glanz *m*

sheep [ʃip] *s* (**sheep**) Schaf *n*

sheep'dog' *s* Schäferhund *m*

sheep'fold' *s* Schafhürde *f*, Schafpferch *m*

sheepish ['ʃipɪʃ] *adj* (*embarrassed*) verlegen; (*timid*) schüchtern

sheep'skin' *s* Schaffell *n*; (coll) Diplom *n*

sheep'skin coat' *s* Schafpelz *m*

sheer [ʃɪr] *adj* rein; (tex) durchsichtig; **by s. force** durch bloße Gewalt ‖ *intr*—**s. off** (naut) abscheren

sheet [ʃit] *s* (*for the bed*) Leintuch *n*; (*of paper*) Blatt *n*, Bogen *m*; (*of metal*) Blech *n*; (naut) Segelleine *f*; **come down in sheets** (fig) in Strömen regnen; **s. of ice** Glatteis *n*; **s. of flame** Feuermeer *n*

sheet' i'ron *s* Eisenblech *n*

sheet' mu'sic *s* Notenblatt *n*

she'-goat' *s* Ziege *f*

sheik [ʃik] *s* Scheich *m*

shelf [ʃelf] *s* (**shelves** [ʃelvz]) Regal *n*; **put on the s.** (fig) auf die lange Bank schieben

shell [ʃel] *s* Schale *f*; (*conch*) Muschel *f*; (*of a snail*) Gehäuse *n*; (*of a tortoise*) Panzer *m*; (*explosive*) Granate *f*; (*bullet*) Patrone *f* ‖ *tr* (*eggs*) schälen; (*nuts*) aufknacken; (mil) beschießen; **s. out money** (coll) mit dem Geld herausrücken ‖ *intr*—**s. out** (coll) blechen

shel'lac [ʃə'læk] *s* Schellack *m* ‖ *v* (*pret* & *pp* –**lacked**; *ger* –**lacking**) *tr* mit Schellack streichen; (sl) verdreschen

shell'fish' *s* Schalentier *n*

shell' hole' *s* Granattrichter *m*

shell' shock' *s* Bombenneurose *f*

shelter ['ʃeltər] *s* Obdach *n*; (fig) Schutz *m* ‖ *tr* schützen

shelve [ʃelv] *tr* auf ein Regal stellen; (fig) auf die lange Bank schieben

shenanigans [ʃɪ'nænɪgənz] *spl* Possen *pl*

shepherd ['ʃepərd] *s* Hirt *m*; (fig) Seelenhirt *m* ‖ *tr* hüten

shep'herd dog' *s* Schäferhund *m*

shepherdess ['ʃepərdɪs] *s* Hirtin *f*

sherbet ['ʃɑrbət] *s* Speiseeis *n*

sheriff ['ʃerɪf] *s* Sheriff *m*

sherry ['ʃeri] *s* Sherry *m*

shield [ʃild] *s* Schild *m*; (fig) Schutz *m*; (rad) Röhrenabschirmung *f* ‖ *tr* (*from*) schützen (vor *dat*); (elec, mach) abschirmen

shift [ʃɪft] *adj* (*worker, work*) Schicht– ‖ *s* Schicht *f*; (*change*) Verschiebung *f*; (*loose-fitting dress*) Kittelkleid *n* ‖ *tr* (*a meeting*) verschieben; (*the blame*) (on) (ab)schieben (auf *acc*); **s. gears** umschalten ‖ *intr* (*said of the wind*) umspringen; **s. for oneself** sich allein durchschlagen; **s. into second gear** in den zweiten Gang umschalten

shift' key' *s* Umschalttaste *f*

shiftless ['ʃɪftlɪs] *adj* träge

shifty ['ʃɪfti] *adj* schlau, gerissen

shimmer ['ʃɪmər] *s* Schimmer *m* ‖ *intr* schimmern, flimmern

shin [ʃɪn] *s* Schienbein *n*

shin'bone' *s* Schienbein *n*

shine [ʃaɪn] *s* Schein *m*, Glanz *m* ‖ *v* (*pret* & *pp shined*) *tr* polieren; (*shoes*) wichsen ‖ *v* (*pret* & *pp shone* [ʃon]) *intr* scheinen; (*said of the eyes*) leuchten; (*be outstanding*) (*in*) glänzen (in *dat*)

shiner ['ʃaɪnər] *s* (sl) blaues Auge *n*

shingle ['ʃɪŋgəl] *s* (*for a roof*) Schindel *f*; (*e.g., of a doctor*) Aushängeschild *n* ‖ *tr* mit Schindeln decken

shin'ing *adj* (*eyes*) leuchtend, strahlend; (*example*) glänzend

shiny ['ʃaɪni] *adj* blank, glänzend

ship [ʃɪp] *s* Schiff *n* ‖ *v* (*pret & pp* **shipped**; *ger* **shipping**) *tr* senden; **s. water** e-e Sturzsee bekommen ‖ *intr*—**s. out** absegeln

ship'board' *s* Bord *m*; **on s.** an Bord

ship'build'er *s* Schiffbauer *m*

ship'build'ing *s* Schiffbau *m*

shipment ['ʃɪpmənt] *s* Lieferung *f*

ship'ping *s* Absendung *f*, Verladung *f*; (*ships*) Schiffe *pl*

ship'ping clerk' *s* Expedient *m*

ship'ping depart'ment *s* Versandabteilung *f*

ship'shape' *adj* ordentlich

ship'wreck' *s* Schiffbruch *m* ‖ *tr* scheitern lassen; **be s.** schiffbrüchig sein ‖ *intr* Schiffbruch erleiden

ship'yard' *s* Werft *f*

shirk [ʃɪrk] *tr* sich drücken vor (*dat*) ‖ *intr* (**from**) sich drücken vor (*dat*)

shirt [ʃʌrt] *s* Hemd *n*; **keep your s. on!** (sl) regen Sie sich nicht auf!

shirt' col'lar *s* Hemdkragen *m*

shirt'sleeve' *s* Hemdsärmel *m*

shirttail' *s* Hemdschoß *m*

shit [ʃɪt] *s* (vulg) Scheiße *f* ‖ *v* (*pret & pp* **shit**) *tr & intr* (vulg) scheißen

shiver ['ʃɪvər] *s* Schauder *m* ‖ *intr* (**at**) schaudern (vor *dat*); (**with**) zittern (vor *dat*)

shoal [ʃol] *s* Untiefe *f*

shock [ʃak] *s* Schock *m*; (*of hair*) Schopf *m*; (agr) Schober *m*; (elec) Schlag *m* ‖ *tr* schockieren; (elec) e-n Schlag versetzen (*dat*)

shock' absorb'er [æb,sɔrbər] *s* Stoßdämpfer *m*

shock'ing *adj* schockierend

shock' troops' *spl* Stoßtruppen *pl*

shock' wave' *s* Stoßwelle *f*

shoddy ['ʃɑdi] *adj* schäbig

shoe [ʃu] *s* Schuh *m* ‖ *v* (*pret & pp* **shod** [ʃɑd]) *tr* beschlagen

shoe'horn' *s* Schuhlöffel *m*

shoe'lace' *s* Schuhband *n*, Schnürsenkel *m*

shoe'mak'er *s* Schuster *m*

shoe' pol'ish *s* Schuhwichse *f*

shoe'shine' *s* Schuhputzen *n*

shoe' store' *s* Schuhladen *m*

shoe' string' *s* Schuhband *m*; **on a s.** mit ein paar Groschen

shoe'tree' *s* Schuhspanner *m*

shoo [ʃu] *tr* (**away**) wegscheuchen ‖ *interj* sch!

shook-up ['ʃuk'ʌp] *adj* (coll) verdattert

shoot [ʃut] *s* Schößling *m* ‖ *v* (*pret & pp* **shot** [ʃɑt]) *tr* (an)schießen, (ab)schießen; (*kill*) erschießen; (*dice*) werfen; (cin) drehen; (phot) aufnehmen; (aer) abschießen; **s. down** *tr* abschießen; **s. the breeze** zwanglos plaudern; **s. up** (*e.g., a town*) zusammenschie-

ßen ‖ *intr* schießen; **s. at** schießen auf (*acc*); **s. by** vorbeisausen an (*dat*); **s. up** (*in growth*) aufschießen; (*said of flames*) emporschlagen; (*said of prices*) emporschnellen

shoot'ing *s* Schießerei *f*; (*execution*) Erschießung *f*; (*of a film*) Drehen *n*

shoot'ing gal'lery *s* Schießbude *f*

shoot'ing match' *s* Preisschießen *n*

shoot'ing star' *s* Sternschnuppe *f*

shoot'ing war' *s* heißer Krieg *m*

shop [ʃɑp] *s* Laden *m*, Geschäft *n*; **talk s.** fachsimpeln ‖ *v* (*pret & pp* **shopped**; *ger* **shopping**) *intr* einkaufen; **go shopping** einkaufen gehen; **s. around for** sich in einigen Läden umsehen aus

shop'girl' *s* Ladenmädchen *n*

shop'keep'er *s* Ladeninhaber –in *mf*

shoplifter ['ʃɑp,lɪftər] *s* Ladendieb –in *mf*

shop'lift'ing *s* Ladendiebstahl *m*

shopper ['ʃɑpər] *s* Einkäufer –in *mf*

shop'ping *s* Einkaufen *n*; (*purchases*) Einkäufe *pl*

shop'ping bag' *s* Einkaufstasche *f*

shop'ping cen'ter *s* Einkaufcenter *n*

shop'ping dis'trict *s* Geschäftsviertel *n*

shop'ping spree' *s* Einkaufsorgie *f*

shop'talk' *s* Fachsimpelei *f*

shop'win'dow *s* Schaufenster *n*

shop'worn' *adj* (fig) abgerissen

shore [ʃor] *s* Küste *f*; (*beach*) Strand *m*; (*of a river*) Ufer *n*; **go to the s.** ans Meer fahren ‖ *tr*—**s. up** abstützen

shore' leave' *s* Landurlaub *m*

shore'line' *s* Küstenlinie *f*; (*of a river*) Uferlinie *f*

shore' patrol' *s* Küstenstreife *f*

short [ʃɔrt] *adj* kurz; (*person*) klein; (*loan*) kurzfristig; **s. time ago** vor kurzem; **be s. of**, *e.g.*, **I am s. of bread** das Brot geht mir aus; **be s. with s.o.** j-n kurz abfertigen; **cut s.** abbrechen; **fall s. of** zurückbleiben hinter (*dat*); **get the s. end** das Nachsehen haben; **I am three marks s.** es fehlen mir drei Mark; **in s.** kurzum; **s. of breath** außer Atem; **s. of cash** knapp bei Kasse ‖ *s* (cin) Kurzfilm *m*; (elec) Kurzschluß *m* ‖ *tr* (elec) kurzschließen

shortage ['ʃɔrtɪdʒ] *s* (**of**) Mangel *m* (**an** *dat*); (com) Minderbetrag *m*

short'cake' *s* Mürbekuchen *m*

short'-change' *tr* zu wenig Wechselgeld herausgeben (*dat*); (fig) betrügen

short' cir'cuit *s* Kurzschluß *m*

short'-cir'cuit *tr* kurzschließen

short'com'ing *s* Fehler *m*, Mangel *m*

short'cut' *s* Abkürzung *f*; **take a s.** den Weg abkürzen

shorten ['ʃɔrtən] *tr* abkürzen

short'ening *s* Abkürzung *f*; (culin) Backfett *n*

short'hand' *adj* stenographisch ‖ *s* Stenographie *f*; **in s.** stenographisch; **take down in s.** stenographieren

short-lived ['ʃɔrt'laɪvd] *adj* kurzlebig

shortly ['ʃɔrtli] *adv* in kurzem; **s. after** kurz nach

short'-or'der cook' *s* Schnellimbißkoch *m*, Schnellimbißköchin *f*

short'-range' *adj* Nah-, auf kurze Sicht

shorts [ʃɔrts] *s* (*underwear*) Unterhose *f*; (*walking shorts*) kurze Hose *f*; (sport) Sporthose *f*

short'-sight'ed *adj* kurzsichtig

short' sto'ry *s* Novelle *f*

short'-tem'pered *adj* leicht aufbrausend

short'-term' *adj* kurzfristig

short'wave' *adj* Kurzwellen– || *s* Kurzwelle *f*

short'wind'ed *adj* kurzatmig

shot [ʃɑt] *adj* (sl) kaputt; (*drunk*) (sl) besoffen; **my nerves are s.** ich bin mit meinen Nerven ganz herunter || *s* Schuß *m*; (*shooter*) Schütze *m*; (*pellets*) Schrot *m*; (*injection*) Spritze *f*; (*snapshot*) Aufnahme *f*; (*of liquor*) Gläschen *n*; **be a good s.** gut schießen; **s. in the arm** (fig) Belebungsspritze *f*; **s. in the dark** Sprung *m* ins Ungewisse; **take a s. at** e-n Schuß abgeben auf (*acc*); (fig) versuchen; **wild s.** Schuß *m* ins Blaue

shot'gun' *s* Schrotflinte *f*

shot'gun wed'ding *s* Mußehe *f*

shot'-put' *s* (sport) Kugelstoßen *n*

should [ʃʊd] *aux* (to express softened affirmation) **I s. like to know** ich möchte wissen; **I s. think so das** will ich meinen; (to express obligation) **how s. I know?** wie sollte ich das wissen?; **you shouldn't do that** Sie sollten das nicht tun; (in conditional clauses) **if it s. rain tomorrow** wenn es morgen regnen sollte

shoulder [ˈʃoldər] *s* Schulter *f*, Achsel *f*; (*of a road*) Bankett *n*; **have broad shoulders** e-n breiten Rücken haben || *tr* (*a rifle*) schultern; (*responsibility*) auf sich nehmen

shoul'der bag' *s* Umhängetasche *f*

shoul'der blade' *s* Schulterblatt *n*

shoul'der strap' *s* (*of underwear*) Trägerband *n*; (mil) Schulterriemen *m*

shout [ʃaʊt] *s* Schrei *m*, Ruf *m* || *tr* schreien, rufen; **s. down** (coll) niederschreien || *intr* schreien, rufen

shove [ʃʌv] *s* Stoß *m*; **give s.o. a s.** j-m e-n Stoß versetzen || *tr* stoßen; (*e.g., furniture*) rücken; **s. around** (coll) herumschubsen; **s. forward** vorschieben || *intr* drängeln; **s. off** (coll) abschieben; (naut) vom Land abstoßen

shov-el [ˈʃʌvəl] *s* Schaufel *f* || *v* (*pret & pp* -el[l]ed; *ger* -el[l]ing) *tr* schaufeln

show [ʃo] *s* (*exhibition*) Ausstellung *f*; (*outer appearance*) Schau *f*; (*spectacle*) Theater *n*; (cin, theat) Vorstellung *f*; **by s. of hands** durch Handzeichen; **make a s. of s.th.** mit etw Staat machen; **only for s.** nur zur Schau || *v* (*pret* showed; *pp* shown [ʃon] & showed) *tr* zeigen; (*prove*) beweisen, nachweisen; (*said of evidence, tests*) ergeben; (*tickets, passport, papers*) vorweisen; **s. around** (*a person*) herumführen; (*a thing*) herumzeigen || *intr* zu sehen sein;

(*said of a slip*) vorgucken; **s. off** (*with*) großtun (mit); **s. up** erscheinen

show' busi'ness *s* Unterhaltungsindustrie *f*

show'case' *s* Schaukasten *m*, Vitrine *f*

show'down' *s* entscheidender Wendepunkt *m*; (*e.g., in a western*) Kraftprobe *f*; (cards) Aufdecken *n* der Karten

shower [ˈʃaʊ·ər] *s* (*rain*) Schauer *m*; (*bath*) Dusche *f*; (*shower room*) Duschraum *m*; (*of stones, arrows*) Hagel *m*; (*of bullets, sparks*) Regen *m*; (*for a bride*) Party *f* zur Überreichung der Brautgeschenke; **take a s.** (sich) duschen || *intr* (*with gifts*) überschütten || *intr* duschen; (meteor) schauern

show'er bath' *s* Dusche *f*, Brausebad *n*

show' girl' *s* Revuegirl *n*

show'ing *s* Zeigen *n*; (cin) Vorführung *f*

show'ing off' *s* Großtuerei *f*

show'man *s* (–men) *s* Schauspieler *m*

show'-off' *s* Protz *m*

show'piece' *s* Schaustück *n*

show'room' *s* Ausstellungsraum *m*

show' win'dow *s* Schaufenster *n*

showy [ˈʃo·i] *adj* prunkhaft

shrapnel [ˈʃræpnəl] *s* Schrapnell *n*

shred [ʃrɛd] *s* Fetzen *m*; (*least bit*) Spur *f*; **tear to shreds** in Fetzen reißen; (*an argument*) gründlich widerlegen || *v* (*pret & pp* shredded & shred; *ger* shredding) *tr* zerfetzen; (*paper*) in Streifen schneiden; (culin) schnitzeln

shredder [ˈʃrɛdər] *s* (*of paper*) Reißwolf *m*; (culin) Schnitzelmaschine *f*

shrew [ʃru] *s* böse Sieben *f*

shrewd [ʃrud] *adj* schlau

shriek [ʃrik] *s* Gekreische *n*, gellender Schrei *m* || *intr* kreischen

shrill [ʃrɪl] *adj* schrill

shrimp [ʃrɪmp] *s* Garnele *f*; (coll) Knirps *m*

shrine [ʃraɪn] *s* Heiligtum *n*

shrink [ʃrɪŋk] *v* (*pret* shrank [ʃræŋk] & shrunk [ʃrʌŋk]; *pp* shrunk & shrunken) *tr* einlaufen lassen || *intr* schrumpfen; **s. back from** zurückschrecken vor (*dat*); **s. from** sich scheuen vor (*dat*); **s. up** einschrumpfen

shrinkage [ˈʃrɪŋkɪdʒ] *s* Schrumpfung *f*

shriv-el [ˈʃrɪvəl] *s* (*pret & pp* -el[l]ed; *ger* -el[l]ing) *intr* schrumpfen; **s. up** zusammenschrumpfen

shriv'eled *adj* schrumpelig

shroud [ʃraʊd] *s* Leichentuch *n*; (fig) Hülle *f*; (naut) Want *f* || *tr* (in) einhüllen (in *acc*)

shrub [ʃrʌb] *s* Strauch *m*

shrubbery [ˈʃrʌbəri] *s* Strauchwerk *n*

shrug [ʃrʌg] *s* Zucken *n* || *v* (*pret & pp* shrugged; *ger* shrugging) *tr* zucken; **s. off** mit e-m Achselzucken abtun; **s. one's shoulders** mit den Achseln zucken || *intr* mit den Achseln zucken

shuck [ʃʌk] *tr* enthülsen

shudder [ˈʃʌdər] *s* Schau(d)er *m* ||

intr (at) schau(d)ern (vor *dat*); **s. at the thought of s.th.** bei dem Gedanken an etw [*acc*] zittern

shuffle ['ʃʌfəl] *s* Schlurfen *n*; (cards) Mischen *n*; **get lost in the s.** (fig) unter den Tisch fallen ‖ *tr* (cards) mischen; (the feet) schleifen; ‖ *intr* die Karten mischen; (walk) schlurfen; **s. along** latschen

shun [ʃʌn] *v* (pret & pp **shunned**; ger **shunning**) *tr* (a person) meiden; (a thing) (ver)meiden

shunt [ʃʌnt] *s* (elec) Nebenschluß *m* ‖ *tr* (shove aside) beiseite schieben; (across) parallelschalten (zu); (rr) rangieren

shut [ʃʌt] *adj* zu ‖ (pret & pp **shut**; ger **shutting**) *tr* schließen, zumachen; **be s. down** stilliegen; **s. down** stilllegen; **s. off** absperren; **s. one's eyes to** hinwegsehen über (*acc*); **s. out** aussperren; **s. s.o. up** j-m den Mund stopfen ‖ *intr* sich schließen; **s. up!** (coll) halt's Maul!

shut'down' *s* Stillegung *f*

shutter ['ʃʌtər] *s* Laden *m*; (phot) Verschluß *m*

shuttle ['ʃʌtəl] *s* Schiffchen *n* ‖ *intr* pendeln, hin- und herfahren

shut'tle bus' *s* Pendelbus *m*

shut'tlecock' *s* Federball *m*

shut'tle serv'ice *s* Pendelverkehr *m*

shut'tle train' *s* Pendelzug *m*

shy [ʃaɪ] *adj* (shyer; shyest) schüchtern; **be a dollar shy** e-n Dollar los sein ‖ *intr* (said of a horse) stutzen; **shy at** zurückscheuen vor (*dat*); **shy away from** sich scheuen vor (*dat*)

shyness ['ʃaɪnɪs] *s* Scheu *f*

shyster ['ʃaɪstər] *s* Winkeladvokat *m*

Siamese' twins' [,saɪ·ə'miz] *spl* Siamesische Zwillinge *pl*

Siberia [saɪ'bɪrɪ·ə] *s* Sibirien *n*

Siberian [saɪ'bɪrɪ·ən] *adj* sibirisch ‖ *s* Sibirier –in *mf*

sibilant ['sɪbɪlənt] *s* Zischlaut *m*

siblings ['sɪblɪŋz] *spl* Geschwister *pl*

sibyl ['sɪbɪl] *s* Sibylle *f*

sic [sɪk] *adv* sic ‖ *v* (pret & pp **sicked**; ger **sicking**) *tr*—**sic 'em!** (coll) faß!; **sic the dog on s.o.** den Hund auf j-n hetzen

Sicilian [sɪ'sɪljən] *adj* sizilianisch ‖ *s* Sizilianer –in *mf*

Sicily ['sɪsɪlɪ] *s* Sizilien *n*

sick [sɪk] *adj* krank; **be s. and tired of s.th.** etw gründlich satt haben; **be s. as a dog** sich hundeelend fühlen; **I am s. to my stomach** mir ist übel; **play s.** krankfeiern

sick' bay' *s* Schiffslazarett *n*

sick'bed' *s* Krankenbett *n*

sicken ['sɪkən] *tr* krank machen; (disgust) anekeln ‖ *intr* krank werden

sick'ening *adj* (fig) ekelhaft

sick' head'ache *s* Kopfschmerzen *pl* mit Übelkeit

sickle ['sɪkəl] *s* Sichel *f*

sick' leave' *s* Krankenurlaub *m*

sickly ['sɪklɪ] *adj* kränklich; (smile) erzwungen

sickness ['sɪknɪs] *s* Krankheit *f*

sick' room' *s* Krankenzimmer *n*

side [saɪd] *adj* Neben–, Seiten– ‖ *s* Seite *f*; (of a team, government) Partei *f*; (edge) Rand *m*; **at my s.** mir zur Seite; **dark s.** Schattenseite *f*; **off sides** (sport) abseits; **on the father's s.** väterlicherseits; **on the s.** (coll) nebenbei; **this s. up** Vorsicht, nicht stürzen; **to be on the safe s.** um ganz sicher zu gehen ‖ *intr*—**s. with s.o.** j-s Partei ergreifen

side' aisle' *s* Seitengang *m*; (of a church) Seitenschiff *n*

side' al'tar *s* Nebenaltar *m*

side'arm' *s* Seitengewehr *n*

side'board' *s* Anrichte *f*, Büffet *n*

side'burns' *spl* Koteletten *pl*

side' dish' *s* Nebengericht *n*

side' door' *s* Seitentür *f*

side' effect' *s* Nebenwirkung *f*

side' en'trance *s* Seiteneingang *m*

side' glance' *s* Seitenblick *m*

side' is'sue *s* Nebenfrage *f*

side' job' *s* Nebenverdienst *m*

side'kick' *s* (coll) Kumpel *m*

side'line' *s* (occupation) Nebenbeschäftigung *f*; (fb) Seitenlinie *f* ‖ *tr* (coll) an der aktiven Teilnahme hindern

side' of ba'con *s* Speckseite *f*

side' road' *s* Seitenweg *m*

side'sad'dle *adv*—**ride s.** im Damensattel reiten

side' show' *s* Nebenvorstellung *f*; (fig) Episode *f*

side'split'ting *adj* zwerchfellerschütternd

side'step' *v* (pret & pp –stepped; ger –stepping) *tr* ausweichen (*dat*)

side' street' *s* Seitenstraße *f*

side'stroke' *s* Seitenschwimmen *n*

side'track' *s* Seitengeleise *n* ‖ *tr* (& fig) auf ein Seitengeleise schieben

side' trip' *s* Abstecher *m*

side' view' *s* Seitenansicht *f*

side'walk' *s* Bürgersteig *m*, Gehsteig *m*

sideward ['saɪdwərd] *adj* nach der Seite gerichtet ‖ *adv* seitwärts

side'ways' *adv* seitlich, seitwärts

sid'ing *s* (of a house) Verkleidung *f*; (rr) Nebengeleise *n*

sidle ['saɪdəl] *intr*—**s. up to s.o.** sich heimlich an j-n heranmachen

siege [sidʒ] *s* Belagerung *f*; **lay s. to** belagern

siesta [si'estə] *s* Mittagsruhe *f*

sieve [sɪv] *s* Sieb *n* ‖ *tr* durchsieben

sift [sɪft] *tr* (durch)sieben; (fig) sichten; **s. out** ausscheiden

sigh [saɪ] *s* Seufzer *m*; **with a s.** seufzend ‖ *intr* seufzen

sight [saɪt] *s* Anblick *m*; (faculty) Sehvermögen *n*; (on a weapon) Visier *n*; **at first s.** auf den ersten Blick; **at s.** sofort; **be a s.** (coll) unmöglich aussehen; **by s.** vom Sehen; **catch s. of** erblicken; **in s.** in Sicht; **lose s. of** aus den Augen verlieren; **out of s.** außer Sicht; **s. for sore eyes** Augentrost *m*; **sights** Sehenswürdigkeiten *pl*; **s. unseen** unbesehen; **within s.** in Sehweite ‖ *tr* sichten

sight′see′ing *s* Besichtigung *f*; **go s. sich** [*dat*] die Sehenswürdigkeiten ansehen

sight′seeing tour′ *s* Rundfahrt *f*

sightseer [′saɪt‚si·ər] *s* Tourist –in *mf*

sign [saɪn] *s* (*signboard*) Schild *n*; (*symbol, omen, signal*) Zeichen *n*; (*symptom, indication*) Kennzeichen *n*; (*trace*) Spur *f*; (math, mus) Vorzeichen *n*; **s. of life** Lebenszeichen *n* ‖ *tr* unterschreiben; **s. away** aufgeben; **s. over (to)** überschreiben (auf *acc*) ‖ *intr* unterschreiben; **s. for** zeichnen für; **s. in** sich eintragen; **s. off** (rad) die Sendung beenden; **s. out** sich austragen; **s. up** (mil) sich anwerben lassen; **s. up for** (*e.g., courses, work*) sich anmelden für

sig·nal [′sɪgnəl] *adj* auffallend ‖ *s* (*by gesture*) Zeichen *n*, Wink *m*; (aut, rad, rr, telv) Signal *n* ‖ *v* (*pret & pp* **-nal[l]ed;** *ger* **-nal[l]ing**) *tr* signalisieren; (*a person*) ein Zeichen geben (*dat*)

sig′nal corps′ *s* Fernmeldetruppen *pl*

sig′nal·man *s* (**–men**) (nav) Signalgast *m*; (rr) Bahnwärter *m*

signatory [′sɪgnə‚tori] *s* Unterzeichner –in *mf*

signature [′sɪgnət∫ər] *s* Unterschrift *f*

sign′board′ *s* Aushängeschild *n*

signer [′saɪnər] *s* Unterzeichner –in *mf*

sig′net ring′ [′sɪgnɪt] *s* Siegelring *m*

significance [sɪg′nɪfɪkəns] *s* Bedeutung *f*

significant [sɪg′nɪfɪkənt] *adj* bedeutsam

signi·fy [′sɪgnɪ‚faɪ] *v* (*pret & pp* **–fied**) bedeuten, bezeichnen

sign′ lan′guage *s* Zeichensprache *f*

sign′ of the cross′ *s* Kreuzzeichen *n*; **make the s.** sich bekreuzigen

sign′post′ *s* Wegweiser *m*

silence [′saɪləns] *s* Ruhe *f*, Stille *f*; (*reticence*) Schweigen *n*; **in s.** schweigend ‖ *tr* zum Schweigen bringen; (*a conscience*) beschwichtigen

silent [′saɪlənt] *adj* (*night, partner*) still; (*movies*) stumm; (*person*) schweigend; **be s.** stillschweigen; **keep s.** schweigen

silhouette [‚sɪlu′ɛt] *s* Schattenbild *n*, Silhouette *f* ‖ *tr* silhouettieren

silicon [′sɪlɪkən] *s* Silizium *n*

silicone [′sɪlɪkon] *s* Silikon *n*

silk [sɪlk] *adj* seiden ‖ *s* Seide *f*

silken [′sɪlkən] *adj* seiden

silk′ hat′ *s* Zylinder *m*

silk′ mill′ *s* Seidenfabrik *f*

silk′ worm′ *s* Seidenraupe *f*

silky [′sɪlki] *adj* seiden, seidenartig

sill [sɪl] *s* (*of a window*) Sims *m & n*; (*of a door*) Schwelle *f*

silliness [′sɪlɪnɪs] *s* Albernheit *f*

silly [′sɪli] *adj* albern, blöd(e)

si·lo [′saɪlo] *s* (**–los**) Getreidesilo *m*; (rok) Raketenbunker *m*, Silo *m*

silt [sɪlt] *s* Schlick *m* ‖ *intr*—**s. up** verschlammen

silver [′sɪlvər] *adj* silbern ‖ *s* Silber *n*; (*for the table*) Silberzeug *n*; (*money*) Silbergeld *n*

sil′verfish′ *s* Silberfischchen *n*

sil′ver foil′ *s* Silberfolie *f*

sil′ver lin′ing *s* (fig) Silberstreifen *m*

sil′ver plate′ *s* Silbergeschirr *n*

sil′ver-plat′ed *adj* versilbert

sil′versmith′ *s* Silberschmied *m*

sil′ver spoon′ *s*—**be born with a s. in one′s mouth** ein Sonntagskind sein

sil′verware′ *s* Silbergeschirr *n*

silvery [′sɪlvəri] *adj* silbern

similar [′sɪmɪlər] *adj* (**to**) ähnlich (*dat*)

similarity [‚sɪmɪ′lærɪti] *s* Ähnlichkeit *f*

simile [′sɪmɪli] *s* Gleichnis *n*

simmer [′sɪmər] *tr* leicht kochen lassen ‖ *intr* brodeln; **s. down** (coll) sich abreagieren

simper [′sɪmpər] *s* selbstgefälliges Lächeln *n* ‖ *intr* selbstgefällig lächeln

simple [′sɪmpəl] *adj* einfach; (*truth*) rein; (*fact*) bloß

sim′ple-mind′ed *adj* einfältig

simpleton [′sɪmpəltən] *s* Einfaltspinsel *m*

simpli·fy [′sɪmplɪ‚faɪ] *v* (*pret & pp* **–fied**) *tr* vereinfachen

simply [′sɪmpli] *adv* einfach

simulate [′sɪmjə‚let] *tr* (*illness*) simulieren; (*e.g., a rocket flight*) am Modell vorführen

sim′ulated *adj* unecht

simultaneous [‚saɪməl′teni·əs] *adj* gleichzeitig, simultan

sin [sɪn] *s* Sünde *f* ‖ *v* (*pret & pp* **sinned;** *ger* **sinning**) *intr* sündigen; **sin against** sich versündigen an (*dat*)

since [sɪns] *adv* seitdem, seither ‖ *prep* seit (*dat*); **s. then** seither; **s. when** seit wann ‖ *conj* (*temporal*) seit(dem); (*causal*) da

sincere [sɪn′sɪr] *adj* aufrichtig

sincerely [sɪn′sɪrli] *adv* aufrichtig, ehrlich; **Sincerely yours** Ihr ergebener, Ihre ergebene

sincerity [sɪn′sɛrɪti] *s* Aufrichtigkeit *f*

sinecure [′saɪnɪ‚kjur] *s* Sinekure *f*

sinew [′sɪnju] *s* Sehne *f*, Flechse *f*; (fig) Muskelkraft *f*

sinewy [′sɪnju·i] *adj* sehnig; (fig) kräftig, nervig

sinful [′sɪnfəl] *adj* sündhaft

sing [sɪŋ] *v* (*pret sang* [sæŋ] *& sung* [sʌŋ]; *pp sung*) *tr & intr* singen

singe [sɪndʒ] *v* (**singeing**) *tr* sengen; (*the hair*) versengen

singer [′sɪŋər] *s* Sänger –in *mf*

single [′sɪŋgəl] *adj* einzeln; (*unmarried*) ledig; **not a s. word** kein einziges Wort ‖ *s*—**s. out** herausgreifen

sin′gle bed′ *s* Einzelbett *n*

sin′glebreast′ed *adj* einreihig

sin′gle file′ *s* Gänsemarsch *m*

sin′gle-hand′ed *adj* einhändig

sin′gle-lane′ *adj* einbahnig

sin′gle life′ *s* Ledigenstand *m*

sin′gle-mind′ed *adj* zielstrebig

sin′gle room′ *s* Einzelzimmer *n*

sin′gle-track′ *adj* (& fig) eingleisig

sing′song′ *adj* eintönig ‖ *s* Singsang *m*

singular [′sɪŋgjələr] *adj* (*outstanding*) ausgezeichnet; (*unique*) einzig; (*odd*) seltsam ‖ *s* (gram) Einzahl *f*

sinister ['sɪnɪstər] adj unheimlich

sink [sɪŋk] s (in the kitchen) Ausguß m; (in the bathroom) Waschbecken n || v (pret sank [sæŋk] & sunk [sʌŋk]; pp sunk) tr (a ship; a post) versenken; (money) investieren; (min) abteufen; s. a well e-n Brunnen bohren || intr sinken; (said of a building) sich senken; he is sinking fast seine Kräfte nehmen rapide ab; s. in (coll) einleuchten; s. into (an easychair) sich fallen lassen in (acc); (poverty) geraten in (acc); (unconsciousness) fallen in (acc)

sink'ing feel'ing s Beklommenheit f

sink'ing fund' s Schuldentilgungsfonds m

sinless ['sɪnlɪs] adj sünd(en)los

sinner ['sɪnər] s Sünder –in mf

sinuous ['sɪnjʊ-əs] adj gewunden

sinus ['saɪnəs] s Stirnhöhle f

sip [sɪp] s Schluck m || v (pret & pp sipped; ger sipping) tr schlürfen

siphon ['saɪfən] s Siphon m, Saugheber m || tr entleeren; s. off absaugen; (profits) abschöpfen

sir [sʌr] s Herr m; yes sir! jawohl!; Dear Sir Sehr geehrter Herr

sire [saɪr] s (& zool) Vater m || tr zeugen

siren ['saɪrən] s (& myth) Sirene f

sirloin ['sʌrlɔɪn] s Lendenbraten m

sissy ['sɪsi] s Schlappschwanz m

sister ['sɪstər] s Schwester f

sis'ter-in-law' s (sisters-in-law) Schwägerin f

sisterly ['sɪstərli] adj schwesterlich

sit [sɪt] v (pret & pp sat [sæt]; ger sitting) intr sitzen; sit down sich (hin)setzen; sit for a painter e-m Maler Modell stehen; sit in on (a meeting) dabeisein bei; sit up and beg Männchen machen

sit'down strike' s Sitzstreik m

site [saɪt] s (position, location) Lage f; (piece of ground) Gelände n

sit'ting—at one s. auf e-n Sitz

sit'ting duck' s wehrloses Ziel n

sit'ting room' s Gemeinschaftsraum m

situated ['sɪtʃʊˌetɪd] adj gelegen; be s. liegen

situation [ˌsɪtʃʊ'eʃən] s Lage f; s. wanted Stelle gesucht

six [sɪks] adj & pron sechs || s Sechs f

sixteen ['sɪks'tin] adj & pron sechzehn || s Sechzehn f

sixteenth ['sɪks'tinθ] adj & pron sechzehnte || s (fraction) Sechzehntel n; the s. (in dates or in series) der Sechzehnte

sixth [sɪksθ] adj & pron sechste || s (fraction) Sechstel n; the s. (in dates or in series) der Sechste

sixtieth ['sɪkstɪ-ɪθ] adj & pron sechzig || s (fraction) Sechzigstel n

sixty ['sɪksti] adj & pron sechzig || s Sechzig f; the sixties die sechziger Jahre

six'ty-four' dol'lar ques'tion s Preisfrage f

sizable ['saɪzəbəl] adj beträchtlich

size [saɪz] s Größe f; (of a book, paper) Format n || tr grundieren; s. up einschätzen

sizzle ['sɪzəl] s Zischen n || intr zischen

skate [sket] s Schlittschuh m || intr Schlittschuh laufen

skat'ing rink' s Eisbahn f

skein [sken] s Strähne f

skeleton ['skɛlɪtən] s Gerippe n

skel'eton crew' s Minimalbelegschaft f

skel'eton key' s Dietrich m

skeptic ['skɛptɪk] s Zweifler –in mf

skeptical ['skɛptɪkəl] adj skeptisch

skepticism [ˈskɛptɪˌsɪzəm] s (doubt) Skepsis f; (philos) Skeptizismus m

sketch [skɛtʃ] s Skizze f; (theat) Sketch m || tr & intr skizzieren

sketch'book' s Skizzenbuch n

sketchy ['skɛtʃi] adj skizzenhaft

skewer ['skjʊ-ər] s Fleischspieß m

ski [ski] s Schi m || intr schilaufen

ski' boot' s Schistiefel m

skid [skɪd] s Rutschen n, Schleudern n; go into a s. ins Schleudern geraten || v (pret & pp skidded; ger skidding) intr rutschen, schleudern

skid' mark' s Bremsspur f

skid'proof' adj bremssicher

skid' row' [ro] s Elendsviertel n

skiff [skɪf] s Skiff n

ski'ing s Schilaufen n

ski' jack'et s Anorak m

ski' jump' s Schisprung m; (chute) Sprungschanze f

ski' jump'ing s Schispringen n

ski' lift' s Schilift m

skill [skɪl] s Fertigkeit f

skilled adj gelernt

skillet ['skɪlɪt] s Bratpfanne f

skillful ['skɪlfəl] adj geschickt

skim [skɪm] v (pret & pp skimmed; ger skimming) tr (milk) abrahmen; (a book) überfliegen; s. off abschöpfen || intr—s. over the water über das Wasser streichen; s. through (a book) flüchtig durchblättern

skim' milk' s entrahmte Milch f

skimp [skɪmp] intr (on) knausern (mit)

skimpy ['skɪmpi] adj (person) knauserig; (thing) knapp, dürftig

skin [skɪn] s Haut f; (fur) Fell n; (of fruit) Schale f; by the s. of one's teeth mit knapper Not; get under s.o.'s s. j-m auf die Nerven gehen || v (pret & pp skinned; ger skinning) tr (an animal) enthäuten; (a knee) aufschürfen; (fleece) das Fell über die Ohren ziehen (dat); (defeat) schlagen; s. alive zur Sau machen

skin'-deep' adj oberflächlich

skin' div'er s Schwimmtaucher –in mf

skin'flint' s Geizhals m

skin' graft' s Hautverpflanzung f

skinny ['skɪni] adj spindeldürr, mager

skin'tight' adj hauteng

skip [skɪp] s Sprung m || v (pret & pp skipped; ger skipping) tr (omit) auslassen; (a page) überblättern; s. it! Schwamm drüber!; s. rope Seil springen; s. school Schule schwänzen || intr springen; s. out abhauen

ski' pole' s Schistock m

skipper ['skɪpər] s Kapitän m
skirmish ['skɜːmɪʃ] s Scharmützel n ‖ intr scharmützeln
skir′mish line′ s (mil) Schützenlinie f
skirt [skɜːt] s Rock m ‖ tr (border) umsäumen; (pass along) sich entlangziehen (an dat)
ski′ run′ s Schipiste f
skit [skɪt] s Sket(s)ch m
skittish ['skɪtɪʃ] adj (lively) lebhaft; (horse) scheu
skull [skʌl] s Schädel m
skull′ and cross′bones s Totenkopf m
skull′cap′ s Käppchen n
skunk [skʌŋk] s Stinktier n; (sl) Saukerl m
sky [skaɪ] s Himmel m; out of the clear blue sky wie aus heiterem Himmel; praise to the skies über den grünen Klee loben
sky′-blue′ adj himmelblau
sky′div′er s Fallschirmspringer –in mf
sky′div′ing s Fallschirmspringen n
sky′lark′ s Feldlerche f
sky′light′ s Dachluke f
sky′line′ s Horizontlinie f; (of a city) Stadtsilhouette f
sky′rock′et s Rakete f ‖ intr in die Höhe schießen
sky′scrap′er s Wolkenkratzer m
sky′writ′ing s Himmelsschrift f
slab [slæb] s Platte f, Tafel f
slack [slæk] adj schlaff; (period) flau ‖ s Spielraum m; slacks Herrenhose f, Damenhose f ‖ intr—s. off nachlassen
slacken ['slækən] tr (slow down) verlangsamen; (loosen) lockern ‖ intr nachlassen
slack′ per′iod s Flaute f
slack′ sea′son s Sauregurkenzeit f
slag [slæg] s Schlacke f
slag′ pile′ s Schlackenhalde f
slake [slek] tr (thirst, lime) löschen
slalom ['slɑləm] s Slalom m
slam [slæm] s Knall m; (cards) Schlemm m ‖ v (pret & pp slammed; ger slamming) tr zuknallen; s. down hinknallen ‖ intr knallen
slander ['slændər] s Verleumdung f ‖ tr verleumden
slanderous ['slændərəs] adj verleumderisch
slang [slæŋ] s Slang m
slant [slænt] s Schräge f; (view) Einstellung f; (personal point of view) Tendenz f ‖ tr abschrägen; (fig) färben
slap [slæp] s Klaps m; s. in the face Ohrfeige f ‖ v (pret & pp slapped; ger slapping) tr schlagen; (s.o.'s face) ohrfeigen; s. together zusammenhauen
slap′stick′ adj Radau– ‖ s Radaukomödie f
slash [slæʃ] s Schnittwunde f ‖ tr aufschlitzen; (prices) drastisch herabsetzen
slat [slæt] s Stab m
slate [slet] s Schiefer m; (to write on) Schiefertafel f; (of candidates) Vorschlagsliste f ‖ tr (a roof) mit Schiefer decken; (schedule) planen; he is slated to speak er soll sprechen
slate′ roof′ s Schieferdach n
slattern ['slætərn] s (slovenly woman) Schlampe f; (slut) Dirne f
slaughter ['slɔtər] s Schlachten n; (massacre) Metzelei f ‖ tr schlachten; (massacre) niedermetzeln
slaugh′terhouse′ s Schlachthaus n
Slav [slɑv], [slæv] adj slawisch ‖ s (person) Slawe m, Slawin f
slave [slev] s Sklave m, Sklavin f ‖ intr (coll) schuften; s. at a job sich mit e-r Arbeit abquälen
slave′ driv′er s (fig) Leuteschinder m
slaver ['slævər] s Geifer m
slavery ['slevəri] s Sklaverei f
slave′ trade′ s Sklavenhandel m
Slavic ['slɑvɪk], ['slævɪk] adj slawisch
slavish ['slevɪʃ] adj sklavisch
slay [sle] v (pret slew [slu]; pp slain [slen]) tr erschlagen
slayer ['sle·ər] s Totschläger –in mf
sled [sled] s Schlitten m ‖ v (pret & pp sledded; ger sledding) intr Schlitten fahren
sledge [sledʒ] s Schlitten m
sledge′ ham′mer s Vorschlaghammer m
sleek [slik] adj (hair) glatt; (cattle) fett ‖ tr glätten
sleep [slip] s Schlaf m; get enough s. sich ausschlafen ‖ v (pret & pp slept [slept]) tr (accommodate) Schlafgelegenheiten bieten für; s. off a hangover seinen Kater ausschlafen ‖ intr schlafen; I didn't s. a wink ich habe kein Auge zugetan; s. like a log wie ein Murmeltier schlafen; s. with (a woman) schlafen mit
sleeper ['sliper] s Schläfer –in mf; (sleeping car) Schlafwagen m; (fig) überraschender Erfolg m
sleepiness ['slipɪnɪs] s Schläfrigkeit f
sleep′ing bag′ s Schlafsack m
Sleep′ing Beau′ty s Dornröschen n
sleep′ing car′ s Schlafwagen m
sleep′ing compart′ment s Schlafabteil n
sleep′ing pill′ s Schlaftablette f
sleep′ing sick′ness s Schlafkrankheit f
sleepless ['sliplɪs] adj schlaflos
sleep′walk′er s Nachtwandler –in mf
sleepy ['slipi] adj schläfrig
sleep′yhead′ s Schlafmütze f
sleet [slit] s Schneeregen m; (on the ground) Glatteis n ‖ impers—it is sleeting es gibt Schneeregen, es graupelt
sleeve [sliv] s Ärmel m; (mach) Muffe f; have s.th. up one's s. etw im Schilde führen; roll up one's sleeves die Ärmel hochkrempeln
sleeveless ['slivlɪs] adj ärmellos
sleigh [sle] s Schlitten m
sleigh′ bell′ s Schlittenschelle f
sleigh′ ride′ s Schlittenfahrt f; go for a s. Schlitten fahren
sleight′ of hand′ [slaɪt] s Taschenspielertrick m
slender ['slendər] adj schlank; (means) gering
sleuth [sluθ] s Detektiv m
slice [slaɪs] s Scheibe f, Schnitte f;

(tennis) Schnittball *m* ‖ *tr* aufschneiden

slicer ['slaɪsər] *s* Schneidemaschine *f*
slick [slɪk] *adj* glatt; (*talker*) raffiniert
slicker ['slɪkər] *s* Regenmantel *m*
slide [slaɪd] *s* (*slip*) Rutsch *m*; (*chute*) Rutschbahn *f*; (*of a microscope*) Objektträger *m*; (phot) Diapositiv *n* ‖ *v* (*pret & pp* **slid** [slɪd]) *tr* schieben ‖ *intr* rutschen; **let things s.** die Dinge laufen lassen
slide′ rule′ *s* Rechenschieber *m*
slide′ valve′ *s* Schieberventil *n*
slide′ view′er *s* Bildbetrachter *m*
slid′ing door′ *s* Schiebetür *f*
slid′ing scale′ *s* gleitende Skala *f*
slight [slaɪt] *adj* gering(fügig); (*illness*) leicht; (*petite*) zart ‖ *tr* mißachten
slim [slɪm] *adj* schlank; (*chance*) gering ‖ *intr*—**s. down** abnehmen
slime [slaɪm] *s* Schlamm *m*; (e.g., *of fish, snakes*) Schleim *m*
slimy ['slaɪmi] *adj* schleimig; (*muddy*) schlammig
sling [slɪŋ] *s* (*to hurl stones*) Schleuder *f*; (*for a broken arm*) Schlinge *f* ‖ *v* (*pret & pp* **slung** [slʌŋ]) *tr* schleudern; **s. over the shoulders** umhängen
sling′shot′ *s* Schleuder *f*
slink [slɪŋk] *v* (*pret & pp* **slunk** [slʌŋk]) *intr* schleichen; **s. away** wegschleichen
slip [slɪp] *s* (*slide*) Ausrutschen *m*; (*cutting*) Ableger *m*; (*underwear*) Unterrock *m*; (*paper*) Zettel *m*; (*pillowcase*) Kissenbezug *m*; (*error*) Flüchtigkeitsfehler *m*; (*for ships*) Schlipp *m*; **give s.o. the s.** j-m entwischen; **s. of the pen** Schreibfehler *m*; **s. of the tongue** Sprechfehler *m* ‖ *v* (*pret & pp* **slipped**; *ger* **slipping**) *tr*—**s. in** (*a remark*) einfließen lassen; (*poison*) heimlich schütten; **s. on** (*a glove*) überstreifen; (*a coat*) überziehen; (*a ring*) auf den Finger streifen; **s. s.o. money** j-m etw Geld zustecken; **s. s.o.'s mind** j-m entfallen ‖ *intr* rutschen; (e.g., *out of or into a room*) schlüpfen; (*lose one's balance*) ausgleiten; **let s. sich** [*dat*] entgehen lassen; **s. by** verstreichen; **s. in** (*said of errors*) unterlaufen; **s. through one's fingers** durch die Finger gleiten; **s. out on s.o.** j-m entschlüpfen; **s. up (on)** danebenhauen (bei); **you are slipping** (coll) Sie lassen in der Leistung nach
slip′cov′er *s* Schonbezug *m*
slip′knot′ *s* Schleife *f*
slipper ['slɪpər] *s* Pantoffel *m*
slippery ['slɪpəri] *adj* glatt
slipshod ['slɪp‚ʃad] *adj* schlampig; **do s. work** schludern
slip′stream′ *s* Luftschraubenstrahl *m*
slip′-up′ *s* (coll) Flüchtigkeitsfehler *m*
slit [slɪt] *s* Schlitz *m* ‖ *v* (*pret & pp* **slit**; *ger* **slitting**) *tr* schlitzen; **s. open** aufschlitzen
slit′-eyed′ *adj* schlitzäugig
slither ['slɪðər] *intr* gleiten
slit′ trench′ *s* (mil) Splittergraben *m*
sliver ['slɪvər] *s* Splitter *m*, Span *m*

slob [slab] *s* (sl) Schmutzfink *m*
slobber ['slabər] *s* Geifer *m* ‖ *intr* geifern
sloe [slo] *s* (bot) Schlehe *f*
sloe′-eyed′ *adj* schlitzäugig
slog [slag] *v* (*pret & pp* **slogged**; *ger* **slogging**) *intr* stapfen
slogan ['slogən] *s* Schlagwort *n*
sloop [slup] *s* Schaluppe *f*
slop [slap] *s* Spülicht *n*; (*bad food*) (sl) Fraß *m* ‖ *v* (*pret & pp* **slopped**; *ger* **slopping**) *tr* (*hogs*) füttern; (*spill*) verschütten
slope [slop] *s* Abhang *m*; (*of a road*) Gefälle *n*; (*of a roof*) Neigung *f* ‖ *tr* abschrägen ‖ *intr* sich neigen; (*said of a road*) abfallen
sloppy ['slapi] *adj* schlampig; (*weather*) matschig
slosh [slaʃ] *intr* schwappen
slot [slat] *s* Schlitz *m*
sloth [sloθ] *s* Faulheit *f*, Trägheit *f*; (zool) Faultier *n*
slothful ['sloθfəl] *adj* faul, träge
slot′ machine′ *s* Spielautomat *m*
slouch [slautʃ] *s* nachlässige Haltung *f*; (*person*) Schlappschwanz *m* ‖ *intr* in schlechter Haltung sitzen; **s. along** latschen
slouch′ hat′ *s* Schlapphut *m*
slough [slau] *s* Sumpf *m*; (*of a snake*) abgestreifte Haut *f*; (pathol) Schorf *m* ‖ *tr* (& fig) abstreifen ‖ *intr* (*said of a snake*) sich häuten
Slovak ['slovak], ['slovæk] *adj* slowakisch ‖ *s* (*person*) Sklowake *m*, Slowakin *f*; (*language*) Slowakisch *n*
slovenly ['slʌvənli] *adj* schlampig
slow [slo] *adj* langsam; (*dawdling*) bummelig; (*mentally*) schwer von Begriff; (com) flau; **be s.** (horol) nachgehen ‖ *adv* langsam ‖ *tr*—**s. down** verlangsamen ‖ *intr*—**s. down** (*in driving*) langsamer fahren; (*in working*) nachlassen; **s. down** (*public sign*) Schritt fahren
slow′down′ *s* Bummelstreik *m*
slow′ mo′tion *s* (cin) Zeitlupe *f*; **in s.** (cin) im Zeitlupentempo
slow′-mo′tion *adj* Zeitlupen—
slow′poke′ *s* (coll) langsamer Mensch *m*
slow′-wit′ted *adj* schwer von Begriff
slug [slʌg] *s* Rohling *m*; (*drink*) Zug *m* (zool) Wegschnecke *f* ‖ *v* (*pret & pp* **slugged**; *ger* **slugging**) *tr* (coll) hart mit der Faust treffen
sluggard ['slʌgərd] *s* Faulpelz *m*
sluggish ['slʌgɪʃ] *adj* träge
sluice [slus] *s* Schleuse *f*
sluice′ gate′ *s* Schleusentor *n*
slum [slʌm] *s* Elendsviertel *n*
slumber ['slʌmbər] *s* Schlummer *m* ‖ *intr* schlummern
slum′ dwell′ing *s* Elendsquartier *n*
slump [slʌmp] *s* (st. exch.) Baisse *f*; **s. in sales** Absatzstockung *f* ‖ *intr* zusammensacken; (*said of prices*) stürzen
slur [slʌr] *s* (*insult*) Verleumdung *f*; (mus) Bindezeichen *n* ‖ *v* (*pret & pp* **slurred**; *ger* **slurring**) *tr* (*words*)

verschleifen; (mus) binden; **s. over** hinweggehen über (acc)

slurp [slʌrp] s Schlürfen n || tr & intr schlürfen

slush [slʌʃ] s Matsch m, Schneematsch m

slush' fund' s Schmiergeld n

slushy ['slʌʃi] adj matschig

slut [slʌt] s Nutte f

sly [slaɪ] adj (slyer & slier; slyest & sliest) schlau || s—on the sly im Verborgenen

sly' fox' s Pfiffikus m

smack [smæk] s (blow) Klaps m; (sound) Klatsch m; (kiss) Schmatz m; **s. in the face** Backpfeife f || tr klapsen; **s. one's lips** schmatzen || intr—s. of riechen nach

small [smɔl] adj klein; (difference) gering; (comfort) schlecht; (petty) kleinlich

small' arms' spl Handwaffen pl

small' busi'ness s Kleinbetrieb m

small' cap'ital s (typ) Kapitälchen n

small' change' s Kleingeld n

small' fry' s kleine Fische pl

small' intes'tine s Dünndarm m

small'-mind'ed adj engstirnig

small' of the back' s Kreuz n

smallpox ['smɔl͵pɑks] s Pocken pl

small' print' s Kleindruck m

small' talk' s Geplauder n

small'-time' adj klein

small'-town' adj kleinstädtisch

smart [smɑrt] adj (bright) klug; (neat, trim) schick; (car) schneidig; (pain) überklug || s Schmerz m || intr weh tun; (burn) brennen

smart' al'eck s [͵ælɪk] s Neunmalkluge mf

smart'-look'ing adj schnittig

smart' set' s elegante Welt f

smash [smæʃ] s (hit) (coll) Bombe f; (tennis) Schmetterschlag m || tr zerschmettern; (e.g., a window) einschlagen; (sport) schmettern; **s. up** zerknallen || intr zerbrechen; **s. into** krachen gegen

smash' hit' s (theat) Bombenerfolg m

smash'-up' s (aut) Zusammenstoß m

smattering ['smætərɪŋ] s (of) oberflächliche Kenntnis f (genit)

smear [smɪr] s Schmiere f; (smudge) Schmutzfleck m; (vilification) Verunglimpfung f; (med) Abstrich m || tr (spread) schmieren; (make dirty) beschmieren; (vilify) verunglimpfen; (trounce) vollständig fertigmachen

smear' campaign' s Verleumdungsfeldzug m

smell [smel] s Geruch m; (aroma) Duft m; (sense) Geruchssinn m || v (pret & pp smelled & smelt [smelt]) tr riechen; (danger, trouble) wittern || intr (of) riechen (nach)

smell'ing salts' pl Riechsalz n

smelly ['smeli] adj übelriechend

smelt [smelt] s (fish) Stint m || tr schmelzen, verhütten

smile [smaɪl] s Lächeln n || intr lächeln; **s. at** anlächeln; (clandestinely) zulächeln (dat); **s. on** lächeln (dat)

smirk [smɪrk] s Grinsen n || intr grinsen

smite [smaɪt] v (pret smote [smot]; pp smitten ['smɪtən] & smit [smɪt]) tr schlagen; (said of a plague) befallen; **smitten with** hingerissen von

smith [smɪθ] s Schmied m

smithy ['smɪθi] s Schmiede f

smock [smɑk] s Kittel m, Bluse f

smog [smɑg] s Smog m

smoke [smok] s Rauch m; (heavy smoke) Qualm m; **go up in s.** (fig) in Dunst und Rauch aufgehen || tr rauchen; (meat) räuchern || intr rauchen; (said of a chimney) qualmen

smoke' bomb' s Rauchbombe f

smoked' ham' s Räucherschinken m

smoker ['smokər] s Raucher –in mf; (sl) obszöner Film m

smoke' screen' s Rauchvorhang m

smoke'stack' s Schornstein m

smok'ing s Rauchen n; **no s.** (public sign) Rauchen verboten

smok'ing car' s Raucherwagen m

smok'ing jack'et s Hausjacke f

smoky ['smoki] adj rauchig

smolder ['smoldər] intr (& fig) schwelen

smooch [smutʃ] intr sich abknutschen

smooth [smuð] adj (surface; talker; landing, operation) glatt; (wine) mild || tr glätten; **s. away** (difficulties) beseitigen; **s. out** glätten; **s. over** beschönigen

smooth'-faced' adj glattwangig

smooth-shaven ['smuð'ʃevən] adj glattrasiert

smooth'-talk'ing adj schönrednerisch

smoothy ['smuði] s Schönredner –in mf

smother ['smʌðər] tr ersticken; **s. with kisses** abküssen

smudge [smʌdʒ] s Schmutzfleck m || tr beschmutzen || intr schmutzig werden

smug [smʌg] adj (smugger; smuggest) selbstgefällig

smuggle ['smʌgəl] tr & intr schmuggeln

smuggler ['smʌglər] s Schmuggler –in mf

smug'gling s Schmuggel m

smut [smʌt] s Schmutz m

smutty ['smʌti] adj schmutzig, obszön

snack [snæk] s Imbiß m

snack' bar' s Imbißstube f, Snack Bar f

snaffle ['snæfəl] s Trense f

snag [snæg] s—hit a s. auf Schwierigkeiten stoßen || v (pret & pp snagged; ger snagging) tr hängenbleiben mit

snail [snel] s Schnecke f; **at a snail's pace** im Schneckentempo

snake [snek] s Schlange f || intr sich schlängeln

snake'bite' s Schlangenbiß m

snake' in the grass' s heimtückischer Mensch m

snap [snæp] s (sound) Knacks m; (on clothes) Druckknopf m; (of a dog) Biß m; (liveliness) Schwung m; (easy work) Kinderspiel n || v (pret & pp snapped; ger snapping) tr (break) zerreißen, entzweibrechen; (a picture) knipsen; **s. a whip** mit der

Peitsche knallen; **s. back** (*words*) hervorstoßen; (*the head*) zurückwerfen; **s. off** abbrechen; **s. one's fingers** mit den Fingern schnalzen; **s. s.o.'s head off** j-n zusammenstauchen; **s. up** gierig an sich reißen; (*buy up*) aufkaufen ‖ *intr* (*tear*) zerreißen; (*break*) entzweibrechen; **s.** at schnappen nach; (*fig*) anfahren; **s. out of it!** komm zu dir!; **s. shut** zuschnappen; **s. to it!** mach zu!

snap'drag'on *s* (bot) Löwenmaul *n*

snap' fas'tener *s* Druckknopf *m*

snap' judg'ment *s* vorschnelles Urteil *n*

snap' per soup' ['snæpər] *s* Schildkrötensuppe *f*

snappish ['snæpɪʃ] *adj* bissig

snappy ['snæpɪ] *adj* (*caustic*) bissig; (*lively*) energisch; **make it s.!** mach schnell!

snap'shot' *s* Schnappschuß *m*

snare [snɛr] *s* Schlinge *f* ‖ *tr* mit e-r Schlinge fangen; (fig) fangen

snare' drum' *s* Schnarrtrommel *f*

snarl [snɑrl] *s* (*tangle*) Verwicklung *f*; (*sound*) Knurren *n* ‖ *tr* verwickeln; **s. traffic** e-e Verkehrsstockung verursachen ‖ *intr* knurren

snatch [snætʃ] *s*—**in snatches** ruckweise; **snatches** (*of conversation*) Bruchstücke *pl* ‖ *tr* schnappen; **s. away from** entreißen (*dat*); **s. up** schnappen

snazzy ['snæzɪ] *adj* (sl) schmissig

sneak [snik] *s* Schleicher –in *mf* ‖ *tr* (*e.g., a drink*) heimlich trinken; **s. in** einschmuggeln ‖ *intr* schleichen; **s. away** sich davonschleichen; **s. in** sich einschleichen; **s. out** sich herausschleichen; **s. up on s.o.** an j-n heranschleichen

sneaker ['snikər] *s* Tennisschuh *m*

sneaky ['snikɪ] *adj* heimtückisch

sneer [snɪr] *s* Hohnlächeln *n* ‖ *intr* höhnisch grinsen; **s. at** spötteln über (*acc*)

sneeze [sniz] *s* Niesen *n* ‖ *tr*—**not to be sneezed at** nicht zu verachten ‖ *intr* niesen

snicker ['snɪkər] *s* Kichern *n* ‖ *intr* kichern

snide' remark' [snaɪd] *s* Anzüglichkeit *f*

sniff [snɪf] *s* Schnüffeln *n* ‖ *tr* (be)riechen; **s. out** ausschnüffeln ‖ *intr* (at) schnüffeln (an *dat*)

sniffle ['snɪfəl] *s* Geschnüffel *n*; **sniffles** Schnupfen *m* ‖ *intr* schniefen

snip [snɪp] *s* (*cut*) Einschnitt *m*; (*small piece snipped off*) Schnippel *m* ‖ *v* (*pret & pp* **snipped;** *ger* **snipping**) *tr & intr* schnippeln

snipe [snaɪp] *intr*—**s. at** aus dem Hinterhalt schießen auf (*acc*)

sniper ['snaɪpər] *s* Heckenschütze *m*

snippet ['snɪpɪt] *s* Schnippelchen *n*; (*small person*) Knirps *m*

snippy ['snɪpɪ] *adj* schroff, barsch

snitch [snɪtʃ] *tr* (coll) klauen ‖ *intr* (coll) petzen; **s. on** (coll) verpfeifen

sniv·el ['snɪvəl] *s* (*whining*) Gewimmer *n*; (*mucus*) Nasenschleim *m* ‖ *v*

(*pret & pp* **–el[l]ed;** *ger* **–el[l]ing**) *intr* (*whine*) wimmern; (*cry with sniffling*) schluchzen; (*have a runny nose*) e-e tropfende Nase haben

snob [snɑb] *s* Snob *m*

snob' appeal' *s* Snobappeal *m*

snobbery ['snɑbərɪ] *s* Snobismus *m*

snobbish ['snɑbɪʃ] *adj* snobistisch

snoop [snup] *s* (coll) Schnüffler –in *mf* ‖ *intr* (coll) schnüffeln

snoopy ['snupɪ] *adj* schnüffelnd

snoot [snut] *s* (sl) Rüssel *m*; **make a s.** e–e Schnute ziehen

snooty ['snutɪ] *adj* hochnäsig

snooze [snuz] *s* (coll) Nickerchen *n* ‖ *intr* (coll) ein Nickerchen machen

snore [snor] *s* Schnarchen *n* ‖ *intr* schnarchen

snort [snɔrt] *s* Schnauben *n* ‖ *tr* wütend schnauben ‖ *intr* prusten; (*said of a horse*) schnauben; (*with laughter*) vor Lachen prusten

snot [snɑt] *s* (sl) Rotz *m*

snotty ['snɑtɪ] *adj* (sl & fig) rotzig

snout [snaʊt] *s* Schnauze *f*, Rüssel *m*

snow [sno] *s* Schnee *m* ‖ *tr* (sl) einwickeln; **s. in** einschneien; **s. under** mit Schnee bedecken ‖ *impers*—**it is snowing** es schneit

snow'ball' *s* Schneeball *m* ‖ *intr* (fig) lawinenartig anwachsen

snow'bank' *s* Schneeverwehung *f*

snow'bird' *s* Schneefink *m*

snow' blind'ness *s* Schneeblindheit *f*

snow' blow'er *s* Schneefräse *f*

snow'bound' *adj* eingeschneit

snow'-capped' *adj* schneebedeckt

snow' chain' *s* (aut) Schneekette *f*

snow'-clad' *adj* verschneit

snow'drift' *s* Schneeverwehung *f*

snow'fall' *s* Schneefall *m*

snow'flake' *s* Schneeflocke *f*

snow' flur'ry *s* Schneegestöber *n*

snow' job' *s*—**give s.o. a s.** (sl) j-n hereinlegen

snow'man' *s* (**–men**) Schneemann *m*

snow'mobile' *s* Motorschlitten *m*

snow'plow' *s* Schneepflug *m*

snow'shoe' *s* Schneeteller *m*

snow' shov'el *s* Schneeschaufel *f*

snow'storm' *s* Schneesturm *m*

snow' tire' *s* Winterreifen *m*

Snow' White' *s* Schneewittchen *n*

snow'-white' *adj* schneeweiß

snowy ['sno·ɪ] *adj* schneeig

snub [snʌb] *s* verächtliche Behandlung *f* ‖ *v* (*pret & pp* **snubbed;** *ger* **snubbing**) *tr* (*ignore*) übersehen; (*treat contemptuously*) verächtlich behandeln

snubby ['snʌbɪ] *adj* (*nose*) etwas abgestumpft; (*person*) abweisend

snub'-nosed' *adj* stupsnasig

snuff [snʌf] *s* Schnupftabak *m*; (*of a candle*) Schnuppe *f*; **up to s.** (sl) auf Draht ‖ *tr*—**s. out** (*a candle*) auslöschen; (*suppress*) unterdrücken

snuff'box' *s* Schnupftabakdose *f*

snug [snʌg] *adj* (**snugger; snuggest**) behaglich; (*fit*) eng angeschmiegt; **s. as a bug in a rug** wie die Made im Speck

snuggle 300 **soliciter**

snuggle ['snʌgəl] *intr*—s. up (to) sich schmiegen (an *acc*)

so [so] *adv* (with adjectives or adverbs) so; (*thus*) so; (*for this reason*) daher; (*then*) also; **and so forth** und so weiter; **or so** etwa, e.g., **ten miles or so** etwa zehn Meilen; **so as to** (*inf*) um zu (*inf*); **so far** bisher; **so far as** soviel; **so far, so good** soweit ganz gut; **so I see!** das seh' ich!; **so long!** (coll) bis bald!; **so much** soviel; **so much the better** um so besser; **so that** damit; **so what?** na, und?

soak [sok] *s* Einweichen *n* || *tr* einweichen; (*soak through and through*) durchnässen; (*overcharge*) (sl) schröpfen; **soaked to the skin** bis auf die Haut durchnäßt || *intr* weichen

so'-and-so' *s* (-sos) Soundso *mf*

soap [sop] *s* Seife *f* || *tr* einseifen

soap'box der'by *s* Seifenkistenrennen *n*

soap'box or'ator *s* Straßenredner –in *mf*

soap' bub'ble *s* Seifenblase *f*

soap' dish' *s* Seifenschale *f*

soap' flakes' *spl* Seifenflocken *pl*

soap' op'era *s* (rad) rührselige Hörspielreihe *f*; (telv) rührselige Fernsehspielreihe *f*

soap' pow'der *s* Seifenpulver *n*

soap'stone' *s* Seifenstein *m*

soap'suds' *spl* Seifenlauge *f*

soapy ['sopɪ] *adj* seifig; (*like soap*) seifenartig

soar [sor] *intr* schweben, (auf)steigen; (*prices*) steigen

sob [sab] *s* Schluchzen *n* || *v* (*pret & pp* sobbed; *ger* sobbing) *intr* schluchzen

sober ['sobər] *adj* nüchtern || *tr* (up) ernüchtern || *intr*—s. up wieder nüchtern werden

sobriety [so'braɪ·əti] *s* Nüchternheit *f*

sob' sto'ry *s* Schmachtfetzen *m*

so'-called' *adj* sogenannt

soccer ['sakər] *s* Fußball *m*

soc'cer play'er *s* Fußballer *m*

sociable ['soʃəbəl] *adj* gesellig

social ['soʃəl] *adj* gesellschaftlich || *s* geselliges Beisammensein *n*

so'cial climb'er *s* Streber –in *m*

socialism ['soʃə,lɪzəm] *s* Sozialismus *m*

socialist ['soʃəlɪst] *s* Sozialist –in *mf*

socialistic [,soʃə'lɪstɪk] *adj* sozialistisch

socialite ['soʃə,laɪt] *s* Prominente *mf*

socialize ['soʃə,laɪz] *intr* (with) verkehren (mit)

so'cialized med'icine *s* staatliche Gesundheitspflege *f*

so'cial reg'ister *s* Register *n* der prominenten Mitglieder der oberen Gesellschaftsklasse

so'cial sci'ence *s* Sozialwissenschaft *f*

so'cial secu'rity *s* Sozialversicherung *f*

so'cial wel'fare *s* Sozialfürsorge *f*

so'cial work'er *s* Sozialfürsorger –in *mf*

society [sə'saɪ·əti] *s* Gesellschaft *f*; (*an organization*) Verein *m*

soci'ety col'umn *s* Gesellschaftsspalte *f*

soci'ety for the preven'tion of cru'elty to an'imals *s* Tierschutzverein *m*

sociological [,sosɪ·ə'lɑdʒɪkəl] *adj* sozialwissenschaftlich, soziologisch

sociologist [,sosɪ'alədʒɪst] *s* Soziologe *m*, Soziologin *f*

sociology [,sosɪ'alədʒi] *s* Soziologie *f*

sock [sak] *s* Socke *f*; (sl) Faustschlag *m* || *tr*—s. it to him! gib's ihm!; **s. s.o.** j-m eine 'runterhauen

socket ['sakɪt] *s* (anat) Höhle *f*; (elec) Steckdose *f*; (mach) Muffe *f*

sock'et joint' *s* (anat) Kugelgelenk *n*

sock'et wrench' *s* Steckschlüssel *m*

sod [sad] *s* Rasenstück *n* || *v* (*pret & pp* sodded; *ger* sodding) *tr* mit Rasen bedecken

soda ['sodə] *s* (*refreshment*) Limonade *f*; (*in mixed drinks*) Selterswasser *n*; (chem) Soda *f & n*

so'da crack'er *s* Keks *m*

so'da wa'ter *s* Sodawasser *n*

sodium ['sodɪ·əm] *s* Natrium *n*

sofa ['sofə] *s* Sofa *n*

soft [sɔft] *adj* (*not hard or tough*) weich; (*not loud*) leise; (*light, music*) sanft; (*sleep, breeze*) leicht; (*effeminate*) verweichlicht; (*muscles*) schlaff; **be s. on** weich sein gegenüber (*dat*)

soft'-boiled egg' *s* weichgekochtes Ei *n*

soft' coal' *s* Braunkohle *f*

soft' drink' *s* alkoholfreies Getränk *n*

soften ['sɔfən] *tr* aufweichen; (*palliate*) lindern; (*water*) enthärten; **s. up** (mil) zermürben || *intr* (& fig) weich werden

soft'-heart'ed *adj* weichherzig

soft' job' *s* Druckposten *m*

soft' land'ing *s* (rok) weiche Landung *f*

soft' pal'ate *s* Hintergaumen *m*

soft'-ped'al *v* (*pret & pp* -al[l]ed; *ger* -al[l]ing) *tr* zurückhaltender vorbringen

soft'-soap' *tr* (coll) schmeicheln (*dat*)

soggy ['sagi] *adj* (*soaked*) durchnäßt; (*ground*) sumpfig

soil [sɔɪl] *s* Boden *m* || *tr* beschmutzen || *intr* schmutzen

soil' pipe' *s* Abflußrohr *n*

sojourn ['sodʒʌrn] *s* Aufenthalt *m* || *intr* sich vorübergehend aufhalten

solace ['salɪs] *s* Trost *m* || *tr* trösten

solar ['solər] *adj* Sonnen-

so'lar plex'us ['plɛksəs] *s* (anat) Sonnengeflecht *n*

solder ['sadər] *s* Lötmetall *n* || *tr* löten

sol'dering i'ron *s* Lötkolben *m*

soldier ['soldʒər] *s* Soldat *m*

sole [sol] *adj* einzig, alleinig || *s* (*of a shoe, foot*) Sohle *f*; (fish) Scholle *f* || *tr* (be)sohlen

solely ['solɪ] *adv* einzig und allein

solemn ['saləm] *adj* feierlich; (*expression*) ernst

solemnity [sə'lɛmnɪti] *s* Feierlichkeit *f*

solicit [sə'lɪsɪt] *tr* (*beg for*) dringend bitten um; (*accost*) ansprechen; (*new members, customers*) werben

solicitor [sə'lɪsɪtər] *s* (com) Agent –in *mf*; (jur) Rechtsanwalt *m*

solicitous [səˈlɪsɪtəs] *adj* fürsorglich

solid [ˈsɑlɪd] *adj* (*hard, firm, e.g., ice, ground*) fest; (*sturdy, e.g., person, furniture; firm, e.g., foundation; learning; financially sound*) solid(e); (*compact*) kompakt, massiv; (*durable*) dauerhaft; (*gold*) gediegen; (*meal, blow*) kräftig; (*hour*) ganz, geschlagen; (*of one color*) einfarbig; (*color*) getönt; (*of one mind*) einmütig; (*grounds, argument*) stichhaltig; (*row of houses*) geschlossen; (*clouds, fog*) dicht; (geom) Raum– || *s* (geom, phys) Körper *m*

solidarity [ˌsɑlɪˈdærɪti] *s* Solidarität *f*, Verbundenheit *f*

sol'id food' *s* feste Nahrung *f*

sol'id geo'metry *s* Stereometrie *f*

solidi·fy [səˈlɪdɪˌfaɪ] *v* (*pret & pp* –fied) *tr* fest werden lassen; (fig) konsolidieren || *intr* fest werden

solidity [səˈlɪdɪti] *s* (*state*) Festigkeit *f*; (*soundness*) Solidität *f*

solidly [ˈsɑlɪdli] *adv*—be s. behind s.o. sich mit j–m solidarisch erklären

sol'id-state' *adj* Transistor–

soliloquy [səˈlɪləkwi] *s* Selbstgespräch *n*

solitaire [ˈsɑlɪˌter] *s* Solitär *m*

solitary [ˈsɑlɪˌteri] *adj* allein; (*life*) zurückgezogen; (*exception*) einzig; (*lonely*) einsam

sol'itary confine'ment *s* Einzelhaft *f*

solitude [ˈsɑlɪˌt(j)ud] *s* Einsamkeit *f*; (*lonely spot*) abgelegener Ort *m*

so·lo [ˈsolo] *adj & adv* solo || *s* (–los) Solo *n*

so'lo flight' *s* Soloflug *m*

soloist [ˈsolo-ɪst] *s* Solist –in *mf*

so'lo part' *s* (mus) Solostimme *f*

solstice [ˈsɑlstɪs] *s* Sonnenwende *f*

soluble [ˈsɑljəbəl] *adj* (fig) (auf)lösbar; (chem) löslich

solution [səˈlu(ʃ)ən] *s* Lösung *f*

solvable [ˈsɑlvəbəl] *adj* (auf)lösbar

solve [sɑlv] *tr* (auf)lösen

solvency [ˈsɑlvənsi] *s* Zahlungsfähigkeit *f*

solvent [ˈsɑlvənt] *adj* zahlungsfähig; (chem) (auf)lösend || *s* Lösungsmittel *n*

somber [ˈsɑmbər] *adj* düster, trüb(e)

some [sʌm] *indef adj* (*with singular nouns*) etwas; (*with plural nouns*) manche; (*sometimes not translated*) e.g., **I am buying s. stockings** ich kaufe Strümpfe; (coll) toll, e.g., **s. girl!** tolles Mädchen!; **at s. time or other** irgendeinmal, irgendwann; **s. ... or other** irgendein; **s. other way** sonstwie || *adv* (*with numerals*) etwa, ungefähr || *indef pron* manche; (*part of*) ein Teil *m*; **s. of these people** einige Leute; **s. of us** manche von uns

some'bod'y *indef pron* jemand, irgendwer; **s. else** jemand anderer || *s*—be a s. etwas Besonderes sein

some'day' *adv* e–s Tages

some'how' *adv* irgendwie; (*for some reason or other*) aus irgendeinem Grunde

some'one' *indef pron* jemand, irgendwer; **s. else** jemand anderer; **s. else's** fremd, e.g., **s. else's property** fremdes Eigentum

some'place' *adv* irgendwo; (*direction*) irgendwohin

somersault [ˈsʌmərˌsɔlt] *s* Purzelbaum *m*; (gym) Überschlag *m*; **do a s. e–n** Purzelbaum schlagen || *intr* sich überschlagen

some'thing *indef pron* etwas; **he is s. of an expert** er ist e–e Art Experte; **s. else** etwas anderes; **s. or other** irgend etwas

some'time' *adv* einmal; **s. today** irgendwann heute

some'times' *adv* manchmal; **sometimes ... sometimes ...** mal ... mal ...

some'way', **some'ways'** *adv* irgendwie

some'what' *adv* etwas

some'where' *adv* irgendwo; (*direction*) irgendwohin; **from s. else** sonstwoher; **s. else** sonstwo

somnambulist [sɑmˈnæmbjəlɪst] *s* Nachtwandler –in *mf*

somnolent [ˈsɑmnələnt] *adj* schläfrig

son [sʌn] *s* Sohn *m*

sonar [ˈsonɑr] *s* Sonar *n*

sonata [səˈnɑtə] *s* Sonate *f*

song [sɔŋ] *s* Lied *n*; (*of birds*) Gesang *m*; **for a s.** (coll) um ein Spottgeld

Song' of Songs' *s* (Bib) Hohelied *n*

sonic [ˈsɑnɪk] *adj* Schall–

son'ic boom' *s* Kopfwellenknall *m*

son'-in-law' *s* (sons-in-law) Schwiegersohn *m*

sonnet [ˈsɑnɪt] *s* Sonett *n*

sonny [ˈsʌni] *s* Söhnchen *n*, Kleiner *m*

Son' of Man', *s* (Bib) der Menschensohn

sonorous [səˈnorəs] *adj* sonor

soon [sun] *adv* bald; **as s. as** sobald; **as s. as possible** sobald wie möglich; **just as s.** (*expressing preference*) genauso gern(e); **no sooner said than done** gesagt, getan; **sooner** (*expressing time*) früher, eher; (*expressing preference*) lieber, eher; **sooner or later** über kurz oder lang; **the sooner the better** je eher, je besser; **too s.** zu früh

soot [sʊt] *s* Ruß *m*

soothe [suð] *tr* beschwichtigen, beruhigen; **have a soothing effect on** beruhigend wirken auf (*acc*)

soothsayer [ˈsuθˌse-ər] *s* Wahrsager *m*

sooty [ˈsuti] *adj* rußig

sop [sɑp] *s* eingetunktes Stück *n* Brot; (*something given to pacify*) Beschwichtigungsmittel *n*; (*bribe*) Schmiergeld *n*; (*spineless person*) Waschlappen *m* || *v* (*pret & pp* sopped; *ger* sopping) *tr* (*dip*) eintunken; **sop up** aufsaugen

sophist [ˈsɑfɪst] *s* Sophist –in *mf*

sophisticated [səˈfɪstɪˌketɪd] *adj* (*person*) weltklug; (*way of life*) verfeinert; (*highly developed*) hochentwickelt

sophistication [səˌfɪstɪˈkeʃən] *s* Weltklugheit *f*

sophistry [ˈsɑfɪstri] *s* Sophisterei *f*

sophomore ['sɑfə͵mɔr] s Student –in mf im zweiten Studienjahr

sop'ping adj klatschnaß || adv—s. wet klatschnaß

sopran·o [sə'præno] adj Sopran– || s (–os) (uppermost voice) Sopran m; (soprano part) Sopranpartie f; (singer) Sopranist –in mf

sorcerer ['sɔrsərər] s Zauberer m

sorceress ['sɔrsəris] s Zauberin f

sorcery ['sɔrsəri] s Zauberei f

sordid ['sɔrdɪd] adj schmutzig; (improper) unlauter

sore [sor] adj wund; (sensitive) empfindlich; (coll) (at) bös (auf acc); be s. weh tun; s. spot (& fig) wunder Punkt m || s Wunde f

sore'head' s (coll) Verbitterte mf

sorely ['sorli] adv sehr

soreness ['sornɪs] s Empfindlichkeit f

sore' throat' s Halsweh n

sorority [sə'rɔriti] s Studentinnenvereinigung f

sorrel ['sɔrəl] adj fuchsrot || s Fuchs m; (bot) Sauerampfer m

sorrow ['sɔro] s Kummer m || intr (for or over) Kummer haben (um)

sorrowful ['sɔrəfəl] adj betrübt

sorry ['sɔri] adj traurig, betrübt; (appearance) armselig; I am s. es tut mir leid; I am (or feel) s. for him er tut mir leid

sort [sɔrt] s Art f, Sorte f; all sorts of alle möglichen; nothing of the s. nichts dergleichen; out of sorts unpäßlich; s. of (coll) (with adjectives) etwas; (with verbs) irgendwie; (with nouns) so 'n, e.g., I had a s. of feeling that ich hatte so 'ne Ahnung, daß; these sorts of derartige; what s. of was für ein || tr sortieren; s. out aussortieren; (fig) sichten

sortie ['sɔrti] s (from a fortress) Ausfall m; (aer) Einzeleinsatz m || intr e–n Ausfall machen

so'-so' adj & adv soso, leidlich

sot [sɑt] s Trunkenbold m

soul [sol] s (spiritual being; inhabitant) Seele f; not a s. (coll) keine Seele f; upon my s.! meiner Seele!

sound [saund] adj Schall–, Ton–; (healthy) gesund; (valid) einwandfrei; (basis) tragfähig; (sleep) fest; (beating) (coll) tüchtig; (business) solid; (judgment) treffsicher || s Laut m, Ton m; (noise) Geräusch n; (of one's voice) Klang m; (narrow body of water) Sund m; (phys) Schall m; (surg) Sonde f || adv—be s. asleep fest schlafen || tr ertönen lassen; (med) sondieren; (naut) loten; s. s.o. out (coll) j–m auf den Zahn fühlen; s. the alarm Alarm schlagen; s. the all-clear entwarnen || intr (er)klingen, (er)tönen; (seem) klingen; (naut) loten; it sounds good to me es kommt mir gut vor; s. off (coll) sich laut beschweren

sound' bar'rier s Schallgrenze f, Schallmauer f

sound' effects' spl Klangeffekte pl

sound' film' s Tonfilm m

sound'ing s Lotung f; take soundings loten

sound'ing board' s (on an instrument) Resonanzboden m; (over an orchestra or speaker) Schallmuschel f; (board for damping sounds) Schalldämpfungsbrett n

soundly ['saundli] adv tüchtig

sound'proof' adj schalldicht || tr schalldicht machen

sound' stu'dio s (cin) Tonatelier n

sound' tech'ni'cian s Tontechniker m

sound' track' s (cin) Tonstreifen m

sound' truck' s Lautsprecherwagen m

sound' wave' s Schallwelle f

soup [sup] s Suppe f; (thick fog) (coll) Waschküche f; in the s. (coll) in der Patsche || tr—s. up (aut) frisieren

soup' kitch'en s Volksküche f

soup'meat' s Suppenfleisch n

soup' plate' s Suppenteller m

soup'spoon' s Suppenlöffel m

sour [saur] adj (& fig) sauer || tr säuern; (fig) verbittern || intr säuern; (fig) versauern

source [sors] s Quelle f

source' lan'guage s Ausgangssprache f

source' mate'rial s Quellenmaterial n

sour' cher'ry s Weichsel f

sour' grapes' spl (fig) saure Trauben pl

sour' note' s (& fig) Mißklang m

sour'puss' s (sl) Sauertopf m

souse [saus] s (sl) Säufer –in mf

soused adj (sl) besoffen

south [sauθ] adj Süd–, südlich || adv (direction) nach Süden; s. of südlich von || s Süd(en) m

South' Amer'ica s Südamerika n

south'east' adj Südost– || adv (direction) südöstlich; s. of südöstlich von || s Südost(en) m

south'east'ern adj südöstlich

southerly ['sʌðərli] adj südlich

southern ['sʌðərn] adj südlich

southerner ['sʌðərnər] s Südländer –in mf; (in the U.S.A.) Südstaatler –in mf

south'paw' adj (coll) linkshändig || s (coll) Linkshänder –in mf

South' Pole' s Südpol m

South' Seas' spl Südsee f

southward ['sauθwərd] adv südwärts

south'west' adj Südwest– || adv südwestlich; s. of südwestlich von || s Südwest(en) m

south'west'ern adj südwestlich

souvenir [͵suvə'nɪr] s Andenken n

sovereign ['sʌvrɪn] adj souverän || s Souverän m, Landesfürst m

sov'ereign rights' spl Hoheitsrechte pl

sovereignty ['sʌvrɪnti] s Souveränität f

soviet ['sovɪ͵ɛt] adj sowjetisch || s Sowjet m; the Soviets die Sowjets pl

So'viet Rus'sia s Sowjetrußland n

So'viet Un'ion s Sowjetunion f

sow [sau] s Sau f || [so] v (pret sowed); pp sowed & sown) tr & intr säen

soybean ['sɔɪ͵bin] s Sojabohne f

spa [spɑ] s Bad n, Badekurort m

space [spes] s Raum m; (between ob-

jects) Zwischenraum *m*; (typ) Spatium *n*; **take up s.** Platz einnehmen || *tr* in Abständen anordnen; (typ) spationieren

space' age' *s* Weltraumzeitalter *n*

space' bar' *s* (typ) Leertaste *f*

space' cap'sule *s* (rok) Raumkapsel *f*

space' craft' *s* Weltraumfahrzeug *n*

space' flight' *s* Raumflug *m*

space'man' *s* (-men) Raumfahrer *m*

space' probe' *s* Sonde *f*

space'ship' *s* Raumschiff *n*

space' shot' *s* Weltraumabschuß *m*

space' shut'tle *s* Raumfähre *f*

space' suit' *s* Raumanzug *m*

space' trav'el *s* Raumfahrt *f*

spacious ['speʃəs] *adj* geräumig

spade [sped] *s* Spaten *m*; (cards) Pik *n*; **call a s. a s.** das Kind beim richtigen Namen nennen

spade'work' *s* (fig) Pionierarbeit *f*

spaghetti [spə'geti] *s* Spahetti *pl*

Spain [spen] *s* Spanien *n*

span [spæn] *s* (& fig) Spanne *f*; (of a bridge) Joch *n*; **s. of time** Zeitspanne *f* || *v* (pret & pp **spanned;** ger **spanning**) *tr* (e.g., the waist) umspannen; (a river) überbrücken; (said of a bridge) überspannen

spangle ['spæŋgəl] *s* Flitter *m* || *tr* mit Flitter besetzen

Spaniard ['spænjərd] *s* Spanier –in *mf*

spaniel ['spænjəl] *s* Wachtelhund *m*

Spanish ['spænɪʃ] *adj* spanisch || *s* Spanisch *n*; **the S.** die Spanier

Span'ish-Amer'ican *s* Amerikaner –in *mf* mit spanischer Muttersprache

Span'ish moss' *s* Moosbärte *pl*

spank [spæŋk] *tr* (ver)hauen

spank'ing *adj* (quick) flink; (breeze) frisch || *adv*—**s.** new funkelnagelneu || *s* Schläge *pl*

spar [spɑr] *s* (aer) Holm *m*; (mineral) Spat *m*; (naut) Spiere *f* || *v* (pret & pp **sparred;** ger **sparring**) *intr* sparren

spare [sper] *adj* Ersatz–; (thin) mager; (time) frei; (leftover) übrig || *s* (aut) Ersatzreifen *m* || *tr* (a person) schonen; (time, money) erübrigen; (expense) scheuen; (do without) entbehren; **have to s.** übrig haben; **s. s.o. s.th.** j-m etw ersparen

spare' bed' *s* Gastbett *n*

spare' part' *s* Ersatzteil *n*

spare' rib' *s* Rippenspeer *f*

spare' time' *s* Freizeit *f*

spare'-time' *adj* nebenberuflich

spare' tire' *s* Ersatzreifen *m*

spar'ing *adj* sparsam; **be s. with** sparsam umgehen mit

spark [spɑrk] *s* Funke(n) *m* || *tr* (set off) auslösen; (stimulate) anregen || *intr* Funken sprühen

spark' gap' *s* Funkenstrecke *f*

sparkle ['spɑrkəl] *s* Funkeln *n* || *intr* funkeln; (said of wine) moussieren

spark' plug' *s* Zündkerze *f*

spar'ring part'ner *s* Übungspartner *m*

sparrow ['spæro] *s* Spatz *m*, Sperling *m*

spar'row hawk' *s* Sperber *m*

sparse [spɑrs] *adj* spärlich

Spartan ['spɑrtən] *adj* spartanisch || *s* Spartaner –in *mf*

spasm ['spæzəm] *s* Krampf *m*, Zukkung *f*

spasmodic [spæz'mɑdɪk] *adj* sprunghaft; (pathol) krampfartig

spastic ['spæstɪk] *adj* spastisch

spat [spæt] *s* (coll) Wortwechsel *m*

spatial ['speʃəl] *adj* räumlich

spatter ['spætər] *s* Spritzen *n*; (stain) Spritzfleck *m* || *tr* verspritzen

spatula ['spætʃələ] *s* Spachtel *m* & *f*

spawn [spɔn] *s* Fischlaich *m* || *tr* hervorbringen || *intr* (said of fish) laichen

spay [spe] *tr* die Eierstöcke entfernen aus

speak [spik] *v* (pret **spoke** [spok]; pp **spoken**) *tr* sprechen; **s. one's mind** sich aussprechen || *intr* (**about**) sprechen (über acc, von); **generally speaking** im allgemeinen; **so to s.** sozusagen; **speaking!** (telp) am Apparat!; **s. to** sprechen mit; (give a speech to) sprechen zu; **s. up** lauter sprechen; (say something) den Mund aufmachen; **s. up!** heraus mit der Sprache!; **s. up for** eintreten für

speak'-eas'y *s* Flüsterkneipe *f*

speaker ['spikər] *s* Sprecher –in *mf*; (before an audience) Redner –in *mf*; (parl) Sprecher –in *mf*; (rad) Lautsprecher *m*

spear [spɪr] *s* Speer *m* || *tr* durchbohren; (a piece of meat) aufspießen; (fish) mit dem Speer fangen

spear'head' *s* Speerspitze *f*; (mil) Stoßkeil *m* || *tr* an der Spitze stehen von

spear'mint' *s* Krauseminze *f*

special ['speʃəl] *adj* besonder, Sonder– || *s* (rr) Sonderzug *m*; **today's s.** Stammgericht *n*

spe'cial deliv'ery *s* Eilzustellung *f*; (tab on envelope) Eilsendung *f*

spec'ial-deliv'ery let'ter *s* Eilbrief *m*

specialist ['speʃəlɪst] *s* Spezialist –in *mf*

specialization [ˌspeʃəlɪ'zeʃən] *s* Spezialisierung *f*

specialize ['speʃəˌlaɪz] *intr* sich spezialisieren; **specialized knowledge** Fachkenntnisse *pl*

spe'cial of'fer *s* (com) Sonderangebot *n*

specialty ['speʃəlti] *s* Spezialität *f*; (special field) Spezialfach *n*

spe'cialty shop' *s* Spezialgeschäft *n*

specie ['spiʃi] *s*—**in s. der Art nach**

spe-cies ['spiʃiz] *s* (-cies) Gattung *f*

specific [spɪ'sɪfɪk] *adj* spezifisch

specification [ˌspesɪfɪ'keʃən] *s* Spezifizierung *f*; **specifications** (tech) technische Beschreibung *f*

specif'ic grav'ity *s* spezifisches Gewicht *n*

speci-fy ['spesɪˌfaɪ] *v* (pret & pp **-fied**) *tr* spezifizieren; (stipulate) bestimmen

specimen ['spesɪmən] *s* (example) Exemplar *n*; (test sample) Probe *f*

specious ['spiʃəs] *adj* Schein–

speck [spek] *s* Fleck *m;* (*in the distance*) Pünktchen *n;* **s. of dust** Stäubchen *n;* **s. of grease** Fettauge *n*

speckle ['spekəl] *s* Sprenkel *m* ‖ *tr* sprenkeln

spectacle ['spektəkəl] *s* Schauspiel *n*, Anblick *m;* **spectacles** Brille *f*

spec'tacle case' *s* Brillenfutteral *n*

spectacular [spek'tækjələr] *adj* sensationell ‖ *s* (cin) Monsterfilm *m*

spectator ['spektetər] *s* Zuschauer –in *mf*

specter ['spetər] *s* Gespenst *n*

spec·trum ['spektrəm] *s* (**–tra** [trə]) Spektrum *n*

speculate ['spekjə,let] *intr* spekulieren; **s. in** spekulieren in (*dat*); **s. on** Überlegungen anstellen über (*acc*)

speculation [,spekjə'le/ən] *s* Spekulation *f*

speculative ['spekjələtɪv] *adj* (com) Spekulations–; (philos) spekulativ

speculator ['spekjə,letər] *s* Spekulant –in *mf*

speech [spit/] *s* Sprache *f;* (*address*) Rede *f;* **give a s.** e–e Rede halten

speech' defect' *s* Sprachfehler *m*

speech' imped'iment *s* Sprachstörung *f*

speechless ['spit/lɪs] *adj* sprachlos

speed [spid] *s* Geschwindigkeit *f;* (*gear*) Gang *m;* **at top s.** mit Höchstgeschwindigkeit; **pick up s.** auf Touren kommen ‖ *v* (*pret & pp* **speeded & sped** [sped]) *tr* beschleunigen; **s. up** forcieren; **s. it up** (coll) ein scharfes Tempo vorlegen ‖ *intr* (aut) rasen; (*above the speed limit*) (aut) zu schnell fahren

speed'boat' *s* Schnellboot *n*

speed'ing *s* (aut) Schnellfahren *n;* **be arrested for s.** wegen Überschreitung der Höchstgeschwindigkeit verhaftet werden; **no s.** (*public sign*) Schnellfahren verboten

speed' lim'it *s* Geschwindigkeitsgrenze *f*

speed' of light' *s* Lichtgeschwindigkeit *f*

speed' of sound' *s* Schallgeschwindigkeit *f*

speedometer [spi'dɑmɪtər] *s* Tachometer *n;* (*mileage indicator*) Meilenzähler *m*, Kilometerzähler *m*

speed' rec'ord *s* Geschwindigkeitsrekord *m*

speed' trap' *s* Autofalle *f*

speed'way' *s* (aut) Rennstrecke *f*

speedy ['spidi] *adj* schnell, schleunig; (*reply*) baldig

speed' zone' *s* Geschwindigkeitsbeschränkung *f*

spell [spel] *s* (*short period*) Zeitlang *f;* (*attack*) Anfall *m;* (*magical influence*) Bann *m;* **be under s.o.'s s.** in j–s Bann stehen; **cast a s.** bannen ‖ *v* (*pret & pp* **spelled & spelt** [spelt]) *tr* buchstabieren; (*in writing*) schreiben; **s. out** Buchstaben für Buchstaben lesen; (fig) auseinanderklamüsern; **s. trouble** Schwie-

rigkeiten bedeuten ‖ *intr* buchstabieren

spell'bind'er *s* faszinierender Redner *m*

spell'bound' *adj* gebannt

spell'ing *s* Schreibweise *f;* (*orthography*) Rechtschreibung *f*

spell'ing bee' *s* orthographischer Wettbewerb *m*

spelt [spelt] *s* Spelz *m*

spelunker [spɪ'lʌŋkər] *s* Höhlenforscher –in *mf*

spend [spend] *v* (*pret & pp* **spent** [spent]) *tr* (*money*) ausgeben; (*time*) verbringen; **s. the night** übernachten; **s. time and effort on** Zeit und Mühe verwenden auf (*acc*)

spend'thrift' *s* Verschwender –in *mf*

spent [spent] *adj* (*exhausted*) erschöpft; (*cartridge*) leergeschossen

sperm [spʌrm] *s* Sperma *n*

sperm' whale' *s* Pottwal *m*

spew [spju] *tr* erbrechen; (fig) ausspeien ‖ *intr* sich erbrechen; (fig) herausströmen

sphere [sfɪr] *s* Kugel *f*, Sphäre *f;* (fig) Bereich *m;* **s. of influence** Einflußsphäre *f*

spherical ['sferɪkəl] *adj* sphärisch, kugelförmig

sphinx [sfɪŋks] *s* (**sphinxes & sphinges** ['sfɪndʒiz]) Sphinx *f*

spice [spaɪs] *s* Gewürz *n*, Würze *f;* (fig) Würze *f* ‖ *tr* würzen

spick-and-span ['spɪkənd'spæn] *adj* blitzblank

spicy ['spaɪsi] *adj* würzig; (fig) pikant

spider ['spaɪdər] *s* Spinne *f*

spi'derweb' *s* Spinnengewebe *n*

spiffy ['spɪfi] *adj* (sl) fesch

spigot ['spɪgət] *s* Wasserhahn *m*

spike [spaɪk] *s* (*nail*) langer Nagel *m;* (*in volleyball*) Schmetterball *m;* (bot) Ähre *f;* (rr) Schwellenschraube *f;* (sport) Dorn *m* ‖ *tr* (*a drink*) e–n Schuß Alkohol tun in (*acc*); (*in volleyball*) schmettern

spill [spɪl] *s* (*spilling*) Vergießen *n;* (*stain*) Fleck *m*, Klecks *m;* (*fall*) Sturz *m;* **take a s.** stürzen ‖ *v* (*pret & pp* **spilled & spilt** [spɪlt]) *tr* verschütten; (*a rider*) abwerfen; **s. out** ausschütten; **s. the beans** (sl) alles ausplaudern ‖ *intr* überlaufen; **s. over into** (fig) übergreifen auf (*acc*)

spill'way' *s* Überlauf *m*

spin [spɪn] *s* (*rotation*) Umdrehung *f;* (*short ride*) kurze Fahrt *f;* (aer) Trudeln *n;* **go for a s.** e–e Spritztour machen; **go into a s.** (aer) ins Trudeln kommen ‖ *v* (*pret & pp* **spun** [spʌn]; *ger* **spinning**) *tr* (*rotate*) drehen; (tex) spinnen; **s. out** (*a story*) ausspinnen; **s. s.o. around** j–n im Kreise herumwirbeln ‖ *intr* kreiseln, sich drehen; (tex) spinnen; **my head is spinning** mir dreht sich alles im Kopf

spinach ['spɪnɪt/] *s* Spinat *m*

spi'nal col'umn ['spaɪnəl] *s* Wirbelsäule *f*

spi'nal cord' *s* Rückenmark *n*

spi'nal flu'id *s* Rückenmarksflüssigkeit *f*

spindle ['spɪndəl] *s* Spindel *f*

spin'-dry' *v* (*pret & pp* **–dried**) *tr* schleudern

spin'-dry'er *s* Trockenschleuder *m*

spine [spaɪn] *s* Rückgrat *n*, Wirbelsäule *f*; (bb) Buchrücken *m*

spineless ['spaɪnlɪs] *adj* (& fig) rückgratlos

spinet ['spɪnɪt] *s* Spinett *n*

spinner ['spɪnər] *s* Spinner –in *mf*; (mach) Spinnmaschine *f*

spin'ning *adj* (*rotating*) sich drehend; (tex) Spinn– || *s* (tex) Spinnen *n*

spin'ning wheel' *s* Spinnrad *n*

spinster ['spɪnstər] *s* alte Jungfer *f*

spi·ral ['spaɪrəl] *adj* spiralig || *s* Spirale *f*; **s. of rising prices and wages** Lohn-Preis-Spirale *f* || *v* (*pret & pp* **–ral[l]ed**; *ger* **–ral[l]ing**) *intr* sich in die Höhe schrauben

spi'ral stair'case *s* Wendeltreppe *f*

spire [spaɪr] *s* Spitze *f*

spirit ['spɪrɪt] *s* Geist *m*; (*enthusiasm*) Schwung *m*; (*ghost*) Geist *m*; **in high spirits** in gehobener Stimmung; **in low spirits** in gedrückter Stimmung; **spirits** Spirituosen *pl*; **that's the right s.!** das ist die richtige Einstellung! || *tr* **s. away** wegzaubern

spir'ited *adj* lebhaft; (*horse*) feurig

spiritless ['spɪrɪtlɪs] *adj* schwunglos

spiritual ['spɪrɪtʃʊ-əl] *adj* (*incorporeal*) geistig; (*of the soul*) seelisch; (*religious*) geistlich || *s* geistliches Negerlied *n*

spiritualism ['spɪrɪtʃʊə‚lɪzəm] *s* Spiritismus *m*

spiritualist ['spɪrɪtʃʊ·əlɪst] *s* Spiritist –in *mf*

spir'itual life' *s* Seelenleben *n*

spit [spɪt] *s* Spucke *f*; (*culin*) Spieß *m* || *v* (*pret & pp* **spat** [spæt] & **spit**; *ger* **spitting**) *tr & intr* spucken

spite [spaɪt] *s* Trotz *m*; **for s.** aus Trotz; **in s. of** trotz (*genit*) || *tr* kränken; **he did it to s. me** er hat es mir zum Trotz getan

spiteful ['spaɪtfəl] *adj* gehässig

spit'fire' *s* (coll) Sprühteufel *m*

spit'ting im'age *s* (coll) Ebenbild *n*

spittoon [spɪ'tun] *s* Spucknapf *m*

splash [splæʃ] *s* Platschen *n*; (*noise of falling into water*) Klatschen *n*; **make a s.** (coll) Aufsehen erregen || *tr* (*a person, etc.*) bespritzen; (*e.g., water*) spritzen || *intr* klatschen, patschen; **s. about** planschen; **s. down** (rok) wassern || *interj* schwaps!, platsch!

splash'down' *s* (rok) Wasserung *f*

splatter ['splætər] *s* *tr & intr* kleckern

spleen [splin] *s* Milz *f*; (fig) schlechte Laune *f*; **vent one's s.** on seiner schlechten Laune Luft machen gegenüber (*dat*)

splendid ['splɛndɪd] *adj* prächtig, herrlich; (coll) großartig

splendor ['splɛndər] *s* Herrlichkeit *f*

splice [splaɪs] *s* Spleiß *m* || *tr* (*a rope*) spleißen; (*film*) zusammenkleben

splint [splɪnt] *s* Schiene *f*; **put in splints** schienen

splinter ['splɪntər] *s* Splitter *m* || *tr* (zer)splittern

splin'ter group' *s* Splittergruppe *f*

split [splɪt] *adj* rissig || *s* Riß *m*, Spalt *m*; (fig) Spaltung *f*; (gym) Spagat *m* || *v* (*pret & pp* **split**; *ger* **splitting**) *tr* spalten || *intr* (*pants*) platzen; (*profits, the difference*) sich teilen in (*acc*); **s. hairs** Haarspalterei treiben; **s. one's sides laughing** vor Lachen platzen; **s. open** aufbrechen || *intr* (**into**) sich spalten (in *acc*); **splitting headache** rasende Kopfschmerzen *pl*; **s. up** (*said of a couple*) sich trennen

split' infin'itive *s* gespaltener Infinitiv *m*

split'-lev'el *adj* mit Zwischenstockwerk versehen

split' personal'ity *s* gespaltene Persönlichkeit *f*

split' sec'ond *s* Sekundenbruchteil *m*

splotch [splatʃ] *s* Klecks *m* || *tr* kleckern

splotchy ['splatʃi] *adj* fleckig

splurge [splʌrdʒ] *s*—**go on a s.** verschwenderischen Aufwand treiben || *tr* verschwenden || *intr* (**on**) verschwenderische Ausgaben machen (für)

splutter ['splʌtər] *s* Geplapper *n* || *tr* (*words*) herausprudeln; (*besplatter*) bespritzen || *intr* plappern; (*said, e.g., of grease*) spritzen

spoil [spɔɪl] *s*—**spoils** Beute *f* || *v* (*pret & pp* **spoiled** & **spoilt** [spɔɪlt]) *tr* (*perishable goods; fun*) verderben; (*a child*) verziehen, verwöhnen || *intr* verderben, schlecht werden; **spoiling for a fight** zanksüchtig

spoilage ['spɔɪlɪdʒ] *s* Verderb *m*

spoil' sport' *s* Spielverderber –in *mf*

spoils' sys'tem *s* Futterkrippensystem *n*

spoke [spok] *s* Speiche *f*

spokes'man *s* (–men) Wortführer –in *mf*

sponge [spʌndʒ] *s* Schwamm *m* || *tr* schnorren || *intr* schnorren; **s. on** (coll) schmarotzen bei

sponge' cake' *s* Sandtorte *f*

sponger ['spʌndʒər] *s* Schmarotzer –in *mf*

sponge' rub'ber *s* Schaumgummi *m* & *n*

spongy ['spʌndʒi] *adj* schwammig

sponsor ['spansər] *s* Förderer –in *mf*; (*of a program*) Sponsor *m*; (*of an immigrant*) Bürge *m*, Bürgin *f*; (*at baptism or confirmation*) Pate *m*, Patin *f* || *tr* fördern; (*a program*) finanziell fördern

spontaneity [spantə'ni·ɪti] *s* Spontaneität *f*

spontaneous [span'teni·əs] *adj* spontan

sponta'neous combus'tion *s* Selbstverbrennung *f*

spontaneously [span'teni·əsli] *adv* von selbst, unaufgefordert

spoof [spuf] *s* (*hoax*) Jux *m*; (*parody*) (*on*) Parodie *f* (*auf acc*) ‖ *intr* albern

spook [spuk] *s* (coll) Spuk *m*

spooky [ˈspuki] *adj* spukhaft

spool [spul] *s* Spule *f*, Rolle *f*

spoon [spun] *s* Löffel *m*; **wooden s.** Kochlöffel *m* ‖ *tr* (out) löffeln

spoonerism [ˈspunə͵rɪzəm] *s* Schüttelreim *m*

spoon'-feed' *v* (*pret & pp* **–fed**) *tr* (fig) es leicht machen (*dat*)

spoonful [ˈspunful] *s* Löffel *m*

sporadic [spəˈrædɪk] *adj* vereinzelt

spore [spor] *s* Spore *f*

sport [sport] *adj* Sport– ‖ *s* Sport *m*; (biol) Spielart *f*; **a good s.** ein Pfundskerl *m*; **go in for sports** sporteln; **in s.** im Spaß; **make s. of** sich lustig machen über (*acc*); **play sports** Sport treiben; **poor s.** Spielverderber –in *mf*; **sports** Sport *m*; (*sportscast*) Sportbericht *m* ‖ *intr* sich belustigen

sport'ing event' *s* Sportveranstaltung *f*

sport'ing goods' *spl* Sportwaren *pl*

sport' jac'ket *s* Sportjacke *f*

sports' car' *s* Sportwagen *m*

sports'cast' *s* Sportbericht *m*

sports'cast'er *s* Sportberichterstatter *m*

sports' fan' *s* Sportfreund –in *mf*

sport' shirt' *s* Sporthemd *m*

sports'man *s* (**–men**) Sportsmann *m*

sports'manlike *adj* sportlich

sports'manship' *s* sportliches Verhalten *n*

sports' news' *s* Sportnachrichten *pl*

sports'wear' *s* Sportkleidung *f*

sports' world' *s* Sportwelt *f*

sports' writ'er *s* Sportjournalist –in *mf*

sporty [ˈsporti] *adj* auffallend

spot [spat] *s* (*stain*) Fleck(en) *m*; (*place*) Platz *m*, Ort *m*; (*as on a leopard*) Tüpfel *m & n*; **be on the s.** (*be present*) zur Stelle sein; (*be in difficulty*) in der Klemme sein; **hit the s.** gerade das Richtige sein; **on the s.** auf der Stelle; **put on the s.** in Verlegenheit bringen ‖ *v* (*pret & pp* **spotted**; *ger* **spotting**) *tr* (*stain*) beflecken; (*espy*) erblicken; (*points in betting*) vorgeben

spot' announce'ment *s* Durchsage *f*

spot' cash' *s* ungebundene Barmittel *pl*

spot' check' *s* Stichprobe *f*

spot'-check' *tr* stichprobenweise prüfen

spotless [ˈspatlɪs] *adj* makellos

spot'light' *s* Scheinwerfer *m*; **in the s.** (fig) im Rampenlicht der Öffentlichkeit ‖ *tr* (fig) in den Vordergrund stellen

spot' remov'er [rɪ͵muvər] *s* Fleckputzmittel *n*

spotty [ˈspati] *adj* fleckig; (*uneven*) ungleichmäßig

spot' weld'ing *s* Punktschweißung *f*

spouse [spaus] *s* Gatte *m*, Gattin *f*

spout [spaut] *s* (*of a pot*) Tülle *f*; (*jet of water*) Strahl *m* ‖ *tr* (& fig) hervorsprudeln ‖ *intr* spritzen; (coll) große Reden schwingen

sprain [spren] *s* Verstauchung *f* ‖ *tr* verstauchen; **s. one's ankle** sich (*dat*) den Fuß vertreten

sprat [spræt] *s* (ichth) Sprotte *f*

sprawl [sprɔl] *intr* (out) alle viere von sich ausstrecken; (*said of a city*) sich weit ausbreiten

spray [spre] *s* (*of ocean*) Gischt *m*; (*from a can*) Spray *n*; (*from a fountain*) Sprühwasser *n*; **s. of flowers** Blütenzweig *m* ‖ *tr* spritzen; (*liquids*) zerstäuben; (*plants*) besprühen

sprayer [ˈspre·ər] *s* Zerstäuber *m*; (*for a garden*) Gartenspritze *f*

spray' gun' *s* Spritzpistole *f*

spray' paint' *s* Spritzfarbe *f*

spread [spred] *s* (*act of spreading*) Ausbreitung *f*; (*extent*) Verbreitung *f*; (e.g., *of a tree*) Umfang *m*; (*on bread*) Aufstrich *m*; (*bedspread*) Bettdecke *f*; (*large piece of land*) weite Fläche *f*; (*of a shot*) Streubereich *m & n*; (*sumptuous meal*) Gelage *n* ‖ *v* (*pret & pp* **spread**) *tr* (*warmth, light, news, rumors*) verbreiten; (*mortar, glue*) auftragen; (e.g., *butter*) aufstreichen; (*the legs*) spreizen; (*manure*) streuen; **s. oneself too thin** sich verzetteln; **s. out over a year** über ein Jahr verteilen ‖ *intr* sich verbreiten; (*said of margarine*) sich aufstreichen lassen

spree [spri] *s* Bummel *m*; (*carousal*) Zechgelage *n*; **go on a buying s.** in e–e Kauforgie stürzen

sprig [sprɪg] *s* Zweiglein *n*

sprightly [ˈspraɪtli] *adj* lebhaft; (*gait*) federnd

spring [sprɪŋ] *adj* Frühlings– ‖ *s* (*of water*) Quelle *f*; (*season*) Frühling *m*; (*resilience*) Sprungkraft *f*; (*of metal*) Feder *f*; (*jump*) Sprung *m*; **springs** (aut) Federung *f* ‖ *v* (*pret* **sprang** [spræŋ] *& pp* **sprung** [sprʌŋ]); *pp* **sprung** [sprʌŋ]) *tr* (*a trap*) zuschnappen lassen; (*a leak*) bekommen; (*a question*) (on) plötzlich stellen (*dat*); (*a surprise*) (on) bereiten (*dat*); **s. the news on s.o.** j–n mit der Nachricht überraschen ‖ *intr* springen; **s. back** zurückschnellen; **s. from** entspringen (*dat*); **s. up** aufspringen; (*said of industry, towns*) aus dem Boden schießen

spring'board' *s* (& fig) Sprungbrett *n*

spring' chic'ken *s* Hähnchen *n*; **she's no s.** (sl) sie ist nicht die Jüngste

spring' fe'ver *s* Frühlingsmüdigkeit *f*

spring'time' *s* Frühlingszeit *f*

spring' wa'ter *s* Quellwasser *n*

springy [ˈsprɪŋi] *adj* federnd

sprinkle [ˈsprɪŋkəl] *s* Spritzen *n*; (*light rain*) Sprühregen *m* ‖ *tr* (*water, streets, lawns, laundry*) sprengen; (e.g., *sugar*) streuen ‖ *intr* sprühen

sprinkler [ˈsprɪŋklər] *s* (*truck*) Sprengwagen *m*; (*for the lawn*) Rasensprenger *m*; (eccl) Sprengwedel *m*

sprin'kling *s* Sprengung *f*; **a s. of** (e.g., *sugar*) ein bißchen; (e.g., *of people*) ein paar

sprin′kling can′ s Gießkanne f
sprin′kling sys′tem s Feuerlöschanlage f

sprint [sprɪnt] s Sprint m ‖ intr sprinten

sprinter ['sprɪntər] s Sprinter –in mf

sprite [spraɪt] s Kobold m, Elfe f

sprocket ['sprɑkɪt] s Zahnrad n

sprout [spraut] s Sproß m ‖ intr sprießen

spruce [sprus] adj schmuck ‖ s (bot) Fichte f ‖ intr—s. up sich schmücken

spry [spraɪ] adj (spryer & sprier; spryest & spriest) flink

spud [spʌd] s (for weeding) Jäthacke f; (potatoe) (coll) Kartoffel f

spume [spjum] s Schaum m

spun′ glass′ s Glasfaser f

spunk [spʌŋk] s (coll) Mumm m

spunky ['spʌŋki] adj (coll) feurig

spur [spʌr] s (on riding boot; on a rooster) Sporn m; (of a mountain) Ausläufer m; (fig) Ansporn m; (archit) Strebe f; (bot) Stachel m; (rr) Seitengleis n; **on the s. of the moment** der Eingebung des Augenblicks folgend ‖ v (pret & pp spurred) ger spurring) tr die Sporen geben (dat); **s. on** anspornen

spurious ['spjurɪ-əs] adj unecht

spurn [spʌrn] tr verschmähen

spurt [spʌrt] s Ruck m; (sport) Spurt m; **in spurts** ruckweise ‖ tr speien ‖ intr herausspritzen; (sport) spurten

sputnick ['spʌtnɪk] s Sputnik m

sputter ['spʌtər] s Stottern n ‖ tr umherspritzen; (words) hervorsprudeln ‖ intr (said of a person, engine) stottern; (said of a candle, fire) flackern

sputum ['spjutəm] s Sputum n

spy [spaɪ] s Spion –in mf ‖ v (pret & pp spied) tr—spy out ausspionieren ‖ intr spionieren

spy′glass′ s Fernglas n

spy′ing s Spionage f

spy′ ring′ s Spionageorganization f

squabble ['skwɑbəl] s Zank m ‖ intr zanken

squad [skwɑd] s (gym) Riege f; (mil) Gruppe f; (sport) Mannschaft f

squad′ car′ s Funkstreifenwagen m

squad′ lead′er s (mil) Gruppenführer m

squadron ['skwɑdrən] s (aer) Staffel f; (nav) Geschwader n

squalid ['skwɑlɪd] adj verkommen

squall [skwɔl] s Bö f

squander ['skwɑndər] tr verschwenden

square [skwer] adj quadratisch; (mile, meter, foot) Quadrat–; (fellow; meal) anständig; (even) quitt; **ten meters s.** zehn Meter im Quadrat; **ten s. meters** zehn Quadratmeter ‖ s Quadrat n; (city block) Häuserblock m; (open area) Platz m; (of a checkerboard or chessboard) Feld n; (carp) Winkel m; (math) zweite Potenz f ‖ tr quadrieren; (a number) ins Quadrat erheben; (accounts) abrechnen ‖ intr—s. off in Kampfstellung gehen; **s. with** (agree with)

übereinstimmen mit; (be frank with) aufrichtig sein zu

square′ dance′ s Reigen m

square′ deal′ s reelles Geschäft n

square′ root′ s Quadratwurzel f

squash [skwɑʃ] s (bot) Kürbis m ‖ tr (a hat) zerdrücken; (a finger, grape) quetschen; (fig) unterdrücken ‖ intr zerdrückt (or zerquetscht) werden

squashy ['skwɑʃi] adj weich, matschig

squat [skwɑt] adj gedrungen, untersetzt ‖ s Hocken n ‖ v (pret & pp squatted; ger squatting) intr hocken; **s. down** sich (hin)hocken

squatter ['skwɑtər] s Ansiedler –in mf ohne Rechtstitel

squaw [skwɔ] s Indianerin f

squawk [skwɔk] s Geschrei n; (sl) Schimpferei f ‖ intr schreien; (sl) schimpfen

squeak [skwik] s (of a door) Quietschen n; (of a mouse) Pfeifen n ‖ intr quietschen; (said of a mouse) pfeifen

squeal [skwil] s Quieken n ‖ intr (said of a pig) quieken; (said of a mouse) pfeifen; (sl) petzen; **s. for joy** vor Vergnügen quietschen; **s. on** (sl) (a pupil) verpetzen; (to the police) verpfeifen

squealer ['skwilər] s (sl) Petze f

squeamish ['skwimɪʃ] adj zimperlich

squeeze [skwiz] s Druck m; **s. of the hand** Händedruck m ‖ tr drücken; (oranges) auspressen; **s. into** (e.g., a trunk) hineinquetschen; **s. out** auspressen; **s. together** zusammenpressen; (e.g., people) zusammenpferchen ‖ intr—s. **in** sich eindrängen; **s. through** sich durchzwängen (durch)

squelch [skwelʧ] s schlagfertige Antwort f ‖ tr niederschmettern

squid [skwɪd] s Tintenfisch m

squill [skwɪl] s (bot) Meerzwiebel f; (zool) Heuschreckenkrebs m

squint [skwɪnt] s Schielen n ‖ intr (look with eyes partly closed) blinzeln; (be cross-eyed) schielen; (look askance) (at) argwöhnisch blicken (auf acc)

squint′-eyed′ adj schielend

squire [skwaɪr] s (hist) Knappe m; (jur) Friedensrichter m

squirm [skwʌrm] intr (through) sich winden (durch); (be restless) zappeln; **s. out of** sich herauswinden aus

squirrel ['skwʌrəl] s Eichhörnchen n

squirt [skwʌrt] s Spritzer m; (boy) (coll) Stöpsel m ‖ tr (ver)spritzen ‖ intr spritzen; **s. out** herausspritzen

S′S′ troops′ ['es'es] spl Schutzstaffel f

stab [stæb] s Stich m; (wound) Stichwunde f; **make a s. at** (coll) probieren ‖ v (pret & pp stabbed; ger stabbing) tr stechen; (kill) erstechen; (a pig) abstechen; **s. s.o. in the back** j-m in den Rücken fallen

stability [stə'brlɪti] s Stabilität f

stabilization [ˌstebɪlɪ'zeʃən] s (e.g., of prices) Stabilisierung f; (aer) Dämpfung f

stabilize ['stebɪ‚laɪz] *tr* stabilisieren

stabilizer ['stebɪ‚laɪzər] *s* (aer) Flosse *f*

stab' in the back' *s* Stoß *m* aus dem Hinterhalt

stable ['stebəl] *adj* stabil || *s* Stall *m* || *tr* unterbringen

sta'ble boy' *s* Stalljunge *m*

stack [stæk] *s* (*of papers, books*) Stapel *m*; (*of wheat*) Schober *m*; (*of a ship*) Schornstein *m*; (*of rifles*) Pyramide *f*; **stacks** (libr) Bücherregale *pl* || *tr* (*wood, wheat*) aufstapeln; (*rifles*) zusammensetzen; (*cards*) packen

stadi·um ['stedɪ·əm] *s* (**-ums** & **-a** [ə]) Stadion *n*

staff [stæf] *s* (*rod*) Stab *m*; (*personnel*) Personal *n*; (*of a newspaper*) Redaktion *f*; (mil) Stab *m*; (mus) Notensystem *n* || *tr* mit Personal besetzen

staff' of'ficer *s* Stabsoffizier *m*

staff' ser'geant *s* Feldwebel *m*

stag [stæg] *adj* Herren– || *adv*—**go s.** ohne Damenbegleitung sein || *s* Hirsch *m*

stage [stedʒ] *s* (*of a theater*) Bühne *f*; (*phase*) Stadium *n*; (*stretch*) Strecke *f*; (*of life*) Etappe *f*; (*of a rocket*) Stufe *f*; (*scene*) Szene *f*; **at this s.** in diesem Stadium; **by easy stages** etappenweise; **final stages** Endstadien *pl* || *tr* (*a play*) inszenieren; (*a comeback*) veranstalten

stage'coach' *s* Postkutsche *f*

stage'craft' *s* Bühnenkunst *f*

stage' direc'tion *s* Bühnenanweisung *f*

stage' door' *s* Bühneneingang *m*

stage' effect' *s* Bühnenwirkung *f*

stage' fright' *s* Lampenfieber *n*

stage' hand' *s* Bühnenarbeiter –in *mf*

stage' light'ing *s* Bühnenbeleuchtung *f*

stage' man'ager *s* Bühnenleiter –in *mf*

stage' play' *s* Bühnenstück *n*

stage' prop'erties *spl* Theaterrequisiten *pl*

stagestruck ['stedʒ‚strʌk] *adj* theaterbegeistert

stagger ['stægər] *s* Taumeln *n* || *tr* (*e.g., lunch hours*) staffeln; (& fig) erschüttern || *intr* taumeln

stag'gering *adj* taumelnd; (*blow, loss*) vernichtend; (*news*) erschütternd

stagnant ['stægnənt] *adj* (*water*) stillstehend; (*air*) schlecht; (fig) träge

stagnate ['stægnet] *intr* stagnieren

stag' par'ty *s* Herrenabend *m*

staid [sted] *adj* gesetzt

stain [sten] *s* Fleck *m*; (*paint*) Beize *f* || *tr* beflecken; (*wood*) beizen

stained'-glass win'dow *s* buntes Glasfenster *n*

stainless ['stenlɪs] *adj* rostfrei

stair [ster] *s* Stufe *f*; **stairs** Treppe *f*

stair'case' *s* Treppenhaus *n*

stair'way' *s* Treppenaufgang *m*

stair'well' *s* Treppenschacht *m*

stake [stek] *s* Pfahl *m*; (*bet*) Einsatz *m*; **be at s.** auf dem Spiel stehen; **die at the s.** auf dem Scheiterhaufen sterben; **play for high stakes** viel riskieren; **pull up stakes** (coll) ab-

hauen || *tr* (*plants*) mit e–m Pfahl stützen; **s. off** abstecken; **s. out a claim** (fig) e–e Forderung umreißen

stake'-out' *s* polizeiliche Überwachung *f*

stalactite [stə'læktart] *s* Stalaktit *m*

stalagmite [stə'lægmart] *s* Stalagmit *m*

stale [stel] *adj* (*baked goods*) altbacken; (*e.g., beer*) schal; (*air*) verbraucht; (*joke*) abgedroschen; **get s.** abstenfen

stale'mate' *s* (fig) Sackgasse *f*; (chess) Patt *n* || *tr* (fig) in e–e Sackgasse treiben; (chess) patt setzen

stalk [stɔk] *s* (*of grain*) Halm *m*; (*of a plant*) Stiel *m* || *tr* beschleichen; **s. game** pirschen

stall [stɔl] *s* (*for animals*) Stall *m*; (*booth*) Bude *f*; (sl) Vorwand *m* || *tr* (*a motor*) abwürgen; (*a person*) aufhalten || *intr* ausweichen; (aut) absterben; **s. for time** Zeit zu gewinnen suchen

stallion ['stæljən] *s* Hengst *m*

stalwart ['stɔlwərt] *adj* stämmig; (*supporter*) treu

stamen ['stemən] *s* Staubfaden *m*

stamina ['stæmɪnə] *s* Ausdauer *f*

stammer ['stæmər] *s* Stammeln *n* || *tr* & *intr* stammeln

stammerer ['stæmərər] *s* Stammler –in *mf*

stamp [stæmp] *s* (*mark*) Gepräge *n*; (*device for stamping*) Stempel *m*; (*for postage*) Briefmarke *f* || *tr* (*e.g., a document*) stempeln; (*a letter*) freimachen; (*the earth*) stampfen; **s. one's foot** mit dem Fuß aufstampfen; **s. out** (*a fire*) austreten; (*a rebellion*) niederschlagen

stampede [stæm'pid] *s* panische Flucht *f* || *tr* in die Flucht jagen || *intr* in wilder Flucht davonrennen

stamped' en'velope *s* Freiumschlag *m*

stamp'ing grounds' *spl* Lieblingsplatz *m*

stamp' machine' *s* Briefmarkenautomat *m*

stamp' pad' *s* Stempelkissen *n*

stance [stæns] *s* Haltung *f*, Stellung *f*

stanch [stɔntʃ] *tr* stillen

stand [stænd] *s* (*booth*) Stand *m*; (*platform*) Tribüne *f*; (*e.g., for bicycles*) Ständer *m*; (*view, position*) Standpunkt *m*; (*piece of furniture*) Ständer *m*; **take a s.** (on) Stellung nehmen (zu); **take one's s.** (*e.g., near the door*) sich stellen; **s. of timber** Waldbestand *m*; **stands** (sport) Tribüne *f*; **take the s.** (jur) als Zeuge auftreten || *v* (*pret* & *pp* **stood** [stʊd]) *tr* (*put*) stellen; (*the cold, hardships*) aushalten; (*a person*) leiden; **s. a chance** e–e Chance haben; **s. guard** Posten stehen; **s. one's ground** sich behaupten; **s. s.o. up** j–n aufsitzen lassen; **s. the test** sich bewähren || *intr* stehen; (*have validity*) gelten; **she wants to know where she stands** sie will wissen, wie sie daran ist; **s. aside** auf die Seite treten; **s. at attention** stillstehen; **s.**

back zurückstehen; **s. behind** s.o. (fig) hinter j-m stehen; **s. by** (in readiness) in Bereitschaft stehen; (a decision) bleiben bei; (e.g., for the latest news) am Apparat bleiben; **s. by** s.o. j-m beistehen; **s. firm** fest bleiben; **s. for** (champion) eintreten für; (tolerate) sich [dat] gefallen lassen; (mean) bedeuten; **s. good for** gutstehen für; **s. idle** stillstehen; **s. on end** sich sträuben, e.g., **my hair stood on end** mir sträubten sich die Haare; **s. on one's head** kopfstehen; **s. out** (project) abstehen; (be conspicuous) hervorstehen; **s. out against** sich abzeichnen gegen; **s. s.o. in good stead** j-m zugute kommen; **s. up** aufstehen; **s. up against** aufkommen gegen; **s. up for** (a thing) verfechten; (a person) die Stange halten (dat); **s. up to** s.o. j-m die Stirn bieten; **s. up under** aushalten

standard ['stændərd] adj Standard-, Normal- ‖ s Standard m; (banner) Banner n

stand'ard-bear'er s Bannerträger m

stand'ard-gauge track' s Normalspur f

standardize ['stændər‚daɪz] tr normen

stand'ard of liv'ing s Lebensstandard m

stand'ard time' s Normalzeit f

stand'-by' s Reserve- ‖ s—**on s.** in Bereitschaft

standee [stæn'di] s Stehplatzinhaber -in mf

stand'in' s (coll) Ersatzmann m; (cin, theat) Double n

stand'ing adj (army, water, rule) stehend; (committee) ständig; (jump) aus dem Stand ‖ s Stehen n; (social) Stellung f; (of a team) Stand m; **in good s.** treu; **of long s.** langjährig

stand'ing or'der s (com) Dauerauftrag m

stand'ing room' s Stehplatz m; **s. only** nur noch Stehplätze

stand'-off' s Unentschieden n

stand-offish ['stænd'ofɪʃ] adj zurückhaltend

stand'out' s Blickfang m

stand'point' s Standpunkt m

stand'still' s Stillstand m; **come to a s.** zum Stillstand kommen

stanza ['stænzə] s Strophe f

staple ['stepəl] adj Haupt-, Stapel- ‖ s (food) Hauptnahrungsmittel n; (product) Hauptprodukt n; (clip) Heftklammer f ‖ tr mit Draht heften

stapler ['steplər] s Heftmaschine f

star [star] adj Spitzen-; (astr) Stern- ‖ s Stern m; (cin, rad, telv, theat) Star m; **I saw stars** (fig) Sterne tanzten mir vor den Augen ‖ v (pret & pp starred) ger starring) tr (cin, rad, sport, telv, theat) als Star herausstellen; (typ) mit Sternchen kennzeichnen ‖ intr Star sein

starboard ['starbərd] adj Steuerbord- ‖ s Steuerbord n

starch [startʃ] s Stärke f ‖ tr stärken

starchy ['startʃi] adj stärkenhaltig

stare [ster] s starrer Blick m ‖ tr—

s. down durch Anstarren aus der Fassung bringen ‖ intr starren; **s. at** anstarren; **s. into space** ins Leere blicken, ins Blaue starren

star'fish' s Seestern m

stargazer ['star‚gezər] s Sterngucker -in mf

stark [stark] adj (landscape) kahl; (sheer) völlig ‖ adv völlig

stark'-na'ked adj splitter(faser)nackt

starlet ['starlɪt] s Sternchen n

star'light' s Sternenlicht n

starling ['starlɪŋ] s (orn) Star m

star'lit' adj sternhell

Star' of Da'vid s David(s)stern m

starry ['stari] adj gestirnt; (night) sternklar; (sky) Stern-

star'ry-eyed' adj verträumt

Stars' and Stripes' spl Sternenbanner n

Star'-Spangled Ban'ner s Sternenbanner n

start [start] s Anfang m; (sudden springing movement) plötzliches Hochfahren n; (lead, advantage) Vorgabe f, Vorsprung m; (of a race) Start m; **give s.o. a s.** j-m auf die Beine helfen ‖ tr anfangen; (a motor) anlassen; (a rumor) in die Welt setzen; (a conversation) anknüpfen; **s. a fire** ein Feuer anmachen; (said of an arsonist) e-n Brand legen ‖ intr anfangen; **s. into** (inf) anfangen zu (inf); **s. out** (begin) anfangen; (start walking) losgehen; **s. out on** (a trip) antreten; **to s. with** zunächst

start'ing gate' s Startmaschine f

start'ing gun' s Startpistole f; **at the s.** beim Startschuß

start'ing point' s Ausgangspunkt m

startle ['startəl] tr erschrecken; **be startled** zusammenfahren

starvation [star've∫ən] s Hunger m; **die of s.** verhungern

starva'tion di'et s Hungerkur f

starva'tion wag'es spl Hungerlohn m

starve [starv] tr verhungern lassen; **s. out** aushungern ‖ intr hungern; (coll) furchtbaren Hunger haben; **s. to death** verhungern

state [stet] adj staatlich, Staats-; (as opposed to federal) bundesstaatlich ‖ s (condition) Zustand m; (government) Staat m; (of the U.S.A.) Bundesstaat m ‖ tr angeben; (a rule, problem) aufstellen; **as stated above** wie oben angegeben

State' Depart'ment s Außenministerium n

stateless ['stetlɪs] adj staatenlos

stately ['stetli] adj stattlich

statement ['stetmənt] s Angabe f; (from a bank) Abrechnung f; (jur) Aussage f

state' of affairs' s Lage f

state' of emer'gency s Notstand m

state' of health' s Gesundheitszustand m

state' of mind' s Geisteszustand m

state' of war' s Kriegszustand m

state'-owned' adj staatseigen; (in communistic countries) volkseigen

state' police' s Staatspolizei f

state'room' s (*in a palace*) Prunkzimmer n; (*on a ship*) Passagierkabine f
states'man s (**-men**) Staatsmann m
states'manlike' adj staatsmännisch
states'manship' s Staatskunst f
static ['stætɪk] adj statisch ‖ s (rad) Nebengeräusche pl
station ['steɪʃən] s (*social*) Stellung f; (*of a bus, rail line*) Bahnhof m; (mil) Standort m ‖ tr aufstellen; (mil) stationieren
stationary ['steɪʃə‚nɛri] adj stationär
sta'tion break' s Werbepause f
stationer ['steɪʃənər] s Schreibwarenhändler –in mf
stationery ['steɪʃə‚nɛri] s Briefpapier n
sta'tionery store' s Schreibwarenhandlung f
sta'tion house' s Polizeiwache f
sta'tion identifica'tion s (rad) Pausenzeichen n
sta'tionmas'ter s Bahnhofsvorsteher m
sta'tions of the cross' spl Kreuzweg s
sta'tion wag'on s Kombiwagen m
statistic [stə'tɪstɪk] s Angabe f; **statistics** (*science*) Statistik f ‖ spl (*data*) Statistik f
statistical [stə'tɪstɪkəl] adj statistisch
statistician [‚stætɪs'tɪʃən] s Statistiker –in mf
statue ['stætʃu] s Statue f
statuesque [‚stætʃu'ɛsk] adj statuenhaft
stature ['stætʃər] s Gestalt f; (fig) Format n
status ['steɪtəs] s (*in society*) Stellung f; (e.g., *mental*) Stand m
sta'tus quo' [kwo] s Status m quo
sta'tus sym'bol s Statussymbol n
statute ['stætʃut] s Satzung f, Statut n
statutory ['stætʃu‚tori] adj statutenmäßig
staunch [stɔntʃ] adj unentwegt
stave [stev] s (*of a barrel*) Daube f; (*of a chair*) Steg m; (*of a ladder*) Sprosse f; (mus) Notensystem n ‖ tr—s. off abwenden
stay [ste] s (*visit*) Aufenthalt m; (prop) Stütze f; (*of execution*) Aufschub m ‖ intr bleiben; **have to s. in** (*after school*) nachsitzen müssen; **s. away** wegbleiben; **s. behind** zurückbleiben; (*in school*) sitzenbleiben
stay'-at-home' s Stubenhocker –in mf
stead [stɛd] s Statt f; **in s.o.'s s. an** j–s Statt
stead'fast' adj standhaft
stead•y ['stɛdi] adj fest, beständig; (*hands*) sicher; (*ladder*) fest; (*pace*) gleichmäßig; (*progress*) ständig; (*nerves*) stark; (*prices*) stabil; (*work*) regelmäßig; **s. customer** Stammkunde m, Stammkundin f; **s. now!** immer langsam! ‖ v (*pret & pp* **-ied**) tr festigen
steak [stek] s Beefsteak n
steal [stil] s—**it's a s.** (coll) das ist geschenkt ‖ v (*pret* **stole** [stol]; *pp* **stolen**) tr stehlen; (*a kiss*) rauben; **s. s.o.'s thunder** j–m den Wind aus den Segeln nehmen; **s. the show** den Vogel abschießen ‖ intr stehlen; **s.**

away wegstehlen; **s. up on s.o.** sich an j–n heranschleichen
stealth [stɛlθ] s—**by s.** heimlich
stealthy ['stɛlθi] adj verstohlen
steam [stim] s Dampf m; (*vapor*) Dunst m; (fig) Kraft f; **full s. ahead!** Volldampf voraus!; **let off s.** Dampf ablassen; (fig) sich [*dat*] Luft machen; **put on s.** (fig) Dampf dahinter machen ‖ tr dämpfen; (culin) dünsten; **s. up beschlagen** ‖ intr dampfen; (culin) dünsten; **s. up** sich beschlagen
steam' bath' s Dampfbad n
steam'boat' s Dampfer m
steam' en'gine s Dampfmaschine f
steamer ['stimər] s Dampfer m
steam' heat' s Dampfheizung f
steam' i'ron s Dampfbügeleisen n
steam' roll'er s (& fig) Dampfwalze f ‖ tr glattwalzen; (fig) niederwalzen
steam'ship' s Dampfschiff n
steam'ship line' s Dampfschiffahrtslinie f
steam' shov'el s Dampflöffelbagger m
steamy ['stimi] adj dampfig, dunstig
steed [stid] s Streitroß n
steel [stil] adj stählern, Stahl– ‖ s Stahl m ‖ tr stählen; **s. oneself against s.th.** sich gegen etw wappnen
steel' wool' s Stahlwolle f
steel'works' spl Stahlwerk n
steely ['stili] adj (fig) stählern
steelyard ['stiljərd] s Schnellwaage f
steep [stip] adj steil; (*prices*) happig ‖ tr (*immerse*) eintauchen; (*soak*) einweichen; **be steeped in** (e.g., *prejudice*) durchdrungen sein von; (*be expert in*) ein Kenner sein (genit); **s. oneself in** sich versenken in (acc)
steeple ['stipəl] s Kirchturm m
stee'plechase' s Hindernisrennen n
steer [stɪr] s Stier m ‖ tr lenken, steuern; **s. a middle course** e–n Mittelweg einschlagen ‖ intr lenken, steuern; **s. clear of** vermeiden
steerage ['stɪrɪdʒ] s Zwischendeck n
steer'ing wheel' s Steuerrad n
stellar ['stɛlər] adj (*role*) Star–; (*attraction*) Haupt–; (astr) Stern(en)–
stem [stem] s (*of a plant*) Halm m; (*of a word; of a tree*) Stamm m; (*of a leaf, fruit; of a glass; of a smoke pipe*) Stiel m; (*of a watch*) Aufziehwelle f; (naut) Steven m; **from s. to stern** von vorn bis achtern ‖ v (*pret & pp* **stemmed**) ger **stemming**) tr (*check*) hemmen; (*fruit*) entstielen; (*the flow*) (an)stauen; (*the blood*) stillen; (*in skiing*) stemmen ‖ intr—**s. from** (ab)stammen von
stench [stɛntʃ] s Gestank m
sten•cil ['stɛnsɪl] s (*for printing*) Schablone f; (*for typing*) Matrize f ‖ v (*pret & pp* **-cil[l]ed**; ger **-cil[l]ing**) tr mittels Schablone aufmalen
stenographer [stə'nɑgrəfər] s Stenograph –in mf
stenography [stə'nɑgrəfi] s Stenographie f
step [stɛp] s Schritt m; (*of a staircase*) Stufe f; (*footprint*) Fußtritt m;

(*measure*) Maßnahme *f;* **be out of s.** nicht Schritt halten; **in. s.** im Takt; **keep in s. with the times** mit der Zeit Schritt halten; **s. by s.** schrittweise; **watch your s.!** Vorsicht! ‖ *v* (*pret & pp* **stepped;** *ger* **stepping**) *tr*—**s. down** (elec) heruntertransformieren; **s. off** abschreiten ‖ *intr* schreiten, treten; **s. aside** beiseitetreten; **s. back** zurücktreten; **s. forward** vortreten; **s. on** betreten; **s. on it** (coll) sich beeilen; **s. on s.o.'s toes** (fig) j–m auf die Zehen treten; **s. out** hinausgehen; **s. out on** (*a marriage partner*) betrügen

step′broth′er *s* Stiefbruder *m*

step′child′ *s* (**–chil′dren**) Stiefkind *n*

step′daugh′ter *s* Stieftochter *f*

step′fa′ther *s* Stiefvater *m*

step′lad′der *s* Stehleiter *f*

step′moth′er *s* Stiefmutter *f*

steppe [stɛp] *s* Steppe *f*

step′ping stone′ *s* Trittstein *m;* (fig) Sprungbrett *n*

step′sis′ter *s* Stiefschwester *f*

step′son′ *s* Stiefsohn *m*

stere·o [′stɛrɪ‚o] *adj* Stereo– ‖ *s* (**–os**) (*sound*) Stereoton *m,* Raumton *m;* (*reproduction*) Raumtonwiedergabe *f;* (*set*) Stereoapparat *m*

stereotyped [′stɛrɪ‑ə‚taɪpt] *adj* (& fig) stereotyp

sterile [′stɛrɪl] *adj* keimfrei

sterility [stɛ′rɪlɪtɪ] *s* Sterilität *f*

sterilize [′stɛrɪ‚laɪz] *tr* sterilisieren

sterling [′stʌrlɪŋ] *adj* (fig) gediegen ‖ *s* (*currency*) Sterling *m;* (*sterling silver*) Sterlingsilber *n;* (*articles of sterling silver*) Sterlingsilberwaren *pl*

stern [stʌrn] *adj* streng; (*look*) finster ‖ *s* (naut) Heck *n*

stethoscope [′stɛθə‚skop] *s* Stethoskop *n*

stevedore [′stivə‚dor] *s* Stauer *m*

stew [st(j)u] *s* Ragout *n,* Stew *n* ‖ *tr & intr* dünsten; (& fig) schmoren

steward [′st(j)u‑ərd] *s* (aer, naut) Steward *m;* (*of an estate*) Gutsverwalter *m;* (*of a club*) Tafelmeister *m*

stewardess [′st(j)u‑ərdɪs] *s* (aer, naut) Stewardeß *f*

stewed′ fruit′ *s* Kompott *n*

stick [stɪk] *s* Stecken *m,* Stock *m;* (*for punishment*) Prügel *pl;* (*of candy or gum*) Stange *f;* **the sticks** (coll) die Provinz *f* ‖ *tr* (*with a sharp point; into one's pocket*) stecken; (*paste*) (**on**) ankleben (an *acc*); **s. it out** durchhalten; **s. one's finger** sich in den Finger stechen; **s. out** herausstrecken; **s. up** überfallen und berauben ‖ *intr* (*adhere*) kleben; (*be stuck, be tight*) klemmen; **nothing sticks in his mind** (coll) bei ihm bleibt nichts haften; **s. around** (coll) in der Nähe bleiben; **s. by** (coll) bleiben bei; **s. close to** sich heften an (*acc*); **s. out** (*said of ears*) abstehen; (*be visible*) heraushängen; **s. to** (fig) beharren auf (*dat*); **s. together** zusammenkleben; (fig) zusammenhalten; **s. up for** sich einsetzen für

sticker [′stɪkər] *s* Klebezettel *m*

stick′-in-the-mud′ *s* (coll) Schlafmütze *f*

stickler [′stɪklər] *s* (**for**) Pedant *m* (in dat)

stick′pin′ *s* Krawattennadel *f*

stick′-up′ *s* (sl) Raubüberfall *m*

sticky [′stɪki] *adj* klebrig; (*air*) schwül; (*ticklish*) heikel

stiff [stɪf] *adj* steif; (*difficult*) schwer; (*drink*) stark; (*opposition*) hartnäckig; (*sentence*) streng; (*bearing*) steif; (*price*) hoch; **s. as a board** stocksteif ‖ *s* (*corpse*) (sl) Leiche *f;* **big s.** (sl) blöder Kerl *m*

stiffen [′stɪfən] *tr* versteifen ‖ *intr* sich versteifen

stiffly [′stɪfli] *adv* gezwungen

stiff′-necked′ *adj* mit steifem Hals; (fig) eigensinnig

stifle [′staɪfəl] *tr* (*a yawn*) unterdrücken; (*a person*) ersticken

stig·ma [′stɪgmə] *s* (**–mas & mata** [mətə]) Brandmal *n;* stigmata Wundmale *pl* Christi

stigmatize [′stɪgmə‚taɪz] *tr* brandmarken

stile [staɪl] *s* Stiege *f*

stilet·to [stɪ′lɛto] *s* (**–os**) Stilett *n*

still [stɪl] *adj* still, ruhig ‖ *adv* (*up to this time, as yet, even*) noch; (*yet, nevertheless*) dennoch; **keep s.** stillbleiben ‖ *s* (*stillness*) Stille *f;* (*for whiskey*) Brennapparat *m;* (cin) Einzelphotographie *f;* (phot) Standphoto *n* ‖ *tr* stillen

still′born′ *adj* totgeboren

still′ life′ *s* (**still lifes & still lives**) Stilleben *n*

stilt [stɪlt] *s* Stelze *f*

stilt′ed *adj* (*style*) geschraubt; (archit) auf Pfeilern ruhend

stimulant [′stɪmjələnt] *s* Reizmittel *n;* **act as a s.** anregend wirken

stimulate [′stɪmjə‚let] *tr* anregen

stimulation [‚stɪmjə′leʃən] *s* Anregung *f*

stimu·lus [′stɪmjələs] *s* (**–li** [‚laɪ]) (& fig) Reizmittel *n;* (fig) Ansporn *m*

sting [stɪŋ] *s* Biß *m,* Stich *m;* (*stinging organ*) Stachel *m* ‖ *v* (*pret & pp* **stung** [stʌŋ]) *tr & intr* stechen

stingy [′stɪndʒi] *adj* geizig

stink [stɪŋk] *s* Gestank *m;* (sl) Krach *m* ‖ *v* (*pret* **stank** [stæŋk]; **stunk** [stʌŋk]) *tr*—**s. up** verstänkern ‖ *intr* stinken

stinker [′stɪŋkər] *s* (sl) Stinker *m*

stinky [′stɪŋki] *adj* stinkend, stinkig

stint [stɪnt] *s* bestimmte Arbeit *f;* **without s.** freigebig ‖ *tr* einschränken ‖ *intr* (**on**) knausern (mit)

stipend [′staɪpənd] *s* (*salary*) Gehalt *n;* (*of a scholarship*) Zuwendung *f*

stipple [′stɪpəl] *tr* punktieren

stipulate [′stɪpjə‚let] *tr* bedingen; **as stipulated** wie vertraglich festgelegt

stipulation [‚stɪpjə′leʃən] *s* Bedingung *f*

stir [stʌr] *s* (*movement*) Bewegung *f;* (*unrest*) Unruhe *f;* (*commotion, ex-*

citement) Aufsehen *n;* **create quite a s.** großes Aufsehen erregen || *v* (*pret* & *pp* **stirred**; *ger* **stirring**) *tr* *e.g.*, *with a spoon*) (um)rühren; (*the fire*) schüren; **s. up** (*hatred*) entfachen; (*trouble*) stiften; (*people*) aufhetzen || *intr* sich rühren

stir′ring *adj* erregend; (*times*) bewegt; (*speech*) mitreißend; (*song*) schwungvoll

stirrup ['stʌrəp] *s* Steigbügel *m*

stitch [stɪtʃ] *s* Stich *m;* (*in knitting*) Masche *f;* **stitches** (*surg*) Naht *f;* **s. in the side** Seitenstechen *n* || *tr* heften; (*surg*) nähen

stock [stɑk] *s* (*supplies*) Lager *n;* (*of a gun*) Schaft *m;* (*lineage*) Zucht *f;* (*of paper*) Papierstoff *m;* (*culin*) Fond *m;* (*st. exch.*) Aktie *f;* **in s.** vorrätig, auf Lager; **not put much s. in** nicht viel Wert legen auf (*acc*); **out of s.** nicht (mehr) vorrätig; (*books*) vergriffen; **stocks** (*hist*) Stock *m;* **take s.** den Bestand aufnehmen; **take s. of** (fig) in Betracht ziehen || *tr* auf Lager halten; (*a stream*) (mit Fischen) besetzen; (*a farm*) ausstatten || *intr*—**s. up** (on) sich eindecken (mit)

stockade [stɑ′ked] *s* Palisade *f;* (mil) Gefängnis *n*

stock′breed′er *s* Viehzüchter –in *mf*

stock′brok′er *s* Börsenmakler –in *mf*

stock′ car′ *s* (aut) Serienwagen *m;* (sport) als Rennwagen hergerichteter Personenkraftwagen *m*

stock′ com′pany *s* (com) Aktiengesellschaft *f;* (theat) Repertoiregruppe *f*

stock′ div′idend *s* Aktiendividende *f*

stock′ exchange′ *s* Börse *f*

stock′hold′er *s* Aktionär –in *mf*

stock′ing *s* Strumpf *m*

stock′ in trade′ *s* Warenbestand *m;* (fig) Rüstzeug *n*

stock′pile′ *s* Vorrat *m* || *tr* aufstapeln

stock′room′ *s* Lagerraum *m*

stocky ['stɑki] *adj* untersetzt

stock′yard′ *s* Viehhof *m*

stodgy ['stɑdʒi] *adj* gezwungen

stogy ['stogi] *s* (coll) Glimmstengel *m*

stoic ['sto·ɪk] *adj* stoisch || *s* Stoiker *m*

stoke [stok] *tr* (*a fire*) schüren; (*a furnace*) heizen

stoker ['stokər] *s* Heizer *m*

stole [stol] *s* (*woman's fur piece*) Pelzstola *f;* (eccl) Stola *f*

stolid ['stɑlɪd] *adj* unempfindlich

stomach ['stʌmək] *s* Magen *m;* (fig) (**for**) Lust *f* (zu) || *tr* (*food*) verdauen; (fig) vertragen

stom′ach ache′ *s* Magenschmerzen *pl*

stone [ston] *adj* steinern || *s* Stein *m;* (*of fruit*) Kern *m;* (pathol) Stein *m* || *tr* steinigen; (*fruit*) entsteinen

stone′ age′ *s* Steinzeit *f*

stone′-broke′ *adj* (coll) völlig abgebrannt

stone′-deaf′ *adj* stocktaub

stone′ ma′son *s* Steinmetz *m*

stone′ quar′ry *s* Steinbruch *m*

stone′s′ throw′ *s* Katzensprung *m*

stony ['stoni] *adj* steinig

stooge [studʒ] *s* Lakai *m*

stool [stul] *s* Schemel *m;* (*e.g., at a bar*) Hocker *m;* (*bowel movement*) Stuhl *m*

stool′ pi′geon *s* Polizeispitzel *m*

stoop [stup] *s* Beugung *f;* (*condition of the body*) gebeugte Körperhaltung *f;* (*porch*) kleine Veranda *f* || *intr* sich bücken; (*demean oneself*) sich erniedrigen

stoop′-shoul′dered *adj* gebeugt

stop [stɑp] *s* (*for a bus or streetcar*) Haltestelle *f;* (*layover*) Aufenthalt *m;* (*station*) Station *f;* (*of an organ*) Register *n;* (ling) Verschlußlaut *m;* **bring to a s.** zum Halten bringen; **come to a s.** anhalten; **put a s. to** ein Ende machen (*dat*) || *v* (*pret* & *pp* **stopped**; *ger* **stopping**) *tr* (*an activity*) aufhören mit; (ger) aufhören (zu *inf*); (*e.g., a thief, car*) anhalten; (*bring to a stop with difficulty*) zum Halten bringen; (*delay, detain*) aufhalten; (*a leak*) stopfen; (*a check*) sperren; (*payment*) einstellen; (*the blood*) stillen; (*traffic*) lahmlegen; **s. down** (phot) abblenden; **s. s.o. from** (ger) j-n davonhalten zu (*inf*) || *intr* (*cease*) aufhören; (*come to a stop; break down*) stehenbleiben; (*said of a person stopping for a short time or of a vehicle at an unscheduled stop*) anhalten; (*said of a vehicle at a scheduled stop*) halten; **s. at nothing** vor nichts zurückschrecken; **s. dead** plötzlich stehenbleiben; **s. in** vorbeikommen; **s. off at e–n kurzen Halt machen bei**

stop′gap′ *adj* Not–, Behelfs– || *s* Notbehelf *m*

stop′light′ *s* (*on a car*) Bremslicht *n;* (*traffic light*) Verkehrsampel *f*

stop′o′ver *s* Fahrtunterbrechung *f;* (aer) Zwischenlandung *f*

stoppage ['stɑpɪdʒ] *s* (*of a pipe*) Verstopfung *f;* (*of payment, of work*) Einstellung *f;* (pathol) Verstopfung *f*

stopper ['stɑpər] *s* Stöpsel *m;* (*made of cork*) Korken *m*

stop′ sign′ *s* Haltezeichen *n*

stop′watch′ *s* Stoppuhr *f*

storage ['storɪdʒ] *s* Lagerung *f*

stor′age bat′tery *s* Akkumulator *m*

stor′age charge′ *s* Lagergebühr *f*

stor′age room′ *s* Rumpelkammer *f;* (com) Lagerraum *m*

stor′age tank′ *s* Sammelbehälter *m*

store [stor] *s* (*small shop*) Laden *m;* (*large shop*) Geschäft *n;* (*supply*) Vorrat *m;* **be in s. for** bevorstehen (*dat*); **have in s. for** bereithalten für; **set great s. by** viel Wert legen auf (*acc*); **s. of knowledge** Wissenschatz *m* || *tr* einlagern; (*in the attic*) auf den Speicher stellen; **s. up** aufspeichern

store′house′ *s* Lagerhaus *n;* (fig) Schatz *m,* Fundgrube *f*

store′keep′er *s* Ladeninhaber –in *mf*

store'room' s Lagerraum m, Vorrats-
raum m

stork [stork] s Storch m

storm [storm] s Sturm m; (thunderstorm) Gewitter n; (fig) Sturm m;
take by s. (& fig) im Sturm nehmen
‖ tr (er)stürmen ‖ intr stürmen

storm' cloud' s Gewitterwolke f

storm' door' s Doppeltür f

storm' warn'ing s Sturmwarnung f

storm' win'dow s Doppelfenster n

stormy ['stormi] adj stürmisch

story ['stori] s Geschichte f; (floor)
Stock m, Stockwerk n; that's another
s. das ist e–e Sache für sich

sto'rybook' s Geschichtenbuch n

sto'rytell'er s Erzähler –in mf

stout [staut] adj beleibt; (heart) tapfer
‖ s Starkbier n

stout'-heart'ed adj beherzt

stove [stov] s Ofen m, Küchenherd m

stove'pipe' s Ofenrohr n; (coll) Angst-
röhre f

stow [sto] tr stauen; s. away verstauen
‖ intr—s. away als blinder Passagier
mitreisen

stowage ['sto·ɪdʒ] s Stauen n; (costs)
Staugebühr f

stow'away' s blinder Passagier m

straddle ['strædəl] tr mit gespreizten
Beinen sitzen auf (dat)

strafe [stref] tr im Tiefflug mit Bord-
waffen angreifen

straggle ['strægəl] intr abschweifen

straggler ['stræglər] s Nachzügler –in
mf; (mil) Versprengte m

straight [stret] adj gerade; (honest)
aufrecht; (candid) offen; (hair) glatt;
(story) wahr; (uninterrupted) ununterbrochen; (whiskey) unverdünnt
‖ adv (directly) direkt; (without interruption) ununterbrochen; give it
to s.o. s. j–m die ungeschminkte
Wahrheit sagen; go s. (fig) seinen
geraden Weg gehen; is my hat on s.?
sitzt mein Hut richtig?; make s. for
zuhalten auf (acc); set the record s.
den Sachverhalt klarstellen; s. ahead
(immer) geradeaus; s. as an arrow
pfeilgerade; s. from the horse's
mouth (coll) aus erster Hand; s.
home schnurstracks nach Hause; s.
off ohne weiteres ‖ s (cards) Buch n

straight'away' adv geradewegs, sofort
‖ s (sport) Gerade f

straighten ['stretən] tr gerade machen;
(e.g., a tablecloth) glattziehen; s. out
(fig) wieder in Ordnung bringen; s.
s.o.'s tie j–m die Krawatte zurecht-
rücken; s. up (a room) aufräumen ‖
intr gerade werden; s. up sich aufrichten

straight' face' s—keep a s. keine
Miene verziehen

straight'for'ward adj aufrichtig

straight' left' s (box) linke Gerade f

straight' man' s Stichwortgeber m

straight' ra'zor s Rasiermesser n

straight' right' s (box) rechte Gerade f

straight'way' adv auf der Stelle

strain [stren] s Belastung f; (of a muscle or tendon) Zerrung f; (task re-
quiring effort) (coll) Strapaze f;
(stock, family) Linie f; (trait) Erbei-
genschaft f; (bot) Art f; without s.
mühelos ‖ tr (filter) durchseihen;
(the eyes, nerves) überanstrengen;
s. oneself (make a great effort) sich
überanstrengen; (in lifting) sich
überheben; s. the truth übertreiben
‖ intr sich anstrengen; s. after sich
abmühen um; s. at ziehen an (dat),
zerren an (dat)

strained adj (smile) gezwungen; (relations) gespannt

strainer ['strenər] s Seiher m, Filter m

strait [stret] s Straße f; financial straits
finanzielle Schwierigkeiten pl; straits
Meerenge f

strait' jack'et s Zwangsjacke f

strait'-laced' adj sittenstreng

strand [strænd] s Strähne f; (beach)
Strand m; s. of pearls Perlenschnur
f ‖ tr auf den Strand setzen; (fig)
stranden lassen; be stranded (fig) in
der Patsche sitzen; get stranded auflaufen; leave s.o. stranded j–n im
Stich lassen

strange [strendʒ] adj (quaint) sonderbar; (foreign) fremd; s. character
Sonderling m ‖ adv—s. to say merkwürdigerweise

stranger ['strendʒər] s Fremde mf

strangle ['stræŋgəl] tr erwürgen ‖ intr
ersticken

stran'glehold' s Würgegriff m

strap [stræp] s Riemen m, Gurt m; (of
metal) Band n f ‖ v (pret & pp
strapped; ger strapping) tr (to) anschnallen (an acc); (a razor) abziehen

strap'ping adj stramm

stratagem ['strætədʒəm] s Kriegslist f

strategic(al) [strə'tidʒɪk(əl)] adj strategisch

strategist ['strætɪdʒɪst] s Stratege m

strategy ['strætɪdʒi] s Strategie f

stratification [ˌstrætɪfɪ'keʃən] s Schich-
tung f

strati·fy ['strætɪˌfaɪ] v (pret & pp
-fied) tr schichten ‖ intr Schichten
bilden

stratosphere ['strætəˌsfɪr] s Strato-
sphäre f

stra·tum ['stretəm], ['strætəm] s (-ta
[tə] & -tums) Schicht f

straw [stro] adj (e.g., hat, man, mat)
Stroh– ‖ s Stroh n; (single stalk; for
drinking) Strohhalm m; that's the
last s.! das schlägt dem Faß den
Boden aus!

straw'ber'ry s Erdbeere f

straw'berry blond' adj rotblond

straw' mat'tress s Strohsack m

straw' vote' s Probeabstimmung f

stray [stre] adj (e.g., bullet) verirrt;
(cat, dog) streunend; s. shell (mil)
Ausreißer m ‖ s verirrtes Tier n ‖
intr herumirren; (fig) abschweifen

streak [strik] s Streifen m; like a s.
wie der Blitz; s. of bad luck Pechsträhne f; s. of luck Glückssträhne
f; s. of light Lichtstreifen m ‖ tr
streifen ‖ intr streifig werden; s.
along vorbeisausen

streaky ['striːki] *adj* gestreift; (*uneven*) (coll) ungleich(mäßig)

stream [striːm] *s* Fluß *m*; (*of people, cars, air, blood, lava*) Strom *m*; (*of words*) Schwall *m*; (*of tears*) Flut *f*; (*of a liquid*) Strahl *m* ‖ *intr* (aus)strömen

streamer ['striːmər] *s* (*pennant*) Wimpel *m*; (*ribbon*) herabhängendes Band *n*; (*rolled crepe paper*) Papierschlange *f*

stream'line' *tr* in Stromlinienform bringen; (fig) reorganizieren

stream'lined' *adj* stromlinienförmig

street [striːt] *s* Straße *f*

street'car' *s* Straßenbahn *f*

street' clean'er *s* Straßenkehrer –in *mf*; (*truck*) Straßenkehrmaschine *f*

street' fight' *s* Straßenschlacht *f*

street'light' *s* Straßenlaterne *f*

street' sign' *s* Straßenschild *n*

street' ven'dor *s* Straßenhändler –in *mf*

street'walk'er *s* Straßendirne *f*

strength [strɛŋθ] *s* Kraft *f*; (*strong point*; *potency of alcohol*; *moral or mental power*) Stärke *f*; (mil) Kopfstärke *f*; bodily s. Körperkraft *f*; on the s. of auf Grund (*genit*)

strengthen ['strɛŋθən] *tr* stärken; (fig) bestärken ‖ *intr* stärker werden

strenuous ['strɛnjʊ·əs] *adj* anstrengend; s. effort Kraftanstrengung *f*

stress [strɛs] *s* (*emphasis, weight*) Nachdruck *m*; (*mental* Belastung *f*; (mus, pros) Ton *m*, Betonung *f*; (phys) Beanspruchung *f*, Spannung *f* ‖ *tr* (& mus, pros) betonen

stress' ac'cent *s* Betonungsakzent *m*

stress' mark' *s* Betonungszeichen *n*

stretch [strɛtʃ] *s* (*of road*) Strecke *f*; (*of the limbs*) Strecken *n*; (*of water*) Fläche *f*; (*of a racetrack*) Gerade *f*; (*of years*) Zeitspanne *f*; do a s. (sl) brummen; in one's. in e–m Zug ‖ *tr* (*a rope*) spannen; (*one's neck*) rekken; (*shoes, gloves*) ausdehnen; (*wire*) ziehen; (*strings of an instrument*) straffziehen; s. a point es nicht allzu genau nehmen; s. oneself sich strecken; s. one's legs sich [*dat*] die Beine vertreten; s. out (*e.g., hands*) ausstrecken ‖ *intr* sich (aus)dehnen; (*said of a person*) sich strecken; s. out on sich ausstrecken auf (*dat*)

stretcher ['strɛtʃər] *s* Tragbahre *f*

stretch'erbear'er *s* Krankenträger *m*

strew [struː] *v* (*pret* strewed; *pp* strewed & strewn) *tr* (aus)streuen; s. with bestreuen mit

stricken ['strɪkən] *adj* (with *e.g.*, *misfortune*) heimgesucht (von); (with *e.g.*, *fear, grief*) ergriffen (von); (*with a disease*) befallen (von)

strict [strɪkt] *adj* streng; in s. confidence streng vertraulich

strictly ['strɪktli] *adv* streng; s. speaking genau genommen

stricture ['strɪktʃər] *s* (on) kritische Bemerkung *f* (über *acc*)

stride [straɪd] *s* Schritt *m*; hit one's. auf Touren kommen; make great

strides große Fortschritte machen; take in s. ruhig hinnehmen ‖ *v* (*pret* strode [stroːd]; *pp* stridden ['strɪdən]) *intr* schreiten; s. along tüchtig ausschreiten

strident ['straɪdənt] *adj* schrill

strife [straɪf] *s* Streit *m*, Hader *m*

strike [straɪk] *s* (*work stoppage*) Streik *m*; (*blow*) Schlag *m*; (*discovery, e.g., of oil*) Fund *m*; (baseball) Fehlschlag *m*; go on s. in Streik treten ‖ *v* (*pret* & *pp* struck [strʌk]) *tr* (*a person, the hours, coins, strings of an instrument*) schlagen; (*a match*) anstreichen; (*a bargain*) schließen; (*a note*) greifen; (go on strike against*) bestreiken; (*a tent*) abbrechen; (*oil*) stoßen auf (*acc*); (*run into*) auffahren auf (*acc*); (*s.o. blind, dumb*) machen; (*s.o. with fear*) erfüllen; (*a blow*) versetzen; (*a pose*) einnehmen; (*seem to s.o.*) erscheinen (*dat*); s. it rich auf e–e Goldader stoßen; s. fear into s.o. j–m e–n Schrecken einjagen; s. up (*a conversation, an acquaintance*) anknüpfen; (*a song*) anstimmen ‖ *intr* (*said of a person or clock*) schlagen; (*said of workers*) streiken; (*said of lightning*) einschlagen; s. home Eindruck machen; s. out (& fig) fehlschlagen

strike'break'er *s* Streikbrecher –in *mf*

striker ['straɪkər] *s* Streikende *mf*

strik'ing *adj* auffallend; (*example*) treffend; (*workers*) streikend

strik'ing pow'er *s* Schlagkraft *f*

string [strɪŋ] *s* Bindfaden *m*; (*row, series*) Reihe *f*; (*of a bow*) Sehne *f*; (*of a musical instrument*) Saite *f*; pull strings (fig) der Drahtzieher sein; s. of pearls Perlenkette *f*; strings (mus) Streicher *pl*; with no strings attached ohne einschränkende Bedingungen ‖ *v* (*pret* & *pp* strung [strʌŋ]) *tr* (*pearls*) auf e–e Schnur (auf)reihen; (*a bow*) spannen; s. along hinhalten; s. up (coll) aufknüpfen

string' band' *s* Streichorchester *n*

string' bean' *s* grüne Bohne *f*; (*tall, thin person*) Bohnenstange *f*

stringed' in'strument *s* Saiteninstrument *n*

stringent ['strɪndʒənt] *adj* streng

string' quartet' *s* Streichquartett *n*

stringy ['strɪŋi] *adj* (*vegetables*) holzig; (*meat*) sehnig; (*hair*) zottelig

strip [strɪp] *s* Streifen *m* ‖ *v* (*pret* & *pp* stripped; *ger* stripping) *tr* (off) abziehen; (*clothes*) (off) abstreifen; (*a thread*) überdrehen; (*gears*) beschädigen; s. down abmontieren; s.o. of office j–n seines Amtes entkleiden ‖ *intr* sich ausziehen

stripe [straɪp] *s* Streifen *m*; (*elongated welt*) Striemen *m*; (mil) Tresse *f* ‖ *tr* streifen

strip' mine' *s* Tagebau *m*

stripper ['strɪpər] *s* Stripperin *f*

strip'tease' *s* Entkleidungsnummer *f*

stripteaser ['strɪp‚tiːzər] *s* Stripperin *f*

strive [straɪv] *v* (*pret* strove [stroːv];

pp **striven** ['strɪvən]) *intr* (**for**) streben (nach); **s. to** (*inf*) sich bemühen zu (*inf*)

stroke [strok] *s* Schlag *m*; (*caress with the hand*) Streicheln *n*; (*of a piston*) Hub *m*; (*of a pen, brush*) Strich *m*; (*of a sword*) Hieb *m*; (*in swimming*) Schwimmstoß *m*; (*of the leg*) Beinstoß *m*; (*of an oar*) Schlag *m*; (*pathol*) Schlaganfall *m*; **at a single s.** mit e-m Schlag; **at the s.** of **twelve** Schlag zwölf Uhr; **not do a s. of work** keinen Strich tun; **she'll have a s.** (coll) dann trifft sie der Schlag; **s. of genius** Genieblitz *m*; **s. of luck** Glücksfall *m*; **with a s. of the pen** mit e-m Federstrich ‖ *tr* streicheln

stroll [strol] *s* Spaziergang *m* ‖ *intr* spazieren

stroller ['strolər] *s* Spaziergänger *m* in *mf*; (*for a baby*) Kindersportwagen *m*

strong [strɔŋ] *adj* kräftig; (*firm*) fest; (*drink, smell, light, wind, feeling*) stark; (*glasses*) scharf; (*wine*) schwer; (*suspicion*) dringend; (*memory*) gut; (*candidate*) aussichtsreich; (*argument*) triftig

strong'-arm' *adj* (*e.g., methods*) Zwangs–

strong'box' *s* Geldschrank *m*

strong'hold' *s* Feste *f*; (fig) Hochburg *f*

strong' lan'guage *s* Kraftausdrücke *pl*

strongly ['strɔŋli] *adv* nachdrücklich; **feel s. about** sich sehr einsetzen für

strong'-mind'ed *adj* willensstark

strontium ['strɑn/ɪ-əm] *s* Strontium *n*

strop [strɑp] *s* Streichriemen *m* ‖ *v* (*pret & pp* **stropped**; *ger* **stropping**) *tr* abziehen

strophe ['strofi] *s* Strophe *f*

structural ['strʌkt/ərəl] *adj* strukturell, Bau–

structure ['strʌkt/ər] *s* Struktur *f*; (*building*) Bau *m*

struggle ['strʌgəl] *s* Kampf *m* ‖ *intr* (**for**) kämpfen (um); **s. against** ankämpfen gegen; **s. to one's feet** sich mit Mühe erheben

strum [strʌm] *v* (*pret & pp* **strummed**; *ger* **strumming**) *tr* klimpern auf (*dat*)

strumpet ['strʌmpɪt] *s* Dirne *f*

strut [strʌt] *s* (*brace*) Strebebalken *m*; (*haughty walk*) stolzer Gang *m* ‖ *v* (*pret & pp* **strutted**; *ger* **strutting**) *intr* stolzieren

strychnine ['strɪknaɪn] *s* Strychnin *n*

stub [stʌb] *s* (*of a checkbook*) Abschnitt *m*; (*of a ticket*) Kontrollabschnitt *m*; (*of a candle, pencil, cigarette*) Stummel *m* ‖ *v* (*pret & pp* **stubbed**; *ger* **stubbing**) *tr*—**s. one's toe** sich an der Zehe stoßen

stubble ['stʌbəl] *s* Stoppel *f*; (*facial hair*) Bartstoppeln *pl*

stubbly ['stʌbli] *adj* stopp(e)lig

stubborn ['stʌbərn] *adj* eigensinnig; (*e.g., resistance*) hartnäckig; (*hair*) widerspenstig

stubby ['stʌbi] *adj* kurz und dick; (*person*) untersetzt

stuc·co ['stʌko] *s* (**-coes & -cos**) Verputz *m* ‖ *tr* verputzen

stuc'co work' *s* Verputzarbeit *f*

stuck [stʌk] *adj*—**be s.** feststecken; (*said, e.g., of a lock*) klemmen; **be s. on** vernarrt sein in (*acc*); **get s.** steckenbleiben

stuck'-up' *adj* (coll) hochnäsig

stud [stʌd] *s* (*ornament*) Ziernagel *m*; (*horse*) Zuchthengst *m*; (archit) Wandpfosten *m* ‖ *v* (*pret & pp* **studded**; *ger* **studding**) *tr* mit Ziernägeln verzieren

stud' bolt' *s* Schraubenbolzen *m*

student ['st(j)udənt] *adj* Studenten– ‖ *s* (*in college*) Student –in *mf*; (*in grammar or high school*) Schüler –in *mf*; (*scholar*) Gelehrte *mf*

stu'dent bod'y *s* Studentenschaft *f*

stu'dent nurse' *s* Krankenpflegerin *f* in Ausbildung

stud' farm' *s* Gestüt *n*

stud'horse' *s* Zuchthengst *m*

stud'ied *adj* gesucht

studi·o ['st(j)udɪ‚o] *s* (**-os**) (fa, phot) Atelier *n*; (cin, fa, phot, telv) Studio *n*

studious ['st(j)udɪ-əs] *adj* fleißig

stud·y ['stʌdi] *s* Studium *n*; (*room*) Studierzimmer *n*; (paint) Studie *f* ‖ *v* (*pret & pp* **-ied**) *tr & intr* studieren

stuff [stʌf] *s* Stoff *m*; (coll) Kram *m*; **do your s.!** (coll) schieß los!; **know one's s.** (coll) sich auskennen ‖ *tr* (*animals*) ausstopfen; (*a cushion*) polstern; (*e.g., cotton in the ears*) sich [*dat*] stopfen; (culin) füllen; **s. oneself** sich vollstopfen

stuffed' shirt' *s* steifer, eingebildeter Mensch *m*

stuff'ing *s* Polstermaterial *n*; (culin) Fülle *f*

stuffy ['stʌfi] *adj* (*room*) stickig; (*nose*) verstopft; (*person*) steif

stumble ['stʌmbəl] *intr* stolpern; (*in reading*) holpern; **s. across** stoßen auf (*acc*)

stum'bling block' *s* Stein *m* des Anstoßes

stump [stʌmp] *s* (*of an arm, tree, cigarette, pencil*) Stummel *m* ‖ *tr* (*a cigarette*) ausdrücken; (*nonplus*) verblüffen; (*a district, state*) als Wahlredner bereisen

stump' speak'er *s* Wahlredner –in *mf*

stun [stʌn] *v* (*pret & pp* **stunned**; *ger* **stunning**) *tr* betäuben

stun'ning *adj* (coll) phantastisch

stunt [stʌnt] *s* Kunststück *n*; **do stunts** Kunststücke vorführen ‖ *tr* hemmen

stunt'ed *adj* verkümmert

stunt' fly'ing *s* Kunstflug *m*

stunt' man' s (**men'**) Sensationsdarsteller *m*

stupe·fy ['st(j)upɪ‚faɪ] *v* (*pret & pp* **-fied**) *tr* verblüffen

stupendous [st(j)u'pɛndəs] *adj* erstaunlich

stupid ['st(j)upɪd] *adj* dumm, blöd

stupidity [st(j)u'pɪdɪti] *s* Dummheit *f*

stupor ['st(j)upər] *s* Stumpfsinn *m*

sturdy ['stʌrdi] *adj* (*person*) kräftig;

(thing) stabil; *(resolute)* standhaft; *(plant)* widerstandsfähig

sturgeon [ˈstɜːdʒən] s Stör m

stutter [ˈstʌtər] s Stottern n ‖ tr & intr stottern

sty [staɪ] s Schweinestall m; *(pathol)* Gerstenkorn n

style [staɪl] s Stil m; *(manner)* Art f; *(fashion)* Mode f; *(cut of suit)* Schnitt m; **be in s.** in Mode sein; **go out of s.** veralten; **live in s.** auf großem Fuße leben ‖ tr *(title)* betiteln; *(e.g., clothes)* gestalten; *(hair)* nach der Mode frisieren

stylish [ˈstaɪlɪʃ] adj modisch; *(person)* modisch gekleidet

stylistic [staɪˈlɪstɪk] adj stilistisch

stymie [ˈstaɪmɪ] tr vereiteln

styp′tic pen′cil [ˈstɪptɪk] s Alaunstift m

suave [swɑːv] adj verbindlich

sub [sʌb] s *(naut)* U-boot n; *(sport)* Ersatzspieler –in mf

sub′chas′er s U-bootjäger m

sub′com·mit′tee s Unterausschuß m

subconscious [sʌbˈkɑnʃəs] adj unterbewußt ‖ s Unterbewußtsein n

sub′con′tinent s Subkontinent m

sub′con′tract s Nebenvertrag m ‖ tr e–n Nebenvertrag abschließen über *(acc)*

sub′con′tractor s Unterlieferant –in mf

sub′divide′, sub′divide′ tr unterteilen ‖ intr sich unterteilen

sub′divi′sion s *(act)* Unterteilung f; *(unit)* Unterabteilung f

subdue [səbˈd(j)u] tr *(an enemy)* unterwerfen; *(one who is struggling)* überwältigen; *(light, sound)* dämpfen; *(feelings, impulses)* bändigen

sub′floor′ s Blindboden m

sub′head′ s Untertitel m

subject [ˈsʌbdʒɪkt] adj *(to)* untertan *(dat)*; **be s. to** *(e.g., approval, another country)* abhängig sein von; *(e.g., colds)* neigen zu; *(e.g., laws of nature, change)* unterworfen sein *(dat)*; **s. to change without notice** Änderungen vorbehalten ‖ s Thema n; *(of a kingdom)* Untertan –in mf; *(educ)* Fach n; *(fa)* Vorwurf m; *(gram)* Satzgegenstand m, Subjekt n; *(libr)* Stichwort n; **change the s.** das Thema wechseln; **get off the s.** vom Thema abkommen ‖ [səbˈdʒɛkt] tr *(& fig)* unterwerfen *(dat)*

subjection [səbˈdʒɛkʃən] s Unterwerfung f

subjective [səbˈdʒɛktɪv] adj subjektiv; **s. case** Werfall m

sub′ject mat′ter s Inhalt m

subjugate [ˈsʌbdʒəˌget] tr unterjochen

subjunctive [səbˈdʒʌŋktɪv] adj konjunktiv(isch) ‖ s Konjunktiv m

sub′lease′ s Untermiete f ‖ **sub′lease′** tr & intr *(to s.o.)* untervermieten; *(from s.o.)* untermieten

sublet [səbˈlet] v *(pret & pp* –let; *ger* –letting) tr & intr *(to s.o.)* untervermieten; *(from s.o.)* untermieten

sublimate [ˈsʌblɪmət] s *(chem)* Sublimat n ‖ [ˈsʌblɪˌmet] tr sublimieren

sublime [səˈblaɪm] adj erhaben ‖ s Erhabene n

submachine′ gun′ s Maschinenpistole f

sub′marine′ adj U-boot– ‖ s U-boot n

sub′marine′ base′ s U-bootstützpunkt m

submerge [səbˈmʌrdʒ] tr & intr untertauchen; **ready to s.** tauchklar

submersion [səbˈmʌrʒən] s Untertauchen n

submission [səbˈmɪʃən] s *(to)* Unterwerfung f *(unter acc)*; *(of a document)* Vorlage f; *(of a question)* Unterbreitung f

submissive [səbˈmɪsɪv] adj unterwürfig

sub·mit′ [səbˈmɪt] v *(pret & pp* –mitted; *ger* –mitting) tr *(a question)* unterbreiten; *(a document)* vorlegen; *(suggest)* der Ansicht sein ‖ intr *(to)* sich unterwerfen *(dat)*

subordinate [səbˈɔrdɪnɪt] adj *(lower in rank)* untergeordnet; *(secondary)* Neben– ‖ s Untergebene mf ‖ [səbˈɔrdɪˌnet] tr *(to)* unterordnen *(dat)*

subor′dinate clause′ s Nebensatz m

suborn [səˈbɔrn] tr verleiten; *(bribe)* bestechen

sub′plot′ s Nebenhandlung f

subpoena [sʌbˈpinə] s Vorladung f ‖ tr *(unter Strafandrohung)* vorladen

subscribe [səbˈskraɪb] tr unterschreiben; *(money)* zeichnen ‖ intr—s. to *(a newspaper)* abonnieren; *(to a series of volumes)* subskribieren; *(an idea)* billigen

subscriber [səbˈskraɪbər] s Abonnent –in mf

subscription [səbˈskrɪpʃən] s *(to)* Abonnement n *(auf acc)*; *(to a series of volumes)* Subskription f *(auf acc)*; **take out a s.** to sich abonnieren auf *(acc)*

sub′sec′tion s Unterabteilung f

subsequent [ˈsʌbsɪkwənt] adj *(nach)*folgend; **s. to** anschließend an *(acc)*

subsequently [ˈsʌbsɪkwəntlɪ] adv anschließend

subservient [səbˈsʌrvɪənt] adj *(to)* unterwürfig *(gegenüber dat)*

subside [səbˈsaɪd] intr nachlassen; *(geol)* sich senken

subsidiary [səbˈsɪdɪˌeri] adj Tochter– ‖ s Tochtergesellschaft f

subsidize [ˈsʌbsɪˌdaɪz] tr subventionieren

subsidy [ˈsʌbsɪdɪ] s Subvention f

subsist [səbˈsɪst] intr *(exist)* existieren; **s. on** leben von

subsistence [səbˈsɪstəns] s *(existence)* Dasein n; *(livelihood)* Lebensunterhalt m; *(philos)* Subsistenz f

subsist′ence allow′ance s Unterhaltszuschuß m

sub′soil′ s Untergrund m

subsonic [səbˈsɑnɪk] adj Unterschall–

sub′spe′cies s Unterart f

substance [ˈsʌbstəns] s Substanz f, Stoff m; **in s.** im wesentlichen

substand′ard adj unter dem Niveau

substantial [səbˈstænʃəl] adj *(sum, amount)* beträchtlich; *(difference)* wesentlich; (meal) kräftig; **be in s. agreement** im wesentlichen übereinstimmen

substantiate [səb'stænʃɪ,et] tr begründen, nachweisen

substantive ['sʌbstəntɪv] adj wesentlich ‖ s (gram) Substantiv m

sub'sta'tion s Nebenstelle f; (postoffice) Zweigpostamt n; (elec) Umspannwerk n

substitute ['sʌbstɪ,t(j)ut] s (person) Stellvertreter –in mf; (material) Austauschstoff m; (pej) Ersatz m; (sport) Ersatzspieler –in mf; **act as a s. for** vertreten; **beware of substitutes** vor Nachamung wird gewarnt ‖ tr—**s. A for B B** durch A ersetzen ‖ intr—**s. for** einspringen für

sub'stitute teach'er s Aushilfslehrer –in mf

substitution [,sʌbstɪ't(j)uʃən] s Einsetzung f; (chem, math, ling) Substitution f; (sport) Auswechseln n

sub'stra'tum s (-ta [tə] & -tums) Unterlage f; (biol) Nährboden m

sub'struc'ture s Unterbau m

subsume [sʌb'sjum] tr unterordnen

subterfuge ['sʌbtər,fjudʒ] s Winkelzug m

subterranean [,sʌbtə'renɪ·ən] adj unterirdisch

subtile ['sʌtəl] adj fein; (poison) schleichend; (cunning) raffiniert

subtlety ['sʌtəlti] s Feinheit f

subtract [səb'trækt] tr subtrahieren

subtraction [səb'trækʃən] s Subtraktion f

suburb ['sʌbʌrb] s Vorstadt f, Vorort m; **the suburbs** der Stadtrand

suburban [sə'bʌrbən] adj Vorstadt-

suburbanite [sə'bʌrbə,naɪt] s Vorstadtbewohner –in mf

subvention [səb'venʃən] s Subvention f

subversion [səb'vʌrʒən] s Umsturz m

subversive [səb'vʌrsɪv] adj umstürzlerisch ‖ s Umstürzler –in mf

subver'sive activ'ity s Wühlarbeit f

subvert [səb'vʌrt] tr (a government) stürzen; (the law) umstoßen; (corrupt) (sittlich) verderben

sub'way' s U-Bahn f, Untergrundbahn f

succeed [sək'sid] tr folgen (dat) ‖ intr (said of persons) (in) Erfolg haben (mit); (said of things) gelingen; **I succeeded in** (ger) es gelang mir zu (inf); **not s.** mißglücken; **s. to the throne** die Thronfolge antreten

success [sək'ses] s Erfolg m; (play, song, piece of merchandise) Knüller m; **be a s.** Erfolg haben; **without s.** erfolglos

successful [sək'sesfəl] adj erfolgreich

succession [sək'seʃən] s Reihenfolge f; (as heir) Erbfolge f; **in s.** nacheinander; **s. to** (e.g., an office, estate) Übernahme f (genit)

successive [sək'sesɪv] adj aufeinanderfolgend

successor [sək'sesər] s Nachfolger –in

mf; **s. to the throne** Thronfolger –in mf

succor ['sʌkər] s Beistand m ‖ tr beistehen (dat)

succotash ['sʌkə,tæʃ] s Gericht n aus Süßmais und grünen Bohnen

succulent ['sʌkjələnt] adj saftig

succumb [sə'kʌm] intr (to) erliegen (dat)

such [sʌtʃ] adj solch; **as s.** als solcher; **no s. thing** nichts dergleichen; **some s. thing** irgend so (et)was; **s. and s.** der und der; **s. as** wie (etwa); **s. a long time** so lange; **s. as it is** wie es nun einmal ist

suck [sʌk] s Saugen n; (licking) Lutschen n ‖ tr saugen; **s. in** einsaugen; (sl) reinlegen ‖ intr saugen; **s. on** (e.g., candy) lutschen

sucker ['sʌkər] s (coll) Gimpel m; (carp) Karpfenfisch m; (bot) Wurzelschößling m; (zool) Saugröhre f

suckle ['sʌkəl] tr stillen; (animals) säugen

suck'ling s Säugling m

suck'ling pig' s Spanferkel n

suction ['sʌkʃən] s Saugen n, Sog m

suc'tion cup' s Saugnapf m

suc'tion pump' s Saugpumpe f

sudden ['sʌdən] adj plötzlich, jäh; **all of a s.** (ganz) plötzlich

suddenly ['sʌdənli] adv plötzlich

suds [sʌdz] spl Seifenschaum m

sudsy ['sʌdzi] adj schaumig

sue [s(j)u] tr (for) verklagen (auf acc) ‖ intr (for) klagen (auf acc)

suede [swed] s Wildleder– ‖ s Wildleder n

suet ['s(j)u·ɪt] s Talg m

suffer ['sʌfər] tr erleiden; (damage) nehmen; (put up with) ertragen ‖ intr (from) leiden (an dat)

sufferance ['sʌfərəns] s stillschweigende Einwilligung f

suf'fering s Leiden n

suffice [sə'faɪs] intr ausreichen

sufficient [sə'fɪʃənt] adj (for) ausreichend (für)

suffix ['sʌfɪks] s Nachsilbe f

suffocate ['sʌfə,ket] tr & intr ersticken

suffrage ['sʌfrɪdʒ] s Stimmrecht n

suffuse [sə'fjuz] tr übergießen

sugar ['ʃugər] s Zucker m ‖ tr zuckern

sug'ar beet' s Zuckerrübe f

sug'ar bowl' s Zuckerdose f

sug'ar cane' s Zuckerrohr n

sug'ar-coat' tr (& fig) überzuckern

sug'ar dad'dy s Geldonkel m

sug'ar ma'ple s Zuckerahorn m

sug'ar tongs' spl Zuckerzange f

sugary ['ʃugəri] adj zuckerig

suggest [səg'dʒest] tr vorschlagen; (hint) andeuten

suggestion [səg'dʒestʃən] s Vorschlag m

suggestive [səg'dʒestɪv] adj (remark) zweideutig; (thought-provoking) anregend; (e.g., dress) hauteng; **be s. of** erinnern an (acc)

suicidal [,su·ɪ'saɪdəl] adj selbstmörderisch

suicide ['su·ɪ,saɪd] s Selbstmord m;

(person) Selbstmörder –in *mf;* **commit s.** Selbstmord begehen

suit [sut] *s (men's)* Anzug *m;* *(women's)* Kostüm *n;* (cards) Farbe *f;* (jur) Prozeß *m;* **bring s.** (against) e-e Klage einbringen (gegen); **follow s.** Farbe bekennen; (fig) sich nach den anderen richten ‖ *tr (please)* passen *(dat); (correspond to)* entsprechen *(dat); (said, e.g., of colors, style)* gut passen *(dat);* **be suited for** sich eignen für; **s. s.th.** to etw anpassen *(dat);* **s. yourself!** wie Sie wollen!

suitable ['sutəbəl] *adj* **(to)** geeignet (für)

suit'case' *s* Handkoffer *m*

suit' coat' *s* Sakko *m & n*

suite [swit] *s (series of rooms)* Zimmerflucht *f; (set of furniture)* Zimmergarnitur *f;* (mus) Suite *f*

suitor ['sutər] *s* Freier *m*

sul'fa drug' *s* Sulfonamid *n*

sulfate ['sʌlfet] *s* Sulfat *n*

sulfide ['sʌlfaɪd] *s* Sulfid *n*

sulfur ['sʌlfər] *adj* Schwefel– ‖ *s* Schwefel *m* ‖ *tr* einschwefeln

sulfur'ic ac'id [sʌl'f(j)urɪk] *s* Schwefelsäure *f*

sul'fur mine' *s* Schwefelgrube *f*

sulk [sʌlk] *intr* trotzen

sulky ['sʌlki] *adj* trotzend, mürrisch ‖ *s* (sport) Traberwagen *m*

sulk'y race' *s* Trabrennen *n*

sullen ['sʌlən] *adj* mißmutig

sul-ly ['sʌli] *v* (*pret & pp* **–lied**) *tr* besudeln

sulphur ['sʌlfər] *var* of **sulfur**

sultan ['sʌltən] *s* Sultan *m*

sultry ['sʌltri] *adj* schwül

sum [sʌm] *s* Summe *f,* Betrag *m;* **in sum** kurz gesagt ‖ *v* (*pret & pp* **summed**; *ger* **summing**)—**sum up** summieren; *(summarize)* zusammenfassen; *(make a quick estimate of)* kurz abschätzen

sumac, sumach ['/umæk] *s* Sumach *m*

summarize ['sʌmə‚raɪz] *tr* zusammenfassen

summary ['sʌməri] *adj* summarisch ‖ *s* Zusammenfassung *f*

sum'mary court'mar'tial *s* summarisches Militärgericht *n*

summer ['sʌmər] *s* Sommer *m*

sum'mer cot'tage *s* Sommerwohnung *f*

sum'mer resort' *s* Sommerfrische *f*

sum'mer school' *s* Sommerkurs *m*

sum'mertime' *s* Sommerzeit *f*

summery ['sʌməri] *adj* sommerlich

summit ['sʌmɪt] *s* (& fig) Gipfel *m*

sum'mit con'ference *s* Gipfelkonferenz *f*

sum'mit talks' *spl* Gipfelgespräche *pl*

summon ['sʌmən] *tr* (e.g., *a doctor*) kommen lassen; *(a conference)* einberufen; (jur) vorladen; **s. up** *(courage, strength)* aufbieten

summons ['sʌmənz] *s* (jur) Vorladung *f*

sumptuous ['sʌmptʃu‑əs] *adj* üppig

sun [sʌn] *s* Sonne *f* ‖ *v* (*pret & pp* **sunned**; *ger* **sunning**) *tr* sonnen; **sun oneself** sich sonnen

sun' bath' *s* Sonnenbad *n*

sun'beam' *s* Sonnenstrahl *m*

sun'burn' *s* Sonnenbrand *m*

sun'burned' *adj* sonnverbrannt

sundae ['sʌnde] *s* Eisbecher *m* mit Sirup, Nüssen, Früchten und Schlagsahne

Sunday ['sʌnde] *adj* sonntäglich; **dressed in one's S. best** sonntäglich gekleidet ‖ *s* Sonntag *m;* **on S.** am Sonntag

Sun'day driv'er *s* Sonntagsfahrer –in *mf*

Sun'day school' *s* Sonntagsschule *f*

sunder ['sʌndər] *tr* trennen

sun'di'al *s* Sonnenuhr *f*

sun'down' *s* Sonnenuntergang *m*

sun'-drenched' *adj* sonnenüberflutet

sundries ['sʌndriz] *pl* Diverses *n*

sundry ['sʌndri] *adj* verschiedene

sun'fish' *s* Sonnenfisch *m*

sun'flow'er *s* Sonnenblume *f*

sun'glass'es *pl* Sonnenbrille *f*

sun' hel'met *s* Tropenhelm *m*

sunken ['sʌŋkən] *adj (ship)* gesunken; *(eyes; garden)* tiefliegend; *(treasure)* versunken; *(cheeks)* eingefallen; **s. rocks** blinde Klippe *f*

sun' lamp' *s* Höhensonne *f*

sun'light' *s* Sonnenlicht *n*

sunny ['sʌni] *adj* sonnig

sun'ny side' *s* Sonnenseite *f*

sun' par'lor *s* Glasveranda *f*

sun'rise' *s* Sonnenaufgang *m*

sun' roof' *s* (aut) Schiebedach *n*

sun'set' *s* Sonnenuntergang *m*

sun'shade' *s* Sonnenschirm *m;* *(awning)* Sonnendach *n;* (phot) Gegenlichtblende *f*

sun'shine' *s* Sonnenschein *m*

sun'spot' *s* Sonnenfleck *m*

sun'stroke' *s* Sonnenstich *m*

sun'tan' *s* Sonnenbräune *f*

sun'tanned' *adj* sonnengebräunt

sun' vis'or *s* (aut) Sonnenblende *f*

sup [sʌp] *v* (*pret & pp* **supped**; *ger* **supping**) *intr* zu Abend essen

super ['supər] *adj (oversized)* Super–; (sl) prima ‖ *s* (theat) Komparse *m*

su'perabun'dance *s* (of) Überfülle *f* (an *dat*)

su'perabun'dant *adj* überreichlich

superannuated [‚supər'ænju‚etɪd] *adj* *(person)* pensioniert; *(thing)* veraltet

superb [su'pərb] *adj* prachtvoll, herrlich

su'perbomb' *s* Superbombe *f*

su'perbomb'er *s* Riesenbomber *m*

supercilious [‚supər'sɪlɪ‑əs] *adj* hochnäsig

superficial [‚supər'fɪʃəl] *adj* oberflächlich

superfluous [su'pʌrflu‑əs] *adj* überflüssig

su'perhigh'way' *s* Autobahn *f*

su'perhu'man *adj* übermenschlich

su'perimpose' *tr* darüberlegen; (elec, phys) überlagern

su'perintend' *tr* die Aufsicht führen über (*acc*), beaufsichtigen

superintendent [‚supərɪn'tendənt] *s* Oberaufseher –in *mf;* *(in industry)*

Betriebsleiter –in *mf; (of a factory)* Werksleiter –in *mf; (of a building)* Hausverwalter –in *mf; (educ)* Schulinspektor –in *mf*

superior [sə'pɪrɪ·ər] *adj (physically)* höher; *(in rank)* übergeordnet; *(quality)* hervorragend; **s. in** überlegen an *(dat); s.* **to** überlegen *(dat)* || *s* Vorgesetzte *mf*

supe′rior court′ *s* Obergericht *n*

superiority [sə‚pɪrɪ'ɑrɪti] *s* (**in**) Überlegenheit *f* (in *dat*, an *dat*); *(mil)* Übermacht *f*

superlative [sʊ'pʌrlətɪv] *adj* hervorragend; *(gram)* superlativisch, Superlativ– || *s* (gram) Superlativ *m*

su′per′man′ *s* (**–men′**) Übermensch *m*

su′per′mar′ket *s* Supermarkt *m*

su′per′nat′ural *adj* übernatürlich || *s* Übernatürliche *n*

supersede [‚supər'sld] *tr* ersctzcn

su′per′sen′sitive *adj* überempfindlich

su′per′son′ic *adj* Überschall–

superstition [‚supər'stɪʃən] *s* Aberglaube *m; (superstitious idea)* abergläubische Vorstellung *f*

superstitious [‚supər'stɪʃəs] *adj* abergläubisch

su′perstruc′ture *s* Überbau *m; (of a bridge)* Oberbau *m; (of a building or ship)* Aufbauten *pl*

supervise ['supər‚vaɪz] *tr* beaufsichtigen

supervision [‚supər'vɪʒən] *s* Beaufsichtigung *f*

supervisor ['supər‚vaɪzər] *s* Vorgesetzte *mf*

su′pine posi′tion ['supaɪn] *s* Rückenlage *f*

supper ['sʌpər] *s* Abendessen *n; eat s.* zu Abend essen

sup′pertime′ *s* Abendbrotzeit *f*

supplant [sə'plænt] *tr* ersetzen

supple ['sʌpəl] *adj* geschmeidig; *(mind)* beweglich

supplement ['sʌplɪmənt] *s (e.g., to a diet)* (**to**) Ergänzung *f (genit); (to a writing)* Anhang *m; (to a newspaper)* Beilage *f* || ['sʌplɪ‚ment] *tr* ergänzen

supplementary [‚sʌplɪ'mentəri] *adj* ergänzend

suppliant ['sʌplɪ·ənt] *adj* flehend || *s* Bittsteller –in *mf*

supplicant ['sʌplɪkənt] *s* Bittsteller –in *mf*

supplicate ['sʌplɪ‚ket] *tr* flehen

supplication [‚sʌplɪ'ke/ən] *s* Flehen *n*

supplier [sə'plaɪ·ər] *s* Lieferant –in *mf*

sup·ply [sə'plaɪ] *s (supplying)* Versorgung *f; (stock)* (**of**) Vorrat *m (an dat); (com)* Angebot *n;* **supplies** Vorräte *pl; (e.g., office supplies, dental supplies)* Bedarfsartikel *pl;* (mil) Nachschub *m* || *v (pret & pp* **–plied**) *tr* (**with**) versorgen (mit); *(deliver)* liefern; *(procure)* beschaffen; *(with a truck)* zuführen; *(equip)* (**with**) versehen (mit); *(a demand)* befriedigen; *(a loss)* ausgleichen; *(missing words)* ergänzen; (mil) mit Nachschub versorgen

supply′ and demand′ *spl* Angebot *n* und Nachfrage *f*

supply′ base′ *s* Nachschubstützpunkt *m*

supply′ line′ *s* Versorgungsweg *m;* (mil) Nachschubweg *m*

support [sə'port] *adj* Hilfs– || *s (prop, brace, stay; person)* Stütze *f; (of a family)* Unterhalt *m;* **in s.** of zur Unterstützung *(genit);* **without s.** *(unsubstantiated)* haltlos; *(unprovided)* unversorgt; **with the s. of** mit dem Beistand von || *tr* stützen, tragen; *(back)* unterstützen; *(a family)* erhalten; *(a charge)* erhärten; *(a claim)* begründen

supporter [sə'portər] *s (of a family)* Ernährer –in *mf; (backer)* Förderer –in *mf; (jockstrap)* Suspensorium *n*

support′ing role′ *s* Nebenrolle *f*

suppose [sə'poz] *tr* annehmen; **be supposed to** sollen; **I s. so** ıch glaube schon; **s. it rains** gesetzt den Fall (or angenommen), es regnet; **s. we take a walk** wie wäre es, wenn wir e–n Spaziergang machten?; **what is that supposed to mean?** was soll das bedeuten? || *intr* vermuten

supposed′ *adj* mutmaßlich

supposedly [sə'pozɪdli] *adv* angeblich

supposition [‚sʌpə'zɪʃən] *s* Annahme *f*

suppository [sə'pɑzɪ‚tori] *s* Zäpfchen *n*

suppress [sə'pres] *tr* unterdrücken; *(news, scandal)* verheimlichen

suppression [sə'preʃən] *s* Unterdrükkung *f; (of news, truth, scandal)* Verheimlichung *f*

suppurate ['sʌpjə‚ret] *intr* eitern

supremacy [sə'preməsi] *s* Oberherrschaft *f*

supreme [sə'prim] *adj* Ober–, höchste

supreme′ author′ity *s* Obergewalt *f*

Supreme′ Be′ing *s* höchstes Wesen *n*

supreme′ command′ *s* Oberkommando *n;* **have s. den** Oberbefehl führen

supreme′ command′er *s* oberster Befehlshaber *m*

Supreme′ Court′ *s* Oberster Gerichtshof *m*

surcharge ['sʌr‚tʃɑrdʒ] *s* (**on**) Zuschlag *m* (zu)

sure [ʃʊr] *adj* sicher, gewiß; *(shot, cure)* unfehlbar; *(shot, footing, ground, way, proof)* sicher; **are you s. you won't come?** kommen Sie wirklich nicht?; **be s. of** sicher sein *(genit);* **be s. to** *(inf)* vergiß nicht zu *(inf);* **feel s. of oneself** s–r selbst sicher sein; **for s.** sicherlich; **she is s. to come** sie wird sicher(lich) kommen; **s. enough** wirklich; **to be s.** *(parenthetically)* zwar

sure′-foot′ed *adj* trittsicher

surely ['ʃʊrli] *adv* sicher(lich), gewiß

surety ['ʃʊr(ɪ)ti] *s* Bürgschaft *f;* **stand s.** (for) bürgen (für)

surf [sʌrf] *s* Brandung *f* || *intr* wellenreiten

surface ['sʌrfɪs] *adj (superficial)* oberflächlich; *(apparent rather than real)*

Schein- || s Oberfläche f; (of a road) Belag m; (aer) Tragfläche f; on the s. oberflächlich (betrachtet) || tr (a road) mit e-m Belag versehen || intr auftauchen

sur′face mail′ s gewöhnliche Post f

sur′face-to-air′ mis′sile s Boden-Luft-Rakete f

sur′face-to-sur′face mis′sile s Boden-Boden-Rakete f

surf′board′ s Wellenreiterbrett n

surf′board′ing s Wellenreiten n

surfeit [′sʌrfɪt] s Übersättigung f || tr übersättigen

surfer [′sʌrfər] s Wellenreiter –in mf

surf′ing s Wellenreiten n

surge [sʌrdʒ] s (forward rush of a wave or crowd) Wogen n; (swelling wave) Woge f; (swelling sea) Wogen n; (elec) Stromstoß m || intr (said of waves or a crowd) wogen; (said of emotions, blood) (up) (auf)wallen

surgeon [′sʌrdʒən] s Chirurg –in mf

surgery [′sʌrdʒəri] s Chirurgie f; (room) Operationssaal m; undergo s. sich e-r Operation unterziehen

surgical [′sʌrdʒɪkəl] adj chirurgisch; (resulting from surgery) Operations–

surly [′sʌrli] adj bärbeißig

surmise [sər′maɪz] s Vermutung f || tr & intr vermuten

surmount [sər′maunt] tr überwinden

surname [′sʌr,nem] s (family name) Zuname m; (epithet) Beiname m || tr e-n Zunamen (or Beinamen) geben (dat)

surpass [sər′pæs] tr (in) übertreffen (an dat)

surplice [′sʌrplɪs] s Chorhemd n

surplus [′sʌrplʌs] adj überschüssig, Über– || s (of) Überschuß m (an dat)

surprise [sər′praɪz] adj Überraschungs– || s Überraschung f; take by s. überraschen; to my (great) s. zu meiner (großen) Überraschung || tr überraschen; be surprised at sich wundern über (acc); be surprised to see how staunen, wie; I am surprised that es wundert mich, daß

surpris′ing adj überraschend

surrealism [sə′ri·ə,lɪzəm] s Surrealismus m

surrender [sə′rɛndər] s (e.g., of a fortress) Übergabe f; (of an army or unit) Kapitulation f; (of rights) Aufgabe f; (of a prisoner) Auslieferung f || tr übergeben; (rights) aufgeben; (a prisoner) ausliefern || intr sich ergeben

surren′der val′ue s (ins) Rückkaufswert m

surreptitious [,sʌrɛp′tɪʃəs] adj heimlich; (glance) verstohlen

surround [sə′raund] tr umgeben; (said of a crowd, police) umringen; (mil) einschließen

surround′ing adj umliegend || surroundings spl Umgebung f

surtax [′sʌr,tæks] s Steuerzuschlag m

surveillance [sər′vel(j)əns] s Überwachung f; keep under s. unter Polizeiaufsicht halten

survey [′sʌrve] s (of) Überblick m (über acc); (of opinions) Umfrage f; (of land) Vermessung f; (plan or description of the survey) Lageplan m || [sʌr′ve] tr überblicken; (a person) mustern; (land) vermessen; (people for their opinion) befragen

sur′vey course′ s Einführungskurs m

survey′ing s Landvermessung f

surveyor [sər′ve·ər] s Landmesser m

survival [sər′vaɪvəl] s Überleben n; (after death) Weiterleben n

surviv′al of the fit′test s Überleben n des Tüchtigsten

survive [sər′vaɪv] tr (a person) überleben; (a thing) überstehen; be survived by hinterlassen || intr am Leben bleiben

surviv′ing adj überlebend

survivor [sər′vaɪvər] s Überlebende mf

susceptible [sə′sɛptɪbəl] adj (impressionable) eindrucksfähig; be s. of zulassen; be s. to (disease, infection) anfällig sein für; (flattery) empfänglich sein für

suspect [′sʌspɛkt] adj verdächtig || s Verdächtige mf || [sə′spɛkt] tr in Verdacht haben; (surmise) vermuten; (have a hint of) ahnen; s. s.o. of j-n verdächtigen (genit)

suspend [sə′spɛnd] tr (from a job, office) suspendieren; (payment, hostilities, proceedings, a game) einstellen; (a rule) zeitweilig aufheben; (a sentence) aussetzen; (a player) sperren; (from a club) zeitweilig ausschließen; (from) hängen (an dat)

suspenders [sə′spɛndərz] spl Hosenträger pl

suspense [sə′spɛns] s Spannung f; hang in s. in der Schwebe sein; keep in s. im ungewissen lassen

suspension [sə′spɛn/ən] s Aufhängung f; (of a sentence) Aussetzung f; (of work) Einstellung f; (e.g., of telephone service) Sperrung f; (aut) Federung f; (chem) Suspension f; s. of driver′s license Führerscheinentzug m

suspen′sion bridge′ s Hängebrücke f

suspen′sion points′ spl (indicating unfinished thoughts) Gedankenpunkte pl; (indicating omission) Auslassungspunkte pl

suspicion [sə′spɪ/ən] s Verdacht m; above s. über jeden Verdacht erhaben; be under s. unter Verdacht stehen; on s. of murder unter Mordverdacht

suspicious [sə′spɪ/əs] adj (person) verdächtig; (e.g., glance) argwöhnisch; (character) zweifelhaft

sustain [sə′sten] tr aufrechterhalten; (a loss, defeat, injury) erleiden; (a family) ernähren; (an army) verpflegen; (a motion, an objection) stattgeben (dat); (a theory, position) erhärten; (a note) dehnen

sustenance [′sʌstɪnəns] s (nourishment) Nahrung f; (means of livelihood) Unterhalt m

swab [swɑb] s (med, surg) Tupfer m;

(*matter collected on a swab*) Abstrich m; (*naut*) Schwabber m ‖ v (*pret & pp* swabbed; *ger* swabbing) tr (*med, surg*) abtupfen; (*naut*) schrubben

Swabia ['sweɪbɪə] s Schwaben n

Swabian ['sweɪbɪən] *adj* schwäbisch ‖ s Schwabe m, Schwäbin f; (*dialect*) Schwäbisch n

swad'dling clothes' ['swɒdlɪŋ] *spl* Windeln pl

swagger ['swægər] s (*strut*) Stolzieren n; (*swaggering manner*) Prahlerei f ‖ *intr* stolzieren; (*show off*) prahlen

swain [swen] s (*lover*) Liebhaber m; (*country lad*) Bauernbursche m

swallow ['swɒlo] s Schluck m; (*orn*) Schwalbe f ‖ tr schlucken; (*fig*) hinunterschlucken ‖ *intr* schlucken; s. **the wrong way** sich verschlucken

swamp [swɒmp] s Sumpf m, Moor n ‖ tr überfluten; (*with work*) überhäufen

swamp'land' s Moorland n

swampy ['swɒmpi] *adj* sumpfig

swan [swɒn] s Schwan m

swan' dive' s Schwalbensprung m

swank [swæŋk], **swanky** ['swæŋki] *adj* (*luxurious*) schick; (*ostentatious*) protzig

swan's'-down' s Schwanendaunen pl

swan' song' s Schwanengesang m

swap [swɒp] s (*coll*) Tauschgeschäft n ‖ v (*pret & pp* swapped; *ger* swapping) tr & *intr* (*coll*) tauschen

swarm [swɔrm] s Schwarm m; (*of children*) Schar f ‖ *intr* schwärmen; s. **around** umschwärmen; s. **into** sich drängen in (*acc*); s. **with** (*fig*) wimmeln von

swarthy ['swɔrθi] *adj* dunkelhäutig

swashbuckler ['swɑʃ͵bʌklər] s Eisenfresser m

swastika ['swɑstɪkə] s Hakenkreuz n

swat [swɒt] s Schlag m ‖ (*pret & pp* swatted; *ger* swatting) tr schlagen

swath [swɒθ] s Schwaden m

swathe [sweð] tr umwickeln, einwikkeln

sway [swe] s Schwanken n, Schwingen n; (*domination*) Herrschaft f ‖ tr (*e.g., tree*) hin- und herbewegen; (*influence*) beeinflussen; (*cause to vacillate*) ins Wanken bringen ‖ *intr* schwanken

sway'-back' s Senkrücken m

swear [swer] v (*pret* swore [swor]; *pp* sworn [sworn]) tr schwören; s. **in** vereidigen; s. **s.o. to secrecy** j-n auf Geheimhaltung vereidigen ‖ *intr* schwören; (*coll*) fluchen; s. **at** schimpfen über (*acc*) *or* auf (*acc*); s. **by** schwören bei; s. **off** abschwören (*dat*); s. **on a stack of Bibles** Stein und Bein schwören; s. **to** (*a statement*) beschwören; s. **to it** darauf schwören

swear'ing-in' s Vereidigung f

swear'word' s Fluchwort n

sweat [swet] s Schweiß m; **break out in s.** in Schweiß geraten ‖ v (*pret & pp* sweat & sweated) tr (*blood*)

schwitzen; (*metal*) seigern; (*a horse*) in Schweiß bringen; s. **off** abschwitzen; s. **out** (sl) geduldig abwarten; s. **up** durchschwitzen ‖ *intr* schwitzen

sweater ['swetər] s Sweater m, Pullover m

sweat'er girl' s vollbusiges Mädchen n

sweat' shirt' s Trainingsbluse f

sweat' shop' s (sl) Knochenmühle f

sweaty ['sweti] *adj* verschwitzt; (*hand*) schweißig

Swede [swid] s Schwede m, Schwedin f

Swedish ['swidɪʃ] *adj* schwedisch ‖ s Schwedisch n

sweep [swip] s (*sweeper*) Kehrer –in mf; (*of the arm, scythe, weapon*) Schwung m; (*of an oar*) Schlag m; (*range*) Reichweite f; (*continuous stretch*) ausgedehnte Strecke f; **in one clean s.** mit einem Schlag; **make a clean s. of it** reinen Tisch machen ‖ v (*pret & pp* swept [swept]) tr kehren, fegen; (*mines*) räumen; (*with machine-gun fire*) bestreichen; (*with a searchlight*) absuchen; **he swept her off her feet** er hat sie im Sturm erobert; s. **clean** reinemachen ‖ *intr* kehren, fegen

sweeper ['swipər] s Kehrer –in mf; (*carpet sweeper*) Teppichkehrer m

sweep'ing *adj* weitreichend ‖ **sweepings** *spl* Kehricht m & n

sweep'-sec'ond s Zentralsekundenzeiger m

sweep'stakes' s & *spl* Lotterie f; (*sport*) Toto m & n

sweet [swit] *adj* süß; (*person*) lieb; (*butter*) ungesalzen; **be s. on** scharf sein auf (*acc*) ‖ **sweets** *spl* Süßigkeiten pl

sweet'bread' s Bries n

sweet'bri'er s Heckenrose f

sweet' corn' s Zuckermais m

sweeten ['switən] tr süßen; (*fig*) versüßen ‖ *intr* süß(er) werden

sweet'heart' s Liebste mf, Schatz m

sweetish ['switɪʃ] *adj* süßlich

sweet' mar'joram s Gartenmajoran m

sweet' meats' *spl* Zuckerwerk n

sweetness ['switnɪs] s Süßigkeit f

sweet' pea' s Gartenwicke f

sweet' pep'per s grüner Paprika m

sweet' pota'to s Süßkartoffel f

sweet'-scent'ed *adj* wohlriechend

sweet' tooth' s—**have a s.** gern naschen

sweet' wil'liam s Fleischnelke f

swell [swel] *adj* (*coll*) prima ‖ s (*of the sea*) Wellengang m; (*of an organ*) Schweller m ‖ v (*pret* swelled; *pp* swelled & swollen ['swolən]) tr zum Schwellen bringen; (*the number*) vermehren; (*a musical tone*) anschwellen lassen ‖ *intr* schwellen

swell'ing s Schwellung f

swelter ['sweltər] *intr* unter der Hitze leiden

swept'-back' *adj* (aer) keilförmig

swerve [swʌrv] s Abweichung f ‖ tr ablenken ‖ *intr* scharf abbiegen

swift [swɪft] *adj* geschwind, rasch

swig [swɪg] s (coll) kräftiger Schluck

m ‖ *v (pret & pp* **swigged;** *ger* **swigging)** *tr* in langen Zügen trinken

swill [swɪl] *s* Spülicht *n*; *(for swine)* Schweinefutter *n*; *(deep drink)* tüchtiger Schluck *m* ‖ *tr & intr* gierig trinken

swim [swɪm] *s* Schwimmen *n*; **take a s.** schwimmen ‖ *v (pret* **swam** [swæm]; *pp* **swum** [swʌm]; *ger* **swimming)** *tr (e.g., a lake)* durchschwimmen; *(cause to swim)* schwimmen lassen; *(challenge in swimming)* um die Wette schwimmen mit ‖ *intr* schwimmen; **my head is swimming** mir schwindelt der Kopf

swimmer [ˈswɪmər] *s* Schwimmer –in *mf*

swim′ming *adj* Schwimm– ‖ *s* Schwimmen *n*; *(sport)* Schwimmsport *m*

swim′ming pool′ *s* Schwimmbecken *n*

swim′ming suit′ *s* Badeanzug *m*

swim′ming trunks′ *spl* Badehose *f*

swindle [ˈswɪndəl] *s* Schwindel *m* ‖ *tr* gaunern; **s. s.th. out of** etw erschwindeln von

swindler [ˈswɪndlər] *s* Schwindler –in *mf*

swind′ling *s* Schwindelei *f*

swine [swaɪn] *s* Schwein *n*

swine′herd′ *s* Schweinehirt *m*

swing [swɪŋ] *s (for children)* Schaukel *f*; *(swinging movement)* Hin– und Herschwingen *n*; *(box)* Schwinger *m*; *(mus)* Swing *m*; **in full s.** in vollem Gang; **take a s. at s.o.** nach j–m schlagen ‖ *v (pret & pp* **swung** [swʌŋ]) *tr* schwingen; *(children on a swing)* schaukeln; *(an election)* entscheidend beeinflussen; **s. (e.g., a car) around** herumdrehen; **we'll s. it somehow** (coll) wir werden es schon schaffen ‖ *intr* pendeln; *(on a swing)* schaukeln; **s. around** sich umdrehen; **s. into action** in Schwung kommen; **things are swinging around here** (coll) hier geht es lustig zu

swing′ing door′ *s* Pendeltür *f*

swinish [ˈswaɪnɪʃ] *adj* schweinisch

swipe [swaɪp] *s* (coll) Hieb *m*; **take a s. at** (coll) schlagen nach ‖ *tr (hit with full force)* (coll) kräftig schlagen; *(steal)* (sl) mausen

swirl [swʌrl] *s* Wirbel *m* ‖ *tr (about)* herumwirbeln ‖ *intr* wirbeln; *(said of water)* Strudel bilden

swish [swɪʃ] *s (e.g., of a whip)* Sausen *n*; *(of a dress)* Rauschen *n* ‖ *tr (a whip)* sausen lassen; **s. its tail** mit dem Schwanz wedeln ‖ *intr (said of a whip)* sausen; *(said of a dress)* rauschen

Swiss [swɪs] *adj* schweizerisch ‖ *s* Schweizer –in *mf*

Swiss′ cheese′ *s* Schweizer Käse *m*

Swiss′ franc′ *s* Schweizerfranken *m*

Swiss′ Guard′ *s* Schweizergarde *f*

switch [swɪtʃ] *s (exchange)* Wechsel *m*, Umschwung *m*; *(stick)* Rute *f*; *(elec)* Schalter *m*; *(rr)* Weiche *f* ‖ *tr* wechseln; *(by mistake)* verwechseln; *(rr)* rangieren; **s. off** (elec, rad, telv) ausschalten; **s. on**

(elec, rad, telv) einschalten ‖ *intr* Plätze wechseln

switch′-blade knife′ *s* feststellbares Messer *n*

switch′board′ *s* Schaltbrett *n*, Zentrale *f*

switch′board op′erator *s* Telephonist –in *mf*

switch′ box′ *s* Schaltkasten *m*

switch′man *s* (–men) (rr) Weichensteller *m*

switch′ tow′er *s* (rr) Blockstation *f*

switch′yard′ *s* Rangierbahnhof *m*

Switzerland [ˈswɪtsərlənd] *s* die Schweiz

swiv•el [ˈswɪvəl] *s* Drehlager *n* ‖ *v (pret & pp* **-el[l]ed;** *ger* **-el[l]ing)** *tr* herumdrehen ‖ *intr* sich drehen

swiv′el chair′ *s* Drehstuhl *m*

swiz′zle stick′ [ˈswɪzəl] *s* Rührstäbchen *n*

swollen [ˈswolən] *adj* (an)geschwollen; *(eyes)* verquollen

swoon [swun] *s* Ohnmacht *f* ‖ *intr* ohnmächtig werden

swoop [swup] *s* Herabstoßen *n*; **in one fell s.** mit e–m Schlag ‖ *intr*—**s. down (on)** herabstoßen (auf *acc*)

sword [sord] *s* Schwert *n*; **put to the s.** mit dem Schwert hinrichten

sword′ belt′ *s* Schwertgehenk *n*

sword′fish′ *s* Schwertfisch *m*

swords′man *s* (–men) Fechter *m*

sworn [sworn] *adj (statement)* eidlich; **s. enemy** Todfeind *m*

sycamore [ˈsɪkəmor] *s* Platane *f*

sycophant [ˈsɪkəfənt] *s* Sykophant *m*

syllabary [ˈsɪlə‚berɪ] *s* Silbenschrift *f*

syllabification [sɪ‚læbɪfɪˈkeʃən] *s* Silbentrennung *f*

syllable [ˈsɪləbəl] *s* Silbe *f*

sylla-bus [ˈsɪləbəs] *s* (–**bai** [‚baɪ] & –**buses**) Lehrplan *m*

syllogism [ˈsɪlə‚dʒɪzəm] *s* Syllogismus *m*

sylvan [ˈsɪlvən] *adj* Wald–

symbol [ˈsɪmbəl] *s* Sinnbild *n*, Symbol *n*

symbolic(al) [sɪmˈbɑlɪk(əl)] *adj* sinnbildlich, symbolisch

symbolism [ˈsɪmbə‚lɪzəm] *s* Symbolik *f*

symbolize [ˈsɪmbə‚laɪz] *tr* symbolisieren

symmetric(al) [sɪˈmetrɪk(əl)] *adj* symmetrisch

symmetry [ˈsɪmɪtrɪ] *s* Symmetrie *f*

sympathetic [‚sɪmpəˈθetɪk] *adj* mitfühlend; *(physiol)* sympathisch

sympathize [ˈsɪmpə‚θaɪz] *intr*—**s. with** mitfühlen mit; *(be in accord with)* sympathisieren mit

sympathizer [ˈsɪmpə‚θaɪzər] *s* Sympathisant –in *mf*

sympathy [ˈsɪmpəθɪ] *s* Mitleid *n*; **be in s. with** im Einverständnis sein mit; **offer one's sympathies to s.o.** j–m sein Beileid bezeigen

sym′pathy card′ *s* Beileidskarte *f*

sym′pathy strike′ *s* Sympathiestreik *m*

symphonic [sɪmˈfɑnɪk] *adj* sinfonisch

symphony [ˈsɪmfənɪ] *s* Sinfonie *f*

symposi·um [sɪm'pozɪ·əm] s (-a [ə] & -ums) Symposion n
symptom ['sɪmptəm] s (of) Symptom n (für)
symptomatic [ˌsɪmtə'mætɪk] adj (of) symptomatisch (für)
synagogue ['sɪnə·gog] s Synagoge f
synchronize ['sɪŋkrə·naɪz] tr synchronisieren
synchronous ['sɪŋkrənəs] adj synchron; (elec) Synchron–
syncopate ['sɪŋkə·pet] tr synkopieren
syncopation [ˌsɪŋkə'pe/ən] s Synkope f
syncope ['sɪŋkə·pi] s Synkope f
syndicate ['sɪndɪkɪt] s Interessengemeinschaft f, Syndikat n || ['sɪndɪ·ket] tr zu e–m Syndikat zusammenschließen; (a column) in mehreren Zeitungen zugleich veröffentlichen || intr ein Syndikat bilden
synod ['sɪnəd] s Synode f
synonym ['sɪnənɪm] s Synonym n
synonymous [sɪ'nɑnəməs] adj sinnverwandt; **s. with** gleichbedeutend mit

synop·sis [sɪ'nɑpsɪs] s (-ses [siz]) Zusammenfassung f
synoptic [sɪ'nɑptɪk] adj synoptisch
syntax ['sɪntæks] s Satzlehre f, Syntax f
synthe·sis ['sɪnθɪsɪs] s (-ses [ˌsiz]) Synthese f
synthesize ['sɪnθɪ·saɪz] tr (& chem) zusammenfügen
synthetic [sɪn'θetɪk] adj künstlich, Kunst– || s Kunststoff m
syphilis ['sɪfɪlɪs] s Syphilis f
Syria ['sɪrɪ·ə] s Syrien n
Syrian ['sɪrɪ·ən] adj syrisch || s Syrer –in mf; (language) Syrisch n
syringe [sɪ'rɪndʒ] s Spritze f || tr (inject) einspritzen; (wash) ausspritzen
syrup ['sɪrəp] s Sirup m
system ['sɪstəm] s System n; (bodily system) Organismus m
systematic(al) [ˌsɪstə'mætɪk(əl)] adj systematisch, planmäßig
systematize ['sɪstəmə·taɪz] tr systematisieren, systematisch ordnen
systole ['sɪstəli] s Systole f

T

T, t [ti] s zwanzigster Buchstabe des englischen Alphabets
tab [tæb] s (label) Etikett n; (on file cards) Karteireiter m; **keep tabs on** (coll) genau kontrollieren; **pick up the tab** (coll) die Zeche bezahlen || v (pret & pp tabbed; ger tabbing) tr (designate) ernennen
tabby ['tæbi] s getigerte Katze f
tabernacle ['tæbər·nækəl] s Tabernakel n
table ['tebəl] s Tisch m; (list, chart) Tafel f, Tabelle f; (geol) Tafel f; **at t.** bei Tisch; **the tables have turned** das Blatt hat sich gewendet || tr (parl) verschieben
tab·leau ['tæblo] s (-leaus & leaux [loz]) Tableau n
ta'blecloth' s Tischtuch n
ta'bleland' s Tafelland n
ta'ble man'ners spl Tischmanieren pl
ta'ble of con'tents s Inhaltsverzeichnis n
ta'ble salt' s Tafelsalz n
ta'ble set'ting s Gedeck n
ta'blespoon' s Eßlöffel m
tablespoonful ['tebəl·spun ˌful] s Eßlöffel m
tablet ['tæblɪt] s (writing pad) Schreibblock m; (med) Tablette f
ta'ble talk' s Tischgespräch n
ta'ble ten'nis s Tischtennis n
ta'bletop' s Tischplatte f
ta'bleware' s Tafelgeschirr n
ta'ble wine' s Tafelwein m
tabloid ['tæblɔɪd] adj konzentriert || s Bildzeitung f; (pej) Sensationsblatt n
taboo [tə'bu] adj tabu || s Tabu n || tr für Tabu erklären

tabular ['tæbjələr] adj tabellarisch
tabulate ['tæbjə·let] tr tabellarisieren
tabulator ['tæbjə·letər] s Tabelliermaschine f
tacit ['tæsɪt] adj stillschweigend
taciturn ['tæsɪtərn] adj schweigsam
tack [tæk] s (nail) Zwecke f, Stift m; (stitch) Heftstich m; (stickiness) Klebrigkeit f; (course of action) Kurs m; (gear for a riding horse) Reitgeschirr n; (course run obliquely to the wind) Schlag m; **be on the wrong t.** (fig) auf dem Holzweg sein || tr (down) mit Zwecken befestigen; (sew) heften; **t. on** (to) anfügen (an acc) || intr (fig & naut) lavieren
tackle ['tækəl] s (gear) Ausrüstung f; (for lifting) Flaschenzug m; (fb) Halbstürmer m; (naut) Takelwerk n || tr (a problem) anpacken; (fb) packen
tacky ['tæki] adj klebrig; (gaudy) geschmacklos
tact [tækt] s Takt m, Feingefühl n
tactful ['tæktfəl] adj taktvoll
tactical ['tæktɪkəl] adj taktisch
tac'tical u'nit s Kampfeinheit f
tactician [tæk'tɪ/ən] s Taktiker m
tactics ['tæktɪks] spl (& fig) Taktik f
tactless ['tæktlɪs] adj taktlos
tadpole ['tæd ˌpol] s Kaulquappe f
taffeta ['tæfɪtə] s Taft m
taffy ['tæfi] s Sahnebonbon n
tag [tæg] s (label) Etikett n; (loose end) loses Ende n; (on a shoestring) Stift m; (loop for hanging up a coat) Aufhänger m; (on a fish hook) Glitzerschmuck m; (game) Haschen n; **play tag** sich haschen; **tags** (aut)

Nummernschild *n* ‖ *v* (*pret & pp* **tagged;** *ger* **tagging**) *tr* (*mark with a tag*) mit e-m Etikett versehen; (*touch*) haschen; (*hit solidly*) heftig schlagen; (*give a traffic ticket to*) e-n Strafzettel geben (*dat*) ‖ *intr*—**tag after s.o.** sich an j-s Sohlen heften

tag′ line′ *s* (*e.g., of a play*) Schlußworte *pl;* (*favorite phrase*) stehende Redensart *f*

tail [tel] *s* Schwanz *m;* (*of a horse, comet*) Schweif *m;* (*of a shirt*) Schoß *m;* (*aer*) Heck *n;* **tails** ein Frack *m;* (*of a coin*) Rückseite *f;* **turn t.** ausreißen; **wag its t.** mit dem Schwanz wedeln ‖ *tr* (coll) beschatten ‖ *intr*—**t. after** nachlaufen (*dat*); **t. off** abflauen

tail′ end′ *s* (*e.g., of a conversation*) Schlußteil *n;* **come in at the t.** end als letzter durchs Ziel gehen

tail′gate′ *s* (*of a station wagon*) Hecktür *f;* (*of a truck*) Ladeklappe *f* ‖ *intr* dicht hinter e-m anderen fahren

tail′ gun′ner *s* (aer) Heckschütze *m*

tail′light′ *s* (aer) Hecklicht *n;* (aut) Rücklicht *n*

tailor [′telər] *s* Schneider *m* ‖ *tr &* *intr* schneidern

tai′loring *s* Schneiderarbeit *f*

tai′lor-made suit′ *s* Maßanzug *m*

tai′lor shop′ *s* Schneiderei *f*

tail′piece′ *s* (*appendage*) Anhang *m;* (*of a stringed instrument*) Saitenhalter *m;* (typ) Zierleiste *f*

tail′ pipe′ *s* (aut) Auspuffrohr *n*

tail′skid′ *s* (aer) Sporn *m*

tail′spin′ *s*—**go into a t.** abtrudeln

tail′ wheel′ *s* (aer) Spornrad *n*

tail′wind′ *s* Rückenwind *m*

taint [tent] *s* Fleck *m;* (fig) Schandfleck *m* ‖ *tr* beflecken; (*food*) verderben

take [tek] *s* (*income*) *s* Einnahmen *pl;* (*loot*) (sl) Beute *f;* (angl) Fang *m;* (cin) Szenenaufnahme *f;* **be on the t.** (sl) sich bestechen lassen ‖ *v* (*pret* **took** [tʊk]; *pp* **taken**) *tr* nehmen; (*in a car*) mitnehmen; (*bring, carry*) bringen; (*subtract*) abziehen; (*require*) erfordern; (*insults, criticism*) hinnehmen; (*bear, stand*) ertragen; (*with a camera*) aufnehmen; (*food, pills*) einnehmen; (*s.o.'s temperature*) messen; (*courage*) schöpfen; (*a deep breath*) holen; (*precautions*) treffen; (*responsibility*) übernehmen; (*an oath, test*) ablegen; (*inventory*) aufnehmen; (*a walk, trip, examination, turn, notes*) machen; (*the consequences*) tragen; (*measures*) ergreifen; (*a certain amount of time to travel*) in Anspruch nehmen; (*a step*) tun; (*advice*) befolgen; (*a game*) gewinnen; (*e.g., third place*) belegen; (*a trick*) (cards) stechen; (gram) regieren; **be able to t. a lot** e-n breiten Rücken haben; **be taken in by s.o.** j-m auf den Leim gehen; **I'm not going to t. that**

das lasse ich nicht auf mir sitzen; **t. along** mitnehmen; **t. aside** beiseitenehmen; **t. at one's word** beim Wort nehmen; **t. away** wegschaffen; **t. away from** wegnehmen (*dat*); **t. back** zurücknehmen; **t.** (*e.g., s.o.'s hat*) **by mistake** verwechseln; **t. down** herunternehmen; (*in writing*) aufschreiben; (*dictation*) aufnehmen; (*minutes*) zu Protokoll nehmen; **t. in** (*money*) einnehmen; (*washing*) ins Haus nehmen; (*as guest*) beherbergen; (*deceive*) täuschen; (*encompass*) umfassen; (*observe*) beobachten; (*sightsee*) besichtigen; (*sew*) enger machen; **t. it out on s.o.** seinen Zorn an j-m auslassen; **t. it that** annehmen, daß; **taken** (*occupied*) besetzt; **t. off** (*subtract*) abziehen; (*clothes*) ausziehen; (*a coat*) ablegen; (*gloves*) abstreifen; (*a hat*) abnehmen; (*a tire, wheel*) abmontieren; (*e.g., a day from work*) sich [*dat*] freinehmen; **t.** (*e.g., wares*) **off s.o.'s hands** j-m abnehmen; **t. on** (*hire*) anstellen; (*passengers*) aufnehmen; **t. out** (*from a container*) herausnehmen; (*a spot*) entfernen; (*a girl*) ausführen; (*a mortgage, loan*) aufnehmen; (*ins*) abschließen; (libr) sich [*dat*] ausleihen; **t. over** übernehmen; **t. s.o. for** j-n halten für; **t. up** aufnehmen; (*absorb*) aufsaugen; (*a profession*) ergreifen; (*room, time*) wegnehmen; (*a collection*) veranstalten; (*a skirt*) kürzer machen; **t. upon oneself** auf sich nehmen; **t. up** (*a matter*) **with** besprechen mit ‖ *intr* (*said of an injection*) anschlagen; (*said of seedlings, skin transplants*) anwachsen; **how long does it t.?** wie lange dauert es?; **how long does it t. to** (*inf*)? wie lange braucht man, um zu (*inf*)?; **t. after** nachgeraten (*dat*); **t. off** (*depart*) (coll) abhauen; (*from work*) wegbleiben; (aer, rok) starten; (aut) abfahren; **t. over for s.o.** für j-n einspringen; **t. to** (*a person*) warm werden mit; (*an idea*) aufgreifen; **t. up with** sich abgeben mit

take′-home pay′ *s* Nettolohn *m*

take′-off′ *s* Karikatur *f;* (aer) Start *m*

take′-off ramp′ *s* (*in skiing*) Schanzentisch *m*

take′o′ver *s* Übernahme *f*

tal′cum pow′der [′tælkəm] *s* Federweiß *n*

tale [tel] *s* Geschichte *f;* **tell tales out of school** aus der Schule plaudern

tale′bear′er *s* Zuträger –in *mf*

talent [′tælənt] *s* Talent *n*

tal′ented *adj* talentiert, begabt

talisman [′tælɪsmən] *s* Talisman *m*

talk [tɔk] *s* Gespräch *n;* (*gossip*) Geschwätz *n;* (*lecture*) Vortrag *m;* (*speech*) Rede *f;* **cause t.** von sich reden machen; **give a t. on** e-n Vortrag halten über (*acc*); **t. of the town** Stadtgespräch *n* ‖ *tr* reden; (*business, politics, etc.*) sprechen über (*acc*); **t. down** zum Schweigen bringen; (aer) heruntersprechen; **t. one-**

self hoarse sich heiser reden; **t. one's way out of** sich herausreden aus; **t.** over **besprechen**; **t. sense** vernünftig reden; **t. s.o. into** (ger) j-n überreden zu (inf); **t. up** Reklame machen für ‖ intr reden; (chat) schwätzen; **t. back** scharf erwidern; **t. big** große Töne reden; **t. dirty** Zoten reißen; **t. down to** herablassend reden zu; **talking of food à propos** Essen; **t. on** (a topic) e-n Vortrag halten über (acc); **t. to the walls** in den Wind reden

talkative ['tɔkətɪv] adj redselig

talker ['tɔkər] s Plauderer –in mf; **big t.** Schaumschläger m

talkie ['tɔki] s (cin) Sprechfilm m

talk'ing-to' s Denkzettel m

tall [tɔl] adj hoch; (person) hochgewachsen; **t. story** Mordsgeschichte f

tallow ['tælo] s Talg m

tal·ly ['tæli] s (reckoning) Rechnung f; (game score) Punktzahl f ‖ v (pret & pp –lied) tr (up) berechnen ‖ intr (with) übereinstimmen (mit)

tallyho [,tæli'ho] interj hallo!

tal'ly sheet' s Zählbogen m

talon ['tælən] s Klaue f

tambourine [,tæmbə'rin] s Tamburin n

tame [tem] adj zahm; (docile) gefügig; (dull) langweilig ‖ tr zähmen; (e.g., lions) bändigen ‖ intr—**t. down** (said of a person) gesetzter werden

tamp [tæmp] tr (a tobacco pipe) stopfen; (earth, cement) stampfen; (a drill hole) zustopfen

tamper ['tæmpər] s Stampfer m ‖ intr —**t. with** sich einmischen in (acc); (machinery) herumbasteln an (dat); (documents) frisieren

tampon ['tæmpən] s Damenbinde f; (surg) Tampon m ‖ tr (surg) tamponieren

tan [tæn] adj gelbbraun ‖ s Sonnenbräunung f ‖ v (pret & pp tanned; ger tanning) tr (the skin) bräunen; (leather) gerben ‖ intr sich bräunen

tandem ['tændəm] adj & adv hintereinander (geordnet) ‖ s Tandem n; **in t.** hintereinander

tang [tæŋ] s Herbheit f; (sound) Geklingel n

tangent ['tændʒənt] adj—**be t. to** tangieren ‖ s Tangente f; **fly off on a t.** plötzlich vom Thema abschweifen

tangerine [,tændʒə'rin] s Mandarine f

tangible ['tændʒɪbəl] adj (& fig) greifbar

tangle ['tæŋgəl] s Verwicklung f; (twisted strands; confused jumble) Gewirr n; (conflict) Auseinandersetzung f ‖ tr verwirren; **get tangled** sich verfilzen ‖ intr sich verwirren; **t. with** sich in e-n Kampf einlassen mit

tango ['tæŋgo] s Tango m ‖ intr Tango tanzen

tangy ['tæŋi] adj herb

tank [tæŋk] s Behälter m; (of a toilet) Spülkasten m; (mil) Panzer m

tank' attack' s Panzerangriff m

tank' car' s (rr) Kesselwagen m, Tankwagen m

tanker ['tæŋkər] s (truck) Tankwagen m; (ship) Tanker m; (plane) Tankflugzeug n

tank' trap' s Panzersperre f

tank' truck' s Tankwagen m

tanned adj gebräunt

tanner ['tænər] s Gerber –in mf

tannery ['tænəri] s Gerberei f

tantalize ['tæntə,laɪz] tr quälen

tantamount ['tæntə,maʊnt] adj—**be t. to** gleichkommen (dat)

tantrum ['tæntrəm] s Koller m; **throw a t.** e-n Koller kriegen

tap [tæp] s (light blow) Klaps m; (on a window or door) Klopfen n; (faucet) Wasserhahn m; (in a cask) Faßhahn m; (elec) Anzapfung f; (mach) Gewindebohrer m; (surg) Punktion f; **on tap** vom Faß; **play taps** (mil) den Zapfenstreich blasen ‖ v (pret & pp tapped; ger tapping) tr (a cask, powerline, telephone) anzapfen; (fluids) abzapfen; (a person on the shoulder) antippen; (a hole) mit e-m Gewinde versehen; **tap one's foot** (to mark time) Takt treten; **tap s.o. for** (money) (coll) j-n anpumpen um; **tap s.o.'s spine** j-n punktieren; **tap the window** am Fenster klopfen ‖ intr tippen

tap' dance' s Steptanz m

tap'-dance' intr steppen

tap' dan'cer s Stepper –in mf

tape [tep] s Band n; (electron) Tonband n; (friction tape) Isolierband n; (of paper) Papierstreifen m; (med) Klebstreifen m; (sport) Zielband n ‖ tr (mit Band) umwickeln; (electron) auf Tonband aufnehmen

tape' meas'ure s Meßband n

taper ['tepər] s Wachsfaden m ‖ tr zuspitzen ‖ intr spitz zulaufen; **t. off** langsam abnehmen

tape' record'er s Tonbandgerät n

ta'pered adj kegelförmig, Keil-

tapestry ['tæpɪstri] s Wandteppich m

tape'worm' s Bandwurm m

tapioca [,tæpɪ'okə] s Tapioka f

tappet ['tæpɪt] s (mach) Stößel m

tap'room' s Ausschank m

tap'root' s Pfahlwurzel f

tap' wa'ter s Leitungswasser n

tap' wrench' s Gewindeschneidkluppe f

tar [tar] s Teer m ‖ v (pret & pp tarred; ger tarring) tr teeren

tardy ['tardi] adj säumig

target ['targɪt] s Ziel n; (on a firing range; of ridicule) Zielscheibe f

tar'get ar'ea s Zielraum m

tar'get date' s Zieltag m

tar'get lan'guage s Zielsprache f

tar'get prac'tice s Scheibenschießen n

tariff ['tærɪf] s Tarif m

tarnish ['tarnɪʃ] tr matt (or blind) machen; (fig) beflecken ‖ intr matt (or blind) werden

tar' pa'per s Teerpappe f

tarpaulin ['tarpəlɪn] s Plane f

tar·ry ['tari] adj teerig ‖ ['tæri] v

(*pret & pp* –ried) *intr* verweilen; (*stay*) bleiben

tart [tɑrt] *adj* sauer; (*reply*) scharf ‖ *s* Tortelett *n*

tartar ['tɑrtər] *s* (dent) Zahnstein *m*

tar'tar sauce' *s* pikante Soße *f*

task [tæsk] *s* Aufgabe *f*; **take to t.** zur Rede stellen

task' force' *s* Sonderverband *m*

task'mas'ter *s* Zuchtmeister *m*

tassel ['tæsəl] *s* Quaste *f*; (*on corn*) Narbenfäden *pl*

taste [test] *s* (& fig) Geschmack *m*; **develop a t. for** Geschmack gewinnen an (*dat*); **have a bad t.** schlecht ‖ *intr*—**t. like** (or of) schmecken nach; **have bad t.** e-n schlechten Geschmack haben; **in bad t.** geschmacklos; **in good t.** geschmackvoll; **to t.** (culin) nach Gutdünken ‖ *tr* schmecken; (*try out*) kosten; (*e.g., the pepper in soup*) herausschmecken; **t. blood** (fig) Blut lecken

taste' bud' *s* Geschmacksknospe *f*

tasteful ['testfəl] *adj* geschmackvoll

tasteless ['testlɪs] *adj* (& fig) geschmacklos

tasty ['testi] *adj* schmackhaft

tatter ['tætər] *s* Lumpen *m* ‖ *tr* zerfetzen

tat'tered *adj* zerlumpt

tattle ['tætəl] *intr* petzen

tattler ['tætlər] *s* Petze *f*

tat'tletale' *s* Petze *f*

tattoo [tæ'tu] *s* Tätowierung *f* ‖ *tr* tätowieren

taunt [tɔnt] *s* Stichelei *f* ‖ *tr* sticheln gegen

taut [tɔt] *adj* straff, prall

tavern ['tævərn] *s* Schenke *f*

tawdry ['tɔdri] *adj* aufgedonnert

tawny ['tɔni] *adj* gelbbraun

tax [tæks] *s* Steuer *f* ‖ *tr* besteuern; (fig) beanspruchen; **tax s.o. with** j-n rügen wegen

taxable ['tæksəbəl] *adj* steuerpflichtig

tax' assess'ment *s* Steuereinschätzung *f*

taxation [tæk'seʃən] *s* Besteuerung *f*

tax' brac'ket *s* Steuerklasse *f*

tax' collec'tor *s* Steuereinnehmer *–in mf*

tax' cut' *s* Steuersenkung *f*

tax' eva'sion *s* Steuerhinterziehung *f*

tax' exemp'tion *s* steuerfreier Betrag *m*

tax-i ['tæksi] *s* Taxi *n*; **go by t.** mit e-m Taxi fahren ‖ *v* (*pret & pp* –ied; *ger* –iing & –ying) *tr* (aer) rollen lassen ‖ *intr* mit e-m Taxi fahren; (aer) rollen

tax'icab' *s* Taxi *n*

tax'i danc'er *s* Taxigirl *n*

taxidermist ['tæksɪˌdʌrmɪst] *s* Tierpräparator –in *mf*

tax'i driv'er *s* Taxifahrer –in *mf*

tax'ime'ter *s* Taxameter *m*

tax'i stand' *s* Taxistand *m*

tax'pay'er *s* Steuerzahler –in *mf*

tax' rate' *s* Steuersatz *m*

tax' return' *s* Steuererklärung *f*

tea [ti] *s* Tee *m*

tea' bag' *s* Teebeutel *m*

tea' cart' *s* Teewagen *m*

teach [titʃ] *v* (*pret & pp* taught [tɔt]) *tr* lehren; (*instruct*) unterrichten; **t. school** an e–r Schule unterrichten; **t. s.o. manners** j–m Manieren beibringen; **t. s.o. music** j–n in Musik unterrichten; **t. s.o.** (to play) tennis j–m das Tennisspielen beibringen ‖ *intr* lehren, unterrichten

teacher ['titʃər] *s* Lehrer –in *mf*

teach'er's pet' *s* Liebling *m* des Lehrers (or der Lehrerin)

teach'ing *s* Lehren *n*; (*profession*) Lehrberuf *m*

teach'ing aid' *s* Lehrmittel *n*

teach'ing staff' *s* Lehrkörper *m*

tea'cup' *s* Teetasse *f*

teak [tik] *s* Teakholz *n*

tea'ket'tle *s* Teekessel *m*

tea' leaves' *spl* Teesatz *m*

team [tim] *s* Team *n*; (*of draught animals*) Gespann *n*; (sport) Mannschaft *f* ‖ *tr* (draft animals) zusammenspannen ‖ *intr*—**t. up with** sich vereinigen mit

team' cap'tain *s* Spielführer –in *mf*

team'mate' *s* Mannschaftskamerad –in *mf*

teamster ['timstər] *s* Fuhrmann *m*; (*trucker*) Lastwagenfahrer *m*

team'work' *s* Gemeinschaftsarbeit *f*; (sport) Zusammenspiel *n*

tea'pot' *s* Teekanne *f*

tear [tɪr] *s* Träne *f*; **bring tears to the eyes** Tränen in die Augen treiben; **burst into tears** in Tränen ausbrechen ‖ [ter] *s* Riß *m* ‖ *v* (*pret* tore [tor]; *pp* torn [torn]) *tr* (zer)reißen; **t. apart** (*meat*) zerreißen; (*a speech*) zerpflücken; **t. away** wegreißen; **t. down** (*a building*) abreißen; (mach) zerlegen; (*a person*) sich [*dat*] das Maul zerreißen über (*acc*); **t. off** abreißen; **t. open** aufreißen; **t. oneself away** sich losreißen; **t. out** ausreißen; **t. up** (*a street*) aufreißen; (*e.g., letter*) zerreißen ‖ *intr* (zer)reißen; **t. along** (at high speed) dahinsausen

teardrop ['tɪrˌdrɑp] *s* Träne *f*

tear' gas' [tɪr] *s* Tränengas *n*

tear-jerker ['tɪrˌdʒʌrkər] *s* (sl) Schnulze *f*

tea'room' *s* Teestube *f*

tease [tiz] *tr* necken; (*e.g., a dog*) quälen; (*hair*) auflockern

teas'ing *s* Neckerei *f*

tea'spoon' *s* Teelöffel *m*

teaspoonful ['tiˌspunˌful] *s* Teelöffel *m*

teat [tit] *s* Zitze *f*

technical ['tɛknɪkəl] *adj* technisch, Fach-

tech'nical in'stitute *s* technische Hochschule *f*

technicality [ˌtɛknɪ'kælɪti] *s* technische Einzelheit *f*

tech'nical school' *s* Technikum *n*

tech'nical term' *s* Fachausdruck *m*

technician [tɛk'nɪʃən] *s* Techniker –in *mf*

technique [tɛk'nik] *s* Technik *f*

technocrat ['tɛknə‚kræt] s Technokrat m

technological [‚tɛknə'ladʒɪkəl] adj technologisch

technology [tɛk'nɑlɪdʒi] s Technologie f

ted'dy bear' ['tedi] s Teddybär m

tedious ['tidɪ-əs] adj langweilig

tee [ti] s (mound) Abschlagplatz m; (wooden or plastic peg) Aufsatz m; **to a tee** aufs Haar ‖ tr—**tee off** (sl) aufregen; **tee up** (golf) auf den Aufsatz stellen ‖ intr—**tee off** (golf) abschlagen

teem [tim] intr (with) wimmeln (von)

teem'ing adj wimmelnd; (rain) strömend

teen-age ['tin‚edʒ] adj halbwüchsig

teen-ager ['tin‚edʒər] s Teenager m

teens [tinz] spl Jugendalter n (vom dreizehnten bis neunzehnten Lebensjahr); **in one's t.** in den Jugendjahren

teeny ['tini] adj (coll) winzig

tee' shot' s (golf) Abschlag m

teeter ['titər] s Schaukeln n ‖ intr schaukeln

teethe [tið] intr zahnen

teeth'ing ring' s Beißring m

teetotaler [ti'totələr] s Abstinenzler –in mf

tele·cast ['tɛlɪ‚kæst] s Fernsehsendung f ‖ v (pret & pp –cast & –casted) tr im Fernsehen übertragen

telecommunications [‚tɛlɪkə‚mjunɪ'keʃəns] spl Fernmeldewesen n

telegram ['tɛlɪ‚græm] s Telegramm n

telegraph ['tɛlɪ‚græf] s Telegraph m ‖ tr & intr telegraphieren

telegrapher [tɪ'legrəfər] s Telegraphist –in mf

tel'egraph pole' s Telegraphenstange f

telemeter [tɪ'lemɪtər] s Telemeter n

telepathy [tɪ'lɛpəθi] s Telepathie f

telephone ['tɛlɪ‚fon] s Telephon n, Fernsprecher m; **be on the t.** am Apparat sein; **by t.** telephonisch; **speak on the t. with** telephonieren mit ‖ tr & intr anrufen

tel'ephone booth' s Telephonzelle f

tel'ephone call' s Telephonanruf m

tel'ephone direc'tory s Teilnehmerverzeichnis n

tel'ephone exchange' s Telephonzentrale f

tel'ephone num'ber s Telephonnummer f

tel'ephone op'erator s Telephonist –in mf

tel'ephone receiv'er s Telephonhörer m

tel'ephoto lens' ['tɛlɪ‚foto] s Teleobjektiv n

telescope ['tɛlɪ‚skop] s Fernrohr n, Perspektiv n ‖ tr ineinanderschieben; (fig) verkürzen ‖ intr sich ineinanschieben

telescopic [‚tɛlɪ'skɑprɪk] adj teleskopisch

telescop'ic sight' s Zielfernrohr n

Teletype ['tɛlɪ‚taɪp] s (trademark) Fernschreiber m ‖ **teletype** tr durch Fernschreiber übermitteln ‖ intr fernschreiben

tel'etype'writ'er s Fernschreiber m

televiewer ['tɛlɪ‚vju-ər] s Fernsehteilnehmer –in mf

televise ['tɛlɪ‚vaɪz] tr im Fernsehen übertragen (or senden)

television ['tɛlɪ‚vɪʒən] adj Fernseh– ‖ s Fernsehen n; **watch t.** fernsehen

tel'evision net'work s Fernsehnetz n

tel'evision screen' s Bildschirm m

tel'evision set' s Fernsehapparat m; **color t.** Farbfernsehapparat m

tel'evision show' s Fernschau f

telex ['tɛlɛks] s Fernschreiber m; (message) Telex n ‖ tr fernschreiben

tell [tɛl] v (pret & pp told [told]) tr (the truth, a lie) sagen; (relate) erzählen; (a secret) anvertrauen; (let know) Bescheid sagen (dat); (inform) bestellen; (express) ausdrücken; (the reason) angeben; (distinguish) auseinanderhalten; **be able to t. time** die Uhr lesen können; **t. apart** auseinanderhalten; **t. me another!** (sl) das machst du mir nicht weis!; **t. s.o. off** j–n abkanzeln; **t. s.o. that** (assure s.o. that) j–m versichern, daß; **t. s.o. to** (inf) j–m sagen, daß er (inf) soll; **t. s.o. where to get off** (sl) j–m e–e Zigarre verpassen; **to t. the truth** erhlich gesagt; **you can t. by looking at her** that man sieht es ihr an, daß ‖ intr—**don't t. me!** na, so was!; **t. on** (betray) verraten; (produce a marked effect on) sehr mitnehmen; **you're telling me!** wem sagst du das!

teller ['tɛlər] s (of a bank) Kassierer –in mf; (of votes) Zähler –in mf

tell'ing adj (blow) wirksam

tell'-tale' adj verräterisch

temper ['tɛmpər] s (anger) Zorn m; (of steel) Härtegrad m; **bad t.** großer Zorn m; **even t.** Gleichmut m; **lose one's t.** in Wut geraten ‖ tr (with) mildern (durch); (steel) härten; (mus) temperieren

temperament ['tɛmpərəmənt] s Temperament n

temperamental [‚tɛmpərə'mɛntəl] adj launisch, temperamentvoll

temperance ['tɛmpərəns] s Mäßigkeit f

temperate ['tɛmpərɪt] adj mäßig; (climate) gemäßigt

Tem'perate Zone' s gemäßigte Zone f

temperature ['tɛmərət/ər] s Temperatur f

tempest ['tɛmpɪst] s Sturm m; **a t. in a teapot** ein Sturm im Wasserglas

tempestuous [tɛm'pɛstʃu-əs] adj stürmisch

temple ['tɛmpəl] s Tempel m; (of glasses) Bügel m; (anat) Schläfe f

tem·po ['tɛmpo] s (–pos & –pi [pi]) Tempo n

temporal ['tɛmpərəl] adj zeitlich

temporary ['tɛmpə‚rɛri] adj zeitweilig; (credit, solution) Zwischen–

temporize ['tɛmpə‚raɪz] intr Zeit zu gewinnen suchen

tempt [tɛmpt] tr versuchen; (said of things) reizen, locken

temptation [temp'teʃən] *s* Versuchung *f*

tempter ['temptər] *s* Versucher *m*

tempt'ing *adj* verlockend

temptress ['temptrɪs] *s* Versucherin *f*

ten [ten] *adj & pron* zehn ‖ *s* Zehn *f*

tenable ['tenəbəl] *adj* haltbar

tenacious [tɪ'neʃəs] *adj* (*obstinate*) nartnäckig; (*memory*) verläßlich

tenacity [tɪ'næsɪtɪ] *s* Hartnäckigkeit *f*

tenant ['tenənt] *s* Mieter –in *mf*

ten'ant farm'er *s* Pächter –in *mf*

tend [tend] *tr* (*flocks*) hüten; (*the sick*) pflegen; (*a machine*) bedienen ‖ *intr*—**t. to** (*attend to*) sich kümmern um; (*inf*) dazu neigen zu (*inf*); **t. toward(s)** neigen zu

tendency ['tendənsɪ] *s* Tendenz *f*

tender ['tendər] *adj* zart ‖ *s* Angebot *n*; (*nav*, rr) Tender *m* ‖ *tr* anbieten

ten'derfoot' *s* Neuankömmling *m*; (*boy-scout*) neu aufgenommener Pfadfinder *m*

ten'derheart'ed *adj* zartfühlend

ten'derloin' *s* Rindslendenstück *n*

tenderness ['tendərnɪs] *s* Zartheit *f*

tendon ['tendən] *s* Sehne *f*

tendril ['tendrɪl] *s* Ranke *f*

tenement ['tenɪmənt] *s* (*dwelling*) Wohnung *f*; (*rented dwelling*) Mietwohnung *f*

ten'ement house' *s* Mietskaserne *f*

tenet ['tenɪt] *s* Grundsatz *m*, Lehrsatz *m*

ten'fold' *adj & adv* zehnfach

tennis ['tenɪs] *s* Tennis *n*

ten'nis court' *s* Tennisplatz *m*

ten'nis rack'et *s* Tennisschläger *m*

tenor ['tenər] *s* (*drift, meaning; singer; voice range*) Tenor *m*

ten'pin' *s* Kegel *m*

tense [tens] *adj* gespannt, straff; **make t.** spannen ‖ *s* (*gram*) Tempus *n*, Zweitform *f*

tension ['tenʃən] *s* (& elec) Spannung *f*; (*phys*) Spannkraft *f*

tent [tent] *s* Zelt *n*

tentacle ['tentəkəl] *s* Fühler *m*; (bot) Tentakel *m*

tentative ['tentətɪv] *adj* vorläufig

tenth [tenθ] *adj & pron* zehnte ‖ *s* (*fraction*) Zehntel *n*; **the t.** (*in dates and in series*) der Zehnte

tent' pole' *s* Zeltstange *f*

tenuous ['tenjʊ-əs] *adj* (*thin*) dünn; (*rarefied*) verdünnt; (*insignificant*) unbedeutend; (*weak*) schwach

tenure ['tenjər] *s* (*possession*) Besitz *m*; (*educ*) Anstellung *f* auf Lebenszeit; **t. of office** Amtsdauer *f*

tepid ['tepɪd] *adj* lauwarm

term [tʌrm] *s* (*expression*) Ausdruck *m*; (*time period*) Frist *f*; (*of office*) Amtszeit *f*; (jur) Sitzungsperiode *f*; (math) Glied *n*; (log) Begriff *m*; **be on good terms with** in guten Beziehungen stehen mit; **come to terms with** handelseinig werden mit; **in plain terms** unverblümt; **in terms of** im Sinne von; **in terms of praise** mit lobenden Worten; **on easy terms zu** günstigen Bedingungen; **on equal terms** auf gleichem Fuß; **on t.** (com) auf Zeit; **not be on speaking terms with** nicht sprechen mit; **tell s.o. in no uncertain terms** j–m gründlich die Meinung sagen; **terms** (*of a contract, treaty, payment*) Bedingungen *pl* ‖ *tr* bezeichnen

termagant ['tʌrməgənt] *s* Xanthippe *f*

terminal ['tʌrmɪnəl] *adj* End-; (*disease*) unheilbar ‖ *s* (aer) Flughafenempfangsgebäude *n*; (*pole*) (elec) Pol *m*; (rr) Kopfbahnhof *m*

terminate ['tʌrmɪ,net] *tr* (*end*) beenden; (*limit*) begrenzen ‖ *intr* enden, endigen; (gram) (**in**) auslauten (auf *acc*)

termination [,tʌrmɪ'neʃən] *s* Beendigung *f*; (gram) Endung *f*

terminology [,tʌrmɪ'nɑlɪdʒɪ] *s* Terminologie *f*

term' insur'ance *s* Versicherung *f* auf Zeit

terminus ['tʌrmɪnəs] *s* (*end*) Endpunkt *m*; (*boundary*) Grenze *f*; (rr) Endstation *f*

termite ['tʌrmaɪt] *s* Termite *f*

term' pa'per *s* Referat *n*

terrace ['terəs] *s* Terrasse *f* ‖ *tr* abstufen, terrassieren

terra cotta ['terə'kɑtə] *s* Terrakotta *f*

ter'ra-cot'ta *adj* Terrakotta–

terrain [te'ren] *s* Gelände *n*, Terrain *n*

terrestrial [tə'restrɪ-əl] *adj* irdisch

terrible ['terɪbəl] *adj* furchtbar

terribly ['terɪblɪ] *adv* (coll) furchtbar

terrier ['terɪ-ər] *s* Terrier *m*

terrific [tə'rɪfɪk] *adj* (*frightful*) fürchterlich; (*intense*) (coll) gewaltig; (*splendid*) (coll) prima

terri-fy ['terɪ,faɪ] *v* (*pret & pp* –**fied**) *tr* Entsetzen einjagen (*dat*)

ter'rifying *adj* schrecklich

territorial [,terɪ'torɪ-əl] *adj* territorial; **t. waters** Hoheitsgewässer *pl*

territory ['terɪ,torɪ] *s* Gebiet *n*, Territorium *n*; (*of a salesman*) Absatzgebiet *n*; (pol) Hoheitsgebiet *n*; (sport) Spielhälfte *f*

terror ['terər] *s* Schrecken *m*; **in t.** vor Schrecken

terrorism ['terə,rɪzəm] *s* Terrorismus *m*

terrorist ['terərɪst] *s* Terrorist –in *mf*

terrorize ['terə,raɪz] *tr* terrorisieren

ter'ror-strick'en *adj* schreckerfüllt

ter'ry cloth' ['terɪ] *s* Frottee *m & n*

terse [tʌrs] *adj* knapp

tertiary ['tʌrʃɪ-ərɪ] *adj* Tertiär–

test [test] *s* Probe *f*, Prüfung *f*; (*criterion*) Prüfstein *m*; (med) Probe *f*; **put to the t.** auf die Probe stellen ‖ *tr* (**for**) prüfen (auf *acc*); (chem) (**for**) analysieren (auf *acc*); **t. out** (coll) ausprobieren

testament ['testəmənt] *s* Testament *n*

testator [tes'tetər] *s* Erblasser –in *mf*

test' ban' *s* Atomstopp *m*

test' case' *s* Probefall *m*; (jur) Präzedenzfall *m*

test' flight' *s* Probeflug *m*

testicle ['testɪkəl] *s* Hoden *m*

testi-fy ['testɪ,faɪ] *v* (*pret & pp* –**fied**)

intr (against) zeugen (gegen), aussagen (gegen); **t. to** bezeugen

testimonial [ˌtestɪˈmonɪ-əl] *adj* (*dinner*) Ehren- ‖ *s* Anerkennungsschreiben *n*

testimony [ˈtestɪˌmonɪ] *s* Zeugnis *n*

test′ pa′per *s* Prüfungsarbeit *f*

test′ pi′lot *s* Versuchsflieger –in *mf*

test′ tube′ *s* Reagenzglas *n*

testy [ˈtestɪ] *adj* reizbar

tetanus [ˈtetənəs] *s* Starrkrampf *m*

tether [ˈteðər] *s* Haltestrick *m*; **be at the end of one's t.** nicht mehr weiter wissen ‖ *tr* anbinden

Teuton [ˈt(j)utən] *s* Teutone *m*, Teutonin *f*

Teutonic [t(j)uˈtɑnɪk] *adj* teutonisch

text [tekst] *s* Text *m*

text′book′ *s* Lehrbuch *n*

textile [ˈtekstaɪl] *adj* Textil- ‖ *s* Webstoff *m*; **textiles** Textilien *pl*

textual [ˈtekst√-əl] *adj* textlich

texture [ˈtekstʃər] *s* (*structure*) Gefüge *n*; (*of a fabric*) Gewebe *n*; (*of a play*) Aufbau *m*

Thai [taɪ] *adj* Thai- ‖ *s* (*person*) Thai –in *mf*; (*language*) Thai *n*

Thailand [ˈtaɪlænd] *s* Thailand *n*

Thames [temz] *s* Themse *f*

than [ðæn] *conj* als; **t. ever** denn je

thank [θæŋk] *s* (*offering*) Dank- ‖ **thanks** *spl* Dank *m*; **give thanks to** danken (*dat*); **many thanks!** vielen Dank!; **return thanks** danksagen; **thanks a lot!** danke vielmals!; **thanks to her,** I ich verdanke es ihr, daß ich ‖ *tr* danken (*dat*); **t. God!** Gott sei Dank!; **t. goodness!** gottlob!; **t. you!** danke schön!; **t. you ever so much!** verbindlichsten Dank!; **you have only yourself to t. for** das hast du dir nur selbst zu verdanken

thankful [ˈθæŋkfəl] *adj* dankbar

thankless [ˈθæŋklɪs] *adj* undankbar

Thanksgiv′ing Day′ *s* Danksagungstag *m*

that [ðæt] *adj* jener, der; **t. one** der da, jener ‖ *adv* (*coll*) so, derart ‖ *rel pron* der, welcher; (*after indefinite pronouns*) was ‖ *dem pron* das; **about t.** darüber; **after t.** danach; **and that's t.** und damit punktum!; **at t.** so, dabei; **by t.** dadurch; **for all t.** trotz alledem; **for t.** dafür; **from t.** daraus; **in t.** darin, daran; **on t.** darauf, drauf; **t.** is das heißt; **that's out** das kommt nicht in Frage!; **t. will do!** genug!, reicht! ‖ *conj* daß

thatch [θætʃ] *s* Dachstroh *n*

thatched′ roof′ *s* Strohdach *n*

thaw [θɔ] *s* Tauwetter *n* ‖ *tr & intr* (auf)tauen

the [ðə], [ðɪ] *def art* der, die, das ‖ *adv*—**so much the better** um so besser; **the … the …** desto, je … um so

theater [ˈθi-ətər] *s* Theater *n*

the′atergo′er *s* Theaterbesucher –in *mf*

the′ater of war′ *s* Kriegsschauplatz *m*

theatrical [θɪˈætrɪkəl] *adj* (& *fig*) theatralisch

thee [ði] *pers pron* dich; **to t.** dir

theft [θeft] *s* Diebstahl *m*

their [ðer] *poss adj* ihr

theirs [ðerz] *poss pron* ihrer

them [ðem] *pron* sie; **to t.** ihnen

theme [θim] *s* Thema *n*; (*essay*) Aufsatz *m*; (*mus*) Thema *n*

theme′ song′ *s* Kennmelodie *f*

themselves′ *intens pron* selbst, selber ‖ *reflex pron* sich

then [ðen] *adv* (*next; in that case*) dann; (*at that time*) damals; **by t.** bis dahin; **from t. on** von da an; **t. and there** auf der Stelle; **till t.** bis dahin; **what t.?** was dann?

thence [ðens] *adv* von da, von dort; (*from that fact*) daraus

thence′forth′ *adv* von da an

theologian [ˌθi-əˈlodʒən] *s* Theologe *m*, Theologin *f*

theological [ˌθi-əˈlɑdʒɪkəl] *adj* theologisch

theology [θiˈɑlədʒɪ] *s* Theologie *f*

theorem [ˈθi-ərəm] *s* Lehrsatz *m*

theoretical [ˌθi-əˈretɪkəl] *adj* theoretisch

theorist [ˈθi-ərɪst] *s* Theoretiker –in *mf*

theorize [ˈθi-əˌraɪz] *intr* theoretisieren

theory [ˈθi-ərɪ] *s* Theorie *f*, Lehre *f*

the′ory of relativ′ity *s* Relativitätstheorie *f*

therapeutic [ˌθerəˈpjutɪk] *adj* therapeutisch ‖ **therapeutics** *s* Therapeutik *f*

therapy [ˈθerəpɪ] *s* Therapie *f*

there [ðer] *adv* (*position*) da; (*direction*) dahin; **down t.** da unten; **not be all t.** (coll) nicht ganz richtig sein; **over t.** da drüben; **t. are** es gibt, es sind; **t. is** es gibt, es ist; **t., t.!** sachte, sachte!; **up t.** da (or dort) oben

there′abouts′ *adv* daherum; **ten people or t.** so ungefähr zehn Leute

there′af′ter *adv* danach

there′by′ *adv* dadurch, damit

therefore [ˈðer‚for] *adv* deshalb, darum

there′in′ *adv* darin

there′of′ *adv* davon

there′to′ *adv* dazu

there′upon′ *adv* daraufhin, danach

there′with′ *adv* damit

thermal [ˈθɑrməl] *adj* Thermal-, Wärme-

thermodynamic [ˌθɑrmodaɪˈnæmɪk] *adj* thermodynamisch ‖ **thermodynamics** *s* Thermodynamik *f*, Wärmelehre *f*

thermometer [θerˈmɑmɪtər] *s* Thermometer *n*

thermonuclear [ˌθermoˈn(j)uklɪ-ər] *adj* thermonuklear

ther′mos bot′tle [ˈθɑrməs] *s* Thermosflasche *f*

thermostat [ˈθɑrmə‚stæt] *s* Thermostat *m*

thesau·rus [θɪˈsɔrəs] *s* (**–ri** [raɪ]) Thesaurus *m*

these [ðiz] *dem adj & pron* diese

the·sis [ˈθisɪs] *s* (**–ses** [siz]) These *f*

they [ðe] *pers pron* sie; **t. say** man sagt

thick [θɪk] *adj* dick; (*dense*) dicht;

(stupid) stumpfsinnig; *(lips)* wulstig; *(intimate)* (coll) dick; **t. with** dust dick bedeckt mit Staub ‖ *adv*—**be in t. with** (coll dicke Beziehungen haben mit; **come t. and fast** Schlag auf Schlag gehen; **lay it on t.** (coll) dick auftragen ‖ *s*—**in the t. of** mitten in *(dat)*; **through t. and thin** durch dick und dünn

thicken ['θɪkən] *tr* verdicken; *(make denser)* verdichten; *(a sauce)* eindicken ‖ *intr* sich verdicken; *(become denser)* sich verdichten; *(said of liquids)* sich verfestigen; *(said of a sauce)* eindicken; **the plot thickens** der Knoten schürzt sich

thicket ['θɪkɪt] *s* Dickicht *n*

thick'head' *s* (coll) Dickkopf *m*

thick'-head'ed *adj* (coll) dickköpfig

thickness ['θɪknɪs] *s* Dicke *f*

thick'-set' *adj* stämmig

thick'skinned' *adj* (coll) dickfellig

thief [θif] *s* (thieves [θivz]) Dieb –in *mf*

thieve [θiv] *intr* stehlen

thievery ['θivəri] *s* Dieberei *f*

thievish ['θivɪ/] *adj* diebisch

thigh [θaɪ] *s* Schenkel *m*, Oberschenkel *m*

thighbone' *s* Oberschenkelknochen *m*

thimble ['θɪmbəl] *s* Fingerhut *m*

thin [θɪn] *adj* (thinner; thinnest) dünn; *(hair)* schütter; *(lean)* mager; *(excuse)* schwach; *(soup)* wäßrig ‖ *v* (pret & pp thinned; ger thinning) *tr* *(a liquid)* verdünnen; *(a forest)* lichten; **t. out** *(plants)* vereinzeln ‖ *intr* *(said of hair)* sich lichten; **t. out** *(said of a crowd)* sich verlaufen

thing [θɪŋ] *s* Ding *n*, Sache *f*; **among other things** unter anderem; **first t.** zu allerest; **how are things?** wie geht's?; **I'll do no such t.!** ich werde mich schön hüten; **of all things!** na sowas!; **the real t.** das Richtige; **things** *(the situation)* die Lage *f*; *(belongings)* Sachen *pl*

think [θɪŋk] *v* (pret & pp thought [θɔt]) *tr* denken; *(regard)* halten; *(believe)* glauben, denken; **he thinks he's clever** er hält sich für klug; **that's what you t.!** ja, denkste!; **t. better of it** sich e-s Besseren besinnen; **t. it best to** *(inf)* es für das Beste halten zu *(inf)*; **t. little of** nicht viel halten von; **t. nothing of it!** es ist nicht der Rede wert!; **t. over** sich *(dat)* überlegen; **t. up** sich *(dat)* ausdenken; **what do you t. you're doing?** was soll das? ‖ *intr* denken; **be thinking of** *(ger)* beabsichtigen zu *(inf)*; **do you t. so?** meinen Sie?; **t. about** *(call to consciousness)* denken an *(acc)*; *(reflect on)* nachdenken über *(acc)*; *(be concerned about)* bedacht sein auf *(acc)*; **t. twice before** es sich *(dat)* zweimal überlegen, bevor

thinker ['θɪŋkər] *s* Denker –in *mf*

thin'-lipped' *adj* dünnlippig

thinner ['θɪnər] *s* Verdünnungsmittel *n*

third [θɪrd] *adj & pron* dritte ‖ *s* *(frac-*

tion) Drittel *n*; *(mus)* Terz *f*; **the third** *(in dates and in series)* der Dritte

third'-class' *adj & adv* dritter Klasse

third' degree' *s*—**give s.o. the t.** j–n e–m Folterverhör unterwerfen

third' par'ty *s* Dritter *m*, dritte Seite *f*

third'-rate' *adj* drittrangig

thirst [θʌrst] *s* (for) Durst *m* (nach); **t. for knowledge** Wissensdurst *m*; **t. for power** Herrschsucht *f* ‖ *intr* (for) dürsten (nach)

thirsty ['θʌrsti] *adj* durstig; **be t.** Durst haben

thirteen ['θʌr'tin] *adj & pron* dreizehn ‖ *s* Dreizehn *f*

thirteenth ['θʌr'tinθ] *adj & pron* dreizehnte ‖ *s* *(fraction)* Dreizehntel *n*; **the t.** *(in dates and in series)* der Dreizehnte

thirtieth ['θʌrtɪ·ɪθ] *adj & pron* dreißigste ‖ *s* *(fraction)* Dreißigstel *n*; **the t.** *(in dates and in series)* der Dreißigste

thirty ['θʌrti] *adj & pron* dreißig ‖ *s* Dreißig *f*; **the thirties** die dreißiger Jahre

thir'ty-one' *adj & pron* einunddreißig

this [ðɪs] *dem adj* dieser; **t. afternoon** heute nachmittag; **t. evening** heute abend; **t. minute** augenblicklich; **one** dieser ‖ *adv* (coll) so ‖ *dem pron* dieser, der; **about t.** hierüber; *(concerning this)* davon; **t. and that** dies und jenes

thistle ['θɪsəl] *s* Distel *f*

thither ['θɪðər] *adv* dorthin, hinzu

thong [θɔŋ] *s* Riemen *m*; *(sandal)* Sandale *f*

tho-rax ['θoræks] *s* (–raxes & –races [rə‚siz]) Brustkorb *m*

thorn [θɔrn] *s* Dorn *m*; **t. in the side** Dorn *m* im Fleisch

thorny ['θɔrni] *adj* dornig; (fig) heikel

thorough ['θʌro] *adj* gründlich; tüchtig

thor'oughbred' *adj* reinrassig ‖ *s* Vollblut *n*; *(horse)* Vollblutpferd *n*, Rassepferd *n*

thor'oughfare' *s* Durchgang *m*; **no t.** (public sign) Durchgang verboten

thor'oughgo'ing *adj* gründlich

thoroughly ['θʌroli] *adv* gründlich

those [ðoz] *dem adj & pron* jene, die da

thou [ðaʊ] *pers pron* du

though [ðo] *adv* immerhin ‖ *conj* obwohl

thought [θɔt] *s* Gedanke(n) *m*; **be lost in t.** in Gedanken versunken sein; **give some t. to** sich *[dat]* Gedanken machen über *(acc)*; **have second thoughts** sich *[dat]* eines Besseren besinnen; **on second t.** nach reiflicher Überlegung; **the mere t.** schon der Gedanke

thoughtful ['θɔtfəl] *adj* *(reflective)* nachdenklich; *(e.g., essay)* gedankenvoll; *(considerate)* aufmerksam; *(gift)* sinnig; **t. of** bedacht auf *(acc)*

thoughtless ['θɔtlɪs] *adj* gedankenlos

thought'-provok'ing *adj* anregend

thousand ['θauzənd] *adj & pron* tausend; **a t. times** tausendmal || *s* Tausend *f;* **by the t.** zu Tausenden

thousandth ['θauzəndθ] *adj & pron* tausendste || *s* (*fraction*) Tausendstel *n*

thrash [θræ∫] *tr* (& *fig*) dreschen; **t. out** (*debate*) gründlich erörten || *intr* dreschen; **t. about** sich hin- und herwerfen

thrash'ing *s* Dreschen *n;* (*beating*) Dresche *f*

thread [θred] *s* Faden *m;* (*of a screw*) Gewinde *n;* (*of a story*) Faden *m;* **hang by a t.** an e-m Faden hängen || *tr* (*a needle*) einfädeln; (*pearls*) aufreihen; (*mach*) Gewinde schneiden in (*acc*)

thread'bare' *adj* fadenscheinig

threat [θret] *s* Drohung *f*

threaten ['θretən] *tr* drohen (*dat*), bedrohen; **t. so. with s.th.** j-m etw androhen || *intr* drohen

three [θri] *adj & pron* drei || *s* Drei *f;* **in threes** zu dritt

three' cheers' *spl* ein dreimaliges Hoch *n*

three'-dimen'sional *adj* dreidimensional

three'-en'gine *adj* dreimotorig

three'-piece' *adj* (*suit*) dreiteilig

three'-ply' *adj* dreischichtig

three'-point land'ing *s* Dreipunktlandung *f*

threnody ['θrenədi] *s* Klagelied *n*

thresh [θre∫] *tr* dreschen; **t. out** (*debate*) gründlich erörten || *intr* dreschen

thresh'ing floor' *s* Dreschtenne *f*

thresh'ing machine' *s* Dreschmaschine *f*

threshold ['θre∫old] *s* Türschwelle *f;* (*psychol*) Schwelle *f*

thrice [θrais] *adv* dreimal

thrift [θrift] *s* Sparsamkeit *f*

thrifty ['θrifti] *adj* sparsam

thrill [θril] *s* Nervenkitzel *m* || *tr* erregen, packen

thriller ['θrilər] *s* Thriller *m*

thrill'ing *adj* packend, spannend

thrive [θraiv] *v* (*pret* **thrived** & **throve** [θrov]; *pp* **thrived** & **thriven** ['θrivən]) *intr* gedeihen

throat [θrot] *s* Kehle *f;* **clear one's t.** sich räuspern; **cut one another's t.** (fig) sich gegenseitig kaputt machen; **cut one's own t.** (fig) sich [*dat*] sein eigenes Grab schaufeln; **jump down s.o.'s t.** j-m an die Gurgel fahren; **sore t.** Halsweh *n*

throb [θrab] *s* Schlagen *n;* (*of a motor*) Dröhnen *n* || *v* (*pret & pp* **throbbed;** *ger* **throbbing**) *intr* schlagen; (*said of a motor or head*) dröhnen

throes [θroz] *spl* Schmerzen *pl;* **be in the t. of death** im Todeskampf liegen

thrombosis [θram'bosis] *s* Thrombose *f*

throne [θron] *s* Thron *m*

throng [θrɔŋ] *s* Menschenmenge *f* || *tr* umdrängen; (*the streets*) sich drängen in (*acc*) || *intr* (**around**) sich drängen (um)

throttle ['θratəl] *s* Drossel(klappe) *f* || *tr* drosseln; (*a person*) erwürgen || *intr*—**t. back** (*aut*) das Gas zurücknehmen

through [θru] *adj* (*traffic, train*) Durchgangs–; (*street*) durchgehend; (*finished*) fertig; (*coll*) quitt || *adv*— **t. and t.** durch und durch || *prep* durch (*acc*)

throughout' *adv* durch und durch || *prep* hindurch (*acc*) (*postpositive*), e.g., **t. the summer** den ganzen Sommer hindurch; **t. the world** in der ganzen Welt

throw [θro] *s* Wurf *m;* (*scarf*) Überwurf *m* || *v* (*pret* **threw** [θru]; *pp* **thrown** [θron]) *tr* werfen; (*a rider*) abwerfen; (*sparks*) sprühen; (*a party, banquet*) geben; (*a game*) absichtlich verlieren; (*into confusion*) bringen; **t. away** wegwerfen; **t. down** niederwerfen; (*overturn*) umwerfen; **t. in** (*e.g., a few extras*) als Zugabe geben; **t. off** (*fig*) aus dem Gleichgewicht bringen; **t. out** hinauswerfen; (*a person*) vor die Tür setzen; (*the chest*) herausdrücken; **t. out of the game** vom Platz verweisen; **t. the book at s.o.** (fig) j-n zur Höchststrafe verurteilen; **t. up to s.o.** j-m vorwerfen || *intr* werfen; **t. up** sich erbrechen

throw'away' *adj* Einweg–

throw'back' *s* (**to**) Rückkehr *f* (zu)

throw' rug' *s* Vorleger *m*

thrum [θrʌm] *v* (*pret & pp* **thrummed;** *ger* **thrumming**) *intr* (**on**) mit den Fingern trommeln (auf *acc*)

thrush [θrʌ∫] *s* (orn) Drossel *f*

thrust [θrʌst] *s* (*shove*) Stoß *m;* (*stab*) Hieb *m;* (aer, archit, geol, rok) Schub *m;* (mil) Vorstoß *m* || *v* (*pret & pp* **thrust**) *tr* stoßen

thud [θʌd] *s* Bums *m* || *v* (*pret & pp* **thudded;** *ger* **thudding**) *tr & intr* bumsen || *interj* bums!

thug [θʌg] *s* Rocker *m*

thumb [θʌm] *s* Daumen *m;* **be all thumbs** zwei linke Hände haben; **be under s.o.'s t.** unter j-s Fuchtel stehen; **thumbs down!** pfui!; **thumbs up!** Kopf hoch! || *tr* (*a book*) abgreifen; **t. a ride** per Anhalter fahren; **t. one's nose at s.o.** j-m e-e lange Nase machen || *intr*—**t. through** durchblättern

thumb' in'dex *s* Daumenindex *m*

thumb'print' *s* Daumenabdruck *m*

thumb'screw' *s* Flügelschraube *f*

thumb'tack' *s* Reißnagel *m*

thump [θʌmp] *s* Bums *m* || *tr & intr* bumsen || *interj* bums!

thump'ing *adj* (coll) enorm

thunder ['θʌndər] *s* Donner *m* || *tr & intr* donnern

thun'derbolt' *s* Donnerkeil *m*

thun'derclap' *s* Donnerschlag *m*

thunderous ['θʌndərəs] *adj* donnernd

thun'dershow'er *s* Gewitterregen *m*

thun'derstorm' *s* Gewitter *n*

thunderstruck ['θʌndər‚strʌk] *adj* (fig) wie vom Schlag getroffen

Thursday ['θʌrzde] *s* Donnerstag *m;* **on T.** am Donnerstag

thus [ðʌs] *adv* so; (*consequently*) also;
t. far soweit

thwack [θwæk] *s* heftiger Schlag *m* ‖
tr klatschen

thwart [θwɔrt] *adj* Quer– ‖ *s* (naut)
Ruderbank *f* ‖ *tr* (*plans*) durchkreuzen; (*a person*) in die Quere
kommen (*dat*)

thy [ðaɪ] *poss adj* dein

thyme [taɪm] *s* Thymian *m*

thy'roid gland' ['θaɪrɔɪd] *s* Schild-
drüse *f*

thyself [ðaɪ'sɛlf] *intens pron* selbst,
selber ‖ *reflex pron* dich

tiara [taɪ'erə] *s* Tiara *f*; (*lady's head-
dress*) Diadem *n*

tibia ['tɪbɪ·ə] *s* Schienbein *n*

tic [tɪk] *s* (pathol) Tick *m*

tick [tɪk] *s* (*of a clock*) Ticken *n*;
(*mattress case*) Überzug *m*; (ent)
Zecke *f*; **on t.** (coll) auf Pump ‖ *tr*—
be ticked off (at) (sl) verärgert sein
(über *acc*); **t. off** (*names, items*) abhaken; (*the minutes*) ticken ‖ *intr*
ticken; **t. by** vergehen

ticker ['tɪkər] *s* (*watch*) (sl) Uhr *f*,
Armbanduhr *f*; (*heart*) (sl) Herz *n*;
(st. exch.) Börsentelegraph *m*

tick'er tape' *s* Papierstreifen *m* (des
Börsentelegraphen)

tick'er-tape parade' *s* Konfettiregen-
parade *f*

ticket ['tɪkɪt] *s* Karte *f*; (*for travel*)
Fahrkarte *f*; (*by air*) Flugkarte *f*;
(*for admission*) Eintrittskarte *f*; (*in
a lottery*) Los *n*; (*for a traffic violation*) Strafzettel *m*; (pol) Wahlliste
f ‖ *tr* etikettieren; (*aut*) mit e–m
Strafzettel versehen

tick'et a'gency *s* Vorverkaufsstelle *f*

tick'et a'gent *s* Fahrkartenverkäufer –in
mf

tick'et of'fice *s* Kartenverkaufsstelle *f*

tick'et win'dow *s* Schalter *m*

tick'ing *s* Ticken *n*

tickle ['tɪkəl] *s* Kitzel *m* ‖ *tr* kitzeln
‖ *intr* jucken

ticklish ['tɪklɪʃ] *adj* kitzlig; (*touchy*)
heikel

ticktock ['tɪk͵tɑk] *adv*—**go t.** ticktack
machen ‖ *s* Ticken *n*

tid'al wave' ['taɪdəl] *s* Flutwelle *f*

tidbit ['tɪd͵bɪt] *s* Leckerbissen *m*

tiddlywinks ['tɪdlɪ͵wɪŋks] *s* Flohhüpf-
spiel *n*

tide [taɪd] *s* Gezeiten *pl*; **against the t.**
(fig) gegen den Strom; **the t. is com-
ing in** die Flut steigt; **the t. is going
out** die Flut fällt ‖ *tr*—**t. s.o. over**
j–n über Wasser halten

tide'land' *s* Watt *n*

tide'wa'ter *s* Flutwasser *n*

tidings ['taɪdɪŋz] *spl* Botschaft *f*

ti·dy ['taɪdi] *adj* ordentlich; (*sum*)
hübsch ‖ *v* (*pret & pp* –**died**) *tr* in
Ordnung bringen; **t. up** aufräumen
‖ *intr*—**t. up** aufräumen

tie [taɪ] *adj* (sport) unentschieden ‖
s (*cord*) Schnur *f*; (*ribbon*) Band *n*;
(*necktie*) Krawatte *f*; (*knot*) Schleife
f; (mus) Ligatur *f*; (parl) Stimmen-
gleichheit *f*; (rr) Schwelle *f*; (sport)

Unentschieden *n*; **end in a tie** punkt-
gleich enden; **ties** (*e.g., of friendship*) Bande *pl* ‖ *v* (*pret & pp* **tied**;
ger **tying**) *tr* binden; **be tied up** (*said
of a person or telephone*) besetzt
sein; **get tied up** (*in traffic*) steckenbleiben; **my hands are tied** mir sind
die Hände gebunden; **tie in with**
verknüpfen mit; **tie oneself down**
sich festlegen; **tie to** festbinden an
(*dat*); **tie up** (*a wound*) verbinden;
(*traffic*) lahmlegen; (*money*) fest anlegen; (*production*) stillegen; (*the
telephone*) blockieren; (*a boat*) festmachen

tie'back' *s* Gardinenhalter *m*

tie'clasp' *s* Krawattenhalter *m*

tie'pin's Krawattennadel *f*

tier [tɪr] *s* Reihe *f*; (theat) Rang *m*

tie'rod' *s* (aut) Zugstange *f*

tie'-up' *s* (*of traffic*) Stockung *f*

tiger ['taɪgər] *s* Tiger *m*

ti'ger shark' *s* Tigerhai *m*

tight [taɪt] *adj* (*firm*) fest; (*clothes*)
eng; (*taut*) straff; (*scarce*) knapp;
(*container*) dicht; (*drunk*) beschwipst; (*with money*) knaus(e)rig;
feel t. in the chest sich beengt fühlen
‖ *adv* fest; **hold t.** festhalten; **sit t.**
sich nicht rühren; **pull t.** stramm-
ziehen ‖ **tights** *spl* Trikot *m & n*

tighten ['taɪtən] *tr* (*a rope*) straff
spannen; (*a belt*) enger schnallen;
(*a jar lid*) festziehen; (*a screw*) anziehen; (*a spring*) spannen; (*a knot*)
zuziehen

tight'-fist'ed *adj* knaus(e)rig

tight'-fit'ting *adj* eng anliegend

tight'-lipped' *adj* verschlossen

tight'rope' *s* Drahtseil *n*; **walk a t.** auf
e–m festgespannten Drahtseil gehen

tight' spot' *s* (coll) Klemme *f*

tight' squeeze' *s* (coll) Zwickmühle *f*

tight'wad' *s* Geizkragen *m*

tigress ['taɪgrɪs] *s* Tigerin *f*

tile [taɪl] *s* (*for the floor or wall*)
Fliese *f*; (*for the roof*) Dachziegel
m; (*glazed tile*) Kachel *f* ‖ *tr* (*a roof*)
mit Ziegeln decken; (*a floor*) mit
Fliesen auslegen; (*a bathroom*)
kacheln

tile' roof' *s* Ziegeldach *n*

till [tɪl] *s* Kasse *f* ‖ *tr* ackern ‖ *prep*
bis (*acc*); **t. now** bisher ‖ *conj* bis

tiller ['tɪlər] *s* (naut) Pinne *f*

tilt [tɪlt] *s* Neigung *f*; **full t.** mit voller
Wucht ‖ *tr* kippen; (*a bottle, the
head*) neigen; **t. back** (*e.g., a chair*)
zurücklehnen; **t. over** umkippen ‖
intr kippen; **t. over** umkippen

timber ['tɪmbər] *s* Holz *n*; (*for structural use*) Bauholz *n*; (*rafter*) Balken
m

tim'berland' *s* Waldland *n*

tim'ber line' *s* Baumgrenze *f*

timbre ['tɪmbər] *s* Klangfarbe *f*

time [taɪm] *s* Zeit *f*; (*limited period*)
Frist *f*; (*instance*) Mal *n*; (mus) Takt
m; **all the t.** ständig; **all this t.** die
ganze Zeit; **any number of times**
x-mal; **at no t.** nie; **at one t.** einst;
at some t. irgendwann; **at that t.**

damals; **at the present t.** derzeit; **at times** manchmal; **at what t.?** um wieviel Uhr?; **by this t.** nunmehr; **do t.** (sl) sitzen; **do you have the t.?** können Sie mir sagen, wie spät es ist?; **for a t.** e–e Zeitlang; **for the last t.** zum letzten Mal; **for the t. being** vorläufig; **give s.o. a hard t.** j–m das Leben schwer machen; **have a good t.** sich gut unterhalten; **have a hard t.** (ger) es schwer haben zu (inf); **in no t.** im Nu; **in t.** zur rechten Zeit; (in the course of time) mit der Zeit; **make good t.** Fortschritte machen; **on one's own t.** in der Freizeit; **on t.** pünktlich; (on schedule) fahrplanmäßig; (com) auf Raten; **several times** mehrmals; **take one's t.** sich [dat] Zeit lassen; **there's t. for that** das hat Zeit; **this t. tomorrow** morgen um diese Zeit; **t.!** (sport) Zeit!; **t. is up!** die Zeit ist um!; **t. of life** Lebensalter n; **times Zeiten** pl; (math) mal, e.g., **two times two** zwei mal zwei; **t. will tell** die Zeit wird es lehren; **what t. is it?** wieviel Uhr ist es? || tr (mit der Uhr) messen; **t. s.th. right** die richtige Zeit wählen für

time′ bomb′ s Zeitbombe f
time′card′ s Stechkarte f
time′ clock′ s Stechuhr f
time′-consum′ing adj zeitraubend
time′ expo′sure s (phot) Zeitaufnahme f
time′ fuse′ s Zeitzünder m
time′-hon′ored adj altehrwürdig
time′keep′er s Zeitnehmer –in mf
time′-lag′ s Verzögerung f
timeless ['taɪmlɪs] adj zeitlos
time′ lim′it s Frist f; **set a t. on** befristen
timely ['taɪmli] adj zeitgerecht; (topic) aktuell
time′ pay′ment s Ratenzahlung f
time′piece′ s Uhr f
timer ['taɪmər] s (person) Zeitnehmer –in mf; (device) Schaltuhr f; (aut) Zündunterbrecher m; (phot) Zeitauslöser m
time′ sig′nal s Zeitzeichen n
time′ stud′y s Zeitstudien pl
time′ta′ble s Zeittabelle f; (aer) Flugplan m; (rr) Fahrplan m
time′work′ s Zeitlohnarbeit f
time′worn′ adj abgenutzt
time′ zone′ s Zeitzone f
timid ['tɪmɪd] adj ängstlich
tim′ing s genaue zeitliche Berechnung f; (aut) Zündeinstellung f
timorous ['tɪmərəs] adj furchtsam
tin [tɪn] adj Zinn– || s (element) Zinn n; (tin plate) Weißblech n
tin′ can′ s Blechdose f
tincture ['tɪŋktʃər] s Tinktur f
tinder ['tɪndər] s Zunder m
tin′derbox′ s (fig) Pulverfaß n
tin′ foil′ s Zinnfolie f
ting-a-ling ['tɪŋə,lɪŋ] s Klingeling m
tinge [tɪndʒ] s (of color) Stich m; (fig) Spur f || v (pret **tingeing** & **tinging**) tr leicht färben

tingle ['tɪŋgəl] s Kribbeln n, Prickeln n || intr kribbeln, prickeln
tinker ['tɪŋkər] s (bungler) Pfuscher m || intr basteln
tinkle ['tɪŋkəl] s Klingeln n || intr klingeln
tin′ mine′ s Zinnbergwerk n
tinsel ['tɪnsəl] s Lametta f; (fig) Flitterkram m
tin′smith′ s Klempner m
tin′ sol′dier s Zinnsoldat m
tint [tɪnt] s Farbton m || tr tönen, leicht färben
tint′ed glass′ s (aut) blendungsfreies Glas n
tiny ['taɪni] adj winzig
tip [tɪp] s Spitze f; (gratuity) Trinkgeld n; (hint) Tip m; **it's on the tip of my tongue** es schwebt mir auf der Zunge || v (pret & pp **tipped**; ger **tipping**) tr schief halten; (a waiter) ein Trinkgeld geben (dat); **tip off** e–n Tip geben (dat); **tip one's hat** auf den Hut tippen (dat) || intr—**tip over** umtippen
tip′-off′ s Tip m, rechtzeitiger Wink m
tipple ['tɪpəl] tr & intr süffeln
tippler ['tɪplər] s Säufer –in mf
tipster ['tɪpstər] s Wettberater m
tipsy ['tɪpsi] adj beschwipst
tip′toe′ s—**on t.** auf den Zehenspitzen || v (pret & pp **–toed**; ger **–toeing**) intr auf den Zehenspitzen gehen
tip′top′ adj tipptopp
tirade ['taɪred] s Tirade f
tire [taɪr] s Reifen m || tr ermüden; **t. out** strapazieren || intr ermüden
tired adj müde; **be t. of** (ger) es satt haben zu (inf); **be t. of coffee** den Kaffee satt haben; **t. out** abgespannt
tire′ gauge′ s Reifendruckmesser m
tireless ['taɪrlɪs] adj unermüdlich
tire′ pres′sure s Reifendruck m
tiresome ['taɪrsəm] adj (tiring) ermüdend; (boring) langweilig
tissue ['tɪʃu] s Gewebe n; (thin paper) Papiertaschentuch n; **t. of lies** Lügengewebe n
tis′sue pa′per s Seidenpapier n
tit [tɪt] s (sl) Brust f; **tit for tat** wie du mir, so ich dir
Titan ['taɪtən] s Titan(e) m
titanic [taɪ'tænɪk] adj titanisch
titanium [taɪ'tenɪ·əm] s Titan n
tithe [taɪð] s Kirchenzehnt m || tr (pay one tenth of) den Zehnten bezahlen von; (exact a tenth from) den Zehnten erheben von
Titian ['tɪʃən] adj tizianrot
titillate ['tɪtɪ,let] tr & intr kitzeln, (angenehm) reizen
title ['taɪtəl] s Titel m; (to a property) Eigentumsrecht n; (claim) Rechtstitel m; (of a chapter) Überschrift f; (honor) Würde f; (aut) Kraftfahrzeugbrief m || tr titulieren
ti′tle bout′ s (box) Titelkampf m
ti′tled adj ad(e)lig
ti′tle deed′ s Eigentumsurkunde f
ti′tle hold′er s Titelverteidiger –in mf
ti′tle page′ s Titelblatt n
ti′tle role′ s Titelrolle f

titter ['tɪtər] s Gekicher n ‖ intr kichern

titular ['tɪtələr] adj Titular–

to [tu], [tʊ] adv—**to and fro** hin und her ‖ prep zu (dat); (a city, country, island) nach (dat); (as far as) bis (acc); (in order to) um ... zu (inf); (against, e.g., a wall) an (dat or acc); **a quarter to eight** viertel vor acht; **how far is it to the town?** wie weit ist es bis zur Stadt?; **to a T** haargenau

toad [tod] s Kröte f

toad'stool' s Giftpilz m

toad·y ['todi] s Schranze m & f ‖ v (pret & pp –ied) intr (to) scharwenzeln (um)

to-and-fro ['tu·ənd'fro] adj Hin– und Her– ‖ adv hin und her

toast [tost] s (bread; salutation) Toast m; **drink a t. to** e–n Toast ausbringen auf (acc) ‖ tr (bread) rösten

toaster ['tostər] s Toaster m

toast'mas'ter s Toastmeister m

tobac·co [tə'bæko] s (–cos) Tabak m

tobac'co pouch' s Tabaksbeutel m

toboggan [tə'bagən] s Rodel m & f ‖ intr rodeln

tocsin ['taksɪn] s Alarmglocke f

today [tu'de] adv heute ‖ s—**from t. on** von heute an; **today's** heutig

toddle ['tadəl] s Watscheln n ‖ intr watscheln

toddler ['tadlər] s Kleinkind n

toddy ['tadi] s Toddy m

to-do [tə'du] s Getue n

toe [to] s Zehe f; **be on one's toes** auf Draht sein; **step on s.o.'s toes** j–m auf die Zehen treten ‖ v (pret & pp toed; ger toeing) tr—**toe the line** nicht aus der Reihe tanzen

toe'dance' s (aut) Spitzentanz m

toe'-in' s (aut) Spur f

toe'nail' s Zehennagel m

together [tu'geðər] adv zusammen; **t. with** mitsamt (dat), samt (dat)

togetherness [tu'geðərnɪs] s Zusammengehörigkeit f

tog'gle switch' ['tagəl] s (elec) Kippschalter m

togs [tagz] spl Klamotten pl

toil [tɔɪl] s Mühe f; **toils** Schlingen pl ‖ intr sich mühen

toilet ['tɔɪlɪt] s (room) Toilette f; (bathroom fixture) Klosett n

toi'let ar'ticle s Toilettenartikel m

toi'let bowl' s Klosettschüssel f

toi'let pa'per s Klosettpapier n

toi'let seat' s Toilettenring m

token ['tokən] adj (payment) symbolisch; (strike) Warn– ‖ Zeichen n; (proof) Beweis m; **by the same t.** aus dem gleichen Grund; **as (or in) t. of** zum Beweis (genit)

tolerable ['talərəbəl] adj erträglich

tolerably ['talərəblɪ] adv leidlich

tolerance ['talərəns] s Duldsamkeit f; (mach) Toleranz f

tolerant ['talərənt] adj (of) duldsam (gegen), tolerant (gegen)

tolerate ['talə,ret] tr dulden

toleration [,talə'reʃən] s Duldung f

toll [tol] adj (road) gebührenpflichtig ‖ s Wegezoll m; (at a bridge) Brückenzoll m; (of bells) Läuten n; (number of victims) Zahl f der Opfer; (fig) Tribut m; (telp) Gebühr f für ein Ferngespräch; **take a heavy t. of life** viele Menschenleben kosten ‖ tr & intr läuten

toll' booth' s Zahlkasse f

toll' bridge' s Zollbrücke f

toll' call' s Ferngespräch n

toll' collec'tor s Zolleinnehmer –in mf

toma·to [tə'meto] s (–toes) Tomate f

toma'to juice' s Tomatensaft f

tomb [tum] s Grab n, Grabmal n

tomboy ['tam ,bɔɪ] s Wildfang m

tomb'stone' s Grabstein m

tomcat ['tam ,kæt] s Kater m

tome [tom] s Band m

tomfoolery [tam'fuləri] s Albernheit f

Tom'my gun' ['tami] s Maschinenpistole f

tom'myrot' s Blödsinn m

tomorrow [tu'məro] adv morgen; **t. evening** morgen abend; **t. morning** morgen früh; **t. night** morgen abend; **t. noon** morgen mittag ‖ s morgen; **tomorrow's** morgig

tom-tom ['tam ,tam] s Hindutrommel f

ton [tʌn] s Tonne f

tone [ton] s Ton m; (of color) Farbton m; (phot) Tönung f ‖ tr tönen; (phot) tönen; **t. down** dämpfen ‖ intr milder werden

tone'-control knob' s (rad) Klangregler m

tongs [tɔŋz] spl Zange f

tongue [tʌŋ] s Zunge f; (language) Sprache f; (of a shoe) Zunge f; (of a buckle) Dorn m; (of a bell) Klöppel m; (of a wagon) Deichsel f; (carp) Feder f; **hold one's t.** den Mund halten

tongue'-tied' adj zungenlahm; (fig) sprachlos

tongue' twist'er s Zungenbrecher m

tonic ['tanɪk] adj tonisch ‖ s (med) Tonikum n; (mus) Tonika f

tonight [tu'naɪt] adv heute nacht; (this evening) heute abend

tonnage ['tʌnɪdʒ] s Tonnage f

tonsil ['tansɪl] s Mandel f

tonsilitis [,tansɪ'laɪtɪs] s Mandelentzündung f

tonsure ['tanʃər] s Tonsur f

too [tu] adv (also) auch; (excessively) zu; **too bad!** Schade!

tool [tul] s (& fig) Werkzeug n ‖ tr (with tools) bearbeiten

tool'box' s Werkzeugkasten m

tool'mak'er s Werkzeugmacher m

tool' shed' s Geräteschuppen m

toot [tut] s (aut) Hupen n ‖ tr (a trumpet) blasen; **t. the horn** (aut) hupen ‖ intr (aut) hupen

tooth [tuθ] s (teeth [tiθ]) Zahn m; (of a rake) Zinke f; **t. and nail** mit aller Gewalt

tooth'ache' s Zahnschmerz m, Zahnweh n

tooth′brush′ s Zahnbürste f
tooth′ decay′ s Zahnfäule f
toothless [′tuθlɪs] adj zahnlos
tooth′paste′ s Zahnpaste f
tooth′pick′ s Zahnstocher m
tooth′ pow′der s Zahnpulver n
top [tɑp] adj oberste; (speed, price, form) Höchst–; (team) Spitzen–; (first-class) erstklassig ‖ s Spitze f; (of a mountain) Gipfel m; (of a tree) Wipfel m; (of a car) Verdeck n; (of a box) Deckel m; (of a garment) Oberteil m & n; (of a bottle) Verschluß m; (of an object) obere Seite f; (of the water) Oberfläche f; (of a turnip) Kraut n; (toy) Kreisel m; **at the top of one's voice** aus voller Kehle; **at the top of the page** oben auf der Seite; **be tops with s.o.** (coll) bei j–m ganz groß angeschrieben sein; **from top to bottom** von oben bis unten; **on top** (& fig) obenauf; **on top of** (position) auf (dat); (direction) auf (acc); **on top of that** obendrein ‖ v (pret & pp **topped; ger topping**) tr (a tree) kappen; (surpass) übertreffen; **that tops everything** das übersteigt alles; **top off** (a meal, an evening) abschließen; **to top it off** zu guter Letzt
topaz [′topæz] s Topas m
top′ brass′ s (mil) hohe Tiere pl
top′coat′ s Überzieher m
top′ dog′ s (coll) Erste mf
top′ ech′elon s Führungsspitze f
top′ hat′ s Zylinder m
top′-heav′y adj oberlastig
topic [′tɑpɪk] s Gegenstand m, Thema n
topical [′tɑpɪkəl] adj aktuell
top′ kick′ s (mil) Spieß m
topless [′tɑplɪs] adj Oben-ohne–
topmast [′tɑp ‚mɛst] s Toppmast m
top′most′ adj oberste
top′notch′ adj erstklassig
top′ of the head′ s Scheitel m
topography [tə′pɑgrəfɪ] s Topographie f
topple [′tɑpəl] tr & intr stürzen
topsail [′tɑpsəl] s Toppsegel n
top′-se′cret adj streng geheim
top′ ser′geant s Hauptfeldwebel m
top′side′ adv auf Deck ‖ s Oberseite f
top′soil′ s Mutterboden m
topsy-turvy [′tɑpsɪ′tʌrvɪ] adj drunter und drüber ‖ adv—**turn t.** durcheinanderbringen
torch [tɔrtʃ] s Fackel f; (Brit) Taschenlampe f; **carry the t. for** (coll) verknallt sein in (acc)
torch′bear′er s (& fig) Fackelträger m
torch′light′ s Fackelschein m
torch′light parade′ s Fackelzug m
torment [′tɔrmɛnt] s Qual f ‖ [tɔr′mɛnt] tr quälen
tormentor [tɔr′mɛntər] s Quäler –in mf
torn [tɔrn] adj zerrissen, rissig
torna·do [tɔr′nedo] s (–does & –dos) Tornado m, Windhose f
torpe·do [tɔr′pido] s (–does) Torpedo m ‖ tr torpedieren

torpe′do boat′ s Torpedoboot n
torpe′do tube′ s Ausstoßrohr n
torpid [′tɔrpɪd] adj träge
torque [tɔrk] s Drehmoment n
torrent [′tɔrənt] s Sturzbach m; (of words) Schwall m; **in torrents** stromweise
torrential [tɔ′rɛntʃəl] adj—**t. rain** Wolkenbruch m
torrid [′tɔrɪd] adj brennend
Tor′rid Zone′ s heiße Zone f
tor·so [′tɔrso] s (–sos) (of a statue) Torso m; (of a human body) Rumpf m
tortoise [′tɔrtəs] s Schildkröte f
tor′toise shell′ s Schildpatt n
torture [′tɔrtʃər] s Folter f, Qual f ‖ tr foltern, quälen
toss [tɔs] s Wurf m; (of the head) Zurückwerfen n; (of a ship) Schlingern n; (of a coin) Loswurf m ‖ tr (throw) werfen; (the head) zurückwerfen; (a ship) hin- und herwerfen; (a coin) hochwerfen; **t. off** (work) hinhauen; **t. s.o. for** mit j–m losen um ‖ intr (naut) schlingern; **t. for** e–e Münze hochwerfen um; **t. in bed** sich im Bett hin –und herwerfen
toss′up′ s Loswurf m; **it's a t. whether** es hängt ganz vom Zufall ab, ob
tot [tɑt] s Knirps m
to·tal [′totəl] adj Gesamt–, total ‖ s Gesamtsumme f ‖ v (pret & pp **-tal[l]ed; ger -tal[l]ing**) tr (add up) zusammenrechnen; (amount to) sich belaufen auf (acc); (sl) (wagen) ganz kaputt machen
totalitarian [to ‚tælɪ′tɛrɪ·ən] adj totalitär
tote [tot] tr schleppen
totem [′totəm] s Totem n
totter [′tɑtər] intr schwanken
touch [tʌtʃ] s Berührung f; (sense of touch) Tastsinn m; (e.g., of a fever) Anflug m; (trace, small bit) Spur f; (of a pianist) Anschlag m; **get in t. with** in Verbindung treten mit; **keep in t. with** in Verbindung bleiben mit; **put in t. with** in Verbindung setzen mit; **with sure t.** mit sicherer Hand ‖ tr berühren; (fig) rühren; **he's a little touched** (coll) er hat e–n kleinen Klaps; **t. bottom** anstoßen; **t. glasses mit den Gläsern** anstoßen; **t. off** auslösen; **t. s.o. for** (coll) j–n anpumpen um; **t. up** (with cosmetics) auffrischen; (paint, phot) retuschieren ‖ intr sich berühren; **t. down** (aer) aufsetzen; **t. on** (a topic) berühren; (e.g., arrogance) grenzen an (acc)
touch′ and go′—**be t.** auf der Kippe stehen
touch′ing adj rührend, herzergreifend
touch′stone′ s (fig) Prüfstein m
touch′-type′ intr blindschreiben
touchy [′tʌtʃɪ] adj (spot, person) empfindlich; (situation) heikel
tough [tʌf] adj (strong) derb; (meat) zäh; (life) mühselig; (difficult) schwierig ‖ s Gassenjunge m
toughen [′tʌfən] tr zäher machen; **t.**

up (*through training*) ertüchtigen || *intr* (up) zäher werden

tough' luck' *s* Pech *n*

tour [tʊr] *s* (*of a country*) Tour *f*; (*of a city*) Rundfahrt *f*; (*of a museum*) Führung *f*; (*mus, theat*) Tournee *f*; **go on t.** auf Tournee gehen || *tr* besichtigen; (*a country*) bereisen || *intr* auf der Reise sein; (*theat*) auf Tournee sein

tour' guide' *s* Reiseführer –in *mf*

tourism ['tʊrɪzəm] *s* Touristik *f*

tournament ['tʊrnəmənt] *s* Turnier *n*

tourney ['tʊrni] *s* Turnier *n*

tourniquet ['tʊrnɪˌket] *s* Aderpresse *f*

tousle ['tauzəl] *tr* (zer)zausen

tow [to] *s*—**have in tow** im Schlepptau haben; **take in tow** ins Schlepptau nehmen || *tr* schleppen; **tow away** abschleppen

toward(s) [tord(z)] *prep* (*with respect to*) gegenüber (*dat*); (*a goal, direction*) auf (*acc*), zu; (*shortly before*) gegen (*acc*); (*for*) für (*acc*); (*facing*) zugewandt (*dat*)

tow'boat' *s* Schleppschiff *n*

tow-el ['tau.əl] *s* Handtuch *n* || *v* (*pret & pp* –el[l]ed; *ger* –el[l]ing) *tr* mit e–m Handtuch abtrocknen

tow'el rack' *s* Handtuchhalter *m*

tower ['tau.ər] *s* Turm *m*; **t. of strength** starker Hort *m* || *intr* ragen; **t. over** überragen

tow'ering *adj* hochragend; (*rage*) rasend

tow'ing serv'ice *s* Schleppdienst *m*

tow'line' *s* Schlepptau *n*

town [taun] *adj* städtisch, Stadt– || *s* Stadt *f*; **in t.** in der Stadt; **out of t.** verreist; **go to t. on** Feuer und Flamme sein für

town' coun'cil *s* Stadtrat *m*

town' hall' *s* Rathaus *n*

town' house' *s* Stadthaus *n*

town'ship' *s* Gemeinde *f*

tow'rope' *s* Schlepptau *n*; (*for a glider*) Startseil *n*

tow' truck' *s* Abschleppwagen *m*

toxic ['taksɪk] *adj* Gift–, toxisch || *s* Giftstoff *m*

toy [tɔɪ] *adj* Spielzeug– || *s* Spielzeug *n*; **toys** Spielsachen *pl*; (com) Spielwaren *pl* || *intr* spielen; **toy with** (fig) herumspielen mit

toy' dog' *s* Schoßhund *m*

toy' shop' *s* Spielwarengeschäft *n*

toy' sol'dier *s* Spielzeugsoldat *m*

trace [tres] *s* Spur *f*; (*of a harness*) Strang *m*; **without a t.** spurlos || *tr* (*a drawing*) durchpausen; (*lines*) nachziehen; (*track*) ausfindig machen; **t. (back) to** zurückführen auf (*acc*)

tracer ['tresər] *s* Suchzettel *m*

trac'er bul'let *s* Leuchtspurgeschoß *n*

trac'ing pa'per *s* Pauspapier *n*

track [træk] *s* Spur *f*; (*of a foot*) Fußspur *f*; (*of a wheel*) Radspur *f*; (*chain of a tank*) Raupenkette *f*; (*parallel rails*) Geleise *n*; (*single rail*) Gleis *n*, Schiene *f*; (*station platform*) Bahnsteig *m*; (*path*) Pfad *m*; (*course*

for running) Laufbahn *f*; (*course for motor and horse racing*) Rennbahn *f*; (*running as a sport*) Laufen *n*; **be off the t.** (fig) auf dem Holzweg sein; **go off the t.** (*derail*) entgleisen; **in one's tracks** mitten auf dem Weg; **jump the t.** aus den Schienen springen || *tr* verfolgen; **t. down** (*game, a criminal*) zur Strecke bringen; (*a rumor, reference*) nachgehen (*dat*); **t. up** (*a rug*) schmutzig treten

track'-and-field' *adj* Leichtathletik–

trackless ['træklɪs] *adj* pfadlos; (*vehicle*) schienenlos

track' meet' *s* Leichtathletikwettkampf *m*

tract [trækt] *s* Strich *m*; (*treatise*) Traktat *n*; **t. of land** Grundstück *n*

traction ['trækʃən] *s* (med) Ziehen *n*; (*of the road*) Griffigkeit *f*

tractor ['træktər] *s* Traktor *m*; (*of a tractor-trailer*) Zugmaschine *f*

trac'tor-trail'er *s* Sattelschlepper *m* mit e–m Anhänger

trade [tred] *s* Handel *m*; (*calling, job*) Gewerbe *n*; (*exchange*) Tausch *m*; **by t.** von Beruf || *tr* (aus)tauschen; **t. in** (*e.g., a used car*) in Zahlung geben || *intr* Handel treiben

trade' agree'ment *s* Handelsabkommen *n*

trade' bar'riers *spl* Handelsschranken *pl*

trade'-in val'ue *s* Handelswert *m*

trade'mark' *s* Warenzeichen *n*

trade' name' *s* (*of products*) Handelsbezeichnung *f*; (*of a firm*) Firmenname *m*

trader ['tredər] *s* Händler –in *mf*

trade' school' *s* Gewerbeschule *f*

trade' se'cret *s* Geschäftsgeheimnis *n*

trades'man *s* (–men) Handelsmann *m*

trade' un'ion *s* Gewerkschaft *f*

trade'wind' *s* Passatwind *m*

trad'ing post' *s* Handelsniederlassung *f*

trad'ing stamp' *s* Rabattmarke *f*

tradition [trə'dɪʃən] *s* Tradition *f*

traditional [trə'dɪʃənəl] *adj* herkömmlich, traditionell

traf-fic ['træfɪk] *s* Verkehr *m*; (*trade*) (in) Handel *m* (in *dat*) || *v* (*pret & pp* –ficked; *ger* –ficking) *intr*—**t. in** handeln in (*dat*)

traf'fic ac'cident *s* Verkehrsunfall *m*

traf'fic cir'cle *s* Kreisverkehr *m*

traf'fic is'land *s* Verkehrsinsel *f*

traf'fic jam' *s* Verkehrsstockung *f*

traf'fic lane' *s* Fahrbahn *f*

traf'fic light' *s* Verkehrsampel *f*; **go through a t.** bei Rot durchfahren

traf'fic sign' *s* Verkehrszeichen *n*

traf'fic tick'et *s* Strafzettel *m*

traf'fic viola'tion *s* Verkehrsdelikt *n*

tragedian [trə'dʒidɪ.ən] *s* Tragiker *m*

tragedy ['trædʒɪdi] *s* (& fig) Tragödie *f*

tragic ['trædʒɪk] *adj* tragisch

trail [trel] *s* (*path*) Fährte *f*; **be on s.o.'s t.** j–m auf der Spur sein; **t. of smoke** Rauchfahne *f* || *tr* (*on foot*) nachgehen (*dat*); (*in a vehicle*) nachfahren (*dat*); (*in a race*) nachhinken (*dat*) || *intr* (*said of a robe*) schleifen

trailer ['treilər] s Anhänger m; (mo-bile home) Wohnwagen m

trail′er camp′ s Wohnwagenparkplatz m

train [tren] s (of railway cars) Zug m; (of a dress) Schleppe f; (following) Gefolge n; (of events) Folge f; **go by t.** mit dem Zug fahren; **t. of thought** Gedankengang m || tr ausbilden; (for a particular job) anlernen; (the memory) üben; (plants) am Spalier auf-ziehen; (an animal) dressieren; (a gun) (on) zielen (auf acc); (sport) trainieren || intr üben; (sport) trai-nieren

trained adj geschult, ausgebildet

trainee [tre'ni] s Anlernling m

trainer ['trenər] s (of domestic ani-mals) Dresseur m, Dresseuse f; (of wild animals) Dompteur m, Domp-teuse f; (aer) Schulflugzeug n; (sport) Sportwart m

train′ing s Ausbildung f; (of animals) Dressur f; (sport) Training n

train′ing school′ s (vocational school) Berufsschule f; (reformatory) Erzie-hungsanstalt f

trait [tret] s Charakterzug m

traitor ['tretər] s Verräter –in mf; (of a country) Hochverräter –in mf

trajectory [trə'dʒɛktəri] s Flugbahn f

tramp [træmp] s Landstreicher –in mf; (loose woman) Frauenzimmer n || tr trampeln; (traverse on foot) durch-streifen || intr vagabundieren; **t. on** herumtrampeln auf (dat)

trample ['træmpəl] s Getrampel n || tr trampeln; **t. to death** tottreten; **t. under foot** (fig) mit Füßen treten || intr—**t. on** herumtrampeln auf (dat); (fig) mit Füßen treten

trampoline ['træmpə,lin] s Trampolin n

trance [træns] s Trance f

tranquil ['træŋkwɪl] adj ruhig

tranquilize ['træŋkwɪ,laɪz] tr beruhi-gen

tranquilizer ['træŋkwɪ,laɪzər] s Beru-higungsmittel n

tranquillity [træn'kwɪlɪti] s Ruhe f

transact [træn'zækt] tr abwickeln

transaction [træn'zækʃən] s Abwick-lung f; **transactions** (of a society) Sitzungsbericht m

transatlantic [,trænsət'læntɪk] adj transatlantisch

transcend [træn'sɛnd] tr übersteigen

transcendental [,trænsən'dɛntəl] adj übersinnlich; (philos) transzendental

transcribe [træn'skraɪb] tr (copy) um-schreiben; (dictated or recorded ma-terial) übertragen; (mus) transkri-bieren; (phonet) in Lautschrift wie-dergeben; (rad) auf Band aufnehmen

transcript ['trænskrɪpt] s Transkript n

transcription [træn'skrɪpʃən] s Um-schrift f; (mus) Transkription f

transept ['trænsɛpt] s Querschiff n

trans-fer ['trænsfər] s (of property) Übertragung f; (of money) Über-weisung f; (of an employee) Ver-setzung f; (of a passenger) Umstei-gen n; (ticket) Umsteigefahrschein

m || [træns'fʌr], ['trænsfər] v (pret & pp –**ferred**; ger –**ferring**) tr (prop-erty) übertragen; (money) über-weisen; (to another account) um-buchen; (an employee) versetzen || intr (to) versetzt werden (nach, zu); (said of a passenger) umsteigen

transfix [træns'fɪks] tr durchbohren

transform [træns'fɔrm] tr (a person) verwandeln; (into) umwandeln (in acc); (elec) umspannen

transformer [træns'fɔrmər] s (elec) Stromwandler m, Transformator m

transfusion [træns'fjuʒən] s (med) Übertragung f, Transfusion f

transgress [træns'grɛs] tr überschreiten

transgression [træns'grɛʃən] s Vergehen n

transient ['trænʃənt] adj vorüberge-hend; (fleeting) flüchtig || s Durch-reisende mf

transistor [træn'sɪstər] adj Transistor-|| s Transistor m

transistorize [træn'sɪstə,raɪz] tr tran-sistorisieren

transit ['trænzɪt] s (astr) Durchgang m; (com) Transit m; **in t.** unterwegs

transition [træn'zɪʃən] s Übergang m

transitional [træn'zɪʃənəl] adj Über-gangs-

transitive ['trænsɪtɪv] adj transitiv

transitory ['trænsɪ,tori] adj vergäng-lich

translate [træns'let] tr übersetzen; **t. into action** in die Tat umsetzen

translation [træns'leʃən] s Übersetzung f

translator [træns'letər] s Übersetzer –in mf

transliterate [træns'lɪtə,ret] tr tran-skribieren

translucent [træns'lusənt] adj durch-scheinend, lichtdurchlässig

transmigration [,trænsmaɪ'greʃən] s—**t. of the soul** Seelenwanderung f

transmission [træns'mɪʃən] s (of a text) Textüberlieferung f; (of news, infor-mation) Übermittlung f; (aut) Ge-triebe n; (rad, telv) Sendung f

trans·mit [træns'mɪt] v (pret & pp –**mitted**; ger –**mitting**) tr (send for-ward) übersenden; (disease, power, light, heat) übertragen; (e.g., cus-toms) überliefern; (by inheritance) vererben; (rad, telp, telv) senden

transmitter [træns'mɪtər] s (rad, telg, telv) Sender m

transmutation [,trænsmju'teʃən] s Um-wandlung f; (biol) Transmutation f; (chem, phys) Umwandlung f

transmute [træns'mjut] tr umwandeln

transoceanic [,trænzoʃɪ'ænɪk] adj überseeisch, Übersee-

transom ['trænsəm] s (crosspiece) Querbalken m; (window over a door) Oberlicht n mit Kreuzsprosse; (of a boat) Spiegel m

transparency [træns'pɛrənsɪ] s Durch-sichtigkeit f, Transparenz f; (phot) Diapositiv n

transparent [træns'pɛrənt] adj durch-sichtig, transparent

transpire [træns'pair] *intr* (*happen*) sich ereignen; (*leak out*) (fig) durchsickern

transplant ['træns,plænt] *s* (bot, surg) Verpflanzung *f* ‖ [træns'plænt] *tr* (bot, surg) verpflanzen

transport ['trænsport] *s* Beförderung *f*, Transport *m*; (nav) Truppentransporter *m* ‖ [træns'port] *tr* befördern

transportation [,trænspor'tefən] *s* Beförderung *f*; (*public transportation*) Verkehrsmittel *n*; **do you need t.?** brauchen Sie e-e Fahrgelegenheit?

trans'port plane' *s* Transportflugzeug *n*

transpose [træns'poz] *tr* umstellen; (math, mus) transponieren

trans-ship [træns'fip] *v* (*pret & pp* **-shipped**; *ger* **-shipping**) *tr* (com, naut) umladen

trap [træp] *s* (& fig) Falle *f*; (*snare*) Schlinge *f*; (*pit*) Fallgrube *f*; (*under a sink*) Geruchsverschluß *m*; (*mouth*) (sl) Klappe *f*; (chem) Abscheider *m*; (golf) Sandbunker *m*; **fall** (or **walk**) **into a t.** in die Falle gehen; **set a trap** e-e Falle stellen ‖ *v* (*pret & pp* **trapped**; *ger* **trapping**) *tr* mit e-r Falle fangen; (fig) erwischen; (mil) einfangen

trap' door' *s* Falltür *f*, Klapptür *f*; (theat) Versenkung *f*

trapeze [trə'piz] *s* Trapez *n*; (gym) Schwebereck *n*

trapezoid ['træpɪ,zɔɪd] *s* Trapez *n*

trapper ['træpər] *s* Fallensteller *m*

trappings ['træpɪŋz] *spl* Staat *m*; (*caparison*) Staatsgeschirr *n*

trap'shoot'ing *s* Tontaubenschießen *n*

trash [træʃ] *s* Abfälle *pl*; (*people*) Schund *m*; (*artistically inferior material*) Kitsch *m*; (*worthless people*) Gesindel *n*

trash' can' *s* Mülleimer *m*, Abfalleimer *m*

trashy ['træʃi] *adj* kitschig; (*literature*) Schund–

travail [trə'vel] *s* Plackerei *f*; (*labor of childbirth*) Wehen *pl*

trav·el ['trævəl] *s* Reisen *n*; (*trip*) Reise *f*; (*e.g., of a bullet, rocket*) Bewegung *f*; (*of moving parts*) Lauf *m*; **travels** Reiseerlebnisse *pl* ‖ *v* (*pret & pp* **-el[l]ed**; *ger* **-el[l]ing**) *tr* bereisen ‖ *intr* reisen; (*said of a vehicle or passenger*) fahren; (astr, aut, mach, phys) sich bewegen

trav'el a'gency *s* Reisebüro *n*

traveler ['trævələr] *s* Reisende *mf*

trav'eler's check' *s* Reisescheck *m*

trav'el fold'er *s* Reiseprospekt *m*

trav'eling bag' *s* Reisetasche *f*

trav'eling sales'man *s* (**-men**) Geschäftsreisende *m*

travelogue ['trævə,lɔg] *s* Reisebericht *m*; (cin) Reisefilm *m*

traverse [trə'vʌrs] *tr* durchqueren ‖ *intr* (*said of a gun*) sich drehen

traves·ty ['trævɪsti] *s* Travestie *f* ‖ *v* (*pret & pp* **-tied**) *tr* travestieren

trawl [trɔl] *s* Schleppnetz *n* ‖ *tr* mit dem Schleppnetz fangen ‖ *intr* mit dem Schleppnetz fischen

trawler ['trɔlər] *s* Schleppnetzboot *n*

tray [tre] *s* Tablett *n*; (phot) Schale *f*

treacherous ['tretʃərəs] *adj* verräterisch; (*e.g., ice*) trügerisch

treachery ['tretʃəri] *s* Verrat *m*

tread [tred] *s* (*step*) Tritt *m*; (*imprint*) Spur *f*; (*on a tire*) Profil *n* ‖ *v* (*pret* **trod** [trɑd]; *pp* **trodden** ['trɑdən] & **trod**) *tr* betreten ‖ *intr* (**on**) treten (*auf acc*)

treadle ['tredəl] *s* Trittbrett *n*

tread'mill' *s* (& fig) Tretmühle *f*

treason ['trizən] *s* Verrat *m*

treasonable ['trizənəbəl] *adj* verräterisch

treasure ['trezər] *s* Schatz *m* ‖ *tr* sehr schätzen

treasurer ['trezərər] *s* Schatzmeister –in *mf*

treasury ['trezəri] *s* Schatzkammer *f*; (*chest*) Tresor *m*; (*public treasury*) Staatsschatz *m*; **Treasury** Finanzministerium *n*

treat [trit] *s* Hochgenuß *m* ‖ *tr* behandeln; (*regard*) (as) betrachten (als); **t. oneself to s.th.** sich [*dat*] etw genehmigen; **t. s.o. to s.th** j–n bewirten mit

treatise ['tritɪs] *s* Abhandlung *f*

treatment ['tritmənt] *s* Behandlung *f*

treaty ['triti] *s* Vertrag *m*

treble ['trebəl] *adj* (*threefold*) dreifach; (mus) Diskant– ‖ *s* Diskant *m*; (*voice*) Diskantstimme *f* ‖ *tr* verdreifachen ‖ *intr* sich verdreifachen

tre'ble clef' *s* Violinschlüssel *m*

tree [tri] *s* Baum *m*

treeless ['trilɪs] *adj* baumlos

tree'top' *s* Baumwipfel *m*

tree' trunk' *s* Baumstamm *m*

trellis ['trelɪs] *s* Spalier *n*; (*gazebo*) Gartenhäuschen *n*

tremble ['trembəl] *s* Zittern *n* ‖ *intr* zittern; (geol) beben; **t. all over** am ganzen Körper zittern

tremendous [trɪ'mendəs] *adj* ungeheuer

tremor ['tremər] *s* Zittern *n*; (geol) Beben *n*

trench [trentʃ] *s* Graben *m*; (mil) Schützengraben *m*

trenchant ['trentʃənt] *adj* schneidend; (*policy*) durchschlagend

trench' war'fare *s* Stellungskrieg *m*

trend [trend] *s* Richtung *f*, Trend *m*

trespass ['trespæs] *s* unbefugtes Betreten *n*; (*sin*) Sünde *f* ‖ *intr* unbefugt fremdes Eigentum betreten; **no trespassing** (public sign) Betreten verboten; **t. on** unbefugt betreten

trespasser ['trespəsər] *s* Unbefugte *mf*

tress [tres] *s* Flechte *f*

trestle ['tresəl] *s* Gestell *n*; (*of a bridge*) Brückenbock *m*

trial ['traɪəl] *s* (*attempt*) Versuch *m*; (*hardship*) Beschwernis *f*; (jur) Prozeß *m*; **a week's t.** e-e Woche Probezeit; **be on t. for** vor Gericht stehen wegen; **be brought up** (or **come up**) **for t.** zur Verhandlung kommen; **new t.** Wiederaufnahmeverfahren *n*; **on t.** (com) auf Probe; **put on t.** vor Gericht bringen

tri′al and er′ror s—by t. durch Aus-probieren

tri′al balloon′ s Versuchsballon m

tri′al by ju′ry s Verhandlung f vor dem Schwurgericht

tri′al or′der s Probeauftrag m

tri′al run′ s Probelauf m

triangle [′traɪ æŋgəl] s Dreieck n

triangular [traɪ′æŋgjələr] adj dreieckig

tribe [traɪb] s Stamm m; (pej) Sipp-schaft f

tribunal [traɪ′bjunəl] s Tribunal n

tributary [′trɪbjə ˌteri] adj zinspflichtig || s Nebenfluß m

tribute [′trɪbjut] s Tribut m, Zins m; pay t. to Anerkennung zollen (dat)

trice [traɪs] s—in a t. im Nu

trick [trɪk] s Trick m; (prank) Streich m; (technique) Kniff m; (artifice) Schlich m; (cards) Stich m; be on to s.o.'s tricks j-s Schliche kennen; be up to one's old tricks sein Unwe-sen treiben; do the t. die Sache schaffen; play a dirty t. on s.o. j-m e-n gemeinen Streich spielen || tr reinlegen; t. s.o. into (ger) j-n durch Kniffe dazu bringen zu (inf)

trickery [′trɪkəri] s Gaunerei f

trickle [′trɪkəl] s Tröpfeln n || intr tröpfeln, rieseln

trickster [′trɪkstər] s Gauner m

tricky [′trɪki] adj (wily) listig; (touchy) heikel; (difficult) verzwickt

trident [′traɪdənt] s Dreizack m

tried [traɪd] adj bewährt, probat

trifle [′traɪfəl] s Kleinigkeit f; a t. (e.g., too big) ein bißchen || tr—t. away vertändeln || intr tändeln

trif′ling adj geringfügig || s Tändelei f

trigger [′trɪgər] s Abzug m; pull the t. abdrücken || tr auslösen

trig′ger-hap′py adj schießwütig

trigonometry [ˌtrɪgə′nɑmətri] s Trigo-nometrie f

trill [trɪl] s Triller m || tr & intr tril-lern

trillion [′trɪljən] s Billion f; (Brit) Trillion f

trilogy [′trɪlədʒi] s Trilogie f

trim [trɪm] adj (trimmer, trimmest) (figure) schick; (well-kept) gepflegt || s (e.g., of a hat) Zierleiste f; (naut) Trimm m; be in t. in Form sein || v (pret & pp trimmed; ger trimming) tr (clip) stutzen; (decorate) dekorie-ren; (a Christmas tree) schmücken; (beat) (coll) schlagen; (naut) trim-men

trim′ming s (e.g., of a dress) Besatz m; (of hedges) Stutzen n; take a t. (coll) e-e Niederlage erleiden; trimmings (decorations) Verzierungen pl; (food) Zutaten pl; (scraps) Abfälle pl; with all the trimmings (fig) mit allen Schikanen

trinity [′trɪnɪti] s Dreiheit f; Trinity Dreifaltigkeit f

trinket [′trɪŋkɪt] s Schmuckgegenstand m

tri·o [′tri·o] s (-os) (& mus) Trio n

trip [trɪp] s Reise f; (on drugs) Trip m; go on (or take) a t. e-e Reise

machen || v (pret & pp tripped; ger tripping) tr ein Bein stellen (dat); t. up (fig) zu Fall bringen || intr stolpern

tripartite [traɪ′pɑrtaɪt] adj Dreipar-teien—; (of three powers) Drei-mächte—

tripe [traɪp] s Kutteln pl; (sl) Schund m

trip′ham′mer s Schmiedehammer m

triple [′trɪpəl] adj dreifach || s Drei-fache n || tr verdreifachen

triplet [′trɪplɪt] s (offspring) Drilling m; (mus) Triole f

triplicate [′trɪplɪkɪt] adj dreifach || s—in t. in dreifacher Ausfertigung

tripod [′traɪpɑd] s Dreifuß m; (phot) Stativ n

triptych [′trɪptɪk] s Triptychon n

trite [traɪt] adj abgedroschen

triumph [′traɪ·əmf] s Triumph m || intr (over) triumphieren (über acc)

triumphal [traɪ′ʌmfəl] adj Sieges—

triumphant [traɪ′ʌmfənt] adj trium-phierend

trivia [′trɪvɪ·ə] spl Nichtigkeiten pl

trivial [′trɪvɪ·əl] adj trivial, alltäglich; (person) oberflächlich

triviality [ˌtrɪvɪ′ælɪti] s Trivialität f, Nebensächlichkeit f

Trojan [′trodʒən] adj trojanisch || s Trojaner —in mf

troll [trol] s (myth) Troll m || tr & intr mit der Schleppangel fischen

trolley [′trɑli] s Straßenbahn f

trollop [′trɑləp] s (slovenly woman) Schlampe f; (prostitute) Dirne f

trombone [′trɑmbon] s Posaune f

troop [trup] s Trupp m; (mil) Truppe f

trooper [′trupər] s Kavallerist m; swear like a t. fluchen wie ein Kutscher

troop′ship′ s Truppentransporter m

trophy [′trofi] s Trophäe f; (sport) Pokal m

tropical [′trɑpɪkəl] adj Tropen—

tropics [′trɑpɪks] spl Tropen pl

trot [trɑt] s Trab m || v (pret & pp trotted; ger trotting) tr—t. out (coll) zur Schau stellen || intr traben

troubadour [′trubə ˌdor] s Minnesänger m

trouble [′trʌbəl] s (inconvenience, bother) Mühe f; (difficulty) Schwie-rigkeit f; (physical distress) Leiden n; (civil disorder) Unruhe f; ask for t. das Schicksal herausfordern; be in t. in Schwierigkeiten sein; (be preg-nant) schwanger sein; cause s.o. a lot of t. j-m viel zu schaffen machen; get into t. in Schwierigkeiten geraten; go to a lot of t. sich (dat) viel Mühe machen; it was no t. at all! gern ge-schehen!; make t. Geschichten ma-chen; take the t. to (inf) sich der Mühe unterziehen zu (inf); that's the t. da liegt die Schwierigkeit; what's the t.? was ist los? || tr (worry) be-unruhigen; (bother) belästigen; (dis-turb) stören; (said of ills) plagen

trou′blemak′er s Unruhestifter —in mf

troubleshooter [′trʌbəl ˌʃutər] s Stö-

rungssucher –in *mf; (in disputes)*
Friedensstifter –in *mf*
troublesome ['trʌbəlsəm] *adj* lästig
trough [trɔf] *s* Trog *m; (of a wave)*
Wellental *n*
troupe [trup] *s* Truppe *f*
trousers ['trauzərz] *spl* Hose *f*
trous·seau [tru'so] *s* (–seaux & –seaus)
Brautausstattung *f*
trout [traut] *s* Forelle *f*
trowel ['trau·əl] *s* Kelle *f*
truant ['tru·ənt] *adj* schwänzend || *s*—
play t. die Schule schwänzen
truce [trus] *s* Waffenruhe *f*
truck [trʌk] *s* Last(kraft)wagen *m; (for luggage)* Gepäckwagen *m* || *tr* mit
Lastkraftwagen befördern
truck'driv'er *s* Lastwagenfahrer *m*
trucker ['trʌkər] *s (driver)* Lastwagenfahrer *m; (owner of a trucking firm)*
Fuhrunternehmer –in *mf*
truck' farm'ing *s* Gemüsebau *m*
truculent ['trʌkjələnt] *adj* gehässig
trudge [trʌdʒ] *intr* stapfen
true [tru] *adj* wahr; *(loyal)* (ge)treu; *(genuine)* echt; *(sign)* sicher; **come t.**
sich verwirklichen; **prove t.** sich als
wahr erweisen; **that's t.** das stimmt
truffle ['trʌfəl] *s* Trüffel *f*
truism ['tru·ɪzəm] *s* Binsenwahrheit *f*
truly ['truli] *adv* wirklich; **Yours t.**
Hochachtungsvoll
trump [trʌmp] *s* Trumpf *m* || *tr* trump-
fen; **t. up** erdichten || *intr* trumpfen
trumpet ['trʌmpɪt] *s* Trompete *f* || *intr
(said of an elephant)* trompeten
truncheon ['trʌntʃən] *s* Gummiknüppel
m
trunk [trʌŋk] *s (chest)* Koffer *m; (of a tree)* Stamm *m; (of a living body)*
Rumpf *m; (of an elephant)* Rüssel *m;
(aut)* Kofferraum *m;* **trunks** (sport)
Sporthose *f*
trunk' line' *s* Fernverkehrsweg *m*
truss [trʌs] *s (archit)* Tragwerk *n;
(med)* Bruchband *n* || *tr (archit)*
stützen; *(bind)* festbinden
trust [trʌst] *s (in)* Vertrauen *n (auf
acc); (com)* Trust *m; (jur)* Treuhand
f || *tr* trauen *(dat); (hope)* hoffen ||
intr—**t.** in vertrauen auf *(acc)*
trust' com'pany *s* Treuhandgesellschaft
f
trustee [trʌs'ti] *s* Aufsichtsrat *m; (jur)*
Treuhänder –in *mf*
trustee'ship *s* Treuhandverwaltung *f*
trustful ['trʌstfəl] *adj* zutraulich
trust' fund' *s* Treuhandfonds *m*
trust'wor'thy *adj* vertrauenswürdig
trusty ['trʌsti] *adj* treu || *s* Kalfaktor
m
truth [truθ] *s* Wahrheit *f;* **in t.** wahrlich
truthful ['truθfəl] *adj (person)* ehrlich; *(e.g., account)* wahrheitsgemäß
try [traɪ] *s* Versuch *m* || *v (pret & pp
tried)* tr versuchen; *(one's patience)*
auf e–e harte Probe stellen; *(a case)*
verhandeln; **be tried for** vor Gericht
kommen wegen; **try on** anprobieren;
(a hat) aufprobieren; **try out** erpro-
ben; *(new food)* kosten; **try s.o. for**

gegen j–n verhandeln wegen || *intr*
versuchen
try'ing *adj* anstrengend
try'out' *s* (sport) Ausscheidungskampf
m
T'-shirt' *s* T-Shirt *m*
tub [tʌb] *s* Wanne *f; (boat)* Kasten *m*
tubby ['tʌbi] *adj* (coll) kugelrund
tube [t(j)ub] *s (pipe)* Rohr *n*, Röhre *f;
(e.g., of toothpaste)* Tube *f; (of rubber)* Schlauch *m; (rad)* Röhre *f*
tuber ['t(j)ubər] *s* (bot) Knolle *f*
tubercle ['t(j)ubərkəl] *s* Tuberkel *m*
tuberculosis [t(j)u ,barkjə'losɪs] *s* Lun-
genschwindsucht *f*
tuck [tʌk] *s* (sew) Abnäher *m* || *tr
(into one's pocket, under a mattress)*
stecken; *(under one's arm)* klemmen;
(into bed) packen; **t. in** reinstecken;
t. up *(trousers)* hochkrempeln; *(a
skirt, dress)* hochschürzen
Tuesday ['t(j)uzde] *s* Dienstag *m;* **on
T.** am Dienstag
tuft [tʌft] *s* Büschel *m* & *n* || *tr (e.g.,
a mattress)* durchheften
tug [tʌg] *s (pull)* Zug *m; (boat)* Schlep-
per *m* || *v (pret & pp tugged)* ger
tugging) *tr* schleppen || *intr (at)*
zerren (an *dat)*
tug'boat' *s* Schleppdampfer *m*
tug' of war' *s* Tauziehen *n*
tuition [t(j)u'ɪʃən] *s* Schulgeld *n*
tulip ['t(j)ulɪp] *s* Tulpe *f*
tumble ['tʌmbəl] *s (fall)* Sturz *m;
(gym)* Purzelbaum *m* || *intr (fall)*
stürzen; *(gym)* Saltos machen; **t.
down the stairs** die Treppe herunter-
purzeln
tum'ble-down' *adj* baufällig
tumbler ['tʌmblər] *s (glass)* Trinkglas
n; (of a lock) Zuhaltung *f; (acrobat)*
Akrobat –in *mf*
tumor ['t(j)umər] *s* Geschwulst *f*
tumult ['t(j)umʌlt] *s* Getümmel *n*
tuna ['tunə] *s* Thunfisch *m*
tune [t(j)un] *s* Melodie *f;* **be in t.**
richtig gestimmt sein; **be out of t.**
falsch singen; *(said of a piano)* verstimmt sein; **change one's t.** e–n an-
deren Ton anschlagen || *tr* stimmen;
t. up *(aut)* neu einstellen || *intr*—
t. in on (rad) einstellen; **t. up** *(said
of an orchestra)* stimmen
tungsten ['tʌŋstən] *s* Wolfram *n*
tunic ['t(j)unɪk] *s* Tunika *f*
tun'ing fork' *s* Stimmgabel *f*
tun·nel ['tʌnəl] *s* Tunnel *m; (min)*
Stollen *m* || *v (pret & pp –nel[l]ed;
ger –nel[l]ing) intr* e–n Tunnel
bohren
turban ['tʌrbən] *s* Turban *m*
turbid ['tʌrbɪd] *adj* trüb(e)
turbine ['tʌrbɪn] *s* Turbine *f*
turboprop ['tʌrbo ,prɑp] *s* Turboprop
m
turbulence ['tʌrbjələns] *s* Turbulenz *f*
tureen [t(j)u'rin] *s* Terrine *f*
turf [tʌrf] *s* Rasendecke *f; (of a gang)*
(sl) Gebiet *n;* **the t.** der Turf
Turk [tʌrk] *s* Türke *m*, Türkin *f*
turkey ['tʌrki] *s* Truthahn *m; (female)*
Truthenne *f;* **Turkey** die Türkei

Turkish ['tʌrkɪʃ] *adj* türkisch ‖ *s* Türkisch *n*

Tur'kish tow'el *s* Frottiertuch *n*

turmoil ['tʌrmɔɪl] *s* Getümmel *n*

turn [tʌrn] *s* (*rotation*) Drehung *f*; (*change of direction or condition*) Wendung *f*; (*curve*) Kurve *f*; (*by a driver*) Abbiegen *n*; (*of a century*) Wende *f*; (*of a spool*) Windung *f*; at every t. bei jeder Gelegenheit; good t. Gunst *f*; it's his t. er ist dran; out of t. außer der Reihe; take turns sich abwechseln ‖ *tr* drehen; (*the page*) umblättern; t. down (*refuse*) ablehnen; (*a radio*) leiser stellen; (*a bed*) aufdecken; (*a collar*) umschlagen; (*an appeal*) (jur) verwerfen; t. in (*an application, resignation*) einreichen; (*lost articles*) abgeben; (*a person*) anzeigen; t. into verwandeln in (*acc*); t. loose frei lassen; t. off (*light, gas*) abdrehen; (rad, telv) abstellen; t. on (*gas, light*) andrehen; (*excite*) (coll) in Erregung versetzen; (rad, telv) anstellen; t. out produzieren; (*pockets*) umkehren; (*eject*) vor die Tür setzen; t. over (*property*) abtreten; (*a business*) übertragen; (*e.g., weapons*) abliefern; t. up (*a card, sleeve*) aufschlagen ‖ *intr* (*rotate*) sich drehen; (*in some direction*) sich wenden; it turned out that es stellte sich heraus, daß; t. against (fig) sich wenden gegen; t. around sich herumdrehen; t. back umdrehen; t. down (*a street*) einbiegen in (*acc*); t. in (*go to bed*) zu Bett gehen; t. into werden zu; t. out ausfallen; t. out for sich einfinden zu; t. out for the best sich zum Guten wenden; t. out in force vollzählig erscheinen; t. out to be sich erweisen als; t. over (*tip over*) umkippen; (aut) anspringen; t. to s.o. for help sich an j–n um Hilfe wenden; t. towards sich wenden gegen; t. up auftauchen

turn'coat' *s* Überläufer –in *mf*

turn'ing point' *s* Wendepunkt *m*

turnip ['tʌrnɪp] *s* Steckrübe *f*

turn'out' *s* Beteiligung *f*

turn'o'ver *s* Umsatz *m*

turn'pike' *s* Autobahn *f*

turnstile ['tʌrn,staɪl] *s* Drehkreuz *n*

turn'ta'ble *s* Plattenteller *m*; (rr) Drehscheibe *f*

turpentine ['tʌrpən,taɪn] *s* Terpentin *n*

turpitude ['tʌrpɪ,t(j)ud] *s* Verworfenheit *f*

turquoise ['tʌrk(w)ɔɪz] *adj* türkisfarben ‖ *s* Türkis *m*

turret ['tʌrɪt] *s* Turm *m*

turtle ['tʌrtəl] *s* Schildkröte *f*

tur'tledove' *s* Turteltaube *f*

tur'tleneck' *s* Rollkragen *m*

tusk [tʌsk] *s* (*of an elephant*) Stoßzahn *m*; (*of a boar*) Hauer *m*

tussle ['tʌsəl] *s* Rauferei *f* ‖ *intr* raufen

tutor ['t(j)utər] *s* Hauslehrer –in *mf*

tuxe·do [tʌk'sido] *s* (**–dos**) Smoking *m*

twang [twæŋ] *s* (*of a musical i̇*̄ *ment*) Schwirren *n*; (*of the vo.*) Näseln *n* ‖ *intr* schwirren; näseln

tweed [twid] *adj* aus Tweed ‖ *s* Tweed *m*

tweet [twit] *s* Gezwitscher *n* ‖ *intr* zwitschern

tweezers ['twizərz] *spl* Pinzette *f*

twelfth [twelfθ] *adj & pron* zwölfte ‖ *s* (*fraction*) Zwölftel *n*; the t. (*in dates or in series*) der Zwölfte

twelve [twelv] *adj & pron* zwölf ‖ *s* Zwölf *f*

twentieth ['twentɪ-ɪθ] *adj & pron* zwanzigste ‖ *s* (*fraction*) Zwanzigstel *n*; the t. (*in dates or in series*) der Zwanzigste

twenty ['twenti] *adj & pron* zwanzig ‖ *s* Zwanzig *f*; the twenties die zwanziger Jahre

twen'ty-one' *adj & pron* einundzwanzig

twice [twaɪs] *adv* zweimal

twiddle ['twɪdəl] *tr* müßig herumdrehen; t. one's thumbs Daumen drehen

twig [twɪg] *s* Zweig *m*

twilight ['twaɪ,laɪt] *adj* dämmerig ‖ *s* Abenddämmerung *f*

twin [twɪn] *adj* (*brother, sister*) Zwillings–; (*double*) Doppel– ‖ *s* Zwilling *m*

twine [twaɪn] *s* (*for a package*) Bindfaden *m*; (sew) Zwirn *m* ‖ *tr*–t. **around** winden um

twin'-en'gine *adj* zweimotorig

twinge [twɪndʒ] *s* stechender Schmerz *m*

twinkle ['twɪŋkəl] *s* Funkeln *n*; in a t. im Nu ‖ *intr* funkeln

twirl [twʌrl] *s* Wirbel *m* ‖ *tr* herumwirbeln ‖ *intr* wirbeln

twist [twɪst] *s* (*turn*) Drehung *f*; (*distortion*) Verdrehung *f*; (*strand*) Flechte *f*; (*bread roll*) Zopf *m*; (*dance*) Twist *m* ‖ *tr* (*revolve*) drehen; (*wind*) winden; (*an arm, words*) verdrehen; t. one's ankle sich [*dat*] den Knöchel vertreten ‖ *intr* sich drehen; (*wind*) sich winden

twister ['twɪstər] *s* (coll) Windhose *f*

twit [twɪt] *s* (sl) Depp *m* ‖ *v* (*pret & pp* **twitted**; *ger* **twitting**) *tr* verspotten; (*upbraid*) rügen

twitch [twɪtʃ] *s* Zucken *n* ‖ *intr* zucken

twitter ['twɪtər] *s* Zwitschern *n* ‖ *intr* zwitschern

two [tu] *adj & pron* zwei ‖ *s* Zwei *f*; by twos zu zweit; in two entzwei; put two and two together Schlußfolgerungen ziehen

two'-edged' *adj* zweischneidig

two'-faced' *adj* doppelzüngig

two' hun'dred *adj & pron* zweihundert

two'-piece' *adj* (*suit*) zweiteilig

twosome ['tusəm] *s* (*of lovers*) Liebespaar *n*; (golf) Einzelspiel *n*

two'-time' *tr* untreu sein (*dat*)

two'-tone' *adj* zweifarbig

two'-way traf'fic *s* Gegenverkehr *m*

tycoon [taɪ'kun] *s* Industriekapitän *m*

type [taɪp] *s* (*kind*) Art *f*; (*of person; of manufacture*) Typ *m*; (typ) Drucktype *f*, Letter *f* ‖ *tr & intr* tippen

type′face′ *s* Schriftbild *n*
type′script′ *s* Maschinenschrift *f*
type′set′ter *s* Schriftsetzer –in *mf*
type′write′ *v* (*pret* **–wrote;** *pp* **–written**) *tr & intr* mit der Maschine schreiben
type′writ′er *s* Schreibmaschine *f*
type′writer rib′bon *s* Farbband *n*
ty′phoid fe′ver [ˈtaɪfɔɪd] *s* Typhus *m*
typhoon [taɪˈfun] *s* Taifun *m*
typical [ˈtɪpɪkəl] *adj* (**of**) typisch (für)
typi·fy [ˈtɪpɪ ˌfaɪ] *v* (*pret & pp* **–fied**) *tr* (*characterize*) typisch sein für; (*exemplify*) ein typisches Beispiel sein für
typ′ing er′ror *s* Tippfehler *m*
typist [ˈtaɪpɪst] *s* Maschinenschreiber –in *mf*
typographic(al) [ˌtaɪpəˈgræfɪk(əl)] *adj* typographisch; (*error*) Druck–
typography [taɪˈpɑgrəfi] *s* (*the skill*) Buchdruckerkunst *f;* (*the work*) Buchdruck *m*
tyrannical [tɪˈrænɪkəl] *adj* tyrannisch
tyrannize [ˈtɪrə ˌnaɪz] *tr* tyrannisieren
tyranny [ˈtɪrəni] *s* Tyrannei *f*
tyrant [ˈtaɪrənt] *s* Tyrann *m*
ty·ro [ˈtaɪro] *s* (**–ros**) Neuling *m*
Tyrol [tɪˈrol] *s* Tirol *n*
Tyrolean [tɪˈrolɪ·ən] *adj* tirolerisch || *s* Tiroler –in *mf*

U

U, u [ju] *s* einundzwanzigster Buchstabe des englischen Alphabets
ubiquitous [juˈbɪkwɪtəs] *adj* allgegenwärtig
udder [ˈʌdər] *s* Euter *n*
ugliness [ˈʌglɪnɪs] *s* Häßlichkeit *f*
ugly [ˈʌgli] *adj* häßlich
Ukraine [juˈkren] *s* Ukraine *f*
Ukrainian [juˈkrenɪ·ən] *adj* ukrainisch || *s* (*person*) Ukrainer –in *mf;* (*language*) Ukrainisch *n*
ulcer [ˈʌlsər] *s* Geschwür *n*
ulcerate [ˈʌlsə ˌret] *intr* eitern
ulte′rior mo′tive [ʌlˈtɪrɪ·ər] *s* Hintergedanke *m*
ultimate [ˈʌltɪmɪt] *adj* äußerste; (*goal*) höchst; (*result*) End– || *s* Letzte *n*
ultima·tum [ˌʌltɪˈmetəm] *s* (**–tums** & **–ta** [tə]) Ultimatum *n*
ul′trahigh fre′quency [ˈʌltrə ˌhaɪ] *s* Ultrahochfrequenz *f*
ultramodern [ˌʌltrəˈmɑdərn] *adj* ultramodern
ultraviolet [ˌʌltrəˈvaɪ·əlɪt] *adj* ultraviolett || *s* Ultraviolett *n*
ultravi′olet lamp′ *s* Höhensonne *f*
umbil′ical cord′ [ʌmˈbɪlɪkəl] *adj* Nabelschnur *f*
umbrage [ˈʌmbrɪdʒ] *s*—**take u. at** Anstoß nehmen an (*dat*)
umbrella [ʌmˈbrelə] *s* Regenschirm *m;* (aer) Abschirmung *f*
umlaut [ˈumlaut] *s* Umlaut *m* || *tr* umlauten
umpire [ˈʌmpaɪr] *s* Schiedsrichter –in *mf* || *tr* als Schiedsrichter leiten || *intr* Schiedsrichter sein
umpteen [ʌmpˈtin] *adj* zig; **u. times** zigmal
UN [ˈjuˈen] *s* (**United Nations**) UNO *f*
unable [ʌnˈebəl] *adj* unfähig
unabridged [ʌnəˈbrɪdʒd] *adj* ungekürzt
unaccented [ˌʌnækˈsentɪd] *adj* unbetont
unacceptable [ˌʌnækˈseptɪbəl] *adj* unannehmbar
unaccountable [ˌʌnəˈkauntəbəl] *adj* nicht verantwortlich; (*strange*) seltsam
unaccounted-for [ˌʌnəˈkauntɪd ˌfɔr] *adj* unerklärt; (acct) nicht belegt
unaccustomed [ˌʌnəˈkʌstəmd] *adj* (**to**) nicht gewöhnt (an *acc*)
unaffected [ˌʌnəˈfektɪd] *adj* nicht affektiert; **u. by** unbeeinflusst von
unafraid [ˌʌnəˈfred] *adj*—**be u.** (**of**) sich nicht fürchten (vor *dat*)
unalterable [ʌnˈɔltərəbəl] *adj* unabänderlich
unanimity [ˌjunəˈnɪmɪti] *s* Stimmeneinheit *f*
unanimous [juˈnænɪməs] *adj* (*persons*) einmütig; (*vote*) einstimmig
unannounced [ˌʌnəˈnaunst] *adj* unangemeldet
unanswered [ʌnˈænsərd] *adj* (*question*) unbeantwortet; (*claim, statement*) unwiderlegt; (*request*) nicht erhört
unappreciative [ˌʌnəˈpriʃɪ·ətɪv] *adj* (**of**) unempfänglich (für)
unapproachable [ˌʌnəˈprotʃəbəl] *adj* unzugänglich
unarmed [ʌnˈɑrmd] *adj* unbewaffnet
unasked [ʌnˈæskt] *adj* (*advice*) unerbeten; (*uninvited*) ungeladen
unassailable [ˌʌnəˈseləbəl] *adj* unangreifbar
unassuming [ˌʌnəˈs(j)umɪŋ] *adj* nicht anmaßend
unattached [ˌʌnəˈtætʃt] *adj* (**to**) nicht befestigt (an *dat*); (*person*) ungebunden; (mil) zur Verfügung stehend
unattainable [ˌʌnəˈtenəbəl] *adj* unerreichbar
unattended [ˌʌnəˈtendɪd] *adj* unbeaufsichtigt
unattractive [ˌʌnəˈtræktɪv] *adj* reizlos
unauthorized [ʌnˈɔθəraɪzd] *adj* unberechtigt
unavailable [ˌʌnəˈveləbəl] *adj* (*person*) unabkömmlich; (*thing*) nicht verfügbar
unavenged [ˌʌnəˈvendʒd] *adj* ungerächt
unavoidable [ˌʌnəˈvɔɪdəbəl] *adj* unvermeidlich

unaware [ˌʌnə'wer] *adj* (**of**) nicht bewußt (*genit*)

unawares [ˌʌnə'werz] *adv* (*unexpectedly*) unversehens; (*unintentionally*) versehentlich; **catch u.** überraschen

unbalanced [ʌn'bælənst] *adj* nicht im Gleichgewicht; (*fig*) unausgeglichen

un·bar [ʌn'bɑr] *v* (*pret & pp* **–barred**; *ger* **–barring**) *tr* aufriegeln

unbearable [ʌn'berəbəl] *adj* unerträglich

unbeaten [ʌn'bitən] *adj* (**&** *fig*) ungeschlagen

unbecoming [ˌʌnbɪ'kʌmɪŋ] *adj* (*improper*) ungeziemend; (*clothing*) unkleidsam

unbelievable [ˌʌnbɪ'livəbəl] *adj* unglaublich

unbeliever [ˌʌnbɪ'livər] *s* Ungläubige *mf*

unbending [ʌn'bendɪŋ] *adj* unbeugsam

unbiased [ʌn'baɪ·əst] *adj* unvoreingenommen

unbidden [ʌn'bɪdən] *adj* ungebeten

un·bind [ʌn'baɪnd] *v* (*pret & pp* **–bound**) *tr* losbinden

unbleached [ʌn'blit/t] *adj* ungebleicht

unbolt [ʌn'bolt] *tr* aufriegeln

unborn ['ʌnbɔrn] *adj* ungeboren

unbosom [ʌn'buzəm] *tr*—**u. oneself to** sich offenbaren (*dat*)

unbowed [ʌn'baud] *adj* ungebeugt

unbreakable [ʌn'brekəbəl] *adj* unzerbrechlich

unbridled [ʌn'braɪdəld] *adj* ungezügelt

unbroken [ʌn'brokən] *adj* (*intact*) ungebrochen; (*line, series*) ununterbrochen; (*horse*) nicht zugeritten

unbuckle [ʌn'bʌkəl] *tr* aufschnallen

unburden [ʌn'bɑrdən] *tr* entlasten; **u. oneself** sein Herz ausschütten

unburied [ʌn'berɪd] *adj* unbeerdigt

unbutton [ʌn'bʌtən] *adj* aufknöpfen

uncalled-for [ʌn'kɔld·fɔr] *adj* unangebracht

uncanny [ʌn'kæni] *adj* unheimlich

uncared-for [ʌn'kerd·fɔr] *adj* verwahrlost

unceasing [ʌn'sisɪŋ] *adj* unaufhörlich

unceremonious [ˌʌnserɪ'moni·əs] *adj* (*informal*) ungezwungen; (*rude*) unsanft

uncertain [ʌn'sʌrtən] *adj* unsicher

uncertainty [ʌn'sʌrtənti] *s* Unsicherheit *f*

unchain [ʌn't/en] *tr* losketten; (*fig*) entfesseln

unchangeable [ʌn't/endʒəbəl] *adj* unveränderlich

uncharacteristic [ˌʌnkærɪktə'rɪstɪk] *adj* wesensfremd

uncharted [ʌn't/ɑrtɪd] *adj* auf keiner Karte verzeichnet

unchaste [ʌn't/est] *adj* unkeusch

unchecked [ʌn't/ekt] *adj* ungehemmt

unchristian [ʌn'krɪst/ən] *adj* unchristlich

uncivilized [ʌn'sɪvɪ‚laɪzd] *adj* unzivilisiert

unclad [ʌn'klæd] *adj* unbekleidet

unclaimed [ʌn'klemd] *adj* nicht abgeholt

unclasp [ʌn'klæsp] *tr* loshaken; (*the arms, hands*) öffnen

unclassified [ʌn'klæsɪ‚faɪd] *adj* nicht klassifiziert; (*not secret*) nicht geheim

uncle ['ʌŋkəl] *s* Onkel *m*

unclean [ʌn'klin] *adj* unsauber; (*relig*) unrein

unclear [ʌn'klɪr] *adj* unklar

un·clog [ʌn'klɑg] *v* (*pret & pp* **–clogged**; *ger* **–clogging**) *tr* von e–m Hindernis befreien

uncombed [ʌn'komd] *adj* ungekämmt

uncomfortable [ʌn'kʌmfərtəbəl] *adj* unbequem; **feel u.** sich nicht recht wohl fühlen

uncommitted [ˌʌnkə'mɪtɪd] *adj* (*troops*) nicht eingesetzt; (*delegates, nations*) unentschieden

uncommon [ʌn'kamən] *adj* ungewöhnlich; (*outstanding*) außergewöhnlich

uncomplaining [ˌʌnkʌm'plenɪŋ] *adj* klaglos

uncompromising [ʌn'kɑmprə‚maɪzɪŋ] *adj* unbeugsam

unconcealed [ˌʌnkən'sild] *adj* unverholen

unconcerned [ˌʌnkən'sʌrnd] *adj* (*about*) unbesorgt (um)

unconditional [ˌʌnkən'dɪ/ənəl] *adj* bedingungslos

unconfirmed [ˌʌnkən'fɪrmd] *adj* unbestätigt, unverbürgt

unconquerable [ʌn'kɑŋkərəbəl] *adj* unüberwindlich

unconquered [ʌn'kɑŋkərd] *adj* unbezwungen

unconscious [ʌn'kanfəs] *adj* bewußtlos; (**of**) nicht bewußt (*genit*) ‖ *s*— **the u.** das Unbewußte

unconstitutional [ˌʌnkɑnstɪ't(j)u/ənəl] *adj* verfassungswidrig

uncontested [ˌʌnkən'testɪd] *adj* unbestritten

uncontrollable [ˌʌnkən'troləbəl] *adj* unkontrollierbar; (*fig*) unbändig

unconventional [ˌʌnkən'vent/ənəl] *adj* unkonventionell

uncork [ʌn'kɔrk] *tr* entkorken

uncouple [ʌn'kʌpəl] *tr* abkoppeln

uncouth [ʌn'kuθ] *adj* ungehobelt; (*appearance*) ungeschlacht

uncover [ʌn'kʌvər] *tr* aufdecken

unctuous ['ʌŋkt/u·əs] *adj* salbungsvoll

uncultivated [ʌn'kʌltɪ‚vetɪd] *adj* unbebaut

uncultured [ʌn'kʌlt/ərd] *adj* (*fig*) unkultiviert

uncut [ʌn'kʌt] *adj* nicht abgeschnitten; (*gem*) ungeschliffen; (*grain*) ungemäht

undamaged [ʌn'dæmɪdʒd] *adj* unbeschädigt, unversehrt

undaunted [ʌn'dɔntɪd] *adj* unverzagt

undecided [ˌʌndɪ'saɪdɪd] *adj* (*person*) unschlüssig; (*thing*) unentschieden

undefeated [ˌʌndɪ'fitɪd] *adj* unbesiegt

undefended [ˌʌndɪ'fendɪd] *adj* unverteidigt

undefiled [ˌʌndɪ'faɪld] *adj* unbefleckt

undefined [ˌʌndɪ'faɪnd] *adj* unklar

undeliverable [ˌʌndɪ'lɪvərəbəl] *adj* unbestellbar

undeniable [ˌʌndɪˈnaɪ·əbəl] *adj* unleugbar

under [ˈʌndər] *adj* Unter– ‖ *adv* unter–, e.g., go u. untergehen ‖ *prep* unter (*position*) (dat); (*direction*) unter (*acc*)

un'derage' *adj* unmündig

un'der·bid' *v* (*pret & pp* –bid; *ger* –bidding) *tr* unterbieten

un'derbrush' *s* Unterholz *n*

un'dercar'riage *s* Fahrgestell *n*

un'derclothes' *spl* Unterwäsche *f*

un'dercov'er *adj* Geheim–; u. agent Spitzel *m*

un'dercur'rent *s* (& *fig*) Unterströmmung *f*

un'dercut' *v* (*pret & pp* –cut; *ger* –cutting) *tr* unterbieten

un'derdevel'oped *adj* unterentwickelt

un'derdog' *s* (coll) Unterlegene *mf*

un'derdone' *adj* nicht durchgebraten

un'deres'timate *tr* unterschätzen

un'derexpose' *tr* (phot) unterbelichten

un'dergar'ment *s* Unterkleidung *f*

un'der·go' *v* (*pret* –went; *pp* –gone) durchmachen; (*an operation*) sich unterziehen (dat)

un'dergrad'uate *s* Collegestudent –in *mf*

un'derground' *adj* unterirdisch; (fig) Untergrund–; (*water*) Grund–; (min) unter Tage ‖ **un'derground'** *s* (*secret movement*) Untergrundbewegung *f*; go u. untertauchen

un'dergrowth' *s* Buschholz *n*, Unterholz *n*

un'derhand' *s* (*throw*) unter Schulterhöhe (ausgeführt)

un'derhand'ed *adj* hinterhältig

un'derline', **un'derline'** *tr* unterstreichen

underling [ˈʌndərlɪŋ] *s* Handlanger *m*

un'dermine' *tr* (& *fig*) untergraben

underneath [ˌʌndərˈniθ] *adj* Unter– ‖ *adv* unten ‖ *s* Unterseite *f* ‖ *prep* (*position*) unter (dat), unterhalb (*genit*); (*direction*) unter (*acc*)

un'dernour'ished *adj* unterernährt

un'dernour'ishment *s* Unterernährung *f*

un'derpad' *s* (*of a rug*) Unterlage *f*

un'derpaid' *adj* unterbezahlt

un'derpass' *s* Straßenunterführung *f*

un'der·pin' *v* (*pret & pp* –pinned; *ger* –pinning) *tr* untermauern

un'derplay' *tr* unterspielen

un'derpriv'ileged *adj* benachteiligt

un'derrate' *tr* unterschätzen

un'derscore' *tr* (& *fig*) unterstreichen

un'dersea' *adj* Unterwasser–

un'dersec'retar'y *s* Untersekretär –in *mf*

un'der·sell' *v* (*pret & pp* –sold; *ger* –selling) *tr* (*a person*) unterbieten; (*goods*) verschleudern

un'dershirt' *s* Unterhemd *n*

un'derside' *s* Unterseite *f*

un'dersigned' *adj* unterschrieben ‖ **un'dersigned'** *s* Unterzeichnete *mf*

un'der·stand' *v* (*pret & pp* –stood) *tr* verstehen; **it's understood that** es ist selbstverständlich, daß; **make oneself understood** sich verständlich machen

understandable [ˌʌndərˈstændəbəl] *adj* verständlich

understandably [ˌʌndərˈstændəbli] *adv* begreiflicherweise

un'derstand'ing *adj* verständnisvoll ‖ *s* (of) Verständnis *n* (für); (*between persons*) Einvernehmen *n*; (*agreement*) Übereinkommen *n*; **come to an u. with s.o.** sich mit j–m verständigen; **it is my u.** that wie ich verstehe

un'derstud'y *s* Ersatzmann *m*; (cin, theat) Ersatzschauspieler –in *mf*

un'der·take' *v* (*pret* –took; *pp* –taken) *tr* unternehmen

undertaker [ˈʌndərˌtekər] *s* Leichenbestatter –in *mf*

un'dertak'ing *s* Unternehmen *n*

un'dertone' *s* leise Stimme *f*; (fig) Unterton *m*

un'dertow' *s* Sog *m*

un'derwa'ter *adj* Unterwasser–

un'derwear' *s* Unterwäsche *f*

un'derweight' *adj* untergewichtig

un'derworld' *s* (*of criminals*) Unterwelt *f*; (myth) Totenreich *n*

un'der·write', **un'der·write'** *v* (*pret* –wrote; *pp* –written) *tr* unterschreiben; (ins) versichern

un'derwrit'er *s* Unterzeichner –in *mf*; (ins) Versicherer –in *mf*; (st. exch.) Wertpapiermakler –in *mf*; **underwriters** Emissionsfirma *f*

undeserved [ˌʌndɪˈzɜrvd] *adj* unverdient

undeservedly [ˌʌndɪˈzɜrvdli] *adv* unverdientermaßen

undesirable [ˌʌndɪˈzaɪrəbəl] *adj* unerwünscht ‖ *s* Unerwünschte *mf*

undeveloped [ˌʌndɪˈveləpt] *adj* unentwickelt; (*land*) unerschlossen

undies [ˈʌndiz] *spl* (coll) Unterwäsche *f*

undigested [ˌʌndɪˈdʒɛstɪd] *adj* (& fig) unverdaut

undignified [ʌnˈdɪgnɪˌfaɪd] *adj* würdelos

undiluted [ˌʌndɪˈlutɪd] *adj* unverdünnt

undiminished [ˌʌndɪˈmɪnɪʃt] *adj* unvermindert

undisciplined [ʌnˈdɪsəplɪnd] *adj* undiszipliniert, zuchtlos

undisputed [ˌʌndɪsˈpjutɪd] *adj* unbestritten, unangefochten

undisturbed [ˌʌndɪsˈtɜrbd] *adj* ungestört

undivided [ˌʌndɪˈvaɪdɪd] *adj* ungeteilt

un·do [ʌnˈdu] *v* (*pret* –did; *pp* –done) *tr* (*a knot*) aufschnüren; (*a deed*) ungeschehen machen

undo'ing *s* Ruin *m*

undone [ʌnˈdʌn] *adj* (*not done*) ungetan; (*ruined*) ruiniert; **come u.** sich lösen; **leave nothing u.** nichts unversucht lassen

undoubtedly [ʌnˈdautɪdli] *adv* zweifellos

undramatic [ˌʌndrəˈmætɪk] *adj* undramatisch

undress [ʌnˈdrɛs] *s*—**in a state of u.** (*nude*) in unbekleidetem Zustand; (*in a negligee*) im Negligé ‖ *tr* ausziehen ‖ *intr* sich ausziehen

undrinkable [ʌn'drɪŋkəbəl] *adj* nicht trinkbar

undue [ʌn'd(j)u] *adj* (*inappropriate*) unangemessen; (*excessive*) übermäßig

undulate ['ʌndjə‚let] *intr* wogen

undulating ['ʌndjə‚letɪŋ] *adj* wellenförmig

unduly [ʌn'd(j)uli] *adv* übermäßig

undying [ʌn'daɪ‚ɪŋ] *adj* unsterblich

un'earned in'come ['ʌnʌrnd] *s* Kapitalrente *f*

unearth [ʌn'ʌrθ] *tr* ausgraben; (fig) aufstöbern

unearthly [ʌn'ʌrθli] *adj* unirdisch; (*cry*) schauerlich; **at an u. hour** (*early*) in aller Herrgottsfrühe

uneasy [ʌn'izi] *adj* (*worried*) ängstlich; (*ill at ease*) unbehaglich

uneatable [ʌn'itəbəl] *adj* ungenießbar

uneconomic(al) [‚ʌnekə'nɑmɪk(əl)] *adj* unwirtschaftlich

uneducated [ʌn'edjə‚ketɪd] *adj* ungebildet

unemployed [‚ʌnem'plɔɪd] *adj* arbeitslos || *s* Arbeitslose *mf*

unemployment [‚ʌnem'plɔɪmənt] *s* Arbeitslosigkeit *f*

unemploy'ment compensa'tion *s* Arbeitslosenunterstützung *f*; **collect u.** (sl) Stempeln gehen

unencumbered [‚ʌnən'kʌmbərd] *adj* unbelastet

unending [ʌn'endɪŋ] *adj* endlos

unequal [ʌn'ikwəl] *adj* ungleich; **u. to** nicht gewachsen (*dat*)

unequaled [ʌn'ikwəld] *adj* ohnegleichen

unequivocal [‚ʌnə'kwɪvəkəl] *adj* eindeutig

unerring [ʌn'erɪŋ] *adj* unfehlbar

UNESCO [ju'nesko] *s* (**United Nations Educational, Scientific, and Cultural Organization**) UNESCO *f*

unessential [‚ʌne'senʃəl] *adj* unwesentlich

uneven [ʌn'ivən] *adj* (*not smooth*) uneben; (*unbalanced*) ungleich; (*not uniform*) ungleichmäßig; (*number*) ungerade

uneventful [‚ʌnɪ'ventfəl] *adj* ereignislos

unexceptional [‚ʌnek'sepʃənəl] *adj* nicht außergewöhnlich

unexpected [‚ʌnek'spektɪd] *adj* unerwartet

unexplained [‚ʌnek'splend] *adj* unerklärt

unexplored [‚ʌnek'splord] *adj* unerforscht

unexposed [‚ʌnek'spozd] *adj* (phot) unbelichtet

unfading [ʌn'fedɪŋ] *adj* unverwelklich

unfailing [ʌn'felɪŋ] *adj* unfehlbar

unfair [ʌn'fer] *adj* unfair; (*competition*) unlauter

unfaithful [ʌn'feθfəl] *adj* treulos

unfamiliar [‚ʌnfə'mɪljər] *adj* unbekannt

unfasten [ʌn'fæsən] *tr* losbinden; (*e.g., a seat belt*) aufschnallen

unfathomable [ʌn'fæðəməbəl] *adj* unergründlich

unfavorable [ʌn'fevərəbəl] *adj* ungünstig

unfeasible [ʌn'fizəbəl] *adj* unausführbar

unfeeling [ʌn'filɪŋ] *adj* unempfindlich

unfilled [ʌn'fɪld] *adj* ungefüllt; (*post*) unbesetzt

unfinished [ʌn'fɪnɪʃt] *adj* unfertig; (*business*) unerledigt

unfit |ʌn'fɪt] *adj* (**for**) ungeeignet (für); (*not qualified*) (**for**) untauglich (für); **u. for military service** wehrdienstuntauglich

unfold [ʌn'fold] *tr* (*a chair*) aufklappen; (*cloth, paper*) entfalten; (*ideas, plans*) offenbaren

unforeseeable [‚ʌnfor'si‚əbəl] *adj* unabsehbar

unforeseen [‚ʌnfor'sin] *adj* unvorhergesehen

unforgettable [‚ʌnfor'getəbəl] *adj* unvergeßlich

unfortunate [ʌn'fortʃ‚ənɪt] *adj* unglücklich

unfortunately [ʌn'fortʃ/ənɪtli] *adv* leider

unfounded [ʌn'faʊndɪd] *adj* unbegründet

un-freeze [ʌn'friz] *v* (*pret* **–froze**; *pp* **–frozen**) *tr* auftauen; (*prices*) freigeben

unfriendly [ʌn'frendli] *adj* unfreundlich

unfruitful [ʌn'frutfəl] *adj* unfruchtbar

unfulfilled [‚ʌnful'fɪld] *adj* unerfüllt

unfurl [ʌn'fʌrl] *tr* (*a flag*) entrollen; (*sails*) losmachen

unfurnished [ʌn'fʌrnɪʃt] *adj* unmöbliert

ungainly [ʌn'genli] *adj* plump

ungentlemanly [ʌn'dʒentəlmənli] *adj* unfein, unedel

ungodly [ʌn'gɑdli] *adj* (*hour*) ungehörig

ungracious [ʌn'greʃəs] *adj* ungnädig

ungrammatical [‚ʌngrə'mætɪkəl] *adj* ungrammatisch

ungrateful [ʌn'gretfəl] *adj* undankbar

ungrudgingly [ʌn'grʌdʒɪŋli] *adv* gern

unguarded [ʌn'gɑrdɪd] *adj* unbewacht; (*moment*) unbedacht

unguent |ʌn'gwent] *s* Salbe *f*

unhandy [ʌn'hændi] *adj* unhandlich; (*person*) unbeholfen

unhappy [ʌn'hæpi] *adj* unglücklich

unharmed |ʌn'hɑrmd] *adj* unversehrt

unharness |ʌn'hɑrnɪs] *tr* abschirren

unhealthful [ʌn'helθfəl] *adj* ungesund

unhealthy [ʌn'helθi] *adj* ungesund

unheard-of [ʌn'hɑrd‚ɑv] *adj* unerhört

unheated [ʌn'hitɪd] *adj* ungeheizt

unhesitating [ʌn'hezɪ‚tetɪŋ] *adj* (*immediate*) unverzüglich; (*unswerving*) unbeirrbar; (*support*) bereitwillig

unhinge [ʌn'hɪndʒ] *tr* (fig) aus den Angeln heben

unhitch [ʌn'hɪtʃ] *tr* (*horses*) ausspannen; (*undo*) losmachen

unholy [ʌn'holi] *adj* unheilig

unhook [ʌn'hʊk] *tr* losmachen; (*a dress*) aufhaken; (*the receiver*) abnehmen

unhoped-for [ˌʌn'hopt ˌfər] *adj* unverhofft

unhurt [ʌn'hʌrt] *adj* unbeschädigt; (*person*) unversehrt

unicorn ['juni ˌkɔrn] *s* Einhorn *n*

unification [ˌjunɪfɪ'keʃən] *s* Vereinigung *f*

uniform ['juni ˌfɔrm] *adj* gleichförmig || *s* Uniform *f*

uniformity [ˌjuni'fɔrmɪti] *s* Gleichförmigkeit *f*

uni·fy ['juni ˌfaɪ] *v* (*pret & pp* –fied) *tr* vereinigen

unilateral [ˌjuni'lætərəl] *adj* einseitig

unimpaired [ˌʌnɪm'perd] *adj* ungeschwächt

unimpeachable [ˌʌnɪm'pitʃəbəl] *adj* unantastbar

unimportant [ˌʌnɪm'pɔrtənt] *adj* unwichtig

uninflected [ˌʌnɪn'flɛktɪd] *adj* (gram) unflektiert

uninhabited [ˌʌnɪn'hæbɪtɪd] *adj* unbewohnt

uninspired [ˌʌnɪn'spaɪrd] *adj* schwunglos

unintelligible [ˌʌnɪn'telɪdʒəbəl] *adj* unverständlich

unintentional [ˌʌnɪn'tenʃənəl] *adj* unabsichtlich

uninterested [ʌn'ɪntə ˌrestɪd] *adj* (**in**) uninteressiert (an *dat*)

uninteresting [ʌn'ɪntə ˌrestɪŋ] *adj* uninteressant

uninterrupted [ˌʌnɪntə'rʌptɪd] *adj* ununterbrochen

uninvited [ˌʌnɪn'vaɪtɪd] *adj* ungeladen

union ['junjən] *s* Gewerkschafts– || *s* Vereinigung *f*; (*harmony*) Eintracht *f*; (*of workers*) Gewerkschaft *f*; (pol) Union *f*

unionize ['junjə ˌnaɪz] *tr* gewerkschaftlich organisieren || *intr* sich gewerkschaftlich organisieren

un'ion shop' *s* Betrieb *m*, der nur Gewerkschaftsmitglieder beschäftigt

unique [ju'nik] *adj* einzigartig

unison ['junɪsən] *s* Einklang *m*

unit ['junɪt] *s* (& mil) Einheit *f*

unite [ju'naɪt] *tr* vereinigen; (chem) verbinden || *intr* sich vereinigen; (chem) sich verbinden

Unit'ed King'dom *s* Vereinigtes Königreich *n*

Unit'ed Na'tions *spl* Vereinte Nationen *pl*

Unit'ed States' *s* Vereinigte Staaten *pl*

unity ['junɪti] *s* (*harmony*) Einigkeit *f*; (*e.g., of a nation*) Einheit *f*; (fa) Einheitlichkeit *f*

universal [ˌjuni'vʌrsəl] *adj* universal, allgemein || *s* Allgemeine *n*; (philos) Allgemeinbegriff *m*

u'niver'sal joint' *s* Kardangelenk *n*

u'niver'sal mil'itary train'ing *s* allgemeine Wehrpflicht *f*

universe ['juni ˌvʌrs] *s* Universum *n*

university [ˌjuni'versɪti] *adj* Universitäts– || *s* Universität *f*

unjust [ʌn'dʒʌst] *adj* ungerecht

unjustified [ʌn'dʒʌstɪ ˌfaɪd] *adj* ungerechtfertigt

unjustly [ʌn'dʒʌstli] *adv* zu Unrecht

unkempt [ʌn'kempt] *adj* ungekämmt; (fig) verwahrlost

unkind [ʌn'kaɪnd] *adj* unfreundlich

unknown [ʌn'non] *adj* unbekannt

un'known quan'tity *s* Unbekannte *f*

Un'known Sol'dier *s* Unbekannter Soldat *m*

unlatch [ʌn'lætʃ] *tr* aufklinken

unlawful [ʌn'lɔfəl] *adj* gesetzwidrig

unleash [ʌn'liʃ] *tr* losbinden; (fig) entfesseln

unleavened [ʌn'levənd] *adj* ungesäuert

unless [ʌn'les] *conj* wenn ... nicht

unlettered [ʌn'letərd] *adj* ungebildet

unlicensed [ʌn'laɪsənst] *adj* unerlaubt

unlike [ʌn'laɪk] *adj* (*unequal*) ungleich; (*dissimilar*) unähnlich || *prep* im Gegensatz zu (*dat*); **be u. s.o.** anders als jemand sein

unlikely [ʌn'laɪkli] *adj* unwahrscheinlich

unlimited [ʌn'lɪmɪtɪd] *adj* unbeschränkt

unlined [ʌn'laɪnd] *adj* (*clothes*) ungefüttert; (*paper*) unliniert; (*face*) faltenlos

unload [ʌn'lod] *tr & intr* ausladen

unload'ing *s* Ausladen *n*; (naut) Löschen *n*

unlock [ʌn'lɑk] *tr* aufsperren

unloose [ʌn'lus] *tr* lösen

unloved [ʌn'lʌvd] *adj* ungeliebt

unlucky [ʌn'lʌki] *adj* unglücklich

un·make [ʌn'mek] *v* (*pret & pp* –made) *tr* rückgängig machen; (*a bed*) abdecken

unmanageable [ʌn'mænɪdʒəbəl] *adj* (*person*, *animal*) widerspenstig; (*thing*) unhandlich

unmanly [ʌn'mænli] *adj* unmännlich

unmanned [ʌn'mænd] *adj* (rok) unbemannt

unmannerly [ʌn'mænərli] *adj* unmännlich

unmarketable [ʌn'mɑrkɪtəbəl] *adj* nicht marktgängig

unmarriageable [ʌn'mærɪdʒəbəl] *adj* nicht heiratsfähig

unmarried [ʌn'mærid] *adj* unverheiratet

unmask [ʌn'mæsk] *tr* (& fig) demaskieren || *intr* sich demaskieren

unmatched [ʌn'mætʃt] *adj* (*not matched*) ungleichartig; (*unmatchable*) unvergleichlich

unmerciful [ʌn'mʌrsɪfəl] *adj* unbarmherzig

unmesh [ʌn'meʃ] *tr* (mach) ausrücken

unmindful [ʌn'maɪndfəl] *adj* uneingedenk

unmistakable [ˌʌnmɪs'tekəbəl] *adj* unmißverständlich

unmitigated [ʌn'mɪtɪ ˌgetɪd] *adj* ungemildert; (*liar*) Erz–

unmixed [ʌn'mɪkst] *adj* ungemischt

unmoor [ʌn'mur] *tr* losmachen || *intr* sich losmachen

unmoved [ʌn'muvd] *adj* (fig) ungerührt

unmuzzle [ʌn'mʌzəl] *tr* den Maulkorb abnehmen (*dat*)

unnatural [ʌn'nætʃərəl] *adj* unnatür-
lich; (*forced*) gezwungen

unnecessary [ʌn'nesə,seri] *adj* unnötig

unneeded [ʌn'nidid] *adj* nutzlos

unnerve [ʌn'nɑrv] *tr* entnerven

unnoticeable [ʌn'notisəbəl] *adj* unbe-
merkbar

unnoticed [ʌn'notist] *adj* unbemerkt

unobserved [ˌʌnəb'zɑrvd] *adj* unbeob-
achtet

unobtainable [ˌʌnəb'tenəbəl] *adj* nicht
erhältlich

unobtrusive [ˌʌnəb'trusiv] *adj* unauf-
dringlich

unoccupied [ʌn'akjə,paɪd] *adj* (*room,
house*) leerstehend; (*seat*) unbesetzt;
(*person*) unbeschäftigt

unofficial [ˌʌnə'fɪʃəl] *adj* inoffiziell

unopened [ʌn'opənd] *adj* ungeöffnet

unopposed [ˌʌnə'pozd] *adj* (*without
opposition*) widerspruchslos; (*unre-
sisted*) unbehindert

unorthodox [ʌn'ɔrθə,daks] *adj* unorthodox; (*relig*) nicht orthodox

unpack [ʌn'pæk] *tr* auspacken

unpalatable [ʌn'pælətəbəl] *adj* unschmackhaft; (fig) widerlich

unparalleled [ʌn'pærə,leld] *adj* unvergleichlich

unpardonable [ʌn'pardənəbəl] *adj* un-
verzeihlich

unpatriotic [ˌʌnpetri'atɪk] *adj* unpatri-
otisch

unpaved [ʌn'pevd] *adj* ungepflastert

unperceived [ˌʌnpər'sivd] *adj* unbemerkt

unpleasant [ʌn'plezənt] *adj* unangenehm; (*person*) unsympathisch

unpopular [ʌn'papjələr] *adj* unbeliebt

unpopularity [ʌn,papjə'læriti] *s* Unbe-
liebtheit *f*

unprecedented [ʌn'presɪ,dentid] *adj*
unerhört; (jur) ohne Präzedenzfall

unpredictable [ˌʌnprɪ'dɪktəbəl] *adj* unberechenbar; (*weather*) wechselhaft

unprejudiced [ʌn'predʒədɪst] *adj* unvoreingenommen

unprepared [ˌʌnprɪ'perd] *adj* unvorbereitet

unpresentable [ˌʌnprɪ'zentəbəl] *adj*
nicht präsentabel

unpretentious [ˌʌnprɪ'tɛnʃəs] *adj* an-
spruchslos

unprincipled [ʌn'prɪnsɪpəld] *adj* haltlos

unproductive [ˌʌnprə'dʌktɪv] *adj* un-
produktiv; (*of*) unergiebig (an *dat*)

unprofessional [ˌʌnprə'fɛʃənəl] *adj*
(*work*) unfachmännisch; (*conduct*)
berufswidrig

unprofitable [ʌn'prafɪtəbəl] *adj* (*useless*) nutzlos; (fi) unrentabel

unpronounceable [ˌʌnprə'naunsəbəl]
adj unaussprechlich

unprotected [ˌʌnprə'tɛktid] *adj* (*place*)
ungeschützt; (*person*) unbeschützt

unpropitious [ˌʌnprə'pɪʃəs] *adj* ungünstig

unpublished [ʌn'pʌblɪʃt] *adj* unveröf-
fentlicht

unpunished [ʌn'pʌnɪʃt] *adj* ungestraft

unqualified [ʌn'kwalə,faɪd] *adj* un-

qualifiziert; (*full, complete*) unbedingt

unquenchable [ʌn'kwentʃəbəl] *adj* un-
stillbar

unquestionably [ʌn'kwestʃənəbli] *adv*
fraglos, unbezweifelbar

unquestioning [ʌn'kwestʃənɪŋ] *adj*
(*obedience*) bedingungslos

unquiet [ʌn'kwaɪ·ət] *adj* unruhig

unrav·el [ʌn'rævəl] *v* (*pret & pp
-el[l]ed; ger -el[l]ing*) *tr* (*a knitted
fabric*) auftrennen; (fig) entwirren ‖
intr sich fasern; (fig) sich entwirren

unreachable [ʌn'ritʃəbəl] *adj* unerreichbar

unreal [ʌn'ri·əl] *adj* unwirklich

unreality [ˌʌnrɪ'æliti] *s* Unwirklich-
keit *f*

unreasonable [ʌn'rizənəbəl] *adj* unver-
nünftig

unrecognizable [ʌn'rekəg,naɪzəbəl] *adj*
unerkennbar

unreel [ʌn'ril] *tr* abspulen

unrefined [ˌʌnrɪ'faɪnd] *adj* roh

unrelated [ˌʌnrɪ'letid] *adj* (*to*) ohne
Beziehung (zu)

unrelenting [ˌʌnrɪ'lentɪŋ] *adj* unerbittlich

unreliable [ˌʌnrɪ'laɪ·əbəl] *adj* unzuverlässig; (fin) unsolid(e)

unremitting [ˌʌnrɪ'mɪtɪŋ] *adj* unablässig

unrepentant [ˌʌnrɪ'pentənt] *adj* unbußfertig

unrequited [ˌʌnrɪ'kwaɪtɪd] *adj* uner-
widert

unreserved [ˌʌnrɪ'zɑrvd] *adj* vorbehaltlos

unresponsive [ˌʌnrɪ'spansɪv] *adj* (*to*)
unempfänglich (für)

unrest [ʌn'rest] *s* Unruhe *f*

unrestricted [ˌʌnrɪ'strɪktid] *adj* uneingeschränkt

unrewarded [ˌʌnrɪ'wərdɪd] *adj* unbe-
lohnt

unrhymed [ʌn'raɪmd] *adj* ungereimt

un·rig [ʌn'rɪg] *v* (*pret & pp -rigged;
ger -rigging*) *tr* abtakeln

unripe [ʌn'raɪp] *adj* unreif

unrivaled [ʌn'raɪvəld] *adj* unübertreff-
lich

unroll [ʌn'rol] *tr* aufrollen; (*e.g., a
cable*) abrollen ‖ *intr* sich aufrollen;
sich abrollen

unromantic [ˌʌnro'mæntɪk] *adj* unro-
mantisch

unruffled [ʌn'rʌfəld] *adj* unerschüttert

unruly [ʌn'ruli] *adj* ungebärdig

unsaddle [ʌn'sædəl] *tr* (*a horse*) ab-
satteln; (*a rider*) aus dem Sattel
werfen

unsafe [ʌn'sef] *adj* unsicher

unsaid [ʌn'sed] *adj* ungesagt

unsalable [ʌn'seləbəl] *adj* unverkäuf-
lich

unsanitary [ʌn'sænɪ,teri] *adj* unhygie-
nisch

unsalted [ʌn'səltid] *adj* ungesalzen

unsatisfactory [ʌn,sætɪs'fæktəri] *adj*
unbefriedigend

unsatisfied [ʌn'sætɪs,faɪd] *adj* unbe-
friedigt

unsavory [ʌn'seʋəri] *adj* unschmackhaft; *(fig)* widerlich

unscathed [ʌn'skeðd] *adj* unversehrt

unscientific [ˌʌnsaɪ-ən'tɪfɪk] *adj* unwissenschaftlich

unscramble [ʌn'skræmbəl] *tr (a message)* entziffern; *(fig)* entflechten

unscrew [ʌn'skru] *tr* aufschrauben

unscrupulous [ʌn'skrupjələs] *adj* skrupellos

unseal [ʌn'sil] *tr* entsiegeln; *(eyes, lips)* öffnen

unseasonable [ʌn'sizənəbəl] *adj* unzeitig; *(weather)* nicht der Jahreszeit entsprechend

unseasoned [ʌn'sizənd] *adj* ungewürzt

unseat [ʌn'sit] *tr (a rider)* aus dem Sattel heben; *(an official)* aus dem Posten verdrängen

unseemly [ʌn'simli] *adj* ungehörig

unseen [ʌn'sin] *adj* ungesehen

unselfish [ʌn'selfɪʃ] *adj* selbstlos

unsettle [ʌn'setəl] *tr* beunruhigen

unsettled [ʌn'setəld] *adj (matter, bill)* unerledigt; *(without a residence)* ohne festen Wohnsitz; *(restless)* unruhig; *(life)* unstet

unshackle [ʌn'ʃækəl] *tr* die Fesseln abnehmen *(dat)*

unshakable [ʌn'ʃekəbəl] *adj* unerschütterlich

unshapely [ʌn'ʃepli] *adj* mißgestaltet

unshaven [ʌn'ʃevən] *adj* unrasiert

unsheathe [ʌn'ʃið] *tr* aus der Scheide ziehen

unshod [ʌn'ʃɑd] *adj* unbeschuht

unsightly [ʌn'saɪtli] *adj* unansehnlich

unsinkable [ʌn'sɪŋkəbəl] *adj* nicht versenkbar

unskilled [ʌn'skɪld] *adj* ungelernt; **u. laborer** Hilfsarbeiter –in *mf*

unskillful [ʌn'skɪlfəl] *adj* ungewandt

unsnarl [ʌn'snɑrl] *tr* entwirren

unsociable [ʌn'soʃəbəl] *adj* ungesellig

unsolicited [ˌʌnso'lɪsɪtɪd] *adj* unverlangt

unsold [ʌn'sold] *adj* unverkauft

unsophisticated [ˌʌnsə'fɪstɪˌketɪd] *adj* unverfälscht; *(naive)* arglos

unsound [ʌn'saund] *adj* ungesund; *(sleep)* unruhig; **of u. mind** geisteskrank

unspeakable [ʌn'spikəbəl] *adj* unsagbar

unspoiled [ʌn'spɔɪld] *adj* unverdorben

unsportsmanlike [ʌn'sportsmən͵laɪk] *adj* unsportlich

unstable [ʌn'stebəl] *adj* unbeständig; *(e.g., ladder)* wacklig; *(hand)* zittrig; *(market, walk)* schwankend; *(inconstant)* unbeständig; *(chem)* unbeständig

unstinted [ʌn'stɪntɪd] *adj* uneingeschränkt

unstinting [ʌn'stɪntɪŋ] *adj* freigebig

unstitch [ʌn'stɪtʃ] *tr* auftrennen

unstressed [ʌn'strest] *adj* unbetont

unsuccessful [ˌʌnsək'sesfəl] *adj* erfolglos

unsuitable [ʌn'sutəbəl] *adj* ungeeignet; *(inappropriate)* unangemessen

unsullied [ʌn'sʌlid] *adj* unbefleckt

unsung [ʌn'sʌŋ] *adj* unbesungen

unsuspected [ˌʌnsəs'pektɪd] *adj* unverdächtig; *(not known to exist)* ungeahnt

unsuspecting [ˌʌnsəs'pektɪŋ] *adj* arglos

unswerving [ʌn'swɜrvɪŋ] *adj* unentwegt

unsympathetic [ˌʌnsɪmpə'θetɪk] *adj* teilnahmslos

unsystematic(al) [ˌʌnsɪstə'mætɪk(əl)] *adj* unsystematisch

untactful [ʌn'tæktfəl] *adj* taktlos

untalented [ʌn'tæləntɪd] *adj* unbegabt

untamed [ʌn'temd] *adj* ungezähmt

untangle [ʌn'tæŋgəl] *tr (& fig)* entwirren

untenable [ʌn'tenəbəl] *adj* unhaltbar

untested [ʌn'testɪd] *adj* ungeprüft

unthankful [ʌn'θæŋkfəl] *adj* undankbar

unthinking [ʌn'θɪŋkɪŋ] *adj* gedankenlos

untidy [ʌn'taɪdi] *adj* unordentlich

un·tie [ʌn'taɪ] *v (pret & pp* **–tied**; *ger* **–tying)** *tr* aufbinden; *(a knot)* lösen; **my shoe is untied** mein Schuh ist aufgegangen

until [ʌn'tɪl] *prep* bis *(acc)*; **u. further notice** bis auf weiteres || *conj* bis

untimely [ʌn'taɪmli] *adj* frühzeitig; *(at the wrong time)* unzeitgemäß

untiring [ʌn'taɪrɪŋ] *adj* unermüdlich

untold [ʌn'told] *adj (suffering)* unsäglich; *(countless)* zahllos

untouched [ʌn'tʌtʃt] *adj* unangetastet; *(fig)* ungerührt

untoward [ʌn'tord] *adj (unfavorable)* ungünstig; *(unruly)* widerspenstig

untrained [ʌn'trend] *adj* unausgebildet; *(eye)* ungeschult; *(sport)* untrainiert

untried [ʌn'traɪd] *adj (unattempted)* unversucht; *(untested)* unerprobt; *(case)* (jur) nicht verhandelt

untroubled [ʌn'trʌbəld] *adj (mind, times)* ruhig; *(peace)* ungestört

untrue [ʌn'tru] *adj* unwahr; *(unfaithful)* un(ge)treu; *(not exact)* ungenau

untrustworthy [ʌn'trʌst͵wɜrði] *adj* unglaubwürdig

untruth [ʌn'truθ] *s* Unwahrheit *f*

untruthful [ʌn'truθfəl] *adj (statement)* unwahr; *(person)* unaufrichtig

untwist [ʌn'twɪst] *tr* aufflechten || *intr* aufgehen

unusable [ʌn'juzəbəl] *adj* nicht verwendbar; *(unconsumable)* unbenutzbar

unusual [ʌn'juʒʊ͵əl] *adj* ungewöhnlich

unutterable [ʌn'ʌtərəbəl] *adj* unaussprechlich

unvarnished [ʌn'vɑrnɪʃt] *adj* nicht gefirnißt; *(truth)* ungeschminkt

unveil [ʌn'vel] *tr (a monument)* enthüllen; *(a face)* entschleiern

unventilated [ʌn'ventɪ͵letɪd] *adj* ungelüftet

unvoiced [ʌn'vɔɪst] *adj* (ling) stimmlos

unwanted [ʌn'wantɪd] *adj* unerwünscht

unwarranted [ʌn'wɑrəntɪd] *adj* ungerechtfertigt

unwary [ʌn'weri] *adj* unvorsichtig

unwavering [ʌn'wevərɪŋ] *adj* standhaft

unwelcome [ʌn'wɛlkəm] *adj* unwillkommen

unwell [ʌn'wɛl] *adj* unwohl

unwept [ʌn'wɛpt] *adj* unbeweint

unwholesome [ʌn'holsəm] *adj* schädlich; (& fig) unbekömmlich

unwieldy [ʌn'wildɪ] *adj* (person) schwerfällig; (thing) unhandlich

unwilling [ʌn'wɪlɪŋ] *adj* (involuntary) unfreiwillig; (reluctant) widerwillig; (obstinate) eigensinnig; **be u. to** (inf) nicht (inf) wollen

unwillingly [ʌn'wɪlɪŋlɪ] *adv* ungern

un·wind [ʌn'waɪnd] *v* (pret & pp **–wound**) *tr* abwickeln ‖ *intr* sich abwickeln; (fig) sich entspannen

unwise [ʌn'waɪz] *adj* unklug

unwished-for [ʌn'wɪʃt͵fər] *adj* unerwünscht

unwitting [ʌn'wɪtɪŋ] *adj* unwissentlich

unworkable [ʌn'wɑrkəbəl] *adj* (plan) unausführbar; (material) nicht zu bearbeiten(d)

unworldly [ʌn'wɑrldlɪ] *adj* nicht weltlich; (naive) weltfremd

unworthy [ʌn'wʌrðɪ] *adj* unwürdig

un·wrap [ʌn'ræp] *v* (pret & pp **–wrapped**; ger **–wrapping**) *tr* auspacken ‖ *intr* aufgehen

unwrinkled [ʌn'rɪŋkəld] *adj* faltenlos

unwritten [ʌn'rɪtən] *adj* ungeschrieben; (agreement) mündlich

unyielding [ʌn'jildɪŋ] *adj* unnachgiebig

up [ʌp] *adj* & *adv* (at a height) oben; (to a height) hinauf; **be up** (be out of bed; said of a shade) aufsein; (baseball) am Schlag sein; **be up and around again** wieder auf den Damm sein; **be up to** (be ready for) gewachsen sein (dat); (e.g., mischief) vorhaben; **from ten dollars and up** von zehn Dollar aufwärts; **it's up to you** es hängt von Ihnen ab; **prices are up** die Preise sind gestiegen; **up and down** (back and forth) auf und ab; (from head to toe) von oben bis unten; **up there** da oben; **up to** (e.g., one hour) bis zu; **up to the ears in debt** bis über die Ohren in Schulden ‖ *v* (pret & pp **upped**; ger **upping**) *tr* erhöhen ‖ *prep* (acc) hinauf (postpositive)

up-and-coming [ˈʌpənˈkʌmɪŋ] *adj* (coll) unternehmungslustig

up-and-up [ˈʌpənˈʌp] *s*—**be on the u.** aufrichtig sein

upbraid′ *tr* Vorwürfe machen (dat)

upbringing [ˈʌp͵brɪŋɪŋ] *s* Erziehung *f*

update′ *tr* aufs laufende bringen

up′**draft**′ *s* Aufwind *m*

upend′ *tr* hochkant stellen

up′**grade**′ *s* Steigung *f*; **on the u.** (fig) im Aufsteigen ‖ **up**′**grade**′ *tr* (reclassify) höher einstufen; (improve) verbessern

upheaval [ʌp'hivəl] *s* Umbruch *m*

up′**hill**′ *adj* ansteigend; (fig) mühsam; **u. struggle** harter Kampf *m* ‖ *adv* bergauf

uphold′ *v* (pret & pp **–held**) *tr* (the law) unterstützen; (a verdict) bestätigen

upholster [ʌp'holstər] *tr* (auf)polstern

upholsterer [ʌp'holstərər] *s* Polsterer –in *mf*

upholstery [ʌp'holstərɪ] *s* Polsterung *f*

up′**keep**′ *s* Instandhaltung *f*; (maintenance costs) Instandhaltungskosten *pl*

upland [ˈʌplənd] *adj* Hochlands–, Berg– ‖ **the uplands** *spl* das Hochland

up′**lift**′ *s* (fig) Aufschwung *m*; **moral u.** moralischer Auftrieb *m* ‖ **up**′**lift**′ *tr* (fig) geistig (or moralisch) erheben

upon [ə'pɑn] *prep* (position) an (dat), auf (dat); (direction) an (acc), auf (acc); **u. my word!** auf mein Wort!

upper [ˈʌpər] *adj* obere, Ober– ‖ **uppers** *spl* Oberleder *n*

up′**per-case**′ *adj* in Großbuchstaben gedruckt (or geschrieben)

up′**per class**′**es** *spl* Oberschicht *f*

up′**percut**′ *s* (box) Aufwärtshaken *m*

up′**per deck**′ *s* Oberdeck *n*

up′**per hand**′ *s* Oberhand *f*

up′**per lip**′ *s* Oberlippe *f*

up′**permost**′ *adj* oberste

uppish [ˈʌpɪʃ] *adj* (coll) hochnäsig

uppity [ˈʌpɪtɪ] *adj* (coll) eingebildet

upraise′ *tr* erheben

up′**right**′ *adj* aufrecht; (fig) redlich ‖ *s* (fb) Torpfosten *m*

up′**rising** *s* Aufstand *m*

up′**roar**′ *s* Aufruhr *m*

uproarious [ʌp'rorɪ·əs] *adj* (noisy) lärmend; (laughter) schallend; (applause) tosend; (very funny) zwerchfellerschütternd

uproot′ *tr* entwurzeln

ups′ **and downs**′ *spl* Auf und Ab *n*

upset′ *adj* (over) verstimmt (über *acc*) ‖ **up**′**set**′ *s* unerwartete Niederlage *f* ‖ **up**′**set**′ *v* (pret & pp **–set**; ger **–setting**) *tr* (throw over) umwerfen; (tip over) umkippen; (plans) umstoßen; (a person) aufregen; (the stomach) verderben

up′**shot**′ *s* Ergebnis *n*

up′**side down**′ *adv* verkehrt; **turn u.** auf den Kopf stellen

up′**stage**′ *adv* in den (or im) Hintergrund der Bühne ‖ *tr* (coll) ausstechen

up′**stairs**′ *adj* im oberen Stockwerk ‖ *adv* (position) oben; (direction) nach oben ‖ *s* oberes Stockwerk *n*

upstanding *adj* aufrecht; (sincere) aufrichtig

up′**start**′ *s* Emporkömmling *m*

up′**stream**′ *adj* weiter stromaufwärts gelegen ‖ *adv* stromaufwärts

up′**stroke**′ *s* Aufstrich *m*; (mach) Hub *m*

up′**surge**′ *s* Aufwallung *f*

up′**sweep**′ *s* Hochfrisur *f*

up′**swing**′ *s* (fig) Aufschwung *m*

upsy-daisy [ˈʌpsɪ'dezɪ] *interj* hopsasa!

up-to-date [ˈʌptə'det] *adj* (modern) zeitgemäß; (with latest information) auf dem neuesten Stand

up′**-to-the-min**′**ute news**′ [ˈʌptəðə'mɪnɪt] *s* Zeitfunk *m*

up′**trend**′ *s* steigende Tendenz *f*

up'turn' s Aufschwung m
upturned' adj nach oben gebogen; **u. nose** Stupsnase f
upward ['ʌpwərd] adj nach oben gerichtet; (tendency) steigend ‖ adv aufwärts
U'ral Moun'tains ['jurəl] spl Ural m
uranium [ju'renɪ·əm] adj Uran– ‖ s Uran n
urban ['ʌrbən] adj städtisch, Stadt–
urbane [ʌr'ben] adj weltgewandt
urbanite ['ʌrbə‚naɪt] s Städter –in mf
urbanize ['ʌrbə‚naɪz] tr verstädtern
ur'ban renew'al s Altstadtsanierung f
urchin ['ʌrt/ɪn] s Bengel m
ure•thra [ju'riθrə] s (–thras & –thrae [θri]) Harnröhre f
urge [ʌrdʒ] s Drang m, Trieb m ‖ tr drängen; **u. on** antreiben
urgency ['ʌrdʒənsi] s Dringlichkeit f
urgent ['ʌrdʒənt] adj dringend
urinal ['jurɪnəl] s (in a toilet) Urinbecken n; (in a sick bed) Urinflasche f
urinary ['jurɪ‚neri] adj Harn–, Urin–
urinate ['jurɪ‚net] intr harnen
urine ['jurɪn] s Harn m, Urin m
urn [ʌrn] s Urne f; (for coffee) Kaffeemaschine f
urology [jɪ'rɑlədʒi] s Urologie f
us [ʌs] per pron uns
U.S.A. ['ju'es'e] s (United States of America) USA pl
usable ['juzəbəl] adj (consumable items) verwendbar; (non-consumable items) benutzbar
usage ['jusɪdʒ] s (using) Gebrauch m; (treatment) Behandlung f; (ling) Sprachgebrauch m; **rough u.** starke Beanspruchung f
use [jus] s (of consumable items) Verwendung f, Gebrauch m; (of non-consumable items) Benutzung f; (application) Anwendung f; (advantage) Nutzen m; (purpose) Zweck m; (consumption) Verbrauch m; **I have no use for him** ich habe nichts für ihn übrig; **in use** in Gebrauch; **it's no use** es nützt nichts; **make use of** ausnutzen; **of use** von Nutzen; **there's no use in** (ger) es hat keinen Zweck zu (inf) ‖ [juz] tr (ge)brauchen, verwenden; (non-consumable items) benutzen; (apply) anwenden; (e.g.,

troops) einsetzen; **use up** verbrauchen ‖ intr—**he used to live here** er wohnte früher hier
used [juzd] adj gebraucht; (car) Gebraucht–; **be u. to** gewöhnt sein an (acc); **be u. to** (ger) gewöhnt sein zu (inf); **get s.o. u. to** j–n gewöhnen an (acc); **get u. to** sich gewöhnen an (acc)
useful ['jusfəl] adj nützlich
usefulness ['jusfəlnɪs] s Nützlichkeit f; (usability) Brauchbarkeit f
useless ['juslɪs] adj nutzlos; (not usable) unbrauchbar
user ['juzər] s (of gas, electric) Verbraucher –in mf; (e.g., of a book) Benutzer –in mf
usher ['ʌ/ər] s Platzanweiser –in mf ‖ tr—**u. in** hereinführen; (a new era) einleiten
U.S.S.R. ['ju'es'es'ɑr] s (Union of Soviet Socialist Republics) UdSSR f
usual ['juʒu·əl] adj gewöhnlich; **as u.** wie gewöhnlich
usually ['juʒu·əli] adv gewöhnlich
usurp [ju'zʌrp] tr usurpieren
usurper [ju'zʌrpər] s Usurpator –in mf
usury ['juʒəri] s Wucher m
utensil [ju'tensɪl] s Gerät n; **utensils** Utensilien pl
uter•us ['jutərəs] s (–i [‚aɪ]) Gebärmutter f
utilitarian [‚jutɪlɪ'teri·ən] adj utilitaristisch, Nützlichkeits–
utility [ju'tɪlɪti] s (usefulness) Nützlichkeit f; (company) öffentlicher Versorgungsbetrieb m; **apartment with all utilities** Wohnung f mit allem Zubehör; **utilities** Gas, Wasser, Strom pl
utilize ['jutɪ‚laɪz] tr verwerten
utmost ['ʌt‚most] adj äußerste, höchste ‖ s—**do one's u.** sein Äußerstes tun; **to the u.** aufs äußerste; **to the u. of one's power** nach besten Kräften
utopia [ju'topɪ·ə] s Utopie f
utopian [ju'topɪ·ən] adj utopisch
utter ['ʌtər] adj völlig, Erz– ‖ tr (a sigh) ausstoßen; (a sound) hervorbringen; (feelings) ausdrücken; (words) äußern
utterance ['ʌtərəns] s Äußerung f
utterly ['ʌtərli] adv ganz und gar, völlig

V

V, v [vi] s zweiundzwanzigster Buchstabe des englischen Alphabets
vacancy ['vekənsi] s (emptiness) Leere f; (unfilled job) freie Stelle f; **no v.** (public sign) kein freies Zimmer
vacant ['vekənt] adj frei; (stare) geistesabwesend; (lot) unbebaut
vacate [ve'ket] tr (a home) räumen; (a seat) freimachen ‖ intr ausziehen
vacation [ve'ke/ən] s Urlaub m; (educ)

Ferien pl; **on v.** auf Urlaub ‖ intr Urlaub machen
vacationer [ve'ke/ənər] s Urlauber –in mf
vaccinate ['væksɪ‚net] tr impfen
vaccination [‚væksɪ'ne/ən] s Impfung f
vaccina'tion certi'ficate s Impfschein m
vaccine [væk'sin] s Impfstoff m

vacillate ['væsɪ ,let] *intr* schwanken

vacuous ['vækju·əs] *adj* nichtssagend

vacu·um ['vækju·əm] *s* (–ums & –a [ə]) Vakuum *n* ‖ *tr & intr* staubsaugen

vac'uum clean'er *s* Staubsauger *m*

vac'uum pump' *s* Absaugepumpe *f*

vac'uum tube' *s* Vakuumröhre *f*

vagabond ['vægə ,bɑnd] *s* Landstreicher –in *mf*

vagary ['vegəri] *s* Laune *f*

vagina [və'dʒaɪnə] *s* Scheide *f*

vagrancy ['vegrənsi] *s* Landstreicherei *f*

vagrant ['vegrənt] *adj* vagabundierend ‖ *s* Landstreicher –in *mf*

vague [veg] *adj* unbestimmt, vage

vain [ven] *adj* (*proud*) eitel; (*pointless*) vergeblich; **in v.** vergebens

vainglo'rious *adj* prahlerisch

valance ['væləns] *s* Quervolant *m*

vale [vel] *s* Tal *n*

valedictory [,vælɪ'dɪktəri] *s* Abschiedsrede *f*

valence ['veləns] *s* Wertigkeit *f*

valentine ['vælən ,taɪn] *s* Valentinsgruß *m*

vale' of tears' *s* Jammertal *n*

valet ['vælɪt] *s* Kammerdiener *m*

valiant ['væljənt] *adj* tapfer

valid ['vælɪd] *adj* (*law, ticket*) gültig; (*argument, objection*) wohlbegründet; (*e.g., contract*) rechtsgültig; **be v.** gelten

validate ['vælɪ ,det] *tr* bestätigen

validation [,vælɪ'deʃən] *s* Bestätigung *f*

validity [və'lɪdɪti] *s* Gültigkeit *f*

valise [və'lis] *s* Reisetasche *f*

valley ['væli] *s* Tal *n*

valor ['vælər] *s* Tapferkeit *f*

valorous ['vælərəs] *adj* tapfer

valuable ['vælju·əbəl] *adj* wertvoll ‖ valuables *spl* Wertsachen *pl*

value ['vælju] *s* Wert *m* ‖ *tr* (at) schätzen (auf *acc*)

val'ue judg'ment *s* Werturteil *n*

valueless ['væljulɪs] *adj* wertlos

valve [vælv] *s* (anat, mach, zool) Klappe *f*; (mach, mus) Ventil *n*

vamp [væmp] *s* (coll) Vamp *m*

vampire ['væmpaɪr] *s* Vampir *m*

van [væn] *s* Möbelwagen *m*; (*panel truck*) Kastenwagen *m*; (fig) Avantgarde *f*; (mil) Vorhut *f*

vandal ['vændəl] *s* Vandale *m*; **Vandal** Vandale *m*

vandalism ['vændə ,lɪzəm] *s* Vandalismus *m*

vane [ven] *s* (*of a windmill, fan, propeller*) Flügel *m*; (*in a turbine*) Schaufel *f*

vanguard ['væn ,gɑrd] *s* (fig) Spitze *f*; (mil) Vorhut *f*

vanilla [və'nɪlə] *s* Vanille *f*

vanish ['vænɪʃ] *intr* (ver)schwinden; **v. into thin air** sich in blauen Dunst auflösen

van'ishing cream' *s* Tagescreme *f*

vanity ['vænɪti] *s* (*arrogance*) Anmaßung *f*; (*emptiness*) Nichtigkeit *f*; (*furniture*) Frisiertisch *m*

van'ity case' *s* Kosmetikköfferchen *n*

vanquish ['væŋkwɪʃ] *tr* besiegen

van'tage point' ['væntɪdʒ] *s* (*advantage*) günstiger Ausgangspunkt *m*; (*view*) Aussichtspunkt *m*

vapid ['væpɪd] *adj* schal, fad(e)

vapor ['vepər] *s* Dampf *m*, Dunst *m*

vaporize ['vepə ,raɪz] *tr & intr* verdampfen

vaporizer ['vepə ,raɪzər] *s* Inhalationsapparat *m*

va'por trail' *s* Kondensstreifen *m*

variable ['verɪ·əbəl] *adj* veränderlich; (*wind*) aus wechselnden Richtungen ‖ *s* (math) Veränderliche *f*

variance ['verɪ·əns] *s* Veränderung *f*; (*difference*) Abweichung *f*; (*argument*) Streit *m*; **be at v. with** (*a person*) in Zwiespalt sein mit; (*a thing*) in Widerspruch stehen zu

variant ['verɪ·ənt] *adj* abweichend ‖ *s* Variante *f*

variation [,verɪ'eʃən] *s* Veränderung *f*; (alg, biol, mus) Variation *f*

var'icose vein' ['verɪ ,kos] *s* Krampfader *f*

varied ['verid] *adj* abwechslungsreich; (*diverse*) verschieden

variegated ['verɪ·ə ,getɪd] *adj* (*diverse*) verschieden; (*in color*) bunt

variety [və'raɪ·əti] *s* (*choice*) Auswahl *f*; (*difference*) Verschiedenheit *f*; (*sort*) Art *f*; (biol) Spielart *f*; **for a v. of reasons** aus verschiedenen Gründen

vari'ety show' *s* Variétévorstellung *f*

various ['verɪ·əs] *adj* verschieden; (*several*) mehrere

varnish ['vɑrnɪʃ] *s* Firnis *m*, Lack *m* ‖ *tr* firnissen

varsity ['vɑrsti] *adj* Auswahl- ‖ *s* Auswahlmannschaft *f*

var·y ['veri] *v* (*pret & pp* –ied) *tr & intr* abwechseln, variieren

vase [ves, vez] *s* Vase *f*

vaseline ['væsə ,lin] *s* (trademark) Vaseline *f*

vassal ['væsəl] *s* Lehensmann *m*

vast [væst] *adj* riesig; (*majority*) überwiegend; **v. amount** Unmasse *f*

vastness ['væstnɪs] *s* Unermeßlichkeit *f*

vat [væt] *s* Bottich *m*

Vatican ['vætɪkən] *adj* vatikanisch; (*city*) Vatikan- ‖ *s* Vatikan *m*

Vat'ican Coun'cil *s* Vatikanisches Konzil *n*

vaudeville ['vodvɪl] *s* Varieté *f*

vaude'ville show' *s* Variétévorstellung *f*

vault [vɔlt] *s* (*underground chamber*) Gruft *f*; (*of a bank*) Tresor *m*; (archit) Gewölbe *n*; **v. of heaven** Himmelsgewölbe *n* ‖ *tr* überspringen

vaunt [vɔnt] *s* Prahlerei *f* ‖ *tr* sich rühmen (genit) ‖ *intr* sich rühmen

veal [vil] *s* Kalbfleisch *n*

veal' cut'let *s* Kalbskotelett *n*

veer [vɪr] *intr* drehen, wenden

vegetable ['vedʒɪtəbəl] *adj* pflanzlich; (*garden, soup*) Gemüse-; (*kingdom, life, oil, dye*) Pflanzen- ‖ *s* Gemüse *n*; **vegetables** Gemüse *n*

vegetarian [ˌvedʒɪˈterɪ·ən] *adj* vegetarisch ‖ *s* Vegetarier –in *mf*
vegetate [ˈvedʒɪˌtet] *intr* vegetieren
vegetation [ˌvedʒɪˈteʃən] *s* Vegetation *f*
vehemence [ˈviː·ɪməns] *s* Heftigkeit *f*
vehement [ˈviː·ɪmənt] *adj* heftig
vehicle [ˈviː·ɪkəl] *s* Fahrzeug *n*
veil [vel] *s* Schleier *m* ‖ *tr* (& fig) verschleiern
veiled *adj* verschleiert; (*threat*) verhüllt
vein [ven] *s* Vene *f*; (geol, min) Ader *f*
vellum [ˈveləm] *s* Velin *n*
velocity [vɪˈlɑsɪti] *s* Geschwindigkeit *f*
velvet [ˈvelvɪt] *adj* Samt– ‖ *s* Samt *m*
velveteen [ˌvelvɪˈtin] *s* Baumwollsamt *m*
velvety [ˈvelvɪti] *adj* samtartig
vend [vend] *tr* verkaufen
vend'ing machine' *s* Automat *m*
vendor [ˈvendər] *s* Verkäufer –in *mf*
veneer [vəˈnɪr] *s* Furnier *n*; (fig) Tünche *f* ‖ *tr* furnieren
venerable [ˈvenərəbəl] *adj* ehrwürdig
venerate [ˈvenəˌret] *tr* verehren
veneration [ˌvenəˈreʃən] *s* Verehrung *f*
Venetian [vɪˈniʃən] *adj* venezianisch ‖ *s* Venezianer –in *mf*
Vene'tian blind' *s* Fensterjalousie *f*
vengeance [ˈvendʒəns] *s* Rache *f*; **take v. on** sich rächen an (*dat*); **with a v.** mit Gewalt
vengeful [ˈvendʒfəl] *adj* rachsüchtig
venial [ˈvinɪ·əl] *adj* (sin) läßlich
Venice [ˈvenɪs] *s* Venedig *n*
venison [ˈvenɪsən] *s* Wildbret *n*
venom [ˈvenəm] *s* Gift *n*; (fig) Geifer *m*
venomous [ˈvenəməs] *adj* giftig
vent [vent] *s* Öffnung *f*; **give v. to** Luft machen (*dat*) ‖ *tr* auslassen
ventilate [ˈventɪˌlet] *tr* ventilieren
ventilation [ˌventɪˈleʃən] *s* Ventilation *f*
ventilator [ˈventɪˌletər] *s* Ventilator *m*
ventricle [ˈventrɪkəl] *s* Ventrikel *m*
ventriloquist [venˈtrɪləkwɪst] *s* Bauchredner –in *mf*
venture [ˈventʃər] *s* Unternehmen *n* ‖ *tr* wagen ‖ *intr* (on) sich wagen (an *acc*); **v. out** sich hinauswagen; **v. to** (*inf*) sich vermessen zu (*inf*)
venturesome [ˈventʃərsəm] *adj* (*person*) wagemutig; (*deed*) gewagt
venue [ˈvenju] *s* zuständiger Gerichtsort *m*; **change of v.** Änderung *f* des Gerichtsstandes
Venus [ˈvinəs] *s* Venus *f*
veracity [vɪˈræsɪti] *s* Wahrhaftigkeit *f*
veranda [vəˈrændə] *s* Veranda *f*
verb [vɜrb] *s* Verb *n*, Zeitwort *n*
verbal [ˈvɜrbəl] *adj* (oral) mündlich; (gram) verbal
verbatim [vərˈbetɪm] *adj* wortgetreu
verbiage [ˈvɜrbɪ·ɪdʒ] *s* Wortschwall *m*
verbose [vərˈbos] *adj* weitschweifig
verdant [ˈvɜrdənt] *adj* grün
verdict [ˈvɜrdɪkt] *s* Urteilsspruch *m* (der Geschworenen); **give a v.** e–n Spruch fällen

verdigris [ˈvɜrdɪˌgris] *s* Grünspan *m*
verge [vɜrdʒ] *s* (fig) Rand *m*; **on the v. of** (*ger*) nahe daran zu (*inf*) ‖ *intr*–**v. on** grenzen an (*acc*)
verifiable [ˌverɪˈfaɪ·əbəl] *adj* nachprüfbar
verification [ˌverɪfɪˈkeʃən] *s* Nachprüfung *f*
veri·fy [ˈverɪˌfaɪ] *v* (*pret* & *pp* –**fied**) *tr* nachprüfen
verily [ˈverɪli] *adv* (Bib) wahrlich
veritable [ˈverɪtəbəl] *adj* echt
vermilion [vərˈmɪljən] *adj* zinnoberrot
vermin [ˈvɜrmɪn] *s* (*objectionable person*) Halunke *m*; **v. spl** Schädlinge *pl*; (*objectionable persons*) Gesindel *n*
vermouth [vərˈmuθ] *s* Wermut *m*
vernacular [vərˈnækjələr] *adj* volkssprachlich ‖ *s* Volkssprache *f*
ver'nal e'quinox [ˈvɜrnəl] *s* Frühlingstagundnachtgleiche *f*
versatile [ˈvɜrsətɪl] *adj* beweglich
verse [vɜrs] *s* (& Bib) Vers *m*; (*stanza*) Strophe *f*
versed [vɜrst] *adj* (in) bewandert in (*dat*)
versification [ˌvɜrsɪfɪˈkeʃən] *s* (*metrical structure*) Versbau *m*; (*versifying*) Verskunst *f*; (*metrical version*) Versfassung *f*
versifier [ˈvɜrsɪˌfaɪ·ər] *s* Verseschmied *m*
version [ˈvɜrʒən] *s* Version *f*
ver·so [ˈvɜrso] *s* (–**sos**) (*of a coin*) Revers *m*; (typ) Verso *n*
versus [ˈvɜrsəs] *prep* gegen (*acc*)
verte·bra [ˈvɜrtɪbrə] *s* (–**brae** [ˌbri] & –**bras**) Rückenwirbel *m*, Wirbel *m*
vertebrate [ˈvɜrtɪˌbret] *s* Wirbeltier *n*
ver·tex [ˈvɜrteks] *s* (–**texes** & –**tices** [tɪˌsiz]) Scheitelpunkt *m*
vertical [ˈvɜrtɪkəl] *adj* senkrecht ‖ *s* Vertikale *f*
ver'tical hold' *s* (telv) Vertikaleinstellung *f*
ver'tical take'off *s* Senkrechtstart *m*
vertigo [ˈvɜrtɪˌgo] *s* Schwindel *m*, Schwindelgefühl *n*
very [ˈveri] *adj*—**that v. day** an demselben Tag; **the v. thought** der bloße Gedanke; **the v. truth** die reine Wahrheit; **the v. man** genau der Mann ‖ *adv* sehr; **the v. best** der allerbeste; **the v. same** ebenderselbe
vesicle [ˈvesɪkəl] *s* Bläschen *n*
vespers [ˈvespərz] *spl* Vesper *f*
vessel [ˈvesəl] *s* (*ship*) Schiff *n*; (*container*) Gefäß *n*
vest [vest] *s* Weste *f*; (*for women*) Leibchen *n* ‖ *tr* (with) bekleiden (mit); **be vested in** zustehen (*dat*)
vest'ed in'terest *s* (*for personal benefits*) persönliches Interesse *n*; (jur) rechtmäßiges Interesse *n*
vestibule [ˈvestɪˌbjul] *s* Vestibül *n*
vestige [ˈvestɪdʒ] *s* Spur *f*
vestment [ˈvestmənt] *s* Gewand *n*
vest'-pock'et *adj* Westentaschen–
vestry [ˈvestri] *s* Sakristei *f*; (*committee*) Gemeindevertretung *f*
vetch [vetʃ] *s* Wicke *f*

veteran ['vetərən] s Veteran m; (sport) Senior m

veterinarian [,vetərı'nerı·ən] s Tierarzt m, Tierärztin f

veterinary ['vetərı ,nerı] adj (college) tierärztlich; **v. medicine** Tierheilkunde f

ve·to ['vito] s (-toes) Veto n || tr ein Veto einlegen gegen

vex [veks] tr ärgern

vexation [vek'seʃən] s Ärger m

V'-forma'tion s (aer) Staffelkeil m

via ['vɪ·ə] prep über (acc)

viable ['vaɪ·əbəl] adj lebensfähig

viaduct ['vaɪ·ə ,dʌkt] s Viadukt m

vial ['vaɪ·əl] s Phiole f

viands ['vaɪ·əndz] spl Lebensmittel pl

vibrate ['vaɪbret] intr vibrieren; **cause to v.** in Schwingung versetzen

vibration [vaɪ'breʃən] s Schwingung f

vicar ['vɪkər] s Vikar m

vicarage ['vɪkərɪdʒ] s Pfarrhaus n

vicarious [vaɪ'kerɪ·əs] adj (pleasure) nachempfunden; (taking the place of another) stellvertretend; **v. experience** Ersatzbefriedigung f

vice [vaɪs] s Laster n

vice'-ad'miral s Vizeadmiral m

vice'-con'sul s Vizekonsul m

vice'-pres'ident s Vizepräsident –in mf

viceroy ['vaɪsrɔɪ] s Vizekönig m

vice' squad' s Sittenpolizei f

vice versa ['vaɪsə'vʌrsə] adv umgekehrt

vicinity [vɪ'sɪnɪtɪ] s Umgebung f; **in the v. of** in der Nähe (genit)

vicious ['vɪʃəs] adj (temper) bösartig; (dog) bissig; (person, gossip) heimtückisch

vi'cious cir'cle s Zirkelschluß m

vicissitudes [vɪ'sɪsɪ ,tjudz] spl Wechselfälle pl

victim ['vɪktɪm] s Opfer n; (animal) Opfertier n; **fall v. to** zum Opfer fallen (dat)

victimize ['vɪktɪ ,maɪz] tr (make a victim of) benachteiligen; (dupe) hereinlegen

victor ['vɪktər] s Sieger –in mf

victorious [vɪk'torɪ·əs] adj siegreich

victory ['vɪktərɪ] adj Sieges– || s Sieg m; (myth) Siegesgöttin f; **flushed with v.** siegestrunken

victuals ['vɪtəlz] spl Viktualien pl

vid'eo sig'nal ['vɪdɪ ,o] s Bildsignal n

vid'eo tape' s Bildband n

vid'eo tape' record'er s Bildbandgerät n

vid'eo tape' record'ing s Bildbandaufnahme f

vie [vaɪ] v (pret & pp **vied**; ger **vying**) intr (with) wetteifern (mit)

Vienna [vɪ'enə] s Wien n

Vien·nese [,vɪ·ə'niz] adj wienerisch || s (-nese) Wiener –in mf

Vietnam [,vɪ·et'nam] s Vietnam n

Vietnam·ese [vɪ ,etnə'miz] adj vietnamesisch || s (-se) Vietnamese m, Vietnamesin f

view [vju] s Aussicht f; (opinion) Ansicht f; **come into v.** in Sicht kommen; **in my v.** meiner Ansicht nach;

in v. of angesichts (genit); **with a v. to** (ger) in der Absicht zu (inf) || tr betrachten; (sights) besichtigen

viewer ['vju·ər] s Zuschauer –in mf

view'find'er s Bildsucher m

view'point s Standpunkt m

vigil ['vɪdʒɪl] s Nachtwache f; **keep v.** wachen

vigilance ['vɪdʒɪləns] s Wachsamkeit f

vigilant ['vɪdʒɪlənt] adj wachsam

vignette [vɪn'jet] s Vignette f

vigor ['vɪgər] s (physical) Kraft f; (mental) Energie f; (intensity) Wucht f

vigorous ['vɪgərəs] adj (strong) kräftig; (act) energisch

vile [vaɪl] adj gemein; (coll) scheußlich

vileness ['vaɪlnɪs] s Gemeinheit f

vili·fy ['vɪlɪ ,faɪ] v (pret & pp **-fied**) tr verleumden

villa ['vɪlə] s Villa f

village ['vɪlɪdʒ] s Dorf n, Ort m

villager ['vɪlɪdʒər] s Dorfbewohner –in mf

villain ['vɪlən] s Bösewicht m, Schurke m

villainous ['vɪlənəs] adj schurkisch

villainy ['vɪlənɪ] s Schurkerei f

vim [vɪm] s Mumm m

vindicate ['vɪndɪ ,ket] tr rechtfertigen

vindictive [vɪn'dɪktɪv] adj rachsüchtig

vine [vaɪn] s Rebe f; (creeper) Ranke f

vinegar ['vɪnɪgər] s Essig m

vine' grow'er [,gro·ər] s Winzer m

vineyard ['vɪnjərd] s Weinberg m

vintage ['vɪntɪdʒ] adj Qualitäts– || s Weinernte f

vin'tage year' s Weinjahr n

vintner ['vɪntnər] s Weinbauer –in mf

vinyl ['vaɪnɪl] adj Vinyl–

viola [vaɪ'olə] s Bratsche f, Viola f

violate ['vaɪ·ə ,let] tr (a law) verletzen; (a promise) brechen; (the peace) stören; (a custom, shrine) entweihen; (a girl) vergewaltigen

violation [,vaɪ·ə'leʃən] s (of the law) Verletzung f; (of a shrine) Entweihung f; (of a girl) Vergewaltigung f

violence ['vaɪ·ələns] s Gewalt f

violent ['vaɪ·ələnt] adj (person) gewalttätig; (deed) gewaltsam; (anger, argument) heftig

violet ['vaɪ·əlɪt] adj violett || s Veilchen n

violin [,vaɪ·ə'lɪn] s Geige f

violinist [,vaɪ·ə'lɪnɪst] s Geiger –in mf

violoncel·lo [,vaɪ·ələn't∫elo] s (-los) Violoncello n

viper ['vaɪpər] s Natter f, Viper f

virgin ['vʌrdʒɪn] adj Jungfern–; (land) unberührt || s Jungfrau f

virginity [vər'dʒɪnɪtɪ] s Jungfräulichkeit f

virility [vɪ'rɪlɪtɪ] s Zeugungskraft f

virology [vaɪ'rɑlədʒɪ] s Virusforschung f

virtual ['vʌrt∫u·əl] adj faktisch; (opt, tech) virtuell

virtue ['vʌrt∫u] s Tugend f; **by v. of** kraft (genit), vermöge (genit)

virtuosity [,vʌrtʃuˈɑsɪti] s Virtuosität f

virtuo·so [,vʌrtʃuˈoso] s (-sos & -si [si]) Virtuose m, Virtuosin f

virtuous [ˈvʌrtʃu-əs] adj tugendhaft

virulence [ˈvɪrjələns] s Virulenz f

virulent [ˈvɪrjələnt] adj virulent

virus [ˈvaɪrəs] s Virus n

visa [ˈvizə] s Visum n

visage [ˈvɪzɪdʒ] s Antlitz n

viscera [ˈvɪsərə] s Eingeweide pl

viscosity [vɪsˈkɑsɪti] s Viskosität f

viscount [ˈvaɪkaunt] s Vicomte m

viscountess [ˈvaɪkauntɪs] s Vicomtesse f

viscous [ˈvɪskəs] adj zähflüssig

vise [vaɪs] s Schraubstock m

visibility [,vɪzɪˈbɪlɪti] s Sichtbarkeit f; (meteor) Sicht f

visible [ˈvɪzɪbəl] adj sichtbar

visibly [ˈvɪzɪblɪ] adv zusehends

vision [ˈvɪʒən] s (faculty) Sehvermögen n; (appearance) Vision f; **of great v.** von großem Weitblick

visionary [ˈvɪʒə,nɛri] adj visionär || s Visionär –in mf

visit [ˈvɪzɪt] s Besuch m; (official) Visite f || tr besuchen; (a museum, town) besichtigen

visitation [,vɪzɪˈteʃən] s Visitation f; **Visitation of our Lady** Heimsuchung f Mariä

vis'iting hours' spl Besuchszeit f

vis'iting nurse' s Fürsorgerin f

visitor [ˈvɪzɪtər] s Besucher –in mf; **have visitors** Besuch haben

visor [ˈvaɪzər] s Schirm m; (on a helmet) Visier n

vista [ˈvɪstə] s (& fig) Ausblick m

Vistula [ˈvɪstʃulə] s Weichsel f

visual [ˈvɪʒu-əl] adj visuell

vis'ual aids' spl Anschauungsmaterial n

visualize [ˈvɪʒu-ə,laɪz] tr sich [dat] vorstellen

vital [ˈvaɪtəl] adj (lebens)wichtig; (signs, functions) Lebens– || **vitals** spl edle Teile pl

vitality [vaɪˈtælɪti] s Lebenskraft f

vitalize [ˈvaɪtə,laɪz] tr beleben

vitamin [ˈvaɪtəmɪn] s Vitamin n

vi'tamin defi'ciency s Vitaminmangel m

vitiate [ˈvɪʃɪ,et] tr verderben

vitreous [ˈvɪtrɪ-əs] adj glasartig

vitriolic [,vɪtrɪˈɑlɪk] adj (fig) beißend; (chem) Vitriol–

vituperate [vaɪˈt(j)upə,ret] tr schelten

vivacious [vɪˈveʃəs] adj lebhaft

vivid [ˈvɪvɪd] adj lebhaft

vivi·fy [ˈvɪvɪ,faɪ] v (pret & pp –fied) tr beleben

vivisection [,vɪvɪˈsɛkʃən] s Vivisektion f

vixen [ˈvɪksən] s Füchsin f

viz. abbr nämlich

vizier [vɪˈzɪr] s Vezier m, Wesir m

vocabulary [voˈkæbjə,lɛri] s (word range) Wortschatz m; (list) Wörterverzeichnis n

vocal [ˈvokəl] adj stimmlich, Stimm–; (outspoken) redselig

voc'al cord' s Stimmband n

vocalist [ˈvokəlɪst] s Sänger –in mf

vocalize [ˈvokə,laɪz] tr (phonet) vokalisieren || intr singen; (phonet) in e–n Vokal verwandelt werden

vocation [voˈkeʃən] s Beruf m; (relig) Berufung f

voca'tional guid'ance [voˈkeʃənəl] s Berufsberatung f

voca'tional school' s Berufsschule f

voca'tional train'ing s Berufsausbildung f

vocative [ˈvɑkətɪv] s Vokativ m

vociferous [voˈsɪfərəs] adj laut

vodka [ˈvɑdkə] s Wodka m

vogue [vog] s (herrschende) Mode f; **be in v.** Mode sein

voice [vɔɪs] s Stimme f; **in a low v.** mit leiser Stimme || tr äußern; (phonet) stimmhaft aussprechen

voiced adj (phonet) stimmhaft

voiceless [ˈvɔɪslɪs] adj stimmlos

void [vɔɪd] adj leer; (invalid) ungültig || s Leere f || tr für ungültig erklären; (the bowels) entleeren

volatile [ˈvɑlətɪl] adj (explosive) jähzornig; (changeable) unbeständig; (chem) flüchtig

volcanic [vɑlˈkænɪk] adj vulkanisch

volca·no [vɑlˈkeno] s (-noes & –nos) Vulkan m

volition [vəˈlɪʃən] s Wollen n; **of one's own v.** aus eigenem Antrieb

volley [ˈvɑli] s (of gunfire) Salve f; (of stones) Hagel m; (sport) Flugschlag m

vol'leyball' s Volleyball m

volt [volt] s Volt n

voltage [ˈvoltɪdʒ] s Spannung f

voluble [ˈvɑljəbəl] adj redegewandt

volume [ˈvɑljəm] s (book) Band m; (of a magazine series) Jahrgang m; (of sound) Lautstärke f; (amount) Ausmaß n; (of a container) Rauminhalt m; **speak volumes** Bände sprechen; **v. of sales** Umsatz m

vol'ume control' s Lautstärkeregler m

voluminous [vəˈluminəs] adj (writer) produktiv; (of great extent or size) umfangreich

voluntary [ˈvɑlən,tɛri] adj freiwillig

volunteer [,vɑlənˈtɪr] adj Freiwilligen– || s Freiwillige mf || tr freiwillig anbieten || intr (for) sich freiwillig erbieten (für, zu)

voluptuary [vəˈlʌptʃu,ɛri] s Wollüstling m

voluptuous [vəˈlʌptʃu-əs] adj wollüstig

vomit [ˈvɑmɪt] s Erbrechen n || tr (er)brechen; (smoke) ausstoßen; (fire) speien; (lava) auswerfen || intr sich erbrechen

voodoo [ˈvudu] adj Wudu– || s Wudu m

voracious [vəˈreʃəs] adj gefräßig

voracity [vəˈræsɪti] s Gefräßigkeit f

vor·tex [ˈvorteks] s (-texes & –tices [tɪ,siz]) (& fig) Wirbel m

votary [ˈvotəri] s Verehrer –in mf

vote [vot] s Stimme f; (act of voting) Abstimmung f; (right to vote) Stimmrecht n; **put to a v.** zur Abstimmung

bringen || *tr (approve of, e.g., money)* (for) bewilligen (für); **v. down** niederstimmen || *intr* stimmen; **v. by acclamation** durch Zuruf stimmen; **v. for** wählen; **v. on** abstimmen über *(acc)*
vote′ get′ter [ˌɡetər] *s* Wahllokomotive *f*
vote′ of con′fidence *s* Vertrauensvotum *n*
vote′ of no′ con′fidence *s* Mißvertrauensvotum *n*
voter [ˈvotər] *s* Wähler –in *mf*
vot′ing booth′ *s* Wahlzelle *f*
vot′ing machine′ *s* Stimmenzählapparat *m*
votive [ˈvotɪv] *adj* Votiv-, Weih–
vo′tive of′fering *s* Weihgabe *f*
vouch [vaʊtʃ] *tr* bezeugen || *intr*—**v. for** bürgen für
voucher [ˈvaʊtʃər] *s* Beleg *m*
vouchsafe′ *tr* gewähren

vow [vaʊ] *s* Gelübde *n;* **take a vow or** geloben || *tr* geloben; *(revenge)* schwören; **vow to** *(inf)* sich *[dat]* geloben zu *(inf)*
vowel [ˈvaʊ·əl] *s* Selbstlaut *m*, Vokal *m*
voyage [ˈvɔɪ·ɪdʒ] *s* Reise *f; (by sea)* Seereise *f* || *intr* reisen
voyager [ˈvɔɪ·ɪdʒər] *s* Reisende *mf; (by sea)* Seereisende *mf*
V′-shaped′ *adj* keilförmig
V′-sign′ *s* Siegeszeichen *n*
vulcanize [ˈvʌlkəˌnaɪz] *tr* vulkanisieren
vulgar [ˈvʌlɡər] *adj* vulgär
vulgarity [vʌlˈɡærɪti] *s* Gemeinheit *f*
Vul′gar Lat′in *s* Vulgärlatein *n*
Vulgate [ˈvʌlɡet] *s* Vulgata *f*
vulnerable [ˈvʌlnərəbəl] *adj* verwundbar; *(position)* ungeschützt; *(fig)* angreifbar; **v. to** anfällig für
vulture [ˈvʌltʃər] *s* Geier *m*

W

W, w [ˈdʌbəlˌju] *s* dreiunzwanzigster Buchstabe des englischen Alphabets
wad [wɑd] *s (of cotton)* Bausch *m; (of money)* Bündel *n; (of papers)* Stoß *m; (of tobacco)* Priem *m*
waddle [ˈwɑdəl] *s* Watscheln *n* || *intr* watscheln
wade [wed] *intr* waten; **w. into** *(fig)* anpacken; **w. through** *(fig)* sich mühsam durcharbeiten durch
wafer [ˈwefər] *s* Oblate *f*
waffle [ˈwɑfəl] *s* Waffel *f*
waf′fle i′ron *s* Waffeleisen *n*
waft [wæft], [wɑft] *tr & intr* wehen
wag [wæɡ] *s (nod)* Nicken *n; (shake)* Schütteln *n; (of the tail)* Wedeln *n; (mischievous person)* Schalk *m* || *v (pret & pp* **wagged**; *ger* **wagging**) *tr (the tail)* wedeln mit; *(nod)* nicken mit; *(shake)* schütteln || *intr (said of a tail)* wedeln; *(said of tongues)* nicht still sein
wage [wedʒ] *adj* Lohn– || *s* Lohn *m;* **wages** Lohn *m* || *tr (war)* führen
wage′ cut′ *s* Lohnabbau *m*
wage′ freeze′ *s* Lohnstopp *m*
wager [ˈwedʒər] *s* Wette *f;* **lay a w.** e–e Wette eingehen || *tr & intr* wetten
waggish [ˈwæɡɪʃ] *adj* schalkhaft
wagon [ˈwæɡən] *s* Wagen *m*
wag′on load′ *s* Wagenladung *f*
waif [wef] *s (child)* verwahrlostes Kind *n; (animal)* verwahrlostes Tier *n*
wail [wel] *s* Wehklage *f* || *intr (over)* wehklagen (über *acc)*
wain·scot [ˈwenskət] *s* Täfelung *f* || *(pret & pp* –**scot[t]ed**; *ger* –**scot-[t]ing)** *tr* täfeln
waist [west] *s* Taille *f;* **strip to the w.** den Oberkörper freimachen
waist′-deep′ *adj* bis an die Hüften (reichend)

waist′line′ *s* Taille *f;* **watch one's w.** auf die schlanke Linie achten
wait [wet] *s* Warten *n;* **an hour's w.** e–e Stunde Wartezeit || *intr* warten; **that can w.** das hat Zeit; **w. for** *(a person)* warten auf *(acc); (e.g., an answer)* abwarten; **w. on** bedienen; **w. up for** aufbleiben und warten auf *(acc)*
wait′-and-see′ pol′icy *s* Politik *f* des Abwartens
waiter [ˈwetər] *s* Kellner *m;* **w.!** Herr Ober!
wait′ing line′ *s* Schlange *f*
wait′ing list′ *s* Warteliste *f*
wait′ing room′ *s* Warteraum *m; (e.g., in a railroad station)* Wartesaal *m*
waitress [ˈwetrɪs] *s* Kellnerin *f*
waive [wev] *tr* verzichten auf *(acc)*
waiver [ˈwevər] *s* Verzicht *m*
wake [wek] *s (at a funeral)* Totenwache *f; (naut)* Kielwasser *n;* **in the w. of** im Gefolge *(genit)* || *v (pret* **waked &** **woke** [wok]; *pp* **waked)** *tr* wecken; **w. up** aufwecken || *intr* erwachen; **w. up** aufwachen; **w. up to** *(fig)* bewußt werden *(genit)*
wakeful [ˈwekfəl] *adj* wachsam
waken [ˈwekən] *tr (auf)wecken || *intr* erwachen
walk [wɔk] *s* Spaziergang *m; (gait)* Gang *m; (path)* Spazierweg *m;* **a five-minute w. to** fünf Minuten zu Fuß zu; **from all walks of life** aus allen Ständen; **go for a w.** spazierengehen; **take for a w.** spazierenführen || *tr (a dog)* spazierenführen; *(a person)* begleiten; *(a horse)* führen; *(the streets)* ablaufen || *intr (zu Fuß)* gehen, laufen; **w. off with** klauen; **w. out on** sitzenlassen; **w. up to** zugehen auf *(acc)*
walk′-away′ *s (coll)* leichter Sieg *m*

walker ['wɔkər] s Fußgänger –in mf

walkie-talkie ['wɔki'tɔki] s Sprechfunk-gerät n

walk'-in' adj (closet) begehbar

walk'ing pa'pers spl Laufpaß m

walk'ing shoes' spl Straßenschuhe pl

walk'ing stick' s Spazierstock m

walk'-on' s (theat) Statist –in mf

walk'out' s Ausstand m

walk'o'ver s (sport) leichter Sieg m

walk'-up' s Mietwohnung f ohne Fahr-stuhl

wall [wɔl] s Mauer f; (between rooms) Wand f || tr—w. up vermauern

wall' brack'et s Konsole f

wall' clock' s Wanduhr f

wallet ['wɑlɪt] s Brieftasche f

wall'flow'er s (coll) Wandblümchen n

wall' map' s Wandkarte f

wallop ['wɑləp] s Puff m; have a w. Schlagkraft haben || tr verprügeln; (defeat) schlagen

wal'loping adj (sl) mordsgroß

wallow ['wɑlo] intr sich wälzen; w. in (fig) schwelgen in (dat)

wall'pa'per s Tapete f || tr tapezieren

walnut ['wɔlnət] s Walnuß f; (wood) Walnußholz n; (tree) Walnußbaum m

walrus ['wɔlrəs] s Walroß n

waltz [wɔlts] s Walzer m || intr Walzer tanzen

wan [wɑn] adj (wanner; wannest) bleich; (smile) schwach, matt

wand [wɑnd] s Stab m; (in magic) Zauberstab m

wander ['wɑndər] intr wandern; (from a subject) abschweifen

wanderer ['wɑndərər] s Wanderer –in mf

wan'derlust' s Wanderlust f

wane [wen] s—be on the w. abnehmen || intr abnehmen

wangle ['wæŋgəl] tr sich [dat] er-schwindeln

want [wɑnt] s Bedürfnis n; for w. of mangels (genit) || tr wollen; wanted (sought, desired) gesucht

want' ad' s Kleinanzeige f

want'ing adj—be w. in ermangeln (genit)

war [wɔr] s Krieg m; at war im Kriege; go to war with e–n Krieg beginnen gegen; make war on Krieg führen gegen || v (pret & pp warred; ger warring) intr kämpfen

warble ['wɑrbəl] s Trillern n || intr trillern

war' bond' s Kriegsanleihe f

war' cry' s Schlachtruf m

ward [wɔrd] s (in a hospital) Station f; (of a city) Bezirk m; (person under protection) Schützling m; (person under guardianship) Mündel n; (guardianship) Vormundschaft f || tr—w. off abwehren

warden ['wɔrdən] s Gefängnisdirektor m

ward'robe' s Garderobe f

ward'room' s (nav) Offiziersmesse f

ware [wer] s Ware f

ware'house' s Lagerhaus n, Warenlager n

ware'house'man s (–men) Lagerist m

war'fare' s Kriegsführung f, Krieg m

war' foot'ing s Kriegsbereitschaft f

war'head' s Gefechtskopf m

war'-horse' s (coll) alter Kämpe m

war'like' adj kriegerisch

war' lord' s Kriegsherr m

warm [wɔrm] adj warm; (friends) in-tim || tr wärmen; w. up aufwärmen || intr—w. up warm werden; (sport) in Form kommen

warm'-blood'ed adj warmblütig

warm'front' s Warmfront f

warm'-heart'ed adj warmherzig

warmonger ['wɔr,mʌŋgər] s Kriegs-hetzer –in mf

warmth [wɔrmθ] s Wärme f

warm'-up' s (sport) Lockerungsübun-gen pl

warn [wɔrn] tr (against) warnen (vor dat)

warn'ing s Warnung f; let this be a w. to you lassen Sie sich das zur War-nung dienen

warn'ing shot' s Warnschuß m

war' of attri'tion s Zermürbungskrieg m

warp [wɔrp] s (of a board) Verziehen n || tr (wood) verziehen; w. s.o.'s mind j–n verschroben machen || intr sich verziehen

war'path' s Kriegspfad m

warped adj (wood) verzogen; (mind, opinion) verschroben

war'plane' s Kampfflugzeug n

warrant ['wɔrənt] s (justification) Rechtfertigung f; (authorization) Berechtigung f; w. for arrest Haft-befehl m || tr (justify) rechtfertigen; (guarantee) garantieren

war'rant of'ficer s (mil) Stabsfeldwebel m; (nav) Deckoffizier m

warranty ['wɔrənti] s Gewährleistung f

war'ranty serv'ice s Kundendienst m

warren ['wɔrən] s Kaninchengehege n

war'ring adj kriegsführend

warrior ['wɔrɪər] s Krieger m

Warsaw ['wɔrsɔ] s Warschau n

war'ship' s Kriegsschiff n

wart [wɔrt] s Warze f

war'time' adj Kriegs– || s Kriegszeit f

war'-torn' adj vom Krieg verwüstet

wary ['weri] adj vorsichtig

war' zone' s Kriegsgebiet n

wash [wɑʃ] adj Wasch– || s Wäsche f; (aer) Luftstrudel m; (paint) dünner Farbüberzug m; do the w. die Wäsche waschen || tr waschen; (metal) schlämmen; (paint) tuschen; (phot) wässern; w. ashore anschwem-men; w. away wegspülen; w. off ab-waschen; w. out auswaschen; (a bridge) wegreißen; w. up aufwaschen || intr waschen; w. ashore ans Land spülen

washable ['wɑʃəbəl] adj waschbar

wash'-and-wear' adj bügelfrei

wash'ba'sin s Waschbecken n

wash'bas'ket s Wäschekorb m

wash'board' s Waschbrett n

wash'bowl' s Waschbecken n

wash'cloth' s Waschlappen m

wash′day′ s Waschtag m

washed′-out′ adj verwaschen; (tired) schlapp

washer [′wɔʃər] s Waschmaschine f; (of rubber) Dichtungsring m; (of metal) Unterlegscheibe f

washed′-up′ adj (coll) erledigt

wash′er-wom′an s (-wom′en) Waschfrau f

wash′ing s Waschen n; (clothes) Wäsche f

wash′ing machine′ s Waschmaschine f

wash′out′ s Auswaschung f; (failure) Pleite f; (person who fails) Versager –in mf

wash′rag′ s Waschlappen m

wash′room′ s Waschraum m

wash′stand′ s Waschtisch m

wash′tub′ s Waschtrog m

wasp [wɔsp] s Wespe f

wasp′ waist′ s Wespentaille f

waste [west] adj (superfluous) überflüssig; (land) öde ‖ s (of material goods, time, energy) Verschwendung f; (waste material) Müll m; (wilderness) Wildnis f; go to w. vergeudet werden ‖ tr verschwenden, vergeuden ‖ intr—w. away verfallen

waste′bas′ket s Papierkorb m

wasteful [′westfəl] adj verschwenderisch

waste′land′ s Ödland n

waste′pa′per s Makulatur f

waste′pipe′ s Abflußrohr n

waste′pro′duct s Abfallprodukt n

wastrel [′westrəl] s Verschwender –in mf

watch [wɑtʃ] s Uhr f; (lookout) Wache f; be on the w. for acht haben auf (acc) ‖ tr (observe) beobachten; (guard) bewachen; (oversee) aufpassen auf (acc); w. how I do it passen Sie auf, wie ich es mache; w. your step! Vorsicht, Stufe! ‖ intr (keep guard) wachen; (observe) zuschauen; w. for abwarten; w. over überwachen; w. out! Vorsicht!; w. out for ausschauen nach; (some danger) sich hüten vor (dat); w. out for oneself sich vorsehen

watch′band′ s Uhrarmband n

watch′case′ s Uhrgehäuse n

watch′ crys′tal s Uhrglas n

watch′dog′ s Wachhund m

watch′dog commit′tee s Überwachungsausschuß m

watchful [′wɑtʃfəl] adj wachsam

watchfulness [′wɑtʃfəlnɪs] s Wachsamkeit f

watch′mak′er s Uhrmacher –in mf

watch′man s (-men) Wächter m

watch′ pock′et s Uhrtasche f

watch′ strap′ s Uhrarmband n

watch′tow′er s Wachturm m

watch′word′ s Kennwort n, Parole f

water [′wɔtər] s Wasser n; (body of water) Gewässer n; pass w. Wasser lassen ‖ tr (& fig), (flowers) begießen; (fields) bewässern; (animals) tränken; (the garden, streets) sprengen; w. down (& fig) verwässern ‖ intr (said of the eyes) tränen; my mouth

waters das Wasser läuft mir im Mund zusammen

wa′ter boy′ s Wasserträger m

wa′ter clos′et s Wasserklosett n

wa′tercol′or s (paint) Aquarellfarbe f; (painting) Aquarell n

wa′tercourse′ s Wasserlauf m

wa′tercress′ s Brunnenkresse f

wa′terfall′ s Wasserfall m

wa′terfront′ s Hafenviertel n

wa′ter heat′er s Warmwasserbereiter m

wa′tering can′ s Wasserkanne f

wa′tering place′ s (for cattle) Tränke f; (for tourists) Badeort m

wa′ter lev′el s Wasserstand m

wa′terlogged′ adj vollgesogen

wa′ter main′ s Wasserleitung f

wa′termark′ s Wasserzeichen n

wa′ter mat′tress s Wasserbett n

wa′termel′on s Wassermelone f

wa′ter me′ter s Wasserzähler m

wa′ter pipe′ s Wasserrohr n

wa′ter po′lo s Wasserball m

wa′ter pow′er s Wasserkraft f

wa′terproof′ adj wasserdicht ‖ tr imprägnieren

wa′ter-repel′lent adj wasserabstoßend

wa′tershed′ s Wasserscheide f

wa′ter-ski′ intr wasserschifahren

wa′terspout′ s (orifice) Wasserspeier m; (pipe) Ablaufrohr n

wa′ter supply′ s Wasserversorgung f

wa′ter ta′ble s Grundwasserspiegel m

wa′ter tank′ s Wasserbehälter m

wa′tertight′ adj wasserdicht; (fig) eindeutig

wa′ter wag′on s—be on the w. Abstinenzler sein

wa′terway′ s Wasserstraße f

wa′ter wheel′ s (for raising water) Schöpfwerk n; (water-driven) Wasserrad n

wa′ter wings′ spl Schwimmkissen n

wa′terworks′ s Wasserwerk n

watery [′wɔtəri] adj wäss(e)rig

watt [wɑt] s Watt n

wattage [′wɑtɪdʒ] s Wattleistung f

wattles [′wɑtəlz] spl Flechtwerk s

watt′me′ter s Wattmeter m

wave [wev] s (fig, meteor, mil, phys, rad) Welle f; w. of the hand Wink m mit der Hand ‖ tr (a hat, flag) schwenken; (a hand, handkerchief) winken mit; (hair) wellen; w. one′s hands about mit den Händen herumfuchteln; w. s.o. away j–n abwinken ‖ intr (said of a flag) wehen; (said of grain) wogen; (with the hand) winken; w. to zuwinken (dat)

wave′length′ s Wellenlänge f

waver [′wevər] intr schwanken, wanken

wavy [′wevi] adj wellenförmig; w. line Wellenlinie f

wax [wæks] adj Wachs– ‖ s Wachs n ‖ tr (the floor) bohnern; (skis) wachsen ‖ intr werden; (said of the moon) zunehmen; wax and wane zu– und abnehmen

wax′ muse′um s Wachsfigurenkabinett n

wax′ pa′per s Wachspapier n

way [we] adv weit; way ahead weit

voraus ‖ *s* Weg *m*; (*manner*) Art *f*; (*means*) Mittel *n*; (*condition*) Verfassung *f*; (*direction*) Richtung *f*; **across the way** gegenüber; **a long way from** weit weg von; **a long way off** weit weg; **by the way** übrigens; **by way of** über (*acc*); **by way of comparison** vergleichsweise; **get s.th. out of the way** etw aus dem Wege schaffen; **get under way** in Gang kommen; **go all the way** aufs Ganze gehen; **go one's own way** aus der Reihe tanzen; **have a way with s.o.** mit j-m umzugehen verstehen; **have in the way of** (*merchandise*) haben an (*dat*); **have it both ways** es sich [*dat*] aussuchen können; **have one's own way** seinen Willen durchsetzen; **I'm on my way!** ich komme schon!; **in a way** gewissermaßen; **in no way** keineswegs; **in the way** im Weg; **in this way** auf diese Weise; **in what way** in welcher Hinsicht; **make one's way through the crowd** sich [*dat*] e-n Weg durch die Menge bahnen; **one way or another** irgendwie· **on the way** unterwegs; **on the way out** (fig) im Begriff unmodern zu werden; **see one's way clear** bereit sein; **that way** auf diese Weise; (*in that direction*) in jener Richtung; **the way it looks** voraussichtlich; **way back** Rückweg *m*; **way here** Herweg *m*; **way out** Ausgang *m*; (fig) Ausweg *m*; **way there** Hinweg *m*
wayfarer ['we‚ferər] *s* Wanderer *m*
way'lay' *v* (*pret & pp* **-laid**) *tr* auflauern (*dat*)
way' of life' *s* Lebensweise *f*
way' of think'ing *s* Denkweise *f*
ways' and means' *spl* Mittel und Wege *pl*
way'side' *adj* an der Straße gelegen ‖ *s* Wegrand *m*; **fall by the w.** dem Untergang anheimfallen
wayward ['weword] *adj* ungeraten
we [wi] *pers pron* wir
weak [wik] *adj* schwach
weaken ['wikən] *tr* (ab)schwächen ‖ *intr* schwach werden
weakling ['wiklɪŋ] *s* Schwächling *m*
weak'-mind'ed *adj* willenlos
weakness ['wiknɪs] *s* (& fig) Schwäche *f*
weak' spot' *s* schwache Stelle *f*
weal [wil] *s* Strieme *f*, Striemen *m*
wealth [welθ] *s* (of) Reichtum *m* (an *dat*)
wealthy ['welθi] *adj* wohlhabend
wean [win] *tr* (from) entwöhnen (*genit*)
weapon ['wepən] *s* Waffe *f*
weaponry ['wepənri] *s* Bewaffnung *f*
wear [wer] *s* (*use*) Gebrauch *m*; (*durability*) Haltbarkeit *f*; (*clothing*) Kleidung *f*; (*wearing down*) Verschleiß *m* ‖ *v* (*pret* **wore** [wor]; *pp* **worn** [worn])*tr* tragen; **w. down** (*a heel*) abtreten; (*a person*) zermürben; **w. out** abnützen; (*tires*) abfahren; (*a person*) erschöpfen; **w. the pants in the family** die Hosen anhaben ‖ *intr* sich tragen; **w. off** sich abtragen; **w.**

out sich abnützen; **w. thin** (*said of clothes*) fadenscheinig werden; (*said of patience*) zu Ende gehen
wearable ['werəbəl] *adj* tragbar
wear' and tear' [ter] *s* Verschleiß *m*; **takes a lot of w.** strapazierfähig sein
weariness ['wɪrɪnɪs] *s* Müdigkeit *f*
wearisome ['wɪrɪsəm] *adj* mühsam
wea·ry ['wɪri] *adj* müde ‖ *v* (*pret & pp* **-ried**) *tr* ermüden ‖ *intr* (of) müde werden (*genit*)
weasel ['wizəl] *s* Wiesel *n* ‖ *intr*—**w. out of** sich herauswinden aus
weather ['weðər] *s* Wetter *n*; **be under the w.** unpäßlich sein; **w. permitting** bei günstiger Witterung ‖ *tr* dem Wetter aussetzen; (*the storm*) (fig) überstehen ‖*intr* verwittern
weath'erbeat'en *adj* verwittert
weath'er bu'reau *s* Wetterdienst *m*
weath'er condi'tions *spl* Wetterverhältnisse *pl*
weath'er fore'cast *s* Wettervoraussage *f*
weath'erman' *s* (**-men'**) Wetteransager *m*
weath'er report' *s* Wetterbericht *m*
weath'erstrip'ping *s* Dichtungsstreifen *pl*
weath'er vane' *s* (& fig) Wetterfahne *f*
weave [wiv] *s* Webart *f* ‖ *v* (*pret* **wove** [wov] & **weaved**; *pp* **woven** ['wovən]) *tr* weben; (*a rug*) wirken; (*a basket*) flechten; (*a wreath*) winden; **w. one's way through traffic** sich durch den Verkehr schlängeln ‖ *intr* weben
weaver ['wivər] *s* Weber –in *mf*
web [web] *s* (*of a spider*) Spinngewebe *n*; (*of ducks*) Schwimmhaut *f*; **web of lies** Lügengewebe *n*
web'-foot'ed *adj* schwimmfüßig
wed [wed] *v* (*pret & pp* **wed & wedded**; *ger* **wedding**) *tr & intr* heiraten
wed'ding *adj* (*cake, present, day, reception*) Hochzeits–; (*ring*) Trau– ‖ *s* Hochzeit *f*; (*ceremony*) Trauung *f*
wedge [wedʒ] *s* Keil *m* ‖ *tr*—**w. in** einkeilen
wed'lock' *s* Ehestand *m*; **out of w.** unehelich
Wednesday ['wenzde] *s* Mittwoch *m*; **on W.** am Mittwoch
wee [wi] *adj* winzig; **a wee bit** ein klein wenig
weed [wid] *s* Unkraut *n*; (*marijuana*) (sl) Marihuana *n*; (*cigarette*) (sl) Zigarette *f*; **pull weeds** jäten ‖ *tr* jäten; **w. out** (fig) aussondern
weed' kill'er *s* Unkrautvertilgungsmittel *n*
week [wik] *s* Woche *f*; **a w. from today** heute in e-r Woche; **a w. ago today** heute vor acht Tagen; **for weeks** wochenlang
week'day' *s* Wochentag *m*
week'end' *s* Wochenende *n*
weekender ['wik‚endər] *s* Wochenendausflügler –in *mf*
weekly ['wikli] *adj* wöchentlich; (*wages*) Wochen– ‖ *s* Wochenblatt *n*
weep [wip] *v* (*pret & pp* **wept** [wept]) *tr & intr* weinen

weep'ing wil'low *s* Trauerweide *f*

weevil ['wiːvəl] *s* Rüsselkäfer *m*

weft [weft] *s* (tex) Schußfaden *m*

weigh [wei] *tr* wiegen; (*ponder*) wägen; (*anchor*) lichten ‖ *intr* wiegen; **w. heavily on** schwer lasten auf (*dat*)

weight [wet] *s* Gewicht *n*; (*burden*) Last *f*; (*influence*) Einfluß *m*; (*importance*) Bedeutung *f*; **carry great w.** sehr ins Gewicht fallen; **lift weights** Gewichte heben; **pull one's w.** das Seine tun; **throw one's w. about** sich breitmachen

weightless ['wetlɪs] *adj* schwerelos

weightlessness ['wetlɪsnɪs] *s* Schwerelosigkeit *f*

weighty ['weti] *adj* (& *fig*) gewichtig

weird [wɪrd] *adj* unheimlich

weir·do ['wɪrdo] *s* (**-dos**) (sl) Kauz *m*

welcome ['welkəm] *adj* willkommen; (*news*) erfreulich; **you're w.!** bitte sehr!; **you're w. to** (*inf*) es steht Ihnen frei zu (*inf*) ‖ *s* Empfang *m*, Willkomm *m* ‖ *tr* empfangen; (*an opportunity*) mit Freude begrüßen ‖ *interj* (**to**) willkommen! (**in** *dat*)

weld [weld] *s* Schweißnaht *n* ‖ *tr* & *intr* schweißen

welder ['weldər] *s* Schweißer *m* –**in** *mf*

weld'ing *s* Schweißen *n*, Schweißarbeit *f*

welfare ['welˌfer] *s* Wohlfahrt *f*

wel'fare work'er *s* Wohlfahrtspfleger –**in** *mf*

well [wel] *adj* gesund; **all is w.** alles ist in Ordnung; **feel w.** sich wohl fühlen ‖ *adv* gut, wohl; **as w.** ebenso; **as w. as** so gut wie; (*in addition to*) sowohl ... als auch; **he is doing w.** es geht ihm gut; **his company is doing w.** seine Firma geht gut; **leave w. enough alone** es gut sein lassen; **w. on in years** schon bejahrt; **w. on the way** mitten auf dem Wege; (*fig*) auf dem besten Wege; **w. over** wohl über ‖ *s* Brunnen *m*; (*hole*) Bohrloch *n*; (*source*) Quelle *f* ‖ *intr*—**w. up** hervorquellen ‖ *interj* na!; (*in surprise*) nanu!

well'-behaved' *adj* artig

well'-be'ing *s* Wohlergehen *n*

well'born' *adj* aus guter Familie

wellbred ['welˌbred] *adj* wohlerzogen

well'-deserved' *adj* wohlverdient

well'-disposed' *adj* (*toward*) wohlgesinnt (*dat*)

well-done ['welˈdʌn] *adj* (culin) durchgebraten ‖ *interj* gut gemacht!

well'-dressed' *adj* gut angezogen

well'-found'ed *adj* wohlbegründet

well'-groomed' *adj* gut gepflegt

well'-heeled' *adj* (coll) steinreich

well'-informed' *adj* wohlunterrichtet

well'-inten'tioned *adj* wohlmeinend

well-kept ['welˈkept] *adj* gut gepflegt; (*secret*) gut gehütet

well'-known' *adj* wohlbekannt

well'-mean'ing *adj* wohlmeinend

well'-nigh' *adv* fast

well'-off' *adj* wohlhabend, vermögend

well'-preserved' *adj* gut erhalten

well-read ['welˈred] *adj* belesen

well'-spent' *adj* (*money*) gut verwendet; (*time*) gut verbracht

well'spring' *s* Brunnquell *m*

well'-thought'-of' *adj* angesehen

well'-timed' *adj* wohl berechnet

well-to-do ['weltəˈdu] *adj* wohlhabend

well-wisher ['welˈwɪʃər] *s* Gratulant –**in** *mf*

well'-worn' *adj* (*clothes*) abgetragen; (*phrase, subject*) abgedroschen

Welsh [welʃ] *adj* walisisch ‖ *s* Walisisch *n*; **the W.** die Walliser *pl* ‖ **welsh** *intr*—**welsh on** (*a promise*) brechen

Welsh' rab'bit or **rare'bit** ['rerbɪt] *s* geröstete Käseschnitte *f*

welt [welt] *s* Striemen *m*

welter ['weltər] *s* Durcheinander *n* ‖ *intr* sich wälzen

wel'terweight' *s* Weltergewichtler *m*

we'lterweight divi'sion *s* Weltergewicht *n*

wench [wentʃ] *s* Dirne *f*, Weibsbild *n*

wend [wend] *tr*—**w. one's way** seinen Weg nehmen

werewolf ['werˌwʌlf] *s* Werwolf *m*

west [west] *adj* westlich ‖ *adv* nach Westen ‖ *s* Westen *m*

western ['westərn] *adj* westlich ‖ *s* (cin) Wildwestfilm *m*

West' Ger'many *s* Westdeutschland *n*

West' In'dies, the ['ɪndiz] *spl* Westindien *n*

Westphalia [ˌwestˈfeljə] *s* Westfalen *n*

westward ['westwərd] *adv* westwärts

wet [wet] *adj* (**wetter; wettest**) naß; **all wet** (coll) auf dem Holzwege ‖ *v* (*pret* & *pp* **wet** & **wetted**; *ger* **wetting**) *tr* naß machen

wet' blan'ket *s* (fig) Miesepeter *m*

wet' nurse' *s* Amme *f*

whack [wæk] *s* (coll) Klaps *m* ‖ *tr* (coll) klapsen

whale [wel] *s* Wal(fisch) *m*; **have a w. of a time** sich großartig unterhalten

whaler ['welər] *s* Walfänger *m*

wharf [wɔrf] *s* (**wharves** ['wɔrvz]) Kaianlage *f*

what [wɑt] *interr adj* welcher, was für ein ‖ *interr pron* was; **so w.?** na und?; **w. about me?** und was geschieht mit mir?; **w. if** was geschieht, wenn; **w. is more** außerdem; **w. next?** was noch?; **w. of it?** was ist da schon dabei?; **what's new?** was gibt es Neues? **what's that to you?** was geht Sie das an? ‖ *interj* was für ein

whatev'er *adj* welch ... auch immer; **no ... w.** überhaupt kein ‖ *pron* was auch immer; **w. I have** alles, was ich habe; **w. you please** was Sie wollen

what'not' *s*—**and w.** und was weiß ich noch (alles)

what's-his-name' *s* (coll) Dingsda *m*

wheal [wil] *s* Pustel *f*; (*welt*) Striemen *m*

wheat [wit] *s* Weizen *m*

wheedle ['hwidəl] *tr*—**w. s.o. into** (*ger*) j-n beschwatzen zu (*inf*); **w. s.th. out of s.o.** j-m etw abschwatzen

wheel [wil] *s* Rad *n*; **at the w.** (aut) am Steuer || *tr* fahren || *intr* sich drehen; **w. around** sich umdrehen

wheelbarrow ['wil‚bæro] *s* Schubkarre *f*

wheel'chair' *s* Krankenfahrstuhl *m*

wheeler-dealer ['wilər'dilər] *s* Drahtzieher –in *mf*

wheeze [wiz] *s* Schnaufen *n* || *intr* schnaufen

whelp [welp] *s* Welpe *m* || *tr* werfen

when [wen] *adv* wann || *conj* (*once in the past*) als; (*whenever; at a future time*) wenn

whence [wens] *adv & conj* woher

whenev'er *conj* wenn, wann immer

where [wer] *adv & conj* wo; (*whereto*) wohin; **from w.** woher

whereabouts ['werə‚bauts] *adv* wo ungefähr || *s & spl* Verbleib *m*

whereas' *conj* während, wohingegen

whereby' *conj* wodurch

where'fore' *adv & conj* weshalb

wherefrom' *adv* woher

wherein' *adv & conj* worin

whereof' *adv & conj* wovon

whereto' *adv* wohin

where'upon' *adv* worauf, wonach

wherever [wer'evər] *conj* wo auch

wherewith' *adv* womit

wherewithal ['werwɪð‚əl] *s* Geldmittel *pl*

whet [wet] *v* (*pret & pp* **whetted**; *ger* **whetting**) *tr* wetzen, schleifen; (*the appetite*) anregen

whether ['weðər] *conj* ob

whet'stone' *s* Wetzstein *m*, Schleifstein *m*

whew [hwju] *interj* hui!; ui!

which [wɪtʃ] *interr adj* welcher || *interr pron* welcher || *rel pron* der, welcher

whichev'er *rel adj & rel pron* welcher

whiff [wɪf] *s* Geruch *m*, Nasevoll *f*

while [waɪl] *s* Weile *f* || *conj* während || *tr*—**w. away** sich [*dat*] vertreiben

whim [wɪm] *s* Laune *f*, Grille *f*

whimper ['wɪmpər] *s* Wimmern *n* || *tr & intr* wimmern

whimsical ['wɪmzɪkəl] *adj* schrullig

whine [waɪn] *s* Wimmern *n*; (*of a siren, engine, storm*) Heulen *n* || *intr* wimmern; heulen

whin·ny ['wɪni] *s* Wiehern *n* || *v* (*pret & pp* **-nied**) *intr* wiehern

whip [wɪp] *s* Peitsche *f* || *v* (*pret & pp* **whipped**; *ger* **whipping**) *tr* peitschen; (*egg whites*) zu Schaum schlagen; (*defeat*) schlagen; **w. out** blitzschnell ziehen; **w. up** (*a meal*) hervorzaubern; (*enthusiasm*) erregen

whip'lash' *s* Peitschenhieb *m*; (fig) Peitschenhiebeffekt *m*

whipped' cream' *s* Schlagsahne *f*

whipper-snapper ['wɪpər‚snæpər] *s* Frechdachs *m*

whip'ping *s* Prügel *pl*

whip'ping boy' *s* Prügelknabe *m*

whip'ping post' *s* Schandpfahl *m*

whir [wʌr] *s* Schnurren *n* || *v* (*pret & pp* **whirred**; *ger* **whirring**) *intr* schnurren

whirl [wʌrl] *s* Wirbel *m*; **give s.th. a w.** (coll) etw ausprobieren || *tr* wirbeln || *intr* wirbeln; **my head is whirling** mir ist schwindlig

whirl'pool' *s* Strudel *m*, Wirbel *m*

whirl'wind' *s* Wirbelwind *m*

whirlybird ['wʌrli‚bʌrd] *s* (coll) Hubschrauber *m*

whisk [wɪsk] *s* Wedel *m*; (culin) Schneebesen *m* || *tr* wischen; **w. away** (fig) eilends mitnehmen; **w. off** wegfegen

whisk' broom' *s* Kleiderbesen *m*

whiskers ['wɪskərz] *spl* Bart *m*; (*on the cheeks*) Backenbart *m*; (*of a cat*) Barthaare *pl*

whiskey ['wɪski] *s* Whisky *m*

whisper ['wɪspər] *s* Flüsterton *m* || *tr & intr* flüstern

whistle ['wɪsəl] *s* (*sound*) Pfiff *m*; (*device*) Trillerpfeife *f*; **wet one's w.** sich [*dat*] die Nase begießen || *tr* pfeifen || *intr* pfeifen; (*said of the wind, bullet*) sausen; **w. for** (coll) vergeblich warten auf (*acc*)

whit [wɪt] *s*—**not care a w. about** sich keinen Deut kümmern um

white [waɪt] *adj* weiß; **w. as a sheet** kreidebleich || *s* Weiß *n*; (*of the eye*) Weiße *f*

white'caps' *spl* Schaumkronen *pl*

white'-col'lar work'er *s* Angestellte *mf*

white'fish' *s* Weißfisch *m*

white'-haired' *adj* weißhaarig

white'-hot' *adj* weißglühend

white' lie' *s* Notlüge *f*

white' meat' *s* weißes Fleisch *n*

whiten ['waɪtən] *tr* weiß machen || *intr* weiß werden

whiteness ['waɪtnɪs] *s* Weiße *f*

white' slav'ery *s* Mädchenhandel *m*

white' tie' *s* Frackschleife *f*; (*formal*) Frack *m*

white'wash' *s* Tünche *f*; (fig) Beschönigung *f* || *tr* tünchen; (fig) beschönigen

whither ['wiðər] *adv* wohin

whitish ['waɪtɪʃ] *adj* weißlich

whittle ['wɪtəl] *tr* schnitzeln; **w. away** (or **down**) verringern || *intr*—**w. away at** herumschnitzeln an (*dat*); (fig) verringern

whiz(z) [wɪz] *s* Zischen *n*; (fig) Kanone *f* || *v* (*pret & pp* **whizzed**; *ger* **whizzing**) *intr* zischen; **w. by** flitzen

who [hu] *interr pron* wer; **who the devil** wer zum Teufel || *rel pron* der; **he who** wer

whoa [wo] *interj* halt!

whoev'er *rel pron* wer, wer auch immer

whole [hol] *adj* ganz || *s* Ganze *n*; **as a w.** im großen und ganzen

whole'-heart'ed *adj* ernsthaft

whole' note' *s* (mus) ganze Note *f*

whole' rest' *s* (mus) ganze Pause *f*

whole'sale' *adj* Massen–; (com) Großhandels– || *adv* en gros || *s* Großhandel *m* || *tr* en gros verkaufen || *intr* im großen handeln

wholesaler ['hol‚selər] *s* Großhändler –in *mf*

wholesome ['holsəm] *adj* gesund; *(food)* zuträglich

whole'-wheat' bread' *s* Vollkornbrot *n*

wholly ['holi] *adv* ganz, völlig

whom [hum] *interr pron* wen; **to w. wem** ∥ *rel pron* den, welchen; **to w. dem, welchem**

whomev'er *rel pron* wen auch immer; **to w.** wem auch immer

whoop [hup], [hwup] *s* Ausruf *m* ∥ *tr*—**w. it up** Radau machen

whoop'ing cough' *s* Keuchhusten *m*

whopper ['wɑpər] *s* Mordsding *n*; *(lie)* (coll) faustdicke Lüge *f*

whop'ping *adj* (coll) enorm, Riesen-

whore [hor] *s* Hure *f* ∥ *intr*—**w. around** huren

whose [huz] *interr pron* wessen ∥ *rel pron* dessen

why [waɪ] *adv* warum; **that's why deswegen; why, there you are!** da sind Sie ja!; **why, yes!** aber ja! ∥ *s* Warum *m*; **the whys and the wherefores** das Warum und Weshalb

wick [wɪk] *s* Docht *m*

wicked ['wɪkɪd] *adj (evil)* böse; *(roguish)* boshaft; *(vicious)* bösartig; *(unpleasant)* ekelhaft; *(cold, pain, storm, wound)* (coll) schlimm; *(fantastic)* (coll) großartig

wicker ['wɪkər] *adj (basket, chair)* Weiden– ∥ *s (wickerwork)* Flechtwerk *n*

wide [waɪd] *adj* breit; *(selection)* reich ∥ *adv* weit

wide'-an'gle lens' *s* Weitwinkelobjektiv *n*

wide'-awake' *adj* hellwach

wide'-eyed' *adj* mit weit aufgerissenen Augen; *(innocence)* naiv

widely ['waɪdli] *adv* weit

widen ['waɪdən] *tr* ausweiten, verbreiten ∥ *intr* sich ausweiten

wide'-o'pen *adj* weit geöffnet

wide' screen' *s* (cin) Breitleinwand *f*

wide'spread' *adj* weitverbreitet; *(damage)* weitgehend

widow ['wɪdo] *s* Witwe *f*

widower ['wɪdo-ər] *s* Witwer *m*

wid'owhood' *s* Witwenstand *m*

width [wɪdθ] *s* Breite *f*; **in w.** breit

wield [wild] *tr (a weapon)* führen; *(power, influence)* ausüben

wife [waɪf] *s (wives* [waɪvz]) Frau *f*

wig [wɪg] *s* Perücke *f*

wiggle ['wɪgəl] *s* Wackeln *n* ∥ *tr* wackeln mit

wigwag ['wɪg,wæg] *s* Winksignal *n*

wigwam ['wɪgwɑm] *s* Wigwam *m & n*

wild [waɪld] *adj* wild; **w. about** scharf auf *(acc)*; **go w.** verwildern; **grow w.** *(become neglected)* verwildern; **make s.o. w.** (coll) j-n rasend machen ∥ *adv*—**grow w.** *(grow in the wild)* wild wachsen; **run w.** verwildern

wild' boar' *s* Wildschwein *n*

wild' card' *s* wilde Karte *f*

wild'cat' *s* Wildkatze *f*

wild'cat strike' *s* wilder Streik *m*

wilderness ['wɪldərnɪs] *s* Wildnis *f*

wild'fire' *s*—**like w.** wie Lauffeuer

wild' flow'er *s* Feldblume *f*

wild'-goose' chase' *s*—**go on a w.** sich *[dat]* vergeblich Mühe machen

wild'life' *s* Wild *n*

wild' oats' *spl*—**sow one's w.** sich *[dat]* die Hörner abstoßen

wile [waɪl] *s* List *f* ∥ *tr*—**w. away** sich *[dat]* vertreiben

will [wɪl] *s* Wille(n) *m*; *(jur)* Testament *n*; **at w.** nach Belieben ∥ *tr (bequeath)* vermachen ∥ *v (pret & cond* **would** [wʊd]) *aux* werden

willful ['wɪlfəl] *adj* absichtlich; *(stubborn)* eigensinnig

William ['wɪljəm] *s* Wilhelm *m*

will'ing *adj* bereitwillig; **be w. to** *(inf)* bereit sein zu *(inf)*

willingly ['wɪlɪŋli] *adv* gern

willingness ['wɪlɪŋnɪs] *s* Bereitwilligkeit *f*

will-o'-the-wisp ['wɪlə'wɪsp] *s (&* fig) Irrlicht *n*

willow ['wɪlo] *s* Weide *f*

willowy ['wɪlo-i] *adj* biegsam

will' pow'er *s* Willenskraft *f*

willy-nilly ['wɪli'nɪli] *adv* wohl oder übel

wilt [wɪlt] *tr* verwelken lassen ∥ *intr* verwelken

wilt'ed *adj* welk

wily ['waɪli] *adj* schlau, listig

wimple ['wɪmpəl] *s* Kinntuch *n*

win [wɪn] *s* Gewinn *m*; (sport) Sieg *m* ∥ *v (pret & pp* **won** [wʌn]; *ger* **winning)** *tr* gewinnen; **win s.o. over to one's side** auf seine Seite ziehen ∥ *intr* gewinnen, siegen

wince [wɪns] *s* Zucken *n* ∥ *intr* zucken

winch [wɪntʃ] *s (windlass)* Winde *f*; *(handle)* Kurbel *f*; (min, naut) Haspel *f & m*

wind [wɪnd] *s* Wind *m*; **break w.** e-n Darmwind lassen; **get w. of** Wind bekommen von; **take the w. out of s.o.'s sails** j-m den Wind aus den Segeln nehmen; **there is s.th. in the w.** es liegt etw in der Luft ∥ [waɪnd] *v (pret & pp* **wound** [waʊnd]) *tr* wickeln, winden; *(a timepiece)* aufziehen; **w. up** aufwickeln; *(affairs)* abwickeln; *(a speech)* abschließen ∥ *intr (said of a river, road)* sich winden; **w. around** *(said of a plant)* sich ranken um

windbag ['wɪnd,bæg] *s* (coll) Schaumschläger –in *mf*

windbreak ['wɪnd,brek] *s* Windschutz *m*

windbreaker ['wɪnd,brekər] *s* Windjacke *f*

winded ['wɪndɪd] *adj* außer Atem, atemlos

windfall ['wɪnd,fɔl] *s (fallen fruit)* Fallobst *n*; (fig) Glücksfall *m*

wind'ing road' ['waɪndɪŋ] *s* Serpentinenstraße *f*; *(public sign)* kurvenreiche Straße *f*

wind'ing sheet' ['waɪndɪŋ] *s* Leichentuch *n*

wind' in'strument [wɪnd] *s* Blasinstrument *n*

windlass ['wɪndləs] *s* Winde *f*

windmill ['wɪnd,mɪl] *s* Windmühle *f*

window ['wɪndo] *s* Fenster *n*; (*of a ticket office*) Schalter *m*; (*for display*) Schaufenster *n*

win'dow display' *s* Schaufensterauslage *f*

win'dow dress'er *s* Schaufensterdekorateur –in *mf*

win'dow dress'ing *s* Schaufensterdekoration *f*

win'dow en'velope *s* Fensterumschlag *m*

win'dow frame' *s* Fensterrahmen *m*

win'dowpane' *s* Fensterscheibe *f*

win'dow screen' *s* Fliegengitter *n*

win'dow shade' *s* Rollvorhang *m*, Rollo *n*

win'dow-shop' *v* (*pret & pp* –**shopped**; *ger* –**shopping**) *intr* e-n Schaufensterbummel machen

win'dow shut'ter *s* Fensterladen *m*

win'dow sill' *s* Fensterbrett *n*

windpipe ['wɪnd‚paɪp] *s* Luftröhre *f*

windshield ['wɪnd‚ʃild] *s* Windschutzscheibe *f*

wind'shield wash'er *s* Scheibenwäscher *m*

wind'shield wip'er *s* Scheibenwischer *m*

windsock ['wɪnd‚sak] *s* Windsack *m*

windstorm ['wɪnd‚stɔrm] *s* Sturm *m*

wind' tun'nel [wɪnd] *s* Windkanal *m*

wind-up ['waɪnd‚ʌp] *s* (*of affairs*) Abwicklung *f*; (*of a speech*) Schluß *m*

windward ['wɪndwərd] *adj* (*side*) Wind– ‖ *adv* windwärts ‖ *s* Windseite *f*; **turn to w.** anluven

windy ['wɪndi] *adj* windig; (*speech*) weitschweifig; (*person*) redselig

wine [waɪn] *s* Wein *m* ‖ *tr* mit Wein bewirten

wine' cel'lar *s* Weinkeller *m*

wine' glass' *s* Weinglas *n*

winegrower ['waɪn‚gro·ər] *s* Weinbauer –in *mf*

wine'grow'ing *s* Weinbau *m*

wine' list' *s* Weinkarte *f*

wine' press' *s* Weinpresse *f*

winery ['waɪnəri] *s* Weinkellerei *f*

wine'skin' *s* Weinschlauch *m*

wing [wɪŋ] *s* (*of a bird, building, party*) Flügel *m*; (*unit of three squadrons*) Geschwader *n*; (*theat*) Kulisse *f* ‖ *tr* (*shoot*) in den Flügel treffen; **w. one' way** dahinfliegen

wing' chair' *s* Ohrensessel *m*

wing' nut' *s* Flügelmutter *f*

wing'spread' *s* Spannweite *f*

wink [wɪŋk] *s* Augenwink *m*; **quick as a w.** im Nu ‖ *intr* blinzeln; **w. at** zublinzeln (*dat*); (*overlook*) ein Auge zudrücken bei (*dat*)

winner ['wɪnər] *s* Gewinner –in *mf*, Sieger –in *mf*; (*e.g., winning ticket*) Treffer *m*

win'ning *adj* (*e.g., smile*) gewinnend; (*sport*) siegreich ‖ **winnings** *spl* Gewinn *m*

winsome ['wɪnsəm] *adj* reizend

winter ['wɪntər] *s* Winter *m* ‖ *intr* überwintern

winterize ['wɪntə‚raɪz] *tr* winterfest machen

wintry ['wɪntri] *adj* winterlich; (fig) frostig

wipe [waɪp] *tr* wischen; **w. clean** abwischen; **w. out** auswischen; (*e.g., a debt*) tilgen; (*destroy*) vernichten; (fin) ruinieren; **w. up** aufwischen

wire [waɪr] *s* Draht *m*; (telg) Telegramm *n*; **get in under the w.** es gerade noch schaffen ‖ *tr* mit Draht versehen; (*a house*) (elec) elektrische Leitungen legen in (*dat*); (*a message*) drahten; (*a person*) telegraphieren (*dat*)

wire' cut'ter *s* Drahtschere *f*

wire'draw' *v* (*pret* –**drew**; *pp* –**drawn**) *tr* drahtziehen

wire' entan'glement *s* Drahtverhau *m*

wire' gauge' *s* Drahtlehre *f*

wire'-haired' *adj* drahthaarig

wireless ['waɪrlɪs] *adj* drahtlos

wire' nail' *s* Drahtnagel *m*

Wire'pho'to *s* (–tos) (trademark) Bildtelegramm *n*

wire' record'er *s* Drahttonaufnahmegerät *n*

wire'tap' *s* Abhören *n* ‖ *v* (*pret & pp* –**tapped**; *ger* –**tapping**) *tr* abhören

wir'ing *s* Leitungen *pl*; **do the w.** die elektrischen Leitungen legen

wiry ['waɪri] *adj* drahtig

wisdom ['wɪzdəm] *s* Weisheit *f*

wis'dom tooth' *s* Weisheitszahn *m*

wise [waɪz] *adj* (*person, decision*) klug; (*impertinent*) naseweis; **be w. to** sich [*dat*] klar werden über (*acc*); **put s.o. w. to** j-n einweihen in (*acc*) ‖ **s—in no w.** keineswegs ‖ *intr*—**w. up** endlich mal vernünftig werden

wise'a'cre *s* Neunmalkluge *mf*

wise'crack' *s* schnippische Bemerkung *f*

wise' guy' *s* (sl) Naseweis *m*

wisely ['waɪzli] *adv* wohlweislich

wish [wɪʃ] *s* Wunsch *m* ‖ *tr* wünschen ‖ *intr*—**w. for** sich [*dat*] wünschen

wish'bone' *s* Gabelbein *n*

wish'ful think'ing ['wɪʃfəl] *s* ein frommer Wunsch *m*

wishy-washy ['wɪʃi‚waʃi] *adj* charakterlos; **be w.** ein Waschlappen sein

wisp [wɪsp] *s* (*of hair*) Strähne *f*

wistful ['wɪstfəl] *adj* versonnen

wit [wɪt] *s* Geist *m*; (*person*) geistreicher Mensch *m*; **be at one's wit's end** sich [*dat*] keinen Rat mehr wissen; **keep one's wits about one** e-n klaren Kopf behalten; **live by one's wits** sich durchschlagen

witch [wɪtʃ] *s* Hexe *f*

witch'craft' *s* Hexerei *f*

witch' doc'tor *s* Medizinmann *m*

witch' ha'zel *s* Zaubernuß *f*; (*ointment*) Präperat *n* aus Zaubernuß

witch' hunt' *s* Hexenjagd *f*

with [wɪð], [wɪθ] *prep* mit (*dat*); (*at the house of*) bei (*dat*); (*because of*) vor (*dat*), e.g., **green w. envy** grün vor Neid; (*despite*) trotz (*genit*); **not be w. it** nicht bei der Sache sein

with'draw' *v* (*pret* –**drew**; *pp* –**drawn**) *tr* zurückziehen; (*money*) abheben ‖ *intr* sich zurückziehen

withdrawal [wɪð'drɔ·əl] *s* Zurückziehung *f*; (*retraction*) Zurücknahme *f*; (*from a bank*) Abhebung *f*; (mil) Rückzug *m*

withdraw'al slip' *s* Abhebungsformular *n*

wither ['wɪðər] *intr* verwelken

with·hold' *v* (*pret & pp* **–held**) *tr* (*pay*) einbehalten; (*information*) (*from*) vorenthalten (*dat*)

withhold'ing tax' *s* einbehaltene Steuer *f*

within' *adv* drin(nen); **from w.** von innen || *prep* (*time*) binnen (*dat*), innerhalb von (*dat*); (*place*) innerhalb (*genit*); **w. walking distance** in Gehweite

without' *adv* draußen || *prep* ohne (*acc*); **w.** (*ger*) ohne zu (*inf*), ohne daß; **w. reason** ohne allen Anlaß

with·stand' *v* (*pret & pp* **–stood**) *tr* widerstehen (*dat*)

witness ['wɪtnɪs] *s* Zeuge *m*, Zeugin *f*; (*evidence*) Zeugnis *n*; **bear w. to** Zeugnis ablegen von; **in w. whereof** zum Zeugnis dessen; **w. for the defense** Entlastungszeuge *m*; **w. for the prosecution** Belastungszeuge *m* || *tr* (*an event*) anwesend sein bei; (*an accident, crime*) Augenzeuge sein (*genit*); (*e.g., a contract, will*) als Zeuge unterschreiben

wit'ness stand' *s* Zeugenstand *m*

witticism ['wɪtɪ‚sɪzəm] *s* Witzelei *f*

wittingly ['wɪtɪŋli] *adv* wissentlich

witty ['wɪti] *adj* geistreich, witzig

wizard ['wɪzərd] *s* Hexenmeister *m*

wizardry ['wɪzərdri] *s* (& fig) Hexerei *f*

wizened ['wɪzənd] *adj* runzelig

wobble ['wɑbəl] *intr* wackeln

wobbly ['wɑbli] *adj* wackelig

woe [wo] *s* Weh *n* || *interj*—**woe is me!** weh mir!

woebegone ['wobɪ‚gɔn] *adj* jammervoll

woeful ['wofəl] *adj* jammervoll

wolf [wʊlf] *s* (**wolves** ['wʊlvz]) Wolf *m*; (coll) Schürzenjäger *m*; **cry w.** blinden Alarm schlagen; **keep the w. from the door** sich über Wasser halten || *tr*—**w. down** verschlingen

wolf'pack' *s* Wolfsrudel *n*; (nav) U-bootrudel *n*

wolfram ['wʊlfrəm] *s* (chem) Wolfram *n*; (mineral) Wolframit *n*

woman ['wʊmən] *s* (**women** ['wɪmən]) Frau *f*

wom'an doc'tor *s* Ärztin *f*

wom'anhood' *s* Frauen *pl*; **reach w.** e-e Frau werden

womanish ['wʊmənɪʃ] *adj* weibisch

wom'ankind' *s* Frauen *pl*

womanly ['wʊmənli] *adj* fraulich

womb [wum] *s* Mutterleib *m*

wom'enfolk' *spl* Weibsvolk *n*

wom'en's dou'bles *spl* (tennis) Damendoppelspiel *n*

wom'en's sin'gles *spl* (tennis) Dameneinzelspiel *n*

wonder ['wʌndər] *s* Wunder *n* || *intr* (*be surprised*) sich wundern; (*ask*

oneself) sich fragen; (*reflect*) überlegen; **wonder at** sich verwundern über (*acc*)

wonderful ['wʌndərfəl] *adj* wunderbar

won'derland' *s* Wunderland *n*

won'der work'er *s* Wundertäter –in *mf*

wont [wʌnt], [wɔnt] *adj*—**be w. to** (*inf*) pflegen zu (*inf*) || *s* Gepflogenheit *f*

wont'ed *adj* gewöhnlich, üblich

woo [wu] *tr* den Hof machen (*dat*)

wood [wʊd] *s* Holz *n*; **out of the woods** (fig) über den Berg; **woods** Wald *m*

wood' al'cohol *s* Methylalkohol *m*

woodbine ['wʊd‚baɪn] *s* Geißblatt *n*; (*Virginia creeper*) wilder Wein *m*

wood' carv'ing *s* Holzschnitzerei *f*

wood'chuck' *s* Murmeltier *n*

wood'cock' *s* Holzschnepfe *f*

wood'cut' *s* (*block*) Holzplatte *f*; (*print*) Holzschnitt *m*

wood'cut'ter *s* Holzfäller *m*

wood'ed *adj* bewaldet

wooden ['wʊdən] *adj* (& fig) hölzern

wood' engrav'ing *s* Holzschnitt *m*

wood'en leg' *s* Stelzbein *n*

wood'en shoe' *s* Holzschuh *m*

woodland ['wʊdlənd] *adj* Wald– || *s* Waldland *n*

wood'man *s* (**–men**) Holzhauer *m*

woodpecker ['wʊd‚pekər] *s* Specht *m*

wood' pi'geon *s* Ringeltaube *f*

wood'pile' *s* Holzhaufen *m*

wood'pulp' *s* Holzfaserstoff *m*

wood' screw' *s* Holzschraube *f*

wood'shed' *s* Holzschuppen *m*

woods'man *s* (**–men**) Förster *m*; (*lumberman*) Holzhauer *m*

wood'winds' *spl* Holzblasinstrumente *pl*

wood'work' *s* Holzarbeit *f*; (*structure in wood*) Gebälk *n*

wood'work'er *s* Holzarbeiter –in *mf*

wood'worm' *s* (ent) Holzwurm *m*

woody ['wʊdi] *adj* waldig; (*woodlike*) holzig

wooer ['wu·ər] *s* Verehrer *m*

woof [wuf] *s* (*of a dog*) unterdrücktes Bellen *n*; (tex) Gewebe *n*

woofer ['wufər] *s* (rad) Tieftöner *m*

wool [wʊl] *adj* wollen || *s* Wolle *f*

woolen ['wʊlən] *adj* wollen, Woll– || **woolens** *spl* Wollwaren *pl*

woolly ['wʊli] *adj* wollig; (*e.g., thinking*) verschwommen

woozy ['wuzi] *adj* benebelt

word [wʌrd] *s* Wort *n*; **be as good as one's w.** zu seinem Wort stehen; **by w. of mouth** mündlich; **get w. from** Nachricht haben von; **give one's w.** sein Wort geben; **have a w. with** ein ernstes Wort sprechen mit; **have words** e–n Wortwechsel haben; **in a w.** mit e–m Wort; **in other words** mit anderen Worten; **in so many words** ausdrücklich; **leave w.** Bescheid hinterlassen; **not another w.!** kein Wort mehr!; **not a w. of truth in it** kein wahres Wort daran; **put in a good w. for s.o.** ein gutes Wort für j–n einlegen; **put into words** in

Worte kleiden; **put words in s.o.'s mouth** j-m Worte in den Mund legen; **send w. to s.o.** j-m benachrichtigen; **take s.o.'s w. for it** j-n beim Wort nehmen; **w. for w.** Wort für Wort ‖ *tr* formulieren

word'-for-word' *adj* wörtlich

word'ing s Formulierung *f*

word' of hon'or s Ehrenwort *n*; **w.!** auf mein Wort!

word' or'der s Wortfolge *f*

wordy ['wardi] *adj* wortreich

work [wark] s Arbeit *f*; (*production, book*) Werk *n*; **be in the works** (coll) im Gang sein; **get to w.** sich an die Arbeit machen; (*travel to work*) zum Arbeitsplatz kommen; **give s.o. the works** (coll) j-n fertigmachen; **have one's w.** cut out zu tun haben; **it took a lot of w. to** (*inf*) es hat viel Arbeit gekostet zu (*inf*); **make short w. of** kurzen Prozeß machen mit; **out of w.** arbeitslos; **works** (horol) Uhrwerk *n* ‖ *tr* (*a machine*) bedienen; (*a pedal*) treten; (*a mine*) abbauen; (*the soil*) bearbeiten; (*metal*) treiben; (*dough*) kneten; (*wonders*) wirken; **w. in** einarbeiten; **w. off** (*a debt*) abarbeiten; **w. oneself to death** sich totarbeiten; **w. one's way up** sich hocharbeiten; **w. out** (*a solution*) ausarbeiten; (*a problem*) lösen; **w. to death** abhetzen; **w. up an appetite** sich [*dat*] Appetit machen ‖ *intr* arbeiten; (*function*) funktionieren; (*succeed*) klappen; **w. against** wirken gegen; **w. away** at losarbeiten auf (*acc*); **w. at** (*a trade*) ausüben; **w. both ways** für beide Fälle gelten; **w. loose** sich lockern; **w. on** (*a person*) bearbeiten; (*a patient, car*) arbeiten an (*dat*); **w. out** (sport) trainieren; **w. out well** gut ausgehen

workable ['warkəbəl] *adj* brauchbar; (*plan*) durchführbar

work'bench' s Werkbank *f*

work'book' s Übungsheft *n*

work' camp' s Arbeitslager *n*

work'day' s Arbeitstag *m*

work' detail' s (mil) Arbeitskommando *n*

worked'-up' *adj* erregt; **get s.o. w.** j-n erregen; **get w.** sich erregen

worker ['warkər] s Arbeiter –in *mf*

work' force' s Belegschaft *f*

work'horse' s Arbeitspferd *n*

work'ing day' s Arbeitstag *m*

work'ing girl' s Arbeiterin *f*

work'ing hours' *spl* Arbeitsstunden *pl*

work'ingman' s (**-men'**) Arbeiter *m*

work'ing or'der s—**in w.** betriebsfähig

work'ingwom'an s (**-wom'en**) Arbeiterin *f*; (*professionally*) berufstätige Frau *f*

work'man s (**-men**) Arbeiter *m*

work'manship' s Ausführung *f*

work'men's compensa'tion insur'ance s Arbeiterunfallversicherung *f*

work' of art' s Kunstwerk *n*

work'out' s Training *n*

work' per'mit s Arbeitsgenehmigung *f*

work'room' s Arbeitszimmer *n*

work' sche'dule s Dienstplan *m*

work'shop' s Werkstatt *f*

work' stop'page s Arbeitseinstellung *f*

world [warld] *adj* Welt– ‖ s Welt *f*; **a w. of** groß; **from all over the w.** aus aller Herren Ländern; **not for all the w.** nicht um die Welt; **see the w.** in der Welt herumkommen; **they are worlds apart** es liegen Welten zwischen den beiden; **think the w. of** große Stücke halten auf (*acc*); **who (where) in the w.** wer (wo) in aller Welt

world' affairs' *spl* internationale Angelegenheiten *pl*

world'-fa'mous *adj* weltberühmt

worldly ['warldli] *adj* (*goods, pleasures*) irdisch; (*person*) weltlich; (*wisdom*) Welt–

world'ly-wise' *adj* weltklug

world's' fair' s Weltausstellung *f*

world'-shak'ing *adj* weltbewegend

world'-wide' *adj* weltweit

worm [warm] s Wurm *m* ‖ *tr*—**w. one's way** sich schlängeln; **w. secrets out of s.o.** j-m die Würmer aus der Nase ziehen

worm-eaten ['warm,itən] *adj* (& fig) wurmstichig

wormy ['warmi] *adj* wurmig

worn [worn] *adj* (*clothes*) getragen; (*tires*) abgenutzt; (*wearied*) müde

worn'-out' *adj* (*clothes*) abgetragen; (*tires*) abgenutzt; (*exhausted*) erschöpft

worrisome ['warisəm] *adj* (*causing worry*) beunruhigend; (*inclined to worry*) sorgenvoll

wor·ry ['wari] s Sorge *f*; (*source of worry*) Ärger *m* ‖ *v* (*pret & pp* **-ried**) *tr* beunruhigen; **be worried** besorgt sein ‖ *intr* (*about*) sich [*dat*] Sorgen machen (um); **don't w.!** keine Sorge!

worse [wars] *comp adj* schlechter, schlimmer; **be w. off** schlimmer daran sein; **he's none the w. for it** es hat ihm nichts geschadet; **what's w.** was noch schlimmer ist

worsen ['warsən] *tr* verschlimmern ‖ *intr* sich verschlimmern

wor·ship ['warʃɪp] s Anbetung *f*; (*services*) Gottesdienst *m* ‖ *v* (*pret & pp* **-shiped**; *ger* **-ship[p]ing**) *tr* (& fig) anbeten ‖ *intr* seine Andacht verrichten

worship(p)er ['warʃɪpər] s Anbeter –in *mf*; (*in church*) Andächtige *mf*

worst [warst] *super adj* schlimmste ‖ *super adv* am schlimmsten ‖ s Schlimmste *n*; **at the w.** schlimmstenfalls; **get the w. of** den kürzeren ziehen bei; **if w. comes to w.** wenn alle Stricke reißen; **the w. is yet to come** das dicke Ende kommt noch ‖ *tr* schlagen

worsted ['wustid] *adj* Kammgarn–

worth [warθ] *adj* wert; **it is w.** (ger) es lohnt sich zu (*inf*); **it is w. the trouble es ist der Mühe wert; ten dollars' w. of meat** für zehn Dollar Fleisch; **w. seeing** sehenswert ‖ s Wert *m*

worthless ['wʌrθlɪs] *adj* wertlos; (*person*) nichtsnutzig

worth′while *adj* lohnend

worthy ['wʌrðɪ] *adj* (**of**) würdig (*genit*)

would [wud] *aux* used to express 1) indirect statements, e.g., **he said he w. come** er sagte, er würde kommen; 2) the present conditional, e.g., **he w. do it if he could** er würde es tun, wenn er könnte; 3) past conditional, e.g., **he w. have paid, if he had had the money** er würde gezahlt haben, wenn er das Geld gehabt hätte; 4) habitual action in the past, e.g., **he w. always buy the morning paper** er kaufte immer das Morgenblatt; 5) polite requests, e.g., **w. you please pass me the butter?** würden Sie mir bitte die Butter reichen; 6) a wish, e.g., **w. that I had never seen it** wenn ich es nur nie gesehen hätte!; **w. rather** möchte lieber, e.g., **I w. rather go on foot** ich möchte lieber zu Fuß gehen

would′-be *adj* angeblich, Möchtegern—

wound [wund] *s* Wunde *f* ‖ *tr* verwunden

wound′ed *adj* verwundet ‖ **the w.** *spl* die Verwundeten *pl*

wow [wau] *s* (coll) Bombenerfolg *m* ‖ *tr* (coll) erstaunen ‖ *interj* nanu!

wrack [ræk] *s*—**go to w. and ruin** untergehen, in Brüche gehen

wraith [reθ] *s* (*apparition*) Erscheinung *f*; (*spirit*) Geist *m*

wrangle ['ræŋgəl] *s* Streit *m* ‖ *intr* streiten

wrap [ræp] *s* Überwurf *m* ‖ *v* (*pret & pp* **wrapped**; *ger* **wrapping**) *tr* wickeln; (*a package*) einpacken; **be wrapped up in** (*e.g., thoughts*) versunken sein in (*dat*); **wrapped in darkness** in Dunkelheit gehüllt; **w. up** (*a deal*) abwickeln

wrapper ['ræpər] *s* Verpackung *f*; (*for mailing newspapers*) Streifband *n*

wrap′ping *s* Verpackung *f*

wrap′ping pa′per *s* Packpapier *n*

wrath [ræθ] *s* Zorn *m*, Wut *f*

wrathful ['ræθfəl] *adj* zornig, wütend

wreak [rik] *tr* (*vengeance*) üben; **w. havoc** schlimm hausen

wreath [riθ] *s* (**wreaths** [riðz]) Kranz *m*; **w. of smoke** Rauchfahne *f*

wreathe [rið] *tr* bekränzen, umwinden

wreck [rek] *s* (*of a car or train*) Unglück *n*; (*wrecked ship, car, person*) Wrack *n* ‖ *tr* (*e.g., a car*) zertrümmern; (*a building*) in Trümmer legen; (*a marriage*) zerrütten; (fig) zum Scheitern bringen; **be wrecked** (fig & naut) scheitern

wreckage ['rekɪdʒ] *s* Wrackgut *n*; (*of an accident*) Trümmer *pl*

wrecker ['rekər] *s* Abschleppwagen *m*

wren [ren] *s* (orn) Zaunkönig *m*

wrench [rentʃ] *s* (*tool*) Schraubenschlüssel *m*; (*of a muscle*) Verrenkung *f* ‖ *tr* verrenken

wrest [rest] *tr* (**from**) entreißen (*dat*)

wrestle ['resəl] *tr* ringen mit ‖ *intr* ringen

wrestler ['reslər] *s* Ringer *m*; (*professional wrestler*) Catcher *m*

wrestling ['reslɪŋ] *s* Ringen *n*; (*professional wrestling*) Catchen *n*

wres′tling match′ *s* Ringkampf *m*

wretch [retʃ] *s* armer Kerl *m*; (*vile person*) Schuft *m*

wretched ['retʃɪd] *adj* elend; (*terrible*) scheußlich

wriggle ['rɪgəl] *s* Krümmung *f*; (*of a worm*) schlängelnde Bewegung *f* ‖ *tr* hin- und herbewegen; **w. one's way** sich dahinschlängeln ‖ *intr* sich winden

wring [rɪŋ] *v* (*pret & pp* **wrung** [rʌŋ]) *tr* (*the hands*) ringen; **w. out** (*the wash*) auswinden; **w. s.o.'s neck** j-m den Hals umdrehen

wringer ['rɪŋər] *s* Wringmaschine *f*

wrinkle ['rɪŋkəl] *s* Falte *f*; **new w.** (fig) neuer Kniff *m*; **take out the wrinkles** (fig) den letzten Schliff geben ‖ *tr* falten, runzeln; (*paper, clothes*) zerknittern ‖ *intr* Falten werfen

wrin′kle-proof′ *adj* knitterfrei

wrinkly ['rɪŋklɪ] *adj* faltig, runzelig

wrist [rɪst] *s* Handgelenk *n*

wrist′band′ *s* Armband *n*

wrist′ watch′ *s* Armbanduhr *f*

writ [rɪt] *s* gerichtlicher schriftlicher Befehl *m*

write [raɪt] *v* (*pret* **wrote** [rot]; *pp* **written** ['rɪtən]) *tr* schreiben; (*compose*) verfassen; **it is written** (*in the Bible*) es steht geschrieben; **it is written all over his face** es steht ihm im Gesicht geschrieben; **w. down** aufschreiben; **w. off** abschreiben; **w. out** ausschreiben; (*a check*) ausstellen ‖ *intr* schreiben; **w. for information** Informationen anfordern

write′-off′ *s* Abschreibung *f*

writer ['raɪtər] *s* Schreiber –in *mf*; (*author*) Schriftsteller –in *mf*

writ′er's cramp′ *s* Schreibkrampf *m*

write′-up′ *s* Pressebericht *m*

writhe [raɪð] *intr* (**in**) sich krümmen (vor *dat*)

writ′ing *s* Schreiben *n*; (*handwriting*) Schrift *f*; **in w.** schriftlich; **put in w.** niederschreiben

writ′ing desk′ *s* Schreibtisch *m*

writ′ing pad′ *s* Schreibblock *m*

writ′ing pa′per *s* Schreibpapier *n*; (*stationery*) Briefpapier *n*

written ['rɪtən] *adj* schriftlich; (law) geschrieben; (*language*) Schrift—

wrong [rɔŋ] *adj* (*incorrect*) falsch; (*unjust*) unrecht; **be w.** (*be incorrect*) nicht stimmen; (*be in error*) Unrecht haben; (*said of a situation*) nicht in Ordnung sein; **be. w. with** fehlen (*dat*); **sorry, w. number!** (telp) falsch verbunden! ‖ *s* Unrecht *n*; **be in the w.** im Unrecht sein; **do w.** ein Unrecht begehen; **do w. to s.o.** j-m ein Unrecht zufügen; **get in w. with s.o.** es sich (*dat*) mit j-m verderben ‖ *adv* falsch, unrecht; **go w.** (*morally*) auf Abwege geraten; (*in walking*) sich verirren; (*in reckoning*)

irregehen; (*in driving*) sich verfahren; (*said of plans*) schief gehen
wrongdoer ['rɔŋ ˌdu·ər] *s* Missetäter –in *mf*

wrong'do·ing *s* Missetat *f*
wrought i'ron [rɔt] *s* Schmiedeeisen *n*
wrought'-up' *adj* aufgebracht
wry [raɪ] *adj* schief

X

X, x [ɛks] *s* vierundzwanzigster Buchstabe des englischen Alphabets
xenophobia [ˌzɛnə'fobɪ·ə] *s* Fremdenhaß *m*
Xerox ['zɪrɑks] *s* (trademark) Xerographie *f* || **xerox** *tr* ablichten
Xer'ox-cop'y *s* Ablichtung *f*

Xmas ['krɪsməs] *adj* Weihnachts– || *s* Weihnachten *pl*
x'-ray' *adj* Röntgen– || *s* (*picture*) Röntgenbild *n;* **x-rays** Röntgenstrahlen *pl* || *tr* röntgen
x'-ray ther'apy *s* Röntgentherapie *f*
xylophone ['zaɪlə ˌfon] *s* Xylophon *n*

Y

Y, y [waɪ] *s* fünfundzwanzigster Buchstabe des englischen Alphabets
yacht [jɑt] *s* Jacht *f*
yacht' club' *s* Jachtklub *m*
yam [jæm] *s* Yamwurzel *f*
yank [jæŋk] *s* Ruck *m;* **Yank** Ami *m* || *tr*—**y. s.th. out of** reißen aus || *intr*—**y. on** heftig ziehen an (*dat*)
Yankee ['jæŋki] *s* Yankee *m*
yap [jæp] *s* (*talk*) (sl) Geschwätz *n;* (*mouth*) (sl) Maul *n;* (*bark*) Gekläff *n* || *v* (*pret & pp* **yapped;** *ger* **yapping**) *intr* (*bark*) kläffen; (*talk*) (sl) schwätzen
yard [jɑrd] *s* (*measure*) Yard *n;* (*ground adjoining a building*) Hof *m;* (naut) Rahe *f;* (rr) Rangierbahnhof *m*
yard'arm' *s* (naut) Nock *f & n*
yard' mas'ter *s* (rr) Rangiermeister *m*
yard'stick' *s* Yardmaß *n;* (fig) Maßstab *m*
yarn [jɑrn] *s* (*thread; story*) Garn *n;* **spin yarns** (fig) Garne spinnen
yaw [jɔ] *s* (aer, rok) Schwanken *n;* (naut) Gieren *n* || *intr* (aer, rok) schwanken; (naut) gieren
yawl [jɔl] *s* (naut) Jolle *f*
yawn [jɔn] *s* Gähnen *n* || *intr* gähnen; (*said, e.g., of a gorge*) klaffen
ye [ji] *pers pron* ihr
yea [je] *s* Jastimme *f* || *adv* ja
yeah [je] *adv* ja
year [jɪr] *s* Jahr *n;* **all y. round** das ganze Jahr hindurch; **a y. from to-day** heute übers Jahr; **for years** seit Jahren; **jahrelang; in years** seit Jahren; **y. in y. out** jahraus jahrein
year'book' *s* Jahrbuch *n*
yearling ['jɪrlɪŋ] *s* Jährling *m*
yearly ['jɪrli] *adj & adv* jährlich
yearn [jɑrn] *intr*—**y. for** sich sehnen nach; **y. to** (*inf*) sich danach sehnen zu (*inf*)
yearn'ing *s* Sehnsucht *f*

yeast [jist] *s* Hefe *f*
yell [jel] *s* Ruf *m*, Aufschrei *m;* (sport) Kampfruf *m* || *tr* (gellend) schreien; **y. one's lungs out** sich tot schreien || *intr* schreien; **y. at** anschreien
yellow ['jelo] *adj* gelb; (sl) feige || *s* Gelb *n* || *tr* gelb machen || *intr* vergilben
yellowish ['jelo·ɪʃ] *adj* gelblich
yel'lowjack'et *s* Wespe *f*
yel'low jour'nalism *s* Sensationspresse *f*
yel'low streak' *s* Zug *m* von Feigheit
yelp [jelp] *s* Gekläff *n* || *intr* kläffen
yen [jen] *s* (*Japanese money*) Yen *m;* (**for**) brennendes Verlangen *n* (nach)
yeo·man ['jomən] *s* (**-men**) (nav) Verwaltungsunteroffizier *m*
yeo'man's serv'ice *s* großer Dienst *m*
yes [jes] *adv* ja; **yes, Sir** jawohl || *s* Ja *n;* **say yes** to bejahen
yes' man' *s* Jasager *m*
yesterday ['jestər ˌde] *adv* gestern; **y. morning** gestern früh || *s* Gestern *n;* **yesterday's** gestrig
yet [jet] *adv* (*still*) noch; (*however*) doch; (*already*) schon; **and yet** trotzdem, dennoch; **as yet** schon; **not yet** noch nicht || *conj* aber
yew [ju] *s* Eibe *f*
Yiddish ['jɪdɪʃ] *adj* jiddisch || *s* Jiddisch *n*
yield [jild] *s* Ertrag *m* || *tr* (*profit*) einbringen; (*interest*) tragen; (*crops*) hervorbringen; (*give up*) überlassen || *intr* (**to**) nachgeben (*dat*)
yo·del ['jodəl] *s* Jodler *m* || *v* (*pret & pp* **-del[l]ed;** *ger* **-del[l]ing**) *intr* jodeln
yodeler ['jodələr] *s* Jodler –in *mf*
yogurt ['jogurt] *s* Yoghurt *m & n*
yoke [jok] *s* (*part of harness; burden*) Joch *n;* **pass under the y.** sich in ein Joch fügen; **y. of oxen** Ochsengespann *n* || *tr* ins Joch spannen

yokel [ˈjokəl] s Bauerntölpel m

yolk [jok] s Dotter m & n

yonder [ˈjɑndər] adv dort drüben

yore [jor] s—**of y.** vormals

you [ju] pers pron du; (plural form) ihr; (polite form) Sie; **to you** dir; (plural form) euch; (polite form) Ihnen; **you of all people!** ausgerechnet Sie! ‖ indef pron man

young [jʌŋ] adj (younger [ˈjʌŋgər]; youngest [ˈjʌŋgɪst]) jung; **y. for one's age** jugendlich für sein Alter ‖ spl (of animals) Jungen pl; **the y.** die Jungen, die Jugend; **with y.** (pregnant) trächtig

young′ la′dy s Fräulein n

young′ man′ s junger Mann m; (boyfriend) Freund m

youngster [ˈjʌŋstər] s Jugendliche mf

your [jur] poss adj dein; (plural form) euer; (polite form) Ihr

yours [jurz] poss pron deiner; (plural form) euerer; (polite form) Ihrer; **y. truly** hochachtungsvoll

your·self [jurˈself] intens pron (–selves [ˈselvz]) selbst, selber ‖ reflex pron dich; (plural form) euch; (polite form) Sich; **to y.** dir; (polite form) Sich; **to yourselves** euch; (polite form) Sich

youth [juθ] s (youths [juθs], [juðz]) (age) Jugend f; (person) Jugendliche mf

youthful [ˈjuθfəl] adj jugendlich

youth′ hos′tel s Jugendherberge f

yowl [jaul] s Gejaule n ‖ intr jaulen

Yugoslav [ˈjugoˈslɑv] adj jugoslawisch ‖ s Jugoslawe m, Jugoslawin f

Yugoslavia [ˈjugoˈslɑvɪ·ə] s Jugoslavien n

yule′ log′ [jul] s Weihnachtsscheit n

yule′tide′ s Weihnachtszeit f

Z

Z, z [zi] s sechsundzwanzigster Buchstabe des englischen Alphabets

zany [ˈzeni] adj närrisch ‖ s Hanswurst m

zeal [zil] s Eifer m

zealot [ˈzelət] s Zelot –in mf

zealous [ˈzeləs] adj eifrig

zebra [ˈzibrə] s Zebra n

zenith [ˈzinɪθ] s Scheitelpunkt m, Zenit m

zephyr [ˈzefər] s Zephir m

zeppelin [ˈzepəlɪn] s Zeppelin m

ze·ro [ˈziro] s (–ros & –roes) Null f ‖ tr—z. **in** a rifle Visier e–s Gewehrs justieren ‖ intr—z. **in on** zielen auf (acc)

ze′ro hour′ s Stunde f Null

zest [zest] s Würze f

Zeus [zus] s Zeus m

zig·zag [ˈzɪgˌzæg] adj Zickzack– ‖ adv im Zickzack ‖ s Zickzack m ‖ (pret & pp **–zagged;** ger **–zagging**) intr im Zickzack fahren

zinc [zɪŋk] s Zink n

Zionism [ˈzaɪ·əˌnɪzəm] s Zionismus m

zip [zɪp] s (coll) Schmiß m ‖ v (pret & pp **zipped;** ger **zipping**) tr (convey with speed) mit Schwung befördern; (fasten with a zipper) mit e–m Reißverschluß schließen ‖ intr sausen; **zip by** vorbeisausen ‖ interj wuppdich!

zip′ code′ s Postleitzahl f

zipper [ˈzɪpər] s Reißverschluß m

zircon [ˈzʌrkɑn] s Zirkon m

zither [ˈzɪθər] s Zither f

zodiac [ˈzodɪˌæk] s Tierkreis m

zombie [ˈzɑmbi] s (sl) Depp m

zone [zon] s (& geol) Zone f; (postal zone) Postbezirk m; (mil) Bereich m

zoo [zu] s Zoo m, Tiergarten m

zoologic(al) [ˌzo·əˈlɑdʒɪk(əl)] adj zoologisch

zoologist [zoˈɑlədʒɪst] s Zoologe m, Zoologin f

zoology [zoˈɑlədʒi] s Zoologie f

zoom [zum] s lautes Summen n; (aer) Hochreißen n ‖ intr laut summen; **z. up** (aer) hochreißen

zoom′ lens′ s Gummilinse f

METRIC CONVERSIONS

Multiply:	By:	To Obtain:
acres	43,560	sq. ft.
	0.4047	hectares
	0.0015625	sq. mi.
ampere-hours	3600	coulombs
atmospheres	76.0	cm. of mercury
	33.90	ft. of water
	14.70	lbs./sq. in.
British thermal units	1054	joules
	777.5	ft.-lbs.
	252.0	gram calories
	0.0003927	horsepower-hrs.
	0.0002928	kilowatt-hrs.
B.T.U./hr.	0.2928	watts
B.T.U./min.	12.96	ft.-lbs./sec.
	0.02356	horsepower
bushels	3523.8	hectoliters
	2150.42	cu. ins.
	35.238	liters
°C + 17.78	1.8	°F
centimeters	0.3937	inches
cm-grams	980.1	cm.-dynes
chains	66	ft.
circumference	6.2832	radians
cubic centimeters	0.0610	cu. ins.
cu. feet	1728	cu. ins.
	62.43	lbs. of water
	7.481	gals. (liq.)
	0.0283	cu. m.
cu. ft./min.	62.43	lbs. water/min.
cu. ft./sec.	448.831	gals./min.
cu. inches	16.387	cu. cm.
	0.0005787	cu. ft.
cu. meters	264.2	gals. (liq.)
	35.3147	cu. ft.
	1.3079	cu. yds.
cu. yards	27	cu. ft.
	0.765	cu. m.
days	86,400	seconds
degrees/sec.	0.1667	revolutions/min.
°F − 32	0.5556	°C
faradays/sec.	96,500	amperes
feet	30.48	cm.
	0.3048	meters
	0.0001894	mi. (stat.)
	0.0001645	mi. (Brit. naut.)

368

Multiply:	By:	To Obtain:
ft. of water	62.43	lbs./sq. ft.
	0.4335	lbs./sq. in.
ft./min.	0.5080	cm./sec.
ft./sec.	0.6818	mi./hr.
	0.5921	knots
fluid ounces	29.573	milliliters
furlongs	660	feet
	0.125	mi.
gallons	231	cu. ins.
	8.345	lbs. of water
	8	pts.
	4	qts.
	3.785	liters
	0.003785	cu. m.
gals./min.	8.0208	cu. ft./hr.
grains	0.0648	grams
grams	980.1	dynes
	15.43	grains
	0.0353	oz. (avdp.)
	0.0022	lbs. (avdp.)
hectares	107,600	sq. ft.
	2.47	acres
hectoliters	2.838	bushels
horsepower	33,000	ft.-lbs./min.
	2545	B.T.U./hr.
	745.7	watts
	42.44	B.T.U./min.
	0.7457	kilowatts
inches	25.40	mm.
	2.540	cm.
	0.00001578	mi.
ins. of water	0.03613	lbs./sq. in.
kilograms	980,100	dynes
	2.2046	lbs. (avdp.)
kg. calories	3086	ft.-lbs.
	3.968	B.T.U.
kg. cal./min.	51.43	ft.-lbs./sec.
	0.06972	kilowatts
kilometers	3280.8	ft.
	0.621	mi.
km./hr.	0.621	mi./hr.
	0.5396	knots
kilowatts	737.6	ft.-lbs./sec.
	56.92	B.T.U./min.
	1.341	horsepower
kilowatt-hrs.	2,655,000	ft.-lbs.
	3415	B.T.U.
	1.341	horsepower-hrs.
knots	6080	ft./hr.
	1.151	stat. mi./hr.
	1	(Brit.) naut. mi./hr.
liters	61.02	cu. ins.
	2.113	pts. (liq.)
	1.057	qts. (liq.)
	0.264	gals. (liq.)
	1.816	pts. (dry)
	0.908	qts. (dry)
	0.1135	pecks
	0.0284	bushels

Multiply:	By:	To Obtain:
meters	39.37	inches
	3.2808	ft.
	1.0936	yds.
	0.0006215	mi. (stat.)
	0.0005396	mi. (Brit. naut.)
miles		
statute	5280	ft.
	1.609	km.
	0.8624	mi. (Brit. naut.)
nautical (Brit.)	6080	ft.
	1.151	mi. (stat.)
mi./hr.	1.467	ft./sec.
milligrams/liter	1	parts/million
milliliters	0.0338	fluid oz.
millimeters	0.03937	inches
ounces		
avoirdupois	28.349	grams
	0.9115	oz. (troy)
	0.0625	lbs. (avdp.)
troy	31.103	grams
	1.0971	oz. (avdp.)
pecks	8.8096	liters
pints		
liquid	473.2	cu. cm.
	28.875	cu. ins.
	0.473	liters
dry	0.550	liters
pounds		
avoirdupois	444,600	dynes
	453.6	grams
	32.17	poundals
	14.58	oz. (troy)
	1.21	lbs. (troy)
	0.4536	kg.
troy	0.373	kg.
lbs. (avdp.)/sq. in.	70.22	g./sq. cm.
	2.307	ft. of water
quarts		
liquid	57.75	cu. ins.
	32	fluid oz.
	2	pts.
	0.946	liters
dry	67.20	cu. ins.
	1.101	liters
quires	25	sheets
radians	3437.7	minutes
	57.296	degrees
reams	500	sheets
revolutions/min.	6	degrees/sec.
rods	16.5	ft.
	5.5	yds.
	5.029	meters
slugs	32.17	lbs. (mass)
square centimeters	0.155	sq. ins.
sq. feet	0.093	sq. m.
sq. inches	6.451	sq. cm.
sq. kilometers	247.1	acres
	0.3861	sq. mi.

Multiply:	By:	To Obtain:
sq. meters	10.76	sq. ft.
	1.1960	sq. yds.
sq. miles	27,878,400	sq. ft.
	640	acres
	2.5889	sq. km.
sq. yards	0.8361	sq. m.
tons		
long	2240	lbs. (avdp.)
	1.12	short tons
	1.0160	metric tons
metric	2204.6	lbs. (avdp.)
	1000	kg.
	1.1023	short tons
	0.9842	long tons
short	2000	lbs. (avdp.)
	0.9072	metric tons
	0.8929	long tons
watts	3.415	B.T.U./hr.
	0.001341	horsepower
yards	36	inches
	3	ft.
	0.9144	meters
	0.0005682	mi. (stat.)
	0.0004934	mi. (Brit. naut.)

LABELS AND ABBREVIATIONS

BEZEICHNUNGEN DER SACHGEBIETE UND ABKÜRZUNGEN

abbr abbreviation—Abkürzung
acc accusative—Akkusativ
(acct) accounting—Rechnungswesen
adj adjective—Adjektiv
(adm) administration—Verwaltung
adv adverb—Adverb
(aer) aeronautics—Luftfahrt
(agr) agriculture—Landwirtschaft
(alg) algebra—Algebra
(Am) American—amerikanisch
(anat) anatomy—Anatomie
(angl) angling—Angeln
(archeol) archeology—Archäologie
(archit) architecture—Architektur
(arith) arithmetic—Rechnen
art article—Artikel
(arti) artillery—Artillerie
(astr) astronomy—Astronomie
(atom. phys.) Atomic physics—Atomphysik
(Aust) Austrian—österreichisch
(aut) automobile—Automobile
aux auxiliary verb—Hilfsverb
(bact) bacteriology—Bakteriologie
(baseball) Baseball
(basketball) Korbball
(bb) bookbinding—Buchbinderei
(Bib) Biblical—biblisch
(billiards) Billard
(biochem) biochemistry—Biochemie
(biol) biology—Biologie
(bowling) Kegeln
(bot) botany—Botanik
(box) boxing—Boxen
(Brit) British—britisch
(cards) Kartenspiel
(carp) carpentry—Zimmerhandwerk
(checkers) Damespiel

(chem) chemistry—Chemie
(chess) Schachspiel
(cin) cinematography—Kinematographie
(coll) colloquial—umgangssprachlich
(com) commercial—Handels-
comb.fm. combining form—Wortbildungselement
comp comparative—Komparativ
conj conjunction—Konjunktion
(crew) Rudersport
(culin) culinary—kulinarisch
(data proc.) data processing—Datenverarbeitung
dem demonstrative—hinweisend
(dent) dentistry—Zahnheilkunde
(dial) dialectical—dialektisch
(dipl) diplomacy—Diplomatie
(eccl) ecclesiastical—kirchlich
(econ) economics—Wirtschaft
(educ) education—Schulwesen
e–e a(n)—eine
e.g. for example—zum Beispiel
(elec) electricity—Elektrizität
(electron) electronics—Elektronik
e–m to a(n)—einem
e–n a(n)—einen
(eng) engineering—Technik
(ent) entomology—Entomologie
e–r of a(n), to a(n)—einer
e–s of a(n)—eines
etw something—etwas
f feminine noun—Femininum
(fa) fine arts—schöne Künste
fem feminine—weiblich
(fencing) Fechtkunst
(fig) figurative—bildlich
(& fig) literal and figurative—buchstäblich und bildlich
(fin) finance—Finanzwesen
(fb) football, soccer—Fußball
fut future—Zukunft
genit genitive—Genitiv
(gcog) geography, Geographie
(geol) geology—Geologie
(geom) geometry—Geometrie
ger gerund—Gerundium
(golf) Golf
(gram) grammar—Grammatik
(gym) gymnastics—Gymnastik
(heral) heraldry—Wappenkunde
(hist) history—Geschichte
(horol) horology—Zeitmessung
(hort) horticulture—Gartenbau
(hum) humorous—scherzhaft
(hunt) hunting—Jagdwesen
(ichth) ichthyology—Ichthyologie

imperf imperfect—Imperfekt
impers impersonal—unpersönlich
ind indicative—Indikativ
indecl indeclinable—undeklinierbar
indef indefinite—unbestimmt
(indust) industry—Industrie
inf infinitive—Infinitiv
(ins) insurance—Versicherungswesen
insep inseparable—untrennbar
intens intensive—verstärkend
interj interjection—Interjektion
interr interrogative—Frage-
intr intransitive—intransitiv
invar invariable—unveränderlich
(iron) ironical—ironisch
j-m to someone—jemandem
j-n someone—jemanden
(journ) journalism—Zeitungswesen
j-s someone's—jemand(e)s
(jur) jurisprudence—Rechtswissenschaft
(libr) library science—Bibliothekswissenschaft
(ling) linguistics—Linguistik
(lit) literary—literarisch
(log) logic—Logik
m masculine noun—Maskulinum
(mach) machinery—Maschinen
(mech) mechanics—Mechanik
(med) medicine—Medizin
(metal) metallurgy—Metallurgie
(meteor) meteorology—Meteorologie
mf masculine or feminine noun according to sex—Maskulinum
    oder Femininum je nach Geschlecht
(mil) military—Militär-
(min) mining—Bergwerkswesen
(mineral) mineralogy—Mineralogie
mod aux modal auxiliary—Modalverb
(mount) mountain climbing—Bergsteigerei
(mus) music—Musik
(myth) mythology—Mythologie
m & f masculine and feminine noun without regard to sex—
    Maskulinum oder Femininum ohne Rücksicht auf Geschlecht
(naut) nautical—nautisch
(nav) navy—Kriegsmarine
neut neuter—sächlich
(obs) obsolete—veraltet
(obstet) obstetrics—Geburtshilfe
(opt) optics—Optik
(orn) ornithology—Ornithologie
(paint) painting—Malerei
(parl) parliamentary—parlamentarisch
(pathol) pathology—Pathologie
(pej) pejorative—pejorativ
pers personal—Personal-

374

(pharm) pharmacy—Pharmazie
(philos) philosophy—Philosophie
(phonet) phonetics—Phonetik
(phot) photography—Photographie
(phys) physics—Physik
(physiol) physiology—Physiologie
pl plural—Plural
(poet) poetical—dichterisch
(pol) politics—Politik
poss possessive—besitzanzeigend
pp past participial—Partizip Perfekt
pref prefix—Präfix
prep preposition—Präposition
pres present—Gegenwart
pret preterit—Präteritum
pron pronoun—Pronomen
pros prosody—Prosodie
(Prot) Protestant—protestantisch
(psychol) psychology—Psychologie
(public sign) Hinweisschild
(rad) radio—Radio
(radar) Radar
recip reciprocal—wechselseitig
ref reflexive verb—Reflexivverb
reflex reflexive—reflexiv
rel relative—relativ
(relig) religion—Religion
(rhet) rhetoric—Rhetorik
(rok) rocketry—Raketen
(rr) railroad—Eisenbahn
s substantive—Substantiv
(sculp) sculpture—Bildhauerkunst
sep separable—trennbar
(sewing) Näherei
sg singular—Einzahl
(sl) slang—Slang
s.o. someone—jemand
s.o.'s someone's—jemand(e)s
spl substantive plural—pluralisches Substantiv
(sport) sports—Sports
(st. exch.) stock exchange—Börse
subj subjunctive—Konjunktiv
suf suffix—Suffix
super superlative—Superlativ
(surg) surgery—Chirurgie
(surv) surveying—Vermessungswesen
(tech) technical—Fachsprache
(telg) telegraphy—Telegraphie
(telp) telephone—Fernsprechwesen
(telv) television—Fernsehen
(tennis) Tennis
(tex) textiles—Textilien
(theat) theater—Theater

(theol) theology—Theologie
tr transitive—transitiv
(typ) typography—Typographie
usw. and so forth—und so weiter
v verb—Verb
var variant—Variante
(vet) veterinary medicine—Veterinärmedizin
(vulg) vulgar—vulgär
(zool) zoology—Zoologie